THE HARSHACARITA OF BĀṆABHAṬṬA

THE HARSHACARITA OF BĀṆABHAṬṬA

(*Text of Uchchhvāsas I — VIII*)

Edited with an Introduction and Notes
by

MAHĀMAHOPĀDHYĀYA
P. V. KANE

MOTILAL BANARSIDASS PUBLISHERS
PRIVATE LIMITED • DELHI

First Edition: Bombay, 1918
Reprint: Delhi, 1965, 1973, 1986, 1997

ISBN: 81-208-0032-x (Cloth)
ISBN: 81-208-0051-6 (Paper)

Also available at:

MOTILAL BANARSIDASS
41 U.A. Bungalow Road, Jawahar Nagar, Delhi 110 007
8, Mahalaxmi Chamber, Warden Road, Mumbai 400 026
120 Royapettah High Road, Mylapore, Madras 600 004
Sanas Plaza, Subhash Nagar, Pune 411 002
16 St. Mark's Road, Bangalore 560 001
8 Camac Street, Calcutta 700 017
Ashok Rajpath, Patna 800 004
Chowk, Varanasi 221 001

PRINTED IN INDIA
BY JAINENDRA PRAKASH JAIN AT SHRI JAINENDRA PRESS,
A-45 NARAINA, PHASE I, NEW DELHI 110 028
AND PUBLISHED BY NARENDRA PRAKASH JAIN FOR
MOTILAL BANARSIDASS PUBLISHERS PRIVATE LIMITED,
BUNGALOW ROAD, DELHI 110 007

PREFACE.

The present edition contains the whole of the text of he Harshacharita (Uchchhvāsas I–VIII). As there is at present no other annotated edition of the Harshacharita in the market, the present edition needs no apology. This edition will, it is hoped, meet all the requirements of the University student. No pains have been spared to make the book useful not only to the college student, but also to the general reader. As the work was published in two parts in two years, the paging of one part is independent of the other.

The commentary of S'aṃkara published by the Nirṇayasāgara Press has been highly useful to me. The elegant and spirited translation of the Harshacharita by Prof. Cowell and Mr. Thomas is a monument of skill and learning. Though I have unfortunately had frequent occasion to differ from them, my sincerest thanks are due to them, particularly for happy renderings of words and phrases. The Harshacharita is a difficult book and I am afraid that many passages have still remained obscure. I crave the indulgence of the reader and will most thankfully receive all suggestions and criticisms.

P. V. KANE.

A list of some of the abbreviations employed in the work.

अ०—The Nirṇaya-sāgara edition of the हर्षचरित.

अम०—अमरकोश.

अलं०—अलंकारसर्वस्व of रुय्यक.

उत्तरराम०—उत्तररामचरित of भवभूति.

क—The Calcutta edition of the Harshacharita by Īs vara-chandra Vidyāsāgara.

का० or **काम०**—कामन्दकीयनीतिसार.

काद०—कादम्बरी (Dr. Peterson's edition).

क्षीर०—क्षीरस्वामी, commentator of the अमरकोश.

चतु०—चतुर्वर्गचिन्तामणि of हेमाद्रि.

पा०—पाणिनि's अष्टाध्यायी.

ब—The edition of the Harshacharita in the Bombay Sanskrit Series.

बृह०—बृहत्संहिता of वराहमिहिर (edited by Prof. Kern).

भागवतपु०—भागवतपुराण. **महा०**—महाभारत (Bombay edition).

मनु०—मनुस्मृति. **मे०**—मेदिनीकोश.

याज्ञ० or **याज्ञवल्क्य०**—याज्ञवल्क्यस्मृति. **रघु०**—रघुवंश.

वायु०—वायुपुराण (Ānandās'rama ed.).

विष्णुपु० or **विष्णु०**—विष्णुपुराण. **शब्द०**—शब्दकल्पद्रुम.

सं०—संकेत, commentary on the हर्षचरित. **सि. कौ.** = सिद्धान्तकौमुदी.

A—The Nirṇaya-sāgara edition of the Harshacharita.

Anand. ed.—Ānandās'rama edition.

B—The edition of the Harshacharita in the Bombay Sanskrit Series.

B. R. W. W.—Beal's Buddhist records of the Western World.

C—Is'varachandra's edition of the Harshacharita.

C. I. or *C. I. I.*—Corpus Inscriptionum Indicarum.

C and *T*.—The translation of the Harshacharita by Prof. Cowell and Mr. Thomas.

E. I.—Epigraphia Indica.

I. A.—Indian Antiquary.

J. B. B. R. A. S.—Journal of the Bombay Branch of the Royal Asiatic Society.

J. R. A. S.—Journal of the Royal Asiatic Society.

P—Dr. Peterson's edition of the Kādambarī.

TABLE OF CONTENTS

Introduction.

I. Personal History of Bâṇa.

About the personal history of Sanskrit authors and especially poets, our knowledge is generally very meagre. In the case of many Sanskrit poets, we know next to nothing beyond their names. Around the names of some (*e. g.* Kâlidâsa), tradition has been busy in weaving such fanciful and bewildering stories that it is no easy task to separate the solid grain of truth from the chaff. In the case of some, the meagre account of themselves contained in their own works has to be eked out with information derived from contemporary or subsequent records in literature, grants and inscriptions. There are a few who have left to posterity a tolerably full account of themselves in their works*. Bâṇa perhaps stands at the head of such Sanskrit authors. To his Kâdambarî is prefixed a brief account of his family. But in his Harshacharita, we find a much fuller account of his ancestors and himself. The first two Uchchhvâsas of the Harshacharita are taken up with the history of Bâṇa's forefathers and Bâṇa himself. The personal narrative is continued even in the third Uchchhvâsa. Space does not permit us to give in detail a full account of Bâṇa as gathered from the Harshacharita. We propose to dwell upon only a few salient points of the narrative of Bâṇa's personal history.

The genealogical tree of Bâṇa's family as constructed

---

* In this connection we may mention Bilhaṇa and Mankha, who, in the Vikramânkadevacharita and the S'rîkaṇṭhacharita respectively, furnish a full account of their lives, their contemporaries &c.

from the Harshacharita* is given in the footnote below. In the introductory verses to the Kâdambarî the genealogy is given as follows. Kubera was a Brâhmaṇa of the Vâtsyâyana gotra and was honoured by many Gupta kings. His son was Arthapati, whose son was Chitrabhânu who was Bâṇa's father. The student will notice that in this narrative, Pâs'upata, who appears to have been the great-grand-father of Bâṇa, if we are to rely upon the Harshacharita, is omitted. It is strange that Bâṇa (or his son who is supposed by some to have written the introductory verses to the Kâdambarî) should have forgotten his own great-grand-father. The only explanation that we offer (of course with great hesitation) is that the verses containing the reference to Pâs'upata were not to be found in the Mss. used for preparing the printed editions of the Kâdambarî.

The progenitor of Bâṇa's family, Vatsa, lived in a place called Prîtikûṭa on the banks of the Hiraṇyabâhu, otherwise called S'oṇa. Bâṇa's mother, Râjadevî, died while he was yet a child. He was all the more dear to his father, who was a very mother to him. Bâṇa had the misfortune to lose his father when he was about fourteen years old. Bâṇa tells us that he thereafter led a wandering life. He mentions as the

---

* वत्स, cousin of सारस्वत who was the son of सरस्वती and दधीच.

कुबेर (a descendant of वत्स).

अच्युत ईशान हर पाशुपत

अर्थपति

भृगु हंस शुचि कवि महीदत्त धर्म जातवेदस् चित्रभानु त्र्यक्ष अहिदत्त विश्वरूप

बाण.

companions of his wanderings a number of persons*. Although Bâṇa had ancestral wealth sufficient to maintain him in ease and comfort, yet his strong curiosity to see differen' lands impelled him to wander from place to place and made him an object of ridicule in the eyes of his elderly contemporaries. After finishing his wanderings in which he gathered a rich harvest of wisdom and experience, he returned to his native place Brâhmaṇâdhivâsa (or Prîtikûṭa) with broadened sympathies and a widened outlook.

One day in the height of summer, when Bâṇa sat in his house after the midday meal his cousin (born of a S'ûdra woman) Chandrasena ushered in a courier who brought a letter from Kṛishṇa, a brother (cousin) of Emperor Harsha. In the letter Kṛishṇa referred Bâṇa to the messenger Mekhalaka and bade him lose no time in carrying out the wishes of the writer. The message was:— "Emperor Harsha's ears have been poisoned against you by some wicked people. But I knew the truth about you and interceded on your behalf with the king and told him that you (Bâṇa) must not have been guilty of anything beyond youthful rashness and folly. The king admits this and so you should come to the emperor's court without delay."

After a good deal of misgiving as to how he would be received at the court of Harsha, Bâṇa performed some auspicious rites and set out from his native place Prîtikûṭa. On the third day he reached the camp of Harsha which was then on the Ajirâvatî near the town Maṇitâra.

---

* "अभवंश्चास्य वयसा समानाः सुहृदः सहायाश्च । तथा च । भ्रातरौ पारशवौ चन्द्रसेनमातृषेणौ, भाषाकविरीशानः परं मित्रं, प्रणयिनौ रुद्रनारायणौ, विद्वांसौ वारबाणवासबाणौ, वर्णकविर्वेणीभारतः, प्राकृतकृत्कुलपुत्रो वायुविकारः, बन्दिनावनङ्गबाणसूचिबाणौ, कात्यायनिका चक्रवाकिका, जाङ्गुलिको मयूरकः, ताम्बूलदायकश्चण्डकः, भिषक्पुत्रो मन्दारकः, पुस्तकवाचकः सुदृष्टिः, कलादश्चामीकरः, हैरिकः सिन्धुषेणः, लेखको गोविन्दकः, चित्रकृद्वीरवर्मा, पुस्तकृत्कुमारदत्तः, मार्दङ्गिको जीमूतः, गायनौ सोमिलग्रहादित्यौ, सैरन्ध्री कुरङ्गिका, वांशिकौ मधुकरपारावतौ, गान्धर्वोपाध्यायो दर्दुरकः, संवाहिका केरलिका, लासकयुवा ताण्डविकः, आक्षिक आखण्डलः, कितवो भीमकः, शैलालियुवा शिखण्डकः, नर्तकी हरिणिका, पाराशरी सुमतिः, क्षपणको वीरदेवः, कथको जयसेनः, शैवो वक्रघोणः, मन्त्रसाधकः करालः, असुरविवरव्यसनी लोहिताक्षः, धातुवादविद्विहङ्गमः, दार्दुरिको दामोदरः, ऐन्द्रजालिकश्चकोराक्षः, मस्करी ताम्रचूडः ।"

When Bâṇa was presented to Harsha who had with him the son of the king of Mâlvâ, the emperor received him at first with mock signs of anger, but afterwards showed him much favour. After basking in the sunshine of royal favour, Bâṇa returned to his native place. He was greeted with a cordial welcome by his friends and relatives. The reader Sudṛishṭi entertained him with a recital of the Vâyupurâṇa. Then the bard Sûchîbâṇa recited two verses (Âryâs), which pointedly referred to the life of Harsha. All were charmed and Bâṇa's cousins (sons of his paternal uncles), Gaṇapati, Adhipaṭi, Târâpati and S'yâmala, looked at one another and the youngest of them, S'yâmala, made bold to ask Bâṇa to tell them from the beginning the wondrous story of Harsha's life. Bâṇa expressed his inability to do justice to the mighty deeds of the emperor and, as the day was far advanced, began the narrative the next morning.

Here ends the autobiographical part of the Harsha-charita with which alone we are concerned at present.

As to the later stages of Bâṇa's life we have no account left. He died leaving his romance of Kâdambarî unfinished. Bâṇa's son tells us in the introduction to the Uttarabhâga that he finished the Kâdambarî as a work of filial duty and not out of pride*. Dr. Buhler says that the name of Bâṇa's son was Bhûshaṇabâṇa†. In some MSS. of the Kâdambarî, the son is called Pulinda‡ or Pulina. Dhana-pâla, while praising Bâṇa in his introduction to the Tilaka-manjarî, seems to suggest that Pulinda was the name of his son§.

---

* "याते दिवं पितरि तद्वचसैव सार्धं विच्छेदमाप भुवि यस्तु कथाप्रबन्धः । दुःखं सतां तदसमाप्तिकृतं विलोक्य प्रारब्ध एव स मया न कवित्वदर्पात् ॥"

† See Dr. Peterson's Introduction to Kâdambarî p. 40.

‡ *Vide* Prof. S. R. Bhandarkar's report on the search for MSS. 1904–5, 1905–6 p. 39; see also Dr. Stein's catalogue of Sanskrit MSS. at Jammu p. 299.

§ केवलोऽपि स्फुरन्बाणः करोति विमदान्कवीन् ।
किं पुनः क्लृप्तसन्धानपुलिन्ध्र (न्द?) कृतसन्निधिः ॥ verse 26.

(It will be noticed that the verse has two meanings).

It is said that the poet Mayûra was a contemporary and father-in-law of Bâṇa. Mayûra praised the sun in hundred verses, which make up the Sûryas'ataka and became free from leprosy. Bâṇa became jealous of him, maimed himself, composed the Chaṇḍîs'ataka in honour of Durgâ, who made him all right. The story of Mayûra's freedom from disease is alluded to in the Kâvyaprakâs'a*. There are Subhâshitas in which Bâṇa and Mayûra are spoken of as contemporaries and as patronized by king Harsha†. Verses from the Sûryas'ataka are quoted in the Dhvanyâloka (latter half of 9th century A. D.)‡. The Kavikaṇṭhâbharaṇa of Kshemendra mentions Mayûra by name and quotes a verse as his which is found in the Sûryas'ataka§. So it is not beyond the bounds of probability that Bâṇa and Mayûra were contemporaries. A Mayûraka is mentioned as one of the companions of Bâṇa in his wanderings (see the passage quoted above on p. III). But as he is mentioned there as a snake-doctor ('Jângulika' = Vishavaidya), it seems to us that he is not the same as the poet Mayûra. The commentators of the Bhaktâmarastotra of the Jain Mânatungâchârya say that Mânatunga lived at the court of Bhoja in Ujjayinî and was a contemporary of Bâṇa and Mayûra. They further narrate various stories about Bâṇa and Mayûra. We believe that those stories have no historic basis and are purely imaginary. We therefore refrain from reproducing them here.

II The date of Bâṇa.

As we are fortunate in possessing some account of Bâṇa from his own pen, so also we are lucky in being able to fix

---

* 'आदित्यादेर्मयूरादीनामिवानर्थनिवारणम्'

† 'अहो प्रभावो वाग्देव्या यन्मातङ्गदिवाकरः ।
श्रीहर्षस्याभवत्सभ्यः समो बाणमयूरयोः ॥'

This verse is ascribed to Râjas'ekhara and is quoted in the Subhâshitâvali and the S'ârngadharapaddhati.

'स चित्रवर्णविच्छित्तिहारिणोरवनीपतिः ।
श्रीहर्ष इव सङ्घट्टं चक्रे बाणमयूरयोः ॥'
नवसाहसाङ्कचरित II. 18.

‡ The verse 'दत्तानन्दाः' &c. (9th in the Nir. ed. of सूर्यशतक.)

§ In the fourth सन्धि of the कविकण्ठाभरण the verse 'अस्तव्यस्तत्वशून्यो' &c. is quoted as Mayūra's (verse 18 of the सूर्यशतक).

(6) Abhinanda wrote the Kâdambarîkathâsâra, in which he faithfully versifies the story of Bâṇa's Kâdambarî. Abhinanda tells us that his great-great-grand-father, S'aktisvâmin was a minister of Muktâpîḍa, a king of the Karkoṭa family*. Abhinanda is praised for the excellence of his Anushṭubh verses by Kshemendra in his Suvṛitta-tilaka†.

(7) The author of the Dhvanyâloka, Ânandavardhana, flourished in the reign of king Avantivarman (855-883 A. D.)‡ of Kashmir. In the Dhvanyâloka, Bâṇa and his two prose compositions are mentioned by name$. From this it follows that in the latter half of the 9th century Bâṇa's works had attained a pre-eminent position in the world of letters.

(8) Vâmana, in his Kâvyâlaṃkârasûtravṛitti seems to quote a few words from the Kâdambarî§. Vâmana flour-

---

* स **शक्तिस्वामिनं** पुत्रमवाप श्रुतशालिनम् । राज्ञः **कर्कोटवंशस्य मुक्तापीडस्य मन्त्रिणम्** ॥ verse 7 of कादम्बरीकथासार.

† 'अनुष्टुप्सततासक्ता साभिनन्दस्य नन्दिनी । विद्याधरस्य वदने गुलिकेव प्रभावभूः ॥'

We wish here to call the attention of the reader to a curious fact. Abhinava-gupta says in his Dhvanyâlokalochana that Bhaṭṭajayantaka wrote Kâdambarîkathâ-sâra; p. 142 "कथातात्पर्ये सर्गबन्धो यथा भट्टजयन्तकस्य कादम्बरीकथासारम्." The question arises whether this is a different work from that of Abhinanda or whether it is a slip on the part of the learned author of the Lochana or whether it is a mistake of the scribe's. We know that Abhinanda was the son of Bhaṭṭajayanta, called Vṛittikâra.

‡ 'मुक्ताकणः शिवस्वामी कविरानन्दवर्धनः । प्रथां रत्नाकरश्चागात्साम्राज्येऽवन्तिवर्मणः ॥' राजतरङ्गिणी V. 34.

$ यथा स्थाण्वीश्वराख्यजनपदवर्णने **भट्टबाणस्य** 'यत्र च मत्तमातङ्गगामिन्यः' ध्वन्यालोक p. 100; यथा **हर्षचरिते** 'समवाय इव विरोधिनां पदार्थानाम्' p. 101; "यथा **हर्षचरिते** सिंहनादवाक्येषु—'वृत्तेऽस्मिन्महाप्रलये' p. 127; 'यथा **कादम्बर्यां** कादम्बरीदर्शनावसरे' p. 87. On p. 99 of the ध्वन्यालोक a passage is quoted from the Harshacharita (उच्छ्वास II) without naming it.

§ "'**अनुकरोति भगवतो नारायणस्य**' इत्यत्रापि, मन्ये, सशब्दः कविना प्रयुक्तो लेखकैस्तु प्रमादान्न लिखित इति" on 'आहेति भूतेऽन्यणलन्तभ्रमाद् ब्रुवो लटि' काव्यालंकारसूत्र V. 2. 44. For the words 'अनुकरोति भगवतो नारायणस्य' see कादम्बरी p. 6 of Dr. Peterson's edition.

ished in the latter half of the 8th century. We shall briefly indicate the data that enable us to arrive at this date for Vâmana. (a) Vâmana quotes from the Uttararâmacharita of Bhavabhûti a verse*. Bhavabhûti flourished before 700 A. D†. So Vâmana is later than 700 A. D. (b) He is often quoted by Pratîhârendurâja, the commentator of Udbhaṭa's Kavyâlaṃkâra‡. Pratîhârendurâja, who was a pupil of Mukula, son of Kallaṭa, flourished in the first half of the 10th century. Therefore Vâmana is earlier than 900 A. D. (c) Abhinavagupta says § that Ânandavardhana, bearing in mind the conflicting views of Vâmana and Bhâmaha as regards Samâsokti and Âkshepa, gave the verse 'Anurâgavatî sandhyâ' (p. 37 Dhvanyâloka) as an example. So according to Abhinavagupta, Vâmana flourished before Ânandavardhana *i. e.* before the latter half of 9th century A. D. (d) A Vâmana is mentioned as the minister ¶ of king Jayâpîḍa (745—776 A. D.) of Kashmir and is identified by Kashmirian Pandits with the author of the Kâvyâlaṃkârasûtra. These four lines of inquiry make it highly probable, if not certain, that Vâmana flourished in the latter half of the 8th century. Bâṇa's Kâdambarî was well-known, as shown above, in the latter half of the 8th century.

Thus from the 12th century backwards to the 8th, we have a host of writers who refer in unmistakable terms to Bâṇa and his works. Besides those mentioned by us above, there are writers of less note such as the authors of the Nalachampû and the Kîrtikaumudî that refer to Bâṇa. We refrain from quoting them for want of space.

The date of Bâṇa is of paramount importance for the chronology of Sanskrit writers. Bâṇa in the introduction to his Harshacharita mentions a number of Sanskrit works

---

* 'इयं गेहे लक्ष्मीरियममृतवर्तिर्नयनयोः' &c. on काव्यालंकारसूत्र IV. 3. 2. (रूपक).

† See Dr. Bhandarkar's preface to the Mâlatîmâdhava p. IX.

‡ See Folios 12, 55, 56, &c. of the Deccan College Ms. of Pratîhârendurâja's commentary.

§ 'वामनाभिप्रायेणायमाक्षेपः, भामहाभिप्रायेण तु समासोक्तिरित्यमुमाशयं हृदये गृहीत्वा समासोक्त्याक्षेपयोरिदमेकमेवोदाहरणं व्यतरद्ग्रन्थकृत्।' लोचन p. 37.

¶ 'मनोरथः शङ्खदत्तश्चटकः सन्धिमांस्तथा। बभूवुः कवयस्तस्य वामनाद्याश्च मन्त्रिणः॥' राजतरंगिणी IV. 497.

and poets*. The first half of the 7th century is the *terminus ad quem* of these poets. In this connection we strongly recommend that the student should read Dr. Peterson's valuable and instructive Introduction to his edition of the Kâdambarî. Although we have the misfortune to differ from the learned author of the Indroduction on a number of points, we feel confident that the Introduction will surely rouse the student's critical faculty†.

As one point (*viz.* the relative position of Subandhu and Bâṇa) on which we differ from Dr. Peterson is of great importance in connection with the date of Bâṇa, we shall discuss it here.

---

* The works and poets mentioned by name are:–Vyâsa, Vâsavadattâ, Bhaṭṭâra–Harichandra, Sâtavâhana, the Setu of Pravarasena, Bhâsa, Kâlidâsa, Bṛihatkathâ and Âḍhyarâja.

† The following are the most important among the points on which we differ from Dr. Peterson, though with the greatest diffidence:—(1) 'it is clear that by *Akhyâyikâ* in the present passage, Bâṇa refers *to metrical stories*, such as furnished him with the material of his own romance' (p. 70); (2) Bhâsa being the contemporary or immediate predecessor of Bâṇa (p. 71); (3) the Vâsavadattâ mentioned in the Harshacharita is not the one that was written by Subandhu; (4) the Nâṭakas, with a sûtradhâra in their beginning, were novelties in Bâṇa's day (p. 80); (5) Kâlidâsa was a contemporary of Bâṇa (p. 81); (6) Aḍhyarâja, mentioned in the Harshacharita, is not a proper noun (p. 96); (7) that Indian Astronomy, as taught by Âryabhaṭa and Varâhamihira and as known to Kâlidâsa and Bâṇa, is of Greek origin. About Âkhyâyikâ, we shall speak later on. It should be noted that in the Mâlavikâgnimitra, Kâlidâsa calls himself 'Vartamânakavi' and styles Bhâsa as of world-wide fame. So Bhâsa, who must have preceded Kâlidâsa by some generations, could not have been a contemporary or immediate predecessor of Bâṇa. We shall try to show that Subandhu preceded Bâṇa. That Âḍhyarâja was a name we know from a verse that occurs in the Sarasvatîkaṇthâbharaṇa (vol.I.p.136 Benares edition) 'केऽभूवन्नाढ्यराजस्य काले प्राकृतभाषिणः। काले श्रीसाहसाङ्कस्य के न संस्कृतभाषिणः ॥'. The commentary explains that आढ्यराज stands for शालिवाहन and साहसाङ्क for विक्रम. It is not possible to dismiss the other points briefly.

Dr. Peterson was inclined to place Subandhu, the author of the extant Vâsavadattâ, after Bâṇa. His reasons are given on pp. 71—73 of his introduction. 'For that after the graceless string of extravagant and indecent puns presented by the present Vâsavadattâ had been received with approval into the national literature, a reversion should have been possible to the chastity, alike of sentiment and of diction, of Bâṇa and Bhavabhûti would be a literary miracle almost incredible.' We have to strike here a note of caution. We should always beware of foisting our modern conceptions of literary style and beauty on authors and critics that flourished centuries before us. How are we to know that the skill of Subandhu in stringing together puns might not have kindled the admiration of Bâṇa who seems to have himself thought very highly of such puzzles as Prahelikâs? It is curious to note that Dr. Peterson, in his preface to the Subhâshitâvali of Vallabhadeva (p. 133), abandons the position taken up by him as to the relative position of Subandhu and Bâṇa in his introduction to the Kâdambarî.

We think that the Vâsavadattâ praised in the Harshacharita so * eloquently is the present work of that name written by Subandhu. Our reasons are:—

(1) In Vâmana's Kâvyâlamkârasûtravṛitti, a passage is quoted which is found in the Harshacharita and the extant Vâsavadattâ of Subandhu with very slight variations †.

---

* कवीनामगलद्दर्पो नूनं **वासवदत्तया** । शक्त्येव पाण्डुपुत्राणां गतया कर्णगोचरम् ॥. The महाभाष्य commenting on the वार्तिक 'अधिकृत्य कृत्ये ग्रन्थे लुबाख्यायिकाभ्यो बहुलम्' mentions three works of the आख्यायिका class, *viz.* वासवदत्ता, सुमनोत्तरा and भैमरथी (Kielhorn vol. II p. 313). In another place he speaks of a person who studies the आख्यायिका वासवदत्ता (vol II p. 284). It is not probable that Bâṇa refers to this work. It is to be noted that the extant वासवदत्ता would have to be called a कथा and not an आख्यायिका as defined below.

† 'कुलिशशिखरखरनखरप्रचयप्रचण्डचपेटापाटितमत्तमातङ्गकुम्भस्थलगलन्मदच्छटाच्छुरितचारुकेसरभारभासुरमुखे केसरिणि' काव्यालंकारसूत्रवृत्ति I. 3. 25. See Vâsavadattâ (p. 331 of the S'rîrangam edition and p. 266 of Hall's). See हर्षचरित (उच्छ्वास VI) p. 40 of our text. In the वासवदत्ता the words are '०चपेटपाटितमत्तमातङ्गकुम्भस्थलरुधिरच्छटाच्छुरितचारुकेसरभारभासुरकेसरिकदम्बेन.' This correspondence between the वासवदत्ता and the हर्षचरित opens up the question whether Bâṇa

We have seen above that Vâmana probably flourished in the latter half of the 8th century and that he quotes the Kâdambarî also. It is difficult to say from what author Vâmana takes his quotation. But from the locative 'Kesariṇi' it seems that the Harshacharita is drawn upon.

(2) Kavirâja, the author of the Râghavapâṇḍavîya, mentions Subandhu, Bâṇa and himself as the masters of Vakrokti *. We think that the three are mentioned by the author in chronological order, placing himself last of all.

(3) Vākpatirâja, the author of Gauḍavaho, a Prakrit poem, refers to the composition of Subandhu †. No other poet bearing the name of Subandhu, except the author of the Vâsavadattâ, is known to us. Therefore we are justified in holding that Vâkpatirâja refers to the author of the extant Vâsavadattâ. Vâkpatirâja was a protégé of Yas'ovarman of Kânyakubja and an admirer (and perhaps friend and pupil) of Bhavabhûti. Pandit comes to the conclusion (Introduction to Gauḍavaho, p. 100) that Vâkpatirâja wrote his poem between 700-725 A. D. It is curious to note that while Vâkpatirâja mentions the work of Subandhu in the same breath with Bhâsa and Kâlidâsa, he is silent as regards Bâṇa who wrote a prose work similar to Subandhu's. What then is the probable conclusion ? It is that when Vâkpatirâja wrote Subandhu was a famous author while Bâṇa was yet unknown to fame.

From the foregoing it seems very probable that Subandhu, the author of the present Vâsavadattâ, preceded Bâṇa.

In Mankha's S'rikanṭhacharita we find a verse where both Bâṇa and Subandhu are praised together ‡.

---

actually borrowed the words of the वासवदत्ता. There are many passages where Bâṇa's words and ideas coincide with those of the Vâsavadattâ. For want of space we refrain from quoting them.

* 'सुबन्धुर्बाणभट्टश्च कविराज इति त्रयः । वक्रोक्तिमार्गनिपुणाश्चतुर्थो विद्यते न वा ॥' राघवपाण्डवीय I. 41.

† 'भासम्मि जलणमित्ते कन्तीदेवे अ जस्स रहुआरे । सोबन्धवे अ बन्धम्मि हारियन्दे अ आणन्दो ॥'

Pandit's Gaudavaho, verse 800.

‡ 'मेण्ठे स्वर्दिरदाधिरोहिणि वशं याते सुबन्धौ विधेः शान्ते हन्त च भारवौ विघटिते बाणे विषादस्पृशः ।' श्रीकण्ठचरित II. 53.

III Bâṇa's works.

Before proceeding with the subject of this section, a few remarks concerning the origin and development of Sanskrit Rhetoric and of Kathâ and Âkhyâyikâ in particular would not be out of place here.

The oldest writer who specifically mentions Âkhyâyikâs is Kâtyâyana*. Kâtyâyana seems to intimate that the Âkhyâyikâs he refers to were not the episodes contained in such books as the Mahâbhârata, but that they were independent and distinct works. Patanjali in his Mahâbhâshya, while commenting upon the above-mentioned Vârtika, gives the names of three Âkhyâyikâs, *viz.* Vâsavadattâ, Sumanottarâ and Bhaimarathî†. In another place Patanjali speaks of one who knows or studies the Âkhyâyikâ Vâsavadattâ or Sumanottarâ‡. Subandhu, who, we saw above, preceded Bâṇa, alludes to some canons of the art of poetry. In one place§ he says that the composition of a good poet should not contain superfluous words such as 'tu', 'hi' &c. In another place he says that the utterances of a good poet should be divided into Uchchhvâsas (chapters) and should contain fine puns and verses in the Vaktra metre¶. This seems to refer to what are called Âkhyâyikâs, as we shall see later on. Daṇḍin,|| who is gene-

---

* 'लुबाख्यायिकाभ्यो बहुलम्' a वार्तिक on 'अधिकृत्य कृते ग्रन्थे' पा० IV. 3. 87.; 'आख्यानाख्यायिकेतिहासपुराणेभ्यश्च' वार्तिक on पा० IV. 2. 60.

† "'अधिकृत्य कृते ग्रन्थे' बहुलं लुग्वक्तव्यः। वासवदत्ता सुमनोत्तरा। न च भवति। भैमरथी।"

‡ Mahâbhāshya (Kielhorn) vol. II. p. 284 'वासवदत्तिकः सौमनोत्तरिकः'. Vide p. XI above.

§ 'सत्कविकाव्यबन्ध इवाबद्धतुहिनः' वासवदत्ता p. 134 (Hall).

¶ 'दीर्घोच्छ्वासरचनाकुलं सुश्लेषवक्त्रघटनापटु सत्कविवचनमिव' वासवदत्ता p. 184 (Hall).

|| A few scholars are inclined to place Daṇḍin later. This is not the place to discuss at length the question. Our reasons for placing him in the 6th century are briefly these:—(1) he is mentioned as an ancient writer along with Bhâmaha and Udbhaṭa (latter half of 8th century) by Jayaratha (p. 3. अलङ्कारसर्वस्व); (2) Namisâdhu speaks of Daṇḍin as follows:— 'ननु दण्डि-मेधाविरुद्र-भामहादिकृतानि सन्त्येवालङ्कारशास्त्राणि' (p. 2 of रुद्रटकाव्यालङ्कार). We believe the authors are arranged chrono-

rally assigned to the 6th century A. D., refers to the distinction drawn between Kathâ and Âkhyâyikâ by certain writers, disapproves of it and finally says that both are different names for the same class of composition*. Daṇḍin further says that an Âkhyâyikâ should exhibit a profusion of compounds†. The lexicon of Amarasiṃha defines‡ Kathâ and Âkhyâyikâ, pointing out that the former is imaginary and has very little historical value, while the latter deals with matters of history. Bâṇa himself often alludes to the two classes of prose compositions§. Bâṇa offers a glowing tribute of praise to the writers of Âkhyâyikâs that preceded him¶. He refers to some peculiarities that distinguished the Âkhyâyikâ from other classes of compositions, *viz.* division into Uchchhvâsas and the occurrence of the Vaktra metre. Bâṇa himself clearly intimates that his Harshacharita is an Âkhyâyikâ||. The introductory verses to the Pûrvabhâga clearly indicate that the Kâdambarî was intended to be a Kathâ ** (technically so called). This makes it clear that Bâṇa *did not* strike out a new path in writing his two prose works, that he had before him certain works which went under the name of Âkhyâyikâ and that criticism had been busy in laying down canons for regulating the two classes of prose compositions.

---

logically, as मेधाविरुद्र is mentioned in Bhâmaha's work; (3) Daṇḍin's treatment appears crude and unscientific as compared with Bhâmaha's; (4) Bhâmaha in a few places refers to the opinions of some (अपरे, अन्ये &c.) and these are found in Daṇḍin's work. (5) Tamil and Canarese writers belonging to the 8th century refer to him.

* See Kâvyâdars'a I. 23–30.

† 'तद्गुरूणां लघूनां च बाहुल्याल्पत्वमिश्रणैः । उच्चावचप्रकारं तद् दृश्यमाख्यायिकादिषु ॥' काव्यादर्श I. 81.

‡ 'आख्यायिकोपलब्धार्था' अमर० I. 6. 5; 'प्रबन्धकल्पना कथा'.

§ 'काव्यनाटकाख्यानकाख्यायिकालेख्यव्याख्यानादिक्रियानिपुणैः' p. 3 of कादम्बरी (Peterson); 'कथासु नाटकेषु आख्यायिकासु काव्येषु' p. 75 (Peterson).

¶ **उच्छ्वासान्तेऽ** प्यखिन्नास्ते येषां **वक्त्रे** सरस्वती । **कथमाख्यायिकाकारा** न ते वन्द्याः **कवीश्वराः** ॥' हर्षचरित.

|| 'तथापि नृपतेर्भक्त्याभीतो निर्वहणाकुलः । **करोम्याख्यायिकाम्भोधौ** जिह्वाप्लवनचापलम् ॥' हर्षचरित.

** 'द्विजेन तेनाक्षतकण्ठकौण्ठ्यया महामनोमोहमलीमसान्धया । अलब्धवैदग्ध्यविलासमुग्धया धिया निबद्धेयमतिद्वयी **कथा** ॥'

It is believed by some Sanskrit scholars that Bâṇa wrote before Sanskrit rhetoricians had done their best to degrade the sublime art of poetry to a pedantic enumeration of set similes and metaphors (*vide* Dr. Peterson's Introduction p. 43). We hold, with the greatest deference, that this is, to a great extent, fallacious. We possess ample evidence to establish that long before Bâṇa flourished, the science of Rhetoric had made great progress. We find that an inscription of Rudradâman (150 A. D.) exhibits a prose containing very long compounds, alliteration (Anuprâsa) and other figures*. In the same inscription reference is made to prose (Gadya) and poetry (Padya) that are ornate, fine on account of the (poetic) conventions observed in them and that contain perspicuous, short, sweet, striking and charming words†. An inscription of the time of Samudragupta (4th century A. D.) contains a prose that vies with that of Bâṇa himself‡. The Mandasor inscription dated in the Mâlava era 529 (*i. e.* 473 A. D.) contains verses that rival in diction and imagery the best efforts of Kâlidâsa, Bhavabhûti and other masters of classical Sanskrit. § Daṇḍin, who, as we said above, is not placed later than the 6th century A. D., gives a tolerably full treatment of Rhetoric. He says that he only improves upon what other Âchâryas that preceded him

---

* See Archaeological Survey, Western India. vol. II (about Kathiawad) p. 128.

† 'स्फुटलघुमधुरचित्रकान्तशब्दसमयोदारालङ्कृतगद्यपद्य'

‡ Dr. Fleet's Corpus Inscriptionum Indicarum vol. III. p. 8. Mark the following 'कृपणदीनानाथातुरजनोद्धरणसमन्त्रदीक्षाद्युपगतमनसः समिद्धस्य विग्रहवतो लोकानुग्रहस्य धनदवरुणेन्द्रान्तकसमस्य स्वभुजबलविजितानेकनरपतिविभवप्रत्यर्पणनित्यव्यापृतायुक्तपुरुषस्य निशितविदग्धमतिगान्धर्वललितैर्व्रीडितत्रिदशपतिगुरुतुम्बुरुनारदादेर्विद्वज्जनोपजीव्यानेककाव्यक्रियाभिः प्रतिष्ठितकविराजशब्दस्य' &c.

§ See Dr. Fleet's Corpus Inscriptionum vol. III p. 76ff. We shall quote only two verses. 'चतुःसमुद्रान्तविलोलमेखलां सुमेरुकैलासबृहत्पयोधराम् । वनान्तवान्तस्फुटपुष्पहासिनीं कुमारगुप्ते पृथिवीं प्रशासति ॥ स्मरवशगतरुणजनवल्लभाङ्गनाविपुलकान्तपीनोरु–स्तनजघनघनालिङ्गननिर्भर्त्सिततुहिन–हिमपाते ॥' It will be noticed that the second verse (an Âryâ) forms a single compound.

had laid down*. Daṇḍin asserts that a profusion of compounds is the very life of prose†. This dictum has been followed by later prose-writers only too well. Bhaṭṭi devotes four *sargas* of his Bhaṭṭikâvya to the illustration of subjects that properly fall to be treated under Rhetoric. He exemplifies more than thirty figures of speech. He wrote in Valabhi under a king named Dharasena. Four kings of the Valabhi dynasty bore the name Dharasena. The dates of the four kings fall between about 500 A. D. and 651 A. D. So Bhaṭṭi was a predecessor or at least a contemporary of Bâṇa. In Subhandhu's Vâsavadattâ we meet with a number of allusions to Rhetoric. Subandhu boasts of his skill in composing a work full of paronomasia on each syllable‡. He refers to S'ṛinkhalâbandha (a peculiar arrangement of words) and mentions the figures of speech Utpreksha and Âkshepa§. Bâṇa refers to such puzzles and conundrums as Prahelikâ and mentions in the introduction to the Harshacharita a few figures of speech such as Jâti (Svabhâvokti), Utprekshâ and S'lesha¶. In the Introduction to the Kâdambarî are mentioned the figures Dîpaka, Upamâ, S'lesha and Jâti.

In this brief *resume* we have shown that, before Bâṇa flourished, Rhetoric had made great progress, though it had not reached perfection.

The Harshacharita $ and the Kâdambarî are well-known as the works of Bâṇa. A third work, the Chaṇḍîs'ataka,

* 'किं तु बीजं विकल्पानां पूर्वाचार्यैः प्रकल्पितम् । तदेव परिसंस्कर्तुमयमसत्परिश्रमः ॥' काव्यादर्श II. 2.

† 'ओजः समासभूयस्त्वमेतद्गद्यस्य जीवितम् ।' काव्यादर्श I. 80.

‡ सरस्वतीदत्तवरप्रसादश्चक्रे सुबन्धुः सुजनैकबन्धुः । प्रत्यक्षरश्लेषमयप्रबन्धविन्यासवैदग्ध्यनिधिर्निबन्धम् ॥

§ 'शृङ्खलाबन्धो वर्णग्रथनासु उत्प्रेक्षाक्षेपौ काव्यालङ्कारेषु' वासवदत्ता p. 126 (Hall).

¶ 'अक्षरच्युतकमात्राच्युतकबिन्दुमतीगूढचतुर्थपादप्रहेलिकाप्रदानादिभिः' p. 3 of कादम्बरी (Peterson); 'बिन्दुमतीं चिन्तयता प्रहेलिकां भावयता' p. 88 of कादम्बरी.

$ The learned translators of the Harshacharita intimate that the Harshacharita was forgotten by Indian writers, though rare copies existed unknown in libraries. They mention only the साहित्यदर्पण and the काव्यप्रकाश as referring to the हर्षचरित. We is ascribed to him. There is nothing improbable in Bâṇa's authorship of a century of verses in honour of Chaṇḍî. We know that he gives in the Kâdambarî a powerful and picturesque description of the temple of Chaṇḍikâ. Still many hesitate to assert that Bâṇa *was* the author of the Chaṇḍîs'ataka*. A drama styled Pârvatîpariṇaya is also ascribed to Bâṇa. In the prelude to the Pârvatîpariṇaya, we are told that the drama was composed by Bâṇa of the Vatsa Gotra†. The author of the Kâdambarî also was descended from Vatsa. The drama, though not of the highest order of merit, has some excellences of its own. The subject is the same as that of the Kumârasambhava of Kâlidâsa. There are remarkable coincidences, both of phrase and thought, between the two works. Hence it is said by some scholars that the Pârvatîpariṇaya is only the work of a plagiarist and not of an eminent author like Bâṇa. We think, however, that this argument does not possess much force. We know that the fine verses of Kâlidâsa were the delight of Bâṇa and had kindled his admiration‡. When the subject was the same, it was quite natural that Bâṇa should unconsciously imitate in thought and expression his favourite author. Even in Kâlidâsa we recognise the words of the Mahâbhârata and the Bhagvatgîtâ. It is further argued that the Pârvatîpariṇaya is, as compared with the Harshacharita and the Kâdambarî, quite common-place. We

---

have quoted above passages from आनन्दवर्धन, नमिसाधु and रुय्यक that mention the हर्षचरित by name. It is clear that, at all events in Kashmir, the Harshacharita was carefully preserved and studied. For Kalhaṇa's indebtedness to the Harshacharita, see Dr. Stein's Kalhaṇa vol. I p. 133.

* We may draw the attention of the reader to the fact that verses from the Chaṇḍîs'ataka occur in the सरस्वतीकण्ठाभरण, in the काव्यप्रकाश and in अर्जुनवर्मदेव's टीका on अमरुशतक. अर्जुनवर्मदेव (p. 3) expressly ascribes the authorship of the चण्डीशतक to बाण "उपनिबद्धं च भट्टबाणेनैवंविध एव संग्रामप्रस्तावे देव्यास्तद्भङ्गिभिर्भगवता भर्गेण सह प्रीतिप्रतिपादनाय बहुधा नर्म-यथा 'दृष्टावासक्तदृष्टिः' &c." (verse 37 of चण्डी०)

† 'अस्ति कविसार्वभौमो वत्सान्वयजलधिसम्भवो बाणः । नृत्यति यद्रसनायां वेधोमुखलासिका वाणी ॥' 4th verse, Act I.

‡ 'निर्गतासु न वा कस्य कालिदासस्य सूक्तिषु । प्रीतिर्मधुरसान्द्रासु मञ्जरीष्विव जायते ॥' Introduction to हर्षचरित.

think that this, even if entirely true, would not militate against Bâṇa's authorship of the work. The work might have been written before Bâṇa had attained the mastery of his mature years. In the Pârvatîpariṇaya we find that Bâṇa is feeling his way. His prose in the drama reminds us of the Kâdambarî and the Harshacharita. Many ideas and turns of expression are common to the drama and the two prose works of Bâṇa. We cite below only one of them for want of space*. Besides we must not forget that Bâṇa was handicapped in verse. We have quoted above a critic's opinion that Bâṇa does not excel so much in verse as in prose. That remark could not have been based on the few verses that occur in the two prose works of Bâṇa. They rather refer to some compositions in verse written by Bâṇa. We suggest that the Pârvatîpariṇaya may be one of them. Chanḍapâla and Guṇavinayagaṇi, the commentators of the Nalachampû of Trivikramabhaṭṭa, inform us that Bâṇa wrote a drama entitled Mukuṭatâḍitaka†. We know nothing about this drama from other sources. Kshemendra quotes a verse as Bâṇa's‡, in which the sad plight of Kâdambarî due to separation from her lover is described. It seems therefore that Bâṇa wrote, according to Kshemendra, the story of Kâdambarî in verse also.

In the Kâvyaprakâs'a we read that Bâṇa obtained money from king Harsha§. A few scholars relying upon Kashmir tradition are of opinion that the drama Ratnâvali was really

---

* Act I 'हिमवान्—देवि कन्यापितृत्वं खलु गृहमेधिनामधिकतरं दुःखमावहति ।...कुचयुगलं परिणद्धं यथा यथा वृद्धिमेति तन्वङ्ग्याः । वरचिन्ताहृतमनसस्तथा तथा कार्श्यमेति मे गात्रम् ॥'. Compare this with the passage in the हर्षचरित (उच्छ्वास IV) 'हृदयमन्धकारयति मे दिवसमिव पयोधरोन्नतिरस्याः ।...सेयं सर्वाभिभाविनी शोकाग्नेर्दाह शक्तिर्यदपत्यत्वे समानेऽपि जातायां दुहितरि दूयन्ते सन्तः' (p. 13 of our text).

† "यदाह मुकुटताडितकनाटके बाणः 'आशाः प्रोषितदिग्गजा इव गुहाः प्रध्वस्तसिंहा इव द्रोण्यः कृत्तमहाद्रुमा इव भुवः प्रोत्खातशैला इव । बिभ्राणाः क्षयकालरिक्तसकलत्रैलोक्यकष्टां दशां जाताः क्षीणमहारथाः कुरुपतेर्देवस्य शून्याः सभाः ॥' "

‡ "यथा वा भट्टबाणस्य-'हारो जलार्द्रवसनं नलिनीदलानि प्रालेयशीकरमुचस्तुहिनांशुभासः । यस्येन्धनानि सरसानि च चन्दनानि निर्वाणमेष्यति कथं स मनोभवाग्निः ॥' अत्र विप्रलम्भभरभग्नधैर्यायाः कादम्बर्या विरहव्यथावर्णना &c." औचित्यविचारचर्चा.

§ 'श्रीहर्षादेर्बाणादीनामिव धनम्.' Many MSS. read धावकादीनाम्.

the work of Bâṇa, who, in return for the money bestowed by king Harsha upon him, published the work in his patron's name. This view seems to us to be entirely wrong. In the first place, there are three dramas, the Ratnâvali, the Priyadars'ikâ and the Nâgânanda, the authorship of which is claimed by Harsha. The Prastâvanâs to all the three dramas are identical almost word for word. In the Prastâvanâ of each of the three dramas Harsha is said to be the author. No one ascribes the Priyadars'ikâ and the Nâgânanda to Bâṇa. Hence the Ratnāvali also is not the work of Bâṇa. The Ratnâvali is quoted by Damodaragupta in his Kuṭṭanîmata (8th century A. D.). The Ratnâvali and the Nâgânanda are quoted by name in the Dhvanyâloka (p. 150, p. 176 respectively). The Ratnâvali is quoted at least a score of times in the Das'arûpa. The Nâgânanda and the Priyadars'ikâ are also quoted in the Das'arûpa but not so frequently. But in none of these writings is there the slightest hint that the author of the Ratnâvali was Bâṇa and not Harsha. It is remarkable that Kshemendra, himself a very erudite Kashmirian scholar, quotes some verses from the Ratnāvali and attributes them to S'rîharsha*.

The introductory verses attached to the Kâdambarî are supposed by some scholars to be the composition not of Bâṇa, but of his son or some one else. We demur to this conclusion on the following grounds. (a) If the verses had been written by Bâṇa's son, he would have referred to his authorship of them, as he does in the case of the introductory verses prefixed to the Uttarabhâga. Moreover he would not have mentioned his father in the colourless way in which the last verse (of the Pûrvabhâga) speaks of Bâṇa as 'Dvijena tena &c.' (b) Kshemendra quotes in his works at least four verses of the Introduction and twice distinctly says that they are Bâṇa's (in Auchityavichâracharchâ†

* In the कविकण्ठाभरण (सन्धि V) "इन्द्रजालपरिच्चयो यथा श्रीहर्षस्य 'एष ब्रह्मा सरोजे' &c. (रत्नावलि IV. 11). In the औचित्यविचारचर्चा he quotes the following verses as श्रीहर्ष's:—'परिम्लानं &c.' (रत्ना० II. 12); 'विश्रान्तविग्रहकथः &c.' (रत्ना० I. 8); 'उद्दामोत्कलिकां &c.' (रत्ना० II. 4); भयानके यथा श्रीहर्षस्य 'कण्ठे कृत्तावशेषं &c.', अपि च 'नष्टं वर्षवरैः' (रत्ना० II. 2–3).

† न तु यथा भट्टबाणस्य 'जयत्युपेन्द्रः स चकार दूरतः' &c.; the कविकण्ठाभरण quotes the verse 'कद्रु क्कणन्तो' &c. as Bāṇa's.

and the Kavikaṇṭhâbharaṇa). (c) It is next to impossible that Bâṇa, an orthodox writer, should have commenced his work without any kind of salutation at the beginning.

IV Kathâ and Âkhyâyikâ.

We shall now briefly indicate the characteristics of these two classes of writings as defined by Sankrit rhetoricians.

The earliest known writer. who puts down the points of difference between Kathâ and Âkhyâyikâ as defined by some rhetoricians (although he himself disapproves of them), is Daṇḍin. (1) In an Âkhyâyikâ, it is the hero himself who tells the whole story; while in a Kathâ, the story is told either by the hero or by someone else. (2) An Âkhyâyikâ is divided into sections named Uchchhvâsas and contains verses in the Vaktra and Aparavaktra metres, while in a Kathâ it is not so. (3) In a Kathâ, such topics as the kidnapping of a girl, battles, separation, the rise of the sun and the moon are described; in an Âkhyâyikâ it is not so. (4) A Kathâ is distinguished by possessing certain catchwords which the author intentionally puts in. Daṇḍin remarks that no hard and fast line of demarcation can be drawn between the two classes of works, and that the points mentioned above have not been invariably followed by writers and that hence Kathâ and Âkhyâyikâ are but two names for the same species of prose composition. Bhâmaha's definitions of Kathâ and Âkhyâyikâ are given below.* In Rudraṭa's Kâvyâlaṃkâra, Kathâ and Âkhyâyikâ are defined†. The author seems to have had in mind the Kâdambarî and the Harshacharita in defining the two species of prose composition. We have seen above that a profusion of compounds was said by Daṇḍin to constitute the very essence of prose and hence long compounds form the ruling characteristic of Kathâ and Âkhyâyikâ. But certain restrictions were laid

* प्रकृतानाकुलश्राव्यं शब्दार्थपदवृत्तिना । गद्येन युक्तोदात्तार्था सोच्छ्वासाऽऽख्यायिका मता ॥ वृत्तमाख्यायते तस्यां नायकेन स्वचेष्टितम् । वक्त्रं चापरवक्त्रं च काले भाव्यर्थशंसि च ॥ कवेरभिप्रायकृतैरङ्कनैः कैश्चिदङ्किता । कन्याहरणसंग्रामविप्रलम्भोदयान्विता ॥ न वक्त्रापरवक्त्राभ्यां युक्ता नोच्छ्वासवत्यपि । संस्कृतं संस्कृता चेष्टा कथाऽपभ्रंशभाक् तथा ॥ अन्यैः स्वचरितं तस्यां नायकेन तु नोच्यते । स्वगुणाविष्कृतिं कुर्यादभिजातः कथं जनः ॥ भामह I. 25–29.

† See Rudraṭa's Kâvyâlaṃkâra XVI. 20–30.

prose.* We give below a few verses containing appreciations of Bâṇa by various Sanskrit writers.†

We shall briefly point out some of the merits and defects of Bâṇa's writings. The student will do well to read Dr. Peterson's eloquent appreciation of Bâṇa in his Introduction to the Kâdambarî (pp. 36-43).

1. He shows great skill and discrimination in characterization. All the characters in the Kâdambarî are life-like and consistent. The gentle and youthful Hârîta; the generous and loving king Târâpîḍa; the trusted S'ukanâsa whose first thought was always for the king; the tender queen Vilâsavatî; the devoted Patralekhâ, who followed the prince Chandrâpîḍa like his shadow; the affectionate yet stern Kapinjala; Mahâs'vetâ, holy in mind as she was fair in body, who serves as the foil for the heroine; these are characters that are bound to make a deep impression on the heart of the reader. Bâṇa, however, lavished all his skill in depicting the hero and the heroine of his romance. We think that Bâṇa, as has been remarked in the case of Shakespeare, was more successful in delineating his heroine than his hero. 'On Kâdambarî in particular, Bâṇa has spent all his wealth of observation, fullness of imagery, and keenness of sympathy.' 'From the moment when for the first

---

* It was said by rhetoricians that prose was the touchstone of poets 'गद्यं कवीनां निकषं वदन्ति' quoted by वामन in his काव्यालङ्कारसूत्रवृत्ति on का. सू. I. 3. 21.

† शश्वद्बाणद्वितीयेन नमदाकारधारिणा ।
धनुषेव गुणाढ्येन निःशेषो रञ्जितो जनः ॥—नलचम्पू.
युक्तं कादम्बरीं श्रुत्वा कवयो मौनमाश्रिताः ।
बाणध्वनावनध्यायो भवतीति स्मृतिर्यतः ॥—कीर्तिकौमुदी I. 15.
जाता शिखण्डिनी प्राग्यथा शिखण्डी तथावगच्छामि ।
प्रागल्भ्यमधिकमाप्तुं वाणी बाणो बभूवेति ॥—आर्यासप्तशती of गोवर्धन.
केवलोपि स्फुरन्बाणः &c. quoted above from धनपाल's तिलकमञ्जरी.
सुबन्धुर्बाणभट्टश्च कविराज इति त्रयः ।
वक्रोक्तिमार्गनिपुणाश्चतुर्थो विद्यते न वा ॥—राघवपाण्डवीय I. 41.
श्लेषे केचन शब्दगुम्फविषये केचिद्रसे चापरेऽ-
लंकारे कतिचित्सदर्थविषये चान्ये कथावर्णने ।
आ सर्वत्र गभीरधीरकविताविन्ध्याटवीचातुरी-
सञ्चारी कविकुम्भिकुम्भभिदुरो बाणस्तु पञ्चाननः ॥—श्रीचन्द्रदेव,
(the last) quoted from Mr. Parakhi's work.

time her eye falls and rests on Chandrâpîḍa, this image of a maiden heart, torn by the conflicting emotions af love and virgin shame, of hope and despondency, of cherished filial duty and a new-born longing, of fear of the world's scorn and the knowledge that a world given in exchange for this will be a world well lost, takes full possession of the reader.

2. Though the Kâdambarî contains glowing descriptions of love, they are chaste and free from grossness of any kind. In this respect the Dasakumâracharita contrasts most unfavourably with the Kâdambarî. In the former, the reader is disgusted with the filthy intrigues of the ruffian heroes of that book.

3. Although Bâṇa was fettered by the canons of Rhetoric which laid down that long compounds were of the essence of prose, he displays considerable variety of style. His diction is generally smooth and graceful and he could write with force and brevity when it suited his purpose to do so. In this connection we may refer to the stern advice of Kapinjala to Punḍarîka. Bâṇa's prose is generally ornate and full of poetic fancies. He revels in the jingling assonance of sounds. Upamâ, Rûpaka and Utprekshâ are met with at every step. Among the other figures of speech may be mentioned Dîpaka, Sahokti, Virodha, Nidars'anâ and Vishama.

4. He seems to have been a close observer not only of courts and kings, but even of the less bright aspects of human life. His description of the old Draviḍa ascetic, though somewhat long-drawn and tedious, shows that he had an eye for the ridiculous and the bizarre. His descriptions of court and life in cities present a vivid picture of the time in which he lived. The advice of S'ukanâsa to Chandrâpîḍa is a masterpiece. It sets out very clearly all the evils that beset not only the path of Chandrâpîḍa, but of all princes in all climes. The Harshacharita of Bâṇa possesses great interest for the antiquarian from the fact that it affords a vivid picture of Indian society in the 7th century and of the manners and customs of those far-off days.

5. Bâṇa seems to have been a great lover of Nature. He is never tired of using for poetic purposes the flora and fauna of India. His references to plants and flowers, though sometimes overdrawn and fanciful, are generally charming.

6. Although most of the characters of the Kâdambarî are shadowy and some of them are in their second or even third birth, the poet's genius is so superb and his power of developing love and pathos is so great that the reader soon forgets the unreal character of the work and his mind is enthralled by the engrossing interest of the woes and happiness of the characters. 'We find ourselves face to face with the story of human sorrow and divine consolation, of death and the passionate longing for a union after death that goes straight from the heart of one who had himself felt the pang and nursed the hope, to us who are of like frame with him'. In the Harshacharita the hero is a historic personage. The author's task is thereby rendered more difficult. Yet Bâṇa acquits himself most creditably. It will be seen later on that he has nowhere stretched any point in favour of his hero and that his version is generally corroborated by independent evidence.

His defects.

One of the greatest flaws of Bâṇa's writings is that they abound in puns on words and recondite allusions. The reader is often at a loss, amidst the array of double-meaning words, bold and fanciful allusions, to grasp the exact meaning of the author. Though this is a blemish according to modern ideas of criticism, ancient India thought otherwise. These by-ways of puns were called Vakrokti (crooked speech), which was raised to the position of an Alaṃkâra. Subandhu, we have seen above, boasts of his skill in puns on each letter.

Another serious blemish is that in the Kâdambarî we meet with a defect in constructive art, which is due to the device of weaving stories within stories. The reader is unable to carry in his head the bewildering turns and convolutions of the story and the confusion of curses and counter curses. The fact that the greater part of the story is put in the mouth of a parrot is a serious drawback to the verisimilitude of the work.

Bâṇa seems to have had very little sense of proportion. In his descriptions of Mahâs'vetā and the temple of Chaṇḍikâ he tires the reader by dwelling too much on every detail. The patience of the reader is exhausted by the overloading of single words with epithets and of the epithets to these epithets. It sometimes so seems that the poet cares only for the gorgeous description of the evening, morning, moonrise or the limbs of the heroine and leaves the plot to take care of itself.

It is necessary to say a few words about Bâṇa's son. It may be at once admitted that the highest praise is due to the dutiful son of Bâṇa for having creditably performed his self-imposed task. He possesses not a few of the excellences of his father. He has almost the same command over the Sanskrit language as his father. His style is as ornate and as full of figures of speech as his father's. But we must not forget that in the son's work the defects of his father are exaggerated and others peculiar to the son alone are added. We miss in the Uttarabhâga the bold and striking fancies of Bâṇa with which we become familiar in the Pûrvabhâga. The description of the love torment of Kâdambarī is insipid and drawn out to a tedious length. The references to mythological and other lore are few and far between in the Uttarabhâga. The different lines of the story are made to converge far more rapidly than Bâṇa would have done. The picturesque descriptions of flora and fauna in which Bâṇa is profuse are lacking in the Uttarabhâga. Such masterpieces of realism as the advice of S'ukanâsa to Chandrâpîḍa are conspicuous by their absence in the Uttarabhâga. The perusal of the Uttarabhâga leaves the reader under the impression that the author was only anxious to bring the story to a close somehow. The touch of genius that appeals to the mind and makes the characters live before the eyes of the reader is altogether wanting.

VI The Harshacharita.

A comparison of the Harshacharita with the Kādambarī is instructive and interesting. Both works are composed in the same ornate and elaborate style. Both exhibit, more or less, the same merits and defects. But the Harshacharita is very much inferior to the Kādambarī as a literary work In the Harshacharita the author cares more for the jingling repetition of the same letters than in the Kādambarī. The puns are generally more laboured in the Harshacharita.

The Kādambarī is much more free from the use of provincial expressions than the Harshacharita. In the Harshacharita the author seems to have consciously employed a very large number of words that are found only in the lexicons. In the Harshacharita we never come across that subtle analysis of human nature that we meet with at every step in the Kādambarī. The characters of the Kādambarī are all of them painted with a finer brush than those in the Harshacharita. In the ease and flow of speech, in the force and vigour of thought and expression, and in the happy description of impulses, emotions and sentiments that sway human conduct, the Kādambarî vastly excels the Harshacharita. In the whole of the Harshacharita there is hardly any passage that approaches, in elegance and grace of language, in the keen observation of human nature and the springs of human action, in apt and happy sentiments, the advice of S'ukanāsa to Chandrāpîḍa or the friendly exhortation of Kapinjala to Puṇḍarîka. But the Harshacharita enjoys certain advantages over the Kādambarī. The Harshacharita is of prime importance to the historian of ancient India. It contains a mass of information on the state of ancient Indian society, on social and religious observances and practices, on military organization, on the actualities of life in camp and city, on the progress of medicine and the various arts and industries.

There is one striking point in which both the Kādambarī and the Harshacharita are similar. The hand of Death prevented the former work from being completed. The latter also comes to an abrupt conclusion. We can only speculate as to the reason why Bāṇa left only a partial account of the career of Harsha. Probably the author never intended to offer to the world a complete account of his patron's life.* Perhaps Bāṇa was swayed by the consideration that the glorious career of his patron after he re-

---

* It should be noted that Bāṇa expressed his inability to do justice to the whole of the career of Harsha and promised his cousins that he would deal only with a portion of it. 'कः खलु पुरुषायुषशतेनापि शक्नुयादविकलमस्य चरितं वर्णयितुम् । एकदेशे तु यदि कुतूहलं वः, सज्जा वयम्' 3rd उच्छ्वास.

covered his sister Rājyas'rī was very fresh in the memory of the people when he wrote and needed no words of praise from him. Bāṇa wrote the Harshacharita rather as a literary work than as a history of Harsha's reign and was satisfied when his Muse had taken a sufficiently long flight. Whatever may have been the reason, the student of Indian antiquities cannot but express his regret and mortification that the work was left incomplete.

Besides the Harshacharita, the writings of Chinese authors, particularly of Hiuen Tsang, supply reliable information about Harsha and his times. Moreover there are several inscriptions of Harsha himself and his contemporaries that shed a flood of light on the topics which the Harshacharita deals with. All this information, when put together, gives us a fairly accurate and life-like picture of the times of Harsha. But several considerations, particularly of space and utility, prevent us from entering into a detailed examination of the data furnished by the authorities indicated above. To those that desire a full treatment of this subject, we would recommend the standard work of Mr. V. A. Smith on the early History of India. All that we can endeavour to do here is to dwell upon some of the salient features of the life and career of Harsha as delineated in the Harshacharita, to note the important points of divergence between the Harshacharita and our other authorities and to supplement the information furnished by the Harshacharita from the other materials mentioned above.

VII The predecessors of Harsha.

The Harshacharita tells us that the remote ancestor of Harsha was Pushpabhūti. Between him and Prabhākaravardhana, father of Harsha, intervened several unnamed kings. The Madhuban and Banskhera copper-plates* of Harsha furnish the following genealogy:—

---

* The following is the text of the Madhuban copper-plate inscription of Harsha (See E. I. vol VII. p. 155 and also E. I. vol. I p. 67). ओम् । स्वस्ति महानौहस्त्यश्वजयस्कन्धावारात् **कपित्थिकाया:** महाराजश्री**नरवर्धन**स्तस्य पुत्रस्तत्पादानुध्यातः श्री**वज्रिणीदेव्या**मुत्पन्नः परमादित्यभक्तो महाराजश्री**राज्यवर्धन**स्तस्य पुत्रस्तत्पादानुध्यातः श्री**अप्सरोदेव्या**मुत्पन्नः परमादित्यभक्तो महाराजश्रीम**दादित्यवर्धन**स्तस्य पुत्रस्तत्पादानुध्यातः श्री**महासेनगुप्तादेव्या**मुत्पन्नश्चतुःसमुद्रातिक्रान्तकीर्तिः प्रतापानुरागोपनतान्यराजो वर्णाश्रमव्यवस्थापनप्रवृत्तचक्र एकचक्ररथ इव प्रजानामार्तिहरः परमादित्यभक्तः परमभट्टारकमहाराजाधिराज-

श्री**प्रभाकरवर्धन**स्तस्य पुत्रस्तत्पादानुध्यातः सितयशःप्रतानविच्छुरितसकलभुवनमण्डलः परिगृहीतधनदवरुणेन्द्रप्रभृतिलोकपालतेजाः सत्पथोपार्जितानेकद्रविणभूमिप्रदानसंप्रीणितार्थिहृदयोऽतिशयितपूर्वराजचरितो देव्याममलयशोमत्यां श्री**यशोमत्या**मुत्पन्नः परमसौगतः सुगत इव परहितैकरतः परमभट्टारकमहाराजाधिराजश्री**राज्यवर्धनः**

राजानो युधि दुष्टवाजिन इव श्री**देवगुप्ता**दयः
कृत्वा येन कशाप्रहारविमुखाः सर्वे समं संयताः ।
उत्खाय द्विषतो विजित्य वसुधां कृत्वा प्रजानां प्रियं
प्राणानुज्झितवानरातिभवने सत्यानुरोधेन यः ॥

तस्यानुजस्तत्पादानुध्यातः परममाहेश्वरो महेश्वर इव सर्वसत्त्वानुकम्पी परमभट्टारकमहाराजाधिराजश्री**हर्षः श्रावस्तीभुक्तौ कुण्डधानी**वैषयिक**सोमकुण्डका**ग्रामे समुपगतान् महासामन्त—महाराज—दौःसाधसाधनिक—प्रमातार—राजस्थानीय—कुमारामात्योपरिक—विषयपति—भटचाटसेवकादीन् प्रतिवासिजनपदांश्च समाज्ञापयति । अस्तु वः संविदितम् । अयं **सोमकुण्डका**ग्रामो ब्राह्मणवामरथ्येन कूटशासनेन भुक्तक इति विचार्य यतस्तच्छासनं भङ्क्त्वा तस्मादाक्षिप्य च स्वसीमापर्यन्तः सोद्रङ्गः सर्वराजकुलाभाव्यप्रत्यायसमेतः सर्वपरिहृतपरिहारो विषयादुद्धृतपिण्डः पुत्रपौत्रानुगश्चन्द्रार्कक्षितिसमकालीनो भूमिच्छिद्रन्यायेन मया पितुः परमभट्टारकमहाराजाधिराजश्री**प्रभाकरवर्धनदेवस्य** मातुः परमभट्टारिकामहादेवीराज्ञीश्री**यशोमतीदेव्याः** ज्येष्ठभ्रातृपरमभट्टारकमहाराजाधिराजश्री**राज्यवर्धनदेव**पादानां च पुण्ययशोभिवृद्धये सावर्णिसगोत्रच्छन्दोगसब्रह्मचारिभट्टवातस्वामि—विष्णुवृद्धसगोत्रबह्वृचसब्रह्मचारि—भट्टशिवदेवस्वामिभ्यां प्रतिग्रहधर्मणाग्रहारत्वेन प्रतिपादितः । विदित्वा भवद्भिः समनुमन्तव्यः प्रतिवासिजनपदैरप्याज्ञाश्रवणविधेयैर्भूत्वा यथासमुचिततुल्यमेयभागभोगकरहिरण्यादिप्रत्याया अनयोरेवोपनेयाः सेवोपस्थानं च करणीयमिति । अपि च

अस्मत्कुलक्रममुदारमुदाहरद्भिरन्यैश्च दानमिदमभ्यनुमोदनीयम् ।
लक्ष्म्यास्तडित्सलिलबुद्बुदचञ्चलाया दानं फलं परयशःपरिपालनं च ॥
कर्मणा मनसा वाचा कर्तव्यं प्राणिने हितम् ।
हर्षेणैतत्समाख्यातं धर्मार्जनमनुत्तमम् ॥

दूतकोऽत्र महाप्रमातार-महासामन्त-श्री**स्कन्दगुप्तः** महाक्षपटलाधिकरणाधिकृतसामन्तमहाराजेश्वरगुप्तसमादेशाच्चोत्कीर्णं गर्जरेण (गुर्जरेण?) । संवत् २० ५ मार्गशीर्ष वदि ६. The Banskhera plate of Harsha (see E. I. vol. IV p. 208 ff) contains the same details as above, except the following:—The charter is issued from Vardhamānakoṭî; the donees are Bālachandra, a Rigvedin of the Bharadvājagotra and Bhadrasvāmin, a Sāmavedin; the village granted is Markaṭasāgara, which was in the *Bhukti* of Ahichchhatrā and in the western *Pathaka* of the Angadîya *Vishaya*; the keeper of the records is one Bhāna or Bhānu and the concluding words are 'उत्कीर्णमीश्वरेणेदमिति संवत् २० २ कार्ति वदि १ स्वहस्तो मम महाराजाधिराजश्रीहर्षस्य ।'.

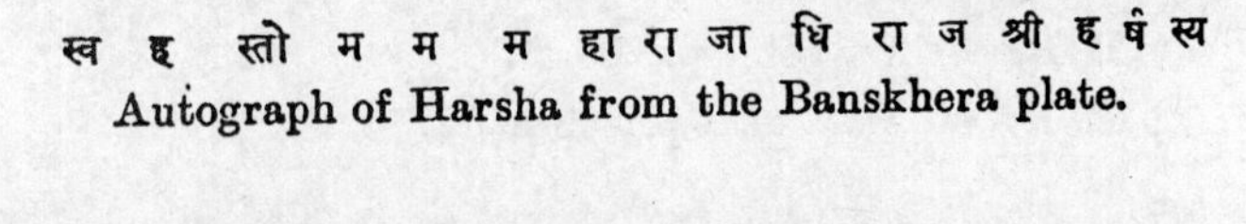

स्व ह स्तो म म म हा रा जा धि रा ज श्री ह र्ष स्य

Autograph of Harsha from the Banskhera plate.

Naravardhana=Vajriṇîdevî
|
Rājyavardhana=Apsarodevī
|
Âdityavardhana=Mahāsenaguptā
|
Prabhākaravardhana=Yas'omatī
|
Rājyavardhana | Harsha | Rājyas'ri

Hiuen Tsang begins with Prabhākaravardhana and informs us that Rājyavardhana was the elder brother of Harsha.* Bāṇa tells us that Harsha's ancestors ruled at Sthāṇvîs'vara (modern Thanesar), while Hiuen Tsang makes Kānyakubja the capital of Harsha.† The explanation probably lies in this fact that when Hiuen Tsang visited Harsha (which was about 643 A. D.), Kānyakubja was one of the capitals of Harsha's vast empire. When Rājyas'ri's husband Grahavarman was killed and she became a Buddhist nun, Harsha might have taken over the kingdom of Kanoj and made the latter his capital as being more in the centre of his dominions than Thanesar.

Hiuen Tsang tells us that the family of Harsha belonged to the Vais'ya caste. It has been rightly pointed out that the learned Chinese traveller confounds the third of the four principal castes with the Bais clan of Rajputs (who were Kshatriyas).‡ Bâṇa nowhere gives the slightest hint that the family of Harsha was not of Kshatriya descent. There are moreover indications to the contrary. Harsha's sister was married to Grahavarman, who came of the ancient Kshatriya family of the Maukharis (for whom see below). Prabhākaravardhana was the son of Mahāsenaguptā, who seems to have been the sister of Mahāsenagupta of Magadha. Unfortunately Bāṇa does not tell us the family from which

---

The Sonpat copper seal inscription of Harshavardhana (C. I. I. vol. III p. 231 ff), though much defaced, confirms the statements made in the two copperplates.

* See B. R. W. W. vol. I p. 210.

† B. R. W. W. vol. I p. 209.

‡ B. R. W. W. Vol. I p. 209 n. 12.

Harsha's mother came. Dr. Hoernle* thinks that her very name indicates that Yas'omatî must have been the daughter of the famous king of Mālava, Yas'odharma Vikramāditya. One fails to see how her very name shows that she was the daughter of Yas'odharman. Some support may be lent to the conjecture of Dr. Hoernle by the words of Yas'omatî that she was born in a family 'rendered glorious by Dharma'.† It further appears from certain words in the Harshacharita that Yas'omatî's father was a mighty warrior and that her parents were living at the time of her death.‡

The kingdom of Thanesar must not originally have been very large. It was surrounded on all sides by petty states, which waged constant wars among themselves. There is small wonder in this. Even Great Britain, which is such a small country, was divided only a few centuries ago into three kingdoms the rulers of which indulged in sanguinary feuds on the slightest pretexts. The inscriptions of Harsha style his ancestors (except Prabhākaravardhana) 'mahārāja'. It is only Prabhākaravardhana who is styled 'Mahārājādhirāja' which was one of the *birudas* of an aspirant for universal sovereignty. The Harshacharita informs us that Prabhākaravardhana fought successfully against the Hûṇas, the kings of Sindhu, Gurjara, Gāndhāra, Lāṭa (Broach) and Mālava. The conquest of the Hûṇas, if effected by Prabhâkaravardhana, must have been very perfunctory, as, a short time before his death, he had to send Râjyavardhana against them.

When Râjyavardhana came to the throne he must have been a very young man (about 19 or 20). We are told in the Harshacharita that the elder of the two Gupta princes named Kumāragupta, who was a companion of Rājyavardhana and Harsha, was about 18 years old. So Rājyavardhana was also of the same age at the time. Further we see that when Rājyavardhana returned after vanquishing

* See J. R. A. S. for 1903 p. 556.

† 'धर्मधवले कुले जाता' text p. 30 (5th उच्छ्वास).

‡ 'वीरजा वीरजाया &c.' text p. 30; 'अम्ब तात न पश्यतं पापां परलोकप्रस्थितां माम् &c.' same page.

the Hûṇas, there was a slight growth of hair on his chin. Harsha was the junior of Rājyavardhana by about four years and Rājyasrî was younger by about six years than her eldest brother. So Harsha and Rājyasrî were respectively about sixteen and fourteen years old when their father died. This is confirmed by the fact that Harsha is in several places* spoken of as '*Bāla*' and Rājyas'rî as 'Bālā.'† It seems that Prabhâkaravardhana died in 605 A. D. and therefore it follows that Harsha was born about 590 A. D. and ascended the throne in 606 A. D.‡ From the astronomical data furnished by Bāṇa about the birth of Harsha, Mr. C.V.Vaidya shows that Harsha was born on 4th June 590 A. D.§ Grahavarmā, the husband of Rājyas'rî, was killed by a king of Mālava. Who this Mālava king was is not quite clear. We are told in the Harshacharita that Rājyavardhana marched against this king with a small but picked force of cavalry under Bhaṇḍin and utterly routed him. In the inscriptions of Harsha we read that Rājyavardhana vanquished a certain king named Devagupta. As Rājyavardhana died very young he could not have waged many wars. Buhler conjectured with great probability that it was this Devagupta that had killed Grahavarman and was therefore chastised by Rājyavardhana. This conjecture is to some extent supported by the fact that the Harshacharita mentions a certain Gupta as having seized Kānyakubja.$ Dr Hoernle does not approve of the conjecture of Buhler. ¶ There are no doubt difficulties in the way of Buhler's guess. The two companions of Harsha and his elder brother are Mālava princes. Harsha is represented in the Harshacharita as very intimate with the younger of the two Mālava princes *viz.* Mâdhavagupta. ‖ In another place we find Harsha talking to 'the son of the

* See text p. 42 'यदि बाल इति नितरां तर्हि न परित्याज्योऽसि'; p. 56 'बाल एवाखण्डलभूमिमारूढः'; p. 85 'इयं नः स्वसा बाला च बहुदुःखखेदिता च.'

† See V. A. Smith's Early History of India p. 312 (2nd edition).

‡ See above p. IV.

§ See J. B. B. R. A. S. vol. 24 pp. 252–254.

$ See text p. 67 'गुप्तनाम्ना गृहीते कुशस्थले'.

¶ J. R. A. S. 1903 p. 561.

‖ See text p. 72 'अवलम्ब्य दक्षिणेन हस्तेन च माधवगुप्तमंसे'.

Mālava king that sat behind (Harsha)'.* So then it could not have been possible that these two princes were in any way related to the Mālava king that killed Grahavarmā. If they had been, they would naturally have been objects of suspicion rather than of trust. It is to be noted that Rājyas'rî is let off from imprisonment by a *certain noble* called Gupta.. † It is remarkable that he is not designated 'Rājaputra' or 'Rāja' but only 'Kulaputra.' So obviously he is not the king of Mālava that killed Grahavarmā nor can he be one of the two Gupta princes, the companions of Harsha, that were 'Rājaputras.' If it was Devagupta that killed Grahavarmā, he could not have been the same as the Mahārājādhirāja Devagupta of Magadha, whose approximate dates according to Dr. Fleet are 680-700 A. D. (see Deo Baranark Inscription pp. 213, 215) and who was the maternal grand-father of the Vākāṭaka king Pravarasena II (*vide* Chammak and Sivani copperplate inscriptions in C. I. vol. III pp. 240 and 247).

Rājyavardhana, young and confiding, was treacherously murdered, according to the Harshacharita, by a Gauḍa king. One MS. of the Harshacharita calls him Narendragupta. ‡ The commentator of the Harshacharita tells us that his name was S'as'ānka. He is corroborated by the statement of Hiuen Tsang that She-shang-kia (S'as'ānka) king of Karṇasuvarṇa (Bengal) murdered Rājyavardhana. § Bāṇa perhaps purposely omitted the express mention of the murderer of the reigning emperor's elder brother.$ But there are passages containing veiled allusions to the name S'as'ānka which we have pointed out in the notes (see *e. g.* text p. 38).

VIII The accession of Harsha and his relations with his contemporaries.

Bāṇa tells us that Harsha quietly ascended the throne

* 'पृष्ठतो निषण्णस्य मालवराजसूनोरकथयत्' 2nd उच्छ्वास.

† 'कान्यकुब्जाद्गौडसंभ्रमे गुप्तितो गुप्तनाम्ना कुलपुत्रेण निष्कासनम्' text p. 81.

‡ See E. I. vol. I. p. 70.

§ B. R. W. W. vol. I. p. 210.

$ Note the verse 'आत्मनाम गुरोर्नाम नामातिकृपणस्य च । श्रेयस्कामो न गृह्णीयाज्ज्येष्ठापत्यकलत्रयोः ॥'.

after the murder of his elder brother. But Hiuen Tsang has surrounded the accession of Harsha in an atmosphere of mystery and suspicion. We are told that the minister Bhaṇḍī asked the ministers to choose Harsha as king and that they accepted his advice; but Harsha had his own scruples and wanted to consult a statue of Avalokites'vara Bodhisattva on the Ganges before accepting the crown offered to him.* It is this account that leads Mr. V. A. Smith to remark that 'some unknown obstacle stood in the way of Harsha's accession and compelled him to rely for his title to the crown upon election by the nobles rather than upon his hereditary claims'.† We believe that the story was probably invented by the Buddhist admirers of Harsha to show that the latter was under the particular care of the Bodhisattva Avalokites'vara. We know from the Harshacharita that Bhaṇḍī, instead of being merely a great minister as Hiuen Tsang says, was a first cousin, being the mother's brother's son of Harsha and a very intimate friend. Bhaṇḍī was about eight years of age when Rājyas'rī was born and was thus slightly senior to Rājyavardhana. After ascending the throne Harsha started on his brilliant career of conquest and within a few years (about six) made himself the overlord of the whole of Northern India including Gujarat from the Himālayas to the Narmadā and from the bay of Bengal to Sindh. He had a long reign of about forty-two years and may fitly be styled the last Hindu Emperor of Northern India.

The Harshacharita contains a few references to these conquests. We are told in the third Uchchhvāsa that he vanquished the king of Sindhu and that he levied tribute from the Himālayan territory which is difficult of access.‡ On his relations with the Guptas we have already made a few remarks above. It seems that Harsha crowned Kumāragupta,§ the elder of the two Mālava princes, the companions

---

* See B. R. W. W. vol. I pp. 211-213.

† See Early History of India p. 312 (2nd edition).

‡ 'अत्र पुरुषोत्तमेन सिन्धुराजं प्रमथ्य लक्ष्मीरात्मीकृता ।...अत्र परमेश्वरेण तुषारशैलभुवो दुर्गाया गृहीतः करः'.

§ 'अत्र देवेनाभिषिक्तः कुमारः' 3rd उच्छ्वास and com. thereon.

of his boyhood. What became of this Kumāragupta we do not know. We saw above that the younger of the two Mālava princes, Mādhavagupta, was in high favour with Harsha. The Aphsad stone Inscription speaks of Mādhavagupta of Magadha who was anxious to meet the glorious Harsha.* The former was most probably the same as the favourite companion of Harsha's early years. Further particulars of the Guptas of Magadha may be learnt from Dr. Fleet's Gupta Inscriptions (pp. 200-218).† Another royal family with whom Harsha came in close contact was the Maukhari. His sister Rājyas'rî was married to Grahavarmā, son of Avantivarman. His capital was Kānyakubja. Bāṇa intimates that the Maukhari family was very ancient and highly honoured and that the Maukharis were great devotees of S'iva. ‡ Particulars of the Maukhari kings and their genealogy will be found in Dr. Fleet's Gupta Inscriptions pp. 219-230. The Maukharis and the Guptas of Magadha went often to war.§ The Harshacharita tells us that Kumāra alias Bhāskaravarman, king of Prāgjyotisha (Assam), formed a close friendship with Harsha on the eve of the latter's career of world conquest. Hiuen Tsang confirms this and tells us how once Harsha followed on the southern bank of the Ganges towards Kanoj while Kumāra-rāja kept pace with him on the northern. $

Harsha's glorious career of conquest suffered one memorable check. Pulakes'in II, the greatest of the

---

* See C. I. vol. III p. 200, 204 'श्रीहर्षदेवनिजसङ्गमवाञ्छया च.'

† Bāṇa says that one of his ancestors was honoured by several Guptas 'अनेकगुप्तार्चितपादपङ्कजः कुबेरनामांश इव स्वयम्भुवः' Introductory verses to the Kādambarî.

‡ The correct form seems to be मौखरि. Mark 'नमामि भर्वोश्चरणाम्बुजद्वयं सशेखरैर्मौखरिभिः कृतार्चनम् ।' Introductory verses to काद०. The Asirgad copper seal of S'arvavarman uses the words 'शर्ववर्मा मौखरिः' (C. I. vol. III. p. 220). But the Jaunpur stone inscription of ईश्वरवर्मन् sanctions the form मौखर 'मौखराणां भूभुजाम्' (C. I. vol. III p. 229).

§ See *e. g.* Aphsad Stone Inscription (C. I. vol. III p. 200, 203).

$ B. R. W. W. vol. I pp. 217-218; see also vol. II pp. 196-198, where Hiuen Tsang relates how he went to the court of Kāmarūpa.

religions in the times of Harsha, viz. Brahmanism, Buddhism and Jainism. Of these the last (particularly the Digambara sect of it) does not appear to have been popular in Northern India. The sight of a naked Jain ascetic is cited as a very bad omen.* The two other religions were in a flourishing state. It should not be supposed that ordinarily Buddhism was looked upon by orthodox Hindus as something to be abhorred. On the contrary Bāṇa everywhere speaks of things Buddhist with fairness and tolerance.† People passed from one persuasion to the other without much fear of persecution. So Divākaramitra is represented as originally being a student of the Maitrāyaṇîya recension of the Yajurveda and as passing over to Buddhism while still young. In spite of his Buddhistic predilections, he is waited upon by persons of various shades of opinions and beliefs, such as S'aivas, Bhāgavatas, Jainas, Paurāṇikas, Mîmāṇsakas, all intent upon arriving at the truth in the giddy whirlpool of opposing doctrines. Bāṇa, though himself an orthodox Brahmin writer, does not gloss over the fact that Rājyavardhana had strong leanings in favour of Buddhism. The companions of Rājyas'rî are represented as invoking the Buddha in their distress.‡ Bāṇa makes even Harsha say that he would don the red robes of the Buddhist order along with his sister after he had fulfilled his vow.§ Harsha describes in his inscription his brother Rājyavardhana as a very devout Buddhist (Paramasaugataḥ) and speaks of him more reverently than even his own father. The inscriptions of Harsha show that even in the royal family there was no strict adherence to a particular deity or form of faith. The three immediate ancestors of Harsha are described as great devotees of the sun (Paramādityabhaktaḥ). Bāṇa tells us that Pushpabhūti, the remote ancestor of Harsha, was a devout worshipper of S'iva.$ But Bāṇa himself describes how Prabhākara-

* *Vide* text p. 20 'अभिमुखमाजगाम शिखिपिच्छलाञ्छनो नग्नाटकः.'

† See *e. g.* text p. 78 ll 4–7.

‡ भगवन् भक्तजने सञ्ज्वरिणि **सुगत** सुप्तोऽसि' text p. 79.

§ 'इयं तु ग्रहीष्यति मयैव समं समाप्तकृत्येन काषायाणि' text p. 85.

$ 'तस्य...सहजैव...अन्यदेवताविमुखी...भगवति...भवे भूयसी भक्तिरभूत्' 3rd उच्छ्वास.

vardhana everyday devoutly worshipped the sun with red flowers. Harsha calls himself a devout worshipper of S'iva (Paramamāhes'varaḥ). The Sonpat seal of Harsha has the emblem of a Nandī. Bāṇa informs us that Harsha set out on his expedition after worshipping S'iva* and that the head accountant of the village where Harsha put up on the first day presented a golden seal with the crest of a bull. From these data one may say that between Brahmin and Buddhist and between the devotee of one deity and that of another there did not exist that great gulf which minds brought up in other environments are apt to suppose as having existed. There were certain root-ideas, certain habits of thought and modes of life, that were common to all. Coming to matters of detail, we find that Prabhākaravardhana celebrated many and elaborate sacrifices.† In describing the houses of his cousins, Bāṇa gives us an instructive picture of their surroundings in the 7th century A. D.‡ When Harsha made fun of Bāṇa by dwelling upon the wild years of his youth, Bāṇa in self-defence mentioned several things which entitled him to be better treated by the king.§ On his return from the court of Harsha, Bāṇa questions his kinsmen on matters that were vital to the Brahmins of his day, viz. the performances of sacrifices, the incessant study of the Vedas, of grammar, logic, the Mīmāṇsā and poetry. Bāṇa tells us that Paurāṇikas were as popular in those days as in these. His friend Sudṛishṭi treated him to a recital of the Vāyupurâṇa. We are told that Paurāṇikas clever in comforting those striken with grief surrounded Harsha after the death of his father. From the Kādambarī we learn that then as now the Mahābhārata was a favourite book with all, especially with women. The Harshacharita also dwells upon the popularity of the great

---

* 'विरचय्य परमया भक्त्या भगवतो नीललोहितस्यार्चाम्' text p. 53.

† Vide text pp. 2 and 38.

‡ Note the first paragraph of the 2nd उच्छ्वास.

§ 'ब्राह्मणोऽस्मि जातः सोमपायिनां वंशे वात्स्यायनानाम् । यथाकालमुपनयनादयः कृताः संस्काराः । सम्यक्पठितः साङ्गो वेदः । श्रुतानि यथाशक्ति शास्त्राणि । दारपरिग्रहादभ्यागारिकोऽस्मि ।...लोकद्वयाविरोधिभिस्तु चापलैः शैशवमशून्यमासीत् । अत्रानपलापोऽस्मि ।' 2nd उच्छ्वास.

epic.* The description of the rites performed when Prabhâkaravardhana was on his deathbed, though somewhat weird, shows us what popular Hindu religious practices and observances were in the 7th century A. D.† When Bâṇa started on his visit to Harsha, he gives us a graphic and entertaining description of the way in which an orthodox Brahmin should make preparations to leave his home on an important undertaking. The long and rather curious list of the companions of Bâṇa in his youth (p. III above) shows us with what a strange medley of people an orthodox Brâhmaṇa could associate without running any serious risk of losing caste or position. It is to be noted that two of his most intimate associates were his cousins born of a S'ûdra mother. We may draw the attention of the student to the elaborate descriptions of the festivities on the birth of Harsha‡ and the marriage of Rājyas'rī. §

Hiuen Tsang dwells at great length on the condition of religion in the times of Harsha. He mentions that towards the end of his career Harsha became a very devout Buddhist and once in every five years he held a great assembly when he emptied his treasury to give away all in charity. $ We hope that the student of the Harshacharita will not fail to read the curious incidents and ancedotes that the Chinese traveller relates conecrning Harsha.

XI. The text of the Harshacharita.

The present edition is based on three editions of the Harshacharita, *viz.* the Nirṇayasāgara edition, that in the Bombay Sanskrit Series and the Calcutta edition of Is'varachandra. The first and third agree closely. The edition of Dr. Fuhrer contains in the footnotes very valuable material derived from eight MSS. We do not follow any particular edition. All important readings have been discussed in the notes. In a few cases the punctuation is wrong in the text, but has been corrected in the notes.

---

* 'महाभारतभावितात्मानः' 3rd उच्छ्वास; 'कस्य न द्वितीयमहाभारते भत्रेदस्य चरिते कुतूहलम्' 3rd उच्छ्वास; 'विविधवीररसवृत्तान्तरामणीयकेन महाभारतमपि लघयन्निव' text p. 45.

† *Vide* text p. 21.

‡ Text pp. 7–9.

§ Text pp. 13–14.

$ B. R. W. W. Vol. I. pp. 214–215.

XII. Commentaries.

The only commentary available is the Sanketa written by S'ankara. The commentary so far as it goes is very valuable, particularly in the explanation of obscure words and puns. But it is very often meagre and passes over whole pages with scarcely a word of comment. So we did not include it in our edition. We know very little concerning the age or native place of the commentator. As the commentary has only been found in Kashmir, it is not unreasonable to suppose that S'ankara was a native of Kashmir. His father's name was Puṇyākara and he invokes Ganes'a at the beginning of his work. Among the authors and works named by him are:—Amarasiṃha, Kālidāsa, Kātyāyana author of the Vārtikas, Kṛishṇa (a Prakrit poet), Kauṭilya, Gāruḍas'āstra, Chāṇakya, Bharatamuni, Bhāmaha, Manu, Mahābhārata, Rājas'ekhara, Lāṭāchārya (an astronomical writer), Vātsyāyana (author of Kāmasūtra), Vyāḍi (author of the grammatical work Saṃgraha). Among the works from which quotations are taken without specifying the author are (besides those mentioned above):—Kāvyālaṃkâra of Udbhaṭa, Dhvanyâloka, Bhagavatgîtā, Meghadūta, Raghuvaṃs'a. The commentator very frequently refers to previous commentators in the words 'kechit', 'anye', 'apare' &c. At the end of his commentary S'ankara tells us that he follows tradition in explaining the difficult Harshacharita.* Hence it is clear that he was preceded by a number of commentaries.

As to the age of the commentator, we can give only an approximate result. As he either names or quotes from Rājas'ekhara, Udbhaṭa and the Dhvanyāloka, he is later than the 9th century A. D. But he is comparatively an early writer. One of the Mss of the commentary was, we are told by Dr. Fuhrer, dated Saṃvat 1520 i. e. 1464 A. D. if it is the Vikrama era to which the date refers, as is likely Besides the fact that, instead of quoting such eminent Âlaṃkārikas as Mammaṭa and Ruyyaka (both Kashmirians), he quotes the ancient Kashmirian rhetoricians Bhāmaha and

---

* 'दुर्बोधे हर्षचरिते संप्रदायानुरोधतः। गूढार्थोन्मुद्रणां चक्रे शङ्करो विदुषां कृते ॥'.

Udbhaṭa goes to strengthen the view that he was an early writer. He may therefore have flourished before the 12th century A. D.

It is to be noted that S'ankara cites a few vernacular words in explaining the Harshacharita. These may furnish some clue to his nationality.*

It appears that Ruyyaka, the famous author of the Alaṃkārasarvasva, wrote a commentary on the Harshacharita called Harshacharitavārtika.† The author of the commentary on the Vyaktiviveka of Mahimabhaṭṭa, who is generally regarded to be the same as Ruyyaka, also refers to his own commentary on the Harshacharita called Harshacharitavārtika.‡ It is a pity that this ancient commentary on the Harshacharita by so able and eminent a critic as Ruyyaka has not yet been brought to light. If it ever comes to light, it will be of great help in explaining many of the difficulties in the Harshacharita and in settling the text which is very corrupt in several places.

XIII The plan of the Notes.

The method adopted in the notes is as follows:—First of all a long passage is taken and is split up into clauses. Each difficult clause in then translated. In order to indicate clearly the meanings of words, Sanskrit words are often enclosed in brackets after their English equivalents. If a clause be difficult, the idea is expanded and clearly explained. Difficult compounds occurring in that clause are dissolved, quotations from kos'as such as that of Amarasiṃha are cited, references to mythology are dealt with at length and difficult words are traced to their origin. All grammatical peculiarities have been carefully noted. Parallel passages from the author's work or from the works of other authors

---

* *e. g.* on the word गुञ्जा he remarks 'सन्ना इति यस्य प्रसिद्धिः' notes p. 168; on प्रौढिक he says 'योग्याशनार्थं प्रसेवकः यो बुक्कण इति प्रसिद्धः'; on लम्बापटहाः he says 'तमिला इति प्रसिद्धाः' notes p. 175.

† p. 61 of अलङ्कारसर्वस्व. *Vide* p. VI above.

‡ 'एतदस्माभिर्हर्षचरितवार्तिके विस्तृत्य प्रतिपादितं तत एवावसेयम्' p. 44 of the commentary of the व्यक्तिविवेक (Trivandrum Sanskrit series).

are given to further elucidate the meaning. Bold type has been employed in the notes to draw attention to important citations. Only easy passages have not been fully translated.

XIV The Appendices.

The first appendix contains an abstract of the Harsha-charita. The second appendix contains the Suprabhâta-stotra. The third appendix is a general index dealing with proper names, mythological references, information of general interest and other kindred matters occurring in the notes.

हर्षचरितम् ।

प्रथम उच्छ्वासः ।

[1]नमस्तुङ्गशिरश्चुम्बिचन्द्रचामरचारवे ।
त्रैलोक्यनगरारम्भमूलस्तम्भाय शम्भवे ॥ १ ॥
हरकण्ठग्रहानन्दमीलिताक्षीं नमाम्युमाम् ।
कालकूटविषस्पर्शजातमूर्छागमामिव ॥ २ ॥
नमः सर्वविदे तस्मै व्यासाय कविवेधसे ।
चक्रे पुण्यं सरस्वत्या यो वर्षमिव भारतम् ॥ ३ ॥
प्रायः कुकवयो लोके रागाधिष्ठितदृष्टयः ।
कोकिला इव जायन्ते वाचालाः कामकारिणः ॥ ४ ॥
सन्ति श्वान इवासंख्या जातिभाजो गृहे गृहे ।
उत्पादका न बहवः कवयः शरभा इव ॥ ५ ॥
अन्यवर्णपरावृत्त्या बन्धचिह्ननिगूहनैः ।
अनाख्यातः सतां मध्ये कविश्चौरो विभाव्यते ॥ ६ ॥
श्लेषप्रायमुदीच्येषु प्रतीच्येष्वर्थमात्रकम् ।
उत्प्रेक्षा दाक्षिणात्येषु गौडेष्वक्षरडम्बरः[2] ॥ ७ ॥
नवोऽर्थो जातिरग्राम्या श्लेषोऽक्लिष्टः स्फुटो रसः ।
विकटाक्षरबन्धश्च कृत्स्नमेकत्र दुष्करम् ॥ ८ ॥
किं कवेस्तस्य काव्येन सर्ववृत्तान्तगामिनी ।
कथेव भारती यस्य न [3]व्याप्नोति जगत्रयम् ॥ ९ ॥
उच्छ्वासान्तेऽप्यखिन्नास्ते येषां वक्त्रे सरस्वती ।
कथमाख्यायिकाकारा न ते वन्द्याः कवीश्वराः ॥ १० ॥
कवीनामगलद्दर्पो नूनं वासवदत्तया ।
शक्त्येव पाण्डुपुत्राणां गतया कर्णगोचरम् ॥ ११ ॥

---

१ अस्मात्प्राक् 'इच्छादिशक्तिनिचयप्रसरक्रमेण विश्वावभासनविधौ प्रथितप्रभावा। याध्यायिनां हृदयकोकनदप्रतिष्ठा रूपं प्रकाशयति नौमि सरस्वतीं ताम्' इत्ययं श्लोको ब-पुस्तके दृश्यते. २ 'डम्बरम्' ब. ३ 'प्राप्नोति दिगन्तरम्' क.

पदबन्धोज्ज्वलो हारी कृतवर्णक्रमस्थितिः ।
भट्टारहरिचन्द्रस्य गद्यबन्धो नृपायते ॥ १२ ॥
अविनाशिनमग्राम्यमकरोत्सातवाहनः ।
विशुद्धजातिभिः कोशं रत्नैरिव सुभाषितैः ॥ १३ ॥
कीर्तिः प्रवरसेनस्य प्रयाता कुमुदोज्ज्वला ।
सागरस्य परं पारं कपिसेनेव सेतुना ॥ १४ ॥
सूत्रधारकृतारम्भैर्नाटकैर्बहुभूमिकैः ।
सपताकैर्यशो लेभे भासो देवकुलैरिव ॥ १५ ॥
निर्गतासु न वा कस्य कालिदासस्य सूक्तिषु ।
प्रीतिर्मधुरसान्द्रा[1]सु मञ्जरीष्विव जायते ॥ १६ ॥
समुद्दीपितकन्दर्पा कृतगौरीप्रसाधना ।
हरलीलेव नो कस्य विस्मयाय बृहत्कथा ॥ १७ ॥
आढ्यराजकृतोत्साहैर्हृदयस्थैः स्मृतैरपि ॥
जिह्वान्तः कृष्यमाणेव न कवित्वे प्रवर्तते ॥ १८ ॥
तथापि नृपतेर्भक्त्याभीतो निर्वहणाकुलः ।
करोम्याख्यायिकाम्भोधौ जिह्वाप्लवनचापलम् ॥ १९ ॥
सुखप्रबोधललिता सुवर्णघटनोज्ज्वलैः ।
शब्दैराख्यायिका भाति शय्येव प्रतिपादकैः ॥ २० ॥
जयति ज्वलत्प्रतापज्वलनप्राकारकृतजगद्रक्षः ।
सकलप्रणयिमनोरथसिद्धिश्रीपर्वतो हर्षः ॥ २१ ॥

एवमनुश्रूयते—पुरा किल भगवान्स्वलोकमधितिष्ठन्परमेष्ठी विकासिनि पद्मविष्टरे समुपविष्टः सुनासीरप्रमुखैर्गीर्वाणैः परिवृतो ब्रह्मोद्याः कथाः कुर्वन्नन्याश्च निरवद्या विद्यागोष्ठीर्भावयन्कदाचिदासाञ्चक्रे । तथासीनं च तं त्रिभुवनप्रतीक्ष्यं मनुदक्षचाक्षुषप्रभृतयः प्रजापतयः सर्वे च सप्तर्षिपुरःसरा महर्षयः सिषेविरे । केचिदृचः स्तुतिचतुराः समुदचारयन् । केचिदपचितिभाञ्जि यजूंष्यपठन् । केचित्प्रशंसासामानि जगुः । अपरे विवृतक्रतुक्रियातन्त्रान्मन्त्रान्व्याचचक्षिरे । विद्याविसंवादकृताश्च तत्र तेषामन्योन्यस्य विद्या[2]विवादाः प्रादुरभवन् ।

अथातिरोषणः प्रकृत्या महातपा मुनिरत्रेस्तनयस्तारापतेर्भ्राता नाम्ना दुर्वासा द्वितीयेन[3] मन्दपालनाम्ना मुनिना सह कलहायमानः साम गायन्क्रोधान्धो विस्वरमकरोत् । सर्वेषु च शापभयप्रतिपन्नमौनेषु मुनिष्वन्यालापलीलयावधीरयति कमलसम्भवे भगवती कुमारी किञ्चिदुन्मुक्तबालभावे

---

१ '०सार्द्रासु' क–ब. २ 'अन्योन्यस्य विवादाः' ब. ३ 'द्वितीयेनोपमन्युनाम्ना' ब.

भूषितनवयौवने वयसि[1] वर्तमाना, गृहीतचामरप्रचलद्भुजलता पितामहमुपवीजयन्ती, निर्भर्त्सनताडनजातरागाभ्यामिव स्वभावारुणाभ्यां पादपल्लवाभ्यां समुद्भासमाना, शिष्यद्वयेनेव पदक्रममुखरेण नूपुरयुगलेन वाचालितचरणा, मर्दन[2]नगरतोरणस्तम्भविभ्रमं बिभ्राणा जङ्घाद्वितयम्, सलीलमुत्कलहंसकुलकलालापप्रलापिनि मेखलाधाम्नि[3] विन्यस्तवामहस्तकिसलया, विद्वन्मानसनिवासलग्नेन गुणकलापेनेवांसावलम्बिना ब्रह्मसूत्रेण पवित्रीकृतकाया, भास्वन्मध्यनायकमनेकमुक्तानुयातमपवर्गमार्गमिव हारमुद्वहन्ती, वदनप्रविष्टसर्वविद्या[4]चरणालक्तकरसेनेव पाटलेन स्फुरता दशनच्छदेन विराजमाना, संक्रान्तकमलासनकृष्णाजिनप्रतिमां साममधुरगीताकर्णनावतीर्णशशिहरिणामिव कपोलस्थलीं दधाना, तिर्यक्सावज्ञमुन्नमितैकभ्रूलता, श्रोत्रमेकं विस्वरश्रवणकलुषितं प्रक्षालयन्तीवापाङ्गनिर्गतेन लोचनाश्रुजलप्रवाहेणेतरश्रवणेन च विकसितसितसिन्धुवारमञ्जरीजुषा हसतेव प्रकटितविद्यामदा, श्रुतिप्रणयिभिः प्रणवैरिव कर्णावतंसकुसुममधुकरकुलैरुपास्यमाना, सूक्ष्मविमलेन प्रज्ञाप्रतानेनेवांशुकेनाच्छादितशरीरा, वाङ्मयमिव निर्मलं दिक्षु दशनज्योत्स्नालोकं विकिरन्ती देवी सरस्वती श्रुत्वा जहास।

दृष्ट्वा च तां तथा हसन्तीं स मुनिः 'आः पापकारिणि, दुर्गृहीतविद्यालवावलेपदुर्विदग्धे, मामुपहससि' इत्युक्त्वा शिरःकम्पशीर्यमाणबन्धविशरारोरुन्मिषत्पिङ्गलिम्नो जटाकलापस्य रोचिषा[5] सिञ्चन्निव रोषदहनद्रवेण दश दिशः, कृतकालसन्निधानामिवान्धकारितललाटपट्टाष्टापदामन्तः[6]पुरमण्डनपत्रभङ्गमकरिकां भ्रुकुटिमाबध्नन्, अतिलोहितेन चक्षुषामर्षदेवतायै स्वरुधिरोपहारमिव प्रयच्छन्, निर्दयदष्टदशनच्छदभयपलायमानामिव वाचं रुन्धन्दन्तांशुच्छलेन, अंसावस्रंसिनः शापशासनपट्टस्येव ग्रथ्नन्ग्रन्थिमन्यथा कृष्णाजिनस्य, स्वेदकणप्रतिबिम्बितैः शापशङ्काशरणागतैरिव सुरासुरमुनिभिः प्रतिपन्नसर्वावयवः, कोपकम्पतरलिताङ्गुलिना करेण प्रसादनलग्नामक्षरमालामिवाक्षमालामाक्षिप्य कामण्डलवेन वारिणा समुपस्पृश्य शापजलं जग्राह।

अत्रान्तरे स्वयम्भुवोऽभ्याशे समुपविष्टा देवी मूर्तिमती पीयूषफेनपटलपाण्डरं कल्पद्रुमदुकूलवल्कलं वसाना, बिसतन्तुमयेनांशुकेनोन्नतस्तनमध्यबद्धगात्रिकाग्रन्थिः, तपोबलनिर्जितत्रिभुवनजयपताकाभिरिव तिसृभिर्भस्मपुण्ड्रकराजिभिर्विराजितललाटाजिरा, स्कन्धावलम्बिना[7] सुधाफेनधवलेन तपःप्रभावकुण्डलीकृतेन गङ्गा[8]स्रोतसेव योगपट्टकेन विरचितवैकक्ष्यका, सव्येन ब्रह्मोत्पत्तिपुण्डरीकमुकुलमिव स्फटिककमण्डलुं करेण कलयन्ती, दक्षिणम-

---

१ '०यौवने नवे वयसि' अ–क. २ 'धर्मनगर' ब. ३ 'धाम्नि' ब. ४ '०विद्यालक्तक०' अ–क. ५ 'शोचिषा' ब–क. ६ 'अन्तकमण्डन०' ब. ७ '०लम्बिना फेन०' ब. ८ 'गगनगङ्गा०' ब.

क्षमालाकृतपरिक्षेपं कम्बुनिर्मितोर्मिकादन्तुरितं तर्जनतरङ्गिततर्जनीकमुत्क्षिपन्ती करम्, 'आः पाप, क्रोधोपहत, दुरात्मन्, अज्ञ, अनात्मज्ञ, ब्रह्मबन्धो, मुनिखेट, अपसद, निराकृत, कथमात्मस्खलितविलक्षः सुरासुरमुनिमनुजवृन्दवन्दनीयां त्रिभुवनमातरं भगवतीं सरस्वतीं शप्तुमभिलषसि' इत्यभिदधाना, रोषविमुक्तवेत्रासनैरोङ्कारमुखरितमुखैरुत्क्षेपदोलायमानजटाभारभरितदिग्भिः परिकरबन्धभ्रमितकृष्णाजिनाटोपच्छायाश्यामायमानदिवसैरमर्षनिःश्वासदोलाप्रेङ्खोलितब्रह्मलोकैः सोमरसमिव स्वेदविसरव्याजेन स्रवद्भिरग्निहोत्रपवित्रभस्मस्मेरललाटैः कुशतन्तुचारुचामरचीरचीवरिभिराषाढिभिः प्रहरणीकृतकमण्डलुमण्डलैर्मूर्तैश्चतुर्भिर्वेदैः सह वृषीमपहाय सावित्री समुत्तस्थौ।

ततो 'मर्षय भगवन्, अभूमिरेषा शापस्य' इत्यनुनाथ्यमानोऽपि विबुधैः, 'उपाध्याय, स्खलितमेकं क्षमस्व' इति बद्धाञ्जलिपुटैः प्रसाद्यमानोऽपि स्वशिष्यैः, 'पुत्र, मा कृथास्तपसः प्रत्यूहम्' इति निवार्यमाणोऽप्यत्रिणा, रोषावेशविवशो दुर्वासाः 'दुर्विनीते, व्यपनयामि ते विद्याजनितामुन्नतिमिमाम्, अधस्ताद्गच्छ मर्त्यलोकम्' इत्युक्त्वा तच्छापोदकं विससर्ज। प्रतिशापदानोद्यतां सावित्रीं 'सखि, संहर रोषम्, असंस्कृतमतयोऽपि जात्यैव द्विजन्मानो माननीयाः' इत्यभिदधाना सरस्वत्येव न्यवारयत्।

अथ तां तथा शप्तां सरस्वतीं दृष्ट्वा पितामहो भगवान्कमलोत्पत्तिलग्नमृणालसूत्रामिव धवलयज्ञोपवीतिनीं तनुमुद्वहन्, उद्गच्छदच्छाङ्गुलीयकमरकतमयूखलताकलापेन त्रिभुवनोपप्लवप्रशमकुशापीडधारिणेव दक्षिणेन करेण निवार्य शापकलकलम्, अतिविमलदीर्घैर्भाविकृतयुगारम्भसूत्रपातमिव दिक्षु पातयन् दशनकिरणैः, सरस्वतीप्रस्थानमङ्गलपटहेनेव पूरयन्नाशाः स्वरेण, सुधीरमुवाच—'ब्रह्मन्, न खलु साधुसेवितोऽयं पन्था येनासि प्रवृत्तः। निहन्त्येष परस्तात्। उद्दामप्रसृतेन्द्रियाश्वसमुत्थापितं हि रजः कलुषयति दृष्टिमनक्षजिताम्। कियद्दूरं वा चक्षुरीक्षते। विशुद्धया हि धिया पश्यन्ति कृतबुद्धयः सर्वानर्थानसतः सतो वा। निसर्गविरोधिनी चेयं पयःपावकयोरिव धर्मक्रोधयोरेकत्र वृत्तिः। आलोकमपहाय कथं तमसि निमज्जसि। क्षमा हि मूलं सर्वतपसाम्। परदोषदर्शनदक्षा दृष्टिरिव कुपिता बुद्धिर्न त आत्मरागदोषं पश्यति। क्व महातपोभारवैवधिकता, क्व पुरोभागित्वम्। अतिरोषणश्चक्षुष्मानन्ध एव जनः। नहि कोपकलुषिता विमृशति मतिः कर्तव्यमकर्तव्यं वा। कुपितस्य प्रथममन्धकारीभवति विद्या, ततो भ्रुकुटिः। आदाविन्द्रियाणि रागः समास्कन्दति, चरमं चक्षुः। आरम्भे तपो गलति, पश्चात्स्वेदसलिलम्। पूर्वमयशः स्फुरति, अनन्तरमधरः। कथं लोकविनाशाय

---

१ 'आक्षेप' ब. २ 'कृष्णाजिनपटच्छाया' क. ३ 'इन्द्रियाधिष्ठानं रागः' ब.

ते विषपादपस्येव जटावल्कलानि जातानि । अनुचिता खल्वस्य मुनिवेशस्य हारयष्टिरिव वृत्तमुक्ता चित्तवृत्तिः । शैलूष इव वृथा वहसि कृत्रिममुपशमशून्येन चेतसा तापसाकल्पम् । अल्पमपि न ते पश्यामि कुशलजातम् । अनेनातिलघिम्नाद्याप्युपर्येव प्लवसे ज्ञानोदन्वतः । न खल्वनेलमूका एडा[1] जडा वा सर्वं एते महर्षयः । रोषदोषनिषद्ये स्वहृदये निग्राह्ये किमर्थमसि निगृहीतवाननागसं सरस्वतीम् । एतानि तान्यात्मप्रमाद[2]स्खलितवैलक्ष्याणि, यैर्याति[3] वाच्यतामविदग्धो जनः' इत्युक्त्वा पुनराह—'वत्से सरस्वति विषादं मा गाः । एषा त्वामनुयास्यति सावित्री विनोदयिष्यति चास्मद्विरहदुःखिताम् । आत्मजमुखकमलावलोकनावधिश्च ते शापोऽयं भविष्यति' इति । एतावदभिधाय विसर्जितसुरासुरमुनिमनुजमण्डलः ससंभ्रमोपगतनारदस्कन्धविन्यस्तहस्तः समुचिताह्निककरणायोदतिष्ठत् । सरस्वत्यपि शप्ता किञ्चिदधोमुखी धवलकृष्णशारां कृष्णाजिनलेखामिव[4] दृष्टिमुरसि पातयन्ती, सुरभिनिःश्वासपरिमललग्नैर्मूर्तैः शापाक्षरैरिव षट्चरणचक्रैराकृष्यमाणा, शापशोकशिथिलितहस्ता, अधोमुखीभूतेनोपदिश्यमानमर्त्यलोकावतरणमार्गेव नखमयूखजालकेन, नूपुरव्याहाराहूतैर्भवनकलहंसकुलैर्ब्रह्मलोकनिवासिहृदयैरिवानुगम्यमाना समं सावित्र्या गृहमगात् ।

अत्रान्तरे सरस्वत्यवतरणवार्तामिव कथयितुं मध्यमं लोकमवततारांशुमाली । क्रमेण च मन्दायमाने मुकुलितबिसिनीविसरव्यसनविषण्णसरसि वासरे, मधुमदमुदितकामिनीकोपकुटिलकटाक्षक्षिप्यमाण इव क्षेपीयः क्षितिधरशिखरमवतरति तरुणतरकपिलपनलोहिते लोकैकचक्षुषि भगवति, प्रस्नुत[5]मुखमाहेयीयूथक्षरत्क्षीरधाराधवलितेष्वासन्नचन्द्रोदयोद्दामक्षीरोदलहरीक्षालितेष्विव दिव्याश्रमोपशल्येषु, अपराह्णप्रचारचलिते चामरिणि चामीकरतटताडना[6]रुणितरदने रदति सुरस्रवन्तीरोधांसि स्वैरमैरावते, प्रसृतानेकविद्याधराभिसारिकासहस्रचरणालक्तकरसानुलिप्त इव प्रकटयति च तारापथे पाटलताम्, तारापथप्रस्थितसिद्धदत्तदिनकरास्तमयार्घ्यावर्जिते रञ्जितककुभि कुसुम्भभासि स्रवति पिनाकिप्रणतिमुदितसंध्यास्वेदसलिल इव रक्तचन्दनद्रवे, वन्दारुमुनिवृन्दारकवृन्दबध्यमानसंध्याञ्जलिवने ब्रह्मोत्पत्तिकमलसेवागतसकलकमलाकर इव राजति ब्रह्मलोके, समुच्चारिततृतीयसवन[7]ब्रह्मणि ब्रह्मणि, ज्वलितवैतानज्वलनज्वालाजटालाजिरेष्वारब्धधर्मसाधनशिबिरनीराजनेष्विव सप्तर्षिमन्दिरेषु, अघमर्षणमुषितकिल्बिषविषगदोल्लाघलघुषु यतिषु, संध्योपासनासीनतपस्विपङ्क्तिपूतपुलिने प्लवमाननलिनयोनियानहंसहासदन्तुरितोर्मिणि मन्दाकिनीजले, जलदेवतातपत्रे पत्त्ररथकुलकलत्रान्तःपुरसौधे

१ 'पण्डा जडा वा' क. २ 'प्रसाद' ब. ३ 'याप्यतां यात्यविदग्धो' अ–क.
४ अस्मातपरं 'तपसे' इत्यधिकं ब–पुस्तके. ५ 'प्रस्तुतमखमाहेयी' ब. ६ '०ताडनरणितरदने' अ–क. ७ 'सवनव्रतब्रह्मणि' ब.

निजमधुमधुरामोदिनि कृतमधुपमुदि मुमुदिषमाणे कुमुदवने, दिवसावसानताम्यत्तामरसमधुरमधुरसपीतिप्रीते सुषुप्सति मृदुमृणालकाण्डकण्डूयनकुण्डलितकन्धरे धुतपक्षराजिवीजितराजीव[१]सरसि राजहंसयूथे, तटलताकुसुमधूलिधूसरितसरिति स[२]रति सिद्धपुरपुरंध्रिधम्मिल्लमल्लिकागन्धग्राहिणि सायन्तने तनीयसि निशानिःश्वासनिभे नभस्वति, सङ्कोचोदञ्चदुच्चकेसरकोटिसङ्कटकुशेशय[३]कोशकोटरकुटीशायिनि षट्चरणचक्रे, नृत्तोद्धूतधूर्जटिजटाटवीकुटजकुड्मलनिकरनिभे नभस्थलं स्तबकयति तारागणे, संध्यानुबन्धताम्रे परिणमत्तालफलत्वक्त्विषि कालमेघमेदुरे मेदिनीं मीलयति नववयसि तमसि, तरुणतरतिमिरपटलपाटनपटीयसि समुन्मिषति यामिनीकामिनीकर्णपूरचम्पककलिकाकदम्बके प्रदीपप्रकरे, प्रतनुतुहिनकिरणकिरणलावण्यालोकपाण्डुन्याश्यानीलनीरमुक्तकालिन्दीकूल[४]वालुकापुलिनायमाने शातक्रतवे क्रशय[५]ति तिमिरमाशामुखे, खमुचि मेचकितविकचितकुवलयसरसि शशधरकरनिकरकचग्रहाविले विलीयमाने मानिनीमनसीव शर्वरीशबरीचिकुरचये चापपक्षत्विषि तमसि, उदिते भगवत्युदयगिरिशिखरकटककुहरहरिखरनखरनिवहहेतिनिहतनिजहरिणगलितरुधिरनिचयनिचितमिव लोहितं वपुरुदयरागधरमधरमिव विभावरीवध्वा धारयति श्वेतभानौ, अचलच्युतचन्द्रकान्तजलधाराधौत इव ध्वस्ते ध्वान्ते, गोलोकगलितदुग्धविसरवाहिनि दन्तमयमकरमुखमहाप्रणाल इवापूरयितुं प्रवृत्ते पयोधिमिन्दुमण्डले, स्पष्टे प्रदोषसमये सावित्री शून्यहृदयामिव किमपि ध्यायन्तीं सास्रां सरस्वतीमवादीत्—

'सखि, त्रिभुवनोपदेशदानदक्षायास्तव पुरो जिह्वा जिह्वेति मे जल्पन्ती। जानास्येव यादृश्यो विसंस्थुला गुणवत्यपि जने दुर्जनवन्निर्दाक्षिण्याः क्षणभङ्गिन्यो दुरतिक्रमणीया[६] न रमणीया दैवस्य वामा वृत्तयः। निष्कारणा च निकारकणिकापि कलु[७]षयति मनस्विनोऽपि मानसमसदृशजनादापतन्ती। अनवरतनयनजलसिच्यमानश्च तरुरिव विपल्लवोऽपि सहस्रधा प्ररोहति शोकः। अतिसुकुमारं च जनं सन्तापपरमाणवो मालतीकुसुममिव म्लानिमानयन्ति। महतां चोपरि निपतन्नणुरपि सृणिरिव करिणां क्लेशः कदर्थनायालम्। सहजस्नेहपाशग्रन्थिबन्धनाश्च बान्धवभूता दुस्त्यजा जन्मभूमयः। दारयति दारुणः क्रकचपात इव हृदयं संस्तुतजनविरहः। सा नार्ह[८]स्येवं भवितुम्। अभूमिः खल्वसि दुःखक्ष्वेडाङ्कुरप्रसवा[९]नाम्। अपि च पुराकृते कर्मणि बलवति शुभेऽशुभे वा फलकृति तिष्ठत्यधिष्ठातरि प्रष्ठे पृष्ठतश्च कोऽ-

१ 'राजीवरजसि' ब. २ एतन्नास्ति अ-क-पुस्तकयोः. ३ 'कुशेशयकोटर०' क; 'कुटीकोटर०' ब. ४ 'बालपुलिना०' अ-क. ५ 'कृशयति' अ. ६ 'क्रमणीया दैवस्य' ब. ७ 'क्लेशयति' ब. ८ एतन्नास्ति अ-क-पुस्तकयोः. ९ 'प्रभावानाम्' ब-क.

णोत् । उपजातकुतूहला च निर्गत्य लतामण्डपाद्विलोकयन्ती विकचकेतकीगर्भपत्रपाण्डुरं रजःसङ्घातं नातिदवीयसि संमुखमापतन्तमपश्यत् । क्रमेण च सामीप्योपजायमानाभिव्यक्ति तस्मिन्महति शफरोदरधूसरे रजसि पयसीव मकरचक्रं प्लवमानं पुरः प्रधावमानेन, प्रलम्बकुटिलकचपल्लवघटितललाटजूटकेन, धवलदन्तपत्रिकाद्युतिहसितकपोलभित्तिना, पिनद्धकृष्णागुरुपङ्ककल्कच्छुरणकृष्णशबलकषायकञ्चुकेन, उत्तरीयकृतशिरोवेष्टनेन, वामप्रकोष्ठनिविष्टस्पष्टहाटककटकेन, द्विगुणपट्टपट्टिकागाढग्रन्थिग्रथितासिधेनुना, अनवरतव्यायामकृशकर्कशशरीरेण, वातहरिणयूथेनेव मुहुर्मुहुः खमुड्डीयमानेन, लङ्घितसमविषमावटविटपेन, कोणधारिणा, कृपाणपाणिना, सेवागृहीतविविधवनकुसुमफलमूलपर्णेन, 'चल चल, याहि याहि, अपसर्पापसर्प, पुरः प्रयच्छ पन्थानम्' इत्यनवरतकृतकलकलेन, युवप्रायेण, सहस्रमात्रेण पदातिबलेन सनाथमश्ववृन्दं सन्ददर्श ।

मध्ये च तस्य सार्धचन्द्रेण मुक्ताफलजालमालिना विविधरत्नखण्डखचितेन शङ्खक्षीरफेनपाण्डुरेण क्षीरोदेनेव स्वयं लक्ष्मीं दातुमागतेन गगनगतेनातपत्रेण कृतच्छायम्, अच्छाच्छेनाभरणद्युतीनां निवहेन दिशामिव दर्शनानुरागलग्नेन चक्रवालेनानुगम्यमानम्, आनितम्बविलम्बिन्या मालतीशेखरस्रजा सकलभुवनविजयार्जितया रूपपताकयेव विराजमानम्, उत्सर्पिभिः शिखण्डखण्डि[१]कापद्मरागमणेररुणैरंशुजालैरदृश्यमानवनदेवताविधृतैर्बालपल्लवैरिव प्रमृज्यमानमार्गरेणु[२]परुषवपुषम्, बकुलकुड्मलमण्डलीमुण्डमालामण्डनमनोहरेण कुटिलकुन्तलस्तबकमालिना मौलिना मीलितातपं पिबन्तमिव दिवसम्, पशुपतिजटामुकुटमृगाङ्कद्वितीयशकलघटितस्येव सहजलक्ष्मीसमालिङ्गितस्य ललाटपट्टस्य मनःशिलापङ्कपिङ्गलेन लावण्येन लिम्पन्तमिवान्तरिक्षम्, अभिनवयौवनारम्भावष्टम्भप्रगल्भदृष्टिपाततृणीकृतत्रिभुवनस्य चक्षुषः प्रथिम्ना विकचकुमुदकुवलयकमलसरःसहस्रसञ्छादितदशदिशं शरदमिव प्रवर्तयन्तम्, आयतनयननदीसीमान्तसेतुबन्धेन ललाटतटशशिमणिशिलातलगलितेन कान्तिसलिलस्रोतसेव द्राघीयसा घोणावंशेन शोभमानम्, अतिसुरभिसहकारकर्पूरकक्कोललवङ्गपारिजातकपरिमलमुचा मत्तमधुकरकुलकोलाहलमुखरेण मुखेन सनन्दनवनं वसन्तमिव [३]वमन्तम्, आसन्नसुहृत्परिहासभावनोत्तानितमुखमुग्धहसितैर्दशनज्योत्स्नास्नपितदिङ्मुखैः पुनःपुनर्नभसि सञ्चारिणं चन्द्रालोकमिव कल्पयन्तम्, कदम्बमुकुलस्थूलमुक्ताफलयुगलमध्याध्यासितमरकतस्य त्रिकण्टककर्णाभरणस्य प्रेङ्खतः प्रभया समुत्सर्पन्त्या कृतसकुसुमहरितकुन्दपल्लवकर्णावतंसमिवोपलक्ष्यमाणम्, आमोदितमृगमदपङ्कलिखितपत्रभङ्गभास्वरं भुजयुगलमुद्दाममकराक्रान्तशिखरमिव म-

---

१ 'गण्डिका' क—ब. २ 'रेणुरूषितपरुष' ब. ३ 'अवतारयन्तम्' ब.

करकेतुकेतुदण्डद्वयं दधानम्, धवलब्रह्मसूत्रसीमन्तितं सागरमथनसामर्षगङ्गास्रोतःसन्दानितमिव मन्दरं देहमुद्वहन्तम्, कर्पूरक्षोदमुष्टिच्छुरणपांशुलेनेव कान्तोच्चकुचचक्रवाकयुगलविपुलपुलिनेनोरःस्थलेन स्थूलभुजायामपुञ्जितं पुरो विस्तारयन्तमिव दिक्चक्रम्, पुरस्तादीपदधोनाभिनिहितैककोणकमनीयेन पृष्ठतः कक्ष्याधिकक्षिप्तपल्लवेनोभयतः संवलनप्रकटितोरुत्रिभागेन हारीतहरिता निबिडनिपीडितेनाधरवाससा विभज्यमानतनुतरमध्यभागम्, अनवरतश्रमोपचितमांस[1]कठिनविकटमकरमुखसंलग्नजानुभ्यां विशालवक्षःस्थलोपलवेदिकोत्तम्भनशिलास्तम्भाभ्यां चारुचन्दनस्थासकस्थूलकान्तिभ्यामूरुदण्डाभ्यामुपहसन्तमिवैरावतकरायामम्, अतिभरितोरुभारवहनखेदेनेव तनुतरजङ्घाकाण्डम्, कल्पपादपपल्लवद्वयस्येव पाटलस्योभयपार्श्वावलम्बिनः पादद्वयस्य दोलायमानैर्नखमयूखैरश्वमण्डनचामरमालामिव रचयन्तम्, अभिमुखमुच्चैरुदञ्चद्भिरतिचिरमुपरि विश्राम्यद्भिरिव वलितविकटं पतद्भिः खुरैः खण्डितभुवि प्रतिक्षणदशन[2]ग्रहमुक्तिखणखणायितखरखलीने दीर्घघ्राण[3]लीनलालिकललाटलुलितचारुचामीकरचक्रके शिञ्जानशात[4]कौम्भजयनशोभिनि मनोरंहसि गोलाङ्गूलकपोलकालकायलोम्नि नीलसिन्धुवारवर्णे वाजिनि महति समारूढम्, उभयतः पर्याणपट्टश्लिष्टहस्ताभ्यामासन्नपरिचारकाभ्यां दोधूयमानधवलचामरिकायुगलम्, अग्रतः पठतो बन्दिनः सुभाषितमुत्कण्टकितकपोलफलकेन लग्नकर्णोत्पलकेसरपक्ष्मशकलेनेव मुखशशिना भावयन्तम्, अनङ्गयुगावतारमिव दर्शयन्तम्, चन्द्रमयीमिव सृष्टिमुत्पादयन्तम्, विलासप्रायमिव जीवलोकं जनयन्तम्, अनुरागमयमिव सर्गान्त[5]रमारचयन्तम्, शृङ्गारमयमिव दिवसमापादयन्तम्, रागराज्यमिव प्रवर्तयन्तम्, आकर्षणाञ्जनमिव चक्षुषोः, वशीकरणमन्त्रमिव मनसः, स्वस्थावेशचूर्णमिवेन्द्रियाणाम्, असन्तोषमिव कौतुकस्य, सिद्धयोगमिव सौभाग्यस्य, पुनर्जन्मदिवसमिव मन्मथस्य, रसायनमिव यौवनस्य, एकराज्यमिव रामणीयकस्य कीर्तिस्तम्भमिव रूपस्य, मूलकोषमिव लावण्यस्य, पुण्यकर्मपरिणाममिव संसारस्य, प्रथमाङ्कुरमिव कान्तिलतायाः, सर्गाभ्यासफलमिव प्रजापतेः; प्रतापमिव विभ्रमस्य, यशःप्रवाहमिव वैदग्ध्यस्य, अष्टादशवर्षदेशीयं युवानमद्राक्षीत्। पार्श्वे च तस्य द्वितीयमपरसंश्लिष्टतुरङ्गम्, प्रांशुमुत्तप्तपनीयस्तम्भाकारम्, परिणतवयसमपि व्यायामकठिनकायम्, नीचनखश्मश्रुकचम्, शुक्तिखलतिम्, ईषत्तुन्दिलम्, रोमशोरःस्थलम्, अनुल्बणोदारवेशतया जरामपि विनयमिव शिक्षयन्तम्, गुणानपि गरिमाणमिवानयन्तम्, महानुभावतामपि शिष्यतामिवानयन्तम्, आचारस्याचार्यकमिव कुर्वाणम्, धवलवारबाणधारिणम्, धौतदुकूलपट्टिकापरिवेष्टितमौलिं पुरुषम्।

---

१ 'मांसबन्धविकट' ब. २ 'दशनविमुक्त' अ–क. ३ 'घ्राणालीनलालिके ललाटपट्टलुठित' ब. ४ 'कुम्भायान' ब. ५ 'मार्गान्तरमानयन्तम्' अ–क.

अथ स युवा पुरोयायिनां यथादर्शनं प्रतिनिवृत्य[1] विस्मितमनसां कथयतां पदातीनां सकाशादुपलभ्य दिव्याकृति तत्कन्यायुगलमुपजातकुतूहलः प्रतूर्णतुरगो दिदृक्षुस्तं लतामण्डपोद्देशमाजगाम दूरादेव च तुरगादवततार। निवारितपरिजनश्च तेन द्वितीयेन साधुना सह चरणाभ्यामेव सविनयमुपससर्प। कृतोपसंग्रहणौ तौ सावित्री समं सरस्वत्या किसलयासनदानादिना सकुसुमफलार्घावसानेन वनवासोचितेनातिथ्येन यथाक्रममुपजग्राह। आसीनयोश्च तयोरासीना नातिचिरमिव स्थित्वा तं द्वितीयं प्रवयसमुद्दिश्यावादीत्—'आर्य, सहजलज्जाधनस्य प्रमदाजनस्य प्रथमाभिभाषणमशालीनता, विशेषतो वनमृगीमुग्धस्य कुलकुमारीजनस्य। केवलमियमालोकनकृतार्थाय चक्षुषे स्पृहयन्ती प्रेरयत्युदन्तश्रवणकुतूहलिनी श्रोत्रवृत्तिः। प्रथमदर्शने चोपायनमिवोपनयति[2] सज्जनः प्रणयम्। अप्रगल्भमपि जनं प्रभवता प्रश्रयेणार्पितं मनो मध्विव वाचालयति। अयत्नेनैव चातिनम्रे साधौ धनुषीव गुणः परां कोटिमारोपयति[3] विस्रम्भः। जनयन्ति च विस्मयमतिधीरधियामप्यदृष्टपूर्वा दृश्यमाना जगति स्रष्टुः सृष्ट्यतिशयाः, यतस्त्रिभुवनाभिभावि रूपमिदमस्य महानुभावस्य। सौजन्यपरतन्त्रा चेयं देवानांप्रियस्यातिभद्रता कारयति कथां न तु युवतिजने सहोत्था तरलता। तत्कथ्यतागमनेनापुण्यभाक्तमो विजृम्भितविरहव्यथः शून्यतां नीतो देशः। क्व वा गन्तव्यम्। कस्य वायमपहृतहरहुङ्काराहङ्कारोऽपर इवानन्यजो युवा। किंनाम्नः समृद्धतपसः पितुरयममृतवर्षी कौस्तुभमणिरिव हरेर्हृदयमाह्लादयति। का चास्य त्रिभुवननमस्या प्रभातसंध्येव महतस्तेजसो जननी। कानि वास्य पुण्यभाञ्जि भजन्त्यभिख्यामक्षराणि। आर्यपरिज्ञानेऽप्ययमेव क्रमः कौतुकानुरोधिनो हृदयस्य'। इत्युक्तवत्यां तस्यां प्रकटितप्रश्रयोऽसौ प्रतिव्याजहार—'आयुष्मति, सतां हि प्रियंवदता कुलविद्या। न केवलमाननं हृदयमपि च ते चन्द्रमयमिव सुधाशीकरशीतलैरानन्दयति वचोभिः। सौजन्यजन्मभूमयो भूयसा शुभेन सज्जननिर्माणशिल्पकला[4] भवादृश्यो जायन्ते। दूरे तावदन्योन्यस्यालापनमभिजातैः सह दृशोऽपि मिश्रीभूता[5] महतीं भूमिमारोपयन्ति। श्रूयताम्—अयं खलु भूषणं भार्गववंशस्य भगवतो भूर्भुवःस्वस्त्रितयतिलकस्य, अदभ्रप्रभावस्तम्भितजम्भारिभुजस्तम्भस्य, सुरासुरमुकुटमणिशिलाशयनदुर्ललितपादपङ्केरुहस्य, निजतेजःप्रसरप्लुष्टपुलोम्नश्च्यवनस्य बहिर्वृत्ति जीवितं दधीचो नाम तनयः। जनन्यस्य जितजगतोऽनेकपार्थिवसहस्रानुयातस्य शर्यातस्य सुता राजपुत्री त्रिभुवनकन्यारत्नं सुकन्या नाम। तां खलु देवीमन्तर्वर्तिनीं विदित्वा वैजनने मासि प्रसवाय पिता पत्युः पार्श्वात्स्वगृहमानाययत्। असूत च सा तत्र देवी

---

१ 'प्रतीत्य' अ. २ '०नयन्ति सज्जनाः' क. ३ 'कटिमारोहन्ति' ब. ४ 'शिल्पकला इव' ब. ५ 'मिश्रीकृता महतीं...पयन्ति प्रणयम्' ब.

दीर्घायुषमेनम् । अनेहसावर्धत तत्रैवायमानन्दितज्ञातिवर्गो बालस्तारकाराज इव राजीवलोचनो राजगृहे । भर्तृभवनमागच्छन्त्यामपि दुहितरि नासेचनकदर्शनमिममुमुञ्चन्मातामहो मनोविनोदनं नप्तारम् । अशिक्षतायं तत्रैव सर्वा विद्याः सकलाश्च कलाः । कालेन चोपारूढयौवनमिममालोक्याहमिवासावप्यनुभवतु मुखकमलावलोकनानन्दमस्येति मातामहः कथंकथमप्येनं पितुरन्तिकमधुना व्यसर्जयत् । मामपि तस्य देवस्य सुगृहीतनाम्नः शर्याततस्याज्ञाकारिणं विकुक्षिनामानं भृत्यपरमाणुमवधारयतु भवती । पितुः पादमूलमायान्तं मया साभिसारमकरोत्स्वामी । तद्धि नः कुलक्रमागतं राजकुलम् । उत्तमानां च चिरन्तनता जनयत्यनुजीविन्यपि जने कियन्मात्रमपि मन्दाक्षम् । अक्षीणः खलु दाक्षिण्यकोशो महताम् । इतश्च गव्यूतिमात्रमिव पारेशोणं तस्य भगवतश्च्यवनस्य स्वनाम्ना निर्मितव्यपदेशं च्यावनं नाम चैत्ररथकल्पं काननं निवासः । तदवधिश्चेयं नौ यात्रा । यदि च गृहीतक्षणं दाक्षिण्यमनवहेलं वा हृदयमस्माकमुपरि भूमिर्वा प्रसादानामयं जनः श्रवणार्हो वा, ततो न विमाननीयोऽयं नः प्रथमः प्रणयः कुतूहलस्य । वयमपि शुश्रूषवो वृत्तान्तमायुष्मत्योः । नेयमाकृतिर्दिव्यतां व्यभिचरति । गोत्रनामनी तु श्रोतुमभिलषति नौ हृदयम् । तत्कथय कतमो वंशः स्पृहणीयतां जन्मना नीतः । का चेयमत्रभवती भवत्याः समीपे समवाय इव विरोधिनां पदार्थानाम् । तथा हि । सन्निहितबालान्धकारा भास्वन्मूर्तिश्च, पुण्डरीकमुखी हरिणलोचना च, बालातपप्रभाधरा कुमुदहासिनी च, कलहंसस्वना समुन्नतपयोधरा च, कमलकोमलकरा हिमगिरिशिलापृथुनितम्बा च, करभोरुर्विलम्बितगमना च, अमुक्तकुमारभावा स्निग्धतारका च' इति । सा त्ववादीत्—'आर्य, श्रोष्यसि कालेन । भूयसो दिवसानत्र स्थातुमभिलषति नौ हृदयम् । अल्पीयांश्चायमध्वा । परिचय एव प्रकटीकरिष्यति । आर्येण न विस्मरणीयोऽयमनुषङ्गदृष्टो जनः' इत्यभिधाय तूष्णीमभूत् । दधीचस्तु नवाम्भोभरगम्भीराम्भोधरध्वाननिभया भारत्या नर्तयन्वनलताभवनभाजो भुजगभुजः सुधीरमुवाच—'आर्य, करिष्यति प्रसादमार्याराध्यमाना । पश्यामस्तावत्तातम् । उत्तिष्ठ । व्रजामः' इति । तथेति च तेनाभ्यनुज्ञातः शनकैरुत्थाय कृतनमस्कृतिरुच्चचाल । तुरगारूढं च तं प्रयान्तं सरस्वती सुचिरमुत्तम्भितपक्ष्मणा निश्चलतारकेण लिखितेनेव चक्षुषा व्यलोकयत् । उत्तीर्य शोणमचिरेणैव कालेन दधीचः पितुराश्रमपदं जगाम । गते च तस्मिन्सा तामेव दिशमालोकयन्ती सुचिरमतिष्ठत् । कृच्छ्रादिव च सञ्जहार दृशम् ।

अथ मुहूर्तमिव स्थित्वा स्मृत्वा च तां तस्य रूपसम्पदं पुनः पुनर्व्यस्मयतास्या हृदयम् । भूयोऽपि चक्षुराचकाङ्क्ष तद्दर्शनम् । अवशेव केनाप्य-

नीयत तामेव दिशं दृष्टिः। अप्रहितमपि मनस्तेनैव सार्धमगात्। अजायत च नवपल्लव इव बालवनलतायाः कुतोऽप्यस्या अनुरागश्चेतसि। ततः प्रभृति सालस्येव शून्येव सनिद्रेव दिवसमनयत्। अस्तमुपयाति च प्रत्यक्पर्यस्तमण्डले लाङ्गलिकास्तबकताम्रत्विषि कमलिनीकामुके कठोरसारसशिरःशोणशोचिषि सवित्रे त्रयीमये तेजसि, तरुणतरतमालश्यामले च मलिनयति व्योम व्योमव्यापिनि तिमिरसञ्चये, सञ्चरत्सिद्धसुन्दरीनूपुररवानुसारिणि च मन्दं मन्दं मन्दाकिनीहंस इव समुत्सर्पति शशिनि गगनतलम्, कृतसंध्याप्रणामा निशामुख एव निपत्य विमुक्ताङ्गी पल्लवशयने तस्थौ। सावित्र्यपि कृत्वा यथाक्रियमाणं सायन्तनं क्रियाकलापमुचिते शयनकाले किसलयशयनमभजत। जातनिद्रा च सुष्वाप।

इतरा तु मुहुर्मुहुरङ्गवलनैर्विलुलितकिसलयशयनतला निमीलितलोचनापि नाभजत निद्राम्। अचिन्तयच्च—'मर्त्यलोकः खलु सर्वलोकानामुपरि, यस्मिन्नेवंविधानि सम्भवन्ति त्रिभुवनभूषणानि सकलगुणग्रामगुरूणि रत्नानि। तथा हि। तस्य मुखलावण्यप्रवाहस्य निष्यन्दबिन्दुरिन्दुः। तस्य च चक्षुषो विक्षेपा विकचकुमुदकुवलयकमलाकराः। तस्य चाधरमणेर्दीधितयो विकसितबन्धूकवनराजयः। तस्य चाङ्गस्य परभागोपकरणमनङ्गः। पुण्यभाञ्जि तानि चक्षूंषि चेतांसि यौवनानि वा स्त्रैणानि, येषामसौ[1] विषयो दर्शनस्य। क्षणं नु दर्शयता च तमन्यजन्मजनितेनेव मे फलितमधर्मेण। का प्रतिपत्तिरिदानीम्' इति चिन्तयन्त्येव कथंकथमप्युपजातनिद्रा चिरात्क्षणमशेत। सुप्ता च तं दीर्घलोचनं स्वप्ने ददर्श। स्वप्नासादितद्वितीयदर्शना चाकर्णाकृष्टकार्मुकेण मनसि निर्दयम[2]ताड्यत प्रतिबुद्धा मकरकेतुना। मदनशरताडितायाश्च तस्या वार्तामिवोपलब्धुमरतिराजगाम। तथा हि। ततः प्रभृति कुसुमधूलिधवलाभिर्वनलताभिरताडितापि वेदनामधत्त। मन्दमन्दमारुतविधुतैः कुसुमरजोभिरदूषितलोचनाप्यश्रुजलं मुमोच। हंसपक्षतालवृन्त[3]वान्तवातविततैः शोणशीकरैरसिक्ताप्यार्द्रतामगात्। प्रेङ्खत्कादम्बमिथुनै[4]रनूढाप्यघूर्णत वनकमलिनीकल्लोलदोलाभिः। विघटमानचक्रवाकयुगलविसृष्टैरस्पृष्टापि श्यामतामाससाद विरहनिःश्वासधूमैः। पुष्पधूलिधूसरैरदष्टापि व्यचेष्टत मधुकरकुलैः।

अथ गणरात्रापगमे निवर्तमानस्तेनैव वर्त्मना तं देशमागत्य तथैव निवारितपरिजनश्छत्रधारद्वितीयो विकुक्षिर्ढुढौके। सरस्वती तु तं दूरादेव संमुखमागच्छन्तं प्रीत्या ससंभ्रममुत्थाय वनमृगीवोद्ग्रीवा विलोकयन्ती मार्गपरिश्रान्तमस्नपयदिव धवलितदशदिशा दृशा। कृतासनपरिग्रहं तु तं प्रीत्या सावित्री पप्रच्छ—'आर्य, कच्चित्कुशली कुमारः' इति। सोऽब्रवीत्—

१ 'येषामसावविषयः' ब. २ 'अताड्यत मकरकेतुना प्रतिबुद्धाया मदन०' अ-क. ३ '०वृन्तव्रात' अ-क. ४ 'मिथुनाभिरनूढा' अ-ब.

'आयुष्मति, कुशली । स्मरति च भवत्योः । केवलममीषु दिवसेषु तनीयसीमिव तनुं बिभर्ति । अविज्ञायमानां चानिमित्तां शून्यतामिवाधत्ते । अपि च । [1]अन्वेक्षमागमिष्यत्येव मालतीति नाम्ना वाणिनी वार्तां वो विज्ञातुम् । उच्छ्वसितं सा कुमारस्य' इति । तच्छ्रुत्वा पुनरपि सावित्री समभाषत—'अतिमहानुभावः खलु कुमारो यदेवमविज्ञायमाने क्षणदृष्टेऽपि जने परिचितिमनुबध्नाति । तस्य हि गच्छतो यदृच्छया कथमप्यंशुकमिव मार्गलतासु मानसमस्मासु मुहूर्तमासक्तमासीत् । अशून्यं हि सौजन्यमाभिजात्येन वः स्वामिसूनोः । अलसः खलु लोको यदेवं सुलभसौहार्दानि येनकेनचिन्न क्रीणाति महतां मनांसि । सोऽयमौदार्यातिशयः कोऽपि महात्मनामितरजनदुर्लभो येनोपकरणीकुर्वन्ति त्रिभुवनम्' इति । विकुक्षिरुच्चावचैरालापैः सुचिरमिव स्थित्वा यथाभिलषितं देशमयासीत् ।

अपरेद्युरुद्यति भगवति द्युमणावुद्दामद्युतावभिद्रुततारके तिरस्कृततमसि तामरस[2]व्यासव्यसनिनि सहस्ररश्मौ शोणमुत्तीर्यायान्ती, तरलदेहप्रभावितानच्छलेनात्यच्छं सकलं शोणसलिलमिवानयन्ती, स्फुटितातिमुक्तककुसुमस्तबकसमत्विषि सटाले महति मृगपताविव गौरी तुरङ्गमे स्थिता, सलीलमुरो[3]वंध्रारोपितस्य तिर्यगुत्कर्णतुरगाकर्ण्यमाननूपुरपटुरणितस्यातिबहलेन पिण्डालक्तकेन पल्लवितस्य कुङ्कुमपिञ्जरितपृष्ठस्य चरणयुगलस्य प्रसरद्भिरतिलोहितैः प्रभाप्रवाहैरुभयतस्ताडनदोहदलोभागतानि किसलयितानि रक्ताशोकवनानीवाकर्षयन्ती, सकलजीवलोकहृदयहठहरणाघोषणयेव रशनया शिञ्जानजघनस्थला, धौतधवलनेत्रनिर्मितेन निर्मोकलघुतरेणाप्रपदीनेन कञ्चुकेन तिरोहिततनुलता, छातकञ्चुकान्तरदृश्यमानैराश्यानचन्दनधवलैरवयवैः स्वच्छसलिलाभ्यन्तरविभाव्यमानमृणालकाण्डेव सरसी, कुसुम्भरागपाटलं पुलकबन्धचित्रं चण्डातकमन्तः[4]स्फुटं स्फटिकभूमिरिव रत्ननिधानमादधाना, हारेणामलकीफलनि[5]स्तलमुक्ताफलेन स्फुरितस्थूलग्रहगणशारा शारदीव श्वेतविरलजलधरपटलावृता द्यौः, कुचपूर्णकलशयोरुपरि रत्नप्रालम्बमालिकामरुणहरितकिरणकिसलयिनीं कस्यापि पुण्यवतो हृदयप्रवेश[6]वनमालिकामिव बद्धां धारयन्ती, प्रकोष्ठनिविष्टस्यैकैकस्य हाट[7]ककटकस्य मरकतमकरवेदिकासनाथस्य हरितीकृतदिगन्ताभिर्मयूखसन्ततिभिः स्थलकमलिनीभिरिव लक्ष्मीशङ्कयानुगम्यमाना, बहलताम्बूलकृष्णिकान्धकारितेनाधरसम्पुटेन मुखशशिपीतं ससंध्यारागं तिमिरमिव वमन्ती, विकचनयनकुवलयकुतूहलालीनयालिकुलसंहत्या नीलांशुकजालिकयेव निरुद्धार्धवदना, नीलीरागनिहितनीलिम्ना [8]शिखिगलशितिना वामश्रवणाश्रयिणा दन्तपत्रेण कालमेघपल्लवेन विद्यु-

१ 'अन्वक्षसमागमिष्यत्येव' क. २ 'तामरसव्याकोश०' क. ३ 'उरोबन्धारोपित०' ब. ४ 'अन्तःस्फुरस्फटिक' ब. ५ 'निस्तुल०' अ. ६ 'वन्दनमालिका०' ब. ७ 'प्रबाल०' ब. ८ 'शिति' अ–क.

दिव द्योतमाना, बकुलफलानुकारिणीभिस्तिसृभिर्मुक्ताभिः कल्पितेन बालिकायुगलेनाधोमुखेनालोकजलवर्षिणा सिञ्चन्तीवातिकोमले भुजलते, दक्षिणकर्णावतंसितया केतकीगर्भपलाशलेखया रजनिकरजिह्वालतयेव लावण्यलोभेन लिह्यमानकपोलतला, तमालश्यामलेन मृगमदामोदनिष्यन्दिना तिलकबिन्दुना मुद्रितमिव मनोभवसर्वस्वं वदनमुद्वहन्ती, ललाटलासकस्य सीमन्तचुम्बिनश्चटुल[1]तिलकमणेरुदञ्चता चटुलेनांशुजालेन रक्तांशुकेनेव कृतशिरोवगुण्ठना, पृष्ठप्रेङ्खदनादरसंयमनशिथिलजूटिकाबन्धा नीलचामरावचूलिनीव चूडामणिमकरिकासनाथा मकरकेतुकेतुपताका, कुलदेवतेव चन्द्रमसः, पुनःसञ्जीवनौषधिरिव पुष्पधनुषः, वेलेव रागसागरस्य, ज्योत्स्नेव यौवनचन्द्रोदयस्य, महानदीव रतिरसामृतस्य, कुसुमोद्गतिरिव सुरततरोः, बालविद्येव वैदग्ध्यस्य, कौमुदीव कान्तेः, धृतिरिव धैर्यस्य, गुरुशालेव गौरवस्य, बीजभूमिरिव विनयस्य, गोष्ठीव गुणानाम्, मनस्वितेव महानुभावतायाः, तृप्तिरिव तारुण्यस्य, कुवलयदलदामदीर्घलोचनया पाटलाधरया कुन्दकुड्मलस्फुटदशनया शिरीषमालासुकुमारभुजयुगलया कमलकोमलकरया बकुलसुरभिनिःश्वसितया चम्पकावदातया कुसुममय्येव ताम्बूलकरङ्कवाहिन्या महाप्रमाणाश्वतरारूढयानुगम्यमाना, कतिपयपरिचारकपरिकरा मालती समदृश्यत। दूरादेव च दधीचप्रेम्णा सरस्वत्या लुण्ठितेव मनोरथैः, आकृष्टेव कुतूहलेन, प्रत्युद्गतेवोत्कलिकाभिः, आलिङ्गितेवोत्कण्ठया, अन्तःप्रवेशितेव हृदयेन, स्नपितेवानन्दाश्रुभिः, विलुप्तेव स्मितेन, वीजितेवोच्छ्वसितैः, आच्छादितेव चक्षुषा, अभ्यर्चितेव वदनपुण्डरीकेण, सखीकृतेवाशया सविधमुपययौ। अवतीर्य च तुरगाद्दूरादेवावनतेन मूर्ध्ना प्रणाममकरोत्। आलिङ्गिता च ताभ्यां सविनयमुपाविशत्। सप्रश्रयं ताभ्यां सम्भाषिता च पुण्यभाजमात्मानममन्यत। अकथयच्च दधीचसन्दिष्टं शिरसि विनिहितेनाञ्जलिना नमस्कारम्। अगृह्णाच्चाकारतः प्रभृत्यग्राम्यतया तैस्तैरपि पेशलैरालापैः सावित्रीसरस्वत्योर्मनसी।

क्रमेण चातीते मध्यन्दिनसमये शोणमवतीर्णायां सावित्र्यां स्नातुमुत्सारितपरिजना साकूता मालती कुसुमप्रस्तरशायिनीं समुपसृत्य सरस्वतीमाबभाषे—'देवि, विज्ञाप्यं नः किञ्चिदस्ति रहसि। अतो मुहूर्तमवधानदानेन प्रसादं क्रियमाणमिच्छामि' इति। सरस्वती तु दधीचसन्देशाशङ्किनी किं वक्ष्यतीति स्तनविनिहितवामकरनखकिरणदन्तुरितमुद्भिद्यमानकुतूहलाङ्कुरनिकरमिव हृदयमुत्तरीयदुकूलवल्कलैकदेशेन सञ्छादयन्ती, गलतावतंसपल्लवेन श्रोतुं श्रवणेनेव धावमानेनानवरतश्वाससन्दोहदोलायितां जीविताशामिव समासन्नलतामवलम्बमाना, समुत्फुल्लस्य मुखशशिनो लावण्यप्रवाहेण शृङ्गाररसेनेव प्लावयन्ती जीवलोकम्, शयनकुसुमपरिमललग्नैर्मधुकरकदम्बकैर्म-

---

१ 'चटुलातिलक' अ-क.

दनानलदाहश्यामलैर्मनोरथैरिव निर्गत्य मूर्तैरुत्क्षिप्यमाणा, कुसुमशयनीयात्स्मरशरसंज्वरिणी मन्दं मन्दमुदगात्। 'उपांशु कथय' इति कपोलतलप्रतिबिम्बितां लज्जयेव कर्णमूलं मालतीं प्रवेशयन्ती मधुरया गिरा सुधीरमुवाच—'सखि मालति किमर्थमेवमभिदधासि। काहमवधानदानस्य शरीरस्य प्राणानां वा। सर्वस्य[1]प्रार्थितोऽपि प्रभवत्ये[2]वातिवेलं चक्षुष्यो जनः। सा न काचिद्या न भवसि मे स्वसा सखी प्रणयिनी प्राणसमा च। नियुज्यतां यावतः कार्यस्य क्षमं क्षोदीयसो गरीयसो वा शरीरकमिदम्। अनवस्करमाश्रवं मे त्वयि हृदयम्। प्रीत्या प्रतिसे[3]रा विधेयास्मि ते। व्यावृणु वरवर्णिनि विवक्षितम्' इति। सा त्ववादीत्—'देवि, जानास्येव माधुर्यं विषयाणाम्, लोलुपतां चेन्द्रियग्रामस्य, उन्मादितां च नवयौवनस्य, पारिप्लवतां च मनसः। प्रख्यातैव मन्मथस्य दुर्निवारता। अतो न मामुपालम्भेनोपस्थातुमर्हसि। न च बालिशता चपलता चारणता वा वाचालतायाः कारणम्। न किंचिन्न कारयत्यसाधारणा स्वामिभक्तिः। सा त्वं देवि यदैव दृष्टासि देवेन तत एवारभ्यास्य कामो गुरुः, चन्द्रमा जीवितेशः, मलयमरुदुच्छ्वासहेतुः, आधयोऽन्तरङ्गस्थानेषु, सन्तापः परमसुहृत्, प्रजागर आप्तः, मनोरथाः सर्वगताः, निःश्वासा विग्रहाग्रेसराः, मृत्युः पार्श्ववर्ती, रणरणकः सञ्चारकः, सङ्कल्पा बुद्ध्युपदेशवृद्धाः। किं वा विज्ञापयामि। अनुरूपो दे[4]व्या इत्यात्मसम्भावना, शीलवानिति प्रक्रमविरुद्धम्, धीर इत्यवस्थाविपरीतम्, सुभग इति त्वदायत्तम्, स्थिरप्रीतिरिति निपुणोपक्षेपः, जानाति सेवितुमित्यस्वामिभावोचितम्, इच्छति दासभावमामरणात्कर्तुमिति धूर्तालापः, भवनस्वामिनी भवसीत्युपप्रलोभनम्, पुण्यभागिनी भजति भर्तारं तादृशमिति स्वामिपक्षपातः, त्वं तस्य मृत्युरित्यप्रियम्, अगुणज्ञासीत्यधिक्षेपः, स्वप्नेऽस्य बहुशः कृतप्रसादासीत्यसाक्षिकम्, प्राणरक्षार्थमर्थयत इति कातरता, तत्रागम्यतामित्याज्ञा, वारितोऽपि बलादागच्छतीति परिभवः। तदेवमगोचरे गिरामसीति श्रुत्वा देवी प्रमाणम्' इत्यभिधाय तूष्णीमभूत्।

अथ सरस्वती प्रीतिविस्फारितेन चक्षुषा प्रत्यवादीत्—'अयि, न शक्नोमि बहु भाषितुम्। एषास्मि ते स्मितवादिनि वचसि स्थिता। गृह्यन्ताममी प्राणाः' इति। मालती तु 'यदाज्ञा[5]पयस्यतिप्रसादः' इति व्याहृत्य प्रहर्षपरवशा प्रणम्य प्रजविना तुरगेण ततार शोणम्। अगाच्च दधीचमानेतुं च्यवनाश्रमपदम्। इतरा तु सखीस्नेहेन सावित्रीमपि विदितवृत्तान्तामकरोत्। उत्कण्ठाभारभृता च ताम्यता चेतसा कल्पायितं कथंकथमपि दिवसशेषमनैषीत्। अस्तमुपगतवति भगवति गभस्तिमति, स्तिमिततरमवतरति तमसि, प्रहसितामिव सितां दिशं पौरन्दरीं दरीमिव केसरिणि मुञ्चति चन्द्रमसि,

---

१ 'प्रार्थितेऽपि' ब. २ 'प्रभवत्येवातिपेशलः' क–ब. ३ 'प्रतिसरास्मि ते' ब, ४ 'देव' ब. ५ 'यथाज्ञापयिष्यसि प्रसादः' ब.

सरस्वती शुचिनि चीनांशुकसुकुमारे तरङ्गिणि दुकूलकोमले शयन इव शोणसैकते समुपविष्टा स्वप्नकृतप्रार्थनापादपतनलग्नां दधीचचरणनखचन्द्रिकामिव ललाटिकां दधाना, गण्डस्थलादर्शप्रतिबिम्बितेन 'चारुहासिनि, अयमसावाहृतो हृदयदयितो जनः' इति श्रवणसमीपवर्तिना निवेद्यमानमदनसन्देशेवेन्दुना, विकीर्यमाणनखकिरणचक्रवालेन बालव्यजनीकृत[1]चन्द्रकलाकलापेनेव करेण वीजयन्ती स्वेदिनं स्पष्टकपोलपट्टम्, 'अत्र दधीचादृते न केनचित्प्रवेष्टव्यम्' इति तिरश्चीनं चित्तभुवा पातितां विलासवेत्रलतामिव बालमृणालिकामधिस्तनं स्तनयन्ती[2] कथमपि हृदयेन वहन्ती प्रतिपालयामास । आसीच्चास्या मनसि—'अहमपि नाम सरस्वती यत्रामुना मनोजन्मना जघन्येव[3] परवशीकृता । तत्र का गणनेतरासु तपस्विनीष्वतितरलासु तरुणीषु' इति ।

आजगाम च मधुमास इव सुरभिगन्धवहः, हंस इव कृतमृणालधृतिः[4], शिखण्डीव घनप्रीत्युन्मुखः, मलयानिल इवाहितसरसचन्दनधवलतनुलतोत्कम्पः, कृष्यमाण इव कृतकरकचग्रहेण ग्रहपतिना, प्रेर्यमाण इव कन्दर्पोद्दीपनदक्षेण दक्षिणानिलेन, उह्यमान इवोत्कलिकाबहलेन रतिरसेन, परिमलसम्पातिना मधुपपटलेन पटेनेव नीलेनाच्छादिताङ्गयष्टिः, अन्तःस्फुरत मत्तमदनकरिकर्णशङ्खायमानेन प्रतिमेन्दुना प्रथमसमागमविलासविलक्षस्मितेनेव धवलीक्रियमाणैककपोलोदरो मालतीद्वितीयो दधीचः । आगत्य च हृदयगतदयितानूपुररवमिश्रयेव हंसगद्गदया गिरा कृतसम्भाषणो यथा मन्मथः समाज्ञापयति, यथा यौवनमुपदिशति, यथानुरागः शिक्षयति, यथा विदग्धताध्यापयति, तथा तामभिरामां रामामरमयत् । उपजातविस्रम्भा चात्मानमकथयदस्य सरस्वती । तेन[5] तु सार्धमेकं दिवसमिवानयत्संवत्सरमधिकम् ।

अथ दैवयोगात्सरस्वती बभार गर्भम् । असूत चानेहसा सर्वलक्षणाभिरामं तनयम् । तस्मै च जातमात्रायैव 'सम्यक्सरहस्याः सर्वे वेदाः सर्वाणि च शास्त्राणि सकलाश्च कलाः मत्प्रसादात्स्वयमाविर्भविष्यन्ति' इति वरमदात् । सद्भर्तृश्लाघया दर्शयितुमिव हृदयेनादाय दधीचं पितामहादेशात्समं सावित्र्या ब्रह्मलोकमारुरोह । गतायां च तस्यां दधीचोऽपि हृदये ह्रादिन्येवाभिहतो भार्गववंशसम्भूतस्य भ्रातुर्ब्राह्मणस्य जायामक्षमालाभिधानां मुनिकन्यकामात्मसूनोः संवर्धनाय नियुज्य विरहातुरस्तपसे वनमगात् । यस्मिन्नेवावसरे सरस्वत्यसूत तनयं तस्मिन्नेवाक्षमालापि सुतं प्रसूतवती । तौ तु सा निर्विशेषं सामान्यस्तन्या शनैः शनैः शिशू समवर्धयत् । एकस्तयोः सारस्वताख्य

१ 'कृतचन्द्रकरेणेव करेण' ब. २ 'स्तनयन्तीम्' क; 'स्तनन्ती' ब. ३ 'जानत्येव' ब. ४ 'घृतिः' ब. ५ 'तया' अ-क.

एवाभवत्, द्वितीयोऽपि वत्सनामाभवत् । आसीच्च तयोः सोदर्ययोरिव स्पृहणीया प्रीतिः ।

अथ सारस्वतो मातुर्महिम्ना यौवनारम्भ एवाविर्भूताशेषविद्यासम्भारस्तस्मिन्सवयसि भ्रातरि प्रेयसि प्राणसमे सुहृदि वत्से वाङ्मयं समस्तमेव सञ्चारयामास । चकार च कृतदारपरिग्रहस्यास्य तस्मिन्नेव प्रदेशे प्रीत्या प्रीतिकूटनामानं निवासम् । आत्मनाप्याषाढी, कृष्णाजिनी, वल्कली, अक्षवलयी, मेखली, जटी च भूत्वा तपस्यतो जनयितुरेव जगामान्तिकम् ।

अथ तस्मात्[१]प्रवर्धमानादिपुरुषजनितात्मचरणोन्नतिनिर्गतप्रघोषः, परमेश्वरशिरोधृतः, सकलकलागमगम्भीरः, महामुनिमान्यः, विपक्षक्षोभक्षमः, क्षितितललब्धायतिः, अस्खलितप्रवृत्तो भागीरथीप्रवाह इव पावनः प्रावर्तत विपुलो[२] वंशः । यस्मादजायन्त वात्स्यायना नाम गृहमुनयः, आश्रितश्रौता अप्यनालम्बितालीकबककाकवः, कृतकुक्कुटवृत्ता अप्यबैडालवृत्तयः, विवर्जितजनपङ्क्तयः, परिहृतकपटकीर[३]कुचीकूर्चाकूताः, अगृहीतगह्वराः, न्यक्कृतनिकृतयः, प्रसन्नप्रकृतयः, विगतविकृतयः, परपरिवादपराचीनचेतसः, वर्णत्रयव्यावृत्तिविशुद्धान्धसः, धीरधिषणा[४]वधूताध्येषणाः, असङ्कसुकस्वभावाः, प्रणतप्रणयिनः, शमितसमस्तशाखान्तरसंशीतयः, उद्घाटितसमग्रग्रन्थार्थग्रन्थयः, कवयः, वाग्मिनः, विमत्सराः, सरस[५]भाषितव्यसनिनः, विदग्धपरिहासवेदिनः, परिचयपेशलाः, नृत्यगीतवादित्रेष्वबाह्याः, ऐतिह्यस्यावितृष्णाः, सानुक्रोशाः, सत्यशुचयः, साधुसंमताः, सर्वसत्त्वसौहार्दद्रवार्द्रहृदयाः, तथा सर्वगुणोपेता राजसेनानभिभूताः, क्षमाभाज आश्रितनन्दनाः, अनिस्त्रिंशा विद्याधराः, अजडाः कलावन्तः, अदोषास्तारकाः, अपरोपतापिनो भास्वन्तः, अनुष्माणो हुतभुजः, अकुसृतयो भोगिनः, अस्तम्भाः पुण्यालयाः, अलुप्तक्रतुक्रिया दक्षाः, अव्यालाः कामजितः, असाधारणा द्विजातयः ।

तेषु चैवमुत्पद्यमानेषु, संसरति संसारे, यात्सु युगेषु, अवतीर्णे कलौ, वहत्सु वत्सरेषु, व्रजत्सु वासरेषु, अतिक्रामति च काले, प्रसवपरम्पराभिरनवरतमापतति विकाशिनि वात्स्यायनकुले, क्रमेण कुबेरनामा वैनतेय इव गुरुपक्षपाती द्विजो जन्म लेभे । तस्याभवन्नच्युत ईशानो हरः पाशुपतश्चेति चत्वारो युगारम्भा इव ब्रह्मतेजोजन्यमानप्रजाविस्तारा नारायणबाहुदण्डा इव सच्चक्रनन्दकास्तनयाः । तत्र पाशुपतस्यैक एवाभवद्भूभार इवाचलकुलस्थितिश्चतुरुदधिगम्भीरोऽर्थपतिरिति नाम्ना समग्राग्रजन्मचक्रचूडामणिर्महात्मा सूनुः । सोऽजनयद्भृगुं हंसं शुचिं कविं महीदत्तं धर्मं जातवेदसं

---

१ 'वत्सात्'ब. २ 'विमलः' ब. ३ 'कौर' क; 'कौर' ब. ४ '०धिषणा विधूताध्येषणा' ब. ५ 'परसुभाषित०' ब.

चित्रभानुं त्र्यंक्ष[1]महिदत्तं विश्वरूपं चेत्येकादश रुद्रानिव सोमामृतरसशीकरच्छुरितमुखान्पवित्रान्पुत्रान् । अलभत च चित्रभानुस्तेषां मध्ये राजदेव्यभिधानायां ब्राह्मण्यां बाणमात्मजम् । स बाल एव विधेर्बलवतो वशादुपसम्पन्नया व्ययुज्यत जनन्या । जातस्नेहस्तु नितरां पितैवास्य मातृतामकरोत् । अवर्धत च तेनाधिकतरमेधी[2]यमानधृतिर्धाम्नि निजे ।

कृतोपनयनादिक्रियाकलापस्य समावृत्तस्य चतुर्दशवर्षदेशीयस्य पितापि श्रुतिस्मृतिविहितं कृत्वा द्विजजनोचितं निखिलं पुण्यजातं कालेनादशमीस्थ एवास्तमगात् । संस्थिते च पितरि महता शोकेनाभीलमनुप्राप्तो दिवानिशं दह्यमानहृदयः कथंकथमपि कतिपयान्दिवसानात्मगृह एवानैषीत् । गते च विरलतां शोके शनैः शनैरविनयनिदानतया स्वातन्त्र्यस्य, कुतूहलबहलतया च बालभावस्य, धैर्यप्रतिपक्षतया च यौवनारम्भस्य, शैशवोचितान्यनेकानि चापलान्याचरन्नित्वरो बभूव । अभवंश्चास्य व[3]यसा समानाः सुहृदः सहायाश्च । तथा च । भ्रातरौ पारशवौ चन्द्रसेनमातृषेणौ, भार्षा[4]कविरीशानः परं मित्रम्, प्रणयिनौ रुद्रनारायणौ, विद्वांसौ वारबाणवासबाणौ[5], वर्णकविर्वेणीभारतः, प्राकृतकृत्कुलपुत्रो वायुविकारः, बन्दिनावनङ्गबाणसूचीबाणौ, कात्यायनिका चक्रवाकिका, जाङ्गुलिको [6]मयूरकः, ताम्बूलदायकश्चण्डकः, भिषक्पुत्रो मन्दारकः, पुस्तकवाचकः सुदृष्टिः, कलादश्चामीकरः, हैरिकः सिन्धुषेणः[7], लेखको गोविन्दकः, चित्रकृद्वीरवर्मा, पुस्तकृत्कुमारदत्तः, मार्दङ्गिको जीमूतः, गायनौ सोमिलग्रहादित्यौ, सैरन्ध्री कुरङ्गिका, वांशिकौ मधुकरपारावतौ, गान्धर्वोपाध्यायो दर्दुरकः, संवाहिका केरलिका, लासकयुवा ताण्डविकः, आक्षिक आखण्डलः, कितवो भीमकः, शैलालियुवा शिखण्डकः, नर्तकी हरिणिका, पाराशरी सुमतिः, क्षपणको वीरदेवः, कथको जयसेनः, शैवो वक्रघोणः, मन्त्रसाधकः करालः, असुरविवरव्यसनी लोहिताक्षः, धातुवादविद्विहङ्गमः, दार्दु[8]रिको दामोदरः, ऐन्द्रजालिकश्चकोराक्षः, मस्करी ताम्रचूडः । स एतैश्चान्यैश्चानुगम्यमानो बालतया निघ्नतामुपगतो देशान्तरालोकनकौतुकाक्षिप्तहृदयः सत्स्वपि पितृपितामहोपात्तेषु ब्राह्मणजनोचितेषु विभवेषु सति चाविच्छिन्ने विद्याप्रसङ्गे गृहान्निरगात् । अगाच्च निरवग्रहो ग्रहवानिव नवं[9]यौवनेन स्वैरिणा मनसा महतामुपहास्यताम् ।

अथ शनैः शनैरत्युदारव्यवहृतिर्मनोहृन्ति बृहन्ति राजकुलानि वीक्षमाणः, निरवद्यविद्याविद्योतितानि च गुरुकुलानि सेवमानः, महार्हालापगम्भीरगुणवद्गोष्ठीश्चोपतिष्ठमानः, स्वभावगम्भीर[10]धीधनानि विदग्धमण्ड-

---

१ 'त्र्यक्षं महिदत्तम्' ब. २ 'आधीयमान०' ब. ३ 'स्ववयसः समानाः' ब. ४ 'कविरीशानः' ब. ५ 'वासधारौ' ब. ६ 'मायूरकः' ब. ७ 'सिद्धसेनः' ब. ८ 'दार्दरिकः' ब. ९ 'यौवनस्वैरिणा' ब. १० '०धीर्धनानि' ब—अ.

कानि च गाहमानः, पुनरपि तामेव वैपश्चितीमात्मवंशोचितां प्रकृतिमभजत्। महतश्च कालात्तामेव भूयो वात्स्यायनवंशाश्रयामात्मनो जन्मभुवं ब्राह्मणाधिवासमगमत्। तत्र च चिरदर्शनादभिनवीभूतस्नेहसद्भावै ससंस्त[1]-वप्रकटितज्ञातेयैराप्तैरुत्सवदिवस इवाभिनन्दितागमनो बालमित्रमण्डलस्य मध्यगतो मोक्षसुखमिवान्वभवदिति।

इति श्रीबाणभट्ट[2]कृतौ हर्षचरिते वात्स्यायनवंशवर्णनं नाम प्रथम उच्छ्वासः।

---

१ 'ससंभ्रम०' क; 'संस्तवप्रकटित' ख. २ 'इति श्रीमहाकविचक्रचूडामणिश्री-बाणभट्टविरचिते हर्षचरिते महाकाव्ये वात्स्यायनवंशवर्णनं नाम प्रथम उच्छ्वासः सम्पूर्णः' ख.

द्वितीय उच्छ्वासः ।

अतिगम्भीरे भूपे कूप इव जनस्य निरवतारस्य ।
दधति समीहितसिद्धिं गुणवन्तः पार्थिवा घटकाः ॥ १ ॥

रागिणि नलिने लक्ष्मीं दिवसो निदधाति दिनकरप्रभवाम् ।
अनपेक्षितगुणदोषः परोपकारः सतां व्यसनम् ॥ २ ॥

अथ तत्रानवरताध्ययनध्वनिमुखराणि, भस्मपुण्ड्रकपाण्डुरललाटैः कपिलशिखाजालजटिलैः कृशानुभिरिव क्रतुलोभागतैर्बटुभिरध्यास्यमानानि, सेकसुकुमारसोमकेदारिकाहरितायमानप्रघनानि, कृष्णाजिनविकीर्णशुष्यत्पुरोडाशीयश्यामाकतण्डुलानि, बालिकाविकीर्यमाणनीवारबलीनि, शुचिशिष्यशतानीयमानहरितकुशपूलीपलाशसमिन्धि, इन्धनगोमयपिण्डकूटसङ्कटानि, आमिक्षीयक्षीरक्षारिणीनामग्निहोत्रधेनूनां खुरवलयैर्विलिखिताजिरवितर्दिकानि, [1]कमण्डलव्यमृत्पिण्डमर्दनव्यग्रयतिजनानि, वैतानवेदीशङ्कव्यानामौदुम्बरीणां शाखानां राशिभिः पवित्रितपर्यन्तानि, वैश्वदेवपि[2]ण्डपङ्क्तिपाण्डुरितप्रदेशानि, हविर्धूमधूसरिताङ्गनविटपिकिसलयानि, [3]वत्सीयवत्सपालकलालितललत्तरलतर्णकानि, क्रीडत्कृष्णशारच्छागशावकप्रकटितपशुबन्धप्रबन्धानि, शुकसारिकारब्धाध्ययनदीयमानोपाध्यायविश्रान्तिसुखानि, साक्षात्त्रयीतपोवनानीव चिरदृष्टानां बान्धवानां प्रीयमाणो भ्रमन्भवनानि सुखमतिष्ठत् ।

तत्रस्थस्य चास्य कदाचित्कुसुमसमययुगमुपसंहरन्नजृम्भत ग्रीष्माभिधानः सम्फुल्लमल्लिकाधवलाट्टहासो महाकालः । प्रत्यग्रनिर्जितस्यास्तमुपगतवतो वसन्तसामन्तस्य बालापत्येष्विव पयःपायिषु नवोद्यानेषु दर्शितस्नेहो मृदुरभूत् । अभिनवोदितश्च सर्वस्यां पृथिव्यां सकलकुसुमबन्धनमोक्षमकरोत्प्रतपन्नुष्णसमयः । स्वयमृतुराजस्याभिषेका[4]र्द्राश्चामरकलापा इवागृह्यन्त कामिनीनां चिकुरचयाः कुसुमायुधेन । हिमदग्धसकलकमलिनीकोपेनेव हिमालयाभिमुखीं यात्रामदादंशुमाली ।

अथ ललाटन्तपे तपति तपने लिखि[5]तललाटिकापुण्ड्रकैरलक[6]चीरचीवरसंवीतैः स्वेदोदबिन्दुमुक्ताक्षवलयवाहिभिर्दिनकराराधननियमा इवागृह्यन्त ललनाललाटेन्दु[7]भिः । चन्दनधूसराभिरसूर्यम्पश्याभिः कुमुदिनीभिरिव दिवसमसुप्यत सुन्दरीभिः । निद्रालसा रत्नालोकमपि नासहन्त दृशः, किमुत जरठमातपम् । अशिशिरसमयेन चक्रवाकमिथुनाभिनन्दिताः सरित इव

१ 'कामण्डलव्य०' अ–क. २ '०पिण्डपाण्डुरित०' ब. ३ 'वत्सीयबालकलालित०' अ–क. ४ '०राजस्यागृह्यन्ताभिषेका०' ब. ५ 'चन्दनलिखित०' ब. ६ 'अलकचीवर०' ब. ७ '०ललाटेन्दुद्युतिभिः' ब.

समूर्धानम्, प्रविशन्तं लेखहारकमद्राक्षीत् । अप्राक्षीच्च दूरादेव—'भद्र, भद्रमशेषभुवननिष्कारणबन्धोस्तत्रभवतः कृष्णस्य' इति । सः 'भद्रम्' इत्युक्त्वा प्रणम्य नातिदूरे समुपाविशत् । विश्रान्तश्चाब्रवीत्—'एष खलु स्वामिनो माननीयस्य लेखः प्रहितः' इति विमुच्य चार्पयत् । अथ बाणः सादरं गृहीत्वा स्वयमेवावाचयत्—'मेखलकात्सन्दिष्टमवधार्य फलप्रतिबन्धी धीमद्भिरपहरणीयः कालातिपात इत्येतावदत्रार्थजातम् । इतरद्वार्तासंवादनमात्रकम्' । अवधृतलेखार्थश्च समुत्सारितपरिजनः सन्देशं पृष्टवान् । मेखलकस्त्ववादीत्—'एवमाह मेधाविनं स्वामी—जानात्येव मान्यो यथैकगोत्रता वा, [1]समानजातिता वा, समं संवर्धनं वा, एकदेशनिवासो वा, दर्शनाभ्यासो वा, परस्परानुरागश्रवणं वा, परोक्षोपकारकरणं वा, समानशीलता वा, स्नेहस्य हेतवः । त्वयि तु विना कारणेनादृष्टेऽपि प्रत्यासन्ने बन्धाविव बद्धपक्षपातं किमपि स्निह्यति मे हृदयं दूरस्थेऽपीन्दोरिव कुमुदाकरे । भवन्तमन्तरेणान्यथा चान्यथा चायं चक्रवर्ती दुर्जनैर्ग्राहित आसीत् । न च तत्तथा । न सन्त्येव ते येषां सतामपि सतां न विद्यन्ते मित्रोदासीनशत्रवः । शिशुचापलपराचीनचेतोवृत्तितया च भवतः केनचिदसहिष्णुना यत्किञ्चिदसदृशमुदीरितमितरो लोकस्तथैव तद्गृह्णाति वक्ति च । सलिलानीव खलु गतानुगति[2]कानि लोलानि भवन्त्यविवेकिनां मनांसि बहुमुखश्रवणनिश्चलीकृतनिश्चयः किं करोतु पृथिवीपतिः । तत्त्वान्वेषिभिश्चास्माभिर्दूरस्थितोऽपि प्रत्यक्षीकृतोऽसि । विज्ञप्तश्चक्रवर्ती त्वदर्थं यथा—प्रायेण प्रथमे वयसि सर्वस्यैव चापलैः शैशवमपराधीति । तथेति च प्रतिपन्नं स्वामिना । अतो भवता राजकुलमकृतकालक्षेपमागन्तव्यम् । अवकोशीवादृष्टपरमेश्वरो बन्धुमध्यमधिवसन्नासि मे बहुमतः । न च सेवावैषम्यविषादिना वा परमेश्वरोपसर्पणभीरुणा वा भवता भवितव्यम् । यतो यद्यपि—

स्वेच्छोपजातविषयोऽपि न याति वक्तुं
देहीति मार्गणशतैश्च ददाति दुःखम् ।
मोहात्समाक्षिपति जीवनमप्यकाण्डे
कष्टं मनोभव इवेश्वरदुर्विदग्धः ॥ ३ ॥

तथाप्यन्ये ते भूपतयः, अन्य एवायं न्यक्कृतनृगनलनिषधनहुषाम्बरीषदशरथदिलीपनाभागभरतभगीरथययातिरमृतमयः स्वामी । नास्याहङ्कारकालकूटविषदिग्धदुष्टा दृष्टयः, न गर्वगुरुगरगलग्रहगदगद्गदा गिरः, नातिस्मयोष्मापस्मारविस्मृतस्थैर्याणि स्थानकानि, नोद्दामदर्पदाहज्वरवेगविक्लवा विकाराः, नाभिमानमहासंनिपातनिर्मिताङ्गभङ्गानि गतानि, न मदार्दितवक्रीकृतौष्ठनिष्ठ्यूतनिष्ठुराक्षराणि जल्पितानि । तथा च, अस्य विमलेषु साधुषु रत्नबुद्धिः, न शिलाशकलेषु । मुक्ताधवलेषु प्रसाधनधीः, नाभरणभारेषु ।

१ 'समानज्ञानता वा' इत्येतदधिकं ब-पुस्तके. २ 'गतागतिकानि' अ-क.

दानवत्सु कर्मसु साधनश्रद्धा, न करिकीटेषु। सर्वाग्रेसरे[1] यशसि महाप्रीतिः, न जीवितजरत्तृणे। गृहीतकरास्वाशासु प्रसाधनैताभियोगः[2], न निजकलत्रचर्मपुत्रिकासु। गुणवति धनुषि सहायबुद्धिः, न पिण्डोपजीविनि सेवकजने। अपि च। अस्य मित्रोपकरणमात्मा, भृत्योपकरणं प्रभुत्वम्, पण्डितोपकरणं वैदग्ध्यम्, बान्धवोपकरणं लक्ष्मीः, कृपणोपकरणमैश्वर्यम्, द्विजोपकरणं सर्वस्वम्, सुकृतसंस्मरणोपकरणं हृदयम्, धर्मोपकरणमायुः[3], साहसोपकरणं शरीरम्, असिलतोपकरणं पृथिवी, विनोदोपकरणं राजकम्, प्रतापोपकरणं प्रतिपक्षः। नास्याल्पपुण्यैरवाप्येत सर्वातिशायिसुखरसप्रसूतिः पादपल्लवच्छाया' इति। श्रुत्वा च तमेव चन्द्रसेनं समादिशत्—'कृतकशिपुं विश्रान्तसुखिनमेनं कारय' इति।

अथ गते च तस्मिन्, पर्यस्ते च वासरे, सङ्घट्टमान[4]रक्तपङ्कजसम्पुटपीयमान इव क्षयिणि क्षामतां व्रजति बालवायसास्यारुणेऽपराह्णातपे, शिथिलितनिजवाजिजवे जपापीडपाटले[5]ऽस्ताचलशिखरस्खलिते खञ्जतीव कमलिनीकण्टकक्षतपादपल्लवे पतङ्गे, पुरः परापतति प्रेङ्खदन्धकारले[6]शलम्बालके शशिविरहशोकश्याम इव श्यामामुखे, कृतसंध्योपासनः शयनीयमगात्। अचिन्तयच्चैकाकी—'किं करोमि। अन्यथा सम्भावितोऽस्मि राज्ञा। निर्निमित्तबन्धुना च सन्दिष्टमेवं कृष्णेन। कष्टा च सेवा। विषमं च भृत्यत्वम्। अतिगम्भीरं महद्राजकुलम्। न च तत्र मे पूर्वजप्रवर्तिता प्रीतिः, न कुलक्रमागता गतिः, नोपकारस्मरणानुरोधः, न बालसेवास्नेहः, न गोत्रगौरवम्[7], न पूर्वदर्शनदाक्षिण्यम्, न प्रज्ञासंविभागोपप्रलोभनम्, न विद्यातिशयकुतूहलम्, नाकारसौन्दर्यादरः, न सेवाकाकुकौशलम्, न विद्वद्गोष्ठीबन्धवैदग्ध्यम्, न वित्तव्ययवशीकरणम्, न राजवल्लभपरिचयः। अवश्यं गन्तव्यम्। सर्वथा भगवान्पुरारातिर्भुवनगुरुर्गतस्य[8] मे[9] सर्वं सांप्रतमाचरिष्यति' इत्यवधार्य गमनाय मतिमकरोत्।

अथान्यस्मिन्नहन्युत्थाय, प्रातरेव स्नात्वा, धृतधौतधवलदुकूलवासाः, गृहीताक्षमालः, प्रास्थानिकानि सूक्तानि मन्त्रपदानि च बहुशः समावर्त्य, देवदेवस्य विरूपाक्षस्य क्षीरस्नपनपुरःसरां सुरभिकुसुमधूपगन्धध्वजबलिविलेपनप्रदीपकबहुलां विधाय पूजां परमया भक्त्या, प्रथमहुततरलतिलत्वग्विघट्टनचटुलमुखरशिखाशेखरं प्राज्याज्याहुतिप्रवर्धितदक्षिणार्चिषं भगवन्तमाशुशुक्षणिं हुत्वा, दत्त्वा द्युम्नं यथाविद्यमानं द्विजेभ्यः, प्रदक्षिणीकृत्य प्राङ्मुखीं नैचिकीम्, शुक्लाङ्गरागः, शुक्लमाल्यः, शुक्लवासाः, रोचनाचित्रदूर्वाग्रपल्लवग्रथितगिरिकर्णिकाकुसुमकृतकर्णपूरः, शिखासक्तसिद्धार्थकः, पितुः कनीयस्या

१ 'सर्वांशाग्रेसरे' ब. २ 'दिक्षु प्रसाधनाभियोगः' ब. ३ 'धर्म' ब. ४ 'संघटमान' ब. ५ 'पाटलिम्नि' ब. ६ 'लेखा' ब. ७ 'तन्त्रगौरवम्' ब. ८ 'भवानीपतिर्भुवनपतिः' ब. ९ 'मे शरणं सर्वं' ब. १० 'विचटन' अ—क.

स्वस्रा मात्रेव स्नेहार्द्रहृदयया श्वेतवाससा साक्षादिव भगवत्या महाश्वेतया मालत्याख्यया कृतसकलगमनमङ्गलः, दत्ताशीर्वादो बान्धववृद्धाभिः, अभिनन्दितः परिजनजरन्तीभिः, वन्दितचरणैरभ्यनुज्ञातो गुरुभिः, अभिवादितैराघ्रातः शिरसि कुलवृद्धैः, वर्धितगमनोत्साहः शकुनैः, मौहूर्तिकमतेन कृतनक्षत्रदोहदः, शोभने मुहूर्ते हरितगोमयोपलिप्ताजिरस्थण्डिलस्थापितमसितेतरकुसुममालापरिक्षिप्तकण्ठं पिष्टपञ्चाङ्गुलपाण्डुरं मुखनिहितनवचूतपल्लवं पूर्णकलशमुदीक्षमाणः, प्रणम्य कुलदेवताभ्यः, कुसुमफलपाणिभिरप्रतिरथं जपद्भिर्निजद्विजैरनुगम्यमानः, प्रथमचलितदक्षिणचरणः, प्रीतिकूटान्निरगात् ।

प्रथमेऽहनि घर्मकालकष्टं निरुदकं निष्पत्रपादपविषमं पथिकजननमस्क्रियमाणप्रवेशपादपोत्कीर्णकात्यायनीप्रतियातनं शुष्कमपि पल्लवितमिव तृषितश्वापदकुललम्बितलोलजिह्वालतासहस्रैः पुलकितमिवाच्छभल्लगोलाङ्गूललिह्यमानमधुगोलचलितसरघासङ्घातै रोमाञ्चितमिव दग्धस्थलीरूढस्थूलाभीरुकन्दलशतैः शनैश्चण्डिकाकाननमतिक्रम्य मल्लकूटनामानं ग्राममगात् । तत्र च हृदयनिर्विशेषेण भ्रात्रा सुहृदा च जगत्पतिनाम्ना सम्पादितसपर्यः सुखमवसत् । अथापरेद्युरुत्तीर्य भगवतीं भागीरथीं यष्टिग्रहकनाम्नि वनग्रामके निशामनयत् । अन्यस्मिन्दिवसे स्कन्धावारमुपमणितारमन्वजिरवति कृतसंनिवेशमाससाद । अतिष्ठच्च नातिदूरे राजभवनस्य ।

निर्वर्तितस्नानाशनव्यतिकरो विश्रान्तश्च मेखलकेन सह याममात्रावशेषे दिवसे भुक्तवति भूभुजि प्रख्यातानां क्षितिभुजां बहून्शिबिरसंनिवेशान्वीक्षमाणः शनैः शनैः पट्टबन्धार्थमुपस्थापितैश्च डिण्डिमाधिरोहणायाहृतैश्चाभिनवबद्धैश्च विक्षेपोपार्जितैश्च कौशलिकागतैश्च नागवीथीपालप्रेषितैश्च प्रथमदर्शनकुतूहलोपनीतैश्च दूतसंप्रेषणप्रेषितैश्च पल्लीपरिवृढढौकितैश्च स्वेच्छायुद्धक्रीडाकौतुककारितैश्च दीयमानैश्चाच्छिद्यमानैश्च मुच्यमानैश्च यामस्थापितैश्च सर्वद्वीपविजिगीषया गिरिभिरिव सागरसेतुबन्धार्थमेकीकृतैर्ध्वजपटपटुपटहशङ्खचामराङ्गरागरमणीयैः पुष्याभिषेकदिवसैरिव कल्पितैर्वारणेन्द्रैः श्यामायमानम्, अनवरतचलितखुरपुटप्रहतमृदङ्गैर्नर्तयद्भिरिव राजलक्ष्मीमुपहसद्भिरिव सृक्किपुटप्रसृतफेनाट्टहासेन जवजडजङ्घां हरिणजातिमाकारयद्भिरिव सङ्घट्टहेतोर्हेषितैनोच्चैःश्रवसमुत्पतद्भिरिव दिवसकररथतुरगरुषा पक्षायमाणमण्डनचामरमालैर्गगनतलं तुरङ्गैस्तरङ्गायमानम्, अन्यत्र प्रेषितैश्च प्रेष्यमाणैश्च प्रेषितप्रतिनिर्वृत्तैश्च बहुयोजनग-

---

१ 'दत्तपिष्ट०' ब. २ 'शुष्कगलगो०' ब. ३ 'चण्डिकायतनकानन०' ब. ४ 'यष्टिगृहक०' ब. ५ 'मणिपुरमन्व०' ब. ६ 'यामावस्थितैश्च' ब. ७ 'हेषितेनोच्चैरुच्चैःश्रवस०' ब. ८ 'प्रतीपनिवृत्तै०' अ-क.

मनगणनसंख्याक्षरावलीभिरिव वराटिकावलीभिर्घटितमुखमण्डनकैस्तारकितै-रिव संध्यातपच्छेदैररुणचामरिकारचितकर्णपूरैः सरक्तोत्पलैरिव रक्तशालि-शालेयैरनवरतझणझणायमानचारुचामीकरघुरुघुरुकमालिकैर्जरत्करञ्जवनैरिव रणितशुष्कबीजकोशीशतैः श्रवणोपान्तप्रेङ्खत्पद्मरागवर्णोर्णाचित्रसूत्रजूटज-टालैः कपिकपोलकपिलैः क्रमेलककुलैः कपिलायमानम्, अन्यत्र शरज्जल-धैररिव सद्यःस्रुतपयःपटलधवलतनुभिः कल्पपादपैरिव मुक्ताफलजाल-कजायमानालोकलुसच्छायामण्डलैर्नारायणनाभिपुण्डरीकैरिवाश्लिष्टगरुडपक्षैः क्षीरोदोद्देशैरिव द्योतमानविकटविद्रुमदण्डैः शेषफणाफलकैरिवोपरिस्फुरत्स्फी-तमाणिक्यखण्डैः श्वेतगङ्गापुलिनैरिव राजहंसोपसेवितैरभिभवद्भिरिव निदा-घसमयमुपहसद्भिरिव विवस्वतः प्रतापमापिबद्भिरिवातपं चन्द्रलोकमयमिव जीवलोकं जनयद्भिः कुमुदमयमिव कालं कुर्वद्भिर्ज्योत्स्नामयमिव वासरं विरचयद्भिः फेनमयीमिव दिवं दर्शयद्भिरकालकौमुदीसहस्राणीव सृजद्भिरु-पहसद्भिरिव शातक्रतवीं श्रियं श्वेतायमानैरातपत्रखण्डैः श्वेतायमानम्[1], क्षण-दृष्टनष्टाष्टदिङ्मुखं च मुष्णद्भिरिव भुवनमाक्षेपोत्क्षेपदोलायितं दिनं गतागता-नीव कारयद्भिरिव कुनृपतिसम्पर्ककलङ्ककालीं कालेयीं स्थितिं विकचविश-दकाशवनपाण्डुरदिशं शरत्समयमिवोपपादयद्भिर्बिसतन्तुमयमिवान्तरिक्षमा-विर्भावयद्भिः शशिकरशुचीनां चलतां चामराणां सहस्रैर्दोलायमानम्, अपि च हंसयूथायमानं करिकर्णशङ्खैः, कल्पलतावनायमानं कदलिकाभिः, माणि-क्यवृक्षकवनायमानं मायूरातपत्रैः, मन्दाकिनीप्रवाहायमानमंशुकैः, क्षीरो-दायमानं क्षौमैः, कदलीवनायमानं मरकतमयूखैः, जन्यमानान्यदिवसमिव पद्मरागबालातपैः, उत्पद्यमानापराम्बरमिवेन्द्रनीलप्रभापटलैः[2], आरभ्यमा-णापूर्वनिशमिव महानीलमयूखान्धकारैः, स्यन्दमानानेककालिन्दीसहस्रमिव गरुडमणिप्रभाप्रतानैः, अङ्गारकितमिव पुष्परागरश्मिभिः, कैश्चित्प्रवेशमल-भमानैरधोमुखैश्चरणनखपतितवदनप्रतिबिम्बनिभेन लज्जया स्वाङ्गानीव वि-शद्भिः कैश्चिदङ्गुलीलिखितायाः क्षितेर्विकीर्यमाणकरनखकिरणकदम्बकव्याजेन सेवाचामराणीवार्पयद्भिः कैश्चिदुरःस्थलदोलायमानेन्द्रनीलतरलप्रभापट्टैः स्वा-मिप्रकोपप्रशमनाय कण्ठबद्धकृपाणपट्टैरिव, कैश्चिदुच्छ्वाससौरभभ्राम्यद्भ्रमर-पटलान्धकारितमुखैरपहृतलक्ष्मीशोकधृतलम्बश्मश्रुभिरिवान्यैः शेखरोड्डीय-मानमधुपमण्डलैः प्रणामविडम्बनाभयपलायमानमौलिभिरिव निर्जितैरपि संमानितैरिवानन्यशरणैरन्तरान्तरा निष्पततां प्रविशतां चान्तरप्रतीहाराणा-मनुमार्गप्रधावितानेकार्थिजनसहस्राणामनुयायिनः पुरुषानश्रान्तैः पुनः पुनः पृच्छद्भिः 'भद्र, अद्य भविष्यति भुक्तास्थानं[3] दास्यति दर्शनं परमेश्वरः, निष्पतिष्यति वा बाह्यां कक्ष्याम्' इति दर्शनाशया दिवसं नयद्भिर्भुजनि-र्जितैः शत्रुमहासामन्तैः समन्तादासेव्यमानम्, अन्यैश्च प्रतापानुरागागतै-

---

१ 'श्वेतद्वीपायमानम्' ब—क. २ 'उत्पाद्यमाना०' ब. ३ 'भुक्त्वा स्थाने' अ—क.

नानादेशजैर्महीपालैः प्रतिपालयद्भिर्नरपतिदर्शनकालमध्यास्यमानम्, एकान्तोपविष्टैश्च जैनैरार्हतैः पाशुपतैः पाराशरिभिर्वर्णिभिश्च सर्वदेशजन्मभिश्च जनपदैः सर्वाम्भोधिवेलावनवलयवासिभिश्च म्लेच्छजातिभिः सर्वद्वीपान्तरागतैश्च दूतमण्डलैरुपास्यमानम्, सर्वप्रजानिर्माणभूमिमिव प्रजापतीनां लोकत्रयसारोच्चयरचितं चतुर्थमिव लोकम्, महाभारतशतैरप्यकथनीयसमृद्धिसम्भारम्, कृतयुगसहस्रैरिव कल्पितसंनिवेशम्, स्वर्गार्बुदैरिव विहितरामणीयकम्, राजलक्ष्मीकोटिभिरिव कृतपरिग्रहं राजद्वारमगमत्।

अभवच्चास्य जातविस्मयस्य मनसि—'कथमिवेदमियत्प्रमाणं प्राणिजातं जनयतां प्रजासृजां नासीत्[1]परिश्रमो महाभूतानां वा परिक्षयः, परमाणूनां वा परि[2]च्छेदः, कालस्य वान्तः, आयुषो वा व्युपरमः, आकृतीनां वा परिसमाप्तिः' इति। मेखलकस्तु दूरादेव द्वारपाललोकेन प्रत्यभिज्ञायमानः 'तिष्ठतु तावत्क्षणमात्रमत्रैव पुण्यभागी' इति तमभिधायाप्रतिहतः पुरः प्राविशत्।

अथ स मुहूर्तादिव प्रांशुना, कर्णिकारगौरेण, वीध्रककञ्चुकच्छन्नवपुषा, समुन्मिषन्माणिक्यपदकबन्धबन्धुरशस्त्[3]बन्धकृशावलग्नेन, हिमशैलशिलाविशालवक्षसा, हरवृषककुदकूटविकटांसतटेन, उरसा चपलहृषीकहरिणकुलसंयमनपाशमिव हारं बिभ्रता, 'कथयतं यदि सोमवंशसम्भवः सूर्यवंशसम्भवो वा भूपतिरभूदेवंविधः' इति प्रष्टुमानीताभ्यां सोमसूर्याभ्यामिव श्रवणगताभ्यां मणिकुण्डलाभ्यां समुद्भासमानेन, वह[4]द्वदनलावण्यविसरवेणिकाक्षिप्यमाणैरधिकारगौरवाद्दीयमानमार्गेणेव दिनकृतः किरणैः, प्रसादलब्धया विकचपुण्डरीकमुण्डमालिकयेव दीर्घया दृष्ट्या दूरादेवानन्दयता, नैष्ठुर्याधिष्ठानेऽपि प्रतिष्ठितेन पदे प्रश्रयमिवावनम्रेण मौलिना पाण्डुरमुष्णीषमुद्वहता, वामेन स्थूलमुक्ताफलच्छुरणदन्तुरत्सरुं करकिसलयेन कलयता कृपाणम्, इतरेणापनीततरलतां ताडितीमिव लतां शातकौम्भीं वेत्रयष्टिमुन्मृष्टां धारयता पुरुषेणानुगम्यमानो निर्गत्यावोचत्—'एष खलु महाप्रतीहाराणामनन्तरश्चक्षुष्यो देवस्य पारियात्रनामा दौवारिकः। समनुगृह्णात्वेनमनुरूपया प्रतिपत्त्या कल्याणाभिनिवेशी' इति। दौवारिकः समुपसृत्य कृतप्रणामो मधुरया गिरा सविनयमभाषत—'आगच्छत। प्रविशत दर्शनाय। कृतप्रसादो देवः' इति। बाणस्तु 'धन्योऽस्मि, यदेवमनुग्राह्यं मां देवो मन्यते' इत्युक्त्वा तेनोपदिश्यमानमार्गः प्राविशदभ्यन्तरम्।

अथ वनायुजैः, आरट्टजैः, काम्बोजैः, भारद्वाजैः, सिन्धुदेशजैः, पारसीकैश्च, शोणैश्च, श्यामैश्च, श्वेतैश्च, पिञ्जरैश्च, हरिद्भिश्च, तित्तिरिकल्माषैश्च, पञ्चभद्रैश्च, मल्लिकाक्षैश्च, कृत्तिकापिञ्जरैश्च, आयतनिर्मांसमुखैः, अनुत्कटक-

---

१ 'नासीन्महाभूतानां' अ–क. २ 'विच्छेदः' ब. ३ 'वस्तबन्धलुप्ताव०' ब. ४ 'बृहद्वदन०' अ.

र्णकोशैः, सुवृत्तश्लक्ष्णसुघटितघण्टिकाबन्धैः, यूपानुपूर्वीवक्रायतोदग्रग्रीवैः, उपचयश्वयत्स्कन्धसन्धिभिः, निर्भुग्नोरःस्थलैः, अस्थूलप्रगुणप्रसृतैर्लोहपीठककठिनखुरमण्डलैः, अतिजवत्रुटनभयादनिर्मितान्त्राणीवोदराणि वृत्तानि धारयद्भिः, उद्यद्द्रोणीविभज्यमानपृथुजघनैः, जगतीदोलायमानबालपल्लवैः, कथमप्युभयतो निखातदृढभूरिपाश[1]संयमननियन्त्रितैः, आयतैरपि पश्चात्पाशबन्धप्रसारितैकाङ्घ्रिभिरायततरैरिवोपलक्ष्यमाणैः, बहुगुणसूत्रग्रथितग्रीवागण्डकैरामीलितलोचनैः, दूर्वारसश्यामलफेनलवशबलान्दशनगृहीतमुक्तान्फरफरितत्वचः कण्डूजुषः प्रतीकान्[2]प्रचालयद्भिः, सालसवलितवालधिभिः, एकशफविश्रान्तिस्रस्तशिथिलितजघनार्धैः, निद्रया प्रध्यायद्भिश्च, स्खलितहुङ्कारमन्दमन्दशब्दायमानैश्च ताडितखुरधरणीरणितमुखरशिखरखुरलिखितक्ष्मातलैर्घासमभिलषद्भिश्च, प्रकीर्यमाणयवसग्रासरसमत्सरोद्धूतक्षोभैश्च, प्रकुपितचण्डचण्डालहुङ्कारकातरतरतरलतारकैश्च, कुङ्कुमप्रमृष्टिपिञ्जराङ्गतया सततसंनिहितनीराजनानलैरिव[3] लक्ष्यमाणैरुपरिविततवितानैः, पुरः पूजिताभिमतदैवतैः, भूपालवल्लभैस्तुरङ्गैरारचितां मन्दुरां विलोकयन्, कुतूहलाक्षिप्तहृदयः किञ्चिदन्तरमतिक्रान्तो हस्तवामेनात्युच्चतया निरवकाशमिवाकाशं कुर्वाणम्, महता कदलीवनेन परिवृतपर्यन्तं सर्वतो मधुकरमयीभिर्मदस्रुतिभिर्नदीभिरिवापतन्तीभिरापूर्यमाणम्, आशामुखविसर्पिणा बकुलवनानामिव विकसतामामोदेन लिम्पन्तं घ्राणेन्द्रियं दूरादव्यक्तमिभधिष्ण्यागारम्[4] अपश्यत्। अपृच्छच्च—'अत्र देवः किं करोति' इति। असावकथयत्—'एष खलु देवस्यौपवाह्यो बाह्यं हृदयं जात्यन्तरित आत्मा बहिश्चराः प्राणा विक्रमक्रीडासुहृद्दर्पशात इति यथार्थनामा वारणपतिः। तस्यावस्थानमण्डपोऽयं महान्दृश्यते' इति। स तमवादीत्—'भद्र, श्रूयते दर्पशातः। यद्येवमदोषो वा पश्यामि तावद्वारणेन्द्रमेव। अतोऽर्हसि मामत्र प्रापयितुम्। अतिपरवानस्मि कुतूहलेन' इति। सोऽभाषत—'भवत्वेवम्। आगच्छतु भवान्। को दोषः। पश्यतु तावद्वारणेन्द्रम्' इति।

गत्वा च तं प्रदेशं दूरादेव गम्भीरगलगर्जितैर्[5]वियति चातककदम्बकैर्भुवि च भवननीलकण्ठकुलैः कलकेकाकलकलमुखरमुखैः क्रियमाणकल[6]कोलाहलम्, विकचकदम्बसंवादिमदसुरासौरभभरितभुवनम्, कायवन्तमिवाकालमेघकालम्[7], अविरलमधुबिन्दुपिङ्गलपद्मजालकितां सरसीमिवाभ्यवगाढां दशां चतुर्थीमुत्सृजन्तम्, अनवरतमवतंसशङ्खैरामन्द्रकर्णतालदुन्दुभिध्वनिभिः पञ्चमीप्रवेशमङ्गलारम्भमिव गायन्तम्[8], अविरतचलनचित्रत्रिपदीललितलास्य-

---

१ 'भूमिपाश' ब. २ 'प्रदेशान्' ब. ३ '°नलरक्ष्यमाणैरिवो०' अ–क.
४ '०दव्यक्तमिव धिष्ण्याकार०' ब; 'धृष्ण्या०' अ. ५ 'गर्जितोर्जितैः' अ–क.
६ 'क्रियमाणाकाल०' ब. ७ 'कायवन्तमिव काल०' ब. ८ 'सूचयन्तम्' ब.

लघ्वैर्दोलायमानदीर्घदेहाभोगतया[1] मेदिनीविदलनभयेन भारमिव लघयन्तं दिग्भित्तितटेषु कायमिव कण्डूयमानम्, आहृचायोदस्तहस्ततया दिग्वारणानिवाह्वयमानम्, ब्रह्मस्तम्भमिव स्थूलनिशितदन्तेन करपत्रेण पाटयन्तम्, अमान्तं भुवनाभ्यन्तरे बहिरिव निर्गन्तुमीहमानम्, सर्वतः सरसकिशलयलतालासिभिर्लेशिकैश्चिरपरिचयोपचितैर्घनैरिव[2] विक्षिप्तसशैवलबिसविसरशबलसलिलैः सरोभिरिव चाधोरणैराधीयमाननिदाघसमयसमुचितोपचारानन्दम्, अपि च प्रतिगजदानपवनादानदूरोत्क्षिप्तेनानेकसमरविजयगणनालेखाभिरिव वलिवलयराजिभिस्तनीयसीभिस्तरङ्गितोदरेणातिस्थवीयसा हस्तार्गलदण्डेनार्गलयन्तमिव सकलं सकुलशैलसमुद्रद्वीपकाननं ककुभां चक्रवालम्, एकं करान्तरार्पितेनोत्पलाशेन कदलीदण्डेनान्तर्गतशीकरसिच्यमानमूलं मुक्तपल्लवमिवापरं लीलावलम्बिना मृणालजालकेन समररसोच्चरोमाञ्चकण्टकितमिव दन्तकाण्डं वहन्तम्, विसर्पन्त्या च दन्तकाण्डयुगलकस्य कान्त्या सरःक्रीडास्वादितानीव कुमुदवनानि बहुधा वमन्तं निजयशोराशिमिव दिशामपर्यन्तं कुकरिकीटपाटनदुर्ललितान्सिंहानिवोपहसन्तं कल्पद्रुमदुकूलमुखपटमिव चात्मनः कल्पयन्तम्[3], हस्तकाण्डदण्डोद्धरणलीलासु च लक्ष्यमाणेन रक्तांशुकसुकुमारतलेन[4] तालुना कवलितानि रक्तपद्मवनानीव वर्षन्तमभिनवकिसलयराशिमिवोद्गिरन्तम्, कमलकवलपीतं मधुरसमिव स्वभावपिङ्गलेन वमन्तं[5] चक्षुषा, चूतचम्पकलवलीलवङ्गकक्कोलवन्स्येलालतामिश्रितानि ससहकाराणि कर्पूरपूरपूरितानि पारिजातकवनानीवोपभुक्तानि[6] पुनः पुनः करटाभ्यां बहलमदामोदव्याजेन विसृजन्तम्, अहर्निशं विभ्रमकृतहस्तस्थितिभिरर्धखण्डितपुण्ड्रेक्षुकाण्डकण्डूयनलिखितैरलिकुलवाचालितैर्दानपट्टकैर्विलभमानमिव सर्वकाननानि करिपतीनाम्, अविरलोदबिन्दुस्यन्दिना हिमशिलाशकलमयेन विभ्रमनक्षत्रमालागुणेन शिशिरीक्रियमाणम्, सकलवारणेन्द्राधिपत्यपट्टबन्धबन्धुरमिवोच्चैस्तरां शिरो दधानम्, मुहुर्मुहुः स्थगितापावृतदिङ्मुखाभ्यां कर्णतालवृन्ताभ्यां वीजयन्तमिव भर्तृभक्त्या दन्तपर्यङ्किकास्थितां राजलक्ष्मीम्, आयतवंशक्रमागतेन गजाधिपत्यचिह्नेन चामरेणेव चलता वालधिना विराजमानम्, स्वच्छशिशिरशीकरच्छलेन दिग्विजयपीताः सरित इव पुनः पुनर्मुखेन मुञ्चन्तम्, क्षणमवधानदाननिस्पन्दीकृतसकलावयवानामन्यद्विरदडिण्डिमाकर्णनाङ्कवलनानामन्ते दीर्घफूत्कारैः परिभवदुःखमिवावेदयन्तम्, अलब्धयुद्धमिवात्मानमनुशोचन्तम्, आरोहाधिरूढिपरिभवेन लज्जमानमिवाङ्गुलीलिखितमहीतलं मदं मुञ्चन्तम्, अवज्ञागृहीतमुक्तकवलकुपितारोहारटनानुरोधेन मदतन्द्रीनिमीलितनेत्रत्रिभागं कथं कथमपि मन्दमन्दमनादरादाददानं कवलान्, अवजग्धतमालपल्लवस्रुतश्यामलरसेन प्रभूततया मद-

१ '०भोगवत्तया' ब. २ '०चितैर्घनै०' अ–क. ३ 'कलयन्तम्' अ–क. ४ '०सुकुमारतरेण' ब. ५ 'गलन्तम्' ब. ६ '०भुक्तानि पुरः करटाभ्याम्' अ–क.

प्रवाहमिव मुखेनाप्युत्सृजन्तम्, दलन्तमिव[1] दर्पेण, श्वसन्तमिव शौर्येण, मूर्च्छन्तमिव मदेन, क्षुभ्यन्तमिव तारुण्येन, द्रवन्तमिव दानेन, वल्गन्तमिव बलेन, माद्यन्तमिव मानेन, उद्यन्तमिवोत्साहेन, ताम्यन्तमिव तेजसा, लिम्पन्तमिव लावण्येन, सिञ्चन्तमिव सौभाग्येन, स्निग्धं नखेषु, परुषं रोमविषये, गुरुं मुखे, सच्छिष्यं विनये, मृदुं शिरसि, दृढं परिचयेषु, ह्रस्वं स्कन्धबन्धे, दीर्घमायुषि, दरिद्रमुदरे, सततप्रवृत्तं दाने, बलभद्रं मदलीलासु, कुलकलत्रमायत्ततासु, जिनं क्षमासु, वह्निवर्षं क्रोधमोक्षेषु, गरुडं नागोद्धृतिषु, नारदं कलहकुतूहलेषु, शुष्काशनिपातमवस्कन्देषु, मकरं वाहिनीक्षोभेषु, आशीविषं दशनकर्मसु, वरुणं हस्तपाशाकृष्टिषु, यमवागुरामरातिसंवेष्टनेषु, कालं परिणतिषु, राहुं तीक्ष्णकरग्रहणेषु, लोहिताङ्गं वक्रचारेषु, अलातचक्रं मण्डलभ्रान्तिविज्ञानेषु, मनोरथसम्पादकं चिन्तामणिपर्वतं विक्रमस्य, दन्तमुक्ताशैलस्तम्भनिवासप्रासादमभिमानस्य, घण्टाचामरमण्डनमनोहरमिच्छासञ्चरणविमानं मनस्वितायाः, मदधारादुर्दिनान्धकारं गन्धोदकधारागृहं क्रोधस्य, सकाञ्चनप्रतिमं महानिकेतनमहङ्कारस्य, सगण्डशैलप्रस्रवणं क्रीडापर्वतमवलेपस्य, सदन्ततोरणं वज्रमन्दिरं दर्पस्य, उच्चकुम्भकूटाट्टालकविकटं सञ्चारि गिरिदुर्गं राज्यस्य, कृतानेकबाणविवरसहस्रं लोहप्राकारं पृथिव्याः, शिलीमुखशतझाङ्कारितं पारिजातपादपं भूनन्दनस्य, तथा च सङ्गीतगृहं[2] कर्णतालताण्डवानाम्, आपानमण्डपं मधुपमण्डलानाम्, अन्तःपुरं शृङ्गाराभरणानाम्, मदनोत्सवं मदलीलालास्यानाम्, अक्षुण्णप्रदोषं नक्षत्रमालामण्डलानाम्, अकालप्रावृट्कालं[3] मदमहानदीपूरप्लवानाम्, अलीकशरत्समयं सप्तच्छदवनपरिमलानाम्, अपूर्वहिमागमं शीकरनीहाराणाम्, मिथ्याजलधरं गर्जिताडम्बराणाम्, दर्पशातमपश्यत्।

आसीच्चास्य चेतसि—'नूनमस्य निर्माणे गिरयो ग्राहिताः परमाणुताम्। कुतोऽन्यथा गौरवमिदम्। आश्चर्यमेतत्। विन्ध्यस्य दन्तावादिवराहस्य करः' इति विस्मयमानमेव[4] तं दौवारिकोऽब्रवीत्—'पश्य।

मिथ्यैवालिखितां मनोरथशतैर्निःशेषनष्टां श्रियं
चिन्तासाधनकल्पनाकुलधियां भूयो वने विद्विषाम्।
आयातः कथमप्ययं स्मृतिपथं शून्यीभवच्चेतसां
नागेन्द्रः सहते न मानसगतानाशागजेन्द्रानपि ॥ ४ ॥

तदेहि। पुनरप्येनं द्रक्ष्यसि। पश्य तावद्देवम्' इत्यभिधीयमानश्च तेन मदजलपङ्किलकपोलपट्टपतितां[5] मत्तामिव मदपरिमलेन मुकुलितां कथमपि तस्माद्दृष्टिमाकृष्य तेनैव दौवारिकेणोपदिश्यमानवर्त्मा समतिक्रम्य भूपालसहस्रसङ्कुलानि त्रीणि कक्ष्यान्तराणि चतुर्थे भुक्तास्थानमण्डपस्य पुरस्तादजिरे

१ 'चलन्तमिव' अ. २ 'गृहकं' ब. ३ 'अकाण्ड' ब. ४ '०मानमेतं' अ–क. ५ '०जलकज्जलकालकपोल०' ब.

स्थितम्, दूरादूर्ध्वस्थितेन प्रांशुना कर्णिकारगौरेण व्यायामव्यायतवपुषा शस्त्रिणा मौलेन शरीरपरिचारकलोकेन पङ्क्तिस्थितेन कार्तस्वरस्तम्भमण्डलेनेव परिवृतम्, आसन्नोपविष्टविशिष्टैष्टलोकम्,[1] हरिचन्दनरसप्रक्षालिते तुषारशीकरशीतलतले दन्तपाण्डुरपादे शशिमय इव मुक्ताशैलशिलापट्टशयने समुपविष्टम्, शयनीयपर्यन्तविन्यस्ते समर्पितसकलविग्रहभारं भुजे, दिङ्मुखविसर्पिणि देहप्रभावितावने विततमणिमयूखे घर्मसमयसुभगे सरसीव मृदुमृणालजालजटिलजले सराजकं रममाणम्, तेजसः परमाणुभिरिव केवलैर्निर्मितम्, अनिच्छन्तमपि[2] बलादारोपयितुमिव सिंहासनं सर्वावयवेषु सर्वलक्षणैर्गृहीतम्, गृहीतब्रह्मचर्यमालिङ्गितं राजलक्ष्म्या, प्रतिपन्नासिधाराधारणव्रतमविसंवादिनं राजर्षिम्, विषमराजमार्गविनिहितपदस्खलनभियेव सुलग्नं धर्मे, सकलभूपालपरित्यक्तेन भीतेनेव लब्धवाचा सर्वात्मना सत्येन सेव्यमानम्, आसन्नवारविलासिनीप्रतियातनाभिश्शरणनखपातिनीभिर्दिग्भिरिव दशभिः[3] प्रणम्यमानम्, दीर्घैर्दिगन्तपातिभिर्दृष्टिपातैर्लोकपालानां कृताकृतमिव प्रत्यवेक्षमाणम्, मणिपादपीठपृष्ठप्रतिष्ठितकरेणोपरिगमनाभ्यनुज्ञां मृगयमाणमिव दिवसकरेण, भूषणप्रभासमुत्सारणबद्धपर्यन्तमण्डलेन प्रदक्षिणीक्रियमाणमिव[4] दिवसेन, अप्रणमद्भिर्गिरिभिरपि[5] दूयमानं शौर्योष्मणा, फेनायमानमिव चन्दनधवलं लावण्यजलधिमुद्वहन्तम्, एकराज्योर्जित्येन[6] निजप्रतिबिम्बान्यपि नृपचक्रचूडामणिधृतान्यसहमानमिव, दर्पदुःखासिकया चामरानिलनिभेन बहुधेव श्वसन्तीं राजलक्ष्मीं दधानम्, सकलमिव चतुःसमुद्रलावण्यमादायोत्थितया श्रिया समुपश्लिष्टम्, आभरणप्रभाजालजायमानानीन्द्रधनुःसहस्राणीन्द्रप्राभृतप्रहितानि विलम्भमानमिव राज्ञाम्, सम्भाषणेषु परित्यक्तमपि मधु वर्षन्तम्, काव्यकथास्वपीतमप्यमृतमुद्वमन्तम्, विस्रम्भभाषितेष्वनाकृष्टमपि हृदयं दर्शयन्तम्, प्रसादेषु निश्चलामपि श्रियं स्थाने स्थाने स्थापयन्तम्, वीरगोष्ठीषु पुलकितेन कपोलस्थलेनानुरागसन्देशमिवोपांशु रणश्रियः शृण्वन्तम्, अतिक्रान्तसुभटकलहालापेषु स्नेहवृष्टिमिव दयिमिष्टे कृपाणे पातयन्तम्, परिहासस्मितेषु गुरुप्रतापभीतस्य राजकस्य स्वच्छमाशयमिव दशनांशुभिः कथयन्तम्, सकललोकहृदयस्थितमपि न्याये तिष्ठन्तम्, अगोचरे गुणानामभूमौ सौभाग्यानामविषये वरप्रदानानामशक्य आशिषाममार्गे मनोरथानामतिदूरे दैवस्यादिश्युपमानानामसाध्ये धर्मस्यादृष्टपूर्वे लक्ष्म्या महत्त्वे स्थितम्, अरुणपादपल्लवेन सुगतमन्थरोरुणा वज्रायुधनिष्ठुरप्रकोष्ठपृष्ठेन वृषस्कन्धेन भास्वद्बिम्बाधरेण प्रसन्नावलोकितेन चन्द्रमुखेन कृष्णकेशेन वपुषा सर्वदेवतावतारमिवैकस्थं दर्शयन्तम्, अपि च मांस-

१ '०विष्टैष्टविशिष्टलोकम्' ब. २ 'अनिच्छन्तं बला०' अ–क. ३ अस्मात्परं 'विग्रहावर्जिताभिः' इत्यधिकं ब–पुस्तके. ४ अस्मात्परं 'गलितोष्मणा' इत्यधिकं ब–पुस्तके. ५ 'गिरिभिरपि भूभृद्भिः' ब. ६ '०राज्योर्जितेन' ब.

लमयूखमालामलिनितमहीतले महति महार्हे माणिक्यमालामण्डितमेखले महानीलमये पादपीठे कलिकालशिरसीव सलीलं विन्यस्तवामचरणमाक्रान्तकालिय.फणाचक्रवालं बालमिव पुण्डरीकाक्षम्, क्षौमपाण्डुरेण चरणनखदीधितिप्रतानेन प्रसरता महीं महादेवीपट्टबन्धेनेव महिमानमारोपयन्तम्, अप्रणतलोकपालकोपेनेवातिलोहितौ सकलनृपतिमौलिमालास्रुतिपीतं पद्मरागरत्नातपमिव वमन्तौ सर्वतेजस्विमण्डलास्तमयसंध्यामिव धारयन्तावशेषराजकशेखरकुसुममधुरसस्रोतांसीव स्रवन्तौ समस्तसामन्तसीमन्तोत्तंसस्रक्सौरभभ्रान्तैर्भ्रमरमण्डलैरमित्रोत्तमाङ्गैरिव मुहूर्तमप्यविरहितौ संवाहनतत्परायाः श्रियो विकचरक्तपङ्कजवनवासभवनानीव कल्पयन्तौ जलजशङ्खमीनमकरसनाथतलतया कथितचतुरम्भोधिभोगचिह्नाविव चरणौ दधानम्, दिङ्नागदन्तमुसलाभ्यामिव विकटमकरमुखप्रतिबन्धबन्धुराभ्यामुद्वेललावण्यपयोनिधिप्रवाहाभ्यामिव फेनाहितशोभाभ्यां चन्[1]दनद्रुमाभ्यामिव भोगिमण्डलशिरोरत्नरश्मिरज्यमानमूलाभ्यां हृदयारोपितभूभारधारणमाणिक्यस्तम्भाभ्यामूरुदण्डाभ्यां विराजमानम्, अमृतफेनपिण्डपाण्डुना मेखलामणिमयूखखचितेन नितम्बबिम्बव्यासङ्गिना विमलपयोधौतेन नेत्रसूत्रनिवेशशोभिनाधरवाससा वासुकिनिर्मोकेणेव मन्दरं द्योतमानम्, अघनेन सतारागणेनोपरिकृतेन द्वितीयाम्बरेण भुवनाभोगमिव भासमानम्, इभपतिदशनमुसलसहस्रोल्लेखकठिनमसृणेनापर्याप्ताम्बरप्रथिम्ना विविधवाहिनीसंक्षोभकलकलसंमर्दसहिष्णुना कैलासमिव महता स्फटिकतटेनोरुणोरःकवाटेन राजमानम्, श्रीसरस्वत्योरुरोवदनोपभोगविभागसूत्रेणेव पातितेन शेषेणेव च तद्भुजस्तम्भविन्यस्तसमस्तभूभारलब्धविश्रान्तिसुखप्रसुप्तेन हारदण्डेन प[2]रिवेष्टितकन्धरम्, जीवितावधिगृहीतसर्वस्वमहादानदीक्षाचीरेणेव हारमुक्ताफलानां किरणनिकरेण प्रावृतवक्षःस्थलम्, अजजिगीषया बालैर्भुजैरिवापरैः प्ररोहद्भिर्बाहूपधानशायिन्याः श्रियः कर्णोत्पलमधुरसधारासन्तानैरिव गलद्भिर्भुजजन्मनः प्रतापस्य निर्गमनमार्गैरिवाविर्भवद्भिररुणैः केयूररत्नकिरणदण्डैरुभयतः प्रसारितमणिमयपक्षवितानमिव माणिक्यमहीधरम्, सकललोकालोकमार्गार्गलेन चतुरुदधिपरिक्षेपख[3]ातशिलाप्राकारेण सर्वराजहंसबन्धवज्रपञ्जरेण भुवनलक्ष्मीप्रवेशमङ्गलमहामणितोरणेनातिदीर्घदोर्दण्डयुगलेन दिशां दिक्पालानां च युगपदायतिमपहरन्तम्, सोदर्यलक्[4]ष्मीचुम्बनलोभेन कौस्तुभमणेरिव मुखावयवतां गतस्याधरस्य गलता रागेण पारिजातपल्लवरसेनेव सिञ्चन्तं दिङ्मुखानि, अन्तरान्तरा सुहृत्परिहासस्मितैः प्रकीर्यमाणविमलदशनशिखाप्रतानैः प्रकृतिमूढाया राजश्रियाः प्रज्ञालोकमिव दर्शयन्तम्, मुखजनितेन्दुसन्देहागतानि कुमुदिनीवनानीव प्रेषयन्तम्, स्फुटस्फटिकधवलदशन-

---

१ 'कल्पचन्दन०' ब. २ 'परिवलित०' अ. ३ 'खातशातकुम्भशिला' ब. ४ 'सौन्दर्य०' ब.

पङ्क्तिकृतकुमुदवनशङ्काप्रविष्टां शरज्ज्योत्स्नामिव विसर्जयन्तम्, मदिरामृतपारिजातगन्धगर्भेण भरितसकलककुभा मुखामोदेनामृतमथनदिवसमिव सृजन्तम्, विकचमुखकमलकर्णिकाकोशेनानवरतमापीयमानश्वाससौरभमिवाधोमुखेन नासावंशेन, चक्षुषः क्षीरस्निग्धस्य धवलिम्ना दिङ्मुखान्यपूर्ववदनचन्द्रोदयोद्वेलक्षीरोदप्लावितानीव कुर्वाणम्, विमलकपोलफलकप्रतिबिम्बितां चामरग्राहिणीं विग्रहिणीमिव मुखनिवासिनीं सरस्वतीं दधानम्, अरुणेन चूडामणिशोचिषा सरस्वतीर्ष्याकुपितलक्ष्मीप्रसादनलग्नेन चरणालक्तकेनेव लोहितायितललाटतटम्[१], आपाटलांशुतन्त्रीसन्तानवलयिनीं[२] कुण्डलमणिकुटिलकोटिबालवीणामनवरतचलितचरणानां वादयतामुपवीणयतामिव स्वरव्याकरणविवेकविशारदं श्रवणावतंसमधुकरकुलानां कलक्वणितमाकर्णयन्तम्, उत्फुल्लमालतीमयेन राजलक्ष्म्याः कचग्रहलीलालग्नेन नखज्योत्स्नावलयेनेव मुखशशिपरिवेशमण्डलेन मुण्डमालागुणेन परिकलितकेशान्तम्, शिखण्डाभरणभुवा मुक्ताफलालोकेन मरकतमणिकिरणकलापेन चान्योन्यसंवलनवृजिनेन प्रयागप्रवाहवेणिकावारिणेवागत्य स्वयमभिषिच्यमानम्, श्रमजलविलीनबहलकृष्णागुरुपङ्कतिलककलङ्ककलिपतेन कालिम्ना प्रार्थनाचाटुचतुरचरणपतनशतश्यामिकाकिणेनेव नीलायमानललाटेन्दुलेखाभिः[३] क्षुभितमानसोद्गतैरुत्कलिकाकलापैरिव हारैरुल्लसद्भिरवष्टभ्यमानाभिर्विलासवल्गनचटुलैर्भ्रूलताकल्पैरीर्ष्यया श्रियमिव तर्जयन्तीभिरायामिभिः श्वसितैरविरलपरिमलैर्मलयमारुतमयैः पाशैरिवाकर्षन्तीभिर्विकटबकुलावलीवराटकवेष्टितमुखैर्बृहद्भिः स्तनकलशैः स्वदारसन्तोषरसमिवाशेषमुद्धरन्तीभिः कुचोत्कम्पिकाविकारप्रेङ्खितानां हारतरलमणीनां रश्मिभिराकृष्य हृदयमिव हठात्प्रवेशयन्तीभिः प्रभामुचामाभरणमणीनां मयूखैः प्रसारितैर्बहुभिरिव बाहुभिरालिङ्गन्तीभिर्जृम्भानुबन्धबन्धुरवदनारविन्दावरणीकृतैरुत्तानैः करकिसलयैः सरभसप्रधावितानि मानसानीव निरुन्धतीभिर्मदलान्धमधुकरकुलकीर्यमाणकर्णकुसुमरजःकणकूणितकोणानि कुसुमशरशरनिकरप्रहारमूर्च्छामुकुलितानीव लोचनानि चतुरं सञ्चारयन्तीभिरन्योन्यमत्सरादाविर्भवद्भङ्गुरभ्रुकुटिविभ्रमक्षिप्तैः कटाक्षैः कर्णेन्दीवराणीव ताडयन्तीभिरनिमेषदर्शनसुखरसराशिं मन्थरितपक्ष्मणा चक्षुषा पीतमिव कोमलकपोलपालीप्रतिबिम्बितं वहन्तीभिरभिलाषलीलानिर्निमित्तस्मितैश्चन्द्रोदयानिव मदनसाहायकाय सम्पादयन्तीभिरङ्गभङ्गवलनान्योन्यघटितोत्तानकरवेणिकाभिः स्फुटनमुखराङ्गुलीकाण्डकुण्डलीक्रियमाणनखदीधितिनिवहनिभेनाकिञ्चित्करकामकार्मुकाणीव रुषा भञ्जतीभिर्वारविलासिनीभिर्विलुप्यमानसौभाग्यमिव सर्वतः, स्पर्शस्विन्नवेपमानकरकिसलयगलितचरणारविन्दां चरणग्राहिणीं विहस्य कोणेन लीलालसं शिरसि ताडयन्तम्, अनवरतकरकलितकोणतया चात्मनः प्रियां वीणामिव श्रिय-

---

१ 'लोहितायत' अ–क. २ 'तनुतन्त्री०' ब. ३ 'ललाटलेखाभिः' अ–क.

मपि शिक्षयन्तम्, निःस्नेह इति धनैरनाश्रयणीय इति दोषैर्निग्रहरुचिरितीन्द्रियैर्दुरुपसर्प इति कलिना नीरस इति व्यसनैर्भीरुरित्ययशसा दुर्ग्रहचित्तवृत्तिरिति चित्तभुवा स्त्रीपर इति सरस्वत्या पण्ढ इति परकलत्रैः काष्ठामुनिरिति यतिभिर्धूर्त इति वेश्याभिर्नेय इति सुहृद्भिः कर्मकर इति विप्रैः सुसहाय इति शत्रुयोधैरेकमप्यनेकधा गृह्यमाणम्, शन्तनोर्महावाहिनीपतिम्, भीष्माज्जितकाशिनम्, द्रोणाच्चापलालसम्, गुरुपुत्रादमोघमार्गणम्, कर्णान्मित्रप्रियम्, युधिष्ठिराद्बहुक्षमम्[1], भीमादनेकनागायुतबलम्, धनञ्जयान्महाभारतरणयोग्यम्, कारणमिव कृतयुगस्य, बीजमिव विबुधसर्गस्य, उत्पत्तिद्वीपमिव दर्पस्य, एकागारमिव करुणायाः, प्रातिवेशिकमिव पुरुषोत्तमस्य, खनिपर्वतमिव पराक्रमस्य, सर्वविद्यासङ्गीतकगृहमिव सरस्वत्याः, द्वितीयामृतमथनदिवसमिव लक्ष्मीसमुत्थानस्य, बलदर्शनमिव वैदग्ध्यस्य, एकस्थानमिव स्थितीनाम्, सर्वस्वकथनमिव कान्तेः, अपवर्गमिव रूपपरमाणुसर्गस्य, सकलदुश्चरितप्रायश्चित्तमिव राज्यस्य, सर्वबलसन्दोहावस्कन्दमिव कन्दर्पस्य, उपायमिव पुरन्दरदर्शनस्य, आवर्तनमिव धर्मस्य, कन्यान्तःपुरमिव कलानाम्, परमप्रमाणमिव सौभाग्यस्य, राजसर्गसमाह्यवभृथस्नानदिवसमिव सर्वप्रजापतीनाम्, गम्भीरं च प्रसन्नं च त्रासजननं च रमणीयं च कौतुकजननं च पुण्यं च चक्रवर्तिनं हर्षमद्राक्षीत् ।

दृष्ट्वा चानुगृहीत इव निगृहीत इव साभिलाष इव तृप्त इव[2] रोमाञ्चमुचा मुखेन मुञ्चन्नानन्दबाष्पवारिबिन्दून्दूरादेव विस्मयस्मेरः समचिन्तयत्—'सोऽयं सुजन्मा सुगृहीतनामा तेजसां राशिः चतुरुदधिकेदारकुटुम्बी भोक्ता ब्रह्मस्तम्भफलस्य सकलादिराजचरितजयज्येष्ठमल्लो देवः परमेश्वरो हर्षः । एतेन च खलु राजन्वती पृथ्वी, नास्य हरेरिव वृषविरोधीनि बालचरितानि, न पशुपतेरिव दक्षोद्वेगकारीण्यैश्वर्यविलसितानि, न शतक्रतोरिव गोत्रविनाशपिशुनाः प्रवादाः, न यमस्येवातिवल्लभानि दण्डग्रहणानि, न वरुणस्येव निस्त्रिंशग्राहसहस्ररक्षिता रत्नालयाः, न धनदस्येव निष्फलाः सन्निधिलाभाः, न जिनस्येवार्थवादशून्यानि दर्शनानि[3], न चन्द्रमस इव बहुलदोषोपहताः श्रियः । चित्रमिदमत्यमरं राजत्वम् । अपि चास्य त्यागस्यार्थिनः, प्रज्ञायाः शास्त्राणि, कवित्वस्य वाचः, सत्त्वस्य साहसस्थानानि, उत्साहस्य व्यापाराः, कीर्तेर्दिङ्मुखानि, अनुरागस्य लोकहृदयानि, गुणगणस्य संख्या, कौशलस्य कला, न पर्याप्तो विषयः । अस्मिंश्च[4] राजनि यतीनां योगपट्टकाः, पुस्तकर्मणां पार्थिवविग्रहाः, षट्पदानां दानग्रहणकलहाः, वृत्तानां पादच्छेदाः, अष्टापदानां चतुरङ्गकल्पना, पन्नगानां द्विजगुरुद्वेषाः, वाक्यविदामधिकरणविचाराः' इति । समुपसृत्य चोपवीती स्वस्तिशब्दमकरोत् ।

---

१ 'बाहुक्षमम्' ब. २ 'इवातृप्त इव' ब. ३ 'विज्ञानदर्शनानि' ब. ४ 'यस्मिंश्च' ब.

अथोत्तरेण[1] नातिदूरे राजधिष्ण्यस्य गजपरिचारको मधुरमपरवक्त्रमुच्चैरगायत्—

'करिकलभ विमुञ्च लोलतां चर विनयव्रतमानताननः।
मृगपतिनखकोटिभङ्गुरो गुरुरुपरि क्षमते न तेऽङ्कुशः' ॥ ५ ॥

राजा तु तच्छ्रुत्वा दृष्ट्वा च तं गिरिगुहागतसिंहबृंहितगम्भीरेण स्वरेण पूरयन्निव नभोभागमपृच्छत्—'एष स बाणः' इति। 'यथाज्ञापयति देवः। सोऽयम्' इति विज्ञापितो दौवारिकेण। 'न तावदेनमकृतप्रसादः[2] पश्यामि' इति तिर्यङ्नीलधवलांशुकशारां तिरस्करिणीमिव भ्रमयन्नपाङ्गनीयमानतरलतारकस्यायामिनीं चक्षुषः प्रभां परिवृत्य प्रेष्ठस्य पृष्ठतो निषण्णस्य मालवराजसूनोरकथयत्—'महानयं भुजङ्गः' इति। तूष्णीम्भावेन त्वगमितनरेन्द्रवचसि तस्मिन्मूके च राजलोके मुहूर्तमिव तूष्णीं स्थित्वा बाणो व्यज्ञापयत्—'देव अविज्ञाततत्त्व इव, अश्रद्दधान इव, नेय इव, अविदितलोकवृत्तान्त इव च कस्मादेवमाज्ञापयसि। स्वैरिणो विचित्राश्च लोकस्य स्वभावाः प्रवादाश्च। महद्भिस्तु यथार्थदर्शिभिर्भवितव्यम्। नार्हसि मामन्यथा सम्भावयितुमविशिष्टमिव। ब्राह्मणोऽस्मि जातः सोमपायिनां वंशे वात्स्यायनानाम्। यथाकालमुपनयनादयः कृताः संस्काराः। सम्यक्पठितः साङ्गो वेदः। श्रुतानि यथाशक्ति शास्त्राणि। दारपरिग्रहादभ्यगारिकोऽस्मि। का मे भुजङ्गता। लोकद्वयाविरोधिभिस्तु चापलैः शैशवमशून्यमासीत्। अत्रानपलापोऽस्मि। अनेनैव च गृहीतविप्रतीसारमिव मे हृदयम्। इदानीं तु सुगत इव शान्तमनसि मनाविव कर्तरि वर्णाश्रमव्यवस्थानां समवर्तिनीव च साक्षाद्दण्डभृति देवे शासति सप्ताम्बुराशिरशनामशेषद्वीपमालिनीं महीं क इवाविशङ्कः सर्वव्यसनबन्धोरविनयस्य मनसाप्यभिनयं कल्पयिष्यति। आसतां तावन्मानुष्यकोपेताः। त्वत्प्रभावादलयोऽपि भीता इव मधु पिबन्ति, रथाङ्गनामानोऽपि लज्जन्त इवाभ्यनुवृत्तिव्यसनैः प्रियाणाम्, कपयोपि चकिता इव चपलायन्ते, शरारवोऽपि सानुक्रोशा इव श्वापदगणाः पिशितानि भुञ्जते। सर्वथा कालेन मां ज्ञास्यति स्वामी स्वयमेव। अनपाचीनचित्तवृत्तिग्राहिण्यो हि भवन्ति प्रज्ञावतां प्रकृतयः' इत्यभिधाय तूष्णीमभूत्।

भूपतिरपि 'एवमस्माभिः श्रुतम्' इत्यभिधाय तूष्णीमेवाभवत्। सम्भाषणासनदानादिना तु प्रसादेन नैनमन्वग्रहीत्। केवलममृतवृष्टिभिः स्नपयन्निव स्नेहगर्भेण दृष्टिपातमात्रेणान्तर्गतां प्रीतिमकथयत्। अस्ताभिलाषिणि च लम्बमाने सवितरि विसर्जितराजलोकोऽभ्यन्तरं प्राविशत्। बाणोपि निर्गत्य धौतारकूटकोमलातपत्विषि निर्वाति वासरे, अस्ताचलकूटकिरीटे निचुलमञ्जरीभांसि तेजांसि मुञ्चति वियन्मुचि मरीचिमति,[3] रोमन्थमन्थरकुरङ्गकुटुम्बकाध्यास्यमानम्रदिष्ठगोष्ठीनपृष्ठास्वरण्यस्थलीषु, शोकाकुलकोककामिनीकूजितक-

---

१ 'अथोत्तरे' अ. २ '०प्रसादं' ब. ३ 'मरीचिमालिनि, अतिरोमन्थ०' अ.

अथ ते तमूचुः—'तात, सन्तोषजुषां सततसन्निहितविद्याविनोदानां वैतानवह्निमात्रसहायानां कियन्मात्रं नः कृत्यं सुखितया सकलभुवनभुजि भुजङ्गराजदेहदीर्घे रक्षति क्षितिं क्षितिभुजो[1] भुजे। सर्वथा[2] सुखिन एव वयम्, विशेषेण तु त्वयि विमुक्तकौसीद्ये परमेश्वरपार्श्ववर्तिनि वेत्रासनमधितिष्ठति। सर्वे च यथाशक्ति यथाविभवं यथाकालं च सम्पाद्यन्ते विप्रजनोचिताः क्रियाकलापाः' इति। एवमादिभिरालापैः स्कन्धावारवार्ताभिश्च शैशवातिक्रान्तक्रीडानुस्मरणैः पूर्वजकथाभिश्च विनोदितमनास्तैः सह सुचिरमतिष्ठत्। उत्थाय च मध्यन्दिने यथाक्रियमाणाः स्थितीरकरोत्। भुक्तवन्तं च तं सर्वे ज्ञातयः पर्यवारयन्।

अत्रान्तरे दुकूलपट्टप्रभवे शिखण्ड्यपाङ्गपाण्डुनी पौण्ड्रे वाससी वसानः, स्नानावसानसमये बन्दितया तीर्थमृदा गोरोचनया च रचिततिलकः, तैलामलकमसृणितमौलिः, अनुच्चचूडाचुम्बिना निबिडेन कुसुमापीडकेन समुद्भासमानः, सकृदुप[3]युक्तताम्बूलविमलाधरकान्तिः, एकशलाकाञ्जनजनितलोचनरुचिः, अचिरभुक्तः, विनीतमार्यं च वेषं दधानः, पुस्तकवाचकः सुदृष्टिराजगाम। नातिदूरवर्तिन्यां चासन्द्यां निषसाद। स्थित्वा च मुहूर्तमिव तत्कालापनीतसूत्रवेष्टनमपि नखकिरणैर्मृदुमृणालसूत्रैरिव वेष्टितं पुस्तकं पुरोनिहितशरशलाकायन्त्रके निधाय, पृष्ठतः सनीडसन्निविष्टाभ्यां मधुकरपारावताभ्यां[4] दत्ते स्थानके, प्राभातिकप्रपाठकच्छेदचिह्नीकृतमन्तरपत्र[5]मुत्क्षिप्य, गृहीत्वा च कतिपयपत्रलघ्वीं कर्पाटिकाम्[6], क्षालयन्निव मषीमलिनान्यक्षराणि दन्तकान्तिभिः, अर्चयन्निव सितकुसुममुक्तिभिर्ग्रन्थम्, मुखसन्निहितसरस्वतीनूपुररवैरिव गमकैर्मधुरैराक्षिपन्मनांसि श्रोतॄणां गीत्या पवमानप्रोक्तं पुराणं पपाठ।

तस्मिंश्च तथा श्रुतिसुभगगीतिगर्भं पठति सुदृष्टौ नातिदूरवर्ती बन्दी सूचीबाणस्तारमधुरेण गीतिध्वनिमनुवर्तमानः स्वरेणेदमार्यायुगलमपठत्[7]—

'तदपि मुनिगीतमतिपृथु तदपि जगद्व्यापि पावनं तदपि।
हर्षचरितादभिन्नं प्रतिभाति हि मे पुराणमिदम्॥ ३॥
वंशानुगमविवादि स्फुटकरणं भरतमार्गभजनगुरु।
श्रीकण्ठविनिर्यातं गीतमिदं हर्षराज्यमिव॥ ४॥'

तच्छ्रुत्वा बाणस्य चत्वारः पितामहमुखपद्मा इव वेदाभ्यासपवित्रितमूर्तयः, उपाया इव सामप्रयोगललितमुखाः, गणपतिरधिपतिस्तारापतिः श्यामल इति पितृव्यपुत्रा भ्रातरः, प्रसन्नवृत्तयो गृहीतवाक्याः कृतगुरुपदन्यासा न्यायवेदिनः[8] सुकृतसंग्रहाभ्यासगुरवो लब्धसाधुशब्दा लोक इव व्याकरणे-

---

१ 'क्षितिपो भुजे' ब. २ 'सर्वदा' ब. ३ 'असकृदुप०' अ–क. ४ अस्मात्परं 'वांशिकाभ्याम्' इत्यधिकं ब–पुस्तके. ५ 'अन्तरं पत्रं' ब. ६ 'कापालिकाम्' ब. ७ 'अगायत्' ब. ८ 'न्यायवादिनः' अ–क.

ऽपि, सकलपुराणराजर्षिचरिताभिज्ञाः, महाभारतभावितात्मानः, विदितसकलेतिहासाः, महाविद्वांसः, महाकवयः, महापुरुषवृत्तान्तकुतूहलिनः, सुभाषितश्रवणरसरसायनाः[1]वितृष्णाः, वयसि वचसि यशसि तपसि महसि वपुषि यजुषि च प्रथमाः, पूर्वमेव कृतसङ्गराः, विवक्षवः स्मितसुधाधवलितकपोलोदराः, परस्परस्य मुखानि व्यलोकयन्।

अथ तेषां कनीयान्कमलदलदीर्घलोचनः श्यामलो नाम बाणस्य प्रेयान्प्राणानामपि वशयिता दत्तसंज्ञस्तैः सप्रणयं दशनज्योत्स्नास्नपितककुभा मुखेन्दुना बभाषे—'तात बाण, द्विजानां राजा गुरुदारग्रहणमकार्षीत्। पुरूरवा ब्राह्मणधनतृष्णया दयितेनायुषा व्ययुज्यत। नहुषः परकलत्राभिलाषी महाभुजङ्ग आसीत्। ययातिराहितब्राह्मणीपाणिग्रहणः पपात। सुद्युम्नः स्त्रीमय एवाभवत्। सोमकस्य प्रख्याता[2] जन्तुवधनिर्घृणता। मान्धाता मार्गणव्यसनेन सपुत्रपौत्रो रसातलमगात्। पुरुकुत्सः कुत्सितं कर्म तपस्यन्नपि मेकलकन्यकायामकरोत्। कुवलयाश्वो भुजङ्गलोकपरिग्रहादश्वतरकन्यामपि न परिजहार। पृथुः प्रथमपुरुषकः परिभूतवान्पृथिवीम्। नृगस्य कृकलासभावे[3] वर्णसङ्करः समदृश्यत। सौदासेन नरक्षिता पर्याकुलीकृता क्षितिः। नलमवशाक्षहृदयं कलिरभिभूतवान्। संवरणो मित्रदुहितरि विक्लवतामगात्। दशरथ इष्टरामोन्मादेन मृत्युमवाप। कार्तवीर्यो गोब्राह्मणातिपीडनेन निधनम[4]यासीत्। मरुत्त इष्टबहुसुवर्णकोऽपि देवद्विजबहुमतो न बभूव। शन्तनुरतिव्यसनादेकाकी वियुक्तो वाहिन्या विपिने विललाप। पाण्डुर्वनमध्यगतो मत्स्य इव मदनरसाविष्टः प्राणान्मुमोच। युधिष्ठिरो गुरुभयविषण्णहृदयः समरशिरसि सत्यमुत्सृष्टवान्। इत्थं नास्ति राजत्वमपकलङ्कमृते देवदेवादमुतः सर्वद्वीपभुजो हर्षात्। अस्य हि बहून्याश्चर्याणि श्रूयन्ते। तथा हि—अत्र बलजिता निश्चलीकृताश्चलन्तः कृतपक्षाः क्षितिभृतः। अत्र प्रजापतिना शेषभोगिमण्डलस्योपरि क्षमा कृता। अत्र पुरुषोत्तमेन सिन्धुराजं प्रमथ्य लक्ष्मीरात्मी[5]कृता। अत्र बलिना मोचितभूभृद्वेष्टनो मुक्तो महानागः। अत्र देवेनाभिषिक्तः कुमारः। अत्र स्वामिनैकप्रहारपातितारातिना प्रख्यापिता शक्तिः। अत्र नरसिंहेन स्वहस्तविशसितारातिना प्रकटीकृतो विक्रमः। अत्र परमेश्वरेण तुषारशैलभुवो दुर्गाया गृहीतः करः। अत्र लोकनाथेन दिशां मुखेषु परिकल्पिता लोकपालाः सकलभुवनकोशश्चाग्रजन्मनां विभक्त इति। एवमादयः प्रथमकृतयुगस्येव दृश्यन्ते महासमारम्भाः। अतोऽस्य[6] सुगृहीतनाम्नः पुण्यराशेः पूर्वपुरुषवंशानुक्रमेणादितः प्रभृति चरितमिच्छामः श्रोतुम्। सुमहान्कालो नः शुश्रूषमाणानाम्। अयस्कान्तमणय इव लोहानि नीरसनि-

---

१ '०रसायनाः, वितृष्णाः,' अ. २ अस्मात्परं 'जगति' इत्यधिकं ब-पुस्तके. ३ '०भावेऽपि' ब. ४ अस्मात्परं 'रामो मनोभवभ्रान्तहृदयो जनकतनयामपि न परिहृतवान्' इत्यधिकं ब-पुस्तके. ५ 'आत्मीया कृता' ब. ६ 'यतो यस्य' ब.

श्रुराणि क्षुल्लकानामप्याकर्षन्ति मनांसि महतां गुणाः, किमुत स्वभावसरसमृदूनीतरेषाम्। कस्य न द्वितीयमहाभारते भवेदस्य चरिते कुतूहलम्। आचष्टां भवान्। भवतु भार्गवोऽयं वंशः शुचिनानेन राजर्षिचरितश्रवणेन सुतरां शुचितरः' इत्येवमभिधाय तूष्णीमभूत्।

बाणस्तु विहस्याब्रवीत्—'आर्य, न युक्त्यनुरूपमभिहितम्। अघटमानमनोरथमिव भवतां कुतूहलमवकल्पयामि। शक्याशक्यपरिसंख्यानशून्याः प्रायेण स्वार्थतृषः। परगुणानुरागिणी प्रियजनकथाश्रवणरसरभसमोहिता च मन्ये महतामपि मतिरपहरति प्रविवेकम्। पश्यत्वार्यः क्व परमाणुपरिमाणं बटुहृदयम्, क्व समस्तब्रह्मस्तम्भव्यापि देवस्य चरितम्, क्व परिमितवर्णवृत्तयः कतिपये शब्दाः, क्व संख्यातिगास्तद्गुणाः। सर्वज्ञस्याप्ययमविषयः, वाचस्पतेरप्यगोचरः, सरस्वत्या अप्यतिभारः, किमुतास्मद्विधस्य। कः खलु पुरुषायुषशतेनापि शक्नुयादविकलमस्य चरितं वर्णयितुम्। एकदेशे तु यदि कुतूहलं वः, सज्जा वयम्। इयमधिगतकतिपयाक्षरलवलघीयसी जिह्वा क्वोपयोगं गमिष्यति। भवन्तः श्रोतारः। वर्ण्यते हर्षचरितम्। किमन्यत्। अद्य तु परिणतप्रायो दिवसः। पश्चाल्लम्बमानकपिलकिरणजटाभारभास्वरो भगवान्भार्गवो राम इव समन्तपञ्चकरुधिरमहाह्रदे निमज्जति संध्यारागपटले पूषा। श्वो निवेदयितास्मि' इति। सर्वे च ते 'तथा' इति प्रत्यपद्यन्त। नातिचिरादुत्थाय संध्यामुपासितुं शोणमयासीत्।

अथ मधुमदपल्लवितमालवीकपोलकोमलातपे मुकुलितेऽह्नि कमलिनीमीलनादिव लोहिततमे तमोलिहि रवौ लम्बमाने, रविरथतुरगमार्गानुसारेण यममहिष इव धावति नभसि तमसि, क्रमेण च गृहतापसकुटीरकपटलावलम्बिषु रक्तातपच्छेदैः सह संहृतेषु वल्कलेषु, कलिकल्मषमुषि पुण्णति[1] गगनमग्निहोत्रधामधूमे, सनियमे यजमानजने मौनव्रतिनि, विहारवेलाविलोले पर्यटति पल्लीजने, विकीर्यमाणहरितश्यामाकशालिपूलिकासु दुग्धासु होमकपिलासु, हूयमाने वैतानतनूनपाति, पूतविष्टरोपविष्टे कृष्णाजिनजटिले जटिनि, जपति बटुजने, ब्रह्मासनाध्यासिनि ध्यायति योगिगणे, तालध्वनिधावमानानन्तान्तेवासिनि अलसवृद्धश्रोत्रियानुमतेन गलद्ग्रन्थदण्डकोद्गारिणि संध्यां समवधारयति[2] वठरविटबटुसमाजे, समुन्मज्जति च ज्योतिषि तारकाख्ये खे, प्राप्ते प्रदोषारम्भे भवनमागत्योपविष्टः स्निग्धैर्बन्धुभिश्च सार्धं तयैव गोष्ठ्या तस्थौ। नीतप्रथमयामश्च गणपतेर्भवने परिकल्पितं शयनीयमसेवत। इतरेषां तु सर्वेषां निमीलितदृशामप्यनुपजातनिद्राणां कमलवनानामिव सूर्योदयं प्रतिपालयतां कुतूहलेन कथमपि सा क्षपा क्षयमगच्छत्।

अथ यामिन्यास्तुर्ये यामे प्रतिबुद्धः स एव बन्दी श्लोकद्वयमगायत्—

---

१ 'मुष्णाति' ब. २ 'समवधीरयति' ब.

'पश्चादङ्घ्रिं प्रसार्य त्रिकनतिविततं द्राघयित्वाङ्गमुच्चै-
रासज्याभुग्नकण्ठो मुखमुरसि सटां धूलिधूम्रां विधूय ।
घासग्रासाभिलाषादनवरतचलत्प्रोथतुण्डस्तुरङ्गो
मन्दं शब्दायमानो विलिखति शयनादुत्थितः क्ष्मां खुरेण ॥ ५ ॥
कुर्वन्नाभुग्नपृष्ठो मुखनिकटकटिः कन्धरामातिरश्चीं
लोलेनाहन्यमानं तुहिनकणमुचा चञ्चता केसरेण ।
निद्राकण्डूकषायं कषति निबिडितश्रोत्रशुक्तिस्तुरङ्ग-
स्त्वङ्गत्पक्ष्माग्रलग्नप्रतनुबुसकणं कोणमक्ष्णः खुरेण ॥ ६ ॥'

बाणस्तु तच्छ्रुत्वा समुत्सृज्य निद्रामुत्थाय प्रक्षाल्य वदनमुपास्य भगवतीं संध्यामुदिते भगवति सवितरि गृहीतताम्बूलस्तत्रैवातिष्ठत् । अत्रान्तरे सर्वेऽस्य ज्ञातयः समाजग्मुः परिवार्य चासाञ्चक्रुः । असावपि पूर्वोद्घातेन विदिताभिप्रायस्तेषां पुरो हर्षचरितं कथयितुमारेभे—

श्रूयताम्—अस्ति पुण्यकृतामधिवासो वासवावास इव वसुधामवतीर्णः, सततमसङ्कीर्णवर्णव्यवहारस्थितिः कृतयुगव्यवस्थः, स्थलकमलबहलतया पोत्रोन्मूल्यमानमृणालैरुद्गीतमेदिनीसारगुणैरिव कृतमधुकरकोलाहलैर्हलैरुल्लिख्यमानक्षेत्रः, क्षीरोदपयःपायिपयोदसिक्ताभिरिव पुण्ड्रेक्षुवाटसन्ततिभिर्निरन्तरः, प्रतिदिशमपूर्वपर्वतकैरिव खलधानधामभिर्विभज्यमानैः सस्यकूटैः सङ्कटसीमान्तः, समन्तादुद्घातघटीसिच्यमानैर्जीरकजूटैर्जटिलितभूमिः, उर्वरावरीयोभिः शालेयैर्[१]रलङ्कृतः, पाकविशरारुराजमाषनिकरकिर्मीरितैश्च स्फुटितमुद्गफलकोशीकपिशितैर्गोधूमधामभिः स्थलीपृष्ठैरधिष्ठितः, महिषपृष्ठप्रतिष्ठितगायद्गोपालपालितैश्च कीटपटलम्पटचटकानुसृतैरवटुघटितघण्टाघटीरटितरमणीयैरटद्भिरटवीं हरवृषभपीतमामयाशङ्कया बहुधा विभक्तं क्षीरोदमिव क्षीरं क्षरद्भिर्बाष्पच्छेद्यतृणतृप्तैर्गोधनैर्धवलितविपिनः, विविधमखहोमधूमान्धशतमन्युमु[२]क्तैर्लोचनैरिव सहस्रसंख्यैः कृष्णशारैः शारीकृतोद्देशः, धवलधूलीमुचां केतकीवनानां रजोभिः पाण्डुरीकृतैः प्रम[३]थनाथोद्धूलनभस्मधूसरैः शिवपुरस्येव प्रवेशैः प्रदेशैरुपशोभितः, शाककन्दलश्यामलितग्रामोपकण्ठकाश्यपीपृष्ठः, पदे पदे करभपालीभिः पीलुपल्लवप्रस्फोटितैः करपुटपीडितमातुलुङ्गीदलरसोपलिप्तैः स्वेच्छाविचितकुङ्कुमकेसरकृतपुष्पप्रकरैः प्रत्यग्रफलरसपानसुखसुप्तपथिकैर्वनदेवतादीयमानामृतरसप्रपागृहैरिव द्राक्षामण्डपैः स्फुर[४]त्फलानां च बीजलग्नशुकचञ्चुरागाणामिव समारूढकपिकुलकपोलसन्दिह्यमानकुसुमानां दाडिमीनां वनैर्विलोभनीयोपनिर्गमः, वनपालपीयमाननारिकेलरसासवैश्च पथिकलोकलुप्यमानपिण्डखर्जूरैर्गोलाङ्गूललिह्यमानमधुरामोदपिण्डीरसैश्चकोरचञ्चुजर्जरितारुकैरुपवनैरभिरामः, तुङ्गार्जुनपालीपरिवृतैश्च गोकुलावतारकलु-

---

१ 'शालीयैः' अ–क. २ 'सक्तैः' ब. ३ 'प्रमथोद्धूलनधूसरैः' अ–क. ४ 'स्फुरत्फलानां' अ–क.

षितकूलकीलालैरध्वगशतशरण्यैररण्य[1]धराबन्धैरवन्ध्यवनरन्ध्रः, करभीयकुमारकपाल्यमानैरौष्ट्रकैरौरभ्रकैश्च कृतसम्बाधः, दिशि दिशि रविरथतुरगविलोभनायेव विलोठनमृदितकुङ्कुमस्थलीरससमालब्धानामुत्प्रोथपुटैरुन्मुखैरुदरशायिकिशोरकजवजननाय प्रभञ्जनमिव चापिबन्तीनां वातहरिणीनामिव स्वच्छन्दचारिणीनां वडवानां वृन्दैर्विचरद्भिराचितः, अनवरतक्रतुधूमान्धकारप्रवृत्तैर्हंसयूथैरिव [2]बाणैर्धवलितभुवनः, सङ्गीतगतमुरजरवमत्तैर्मयूरैरिव विभवैर्मुखरितजीवलोकः, शशिकरावदातवृत्तैर्मुक्ताफलैरिव गुणिभिः प्रसाधितः, पथिकशतविलुप्यमानस्फीतफलैर्महातरुभिरिव सर्वातिथिभिरभिगमनीयः, मृगमदपरिमलवाहिमृगरोमाच्छादितैर्हिमवत्पादैरिव महत्तरैः स्थिरीकृतः, प्रोद्दण्डसहस्रपत्रोपविष्टद्विजोत्तमैर्नारायणनाभिमण्डलैरिव तोयाशयैर्मण्डितः, मथितपयःप्रवाहप्रक्षालितक्षितिभिः क्षीरोदमथनारम्भैरिव महाघोषैः पूरिताशः श्रीकण्ठो नाम जनपदः।

यत्र त्रेताग्निधूमाश्रुपातजलक्षालिता इवाक्षीयन्त कुदृष्टयः। पच्यमानचयनेष्टकादहनदग्धानीव नादृश्यन्त दुरितानि। छिद्यमानयूपदारुपरशुपाटित इव व्यदीर्यताधर्मः। मखशिखिधूमजलधरधाराधौत इव ननाश वर्णसङ्करः। दीयमानानेकगोसहस्रशृङ्गखण्ड्यमान इवापलायत कलिः। सुरालयशिलाघट्टनटङ्कनिकरनिकृत्ता इव व्यदीर्यन्त विपदः। महादानविधानकलकलाभिद्रुता इव प्राद्रवन्नुपद्रवाः। दीप्यमानसत्रमहानससहस्रसन्तापिता इव व्यलीयन्त व्याधयः। वृषविवाहप्रहतपुण्यपटहपटुरवत्रासिता इव नोपासर्पन्नपमृत्यवः। सन्ततब्रह्मघोषबधिरीकृता इवापजग्मुरीतयः। धर्माधिकारपरिभूतमिव न प्राभवद्दुर्दैवम्।

तत्र चैवंविधे नानारामाभिरामकुसुमगन्धपरिमलसुभगो यौवनारम्भ इव भुवनस्य, कुङ्कुममलनपि[3]ञ्जरितबहुमहिषीसहस्रशोभितोऽन्तःपुरनिवेश इव धर्मस्य, मरुदुद्धूयमानचमरीबालव्यजन[4]शतधवलितप्रान्त एकदेश इव सुरराज्यस्य, ज्वलन्मखशिखिसहस्रदीप्यमानदशदिगन्तः शिबिरसन्निवेश इव कृतयुगस्य, पद्मासनस्थितब्रह्मर्षिध्यानाधीयमानसकलाकुशलप्रशमः प्रथमोऽवतार इव ब्रह्मलोकस्य, कलकलमुखरमहावाहिनीशतसङ्कुलो विप[5]क्ष इवोत्तरकुरूणाम्, ईश्वरमार्गणसन्तापानभिज्ञसकलजनो विजिगीषुरिव त्रिपुरस्य, सुधारससिक्तधवलगृहपङ्क्तिपाण्डुरः प्रतिनिधिरिव चन्द्रलोकस्य, मधुमत्त[6]मत्तकाशिनीभूषणरवभरितभुवनो नामाभिहार इव कुबेरनगरस्य, स्थाण्वीश्वराख्यो जनपदविशेषः।

यस्तपोवनमिति मुनिभिः, कामायतनमिति वेश्याभिः, सङ्गीतशालेति लासकैः; यमनगरमिति शत्रुभिः, चिन्तामणिभूमिरित्यर्थिभिः, वीरक्षेत्रमिति

---

१ 'अरण्यवरुणधरा०' ब. २ 'गुणैः' ब. ३ '०मलनापञ्जरित०' ब. ४ 'व्यजनधवलित०' अ–क. ५ 'विक्षेपः' ब–क. ६ 'मधुमदमत्तकासिनी' ब.

शस्त्रोपजीविभिः, गुरुकुलमिति विद्यार्थिभिः, गन्धर्वनगरमिति गायनैः, विश्वकर्ममन्दिरमिति विज्ञानिभिः, लाभभूमिरिति वैदेहकैः, द्यूतस्थानमिति बन्दिभिः, साधुसमागम इति सद्भिः, वज्रपञ्जरमिति शरणागतैः विटगोष्ठीति विदग्धैः, सुकृतपरिणाम इति पथिकैः, असुरविवरमिति वातिकैः, शाक्याश्रम इति शमिभिः, अप्सरःपुरमिति कामिभिः, महोत्सवसमाज इति चारणैः, वसुधारेति च विप्रैरगृह्यत।

यत्र च मातङ्गगामिन्यः शीलवत्यश्च, गौर्यो विभवरताश्च, श्यामाः पद्मरागिण्यश्च, धवलद्विजशुचिवदना मदिरामोदिश्वसनाश्च, चन्द्रकान्तवपुषः शिरीषकोमलाङ्ग्यश्च, अभुजङ्गगम्याः कञ्चुकिन्यश्च, पृथुकलत्रश्रियो दरिद्रमध्यकलिताश्च, लावण्यवत्यो मधुरभाषिण्यश्च, अप्रमत्ताः प्रसन्नोज्ज्वलरागाश्च[1], अकौतुकाः प्रौढाश्च प्रमदाः।

यत्र च प्रमदानां चक्षुरेव सहजं मुण्डमालामण्डनं भारः कुवलयदलदामानि। अलकप्रतिबिम्बान्येव कपोलतलगतान्यक्लिष्टाः श्रवणावतंसाः पुनरुक्तानि तमालकिसलयानि। प्रियकथा एव सुभगाः कर्णालङ्कारा आडम्बरः कुण्डलानि[2]। कपोला एव सततमालोककारका विभवो[3] निशासु मणिप्रदीपाः। निःश्वासाकृष्टमधुकरकुलान्येव रमणीयं मुखावरणं कुलस्त्रीजनाचारो जालिका। वाण्येव मधुरा वीणा बाह्यविज्ञानं तन्त्रीताडनम्। हासा एवातिशयसुरभयः पटवासा निरर्थकाः कर्पूरपांसवः। अधरकान्तिविसर एवोज्ज्वलतरोऽङ्गरागो निर्गुणो लावण्यकलङ्कः कुङ्कुमपङ्कः। बाहव एव कोमलतमाः परिहासप्रहारवेत्रलता निष्प्रयोजनानि मृणालानि। यौवनोष्मस्वेदबिन्दव एव विदग्धाः कुचालङ्कृतयो हारास्तु भाराः। श्रोण्य एव विशालस्फाटिकशिलातलचतुरस्रा रागिणां विश्रमकारणमनिमित्तं भवनमणिवेदिकाः। कमललोभनिलीनान्यलिकुलान्येव मुखराणि पदाभरणकानि निष्फलानीन्द्रनीलनूपुराणि। नूपुररवाहूता[4] भवनकलहंसा एव समुचिताः सञ्चरणसहाया ऐश्वर्यप्रपञ्चाः परिजनाः।

तत्र च साक्षात्सहस्राक्ष इव सर्ववर्णधरं धनुर्दधानः, मेरुमय इव कल्याणप्रकृतित्वे, मन्दरमय इव लक्ष्मीसमाकर्षणे, जलनिधिमय इव मर्यादायाम्, आकाशमय इव शब्दप्रादुर्भावे, शशिमय इव कलासंग्रहे, वेदमय इवाकृत्रिमालापत्वे, धरणिमय इव लोकधृतिकरणे, पवनमय इव सर्वपार्थिवरजोविकारहरणे, गुरुर्वचसि, पृथुरुरसि, विशालो मनसि, जनकस्तपसि, सुयात्रस्तेजसि, सुमन्त्रो रहसि, बुधः सदसि, अर्जुनो यशसि, भीष्मो धनुषि, निषधो वपुषि, शत्रुघ्नः समरे, शूरः शूरसेनाक्रमणे, दक्षः प्रजाकर्मणि, सर्वादिराजतेजःपुञ्जनिर्मित इव राजा पुष्पभूतिरिति नाम्ना बभूव।

---

१ '०मुखरागाश्च' ब. २ 'कुण्डलादिः' अ–क. ३ 'विभवो निश्वासमणि०' ब. ४ 'रवोहृताः' ब.

पृथुना गौरियं[1] कृतेति यः स्पर्धमान इव महीं महिषीं चकार। निसर्गस्वैरिणी स्वरुच्यनुरोधिनी च भवति हि महतां मतिः। यतस्तस्य केनचिदनुपदिष्टा सहजैव शैशवादारभ्यान्यदेवता[2]विमुखी भगवति भक्तिसुलभे भुवनभृति भूतभावने भवच्छिदि भवे भूयसी भक्तिरभूत्। अकृतवृषभध्वजपूजाविधिर्न स्वप्नेऽप्याहारमकरोत्। अजम्, अजरम्, अमरगुरुम्, असुरपुररिपुम्, अपरिमितगणपतिम्, अचलदुहितृपतिम्, अखिलभुवनकृतचरणनतिम्, पशुपतिं प्रपन्नोऽन्यदेवताशून्यममन्यत त्रैलोक्यम्। भर्तृचित्तानुवर्तिन्यश्चानुजीविनां प्रकृतयः। तथा हि। गृहे गृहे भगवानपूज्यत खण्डपरशुः। ववुरस्य होमालवा[3]लविलीयमानबहलगुग्गुलुगन्धगर्भाः स्नपनक्षीरशीकरक्षोदक्षारिणो बिल्वपल्लवदामदलोद्वाहिनः पुण्य[4]विषयेषु वायवः। शिवसपर्यासमुचितैरुपायनैः प्राभृतैश्च पौराः पादोपजीविनः सचिवा भुजबलनिर्जिताश्च करदीकृता महासामन्तास्तं सिषेविरे। तथा हि। कैलासकूटधवलैः कनकपत्रलतालङ्कृतविषाणकोटिभिर्महाप्रमाणैः संध्याबलिवृषैः सौवर्णैश्च स्नपनकलशैरर्घभाजनैश्च धूपपात्रैश्च पुष्पपट्टैश्च मणियष्टिप्रदीपैश्च ब्रह्मसूत्रैश्च महार्हमाणिक्यखण्डखचितैश्च मुखकोषैः परितोषमस्य मनसि चक्रुः। अन्तःपुराण्यपि स्वयमारब्धबालेयतण्डुलकण्[5]डनानि देवगृहोपलेपनलोहिततरकरकिसलयानि कुसुमग्रथनव्यग्रसमस्तपरिजनानि तस्याभिलषितमन्ववर्तन्त। तथा च। परममाहेश्वरः स भूपालो लोकतः शुश्राव भुवि भगवन्तमपरमिव साक्षाद्दक्षमखमथनं दाक्षिणात्यं बहुविधविद्याप्रभावप्रख्यातैर्गुणैः शिष्यैरिवानेकसहस्रसंख्यैर्व्याप्तमर्त्यलोकं भैरवाचार्यनामानं महाशैवम्। उपनयन्ति हि हृदयमदृष्टमपि जनं शीतलसंवादाः। यतः स राजा श्रवणसमकालमेव तस्मिन्भैरवाचार्ये भगवति द्वितीय इव कपर्दिनि दूरगतेऽपि गरीयसीं बबन्ध भक्तिम्। आचकाङ्क्ष च मनोरथैरप्यस्य सर्वथा दर्शनम्।

अथ कदाचित्पर्यस्तेऽस्ताचलचुम्बिनि वासरेऽन्तःपुरवर्तिनं राजानमुपसृत्य प्रतीहारी विज्ञापितवती—'देव, द्वारि परिव्राडास्ते कथयति च भैरवाचार्यवचनाद्देवमनुप्राप्तोऽस्मि' इति। राजा तु तच्छ्रुत्वा सादरम्—'क्वासौ आनयात्रैव। प्रवेशयैनम्' इति चाब्रवीत्। तथा चाकरोत्प्रतीहारी। न चिराच्च प्रविशन्तं प्रांशुमाजानुभुजम्, भैक्षक्षाममपि स्थूलास्थिभिरवयवैः पीवरमिवोपलक्ष्यमाणम्, पृथूत्त[6]माङ्गमुत्तुङ्गवलिभङ्गस्थपुटललाटम्, निर्मांसगण्डकूपकम्, मधुबिन्दुपिङ्गलपरिमण्डलाक्षम्, ईषदावक्रघोणम्, अतिप्रलम्बैककर्णपाशम्, अलाबुबीजविकटोन्नतदन्तपङ्क्तिम्, तुरगानूकश्लथाधरलेखम्, लम्बचिबुकायततरलपनम्, अंसावलम्बिना काषायेण योगपट्टकेन विरचितवैकक्षकम्, हृदयमध्यनिबद्धग्रन्थिना च रागेणेव खण्डशः कृतेन धातुरसारुणेन

---

१ 'गौरिवेयं' ब. २ 'अनन्यदेवता भगवति' ब. ३ 'होमालवालानलविलीय०' ब. ४ 'पुण्याविषयेपु' ब. ५ 'खण्डनानि' ब. ६ 'पृथुत्तमाङ्गम्' ब.

कर्पटेन कृतोत्तरासङ्गम्, पुनरुक्तव्यालप्रग्रहवेष्टननिश्चलमूलेन बद्धमृत्परिशोधनवंशत्वक्तितउना कौपीनसनाथशिखरेण खर्जूरपुटसंमुद्गकगर्भीकृतभिक्षाकपालकेन दारवफलकत्रयत्रिकोणत्रियष्टिनिविष्टकमण्डलुना बहिरुपपादितपादुकावस्थानेन स्थूलदशासूत्रनियन्त्रितपुस्तिकापूलिकेन वामकरधृतेन योगभारकेणाध्यासितस्कन्धम्, इतरकरगृहीतवेत्रासनं मस्करिणमद्राक्षीत्। क्षितिपतिरप्युपगतमुचितेन चैनमादरेणान्वग्रहीत्। आसीनं च पप्रच्छ—'क्व भैरवाचार्यः' इति। सादरनरपतिवचनमुदितमनास्तु परिव्राट् तमुपनगरं सरस्वतीतटवनावलम्बिनि शून्यायतने स्थितमाचचक्षे। भूयश्चाबभाषे—'अर्चयति हि महाभागं भगवानाशीर्वचसा' इत्युक्त्वा चोपनिन्ये योगभारकादाकृष्य भैरवाचार्यप्रहितानि रत्नवन्ति बहलालोकलिप्तान्तःपुराणि पञ्च राजतानि पुण्डरीकाणि।

नरपतिस्तु प्रियजनप्रणयभङ्गकातरो[1] दाक्षिण्यमनुरुध्यमानो ग्रहणलाघवं च लङ्घयितुमसमर्थो दोलायमानेन मनसा स्थित्वा कथं कथमप्यतिसौजन्यनिघ्नस्तानि जग्राह। जगाद च—'सर्वफलप्रसवहेतुः शिवभक्तिरियं नो मनोरथदुर्लभानि फलति फलानि। येनैवमस्मासु प्रीयते तत्रभगवान्भुवनगुरुर्भैरवाचार्यः। श्वो द्रष्टास्मि भगवन्तम्' इत्युक्त्वा च मस्करिणं व्यसर्जयत्। अनया च वार्तया परां मुदमवाप। अपरेद्युश्च प्रातरेवोत्थाय[2] वाजिनमधिरुह्य समुच्छ्रितश्वेतातपत्रः समुद्धूयमानधवलचामरयुगलः कतिपयैरेव राजपुत्रैः परिवृतो भैरवाचार्यं सवितारमिव शशी द्रष्टुं प्रतस्थे। गत्वा च किञ्चिदन्तरं तदीयमेवाभिमुखमापतन्तमन्यतमं शिष्यमद्राक्षीत्। अप्राक्षीच्च—'क्व भगवानास्ते' इति। सोऽकथयत्—'अस्य जीर्णमातृगृहस्योत्तरेण बिल्ववाटिकामध्यास्ते' इति। गत्वा च तं प्रदेशमवततार तुरगात्। प्रविवेश च बिल्ववाटिकाम्।

अथ महतः कार्पटिकवृन्दस्य मध्ये प्रातरेव स्नातम्, दत्ताष्टपुष्पिकम्, अनुष्ठिताग्निकार्यम्, कृतभस्मरेखापरिहारपरिकरे हरितगोमयोपलिप्तक्षितितलवितते व्याघ्रचर्मण्युपविष्टम्, कृष्णकम्बलप्रावरणनिभेनासुरविवरप्रवेशाशङ्कया पातालान्धकारावासमिवाभ्यस्यन्तम्, उन्मिषता विद्युत्कपिलेनात्मतेजसा महामांसविक्रयक्रीतेन मनःशिलापङ्केनेव शिष्यलोकं लिम्पन्तम्, जटीकृतैकदेशलम्बमानरुद्राक्षशङ्खगुटिकेनोर्ध्वबद्धेन शिखापाशेन बध्नन्तमिव विद्यावलेपदुर्विदग्धानुपरि सञ्चरतः सिद्धान्, धवलकतिपयशिरोरुहेण वयसा पञ्चपञ्चाशतं वर्षाण्यतिक्रामन्तम्, खालित्यक्षीयमाणशङ्खलोमलेखम्, लोमशकर्णशष्कुलीप्रदेशम्, पृथुललाटतटम्, तिरश्च्या भस्मललाटिकया बहुशः शिरोर्ध्वधृतदग्धगुग्गुलुसन्तापस्फुटितकपालास्थिपाण्डुरराजिशङ्कामिव जनयन्तम्, सहजललाटवलिभङ्गसङ्कोचितकूर्चभागां बभ्रुभासं भ्रूसङ्गत्या

---

१ 'कातरम्' ब. २ अस्मात्परं 'कृतकृत्यः' इत्यधिकं ब-पुस्तके.

निरन्तरामायामिनीमेकामिव[1] भ्रूलेखां बिभ्राणम्, ईषत्काचकाचरकनीनिकेन[2] रक्तापाङ्गनिर्गतांशुप्रतानेन मध्यधवलभासेन्द्रायुधेनेवातिदीर्घेण लोचनयुगलेन परितो महामण्डलमिवानेकवर्णरागमालिखन्तं सितपीतलोहितपताकावलीशबलं शिवबलिमिव दिक्षु विक्षिपन्तम्, तार्क्ष्यतुण्डकोटिकुब्जाग्रघोणम्, दूरविदीर्णसृक्किसंक्षिप्तकपोलम्, किञ्चिद्दन्तुरतया सदाहृदयसन्निहितहरमौलिचन्द्रातपेनेव निर्गच्छता दन्तालोकेन धवलयन्तं दिशां जालकम्, जिह्वाग्रस्थितसर्वशैवसंहितातिभारेणेव मनाक्प्रलम्बितौष्ठम्, प्रलम्बश्रवणपालीप्रेङ्खिताभ्यां स्फाटिककुण्डलाभ्यां शुक्रबृहस्पतिभ्यामिव सुरासुरविजयविद्यासिद्धिश्रद्धयानुबध्यमानम्, बद्धविविधौषधिमन्त्रसूत्रपङ्क्तिना सलोहवलयेनैकप्रकोष्ठेन शङ्खखण्डं पूष्णो दन्तमिव भगवता भवेन भग्नं भक्त्या भूषणीकृतं कलयन्तम्, अखिलरसकूपोदञ्चनघटीयन्त्रमालामिव रुद्राक्षमालां दक्षिणेन पाणिना भ्रमयन्तम्, उरसि दोलायमानेनापिङ्गलाग्रेण कूर्चकलापेन संमार्जयन्तमिवान्तर्गतं निजरजोनिकरम्, अतिनिबिडनीललोममण्डलनिचितं च ध्यानलब्धेन ज्योतिषा दग्धमिव हृदयदेशं दधानम्, ईषत्प्रशिथिलवलिवलयबध्यमानतुन्दम्, उपचीयमानस्फिङ्मांसपिण्डकम्, पाण्डुरपवित्रक्षौमावृतकौपीनम्, सावष्टम्भपर्यङ्कबन्धमण्डलितेनामृतफेनश्वेतरुचा योगपट्टकेन वासुकिनेवाप्रतिहतानेकमन्त्रप्रभावाविर्भूतेन प्रदक्षिणीक्रियमाणम्, अरुणतामरससुकुमारतलस्य पादयुगलस्य निर्मलैर्नखमयूखजालकैर्जर्जरयन्तमिव महानिधानोद्धरणरसेन रसातलम्, तोयक्षालितशुचिना धौतपादुकायुगलेन हंसमिथुनेनेव भागीरथीतीर्थयात्रापरिचयागतेनामुच्यमानचरणान्तिकम्, शिखरनिखातकुब्जकालायसकण्टकेन वैणवेन विशाखिकादण्डेन सर्वविद्यासिद्धिविघ्नविनायकापनयनाङ्कुशेनेव सततपार्श्ववर्तिना विराजमानम्, अबहुभाषिणम्, मन्दहासिनम्, सर्वोपकारिणम्, कुमारब्रह्मचारिणम्, अतितपस्विनम्, महामनस्विनम्, कृशक्रोधम्, अकृशानुरोधम्, महानगरमिवादीनप्रकृतिशोभितम्, मेरुमिव कल्पतरुपल्लवराशिसुकुमारच्छायम्, कैलासमिव पशुपतिचरणरजःपवित्रितशिरसम्, शिवलोकमिव माहेश्वरगणानुयातम्, जलनिधिमिवानेकनदनदीसहस्रप्रक्षालितशरीरम्, जाह्नवीप्रवाहमिव बहुपुण्यतीर्थस्थानशुचिम्, धाम धर्मस्य, तीर्थं तथ्यस्य, कोशं कुशलस्य, पत्तनं पूततायाः, शालां शीलस्य, क्षेत्रं क्षमायाः, शालेयं शालीनतायाः, स्थानं स्थितेः, आधारं धृतेः, आकरं करुणायाः, निकेतनं कौतुकस्य, आरामं रामणीयकस्य, प्रासादं प्रसादस्य, अगारं गौरवस्य, समाजं सौजन्यस्य, सम्भवं सद्भावस्य, कालं कलेः, भगवन्तं साक्षादिव विरूपाक्षं भैरवाचार्यं ददर्श। भैरवाचार्यस्तु दूरादेव राजानं दृष्ट्वा शशिनमिव जलनिधिश्चचाल। प्रथमतरोत्थितशिष्यलोकश्चोत्थाय प्रत्युजगाम

---

१ 'एकामेव' ब. २ 'ईषत्काचर०' ब.

समर्पितश्रीफलोपायनश्च जह्नुकर्णसमुद्गीर्यमाणगङ्गाप्रवाहह्रादगम्भीरया गिरा स्वस्तिशब्दमकरोत्।

नरपतिरपि प्रीतिविस्तार्यमाणधवलिम्ना चक्षुषा प्रत्यर्पयन्निव बहुतराणि पुण्डरीकवनानि ललाटपट्टपर्यस्तेन चोदंशुना शिखामणिना महेश्वरप्रसादमिव तृतीयनयनोद्गमेन प्रकाशयन्नावर्जितकर्णपल्लवपलायमानमधुकरः शिवसेवा-समुन्मूलिताशेषपापलवमुच्यमान[1] इव दूरावनतः प्रणाममस्मिनवं चकार। आचार्योऽपि—'आगच्छ। अत्रोपविश' इति शार्दूलचर्मात्मीयमदर्शयत्। उप-दर्शितप्रश्रयस्तु राजा मत्तहंसकलगद्गदस्वरसुभगां मधुरसमर्यीं महानदीमिव प्रवर्तयन्वाचं व्याजहार—'भगवन्, नार्हसि मामन्यनृपस्खलितैः खलीक-र्तुम्। अशेषराजकोपेक्षितताया हतलक्ष्म्याः खल्वयं शीलापराधो द्रविणदौ-रात्म्यं वा यदेवमाचरति मयि गुरुः। अभूमिरयमुपचाराणाम्। अलमतिय-न्त्रणया। दूरस्थितोऽपि मनोरथशिष्योऽयं जनो भवताम्। माननीयं च गुरु-वचोल्लङ्घनमर्हति गुरोरासनम्। आसतां च भवन्त एवात्र' इति व्याहृत्य परिजनोपनीते वाससि निषसाद। भैरवाचार्योऽपि प्रीत्यानतिक्रमणीयं नृपव-चनमनुवर्तमानः पूर्ववत्तदेव व्याघ्राजिनमभजत।

आसीने च सराजके परिजने शिष्यजने च समुचितमर्घ्यादिकं चक्रे। क्रमेण च नृपमाधुर्यहृतान्तःकरणः शशिकरनिकरविमला दशनदीधितीः स्फुरन्तीः शिवभक्तीरिव साक्षाद्दर्शयन्नुवाच—'तात, अतिनम्रतैव ते कथयति गुणानां गौरवम्। सकलसम्पत्पात्रमसि। विभवानुरूपास्तु प्रतिपत्तयः। जन्मनः प्रभृत्यदत्तदृष्टिरस्मि स्वापतेयेषु। यतः सकलदोषकलापानलेन्धनैर्ध-नैरविक्रीतं क्वचिच्छरीरकमस्ति। भैक्षरक्षिताः सन्ति प्राणाः। दुर्गृहीतानि कतिचिद्विद्यन्ते विद्याक्षराणि। भगवच्छिवभट्टारकपादसेवया समुपार्जिता[2] कियत्यपि सन्निहिता पुण्यकणिका। स्वीक्रियतां यदत्रोपयोगार्हम्। प्रतनुगु-णग्राह्याणि कुसुमानीव हि भवन्ति सतां मनांसि। अपि च। विद्वत्संमताः श्रूयमाणा अपि सुखयन्ति[3] साधवः शब्दा इव, सुधीरेऽपि हि मनसि यशांसि कुर्वन्ति विवरं, विशतः कुतूहलस्य फेनधवलैः स्रोतोभिरिवापह्रिय-माणो गुणगणैरानीतोऽस्मि कल्याणिना' इति।

राजा तु तं प्रत्यवादीत्—'भगवन्, अनुरक्तेष्वपि शरीरादिषु साधूनां स्वामिन एव प्रणयिनः। युष्मद्दर्शनादुपार्जितमेव चापरिमितं कुशलजातम्। अनेनैवागमनेन[4] स्पृहणीयं पदमारोपितोऽस्मि गुरुणा।' इति विविधाभिश्च कथाभिश्चिरं स्थित्वा गृहमगात्।

अन्यस्मिन्दिवसे भैरवाचार्योऽपि राजानं द्रष्टुं ययौ। तस्मै च राजा सान्तःपुरं सपरिजनं सकोषमात्मानं निवेदितवान्। स च विहस्योवाच—

---

१ 'पापमललव०' ब. २ 'समुपार्जिताः कियत्योपि सन्निहिताः पुण्यकणिकाः' ब ३ 'सुखयन्ति' इति नास्ति अ-क—पुस्तकयोः. ४ 'कृतमनेनैवानुगमनेन' ब.

'तात, क्व विभवः, क्व च वयं वनवर्धिताः। धनोष्मणा म्लायत्यलं लतेव मनस्विता। खद्योतानामिवास्माकमियमपरोपतापिनी राजते तेजस्विता। भवादृशा एव भाजनं भूतेः' इति स्थित्वा च कञ्चित्कालं जगाम।

परिव्राट् तेनैव क्रमेण पञ्च पञ्च राजतानि पुण्डरीकाण्युपायनीचकार। एकदा तु श्वेतकर्पटावृतं किमप्यादाय प्राविशत्। उपविश्य च पूर्ववत्स्थित्वा मुहूर्तमब्रवीत्—'महाभाग, भवन्तमाह भगवान्यथास्मच्छिष्यः पातालस्वामिनामा ब्राह्मणः। तेन ब्रह्मराक्षसहस्तादपहृतो महासिरट्टहासनामा। सोऽयं भवद्भुजयोग्यो गृह्यताम्'। इत्यभिधायापहृतकर्पटावच्छादनात्परिवारादाचकर्ष शरद्गगनमिव पिण्डतां नीतम्, कालिन्दीप्रवाहमिव स्तम्भितजलम्, नन्दकजिगीषया कृष्णकोपितं कालियमिव कृपाणतां गतम्, लोकविनाशाय प्रकाशितधारासारं प्रलयकालमेघखण्डमिव नभस्तलात्पतितम्, दृश्यमानविकटदन्तमण्डलं हासमिव हिंसायाः, हरिबाहुदण्डमिव कृतदृढमुष्टिग्रहम्, सकलभुवनजीवितापहरणक्षमेण कालकूटेनेव निर्मितम्, कृतान्तकोपानलतप्तेनेवायसा घटितम्, अतितीक्ष्णतया पवनस्पर्शेनापि रुषेव क्वणन्तम्, मणिसभाकुट्टिमपतत्प्रतिबिम्बच्छद्मनात्मानमपि द्विधेव पाटयन्तम्, अरिशिरश्छेदलग्नैः कचैरिव किरणैः करालितधारम्, मुहुर्मुहुस्तडिदुन्मेषतरलैः प्रभाचक्रच्छुरितैर्जर्जरितातपम्, खण्डशश्छिन्दन्तमिव दिवसम्, कटाक्षमिव कालरात्रेः, कर्णोत्पलमिव कालस्य, ओङ्कारमिव क्रौर्यस्य, अलङ्कारमहङ्कारस्य, कुलमित्रं कोपस्य, देहं दर्पस्य, सुसहायं साहसस्य, अपत्यं मृत्योः, आगमनमार्गं लक्ष्म्याः, निर्गमनमार्गं कीर्तेः, कृपाणम्।

अवनिपतिस्तु तं गृहीत्वा करेणायुधप्रीत्या प्रतिमानिभेनालिङ्गन्निव सुचिरं ददर्श। सन्दिदेश च—'वक्तव्यो भगवान्परद्रव्यग्रहणावज्ञादुर्विदग्धमपि हि मे मनो युष्मद्विषये न शक्नोति वचनव्यतिक्रमव्यभिचारमाचरितुम्' इति। परिव्राट् तु गृहीते तस्मिन्परितुष्टः 'स्वस्ति भवते, साधयामः' इत्युक्त्वा निरयासीत्। नृपश्च प्रकृत्या वीररसानुरागी तेन कृपाणेनामन्यत करतलवर्तिनीं मेदिनीम्।

अथ व्रजत्सु दिवसेष्वेकदा भैरवाचार्यो राजानमुपह्वरे सोपग्रहमवादीत्—'तात, स्वार्थालसाः[1] परोपकारदक्षाश्च प्रकृतयो भवन्ति भव्यानाम्। भवादृशां चार्थिदर्शनं महोत्सवः प्रणयनमाराधनमर्थग्रहणमुपकारः। भूमिरसि सर्वलोकमनोरथानां येनाभिधीयसे। श्रूयताम्। भगवतो महाकालहृदयनाम्नो महामन्त्रस्य कृष्णस्रगम्बरानुलेपेनाकल्पेन कल्पकथितेन महाश्मशाने जपकोट्या कृतपूर्वसेवोऽस्मि। तस्य वेतालसाधनावसाना सिद्धिः। असहायैश्च सा दुरवापा। त्वं चालमस्मै कर्मणे। त्वयि च गृहीतभरे भविष्यन्त्यपरे

१ 'स्वार्थलालसाः' ब.

सहायास्त्रयः। एकः स एवास्माकं टीटिभनामा बालमित्रं मस्करी यो भवन्तमुपतिष्ठते। द्वितीयः स पातालस्वामी। अपरो मच्छिष्य एव कर्णतालनामा द्राविडः। यदि साधु मन्यसे ततो नीयतामयं दिङ्नागहस्तदीर्घो गृहीताट्टहासो निशामेकामेकदिङ्मुखार्गलतां बाहुः' इति। कृतवचसि च तस्मिन्नन्धकारं प्रविष्ट इव दृष्टप्रकाशः प्राप्तोपकारावकाशः प्रमुदितेनान्तरात्मना नरेन्द्रः समभाषत—'भगवन्, परमनुगृहीतोऽस्म्यनेन शिष्यजनसामान्येन निदेशेन कृतपरिग्रहमिवात्मानमवैमि' इति। ननन्द च तेन नरेन्द्रव्याहृतेन भैरवाचार्यः। चकार च सङ्केतम्—'अस्यामेवागामिन्यामसितपक्षचतुर्दशीक्षपायामियत्यां वेलायाममुष्मिन्महाश्मशानसमीपभाजि शून्यायतने शस्त्रद्वितीयेनायुष्मता द्रष्टव्या वयम्' इति।

अथातिक्रान्तेष्वहःसु प्राप्तायां च तस्यामेव कृष्णचतुर्दश्यां शैवेन विधिना दीक्षितः क्षितिपो नियमवानभूत्। कृताधिवासं च सम्पादितगन्धधूपमाल्यादिपूजं खड्गमट्टहासमकरोत्। ततः परिणते दिवसे केनापि कर्मसाधनाय कृतरुधिरबलिविधानास्विव लोहितायमानासु दिक्षु, रुधिरबलिलम्पटासु च वेतालजिह्वास्विव लम्बमानासु च रविदीधितिषु, नरेन्द्रानुरागेण गृहीतापरदिशि स्वयमिव दिक्पालतां चिकीर्षति सवितरि, यातुधानीष्विव वर्धमानासु तरुच्छायासु, पातालतलवासिषु विज्ञाय दानवेष्विवोत्तिष्ठत्सु तमोमण्डलेषु, नभसि पुञ्जीभवति रौद्रं कर्म दिदृक्षमाण इव नक्षत्रगणे, विगाढायां शर्वर्याम्, सुप्तजने निःशब्दस्तिमिते निशीथे, राजा सान्तःपुरं परिजनं वञ्चयित्वा वामकरस्फुरत्सरुर्दक्षिणकरेणोत्खातं खड्गमट्टहासमादाय विसर्पता च खड्गप्रभापटलेन नीलांशुकपटेनेव दर्शनभयादवगुण्ठितनिखिलगात्रयष्टिरनादिष्टयाप्यनुगम्यमानो राजलक्ष्म्या पृष्ठतः परिमललग्नमधुकरवेणिव्याजेन केशेष्विव कर्मसिद्धिमाकर्षन्नेकाकी नगरान्निरगात्। अगाच्च तमुद्देशम्।

अथ प्रत्युज्जग्मुस्ते त्रयो द्रौणिकृपकृतवर्माण इव सौप्तिके सन्नद्धाः, स्नाताः, स्रग्विणो गृहीतविकटवेशाः, कुसुमशेखरसञ्चारिभिः क्रियमाणमन्त्रशिखाबन्धा इव गुञ्जद्भिः षट्चरणैः, उष्णीषपट्टकाँल्ललाटमध्यवटितविकटस्वस्तिकाग्रन्थीन्महामुद्राबन्धानिव धारयन्तो मूर्धभिः, एकश्रवणविवरविततविमलदन्तपत्रप्रभालोकलेपधवलितकपोलैर्मुखैरापिबन्त इव निशाचरापचयचिकीर्षया शार्वरमन्धकारम्, इतरकर्णावलम्बिनां रत्नकुण्डलानामरुणच्छाच्छया रुचा गोरोचनयेव मन्त्रपरिजप्तया समालब्धाः[2], स्वप्रतिबिम्बगर्भान्कर्मसिद्धये दत्तपुरुषोपहारानिवोल्लासयन्तो निशितान्निस्त्रिंशान्, निस्त्रिंशांशुसन्तानसीमन्तिततिमिरामात्मीयात्मीयदिग्भागसंरक्षणाय त्रिधेव त्रियामां पाटयन्तः, सार्धचन्द्रैः कलधौतबुद्बुदावलितरलतारागणैर्निशाया इव परुषासिधारानिकृत्तैः खण्डैर्गृहीतैश्चर्मफलकैरकाण्डशर्वरीमपरां घटयन्तः, काञ्चनशृङ्खलाकलापनियमित-

१ 'जननिःशब्द०' अ-क. २ '०लब्धाङ्गाः' ब.

निबिडनिष्प्रवाणयः, बद्धासिधेनवः, टीटिभकर्णतालपातालस्वामिनो निवेदितवन्तश्चात्मानम्। अवनिपतिस्तु—'कोऽत्र कः' इति त्रीनपृच्छत्। आचचक्षिरे च स्व स्वं नाम त्रयोऽपि ते। तैरेव चानुगम्यमानो जगाम तां बलिदीपालोकजर्जरितगुग्गुलुधूपधूमगृह्यमाणदिग्भागतया विक्षिप्यमाणरक्षासर्षपाधैदग्धान्धकारपलायमाननिशामिव समुपकल्पितसर्वोपकरणां निःशब्दां च गम्भीरां च भीषणां च साधनभूमिम्।

तस्यां च कुमुदधूलिधवलेन भस्मना लिखितस्य महतो मण्डलस्य मध्ये स्थितं दीप्ततरतेजःप्रसरम्, पृथुपरिवेशपरिक्षिप्तमिव शरत्सवितारम्, मथ्यमानक्षीरोदावर्तवर्तिनमिव मन्दरम्, रक्तचन्दनानुलेपिनो रक्तस्रगम्बराभरणस्योत्तानशयस्य शवस्योरस्युपविश्य जातजातवेदसि मुखकुहरे प्रारब्धाग्निकार्यम्, कृष्णाङ्गरागम्, कृष्णप्रतिसरम्, कृष्णवाससम्, कृष्णतिलाहुतिनिभेन विद्याधरत्वतृष्णया मानुषनिर्माणकारणकालुष्यपरमाणूनिव क्षयमुपनयन्तम्, आहुतिदानपर्यस्ताभिः प्रेतमुखस्पर्शदूषितं प्रक्षालयन्तमिवाशुशुक्षणिं करनखदीधितिभिः, धूमालोहितेन चक्षुषा क्षतजाहुतिमिव हुतभुजि पातयन्तम्, ईषद्विवृताधरपुटप्रकटितसितदशनशिखरेण दृश्यमानमूर्तमन्त्राक्षरपङ्क्तिनेव मुखेन किमपि जपन्तम्, होमश्रमस्वेदसलिलप्रतिबिम्बिताभिरासन्नदीपिकाभिर्दहन्तमिव सिद्धये सर्वावयवान्, अंसावलम्बिना बहुगुणेन विद्याराजेनेव ब्रह्मसूत्रेण परिगृहीतं भैरवाचार्यमपश्यत्। उपसृत्य चाकरोन्नमस्कारम्। अभिनन्दितश्च तेन स्वव्यापारमन्वतिष्ठत्।

अत्रान्तरे पातालस्वामी शातक्रतवीमाशामङ्गीचकार। कर्णतालः कौबेरीम्। परिव्राट् प्राचेतसीम्। राजा तु त्रैशङ्कवेन ज्योतिषाङ्कितां ककुभमलङ्कृतवान्।

एवं चावस्थितेषु दिक्पालेषु दिक्पालभुजपञ्जरप्रविष्टे विस्रब्धं कर्म साधयति भैरवं भैरवाचार्येऽतिचिरं कृतकोलाहलेषु निष्फलप्रयत्नेषु प्रत्यूहकारिषु शान्तेषु कौणपेषु गलत्यर्धरात्रसमये मण्डलस्य नातिदवीयस्युत्तरेणाकस्मात्प्रलयमहावराहदंष्ट्राविवरमिव दर्शयन्ती क्षितिरदीर्यत। सहसैव च तस्माद्विवरादाशावारणोत्क्षिप्त इवालानलोहस्तम्भः, महावराहपीवरस्कन्धपीठो नरकासुर इव भुवो गर्भादुद्भूतः, बलिदानव इव भित्त्वोत्थितः पातालम्, इन्द्रनीलप्रासाद इवोपरिज्वलितरत्नप्रदीपः, स्निग्धनीलघननिबिडकुटिलकुन्तलकान्तमौलिरुन्मीलन्मालतीमुण्डमालः, गद्गदतया स्वरस्य स्वभावपाटलतया च चक्षुषः क्षीब इव यौवनमदेन, वल्गद्गलदामकः, करसम्पुटमृदितया मृदा दिङ्नागकुम्भाभावंसकूटौ पुनः पुनः परिपङ्कयन्, सान्द्रचन्दनकर्दमदत्तैरव्यवस्थास्थासकैरतिसितजलधरशकलशारित इव शारदाकाशैकदेशः, केतकीगर्भपत्रपाण्डुरस्य चण्डातकस्योपरि क्षामतरीकृतकुक्षिः कक्ष्याबन्धं विधाय

णया भवान्भुवि सूर्याचन्द्रमसोरतृतीय इवाविच्छिन्नस्य प्रतिदिनमुपचीयमानवृद्धेः शुचिसुभगसत्यत्यागधैर्यशौण्डपुरुषप्रकाण्डप्रायस्य[1] महतो राजवंशस्य कर्ता भविष्यति। यस्मिन्नुत्पत्स्यते सर्वद्वीपानां भोक्ता हरिश्चन्द्र इव हर्षनामा चक्रवर्ती त्रिभुवनविजिगीषुर्द्वितीयो मान्धातेव।यस्यायं करः स्वयमेव कमलमपहाय ग्रहीष्यति चामरम्' इति वचसोऽन्ते तिरोबभूव।

भूमिपालस्तु तदाकर्ण्य हृदयेनातिमात्रमप्रीयत। भैरवाचार्योऽपि तस्या देव्यास्तेन वचसा कर्मणा च सम्यगुपपादितेन सद्य एव कुन्तली किरीटी हारी केयूरी मेखली मुद्गरी खड्गी[2] च भूत्वावाप विद्याधरत्वम्। प्रोवाच च—'राजन्, अदूरव्यापिनः फल्गुचेतसामलसानां मनोरथाः। सतां तु भुवि विस्तारवत्यः स्वभावेनैवोपकृतयः। स्वप्नेऽप्यसम्भावितां दातुमिमां दक्षिणां क्षमः कोऽन्यो भवन्तमपहाय। सम्पत्कणिकामपि प्राप्य तुलेव लघुप्रकृतिरुन्नतिमायाति। त्वदीयैर्गुणैरुपकरणीकृतस्य त्वत्त एव च लब्धात्मलाभस्य निर्लज्जतेयमस्य मूढहृदयस्य यदिच्छामि[3] येन केनचित्कार्यलवोपपादनोपयोगेन स्मरयितुमात्मानम्' इति। प्रत्युपकारदुष्प्रवेशास्तु भवन्ति धीराणां हृदयावष्टम्भाः। यतस्तं राजा 'भवत्सिद्ध्यैव परिसमाप्तकृत्योऽस्मि। साधयतु मान्यो यथासमीहितं स्थानम्' इति प्रत्याचचक्षे।

तथोक्तश्च भूभुजा जिगमिषुः सुदृढं समालिङ्ग्य टीटिभादीन्कुवलयवनेनेवावश्यायशीकरस्राविणा सास्रेण चक्षुषा वीक्षमाणः क्षितिपतिं पुनरुवाच—'तात, ब्रवीमि—यामीति न स्नेहसदृशम्। त्वदीयाः प्राणा इति पुनरुक्तम्। गृह्यतामिदं शरीरकमिति व्यतिरेकेणार्थकरणम्। तिलशः क्रीता वयमिति नोपकारानुरूपम्। बान्धवोऽसीति दूरीकरणमिव। त्वयि स्थितं हृदयमित्यप्रत्यक्षम्। त्वद्विरहकारिणी[4] कारणेयं नः सिद्धिरित्यश्रद्धेयम्। निष्कारणस्तवोपकार इत्यनुवादः। स्मर्तव्या वयमित्याज्ञा। सर्वथा कृतघ्नालापेष्वसज्जनकथासु च चेतसि कर्तव्योऽयं स्वार्थनिष्ठुरो जनः' इत्यभिधाय वेगच्छिन्नहारोच्छलितमुक्ताफलनिकरताडिततारागणं गगनतलमुत्पपात। ययौ च सीमन्तितग्रहग्रामः सिद्धोचितं धाम। श्रीकण्ठोऽपि—'राजन्, पराक्रमक्रीतः कर्तव्येषु नियोगेनानुग्राह्यो ग्राहितविनयोऽयं जनः[5]' इत्यभिधाय राजानुमोदितस्तदेव भूयो भूविवरं विवेश।

नरपतिस्तु क्षीणभूयिष्ठायां क्षपायां, प्रवातुमारब्धे प्रबुध्यमानकमलिनीनिःश्वाससुरभौ वनदेवताकुचांशुकापहरणपरिहासस्वेदिनीव सावश्यायशी-

---

१ '०सुभगमान्यसत्यत्यागशौर्यशौण्डि०' ब. २ अस्मात्परं 'कवची' इत्यधिकं ब-पुस्तके. ३ 'तदिच्छामि' अ-क. ४ '०रहानुकारिणी' ब. ५ 'परिजनः' ब.

करे परिमलाकृष्टमधुकृति कुमुदनिद्रावाहिनि निशापरिणतिजडे तुषारलेशिनि[1] वनानिले, विरहविधुरचक्रवाकचक्रनिःश्वसितसन्तापितायामिवापरजलनिधिमवतरन्त्यां त्रियामायां, साक्षादागतलक्ष्मीविलोकनकुतूहलिनीष्विव समुन्मीलन्तीषु नलिनीषु, उन्निद्रपक्षिणि क्षरति कुसुमविसरमिव तुहिनकणनिकरं मृदुपवनलासितलते कानने, कमललक्ष्मीप्रबोधमङ्गलशङ्खेष्विव रसत्स्वन्तर्बद्धध्वनन्मधुकरेषु मुकुलायमानेषु कुमुदेषु, उज्जिहानरविरथवाजिविसृष्टैः प्रोथपवनैः प्रोत्सार्यमाणास्विव वारुण्यां ककुभि पुञ्जीभवन्तीषु श्यामालताकलिकासु तारकासु, मन्दरशिखराश्रयिणि मन्दानिललुलितकल्पलतावनकुसुमधूलिविच्छुरित इव धूसरीभवति सप्तर्षिमण्डले, सुरवारणाङ्कुश इव च्युते गलति तारामये मृगे, त्रीनपि टीटिभादीन्गृहीत्वा नागयुद्धव्यतिकरमलीमसानि शुचिनि वनवापीपयसि प्रक्षाल्याङ्गानि नगरं विवेश । अन्यस्मिन्नहनि तेषामात्मशरीरानन्तरस्नान[2]भोजनाच्छादनादिना प्रीतिमकरोत् ।

कतिपयदिवसापगमे च परिव्राट् भूभुजा वार्यमाणोऽपि वनं ययौ । पातालस्वामिकर्णतालौ तु शौर्यानुरक्तो तमेव सिषेवाते । सम्पादितमनोरथातिरिक्तविभवौ च सुभटमण्डलमध्ये निष्कृष्टमण्डलाग्रौ समरमुखेषु प्रथममुपयुज्यमानौ कथान्तरेषु चान्तरान्तरा राज्ञा समादिष्टौ विचित्राणि भैरवाचार्यचरितानि शैशववृत्तान्तांश्च कथयन्तौ तेनैव सार्धं जरामाजग्मतुरिति ।

इति श्रीबाणभट्टकृते[3] हर्षचरिते राजवंशवर्णनं नाम

तृतीय उच्छ्वासः ।

१ 'तुषारलेखिनि' ब. २ 'शरीरानन्तरं स्नान' ब. ३ 'इति श्रीमहाकविचक्रचूडामणि–श्रीबाणभट्टविरचिते हर्षचरिते महाकाव्ये राजवंशवर्णनं नाम तृतीय उच्छ्वासः सम्पूर्णः' ब.

चतुर्थ उच्छ्वासः ।

योगं स्वप्नेऽपि नेच्छन्ति कुर्वते न करग्रहम् ।
महान्तो नाममात्रेण भवन्ति पतयो भुवः ॥ १ ॥

सकलमहीभृत्कम्पकृदुत्पद्यत एक एव नृपवंशे ।
विपुलेऽपि पृथुप्रतिमो दन्त इव गणाधिपस्य मुखे ॥ २ ॥

अथ तस्मात्पुष्प[1]भूतेर्द्विजवरस्वेच्छागृहीतकोषो नाभिपद्म इव पुण्डरीकेक्षणात्, लक्ष्मीपुरःसरो रत्नसञ्चय इव रत्नाकरात्, गुरुबुधकविकला[2]वत्तेजस्विभूनन्दनप्रायो ग्रहगण इवोदयस्थानात्, महाभारवाहनयोग्यः सागर इव सगरप्रभावात्, दुर्जयबलसनाथो हरिवंश इव शूरान्निर्जगाम राजवंशः । यस्मादविनष्टधर्मधवलाः प्रजासर्गा इव कृतमुखात्, प्रतापाक्रान्तभुवनाः किरणा इव तेजोनिधेः, विग्रहव्याप्तदिङ्मुखा गिरय इव भूभृत्प्रभ[3]वात्, धरणिधारणक्षमा दिग्गजा इव ब्रह्मकरात्, उदधीन्पातुमुद्यता जलधरा इव घनागमात्, इच्छाफलदायिनः कल्पतरव इव नन्दनात्, सर्वभूताश्रया विश्वरूपप्रकारा इव श्रीधरादजायन्त राजानः ।

तेषु चैवमुत्पद्यमानेषु क्रमेणोदपादि हूर्ण[4]हरिणकेसरी सिन्धुराजज्वरो गुर्जरप्रजागरो गान्धाराधिपगन्धद्विपकूट[5]पाकलो लाटपाटव[6]पाटच्चरो मालवलक्ष्मीलतापरशुः प्रतापशील इति प्रथितापरनामा प्रभाकरवर्धनो नाम राजाधिराजः । यो राज्याङ्गसङ्गीन्यभिषिच्यमान एव मलानीव मुमोच धनानि । यः परकीयेणापि कातरवल्लभेन रणमुखे तृणेनेव धृतेनालज्जत जीवितेन । यः करधृतधौतासिप्रतिबिम्बितेनात्मनाप्यदूयत समितिषु सहायेन रिपूणां पुरः प्रध्वनेषु धनुषापि नमता । यो मानी मानसेनाखिद्यत । यश्चान्तर्गता[7]परिमितरिपुशल्यशङ्कुकीलितामिव निश्चलामुवाह राजलक्ष्मीम् । यश्च सर्वासु दिक्षु समी[8]कृतसरित्तटावटविटपाटवीतरु[9]तृणगुल्मवल्मीकगिरिगहनैर्दण्डयात्रापथैः पृथुभिर्भृत्योपयोगाय व्यभजतेव वसुधां बहुधा । यं चालब्धयुद्धदोहदमात्मीयोऽपि सकलरिपु[10]समुत्सारकः परकीय इव ततापः प्रतापः । यस्य च वह्निमयो हृदये-

१ 'पुष्यभूतेः' ब. २ 'कलाभृत्' ब. ३ 'भूभृत्प्रवरात्' ब. ४ 'हून०' ब. ५ '०कूटहस्तिज्वरः पाकलो' ब. ६ 'पाटज्वरः' ब. ७ 'अन्तर्गतामपरि०' ब. ८ 'समीकृततटावट' अ. ९ 'तरुकण्टकतृण' ब. १० 'रिपुसमूहसमु०' ब.

षु जलमयो लोचनपुटेषु मारुतमयो निःश्वसितेषु क्षमामयोऽङ्गेषु आकाशमयः शून्यतायां पञ्चमहाभूतमयो मूर्त इवादृश्यत निहतप्रतिसामन्तान्तःपुरेषु प्रतापः। यस्य चासन्नेषु भृत्यरत्नेषु प्रतिबिम्बितेव तुल्यरूपा समलक्ष्यत लक्ष्मीः। तथा च यस्य प्रतापाग्निना भूतिः शौर्योष्मणा सिद्धिरसिधाराजलेन वंशवृद्धिः शस्त्रव्रणमुखैः पुरुषकारोक्तिर्धनुर्गुणकिणेन करगृहीतिरभवत्। यश्च वैरमुपायनं विग्रहमनुग्रहं समरागमं महोत्सवं शत्रुं निधिदर्शनमरिबाहुल्यमभ्युदयमाहवाह्वानं वरप्रदानमवस्कन्दपातं दिष्टवृद्धिं शस्त्रप्रहारपतनं वसुधा[1]राममन्यत। यस्मिंश्च राजनि निरन्तरैर्यूपनिकरैरङ्कुरितमिव कृतयुगेन, दिङ्मुखविसर्पिभिरध्वरधूमैः पलायितमिव कलिना, ससुधैः सुरालयैरवतीर्णमिव स्वर्गेण, सुरालयशिखरोद्धूयमानैर्धवलध्वजैः पल्लवितमिव धर्मेण, बहिरुपरचितविकटसभासत्रप्रपाप्राग्वंशमण्डपैः प्रसू[2]तमिव ग्रामैः, काञ्चनमयसर्वोपकरणैर्विभवैर्विशीर्णमिव मेरुणा, द्विजदीयमानैरर्थकलशैः फलितमिव भाग्यसम्पदा।

तस्य च जन्मान्तरेऽपि सती पार्वतीव शङ्करस्य, गृहीतपर[3]हृदया लक्ष्मीरिव लोकगुरोः, स्फुरत्तरलतारका रोहिणीव कलावतः, सर्वजनजननी बुद्धिरिव प्रजापतेः, महाभूभृत्कुलोद्गता गङ्गेव वाहिनीनायकस्य, मानसानुवर्तनचतुरा हंसीव राजहंसस्य, सकललोकार्चितचरणा त्रयीव धर्मस्य, दिवानिशममुक्तपार्श्वस्थितिररुन्धतीव महामुनेः, हंसमयीव गतिषु, परपुष्टमयीवालापेषु, चक्रवाकमयीव पतिप्रेम्णि, प्रावृण्मयीव पयोधरोन्नतौ, मदिरामयीव विलासेषु, निधिमयीवार्थसञ्चयेषु, वसुधारामयीव प्रसादेषु, कमलमयीव कोषसंग्रहेषु, कुसुममयीव फलदानेषु, संध्यामयीव वन्द्यत्वे, चन्द्रमयीव निरूष्मत्वे, दर्पणमयीव प्रतिप्राणिग्रहणेषु, सामुद्रमयीव परचित्तज्ञानेषु, परमात्ममयीव व्याप्तिषु, स्मृतिमयीव पुण्यवृत्तिषु, मधुमयीव सम्भाषणेषु, अमृतमयीव तृष्यत्सु, वृष्टिमयीव भृत्येषु, निर्वृतिमयीव सखीषु, वेतसमयीव गुरुषु, गोत्रवृद्धिरिव विलासानाम्, प्रायश्चित्तशुद्धिरिव स्त्रीत्वस्य, आज्ञासिद्धिरिव मकरध्वजस्य, व्युत्थानबुद्धिरिव रूपस्य, दिष्टवृद्धिरिव रतेः, मनोरथसिद्धिरिव रामणीयकस्य, दैवसम्पत्तिरिव लावण्यस्य, वंशोत्पत्तिरिवानुरागस्य, वरप्राप्तिरि[4]व कान्तेः, सर्गसमाप्तिरिव सौन्दर्यस्य, आयतिरिव यौवनस्य, अनभ्रवृष्टिरिव वैदग्ध्यस्य, अयशःप्रमृष्टिरिव लक्ष्म्याः, यशःपुष्टिरिव चारित्रस्य, हृदयतुष्टिरिव धर्मस्य, सौभाग्य[5]परमाणुसृष्टिरिव प्रजापतेः, शमस्यापि शान्तिरिव, विनयस्यापि विनीतिरिव, आभिजात्यस्याप्यभिजातिरिव, संयमस्यापि संयतिरिव, धैर्यस्यापि धृतिरिव, विभ्रमस्यापि विभ्रान्तिरिव यशोमती नाम महा-

---

१ '०धारारसममन्यत' अ. २ 'प्रसुतमिव' ब. ३ 'गृहीतहृदया' ब. ४ 'वरप्राप्तिरिव सौभाग्यस्य, उत्पत्तिभूमिरिव कान्तेः' ब. ५ 'सौहार्दम्य भागयरूपपरमाणु०' ब.

देवी प्राणानां प्रणयस्य विस्रम्भस्य धर्मस्य सुखस्य च भूमिरभूत्। यास्य वक्षसि नरकजितो लक्ष्मीरिव ललास।

निसर्गत एव च स नृपतिरादित्यभक्तो बभूव। प्रतिदिनमुदये दिनकृतः स्नातः सितदुकूलधारी धवलकर्पटप्रावृतशिराः प्राङ्मुखः क्षितौ जानुभ्यां स्थित्वा कुङ्कुमपङ्कानुलिप्ते मण्डलके पवित्रपद्मरागपात्रीनिहितेन स्वहृदयेनेव सूर्यानुरक्तेन रक्तकमलषण्डेनार्घं[1] ददौ। अजपच्च जप्यं सुचरितः प्रत्युषसि मध्यन्दिने दिनान्ते चापत्यहेतोः प्राध्वं प्रयतेन मनसा जञ्जपूको मन्त्रमादित्यहृदयम्।

भक्तजनानुरोधविधेयानि तु भवन्ति देवतानां मनांसि। यतः स राजा कदाचिद्ग्रीष्मसमये यदृच्छया सितकरकरसितसुधाधवलस्य हर्म्यस्य पृष्ठे सुष्वाप। पार्श्वे चास्य द्वितीयशयने देवी यशोमती शिश्ये। परिणतप्रायायां तु श्यामायाम्, आसन्नप्रभातवेलाविलुप्यमानलावण्ये लिलम्बिषमाणे सीदत्तेजसि तारकेश्वरे, कराग्रस्पृष्टकुमुदिनीप्रमोदजन्मनि शशधरस्वेद इव गलत्यतिशीतलेऽवश्यायपयसि, मधुमदमत्तप्रसुप्तसीमन्तिनीनिःश्वासाहतेषु संक्रान्तमदेष्विव घूर्णमानेष्वन्तःपुरप्रदीपेषु, राजनि च विमलनखप्रतिबिम्बिताभिः संवाह्यमानचरण इव तारकाभिर्विस्रब्धप्रसारितैर्दिगङ्गनानामिवार्पितैरङ्गैर्मधुसुगन्धिभिः स्वहस्तकमलतालवृन्तवातैरिव श्वसितैर्मुखश्रिया वीज्यमाने विमलकपोलस्थलस्थितेन सितकुसुमशेखरेणेव रतिकेलिकचग्रहलम्बितेन प्रतिमाशशिबिम्बेन विराजिते स्वपति देवी यशोमती सहसैव 'आर्यपुत्र, परित्रायस्व परित्रायस्व' इति भाषमाणा भूषणरवेण व्याहरन्तीव परिजनमुत्कम्पमानाङ्गयष्टिरुदतिष्ठत्।

अथ तेन सर्वस्यामपि पृथिव्यामश्रुतपूर्वेण किमुत देवीमुखे परित्रायस्वेति ध्वनिना दग्ध इव श्रवणयोरेकपद एव निद्रां तत्याज राजा। शिरोभागाच्च कोपकम्पमानदक्षिणकराकृष्टेन कर्णोत्पलेनेव निर्गच्छताच्छधारेण धौतासिना सीमन्तयन्निव निशामन्तरालव्यवधायकमाकाशमिवोत्तरीयांशुकं विक्षिपन्वामकरपल्लवेन करविक्षेपवेगगलितेन हृदयेनेव भयनिमित्तान्वेषिणा भ्रमता दिक्षु कनकवलयेन विराजमानः, सत्वरावतारितवामचरणाक्रान्तिकम्पितप्रासादः, पुरःपतितेनासिधारागोचरगतेन शशिमयूखखण्डेनेव खण्डितेन हारेण राजमानः, लक्ष्मीचुम्बनलग्नताम्बूलरसरञ्जिताभ्यामिव निद्रया कोपेन चातिलोहिताभ्यां लोचनाभ्यां पाटलयन्[2]पर्यन्तानाशानाम्, बद्धान्धकारया त्रिपताकया भ्रुकुट्या पुनरिव त्रियामां परिवर्तयन् 'देवि, न भेतव्यम्, न भेतव्यम्' इत्यभिदधानो वेगेनोत्पपात। सर्वासु च दिक्षु विक्षिप्तचक्षुर्यदा नाद्राक्षीत्किंचिदपि तदा पप्रच्छ तां भयकारणम्।

---

१ 'अर्घं' ब. २ 'पटलयन्' ब.

अथ गृहदेवतास्विव प्रधावितासु यामिकिनीषु, प्रबुद्धे च समीपशायिनि परिजने, शान्ते च हृदयोत्कम्पकारिणि साध्वसे सा समभाषत—'आर्यपुत्र, जानामि स्वप्ने भगवतः सवितुर्मण्डलान्निर्गत्य द्वौ कुमारकौ तेजोमयौ बालातपेनेव पूरयन्तौ दिग्भागान् वैद्युतमिव जीवलोकं कुर्वाणौ मुकुटिनौ कुण्डलिनौ अङ्गदिनौ कवचिनौ गृहीतशस्त्रौ इन्द्रगोपकरुचा रुधिरेण[1] स्नातौ उन्मुखेनोत्तमाङ्गघटमानाञ्जलिना जगता निखिलेन प्रणम्यमानौ कन्ययैकया च चन्द्रमूर्त्येव सुषुम्णरश्मिनिर्गतयानुगम्यमानौ क्षितितलमवतीर्णौ । तौ च मे विलपन्त्याः शस्त्रेणोदरं विदार्य प्रवेष्टुमारब्धौ । प्रतिबुद्धास्मि चार्यपुत्रं विक्रोशयन्ती वेपमानहृदया' इति ।

एतस्मिन्नेव च कालक्रमे राजलक्ष्म्याः प्रथमालापः प्रथयन्निव स्वप्नफलमुपतोरणं रराण प्रभातशङ्खः । भाविनीं भूतिमिवाभिदधाना दध्वनुरमन्दं दुन्दुभयः । चकाण कोणाहतानन्दादिव[2] प्रत्यूषनान्दी । जय जयेति प्रबोधमङ्गलपाठकानामुच्चैर्वाचोऽश्रूयन्त । पुरुषश्च वल्लभतुरङ्गमन्दुरामन्दिरे मन्दमन्दं सुप्तोत्थितः सप्तीनां कृतमधुरहेषारवाणां पुरश्च्योतत्तुषारसलिलशीकरं किरन्मरकतहरितं यवसं वक्त्रापरवक्त्रे पपाठ—

'निधिस्तरुविकारेण सन्मणिः स्फुरता धाम्ना ।
शुभागमो निमित्तेन स्पष्टमाख्यायते लोके ॥ ३ ॥
अरुण इव पुरःसरो रविं पवन इवातिजवो जलागमम् ।
शुभमशुभमथापि वा नृणां कथयति पूर्वनिदर्शनोदयः' ॥ ४ ॥

नरपतिस्तु तच्छ्रुत्वा प्रीयमाणेनान्तःकरणेन तामवादीत्—'देवि, मुदोऽवसरे विषीदसि । समृद्धास्ते गुरुजनाशिषः पूर्णा नो मनोरथाः परिगृहीतासि कुलदेवताभिः प्रसन्नस्ते भगवानंशुमाली नचिरेणैवातिगुणवदपत्यत्रयलाभेनानन्दयिष्यति भवतीम्' इति । अवतीर्य च यथाक्रियमाणाः क्रियाश्चकार । यशोमत्यपि[3] तुतोष तेन पत्युर्भाषितेन ।

ततः समतिक्रान्ते कस्मिंश्चित्कालांशे देव्यां च यशोमत्यां देवो राज्यवर्धनः प्रथममेव सम्बभूव गर्भे । गर्भस्थितस्यैव च यस्य यशसेव पाण्डुतामादत्त जननी । गुणगौरवक्लान्तेव गात्रमुद्वोढुं न शशाक । कान्तिविसरामृतरसतृप्तेवाहारं प्रति पराङ्मुखीबभूव । शनैः शनैरुपचीयमानगर्भभरालसा च गुरुभिर्वारितापि वन्दनाय कथमपि सखीभिर्हस्तावलम्बेनानीयत । विश्राम्यन्ती सालभञ्जिकेव समीपगतस्तम्भभित्तिष्वलक्ष्यत । कमललोभनिलीनैरलिभिरिव वृतावुद्धर्तुं नाशकच्चरणौ । मृणाललोभेन च चरणनखमयूखलग्नैर्भवनहंसैरिव सञ्चार्यमाणा मन्दमन्दं बभ्राम । मणिभित्तिपातिनीषु प्रतिमास्वपि हस्तावलम्बनलोभेन प्रसारयामास करकमलम्, किमुत सखीषु ।

---

१ 'रुधिरेण धाम्ना स्नातौ' ब. २ 'कोणाभिहता०' ब. ३ 'यशोवत्यपि' अ.

माणिक्यस्तम्भदीधितीरप्यालम्बितुमाचकाङ्क्ष, किं पुनर्भवनलताः। समादेष्टुमप्यसमर्थासीद्गृहकार्याणि कैव कथा कर्तुम्। आस्तां नूपुरभारखेदितं चरणयुगलं मनसापि नोदसहत सौधमारोढुम्। अङ्गान्यपि नाशक्नोदुद्धारयितुं दूरे भूषणानि। चिन्तयित्वापि क्रीडापर्वताधिरोहणमुत्कम्पितस्तनी तस्तान। प्रत्युत्थानेषूभयजानुशिखरविनिहितकरकिसलयापि गर्वादिव गर्भेणाधार्यत। दिवसं चाधोमुखी स्तनपृष्ठसंक्रान्तेनापत्यदर्शनौत्सुक्यादन्तःप्रविष्टेनेव मुखकमलेनैवं प्रीयमाणा ददर्श गर्भम्। उदरे तनयेन हृदये च भर्त्रा तिष्ठता द्विगुणितामिव लक्ष्मीमुवाह। सख्युत्सङ्गमुक्तशरीरा च शरीरपरिचारिकाणामङ्केषु सपत्नीनां. तु शिरःसु पादौ चकार। अवतीर्णे च दशमे मासि सर्वोर्वीभृत्पक्षपाताय वज्रपरमाणुभिरिव निर्मितम्, त्रिभुवनभारधारणसमर्थ शेषफणामण्डलोपकरणैरिव कल्पितम्, सकलभूभृत्कम्पकारिणं दिग्गजावयवैरिव विहितमसूत देवं राज्यवर्धनम्। यस्मिञ्जाते जातप्रमोदा नृत्यमय्य इवाजायन्त प्रजाः। पूरितासंख्यशङ्खशब्दमुखरं प्रहतपटहशतपटुरवं गम्भीरभेरीनिनादनिर्भरभरितभुवनं प्रमोदोन्मत्तमर्त्यलोकमनोहरं मासमेकं दिवसमिव महोत्सवमकरोन्नरपतिः।

अथान्यस्मिन्नतिक्रान्ते कस्मिंश्चित्काले कन्दलिनि कुड्मलितकदम्बतरौ रूढतोक्मतृण[1]स्तम्बे स्तम्भिततामरसे विकसितचातकचेतसि मूकमानसौकसि नभसि मासि[2] देव्या देवक्या इव चक्रपाणिर्यशोमत्या हृदये गर्भे च सममेव सम्बभूव हर्षः। शनैः शनैश्चास्याः सर्वप्रजापुण्यैरिव परिगृहीता भूयोऽप्यापाण्डुतामङ्गयष्टिर्जगाम। गर्भारम्भेण श्यामायमानचारुचूचुकचूलिकौ चक्रवर्तिनः पातुं मुद्रिताविव[3] पयोधरकलशौ बभार[4]। स्तन्यार्थमाननिहिता दुग्धनदीव दीर्घस्निग्धधवला माधुर्यमधत्त दृष्टिः। सकलमङ्गलगणाधिष्ठितगात्रगरिम्णेव गतिरमन्दायत। मन्दं मन्दं सञ्चरन्त्या निर्मलमणिकुट्टिमनिमग्नप्रतिबिम्बनिभेन गृहीतपादपल्लवा पूर्वसेवामिवारेभे पृथिव्यस्याः। दिवसमधिशयानायाः शयनीयसपाश्रयपत्त्रभङ्गपुत्रिकाप्रतिमा विमलकपोलोदरगता प्रसवसमयं प्रतिपालयन्ती लक्ष्मीरिवालक्ष्यत। क्षपासु सौधशिखराग्रगताया गर्भोन्माथमुक्तांशुके स्तनमण्डले संक्रान्तमुडुपतिमण्डलमुपरि गर्भस्य श्वेतातपत्रमिव केनापि धार्यमाणमदृश्यत। सुप्ताया वासभवने चित्रभित्तिचामरग्राहिण्योऽपि चामराणि चालयांचक्रुः। स्वप्नेषु करविधृतकमलिनीपलाशपुटसलिलैश्चतुर्भिरपि दिक्करिभिरक्रियताभिषेकः। प्रतिबुध्यमानायाश्च चन्द्रशालिकासालभञ्जिकापरिजनोऽपि जयशब्दमसकृदजनयत्। परिजनाह्वानेष्वादिशेत्यशरीरा वाचो निश्चेरुः। क्रीडायामपि नासहताज्ञाभङ्गम्। अपि च चतुर्णामपि महार्णवानामेकीकृतेनाम्भसा स्नातुं वाञ्छा बभूव। वेला-

---

१ अ omits रूढ. २ अ omits मासि. ३ 'मुद्रिताविव जतुना' ब. ४ 'बभारोरुस्थलम्' ब.

वनलतागृहोदरपुलिनपरिसरेषु पर्यटितुं हृदयमभिललाष । आत्ययिकेष्वपि कार्येषु सविभ्रमं भ्रूलता चचाल । सन्निहितेष्वपि मणिदर्पणेषु मुखमुत्खाते खड्गपट्टे वीक्षितुं व्यसनमासीत् । उत्सारितवीणाः स्त्रीजनविरुद्धा धनुर्ध्वनयः श्रुतावसुखायन्त । पञ्जरकेसरिषु चक्षुररमत । गुरुप्रणामेष्वपि स्तम्भितमिव शिरः कथमपि ननाम । सख्यश्चास्याः प्रमोदविस्फारितैर्लोचनपुटैरासन्नप्रसवमहोत्सवधियेव धवलयन्त्यो भवनं विकचकुमुदकमलकुवलयपलाशवृष्टिमयं रक्षाबलिविधिमिवानवरतं विदधाना दिक्षु क्षणमपि न मुमुचुः पार्श्वम् । आत्मोचितस्थाननिषण्णाश्च महान्तो विविधौषधिधरा भिषजो भूधरा इव भुवो धृतिं चक्रुः । पयोनिधीनां हृदयानीव लक्ष्म्या सहागतानि ग्रीवासूत्रग्रन्थिषु प्रशस्तरत्नान्यबध्यन्त ।

ततश्च प्राप्ते ज्येष्ठामूलीये मासि बहुलासु बहुलपक्षद्वादश्यां व्यतीते प्रदोषसमये समारुरुक्षति क्षपायौवने सहसैवान्तःपुरे समुदपादि कोलाहलः स्त्रीजनस्य । निर्गत्य च ससंभ्रमं यशोमत्याः स्वयमेव हृदयनिर्विशेषा धात्र्याः सुता सुयात्रेति[1] नाम्ना राज्ञः पादयोर्निपत्य 'देव, दिष्ट्या वर्धसे द्वितीयसुतजन्मना' इति व्याहरन्ती पूर्णपात्रं जहार ।

अस्मिन्नेव च काले राज्ञः परमसंमतः शतशः संवादितातीन्द्रियादेशो दर्शितप्रभावः सङ्कलिती[2] ज्योतिषि सर्वासां ग्रहसंहितानां पारदृश्वा सकलगणकमध्ये महितो हितश्च त्रिकालज्ञानभाग्भोजकस्तारको नाम गणकः समुपसृत्य विज्ञापितवान्—'देव, श्रूयताम्[3] । मान्धाता किलैवंविधे व्यतीपातादिसर्वदोषाभिषङ्गरहितेऽहनि सर्वेषूच्चस्थानस्थितेष्वेवं ग्रहेष्वीदृशि लग्ने भेजे जन्म । अर्वाक्ततोऽस्मिन्नन्तराले पुनरेवंविधे योगे चक्रवर्तिजनने नाजनि जगति कश्चिदपरः । सप्तानां चक्रवर्तिनामग्रणीश्चक्रवर्तिचिह्नानां महारत्नानां च भाजनं सप्तानां सागराणां पालयिता सप्ततन्तूनां सर्वेषां प्रवर्तयिता सप्तसप्तिसमः सुतोऽयं देवस्य जातः' इति ।

अत्रान्तरे स्वयमेवानाध्माता अपि तारमधुरं शङ्खा विरेसुः । अताडितोऽपि क्षुभितजलनिधिजलध्वनिधीरं जुगुञ्जाभिषेकदुन्दुभिः । अनाहतान्यपि मङ्गलतूर्याणि रेणुः । सर्वभुवनाभयघोषणापटह इव दिगन्तरेषु बभ्राम तूर्यप्रतिशब्दः । विधुतकेसरसटाश्च साटोपगृहीतहरितदूर्वापल्लवकवलप्रशस्तैर्मुखपुटैः समहेषन्त हृष्टा वाजिनः । सलीलमुत्क्षिप्तैर्हस्तपल्लवैर्नृत्यन्त इव श्रवणसुभगं जगर्जुर्गजाः । ववौ चाचिराच्चक्रायुधमुत्सृजन्त्या लक्ष्म्या निःश्वास इव सुरामोदसुरभिर्दिव्यानिलः । यज्वनां मन्दिरेषु प्रदक्षिणशिखाकलापकथितकल्याणागमाः प्रजज्वलुरनिन्धना वैतानवह्नयः । भुवस्तलात्तपनीयशृङ्खलाबन्धबन्धुरकलशीकोशाः समुदगुर्महानिधयः । प्रहतमङ्गलतूर्यप्रतिशब्दनिभेन दिक्षु दिक्पालैरपि प्रमोदादक्रियतेव दिष्टवृद्धिकलकलः । तत्क्षण एव च शुक्लवाससो

---

१ 'सुपात्रेति' ब. २ 'सङ्कलितो' ब. ३ 'श्रूयते' ब.

ब्रह्ममुखाः कृतयुगप्रजापतय इव प्रजावृद्धये समुपतस्थिरे द्विजातयः। साक्षाद्धर्म इव शान्त्युदकफलहस्तस्तस्थौ पुरः पुरोधाः। पुरातन्यः स्थितय इवादृश्यन्तागता बान्धववृद्धाः। प्रलम्बश्मश्रुजालजटिलाननानि बहलमलपङ्ककलङ्ककालकायानि नश्यतः कलिकालस्य बान्धवकुलानीवाकुलान्यधावन्त मुक्तानि बन्धनवृन्दानि। तत्कालापक्रान्तस्याधर्मस्य शिबिरश्रेणय इवालक्ष्यन्त लोकविलुण्ठिता विपणिवीथ्यः। विलसदुन्मुखवामनकबधिरवृन्दवेष्टिताः साक्षाज्जातमातृदेवता इव बहुबालकव्याकुला ननृतुर्वृद्धधात्र्यः। प्रावर्तत च विगतराजकुलस्थितिरधःकृतप्रतीहाराकृतिरपनीतवेत्रिवेत्रो निर्दोषान्तःपुरप्रवेशः समस्वामिपरिजनो निर्विशेषबालवृद्धः समानशिष्टाशिष्टजनो दुर्ज्ञेयमत्तामत्तप्रविभागस्तुल्यकुलयुवतिवेश्यालापविलासः प्रनृत्तसकलकटकलोकः पुत्रजन्मोत्सवो महान्।

अपरेद्युरारभ्य सर्वाभ्यो दिग्भ्यः स्त्रीराज्यानीवावर्जितानि, असुरविवराणीवापावृतानि, नारायणावरोधानीव प्रचलितानि, अप्सरसामिव महीमवतीर्णानि कुलानि, परिजनेन पृथुकरण्डपरिगृहीताः स्नानीयचूर्णावकीर्णकुसुमाः सुमनःस्रजः, स्फटिकशिलाशकलशुक्लकर्पूरखण्डपूरिताः पात्रीः, कुङ्कुमाधिवासभाञ्जि भाजनानि च मणिमयानि, सहकारतैलतिम्यत्तनुखदिरकेसरजालजटिलानि चन्दनधवलपूगफलफालीदन्तुरदन्तशफरुकाणि, गुञ्जन्मधुकरकुलपीयमानपारिजातपरिमलानि पाटलकानि[1] च, सिन्दूरपात्राणि च पिष्टातकपात्राणि च बाललतालम्बमानविटकवीटकांश्च ताम्बूलवृक्षकान्बिभ्राणेनानुगम्यमानानि चरण[2]निकुट्टनरणितमणिनूपुरमुखरितदिङ्मुखानि नृत्यन्ति राजकुलमागच्छन्ति समन्तात्सामन्तान्तःपुरसहस्राण्यदृश्यन्त।

शनैः शनैर्व्यजृम्भत च क्वचिन्नृत्तानुचितचिरन्तनशालीनकुलपुत्रकलोकलास्यप्रथितपार्थिवानुरागः क्वचिदन्तःस्मितक्षितिपालापेक्षितक्षीबक्षुद्रदासीसमाकृष्यमाणराजवल्लभः क्वचिन्मत्तकटककुट्टनीकण्ठलग्नवृद्धार्यसामन्तनृत्तनिर्भरहसितनरपतिः क्वचित्क्षितिपाक्षिसंज्ञादिष्टदुष्टदासेरकगीतसूच्यमानसचिवचौर्यरतप्रपञ्चः क्वचिन्मदोत्कटकुटहारिकापरिष्वज्यमानजरत्प्रव्रजितजनितजनहासः क्वचिदन्योन्यनिर्भरस्पर्धोद्धुरविटचेटका[3]रब्धावाच्यवचनयुद्धः क्वचिन्नृपाबलाबलात्कारनर्त्यमाननृत्यानभिज्ञान्तःपुरपालभावितभुजिष्यः, सपर्वत इव कुसुमराशिभिः, सधारागृह इव सीधुप्रपाभिः, सनन्दनवन इव पारिजातकामोदैः, सनीहार इव कर्पूररेणुभिः, साट्टहास इव पटहरवैः, सामृतमथन इव कलकलैः, सावर्त इव रासकमण्डलैः, सरोमाञ्च इव भूषणमणिकिरणैः, सपट्टबन्ध इव चन्दनललाटिकाभिः, सप्रसव इव प्रतिशब्दकैः, सप्ररोह इव प्रसाददानैरुत्सवामोदः।

---

१ 'पाटलानि पोटलकानि च सिन्दूर०' अ. २ 'चरणानि कुट्टन० ब. ३ 'चेटकपेटकारब्ध' ब.

स्कन्धावलम्बमानकेसरमालाः काम्बोजवाजिन इवास्कन्दन्तस्तरलतारका हरिणा इवोड्डीयमानाः सगरसुता इव खनित्रैर्निर्दयैश्चरणाभिघातैर्दारयन्तो भुवमनेकसहस्रसंख्याश्चिक्रीडुर्युवानः। कथमपि तालावचरचारणचरणक्षोभं चक्षमे क्षमा। क्षितिपालकुमारकाणां खेलतामन्योन्यास्फालैराभरणेषु मुक्ताफलानि फेलुः। सिन्दूररेणुना पुनरुत्पन्नहिरण्यगर्भगर्भशोणितशोणाशमिव ब्रह्माण्डकपालमभवत्। पटवासपांशुपटलेन प्रकटितमन्दाकिनीसैकतसहस्रमिव शुशुभे नभस्तलम्। विप्रकीर्यमाणपिष्टातकपरागपिञ्जरितातपा भुवनक्षोभविशीर्णपितामहकमलकिञ्जल्करजोराजिरञ्जिता इव रेजुर्दिवसाः। सङ्घट्टविघटितहारपतितमुक्ताफलपटलेषु चस्खाल लोकः।

स्थानस्थानेषु च मन्दमन्दमास्फाल्यमाना[1]लिङ्ग्यकेन शिञ्जानमञ्जुवेणुना झणझणायमानझल्लरीकेण ताड्यमानतन्त्रीपटहिकेन वाद्यमानानुत्ताना[2]लाबुवीणेन कलकांस्यकोशीक्वणितकाहलेन समकालदीयमानानुत्तालताल[3]केनातोद्यवाद्येनानुगम्यमानाः, पदेपदे झणझणितभूषणरवैरपि सहृदयैरिवानु[4]वर्तमानताललयाः, कोकिला इव मदकलकाकलीकोमलालापिन्यो विटानां कर्णामृतान्यश्लीलरासकपदानि गायन्त्यः, समुण्डमालिकाः, सकर्णपल्लवाः, सचन्दनतिलकाः, समुच्छ्रिताभिर्वलयावलीवाचालाभिर्बाहुलतिकाभिः सवितारमिवालिङ्गयन्त्यः, कुङ्कुमप्रमृष्टिरुचिरकायाः काश्मीरकिशोर्य इव वल्गन्त्यः, नितम्बबिम्बलम्बिविकटकुरण्टकशेखराः प्रदीप्ता इव रागाग्निना, सिन्दूरच्छटाच्छुरितमुखमुद्राः शासनपट्टपङ्क्तय इवाप्रतिहतशासनस्य कन्दर्पस्य, मुष्टिप्रकीर्यमाणकर्पूरपटवासपांसुलमनोरथसञ्चरणरथ्या इव यौवनस्योद्दामकुसुमदामताडिततरुणजनाः प्रतीहार्य इव तरुणमहोत्सवस्य, प्रचलत्पत्रकुण्डला लसन्त्यो लता इव मदनचन्दनद्रुमस्य, ललितपदहंसकरवमुखराः समुल्लसन्त्यो वीचय इव शृङ्गारर[5]ससागरस्य, वाच्यावाच्यविवेकशून्या बालक्रीडा इव सौभाग्यस्य, घनपटहरवोत्कण्टकितगात्रयष्टयः केतक्य इव कुसुमधूलिमुद्गिरन्त्यः, कमलिन्य इव दिवसमुत्फुल्लाननाः, कुमुदिन्य इव रात्रावनुपजातनिद्राः, आविष्टा इव नरेन्द्रवृन्दपरिवृताः, प्रीतय इव हृदयमपहरन्त्यः, गीतय इव रागमुद्दीपयन्त्यः, पुष्टय इवानन्दमुत्पादयन्त्यः, मदमपि मदयन्त्य इव, रागमपि रञ्जयन्त्य इव, आनन्दमपि आनन्दयन्त्य इव, नृत्यमपि नर्तयमाना इव, उत्सवमप्युत्सुक[6]यन्त्य इव, कटाक्षेक्षितेषु पिबन्त्य इवापाङ्गशुक्तिभिः, तर्जनेषु संयमयन्त्य इव नखमयूखपाशैः, कोपाभिनयेषु ताडयन्त्य इव भ्रूलताविभागैः, प्रणयसम्भाषणेषु वर्षन्त्य इव सर्वरसान्, चतुरचङ्क्रमणेषु विकिरन्त्य इव विकारान्, पण्यविलासिन्यः प्रानृत्यन्।

---

१ '०मानलिङ्गकेन' ब. २ 'अनुत्तालालाबु०' ब. ३ ०'तालिकेन' ब. ४ 'अनुवर्त्यमान०' ब. ५ 'शृङ्गाररसस्य' अ. ६ 'उत्सवयन्त्यः' ब.

अन्यत्र वेत्रिवेत्रवित्रासितजनदत्तान्तरालाः, ध्रियमाणधवलातपत्रवना वनदेवता इव कल्पतरुतलविचारिण्यः, काश्चित्स्कन्धोभयपालीलम्बमानलम्बोत्तरीय[1]लग्नहस्ता लीलादोलाधिरूढा इव प्रेङ्खन्त्यः, काश्चित्कनककेयूरकोटिपाट्यमानपट्टांशुकोत्तरङ्गास्तरङ्गिण्य इव तरच्चक्रवाकसीमन्त्यमानस्रोतसः, काश्चिदुद्धूयमानधवलचामरसटालग्नत्रिकण्टकवलितविकटकटाक्षाः सरस्य इव हंसाकृष्यमाणनीलोत्पलवनाः, काश्चिच्चलच्चरणच्युतालक्तकारुणस्वेदशीकरसिच्यमानभवनहंसाः संध्यारागरज्यमानेन्दुबिम्बा इव कौमुदीरजन्यः, काश्चित्कण्ठनिहितकाञ्चनकाञ्चीगुणाञ्चितकञ्चुकिविकारा[2]कुञ्चितभ्रुवः कामवागुरा इव प्रसारितबाहुपाशा राजमहिष्यः प्रारब्धनृत्या विलेसुः[3]।

सर्वतश्च नृत्यतः स्त्रैणस्य गलद्भिः पदालक्तकैररुणिता रागमयीव शुशोण क्षोणी। समुल्लसद्भिः स्तनमण्डलैर्मङ्गलकलशमय इव बभूव महोत्सवः। भुजलताविक्षेपैर्मृणालवलयमय इव रराज जीवलोकः। समुल्लसद्भिर्विलासस्मितैस्तडिन्मय इवाक्रियत कालः। चञ्चलानां चक्षुषामंशुभिः कृष्णसार[4]मया इवासन्वासराः। समुल्लसद्भिः शिरीषकुसुमस्तबककर्णपूरैः शुकपिच्छमय इव हरितच्छायोऽभूदातपः। विस्रंसमानैर्धम्मिल्लतमालपल्लवैः कज्जलमयमिवालक्ष्यतान्तरिक्षम्। उत्क्षिप्तैर्हस्तकिशलयैः कमलिनीमय्य इव बभासिरे सृष्टयः। माणिक्येन्द्रायुधानामर्चिषा चाषपत्रमया इव चकाशिरे रविमरीचयः। रणतामाभरणगणानां प्रतिशब्दकैः किङ्किणीमय्य इव शिशिञ्जिरे दिशः। जरत्योऽप्युन्मादिन्य इव रमण्यो रेणुः। वर्षीयांसोऽपि ग्रहगृहीता इव नापत्रेपिरे। विद्वांसोऽपि मत्ता इवात्मानं विसस्मरुः। निनर्तिषया मुनीनामपि मनांसि विपुस्फुलुः। सर्वस्वं च ददौ नरपतिः। दिशि दिशि कुबेरकोषा इवालुप्यन्त लोकेन द्रविणराशयः।

एवं च वृत्ते तस्मिन्महोत्सवे शनैः शनैः पुनरप्यतिक्रामति काले, देवे चोत्तमाङ्गनिहितरक्षासर्षपे[5], समुन्मिषत्प्रतापाग्निस्फुलिङ्ग इव गोरोचनापिञ्जरितवपुषि, समभिव्यज्यमानसहजक्षात्रतेजसीव हाटकबद्धविकटव्याघ्रनखपङ्क्तिमण्डितग्रीवके, हृदयोद्भिद्यमानदर्पाङ्कुर इव प्रथमाव्यक्तजल्पितेन सत्यस्य शनैः शनैरोंकारमिव कुर्वाणे, मुग्धस्मितैः कुसुमैरिव मधुकरकुलानि बन्धुहृदयान्याकर्षति, जननीपयोधरकलशपयःशीकरसेकादिव जायमानैर्विलासहसिताङ्कुरैर्दशनकैरलंक्रियमाणमुखकमलके, चारित्र इवान्तःपुरस्त्रीकदम्बकेन पाल्यमाने, मन्त्र इव सचिवमण्डलेन रक्ष्यमाणे, वृत्त इव कुलपुत्रकलोकेनामुच्यमाने, यशसीवात्म[6]वंशेन संवर्ध्यमाने, मृगपतिपोत इव रक्षिपुरुषशस्त्रपञ्जरमध्यगते, धात्रीकराङ्गुलिलग्ने पञ्चषाणि पदानि प्रयच्छति हर्षे, षष्ठं

१ '०लग्ना लीला०' अ. २ 'विकारकुञ्चितभुवः' ब. ३ 'विरेसुः' ब. ४ 'कृष्णशार०' भ. ५ '०सर्षपकणे' ब. ६ 'आत्मवशेन' ब.

वर्षमवतरति च राज्यवर्धने देवी यशोमती गर्भेणाधत्त नारायणमूर्तिरिव वसुधा देवीं राज्यश्रियम् ।

पूर्णेषु च प्रसवदिवसेषु दीर्घरक्तनालनेत्रामुत्पलिनीमिव सरसी, हंसमधुरस्वरां शरदमिव प्रावृट्, कुसुमसुकुमारावयवां वनराजिमिव मधुश्रीः, महाकनकावदातां वसुधारामिव द्यौः, प्रभावर्षिणीं रत्नजातिमिव वेला, सकलजननयनानन्दकारिणीं चन्द्रलेखामिव प्रतिपत्, सहस्रनेत्रदर्शनयोग्यां जयन्तीमिव शची, सर्वभूभृदभ्यर्थितां गौरीमिव मेना, प्रसूतवती दुहितरम्। यया द्वयोः सुतयोरुपरि स्तनयोरिवैकावलीलतया नितरामराजत ।

अस्मिन्नेव तु काले देव्या यशोमत्या भ्राता सुतमष्टवर्षदेशीयमुद्धूयमानकुटिलकाकपक्षकशिखण्डं खण्डपरशुहुंकाराग्निधूमलेखानुबद्धमूर्धानं मकरध्वजमिव पुनर्जातम्, एकेनेन्द्रनीलकुण्डलांशुश्यामलितेन शरीरार्धेनेतरेण च त्रिकण्टकमुक्ताफलालोकधवलितेन संपृक्तावतारमिव हरिहरयोर्दर्शयन्तम्, पीनप्रकोष्ठप्रतिष्ठितपुष्पलोहवलयं परशुराममिव क्षत्रक्षपणक्षीणपरशुपाशचिह्नितं बालतां गतम्, कण्ठसूत्रग्रथितभङ्गुरप्रवालाङ्कुरं हिरण्यकशिपुमिवोरःकाठिन्यखण्डितनरसिंहनखरखण्डम्, गृहीतजन्मान्तरं शैशवेऽपि सावष्टम्भं बीजमिव वीर्यद्रुमस्य भण्डिनामानमनुचरं कुमारयोरर्पितवान् ।

अवनिपतेस्तु तस्योपरि पुत्रयोस्तृतीयस्य नेत्रयोरिवेश्वरस्य तुल्यं दर्शनमासीत् । राजपुत्रावपि सकलजीवलोकहृदयानन्ददायिनौ तेन प्रकृतिदक्षिणेन मधुमाधवाविव मलयमारुतेनोपेतौ नितरां रेजतुः । क्रमेण चापरेणेव भ्रात्रा प्रजानन्देन सह वर्धमानौ यौवनमवतेरतुः स्थिरोरुस्तम्भौ च पृथुप्रकोष्ठौ दीर्घभुजार्गलौ विकटोरःकपाटौ प्रांशुसालाभिरामौ महानगरसंनिवेशाविव सर्वलोकाश्रयक्षमौ बभूवतुः ।

अथ चन्द्रसूर्याविव स्फुरज्ज्योत्स्नायशःप्रतापाक्रान्तभुवनावभिरामदुर्निरीक्ष्यौ, अग्निमारुताविव समभिव्यक्ततेजोबलावेकीभूतौ, शिलाकठिनकायबन्धौ हिमवद्विन्ध्याविवाचलौ, महावृषाविव कृतयुगयोग्यौ, अरुणगरुडाविव हरिवाहनविभक्तशरीरौ, इन्द्रोपेन्द्राविव नागेन्द्रगतौ,कर्णार्जुनाविव कुण्डलकिरीटधरौ, पूर्वापरदिग्भागाविव सर्वतेजस्विनामुदयास्तमयसम्पादनसमर्थौ, अमान्ताविवातिमानेनासन्नवेलार्गलनिरोधसङ्कटे कुकुटीरके तेजःपराङ्मुखीं छायामपि जुगुप्समानौ, स्वात्मप्रतिबिम्बेनापि पादनखलग्नेन लज्जमानौ, शिरोरुहाणामपि भङ्गेन दुःखमवतिष्ठमानौ, चूडामणिसंक्रान्तेनापि द्वितीयेनातपत्रेणापत्रपमाणौ, भगवति षण्मुखेऽपि स्वामिशब्देनासुखायमानश्रवणौ, दर्पणदृष्टेनापि प्रतिपुरुषेण दूयमाननयनौ, संध्याञ्जलिघटनेष्वपि शूलायमानोत्तमाङ्गौ, जलधरधृतेनापि धनुषा दोदूयमानहृदयौ, आलेख्यक्षितिपतिभिरप्यप्रणमद्भिः सन्तप्यमानचरणौ, परिमितमण्डलसन्तुष्टं तेजः सवितुरप्यबहुमन्यमानौ,

१ 'अमान्ताविवाभिमानेन' ब. २ 'दोधूयमान०' ब.

भूभृदपहृतलक्ष्मीकं सागरमप्युपहसन्तौ, बलवन्तमकृतविग्रहं मारुतमपि निन्दन्तौ, हिमवतोऽपि चमरीबालव्यजनवीजितेन दह्यमानौ, जलधीनामपि शङ्खैः खिद्यमानौ, चतुःसमुद्राधिपतिमपरं प्रचेतसमप्यसहमानौ, अनपहृतच्छत्रानपि विच्छायानवनिपालान्कुर्वाणौ, साधुष्वप्यसेवितप्रसन्नौ, मुखेन मधु क्षरन्तौ, दुष्टराजवंशानूष्मणा दूरस्थितानपि म्लानिमानयन्तौ, अनुदिवसं शास्त्राभ्यासश्यामिकाकलङ्कितमशेषराजकप्रतापाग्निनिर्वापणमलिनमिव करतलमुद्वहन्तौ, योग्याकालेषु धीरैर्धनुर्ध्वनिभिरभ्यर्णोपभोगाद्दिग्वधूभिरिवालपन्तौ, राज्यवर्धन इति हर्ष इति सर्वस्यामेव पृथिव्यामाविर्भूतशब्दप्रादुर्भावौ, स्वल्पीयसैव कालेन द्वीपान्तरेष्वपि प्रकाशतां जग्मतुः ।

एकदा च तावाहूय भुक्तवानभ्यन्तरगतः पिता सस्नेहमवादीत्—'वत्सौ, प्रथमं राज्याङ्गं दुर्लभाः सद्भृत्याः । प्रायेण परमाणव इव समवायेष्वनुगुणीभूय द्रव्यं कुर्वन्ति पार्थिवं क्षुद्राः । क्रीडारसेन नर्तयन्तो मयूरतां नयन्ति बालिशाः । दर्पणमिवानुप्रविश्यात्मीयां प्रकृतिं संक्रामयन्ति पल्लविकाः[1] । स्वप्ना इव मिथ्यादर्शनैरसद्बुद्धिं जनयन्ति विप्रलम्भकाः । गीतनृत्यहसितैरुन्मत्ततामावहन्त्युपेक्षिता विकारा इव वातिकाः । चातका इव तृष्णावन्तो न शक्यन्ते ग्रहीतुमकुलीनाः । मानसे मीनमिव स्फुरन्तमेवाभिप्रायं गृह्णन्ति जालिकाः । यमपट्टिका इवाम्बरे चित्रमालिखन्त्युद्गीतकाः । शल्यं हृदये निक्षिपन्त्यतिमार्गणाः । यतः सर्वैर्दोषाभिष्वङ्गैरसङ्गतौ बहुधोपधाभिः परीक्षितौ शुची विनीतौ विक्रान्तावभिरूपौ मालवराजपुत्रौ भ्रातरौ भुजाविव मे शरीरादव्यतिरिक्तौ कुमारगुप्तमाधवगुप्तनामानावस्माभिर्भवतोरनुचरत्वार्थमिमौ निर्दिष्टौ, अनयोरुपरि भवद्भ्यामपि नान्यपरिजनसमवृत्तिभ्यां भवितव्यम्' इत्युक्त्वा तयोराह्वानाय प्रतीहारमादिदेश ।

नचिराद्द्वारदेशनिहितलोचनौ राज्यवर्धनहर्षौ प्रतीहारेण सह प्रविशन्तम्, अग्रतो ज्येष्ठमष्टादशवर्षवयसं नात्युच्चं नातिखर्वमतिगुरुभिः पदन्यासैरनेकनरपतिसञ्चरणचलां निश्चलीकुर्वाणमिवोर्वीम्, अनवरताभ्यस्तलङ्घनघनोपचयकठिनमांसमेदुरादूरुद्वयान्निष्पततेवानुल्बणजानुग्रन्थिप्रसूतेन तनुतरजङ्घाकाण्डयुगलेन भासमानम्, उल्लिखितपार्श्वप्रकाशितकशिम्ना मन्दरमिव सुरासुरभसभ्रमितवासुकिकषणक्षीणेन मध्येन लक्ष्यमाणम्, अतिविस्तीर्णेनोरसा स्वामिसम्भावनानामपरिमितानामवकाशमिव प्रयच्छन्तम्, प्रलम्बमानस्य भुजयुगलस्य निभृतललितैर्विक्षेपैरतिदुस्तरं तरन्तमिव यौवनोदधिम्, वामकरकटकमाणिक्यमरीचिमञ्जरीजालिन्या समुद्भिद्यमानप्रतापानलशिखापल्लवयेव चापगुणकिणलेखयाङ्कितपीवरप्रकोष्ठम्, आलोहिनीमुच्चांसतटावलम्बिनीमस्त्रग्रहणव्रतविधृतां रौरवीमिव त्वचं कर्णाभरणमणेः प्रभां बिभ्राणम्, उत्कोटिकेयूरप-

[1] 'पल्लवकाः' ब.

मुखाविर्भूतचारणपरम्परापूर्यमाणप्र[1]कोष्ठं प्रतिष्ठाप्यमानेन्द्राणीदैवतम्, सितकुसुमविलेपनवसनसत्कृतैः सूत्रधारैरादीयमानविवाहवेदीसूत्रपातम्, उत्कूर्चककरैश्च सुधाकर्परस्कन्धैरधिरोहिणीसमारूढैर्धवैर्धवलीक्रियमाणप्रासादप्रतोलीप्राकारशिखरम्, क्षुण्णक्षाल्यमानकुसुम्भकसम्भाराम्भःप्लवपूररज्यमानजनपादपल्लवम्, निरूप्यमाणयौतकयोग्यमातङ्गतुरङ्गतरङ्गिताङ्गनम्, गणनाभियुक्तगणकगणगृह्यमाणलग्नगुणम्, गन्धोदकवाहिमकरमुखप्रणालीपूर्यमाणक्रीडावापीसमूहम्, हेमकारचक्रप्रक्रान्तहाटकघटनटाङ्कारवाचालितालिन्दकम्, उत्थापिताभिनवभित्तिपात्यमानबहलवालुकाकण्ठकालेपाकुलालेपकलोकम्, चतुरचित्रकरचक्रवाललिख्यमानमङ्गल्यालेख्यम्, लेप्यकारकदम्बकक्रियमाणमृण्मयमीनकूर्ममकरनारिकेलकदलीपूगवृक्षकम्, क्षितिपालैश्च स्वयमाबद्धकक्ष्यैः स्वाम्यर्पितकर्मशोभासम्पादनाकुलैः सिन्दूरकुट्टिमभूमीश्च मसृणयद्भिर्विनिहितसरसातर्पणहस्तान्विन्यस्तालक्तकपाटलांश्च चूताशोकपल्लवलाञ्छितशिखरानुद्वाहवितर्दिकास्तम्भानुत्तम्भयद्भिः प्रारब्धविविधव्यापारम्, आसूर्योदयाच्च प्रविष्टाभिः सतीभिः सुभगाभिः सुरूपाभिः सुवेशाभिरविधवाभिः सिन्दूररजोराजिराजितललाटाभिर्वधूवरगोत्रग्रहणगर्भाणि श्रुतिसुभगानि मङ्गलानि गायन्तीभिर्बहुविधवर्णकादिग्धाङ्गुलीभिर्ग्रीवासूत्राणि च चित्रयन्तीभिश्चित्रपत्रलतालेख्यकुशलाभिः कलशांश्च धवलिताञ्शीतलशाराजिरश्रेणीश्च मण्डयन्तीभिरभिन्नपुटकर्पासतूलपल्लवांश्च वैवाहिककङ्कणोर्णासूत्रसंनाहांश्च रञ्जयन्तीभिर्बलाशनाघृतघनीकृतकुङ्कुमकल्कमिश्रितांश्चाङ्गरागांल्लावण्यविशेषकृन्ति च मुखालेपनानि कल्पयन्तीभिः कक्कोलमिश्राः सजातीफलाः स्फुरत्स्फीतस्फाटिककर्पूरशकलखचितान्तराला लवङ्गमाला रचयन्तीभिः समन्तात्सामन्तसीमन्तिनीभिर्व्याप्तम्, बहुविधभक्तिनिर्माणनिपुणपुराणपौरपुरंध्रिबध्यमानैर्बद्धैश्चाचारचतुरान्तःपुरजरतीजनितपूजाराजमानर[2]ञ्जकरज्यमानै रक्तैश्चोभयपटान्तलग्नपरिजनप्रेङ्खोलितैश्छायासु शोष्यमाणैः शुष्कैश्च कुटिलक्रमरूपक्रियमाणपल्लवपरभागैरपरैरारब्धकुङ्कुमपङ्कस्थासकच्छुरणैरपरैरुद्भुजभुजिष्याभज्यमानभङ्गुरोत्तरीयैः क्षौमैश्च बादरैश्च दुकूलैश्च लालातन्तुजैश्चांशुकैश्च नेत्रैश्च निर्मोकनिभैरकठोररम्भागर्भकोमलैर्निःश्वासहार्यैः स्पर्शानुमेयैर्वासोभिः सर्वतः स्फुरद्भिरिन्द्रायुधसहस्रैरिव सञ्छादितम्, उज्ज्वलनिचोलकावगुण्ठ्यमानहंसकुलैश्च शयनीयैस्तारामुक्ताफलोपचीयमानैश्च कञ्चुकैरनेकोपयोगपाट्यमानैश्चापरिमितैः पट्टपटीसहस्रैरभिनवरागकोमलै[3]र्दुकूलराजमानैश्च पटवितानैः स्तवरकनिवहनिरन्तरच्छाद्यमानसमस्तपटलैश्च मण्डपैरुच्छ्रिन्ननेत्रपटवेष्ट्यमानैश्च स्तम्भैरुज्ज्वलं रमणीयं चौत्सुक्यदं च मङ्गल्यं चासीद्राजकुलम्।

१ 'प्रकोष्ठप्रतिष्ठाप्य०' अ. २ 'रजकमहादारजतरज्यमानैः' ब. ३ '०कोमलैर्दुकूल०' ब.

देवी तु यशोमती विवाहोत्सवपर्याकुलहृदया हृदयेन भर्तरि कुतूहलेन जामातरि स्नेहेन दुहितरि उपचारेण निमन्त्रितस्त्रीषु आदेशेन परिजने शरीरेण सञ्चरणे चक्षुषा कृताकृतप्रत्यवेक्षणेषु आनन्देन महोत्सवे एकापि बहुधा विभक्तेवाभवत्। भूपतिरप्युपर्युपरि विसर्जितोष्ट्रवामीजनितजामातृजोषः सत्यप्याज्ञासम्पादनदक्षे मुखेक्षणपरे परिजने समं पुत्राभ्यां दुहितृस्नेहविक्लवः सर्वं स्वयमकरोत्।

एवं च तस्मिन्नविधवामय[1] इव भवति राजकुले, मङ्गलमय इव जायमाने जीवलोके, चारणमयेष्विव लक्ष्यमाणेषु दिङ्मुखेषु, पटहमय इव कृतेऽन्तरिक्षे, भूषणमय इव भ्रमति परिजने, बान्धवमय इव दृश्यमाने सर्गे, निर्वृत्तिमय इवोपलक्ष्यमाणे काले, लक्ष्मीमय इव विजृम्भमाणे महोत्सवे, निधान इव सुखस्य फल इव जन्मनः परिणाम इव पुण्यस्य यौवन इव विभूतेर्यौवराज्य इव प्रीतेः सिद्धिकाल इव मनोरथस्य वर्तमाने, गण्यमान इव जनाङ्गुलीभिः, आलोक्यमान इव मार्गध्वजैः, प्रत्युद्गम्यमान इव मङ्गल्यवाद्यप्रतिशब्दकैः, आहूयमान इव मौहूर्तिकैः, आकृष्यमाण इव मनोरथैः, परिष्वज्यमान इव वधूसखीहृदयैराजगाम विवाहदिवसः। प्रातरेव प्रतीहारैः समुत्सारितनिखिलानिबद्धलोकं विविक्तमक्रियत राजकुलम्।

अथ महाप्रतीहारः प्रविश्य नृपसमीपम् 'देव, जामातुरन्तिकात्ताम्बूलदायकः पारिजातकनामा संप्राप्तः' इत्यभिधाय स्वाकारं युवानमदर्शयत्। राजा तु तं दूरादेव जामातृबहुमानाद्दर्शितादरः 'बालक, कच्चित्कुशली ग्रहवर्मा' इति पप्रच्छ। असौ तु समाकर्णितनराधिपध्वनिर्धावमानः कतिचित्पदान्युपसृत्य प्रसार्य च बाहू सेवाचतुरश्चिरं वसुन्धरायां निधाय मूर्धानमुत्थाय 'देव, कुशली यथाज्ञापयस्यर्चयति च देवं नमस्कारेण' इति व्यज्ञापयत्। आगतजामातृनिवेदनागतं च तं ज्ञात्वा कृतसत्कारं राजा 'यामिन्याः प्रथमे यामे विवाहकालात्ययकृतो यथा न भवति दोषः[2]' इति सन्दिश्य प्रतीपं प्राहिणोत्।

अथ सकलकमलवनलक्ष्मीं वधूमुख इव सञ्चार्य समवसिते वासरे, विवाहदिवसश्रियः पादपल्लव इव रज्यमाने सवितरि, वधूवरानुरागलघूकृतप्रेमलज्जितेष्विव विघटमानेषु चक्रवाकमिथुनेषु, सौभाग्यध्वज इव रक्तांशुकसुकुमारवपुषि नभसि स्फुरति संध्यारागे, कपोतकण्ठकर्बुरे वरयात्रागमनरजसीव कलुषयति दिङ्मुखानि तिमिरे, लग्नसम्पादनसज्ज इवोज्जिहाने ज्योतिर्गणे, विवाहमङ्गलकलश इवोदयशिखरिणा समुत्क्षिप्यमाणे वर्धमानधवलच्छाये ताराधिपमण्डले वधूवदनलावण्यज्योत्स्नापरिपीततमसि प्रदोषे वृथोदितमुपहसत्स्विव रजनिकरमुत्तानितमुखेषु कुमुदवनेष्वाजगाम मुहुर्मुहु-

१ 'अविधवाधवे' ब. २ 'दोषस्तथा विधीयतामिति' ब.

रुल्लासितस्फारस्फुरितारुणचामरैर्मनोरथैरिवोत्थितरागाग्रपल्लवैः पुरो धावमानैः पादातैरुत्कर्णकटकहयप्रतिहेषितदीयमानस्वागतैरिव वाजिनां वृन्दैश्चापूरितदिग्भागश्चलकर्णचामराणां चामीकरमयसर्वोपकरणानां वर्ष्मकलम्बिनां बलिनां घण्टाटाङ्कारिणां करिणां घटाभिः घटयन्निव पुनरिन्दूदयविलीनमन्धकारं नक्षत्रमालामण्डितमुखीं करिणीं निशाकर इव पौरन्दरीं दिशमारूढः प्रकटितविविधविहगविरुतैस्तालावचरचारणैः पुरःसरैर्बालो वसन्त इवोपवनैः क्रियमाणकोलाहलो गन्धतैलावसेकसुगन्धिना दीपिकाचक्रवालस्यालोकेन कुङ्कुमपटवासधूलिपटलेनेव पिञ्जरीकुर्वन्सकलं लोकमुत्फुल्लमल्लिकामुण्डमालामध्याध्यासितकुसुमशेखरेण शिरसा हसन्निव सपरिवेशक्षपाकरं कौमुदीप्रदोषमात्मरूपनिर्जितमकरकेतुकरापहृतेन कार्मुकेणेव कौसुमेन दाम्ना विरचितवैकक्ष्यकविलासः कुसुमसौरभगर्वभ्रान्तभ्रमरकुलकलप्रलापसुभगः पारिजात इव जातः श्रिया सह पुनरवतारितो मेदिनीं नववधूवदनावलोकनकुतूहलेनेव कृष्यमाणहृदयः पतन्निव मुखेन प्रत्यासन्नलग्नो ग्रहवर्मा ।

राजा तु तमुपद्वारमागतं चरणाभ्यामेव राजचक्रानुगम्यमानः ससुतः प्रत्युज्जगाम । अवतीर्णं च तं कृतनमस्कारं मन्मथमिव माधवः प्रसारितभुजो गाढमालिलिङ्ग । यथाक्रमं परिष्वक्तराज्यवर्धनहर्षं च हस्ते गृहीत्वाभ्यन्तरं निन्ये । स्वनिर्विशेषासनदानादिना चैनमुपचारेणोपचचार ।

नचिराच्च गम्भीरनामा नृपतेः प्रणयी विद्वान्द्विजन्मा ग्रहवर्माणमुवाच—'तात, त्वां प्राप्य चिरात्खलु राज्यश्रिया घटितौ तेजोमयौ सकलजगद्गीयमानबुधकर्णानन्दकारिगुणगणौ सोमसूर्यवंशाविव पुष्पभूतिमुखरवंशौ । प्रथममेव कौस्तुभमणिरिव गुणैः स्थितोऽसि हृदये देवस्य । इदानीं तु शशीव शिरसा परमेश्वरेणाऽसि वोढव्यो जातः' इति । एवं वदत्येव तस्मिन्नृपमुपसृत्य मौहूर्तिकाः 'देव, समासीदति लग्नवेला व्रजतु जामाता कौतुकगृहम्' इत्यूचुः । अथ नरेन्द्रेण 'उत्तिष्ठ गच्छ' इति गदितो ग्रहवर्मा प्रविश्यान्तःपुरं जामातृदर्शनकुतूहलिनीनां स्त्रीणां पतितानि लोचनसहस्राणि विकचनीलकुवलयवनानीव लङ्घयन्नाससाद कौतुकगृहद्वारम् । निवारितपरिजनश्च प्रविवेश ।

अथ तत्र कतिपयाप्तप्रियसखीस्वजनप्रमदाप्रायपरिवाराम्, अरुणांशुकावगुण्ठितमुखीं प्रभातसंध्यामिव स्वप्रभया निष्प्रभान्प्रदीपकान्कुर्वाणाम्, अतिसौकुमार्यशङ्कितेनेव यौवनेन नातिनिर्भरमुपगूढाम्, साध्वसनिरुध्यमानहृदयदेशदुःखमुक्तैर्निभृतायतैः श्वसितैरपयान्तं कुमारभावमिवानुशोचन्तीम्, अत्युत्कम्पिनीं पतनभियेव त्रपया निष्पन्दं धार्यमाणाम्, हस्तं तामरसप्रतिपक्षमासन्नग्रहणं शशिनमिव रोहिणीं भयवेपमानमानसामवलोकयन्तीम्,

चन्दनधवलतनुलतां ज्योत्स्नादानसञ्चितलावण्यात्कुमुदिनीगर्भादिव प्रसूताम्, कुसुमामोदनिर्हारिणीं वसन्तहृदयादिव निर्गताम्, निःश्वासपरिमलाकृष्टमधुकरकुलां मलयमारुतादिवोत्पन्नाम्, कृतकन्दर्पानुसरणां रतिमिव पुनर्जाताम्, प्रभालावण्यमदसौरभमाधुर्यैः कौस्तुभशशिमदिरापारिजातामृतप्रभवैः सर्वैरत्नगुणैरपरामिव सुरासुररुषा रत्नाकरेण कल्पितां श्रियम्, स्निग्धेन बालिकालोकेन सितसिन्धुवारकुसुममञ्जरीभिरिव मुक्तादीधितिभिः कल्पितकर्णावतंसाम्, कर्णाभरणमरकतप्रभाहरितशाद्वलेन कपोलस्थलीतलेन विनोदयन्तीमिव हारिणीं लोचनच्छायाम्, अधोमुखीं वरकौतुकालोकनाकुलं मुहुर्मुहुः कृतमुखोन्नमनप्रयत्नं सखीजनं हृदयं च निर्भर्त्सयन्तीं वधूमपश्यत्।

प्रविशन्तमेव तं हृदयचौरं वध्वा समर्पितं जग्राह कन्दर्पः। परिहासस्मेरमुखीभिश्च नारीभिः कौतुकगृहे यद्यत्कार्यते जामाता तत्तत्सर्वमतिपेशलं चकार। कृतपरिणयानुरूपवेशपरिग्रहां गृहीत्वा करे वधूं निर्जगाम। जगाम च नवसुधाधवलां निमन्त्रितागतैस्तुषारशैलोपत्यकामिव त्र्यम्बकाम्बिकाविवाहाहूतैर्भूभृद्भिः परिवृताम्, सेकसुकुमारयवाङ्कुरदन्तुरैः पञ्चास्यैः कलशैः कोमलवर्णिकाविचित्रैरमित्रमुखैश्च मङ्गल्यफलहस्ताभिरञ्जलिकारिकाभिरुद्भासितपर्यन्ताम्, उपाध्यायोपश्रीयमानेन्धनधूमायमानाग्निसन्धुक्षणाक्षणिकोपद्रष्टृद्विजाम्, उपकृशानुनिहितानुपहतहरितकुशाम्, संनिहितदृषदजिनाज्यस्रुक्समित्पूलीनिवहाम्, नूतनशूर्पार्पितश्यामलशमीपलाशमिश्रलाजहासिनीं वेदीम्। आरुरोह च तां दिवमिव सज्योत्स्नः शशी। समुत्ससर्प च वेल्लितारुणशिखापल्लवस्य शिखिनः कुसुमायुध इव रतिद्वितीयो रक्ताशोकस्य समीपम्। हुते च हुतभुजि दक्षिणावर्तप्रवृत्ताभिर्वधूवदनविलोकनकुतूहलिनीभिरिव ज्वालाभिरेव सह प्रदक्षिणं बभ्राम। पात्यमाने च लाजाञ्जलौ नखमयूखधवलिततनुरदृष्टपूर्ववधूवररूपविस्मयस्मेर इवादृश्यत विभावसुः।

अत्रान्तरे स्वच्छकपोलोदरसंक्रान्तमनलप्रतिबिम्बमिव निर्वापयन्ती स्थूलमुक्ताफलविमलबाष्पबिन्दुसन्दोहदर्शितदुर्दिना निर्वेदनविकारं रुरोद वधूः। उदश्रुविलोचनानां च बान्धववधूनामुदपादि महानाक्रन्दः। परिसमापितवैवाहिकक्रियाकलापस्तु जामाता वध्वा समं प्रणनाम श्वशुरौ। प्रविवेश च द्वारपक्षलिखितरतिप्रीतिदैवतं प्रणयिभिरिव प्रथमप्रविष्टैरलिकुलैः कृतकोलाहलम्, अलिकुलपक्षपवनप्रेङ्खोलितैः कर्णोत्पलप्रहारभयप्रकम्पितैरिव मङ्गलप्रदीपैः प्रकाशितम्, एकदेशलिखितस्तबकितरक्ताशोकतरुतलभाजाधिज्यचापेन तिर्यक्कूणितनेत्रत्रिभागेण शरमृजूकुर्वता कामदेवेनाधिष्ठितम्, एकपार्श्वन्यस्तेन काञ्चनाचामरुकेणेतरपार्श्ववर्तिन्या च दान्तशफरुकधारिण्या कनकपुत्रिकया साक्षाल्लक्ष्म्येवोद्दण्डपुण्डरीकहस्तया सनाथेन सोपधानेन स्वास्तीर्णेन

१ 'प्रदक्षिणा०' ब. २ 'काञ्चनावामनकेन' ब.

शयनेन शोभमानम्, शयनशिरोभागस्थितेन च कृतकुमुदशोभेन कुसुमायुधसाहायककायागतेन शशिनेव निद्राकलशेन राजतेन विराजमानं वासगृहम्।

तत्र च ह्रीताया नववधूकायाः पराङ्मुखप्रसुप्ताया मणिभित्तिदर्पणेषु मुखप्रतिबिम्बानि प्रथमालापाकर्णनकौतुकागतगृहदेवताननानीव मणिगवाक्षकेषु वीक्षमाणः क्षणदां निन्ये। स्थित्वा च श्वशुरकुले शीलेनामृतमिव श्वश्रूहृदये वर्षन्नभिनवाभिनवोपचारैरपुनरुक्तान्यानन्दमयानि दश दिनानि स्थित्वा दत्त्वा राजदौवारिकमिव राजकुले रणरणकं यौतकनिवेदितानीव शम्बलान्यादाय हृदयानि सर्वलोकस्य कथं कथमपि विसर्जितो नृपेण वध्वा सह स्वदेशमगमदिति।

इति श्रीबाणभट्टकृतौ हर्षचरिते चक्रवर्तिजन्मवर्णनं नाम
चतुर्थ उच्छ्‌वासः।

पञ्चम उच्छ्वासः।

नियतिर्विधाय पुंसां प्रथमं सुखमुपरि दारुणं दुःखम्।
कृत्वालोकं तरला तडिदिव वज्रं निपातयति ॥ १ ॥

पातयति महापुरुषान्सममेव बहूननादरेणैव।
परिवर्तमान एकः कालः शैलानिवानन्तः ॥ २ ॥

अथ कदाचिद्राजा राज्यवर्धनं कवचहरमाहूय हूणान्हन्तुं हरिणानिव हरिर्हरिणेशकिशोरकमपरिमितबलानुयातं चिरन्तनैरमात्यैरनुरक्तैश्च महासामन्तैः कृत्वा साभिसरमुत्तरापथं प्राहिणोत्।

प्रयान्तं च तं देवो हर्षः कतिचित्प्रयाणकानि तुरङ्गमैरनुवव्राज। प्रविष्टे च कैलासप्रभाभासिनीं ककुभं भ्रातरि वर्तमानो नवे वयसि विक्रमरसानुरोधिनि केसरिशरभशार्दूलवराहबहुलेषु तुषारशैलोपकण्ठेषूत्कण्ठमानवनदेवताकटाक्षांशुशारितशरीरकान्तिः क्रीडन्मृगयां मृगलोचनः कतिपयान्यहानि बहिरेव व्यलम्बत। चकार चाकर्णान्ताकृष्टकार्मुकनिर्गतभासुरभल्लवर्षी स्वल्पीयोभिरेव दिवसैर्निःश्वापदान्यरण्यानि। एकदा तु वासतेय्यास्तुरीये यामे प्रत्युपस्येव स्वप्ने चटुलज्वालापुञ्जपिञ्जरीकृतसकलककुभा दुर्निवारेण दवहुतभुजा दह्यमानं केसरिणमद्राक्षीत्। तस्मिन्नेव च दावदहने समुत्सृज्य शावकानुप्लुत्य चात्मानं पातयन्तीं सिंहीमपश्यत्। आसीच्चास्य चेतसि—'लोके हि लोहेभ्यः कठिनतराः खलु स्नेहमया बन्धनपाशाः, यदाकृष्टास्तिर्यञ्चोऽप्येवमाचरन्ति' इति। प्रबुद्धस्य चास्य मुहुर्मुहुर्दक्षिणेतरमक्षि पस्पन्दे। गात्रेषु चाकस्मादेव वेपथुर्विपप्रथे। निर्निमित्तमेवान्तर्बन्धनस्थानाच्चचालेव हृदयम्। अकारणादेव चाजायत गरीयसी दुःखासिका। किमिदमिति च समुत्पन्नविविधविकल्पविमथितमतिरपगतधृतिश्चिन्तावनमितवदनः स्तिमिततारकेण चक्षुषा समुद्विद्यमानस्थलकमलिनीवनामिव चकार चकोरेक्षणः क्षणं क्षौणीम्। अह्नि च तस्मिञ्शून्येनैव च चेतसा चिक्रीड मृगयाम्। आरोहति च हरितहये मध्यमह्नो भवनमागत्योभयतो मन्दमन्दं संवाह्यमानतनुतालवृन्तः क्षितितलविततामतिशिशिरमलयजरसलवलुलितवपुषमिन्दुधवलोपधानधारिणीं वेत्रपट्टिकामधिशयानः साशङ्क एव तस्थौ।

अथ दूरादेव लेखगर्भया नीलीरागमेचकरुचा चैलचीरिकया रचितमुण्डमालकम्, श्रमातपाभ्यामारोप्यमाणकायकालिमानमन्तर्गतेन शोकशिखिनाङ्गारतामिव नीयमानम्, अतित्वरागमनद्रुततरपदोद्धूयमानधूलिराजिव्याजेन राजवार्ताश्रवणकुतूहलिन्या मेदिन्येवानुगम्यमानम्, अभिमुखपवन-

१ 'हूनान्' ब. २ 'निवर्तमानो' ब. ३ 'निःश्वासप्रदानि' ब. ४ 'चीरचीरिकया' अ.

प्रेङ्खत्प्रवितततोत्तरीयपटप्रान्तवीज्यमानोभयपार्श्वमतित्वरया कृतपक्षमिवाशु परापतन्तम्, प्रेर्यमाणमिव पृष्ठतः स्वाम्यादेशेन, कृष्यमाणमिव पुरस्तादायतैः श्रमश्वाससमोक्षैः, स्विद्यल्ललाटतटघटमानप्रतिबिम्बकेन कार्यकौतुकादुपह्रियमाणलेखमिव भास्वता, संभ्रमभ्रष्टैरिवेन्द्रियैः शून्यीकृतशरीरम्, लेखार्पितप्रयोजनगौरवादिव समेऽपि वर्त्मनि शून्यहृदयतया स्खलन्तम्, कालमेघशकलमिव पतिष्यतो दुर्वार्तावज्रस्य, धूमपल्लवमिव ज्वलिष्यतः शोकज्वलनस्य, वीजमिव फलिष्यतो दुष्कृतशालेरनिमित्तभूतदीर्घाध्वगं कुरङ्गकनामानमायान्तमद्राक्षीत्।

दृष्ट्वा च पूर्वनिमित्तपरम्पराविर्भावितभीतिरभिद्यत हृदयेन। कुरङ्गकस्तु कृतप्रणामः समुपसृत्य प्रथममाननलग्नं विषादमुपनिन्ये, पश्चाल्लेखम्। तं च देवो हर्षः स्वयमेवादायावाचयत्। लेखार्थेनैव च समं गृहीत्वा हृदयेन सन्तापमवग्रहरूपोऽभ्यधात्—'कुरङ्गक, किं मान्द्यं तातस्य' इति। स चक्षुषा वाष्पजलबिन्दुभिर्मुखेन च खञ्जाक्षरैः क्षरद्भिर्युगपदाचचक्षे—'देव दाहज्वरो महान्' इति। तच्चाकर्ण्य सहसा सहस्रधेवास्य हृदयं पफाल। कृताचमनश्च जनयितुरायुष्कामोऽपरिमितमणिकनकरजतजातमात्मपरिबर्हमशेषं ब्राह्मणसादकरोत्। अभुक्त एवोच्चचाल। 'दापय वाजिनः पर्याणम्' इति च पुरःस्थितं शिरःकृपाणं बिभ्राणं बभाण युवानम्। वेपमानहृदयश्च संभ्रमप्रधावितपरिवर्धकोपनीतमारुह्य तुरङ्गमेकाक्येव प्रावर्तत।

अकाण्डप्रयाणसंज्ञाशङ्खक्षुभितं तु संभ्रमात्सज्जीभूतमुद्भूतमुखरखुररवभरितसकलभुवनविवरमागत्यागत्य सर्वाभ्यो दिग्भ्यो धावमानमश्वीयमढौकत। प्रस्थितस्य चास्य प्रदक्षिणेतरं प्रयान्तो विनाशमुपस्थितं राजसिंहस्य हरिणाः प्रकटयांबभूवुः। अशिशिररश्मिमण्डलाभिमुखश्च हृदयमवदारयन्निव दावशुष्के दारुणि दारुणं रराण वायसः। कज्जलमय इव बहुदिवसमुपचितबहलमलपटलमलिनिततनुरभिमुखमाजगाम शिखिपिच्छालाञ्छनो नग्नाटकः। दुर्निमित्तैरनभिनन्द्यमानगमनश्च नितरामशङ्कत हृदयेन पितृस्नेहाहितम्रदिम्ना च तत्तदुपेक्षमाणस्तुरङ्गमस्कन्धबद्धलक्ष्यं चक्षुरविचलं दधानो दुःसमवसितहसितसङ्कथस्तूष्णींभूतेन भूपाललोकेनानुगम्यमानो बहुयोजनसम्पिण्डितमध्वानमेकेनैवाह्ना समलङ्घयत्।

उपलब्धनरेन्द्रमान्द्यवार्ताविषण्ण इव नष्टतेजस्यधोमुखीभवति भगवति भानुमति भण्डिप्रमुखेन प्रणयिना राजपुत्रलोकेन बहुशो विज्ञाप्यमानोऽपि नाहारमकरोत्। पुरःप्रवृत्तप्रतीहारगृह्यमाणग्रामीणपरम्पराप्रकटितप्रगुणवर्त्मा च वहन्नेव निन्ये निशाम्।

अन्यस्मिन्नहनि मध्यन्दिने विगतजयशब्दम्, अस्तमिततूर्यनादम्, उपसंहृतगीतम्, उत्सारितोत्सवम्, अप्रगीतचारणम्, अप्रसारितापणपण्यम्,

१ 'उत्तरीयकर्पट' ब.

स्थानस्थानेषु पवनबलकुटिलाभिः कोटिहोमधूमलेखाभिरुल्लसन्तीभिर्यममहिषविषाणकोटिभिरिवोल्लिख्यमानम्, कृतान्तपाशवागुराभिरिवावेष्ट्यमानम्, उपरि कालमहिषालङ्कारकालायसकिङ्किणीभिरिव कटु क्वणन्तीभिर्दिवसं वायसमण्डलीभिर्भ्रमन्तीभिरावेद्यमानप्रत्यासन्नाशुभम्, क्वचित्प्रतिशायितस्निग्धबान्धवाराध्यमानाहिर्बुध्न्यम्, क्वचिद्दीपिकां[1]दह्यमानकुलपुत्रकप्रसाद्यमानमातृमण्डलम्, क्वचिन्मुण्डोपहाराहरणोद्यतद्रविडप्रार्थ्यमानामर्दकम्, क्वचिदान्ध्रोद्ध्रियमाणबाहुवप्रोपयाच्यमानचण्डिकम्, अन्यत्र शिरोविधृतविलीयमानगु[2]ग्गुलुविकलनवसेवकानुनीयमानमहाकालम्, अपरत्र निशितशस्त्रीनिकृत्तात्ममांसहोमप्रसक्तासवर्गम्, अपरत्र प्रकाशनरपतिकुमारक्रियमाणमहामांसविक्रयप्रक्रमम्, उपहतमिव श्मशानपांशुभिरमङ्गलैरिव परिगृहीतम्, यातुधानैरिव विध्वस्तम्, कलिकालेनेव कवलितम्, पापपटलैरिव सञ्छादितम्, अधर्मविक्षेपैरिव लुण्ठितम्, अनित्यताधि[3]कारैरिवाक्रान्तम्, नियतिविलासैरिवात्मीकृतम्, शून्यमिव सुप्तमिव मुषितमिव विलक्षितमिव छलितमिव मूर्छितमिव स्कन्धावारं समाससाद।

प्रविशन्नेव च विपणिवर्त्मनि कुतूहलाकुलबहलबालकपरिवृतमूर्ध्वयष्टिविष्कम्भवितते वामहस्तवर्तिनि भीषणमहिषाधिरूढप्रेतनाथसनाथे चित्रवति पटे परलोकव्यतिकरमितरकरकलितेन शरकाण्डेन कथयन्तं यमपट्टिकं ददर्श। तेनैव च गीयमानं श्लोकमश्रृणोत्—

'मातापितृसहस्राणि पुत्रदारशतानि च।
युगे युगे व्यतीतानि कस्य ते कस्य वा भवान्॥ ३॥' इति

तेन चाधिकतरमवदीर्यमाणहृदयः क्रमेण राजद्वारं प्रतिषिद्धसकललोकप्रवेशं ययौ। तुरगादवतीर्णश्चाभ्यन्तरान्निष्क्रामन्तमप्रसन्नमुखरागमुन्मुक्तमिवेन्द्रियैः सुषेणनामानं वैद्यकुमारकमद्राक्षीत्। कृतनमस्कारं चाप्राक्षीत्—'सुषेण, अस्ति तातस्य विशेषो न वा' इति। सोऽब्रवीत्—'नास्तीदानीं यदि भवेत्कुमारं दृष्ट्वा' इति। मन्दं मन्दं द्वारपालैः प्रणम्यमानश्च दीयमानसर्वस्वम्, पूज्यमानकुलदेवतम्, प्रारब्धामृतचरुपचनक्रियम्, क्रियमाणषडाहुतिहोमम्, हूयमानपृषदाज्यलवलिप्तप्रचलदूर्वापल्लवम्, पठ्यमानमहामायूरीप्रवर्त्यमानगृहशान्तिनिर्वर्त्यमानभूतरक्षाबलिविधानम्, प्रयतविप्रप्रस्तुतसंहिताजपम्, जप्यमानरुद्रैकादशीशब्दायमानशिवगृहम्, अतिशुचिशैवसम्पाद्यमानविरूपाक्षक्षीरकलशसहस्रस्नपनम्, अजिरोपविष्टैश्चानासादितस्वामिदर्शनदूयमानमानसैरभ्यन्तरनिष्पतितनिकटवर्तिपरिजननिवेद्यमानवा[4]र्तैर्वार्तीभूतस्नानभोजनशयनैरुज्झितात्मसंस्कारमलिनवेशैर्लिखितैरिव निश्चलैर्नरपतिभिर्नीयमाननक्तन्दिवं दुःखदीनवदनेन च प्रघनेषु बद्धमण्डलेनोपांशुव्याहृतैः

१ 'दीपिकादहनदह्यमान०' ब. २ 'विलीयमानबहलगलद्गुग्गुलु०' ब. ३ 'अनित्यताधिकारैः' ब. ४ '०वान्तैः' ब.

केनचिच्चिकित्सकदोषानुद्भावयता, केनचिदसाध्यव्याधिलक्षणपदानि पठता, केनचिद्दुःस्वप्नानावेदयता, केनचित्पिशाचवार्तां विवृण्वता, केनचित्कार्तान्तिकादेशान्प्रकाशयता, केनचिदुपलिङ्गानि गायता, अन्येनानित्यतां भावयता संसारं चापवदता कलिकालविलसितानि च निन्दता दैवं चोपालभमानेनापरेण धर्माय कुप्यता राजकुलदेवताश्चाधिक्षिपता, अपरेण क्लिष्टकुलपुत्रकभाग्यानि गर्हयता, बाह्यपरिजनेन कथ्यमानकष्टपार्थिवावस्थं राजकुलं विवेश।

अविरलबाष्पपयःपरिप्लुतलोचनेन पितृपरिजनेन वीक्ष्यमाणो विविधौषधिद्रव्यद्रवगन्धगर्भमुत्क्वथतां क्वाथानां सर्पिषां तैलानां च पच्यमानानां गन्धमाजिघ्रन्नवाप तृतीयं कक्ष्यान्तरम्।

तत्र चातिनिःशब्दे गृहावग्रहणीग्राहिबहुवेत्रिणि, त्रिगुणतिरस्करिणीतिरोहितसुवीथीपथे, पिहितपक्षद्वारके, परिहृतकपाटरटिते, घटितगवाक्षरक्षितमरुति, दूयमानपरिचारके, चरणताडनस्वनत्सोपानप्रकुपितप्रतीहारे, निभृतसंज्ञानिर्दिश्यमानसकलकर्मणि, नातिनिकटोपविष्टकञ्चुकिनि, कोणस्थिताह्वानचकिताचमनवाहिनि, चन्द्रशालिकालीनमूकमौलिलोके, महाधिविधुरबान्धवाङ्गनावर्गगृहीतप्रच्छन्नप्रग्रीवके, सञ्जवनपुञ्जितोद्विग्नपरिजने, प्रविष्टकतिपयप्रणयिनि, गम्भीरज्वरारम्भभीतभिषजि, दुर्मनायमानमन्त्रिणि, मन्दायमानपुरोधसि, सीदत्सुहृदि, विद्राणविपश्चिति, सन्तप्तासामन्ते, विचित्तचामरग्राहिणि, दुःखक्षामशिरोरक्षिणि, क्षीयमाणप्रसादवित्तमनोरथसम्पदि, स्वामिभक्तिपरित्यक्ताहारहीयमानबलविकलवल्लभभूभृति, क्षितितलपतितसकलरजनीजागरूकराजपुत्रकुमारके, कुलक्रमागतकुलपुत्रकनिवहोह्यमानशुचिशोकसङ्कुचितकञ्चुकिनि, निरानन्दवन्दिनि, निःश्वसन्निराशासन्नसेवके, निःसृतताम्बूलधूसराधरवारयोषिति, विलक्षवैद्योपदिश्यमानपथ्याहरणावहितपौरोगवे, अनुजीविपीयमानोच्चंपक[1]धारावारिविनोद्यमानास्यशोषरुजि, राजाभिलापभोज्यमानबहुभुजि, भेषजसामग्रीसम्पादनव्यग्रसमग्रव्यवहारिणि, मुहुर्मुहुराहूयमानतोयकर्मान्तिकानुमितघोरातुरतृषि, तुषारपरिकरितकरकशिशिरीक्रियमाणोदश्विंति[2], श्वेतार्द्रकर्पटार्पितकर्पूरपरागशीतलीकृतशलाके, नाश्यमानपङ्कलिप्यमाननवभाण्डगतगण्डूषग्रहणमस्तुनि, निम्यत्कोमलकमलिनीपलाशप्रावृतमृदुमृणालके, सनालनीलोत्पलपूलीसनाथसलिलपानभाजनभुवि, धारानिपातनिर्वाप्यमाणक्वथिताम्भसि, पटुपाटलशर्करामोदमुचि, मञ्चकाश्रितसिकतिलकर्करीविश्रान्तान्तरचक्षुषि, सरस[3]शैवलवलयितगलद्गोलयन्त्रके, गल्वर्कशालाजिरोल्लासितलाजसक्तुनिपीतमसारपारीपरिगृहीतकर्कशर्करे, शिशिरौषधरसचूर्णावकीर्णस्फटिकशुक्तिशङ्खसञ्चये, सञ्चितप्रचुरप्राचीनामलकमातुलुङ्गद्राक्षादाडिमादिफले, प्रतिग्राहितविप्रविप्रकीर्यमाणशान्त्युदकविप्रुषि, प्रेष्यापेयमाणल-

[1] 'पीयमानोच्चचपक' ब. [2] '°श्विनि' ब. [3] 'सरल' अ.

ललाटलेपोपदिग्धद्वपदि धवलगृहे स्थितम्, परलोकविजयाय नीराज्यमानमिव ज्वरज्वलनेनानवरतपरिवर्तनैस्तरङ्गिणि शयनीये शेषमिव विषोष्मणा क्षीरोदन्वति विचेष्टमानम्, मुक्ताफलवालुकाधूलिधवलितं जलधिमिव क्षयकाले शुष्यन्तम्, कालेन कैलासमिव दशाननेनोद्ध्रियमाणम्, अविरतचन्दनचर्चापराणां परिचारकाणामत्युष्णावयवस्पर्शभस्मीभूतोदरैरिव धवलैः करैः स्पृश्यमानं लोकान्तरप्रस्थितम्, स्थास्नुना स्वयशसैव चन्दनानुलेपनच्छलेनापृच्छ्यमानम्, अविच्छिन्नदीयमानकमलकुमुदेन्दीवरदलं कालकटाक्षपतनशबलमिव शरीरमुद्वहन्तम्, निबिडदुकूलपट्टनिपीडितकेशान्तकथ्यमानकष्टवेदनानुबन्धं मूर्धानं धारयन्तम्, दुर्धरवेदनोन्नमन्नीलशिराजालककरालेन च कालाङ्गुलिलिख्यमानलेखाख्यातमरणावधिदिवससंख्यानेनेव ललाटफलकेन भयमुपजनयन्तम्, आसन्नयमदर्शनोद्वेगादिव च किंचिदन्तःप्रविष्टतारकं चक्षुर्दधानम्, शुष्यद्दशनपङ्क्तिप्रसूतधूसरदीधितितरङ्गिणीं मृगतृष्णिकामिवोष्णां निश्वासपरम्परामुद्वहन्तम्, अत्युष्णनिश्वासदग्धयेव श्यामायमानया रसनया निवेद्यमानदारुणसन्निपातारम्भम्, उरःस्थलस्थापितमणिमौक्तिकहारचन्दनचन्द्रकान्तं कृतान्तदूतदर्शनयोग्यमिवात्मानं कुर्वाणम्, अङ्गभङ्गवलनोत्क्षिप्तभुजयुगलम्, पर्यस्तहस्तनखमयूखैर्धारागृहमिव तापशान्तये रचयन्तम्, नेदिष्ठसलिलमणिकुट्टिमादर्शोदरेषु निपतद्भिः प्रतिबिम्बैरपि सन्तापातिशयमिव कथयन्तम्, स्पृशन्तीं प्रणयिनीमिव विश्रामभूमिं मूर्छामपि बहु मन्यमानम्, अन्तकाह्वानाक्षरैरिव सभयभिषग्दृष्टैररिष्टैराविष्टम्, महाप्रस्थानकाले स्वसन्तापसन्तानमाप्तहृदयेषु सञ्चारयन्तम्, अरतिपरिगृहीतमीर्ष्ययेव छायया मुच्यमानम्, उद्योगमिवोपद्रवाणाम्, सर्वाश्रमोक्षमिव क्षामतायाः, हस्तीकृतं विहस्ततया, विषयीकृतं वैषम्येण, क्षेत्रीकृतं क्षयेण, गोचरीकृतं ग्लान्या, दृष्टं दुःखासिकया, आत्मीकृतमस्वास्थ्येन, विधेयीकृतं व्याधिना, क्रोडीकृतं कालेन, लक्ष्यीकृतं दक्षिणाशया, पीतमिव पीडाभिः, जग्धमिव जागरेण, निगीर्णमिव वैवर्ण्येन, ग्रासीकृतं गात्रभङ्गेन, ह्रियमाणमिव विपद्भिः, वण्ट्यमानमिव वेदनाभिः, लुण्ठ्यमानमिव दुःखैः, आदिष्टं दैवेन, निरूपितं नियत्या, घ्रातमनित्यत्वेन, अभिभूयमानमभावेन, परिकलितं परासुतया, दत्तावकाशं क्लेशस्य, निवासं वैमनस्यस्य, समीपे कालस्य, अन्तिकेऽन्त्योच्छ्वा[1]सस्य, मुखे महाप्रवासस्य[2], द्वारि दीर्घनिद्रायाः, जिह्वाग्रे जीवितेशस्य वर्तमानम्, विरलं वाचि, चलितं चेतसि, विह्वलं वपुषि, क्षीणमायुषि, प्रचुरं प्रलापे, सन्ततं श्वसिते, जितं जृम्भिकाभिः, पराधीनमाधिभिः, अनुबद्धमनुबन्धिकाभिः, पार्श्वोपविष्टयानवरतरोदनोच्छूननयनया गृहीतचामरिकयापि निश्वसितैरेव वीजयन्त्या विविधौषधिधूलिधूसरितशरीरया मुहुर्मुहुः 'आर्यपुत्र स्वपिषि' इति व्याहरन्त्या देव्या यशोमत्या शिरसि वक्षसि च स्पृश्यमानं पितरमद्राक्षीत्।

---

१ 'विश्वास०' अ. २ '०प्रयासस्य' अ.

दृष्ट्वा च प्रथमदुःखसम्पातमथ्यमानमतिराशङ्कित इव भागधेयेभ्यः समभवत् । अन्तकपुरवर्तिनमेव च पितरममन्यत । निराकृत इव चान्तःकरणेन क्षणमासीत् । अवधूतश्च धैर्येण, क्षेत्रीकृतः क्षोभेण, रिक्तीकृतो रत्या, विषयीकृतो विषादेन, पावकमयमिव हृदयमुद्वहन्, विषमविषदूषितानीव मुह्यन्तीन्द्रियाणि बिभ्राणः, तमसा रसातलमपि विशेषयन्, शून्यत्वेनाकाशमप्यतिशयानो नाविन्दत कर्तव्यम् । पस्पर्श च हृदयेन भियमुत्तमाङ्गेन च गाम् ।

अवनिपतिस्तु दूरादेव दृष्ट्वातिदयितं तनयं तदवस्थोऽपि निर्भरस्नेहावर्जितः प्रधावमानो मनसा प्रसार्य भुजौ 'एह्येहि' इत्याह्वयञ्शरीरार्धेन शयनादुदगात् । ससंभ्रममुपसृतं चैनं विनयावनम्रमुन्नमय्य बलादुरसि निवेश्य विशन्निव प्रेम्णा निशाकरमण्डलमध्यम्, मज्जन्निवामृतमये महासरसि, स्नापयन्निव[1] महति हरिचन्दनरसप्रस्रवणे, अभिषिच्यमान इव तुषाराद्रिद्रवेण, पीडयन्नङ्गैरङ्गानि, कपोलेन कपोलमवघट्टयन्, निमीलयन्पक्ष्माग्रग्रथिताजस्रास्रविस्राविणी विलोचने विस्मृतज्वरसंज्वरः सुचिरमालिलिङ्ग कथं कथमपि चिराद्विमुक्तमपसृत्य[2] कृतनमस्कारं प्रणतजननीकमुपागतमासीनं च शयनान्तिके पिबन्निव विगतनिमेषनिश्चलेन चक्षुषा व्यलोकयत् । पस्पर्श च पुनः पुनर्वेपथुमता पाणितलेन क्षयक्षामकण्ठश्च कृच्छ्रादिवावादीत्—'वत्स, कृशोऽसि' इति । भण्डिस्त्वकथयत्—'देव, तृतीयमहः कृताहारस्यास्याद्य' इति ।

तच्छ्रुत्वा बाष्पवेगगृह्यमाणाक्षरं कथं कथमप्यायतं निःश्वस्योवाच—'वत्स, जानामि त्वां पितृप्रियमतिमृदुहृदयम् । ईदृशेषु विधुरयति धीमतोऽपि धियमतिदुर्धरो बान्धवस्नेहः सर्वप्रमाथी यतो[3] नार्हस्यतिमात्रमात्मानं शुचे दातुम् । उद्दामदाहज्वरदग्धोऽपि दह्ये खल्वहमधिकतरमनेनायुष्मदाधिना । निशितमिव शस्त्रं तक्ष्णोति मां त्वदीयस्तनिमा । सुखं च राज्यं च वंशश्च प्राणाश्च परलोकश्च त्वयि मे स्थिताः । यथा मम तथा सर्वासां प्रजानाम् । त्वद्विधानां पीडाः पीडयन्ति सकलमेव भुवनतलम् । न ह्यल्पपुण्यभाजां वंशमलङ्कुर्वन्ति भवादृशाः । फलमस्यनेकजन्मान्तरोपार्जितस्याकलुषस्य कर्मणः । करतलगतमिव कथयन्ति चतुर्णामप्यर्णवानामाधिपत्यं ते लक्षणानि । त्वज्जन्मनैव कृतार्थोऽस्मि । निरभिलाषोऽस्मि जीवितव्ये । भिषगनुरोधः पाययति मामौषधम् । अपि च सर्वप्रजापुण्यैः सकलभुवनतलपरिपालनार्थमुत्पत्स्यमानानां भवादृशां जन्मग्रहणोपायः पितरौ । प्रजाभिस्तु बन्धुमन्तो राजानः, न ज्ञातिभिः । तदुत्तिष्ठ । कुरु पुनरेव सर्वाः क्रियाः । कृताहारे च त्वय्यहमपि स्वयमुपयोक्ष्ये पथ्यम्' इत्येवमभिहितस्य चास्य धक्ष्यन्निव हृदयमतितरां शोकानलः सन्दुधुक्षे । क्षणमात्रं च स्थित्वा पित्रा पुनराहारार्थमादिश्यमानो धवलगृहादवततार । चकार च चेतसि—'अकाण्डे खल्वयं समु-

१ 'स्नानिव' अ. २ 'उपसृत्य' अ. ३ 'अतो नार्हस्यात्मानम्' अ. ४ A omits this.

पस्थितो महाप्रलयो व्यभ्र इव वज्रपातः। सामान्योऽपि तावच्छोकः सोच्छ्वासं मरणम्, अनुपदिष्टौषधो महाव्याधिः, अभस्मीकरणोऽग्निप्रवेशः, अनुपरतश्चैव नरकवासः, निर्ज्योतिरङ्गारवर्षम्, अशकलीकरणं क्रकचदारणम्, अव्रणो वज्रसूचीपातः। किमुत विशेषाश्रितः। किमत्र करवाणि' इति।

राजपुरुषेणाधिष्ठितश्च गत्वा स्वधाम धूममयानिव कृताश्रुपातान्, अग्निमयानिव जनितहृदयदाहान्, विषमयानिव दत्तमूर्छावेगान्, महापातकमयानिवोत्पादितघृणान्, क्षारमयानिवानीतवेदनान्, कतिचित्कवलानगृह्णात्। आचामंश्च चामरग्राहिणमादिदेश—'विज्ञायागच्छ कथमास्ते तातः' इति। गत्वा च प्रतिनिवृत्य च 'देव तथैव' इति विज्ञापितस्तेनागृहीतताम्बूल एवोत्ताम्यता मनसास्ताभिलाषिणि सवितरि सर्वानाहूयोपह्वरे वैद्यान् किमस्मिन्नेवंविधे विधेयमधुनेति विषण्णहृदयः पप्रच्छ। ते तु व्यज्ञापयन्—'देव, धैर्यमवलम्बस्व। कतिपयैरेव वासरैः पुनः स्वां प्रकृतिमापन्नं श्रोष्यसि पितरम्' इति।

तेषां तु भिषजां मध्ये पौनर्वसवो युवाष्टादशवर्षदेशीयस्तस्मिन्नेव राजकुले कुलक्रमागतो गतः पारमष्टाङ्गस्यायुर्वेदस्य भूभुजा सुतनिर्विशेषं लालितः प्रकृत्यैवातिपटीयस्या प्रज्ञया यथावद्विज्ञाता व्याधिस्वरूपाणां रसायनो नाम वैद्यकुमारकः सास्रस्तूष्णीमधोमुखोऽभूत्। पृष्टश्च राजसूनुना—'सखे रसायन, कथय तथ्यं यद्यसाध्विव पश्यसि' इति। सोऽब्रवीत्—'देव, श्वः प्रभाते यथावस्थितमावेदयितास्मि' इति।

अत्रैव चान्तरे भवनकमलिनीपालः कोकमाश्वासयन्नपरवक्त्रमुच्चैरपठत्—

'विहग कुरु दृढं मनः स्वयं त्यज शुचमास्स्व विवेकवर्त्मनि।
सह कमलसरोजिनीश्रिया श्रयति सुमेरुशिरो विरोचनः ॥ ४ ॥'

तच्चाकर्ण्य, वाङ्गिमित्तज्ञः पितरि सुतरां जीविताशां शिथिलीचकार। गतेषु च भिषक्षु क्षतधृतिः क्षपामुखे क्षितिपालसमीपमेव पुनरारुरोह। तत्र च—'दाहो महान्। आहर हारान्हरिणि, मणिदर्पणान्मे देहे देहि वैदेहि, हिमलवैर्लिम्प ललाटं लीलावति, घनसारक्षोदधूलीर्निधेहि धवलाक्षि, निक्षिप चक्षुषि चन्द्रकान्तं कान्तिमति, कपोले कलय कुवलयं कलावति, चन्दनचर्चां रचय चारुमति, पाटय पटमारुतं पाटलिके, मन्दय दाहमिन्दुमति, अरविन्दैर्जनय जलार्द्रया मुदं मदिरावति, समुपनय मृणालानि मालति, तरलय तालवृन्तमावन्तिके, मूर्धानं धावमानं बधान बन्धुमति, कन्धरां धारय धारणिके, उरसि सशीकरं करं कुरु कुरङ्गवति, संवाहय बाहू बलाहिके, पीडय पादौ पद्मावति, गृहाण गाढमनङ्गसेने, का वेला विलासवति नैति निद्रा, कथाः कथय कुमुद्वति' इत्येवंप्रायान्पितुरालापाननवरतमाकर्णयन्दूयमानहृदयो दुःखदीर्घां जाग्रदेव निशामनैषीत्।

उषसि चावतीर्य राजद्वारदेशोपसर्पिणा परिवर्धकेनोपस्थापितेऽपि तुरङ्गे चरणाभ्यामेवाजगाम स्वमन्दिरम् । तत्र च त्वरमाणो भ्रातुरागमनार्थमुपर्युपरि क्षिप्रपातिनो दीर्घाध्वगान्प्रजविनश्चोष्ट्रपालान्प्राहिणोत् । प्रक्षालितवदनश्च परिजनोपनीतमपि प्रतिकर्म नाग्रहीत् । अग्रतः स्थितानां राजपुत्रयूनां विमनसां 'रसायनो रसायनः' इति जल्पितमव्यक्तमश्रौषीत् । पर्यपृच्छच्च तान्—'भद्राः, कथयत किं रसायनः' इति । पृष्टाश्च ते सर्वे सममेव तूष्णींबभूवुर्भूयोभूयश्चानुबध्यमाना दुःखेन कथंकथमप्याचचक्षिरे—'देव, पावकं प्रविष्टः' इति । तच्च श्रुत्वा क्षुष्ट इवान्तस्तापेन सद्यो विवर्णतामगात् । उत्पाट्यमानमिव च न शशाक शोकान्धं धारयितुं हृदयम् । आसीच्चास्य चेतसि 'कामं स्वयं न भवति न तु श्रावयत्यप्रियं वचनमरतिकरमितर इवाभिजातो जनः । कृच्छ्रे च यथानेनानुष्ठितमुज्ज्वलीकृतमधिकतरं ज्वलनप्रवेशेन कल्याणप्रकृति कार्तस्वरमिव कौलपुत्रमस्य' इति । पुनश्चाचिन्तयत्—'समुचितमेवाथवा स्नेहस्येदम् । किमस्य तातो न तातः, किं वाम्बा न जननी, वयं न भ्रातरः । अन्यस्मिन्नपि तावत्स्वामिनि दुर्लभीभवति भवन्त्यसवो ध्रियमाणा ह्रीहेतवो लोके किमुतामृतमयेऽनुजीविनां निर्व्याजबान्धवेऽवन्ध्यप्रसादे सुगृहीतनाम्नि ताते । संप्रति सांप्रतमाचरितमनेनात्मानं दहता किं वास्याकल्पमवस्थितस्य स्थेयसो यशोमयस्य दह्यते । पतितः स केवलं दहने । दग्धास्तु वयम् । धन्यः खल्वसावग्रणीः पुण्यभाजाम् । अपुण्यभाक्त्विदमेव राजकुलं कुलपुत्रेण यत्तादृशा वियुक्तम् । अपि च ममापि कः खल्वेतेषां प्राणानां कार्यातिभारः कृतशेषो वा, का वा व्यापृतता, येन नाद्यापि निष्ठुराः प्राणाः प्रतिष्ठन्ते, को वान्तरायो हृदयस्य येन सहस्रधा न दलति' इति । दुःखार्तश्च न जगाम राजसद्म । समुत्ससर्ज च सर्वकार्याणि । शयनीये निपत्य उत्तरीयवाससा सोत्तमाङ्गमात्मानमवगुण्ठ्यातिष्ठत् ।

इत्थंभूते च देवे हर्षे राजनि च तदवस्थे सर्वस्य लोकस्य कपोलेषु कीलिता इव कराः, लोचनेषु लेप्यमय्य इवाश्रुस्रुतयः, नासाग्रेषु ग्रथिता[1] इव दृष्टयः, कर्णेषूत्कीर्णा इव रुदितध्वनयः, जिह्वासु सहजानीव हाकष्टानि, लपनेषु पल्लवितानीव श्वसितानि, अधरेषु लिखितानीव परिदेवितपदानि, हृदयेषु निधानीकृतानीव दुःखान्यभवन् । उष्णाश्रुदाहभीतेव नाभजत नेत्रोदराणि निद्रा । निःश्वासवातविधुता इव व्यलीयन्त हासाः । निरवशेषदग्धेव च सन्तापेन न प्रावर्तत वाणी । कथास्वपि नाश्रूयन्त परिहासाः । क्वागमन्निति नाज्ञायन्त गीतगोष्ठ्यः । जन्मान्तरातीतानीव नास्मर्यन्त लास्यानि । स्वप्नेऽपि नागृह्यन्त प्रसाधनानि । वार्तापि नालभ्यतोपभोगानाम् । नामापि नाकीर्त्यताहारस्य । खपुष्पप्रतिमान्यासन्नापानमण्डलानि । लोकान्तरमिवानीयन्त बन्दिवाचः । युगान्तर इवावर्तन्त निर्वृतयः[2] । पुनरिवादह्यत शोकाग्निना मकरकेतुः ।

---

१ 'प्रथिताः' ब. २ 'निवृत्तयः' ब.

नार्द्रदेहतया श्रियमिव भगवतीं सद्यः समुद्रादुत्थिताम्, कुसुम्भबभ्रुणी वाससी दिवमिव तेजसी सांध्ये दधानाम्, ताम्बूलदिग्धरागान्धकाराधरप्रभापटलपाटलं पट्टांशुकमिव विधवामरणचिह्नमङ्गलग्नमुद्वहन्तीम्, रक्तकण्ठसूत्रेण कुचान्तरावलम्बिना स्फुटितहृदयविगलितरुधिरधाराशङ्कां कुर्वतीम्, तिर्यक्कुटिलकुण्डलकोटिकण्टकाकृष्टतन्तुना हारेण वलितेन सितांशुकपाशेनेव कण्ठमुत्पीडयन्तीम्, सरसकुङ्कुमाङ्गरागतया कवलितामिव दिधक्षता चितार्चिष्मता, चितानलार्चनकुसुमैरिव धवलधवलैरश्रुबिन्दुभिरंशुकोत्सङ्गमापूरयन्तीम्, गृहदेवतामन्त्रणबलिमिव वलयैर्विगलद्भिः पदे पदे विकिरन्तीम्, आप्रपदीनां कण्ठे गुणकुसुममालां यमदोलामिवारूढाम्, अन्तर्गुञ्जन्मधुकरमुखरेणामन्त्र्यमाणलोचनोत्पलामिव कर्णोत्पलेन, प्रदक्षिणीक्रियमाणामिव मणिनूपुरबन्धुभिर्बद्धमण्डलं भ्रमद्भिर्भवनहंसैः, संनिहितप्राणसमं मरणाय चित्तमिव चित्रफलकमविचलं धारयन्तीम्, अर्चाबद्धोद्धूयमानधवलपुष्पदामकाम्, पतिव्रतापताकामिव पतिप्रासयष्टिमिष्टामुपगूहमानाम्, बन्धोरिव निजचारित्रधवलस्य नृपातपत्रस्य पुरो नेत्रोदकमुत्सृजन्तीम्, पत्युः पादपतनसमुद्गमदभ्यधिकबाष्पाम्भःप्रवाहप्रतिरुद्धदृशः कथमपि प्रतिपन्नादेशान्सचिवान्सन्दिशन्तीम्, अनुनयनिवर्तितविधुरवृद्धबन्धुवर्गवर्धमानध्वनिभिर्गृहाक्रन्दैराकृष्यमाणश्रवणाम्, भर्तृभाषितनिभैः पञ्जरसिंहबृंहितैर्ह्रियमाणहृदयाम्, धात्र्या भर्तृभक्त्या च निजया प्रसाधिताम्, जरत्या मूर्च्छया च संस्तुतया धार्यमाणाम्, सख्या पीडया च व्यसनसङ्गतया समालिङ्गिताम्, परिजनेन सन्तापेन च गृहीतसर्वावयवेन परीताम्, कुलपुत्रैरुच्छ्वसितैश्च[1] महत्तरैरधिष्ठिताम्, कञ्चुकिभिर्दुःखैश्चातिवृद्धैरनुगताम्, भूपालवल्लभान्कौलेयकानपि सास्रमालोकयन्तीम्, सपत्नीनामपि पादयोः पतन्तीम्, चित्रपुत्रिका अप्यामन्त्रयमाणाम्, गृहपतत्रिणामप्यञ्जलिं पुरस्तादुपरचयन्तीम्, पशूनप्यापृच्छथमानाम्, भवनपादपानपि परिष्वजमानां मातरं ददर्श।

दूरादेव च बाष्पायमाणदृष्टिरभ्यधात्—'अम्ब, त्वमपि मां मन्दपुण्यं त्यजसि। प्रसीद। निवर्तस्व' इत्यभिदधान एव च सस्नेहमिव नूपुरमणिमरीचिमिश्चुम्ब्यमानचूडश्चरणयोर्न्यपतत्। देवी तु यशोमती तथा तिष्ठति पादनिहितशिरसि विमनसि कनीयसि प्रेयसि तनये गुरुणा गिरिणेवोद्वेगावेगेनावष्टभ्यमाना, मूर्च्छान्धतमसं रसातलमिव प्रविशन्ती, बाष्पप्रवाहेणेव चिरनिरोधसम्पिण्डितेन स्नेहसम्भारेण निर्भराविर्भूतेनाभिभूयमाना, कृतप्रयत्नापि निवारयितुं न शशाक बाष्पोत्पतनम्। उत्कटकुचोत्कम्पप्रकटितासह्यशोकाकूता च गद्गदिकागृह्यमाणगलविकला निःसामान्यमन्युतरलीक्रियमाणाधरोद्देशा पुनरुक्तस्फुरणनिबिडितनासापुटा निमील्य नयने नयनाम्भःसेकप्लवेन प्लावयन्ती विमलौ कपोलौ सञ्छाद्य करनखमयूखमालाखचिततनुना

१ 'कुलपुत्रोच्छ्वसितैश्च' ब.

तन्वन्तरनिर्गच्छदच्छास्रस्रोतसेवांशुकपटान्तेन किंचिदुत्तानितं वदनेन्दुं दूयमानमानसा स्मरन्ती प्रस्नुतस्तनी प्रसवदिवसादारभ्य सकलमङ्कशायिनः शैशवमस्य ज्ञातिगृहगतहृदया 'अम्ब, तात, न पश्यतं पापां परलोकप्रस्थितां मामेवमतिदुःखिताम्' इति मुहुर्मुहुराक्रन्दन्ती पितरौ, 'हा वत्स, विश्रान्तभागधेयया न दृष्टोऽसि' इति प्रेष्ठं ज्येष्ठं तनयमसंनिहितं क्रोशन्ती, 'अनाथा जाता' इति श्वशुरकुलवर्तिनीं दुहितरमनुशोचन्ती, 'निष्करुण, किमपराद्धं तवामुना जनेन' इति दैवमुपालभमाना, 'नास्ति मत्समा सीमन्तिनी दुःखभागिनी' इति निन्दन्ती बहुविधमात्मानम्, 'मुषितास्मि नृशंस त्वया' इत्यकाण्डे कृतान्तं गर्हमाणा मुक्तकण्ठमतिचिरं प्राकृतप्रमदेव प्रारोदीत्।

प्रशान्ते च मन्युवेगे सस्नेहमुत्थापयामास सुतम्। हस्तेन चास्य प्ररुदितस्य पक्ष्मपालीपुञ्ज्यमाननखकिरणनिवहां द्रुतामिवाधिकतरं क्षरन्तीं दृष्टिमुन्ममार्ज। स्वयमपि कठोररागपरिपीयमानेन धवलिम्ना मुच्यमानोदरे क्वथदस्रश्रयत्पर्यन्ते शुक्रशीकरतारतारकितपक्ष्मणी सूक्ष्मतराश्रुबिन्दुपरिपाटीपतनानुबन्धविधुरे लोचने पुनः पुनरापूर्यमाणे प्रमृज्य बाष्पार्द्रगण्डगृहीतां च श्रवणशिखरमारोप्य शोकलम्बामलकलतामधःस्रस्तविलोलबालिकाव्याकुलितां च समुत्सार्य तिरश्चीं चिकुरसटामश्रुप्रवाहपूरितमार्द्रं च किंचिच्च्युतमुत्क्षिप्य हस्तेन स्तनोत्तरीयं तरङ्गितमिव[1] मग्नांशुकपटान्ततनुताम्रलेखालाञ्छितलावण्यकुञ्जिका[2]वर्जितराजतराजहंसास्यसमुद्गीर्णेन पयसा प्रक्षाल्य मुखकमलं कलमूकलोकविधृते वासःशकले शुचिनि समुन्मृज्य पाणौ सुतवदनविनिहितनिभृतनयनयुगला चिरं स्थित्वा पुनः पुनरायतं निश्वस्यावादीत्—'वत्स, नासि न प्रियो निर्गुणो वा परित्यागार्हो वा। स्तन्येनैव सह त्वया पीतं मे हृदयम्। अस्मिंश्च समये प्रभूतप्रभुप्रसादान्तरिता त्वां न पश्यति दृष्टिः। अपि च पुत्रक, पुरुषान्तरविलोकनव्यसनिनी राज्योपकरणमकरुणा वा नास्मि लक्ष्मीः क्षमा वा। कुलकलत्रमस्मि चारित्रमात्रधना धर्मधवले कुले जाता। किं विस्मृतोऽसि मां समरशतशौण्डस्य पुरुषप्रकाण्डस्य केशरिण इव केशरिणीं गृहिणीम्। वीरजा वीरजाया वीरजननी च मादृशी पराक्रमक्रीता कथमन्यथा कुर्यात्। एवंविधेन पित्रा ते भरतभगीरथनाभागनिभेन नरेन्द्रवृन्दारकेण गृहीतः पाणिः। आसेवितः सेवासंभ्रान्तानन्तसामन्तसीमन्तिनीसमावर्जितजाम्बूनदघटाभिषेकः शिरसा। लब्धो मनोरथदुर्लभो महादेवीपट्टबन्धसत्कारलाभो ललाटेन। आपीतौ युष्मद्विधैः पुत्रैरमित्रकलत्रबन्दीवृन्दविधूयमानचामरमरुच्चलचीनांशुकधरौ पयोधरौ। सपत्नीनां शिरःसु निहितं नमन्निखिलकटककुटुम्बिनीकिरीटमाणिक्यमालार्चितं चरणयुगलकम्। एवं कृतार्थसर्वावयवा किमपरमपेक्षे क्षीणपुण्या। मर्तुमविधवैव

---

१ 'तरङ्गितमिव नखांशुपटलेन' ब. २ 'कुञ्जिका' ब.

वाञ्छामि। न च शक्नोमि दग्धस्य भर्तुरार्यपुत्रविरहिता रतिरिव निरर्थकान्प्रलापान्कर्तुम्। पितुश्च ते पादधूलिरिव प्रथमं गगनगमनमावेदयन्ती बहुमता भविष्यामि शूरानुरागिणीनां सुराङ्गनानाम्। प्रत्यग्रदृष्टदारुणदुःखदग्धायाश्च मे किं धक्ष्यति धूमध्वजः। मरणाच्च मे जीवितमेवास्मिन्समये साहसम्। अतिशीतलः पतिशोकानलादक्षयस्नेहेन्धनादस्मादनलः। कैलासकल्पे प्रवसति जीवेश्वरे जरत्तृणकणिकालघीयसि जीविते लोभ इति क्व घटते। अपि च जीवन्तीमपि मां नरपतिमरणावधीरणमहापातकिनीं न स्प्रक्ष्यन्ति पुत्र पुत्रराज्यसुखानि। दुःखदग्धानां च भूतिरमङ्गला चाप्रशस्ता च निरुपयोगा च भवति। वत्स, विश्वस्तानां यशसा स्थातुमिच्छामि लोके न वपुषा। तदहमेव त्वां तावत्तात प्रसादयामि न पुनर्मनोरथप्रातिकूल्येन कदर्थनीयास्मि।' इत्युक्त्वा पादयोरपतत्।

स तु ससंभ्रममपनीय चरणयुगलमवनमिततनुरुभयकरविधृतवपुषमवनितलगतशिरसमुदनमयन्मातरम्। दुर्निवारतां च शुचः समवधार्य कुलयोषिदुचितां च तामेव श्रेयसीं मन्यमानः क्रियां कृतनिश्चयां च तां ज्ञात्वा तूष्णीमधोमुखोऽभवत्।

अभिनन्दति हि स्नेहकातरापि कुलीनता देशकालानुरूपम्। देव्यपि यशोमती परिष्वज्य समाघ्राय च शिरसि निर्गत्य चरणाभ्यामेव चान्तःपुरात्पौराक्रन्दप्रतिशब्द[1]निर्भराभिरुपरुध्यमानेव दिग्भिः सरस्वतीतीरं ययौ। तत्र च स्त्रीस्वभावकातरैर्दृष्टिपातैः प्रविकसितरक्तपङ्कजपुञ्जैरिवार्चयित्वा भगवन्तं भानुमन्तमिव मूर्तिरैन्दवी चित्रभानुं प्राविशत्। इतरोऽपि मातृमरणविह्वलो बन्धुवर्गपरिवृतः पितुः पार्श्वं प्रायात्। अपश्यच्च स्वल्पावशेषप्राणवृत्तिं परिवर्त्यमानतारकं तारकराजमिवास्तमभिलषन्तं जनयितारम्। असह्यशोकोद्रेकाभिद्रुतश्च त्याजितः स्नेहेन धैर्यम्। आश्लिष्यास्य सकलदुर्मदमहीपालमौलिमालालालितौ पादपद्मावन्तस्तापान्मुखचन्द्रमिव द्रवीभवन्तं दशनज्योत्स्नाजालमिव जलतामापद्यमानं लोचनलावण्यमिव विलीयमानं मुखसुधारसमिव स्यन्दमानमच्छाच्छमश्रुस्रोतसां सन्तानं महामेघमयविलोचन इव वर्षन्नितरवद्विमुक्तारावश्चिरं रुरोद।

राजा तु तमुपरुध्यमानदृष्टिरविरतरुदितशब्दाश्रितश्रवणः प्रत्यभिज्ञाय शनैः शनैरवादीत्—'पुत्र, नार्हस्येवं भवितुम्। भवद्विधा न ह्यमहासत्त्वाः। महासत्त्वता हि प्रथममवलम्बनं लोकस्य पश्चाद्राजबीजिता। सत्त्ववतां चाग्रणीः सर्वातिशयाश्रितः क्व भवान्, क्व वैक्लव्यम्। 'कुलप्रदीपोऽसि' इति दिवसकरसदृशतेजसस्ते लघूकरणमिव। 'पुरुषसिंहोऽसि' इति शौर्यपटुप्रज्ञोपबृंहितपराक्रमस्य निन्देव। 'क्षितिरियं तव' इति लक्षणाख्यातचक्रवर्तिपदस्य पुनरुक्तमिव। 'गृह्यतां श्रीः' इति स्वयमेव श्रिया गृहीतस्य विपरीतमिव।

१ 'पौराक्रन्दनिर्भराभिः' अ.

'अध्यास्यतामयं लोकः' इत्युभयलोकविजिगीषोरपुष्कलमिव। 'स्वीक्रियतां कोषः' इति शशिकरनिकरनिर्मलयशःसञ्चयैकाभिनिवेशिनो निरुपयोगमिव। 'आत्मीक्रियतां राजकम्' इति गुणगणात्मीकृत[1]जगतो गतार्थमिव। 'उह्यतां राज्यभारः' इति भुवनत्रयभारोचितस्यानुचितनियोग इव। 'प्रजाः परिरक्ष्यन्ताम्' इति दीर्घदोर्दण्डार्गलितदिङ्मुखस्यानुवाद इव। 'परिजनः परिपाल्यताम्' इति लोकपालोपमस्यानुषङ्गिकमिव। 'शस्त्राभ्यासः कार्यः' इति धनुर्गुणकिणकलङ्ककालीकृतप्रकोष्ठस्य किमादिश्यते। 'निग्राह्यतां चापलम्' इति नूतनतरवयसि निगृहीतेन्द्रियस्य निरवकाशेव मे वाणी। 'निरवशेषतां शत्रवो नेयाः' इति सहजस्य तेजस एवेयं चिन्ता।' इत्येवं वदन्नेवापुनरुन्मीलनाय निमिमील राजसिंहो लोचने[2]।

अस्मिन्नेवान्तरे पूषाप्यायुषेव तेजसा व्ययुज्यत। ततश्च लज्जमान इव नरपतिजीवितापहरणजनितादात्मापराधादधोमुखः समभवत्। भूपालाभावशोकशिखिनेव चान्तस्ताप्यमानस्ताम्रतां प्रपेदे। मन्दं मन्दमप्रियप्रश्नार्थमिव स्थितिमनुवर्तमानो लौकिकीमवातरद्दिवः। दित्सुरिव जनेशाय जलाञ्जलिमपरजलनिधिसमीपमुपससर्प। सद्योदत्त[3]नृपजलाञ्जलिर्दुःखदहनदग्धमिव करसहस्रमालोहितमधत्त।

एवं च महानराधिपनिधननिधीयमानविपुलवैराग्य इव शान्तवपुषि विशति गिरिगुहागह्वरं गभस्तिमालिनि, समुपोह्यमानमहाजनाश्रुदुर्दिनार्द्रीकृत इव निर्वात्यातपे, रोदनताम्रसकललोकलोचनरुचेव लोहितायति जगति, उष्णायमानानेकनरनिश्वाससन्तापप्लुष्ट इव च नीलायमाने दिवसे, नृपानुगमनप्रचलितयेव लक्ष्म्या मुच्यमानासु कमलिनीषु, पतिशुचेव परिवृतच्छायायां श्यामायमानायां भुवि, कुलपुत्रेष्विव परित्यक्तकलत्रेषु कृतकरुणप्रलापेषु वनान्तानाश्रयत्सु दुःखितेषु चक्रवाकेषु, छत्रभङ्गभीतेष्विव निगूढकोशेषु कुशेशयेषु, स्फुटितदिग्वधूहृदयरुधिरप्लव इव गलिते रक्तातपे, क्रमेण च लोकान्तरमुपगतवत्यनुरागशेषे जाते तेजसामधीशे, गगनतलवितन्यमानबहलरायपाटल[4]ायां प्रेतपताकायामिव प्रवृत्तायां संध्यायाम्, शवशिबिकालङ्कारकृष्णचामरमालास्विव स्फुरन्तीषु दर्शनप्रतिकूलासु तिमिरलेखासु, असितागुरुकालकाष्ठायां केनापि चितायामिव रचितायां रजन्याम्, दन्तामलपत्त्रप्रसाधितकर्णिकासु केसरमालाकल्पितमुण्डमालिकासु अनुमर्तुमिवोद्यतासु प्रहसितमुखीषु कुमुदलक्ष्मीषु, अवतरत्त्रिदशविमानकिङ्किणीक्वणित इव श्रूयमाणे शाखिशिखरकुलायलीयमानशकुनिकुलकूजिते, नाकपथप्रस्थितपार्थिवप्रत्युद्गतपुरुहूतातपत्र इव पूर्वस्यां दिशि दृश्यमाने चन्द्रमसि, नरेन्द्रः स्वयं समर्पितस्कन्धैर्गृहीत्वा शवशिबिकां शिबिसमः सामन्तैः पौरैश्च पुरोहितपुरःसरैः सरितं

१ '०गणात्मीकृतं जगतो' ब. २ 'प्रलपयत च पूषात्मजः' इत्यधिकं ब-पुस्तके. ३ '०दत्तजला०' अ. ४ '०पटलायाम्' अ.

सरस्वतीं नीत्वा नरपतिसमुचितायां चितायां हुताशसत्क्रियया यशः-शेषतामनीयत ।

देवोऽपि हर्षः पुञ्जीभूतेन सकलेनेव जीवलोकेन लोकेन राजकुलसम्बद्धेनाशेषेण शोकमूकेन परिवृतोऽन्तर्वर्तिनापि शोकानलतप्तेन स्नेहद्रवेण बहिरिव सिच्यमानो निर्व्यवधानायां धरण्यामुपविष्ट एव तां निशीथिनीं भीमरथीभीमामखिलां सराजको जजागार । अजनि चास्य चेतसि । 'ताते दूरीभूते संप्रत्येतावान्खलु जीवलोकः, लोकस्य भग्नाः पन्थानः, मनोरथानां खिलीभूतानि भूतिस्थानानि, स्थगितान्यानन्दस्य द्वाराणि, सुप्ता सत्यवादिता, लुप्ता लोकयात्रा, विलीना बाहुशालिता, प्रलीना प्रियालापिता, प्रोषिताः पुरुषकारविहारविकाराः, समाप्ता समरशौण्डता, ध्वस्ता परगुणप्रीतिः, विश्रान्ता विश्वासभूमयः, अपदान्यपदानानि, निरुपयोगानि शास्त्राणि, निरवलम्बना विक्रमैकरसता, कथावशेषा विशेषज्ञता, ददातु जनो जलाञ्जलिमौर्जित्याय, प्रतिपद्यतां प्रव्रज्यां प्रजापालता, बध्नातु वैधव्यवेणीं वरमनुष्यता, समाश्रयतु राजश्रीराश्रमपदम्, परिधत्तां धवले वाससी वसुमती, वहतु वल्कले विलासिता, तपस्यतु तपोवनेषु तेजस्विता, प्रावृणोतु चीवरे वीरता, क्व गम्यतां पुनस्तस्य कृते कृतज्ञतया, क्व पुनः प्राप्स्यति तादृशान्महापुरुषनिर्माणपरमाणून्परमेष्ठी, शून्याः संवृत्ता दश दिशो गुणानाम्, जगज्जातमन्धकारं धर्मस्य, निष्फलमधुना जन्म शस्त्रोपजीविनाम् । तातेन विना कुतस्त्यास्तादृश्यो दिवसमसमसमररससमारब्धकलहकथाकण्टकितसुभटकपोलभित्तयो वीरगोष्ठ्यः । अपि नाम स्वप्नेऽपि दृश्येत दीर्घरक्तनयनं पुनस्तन्मुखसरोजम्, जन्मान्तरेऽपि पुनः परिष्वज्येत तल्लोहस्तम्भाभ्यधिकगरिमगर्भं भुजयुगलम् । लोकान्तरेऽपि पुत्रेत्यालपतः श्रूयेत सा सुधारसमुद्गिरन्ती मथ्यमानक्षीरसागरोद्गारगम्भीरा भारती' इति । एतानि चान्यानि च चिन्तयत एवास्य कथमपि सा क्षयमियाय यामिनी ।

ततः शुचेव मुक्तकण्ठमारटत्सु कृकवाकुकुलेषु, गृहगिरितरुशिखरेभ्यः पातयत्स्वात्मानं मन्दिरमयूरेषु परित्यक्तनिवासेषु च वनाय प्रस्थितेषु पत्ररथेषु, सद्यस्तनूभूते ताम्यति तमसि, मन्दीभूतात्मस्नेहेष्वभावमभिलषत्सु प्रदीपेषु, स्फुरदरुणकिरणवल्कलप्रावृतवपुषि प्रव्रज्यामिव प्रतिपन्ने नभसि, प्रभातसमयेन समुत्तीर्यमाणासु पार्थिवास्थिशकलकलास्विव कलविङ्ककन्धराधूसरासु तारकासु, भूभृद्धातुगर्भकुम्भधारिषु विविधसरःसरित्तीर्थाभिमुखेषु प्रस्थितेषु वनकरिकुलेषु, शावशुचिसिक्थपटलपाण्डुरे पिण्ड इवापरपयोनिधिपुलिनपरिसरे पात्यमाने शशिनि, क्रमेण नृपचितानलधूमविसरधूसरीकृततेजसीव नरपतिशोकपावकदाहकिणकलङ्ककालीकृतचेतसीव प्रोषितसमस्तान्तःपुरपुरंध्रिमुखचन्द्रवृन्दोद्वेगविद्राणवपुषीव प्रथमास्तमितरोहिणीरणरणकविमनसीव चास्तमुपगते रजनिकरे, राजतीव देवे दिवमारूढे सवितरि, परिवृत्ते

राज्य इव रजनीप्रबन्धे प्रबुद्धराजहंसमण्डलप्रबोध्यमानः पङ्कजाकर इव चचाल[1] चोपस्नानाय देवो हर्षः। ततश्च नूपुररवविराममूकमन्दमन्दिरहंसेषु, शोकाकुलकतिपयकञ्चुकिमालावशेषेषु शुद्धान्तेषु, पतितयूथप इव वनगजयूथे कक्ष्यान्तरवर्तिनि पितृपरिजने, विषादिन्युपरिरुदन्निषादिनि च स्तम्भनिषण्णे निष्पन्दमन्दे राजकुञ्जरे, मन्दुरापालकाक्रन्दकथिते चाजिरभाजि राजवाजिनि, विश्रान्तजयशब्दकलकले च शून्ये च महास्थानमण्डपे दह्यमानदृष्टिर्निर्जगाम राजकुलात्। अगाच्च सरस्वतीतीरं तस्यां स्नात्वा पित्रे ददावुदकम्। अपस्नातश्चानिष्पीडितमौलिरेव परिधायोद्गमनीयदुकूलवाससी निश्वासपरो निरातपत्रो निरुत्सारणः समुपनीतेऽपि सप्तौ चरणाभ्यामेव नासाग्रासक्तेन रक्ततामरसताम्रेण चक्षुषा हृदयावशेषस्यापि पितुर्दाहशङ्कया शोकाग्निमिव उद्गिरन्नताम्बूलस्यापि सुचिरप्रक्षालितस्य कल्पतरुकिसलयस्येव[2] स्वभावपाटलस्याधरपल्लवस्य प्रभया मांसरुधिरकवलानिव हृदयाभिघातादुद्वमन्नुष्णनिश्वासमोक्षैर्भवनमाजगाम।

राजवल्लभास्तु भृत्याः सुहृदः सचिवाश्च तस्मिन्नेवाहनि निर्गत्य प्रियं पुत्रदारमुत्सृज्योद्बाष्पैर्बन्धुभिर्वार्यमाणा अपि बहुनृपगुणगणहृतहृदयाः केचिदात्मानं भृगुषु बबन्धुः, केचित्तत्रैव तीर्थेषु तस्थुः, केचिदनशनैरास्तीर्णतृणकुशा व्यथमानमानसाः शुचमसमामर्शमयन्, केचिच्छलभा इव वैश्वानरं शोकावेगविवशा विविशुः, केचिद्दारुणदुःखदहनदह्यमानहृदया. गृहीतवाचस्तुषारशिखरिणं शरणमुपययुः, केचिद्विन्ध्योपत्यकासु वनकरिकुलकरशीकरासारसिच्यमानतनवः पल्लवशयनशयिनः सन्तापमशमयन्, केचित्संनिहितानपि विषयानुत्सृज्य सेवाविमुखाः परिच्छिन्नैः पिण्डकैरटवीभुवः शून्या जगृहुः, केचित्पवनाशना धर्मधना धमद्धमनयो मुनयो बभूवुः, केचिद्गृहीतकाषायाः कापिलं मतमधिजगिरे गिरिषु, केचिदाचोटितचूडामणिषु शिरःसु शरणीकृतधूर्जटयो जटा जघटिरे। अपरे परिपाटलप्रलम्बचीवराम्बरसंवीताः स्वाम्यनुरागमुज्ज्वलं चक्रुः। अन्ये तपोवनहरिणजिह्वाञ्चलोल्लिह्यमानमूर्तयो जरां ययुः। अपरे पुनः पाणिपल्लवप्रमृष्टैराताम्रगैर्नयनपुटैः कमण्डलुभिश्च वारि वहन्तो गृहीतव्रता मुण्डा विचेरुः।

देवमपि हर्षं तदवस्थं पितृशोकविह्वलीकृतम्, श्रियं शाप इति महीं महापातकमिति राज्यं रोग इति भोगान्भुजङ्गा इति निलयं निरय इति बन्धुं बन्धनमिति जीवितमयश इति देहं द्रोह इति कल्यतां कलङ्क इति आयुरपुण्यफलमिति आहारं विषमिति विषममृतमिति चन्दनं दहन इति कामं क्रकच इति हृदयस्फोटनमभ्युदय इति च मन्यमानम्, सर्वासु क्रियासु विमुखम्, पितृपितामहपरिग्रहागताश्चिरन्तनाः कुलपुत्राः वंशक्रमाहितगौरवाश्च प्राह्यगिरो गुरवः श्रुतिस्मृतीतिहासविशारदाश्च जरद्द्विजातयः श्रुताभि-

१ 'चचाल देवो हर्षः' अ. २ 'किसलयकोमलस्येव' ब.

जनशीलशालिनो मूर्धाभिषिक्ताश्चामात्या राजानो यथावदधिगतात्मतत्त्वाश्च संस्तुता मस्करिणः समदुःखसुखाश्च[1] समाश्रिताः सनाभयश्चित्तज्ञाश्च प्रधाना सचिवाः निष्कारणबान्धवाश्च मुनयः संसारासारत्वकथनकुशला ब्रह्मवादिनः शोकापनयननिपुणाश्च पौराणिकाः पर्यवारयन् ।

अस्वतन्त्रीकृतश्च तैर्मनसापि नालभत शोकानुप्रवणमाचरितुम् । अनुनीयमानश्च कथं कथमप्याहारादिकासु क्रियास्वाभिमुख्यमभजत । भ्रातृगतहृदयश्चाचिन्तयत्–अपि नाम तातस्य मरणं महाप्रलयसदृशमिदमुपश्रुत्य आर्यो बाष्पजलस्नातो न गृह्णीयाद्वल्कले, नाश्रयेद्वा राजर्षिराश्रमपदम्, न विशेद्वा पुरुषसिंहो गिरिगुहाम्, अस्रसलिलनिर्भरभरितनयननलिनयुगलो वा पश्येदनाथां पृथिवीम्, प्रथमव्यसनविषमविषविह्वलः स्मरेदात्मानं वा पुरुषोत्तमः, अनित्यतया जनितवैराग्यो वा न निराकुर्यादुपसर्पन्तीं राज्यलक्ष्मीम्, दारुणदुःखदहनप्रज्वलितदेहो वा प्रतिपद्येताभिषेकम्, इहागतो वा राजभिरभिधीयमानो न पराचीनतामाचरेत् । अतिपितृपक्षपाती खल्वार्यः । सर्वदा तातश्लाघया[2] मामभिधत्ते—'तात हर्ष, कस्यचिद्भूद्भविष्यति वा पुनः काञ्चनतालतरुप्रांशु कायप्रमाणमिदम्[3] । ईदृक्च दिवसकरप्रीत्या दिवसमुन्मुखविकसितं मुखमहाकमलम् । एतौ च वज्रस्तम्भभास्वरौ भुजकाण्डौ । एते च हसितमदालसहलधरविभ्रमा विलासाः । कोऽन्यो मानी विक्रान्तो वदान्यो वा' इति । एतानि चान्यानि च चिन्तयन्दर्शनोत्सुकहृदयो भ्रातुरागमनमुदीक्षमाणः कथं कथमप्यतिष्ठदिति ।

इति श्रीबाणभट्टकृतौ हर्षचरिते महाराजमरणवर्णनं
नाम पञ्चम उच्छ्वासः ।

---

१ '०सुखाश्च मुनयः' अ. २ 'तातश्लाघायाम्' ब. ३ '०प्रांशु प्रमाण०' ब.

षष्ठ उच्छ्वासः ।

उच्चित्योच्चित्य भुवि प्रहितनिगूढात्मदूतनीतानाम् ।
विजिगीषुरिव कृतान्तः शूराणां संग्रहं कुरुते ॥१॥
विस्रब्धघातदोषः स्ववधाय खलस्य वीरकोपकरः ।
नवतरुभङ्गध्वनिरिव हरिनिद्रातस्करः करिणः ॥ २ ॥

अथ प्रथमप्रेतपिण्डभुजि भुक्ते द्विजन्मनि, गतेषूद्वेजनीयेष्वशौचदिवसेषु, चक्षुर्दाहदायिनि दीयमाने द्विजेभ्यः शयनासनचामरातपत्रामत्रपत्रशस्त्रादिके नृपनिकटोपकरणकलापे, नीतेषु तीर्थस्थानानि सह जनहृदयैः कीकसेषु, कल्पितशोकशल्ये सुधानिचयचिते चिताचैत्यचिह्ने, वनाय विसर्जिते महाजिजिति राजगजेन्द्रे, क्रमेण च मन्देष्वाक्रन्देषु, विरलीभवत्सु च विलापेषु, विश्राम्यत्यश्रुणि, शिथिलीभवत्सु श्वसितेषु, अविस्पष्टेषु हाकष्टाक्षरेषु, उत्सार्यमाणासु च व्यसनशय्यासु, उपदेशश्रवणक्षमेषु श्रोत्रेषु, अनुरोधावधानयोग्येषु हृदयेषु, गणनीयेषु नृपगुणेषु, प्रदेशवृत्तितामाश्रयति शोके, कृतेषु कविरुदितकेषु, जाते च स्वप्नावशेषदर्शने हृदयावशेषावस्थाने, चित्रावशेषाकृतौ काव्यावशेषनाम्नि नरनाथे देवो हर्षः कदाचिदुत्सृष्टव्यापारः पुञ्जीभूतवृद्धबन्धुवर्गाग्रेसरेणावनतमूकमुखेन महाजनेन मौलेनाकाल आत्मानं वेष्ट्यमानमद्राक्षीत् । दृष्ट्वा चाकरोन्मनसि—'किमन्यदार्यमागतमावेदयत्ययं शोकपराभूतो लोकाकरः' इति । वेपमानहृदयश्च पप्रच्छ प्रविशन्तमधिकतरप्रचारमन्यतमं पुरुषम् 'अङ्ग, कथय किमार्यः प्राप्तः' इति । स मन्दमब्रवीत्—'देव, यथादिशसि द्वारि' इति श्रुत्वा च सोदर्यस्नेहनिहितनिरतिशयमन्युमृदूकृतमनाः कथमपि न ववाम बाष्पवारिप्रवाहोत्पीडेन सह जीवितम् ।

अनन्तरं च द्वारपालमुक्तेन प्रथमप्रविष्टेन परिजनेनेवाक्रन्देन कथ्यमानम्, दूरद्रुतागमनमुषितवाहुल्येन विच्छिन्नच्छत्रधारेण लम्बिताम्बरवाहिना भ्रष्टभृङ्गारग्राहिणा च्युताचमनधारिणा ताम्यत्ताम्बूलिकेन खञ्जत्खड्गग्राहिणा कतिपयप्रकाशदासेरकप्रायेण बहुवासरान्तरितस्नानभोजनशयनश्यामक्षामवपुषा परिजनेन परिवृतम्, अविरलमार्गधूलिधूसरितशरीरतया शरणीकृतमिवाशरणया क्रमागतया वसुन्धरया, हूणनिर्जयसमरशरव्रणबद्धपट्टकैर्दीर्घधवलैः समासन्नराज्यलक्ष्मीकटाक्षपातैरिव शबलीकृतकायम्, अवनिपतिप्राणपरित्राणार्थमिव च शोकहुतभुजि हुतमांसैरतिकृशैरवयवैरावेद्यमानदुःखभारम्, अपगतचूडामणिनि मलिनाकुलकुन्तले शेखरशून्ये शिरसि शुचमारूढां मूर्तिमतीमिव दधानम्, आतपगलितस्वेदराजिना रुदतेव पितृपादपतनोत्कण्ठितेन ललाटपट्टेन लक्ष्यमाणम्, प्रथीयसा बाष्पपयःप्रवाहेनामिमतपतिमरणमूर्च्छ-

तामिव महीमनवरतं सिञ्चन्तम्, अनन्तसन्तताश्रुप्रवाहनिपतननिम्नीकृताविव दुःखक्षामौ कपोलावुद्वहन्तम्, अत्युष्णमुखमारुतमार्गगतेन द्रवतेव गलितताम्बूलरागेणाधरबिम्बेनोपलक्षितम्, पवित्रिकामालावशेषेन्द्रनीलिकांशुश्यामायमानमचिरश्रुतपितृमरणमहाशोकाग्निदग्धमिव श्रवणप्रदेशमुद्वहन्तम्, अस्फुटाभिव्यक्तव्यञ्जनेनाप्यधोमुखस्तिमितनयननीलतारकामयूखमालाखचितेन शोकप्ररूढश्मश्रुश्यामलेनेव मुखशशिना लक्ष्यमाणम्, केशरिणमिव महाभूभृद्विनिपातविह्वलं निरवलम्बनम्, दिवसमिव तेजःपतिपतनपरिम्लानश्रियं श्यामीभूतम्, नन्दनमिव भग्नकल्पपादपं विच्छायम्, दिग्भावमिव प्रोषितदिक्कुञ्जरं शून्यम्, गिरिमिव गुरुवज्रपातदारितं कम्पमानम्, क्रीतमिव कशिम्ना, किङ्करीकृतमिव कारुण्येन, दासीकृतमिव दौर्मनस्येन, शिष्यीकृतमिव शोचितव्येन, आत्मीकृतमिवाधिना[1], मूकीकृतमिव मौनेन, पिष्टमिव पीडया, स्विन्नमिव सन्तापेन, उच्चितमिव चिन्तया, लुप्तमिव विलापेन, धृतमिव वैराग्येण, प्रत्याख्यातमिव प्रतिसंख्यानेन, अवज्ञातमिव प्रज्ञया, दूरीकृतमिव दुरभिभवत्वेन, अबोध्येन वृद्धबुद्धीनाम्, असाध्येन साधुभाषितानाम्, अगम्येन गुरुगिराम्, अशक्येन शास्त्रशक्तीनाम्, अपथेन प्रज्ञाप्रयत्नानाम्, अगोचरेण सुहृदनुरोधानाम्, अविषयेण विषयोपभोगानाम्, अभूमिभूतेन कालक्रमोपचयानां शोकेन कवलीकृतं ज्येष्ठं भ्रातरमपश्यत्। आवेगोद्गतकृत्स्नस्नेहोत्कलिकाकलापोत्क्षिप्यमाणकाय इव च परवशः समुदगात्।

अथ तं दूरादेव दृष्ट्वा देवो राज्यवर्धनश्चिरकालकलितं बाष्पवेगं मुमुक्षुः सुदूरप्रसारितेन सङ्कल्पयन्निव सर्वदुःखानि दीर्घेण दोर्दण्डद्वयेन गृहीत्वा कण्ठे मुक्तकण्ठं पुनः पतितक्षौमे क्षामे वक्षसि पुनः कण्ठे पुनः स्कन्धभागे पुनः कपोलोदरे निधाय तथा तथा रुरोद यथा सबन्धनानीवोदपाट्यन्त हृदयानि। अश्रुस्रोतःशिरा इव अमुच्यत लोचनेषु लोकेन[2]। स्मृतनृपतिना राजवल्लभेनापि प्रतिशब्दनिभेन निर्भरमिवारुद्यत। सुचिराच्च कथं कथमपि निर्वृष्टनयनजलः पर्जन्य इव शरदि स्वयमेवोपशशाम। उपविष्टश्च परिजनोपनीतेन तोयेन तत्करनखमयूखपुञ्जतया[3] महाजलप्लवजायमानफेनलेखमिव पुनः पुनः प्रमृष्टमपि पक्ष्माग्रसङ्गलद्बिन्दुवृन्दमन्दोन्मेषमुषितदर्शनं कथं कथमपि चक्षुरक्षालयत्। ताम्बूलिकोपस्थापितेन च वाससा चन्द्रातपशकलेनेवोष्णोष्णबाष्पदग्धं वदनमुन्ममार्ज। तूष्णीमेव च चिरं स्थित्वोत्थाय स्नानभूमिमगात्। तस्यां च स्थित्वा विभूषं विलस्तव्यस्तकुन्तलं मौलिमनादरान्निष्पीड्य सावशेषमन्युस्फुरितेन जिजीविषतेव जलधौतसुभगमात्मानमपि चुचुम्बिषतेवाधरेण क्षालितस्य चक्षुषः श्वेतिम्ना च शारदशशिकरविकासित-

---

१ 'अन्धीकृत०' ब. २ एतद्वाक्यं नास्ति अ-पुस्तके. ३ 'तरत्कर०' ब.

विशदकुमुदवनदलावलिबलिविक्षेपैरिव दिग्देवतार्चनकर्म कुर्वाणश्चतुःशालवितर्दिकायां[1] नीचापाश्रयविनिहितैकोपबर्हायां पर्यङ्किकायां निपत्य जोषमस्थात्।

देवोऽपि हर्षस्तथैव स्नात्वा धरणितलनिहितकुथाप्रसारितमूर्तिरदूर एवास्य तूष्णीमेव समवातिष्ठत। दृष्ट्वा दृष्ट्वा दूयमानमानसमग्रजन्मानं समस्फुटदिवास्य सहस्रधा हृदयम्। औरसदर्शनं हि यौवनं शोकस्य। लोकस्य तु नरपतिमरणदिवसादपि दारुणः स बभूव दिवसः। सर्वस्मिन्नेव नगरे न केनचिदपाचि न केनचिदस्नायि नाभोजि सर्वत्र सर्वेणारोदि। केवलमनेन क्रमेणातिचक्राम दिवसः। स च प्रत्यग्रत्वष्टृटङ्कतष्टतनुरिव वहद्बहलरुधिररसमांसच्छविरपरपारावारपयसि ममज्ज मञ्जिष्ठारुणोऽरुणसारथिः। मुकुलायमानकमलिनीकोषविकलं चकाण चञ्चरीककुलं कमलसरसि। सविधविरहव्याधिविधुरवधूवाध्यमानं बबन्ध बन्धाविव विबुद्धबन्धूकभासि भास्वति सास्रां दृशं चक्रवाकचक्रवालम्। सञ्चरन्त्याः समधुकररवं कैरवाकरं कलहंसरमणीरमणीयं माणिक्यकाञ्चीकिङ्किणीजालमिवाण[2] श्रियः। प्रकटकलङ्कमुदयमानं विशङ्कटविषाणोत्कीर्णपङ्कसङ्करशङ्करशर्कुर[3]शक्करककुदकूटसङ्काशमकाशताकाशे शशाङ्कमण्डलम्।

अस्यां च वेलायामनतिक्रमणवचनैरुपसृत्य प्रधानसामन्तैर्विज्ञाप्यमानः कथं कथमप्यभुक्त। प्रभातायां च शर्वर्यां सर्वेषु प्रविष्टेषु राजसु समीपस्थितं हर्षदेवमुवाच—'तात, भूमिरसि गुरुनियोगानाम्। शैशव एवाग्राहि गुणवत्पताकेव भवता तातस्य चित्तवृत्तिः। यतो भवन्तमेवंविधं विधेयं विधिविधानोपनतनैर्घृण्यमिदं किमपि बिभणिषति मे हृदयम्। नावलम्बनीया बालभावसुलभा प्रेमविलोपा वामता। वैधेय इव मा कृथाः प्रत्यूहमीहितेऽस्मिन्। शृणु। न खलु न जानासि लोकवृत्तम्। लोकत्रयत्रातरि मान्धातरि मृते किं कृतं पुरुकुत्सेन भ्रूलतादिष्टाष्टादशद्वीपे दिलीपे वा रघुणा महासुरसमरमध्याध्यासितत्रिदशरथे दशरथे वा रामेण गोष्पदीकृतचतुरुदन्वदन्ते दुष्यन्ते वा भरतेन। तिष्ठन्तु तावदेते तातेनैव शतसमधिकाध्वरधूमविसरधूसरितवासववयसि सुगृहीतनाम्नि तत्रभवति परासुतां गते पितरि किं नाकारि राज्यम्। यं च किल शोकः समभिभवति तं कापुरुषमाचक्षते शास्त्रविदः। स्त्रियो हि विषयः शुचाम्। तथापि किं करोमि। स्वभावस्य सेयं कापुरुषता वा स्त्रैणं वा यदेवमास्पदं[4] पितृशोकहुतभुजो जातोऽस्मि। मम हि भूभृति पर्यस्ते निरवशेषतः प्रस्रवणानीव स्रुतान्यश्रूण्यस्तमिते महति तेजस्यन्धकारीभूतदशाशस्य प्रणष्टः प्रज्ञालोकः[5] प्रज्वलितं हृदयम्, आत्मदाहभीत इव स्वप्नेऽपि नोपसर्पति विवेकः, बली-

---

१ 'वितर्दिकाविनिवेशितायामप्रतिपादिकायां चापाश्रय०' ब. २ 'जालमिवाचकाण' अ. ३ 'बर्कुरशक्कर' ब. ४ 'यदेवमसादपि' ब. ५ 'प्रज्ञानलोकः' अ.

यस्या सन्तापेन जातुषमिव विलीनमखिलं धैर्यम्, पदे पदे दिग्धरोपाहतेव हरिणी मुह्यति मतिः, पुरुषद्वेषिणीव दूरेण[१] भ्रमति परिहरन्ती स्मृतिः, अम्बेव तातेनैव सह गता धृतिः, वार्द्धुषिकप्रयुक्तानीव वित्तानि प्रतिदिवसं वर्धन्ते दुःखानि, शोकानलधूमसम्भारसम्भूताम्भोधरभरितमिव वर्षति नयनवारिधाराविसरं शरीरम्। सर्वः पञ्चजनः पञ्चत्वमुपरतः[२] प्रयाति वितथमेतद्वदति बालो लोकः। तातो हुताशनतामेव केवलामापन्नो[३] येनैवं दहति माम्। इदमसाम्परायिकमिव हृदयमवष्टभ्य व्युत्थितः शोको दुर्निवारः वाडव इव वारिराशिम्, पविरिव पर्वतम्, क्षय इव क्षपाकरम्, राहुरिव रविम्, दहति दारयति तनूकरोति कवलयति च माम्। न शक्नोति मे हृदयं तादृशस्य सुमेरुकल्पस्य कल्पमहापुरुषस्य विनिपातमश्रुभिरेव केवलैरतिवाहयितुम्। राज्ये विष इव चकोरस्य मे विरक्तं चक्षुः। बहुमृतपटावगुण्ठनां रञ्जितरङ्गां जनङ्गमानामिव वंशबाह्यामनार्यां श्रियं त्यक्तुमभिलषति मे मनः। क्षणमपि दग्धगृहे शकुलिरिव न पारयामि स्थातुम्। सोऽहमिच्छामि मनसि वाससीव सुलग्नं स्नेहमलमिदममलैः शिखरिशिखरप्रस्रवणस्वच्छस्रोतोऽम्बुभिः क्षालयितुमाश्रमपदे। यतस्त्वमन्तरितयौवनसुखामनभिमतामपि जरामिव पूरुराज्ञया गुरोर्गृहाण मे राज्यचिन्ताम्। त्यक्तसकलबालक्रीडेन हरिणेव दीयतामुरो लक्ष्म्यै। परित्यक्तं मया शस्त्रम्।' इत्येवमभिधाय खड्गग्राहिणो हस्तादादाय निजं निस्त्रिंशमुत्ससर्ज धरण्याम्।

अथ तच्छ्रुत्वा निशितशिखेन शूलेनेवाहतः प्रविदीर्णहृदयो देवो हर्षः समचिन्तयत्—किं नु खलु मामन्तरेणार्यः केनचिदसहिष्णुना किंचिद्ग्राहितः कुपितः स्यात्। उतानया दिशा परीक्षितुकामो माम्। उत शोकजन्मा चेतसः समाक्षेपोऽयमस्य। आहोस्विदार्य एवायं न भवति। किं वार्येणान्यदेवाभिहितमन्यदेवाश्रावि मया शोकशून्येन श्रवणेन्द्रियेण। आर्यस्य वान्यदेव विवक्षितमन्यदेवापतितं मुखेन। अथवा सकलवंशविनाशाय निपातनोपायोऽयं विधेः, मम वा निखिलपुण्यपरिक्षयोपक्षेपः कर्मणामननुकूलसमग्रग्रहचक्रवालविलसितं वा, अथवा तातविनाशनिःशङ्ककलिकालक्रीडितं येनायं यः कश्चिदिव यत्किंचनकारिणं मामपुष्पभूतिवंशसम्भूतमिव, अताततनयमिव, अनात्मानुजमिव, अभक्तमिव, अदृष्टदोषमपि[४] श्रोत्रियमिव सुरापाने सद्भृत्यमिव स्वामिद्रोहे सज्जनमिव नीचोपसर्पणे सुकलत्रमिव व्यभिचारे, अतिदुष्करे कर्मणि समादिष्टवान्। तदेतत्तावदनुरूपं यच्चौर्योन्मादमदिरोन्मत्तसमस्तसामन्तमण्डलसमुद्रमथनमन्दरे[५] तादृशि पितरि मृते तपोवनं वा गम्यते वल्कलानि वा गृह्यन्ते तपांसि वा सेव्यन्ते। या तु मयि राज्याज्ञा सा दग्धेऽपि दाहकारिणी मय्यवग्रहग्लपिते धन्वनीवाङ्गार-

---

१ 'दूरत एव भ्रमन्ती परिहरति' अ. २ 'उपरतः' इति नास्ति ब-पुस्तके. ३ 'आपन्नोऽपि नैवं मां दहति.' ब. ४ 'दृष्टदोषमिव' अ. ५ 'मन्दिरे' ब.

वृष्टिः। तदसदृशमिदमार्यस्य। यद्यपि च विभुरनभिमानः, द्विजातिरनेषणः, मुनिररोषणः, कपिरचपलः, कविरमत्सरः, वणिगतस्करः, प्रियजानिरकुहनः, साधुरदरिद्रः, द्रविणवानखलः, कीनाशोऽनक्षिगतः, मृगयुरहिंस्रः, पाराशरी ब्राह्मण्यः, सेवकः सुखी, कितवः कृतज्ञः[1], गोप्यः प्रियवाक्, अमात्यः सत्यवादी, राजसूनुरदुर्विनीतश्च जगति दुर्लभः, तथापि ममार्य एवाचार्यः। को हि नाम तद्विधे निपतिते राजगन्धकुञ्जरे जनयितरि ईदृशे च विफलीकृतविशालशिलास्तम्भोरुभुजे भूपजिति भ्रातरि त्यक्तराज्ये ज्यायसि नववयसि तपोवनं गच्छति सकललोकलोचनजलपातापवित्रं मृद्गोलकं वसुधाभिधानं धनमदखेलनिखिलखलमुखविकारलक्षणाख्यायमाननीचाचरणां श्रीसंज्ञिकां सुभटकुटुम्बकर्मकुम्भदासीं चण्डालोऽपि कामयेत। कथमिव सम्भावितमत्यन्तमनुचितमिदमार्येण। किमुपलक्षितमनवदातमिदं मयि। किं वास्य चेतसश्च्युतः सौमित्रिर्विस्मृता वा वृकोदरप्रभृतयः। अनपेक्षितभक्तजना स्वार्थैकनिष्पादननिष्ठुरा नासीदियमार्यस्येदृशी प्रभविष्णुता। अपि चार्ये तपोवनं गते जिजीविषुः को हि नाम महीं मनसापि ध्यायेत्। कुलिशशिखरखरनखरप्रचयप्रचण्डचपेटापाटितमत्तमातङ्गोत्तमाङ्गमदच्छटाच्छुरितचारुकेसरभारभास्वरमुखे केसरिणि वनविहाराय विनिर्गते निवासं गिरिगुहां कः पाति पृष्ठतः। प्रतापसहाया हि सत्त्ववन्तः। कश्चपलां लक्ष्मीं प्रत्यनुरोधोऽयमार्यस्य यदीयमपि न चीवरान्तरितकुचा कुशकुसुमसमित्पलाशपूलिकां वहन्ती तत्रैव तपोवने वनमृगीव नीयते जराजालिनी। किं वा ममानेन वृथा बहुधा विकल्पितेन। तूष्णीमेवार्यमनुगमिष्यामि। गुरुवचनातिक्रमकृतं च किल्बिषमेतत्तपोवने तप एवापास्यति। इत्यवधार्य मनसा प्रथमतरं गतस्तपोवनमधोमुखस्तूष्णीमवातिष्ठत।

अत्रान्तरे पूर्वादिष्टेनैव रुदता वस्त्रकर्मान्तिकेन समुपस्थापितेषु वल्कलेषु निर्दयकरतलताडनमिव क्वापि गते हृदये रटति राजस्त्रैणे तारमब्रह्मण्यमूर्ध्वदोष्णि विरुदति विप्रजने, पादप्रणतिपरे फूत्कुर्वति पौरवृन्दे, विद्राति विद्रुतचेतसि चिरन्तने परिजने, परिजनावलम्बिते[2] वेपमानवपुषि पर्याकुलवाससि शोकगद्गदवचसि गलितनयनपयसि निवारणोद्यतमनसि[3] वर्षीयसि विशति बन्धुवर्गे, निराशेषु नखलिखितमणिकुट्टिमेष्ववाङ्मुखेषु निश्वसत्सु सामन्तेषु, सबालवृद्धासु तपोवनाय प्रस्थितासु सर्वासु प्रजासु सहसैव प्रविश्य शोकविक्लवः प्रक्षरितनयनसलिलो राज्यश्रियः परिचारकः संवादको नाम प्रज्ञाततमो विमुक्ताक्रन्दः सदस्यात्मानमपातयत्।

अथ संभ्रान्तो भ्रात्रा सह स्वयं देवो राज्यवर्धनस्तं पर्यपृच्छत्—'भद्र, भण भण किमस्मद्व्यसनव्यवसायवर्धनबद्धधृतिः[4], अवनिपतिमरणमुदित-

---

१ 'कृतघ्नः, परिव्राडबुभुक्षुः, नृशंसः प्रियवाक्' अ. २ '०लम्बिते गते वर्षीयसि' ब.
३ '०मनसि विशति' ब. ४ '०व्यसनमभ्यवसाय' अ.

मतिः, अधृतिकरमपरमधिकतरमितः दुःखातिशयं समुपनयति विधिः' इति। स कथं कथमप्यकथयत्—'देव, पिशाचानामिव नीचात्मनां चरितानि छिद्रप्रहारीणि प्रायशो भवन्ति। यतो यस्मिन्नहन्यवनिपतिरुपरत इत्यभूद्वार्ता तस्मिन्नेव देवो ग्रहवर्मा दुरात्मना मालवराजेन जीवलोकमात्मनः सुकृतेन सह त्याजितः। भर्तृदारिकापि राज्यश्रीः कालायसनिगडयुगलचुम्बितचरणा चौराङ्गनेव संयता कान्यकुब्जे कारायां निक्षिप्ता। किंवदन्ती च यथा किलानायकं साधनं मत्वा जिघृक्षुः सुदुर्मतिरेतामपि भुवमाजिगमिषतीति विज्ञापिते प्रभुः प्रभवति' इति।

ततश्च तादृशमनुपेक्षणीयमसम्भावितमाकस्मिकमपरं व्यतिकरमाकर्ण्याश्रुतपूर्वत्वात्परिभवस्य, परपरिभवासहिष्णुतया च स्वभावस्य, दर्पबहुलतया च नवयौवनस्य, वीरक्षेत्रसम्भवत्वाच्च जन्मनः, कृपाभूमिभूतायाश्च स्वसुः स्नेहात्स तादृशोऽपि बद्धमूलोऽप्यत्यन्तगुरुरेकपद एवास्य ननाश शोकावेगः। विवेश च सहसा केसरीव गिरिगुहागृहं गम्भीरं हृदयं भयङ्करः कोपावेगः। केशिनिषूदनशङ्काकुलकालियकुलभङ्गुरभ्रूभङ्गतरङ्गिणी श्यामायमाना यमस्वसेव प्रथीयसि ललाटपट्टे भीषणा भ्रुकुटिरुदभिद्यत। दर्पात्परामृशन्नखकिरणसलिलनिर्झरैः समरभारसम्भावनाभिषेकमिव चकार दिङ्नागकुम्भकूटविकटस्य बाहुशिखरकोषस्य वामः पाणिपल्लवः। सञ्जलत्स्वेदसलिलपूरितोदरो निर्मूलं मालवोन्मूलनाय गृहीतकेश इव दुर्मदश्रीकचग्रहोत्कण्ठयेव च कम्पमानः पुनरपि समुत्ससर्प भीषणं कृपाणं पाणिरपरः। शस्त्रग्रहणमुदितराजलक्ष्मीक्रियमाणदिष्टवृद्धिविधुतसिन्दूरधूलिरिव कपिलः कपोलयोरदृश्यत रोपरागः। समासन्नसकलमहीपालचूडामणिचक्राक्रमणजाताहङ्कार इव च समारुरोह वाममूरुदण्डमुत्तानितश्चरणो दक्षिणः। निष्ठुराङ्गुष्ठकषणनिष्ठ्यूतधूमलेखो निर्वीरोर्वीकरणाय विमुक्तशिख इव लिलेख मणिकुट्टिममितरः पादपद्मः। दर्पस्फुटितसरसव्रणोच्छलितरुधिरच्छटावसेकैः शोकविषप्रसुप्तं प्रबोधयन्निव पराक्रममनुजमवादीत्—'आयुष्मन्, इदं राजकुलम्, अमी बान्धवाः, परिजनोऽयम्, इयं भूमिः, भूपतिभुजपरिघपालिताश्चैताः प्रजाः गतोऽहमद्यैव मालवराजकुलप्रलयाय। इदमेव तावद्वल्कलग्रहणमिदमेव तपः शोकापगमोपायश्चायमेव यदत्यन्ताविनीतारिनिग्रहः। सोऽयं कुरङ्गकैः कचग्रहः केशरिणः, भेकैः करपातः कालसर्पस्य, वत्सकैर्बन्दिग्रहो व्याघ्रस्य, अलगर्दैर्गलग्रहो गरुडस्य, दारुभिर्दाहादेशो दहनस्य, तिमिरैस्तिरस्कारो रवेः, [२]यो मौखराणां मालवैः परिभवः पुष्पभूतिवंशस्य च। अन्तरितस्तापो मे महीयसा मन्युना। तिष्ठन्तु सर्व एव राजानः करिणश्च त्वयैव सार्धम्। अयमेको भण्डिरयुतमात्रेण तुरङ्गमाणामनुयातु माम्।' इत्यभिधाय चानन्तरमेव प्रयाणपटहमादिदेश।

---

१ 'इतः समुपनयति' अ. २ 'यो मालवैः' अ.

धावितः, पूर्वागम इव पौरुषस्य, उन्माद इव मदस्य, आवेग इवावलेपस्य, तारुण्यावतार इव तेजसः, सर्वोद्योग इव दर्पस्य, युगागम इव यौवनोष्मणः, राज्याभिषेक इव रणरसस्य, नीराजनदिवस इवासहिष्णुतायाः, परां भीषणतामयासीत् ।

अवादीच्च । 'गौडाधिपाधममपहाय कस्तादृशं महापुरुषं तत्क्षण एव निर्व्याजभुजवीर्यनिर्जितसमस्तराजकं मुक्तशस्त्रं कलशयोनिमिव कृष्णवर्त्मप्रसूतिरीदृशेन सर्ववीरलोकविगर्हितेन मृत्युना शमयेदार्यम् । अनार्यं च तं मुक्त्वा भागीरथीफेनपटलपाण्डुराः केषां मनःसु सरःसु राजहंसा इव परशुरामपराक्रमस्मृतिकृतो न कुर्युरार्यशौर्यगुणाः पक्षपातम् । कथमिवात्युग्रस्यास्यार्यजीवितहरणे निदाघरवेरिव कमलाकरसलिलशोषणेऽनपेक्षितप्रीतयः प्रसृताः कराः । कां नु गतिं गमिष्यति, कां वा योनिं प्रवेक्ष्यति, कस्मिन्वा नरके निपतिष्यति । श्वपाकोऽपि क इदमाचरेत् । नामापि गृह्णतोऽस्य पापकारिणः पापमलेन लिप्यत इव मे जिह्वा । किं वाङ्गीकृत्य कार्यमार्यस्तेन क्षुद्रेणानुप्रविश्य विगतघृणेन घुणेनेव सकलभुवनाह्लादनचतुरश्चन्दनस्तम्भः क्षयमुपनीतः । नूनं नानेन मूढेन मधुरसास्वादलुब्धेन मध्विवार्यजीवितमाकर्षता भावी दृष्टः[1] कष्टशिलीमुखसम्पातोपद्रवः । निजगृहदूषणं जालमार्गप्रदीपकेन कज्जलमिवातिमलिनं केवलमयशः सञ्चितं[2] गौडाधमेन । न त्वाश्वेवास्तमुपगतवत्यपि त्रिभुवनचूडामणौ सवितरि वेधसादिष्टः[3] सत्पथशत्रोरन्धकारस्य निग्रहाय ग्रहषण्डविहारैकहरिणाधिपः शशी । विनयविधायिनि भग्नेऽपि चाङ्कुशे विद्यत एव व्यालवारणस्य विनयाय सकलमत्तमातङ्गकुम्भस्थलस्थिरशिरोभागभिदुरः खरतरः केसरिनखरः । तादृशाः कुवैकटिका इव तेजस्विरत्नविनाशकाः कस्य न वध्याः । क्वेदानीं यास्यति दुर्बुद्धिः ।' इत्येतदभिदधत एवास्य पितुरपि मित्रं सेनापतिः समग्रविग्रहप्राग्रहरो हरितालशैलावदातदेहः, परिणतप्रगुणसालप्रकाण्डप्रकाशः, प्रांशुरतिशौर्योष्मणेव परिपाकमागतो गतभूयिष्ठे वयसि वर्तमानः, बहुशरशयनसुप्तोत्थितोऽपि हसन्निव शान्तनवमतिदीर्घेणायुषा, दुरभिभवशरीरतया जरयापि भीतभीतयेव प्रकटितप्रकम्पया परामृष्टः कथमपि सारमयेषु शिरोरुहेषु, शशिकरनिकरसितसरलशिरोरुहसटालः[4] सैंहीमिव निष्कपटपराक्रमरसरचितां संक्रान्तो जीवन्नेव जातिम्, अपरस्वामिमुखदर्शनमहापातकपरिजिहीर्षयेव भ्रूयुगलेन वलिन[5]शिथिलप्रलम्बचर्मणा स्थगितदृष्टिः, धवलस्थूलगुञ्जापिच्छप्रच्छादितकपोलभागभास्वरेण वमन्निव विक्रमकालमकालेऽपि विकाशिकाशकाननविशदं शरदारम्भं भीमेन मुखेन, मृतमपि हृदयस्थितं स्वामिनमिव सितचामरेण वीजयन्नाभिलम्बेन कूर्चकलापेन, परिणामेऽपि धौतासिधाराजलपानतृषितैरिव विवृतवदनैर्बृहद्भिर्व्रणविदारैर्विषमितविशालवक्षाः, निशितशस्त्रटङ्ककोटि-

---

१ 'दृष्टः शिली'-अ. २ 'सञ्चितं नत्वाश्वेवास्त' ब. ३ 'वेधसादिसृष्टः' ब.
४ 'सटालाम्' अ. ५ 'वलित' अ.

कुट्टितबहुबृहद्व्रणाक्षरपङ्क्तिनिरन्तरतया च सकलसमरविजयपर्वगणनामिव कुर्वन्पूर्वपर्वत इव पादचारी, विविधवीररसवृत्तान्तरामणीयकेन महाभारतमपि लघयन्निव, प्रतिपक्षक्षपणातिनिर्बन्धेन परशुराममपि शिक्षयन्निव, अब्भ्रमणेनानादरश्रीसमाकर्षणविभ्रमेण मन्दरमपि मन्दयन्निव, वाहिनीनायकमर्यादानुवर्तनेनाम्भोधिमप्यभिभवन्निव, स्थैर्यकार्कश्योन्नतिभिरचलानपि ह्रेपयन्निव, सहजप्रचण्डतेजःप्रसरपरिस्फुरणेन सवितारमपि तृणीकुर्वन्निव, ईश्वरभारोद्वहनघृष्टपृष्ठतया हरवृषभमपि हसन्निव, अरणिरमर्षाग्नेः, ऐश्वर्यं शौर्यस्य, मदो मदस्य, विसर्पो दर्पस्य, हृदयं हठस्य, जीवितं जिगीषुतायाः, उच्छ्वसितमुत्साहस्य, अङ्कुशो दुर्मदानाम्, नागदमनो दुष्टभोगिनाम्, विरामो वरमनुष्यतायाः, कुलगुरुर्वीरगोष्ठीनाम्, तुला शौर्यशालिनाम्, सीमान्तदृश्वा शस्त्रग्रामस्य, निर्वोढा प्रौढवादानाम्, संस्तम्भयिता भग्नानाम्, पारगः प्रतिज्ञायाः, मर्मज्ञो महाविग्रहाणाम्, आघोषणापटहः समरार्थिनाम्, सन्निधावेव समुपविष्टः सिंहनादनामा स्वरेणैव दुन्दुभिनिर्घोषगम्भीरेण सुभटानां समररसमानयन्विज्ञापितवान्—'देव, न क्वचित्कृताश्रयया मलिनया मलिनतराः कोकिलया काका इव कापुरुषा हतलक्ष्म्या विप्रलभ्यमानमात्मानं न चेतयन्ते। श्रियो हि दोषान्धतादयः कामला विकाराः। छत्रच्छायान्तरितरवयो विस्मरन्त्यन्यं तेजस्विनं जडधियः। किं वा करोतु वराकः येनातिभीरुतया नित्यपराङ्मुखेन न तु दृष्टान्येव सर्वातिशायिशौर्यातिशयश्वयथुकपिलकपोलपुलकपल्लवितकोपानलानि कुपितानां तेजस्विनां मुखानि। नासौ तपस्वी जानात्येवं यथाभिचारा इव विप्रकृताः सद्यः सकलकुलप्रलयमुपाहरन्ति मनस्विनः। जलेऽपि ज्वलन्ति ताडितास्तेजस्विनः। सकलवीरगोष्ठीबाह्यस्य तस्यैवेदमुचितमनुत्तारनिरयनिपातनिपुणं कर्म। मनस्विनां हि प्रधनप्रधानधने धनुषि ध्रियमाणे सति च कमलाकलहंसीकेलिकुवलयकानने कृपाणे कृपणोपायाः पयोधिमथनप्रभृतयोऽपि श्रीसमुत्थानस्य किं पुनरीदृशाः। येषां च धात्रा धरित्रीं त्रातुं नियुक्ताः स्वयमसमर्था इव कुलिशकर्कशभुजपरिघप्रहरणहेतोरुद्गिरन्ति गिरयोऽपि लोहानि ते कथमिव बाहुशालिनो मनसापि विमलयशोबान्धवा ध्यायेयुरकार्यम्। सर्वग्रहाभिभवभास्वराणां हि सुभटकराणामग्रतो दिग्ग्रहणे पङ्गवः पतङ्गकराः। महामहिषशृङ्गतरङ्गभङ्गभङ्गुर[2]भीषणान्तराला लोकप्रवादमात्रेण दक्षिणाशा परमार्थतो भटभ्रुकुटिरधिवासो यमस्य। चित्रं च यदुन्मुक्तसिंहनादानां सहसासाहसरसरोमाञ्चकण्टकनिकरेण सह न निर्यान्ति सटाः शूराणां रणेषु। द्वयमेव च चतुःसागरसम्भूत[3]स्य भूतिसम्भारस्य भाजनं प्रतिपक्षदाहि दारुणं वडवामुखं वा महापुरुषहृदयं वा। तेजस्विनः सकलाननवाप्य पयोराशीन्सहजस्य कुतो निवृत्तिरूष्मणः। वृथावितविपुलफणाभारो भुजङ्गानां भर्ता

---

१ 'पर्वपूर्वपर्वत इव' ब. २ 'भङ्गुरभङ्गिभीषणा—' ब. ३ 'सम्भृतस्य' ब.

बिभर्ति यो भोगीन मृत्पिण्डमेव केवलम् । अप्रतिहतशासनाक्रान्त्युपभोगसुखरसं तु रसाया दिक्कुञ्जरकरभारभास्वरप्रकोष्ठा वीरबाहव एव जानन्ति । रविरिवोन्मुखपद्माकरगृहीतपादपल्लवः सुखेनाखण्डिततेजा दिवसान्नयति शूरः । कातरस्य तु शशिन इव हरिणहृदयस्य पाण्डुरपृष्ठस्य कुतो द्विरात्रमपि निश्चला लक्ष्मीः । अपरिमितयशःप्रकरवर्षी विकासी वीररसः । पुरःप्रवृत्तप्रतापप्रहताः पन्थानः पौरुषस्य । शब्दविद्रुतद्विषन्ति भवन्ति द्वाराणि दर्पस्य । शस्त्रालोकप्रकाशिताः शून्या दिशः शौर्यस्य । रिपुरुधिरशीकरासारेण भूरिव श्रीरप्यनुरज्यते । बहुनरपतिमुकुटमणिशिलाशाणकोणकषणेन चरणनखराजिरिव राजताप्युज्ज्वलीभवति । अनवरतशस्त्राभ्यासेन करतलानीव रिपुमुखानि श्यामीभवन्ति । विविधव्रणबद्ध[1]पट्टकशतैः शरीरमिव यशोऽपि धवलीभवति । कवचिषु रिपूरःकपाटेषु पात्यमानाः पावकशिखामिव श्रियमपि वमन्ति निष्ठुरा निस्त्रिंशप्रहाराः । यश्चाहितहतस्वजनो मनस्विजनो द्विषद्योषिदुरस्ताडनेन कथयति हृदयदुःखम् । परुषा[2]सिलतानिपातपवने[3]नोच्छ्वसिति निरुच्छ्वसितशत्रुशरीराश्रुधारापातेन रोदिति विपक्षवनिताचक्षुषा ददाति जलं स श्रेयान्नेतरः । न च स्वप्नदृष्टनष्टेष्विव क्षणिकेषु शरीरेषु निबध्नन्ति बन्धुबुद्धिं प्रबुद्धाः । स्थायिनि यशसि शरीरधीर्वीराणाम् । अनवरतप्रज्वलिततेजःप्रसरभास्वरस्वभावं च मणिप्रदीपमिव कलुषः कज्जलमलो न स्पृशत्येव तेजस्विनं शोकः । स त्वं सत्त्ववतामग्रणीः प्राग्रहरः प्राज्ञानां प्रथमः समर्थानां प्रष्ठोऽभिजातानामग्रेसरस्तेजस्विनामादिरसहिष्णूनाम् । एताश्च सततसन्निहितधूमायमानकोपाग्नयः सुलभासिधारातोयतृष्णयो विकटबाहुवनच्छायोपगूढा धीरताया निवासशिशिरभूमयः स्वायत्ताः सुभटानामुरःकवाटभित्तयः । यतः किं गौडाधिपाधमेनैकेन । तथा कुरु यथा नान्योऽपि कश्चिदाचरत्येवं भूयः । सर्वोर्वीश्रद्धाकामुकानामलीकविजिगीषूणां सञ्चारय चामराण्यन्तःपुरपुरंध्रिनिश्वसितैः । उच्छिन्धि रुधिरगन्धान्धगृध्रमण्डलाच्छादनैश्छत्रच्छायाव्यसनानि । अपाकुरु कदुष्णशोणितोदकस्वेदैः कुलक्ष्मीकुलटाकटाक्षचक्षूरागरोगान् । उपशमय निशितशरशिरावेधै[4]र्वैरकार्यशौर्यश्वयथून् । उन्मूलय लोहनिगडापीडमालामलं[5]महौषधैः पादपीठदोहददुर्ललितपादपटुमान्द्यानि । क्षपय तीक्ष्णाज्ञाक्षरक्षारपातैर्जयशब्दश्रवणकर्णकण्डूः । अपनय चरणनखमरीचिचन्दनचर्चाललाटलेपैरनमितस्तिमितमस्तकस्तम्भविकारान् । उद्धर करदानसन्देशसन्दंशैर्द्रविणदर्पोष्मायमाणदुःशीललीलाशल्यानि । भिन्धि मणिपादपीठदीधितिप्रदीपिकाभिः शुष्कसुभटाटोपभ्रुकुटिबन्धान्धकारान् । जय चरणलङ्घनलाघवगलितशिरोगौरवारोग्यैर्मिथ्याभिमानमहासन्निपातान् । म्रदय सततसेवाञ्जलिमुकुलितकरसम्पुटोष्मभिरिष्वसनगुणकिण-

१ 'बन्ध' ब. २ 'परुषानसि' ब. ३ 'निपातवनेन' अ. ४ 'वेधैर्वीरकार्य'- ब.
५ 'मालामलयमहोषधैः' ब.

कार्कश्यानि। येनैव ते गतः पिता पितामहः प्रपितामहो वा तमेव मा हासीस्त्रिभुवनस्पृहणीयं पन्थानम्। अपहाय कुपुरुषोचितां शुचं प्रतिपद्यस्व कुलक्रमागतां केसरीव कुरङ्गीं राजलक्ष्मीम्। देव, देवभूयं गते नरेन्द्रे दुष्टगौडभुजङ्गजग्धजीविते च राज्यवर्धने वृत्तेऽस्मिन्महाप्रलये धरणीधारणायाधुना त्वं शेषः। समाश्वासय अशरणाः प्रजाः क्ष्मापतीनां शिरःसु शरत्सवितेव ललाटंतपान्प्रयच्छ पादन्यासान्। अहितानामभिनवसेवादीक्षादुःखसन्तप्तश्वासधूममण्डलैर्नखम्पचैः प्रचलितचूडामणिचक्रवालबालातपैश्चायाहि कल्माषपादताम्। अपि च हते पितर्येकाकी तपस्वी मृगैः सह संवर्धितः सहजब्राह्मण्यमार्दवसुकुमारमनाः कृतनिश्चयश्चण्डचापवनाटनिटांकारनादनिर्मदीकृतदिग्गजं गुञ्जज्ज्याजालजनितजगज्ज्वरं समग्रमुद्यतमेकविंशतिकृत्वः कृत्त[1]वंशमुत्खातवान्राजन्यकं परशुरामः। किं पुनर्नैसर्गिककायकार्कश्यकुलिशायमानमानसो मानिनां मूर्धन्यो देवः। तदद्यैव कृतप्रतिज्ञो गृहाण गौडाधमजीवितध्वस्तये जीवितसङ्कलनाकुलकालाकाण्डयात्राचिह्नध्वजं धनुः। न ह्ययमरातिरक्तचन्दनचर्चाशिशिरोपचारमन्तरेण शाम्यति परिभवानलपच्यमानदेहस्य देवस्य दुःखदाहज्वरः सुदारुणः। निकारसन्तापशान्त्युपायपरिक्षये हि हिडिम्बाचुम्बनास्वादितमिव रिपुरुधिरामृतममन्दरोपायमपायि पवनात्मजेन। जामदग्न्येन च शाम्यन्मन्युशिखिशिखासंज्वरसुखायमानस्पर्शशीतलेपु क्षत्रियक्षतजह्रदेष्वस्नायि।' इत्युक्त्वा व्यरंसीत्।

देवस्तु हर्षस्तं प्रत्यवादीत्—'करणीयमेवेदमभिहितं मान्येन। इतरथा हि मे गृहीतभुवि भोगिनाथेऽपि दायाददृष्टिरीर्ष्यालोर्भुजस्य। उपरि गच्छतीच्छति निग्रहाय ग्रहगणेऽपि भ्रूलता चलितुम्। अनमत्सु शैलेष्वपि कचग्रहमभिलषति दातुं करः। तेजोदुर्विदग्धानर्ककरानपि चामराणि ग्राहयितुमीहते हृदयम्। राजशब्दरुषा मृगराजानामपि शिरांसि वाञ्छति पादः पादपीठीकर्तुम्। स्वच्छन्दलोकपालस्वेच्छागृहीतानामाक्षेपादेशाय दिशामपि स्फुरत्यधरः। किं पुनरीदृशे दुर्जाते जाते जातामर्षनिर्भरे च मनसि नास्त्येवावकाशः शोकक्रियाकरणस्य। अपि च हृदयविषमशल्ये मुसल्ये जीवति जाल्मे जगद्विगर्हिते गौडाधिपाधमचण्डाले जिहेमि शुष्काधरपुटः पोटेव प्रतिकारशून्यं शुचा सूत्कर्तुम्। अकृतरिपुबलाबलाविलोललोचनोदकदुर्दिनस्य मे कुतः करयुगलस्य जलाञ्जलिदानम्। अदृष्टगौडाधमचिताधूममण्डलस्य वा चक्षुषः स्वल्पमप्यश्रुसलिलम्। श्रूयतां मे प्रतिज्ञा। शपाम्यार्यस्यैव पादपांशुस्पर्शेन यदि परिगणितैरेव वासरैः सकलचापचापलदुर्ललितनरपतिचरणरणरणायमाननिगडां निर्गौडां न करोमि मेदिनीं ततस्तनूनपाति पीतसर्पिषि पतङ्ग इव पातकी पातयाम्यात्मानम्।' इत्युक्त्वा च महासन्धिविग्रहाधिकृतमवन्तिमन्तिकस्थमादिदेश—'लिख्यताम्। आ रविरथच-

१ 'कृतवंशं' ब.

क्रचीत्कारचकितचारणमिथुनमुक्तसानोरुदयाचलात्, आ त्रिकूटकटककुट्टाकटङ्कलिखितकाकुत्स्थलङ्कालुण्ठनव्यतिकरात्सुवेलात्, आ वारुणीमदस्खलितवरुणवरनारीनूपुररवमुखरकुहरकुक्षेरस्तगिरेः, आ गुह्यकगेहिनीपरिमलसुगन्धिगन्धपाषाणवासितगुहागृहाच्च गन्धमादनात्, सर्वेषां राज्ञां सज्जीक्रियन्तां कराः करदानाय शस्त्रग्रहणाय वा, गृह्यन्तां दिशश्चामराणि वा, नमन्तु शिरांसि धनूंषि वा, कर्णपूरीक्रियन्तामाज्ञा मौर्व्यो वा, शेखरीभवन्तु पादरजांसि शिरस्त्राणि वा, घटन्तामञ्जलयः करिघटाबन्धा वा, मुच्यन्तां भूमय इषवो वा, समालम्ब्यन्तां वेत्रयष्टयः कुन्तयष्टयो वा, सुदृष्टः क्रियतामात्मा मच्चरणनखेषु कृपाणदर्पणेषु[1] वा परागतोऽहमिति। पङ्गोरिव मे कुतो निवृत्तिस्तावद्यावन्न कृतः सर्वद्वीपान्तरसञ्चारी सकलनरपतिमुकुटमणिशिलालोकमयः पादलेपः।' इति कृतनिश्चयश्च मुक्तास्थानो विसर्जितराजलोकः स्नानारम्भाकाङ्क्षी सभामत्याक्षीत्। उत्थाय च स्वस्थवन्निःशेषमाह्निकमकार्षीत्। अगलच्च दर्पप्रसर इव श्रुतप्रतिज्ञस्य शाम्यदूष्मा दिवसस्त्रिभुवनस्य।

ततश्च निजाधिकारापहारभीत इव भगवत्यपि क्वापि गते गततेजस्यहिमतामरसवनेष्वपि निगूढशिलीमुखालापेषु त्रासादिव सङ्कुचत्सु, विहगगणेष्वपि समुपसंहृतनिजपक्षविक्षेपनिश्चलेषु भियेवाप्रकटीभवत्सु, भुवनव्यापिनीं संध्यां प्रतिज्ञामिव मानयति नतशिरसि घटिताञ्जलिवने जने सकले, स्वपदच्युतिचकितदिक्पालदीयमानाभ्रंलिहलोहप्राकारवलयास्विव[2] बहलतिमिरमालातिरोधीयमानासु दिक्षु प्रदोषास्थाने नातिचिरं तस्थौ। नमन्नृपलोकलोलांशुकपवनकम्पितशिखैर्दीपिकाचक्रवालैरपि प्रणम्यमान इव प्राहिणोल्लोकं प्रतिषिद्धपरिजनप्रवेशश्च शयनगृहं प्राविशत्। उत्तानश्च मुमोचाङ्गानि शयनतले। दीपद्वितीयं च तमभिसर इव लब्धावसरस्तरसा भ्रातृशोको जग्राह। जीवन्तमिव हृदये निर्मीलितलोचनो ददर्शाग्रजम्। उपर्युपरि भ्रातृजीवितान्वेषिण इव प्रसस्रुः श्वासाः। धवलांशुकपटान्तेनेव चाश्रुजलप्लवेन मुखमाच्छाद्य निःशब्दमतिचिरं रुरोद। चकार च चेतसि। कथं नामाकृतेस्तादृश्या युक्तः परिणामोऽयमीदृशः। पृथुशिलासङ्घातकर्कशकायबन्धात्तातादचलादिव लोहधातुः कठिनतर आसीदार्यः। कथं चास्य मे हतहृदयस्यार्यविरहे सकृदपि युक्तमुच्छ्वसितुम्। इयं सा प्रीतिर्भक्तिरनुवृत्तिर्वा। बालिशोऽपि कः सम्भावयेदार्यमरणे मज्जीवितम्। तत्तादृशमैक्यमेकपद एव क्वापि गतम्। अयत्नेनैव हतविधिना पृथक्कृतोऽस्मि। दग्धरोषान्तरितशुचा सुचिरं रुदितमपि न मुक्तकण्ठं गतघृणेन मया। सर्वथा लूतातन्तुच्छटाच्छिदुरास्तुच्छाः प्रीतयः प्राणिनाम्। लोकयात्रामात्रनिबन्धना बान्धवता यतोऽहमपि नाम पर इवार्ये स्वर्गस्थे स्वस्थ इवासे। किं च दैवहतकेन फलमासादितमीदृशि परस्परप्रीतिबन्धनिर्वृतहृदये सुखभाजि भ्रातृमिथुने विघटिते। तथा

१ 'मणिदर्पणेषु' ब. २ 'वलयकलितास्विव' ब.

चन्द्रमया इव जगदाह्लादिनो लोकान्तरीभूतस्य लग्नचिताग्नय इवार्यस्य त एव दहन्ति गुणाः। इत्येतानि चान्यानि च हृदयेन पर्यदेवत। प्रभातायां च शर्वर्यां प्रातरेव प्रतीहारमादिदेशाशेषगजसाधनाधिकृतं स्कन्दगुप्तं द्रष्टुमिच्छामीति।

अथ युगपत्प्रधावितबहुपुरुषपरम्पराहूयमानः, स्वमन्दिरादप्रतिपालितकरेणुश्चरणाभ्यामेव संभ्रान्तः, ससंभ्रमैर्दण्डिभिरुत्सार्यमाणजनपदः, पदे पदे प्रणमतः प्रतिदिशमिभभिषग्वरान्वरवारणानां विभावरीवार्ताः पृच्छन् उच्छ्रितशिखिपिच्छलाञ्छितवंशलतावनगहनगृहीतदिगायामैर्विन्ध्यवनैरिव वारणबन्धविमर्दोद्योगागतैः पुरःप्रधावद्भिरनायतमण्डलैराधोरणगणैश्च मरकतहरितघासमुष्टीश्च दर्शयद्भिर्नवग्रहगजपतींश्च प्रार्थयमानैश्च लब्धाभिमतमत्तमातङ्गमुदितमानसैश्च सुदूरमुपसृत्य नमस्यद्भिरात्मीयमातङ्गमदागमांश्च निवेदयद्भिः, डिण्डिमाधिरोहणाय च विज्ञापयद्भिः, प्रमादपतितापराधापहृतद्विरददुःखधृतदीर्घश्मश्रुभिरग्रतो गच्छद्भिः, अभिनवोपसृतैश्च कर्पटिभिर्वारणाप्तिसुखप्रत्याशया धावमानैः, गणिकाधिकारिगणैश्चिरलब्धान्तरैरुच्छ्रितकरैः, कर्मण्यकरेणुकासङ्कथनाकुलैरुल्लासितपल्लवचिह्नाभिररण्यपालपङ्क्तिभिश्च, निष्पादितनवग्रहनागनिवहनिवेदनोद्यताभिरुत्तम्भिततुङ्गतोत्रवनाभिर्महामात्रपेटकैश्च प्रकटितकरिकर्मचर्मपुटैः, अभिनवगजसाधनसञ्चरणवार्तानिवेदनविसर्जितैश्च नागवनवीथीपालदूतवृन्दैः, प्रतिक्षणप्रत्यवेक्षितकरिकवलकूटैः, कटभङ्गसंग्रहं ग्रामनगरनिगमेषु निवेदयमानैः, कटककदम्बकैः क्रियमाणकोलाहलः, स्वामिप्रसादसम्भृतेन महाधिकाराविष्कारेण स्वाभाविकेन चावष्टम्भाभोगेनोदासीनोऽप्यादिशन्निव, असंख्यकरिकर्णशङ्खसम्पत्सम्पादनाय समुद्रानाज्ञापयन्निव, शृङ्गारगैरिकपङ्काङ्गरागसंग्रहाय गिरीन्मुष्णन्निव, दिग्गजाधिकारं ककुभामैरावतमिवापहरन्हरेर्हरपदभारनमितकैलासगिरिगुरुभिः पादन्यासैर्गुरुभारग्रहणगर्वमुर्व्याः संहरन्निव, गतिवशविलोलस्य चाजानुलम्बस्य बाहुदण्डद्वयस्य विक्षेपैरालानशिलास्तम्भमालामिवोभयतो निखनन्, ईषदुत्तुङ्गलम्बेनाधरबिम्बेनामृतरसस्वादुना नवपल्लवकोमलेन कवलेनेव श्रीकरेणुकां विलोभयन्, निजनृपवंशदीर्घं नासावंशं दधानः, अतिस्निग्धमधुरधवलविशालतया पीतक्षीरोदेनेव पिबन्नीक्षणयुग्मायामेन दिशामायामम्, मेरुतटादपि विकटविपुलालिकः, सततमविच्छिन्नच्छत्रच्छायाप्ररूढिवशादिव नितान्तायतनीलकोमलच्छविसुभगेन स्वभावभङ्गुरेण कुन्तलबालवल्लरीवेल्लितविलासिना लुनन्निव लुप्तालोकानर्ककरान्बर्बरकेण, अरिपक्षपरिक्षयपरित्यक्तकार्मुककर्मापि सकलदिगन्तश्रूयमाणगुरुगुणध्वनिः, आत्मस्थसमस्तमत्तमातङ्गसाधनोऽप्यस्पृष्टो मदेन, भूतिमानपि स्नेहमयः, पार्थिवोऽपि गुणमयः, करिणामिव दानवतामुपरि स्थितः, स्वामितामिव स्पृहणीयां भृत्यतामप्यपरिभूतामुद्वहन्नेकभर्तृभक्तिनिश्चलां कुलाङ्गनामिवान-

१ 'प्रमादापतित' ब.

न्यगम्यां प्रभुप्रसादभूमिमारूढः, निष्कारणबान्धवो विदग्धानाम्, अभृतभृत्यो भजताम्, अक्रीतदासो विदुषाम्, स्कन्दगुप्तो विवेश राजकुलम्। दूरादेव चोभयकरकमलावलम्बितं स्पृशन्मौलिना महीतलं नमस्कारमकरोत्।

उपविष्टं नतिनिकटे तं तदा जगाद देवो हर्षः—'श्रुतो विस्तर एवास्यार्यव्यतिकरस्यास्मच्चिकीर्षितस्य च। अतः शीघ्रं प्रवेश्यन्तां प्रचारनिर्गतानि गजसाधनानि। न क्षाम्यत्यतिस्वल्पमप्यार्यपरिभवपीडापावकः प्रयाणविलम्बम्[1]।' इत्येवमभिहितश्च प्रणम्य व्यज्ञापयत्—'कृतमवधारयतु स्वामी समादिष्टं किंतु स्वल्पं विज्ञाप्यमस्ति भर्तृभक्तेः। तदाकर्णयतु देवः। देवेन हि पुष्पभूतिवंशसम्भूतस्याभिजनस्याभिजात्यस्य[2] सहजस्य तेजसो दिक्करिकरप्रलम्बस्य बाहुयुगलस्यासाधारणस्य च सोदरस्नेहस्य सर्वं सदृशमुपक्रान्तम्। काकोदराभिधानाः कृपणाः कृमयोऽपि न मृष्यन्ति निकारं[3] किमुत भवादृशास्तेजसां राशयः। केवलं देवराज्यवर्धनोदन्तेन कियदपि दृष्टमेव देवेन दुर्जनदौरात्म्यम्। ईदृशाः खलु लोकस्वभावाः प्रतिग्रामं प्रतिनगरं प्रतिविषयं प्रतिदेशं प्रतिद्वीपं प्रतिदिशं च भिन्ना वेशाश्चाकाराश्चाहाराश्च व्याहाराश्च व्यवहाराश्च जनपदानाम्। तदियमात्मदेशाचारोचिता स्वभावसरलहृदयजा त्यज्यतां सर्वविश्वासिता। प्रमाददोषाभिषङ्गेषु श्रुतबहुवार्त एव प्रतिदिनं देवः। यथा नागकुलजन्मनः सारिकाश्रावितमन्त्रस्य[4] आसीन्नाशो नागसेनस्य पद्मावत्याम्। शुकश्रुतरहस्यस्य च श्रीरशीर्यत श्रुतवर्मणः श्रावस्त्याम्। स्वप्नायमानस्य च मन्त्रभेदोऽभून्मृत्यवे मृत्तिकावत्यां सुवर्णचूडस्य। चूडामणिलग्नलेखप्रतिबिम्बवाचिताक्षरा च चारुचामीकरचामरग्राहिणी यमतां ययौ यवनेश्वरस्य। लोभबहुलं च बहुलनिशि निधानमुत्खनन्तमुत्खातखड्गप्रमाथिनी ममन्थ माथुरं बृहद्रथं विदूरथवरूथिनी। नागवनविहारशीलं च मायामातङ्गाङ्गान्निर्गता महासेनसैनिका वत्सपतिं न्ययंसिषुः। अतिदयितलास्यस्य च शैलूषमध्यमध्यास्य मूर्धानमसिलतया मृणालमिवालुनादग्निमित्रात्मजस्य सुमित्रस्य मित्रदेवः। प्रियतन्त्रीवाद्यस्यालाबूवीणाभ्यन्तरशुषिरनिहितनिशिततरवारयो गान्धर्वच्छात्रच्छद्मानः चिच्छिदुरश्मकेश्वरस्य शरभस्य शिरो रिपुपुरुषाः। प्रज्ञादुर्बलं च बलदर्शनव्यपदेशदर्शिताशेषसैन्यः सेनानीरनार्यो मौर्यं बृहद्रथं पिपेष पुष्यमित्रः स्वामिनम्। आश्चर्यकुतूहली च चण्डीपतिर्दण्डोपनतयवननिर्मितेन नभस्तलयायिना यन्त्रयानेनानीयत क्वापि। काकवर्णः शैशुनागिश्च नगरोपकण्ठे कण्ठे निचकृते निस्त्रिंशेन। अतिस्त्रीसङ्गरतमनङ्गपरवशं शुङ्गममात्यो वसुदेवो देवभूतिदासीदुहित्रा देवीव्यञ्जनया वीतजीवितमकारयत्। असुरविवरव्यसनिनं चापजहुरपरिमितरमणीमणिनूपुरझणझणाह्लादरम्यया मागधं गोधनगिरिसुरुङ्गया स्वविषयं मेकलाधिपमन्त्रिणः। महाकालमहे च महा-

---

१ 'प्रणयविलम्बम्' ब. २ 'सम्भूतस्याजात्यस्य' अ-क. ३ 'विकारम्' अ-क. ४ 'प्लावितमन्त्रस्य' ब.

मांसविक्रयवादवातूलं वेतालस्तालजङ्घो जघान जघन्यजं प्रद्योतस्य पौणकिं कुमारं कुमारसेनम्। रसायनरसाभिनिवेशिनश्च वैद्यव्यञ्जनाः सुबहुपुरुषान्तरप्रकाशितौषधगुणा गणपतेर्विदेहराजसुतस्य राजयक्ष्माणमजनयन्। स्त्रीविश्वासिनश्च महादेवीगृहगूढभित्तिभाग्भ्राता भद्रसेनस्याभवन्मृत्यवे कालिङ्गस्य वीरसेनः। मातृशयनीयतूलिकातलनिषण्णश्च तनयोन्यं तनयमभिषेक्तुकामस्य दध्रस्य करूषाधिपतेरभवन्मृत्यवे। उत्सारकरुचिं च रहसि ससचिवमेव दूरीचकार चकोरनाथं शूद्रकदूतश्चन्द्रकेतुं जीवितात्। मृगयासक्तस्य च मध्नतो गण्डकानुद्दण्डनड्वलनलवननिलीनाश्च चम्पाधिपचमूचरभटाश्चामुण्डीपतेराचेमुः प्राणान्पुष्करस्य। बन्दिरागपरं च परप्रयुक्ता जयशब्दमुखरमुखा मङ्क्षु मौखरिं मूर्खं क्षत्रवर्माणमुदखनन्। अरिपुरे च परकलत्रकामुकं कामिनीवेशगुप्तश्च चन्द्रगुप्तः शकपतिमशातयदिति। प्रमत्तानां प्रमदाकृताः प्रमादाः श्रुतिविषयमागता एव देवस्य। यथा मधुमोदितं मधुरकसंलिप्तैर्लाजैः सुप्रभा पुत्रराज्यार्थं महासेनं काशिराजं जघान। व्याजजनितकन्दर्पदर्पा च दर्पणेन क्षुरधारापर्यन्तेनायोध्याधिपतिं परन्तपं रत्नवती जारूथम्, विषचूर्णचुम्बितमकरन्देन च कर्णेन्दीवरेण देवकी देवरानुरक्ता देवसेनं सौह्मम्, योगपरागविसरवर्षिणा च मणिनूपुरेण वल्लभा सपत्नीरुषा वैरन्त्यं[1] रन्तिदेवम्, वेणीनिगूढेन च शस्त्रेण बिन्दुमती वृष्णिं विदूरथम्, रसदिग्धमध्येन च मेखलामणिना हंसवती सौवीरं वीरसेनम्, अदृश्यागदलिप्तवदना च विषवारुणीगण्डूषपायनेन पौरवी पौरवेश्वरं सोमकम्।' इत्युक्त्वा विरराम स्वाम्यादेशसम्पादनाय च निर्जगाम।

देवोऽपि हर्षः सकलराज्यस्थितीश्चकार। ततश्च तथा कृतप्रतिज्ञे प्रयाणं विजयाय दिशां समादिशति[2] देवे हर्षे गतायुषां प्रतिसामन्तानामुदवसितेषु बहुरूपाण्युपलिङ्गानि वितेनिरे। तथा ह्यविप्रकृष्टाः[3] कालदूतदृष्टय इवेतस्ततश्चेरुश्चटुलाः कृष्णशारश्रेणयः। प्रचलितलक्ष्मीनूपुरप्रणादप्रतिमा मधुसरघासंघातझंकारा जह्रादिरेऽजिरे[4]। विवृतविकृतवदनविवरविसृतवह्निविसरा वासरेऽपि विरसं विरेसुश्चिरमशिवार्थमशिवाः[5] शिवाः। शवपिशितप्ररूढप्रसरा[6] इव कपिपोतकपोलकपिलपक्षतयः काननकपोताः पेतुः। आमन्त्रयमाणा इव दधुरकालकुसुमानि सममुपवनतरवः। तरलकरतलप्रहारप्रहतपयोधरा रुरुदुः प्रसभं सभाशालभञ्जिकाः। ददृशुरासन्नकचग्रहभयोत्क्रान्तोत्तमाङ्गमिवात्मानं कबन्धमादर्शोदरेषु योधाः। चूडामणिषु चक्रशङ्खकमललक्ष्माणः प्रादुरभवन्पादन्यासा राजमहिषीणाम्। चेटीचामराण्यकस्मादधावन्त पाणिपल्लवात्। प्रणयकलहेऽपि दत्तपृष्ठाश्चिरमभवन्भटाः पराङ्मुखा मानिनीनाम्। करिकपोलेषु[7] व्यघटन्त मधुलिहां मधुमदिरापानगोष्ठ्यः। समाघ्राततयममहिषगन्धा

१ 'वैरन्त्या' ब. २ 'दित्सति' ब. ३ 'प्रविष्टकाल०' ब. ४ 'जहादिरे। चिरम्' ब.
५ 'विरेसुरुपशिबिरं शवार्थम्' ब. ६ 'प्ररूढप्रणयेव' अ-क. ७ '०करिणीकपोलेषु' ब.

इव ताम्यन्तः स्तम्बकरिमपि हरयो हरितं नवयवसं न चेरुः। चलवलयावलीवाचालबालिकातालिकातोद्यलालिता अपि न ननृतुर्मन्दा मन्दिरमयूराः। निशि निशि रजनिकरहरिणनिहितनयन इवोन्मुखस्तारमुपतोरणमकारणमकाणीत्कौलेयकगणः। गणयन्तीव गतायुषस्तर्जनतरलया तर्जन्या दिवसमाट वाटकेषु कोटवी। कुट्टिमेषु कुटिलहरिणखुरवेणीतरङ्गिण्यः शष्पराजयोऽजायन्त। जनितवेणीबन्धानि निरञ्जनरोचनारोर्चीषि चषकमधुनि मुखकमलप्रतिबिम्बान्यदृश्यन्त भटीनाम्। समासन्नात्मापहारचकिता इव चकम्पिरे भूमयः। वध्यालङ्काररक्तचन्दनरसच्छटा इवालक्ष्यन्त शूराणां पतिताः शरीरेषु विकसितबन्धूककुसुमशोणितशोचिषः शोणितवृष्टयः। पर्यग्नीकुर्वाणा इव विनश्वरीं श्रियमविरलस्फुरत्स्फुलिङ्गाङ्गारोद्गारदग्धतारागणा गणशः पतन्तः प्रज्वलन्तो न व्यरंसिषुरुल्कादण्डाः। प्रथममेव प्रतीहारीवापहरन्ती प्रतिभवनं चामरातपत्रव्यजनानि परुषा बभ्राम वात्येति।

इति श्रीबाणभट्टकृतौ हर्षचरिते राजप्रतिज्ञावर्णनं नाम षष्ठ उच्छ्वासः।[1]

---

१ '०कृते हर्षचरिते षष्ठ' क; 'इति श्रीमहाकविचक्रचूडामणिश्रीबाणभट्टविरचिते हर्षचरिते महाकाव्ये राजप्रतिष्ठा नाम षष्ठ उच्छ्वासः सम्पूर्णः' ब.

सप्तम उच्छ्वासः।

अङ्गनवेदी वसुधा कुल्या जलधिः स्थली च पातालम्।
वल्मीकश्च सुमेरुः कृतप्रतिज्ञस्य वीरस्य ॥ १ ॥
धृतधनुषि बाहुशालिनि शैला न नमन्ति यत्तदाश्चर्यम्।
रिपुसंज्ञकेषु गणना कैव वराकेषु काकेषु ॥ २ ॥

अथ व्यतीतेषु च केषुचिद्दिवसेषु मौहूर्तिकमण्डलेन शतशः सुगणिते सुप्रशस्तेऽहनि दत्ते चतसृणामपि दिशां विजययोग्ये दण्डयात्रालग्ने सलिलमोक्षविशारदैः शारदैरिवाम्भोधरैः कालधौतैः शातकौम्भैश्च[1] कुम्भैः स्नात्वा विरचय्य परमया भक्त्या भगवतो नीललोहितस्यार्चामुदर्चिपं हुत्वा प्रदक्षिणावर्तशिखाकलापमाशुशुक्षणिं दत्त्वा द्विजेभ्यो रत्नवन्ति राजतानि जातरूपमयानि च सहस्रशस्तिलपात्राणि कनकपत्रलतालङ्कृतशफशृङ्गशिखरा गाश्चार्बुदशः समुपविश्य विततव्याघ्रचर्मणि भद्रासने विलिप्य प्रथमविलिप्तायुधो निजयशोधवलेनाचरणतश्चन्दनेन शरीरं परिधाय राजहंसमिथुनलक्ष्मणी सदृशे दुकूले परमेश्वरचिह्नभूतां शशिकलामिव कल्पयित्वा सितकुसुममुण्डमालिकां शिरसि नीत्वा कर्णाभरणमरकतमयूखमिव कर्णगोचरतां[2] गोरोचनाच्छुरितमभिनवं दूर्वापल्लवं विन्यस्य सह शासनवलयेन गमनमङ्गलप्रतिसरं प्रकोष्ठे परिपूजितप्रहृष्टपुरोहितकरप्रकीर्यमाणशान्तिसलिलसीकरनिकराभ्युक्षितशिराः संप्रेष्य महार्हाणि वाहनानि बहलरत्नालोकलिप्तककुम्भि च भूषणानि भूभुजां संविभज्य क्लिष्टकार्पटिककुलपुत्रलोकमोचितैः प्रसाददानैश्च विमुच्य बन्धनानि नियुज्य तत्कालस्मरणस्फुरणेन कथितात्मानमिव चाष्टादशद्वीपजेतव्याधिकारे दक्षिणं भुजस्तम्भमहमहमिकया सेवकैरिव सुनिमित्तैरपि समग्रैरग्रतो भवद्भिः प्रमुदितप्रजाजन्यमानजयशब्दकोलाहलो हिरण्यगर्भ इव ब्रह्माण्डात्कृतयुगकरणाय भवनान्निर्जगाम।

नातिदूरे च नगरादुपसरस्वति निर्मिते महति तृणमये, समुत्तम्भिततुङ्गतोरणे, वेदीविनिहितपल्लवललामहेमकलशे, बद्धवनमालादाम्नि[3], धवलध्वजमालिनि, भ्रमच्छुक्लवाससि, पठद्विजन्मनि, मन्दिरे प्रस्थानमकरोत्। तत्रस्थस्य चास्य ग्रामाक्षपटलिकः सकलकरणिपरिकरः 'करोतु देवो दिवसग्रहणमद्यैवावन्ध्यशासनः शासनानाम्' इत्यभिधाय वृषाङ्कामभिनवघटितां हाटकमयीं मुद्रामुपनिन्ये। जग्राह च तां राजा। समुपस्थापिते च प्रथमत एव मृत्पिण्डे परिभ्रश्य करकमलादधोमुखी महीतले पपात मुद्रा। मन्दाश्यानपङ्कपटले मृदुमृदि सरस्वतीतीरे स्फुटं व्यराजन्त राजयो वर्णानाम्।

---

१ 'शातकुम्भैश्च' क. २ 'कर्णपूरगोचरताम्' ब. ३ 'धाम्नि' ब.

अमङ्गलाशङ्किनि च विषीदति परिजने नरपतिरकरोन्मनस्येतत्—'अतत्त्व[1]-दर्शिन्यो हि भवन्त्यविदग्धानां धियः। तथाहि एकशासनमुद्राङ्का भूर्भवतो भविष्यतीति निवेदितमपि निमित्तेनान्यथा गृह्णन्ति ग्राम्याः।' इत्यभिनन्द्य मनसा महानिमित्तं तत्सीरसहस्रसंमितसीम्नां ग्रामाणां शतमदाद्द्विजेभ्यः। निनाय च तत्र तं दिवसम्। प्रतिपन्नायां शर्वर्यां संमानितसर्वराजलोकः सुष्वाप।

अथ गलति तृतीये यामे सुप्तसमस्तसत्त्वनिःशब्दे दिक्कुञ्जरजृम्भमाणगम्भीरध्वनिरताड्यत प्रयाणपटहः। अग्रतः स्थित्वा च मुहूर्तमिव पुनः प्रयाणक्रोशसंख्यापकाः स्पष्टमष्टावदीयन्त प्रहाराः पटहे पटीयांसः।

ततो रटत्पटहे, नन्दन्नान्दीके, गुञ्जत्कुञ्जे, कूजत्काहले, शब्दायमानशङ्खे, क्रमोपचीयमानकटककलकले, परिजनोत्थापनव्यापृतव्यवहारिणि, द्रुतद्रुघनघातघट्यमानकोणिकाकीलकोलाहलकलितककुभि, बलाधिकृतबध्यमानपाटीपतिपेटके, जनज्वलितोल्कासहस्रालोकलुप्यमानत्रियामातमसि, यामचेटीचरणचलनोत्थाप्यमानकामिमिथुने, कटुक[2]टुकनिर्देशनश्यन्निद्रोन्मिषन्निषादिनि, प्रबुद्धहास्तिकशून्यीक्रियमाणशय्यागृहे, सुप्तोत्थिताश्वीयविधूयमानसटे, रटत्कटकमुखरखनित्रखन्यमानक्षोणीपाशे, समुत्कील्यमानकीलशिञ्जानहिञ्जीरे, उप[3]नीयमाननिगडतालककलरवोत्तालतुरङ्गतरङ्ग्यमाणखुरपुटे, लेशिकमुच्यमानमदस्यन्दिदन्तिसन्दानशृङ्खलाखनखननिनादनिर्भरभरितदशदिशि, घासपूलक[4]प्रहारप्रमृष्टपांसुलकरिपृष्ठप्रसार्यमाणप्रस्फोटित[5]प्रमृष्टचर्मणि, गृहचिन्तकचेटकसंवेष्ट्यमानपटकुटीकाण्डपटमण्डपपरिवस्त्रावितानके, कीलककलापापूर्यमाणचिपिटचर्मपुटे, सम्भाण्डायमानभाण्डागारिणि, भाण्डागारवहनवाह्यमानबहुनालीवाहिके, निषादिनिश्चलानेकानीक[6]पारोप्यमाणकोशकलशपीडापीडसङ्कटायमानसामन्तौकसि, दूरगतदक्षदासेरकक्षिप्रप्रक्षिप्यमाणोपकरणसम्भारध्रियमाणदुष्टदन्तिनि, तिर्यगानमज्जा[7]घनिककरकृच्छ्राकृष्टलम्बमानपरतन्त्रतुन्दिलचुन्दीजनजनितजनहासे, पीड्यमानशारशारिवरत्रागुणग्राहितगात्रविहारबृंहद्बहुबृहदुन्मदकरिणि, करिघटाघटमानघण्टाटांकारक्रियमाणकर्णज्वरे, पृष्ठप्रतिष्ठाप्यमानकण्ठालककदर्थितकूजत्करभे, अभिजातराजपुत्रप्रेष्यमाणकुप्रयुक्ताकुलकुलीनकुलपुत्रकलत्रवाहने, गमनवेलाविप्रलब्धवारणाधोरणान्विष्यमाणनवसेवके, प्रसादवित्तपत्तिनीयमाननरपतिवल्लभवारवाजिनि, चारुचारभटसैन्यन्यस्यमाननासीरमण्डलाडम्बरस्थूलस्थासके, स्थानपालपर्याणलम्बमानलवणकलायी[8]किङ्किणीनालीसनाथसङ्कलिततलसारके, कुण्डलीकृतावरक्षणीजालजटिलवल्लभपालाश्वघटानिवेश्यमानशाखामृगे, परिव-

१ 'तत्त्व-' अ. २ 'कटुककटुक-' अ-क. ३ 'पनीयमान' ब. ४ 'पूलिक' ब. ५ 'प्रस्फोटितचर्मणि' अ-क. ६ 'अनेकानेकपा-' अ-क. ७ 'घनिकर' अ. ८ 'कलापि' क.

र्धकाकृष्यमाणार्धजग्धप्राभातिकयोग्याशनप्रारोहके, व्याक्रोशीविजृम्भमाणघासिकाघोषे, गमनसंभ्रमभ्रष्टभ्रमदुत्तुण्डतरुणतुरङ्गमतन्यमानानेकमन्दुराविमर्दे, सज्जीकृतकरेणुकारोहाह्वानसत्वरसुन्दरीदीयमानमुखालेपने, चलितमातङ्गतुरङ्गप्रधावितप्राकृतप्रातिवेश्यकलोकलुण्ठ्यमाननिर्घो[1]ससस्यसञ्चये, सञ्चरच्चेलचक्राक्रान्तचक्रीवति, चक्रचीत्कारिगन्त्रीगणगृह्यमाणप्रहतवर्त्मनि, अकाण्डदीयमा[2]नभाण्डभरितानडुहि, निकटघासलाभलुभ्यल्लम्बमानप्रथमप्रसार्यमाणसारसौरभेये, प्रमुखप्रवर्त्यमानमहासामन्तमहानसे, पुरःप्रधावद्धुजवाहिनि, प्रियशतोपलभ्यमानासङ्कटकुटीरकान्तरालनिःसरणे, करिचर[3]णचलितमठिकोत्थितलोकलोष्टहन्यमानमेण्ठक्रियमाणासन्नसाक्षिणि, सङ्घट्टविघट्टमानव्याघ्रपल्लीपलायमानक्षुद्रकुटुम्बके, कलकलोपद्रवद्द्रवद्द्रविणबलीवर्दविद्राणवणिजि, पुरःसरदीपिकालोकविरलायमानलोकोत्पीड[4]प्रस्थितान्तःपुरकरिणीकदम्बके, हयारोहाहूयमानलम्बितशुनि, सरभसचरणनिपतननिश्चलगमनसुखायमानखक्खटै[5]स्तूयमानतुङ्गतुङ्ग[6]णगुणे, त्रस्तवेसरविसंवादिसीदद्दाक्षिणात्यसादिनि, रजोजग्धजगति प्रयाणसमये, प्रतिदिशमागच्छद्भिर्गजवधूसमारूढैराधोरणैरूर्ध्वध्रियमाणहेमपत्रभङ्गशारशार्ङ्गैः, अन्तरासनासीनान्तरङ्गगृहीतासिभिः, ताम्बूलिकविधूयमानचामरपल्लवैः, पश्चिमासनिकार्पितभस्त्राभरणभिन्दिपालपूलिकैः, पत्रलताकुटिलकलधौतनलकपल्लवितपर्याणैः, पर्याणपक्षकपरिक्षेपपट्टिकाबन्धनिश्चलपट्टोपधानस्थिरावधानैः, प्रचलपादफलिकास्फालनस्फायमानपदबन्धमणिशिलाशब्दैः, उच्चित्रनेत्रसुकुमारस्वस्था[7]नैस्थगितजङ्घाकाण्डैश्च कार्दमिकपटकल्माषितपिशङ्गपिङ्गैः, अलिनीलमसृणसतुलासमुत्पादितसितसमायोगपरभागैश्चावदातदेहवर्णविराजमानराजावर्तमेचकैः, कञ्चुकैश्चा[8]पचितचीनचोलकैश्च तारमुक्तास्तबकितस्तवरकवारबाणैश्च नानाकषायकर्बुरकूर्पासकैश्च शुकपिच्छच्छायाच्छादनकैश्च व्यायामोल्लुप्तपार्श्वप्रदेशप्रविष्टचारुशं[9]स्त्रैश्च गतिवशवेल्लितहारलतागलल्लोलकुण्डलोन्मोचनप्रधावितपरिजनैश्च चामीकरपत्राङ्कुरकर्णपूरकविघट्टमानवाचालबालपाशैश्चोष्णीषपट्टविष्ट[10]ब्धकर्णोत्पलनालैश्च कुङ्कुमरागकोमलोत्तरीयान्तरितोत्तमाङ्गैश्च चूडामणिखण्डखचितक्षौमखोलै[11]श्च मायू[12]रातपत्रायमाणशेखरषट्पदपटलैश्च मार्गागतशारिकशा[13]रिवाहवेगदण्डैः, पुरश्चञ्चच्चामरकिर्मीरकार्दरङ्गचर्ममण्डलमण्डनोड्डीयमानचटुलडामरचारभटभरितभुवनान्तरैः, आस्कन्दत्काम्बोजवाजिशतशिञ्जानजातरूपायानरवमुखरितदिङ्मुखैश्च निर्दयप्रहतलम्बापटहशतपटुरवबधिरीकृतश्रवणविवरैः, उ-

---

१ 'निघाससञ्चये' ब. २ 'अकाण्डोड्डीयमान-' ब. ३ 'चरणदलित' अ-क. ४ 'लोकोत्पीडा' ब. ५ 'खक्खटक्षत्रियस्तूय०' ब. ६ 'तङ्गण' ब. ७ 'स्वस्थगनस्थगित' अ-क. ८ 'कञ्चुकैश्चोप' अ-क. ९ '०शस्तैश्च' ब. १० 'पट्टावष्टब्ध' अ-क. ११ 'चोलैश्च' अ-क. १२ 'मायूरपत्राय'-अ-क. १३ 'शारीरिकशारिवाह' ब.

द्घोष्यमाणनामभिः, उन्मुखपादातप्रतिपाल्यमानाज्ञापातै राजभिरापुपूरे राजद्वारम् ।

उदिते च भगवति दिनकृति राज्ञः समायोगग्रहणसमयशंसी सस्वान संज्ञाशङ्खो मुहुर्मुहुः । अथ नचिरादिव प्रथमप्रयाण एव दिग्विजयाय दिग्गजसमागममिव गमनविलोलकर्णतालदोलाविलासैः कुर्वाणया करेणुकया[1] सिद्धयात्रयोह्यमानः, वैदूर्यदण्डविकटेनोपरि प्रत्युसपद्मरागखण्डखचिततया सूर्योदयदर्शनकोपादिव लोहितायतया ध्रियमाणेन मङ्गलातपत्रेण, कदलीगर्भाभ्यधिकम्रदिम्ना नवनेत्रनिर्मितेन द्वितीय इव भोगिनामधिपतिरङ्गलग्नेन कञ्चुकेन, अमृतमथनदिवस इव क्षीरोदफेनपटलधवलाम्बरवाही, बाल एव पारिजातपादप इवाखण्डलभूमिमारूढः, विधूयमानचामरमरुद्विधूतकर्णपूरकुसुममञ्जरीरजसा सकलभुवनवशीकरणचूर्णेनेव दिशश्छुरयन्, अभिमुखचूडामणिघटमानपाटलप्रतिबिम्बमुदयमानं सवितारमपि पिबन्निव तेजसा, बहलताम्बूलसिन्दूरच्छुरितया विलभमान इव द्वीपान्तराण्योष्ठमुद्रयानुरागस्य स्फुरन्महाहारमरीचिचक्रवालानि चामराणीव दिशोऽपि ग्राहयन्, राजकेक्षणोत्क्षिप्तत्रिभागया त्रीनपि लोकान्करदानायाज्ञापयन्निव सविभ्रमं भ्रूलतया, द्राघीयसा बाहुप्राकारेण परिक्षिपन्निव रिरक्षया सप्तापि सागरमहाखातान्, अखिलमिव क्षीरोदमाधुर्यमादायोद्गतया लक्ष्म्या समुपगूढः, गाढममृतमय इव पीयमानः कुतूहलोत्तानकटकलोकलोचनसहस्रैः, स्नेहार्द्रेषु राज्ञां हृदयेषु गुणगौरवेण मज्जन्निव, मज्जामपि[2] लिम्पन्निव सौभाग्यद्रवेण द्रष्टॄणाम्, अमरपतिरिवाग्रजवधकलङ्कप्रक्षालनाकुलः, पृथुरिव पृथिवीपरिशोधनावधानसङ्कलितसकलमहीभृत्समुत्सारणः, पुरःसैरालोककारकैः सहस्रसंख्यैरर्क इव किरणैरधिकारचातुर्यचञ्चलचरणैर्व्यवस्थास्थापननिष्ठुरैः भयपलायमानलोकोत्पीडान्तरिता दशापि दिशो ग्राहयद्भिरिव चलितकदलिकासम्पातपीतप्रचारं पवनमपि विनये स्थापयद्भिरिव द्रुतचरणोद्धूतधूलिपटलावधूतान्दिनकरकिरणानप्युत्सारयद्भिरिव कनकवेत्रलतालोकविक्षिप्यमाणं दिनमपि दूरीकुर्वद्भिरिव दण्डिभिरितस्ततः समुत्सार्यमाणजनसमूहो निर्जगाम नरपतिः ।

अवनमति च विनयनमितवपुषि भयचकितमनसि चलनशिथिलमणिकनकमुकुटकिरणनिकररुचिरशिरसि विलुलितकुसुमशेखररजसि राजचक्रे, प्रभामुचां चूडामणीनामवाञ्चस्तिर्यञ्च उदञ्चश्च चञ्चन्तो मरीचयश्चाषराशय इव सुशकुनसम्पादनाय चेलुः । मेघायमानरेणुमेदुरं मन्दिरशिखण्डिन इव खमुड्डीयमानाः कोमलकल्पपादपपल्लववन्दनमाला[3]कलापा इवाबध्यन्त दिग्द्वारेषु

---

१ 'करेणुकयोह्य०' अ-क. २ 'मज्जामपि' इति नास्ति अ-क- पुस्तकयोः. ३ 'चन्दनमाला' अ-क.

चण्डदण्डपाणिपेटकानुबद्धैर्गिरिगुडकैरिव हन्यमानैरितस्ततः सञ्चरद्भिरपरैर्युगपत्परापतितमहाजनग्रस्तैस्तिलशो विलुप्यमानैरनेकजन्तुजङ्घान्तरालनिःसरणकुशलिभिः कुटिलिकाव्यंसितसादिबहुश्वभिः पतल्लोष्टलगुडकोणकुठारकीलकुद्दालखनित्रदात्र[1]यष्टिभिरपि निःसरद्भिरायुषो बलात्कृतकलकलम्, अन्यत्र सङ्घशो घासिकैर्बुसधूलीधूसरितघासजालजालकितजघनैश्च पुराणपर्याणैकदेशदोलायमानदात्रैश्च शीर्णोर्णाशकलशिथिलमलिनमलकुथैश्च प्रभुप्रसादीकृतपाटितपटच्चरचलच्चोलकधारिभिश्च धावमानैरुद्धूयमानधूलिपटलम्, क्वचिदेकान्तप्रवृत्ताश्ववारचक्रचर्व्यमाणागामिगौडविग्रहम्, क्वचित्पङ्किलप्रदेशपूरणादेशाकुलसकललोकलूयमानतृणपूलकम्, क्वचित्तलवर्तिवेत्रिवेत्रवित्रास्यमानशाखिशिखरगतविक्रोशद्विवादिब्राह्मणम्, क्वचित्[2]कुलुण्ठकपाशविवेष्ट्यमानग्रासीणकग्रामाकृष्टकौलेयकम्, क्वचिदन्योन्य[3]विभवस्पर्धोद्धुरराजपुत्रवाह्यमानवाजिसङ्घट्टमण्डितम्, अनेकवृत्तान्ततया कौतुकजननम्, प्रलयजलधिमिव जगद्ग्रासग्रहणाय प्रवृत्तम्, पातालमिव महाभोगिनां गुप्तये समुत्पादितम्, कैलासमिव परमेश्वरवसतये सृष्टम्, दृश्यमानसकलप्राणिपर्यायं चतुर्युगसर्गकोशमिव प्रजापतीनाम्, क्लेशबहुलमपि तपःकरणमिव क्रम[4]कारणं कल्याणानाम्, एवं च वीक्षमाणः कटकं जगाम।

आसन्नवर्तिनां च तत्रभवताम्, 'मान्धात्रा प्रवर्तिताः पन्थानो दिग्विजयाय। अप्रतिहतरथरंहसा रघुणा लघुनैव कालेनाकारि ककुभां प्रसादनम्। शरासनद्वितीयः करदीचकार चक्रं क्रमागतभुजबलाभिजनधनमदावलिप्तानां भूभुजां पाण्डुः। पाण्डवः सव्यसाची चीनविषयमतिक्रम्य राजसूयसम्पदे क्रुध्यद्गन्धर्वधनुष्कोटिटांकारकूजितकुञ्जं हेमकूटपर्वतं पराजैष्ट। सङ्कल्पान्तरितो विजयस्तरस्विनाम्। सहिमहिमवद्व्यवहितोऽप्युवाह बाहुबलव्यतिकरकातरः करं कौरवेश्वरस्य किङ्कर इवाकृती द्रुमः। नातिजिगीषवः खलु पूर्वे येनाल्प एव भूभागे भूयांसो भगदत्तदन्तवक्त्रक्राथकर्णकौरवशिशुपालसाल्वजरासन्धसिन्धुराजप्रभृतयोऽभवन्भूपतयः। सन्तुष्टो राजा युधिष्ठिरो यो ह्यसहत समीप एव धनञ्जयजयजनितजगत्कम्पः किंपुरुषाणां राज्यम्। अलसश्चण्डकोशो यो न प्राविक्षत्क्ष्मां जित्वा स्त्रीराज्यम्। ह्रसीय एवान्तरं तुषारगिरिगन्धमादनयोः उत्साहिनः किष्कुस्तुरुष्कविषयः, पारसीकदेशः प्रादेशः, शशपदं शकस्थानम्, अदृश्यमानप्रतिप्रहारे पारियात्रे यात्रैव शिथिला, शौर्यशुल्कः सुलभो दक्षिणापथः, दक्षिणार्णवकल्लोलानिलचलितचन्दनलतासौरभसुन्दरीकृतदरीमन्दिराद्दर्दुरादद्रेर्नेदीयसि मलयो मलयलग्न एव च महेन्द्रः।' इत्येवंप्रायानुद्योगद्योतकानामालापान्पार्थिवकुमाराणां बाहुशालिनां शृण्वन्नेवासससादावासम्। मन्दिरद्वारि चोभयतः सबहुमानं भ्रूलताभ्यां विसर्जितराजलोकः

१ 'यष्टिवृष्टिभिरपि' ब. २ 'कुलुण्डकपाशविवेद्य' क. ३ 'विभाव' ब. ४ 'कारिणम्' क.

प्रविश्य चावततार बाह्यास्थानमण्डपस्थापितमासनमाचक्राम। प्रास्तसमायोगश्च क्षणमासिष्ट।

अथ तत्र प्रतीहारः पृथ्वीपृष्ठप्रतिष्ठापितपाणिपल्लवो विज्ञापितवान्—'देव, प्राग्ज्योतिषेश्वरेण कुमारेण प्रहितो हंसवेगनामा दूतोऽन्तरङ्गस्तोरणमध्यास्ते' इति। राजा तु 'तमाशु प्रवेशय' इति सादरमादिदेश। अथ दक्षतया क्षितिपालादराच्च प्रतीहारः स्वयमेव निरगात्। अनन्तरं च हंसवेगः सविनयमाकृत्यैव नयनानन्दसम्पादनसुभगाभोगभद्रया समुल्लङ्घ्यमानगुणगरिमा प्रभूतप्राभृतभृतां पुरुषाणां समूहेन महतानुगम्यमानः प्रविवेश राजमन्दिरम्। आरादेव पञ्चाङ्गालिङ्गिताङ्गनः प्रणाममकरोत्। 'एह्येहि' इति सबहुमानमाहूतश्च प्रधावितोऽपसृतः पादपीठलुठितललाटलेखो न्यस्तहस्तः पृष्ठे पार्थिवेनोपसृत्य भूयो नमश्चक्रे। स्निग्धनरेन्द्रदृष्ट्या निर्दिष्टमविप्रकृष्टं स प्रदेशमध्यास्त। ततो राजा तिरश्चीं तनुमीषदिव दधानश्चामरग्राहिणीमन्तरालवर्तिनीं समुत्सार्य संमुखीनस्तं सप्रश्रयं पप्रच्छ—'हंसवेग, श्रीमान्कच्चित्कुशली कुमारः' इति। स तमन्ववादीत्—'अद्य कुशली येनैवं स्नेहस्नपितया सौहार्दद्रवार्द्रया सगौरवं गिरा पृच्छति देवः' इति।

स्थित्वा च मुहूर्तमिव पुनः स चतुरम्भोधिभोगभूतिभाजनभूतस्य देवस्य सद्भावगर्भमपहाय हृदयमेकमन्यदनुरूपं प्राभृतमेव दुर्लभं लोके तथाप्यस्मत्स्वामिना सन्देशमशून्यतां नयता पूर्वजोपार्जितं वारुणातपत्रमाभोगाख्यमनुरूपस्थानन्यासेन कृतार्थीकृतमेतत्। अस्य च कुतूहलकृन्ति बहूनि आश्चर्याणि दृश्यन्ते। तथाहि प्रतिदिवसं प्रविशति शैत्यहेतोश्छायायाः किरणसहस्रादेकैकः सोमस्य रश्मिरस्मिन्। यस्मिन्प्रविष्टे प्रध्यानानन्तरं स्वादवो दन्तवीणोपदेशाचार्याश्च्योतन्ति चन्द्रभासामम्भसां मणिशलाकाभ्यो यावदिच्छमच्छा धाराः। प्रचेता इव यश्चतुर्णामर्णवानामधिपतिर्भूतो भावी वा तमिदमनुगृह्णाति च्छायया नेतरम्। इदं च न सप्तार्चिर्दहति, न पृषदश्वो हरति, नोदकमार्द्रयति, न रजांसि मलिनयन्ति, न जरा जर्जरयति। एतत्तावदनुगृह्णातु दृशा देवः सन्देशमपि विस्रब्धं श्रोष्यति।' इत्येवमभिधाय विवृत्यात्मीयं पुरुषमभ्यधात्—'उत्तिष्ठ दर्शय देवस्य' इति।

स वचनानन्तरमुत्थाय पुमानूर्ध्वीचकार तद्धौतदुकूलकल्पिताच्च निचोलकादकोषीत्। आकृष्यमाण एव च यस्मिन्नतिसितमहसि सरभसमहासीव हरेण, रसातलादुदलासीव शेषफणिफणाफलकमण्डलेन, अस्थायीव चक्रीभूयान्तरिक्षे क्षीरोदेन, अघटीव गगनाङ्गने गोष्ठीबन्धः शारदेन बलाहकव्यूहेन, विश्रान्तमिव विततपक्षतिना वियति पितामहविमानहंसयूथेन, अत्रिनेत्रनिर्गतस्य धवलधाममण्डलमनोहरो दृष्ट इव जनेन जन्मदिवसः कुमुदबन्धोः, प्रत्यक्षीकृत इवोद्गमनक्षणो नारायणनाभिपुण्डरीकस्य, आहितेव कौमुदीप्रदोषदर्शनानन्दतृप्तिरक्षणाम्, उदमाङ्क्षीदिव मन्दाकिनीपुलिनमण्डलं

महदम्बरोदरे, परिवर्तित इव दिवसः पौर्णमासीनिशया, मन्दमन्दमिन्दूदय-सम्देहदूयमानमानसैर्विघटितं विघटमानचञ्चुच्युतमृणालकोटिभिरासन्नकमलिनीचक्रवाकमिथुनैः, शरज्जलधरपटलाशङ्कासङ्कोचितकेकारवमूकमुखपुटैः पराङ्मुखीभूतं भवनशिखण्डिमण्डलैः, प्रबुद्धमाबद्धचन्द्रानन्दोद्दामोद्दलद्दलपुटाट्टहासविशदं कुमुदषण्डैः ।

चित्रीयमाणचेताश्च सराजको राजा दण्डानुसाराधिरोहिण्या दृष्ट्या सादरमैक्षिष्ट तत्तिलकमिव त्रिभुवनस्य, शैशवमिव श्वेतद्वीपस्य, अंशावतारमिव शरदिन्दोः, हृदयमिव धर्मस्य, निवेशमिव शशिलोकस्य, दन्तमण्डलकद्युतिधवलं मुखमिव चक्रवर्तित्वस्य, मौक्तिकजालपरिकरसितं सीमन्तचक्रमिव दिवः, बहलज्योत्स्नाशुक्लोदरमैन्दवमिव परिवेशवलयम्, शौक्ल्यापहसितशङ्खश्रीकं श्रवणमण्डलमिव निश्चलतां गतमैरावतस्य, श्वेतगङ्गावर्तपाण्डुरं पदमिव त्रिभुवनवन्दनीयं त्रिविक्रमस्य, प्रचेतसश्चूडामणिमरीचिशिखाभिरिव श्लिष्टाभिर्मानसबिसतन्तुमयीभिश्चामरिकावलीभिर्विरचितपरिवेशम्, उपरि चक्रवर्तिलक्ष्मीनूपुरस्वनश्रवणदोहदनिश्चलेनेव लक्ष्मणा विततपत्रेण हंसेन सनाथीकृतशिखरम्, स्पर्शवता च प्रभावस्तम्भितेन मन्दाकिनीमृणालेन मुकुलितफणेन वासुकिनेव नीतेन दण्डतां द्योतमानम्, धवलिम्ना क्षालयदिव नक्षत्रपथम्, प्रभाप्रवाहप्रथिम्ना प्रावृण्वदिव दिवसम्, समुच्छ्रायेणाधःकुर्वदिव दिवम्, उपरिस्थितमिव सर्वमङ्गलानाम्, श्वेतमण्डपमिव श्रियः, स्तबकमिव ब्रह्मस्तम्भस्य, नाभिमण्डलमिव ज्योत्स्नायाः, विशदहासमिव कीर्तेः, फेनराशिमिव खड्गधाराजलानाम्, यशःपटलमिव शौर्यशालितायाः, त्रैलोक्याद्भुतं महच्छत्रम् ।

दृष्टे च तस्मिन्राज्ञा प्रथमं शेषमपि प्राभृतं प्रकाशयांचक्रुः क्रमेण कार्माः । तद्यथा परार्ध्यरत्नांशुशोणीकृतदिग्भागान्, भगदत्तप्रभृतिख्यातपार्थिवपरागतानाहतलक्षणानलङ्कारान्, प्रभालेपिनां च चूडामणीनां समुत्कर्षान्, क्षीरोदधेर्धवलताहेतूनिव हारान्, अनेकरागरुचिरवेत्रकरण्डकुण्डलीकृतानि शरच्चन्द्रमरीचिरुञ्चि शौचक्षमाणि क्षौमाणि कुशलशिल्पिलोकोल्लिखितानां च शुक्तिशङ्खगल्वर्कप्रमुखानां पानभाजनानां निचयान्, निचोलकरक्षितरुचां च रुचिरकाञ्चनपत्रभङ्गभङ्गुराणामतिबन्धुरपरिवेशानां कार्दरङ्गचर्मणां सम्भारान्, भूर्जत्वक्कोमलाः स्पर्शवतीः जातीपट्टिकाः, चित्रपटानां च म्रदीयसां समूरुकोपधानादीन्विकारान्, प्रियङ्गुप्रसवपिङ्गलत्वञ्चि चासनानि वेत्रमयान्यगुरुवल्कलकल्पितसञ्चयानि च सुभाषितभाञ्जि पुस्तकानि, परिणतपाटलपटोलत्विषि च तरुणहारीतहरिन्ति क्षीरक्षारीणि च पूगानां पल्लवलम्बीनि सरसानि फलानि, सहकारलतारसानां च कृष्णागुरुतैलस्य च कुपितकपिकपोलकपिलकापोतिकापलाशकोशीकवचिताङ्गीः स्थवीयसीर्वैणवीर्नाडीश्च, पट्टसूत्रप्रसेव-

१ 'हूयमान' अ-क. २ 'मण्डलधवलं' अ-क. ३ '०तैलस्य च कपोतकपिल०' ब.

कार्पितांश्च भिन्नाञ्जनकृष्णस्य कृष्णागुरुणो गुरुपरितापमुषश्च गोशीर्षचन्दनस्य तुषारशिलाशकलशिशिरस्वच्छसितस्य च कर्पूरस्य कस्तूरिकाकोशकानां च पक्कफलजूटजटिलानां च कक्कोलपल्लवानां लवङ्गपुष्पमञ्जरीणां जातीफलस्तबकानां च राशीन्, अतिमधुरमधुरसामोदनिर्हारिणीश्चोल्लककलशीः सितासितस्य च चामरजातस्य निचयान्, अवलम्बमानतूलिकालाबुकांश्च लिखिताने[2]लेख्यफलकसम्पुटान्, कुतूहलकृन्ति कनकशृङ्खलानियमितग्रीवाणां किंनराणां च वनमानुषीणां च जीवञ्जीवकानां च जलमानुषाणां च मिथुनानि, परिमलामोदितककुभश्च कस्तूरिकाकुरङ्गान्, गेहपरिसरणपरिचिताश्च चमरीः, चामीकररसचित्रवेत्रपञ्जरान्तर्गतांश्च बहुसुभाषितजल्पाकजिह्वांश्च[3] शुकशारिकाप्रभृतीन्पक्षिणः प्रवालपञ्जरगतांश्च चकोरान्, जलहस्तिनामुदग्रकुम्भमुक्ताफलदामदन्तुराणि च दन्तकाण्डकुण्डलानि।

राजा तु छत्रदर्शनात्प्रहृष्टहृदयः प्रथमप्रयाणे शोभननिमित्तमिति मनसा जग्राह। हंसवेगं च प्रीयमाणो बभाषे—'भद्र, सकलरत्नधाम्नः परमेश्वरशिरोधारणार्हस्यास्य महातपत्रस्य महार्णवादिव कुमुदबान्धवस्य कुमाराल्लाभो न विस्मयाय। बालविद्याः खलु महतामुपकृतयः' इति। अपनीते च तस्मात्प्रदेशात्प्राभृतसम्भारे क्षणमिव स्थित्वा 'हंसवेग, विश्रम्यताम्' इति प्रतीहारभवनं विसर्जयांबभूव। स्वयमप्युत्थाय स्नात्वा मङ्गलाकाङ्क्षी प्राङ्मुखः प्राविशदाभोगस्य छायाम्।

अथ विशत एवास्य छायाजन्मना जडिम्ना चूडामणितामनीयतेव शशिबिम्बमम्बुबिन्दुमुचश्चुचुम्बुरिव चन्द्रकान्तमणयो ललाटतटं कर्पूररेणव इव व्यलीयन्त लोचनयुगले गलत्तुहिनकणनिकरकृतनीहारा हारा इवाबध्यन्त हरिचन्दनरसासारेणेवापाति सन्ततमुरसि कुमुदमयमिव हृदयमभवदतिशिशिरमन्तर्हितहिमशिलेव विलीयमाना व्यलिम्पदङ्गानि। जातविस्मयश्चाकरोन्मनसि एकमजर्यं[4] सङ्गतमपहाय कास्त्यन्या प्रतिकौशलिकेति। आहारकाले च हंसवेगाय धवलकर्पटप्रावृतधौतनालिकेरपरिगृहीतं विलिप्तशेषं चन्दनमङ्गस्पृष्टे च वाससी शरत्तारकाकारतारमुक्तास्तबकितपदं परिवेशं नाम कटिसूत्रमतिमहार्हपद्मरागालोकलोहितीकृतदिवसं च तरङ्गकं नाम कर्णाभरणं प्रभूतं च भोज्यजातं प्राहिणोत्। एवंप्रायेण च क्रमेण जगाम दिवसः।

ततः कटकस्थबलबहलधूलिधूसरितवपुरंशुमाली मलीमसमङ्गमिव क्षालयितुमपरजलनिधिमवातरत्। आभोगातपत्रप्रदानवार्तामिव निवेदयितुं वरुणाय वारुणीं दिशमयासीत्। मुकुलायमानसकलकमलवना प्रमुख एव बद्धसेवाञ्जलिपुटेव सद्वीपा भूरभूद्भूपतेः। नृपानुरागमय इव निखिलजीवलोकलोकाञ्जलिबन्धबन्धुर्जगज्जग्राह संध्यारागः[6]। गौडापराधशङ्किनीव श्या-

---

१ 'वर्णस्य' ब. २ 'लिखितानेकलेख्य०' ब. ३ '०जिह्वांश्च जातीः कौशिकशुक०' ब. ४ 'अजर्यं' ब. ५ 'भूपालानुरागराशिमय' ब. ६ 'बद्ध' ब.

मतां प्रपेदे दिक्प्राची। प्रचिततिमिरनिवहा[1] निर्वाणान्यनृपप्रतापानलकलापेव कालिमानमतानीन्मेदिनी। मेदिनीशप्रदोषास्थानपुष्पनिकरमिव विकचतगर[2]-रुचिरमवचकरुरुडुनिकरमविरलं ककुभः। स्कन्धावारगन्धगजमदामोदधावितस्येव मार्गो वियति विरराज रजःपाण्डुरैरावतस्य। कुपितनृपव्याघ्राघ्रातामुपसृष्टामिव पौरुष्टुतीं विहाय विहायस्तलमारुरोह रोहिणीरमणः। प्रयाणवार्ता इव मानिनीनां हृदयभेदिन्यो ययुरिन्दुदीधितयो दश दिशः। नवनृपदण्डयात्रात्रासातुरा इव तरलितसत्त्ववृत्तयश्चक्षुभुः पतयो वाहिनीनाम्। चिन्तेव भूभृतां हृदयानि विवेश गुहाविवराणि विमुक्तसर्वाशा तिमिरसन्ततिः। प्रतिसामन्तचक्षुषामिव ननाश निद्रा कुमुदवनानाम्।

अस्यां च वेलायां विततवितानतलवर्ती नरेन्द्रो 'यात तावत्' इति विसर्ज्यानुजीविनो हंसवेगमादिष्टवान्—'कथय सन्देशम्' इति। प्रणम्य स कथयितुं प्रास्तावीत्—'देव, पुरा महावराहसम्पर्कसम्भृतगर्भया भगवत्या भुवा नरको नाम सूनुरसावि रसातले। वीरस्य यस्याभवन्बाल्य एव पादप्रणामप्रणयिनश्चूडामणयो लोकपालानाम्। यस्य च त्रिभुवनभुजो भुजशौण्डस्य भवनकमलिनीचक्रवाकीकोपकुटिलकटाक्षेक्षितोऽपि भयचकितारुणपरिवर्तितरथो नाज्ञया विना रविरस्तमव्राजीत्। यश्च वरुणस्य बहिर्वृत्ति हृदयमिदमातपत्रमहार्षीत्। महात्मनस्तस्यान्वये भगदत्तपुष्पदत्तवज्रदत्तप्रभृतिषु व्यतीतेषु बहुषु मेरूपमेषु महत्सु महीपालेषु प्रपौत्रो महाराजभूतिवर्मणः पौत्रश्चन्द्रमुखवर्मणः पुत्रो देवस्य कैलासस्थिरस्थितेः स्थितिवर्मणः सुस्थिरवर्मा नाम महाराजाधिराजो जज्ञे तेजसां राशिर्मृगाङ्क इति [3]यं जना जगुः। योऽयमग्रजेनेवाजायत[4] सहैवाहंकारेण। यश्च बाल एव प्रीत्या द्विजातीनप्रीत्या चारातीन्समग्रान्प्रतिग्रहानग्राहयत्। यत्र चातिदुर्लभं लवणालयसम्भूतायाः परं माधुर्यमभूल्लक्ष्म्याः। तथा च यो वाहिनीनाथानां शङ्खाञ्जहार न रत्नानि, पृथिव्याः स्थैर्यं जग्राह न करम्, अवनिभृतां गौरवमादत्त न नैष्ठुर्यम्। तस्य च सुगृहीतनाम्नो देवस्य देव्यां श्यामादेव्यां भास्करद्युतिर्भास्करवर्मापरनामा तनयः शन्तनोर्भागीरथ्यां भीष्म इव कुमारः समभवत्। अयमस्य च शैशवादारभ्य सङ्कल्पः स्थेयान्स्थाणुपादारविन्दद्वयादृते नाहमन्यं नमस्कुर्यामिति। ईदृशश्चायं मनोरथस्त्रिभुवनदुर्लभस्त्रयाणामन्यतमेन सम्पद्यते सकलभुवनविजयेन वा मृत्युना वा यदि वा प्रचण्डप्रतापज्वलने[5]जनितदिग्दाहेन जगत्येकवीरेण देवोपमेन मित्रेण। मैत्री च प्रायः कार्यव्यपेक्षिणी क्षोणीभृताम्। कार्यं च कीदृशं नाम तद्भवेद्यदुपन्यस्यमानमुपनयेन्मित्रतां देवम्। देवस्य हि यशांसि सञ्चिचीषतो बहिरङ्गभूतानि धनानि। बाहावेव च केवले निषण्णस्य शेषावयवानामपि साहायकसम्पादनमनोरथो निरवकाशः किमुत बाह्यजन-

१ 'निर्वाहा' ब. २ 'तवर' ब. ३ 'प्रियं जना' ब. ४ 'योऽयमजेनेवा०' अ-क.
५ 'ज्वलनदिग्दाहेन' अ-क.

स्य। चतुःसागरग्रामग्रहणघस्मरस्य पृथिव्येकदेशदानोपन्यासेनापि का तुष्टिः। अभिरूपकन्याविश्राणनविलोभनमपि लक्ष्मीमुखारविन्ददर्शनदुर्ललितदृष्टेरकिंचित्करम्। एवमघटमानसकलोपायसम्पादितपदार्थेऽस्मिन्प्रार्थनामात्रकमेव केवलमनुरुध्यमानः शृणोतु देवः। प्राग्ज्योतिषेश्वरो हि देवेनैकपिङ्ग इवानङ्गद्विषा, दशरथ इव गोत्रभिदा, धनञ्जय इव पुष्कराक्षेण, वैकर्तन इव दुर्योधनेन, मलयानिल इव माधवेन, अजर्यं सङ्गतमिच्छति। यदि च देवस्यापि मैत्रीयति हृदयमवगच्छति च पर्यायान्तरितं दास्यमनुतिष्ठन्ति सुहृद इति ततः किमास्यते समाज्ञाप्यतामनुभवतु विष्णोर्मन्दरगिरिरिव विकटकेयूरकोटिमणिविघट्टनकणितकटकमणिशिलाशकलानि गाढोपगूढानि देवस्य कामरूपाधिपतिः। अस्मिन्नातृप्तेरनवरतविमललावण्यसौभाग्यसुधानिर्झरिणि मुखशशिनि चिराच्चक्षुषी लालयतु प्राग्ज्योतिषेश्वरश्रीः। नाभिनन्दति चेद्देवः प्रणयमाज्ञापयतु किं कथनीयं मया स्वामिनः' इति।

विरतवचसि तस्मिन्भूपालः पूर्वोपलब्धैरेव गुरुभिर्गुणैरारोपितबहुमानः कुमारे सुदूरमाभोगातपत्रव्यतिकरेण तु परां कोटिमारोपिते प्रेम्णि लज्जमान इव सादरं जगाद—'हंसवेग, कथमिव तादृशि महात्मनि महाभिजने पुण्यराशौ गुणिनां प्राग्रहरे परोक्षसुहृदि स्निह्यति मद्विधस्यान्यथा स्वप्नेऽपि प्रवर्तेत मनः। सकलजगदुत्तापनपटवोऽपि शिशिरायन्ते त्रिभुवननयनानन्दकरे कमलाकरे करास्तिग्मतेजसः। सुबहुगुणगणक्रीताश्च के वयं सख्यस्य। सज्जनमाधुर्याणामभृतदास्यो दश दिशः। एकान्तावदातोत्तानस्वभावसम्भृतसादृश्यस्य कुमुदस्य कृते केनाभिहितः शिशिररश्मिः। श्रेयांश्च सङ्कल्पः कुमारस्य। स्वयं बाहुशाली मयि च समालम्बितशरासने सुहृदि हराद‍ृते कमन्यं नमस्यति। संवर्धिता मे प्रीतिरमुना सङ्कल्पेन। अवलेपिनि पशावपि केसरिणि बहुमानो हृदयस्य किं पुनः सुहृदि। तत्तथा यतेथा यथा न चिरमियमस्मान्क्लेशयति कुमारदर्शनोत्कण्ठा' इति।

हंसवेगस्तु विज्ञापयाम्बभूव—'देव, किमपरमिदानीं क्लेशयत्यभिजातमभिहितं देवेन। सेवाभीरवो हि सन्तः, तत्रापि विशेषेणायमहङ्कारधनो वैष्णवो वंशः। आस्तां तावदस्मत्स्वामिवंशः। पश्यतु देवः पुरुषस्य हि सेवां प्रति दुर्जनन्येवातिवृद्धया दुर्गत्या वाभिमुखीक्रियमाणस्य, कुटुम्बिन्येवासन्तुष्टया तृष्णया वा प्रेर्यमाणस्य, दुरपत्यैरिव यौवनजनितैर्नानाभिलाषिभिरसत्सङ्कल्पैर्वाकुलीक्रियमाणस्य, जरत्कुमारीमिव परमार्गणयोग्यामतिमहतीं वा अवस्थां पश्यतः, स्वगृहे दुर्बन्धुभिरिव दुःस्थितैः समग्रैर्ग्रहैर्वा ग्राह्यमाणस्याभियोगं, पुरातनैररतिदुस्त्यजैर्भृत्यैरिव मलिनैः कर्मभिर्वानुवर्त्यमानस्य, सकलशरीरसन्तापकरं कारीषाग्निमिव दुष्कृतिनः कृतचित्तस्य संप्रवेष्टुं राजकुलम्, उपहतसकलेन्द्रियशक्तेरिव मिथ्यैव हृदयगतविषयग्रामग्रहणाभिलाषस्य, प्रथममेव तोरणतले वन्दनमालाकिशलयस्येव शुष्यतो द्वाररक्षिभिर्निरुद्धस्य, पीडितस्य

प्रविशतो द्वारे हरिणस्येवापरैर्हन्यमानस्य, करिकर्मचर्मपुटस्येव मुहुर्मुहुः प्रतिहारमण्डलकरप्रहारैर्निरस्यमानस्य, निधिपादपप्ररोहस्येव[1] द्रविणाभिलाषादधोमुखीभवतः, दूरममार्गणस्याप्यतिविप्रकृष्टविवृत्त[2]विसर्जितस्योद्वेगं व्रजतः, अकण्टकस्यापि चरणतललग्नस्याकृष्य क्षेपीयः क्षिप्यमाणस्य, अमकरकेतोरप्यकालोपसर्पणप्रकुपितेश्वरदृष्टिदग्धस्य प्रलयमुपगच्छतः, कपेरिव कोपनिर्भर्त्सितस्याप्यभिन्नमुखरागस्य, ब्रह्मघ्न इव प्रतिदिवसवन्दनोद्घृष्टशिरःकपालस्य, स्पर्शरहितस्याशुभकर्माणि निर्वहतः, त्रिशङ्कोरिवोभयलोकभ्रष्टस्य नक्तन्दिनमर्वाक्शिरसस्तिष्ठतः, वाजिन इव कवलवशेन सुखवाह्यमात्मानं विदधानस्य, अनशनशायिन इव हृदयस्थापितजीवनाशस्य शरीरं क्षपयतः, शुन इव निजदारपराङ्मुखस्य जघन्यकर्मलग्नमात्मानं ताडयतः, प्रेतस्येवानुचितभूमिदीयमानान्नपिण्डस्य, बलिभुज इव जिह्वालौल्योपयुक्तपुरुषवर्चसो वृथा विहितायुषो जीवतः, श्मशानपादपानिव पिशाचस्य दग्धभूत्या परुषीकृतान्राजवल्लभानुपसर्पतः, विपरीतजिह्वाजनितमाधुर्यैरोष्ठमात्रप्रकटितरागै राजशुकालापैः शिशोरिव मुग्धविलोभ्यमानस्य, वेतालस्येव नरेन्द्रप्रभावाविष्टस्य न किंचिन्नाचरतः, चित्रधनुष इवालीकगुणाध्यारोपणैकक्रियानित्यनम्रस्य निर्वाणतेजसः, संमार्जनीसमुपार्जितरजसोऽवकरकूटस्येव निर्माल्यवाहिनः, कफविकारिण इव दिने दिने कटुकैरुद्वेज्यमानस्य, सौगतस्येवार्थशून्यविज्ञप्तिजनितवैराग्यस्य काषायाण्यभिलषतः, निशास्वपि मातृबलिपिण्डस्येव दिक्षु विक्षिप्यमाणस्य, अशौचगतस्येव कुशयनजनितसमधिकतरदुःखवृत्तेः, तुलायन्त्रस्येव पश्चात्कृतगौरवस्य तोयार्थमपि नमतः, अतिकृपणस्य शिरसा केवलेनासन्तुष्टस्य वचसापि पादौ स्पृशतः, निर्दयवेत्रिवेत्रताडनत्रस्तयेव त्रपया त्यक्तस्य, दैन्यसङ्कोचितहृदयहृतावकाशयेवाहोपुरुषिकया परिवर्जितस्य, कुत्सितकर्माङ्गीकरणकुपितयेवोन्नत्या वियुक्तस्य, धनश्रद्धया क्लेशानुपार्जयतः, स्ववृद्धिबुद्ध्यावमानं वर्धयतो मूढस्य, सत्यपि विविधकुसुमाधिवाससुरभिणि वने तृष्णाञ्जलिमुपरचयतः, कुलपुत्रस्यापि कृतागस इव भीतभीतस्य समीपमुपसर्पतः, दर्शनीयस्याप्यालेख्यकुसुमस्येव निष्फलजन्मनः, विदुषोऽपि वैधेयस्येवापशब्दमुखस्य, शक्तिमतोऽपि श्वित्रिण इव सङ्कोचितकरयुगलस्य, समसमुत्कर्षेषु निरघ्निपच्यमानस्य, नीचसमीकरणेषु निरुच्छ्वासं म्रियमाणस्य, परिभवैस्तृणीकृतस्य, दुःखानिलेनानिर्वृतेः, ज्वलतो भक्तस्याप्यभक्तस्य, निरूष्मणः सन्तापयतो बन्धून्विमानस्याप्यगतिकस्य, च्युतगौरवस्याप्यधस्ताद्गच्छतः, निःसत्त्वस्यापि महामांसविक्रयं कुर्वतः, निर्मदस्याप्यस्वतन्त्रवृत्तेरयोगिनोऽपि ध्यानवशीकृतात्मनः शय्योत्थायं प्रणमतो दग्धमुण्डस्य गोत्रविदूषकस्य नक्तंदिनं नृत्यतो मनस्विजनं हासयतः, कुलाङ्गारस्य वंशं दहतः, नृपशोः तृणेऽपि लब्धे कन्धरामवनमयतः, जठरपरिपूरणमात्रप्रयोजनजन्मनो मांसपिण्डस्य गर्भरोगस्य

---

१ '०प्ररोठदारुमयदेहस्येव द्रविणा–' ब. २ 'विवृत' ब.

मातुः,अपुण्यानां कर्मणामाचरणाद्भृतकस्य किं प्रायश्चित्तम्, का प्रतिपत्तिक्रिया, क्व गतस्य शान्तिः, कीदृशं जीवितम्, कः पुरुषाभिमानः, किंनामानो विलासाः, कीदृशी भोगश्रद्धा, प्रबलपङ्क इव सर्वमधस्तान्नयति दारुणो दासशब्दः। धिक्तदुच्छ्वसितमुपयातु[1] तद्धनं निधनमभवनिर्भूतेरस्तु तस्याः नमो भगवद्भ्यस्तेभ्यः सुखेभ्यस्तस्यायमञ्जलिरैश्वर्यस्य तिष्ठतु दूर एव सा श्रीः शिवं स परिच्छदः करोतु यदर्थमुत्तमाङ्गं गां गमिष्यति[2] मुखप्रियरतः क्लीबः पूतिमांसमयः कृमिरगण्यमानो नरकः, पादरजोधूसरोत्तमाङ्गो जङ्गमः पादपीठः, पुंस्कोकिलः काकुक्वणितेषु, शिखी सुखकरकेकासु, स्थूलकूर्मः क्रोडकषणेषु, श्वा नीचचाटुकरणेषु, वेणुर्मूर्च्छनासु, वेश्याकायः करणबन्धक्लेशेषु, पलालं सत्त्वशालिषु, कृकलासः[3] शिरोविडम्बनासु, जाहक आत्मसङ्कोचनेषु, प्रतिपादकः पादसंवाहनासु, कन्दुकः करतलताडनेषु, वीणादण्डः कोणाभिघातेषु, वराकः सेवकोऽपि मर्त्यमध्ये राजिलोऽपि वा भोगी पुलाकोऽपि वा कलमः वरं क्षणमपि कृता मानवर्ता[4] मानवता न मतो नमतस्त्रैलोक्याधिराज्योपभोगोऽपि मनस्विनः। तदेवमभिनन्दितास्मदीयप्रणयो देवोऽपि दिवसैः कतिपयैरेव परागतः प्राग्ज्योतिषेश्वर इति करोतु चेतसि' इत्युक्त्वा तूष्णीमभूदचिराच्च नमस्कृत्य निर्जगाम।

राजापि रजनीं तां कुमारदर्शनौत्सुक्यस्वीकृतहृदयः समनैषीत्। आत्मार्पणं हि महताममूलमन्त्रमयं वशीकरणम्। प्रभाते च प्रभूतं प्रतिप्राभृतं प्रधानप्रतिदूताधिष्ठितं दत्त्वा हंसवेगं प्राहिणोत्। आत्मनापि ततः प्रभृति प्रयाणकैरनवरतैरभ्यमित्रं प्रावर्तत। कदाचित्तु राज्यवर्धनभुजबलोपार्जितमशेषं मालवराजसाधनमादायागतं समीप एवावासितं लेखहारकाद्भण्डिमश्रृणोत्। श्रुत्वा चाभिनवीभूतभ्रातृशोकहुताशनः कातरहृदयो बभूव मूर्च्छान्धकारमिव विवेशातिष्ठच्च समुत्सृष्टसकलव्यापारः प्रतीहारनिवारणनिभृतनिःशब्दपरिजने निजमन्दिरे सराजकपरिवारस्तदागमनमुदीक्षमाणो मुहूर्तम्।

अथ भण्डिरेकेनैव वाजिना कतिपयकुलपुत्रपरिवृतो मलिनवासा रिपुशरशल्यपूरितेन निखातबहुलोहकीलकपरिकररक्षितस्फुटनेनेव हृदयेन, हृदयलग्नैः स्वामिसत्कृतैरिव श्मश्रुभिः शुचं समुपदर्शयन्, दूरीकृतव्यायामशिथिलभुजदण्डदोलायमानमङ्गलवलयैकशेषालङ्कृतिः, अनादरोपयुक्तताम्बूलविरलरागेण शोकदहनदह्यमानस्य हृदयस्याङ्गारेणेव दीर्घनिश्वासवेगनिर्गतेनाधरेण शुष्यता, स्वामिविरहविधृतजीवितापराधवैलक्ष्यादिव बाष्पवारिपटलेन पटेनेव प्रावृतवदनः, विशन्निव दुर्बलीभूतैः स्वाङ्गमपत्रपयाङ्गैः, वमन्निव च व्यर्थीभूतभुजोष्माणमायतैर्निश्वसितैः, पातकीव, अपराधीव, द्रोहीव, मुषित

---

१ 'उपयातु निधनं धनम्' ब. २ 'गमिष्यत्यशापानुग्रहक्षमस्तपस्वी मुख–' ब.
३ 'कृकलासः······सङ्कोचनेषु' इत्येतत् 'नीचचाटुकरणेषु' इत्यस्यानन्तरं ब–पुस्तके.
४ 'मानवताम्' ब.

इव, छलित इव, यूथपतिपतनविषण्ण इव वेगदण्डवारणः, सूर्यास्तमयनिःश्रीक इव कमलाकरः, दुर्योधननिधनदुर्मना इव द्रौणिः, अपहृतरत्न इव सागरो राजद्वारमाजगाम। अवतीर्य च तुरङ्गमादवनतमुखो विवेश राजमन्दिरम्। दूरादेव च विमुक्ताक्रन्दः पपात पादयोः।

अवनिपतिरपि दृष्ट्वा तमुत्थाय विरलैः पदैः प्रत्युद्गम्योत्थाप्य च गाढमुपगुह्य कण्ठे करुणमतिचिरं रुरोद। शिथिलीभूतमन्युवेगश्च पुरेव पुनरागत्य निजासने निषसाद। प्रथमप्रक्षालितमुखे च भण्डौ मुखमक्षालयत्। समतिक्रान्ते च कियत्यपि काले भ्रातृमरणवृत्तान्तमप्राक्षीत्। अथाकथयच्च यथावृत्तमखिलं भण्डिः। अथ नरपतिस्तमुवाच—'राज्यश्रीव्यतिकरः कः' इति। स पुनरवादीत्—'देव, देवभूयं गते देवे राज्यवर्धने गुप्तनाम्ना च गृहीते कुशस्थले देवी राज्यश्रीः परिभ्रश्य बन्धनाद्विन्ध्याटवीं सपरिवारा प्रविष्टेति लोकतो वार्तामश्रृणवम्। अन्वेष्टारस्तु तां प्रति प्रभूताः प्रहिता जना नाद्यापि निवर्तन्ते' इति। तच्चाकर्ण्य भूपतिरब्रवीत्—'किमन्यैरनुपदिभिः यत्र सा तत्र परित्यक्तान्यकृत्यः स्वयमहं यास्यामि। भवानपि कटकमादाय प्रवर्ततां गौडाभिमुखम्।' इत्युक्त्वा चोत्थाय स्नानभुवमगात्। कारितशोकश्मश्रुवपनकर्मणा च महाप्रतीहारभवनस्नातेन शारीरिकवसनकुसुमाङ्गरागालङ्कारप्रेषणप्रकटितप्रसादेन भण्डिना सार्धमभुक्त निनाय च तेनैव सह वासरम्।

अथापरेद्युरुषस्येव भण्डिर्भूपालमुपसृत्य व्यज्ञापयत्—'पश्यतु देवः श्रीराज्यवर्धनभुजबलार्जितं साधनं सपरिबर्हं मालवराजस्य' इति। नरपतिना स 'एवं क्रियताम्' इत्यभ्यनुज्ञातो दर्शयाम्बभूव। तद्यथा—अनवरतगलितमदमदिरामोदमुखरमधुकरजूटजटिलकरटपट्टपङ्किलगण्डान् गण्डशैलानिव जङ्गमान् गम्भीरगर्जितरवाञ्जलधरानिव महीमवतीर्णानुत्फुल्लसप्तच्छदवनामोदमुचः शरद्दिवसानिव पुञ्जीभूताननेकसहस्रसंख्यान्करिणः, चारुचामीकरचित्रचामरमण्डलमनोहरांश्च हरिणरंहसो हरीन्, बालातपविसरवर्षिणां च किरणैरनेकेन्द्रायुधीकृतदशदिशामलङ्काराणां विशेषान्, विस्मयकृतः स्मरोन्मादितमालवीकुचपरिमलदुर्ललितांश्च[1] निजज्योत्स्नापूरप्लावितदिगन्तानपि तारान्हारान्, उडुपतिपादसञ्चयशुचीनि निजयशांसीव बालव्यजनानि, जातरूपमयनालं च निवासपुण्डरीकमिव श्रियः श्वेतातपत्रम्, अप्सरस इव बहुसमररससाहसानुरागावतीर्णा वारविलासिनीः, सिंहासनशयनासन्दीप्रभृतीनि राज्योपकरणानि, कालायसनिगडनिश्चलीकृतचरणयुगलं च सकलं मालवराजलोकमशेषांश्च ससंख्यालेख्यपत्रान् सालङ्कारापीडपीडान्[2] कोषकलशान्। अथालोच्य तत्सर्वमवनिपालः स्वीकर्तुं यथाधिकारमादिक्षदध्यक्षान्। अन्यस्मिंश्चाहनि हयैः स्वसारमन्वेष्टुमुच्चचाल विन्ध्याटवीमवाप च परिमितैरेव प्रयाणकैस्ताम्।

---

१ 'कालकलाकलापे' ब. २ सालङ्कारपेडापीडान्' ब.

अथ प्रविशन्दूरादेव दह्यमानषष्टिकबुसविसरविसारिविभावसूनां वन्यधान्यबीजधानीनां धूमेन धूसरिमाणमादधानैः, शुष्कशाखासञ्चयरचितगोवाटवेष्टितविकटवटैः, व्यापादितवत्सरूपकरोषरचितै[1]र्व्याघ्रयन्त्रैः, [2]अयन्त्रितवनपालहठह्रियमाणपरग्रामीणकाष्ठिककुठारैः, गहनतरुषण्डनिर्मितचामुण्डामण्डपैर्वनप्रदेशैः प्रकाश्यमानम्, अटवीप्रायप्रान्ततया कुटुम्बभरणाकुलैः कुद्दालप्रायकृषिभिः कृषीवलैरबलीवर्दैरवलद्भिरुच्चभागभाषितेन भज्यमानभूरि[3]शालिखलक्षेत्रखण्डलकम्, अल्पावकाशैश्च [4]काशिलैः कालायसैरिव कृष्णमृत्तिकाकठिनैः स्थानस्थानस्थापितस्थाणूत्थितस्थूलपल्लवैः दुरुपगमश्यामाकप्ररूढिभिरलम्बुसबहुलैरविरहितकोकिलाक्षक्षुपैर्विरलविरलैः केदारैः कृच्छ्रकृष्यमाणैर्नातिप्रभूतप्रवृत्तगतागताप्रहतभुवमुपक्षेत्रमुपरचितैरुच्चैर्मञ्चैश्च सूच्यमानश्वापदोपद्रवम्, दिशि दिशि च प्रतिमार्गद्रुमकृतानां पथिकपादप्रस्फोटनधूलिधूसरैर्नव[5]पल्लवैर्लाञ्छितच्छायानाम्, अटवीसुलभसालकुसुमस्तबकाञ्चितनवखातकूपिकोपकण्ठप्रतिष्ठितनागस्फुटानामच्छिद्रकटकल्पितकुटीरकाणाम्, कुटिलकीटवेणीवेष्ट्यमानशक्तुशारशरावश्रेणीश्रितानामध्वगजनजग्धजम्बूफलास्थिशबलसमीपभुवामुद्धूलितधूलीकदम्बस्तबकप्रकरपुलकिनीनाम्, कण्टकितकर्करीचक्राक्रान्तकाष्ठमञ्चिकामुषिततृषाम्, तिम्यत्तलशीतलसिकतिलकलशीशमितश्रमाणामाश्यानशैवलश्यामलितालिञ्जरजायमानजलजडिम्नामुदकुम्भाकृष्टपाटलशर्कराशकलशिशिरीकृतदिशाम्, घटमुखघटितकटह्रारपाटलापुष्पपुटानाम्, शीकरपुलकितपल्लवपूलीपाल्यमानशोष्यसरसशिशुसहकारफलजूटीजटिलै[6]स्स्थाणूनाम्, विश्राम्यत्कार्पटिकपेटकपरिपाटीपीयमानपयसामटवीप्रवेशप्रपाणां शैत्येन त्याजयन्तमिव ग्रैष्ममुष्माणं क्वचिदन्यत्र ग्राहयन्तमिवाङ्गारीयदारुसंग्रहदाहिभिः व्योकारैः, सर्वतश्च प्रातिवेश्यविषयवासिनां समासन्नग्राम[7]गृहस्थापितस्थविरपरिपाल्यमानपाथेयस्थगितेन कृतदारुणदारुव्यायामयोग्याङ्गाभ्यङ्गेन स्कन्धाध्यासितकठोरकुठारकण्ठलम्बमानप्रातराशपुटेन पाटच्चरप्रत्यवायप्रतिपन्नपटच्चरेण कालवेत्रकत्रिगुणव्रततिवलयपाशग्रथितग्रीवाग्रथितैः पत्रवीटावृतमुखैः पीतकूटैरूढवारिणा पुरःसरवलद्बलीवर्दयुगसरेण नैकटिककुटुम्बिकलोकेन काष्ठसंग्रहार्थमटवीं प्रविशता, श्वापदव्यधनव्यवधानबहलीसमारोपितकुटीकृतकूटपाशैश्च गृहीतमृगतन्तुतन्त्रीजालवलयवागुरैः बहिर्व्याधैर्विचरद्भिः, अंसावसक्तवीतंसव्यालम्बमानबालपाशिकैश्च संगृहीतग्राहकक्रकरकपिञ्जलादिपञ्जरकैः शाकुनिकैः सञ्चरद्भिः, च्युत[8]लासकलेशलिप्तलतावधूलट्वालम्पटानां च पेटकैः पाशिकशिशूनामटद्भिः, तृणस्तम्बान्तरिततित्तिरितरलायमानकौलेयककुलचाटुकारैश्च विहगमृगयां मृगयुयुवभिः क्रीडद्भिः, परिणतचक्रवाककण्ठकषायरुचां शीधव्यानां वल्कलानां

---

१ 'रोषाविष्टगोपालकल्पितव्याघ्र–' ब. २ 'यन्त्रित' अ–क. ३ 'भूरिखिलक्षेत्र०' ब. ४ 'कापिलैः' अ. ५ 'वनपल्लवैः' ब. ६ 'स्थूणानाम्' ब. ७ 'ग्रामगृहस्थगृह०' ब. ८ 'संचरद्भिश्च्युतच्युत' ब.

कलापान्, नातिचिरोद्धृतानां च धातुत्विषां धातकीकुसुमानां गोणीरगणिताः पिचव्यानां चातसीगणपट्टमूलकानां पुष्कलान्सम्भारान्, भारांश्च मधुनो माक्षिकस्य मयूराङ्गजस्याक्लिष्टमधूच्छिष्टचक्रमालानां लम्बमानलामज्जक[1]जूटजटानामपत्वचां खदिरकाष्ठानां कुष्ठस्य कठोरकेशरिसटाभारबभ्रुणश्च रोध्रस्य भूयसो भारकान् लोकेनादाय व्रजता प्रविचितविविधवनफलपूरितपिटकमस्तकाभिश्चाभ्यर्णग्रामगत्वरीभिस्त्वरमाणाभिर्विक्रयचिन्ताव्यग्राभिर्ग्रामेयिकाभिर्व्याप्तदिगन्तरम्, इतस्ततश्च युक्तशूरशकुरशाक्कराणां पुराणपांसूत्किरकरीषकूटवाहिनीनां धूर्गतधूलिधूसरसैरि[2]कसरोषस्वरसार्यमाणानां संक्रीडच्चटुलचक्रचीत्कारिणीनां शकटश्रेणीनां सम्पातैः सम्पाद्यमानदुर्बलोर्वीविरूक्षक्षेत्रसंस्कारम्, आरक्षक्षिप्तक्षिप्रदान्तवाहकदण्डोड्डीयमानहरिणहेलालङ्घिततुङ्गवैणववृतिभिश्च निखातगौरकरङ्कशङ्कुशङ्कितशशकशकलिततुङ्गशुङ्गैः प्रयत्नप्रभृतविशङ्कटविटपैर्वाटैरैक्षवैर्बहुभिः श्यामायमानोपकण्ठम्, अतिविप्रकृष्टान्तरैर्मरकतस्निग्धस्नुहावाटवेष्टितैः कार्मुककर्मण्यवंशविटपसङ्कटैः कण्टकितकरञ्जराजिदुष्प्रवेश्यैः उरुबूकवचावङ्ककसुरससूरणशिग्रुग्रन्थिपर्णगवेधुकागर्मुद्गुल्मगहनगृहवाटिकैः, निखातोच्चकाष्ठारोपितकाष्ठालुकलताप्रतानविहितच्छायैः, परिमण्डलबदरीमण्डपकतलनिखातखादिरकीलबद्धवत्सरूपैः; कथमपि कुक्कुटरटितानुमीयमानसंनिवेशैरङ्ग[3]नागस्तिस्तम्बतलविरचितक्षिप्रपक्षिपूपिकावापिकैर्विकीर्णबदरपाटलपटलैः, वेणु[4]पोटदलनलशरमयवृतिविहितभित्तिभिः, किंशुकरोचनारचितमण्डलमण्डपबल्वजबद्धाङ्गारराशिभिः, शाल्मलिफलतूलसञ्चयबहुलैः, संनिहितनलशालिशालूकखण्डकुमुदबीजवेणुतण्डुलैः, सङ्गृहीतमालबीजैः, भस्त्रमलिनम्लानकाश्मर्यकूटव्याधतकटैराश्यानराजादनमदनफलस्फीतैर्मधूकासवमद्यप्रायैः, कुसुम्भकुम्भगण्डकुसूलैरविरहितराजमाषत्रपुषकर्कटिकाकूष्माण्डालाबुबीजैः, पोष्यमाणवनबिडालमालुधाननकुलशालिजातजातकादिभिरटवीकुटुम्बिनां गृहैरुपेतं वनग्रामकं ददर्श तत्रैव[5] चावसदिति।

इति श्रीबाणभट्टकृतौ [6]हर्षचरिते छत्रलब्धिर्नाम

सप्तम उच्छ्वासः।

---

१ 'लामज्जकमुञ्जजूटक' ब. २ 'सैरिभ' अ-क. ३ 'अङ्गनाशस्तिस्तम्भ...क्षिप्रपूपिका' अ-क. ४ 'पोटपटलनलकलितशरमय' ब. ५ 'तत्रैव च तं दिवसमत्यवाहयत्' ब. ६ '०कृते हर्षचरिते सप्तम' क; 'इति श्रीमहाकविचक्रचूडामणिश्रीबाणभट्टविरचिते श्रीहर्षचरिते महाकाव्ये छत्रलब्धिर्नाम सप्तम उच्छ्वासः सम्पूर्णः' ब.

अष्टम उच्छ्वासः।

सहसा सम्पादयता मनोरथप्रार्थितानि वस्तूनि।
दैवेनापि क्रियते भव्यानां पूर्वसेवेव ॥ १ ॥
विद्वज्जनसम्पर्को नष्टेष्टज्ञातिदर्शनाभ्युदयः।
कस्य न सुखाय भवने भवति महारत्नलाभश्च ॥ २ ॥

अथापरेद्युरुत्थाय पार्थिवस्तस्माद्ग्रामकान्निर्गत्य विवेश विन्ध्याटवीम्। आट च तस्यामितश्चेतश्च सुबहून्दिवसान्। एकदा तु भूपतेर्भ्रमत एवाटविकसामन्तशरभकेतोः सूनुर्व्याघ्रकेतुर्नाम कुतोऽपि कज्जलश्यामलश्यामलतावलयेनाधिललाटमुच्चैः कृतमौलिबन्धम्, अन्धकारिणीमकारणभुवा भ्रुकुटिभङ्गेन त्रिशाखेन त्रियामामिव साहससहचारिणीं ललाटस्थलीं सदा समुद्वहन्तम्, अवतंसितैकशुकपक्षकप्रभाहरितायमानेन पिनद्धकाचरकाचमणिकर्णिकेन श्रवणेन शोभमानम्, किंचिच्चुल्लस्य प्रविरलपक्ष्मणश्चक्षुषः सहजेन रागरोचिषा रसायनरसोपयुक्तं तारक्षवं क्षतजमिव क्षरन्तम्, अवनाटनासिकम्, चिपिटाधरम्, चिकिनचिबुकम्, अहीनहनूत्कटकपोलकूटास्थिपर्यन्तमीषदवाग्रग्रीवाबन्धम्, स्कन्नस्कन्धार्धभागम्, अनवरतकोदण्डकुण्डलीकरणकर्कशव्यायामविस्तारितेनांसलेनोरसा हसन्तमिव तटशिलाप्रथिमानं विन्ध्यगिरेः, अजगरगरीयसा च भुजयुगलेन लघयन्तं तुहिनशैलशालद्रुमाणां द्राघिमाणम्, वराहबालवलितबन्धनाभिर्नागदमनजूटिकावाटिकाभिर्जटिलीकृतपृष्ठे प्रकोष्ठे प्रतिष्ठां गतं गोदन्तमणिचित्रं त्रापुपं वलयं बिभ्राणम्, अतुन्दिलमपि तुण्डिभम्, अहीरमणीचर्मनिर्मितपट्टिकयोश्चित्रचित्रकत्वक्त्सारकितपरिवारया सङ्कुब्जाजिनजालकितया शृङ्गमयमसृणमुष्टिभागभास्वरया पारदरसलेशलिप्तसमस्तमस्तकया कृपाण्या करालितविसङ्कटकटिप्रदेशम्, प्रथमयौवनोल्लिख्यमानमध्यभागभ्रष्टमांसभरिताविव स्थवीयसावूरुदण्डौ दधतम्, अच्छभल्लचर्ममयेन भल्लीप्रायप्रभूतशरभृता शबलशार्दूलचर्मपट्टपीडितेनालिकुलकालकम्बललोम्ना पृष्ठभागभाजा भस्त्राभरणेन पल्लवितमिव कार्श्यमुपदर्शयन्तम्, उत्तरत्रिभागोत्तंसितचाषपिच्छचारुशिखरे खदिरजटानिर्माणे खरप्राणे प्रचुरमयूरपित्तपत्रलताचित्रितत्वचि त्वचिसारगुरुणि वामस्कन्धाध्यासितधनुषि दोषि लम्बमानेनावाक्शिरसा शितशरकृतैकनलकविवरप्रवेशितेतरजङ्घाजनितस्वस्तिकबन्धेन बन्धूकलोहितरुधिरराजिरञ्जितघ्राणवर्त्मना वपुर्विततिव्यक्तविभाव्यमानकोमलक्रोडरोमशुक्लिम्ना शशेन शिताटनीशिखाग्रग्रथितग्रीवेण चापावृतचञ्चूत्तानतान्त्रतालुना तित्तिरिणा वर्णकमुष्टिमिव मृगयाया दर्शयन्तम्, विषमविषदूषितवदनेन च विकर्णेन कृष्णाहिनेव मूलगृहीतेन व्यग्रदक्षिणकराग्रम्, जङ्गममिव

---

१ 'पूर्वसेवैव' ब. २ 'अहीरणि०' क. ३ 'अच्छवलचर्मयेन (?)' ब. ४ 'विवर्णेन' अ.

गिरितटतमालपादपम्, यन्त्रोल्लिखितमश्मसारस्तम्भमिव भ्रमन्तम्, अञ्जनशिलाच्छेदमिव चलन्तम्, अयःसारमिव गिरेर्विन्ध्यस्य गलन्तम्, पीकलं करिकुलानाम्, कालपाशं कुरङ्गयूथानाम्, धूमकेतुं मृगराजचक्राणाम्, महानवमीमहं महिषमण्डलानाम्, हृदयमिव हिंसायाः, फलमिव पापस्य, कारणमिव कलिकालस्य, कामुकमिव कालरात्रेः, शबरयुवानमादायाजगाम। दूरे च स्थापयित्वा विज्ञापयांबभूव—'देव, सर्वस्यास्य विन्ध्यस्य स्वामी सर्वपल्लीपतीनां प्राग्रहरः शबरसेनापतिर्भूकम्पो नाम। तस्यायं निर्घातनामा स्वस्त्रीयः सकलस्यास्य विन्ध्यकान्ताराररण्यस्य पर्णानामप्यभिज्ञः किमुत प्रदेशानाम्। एनं पृच्छतु देवः योग्योऽयमाज्ञां कर्तुम्।' इति कथिते च निर्घातस्तु क्षितितलनिहितमौलिः प्रणाममकरोदुपनिन्ये च तित्तिरिणा सह शशोपायनम्। अवनिपतिस्तु संमानयन्स्वयमेव तमप्राक्षीत्—अङ्ग, अभिज्ञा यूयमस्य सर्वस्योद्देशस्य। विहारशीलाश्च दिवसेष्वेतेषु भवन्तः। सेनापतेर्वान्यस्य वा तदनुजीविनः कस्यचिदुदाररूपा नार्यागता भवेद्दर्शनगोचरम्' इति।

निर्घातस्तु भूपालालापनप्रसादेनात्मानं बहुमन्यमानः प्रणनाम दर्शितादरं च व्यज्ञापयत्—'देव प्रायेणात्र हरिण्योऽपि नापरिगताः सञ्चरन्ति सेनापतेः कुत एव नार्यो नाप्येवंरूपा काचिदबला। तथापि देवादेशादिदानीमन्वेषणं प्रति प्रतिदिनमनन्यकृत्यैः क्रियते यत्नः। इतश्चार्धगव्यूतिमात्र एव मुनिमहिते महति महीधरमालामूलरुहि महीरुहां षण्डे पिण्डपाती प्रभूतान्तेवासिपरिवृतः पाराशरी दिवाकरमित्रनामा गिरिनदीमाश्रित्य प्रतिवसति स यदि विन्देद्वार्ताम्' इति। तच्छ्रुत्वा नरपतिरचिन्तयत्—'श्रूयते हि तत्रभवतः सुगृहीतनाम्नः स्वर्गतस्य ग्रहवर्मणो बालमित्रं मैत्रायणीयस्त्रयीं विहाय ब्राह्मणायनो विद्वानुत्पन्नसमाधिः सौगते मते युवैव काषायाणि गृहीतवानिति। प्रायशश्च जनस्य जनयति सुहृदपि दृष्टो भृशमाश्वासम्। अभिगमनीयाश्च गुणाः सर्वस्य। कस्य न प्रतीक्ष्यो मुनिभावः। भगवती वैधेयेऽपि धर्मगृहिणी गरिमाणमापादयति प्रव्रज्या किं पुनः सकलजनमनोमुषि विदुषि जने। यतो नः कुतूहलि हृदयमभूत्सततमस्य दर्शनं प्रति प्रासङ्गिकमेवेदमापतितमतिकल्याणं पश्यामः प्रयत्नप्रार्थितदर्शनं जनम्' इति। प्रकाशं चाब्रवीत्—'अङ्ग, समुपदिश तमुद्देशं यत्रास्ते स पिण्डपाती' इति। एवमुक्त्वा च तेनैवोपदिश्यमानवर्त्मा प्रावर्तत गन्तुम्।

अथ क्रमेण गच्छत एव तस्य अनवकेशिनः, कुड्मलितकर्णिकाराः, प्रचुरचम्पकाः, स्फीतफलेग्रहयः, फलभरभरितनमेरवः, नीलदलनलदनारिकेलनिकराः, हरिकेसरसरलपरिकराः, कोरकनिकुरुम्बरोमाञ्चितकुरबकराजयः, रक्ताशोकपल्लवलावण्यलिप्यमानदशदिशः, प्रविकसितकेसररजोविसरबध्यमानवासरधूसरिमाणः, स्वरजःसिकतिलतिलकतलाः, प्रविचलितहिङ्गवः,

१ 'पालकम्' ख. २ 'बध्यमानघारुधू०' अ-क.

लोकोचितेन सर्वाभिभाविना महानुभावाभोगभाजा भ्राजिष्णुना भूपतेरप्राकृतेनाकारविशेषेण तेन चाभिजात्यप्रकाशकेन गरीयसा प्रश्रयेण चाह्लादितश्चक्षुषि च चेतसि च युगपदग्रहीत् । वीरस्वभावोऽपि च सम्पादितससंभ्रमाभ्युत्थानः सङ्कलय्य किंचिदुद्गमनकेन विलोलं विलम्बमानं वामांसाच्चीवरपटान्तमुत्क्षिप्यानेकाभयदानदीक्षादक्षिणो दक्षिणं महापुरुषलक्षणलेखाप्रशस्तं हस्तं स्निग्धमधुरया वाचा सगौरवमारोग्यदानेन राजानमन्वग्रहीत् । अभ्यनन्दच्च स्वागतगिरा गुरुमिवाभ्यागतं बहु मन्यमानः स्वेनासनेनाध्वमत्रेति निमन्त्रयांचक्रे । पार्श्वे स्थितं च शिष्यमब्रवीत्—'आयुष्मन्, उपानय कमण्डलुना पादोदकम्' इति । राजा त्वचिन्तयत्—'अलोहः खलु संयमनपाशः सौजन्यमभिजातानाम् । स्थाने खलु तत्रभवान्गुणानुरागी ग्रहवर्मा बहुशो वर्णितवानस्य गुणान्' इति । प्रकाशं चावभाषे—'भगवन्, दर्शनपुण्यानुगृहीतस्य मम पुनरुक्त इवायमार्यप्रयुक्तः प्रतिभात्यनुग्रहः । चक्षुष्प्रमाणप्रसादस्वीकृतस्य च परकरणमिवासनादिदानोपचारचेष्टितम् । अतिभूमिर्भूमिरेवासनं भवादृशां[1] पुरः सम्भाषणामृताभिषेकप्रक्षालितसकलवपुषश्च मे प्रदेशवृत्तिः । पाद्यमप्यपार्थकम् । आसतां भवन्तो यथासुखम् । आसीनोऽहम्' इत्यभिधाय क्षितावेवोपाविशत् ।

'अलंकारो हि परमार्थतः प्रभवतां प्रश्रयातिशयः, रत्नादिकस्तु शिलाभारः' इत्याकलय्य पुनः पुनरभ्यर्थ्यमानोऽपि यदा न प्रत्यपद्यत पार्थिवो वचनं तदा स्वमेवासनं पुनरपि भेजे भदन्तः । भूपतिमुखनलिननिहितनिभृतनयनयुगलनिगडनिश्चलीकृतहृदयश्च स्थित्वा कांचित्कालकलां[2] कलिकालकल्मषकालुष्यमिव क्षालयन्नमलाभिर्दन्तमयूखमालाभिर्मूलफलाभ्यवहारसम्भवमुद्वमन्निव च परिमलसुभगं विकचकुसुमपटलपाण्डुरं लतावनमवादीत्—'अद्यप्रभृति न केवलमयमनिन्द्यो वन्द्योऽपि प्रकाशितसत्सारः संसारः । किं नाम नालोक्यते जीवद्भिरद्भुतं येन रूपमचिन्तितोपनतमिदं दृक्पथमुपगतम् । एवंविधैरनुमीयन्ते जन्मान्तरावस्थितसुकृतानि हृदयोत्सवैः । इहापि जन्मनि दत्तमेवास्माकममुना तपःक्लेशेन फलमसुलभदर्शनं दर्शयता देवानां प्रियम् । आ तृप्तेः पीतममृतमीक्षणाभ्याम् । जातं निरुत्कण्ठं मानसं निर्वृत्तिसुखस्य । महद्भिः पुण्यैर्विना न विश्राम्यन्ति सज्जने त्वादृशि दृशः । सुदिवसः स यस्मिञ्जातोऽसि । सा सुजाता जननी या सकलजीवलोकजीवितजनकमजनयदायुष्मन्तम् । पुण्यवन्ति पुण्यान्यपि तानि येषामसि परिणामः । सुकृततपसस्ते परमाणवो ये तव परिगृहीतसर्वावयवाः । तत्सुभगं सौभाग्यमाश्रितोऽसि येन । भव्यः स पुरुषभावो भवत्यवस्थितो यः । यत्सत्यं मुमुक्षोरपि मे पुण्यभाजमालोक्य पुनः श्रद्धा जाता मनुजजन्मनि । नेच्छद्भिरप्यस्माभिर्दृष्टः कुसुमायुधः । कृतार्थमद्य चक्षुर्वनदेव-

---

१ 'अतिभूमिरेव भवादृशाम्' अ-क. २ 'कालकक्ष्याम्' ब.

तानाम् । अद्य सफलं जन्म वनपादपानां येषामसि गतो गोचरम् । अमृतमयस्य भवतो वचसां माधुर्यं कार्यमेव । अस्य त्वीदृशे शैशवे विनयस्योपाध्यायं ध्यायन्नपि न सम्भावयामि । भुवि सर्वथा शून्य आसीदजाते दीर्घायुषि गुणग्रामः । धन्यः स भूभृद्यस्य वंशे मणिरिव मुक्तामयः सम्भूतोऽसि । एवंविधस्य च पुण्यवतः कथंचित्प्राप्तस्य केन प्रियं समाचराम इति पारिप्लवं चेतो नः । सकलवनचरसार्थसाधारणस्य[1] कन्दमूलफलस्य गिरिसरिदम्भसो वा के वयम् । अपरोपकरणीकृतस्तु कायकलिरयमस्माकम् । सर्वस्वमवशिष्टमिष्टातिथ्याय । स्वायत्ताश्च विद्यन्ते विद्याबिन्दवः कतिचित् । उपयोगं तु न प्रीतिर्विचारयति । यदि च नोपरुणद्धि कश्चित्कार्यलवमरक्षणीयाक्षरं वा कथनीयं तत्कथयतु भवाञ्छ्रोतुमभिलषति हृदयं सर्वमिदं नः । केन कृत्यातिभारेण भव्यो भूषितवान्भूमिमेतामभ्रमणयोग्याम् । कियदवधिर्वायं शून्याटवीपर्यटनक्लेशः कल्याणराशेः । कस्माच्च सन्तप्तरूपेव ते तनुरियमसन्तापार्हा विभाव्यते' इति ।

राजा तु सादरतरमब्रवीत्—'आर्य, दर्शितसंभ्रमेणानेन मधुरसविसरमसृतमिव[2] हृदयधृतिकरमनवरतं वर्षता वचसैव ते सर्वमनुष्ठितम् । धन्योऽस्मि यदेवमभ्यर्हितमनुपचरणीयमपि मान्यो मन्यते माम् । अस्य च महावनभ्रमणपरिक्लेशस्य कारणमवधारयतु मतिमान् । मम हि विनष्टनिखिलेष्टबन्धोर्जीवितानुबन्धस्य निबन्धनमेकैव यवीयसी स्वसावशेषा[3] । सापि भर्तुर्वियोगाद्वैरिपरिभवभयाक्रमन्ती कथमपि विन्ध्यवनमिदम्, अशुभशबरबलबहुलम्, अगणितगजकुलकलिलम्, अपरिमितमृगपतिशरभभयम्, उरुमहिषमुषितपथिकगमनम्, अतिनिशितशरकुशपरुषम्, अवटशतविषममविशत् । अतस्तामन्वेष्टुं[4] वयमनिशं निशिनिशि च सततमिमामटवीमटामः । न चैनामासादयामः । कथयतु च गुरुरपि यदि कदाचित्कुतश्चिद्वने चरतः श्रुतिपथमुपगता तद्वार्ता' इति ।

अथ तच्छ्रुत्वा जातोद्वेग इव भदन्तः पुनरभ्यधात्—'धीमन्, न खलु कश्चिदेवंरूपो वृत्तान्तोऽस्मानभ्युपगतवान् । अभाजनं हि वयमीदृशानां प्रियाख्यानोपायनानां भवताम्[5] ।' इत्येवं भाषमाण एव तस्मिन्नकस्मादागत्यापरः शमिनि वयसि वर्तमानः संभ्रान्तरूप इव पुरस्तादुपरचिताञ्जलिर्जातकरुणः प्रक्षरितचक्षुर्भिक्षुरभाषत—'भगवन्भदन्त, महत्करुणं वर्तते । बालैव बलवद्व्यसनाभिभूता भूतपूर्वापि कल्याणरूपा स्त्री शोकवेगविवशा वैश्वानरं विशति । सम्भावयतु तामप्रोषितप्राणां भगवान् । अभ्युपपद्यतां समुचितैः समाश्वासनैः । अनुपरतपूर्वं कृमिकीटमपि दुःखितं दयाराशेरार्यस्य गोचरगतम्' इति ।

---

१ 'सार्थासाधारणस्य' ब. २ 'विसरं धृतमिव हृदय-' ब. ३ 'अवशेषात्' ब. ४ 'अयोगादतस्ताम्' ब. ५ 'भवतम्' ब.

राजा तु जातानुजाशङ्कः सोदर्यास्नेहाद्यान्तङ्कुत इव दुःखेन दोदूयमानहृदयः कथमपि गद्गदिकागृहीतकण्ठो विकलवाग्बाष्पायमाणदृष्टिः पप्रच्छ—"पाराशरिन्, कियद्दूरे सा योषिदेवंजातीया जीवेद्वा कालमेतावन्तमिति। पृष्टा वा त्वया 'कासि, कस्यासि, कुतोऽसि, किमर्थं वनमिदमभ्युपगतासि, विशसि च किंनिमित्तमनलम्' इत्यादितः प्रभृति कात्स्न्र्येन कथ्यमानमिच्छामि श्रोतुं कथमार्यस्य गता गोचरमाकारतो वा कीदृशी" इति।

तथाभिहितस्तु भूभुजा भिक्षुराचचक्षे—'महाभाग, श्रूयताम्। अहं हि प्रत्यूषस्येवाद्य वन्दित्वा भगवन्तमनेनैव गिरिनदीरोधसा सैकतसुकुमारेण यदृच्छया विहृतवानतिदूरम्। एकस्मिंश्च वनलतागहने गिरिनदीसमीपभाजि भ्रमरीणामिव हिमहतकमलाकरकातराणां रसितं सार्यमाणानामतितारतानवर्तिनीनां वीणा[1]तन्त्रीणामिव झांकारमेकतानं नारीणां रुदितमध्रतिकरमतिकरुणमाकर्णितवानस्मि। समुपजातकृपश्च गतोऽस्मि तं प्रदेशम्। दृष्टवानस्मि च दृषत्खण्डखण्डिताङ्गुलिगलल्लोहितेन च पार्ष्णिप्रविष्टशरशलाकाशल्यशूलसङ्कोचितचक्षुषा चाध्वनीनश्रमश्वयथुनिश्चलचरणेन च स्थाणवव्रणव्यथितगुल्फबद्धभूर्जत्वचा च वातखुडखेदखञ्जजङ्घाजातज्वरेण च पांसुपाण्डुरपिण्डिकेन च खर्जूरजूटजटाजर्जरितजानुना च शतावरीविदारितोरुणा च विदारीदारिततनुदुकूलपल्लवेन चोत्कटवंशविटपकण्टककोटिपाटितकञ्चुककर्पटेन च फललोभालम्बितानम्रबदरीलताजालकैरुत्कण्टकैरुल्लिखितसुकुमारकरोदरेण च कुरङ्गशृङ्गोत्खातैः कन्दमूलफलैः कदर्थितबाहुना च ताम्बूलविरहविरसमुखखण्डितकोमलामलकीफलेन च कुशकुसुमाहतिलोहितानां श्वयतां[2]मक्ष्णां लेपीकृतमनःशिलेन च कण्टकिलताल्लूनालकक्लेशेन च केनचित्किसलयोपपादितातपत्रकृत्येन केनचित्कदलीदलव्यजनवाहिना केनचित्कमलिनीपलाशपुटगृहीताम्भसा केनचित्पाथेयीकृतमृणालपूलिकेन केनचिच्चीनांशुकदशाशिक्यनिहितनालिकेरकोशकलशीकलितरसालतैलेन[3], कतिपयावशेषशोकविक्ल[4]वकलामूककुब्जवामनबधिरबर्बराविरलेनाबलानां चक्रवालेन परिवृताम्, आपत्कालेऽपि कुलोद्गतेनेवामुच्यमानां प्रभालेपिना लावण्येन, प्रतिबिम्बितैरासन्नवनलताकिसलयैः सरसैर्दुःखक्षतैरिवान्तःपटलीक्रियमाणकायाम्, कठोरदर्भाङ्कुरक्षतक्षारिणा क्षतजेनानुसरणालक्तकेनेव रक्तचरणाम्, उष्णालेनान्यतरनारीधृतेनारविन्दिनीदलेन कृतच्छायमपि विच्छायं मुखमुद्वहन्तीम्, आकाशमपि शून्यतयातिशयानाम्, मृण्मयीमिव निश्चेतनतया, मरुन्मयीमिव निश्वाससम्पदा, पावकमयीमिव सन्तापसन्तानेन, सलिलमयीमिवास्रप्रस्रवणेन, वियन्मयीमिव निरवलम्बनतया, तडिन्मयीमिव पारिप्लवतया, शब्दमयीमिव

१ 'वर्णातन्त्रीणाम्' ब. २ 'श्वयथ्युमता–' ब. ३ 'कलितसरलतैलेन' ब. ४ 'विकलमूक' अ–क.

परिदेवितवाणीबाहुल्येन, मुक्तमुक्तांशुकरत्नकुसुमकनकपत्त्राभरणां कल्पलतामिव महावने पतिताम्, परमेश्वरोत्तमाङ्गपातदुर्ललिताङ्गां गङ्गामिव गां गताम्, वनकुसुमधूलिधूसरितपादपल्लवाम्, प्रभातचन्द्रमूर्तिमिव लोकान्तरमभिलषन्तीम्, निजजलमोक्षकदर्थितदर्शितधवलायतनेत्रशोभाम्[1], मन्दाकिनीमृणालिनीमिव परिम्लायमानाम्, दुःसहरविकिरणसंस्पर्शखेदनिमीलितां कुमुदिनीमिव दुःखेन दिवसं नयन्तीम्, दग्धदशाविसंवादितां प्रत्यूषप्रदीपशिखामिव क्षामक्षामां पाण्डुवपुषम्, पार्श्ववर्तिवारणाभियोगरक्ष्यमाणां वनकरिणीमिव महाह्रदे निमग्नाम्, प्रविष्टां वनगहने[2] ध्याने च, स्थितां तरुतले मरणे च, पतितां धात्र्युत्सङ्गे महानर्थे च, दूरीकृतां भर्त्रा सुखेन च, विरेचितां श्रमणेनायुषा च, आकुलां केशकलापेन मरणोपायेन च, विवर्णितामध्वधूलिभिरङ्गवेदनाभिश्च, दग्धां चण्डातपेन वैधव्येन च, धृतमुखीं पाणिना मौनेन च, गृहीतां प्रियसखीजनेन मन्युना च, तथा च भ्रष्टैर्बन्धुभिर्विलासैश्च, मुक्तेन श्रवणयुगलेनात्मना च, परित्यक्तैर्भूषणैः सर्वारम्भैश्च, भग्नैर्वलयैर्मनोरथैश्च, चरणलग्नाभिः परिचारिकाभिर्दर्भाङ्कुरसूचीभिश्च, हृदयविनिहितेन चक्षुषा प्रियेण च, दीर्घैः शोकश्वसितैः केशैश्च, क्षीणेन वपुषा पुण्येन च, पादयोः पतन्तीभिर्वृद्धाभिरश्रुधाराभिश्च, स्वल्पावशेषेण परिजनेन जीवितेन च, अलसामुन्मेषे, दक्षामश्रुमोक्षे, सन्ततां चिन्तासु, विच्छिन्नामाशासु, कृशां काये, स्थूलां श्वसिते, पूरितां दुःखेन, रिक्तां सत्त्वेन, अध्यासितामायासेन, शून्यां हृदयेन, निश्चलां निश्चयेन, चलितां धैर्यात्, अपि च वसतिं व्यसनानाम्, आधानमाधीनाम्, अवस्थानमनवस्थानाम्, आधारमधृतीनाम्, आवासमवसादानाम्, आस्पदमापदाम्, अभियोगमभाग्यानाम्, उद्वेगमुद्वेगानाम्, कारणं करुणायाः, पारं[3] परायत्ततायाः योषितम्। चिन्तितवानस्मि च चित्रमीदृशीमप्याकृतिमुपतापाः स्पृशन्तीति। सा तु समीपगते मयि तदवस्थापि सबहुमानमानतमौलिः प्रणतवती। अहं तु प्रबलकरुणाप्रेर्यमाणस्तामालपितुकामः पुनः कृतवान्मनसि—कथमिव महानुभावामेनामामन्त्रये। 'वत्से' इत्यतिप्रणयः, 'मातः' इति चाटु, 'भगिनि' इत्यात्मसम्भावना, 'देवि' इति परिजनालापः, 'राजपुत्रि' इत्यस्फुटम्, 'उपासिके' इति मनोरथः, 'स्वामिनि' इति भृत्यभावाभ्युपगमः, 'भद्रे' इतीतरस्त्रीसमुचितम्, 'आयुष्मति' इत्यवस्थायामप्रियम्, 'कल्याणिनि' इति दशायां विरुद्धम्, 'चन्द्रमुखि' इत्यमुनिमतम्, 'बाले' इत्यगौरवोपेतम्, 'आर्ये' इति जरारोपणम्, 'पुण्यवति' इति फलविपरीतम्, 'भवति' इति सर्वसाधारणम्। अपि च 'कासि' इत्यनभिजातम्, 'किमर्थं रोदिषि' इति दुःखकारणस्मरणकारि, 'मा रोदीः' इति शोकहेतुमनपनीय न शोभते, 'समाश्वसिहि' इति किमाभिख्य, 'स्वागतम्' इति यातयामम्, 'सुखमास्यते' इति मिथ्या। इत्येवं

१ '०धवलायित०' ब. २ 'गहनं ध्यानं च' अ-क. ३ 'पदं परायत्तयत्तताया' ब.

चिन्तयत्येव मयि तस्मात्क्षणादुत्थायान्यतरा योषिदार्यरूपेव शोकविक्लवा समुपसृत्य कतिपयपलितशारं शिरो नीत्वा महीतलमतुलहृदयसन्तापसूचकैरश्रुबिन्दुभिश्चरणयुगलं दहन्ती ममातिकृपणैरक्षरैश्च हृदयमभिहितवती—'भगवन्, सर्वसत्त्वानुकम्पिनी प्रायः प्रव्रज्या । प्रतिपन्नपरदुःखक्षपणदीक्षादक्षाश्च भवन्ति सौगताः। करुणाकुलगृहं च भगवतः शाक्यमुनेः शासनम्। सकलजनोपकारसज्जा सज्जनता जैनी। परलोकसाधनं च धर्मो मुनीनाम्। प्राणरक्षणाच्च न परं पुण्यजातं जगति गीयते जनेन । अनुकम्पाभूमयः प्रकृत्यैव युवतयः किं पुनर्विपदभिभूताः । साधुजनश्च सिद्धक्षेत्रमार्तवचसाम्[1]। यत इयं नः स्वामिनी मरणेन[2] पितुरभावेन भर्तुः प्रवासेन च भ्रातुः भ्रंशेन च शेषस्य बान्धववर्गस्यातिमृदुहृदयतयानपत्यतया च निरवलम्बना, परिभवेन च नीचारातिकृतेन प्रकृतिमनस्विनी, अमुना च महाटवीपर्यटनक्लेशेन कदर्थितसौकुमार्या, दग्धदैवदत्तैरेवंविधैर्बहुभिरुपर्युपरि व्यसनैर्विक्लवीकृतहृदया, दारुणं दुःखमपारयन्ती सोढुं निवारयन्तमनतिक्रान्तपूर्वं स्वप्नेऽप्यवगणय्य गुरुजनमनुनयन्तीरखण्डितप्रणया नर्मस्वपि समवधीर्य प्रियसखीर्विज्ञापयन्तमशरणमश्रुव्याकुलनयनमपरिभूतपूर्वं मनसापि परिभूय भृत्यवर्गमग्निं प्रविशति । परित्रायताम् । आर्योऽपि तावदसह्यशोकापनयनोपायोपदेशनिपुणां व्यापारयतु वाणीमस्याम्' इति चातिकृपणं व्याहरन्तीमहमुत्थाप्योद्विग्नतरः शनैरभिहितवान्—'आर्ये, यथा कथयसि तथा अस्मद्विरामगोचरोऽयमस्याः पुण्याशयायाः शोकः। शक्यते चेन्मुहूर्तमात्रमपि त्रातुमुपरिष्टान्न व्यर्थेयमभ्यर्थना भविष्यति। मम हि गुरुरपर इव भगवान्सुगतः समीपगत एव। कथिते मयास्मिन्नुदन्ते नियतमागमिष्यति परमदयालुः। दुःखान्धकारपटलभिदुरैश्च सौगतैः सुभाषितैः स्वकैश्च दर्शितनिदर्शनैर्नानागमगुरुभिर्गिरां कौशलैः कुशलशीलामेनां प्रबोधपदवीमारोपयिष्यति' इति । तच्च श्रुत्वा 'त्वरतामार्यः' इत्यभिदधाना सा पुनरपि पादयोः पतितवती। सोऽहमुपगत्य त्वरमाणो व्यतिकरमिममद्यतिकरमशरण[3]कृपणबहुयुवतिमरणमतिकरुणमत्रभवते गुरवे निवेदितवान्' इति।

अथ भूभृद्भैक्षवं समवधार्य तद्भाषितमश्रुमिश्रितमश्रुतेऽपि स्वसुर्नाम्नि निम्नीकृतमना मन्युना सर्वाकारसंवादिन्या दशयैव दूरीकृतसन्देहो दग्ध इव सोदर्यावस्थाश्रवणेन श्रवणयोः श्रमणाचार्यमुवाच—'आर्य, नियतं सैवेयमनार्यस्यास्य जनस्यातिकठिनहृदयस्यातिनृशंसस्य मन्दभाग्यस्य भगिनी भागधेयैरेतामवस्थां नीता निष्कारणवैरिभिर्वराकी विदीर्यमाणं मे हृदयमेवं निवेदयति' इत्युक्त्वा तमपि श्रमणमभ्यधात्—'आर्य, उत्तिष्ठ। दर्शय क्वासौ।

---

१ 'आर्यवचसाम्' ब. २ 'मरणेन च मातुः प्रवसनेन च पितुरभावेन च भर्तुः परलोकगमनेन च भ्रातुर्भ्रंशेन च' ब. ३ 'अशरणम्' ब.

यतस्व प्रभूतप्राणिपरित्राणपुण्योपार्जनाय[1]। यामः। यदि कथंचिज्जीवन्तीं सम्भावयामः' इति भाषमाण एवोत्तस्थौ।

अथ समग्रशिष्यवर्गानुगतेनाचार्येण तुरगेभ्यश्चावतीर्य समस्तेन सामन्तलोकेन पश्चादाकृष्यमाणाश्वीयेनानुगम्यमानः पुरस्ताच्च तेन शाक्यपुत्रीयेण प्रदिश्यमानवर्त्मा पद्भ्यामेव तं प्रदेशमविरलैः पदैः पिबन्निव प्रावर्तत। क्रमेण च समुपगतः शुश्राव लतावनान्तरितस्य मुमूर्षोर्महतः स्त्रैणस्य तत्कालोचितानेकप्रकारानालापान्—'भगवन्धर्म, धाव शीघ्रम्। क्वासि कुलदेवते। देवि धरणि, धीरयसि न दुःखितां दुहितरम्। क्व नु खलु प्रोषिता पुष्पभूतिकुटुम्बिनी लक्ष्मीः। अनाथां नाथ मुखरवंश्य विविधाधिविधुरां वधूं विधवां विबोधयसि किमिति नेमाम्। भगवन्, भक्तजने संज्वरिणि सुगत सुप्तोऽसि। राजधर्म पुष्पभूतिभवनपक्षपातिन्, उदासीनीभूतोऽसि कथम्। त्वय्यपि विपद्बान्धव विन्ध्य वन्ध्योऽयमञ्जलिबन्धः। मातर्महाटवि, रटन्तीं न शृणोषीमामापत्पतिताम्[2]। पतङ्ग, प्रसीद पाहि पतिव्रतामशरणाम्। प्रयत्नरक्षित कृतघ्न चारित्रचण्डाल, न रक्षसि राजपुत्रीम्। किमवधृतं लक्षणैः। हा देवि दुहितृस्नेहमयि यशोमति, मुषितासि दग्धदैवदस्युना। देव, दुहितरि दह्यमानायां नापतसि प्रतापशील, शिथिलीभूतमपत्यप्रेम। महाराज राज्यवर्धन, न धावसि मन्दीभूता भगिनीप्रीतिः। अहो निष्ठुरः प्रेतभावः। व्यपेहि पाप पावक स्त्रीघातनिर्घृण, ज्वलन्न लज्जसे। भ्रातर्वात, दासी तवास्मि। संवादय द्रुतं देवीदाहं देवाय दुःखितजनार्तिहराय हर्षाय। नितान्तनिःशूक शोकश्वपाक, सकामोऽसि। दुःखदायिन्वियोगराक्षस, तुष्टोसि। विजने वने कमाक्रन्दामि, कस्मै कथयामि, कमुपयामि शरणम्, कां दिशं प्रतिपद्ये, करोमि किमभागधेया। गान्धारि, गृहीतोऽयं लतापाशः। पिशाचि मोचनिके, मुञ्च शाखाग्रहणकलहम्। कलहंसि, हंसि किमतःपरमुत्तमाङ्गम्[3]। मङ्गलिके, मुक्तगलं किमद्यापि रुद्यते। सुन्दरि, दूरीभवति सखीसार्थः। स्थास्यसि कथमिवाशिवे शवशिबिरे शबरिके। सुतनु, तनूनपाति पतिष्यसि त्वमपि। मृणालकोमले मालावति, म्लानासि। मातर्मातङ्गिके, अङ्गीकृतस्त्वयापि मृत्युः। वत्से वत्सिके, वत्स्यसि कथमनभिप्रेते[4] प्रेतनगरे। नागरिके, गरिमाणमागतास्यनया स्वामिभक्त्या। विराजिके, विराजितासि राजपुत्रीविपदि जीवितव्ययव्यवसायेन। भृगुपतनाभ्युद्यमभागाभिज्ञे भृङ्गारधारिणि, धन्यासि। केतकि, कुतः पुनरीदृशी सुस्वामिनी[5]। मेनके, जन्मनि जन्मनि देवीदास्यमेव ददातु देवो देहं दहन्दहनः। विजये वीजय कृशानुम्। सानुमति, नमतीन्दीवरिका दिवं गन्तुकामा। कामदासि, देहि दहनप्रदक्षिणावकाशम्। विचरिके, विरचय वह्निम्। विकिर किरातिके कुसुमप्रकरम्। कुररिके, कुरु

---

१ 'यतः सुप्रभूतप्राण०' अ-क. २ 'शृणोषि मामापत०' ब. ३ 'किमपरमुत्त०' ब. ४ 'कथनमभि-' अ-ब. ५ 'स्वस्वामिनी' ब.

कुरुबककोरकाचितां चिताम्। चामरं चामरग्राहिणि गृहाण। पुनरपि कण्ठे मर्षयितव्यानि नर्मदे नर्मनिर्मितानि निर्मर्यादहसितानि। भद्रे सुभद्रे, भद्रमस्तु ते परलोकगमनम्। अग्रामीणगुणानुरागिणि ग्रामेयिके, गच्छ सुगतिम्। वसन्तिके, अन्तरं प्रयच्छ। आपृच्छते छत्रधारी देवि देहि दृष्टिम्। दृष्टा तव जहाति जीवितं विजयसेना। सेयं मुक्तिका मुक्तकण्ठमारटति निकटे नाटकसूत्रधारी। पादयोः पतति ते ताम्बूलवाहिनी बहुमता राजपुत्रि पत्रलता। कलिङ्गसेने, अयं पश्चिमः परिष्वङ्गः पीडय निर्भरमुरसा माम्। असवः प्रवसन्ति वसन्तसेने। मञ्जुलिके, मार्जयसि कतिकृत्वः सुदुःसहदुःखसहस्रास्रदिग्धं दग्धचक्षुरिदं रोदिषि कियदाश्लिष्य च माम्। निर्माणमीदृशं प्रायशो यशोधने। धीरयस्यद्यापि किं मां माधविके। केयमवस्था संस्थापनानाम्। गतः कालः कालिन्दि सखीजनानुनयाञ्जलीनाम्। उन्मत्तिके मत्तपालिके, कृताः पृष्ठतः प्रणयिनीप्रणिपातानुरोधाः। शिथिलय चकोरवति चरणग्रहणं ग्रहिणि। कमलिनि, किमनेन पुनः पुनर्दैवोपालम्भेन। न प्राप्तं चिरं सखीजनसङ्गमसुखम्। आर्ये महत्तरिके तरङ्गसेने नमस्कारः। सखि सौदामिनि, दृष्टासि। समुपनय हव्यवाहनार्चनकुसुमानि कुमुदिके। देहि चितारोहणाय रोहिणि हस्तावलम्बनम्। अम्ब धात्रि, धीरा भव। भवन्त्येवंविधा एव कर्मणां विपाकाः पापकारिणीनाम्। आर्यचरणानामयमञ्जलिः। परः परलोकप्रयाणप्रणामोऽयं मातः। मरणसमये कस्माल्लवलिके हलहलको बलीयानानन्दमयो हृदयस्य मे। हृष्यन्त्युच्चरोमाञ्चमुञ्चि किमङ्गीकृत्याङ्गानि। वामनिके, वामेन मे स्फुरितमक्ष्णां। वृथा विरमसि वयस्य वायस वृक्षे[1] क्षीरिणि क्षणे क्षणे क्षीणपुण्यायाः पुरः। हरिणि, हेषितमिव हयानामुत्तरतः। कस्येदमातपत्रमुच्चमत्र पादपान्तरेण प्रभावति विभाव्यते। कुरङ्गिके, केन सुगृहीतनाम्नो नाम गृहीतममृतमयमार्यस्य। देवि, दिष्ट्या वर्धसे देवस्य हर्षस्यागमनमहोत्सवेन।' इत्येतच्च श्रुत्वा सत्वरमुपससर्प। ददर्श च मुह्यन्तीमग्निप्रवेशायोद्यतां राजा राज्यश्रियम्। आललम्बे च मूर्च्छामीलितलोचनाया ललाटं हस्तेन तस्याः ससंभ्रमम्।

अथ तेन भ्रातुः प्रेयसः प्रकोष्ठबद्धानामोषधीनां रसविसरमिव प्रत्युज्जीवनक्षमं क्षरता वमतेव पारिहार्यमणीनामचिन्त्यं प्रभावममृतमिव नखचन्द्ररश्मिभिरुद्गिरता बध्नतेव चन्द्रोदयच्युतशिशिरशीकरं चन्द्रकान्तचूडामणिं मूर्धनि मृणालमयाङ्गुलिनेवातिशीतलेन निर्वापयता दह्यमानं हृदयं प्रत्यानयतेव कुतोऽपि जीवितमाह्लादकेन हस्तसंस्पर्शेन सहसैव समुन्मिमील राज्यश्रीः। तथा चासम्भावितागमनस्याचिन्तितदर्शनस्य सहसा प्राप्तस्य भ्रातुः स्वप्नदृष्टदर्शनस्येव कण्ठे समाश्लिष्य तत्कालाविर्भावनिर्भरेणाभिभूतसर्वात्मना दुःखसम्भारेण निर्दयं नदीमुखप्रणालाभ्यामिव मुक्ताभ्यां स्थूलप्रवाहमुत्सृजन्ती

---

[1] 'प्लक्षवृक्षे' ब.

बाष्पवारि विलोचनाभ्याम् 'हा तात, हा अम्ब, हा सख्यः' इति व्याहरन्ती मुहुर्मुहुरुच्चैस्तरां च, समुद्भूतभगिनीस्नेहसद्भावभारभावितमन्युना मुक्तकण्ठमतिचिरं विक्रुश्य 'वत्से, स्थिरा भव त्वम्' इति भ्रात्रा करस्थगितमुखी समाश्वास्यमानापि, 'कल्याणिनि, कुरु वचनमग्रजस्य गुरोः' इत्याचार्येण याच्यमानापि, 'देवि, न पश्यसि देवस्यावस्थाम् । अलमतिरुदितेन' इति राजलोकेनाभ्यर्थ्यमानापि, 'स्वामिनि, भ्रातरमवेक्षस्व' इति परिजनेन विज्ञाप्यमानापि, 'दुहितः, विश्रम्य पुनरारटितव्यम्' इति निवार्यमाणापि बान्धववृद्धाभिः, 'प्रियसखि, कियद्रोदिषि । तूष्णीमास्स्व । दृढं दूयते देवः' इति सखीभिरनुनीयमानापि, चिरसम्भावितानेकदुःखनिवहनिर्वहणबाष्पोत्पीडपीड्यमानकण्ठभागा, प्रभूतमन्युभारभरितान्तःकरणा करुणं काहलेन[1] स्वरेण कालमतिदीर्घं रुरोद । विगते च मन्युवेगे वह्नेः समीपादाक्षिप्य भ्रात्रा नीता निकटवर्तिनि तरुतले निषसाद ।

शनैराचार्यस्तु तथा हर्ष इति विज्ञाय विवर्धितादरः सुतरां मुहूर्तमिवातिवाह्य निभृतसंज्ञाज्ञापितेन शिष्येणोपनीतं नलिनीदलैः स्वयमादाय नम्रो मुखप्रक्षालनायोदकमुपनिन्ये । नरेन्द्रोऽपि सादरं गृहीत्वा प्रथममनवरतरोदनाताम्रं चिरप्रवृत्ताश्रुजलजालं रक्तपङ्कजमिव स्वसुश्चक्षुरक्षालयत्पश्चादात्मनः । प्रक्षालितमुखशशिनि च महीपाले सर्वतो निःशब्दः सम्बभूव सकलो लिखित इव लोकः । ततो नरेन्द्रो मन्दमन्दमब्रवीत्स्वसारम्—'वत्से, वन्दस्वात्रभवन्तं भदन्तम् । एष ते भर्तुर्हृदयं द्वितीयमस्माकं च गुरुः' इति । राजवचनात्तु राजदुहितरि पतिपरिचयश्रवणोद्घातेन पुनरानीतनेत्राम्भसि नमन्त्यामाचार्यः प्रयत्नरक्षितागतबाष्पाम्भःसम्भारभज्यमानधैर्यार्द्रलोचनः किंचित्परावृत्तनयनो दीर्घं निशश्वास । स्थित्वा च क्षणमेकं प्रदर्शितप्रश्रयो मृदुवादी मधुरया वाचा व्याजहार—'कल्याणराशे, अलं रुदित्वातिचिरम् । राजलोको नाद्यापि रोदनान्निवर्तते । क्रियतामवश्यकरणीयः स्नानविधिः । स्नात्वा च गम्यतां तामेव भूयो भुवम्' इति ।

अथ भूपतिरनुवर्तमानो लौकिकमाचारमाचार्यवचनं चोत्थाय स्नात्वा गिरिसरिति सह स्वस्रा तामेव भूमिमयासीत् । तस्यां च सपरिजनां प्रथममाहितावधानः पार्श्ववर्ती परवतीं शुचा पतिपिण्डप्रदर्शितप्रयत्नप्रतिपन्नाभ्यवहारकरणां[2] भगिनीमभोजयत् । अनन्तरं च स्वयमाहारस्थितिमकरोत् । भुक्तवांश्च बन्धनात्प्रभृति विस्तरतः स्वसुः कान्यकुब्जाद्गौडसंभ्रमं गुप्तितो गुप्तनाम्ना कुलपुत्रेण निष्कासनं निर्गतायाश्च राज्यवर्धनमरणश्रवणं श्रुत्वा चाहारनिराकरणमनाहारपराहतायाश्च विन्ध्याटवीपर्यटनखेदं जातनिर्वेदायाः पावकप्रवेशोपक्रमणं यावत्सर्वमशृणोद्व्यतिकरं परिजनतः । ततः सुखासीनमेकत्र तरुतले विविक्तभुवि भगिनीद्वितीयं दूरस्थितानुजीविजनं राजान-

---

१ 'करुणकाहलेन' अ-क. २ '०हारकारणाम्' ब.

माचार्यः समुपसृत्य शनैरासांचक्रे। स्थित्वा च कंचित्कालांशं लेशतो वक्तुमुपचक्रमे—'श्रीमन्, आकर्ण्यताम्। आख्येयमस्ति नः किंचित्—

अयं हि यौवनोन्मादात्परिभूय भूयसीर्भार्या यौवनावतारतरलतरास्तारा-राजो रजनीकर्णपूरः पुरुहूतपुरोधसो धिषणस्य पुरंध्रीं धर्मपत्नीं पत्नीयन्नतितरलस्तारां नामापजहार। नाकतश्च पलायांचक्रे। चकितचकोरलोचनया तया सहातिकामया सर्वाकाराभिरामया रममाणो रमणीयेषु देशेषु चचार। चिराच्च कथंचित्सर्वगीर्वाणवाणीगौरवाद्गिरां पत्युः पुनरपि प्रत्यर्पयामास ताम्। हृदये त्वनिन्धनमदह्यत विरहाद्वरारोहायास्तस्याः सततम्।

एकदा तु शैलादुदयादुदयमानो विमले वारिणि वारुणालयस्य संक्रान्तमात्मनः प्रतिबिम्बं विलोकितवान्। दृष्ट्वा च तदा सस्मार स्मरः स्मेरगण्डस्थलस्य ताराया मुखस्य। मुमोच च मन्मथोन्मादमथ्यमानमानसः स्वःस्थोऽप्यस्वस्थः स्थवीयसः पीतसकलकुमुदवनप्रभाप्रवाहधवलताराभ्यामिव लोचनाभ्यां बाष्पवारिबिन्दून्। अथ पततस्तानुदन्वति समस्तानेवाचेमुर्मुक्ताशुक्तयः। तासां च कुक्षिकोषेषु मुक्ताफलीभूतानवाप तान्कथमपि रसातलनिवासी वासुकिर्नाम विषमुचामीशः। स च तैर्मुक्ताफलैः पातालतलेऽपि तारागणमिव दर्शयद्भिरेकावलीमकल्पयत्। चकार च मन्दाकिनीति नाम तस्याः। सा च भगवतः सोमस्य सर्वासामोषधीनामधिपतेः प्रभावादत्यन्तविषघ्नी हिमामृतसम्भवत्वाच्च स्पर्शेन सर्वसत्त्वसन्तापहारिणी बभूव। यतः स तां सर्वदा विषोष्मशान्तये वासुकिः पर्यधत्त।

समतिक्रामति च कियत्यपि काले कदाचित्तामेकावलीं तस्मान्नागराजान्नागार्जुनो नाम नागैरेवानीतः पातालतलं भिक्षुरभिक्षत लेभे च। निर्गत्य रसातलात्त्रिसमुद्राधिपतये सातवाहननाम्ने नरेन्द्राय सुहृदे स ददौ ताम्। सा चास्माकं कालेन शिष्यपरम्परया कथमपि हस्तमुपगता। यद्यपि च परिभव इव भवति भवादृशां दत्रिम उपचारस्तथाप्योषधिबुद्ध्या बुद्धिमता सर्वसत्त्वराशिरक्षाप्रवृत्तेन रक्षणीयशरीरेणायुष्मता विषरक्षापेक्षया गृह्यताम्। इत्यभिधाय भिक्षोरभ्याशवर्तिनश्चीवरपटान्तसंयतां मुमोच तामेकावलीं मन्दाकिनीम्।

उन्मुच्यमानाया एव यस्याः प्रभालेपिनि लब्धावकाशे विशदमहसि[1] महीयसि विसर्पति रश्मिमण्डले युगपद्धवलायमानेषु दिङ्मुखेषु मुकुलितलतावधूत्कण्ठितैरामूलाद्विकसितमिव तरुभिः, अभिनवमृणाललुब्धैर्धावितमिव धुतपक्षपुटपटलधवलितगगनं वनसरसीहंसयूथैः, स्फुटितमिव भरवशविशीर्यमाणधूलिधवलैर्गर्भभेदसूचितसूचीसञ्चयशुचिभिः केतकीवाटैः, उद्दलितद[2]लदन्तुराभिः प्रबुद्धमिव कुमुदिनीभिः, विधुतासितसठाभारभरितदिक्चक्रैश्च-

---

१ 'विषद' अ-क. २ 'उद्दलित-' ब.

लितमिव केसरिकुलैः, प्रहसितमिव सितदशनांशुमालालोकलिप्यमानवनं वनदेवताभिः, विकसितमिव शिथिलितकुसुमकोशकेसराट्टहासनिरङ्कुशं काशकाननैः, भ्रान्तमिव संभ्रमभ्रमितबालपल्लवपरिवेशश्वेतायमानैश्चमरीकदम्बकैः, प्रसृतमिव स्फायमानफेनिलतरलतरतरङ्गोद्गारिणा गिरिनदीपूरेण, अपरतारागणलाभमुदितेनोदितमिव विकचमरीचिचक्राक्रान्तककुभा पूर्णचन्द्रेण, प्रक्षालित इव दावानलधूलिधूसरितदिगन्तो दिवसः, पुनरिव धौतान्यश्रुजलक्लिष्टानि नारीणां मुखानि।

राजा तु मांसलैस्तस्याः संमुखैर्मयूखैराकुलीक्रियमाणं मुहुर्मुहुरुन्मीलयन्निमीलयंश्च चक्षुः कथमपि प्रयत्नेन ददर्श सर्वाशापूर्णीं पङ्क्तीकृतामिव दिङ्नागकरशीकरसंहतिम्, घनमुक्तां शारदीमिव लेखीकृतां ज्योत्स्नाम्, प्रकटपदकचिह्नां सञ्चारणवीथीमिव बालेन्दोर्निश्चलीभूतां सप्तर्षिमालामिव हस्तमुक्ताम्, अभिभूतसकलभुवनभूषणभूतिप्रभावा[२]मैशानीमिव शशिकलाम्, धवलतागुणपरिगृहीतां कान्तिमिव निर्गतां क्षीरराशेः, अनेकमहामहीभृत्परम्परागतां गङ्गामिव दुर्गतिहराम्, अनवरतस्फुरिततरलांशुकां पुरःसरपताकामिव महेश्वरभावागमस्य, घनसारशुक्लां दन्तपङ्क्तिमिवाभिमुखस्येश्वरस्य, वरमनोरथपूरणसमर्थां स्वयंवरस्रजमिव भुवनश्रियः, निजकरपल्लवावरणदुर्लक्ष्यां चक्षूरागविहसतिकामिव वसुधायाः, मन्त्रकोषसाधनप्रवृत्तस्याक्षमालामिव राजधर्मस्य, समुद्रालङ्कारभूतां संख्यालेख्यपट्टिकामिव कुबेरकोशस्य। पश्यंश्चैतां विस्मयमाजगाम मनसा सुचिरम्। आचार्यस्तु तामुद्धृत्य बबन्ध बन्धुरे स्कन्धभागे भूपतेः। अथ नरपतिरपि प्रीतिमुपदर्शयन्प्रत्यवादीत्—'आर्य, रत्नानामीदृशानामनर्हाः प्रायेण पुरुषाः। तपःसिद्धिरियमार्यस्य देवताप्रसादो वा। के च वयमिदानीमात्मनोऽपि किमुत ग्रहणस्य प्रत्याख्यानस्य वा। दर्शनात्प्रभृति प्रभूतगुरुगुणगणहृतेन हृदयेन परवन्तो वयम्। सङ्कल्पितमिदमा मरणादार्योपयोगाय शरीरम्। अत्र कामचारो वः कर्तव्यानाम्' इति।

समतिक्रान्ते च कियत्यपि काले गते चैकावलीवर्णनालापे लोकस्यानन्तरं लब्धविश्रम्भा राज्यश्रीस्ताम्बूलवाहिनीं पत्रलतामाहूयोपांशु किमपि कर्णमूले शनैरादिदेश। दर्शितविनया च पत्रलता पार्थिवं व्यज्ञापयत्—देव, देवी विज्ञापयति न स्मराम्यार्यस्य पुरः कदाचिदुच्चैर्वचनमपि। कुतो विज्ञापनम्। इयं हि शुचामसह्यतां[३] व्यापारयन्ती हतदैव[४]दत्तादेशा शिथिलयति विनयम्। अबलानां हि पतिरपत्यं वावलम्बनम्। उभयविकलानां तु दुःखानलेन्धनायमानं प्राणितमशालीनत्वमेव केवलम्। आर्यागमनेन च

१ 'लोभ' ब. २ 'प्रभावामिवैशानीम्' ब. ३ 'असह्यतां...हतदैवदत्ता च दशा' ब. ४ 'देव०' अ.

कृतोऽपि प्रतिहतो मरणप्रयत्नः । अतः काषायग्रहणाभ्यनुज्ञयानुगृह्यतामयमपुण्यभाजनं जनः' इति । जनाधिपस्तु तदाकर्ण्य तूष्णीमेवावातिष्ठत ।

अथाचार्यः सुधीरमभ्यधात्—'आयुष्मति, शोको हि नाम पर्यायः पिशाचस्य रूपान्तरमाक्षेपस्य तारुण्यं तमसो विशेषणं विषस्यानन्तकः प्रेतनगरनायकः । अयमनिर्वृतिधर्मा दहनः । अयमक्षयो राजयक्ष्मा । अयमलक्ष्मीनिवासो जनार्दनः । अयमपुण्यप्रवृत्तः क्षपणकः । अयमप्रतिबोधो निद्राप्रकारः । अयमनलसधर्मा सन्निपातः । अयमशिवसहचरो विनायकः । अयमबुधसेवितो ग्रहवर्गः । अयमयोगसमुत्थो ज्योतिःप्रकारः । अयं स्नेहाद्वायुप्रकोपः, मानसादग्निसम्भवः, आर्द्रभावाद्रजःक्षोभः, रसादभिशोष[1]:, रागात्कालपरिणामः । तदस्याजस्रस्राविणो हृदयमहाव्रणस्य बहुलदोषान्धकारलब्धप्रवेशप्रसरस्य प्राणतस्करस्य शून्यताहेतोर्महाभूतग्रामघातकस्य सकलविग्रहक्षपणदक्षस्य दोषचक्रवर्तिनः कार्श्यश्वासप्रलापोपद्रवबहलस्य दीर्घरोगस्यासद्ग्रहस्य सकललोकक्षयधूमकेतोर्जीवितापहारदक्षस्याक्षणरुचेरनभ्रवज्रपातस्य स्फुरदनवद्यविद्याविद्युदुद्द्योतमानानि गहनग्रन्थग्रन्थिगूढगर्भग्रहणगम्भीराणि भूरिकाव्यकथाकठोराणि बहुशास्त्रोद्वहनबृहन्ति विदुषामपि हृदयानि नालं सोढुमापातं किमुत नवनवमालिकाकुसुमकोमलानां सरसबिसतन्तुदुर्बलकमबलानां हृदयम् ।

एवं सति सत्यव्रते, वद किमत्र क्रियते, कतम उपालभ्यते, कस्य पुर उच्चैराक्रन्द्यते, हृदयदाहि दुःखं वा ख्याप्यते । सर्वमक्षिणी निमील्य सोढव्यममूढेन मर्त्यधर्मणा । पुण्यवति, पुरातन्यः स्थितय एताः केन शक्यन्तेऽन्यथाकर्तुम् । संसरन्त्यो नक्तंदिवं द्राघीयस्यो जन्मजरामरणघटनघटीयन्त्रराजिरजवः पञ्चजनानाम् । पञ्चमहाभूतपञ्चकुलाधिष्ठितान्तःकरणव्यवहारदर्शननिपुणाः सर्वंकषा विषमा धर्मराजस्थितयः । क्षणमपि क्षममाणा गलन्त्यायुष्कलाकलनकुशला निलये निलये कालनालिकाः । जगति सर्वजन्तुजीवितोपहारपातिनी सञ्चरति झटिति चण्डिका यमाज्ञा । रटन्त्यनवरतमखिलप्राणिप्रयाणप्रकटनपटवः प्रेतपतिपटहाः । प्रतिदिशं पर्यटन्ति पेटकैः प्रतिपुरं प्रतप्तलोहलोहिताक्षाः कालकूटकान्तिकालकायाः कालपाशपाणयः कालपुरुषाः । प्रतिभवनं भ्रमन्ति भीषणकिङ्करकरघट्टितयमघण्टापुटपटुटांकारभयङ्कराः सर्वसत्त्वसङ्घसंहरणाय घोराघातघोषणाः । दिशि दिशि वहन्ति बहुचिताधूमधूसरितप्रेतपतिपताकापटुपतितगृध्रदृष्टयः शोककृतकोलाहलाकुलकुटुम्बिनीविकीर्णकेशकलापशबलशवशिबिकासहस्रसङ्कुलाः किलकिलायमानश्मशानशिबिरशिवाशावकाः परलोकावसथपथिकसार्थप्रस्थानविशिखावीथयः । सकललोककवलावलेहलम्पटा बहला वहंलिहा लेढि लोहिताचिता चिताङ्गारकाली कालरात्रीजिह्वा जीवितानि जीविनाम् । तृप्तिमशिक्षिता च

१ 'अतिशोषः' ब.

भगवतः सर्वभूतभुजो बुभुक्षा मृत्योः । अतिद्रुतवाहिनी चानित्यतानदी । क्षणिकाश्च महाभूतग्रामगोष्ठ्यः । रात्रिषु भङ्गुराणि गात्रयन्त्रपञ्जरदारूणि[1] देहिनाम् । अशुभशुभावेशविवशा विशरारवः शरीरनिर्माणपरमाणवः । छिदुरा जीवबन्धनपाशतन्त्रीतन्तवः । सर्वमात्मनोऽनीश्वरं विश्वं नश्वरम् । एवमवधृत्य नात्यर्थमेवार्हसि मेधाविनि मृदुनि मनसि तमसः प्रसरं दातुम् । एको हि प्रतिसंख्यानक्षण आधारीभवति धृतेः । अपि च दूरगतेऽपि हि शोके नन्विदानीमपेक्षणीय एवाय ज्येष्ठः पितृकल्पो भ्राता भवत्या गुरुः । इतरथा को न बहु मन्येत कल्याणरूपमीदृशं सङ्कल्पमत्रभवत्याः काषाय-ग्रहणकृतम् । अखिलमनोज्वरप्रशमनकारणं हि भगवती प्रव्रज्या । ज्यायः खल्विदं पदमात्मवताम् । महाभागस्तु भिनत्ति मनोरथमधुना । यदयमा-दिशति तदेवानुष्ठेयम् । यदि भ्रातेति यदि ज्येष्ठ इति यदि वत्सल इति यदि गुणवानिति यदि राजेति सर्वथा स्थातव्यमस्य नियोगे ।' इत्युक्त्वा व्यरंसीत् ।

उपरतवचसि च तस्मिन्निजगाद नरपतिः—'आर्यमपहाय कोऽन्य एव-मभिदध्यात् । अनभ्यर्थितदैवनिर्मिता हि विषमविपदवलम्बनस्तम्भा भवन्तो लोकस्य । स्नेहार्द्रमूर्तयो मोहान्धकारध्वंसिनश्च धर्मप्रदीपाः । किंतु प्रणयप्र-दानदुर्ललिता दुर्लभमपि मनोरथमांतिप्रीतिरभिलषति । धीरस्यापि धाष्टर्य-मारोपयति हृदयलघिमलङ्घितमतिवल्लभत्वम् । युक्तायुक्तविचारशून्यत्वाच्च शालीनमपि शिक्षयन्ति स्वार्थतृष्णाः प्रागल्भ्यम् । अभ्यर्थनाया रक्षन्ति च जलनिधय इव मर्यादामार्याः ।दत्तमेव च शरीरमिदमनभ्यर्थितेन प्रथममेवा-तिथ्याय माननीयेन भवता मह्यम् । अतः किंचिदर्थये भदन्तम्-इयं नः स्वसा बाला च बहुदुःखखेदिता च सर्वकार्यावधीरणोपरोधेनापि यावल्लाल-नीया नित्यम् । अस्माभिश्च भ्रातृवधापकारिरिपुकुलप्रलयकरणोद्यतस्य बाहो-र्विधेयैर्भूत्वा सकललोकप्रत्यक्षं प्रतिज्ञा कृता । पूर्वावमाननाभिभवमसह-मानैरर्पित आत्मा कोपस्य । अतो नियुङ्क्ष्व कियन्तमपि कालमात्मानमार्यो-ऽपि कार्ये मदीये । दीयतामतिथये शरीरमिदम् । अद्यप्रभृति यावदयं जनो लवयति प्रतिज्ञाभारमाश्वासयति च तातविनाशदुःखविक्लवाः प्रजाः, ताव-दिमामत्रभवतः कथाभिश्च धर्म्याभिः, कुशलप्रतिबोधविधायिभिरुपदेशैश्चार-[2]जोभिः, शीलोपशमदायिनीभिश्च देशनाभिः, क्लेशप्रहाणहेतुभूतैश्च तथागतैर्द-र्शनैः, अस्मत्पार्श्वोपयायिनीमेव प्रतिबोध्यमानामिच्छामि । इयं तु ग्रहीष्यति मयैव समं समाप्तकृत्येन काषायाणि । अर्थिजने च किमिव नातिसृजन्ति महान्तः । सुरनाथमात्मास्थिभिरपि यावत्कृतार्थमकरोद्धैर्योदधिर्दधीचः । मु-निनाथोऽप्यनपेक्षितात्मस्थितिरनुकम्पेति कृत्वा कृपावानात्मानं वठरसत्त्वेभ्यः कतिकृत्वो न दत्तवान् । अतः परं भवन्त एव बहुतरं जानन्ति ।' इत्युक्त्वा तूष्णींबभूव भूपतिः ।

---

१ 'पात्र' अ-क. २ '°विधायिनीभिरुपदेशैश्च दूरापसारितरजोभिः' ब.

भूयस्तु बभाषे भदन्तः—'भव्या न द्विरुच्चारयन्ति वाचम्। चेतसा प्रथममेव प्रतिग्राहिता गुणास्तावकाः कायबलिमिमाम्। अमुना जनेनोपयोगस्तु निरुपयोगस्यास्य लघुनि गुरुणि वा कृत्ये गुणवदायत्तः' इति। अथ तथा तस्मिन्नभिनन्दितप्रणये प्रीयमाणः पार्थिवस्तत्र तामुषित्वा विभावरीमुषसि वसनालङ्कारादिप्रदानपरितोषितं विसर्ज्य निर्घातमाचार्येण सह स्वसारमादाय प्रयाणकैः कतिपयैरेव कटकमनुजाह्नवि निविष्टं प्रत्याजगाम।

तत्र च राज्यश्रीप्राप्तिव्यतिकरकथां कथयत एव प्रणयिभ्यो रविरपि ततार गगनतलम्। बहलमधुपङ्कपिङ्गलः पङ्कजाकर इव सञ्चुकोच चक्रवाकवल्लभो वासरः। प्रकीर्णानि नवरुधिररसारुणवर्णानि लोकालोकजूंषि यजूंषीव कुपितयाज्ञवल्क्यवक्त्रवान्तानि निजवपुषि पूषा पापमूंषि पुनरपि सञ्जहार जालकानि रोचिषाम्। क्रमेण च समुपोह्यमानमांसलरागरोचिष्णुरुष्णांशुः, उष्णीषबन्धसहजचूडामणिरिव वृकोदरकरपुटोत्पाटितः प्रत्यग्रशोणितशोणाङ्गरागरौद्रो द्रौणायनस्य, रुद्रभिक्षादानशौण्डपुरमथनमुक्तमुण्डशिरानाडिरुधिरपूरणशोणितकपिलः[1] कपालकर्पर इव च पैतामहः, पितृवधरुषितरामरागरचितः पृथुविकटकार्तवीर्यांसकूटकुट्टाककुठारतुण्डतष्टदुष्टक्षत्रियकण्ठकुहररुधिरकुल्याप्रणालसहस्रपूरितो ह्रद इव दूररोधी रौधिरः, भयनिगूढकरचरणमुण्डमण्डलाकृतिर्गुल्गारुडनखपञ्जराक्षेपक्षपणक्षिप्तक्षतजोक्षितो व्यसुर्विभावसुः[2], कमठ इव च लोठ्यमानो नभसि, अरुणगर्भमांसपिण्डाण्ड इव च खण्डिमानमानीतो नियतकालातिपातदूयमानदाक्षायणीक्षिप्तः, धातुतट इव च सुमेरोरसुरवधाभिचारचरुपचनपिशुनः, शोणितक्वाथकषायितकुक्षिरतिविसङ्कटः कटाह इव च बार्हस्पत्य ;सद्योगलितगजदानवदेहलोहितोपलेपभीषणो मुखमण्डलाभोग इव महाभैरवस्य मुहूर्तमदृश्यत। जलनिधिजलप्रतिबिम्बितरविबिम्बराजिभास्वराभ्रावलम्बिनी गृहीतार्द्रमांसभारेव चाबभासे वासरावसानवेला वेतालनिभा। ज्वलत्संध्यारागरज्यमानजलप्रवाहः पुनरिव पुराणपुरुषपीवरोरुसम्पुटपिष्टमधुकैटभरुधिरपटलपाटलवपुरभवदधिपतिरर्णसाम्। अवसिते संध्यासमये समनन्तरमपरिमितयशःपानतृषिताय मुक्ताशैलशिलाचषक इव निजकुलकीर्त्या, कृतयुगकरणोद्यतायादिराजराजतशासनमुद्रानिवेश इव राज्यश्रिया, सकलद्वीपजिगीषाचलिताय श्वेतद्वीपदूत इव चायत्या, श्वेतभानुरुपानीयत निशया नरेन्द्रायेति॥

इति श्रीबाणभट्टकृतौ[3] हर्षचरितेऽष्टम उच्छ्वासः।

---

१ 'पूरणकपिलः' अ—क. २ 'विभावसुकमट इव' ब. ३ '०कृते' ब; 'श्रीचित्रभानुसुनुमहाकविचक्रचूडामणिश्रीबाणभट्टकृतौ श्रीहर्षचरिते महाकाव्ये विन्ध्याद्रिनिवेशनं नामाष्टम उच्छ्वासः सम्पूर्णः। समाप्तमिदं श्रीहर्षचरितमहाकाव्यम्' ब.

Verse 3. The poet in this verse after invoking deities salutes Vyāsa the author of the महाभारत and thereby shows his great reverence for him. सर्वं वेत्तीति सर्वविद् तस्मै. कविवेधसे—who is Brahmā among poets. Brahmā is called सुरज्येष्ठ; so व्यास is the best of poets. The word may also mean 'who is the creator of (the effusions of) poets.' The idea is that later poets derive their inspiration from his work. The महाभारत itself gives expression to this idea. 'इतिहासोत्तमादस्माज्जायन्ते कविबुद्धयः' आदिपर्व 2. 385; 'इदं कविवरैः सर्वैराख्यानमुपजीव्यते' आदि० 2. 389; 'यदिहास्ति तदन्यत्र यन्नेहास्ति न तत्क्वचित्'. यः सरस्वत्याः वर्षमिव पुण्यं भारतं चक्रे who composed the sacred (work called) Bhārata which is as it were a shower of speech. The भारत contains the choicest speech in abundance. The poet conveys another idea. यः सरस्वत्या (वाचा) भारतं पुण्यं चक्रे सरस्वत्या (नद्या) भारतं वर्षमिव. Vyāsa by his holy words sanctified भारतवर्ष (India) as the sacred river सरस्वती sanctifies भारतवर्ष. According to ancient ideas of Geography, the earth was divided into seven द्वीपs (जम्बु, प्लक्ष, शाल्मल, कुश, क्रौञ्च, शाक and पुष्कर). Each of these द्वीपs was subdivided into 9 वर्षs, had its own mountains and was surrounded by a sea. जम्बुद्वीप had 9 वर्षs (कुरु, हिरण्मय, रम्यक, इलावृत, हरि, केतुमाल, भद्राश्व, किन्नर and भारत). Vide विष्णुपुराण II. 1-3 and मार्कण्डेय chap. 54 ff. भारतवर्ष is defined as 'उत्तरं यत्समुद्रस्य हिमाद्रेश्चैव दक्षिणम् । वर्षं तद्भारतं नाम भारती यत्र सन्ततिः ॥'. सरस्वती was a sacred river in the Panjab now lost in the sands of the great desert of India. We may also interpret 'who sanctified the line descended from भरत by his speech.' The महाभारत narrates the story of the Kauravas and Pāṇḍavas who were descendants of भरत, son of दुष्यन्त and शकुन्तला. Vide आदिपर्व chap. 74. 'भरताद्भारती कीर्तिर्येनेदं भारतं कुलम् ॥' verse 131. The word कविवेधसे may also mean 'who is a creator in the form of a poet.' A poet is often spoken of as a creator (of high thoughts and aspirations). Compare the first verse of काव्यप्रकाश and 'अपारे काव्यसंसारे **कविरेव प्रजापतिः** । यथास्मै रोचते विश्वं तथेदं परिवर्तते' ॥ ध्वन्यालोक III. p. 222 and also अग्निपुराण chap. 339. 10.

Verse 4. कुकवयः bad poets, poetasters. रागेण अधिष्ठिता दृष्टिः येषाम्—whose vision (intellect) is dominated by (evil) passions (with कुकवयः); whose eye is dominated by redness (with कोकिलाः). Poetasters are not inspired by noble ideals and thoughts; but their effusions are due to the envy of good poets and such other evil tendencies. The three words रागा०,

वाचालाः and °कारिणः apply equally to bad poets and cuckoos and so the author compares bad poets with cuckoos. वाचालाः loquacious (with poets); making a noise (with cuckoos). कामकारिणः doing just as they please; that excite passion (with कोकिलाः). Poetasters compose poems throwing to the winds all canons of good taste and sound criticism. The notes of the cuckoo are an excitant of love. According to the terminology of Sanskrit rhetoricians रति is the स्थायिभाव of शृङ्गाररस; the नायक and नायिका are the आलम्बनविभाव; वसन्त, the moon, the notes of the cuckoo are the उद्दीपनविभाव; external indications such as स्वेद are the अनुभावs and चिन्ता, जडता &c. are व्यभिचारिभावs. Bāṇa in this verse finds fault with poetasters and says that the voice of a true poet is very rarely heard amidst the din of poetasters. The com. suggests another meaning; 'such is the natural charm of poetry; even bad poets give pleasure; how much more will those who are specially gifted ?' But this is rather strained and not in keeping with the next verse. सं० gives another sense of कुकवयः 'कुकन्ति गृह्णन्ति चेतांसि इति कुकाः ते च वयो मयूरप्रवराः पक्षिणः'.

Verse 5. This verse is full of puns. The plain meaning is 'Innumerable are the poets to be found in each house that can write only plain and matter of fact descriptions, like dogs (that are also numberless). Poets that possess creative genius are not many, like शरभs'. जाति is another name for स्वभावोक्ति. It consists in describing objects (particularly the doings of children, lower animals &c.) as they are in their various positions. 'नानावस्थं पदार्थानां रूपं साक्षाद्विवृण्वती । स्वभावोक्तिश्च जातिश्चेत्याद्या सालङ्कृतिर्यथा ॥' काव्यादर्श II. 8. See also भोज's सरस्वतीकण्ठाभरण III and रुद्रट's काव्यालंकार 7. 30–31. जाति (or स्वभावोक्ति) is opposed to वक्रोक्ति, which latter was often looked upon as the soul of poetry and as something which a poet should strive for. Note 'सैषा सर्वत्र वक्रोक्तिरनयार्थो विभाव्यते । यत्नोऽस्यां कविना कार्यः कोऽलङ्कारोऽनया विना ॥' भामह II. जातिभाजः also means 'possessed of the common characteristic' (श्वत्व or कवित्व). The idea is:—the most wretched cur and the best hound are both dogs *i. e.* they possess the जाति (species) श्वत्व in common; but there is great disparity in their worth; so poetasters (कुकवयः) possess the जाति कवित्व in common with poets of genius. असंख्याः also means 'of no account, useless (with poets); that do not fight' (with dogs). 'मृधमास्कन्दनं संख्यं समीकं सांपरायिकम्' इत्यमरः. उत्पादकाः उद्गताः पादकाः (पादाः)

येषां that have feet upwards (growing on their backs). शरभाः—शरभ is a fabulous animal with eight legs and stronger than a lion. See वनपर्व chap. 119 for the story of a dog that was successively turned into a leopard, a tiger, an elephant, a lion and lastly into a शरभ 'अष्टपादूर्ध्वनयनः शरभो वनगोचरः। स सिंहं हन्तुमागच्छन्मुनेस्तस्य निवेशनम् ॥' verse 13.

Verse 6. In this verse Bāṇa speaks of so-called poets that are merely plagiarists. अन्य—वृत्त्या by (merely) changing the words of other (poets). बन्ध...गूहनैः by concealing the distinctive marks of their compositions. अना...भाव्यते a poet without being (expressly) declared (to be so) is revealed to be a thief (a plagiarist) in the midst of the good. The idea is:—the composition of a plagiarist is seen in its true light by the good, though there is no express declaration that it is merely a patchwork. The words अना...मध्ये may also mean 'who is not esteemed among the good.' This meaning also suits the word चौरः. We can also separate as अ-ना आख्यातः 'he (the plagiarist or the thief) is not counted a man'. ना is the nom. sing. of नृ. बन्ध...गूहनैः—the idea (according to the com.) is:—great poets compose works containing particular words like श्री, लक्ष्मी in particular verses or in some particular order. The plagiarist in copying suppresses such indications. बन्धः also means the arrangements of the letters of a stanza in a particular way, such as खड्गबन्ध, शृङ्खलाबन्ध, सर्वतोभद्र. Or बन्धचिह्न may be used in a general sense *viz.* 'the characteristic style of a good composition.' 'बन्धः पदरचना' वामन's काव्यालंकारसूत्रवृत्ति 3. 1. 4. A thief also changes colour *i. e.* his face becomes pale (when challenged in the midst of the good). He also tries to conceal the marks left (in his flesh) by the chains (with which he was bound when caught). Although a thief conceals these marks and so is not declared to be a thief (अनाख्यात), yet by the pallor that comes over his face when challenged he is revealed in his true light.

Verse 7. The author in this verse points out that the poets of particular countries exhibit only a few poetic excellences in their works and not all. श्लेष...च्येषु Among the northern (poets), a work most exhibits puns. श्लेष is of two kinds, शब्दश्लेष and अर्थश्लेष. In the first a particular word when used gives rise to different senses; but if that word be omitted and a synonym substituted, then the double meaning vanishes *e. g.* बालेवोद्यानमालेयं **सालकाननशोभिनी.** Here take the word साल० as meaning सालकं (अलकैः सह) आननं तेन शोभिनी (with बाला) and सालानां काननं तेन शोभिनी (with उद्यानमाला). If for सालक we substitute सकुन्तल then the श्लेष vanishes. In अर्थश्लेष, even if we change the words, there are two meanings; *e. g.* 'उदयमयते दिङ्मालिन्यं निराकुरुतेतरां नयति निधनं निद्रामुद्रां प्रवर्तयति क्रियाः । रचयतितरां स्वैराचारप्रवर्तनकर्तनं बत बत लसत्तेजःपुञ्जो विभाति विभाकरः ॥' काव्यप्रकाश X. (Here a king called विभाकर and the Sun are both praised). अर्थमात्रकम्—The poets of the west care only for the meaning (they do not exhibit charm of style or figures of speech). उत्प्रेक्षा is a figure of speech. To explain it briefly, it consists in representing (poetically, not through mistake) one thing as another thing or in representing a particular effect as due to some cause other than the real one or representing something done with one motive as due to another. It is generally introduced by such words as मन्ये, शङ्के, ध्रुवं or इव (as it were). Bāṇa's works bristle at every step with this figure. The verse 'हरकण्ठ' is a good example of उत्प्रेक्षा. गौडे...डम्बरः among Gauda poets there is only show of words (high-flown language). Their works do not contain charming thoughts or such qualities as perspicuity &c. Daṇḍin, who was at least a contemporary of Bāṇa, if he was not earlier still, speaks of two literary styles. (रीति), *viz.*, वैदर्भी and गौडी. He says that ten Guṇas (such as प्रसाद, माधुर्य and ओजः) are the essence of the Vaidarbhî style, while the Gauḍî style is the reverse of the Vaidarbhî (काव्यादर्श I. 41–42). He tells us that the Gauḍas were very fond of अनुप्रास (काव्यादर्श I. 54) and that even in verse they employed long compounds (काव्यादर्श I. 80). वामन says in his काव्यालङ्कारसूत्रवृत्ति (I. 2. 12.) 'समस्तात्युद्भटपदामोजःकान्तिगुणान्विताम् । गौडीयामपि गायन्ति रीतिं रीतिविचक्षणाः ॥'. गौड is the district of Gaur, central part of Bengal; formerly it extended from वङ्ग to the borders of Orissa.

Verse 8. नवोर्थः—a new topic (*i. e.* a subject not dealt with by former writers) or a striking subject or meaning. This refers to the imaginative side of a poet's mind, called प्रतिभा by Sanskrit rhetoricians. 'प्रज्ञा नवनवोन्मेषशालिनी **प्रतिभा** मता'. जातिरग्राम्या description of nature or objects that is not vulgar. For जाति, see above p. 4. दण्डी gives the following as examples of ग्राम्य and अग्राम्य ways of description respectively, although the meaning is the same. 'कन्ये कामयमानं मां न त्वं कामयसे कथम्। इति ग्राम्योऽयमर्थात्मा वैरस्याय प्रकल्पते ॥ कामं कन्दर्पचाण्डालो मयि वामाक्षि निर्दयः । त्वयि निर्मत्सरो दिष्ट्येत्यग्राम्योऽर्थो रसावहः ॥' (काव्या० I. 63-64). जाति also means a particular class of metres regulated by Mātrās, such as आर्या. Compare 'पद्यं चतुष्पदी तच्च वृत्तं जातिरिति द्विधा' काव्या० I. 11. जाति also means 'a composition or verse in which the same words represent Sanskrit or Prakrit.' Both these meanings are not suitable here. श्लेषः—for explanation, see the preceding verse. अक्लिष्टः not laboured. 'व्यवहितार्थप्रत्ययं क्लिष्टम्' काव्यालङ्कारसूत्र II. 1. 21. स्फुटो रसः A sentiment (which is the subject matter of a poem) that is easily understood. रस is the soul of Kāvya. It is that sentiment which rules a composition and which is the object of the poem to present to the mind of the reader. Rasas are eight शृङ्गार, वीर, करुण, हास्य, रौद्र, भयानक, बीभत्स, अद्भुत. Some add a ninth रस *viz.* शान्त. विक...बन्धः—The Com. says 'उदारतालक्षणबन्धगुणयुक्तः यत्र सति नृत्यन्तीव पदानि प्रतिभासन्ते.' In this he follows वामन's काव्यालङ्कारसूत्र III. 1. 22 'विकटत्वमुदारता'—वृत्ति "बन्धस्य विकटत्वं यदसौ उदारता । यस्मिन्सति नृत्यन्तीव पदानीति जनस्य वर्णभावना भवति तत् विकटत्वं लीलायमानत्वमित्यर्थः । यथा 'स्वचरणविनिविष्टैर्नूपुरैर्नर्तकीनां झणिति रणितमासीत्तत्र चित्रं कलं च' । न पुनः 'चरणकमलकलग्नैर्नूपुरैर्नर्तकीनां झटिति रणितमासीन्मञ्जु चित्रं च तत्र.'" This means that in विकटत्व the sound must be an echo to the sense. C and T translate 'language rich in sonorous words.' The author in our opinion rather refers to ओजोगुण about which दण्डी says 'ओजः समासभूयस्त्वमेतद्गद्यस्य जीवितम् । पद्येऽप्यदाक्षिणात्यानामिदमेकं परायणम् ॥' काव्या. I. 80. कृत्स्न...ष्करम् all this it is difficult to find in one composition.

Verse 9. किं...काव्येन what is the use of the poetry of that poet? C and T translate 'what has that poet to do with poetry?' This does not yield a good sense. Construe यस्य सर्ववृत्तान्तगामिनी भारती जगत्त्रयं न व्याप्नोति सर्ववृत्तान्तगामिनी भारती कथेव (सा यथा जगत्त्रयं व्याप्नोति)—whose Muse comprehending the furthest limit of metrics does not cover the three worlds (*i. e.* does not become well-known in the world) like the Bhārata story. सर्वेषां वृत्तानां (metres) अन्तं गच्छति इति (with Muse); सर्वान् वृत्तान्तान् (इतिहासान्) गमयतीति that conveys all sorts of narratives (with भारती कथा). The Mahābhārata contains numerous episodes.

Verse 10. Here Bāṇa offers his meed of praise to the authors of आख्यायिकाs that preceded him. आख्यायिकाs were composed from very ancient times. Vide Introduction p. XIII.

For a definition of आख्यायिका given by भामह, see Introduction p. XX. The salient points are that it is in prose, has a high topic, is divided into sections called उच्छ्वासs, contains verses in the वक्त्र and अपरवक्त्र metres which suggest coming events. The साहित्यदर्पण (परिच्छेद VI) calls the sections आश्वासs. कथ...श्वराः how are those princes among poets, *viz.* the authors of आख्यायिकाs, not to be praised? (*i. e.* they deserve the highest praise). उच्छ्वा...न्नाः unwearied even at the end of an उच्छ्वास *i. e.* who are able to compose another उच्छ्वास equal in merit to its predecessor. येषां...स्वती in whose verses (in the वक्त्र metre) the goddess of speech dwells. In the वक्त्र metre, there are eight syllables in each पाद as in अनुष्टुभ्. It is defined as 'नाद्यान्नसौ स्यातामब्धेर्योऽनुष्टुभि ख्यातम्'. After the first letter in each पाद there should be no नगण nor सगण and after the first four letters there should be a यगण. उच्छ्वा...खिन्नाः—conveys another idea. A man who is tired heaves out a deep breath. There is an apparent विरोध in saying that they are not exhausted even when they are breathing hard. कवीश्वराः may also mean 'the omniscient gods' *i. e.* the creator (the plural being used for श्लेष or to show respect). The supreme spirit is often called कवि in the Upanishads and the Gîtā. 'कविं पुराणमनुशासितारं' &c. गीता 8. 9; 'कविर्मनीषी परिभूः स्वयम्भूः' ईशावास्योपनिषद् 8. उच्छ्वा...खिन्नाः would mean 'not exhausted or afflicted even at the end of the Universe.' In the Upanishads the Universe containing the Vedas, the Heavens, the earth &c. is said to be the निःश्वसित of the Supreme. 'अस्य महतो भूतस्य निःश्वसितमेतद्यदृग्वेदो... अस्यैवैतानि निःश्वसितानि' बृहदारण्यकोपनिषद् II. 4. 10. वक्त्रे...सरस्वती The goddess of speech is often poetically described as dwelling in the mouth of Brahmā. Compare 'चतुर्मुखमुखाम्भोजवनहंसवधूर्मम । मानसे रमतां नित्यं सर्वशुक्ला सरस्वती ॥' काव्यादर्श I. 1.

Verse 11. Construe कर्णगोचरं गतया वासवदत्तया नूनं कवीनां दर्पः अगलत् कर्णगोचरं गतया पाण्डुपुत्राणां शक्त्या इव कवीनां (दर्पः अगलत्). The pride of poets indeed melted away on account of वासवदत्ता when it reached their ears, just as the pride of Droṇa vanished when the missile of the sons of Pāṇḍu given by Vāsava (Indra) came near Karṇa. वासवदत्ता—This seems to be the work of Subandhu. It is a कथा technically so called. Vide Introduction p. XX. It cannot be the आख्यायिका वासवदत्ता mentioned by Patañjali (Introduction p. XIII). The authors of आख्यायिकाs came in for high praise in the preceding verse. We naturally expect that in this verse the author should refer to another class of works. In this Introduction Bāṇa assigns only one verse to each of the poets or works mentioned below. There is no reason why he should depart from that rule in the case of आख्यायिका. A कथा is very much like an आख्यायिका and so it is but proper that the वासवदत्ता of सुबन्धु (being a कथा) should receive encomiums after the authors of आख्यायिकाs, if सुबन्धु preceded Bāṇa, as we hold. कवि also means द्रोण. The plural कवीनां may be explained as due to the exigencies of श्लेष or as expressing respect. द्रोण was the son of भरद्वाज 'भरद्वाजस्य च स्कन्नं द्रोण्यां शुक्रमवर्धत । महर्षेरुग्रतपसस्तस्माद् द्रोणो व्यजायत ॥' आदिपर्व 63. 6. कवि is a name for शुक्र and so indicates द्रोण. The story of कर्ण, the son of कुन्ती, is well-known. The reference seems to be to the defeat of कर्ण by भीम (vide द्रोणपर्व chap 129, 131, 133). We may also construe कवीनां पाण्डुपुत्राणां (दर्पः) कर्णगोचरं गतया वासवदत्तया शक्त्या इव (अगलत्) 'as the pride of the wise sons of Pâṇḍu melted away through the javelin that was given by इन्द्र and that came to the hands of Karṇa. Karṇa was a generous man. Once Indra who was interested in Arjuna came to Karṇa as a Brāhmaṇa and begged of him his divine armour and ear-rings. Karṇa true to his word gave Indra what he wanted. Indra being pleased with Karṇa gave him a शक्ति that would kill one महारथी whoever he might be. See आदिपर्व chap. 111. 'ददौ शक्तिं सुरपतिर्वाक्यं चेदमुवाच ह ॥ देवासुरमनुष्याणां गन्धर्वोरगरक्षसाम् । यमेकं जेतुमिच्छेथाः सोऽन्यया न भविष्यति ॥' verses 29–30.

Verse 12. भट्टार...यते the prose composition of the revered हरिचन्द्र acts like a king *i. e.* is pre-eminent like a king. भट्टारः or भट्टारकः is a term of respect applied to kings in dramas and inscriptions. 'राजा भट्टारको देवः' इत्यमरः. It was also applied by Jain writers to those who abandoned the worldly life. नृप इव आचरति नृपायते according to 'कर्तुः क्यङ् सलोपश्च' पा. 3. 1. 11. पद...ज्ज्वलः charming or brilliant on account of the arrangement of words (with गद्यबन्ध); splendid on account of the firmness of his position (with नृप). पदानां शब्दानां बन्धेन (रचनया) उज्ज्वलः; पदस्य बन्धेन &c. हारी charming (with गद्यबन्ध); wearing a necklace (with नृप). We may also separate as ०ज्ज्वलो अहारी (with गद्यबन्ध). अहारी not stealing (from the works of others). कृत...स्थितिः—कृता वर्णानां क्रमेण (अलङ्कारशास्त्रानुसारेण) स्थितिः यस्मिन्; कृता वर्णानां ब्राह्मणादीनां क्रमेण (शास्त्रक्रमेण) स्थितिः येन—In which letters are employed in accordance with the rules of poetics (with गद्यबन्ध); who makes the four Varṇas follow the rules prescribed for each (with नृप). It was the canon of rhetoricians that माधुर्यगुण was most appropriate in शृङ्गार and करुण, and ओजः in वीररस. माधुर्य consists in employing letters from क् to म्, except टवर्ग, preceded by the nasals of their class, and that in ओजः one should employ conjunct consonants joining the first and second or third and fourth letters of each class, टवर्ग, श् and ष्. 'टवर्गवर्जिताः स्पर्शाः स्वस्ववर्गान्तशेखराः। लघुरेफलकारौ च कोमलाः परिकीर्तिताः॥ रेफेन यस्य कस्यापि योग आद्यतृतीययोः। स्वोत्तराभ्यां तुल्ययोर्वा परुषाष्टगणः शषौ॥' रत्नापण on प्रतापरुद्र. भट्टारहरिचन्द्र is no more than a mere name to us. His prose composition has not yet been discovered. There is a *poem* called धर्मशर्माभ्युदय written by a Jain writer हरिचन्द्र. A verse of the Gauḍavaho (Vide Intro. p. XII) speaks of a हारियन्द (Prakrit for हारिचन्द्र) बन्ध. Is this a reference to this हरिचन्द्र ?

Verse 13. The principal sentence is सातवाहनः सुभाषितैः रत्नैरिव कोशमकरोत्—सातवाहन made a treasure with fine sayings as with jewels. अविनाशिनम् Immortal (as applied to the collection of सुभाषितs); inexhaustible (with the treasure of jewels). अग्राम्यम्—not vulgar or indecent *i. e.* refined (with सुभाषितकोश); not produced in villages (with रत्नकोश). Jewels are found in the sea or in mines (not in villages). विशुद्धा जातिः स्वभावोक्तिः येषु (with सुभाषितैः); विशुद्धा जातिः येषां (with रत्नैः) of purest character. विशुद्धजातिभिः means the same thing as 'जातिरग्राम्या' above. कोशं—a collection of verses that are unconnected with one another *i. e.* the same subject does not run through them all. It also means 'a treasure.' 'कोशः श्लोकसमूहस्तु स्यादन्योन्यानपेक्षकः' साहित्यदर्पण VI. See also काव्यादर्श I. 13. "मुक्तकं कुलकं कोशः सङ्घात इति तादृशः। सर्गबन्धाङ्गरूपत्वादनुक्तः पद्यविस्तरः॥". In this verse the author seems to praise the गाथासप्तशती of हाल. That work consists of 700 Prakrit verses. It is a collection of verses composed by हाल (सप्तशती I. 3) in the Āryā metre (which is a subdivision of जाति for which see p. 7). 'मात्राभिर्गणना यत्र सा जातिरिति काश्यप।' अग्निपुराण chap. 337. 22. सातवाहन (Prakrit सालाहण) is identified by हेमचन्द्र with हाल 'सालाहणम्मि हालो' देशीनाममाला VIII. 66. In the अभिधानचिन्तामणि we have 'हालः स्यात्सातवाहनः'. हाल seems to us to be an abbreviated form of the Prakrit सालाहण (स् and ह् being often interchanged even in modern vernaculars like the Gujarati). क्षीरस्वामी quotes several verses enumerating the names of famous emperors of old among whom occurs हाल 'हालः स्याच्छालिवाहनः'. A king सातवाहन is connected with गुणाढ्य the author of the बृहत्कथा, for which see verse 17. सुभाषित is defined as 'पुराणेष्वितिहासेषु तथा रामायणादिषु । वचनं सारभूतं यत्तत्सुभाषितमुच्यते ॥'.

Verse 14. प्रवरसेनस्य कुमुदोज्ज्वला (कुमुदवत् उज्ज्वला) कीर्तिः सेतुना सागरस्य परं पारं प्रयाता कुमुदोज्ज्वला (कुमुदेन तदाख्येन वानरसेनापतिना) उज्ज्वला कपिसेना सेतुना सागरस्य परं पारमिव प्रयाता. The author here praises the Prakrit poem called सेतुबन्ध or रावणवध. Bāṇa is engaged in this Introduction in celebrating the names of *authors* and their works. Hence it follows that प्रवरसेन was the author of सेतुबन्ध. There is a tradition that the सेतुबन्ध was composed by कालिदास and that प्रवरसेन was only the patron of that great poet. Bāṇa's words at least do not lend any support to this tradition. The Rājataranginī speaks of several kings of Kashmir that bore the name प्रवरसेन. At the command of हर्ष-विक्रमादित्य of उज्जयिनी the kingdom of काश्मीर was offered to a poet मातृगुप्त who is often identified with कालिदास without any reason beyond the fact that both names mean the same thing. When at Harsha's death मातृगुप्त abdicated the throne, प्रवरसेन (II) ascended it and generously treated मातृगुप्त; vide राजतरङ्गिणी III. 125-323. Daṇḍin says that the language of the country of Mahārāshṭra is Prakrit *par excellence* and that the सेतुबन्ध is composed in (महाराष्ट्री) प्राकृत. 'महाराष्ट्राश्रयां भाषां प्रकृष्टं प्राकृतं विदुः । सागरः सूक्तिरत्नानां सेतुबन्धादि यन्मयम् ॥' काव्यादर्श I. 34. If, as tradition says, the author of the सेतुबन्ध was a king, may we hazard a conjecture that he may have been one of the Vākāṭaka kings? In the Chammak and Sivani copperplate grants (C. I. I. III pp. 235, 243) we have two प्रवरसेनs of the Vakāṭaka family. In the army of the monkeys कुमुद was a commander. 'शरभः कुमुदो वह्निर्वानरो रम्भ एव च ॥ एते चान्ये च बहवो वानराः कामरूपिणः ।' रामायण किष्किन्धा 39. 37-38. The monkeys under the supervision of their leader नल, son of विश्वकर्मा, constructed the bridge by means of which they crossed over to लङ्का. See युद्धकाण्ड chapter 22. 74-75 'तानि कोटिसहस्राणि वानराणां महौजसाम् ॥ बध्नन्तः सागरे सेतुं जग्मुः पारं महोदधेः ।'. The Com. construes प्रवरसेनस्य also with कपिसेना 'प्रवे प्लुते रसो येषां ते प्रवरसाः वानरास्तेषामिनः स्वामी, प्रवरा च सेना यस्य स सुग्रीवश्च'. According to this प्रवरसेन is सुग्रीव (प्रव-रस-इन), because he was the master of monkeys who have a liking for leaping or because he had an excellent army. कुमुद is a white lotus and कीर्ति is poetically represented as white.

Verse 15. Bāṇa here eulogises the dramatist Bhāsa. Kālidāsa speaks of him in his मालविकाग्निमित्र as very famous. For a reference to him in the Gauḍavaho see p. XII of the Introduction. The सरस्वतीकण्ठाभरण quotes the verse 'भासवत्यपि भासादी कविवर्गे जगत्रयीम् । के न यान्ति निबन्धारः कालिदासस्य दासताम् ॥'. The सूक्तिमुक्तावलि quotes a verse of राजशेखर about भास 'भासनाटकचक्रेऽपि छेकैः क्षिप्ते परीक्षितुम् । स्वप्नवासवदत्तस्य दाहकोऽभून्न पावकः ॥' Peterson's Intro. to सुभाषितावलि pp. 80-81. Until very recently it was believed by all that Bhāsa's dramas were lost. Mr. T. Ganapatis astri of Trivandrum has published about thirteen plays the authorship of which he ascribes to Bhāsa on several grounds. We have our own doubts as to whether the plays now put forward are the genuine works of Bhāsa. But obvious considerations prevent us from entering into that question here. The principal sentence is भासः नाटकैः देवकुलैरिव यशो लेभे. सूत्र...रम्भैः—सूत्रधारेण कृतः आरम्भः येषाम्—that had an introduction spoken by the manager of the stage (with नाटकैः); that were constructed by architects (with देवकुलैः). बहवो भूमिकाः येषु; बहवः भूमयः येषु—in which there are numerous characters (with नाटकैः); in which there are several stories. The affix क is optionally added to all बहुव्रीहि compounds. सपताकैः containing पताकाs (with नाटकैः); possessed of banners (with देवकुलैः). पताका is a term in dramaturgy. There are five अर्थप्रकृतिs (the leading sources of the principal object in a drama) *viz.*, बीज, बिन्दु, पताका, प्रकरी and कार्य. पताका is defined by भरत 'यद्वृत्तं हि परार्थं स्यात्प्रधानस्योपकारकम् । प्रधानवच्च कल्प्येत सा पताकेति कीर्तिता ॥' नाट्यशास्त्र. 19. 23. It is an episode which has no purpose in itself, but is put in by the author for serving as a foil to the principal theme; *e. g.* the representation of the career of सुग्रीव when the principal theme is रामचरित. The दशरूप says 'प्रासङ्गिकं परार्थस्य स्वार्थो यस्य प्रसङ्गतः । सानुबन्धं पताकाख्यं प्रकरी च प्रदेशभाक् ॥' I. 13. On this धनिक's comment is 'दूरं यदनुवर्तते प्रासङ्गिकं सा पताका । सुग्रीवादिवृत्तान्तवत् । पताकेवासाधारणनायकचिह्नवत्तदुपकारित्वात् । यदल्पं सा प्रकरी श्रवणादिवृत्तान्तवत्.' The साहित्यदर्पण defines पताका as 'व्यापि प्रासङ्गिकं वृत्तं पताकेत्यभिधीयते.' This is quite different from पताकास्थानक, which is of four kinds. See साहित्यदर्पण VI. for it. It is not to be supposed that Bhāsa alone among the dramatists before Bāṇa wrote plays that were commenced by सूत्रधारs or that contained varied dramatis personae or पताकाs. Bāṇa's only object is to show, by taking three paronomastic clauses, similarity between temples and dramas.

Verse 16. In this verse Bāṇa offers a very glowing tribute of praise to the prince of Sanskrit poets. Translate 'who indeed does not feel delight the moment the fine sayings of Kālidāsa are uttered, sayings which are sweet and agreeable (सान्द्र) like sprays of flowers?' The idea is that even men of ordinary intelligence are delighted with Kālidāsa's sayings, much more therefore will those possessed of high critical faculty find delight in them. वा does not mean 'or' here. It is to be connected with कस्य (कस्य वा न प्रीतिर्जायते), the meaning being 'I should like to know who is not &c.' Compare for this use of वा 'परिवर्तिनि संसारे मृतः को वा न जायते.' Note also the use of इव in a similar way 'परैस्त्वदन्यः क इवापहारयेन्मनोरमामात्मवधूमिव श्रियम् ॥' किरातार्जुनीय I. 31. निर्गतासु when uttered by anyone (with सूक्तिषु); come out (मञ्जरीषु). The मञ्जरी also is fragrant and thick or glossy (सान्द्र). The reading मधुरसार्द्रासु (wet with sweet juice) is not so good, as it cannot be well construed with सूक्तिषु. This verse indicates, in our humble opinion, that Kālidāsa was an household word in the days of Bāṇa and that therefore the former preceded the latter by a long interval of time.

Verse 17. The principal sentence here is–बृहत्कथा हरलीला इव कस्य विस्मयाय नो (भवेत्)—In whom would the बृहत्कथा not cause marvel, as the sportive action of S'iva does? The बृहत्कथा here spoken of is a work in a Prakrit dialect called पैशाची ascribed to गुणाढ्य. The original work in पैशाची is not now extant. But it is certain that in the 11th and 12th centuries of the Christian era it was available. We have abridgments of the work in Sanskrit compiled by two Kashmirian Pandits, Kshemendra (11th century) and Somadeva (12th century). सोमदेव tells us in the कथासरित्सागर 'यथामूलं तथैवैतन्न मनागप्यतिक्रमः । ग्रन्थविस्तरसंक्षेपमात्रं भाषा च भिद्यते ॥' I. 1. 10. A third redaction of the ancient बृहत्कथा was issued by a French Scholar M. Lacôte. See J. R. A. S. for 1906 p. 689 for a Tamil work based upon the बृहत्कथा. Why the book was written in पैशाची is explained in the 6th and 7th chapters (तरङ्ग) of the first लम्बक of the कथासरित्सागर. The story resembles that of the sibylline books. गुणाढ्य was originally a minister of शातवाहन king of the Deccan. Being defeated in a wager he went to the विन्ध्य forest, learnt पैशाची, wrote a work in his own blood containing seven lakhs of verses. When the king would not receive a strange work like that, गुणाढ्य read each page and burnt it. Ultimately the king sent for गुणाढ्य when only a lakh of verses remained. For references to गुणाढ्य and his बृहत्कथा see Introduction p. XXII (footnote). According to the कथासरित्सागर, गुणाढ्य had to forego संस्कृत, प्राकृत and देशभाषाs. We hazard the conjecture that पैशाची was the name given to Pâli or some dialect similar to it by गुणाढ्य to prove true to his word or by others before him in derision as the language of the Buddhistic heretics (who would be no better than पिशाचs to orthodox Indians). The बृहत्कथा excites wonder on account of the marvellous stories it contains. समुद्दीपितः कन्दर्पः यया by which passion is excited (with बृहत्कथा). The बृहत्कथा, to judge from its abridgments, contained numerous stories of love and intrigue. The Com. explains in another way also 'समुद्दीपितः प्रकाशितः ख्यातिं नीतः कन्दर्पो नरवाहनदत्तो यस्यामिति । स हि कामांश इति आगमः'. नरवाहनदत्त was the son of वत्सराज and वासवदत्ता and was crowned king of the विद्याधरs. 'गगनादुच्चचारैव काले तस्मिन्सरस्वती ॥ कामदेवावतारोऽयं राजञ्जातस्तवात्मजः । नरवाहनदत्तं च जानीह्येनमिहाख्यया ॥' कथासरित्सागर 4th लम्बक 3rd तरङ्ग verses 72-73. समुद्दीपितः कन्दर्पः यस्याम् or यया (with हरलीला) by which Cupid was burnt up. Or we may separate समुत् and दीपितकन्दर्पा. समुद् (मुदा सह) = सहर्षा full of joy. मदन wanted to help the gods against the demon तारक who was destined to be killed by the son of शिव. In order to induce शिव to marry पार्वती Cupid was about to shoot his flowery arrow, when S'iva, coming to know his intention, burnt him to ashes in wrath with the fire from his third eye. कृतं गौर्याः प्रसाधनं (*lit.* accomplishment *i. e.* propitiating) यस्याम्. The Com. explains in two ways. गौरी was a goddess presiding over some विद्या which was propitiated by नरवाहनदत्त. The other is a strained explanation 'गौरीं प्राति पूरयति गौरीप्रः । साधनं परिकरबन्धो यथाप्रस्तावो यस्याम् । गौरीप्रेरितेन हि हरेण तथा तस्यां परिकरबन्धः कृतो यथा साऽतीव पिप्रिये'. The story narrated in the बृहत्कथा was first given to पार्वती by शिव. *Vide* बृहत्कथामञ्जरी I. 1. There is no necessity to divide the words in an unusual way (as गौरीप्र and साधन). The simple meaning is:—शिव propitiated गौरी by telling her the original story of the बृहत्कथा. प्रसाधन also means 'decoration' (with हरलीला).

Verse 18. This is a very hard verse. Various interpretations have been proposed. The Com. takes आढ्यराज to be some poet and explains उत्साह as 'beating time in dancing' and then quotes the explanations of others. 'उत्साहो नृत्ते तालवि-

श्लेषः । उदीर्यमाणगीत्याधारभूतपदोपचारात्काव्यमप्युत्साह इति केचित् । यत्र पूर्वं श्लोकेनार्थं उपक्षिप्यते पश्चात्स एव गद्येन वितन्यते मध्ये वृत्तनिबन्धश्च भवति स परिसमाप्तार्थ उत्साह उच्यते इत्यन्ये'. In construing this verse we have to remember two things. Firstly, in the preceding verses Bâṇa eulogises eminent poets and their works; so it is not unnatural to expect that आढ्यराज is the name of a poet. Secondly, in the following verse the author in a strain of humility says that he is taking a bold step in writing an Âkhyâyikâ about his patron Harsha. He intimates that he has no intention to rival the works of the great poets of old, but that his sole motive is to give expression to his admiration for his patron The plain meaning is 'my tongue, as if drawn inwards by the Utsâhas composed by Âḍhyarâja, does not set about to write a poem'. The idea is that the Utsâhas of आढ्यराज are such works of genius that I (बाण) cannot embark on making an effort in the same direction for fear of being ridiculed when my puny gifts are compared by people with the giant intellect of आढ्यराज. The idea conveyed by हृदयस्थैः स्मृतैरपि is this—Bâṇa had studied the उत्साहs of आढ्यराज and so they were हृदयस्थ. As they were हृदयस्थ (and so inside the body) they may be fancied as able to draw his tongue in. But the works of आढ्यराज were not bodily present in Bâṇa's heart. They were only remembered. In order to draw anything, the presence of the person drawing is necessary. But in the case of the उत्साहs their very memory (the mere memory of their worth and greatness) is sufficient to draw his tongue in (*i. e.* to prevent Bāṇa from writing any poetic work). This is the force of the word अपि in स्मृतैरपि.

Who आढ्यराज was and what were the उत्साहs he composed it is difficult to say. The alternative explanations given by the com. convey some idea of what they may have been. According to the commentator रत्नेश्वर on the सरस्वतीकण्ठाभरण, आढ्यराज is another name of शालिवाहन who encouraged the study of Prakrit (*vide* Intro. p. X footnote). Against accepting this interpretation the only objection is that Bâṇa has already praised सातवाहन (who is the same as शालिवाहन) in verse 13. Peterson thinks that it is a mistake to take आढ्यराज as a proper noun (Intro. to Kâdambarî p. 96). He regards आढ्यराज as almost the same as आद्यराज. He takes उत्साह to mean 'brave deeds'. Some MSS. read आद्यराज but that

also written as शुनासीर; क्षीरस्वामी derives as 'शोभना नासीरा अग्रेसरा अस्य शुनासीरयोरपत्यमित्येके'. गीर्वाणैः = देवैः. गीः (वाक्) एव वाणः (बवयोरभेदात्) बाणः येषाम्. सं. also explains as 'गिरः स्तुतिरूपा वणन्ति भजन्तीति'. ब्रह्मो...कुर्वन् engaged in philosophical discussion about ब्रह्म. ब्रह्मोद्यं = ब्रह्मणः वदनं उक्तिः. ब्रह्मोद्य is generally used as a noun in the neuter, but here it is an adjective of कथाः. ब्रह्म means either Veda or the supreme all-pervading apirit which is the subject–matter of the Upanishads. 'वदः सुपि क्यप् च' पा. 3.1.106 (वदेर्भावे क्यप् स्यात् चात् यत् अनुपसर्गे सुपि उपपदे । ब्रह्मोद्यम् । ब्रह्मवद्यम् । सि. कौ.). सं० explains 'ब्रह्मोद्या सा कथा यस्यामुच्यते ब्रह्म शाश्वतम्.' See मनुस्मृति 3.231 'यद्यद्रोचेत विप्रेभ्यस्तत्तद्दद्यादमत्सरः । ब्रह्मोद्याश्च कथाः कुर्यात्पितॄणामेतदीप्सितम् ॥'. मेधातिथि on मनु० explains 'ब्रह्मोद्या ब्रह्मणि वेदे या उद्यन्ते कथ्यन्ते ता ब्रह्मोद्याः देवासुरयुद्धं वृत्रवधः सरमादूत्यमित्याद्याः । अथवा कः स्विदेकाकी चरतीत्यादि'. अन्याश्च...भावयन् engaged in (*lit.* causing to be, putting forward) other blameless (निरवद्य) discussions on various lores. विद्याs were either four or fourteen. The four are आन्वीक्षिकी (metaphysics), त्रयी (the three Vedas), वार्ता (agriculture and trade), दण्डनीति (science of Government). See चाणक्य's अर्थशास्त्र p. 6. 'पुराणन्यायमीमांसाधर्मशास्त्राङ्गमिश्रिताः । वेदाः स्थानानि विद्यानां धर्मस्य च चतुर्दश ॥' याज्ञ० I. 3 (*i. e.* four Vedas, six वेदाङ्गs, पुराण, न्याय, मीमांसा and धर्मशास्त्र). These are the fourteen Vidyâs. गोष्ठी an assembly or discourse. In ancient times गोष्ठी was somewhat like a modern club. 'समानविद्यावित्तशीलबुद्धिवयसामनुरूपैरालापैरेकत्रासनबन्धो गोष्ठी' सं. If we read निरवद्यविद्या as one word, then we shall have to separate as निरवद्य अविद्या०, which does not yield a good sense. If we read निरवद्यविद्या० the meaning will be the same or we may interpret as 'discussion about the knowledge of the Blameless One' (*i. e.* ब्रह्म). निरवद्य is an epithet of ब्रह्म. Compare 'निष्कलं निष्क्रियं शान्तं निरवद्यं निरञ्जनम्' श्वेताश्वतरोपनिषद् 6.19. Note the words 'निरवद्यविद्याविद्योतितानि' in the last para. of the first उच्छ्वास (p. 19 text). Separate तथा आसीनं (sitting). त्रिभुवनेन प्रतीक्ष्यं पूज्यम् (from ईक्ष् with प्रति). प्रजापतयः—In the मनुस्मृति the ten प्रजापतिs enumerated do not include मनु, दक्ष and चाक्षुष. 'पतीन्प्रजानामसृजं महर्षीनादितो दश ॥ मरीचिमत्र्यङ्गिरसौ पुलस्त्यं पुलहं क्रतुम् । प्रचेतसं वसिष्ठं च भृगुं नारदमेव च ॥' मनु० I. 34-35. In the मनुस्मृति (I. 36) we are told that these ten प्रजापतिs created seven Manus of whom चाक्षुष is the sixth (मनु० I. 62). The रामायण gives a slightly different list (अरण्यकाण्ड 14.7-9). दक्ष is a well-known प्रजापति. He was born from the right अङ्गुष्ठ of ब्रह्मा (*vide* आदिपर्व 66.10). Probably the author uses the word प्रजापति not in a technical sense, but in a general sense 'progenitors.' सप्तर्षयः पुरःसराः (मुख्याः) येषाम्. The seven sages are मरीचि, अत्रि, अङ्गिरस्, पुलस्त्य, पुलह, क्रतु, वसिष्ठ. के...चारयन् some uttered with proper accents hymns from the Rigveda that are appropriate for praising (God). The Rigveda mostly consists of verses praising various deities, describing their wondrous works and soliciting the gods for various boons. केचि... पठन् some recited the Yajus formula containing worship. 'क्ष्यार्चयोरपचितिः' इत्यमरः. अपचितिं पूजां भजन्ते इति. प्रशंसासामानि Sāman hymns containing praise. साम verses are to be sung. Almost the whole of the सामवेद is taken from the Rigveda. A Yajus is in prose, while a ऋक् is in a metrical form. Bāṇa uses appropriate verbs and descriptive words with reference to the ऋग्वेद, the यजुर्वेद and the सामवेद. विवृतं क्रतुक्रियातन्त्रं यैः that explained (*lit.* laid bare) the doctrines (or dogmas) of the performance of sacrifice. 'तन्त्रं प्रधाने सिद्धान्ते' इत्यमरः. व्याचचक्षिरे expounded (3rd plu. Perfect of चक्ष् with वि and आ). विद्यानां विसंवादः (difference) तेन कृताः due to the difference of the lores they had studied. It is better to read with B 'अन्योन्यस्य विवादाः.' प्रादुरभवन्—(naturally or spontaneously) arose. What the author means is:—The sages had each of them made a profound study of some particular विद्या and so disputes arose among them not out of envy or pride, but because each was specially devoted to a particular विद्या and so gave expression to his views without meaning any offence to other personages present.

P. 2 l. 29–p. 3 l. 15 **अथाति...जहास.** अति...प्रकृत्या by nature extremely irritable. अत्रेस्तनयः–अत्रि's wife was अनसूया a daughter of दक्ष. अत्रि had three sons सोम, दुर्वासस् and दत्तात्रेय. See विष्णुपुराण I. 10. तारापतेः (चन्द्रमसः) भ्राता. The moon is said to have sprung from the lustre of Atri's eye. See हरिवंश 25 'नेत्राभ्यां वारि सुस्राव दशधा द्योतयद्दिशः। तं गर्भं विधिना हृष्टा दश देव्यो दधुस्तदा॥ समेत्य धारयामासुर्न च ताः समशक्नुवन्॥ स ताभ्यः सहसैवाथ दिग्भ्यो गर्भः प्रभान्वितः। पपात भासयँल्लोकाञ्शीतांशुः सर्वभावनः॥' verses 6–8. Note 'अत्रिनेत्रनिर्गतस्य... दृष्ट इव जनेन जन्मदिवसः कुमुदबन्धोः' हर्षचरित 7th उच्छ्वास. मन्दपालः नाम यस्य सः मन्दपालनामा तेन. कलहं करोति इति कलहायते according to 'शब्द-वैरकलहाभ्रकण्वमेघेभ्यः करणे' पा. 3.1.17 (एभ्यः कर्मभ्यः करोत्यर्थे क्यङ् स्यात्। सि. कौ.). विस्वरमकरोत् he struck a discordant note. विस्वरम् may be taken as an adjective of साम or as an adverb. सर्वेषु goes with मुनिषु. शापभयात् प्रतिपन्नं मौनं यैः that took to silence through fear of a curse. दुर्वासस् was well-known for cursing persons at the slightest offence. अन्या...सम्भवे while Brahmâ paid no heed (to the lapse of दुर्वासस्) being engaged in conversing with some one else. ब्रह्मा is supposed to have sprung from the lotus in the navel of Vishṇu. Compare first para of the 4th उच्छ्वास 'द्विजवरस्वेच्छागृहीतकोषो नाभिपद्म इव पुण्डरीकेक्षणात्.' भगवती कुमारी—connect these with देवी सरस्वती below. The principal sentence is भगवती कुमारी देवी सरस्वती श्रुत्वा जहास. किञ्चित् उन्मुक्तः बालभावः यस्मिन् or येन (*adj.* of वयसि) which had just cast aside childhood *i. e.* which had just passed the stage of being a mere girl. भूषितं नवयौवनं येन—The idea is:—she was so charming at that age that youth itself had its charms heightened by claiming her as one of its owners. गृहीतचामरा प्रचलन्ती भुजलता यस्याः whose creeperlike hand held a chowrie and was waving. पितामहं = ब्रह्माणम्. उपवीजयन्ती fanning. निर्भर्त्सनार्थं ताडनं तेन जातः रागः (रक्तवर्णः) ययोः. निर्भर्त्सन... समाना brilliant with her spray-like feet naturally red, that as if seemed to have grown red by stamping (on the ground) for censuring (दुर्वासस्). Her feet were naturally red; the poet fancies that they grew red because she stamped with her feet on the ground by way of finding fault with दुर्वासस् who had committed a mistake in singing a साम verse. शिष्य... चरणा whose feet were musical with two anklets that jingled in accordance with the movements (क्रमः) of her steps, as if they (नूपुरयुगल) were two pupils. वाचालितौ चरणौ यस्याः. As she moved about, the anklets on the feet jingled. The words पद० and वाचा० yield another sense with शिष्यद्वय. The पदपाठ of the Rigveda is ascribed to शाकल्य in the निरुक्त. क्रम, जटा and घन are certain arrangements of the verses of the Rigveda intended to preserve the purity of the text. The क्रमपाठ is ascribed to पाञ्चाल बाभ्रव्य. See शान्तिपर्व 343.103. The अनुशासनपर्व (85.90) mentions both पद and क्रम. The क्रमपाठ of the verse 'इदं विष्णुर्विचक्रमे त्रेधा निदधे पदम्' would be 'इदं विष्णुः। विष्णुर्वि। वि चक्रमे। चक्रमे त्रेधा। त्रेधा नि। नि दधे। दधे पदम्। पदमिति पदम्।'. शिष्यs would be noisy (मुखर) by repeating the पदपाठ and the क्रमपाठ. The words चरण and शाखा are sometimes used as synonyms; चरण means 'शाखाध्येतृ' *i. e.* 'those who study a particular शाखा of the Veda, an ideal succession of teachers and pupils.' This latter sense is required here (with शिष्य०). मदन... द्वितयम् who (सरस्वती) had legs appearing like the pillars of the arched portal of the city of love. मदननगरस्य तोरणं तस्य स्तम्भयोः इव विभ्रमः यस्य (*adj.* of °द्वितयम्). Her legs were straight and delicately proportioned. Therefore they as if supported (*i. e.* excited) love, as pillars support the portal of a city. This is not a very elegant way of describing सरस्वती. The reading धर्मनगर० would make सरस्वती the support of धर्म. This is somewhat better. सलीलं is to be connected with विन्यस्त०. उत्काः कलहंसाः तेषां कुलं तस्य कलः आलापः तद्वत् प्रलपति इति °प्रलापिनि. सलील...किसलया who had sportively placed her sprout-like left hand on the string of her girdle that jingled like the sweet murmur of the swarms of love-sick कलहंसs. उत्कः= उत्कण्ठितः. 'उत्क उन्मनाः' पा. 5.2.80. Small bells were attached to girdles. विन्यस्तं वामहस्त एव किसलयं यया. विद्व... काया whose body was rendered pure by the Brahmanical thread hanging down from her shoulder, as if it (ब्रह्मसूत्र) were a coil of virtues that stuck to her on account of dwelling in the heart of the wise. ब्रह्मसूत्रं=यज्ञोपवीतम् (ब्रह्मणि वेदग्रहणकाले धृतं सूत्रम्). सरस्वती dwells in the mind of the wise; गुणs (virtues) also occupy the heart of the wise. The मानस lake was created by ब्रह्मा whose daughter was सरस्वती; so she may be said to be dwelling on the मानस lake. ब्रह्मसूत्र is a coil of गुणs (threads). 'कैलासशिखरे राम मनसा निर्मितं सरः । ब्रह्मणा प्रागिदं यस्मात्तदभून्मानसं सरः ॥' रामायण. Compare the description of महाश्वेता 'मण्डलीकृतेन ब्रह्मसूत्रेण पवित्रीकृतकायाम्' कादम्बरी p. 130 of P. भास्वान् मध्यनायकः (मध्यरत्नं) यस्य— the central gem of which is brilliant. अने... यातं inlaid with many pearls (अनेकमुक्ताभिः अनुयातम्). अपवर्गमार्गम्=मोक्षमार्गम्. हार is fancied to be मोक्षमार्ग because the two epithets भास्व० and अनेक० apply to both. भास्वतः सूर्यस्य मध्यं नयतीति ०नायकः—the path of final beatitude leads through the sun. The Upanishads speak of two paths, देवयान and पितृयाण. Those who follow the doctrine of works, reach by various stages the moon and after enjoying the fruits of their good works there, they have to be born again. Those who follow the path of knowledge were supposed to reach by various stages the sun and thence to attain to मोक्ष. When there is मोक्ष, the cycle of births and deaths ceases. 'ते य एवमेतद्विदुर्ये चामी अरण्ये श्रद्धां सत्यमुपासते तेऽर्चिरभिसम्भवन्ति, अर्चिषोऽहः, अह्न आपूर्यमाणपक्षमापूर्यमाणपक्षाद्यान्षण्मासानुदङ्ङादित्य एति मासेभ्यो देवलोकं देवलोकादादित्यमादित्याद्वैद्युतं तान्वैद्युतान्पुरुषोऽमानव एत्य ब्रह्मलोकान् गमयति तेषु ब्रह्मलोकेषु पराः परावतो वसन्ति तेषां न पुनरावृत्तिः' बृहदारण्यकोपनिषद् XI. 2. 14. In the गीता, they are called शुक्लगति and कृष्णगति. 'शुक्लकृष्णे गती ह्येते जगतः शाश्वते मते । एकया यात्यनावृत्तिमन्ययावर्तते पुनः ॥' VIII. 26. The com. quotes the verse 'परिव्राड् योगयुक्तश्च शूरश्चाभिमुखं हतः । द्वाविमौ पुरुषौ लोके सूर्यमण्डलभेदिनौ ॥' which is महा० उद्योगपर्व

33. 61 with slight variations. वदन...राजमाना resplendent with her quivering lip that was red as if with the Alaktaka dye from the feet of all the Vidyās that had entered her mouth. Alaktaka dye was applied to the feet by young ladies. Her lip was naturally red. The poet fancies that the redness was due to the fact that Vidyâs (ladies) in entering her mouth left some lac sticking to her lip. A very learned person is often spoken of as one on the tip of whose tongue dance Vidyâs. Compare 'अमुष्य विद्या रसनाग्रनर्तकी.' सरस्वती, as presiding over all Vidyâs, would naturally have them at the tip of her tongue. 'ओष्ठाधरौ तु रदनच्छदौ दशनवाससी' इत्यमरः. सं... प्रतिमाम् (her cheek) on which was reflected (संक्रान्त) an image of the black antelope skin of Brahmâ. साम... हरिणामिव as if the deer in the moon had got down on it for listening to her singing sweet with Sâman (hymns). सामभिः or साम्नां मधुरं गीतं तस्य आकर्णनाय अवतीर्णः शशिहरणः यस्याम् (*adj.* of कपोलस्थलीम्). Deer are very found of music. The spots on the moon were supposed to be either a deer or hare. Compare the verse 'अङ्कं केऽपि शशङ्किरे जलनिधेः पङ्कं परे मेनिरे सारङ्गं कतिचिच्च सञ्जगदिरे भूच्छायमैच्छन्परे ॥ इन्दौ यद्दलितेन्द्रनीलशकलश्यामं दरीदृश्यते तत्सान्द्रं निशि पीतमन्धतमसं कुक्षिस्थमाचक्ष्महे ॥.' The reflection of the deerskin of Brahmâ on her bright cheek is fancied as being the deer in the moon. The bright cheek was like the moon. As the goddess was in heaven, it is appropriate that the deer in the moon is spoken of (and not an ordinary one). ति... लता One of whose creeper—like eyebrows was raised in a curve (तिर्यक्) and with contempt (सावज्ञम्). अवज्ञया सह यथा स्यात्तथा. She felt contempt for दुर्वासस् when the latter committed a mistake through wrath. श्रोत्र... प्रवाहेण as if washing one ear that was soiled by hearing the discordant note (of दुर्वासस्) with a stream of tears issuing out of the corner (अपाङ्गः) of her eye. The poet fancies that, her ear being soiled, she wanted to wash it clean with water. The curved eyebrow looked like a stream of water issuing from the corner of the eye and proceeding towards its neighbour the ear to free it of its taint. It is not to be supposed that she had tears in her eyes. इतर... मदा who, with the other ear that had on it a white full-blown सिन्धुवार bunch and that looked as if it were smiling, manifested her pride of knowledge. Smiles are poetically represented as white. The सिन्धुवार flower on her ear is fancied as the smile of सरस्वती. We smile at the fall

of others. सरस्वती under the garb of the white flower smiled at the lapse of दुर्वासस्. श्रुति...समाना who was attended upon by swarms of bees in the flowers of her ear-ornament that (bees) besought her ear, as if they (bees) were Oṃkâras. The bees hovering round the flowers on her ear seemed to be making requests (प्रणय) to her ear. प्रणव (*i. e.* the syllable Om) also is श्रुतिप्रणयि (*i. e.* the friend or constant attendant of Veda). The mystic syllable ओम् precedes the study of the Veda or a Vedic text. Compare 'ओङ्कारः स्वर्गद्वारं तस्माद् ब्रह्म अध्येष्यमाणः एतदादि प्रतिपद्येत' आपस्तम्बधर्मसूत्र I. 13.6; 'आसीन्महीक्षितामाद्यः प्रणवश्छन्दसामिव' रघु. I. 11. श्रुतिं वेदं प्रणयन्ति that lead forth *i. e.* introduce Veda. सूक्ष्म...शरीरा whose figure was covered with a spotless silken robe of fine texture (सूक्ष्म) as if with a flash of intellect. प्रतानः shoot or tendril. सूक्ष्म subtle (with प्रज्ञा). विमल pure (and not wicked or sinful), with प्रज्ञा. Her fine robe was like the subtle flashes of intellect. वाङ्मयं...किरन्ती spreading in all directions the pure moon-light of her teeth, as if it were literature. ज्योत्स्नायाः आलोकः तम्. The bright teeth of सरस्वती gleamed forth when she laughed at दुर्वासस्. The teeth, as they belonged to सरस्वती, were really वाङ्मय (वाचः सरस्वत्याः विकारः). वाङ्मयं also means 'literature.' Pure literature spreads enlightenment in the world.

P. 3 ll. 16-25 **दृष्ट्वा...जग्राह.** The principal sentence is दृष्ट्वा च तां तथा हसन्तीं स मुनिः...वारिणा समुपस्पृश्य शापजलं जग्राह. दुर्गृहीतः विद्यालवः तेन अवलेपः तेन दुर्विदग्धे (vocative) that are puffed up with vanity at the (acquisition of) particle of ill-understood knowledge. शिरः...शरारोः (*adj.* of ०कलापस्य) that fell dishevelled as the knot was unloosened when he shook his head. शिरःकम्पेन शीर्यमाणः बन्धः तेन विशरारुः (from शॄ with वि) तस्य. 'शॄवन्द्योरारुः' पा. 3.2.173 (शरारुः, वन्दारुः). उन्मिषन् पिङ्गलिमा यस्य the yellow colour of which flashed forth. पिङ्गलिमन् *m.* from पिङ्गल with affix इमन्. 'पृथ्वादिभ्य इमनिज्वा' पा. 5.1.122. रोचिषा = तेजसा कान्त्या वा. सिञ्च...दिशः as if sprinkling the ten quarters with the fluid of the fire of his wrath. The reddish—yellow gleam of his matted hair is fancied to be a fluid spreading over the world. Fire has a reddish flame. The reddish जटा is like a flame of fire (here identified with wrath). कृत...बध्नन्—This clause contains a complicated pun. The plain sense is that Durvāsas knit his eyebrow into a terrific curve whereby his broad forehead was contracted into wrinkles. These wrinkles looked like the lines on a chessboard (अष्टापदम्). अन्धकारितं ललाटपट्टमेव अष्टापदं यया (*adj.* of भ्रुकुटिम्). This is one of the earliest allusions to the game of chess, which was invented in India. 'अष्टापदं शारिफलम्' इत्यमरः (अष्टौ पदान्यस्य). It is a board divided into eight rows, each row having eight squares. It is a question with some whether अष्टापद is a chess board or only a draught board (Marathi सोंगट्यांचा पट). We incline to the former view. Bâṇa at all events associates it with the game of chess. Compare 'अष्टापदानां चतुरङ्गकल्पना' हर्षचरित 2nd उच्छ्वास. चतुरङ्ग refers to the four arms of the ancient Indian army *viz.* infantry, cavalry, elephant riders and chariots. Pâṇini was aware of the word अष्टापद being used in a technical sense 'अष्टनः संज्ञायाम्' पा. 6.3.125 (उत्तरपदे दीर्घः। अष्टापदम्। सि. कौ.). Moreover Pâṇini refers to a particular position of S'āras (chessmen) in 'अनुपद-सर्वान्न-अयानयं बद्धा-भक्षयति-नेयेषु' पा. 5.2.9 (अयानयः स्थलविशेषः तं नेयः आयानयीनः शारः। सि. कौ.). पतञ्जलि comments on this सूत्र and explains the technical meaning of अय and अनय (see Kielhorn's महाभाष्य vol. II. p. 373). In कादम्बरी we have 'अष्टापदपरिचयचतुराभिः' (p. 196 of P.). कृत...धानाम् has three senses· (1) कृतं कालस्य कृष्णवर्णस्य सन्निधानं यया that had blackness near it (with भ्रुकुटि, which was dark); (2) कृतं कालस्य कृष्णवर्णशारस्य सन्निधानं येन (with अष्टापद)—That had black chessmen on it. Chessmen were grouped into black and white or red to mark the opposing sides. कृतं कालस्य यमस्य सन्निधानं यया (with अन्तःपुर... मकरिका) that was near यम or that took persons in the presence of यम. दुर्वासस् by his curses made people perish and so brought them before यम. So his भ्रुकुटि is properly spoken of as driving people into the presence of यम. अन्तः...मकरिकाम् that (frowning eyebrow) was the crocodile ornament painted on the (faces of the) wives (of यम). पत्रभङ्ग–drawings of ornamental figures on the face, bosom etc. The knit brow resembled the figure of a crocodile drawn on the cheeks of Yama's wives. A crocodile is an emblem of death and so is an appropriate decoration for Yama s wives. अति... प्रयच्छन् with his extremely red eye offering as it were the oblation (उपहारः) of his own blood to the goddess of wrath (अमर्षः). His eyes were suffused red with wrath and seemed to drop down blood. So the poet fancies that he was going to offer an oblation of blood to अमर्षदेवता. निर्दयं दष्टः दशनच्छदः तस्मात् भयं तेन पलायमानाम्. निर्दय...च्छलेन under the guise of the rays of his teeth, confining his speech that was as if fleeing through fear at the merciless biting of his lip. The idea is:-दुर्वासस् being enraged bit his lips and when he did so his bright teeth gleamed forth. The poet fancies that his speech was afraid of being mercilessly dealt with as his lip was and so wanted to run away, but was confined inside by the rays of his gleaming teeth. अंसा...जिनस्य tying in another way the knot of his deerskin that slipped from his shoulder, as if it were an edict (giving him authority) for cursing. As the skin slipped from his shoulder he tied it in another way so as not to allow it to drop down. The deerskin had a brownish surface with dark spots. A शासनपट्ट is a grant (generally on copperplate or silk cloth) of land or it is a proclamation announcing the orders of a king. The brown deerskin resembled a copperplate or silken charter and the dark spots resembled the letters. In the case of दुर्वासस् it is fancied to be a charter giving him the authority to curse others. स्वेद...यवः held in all limbs by gods, demons and sages that were reflected in the drops of perspiration (on his body) and that had as if come in refuge to him out of fear of the curse (that he might pronounce). प्रतिपन्नाः सर्वे अवयवाः यस्य. दुर्वासस् perspired on account of his intense rage and the assembly of gods was reflected in the bright drops. The poet fancies that they out of fear of a curse came beseeching him to be merciful. कोपात् कम्पः तेन तरलिताः (tremulous) अङ्गुलयः यस्य (*adj.* of करेण). करेण... क्षिप्य tossing aside his rosary (अक्षमाला) as if it were a string of letters that stuck (to his hand) for propitiating (प्रसादनं) him. He had his rosary in his hand, but, when he began to shake with wrath, he threw it away. The poet fancies that it was not the अक्षमाला that was thrown away, but the letters of the alphabet. The letters of the alphabet are here represented as the partisans of सरस्वती and as interceding with दुर्वासस् for सरस्वती (who presides over all learning and therefore also over letters). The sage as if intimated that he would listen to no intercession. अक्षरमाला suggests अक्षमाला for two reasons. Letters constitute a string as beads do. Besides अक्ष may be used as an abbreviated way of indicating all the letters from अ to क्ष. कामण्डलव (from कमण्डलु with the affix अण्) contained in his water pot. समुपस्पृश्य having sipped water and ejected it. A curse was generally pronounced with the pouring of water.

P. 3 l. 26—**P. 4.** l. 10 **अत्रान्तरे...समुत्तस्थौ.** The principal sentence is अत्रान्तरे स्वयम्भुवोऽभ्याशे समुपविष्टा देवी सावित्री चतुर्भिर्वेदैः सह समुत्तस्थौ. स्वयम्भुवः ब्रह्मणः अभ्याशे समीपे. मूर्तिमती in a corporeal form. पीयूष...वसाना wearing a fine bark robe of the tree of paradise that (robe) was as white as the mass of the foam of nectar. This and the following clauses in the nominative qualify सावित्री. बिस...ग्रन्थिः that had tied between her high breasts a knot with an upper garment (a shawl) made of lotus filaments. उन्नतस्तनयोर्मध्ये बद्धा गात्रिक ग्रन्थिः यया. सं० remarks 'गात्रिकाग्रन्थिर्ग्रन्थिविशेषः स्वस्तिकाकारः स्त्रीणामुत्तरीयस्य स्तनोद्देशे भवति.' She had tied the knot of her shawl in the form of a स्वस्तिक on her bosom. तपोबलेन निर्जितं त्रिभुवनं तस्य जयः तस्य पताकाभिः. भस्म...राजिभिः with lines of the marks of ashes. पुण्ड्रकः a mark on the forehead made with sandal &c., showing the particular sect to which the votary belongs. विराजितं ललाटाजिरं (ललाटं अजिरमिव) यस्याः Her forehead being broad is compared to a court-yard. The three lines of ashes on her forehead are compared to banners indicating her conquest of the worlds by the power of her austere penance. The worlds are three and पताकाs may be fluttering on an open space (अजिरं). 'वक्रा ललाटगास्तिस्रो भस्मरेखास्त्रिपुण्ड्रकम् ॥' हारावली. 'ऊर्ध्वपुण्ड्रं मृदा कुर्यात् त्रिपुण्ड्रं भस्मना सदा । तिलकं वै द्विजः कुर्याच्चन्दनेन यदृच्छया ॥'. योग...कक्ष्यका whose वैकक्ष्यक scarf was made up of an ascetic's wrap. वैकक्ष्यकम् or वैकक्षकम् (विकक्षायां भवं) is primaring a garland (and secondarily an ornamental robe) worn over one shoulder and under the other like a यज्ञोपवीत. 'वैकक्षकं तु तत् । यत्तिर्यक् क्षिप्तमुरसि' इत्यमरः. योगपट्टकं a cloth thrown over the back and knees of an ascetic during contemplation. 'पृष्ठजान्वोः समायोगे वस्त्रं वलयवद् दृढम् । परिवेष्ट्य यदूर्ध्वज्ञुस्तिष्ठेत्तद्योगपट्टकम् ॥'. स्कन्धा ... ना hanging down from her shoulder (with पट्टकेन); that supports itself on a section of the wind (with ०स्रोतसा). The wind (वायु) is believed to be divided in-to seven स्कन्धs, one of which called परिवह supports the Ganges. Compare शाकुन्तल VII '**त्रिस्रोतसं** वहति यो गगनप्रतिष्ठां...वायोरिमं परिवहस्य वदन्ति मार्गम् ॥'. See विष्णुपु. II. 12. 28 also. सुधाफेनवत् धवलेन (with both पट्टकेन and स्रोतसा). तपः...स्रोतसेव—The idea is :—The white योगपट्टक passing over her shoulder and underneath is fancied to be the stream of the Ganges (both being white and both being ०लम्बिन्) that had been coiled round her body by the power of her austerities. सव्येन goes with करेण. कलयन्ती holding. **ब्रह्मो... कमण्डलुं**—the crystal vessel resembled the white lotus bud from which Brahmā was supposed to spring. दक्षिणं goes with **करं**

(p. 4 l. 2) which is the object of उत्क्षिपन्ती. अक्षमालया कृतः परिक्षेपः यस्य—that (कर) was encircled by a rosary. कम्बुनिर्मिताः (made of conch-shell) ऊर्मिकाः (rings) ताभिः दन्तुरितं (bristling). On her right hand she had bright rings of conch-shell (instead of glass bangles as at present). 'कम्बुर्ना वलये शङ्खे' इति, 'अङ्गुलीयकमूर्मिका' इति चामरः. तर्जने तरङ्गिता तर्जनी यस्य the fore-finger of which was waved in chiding (दुर्वासस्). For क see above p. 12. उत्क्षिपन्ती raising or tossing up. क्रोधोपहत overwhelmed by wrath. अनात्मज्ञ not knowing thyself. ब्रह्मबन्धु is a term of reproach meaning 'a ब्राह्मण only by caste or in name and not in deeds.' 'ब्रह्मबन्धुरधिक्षेपः' इत्यमरः (ब्राह्मणस्य बन्धुः परमनुष्ठानाभावाज्जातिब्राह्मणः—क्षीरस्वामी). मुनिखेट miserable or villainous sage. खेट added to words gives the sense of 'अधम.' अपसदः = नीचः. निराकृत an abandoned wretch (lit. expelled). The com. explains 'निराकृतोऽस्वाध्यायः' *i. e.* one who does not study the Vedas. आत्मनः स्खलितेन (mistake) विलक्षः (dismayed or ashamed). 'विलक्षो विस्मयान्विते' इत्यमरः. रोषात् विमुक्तं वेत्रासनं यैः. This and the following words in the instrumental qualify वेदैः (l. 9). ओङ्कारेण मुखरितं (noisy) मुखं येषाम्. The Vedas are represented as repeating loudly the sacred syllable ओम्. उत्क्षेपेण (by their rapid rising up) दोलायमानः (waving to and fro) जटाभारः तेन भरिताः दिशः यैः. The reading आक्षेप० (snatching) does not yield a good sense. परिकरबन्धे भ्रमितं कृष्णाजिनं तस्य आटोपः (expanse) तस्या छाया तया श्यामायमानः दिवसः येषाम् who made the day look dark with the colour of their expanded deer skins that were flung round (their body) in girding up their loins. They girt up their loins out of impatience at Durvāsas' conduct. The reading कृष्णाजिनपटच्छाया० is not bad. It means 'the colour of their deer skin garments.' अमर्षात् क्रोधात् निःश्वासाः एव दोलाः (swings) तासु प्रेङ्खोलितः (tossed, swung) ब्रह्मलोकः यैः—the whole ब्रह्मलोक vibrated with their rapid breaths. सोम...स्रवद्भिः—They perspired through wrath. The poet fancies that it was सोमरस that oozed from their body and not perspiration. विसरः = समूहः. अग्निहोत्रस्य पवित्रं भस्म तेन स्मेरं ललाटं येषाम् whose forehead was bright with the holy ashes of oblations offered into fire. कुश...वरिभिः—कुशतन्तूनां चारु चामरं चीरचीवरं च ते ०चीवरे स्तः एषां—who had a charming chowrie of Kus'a threads (*i. e.* slender कुश grass) and were clad in bark garments. The affix इन् is added to the द्वन्द्व compound ०चीवरे. आषाढिभिः bearing a staff of the पलाश wood. 'पालाशो दण्ड आषाढः' इत्यमरः (आषाढासु जातः—क्षीर०). 'विशाखाषाढादण् मन्थदण्डयोः' पा. 5. 1. 110 (वैशाखो मन्थः, आषाढो दण्डः). A ब्रह्मचारी of each of the three Varṇas was to carry a staff of a particular tree 'ब्राह्मणो बैल्वपालाशौ क्षत्रियो वाटखादिरौ । पैलवौदुम्बरौ वैश्यो दण्डानर्हन्ति धर्मतः ॥' मनुस्मृति II. 45. प्रहरणीकृतं कमण्डलुमण्डलं यैः. They seized their water vessels in their hands as their weapons. मूर्तैः in a corporeal form. वृषीमपहाय abandoning their seats. बृषी or वृषी ('व्रतिनामासनं बृषी' इत्यमरः) a seat of कुश grass for ascetics.

P. 4 ll. 11–17 **ततो...न्यवारयत्.** मर्षय forgive. अभू...शापस्य she is not a fit person for a curse. अनु...बुधैः though besought by the gods. नाथ् 1 P to solicit, but A when it means 'to bless'. बद्धं अञ्जलिपुटं यैः that folded their hands. मा...द्वम् Do not cause loss to your austerities. **'विघ्नोऽन्तरायः प्रत्यूहः'** इत्यमरः. It was supposed that by pronouncing a curse a person lost his merit. रोषस्य आवेशेन विवशः beside himself with the emotion of wrath. दुर्विनीत impudent, ill-mannered. व्यपनयामि I shall remove. उन्नतिम्—is used in two senses; (1) going up, (2) exalted or proud position. The first meaning contrasts well with the words 'अधस्ताद्गच्छ.' प्रति...यतां who was ready to give a curse in return. सावित्रीम्—is the object of न्यवारयत्. असं...माननीयाः Brāhmaṇas, though their minds are not well disciplined, deserve respect solely for their very birth (caste). Compare वनपर्व 200. 89 'यथा श्मशाने दीप्तौजाः पावको न प्रदुष्यति । एवं विद्वानविद्वान्वा ब्राह्मणो दैवतं महत् ॥'.

P. 4 l. 18—**P. 5** l. 16 **अथ तां...मगात्.** पितामहः is the subject of उवाच (l. 23). कम...द्वहन् having a body wearing a white sacrificial thread as if lotus fibres stuck to it when it (body) sprang from the lotus. कमलात् उत्पत्तौ लग्नानि मृणालसूत्राणि यस्याः. For the birth of ब्रह्मा from the lotus in the navel of Vishṇu, see above p. 20. The fibres and यज्ञोपवीत are both white. The poet fancies that lotus fibres stuck to the body of Brahmā when he sprang from a lotus. उद्ग...कलम् having stopped the tumult consequent upon the curse with his right hand, from which shot up a pencil of the rays of the clear emerald on his ring and which therefore seemed to hold a bundle of Kus'a grass for warding off the calamity of the three worlds. उद्गच्छन् अच्छस्य अङ्गुलीयकमरकतस्य मयूखलताकलापः यस्मिन्. त्रिभुवनस्य उपप्लवः (calamity, injury) तस्य प्रशमाय कुशानां आपीडः समूहः तं धारयतीति. The rays of the emerald resemble green blades of कुश grass. कुश grass was supposed to ward off evil. It was a calamity for the three worlds that सरस्वती was cursed. C and T refer to अथर्ववेद 19. 30. 4 and 6. 43. 1 (where दर्भ is called मन्युशमन) for showing that कुश grass originated from a world convulsion and that कुश had power to allay passion. अति... किरणै: with the pure and far-reaching rays of his teeth he as if let fall in all directions lines for constructing the coming कृतयुग. In constructing a building a carpenter takes measurements with plumblines that are also long (दीर्घ) and white (with chalk). The rays of Brahmā's teeth resembled such lines. The poet fancies that ब्रह्मा measured with lines the directions for constructing the future कृतयुग. कृतयुग is the first of the four Yugas (कृत, त्रेता, द्वापर and कलि). At the time about which बाण spoke, it was कलियुग and hence he uses the word भावि. सर...पटहेनेव—his voice resembled the sound of an auspicious drum beaten at the time of starting on a journey. सरस्वती, being cursed, was to start on her journey to the world of mortals. निह...स्तात् It will ruin you hereafter. उद्दामं प्रसृता: इन्द्रियाण्येव अश्वा: तै: समुत्थापितं raised by the steeds of senses that rush unchecked. रज: (1) dust (with अश्व); passion (with इन्द्रिय). रज...जिताम्—Rajas clouds the vision of those that have not conquered the अक्षs (senses, axles). Dust raised by horses when the charioteer cannot control the chariot (the axle) enters the eye and obscures the vision. If proper control be not exercised over the senses, passion clouds the intellect. Compare 'यस्त्वविज्ञानवान्भवत्ययुक्तेन मनसा सदा। तस्येन्द्रियाण्यवश्यानि दुष्टाश्वा इव सारथे:॥' कठोपनिषद् I. 3. 5. अक्ष: axle, cart. अक्षं = इन्द्रियं. कि...क्षते How far indeed can the (physical) eye see? The idea is that it has only a limited scope. For the use of वा, see verse 16 above. कृतबुद्धय: whose minds are perfect or educated. असत: सतो वा good or bad; or the meaning is 'actually existent before the eye or not so existent' (*i. e.* absent). निसर्गविरोधिनी opposed by nature. धर्म means 'performance of one's duties enjoined by the S'āstras'. एकत्र वृत्ति: = एकत्र अवस्थानम्. आलोक: (1) light, (2) enlightenment. तमसि (1) in darkness, (2) in ignorance, delusion. पर...दक्षा clever in detecting the defects of others (applies to both दृष्टि and बुद्धि). दृष्टि... पश्यति your angry mind, like the inflamed eye, does not observe your own sin *viz.* your flying into passion. दुर्वासस् saw the fault of सरस्वती *viz.* laughing at him, but his mind did not dwell upon the mistake he had committed nor did he observe that he was swayed by passion (राग). When the eye is inflamed (कुपित) it cannot see its own redness (राग). The word कुपित in medicine means 'suffering from a deranged state of the three humours वात, पित्त and कफ.' क...क—two कs denote great incongruity or inconsistency between two things. वैवधिक one who carries loads on a pole. 'विभाषा विवधात्' पा. 4. 4. 17. (विवधेन हरति विवधिकः, पक्षे ठक् । वैवधिकः । विवधवीवधशब्दौ उभयतो बद्धशिक्ये स्कन्धवाह्ये काष्ठे वर्तेते । सि. कौ.). पुरोभागित्वम्—finding only the faults of others, censoriousness. 'दोषैकदृक् पुरोभागी' इत्यमरः. चक्षुष्मा...जनः that man though possessed of eye-sight is really blind. नहि...कर्तव्यं वा obscured by rage, the mind does not discriminate between what should and should not be done. कुपितस्य...भ्रुकुटिः of the man flying into a passion, wisdom first becomes clouded and then his eyebrow. In this and the three following sentences, the verbs अन्धकारीभवति and others are used in a literal physical sense and also in a secondary sense. When a man is angered his brow becomes dark (threatening) and his wisdom forsakes him for the moment. रागः passion ; redness. समास्कन्दति overwhelms; attacks. चरमं चक्षुः lastly (redness attacks) the eye *i. e.* the eye becomes red when a man is angry. तपो गलति the austerities (performed by the angry man) are dissolved *i. e.* have to give way before the wave of passion. पश्चा...लिलम्—the angry man perspires. पूर्व...धरः—If a person becomes angry, that gives rise to an evil reputation; the angry man's lips quiver. ०नाशाय—the dative shows the effect wrought by दुर्वासस्. A poisonous tree also kills people and has fibrous roots (जटा) and bark. मूले लग्नकचे जटा' इत्यमरः (वृक्षादिमूलं जटा). अनुचिता...वृत्तिः this tendency of your mind is not in keeping with this garb of a sage (that you wear) as a necklace of pearls (is not appropriate to मुनिवेश). वृत्तमुक्ता (वृत्तेन मुक्ता) devoid of good conduct (with ०वृत्तिः); (वृत्ताः मुक्ताः यस्याः) the pearls of which are round (with ०यष्टिः). शैलूषः इव like an actor. 'शिलूषस्य ऋषेः अपत्यं शैलूषः' क्षीरस्वामी. कृत्रिमम् not natural, counterfeit. उपशमशून्येन—the actor dressed as an ascetic has no restraint over his senses (उपशम) nor had दुर्वासस्. आकल्पः dress. अल्प...जातम् I do not see even the slightest virtue in you. The words may also mean 'I don't see the slightest happiness in you (*i. e.* proceeding from you to others)'. अतिलघिम्ना (1) by great levity; (2) by extreme lightness (in weight). उपर्येव...प्लवतः you are floating only on the surface of the ocean of knowledge (*i. e.* you have not penetrated deep into the mysteries of knowledge). What is light floats on the sea. अनेलमूकाः deaf and dumb. 'जडोऽज्ञेऽनेडमूकस्तु वक्तुं श्रोतुमशिक्षिते' इत्यमरः. ड and ल are often interchanged. एडाः deaf. The meaning is:—All these sages are not deaf and dumb nor are they fools. They also

heads of elephants and horses. चामीकरतटे (सुवर्णतटे) ताडनेन अरुणिताः रदनाः (दन्ताः) यस्य. रदति pr. p. of रद् 1 P to split. सुरस्रवन्ती the Ganges. ऐरावत is the elephant of Indra. His tusks became red because some of the gold stuck to them after the impact. Elephants are represented as fond of butting against banks and mounds. The reading ०ताडनरणितरदने would mean 'whose tusks resounded by striking etc.' प्रसृ...पाटलताम् when the sky (तारापथः) presented a rosy colour, as if it (sky) were besmeared (अनुलिप्त) with the Alaktaka dye of the feet of the several thousands of विद्याधर damsels that were moving about (towards their rendezvous). The sky was suffused red in the evening; the poet fancies that the rosy colour was due to the अलक्तक etc. विद्याधर is a class of semi-divine beings. अभिसारिका a young woman who goes out to meet her lover or keeps on appointment made by him. 'कान्तार्थिनी तु या याति सङ्केतं साऽभिसारिका' इत्यमरः. तारापथ...द्रवे when red sandal juice, poured out (आवर्जित) in the sun-set worship offered by the Siddhas journeying in the sky, flowed colouring the quarters and possessing the hue of safflower (कुसुम्भं) as though it (juice) were the perspiration of the Evening delighted at her obeisance to S'iva. तारापथे प्रस्थिताः सिद्धाः (semidivine beings) तैः दत्तं दिनकरस्य अस्तमये अर्घ्यं तस्मिन् आवर्जिते (*adj.* of द्रवे). अर्घ्यम्--materials of worship, such as water, sandal &c. रञ्जिताः ककुभः (दिशः) येन (*adj.* of ०द्रवे). कुसुम्भस्य इव भाः यस्य. Connect स्रवति (pr.p. loc. sing.) with ०द्रवे. पिनाकिने प्रणतिः तया मुदिता &c. As सन्ध्या is red, her perspiration also would look red. The red sandal juice is fancied to be the perspiration of Evening. वन्दारु...लोके when the world of ब्रह्मा, where crowds of the best of worshipping sages folded their hands in evening adoration, seemed as though all the lotus beds had come to wait upon that from which Brahmā sprang. For वन्दारु see शरारु above p. 23. वन्दारूणां (bowing) मुनीनां वृन्दारकाः (श्रेष्ठाः) तेषां वृन्दं तेन बध्यमानं सन्ध्याञ्जलिवनं यस्मिन्. ब्रह्मणः उत्पत्तिः यस्मात् तत् ब्रह्मोत्पत्ति कमलं तस्य सेवायै आगतः सकलानां कमलानां आकरः यस्मिन्. The hands folded in सन्ध्या adoration look like lotus buds; hence the उत्प्रेक्षा in ब्रह्मोत्पत्ति०. समुच्चा...ब्रह्मणि when Brahmā had uttered the Vedic hymns of the third Savana. समुच्चारितं तृतीयसवनस्य ब्रह्म (वेदः) येन. There were three सवनs (sacrifices at which libations of सोम were offered) प्रातःसवन, माध्यन्दिनसवन and तृतीयसवन. The meaning may also be 'when Brāhmaṇas had uttered &c.' Here the singular ब्रह्मणि is used for the whole class. Some taken सवन in the sense of स्नान.

ज्वलित...मन्दिरेषु when the houses of the seven sages had their courts full (जटाल) of the flames of blazing sacrificial (वैतान) fires, as if in them (houses) was begun the lustration of the camp that was a means of securing the performance of one's duties. ज्वलिताः वैतानाः ज्वलनाः तेषां ज्वालाः ताभिः जटालानि अजिराणि येषाम्. आरब्धं धर्मसाधनस्य शिबिरस्य नीराजनं येषु or आरब्धं धर्मसाधनाय शिबिरस्य &c. नीराजन was a religious and military ceremony, performed by kings and generals before they took the field; it consisted in waving lights before the components of an army. As sacrificial fires blazed in the houses, the poet fancies that नीराजन was being performed over the houses (which looked like camps), the object for which the houses were erected being धर्मसाधन and not जयसाधन or अर्थसाधन. Another sense also is suggested. साधन means 'army'. An army is housed in a camp (शिबिरं) over which नीराजन may be performed. For सप्तर्षि see above p. 19. C and T translate 'as though a camp lustration had commenced in an army devoted to Dharma'. This is not correct and does not bring out the उत्प्रेक्षा properly. अघमर्षणेन मुषितः किल्बिषविषगदः (किल्बिषं पापं एव विषगदः) येषां ते ०गदाः उल्लाघाः लघवश्च. अघ...यतिषु when the hermits had light hearts, being free from the poison disease of sin that was removed by the अघमर्षण hymn. उल्लाघ convalescent. 'उल्लाघो निर्गतो गदात्' इत्यमरः. A person who has been taking medicines against poison becomes convalescent and light—hearted. अघमर्षण is a term applied to the hymn (of three verses) beginning with 'ऋतं च सत्यं चाभीद्धात्तपसोऽध्यजायत' (ऋग्वेद X. 190). 'सर्वैनसामपध्वंसि जप्यं त्रिष्वघमर्षणम्' इत्यमरः. सन्ध्योपासनाय आसीनानां तपस्विनां पङ्क्त्या (row, line) पूतं पुलिनं (sandy bed) यस्य (*adj.* of ०जले). प्लवमानाः नलिनयोनियानहंसाः एव हासः तेन दन्तुरिताः ऊर्मयः यस्य the waves of which were furrowed by the smile-like हंसs, the vehicles of ब्रह्मा, floating thereon. हंस is the वाहन of ब्रह्मा. हंसs are white and so resemble हास which is poetically described as white. One who smiles shows his teeth. The हंसs sailing on the waves divide them into crests that look like teeth. जल...वने when the beds of कुमुदs (night-lotuses) were about to expand, causing delight to bees and sweetly perfumed with their own honey, that (beds) were the umbrellas of water nymphs and were the private mansions of the wives of the tribes of birds. Water nymphs dwelt under the shelter of कुमुदs and birds also made them their haunts. कृता मधुपानां मुत् येन. There is another sense also. When Kumudas open (*i. e.* at night) those who drink wine (मधुप) are exhilarated. मुमुदिषमाणे *pr. p.* of the desiderative of मुद् to delight or expand with joy. दिवसा...यूथे when the crowds of flamingoes, delighted by their drinking bout on the sweet honey of the day-lotuses that were going to languish as the day closed, were about to sleep, fanning the blue-lotus (राजीवं) lakes with rows of their flapping (धुत) wings and turning their necks into coils in order to be scratched by the soft lotus stalks. दिवसस्य अवसाने ताम्यतां तामरसानां मधुरं मधु तस्य सपीतिः (सहपानं) तया प्रीते. 'सपीतिः स्त्री तुल्यपानम्' इत्यमरः. सुषुप्सति *pr. p.* loc. sing. of the desiderative base of स्वप्. ०काण्डेन कण्डूयनं तदर्थं कुण्डलिता कन्धरा येन. The flamingoes bent their neck in a circle round the lotus stalks in order to get it scratched. धुतानां पक्षाणां राज्या वीजितं राजीवसरः येन. तट...नभस्वति when a slight (तनीयस्) evening breeze, resembling the sigh of Night, began to blow, making the river grey with the pollen of the flowers of creepers growing on the bank, and bearing the perfume of the jasmine flowers in the braids (धम्मिल्लः) of the matrons (पुरन्ध्रि) of the city of Siddhas. ०धूलिभिः धूसरिता सरित् येन (qualifies नभस्वति). सरति *pr. p. loc. sing.* of सृ. ०पुरन्ध्रीणां धम्मिल्लेषु मल्लिकाः तासां गन्धं गृह्णन्ति इति. मल्लिका is a flower that opens in the evening. सङ्कोचेन उदभ्रान्तः (erected) उच्चाः (stiff) केसराः तेषां कोटिभिः सङ्कटः कुशेशयानां कमलानां कोशः तस्य कोटरः एव कुटी तस्यां शेते इति—that lay in the hut in the form of the cavity of the lotuses that were full of the tips of filaments high and stiff by the closing (of the petals). As the lotuses contracted at sunset, their filaments that were loose became straightened up and barred the way of escape out of the lotuses, the bees being confined inside as in a hut. नृत्तो...गणे the constellations of stars, presenting the appearance of the bunches of कुटज buds in the forest of the matted hair of S'iva tossed up in dance, were scattered in clusters in the sky. स्तबकयति a denominative verb from स्तबक. The clusters of stars looked like कुटज buds, which are white. कुटज is a wild flower and hence the word अटवी is put in. The stars appeared scattered about. शिव is represented as fond of dancing. When शिव danced, the flowers in his hair would be scattered about. सन्ध्या...तमसि darkness, that was not yet full grown, that was reddish with the continuance of twilight, that had the colour of the skin of a ripe Tāla fruit and that was thick (मेदुर) like a dark cloud, closed round the earth. सन्ध्यायाः अनुबन्धः तेन ताम्रे—twilight had not yet completely vanished and so a slight rosy hue still persisted and was mixed up with the darkness. परिणमत् तालफलं तस्य त्वचः इव त्विट् (कान्तिः) यस्य. कालमेघ also means 'the clouds at the end of the world.' नवं वयः यस्य. तरुण...प्रकरे when numerous lamps, capable of piercing (पाटनं) the veil of fresh (not yet fullgrown *i. e.* not deep or pitchy) darkness, began to blaze forth, being a cluster of champaka buds serving as the ear-ornaments of the lady of Night. The flame of a lamp is like a चम्पक bud. Therefore the lamps lit at night are said to be the कर्णपूरs of the lady (Night). प्रतनु...मुखे when the region of Indra (*i. e.* the east), pale with the lovely light of the few rays of the moon and appearing like the sandy islet of the Jumna slightly dry and free from its blue waters, reduced the darkness. In the east the moon was about to rise. The first rays of the moon lessened the darkness and the east lookd grey (white-dark). The east therefore resembled the sandy bed of the Jumna from which the waters had just receded, the sand being white, but the remnants of water being dark. The water of the Jumna is dark as compared with the Ganges. प्रतनु (slight) तुहिनकिरणस्य शीतरश्मेः किरणाः तेषां लावण्यं तस्य आलोकेन पाण्डुनि. आश्यानं (partially dried) नीलनीरेण मुक्तं कालिन्दीकूलं तस्य वालुकायुक्तं पुलिनं, पुलिनं इव आचरति पुलिनायते. The reading बालपुलिनायमाने for वालुका॰ is better, as in कूलवालुका॰ there are too many words. बालपुलिनं would mean 'a sandy spot just raised out of water.' शतक्रतोः (इन्द्रस्य) इदं शातक्रतवम्. कृशयति *pr. p. loc.* sing. of कृशयति denominative verb from कृश. खमुचि...तमसि when darkness that had blackened (मेचकित) the lake of expanded blue lotuses, that (तमः) was a veritable cluster of the tresses of the S'abarî in the form of the night, that (तमः) had the colour of the wings of a jay (चाषः), was leaving the sky and was being dissolved, being disturbed by having its hair seized by the rays of the moon, like the mind of a proud beauty. खं आकाशं मुञ्चति इति ख॰. At the approaching rise of the moon darkness left the sky and was massed on the earth. मेचकितं ॰सरः येन. शश...विले and विलीयमाने apply both to तमसि and ॰मनसि. शशधरस्य कराणां (किरणानां) निकरेण कचग्रहः तेन आविले. When a person is seized by the hair, he is harshly and forcibly dealt with. The moon's rays forcibly drove away darkness. आविल turbid, muddy. शशधर...मनसि—the idea here is:—a proud young lady, being offended with her husband, resolved upon accepting no reconciliation. When the moon caressed her hair with its rays, her resolve began to waver and at last her proud mind gave way (विलीयमान) and she was quickly reconciled. The word कर also means 'hand' and the clause suggests 'when her tresses were stroked by the gentle hand of her husband by way of reconciliation, she wavered'. शर्वरी (निशा) एंव शबरी तस्याः चिकुरचयः कुन्तलभारः. शबरी is a woman of an aboriginal tribe, such as the Bhils. Both शर्वरी and शबरी are dark and further the two words are almost the same in sound. चाषपक्षस्य इव त्विट् यस्य. उदिते...श्वेतमानौ when the moon (श्वेतभानुः), now risen, assumed a red form (वपुः) as though covered (निचित) with the mass of blood dropping from his own deer slain by the weapon (हेति) of the sharp paw of the lion (हरिः) in the cave of the slopes (कटकं) of the peaks of the Rising Mountain, a red form that was as though the lower lip of the damsel of Night possessed of glow at the rise (of the moon). The disc of the moon was red when it rose. There are two उत्प्रेक्षाs in this clause. The first up to निचितमिव is concerned with redness and the second (in उदय...धरमिव) is concerned with the red orb of the moon. The poet fancies that the natural redness of the disc at moon-rise is due to the blood &c. For the deer in the moon see notes p. 22. उदयगिरि a fabulous mountain in the east from behind which the sun and the moon were supposed to come up. The red and round orb of the moon appears like the red and full lip of a young lady. So the poet fancies it to be the lip of the lady of Night. The word उदयरागधरम् conveys two ideas. The lip of a fair woman possesses the same redness (रागः) as is seen (in the moon) at moon-rise. The night also possesses rosy hue (राग) at moon-rise (on the eastern horizon). C and T translate 'the form of the Lord of white splendour... assumed the glow of the Udaya mountain, resembling the lip of the nymph of night'. This does not appear to us to be correct. वपुः is the object of धारयति and ०धरमधरम् is in apposition to वपुः. अचलात् (पर्वतात् अर्थात् उदयगिरेः) च्युताः चन्द्रकान्तस्य जलधाराः ताभिः धौते. From the चन्द्रकान्त stone water oozes at the rise of the moon. ध्वान्ते=तमसि. गो...मण्डले when the orb of the moon had begun to fill the ocean, as though it (orb) were a great ivory conduit with the shape of a crocodile's mouth bearing a stream of milk dropping from the world of cows. The bright rays of the moon fell on the ocean which rose in a high tide. The streaming rays of the moon looked like a stream of milk. The pale white moon looked like ivory (hence दन्तमय). The orb of the moon presented the appearance of the end of a conduit pipe (प्रणालः) as large as the mouth of a crocodile. गो also means 'rays'. दन्तमयः मकरमुखः (मकरस्य इव मुखं यस्य) महाप्रणालः तस्मिन्. स्पष्टे... समये when the evening time was clear *i. e.* when the night had advanced beyond the stage of dusk or twilight. त्रि...जल्पन्ती my tongue prattling to thee feels shame before thee that are clever enough to instruct the three worlds. यादृश्यः—connect with दैवस्य वामाः वृत्तयः. जानास्येव...वृत्तयः thou knowest already what the crooked actions (वृत्तयः, ways) of Fate are, actions that are unsteady (विसंस्थुल), that are unkind like the wicked even to worthy men, changing in a moment, not to be resisted and unpleasant. The word वामाः also means 'handsome women, or women in general'. Women also, according to the estimation of many people, are unsteady, changeful to a degree, heartless hard to be resisted (when once they set their heart on achieving an object). Compare 'विमुक्तधर्माश्चपलास्तीक्ष्णा भेदकराः स्त्रियः॥' अरण्यकाण्ड 45.30. 'पौंश्चल्याच्चलचित्ताच्च नैस्नेह्याच्च स्वभावतः ।' मनुस्मृति 9.15. न रमणीयाः does not well apply to women. Hence the words should have been omitted in the text (as B does). निष्कारणा...पतन्ती even the slightest insult, when without cause, coming from an inferior person, disturbs the mind even of a high-souled person. निकारः insult or wrong. कणिका a particle. Here सरस्वती is the high-souled person and दुर्वासस the inferior man. मानस means also 'the मानस lake.' It may become turbid by a particle (of dust) falling in it. अन...सिच्यमानः—sprinkled with ceaseless tears (with शोकः); अनवरतं नयनं यस्य एतादृशं जलं तेन सिच्यमानः sprinkled with water that is carried incessantly (with तरुः). विपल्लवः—विपदः (of adversity) लवः यस्मिन् in which there is a slight misfortune *i. e.* caused by slight misfortune (with शोकः); विपल्लवः void of foliage (with तरुः). प्ररोहति increases (with शोकः); puts forth shoots. The more one dwells on one's misfortune and sheds tears, the greater the pangs of it. अतिसुकुमारं applies both to जनं and ०कुसुमम्. सन्तापपरमाणवः atoms of affliction *i. e.* slight affliction (with जनम्); atoms of heat *i. e.* slight heat (with ०कुसुमम्). महतां on the great; of large size (elephants). अणुः small (with क्लेशः); with a fine edge (with सृणिः). अणुरपि...लम् even a slight affliction is sufficient to torment them (the great) as the piercing goad is sufficient to humble (the big elephants). कदर्थनम् is a noun from the denominative verb कदर्थयति, which is formed from कदर्थ.

'कोः कत्तत्पुरुषेऽचि' पा. 6. 3. 101 (कु when followed in a तत्पुरुष by a word beginning with a vowel becomes कत्). कुत्सितः अर्थः कदर्थः. अलम् in the sense of 'sufficient or able' governs the dative. सहजः स्नेहपाशः (स्नेहः पाशः इव) तस्य ग्रन्थिना बन्धनं येषां or यासाम्. सहज...भूमयः our native home, which is linked to us like a kinsman by fast (*lit.* knotted) ties of natural affection, is hard to give up. जन्मभूमिः also means 'mother'. दारुणः terrible (with ०विरहः); of wood (with ०पातः). Construe दारुणः ०विरहः हृदयं दारयति ०पातः दारुणः हृदयं (central part) इव. क्रकचपातः the stroke of a saw. संस्तुत familiar, dear. अभूमि...सवानाम् you are not the soil for the shoots of the poison plant of sorrow. The idea is that sorrow should not take a footing in you. 'क्ष्वेडस्तु गरलं विषम्' इत्यमरः. अपि च...शुचाम् what occasion have the wise for grief, when in front of and behind us stand our powerful deeds, whether good or bad, that rule us and yield fruit to us? It is our own actions, good or bad, that produce the vicissitudes of our lives. If adversities assail us, that is due to the bad actions of our former lives. If we were put into trouble without any fault on our part, then there would be room for sorrow. But we know that under the inexorable law of *Karma* there is no such thing as chance. The idea of तिष्ठ...पृष्ठतश्च is:—It is our own *Karma* that determines the rewards that we are to enjoy and *Karma* encompasses us on all sides. शुचाम् is genitive plural of शुच्. प्रष्ठ = पुरःसर. 'प्रष्ठोऽग्रगामिनि' पा. 8. 3. 92 (प्रतिष्ठते इति प्रष्ठो गौः। अग्रतो गच्छतीत्यर्थः। सि.कौ.). Compare for the idea 'यादृशं कुरुते कर्म तादृशं फलमश्नुते' रामायण उत्तरकाण्ड 15. 23. त्रिभुवनस्य मङ्गलं तदर्थं एकं (केवलं) कमलम्. अपवित्रं कुर्वन्ति अपवित्रयन्ति. तदलम् therefore enough (of this weeping). अवतितीर्षति desires to descend. पुण्यभाजि—that will be blest (by your descent thereon). तपोवनधामसु = तपोवनस्थानेषु. तपस्यन्ती performing austerities. अयं सखीजनः means सावित्री herself. उप...पेशलः skilful in serving you and agreeable (पेशल) on account of familiarity with you (commencing from) playing in the dust together. The idea is they were intimate playmates since early childhood. न अन्यत् शरणं (रक्षितृ) यस्याः सा ०शरणा who seeks no other refuge (than S'iva). प्रतिपद्यस्व resort to (the object being त्र्यम्बकम्). सर्व...तारम् the author of all lores. धातारम् the supporter of all. स्वश्रेयसे for your own welfare. Connect this with प्रतिपद्यस्व. स्वचरणरजसा पवित्रिताः त्रिदशाः असुराश्च येन (adj. of त्र्यम्बकम्). सुधासूतिः (सुधायाः अमृतस्य सूतिः यस्मात्) चन्द्रः एव कलिका तया कल्पितः कर्णावतंसः यस्य (adj. of त्र्यम्बकम्)—whose ear-ornament is formed by the crescent (*lit.* bud) of the moon. त्रिभुवनगुरुम् to be honoured by the three worlds. त्र्यम्बकं = शिवम्. The reading of A and C दातारं श्वःश्रेयसस्य means 'who bestowes future happiness'. श्वः tomorrow *i. e.* future. From Bāṇa's usual style we can infer that he wrote as in the text (repeating धातारम्). श्वः-श्रेयसस्य is rather an unusual combination and ungrammatical. ते = तुभ्यम्. शापेन शोकः तस्य विरतिम् (cessation). वितरिष्यति दास्यति. ब्रह्मा had already declared (text p. 5 l. 9) that the curse would end with the birth of a son. By S'iva's favour that happy event would follow in a very short time.

P. 7 ll. 11–27 **एवमुक्त्वा…निर्जगाम.** मुक्ताः मुक्ताफलवत् धवलाः लोचनजललवाः यया that shed tears bright like pearls. केवलं…हृदयम् it is only the happiness of serving Brahmā (to which I shall be a stranger till the curse lasts) that makes my heart soft (*i. e.* makes my heart wistful and sad). भुवि…धामानि the places on the earth where Dharma can be performed. समाधि-साधनानि means of abstract meditation; or the word may be taken as in apposition to स्थानानि, meaning 'places that will help in abstract meditation'. समाधि is the eighth and last अङ्ग of योग. 'यमनियमासनप्राणायामप्रत्याहारधारणाध्यानसमाधयोऽष्टावङ्गानि' योगसूत्र II. 29. योग is defined as 'योगश्चित्तवृत्तिनिरोधः' योगसूत्र. I. 2. रणरणकेन उपनीतः प्रजागरः यस्यै who was kept awake by agitation. अनिमीलिते (not closed) लोचने यस्याः. त्रिभुवनशेखरे head jewel of the three worlds. खण…वपुषि whose form was red, as though with the blood (क्षतजम्) scattered from the mouths of his (the sun's) own horses pierced by the rough (खर) and clanking bit (खलीनः-नम्). The redness of the morning sun is fancied to be due to the blood &c. Vide a similar conceit above in the case of the moon (text p. 6 l. 15). उद…मणौ—the resplendent sun appeared like a crest jewel of the eastern mountain. जरन् कृकवाकुः (कुक्कुटः) तस्य चूडा तद्वत् अरुणः अरुणः पुरःसरः यस्य who is ushered by Aruṇa rosy like an old cock's comb. Aruṇa is a personification of the ruddy sky before sunrise. He is the charioteer of the sun. 'कृकवाकुस्ताम्रचूडः कुक्कुटश्चरणायुधः' इत्यमरः (कृकेण शीरोग्रीवेण वक्ति—क्षीर०). विरोचने = सूर्ये. नाति…र्तीं not being far away (from the place where सरस्वती passed a sleepless night). विविच्य having reflected. पिता…पालः the keeper of the tribe of Haṁsas that are the conveyances (विमानः-नम्) of Brahmā. अपरवक्त्र is a metre defined as 'अयुजि ननरला गुरुः समे तदपर-

वक्त्रमिदं नजौ जरौ' (in the first and third pādas there are eleven letters *i. e.* two तगणs, a रगण, one लघु letter and one गुरु letter and in the 2nd and 4th पादs there are twelve letters, the गणs being न, ज, ज, र). An आख्यायिका must contain verses in the वक्त्र and अपरवक्त्र metres. Vide Intro. XX. तर...त्सुकाम् why do you make thy anxious eye tremulous ? अक...लालिते (vocative) you that are fondled by dwelling with Brahmā whose mind is pure (with सरस्वती); that are fondled by dwelling in the pure मानस lake (with कलहंसी). अकलुषं मानसं यस्य स ०मानसः ब्रह्मा तेन वासः &c. अकलुषं मानसं (सरः) तस्मिन् वासः &c. अवतर वापिकाम् descend into the well (with कलहंसी). The word वापिका suggests the world of mortals where we have to reap as we sow (वप्). The कलहंसी finds it hard to descend into a pond after being long familiar with the pure मानस lake; so सरस्वती found it hard to descend to earth after enjoying the pure atmosphere of Heaven. पङ्कजालयम् the abode of lotuses *i. e.* the lake (with ०हंसी); Brahmā (with सरस्वती). पङ्कजं आलयः यस्य. Brahmā sprang from a lotus. अह...युक्ता it was as if I that was asked by him (or censured by him). कृतः महीतलावतरणस्य सङ्कल्पः (resolve) यया. वियोगेन विक्लवम् (distressed). परित्यज्य—the object is ०परिजनम्. ज्ञाति...गणय्य not minding her kindred. अवगणा (*adj.* of सरस्वती) separated from her companions (अवयुक्ता गणात्). कथमपि with great difficulty. अनुनयेन निवर्तितः अनुयायिव्रातः यया—who sent back with courteous words the crowd of devotees that followed her.

P. 7 l. 28—**P. 8** l. 30 **ततः क्रमेण...वाहयत्.** The first sentence is ततः क्रमेण...मन्दाकिनीमनुसरन्ती मर्त्यलोकमवततार (P. 8 l. 12). ध्रुव...धराम्—this and the following clauses qualify मन्दाकिनीम् below. ध्रुवप्रवृत्ताम् (1) that springs from Vishṇu or that flows from the firmament or from the ध्रुव constellation; that starts from a post. The Ganges is said to have sprung from the toe of Vishṇu. See 'श्वेतगङ्गावर्तपाण्डुरं पदमिव त्रिविक्रमस्य' हर्ष० 7th उच्छ्वास. Compare 'वामपादाम्बुजाङ्गुष्ठे नखस्रोतोविनिर्गता । विष्णोर्बिभर्ति यां भक्त्या शिरसाहर्निशं ध्रुवः ॥' विष्णुपु० II. 8. 10; see also मार्कण्डेयपु० 56. 1. ध्रुव is a name of विष्णु. Vide विष्णुसहस्रनाम in अनुशासनपर्व 149. 'स्थविष्ठः स्थविरो ध्रुवः' verse 19. विष्णु's third step is ध्रुव (constellation) and as the Ganges springs from the foot of विष्णु, it may be said to be ध्रुवप्रवृत्त. 'ऊर्ध्वोत्तरमृषिभ्यस्तु ध्रुवो यत्र व्यवस्थितः । एतद्विष्णुपदं दिव्यं तृतीयं व्योम्नि भास्वरम् ॥' विष्णुपुराण 2. 8. 99. आकाश is ध्रुव (*i. e.* नित्य) according to the नैयायिकs. A cow also starts from a post (ध्रुवः) to which it is tied. 'स्थाणुर्वा ना ध्रुवः शङ्कुः' इत्यमरः. अधो धावमानाः

धवलाः पयोधराः (मेघाः यस्याः) the clouds from which (celestial Ganges) are white and stream downwards (towards the earth). The water of the Ganges being white, the clouds are supposed to be white. अधो...धराम् (with धेनु) the white udders of which stream downwards. The Ganges is called धर्मधेनु because it enables one to secure holiness and merit. उद्धुरः (unchecked, loud) ध्वनिः यस्याः. अन्धकमथनः शिवः तस्य मौलिः (शिरः) तस्मिन् मालतीमालिकाम्. The celestial Ganges fell on the head of शिव in its descent to the earth to purify the sons of सगर reduced to ashes by Kapila. Both the Ganges and a wreath of Mālatî are white. The demon अन्धक was slain by S'iva when the former attempted to carry off पारिजात from heaven. See रामायण III. 30. 27 'रुद्रेणेव विनिर्दग्धः श्वेतारण्ये यथान्धकः.' आलीयमानैः वालखिल्यैः रुद्धं रोधः यस्याः the banks of which were covered (or obstructed) by the वालखिल्यs that settled down upon it. The वालखिल्यs were 60000 diminutive sages born of the प्रजापति क्रतु and his wife सन्नति as large as a man's thumb. 'षष्टिर्यानि सहस्राणि मुनीनामूर्ध्वरेतसाम् । अङ्गुष्ठपर्वमात्राणां ज्वलद्भास्करतेजसाम् ॥' विष्णुपुराण I. 10. 12. Vide मार्कण्डेयपुराण 52. 24-25. Compare 'अनेकशो वालखिल्यकदम्बककृतसन्ध्योपासनं (सरः)' कादम्बरी p. 123 (of P.). अरुन्धत्या धौता तारवी (तरोः इयं) त्वक् यस्याम्. तारवत्वक् bark of a tree (used as a garment). अरुन्धती, the wife of वसिष्ठ, is a type of holiness and conjugal fidelity. Note the high praise of her in the उत्तररामचरित IV. 10. 'यया पूतंमन्यो निधिरपि पवित्रस्य महसः &c'. Read त्वङ्गत्तुङ्ग for त्वङ्गत्तङ्ग. त्वङ्गन्तः तुङ्गाः तरङ्गाः तेषु तरन्तः तरलतराः ताराः तारकाः यस्याम्—that had the tremulous bright (तार) stars crossing over high surging (त्वङ्गत्) waves. It should be remembered that it is the celestial Ganges that is being described. तापसैः विकीर्णं (scattered) विरलं तिलोदकं तेन पुलकितानि (bristling) पुलिनानि यस्याः. तिलाश्च उदकं च तिलोदकं तेषां समाहारः (समाहारद्वन्द्व). पुलकित—from पुलक (=रोमाञ्च) with the affix इत according to 'तदस्य सञ्जातं तारकादिभ्य इतच्' पा. 5. 2. 36. Sesame and water were offered to the dead. वितीर्ण (given) is also a good reading. Note मनुस्मृति III 207 and 210. 'अवकाशेषु चोक्षेषु नदीतीरेषु चैव हि । विविक्तेषु च तुष्यन्ति दत्तेन पितरः सदा ॥ तेषामुदकमानीय सपवित्रांस्तिलानपि । अग्नौ कुर्यादनुज्ञातो ब्राह्मणो ब्राह्मणैः सह ॥'. आप्लवनेन (स्नानेन) पूतः पितामहः (ब्रह्मा) तेन पातिताः पितृपिण्डाः (पितृभ्यो दत्ताः पिण्डाः) तैः पाण्डुरितः पारः यस्याः. पितृ here must be taken in the sense of 'a particular class of divine beings' and not in the sense of 'father' or 'dead ancestors'. There is some incongruity in ascribing to Brahmā human actions such as पितृपिण्डदान. The balls of rice are white and hence the word पाण्डुरित is used. 'अक्रोधनाः शौचपराः सततं ब्रह्मचारिणः । न्यस्तशस्त्रा महाभागाः पितरः **पूर्वदेवताः** ॥' मनु॰ III. 192. See the following verses for various classes of Pitṛis. पर्यन्ते सुप्ताः सप्तर्षयः तेषां कुशशयनेन सूचितः सूर्यग्रहसूतके उपवासः यस्याम्—on which the fast due to the impurity (सूतकं) caused by a solar eclipse was indicated by the Kus'a bed of the seven sages sleeping nearby. An eclipse causes impurity and people observe a fast before it and on the day of eclipse. Compare धर्मसिन्धु (परिच्छेद I) 'त्रिरात्रमेकरात्रं वा समुपोष्य ग्रहणे स्नानदानाद्यनुष्ठाने महाफलम्, एकरात्रपक्षे ग्रहणदिनात्पूर्वदिने उपवास इति केचित् ग्रहणसम्बन्धाहोरात्र उपवास इत्यपरे'. So निर्णयसिन्धु (परिच्छेद I) says 'सर्वेषामेव वर्णानां **सूतकं** राहुदर्शने । स्नात्वा कर्माणि कुर्वीत शृतमन्नं विवर्जयेदिति हेमाद्रौ षट्त्रिंशन्मतात्'. A person in impurity was to sleep on a spare bed of mats, grass &c. Note धर्मसिन्धु (परिच्छेद III) 'तृणकटास्तीर्णभूमौ पृथक्शयीरन्कम्बलाद्यास्तीर्णभूमौ.' आचमनेन शुचिः शचीपतिः (इन्द्रः) तेन मुच्यमानः अर्चनकुसुमानां निकरः (समूहः) तेन शाराम्. The flowers being of various colours, the river looked variegated. The voluptuous Indra did not care to bathe, as Brahmā did. शिवपुरात् आपतितं निर्माल्यमन्दारदाम यस्याम् in which was dropped from the city of S'iva a garland of मन्दार flowers that had been already offered in worship. For क, see above p. 12. निर्माल्यं remains of flowers and other things offered to deities, flowers that are used and cast off. मन्दार is one of the five trees of Paradise. 'पञ्चैते देवतरवो **मन्दारः** पारिजातकः । सन्तानः कल्पवृक्षश्च पुंसि वा हरिचन्दनम् ॥' इत्यमरः. अना...दृषदम् that cleft with ease the stones in the caves of Mandara. The celestial Ganges had such a powerful stream that it cleft stones. मन्दर is a mountain to the east of Meru. Compare मार्क॰ 56. 3-5 'मेरुकूटतटान्तेभ्यो निपतन्ती विवर्तिता ॥ विकीर्यमाणसलिला निरालम्बा पपात सा । **मन्दराद्येषु पादेषु** प्रविभक्तोदका समम् ॥ चतुर्ष्वपि **पपाताम्बु**विभिन्नाद्रिशिलोच्चया ॥.' अनेकनाकनायकानां निकायाः तेषां कामिन्यः तासां कुचकलशैः विलुलितः विग्रहः (शरीरं) यस्याः which was tremulous with the jar-like bosoms of the beautiful wives of the hosts (निकायः) of the chief leaders of heaven. The beauties bathed in the Ganges and caused ripples. ग्राहाणां ग्राव्णां च ग्रामः (समूहः) तस्मिन् स्खलनं तेन मुखरितं स्रोतः यस्याः the stream of which resounded as it stumbled over numerous crocodiles and stones. सुषुम्णास्रुता शशिनः सुधा तस्याः शीकराणां स्तबकेन तारकितं तीरं यस्याः—the banks of which were spotted with clusters of the spray of the nectar of the moon flowing from the सुषुम्णा ray. It was believed that the waxing of the moon was due to a ray of the sun called सुषुम्ण. We should read सुषुम्ण॰,

as the quotations below require. 'सूर्यरश्मिः सुषुम्नो यस्तर्पितस्तेन चन्द्रमाः । कृष्णपक्षेऽमरैः शश्वत्पीयते वै सुधामयः ॥' विष्णुपु० II. 11. 22. यास्क has an interesting note on this ray "अथाप्यस्यैको रश्मिश्चन्द्रमसं प्रति दीप्यते तदेतेनोपेक्षितव्यमादित्यतोऽस्य दीप्तिर्भवतीति । 'सुषुम्णः सूर्यरश्मिश्चन्द्रमा गन्धर्वः' इत्यपि निगमो भवति ।" (निरुक्त II. 2. 2.). बाण frequently refers to सुषुम्ण 'कन्यया एकया च चन्द्रमूर्त्येव सुषुम्णरश्मिनिर्गतयानुगम्यमानौ' हर्ष० 4th उच्छ्वास; 'अलीकं चेदं यथा किल सकलाः कलाः कलावतो बहुलपक्षे क्षीयमाणस्य सुषुम्णनाम्ना रश्मिना रविरापिबतीति' कादम्बरी p. 141 of P. धिषणस्य (बृहस्पतेः) अग्निकार्यं (offering oblations to fire) तस्य धूमः तेन धूसरितं सैकतं यस्याः. सैकत *adj.* 'sandy,' according to 'सिकताशर्कराभ्यां च' पा. 5. 2. 104 (सैकतो घटः). But in the sense of 'a sandy tract,' we have सिकता, सिकतिल, सैकत and सिकतावत् 'देशे लुबिलचौ च' पा. 5. 2. 105 (चात् अण् मतुप् च। सिकताः सन्त्यस्मिन् देशे इति सिकताः सिकतिलः &c.). सिद्ध...धराम् where the विद्याधरs ran away in fear (त्रासः) of crossing over (or treading upon) the sandy *lingas* made by *Siddhas.* To cross over or tread upon a sacred object is sinful. विद्याधरs were afraid of unwarily crossing over the लिङ्गs and thus incurring sin and the wrath of शिव. निर्मो...रगस्य as though it (Ganges) were the cast-off slough of the sky serpent. It is the celestial Ganges that is described; hence the word गगनोरगस्य (गगनमेव उरगः). Both the slough and the Ganges are white. गगन which is blue resembles a dark serpent. त्रिविष्टपः (सुरलोकः) एव विटः. ललाटिका a mark of sandal or other fragrant powder on the forehead. 'कर्णललाटात्कनलङ्कारे' पा. 4. 3. 65. Both the Ganges and sandal are white. A विट is a voluptury, a companion of a prince or dissolute young man in dramas. He decks himself with sandal marks on the forehead. विक्रय...पण्यस्य as if it (Ganges) were a stall for the sale of the merchandise of merit. पुण्यमेव पण्यं तस्य. As wares are exhibited in a row of shops, so the Ganges flowed, on both banks of which पुण्य could be acquired. दन्ता...द्वारस्य the ivory bolt against the gate of the city of Hell. The current of the white Ganges looked like an ivory bolt. The Ganges prevents people from falling into Hell for their sins, just as a bolt fastening the gate prevents entrance into a city. All the clauses indicate either the whiteness or holiness of the Ganges. अंशु... नृपस्य as if it were the silken turban fold of the king—Meru. 'मेरुः सुमेरुर्हेमाद्री रत्नसानुः सुरालयः' इत्यमरः. सुमेरुः एव नृपः तस्य. The celestial Ganges flows from the slopes of Meru. See above p. 43. A king's head may be wrapped in a white silken turban. सुमेरुनृप may also mean 'the lord of Meru *i. e.* S'iva.' The Ganges is placed on the head of S'iva and looks like a white turban fold. दुकूल...कुञ्जरस्य as if it were the fine-textured banner (कदलिका) of the elephant—the Kailāsa range. पद्धति...वर्गस्य as if it were the beaten road to *Moksha*. नेमि...चक्रस्य as if it were the ring of the wheel of the Kṛita age. कृतयुगमेव चक्रं तस्य. A wheel has a rim (which is its centre). The Ganges is the centre of कृतयुग (*i. e.* of holiness and righteousness). The कृतयुग is an era of unmixed holiness and righteousness. 'चतुष्पात्सकलो धर्मः सत्यं चैव कृते युगे । नाधर्मेणागमः कश्चिन्मनुष्यान्प्रति वर्तते ॥' मनु० I. 81. सप्त...महिषीं the queen of the lord of seven oceans *i. e.* of क्षीरसमुद्र. All rivers are poetically represented as the wives of the ocean. क्षीरसागर being the last and best of the seven may be called the king of oceans. For the seven oceans, see above p. 32. The com. says 'सप्तसागरराजः क्षीरसमुद्रः । चन्द्राख्यपर्वत इति केचित्'. अपश्यत्—the object is महानदम् (l. 16). हारमिव—this and the following clauses are intended to convey the crystal-like pellucid waters of the शोण. वरुण is the lord of the ocean, in which pearls are found. चन्द्रः एव अचलः (पर्वतः). The moon is supposed to be full of अमृत. From a mountain springs (निर्झरः) proceed. शशिमणि = चन्द्रकान्तमणि. विन्ध्यस्य—the शोण springs in the Vindhya range. कर्पूर...रण्यस्य as if it were a flood of the sap of camphor trees from the Daṇḍakā forest. Camphor is white. This clause shows that the शोण flowed through the दण्डका forest. The precise extent of the दण्डकारण्य is far from certain. It seems to have been a general name comprising all forests from the Jumna to the Krishṇā. गुह who helped भरत to cross the Ganges is described as well-acquainted with दण्डकारण्य. So it seems that दण्डकारण्य stretched right up to the Ganges. 'एष ज्ञातिसहस्रेण स्थपतिः परिवारितः । कुशलो दण्डकारण्ये वृद्धो भ्रातुश्च ते सखा ॥ तस्मात्पश्यतु काकुत्स्थ त्वां निषादाधिपो गुहः ।' अयोध्याकाण्ड 84. 12-13. हेमाद्रि in his व्रतखण्ड says that देवगिरि (modern Daulatabad) was in सेउणदेश which was on the confines of दण्डकारण्य (*Vide* Bombay Gazetteer part II p. 231). लावण्यं bright complexion. स्फाटिक...श्रियाः as if it were the crystal couch of the Beauty of the sky. A beauty reclines on a couch white like crystal. The sky was reflected in the pellucid waters of the शोण. रामणीयकेन (loveliness) हृतं हृदयं यस्याः. मधुराः मयूराणां विरुतयः (केकाः) यासु (*adj.* of ०भूमयः, l. 20). ०पटलेन सिकतिलानि (sandy) तरुतलानि यासु. For सिकतिल, see सैकत above p. 44. परिमलेन मत्तानां मधुपानां वेणी (string, line) एव वीणा तस्याः रणितेन रमणीयाः. The humming of the rows of bees was like the

and again as if they were a herd of swift deer. वातहरिण is a very swift deer (called also वातप्रमी). लङ्घित...विटपेन that jumped over even and uneven ground, pits (अवटः) and bushes (विटपः). कोणः a stick, club. सेवायै (for worship) गृहीतानि विविधानि वन... पर्णानि येन. अनवरतं कृतः कलकलः येन. युवप्रायेण consisting mostly of young men. सनाथम् accompanied by.

P. 9 l. 13—**P. 10** l. 33 **मध्ये च...पुरुषम्.** The sentence is मध्ये च तस्य (अश्ववृन्दस्य) अष्टादशवर्षदेशीयं युवानमद्राक्षीत् (p.10 l. 27). ०चन्द्रेण, ०मालिना, ०खचितेन and ०पाण्डुरेण qualify both क्षीरोदेन and आतपत्रेण. सार्धचन्द्रेण—the umbrella had the figure of a crescent-shaped moon on it; the sea is सार्धचन्द्र, as the moon sprang from it at the time of the churning. मुक्ता...मालिना that (umbrella) was encircled by a heap of pearls. अर्धचन्द्र also means 'the semi-circular marks on a peacock's tail.' The umbrella might have such marks by way of ornament. The sea also has in it heaps of pearls. रत्न...खचितेन—the umbrella was inlaid with precious stones; the sea also is called रत्नाकर. शङ्ख...पाण्डुरेण white like a conch, milk and foam (with umbrella); white with conches, milk and foam (with क्षीरोदेन). क्षीरोदेनेव—The umbrella being सार्धचन्द्र, मुक्ता...मालिन् &c., the poet fancies it to be क्षीरसागर. स्वयं...तेन—the umbrella lent a charm (लक्ष्मी) to the youth over whom it was held. The force of स्वयं in the case of क्षीरोद is this:—when the three worlds became devoid of श्री by the curse of दुर्वासस् pronounced against Indra, the gods had to churn the ocean to find out the jewels including लक्ष्मी. The ocean did not of his own accord yield up लक्ष्मी. But the umbrella fancied to be क्षीरोद lent a लक्ष्मी (charm) to the young man without the latter making any effort to acquire it. गगनगतेन raised high in the air. आतपत्रेण—an umbrella is among the insignia of royalty. कृता छाया यस्य. कृतच्छायम्—this and the following clauses in the accusative qualify युवानं below (p. 10 l. 27). अच्छाच्छेन...गम्यमानम्—the idea is:—the youth was surrounded by a bright circle of the rays of the brilliant ornaments he wore. The poet fancies that it was a ring (चक्रवालं) of the quarters that stuck very close round him, because the quarters were very fond of seeing him (who was so young and handsome). Ordinarily चक्रवाल (horizon) is far from a person. आनितम्ब... राजमानम् who was decked with a wreath of Mālatī flowers on his head that hung down to his hips, as if it (wreath) were the banner of his beauty won by the conquest of the whole world. He surpassed by his beauty everyone in the world. A conqueror triumphantly carries away the banner from his vanquished rivals. The long wreath looked like a waving pennon. उत्सर्पिभिः...वपुषम् whose body rendered dirty by the dust on the road was being rubbed by the red up-shooting (उत्सर्पिभिः) rays of the ruby in his crest, as if with tender leaves held by invisible nymphs of the forest. 'शिखण्डखण्डिका चूडाभरणम्' com. The red rays resemble slender and reddish fresh leaves. प्रमृज्यमानं मार्गरेणुना परुषं वपुः यस्य. Dust may be rubbed off with पल्लवs. The reading रूषित would mean 'covered or soiled'. बकुल...दिवसम् with his head lovely by being decked with a wreath (मुण्डमाला) of Bakula buds and having a profusion of curling hair, he seemed as though drinking the day, the light of which was contracted. मीलितः आतपः यस्य (*adj.* of दिवसम्). The brilliance of the day is lessened by the approach of night. The white Bakula is like the light of day and his dark hair in contact with the white Bakula buds is like night. With his dark hair he as though lessened the light of day, which remained only in a scattered form in the shape of Bakula buds. पशु रिक्षम् with the brilliance, yellowish red like arsenic paste, of his broad forehead that was possessed of natural (सहज) loveliness (लक्ष्मी), he as though smeared the sky as if it (the forehead) were composed of the second portion of the moon that is the crown of the matted hair of S'iva. He had a bright and naturally lovely forehead. It was bright like the moon and so the poet fancies that it was made of the moon. The propriety of द्वितीय॰ is this:—शिव placed the crescent of the moon on his head. So if his ललाट was made of the moon, it could not have been that (part of the) moon that was placed by शिव on his head and so the forehead must have been made of the remaining portion of the moon (the second piece). The forehead being thus fancied to be मृगाङ्कघटित, it would be naturally embraced by लक्ष्मी that was born of the ocean along with the moon (सहज). For the churning of the ocean, see विष्णुपुराण I. 9 and रामायण I. 44. अभिनवं यौवनं तस्य आरम्भेण अवष्टम्भः (pride) तेन प्रगल्भाः दृष्टिपाताः तैः तृणीकृतं त्रिभुवनं येन. He was proud and his eye seemed to look upon the world as of no account. Compare 'दृष्टिस्तृणीकृतजगत्त्रयसत्त्वसारा' उत्तररामचरित VI. 19. प्रथिम्ना (instru. sing. of प्रथिमन् from पृथु)—vide notes on पिङ्गलिमा p. 23. ॰सहस्रैः सञ्छादिताः दश दिशः यया (*adj.* of शरदम्). In शरद् lotuses of various sorts abound. कुमुद is a white lotus, while कुवलय is dark and कमल is red. When he cast glances from his large eyes, the white of his eyes looked like कुमुदs and the dark pupils like कुवलयs and the red corners looked like कमलs. शर...तैयन्तम् who as though caused the season of autumn. आयत...शोभमानम्—the idea is:—his long nose is deemed to be a dam (सेतुबन्धः) over the borders (सीमान्त) of the two rivers *viz.*, the two eyes. His nose separated the two eyes, as a dam would separate a river in two. Further the nose is fancied to be a stream of the water of beauty dropping from the slab of moonstone in the form of the forehead. His bright forehead resembled चन्द्रकान्त, from which water oozes when the moon rises. The nose also rises up after there is a depression from the forehead. His nose was charming and so is fancied to be the stream of the water of loveliness. अति...वमन्तम् with his mouth emitting the perfume of very fragrant mango, camphor, *kakkola*, cloves and Pârijātaka and resounding with the hum of the swarms of intoxicated bees, he vomited as if the season of spring together with the Nandana garden. Even now camphor, कक्कोल (Marathi कंकोळ) and cloves are taken with ताम्बूल. सहकार and पारिजातक are explained by the com. as certain fragrant substances, 'सहकारः सुगन्धद्रव्यभेदः सहकारफलेनैव क्रियते पारिजातकोऽनेकद्रव्यसंस्कृतो मुखवासविशेषः'. The youth had partaken of कर्पूर, कक्कोल &c. with his ताम्बूल and emitted their fragrance with his breath. In वसन्त also, there is the fragrance of mango blossoms and of other flowers and the humming of bees. नन्दन is the garden of Indra. पारिजातक is one of the five trees of Paradise. *Vide* notes p. 43. Hence the poet says 'सनन्दनवनं'. The reading अवतारयन्तम् is more striking than वमन्तम्, but is probably an emendation. It means 'he made वसन्त descend to the earth together with नन्दनवन'. The critics had laid down that the use of words like वान्त (*past p. p.* of वम्) and उद्गीर्ण in their literal sense was against good taste (ग्राम्य) and so the copyists thinking that the word वमन्तं was so used here probably changed it to अवतारयन्तम्. But it is to be noted that Bāna uses it only in a figurative sense. 'निष्ठ्यूतोद्गीर्णवान्तादि गौणवृत्तिव्यपाश्रयम्। अतिसुन्दरमन्यत्र ग्राम्यकक्षां विगाहते॥' काव्या० I. 95. आसन्नाः सुहृदः तेषां परिहासाः (jests) तेषां भावनया (appreciation, understanding) उत्तानितं मुखं तस्य मुग्धैः हसितैः. दशनज्योत्स्नया स्नपितानि दिङ्मुखानि यैः that bathed the quarters in the moonlight of his teeth. Whenever he smiled at the jests of his friends, his bright teeth gleamed forth and cast their lustre all round. That lustre resembled moonlight. पुनः पुनः...कल्पयन्तम् who again and again created the light of the moon moving about in the sky. As he smiled now and then (and not continuously), he seemed to create moonlight at different times and so the poet uses the word पुनःपुनः. There is a pun on the word नभसि (in the sky; in the month of श्रावण). In श्रावण, the moon is seen now and then on account of the clouds and not continuously (just like his bright smiles). कदम्बमुकुलवत् स्थूलं मुक्ताफलयुगलं तस्य मध्ये अध्यासितं (placed) मरकतं यस्मिन् (*adj.* of ०भरणस्य). त्रि... भरणस्य three-pointed ear-ornament. His ear-ornament was made of two big pearls between which was inserted an emerald. This ornament seems to be somewhat like the भिकबाळी worn by men in Mahārāshṭra. त्रिकण्टक 'त्रिकण्टकस्तु त्र्यश्रः स्यात्रिभी रत्नैश्च भूषणम्'. Compare 'काश्चिदुद्धूयमानधवलचामरसटालग्नत्रिकण्टकवलितविकटकटाक्षाः' हर्ष० 4th उच्छ्वास. प्रेङ्खतः (*adj.* of ०भरणस्य) dangling. प्रभया... लक्ष्यमाणम् by the up-spreading lustre (of the ear-ornament) it seemed as though he had an ear-ornament made of green *Kunda* leaves together with their flowers. *Kunda* flowers, being white, are like pearls and the leaves are green like emerald. कृतः सकुसुमेन हरितकुन्दपल्लवेन कर्णावतंसः यस्य. आमोदितः (आमोदः सञ्जातः अस्य) मृगमदपङ्कः तेन लिखितः पत्रभङ्गः तेन भास्वरम् adorned with ornamental lines drawn with very fragrant musk paste. 'मृगनाभिर्मृगमदः कस्तूरी च' इत्यमरः. For पत्रभङ्ग see notes p. 24. भुजयुगलम्—object of दधानम्. उद्दाम...दधानम् possessing (arms) that seemed to be the two poles of the banner of Cupid (मकरकेतुः), that (poles) had on their tops (the figure of) a formidable crocodile. उद्दामेन मकरेण आक्रान्तं शिखरं यस्य. This may apply to भुजयुगलं also, meaning '(arms) the tops of which had on them a loose (or formidable) crocodile-shaped ornament'. Long arms are a sign of good fortune and high position. As he was handsome like Cupid and had long arms, they (arms) are said to be poles. The marks of the black musk on the arms looked like the dark crocodile, which is the emblem on the banner of Cupid. सीमन्तितं parted (*adj.* of देहम्). सीमन्त is the parting line of the hair of women. It is white. His ब्रह्मसूत्र also was white and was placed across his body like a line. He had a formidable body which was encircled by the white यज्ञोपवीत. The white यज्ञोपवीत is like the fair Ganges. So the poet fancies that his body was the मन्दर mountain chained (encircled) by the stream of the Ganges indignant at the churning of the ocean. When the ocean was churned for jewels, मन्दर was made the churning handle. The ocean is poetically spoken of as the husband of the Ganges (and also of all other rivers). The Ganges (ब्रह्मसूत्र) was as if angry at the harassment of her husband and bound down मन्दर (his body) in order to stay the churning. **'मन्थानं मन्दरं** कृत्वा नेत्रं कृत्वा तु वासुकिम्। मथ्यतामभृतं देवाः साह्यये मय्यवस्थिते ॥' विष्णुपु० I. 9. 76. 'बद्धे सन्दानितम्' इत्यमरः. कर्पूर... पांशुलेन rendered dusty, being smeared with a handful of camphor powder (क्षोदः). कान्तायाः उच्चौ कुचौ एव चक्रवाकौ तयोः युगलं तस्य विपुलं पुलिनं तेन. His broad chest was like a vast sandy beach for the चक्रवाकs—*viz.*, the high breasts of his (future) wife. His wife would rest on his broad chest, as the चक्रवाक does on a पुलिन. A beach also is dusty (पांशुल) with white sand (resembling camphor). उरःस्थलेन...क्रम्—the idea is:—He had a very broad chest and stout long arms. The poet fancies that by his long arms he embraced the distant quarters and brought them together in a heap (पुञ्जित). The heaped up quarters were allowed expansion on his broad chest. आयामः length. पुरस्ता...भागम्—the author describes here the under-garment (something like modern मांडचोळणा) of the youth. पुरस्ता...कमनीयेन that was charming because one end (कोणः) of it was set in front a little below his navel. पृष्ठत...पल्लवेन the hem of which hung behind over his girdle (कक्ष्या). पल्लव (Marathi गोंडा) the hem of the strings with which the garment was made fast. उभय...भागेन that was so wound on both sides as to display a third part of his thighs. हारीत...वाससा by his lower garment that was green like the हारीत (pigeon) bird and that tightly (निबिड) pressed (his waist). विभ...भागम् whose very slender waist was divided (from the upper part of his body). अनवरतव्यायामेन उपचितमांसे कठिने विकटे मकरमुखसंलग्ने जानुनी ययोः (*adj.* of ऊरुदण्डाभ्याम्) the knees of which had flesh accumulated by incessant exercise, were hard, formidable and firmly knit to the parts above them. 'मकरमुखं जानुनोरुपरिभागः' सं०. We may also explain मकरमुखसंलग्न as 'knees that had a crocodile shape and that were thick-set (and not loose or flabby)'. विशाल... स्तम्भाभ्याम् (thighs) that were stone pillars for supporting (उत्तम्भन) the stone platform of his broad chest. The image here is taken from architecture. His long and tapering thighs were like stone columns. His broad chest was like the entablature (constituting the architrave, frieze and cornice) resting on slender pillars. चारु...कान्तिभ्याम् the beauty of which was rendered patent by the lovely marks of sandal thereon. Sandal paste had been applied to that part of the thighs that was not covered. स्थासकः perfuming the body with unguents. 'चर्चा तु चार्चिक्यं स्थासकः' इत्यमरः. ऊरु...यामम् with his long thighs, he as if laughed in scorn at the length of the trunk of ऐरावत. The trunk of an elephant is long and tapering downwards like the thigh. ऐरावत is white and the youth's thigh also was besmeared with white sandal paste. अति...काण्डम् his shanks (जङ्घा) were very slender, as though through the fatigue (खेदः) caused by bearing the burden of his very stout (भरित) thighs (ऊरु). One who carries burdens is slim (and not fat). कल्प...पाटलस्य—his feet were red like the fresh shoots of the tree of Paradise. The shoots of a tree are red; much more of a कल्पवृक्ष. उभय...लम्बिनः His feet hung on both sides (of the horse he was riding). दोला...रचयन्तम्—the idea is:—the motion of the horse caused the rays from his toe-nails to move about. The bright rays of the nails resemble a white chowrie. As he was riding the nails appeared to be a chowrie placed on the horse. Chowries were placed on horses and elephants. Compare शाकुन्तल I 'निष्कम्पचामरशिखा निभृतोर्ध्वकर्णाः । ...धावन्त्यमी मृगजवाक्षमयेव रथ्याः ॥'. अभि...भुवि that (horse) tore the earth with its hoofs that were raised (उदञ्चत्) aloft in front, that seemed as though to rest long in the air and that fell forcibly on account of their curvetting (वलितं). The high spirited steed pranced, remained standing on its hind legs for a long time as if it wanted to give them rest and then came down on the earth with force with its front legs, thereby raising dust from the earth. वलितेन विकटं यथा स्यात्तथा (अव्ययीभाव)—to be taken with पतद्भिः. ०भुवि and the following locatives qualify वाजिनि (l. 15). प्रतिक्षणं दशनैः (आदौ) ग्रहः (पश्चात्) मुक्तिश्च ताभ्यां खणखणायितं खरं खलीनं (खे तालुनि लीनम्) येन. The hard bridle-bit made a sound when the horse bit it between its teeth and then let it off. The reading दशनविमुक्त conveys almost the same sense. दीर्घघ्राणे लीना लालिका यस्य सः ०लालिकः स चासौ ललाट...चक्रकश्च. ललाटे लुलितानि (tossed, waving) चारूणि चामीकरस्य (सुवर्णस्य) चक्रकाणि (rings) यस्य. लालिका is explained by सं० as 'the end of the bit'. It is better to read with B 'दीर्घ...लालिके ललाट०,' as then it is easier to dissolve the compounds. शिञ्जान...शोभिनि

adorned with tinkling (शिञ्जान) golden trappings. 'तपनीयं शातकौम्भम्' इत्यमरः ('शतकुम्भे गिरौ भवं शातकौम्भम्, अनुशतिकादित्वादुभयपद-वृद्धिः, शातकुम्भमित्येके' क्षीर०). शातकौम्भम् (or—कुम्भम् according to some) gold. 'जयनं हयमण्डनमाला' सं०. 'अश्वादीनां च सन्नाहे जये च जयनं मतम्' शाश्वत 515. मनसः इव रंहः (वेगः) यस्य. गोलाङ्गूलस्य कपोलवत् कालानि (dark) कायलोमानि यस्य. गोलाङ्गूलः an ape with a dark face and a tail like a cow's. 'कृष्णमुखो गोलाङ्गूलः' क्षीर०. उभय...हस्ताभ्याम् whose hands gripped the saddle (पर्याणं) cloth on both sides. आसन्नपरिचारकः body-guard. दोधूयमानं (*pr. p.* of the frequentative base of धू to shake) चामरिकायुगलं यस्य. बन्दिनः of the bard. 'बन्दिनः स्तुतिपाठकाः' इत्यमरः. सुभाषितम्—object of भावयन्तम्. उत्कण्टकितः (रोमाञ्चितः) कपोलफलकः यस्य. लग्न...कलेनेव—the idea is:—his cheek had hair standing on end on account of emotion roused by the song of the bard; the poet fancies the रोमाञ्च to be pieces of the fine hairy growth (पक्ष्म) on the filaments (केसरम्) of the lotus on his ear. भावयन्तम् reflecting over, appreciating. अनङ्ग...दर्शयन्तम् who as if showed (in his person) the advent of the *yuga* (the era) of Cupid. He was charming like Cupid. सं० says 'अनङ्गजन्मना यदुपलक्षितं युगं कालविशेषः, तस्य नूतनमदनसादृश्यात्, यद्वा अनङ्गयोर्युगं तदवतारमिव । द्वित्वसंख्यापूर्वकत्वात्'. This and the following clauses lay stress on the extreme loveliness of the youth in various ways and the effects he produced on others. चन्द्र...यन्तम् who as though created a world full of moonlight. He was bright like the moon and shed his lustre over the whole world. विलासप्रायम्—his youthful smiles and gestures were to be seen everywhere. अन्यः सर्गः (सृष्टिः) सर्गान्तरम्. अनु...रचयन्तम्—this world is full of love and hatred; but he was the centre of the affection of all; no one hated him. So he brought about another world as it were, where there was nothing but affection. The student will note Bāṇa's command over language. He uses different words like उत्पादयन्तं, जनयन्तं &c., to convey the same sense. शृङ्गारमयम्—full of love. He was the cynosure of all eyes the whole day. राग...यन्तम् inaugurating a reign of affection. आक...चक्षुषोः he was to the eyes as though the infatuating collyrium. It was supposed that some magical collyrium when applied to the eye by a person made that person attractive to every spectator. He by his beauty fascinated the eyes of all. वशी०—certain incantations were supposed to have the power of subduing the will of others. Note the following मन्त्र credited with great power. 'ॐ

गणपतये स्वाहेति । अयं गणपतेर्मन्त्रो धनविद्याप्रदायकः । इममष्टसहस्रं च जप्त्वा बद्ध्वा शिखां ततः । व्यवहारे जयः स्याच्च शतजाप्यान्नृणां प्रियः ॥.' स्वस्था...णाम् he was as though a powder that influences the senses to be comfortable. The idea is:—in his presence, the senses of the spectators were lulled into pleasure. C and T translate 'to the senses a powder able to affect the healthiest'. This is not so good as the meaning we suggest. अस...कस्य—the curiosity to see him is never satiated. सिद्ध...ग्यस्य he was as though the never-failing remedy of blessedness. The moment he was seen, everyone felt blessed. पुनर्ज०—Cupid was once burnt by S'iva; but on seeing that handsome youth, hearts fell under the sway of Love (*i. e.* love was born again). रसायनमिव यौवनस्य—रसायनम् (रसः mercury + अयनम्) a medical preparation containing mercury. In ancient India, it was believed, as in many other countries, that mercury, if properly prepared, would make men immortal and free from old age. Note the passages 'संसारस्य परं पारं दत्तेऽसौ पारदः स्मृतः'; 'एकोऽसौ रसराजः शरीरमजरामरं कुरुते'. The सर्वदर्शनसंग्रह devotes a chapter to रसेश्वरदर्शन 'the philosophy of Mercury' (रस being identified with शिव). As रसायन produces perfect health, so youth attained perfection in the young man. एक...रामणीयकस्य—रामणीयक shared the youth with nothing else *i. e.* loveliness reigned supreme in him. कीर्ति...रूपस्य.—He was so charming that he seemed to be a pillar set up for all time to commemorate the triumph of beauty. मूल...लावण्यस्य as the principal amount of loveliness. The loveliness in others is like interest *i. e.* it is subsidiary (inferior) to the principal (the youth's charms). पुण्य...संसारस्य—the good deeds of the world bore fruit in the splendid form of the youth. कान्तिः (beauty) एव लता तस्याः प्रथमाङ्कुरम्—none as handsome as the youth had preceded him. सर्गा...पतेः—Brahmā had created the world several times. By practice one acquires great skill and perfection. So the beauty of the youth was the result of the skill acquired by Brahmā. प्रतापः glory, greatness. विभ्रमः amorous or sportive movements. यशः...ग्ध्यस्य—learning had attained the highest pitch of excellence in him. अष्टा...देशीयम् about 18 years old. The affixes कल्प, देश्य and देशीय are added in the sense ef 'a little less than, about'. 'ईषदसमाप्तौ कल्पब्देश्यदेशीयरः' पा. 5. 3. 67. (ईषदूनो विद्वान् विद्वत्कल्पः विद्वद्देशीयः । सि. कौ.). द्वितीयम्—This and the following clauses in the accusative qualify पुरुषम् (l. 33). अपर...तुरङ्गम्—न परेण संश्लिष्टः तुरङ्गः यस्य whose horse was not touched by another. This may mean that his saddle was not held by any attendants as that of the youth was or that his horse was not closely followed by another *i. e.* other riders kept at a respectful distance. We prefer the former meaning. From the fact that the young man was cracking jokes with his companions, it seems that they were close to him (and so to the old man also). उत्तप्त...कारम् whose form was like a pillar of heated (molten) gold (तपनीयं) *i. e.* he was bright and red in complexion. परिणतं वयः यस्य—old. नीच...कचम् who had short nails, beard and hair. He did not allow these to grow. शुक्तिखलतिम् bald-headed as a shell. His head had no hair and the skin was white and glossy like mother-o'-pearl. रोमशं उरःस्थलं यस्य. 'लोमादिपामादि—पिच्छादिभ्यः श-न-इलचः' पा. 5. 2. 100 (लोमादिभ्यः शः । लोमशः । रोमवान् । पामादिभ्यो नः । पामनः । सि. कौ.). र् and ल् are often interchanged as in रोमन् and लोमन्. अनु...शिक्षयन्तम् who, being dressed elegantly but not gaudily, seemed as though to teach even old age decorousness. It is old age that makes men decorous. He was old and such an embodiment of decorum that old age might have taken lessons from him. उल्बण showy, gaudy. गुणा...नयन्तम् who seemed as though lending weight (importance or greatness) even to virtues. He was so virtuous that he seemed to heighten the worth of the virtues themselves. गरिमा—from गुरु. Vide notes on पिङ्गलिमा p. 23. महानुभावता dignity or nobility. He was so noble or dignified that even Dignity may have something to learn from him. आचारः correct deportment. आचार्यकम् teaching, instruction. आचार्यस्य भावः कर्म वा—according to 'योपधाद्गुरूपोत्तमाद्वुञ्' पा. V. 1. 132 (रामणीयकम् । आभिधानीयकम् । सि. कौ.). वारबाणः or-वाणः a coat of mail, jacket. 'कञ्चुको वारवाणोऽस्त्री' इत्यमरः (वारं आच्छादकं वानमस्य इति वारवाणः—क्षीर०). ०पट्टिकया परिवेष्टितः मौलिः यस्य. पुरुषम्—is to be connected with अद्राक्षीत् (l. 27) above.

P. 11 l. 1—**P. 12** l. 32 **अथ स...दशम्.** पुरोयायिनाम् soldiers that had gone ahead, vanguard. यथा...कथयताम् who, having come back, narrated all as they saw with astonished minds. The vanguard was deep in wonder at the superhuman beauty of the two maidens. The reading प्रतीत्य may mean प्रतिनिवृत्य and also 'having approached'. उपलभ्य having learnt. दिव्या आकृतिः यस्य (*adj.* of ०युगलम्). ०युगलम्—object of उपलभ्य. प्रतूर्णतुरगः whose horse began to gallop (*i. e.* he urged his horse to greater speed). निवारितः परिजनः येन who prohibited his servants (to follow him).

तेन—refers to the old companion of the youth described above. कृतं उपसङ्ग्रहणं याभ्याम् who made a respectful salutation. तौ—object of उपजग्राह. किस...जग्राह received them according to their precedence with hospitality usual in forest life beginning with the offering of a seat of tender foliage and ending with the present of fruit and flowers. सकुसुमैः फलैः अर्घः (पूजाविधिः) अवसानं (अन्तः) यस्य (*adj.* of आतिथ्येन). आसीनयोश्च तयोः when they sat. प्रवयस् an old man. प्रगतं वयः यस्य. 'प्रवयाः स्थविरो वृद्धः' इत्यमरः. सहजा (inborn) लज्जा धनं यस्य. सहज...जनस्य to address (another man) first (*i. e.* before he addresses) is (seems) an immodest act in the case of young women to whom innate bashfulness is all-in-all, particularly in the case of highborn maidens that are simple like the does of the forest. शालीन—bashful, shy–from शाला with the affix ख (ईन). 'शालीनकौपीने अधृष्टाकार्ययोः' पा. 5. 2. 20 (शालाप्रवेशमर्हति शालीनः अधृष्टः । सि. कौ. । अप्रागल्भ्यादन्यत्र गन्तुमशक्तः शालामेव प्रवेष्टुमर्हतीत्यर्थः । तत्त्वबोधिनी). The propriety of the word वन is this. A doe, by contact with human beings, may become bold; but one brought up in the forest far from human habitation will retain its original shyness and innocence. केवल...वृत्तिः But this (my) sense of hearing, envious of (my) eye that is blest (कृतार्थ) by seeing you, urges me, being eager to hear the news (of you). What सावित्री means is:—on seeing this extremely handsome young man, our eyes have been rewarded and gratified; but our ears have not yet heard anything concerning him and are therefore envious of the eye. चक्षुषे स्पृहयन्ती (०वृत्तिः)—स्पृह् governs the dative of the object of desire or envy. 'स्पृहेरीप्सितः' पा. 1. 4. 36. 'वार्ता प्रवृत्तिर्वृत्तान्त उदन्तः स्यात्' इत्यमरः. प्रथम...प्रणयम् a good man at first sight offers his affection (प्रणयः) as though it were a present. She means that both the men, being good, have given their good will to the two maidens even at the first meeting. अप्र...वाचालयति *lit.* the heart offered by the great (प्रभवत्) with courtesy (प्रश्रयः) makes even a timid person talkative, as wine does. She means:—we are timid. You are great and courteously offered your heart (*i. e.* your regard) to us. This your regard for us makes us bold enough to address you. Wine also makes even a timid person garrulous, when he gets drunk. प्रभ...र्पितं (with मधु) means 'proffered with over-powering courtesy' or 'proffered by a great man with courtesy'. अति...विस्रम्भः confidence easily reaches its highest pitch in the case of a very yielding good man, as the bowstring on the bow. She means:—you are very good and yielding. So we treat you with the greatest confidence. The words नम्र and कोटि are श्लिष्ट. The bow-string easily reaches the furthest tip (कोटि) when the bow is extremely bent (नम्र). It is better to read आरोहति with B. With आरोपयति (causal of रुह् with आ) we naturally expect one more noun in the accusative (besides कोटिम्). आरोपयति will yield a very good sense, if we could read विस्रम्भम् and in that case गुणः (virtue, string) will be श्लिष्ट and will be construed with both साधौ and धनुषि. अति... धियाम् in those whose minds are steady or who are very wise. स्रष्टुः...शयाः master-pieces of creation from the Creator's hands. त्रि...भावि surpassing (everything) in the three worlds. अस्य—refers to the young man. सौजन्य...तरलता it is not fickleness that is natural to young women that causes me to speak, but it is the great beauty of this one dear to the gods, which (भद्रता) is under the control of kindness (that makes me talk). She means:—this young man is extremely handsome and yet very considerate (and not capricious in the vanity of his charms). It is this that urges me to know something more about him. सावित्री very much desired that सरस्वती should be married to such a young man if otherwise eligible. सह उत्तिष्ठति इति सहोत्था. The word देवानां प्रिय is used by Bâṇa in a good sense *i. e.* as meaning 'worthy, honourable'. Compare 'इहापि जन्मनि दत्तमेवास्माकममुना तपःक्लेशेन फलमसुलभदर्शनं दर्शयता देवानां प्रियम्' हर्षचरित 8th उच्छ्वास. As'oka in his edicts calls himself देवानां प्रिय. The महाभाष्य uses it in a good sense 'के पुनर्भवदादयः। भवान् दीर्घायुः देवानां प्रियः आयुष्मानिति' on पा. 5. 3. 14 (Kielhorn vol. II. p. 405). But later Sanskrit grammarians assign the meaning of 'fool' to this Aluk compound. Mr. R. R. Kale takes देवानां प्रिय in this sense and applies it to सावित्री, but that is not correct. Besides the sense becomes involved. We may also take देवानां प्रियस्य as referring to the old courtier. आगमनेन—connect with शून्यतां नीतः. अपुण्यभाक् unhappy. विजृम्भिता विरहव्यथा यस्य in which the pain of separation is growing. अपहृतः हरस्य हुङ्काराहङ्कारः येन who humbles the pride of the defiant roar of S'iva. A wrathful man makes the sound हुम्. शिव in wrath burnt मदन by the fire from his third eye. Vide p. 14 (notes). But the youth, who was as handsome as Cupid, humbled S'iva's pride by his very existence. This passage is reminiscent of the verse 'असह्यहुङ्कारनिवर्तितः पुरा पुरारिमप्राप्तमुखः शिलीमुखः। इमां हृदि व्यायतपातमक्षिणोद्विशीर्णमूर्तेरपि पुष्पधन्वनः॥

कुमारसम्भव V. 54. अनन्यजः—न अन्यस्मात् जायते इति—Love is mind-born and has no physical birth. So Cupid is called अनन्यज or अनन्यजन्मा. किं नाम यस्य सः किंनामा तस्य. समृद्धं तपः यस्य—her idea is that none who does not possess a store of merit or austerities can be blest with such a son. अमृतवर्षी showering nectar *i. e.* great delight (with the youth); कौस्तुभ sprang from the ocean along with अमृत. कौस्तुभ...ह्लादयति—The कौस्तुभ jewel churned from the ocean was placed on his chest by Vishṇu. 'कौस्तुभाख्यमभूद्रत्नं पद्मरागो महोदधेः। तस्मिन्हरिः स्पृहां चक्रे वक्षोऽलङ्करणे मणौ॥' भागवतपुराण VIII. 8. 5. The word is derived as 'कुं भुवं स्तुभ्नाति व्याप्नोति कुस्तुभः सागरः तत्र भवः'. त्रि.. स्या deserving to be worshipped by the three worlds. महतस्तेजसः of this very brilliant man. प्रभातसन्ध्येव—The morning twilight gives birth to the sun, the great luminary, and people perform their adoration in the morning. कानि...क्षराणि what fortunate letters come to be his name (अभिख्या)? 'अभिख्या नामशोभयोः' इत्यमरः. The student will notice how politely सावित्री asks for information concerning the young man's country of birth, his destination, his parentage and his name. आर्य...हृदयस्य in seeking to know your honour, the same order is followed by my heart that acts as curiosity dictates. She wants to know the same four things (country of birth &c.) about the old man. प्रकटितः प्रश्रयः (courtesy) येन. सतां...विद्या to speak what is agreeable is a hereditary art with the good (*i. e.* they are past masters in that). न...वचोभिः—handsome women are described as चन्द्रानना. सावित्री had not only a moon-like face, but her words also were चन्द्रमय, were such as gladdened the heart of the listener by their ambrosial sweetness. चन्द्रमय—made of the moon. सुधा॰—The moon is said to shower down nectar with his rays, being called सुधांशु. सौजन्य...जायन्ते women like you, who are the birthplace of goodness, come into the world as the arts for moulding good men after a great deal of merit (शुभ *i. e.* पुण्य). He means:—It is due to the accumulation of the good deeds of the world that noble women like you are born. Such noble women fashion men into good men, as the study of the arts enables a person to fashion from raw materials finished articles. दूरे...पयन्ति let alone mutual conversation, even the interchange of glances with the noble (अभिजात) raises a man to the highest pitch (of goodness or glory). भूषणं goes with दधीचः. भार्गववंशस्य—च्यवन the father of दधीच belonged to the भृगुगोत्र. The story of च्यवन and his wife सुकन्या is alluded to in विष्णुपुराण IV.1. In रामायण सुन्दरकाण्ड chap. 24 she is mentioned in a list of पतिव्रताs (verse 1.). The story is given in great detail in पद्मपुराण 4th खण्ड (पातालखण्ड) chap. 14 ff. च्यवन was the son of भृगु. He performed such severe austerities that an ant-hill grew upon him. The daughter of king शर्याति in play thrust a pin in the anthill and put out च्यवन's eye. In order to propitiate the sage he gave that daughter to him in marriage. भू...लकस्य who is an ornament of the three worlds भूः, भुवः and स्वः. These are the first three out of the seven worlds (भूः, भुवः, स्वः, महः, जनः, तपः, सत्यम्). अदभ्रेण (प्रचुरेण) प्रभावेण स्तम्भितः (paralysed) जम्भारेः (इन्द्रस्य) भुजस्तम्भः येन. The As'vins cured च्यवन of old age and blindness. च्यवन gave सोम at a sacrifice to the As vins who were never before allowed that honour. Indra becoming angry at this raised his hand to strike the sage with his वज्र. च्यवन paralysed the hand of Indra. Vide पद्मपुराण 4th खण्ड chap. 16. 'शक्रं वज्रधरं दृष्ट्वा मुनिः स्वहननोद्यतम् ॥ हुङ्कारमकरोद्धीमान् स्तम्भयामास तद्भुजम् ॥' verses 15-16. ०शिलासु शयनं तेन दुर्ललितं पादपङ्केरुहं यस्य- Gods and demons bowed their crowned heads at his feet, which were thus over-fondled (दुर्ललित) by treading on the jewels in their crowns. निजतेजःप्रसरेण (by the spreading of his own lustre) प्लुष्टः (scorched) पुलोमा येन. When भृगु went out leaving his pregnant wife alone, the demon पुलोमा made bold to lay hands on her, when her foetus slipped from her womb. On seeing that foetus so fallen, the demon was burnt to ashes. See आदिपर्व chap. 5-6. बहिर्वृत्ति जीवितं *lit.* his life existing outside *i. e.* the son was dear to his father as his own life. Separate जननी अस्य. जितं जगत् येन. शर्यातस्य—In विष्णुपुराण (IV. 1) king शर्याति is said to be the son of मनु. अन्तर्वत्नीं pregnant ('अन्तर्वत्नी च गर्भिणी' इत्यमरः) from अन्तर् with the affix वत्. 'अन्तर्वत्पतिवतोर्नुक्' पा. 4. 1. 32 (एतयोः स्त्रियां नुक् स्यात् । अन्तरस्त्यस्यां गर्भ इति...अन्तर्वत्नी । पतिवत्नी । सि. कौ.). वैजनने मासि in the month in which the child was expected 'सूतिमासो वैजननः' इत्यमरः. विजनने भवः or विजननस्य अयं वैजननः. पिता...नाययत्—Even now a woman is brought to her father's house particularly when it is the first delivery. Separate अनेहसा (by time, in course of time) अवर्धत. अनेहस् *m.* time. तत्रैव—in the palace of king शर्यात. बालः young (applies to the child दधीच as well as to the moon). The young moon gives delight to all. राजीवलोचनः lotus-eyed. भर्तृ...दुहितरि even when his daughter (सुकन्या) returned to her husband's house. आसेचनकदर्शनम्

at the approach of the rains हंसs were supposed to migrate to the मानस lake. Or the विरोध may be this:—if there is thunder in her, how can she have the low cackling of कलहंसs? कमल...करा (1) possessing the delicate lustre of lotuses; (2) whose hand is delicate like a lotus. हिम...तम्बा (1) whose hips are broad with slabs of the Himālaya mountain; (2) whose hips are broad like &c. Lotuses and slabs of snow cannot exist together, as snow blights lotuses. Compare 'हिमसेकविपत्तिरत्र मे नलिनी पूर्वनिदर्शनं मता' रघु० VIII. 45. करभोरुः (1) having the thigh of a camel; (2) having a thigh round and tapering like the trunk of an elephant. करभः a young camel; also 'the back portion of the hand from the wrist to the root of the fingers.' वि...मना (1) whose gait is slow; (2) whose gait is languidly sportive. A camel is well-known to be a fast animal. One who has the camel's thigh cannot be slow. अमु...भावा (1) who has not given up devotion to Kumāra *i. e.* कार्तिकेय; (2) who has not yet passed the stage of girlhood. अमुक्तः कुमारे स्कन्दे भावः भक्तिः यया. अमुक्तः कुमारभावः यया. स्निग्धः (affectionate) तारकः (तदाख्यः असुरः) यस्याम्. स्निग्धा (charming) तारका (pupil of the eye) यस्याः. The demon तारक was killed by स्कन्द. One who is devoted to स्कन्द cannot secure the affection of तारक. अध्वा the road *i. e.* the distance. परि...रिष्यति Familiarity (with us) will surely make (everything) clear. अनुषङ्गे दृष्टः seen by chance. अनुषङ्गः incidental connection. नवः अम्भसां भरः (burden) तेन गम्भीरः अम्भोधराणां (मेघानां) ध्वानः (ध्वनिः) तन्निभया तत्सदृश्या. भारत्या in a voice. नर्तयन् भुजगभुजः making the peacocks dance. Peacocks subsist on reptiles and dance when clouds thunder. The voice of दधीच was mistaken by the peacocks to be the thunder of clouds. भुजगभुजः (with दधीच) would mean 'whose arms were (long and lithe) like snakes.' Separate प्रसादम् आर्या आराध्य०. कृता नमस्कृतिः येन. उच्चचाल started away. उत्तम्भितं पक्ष्म यस्य the eyelashes of which were raised up. निश्चला तारका यस्य. लिखितेनेव चक्षुषा with an eye that was as though drawn in a picture (*i. e.* that was quite motionless). कृच्छ्रा...दृशम् with difficulty she withdrew her eye (from that direction).

P. 12 l. 33—**P. 13** l. 10. अथ...सुष्वाप. तस्य=दधीचस्य. रूपसम्पदम् perfection of beauty. अवशेव as though helpless. अप्रहितमपि though not sent. कुतोऽपि (1) from some indescribable cause; (2) from the earth. The creeper with its shoots springs from the earth. सालस्या इव—आलस्येन सह (बहुव्रीहि). शून्या vacant in mind.

सनिद्रा sleepy, dreamy. अस्तमुपयाति—connect with तेजसि. प्रत्यक् पर्यस्तं मण्डलं यस्य whose orb was thrown westward. लाङ्ग...त्विषि the brilliance of which was rosy like a bunch of लाङ्गलिका. कमलिनीकामुक the lover of lotuses plants. कमलिनी plants bloom at the advent of the sun. कठोर...शोचिषि the lustre (शोचिः) of which was red like the head of a fully developed (कठोर) crane. सावित्रं सवितुः इदं सावित्रम्. त्रयीमये—त्रयीमय is an appellation of the sun. त्रयी means 'the three Vedas'. As the sun is worshipped with the Veda or as the most sacred verse of the Rigveda, the गायत्री, is addressed to the sun, the latter is called त्रयीमय or त्रयीतनु. Compare भागवतपुराण 5. 20. 4. '**त्रय्या विद्यया** भगवन्तं **त्रयीमयं** सूर्यमात्मानं यजन्ते'. तमाल is a tree the leaves of which are dark. मलिनयति *loc. sing.* of the *pr. p.* of the denominative verb मलिनयति from मलिन. व्योम is the object of मलिनयति. सञ्च...तलम् when the moon very slowly crept up the sky, like a swan of the Ganges following the tinkling of the anklets of the roaming Siddha damsels. For सिद्ध, see above (text p. 5 l. 25). सिद्ध does not mean 'saint' here as C and T think. A हंस is white and hence the moon is compared to हंस. The moon sailed in the Milky Way, which is white and resembles the मन्दाकिनी. कृतः सन्ध्यायै प्रणामः यया. निशामुखे at the very beginning of night. She was languid and tired and so took the first opportunity to lie down. This contrasts with उचिते शयनकाले below. विमुक्तानि अङ्गानि यस्याः whose limbs were drooping or languid. कृत्वा...कलापम् having gone through her evening ritual as it was being usually performed by her. कलापः = समूहः. This shows that she was unaffected, while सरस्वती was perturbed by the wave of passion.

P. 13 ll. 11—28 इतरा...कुलैः. अङ्ग...तला whose bed of tender leaves was disarranged (विलुलित) by the tossing of her limbs. निमीलित closed. मर्त्य...परि the world of mortals is surely above (*i. e.* superior to) all worlds. एवंविधानि—refers to दधीच. सक...गुरूणि (1) worthy of respect on account of (the possession of) all virtues (with दधीच); (2) heavy even to the collection of all threads (with रत्नानि). Even numerous threads may not bear the burden of a big jewel; what of a single thread? ग्रामः = समूहः. She explains in the following clauses how he possesses all the qualities and is an ornament to त्रिभुवन. तस्य...न्दुः—the moon is but a drop oozing from the stream of the beauty of his face. The moon is round and bright like a drop. His face is so much more charming than the moon, that the latter seems but a drop as compared with the stream of his beauty. Explain the following clauses similarly. विक्षेपाः glances. For विकच...कराः, compare above 'चक्षुषः प्रथिम्ना विकचकुमुदकुवलयकमलसरःसहस्रसञ्छादितदशदिशं' (text p. 9. ll. 23–24 and notes p. 50). आकरः = समूहः. अधरमणेः of. his jewel-like lip. His red lip is like a red jewel. दीधितयः = किरणाः. बन्धूकम् is a red flower. The word विकसित is put in to indicate deep red. तस्य...नङ्गः The disembodied one (Cupid) is only a means (उपकरणं) of enhancing the beauty of his body. There is a picturesque effect in saying that his अङ्ग has its beauty enhanced by अनङ्ग (one who is without body). 'परभागो गुणोत्कर्षः' क्षीरस्वामी. बाण is fond of this word. Compare 'उपहितकान्तिपतिपरभागा लक्ष्मच्छायेव चन्द्रमसः' कादम्बरी p. 267 of P; "कुटिलक्रमरूपक्रियमाणपल्लवपरभागैरपरैः' हर्षचरित 1st उच्छ्वास. Connect स्त्रैणानि with the three, चक्षूंषि, चेतांसि and यौवनानि. स्त्रैणानि of women (from स्त्री). 'स्त्रीपुंसाभ्यां नञ्स्नञौ भवनात्' पा. 4. 1. 87. येषा...दर्शनस्य within whose vision be comes. The reading अविषयः is explicable. The meaning then would be 'the eyes, minds and youths of those women are blessed who do not see him', the idea perhaps being that it is better that he be not seen at all rather than suffer for his sake an insatiable longing. क्षणं...धर्मेण in showing him to me only for a moment, my evil deeds of former lives have as though borne their fruit. She means that if he could be seen continuously, there would then be no distress, but only bliss. This sentence has been explained differently. 'My misconduct (in laughing at दुर्वासस्), though done in this very life, has borne fruit, as though it were done in a previous life, by showing that rare young man to me, though for a moment'. It is generally the actions of past lives that bear fruit in this life. But this is not a very happy explanation. We think that the mere fact of laughing at a mistake would hardly be called an अधर्म even by सरस्वती. It will be noticed that from the words अजायत च नवपल्लव &c. (p. 13 l. 1 ff), Bāṇa describes the various stages of Love in strict accordance with writers on Rhetoric. 'अभिलाषश्चिन्ता-स्मृति-गुणकथनोद्वेगसम्प्रलापश्च । उन्मादोऽथ व्याधिर्जडता मृतिरिति दशाऽत्र कामदशाः ॥' साहित्यदर्पण III. 190. The sentence अजायत॰ shows अभिलाष; the next shows चिन्ता. The sentence 'कृतसन्ध्याप्रणामा...तस्थौ' indicates स्मृति and in 'मर्त्यलोकः खलु' we have the fourth अवस्था 'गुणकथन.' In the sentence 'मदनशर॰' (l. 21) we have the 5th stage of उद्वेग. प्रतिपत्तिः course of action; means. का...दानीम् what should I do now? स्वप्ने आसादितं द्वितीयं दर्शनं यया. आकर्णे आकृष्टं

कार्मुकं (धनुः) येन. Cupid smote her with all his power. प्रतिबुद्धा when she awoke. At his very first sight she fell in love with him. But when she saw him again in her dreams, she was hopelessly smitten by love. मदन...जगाम unrest came to her who was struck by the arrows of Cupid, as though to learn the news (of her state). The plain meaning is:— being smitten by love, she became restless. When a person falls ill or is beaten or meets with an accident, people call on him to express their sympathy or regard. So here अरति is fancied to have made a call on her. अरतिः—'स्वाभीष्टवस्त्वलाभेन चेतसो याऽनवस्थितिः । अरतिः सा'. Another sense also is hinted. रति is the wife of मदन. As मदन struck her (सरस्वती), अरति (one who is opposed to रति, the wife of the offending मदन) made a call on her. The meanings of नञ् (अ) are six 'तत्सादृश्यमभावश्च तदन्यत्वं तदल्पता । अप्राशस्त्यं विरोधश्च नञर्थाः षट् प्रकीर्तिताः ॥'. कुसुम...धत्त— one who is beaten feels pain. But she felt pain though not beaten. The cause of pain was really her love-sick condition. In this and the following five sentences Bāṇa describes her condition by employing the figure of speech called विभावना. It consists in stating that an effect follows though its cause is non—existent. 'क्रियायाः प्रतिषेधेऽपि फलव्यक्तिर्विभावना' काव्यप्रकाश X. In such cases only the well-known cause is absent; while some other cause works to bring about the effect. Compare for this and the last clause 'कुसुमितलताभिरहताप्यधत्त रुजमलिकुलैरदष्टाऽपि ।' परिवर्तते स्म नलिनीलहरीभिरलोलिताप्यघूर्णत सा ॥'. मन्द... मुमोच when dust (रजः) enters one's eyes, tears fall. She shed tears through love-pangs, though the pollen (रजः) of flowers did not soil her eyes. हंसपक्षाः एव तालवृन्तानि (fans) तै वान्ताः (emitted) वाताः तैः वितताः (spread) तैः. शोणशीकरैः the spray of the S'oṇa river. आर्द्रता (1) becoming wet; (2) becoming full of soft feeling. प्रेङ्ख...दोलाभिः though not borne on the pairs of roving (प्रेङ्खत्) Kādambas she rolled on the swinging waves of the sylvan lotus ponds. 'कादम्बः कलहंसः स्यात्' इत्यमरः. कमलिनी—a place abounding in कमलs. 'पुष्करादिभ्यो देशे' पा. 5. 2. 135 (पुष्करिणी । पद्मिनी । सि. कौ.). The ripples of the pond wafting the scent of lotuses excited her and made her roll on her bed. विघटमानानि (separating) चक्रवाकयुगलानि तैः विसृष्टैः (*adj.* of धूमैः). श्यामतामाससाद she became dark (*i. e.* lost the colour of her complexion as she was love-sick). One is darkened by smoke. The sighs heaved by the separated चक्रवाकs are like धूम. The चक्रवाक male was poetically supposed to become separated from its mate at the approach of night. व्यचेष्टत she wriggled. A man stung by bees would fling his body about.

P. 13 l. 29—**P. 14** l. 11 **अथ...यासीत्.** गण...गमे after the lapse of many nights. 'गणरात्रं निशा बह्वयः' इत्यमरः. निवर्तमानः—विकुक्षि returned after accompanying दधीच to his father's place. तथैव—as before (when दधीच left his attendants behind). छत्रधारः (umbrella-bearer) द्वितीयः यस्य. डुढौके Perfect of ढौक् 1 A to approach. वन...ग्रीवा stretching her neck like a woodland doe. मार्ग...दृशा she as though bathed him who was tired by the journey with her glance that whitened the ten quarters. One's fatigue is lessened by a bath. She steadfastly looked at him. The glances of her bright eye were like water. कृतः आसनपरिग्रहः येन. कच्चि...कुमारः is the prince well? कच्चित् (*ind.*) indicates 'I hope'. स्मरति भवत्योः—the genitive is used in accordance with 'अधीगर्थदयेशां कर्मणि' पा. 2. 3. 52 (words having the sense of इ with अधि 'to remember' and दय् and ईश् govern the genitive of the object). केव...बिभर्ति only he is somewhat emaciated in body in these days. अवि...धत्ते he has a certain vacantness (of mind) which is inexplicable and without any (apparent) cause. अन्वक्षम् *adv.* immediately, forthwith. अक्षस्य (रथस्य इन्द्रियस्य वा) पश्चात् अन्वक्षम् (अव्ययीभाव). The reading अन्वक् means the same thing. 'अन्वगन्वक्षमनुगेऽनुपदं क्लीबमव्ययम्' इत्यमरः. The meaning प्रत्यक्षं assigned by the com. does not suit the context. वाणिनी = दूती. 'वाणिन्यौ नर्तकीदूत्यौ' इत्यमरः. उच्छ्वसितं—the breath or life (*i. e.* she is a great confidante of the prince). महानुभावः magnanimous, noble. यदे...बध्नाति that he thus keeps up familiarity with a person not known to him and seen only for a moment. तस्य...मासीत् his mind was somehow by chance fixed on us (caught by us) while he passed (on his way), as a shawl may be caught by wayside creepers (in the case of a traveller). अशून्यं...सूनोः the nobility of your prince is not devoid of high birth *i. e.* in the prince high birth and nobility of character are combined. अशून्यम् not devoid of, full. स्वामिसूनु must mean prince here. विकुक्षि was the servant of शर्यात, whose *grandson* (and not son) दधीच was. Or सूनु may be used in the sense of 'off-spring in general'. A daughter's son was in ancient times like a son of the body. 'औरसो धर्मपत्नीजस्तत्समः पुत्रिकासुतः ।' याज्ञ० II. 128. अलसः...मनांसि people are indeed lazy that they do not make their own (*lit.* buy) the hearts of the great that are easily befriended by offering something or other. सुलभं सौहार्दं (मैत्री) येषाम्. She means:—she and her friend did very little for the prince; but he being great and noble offered his affection to them in return for what little they did. If the world will also offer something ever so little to the great, the latter will befriend them. सो... भुवनम् it is this excess of magnanimity in the great, not found in ordinary people, that makes the three worlds the instruments (of the great). The three worlds come under the control (are willing to abide by the orders) of the great on account of the latter's औदार्य. उच्चावचैः high and low, various. 'उच्चावचैः प्रकृतवस्त्वसंस्पर्शिभिः, विचित्रैरिति वा' सं०. 'उदक् च अवाक् च उच्चावचं उन्नतं चावनतं च वा' क्षीरस्वामी. It is a compound of the मयूरव्यंसकादि class (पा. II. 1. 72.).

P. 14 l. 12—**P. 15** l. 25. **अपरे...मनसी.** The first sentence is अपरेद्युः मालती समदृश्यत (p. 15. l. 17). उद्यति loc. sing. of *pr. p.* of इ with उद्. द्युमणौ—the jewel of the heavens. उद्दामा द्युतिः यस्य. अभिद्रुताः (attacked) तारकाः येन. तामरसानां व्यासः (विकासः) तस्य व्यसनं (intent application) अस्ति अस्य इति व्यसनिन् तस्मिन्. Red lotuses open at sunrise. आयान्ती this and the following adjectives (in the *nom. sing. f.*) qualify मालती (p. 15. l. 17). तरल...नयन्ती under the guise (छलं) of the covering of the sparkling (तरल) complexion of her body, she seemed to bring all the very clear water of the S'oṇa. The poet fancies that her sparkling complexion was really the transparent water of the शोण which she brought with her when crossing it. वितानः—म् canopy. Here the figure is अपह्नुति, which consists in the poetic denial of the real character of a thing and establishing in its place something else resembling it. 'प्रकृतं यन्निषिध्यान्यत्साध्यते सा त्वपह्नुतिः' काव्यप्रकाश X. स्फुटितानां (opened, expanded) अतिमुक्तककुसुमानां स्तबकेन समा त्विट् (कान्तिः) यस्य—*adj.* of तुरङ्गमे and मृगपतौ. सटाल having a mane (*adj.* of both मृगपतौ and तुरङ्गमे). मृगपतौ इव गौरी as पार्वती rides a lion. गौरी also means 'fair' (as applied to मालती). सिंह is the वाहन of दुर्गा. सली...तस्य (*adj.* of ०युगलस्य) that were gracefully placed on the girth of the horse. उरोबध्रम्—the leathern strap passing round the horse's chest. तिर्य...रणितस्य (*adj.* of ०युगलस्य) the sharp jingle (रणितं) of the anklets on which was listened to by the horse with slantingly upraised ears. अति... वितस्य that were decked with very thick Alaktaka dye. 'पिण्डालक्तकः कथितोऽलक्तकरसः' सं०. पल्लवितस्य—पल्लवाः सञ्जाताः अस्य सः पल्लवितः—the soles of the feet were so dyed with Alaktaka as to look like the new leaves (which are reddish) of trees. कु...पृष्ठस्य the upper surface of which (feet) was reddened with saffron. उभयतः—as she rode astride, her feet were on both sides of the horse. ताडन...गतानि come out of their craving for her kicks. It was a convention among Sanskrit poets that the red As'oka tree put forth blossoms when kicked by handsome young ladies. Such conventions are summarised in the following verse 'स्त्रीणां स्पर्शात् प्रियङ्गुर्विकसति बकुलः सीधुगण्डूषसेकात् पादाघातादशोकस्तिलककुरबकौ वीक्षणालिङ्गनाभ्याम् । मन्दारो नर्मवाक्यात्पटुमृदुहसनाच्चम्पको वक्त्रवाताच्चूतो गीतान्नमेरुर्विकसति च पुरो नर्तनात्कर्णिकारः ॥' quoted by मल्लिनाथ on मेघदूत' II. 17. 'रक्ताशोकश्चलकिसलयः'. दोहदम् longing. 'अथ दोहदम् । इच्छाकाङ्क्षा स्पृहेहा तृट्' इत्यमरः. Her feet being dyed red both beneath and above and being on both sides of the horse, the poet fancies that she as if drew along with her forests of red As'oka trees that had put forth foliage (किसलयित) and that accompanied her in the desire of being kicked by her. The lines (पल्लवs) of अलक्तक dye on her soles correspond to the किसलयs of the रक्ताशोक. सकल...स्थला on whose hips jingled a girdle as though it were a proclamation (आघोषणा) for forcibly seizing the hearts of the whole mortal world. She was so handsome that she forcibly captivated the hearts of all. The jingling रशना was the proclamation announcing this pillage of the hearts. C and T translate 'a proclamation devoting to murder and rapine the hearts'. It is difficult to see how 'murder' comes in here. धौत...लता whose creeper-like form was covered by a gown (कञ्चुकः) made of washed and white silk and reaching up to her toes and lighter than even serpent's slough (निर्मोकः). नेत्रम्—silk cloth. 'स्याज्जटांशुकयोर्नेत्रम्' इत्यमरः. निर्मोकात् लघुतरेण. आप्रपदीन—from आप्रपद with the affix ख (ईन), according to 'आप्रपदं प्राप्नोति' पा. 5. 2. 8. (पादस्याग्रं प्रपदं तन्मर्यादीकृत्य आप्रपदम्). छात...सरसी who, with her limbs white with slightly dried (आश्यान) sandal and visible through the fine (छात) gown, seemed as though she were a lotus plant, the stalks of which were clearly visible (विभाव्यमान) in the transparent water. 'अमांसो दुर्बलश्छातः' इत्यमरः. छात lean, thin (from छो to cut). अवयवैः—understand उपलक्षिता after it. The instrumental is used in accordance with 'इत्थम्भूतलक्षणे' पा. 2. 3. 21 (जटाभिस्तापसः । सि. कौ.). कुसुम्भ...दधाना wearing a petticoat (चण्डातकं) red with safflower dye, variegated with spots (पुलकः) of different colours and gleaming inside (the gown), as thoush she were a crystal spot bearing a treasure (निधानं) of jewels. Her gown was white and glossy like crystal. Inside it was the red चण्डातक as inside the crystal ground red gems may be found. Jewels are red like safflower dye (कुसुम्भरागवत् पाटलं). The spots of various colours on the petticoat looked like precious stones called पुलक. पुलक also means 'yellow orpiment.' "नानावर्णबिन्दुविन्यासः पुलकबन्धः, मणिविशेषाश्च पुलकाः' सं०. 'कृमिप्रभेदे रोमाञ्चे पुलकं प्रस्तरे विदुः' शाश्वत 373. चण्डातकं—a petticoat reaching to the middle of the thighs. 'अर्धोरुकं वरस्त्रीणां स्याच्चण्डातकमंशुकम्' इत्यमरः. हारेणा...चौः with a necklace having pearls round like Āmalakī fruit, she seemed to be the autumnal sky variegated (शार) with bright (स्फुरित) and large clusters of stars and overcast with a veil of thin white clouds. She was like the autumnal sky; her white silken कञ्चुक like the white thin clouds of शरद् and the large and round pearls like the stars in the sky. आमलकीफलवत् निस्तलानि (without a bottom *i. e.* round) मुक्ताफलानि यस्य. The reading निस्तुल (incomparable) is not good. कुच...धारयन्ती over her breasts resembling full jars, she had tied a jewelled necklace shooting forth red and green rays, as though it (necklace) were a garland of wild flowers (indicating) the entrance into her heart of some (indescribable) happy man. कुचौ पूर्णकलशौ इव. प्रालम्बमालिका is a garland or necklace reaching from the neck to the chest. 'प्रालम्बमृजुलम्बि स्यात्कण्ठात्' इत्यमरः. The jewels were red and green (emerald) and so resembled red and green leaves (किसलय). Jars full of water were placed at the entrance of houses as auspicious. पल्लवs were placed on the tops of such jars and garlands were tied round the necks of jars and on gates. Hence the poet fancies that her breasts on which rolled a necklace were jars with leaves and flowers indicating the auspicious entrance of some one in her heart. He whoever swayed her heart with love must be called blessed (पुण्यवत्). 'वनमाला विधातव्या पल्लवैः कुसुमैः फलैः' विष्णुरहस्य. Compare for the ideas 'उभयपार्श्वस्थापितोत्पल्लवमुखपूर्णहेमकलशं (कायमानं)' कादम्बरी p. 281 of P; 'वेदीविनिहितपल्लवललामहेमकलशे बद्धवनमालादाम्नि ...मन्दिरे' हर्षचरित 7th उच्छ्वास (2nd para); 'समुल्लसद्भिः स्तनमण्डलैर्मङ्गलकलशमय इव बभूव लोकः' हर्षचरित IV. एकैकस्य of each one (out of the many she wore). हाटककटकस्य of the golden bracelet. मर...नाथस्य—the golden bracelets were inlaid with emerald stones cut into the shape of a crocodile. वेदिका—level ground (on which the stone was set). स्थल...माना who was as though followed by land lotus plants under the belief that she was लक्ष्मी. The emeralds on her bracelets emitted pencils (सन्तति) of green rays in all directions, which (pencils) the poet fancies to be स्थलकमलिनीs that are also green (with leaves). Lotus plants are ordinarily in water. As she moved on land the मयूखसन्तति is fancied to be स्थलकमलिनी. लक्ष्मी dwells in lotus beds. मालती resembled लक्ष्मी in her beauty. बहल...वमन्ती from her lips darkened by the dark streak (कृष्णिका) of plenty of betel, she as though emitted darkness mixed with the glow of evening that was drunk by the moon of her face. The moon swallows darkness. Her face was like the moon. The dark-red tint of ताम्बूल taken by her in abundance resembled darkness mingled with evening radiance. मुखमेव शशी तेन पीतम्. विकचं नयनकुवलयं तस्मिन् कुतूहलेन आलीनया (settling or sitting upon). संहत्या = समूहेन. निरुद्धं अर्धवदनं यस्याः. Bees followed her dark eyes, thinking them to be lotuses and covered the upper part of her face, as though with a veil (जालिका) of blue silk. नीलीरागेण निहितः नीलिमा यस्मिन् (*adj.* of दन्तपत्रेण) which was made blue with indigo-colour. नीलिमा is formed from नील like पिङ्गलिमा (p. 23). शिखि...शितिना as blue as the throat of a peacock. The reading शितिगल॰ would mean 'as blue as (the throat of) शिव.' शिव is called शितिकण्ठ, as his throat grew dark when he drank कालकूट. See notes p. 2. दन्तपत्रं an ear-ornament. काल...माना— she was fair and bright like lightning and the dark दन्तपत्र was like a streak of dark (काल) cloud. पल्लवs also are placed on the ear as ornament. कल्पितेन made. बालिका—an ear-ornament dangling from the lobe of the ear. '**बालिका** । बालायां वालुकापत्रकाद्दला- **कर्णभूषणे** ।।' मेदिनी (कान्तवर्ग 130). आलोकः (light) एव जलं or जल- मिव तत् वर्षतीति. The bright light of the pearl pendants hanging downwards (अधोमुख) fell on her creeperlike arms. Tender creepers may be watered by two girls (बालिकायुगल) bending down. The bright light resembles clear water. दक्षिण...तला with the inner leaf of Ketakī flower placed on her right ear as an ear-ornament, she seemed to have her cheek licked through greed for beauty by the creeperlike tongue of the moon. The long and white केतकी leaf dangling on her cheek is fancied to be the tongue of the moon. The moon desired more grace and licked her cheek, which was very bright and fair. मृग...ष्यन्दिना that emitted the perfume of musk. तिलक... दहन्ती with the round mark on her forehead she bore a face which seemed to be the all-in-all of Cupid kept under a seal. The dark round तिलक of कस्तूरी resembled the mark of a seal.

One keeps one's treasure under seal. Her beautiful face was the सर्वस्व of Cupid *i. e.* she was calculated to inspire love in anyone. लला...चुम्बिनः dancing on her forehead and touching the parting line of her hair. The com. reads 'चटुलातिलक' and explains 'सुवर्णशृङ्खलाबद्धो नानारत्नौघमण्डितः। ललाटलम्ब्यलङ्कारश्चटुलातिलको मतः॥'. चटुलतिलकमणि may mean 'a jewel dangling on the forehead' (where the तिलक mark is made). उदञ्चता shooting up. कृतं शिरोऽवगुण्ठनं यस्याः. The red rays of the jewel on the forehead shooting round her head are fancied to be a red veil of silk. पृष्ठे प्रेङ्खन् अनादरसंयमनेन शिथिलश्च जूटिकाबन्धः यस्याः—whose thick hair dangled on her back, being loose as she tied it carelessly. नील... पताका as though she, who had a crocodile-like crest jewel (in her hair), was the banner of Cupid, with the ornament of a blue chowrie. Her loose and dangling hai was like a dark chowrie, which is placed as an ornament on banners; chowries are generally white, but her hair being dark, we have नीलचामर here. On the banner of Cupid (who is called मकरकेतु) there would be figures of crocodiles. Her चूडामणि was of the shape of a crocodile. A banner indicates the approach of a conquering general. She would help Cupid to subdue anybody by her charms. 'अवचूलं चिह्नम्' सं०. अवचूलः—a pendant tuft or garland, an ornament hanging from the top of a banner. मल्लिनाथ on शिशुपालवध 5. 13. says '"अस्योच्चूडावचूडाख्यावूर्ध्वाधोमुखचूडकौ' इति ध्वजाङ्गेषु हलायुधः'. बाण is very fond of this word. Compare 'दिवसकरवारणस्यावचूलचामरकलाप इवोपलक्ष्यमाणे...किरणजाले' का० p. 26; 'समदगजघटावचूलसहस्रसंरुद्धम्' p. 114. 'बहलरजोधूसरितमशिशिरकिरणबिम्बमवचूलचामरमिव निष्प्रभमभवत्' का० p. 116; केशकलापकान्तिना च कृष्णचामरावचूलेन... उपरचितदण्डं (ध्वजम्)' का० p. 224. कुल...मसः—As one worships one's कुलदेवता everyday and on every important undertaking, so the moon, by honouring her, would obtain her charms (in which the moon falls far short of her). पुनः०—Cupid was once burnt by S'iva; but she would revive him again (*i. e.* she inspires love in anyone). सञ्जीवनौषधि brings a person back to life. 'पुष्पधन्वा रतिपतिः' इत्यमरः. वेले...गरस्य As the ocean cannot go beyond the shore, so love reaches its high water-mark in her. Or the meaning is 'As the ocean beats with the greatest fury on the shore, so she creates the most furious passion by her charm.' ज्योत्स्ने...दयस्य as at moonrise, moonlight covers everything, so her charming youth brings under its sway everything. रतिरसः एव अमृतं तस्य—A great river has plenty of water

('पयः कीलालममृतम्' इत्यमरः). She was full of ambrosial (*i. e.* delightful) love. कु...तरोः a tree reaches its perfection by putting forth flowers. बाल...ज्ध्यस्य what one learns in boyhood, one hardly forgets. So she was never left by cleverness. कौमुदीव कान्तेः—even Grace may derive charms from her, as the mellow moonlight lends beauty to everything. धृ...र्यस्य she was the strength of firmness *i. e.* she was so firm of resolve that even Firmness may draw upon her to add to itself. सं० gives another curious explanation 'यद्वा धृतिः प्रवेशरक्षणम् । यथा प्रविशन्कश्चिद्राजनिकटं ध्रियते केनचित्तथा धैर्यं तावत्प्रसरति यावदेषा न दृष्टा । एतस्यां दृष्टायां सर्वे धैर्यशून्या इति.' गुरु...वस्य she is as though the teacher's hall for reverence. Even Reverence would respect her or even reverence would learn from her as one learns in a teacher's house. बीज...नयस्य modesty would be nursed in her *i. e.* she would be the source of all modesty. गोष्ठी०—all virtues met in her, as persons meet at an assembly or in a club. मन...भावतायाः—Those who are noble are always spirited and yet they would have to take lessons from her in मनस्विता. मनस्विता high-spirited nature. तृप्ति...ण्यस्य—तारुण्य after reaching her was satisfied *i. e.* did not find another, who could surpass her in charms. ०दामवत् दीर्घे लोचने यस्याः. This and the following words in the instru. qualify ०करङ्कवाहिन्या. पाटलः (red) अधरः यस्याः. पाटल is also a kind of flower. कुन्दकुड्मलवत् स्फुटाः (bright) दशनाः यस्याः. कुन्द buds are white. शिरीष is one of the most delicate of flowers. चम्पकवत् अवदातया who was bright and fair (in complexion) like the *champaka*. 'अवदातः सिते पीते' इत्यमरः. कुसुममय्या इव—It will be noticed that her limbs, body and breath are compared to various flowers and hence the poet fancies that she was made of flowers. ताम्बूलकरङ्कवाहिनी the bearer of betel-box. महाप्रमाणः अश्वतरः (mule) तमारूढया. कतिपये परिचारकाः (attendants) परिकरः (retinue) यस्याः. दधीचप्रेम्णा on account of the love she bore for दधीच (whose confidante मालती was). This is to be connected with the words लुण्ठिता, आकृष्टा &c. लुण्ठि...रथैः she (मालती) was plundered by सरस्वती with her desires. Although मालती was far away, from her face सरस्वती's longing and loving heart understood what मालती had to say. So the poet says that मनोरथs of सरस्वती looted from मालती what she came to convey. प्रत्युद्ग...काभिः she (मालती) was received with welcome by her (सरस्वती's) longings. 'उत्कण्ठोत्कलिके समे' इत्यमरः. Though she was far off, on seeing her सरस्वती became eager to know her message and her eager heart went forward to meet मालती, though she herself sat where she was. विलुप्तेव स्मितेन she (मालती) was as though seized by her (सरस्वती's) smile. Her bright smile reached (was seen by मालती) and brought her hurriedly. The reading विलिप्ता adopted by C and T is much better. Her bright smile resembled sandal with which a person is anointed. आच्छा...पुण्डरीकेण—she cast continuous glances at her (मालती) and her face was fixed on her When one's friend comes to one's house, one welcomes him, embraces him, fans him, honours him &c. The poet represents that all these actions were done by सरस्वती, though मालती was yet far off. स...शया—मालती appeared to her a friend, as she (सरस्वती) hoped that मालती was the harbinger of good news from दधीच. सविधम् = समीपम्. अगृह्णा...तया she captured (their hearts) by her polish (in all things) beginning with her (majestic) form. पेशलैः clever or soft.

P. 15 l. 26—**P. 16** l. 25 **क्रमेण...मभूत्.** शोण...स्नातुम् when Sâvitrī had gone to the S'oṇa to bathe.. साकूता with feeling. प्रस्तरः couch. वि...रहसि I have to make you a request in private. किं वक्ष्यति what would she (मालती) say ? स्तने विनिहितः वामकरः तस्य नखानां किरणैः दन्तुरितं (bristling). To calm down the turmoil of her bosom she placed her hand on it. उद्भिद्यमानाः कुतूहलस्य अङ्कुरनिकराः यस्मात्. Her heart was curious to know what she would say. The poet fancies that the rays of her nails were the shoots of curiosity bursting out of her heart. गलता...धावमानेन—(understand उपलक्षिता after ०पल्लवेन) the tender leaves on her ear used as an ornament dropped down (in her flurry), as though it were her ear running to hear (what मालती was going to say). अनव...लम्बमाना supporting herself on a neighbouring creeper, as though it were the hope of her life that was made to sway by her incessant sighs. ०सन्दोहेन (समूहेन) दोलायिता. दोलायिता placed in a swing *i. e.* moved to and fro. The creeper swayed to and fro on account of her incessant sighs. दोलायित also means 'held in suspense' (with जीविताशा). The hope for her life was also in suspense *i. e.* her life was in suspense on account of the incessant sighs. It seemed that life would depart from her body which was so much agitated. समु...लोकम्—her moonlike face became bright at the sight of a messenger from her lover and bathed the world in its brilliance. That brilliance being due to love, the poet fancies that she flooded the world with शृङ्गाररस (the sentiment of love; the fluid of love). ०लग्नैः

sticking or attracted by. कदम्बकैः = समूहैः. मदना...प्यमाणा—the idea is:—she got up from her flowery bed, on which bees clustered. The poet fancies that the dark bees were her longings (for union with दधीच) that came out of her in a visible form and lifted her up, being scorched by the fire of love (in her) and so being rendered dark. What is scorched becomes black. कुसुम...गात् she very slowly got up from her flowery bed, being in a high fever due to the darts of love. One who is laid up with fever rises slowly from his bed. Flowers are the darts of Cupid and as she slept on them they tormented her. 'अरविन्दमशोकं च चूतं च नवमल्लिका। नीलोत्पलं च पञ्चैते पञ्चबाणस्य सायकाः॥'. 'सन्तापः सञ्ज्वरः समौ' इत्यमरः. उपांशु *adv.* in a whisper, secretly. कपोल...वेशयन्ती—In her bright cheek Mālatī was reflected. The poet fancies that she placed मालती (reflected in her cheek) near her ear that she (मालती) may deliver her message in a whisper. She would have felt ashamed (लज्जयेव) if people had heard what मालती would have said loudly. काह...प्राणानां वा who am I as to paying attention or as to the body or life? मालती requested her above to pay attention (text p. 15, l. 28). सरस्वती says that she has no control over her attention or body or even life and that all of them are at the disposal of Mālatī and her prince. C and T take शरीरस्य प्राणानां वा with the next sentence; but in that case we expect that वा should follow सर्वस्य. सर्व...जनः even without a request, an extremely handsome man is master of everything. अविद्यमानं प्रार्थितं (प्रार्थना) यस्य—A handsome man has not to make a request for anything; he gets it without a request. The reading अप्रार्थितेऽपि would convey the same sense. अतिवेलम् = अत्यर्थम्. अतिक्रान्तं वेलां यथा स्यात्तथा. The reading अतिपेशलः means 'very fine or graceful'. चक्षुष्यः (चक्षुषि साधुः) = प्रियदर्शनः. सा...समा च There is nothing that you are not to me, a sister, a loving (प्रणयिनी) friend, a second self. She says:—you are to me in place of whatever relationship I may think of. Then she specifies some of these *viz.* स्वसा, सखी, प्राणसमा. नियुज्य...मिदम् Appoint this my frail body to (do) whatever task, great or small, it is capable (क्षम) of. क्षोदीयस् and गरीयस् are respectively the comparative forms of क्षुद्र and गुरु. क is added to शरीर in the sense of अनुकम्पा or कुत्सा (contempt). 'कुत्सिते' पा. 5. 3. 74. (कुत्सितं शरीरं शरीरकम्); 'अनुकम्पायाम्' पा. 5. 3. 76. अविद्यमानः अवस्करः (गुह्यं) यस्य—that has no secrets. आश्रव *adj.* obedient. 'वचने स्थित आश्रवः' इत्यमरः (आशृणोति वाक्यमिति). प्रतिसर dependent.

in securing the love of the woman he loves.' स्थिर...क्षेप: If I say 'he is constant in his affection,' that would be a clever hint or statement. Those words would insinuate that other handsome young men are not constant in their affections. जानाति...चितम् If I say 'he knows how to serve (his fiancee),' that would not be appropriate to his position as a prince. A prince does not ordinarily know how to serve; he only knows how to command. इच्छति...लाप: to say 'he desires to be your slave till death' would be the words of a rogue (*i. e.* all false). Being a prince, he cannot be a *slave*. भवन...लोभनम् 'you would be the mistress of his home' would be offering an allurement. A noble lady like you would not be tempted by the allurements of pomp and wealth and palaces. You would accept him only for his intrinsic worth. पुण्य...पात: 'blessed is she who secures such a husband' would be (sheer) partiality for one's master. त्वं...प्रियम् 'you are his death' is unpleasant (speech). अगु...क्षेप: 'you do not know his worth' would be a censure (of you). स्वप्ने...क्षिकम् 'you have often shown him favours in his dreams' would be without a witness. She means:—he is so deep in love with you, that he often sees you in his dreams. But that statement cannot be corroborated by producing any witness, as no one saw him dreaming of you. अविद्यमान: साक्षी यस्य. For क, see above p. 12. प्राण...तरता 'he solicits you for his life' would be cowardliness. A prince like him should not beg even for his life. She intimates by this how deep his love is. तत्रा...ज्ञा 'come there' would be a command. She means she has no authority nor right to command her (सरस्वती). वारि...भव: 'even though forbidden (by you), he will perforce come' would be an insult to you. तदे...मसि you are thus beyond the range of words. She means that she (मालती) has not words that would appropriately describe what दधीच feels for her and what she (सरस्वती) should do for him. The words she may employ are defective in some way or other.

P. 16 l. 26—**P. 17** l. 11 **अथ सरस्वती...इति.** विस्फारित wide, expanded. स्मितेन वदतीति ०वादिनी. ०वादिनि O lady of smiling speech. यदा...साद: what you order is a great favour (*i. e.* even your orders are &c.). प्र...वशा beside herself with joy. विदित: वृत्तान्त: यया. उत्कण्ठाया: भारं बिभर्ति इति ०भृत् तेन—that laboured under the burden of longing. ताम्यता languishing. One carrying a burden feels fatigue. कल्पायितम्—*past p. p.* of कल्पायते

denominative verb from कल्प (कल्प इव आचरति). The rest of the day seemed to her as long as a कल्प on account of her longing. कल्प is a day of Brahmā, and is a period of 1000 महायुगs (कृत, त्रेता, द्वापर and कलि being one महायुग). Each महायुग has 4320000 human years. गभस्तिमति = रवौ. The sentence here is सरस्वती (p. 17 l. 1) प्रतिपालयामास (l. 8). स्तिमिततरम् noiselessly. प्रहसि... चन्द्रमसि when the moon came up from the eastern quarter that was now bright as if smiling, as a lion comes out of a cave. The east gleamed with moonlight and hence is said to be प्रहसिता (smiles being described as white). पुरन्दरः इन्द्रः तस्य इयं पौरन्दरी. इन्द्र is the lord of the East. *Vide p.* 36. above. The words शुचिनि...कोमले may apply to both शयने and ०सैकते. But there would be repetition in ची...मारे and ०कोमले. So it is better to take the first three words with सैकते and ०कोमले alone with शयने as the com. does. शुचिनि white; pure. ची...मारे (1) soft with china silk; (2) soft like &c. तरङ्गिणि (1) that has waves *i. e.* is crumpled up or has a shining coverlet; (2) that has ripples (marks left by receding ripples). स्वप्न...दधाना having an ornamental mark on her forehead that (mark) seemed to be the lustre (चन्द्रिका) of the toe-nails of दधीच, that (चन्द्रिका) stuck (to her forehead) when she in her dream fell at his feet in supplication. स्वप्ने कृता प्रार्थना तस्यां पादपतनं तस्मिन् लग्नाम्. The white mark of sandal on her forehead is fancied to be the light of दधीच's toes sticking to her forehead &c. गण्डस्थलमेवादर्शः तस्मिन् प्रति० *(adj.* of इन्दुना). अय...जनः Here have I brought the person (दधीच) dear to you. निवेद्यमानः मदनसन्देशः यस्यै—The moon was reflected in her bright cheek. The poet fancies that that moon as if whispered in her ear this message of Love 'अयमसौ &c.' विकीर्य...पट्टम् fanning her perspiring bright (स्पष्ट) cheek with her hand that scattered pencils (चक्रवालं) of the rays of her nails, as though it (hand) had turned into a yak-tail fan the digits of the moon. She had no fan; therefore she fanned her cheek with her hand. Her cheek perspired on account of the deep emotion agitating her heart. स्वेद is one of the eight सात्त्विकभावs that are indicative of deep feeling. 'स्तम्भः स्वेदोऽथ रोमाञ्चः स्वरभङ्गोऽथ वेपथुः। वैवर्ण्यमश्रु प्रलय इत्यष्टौ सात्त्विकाः स्मृताः ॥'. When she moved her hand to and fro, the rays of her bright nails were tossed about. Those rays resemble the digits of the moon. A yak's tail is also white. बालव्यजनीकृतः चन्द्रकलाकलापः येन. Connect ०मृणालिकां with वहन्ती. She had placed across her breasts a fresh lotus-stalk to allay the fever of love. She placed the stalk across the breasts as they were plump and not between them. सं० explains 'स्तनमध्ये प्रवेशाभावात्तिरश्चीनमित्युक्तम्.' स्तनयोरधि अधिस्तनम् (अव्ययीभाव). The white lotus-stalk resembled a cane. The poet fancies that the lotus-stalk was a cane sportively let fall on her bosom by Cupid (चित्तभू) intimating that no one but दधीच was to enter her heart (*i. e.* only दधीच was to be her lover). A doorkeeper also uses his cane and prevents people from entering the royal gate. स्तनयन्ती murmuring (to herself). If we read स्तनयन्तीम्, the meaning is 'the lotus-stalk on her bosom made a sound'. मनोजन्मना=कामेन. जघन्या इव like a low woman. 'जघन्योन्त्येऽधमेपि च' इत्यमरः. का...तरुणीषु of what account are other poor (तपस्विनी) extremely excitable young women?

P. 17 ll. 12—23 **आजगाम...धिकम्.** The sentence is आजगाम च...मालतीद्वितीयो दधीचः (l. 18.). मधुमासः—the month of चैत्र, the first month of वसन्त. **'स्याच्चैत्रे** चैत्रिको **मधुः'** इत्यमरः. In this and the following clauses, the poet compares दधीच, who was accompanied by मालती, to several things by paronomastic words. मधुमास is an excitant of love. The poet hints by reference to मधुमास, मलयानिल &c., that the love of both दधीच and सरस्वती had reached the highest pitch through exciting surroundings. सु...वहः which has sweet breezes (with मधुमासः); who bore (on his body) sweet perfumes (with दधीच). Spring is the season of flowers and hence the breezes are charged with fragrance. सुरभिः गन्धवहः (वायुः) यस्मिन्; सुरभिं गन्धं वहतीति. कृता मृणालानां धृतिः (धारणं) येन—who bore lotus-stalks; कृता मृणालैः धृतिः (प्राणधारणं) येन that subsists on lotus-stalks. दधीच bore lotus-stalks to alleviate the burning torment of love. Haṁsas subsist on lotus-stalks. Compare 'मृणाललोभेन च चरणनखमयूखलग्नैर्भवनहंसैरिव सञ्चार्यमाणा मन्दमन्दं बभ्राम' हर्षचरित 4 उच्छ्वास. शिखण्डी peacock. घनप्रीत्या उन्मुखः—that uplifts its face in joy at (seeing) a cloud (with शिखण्डी); whose face was upturned (in expectation) on account of his deep (घन) love (with दधीच). आहितः सरसायाः चन्दनस्य धवलायाः तनुलतायाः उत्कम्पः येन that shakes a juicy tender white creeper (growing) on a sandal tree (with मलयानिल). Or we may explain as the com. does. 'सरसान् चन्दनान् धवांश्च लान्ति इति सरस...लाः तनुलताः' *i. e.* tender creepers that hang upon juicy sandal and धव trees. आहितः सरसेन चन्दनेन धवलायाः तनुलतायाः उत्कम्पः यस्मिन् whose delicate body white with viscous sandal had a tremor (with दधीच). We may also dissolve as आहितः...उत्कम्पः येन who caused the delicate body (of

सरस्वती) to shake (through love for him). But this is rather far-fetched. The poet is describing the personal appearance of दधीच and not of सरस्वती. दधीच's body shook with the emotion of love. कम्प is one of the eight सात्त्विकभावs, for which see above p. 79. कृष्य...पतिना as if drawn forward by the lord of planets (the moon) that as though seized his hair by his करs (rays, hands). When we want to drag a man, we may do so by seizing his hair with our hands. The moon's rays fell on his head. The moon is an excitant of love and urged him forward. कृतः करैः (रश्मिभिः) करेण (हस्तेन) वा कचग्रहः येन. कन्दर्पस्य उद्दीपने (exciting) दक्षेण. उह्यमान...रसेन as though he was borne by the रस (sentiment, water *i. e.* flood) of love abounding in उत्कलिकाs (agitation, waves). The student will notice the appropriate words कृष्यमाण, प्रेर्यमाण, उह्यमान used by the author in each clause. परि...यष्टिः whose body was covered with a swarm of bees that crowded (over him) on account of the perfumes (his body bore), as though it (swarm) was a blue piece of cloth. अन्तः...दरः one of whose cheeks was whitened by the reflection of the moon gleaming inside it, which (reflected moon) appeared like the temporal bone over the ear of the intoxicated cupid—elephant, as though by the graceful embarrassed smile of the first union (of a loving couple). 'शङ्खो निधौ ललाटास्थि' इत्यमरः. मत्तः मदनकरी (मदनः एव करी) तस्य कर्णशङ्खवत् आचरति ०शङ्खायते तेन. His bright cheek had a reflection of the moon. The bright image of the moon on his cheek looked like the temporal bone over the ears of an elephant. Bones are white. An intoxicated elephant, from whose temples मद flows, might expose the temporal bone to view. The moon is a friend and excitant of Love. Hence the poet says मत्तमदनकरी. Or we may explain in another way. The reflection of the moon was like the temporal bone and her broad cheek was like the broad ear of an elephant. Smiles are bright and so resemble the image of the moon. The poet probably puts in the word एक in एककपोलोदरः by way of a picturesque contrast to मालतीद्वितीयः. Or perhaps the idea is that only one of his cheeks was turned towards the rising moon. हृदय...गिरा in a voice broken like that of Haṁsas, as though mingled with the tinkling of the anklets of his beloved enshrined in his heart. His voice was broken by emotion. The poet fancies that it was interrupted by the tinkling &c. कृतं सम्भाषणं येन. यथा...ज्ञापयति—connect this and the following clauses with तथा तां...रामाम् अरमयत्. उपजातः विस्रम्भः (confidence) यस्याम्. आत्मानमकथयत्—she declared to him who she really was (*i. e.* she told him that she was सरस्वती). संवत्सरमधिकम् a year or more. It will be noticed how Bāṇa very appropriately draws the veil of silence over the amorous sports of the meeting of सरस्वती and दधीच. It is a canon of rhetoricians that the love sports of divinities are not to be dwelt upon in a poem. In this respect Bāṇa offers a pleasing contrast to Kālidāsa who could not resist the temptation of describing the S'ṛingāra of S'iva and Pārvatī in the कुमारसम्भव (VIII). Vide ध्वन्यालोक (उद्द्योत III under verse 14) 'तस्मादभिनेयार्थे च काव्ये यदुत्तमप्रकृते राजादेरुत्तमप्रकृतिभिर्नायिकाभिः सह ग्राम्यसम्भोगवर्णनं तत्पित्रोः सम्भोगवर्णनमिव सुतरामसभ्यम्। तथैवोत्तमदेवताविषयम्। **न च सम्भोगशृङ्गारस्य सुरतलक्षण एवैकः प्रकारः**, यावदन्येऽपि प्रभेदाः परस्परप्रेमदर्शनादयः सम्भवन्ति। ते कस्मादुत्तमप्रकृतिविषये न वर्ण्यन्ते।...**यत्त्वेवंविधे विषये महाकवीनामप्यसमीक्ष्यकारिता लक्ष्ये दृश्यते स दोष एव।**'.

P. 17 l. 24—**P. 18** l. 8 **अथ दैव...मान्तिकम्.** सर्व...रामम् lovely on account of possessing all (auspicious) characteristics. The following verse summarises most of them 'त्रिषु विपुलो गम्भीरस्त्रिष्वेव षडुन्नतश्चतुर्ह्रस्वः। सप्तसु रक्तो राजा पञ्चसु दीर्घश्च सूक्ष्मश्च॥' बृहत्संहिता 68. 84. जातमात्रायैव the moment he was born. सरहस्याः together with the esoteric or mystical meaning. Or सरहस्याः may mean 'together with the esoteric portion *viz.* the Upanishads.' वेद is often defined as 'मन्त्रब्राह्मणात्मकः'. Compare 'वेदः कृत्स्नोऽधिगन्तव्यः सरहस्यो द्विजन्मना॥' मनु II. 165, where मेधातिथि says 'रहस्यमुपनिषदः'. स्वय...ष्यन्ति will spontaneously manifest themselves. सद्भर्तृ...दधीचम् The idea is:—when सरस्वती left the mortal world at the bidding of ब्रह्मा, she started, enshrining her husband दधीच in her heart. The poet fancies that she carried him in her heart for the purpose of boastfully displaying to the heavenly assembly that she had secured an ideal husband. श्लाघा boast. पिता...देशात्—her curse was to end, according to Brahmā, when she bore a son. Vide text p. 5. l. 9. हृदये...हतः struck in the heart as though by a thunderbolt or by a lightning flash. 'ह्रादिन्यौ वज्रतडितौ' इत्यमरः. भ्रातुः of his cousin (as दधीच had no brother). C and T think that भ्रातृ was a proper name, as it would be unnecessary to describe दधीच's brother or cousin as a Brāhmaṇa. In our opinion ब्राह्मणस्य is purposely put in. दधीच was the son of च्यवन and सुकन्या (the daughter of a क्षत्रिय) and so was only ब्राह्मणसदृश. Vide मनु० 10. 6 'स्त्रीष्वनन्तरजातासु द्विजैरुत्पादितान्सुतान्। सदृशानेव तानाहुर्मातृदोषविगर्हितान्॥'. बाण wants to intimate that

दधीच's cousin was the offspring of Brâhmaṇa parents. अक्षमाला अभिधानं यस्याः. निर्विशेषम् *adv.* without making any difference (connect with समवर्धयत्). सामान्यं स्तन्यं ययोः who were fed alike with the same milk. सारस्वतः (सरस्वत्याः अपत्यं पुमान्) आख्या यस्य. सोदर्ययोरिव like that of brothers. समानोदरे शयितः सोदर्यः according to 'विभाषोदरे' पा. 6. 3. 88 and 'सोदराद्यः' पा. 4. 4. 109. आविर्भूतः अशेषाणां (सकलानां) विद्यानां सम्भारः (समूहः) यस्मिन्. सवयसि—of the same age. समानं वयः अस्य सवयाः. वाङ्मयं...यामास imparted the whole literature. प्राचुर्येण प्रस्तुता वाक् अत्र इति वाङ्मयम् according to 'तत्प्रकृतवचने मयट्' पा. 5. 4. 21. कृतः दाराणां परिग्रहः येन who took a wife. अस्य...वासम् he out of affection made for him in that very place a dwelling named प्रीतिकूट. प्रीतिकूट seems to be the name given to the house of Bāṇa's ancestors. It was so called because सारस्वत built it out of love (प्रीति) for his cousin. आत्मनाऽपि as for himself. आषाढी—see above p. 27. कृष्णाजिनं अस्ति अस्य. These and the following words show that he remained a ब्रह्मचारी. मेखला is a girdle made of grass (मुञ्ज &c). तपस्यतः—*geni. sing.* of the *pr. p.* of तपस्यति denominative verb from तपस् (तपः आचरति).

P. 18 ll. 9--25 **अथ तस्मात्...द्विजातयः.** The first sentence is अथ तस्मात् (वत्सात्)...प्रावर्तत विपुलो वंशः. All the adjectives apply to भागीरथीप्रवाह and वंश. The reading वत्सात् is good. प्रवर्धमानः आदिपुरुषैः (भार्गवादिभिः) जनिता या आत्मचरणस्य उन्नतिः तया निर्गतः प्रघोषः यस्य whose noisy fame went on increasing on account of the eminence of the school (चरणः) established by the first founders (with वंश). वत्स belonged to भार्गवगोत्र. For चरण see above p. 20. Or प्रवर्धमान may be connected with आदिपुरुष, meaning 'who increased *i. e.* had progeny'. प्रवर्धमानः आदिपुरुषः (विष्णुः) तेन जनिता आत्मचरणात् उन्नतिः यस्य ०न्नतिः स चासौ निर्गतप्रघोषश्च (with ०प्रवाहः)—that emitted a loud uproar, issuing from the foot of Vishṇu. The com. sees here (in प्रवर्धमान) a reference to the वामनावतार, when विष्णु, first coming to बलि as a dwarf, assumed a huge form and covered the worlds. 'किल त्रैलोक्याक्रान्तिकाले ब्रह्मलोकप्राप्ताद्विष्णुपदाद् ब्रह्मणा कमण्डलुजलक्षालितात् गङ्गा समभवदिति वार्ता'. For the Ganges rising from the foot of विष्णु, see above p. 41. परमेश्वरेण (शिवेन) शिरसि धृतः (०प्रवाहः); परमेश्वरैः (नृपैः) शिरसि धृतः honoured by kings (with वंश). The Ganges in her descent at भगीरथ's request to purify his ancestors fell on S'iva's head. सकलकलः (कलकलेन सह) आगमः (आगमनं) तेन गम्भीरः—deep (in stream) on account of its coming (from heaven) with an uproar (with ०प्रवाहः); सकलानां कलानां (नृत्यादीनां) आगमेन (by the acquisition) गम्भीरः deep *i. e.* well versed (with

वंशः). महा...मान्यः applies in the same sense to both. Or महामुनि may refer to जह्नु, whose daughter the Ganges became by being let off from his ear. Note रामायण I. 43. 'ततो हि यजमानस्य जह्नोरद्भुतकर्मणः । गङ्गा संप्लावयामास यज्ञवाटं महात्मनः ॥ 35 तस्यावलेपनं ज्ञात्वा क्रुद्धो जह्नुश्च राघव । अपिबत्तु जलं सर्वं गङ्गायाः परमाद्भुतम् ॥ 36...गङ्गां चापि नयन्ति स्म दुहितृत्वे महात्मनः । ततस्तुष्टो महातेजाः श्रोत्राभ्यामसृजत्प्रभुः ॥ 38.' विपक्षाणां शत्रूणां क्षोभः तस्य क्षमः (with वंशः); विपक्षाणां (विगताः पक्षाः येषां ते विपक्षाः पर्वताः तेषां) क्षोभः &c. The Ganges wears out mountains by its flood. Mountains had once wings and harassed the earth by flying anywhere. Indra cut off their wings. Compare 'उदधिमिव भयान्तःप्रविष्टसपक्षभूमिभृत्सहस्रसङ्कुलम्' काम्दबरी p. 90 of P; also रघु० 13. 7. क्षितितले लब्धा आयतिः (दैर्घ्यं प्रभावश्च) येन. The Ganges stretches for a long distance over the earth. The family attained dignity (आयति). अस्ख...त्तः that proceeded without stumbling *i. e.* without minding any obstacle (with गङ्गा); that conducted itself without deviating (from the path of right). The sentence is यस्माद् अजायन्त वात्स्यायना नाम...द्विजातयः. गृहमुनयः who were sages dwelling in houses (and not in forests). A मुनि is a sage or a recluse, who has given up worldly life. The ancestors of Bāṇa were householders but their conduct was so pure that they might be as well styled *munis.* Compare भगवद्गीता 2. 56 for a description of a मुनि. आश्रितं श्रौतं यैः that had recourse to ritual prescribed by the Vedas. अनालम्बिता अलीका बककाकुः यैः (1) that did not resort to the crane-like disagreeable (अलीक) tones; (2) that did not assume false hypocritical tones. There is an apparent contradiction between आश्रितश्रौताः and अना...काकवः in the first sense. Those who studiously perform the ritual of the Vedas have to recite in disagreeable tones the Vedic texts. This विरोध is got over by taking the second sense of अना०. A बक is a symbol of hypocrisy, as it stands on one leg as though deep in meditation and then pounces down upon a fish. काकुः is a change of voice due to fear, sorrow &c. 'काकुः स्त्रियां विकारो यः शोकभीत्यादिभिर्ध्वनेः' इत्यमरः. For बकवृत्ति, note मनु० 'बकवच्चिन्तयेदर्थान्' VII. 106. Explain the विरोध in the following clauses similarly. Read ०व्रता for ०वृता. कृतं कुक्कुटव्रतं यैः (1) that observed the vow of fasting called कुक्कुटव्रत; (2) that devoured cocks. अवैडाला वृत्तिः येषाम् (1) whose conduct was not ferocious, (2) whose conduct was not cat-like. Cats (बिडाल) pounce upon cocks. There is विरोध in the second senses of both compounds; but none if the first sense of each be taken. In कुक्कुटव्रत, one is to subsist on a lump of food not bigger than the egg of a hen. विवर्जिता जनपङ्क्तिः यैः (1) that avoided the cooking of (ordinary or low) people *i. e.* who did not take food cooked by common people; (2) that avoided the company of their castemen at dinner (*i. e.* that avoided a life of bustle and luxury). C and T translate 'averse to worldly pretence.' We cannot understand how this sense is arrived at. परि...कूताः that were free from thoughts (आकूतं) of fraud, bragging and hypocrisy (कूर्चं). It is difficult to say what the words कीर and कुची mean. कीर means a parrot and so might stand for 'uttering words without understanding the meaning, bragging.' अगृहीतं गह्वरं यैः (1) that did not resort to caves (*i. e.* remained householders and did not become recluses); (2) that were not hypocrites. 'गुहादम्भौ गह्वरे द्वे' इत्यमरः. न्यक्कृता निकृतिः (शाठ्यं) यैः that disdained dishonesty. प्रसन्ना (tranquil) प्रकृतिः (स्वभावः) येषाम्. We may also dissolve प्रसन्नाः प्रकृतयः (राजामात्याः) येषु. 'अमात्याद्याश्च पौराश्च सद्भिः प्रकृतयः स्मृताः' क्षीर० quoting कात्य. विगताः विकृतयः (changes of mind) येभ्यः. परेषां परिवादः (निन्दा) तस्मात् पराचीनं (पराङ्मुखं) चेतः येषाम्. वर्णत्रयस्य व्यावृत्त्या विशुद्धं अन्धः (अन्नं) येषाम् whose food was pure, the three Varnas being excluded *i. e.* they did not take food with people of the three Varṇas other than that to which they belonged. व्यावृत्तिः exclusion. C and T suggest another sense. 'Whose darkness *i.e.* delusion was corrected by sublating the three colours'. In the श्वेताश्वतरोपनिषद्, (IV. 5. अजामेकां लोहितशुक्लकृष्णां &c.) the three colours शुक्ल, लोहित and कृष्ण represent सत्त्व, रजः and तमः and stand for the material world as opposed to the spirit. Having excluded the material world, their error was at an end and they properly understood the Reality underlying the material world. धीरया धिषणया (बुद्ध्या) अवधूताः अध्येषणाः यैः—who disregarded desires by their firm intellect. 'सनिस्त्वध्येषणा याच्ञा' इत्यमरः. The reference is probably to बृहदारण्यकोपनिषद् 4. 4. 22 'ते ह स्म पुत्रैषणायाश्च वित्तैषणायाश्च लोकैषणायाश्च व्युत्थायाथ भिक्षाचर्यं चरन्ति' or to desires in general. असङ्कसुकः—स्थिरः. 'सङ्कसुकोऽस्थिरे' इत्यमरः (from कस् 10 'to move' with सम्). प्रणत०—who befriended those that came seeking their help (*lit.* that bowed to them). शमिताः समस्तानां शाखान्तराणां संशीतयः (संशयाः) यैः that removed (explained) all the doubts of other schools. शाखा is a traditional recension of a particular Veda, as शाकल of the ऋग्वेद. Here it seems to be used in the sense of शाखाध्येतृ. उद्घाटिताः (opened *i. e.* expounded) समग्राः

ग्रन्थार्थानां ग्रन्थयः (knotty or difficult points) यैः. वाग्मिनः eloquent. वाग्मिन् is used in a good sense, while वाचाल and वाचाट (derived from the same word वाच्) are used in a bad sense. स...निनः fond of clever speech. If we read परसुभा० then the meaning is 'fond of the good sayings of others'. विद...वेदिनः appreciating clever jokes. They did not *themselves crack* jokes, but could appreciate them; they, though वेदाभ्यासरत, were not devoid of a sense of wit and humour. परि...बाह्याः they were charming in their intercourse (with others) and not strangers to dancing, singing and music. They knew a little of नृत्य and other arts, but were not solely devoted to them. ऐति...तृष्णाः who were never surfeited with traditional tales. 'पारम्पर्योपदेशे स्यादैतिह्यमितिहाव्ययम्' इत्यमरः. ऐतिह्यम् from इति ह with the affix ञ्य (य), according to 'अनन्तावसथेतिहभेषजाञ्ञ्यः' पा. 5. 4.23. (आनन्त्यम्, ऐतिह्यम्). सानुक्रोशाः = सदयाः. सत्येन शुचयः pure on account of truthfulness. सर्वसत्त्वेषु सौहार्दं (good will, friendship) एव द्रवः तेन आर्द्रं हृदयं येषाम्. तथा सर्व० the clauses from this downwards are to be taken singly and also in pairs. Taken singly each is construable by itself; if they are taken in pairs, there is an apparent विरोध. सर्व...पेताः possessed of all virtues. सर्व...भूताः possessed of all Guṇas (सत्त्व, रजः and तमः) and (yet) not overwhelmed by the quality of रजस्. राजसेन (गुणेन) अनभिभूताः. राजस is from रजस्. राज...भूताः is construable by itself; but in avoiding the विरोध with सर्व...पेताः, we may explain it as राजसेनया अनभिभूताः—not treated with dishonour by the royal army (०सेना अनभि०). Explain the following clauses similarly. क्षमाभाजः who are forbearing. क्षमा...नन्दनाः who resort to the earth and have recourse to the Nandana garden. नन्दन is the garden of Indra. Those who resort to it cannot be on the earth. आ...नन्दनाः also means 'who delight their dependents'. अनिस्त्रिंशाः = अक्रूराः. विद्याधराः—those that possess Vidyās. अनि...धराः—that are without swords and (yet) विद्याधरs. निस्त्रिंशः a sword. निष्क्रान्तस्त्रिंशतोङ्गुलिभ्यः—that which is longer than 30 finger-breadths. विद्याधरs are semi-divine beings that are always armed with swords. 'मालाखड्गगुलिकाञ्जनादिना भेदेन भिन्नानामपि विद्याधराणां खड्गहस्तत्वं न व्यभिचरति' सं०. अज...वन्तः not dull and well-versed in the arts. अज...वन्तः not cold and (yet) moons. 'शिशिरो जडः' इत्यमरः. अदो...काः free from faults (sins) and helping others (against difficulties or sins). तारयन्तीति तारकाः. अदो...काः without nights (दोषा) and yet constellations. Stars cannot be seen without night. अप...

स्वन्तः not causing distress to others and brilliant (in appearance); not heating others and yet suns. अनु...भुजः without pride (ऊष्मन् *m.*) and sacrificers; without heat and (yet) fires. हुतं भुञ्जते those who enjoy (the fruit of) what they offer as an oblation. अकु...गिनः who had no deceit and were not addicted to pleasure; who did not creep on the earth and (yet) were serpents. अविद्यमाना कुसृतिः शाठ्यं येषाम्. 'कुसृतिर्निकृतिः शाठ्यम्' इत्यमरः. अविद्यमाना कौ (पृथिव्यां) सृतिः (सरणं) येषाम्. भोगिन् *m.* 'a serpent' (from भोगः hood + इन्). अस्त...लयाः who were free from stiffness (arrogance) and were abodes of good deeds; without pillars and (yet) holy places (temples &c.) A house cannot be without a pillar. अलुप्त...दक्षाः who never ceased in the performance of sacrifices and were skilful; the performance of their sacrifice was not disturbed and (yet) they were दक्षs. दक्ष was a famous प्रजापति. He once celebrated a sacrifice at which he did not invite his own daughter सती and her husband शिव. She went uninvited, was insulted and threw herself into fire. S'iva destroyed the sacrifice of दक्ष, pursued the latter and killed him. Compare 'न पशुपतेरिव दक्षोद्वेगकारीण्यैश्वर्यविलसितानि' हर्षचरित II;'दक्षाध्वरक्रियामिवोद्धतगणकचग्रहभयोपसेवितत्र्यम्बकाम्' कादम्बरी p. 128 of P. and कुमारसम्भव I. 21. अ...जितः who were not deceitful and had restrained desires; without serpents and vanquishers of Cupid (*i. e.* S'ivas). S'iva has serpents encircling his body. कामान् जयन्तीति or कामं कन्दर्पं जयन्तीति. 'भेद्यलिङ्गे शठे व्यालः पुंसि श्वापदसर्पयोः' इत्यमरः. असा...जातयः who were pre-eminent and Brāhmaṇas; who had nothing in common (with others) and (yet) had two jātis. A जाति (genus) is defined as 'नित्यमेकमनेकानुगतम्'. A जाति like गोत्व is common to all cows. So if they had two जातिs they must have certain characteristics in common with others and so could not be असाधारण.

P. 18 l. 26–**P. 19** l. 5 तेषु...निजे. संसरति संसारे the world went on or revolved. वहत्सु वत्सरेषु as years rolled. प्रसवः... कुले as the वात्स्यायन family incessantly went on growing in an unbroken chain of progeny. वैनतेयः = गरुडः. गुरु...पाती (1) who was devoted to (had a liking for) his teachers or parents (with कुबेरनामा); that flies on his big wings (with गरुड). द्विजः (1) a Brāhmaṇa; a bird. गरुड was the son of विनता one of the wives of कश्यप. विनता lost a wager with her co-wife कद्रू and had to be the latter's slave. She was released from slavery by Garuda who gave nectar as a ransom after vanquishing Indra. युगा...विस्तारः (1) whose progeny expanded by their Brāhmanical lustre (*i. e.* by their knowledge of the Vedas); (2) which have a vast creation of beings produced from Brahmā's lustre (with युगारम्भाः.). In the beginning of the कृतयुग, ब्रह्मा was alone and from him sprang the creation. चत्वारः may be connected also with युगारम्भाः as there are four Yugas. स...नन्दकाः— (1) that delighted the assembly of the good (with sons); that have the discuss and the नन्दक sword (with नारायणबाहु०). सतां (साधूनां) चक्रं नन्दयन्तीति; सतौ चक्रनन्दकौ येषाम्. चक्र is one of the weapons of नारायण, who also has four arms. नन्दक is the sword of विष्णु. भूभारः इव like the heavy earth. अचल...स्थितिः (1) who never swerved from the usages of his family (with सूनुः); (2) that obtained steadiness by the group of mountains. अचला कुलस्थितिः यस्य; अचलकुले (पर्वतसमूहे) स्थितिः यस्य. It was believed that the earth, which was at first unsteady, was made steady by the mountains. Compare 'भिषजो भूधरा इव भुवो धृतिं चक्रुः' हर्षचरित IV; 'अनुजीविभूभृच्छतसहस्रकल्पिताष्टम्भं सञ्चारिणं द्वितीयमिव मेदिनीसंनिवेशम्' कादम्बरी. Each वर्ष has its कुलपर्वतs; for the seven कुलपर्वतs of भरतवर्ष, see above p. 76. In अचलकुल, the author refers to the कुलपर्वतs. चतुरुदधिवत् गम्भीरः (सूनुः), चतुरुदधिभिः गम्भीरः (भूभारः). समग्राणां अग्रजन्मनां (ब्राह्मणानां) चक्रं समूहः तस्य चूडामणिः. एकादश—the eleven sons are compared to the Rudras that are also eleven. They are manifestations of शिव. सोमा...मुखान् (1) whose mouths were full of the spray of the nectar-like Soma juice (with पुत्रान्); whose faces are covered with the spray of the nectar from the moon (with रुद्रान्). सोम juice was drunk in sacrifices. सोमः अमृतरस इव तस्य शीकरैः च्छुरितानि मुखानि येषाम्; सोमस्य (चन्द्रमसः) अमृतरसः तस्य शीकरः तेन &c. शिव has the moon on his head and, as the moon was full of nectar, शिव's face would be covered with nectar spray. राजदेवी अभिधानं यस्याः. उपसम्पन्नया who died (connect with विधेर्वशात्). एधीयमाना (increasing) धृतिः (energy, steadiness) यस्य. धाम्नि = गृहे.

P. 19 ll. 6–28 **कृतोप...हास्यताम्.** कृतः उपनयनादिक्रियाकलापः यस्य. समावृत्त *lit.* 'returned' *i. e.* one who returns from his teacher's house to his home after finishing his study. Compare मनु० III. 4. 'गुरुणानुमतः स्नात्वा समावृत्तो यथाविधि। उद्वहेत द्विजो भार्यां सवर्णां लक्षणान्विताम्॥.' समावर्तन is what is now symbolised in सोडमुंज (in Marathi). For देशीय, see above (notes p. 55). चतुर्दश०–fourteen was rather an early age for समावर्तन, but it contrasts most favourably with the unseemly haste with which समावर्तन is now performed. श्रुति means the Vedas and Smṛitis are woks like the मनुस्मृति, which contain the traditional laws and usages of the Āryas. 'श्रुतिस्तु वेदो विज्ञेयो धर्मशास्त्रं तु वै स्मृतिः' मनु० 2. 10. पुण्यजातम्—is the object of कृत्वा. अदशमीस्थ एव *lit.* 'without reaching the tenth decade of life' *i. e.* not in ripe old age. The full period of human life is 100 years, as expressed in the Vedic words 'शतायुर्वै पुरुषः.' This was divided into ten decades. दशमीस्थ would be one between 90 and 100 years of age. 'दशमीस्थौ क्षीणरागवृद्धौ' इत्यमरः—दशम्यां वयोवस्थायां तिष्ठतीति. संस्थिते = मृते. आ...प्राप्तः overwhelmed with great distress. 'स्यात्कष्टं कृच्छ्रमाभीलम्' इत्यमरः—आ समन्तात् भियं लातीति (क्षीरस्वामी). अवि... तन्त्र्यस्य as independence is the prime source (निदानं) of misconduct. Bāṇa became his own master at the tender age of fourteen. 'निदानं त्वादिकारणम्' इत्यमरः. This and the following clauses assign reasons as to why he became इत्वर. कुतू...भावस्य as adolescence is a period when curiosity predominates. 'बाल आ षोडशाद्वर्षात्'. Bāṇa wanted to gratify the curiosity he felt as to various things in the world. धैर्य...रम्भस्य as the first stage of youth is opposed to steadiness. शैश... चरन् doing many rash acts in keeping with his youth. इत्वरः—from इ to go, according to 'इण्-नश्-जि-सर्तिभ्यः क्वरप्' पा. 3. 2. 163 (इत्वरः, नश्वरः, जित्वरः)—a wanderer, a wild man. वयसा...याश्च friends and companions of the same age (as himself). The list shows that Bāṇa must have been in very affluent circumstances and must have led a life of ease and luxury. पारशवौ—they were the sons of his uncles from wives of the S'ūdra caste. Note मनु० 9. 178. 'यं ब्राह्मणस्तु शूद्रायां कामादुत्पादयेत्सुतम्। स पारयन्नेव शवस्तस्मात्पारशवः स्मृतः ॥'. पारयन्नेव (जीवन्नेव) शवः (a corpse) पारशवः—this kind of son was so called because he was no better than a corpse for conferring the spiritual benefits which a son was expected to confer. भाषाकविः a vernacular poet. The word भाषा was often applied to the spoken vernaculars as opposed to संस्कृत, when the latter ceased to be spoken by the masses. The com. also explains as 'a composer of songs.' 'भाषा गेयवस्तुवाचः तेषु (?) कविः' सं०. प्रणयिनौ loving (dependents). विद्वांसौ = पण्डितौ. वर्णकविः probably means 'a poet celebrating the renown of others, a bard or panegyrist.' But we have 'बन्दिनौ' a little later on. The com. takes the word to mean 'a poet of Gāthās or versifier in the अपभ्रंश dialects.' 'वर्णकविर्गाथादिषु गीतिदः। अपभ्रष्टगीतविद्यः' सं०. प्रा...पुत्रः a young noble composing Prâkrit poems. महाराष्ट्री was the Prākrit *par excellence*, the other important प्राकृत dialects being शौरसेनी, मागधी and पैशाची. प्राकृत is derived as 'प्रकृतिः संस्कृतं तत्र भवं तत आगतं वा;' while some take it as meaning the language of the masses as opposed to संस्कृत, the speech of polished society. कात्यायनिका—'कात्यायन्यर्धवृद्धा या काषायवसनाधवा' इत्यमरः—an elderly widow dressed in the ascetic's red robes. जाङ्गुलिकः = विषवैद्यः—a dealer in antidotes or a snake-doctor. भिषक्पुत्रः a young physician. 'कलादो रुक्मकारके' इत्यमरः. कलादः a goldsmith. 'कलामादत्ते, कलं सुवर्णकालिकामाचति आखण्डयति वा' क्षीर०. हैरिकः supervisor (of goldsmiths), according to सं०. लेखकः scribe. चित्रकृत् a painter. पुस्तकृत् a model-maker, a manufacturer of dolls 'पुस्तकृल्लेप्यकारः.' 'मृदा वा दारुणा वाथ वस्त्रेणाप्यथ चर्मणा । लोहरत्नैः कृतं चापि पुस्तमित्यभिधीयते ॥'. मार्दङ्गिकः versed in playing on a drum (मृदङ्ग). 'मृदङ्गवादनं शिल्पमस्य मार्दङ्गिकः' according to 'शिल्पम्' पा. 4. 4. 55. गायनौ singers. सैरन्ध्री—a female who, not being a regular servant, is employed in others' houses for doing things requiring skill, such as decoration of the hair &c. 'सैरन्ध्री परवेश्मस्था स्ववशा शिल्पकारिका' इत्यमरः. वांशिकौ—a flute-player, piper. गान्धर्वम् music. संवाहिका shampooer. लासकयुवा a young dancer. ताण्डविक—It will be noticed that many of the names of Bāna's associates such as सुदृष्टि, चामीकर, जीमूत are very appropriate to the art they cultivated or the profession they followed. This is rather suspicious. आक्षिकः one who plays at dice. अक्षैर्दीव्यति or जयति इति आक्षिकः, according to 'तेन दीव्यति खनति जयति जितम्' पा. 4. 4. 2. कितवः a gambler. 'धूर्तोऽक्षदेवी कितवोऽक्षधूर्तो द्यूतकृत्समाः' इत्यमरः. शैलालियुवा a young actor. 'पाराशर्यशिलालिभ्यां भिक्षुनटसूत्रयोः' पा. 4. 3. 110 (शिलालिना प्रोक्तं नटसूत्रमधीयते शैलालिनो नटाः). पाराशरी—an ascetic that has studied the Sûtra of Parās'ara. पाराशर्येण प्रोक्तं भिक्षुसूत्रं अधीयते पाराशरिणो भिक्षवः. See Pāṇini's sūtra quoted above. क्षपणकः—a Jain monk. कथकः a narrator or story—teller; one who publicly reads and expounds the Purāṇas. मन्त्रसाधकः a magician, one who is an adept in incantations. असुर... सनी-treasure—seeker. Bāṇa very frequently uses this word; but it is not easy to give the exact sense. On considering all the passages where the word occurs, we think that असुरविवर was a term applied to shafts of mines that had already been worked up in bygone days. They were believed to be the work of Asuras and to lead to the treasures of पाताल, in hopes of reaching which many people must have endangered their lives. Note 'यः (जनपदविशेषः) असुरविवरमिति वातिकैः (अगृह्यत)' हर्ष० 3rd उच्छ्वास; 'असुरविवराणीवापावृतानि' हर्ष० 4th उच्छ्वास; 'असुरविवरव्यसनिनं चापजहुः... मागधं गोधनगिरिसुरङ्गया स्वविषयं मेकलाधिपमन्त्रिणः;' हर्ष० 6th उच्छ्वास; 'लग्नासुरविवरप्रवेशपिशाचेन' कादम्बरी p. 227 of P. धातु...वित् who knew

Uchchhvāsa II

Verse 1. The verse contains many श्लिष्ट words. The sentence is अतिगम्भीरे भूपे निरवतारस्य जनस्य समीहितसिद्धिं गुणवन्तः घटकाः पार्थिवाः दधति कूपे इव--with a very profound king it is the virtuous and energetic princes that bring about the fulfilment of what is desired by people who have no entrance (to the king), as with a well. The idea is that good princes that are about the person of an emperor intercede with the latter for bestowing favours on people. This and the next verse suggest how कृष्ण the cousin of हर्ष introduced बाण to the favour of हर्ष. गम्भीर means one whose feelings of anger &c. are not indicated by his gestures or appearance. अवतारः entrance or access. घटकाः those that accomplish. अतिगम्भीरे कूपे निरवतारस्य जनस्य गुणवन्तः पार्थिवाः घटकाः ०सिद्धिं दधति in the case of a deep well, small earthen (पार्थिव) jars to which strings (गुण) are attached bring about the fulfilment of the desires of people who have no means of descending (into the well). अवतारः a flight of steps. The metre is Âryā. From the definition of आख्यायिका (Intro. p. XX) it will be seen that the verses occurring therein were to suggest future events.

Verse 2. रागि...भवाम्—the day plants in the red lotus beauty that is due to the sun. रागिन् also means 'affectionate, devoted.' लक्ष्मी wealth. This suggests how कृष्ण (who was like दिवस) planted wealth in Bāṇa who was devoted to the king हर्ष (who corresponds to the sun), the wealth being the gift of हर्ष and he (कृष्ण) being only the intercessor. अनपेक्षिताः गुणदोषाः यस्मिन् in which no regard is paid to merits or faults. The good are passionately devoted to the task of helping others, irrespective of their merits or faults. Here there is a veiled reference to the चापल of Bāṇa's youth.

P. 21 ll. 5-16 **अथ...तिष्ठत्.** The principal sentence is अथ तत्र...बान्धवानां भवनानि भ्रमन् सुखमतिष्ठत्. भस्मपुण्ड्रकैः पाण्डुराणि ललाटानि येषाम् (*adj.* of बटुभिः). For पुण्ड्रक, see notes p. 26. कपि... टिलैः that had tawny hair (with बटुभिः); that were full of tawny flames (with कृशानुभिः). कृशानुभिः = अग्निभिः. क्रतु०—The boys had come to see the sacrifices and partake of the दक्षिणा. They are fancied to be fires coming with the desire that sacrifices may be offered to them. अध्यास्यमानानि inhabited. This and the following nouns in the accusative qualify भवनानि below. सेकेन सुकुमारा सोमकेदारिका तया हरितायमानाः प्रघनाः येषाम् the porches in front of the doors of which were green with the small beds of Soma plants that looked fine (fresh) on account of being (recently) watered. केदारिका small field. 'प्रघाणप्रघणालिन्दा बहिर्द्वारप्रकोष्ठके' इत्यमरः. The juice of Soma plants was required in sacrifices. कृष्णाजिनेषु विकीर्यमाणाः (spread) शुष्यन्तः पुरोडाशीयाः श्यामाकतण्डुलाः येषु. पुरोडाशीय (from पुरोडाश with the affix छ *i. e.* ईय) useful for पुरोडाश, which means 'a sacrificial oblation made of ground rice and offered in vessels.' 'विभाषा हविरपूपादिभ्यः' पा. 5. 1. 4. (पुरोडाश्याः तण्डुलाः, पुरोडाशीयाः वा). श्यामाकः a kind of grain (called सांवे in Marathi). बालिकाभिः विकीर्यमाणाः नीवार—बलयः येषु. नीवार is a kind of wild rice growing without cultivation. The girls offered the grain to the birds and their pets. ०शतैः आनीयमानाः ०समिधः येषु. पूली a bundle. पलाशम् a leaf. समिध् *f.* fuel. They brought green Kus'a grass, leaves and fuel. Or we make take पलाशसमिधः as meaning 'small twigs of the पलाश tree' that were required for being thrown into the fire. इन्ध... कूटानि full of heaps (कूटः) of fuel (इन्धनं) and cowdung cakes. आमिक्षा a mixture of curds and boiled milk, offered in the वैश्वदेव oblation. 'पक्के पयसि दध्यानयति सा वैश्वदेव्यामिक्षा' quoted by क्षीर० as a श्रुति. For आमिक्षीय (आमिक्षायै हित) see पुरोडाशीय above. खुर...र्दिकानि the covered platforms (वितर्दिः) in the court-yards of which were rubbed by the round hoofs. 'स्याद्वितर्दिस्तु वेदिका' इत्यमरः (दारुपरिष्कृता चतुरस्रा विश्रान्तिभूः' क्षीर०). कमण्डलव्य useful or fit for making pots (कमण्डलु). 'उ—गवादिभ्यो यत्' पा. 5. 1. 2. मर्दनम् pounding. वै...व्यानाम् useful for making pegs for measuring the sacrificial (वैतान) altar. शङ्कव्य from शङ्कु with affix यत्, according to 'तस्मै हितम्' पा. 5. 1. 5. (शङ्कवे हितं शङ्कव्यम्). Pegs of the branches of उदुम्बर trees were used in measuring altars. पवित्रिताः पर्यन्ताः (borders, outskirts) येषाम्. वैश्वदेवपिण्ड—the offerings of boiled rice made to all the deities (विश्वेदेवाः) before taking one's dinner. हवि...लयानि the tender leaves of the trees (विटपिन् *m.*) in the courts of which were darkened with the smoke of the oblations. वत्सीय...तर्णकानि where the newly born calves, being caressed (लालित) by the cowherds (वत्सपालकः) that were fond of them, frisked about. वत्सीयः (वत्सेभ्यो हितः) is formed like शङ्कव्य. From the numerous words formed with the affixes छ (ईय) and यत् it seems as though बाण wanted to illustrate the first Pāda of the 5th अध्याय of the अष्टाध्यायी. 'सद्योजातस्तु तर्णकः' इत्यमरः. ०पालकैः लालिताः ललन्तः (sportive) तरलाः (चञ्चलाः) तर्णकाः येषु. क्रीडद्भिः कृष्णशारच्छागशावकैः प्रकटितः पशुबन्धानां (यज्ञानां) प्रबन्धः (सन्ततिः) येषु where the continuous performance of animal sacrifices was indicated by the young goats, dark and variegated (शार), playing about. This shows that in Bāṇa's day animal sacrifices were frequently performed. शुक...सुखानि where the teachers were given rest by the fact that parrots and *mainas* (सारिका) commenced to repeat (the Vedas). The idea is:—the parrots and सारिकाs, having repeatedly heard the teachers reciting the Vedas, themselves correctly repeated them and the students could take lessons from them, instead of from the teachers, who thus got rest. Compare 'स्वतःप्रमाणं परतः प्रमाणं कीराङ्गना यत्र गिरं गिरन्ति । द्वारस्थनीडान्तरसंनिरुद्धा जानीहि तन्मण्डनपण्डितौकः ॥' माधवाचार्य's शङ्करदिग्विजय VIII. 6. सा...नीव as though they were the penance groves of the three Vedas incarnate. भवनानि—is the object of भ्रमन्.

P. 27 ll. 17–23 **तत्र...माली.** Bāṇa now describes the advent of summer in highly paronomastic sentences, the season (कालः) being identified with शिव in his terrific form (महाकाल). तत्रस्थस्य while staying in the houses of his kinsmen. कुसुमसमयः (वसन्तः) एव युगम्. उपसंहरन् bringing to an end. ग्रीष्म brings to an end the season of spring. शिव when destroying the world brings the युग to an end. अजृम्भत *lit.* yawned *i. e.* increased. ग्रीष्मः अभिधानं यस्य. सम्फुल्लमल्लिकाभिः धवलाः अट्टाः (market stalls) एव हासाः यस्य where the stalls smiled with white full blown jasmine flowers. The मल्लिका is a flower of the hot season. ०मल्लिकावत् धवलः अट्टहासः यस्य. The loud laugh of शिव is called अट्टहास. महाकालः the great season (of summer); S'iva. प्रत्य...तस्य recently conquered. The poet now changes the metaphor. ग्रीष्म is a conqueror that subdues the prince वसन्त, but at first treats kindly the children of his vanquished rival. वसन्तः एव सामन्तः तस्य. पयः पायिषु that drink milk (with बालापत्येषु); that drink water *i. e.* are thirsty (with नवोद्यानेषु). दर्शितः स्नेहः येन. स्नेहः affection; moisture. नवोद्यानेषु (with ०पत्येषु) would also mean 'who have just begun to walk.' मृदुरभूत्—summer did not at once scorch the gardens, but was mild at first. सकल...रोत् made the stalks of all flowers loose *i. e.* summer scorched the flowers of spring which easily dropped down from the stem.

A king at his accession (अभिनवोदितः) lets loose prisoners from his jails. It was usual to set prisoners free on the accession of a king or at the birth of a prince or on other great occasions. Compare हर्ष० 4th उच्छ्वास 'अधावन्त मुक्तानि बन्धनवृन्दानि' and notes thereon. प्रतपन् showing his valour; very hot. ऋतुः एव राजा तस्य. अभिषेकार्द्राः wet after a bath (with कामिनीनां ०चयाः); wet at the time of the coronation (with चामरकलापाः). At a king's coronation, holy water is poured over him. Chowries are a symbol of royalty; they may become wet at a coronation. In ग्रीष्म, young women bathe their heads with water; their hair looks very charming after the bath and excites love. In वसन्त, love is excited spontaneously, but in the scorching heat of ग्रीष्म, such extraneous aids as charming tresses are required. This is spoken of as कामिनीनां ०चयाः कुसुमायुधेन स्वयमगृह्यन्त. The hair of the women is fancied to be the chowrie of the king-summer, that is held in his own hand by Cupid. Bāṇa seems to follow the रघुवंश in this description as suggested by the com. Compare 'स्नानार्द्रमुक्तेष्वनुधूपवासं विन्यस्तसायन्तनमल्लिकेषु । कामो वसन्तात्ययमन्दवीर्यः केशेषु लेभे रतिमङ्गनानाम् ॥' रघु० 16. 50. हिमा...माली the sun made his expedition towards the Himālaya (*i. e.* towards the north). यात्रा journey, expedition. It is in ग्रीष्म that the sun reaches the northernmost point in his apparent yearly motion. This natural phenomenon is fancied to be due to the wrath which the sun feels at the fact that the lotuses (that open by day-light) are blighted by snow. For the effect of हिम on कमलिनी, see notes p. 63.

P. 21 l. 24—**P. 22** l. 2 **अथ...सन्तापात्.** ललाटं तपतीति ललाटन्तपः scorching the brow (*lit.* forehead), according to 'असूर्यललाटयोर्दृशितपोः' पा. 3. 2. 36 (असूर्यपश्या राजदाराः, ललाटन्तपः सूर्यः । सि. कौ.), a nasal being inserted after ललाट in accordance with 'अरुर्द्विषदजन्तस्य मुम्' पा. 6. 3. 67. तपने = सूर्ये. लिखितः ललाटिका एव पुण्ड्रकः यैः. For ललाटिका, see p. 44 and for पुण्ड्रक, see p. 26. अलकाः (curls) एव चीरचीवरं (ragged dress of a mendicant) तेन संवीतैः (covered). दिन...न्दुभिः the foreheads of ladies as though undertook vows (नियमाः) for propitiating the sun. One who observes a व्रत has a पुण्ड्रक on his forehead, wears ragged garments and a rosary; ladies (on account of the fierce heat) had sandal mark on their foreheads, allowed their curls to play about their foreheads and had drops of perspiration (resembling pearls in their brightness). चन्दनेन धूसराभिः (with सुन्दरीभिः); चन्दनवत् धू० (with कुमुदिनीभिः). असूर्यम्पश्या—see notes above on ललाटन्तप. The women did not come out in the sun; the कुमुद plants close their buds in the day. कुमुदs are white and so the plants are called चन्दनधू०. दिवसमसुप्यत—the ladies slept the whole day; the कुमुद plants closed their petals in the day. निद्रा...तपम् the eyes, heavy with sleep, could not bear even the light of the jewels; what of the fully grown heat? अशि...शर्वर्यः In the season of summer the moonlit nights became shorter and shorter, being esteemed by pairs of चक्रवाकs, like rivers. चक्रवाक is separated from its mate at night and so they welcome the shortness of the nights. सोडुपाः possessed of the moon (with शर्वर्यः); with rafts (with सरितः). There are boats on rivers, which are welcomed by चक्रवाकs, as they live near them. उडुपः lord of stars (उडु *f. n.*) *i. e.* the moon. उडुपः–पम् raft. अभिनवः पटुः (strong) पाटलानां आमोदः तेन सुरभिः परिमलः यस्य (*adj.*of जलं and पवनं also). पाटल (trumpet flower) is a kind of fragrant summer flower. Compare शाकुन्तल I 'सुलभसलिलावगाहाः पाटलसंसर्गसुरभिवनवाताः ।'.

P. 22 l. 3–**P. 23** l. 5. **क्रमेण......मातरिश्वानः.** The sentence is क्रमेण च ...प्रावर्तन्त...मातरिश्वानः. खराः (fierce) खगस्य (सूर्यस्य) मयूखाः यस्मिन्. 'शरार्कविहगाः खगाः' इत्यमरः. This and the following clauses in the locative qualify निदाघकाले (l. 12). खण्डितं शैशवं यस्य whose childhood was gone *i. e.* when the season had far advanced. सीदन्ति स्रोतांसि यस्मिन् when the streams sank low *i. e.* had hardly any water left in them. झिल्लि...रिणि resounding with the cries of crickets. कातर...विश्वे when the world was deafened by the continued cooing of the distressed doves. वि...त्रिणि when the birds breathed very heavily. करीषङ्कषः मरुत् यस्मिन् when the wind swept dried cowdung. 'सर्वकूलाभ्रकरीषेषु कषः' पा. 3–2–42. (सर्वङ्कषः खलः । कूलङ्कषा नदी । करीषङ्कषा वात्या । सि. कौ). 'गोविड् **गोमय**मस्त्रियाम् । तत्तु **शुष्कं करीषो**ऽस्त्री' इत्यमरः. विरलाः वीरुधः (लताः) यस्मिन्. As the leaves fell off through heat, the creepers grew less dense. रुधिर...स्तबके when the bunches of fullgrown (कठोर) धातकी flowers were licked by the young of lions in their greed for blood. धातकी flowers are very red. ताम्यत् स्तम्बेरमानां यूथं तस्य वमथुः तेन तिम्यन्तः महामहीधराणां नितम्बाः यस्मिन् where the slopes (नितम्बः) of large mountains became wet with the spray spouted from the trunks of languid elephants. स्तम्बेरमः हस्ती

स्तम्बे (तृणे) रमते इति (अलुक्समास) according to 'स्तम्बकर्णयो रमिजपोः' पा. 3-2-13. (स्तम्बेरमः कर्णेजपः). 'वमथुः करशीकरः' इत्यमरः. दिनकरेण दूयमानाः द्विरदाः तेषां दीनेषु (distressed) वदनेषु आश्याना (partially dried) दानस्य (ichor) श्यामिका (dark streak) तस्यां आलीनाः मूकाः मधुलिहः (bees) यस्मिन्. The thirsty bees stuck to whatever was left of the ichor. लोहितायमानाः मन्दारैः सिन्दूरिताः सीमानः यस्मिन् when the boundaries (of villages) looked red, being as though smeared with vermilion by the मन्दार flowers. मन्दार trees were planted on the boundaries. Their red flowers looked like सिन्दूर. Even now boundary stones are smeared with सिन्दूर. स्यन्दः stream, trickling line. सन्दोहः mass. ०सन्दोहस्य सन्देहेन मुञ्चन्तः महामहिषाः तेषां विषाणकोटिभिः विलिख्यमानाः (scratched) स्फुटन्त्यः स्फाटिकदृषदः यस्मिन्—The crystal slabs looked like trickling water; so the buffaloes in hopes of getting more water vehemently struck them with their horns. घर्मेण (by heat) मर्मरिताः (rustled) गर्मुतः (creepers) यस्मिन्. The leaves being dry, the creepers produced a rustle. त...किरे when the scratching cocks were afraid of scratching (for food) in husk-fire due to the heated dust. कुकूलः-लम् fire burning in chaff. Cocks ordinarily scratch for food in chaff, which is heaped up in dust. The dust being heated set fire to a portion of the chaff and so cocks became afraid to scratch near it. विकिरः a bird, particularly, a cock (from कॄ with वि). 'विष्किरः शकुनिर्विकिरो वा' पा. 6. 1. 150. विवरशरणाः (विवरं शरणं येषां) श्वाविधाः (porcupines) यस्मिन्. Generally the word is श्वाविध्, but Bāṇa uses the form श्वाविध. तटा...म्भसि when the waters of the ponds (being dried up) left only mud and were coloured by the fish rolling (विवर्तमान) on their backs, the fish being distressed by the cries (कूजा) of the ospreys (कुरराः) on the Arjuna trees on the banks of the ponds. The com. reads कूटज्वर० and explains 'कूटः शब्द एव सन्तापकारित्वात् ज्वरः.' ०वर्तमानाः उत्तानाः शफराः तैः शारं पङ्कशेषं (पङ्कः शेषः यस्य) पल्वलाम्भः यस्मिन्. On the connection between the cries of ospreys and the distress of fishes, the com. remarks 'कुररास्तटस्था यदा कूजन्ति तदा मत्स्याः पीडिताः सन्तः उत्प्लवन्तीति वस्तुधर्मोऽयम्.' दावेन जनितं जगन्नीराजनं यस्मिन्. The forest conflagration as though performed the नीराजन rite of the world. For नीराजन, see above p. 34. रज...यक्ष्मणि which was the (cause of) the consumption of night. In summer night slowly dwindles, as a man gradually becomes emaciated in consumption. Compare 'घर्मवृद्धिरपां प्रस्थः क्षपाह्रास उदग्गतौ' वेदाङ्गज्योतिष. कठो...काले when the season of summer was far advanced. प्रति...लुण्ठका: that openly carried off in desert places the roofs (पटलं) of water-sheds (प्रपा), garden enclosures (वाट:) and huts, as though they were leaping in all directions. This and the following nouns in the nominative qualify उन्मत्ता मातरिश्वान: below. A mad man (उन्मत्त) also wanders (आटीकमान) everywhere. ऊषर: a desert. प्रपा is Marathi पाणपोई. लुण्ठक: robber. प्रपक्व...स्थली: rubbing against sandy (शर्करिल) hard (कर्कर) places, as though they (the winds) were all of a sudden itching on account of their rashness in cracking (आच्छोटनं) the lines of the bushes of ripe कपिकच्छू. A person whose skin is itching rubs it against a hard substance. The wind broke the bushes of the prickly कपिकच्छू plant (that causes itch) and also dragged the sand off hard stony places. 'स्त्री शर्करा शर्करिल: शार्कर: शर्करावति । देश एवादिमौ' इत्यमर:. Vide notes on सैकत above p. 44. A mad man also may break the bush of the prickly कपिकच्छू, have itch thereby and rub his hands against stones. कपीनामपि कच्छू: यस्या: सा कपिकच्छू:. स्थूल...मुच:—The strong winds carried off gravel of comparatively large size. मुचु...दन्तुरा: bristling with the shoots (कन्दल:-लम्) of मुचुकुन्द broken by them. दलनं breaking. The broken shoots looked like teeth. A mad man also shows his teeth. In most of the following clauses reference is made to a mad man's appearance and actions. We shall not explain all of them, as almost all can be easily understood. समन्त...तनव: that were moistened by the spray from the mouths of the noisy tribes of crickets (चीरी) flying all round. 'भृङ्गारी चीरुका चीरी झिल्लिका च स्त्रियामिमा:' इत्यमर:. ०शीकरे शीक्यमाना तनु: येषाम्. शीक् 10th *conj.* to moisten. तरुणतर: तरणि: (सूर्य:) तस्य तापेन तरले चञ्चले (*adj.* of ०वारिणि). तरुण...वारिणि as though floating on the illusory and tremulous waters of the mirage, as they (waters) trembled with the heat of the fierce (*lit.* young) sun. The heat of the sun produced the appearance of a mirage on sandy deserts. The air being set in motion by the heat produced the appearance of waves. As the winds swept over the desert while the mirage lasted, they are fancied to be floating in the false water &c. तरङ्गिणी a stream. A mad man also may lie on a sandy bank and pretend to be swimming though there be no water. शुष्य...जङ्घाला: (winds) that blew with velocity easily crossing the desert tracks rustling (मर्मर) with dry S'amī trees. The winds swept with violence over deserts. मारव from मरु with the affix अ. मरो: अयं मारव: मार्ग: तस्य लङ्घने लाघवं (नैपुणं) तेन

जवः तेन जङ्घालाः (rapid). A mad man also runs rapidly. 'जङ्घालोऽतिजवस्तुल्यौ' इत्यमरः. रैणवः (रेणूनां अयं) आवर्तः (circular motion, eddy) तेषां मण्डली (समूहः) तस्याः रेचकं रासे रसेन रभसारब्धं नर्तनं तस्य आरम्भे आरभटीनटाः (winds) that were wild actors in beginning a dance commenced with violence through liking (रसः) for the circular dance (रासः), that (नर्तनं) purged (swept away) whirling columns of dust. The idea is that whirl-winds arose, raised moving columns of dust and carried the dust columns from place to place. This clause contains several technical words pertaining to the science of dramaturgy. आरभटी is one of the four styles (वृत्ति) in dramatic compositions, the other three being भारती, सात्वती and कैशिकी. It is defined in Bharata's नाट्यशास्त्र as follows:—'आरभटप्रायगुणा तथैव बहुकपटवञ्चनोपेता। दम्भानृतवचनवती त्वारभटी नाम विज्ञेया॥ प्रस्तावपातप्लुतलङ्घितानि छेद्यानि मायाकृतमिन्द्रजालम्। चित्राणि युद्धानि च यत्र नित्यं तां तादृशीमारभटीं वदन्ति॥' chap 20. 25–26. The साहित्यदर्पण (VI. 132–133) says 'मायेन्द्रजालसंग्रामक्रोधोद्भ्रान्तादिचेष्टितैः॥ संयुक्ता वधबन्धाद्यैरुद्धतारभटी मता।.' This style consists in representing intrigues, deceits, falsehoods, illusions, fight, imprisonments &c. The com. derives as 'इरयन्तीति (*v. l.* इयरतीति) अरा अराश्च ते भटाश्च अरभटास्तेषामियमारभटी.' रास is a dance in a circle in which men and women join, holding one another's hands. It is frequently mentioned in connection with कृष्ण and the Gopīs. See भागवतपुराण X. 33. 'तत्रारभत गोविन्दो रासक्रीडामनुव्रतैः। स्त्रीरत्नैरन्वितः प्रीतैरन्योन्याबद्धबाहुभिः॥' 2. The com. quotes 'अष्टौ षोडश द्वात्रिंशद्यत्र नृत्यन्ति नायकाः। पिण्डीबन्धानुसारेण तन्नृत्तं रासकं स्मृतम्॥.' In a रास, there is आवर्तमण्डली *i. e.* a ring of dancers that moves round and round. Compare 'सावर्त इव रासकमण्डलैः' हर्ष० 4th उच्छ्वास. रेचक means 'movements of the eye, brows &c. which indicate love'. 'तत्राक्षिभ्रूविकाराश्च शृङ्गाराकारसूचकाः। सग्रीवा रेचका ज्ञेयो हावश्चित्तसमुत्थितः॥' नाट्यशास्त्र chap. 22. 10. As to रेचक, the com. says that they are three कटीरेचक, हस्तरेचक and ग्रीवारेचक. Mad men also dance. मलनं crushing. Mad men also are मलिन. We may connect this clause with the next. A क्षपणक remained as मलिन as soot. Compare 'कज्जलमय इव बहुदिवससमुपचितबहलमलपटलमलिनिततनुरभिमुखमाजगाम शिखिपिच्छालाञ्छनो नग्नाटकः' हर्ष० 5th उच्छ्वास. Note the आचाराङ्गसूत्र (Sacred Books of the East Vol. XXII. p. 124) II. 2. 2. 1. 'Some householders are of clean habits and the mendicants, because they never bathe, are covered with uncleanliness.' शिक्षित...च्छिन्वतः that (winds) gathered up the feathers of the forest peacocks, as though they had learnt the ways of Jain ascetics. Jain ascetics (Digambara) carry peacock's feathers to sweep insects from their path. 'लुञ्चिताः पिच्छिकाहस्ताः पाणिपात्रा दिगम्बराः' सर्वदर्शनसंग्रह (आर्हतदर्शन). सप्र...जालकैः—करञ्ज is a wild tree so called even in Marathi. The dried seeds in its pods (मञ्जरी) rattle when the wind violently blows against them. That rattling resembles the noise of drums (गुञ्जा) beaten to announce the march of a prince &c. 'गुञ्जा तु काकचिञ्चायां पटहे च कलध्वनौ' मेदिनी. See भट्टिकाव्य XIV. 2. 'वेणून् पुपूरिरे गुञ्जा जुगुञ्जुः करघट्टिताः.' आतपेन आतुराः (distressed) वनमहिषाः तेषां नासाः निकुञ्जाः (bowers) इव तेषां स्थूलनिश्वासैः—the buffaloes heavily snorted. Their noses being compared to bowers, their deep breaths are properly fancied to be shoots (प्ररोहः). वातहरिण very swift deer. परिपाटी row, line. पेटकैः = समूहैः. The very swift deer springing up in the air seemed to be the children of the winds, as they equalled the wind in velocity. सभ्रु...कोटिभिः with the curling (कुटिल) lines of the smoke of the burning heaps of chaff (बुसं) on the threshing floor (खलधानं), they (winds) as though seemed to knit their brows. The curved lines of smoke resemble dark and curved eyebrows. सा...मुक्तिभिः by the emission of great heat, they (winds) seemed as though possessed of the waves of the अवीचि hell. Hell is a place of torments. अवीचि is one of the numerous hells mentioned in the Purāṇas. 'स्यान्नारकस्तु नरको... । तद्भेदास्तपनावीचिमहारौरवरौरवाः' इत्यमरः. अवीचिवीचिभिः सह सावीचि° (*adj.* of मातरिश्वानः). The waves are of fire burning in them. मनुस्मृति (IV. 87-90) enumerates 21 hells of which महावीचि is one. लोम...तन्तुभिः with the threads of the cotton of the silk-cotton pods that were cleft (by the heat), they (winds) seemed as though they were shaggy. Mad men do not shave and so are लोमश. दद्रुणा...ष्टिभिः by the carrying of the heaps of dried leaves, they seemed as though suffering from leprosy or cutaneous eruptions. The dry leaves present the appearance of दद्रू. Or we may explain that those who suffer from दद्रू cover the skin with leaves to ward off flies. दद्रुण is formed from दद्रू with the affix न like पामन from पामन्, according to 'रोमादिपामादिपिच्छादिभ्यः शनेलचः' पा. 5. 2. 100. दद्रू is one of the eleven क्षुद्रकुष्ठकs. It is a name for skin diseases such as Eczema, Erysipelas. 'सकण्डुरागपिटिकं दद्रुमण्डलमुद्गतम्.' सिरा...करणैः by scattering the long lines of grass, they seemed to have exposed their veins. वेणी and veins are both dark. Mad men, being underfed, may expose their veins. उच्छम...शङ्कुभिः with the shaking points (शङ्कुः) of the pieces of barley awns (शूकः—

कम्), they seemed to have long beards. उद्गतं श्मश्रु येषाम्. दंष्ट्रा... शतैः—The pointed quills (शललं) of porcupines resemble teeth. जिह्वा...खाभिः—the flames of fire resemble tongues. उत्स...लाः possessed of crests in the serpents' sloughs that were whirled up by them. ब्रह्म...स्यन्तः that, with the hot honey of lotuses, practised the taking of mouthfuls for the purpose of swallowing up the moisture in the whole universe. The winds carried away the hot honey of lotuses. They made a mouthful of it. The poet fancies that the winds were only practising in order to be able to swallow the fluid *(i. e.* to dry up) of the whole universe. अभ्यवहरणं भोजनम्. Another sense is suggested. There are six *rasas* मधुर, अम्ल, लवण, कटु, कषाय and तिक्त. The winds took the sweet (मधुर) honey, the first रस, in order gradually to be able to taste all the six. ब्रह्मस्तम्भः the universe. The word is usually written as ०स्तम्ब. 'स्तम्बशब्देनोर्ध्वत्वादिसादृश्याद्रौण्या भुवनाण्डान्युच्यन्ते' वीरराघव on महावीरचरित 3. 48. For ब्रह्मस्तम्भ, see text p. 30 l. 3. सकल... यन्तः producing an alarm (विभीषिका) for the three worlds by the sharp sounds of the cracking of dried bamboo forests, as though they (sounds) were drums announcing the (might) of heat (घर्मः) that dries up all water. ०च्छोषणः घर्मः तस्य घोषणा तदर्थं पटहैः. Read त्रिभुवनविभीषिका०. च्युत...सृतयः that made the roads (सृतिः) variegated by the rows of the falling feathers of moving jays. The feathers of चाष are dark. त्विषि...ताङ्गाः that (winds) were marked with sparks (स्फुलिङ्गः) and cold cinders in the bursting Gunjā berries, as though their bodies were dark-red by being scorched with the firebrand of the rays of the sun. Small round Gunjā berries are red with a patch of black. The red represents sparks and the dark stands for charcoal (अङ्गारः). A firebrand (अलातं) is red and the scorched skin is dark. त्विषिमान् सूर्यः तस्य मयूखलता एव अलातं तेन प्लोषः (burning) तेन कल्माषं (variegated) वपुः येषाम्. By the sun's rays the Gunjā berries were split up. The bursting berries look like patches of skin scorched by contact with firebrands. गिरिगुहासु गम्भीराः झाङ्काराः तैः भीषणा भ्रान्तिः (भ्रमणं) येषाम् the movements of which were terrible as they roused echoes in the mountain caves (by their fierce velocity). Mad men also wander among mountains. भुवनभस्मीकरणार्थं अभिचारः तस्य चरुः तस्य पचने चतुराः. अभिचारः a magical spell for securing some malevolent purpose. चरुः an oblation of rice. One who wants to effect some evil object offers a चरु with red powder sprinkled thereon or offers even blood. The bunches of the पारिभद्र flowers, being red, resemble oblations of blood. तारवः—तरोः अयम्. तर्पय... वसून् propitiating the forest fires (feeding) on trees. Oblations are thrown into fire. The winds carried the red पारिभद्र flowers and there were forest fires also. The poet fancies that the winds propitiated fires with oblations of blood. पारिभद्र is निम्बतरु. Compare हर्ष० 8th उच्छ्वास last para. 'असुरवधाभिचारचरुपिशुनः शोणितक्वाथकषायितकुक्षिः...कटाह इव च बार्हस्पत्यः.' अशि...रंहसः the velocity (the path) of which was bestarred with hot sand. शिलाजतुः bitumen. It is used as a medicine. ०रसलवैः लिप्ताः दिशः यैः. दावदहनेन पच्यमानानि चटकाण्डानि तेषां खण्डैः खचितानि तरुकोटरकीटपटलानि तेषां पुटपाकः तेन गन्धः तेन कटवः. The forest fires made the sparrow's eggs burst open. The shells of the eggs fell all round the insects in the hollows of trees and covered them as in a vessel of leaves. Inside them the insects were baked. That produced a strong smell. पुटपाक is a particular method of preparing drugs. The ingredients are wrapped up in leaves and then plastered over with clay. The whole is then roasted in the fire of cowdung cakes. मातरिश्वानः =वायवः. मातरि आकाशे श्वयति or श्वसिति or मातरि शु (आशु) अनिति.

P. 23 ll. 6–22. **सर्वतश्च...दावाग्नयः.** The sentence is सर्वतश्च... प्रत्यदृश्यन्त दावाग्नयः. भूरि...वायुभिः with the breaths blowing from the deep cavern-like jaws of old huge serpents, they (forest fires) seemed to be as though kindled by being fanned with thousands of bellows (भस्त्रा). क्वचि...हरिणाः—fires are yellowish (हरिण) and burn grass. Deer (हरिणाः) also subsist on grass. 'हरिणः पाण्डुरः पाण्डुः' इत्यमरः. In this and the following clauses up to ०स्थितयः (l. 14) there are pairs of words that serve to qualify दावाग्नयः and also serve another purpose. The latter in each pair of words is a noun with which the former can be construed as an adjective. क्वचित्—क्वचित् in some places—in other places. ०विवर्तिनः rolling. बभ्रवः yellowish-red; ichneumons. 'विपुले नकुले विष्णौ बभ्रुः स्यात्पिङ्गले त्रिषु' इत्यमरः जटा...कपिलाः resting on fibrous roots and tawny. जटा also means 'matted hair.' कपिलाः the sage Kapila, the founder of the सांख्य system, the plural being used to show respect. Or कपिलाः may stand for 'followers of कपिल'. शकु...श्येनाः that make the nests (कुलायः) of birds fall and are white (श्येन). Hawks (श्येनाः) bring down the nests of smaller birds. विलीनलाक्षारसवत् लोहिता छविः (कान्तिः) येषाम्. अधराः that could not be controlled. The lips of ladies are red like melting lac and also red with lac. आसा...

शिखाः the motion of which became greater by the wings of the birds that were overtaken (by the fires) and that (fires) had flames blazing up. The oily wings of the birds added to the strength of the conflagration. विगताः शिखाः (flames) येषाम्. विशिखाः also 'arrows.' आसा...गतयः (with arrows) 'the velocity of which was increased by obtaining the feathers of birds.' Arrows have feathers attached to them. दग्धाः निःशेषाः जन्महेतवः यैः. दग्ध...र्वाणाः—The fires burnt up the woods, leaves &c., from which they were produced and then became extinguished. निर्वाण from वा with निर्. निर्वाणम् also means 'मोक्ष' and निर्वाणाः would mean 'those that are liberated from संसार, the cycle of births and deaths.' दग्ध...हेतवः (with 'liberated') 'that have completely burnt up the causes of birth, *viz.* all actions.' Actions done for gratifying this or that desire produce their results for enjoying which one has to go through the cycle of births and deaths. When correct knowledge of the nature of the soul and the Supreme is acquired, then the ज्ञानी does not desire the fruits of his actions. No man can be free from actions; but what he can be free from and what he is advised to be free from is the desire to obtain for himself the fruits of his actions. Compare the following from the भगवद्गीता 'ज्ञानाग्निः सर्वकर्माणि भस्मसात्कुरुते तथा ॥' chap. 4. 37; अनाश्रितः कर्मफलं कार्यं कर्म करोति यः। स संन्यासी च योगी च न निरग्निर्न चाक्रियः ॥ chap. 6. 1; त्यक्त्वा कर्मफलासङ्गं नित्यतृप्तो निराश्रयः। कर्मण्यभिप्रवृत्तोऽपि नैव किञ्चित्करोति सः ॥ chap. 4. 20. कुसुम...रागिणः that are charged with the fragrance of the sky (अम्बरं) perfumed with flowers and are of rosy hue (रागिणः); also 'lovers, that give out the perfume of garments (अम्बरं) scented with flowers'. The com. takes कुसुम to mean 'smoke' in the first case (with fires). स...रुचयः that emit smoke and have a faint lustre (रुचिः); those that have no taste for food (suffering from indigestion) emit smoky (foul) eructations. धूमस्य उद्गारः तेन सह स० (बहुव्रीहि) with दावाग्नयः; सधूमः उद्गारः (eructation) येषाम् (with मन्दरुचयः). सकल...स्मकाः that swallow the whole world as a morsel and have ashes; those that suffer from the disease called भस्मकरोग are prepared to devour the food in the whole world. घस्मर=भक्षक. ग्रासः mouthful, food. 'कट्वादिरूक्षान्नभुजो नराणां क्षीणे कफे मारुतपित्तवृद्धौ। अतिप्रवृद्धः पवनान्वितोऽग्निः क्षणाद्रसं शोषयति प्रसह्य ॥ भुक्तं क्षणाद्भस्म करोति यस्मात्तस्मादयं भस्मकसंज्ञकोऽभूत्।' योगरत्नाकर. वेणु...वृद्धाः that were seen (blazing) on the tops of bamboos and had assumed large proportions; very old persons rest their bodies on the tops of bamboo sticks (*i. e.* they cannot walk without the support of a stick). अचलो...क्षयिणः that consumed (उपयुक्त) bitumen on mountains and wrought destruction; consumptives (क्षयिणः) consume bitumen continuously. शिलाजतु was supposed to cure consumption. '**शिलाजतु** रसायनं कटुकतिक्तमुष्णं कृमिक्षयोदरभिदश्मरीश्वयथुपाण्डुकण्डूहरम् ।' योगरत्नाकर. Compare com. 'शिलाधातुप्रयोगाद्वा प्रसादाद्वाथ शाङ्करात् अजामूत्रप्रयोगाद्वा क्षयः क्षीयेत नान्यथा ॥.' सर्व...पीवानः destroyed all fluidity and had assumed vast proportions; those that eat all kinds of food become plump and fat. पीवत् fat. For the six *Rasas* see above p. 102. रौद्राः terrible; worshippers of Rudra (शिव). गुग्गुलु (Marathi गुग्गुळ) is a kind of fragrant gum, burnt in the temples of शिव. Compare 'शिरोविधृतविलीयमानगुग्गुलुविकलनवसेवकानुनीयमानमहाकालम्' हर्ष० 5th उ०. ज्वलित...स्थितयः (fires) that burnt the reeds and Madana trees together with flowers by the fire of the blazing roots and stood (blazing) on the stumps of trees. ज्वलितानि नेत्राणि (मूलानि) तेषां दहनेन दग्धाः सकुसुमाः शराः मदनाश्च येषु. कृता स्थाणुषु स्थितिः यैः. ज्वलित...स्थितयः that behaved like S'iva, who burnt up Cupid together with his flowery arrows by the blazing fire from his eye. ज्वलितेन नेत्रदहनेन दग्धः सकुसुमशरः मदनः यैः. कृता स्थाणोः शिवस्य स्थितिः व्यवहारो यैः. For the burning of मदन, *vide* p. 14. Separate ०शिखा नर्तनारम्भ०. चटुल...नटाः the flames of which quivered and which (therefore) looked like wild dancers at the beginning of their dance. चटुल०—The dancers in the आरभटी style have their hair waving when they begin to dance. For आरभटी see above p. 100. शुष्केषु कासारेषु सृतिः (सरणं येषाम्) that pass over dried up tanks. The com. connects this with the preceding clause. "कासाराणि नड्वलास्तेषु याः सृतयः क्वचित् स्मृतय इति पाठः । इतरत्र तु शुष्ककं शुष्कगीतं झण्ठुमादि । आसार्यन्ते इति आसाराः । आसारितानि यद्यपि गीयन्त एव तथापि 'वर्धमानमथापीह ताण्डवं यत्र योज्यते' इति ताण्डवं हि आरभटीप्रधानम्' सं०. स्फुट...घृणिम् with their flames—hands, that showered the bursting dry grains of wild rice, they seemed as though worshipping the sun. One may make an offering of parched grain (लाज) to the sun. When the fires made their way over dried up tanks, they parched up the seeds of नीवार rice growing there. घर्मघृणिः means 'one whose rays (घृणिः) are very hot' *i. e.* the sun. अघृणाः without disgust. '**जुगुप्साकरुणे घृणे**' इत्यमरः. हठ...गृध्नवः greedy (गृध्नु) for the stinking smell of the fat (वसा) of the full—grown (कठोर) land tortoises that were forcibly offered (in the fires). One

sentence *viz.* that Bāṇa should start at once. All else in the letter was of a complimentary character. अवधृतः (understood) लेखार्थः येन. समुत्सारितः (sent away) परिजनः येन. मेधाविनं refers to बाण. स्वामी refers to कृष्ण. एकगोत्रता belonging to the same family. In this sentence are collected most of the circumstances that give rise to friendship and affection. समानजातिता belonging to the same caste. The words समानज्ञानता in B would mean 'pursuing the same subject of study'. दर्शनाभ्यासः repeatedly seeing each other. परो...करणं conferring benefits in one's absence. प्रत्यासन्न near. बद्धः पक्षपातः (liking) येन. किमपि in an indescribable way. कुमुदानाम् आकरे. भवन्त...आसीत् with reference to you, this (our) emperor had been informed by bad men in various ways *i. e.* he had been prejudiced by them against you. न...था but that is not so *i. e.* there is no truth in what the wicked said about you. न...शत्रवः there exist no persons who, even though they may be good, will not have friends, neutrals and enemies. सतामपि सताम्—this has a picturesque effect. The first सताम् means 'साधूनाम्.' शिशु...भवतः as your mind was not averse to boyish follies. Read चापलापराचीन. °चापलेभ्यो अपराचीना चित्तवृत्तिः यस्य सः °वृत्तिः तस्य भावः °वृत्तिता तया. 'पराङ्मुखः पराचीनः' इत्यमरः. असदृशम् not worthy of or deserved by you. इतरो...वक्ति च other people take it up and repeat it. सलि...मनांसि the minds of the unreflecting (public) are blind and fickle, like water. गतस्य अनुगतिर्यस्य. The unreflecting people blindly follow what others say. Water also rushes in a continuous stream. Put a vertical line after मनांसि. बहु...श्चयः who arrives at a firm conclusion after listening to many people. A king has to form his opinion as best as he can after listening to the various opinions of other people about things and individuals. पृथिवीपतिः refers to हर्ष. तत्त्वान्वेषिभिः who seek to know the truth. दूर...कृतोऽसि though you are far off, I know you as well as if you were before me. सर्वे... राधि the youth of every one is guilty of follies. It is unfortunate that Bāṇa nowhere specifies clearly the follies he was guilty of. He merely makes a vague reference to 'चापल.' In the penultimate paragraph of the first उच्छ्वास also, he vaguely alludes to 'चापलानि'. Again in the last para of this chapter, he speaks of 'बालचरितचापल'. Later on हर्ष accuses him of being a भुजङ्ग (a gallant, a dissolute person) but he repudiates that charge. तथे...मिना and the king accepted it to be so *i. e.* he accepted that proposition or excuse (about बाण). अकृतः कालस्य क्षेपः यथा स्यात्तथा

(अव्ययीभाव) without loss of time. Read अवकेशी &c. अवके...मतः I do not approve of your dwelling in the midst of your kindred without seeing the great king (हर्ष), like a tree without fruit. अवकेशी इव. 'वन्ध्योऽफलोऽवकेशी च' इत्यमरः (अवके शून्ये ईष्टे इति—क्षीर०). A tree without fruits is not liked by anybody. अदृष्टः परमेश्वरः येन that does not see the god (sun). बन्धु...वसन् being in the midst of (*i. e.* in the shade of) other trees. न च...भवितव्यम् you should not be despondent (विषादिन्) by the difficulties of attendance in court nor should you be afraid of waiting upon the lord. यतो०–There is one sentence from यतो to स्वामी (including the verse). The words in the verse are capable of three meanings, one applying to Cupid (मनोभव), the second to a vain master and the third to S'iva (ईश्वर). The first and second are those principally intended. स्वस्य इच्छया सङ्कल्पेन उपजातः उत्पन्नः विषयः यस्य the realm of which (Cupid) springs from one's own fancy. काम is called सङ्कल्पज. Compare दशकुमारचरित 'कः कामः सङ्कल्पः'. स्वेच्छोपजाताः विषयाः यस्य (with a bad king) that has under his rule as many countries as he desires. स्वेच्छायाः उपजाताः विषयाः यस्य from whose mere will, this world of objects springs up (with शिव). न...देहीति who cannot be described as possessing a body (with काम). काम is अनङ्ग and so he cannot be called देही. न...देहि इति who cannot be addressed with the words 'give' (with a bad king). A bad king, though possessed of vast territory, cannot be thus addressed for fear of his punishing the suppliant. शिव cannot be described as देही, because thereby one would detract from his all-pervading nature. मार्ग...दुःखम् he causes pain with numerous darts (with काम). मार्गणाः बाणाः. मार्गण also means याचक (with bad king). मार्गण will mean 'search for truth' or begging (with शिव). One has to pray to शिव with hundreds of requests; or one has to search for truth about God in various ways. This causes trouble. मोहा...काण्डे all of a sudden he snatches life (of lovers) by producing infatuation (with काम). मोहा...काण्डे (a bad king) takes away livelihood (such as grants of villages &c.) through his folly. मोहात्...काण्डे—शिव, who typifies the principle of destruction, takes away the lives of all, when मोह (*i. e.* तमोगुण) predominates. कष्टं alas. ईश्वरदुर्विदग्धः (with काम) badly burnt by शिव. ईश्वरश्चासौ दुर्विदग्धश्च a conceited king. C and T understand the verse differently. They take ईश्वर...ग्ध as 'one who is unskilled in waiting upon a king' (ईश्वरे दुर्विदग्धः). This sense may possibly be extracted from the words, but to regard that sense as the principal one (as C and T do) is wrong. The subject matter of discussion is the conduct of kings and not the want of skill of courtiers. न्यकृताः... ०ययातयः येन who humbles, puts into the shade Yayāti &c. Here is a long list of famous ancient emperors. The story of नृग who was cursed for making delay in deciding a disputed claim is narrated in रामायण उत्तरकाण्ड chap. 53. नल is well-known. नल was king of निषध. What king is meant by निषध is not clear. It is probably निषध the great-grandson of राम. Vide रघु० 18. 1 and हरिवंश 15. 26. नहुष son of आयुः and father of ययाति. He was cursed to be अजगर. See विष्णुपुराण IV. 10. अम्बरीष is referred to in कौटिल्य's अर्थशास्त्र as a king that had conquered the six enemies (काम &c.). दिलीप was an ancestor of Rāma. नाभाग—See विष्णुपु० IV. 1. and मार्कण्डेय chap. 113. ff. भरत—the son of दुष्यन्त and शकुन्तला. भगीरथ who brought down the Ganges is well-known. ययाति, son of नहुष, transferred his old age to पूरु. अहङ्कारः एव कालकूटविषं तेन दिग्धाः अत एव दुष्टाः. ना...दृष्टयः. his eyes are not polluted and stained with the deadly poison of conceit. As he is called अमृतमय, कालकूट, which is the opposite of अमृत, is naturally suggested and अहङ्कार is compared to it. न...गिरः his speech is not choked by the disease of the throat due to the terrible poison (गरः) of pride *i. e.* he does not speak proudly. गर्वः गुरुगरः तेन गलग्रहगदः तेन गद्गदाः. गलग्रहः inflammation of the throat due to various causes. अतिस्मयेन ऊष्मा एव अपस्मारः तेन विस्मृतं स्थैर्यं येषु. नाति...स्थानकानि his postures are not such that he will forget his serenity by the epilepsy of puffed up pride. स्मयः pride. ऊष्मा stiffness. In epilepsy there is loss of consciousness (विस्मृतं) and the body becomes stiff (*i. e.* the man falls down in a fit). उद्दामः (overbearing) दर्पः एव दाहज्वरः (burning fever) तस्य वेगेन (operation) विक्लवाः (distressed, overwhelmed). अभिमानः एव महासन्निपातः तेन निर्मितः अङ्गभङ्गः यस्मिन्. गतानि movements. सन्निपात is a fatal fever in which there is a combined derangement of the three humours वात, पित्त and कफ. The योगरत्नाकर (आनन्दाश्रम ed. p. 98) gives the general symptoms. In it there is अङ्गभङ्ग (the limbs become stiff and painful). मदः एव अर्दितं तेन वक्रीकृतः ओष्ठः तस्मात् निष्ठ्यूतानि (emitted) निष्ठुराणि अक्षराणि येषु. A haughty man may curl up his lips and utter harsh words. अर्दित is a वातव्याधि, which may affect the lips. 'उच्चैर्व्याहरतोत्यर्थं खादतः कठिनानि च । हसतो जृम्भतो भाराद्विषमाच्छयनासनात् ॥ शिरोनासौष्ठचिबुकललाटेक्षणसन्धिषु । अर्दयत्यनिलो वक्त्रमर्दितं जनयेत्ततः ॥'. अस्य...

शकलेषु he looks upon good men of unblemished character as jewels and not on pieces of stone. He cares for नररत्नs and not for ordinary jewels. In this and the following clauses बाण employs the figure of speech called परिसंख्या, of which he is very fond. It occurs where an express specification of one thing, either made in answer to a question or not, tends to exclude either expressly or impliedly other similar things; *i. e.* किं भूषणं सुदृढमत्र यशो न रत्नं किं कार्यमार्यचरितं सुकृतं न दोषाः ।. In the text, the figure occurs without a preceding question. 'किंचित्पृष्टमपृष्टं वा कथितं यत्प्रकल्पते । तादृगन्यव्यपोहाय परिसंख्या तु सा स्मृता ॥' काव्यप्रकाश X. Read ०धवलेषु गुणेषु. मुक्ता...भारेषु He looks upon virtues pure like pearls as decorations and not on loads of ornaments white with pearls. दान...कीटेषु he believes in deeds of liberality as साधन and not in the worms of elephants that are दानवत्. दानवत् endowed with gifts; possessed of ichor. 'मदो दानम्' इत्यमरः. साधनम् a means of accomplishing one's object; army. Elephants were one of the four component parts of the ancient Indian army. सर्वाग्रेसरे that is the foremost of all. He wanted such fame as would make him the most pre-eminent man. जीवितं एव जरत्तृणम्—to him life was like rotten grass; glory was everything. Life (with ordinary men) is the foremost of all (things). If we read सर्वाशा० then आशा means 'quarters, hopes'. It is a good reading. गृहीतः करः (tribute) याभ्यः; गृहीतः करः (पाणिः) यासाम् (with ०पुत्रिकासु). गृहीत...योगः he exerts himself to subdue (*lit.* to accomplish) the quarters from which he levies tribute. अभियोगः exertion, perseverance. He makes no प्रसा...योगः (effort to adorn) the dolls *viz.* his wives whose hand he took (in marriage). चर्मपुत्रिका dolls of leather. गुणवति strung (with धनुषि); possessed of good qualities (with ०जने). पिण्डो० that live on the crumbs that he gives. अस्य...मात्मा His soul is for serving his friends *i. e.* he is devoted heart and soul to his friends. उपकरणम् what helps; an instrument, means *i. e.* something subservient or subsidiary. भृत्यो...भुत्वम् his sovereignty is for helping his servants. पण्डित...ग्ध्यम्—his learning enables him to understand the worth of learned men and to help them. कृपण wretched. सु...हृदयम् his heart is to him a means to remember the good deeds of others or to gratefully remember the benefits received from others. साह...शरीरम्—the one use that he makes of his body is to plunge in bold undertakings. असि...थिवी the earth enables him to show his skill in sword-play *i. e.* he vanquishes everyone in the world with his sword. वि...जकम् he requires the circle of kings (attending on him) for amusing himself (he does not require their help in battle). 'अथ **राजकम्।** राजन्यकं च **नृपतिक्षत्रियाणां गणे** क्रमात् ॥' इत्यमरः. प्र...पक्षः his enemies only serve to show his valour (or glory). सर्वम् अतिशेते ०शायि सुखमेव रसः तस्य प्रसूतिः यस्याः from which flows happiness that excels other pleasures. As his feet are compared to पल्लव, the happiness of serving him is compared to रस. पल्लवs give shade. His feet afford protection. पाद...च्छाया may also mean the brilliance of his sprout-like (*i. e.* red) feet. कृतं कशिपु (food and clothing) यस्य. 'कशिपु त्वन्नमाच्छादनं द्वयम्' इत्यमरः. विश्रान्तश्चासौ सुखी च that has taken rest and feels refreshed.

P. 25 ll. 11–24. **अथ गते···मकरोत्.** पर्यस्ते वासरे when the day was scattered about (was drawing to a close). सङ्घट्ट...तपे when the afternoon sunlight, red like a young crow's mouth, was growing fainter and fainter (क्षाम *lit.* emaciated), as though drunk by the cavities (सम्पुटः) of the closing red lotuses. सङ्घट्ट् or सङ्घट् 1 A to unite or join. क्षयिणि decreasing; consumptive. A consumptive also becomes emaciated. Red lotuses close their cups in the evening. The poet fancies that the sunlight grew faint because it was drunk the whole day by the red lotuses that were fully expanded. One may drink water with हस्तसम्पुट. शिथिलितः (lessened) निजवाजिजवः येन (*adj.* of पतङ्ग). The sun is represented as drawn by seven horses. जपा...ले as rosy as a bunch (आपीडः) of china roses. अस्ता...पतङ्गे when the sun stumbled (स्खलित) on to the top of the setting mountain, as though he was limping, having tender feet pierced by the thorns of lotus plants. The hairy growth on the stems of lotus plants is like thorns. One whose feet are pierced by thorns limps and may stumble if he has to ascend to the tops of mountains. ०कण्टकैः क्षतः पादपल्लवः यस्य. पुरः...मुखे when the first part (मुखं) of the night (श्यामा) came hurrying in the east (पुरः), having her long tresses of slight darkness dangling about, and being dark through grief at the absence of the moon. अन्धकारलेशः एव लम्बालकाः, प्रेङ्खन्तः ०लकाः यस्मिन्. The idea is that it was a moonless night and the east began to look dark. श्यामा also 'a handsome young woman.' खञ्जति *loc. sing.* of *pr. p.* of खञ्ज् 1 P to limp. A lady's face (मुखं) also may lose its brightness through separation and she might have her hair rolling on her back, because not tied up. A woman, whose husband had gone on a journey, was not to decorate her body &c. 'हास्यं परगृहे यानं समाजोत्सवदर्शनम् । क्रीडां शरीरसंस्कारं त्यजेत्प्रोषितभर्तृका ॥.' कृतं सन्ध्योपासनं येन. अन्य...राज्ञा I have been misunderstood by the king. निर्निमित्त = निष्कारण. कष्टा distressing. विषमम् full of difficulties. तत्र = राजकुले. न...गतिः I cannot claim to have affection for the royal family first started by my ancestors, nor have I access to it from their time. In these and the following clauses he intimates that neither his ancestors nor himself had ever before visited the court and so he is diffident as to how he might acquit himself when once there. नो...रोधः nor do I possess that regard (of the king) which comes of remembering (former) benefits. अनुरोधः consideration. बाल...स्नेहः affection that springs from serving (the king) from one's childhood. गोत्रगौरवम् family position or importance. पूर्व...ण्यम् the courtesy due to old acquaintance. न प्रज्ञा...लोभनम् nor can I offer the allurement of the exchange of thoughts. विद्या...हलम् nor can I claim the admiration due to vast learning. आ...दरः—regard paid to fine appearance. सेवा...लम् skill in the changes of tones necessary in service. A servant has to assume tones of humility even when exasperated. For काकु, see above p. 84. वि...ग्ध्यम् the cleverness requisite in the meeting of the learned. वित्तव्ययेन वशीकरणम् winning over (people about the court) by expenditure of money. अवश्यं गन्तव्यम्—In spite of all these drawbacks I must go. पुरारातिः 'enemy of the cities' *i. e.* शिव. He was so called because he burnt down the three cities of gold, silver and iron built by Maya for demons in the sky, air and earth. 'असुराणां पुराण्यासंस्त्रीणि वीर्यवतां दिवि । आयसं राजतं चैव सौवर्णं परमं महत् ॥' द्रोणपर्व chap. 202. 64. भुवनगुरुः the object of worship to the world. गतस्य...ष्यति will do everything that is proper (सांप्रत) when I go there.

P. 25 l. 25—**P. 26** l. 9 **अथान्य...रगात्.** The sentence is अथ अन्यस्मिन्नहनि...प्रीतिकूटात् निरगात्. In this paragraph we have a very interesting and instructive account of how an orthodox Brāhmaṇa left his home on an important undertaking. धृतं धौतं धवलं दुकूलवासः येन. गृहीता अक्षमाला (rosary) येन. प्रास्था...वर्त्य having many times recited the Vedic hymns and portions of *mantras* suited to one starting on a journey. प्रस्थाने भवं or प्रस्थानं प्रयोजनमस्य इति प्रास्थानिकम्, according to 'प्रयोजनम्' पा. 5. 1. 109. विरूपाक्षः शिवः. He is so called because he has three eyes. क्षीरस्नपनं पुरःसरं यस्याः

(*adj.* of पूजा) preceded by a bath of milk. The image of शिव was washed with milk by Bāṇa. क्षीराभिषेक is even now resorted to to propitiate Rudra. Compare 'अतिशुचिशैवसम्पाद्यमानविरूपाक्षक्षीरकलश-सहस्रस्नपनं (राजकुलं)' हर्ष० 5th उच्छ्वास. सुर...बहुलां mostly consisting of or abounding in sweet flowers &c. विलेपनं sandal ointment. प्रथमहुताः तरलाः तिलाः तेषां त्वचः विघटनं तेन चटुलाः मुखराः शिखा एव शेखरः यस्य—whose crest was formed by the rolling and crackling flames that split open the husks of the sesame that were offered first of all and hurled about (being heated by the fire). प्राज्यं (plentiful) आज्यं (ghee) तस्य आहुत्या प्रवर्धिता दक्षिणार्चिः यस्य whose right flame was kindled &c. Flames of fire curving to the right were regarded as indicating good luck. Compare 'तस्मै सम्यग्घुतो वह्निर्वाजिनीराजनाविधौ । प्रदक्षिणार्चिर्व्याजेन हस्तेनेव जयं ददौ ॥' रघु० IV. 25; 'प्रदक्षिणार्चिर्हविरग्निराददे । बभूव सर्वं शुभशंसि तत्क्षणं' रघु० III. 14; 'उदर्चिषं हुत्वा प्रदक्षिणावर्तशिखाकलापमाशुशुक्षणिं' हर्ष० 7th उ० 1st para. आशुशुक्षणिं = अग्निम्. This is a Vedic word rarely used in classcial literature. It is variously derived from शुच् or शुष्. द्युम्नं = धनम् This is again a word very frequently used in the Vedas. यथाविद्यमानं according to his means. प्राङ्मुखीं facing the east. नैचिकी an excellent cow or a sacrificial cow. 'उत्तमा गोषु नैचिकी' इत्यमरः. शुक्लः अङ्गरागः (ointment) यस्य. शुक्लं माल्यं (garland) यस्य. रोचनया चित्राः दूर्वाग्रपल्लवाः तैः ग्रथितानि ०कुसुमानि तैः कृतः कर्णपूरः यस्य whose ear was adorned with गिरिकर्णिका flowers that were interwoven with the tips of दूर्वा grass that was smeared with रोचना. रोचना—bright yellow pigment prepared from the urine or bile of a cow or found in its head. All the three रोचना, दूर्वा and गिरिकर्णिका (a kind of white flower) are auspicious. रोचना was used to ward off evil spirits and the evil eye. शिखायां आसक्ताः सिद्धार्थकाः (white mustard) येन. The white mustard was believed to protect against evil spirits. सिद्धः अर्थः यस्मात्. मात्रे...यया whose heart overflowed with affection, as if she were his mother. श्वेतं वासः यस्याः. कनीयस्या स्वस्रा this is a personal matter mentioned only casually by the author. महाश्वेतया—it is difficult to say what goddess is alluded to. Both दुर्गा and सरस्वती are fair and may be called महाश्वेता. We believe it is दुर्गा that is meant. दुर्गा is also named गौरी and सर्वमङ्गला. Here the chief point is the auspicious rites performed when Bāṇa started. The देवीभागवत says 'श्वेतं शुक्लं शिवस्थानं यस्माच्चेह समागता । महाभावसमुत्पन्ना महाश्वेता ततः स्मृता ॥'. सं० says 'महाश्वेता देवताविशेषः रविस्थदेवतेत्यन्ये'. महाश्वेतया would also mean 'who (मालती) was very fair'. अभि...जरन्तीभिः congratulated or applauded by the old female servants. वन्दितौ चरणौ येषाम्. अभि... वृद्धैः kissed on the head by the elders in the family at whose feet he fell. वर्धितः गमनोत्साहः यस्य. मौहू...हृदः having made, in accordance with the opinions of astrologers, offerings to the lunar mansions to satisfy their desires *i. e.* he offered such things as were calculated to propitiate the नक्षत्र on which he started. मुहूर्तं वेद मौहूर्तिकः (with affix ठक्), according to 'तदधीते तद्वेद' पा. 4. 2. 59. कृतं नक्षत्रदोहदं येन. हरितगोमयेन उपलिप्तं (plastered) अजिरं तस्मिन् स्थण्डिलं (a raised plot for sacrifice) तस्मिन् स्थापितम् (*adj.* of ०कलशं). असितेतराणां (धवलानां) कुसुमानां मालया परिक्षिप्तः (encircled) कण्ठः यस्य (*adj.* of ०कलशं). पिष्ट...पाण्डुरं white with five finger marks of flour. The five fingers were dipped in some powder (or flour) mixed with milk and the jar was smeared with the finger—marks by way of मङ्गल. Compare 'पिष्टपञ्चाङ्गुल--मण्ड्यमानोलूखल-मुसलशिलाद्युपकरणम्' हर्ष० 4th उ० below. मुख...पल्लवम् even now आम्रपल्लवs are placed in the mouth of jars as auspicious. For पूर्णकलश as being auspicious, *vide* notes above p. 70. कुसुमानि फलानि च पाणिषु येषाम्. अप्र...पद्भिः that recited the *apratiratha* hymn. It is ऋग्वेद X. 103. अप्रतिरथ is the name of the sage who composed the hymn. निजद्विजैः by the Brāhmaṇas that were his dependents. प्रथम...चरणः putting forward his right foot first. The right foot, eye, hand in the case of males and the left foot, eye, hand in the case of females are auspicious.

P. 26 ll 10–18 प्रथमे...भवनस्य. घर्म...कष्टं very distressing owing to summer. This and the clauses up to रोमाञ्चितमिव qualify ०काननम् (l. 14). निष्प...षमं terrible on account of the leafless trees. पथिकजनेन नमस्क्रियमाणाः प्रवेशपादपे उत्कीर्णाः कात्यायनीप्रतियातनाः यस्मिन् in which the images of Durgā carved under (or on) the trees at the entrance (of the forest) were paid homage by travellers. 'प्रतिमा प्रतियातना प्रतिच्छाया' इत्यमरः. शुष्क...सहस्रैः though dried up, it (forest) seemed as though full of sprouts with thousands of tremulous long tongues that hung from (the mouths of) thirsty beasts. The red and tremulous tongues resemble red and restless पल्लवs. पुलकित...सङ्घातैः seemed to be spotted with the swarms of bees (सरघा) flying from the honey combs (मधुगोलः) that were licked by bears and monkeys. अच्छाः निर्मलाः भल्लाः शस्त्राणि नखानि यस्य. For पुलक in the sense of 'spots,' see above notes pp. 69–70. As रोमाञ्चित follows immediately afterwards, we cannot take पुलकित in the sense of रोमाञ्चित. For गोलाङ्गूल see p. 54. 'सरघा मधुमक्षिका' इत्यमरः.

रोमा... शतैः bristling with horripilation with the hundreds of the stout shouts of asparagus (अभीरु) that grew on the soil burnt (by forest fires). दग्धस्थलीषु रूढा अभीरुः तस्याः कन्दलशतैः. अभीरु is a plant called शतावरी or नारायणी. When soil is burnt, it becomes more fertile; hence the word स्थूल. Seeds that are lying deep down in the debris spring up vigorously after the burning of forest trees by conflagration. हृदयनिर्विशेषेण not different from (*i. e.* as dear as) his own heart. The com. takes भ्रात्रा to refer to चन्द्रसेन. सुहृदा is to be connected with जगत्पतिनाम्ना. We may possibly take भ्रात्रा (cousin) also with जगत्पति. We are not told anywhere that चन्द्रसेन accompanied Bāṇa. सम्पादिता सपर्या (पूजा) यस्य. स्कन्धावारम् (object of आससाद) army. मणितारस्य समीपे उप० (अव्ययीभाव). मणितार was a town. अजिरवतीमन्वायतम् अन्व० (अव्ययीभाव) along the river अजिरवती. कृतः सन्निवेशः येन encamped.

P. 26 l. 19—**P. 28** l. 7. **निर्वर्तित...गमत्.** The principal sentence is निर्वर्तित...करः मेखलकेन सह...राजद्वारमगमत्. निर्वर्तितः ०करः येन who carried out the usual incidents of bathing and taking his meals. याममात्रं अवशेषः यस्य when only one watch (of three hours) remained. पट्ट...पितैः that were brought (near the royal gate) for tying on their heads the fillets of honour. This and the following nouns in the instrumental qualify वारणेन्द्रैः (p. 26. l. 27). A पट्टबन्ध was a mark of great honour. Compare 'लब्धो मनोरथदुर्लभो महादेवीपट्टबन्धसत्कारलाभो ललाटेन' हर्ष० 5th उ०. डिण्डि...हृतैश्च (some) brought for mounting drums (डिण्डिमः) on their backs. विक्षे...प्रेषितैः some acquired by way of tribute, some received as presents and some sent by the rangers of the elephant depots. सं० says 'विक्षेपः करः;' we may translate 'वि०...र्जितैः' as 'collected for being despatched to various places'. कौशलिकं or–का a present (from कुशलम्). नागवीथी rows of elephants or place where elephants were caught and trained. प्रथम...ढौकितैः that were brought near for being seen with curiosity (or admiration) for the first time, that were sent at the time of despatching an envoy, and that were presented (ढौकित) by the chiefs of small villages (in forests). पल्ली a small village or settlement. परिवृढः Head. 'प्रभुः परिवृढोऽधिपः' इत्यमरः. स्वेच्छा...कारितैः that were called for the pleasure. (कौतुक) of a mimic fight at will. दीय...मानैश्च that were given (*i. e.* put together for a sham fight), that were separated (when they had faught for some time) and were led off. यामस्थापितैः that were placed at the watch (at the place where the hours of the watch were marked). सर्व...कृतैः that were collected together, as though they were mountains, for constructing a dam across the ocean in order to conquer all continents. The elephants were dark and big like mountains. The king wanted to conquer the continents beyond the sea. He would cast the hills of elephants into the sea and would thereby cross over to the other side. In the Purāṇas, the द्वीपs are seven (जम्बु, प्लक्ष, शाल्मल, कुश, क्रौञ्च, शाक and पुष्कर). See विष्णुपु. II. 1. 11. *ff*. Sometimes they are spoken of as eighteen. 'अष्टादशद्वीपनिखातयूपः' रघु० 6. 38; 'भ्रूलतादिष्टाष्टादशद्वीपे दिलीपे' and 'अष्टादशद्वीपाष्टमङ्गलकमालिनी मेदिनी' हर्ष० 6th उ०. ध्वज...कल्पितैः that were made like so many festive days of पुष्याभिषेक, charming with banner-cloths, sharp drums, conches, chowries and unguents. पुष्याभिषेक is the day when the king takes a ceremonial bath, the moon being in the Pushya asterism. On these days the king is accompanied by ध्वज &c., which are the insignia of royalty. The elephants also had these on their body. श्यामायमानम्—this qualifies राजद्वारम् (p. 28. l. 7). The dark elephants made the gate look dark. There is another sense suggested. 'The day looked like night on account of the dark elephants.' अनवरतचलितैः खुरपुटैः प्रहतं मृदः (पृथिव्याः) अङ्गं यैः—that struck the earth with their hoofs that pranced ceaselessly. ०पुटैः प्रहतः मृदङ्गः यैः the sound of the hoofs resembled the beating of a tabor to the accompaniment of dancing. Hence the poet says 'न...लक्ष्मीम्'—that made Royal Glory to dance (while they themselves beat the drum). उप...जातिम् with the laugh-like foam spreading over the the corners of their lips, they seemed as though mocking the tribe of deer that (compared with the horses) had slow legs. The idea is that the horses were swifter than deer. Both फेन and हास are white. सृक्किन् *n.* corner of the lip. आका...श्रवसम् that challenged with their joyous neighing the horse of Indra to a combat (सङ्घट्टः). उच्चैःश्रवस् is the horse of Indra, one of the 14 jewels churned from the ocean. उत्पत...तलं that as though flew up into the sky in anger against the horses of the sun, their ornamental chowries serving them as wings. पक्षायमाणा मण्डनचामरमाला येषाम्. पक्षः इव आचरति पक्षायते. तुरङ्गै...मानम् (राजद्वारम्) that was as though in waves with horses. प्रे...वृत्तैः returning after being sent. From प्रेषितैश्च to ०कपिलैः (p. 27 l. 5) we have words qualifying क्रमेलककुलैः. बहु...मण्डनकैः their mouths were ornamented with rows of cowries (वराटिका) as though they (cowries) were rows of numerical figures in counting the distance of many *yojanas* they had travelled. तार...च्छेदैः that looked as though they were patches (छेद) of evening light marked with stars. The white cowries on the mouths of the camels looked like stars and their tawny skins like the yellow glow of sunlight in the evening. अरुण...लेयैः that, having their ears ornamented with red chowries, looked as though they were fields of red rice covered with red lotuses. The अरुण-चामरिका looked like red chowrie and the tawny skin like a field of red rice. 'क्षेत्रं त्रैहेयशालेयं व्रीहिशाल्युद्भवोचितम्' इत्यमरः. 'व्रीहिशाल्योर्ढक्' पा. 5. 2. 2. (शालीनां भवनं क्षेत्रम् । ढक्). अनव...शतैः having strings of charming golden bells tinkling incessantly, they seemed to be groves of old *karanja* trees with hundreds of dry pods of seed rattling on them. घुरुघुरुक a small bell (Marathi घुंगुर). For करञ्जबीज see text p. 22 l. 20. श्रव...जटालैः that were full of beautiful (चित्र) tufts of woollen threads of five colours, dangling near their ears. The next clause is अन्यत्र...आतपत्रखण्डैः श्वेतायमानम् (l. 13). शर...तनुभिः (umbrellas) that were white like milk freshly flowing, as though they were autumnal clouds. Autumnal clouds are white when a mass of water (पयःपटल) drops from them. कल्प...मण्डलैः the circular shadow of which was annihilated by the light (आलोकः) due to a mass of pearls (which encircled the umbrellas), as though they were trees of paradise. A कल्पपादप yields whatever one desires and so it may yield pearls. नारा...पक्षैः had jewels (emeralds) sticking to them, as though they (आतपत्र) were the lotuses in the navel of Vishṇu. पुण्डरीकs and the umbrellas are white. The lotus in Vishṇu's navel may touch the wings of गरुड who is the वाहन of विष्णु. आश्लिष्टाः गरुडपक्षाः येषु. गरुडपक्ष is a kind of gem, otherwise called गारुत्मत. 'गारुत्मतं मरकतम्' इत्यमरः. क्षीरो...दण्डैः that had brilliant and large rods of coral, as though they were regions (उद्देशः) of the milky ocean. The umbrellas were white like milk. Coral is found in the sea. शेष...खण्डैः that had large (स्फीत) rubies sparkling on them, as though they were the board-like (*i. e.* broad) hoods of शेष. It was supposed that serpents had red gems in their hoods. शेष has a 1000 hoods and is as white as the umbrellas. श्वेत...सेवितैः that were resorted to by swanlike kings, as though they were the islands of the heavenly Ganges.

Swans (राजहंस) resort to the celestial Ganges. अभि...तपम् overpowering the season of summer, laughing at the splendour (or heat) of the sun, and drinking up the light of the sun. The umbrellas did not allow the heat to be felt. चन्द्र...जनयद्भिः in the shade of the umbrellas people felt as cool as in moonlight. There is an apparent विरोध *viz.* how can जीवलोक be turned into चन्द्रलोक? कुमुद...कुर्वद्भिः the (white) umbrellas made the season full of white lotuses. The umbrellas look like कुमुदs. There is विरोध in saying that umbrellas turned the season (it was ग्रीष्म then) into कुमुदमयकाल (*i. e.* the season of शरद्). There is another विरोध. काल means 'dark.' What is कुमुदमय (and so white) cannot be dark. There is विरोध between ज्योत्स्ना and वासर, फेन and sky (there can be no foam in the sky). अकाल...सृजद्भिः—the white umbrellas in the day looked like moonlight. कौमुदी means 'the full-moon day in आश्विन.' It was ग्रीष्म then and so the poet uses the word अकाल. उप...श्रियम् laughing at the glory of Indra. शतक्रतोः इयं शातक्रतवी. खण्डः-म् Mass. श्वेतायमानैः resembling conch-shell. The reading श्वेतद्वीपायमानम् is better than श्वेतायमानम्. The royal gate seemed on account of the numerous white umbrellas to be like श्वेतद्वीप (where everything is white). For a description of it see शान्तिपर्व chap. 336. 'क्षीरोदधेर्योत्तरतो हि द्वीपः श्वेतः स नाम्ना प्रथितो विशालः ॥ 8...श्वेताः पुमांसो गतसर्वपापाः' 10. The next clause is क्षण... दोलायमानम् (l. 17). क्षण...भुवनम् that (chowries) as though seemed to steal away the world, the eight regions of which were seen for a moment and then lost to view. क्षणदृष्टनष्टानि (क्षणदृष्टानि पश्चान्नष्टानि) अष्टदिङ्मुखानि यस्य. The idea is:—thousands of chowries were waved to and fro. So the people could see the regions beyond where they were standing between one waving of the chowries and another. That interval being very short, the author says that the worlds disappeared from view after being seen for a moment. आक्षे...कारयद्भिः—the idea is:—when the chowries were uplifted (उत्क्षेप) they shaded the sun from view and so caused darkness (*i. e.* the day went away); when the were lowered down (आक्षेप), the sun again came into view (*i. e.* the day came). The poet fancies that the day was as if placed on a swing by the chowries and was made to come near and then go away as a person sitting on a swing does. Mark they two accusatives दिनं and ०गतानि. दिनं गतागतानि करोति (primitive sense of कृ); दिनेन दिनं वा ०गतानि कारयन्ति चामराणि (causal). 'हृक्रो-

रन्यतरस्याम्' पा. 1. 4. 53 (the subject of हृ and कृ in the primitive sense is put in the instrumental or accusative in the causal). उत्सारयद्भिः has been omitted by oversight after कारयद्भिः. उत्सा°... स्थितिम् that as though drove away the rule of *Kali* rendered dark (काली) by the stain of the contact of bad kings. *Kaliyuga* had set in long before हर्ष began to rule. Bad kings ruled in Kali. Everything that is evil and sinful is represented as dark. Kali's rule must be dark with the misdeeds of bad kings. The white चामरs as though removed this darkness. कालेय is derived from कलि with the affix ढक्. विकचैः विशदैः (bright) काशवनैः पाण्डुराः दिशः यस्मिन् (*adj.* of °समयम्). विकच...पादयद्भिः—The white काश flowers are seen in शरद्. The white chowries resemble काशs and so are fancied as bringing about autumn. बिस...र्भावयद्भिः—chowries are white like lotus fibres and are waved in the air. So the poet fancies that chowries made the sky बिसमय. शशिकरवत् शुचीनां (pure, bright). हंस...शङ्खैः that (राजद्वार) seemed like a flock of Haṁsas with the conchshells in the ears of elephants. Both हंसs and शङ्ख are white. Rings of conchshell were suspended from the ears of elephants for ornamentation or as auspicious. This explanation of करिकर्णशङ्ख will do in 'अन्तःस्फुरता मत्तमदनकरिकर्णशङ्खायमानेन प्रतिमेन्दुना' (text p. 17 ll. 16-17). See below अनवरतमवतंसशङ्खैः &c. (text p. 29 l. 30). कल्प...काभिः—the कदलिकाs (banners; plantain trees) were so many that there seemed to be a forest of कल्पलताs. माणिक्य...पत्रैः—the umbrellas of peacock's feathers looked like a forest of ruby trees (on account of the reddish tinge of the eyes). मन्दा...क्षौमैः—the white and flowing silken dresses looked like the stream of the Ganges and the white linen dresses like the milky ocean. कद...यूखैः—emeralds are green like plantain trees. जन्य...तपैः that seemed to create as though a second day by the (rosy) morning hues of rubies. It was afternoon when बाण saw the राजद्वार. The red light shed by the rubies there was like बालातप and hence there seemed to be morning in the afternoon. जन्यमानः अन्यदिवसः यस्मिन्. उत्पद्यमानं अपरं अम्बरं (आकाशं) यस्मिन्. उत्पद्य...पटलैः—Sapphires are blue like the sky. आरभ्यमाणा अपूर्वा निशा यस्मिन्. The dark महानील stones produced the appearance of night in the day; hence the author uses the word अपूर्व. स्यन्दमानं अनेककालिन्दीसहस्रं यस्मिन्. The Jumna is dark like गरुडमणि. See गरुडपक्ष above (text p. 27, l. 7). अङ्गा... रश्मिभिः with the rays of topaz it seemed to be full of charcoal.

प्रजापतिs that created everything. *Vide* मनु I. 36-41. लोक...रचितं made by gathering together the essence of the three worlds. अकथनीयः समृद्धिसम्भारः यस्य. The महाभारत is the biggest work in the Sanskrit language and yet a work of that vast extent would have fallen far short of adequately describing the glory of Harsha's gate. कृत...वेश्म the position of which was effected by a thousand कृतयुगs. Various meanings are possible. The royal gate was so gorgeous that it would seem to an observer to have been the work of long ages. Or the royal gate conveyed an atmosphere of so much purity and righteousness that as though a thousand कृतयुगs had combined to form it. For कृतयुग as an era of unmixed virtue, *vide* p. 45. स्वर्गाणां अर्बुदैः. अर्बुद is equal to 10 कोटिs. 'लक्षं च नियुतं चैव कोटिरर्बुदमेव च । वृन्दः खर्वो निखर्वश्च शङ्खपद्मौ च सागरः । अन्त्यं मध्यं परार्धं च दशवृद्ध्या यथाक्रमम् ॥'. विहितं रामणीयकं यस्य. राज...ग्रहं that was surrounded or resorted to (*lit.* accepted) by crores of royal glories.

P. 28 ll. 8–13 **अभव...प्राविशत्.** जातः विस्मयः यस्मिन्. इयत् प्रमाणं यस्य (*adj.* of ०जातं) of this (vast) extent. प्रजासृजां of those (प्रजापतिs) that created beings. महा...क्षयः how is it that the great elements were not exhausted (in creating these numerous beings)? महाभूतs are the five gross elements *viz.* पृथिवी, अप्, तेजः, वायु and आकाश, from which the bodies of all beings are created. परिच्छेदः limit. The idea is that in creating so many beings, the furthest limit of the number of atoms must have been reached and exhausted. विच्छेदः is a better reading, but is probably an emendation. परमाणूनां परिच्छेदः is more in accordance with the style of Bāṇa who cares for अनुप्रास more than for anything else. व्युपरमः cessation, end. आकृ...तिः the exhaustion of all forms. पुण्यभागी (refers to बाण)—because he was soon to be ushered into the presence of the glorious हर्ष. तम् = बाणम्. अप्रतिहतः without being obstructed.

P. 28 ll. 14–30 **अथ स...भ्यन्तरम्.** The first sentence is अथ स मुहूर्तादिव...पुरुषेणानुगम्यमानः निर्गत्य अवोचत्. सः = मेखलकः. The instrumentals from प्रांशुना qualify पुरुषेण. कर्णिकारवत् गौरेण. वीध्रकेन (विमलेन) कञ्चुकेन छन्नं वपुः यस्य. समु...लग्नेन whose waist (अवलग्नं) was small, being bound by a belt (शस्तं) that was studded (बन्धुर) with ornaments of flashing rubies. पदकं metal plate studded with stones. ०पदकबन्धेन बन्धुरं शस्तं तस्य बन्धेन कृशं अवलग्नं यस्य. In the lexicons the meaning assigned to शस्त is 'finger-guard'

'अङ्गुलित्रं शस्तकं च तथा चाङ्गुष्ठरक्षकम्'. But that meaning will not do here. If we read वस्तबन्ध, the meaning is 'by a strap of goat-skin.' ०शिलावत् विशालं वक्षः यस्य. हरस्य (शिवस्य) वृषः तस्य ककुदं (hump) तस्य कूटो (राशिः) तद्वत् विकटः (formidable) अंसतटः. He was fair and formidable like हरवृष. उरसा...बिभ्रता wearing on his chest a necklace as though it (हार) were a rope to restrain the tribe of deer in the form of restless organs of sense. हृषीकं = इन्द्रियम्. इति... समानेन—the jewelled rings in his ear are fancied to be the sun and the moon brought there to inquire of them whether there existed any one in their families equal to हर्ष. वह...किरणैः for whom room was as though made by the rays of the sun out of regard for his (पुरुष's) position, the rays being eclipsed (*lit.* pulled away) by the flowing (वहत्) stream (वेणिका) of the beauty of his face. विसरः = समूहः. When there is a crowd and a way has to be made for a great man, people have to be dragged out (आक्षिप्यमाण). The bright lustre of his face surpassed the sun's rays. प्रसादेन लब्धया obtained through the favour of his master (with ०मालिकया); serene (with दृष्टया). लब्धः प्रसादः (serenity) यया सा लब्धप्रसादा or प्रसादलब्धा, according to 'वाहिताग्न्यादिषु' पा. 2. 2. 37 (आहिताग्निः । अग्न्याहितः). आहिताग्नि is an आकृतिगण (illustrative list only and not exhaustive). मुण्डमालिका a chaplet. नैष्ठु...हता bearing on his bent head a white turban as if it (turban) were courtesy itself, though he occupied a position that was the centre (अधिष्ठानं) of sternness. As the chief of all doorkeepers his position required him to be stern in keeping discipline; yet he was courteous and had bent his head when approaching Bāṇa. C and T translate 'lifting his white turban as a token of respect'. This is quite wrong. No one in India would lift his turban *as a token of respect*. The learned authors are misled by western notions. वामेन goes with ०लयेन and ०त्सरुं with कृपाणम्, which latter is the object of कलयता. स्थूलमुक्ताफलानां छुरणेन (inlaying) दन्तुरः (uneven, jagged) त्सरुः (handle) यस्य. कलयता (goes with पुरुषेण) holding. 'त्सरुः खड्गादिमुष्टौ स्यात्' इत्यमरः. इतरे...धारयता holding in the other (*i. e.* right) hand a polished (उन्मृष्टां) golden staff, as though it (staff) were a streak of lightning without its unsteadiness. अपनीता तरलता यस्याः. For शातकौम्भ see above p. 54. ताडिती is from तडित्. अप...रलतां (with वेत्रयष्टिम्) also means 'that prevents wanton actions' (of the crowd at the door). अपनीता तरलता यया. अनन्तरः = मुख्यः. चक्षुष्यः = प्रियः. See above p. 75. द्वारे नियुक्तः

दौवारिकः. सम...वेशी let your honour (Bāṇa) who is intent on welfare treat him with befitting behaviour. प्रतिपत्तिः respectful behaviour, course of conduct. कल्याणे अभिनिवेशः अस्य ०शिन्. The word means the same thing as कल्याणिन्. Compare 'आलोकयतु तावत्कल्याणाभिनिवेशी लक्ष्मीमेव प्रथमाम्' का० p. 104 of P; 'एतत्प्रायेण कल्याणाभिनिवेशिनः श्रुतिविषयमापतितमेव' का० p. 136 (P). आगच्छत—the plural shows the respect he paid to बाण. एव...ग्राह्यं worthy to be thus favoured.

P. 28 l. 31—**P. 29** l. 25. **अथ...इति.** The first sentence is अथ...तुरङ्गैः आरचितां मन्दुरां विलोकयन् (l. 14)...अव्यक्तं इभधिष्ण्यागारमपश्यत् (l. 19). वनायुजैः born in the country of वनायु. The words in the instrumental from वनायुजैः qualify तुरङ्गैः below (l. 14). From वनायुजैः to पारसीकैः we have the breeds of horses from various countries. हलायुध and विश्व give वनायुज and पारसीक as synonyms. But that will not do here as पारसीक follows. आरट्ट—'पञ्च नद्यो वहन्त्येता यत्र निःसृत्य पर्वतात्। आरट्टा नाम वाहीका न तेष्वार्यो द्व्यहं वसेत्॥'. The country of कम्बोज was beyond the Hindookush mountains (probably eastern Persia) and was known in very ancient times. It produced one of the best breeds of horses. See रघु० IV. 69–70. यास्क refers to the country 'शवतिर्गतिकर्मा कम्बोजेष्वेव भाष्यते विकारमस्यार्येषु भाषन्ते शव इति' निरुक्त. See पाणिनि IV. 1. 75. पारसीक is Persia. From शोणैः, we have horses of various colours. ति...षैः dappled like partridges. In this para, the author shows his familiarity with शालिहोत्र, the science of horses. पञ्चभद्रः–horse having on the head and four hoofs five auspicious marks. According to सं०, it is a horse whose face together with the head and four hoofs is white.' 'सिताश्च यस्य वाजिनः शफाः समस्तकं मुखं स पञ्चभद्रनामको नृपस्य राज्यसौख्यदः।.' 'पञ्चभद्रस्तु हृत्पृष्ठमुखपार्श्वेषु पुष्पितः' हेमचन्द्र. On मल्लिकाक्षैः, सं० says "शुक्लपर्यन्ते असिततारके नयने येषां ते मल्लिकाक्षाः। उक्तं च 'पृथुस्निग्धाः समा चैव मल्लिकाकुसुमप्रभा। राजी यस्य तु पर्यन्ते परिक्षिप्ये तु लोचने। स हयो मल्लिकाक्षस्तु दृष्टिपर्यन्ततारकः॥' इति." They are horses on the corners of whose eyes there are spots of white hair. कृत्तिकापिञ्जरैः—सं० 'तारकाकदम्बककलपानेकबिन्दुकल्माषितत्वचः'—horses the coat of which is marked with numerous starlike spots. कृत्तिका is a cluster of six stars. आयतं (long) निर्मांसं मुखं येषाम्. अनुत्कटः (ह्रस्वः) कर्णकोशः येषाम्. सुवृत्तः (well rounded) श्लक्ष्णः (soft or delicate) सुघटितः (well proportioned) घण्टिकाबन्धः येषाम्. घण्टिकाबन्ध–that part of the neck where bells are tied. The com. says "शिरसो ग्रीवायाश्च यन्मध्यं स घण्टिकाबन्धः यो निगाल इत्युच्यते। तस्य सुवृत्तादि शस्यते। यदाह 'ग्रीवाशिरोन्तर-

श्लिष्टो दीर्घवृत्तः समाहितः। नोद्वर्तो नार्धितो नातिदुर्नाह्रोऽतिविधानतः। सुदिग्धोनुपदिग्धश्च निगालो गदितः शुभः ॥' इति". यूपानुपूर्व्या वक्रा आयता उदग्रा ग्रीवा येषाम् with curved, long and up-turned necks resembling a sacrificial post in their contour. आनुपूर्वी order, regular succession of parts. पूर्वानुक्रमेण अनुपूर्वं तस्य भावः आनुपूर्वी or ०पूर्व्यम्. उपचयेन श्वयन्तः स्कन्धसन्धयः येषाम् whose shoulder joints were stout (swelling) on account of the accumulation (of flesh). निर्भुग्नं (projecting, convex) उरःस्थलं येषाम्. The com. says 'स्थूलास्थि महदच्छिद्रं पृथुलं यच्च निर्वलि। उर ईदृक्प्रशंसन्ति स्थूलक्रोडं महत्तरम् ॥'. अस्थूलाः (not thick) slender प्रगुणाः (straight) प्रसृताः (legs) येषाम्. लोहपीठवत् कठिनं खुरमण्डलं येषाम्. अति...धारयद्भिः that had bellies round and as though without entrails through fear of their being broken through great speed. अनिर्मिताणि अन्त्राणि येषु. अन्त्राणि suggests the idea of interstices or ups and downs. What is वृत्त (well rounded) cannot have ups and downs. उद्यन्त्या (large) द्रोण्या विभज्यमानं पृथुजघनं येषाम् whose broad flanks were divided by a large depression. द्रोणी is a feature of beauty in a horse. It is a depression on the chest, back and flanks of a horse. The com. quotes 'पृष्ठोरःकटिपार्श्वस्य मांसोत्कर्षणनिर्मिता। द्रोणिकेति प्रशंसन्ति शोभा वाजिनि पञ्चमी ॥'. जगती...पल्लवैः whose leaf-like tails rolled on the ground (जगती). C and T translate 'with the hairs like new shoots swaying about in the wind'. कथ...यन्त्रितैः that were restrained with difficulty by the numerous firm ropes fixed (in the earth) on both sides. The ropes held their necks. If we read भूमिपाश०, then the meaning is 'ropes in the ground firmly fixed &c'. We then expect the order to be भूमिनिरवात &c. आय...माणैः although already long enough, they (horses) seemed to be longer still as one of their hinder legs was stretched because it was tied with a rope. पाशबन्ध is Marathi पायबन्द. बहुगुणेन सूत्रेण ग्रथितः ग्रीवागण्डकः येषाम् the neck-ornament of which was suspended with a cord of many strings. आमीलिते (closed) लोचने येषाम्. दूर्वा...चालयद्भिः that kept moving their limbs that were itching, the skin of which twitched, that were held between the teeth and then let go, that were spotted with bits of foam darkened by Dūrvā juice. दशनैः आदौ गृहीताः पश्चात् मुक्ताः. फरफरिता पुनः पुनः ईषत्कम्पिता त्वक् येषाम्. When their limbs had itch, the skin twitched and they held the itching skin between their teeth to ease the itching sensation. This caused the foam and the juice of the Dūrvās they were grazing upon to stick to their bodies. 'प्रतीकोऽवयवेऽपि स्यात्' मेदिनी.

C and T take the word as meaning 'mouths'. But we cannot then construe ०मुक्तान् with प्रतीकान्, as mouths cannot be bitten by teeth. सालसं वलितः वालधिः (पुच्छं) यैः that lazily moved their tails. बाला धीयन्ते अस्मिन् इति बालधिः (वालधिः also). एक...घनार्धैः half of whose flanks was drooping (स्रस्त) and relaxed as they rested on one hoof. निद्र...यद्भिः that seemed to ponder when they slept. स्खलित...यमानैः that emitted low rumbling neighing when they stumbled. ताडिता खुरधरणी तस्याः रणितेन मुखरं शिखरं येषां ते ०शिखराः खुराः तैः लिखितं क्ष्मातलं यैः. खुरधरणी is a wooden foot-rest. The object may be to allow the urine to pass through a hole in the foot-rest into a gutter underneath over which the plank is placed. प्रकीर्यमाणाः यवसग्रासाः तेषु रसः (liking) तेन or तस्मात् मत्सरः तेन उद्भूतः क्षोभः येषाम्. When fodder was scattered before other horses, they became enraged and jealous. प्रकुपिताः चण्डाः चण्डालाः (अश्वपालाः) तेषां हुङ्कारैः (threatening words) कातरतराः तरलाः तारकाः (pupils) येषाम्. कुङ्कुम...लक्ष्यमाणैः As their bodies were yellowish red because saffron was rubbed over them, they seemed to have always near them the lustration-fires. Both कुङ्कुम and fire are red. For नीराजन, see above p. 34. उपरिविततं वितानं (canopy) येषाम्. पुरः पूजितं अभिमतदैवतं येषाम्. The अभिमत-दैवत according to the com. is गोविन्द. आरचितां filled. मन्दुरा stable. 'वाजिशाला तु मन्दुरा' इत्यमरः. हस्तवामेन to the left of his hand. अत्युच्च...कुर्वाणम्—this and the following clauses qualify ०गारम्. अत्युच्च०—which, on account of its great height, as though left the sky no room. The elephant stable was very high and crowded the whole sky. कदली plantain tree; banner. परिवृताः पर्यन्ताः यस्य the outskirts of which were surrounded. सर्व...पूर्यमाणम् that was filled on all sides with streams (स्रुति) of ichor full of bees, as though with rivers. आशा...न्द्रियं that filled the nostrils with the odour, as though of blooming Bakula trees, spreading in all directions. The odour of the ichor of the best elephants was said to be like that of Bakula. Separate विकसताम् + आमोदेन. The com. says "तदुक्तम्। 'मालतीमुक्तपुन्नागबकुलोपमसौरभम्। दानं पि(मि?)ष्टाम्बुसदृशं मुञ्चच्छ्रेष्ठं तु शीतलम्॥.' दूराद्व्यक्तम् not quite distinct owing to distance. इभ...गारम् a stable where elephants were housed. 'धिष्ण्यं स्थाने गृहे' इत्यमरः. अत्र...करोति—the elephant—stable looked from a distance like a palace. So बाण asked this question. औपवाह्यः—'राजवाह्यस्त्वौपवाह्यः सन्नाह्यः समरोचितः' क्षीरस्वामी—a king's elephant meant for riding only (and not for fighting). जात्यन्तरितः आत्मा his very soul separated from him by another species. The king's soul was in a human body, while in दर्पशात it was in an elephantine body. दर्पशातः—literally means 'one who destroys the pride' (of other elephants). दर्पं शातयति इति. C and T strangely enough explain it as 'keen (or perhaps attenuated and lacking) in pride'. श्रूयते—I have only *heard*, but never seen. यद्ये...न्द्रमेव If it be so (*i. e.* if दर्पशात is housed here) and if there be no objection (in seeing it), then I shall first of all see the great elephant. अतिपरवान् overcome.

P. 29 l. 26—**P. 31** l. 22. **गत्वा च...पश्यत्.** The principal sentence is गत्वा च दूरादेव...दर्पशातमपश्यत्. गम्भीर...गर्जितैः—by the deep sounds issuing from his throat. कल low, sweet. गम्भीर... हलम्—the idea is :—The big elephant trumpeted in deep grunts (as is usual with these animals); that sound resembled the rumbling of a cloud. So the चातक and the peacock welcomed the sound (thinking that a cloud was near) with vociferous notes. A चातक was supposed not to be able to drink the water flowing on the earth; it had to rest content with a few drops from the cloud falling direct into its mouth. Hence the word वियति with चातककदम्बकैः and भुवि with peacocks (नीलकण्ठ). Compare 'चातका इव तृष्णावन्तो न शक्यन्ते ग्रहीतुमकुलीनाः' हर्ष० 4th उ०. See for peacocks dancing when it thunders, p. 63. क्रियमाणः कलः कोलाहलः यस्य. This and the following words in the accusative singular qualify दर्पशातं below. विकचानि कदम्बानि संवदति (resembling) इति ०संवादी मदः सुरा इव तस्याः सौरभेण भरितं भुवनं येन. काय...कालम् that seemed as though he were the premature season of clouds wearing an embodied form. Both the elephant and clouds are dark. In the season of clouds (rains) one sees चातकs, peacocks dancing and the कदम्ब tree putting forth buds. Therefore the elephant (whose ichor resembled the odour of *Kadamba* buds) is fancied to be the season of clouds incarnate. It was then the middle of ग्रीष्म and not वर्षा. So the word अकाल is put in. अविरल...त्सृजन्तम् leaving (about to leave) the fourth stage of life that had reached its perfection by his skin being marked with spots brown like thick drops of honey as though it were a lake. अभ्यवगाढाम् full developed (with दशाम्); deep (with सरसीम्). अविरलमधुबिन्दुवत् पिङ्गलानि पद्मजालकानि सञ्जातानि अस्याः इति ०जालकिताम् (with दशाम्). *Vide* notes on तारकित p. 42. पद्मजालकम्—marks of reddish spots on the elephant's skin. 'पद्मकं बिन्दुजालकम्' इत्यमरः (पद्मप्रतिकृति

रक्तत्वात्पद्मकम् तारुण्ये हि हस्तिनां देहे रक्तबिन्दवः स्युः। क्षीर०). 'चतुर्थ्यामवगाढायां लेखाबिन्दुभिराचितः' सं०. ०बिन्दुभिः पिङ्गलानि पद्मानि (कमलानि) तैः जालकिताम् (with सरसीम्). There is brown honey in lotuses. सरसीम्—'दक्षिणापथे हि महान्ति सरांसि सरस्य इत्युच्यन्ते' महाभाष्य (Kielhorn Vol I. p. 73.). चतुर्थीदशा means 'the age between 30 and 40'; compare कौटिल्य's अर्थशास्त्र 'That which is seven अरत्नि*s* in height, nine in length, ten in circumference and is 40 years old is the best' (translation p. 207). आमन्द्रः कर्णताल एव दुन्दुभिध्वनिः येषु (*adj.* of शंखैः). अन...गायन्तम् that chanted (the tune suited to) the beginning of his auspicious entrance into the fifth stage with the conch-shell ornaments on his ears that were blended with the low drum-like rumbling of the flapping of his ears. For शङ्ख*s* on elephant's ears, see above text p. 27 l. 18. At an auspicious ceremony such as the first entrance in a new house, there is the music of drums (दुन्दुभि) and conches may be blown. पञ्चमी stands for पञ्चमीदशा. अविरतचलने चित्रा (charming) त्रिपदी एव ललितं (fine) लास्यं (dancing) तस्य लयैः (harmony). त्रिपदी standing on three legs, while one is lifted up. This is a characteristic action with the elephant. 'गानगेययोरन्यूनाधिक्ये श्लिष्टता लयो द्रुतादिः वाद्यादीनामन्योन्यं समत्वमिति यावत्' क्षीरस्वामी. The elephant moved incessantly and he rested his body on three legs. So he seemed to be engaged in dancing and there was a certain rhythmical method in his movements. दोलायमानः दीर्घदेहस्य आभोगः (expanse) यस्य सः ०भोगः तस्य भावः ०भोगता तया. मेदिनी...यमानम्—the idea is:—by his incessantly standing on three legs, he seemed to be lessoning his weight on the earth for fear of (otherwise) breaking it (विदलन). His incessant movements to and fro looked like rubbing the itching body against the quarters. Buffaloes and elephants may rub their bodies against walls. लघयन्तम् *pr. p.* of लघयति denominative verb from लघु. आहवः fight. उदस्तहस्ततया because he threw up his trunk (into space). उदस्त *past p. p.* of अस् to throw with उद्. There are eight guardian elephants of the eight quarters. 'ऐरावतः पुण्डरीको वामनः कुमुदोऽञ्जनः। पुष्पदन्तः सार्वभौमः सुप्रतीकश्च दिग्गजाः॥' इत्यमरः. ह्वे with आ in the sense of 'to challenge to a fight' takes the आत्मनेपद only. 'स्पर्धायामाङः' पा. 1. 3. 31. (कृष्णश्चाणूरमाह्वयते). करपत्रम् saw (Marathi करवत); saw-like trunk (करः पत्रमिव). स्थूलाः निशिताः दन्ताः यस्य. A saw has teeth and cleaves pillars (स्तम्भः). स्थूलौ निशितौ दन्तौ बस्मिन् (with trunk). He moved his trunk armed with sharp tusks and seemed to cleave the world (ब्रह्मस्तम्भः). See above

p. 102 for ब्रह्मस्तम्भ. अमा...मानम् he seemed to desire to go out, as though the world could not contain him. His incessant movements and large body give rise to this conceit. The next clause is सर्वतः...नन्दम्, the chief portion of which is सर्वतः लेशिकैः आधोरणैः च आधीय...नन्दम्—to whom delight was caused by riders (लेशिक) and keepers (आधोरण) who treated him with remedies (उपचारः) appropriate to summer. आधीयमानः ०समयसमुपचितोपचारैः आनन्दः यस्मिन्. 'आधोरणा हस्तिपकाः' इत्यमरः. सरस...वनैरिव by riders who tossed (over the elephants) creepers full of juice and sprouts and who seemed as though they were forests gathered together through long familiarity. In forests also there are dancing creepers full of juice &c. The elephant roamed in forests which as though came there in crowds (उपचित) to alleviate his torment. If we read घनैः, the words चिर...चितैः cannot be well-explained; clouds also cause creepers to dance when they pour water over them. विक्षिप्त...धोरणैः keepers that threw water mixed with juicy moss and bundles (विसरः) of lotus stalks (on them) looked like lakes. In lakes also there are waters, moss and lotus stalks. The chief words in the next clause are अपि च अतिस्थवीयसा ०दण्डेन अर्गलयन्तमिव सकलं ककुभां चक्रवालम्—and who seemed to chain the circle of the quarters by his very stout bolt-like trunk. स्थवीयस् comparative of स्थूल. प्रति...क्षिप्तेन (*adj.* of ०दण्डेन) that was tossed aloft as though he smelt (*lit.* took the wind) the ichor of some rival elephants. प्रतिगजदानपवनस्य आदानेन दूरक्षिप्तः तेन. अनेक...दरेण which was wavy with small lines of wrinkles (वलिः) round it as though with marks (lines) to reckon his victories in many battles. Ignorant persons reckon by drawing lines on the earth or wall &c. The wrinkles on the trunk are fancied to be such lines. Compare 'बहुयोजनगमनगणनसंख्याक्षरावलीभिरिव' &c. (text p. 27 l. 1). कुलशैलाः समुद्राः द्वीपाः काननानि च तैः सह (बहुव्रीहि)—*adj.* of चक्रवालम्. For the कुलपर्वतs, see above p. 76, for the seven seas p. 32 and the seven continents p. 3. एकं and अपरं qualify दन्तकाण्डम्. करा...पल्लवमिव—When a plant is watered it puts forth पल्लवs. The leaves of the कदली held in the trunk seemed to be the पल्लवs of his tusk, the tusk being watered by the juice oozing from the कदली stem. करान्तरे अर्पितेन. उद्गतानि पलाशानि यस्य. मुक्ताः पल्लवाः येन. It is not correct to understand मुक्तपल्लव as 'a shooting twig of pearls.' In that case मुक्तपल्लव cannot be properly dissolved and the उत्प्रेक्षा is not properly worked out. अपर...दन्तकाण्डं—From the other tusk hung down lotus fibres, which resembled रोमाञ्च due to his great zest for fighting. 'विसर्पन्त्या...कान्त्या'-these words are to be connected with वमन्तं, अर्पयन्तं, ०हसन्तं and कल्पयन्तम्. सर...वमन्तम्—His tusks were very white. कुमुद्s also are white. When the brilliance of the tusks spread all round, the poet fancies that he vomitted the कुमुद् bed that he had eaten when he sported in the lakes. On the use of वान्त in poetry, *vide* p. 50. निज...र्पयन्तम्—the brilliance of tusks spreading in the world is fancied to be his fame (which is white) spreading in all directions. कु...हसन्तम्—he seemed to laugh at lions that were naughty (दुर्ललित) because they had broken down some wretched worms of elephants. हास is white. कल्प...कल्पयन्तम् he seemed to make for himself a silken veil manufactured from the heavenly tree. The brilliance of his tusks spreading round his face looked like a fine white silken veil. हस्त...लक्ष्यमाणेन which (palate) was seen when he gracefully lifted up his trunk. रक्ता...वर्षन्तम् when he showed his red palate, he seemed to vomit the red lotuses he had devoured. His तालु was red like रक्तांशुक and fresh किसलय. A red तालु showed an excellent elephant and so did a brown (पिङ्गल) eye. Compare बृहत्संहिता 'ताम्रोष्ठतालुवदनाः' 67. 6. चूत...विसृजन्तम्—the plain idea is that the ichor flowing from his cheeks (करटः) was as fragrant as चूत, पारिजातक &c. 'काकेभगण्डौ करटौ' इत्यमरः. अहर्निशं...पतीनाम् that seemed to bestow on the elephants all the forests by दानपट्टकs, on which he gracefully placed his trunk, that were rubbed with a half-cut sugarcane reed, and that resounded with a swarm of bees. विभ्रमेण (लीलया) कृता हस्तस्य शुण्डायाः स्थितिः येषु. अर्धखण्डितं पुण्ड्रेक्षुकाण्डं तेन कण्डूयनं तस्मिन् लिखितैः. पुण्ड्र is a kind of very sweet red sugarcane. करिपतीनाम्—the genitive is used in the sense of the dative. दानपट्टकैः is used in two senses; (1) streams of ichor; (2) royal grants declaring a gift. All the clauses have an application to royal grants. विभ्रम...स्थितिभिः on which (royal copperplates or other edicts) the hand (royal signature) is gracefully (or hastily) made. Mark the use of the word हस्त in inscriptions as in 'स्वहस्तो मम &c'. Intro. p. XXIX footnote. लिखितैः suggests that royal orders are written with a pen (लेखनी) of reed (resembling इक्षुकाण्ड). वाचालितैः—royal grants are loudly read by the donees (who resemble bees that seek the दान). Take away the comma after क्रियमाणम्. शिशिरी० qualifies शिरः. अविरल...दधानम्—the idea is:—As the heat was intense, his high head was cooled with a garland made of pieces of ice. His head on which the white pieces of ice were placed seemed to be covered with a पट्टबन्ध (fillet) studded with bright jewels. The jewels resemble stars, as do the pieces of ice. A पट्टबन्ध indicated authority. *Vide* notes p. 116. 'बन्धुरं तून्नतानतम्' इत्यमरः. 'सैव नक्षत्रमाला स्यात्सप्तविंशतिमौक्तिकैः' इत्यमरः. As there were no pearls, but only icy pieces, the author says विभ्रमन० &c. आदौ स्थगितानि (covered, concealed) पश्चात् अपावृतानि (opened, laid bare) दिङ्मुखानि याम्यां. कर्णौ तालवृन्ते (fans) इव. As he flapped his large ears, he screened from view for sometime the worlds and then again allowed them to be seen. Compare for a similar conceit 'क्षणदृष्टनष्टाष्टदिङ्मुखं' &c. (text p. 27 l. 13). कर्ण...क्ष्मीम् out of devotion to his master, he, as though fanned Royal glory resting on the couch of his tusks. A lady resting on a couch of ivory (in summer) may be fanned by a servant. The elephant is a symbol of लक्ष्मी. Further the elephant helped the king to secure राजलक्ष्मी. The flapping ears would fan his tusks. आ...गतेन (1) that descended in a well-proportioned shape from the backbone (with बालधिना); that was handed down through a long family in succession (with चामरेण). A chowrie was one of the signs of royalty (आधिपत्यचिह्न) and may be handed down from father to son. चलता waving (applies to both चामर and बालधि). वंशः family; back-bone. आयत long. On आयत-वंश०, सं० remarks "आयतवंशः, वक्रवंशः, शरवंशः, बालवंशश्चेति चत्वारो वंशाः। तेषु बालवंश आयत एव शास्त्रकृतामभिप्रेतः। तथा च 'यावत्पूरितपाशश्च वंशश्चापलताकृतिः। शुभो क्षेयो गजेन्द्राणामायतः कुरुते सुखम् ॥' इति तैरुक्तम्। आयताद्वंशात्तत्क्रमेण गोपुच्छवदायत इति विग्रहः। समानार्हो हि बालधिः शोकं करोति। यदुक्तम् 'वक्रं स्थूलं च ह्रस्वं च पुच्छं कचविवर्जितम्। समानार्हं हि नागस्य भर्तुः शोककरं स्मृतम् ॥.' शीकर the spray from the elephant's trunk. दिग्विजयपीताः—he had drunk the waters of several rivers when he accompanied his master Harsha on the latter's दिग्विजय. अवधानदानेन निस्पन्दीकृताः (made motionless) सकलावयवाः येषु (*adj.* of वलनानां). अन्य...वलनानाम् of the twistings of his body when he heard the sound of the drum borne by other elephants. क्षण...शोचन्तम्–the idea is:—When he heard the sound of drums on other elephants, he attentively listened for a moment and then again became restless and trumpeted. A person, when insulted, heaves deep sighs. The author fancies that the elephant trumpeted because it wanted to convey that it was insulted by there being other elephants carrying drums and that it bewailed its own lot that it could not fight with those elephants. आरो...मुञ्चन्तम्—the elephant scratched the ground and dropped ichor (मद). The poet fancies that the elephant did these actions through shame at the humiliation of having to bear on his back the riders (आरोहाः). A person who feels ashamed scratches the ground and gives up pride (मद). अवज्ञया (आदौ) गृहीताः (पश्चात्) मुक्ताः कवलाः तैः कुपिताः आरोहाः तेषां आरटनस्य अनुरोधेन in obedience to the shouts of the riders &c. The riders shouted angrily when the elephant took up mouthfuls and then dropped them. मदस्य तन्द्रा (drowsiness) निमीलितः नेत्रत्रिभागः यथा स्यात्तथा. अनादरात् unwillingly. अवजग्धेभ्यः (eaten) तमालपल्लवेभ्यः स्रुतः श्यामलः रसः यस्मिन् (*adj.* of मुखेन). As the juice of तमाल leaves was dark, it resembled मद. मुखेनापि—it is from the temples that ichor flows. दल...र्पेण he seemed as though splitting with pride. It will be noticed that from these words up to सिञ्चन्तमिव सौभाग्येन, there are pairs of words, each of which begins with the same letter. So the reading दलन्तं is better than चलन्तम्. श्व...मदेन who breathed heavily as though through bravery (that finds no outlet), who swelled as though through pride. मूर्च्छन्तम् also means 'fainting.' मदेन through intoxication. स्फु...दानेन breaking through youth, flowing with ichor. He was so full of youthful energy that it, not being contained within him, as though split him up. वल्गन्तम् prancing. माद्य...त्साहेन he was as though intoxicated through arrogance and seemed to rise aloft through his energy. ताम्य...सौभाग्येन he gasped on account of his own brilliance, he smeared (everything) with his grace, he sprinkled (the world) with his loveliness. Heat (तेजस्) makes one languid (ताम्यत्). स्निग्धं smooth; affectionate. Smooth nails in elephants were highly thought of. "उक्तं च 'नखाः स्निग्धाः सिताः शस्ताः' इति" सं०. परुष rough; unkind. It will be noticed that the first words in each pair of clauses are contradictory as in स्निग्धं परुषं and गुरुं सच्छिष्यम्. गुरुम् large; teacher. सच्छिष्यं विनये a good disciple in modesty or discipline. मृदुं soft; affectionate. दृढं hard; firm (in friendship). ह्रस्वं...बन्धे short of neck. दरिद्रं slender; poverty-stricken. सत...दाने ceaselessly flowing with ichor; ceaselessly giving gifts. बलभद्र is बलराम, the elder brother of कृष्ण. मदलीलासु in pranks due to being in rut; pranks due to drink. भद्र is an elephant of the best type. *Vide* चाणक्य's अर्थशास्त्र II. chap. 31 for भद्र and मन्द्र elephants and बृहत्सं-

ह्निता 67. 1. 'भद्रो मन्द्रो मृगश्चेति विज्ञेया त्रिविधा गजाः.' बलराम was notorious for drinking. See विष्णुपु० V. 25. कुल...तासु who was like a high-born wife in his obedient nature. आयत्तता obedience, docility. जिनं क्षमासु a Jina in patience जिन may stand for Buddha or Mahāvīra, the founder of Jainism, both of whom laid emphasis on क्षमा. वह्नि...मोक्षेषु he was a very shower of fire, when he let loose his wrath. ना...षु (1) pulling out or lifting serpents; (2) in destroying elephants. Garuḍa is the implacable foe of serpents. दर्पशात destroyed his rivals in battle. कलहकुतूहलेषु in his eagerness for quarrels (or fights). नारद–*vide* p. 18. नारद is represented as always proceeding from heaven to earth and *vice versa* with some mission or news and as fond of quarrels. Note the Marathi expression 'कळीचा नारद'. He is therefore styled कलिप्रिय. शुष्का...स्कन्देषु—In the rains one expects अशनिपात. But a thunderbolt when there is no rain (no cloud) is unexpected. So दर्पशात made sudden (and hence terrific) attacks (अवस्कन्दः). वाहिनीक्षोभेषु (1) in agitating rivers; (2) in terrifying armies. आश्यां विषं यस्य सः आशीविषः सर्पः. दशनकर्मसु (1) in biting; (2) in using his tusks. पाश...ष्टिषु (1) in drawing (sinners) with the noose in his hand; (2) in drawing with his charming trunk. The word पाश at the end of compounds conveys the idea of 'beauty' as in केशपाश. प्रशस्तः हस्तः हस्तपाशः. The god Varuṇa, who in the Rigveda is represented as ruling over the moral laws of the world, has a पाश as his weapon. Compare 'उदुत्तमं मुमुग्धि नो वि पाशं मध्यमं चृत । अवाधमानि जीवसे' ऋग्वेद I. 25. 21. यम...वेष्टनेषु he is the net of Yama in entangling his enemies. 'वागुरा मृगबन्धनी' इत्यमरः. यम is represented as drawing the soul of a dying man with his पाश. Compare सावित्र्युपाख्यान (वनपर्व 297. 17) 'ततः सत्यवतः कायात्पाशबद्धं वशङ्गतम् । अङ्गुष्ठमात्रं पुरुषं निश्चकर्ष यमो बलात् ॥.' कालम् (1) dark; (2) time. परिणतिषु (1) in butting with his tusks; (2) in maturity or old age. Time makes one old or time brings to maturity one's actions. The elephant was dark and butted with his tusks or the elephant meant death (destruction) when परिणत as he butted against anything. परिणत when applied to an elephant has a technical sense. 'तिर्यग्दन्तप्रहारस्तु गजः परिणतो मतः' हलायुध quoted by मल्लिनाथ on शिशुपालवध 4. 29. तीक्ष्णकरः सूर्यः तस्य ग्रहेषु in eclipsing the Sun; तीक्ष्णं करेण ग्रहणं तेषु in seizing forcibly with his trunk. लोहिताङ्ग the planet Mars (that is red in appearance). वक्रचारेषु (1) in crooked movements; (2) in retrograde motion. The movements of the earth and the other planets round the sun give rise at times to an apparent retrograde motion. This occurs very often in the case of Mars and therefore वक्र itself means 'Mars.' When Mars is retrograde, it is an evil sign. अलातचक्रं a firebrand. मण्डल...ज्ञानेषु (1) in the knowledge of moving in a circle; (2) in the false knowledge of a circle of fire. If a firebrand is quickly revolved round, it produces the appearance of a circle of fire. The elephant knew how to move in a circle. The com. sees here a reference to difficult combinations of letters in a verse that were indulged in by certain poets like भारवि and माघ and were called चित्रबन्धs such as गोमूत्रिका. 'गोमूत्रिकामण्डले त्रिविधा हि गतिः। तत्रालातचक्रमुल्मुकचक्रं भ्रमणं करोति'. मनो...क्रमस्य—The elephant was big like a hill and he was very heroic, the result being that the king succeeded in whatever he desired. A चिन्तामणि was a fabulous jewel supposed to yield whatever one desired. दन्त...मानस्य the elephant is now called a palace of pride or high-mindedness. A palace may have columns of ivory and pearls. The elephant had tusks resembling (in whiteness) pillars of pearl stones. दन्तानां मुक्ताशैलानां च स्तम्भाः यस्मिन् स ०स्तम्भः निवासप्रासादः; दन्तौ मुक्ताशैलस्य स्तम्भौ इव तयोः निवासप्रासादः. घण्टा...हरम् charming with bells, chowries and ornaments. Both the elephant and the celestial car are so adorned. इच्छा...स्वितायाः the heavenly car of nobility or high spirits moving at will. The elephant conveys his master where he wishes. मद...क्रोधस्य to irritability he is a shower-bath of scented water, dark with a cloud of ichor-stream. मदधारा एव दुर्दिनं (rainy day) तस्य अन्धकारः यस्मिन्. 'मेघच्छन्नेऽह्नि दुर्दिनम्' इत्यमरः. धारागृह is comparatively dark and has scented water. The ichor is dark and has odour. सकाञ्चना प्रतिमा (image) यस्मिन्. A big temple is स...प्रतिम (has a golden image). The elephant also was स...प्रतिम; he had a head marked with gold. प्रतिमा is the part of an elephant's head between the tusks. Compare 'विपुलेऽपि पृथुप्रतिमो दन्त इव गणाधिपस्य मुखे' हर्ष० 4th उच्छ्वास, 2nd verse. निकेतनम् a house, (here) temple. क्रीडापर्वत has प्रस्रवणs (streams) and गण्डशैलs (boulders). The elephant also had प्रस्रवण (the flow of ichor) from his hill-like cheeks. गण्डौ शैलौ इव तौ च प्रस्रवणं (दानं) च तैः सह (with दर्पशातं); गण्डशैलाश्च प्रस्रवणानि (वारिप्रवाहाः) च तैः सह. 'गण्डशैलास्तु च्युताः स्थूलोपला गिरेः' इत्यमरः ('च्युताः भूकम्पादिना' क्षीर०). The elephant was hard like adamant (वज्र) and had tusks and neck (तोरणम्). A मन्दिर has an arched

क्ष्यान्तराणि courts (object of समतिक्रम्य). भुक्ते आस्थानमण्डपः तस्य पुरस्तात् in front of an audience-pavilion after he had taken his meal. For भुक्तास्थान, see above text p. 27. l. 32. स्थितम्—the principal sentence is स्थितं...चक्रवर्तिनं हर्षमद्राक्षीत् (p. 35. l. 17). The next clause is दूरा...वृतम्. दूरात् (surrounded) at a distance. ऊर्ध्वस्थितेन standing erect. All the adjectives qualify ०लोकेन ard ०स्तम्भमण्डलेन. प्रांशुना tall; the rays of which spread all round. प्रकृष्टाः or प्रसृताः अंशवः यस्य. व्यायामेन व्यायतं (firm, powerful) वपुः यस्य (with ०लोकेन); व्यायामव्यायतं वपुः यस्य that were as long (व्यायत) as the distance between the outstretched hands (about six feet). शस्त्रिणा armed; on which weapons were tied or that were shaped with instruments (with स्तम्भमण्डलेन). व्यायाम is the same as व्याम (Marathi वांव). 'व्यामो बाह्वोः सकरयोस्ततयोर्तिर्यगन्तरम्' इत्यमरः. मौलेन hereditary (मूलं वेत्ति मूलादागतो मूले भवो वा); placed on a base or pedestal. As the attendants were of ruddy complexion they are compared to golden pillars. आ...लोकम् near whom were sitting his distinguished (विशिष्ट) favourites. हरिचन्दन is a kind of very fragrant sandal. तुषारः ice. दन्त...पादे the feet of which (bedstead) were white being made of ivory; the rays of which are white like ivory. The words ०तले and ०पादे furnish the reason why the bedstead of pearl-stone is fancied to be made of the moon. शय...भुजे who rested the whole weight of his body on his arm that was placed on the end of the bedstead. दिङ्मुख...रममाणम्—the idea is:—The lustre of his body spread all round like a canopy (वितानं), being blended with the rays of jewels. As the Emperor with his vassal kings was bathed in the brilliance, he seemed to be bathing in a lake, the lustre being the water and the rays of jewels lotus fibres. A bath is very agreeable (सुभग) in summer. वितताः मणिमयूखाः यस्मिन् (*adj.* of ०विताने). राजकेन सह. For राजक, see p. 112. तेजसः...र्मितम्—Ordinarily every being is पञ्चमहाभूतात्मक. But he, being all brilliance, seemed to be created from the atoms of तेजस् alone. अनि...गृहीतम् he was seized by all auspicious marks in all limbs as though in order to place him on the throne, though he was unwilling to occupy it. The idea is—all his limbs had the auspicious signs as required by the सामुद्रिकशास्त्र. One who has such signs becomes a king. If a person be unwilling to sit in a place, he has to be made to occupy the place by being seized. The word गृहीत has two senses 'seized, accepted.' C and T think that in this clause there is probably a reference to the facts underlying Hiuen Tsang's story that Harsha at the advice of a Bodhisattva refrained from mounting the '*siṁhāsana.*' We do not think there is any such reference. The author indulges in an उत्प्रेक्षा on seeing the king occupying the throne and his great brilliance. Compare 'लक्षणैरपि रागाविष्टैरिवाधिष्ठितसर्वाङ्गाम्' (कादम्बरीम्) का० p. 186 of P. गृहीतं ब्रह्मचर्यं येन who was observing the vow of celibacy. There is विरोध between गृही...चर्यम् and आ...क्ष्म्या. Compare 'द्यूतं च जनवादं च परिवादं तथानृतम् । स्त्रीणां च प्रेक्षणालम्भमुपघातं परस्य च ॥' मनु० 2. 179 (ब्रह्मचारी वर्जयेत्). The विरोध can be got over by taking आ...क्ष्म्या as meaning 'who was possessed of royal glory.' गृ० may be explained in this way. According to Manu, a householder who was devoted solely to his wife and observed certain rules about cohabitation was as good as a ब्रह्मचारी. 'ऋतुकालाभिगामी स्यात्स्वदारनिरतः सदा । पर्ववर्जं व्रजेच्चैनां तद्व्रतो रतिकाम्यया ॥ निन्द्यास्वष्टासु चान्यासु स्त्रियो रात्रिषु वर्जयन् । ब्रह्मचार्येव भवति यत्र तत्राश्रमे वसन् ॥' मनु० III. 45 and 50. The com. refers to a curious tradition "था त्वेवमनुश्रूयते 'यावन्मया न सकला जिता भूमिस्तावन्मे ब्रह्मचर्यम्' इति श्रीहर्षः प्रतिज्ञातवान् । द्वादशभिश्च वर्षैर्जित्वा तां महिषीमब्रवीत् 'प्रतिज्ञा मे निर्व्यूढा' इति । ततो रोषात् 'अहमपि द्वादशवर्षं ब्रह्मचर्यं चरामि' इति सा प्रतिज्ञामकरोत् । इति ब्रह्मचर्येणाशाकालोऽतिवाहितः." We may expllain गृहीत० as गृहीता ब्रह्मणः वेदस्य चर्या येन 'who practised the study of the Veda.' In the next clause also there is an apparent विरोध. प्रतिपन्नं (accepted) असिधाराधारणव्रतं येन. A ऋषि has nothing to do with wielding a sword. So he could not be called a consistent (अविसंवादिन्) ऋषि, as he wielded a sword. But there is no inconsistency in his wielding the sword for protecting the good and the distressed and in being a saintly king (राजर्षि). प्रति० suggests another sense 'who wields the sword against those that come to him for protection'. प्रतिपन्नेषु असिधाराधारणं व्रतं यस्य. If he does so, how can he be called a राजर्षि (whose first duty is to protect)? Compare मनु I. 89 and 10. 80. प्रति० also means 'who observes the vow called असिधाराव्रत.' A ऋषि would observe such a व्रत. It is explained as 'यत्रैकशयनस्थापि प्रमदा नोपभुज्यते । असिधाराव्रतं नाम वदन्ति मुनिपुङ्गवाः ॥.' *Vide* मल्लिनाथ on रघु 13. 67. विषम...धर्मे who firmly clung to धर्म as though through fear of stumbling in his steps placed on the uneven path of kings. विषमः (uneven, difficult to carry out) राजमार्गः (royal road, the duties of kings) तस्मिन् विनिहितं पदं (foot, position) तस्य स्खलनं (stumbling, deviating)

तस्य भिया (भीत्या). One who is afraid of stumbling on a public road supports himself (दुलम्ब) on a stick. भीते...सेव्यमानम् who was attended whole-heartedly by Truth that had obtained his word, as though it (truth) were afraid. The idea is:– all kings had given up truth; हर्ष alone stuck to it whole-heartedly. One who is abandoned by others becomes afraid and goes to another who would promise to protect him. लब्धा वाक् (रक्षणरूपा येन). Truth resorts to speech *i. e.* it is word that must be kept. वारविलासिनी nautch girl. प्रतियातना reflection. In the ten toe-nails of his feet the girls were reflected. The poet fancies that the ten quarters (the ten reflections) were bowing to him. दीर्घैः...वेक्षमाणम् with his long glances that reached the ends of the quarters he seemed as though to examine what the regents of the worlds had done or left undone. Bāṇa seems to use the word लोकपाल in the sense of दिक्पाल. The दिक्पालs and लोकपालs are eight, but slightly differ. 'इन्द्रो वह्निः पितृपतिर्नैर्ऋतो वरुणो मरुत् । कुबेर ईशः पतयः पूर्वादीनां दिशां क्रमात् ॥' इत्यमरः. 'सोमाग्न्यर्कानिलेन्द्राणां वित्ताप्पत्योर्यमस्य च । अष्टानां लोकपालानां वपुर्धारयते नृपः ॥' मनु 5. 96. मणि...करेण—मणि...पृष्ठे प्रतिष्ठिताः कराः (किरणाः, हस्ताः) यस्य. The sun's rays were reflected in his footstool (पादपीठ). One who makes a request may fold his hands at the feet of the king. भूषणप्रभया समुत्सारणं (driving away) तेन बद्धं पर्यन्ते मण्डलं (circle, ring) येन. The idea is:—daylight was eclipsed by the brilliance of his ornaments up to a certain distance from the king on all sides; beyond that he was surrounded by daylight as in a circle. So the poet fancies that daylight performed प्रदक्षिणा round him. The reading गलितोष्मणा would mean 'whose pride (or heat) was gone.' शौर्यमेव ऊष्मा तेन. He was so brave that he could not endure that the mountains should remain stiff before him. Heat (ऊष्मा) causes distress. फेना...इन्तम्—his personal grace being compared to the ocean, the white sandalwood paste applied to his body to alleviate heat is compared to the foam of the ocean. The reading भूभृद्भिः would mean 'that support the earth; kings.' The com. connects शौर्योष्मणा with फेनायमानम् 'जलं सन्तापेन सफेनं भवति'. This is not bad. एक...र्जित्येन on account of his greatness in wielding the sole sovereignty of the world. ऊर्जितस्य भावः और्जित्यम्. When the vassal kings fell at his feet, his image was reflected in their crest jewels. He could not endure that the kings should honour anyone else (even though his own reflection). Compare 'यः करधृतधौतासिप्रतिबिम्बितेनात्मनाप्यदूयत समितिषु सहायेन' हर्ष० 4th उ० 2nd para. दर्प...दधानम् who bore royal glory that, under the guise of the breezes of chowries, as though heaved many sighs through the pain of pride. He had snatched the राजलक्ष्मी of other kings. This rankled in her heart and she heaved deep sighs—the breezes set in motion by chowries. दुःखमासते अस्यामिति or दुःखं असिका इव poignant pain or grief. सकल...श्लिष्टम्—At the time of the churning, लक्ष्मी (the wife of विष्णु) rose from the *single ocean;* but he was embraced by लक्ष्मी that came to him bringing the *entire* लावण्य (beauty, salt) of the *four* oceans. This shows his superiority over विष्णु. In the case of विष्णु, लक्ष्मी did not bring all लावण्य (as the sea is still very salt).लवणस्य भावः लावण्यम्. In his case, लक्ष्मी brought all the लावण्य (beauty). आभरण...राज्ञाम् he as though distributed among the vassal kings thousands of rainbows produced from the radiance of his ornaments, as though they were sent by Indra as a present to him (हर्ष). The rays of his jewels presented rainbow colours and spread over his vassals. The poet insinuates that even Indra sent presents (इन्द्रधनुः) to हर्ष. प्राभृतम् present. 'प्रकर्षेण आराधनार्थं आभ्रियते ढौक्यते स प्राभृतम्' क्षीर०. For वि...राज्ञाम् compare above 'विलभमानमिव सर्वकाननानि करिपतीनाम्' text p. 30 ll. 21-22. मधु honey, wine. सम्भा...वर्षन्तम्—There is विरोध in his showering मधु when he had given it up. But he had given up (drinking) wine and he was very sweet in conversation. परित्यक्तमपि (as an *adj.* of the king) would mean 'though he was so poor, (still he showered मधु)'. The words अमृतं, हृदयं and श्रियम् in the three following clauses are similarly श्लिष्ट. काव्य...मन्तम्—One vomits what one has eaten or drunk. In discussion about poetry he poured out sweet words that were all his own (which he had not copied from anyone else). He had not drunk अमृत (only the gods did so) and yet he poured it out. विश्रम्भ०—In confidential conversations, he exhibited his हृदय though he did not draw it out (of his body). What is meant is he showed his real thoughts, though the persons speaking with him did not draw him out. प्रसादेषु...पयन्तम्—लक्ष्मी is निश्चल in him (and not चञ्चल as in other kings) and yet in showing favours he distributed it in various places (that is made लक्ष्मी leave himself). What is meant is that he distributed श्री (wealth) among worthy objects (स्थाने). वीरगोष्ठीषु in meetings of heroes. When he heard about the heroic deeds of his soldiers that had secured a victory his cheek became thrilled. The poet fancies that the thrill (रोमाञ्च) was due to the message of love whispered in his ear by रणश्री (victory). Love causes रोमाञ्च, which is one of the eight सात्त्विकभावs. *Vide* p. 79. उपांशु *adv.* secretly. अति...पातयन्तम् in talking about his past fights with warriors, he cast his glance at his favourite sword, as though it (दृष्टि) were a shower of स्नेह (affection, oil). He lovingly looked at his sword as his trusty companion in battles. When fighting is over (अतिक्रान्त) oil is applied to swords in order that they may not get rusty. परिहास...यन्तम्—when he smiled at jests, the rays of his teeth spread round the kings. The pure rays of teeth are fancied to be his good will (pure meaning) towards them. One who is afraid of great heat (प्रताप) will gain confidence, if a clear reservoir (of water) be shown to him. सकल...तिष्ठन्तम्—there is विरोध in saying that he was सकल० and yet stood in न्याय alone. न्याये तिष्ठन्तम् means (in a secondary sense) 'he held fast to the path of right'. The words अगोचरे, अभूमौ, अविषये, अमार्गे, अतिदूरे, अदिशि all mean the same thing and all the clauses are to be explained similarly, connecting स्थितम् with each. अगोचरे गुणानाम् (स्थितम्) who stood beyond the reach of गुणs. The idea is:—he was perfect in virtues; he was wanting in none and so there was no scope for any गुण to come to him and make him perfect. अवि...नाम् boons could not make him more prosperous than he already was. अदि...धर्मस्य he was beyond all comparison and there was nothing which धर्म could accomplish for him. अदृष्ट...स्थितम् he had an unprecedented vastness of glory (or wealth). All the words from अरुण to कृष्णकेशेन have two meanings, one referring to his body and the other to some देवता. अरुणाः (red) पादपल्लवाः यस्य. All the instrumentals qualify वपुषा. अरुणः (the charioteer of the sun) पादपल्लवे यस्य. सुगतौ (of graceful gait) मन्थरौ (slow) ऊरू (thighs) यस्य; सुगतः (बुद्धः) मन्थरयोः ऊर्वोः यस्य. वज्रायुधवत् (like the weapon thunderbolt) निष्ठुरं (hard) प्रकोष्ठस्य (forearm) पृष्ठं यस्य; वज्रायुधः इन्द्रः (वज्रं आयुधं यस्य) निष्ठुरे प्रकोष्ठपृष्ठे यस्य. वृषस्य इव स्कन्धः यस्य whose shoulder was stout like that of a bull; वृषः (धर्मः) स्कन्धे यस्य. 'वृषो हि भगवान्धर्मः' मनु० VIII. 16. भास्वान् (bright) बिम्बवत् अधरः (lip resembling the ripe *bimba* fruit) यस्य. भास्वान् (रविः) तस्य बिम्बं अधरे यस्य. प्रसन्नं (mild, gracious) अवलोकितं (glance) यस्य; प्रसन्नः अवलोकितः (अवलोकितेश्वरः) यस्य. अवलोकितेश्वर is a बोधिसत्त्व specially worshipped in northern Buddhism. Compare 'परमसौगतमप्यवलोकितेश्वरम्' हर्ष० 8th उ० 4th para. There is another possible explanation. प्रसन्ना अवलोकिते यस्य. This explanation keeps the symmetry of the passage. The first word in each clause is a देवता. That will be departed from if we take अवलोकित as the देवता. प्रसन्ना means 'wine', which is generally personified as वारुणी देवता. 'बभूव वारुणी देवी मदाघूर्णितलोचना ।' विष्णुपु० I. 9, 92. 'गन्धोत्तमा प्रसन्नेरा' इत्यमरः. The only objection is that वारुणी is not a देवता to which any honour would be paid by बाण and who would hardly be enumerated along with धर्म, कृष्ण &c. कृष्णाः केशाः यस्य; कृष्णः केशेषु यस्य. **P. 33.** मांसलाभिः (thick) मयूखमालाभिः मलिनितं (darkened) महीतलं येन (*adj.* of ०पीठे). माणिक्यमालया मण्डिता मेखला (girdle, centre) यस्य. महानील was a kind of blue gem. कलि...चरणम्—to plant one's left foot on another's head is symbolical of utterly humiliating him. कलि, being an age of sin, is dark. The poet fancies that the blue footstool on which the king's foot rested was the head of कलि, the idea being that Harsha's reign ousted the evil age of sin. आक्रान्त...क्षम्—who looked like the child Krishna (पुण्डरीकाक्ष) that trod on the line of the hoods of कालिय. The foot-stool of blue gems looked like the dark hoods of कालिय. हर्ष was lotus-eyed (पुण्डरीकाक्ष). The serpent कालिय was in the waters of the Jumna and rendered it poisonous. No tree except a कदम्ब grew on its banks. कृष्ण threw himself from the कदम्ब into the river and trampled upon the hoods of the serpent. The serpent and its wives begged कृष्ण to be merciful. कृष्ण said 'नात्र स्थेयं त्वया सर्प कदाचिद्यमुनाजले । सभृत्यपरिवारस्त्वं समुद्रसलिलं व्रज ॥ मत्पदानि च ते सर्प दृष्ट्वा मूर्धनि सागरे । गरुडः पन्नगरिपुस्त्वयि न प्रहरिष्यति ॥' विष्णुपु० V. 7. 75-76. क्षौमवत् पाण्डुरेण pale like fine linen (with प्रतानेन); क्षौमेण पाण्डुरः तेन pale-white with fine linen (with ०बन्धेन). ०प्रतानेन...यन्तम्—The bright rays of the toe-nails spread over the earth; the poet fancies that they were the पट्टबन्ध, which he conferred on the earth and thus raised her to high rank. The earth is often spoken of as the wife of a king. A crowned queen wears a पट्टबन्ध (tiara) of fine silk or linen. *Vide* notes on पट्टबन्ध p.116. All the words from ०लोहितौ to ०चिह्नौ qualify चरणौ. अप्र...लोहितौ-his feet were naturally red. The poet fancies that they became red because the लोकपालs did not bow to them. For लोकपाल see above p. 140. सकल...धारयन्तौ—the idea is:—when the vassal chiefs bowed their heads at his feet, the yellowish (अतिपीत) brilliance of his feet resembling the पद्मराग (rubies) spread over them; the rosy light of his feet resembled the rosy hues of evening, when the disc of the luminary (the sun) sets. His feet also deprived all powerful persons (तेजस्विन्) of their might. His feet as though drank (पीत) the light of rubies अशेष...स्नवन्तौ—the hue of his feet was like that of the honey in the flowers of the chaplets on the heads of kings (which heads were placed on his feet). समस्त...रहितौ—his feet were never left by bees because they were attracted by the fragrance of the chaplets (उत्तंस) of the chieftains who bowed their heads. The dark bees looked like the heads of his enemies covered with hair (their crowns being wrested from them). पुंस्युत्तंसावतंसौ द्वौ कर्णपूरेऽपि शेखरे' इत्यमरः. संवाहनं shampooing. श्रियो...कल्पयन्तौ—his red feet resembled red lotuses and were charming (*i. e.* लक्ष्मी waited on them to shampoo them). लक्ष्मी is represented as dwelling in a red lotus. Mark the name पद्मालया given to लक्ष्मी. Compare 'अधोमुखेन चक्षुषा शिक्षयन्तमिव लक्ष्मीलाभोत्तानितमुखानि पङ्कजवनानि विनयम्' हर्ष० 4th उ०. जलजशङ्खमीनमकराः तैः सनाथं तलं ययोः तयोः भावः ०तलता तया. जलजं कमलम्. The soles of his feet were marked with lines that resembled a lotus, conch &c. These are looked upon as very auspicious signs and as indicative of greatness. कथित...चिह्नौ इव that had marks announcing his sovereignty of the four oceans. There were four marks जलज, शङ्ख, मीन and मकर and these four indicated that he would rule over the four oceans (*i. e.* the whole world). ०मुसलाभ्याम् and the following instrumentals are to be connected with ऊरुदण्डाभ्याम्. ०मुसलाभ्याम् his thighs were like huge (pestle-like) tusks of दिग्गज. विकट...बन्धुराभ्याम् that were uneven (or charming) on account of the obstruction caused by the block of flesh over the knees. For मकरमुख see notes p. 52. The evenness of his thigh was broken by the protuberant (fleshy) part above the knee. उद्वेलः (going beyond the usual water line) लावण्यपयोनिधिः. फेनेन आहिता शोभा ययोः. His thighs that were charming looked more beautiful by being rubbed over with the polishing powder of white cuttle-fish bone (फेनः). The ocean also looks charming with foam. चन्दन...मूलाभ्याम्—at the foot of sandal trees, serpents (भोगिन्) dwell, in whose hoods jewels were supposed to exist. The roots of his thighs were coloured by the head jewels of kings (भोगिन्) that bowed ot his feet. ०रश्मिभिः रज्यमानं मूलं ययोः. 'भोगी भुजङ्गमेऽपि स्यादाममात्रे नृपे पुमान्' मेदिनी. हृदये आरोपितः भूभारः तस्य धारणाय माणिक्यस्तम्भौ. His fair thighs were like ruby pillars. Pillars support weight. His thighs supported his broad chest (हृदय) on which rested the earth. His mind cared for the government of his kingdom. Compare for a similar conceit 'विशालवक्षःस्थलोपलवेदिकोत्तम्भनशिलास्तम्भाभ्यां...ऊरुदण्डाभ्याम्' (text p. 10 ll. 7–8). The words from अमृत...पाण्डुना to ०शोभिना qualify both अधरवाससा (lower garment) and ०निर्मोकेण (slough of the serpent वासुकि). For mountain मन्दर as the churning handle and the serpent वासुकि as the rope (नेत्रम्), see notes p. 52. The king looked like मन्दर and his lower garment like slough. ०पिण्डवत् पाण्डुना (०वाससा); ०पिण्डेन पाण्डुना (with ०निर्मोकेण). As अमृत was churned out of the ocean, its foam might have stuck to मन्दर. मेखला girdle; the central part of a mountain. The garment was covered with the jewels of the girdle she wore. The slough had the rays of the jewels on the centre of मन्दर. नितम्बः hips; slopes. व्यासङ्गिन् in contact with, clinging. पयः water, milk. It was the क्षीरसागर that was churned. नेत्र...शोभिना charming by the texture of the silken (नेत्रं) threads; charming on account of being placed on the rope. 'स्याज्जटांशुकयोर्नेत्रम्' इत्यमरः, 'नेत्रं मन्थगुणे वस्त्रभेदे मूले द्रुमस्य च' मेदिनी. अघनेन...मानम्—the king looked like the expanse (आभोगः) of the world. He had a second garment (upper one). The world also has अम्बर (the sky). अघनेन not thick (*i. e.* fine); without clouds. स...गणेन spotted with stars of various colours; full of stars (sky). उपरिकृतेन that he wore on the upper part of his body; that is overhead. इभ...राजमानम्—his broad (उरु) chest (उरःकवाटं panel-like chest) is compared to स्फटिकतट and he himself is compared to कैलास. इभ...मसृणेन (applies both to ०कवाटेन and ०तटेन in the same sense) glossy though hardened by being struck with the tusks of elephants. The king was struck in battles and elephants are found in the कैलास range. अपर्याप्तः अम्बरप्रथिमा यस्य which was not contained within the limits of his dress (coat); which was not contained within the limits of the sky. वाहिनी army; river. संक्षोभः shock; agitation. कैलास is white and very high and so is chosen for comparison. श्री...पातितेन (हारदण्डेन)—his long neklace looked like a dividing line for separating the respective realms of glory and learning. The proper sphere of सरस्वती is the mouth and of राज्यश्री the chest (on which it is represented as resting). So the necklace at the neck serves to separate these two. शेषेणेव—the necklace resembled in colour the शेष serpent. तस्य (हर्षस्य) भुजस्तम्भे विन्यस्तः समस्तः भूभारः तेन लब्धं विश्रान्तिसुखं तेन प्रसुप्तेन. शेष is supposed to support the earth. Compare 'त्रिभुवनभारधारणसमर्थं शेषफणामण्डलोपकरणैरिव कल्पितम्' हर्ष० 4th उ० and notes thereon. The poet fancies that the necklace lying on his chest is the serpent शेष gone to sleep because it has no longer to support the earth. परिवेष्टिता कन्धरा यस्य. जीविता...स्थलम्—His chest was covered with the pure rays of the pearls of the necklace. They looked like a bark garment (चीरं) which is worn when a person carries out the vow (दीक्षा) of making a gift of all he possessed as long as he lived. In this one may see a reference to the practice of Harsha, as narrated by Hiouen Tsang, of giving everything in charity once every five years. *Vide* Intro. XL. In the विश्वजित् sacrifice, everything was given away. **'स विश्वजितमाजह्रे यज्ञं सर्वस्वदक्षिणम् ।'** रघु० IV. 86. अज...महीधरम्—In this clause, the principal part is अरुणैः...धरम्—with the reddish rays of the jewels of the armlets (he wore on the upper arms) he seemed to be a mountain of rubies having as though outstretched canopy-like wings of jewels. Formerly Mountains had wings; *vide* p. 84. प्रसारितं मणिमयं पक्षवितानं यस्मिन्. In अज...र्भवद्भिः there are three उत्प्रेक्षाs suggested by the spreading rays of the jewels on the armlets. अज...रोहद्भिः as if they (rays) were other arms freshly growing with the desire of vanquishing Vishṇu. Vishṇu has four arms; so the king in order to rival him had as if growing on his arms others in the form of the rays. **'अजा विष्णुहरच्छागाः'** इत्यमरः. बाहुरेव उपधानं (pillow) तस्मिन् शेते इति ०शायिनी. बाहू...गलद्भिः-लक्ष्मी is poetically represented as resting on the arm of a king. Women used to place a lotus as an ornament on the ear. The rays of the jewels resembled the honey in a lotus (which is yellowish red). भुज...र्भवद्भिः—the pencils of rays looked like long avenues that served as the outlets for the प्रताप (prowess; bright light) of his arms. भुजात् जन्म यस्य. In the next clause the principal part is अति...हरन्तम्—with his very long arms he simultaneously deprived the regions and their guardians of their आयति (length; might or greatness). 'स्यात्प्रभावेऽपि **चायतिः'** इत्यमरः. Long arms were looked upon as a sign of greatness. For दिक्पाल, see above p. 140. सकल...र्गलेन which (arms) were the bolts to all the paths of लोकालोक. A bolt blockades the path leading to a destination beyond the door. लोकालोक is a mythical mountain in पुष्करद्वीप, the last of the seven द्वीपs. On the other side of the mountain there was complete darkness and on this side, the sun and light. See विष्णु पु० II. 4. 'लोकालोकस्ततः शैलो योजनायुतविस्तृतः । ततस्तमः समावृत्य तं शैलं सर्वतः स्थितम् । तमश्चाण्डकटाहेन समन्तात् परिवेष्टितम् ॥' 95-96. Note 'लोकालोकजूंषि...पूषा पुनरपि

सज्जहार जालकानि रोचिषाम्' हर्ष० 8th उ० last para. His arms protected the world up to लोकालोक. सकल...र्गलेन also means 'that were the bolts to the vision of all people *i. e.* that arrested the sight of all people by their prowess'. चतु...कारेण that were the stone wall to the ditch (खातं) of the circle of the four oceans. He ruled over (*i. e.* protected the earth girt by) the four oceans. Ordinarily it is the ditch that surrounds the wall. But his wall-like arms protected (surrounded) the ditch-like oceans. सर्व...पञ्जरेण—He had vanquished all great kings by the adamantine power of his arms. A राजहंस (swan) may be confined in a cage (पञ्जरं). भुवन...तोरणेन—The लक्ष्मी (*i. e.* the dominion) of the worlds came to him (*lit.* entered him) by the power of his arms. A person makes an entrance under an auspicious तोरण (arch). His arms were decked with jewels and so are said to be मणितोरण. सोदर्य...दिङ्मुखानि—the idea is:—his red lip cast its red lustre in all directions. The poet fancies that the red lip was कौस्तुभमणि that had become a part of his mouth with the desire of kissing लक्ष्मी, its sister, (that dwelt with the king). Both लक्ष्मी and कौस्तुभ were born of the ocean, when the fourteen jewels were churned out and so are here said to be सोदर्य. दिङ्मुखानि is the object of सिञ्चन्तम्, which qualifies हर्षम् below. The redness (राग) of the lips spreading all round is fancied to be the exudation of the पल्लवs (that are red) of पारिजात. अन्तरान्तरा at intervals. प्रकीर्यमाणः विमलानां दशनशिखानां प्रतानः येषु (*adj.* of स्मितैः). शिखा ray of light. अन्तरा...दर्शयन्तम्—the idea is:—when he smiled at the jests of his friends, bright rays from his white teeth shot forth. The poet fancies that the king displayed the light of intelligence to लक्ष्मी that is by nature dull. The two clauses ending with प्रेषयन्तम् and विसर्जयन्तम् are to be connected with सुहृ...स्मितैः. मुखेन जनितः इन्दुसन्देहः तेन आगतानि. His face was like the moon. कुमुदs are white like स्मित and open at night. The poet fancies that कुमुद lotus plants in the form of smiles had come mistaking his face to be the moon. He sent them away in the form of the spreading rays of his teeth. स्फटिकवत् धवलाः दशनाः तेषां पङ्क्तिः तया कृता कुमुदवनशङ्का तया प्रविष्टाम्. His smile was like autumnal moonlight, which rests on कुमुदs blooming at night. मदिरा...जातानां गन्धः गर्भे यस्य. भरिताः सकलाः ककुभः दिशः येन. His mouth (that had partaken of ताम्बूल) emitted a fragrance like that of wine, अमृत and पारिजात. मदिरा, अमृत and पारिजात were among the jewels churned out of the ocean, when their combined fragrance must have spread over the world. मदिरा...गर्भेण may also mean '(his mouth) that had the fragrance of ambrosial wine and पारिजात (a fragrant powder).' For पारिजात in this sense, see text p. 9. l. 27 'अतिसुरभि...पारिजातकपरिमलमुचा...मुखेन... वसन्तमिव वमन्तम्.' विकच...वंशेन—the fragrance of his breath was as though continuously inhaled by his high overhanging nose which was the pericarp cup of his lotus-like face. चक्षुषः... कुर्वाणम्—the brilliance of the white of his eye spread all round. It seemed as though the world was flooded by the Milky Ocean rising high (उद्वेल) at the rise of the moon of his unsurpassed face. अपूर्वः वदनमेव चन्द्रः तस्य उदयेन उद्वेलः क्षीरोदः तेन प्लावितानि. विग्रहिणी = शरीरिणी. The female chowrie-bearer was reflected in his bright cheek. The poet fancies that in the form of reflection he bore the embodied सरस्वती in his mouth. सरस्वती is described as मुखनिवासिनी or रसनाग्रनर्तकी. ०शोचिषा = कान्त्या. लोहितायितः ललाटतटः यस्य. लोहितायित *past p. p.* of लोहितायति (or-ते) denominative verb from लोहित, according to 'लोहितादि-डाज्भ्यः क्यष्' पा. 3. 1. 13 and 'वा क्यषः' पा. 1. 3. 90. सरस्वतीर्ष्याकुपिता लक्ष्मीः तस्याः प्रसादने लग्नेन. The idea is:—The red rays of his crest jewel rendered his forehead red. The poet fancies that the redness of the forehead was due to the अलक्तक dye of the feet of लक्ष्मी sticking to his forehead when he bowed at her feet to appease her. लक्ष्मी was angry because he showed preference to सरस्वती. Sanskrit poets delight in dwelling upon the feud between लक्ष्मी and सरस्वती. आ...यन्तम् the principal idea is 'he was listening to the sweet (कल) song of bees that served as an ornament (अवतंसः) to his ear.' The author indulges in a metaphor derived from playing on a lute. आपाट...वादयताम् (of bees) that played on the small lute made up by the curved ends (कोटिः) of the jewel in his ear-ring and which (lute) was surrounded (वलयिनी) by a web of strings (तन्त्री) in the form of slightly red rays (of the jewels). The reddish rays resemble the copper strings of a वीणा. अन...चरणानाम् the bees constantly moved their feet (*i. e.* they hovered round the कुण्डलमणि). One playing on a lute has constantly to move his fingers. उप...मिव—as if they worshipped him by playing on a lute. It is from उपवीणयति a denominative verb. स्वर...शारदं (may be construed both with the king and with क्वणित) who was proficient in the understanding of the analysis of notes (with हर्ष); that (क्वणित) was eminent by its judicious evolution of the notes. The musical notes are seven. 'निषादर्षभगान्धारषड्ज-मध्यमधैवताः । पञ्चमश्चेत्यमी सप्त तन्त्रीकण्ठोत्थिताः स्वराः ॥' इत्यमरः. The next clause 'उत्फुल्ल...केशान्तम्' describes a wreath of full-blown मालती flowers that was placed on his locks. परिकलितः केशान्तः यस्य. For मुण्डमाला, see text p. 9. l. 19. राज...वलयेनेव—the wreath of white मालती flowers was like moonlight and bright rays of nails. The poet fancies that it (मालती wreath) was the moonlight of the nails of राजलक्ष्मी when the latter took hold of his hair in playful dalliance. मुख...मण्डलेन—the मालती wreath was like the halo (परिवेशः) of the moon, *viz.* his face. शि...भुवा proceeding from the ornament in his top-knot. शिखण्डः = चूडा. शिखण्ड...मानम् The blending of the bright light of pearls and of the rays of dark-green emerald in his top-knot presented the appearance of the braidlike stream of the Ganges and the Jumna at Prayāga (Allahabad). The poet fancies that the confluence of the holy rivers came of its own accord for anointing him as king. At a king's coronation (अभिषेक) the water of holy rivers is used. The water of the Ganges is white and of the Jumna dark. अन्यो...वृजिनेन turbid by being mixed with each other (with ०वारिणा and ०कलापेन). वृजिन also means 'curved' (with वारिणा). In the next clause 'श्रमजल...सर्वतः' (l. 32), the chief part is 'वार...सर्वतः'—whose loveliness was being eclipsed on all sides by dancing girls. All the words in the instrumental plural (feminine) are to be connected with ०विलासिनीभिः. श्रम...लेखाभिः whose crescent-like foreheads were blackened by the darkness (कालिमन् *m.*) produced through the mark of thick black agallochum *tilaka* that melted by the drops of perspiration, as though it (darkness) were a dark callosity (किणः) due to their repeated prostrations at his feet that were agreeable on account of their coaxing requests. If one's forehead is rubbed repeatedly in prostrations, a dark mark (किण) may be produced. चाटु *m. n.* endearing words. क्षुभित...मानाभिः enveloped by their flashing necklaces (or garlands) that rose up from their agitated hearts, as if they were masses of उत्कलिकाs. The word मानस has three senses here. The हारs rolled (through dancing) on their swelling bosoms (मानस). उत्कलिका longing; wave. Their minds were agitated with longings. The मानस lake is tossed by waves. विलास...र्जयन्तीभिः that as though rebuked Lakshmî herself in jealousy with their charming creeper-like eyebrows that were tremulous (चटुल) with their playful movements (वल्गनं). भ्रूः एव लता तस्याः आकल्पैः (ornamentation). The eyebrow becomes curved in threatening a person. The reading भ्रूलताकम्पैः of B is more easy. आ...कर्षन्तीभिः drawing (captivating) him (हर्ष) by their long (deep) sighs thick with perfume as though they (sighs) were bonds made of the *malaya* breeze. अविरलः परिमलः येषाम् (goes with श्वसितैः and पाशैः). They breathed hard through the effort of dancing. For मलयमारुत, see p. 76. मलयमारुत is redolent with the perfume of sandal and excites love. विकट...द्धरन्तीभिः. विकट large. वराटकः rope **'वराटकः पद्मबीजकोशे रज्जौ कपर्दके'** मेदिनी. ०लावली एव वराटकः तेन वेष्टितं मुखं येषाम्. स्तनौ एव कलशौ. रसः feeling; water. Water is taken out by means of jars to which ropes are attached. On their breasts rolled garlands of *Bakula* flowers which resembled ropes. कुचो... शयन्तीभिः forcibly (हठात्) making him enter their hearts after dragging him with the rays of the central gems of their necklaces which shook to and fro on account of the trembling of their bosoms. 'तरलो हारमध्यगः' इत्यमरः. प्रभां मुञ्चन्तीति तेषां प्रभामुचाम्. The spreading rays of their jewels looked like out-stretched arms. जृम्भानां अनुबन्धेन वन्धुरं वदनं एव अरविन्दं तस्य आवरणीकृतैः that covered their lotus-like mouths that looked charming (वन्धुर) by continuous yawning (जृम्भा). They yawned on account of the heat and the fatigue of dancing. उत्तानैः open. सर...रुन्धतीभिः—the idea is:- They closed their yawning mouths with their open hands. The poet fancies that they did so because they wanted to confine their hearts that started hastily in order to come out of their mouths. The heart is inside the body and as though wanted to come out of the opening mouth. Their minds were impetuous in their love for the king. A lotus flower also opens (जृम्भा) and is covered with the rays (कर) of the sun. मानस means also the मानस lake in which there are lotuses. मदनेन अन्धं ०कुलं तेन कीर्यमाणाः कर्णकुसुमस्य (of the flower placed on the ear as ornament) रजःकणाः तैः कूणितः (contracted) कोणः (corner) येषाम्. कुसुमशरः मदनः तस्य शरैः प्रहारः तेन मूर्छा तया मुकुलितानि (closed). One who receives a terrific blow faints and closes his eyes. Their eyes were contracted because pollen entered them; the poet fancies that they were closed by the swoon due to their being struck by the arrows of Cupid. चतु...न्तीभिः that skilfully cast (their eyes at the king). अन्योन्य...डयन्तीभिः that struck the blue lotuses on their ears with their glances playfully shot u

i. e. the Ganges. In this and the following clauses, the poet establishes by श्लिष्ट words that Harsha deserved certain epithets far better than many heroes of old to whom they were applied. शन्तनु married the Ganges. Their son was भीष्म. Vide महाभारत आदिपर्व chap. 98-99. गङ्गा married for the sake of the eight Vasus who were cursed by वसिष्ठ. She plunged in water each son as he was born. When the 8th was born, she spared him at the pressing request of शन्तनु and left him. The ablative शन्तनोः is used in accordance with 'पञ्चमी विभक्ते' पा. 2. 3. 42 (विभागो विभक्तम् । निर्धार्यमाणस्य यत्र भेद एव तत्र पञ्चमी स्यात् । माथुराः पाटलिपुत्रकेभ्य आढ्यतराः । सि. कौ.). जितकाशिनम्—has several senses. भीष्म vanquished काशिराज and married his daughters अम्बिका and अम्बालिका to विचित्रवीर्य, son of शन्तनु and सत्यवती. See आदिपर्व chap 102. जितः काशी (काशिराजः) येन. जितकाशी also means 'जितेन्द्रिय.' शन्तनु fell in love with सत्यवती, the daughter of a fisherman. Out of fear of Bhīshma, he would not allow शन्तनु to marry her. भीष्म promised to resign the kingdom in favour of the son of सत्यवती. Then the fisherman said that he feared that भीष्म's sons would contest the claims of सत्यवती's son. Thereupon भीष्म promised to remain a celibate all his life and carried out the promise. See महाभारत आदिपर्व chap 103. जितकाशी also means 'proud of victories' (जितेन जयेन काशते शोभते इति जययुक्तः). द्रोण was the teacher of the कौरव and पाण्डव princes in धनुर्वेद. See p. 9 for the story of his birth. चापे लालसम् fond of the bow. We may also explain चापले अलसम् (with the king) 'who was averse to follies'. We may separate as च अपलालसम् (अपगता लालसा यस्मात्) 'who was free from desires'. गुरुपुत्र is a term applied to अश्वत्थामा, the son of द्रोण, who was the गुरु of the कौरवs and पाण्डवs. अमोघाः (unerring, reaching the mark) मार्गणाः बाणाः यस्य. अमोघं मार्गणं (याचनं) यस्मिन् requests made to whom were never fruitless. The point of the allusion in the case of अश्वत्थामा is this:-When भीमसेन ran after अश्वत्थामा to kill the latter for his night attack, he discharged a terrible missile called ब्रह्मशिरः for the destruction of all the पाण्डवs. अर्जुन discharged an equally terrible अस्त्र, but only for the purpose of nullifying the effect of अश्वत्थामा's missile and not for killing अश्वत्थामा. Later on अर्जुन withdrew his अस्त्र, but अश्वत्थामा could not do so. The अस्त्र, being अमोघ, deprived अश्वत्थामा of his jewel on the head and killed the गर्भ of उत्तरा by way of a compromise at the desire of Vyāsa. *Vide* सौप्तिकपर्व chap. 13-15. 'गर्भेषु पाण्डवेयानाममोघं चैतदुत्तमम् । न च शक्तोऽसि भगवन्संहर्तुं पुनरुद्यतम् ॥'

chap. 15. 32. कर्ण was the son of कुन्ती, born mysteriously from repeating a Mantra sacred to the Sun. See आदिपर्व chap. 111. So he is represented as the son of the Sun who took special interest in him. मित्रप्रियम् dear to his friends (with the king). कर्ण also was dear to his friend दुर्योधन. बह्वी क्षमा (forbearance, patience) यस्य (with युधिष्ठिर). बहुक्षमम् who ruled over plenty of land (with हर्ष). क्षमा earth. युधिष्ठिर was very patient even under the gravest of provocations (*viz.* द्रौपदीवस्त्रहरण). अनेकनागायुतानां बलं यस्य who had the strength of several thousands of Nāgas (with भीम); who had an army consisting of several thousands of elephants (with हर्ष). अयुतम् ten thousand. भीम was poisoned by दुर्योधन and thrown into water. He was taken to नागलोक, where through the favour of वासुकि he became endowed with the strength of thousands of नागs. *Vide* आदिपर्व chap. 128–129. 'यत्ते पीतो महाबाहो रसोऽयं वीर्यसम्भृतः । तस्मान्नागायुतबलो रणेऽधृष्यो भविष्यसि ॥' chap. 129. 22. धनञ्जय is अर्जुन, the greatest warrior in the great Bhārata war. महाभारत-रण-योग्यम् fit to figure in the great war of the महाभारत. महा-भार-तरण-योग्यम् worthy of wielding (*lit.* crossing) great responsibility (of governing the world). कारण...युगस्य—कृतयुग is an age of complete virtue and righteousness. Under Harsha also these reigned supreme. विबुधसर्गस्य (1) of the creation of gods (विबुधः); of the creation of wise men. He encouraged learned men. उत्पत्ति... दर्पस्य he was the first among the proud or confident. एकागारम् the only house. प्रातिवेशिकः a next door neighbour *i. e.* a very intimate friend; also 'closely resembling.' पुरुषोत्तमस्य of the best of men; of विष्णु. हर्ष befriended good men and resembled विष्णु. खनिपर्वत—a mountain where mines are opened (for jewels &c). सर्व...त्याः the music hall where all lores meet for सरस्वती. सरस्वती was delighted with him as one is delighted in a सङ्गीतगृह. He was the meeting place of all विद्याs. लक्ष्मीसमुत्थान (1) the rising of लक्ष्मी (out of the ocean); increase of royal glory. As there was already one लक्ष्मीसमुत्थान at the time of churning, the author uses the word द्वितीया°. बल...ग्ध्यस्य it was in him that cleverness exhibited its utmost strength. एक... तीनाम् in him all rules of good conduct were to be found in one place. सर्व...कान्तेः Beauty announced in his person her all-in-all *i. e.* he was the *beau ideal*, the *ne plus ultra* of loveliness. अप... सर्गस्य who was the perfection of the creation of the atoms of beauty. अपवर्गः completion, highest point. 'स्यादपवर्गस्त्यागे मोक्षे

कार्यावसानसाफल्ये' मेदिनी. There is another sense hinted at. Where there is अपवर्ग (*i. e.* मोक्ष), सर्ग (birth) comes to an end (अपवर्ग). सकल...राज्यस्य—the idea is:—he was so holy and pure that all the misdeeds of the kings (of all ages in securing kingdoms) were altogether got rid of by expiation. It is not proper to explain that his merit was sufficient to expiate all the sins of subjects put together (as Mr Kale does). सर्व...पैस्य he was as though the surprise attack of Cupid with all his forces *i. e.* he was irresistible in his charms. उपा...र्शनस्य he was a means of seeing पुरन्दर *i. e.* in him one saw पुरन्दर. पुरन्दर—Indra; one who storms cities. आवर्तनम् fusing together; practising. धर्म was as though put into a crucible and moulded into his form. He practised धर्म incessantly. कन्या...लानाम् as women confined in the अन्तःपुर move about freely there, so the कलाs were to be found only in him and to the fullest extent. परमप्रमाणं highest authority. राज...पतीनाम्—For प्रजापतिs, see above p. 18. When a sacrifice was finished, the sacrificer took a ceremonial bath called अवभृथस्नान. The प्रजापतिs, to whom was entrusted the task of creation, produced Harsha as the highest point (समाप्ति) of perfection in the creation of kings. गम्भीरं च प्रसन्नं च. There are three pairs of adjectives in each of which there is an apparent विरोध. गम्भीरम् (deep; serene). प्रसन्न transparent; gracious. When water is deep, we cannot see the bottom (it is not transparent). त्रासजननं—he produced fear in the irreverent or sinful. The com. refers to रघु I. 16. 'भीमकान्तैर्नृपगुणैः स बभूवोपजीविनाम् । अधृष्यश्चाभिगम्यश्च यादोरत्नैरिवार्णवः ॥'. कौतुकम् curiosity; admiration. What rouses one's curiosity may be sinful.

P. 35 ll. 18—33 दृष्ट्वा...करोत्. अनुगृहीत इव as though blessed (by the sight of such a holy king). निगृहीत इव as though checked (by the august appearance of the king). साभि...तृप्त इव eager (to see him more) and yet satisfied (by feeling blessed on seeing him). रोमाञ्चं मुञ्चतीति ०मुच् तेन. विस्मयेन स्मेरः (smiling). शोभनं जन्म यस्य. सुगृहीतं नाम यस्य whose name is honoured. चत्वारः उदधयः एव केदारं तेन कुटुम्बी who is a house-holder of the field in the form of the four oceans *i. e.* who looks upon the whole world as his family. Compare 'उदारचरितानां तु वसुधैव कुटुम्बकम् ।'. For ब्रह्मस्तम्भ, see above p. 102. हर्ष enjoyed the best the universe could yield. A केदारकुटुम्बी (*i. e.* an humble farmer) enjoys the standing crops. सकलानां आदिराजानां चरितं तस्य जये ज्येष्ठः (प्रधानः) मल्लः the foremost protagonist in vanquishing (*i. e.*

eclipsing) the deeds of the primeval kings (like मनु, पृथु). राजन्वती ruled by a good king. राजवती ruled by a king. 'सुराज्ञि देशे राजन्वान् स्यात्ततोऽन्यत्र राजवान्' इत्यमरः. 'राजन्वान् सौराज्ये' पा. 8. 2. 14. नास्य...चरितानि his youthful actions are not opposed to वृष (धर्म), as those of Kṛishṇa were. Even as a boy he did not do any rash act. कृष्ण killed a demon अरिष्ट that had assumed the form of a bull (वृष). *Vide* विष्णुपु० V. 14. In these and the following clauses up to न...श्रियः, the author shows by श्लिष्ट words the superiority of हर्ष to various deities. न...लसितानि the manifestations of his ऐश्वर्य (greatness, prosperity) do not cause sorrow to दक्ष (clever men), as those of शिव did. The king, though prosperous, does not offend the clever. ऐश्वर्य also means 'ईश्वरस्य शिवस्य भावः'. For दक्ष whose sacrifice was destroyed by शिव, *vide* p. 87. There is an emphasis on the word पशुपति. शिव acted very brutally in destroying his own father-in-law. न...वादाः There are no प्रवाद्s (rumours) about him indicating (पिशुन) the ruin of his गोत्र (family), as in the case of Indra. प्रवादाः also 'myths.' गोत्राः mountains (गां पृथ्वीं त्रायन्ते इति). There are myths relating that Indra destroyed the wings of mountains. Indra is therefore called गोत्रभिद्. *Vide* p. 84. 'पिशुनौ खलसूचकौ' इत्यमरः. दण्डग्रहणानि (1) taking of fines (as punishment); (2) holding the rod. दण्डधर is one of the names of यम. The king did not like to be too severe in exacting fines. नि...रक्षिताः guarded by thousands of pitiless (निस्त्रिंश)sea-monsters (ग्राहः). रत्नालयाः treasure-houses; the seas. In the sea we have cruel ग्राह्s. वरुण is the lord of the sea. निस्त्रिंशग्राह would mean 'swordsman.' धनदः = कुबेरः. न निष्फला...लाभाः obtaining his presence (*i. e.* an interview with him) is never fruitless *i. e.* he bestows gifts on those who come near him. In the case of कुबेर, the excellent निधिs (treasures) that he has secured are lying idle (he does not make a gift of anything). कुबेर is the lord of the nine निधिs. 'महापद्मश्च पद्मश्च शङ्खो मकरकच्छपौ । मुकुन्दकुन्दनीलाश्च खर्वश्च निधयो नव ॥'. न अर्थ...दर्शनानि the sight of him (हर्ष) is never bereft of solid gain *i. e.* when anyone sees him, one gets अर्थ (wealth) and people talk (वाद) about it. जिन must mean here बुद्ध. दर्शनानि means 'systems of philosophy'. अर्थ...शून्यानि not recognising the doctrine of the existence of (material) objects. There are four Buddhistic schools, सौत्रान्तिक, वैभाषिक (both of which maintained that thoughts as well objects are real), योगाचार and माध्यमिक (that maintained the unreality of thoughts, as well as objects). What is common to all these schools is the idea of क्षणिकत्व. The author here refers to the योगाचार school. That school holds that the only reality is विज्ञान (thought); there are no real entities (अर्थ or बाह्यार्थ) in the external world corresponding to the thoughts that a person is conscious of. This theory is called विज्ञानवाद. *Vide* वेदान्तसूत्र II. 2. 28 and S'aṅkara's Bhāshya thereon. Compare 'बौद्धबुद्धिमिव निरालम्बनाम्' कादम्बरी p. 131 of P. बहुलैः दोषैः उपहताः marred by many sins. श्रियः = लक्ष्म्यः. बहुलस्य कृष्णपक्षस्य दोषा (रात्रिः) तस्यां उपहताः (reduced). श्रियः—beauty. चित्रम् wonderful. अत्यमरम् surpassing the gods. अमरान् अतिक्रान्तं अत्यमरम्. 'अत्यादयः क्रान्ताद्यर्थे द्वितीयया' वार्तिक on पा. I. 4. 79. अपि...र्थिनः (न पर्याप्तो विषयः) and moreover suppliants do not afford a sufficient (पर्याप्त) scope for his liberality *i. e.* there is not a sufficient number of suppliants to enable him to exercise his liberality to the fullest. Understand 'न पर्याप्तो विषयः' in each of the following clauses and explain similarly. प्रज्ञायाः शास्त्राणि all the शास्त्रs do not give sufficient employment to his intellect. कवित्वस्य वाचः language fails to give adequate expression to his poetic gifts. सत्त्वं spirit, courage. उत्साह (energy) is one of the three शक्तिs of a king *viz.* प्रभुशक्ति, उत्साहशक्ति and मन्त्रशक्ति. व्यापाराः undertakings. कीर्तेर्दिङ्मुखानि the ten regions are not sufficient to contain his fame. गुण...संख्या—*i. e.* his virtues were beyond enumeration. कौशलस्य कला the 64 *kalās* did not exhaust his skill. अस्मिंश्च राजनि while this king rules. यती...ट्टकाः—योगपट्टक was to be seen only with यतिs and nowhere else (in another sense). For the योगपट्टक of ascetics, see p. 26 above. योगपट्टकाः—योगेन कूटकर्मणा युक्ताः पट्टकाः false or forged grants. For योग in the sense of 'deceit', *vide* the first verse of the 4th उच्छ्वास. There are numerous examples of परिसंख्यालङ्कार here. पुस्त...ग्रहाः—पार्थिवविग्रहs (earthen bodies; fights among princes) were to be seen in पुस्तकर्म only (in the manufacture of dolls). *Vide* notes on पुस्तकृत् above p. 90. षट्पदः = भ्रमरः. दान...लहाः the quarrels over receiving ichor; quarrels about the recovery of debts. As nobody incurred debts there were no quarrels about the recovery of money lent. वृत्तानां of metres. पादच्छेदाः division into four parts; the cutting off of feet. अष्टापदानाम्—*Vide* notes p. 24. चतु...ल्पना arrangement of the four members (*i. e.* chess); the cutting off of the four limbs (hands and feet). No one committed grave offences for which hacking of limbs was

14

prescribed by the Smṛitis. द्विज...द्वेषाः hatred of the chief of birds (*i. e.* गरुड); hatred of Brāhmaṇas and teachers. वाक्यविदाम् those who know the rules of the interpretation of Vedic sentences *i. e.* मीमांसकs. अधिकरणविचाराः examination of अधिकरणs (cases for discussion); considerations in a court of justice. No one resorted to the courts of justice, as there were no disputes. Or we may separate as अधिक-रण-विचाराः (thoughts of great fights). The पूर्वमीमांसा of जैमिनि and the उत्तरमीमांसा of बादरायण are divided into अध्यायs, each अध्याय into पादs and each पाद into अधिकरणs, each अधिकरण containing one or more सूत्रs and completely treating of one topic. अधिकरण has five members. 'विषयो विशयश्चैव पूर्वपक्षस्तथोत्तरम् । निर्णयश्चेति सिद्धान्तः शास्त्रेऽधिकरणं स्मृतम् ॥'. According to others the five members are विषय, सन्देह (or विशय), सङ्गति, पूर्वपक्ष and सिद्धान्त. उपवीती—'प्रोद्धृते दक्षिणे पाणावुपवीत्युच्यते द्विजः'—क्षीरस्वामी quoting from मनु-wearing the sacred cord in the usual manner (over the left shoulder and under the right arm). 'उपवीतं यज्ञसूत्रं प्रोद्धृते दक्षिणे करे' इत्यमरः.

P. 36 ll. 1-27. **अथोत्तरेण...मभूत्.** उत्तरेण...धिष्ण्यस्य not far to the north of the royal seat. Words ending in एन like दक्षिणेन and उत्तरेण govern the accusative or genitive. अपरवक्त्रम्—*Vide* notes p. 40. **Verse 5.** करिकलभ (vocative) young elephant ! लोलता = चञ्चलता. चर...व्रतम् observe the vow of discipline (humility). आनतं आननं यस्य whose head is bent (not held high in pride). मृगपतिनखवत् भङ्गुरः (curved). गुरुः formidable. उपरि held above (the elephant's head). क्षमते...शः the hook would not tolerate your लोलता. The अङ्कुश brought round the elephant when it became restless and disobedient. This verse contains a veiled rebuke of Bāṇa for his लोलता in his youth, when he was like करिकलभ. The words मृगपति and गुरुः (who teaches or chastises) refer to the king. The verse reminds the king of the presence of बाण, about whose चापल he had heard reports. Mr. R. R. Kale sees a veiled allusion to the king even in the words करिकलभ &c., but that does not seem to us to be proper. He takes गुरु as referring to the preceptor of the king. तं = बाणम्. गिरि...गम्भीरेण as deep as the roar (बृंहितं) of a lion in a mountain cave. एष... बाणः is he that बाण ? न...पश्यामि I shall not see him without showing him favour. Bāṇa conveys that the very way in which the king addressed him (महानयं भुजङ्गः) showed that the king had favoured him. The king spoke the words to the मालव

prince and then looked बाण in the face. The reading अकृतप्रसादम् (अकृतः प्रसादः यस्मिन्) would convey the same sense. नीलैः धवलैः अंशुकैः (किरणैः, वस्त्रैः) शाराम् (variegated) *adj.* of प्रभाम् and तिरस्करिणीम्. भ्रमयन्—the object is प्रभाम्. अपाङ्गे नीयमाना तरला तारका (pupil) यस्य. आयामिनीं long *i. e.* spreading. परिवृत्य having turned (his body). In order to look at the मालव prince, he turned his eye sideways (तिर्यक्). The rays of the dark pupil became mixed with the lustre of the white eye and so the lustre of the whole eye looked शार. The rays of the eye resembled a curtain made of white and dark silk. His pupil was moved towards the corner of the eye. A curtain may have stars on the borders (अपाङ्ग). प्रेष्ठ superlative of प्रिय. मालवराजसूनोः—(*Vid.* Intro. p. XXXII) this seems to have been माधवगुप्त the younger of the two princes that were the companions of Harsha and his elder brother. भुजङ्ग: a gallant, a man of dissolute habits. 'भुजङ्गः सर्पषिङ्गयोः' हेमचन्द्रः. तूष्णी...तस्मिन् when that (मालव prince) showed by his silence that he had not understood the king's words. अगमितं नरेन्द्रवचः येन. अविज्ञातं तत्त्वं येन who does not know the truth. अश्रद्दधान इव as if you do not believe me (in my real character). नेय इव like one led (by others). आज्ञापयसि—this and the correlative विज्ञापयामि or विज्ञापयति are employed by ordinary persons in addressing a person very much superior in the sense of वदसि, कथयामि &c. स्वैरिण: capricious, unrestrained. विचित्रा: various, strange. प्रवादाः rumours. महद्भि...तव्यम् but the great ought to see things as they are. नार्ह...शिष्टमिव you will please not misunderstand me, as if I were an ordinary man. अविशिष्टम् without anything to distinguish him. सोमपायिनाम् that drink सोम *i. e.* that performed the सोमयागs. संस्काराः the purificatory ceremonies performed in the case of a द्विज from conception to death, such as जातकर्म, नामकरण, उपनयन &c. साङ्गः—the अङ्गs (auxiliary branches of study) of the वेद are six, *viz.* शिक्षा (phonetics), कल्प (ritual of sacrifices), व्याकरण (grammar), निरुक्त (etymology and exegesis), छन्दः (metrics) and ज्योतिष (astronomy). In these three sentences बाण seems to have in view the well-known verse 'जन्मना ब्राह्मणो ज्ञेयः संस्कारैर्द्विज उच्यते। विद्यया याति विप्रत्वं त्रिभिः श्रोत्रिय उच्यते॥'. शास्त्राणि—such as अलङ्कार, न्याय, वेदान्त &c. दार...रिकोऽस्मि since my marriage I have been a diligent householder. 'कुटुम्बव्यापृतस्तु यः। स्यादभ्यागारिकः' इत्यमरः. 'अभितोऽगारे भवः अभ्यागारिकः' क्षीर०. कामे भुजङ्गता—this sentence is capable of three senses, two of which are principally intended. (1) Wherein consists my भुजङ्गता (being a lewd person)? What is there in all my life which deserves to be referred to in the words 'महानयं भुजङ्गः?' (2) भुजङ्गता is to be found only in काम (Cupid) and not in me. (3) What woman was embraced by me? (का मे भुजं गता). लोक... मासीत् but (I must admit) that my youth was not without those follies which are not inconsistent with the two worlds (*i. e.* this world and the next). He says he was guilty of trifling follies that would not be very much censured in this world or would not come in the way of his attaining heaven. अविद्यमानः अपलापः (concealment, denial) यस्य. अत्रा...स्मि I do not deny this much. अनेनै...हृदयम् my heart does feel repentance (विप्रतीसारः) for this. सुगतः = बुद्धः. शान्तमनसि—this, कर्तरि and दण्डभृति are to be connected with देवे. मना...स्थानाम् who carries out all the rules of the (four) Varṇas and the (four) *ās'ramas*, like Manu. Bāṇa refers probably to the मनुस्मृति wherein are laid down the rules of वर्णs and आश्रमs that were supposed to have been promulgated by Manu. *Vide* मनुस्मृति I. 2 and 107. सम...भृति when you wield the rod of punishment like यम. 'धर्मराजः पितृपतिः समवर्ती परेतराट्' इत्यमरः. Death deals equally with all; यम is also called दण्डधर. The king also is दण्डधर (he punishes wrongdoers). सप्ता...रशनाम् whose girdle is formed of the seven oceans. For the seven oceans, see p. 32. For the द्वीपs, see p. 3. अविशङ्कः without fear. क इव सर्व...कल्पयिष्यति what man possibly will act the part of improper conduct even in his mind, improper conduct which is closely related to all calamities. From अविनय spring all calamities. Even the *acting* of improper conduct is impossible; much more actual performance. आसतां...पेताः let alone human beings. मनुष्यस्य भावः मनुष्याणां समूहो वा मानुष्यकम्. त्वत्प्र...पिबन्ति In consequence of your power, even bees drink honey in fear. To drink मधु (wine) was a महापातक. So the bees are as though afraid of the punishment that may be meted out to them. 'ब्रह्महत्या सुरापानं स्तेयं गुर्वङ्गनागमः। महान्ति पातकान्याहुः संसर्गश्चापि तैः सह ॥' मनु० 11. 54. रथाङ्गं (चक्रं) नाम येषाम् (चक्रवाकाः). लज्जन्ते...प्रियाणाम् are ashamed of their great attachment to their mates. अभ्यनुवृत्तिः (pleasing, following) एव व्यसनं (vice; attachment). A चक्रवाक is a type of love. चपलायन्ते play their tricks. शरारवः destructive, ferocious. For शरारु see p. 23. सानुक्रोशा इव as though compassionate. पिशितानि = मांसानि. अन...ग्राहिण्यः understanding the minds of others as they are. अनपाचीन not opposite (to the real state of things).

P. 36 l. 28—**P. 37.** l. 32. **भूपति...णेति.** केवल...कथयत् he only revealed his inward pleasure by merely casting at him an affectionate glance which seemed to bathe him in a shower of nectar. The king did not show him any *outward* marks of favour such as सम्भाषण; but बाण understood from the king's look that *inwardly* the king was pleased with him. लम्बमाने hanging (on the western horizon). The next sentence is बाणोऽपि... निवासस्थानमगात् (l. 21). धौतः (washed, polished) आरकूटः (brass) तस्य इव कोमला आतपत्विट् यस्मिन् (*adj.* of वासरे). The light of the sun in the evening (on trees and mountains) looked like polished brass. निर्वाति *loc. sing.* of *pr. p.* of वा with निर्—to be extinguished. अस्ता...मति when the sun (मरीचिमत्), leaving the sky, the diadem (किरीटं) of the crest of the setting mountain, let fall his rays like the sprays of *Nichula* trees. 'कूटोऽस्त्री शिखरं शृङ्गं' इत्यमरः. निचुलमञ्जरीणामिव भाः येषाम्. निचुल is a tree with scarlet flowers. 'निचुलो हिज्जलोऽम्बुजः' इत्यमरः. रोमन्थेन मन्थराणि कुरङ्गकुटुम्बकानि तैः अध्यास्यमानं म्रदिष्ठं गोष्ठीनपृष्ठं यासु. रोमन्थ... स्थलीषु when the soft surfaces of deserted cowpens in the forests had families of deer sitting on them lazily ruminating. म्रदिष्ठ—superlative of मृदु. We must read गौष्ठीन. गोष्ठः भूतपूर्वः (that was formerly a cow-pen) गौष्ठीनं, according to 'गोष्ठात् खञ् भूतपूर्वे' पा. 5. 2. 18. शोका...तटीषु when the banks of rivers were plaintive with the cries (कूजितं) of the female चक्रवाक birds overwhelmed with sorrow. At the approach of night the चक्रवाकs were supposed to be separated from their mates. वासविटपेषु (on branches where they had made their nests) उपविष्टानि वाचाटानि चटकानां चक्रवालानि येषु. आलवालेषु (basins round trees) आवर्जिताः (emptied) सेकार्थं जलकुटाः (water pots) येषु—*adj.* of निष्कुटेषु (pleasure groves). 'घटः कुटनिपावस्त्री' इत्यमरः. 'गृहारामास्तु निष्कुटाः' इत्यमरः (कुटात् गृहात् निष्क्रान्ताः निष्कुटाः). दिवस...व्राते when herds of hungry calves (तर्णकः) began to suck the flowing udders of cows that returned after wandering (विहृतिः) the whole day. प्रस्नुताः स्तनाः यस्य (*adj.* of वर्गम्). स्तनन्धय—from स्तन and the root धे 1 P. to suck (स्तनं धयतीति), a nasal being inserted according to 'नासिकास्तनयोर्ध्माधेटोः' पा 3. 2. 29. उद्धृतं क्षीरं यस्मात्. Read चास्तधराधर°. अस्त...मण्डले when the disc of the sun, the boat in the ocean of evening (twilight), with red hue, sank (below the horizon), as though it were plunged into the flood of the stream (धुनी) of the minerals (धातुः) on the western mountain. गैरिक (red chalk) is particularly known as धातु (in the case of mountains). 'धातुर्मनःशिलाद्यद्रेर्गैरिकं तु विशेषतः' इत्यमरः. पतङ्गस्य इदं पातङ्गम्. The sun's disc became extremely red when about to dip into the ocean. The poet fancies that it was swept into the stream of red chalk. The disc resembles a small boat and the rosy hues of the evening sky resemble the sea. पानपात्रे is not so good as यानपात्रे. It will mean 'the disc of the sun looked like a goblet for drinking the ocean of evening.' The evening being red, the goblet containing it would also look red. ०जलेन शुचयः शयचरणाः येषाम्. 'पञ्चशाखः शयः पाणिः' इत्यमरः. Brāhmanical ascetics washed their hands and feet before worshipping in the shrine. चैत्यः a sanctuary; a temple; a holy tree (growing by the side of a road). 'चैत्यमायतनं तुल्ये' इत्यमरः ('चित्यायामिदं चैत्यं देवकुलमहावृक्षाद्युपाश्रयः' क्षीर०). पाराशरिषु—see above p. 90. यज्ञपात्रैः पवित्राः पाणयः येषाम् (*adj.* of ०जने). प्रकीर्णाः (spread round) बर्हिषः (कुशाः) यस्य (*adj.* of ०वेदसि). उद्गतं तेजः यस्य the flames of which leapt up (when oblations were thrown into it). वषट्कृ to offer (an oblation) with the cry वषट्. वषट् is an exclamation on offering an oblation (the name of the deity being put in the dative) *e. g.* इन्द्राय वषट्. यायजूकः—one who frequently performs sacrifices—from यज् with affix ऊक, according to 'यजजपदशां यङः' पा. 3. 2. 166 (यायजूकः, जञ्जपूकः, दन्दशूकः). निद्राविद्राणानि द्रोणकुलानि तैः कलिलाः (full of) कुलायाः येषु. द्रोणाः काकाः. The com. explains निद्राविद्राण as 'dull with sleep'. But elsewhere विद्राण is used in the sense of 'awake'. Compare 'विद्राणविपश्चिति' हर्ष० 5th उ० 11th para. So we take 'निद्राविद्राण' as 'not yet gone to sleep' (though crowding in their nests). Or we may separate as निद्रा-अविद्राण meaning 'not awake through sleep'. कापेयविकलानि (free from their pranks) कपिकुलानि येषु. At night the monkeys desist from their pranks. 'कापेयं चापलादिकम्' क्षीर० (कपेः भावः कर्म वा). आरामतरुषु on the trees in the gardens. निर्जि...कुले when the swarms of owls (कौशिकः), settled (*lit.* householders) in their huts *viz.* the hollows of old trees, were about to go out. मुनि...रम्बे—The clusters of bright stars looked like the bright drops of water scattered about in सन्ध्यावन्दन by the sages. दन्तुरयति *loc. sing.* of *pr. p.* of दन्तुरयति (make indented or serrated) denominative verb from दन्तुर. The clusters also looked like the bright teeth (of a lady *viz.* the sky). As drops are scattered on the ground (स्थली), so the stars were scattered in the sky. स्थवीयस्—comparative of स्थूल. 'निकुरम्बं कदम्बकम्' इत्यमरः. अम्बरा...शिखण्डे when the topknot of the S'abarî of night rose in the sky *i. e.* when the sky was overcast with darkness. For शर्वरीशबरी compare 'शर्वरीशबरीचिकुरचये...तमसि' text p. 6. l. 13. अम्बरा०—The topknot of a शबरी may be dangling on her garment (अम्बरं). खण्डपरशुः (शिवः) तस्य कण्ठवत् काले (dark)-goes with ०तारे. For S'iva's dark throat, see notes p. 2. कव...तारे when the young (fresh, recent) *avatara* (advent) of darkness swallowed all that remained of the evening light. सान्ध्यम्–सन्ध्यायाः अयं सान्ध्यः (०शेषः) तम्. तिमिर... र्गतासु (०तर्जनाय निर्गतासु) that came forth as if to chide darkness. दहनं प्रविष्टः दिनकरः तस्य करशाखासु (fingers; branch-like rays). The blazing lamps are fancied to be the fingers of the sun. Fingers start from the hand and one of them (called तर्जनी) is employed in threatening or chiding a person. Flames are tapering like fingers. It was believed that the sun, when setting, entered fire. Compare रघु० IV. 1. 'स राज्यं गुरुणा दत्तं प्रतिपद्याधिकं बभौ। दिनान्ते निहितं तेजः सवित्रेव हुताशनः ॥'. अररसम्पुटसंक्रीडनेन कथिता आवृत्तिः यैः. अररं panel. 'कवाटमररं तुल्ये' इत्यमरः. 'पुरद्वारं तु गोपुरम्' इत्यमरः. अरर...पुरेषु when the city gates as though announced their clo sing (आवृत्ति) by the creaking of their folding panels. It would be better if we could read ०वृतिषु. आवृति means 'shutting', while आवृत्ति usually means 'revolving.' शय...जुषि enjoying the pleasure (उपजोषः) of lying on their beds. They first lay on their beds for some time and then went to sleep. जरतीभिः कथिताः कथाः यस्मै. शिशयिषमाणे (*pr. p.* of the desiderative of शी) was about to sleep. जरन् महिषः मषी (lamp-black, ink) च तद्वत् मलीमसं (dark) तमः यस्य. जनितः पुण्यजनानां (goblins) प्रजागरः येन. 'यातुधानाः पुण्यजनाः' अमरः. Goblins stalk abroad at night. पुण्यजन also means 'यक्ष'. They are guardians of कुबेर's treasures and as such must be awake at night. विजृम्भमाणे (growing, yawning). तमीमुखे the mouth (or first part) of Night. 'रजनी यामिनी तमी' अमरः मुखरितं (twanging) विततज्यं (वितता ज्या यस्य) धनुः यस्य (*adj.* of ०ध्वजे). अशेषस्य संसारस्य शेमुषीं (मतिं) मुष्णाति इति ०मुष् तस्मिन्—Cupid blinds the intellect of every one in the world. रतस्य आकल्पः (dress) तस्य आरम्भेण शोभते इति. शम्भलीनां (procuress) भाषितं भजते इति. 'कुट्टनी शम्भली समे' अमरः. भूषा ornaments, decoration. भुजिष्या a maid harlot. सैरन्ध्या बध्यमानं रशनाजालं तेन जल्पाकं (noisy, jingling) जघनं (loins) यासाम्. 'स्याज्जल्पाकस्तु वाचालः' अमरः. For सैरन्ध्री, see notes p. 90. जनीषु young ladies. 'समाः स्नुषा जनी वध्वः' अमरः. वशिकासु (empty) विशिखासु (roads) विहरन्तीति विहारिण्यः (wandering) तासु. 'वशिकं तुच्छरिक्तके' अमरः. 'रथ्या प्रतोली विशिखा' अमरः (विगतशिखा मुण्डितेव, समन्ताद्विशीर्यते जनसंमर्देन वा' क्षीर०). अनन्यजः (कामः) अनुप्लवः

यासाम्. 'अनुप्लवः सहायश्च' अमरः. They went alone, with hearts aflame. अभिसारिकासु—see notes p. 33. विरली...जल्पिते when the sweet (मञ्जु) chatter of the females of *Haṁsas* lying in the ponds, as dull (low) as the jingling of anklets (मञ्जीरः-रम्), gradually ceased. 'हंसस्य योषिद्वरटा' अमरः; 'वेशन्तः पल्वलं चाल्पसरः' अमरः. For निद्राविद्राण, see notes above p. 162. निद्रा...रसिते when the notes of cranes, appearing to grow longer to those that were kept awake, as though melted the hearts of separated lovers. In the stillness of night, the notes appeared longer. भावि...निकरे इव—the lamps scattered about were like the shoots of the seeds of the coming day. From shoots large trees grow. The flickering lamps contained in them the potential day that was to dawn. अनेकानि बालचरित-चापलानि तस्य उचितं (appropriate to) कौलीनं (evil report) तेन कोपितः. 'कौलीनं पशुभिर्युद्धे कुलीनत्वापवादयोः' इति धरणिः. कौलीन (कुलीनस्य कर्म भावो वा) according to 'हायनान्तयुवादिभ्योऽण्' पा. 5. 1. 130. If we read 'चापलोपचित' the meaning is 'the scandals that grew on account of my follies'. मनसा—there is emphasis on this word. *Vide* notes p. 161. यद्य...स्याम् if I were an eye-sore to him, if he were displeased with me. इच्छति...वन्तम् but he wishes me to be virtuous. उप...स्वामिनः for masters teach their dependents proper conduct even without words by granting them an honour (प्रतिपत्तिः) suited to them. स्वदोषेण अन्धं मानसं यस्य. अनादरपीडितम् who am pained by the absence of (outward) respect (shown by the king). अति...चिन्तयन्तम् who entertain various fancies about this most virtuous king. यथा...स्थितम् as I really am. कटकात्—It will be remembered that Harsha was encamped on the अजिरवती (text p. 26. l. 17). गृहीतः (understood) स्वभावः येन. परमप्रीतेन—qualifies नरेन्द्रेण. प्रसादात् जन्म यस्य springing from the favour (of the king). This qualifies all the words from मानस्य to प्रभावस्य. नर्मन् *n.* amusement, merriment.

Uchchhvāsa III

Verse 1. The principal sentence is सु...भूभुजः—kings (of the character described in the first half of the verse) are born like fine seasons (prosperous times) through the merit of the subjects (of the people). निज...स्नेहाः (निजे वर्षे देशे आहितः स्नेहः यैः) that plant their affection in their kingdom *i. e.* that love their kingdoms; (निजेन वर्षेण वृष्टया आहितः स्नेहः रसः घृतं वा यैः) that produce moisture (or ghee) by rain. वर्ष is a subdivision of द्वीप (as in भरतवर्ष). बहु...न्विताः (बहुभिः भक्तजनैः अन्विताः) followed by many devoted persons; (बहूनां भक्तानां अन्नानां ओदनानां वा जनेन समूहेन अन्विताः) that are marked by plenty of rice-crops or plenty of food. 'भक्तमन्धोऽन्नमोदनोऽस्त्री स दीदिविः' अमरः. This verse foreshadows the greatness of पुष्पभूति, the founder of Harsha's family, the treatment he gave to his subjects and the prosperity of his kingdom. The metre is अनुष्टुभ्.

Verse 2. लक्ष्मीं द्रष्टुम् to see लक्ष्मी; to obtain wealth. विहायसा गन्तुम् to sail in the sky; to rise high. न...मनः whose mind is not eager ? This verse shadows forth the four principal topics of this उच्छ्वास. Here also the king पुष्पभूति conferred an obligation on भैरवाचार्य; the king had a vision of लक्ष्मी in flesh and blood; भैरवाचार्य assumed a semi-divine form and the cousins of बाण became eager to hear the story of Harsha's life. The metre is आर्या.

P. 38 ll. 2–16 **अथ...समगात्.** The principal sentence is अथ...शरत्समयारम्भे वाणः बन्धून् द्रष्टुं पुनरपि तं ब्राह्मणाधिवासमगात्. Here we have a description of autumn. All the words in the locative (singular) qualify शरत्समयारम्भे. विरलिताः बलाहकाः (मेघाः) यस्मिन्. चातकस्य आतङ्कं करोतीति. 'रुक्तापशङ्कास्वातङ्कः' अमरः. For चातक, see above p. 128. When the clouds disappeared the चातक would not get even a drop of water. क्वणन्तः कादम्बाः (कलहंसाः) यस्मिन्. कलहंसs are at ease in the rainy season. दर्दुरद्विषि—which is an enemy to frogs. मयूरस्य मदं मुष्णाति इति. The peacock dances at the appearance of clouds and so in शरद् when clouds become rare it pines away. हंसा एव पथिकसार्थः सर्वः अतिथिः यस्य whose only guest is the swarm of travellers-the swans. At the approach of the rains, हंसs were supposed to leave the plains and run to the मानस lake, whence they returned after the rains were over. शरद् welcomes to the पूर्वमीमांसा of जैमिनि and to the उत्तरमीमांसा of बादरायण. In these three clauses बाण suggests that his cousins were पदवाक्यप्रमाणज्ञ, पद standing for grammar, वाक्य for मीमांसा and प्रमाण for न्यायशास्त्र. अभिनवं सुभाषितं एव सुधा तां वर्षन्तीति. For सुभाषित see p. 11.

P. 39 ll. 1–9 **अथ...वारयन्.** तात a term of endearment applied even by elders to youngsters and by friends to friends. Compare 'नहि कल्याणकृत्कश्चिद्दुर्गतिं तात गच्छति' गीता. 6. 40. सन्तोषजुषां who are contented (*adj.* of नः). सततं सन्निहितः विद्याविनोदः (intellectual diversion) येषाम्. वैतानः वह्निः एव ०वह्निमात्रं सहायः येषाम्. किय...तया what have we to do with being happy (we have but little concern with being happy)? It should be noticed that the first question asked by बाण was 'कच्चित्...सुखिनो यूयम्.' They reply by saying that they have all those things that make for happiness *viz.* friends (वैतानवह्नि), amusements and contentment and that they need not bother themselves further, as king हर्ष will look to the rest (to their protection &c.). सकलभुवनानि भुनक्ति (protects). भुजङ्गराजः शेषः तस्य देहवत् दीर्घे. शेष also supports (protects) the earth. क्षितिभुजः = हर्षस्य. विमुक्तं कौसीद्यं येन. कौसीद्य— from कुसीद (कुत्सितं सीदति अस्मिन्) with affix ष्यञ्. The kinsmen of बाण administer him a delicate rebuke. यथाविभवं as our wealth permits. शैश...कथाभिः remembrances of past boyish sports and stories of their ancestors. यथा...करोत् he performed the usual observances.

P. 39 ll. 10—22 **अत्रान्तरे...पपाठ.** दुकू...वसानः wearing a pair of silken Pauṇḍra garments, as white as the corner of the peacock's eye, and cut off from a long piece of silk cloth. पट्ट here stands for what is called तागा in Marathi. He had cut off two pieces from a long roll of silk cloth. पौण्ड्र–Manufactured in the Puṇḍra country. पुण्ड्र would correspond to modern Bengal and Bihar. शिखण्डिनः अपाङ्गवत् पाण्डुनी. अवसानं end. बन्दितया because he was a bard. The bards formed a distinct class, sprung from क्षत्रिय father and S'ūdra mother. तीर्थ...तिलकः whose *tilaka* (on the forehead) was made of *gorochanā* and clay from a sacred spot (river &c.). Various substances were prescribed as affording fit material for making a तिलक. **'तीर्थमृ**द्यज्ञकाष्ठं च बिल्वो मलयसम्भवम् । जाह्नवीमृन्महानिम्बतुलसीकाष्ठमेव च । ...**गोरोचना** गन्धकुष्ठं जलं चागुरुगोमयम् ।...स्नानान्ते सर्ववर्णानामाश्रमाणां तथैव च । एतानि तिलकान्याहुः सन्ध्यादिसर्वकर्मसु ॥.' तैलामलकाभ्यां मसृणितः (made smooth and glossy) मौलिः (केशाः) यस्य. अनु...चुम्बिना kissing his short topknot. निबिडेन dense with flowers. सकृ...कान्तिः the colour of his lip was bright because he had chewed betel only once. If he had taken betel very often, his lip would have been dark-red and not विमल. So the reading असकृदुपयुक्त is not good. एक...रुचिः the lustre of whose eye was heightened by the application of an eye-salve with a pin. विनी...दधानः wearing a simple (not gaudy) and respectable dress. आसन्दी = पीठिका—a chair. तत्कालं अपनीतं सूत्रवेष्टनं यस्य (*adj.* of पुस्तकं). तत्काला...निधाय having laid, on a stand (यन्त्रकं) made of reedstalks placed in front, his book which seemed as if bound with soft lotus fibres on account of the rays of his nails, although its band was removed at that very moment. His nails were bright and the rays from them resembled lotus-fibres. When he passed his hand round the book in unloosening the string in which it was wrapped, he as though seemed to be tying it up again. पृष्ठतः... स्थानके when a place was assigned behind him to मधुकर and पारावत that sat near (सनीड). The two seem to have been persons that played upon flutes by way of accompaniment. So the reading of B 'वांशिकाभ्यां' is good. C and T translate मधुकर and पारावत as bee and dove. What purpose these served is not clear. Perhaps they were pets. वांशिक-वंशवादनं शिल्पमस्य (from वंश + ठक्) according to 'शिल्पम्' पा. 4. 4. 55. It would mean 'that served as flute-players.' प्राभातिक...त्क्षिप्य having taken out the leaf inserted inside as a mark to indicate the portion read in the morning. प्राभातिकः प्रपाठकः (section) तस्य छेदः (end) तस्य चिह्नीकृतम्. प्रपाठक also means 'reader', the meaning being 'made as a mark to denote the portion read by the morning reader.' गृहीत्वा...पाटिकां he took a small block (*lit.* panel) light (not heavy) because there were a few leaves only. क्षालय...ग्रन्थम्—the idea is:—the bright rays of his teeth when he recited the verses looked like bright water and like white flowers. मुख...श्रोतृणाम् captivating the hearts of his hearers by the sweet intonations of his voice, as though they were the jinglings of the anklets of सरस्वती residing in his mouth (tongue). सरस्वती is spoken of as dwelling in the mouth of a learned man. On गमक the com. says 'गमयन्ति रागस्वरूपमिति गमकाः असाधारणानि स्वराणां निमीलनानि यानि लक्ष्येष्वान्तरमार्गे इति प्रसिद्धास्तैर्गमकैः स्वरयतिविशेषैः.' गमक is thus defined 'गमकः स्वश्रुतिस्थानच्छायां श्रुत्यन्तराश्रयाम्। स्वरो यो मूर्छनामेति गमकः स इहोच्यते॥ कम्पितः स्फुरितो नीलो भिन्नः स्थविर एव च। आहतान्दोलितौ चेति गमकाः सप्त कीर्तिताः॥.' According to the सङ्गीतरत्नाकर, गमक

is a certain कम्प of the voice; it enumerates 15 kinds of it 'स्वरस्य कम्पो गमकः श्रोतृचित्तसुखावहः ।' 3rd chap. 45. गीत्या पपाठ he sang or chanted. पवमानप्रोक्तं पुराणं the Purāṇa promulgated by Vāyu *i. e.* the वायुपुराण. सूत says in the वायुपुराण I. 47–48. 'पुराणं संप्रवक्ष्यामि यदुक्तं मातरिश्वना ॥ पृष्टेन मुनिभिः पूर्वं नैमिषीयैर्महात्मभिः ।'. सूत had learnt it from व्यास (verse 46). The वायुपुराण is one of the most ancient of Purāṇas. The topics generally treated of in a पुराण are summarised in the following verse 'सर्गश्च प्रतिसर्गश्च वंशो मन्वन्तराणि च । वंशानुचरितं चैव पुराणं पंचलक्षणम् ॥'.

P. 39 l. 23—**P. 40** l. 5 **तस्मिंश्च...लोकयन्.** श्रुतिभिः सुभगा गीतिः गर्भे यथा स्यात् तथा. श्रुति is a technical term in music. It means 'a particular division of the octave, a quarter tone or interval.' They are 22 in number. श्रुतिs are those elementary नादs from which the seven स्वरs (सरिगमपधनि) are evolved. 'हृद्यूर्ध्वनाडिकास्थ-द्वाविंशत्यणुतिरोजनाडीषु । तावन्तः श्रुतिसंज्ञाः स्युर्नादाः परपरोच्चोच्चाः ॥ एवं गले च शीर्षे ताभ्यः सप्त स्वराः श्रुतिभ्यः स्युः ।' रागविबोध verses 13–14. तार...स्वरेण accompanying the note of the chant in a voice loud (तार) and sweet. **Verse 3.** The first half contains words that apply both to हर्षचरित and पुराण. तदपि that also. मुनिगीतम् sung by sages. अतिपृथु very large. The वायुपुराण contains several thousand verses. अतिपृथु surpassing पृथु, the first king (पृथुमतिक्रान्तं). For पृथु vide notes on the 2nd verse in the 4th उ०. पावनं holy (applies to both). पावनं also means 'composed by पवन *i. e.* by वायु'. हर्ष...मिदम् this Purāṇa does not seem to me to differ from the career of Harsha. **Verse 4.** The four adjectives qualify both गीत and हर्षराज्य. वंशा...वादि that is chanted in notes that are in harmony with the flute (with गीत); where disputants follow their family *i. e.* where there are no disputes among members of the same family. वंशस्य (flute) अनुगमः ययोः तौ ०गमौ विवादिनौ (स्वरौ) यत्र; वंशस्य (family) अनुगमः येषां ते ०गमाः विवादिनः यस्मिन्. The seven स्वरs are gruped into four classes in भरत's नाट्यशास्त्र (Chap. 28. 23.) 'चतुर्विधत्वमेतेषां विज्ञेयं श्रुतियोगतः । वादी चैवाथ संवादी ह्यनुवादी विवाद्यपि ॥'. Then he says 'विवादिनस्तु ये तेषां स्याद्विंशतिकमन्तरम् । तद्यथा ऋषभगान्धारौ धैवतनिषादौ'. Those are विवादिस्वरs (*viz.* ऋषभ and गान्धार, धैवत and निषध) between which there is a difference of 20 श्रुतिs. The रागविबोध (verse 38) puts the matter differently 'एकश्रुत्यन्तरितौ विवादिनौ वैरिणौ मिथो भवतः ।'. Those are विवादिs that are separated by one श्रुति (*i. e.* ultimately 20 श्रुतिs, as there are only 22 श्रुतिs) and are destructive of the harmony of each other. स्फुटकरणं which is clearly pronounced or the rhythmie pauses of which are clear

(with गीत). स्फुटं करणं (pronunciation) यस्मिन् or स्फुटानि करणानि यस्मिन्. करणं means 'the beating of the hands to indicate the proper ताल'. मल्लिनाथ on कुमारसम्भव 6. 40 says "करणैस्तालव्यवस्थापकैस्ताडनविशेषैः । तदुक्तं राजकन्दर्पेण 'नृत्यवादित्रगीतानां प्रयोगवशभेदिनाम् । संस्थानं ताडनं रोधः करणानि प्रचक्षते ॥' इति". स्फुटानि करणानि यस्मिन् (with ०राज्यम्) in which the documents (of sale &c.) were clear (and not ambiguous). For this meaning of करण see मनु० VIII. 145. भरत... गुरु weighty (important) because of its conforming to the path of Bharata (with गीत). भरत is the reputed author of the science of dancing and music. The extant नाट्यशास्त्र claims to be his work. The chant of सुदृष्टि conformed to the rules laid down by भरत. भरत...गुरु (with राज्यं) 'that was wide because it embraced the path (the region) of Bharata.' Here there is a reference to भरतवर्ष (India) which was so named according to the वायुपुराण (chap. 33. 50-52) and the भागवतपुराण (V. 4. 9. and XI. 2. 15-17) after भरत, son of ऋषभ. According to ब्रह्मपुराण (13. 57) भरतवर्ष was named after भरत son of दुष्यन्त and शकुन्तला. श्री... यीतम्—(1) issuing from a sweet throat (with गीत); issuing from श्रीकण्ठ. श्रीकण्ठ was the name of the country where हर्ष's ancestors ruled. श्रीयुक्तः कण्ठः श्रीकण्ठः. Or श्रीकण्ठ means शिव. Then गीत would refer to the वायुपुराण and not the chanting of it by सुदृष्टि. As all learning springs from शिव, the पुराण may also be called श्री०. हर्षराज्यम् (with गीतम्) would mean 'which is the realm of joy'. These verses serve to introduce the request made by Bāṇa's cousins. चत्वारः qualifies ०पद्माः and भ्रातरः. पितामहमुखानि एव पद्माः. Brahmā has four mouths. वेदाभ्यासेन पवित्रिताः मूर्तयः येषाम् (applies to both ०पद्माः and भ्रातरः). Each of the four Vedas was promulgated by a special mouth of Brahmā. *Vide* विष्णुपुराण I. 5. ऋग्वेद, यजुर्वेद, सामवेद and अथर्ववेद were respectively created from his four mouths beginning with the eastern. उपायाः—these are the four methods of policy in politics *viz.* साम (reconciliation), दान (bribery), भेद (internal dissensions) and दण्ड (open attack). साम...मुखाः whose mouths are charming by the repeating of the सामवेद or by adopting the policy of conciliation (with भ्रातरः); the commencement of which is charming by the employment of reconciliation (with उपायाः). साम is the first उपाय. गणपति—These are the names of बाण's cousins. भ्रातरः—connect this with परस्परस्य मुखानि व्यलोकयन्. प्रसन्न...व्याकरणेऽपि—In the world as well as in grammar they were प्रसन्नवृत्तयः &c. The words in this clause have two meanings throughout. प्रसन्ना वृत्तिः येषाम् whose conduct is gracious or mild (with लोके); whose exposition (of पाणिनि's सूत्रs) is clear (with व्याकरणे). It is not posssible to suppose that the काशिकावृत्ति of वामन and जयादित्य is referred to here. According to Itsing's statement, the काशिकावृत्ति was composed about 660 A. D. But Itsing's statements are rather confused and in our humble opinion not entitled to the weight given to them by western scholars. *Vide* Dr. Takakusu's translation of Itsing's work (Oxford 1896 pp. 175–176 for what is called वृत्तिसूत्र there). गृहीतं वाक्यं (गुरुवाक्यं आप्तवाक्यं वा) यैः that listened to the words of relatives or elders (with लोके); that had understood the Vārtikas of कात्यायन (according to the com.). वाक्य may refer also to the वाक्यपदीय of भर्तृहरि. कृतः गुरुपदे न्यासः यैः that followed in the footsteps of their teachers or that had planted their feet on *(i. e.* had attained) an eminent position (with लोके); कृतः (अभ्यस्तः) गुरुपदेषु न्यासः यैः that studied the न्यास on difficult words (in the Sūtras of पाणिनि). न्यास is a name applied to the commentary of जिनेन्द्रबुद्धि on the काशिकावृत्ति. But it is hardly possible that Bāṇa refers to it. न्यास was a name given to several grammatical works. Bhāmaha (8th century A. D.) mentions a न्यास, which seems to be जिनेन्द्रबुद्धि's work. 'शिष्टप्रयोगमात्रेण न्यासकारमतेन वा । तृचा समस्तषष्ठीकं न कथञ्चिदुदाहरेत् ॥'. माघ in शिशु० II. 112. refers to a न्यास, वृत्ति and निबन्धन *(i. e.* महाभाष्य). न्यायवेदिनः who knew what was proper; who knew the maxims of grammar. The महाभाष्य mentions many न्यायs like the कूपखानकन्याय (vol I. p. 11), कुम्भीधान्यन्याय (vol I p. 265), अर्धजरतीयन्याय (vol II p. 231), अविरविकन्याय (vol. III. p. 124). Or न्याय means 'rules for the interpretation of the Sūtras', such as 'असिद्धं बहिरङ्गमन्तरङ्गे' (vol I. p. 26) or 'छंदोवत्सूत्राणि भवन्ति' (vol I. p. 37). सु...गुरवः (सुकृतं पुण्यं तस्य संग्रहः (सञ्चयः) तस्य अभ्यासे गुरवः) that were great in the repeated accumulation of merit ; सुकृतः संग्रहस्य अभ्यासः तेन गुरवः who became teachers (of grammar) because they had well studied the संग्रह (a work of व्याडि). In the महाभाष्य, the work called संग्रह is frequently referred to 'संग्रहे एतत्प्राधान्येन परीक्षितं नित्यो वा स्यात्कार्यो वेति' (vol I. p. 6). In the days of भर्तृहरि, author of the वाक्यपदीय, the work was lost. 'प्रायेण संक्षेपरुचीनल्पविद्यापरिग्रहान् । सम्प्राप्य वैयाकरणान् संग्रहेऽस्तमुपागते ॥' वाक्यपदीय II. 484. Therefore it seems unlikely that बाण is serious when he says that his cousins had studied the संग्रह. His sole aim is to bring out similarity between लोक and व्याकरण by puns. लब्ध...शब्दाः that were called 'good' by the people; that employed only grammatically correct words. महाभारतेन भाविताः (purified) आत्मानः येषाम्. 'आर्षादिबहुधाख्यानं देवर्षिचरिताश्रयम् । इतिहासमिति प्रोक्तं भविष्यद्भूतधर्मयुक् ॥.' महा...हलिनः eager to know the stories of heroes. सुभाषितश्रवणे रसः एव रसायनं तस्मिन् अवितृष्णाः not free from desire as to the elixir *viz.* pleasure of listening to सुभाषितs. For रसायन, see p. 55. They had no desires except this. वयसि प्रथमाः foremost in years. वचसि in eloquence. महसि in (Brahmanical) lustre. यजुषि in sacrificial prayers, or in the (study of) the यजुर्वेद. पूर्व...ङ्कराः who had already made an agreement (सङ्करः) (to request बाण to tell the story of Harsha's life). विवक्षवः=वक्तुम् इच्छवः. सितं एव सुधा तया धवलितं कपोलोदरं येषाम्

P. 40 l. 6–**P. 41** l. 4. **अथ...मभूत्.** कमलदलवत् दीर्घे लोचने यस्य. दत्ता संज्ञा यस्मै to whom a signal was given. दशनानां ज्योत्स्नया स्नपिताः ककुभः येन. The rays of his white teeth resembled moonlight. द्विजानां...कार्षीत् The moon, lord of *dvijas*, carried off the wife of his preceptor. In this and the following sentences, the author finds various faults in the kings and heroes of old to show that only Harsha is spotless. Some of the blemishes, however, are merely verbal. 'द्विजराजः शशधरः नक्षत्रेशः क्षपाकरः' इत्यमरः. गुरुदारग्रहण is a महापातक. *Vide* notes p. 160. It is to be noted that this passage up to युधिष्ठिरः &c. corresponds almost *verbatim* with a passage in the वासवदत्ता of सुबन्धु, where however there is no reference to मान्धाता, सौदास, मरुत्त, पाण्डु and पृथु. Our humble opinion is that examples had already been collected in works that preceded सुबन्धु and बाण and that both derived their inspiration from them. If there is any borrowing between the two, then it is बाण that borrows. बाण adds to the list and also to the phraseology employed in the वासवदत्ता, as we shall show later on. *Vide* Hall's Vāsavadattā pp. 273-276 and pp. 337-340 of the Srīrangam edition. सोम performed राजसूय and became conceited. He carried away तारा, the wife of बृहस्पति, and did not give her back though asked by Brahmā to do so. He had a son from her named बुध. *Vide* विष्णुपु० IV. 6. See 'सकलजगद्गीयमानबुधकर्णानन्दकारिणौ सोमसूर्यवंशाविव' हर्ष० 4th उ० and notes thereon. दयिते...त was separated from Āyus, dear to him. आयुस् means 'life' also. आयुस् was the son of पुरूरवस् and उर्वशी. The com. gives the story alluded to here as follows:—'पुरूरवाः पूर्वां दिशं जेतुं गच्छन्केनाप्याहृतप्रभूतधनेन विप्रेण यज्ञे निमन्त्रितो लोभाक्षिप्तस्तद्धनं जिहीर्षुस्तच्छापान्नष्टः । तस्मिन्मृते स विप्रो नृपं विना प्रजा

निवर्तते इति ज्ञात्वा तदायुषा राजर्षिमायुर्नामानमजीजनदिति'. In the वासवदत्ता we have 'पुरूरवा ब्राह्मणधनतृष्णया विननाश.' नहुष...आसीत्—नहुष, desiring another's wife, became a great serpent. Note that भुजङ्ग also means 'a lewd or dissolute person'. नहुष was the eldest son of आयुः. When Indra ran away through fear of the sin of ब्रह्महत्या in killing वृत्र, नहुष, who had performed numerous sacrifices, was appointed इन्द्र by the gods. In his vanity he cast lustful eyes on शची, the wife of इन्द्र. At the advice of बृहस्पति, she agreed to yield to his wishes if he would come to her in a palanquin carried by sages. While coming in that way, he struck अगस्त्य, who was slow, with his foot urging him to greater speed with the words 'सर्प सर्प'. Then अगस्त्य cursed him to be a सर्प. *Vide* महाभारत वनपर्व Chapter 181. Compare रघु० 13. 36. 'भ्रूभेदमात्रेण पदान्मघोनः प्रभ्रंशयां यो नहुषं चकार ।'. ययाति was the second son of नहुष and married देवयानी, the daughter of शुक्र, who was a ब्राह्मण. आहितं ब्राह्मण्याः पाणिग्रहणं येन—Who took the hand of a Brāhmaṇa girl (*i. e.* married her); who held a ब्राह्मणी (देवयानी) in his hand (when rescuing her from a well). पपात fell off from caste usages; perished (*i. e.* became prematurely old). A male belonging to any one of the four Varṇas could marry a girl of the same Varṇa as himself or of a lower Varṇa; but was forbidden to marry one of a higher वर्ण. Compare what ययाति himself says 'अविवाह्या हि राजानो देवयानि पितुस्तव ।' आदि० 81. 18. ययाति being a क्षत्रिय, there could be no marriage between him and देवयानी, who was a ब्राह्मणी, according to caste usages. Therefore he incurred sin. शुक्र was the preceptor of वृषपर्वा, king of the असुरs. The latter's daughter शर्मिष्ठा quarrelled with देवयानी and threw her in a well. ययाति, while hunting, found her there and took her out with his hand. वृषपर्वा, afraid of शुक्र's curse, wanted to please her. She demanded that his daughter शर्मिष्ठा should be her slave. शुक्र, seeing that his daughter loved ययाति, consented to their marriage. Seeing शर्मिष्ठा in her service, he secretly married her also. When देवयानी complained to her father of ययाति's faithlessness he cursed him to be prematurely old. It will be seen from the above that marrying a ब्राह्मणी was not the *cause* of ययाति's premature old age; but that the latter was only an incident that occurred later on. बाण of course presses it in his service to find fault with ययाति. *Vide* महाभारत आदिपर्व chap. 78–83. Note 'तामथो ब्राह्मणीं राजा विज्ञाय नहुषा-

त्मजः। गृहीत्वा दक्षिणे पाणावुज्जहार ततोऽवटात् ॥ chap. 78. 22. स्त्रीमय एवाभवत्—there are three senses; (1) he was born a woman; (2) he became a woman; (3) he could think of nothing but women *i. e.* he was extremely lascivious. The last is the fault found in him. The first two are matters of mythology. See the following from विष्णुपुराण IV. 1. 8. *ff.* 'इष्टिं च मित्रावरुणयोर्मनुः पुत्रकामश्चकार। तत्रापहृते होतुरपचारादिला नाम कन्या बभूव॥ सैव मित्रावरुणप्रसादात्सुद्युम्नो नाम मनोः पुत्रो मैत्रेयासीत्पुनश्चेश्वरकोपात् स्त्री सती सोमसूनोर्बुधस्याश्रमसमीपे बभ्राम।' *Vide* also मार्कण्डेयपु० chap. 111. सुद्युम्न, when hunting, trespassed upon a grove sacred to पार्वती who was promised by शिव that whoever trespassed on the spot where it was would become a female. सुद्युम्न then again became a female. See भागवत पुराण 9.1. जन्तु...निर्घृणता cruelty of killing living beings; cruelty in killing (his own son) जन्तु. सोमक had 100 wives and only one son in old age. The son जन्तु was once bitten by an ant and the whole royal family was very much distressed and therefore he wanted a hundred sons. 'धिगस्त्विहैकपुत्रत्वमपुत्रत्वं वरं भवेत्।' वनपर्व chap. 127. 12. He sacrificed his only son and after smelling the smoke of his fat his queens gave birth to a 100 sons. The com. gives the story "सोमकस्य राज्ञो जन्तुर्नाम एकः पुत्रोऽभूत्। स च एकपुत्रत्वादपुत्रत्वं वरमिति जानन्नुद्विग्नः पुरोधसा अभ्यधायि 'बहून्पुत्रांश्चेदिच्छसि तदस्य सुतस्य वपया होमः क्रियताम्। ततो यावत्यो धूममाजिघ्रन्ति ताः पुत्रैर्युज्यन्ते' इति। स चापि घृणामपहाय तथा कारितवानिति।" See वनपर्व chap. 127–128. मार्गणव्यसनेन—by his great liking for arrows (*i. e.* for fighting); by his vice of begging. रसातलमगात्—went to पाताल; perished. रसातल is one of the seven पातालs, अतल, वितल, सुतल, महीतल, रसातल, तलातल and पाताल. मान्धाता, son of युवनाश्व, conquered the earth and wanted to vanquish इन्द्र. Indra offered to hand over his kingdom when he would conquer the demon लवण. So मान्धाता attacked लवण, who had secured a शूल of miraculous powers from शिव. मान्धाता perished with all his army in the fight against लवण. *Vide* रामायण उत्तरकाण्ड chap. 67. The रामायण does not mention that the son and grandson of मान्धाता accompanied him in the fight. पुरुकुत्सः...करोत्—पुरुकुत्स, though practising penance, committed a bad deed on the daughter of मेकल (the suggestion being that he had intercourse with a कन्यका a maiden). मेकलकन्यका means the river नर्मदा. पुरुकुत्स was guilty of bad conduct while practising penance on the Narmadâ. The com. says 'पुरुकुत्सः पुरा तपश्चरन्नर्मदायां स्नानं कुर्वन्कामप्यङ्गनामालोक्य कामाविष्टो नीतिमुत्ससर्ज'. The वासदत्ता has 'पुरुकुत्सः

कुत्सित एवाभवत्.' कुवलयाश्वः—According to the मार्कण्डेयपुराण (chap. 20 ff.) the king ऋतध्वज had secured a horse named कुवलय. He pursued a demon that had disturbed the sage गालव in his austerities and went to पाताल. After various incidents which need not be detailed here, he married मदालसा, daughter of a नाग अश्वतर. भुज...ग्रहात् by resorting to the world of नागs (*viz.* पाताल); by associating with भुजङ्गs (rakes). अश्वतरकन्या means 'the daughter of a mule'. न परिजहार did not omit. The com. gives the story differently 'कुवलयाश्वो राजा मृगयाक्रीडनप्रसङ्गेन घर्मातुरो मज्जनरभसेन सरसीमवतीर्णो रसातलं प्राप्तोऽश्वतराभिधां नागकन्यामूढ-वानिति'. The वासदत्ता has 'कुवलयाश्वो अश्वतरकन्यामपि जगाम.' प्रथमपुरुषकः the first man; foremost of bad men. क is added according to 'कुत्सिते' पा. 5. 3. 74. कुत्सितः पुरुषः पुरुषकः. परि... पृथिवीम् violated पृथिवी; humbled the earth. पृथु was the first king. During his reign, on account of a draught, people were dying of hunger and the earth yielded nothing. People came to him. He took his bow, when the earth assumed the form of a cow and ran away. Then पृथु pursued her and got from her whatever he desired. *Vide* विष्णुपु० I. 13. कृकलासभावे in being a chameleon (Marathi सरडा). वर्णसङ्करः—a combination of colours; confusion of castes (by intermarriage). It is well-known that the chameleon changes the colours of its skin. वर्णसङ्कर was looked upon as sinful. Compare गीता I. 42. 'सङ्करो नरकायैव.' नृग gave by mistake the cow belonging to one ब्राह्मण to another. The real owner and the donee had a dispute and came to the king's palace to get it settled. नृग, being absorbed in pleasures, did not see them for many days. They cursed him. 'अर्थिनां कार्य-सिद्ध्यर्थं यस्मात्त्वं नैषि दर्शनम् । अदृश्यः सर्वभूतानां कृकलासो भविष्यसि ॥' रामायण उत्तरकाण्ड Chap. 53. 18. The वासदत्ता says 'नृगः कृकलासतामगमत्.' सौदा...क्षितिः by सौदास the earth was not protected but (only) disturbed or agitated. न रक्षिता (goes with क्षितिः). नरक्षिता (instru. sing. of नरक्षित्) will also mean 'who killed human beings' (with सौदासेन). To protect the earth is the first duty of a king. 'क्षत्रियस्य परो धर्मः प्रजानामेव पालनम्' मनु० 7. 144. King सौदास also called कल्माषपाद, when tired by hunting, asked a sage named शक्ति the eldest son of वसिष्ठ to make way for him on a road. When he did not move the king whipped him, whereupon the sage cursed him to be a राक्षस subsisting on human flesh. नरान् क्षिणोति इति नरक्षित्. See महाभारत आदिपर्व chap. 176. नलम्—the story of नल is well-known. अवशं अक्षहृदयं यस्य who was not master of the secret of managing dice. गृहीत्वा चाश्वहृदयं राजन्भाङ्गासुरिर्नृपः ॥ निषधाधिपतेश्चापि दत्वाक्षहृदयं नृपः ।' वनपर्व Chap. 77. 18-19. अवशानि अक्षाणि हृदयं च यस्य whose heart and senses were not under his control. This is the fault found in him and also that कलि overcame him (while हर्ष had controlled his senses and his reign was an era of righteousness). दमयन्ती chose नल, though even gods like इन्द्र had attended the स्वयंवर. कलि enraged at this entered the body of नल. नल became addicted to gambling, lost his kingdom in favour of his brother who was an expert in gambling, and had to leave his country. After various vicissitudes, he learnt अक्षहृदय from ऋतुपर्ण and regained his wife, kingdom &c. *Vide* वनपर्व Chap. 53-77. The वासवदत्ता has 'नलः कलिनाभिभूतः.' मित्र ...गात् had his mind disturbed in regard to the daughter of मित्र; had a weakness for his friend's daughter. The last is the fault found in him. One's friend's daughter should be like one's own daughter. संवरण—सूर्य had a daughter named तपती, who was married by king संवरण who was a devotee of the sun. *Vide* आदिपर्व Chap. 171-173. इष्टः (प्रियः) रामः तस्य उन्मादेन (intense love); इष्टा रामा (a handsome woman) तस्याः उन्मादेन (by his mad love for). The latter is the fault found in दशरथ. दशरथ died when राम left for the forest to keep his father's promise given to कैकेयी. कार्तवीर्यः refers to सहस्त्रार्जुन. A king, according to ancient ideas, should be गोब्राह्मणप्रतिपालक and not ०पीडक. गो...पीडनेन also means 'by troubling a ब्राह्मण for a cow'. कार्तवीर्य, a king of माहिष्मती on the नर्मदा, took away the calf of the कामधेनु of जमदग्नि, father of परशुराम. परशुराम killed him. His sons killed जमदग्नि when परशुराम in revenge took the vow of destroying the क्षत्रिय race. *Vide* वनपर्व chap. 115-117. इष्टं बहु सुवर्णं यस्य to whom plenty of gold was dear. इष्टः बहुसुवर्णकः येन who performed a sacrifice called बहुसुवर्णक (in which there was gold and nothing else. *i. e.* in which the utensils were of gold and gold was distributed like water). देवानां द्विजः बृहस्पतिः तस्य बहुमतः (liked); देवानां द्विजानां च बहुमतः. The fault found in him is that he was not देव...मतः (while हर्ष was देवद्विजबहुमत). *Vide* विष्णुपु० IV. 1. 'मरुत्तस्य यथा यज्ञस्तथा कस्याभवद्भुवि । सर्वं हिरणमयं यस्य यज्ञवस्त्वतिशोभितम् ॥ अमाद्यदिन्द्रः सोमेन दक्षिणाभिर्द्विजातयः । मरुतः परिवेष्टारः सदस्याश्च दिवौकसः ॥ 18-19. The verse मरुतः परिवेष्टारो मरुत्तस्या &c. is well-known to every Brāhmaṇa. मरुत्त desiring to rival इन्द्र asked बृहस्पति to officiate at his sacrifice, but the latter refused. So he had it performed by बृहस्पति's brother संवर्त. बृहस्पति was very much pained at the prosperity of मरुत्त. *Vide* chap. 8. 36. *Vide* महाभारत आश्वमेधिकपर्व chap. 6–10. For शन्तनु see above p. 153. अतिव्यसनात् through extreme attachment. वियुक्तो वाहिन्या separated from the river (Ganges); separated from his army. One who is separated from an army is left all alone (एकाकी). To cry because he was left alone does not become a great king. The वासवदत्ता has 'शन्तनुरतिव्यसनाद्वने विललाप.' वन—means 'forest' (with पाण्डु) and 'water' (with मत्स्य). मदनरसेन आविष्टः overwhelmed by the passion of love; that has tasted the fruit of the मदन tree. For this story see आदिपर्व chap. 125. He had been cursed by sage किन्दम that he would die when he had intercourse with his wife. गुरु...हृदयः whose heart was despondent through fear (of the prowess) of his teacher (द्रोणाचार्य). गुरुभय also means 'great fear'. It does behove a king to give up truth through fear, however great it may be. When द्रोण made a terrible havoc in the Pāṇḍava hosts, a rumour spread that अश्वत्थामा (son of द्रोण) was killed. द्रोण who believed implicitly in the truthfulness of युधिष्ठिर asked him what the truth was. यु०, who knew that it was only an elephant named अश्वत्थामा that was killed, said 'हतः कुञ्जरः,' the latter word being uttered in a very low tone. The old man heard only the first word, laid aside his weapon in grief, when धृष्टद्युम्न killed him. *Vide* द्रोणपर्व chap. 190. Compare 'मुक्तशस्त्रं कलशयोनिमिव कृष्णवर्त्मप्रसूतिः' हर्ष० 6thउ०. The वासवदत्ता omits 'गुरु...हृदयः'. इत्थ...कलङ्कम् thus there has been no king without (some) stain. अपगतः कलङ्कः यस्मात्. ऋते except (governs the ablative). तथाहि—Here follow several sentences in which बाण shows by श्लिष्ट words how हर्ष emulates the deeds of gods and heroes of old. बल...भृतः (1) by Indra, the moving mountains possessed of wings (पक्षः) were made steady; by Harsha who subdues armies, fickle kings, that had formed coalitions, were paralysed. In this sentence the king is shown as doing what इन्द्र did. For the cutting off of the wings of mountains, see p. 84. अत्र...कृता (1) By Brahmā (प्रजापति) the earth (क्ष्मा) was placed over the hoods of the serpent (भोगिन्) शेष; by (हर्ष) the lord of the people, forgiveness was shown to the circle of the remaining kings. For शेष, see above p. 145. अत्र पुरु...कृता (1) Vishṇu, having churned the ocean-king (*viz.* क्षीरसागर), made लक्ष्मी his own (wife); by (हर्ष) the best of men, glory was made his by vanquishing the king of सिन्धु. सिन्धु—country on the Sindhu river. There is a reference to the conquests of हर्ष

in this and some of the following sentences. बलिना...नागः By Bali (king of असुरs) the great serpent (वासुकि) was let loose, who (वासुकि) had unloosened up his coils round the mountain (मन्दर); by the powerful Harsha, the great elephant (दर्पशात) was abandoned (in the forest), having loosened a king from the coils (of the trunk). वासुकि was the rope in the सागरमथन, while मन्दर mountain (भूभृत्) was the churniug handle, which must have had round it the coils of वासुकि. The churning was done both by gods and demons. Compare 'मन्दरमिव सुरासुररभसभ्रमितवासुकिकषणक्षीणेन' हर्ष० 4th उ०. मोचितं भूभृतः वेष्टनं येन. As to the reference to हर्ष the com. says 'श्रीकुमारो नाम राजा किल दर्पशातेनोपजातमदेन हस्तिना वेष्टितः ततः श्रीहर्षेणाकृष्य खड्गं तस्मान्मोचितोऽसौ दन्ती च रोषाद्वने परित्यक्त इति वार्ता.' देवे...कुमारः—by God, कार्तिकेय was crowned (as the commander-in-chief of the gods against the demon तारक); by the Lord (हर्ष), कुमार was crowned. This may refer to the fact that हर्ष crowned his own son in his life-time. We think, however, that the reference is rather to some other prince. It may be कुमारगुप्त, the elder of the two princes of Mālava, that were the companions of Harsha in his boyhood. Or कुमार may be the king of प्राग्ज्योतिष referred to in the 7th उच्छ्वास. स्वामि...शक्तिः by कार्तिकेय who felled the enemy with one stroke, his weapon (called शक्ति) was made famous; by the lord (हर्ष) who destroyed his enemies at one stroke, his prowess was made known. स्वामी is a name of कार्तिकेय. He wielded a weapon called शक्ति and killed the demon तारक. कार्तिकेय is also called शक्तिधर. नरासिंहेन...क्रमः—नरसिंह (Vishṇu in his man-lion *avatara*) that killed his foe (हिरण्यकशिपु) with his own hand (not with weapons) manifested his valour; the best of men (हर्ष), who destroyed his enemies in person (not with the help of an army), showed his might. Perhaps the word विक्रम (which means 'a footstep') contains an allusion to the वामनावतार. परमेश्व...करः—the great शिव took the hand of (*i. e.* married) Durgā the daughter of Himālaya; by the great Lord (हर्ष) tribute (करः) was levied from the inaccessible (दुर्ग) Himālaya regions. According to Buhler this passage refers to Harsha's conquest of Nepal. लोक... विभक्तः by Brahmā guardians of the world were appointed in the quarters and the treasures of the world were divided among the first-born (kings). 'हिरण्यगर्भो लोकेशः स्वयम्भूश्चतुराननः' इत्यमरः. For लोकपाल, see above p 140. भुवनकोश means the whole universe or world. अग्रजन्मनाम् the kings like मनु and पृथु that were first born. लोक...विभक्तः by the lord of the world (हर्ष), guardians of the people (great officers) were appointed in the regions and the treasure collected (by taxation) from the whole world was distributed among Brāhmaṇas. For this distribution, vide Intro. XL and notes p. 146. There is a third meaning suggested. लोकनाथ means बुद्ध. कोश is the Buddhist dictionary of वसुबन्धु. Compare 'शुकैरपि शाक्यशासनकुशलैः कोशं समुपदिशद्भिः' हर्ष० 8th उ० 5th para. महासमारम्भाः Great beginnings (with कृतयुग); great undertakings or efforts (with हर्ष). The propriety of प्रथम is this. According to Pauranic accounts, the present is the 7th Manu called वैवस्वत. Fourteen Manus are equal to a day of ब्रह्मा, which latter again is equal to 1000 महायुगs (constituted by the four युगs, कृत, त्रेता, द्वापर and कलि). A day of ब्रह्मा is called कल्प. It will be seen therefore that numerous कृतयुगs have passed away since the world began. In the first कृतयुग, however, very great beginnings had to be made as everything was new; the earth had to be made steady &c.; in the succeeding ones there were no such great beginnings. पूर्व...क्रमेण in the order of the lineage of his ancestors. सु...माणानाम् It is long since we entertained the desire to hear. अयस्कान्तमणयः magnets. नीरस-निष्ठुराणि—dry and hard (with लोहानि); without taste (apprecia-tion) and harsh (with मनांसि). क्षुल्लकानाम् of insignificant (or mean) persons. स्वभावेन सरसानि (affectionate, appreciative) मृदूनि च. These two words are the opposite of नीरस and निष्ठुर. इतरेषाम् of those who are not क्षुल्लक. भार्गवो वंशः—we saw above (text p. 17 l. 29) that Bāṇa's ancestor वत्स belonged to the भार्गववंश.

P. 41 ll. 5—18 बाणस्तु...यासीत्. न...हितम् you did not say what would be reasonable (or fit). The idea is that it does not stand to reason that a puny narrator like बाण could narrate the wondrous tale of Harsha's life. अघटमानः मनोरथः यस्मिन्. अघट...कल्पयामि I am of opinion that your curiosity cannot secure its object. शक्या...तृषः those who are eager to secure their object are generally wanting in the proper estimate as to what is possible and what is not possible. स्वार्थे तृट् येषां ते ०तृषः or स्वार्थाय तृष्यन्ति ते ०तृषः or तृषः may mean simply 'desires'. प्रियजनकथायाः श्रवणे रसः (passion, liking) तस्य रभसेन (excess) मोहिता. प्रविवेक—judgment. क्व-क्व Two क्वs show great disparity or incongruity between two things. परमाणोरिव परिमाणं यस्य the capacity of which is as small as

स्युः तथा उद्गिरति इति that recited (*lit.* emitted) disconnected lines (दण्डकः) of the text or that recited the texts in such a way that many lines were dropped (in the effort to recite). The idea seems to be this:—naughty and dull boys were called upon by their wearied old teachers to perform सन्ध्यावन्दन either by repeating what the teacher would himself first pronounce or by repeating what they had been taught before. In this process the careless boys omitted certain portions and loudly repeated the rest. The old and wearied preceptors did not seem to notice the lapses of the students. सन्ध्यां...यति that listened to the evening prayer. The reading समवधीरयति is in one way better, meaning 'that treated with contempt the evening prayer.' बठरः dullard ; compare 'मुनिनाथोऽपि...कृपावानात्मानं बठरसत्त्वेभ्यः कतिकृत्वो न दत्तवान्' हर्ष० 8th उ०. विटः sensualist, dandy. तारका आख्या (name) यस्य (*adj.* of ज्योतिषि). समुन्म...खे (*lit.*) when in the sky (खं) emerged the lights called stars *i. e.* when the stars began to twinkle. तयै...तस्थौ he stood in the same company (as before). नीतः प्रथमः यामः (प्रहरः) येन who passed the first part of the night. गणपतेः—गणपति was one of the four cousins of बाण mentioned above (text p. 39 l. 30). निमीलिता (closed) दृक् (eye) येषां. अनुपजाता निद्रा येषाम्—They could not sleep (through expectant curiosity) though they closed their eyes. सूर्यो...लयताम् that waited for the rise of the sun. कमलs also close their buds at night and wait for सूर्योदय when they bloom.

P. 41 l. 33—**P. 42** l. 12 अथ...रेभे. तुर्ये चतुर्थे. प्रतिबुद्धः waking up. **Verse 5.** This is cited by the काव्यप्रकाश as an instance of the figure स्वभावोक्ति. For जाति or स्वभावोक्ति *vide* notes p. 4. The principal sentence is तुरङ्गः क्ष्मां (पृथ्वीं) खुरेण विलिखति (paws, scratches). पश्चा...सार्थे having stretched his foot behind. त्रिक...मुच्चैः having lengthened out upwards his body that was stretched (to full length) by bending the lower part of the spine. 'पृष्ठवंशाधरे त्रिकम्' अमरः (पृष्ठास्थ्नोऽध ऊर्वोः सन्धौ त्रिसङ्घट्टस्त्रिकम्—क्षीर०). विततं *adj.* of अङ्गम् or we may take it as an अव्ययीभाव. त्रिकस्य नत्या विततं यथा स्यात्तथा. द्राघयति is a denominative verb from दीर्घ. आस...रसि with bent (आभुग्न) neck having rested his mouth on his chest. सटां...धूय having tossed his mane grey with dust. घासः fodder. अनवरतं चलत् प्रोथं यस्य तत् अ...प्रोथं ०त्प्रोथं तुण्डं यस्य सः ०तुण्डः (nostril). 'घोणा तु प्रोथमस्त्रियाम्' अमरः. मन्दं शब्दायमानः gently neighing. शब्दं करोति इति शब्दायते, according to 'शब्दवैरकलहाभ्रकण्वमेघेभ्यः करणे' पा. 3. 1. 17. The metre is स्रग्धरा. **Verse 6.**

कुर्वन् (तुरङ्गः)—the object is कन्धराम् (neck). आभुग्नं पृष्ठं यस्य. मुख...कटिः bringing his loins near his mouth. आतिरश्चीम् curved sideways. लोलेना...केसरेण that (कोण) was struck with his restless and waving mane that dropped down particles of dew (तुहिनं). केसर is that part of the mane which is on the forehead. निद्रा...कषायम् that was reddish through the itch after sleep (or through sleep and itch). कषति—the subject is तुरङ्गः and the object is कोणम्. निबिडिता श्रोत्रशुक्तिः येन that closed his shell-like ears (with his mane). त्वङ्गन्ति पक्ष्माग्राणि तेषु लग्नाः प्रतनुबुसकणाः यस्मिन् (the corner of the eye) on the restless lashes of which stuck small particles of chaff. खुरेण—is to be connected with कषति. The metre is स्रग्धरा. ज्ञातयः=बान्धवाः. पूर्वो...प्रायः who understood their intention by the discussion that had already taken place. उद्घातः allusion, reference.

P. 42 l. 13—**P. 43** l. 12. **श्रूयताम्...जनपदः.** The principal sentence is अस्ति...श्रीकण्ठो नाम जनपदः. पुण्य...तीर्णः which was inhabited by the meritorious, as though it were the abode (आवासः) of Indra descended upon the earth. पुण्यकृत् also means 'gods'. It was believed that those who accumulated merit by the performance of sacrifices went to Indra's heaven and returned to the earth when their merit was exhausted. Compare 'त्रैविद्या मां सोमपाः पूतपापा यज्ञैरिष्ट्वा स्वर्गतिं प्रार्थयन्ते । ते **पुण्यमासाद्य सुरेन्द्रलोक**मश्नन्ति दिव्यान्दिवि देवभोगान् ॥ ते तं भुक्त्वा स्वर्गलोकं विशालं क्षीणे पुण्ये मर्त्यलोकं विशन्ति ।' भगवद्गीता Chap. IX. 20–21. असङ्कीर्णे वर्णानां व्यवहारस्थिती (व्यवहारः स्थितिश्च) यस्मिन् where the practices and usages of the (four) Varṇas were not confused. कृतयुगस्येव व्यवस्था यस्मिन्. In कृतयुग there was no वर्णसङ्कर, nor was there any in the country of श्रीकण्ठ. If we read कृतकृत०, then we dissolve as कृता कृतयुगस्य व्यवस्था यस्मिन्. स्थल...क्षेत्रः abounding as it did in land lotuses, its fields were broken by ploughs (हलम्) the points (पोत्रं) of which uprooted lotus fibres and which caused a humming of bees, as though they (हल) sang the excellent (सार) qualities of the soil. स्थलकमल—distinguish them from water-lotuses, that are simply कमलs. पोत्रैः उन्मूल्यमानानि मृणालानि येषाम्. '**मुखाग्रे** क्रोड**हलयोः** पोत्रम्' अमरः. उद्गीताः मेदिन्याः साराः गुणाः यैः. There is a श्लेष on the word गुण (quality, string). The मृणालs are गुणs. The poet fancies that the hum of bees on the lotuses that were uprooted is a song declaring the fertility of the soil. उल्लिख्यमानानि क्षेत्राणि यस्य. क्षीरो...न्तरः that was dense with rows of plantations (वाटः-टम्) of Puṇḍra sugarcane, as though they

(rows) were watered by clouds that had drunk the waters of the milky ocean. पुण्ड्र is a very sweet variety of sugar-cane. The poet fancies that the sweetness must be due to their being watered by clouds from क्षीरसागर (and not from the salt ocean). It is a general rule that the qualities of effects arise from similar qualities in their causes. Compare 'कारणगुणपूर्वकः कार्यगुणो दृष्टः' वैशेषिकसूत्र II. 1. 24 or the न्याय 'कारणगुणा हि कार्यगुणानारभन्ते.' प्रति...सीमान्तः the borders of which were in every direction crowded (सङ्कट) with heaps of corn, as though they were strange hills, separated (from each other) by threshing floors. खलधानं threshing floor. धामन् *n.* place. The heaps were big like hills. The com. says 'खलधानधामभिः खलपालैः' *i. e.* it takes it to mean 'by the owners or watchmen of the threshing floors.' (खलधानं धाम येषाम्). This is not good. सम...भूमिः the ground of which was thickly covered (जटिलित) with beds of cumin seed (जीरकः) being watered by the pots of the water-wheel. क्षीर० says that, according to कौटिल्य, उद्घातन means 'घटीयन्त्र.' We must ascribe the same sense to उद्घात. 'उद्घाटनं घटीयन्त्रम्' अमरः. उर्वरा...कृतः adorned with rice fields extending (beyond their proper limits) on account of the very fertile soil. 'उर्वरा सर्वसस्याढ्या' अमरः. For शालेय see p. 118. वरीयः is the comparative of उरु. The idea is:—the land surrounding the rice fields also was fertile and so beyond the fields proper grew ricecrops due to the fact that some grains were carried away by the birds or by the ants and grew luxuriantly there. पाक...छितः that had stretches of wheat fields (गोधूमधामन्) variegated (किर्मीरित) by heaps of *Rājamāsha* beans bursting as they were ripe and rendered brown (कपिशित) by the split pods of *mudga*. मुद्ग is Marathi मूग. पाकेन विशरारवः राजमाषाः तेषां निकरैः किर्मीरितानि तैः. The next clause is महिष...विपिनः. महिषपृष्ठे प्रतिष्ठिताः (mounted) गायन्तः गोपालाः तैः पालितानि तैः (*adj.* of गोधनैः). कीट...सृतैः (गोधनैः) that were followed by sparrows greedy (लम्पट) for the swarms of insects. The insects (probably flies) pursued the cows (as they had ulcers on their backs or feet &c.) and were in their turn pursued by चटकाs. अवटुः (ग्रीवा) तस्यां घटिताः घण्टाः एव घट्यः तासां रटितेन रमणीयैः charming with the tinkling of jar-like bells bound round their necks. 'कम्बुग्रीवा त्रिरेखा सावटुर्घाटा कृकाटिका' अमरः. अटद्भिरटवीं that wandered over the forest. क्षर...क्षरद्भिः that dropped milk (from their udders), as though it (milk) were the milky ocean drunk by the bull of S'iva and then distributed in many places (*viz.* the cows) for fear of disease (*i. e.* indigestion). बाष्प...तृप्तैः that were fed on very tender grass. बाष्प...तृण means 'grass that can be cut with tears' *i. e.* very soft and tender. Note 'कृत्यैरधिकार्थवचने' पा. 2. 1. 33. (स्तुतिनिन्दाफलकमर्थवादवचनमधिकार्थवचनं तत्र कर्तरि करणे च तृतीया कृत्यैः सह प्राग्वत्। वातच्छेद्यं तृणम्। काकपेया नदी। सि. कौ.). कृत्य means potential participles. 'गोधनं स्याद्गवां व्रजे' अमरः. धवलितानि विपिनानि यस्य. The cows were white. विविध...देशः the districts (उद्देशः) of which were variegated with black antelopes in thousands, as though they were the eyes let fall (from heaven on earth) by Indra (शतमन्युः) blinded by the smoke of the offerings of various sacrifices. शतं मन्यवः क्रतवः अस्य इति शतमन्युः. Indra also has a 1000 eyes; eyes are कृष्णशार (dark and variegated). The pupil is dark, while the corners of the eye are reddish and the other part is white; hence the word कृष्णशार. For the 1000 eyes of इन्द्र *vide* 'सहस्रनेत्रदर्शनयोग्यां जयन्तीमिव शची' हर्ष० 4th उ० and notes thereon. धवल...शोभितः adorned with regions whitened with the pollen of *Ketakī* groves that scattered about white dust, as though they (regions) were the entrances of the city of S'iva grey with the ashes sprinkled over the lord of प्रमथs. प्रमथs are the attendants of शिव. उद्धूलनम् smearing the body with ashes. शिव is represented as fond of this. शाककन्दलैः श्यामलितानि ग्रामाणां उपकण्ठे (समीपे) काश्यपीपृष्ठानि यस्मिन्. शाककन्दलैः with the shoots of vegetables; or 'with vegetables and plantains.' काश्यपी—the earth, so called because परशुराम, after vanquishing the क्षत्रियs, made a gift of it to कश्यप. 'क्षोणी ज्या काश्यपी क्षितिः' अमरः. करभपालीभिः with rows of young camels. Understand उपलक्षितः after this, in accordance with the Sūtra 'इत्थम्भूतलक्षणे' पा. 2. 3. 21. For करभ, mark the Sūtra 'शृङ्खलमस्य बन्धनं करभे' पा. 5. 2. 79. (शृङ्खलकः करभः). The instrumentals from ०प्रस्फोटितैः to ०पथिकैः qualify द्राक्षामण्डपैः. पीलुपल्लवैः प्रस्फोटितं येषु—where (the dust on the feet of travellers) was rubbed off with the tender leaves of the Pīlu tree. For this use of प्रस्फोटित compare 'पथिकपादप्रस्फोटनधूलिधूसरैर्नवपल्लवैर्लाञ्छितच्छायानाम् (अटवीप्रवेशप्रपाणां)' हर्ष० 7th उ० last para; 'विश्रान्तकार्पटिकप्रस्फोटितचरणधूलिधूसरकिसलयलाञ्छितोपकण्ठैः' कादम्बरी p. 223 of P. प्रस्फोटित may also mean 'pierced.' The com. says 'प्रस्फोटितैर्नीराजनीकृतैः.' करपुटैः पीडितानि (squeezed) मातुलुङ्गीदलानि (citron leaves) तेषां रसेन उपलिप्तैः besmeared. मातुलुङ्गी is Marathi महाळुंग. स्वेच्छया विचिताः कुङ्कुमकेसराः तैः कृतः पुष्पप्रकरः येषु—where the saffron filaments gathered at their pleasure (by the travellers) served as the offering of flowers. प्रत्यग्राणां (fresh) फलानां रसः तस्य पानेन सुखसुप्ताः पथिकाः येषु. वन...गृहैरिव—the poet fancies that the vine arbours under which the travellers rested were as though the water-hostels where nectar was given by wood nymphs. The juice of the sweet grapes that the travellers eat is like nectar. The words from ०प्रस्फोटितैः to ०पथिकैः suggest certain characteristics of a प्रपागृह (Marathi पाणपोई). The dust in a प्रपा may be cleared away with पल्लवs; it may be उपलिप्त with cowdung as green as मातुलुङ्गीदलरस. Offerings of flowers (पुष्पप्रकरः) are made on the floor of प्रपाs. Travellers take rest after drinking water (रसपान) there. द्राक्षामण्डपैः—is to be connected with विलो... र्गमः. स्फुटन्ति (bursting open) फलानि यासाम्—*adj.* of दाडिमीनां. बीजलग्नः शुकचञ्चुरागः यासाम्. The reddish grains of the pomegranate look like the red beaks of parrots. The poet fancies that the redness of beaks stuck to the seeds, when parrots pecked the फलs. समारूढं कपिकुलं तस्य कपोलैः सन्दिह्यमानानि कुसुमानि यासाम्. The flowers of the pomegranate trees looked like the cheeks of the monkeys that had climbed them, so that one had difficulty in distinguishing them. विलोभनीयाः उपनिर्गमाः यस्य the approaches to which (country of श्रीकण्ठ) were fascinating. वनपालैः पीयमानः नारिकेलरसासवः (the wine of cocoanut juice) येषु—*adj.* of उपवनैः. पथिकलोकेन लुप्यमानाः (pillaged) पिण्डखर्जूराः (datetrees) येषु *adj.* of उपवनैः. गोलाङ्गूलैर्लिह्यमानः मधुरामोदः (मधुरः आमोदः यस्य) पिण्डीरसः येषु. पिण्डी is a kind of palm tree. For गोलाङ्गूल, see p. 54. ०चञ्चुभिः जर्जरिताः आरुकाः येषु. आरुकः a plant growing in the हिमालय with cooling properties. ०वृतैः—*adj.* of ०बन्धैः. अर्जुन is a kind of tree. गोकुलानां अवतारेण कलुषितं कूलकीलालं येषाम्—the water on the edges of which was rendered turbid by the descent of herds of kine. अध्वगः a traveller. शरण्य that afforded refuge. शरणे साधुः शरण्यः, according to 'तत्र साधुः' पा. 4. 4. 98. अरण्यधराबन्धैः forest pools. अवन्ध्यानि वनरन्ध्राणि यस्मिन् the hollows (or valleys) in the forests of which are not barren (on account of pools). करभेभ्यो हितः करभीयः; *vide* notes on शङ्कव्य and वत्सीय p. 94. उष्ट्राणां (camels) समूहः औष्ट्रकम्, उरभ्राणां (rams) समूहः औरभ्रकम्, according to 'गोत्रोक्षोष्ट्रोरभ्रराजराजन्यराजपुत्रवत्समनुष्याजाद्वुञ्' पा. 4. 2. 39 (एभ्यः समूहे वुञ् स्यात्). *Vide* औक्षक p. 166. कृतः सम्बाधः (crowd) यस्मिन्. In the next clause दिशि...चितः, the principal part is वडवानां...चितः full of the wandering droves of mares (वडवा). विलो...लब्धानाम् that were smeared with the juice of saffron plots that were crushed

(मृदित) by their rolling (विलोठनं) on them. समालब्ध 'smeared with unguents'. For the rolling of horses on saffron spots, compare रघु. 4. 67. विनीताध्वश्रमास्तस्य सिन्धुतीरविचेष्टनैः । दुधुवुर्वाजिनः स्कन्धाँल्लग्नकुङ्कुमकेसरान् ॥.' The poet fancies that the mares were smeared with saffron and wandered about (as अभिसारिकाs would do) for seducing the horses (seven) of the Sun. उत्प्रोथपुटैः and उन्मुखैः are equivalent to उद्गतप्रोथ० and उद्गतमुखैः—with their up-turned nostrils and mouths. उदर...पिबन्तीनाम्—the poet fancies that the mares turned up their noses because they wanted to take in the wind (प्रभञ्जनः) for the purpose of producing speed in the young lying in their wombs. वातहरिणीनामिव–This word has several senses. वातहरिण is a very swift kind of deer. The wind-gods (Maruts) are supposed to be drawn by deer. पृषदश्व is a synonym of वात. The word may also suggest the sense 'that surpass the wind (in speed)'. अनवरतानां क्रतूनां धूमः तेन अन्धकारः तस्मिन् प्रवृत्तैः that were produced (kindled) in the darkness of the smoke of &c. बाणैः—fires. हंसs have white wings and hence the fires are fancied to be हंसयूथs. हंसs move about in the dark (अन्धकार) resembling the smoke &c. There is an apparent विरोध between अन्धकारप्रवृत्तैः and धवलितभुवनः. What springs from darkness cannot whiten the world. If we read गुणैः for बाणैः, then the meaning is similar. By the performance of क्रतुs, merit is produced. पुण्य and यशः are poetically said to be white. सङ्गीत...लोकः with the vast resources (prosperity) of which the mortal world resounded, as though with peacocks intoxicated by the sound of drums. ०मुरजः a drum beaten in a concert. Peacocks are overjoyed when it thunders. They mistook मुरजरव for thunder. Another sense is suggested by सङ्गीत...मत्तैः—the wealth of the people was so vast that they were mad after singing &c. शशि...वृत्तैः whose conduct was as pure (अवदात) as the rays of the moon (with virtuous men); that were round (वृत्त) and bright like the rays of the moon (with pearls). गुणिभिः (with pearls) would also mean 'that were strung together.' प्रसाधितः adorned. पथिकशतैः विलुप्यमानानि (pillaged) स्फीतानि (abundant) फलानि येषाम् (with trees); ०विलुप्यमानं स्फीतं फलं (ऐश्वर्यं येषाम्)—the guests obtained plenty of money in that country, which (money) was distributed by them among other travellers. अभिगमनीयः sought for (by all guests); inviting (with big trees). मृग...कृतः that was steadied (protected) by the headmen of villages (महत्तरः) clad in garments of deer-skin bearing the fragrance of musk, as though they were the hills at the foot of the हिमालय. For मृगमद, see p. 51. मृग...दितैः (with ०पादैः) means 'covered with the hair of the deer scented with' &c. The musk-deer is found in the Himālaya range. महत्तरैः with ०पादैः means 'very large.' 'पादाः प्रत्यन्तपर्वताः' अमरः. महत्तर as the name of an officer occurs in numerous grants (compare I. A. vol. VIII p. 20 and vol. XII p. 25). The word occurs in the 7th उच्छ्वास also. प्रोद्दण्ड...त्तमैः on the lotuses of which with upraised stalks were seatd the best of birds (with reservoirs of water); on the lotus of which with upraised stalk was seated Brahmā (with the navel of Vishṇu). 'सहस्रपत्रं कमलम्' इत्यमरः. For नारायणनाभि, see notes pp. 20 and 28 above. For द्विजोत्तम as meaning ब्रह्मा, see 'द्विजवरस्वेच्छागृहीतकोषो नाभिपद्म इव' हर्ष० 4th उ० first para. प्रोद्दण्ड...मण्डितः also conveys another sense. The best of Brāhmanas in thousands sat on thousands of leaves near the lakes in that country for perfoming सन्ध्यावन्दन &c. मथितः...क्षितिभिः where the ground (or earth) was washed with streams of churned milk (with महाघोषैः aud ०रम्भैः). मथितं also means 'buttermilk.' 'तक्रं ह्युदश्विन्मथितं पादाम्बर्धाम्बु निर्जलम्' अमरः. महाघोषः a big hamlet of cowherds. महान् घोषः (uproar) येषु (*adj.* of रम्भैः). At the time when the gods and demons began to churn there must have been a great uproar. पूरिताशः the regions of which were filled (with जनपदः). The directions were filled with great uproar at the time of churning or the effort of churning satisfied the hopes (of the gods and demons). जनपदः a country.

P. 43 ll. 13—21. **यत्र...दैवम्.** यत्र...दृष्टयः where wrong doctrines faded away, as though washed by the water of the tears due to the smoke of the three fires. 'दक्षिणाग्निर्गार्हपत्याहवनीयौ त्रयोऽग्नयः । अग्नित्रयमिदं त्रेता' अमरः. As the people stuck to Vedic rites, heresies departing from the Veda ceased to exist. कुदृष्टयः also 'weak eyesight.' Weak eyesight may be cured by medicines applied to the eye, which cause the eye to drop tears. पच्य...दुरितानि sins were not seen (*i. e.* vanished) as though burnt by the fire of the bricks (इष्टका) that were being baked for constructing altars. As the people were virtuous, no sins were committed. The poet fancies that sins vanished because they were consumed &c. Explain the following उत्प्रेक्षाs similarly. छिद्यमानं यूपाय दारु येन सः ०दारुः परशुः तेन पाटितः cleft. मख...धौत इव as though washed by the streams of the clouds made up of the smoke of sacrificial fires (शिखिन् *m.*). For clouds being formed of smoke, see notes p. 106. वर्णसङ्करः (a combination of colours) may be washed with water and then no colour would remain. सुरा...इव as though cut up by numerous chisels (टङ्कः) for shaping (घट्टनं) the stones of the temples. 'टङ्कः पाषाणदारणः' अमरः. महा...द्रवाः calamities ran away, as though routed by the tumult of the making of महादानs. महादान is a name of certain very munificent gifts (16 in number), the first being तुलापुरुषदान. उपद्रवः a misfortune or national calamity (such as a famine). दीप्य...पिता इव as though heated by thousands of blazing kitchens in the great sacrifices. 'सत्रमाच्छादने यज्ञे' अमरः. वृष...त्रासिताः इव as though frightened by the sharp sound of the holy drums beaten at the marriages of bulls. On the eleventh day after the death of a person, a bull is let loose along with cows, which is called वृषोत्सर्ग or वृषविवाह. 'एकादशाहे प्रेतस्य यस्य चोत्सृज्यते वृषः । प्रेतलोकं परित्यज्य स्वर्गलोकं स गच्छति ॥.' अपमृत्यवः untimely deaths. ब्रह्मघोष = वेदघोष. 'वेदस्तत्त्वं तपो ब्रह्म' अमरः. ईतयः—Distress or calamity. ईतिs are usually said to be six. 'अतिवृष्टिरनावृष्टिर्मूषिकाः शलभाः शुकाः । अत्यासन्नाश्च राजानः षडेता ईतयः स्मृताः ॥.' क्षीर॰. शलभाः locusts. अत्यासन्नाः राजानः extreme proximity of kings (*i. e.* encampment of soldiers, whether hostile or friendly). धर्मा... दैवम् As the sole अधिकार (power) rested with धर्म, दुर्दैव could not become a प्रभु (lord) in that country.

P. 43 ll. 22—31. तत्र...विशेषः. The principal sentence is तत्र च एवंविधे...स्थाण्वीश्वराख्यो जनपदविशेषः. नाना आरामाः (gardens) तेषां अभिरामः ॰परिमलः तेन सुभगः (with ॰विशेषः). नाना रामाः (beautiful women) अभिरामाः ॰परिमलाश्च तैः सुभगः (with यौवनारम्भः). As youth is the most charming period of one's life, so the country was the most charming in the world. कुङ्कुम...शोभितः decked with many thousands of buffaloes reddened (पिञ्जरित) by crushing (*i. e.* rolling in) saffron (with country); decked with many thousands of crowned queens (महिषी) reddened with saffron unguents (with अन्तःपुरनिवेशः). अन्तः...धर्मस्य—As the अन्तःपुर is a spot loved by a king, where he moves about freely and confidently, so in that country धर्म reached its highest pitch. मरुता (वातेन) उद्धूयमानानि ॰व्यजनानि तेषां शतैः धवलिताः प्रान्ताः यस्य (with the country); मरुत्सु (देवेषु) उद्धूयमानानि (being waved) ॰व्यजनानि &c. In the country roamed चमरी deer the tails of which were shaken by the wind. In heaven (सुरराज्य) chowries are waved before gods. ज्वलन्तः मखशिखिनः तेषां सहस्रैः दीप्यमानाः दश दिगन्ताः

यस्मिन्. As thousands of sacrifices were performed, a vast store of merit was accumulated. In कृतयुग also there was vast merit. So the country is fancied to be an encampment. In a camp also fires blaze forth at night. Or the reference may be to the fires in the नीराजन ceremony of the camp. *Vide* p. 34. The com. shows that कृतयुग also means 'king'. 'कृतं प्रतिसमाहितं युगं द्वयं स्वपक्षपरपक्षरूपं येन स राजोच्यते.' पद्ममेव आसनं तस्मिन् स्थितः ब्रह्मर्षिः(ब्रह्मा चासौ ऋषिश्च) तस्य ध्यानेन आधीयमानः (brought about) सकलस्य अकुशलस्य (evil, calamity) प्रशमः यस्मिन् (with अवतारः); पद्मासनं आसनभेदः तस्मिन् स्थिताः ब्रह्मर्षयः तेषां ध्यानेन &c. Brahmā sits on the lotus in the navel of विष्णु. For ब्रह्मा warding off evil, compare 'त्रिभुवनोपप्लवप्रशमकुशापीडधारिणेव दक्षिणेन करेण' (text) p. 4. l. 20. In the country there were ब्रह्मर्षिs (saintly Brāhmaṇas) sitting in the *yogic* posture called पद्मासन. In this आसन the right foot is placed on the left thigh and the left foot on the right thigh; the toes are to be firmly held by the hands; the chin is to be on the heart and one has to look at the tip of the nose. 'वामोरूपरि दक्षिणं च चरणं संस्थाप्य वामं तथा दक्षोरूपरि पश्चिमेन विधिना धृत्वा कराभ्यां दृढम् । अङ्गुष्ठौ हृदये निधाय चिबुकं नासाग्रमालोकयेदेतद्व्याधिविनाशकारि यमिनां पद्मासनं प्रोच्यते ॥ हठयोगप्रदीपिका. महावाहिनी great river; great army. विपक्ष...कुरूणाम् that was as though the enemy (*i. e.* the rival) of the country of उत्तरकुरु. An enemy (विपक्ष) has large armies. In the country described there were both large armies and large rivers. उत्तरकुरु is one of the four द्वीपs near मेरु (भीष्मपर्व 6. 13). The great river there is the Ganges. 'दक्षिणेन तु नीलस्य मेरोः पार्श्वे तथोत्तरे । उत्तराः कुरवो राजन् पुण्याः सिद्धनिषेविताः॥' भीष्मपर्व 7. 2. If we read विक्षेपः the meaning is 'that throws off (into the background) *i. e.* surpasses.' वि...पुरस्य like the conqueror of the three cities *i. e.* like S'iva; that desired to conquer (*i. e.* that equalled in splendour) the three cities of the Asuras (with the country). For त्रिपुरदाह, see p. 113 above. ईश्वरः शिवः तस्य मार्गणाः बाणाः तैः सन्तापः तस्य अनभिज्ञाः सकलजनाः यस्मिन्; ईश्वरस्य नृपस्य मार्गणं तस्य &c. The idea in the latter case is either that the people of that country did not know the harassment due to the exacting demands of the king or that they did not know how to solicit favours from the king. सुधारसेन (by *chunam* or whitewash) सिक्तानि धवलगृहाणि तेषां पङ्क्त्या पाण्डुरः. The country had whitewashed houses and so resembled moonlight. In चन्द्रलोक there must be houses sprinkled with nectar (as the moon is full of सुधा). मधुमत्ताः (intoxicated by drink) मत्तकाशिन्यः (handsome and fascinating women) तेषां भूषणरवेण भरितं भुवनं यस्मिन्. मत्तकाशिनी—मत्ता क्षीबा इव काशते भाति इति मत्तकाशिनी. The com. says that मत्तकाशिनी also means 'यक्षिणी'. यक्षs are the servants of कुबेर. नामाभिहारः carrying away the name (and depositing it in another place) *i. e.* a synonym. As there was the jingling of the ornaments of मत्तकाशिनीs, the country was a synonym of कुबेरनगर. स्थाण्वीश्वरः—the modern Thanesar. जन...शेषः—श्रीकण्ठ was a large country of which स्थाण्वीश्वर was a part.

P. 43 l. 32—**P. 44** l. 6. **यस्तपो...गृह्यत.** The principal sentence is यः...अगृह्यत. We have to supply अगृह्यत in each clause. कामायतनम् abode of Cupid or the temple of Cupid. लासकैः = नटैः. यम...शत्रुभिः—the country was so well guarded that enemies were as much afraid of it as of Death. For चिन्तामणि, see above p. 135. वीरक्षेत्रम् It was the home of heroes. गन्धर्वनगरम्–गन्धर्वs are the musicians of the gods. गायनैः by singers. विश्वकर्मा—is the architect of the gods and presides over all arts. विज्ञानिभिः by artisans, by those skilled in the 64 arts. 'मोक्षे धीर्ज्ञानमन्यत्र विज्ञानं शिल्पशास्त्रयोः' अमरः. वैदेहकैः = वणिग्भिः. 'वैदेहकः सार्थवाहो नैगमो वाणिजो वणिक्' अमरः. द्यूत...बन्दिभिः—bards looked upon it as a gambling house. In a gambling house fortunes are made (and also lost) in a day. Bards were richly rewarded in that country. विट...दग्धैः by sharpwitted men (or crafty) it was looked upon as a club of clever voluptuaries. सुकृतपरिणामः as the fulfilment (ripening) of their good deeds. Travellers got there everything they desired. It is only through one's good deeds in former lives that one is so fortunate as to secure whatever one desires. असुरविवरम्—*vide* notes p. 90. वातिकैः—com. paraphrases as 'विवरव्यसनिभिराचार्यैः.' Probably there is a pun on the word वातिक which means 'mad' and 'those whose heads are turned by the thought of amassing money.' Mad men are confined in dark places. That country gave as much money to fortune-hunters as असुरविवर was supposed to yield. शा...भिः it was looked upon as a Buddhist monastery by those who wanted tranquility of mind. महोत्सवसमाजः concourse of people on a great festival. चारणैः wandering actors (देशान्तरभ्रमणाज्जीवति इति चारणः). वसुधारा stream of wealth. Munificent gifts were made to Brāhmaṇas in that country.

P. 44 ll. 7—11 **यत्र च...प्रमदाः.** In this paragraph, each adjective independently qualifies प्रमदाः. Further in each pair of adjectives there is an apparent contradiction due to श्लेष. मातङ्गगामिन्यः possessing the gait of elephants; having sexual intercourse with chaṇḍālas. **'चण्डालप्लवमातङ्ग**दिवाकीर्तिजनङ्गमाः।' अमरः. If they were मातङ्ग॰ (in the 2nd sense), they could not be शीलवत्यः (of pure conduct). गौर्यः fair; Gaurîs (पार्वती). विभवरताः attached to pomp and luxury; attached to a place where no शिव existed. विगतः भवः यस्मात् तस्मिन् रताः. If they were पार्वती, they must be भवरत (and not विभवरत). श्यामाः handsome; dark. श्यामा is a handsome lady described as 'शीते सुखोष्णसर्वाङ्गी ग्रीष्मे या सुखशीतला। तप्तकाञ्चनवर्णाभा सा स्त्री श्यामेति कथ्यते॥'. पद्म॰ decked with rubies; having the colour of (red) lotus. What is dark cannot be red. श्यामाः also means 'nights' and पद्मरागिण्यः would mean 'loving lotuses.' Nights cannot love day lotuses. धवल... वदनाः whose faces are bright with white teeth; whose mouths are pure like those of pure Brāhmaṇas. मदि...सनाः whose breath is fragrant like wine; whose breath...with wine. If they drank wine, their mouths could not be pure. Wine-drinking was forbidden to all, particularly to Brāhmaṇas. *Vide* notes above p. 160. चन्द्र...वपुषः whose bodies are charming like the moon; whose bodies are (hard) like the चन्द्रकान्त stone. शिरीष is a very delicate flower. अ...गम्याः not to be approched by gallants; not to be approached by serpents. कञ्चुकिन्यः wearing a bodice; female serpents (*lit.* possessed of slough). कञ्चुकिन्यः also means 'libidinous.' पृथु...श्रियः whose glory as wives spread far and wide (also 'whose beautiful hips are broad'); whose retinue of women is large. **'कलत्रं** श्रोणिभार्ययोः' अमरः. दरिद्र...लिताः possessed of a slender waist; counted among the poor. लावण्यवत्यः possessed of beauty; possessed of salt. अप्रमत्ताः not rash or careless; not intoxicated. प्रसन्नः (clear) उज्ज्वलः रागः (colour) यासाम्; प्रसन्नावत् उज्ज्वलः रागः येषाम्. प्रसन्ना means 'wine.' *Vide* notes p. 143 on प्रसन्ना. अकौतुकाः that did not wear the marriage thread; that were free from (girlish) curiosity. For the meaning of कौतुक compare रघु॰ 8. 1 'अथ तस्य **विवाहकौतुकं** ललितं बिभ्रत एव पार्थिवः'. Being grown up (प्रौढ) they must once have worn the marriage thread.

P. 44 l. 12—24 **यत्र च...परिजनाः.** In this passage the poet describes that the women possessed naturally those things which they had added by way of decoration and so the latter were really superfluous. चक्षु...दामानि their very eyes are a natural wreath for the head, the garlands of lotus petals are a mere burden. Their eyes were darker than the blue कुवलयs. अलक...किसलयानि the images of their tresses reflected in their (bright) cheeks were ear-ornaments unimpaired (in beauty); the tender leaves of the *Tamāla* (placed on the ear as ornament) were superfluous. Their tresses were darker and more glossy than तमाल leaves. प्रियकथा: talk about their husbands. आडम्बर: show, external appendage. कपोला...दीपा: their (bright) cheeks alone caused continuous light (आलोक:); the jewelled lamps at night were merely (for the sake of) pomp. कुल...जालिका the veil (जालिका) was merely an appendage worn because it was the custom of high-born ladies to wear one. बाह्य...ताडनम् playing on the lute was an external accomplishment (*i. e.* an accomplishment for display). पटवास: perfumed powder. Their smile was bright like camphor and when they smiled their breath was also fragrant like camphor. 'पिष्टातः पटवासकः' अमरः (पटो वास्यतेऽनेन). अधर०—The redness of their lips surpassed that of saffron. निर्गुण: useless. लावण्यकलङ्क: a stain on their beauty. The paste of saffron only marred the beauty of their complexion. परि... लता: canes for striking in joke. Their arms were fair and slender like cane. यौ...बिन्दव: drops of perspiration due to the warmth of youth. विदग्धा: fine, artful. विशाल...रस्रा square like broad crystal slabs. रागिणाम् of their lovers. Construe श्रोण्य: विश्रमकारणम्. अनि...वेदिका: the jewelled couches in their houses were useless (for giving rest to their lovers). कमल... भरणकानि—bees hovered round their feet (that resembled red lotuses) mistaking them to be lotuses and so looked like sapphire anklets. समुचि...सहाया: the proper (or usual) companions of their strolls. For Haṁsas following the tinkling anklets of ladies, see p. 31 above. ऐ...जना: attendants were but the details of their prosperity.

P. 44 ll. 25—32 **तत्र च...बभूव.** The principal sentence is तत्र च...राजा पुष्पभूतिरिति नाम्ना बभूव. सह...दधानः—इन्द्रधनुः possesses all colours. The king supported all (the four) castes. As to Indra's 1000 eyes, see above notes p. 186. कल्याणप्रकृतित्वे in being by nature well disposed to all (with पुष्पभूति); in being the source (प्रकृतिः) of gold (with मेरु). Meru is a mountain of gold. 'मेरुः सुमेरुर्हेमाद्रिः रत्नसानुः सुरालयः' अमरः. लक्ष्मीसमाकर्षणे in drawing Glory or prosperity towards himself; in drawing out लक्ष्मी (with मन्दर). For मन्दर see p. 52. मर्यादायाम् in propriety of conduct; in the boundary or shore. The sea does not pass beyond the shore. The king never transgressed the rules of decorum. शब्दप्रादुर्भावे in the diffusion of his fame or in the knowledge of grammar; in manifesting sound (with आकाश). According to the writers on Sanskrit logic, गन्ध, रस, रूप, स्पर्श and शब्द are respectively the special qualities of पृथिवी, अप्, तेजः, वायु and आकाश. आकाश is defined by them as 'शब्दगुणमाकाशम्'. कलासंग्रहे in the comprehension of the (64) arts; in the accumulation of the (16) digits (with शशी). अकृत्रिमालापत्वे in employing speech that is not false; in having its words not created (composed) by anyone. According to the मीमांसकs वेद is self-existent and eternal. It is अपौरुषेय. धरणिः the earth. लोक...करणे in steadying or supporting the people; in supporting (on its surface) the people (with धरणिः). सर्व...हरणे in removing the effects of *Rajas* in the case of all kings; in carrying away all the dust of the earth. The wind carries off the dust. रजः is one of the three Guṇas of the सांख्य system, *viz.* सत्त्व, रजः and तमः. Its effects are काम, क्रोध &c. Compare 'काम एष क्रोध एष रजोगुणसमुद्भवः' गीता 3. 37. पुष्पभूति subdued all kings (पार्थिव) and their passions. गुरुर्वचसि weighty or great in speech; Bṛihaspati in speech. It should be noted that the words from गुरु up to दक्ष are adjectives as well as proper nouns. पृथुरुरसि wide in the chest. पृथु also was a famous king. Note the 2nd verse of the 4th उच्छ्वास and *vide* the notes thereon. विशालो मनसि comprehensive in intellect. The com. says that विशाल was also the name of a बोधिसत्त्व. विशाल was also a son of इक्ष्वाकु and founder of the city विशाला. जनकस्तपसि—he performed various austerities. जनक, king of मिथिला, was famous for his holiness and spiritual knowledge. सुयात्रः whose expedition (or invasion) is grand. सुयात्र seems to be the name of a king. सुमन्त्रः whose policy is good; सुमन्त्र was the charioteer of दशरथ. शोभनः मन्त्रः यस्य. Works on politics lay down that a king should keep his line of policy secret till it bears fruit. Compare 'मन्त्र इव सचिवमण्डलेन रक्ष्यमाणे' हर्ष० 4th उ० and notes thereon. बुधः wise; Mercury (the son of the Moon). अर्जुनः white; the hero अर्जुन. भीष्मः terrific; the great warrior भीष्म. निषधः is the name of a mountain and also of a king, who was father of नल. निषधः hard, solid. शत्रुघ्नः who killed his enemies; the brother of Rāma. शूरः brave; a king of the यादवs, who was grand-father of कृष्ण. शूर...क्रमणे in vanquishing brave armies; in occupying the country of शूरसेन (*i. e.* मथुरा). दक्ष...र्मणि vigilant or clever in discharging his duty to his subjects. दक्ष is a well-known

उत्तमाङ्गं (शिरः) यस्य. If we read पृथुतमाङ्गम्, then dissolve as पृथुतमं अङ्गं (शरीरं) यस्य. उत्तुङ्गेन वलिभङ्गेन स्फुटं ललाटं यस्य—whose forehead was undulating with prominent folds of wrinkles. 'स्फुटं तु नतोन्नतम्' क्षीरस्वामी. निर्मांसः गण्डकूपकः यस्य. गण्डकूपक is the hollow beneath the eye and above the cheek. मधु...क्षम् whose eyes were round and brown like drops of honey. ई...घोणम whose nose (घोणा) was slightly curved. अतिप्रलम्बः एकः कर्णपाशः (प्रशस्तः कर्णः) यस्य one of whose ears hung down very much. अलाबु... पङ्क्तिम् the row of whose teeth was prominent and formidable (विकट) like the seeds of bottle-gourd. These seeds are white and long. तुरगानूकवत् श्लथा अधरलेखा यस्य whose lip was loose like the अनूक of a horse. According to the com. अनूक is the lower lip of a horse. अनूकः-कम् means 'backbone or spine.' लम्बेन चिबुकेन आयततरं लपनं (मुखं) यस्य whose mouth looked elongated on account of a hanging chin. काषाय red. For योगपट्टक, see p. 26 above. विरचितः वैकक्षकः यस्य. For वैकक्षक see p. 26. हृदयमध्ये निबद्धः ग्रन्थिः (knot) यस्य. धातुरसारुणेन red because dyed with red chalk. *Vide* notes p. 161 for धातु. रागेणेव...कृतेन—the poet fancies that the red piece of cloth was राग (passion, redness) which he had cut into pieces. The ascetic had uprooted passions (राग) which sway the human heart (हृदय) and had as though tied into a knot on the chest the pieces of passion as red garment. कर्पटः a ragged garment. कृतः उत्तरासङ्गः यस्य. उत्तरासङ्गः upper garment (उत्तरे ऊर्ध्वाङ्गे आसज्यते उत्तरासङ्गः). पुन...मूलेन—this and the following instrumentals qualify योगभारकेण. What a योगभारक means is not quite clear. It seems to have been something like an 'hold-all,' a bag tied to a pole. C and T render it as 'yoke pole'. पुनरुक्तं ०वेष्टनं तेन निश्चलं मूलं यस्य the root of which was made firm with fastenings (प्रग्रहः) of hair tied over and over again. The bag was tied to the pole by hair ropes. बद्धः मृत्परिशोधनाय वंशत्वचः तितउः यस्मिन् on which was tied a sieve (तितउः) of bamboo bark for straining earth. 'चालनी तितउः पुमान्' अमरः. कौपीनेन सनाथं शिखरं यस्य. कौपीनम्—loin-cloth (from कूप) according to 'शालीनकौपीने अधृष्टाकार्ययोः' पा. 5. 2. 20 (कूपपतनमर्हति कौपीनं पापं तत्साधनत्वात्तद्वद्गोप्यत्वात्पुरुषलिङ्गमपि । तत्सम्बन्धात्तदाच्छादनमपि । सि. कौ.). खर्जूर...कपालके whose alms bowl was placed inside a box (समुद्गकः) made of date leaves. दारव...कमण्डलुना that had his water pot placed on a stool of three sticks inserted into the corners of three wooden planks. दारव-from दारु. Three planks were joined together to make a triangular base. In their corners a stick was fixed.

दहिरुपपादितं ०स्थानं यस्मिन् outside which a place was found for his slippers (of wood). स्थूलेन दशासूत्रेण नियन्त्रिता पुस्तिकापूलिका यस्मिन्—that had his bundle of manuscripts tied by a stout rope made of the hems of garments. अध्यासितः स्कन्धः यस्य. इतरकरेण (दक्षिणेन करेण) गृहीतं वेत्रासनं (caneseat) येन. मस्करिणम्—*vide* notes p. 91. This clause gives a vivid and picturesque description of an ascetic and reminds us of modern *Gosavis* and *Sādhus*. उपगतम् when he came near. नगरस्य समीपे उपनगरम् (अव्ययीभाव). शून्यायतने in a deserted house or temple. उपनिन्ये presented. बहलेन आलोकेन लिप्तं अन्तःपुरं यैः. राजतानि made of silver.

P. 46 ll. 12—23 **नरपति...वाटिकाम्.** प्रिय...कातरः afraid to go contrary to the request or love of a person dear to him. दाक्षिण्यमनुरुध्यमानः following the dictates of courtesy. ग्रहण...समर्थः not able to get free from the (charge of) mean-mindedness if he accepted them. दोलायमानेन—vacillating. The king was afraid that if he refused the present, he would offend the ascetic for whom he had high regard; but the king also felt that if he being a king accepted from a poor mendicant a gift, that would be an act deserving to be censured by the people. अति...निघ्नः yielding to his own extreme goodness. सर्व...हेतुः the cause of the production of all rewards (goes with ०भक्तिः).शिव...फलानि It is our devotion to शिव that yields rewards that could not (otherwise) have been secured even in desires. येन since. समुच्छ्रितं श्वेतातपत्रं यस्य whose white umbrella was held high over him. समुद्धूयमानं (being waved) धवलं चामरयुगलं यस्य. The white umbrella and two chowries were indispensable insignia of royalty in ancient India. Compare 'अदेयमासीत् त्रयमेव भूपतेः **शशिप्रभं छत्रमुभे च चामरे**' रघु० 3. 16. राजपुत्रैः nobles. अन्तरं distance. अभि...शिष्यं another pupil coming towards (the king). He was other than the one that had come before with the five silver lotuses. अस्य...त्तरेण to the north of this dilapidated temple of the Mātṛis. The Mātris are eight (or seven, according to others) divinities said to be the attendants of शिव. 'ब्राह्मी माहेश्वरी चैन्द्री वाराही वैष्णवी तथा। कौमारी चर्ममुण्डा च कालसङ्कर्षणीति च ॥'. *Vide* 'साक्षाज्जातमातृदेवता इव बहुबालकव्याकुला ननृतुर्वृद्धधात्र्यः' हर्ष० 4th उ० and notes thereon. For उत्तरेण, *vide* notes p. 158.

P. 46 l. 24—**P. 48** l. 2 **अथ महतः...मकरोत्.** The first sentence is अथ...भगवन्तं...भैरवाचार्यं ददर्श (p. 47 l. 32). महत...मध्ये in the midst of a large crowd of pilgrims. कार्पटिक is derived from कर्पट with the affix ठक् (कर्पटेन चरति). स्नातम्—this and the following adjectives in the accusative singular qualify भैरवाचार्य below. दत्ता अष्टपुष्पिका येन. For अष्टपुष्पिका, *vide* notes p. 46. पुष्पाणामष्टकमष्टपुष्पिका. अनुष्ठितं अग्निकार्यं येन. कृतः भस्मरेखापरिहारेण परिकरः यस्य that was surrounded by a circle of ashes. परिहारः a tract of common land round a village; hence, here 'a tract or circle'. Compare 'धनुःशतं परीहारो ग्रामस्य स्यात्समन्ततः ।' मनु० 8. 237. The com. says 'परिहारोऽत्र मर्यादा'. हरितेन गोमयेन उपलिप्तं ०तलं तस्मिन् वितते (spread). कृष्ण...भ्यस्यन्तम् under the guise (निभः) of wrapping himself in a dark woollen blanket, he as though was practising residence (आवासः) in the darkness of *pātāla* in the apprehension that he might have to enter into an *Asura* cavern. For असुरविवर, *vide* notes p. 90. Pātāla as the haunt of demons and sinners is supposed to be dark. An असुरविवर must also be very dark, if our explanation of it be correct. He did not want to enter असुरविवर; but the poet fancies that he was familiarising himself with darkness because he feared that he might one day have do so. उन्मिषता...लिम्पन्तम् who covered his disciples with the flashing lustre of his body as tawny as lightning, as though with red arsenic paste purchased by the sale of human flesh. मनःशिला is red and therefore would be like the glow of his body. मनःशिला costs money and so the question arises how the poor ascetic got it. The words महा...क्रीतेन explain this. They suggest that भैरवाचार्य was a शाक्त, had offered human flesh to शक्ति and the पिशाचs and thereby secured super-human powers. Compare 'अपरत्र प्रकाशनरपतिकुमारकक्रियमाणमहामांसविक्रयप्रक्रमम्' हर्ष० 4th उ० 7th para. The शाक्तs say 'अष्टम्यां रुधिरैर्मांसैर्महामांसैः सुगन्धिभिः । पूजयेद्बहुजातीयैर्बलिभिर्भोजनैः शिवाम् ॥.' जटी...सिद्धान् with his hair tied in a lump so as to peep upwards from a portion of which that was matted hung down the round globes of conch-shell and his rosary beads, he seemed to be imprisoning the Siddhas conceited by the pride of knowledge and roaming overhead (in the sky). जटीकृतः एकदेशः तस्मात् लम्बमानाः रुद्राक्षाणां शंखानां च गुटिकाः यस्मिन्. प्रशस्ता शिखा शिखापाशः. The शिखा was long (like a cord) and ऊर्ध्वबद्ध hence the उत्प्रेक्षा 'बध्नन्तमिव &c.' For सिद्धs, see above p. 83. The poet wants to suggest that he had secured superhuman powers (सिद्धिs) which enabled him even to imprison the सिद्धs. धवलाः कतिपये शिरोरुहाः (hair) यस्मिन् (*adj* of वयसा). वयसा...क्रामन्तम् in age he had passed beyond 55 years. खालित्येन क्षीयमाणा शङ्खलोम्नां लेखा यस्य the line of the hair on the front part of his head was faint owing to baldness. We expect खालत्य (from खलति) for खालित्य. 'शङ्खो निधौ ललाटास्थ्नि' अमरः. लोमशः (hairy) कर्णशष्कुलिप्रदेशः (the outer part of the ear) यस्य. तिरश्च्या...जनयन्तम् with his slanting forehead mark made with ashes, he led one to think that it was the white line of his skull-bone burst by the heat of the burnt *guggulu* repeatedly held over his head. It is better to read शिरोविधृत with some MSS. For ललाटिका, see p. 44. For the burning of गुग्गुलु in the temple of शिव and on the head, *vide* notes p. 105. Bones are white. The line of white ashes on the forehead is fancied to be the skull bone split up by heat. सहज...बिभ्राणम् who had as though a single, long (आयामिनी) and unbroken (निरन्तरा) brow by the meeting together of his brows, as the part between the brows was contracted by the natural folds of the wrinkles on his forehead, the brow being tawny in colour. ०भङ्गैः सङ्कोचितः कूर्चभागः यस्याः. 'कूर्चमस्त्री भ्रुवोर्मध्यम्' अमरः. बभ्रुः भाः यस्याः. Between the brows there is ordinarily a part of the head. But as his forehead was deeply wrinkled, the two brows presented a continuous line. निरन्तराम् leaving no intervening space. ईषत् काचवत् काचरा कनीनिका यस्य the pupil of which was greenish like glass. रक्तापाङ्गाभ्यां निर्गतः अंशुप्रतानः यस्य from the red corners of which shot forth rays. मध्ये धवला भाः यस्य तेन ०भासा. These three qualify ०युगलेन. इन्द्रायुधेनेव—The rainbow also presents red and green colours and so his eyes are fancied to be इन्द्रायुध. Then there are two more उत्प्रेक्षाs. लोचन...लिखन्तम्—the idea is:—when he cast glances all round from his eyes that were white, red (in the corners) and greenish-yellow (in the pupil), he seemed to draw all round a large circle tinged with various colours. A मण्डल is drawn on the ground in worshipping a deity. Compare 'कुङ्कुमपङ्कानुलिप्ते मण्डलके...रक्तकमलषण्डेनार्चां ददौ' हर्ष० 4th उ०, 4th para. सित...क्षिपन्तम् he seemed to scatter in all directions an oblation to शिव variegated with rows of white, yellow and red flags (or marks). That flags were used in the worship of शिव we see from the 2nd उ० 'सुरभिकुसुमधूपगन्धध्वजबलिविलेपनप्रदीपकबहुलां विधाय पूजाम्' (text p. 25). If we take पताका as meaning 'mark' (in a secondary sense), then there is a reference to an oblation of rice (which is white) smeared with red powder and yellow turmeric. Such oblations are even now placed where four roads meet. तार्क्ष्यतुण्डकोटिवत् कुब्जा अग्रघोणा (घोणायाः अग्रं or rather अग्रं चासौ घोणा च) यस्य the tip of whose nose was curved like the end of Garuḍa's beak. 'गरुत्मान्गरुडस्तार्क्ष्यः' अमरः. For the form अग्रघोणा, mark वामन's काव्यालङ्कारसूत्र 5. 2. 20 'हस्ताग्राग्रहस्तादयो गुणगुणिनोर्भेदाभेदात्'. दूर...कपोलम् whose cheeks looked narrow on account of the corners of his mouth being very far gashed. दूरविदीर्णे सृक्किणी ताभ्यां संक्षिप्तौ कपोलौ यस्य. किञ्चिद्दन्तुरतया because he had slightly prominent teeth. सदा हृदये सन्निहितः हरः तस्य मौलौ चन्द्रः तस्य आतपेन इव. He had white and prominent teeth, the brilliance of which brightened the circle of the quarters. The poet fancies that it was the light of S'iva's crescent issuing out of his mouth, शिव being always present in his heart. जिह्वाग्र...तौष्ठम्—his lip naturally hung down a little. He knew by heart (जिह्वाग्रस्थित) all the canonical works (संहिता) of the S'aivite sect. The poet fancies that his lip hung down as though on account of the weight of the संहिताs that were on the tip of the tongue. प्रलम्ब...बध्यमानम् with his crystal ear-rings dangling from his pendulous (प्रलम्ब) ear-lobes, he seemed as though pursued by Venus and Jupiter in the belief of acquiring (from him) a lore which would enable them to conquer the gods and demons (respectively). शुक्र and गुरु were respectively the preceptors of the असुरs and देवs. Venus and Jupiter, with which the two are identified, are the brightest of the planets. So the crystal ear-rings are fancied to be शुक्र and गुरु. बद्ध... कलयन्तम् wearing, on one of his forearms (प्रकोष्ठः) that had an iron bracelet and on which was tied a bundle of magic threads with various herbs, a piece of conchshell, as though it were the tooth of Pūshan broken by S'iva and turned by him (भैरवाचार्य) into an ornament out of devotion to शिव. The piece of शङ्ख was white like teeth. विविधौषधिभिः मन्त्रैः च युक्ता सूत्रपङ्क्तिः, बद्धा ॰पङ्क्तिः यस्मिन्. Even now people wear dark thread on their forearms supposed to have magical properties. पूष्णो दन्तमिव— When वीरभद्र produced from S'iva's matted hair destroyed the sacrifice of दक्ष, some of the gods were severely dealt with. भग lost his eye, while one of the teeth of पूषन् was broken. *Vide* for the story भागवतपुराण 4. 5. 'भगस्य नेत्रं भगवान्पातितस्य रुषा भुवि। उज्जहार सदःस्थोऽक्ष्णो यः शपन्तमसूसुचत् ॥ पूष्णश्चापातयद्दन्तान् कालिङ्गस्य यथा बलः। शप्यमाने गरिमणि योऽहसद्दर्शयन्दतः ॥' verses 20-21. As the दन्त became holy by the touch of वीरभद्र, the ascetic is fancied as wearing it with भक्ति. There seems to be some faint reference even in the Rigveda to the story about the loss of the tooth of पूषन्. Compare 'वामं पूषा वामं भगो वामं देवः करूळती' (which last is explained as कृत्तदन्त) Rigveda IV. 30. 24. अखिल...मालामिव—The beads of the rosary looked like the pots for throwing up (उदञ्चन) the water (रस) in a well and the string of the rosary like the rope on which the pots are placed at intervals. He revolved the rosary in his right hand. A water-wheel also is turned with the right hand. अखिलस्य रसस्य कूपात् उदञ्चनं तदर्थं घटीयन्त्रमाला. The रुद्राक्षमाला also threw out all pleasures (रस) from his heart (which was concentrated solely on शिव). आ (ईषत्) पिङ्गलानि अग्राणि यस्य. कूर्चकलापेन by his thick beard. संमार्जे...निकरम्—the idea is:—a कूर्च (brush, peacock's feathers) is used in sweeping off a heap (निकरः) of dust (रजः); his beard that rubbed his chest. is fancied as sweeping off रजः (passion) contained in the heart. रजः is one of the three Guṇas according to the सांख्यs. It is रजोगुण that gives rise to काम and क्रोध and leads a person into sin. 'सत्त्वं लघु प्रकाशकमिष्टमुपष्टम्भकं चलं च रजः । गुरु वरणकमेव तमः' सांख्यकारिका; 'अथ केन प्रयुक्तोऽयं पापं चरति पूरुषः । अनिच्छन्नपि वार्ष्णेय बलादिव नियोजितः ॥ काम एष क्रोध एष **रजोगुणसमुद्भवः।**' गीता chap. 3. 36–37. निचितं full of (*adj.* of ०देशं). ध्यान...दधानम्—the idea is:—By meditation he had acquired the illumination (ज्योतिः) of knowledge. Light (ज्योतिः) such as that of fire or the sun burns; what is burnt up becomes dark. The dark hair on his chest is fancied to be the effect of ज्योतिः which illumines his heart. ईषत्प्रशिथिलेन वलिवलयेन बध्यमानं तुन्दं (उदरं) यस्य. उपचीयमानः (protuberant) स्फिङ्मांसपिण्डकः यस्य. स्फिच् *f.* buttocks, hips. 'स्त्रियां **स्फिचौ कटिप्रोथौ'** अमरः. पाण्डुरेण पवित्रेण क्षौमेण (linen cloth) आवृतं कौपीनं (private parts) यस्य. For कौपीन see above notes p. 198. सा...मण्डलितेन that was passed round (his body) while he sat in a dignified पर्यङ्क posture. When a person sits on his hams with legs cross-wise and a piece of cloth is firmly tied round his knees, loins and back, it is called पर्यङ्कबन्ध (Marathi जेठा मारून बसणें). बाण's description leaves no doubt about the meaning of पर्यङ्कबन्ध. But मल्लिनाथ commenting on the words 'पर्यङ्कबन्ध-स्थिरपूर्वकायम्' (कुमारसम्भव 3. 45) explains it as वीरासन and quotes two definitions of the latter, which do not agree with our explanation. *Vide* मल्लिनाथ's comment. अमृतफेनवत् श्वेता रुक् (कान्तिः) यस्य (with योगपट्टकेन); ०फेनेन श्वेता रुक् यस्य (with वासुकिना). For योगपट्टक, see p. 26. For वासुकि being the rope in churning, *vide* p. 52. वासुकि must have been sprinkled with the foam of अमृत as it came out of the churned ocean. अप्रतिहतः (irresistible) अनेकमन्त्राणां प्रभावः तेन आविर्भूतः तेन. The poet fancies that the योगपट्टक encircling his body was वासुकि manifesting itself through the irresistible might of the ascetic's incantations and then performing a प्रदक्षिणा round him. Even now it is believed that a मान्त्रिक can call out a serpent from its hiding place by the power of मन्त्रs. The suggested meaning is that, as वासुकि is the king of serpents, the ascetic must have been a great magician indeed. Compare for the conceit 'सुधाफेनधवलेन तपः-प्रभावकुण्डलीकृतेन गङ्गास्रोतसेव योगपट्टकेन विरचितवैकक्ष्यका' (text p. 3 ll. 29–30 above). अरुणतामरसवत् सुकुमारं तलं यस्य. जर्जरयन्त...तलम्—the idea is:—the bright rays of his reddish soles spread on the surface (तल) of the earth (रसा). The poet fancies that he crushed the earth (with the rays) in his passion or zeal (रसः) for bringing out the great treasures (supposed to be lying in the earth). The person who is believed to be able to see treasures hidden in the earth is called (in Marathi) पायाळु. तोयेन क्षालितं अत एव शुचि तेन (applies to both युगलेन and ०मिथुनेन). हंस...गतेन as though they were two हंसs that had come there in order to become familiar with the pilgrimage to holy places on the Ganges. He had often been to the holy Ganges and would again go there. Therefore हंसs (in the form of the wooden slippers) never left his feet. In the next clause the principal part is वैणवेन विशाखिकादण्डेन सततपार्श्ववर्तिना विराजमानम्—who had constantly at his side a bamboo विशाखिका staff. What विशाखिका means is not quite clear. Probably it is a staff the upper part of which branches off into two and forms a loop. Compare 'विशाखिकाशिखरनिबद्धनालिकेरीफलवल्कलमयधौतोपानद्युगोपेताम्' कादम्बरी p. 133 of P. The commentators of the कादम्बरी explain it variously as 'विशाखिका भूमिशुद्ध्यर्थमाद्रियमाणा लोहयष्टिरूपा शिक्यभेदो वा;' 'विशाखिका रुद्राङ्कुशः; विशाखिका विशाखा सा तरोरवयवान्तरम्'. शिखरे निखाताः (imbedded) कुब्जाः (curved) कालायसकण्टकाः (iron hooks) यस्य. Even now people in the Konkan use a staff that has a few iron hooks fixed at the top, which rattle when a man walks and frighten away reptiles. ०कण्टकेन applies to ०ङ्कुशेन also. An अङ्कुश (goad) also has an iron barb imbedded in it. सर्व...ङ्कुशेनेव as though it were a goad for driving away Ganes'a who causes obstacles in the mastery of all the lores. It should be remembered that an elephant is controlled by a goad and that गणेश has the head of an elephant. विनायक is called विघ्नराज (he controls as well as causes obstacles). विनायक also presides over learning. The suggestion is:—the ascetic had mastered all विद्याs; he had the goad-like staff always with him by way of a threat to गणेश if the latter wanted to cause any obstacle. बाण often uses विनायक for श्लेष. Compare 'अयमशिवसहचरो विनायकः' हर्ष० 8th उ०; 'अशिवमूर्तयो महाविनायकाधिष्ठिताः' कादम्बरी p. 287 of P. The words सर्व० would also mean 'with a goad that drives away the chief (विनायक) obstacles &c.' or 'with a goad that subdues (विनायक) and drives away the obstacles &c.' कुमारब्रह्मचारिणम् who had observed the vow of celibacy all his life from boyhood (*i. e.* he was a नैष्ठिकब्रह्मचारी 'a perpetual student' and not उपकुर्वाण). कृशः (thin *i. e.* restrained) क्रोधः यस्य. अकृशः (not thin *i. e.* great) अनुरोधः (complying with another's request, kindness) यस्य. 'अनुरोधोऽनुवर्तनम्' अमरः. अदीना (not wretched *i. e.* noble) प्रकृतिः (nature) तया शोभितम्. अदीन...शोभितम् (with महानगर 'capital') means 'adorned by noble ministers &c. or rich guilds'. प्रकृति means 'the constituent elements of a kingdom' or 'guilds of citizens.' 'स्वाम्यमात्यसुहृत्कोशराष्ट्रदुर्गबलानि च । **राज्याङ्गानि प्रकृतयः पौराणां श्रेणयोऽपि च ॥**' अमरः. क्षीर० quotes कात्य as "यत्कात्यः 'अमात्याद्याश्च पौराश्च सद्भिः प्रकृतयः स्मृताः.'" There is another sense possible. प्रकृति means 'the base' or 'the original accent of a word.' Each word (whether single or compounded with another word) has generally only one उदात्त accent. If a word be compounded with another, it may lose its accent and take the accent for the whole compound as determined by the rules. There is a rule that 'when नगर is the second member of a समास, the first letter of the first member has the उदात्त accent, except when the first word is महत् or नवन्.' 'अमहन्नवन्नगरेऽनुदीचाम्' पा. 6. 2. 89. In महानगर, the first word is महत्; therefore नगर retains its original accent (प्रकृतिस्वर) and the first letter has not the उदात्त accent. Thus in महानगर the प्रकृति (स्वर) is अदीन (not low-pitched; but is high-pitched, as उदात्त is). 'उच्चैरुदात्तः' and 'नीचैरनुदात्तः' पा. 1. 2. 29–30. कल्प...च्छायम्—०राशिवत् सुकुमारा छाया (कान्तिः) यस्य (with भैरवाचार्य); ०राशिभिः सुकुमारा छाया (shade) यस्य (with मेरु). मेरु is shaded with the delicate leaves of the trees of paradise. ०रजसा पवित्रितं शिरः (head, top) यस्य. On the top of कैलास dwells शिव. He had bowed his head at the feet of the image of शिव. मा...यातम् followed by a crowd (गणः) of Saivas (with भैरवाचार्य); peopled with the attendants (गणाः) of शिव. महेश्वरस्य इमे माहेश्वराः गणाः (प्रमथाः). **'सङ्घाते प्रमथे गणः'** अमरः. ०सहस्रे प्रक्षालितं शरीरं येन; ०स्रेण प्रक्षालितं शरीरं यस्य (with जलनिधि). The ascetic had bathed in numerous rivers. Numerous rivers fall into the ocean. बहु...शुचिम् pure by residing in many holy spots (with भैरवाचार्य); pure with many holy तीर्थs situated on it (with ०प्रवाहम्). धाम place, dwelling. तीर्थं तथ्यस्य the sacred place of truth. कुशलस्य of welfare or prosperity. पूतता holiness. शालेयं शालीनतायाः the ricefield of modesty. For शालेय, see p. 118 and for शालीन p. 57. स्थानं स्थितेः abode of all propriety or decorum. आधारं धृतेः support of steadiness. आकरः mine. निकेतनं कौतुकस्य the house of admiration. All admired him. आरामं रामणीयकस्य the garden of loveliness. प्रासादं प्रसादस्य the palace of good-will (towards all). अगारं गौरवस्य house of respect. All respected him. समाजं सौजन्यस्य the conference of goodness. सम्भवं सद्भावस्य the source of amiability. कालं कलेः the death of Kali. He nullified the effects of Kali, the age of sin and discord. विरूपाक्षम् = शिवम्. शशि...चाल he got up, as the ocean rises up on seeing the moon. At moonrise, the waters of the ocean begin to rise in a tide. प्रथमतरं उत्थितः शिष्यलोकः यस्य. प्रत्युज्जगाम went forward to receive. समर्पितं श्रीफलोपायनं येन who gave him the present of Bilva fruit. **'बिल्वे** शाण्डिल्यशैलूषौ मालूरश्री- **फला**वपि' अमरः. The बिल्व tree is sacred to शिव. जह्नुकर्णात् समुद्गीर्यमाणः (emitted) गङ्गाप्रवाहः तस्य ह्रादः (roar) तद्वत् गम्भीरया. For Jahnu, see p. 84.

P. 48 ll. 3–15 **नरपति...भजत.** प्रीत्या विस्तार्यमाणः धवलिमा यस्य the whiteness of which increased through the joy he felt. प्रत्यर्प...वनानि—When he bowed, he cast glances from the whites of his eyes. These resembled the silver lotuses that भैरवाचार्य had sent. The poet fancies that he returned in the form of his glances the lotuses that he had received. The only difference was that he returned many (as he cast many glances), while he had received only five. ललाट...प्रकाशयन् with his crest-jewel dangling about on his forehead and having its rays shooting up he as though manifested the favour of S'iva by the appearance of a third eye. उद्गताः अंशवः यस्य. शिव has a third eye on the forehead. The red jewel dangling on the forehead of the king, when he bowed to भैरव, is fancied to be the third eye that appeared (उद्गमः) just at that moment. शिव favoured the king so much that he made him त्रिनेत्र like himself. आवर्जितः (bent down) कर्णपल्लवः तस्मात् पलायमानाः मधुकराः यस्य. When he bent down to bow, the bees ran away from his ear-ornament of flowers. शिवसेवया समुन्मूलिताः अशेषपापलवाः तैः मुच्यमानः. The dark bees look like sins (which are supposed to be dark). दूरावनतः bending very low. अभिनवम्—his bow is called अभिनव (a new or unique one), because it is accompanied by all the wonderful results described above. शार्दूल...दर्शयत्—the ascetic desired the king to be seated on his own tiger skin. To seat a person on one's आसन is a mark of great respect and friendship. It shows that the person so treated is at least the equal, if not the superior, of the person so treating. उपदर्शितः प्रश्रयः (humility) येन. मत्तहंसस्य कलः गद्गदः स्वरः तेन सुभगां (with नदीम्); तद्वत् सुभगां (with वाचम्). मधुरसमयीम् full of sweetness (with वाचम्); full of sweet water (with नदीम्). प्रवर्तयन् making flow; uttering. नार्हसि...कर्तुम् you will please not ill-treat me on account of the misdeeds of other kings. His meaning is:—Other kings might not have reverence for holy ascetics like you and might sit on the seat occupied by you. But I cannot occupy that seat honouring you as I do; and I do not like such formal treatment from you. अशेष...गुरुः that the teacher (your reverence) so deals with me is the fault of the character of that wretched Lakshmî (royalty) that is looked up to by all kings or is the ill-natured-ness of lucre. All kings care too much for लक्ष्मी and become wicked through wealth. You think that I am also one of those kings and would take umbrage if you did not offer me your own seat. The usual meaning of उपेक्षित is 'neglected, slighted.' But that meaning does not suit the context. अभूमि...चाराणाम् this person (*i. e.* I) is not a fit subject for ceremonious behaviour (उपचारः). अल...णया enough of great restraint (*i. e.* formality). मनोरथशिष्यः a pupil in wishes (*i. e.* I desired to be your disciple). नोल्लङ्घनमर्हति does not deserve to be trodden. परिजनेन उपनीते (brought). वाससि on a garment. अनतिक्रमणीय irresistible. अनुवर्तमानः acceding to, complying with.

P. 48 ll. 16—31 **आसीने...मगात्.** राजकेन सह सराजके (*adj.* of परिजने). अर्घ्यम् respectful offering of flowers, water &c. अर्घः पूजाविधिः तदर्थं द्रव्यं अर्घ्यम्. 'पादार्घाभ्यां च' पा. 5. 4. 25 (यत्). नृपमाधुर्येण हृतं (captivated) अन्तःकरणं यस्य. शशि...मलाः pure like the rays of the moon (with दशनदीधितीः); pure with the rays of the moon (with ०भक्तीः). शिवभक्तीः (*accu. plu.* of ०भक्ति)—if one were to worship शिव, then one's devotion would be illumined by the light of the moon that is on the head of शिव. अति...गौरवम् your very modesty declares the greatness (vast extent) of your qualities. The more the virtues that a man possesses, the more modest does he become, as he comes to know of his defects. It is only those that are shallow that become puffed up. गौरव also means 'weight'. What is heavy makes the carrier bend down. सकल...मसि you are a fit receptacle for all prosperity. विभ...पत्तयः your conduct (or undertakings) is quite in keeping with your greatness. जन्मनः...तेयेषु since my birth I never cast my eyes on wealth (*i. e.* I never paid any regard to it). स्वापतेयं wealth, from स्वपति, according to 'पथ्यतिथिवसतिस्वपतेर्ढञ्' पा. 4. 4. 104 (पथि साधु पाथेयम्।...स्वापतेयं धनम्। सि. कौ.). यतः...मस्ति since I possess this poor body not sold for money that is the fuel to the fire of all sins. He says that he is master of his own body, poor though it be. All persons sell their bodies to others for amassing money. As fuel feeds fire, so money feeds sins. So he never cared for money. क is added to शरीर to indicate that he does not care much even for that body. कुत्सितं शरीरं शरीरकम्. दुर्गृ...क्षराणि I have a few ill-understood syllables of knowledge. This he speaks in great humility. भट्टारक *adj.* venerable; *m.* god. पुण्यकणिका particle of merit. अत्र—out of the things enumerated (by him) *viz.* body, प्राणाः, विद्या and पुण्य. प्र...ग्राह्याणि to be captivated by a few virtues (with मनांसि); to be bound by a fine (प्रतनु) thread (with कुसुमानि). The comparison shows that the minds of the good are tender like flowers. विद्वत्संमताः highly thought of by the learned (with साधवः); approved by the learned (with शब्दाः). श्रूयमाणा अपि even when merely heard (though not actually seen). साधवः the good; grammatically pure (with words). सुधीरे...विवरम् fame makes a hole (*i. e.* an impression) in a mind even though it be very steady. A hole (विवर) cannot be easily made on what is firm. विशतः...कल्याणिना I, who was being borne away by the currents, white with foam, of curiosity that entered my heart, am now brought back by your auspicious self with your virtues. The idea is:—so long, not having seen you, my heart overflowed with curiosity to see you; but now that I see you, *you* occupy my heart and not *mere curiosity* about you. A stream becomes white with foam. गुणगण is white like foam. A person who is borne away by a flood is brought back by ropes (गुणगण). If we omit सुखयन्ति, then this passage becomes involved and difficult to explain. Then we must stop at कुर्वन्ति and take विवरं with विशतः. अनु...प्रणयिनः In the case of the bodies &c. of the good, though they be dear to them, friends are the masters *i. e.* friends can dispose of the bodies of the good just as they like, though the good may love their bodies. Here अनुरक्त has to be taken in an unusual sense. It is not शरीर that is अनुरक्त. It is the good that are अनुरक्त so far as their शरीर is concerned. So अनुरक्त means 'प्रिय' here. The com. seems to read 'अनुक्तेष्वपि.' This is a better reading. The meaning then is 'friends are the masters of the bodies &c. of the good, even though it be not declared in so many words.' अने...गुरुणा on this my coming here I am placed in an enviable position by the teacher. He means:—the mere fact that on my arrival here I was treated so well by you has given me great pleasure and has raised me to an exalted position.

P. 48 l. 32—**P. 49** l. 20 **अन्य...कृपाणम्.** तस्मै...वेदितवान् the king placed himself, his harem, his servants, and his treasury at his disposal. Mark this use of the word निवेदितवान्. निवेदय् to offer, to present. आत्मनिवेदन is the last stage in नवविधा भक्ति. 'श्रवणं कीर्तनं विष्णोः स्मरणं पादसेवनम् । अर्चनं वन्दनं दास्यं सख्यमात्मनिवेदनम् ॥ इति पुंसार्पिता विष्णौ भक्तिश्चेन्नवलक्षणा ॥' भागवतपु० 7. 5. 23-24. For two क्तs, see above notes p. 180. धनो...स्विता high-mindedness surely withers away, like a creeper, by the heat of wealth. अलं is used here in the sense of 'excessively' or 'surely.' खद्यो...तेजस्विता The brilliance that we possess is like that of fire-flies, scorching no one else. अ...तापिन् not causing harm to others (with भैर०); not setting on fire any other thing (with खद्योत). Fireflies have a centre of light in their bodies, but it does not burn anyone. भैरवाचार्य says he prefers to have the तेजस्विता of moneyless asceticism, which has no power to hurt others and which is purely spiritual; while the तेजस्विता of wealth has great potentialities for evil. भाजनं = पात्रं. भूतेः = ऐश्वर्यस्य. तेनैव क्रमेण as before, as was his wont. श्वेत...वृतं wrapped in a white piece of cloth. ब्रह्मराक्षसः the ghost of a wicked ब्राह्मण, who, when living, used to commit sins such as carrying away the wives of others and the property of Brāhmaṇas. 'परस्य योषितं हृत्वा ब्रह्मस्वमपहृत्य च । अरण्ये निर्जले देशे भवति ब्रह्मराक्षसः ॥' याज्ञ० 3. 212. अपहृतं कर्पटावच्छादनं यस्य (*adj.* of परिवारात्) from which the covering of cloth was removed. परिवारः sheath. आचकर्ष—the object is कृपाणम् (l. 20). शर...नीतम् as though it were the autumnal sky turned into a solid mass. The author indulges here into many उत्प्रेक्षाs to convey the clearness, brightness and formidableness of the sword. पिण्डं also means 'steel.' 'लोहोऽस्त्री शस्त्रकं

तीक्ष्णं पिण्डं कालायसायसी' अमरः. The com. explains 'पिण्डं' as 'शस्त्रम्' (weapon) and quotes the above words of Amara in support. The sky is clear and bright like a sword in autumn. कालिन्दी... जलम् as though it were the stream of the Jumna with the water benumbed (*i. e.* not allowed to flow). The waters of the Jumna are dark and hence the उत्प्रेक्षा. नन्दक...गतम् as though Kāliya, irritated by Kṛishṇa, had assumed the form of a sword for conquering (*i. e.* surpassing) Nandaka (the sword of Vishṇu). For नन्दक, see p. 88 and for कालिय p. 143. The serpent कालिय was dark. लोक...तितम् as though it were a piece of cloud at the time of *pralaya* fallen from the sky, manifesting a heavy down-pour of water for the destruction of the world. प्रकाशितः धाराणां आसारः येन. 'धारासम्पात आसारः' अमरः. प्रकाशितः धारायाः सारः (बलं) येन that manifests the strength of its edge (with the sword). Or we may dissolve as प्रकटितः धारा एव आसारः येन. We speak of the 'water' of the edge of a sword. काल time; dark. A कल्प is a period of 1000 महायुगs and equal to 4320000000 human years. It is equal to a day of ब्रह्मा, the night being also of the same duration. At the end of one कल्प the whole universe is dissolved and merges in the supreme spirit and remains there for one कल्प and is then again produced. Note भगवद्गीता 8. 17–18. At the time of कल्पान्त or प्रलय, it was believed that the 49 winds began to blow, the twelve suns rose and dark clouds called पुष्कर and आवर्तक enveloped the sky. Compare 'महाप्रलयेषु प्रलयपयोदाः प्रलयदुर्दिनान्धकारितदशदिशः प्लावयन्ति भुवनान्तराणि' कादम्बरी p. 125 of P. The sword also manifests its धारासार for destroying people. दृश्यमानं विकटं दन्तमण्डलं यस्मिन्. दृश्य...हिंसायाः as though it were the laugh of destruction showing a terrible circle of teeth. In laughing one shows one's teeth. हिंसा (killing beings), if personified, must have terrible teeth. The sword was bright like a laugh (but of हिंसा, because it killed). The sword also had terrible दन्तs (indentations). हरि...ग्रहम् as though it were the stout arm of Hari, holding fast मुष्टि. कृतः दृढः मुष्टिग्रहः येन that tightly clinched the fist (with बाहुदण्ड); कृतः दृढः मुष्टिग्रहः यस्य the hilt of which was firmly held (with कृपाणम्); also 'that firmly seized the demon मुष्टि'. मुष्टिक was a demon killed by बलराम who is supposed to be an incarnation of Vishṇu. Compare 'केशव धृतहलधररूप जय जगदीश हरे' गीतगोविन्द. For मुष्टिक see भागवतपु॰ 10. 44. 24. सकल...क्षमेण capable of destroying the lives of all the worlds. This applies both to the sword and to कालकूट. कालकूट

the subduing of a goblin. वेतालः ghost occupying a dead body. त्वं...कर्मणे you are quite a match for that deed (*i. e.* you will be able to achieve this). अलं in the sense of 'being sufficient for a thing or able to do a thing' governs the dative. 'नमः—स्वस्तिस्वाहास्वधाऽलंवषड्योगाच्च' पा. 2. 3. 16 (अलमिति पर्याप्त्यर्थग्रहणम्। दैत्येभ्यो हरिरलम्। सि. कौ.). गृहीतः भरः येन. त्वयि...भरे when you undertake the responsibility. भवन्तमुपतिष्ठते who waits upon you (who brought the silver lotuses). The Ātmanepada is in accordance with the वार्तिक 'उपाद्देवपूजासङ्गतिकरणमित्रकरणपथिष्विति वाच्यम्' (on 'उपान्मन्त्रकरणे' पा. 1. 3. 25). द्राविडः inhabitant of the द्रविड country. द्रविड was roughly between the कृष्णा and the कावेरी. Its capital was काञ्ची. यदि...मन्यसे If you approve. दिङ्नागः दिग्गजः तस्य हस्तवत् दीर्घः. गृहीतः अट्टहासः येन. नीयतामयं निशा...बाहुः let this arm (of yours) be made a bolt of one of the quarters for one night *i. e.* you must guard one of the (four) quarters on one night (that I shall appoint). The student will find that the king and the three others mentioned here guarded the four quarters while भैरवाचार्य was engaged in grim rites. कृतं वचः येन—when he had finished his words. अन्ध...प्रकाशः (delighted) like one in darkness that sees a light. प्राप्तः उपकारस्य अवकाशः (opportunity) येन—The king had been obliged by the ascetic who had made him a present of the sword called अट्टहास and of several silver lotuses. The king desired to oblige the ascetic in return. And this was the first opportunity he found to do so. अनेन...वैमि I look upon myself as accepted by you (as yours) by this task (निदेशः) which is shared by me in common with your pupils. कृतः परिग्रहः (स्वीकारः) यस्य. निदेशः order; appointed task. व्याहृतं utterance. सङ्केतः an appointment; a place of meeting. असितपक्ष dark fortnight. The 14th day of the dark fortnight (particularly of माघ) is sacred to शिव. इयत्यां वेलायां at this hour or at such an hour.

P. 50 ll. 11–23. **अथाति...तमुद्देशम्.** शैवेन...दीक्षितः being initiated into the S'aiva ritual. नियमवान्—observing a fast (or other rules of a दीक्षा). कृतः अधिवासः यस्य—on which purificatory ceremonies were performed. अधिवासः or अधिवासनम् application of scents and perfumes 'संस्कारो गन्धमाल्याद्यैर्यः स्यात्तदधिवासनम्' अमरः. But बाण immediately afterwards says 'समाहित...पूजम्.' So अधिवास must be taken in the sense of 'preliminary consecration of an object of worship with suitable *mantras* before the commencement of a sacrifice.' 'अधिवासो नियमदिवसादाद्येऽहनि यथाशास्त्रं विधिना

मश्रन्यासादिः' सं०. सम्पादिता गन्ध...माल्यादिना पूजा यस्य. The next sentence is ततः परिणते दिवसे...एकाकी नगरान्निरगात्. परिणते दिवसे when the day came to a close. केनापि...दिक्षु when the regions put on a rosy hue as though someone had made offerings of blood for the purpose of securing success in his undertaking. कृतं रुधिरबलिविधानं यासु. The natural redness of the regions in the evening is fancied to be due to the offerings of blood. रुधिर... दीधितिषु when the rays of the sun hung down as though they were the tongues of goblins greedy (लम्पट) for the offering of blood. Blood is scattered about to propitiate वेतालs. लम्बमानासु applies to 'tongues' also, as they also loll out when greedy. रुधिर...लम्पटासु may apply to the rays of the sun. 'That are greedy (*i. e.* that fall upon) for red offerings' (smeared with red powder). Such offerings are placed on roads in the evening. नरेन्द्रा... सवितरि when the sun, that resorted to the west, as though himself desired to do duty as a guardian of the quarters out of affection for the king. The king had been asked to guard one direction. The sun set in the west. The poet fancies that the sun, seeing that his friend (the king) was to be दिक्पाल, himself wanted to be दिक्पाल and so resorted to the west. गृहीता अपरदिक् (west) येन; गृहीता अपरा (another, other than the one the king would accept) दिक् येन. यातुधानी = राक्षसी. The long and dark shadows of trees looked like demons. पाताल...मण्डलेषु—It was believed that demons infested पाताल, stalked abroad at night and caused obstacles to यज्ञ. पाताल is also supposed to be a region of darkness. पाताल०—this applies both to दानवेषु and ०मण्डलेषु. नभसि...गणे when the clusters of stars formed groups in the sky, as though they desired to witness the terrible rite. On कृष्णचतुर्दशी the night is very dark and so the clusters of stars appear very clear. Sight-seers gather together in small groups. रौद्रं कर्म may also mean 'rite of which the देवता is रुद्र (*i. e.* शिव).' विगाढा dense, deep. विगाढायां शर्वर्याम् in the depth of night *i. e.* when the night had advanced a great deal. सुप्ताः जनाः यस्मिन् (*adj.* of निशीथे). निःशब्दस्तिमिते noiseless and motionless. निशीथे at midnight. 'अर्धरात्रनिशीथौ द्वौ' अमरः. वञ्चयित्वा deceiving *i. e.* eluding. वामकरे स्फुरन् त्सरुः (hilt) यस्य (*adj.* of राजा). उत्खात drawn. विसर्पता...यष्टिः by the spreading radiance of the sword, his whole body was concealed as in a blue silken robe for fear that he might be seen. The king wanted to go unobserved. The dark hue of his sword surrounded his body as in a dark robe and effected his object. अनादिष्टया अपि although not ordered by him. पृष्ठतः...कर्षन् in the shape of the rows (*lit.* braids) of bees pursuing him on account of the fragrance (of his body) he dragged behind him by the hair success in the rite. The dark bees resemble the dark braid of a woman. The bees came behind him. The poet fancies that he seized by the hair कर्मसिद्धि and dragged her behind him (made her follow him), the suggestion being that it was a foregone conclusion that the undertaking was to be successful. उद्देशः spot.

P. 50 l. 24—**P. 51** l. 6. **अथ...भूमिम्.** The first sentence is अथ प्रत्युज्जग्मुस्ते त्रयः...टीटिभ...स्वामिनः (p. 51 l. 1) निवेदितवन्तश्चात्मानम्. द्रौणि...सौप्तिके like the son of द्रोण (*i. e.* अश्वत्थामा), कृप and कृतवर्मन् in the night attack. सुप्तेषु भवं सौप्तिकम्. The reference is to the सौप्तिकपर्व of the महाभारत. While कृप and कृतवर्मा lay under a न्यग्रोध tree at night towards the close of the great war, अश्वत्थामा saw an owl killing crows at night when they were asleep in their nests. This suggested to him a night attack on the Pāṇḍava camp. कृप and कृतवर्मा followed him. अश्वत्थामा entered into the camp and stationed the other two at the door. He killed almost all and those that ran towards the door were killed by कृप and कृतवर्मा. सन्नद्धाः wearing armour. गृहीतः विकटः (frightful, gaudy) वेशः यैः. क्रियमाणः मन्त्रैः शिखाबन्धः येषाम्. कुसुम... चरणैः—bees hovered over the flowers they wore in their top-knot and hummed. The poet fancies that the humming was the reciting of *mantras* and the dark bees were themselves the knot of their hair that was being tied to the accompaniment of mystic *mantras* (in order that they may come unscathed out of the perilous undertaking). उष्णीष...मूर्धभिः on their heads they wore turban wraps that were tied in a knot in the form of a large *svastika* on the middle part of their forehead, as though they were sectarial marks (on the forehead). ललाटमध्ये घटितः (formed) विकटः स्वस्तिकाग्रन्थिः यैः. We rather expect स्वस्तिकग्रन्थीन्. स्वस्तिक is a mystical figure and so the author indulges in the उत्प्रेक्षा 'महामुद्राबन्धानिव.' The *svastika*-like knot of the turban on the forehead seemed to be some mystic मुद्रा on the forehead. For another meaning of मुद्रा (which also may be applicable here) see p. 46. The figure of स्वस्तिक due to wrapping of the turban looks like the intertwining of the hands and figures practised in worship. 'अन्योन्यग्रथिताङ्गुष्ठा प्रसारितपराङ्गुली । **महामुद्रे**यमुदिता परमीकरणे बुधैः ॥'. एकश्रवणविवरे विततं

(spread, stretching) विमलं दन्तपत्रं (ear-ring) तस्य प्रभालोकलेपेन धवलितः कपोलः येषाम् (*adj.* of मुखैः). आपिबन्तः—governs अन्धकारम् as its object. निशा...र्षया from the desire to thin the (numbers of) goblins. निशाचराणां अपचयः (reducing) शर्वर्याः इदं शार्वरम्. If they swallowed up the darkness of night, the goblins would vanish. अच्छाच्छया रुचा by the very clear brilliance. गो...लब्धाः anointed as though with *gorochanā* (yellow pigment) over which *mantras* were muttered. For गोरोचना *vide* notes on रोचना p. 114. स्व...स्त्रिंशान् brandishing sharp swords in which their images were reflected, they seemed to make offerings of human beings for the success of their undertaking. The images reflected in the bright sword-blade are fancied to be human beings killed by the sword-blade for ensuring success. निस्त्रिंशस्य अंशवः तेषां सन्तानेन सीमन्तितं तिमिरं यस्याः (*adj.* of त्रियामाम्). निस्त्रिंशांशु...पाटयन्तः—the idea is:—by the rays of their swords they (being three) parted (सीमन्तित) the darkness of night into three parts. The poet fancies that they cut up the night into three parts in order to guard their several regions. Read खण्डैः for खड्गैः. सार्ध...घटयन्तः with their shields that had crescents on them and had flashing on them star-like silver knobs, which (shields) looked like pieces of night sheared (निकृत्त) by the sharp edge of their swords, they seemed to create another night all of a sudden. In a night there is generally the moon; on that particular night there could be no moon as it was कृष्णचतुर्दशी. Their shields had bright crescent-shaped figures. कलधौतं gold or silver 'कलधौतं रूप्यहेम्नोः' अमरः. ०वलिः एव तरलः तारागणः येषाम्. Stars twinkle in the night; on the shields there were star-like silver patches. The shields were dark. For these three reasons the poet fancies them to be pieces of night. They walked in a line holding their dark shields; and so the author fancies that they created another night. For बुद्बुद (a sphere or knob) compare 'परिणतवराटकघटितबुद्बुदार्धचन्द्रखण्डखचितं (ध्वजं)' काद० p. 224. काञ्चनशृङ्खलाकलापेन नियमितं (fastened) निबिडं (thick or close-fitting) निष्प्रवाणि (new unbleached cloth) येषाम्. 'अनाहतं निष्प्रवाणि' अमरः (छेदः क्षालनं भोगश्च आहननं तद्रहितमनाहतम्-क्षीर०). 'निष्प्रवाणिश्च' पा. 2. 2. 160 (कबभावोऽत्र निपात्यते। प्रवाणी तन्तुवायशलाका। निर्गता प्रवाणी अस्य निष्प्रवाणिः पटः। समाप्तवानः नवः इत्यर्थः। सि.कौ.). बद्धा असिधेनुः यैः that had daggers fixed (in their waist-belt). निवे...दमानम् they announced themselves. ताम्—this and the following adjectives in the accu. sing. (*f.*) qualify ०भूमिम्. बलि...

दिग्भागतया the regions being filled with the smoke of *guggulu* and incense that was overspread with the light of the lamps (that were lit in worship). विक्षिप्य...निशामिव—the idea is:—white mustard was being scattered in all directions for protection from evil spirits. The poet fancies that the smoke of गुग्गुलु and धूप looking glossy on account of बलिदीप was really the night running away, having its darkness half burnt by the mustard seeds. One whose limbs are half burnt runs away (not one who is completely burnt). For white mustard, see p. 114. समुपकल्पितानि (got ready) सर्वाणि उपकरणानि यस्याम्. साधनभूमिः place of accomplishing an object by magic *i. e.* cemetery.

P. 51 ll. 7—22 **तस्यां च...ङ्कृतवान्.** The first sentence is तस्यां च...भैरवाचार्यमपश्यत् (l. 18). कुमु...धवलेन as white as the pollen of कुमुद्s (white night lotus). दीप्ततरः तेजःप्रसरः यस्य whose radiance was very much aglow. Remove the comma after ०प्रसरम्. पृथु...सवितारम् like the sun in autumn surrounded by a broad halo (परिवेशः). In शरद्, the sun's disc is clear and not clouded (as it often is in summer). भैरवाचार्य looked like the sun and the circle of ashes like the halo. मथ्य...मन्दरम्—भैरवाचार्य looked like the मन्दर mountain and the circle of ashes like the whirlpool of the milky ocean. For मन्दर as the churning handle, *vide* p. 52. रक्तानि स्रक् अम्बरं आभरणानि च यस्य (*adj.* of शवस्य). उत्तानशयस्य lying on its back. जातः जातवेदाः अग्निः यस्मिन् (*adj.* of मुखकुहरे). प्रारब्धं अग्निकार्यं येन. भैरवाचार्य sat on the chest of a corpse and offered oblations to fire kindled (by magic power) in the mouth of the corpse. कृष्णः अङ्गरागः (unguents) यस्य. कृष्णः प्रतिसरः (amulet) यस्य. 'भवेत्प्रतिसरो मन्त्रभेदे माल्ये च कङ्कणे ।...आरक्षे करसूत्रे च' मेदिनी. कृष्ण...नयन्तम् under the guise of the oblation of black sesame, he seemed as though annihilating the defiled atoms that were the cause of his being born a man, with the desire of becoming a विद्याधर. The black sesame are fancied to be the atoms that go to make up the human body. They are supposed to be कलुषित (defiled) as compared with the constituents of the body of विद्याधरs. The तिलs being कृष्ण, the atoms are said to be कालुष्यपरमाणुs. आहुति...दीधितिभिः with the rays of his nails that were scattered about when he offered the oblations, he seemed to cleanse the fire that was polluted by contact with the mouth of a corpse. The bright rays resemble water used for cleansing. धूमेन आलोहितः (slightly red) तेन. क्षतजं blood.

The glances of his red eyes are fancied to be offerings of blood. ईषत् विवृतं (open) अधरपुटं तेन प्रकटितानि सितानि दशनशिखराणि यस्मिन् (*adj.* of मुखेन). दृश्य...पङ्क्तिना इव–the white tips of his teeth are fancied to be the lines of the syllables of the *mantras* he was muttering. होम...यवान्—the lamps that were lighted near him were reflected in the perspiration due to his efforts in offering oblations. The poet fancies that he burnt his body with those lamps to ensure success. बहुगुणेन consisting of many threads (with ब्रह्मसूत्रेण); of great efficacy (with विद्याराजेन). विद्याराज is a particular *mantra*. बहुगुणेन may also mean 'repeated many times' (with विद्याराजेन). There is another sense suggested. ब्रह्मसूत्र is the work of बादरायण dealing with the Vedānta philosophy. ब्रह्मविद्या is the king of विद्याs (विद्याराज). Compare गीता 9. 2 **'राजविद्या** राजगुह्यं पवित्रमिदमुत्तमम्'. शातक्रतवीमाशाम् the quarter of Indra (*i. e.* the east). For the guardians of the eight quarters, see p. 140. कौबेरीम् the north presided over by कुबेर. प्राचेतसीम् west presided over by प्रचेतस् (*i. e.* वरुण). त्रै...ककुभम् the quarter marked with the constellation of त्रिशङ्कु *i. e.* the south. त्रिशङ्कु was father of हरिश्चन्द्र. He wished to go to heaven with his mortal body. He went to his family priest वसिष्ठ who declared it to be impossible. He then went to वसिष्ठ's sons who also rejected his proposal. त्रिशङ्कु then went to विश्वामित्र who raised him towards heaven, when Indra refused to admit him and made him fall headlong. Then विश्वामित्र called upon him to stay where he was and created new worlds, नक्षत्रs &c. The gods intervened and made विश्वामित्र's creations as eternal as those of ब्रह्मा and त्रिशङ्कु blazed forth as a constellation. *Vide* रामायण बालकाण्ड 57–60. Compare 'त्रिशङ्कोरिवोभयलोकभ्रष्टस्य नक्तन्दिवमर्वाक्शिरसस्तिष्ठतः' हर्ष० 7th उ०; 'सुरलोकमारोहतस्त्रिशङ्कोरिव कुपितशतमखहुङ्कारनिपतिता राजलक्ष्मीः' कादम्बरी p. 8 of P. The author avoids the use of the words दक्षिणां दिशम्, as they are inauspicious.

P. 51 l. 23—**P. 52** l. 14. **एवं...पातयत्.** दिक्पाल...चार्ये while भैर० fearlessly performed his terrific work, being inside the cage of the arms of the four guardians of the quarters (*viz.* the king and the three others). अति...कौणपेषु when the demons causing obstacles, after making much noise for a long time and after having found that their efforts (to frighten the guardians and cause obstacles) proved futile, became quiet (*i. e.* vanished). **'राक्षसः कौणपः** क्रव्यात्' अमरः (कुणपमत्ति कौणपः). गल...समये when midnight had just passed. मण्डल...रेण not far to the north of the circle (of ashes in which भैर० was sitting). प्रलय...दीर्यत the earth was rent open, as though exhibiting a chasm of the jaws of the Great Boar at the time of *pralaya*. For प्रलय see above p. 210. The demon हिरण्याक्ष, on the strength of a boon from Bramhā, became insolent and carried the earth into the ocean. Vishṇu assumed the form of a boar and brought it up. See भागवतपुराण 3rd स्कन्ध chap. 13–19. Compare 'येन **प्रलयवराह**घोणाभिघातभीता भूतधात्री... सागरमवतीर्णा' कादम्बरी p. 124 of P; 'वसति दशनशिखरे धरणी तव लग्ना। शशिनि कलङ्ककलेव निमग्ना। केशव धृतसूकररूप जय जगदीश हरे॥' गीतगोविन्द. The next sentence is सहसैव...तस्मात् विवरात्...कुवलयश्यामलः पुरुष उज्जगाम (p. 52 l. 6). आशावारणैः (दिग्गजैः) उत्क्षिप्तः (tossed up, uprooted). आ...स्तम्भः इव as though he were the iron post for tying elephants. 'आलानं बन्धस्तम्भे' अमरः. The post is fixed in the earth. As the पुरुष was dark-coloured, formidable and suddenly rose up from the earth, he is fancied to be आ...स्तम्भ. महावराहस्य इव पीवरं स्कन्धपीठं यस्य (*adj*. of पुरुषः) whose square shoulders were stout like those of the Great Boar. नर...द्भूतः—By the contact of महावराह with the earth at the time of raising it up out of the ocean, a demon was born of the earth, named नरक. He was very powerful and deprived वरुण of his umbrella, took away the ear-rings of अदिति. 'यदाहमुद्धृता नाथ त्वया सूकरमूर्तिना। त्वत्स्पर्शसम्भवः पुत्रस्तदायं मय्यजायत॥' विष्णुपुराण 5. 59. 23. The पुरुष also rose from the bowels (गर्भात्) of the earth. Compare 'पुरा महावराहसम्पर्कसम्भृतगर्भया भगवत्या भुवा नरको नाम सूनुरसावि रसातले' हर्ष० 7th उ०. बलि...पातालम् he seemed to be the demon Bali rising up after cleaving asunder *Pātāla*. When Bali became very powerful, Vishṇu assumed the form of a Brāhmaṇa boy and begged of him land measuring his three steps. Then Vishṇu assumed a universal form, covered heaven and earth in two steps and placed the third on Bali's head and sent him down to पाताल where he is supposed to reign even now, as he is one of the seven चिरजीविन्s. *Vide* भागवतपुराण 8th स्कन्ध chap. 20–23. Note 'तावत्सुतलमध्यास्तां विश्वकर्मविनिर्मितम्।' chap. 22. 32. उपरि ज्वलितः रत्नप्रदीप यस्य. Remove the comma after ०प्रदीपः. As his body and hair were dark, he is said to be a mansion of sapphire. As he had a brilliant मालती wreath on his head we have the words उपरि...दीपः. Jewelled lamps are lighted in palaces. स्निग्ध...मौलिः the top (मौलिः) of whose head was charming with glossy, dark, thick and curling hair. उन्मीलन्ती (gleaming) मालतीमुण्डमाला यस्य. गद्गद...मदेन by his gurgling (faltering) voice and his naturally red eye, he seemed as though drunk by the pride (or 'intoxication') of youth. One who has drunk wine has a red eye and hoarse voice. **'मत्ते शौण्डोत्कटक्षीबाः'** अमरः. वल्गत् गलदाम यस्य whose necklace dangled about his throat. For क added to बहुव्रीहि compounds, *vide* p. 12. कर...पङ्कयन् with the mud crushed in his clenched hands he again and again smeared his big shoulders resembling the foreheads of the elephants of the quarters. ०कुम्भस्य इव आभा ययोः. कुम्भः frontal globe on the temple of an elephant. This action is characteristic of our wrestlers even now. सान्द्र... देशः with the irregularly made marks of moist-(सान्द्र) sandal paste, he seemed to be a part of the autumnal sky variegated (शारित) with pieces of very white clouds. 'अविद्यमाना व्यवस्था येषु ते अव्यवस्थाः स्थासकाः तैः. For स्थासक, see p. 53 above. He had applied white sandal paste to his body in various places without any order. His body was dark like the clear blue sky of शरद्. In the sky also irregular patches of clouds are seen in शरद्. शारदं (शरदः इदं) आकाशं तस्य एकदेशः. For चण्डातक, see above p. 69. क्षामतरीकृतः कुक्षिः यस्य whose flanks looked small (by his waist being tightly bound). कक्ष्या...शेषेण after having tightly girt his waist, he gracefully let loose on the ground the fringe of his white cotton cloth used at exercise time and thereby he appeared as though supported from behind by शेष. The idea is:—over his चण्डातक, he had firmly tied his waist with the coils of a long white piece of cotton cloth which he used at the time of taking exercise. A portion of that cloth remained, which he allowed to reach the ground behind him. Being white, it resembled the serpent शेष that is also white. शेष also is धरणितलग *i. e.* it supports the earth. 'फाली कक्ष्याबन्धः' सं०. **'फालः** पुंसि महादेवे कालिन्दीभेदनेपि च । क्लीबं सीरोपकरणे **त्रिषु कार्पासवाससि** ॥' मेदिनी. स्थिरौ स्थूलौ ऊरुदण्डौ यस्य. भूमि...पदानि he planted his steps slowly as though he feared that the earth would break (if he walked faster). निर्भर...गुरु heavy with great pride. A शैल (mountain) also is heavy (गुरु). मुहुर्मुहुः... टाङ्कारैः by the terrible and twanging slapping (with his hand) of his left arm that was doubled (द्विगुणित) on his chest and of his right thigh, put forward slantingly and thus appearing to be coiled up. टाङ्कार is an onomatopoetic word. It is better to read चण्डास्फोटन. The पुरुष smote loudly his left arm doubled on his chest and his right thigh with his hand. This is a characteristic action for wrestless and is a sort of challenge. कर्म...कुर्वन्—The noise made by the slapping was so terrific that it seemed as though the पुरुष sent down निर्घात s for hindering the rite on which भै० was embarked and as though depriving the mortal world of one organ (*i. e.* of the sense of hearing). The noise of the आस्फोटन was deafening. निर्घात: 'noise of contending winds in the sky; a whirlwind.' 'पवनः पवनाभिहतो गगनादवनौ यदा समापतति । भवति तदा निर्घातः स च पापो दीप्तविहगरुतः ॥' बृहत्संहिता 39. 1. कुवलय is a blue lotus. नर...भारत्या in a voice as terrific as the echo (निर्घोष:) of the roar of the Man-lion. This is a reference to the 5th incarnation of Vishṇu when the latter tore off with his nails the chest of हिरण्यकशिपु विद्या...कामुक confident lover of विद्याधरी s. This is said in derision भैर० wanted to be a विद्याधर and believed that he would become one by the successful performance of the rite he was engaged in The emphasis is on the word श्रद्धा, the idea being 'you are sure that you would be a विद्याधर, but I shall show that your belief is worthless.' किम...लषसि Is this pride due to (the possession of) a little knowledge or the arrogance due to being helped by friends that without making an offering to this person (*i. e.* myself) you desire success (in this rite) like a fool? एतावता कालेन during all this time. क्षेत्राधिपति: lord or tutelary deity of a place. अस्य... देशस्य (to be connected with ०पतिः) of this country that is styled (श्रीकण्ठ) after me. लब्धः व्यपदेशः (नाम) येन. नागोहम्—even now the belief in the existence of guardian नाग s presiding over various places is very common. अनि...गगने what power have the planets to move in the sky against my will? Even the planets cannot act against his wishes. What of भै० who wanted to go to heaven as विद्याधर? भूनाथो...क्रियते Though a king, he is no king and is wretched since he is made a tool by vile S'aivas like you. 'निहीनोऽपसदो जाल्मः' अमरः. The word अपसद is generally used at the end of compounds as a term of abuse. The contrast is between भूनाथः and अनाथः (no king; helpless in the hands of भै०). सहस्वे...फलम् now receive along with this bad king the fruit of the bad conduct of a bad snake-charmer. नरेन्द्र means 'a snake-doctor.' भैरवाचार्य was a bad नरेन्द्र in that he did not propitiate the नाग. A and C read दुर्नरेन्द्रेण दुर्नयस्य, but the reading in the text is preferable, as it is more in keeping with Bāṇa's style. नरेन्द्र—compare 'आविष्टा इव नरेन्द्रवृन्दपरिवृताः' हर्ष० 4th उ० and notes thereon; compare also 'महाशीविष इव दुर्नरेन्द्राभिभवरोषितः' हर्ष० 6th उ०. प्रकोष्ठप्रहारैः by the strokes of his forearms. स... कृपाणान् together with their armours and swords.

P. 52 l. 15—**P. 53** l. 2 **अथापूर्व...दृष्टिम्.** अपू...श्रवणात् on hearing the unprecedented insult. This was the first time that the king heard such insulting language. अविद्यमानः शस्त्रव्रणः येषाम् (*adj.* of अवयवैः). अशस्त्र...वमद्भिः that (limbs), though unwounded (then), as though vomitted, under the guise of the sweat due to wrath, the dark water of sword-edges drunk in many battles. The idea is:—He was sorely pained at heart by the insulting words of the नाग, though he was not physically wounded. Sweat due to fury appeared on his body. The poet fancies that the sweat was the 'water' of the sword edges (of his enemies) which had struck him in former battles. अवय...कुर्वद्भिः with his limbs, that under the guise of horripilation, made him light for battle by shooting out an array of arrow-points. His body had रोमाञ्च due to rage. The hair looked like arrow-points. The poet fancies that the hair were arrowheads, planted in his body in former battles but now taken out in order to make his body fit for combat. प्रतिबिम्बितः तारागणः यस्मिन् (*adj.* of अट्टहासेन). स्पष्टं दृष्टा धवला दन्तमाला यथा स्यात्तथा. अवज्ञया in contempt. हसता इव—The stars reflected in the blade looked like white teeth seen when one laughs. कथ्यमानः सत्त्वस्य (courage, spirit) अवष्टम्भः (pride, majesty) यस्य. The three clauses ०वमद्भिः, ०कुर्वद्भिः and ०हसता इव are to be connected with कथ्यमान. These three indicated the greatness of his courage, in spite of the fact that his three companions had been brought to the ground in no time. परिकरबन्धे विभ्रमेण भ्रमितः करः तस्य नखानां किरणचक्रवालेन. व्यप...दिशः—the idea is:—the king girded up his loins as a preparation for the impending fight. The rays of his hand gracefully girding up spread round. The poet fancies that the circle of rays was a charmed circle which the king drew for imprisoning the नाग and preventing it from running in the ten directions (which the king thought the नाग would do). For परिकरबन्ध, see text p. 4. l. 6 and notes thereon. नागदमनाय मन्त्रैः मण्डलबन्धः तेन. The com. says 'मण्डलं गारुडशास्त्रप्रसिद्धमैन्द्रादिकम्.' 'कुण्डली गूढपाच्चक्षुःश्रवाः **काकोदरः फणी'** अमरः (काकस्येव उदरमस्य). The king addressed the नाग as काक out of contempt. It is only a crow that asks for a बलि (as the नाग did above). Further the word is in contrast with the word राजहंस below. राजहंसे swan-like king; a राजहंस. A crow is a nonentity before राजहंसs. अमी...भाषितैः what is the use of these harsh words? अयं न भवसि you will be no more *i. e.* I shall kill you. अगृहीता हेतिः (weapon) यैः. अगृही...हर्तुम्

my arm has not been taught to strike the unarmed. It is better to take अनादृततरं outside the quotation marks. Connect अनादृततरम् (with great unconcern or disdain) with अभिधाय. आस्फोटयामास he slapped (his arm and thigh). निरायुधम्—object of जेतुम्. चर्मफलकेन सह स...फलकम् (*adj.* of असिम्) together with the shield. अर्धो...कक्ष्याम् above his cloak he girt up his loins for a fight with fists. अर्धोरुक is the same as चण्डातक. **'अर्धोरुकं वरस्त्रीणां स्याच्चण्डातकमंशुकम्'** अमरः (ऊर्वोरर्धोच्छादकमंशुकमर्धोरुकं—क्षीर०). कक्ष्या girdle, waist. निर्दयेन आस्फोटनेन स्फुटितौ भुजौ तयोः रुधिरं तस्य शीकरेण सिच्यमानौ. The furious slapping of their arms caused blood to come out of them. शब्द...भुवनम्—the incessant slapping of their arms filled the world with the sound. उच्चखान drew out (of the sheath). अपश्य...वीतम् the king saw inside the wreath his sacred thread. For वैकक्षक, see p. 26. It is worn like the यज्ञोपवीत and hence the king did not notice it before. उपसंहृतः (stopped) शस्त्रव्यापारः येन. दुर्विनीत impudent. अस्ति...मिदम् you possess this seed (*i. e.* means) which (safely) carries you over your bad deeds. विश्रब्धम् *adv.* confidently. The यज्ञोपवीत showed that the नाग was a ब्राह्मण. A ब्राह्मण was never to be killed, however great his offence might be. ब्रह्महत्या was a महापातक; *vide* p. 160 above. Hence the king laid aside his weapon. घ्राणावलेपिनम् smearing his nose (*i. e.* overpowering it).

P. 53 ll. 3–28. **अथ...इति.** The first sentence is अथ... अट्टहासस्य मध्ये...स्फुरन्तीं...स्त्रियमपश्यत् (l. 20). तडि...स्फुरन्तीम्—the lady was fair like a flash of lightning and the sword was like a dark cloud. प्रभया...यामाम् that as though swallowed up the night by her radiance. तामरसं (red lotus) हस्ते यस्याः. The woman of whom the king had a vision was लक्ष्मी. So she was तामरसहस्ता. कोमला...कर्षन्तीम् that drew the webs of the glow of her delicate toes, as though they were the coral creepers on the seaside sticking to her feet. Her toes were red like coral. कर...बिभ्रतीम्—पद्म closes its petals in moonlight. Her toe-nails were bright like moonlight. Therefore the poet fancies that लक्ष्मी desiring to have the lotus in her hand always blooming carried the moon cut into pieces (*viz.* her toe-nails). To explain (as C and T and Mr. Kale do) that it was a night lotus and that therefore she carried the pieces of the moon is not happy. गुल्फा...गताम् as her anklets lay about her ankles (गुल्फः) she appeared to have escaped from fetters (or imprisonment) in which there were many thick links. कटकं a link. स्थिता निबिडा

कटकावलिः यस्मिन् तत् ०वलि बन्धनं तस्मात्. The anklet appeared to be the single link remaining on her ankle after she had burst asunder the chain with which she was imprisoned. बहु...शोभितात् ornamented with various flowers and birds (painted on or woven into the texture of the garment). On the waters of the ocean also are birds and flowers (offered by people in worship). पव... तरङ्गात् over which there were slight folds worked up by the breeze (with अंशुकात्); that had slight ripples caused by the wind (with ०सलिलात्). अंशु...रन्तीम् coming out (into view) from under her garment, as though from the water of the ocean. The garment was fine and bright like sea-water. उदधि... मध्याम् under the disguise of the three folds of skin (on her waist), her waist was as though embraced by the Ganges out of love for her because she was born of the ocean. The Ganges is represented as the queen of the ocean. It is called त्रिपथगा because it flows in heaven, on the earth and in पाताल. Three folds of skin are a sign of beauty among women. लक्ष्मी sprang out of the ocean at the time of churning. The poet fancies that the three folds of लक्ष्मी are the Ganges clasping her waist because she was the daughter of her husband, the ocean. Remove the comma after ०मण्डलाम्. दृश्यमानौ दिङ्नागकुम्भौ यस्याम् (*adj.* of ककुभम्). She with her swelling bosom looked like the quarter with the prominent frontal bones of its guardian elephant. मदलग्नः (समदः) ऐरावतः &c. The pearls of the necklace she wore appeared like the spray from the trunk of ऐरावत when in rut. ऐरावत is white and her bosom also was fair. The necklace was brilliant (तार) like the stars in autumn. धवल...वीज्यमानाम्—the rays of the necklace as it heaved up and down with her soft breathing resembled white chowries. मदान्धः गन्धेभः (गन्धगजः) तस्य कुम्भस्य आस्फालनेन संक्रान्तं सिन्दूरं यस्य. It is to be noted that the woman described here is लक्ष्मी. In India an elephant was the symbol of prosperity (लक्ष्मी). So लक्ष्मी is represented as riding an elephant. Red lead is applied to the temples of elephants by way of decoration. The poet fancies that the hands of लक्ष्मी (that were naturally red) became red because red lead was transferred to them when she rubbed the temple of her elephant. For गन्धेभ, compare 'गान्धाराधिपगन्धद्विपकूटपाकलः' हर्ष० 4th उ० 2nd para and notes thereon. The com. says 'श्रीर्हस्तिपृष्ठेन यातीति मदान्धेत्याद्युक्तम् । हस्तिवाहित्वाल्लक्ष्म्या एवमुक्तम्.' हरशिखण्डे इन्दुः तस्य द्वितीयखण्डेन इव. हर...भ्राजमानम्—the idea is:—her brilliant (*lit.* shedding moonlight) ear-ornament looked like the second piece of the moon on the top-knot of शिव turned into a ring. शिव has the crescent of the moon on his head. The remaining portion (the other half) of the moon was as though bent into a ring and made her ear-ornament. For a similar conceit, *vide* text p. 9 l. 21. कौस्तुभ...ङ्कृताम्—the shoots of अशोक on her ear resembled the cluster of the rays of the कौस्तुभ gem. महता...ललाटाम् on whose forehead was present a large *tilaka* of elephant's ichor, as thought it were the round shadow of an invisible umbrella. Her तिलक was large, round and dark (as ichor is dark). The shadow of an umbrella would be round and dark. An umbrella is a sign of sovereignty (राजलक्ष्मी). So लक्ष्मी must be accompanied by it, though it may not be actually visible. आपाद...सीमन्ताच्च from the soles of her feet to the parting line of her hair. यशस् is white. धरणि...नीभिः kissing (*i. e.* touching) the ground (with ०मालाभिः); flowing over the earth (with सरिद्भिः). सागराधिष्ठाभिः (सागरमधितिष्ठन्तीति ताभिः) that repose in the ocean. Rivers fall into the ocean. The long wreaths she wore were rivers that wafted her into the ocean from which she sprang at the time of churning. मृणाल...चक्षाणाम् with her limbs delicate like lotus fibres she declared her birth in a lotus without words. अनक्षरम्—अविद्यमानानि अक्षराणि यथा स्युः (अव्ययीभाव). लक्ष्मी is represented as rising from an expanded lotus. Compare 'चक्षुषा शिक्षयन्तमिव लक्ष्मीलाभोत्तानितमुखानि पङ्कजवनानि विनयम्' हर्ष० 4th उ०. असंभ्रान्तः not agitated. कस्यासि whose (wife) art thou? स्त्री...भवन्तीव as though overpowering him with a boldness (or dignity) at variance with her sex. नारायणस्य उरः एव स्थली तस्यां लीलया विहारे हरिणीम्—लक्ष्मी is represented as reclining on the chest of Vishṇu. Compare 'यास्य वक्षसि नरकजितो लक्ष्मीरिव ललास' हर्ष० 4th उ० 3rd para. A female deer also wanders at will on sylvan spots. पृथु...पताकाम् the banner of the families of the kings of old such as पृथु, भरत and भगीरथ. As a पताका is very prominent, so लक्ष्मी was very prominent in the families of these kings. A पताका (pennon) flutters from a वंश (bamboo pole). सुभटानां भुजाः एव जयस्तम्भाः तेषु विलासशालभञ्जिका—the idea is:—लक्ष्मी loves great heroes. In ancient India triumphal columns were often erected to proclaim the victories won by great kings. C and T call attention to the Mandasor stone pillar which has an inscription of Yas'odharman (*vide C. I. I.* Vol III p. 142). A शालभञ्जिका (doll, female

bright tears dew-drops. ब्रवीमि...सदृशम् if I say 'I am going', that would not be suitable to the affection I bear to you. The roots या and गम् were inauspicious and would not be used by a person parting from his friend. In these and the following clauses, भैरवाचार्य puts forward various sentences and dismisses each of them as not suited to adequately express his sentiments when parting from his friend, the king. त्वदीयाः...सक्तम् If I say 'my life is at thy disposal,' that is merely superfluous. His meaning is 'without my saying so, my life is already at your service; so those words need not be uttered.' गृह्यता...करणम् 'take this wretched body' would be to keep things distinct (which are not so). You and I are one. Therefore what is mine is already yours. To ask you to receive my body would be to make a distinction (व्यतिरेकः) between you and me which does not exist. तिल...रूपम् 'I am purchased by you bit by bit' would not be appropriate to your obligations. Your obligations are so many and so great, that even if I were cut up into small particles the number of those particles would be too small as compared with them. बान्ध...करणमिव 'you are my kinsman' would be placing you at a distance. One is not necessarily very friendly and affectionate to one's kinsman. त्वयि...प्रत्यक्षम् 'my heart remains with you' cannot be directly perceived. I cannot show by प्रत्यक्षप्रमाण (by the testimony of the eye) that my heart is bound to yours. त्व...श्रद्धेयम् 'this my success (or attainment of superhuman power) that causes separation from you is a veritable torment (कारणा)' cannot be believed. As I aspired to be विद्याधर and worked hard to secure my object, no one will believe me if I say that my सिद्धि is a torment to me. 'कारणा तु यातना तीव्रवेदना' अमरः. निष्का...वादः 'your kindness was disinterested' is a mere repetition (or praise). निष्कारणः would also mean 'without any merit in me (to deserve such kindness).' He means:—if I say 'निष्का...कारः,' I do not say anything new; it is your nature to do kind deeds without any merit in those whom you so benefit. So my words will repeat what already exists and I may be looked upon as simply praising you. Vedic sentences are divided into विधि and अर्थवाद. A विधि is that which lays down a rule or injunction or a religious commandment such as स्वर्गकामो ज्योतिष्टोमेन यजेत. An अर्थवाद is a sentence which recommends a विधि, which illustrates it, praises those that followed the विधि and points out the evils of not following a विधि. अनुवाद is one of the three kinds of अर्थवादs. अनुवाद is explained as 'सिद्धस्य उपन्यासः' or as 'विधिविहितस्य अनुवचनमनुवादः.' स्मर्तव्या...ज्ञा 'I should be remembered' sounds as a command. He says—'you are so great that it would be presumptuous on my part to command you.' सर्वथा...जनः At all events this person (*i. e.* I), remorseless in pursuing his own selfish purpose, should be kept in mind in talking about ungrateful persons and in narrating the accounts of bad men. He requests the king to remember him at least among ungrateful and bad men. वेगेन छिन्नः हारः तस्मात् उच्छलितः (shaken, tossed about) मुक्ताफलनिकरः तेन ताडितः तारागणः यस्मिन् (*adj.* of ०तलम्) or we may take it as an adverb (ताडितः तारागणः यथा स्यात्तथा). As he rose up with violent speed, his necklace was rent asunder and he struck the stars with the falling pearls. सीमन्तितः (parted) ग्रहग्रामः ग्रहसमूहः येन. As the white line parts the hair of women so he parted the planets while going through them. ग्राहितः विनयः येन who was taught modesty. श्रीकण्ठ had been humbled by the king. कर्तव्येषु...ग्राह्यः अयं जनः I should be favoured with a command whenever necessary.

P. 54 l. 29—**P. 55** l. 12 **नरपति...करोत्.** The principal sentence is नरपतिः...नगरं विवेश. क्षीण...क्षपायाम् when the night had almost run out. प्रवातुमारब्धे (connect with वनानिले) began to blow. प्रबुध्य...सुरभौ fragrant with the exhalations of the opening lotus plants; fragrant like the breaths of waking handsome women. कमलिनी = पद्मिनी. Writers on erotics divide women into four classes पद्मिनी, चित्रिणी, हस्तिनी and शङ्खिनी, the first being the best. ०परिहासेन स्वेदिनि इव. अवश्यायशीकरेण सह साव० (बहुव्रीहि). वन...शीकरे—the idea is:—the wind was charged with the dew of dawn; the poet fancies that the wind was a lover who was covered with sweat (in the form of dew drops) at the joke of removing the shawls from the bosoms of forest nymphs. परिमलेन आकृष्टाः मधुकृतः (मधुकराः) येन. कुमुद...वाहिनि that brought sleep to moon-lotuses. At the advent of morn कुमुदs close their petals. निशा...जडे chilled by the end of night; void of the warmth (of love) on account of the old age of Night. तुषारलेशिनि having particles of frost or snow. विरहेण विधुरं (helpless) चक्रवाकचक्रं तस्य निःश्वसितैः सन्तापितायाम् इव. विरह...त्रियामायाम्—the idea is:—चक्रवाक pairs are separated at night. Throughout the night they heaved hot sighs. The poet fancies that the night was corched by those hot sighs and entered the western ocean to allay the heat. One that is heated enters into water. As a matter of fact there is a glow of light in the east at dawn, while the west is still dark. Hence the words 'अपरजल०.' For चक्रवाक, *vide* notes pp. 67, 97. साक्षा... नलिनीषु when the lotus plants began to open (their eyes) as though curious to see Lakshmī that was bodily present. लक्ष्मी had showed herself to the king. As night was drawing to a close, the lotuses began to open. The poet fancies that they were curious to see the bodily presence of लक्ष्मी. उन्निद्राः पक्षिणः यस्मिन् (*adj.* of कानने) the birds in which awoke from sleep. क्षरति...कानने when the forests, the creepers in which were made to dance by a soft breeze, dropped down a mass of particles of frost as though it were a heap of flowers. Both flowers and particles of frost are bright. मृदुपवनेन लासिताः लताः यस्मिन्. कमल...कुमुदेषु when the closing *kumudas* (night lotuses) inside which were imprisoned buzzing bees hummed forth, as though they were auspicious conches (blown) to awaken the glory of day lotuses. Kings and great persons are aroused from sleep in the morning by the blowing of conches, by the lays of bards &c. अन्तर्बद्धाः ध्वनन्तः मधुकराः येषु. कुमुदs began to close in the morning and the bees were confined in them and made a noise inside. This noise is fancied to be the blowing of a conch. उज्जिहानाः (getting up from their beds) रविरथवाजिनः तैः विसृष्टैः. प्रोथपवनैः the breaths of their nostrils. प्रोत्सार्य...तारकासु when the stars, the buds of the creeper of Night, clustered together in the west, as though they were driven away (by the breaths of the sun's horses). श्यामा (रात्रिः) एव लता तस्याः कलिकासु or श्यामालता प्रियङ्गुलता तस्याः कलिकासु. The stars were like buds. In the east no stars were visible on account of the glow of day-break. The poet fancies that on the breaths of the sun's horses, stars were wafted towards the west and there clustered together. वारुण्यां ककुभि—वरुण is the lord of the west. मन्दानिलेन लुलितानि (shaken) ०कुसुमानि तेषां धूल्या विच्छुरिते (inlaid, covered). मन्दानिल... मण्डले—the constellation of the Great Bear looked grey in the light of morn. The poet fancies that it looked grey being covered with pollen &c. मन्दर...श्रयिणि—मन्दर is a mountain to the east of Meru. *Vide* notes above p. 43. The Sun, the Moon and the stars were supposed to revolve round Meru. Compare भागवत-पुराण 5. 22. 'यथा कुलालचक्रेण भ्रमता सह भ्रमतां तदाश्रयाणां पिपीलिकादीनां गतिरन्यैव प्रदेशान्तरेष्वप्युपलभ्यमानत्वादेवं **नक्षत्रराशिभिरुपलक्षितेन कालचक्रेण ध्रुवं मेरुं च प्रदक्षिणेन** परिधावता सह &c.' सुर...मृगे when the starry deer sank (towards the west) as though it were the fallen goad of the elephant of the gods (*i. e.* of ऐरावत). The reference is to the constellation of मृगशीर्ष, particularly to the three stars (constituting the belt of Orion) that look like a dart. Those dart–like stars seemed to be the goad of ऐरावत fallen from the rider's hand. नाग...मलीमसानि (*adj.* of अङ्गानि) soiled by the incident (व्यतिकरः) of the fight with the Nāga. शुचिनि *adj.* of ०पयसि. आत्म...करोत् pleased all the three with bath, food and clothing that did not differ from his own. आत्मशरीरात् अनन्तरं (अविद्यमानं अन्तरं विशेषः यस्य) स्नान...च्छादनादि तेन. He gave them the same food that he partook of, the same rich clothing that he wore &c. The com. explains differently. The king made them bathe, take food &c. before himself and then took his bath, food &c. 'आत्मशरीरमनन्तरं यस्य तादृशेन स्नानभोजनाच्छादिना। तेषु कृत्वा पश्चादात्मनः करोतीत्यर्थः' सं०. C and T translate 'with unguents, food and clothing immediately after his own person.'

P. 55 ll. 13–17 **कतिपय...जग्मतुरिति.** परिव्राट् refers to टीटिभ. शौर्यानुरक्तौ devoted to the king on account of his bravery. सम्पादितः मनोरथात् अतिरिक्तः विभवः ययोः on whom was bestowed wealth exceeding even their desires. सुभ...मण्डलाग्रौ who drew out their swords in the midst of the guard of warriors. They were allowed, on account of their rank and devotion to the king, to walk with drawn swords in the midst of the king's guard or in the midst of the king's warlike courtiers. 'कौक्षेयको मण्डलाग्रः करवालः कृपाणवत्' अमरः (मण्डलाकृति अग्रमस्य). समर... युज्यमानौ they occupied the foremost rank in battle. अन्तरान्तरा now and then. राज्ञा समादिष्टौ when ordered by the king. शैशववृत्तान्तान् the incidents of their boyhood.

Uchchhvāsa IV

For a brief analysis of the contents of the first three Uchchhvāsas, see Appendix A. In the third Uchchhvāsa Bāṇa narrated how Pushpabhûti, king of Sthāṇvîs'vara (modern Thanesar) and the ancestor of Emperor Harsha, made the friendship of a S'aiva ascetic Bhairavāchārya, how the latter presented a miraculous sword to the king, and how the king helped the ascetic in the practice of magic for attaining a divine form.

P. 56 Verse 1 The words योग and करग्रह have two meanings. The great even in dreams do not desire to employ deceitful tricks (योग) nor do they take कर (tribute). In these two respects they are distinguishable from others who become *Pati*. Husbands desire union with their wives and take the hand of their wives (at the time of marriage). Without these two (योग and करग्रहण) the great become the masters (पति) of the world by their mere name *i. e.* their very name is sufficient to bring to them the devoted allegiance of the world.

Verse 2 Construe विपुलेऽपि नृपवंशे सकल...कृत् पृथुप्रतिमः एक एव उत्पद्यते विपुलेऽपि गणाधिपस्य मुखे पृथुप्रतिमः एक एव दन्त इव. सकल...कृत् One who strikes terror in (the heart of) all kings. पृथुप्रतिमः— resembling the (ancient king) Pṛithu. Pṛithu was the son of वेन. Formerly the mountains were rebellious and covered the earth just as they pleased. As no corn grew, people became famished and prayed to Pṛithu for deliverance. He levelled the earth by casting away the mountains with his bow and made it fertile. So पृथु also was सकल...कृत् (as महीभृत् means 'mountain' also). See विष्णुपुराण I. 13 'तत उत्सारयामास शैलान् शतसहस्रशः । धनुष्कोट्या तदा वैन्यस्तेन शैलविवर्धिताः' ॥ 82. Compare कादम्बरी (p. 5 of P) 'वैन्य इव चापकोटिसमुत्सारितसकलारातिकुलाचलः'. गणाधिप is the god गणेश, one of whose names is एकदन्त. 'सुमुखश्चैकदन्तश्च कपिलो गजकर्णकः । लम्बोदरश्च विकटो विघ्ननाशो गणाधिपः ॥ धूम्रकेतुर्गणाध्यक्षो भालचंद्रो गजाननः ॥' गणेशपुराण I chap. 92. पृथुः प्रतिमा यस्य (with दन्त) the size of which is great. प्रतिमा also means 'the part of an elephant's head between the tusks'. How Ganes'a became

एकदन्त is explained by the ब्रह्मवैवर्तपुराण. The story is:—'एकदा रहसि स्थितयोः पार्वतीपरमेश्वरयोर्द्वारपालत्वमङ्गीकृतं गजाननेन । एतस्मिन्नन्तरे परशुरामः शिवं द्रष्टुमागतः । शिवदर्शनोत्सुकस्यान्तर्जिगमिषोर्द्वाररोधे कृते गणपतिना सह तस्य तुमुलं युद्धमभवत् । परशुरामक्षिप्तेन परशुना च गजाननस्य एको दन्तो भग्नः'.

In these two verses the poet suggests the greatness of Harsha whose birth forms the principal topic of the fourth Uchchhvāsa.

अथ...राजवंशः The principal sentence is अथ तस्मात् पुष्पभूतेः राजवंशः निर्जगाम. There are five dependent clauses containing comparisons. It is to be noted that all the words in these five clauses except the उपमानपद्s apply also to राजवंश and पुष्पभूति (according to their respective cases). द्विज...क्षणात् as the navel lotus, the calix of which was resorted to of his own will by Brahmā, (springs) from विष्णु (पुण्डरीकेक्षण). द्विजवरेण ब्रह्मणा स्वेच्छया गृहीतः कोषः (कर्णिका) यस्य (स नाभिपद्मः). 'वा पुंसि पद्मं नलिनम्' इत्यमरः. In the Purāṇas Brahmā is represented as being born in a lotus which springs from the navel of विष्णु. Being स्वयम्भू, his birth must be said to be due to his own will. राजवंश also was द्विज... कोषः (द्विजवरैः ब्राह्मणश्रेष्ठैः स्वेच्छया गृहीतः कोषः यस्य). The kings of पुष्पभूति's line allowed learned Brahmins to take from their treasury as much as they liked. पुष्पभूति was पुण्डरीकेक्षण (कमलनयन). Dr. Buhler (E. I. I. p. 68) says that पुष्यभूति must have been the name of the king (after the constellation of पुष्य) and that the Mss. make little distinction between य and प. लक्ष्मी...रत्नाकरात् as the series of (14) jewels, chief of which was लक्ष्मी, (sprang) from the ocean. लक्ष्मीः पुरःसरा यस्य. This refers to the churning of the ocean, for which see विष्णुपुराण I. 9 and रामायण I. 44. राजवंश was favoured by लक्ष्मी (prosperity) and पुष्पभूति was रत्नाकर (रत्नानां आकरः mine of jewels, *i. e.* possessed all the best things in the world). गुरु...स्थानात् as the assembly of planets mostly consisting of Jupiter (गुरु), mercury (बुध), Venus (कवि), the moon (कलावत्), the sun (तेजस्विन्) and Mars (भूनन्दन) comes up from the mount in the east. गुरु...प्रायः (with राजवंशः) means 'mostly consisting of teachers, wise men, poets, artists (कलावत्), brave men and princes' (भूनन्दन). According to ancient Hindu astronomy there were nine ग्रहs (including the sun). उदयस्थानात् the sun, the moon and the planets were supposed to rise from a mountain in the east, more often called उदयगिरि. But for श्लेष, the word उदयस्थान is used here. कला 'digits of the moon'; 'the 64 arts, such as painting, dancing &c.' पुष्पभूति was the source of prosperity (उदयस्थान) to गुरुबुध०. महा...प्रभावात् as the ocean fit for bearing the great burden sprang from the might of the Sagaras (sons of सगर). By महाभार may be meant विष्णु who sleeps on the ocean or the reference may be to the ocean's keeping the earth inviolate. When the sacrificial horse of सगर was stolen away by इन्द्र, his sixty thousand sons dug the whole earth. The void thus created was filled by the rush of the Ganges brought from heaven by भगीरथ, descendant of सगर. राजवंश was महा...योग्यः (fit to bear the great responsibility of protecting the world). पुष्पभूति was सगरप्रभाव (सगरस्य इव प्रभावः यस्य). दुर्जय...शूरात् as the हरिवंश which comprises Vishṇu (दुर्जय) and Balarāma (sprang) from शूर. दुर्जयः बलश्च ताभ्यां सनाथः. दुर्जय is given as one of the thousand names of विष्णु in the अनुशासनपर्व (महाभारत 13.149.96 समावर्तो निवृत्तात्मा दुर्जयो दुरतिक्रमः). शूर was a descendant of यदु and grandfather of कृष्ण. राजवंशः दुर्जयेन बलेन सैन्येन सनाथः. पुष्पभूति was brave (शूर).

P. 56 यस्मा...राजानः The principal sentence is यस्मात् अजायन्त राजानः. Syntax requires that यस्मात् must be taken with राजवंशः. But it would be better to take it with पुष्पभूतेः, if the sense of what follows be carefully considered. Here again there are numerous dependent clauses containing comparisons. अविनष्ट...मुखात् As the creations of beings, rendered glorious by (the existence of) धर्म in its unimpaired state, are produced in the beginning of the Kṛita age. अविनष्टः (सकलः) धर्मः तेन धवलाः. According to ancient Hindu ideas, in the कृतयुग धर्म existed in its fullest splendour and there was not a trace of अधर्म. In each of the other three युगs (त्रेता, द्वापर and कलि) धर्म decreased by one quarter, and अधर्म increased by one quarter in an ascending scale. 'चतुष्पात्सकलो धर्मः सत्यं चैव कृते युगे। नाधर्मेणागमः कश्चिन्मनुष्यान्प्रति वर्तते ॥ इतरेष्वागमाद्धर्मः पादशस्त्ववरोपितः। चौरिकानृतमायाभिर्धर्मश्चापैति पादशः ॥' मनु० I. 81–82. The kings (राजानः) were also rendered glorious by the fact that in their regime धर्म was never on the wane. कृतं संस्कृतं मुखं यस्य (goes with यस्मात्). प्रतापेन (by light; by valour) आक्रान्तं भुवनं यैः. तेजोनिधेः (from the sun; from the राजवंश that is the centre of bravery). विग्रहेण व्याप्तानि दिङ्मुखानि यैः that covered the quarters with their bodies (with गिरयः); that filled the world with their battles (with राजानः). भूभृत्प्रभवात् from ब्रह्मा who is the creator of mountains (with गिरयः); from that which is the source of kings. Mountains had at first wings and they went where they pleased. The reading भूभृत्प्रवरात् would mean 'from the best of mountains (हिमकर); from the best of kings'. The latter meaning is unsuitable if we take यस्मात् as referring to राजवंश. भर...क्षमा capable of bearing the earth (applies to both दिग्गजाः and राजानः). There are eight guardian elephants of the quarters. They are supposed to support the earth. 'कमठकुलाचलदिग्गजफणिपतिविधृतापि चलति वसुधेयम्' भर्तृहरि. On the birth of the दिग्गजs from ब्रह्मकर, the हस्त्यायुर्वेद of पालकाप्य tells us 'सूर्यस्याण्डकपाले द्वे समानीय प्रजापतिः । हस्ताभ्यां परिगृह्यादौ सप्त सामान्यगायत ॥ गायतो ब्रह्मणस्तस्य समुत्पन्ना मतङ्गजाः । chap I. 218–219 (Anand. ed). ब्रह्मकरात् from that which produces ब्रह्म *i. e.* learning (with यस्मात्). 'वेदस्तत्त्वं तपो ब्रह्म' इत्यमरः. पातुम् to drink (with जलधराः); to protect (with राजानः). घनागमः वर्षाकालः तस्मात्. घनः (दृढः) आगमः (sacred knowledge) यस्य or यस्मिन् (with यस्मात्). इच्छा...यिनः applies to both तरवः and राजानः. कल्पतरु was one of the five trees of Paradise. 'पञ्चैते देवतरवो मन्दारः पारिजातकः । सन्तानः कल्पवृक्षश्च पुंसि वा हरिचन्दनम् ॥'. नन्दनात् from the garden of Indra; from that which gladdened. सर्व...धरात् as the various forms in the universe having for their substrata all the beings spring from Hari. सर्वभूतानि आश्रयाः येषाम् (with प्रकाराः); सर्वभूतानामाश्रयाः that gave shelter to all beings (with राजानः). विश्वस्य रूपाणि तेषां प्रकाराः. श्रीधरात् (with यस्मात्) that was possessed of prosperity.

P. 56 l. 16—**P. 2** l. 13 **तेषु...सम्पदा.** तेषु—supply राजसु. उदपादि 3rd sing. Aorist of पद् with उद्. हूण...केसरी a very lion to the deer in the form of the Hûṇas. हूणाः एव हरिणाः तेषां केसरी. Huns—This is a name given to several peoples:—(1) the Huns who invaded the Roman Empire between 372–453 A. D. and were most formidable under Attila; (2) the White Huns or Ephthalites who troubled Persia from 420 to 557 A. D.; they are probably the सितहूणs mentioned by वराहमिहिर (बृहत्संहिता 11.61); (3) the Hûṇas who invaded India about the same period. See the Mandasor stone inscription of यशोधर्मन् (C. I. III p. 146) and the Bhitari stone pillar inscription of स्कन्दगुप्त (C. I. III p. 54) of whom it is said, 'हूणैर्यस्य समागतस्य समरे दोर्भ्यां धरा कम्पिता'. गुर्जरप्रजागरः—who caused loss of sleep (through fear) to the Gurjara king (*i. e.* king of Bhinmal in Rajputana). गान्धाराधिपः एव गन्धद्विपः तस्य कूटपाकलः. गान्धार was the country round modern Kandahar. गन्धद्विपः an elephant of the best type. यस्य गन्धं समाघ्राय न तिष्ठन्ति प्रतिद्विपाः । स वै गन्धगजो नाम नृपतेर्विजयावहः ॥. कूटपाकलः

is a fever which attacks elephants. The reading in the text is better than 'कूटहस्तिज्वरः पाकलः'. The हस्त्यायुर्वेद of पालकाप्य tells us that all the fevers of elephants are called पाकल and that there are ten varieties of them. See अध्याय 9, which is styled पाकलाध्याय. कूट is one of the varieties and it is the deadliest of all. पालकाप्य says that it is called कूट because it kills elephants at once. 'तत्र गजस्याभीक्ष्णशो रूक्षान्नयवसकवलकुवलतिक्तकटुकषायलघुविषम-रूक्षबह्वन्नभोजनात्, अथवातिगुरुभारहरणतरणविलङ्घनात्कुप्यति अनिलः । तदात्मकश्च कूटः । कूटो नामाशुघातनम् आशुघातनाद् द्विरदानाम् । तस्मात्कूटपाकलमाचक्ष्महे । तत्र श्लोकः । यथा हि हन्यात्कूटेन मृगशावं वनेचरः । तथा वातात्मको नागं हन्ति वै कूटपाकलः ॥'. The other reading would mean 'who was पाकल, that is a fever of elephants, working secretly'. This does not bring out the force and terror of the king's attack upon his enemies. Every fever (पाकल) is not equally dangerous to elephants. Compare 'अचिरेण वैकृतविवर्तदारुणः कलभं कठोर इव कूटपाकलः ॥' (मालतीमाधव I). लाट...चरः who steals (*i. e.* removes, renders nugatory) the skill of the king of Lāṭa (country about Broach *i. e.* Southern Gujerat). C and T translate 'a looter to the lawlessness of the Lāts.' This does not seem to be correct. मालवलक्ष्मीः एव लता तस्याः परशुः. मालव is modern Malva. प्रथितं (well-known) अपरनाम यस्य. The author means to say that प्रभाकरवर्धन had conquered the Huns, the Gurjaras &c. See Introduction. यो... धनानि who, the moment he was crowned, gave up wealth that sticks to the राज्याङ्गs (constituent elements of a state), as if it were dirt. One who bathes removes the dirt (मल m. n.) from his body (अङ्ग). In a coronation a king is bathed with the waters of sacred rivers and in commemoration of it money is distributed among Brahmins. राज्याङ्गानि सप्त 'स्वाम्यमात्यसुहृत्कोशराष्ट्र-दुर्गबलानि च । राज्याङ्गानि' इत्यमरः. यः...जीवितेन who felt ashamed even when others clung to life in the first rush of battle, life which is dear to the cowardly, as if it were grass held in the mouth. To hold grass in the mouth is a sign of defeat and abject submission. Note the Marathi proverb 'दांतीं तृण धरून'. It is only the chickenhearted that will cling to life and save it at the cost of self-respect. When the king's enemies submitted to him in battle, he felt ashamed at *their* abject submission to save life, which to the brave is as तृण. कातरवल्लभेन goes with both तृणेन and जीवितेन. करे धृतः धौतः असिः तस्मिन् प्रतिबिम्बितेन. समितिषु सहायेन that (reflection of self) was his (only) companion in battles. प्रधनेषु in battles. The idea is this:—When the king fought with his enemies, he bent his bow for discharging arrows. In his bright sword-blade appeared the reflection of the king bending his bow. It appeared as if the king was helped by his reflection and even this made him uneasy (with the thought of having to receive another's help in battle). Further he was pained by the fact that his bow bent before his foes (though only for killing them). यो...खिद्यत there seems to be a pun, giving two opposite senses. यो मानी (proud) मानसेन अखिद्यत (was troubled by mind *i. e.* by the high soaring desires of his mind); यो मानी मानसे न अखिद्यत—who, proud as he was, was never troubled in mind (by difficulties). अन्तर्गताः अपरिमिताः रिपवः एव शल्यानि शङ्कवश्च तैः कीलिताम् nailed with the inserted (अन्तर्गत) points of darts in the form of numberless enemies in his empire. लक्ष्मी is said to be चंचल. But in his case it was निश्चल *i. e.* never left him. What is nailed becomes fixed. His sovereignty extended over many kings—his enemies whom he had subdued; so though they were like so many thorns in his side, yet they served the purpose of nails and made his sovereignty निश्चल. The reading in the text seems better than अन्तर्गताम्. Nails are inside; so the subdued kings were inside his empire. C and T take अन्तर्गत to mean 'dead' (with foes). यश्च...बहुधा who, by the numerous (पृथु) roads for the march (यात्रा) of his troops (दण्डः) as it were cut up the earth in many parts in all directions for the benefit of his servants, (roads) by which (*i. e.* in making which) the river-banks, pits, trees with luxuriant branches, clumps of grass, anthills and forests were levelled up. समीकृतानि सरित्तटाः अवटाः, विटपानामटवी (समूहः) तया युक्ताः तरवः, तृणानां गुल्माः (समूहाः), वल्मीकगिरयः, गहनानि (वनानि) च—यैः (०पथैः). The king's victorious armies marched in various directions and so roads had to be prepared for them or were made by the very fact of marching in large numbers. Rivers, banks, clumps of trees and grass, and hills and forests-these serve as boundaries to demarcate one province from another. But these were all removed by his armies. It was only the broad roads that separated the several provinces which the king apportioned among his own servants. See मनु० 8. 246—47 '**सीमावृक्षांश्च** कुर्वीत न्यग्रोधाश्वत्थकिंशुकान् । गुल्मान्वेणूंश्च विविधाञ्छमीवल्लीस्थलानि च । शरान् कुब्जकगुल्मांश्च तथा सीमा न नश्यति ॥.' याज्ञवल्क्य II. 151 '**नयेयुरेते सीमानं स्थलाङ्गारतुषद्रुमैः । सेतुवल्मीक**निम्नास्थिचैत्याद्यैरुपलक्षिताम् ॥'. **अलब्धं युद्धस्य दोहदं येन** whose longing or thirst for battle was not gratified. **यं चा...**

प्रताप: the idea is—his prowess was so great that nobody dared oppose him; the result was that his desire to fight was never gratified and his own prowess in this way caused him uneasiness, as if it were the prowess of another. If anyone else had great prowess that would have been a source of trouble to him. **P. 57** यस्य च...प्रताप:—the principal sentence is यस्य प्रताप: निहत... पुरेषु पञ्च...मयो मूर्त इवादृश्यत—whose prowess appeared as if it had an embodied existence made up of the five great elements in the wives of the chieftains that were slain in opposing him. निहता: प्रतिसामन्ता: तेषां अन्त:पुराणि तेषु. By his prowess the princes that opposed him were killed and their wives' hearts burnt through anguish, their eyes shed tears, they waved deep sighs, they had earth on their bodies because they rolled on the ground through grief, they felt the world a void (शून्य), as their husbands were dead. The author fancies that प्रताप was identical with the effects it produced on the widows of the princes that were killed. As these effects were perceptible, he says प्रताप was मूर्त. The word क्ष्मा means 'the earth'. All visible bodies are made up of the five elements पृथ्वी (here the word क्ष्मा is used for a pun), अप्, तेज:, वायु and आकाश. क्ष्मा also means 'patience'. The women had to suffer. यस्य...लक्ष्मी:—The idea is:—The best of his servants that were near him (*i. e.* high officers of state) were endowed by him with so much wealth and splendour that they appeared like him. A reflection is generally seen in objects that are near (आसन्न) and bright like jewels &c. 'जातौ जातौ यदुत्कृष्टं तद्रत्नमभिधीयते.' यस्य...भवत् Here the words भूति, सिद्धि, वंश, उक्ति, कर have double meanings. प्रताप: अग्निरिव तेन; also प्रतापसदृश: अग्नि: तेन. Dissolve शौर्योष्मणा and असिधाराजलेन similarly. यस्य प्रता...भूति: अभवत् who had भूति (prosperity, ashes) by the fire of his prowess. He became prosperous by his prowess; fire produces भूति (ashes). Explain the following similarly. शौर्योष्मणा सिद्धि: he attained his objects by the heat of his bravery. सिद्धि also means 'cooking', which is effected by ऊष्मन् (heat). असि...वृद्धि: his family (वंश) prospered by the water of his sword—blade. वंश (bamboo) when watered grows. शस्त्र...रोक्ति: his manliness (पुरुषकार:) was proclaimed by the mouths of the wounds received by him from weapons. उक्ति (utterance) can be made only by the mouth (मुख). धनु...गृहीति:—he levied tribute by the scar made by the string of his bow *i. e.* fought his enemies with the bow, vanquished them and took tribute from them. By constantly wielding the bow his hands (कर) became hard and had scars, *i. e.* किण (corn) seized his hand. यश्च...मन्यत who looked upon enmity as a present, fight (विग्रह) as a blessing, the advent (आगम) of battle as a great festival. शत्रुं निधिदर्शनम् he regarded an enemy as the discovery of a treasure (because by conquering him, he would secure booty and tribute). अवस्क...वृद्धिम् a sudden attack as an auspicious event. वसुधारा—a stream of wealth. निरन्तरै...कृतयुगेन On account of the multitude of sacrificial posts that were erected close to each other it seemed as if the कृत age had put forth sprouts. The king performed numerous sacrifices, in each of which a यूप was required. There was thus a thick row of यूपs. In the कृतयुग also, people performed many sacrifices. Therefore it seemed as though कृतयुग, that had vanished (the present being कलियुग), had again come to life. दिक्षु...कलिना On account of the clouds of sacrificial smoke that spread in all directions, it seemed as if Kali had run away. Kali (being the age of sin and vice) is contemplated as dark; smoke is also dark. As the clouds of smoke were wafted hither and thither by the breeze, the poet fancies that it was Kali that was flying the country. ससुधैः plastered with chunam; possessed of सुधा (nectar). स्वर्ग which is the abode of the gods has सुधा. सुरालयशिखरेषु उद्धूयमानैः (that were being tossed to and fro). The fluttering banners on the spires of temples resemble the leaves पल्लव) of trees shaken by the wind. धर्म is contemplated as white. बहि...ग्रामैः—the idea is:—the king erected, when he performed sacrifices, outside the villages, large (विकट) सभामण्डपs, सत्रमण्डपs, प्रपाम° and प्राग्वंशमण्डपs. It seemed as if the ग्रामs had given birth to them. We take मण्डप with each of the four. सभा is the hall where the sacrificer, the priests and other learned men meet. सत्र is the room where food is distributed to all. प्रपा (Marathi पाणपोई) where water is given to travellers &c. प्राग्वंश is a room to the east of the अग्निशाला to be occupied by the wife and the household of the sacrificer. 'प्राग्वंशो प्राग्धविर्गेहात्' on which क्षीरस्वामी remarks 'प्राग्वंशः पत्नीशालाख्योऽग्निशालायाः प्राग्यो भागः.' काञ्चनमयानि सर्वाणि उपकरणानि (materials, utensils) येषु. विशीर्णमिव मेरुणा as if मेरु had been shattered into pieces. The golden utensils were so many that it seemed as if मेरु had been broken up into pieces which were turned into utensils. मेरु is said to be the mountain of gold. 'मेरुः सुमेरुर्हेमाद्री रत्नसानुः सुरालयः' इत्यमरः. द्विजेभ्यो दीयमानैः.

P. 57 l. 14—P. 58 l. 2 तस्य च … ललास. The principal sentence is तस्य च यशोमती नाम महादेवी प्राणानां…भूमिरभूत्. All the genitives from शङ्करस्य (l. 14) to महामुनेः (l. 18) apply to the king also and all the nominatives in those clauses apply to यशोमती also. जन्मा…शङ्करस्य as पार्वती, who was called सती in her former life, was to S'iva. The queen was सती (पतिव्रता) and the king was शङ्कर (one who caused happiness). The word सती may also suggest (as the com. points out) that यशोमती was fair while पार्वती was श्यामा. दक्ष once celebrated a great sacrifice at which he did not invite his daughter सती nor her husband शिव. She went uninvited, but being greatly insulted, threw herself into the fire and perished. S'iva when he heard of this destroyed Daksha's sacrifice. सती was afterwards born as पार्वती. Compare कुमारसंभव I. 21. 'अथावमानेन पितुः प्रयुक्ता दक्षस्य कन्या भवपूर्वपत्नी । सती सती योगविसृष्टदेहा तां जन्मने शैलवधूं प्रपेदे ॥'. बाण refers often to the story of दक्ष. See कादम्बरी 'दक्षाध्वरक्रियामिवोद्धतगणकचग्रहभयोपसेवितत्र्यम्बकाम्' (महाश्वेताम्). गृहीतं परस्य (विष्णोः) हृदयं वक्षः यया—who rests on the bosom of विष्णु. Compare कादम्बरी 'उरःस्थलनिवाससंक्रान्तनारायणदेहप्रभाश्यामलितामिव श्रियम्' (p. 10–11 of P). The king was लोकगुरु (*i. e.* to be honoured by the world) and the queen was गृ…या (who had captivated the heart of the king). हृदय here means अन्तःकरण and पर means 'the last.' There are four अन्तः—करणs of which चित्त is the last. गृहीतं परं हृदयं (चित्तं) यया. 'मनोबुद्धिरहङ्कारश्चित्तं करणमान्तरम्.' The reading गृहीतहृदया seems to be due to an effort to make good sense. बाण perhaps intended to suggest another sense also (by putting the word पर) *viz.* Lakshmî transfers her affections to many kings. स्फुरन्ती तरला तारका यस्याः the star of which is brilliant and twinkling (with रोहिणी); the pupil (तारका) of whose eye was bright and unsteady (with यशोमती). रोहिणी is said in mythology to be the special favourite of the moon out of his 27 wives (the नक्षत्रs). The king also was कलावत् (well-versed in the arts). सर्वलोक…प्रजापतेः—ब्रह्मा desired to create all the beings and then they were produced. So the बुद्धि (thought) of ब्रह्मा is सर्वलोकजननी. The king was the lord of his subjects and the queen was like a mother to all her people. महा…नायकस्य—The Ganges springs from tha great mountain (हिमालय) and is looked upon as the queen of the ocean (the lord of rivers). The king was the lord of वाहिनी (an army) and यशोमती was born in the family of great kings. मान…तुरा clever in follow

person of the queen. वंशो...रागस्य she was the root of the ancestry of love. As a family traces its ancestry back to some founder, so true love started with her and was then propagated through succeeding generations of loving women. The readings of B also make good sense. सर्ग...सौन्दर्यस्य she was the utmost limit of the creation of loveliness. In her loveliness found its perfection. आयति...यौवनस्य she was as if the majesty of youth. 'प्रभावेपि चायतिः' इत्यमरः. अनभ्र...वैदग्ध्यस्य she was the cloudless rain of intelligence. Rainfall requires clouds; hence rain without clouds is looked upon as an extraordinary thing, a wonder. Her intelligence was wonderful. अयशः...लक्ष्म्याः. लक्ष्मी is said to be चञ्चल. This bad name that लक्ष्मी had acquired was wiped off by the queen, in whom लक्ष्मी was स्थिर. Compare 'येन श्रियः संश्रयदोषरूढं स्वभावलोलेत्ययशः प्रमृष्टम्' रघु० VI. 41. यशः... चारित्रस्य she was the fulness of the fame of chastity. C and T translate 'goodness' bloom of beauty', which is not correct. सौभाग्य...पतेः she was Brahmā's creation of the atoms of beauty. The idea seems to be this:—By creating her, Brahmā created the परमाणुs of beauty; whenever he wants to create another lovely form he would draw upon her beauty (the परमाणुs). According to the Vais'eshika philosophy, from atoms the whole world is produced. शम...शान्तिरिव the quietude of quiescence. शमः is restraint of passions or of the mind. The idea is that even शम would derive शान्ति from her. Explain the remaining clauses similarly. आभिजात्यम् (अभिजातस्य भावः) high birth. संयमः restraint. धैर्यम्—steadiness (of mind). विभ्रमः sportive or amorous action. यशोमती—From the Sonpat seal we see that the name of हर्ष's mother was यशोमती and not यशोवती. See Introduction. प्राणानां भूमिः she was the centre of the life of the king, she was the very life of the king. विश्रामस्य भूमिः—the king confided everything to her. धर्मस्य भूमिः she was the source of the righteousness of the king. A wife is the source of धर्माचरण, as said by आपस्तम्ब 'धर्मप्रजासम्पत्तिः प्रयोजनं दारसंग्रहस्य.' No यज्ञ could be performed without her. See तैत्तिरीय ब्राह्मण III. 3. 3. 1 'अयज्ञो वा एष योऽपत्नीकः'. The महाभारत says that the wife is the source of त्रिवर्ग (धर्म, अर्थ and काम) 'अर्धं भार्या मनुष्यस्य भार्या श्रेष्ठतमः सखा। भार्या मूलं त्रिवर्गस्य भार्या मूलं तरिष्यतः॥' आदिपर्व 74.40. C and T render 'the centre of all creatures' love, confidence, duty and felicity'. This is not correct. अस्य=राज्ञः प्रभाकरवर्धनस्य. नरकजितः (1) of the conqueror of the demon नरक (*i. e.* of

विष्णु); (2) of the vanquisher of Hell. The king by his धर्माचरण had removed the possibility of going to Hell. लक्ष्मी is represented as resting on the bosom of Vishṇu. कृष्ण killed नरक who was the son of भूमि (the earth) and was king of प्राग्ज्योतिष; see विष्णुपुराण V. 29.

P. 58 ll. 3–8 निसर्गत...हृदयम्. उदये...कृतः at the rise of the sun (दिनकृत्). धवलेन कर्पटेन (piece of cloth) प्रावृतं शिरः यस्य. प्राङ्मुखः with his face towards the east. कुङ्कुममण्डलके in a circle that was smeared with saffron paste. C and T translate 'kneeling eastward upon the ground in a circle.' This is wrong. The king did not *kneel in a circle*. He had drawn up a circle with saffron paste on to which he put his offerings. पद्मराग—ruby (which is red in colour). स्व...ददौ he offered worship (अर्चा) with a bunch (षण्ड *m. n.*) of red lotuses that were reddened (अनुरक्त) by the sun, as if it (bunch) were his own heart devoted to the sun. सूर्ये अनुरक्तम् (हृदयम्); सूर्येण अनुरक्तम् (षण्डम्). The heart and the bunch of lotuses are both red and ०नुरक्त. जप्यम्—muttered prayer. शोभनं चरितं यस्य स सुचरितः· अपत्यहेतोः for the purpose of (securing) issue. प्राध्वम् *ind.* favourably, suitably. 'आनुकूल्यार्थके प्राध्वम्' इत्यमरः. Here it may be taken as an adjective of मन्त्रम् meaning 'favourable.' प्रयत restrained, devout. जञ्जपूकः one who mutters prayers. 'यजजपदशां यङः' पा. 3. 2. 166 (The affix ऊक is applied to the frequentative base of यज्, जप् and दश्. यायजूक, दन्दशूक, जञ्जपूक). मन्त्रमादित्यहृदयम्—आदित्यः हृदयं (रहस्यं) यस्य. The आदित्यहृदय is a well-known स्तोत्र declared by कृष्ण to अर्जुन (see बृहत्स्तोत्ररत्नाकर Nir. ed.). For some of the details given in the text, note the following from the स्तोत्र. 'वृत्तं वा चतुरस्रं वा लिप्तभूमौ न्यसेच्छुचिः। त्रिधा तत्र लिखेत्पद्ममष्टपत्रं सकर्णिकम् ॥ 99...सकेसराणि पद्मानि करवीराणि चार्जुन। रक्तचन्दनमिश्राणि कृत्वा वै ताम्रभाजने। धृत्वा शिरसि तत्पात्रं जानुभ्यां धरणीं स्पृशेत् ॥ 104–5.

P. 58 ll. 9–21 भक्त...तिष्ठत्. भक्तजनानां अनुरोधः (entreaty) तेन विधेयानि—influenced by the entreaties of their devotees. सितकरस्य (चन्द्रमसः) कराः तद्वत् सिता (शुभ्रा) सुधा *(chunam)* तया धवलस्य. द्वितीयशयने on a second couch. On the propriety of this, see the com. 'द्वितीयेत्यादिनास्य सदाचारनिष्ठोक्ता। उक्तं हि नाश्नीयाद्भार्यया साकं न च सुप्यात्तया समम्॥'. See मनु० 'समानशयने चैव न शयीत तया सह॥' IV. 40. शिश्ये—Perfect 3rd sing. of शी. परिणत...तिष्ठत्—the principal sentence is देवी यशोमती सहसैव 'आर्यपुत्र परित्रायस्व' इति भाषमाणा उदतिष्ठत्. परिण...श्यामायाम् when the night had reached its close. आसन्ना

(approaching) प्रभातवेला तया विलुप्यमानं लावण्यं यस्य. लिलम्बिषमाणे (*loc. pr. p.* of the desiderative of लम्ब्) when (the moon) was declining (*lit.* about to hang down). सीदत् (sinking, waning) तेजः यस्य. तारकाणां ईश्वरः चन्द्रः. कराग्रैः स्पृष्टा कुमुदिनी तया प्रमोदः तस्मात् जन्म यस्य (with ०स्वेदे). कराग्र...पयसि when very cool drops of dew (अवश्यायः) were falling as if they were the perspiration of the moon (शशधरः) evoked by the joy of touching the night lotuses with the tips of his करs (rays, hands). The poets represent that when a young person intensely in love touches his sweetheart, he perspires. स्वेद is one of the eight सात्त्विकभावs. मधु... प्रदीपेषु when the lamps in the harem, being smitten (आहत *lit.* struck) by the breath of the sleeping beauties that were intoxicated by wine, flickered as if intoxication had been transferred to them. The lamps flickered owing to the breaths of sleeping women. The author represents this flickering as the staggering of intoxication. The lamps caught intoxication from the breath of women wafting the smell of wine. संक्रान्तः मदः येषु. राजनि—construe this with स्वपिति below. विमल...तारकाभिः whose feet were as if shampooed by the stars that were reflected in his white nails. संवाह्यमानौ चरणौ यस्य तस्मिन् (राजनि). It should be remembered that the king is represented as sleeping on the roof of his palace in the summer. Hence the stars were reflected in his nails. विस्रब्ध...अङ्गैः he had his limbs spread carelessly as if they were consigned to the women in the form of the quarters. Understand लक्षिते after अङ्गैः, the instrumental being used in accordance with the Sûtra 'इत्थंभूतलक्षणे' पा. 2. 3. 21. (जटाभिस्तापसः). दिश एव अङ्गनाः. मधु...वीज्यमाने who was fanned by the beauty (श्री) of his face with breath that was scented with मधु (wine, honey), as if the (breaths) were the breezes of the fan *viz.* the lotus in her hand. The king had drunk wine and his breath was charged with its odour. The poet fancies that he was fanned by the लक्ष्मी of his face with the breath. लक्ष्मी is represented as having a lotus in her hand. कमल would have मधु (honey in it). If the lotus were used as a fan the breeze would be charged with the scent of honey. ०गन्धिभिः goes with ०वातैः as well as श्वसितैः. स्वहस्ते यत्कमलं तदेव तालवृन्तं तस्य वातैः. विमल...विराजिते who was adorned by the image of the moon's disc reflected on his bright (विमल) cheek which (image) looked like a chaplet (शेखरः) of white flowers displaced by the seizing of hair in amorous sports. The reflection of the white moon looked like a white garland. A शेखर (which is worn on the head) may be displaced and dangle on the cheek when seized in रतिकेलि. रतिकेल्यां कचग्रहः तेन लम्बितः तेन. भूषण...जनम् as if calling on her attendants by the tinkling of her ornaments. उत्कम्पमाना (trembling) अङ्गयष्टिः यस्याः.

P. 58 ll. 22–33 अथ तेन...कारणम्. तेन—connect this with ध्वनिना. सर्वस्या...मुखे which (cry) was never heard before even in the whole world, much less in the queen's mouth. The king protected the world so well that not even the meanest had ever to cry 'help.' एकपदे *ind.* at once. शिरो...निशाम् who as if drew a parting line in the night with his bright (धौत) sword having a glittering edge, which (sword) was snatched from that part of his bed on which his head rested with his right hand that quivered with wrath, as if it (sword) were the white lotus in his ear coming out. सीमन्त the parting line in the hair on the head of women. सीमन्तयन् is the *pr. p.* of the denominative verb from सीमन्त. Night is dark as hair. The flash of the bright sword made a सीमन्त in the hair of the woman (night) *i. e.* darkness was parted by the white streak. The sword was kept below his pillow to be taken out in case of necessity. Being taken from under his head, the bright sword resembled a white lotus which is often placed on the ear as an ornament. अच्छा धारा यस्य. C and T translate 'whose glittering edge drew a line like a prolongation of his ear-wreath across the night.' This is obscure and does not bring out the sense. अन्तराल... पल्लवेन tossing aside with his left hand his upper garment, as if it were the ether that intervened in space. The garment was very fine and thin and hence is compared to आकाश. The fine garment screened his limbs. आकाश also screens from our view the things in space (अन्तराल). कर...राजमानः—his golden bracelet (worn on the left hand with which he tossed aside his upper garment) dropped down (from his hand) by the violent tossing of his hand and went rolling in all directions on the ground. The poet fancies that the वलय was his heart which wandered about in search of the cause of the alarm (of the queen). Some rich men even now wear golden वलयs on their left hand. सत्वरं अवतारितः (brought down) वामचरणः तस्य आक्रान्तिः (placing) तया कम्पितः प्रासादः येन. पुरः...मानः—his necklace was torn asunder by his violent movements, fell down before him and was reflected in the edge of his sword and looked like a piece of the rays of the moon. लक्ष्मी...आशानाम् he made the ends (पर्यन्त *m.*) of the quarters ruddy with his eyes that were red owing to sleep and rage, as if they (eyes) were coloured with betel juice when kissed by Lakshmî. The poet fancies that लक्ष्मी (sovereignty) had chewed betel and then out of love kissed his eyes. पाटलयन् is *pr. p.* of the denominative verb from पाटल (red). The reading पटलयन् means 'veiling or covering' and does not yield a good sense. बद्धा...वर्तयन् as if again bringing back the night (त्रियामा) by his frowning brow that was trident—shaped and that caused darkness. बद्धः अन्धकारः यया. तिस्रः पताकाः (रेखा) यस्याः. His forehead was wrinkled into three lines by rage and his brows were dark. The author lays emphasis on त्रि in त्रिपताकया and त्रियामां. विक्षिप्तं चक्षुः येन.

P. 59 ll. 1–9 **अथ...इति.** यामिकिनी—a woman of the night watch (from यामिका meaning night). 'साध्वसं भयम्' इत्यमरः. बाला ...भागान् filling the different quarters as if with the glory of morn. कुण्डलिनौ...कवचिनौ wearing earrings, armlets and coat of mail. इन्द्र...स्नातौ bathed in saffron (juice) of the hue of the इन्द्रगोपक insect. The इन्द्रगोपकs are red insects that are seen at the beginning of the rainy season. इन्द्रगोपकस्येव रुक् (कान्तिः) यस्य. Saffron is auspicious and women used to apply saffron तिलक on their forehead as a mark of auspiciousness. C and T translate 'bathed in blood cochineal red'. This is bad. To see in a dream a person bathed in blood is not a good omen. The author intends the whole description to indicate good fortune. 'अथ कुङ्कुमम् ॥...रक्तसङ्कोचपिशुनं वीरलोहितचन्दनम् ॥' इत्यमरः (on which क्षीरस्वामी says 'रञ्जनाद्रक्तम् । अत एवासृक्संज्ञम्'). On the two meanings of रुधिर, note रघु 11. 20 'राममन्मथशरेण ताडिता दुःसहेन हृदये निशाचरी । गन्धवद्रुधिरचन्दनोक्षिता जीवितेशवसतिं जगाम सा ॥'. उत्तमाङ्गे (शिरसि) घटमानः अञ्जलिः यस्य that folded their hands on their heads (in token of submission and adoration). चन्द्रं...निर्गतया as if she were the moon issuing out from the सुपुम्ण ray. It was believed that the waxing of the moon was due to a ray of the sun called सुषुम्ण and that the waning was due to the digits of the moon being drunk by the gods. 'सूर्यरश्मिः सुपुम्नो यस्तर्पितस्तेन चन्द्रमाः । कृष्णपक्षेऽमरैः शश्वत्पीयते वै सुधामयः॥' विष्णु० II. 11. 22. यास्क has a very interesting note on this "अथाप्यस्यैको रश्मिश्चन्द्रमसं प्रति दीप्यते तदेतेनोपेक्षितव्यमादित्यतोऽस्य दीप्तिर्भवतीति। 'सुपुम्णः सूर्यरश्मिश्चन्द्रमा गन्धर्वः' इत्यपि निगमो भवति ।" निरुक्त II. 2. 2. Bāṇa frequently refers to this belief. See कादम्बरी 'अलीकं चेदं यथा किल सकलाः कलाः कलावतो बहुलपक्षे क्षीयमाणस्य

सुषुम्णनाम्ना रश्मिना रविरापिबतीति;' हर्षचरित 'सुषुम्णास्रुतिशशिसुधाशीकरस्तबकतारकिततीराम्' (मन्दाकिनीम्). It should be noted that in the passage from कादम्बरी Bāṇa attributes the waning of the moon to सुषुम्णरश्मि. मे विलपन्त्याः In spite of the fact that I was weeping.

P. 59 ll. 10–24 **एतस्मिन्नेव...पत्युर्भाषितेन.** तोरणस्य समीपे उपतोरणम् (अव्ययीभाव)—near the royal porch. रराण *perfect 3rd. p. sing.* of रण् to sound. राज...फलम् as if it were the first utterance of royal splendour (personified) proclaiming the result of (*i. e.* indicated by) the dream. भाविनीं भूतिम् future prosperity. अमन्दम् violently. चकाण *perfect* of कण् *1. P.* to sound. कोणेन (drum-stick) आहता. Separate हता आनन्दात्. नान्दी—This has been explained as 'the symphony of twelve drums beaten simultaneously' ('एकदा द्वादशमृदङ्गघोषो नान्दी' रङ्गराज on उत्तररामचरित). प्रबोध...पाठकानाम् of (minstrels) that recited auspicious (verses or words) that rouse from sleep. वल्लभाः तुरङ्गाः तेषां मन्दुरामन्दिरम् (stables). आदौ सुप्तः पश्चादुत्थितः सुप्तोत्थितः. सप्ति...पुरः in front of the horses (सप्ति *m*) that neighed sweetly (कृतः मधुरहेषारवः यैः). च्योतन्तः तुषारसलिलस्य शीकराः यस्मात् (*adj.* of यवसम्) from which oozed out the spray of frost—water. किरन् *nom. sing. m.* of *pr. parti.* of कॄ (qualifies पुरुषः and has यवसं for its object). वक्त्रा ...वक्त्रे two verses in the वक्त्र and अपरवक्त्र metres respectively. According to some writers the species of composition called आख्यायिका (the हर्षचरित is one) should be divided into sections called उच्छ्वासs and should contain verses in the वक्त्र and अपरवक्त्र metres foreshadowing coming events. See the quotation from भामह in the Introduction. अपरवक्त्र is an अर्धसमवृत्त having eleven letters (न, न, र, ल, ग) in the 1st and 3rd Pāda and twelve letters (न, ज, ज, र) in the 2nd and 4th. 'अयुजि ननरला गुरुः समे तदपरवक्त्रमिदं नजौ जरौ ॥'. It is also called वैतालीय, as said by the वृत्तरत्नाकर 'वदन्त्यपरवक्त्राख्यं वैतालीयं विपश्चितः'. वक्त्र is defined as 'नाद्यान्नसौ स्यातामब्धेर्योऽनुष्टुभि ख्यातम्.' Like the अनुष्टुभ् it has eight letters in a पाद. After the first four letters in each पाद there is a यगण. C and T take वक्त्रा and अपरवक्त्रा to be the names of the metres. निधिस्तरुविकारेण स्पष्टमाख्यायते a hidden treasure is clearly indicated by the change in a tree (*i. e.* by some singular or remarkable thing about a tree). The com. says 'यत्राधो निधिस्तत्र परिणाहोद्गताधोमुखशाखामूलादिभाजो वृक्षा भवन्ति.' शुभस्य आगमः the advent of luck. अरुण is the charioteer of the sun in mythology and is a personification of the radiant sky at daybreak; compare 'यावत्प्रतापनिधिराक्रमते न भानु-रह्राय तावदरुणेन तमो निरस्तम्.' अतिजवः very rapid. पूर्व...दयः the previous appearance of an omen. मुदो...षीदसि you feel dejected when it is a time of joy. परिगृहीतासि thou art accepted (*i. e.* favoured). अंशुमाली = सूर्यः. अवतीर्य descending (from the roof where the king had slept).

P. 59 l. 25—**P. 60** l. 15 **ततः समति...पतिः.** गर्भ...जननी his mother took upon herself pallor as if on account of his glory though he was only in the womb yet. Being pregnant, she became pale. यशः is represented by poets as white. The poet fancies that her pallor (really) due to pregnency was due to the glory the son in the womb was to attain in future. गुण... क्लान्तेव as if exhausted by the weight of his virtues. कान्ति...बभूव she became averse to food as if she were satiated with the nectar of the expanding brilliance. On account of pregnancy, she became more brilliant in complexion and lovely. This the poet compares to अमृत. One who has taken अमृत would have no appetite for ordinary food. उपचीयमानः (increasing) गर्भः तस्य भरः तेन अलसा. गुरुभिर्वारितापि although dissuaded by her elders. C and T translate गुरु as parents. This is not necessary. She would have to bow to all elderly persons including her parents. Further it seems questionable whether her parents would be at her husband's palace ordinarily. वन्दनाय...अनीयत she was taken by her friends for saluting (her elders) with difficulty by supporting her with their hands. सालभञ्जिकेव The queen would support herself against walls and pillars and would look like a doll. कमल...रणौ she could not lift up her feet as if they were surrounded by bees that had sat upon them out of their greed for a lotus. Her feet were radiant like lotuses. She could not walk swiftly because she was गर्भभरालसा. The poet represents that this was due to the weight of bees. The rays from her bright toenails resembled the delicate fibres of lotus plants. हंसs subsist upon मृणालs. मणि...कमलम्—the idea is that she was so eager for support that she would stretch out her hand expecting support even from her own images reflected in the jewelled walls. समा ...कर्तुम् she was unable even to issue commands for the performance of household duties, much less to do them herself. आस्तां... रोढुम्—The idea is:—she could not bear to mount to the roof of the palace even in thought, much less with her feet that were oppressed by the weight of the anklets. उत्कम्पितौ स्तनौ यस्याः (on account of hard breathing). तस्तान (perfect of स्तन्) she groaned, breathed hard. प्रत्युत्थानेषु at times of rising to receive (some person worthy of honour). उभयजानुशिखरविनिहितौ करकिसलयौ यस्याः. गर्वा...र्यंत she was held up by the child in the womb as if through pride. The idea is:—she wanted to rise to receive and tried to get up by placing her hands upon her knees. But she did not after all get up. The poet fancies that the child in the womb, being proud, did not like to bow to any body, as it would have to do if its mother bowed and so prevented her from rising. दिवसं all day long (accu. of time). The sentence is दिवसं अधोमुखी ददर्श गर्भम्. Her face was reflected in her bright bosom. The poet fancies that her face had entered inside her body (in the form of the reflection) because it was anxious to see the child. सखीनामुत्सङ्गेषु मुक्तं शरीरं यया. निर्मितं, कल्पितं and विहितं qualify राज्यवर्धनम्. सर्वोर्वी...र्मितम् composed as if with the atoms of वज्र for destroying the alliances of all kings. सर्वेषां उर्वीभृतां (राज्ञां) पक्षः (समूहः) तस्य पाताय (with राज्यवर्धन); सर्वेषां उर्वीभृतां पर्वतानां पक्षाः (wings) तेषां पाताय (with इन्द्र understood). The mountains had once wings and troubled the earth by flying anywhere. Indra cut off their wings with his वज्र. बाण refers to this story very often. कादम्बरी 'अशनिभयपुञ्जितकुलशैलमध्यगतमिव कनकशिखरिणम्'; 'मैनाकेनेवाविदितपक्षपातेन'. शेष...कल्पितम् as if made with the means, *viz.* the numerous hoods of शेष. It is supposed that the earth is borne by the serpent शेष on its hoods. Compare 'किं शेषस्य भरव्यथा न वपुषि क्ष्मां न क्षिपत्येष यत्' भर्तृहरि. राज्यवर्धन also would be able to bear the responsibility of the world. सकल...विहितम् (she gave birth to रा०) who caused tremor to all भूभृत्s (kings, mountains) and who was as if made with the limbs of the elephants of the quarters. ०मुखरं, ०रवं, ०भुवनं and मनोहरं qualify महोत्सवम्. पूरिताः असंख्याः शङ्खाः तेषां शब्दैः मुखरम् (resounding). प्रहतानि पटहशतानि तैः पटुः रवः यस्मिन्. गम्भीरेण भेरीनिनादेन निर्भरं भरितं भुवनं यस्मिन्. प्रमोदेन उन्मत्तः मर्त्यलोकः तेन मनोहरम्. मास...दिवसमिव for one month as if it were a single day.

P. 60 l. 16—**P. 61** l. 10 अथान्य...बध्यन्त. The locatives from कन्दलिनि to ०कसि qualify नभसि (*i. e.* the month of श्रावण). कन्दलिनि abounding in plantain trees. Wild plantain plants grow up spontaneously in the rainy season. कुड्मलिताः कदम्बतरवः यस्मिन् in which the *Kadamba* trees have put forth buds. The कदम्ब tree is said to put forth buds at the advent of thunder and rain;

compare 'मरुन्नवाम्भःप्रविधूतसिक्ता कदम्बयष्टिः स्फुटकोरकेव' उत्तरराम० III. कुड्मलाः सञ्जाताः अस्य इति कुड्मलितः according to 'तदस्य सञ्जातं तारकादिभ्य इतच्' पा. 5. 2. 36. रूढाः तोक्मतृणस्तम्बाः यस्मिन् in which the clusters (स्तम्बः) of barley blades had taken firm root. 'शितशूकयवौ समौ ॥ तोक्मस्तु तत्र हरिते' इत्यमरः. स्तम्भितानि तामरसानि यस्मिन् in which the red lotuses were supported (*i. e.* stood firm and erect, being nourished with plenty of water). विकसितं (delighted) चातकचेतः यस्मिन्. It was believed that the चातक could not drink water on the earth, but subsisted on a few drops from the clouds. मूकाः मानसौकसः (हंसाः, मानसे ओकः सद्म येषां) यस्मिन्. हंसs are said to migrate to the मानस lake at the commencement of the rainy season and so on the plains the cackling of हंसs was not heard. नभसि मासि—कृष्ण was born in श्रावण; while the poet says that हर्ष was conceived in श्रावण. चक्रं पाणौ यस्य = विष्णु (*i. e.* कृष्ण). हर्ष also was चक्रपाणि *i. e.* on his hand there were lines resembling a चक्र, which was looked upon as one of the चक्रवर्तिलक्षणs. See बृहत्संहिता 67. 47 'चक्रासिपरशुतोमरशक्तिधनुःकुन्तसन्निभा रेखाः । कुर्वन्ति चमूनाथं' &c. सममेव at the same time. हृदये हर्षः—यशोमती was delighted at heart and conceived the future हर्ष. सर्व...गृहीता as if accepted (*i. e.* endowed with) by all the merits of her subjects. पुण्य is represented as white. The queen's body became slightly pallid (आपाण्डु) on account of pregnancy; the poet fancies that it was the पुण्य of the subjects that had assumed shape and come to her in the form of her गर्भ, the idea being that the birth of a good Emperor like हर्ष is due to the पुण्य of the subjects. गर्भारम्भेण as pregnancy came on. श्यामायमाने चारुचूचुकचूलिके ययोः (also श्यामायमाना चारुचूचुकसदृशी चूलिका ययोः) चूचुक nipple. चूलिका crest. पयोधरौ कलशौ इव (also पयोधरसदृशौ कलशौ or पयसः धरौ पयोधरौ कलशौ). The queen's breasts had nipples growing dark on account of pregnancy. They would be sucked by an emperor (चक्रवर्तिन् *i. e.* हर्ष). Drinking *water* was brought for emperors in sealed (मुद्रित) jars in order to prevent poisoning. The dark crest of the seal resembled the crest of the nipple. स्तन्यार्थं...दृष्टिः her eye, long, glossy (स्निग्ध) and white became sweeter as if it were a stream of milk placed in her face for (supplying) milk (to her breast). दुग्धनदी also would be दीर्घ, स्निग्ध (viscous) and धवल. See for the same simile 'स्नपयति हृदयेशं स्नेहनिष्यन्दिनी ते धवलमधुरमुग्धा दुग्धकुल्येव दृष्टिः ॥' उत्तरराम III. 23. सकलमङ्गलानां गणेन अधिष्ठितं (occupied) गात्रं (body) तस्य गरिम्णा (by the weight). अमन्दायत became slow (from the denominative verb मन्दायते). Her gait became slow owing to pregnancy. The poet fancies that the slowness was due to the weight of the numerous auspicious signs due to the conception of a चक्रवर्तिन्. निर्मलं मणिकुट्टिमं (floor inlaid with gems) तस्मिन् निमग्नं प्रतिबिम्बं (reflection of the queen) तस्य निभेन (under the guise). गृहीतौ पादपल्लवौ यया. पूर्वं ... पृथिवी अस्याः (यशोमत्याः)—The queen was reflected in the brilliant pavement. The poet fancies that the earth was worshipping her feet by way of a prelude to what would follow when her son became the emperor of the world. दिवसम् *accu.* of time. शयनीयं is the object of अधिशयानायाः (यशोमत्याः). अपाश्रयः awning. पत्रभङ्गः drawing of lines or figures. ०प्रतिमा image of a figure drawn on the awning. विमलकपोलोदरे गता reflected in the bright cheek (of the queen). गर्भो...संक्रान्तम् reflected in her round bosom from which the garment had been taken away on account of the agitation (उन्माथः) of pregnancy. गर्भस्य उन्माथेन मुक्तं अंशुकं यस्मात्. उडुपतिः the moon. The reflection of the moon in the bosom appeared like a white umbrella held over the गर्भ. A white umbrella is an emblem of चक्रवर्तित्व; compare रघुवंश 3. 16. 'अदेयमासीत्रयमेव भूपतेः शशिप्रभं छत्रमुभे च चामरे.' चित्र...ग्राहिण्योपि even the women holding chowries on the painted walls (*i. e.* even pictures moved chowries). चामरs are among the insignia of royalty. करे (by the trunk) विधृतं कमलिन्याः पलाशानां (पत्राणां) पुटं तस्मिन् सलिलानि तैः. She dreamt that the four दिग्गजs bathed her with water. This was a precursor of the future sovereignty of her son. प्रतिबुध्यमानायाश्च and when she woke up. चन्द्रशालिका—a chamber on the roof. 'चन्द्रशाला शिरोगृहम्' क्षीरस्वामी. Even the puppets cried 'victory.' परिज...निश्चेरुः When she called out to her attendants, incorporeal voices issued forth saying 'command.' क्रीडा...भङ्गम्—This sentence and the following give expression to the popular notion that the mother's mind is influenced by the potential thoughts of the child in the womb, as said by the com. 'गर्भस्थजनचित्तवृत्त्यनुसारेण गर्भिण्या अपि चित्तवृत्तिर्भवति'. चतुर्णामपि—This indicates that हर्ष's empire would extend up to the four oceans. The oceans are sometimes spoken of as four or as seven. वेला...सरेषु in the vicinity (परिसरः) of sandy banks (पुलिनं, 'तोयोत्थितं तत्पुलिनम्' इत्यमरः) inside the bowers of creepers on the seashore. आत्य...चचाल Even as regards business of extreme importance, her eyebrow moved playfully. The idea is that she felt no concern or anxiety even as regards serious matters; so calm and collected she was. आत्ययिक—अत्ययः प्रयोजनं अस्य 'प्रयोजनम्' पा. 5. 1. 109 (प्रयोजनं फलं कारणं च). सन्नि...सीत् though jewelled mirrors were near her, she had a strong liking (व्यसनम्) for seeing her face in a drawn (उत्खात) sword blade. उत्सारिता वीणा यैः. श्रुतौ असुखायन्त gave pleasure to her ear. स्तम्भितम् stiffened. सख्यश्चास्याः &c.—construe सख्यश्च अस्याः पार्श्वं क्षणमपि न मुमुचुः. विस्फारित stretched wide. आसन्न...भवनम् brightening the house as if with the idea of celebrating the festival of her delivery that was approaching. At जन्ममहोत्सव houses are washed with chunam. The friends whitened the house with their eyes expanded wide. विकच...विदधाना—The friends cast glances in all directions from their widely expanded eyes (that were white). The author fancies that the glances were so many white and blue flowers of various kinds of lotuses, offered in worship to protect the queen from evil. कुमुद is a white night lotus. कुवलय is a blue lotus. कमल is pale red. The white of the eye was mixed with the blue of the pupil and the white—red of the corners. आत्मो...चक्रुः eminent physicians holding various drugs and sitting in their proper places supported the queen like high mountains (occupying their proper places and having various plants growing on them and that made the earth steady). It was believed that the earth, which was formerly unsteady, was made steady by the mountains. Compare कादम्बरी 'अनुजीविभूभृच्छतसहस्रकल्पितावष्टम्भं सञ्चारिणं द्वितीयमिव मेदिनीसंनिवेशम्.' ग्रीवा...बध्यन्त in the knots of her necklace cord were tied excellent jewells. लक्ष्म्या...गतानि that had come with लक्ष्मी (*i. e.* royal splendour). She being a queen could command jewels. There is a pun on these words. Jewels were also produced from the oceans (पयोनिधि) at the time of the churning along with लक्ष्मी who was one of them. See above for सागरमन्थन.

P. 61 ll. 11–15 ततश्च...जहार. ज्येष्ठामूलीये मासि in the month of ज्येष्ठ. ज्येष्ठा मूलं च ज्येष्ठामूले. 'द्वन्द्वाच्छः' पा. 4. 2. 6 नक्षत्रद्वन्द्वाद्युक्ते काले छः स्यात्. बहुलासु = कृत्तिकासु—when the moon was in the कृत्तिका constellation. बहुलपक्ष = कृष्णपक्ष. समा...यौवने when the youth of the night was about to climb up (*i. e.* when night was just beginning). समारुरुक्षति *loc. sing.* of the *desiderative part.* of रुह् with सम् and आ. हृदयनिर्विशेषा not different from her own heart *i. e.* who was as dear to यशोमती as her own self. दिष्ट्या... जन्मना you are to be congratulated on the birth of a second son.

पूर्णपात्रम् a present given to or taken by one who brings some happy news. The com. defines पूर्णपात्र as 'आनन्ददो हि सौहार्दादित्य वस्त्रादिकं बलात् । अजानतो हरत्येव पूर्णपात्रं तु तत्स्मृतम् ॥.' Another definition given in the शब्दकल्पद्रुम is 'हर्षादुत्सवकाले यदलंकारांशुकादिकम् । आकृष्य गृह्यते पूर्णपात्रं पूर्णालकं च तत् ॥'.

P. 61 ll. 16–24 **अस्मिन्नेव...जातः इति.** संवादिताः अतीन्द्रियादेशाः यस्य whose extraordinary predictions had come true. अतीन्द्रिय beyond the reach of the senses. दर्शितः प्रभावः येन. सङ्कलिती ज्योतिषी—who had grasped the science of astronomy. सङ्कलितमनेन इति सङ्कलितिन्—Words like अधीतिन् take the *loc.* of the object of study, according to वार्तिक 'सप्तमीविधाने क्तस्येन्विषयस्य कर्मण्युपसंख्यानम्' on 'सप्तम्यधिकरणे च' पा. 2. 3. 36 (अधीती व्याकरणे आम्नाती छन्दसि । महाभाष्य). सर्वासां...दृष्ट्वा who had mastered all the treatises on planets. महितः = पूजितः. The बृहत्संहिता of वराहमिहिर refers to three branches of ज्योतिष *viz.* ग्रहगणित, संहिता and होराशास्त्र and remarks 'संहितापारगश्च दैवचिन्तको भवति'. It then gives a long list of the topics of संहिता (2nd chap.). हितः who was favourable to (the royal family). भोजकः—The com. says 'रविमर्चयित्वा पूजका हि भूयसा गणका भवन्ति । ये मगा इति प्रसिद्धाः भागवता इत्यन्ये.' This means that the astrologer was a Maga, a worshipper of the sun. The बृहत्संहिता tells us that in a temple of the sun, a मग should be placed in charge of the worship 'विष्णोर्भागवतान्मगांश्च सवितुः शम्भोः सभस्मद्विजान् &c.' (60. 19). C and T refer to Wilson's Vishṇu—purāṇa (Hall's ed) vol. V. p. 382 where an analysis of the last 12 chapters of the भविष्यपुराण is given concerning the मगs. साम्ब son of कृष्ण became a leper by the curse of दुर्वासस् and was cured by worshipping the sun. He gratefully built a temple of the sun and brought 18 families of मगs from शकद्वीप as priests and induced the भोजs of द्वारका, a branch of the यादवs, to give their daughters in marriage to the मगs. Hence the मगs were styled भोजकs. मान्धाता—He was a king of the solar race. युवनाश्व had no son and therefore the sages performed a sacrifice for him and placed a jar full of holy water on a *Vedī* and slept. युवनाश्व being thirsty drank the water and then a son was born from his side. The विष्णुपु० (IV. 2.) gives the origin of the name मान्धातृ as follows "गर्भश्च युवनाश्वोदरेऽभवत् । ...दक्षिणकुक्षिमवनिपतेर्निर्भिद्य निश्चक्राम नासौ ममार । जातो नामैष कं धास्यतीति ते मुनयः प्रोचुः ॥ 17 अथागत्य देवराजोऽब्रवीन्मामयं धास्यतीति ततो मान्धाता नामतोऽभवत् ।". About मान्धाता the रामायण says 'अयोध्यायां पुरा राजा युवनाश्वसुतो बली । मान्धाता इति विख्यातस्त्रिषु लोकेषु वीर्यवान् ॥ स कृत्वा पृथिवीं कृत्स्नां शासने पृथिवीपतिः । सुरलो-

कमितो जेतुमुद्योगमकरोन्नृपः ।' उत्तरकाण्ड 67. 5–6. व्यती...रहिते free from the contact (अभिषङ्गः) of all evil positions such as व्यतीपात. व्यतीपात is the 17th योग out of the 27, beginning with विष्कम्भ. The धर्मसिन्धु says 'कुमारजन्मकाले तु व्यतिपातश्च वैधृतिः । संक्रमश्च रवेस्तत्र जातो दारिद्र्यकारकः ॥ अश्रियं मृत्युमाप्नोति नात्र कार्या विचारणा ॥'. उच्चस्थानस्थितेषु ग्रहेषु when the planets were in their places of exaltation. It is said that मेष, वृषभ, मकर, कन्या, कर्क, मीन and तुला are the उच्चs respectively of रवि, चंद्र, भौम, बुध, गुरु, शुक्र and शनि. See बृहज्जातक 'अजवृषभमृगाङ्गनाकुलीरा झषवणिजौ च दिवाकरादितुङ्गाः ।'. लग्नम् is that sign of the zodiac that is on the eastern horizon at the time of birth. अर्वाक् ततः after that *i. e.* since that time. योगः conjunction (in astrology). It seems to us impossible from an astrological point of view that all the planets were in their exaltation at the time of Harsha's birth. The day being the 12th of the dark half of ज्येष्ठ, the sun could not have been in मेष (which is the उच्च of the sun). सप्तानां चक्रवर्तिनाम्—the seven चक्रवर्तिs are 'भरतार्जुनमान्धातृभगीरथयुधिष्ठिराः । सगरो नहुषश्चैव सप्तैते चक्रवर्तिनः ॥'. अर्जुन must be सहस्रार्जुनकार्तवीर्य. चक्रवर्तिचिह्नानाम्—such as चक्र on the hand, जालग्रथितांगुलिकरत्व (mentioned in the 7th Act of शाकुन्तल). The great रत्नs are said to be fourteen in the विष्णुपुराण IV. 12. The शब्दकल्पद्रुम gives them as follows 'चक्रं रथो मणिः खड्गश्चर्म रत्नं च पञ्चमम् । केतुर्निधिश्च सप्तैवमप्राणानि प्रचक्ष्यते ॥ भार्या पुरोहितश्चैव सेनानी रथकृच्च यः । पत्त्यश्वौ कलभश्चेति प्राणिनः सप्त कीर्तिताः ॥ चतुर्दशैतानि रत्नानि सर्वेषां चक्रवर्तिनाम् ॥'. The great रत्नs according to the com. are six. 'मण्यश्वकरिचक्राणि वरा स्त्री परिनायकः । षडेतानि तु रत्नानि कीर्तितानि मनीषिभिः ॥'. The seven oceans are 'एते द्वीपा समुद्रैस्तु सप्त सप्तभिरावृताः । लवणेक्षुसुरासर्पिर्दधिदुग्धजलैः समम् ॥' विष्णुपु० II. 2. 6. सप्ततन्तुः means a 'sacrifice.' सप्तसप्तिः = सूर्यः (सप्त सप्तयः अश्वाः यस्य).

P. 61 l. 25—**P. 62** l. 11 **अत्रान्तरे...महान्.** अनाध्माताः—though not blown or filled with wind from the mouth. तारमधुरम् loudly and sweetly. विरेसुः perfect of रस् with वि. क्षुभितं जलनिधिजलं तस्य ध्वनिः तद्वत् धीरम् (deep). अभिषेकदुन्दुभिः—the drum that is beaten at the time of crowning a king. The author wants to indicate that the whole world, animate and inanimate, rejoiced at the birth of हर्ष who was destined to be a great emperor and vied in spontaneously manifesting its joy. सर्वभुवनस्य अभयं तस्य आघोषणा तस्याः पटहः—The echo of the tabors spread in all directions. The poet fancies that it was the kettledrum (पटहः) that proclaimed immunity from danger to the whole world. The idea is that हर्ष would give security against danger to the whole

P. 62 ll. 12–21 **अपरेद्यु...दृश्यन्त.** The principal sentence is अपरेद्युः...बिभ्राणेन परिजनेन अनुगम्यमानानि...समन्तात् सामन्तान्तःपुरसहस्राणि अदृश्यन्त. अपरेद्युरारभ्य beginning from the next day. स्त्रीरा...तानि as if they (*i. e.* the wives of the सामन्तs) were the kingdoms of amazons brought together or poured forth (आवर्जित). The idea is that the women were so many. In the महाभारत, we read of प्रमीला, who fought with Arjuna, as being at the head of a स्त्रीराज्य. असुर...वृतानि as if they were the mines opened wide. For असुरविवर, see the description of स्थाण्वीश्वर in the 3rd उच्छ्वास, where we have 'असुरविवरमिति वार्तिकैः.' नारा...लितानि as if they were the wives of Vishṇu (*i. e.* Kṛishṇa) moving onwards. अवरोध is m., while अवरोधन is *n;* we should therefore read॰रोधनानि. In the विष्णुपुराण, कृष्ण is said to have had 16101 wives 'षोडशसहस्राण्येकोत्तरशताधिकानि स्त्रीणामभवन्' विष्णु॰ 4. 15; 'षोडशात्र सहस्राणि स्त्रीणामन्यानि चक्रिणः।...निशासु जगतः स्रष्टा तासां गेहेषु केशवः। उवास विप्र सर्वासां विश्वरूपधरो हरिः॥' विष्णु॰ 5. 28. 5 and 18. Besides these, रुक्मिणी and seven others were his chief wives. The भागवतपु॰ gives the number of 16000 in various places (see X. 59. 33; X. 69. 8 and 44). अप्स...कुलानि—The Apsarases are the damsels of heaven and have fourteen कुलs as described by बाण himself in कादम्बरी 'एतत्प्रायेण कल्याणाभिनिवेशिनः श्रुतिविषयमापतितमेव यथा विबुधसद्मन्यप्सरसो नाम कन्यकाः सन्ति। तासां चतुर्दश कुलानि.' This clause shows that the wives of सामन्तs were very handsome. परिजनेन—this word is to be read with बिभ्राणेन below. स्रजः, पात्रीः and others are the objects of बिभ्राणेन. पृथु...स्रजः (carrying garlands of flowers (सुमनस् *f n*) contained in a large bamboo box (करण्डः) and which were sprinkled over (अवकीर्ण) with bath powder. स्नानीयं (स्नानाय हितं चूर्णं) तेन अवकीर्णानि कुसुमानि यासाम्. स्फटिकशिलायाः शकलवत् शुक्लं कर्पूरखण्डं तेन पूरिताः. पात्रीः dishes. कुङ्कुमा...मयानि jewelled pots containing the fragrant powder (अधिवासः) of saffron. सह...रुकाणि ivory boxes (दन्तशफरुकम्) jagged (दन्तुर) with rows (फाली) of arecanuts white like sandalwood and tufted (जटिल) with masses of small खदिर fibres wet (तिम्यत्) with mango-oil. सहकारतैलेन तिम्यत् तनुखदिरकेसरजालं तेन जटिलानि चन्दनवत् धवलानि पूगफलानि (the dry areca nut with the upper coating peeled off is white) तेषां फाली तेन दन्तुराणि दन्तशफरुकाणि. तिम् 4th P. to become wet. The solid extract of खदिर called खदिरसार (catechu) is now used for ताम्बूल. It seems that tender and small fibres of खदिर were so used in Bāṇa's time. गुञ्जन्तः मधुकराः तेषां कुलं तेन पीयमानः पारिजातपरिमलः येषाम्. पाटलकानि च—take away the comma after this. पाटलकानि pink red (*adj.* of ०पात्राणि). सिन्दूर...पात्राणि boxes of vermilion and fragrant powder (for perfuming garments). 'पिष्टातः पटवासकः' इत्यमरः. The reading of B, पोटलकानि, does not make much sense. पोटलक means 'bundle, packet.' बाल...बिभ्राणेन carrying betel trees with bundles of rolls of betel leaves hanging from young creepers. We must read वीटिकावीटकांश्च as suggested by C and T. विटक makes no sense. वीटिका is the same as Marathi विडा. बाललताभ्यः लम्बमानाः वीटिकावीटकाः येषु. The com. remarks 'विटकवीटकं पञ्चाशत्ताम्बूलपत्रैः क्रियते.' चरणनिकुट्टनेन रणिताः मणिनूपुराः तैः मुखरितानि दिङ्मुखानि यैः—that made the quarters to resound with the jewelled anklets that jingled when they stamped the earth with their feet (in dancing). The reading of B makes no sense.

P. 62 ll. 22–33 शनैः...मोदः. The principal sentence is शनैः शनैः व्यजृम्भत...उत्सवामोदः. क्वचित्—क्वचित् in one place, in another place. नृत्तस्य अनुचितः (not accustomed) चिरन्तनः (of ancient families) शालीनः (high born) कुलपुत्रकलोकः तस्य लास्यं तेन प्रथितः (shown) पार्थिवे अनुरागः यस्मिन्. This and the following nominatives qualify ०मोदः. शालीन not bold, bashful (usually applied to high born ladies) 'स्यादधृष्टे तु शालीनः' इत्यमरः. शालीन formed from शाला with the affix ख (ईन) according to 'शालीनकौपीने अधृष्टाकार्ययोः' पा. 5. 2. 20 (शालाप्रवेशमर्हति शालीनः अधृष्टः। सि. कौ.। अप्रागल्भ्यादन्यत्र गन्तुमशक्तः शालामेव प्रवेष्टुमर्हतीत्यर्थः। तत्वबोधिनी). कुलपुत्रकः a nobly born young man. लास्यम् is a peculiar kind of dance 'ललिताङ्गहाराभिनयं कैशिकीवृत्तिप्रधानं वासकसज्जादिनायिकाचरितं डोम्बिल्लिकादिनिबद्धं श्लिष्टत्वाल्लास्यम्। नृत्तं त्वङ्गविक्षेपमात्रं विवाहाभ्युदयादौ' क्षीरस्वामी. अन्तः सितं यस्य तेन क्षितिपालेन (प्रभाकरवर्धनेन) अपेक्षिताः क्षीबाभिः (drunk) क्षुद्रदासीभिः समाकृष्यमाणाः राजवल्लभाः यस्मिन्. The king smiled to himself when the drunken maids caught hold of his favourites. We expect अवेक्षिताः for अपेक्षिताः. The reading of two MSS. of B, उपेक्षित, would be also good. मत्ता कटककुट्टनी (bawd of the capital) तस्याः कण्ठे लग्नः वृद्धः आर्यः (noble, respectable) सामन्तः (chieftain, feudatory) तस्य नृत्तेन निर्भरं (much, loudly) हसितः नरपतिः यस्मिन्. क्षितिपस्य (प्रभाकरवर्धनस्य) अक्षिसंज्ञा (sign or hint given by the eye or glance) तया आदिष्टाः (ordered, instigated) दुष्टाः दासेरकाः (भृत्याः) तेषां गीतैः सूच्यमानः सचिवानां चौर्यरतप्रपञ्चः (numerous secret amours) यस्मिन्. दासेरक son of a दासी. दासेर is formed from दासी according to 'क्षुद्राभ्यो वा' पा. 4. 1. 131 (अङ्गहीनाः शीलहीनाश्च क्षुद्रास्ताभ्यो वा ढ्रक्। पक्षे ढक्। दासेरः दासेयः। सि. कौ.). मदोत्कटा कुटहारिका (water-girl) तया परिष्वज्यमानः जरन् (old) प्रव्रजितः (ascetic, संन्यासिन्) तेन जनितः जन-

हासः यस्मिन्. कुटः—टम् a water-jar + हारिका carrier. 'घटः कुटनिपावल्ली' इत्यमरः. अन्योन्यस्य निर्भरा (excessive) स्पर्धा तया उद्धुराः (unrestrained, उद्गता धूः येभ्यः) विटचेटकाः तैः आरब्धं अवाच्यवचनयुद्धं यस्मिन्. विटः is a voluptuary and companion of a dissolute young man or courtezan. See the मृच्छकटिक for a specimen. चेटकः a servant. अवाच्यं वचनम् words that should not be uttered *i. e.* foul words. The servants engaged in a war of choice Billingsgate. नृपाबलाभिः (royal ladies) बलात्कारेण (by force) नर्त्यमानाः (made to dance) नृत्ये अनभिज्ञाः अन्तःपुरपालाः (chamberlains) तैः भाविताः (enlivened, entertained) भुजिष्याः परिचारिकाः यस्मिन्. 'नियोज्यकिङ्करप्रैष्यभुजिष्यपरिचारकाः' इत्यमरः ('भुङ्क्ते स्वाम्युच्छिष्टं भुजिष्यः' क्षीरस्वामी). स...राशिभिः with heaps of flowers it looked as if it were a mountain. Mountains have trees full of flowers. In the festival also heaps of flowers were used. स...प्रपाभिः with rum-booths it looked as if it had a showerbath. धारागृहम् is a showerbath or house furnished with jets of water. सीधुः rum. प्रपा lit. a place where water is distributed to travellers. In the festival rum flowed like water. पारि...मोदैः with the fragrance of पारिजातक. The पारिजातक is one of the five trees of Indra's garden (नन्दनवन). नीहारः frost. The dust of camphor spread in the उत्सव looked like frost. अट्टहासः the laugh of शिव in his ताण्डव dance. The sounds of drums beaten in the birth festival resembled the अट्टहास of शिव. अमृतमथनेन सह सा० (बहुव्रीहि). The uproar was so great that it resembled the noise made by the gods and demons at the time of the churning of the ocean as the रत्नs came out of the ocean. रास or—क is a dance (in a ring) practised by कृष्ण and गोपीs. See भागवतपुराण X. 33 'तत्रारभत गोविन्दो रासक्रीडामनुव्रतैः। स्त्रीरत्नैरन्वितः प्रीतैरन्योन्याबद्धबाहुभिः॥ 2'. आवर्तः a whirlpool 'स्यादावर्तोऽम्भसां भ्रमः' इत्यमरः. The ring of dancers resembled a vortex. सरो...किरणैः—the rays shooting from the jewelled ornaments resembled hair standing on end. पट्टबन्धः tying of a piece of cloth on the head (a tiara, turban &c.). चन्दनललाटिका sandal marks on the forehead. Sandal is white and is compared to white cloth tied round the head. 'कर्णललाटात्कनलङ्कारे' पा. 4. 3. 65 (कर्णिका, ललाटिका). प्रसवः progeny, offspring. The echoes were as if the progeny of the original sounds. प्ररोहः sprout, leaf. The gifts of favour were given and appeared to spring forth like so many sprouts shooting forward in all directions.

P. 63 ll. 1–9 **स्कन्धा...लोकः** स्कन्धा...मालाः—स्कन्धे अवलम्बमानाः केसरमालाः (बकुलपुष्पमालाः) येषाम् (युवानः); स्कन्धे अवलम्बमानाः केसरमालाः

(केसराः माला इव) येषाम् (with ०वाजिनः). The manes of the horses are compared to garlands. काम्बोजवाजिनः horses from the country of Kamboja. This country was looked upon as producing one of the best breeds of horses. See रघुवंश IV. 69–70 **'काम्बोजाः** समरे सोढुं तस्य वीर्यमनीश्वराः ।...तेषां **सदश्वभूयिष्ठास्तुङ्गा** द्रविणराशयः ।'. 'वनायुजाः पारसीकाः काम्बोजा वाह्लिका हयाः ।' इत्यमरः. The country of कम्बोज was beyond the Hindookush mountain (probably eastern Persia) and it was known from very ancient times. See पाणिनि IV. 1. 75. Yāska refers to it 'शवतिर्गतिकर्मा कम्बोजेष्वेव भाष्यते... विकारमस्यार्येषु भाषन्ते शव इति' (निरुक्त II). आस्कन्दन्तः—treading the ground (with youths); leaping (with horses). तरलाः (unsteady) तारकाः (pupil of the eye) येषाम्—applies to both the youths and deer. सगर...भुवम्—who rent the earth with the violent stamping (अभिघातः) of their feet, as the sons of सगर did with spades. See p. 3 for the story of the sons of सगर. See विष्णुपुराण IV. 4 and रामायण I. 38–44. अनेक...संख्याः may apply also to the sons of सगर (who were 60000). कथमपि...क्षमा the earth bore with difficulty the agitation caused by the feet of the bards (चारणाः) dancing to time. तालः keeping time (in music) + अवचरः one who moves. अन्योन्यास्फालैः striking each other (in play). आभ... फेलुः the pearls in the ornaments were cleft asunder. फेलुः *perfect* of फल् 1 P. ब्रह्माण्डकपालम्—the world. पुनः उत्पन्नः हिरण्यगर्भस्य गर्भः तस्य शोणितेन शोणाः (रक्ताः) आशाः (दिशः) यस्मिन्. स्वयम्भू first of all produced waters and cast the seed in them. That seed became an egg and in it हिरण्यगर्भ remained for a year and then the egg was split into two parts. See मनुस्मृति 'सोभिध्याय शरीरात्स्वात्सिसृक्षुर्विविधाः प्रजाः । अप एव ससर्जादौ तासु बीजमवासृजत् ॥ तदण्डमभवद्धैमं सहस्रांशुसमप्रभम् । तस्मिञ्जज्ञे स्वयं ब्रह्मा सर्वलोकपितामहः ॥ तस्मिन्नण्डे स भगवानुषित्वा परिवत्सरम् । स्वयमेवात्मनो ध्यानात्तदण्डमकरोद्द्विधा ॥' मनुस्मृति I. 8–9, 12. The world was reddened by the vermilion powder. Blood is red. The poet fancies that हिरण्यगर्भ was again being born in ब्रह्माण्डकपाल. पट...पटलेन by the cloud of the fragrant powder (used in perfuming garments). The fragrant powder resembled the sandy banks of the celestial Ganges. प्रकटितं मन्दाकिन्याः (वियद्गङ्गायाः) सैकतसहस्रं यस्मिन्. सैकतम् (from सिकता) according to 'सिकताशर्कराभ्यां च' and 'देशे लुबिलचौ च' पा. 5. 2. 104–5 (सिकताः सन्त्यस्मिन् देशे इति सिकताः । सिकतिलः । सैकतिलः । सि. कौ.). विप्रकीर्यमाणः पिष्टातकः (पटवासकः) तस्य परागः (pollen) तेन पिञ्जरितः (rendered yellow) आतपः (light) येषाम् (with दिवसाः). भुवनस्य क्षोभः तेन विशीर्णं पितामहस्य (ब्रह्मणः) कमलं तस्य किञ्जल्काः (filaments) तेषां रजोराजिः तया रञ्जिताः

इव. The world was disturbed by the riotous festival days. The poet fancies that the lotus on which ब्रह्मा sits was shattered by the भुवनs being shaken by the birth festivities. सङ्घट्ट...लोकः people tripped over masses of pearls that had fallen from necklaces rent asunder (विघटित) in collision (when people running in haste jostled against each other).

P. 63 ll. 10–33 **स्थान...प्रानृत्यन्.** The principal sentence is स्थानस्थानेषु च...वाद्येन अनुगम्यमानाः...पण्यविलासिन्यः प्रानृत्यन्. The instrumentals from ०लिङ्गयकेन to तानकेन qualify ०वाद्येन. मन्द... लिङ्गयकेन in which tambourines were struck gently. आलिङ्गयकः a drum having the shape of a barley-corn. According to the अमरकोश, it is a kind of मृदङ्ग 'मृदङ्गा मुरजा भेदास्त्वङ्क्यालिङ्ग्योर्ध्वकास्त्रयः'. 'चतुरङ्गुलहीनोऽङ्क्यान्मुखे चैकाङ्गुलेन यः । यवाकृतिः स आलिङ्ग्य आलिङ्ग्य स हि वाद्यते ॥' शब्दार्णवः. शिञ्जानः (jingling) मञ्जुः (sweet) वेणुः (flute) यस्मिन्. झणझणायमाना झल्लरी यस्मिन् in which cymbals tinkled. झणझणायमाना pr. p. of the onomatopoetic verb ०णायते. क (in ०झल्लरीक) is affixed to बहुव्रीहि compounds having as the last member a feminine noun ending ई, ऊ, ॠ or a noun ending in ऋ. 'नद्यृतश्च' पा. 5. 4. 153. ताड्यमाना तन्त्रीपटहिका यस्मिन्—in which a stringed drum was played upon. वाद्यमाना अनुत्ताना अलाबुवीणा यस्मिन् in which the gourd lute that had its mouth turned downwards (अनुत्तान) was being played. This seems to have been some instrument like the बीन of these days. The reading of B 'अनुत्ताला०' makes a good sense. अनुत्ताल means 'low-pitched.' कलक्वांस्यकोश्या क्वणिताः काहलाः (बृहड्ढक्काः) यस्मिन् in which there were kāhalas booming sweetly and indistinctly on account of the sounding boxes of bell-metal. समकाले दीयमानः अनुत्तालः तानकः यस्मिन् in which a protracted tone was indulged in at the interval called सम. The reading of B is better and should have been kept in the text. ०दीयमाना अनुत्ताला तालिका यस्मिन् in which the hands were clapped gently at the interval called सम. सम is the principal interval in a ताल. C and T translate 'while all the time a subdued clapping proceeded.' आतोद्यवाद्येन by instrumental music. 'ततं चैवावनद्धं च घनं सुषिरमेव । चतुर्विधं तु विज्ञेयमातोद्यं लक्षणान्वितम् ॥' नाट्यशास्त्र 28. 1. According to अमरकोश, आतोद्य and वाद्य are synonyms. अनुगम्यमानाः adj. of पण्यविलासिन्यः (harlots). अनुवर्तमानौ ताललयौ यासाम्. तालः keeping time. लयः harmony. Even the ornaments of the *naikins* kept time and jingled in harmony with their singing and thus looked as if they were intelligent beings (सहृदय).

There is another idea. Those who are masters in singing (सहृदय = मार्मिक) will unconsciously keep time when another person is singing. मदेन कला काकली तया कोमलः आलापः अस्ति आसां इति० लापिन्यः—who sang delicate tunes in a voice sweet but low on account of passion. 'काकली तु कले सूक्ष्मे ध्वनौ तु मधुरास्फुटे' इत्यमरः. विटानां...गायन्त्यः who sang the vulgar words of रासकs that were the nectar of the ear of dissolute young men. रासक here means either (1) a particular kind of dance (for which see above p. 29); or (2) a species of dramatic composition. See for a definition of the latter the साहित्यदर्पण VI. It has only five characters, it is in various dialects; there is no सूत्रधार; there is a single Act; the hero is a fool, while the heroine is famous. स... मालिकाः they had wreaths on their heads. समुच्छ्रित raised up (past p. p. of श्रि with सम् and उद्). कुङ्कुम...वल्गन्त्यः like Kashmir fillies they pranced, having bodies radiant with the stains of saffron. कुङ्कुमेन प्रमृष्टिः (rubbing the body) तया रुचिरः कायः येषाम् (with ०विलासिन्यः); कुङ्कुमे प्रमृष्टिः (rolling in) तया &c. (with किशोर्यः). नितम्बबिम्बे लम्बमानाः विकटाः (large) कुरण्टकशेखराः यासाम्. कुरण्टकः Amaranth. The glow cast on their bodies by the flowers is fancied to be due to the fire of राग (passion). सिन्दूरस्य छटाभिः (streaks) छुरिता (overspread) मुखमुद्रा (colour of their face) यासाम्. The women had marked their faces with vermilion streaks. These are fancied to be the lines of the plates (पट्टः) of the edict (शासन) of cupid. The plates were smeared with सिन्दूर in order that the letters of the seal might look prominent. सिन्दू...छुरिता मुखे मुद्रा (seal) यासाम् (with ०पङ्क्तयः). अप्रतिहतं शासनं यस्य whose command is irresistible. मुष्ट्या प्रकीर्यमाणौ कर्पूरपटवासौ ताभ्यां पांसुलाः. Read ०पांसुला मनो०. मनो...यौवनस्य they were as if the roads for the wandering of the desires of youth *i. e.* the desires of young men converged in them. There is a pun. A रथ (in मनोरथ) requires a road for सञ्चरण and the road may be पांसुल (dusty.) प्रतीहार्य इव—It is the business of door-keepers in any festival to use their canes when people make a rush. The women are fancied to be प्रतीहारीs of तरुणमहोत्सव. All young men would flock to them. Hence the propriety of the word तरुण. C and T translate तरुण० as 'of a children's festival'. This is wrong. प्रचलन्ति पत्रसदृशानि कुण्डलानि यासां—whose ear-rings resembling leaves dangled about (when they danced); प्रचलन्ति पत्राणि कुण्डलानीव यासाम् (with लताः) whose leaves resembling ear-rings tossed about. लसन्त्यः dancing;

moving (with लताः). मदनः चन्दनद्रुम इव; मदनसदृशः चन्दनद्रुमः. The harlots danced out of passion. The creeper clinging to a sandal tree would also move about when tossed by the wind. ललिते पदे हंसकः (पादकटकः anklet) तस्य रवेण मुखराः (with ०विलासिन्यः); ललितं पदं (gait) येषां ते ललितपदाः हंसकाः (हंसाः) तेषां रवेण मुखराः (with वीचयः). शृङ्गाररसः सागर इव. The harlots were the ripples of the ocean of passion. हंसs may be cackling near the waves of a lake. वाच्या...शून्याः void of discrimination as to what was to be said or not said (applies to both ०विलासिन्यः and ०क्रीडाः). घनः (deep) पटहरवः तेन उत्कण्टकिताः (thrilled) गात्रयष्टयः यासाम् (with ०विलासिन्यः); घनः मेघः पटहः इव तस्य रवः तेन उत्कण्टकिताः (सञ्जातकण्टकाः) गात्रयष्टयः यासाम् (with केतक्यः). The pollen from the flowers worn by the women was carried about. The केतकी flower also has pollen. The केतक blossoms forth when the cloud thunders (in the rainy season (and there are कण्टकs on the केतक petals). दिवसम् (acc. of time) the whole day. उत्फुल्लं आननं यासाम्. The कविसमय is that the कमल expands in the day and the कुमुद at night. अनुपजाता निद्रा यासाम्. The women had no sleep at night. The कुमुद plants open their buds at night. आविष्टाः इव like persons possessed. नरेन्द्र...वृताः surrounded by a host of princes; surrounded by a host of magicians. नरेन्द्रः means generally a विषवैद्य and not one who exorcises evil spirits. See शिशुपालवध II. 88. 'सुनिग्रहा नरेन्द्रेण फणीन्द्रा इव शत्रवः' (where also there is a pun). रागमुद्दीपयन्त्यः kindling passion (with women); heightening the melody. The principal रागs are six. पुष्टयः fatness. मदमपि मदयन्त्य इव who as if intoxicated intoxication itself. Even मद could draw upon them for adding to itself. The reading उत्सवयन्त्यः would be more in keeping with what precedes. कटाक्षे...शुक्तिभिः in casting sidelong eyes, they seemed to be drinking with the shells (शुक्ति) of the corners of their eyes. The idea is:—when they cast glances, they took the pupil of the eye far away and exposed only the white portion of the eye. The white of the eye resembles mother-o'-pearl which is used in drinking (particularly milk &c.). तर्जनेषु in frightening a person they seemed as if to fetter him with the chains of the rays of their nails. They used the forefinger (तर्जनी) in chiding people. Naturally their nails flashed. The rays are fancied to be पाशs with which to bind the person chid. कोपाभिनयेषु—when a person is angry or wants to convey that he is angry, he knits his brows. चतुर...विकारान् in their clever movements they seemed to scatter about emotions. Their various movements caused the spectators to be roused to various emotions.

P. 64 ll. 1–9 **अन्यत्र...विलेसुः.** The principal sentence is अन्यत्र...राजमहिष्यः...विलेसुः. वेत्रिणां वेत्रेण वित्रासिताः जनाः तैः दत्तं अन्तरालं यासाम् for whom room was made by people that had been terrified away by the cane of the warders or chamberlains. A cane is the symbol of the authority of a कञ्चुकिन्. Note 'आचार इत्यवहितेन मया गृहीता या वेत्रयष्टिरवरोधगृहेषु राज्ञः' शाकुन्तल II. This and the following adjectival clauses qualify राजमहिष्यः. ध्रियमाणं धवलातपत्राणां वनं (समूहः) यासु over whom was held a forest of white parasols. कल्प...रिण्यः wandering under the tree of paradise. The queens resembled the nymphs of the woods. स्कन्धयोः उभयपालीभ्यां लम्बमानं लम्बं उत्तरीयं तस्मिन् लग्नौ हस्तौ यासाम् whose hands clung to the waving upper garment hanging down from both sides of their shoulders. लीला...प्रेङ्खन्त्यः who swung as if mounted on a swing in play. The shawls of the queens when they danced fluttered on their shoulders and they tried to hold them with both their hands. This looked as if they held the ropes of a swing with their hands. कनककेयूर-कोट्या पाट्यमानं पट्टांशुकं तेन उत्तरङ्गाः that were waving because the fine cloth they wore was torn by the ends of the golden armlets. तरन्तः चक्रवाकाः तैः सीमन्त्यमानं स्रोतः यासाम् (rivers) the water of which was separated into two by the चक्रवाक birds that floated in them. सीमन्त्यमान (from the noun सीमन्तः) *pr. p.* of the passive of the denominative verb सीमन्तयति. The golden armlet was like चक्रवाक, the fine cloth was like the stream and the queens therefore resembled rivers. उद्धूयमाना (being waved) धवला चामरसटा तस्यां लग्नः त्रिकण्टकः तस्मिन् वलिताः (turned) विकटाः कटाक्षाः यासाम्. हंसैः आकृष्यमाणं नीलोत्पलवनं यासु. सरस्यः lakes. त्रिकण्टकः an ear-ornament containing three gems 'त्रिकण्टकस्तु त्र्यश्रः स्यात्रिभी रत्नैश्च भूषणम्' quoted by the com. Their chowries stuck to their ear-ornament. When this happened they looked at the ornament to disentangle them. Their dark eyes resembled blue lotuses and the ornament with three gems resembled हंसs with their two feet and long beak; and the white chowries resembled the white body of the swans. The resemblance may also be due to the red colour of the gems and the redness of the feet and beak of राजहंसs. 'राजहंसास्तु ते चञ्चुचरणैर्लोहितैः सिताः' इत्यमरः. चलन्तौ चरणौ ताभ्यां च्युतः अलक्तकः तेन अरुणाः स्वेदशीकराः तैः सिच्यमानाः भवनहंसाः याभिः. सन्ध्यारागेण रज्यमानमिन्दुबिम्बं यासु. कौमुदीरजन्यः nights of the full moon in कार्तिक (which is in शरदृतु). In शरदृतु moon-light is at its best. The fair queens are like कौमुदी nights, the white हंसs like the moon's disc and the sweat reddened by lac-dye like the glow of evening. कण्ठे निहितः काञ्चनकाञ्चीगुणः तेन अञ्चितः (bent) कञ्चुकी तस्य विकाराः तै आकुञ्चिताः भ्रुवः यासाम्. The queens put their golden girdles round the neck of the chamberlain and bent him. The कञ्चुकिन् made contortions when so treated, at which the women knit their brows (in derision). वागुरा net. प्रसारितौ बाहुपाशौ याभिः. The out-stretched arms resemble the cords of the net (of love).

P. 64 ll. 10–22 **सर्वतश्च...राशयः.** स्त्रैणम् bevy of women. 'स्त्रीपुंसाभ्यां नञ्स्नञौ भवनात्' पा. 4. 1. 87. रागमयी full of राग (redness, love). शुशोण perfect of शोण् I P to become red. मङ्गलकलशमयः—jars full of water are looked upon as a good omen. विक्षेपः tossing. Their tender arms resembled the filaments of lotuses. विलासस्मितैः—Their flashing smiles appeared like the flashes of lightning. The word कालः means 'time (such as day &c.) or dark.' With the last meaning there is a विरोध in saying that काल became तडिन्मय (bright). Both smiles and lightning are bright. अंशुभिः = किरणैः. कृष्ण...वासराः the days seemed as if dappled. कृष्णसारः (1) spotted antelope; (2) dark and variegated. शिरीष...पुरैः by the bunches of शिरीष flowers used as ornaments of the ear. The शिरीष is a very delicate flower and used as ear-ornament. See शाकुन्तल I 'अवतंसयन्ति प्रमदा दयमानाः शिरीषकुसुमानि'. हरिता (green) छाया (कान्तिः) यस्य. आतपः daylight. विस्रंस...रिक्षम् the sky seemed as if full of collyrium by the sprays of तमाल in the braided hair becoming loose (by dancing). The तमाल leaf is dark and was used as decoration for the hair. 'धम्मिल्लः संयताः कचाः' इत्यमरः. हस्तकिशलयैः—their hands were delicate like tender leaves. माणिक्ये...षा by the radiance of the rain-bow in the gems. चाषपत्रमयाः full of the wings of चाष (blue jay). The sun's rays falling upon the gems of the women gave rise to rain-bow colours. ग्रहगृहीताः seized by a ghost. निनर्तिषया with the desire to dance (निनर्तिषा noun from the desiderative base of नृत्). विपुस्फुलुः *perfect* of स्फुल् 6 P with वि to throb, to vibrate. कुवेरकोषाः the treasures of कुबेर. कुबेर is the lord of riches and treasures. अलुप्यन्त were plundered.

P. 64 l. 23—**P. 65** l. 2 **एवं च...श्रियम्.** The principal sentence is देवी यशोमती गर्भेणाधत्त...राज्यश्रियम्. वृत्ते concluded. देवे—

11

this is to be connected with हर्षे below (last line of p. 9). उत्तमाङ्गे निहिताः रक्षासर्षपाः यस्य on whose head were placed mustard seeds to ward off (evil). This and the following words in the locative qualify हर्षे. समुन्मिषन्तः प्रतापः एव अग्निः तस्य स्फुलिङ्गाः यस्मिन् In whom the sparks of the fire of prowess were as if bursting forth. The idea is that the सर्षपs on the head were so many sparks of fire &c. The punctuation in the text is wrong. Take away the comma after सर्षपे, वपुषि and ग्रीवके and put it after स्फुलिङ्ग इव, तेजसीव, दर्पाङ्कुर इव. The सर्षपs employed were probably red. The white सर्षप is usually called सिद्धार्थ and is used as a protection against evil spirits. गोरोचनया पिञ्जरितं वपुः यस्य whose body was rendered yellow with गोरोचना. गोरोचना is a bright yellow pigment prepared from the urine or bile of a cow or found in the head of a cow; it is used as a medicine and to ward off the evil eye and evil spirits. समभिव्यज्यमानं सहजं क्षात्रतेजः यस्य. The yellow गोरोचना resembles तेजः. हाटके (सुवर्णे) बद्धा विकटा (large) व्याघ्रनखपङ्क्तिः तया मण्डिता ग्रीवा यस्य स ०ग्रीवकः तस्मिन्. Even now the same ornament is tied round the necks of children. When क is added at the end of बहुव्रीहि compounds, the preceding vowel, if long, is shortened. 'केऽणः' पा. 7. 4. 13. (के परे अणो ह्रस्वः स्यात्). हृदयात् उद्भिद्यमानाः दर्पाङ्कुराः यस्मिन्. The poet fancies that the tiger's claws worn on the chest were the buds of pride bursting out of his heart. प्रथ...कुर्वाणे by his first indistinct prattle he seemed to make a beginning of truth. ओंकारं कृ (lit.) to utter Om *i. e.* to make a beginning. The syllables ओम् and अथ are very auspicious and are therefore uttered at the beginning of many things. A child even now is first taught the words 'ओं नमः सिद्धम्'. प्रणव or ओंकार precedes the study of the Veda. 'ओङ्कारः स्वर्गद्वारं तस्माद् ब्रह्माध्येष्यमाण एतदादि प्रतिपद्येत' आपस्तम्ब I. 13. 6. Compare रघु० I. 11 'आसीत्महीक्षितामाद्यः प्रणवश्छन्दसामिव'. Connect मुग्धस्मितैः with आकर्षति, which qualifies हर्षे. Smiles and flowers are both white. जनन्याः पयोधरौ कलशौ इव तयोः पयः दुग्धं तस्य शीकरः तस्य सेकः. वदन is compared to कमल, small teeth to अङ्कुर. पयोधर also means मेघ and पयः means 'water.' The child smiled a happy smile when nursed at the breast and showed its teeth, which looked like buds. चारित्र...पाल्यमाने—he was as much guarded by the women in the seraglio as their own chastity. मन्त्रः state policy determined upon by a king in consultation with his ministers. 'मन्त्रो विजयमूलं हि राज्ञो भवति राघव' अयोध्याकाण्ड 100. 16; 'विजयो मन्त्रमूलो हि राज्ञो भवति भारत' सभापर्व 5. 27. The मनुस्मृति says

'यस्य मन्त्रं न जानन्ति समागम्य पृथग्जनाः । स कृत्स्नां पृथ्वीं भुङ्क्ते कोशहीनोऽपि पार्थिवः ॥' VII. 148. 'मन्त्रमूलं यतो राज्यं तस्मान्मन्त्रं सुरक्षितम् । कुर्याद्यथास्य न विदुः कर्मणामा फलोदयात् ॥ याज्ञ० I. 344. वृत्तम् good conduct. यश...वर्ध्यमाने who was cherished by his kindred like their own good name. पञ्च वा षड् वा पञ्चषाणि (बहुव्रीहि). गर्भेणाधत्त राज्यश्रियम् became pregnant with राज्यश्री. Read वसुधां for वसुधा. गर्भे...वसुधाम् as the form of नारायण produced the earth through गर्भ (*i. e.* हिरण्यगर्भ). We have seen above (p. 30) that स्वयम्भू cast seed in the water, which became an egg in which हिरण्यगर्भ was produced. This हिरण्यगर्भ in his turn created heaven and earth. 'ताभ्यां स शकलाभ्यां च दिवं भूमिं च निर्ममे ।' मनु० I. 13. नारायण is identified in the मनुस्मृति with ब्रह्मा (see I. 10). If we take गर्भेणाधत्त in its ordinary sense (*viz.* 'conceived') it is difficult to point out the particular story to which Bāṇa alludes. We may explain thus:—the whole universe at the time of प्रलय lies in नारायणोदर and comes out of it at the time of creation; so पृथिवी is in the गर्भ (उदर) of नारायण.

P 65 ll. 3–8 **पूर्णेषु...राजत.** The principal sentence is (देवी यशोमती) प्रसूतवती दुहितरम्. दीर्घ...सरसी as the lake gives birth to a lotus plant that has long and red stalks and roots. दीर्घाणि रक्तानि नालानि नेत्राणि (मूलानि) च यस्याः (with उत्पलिनी). This and the adjectives in the following clauses apply to दुहितरं also. दीर्घरक्ते नालवत् नेत्रे यस्याः whose eyes are red and long like a lotus-stalk. Redness of the corner of the eye was looked upon as a sign of beauty. हंसैः मधुरः स्वरः यस्याम् (with शरदम्); हंसवत् मधुरः स्वरः यस्याः (with दुहितरम्). कुसुमैः सुकुमाराः अवयवाः भागाः यस्याः (वनराजिम्); कुसुमवत् सुकुमाराः अवयवाः हस्तादयः यस्याः (दुहितरम्). मधुश्रीः vernal beauty. महाकनकेन (grains of gold) अवदाता (resplendent); महाकनकवत् अवदाता. The com. says 'महाकनकं तिलसुवर्णं वसुधारा धनवृष्टिः । इयं च महाभ्युदयसूचनाय दिवा पतति ।'. वेला the shore of the sea. The sea is called रत्नाकर. सहस्रनेत्रः इन्द्रः तेन दर्शनं तस्य योग्याम्; सहस्रनेत्रैः दर्शनस्य योग्याम्. शची is the wife of इन्द्र. अहल्या the wife of the sage गौतम was seduced by इन्द्र who assumed the form of the sage. For this the sage cursed अहल्या to be a stone and इन्द्र had a thousand marks on his body, which were afterwards turned into eyes. See रामायण I. 48 and VII. 30 for the story. The कथासरित्सागर contains the story 'वराङ्गलुब्धस्याङ्गे ते तत्सहस्रं भविष्यति । दिव्यस्त्रीं विश्वकर्मा यां निर्मास्यति तिलोत्तमाम् ॥ तां विलोक्य तदैवाक्ष्णां सहस्रं भविता च ते ।' III. 3. 144–145. कुमारिलभट्ट in his तन्त्रवार्तिक explains this story along with others in a rationalistic manner. सर्वैः भूभृद्भिः

(पर्वतैः, राजभिः) अभ्यर्थिताम् solicited, wooed. गौरी=पार्वती. मेना the wife of हिमालय. See above p. 9 (notes) as to the birth of पार्वती. एकावली a single string of pearls. 'एकावल्येकयष्टिका' इत्यमरः.

P 65 ll. 9–16 अस्मिन्नेव...र्पितवान्. The principal sentence is अस्मिन्नेव तु काले...यशोमत्या भ्राता सुतम्...भण्डिनामानमनुचरं कुमारयोरर्पितवान्. अष्ट...देशीयम् about eight years old. The affixes कल्प, देश्य and देशीय are added in the sense of 'a little less than.' 'ईषदसमाप्तौ कल्पब्देश्यदेशीयरः' पा. 5. 3. 67. उद्धूयमानः कुटिलः काकपक्षकशिखण्डः यस्य. The अमरकोश gives काकपक्ष and शिखण्डक as synonyms. Therefore we may take शिखण्ड as meaning 'tuft of hair' and काकपक्षक as 'the side-locks of hair on the temples.' खण्डपरशोः (शिवस्य) हुंकारेणाग्निः तस्य धूमलेखा तया अनुबद्धः मूर्धा यस्य. खण्ड...जातम् who looked like cupid born again with his head encircled (अनुबद्ध) by the streak of smoke of the fire of S'iva's wrath. The boy was handsome and had dark curling hair. The poet fancies him to be मदन with धूम on his head. धूम is dark and waving. मदन wanted to help the gods against the demon तारक who was to be killed by the son of शिव. In order to induce शिव to marry पार्वती, Cupid was about to shoot his flowery arrow, when S'iva came to know Cupid's intention and in wrath burnt him to ashes by the fire from his third eye. Compare कुमारसम्भव III 'क्रोधं प्रभो संहर संहरेति यावद्गिरः खे मरुतां चरन्ति । तावत्स वह्निर्भवनेत्रजन्मा भस्मावशेषं मदनं चकार ॥'. त्रिकण्टके मुक्ताफलं तस्य आलोकः (light) तेन धवलितं तेन. संपृ...दर्शयन्तम् who exhibited as it were the compound *Avatara* of Vishṇu and S'iva. For त्रिकण्टक as an ear-ornment, see above p. 34. This refers to the mythological story that विष्णु is dark in colour and शिव bright. पीने प्रकोष्ठे (fore-arm) प्रतिष्ठितं पुष्पलोहस्य वलयं यस्य. The com. says 'पुष्पलोहं मणिभेदः'. क्षत्रस्य क्षपणे क्षीणः परशुः तस्य पाशः तेन चिह्नितं marked with the ring of the axe that had been worn away in destroying the क्षत्रियs. The idea is that in killing the क्षत्रियs the blade became worn out and what remained was the iron ring behind the blade. The वलय resembled the ring of the परशु thus worn away. बाण very frequently refers to the story of the slaughter of the क्षत्रियs by परशुराम. See pp. 44, 47 of the text. परशुराम killed कार्तवीर्य for carrying away the cow of his father जमदग्नि. The sons of कार्तवीर्य killed जमदग्नि in the absence of परशुराम. परशुराम on knowing this took the vow of exterminating the क्षत्रियs and fulfilled it 21 times. कण्ठसूत्रे ग्रथिताः भङ्गुराः (कुटिलाः) प्रवालाङ्कुराः (coral) यस्य. उरःकाठिन्येन खण्डितानि नरसिंहनखरस्य खण्डानि येन. The corals were red and curved. They are fancied to be the pieces of the nails of नरसिंह which stuck to the chest of हिरण्यकशिपु. प्रवाल is worn as an auspicious thing. Put the comma after ०न्तरं and not after ०खण्डम्. गृहीतं जन्मान्तरं येन. The boy looked like हिरण्यकशिपु born again. For persecuting his son प्रह्लाद who was a devotee of विष्णु, the latter assumed the man-lion form and killed हिरण्यकशिपु. The story is given in the भागवतपुराण (VII). शैश...ष्टम्भम् even in boyhood he bore himself proudly. बीज...द्रुमस्य—being a boy yet, he is styled 'the seed of the tree of valour'. अनुचरं कुमारयोः as an attendant of the two princes (राज्यवर्धन and हर्ष).

P. 65 ll. 17-22 अवनि...बभूवतुः. तस्य refers to भण्डि. ईश्वरस्य = शिवस्य. तुल्यं...सीत् he looked upon (his two sons and the third Bhaṇḍi) equally *i. e.* he bestowed equal care on all the three. दर्शन means also 'sight'. शिव saw with the third eye as well as with the other two. ईश्वरस्य applies to the king also. सकल... दायिनौ applies to राजपुत्रौ and मधुमाधवौ. तेन = भण्डिना. प्रकृतिदक्षिणेन courteous by nature (with तेन); blowing from the south by nature (with ०मारुतेन). मधुमाधवौ—चैत्र and वैशाख, the months of spring. 'मधुश्च माधवश्च वासन्तिकावृतू' तै. सं. 4. 4. 11. 1. मलय is one of the seven principal mountains of India. It is to be identified with the southern portion of the ghauts running from the south of Mysore and forming the eastern boundary of Travancore. मधुमास and मलयमारुत are both excitants of Love. The seven कुलपर्वतs are 'महेन्द्रो मलयः सह्यः शुक्तिमानृक्षपर्वतः । विन्ध्यश्च पारियात्रश्च सप्तैते कुलपर्वताः ॥' वायु० 45. 88. Compare for the श्लेष on दक्षिण and the idea also 'उत्पादयति लोकस्य प्रीतिं मलयमारुतः । ननु दाक्षिण्यसम्पन्नः सर्वस्य भवति प्रियः ॥' काव्यादर्श II. 174. अपरे...सह वर्धमानौ growing together with the joy of the subjects, as if it (joy) were another brother (of the two princes हर्ष and राज्यवर्धन). The idea is that as the princes became endowed with youth and all the esteemed qualities of young princes, the joy of the people also grew *pari passu.* The adjectives from ०स्तम्भौ to क्षमौ apply to the princes and to ०संनिवेश. स्थिरौ ऊरुस्तम्भौ (ऊरू स्तम्भौ इव) ययोः whose pillar-like thighs were firm (with princes); स्थिराः उरवः स्तम्भाः ययोः whose pillars are firm and big (with ०सन्निवेशौ). पृथुः प्रकोष्ठः ययोः (applies to both). प्रकोष्ठः the forearm; the room near the gate or a quadrangle. दीर्घौ भुजार्गलौ ययोः that had long bar-like arms. A city-gate has large bars to fasten it. विकटं उरःकपाटं ययोः whose chest was broad like the panel of a gate. The word is कपाट; but is also written कवाट. 'कं शिरः पाटयति प्रविशताम्' क्षीरस्वामी.

the demon तारक whom he slew. See रामायण बालकाण्ड 36 and 37, कथासरित्सागर III. 6. and बृहत्कथामञ्जरी III. 1. 142. ff. प्रतिपुरुष (1) reflection; (2) rival. सन्ध्या...माङ्गौ Even in folding their hands at the morning and evening adoration, their heads ached. शूलायमानं उत्तमाङ्गं (शिरः) येषाम्. To fold the hands is a sign of humility and submission. They had to fold hands in सन्ध्यावन्दन. Even this caused them मस्तकशूल. जल...हृदयौ their hearts were pained even by the bow borne by the cloud. They could not tolerate any one wielding a bow and hence were distressed when they saw the rain-bow in the cloud. दोदूयमान *pr. p.* of the intensive base of दू. The reading दोधूयमान is not so good as दोदूयमान. It would mean 'whose hearts were shaken.' आले... पतिभिः by the kings painted in pictures. They were accustomed to the fact that ordinary rulers bowed at their feet. परिमितं मण्डलं (disc) तेन सन्तुष्टम्. The sun has only a limited मण्डल (disc); they wanted an unlimited मण्डल (sphere of influence extending over numerous neighbouring and distant kings). The कामन्दकीयनीतिसार (in the 8th Sarga) gives the views of several authors on the number of kings constituting a मण्डल. Ordinarily मण्डल comprises twelve near and distant kings. 'इतिप्रकारं बहुधा मण्डलं परिचक्षते। सर्वलोकप्रतीतं हि स्फुटं द्वादशराजकम् ॥' का. 8. 41. See the मिताक्षरा on याज्ञवल्क्य॰ I. 345 'अरिर्मित्रमुदासीनोऽनन्तरस्तत्परः परः। क्रमशो मण्डलं चिन्त्यं सामादिभिरुपक्रमैः ॥'. भूभृता (पर्वतेन मन्दरेण) अपहृता लक्ष्मीः यस्य. In churning the ocean the gods made मन्दर the churning handle. 'मन्थानं मन्दरं कृत्वा नेत्रं कृत्वा तु वासुकिम्। मथ्यताममृतं देवाः साहाय्ये मय्यवस्थिते ॥' विष्णु॰ I. 9. 76. लक्ष्मी was one of the 14 jewels churned out. The princes (हर्ष and राज्य॰) never allowed any भूभृत् (king) to carry off their लक्ष्मी (glory) and therefore laughed at the ocean that allowed its लक्ष्मी (the goddess) to be carried off by a भूभृत् (mountain). For क in ॰लक्ष्मीकं see above p. 31. अकृतः विग्रहः (शरीरं) येन. A powerful person would offer विग्रह (battle); the wind though powerful offered no विग्रह (it had no body). चमरीणां बालव्यजनेन वीजितं तेन. चमरी deer, of the tails of which chowries are made, are to be found in the Himālayas. The चामर is an emblem of sovereignty. Therefore they could not bear that the mountain should be fanned by the tails of चमरीs. जल... खिद्यमानौ—conches are found on the seashore. Conches were blown by great warriors only. There is perhaps another idea. शङ्ख is one of the nine निधिs. They could not allow शङ्ख (treasure) to remain with जलधि. The author perhaps intends also a picturesque effect. शङ्ख and जलधि are words meaning enormous numbers. 'लक्षं च नियुतं चैव कोटिरर्बुदमेव च । वृन्दः खर्वो निखर्वश्च शङ्खपद्मौ च सागरः । अन्त्यं मध्यं परार्धं च दशवृद्ध्या यथाक्रमम् ॥'. चतु...सहमानौ. वरुण (प्रचेतस्) is the lord of the ocean in mythology. हर्ष's sovereignty extended over the earth bounded by the four oceans. अनपहृतानि छत्राणि येषाम्. विगता छाया (shade; splendour) येषाम्. Parasols shade one from the sun. Though they did not carry away the parasols of kings whom they vanquished, they made them विच्छाय (*i. e.* void of splendour; void of shade against the sun). There is an apparent contradiction which is removed by taking the other sense of छाया. साधु...क्षरन्तौ they were pleased with (*i. e.* they bestowed favours upon) the good, though not courted by them (the good), and poured nectar (sweet words) with their lips on them. There is another meaning due to श्लेष, which gives rise to विरोधाभास. प्रसन्न means 'transparent, clear' (as applied to wine). मधु means 'wine'. 'Even on good (*i. e.* teetotallers) people they poured wine with their lips, they being प्रसन्न without having taken (wine)'. Remove the comma after ०प्रसन्नौ. वंशः (1) family; (2) bamboo. ऊष्मणा (1) by their pride; (2) by heat. म्लानि (1) decline; (2) withering. दूरस्थितानपि. The force of अपि lies in this—if bamboos were to be destroyed fire would have to be brought near them; but the two princes brought about the decline of even *distant* kings. दिवसे दिवसे अनुदिवसं (अव्ययीभाव). Read शस्त्राभ्यास० for शास्त्राभ्यास०. शस्त्राभ्यासेन श्यामिका (darkness) तया कलङ्कितम्. अशेषं राजकं (राज्ञां समूहः) तस्य प्रतापः एव अग्निः तस्य निर्वापणं तेन मलिनम्. 'अथ राजकम् ॥ राजन्यकं च नृपतिक्षत्रियाणां गणे क्रमात् ।' इत्यमरः. Their hands were darkened by the practice of sword play. That darkness is fancied to be due to the extinguishing of the fire of the prowess of kings. योग्याकालेषु at the times of (martial) exercise. धीर deep. अभ्यर्णोपभोगात् after enjoyment that was near (*i. e.* that occurred a short while before). दिग्...लपन्तौ— the twang of their bows spread in all directions. The author fancies that the twang was the talk of the princes with the damsels (the quarters). आविर्भूतः शब्दस्य प्रादुर्भावः ययोः—whose names became known. द्वीपान्तरेषु—The द्वीपs are either spoken of as seven (जम्बु, प्लक्ष, शाल्मल, कुश, क्रौञ्च, शाक and पुष्कर) or eighteen. See विष्णुपुराण II. 1. 11 ff. and व्यासभाष्य on योगसूत्र III. 25 (for सप्तद्वीपा वसुमती) and रघुवंश for 'अष्टादशद्वीपनिखातयूपः' 6. 38.

P. 66 ll. 10–22 **एकदा...दिदेश.** भुक्तवान् that had taken his dinner. प्रथमं...भृत्याः good servants, the first essential of sovereignty, are difficult to obtain. For the seven Angas of राज्य see above p. 5. प्रायेण...क्षुद्रा: generally mean persons, being agreeable in company, make the king their wealth, like atoms. The idea is that mean persons are agreeable to whatever the king says when they are in his company and thus by flattery make him the source of wealth to themselves. There are double meanings. It is the atoms that produce the पार्थिव द्रव्य (earthy substance). द्रव्य and समवाय are technical words in the न्यायवैशेषिक philosophy. The द्रव्यs are 'पृथिव्यप्तेजोवाय्वाकाशकालदिगात्ममनांसि नवैव.' समवाय is one of the seven categories of the न्यायवैशेषिक system 'द्रव्यगुणकर्मसामान्यविशेषसमवायाभावा: सप्त पदार्था:'. समवाय is defined as 'नित्यसम्बन्ध: समवायोऽयुतसिद्धवृत्ति:' *i. e.* it is an inseparable connection of such things as the whole and its parts, qualities and actions and their abode &c. Action is produced in the atoms by the will of God; two परमाणुs give rise to a द्व्यणुक and three द्व्यणुकs to a चतुरणुक and so on, when the earthy and other substances are ultimately evolved. The परमाणुs are the causes of द्व्यणुक &c. and between these latter and the परमाणुs there is समवाय. So सम...भूय means (in the case of atoms) 'being favourable to समवाय (*i. e.* entering into समवाय relation with their effects, the द्व्यणुक &c.). क्रीडारसेन on account of their liking for play. नर्तयन्त: making to dance. बालिशा: (1) children (2) triflers. Children in play make the peacock dance. Rogues, in whose hands the king becomes a puppet, make him dance (act) as they please. The com. gives another sense of मयूर 'धूर्तजनयोग्यो हास:'. But this is not absolutely necessary. दर्पण...पल्लविका: rogues having entered into the heart (*i. e.* having secured influence over the prince's mind) transfer their disposition to him, as in a mirror. In a mirror also tendrils transfer bodies (*i. e.* the forms of tendrils are reflected). 'पल्लविको विट:' क्षीरस्वामी. The शब्दकल्पद्रुम gives वेश्यापति as the meaning of पल्लवक and कामुक as the meaning of पल्लविक. विप्रलम्भका: deceivers, impostors. मिथ्यादर्शनै: (1) by false sights; (2) by false doctrines. असद्बुद्धिं (1) ideas about things that have no existence (असत: अविद्यमानस्य बुद्धि:, with स्वप्न:); (2) false notions. Impostors warp the mind of the prince with false doctrines; dreams delude us by presenting things to our vision that do not exist. गीत...वातिका: rogues, not being watched, bring about intoxication by singing, dancing and laughter. उपेक्षिता: वातिका: विकारा:—as diseases of wind when neglected bring on madness. वात is one of the three humours of the body (वात, पित्त and कफ).

A mad man sings, dances and laughs. तृष्णावन्तः (1) thirsty; (2) greedy (for wealth). अकुलीनाः (1) not lying on the earth; (2) low-born. न शक्यन्ते ग्रहीतुम्—(1) cannot be seized; (2) cannot be reconciled. The चातक bird always feels thirst because it cannot drink the water on the earth, but subsists on a few drops from the cloud. Sailing as it does through the sky (कौ पृथिव्यां लीनो न भवति इति अकुलीनः) it cannot be seized. मानसे (1) in the मानस lake; (2) in the mind. स्फुरन्तम् (1) moving about; (2) appearing. जालिकाः (1) fishermen; (2) cheats. जालेन चरतीति जालिकः. Fishermen catch fish in the मानस lake. Cheats are so clever that they grasp the thought (of the prince) the moment it rises in his mind. Ordinarily one's thoughts are understood by their effects. यमपट्टिकाः—those who exhibit canvas on which are drawn the torments of Hell inflicted by Yama on sinners. See मुद्राराक्षस Act I where we have a person showing यमपट. अम्बरे (1) on canvas; (2) in the sky. उद्गीतकाः who sing loudly. Rogues draw paintings in the sky *i. e.* build castles in the air, represent to the king as possible what is impossible. शल्यम् (1) the point of an arrow, barb; (2) pain. अतिमार्गणाः (1) very keen arrows; (2) importunate in their demands. Read अभिषङ्गैः for ०ष्वङ्गैः. अभिषङ्गः contact. उपधाभिः परीक्षितौ tested by trials of honesty. 'उपधा धर्माद्यैर्यत्परीक्षणम्' इत्यमरः. The अर्थशास्त्र of कौटिल्य contains a chapter styled 'उपधाभिः शौचाशौचज्ञानममात्यानाम्' (I. 6.) and details four kinds of उपधा called धर्मोपधा, अर्थो०, कामो० and भयोपधा. विक्रान्तौ valiant. अभिरूपौ handsome or learned. मालव...पुत्रौ sons of the king of Malva, or Rajputs from Malva. भुजा...रिक्तौ not separable from my body like my two arms (*i. e.* I regard them as my own body). कुमारगुप्त०—for these see Introduction. भव ... भवितव्यम्—You two should not behave towards them on the same footing as other attendants.

P 66 l. 22—**P. 67** l. 17 नचिरात्...ददृशतुः. The principal sentence is नचिरात्...राज्यवर्धनहर्षौ प्रतीहारेण सह प्रविशन्तं अग्रतो ज्येष्ठं...कुमारगुप्तं (p. 12 l. 9) पृष्ठतस्तस्य कनीयांसं ... माधवगुप्तं ददृशतुः. प्रविशन्तम्—this and the following adjectives in the accusative qualify कुमारगुप्तं below. अग्रतो ज्येष्ठम्—the eldest of the two brothers was in front, as was proper. अष्टादशवर्षाणि वयः यस्य. अतिखर्वम् very low in stature. अति...र्वीम् who, with very heavy steps, as if steadied the earth that was unsteady on account of being transferred to numerous kings. The earth has passed through the hands of several kings and so is चञ्चल like लक्ष्मी. ०नृपतिषु सञ्चरणं तेन चला. C and T translate 'which trembled with the movements of numerous kings.' This is not so striking as the sense given by us. अनवरताभ्यस्तं लङ्घनं (leaping) तेन घनः उपचयः (growth or mass) यस्य एतादृशं मांसं तेन मेदुरात् (fat). अन... भासमानम् endowed with a pair of very thin shanks (जङ्घा) issuing from the knee joints that were not prominent and that (therefore) appeared as if to fall down from a pair of thighs that were plump with hard flesh of tough growth due to leaping constantly practised. His thighs were muscular and round, while the knee bones were not prominent (as they would be n the case of one who was not muscular) and his legs were thin. The shanks therefore appeared to jump out of his rounded thighs. उल्लिखिताभ्यां पार्श्वाभ्यां (sides) प्रकाशितः कृशिमा यस्य तेन (with मध्येन). सुरासुरैः रभसेन (with force) भ्रमितः वासुकिः तेन कषणं (rubbing) तेन क्षीणेन. कुमारगुप्त had a waist the smallness of which was laid bare by his sides that were hollowed (being void of fatty layers). At the time of churning the ocean for the 14 jewels, मन्दर became the handle and वासुकि was the rope. See above (notes) p. 42. The sides of मन्दर were scratched off by the violent rubbing of the rope Vāsuki and so its मध्य became slight. स्वामि...यच्छन्तम् giving room to innumerable (tokens of) regard received from his master. Even now it is usual to wear on the chest medals awarded to a person for excelling in anything. C and T render 'offered room for unbounded feelings of respect for his master.' This is not good. The poet is giving the good points in the physique of कुमारगुप्त and not the largeness of his heart. The plural सम्भावनानाम् is also against the latter interpretation. निभृत...क्षेपैः by the quiet and graceful movements. One who swims has to move his arms backwards and forwards as in walking. Youth is a period that can scarcely be crossed without pit-falls. वामकरे कटकं (वलयं) तस्य माणिक्यं तस्य. मरीचीनां मञ्जरी तस्याः जालमस्याः अस्तीति ०जालिन्या (with ०लेखया). समुद्भिद्यमानः प्रतापानलस्य शिखापल्लवः यस्याः (with ०लेखया). अङ्कितः पीवरः प्रकोष्ठः यस्य वामकर...प्रकोष्ठम् whose round fore-arm was marked by the line of the scar of the bow-string, the scar that had a pencil of rays from the ruby in the bracelet of the left hand and from which (therefore) the budlike flame of the fire of valour seemed to shoot forward. As to the wearing of वलय on the left forearm, see notes above p. 15. His forearm had a scar made by the bowstring and on the scar rays from the jewelled bracelet fell, which appeared like flames of fire. आलोहिनीम् slightly red. उच्चं अंसतटं अवलम्बते इति that hung down from his high shoulder. On his shoulder fell the reddish light of the jewel in his ear-ornament. It resembled the skin of the Ruru deer, which is worn across the chest and shoulder by a क्षत्रियब्रह्मचारिन्. Hence the word ब्रह्मग्रहणव्रतविधृताम्. See बौधायनस्मृति I. 2. 14 'कृष्णरुरुबस्ताजिनान्यजिनानि.' For a graphic description of the equipment of a क्षत्रियब्रह्मचारिन्, see उत्तररामचरित IV. 20. उद्गता कोटिः यस्य सः उत्कोटिः केयूरः तस्य पत्रभङ्गे पुत्रिका तस्याः प्रतिबिम्बं गर्भे यस्य सः ०गर्भः, ०गर्भः कपोलः यस्य. हृदये स्थिता रोहिणी यस्य. ०कपोलं मुखं—a face on the cheeks of which there was a reflection of a female figure drawn in lines on the armlets that had projecting points. His face was like the moon. रोहिणी is said to be the special favourite of the moon. On his cheek there was the reflection of a पुत्रिका. The moon's heart thinks of रोहिणी. The star रोहिणी has flashing light, as the points of the केयूर flash light. For क at the end of बहुव्रीहि compounds, see above. p. 31. अचपला स्तिमिता च तारका (pupil) यस्य. लक्ष्म्याः लाभः तदर्थं उत्तानितानि मुखानि येषाम्. He had a downcast eye (by way of showing his humility) and therefore taught humility to lotus beds. लक्ष्मी is represented as standing in an expanded lotus. He, though desirous of लक्ष्मी (glory), had a downcast look and not an uplifted face like the lotuses. उत्तंसः crest, ornament worn on the crown of the head. अम्लातक is a kind of red flower. स्वाम्यनुरागः loyalty. रागः means 'redness' also. नम्रता (1) humility; (2) capacity to bend, flexibility. कङ्कणभङ्गात् भीतानि सकलानि कार्मुकाणि तैः अर्पिताम्—presented by all the bows that were afraid of being broken in their rings (*i. e.* their crests). Connect निर्दयग्र with भङ्ग. But to connect separate words with part of a समास is rather unusual. The reading of some of the MSS of B 'निर्दयाकर्षणभङ्ग' is much better, but seems to be a conscious improvement. Bows have नम्रता (they bend) and transferred it to him. संयतैः confined, restrained. प्रण...वर्तमानम् who acted according to the status of a nobly born youth, that (status) is the seat of trust, as if it were his sweet-heart. तेजस्विन् (1) brilliant ; (2) high-spirited. आह्लादक applies to both शीलेन and शशिना. He was high-spirited and had a winning disposition and therefore resembled the sun, having a moon inside it. गन्धनम्—hurting, rubbing. दर्शन...सौभाग्येन who by the charm of his person purchased the people at sight and sold them into the hands of joy. The moment the people saw him, they gave their allegiance to him and were further delighted. What one buys, one may sell to another. कुमारगुप्तम्—connect with ददृशतुः. प्रांशु tall. गौर fair, white-red. मनःशिला (Mar. मनशीळ) red arsenic. अनुल्बण...निभेन under the guise of a crest of मालती flowers, that (crest) was not very prominent. This shows his विनय. निर्जिगमिषता = गन्तुमिच्छता. The white मालती crest resembled his great (गुरु) यशः which is poetically represented to be white. His यशः wanted to go out (*i. e.* spread in the world) and therefore kissed him on the head (as मालती flower) as a father (गुरु) when leaving the house on a journey may kiss his son on the head. भ्रूसङ्गतकेन by the meeting of his eyebrows. विनय and यौवन were united in him for the first time after a long interval. यौवन and विनय are rarely found together. His eyebrows that met were as it were the first sign of this union. हृदयनिहिता (1) placed in the heart (with ०भक्ति); (2) fixed on his chest (with ०दृष्टि). अच्छाच्छस्य अतिशुभ्रस्य चन्दनरसस्य अनुलेपेन शीतलम् (वक्षःस्थलं, which is the object of बिभ्राणम्). संनिहितं हारः एव उपधानं (pillow) यस्य. अनन्त...श्रान्तायाः tired by passing to innumerable chieftains. शशि...शयनम् a bed of the slabs of चद्रकान्त stones. His chest was smeared with cool चन्दन paste and therefore resembled the चन्द्रकान्त stone, which is also white and शीतल. His chest had a necklace of pearls which resembled a white pillow. His chest was broad like a slab. लक्ष्मी rested on his chest after being tired &c. चक्षुः and the other words in the accusative up to गमनं are governed by दर्शयन्तम्. चक्षुः कुरङ्गकैः भीतैरुत्कोचमिव दत्तं—eye which was given to him as a bribe (उत्कोचः) by the terrified deer. The same words are to be understood after वराहैः &c. The idea is that his eye was beautiful like that of the deer; the rest to be construed similarly. घोणावंशं bamboo-like (*i. e.* high) nose. स्कन्धपीठं broad shoulders. मृगया...शेषैः that remained out of those that were left after being hunt down in chase.

P. 67 ll. 18–28 **प्रविश्य...बभूवतुः.** चतुर्भिः अङ्गैः with four limbs *i. e.* hands and knees. गाम् the earth. स्निग्धा (affectionate) नरेन्द्रस्य दृष्टिः तया निर्दिष्टाम् (indicated). अस्तः (cast aside) अपरः व्यापारः याभ्याम्. सङ्कल्पाः...भविष्यन्ति your desires will give you this special distinction that the result will follow in all its fulness, like the trees of Paradise. मेदिन्यां दोलायमानः मौलिः ययोः whose head hung on the earth *i. e.* who prostrated themselves. युगपत् at the same time. ताभ्याम् by कुमारगुप्त and माधवगुप्त. उत्थाय—रा० and हर्ष got up. The reading of A 'उत्थाय राज्यवर्धनहर्षौ प्रणेमतुः तौ च पितरम्' means they (कुमारगुप्त and माधवगुप्त) got up and bowed to रा० and हर्ष and these two latter bowed to their father. It is better to suppose that राज्यवर्धन and हर्ष did not allow the young men any time to bow to themselves. निमेषो...यान्तौ not going away from the range of the (prince's) eye, like the opening and shutting of the eye. निमेष and उन्मेष are always present in the eye. The two princes always stood before हर्ष and राज्यवर्धन. उच्छ्वास (exhalation) and निश्वास (inhalation) are also अभिमुख (done through the mouth). भुजाविव पार्श्ववर्तिनौ our hands are constantly at our side.

P. 67 l. 29—**P. 68** l. 24 **अथ राज्यश्री...जानातीति.** विदग्धासु (applies to both सखीषु and कलासु)—clever; fine. कलासु—The कामसूत्र of वात्स्यायन (I. 3.) enumerates the 64 arts such as गीत, वाद्य, नृत्य, आलेख्य &c. उपचीयमानः परिचयः यस्याः whose familiarity (with सखीs and कलाs) was on the increase. शरा...भुवि as arrows on the target. बाह्य...स्थितेन occupying the outer court. स्व...गताम् that came (*i. e.* occurred to him) in its own context. The man was thinking on some topic or story and in connection with it he remembered a verse which he sang loudly. आर्या—'यस्याः प्रथमे पादे द्वादश मात्रास्तथा तृतीयेऽपि । अष्टादश द्वितीये चतुर्थके पञ्चदश साऽऽर्या ॥'. *Verse 5.* The sentence is विवर्धमाना सुता पितरं उद्वेगमहावर्ते पातयति सरित् तटमिव—a growing daughter casts her father in the whirlpool of gloom, as a rising river casts its bank in a whirlpool. उद्वेगः महावर्तः इव (with सुता); उद्वेगसदृशः महावर्तः (with सरित्). पयोधराणां (मेघानां) उन्नमनं तस्य काले at the time of the impending clouds; पयोधरयोः स्तनयोः उन्नमनं (elevation) तस्य काले. अनुवर्षम्—(वर्षे वर्षे इति अव्ययीभाव) each year (with सुता). वर्षमनु after rainfall. अनु as a कर्मप्रवचनीय governs वर्ष in the accusative. Or we may also take अनुवर्षम् in the sense of 'at each rainy season.' It should be noted that the verse fits in with the topic of the youth of राज्यश्री and the seeking of her hand by various kings. उत्सारितः परिजनः येन. गुणवत्ता possession of good qualities. चिन्ता—anxiety (as to finding a proper husband for her) never left his heart, just as her गुणवत्ता never left him (*i. e.* he was always dwelling upon her good qualities). The reading गुणवृत्तेव makes no sense. C and T say in the appendix that गुणवृत्ता is an easier reading. We fail to see how. They render गुणवृत्ता as 'as if become an attribute' and therefore take it as an adjective of चिन्ता इन्धनीभवन्ति become the fuel (of the fire of torment). अस्याः पयोधरोन्नतिः (पयोधरयोः स्तनयोः उन्नतिः) मे हृदयमन्धकारयति. पयोधराणां मेघानां उन्नतिः दिवसमन्धकारयति. केना...रियं this rule of conduct (regarded as) right, by whomsoever it may have been made, is not approved of by me. धर्म्या—धर्मादनपेता—according to 'धर्मपथ्यर्थ—न्यायादनपेते' पा. 4. 4. 92. अङ्कलालितानि fondled on our knees. अकाण्ड एव...नीयन्ते are taken away by strangers (असंस्तुत) who come all of a sudden. एतानि...संसारस्य these indeed are the branded spots of this worldly existence *i. e.* these are the most painful of the events of this संसार. सर्वाभिभाविनी overwhelming all. अपत्य... सन्तः good men are grieved at the birth of a daughter though both (son and daughter) are equally (their) offspring. जन्मकाल...साधवः good men offer water by their tears to their daughters even at the time of their birth. Emphasis is laid on the word जन्मकाले, because water is offered to the dead. Good men shed tears when a daughter is born. अकृतः दाराणां परिग्रहः (acceptance) यैः. परिहृता (avoided) गृहे वसतिः यैः. अरण्यानि is the object of अधिशेरते. The roots शी, स्था, and आस्, when preceded by अधि, govern the accusative of the abode (आधार). 'अधिशीङ्—स्थासां कर्म' पा. 1. 4. 46. यथा...हृदयम् the more do the envoys of the suitors come in, the more does wretched anxiety enter deep into my heart, like a woman abashed. लज्जमानेव—a woman that feels abashed will run inside the house. गृहगतैः=गृहस्थैः. लोकवृत्तयः—the ways of the world. वरगुणेषु qualities in a bridegroom (or 'excellent qualities'). अभि...धीमन्तः the wise follow (*i. e.* pay great regard to) noble birth alone. Mark the verse 'कन्या वरयते रूपं माता वित्तं पिता श्रुतम् । बान्धवाः कुलमिच्छन्ति मृष्टान्नमितरे जनाः ॥' quoted by commentators on कुमारसम्भव V. 72. धर...स्थितः standing at the head of all kings. धरणीधराणां= पर्वतानाम्. माहेश्वरः पादन्यासः the foot-print of महेश्वर (शिव). शिव is said to reside on the top (मूर्धन्) of the कैलास mountain. माहेश्वरः with मौखरिवंशः would mean 'that was devoted to महेश्वर (*i. e.* शिव)'. मौखरिवंशः—for the Maukharis, see Introduction. From the inscriptions it appears that the correct form is either मौखरि or मौखर. The reading of A 'भौखरीवंशः' is therefore bad. Bāṇa in his introduction to the कादम्बरी has 'नमामि भर्वोश्चरणाम्बुजद्वयं सशेखरैर्मौखरिभिः कृतार्चनम् ।'. ग्रह...गतः as if he were the sun (ग्रहपति) come to the earth. पितु...गुणै. not inferior to his father in his virtues. एनाम्—refers to राज्यश्री. दुहितृस्नेहेन कातरतरं हृदयं यस्याः.

संवर्धन...गिन्य: useful only in nursing them (and not in determining such delicate questions as their disposal in marriage). धात्रीनिर्विशेषा: not different from (*i. e.* no better than) their nurses. प्रदाने...पितर: in bestowing them (in marriage) their fathers are the (sole) authority. कृपया कृत: विशेष: यस्मिन्—the difference being made by pity. कृपा...स्नेह:—यशोमती gives expression to the general feeling of Indian mothers that they love their daughters more than their sons and assigns the reason for this. The position of the daughter in society excites the pity of the mother more than that of the sons. Read आर्तिता for आर्तिता. यथा...जानाति my lord knows how to act so that she (राज्यश्री) will not become a lifelong (source of) anxiety to us. The reading of A 'यथा यावज्जीवमावयोरार्तिता' is not good. The meaning then would be ' my lord knows how lifelong anxiety would be caused to us '. C reads 'आवयोर्नाधितां प्रतिपद्यते', which yields the same sense as the text (न + आधिताम्).

P. 68 l. 25—**P. 69** l. 32 **राजा तु ... कुलम्.** प्रति governs the accusative according to the वार्तिक 'अभित:परित:समयानिकषाहाप्रतियोगेऽपि' on 'उपान्वध्याङ्वस:' I. 4. 48. विदित: अर्थ: याभ्याम्. जाता मुद् (delight) यस्य—qualifies तस्मिन्, which refers to प्रधानदूतपुरुष. The principal sentence is जातमुदि...गते तस्मिन् आसन्नेषु विवाहदिवसेषु... ०लोकम्...आसीत् राजकुलम्. The author now gives a graphic description of the preparations of a marriage in a royal family. उद्दामं दीयमानानि ताम्बूलपटवासकुसुमानि तै: प्रसाधित: सर्वलोक: यस्मिन् all the people in which were decked by the betel, fragrant powders and flowers that were being given with an unrestrained hand. सकलदेशेभ्य: आदिश्यमानं शिल्पिनां सार्थस्य (समूहस्य) आगमनं यस्मिन्. Skilled artisans were invited from all countries. अवनिपालपुरुषै: (king's officers) गृहीत: समग्रै: ग्रामीणै: (villagers) आनीयमानानां उपकरणानां (useful materials) सम्भार: (collection) यस्मिन्. ग्रामे भव: ग्रामीण:. राजदौवारिकै: उपनीयमानानि अनेकनृपाणां उपायनानि यस्मिन् where the presents sent by numerous chiefs were brought (to the royal presence) by the doorkeepers of the king (प्रभाकरवर्धन). दौवारिक:— द्वारे नियुक्त: according to ' तत्र नियुक्त:' पा. 4. 4. 69. उपनिमन्त्रिता: (invited) आगता: बन्धुवर्गा: तेषां संवर्गणं (attracting, winning) तस्मिन् व्यग्रा: राजवल्लभा: यस्मिन्. लब्धं मधु (wine) तस्य मदेन प्रचण्डा: (wild) चर्मकारा: तेषां करपुटै: उल्लालिता: (shaken, moved) कोणा: (drumsticks) तै: पटु (sharp) विघट्टनं (striking) तेन रणन्त: मङ्गलपटहा: यस्मिन्. Leather workers had been summoned to make drums and were plied with wine. In their intoxication they struck the drums lustily. पिष्टपञ्चागुलेन मण्ड्यमानानि उलूखलमुसलशिलाद्युपकरणानि यस्मिन् in which such utensils as mortar, pestle and grinding stones were decked with five finger-prints of powder (of turmeric probably). The five fingers were dipped in turmeric mixed with water and the mortar &c. were smeared with the finger-marks by way of मङ्गल. In the 2nd उच्छ्वास we read 'पिष्टपञ्चाङ्गुलपाण्डुरं मुखनिहितनवचूतपल्लवं पूर्णकलशमुदीक्षमाणः...प्रीतिकूटान्निरगात्' on which the Com. says 'पिष्टपञ्चाङ्गुलमाजकोक्ताभिः पंचभिरङ्गुलिभिर्मङ्गल्याय दीयते'. Even now the pestle and grinding stones are so marked. अशेषेभ्यः आशामुखेभ्यः आविर्भूता चारणानां (bards) परम्परा तया आपूर्यमाणाः प्रकोष्ठाः (quadrangles) यस्मिन्. प्रतिष्ठाप्यमानं इन्द्राणीदैवतं यस्मिन् where images of इन्द्राणी (wife of इन्द्र) were being set up. A reads ०प्रकोष्ठप्रतिष्ठाप्य०, which would mean that 'images of इन्द्राणी were being set up in quadrangles.' The works on marriage ritual lay down that शची should be worshipped. "विवाहे शचीपूजनं नारदीयसंहितायाम् 'सम्पूज्य प्रार्थयित्वा तां शचीदेवीं गुणाश्रयाम्' इति। तथा च प्रयोगरत्नाकरे। ततो दाता पात्रस्थसिततण्डुलपुञ्जे शचीमावाह्य षोडशोपचारैः पूजयेत्तां च कन्यैवं प्रार्थयेत् 'देवेन्द्राणि नमस्तुभ्यं देवेन्द्रप्रियभामिनि। विवाहं भाग्यमारोग्यं पुत्रलाभं च देहि मे।'" quoted from Mr. Nardurgikar's notes on रघु० VII. 3. The धर्मसिन्धु says 'अन्योन्यालिङ्गितगौरीहरयोः प्रतिमां सुवर्णरौप्यादिनिर्मितां कात्यायनीमहालक्ष्मीशचीभिः सह पूजयेत्।'. सूत्रधारैः (carpenters) आदीयमानः विवाहवेद्याः सूत्रपातः यस्मिन् where carpenters began to measure with their measuring line the marriage altar. सित...सत्कृतैः—the carpenters were honoured for their trouble by presents of white flowers, unguents and clothes. उत्कूर्चकः (उद्गतः कूर्चकः यस्मिन्) करः येषाम्—whose hands had brushes held up (in whitewashing). सुधायाः *(chunam)* कर्परः (pail) स्कन्धे येषाम्. अधि...रूढैः mounted on ladders. धवैः = पुरुषैः. धवलीक्रियमाणं प्रासादस्य प्रतोलीप्राकारशिखरं यस्मिन् where the top of the palace wall (प्राकारः) on the street (प्रतोली) was being whitened. आदौ क्षुण्णं पश्चात् क्षाल्यमानं कुसुम्भकं तस्य सम्भारः तस्य अम्भः—प्लवपूरेण रज्यमानाः जनपादपल्लवाः यस्मिन् where the feet of the people were coloured by the flood of the torrents of water from the heap (सम्भारः) of safflower that was powdered (क्षुण्ण) and then washed. निरूप्यमाणाः यौतकयोग्याः मातङ्गाः (गजाः) तुरङ्गाश्च तैः तरङ्गितं अङ्गनं यस्मिन् where the courtyard was surging with horses and elephants that were being examined as suitable bridal gifts. यौतक (n) is a kind of स्त्रीधन. यौतक means the gifts that are given to a woman at the time of marriage when she is seated with her husband. 'यौतकं विवाहादिकाले पत्या सहैकासने प्राप्तं युतयोर्यौतकमिति निघण्टूक्तेरिति मदनः' व्यवहारमयूख. गणने अभियुक्तः (engaged in)

गणकानां गणः तेन गृह्यमाणाः लग्नगुणाः यत्र. For लग्न see notes p. 24. A marriage was to be performed only when certain signs of the Zodiac were on the horizon and when there were no evil aspects of the planets. For example, the धर्मसिन्धु says 'त्रिषष्ठाष्टस्वर्कस्त्रिजलधनगोऽब्जः क्षितिसुतस्त्रिषष्ठस्थो शेज्यौ व्ययनिधिनवर्ज्यौ भृगुसुतः। द्वितीयाब्धीष्वङ्काभ्रतनुषु रिपुत्र्यष्टसु शनिस्तमः केतुश्चाये भवति सुखहेतुश्च सकलः॥'. This verse gives the evil aspects of the planets with the लग्न. गन्धोदकवाहिमकरमुखाः (crocodile—shaped) प्रणाल्यः (conductors Marathi पन्हळ) ताभिः पूर्यमाणः क्रीडावापीसमूहः यस्मिन्. हेमकाराणां (goldsmiths) चक्रं (समूहः) तेन प्रक्रान्तं (carried on) हाटकस्य (सुवर्णस्य) घटनं (shaping, hammering) तस्य टाङ्कारः तेन वाचालिताः अलिन्दकाः यत्र. अलिन्दकः a terrace before an outer door. उत्थापिता (constructed) अभिनवा भित्तिः तस्याः पात्यमाना बहला वालुका तस्याः कण्टकानां आलेपः तेन आकुलः आलेपकलोकः (plasterers) यस्मिन्. Read कण्टका० for कण्ठका०. चतुराणां चित्रकराणां चक्रवालं (समूहः) तेन लिख्यमानानि माङ्गल्यानि आलेख्यानि यत्र. लेप्य...वृक्षकम् where groups of clay—workers were engaged in making clay figures of fishes, tortoises, crocodiles, cocoanuts, plantain and betel trees. क्षितिपालैश्च—connect this with प्रारब्धविविधव्यापारम् four lines below. स्वय...कक्ष्यैः who girt up their own loins *i. e.* who personally engaged in physical labour. स्वामिना (प्रभाकरवर्धनेन) अर्पितानि (assigned) कर्माणि तेषां शोभा तस्याः सम्पादने आकुलैः. सिन्दू...मसृणयद्भिः who rendered glossy the pavements besmeared with red lead. विनिहिताः सरसाः आतर्पणहस्ताः येषु on which were placed sticky hand-marks of pigment for white-washing. 'आतर्पणं प्रीणने स्यान्मङ्गलालेपनेऽपि च' मेदिनी. विन्य...उत्तम्भयद्भिः who raised the pillars of the marriage (उद्वाहः) platforms, the tops of which were marked with tender mango and As'oka leaves, and which (pillars) were red with the Alaktaka dye placed on them. 'वितर्दिस्तु वेदिका' इत्यमरः. Even now mango leaves are hung up from pillars &c. as auspicious. प्रविष्टाभिः—this and the following instrumentals qualify ०सीमन्तिनीभिः below. आ सूर्योदयात् from early morn. The wives of chieftains were in the palace from the early morn engaged in various occupations. C and T translate 'from the furthest orient,' which seems far—fetched. सुवेशाभिः finely dressed. वधू...गायन्तीभिः singing auspicious (songs) pleasing to the ear (श्रुतिः) and containing in them mention of the families of the bride and bridegroom. बहु...चित्रयन्तीभिः dying neck-strings with their fingers that were smeared (आदिग्ध) with various paints (वर्णकः). चित्र...मण्डयन्तीभिः who, being clever in painting and drawing figures, decorated polished jars and groups of raw (शीतल) clayware. शालाजिर means a शराव according to हेमचन्द्र. र and ल are often interchanged in words. अभिन्न...रञ्जयन्तीभिः who reddened the threads of cotton that had not been taken out from its pod and the collections of woollen threads for making a marriage bracelet. Cotton is contained in pods. They took such cotton as had not yet been taken out of the pod, spun it into thread, which thread they dyed red. Such thread dyed red is even now required in marriage ceremonies. The Com. says 'अभिन्नपुटो वंशादिमयश्चतुष्कोणः पाटलाकृतिर्जालकैः क्रियते। तच्छिद्रान्तरपूरणाय कर्पासतूलपल्लवा रज्यन्ते'. What this means is not quite clear. It seems to mean—a square box of bamboo &c. is prepared, the interstices of which are filled in with dyed cotton thread. C and T following the Com. translate 'stained skeins of cotton thread for bamboo baskets.' The cotton and शाल्मलि both yield wool and hence the words कर्पासतूल are employed. बलाशनाघृतेन घनीकृतः कुङ्कुमकल्कः (saffron paste) तेन मिश्रिताम्. On बलाशना०, the Com. says 'बलाशना पुष्पाख्यौषधिः। तत्पक्वं घृतं रक्षार्थं क्रियते'. अङ्गरागः cosmetic. लावण्य...कल्पयन्तीभिः who were preparing unguents for the face that produced special beauty. कक्कोलम् (Marathi कंकोळ) is a kind of fragrant berry. जातीफलम् nutmeg. स्फुरन्ति स्फीतानि (abundant) स्फाटिककर्पूरशकलानि तैः खचितं अन्तरालं यासाम्. बहु...बध्यमानैः—this and the following instrumentals qualify वासोभिः (in l. 27). बहुविधानां भक्तीनां निर्माणे निपुणाः पुराणाः (old) पौरपुरन्ध्रियः (city matrons) ताभिः बध्यमानानि तैः. भक्तिः means 'texture, decoration.' बध्यमानैः बद्धैश्च many garments were in course of weaving and many were already woven. Those that were woven were dyed by रजकs. आचारे चतुराः अन्तःपुरजरत्यः ताभिः जनिता पूजा तया राजमानाः रजकाः (washermen) तैः रज्यमानैः. The old women honoured the washermen who thereupon beamed with self-complacency. उभय...शोष्यमाणैः that were waved to and fro by servants holding them by the two ends and were dried in shade. Those that were dyed were being dried. कुटिलः क्रमः यस्य तत् कुटिलक्रमं रूपं तेन क्रियमाणः पल्लवानां परभागः येषु. 'परभागः गुणोत्कर्षे' क्षीरस्वामी. Compare for परभाग, कादम्बरी उत्तरभाग (p. 267 of P) 'उपहितकान्तिपतिपरभागा लक्ष्मच्छायेव चन्द्रमसः' (श्मश्रुराजिलेखा). What the author means is not quite clear. The meaning seems to be—on the dyed and dried cloth, some paintings of the leaves of various trees were being drawn. The paintings had very great beauty (परभागः). The paintings were being drawn

ous and splendid. निधाने (treasure)—connect this and the following locatives with वर्तमाने below. यौवने...प्रीतेः it seemed as if there was a youth of prosperity and as if there was a new regime of pleasure (प्रीति). यौवराज्यम्—from युवराज—the heir-apparent. The installation of an heir-apparent is a very important function, as will appear from the रामायण. गण्यमानः—one counts with the aid of one's fingers. आलो...ध्वजैः—the unfurled banners seemed to be looking out for the arrival (of the marriage day), as a person stretches his neck and tries to descry a person coming from a distance. प्रत्यु...शब्दकैः the echoes of the drums beaten in the palace spread far and wide. The echoes went so far, the poet fancies, to receive the coming विवाहदिवस. मौहूर्तिकैः—मुहूर्तं वेद मौहूर्तिकः (astrologer). समुत्सारितः निखिलः अनिबद्धलोकः यस्मात्. अनिबद्ध—unconnected *i. e.* strangers. विविक्तम् lonely.

P. 70 ll. 16–25 **अथ...प्राहिणोत्.** शोभनः आकारः यस्य सः स्वाकारः तम्. त—object of पप्रच्छ. दर्शितः आदरः येन. कच्चित्—this is a particle indicating 'I hope.' यथाज्ञापयसि—servants were to use the verb आज्ञापय् with reference to whatever the king said or asked. आगत...ज्ञात्वा knowing him to have come to intimate the arrival of the bridegroom. यामे = प्रहरे. विवाह...दोषः (so act) that there will be no defect due to the passing away of the hour fixed for marriage. The reading of B is better, but seems to be an emendation purposely mode. प्रतीपं प्राहिणोत् sent him back.

P. 70 l. 26—**P. 71** l. 14 **अथ...ग्रहवर्मा.** The principal sentence is अथ...समवसिते वासरे...आजगाम (p. 15 l. 33)...ग्रहवर्मा. सकल...वासरे—कमलs fade in the evening. The bride's face glowed with expectation of the hour of marriage. The poet fancies that the glory of the fading कमलs was transferred to the beaming face of the bride. समवसित ended (*past. p. p.* of सो with सम् and अव). विवाह...सवितरि when the sun looked radiant like the tender feet of the Glory of the bridal day. The sun looks red when setting. The feet of handsome young ladies are red. वधूवरयोः अनुरागः तेन लघूकृतं प्रेम तेन लज्जितेषु. विघटमानेषु separating. The ruddy goose becomes separate from its mate at the close of day and is a type of abiding love. See notes p. 10. This separation is fancied to be due to the shame felt at the fact that the चक्रवाक pairs were eclipsed in love by the bride and bridegroom. सौभाग्य...रागे when the radiance of the evening looking as delicate as a red silken garment flashed in the sky as if it were the banner of marital felicity. A banner also waves in the sky and may be of red silk. रक्तांशुकस्य इव सुकुमारं वपुः यस्य; रक्तांशुकेन &c. कपोत...तिमिरे when darkness variegated like the pigeon's throat began to obscure the faces of the quarters as if it were the dust (raised) by the arrival of the bridegroom's procession. Both तिमिर and dust are dark and obscure the face. कपोत...कबुरे should be construed with तिमिर and *not* with सन्ध्यारागे, as C and T do. कर्बुर according to अमरसिंह is a synonym of कल्माष, शबल &c., 'चित्रं किर्मीरकल्माषशबलैताश्च कर्बुरे'. कर्बुर means 'dark-white' and not 'yellow'. See उत्तरराम VI. 4 'अवदग्धकर्बुरितकेतुचामरैः &c.' लग्न... सज्जे ready to effect the लग्न (the auspicious aspect of the heavenly bodies). This applies to both the stars and the astrologers. उज्जिहान *pr. p.* of हा 3 A with उद् going up, rising. ज्योतिर्गणे (1) galaxy of luminaries; (2) astrologers. A person who is सज्ज gets up. वर्धमाना धवला छाया यस्य. The round disc of the moon resembles a round मङ्गलकलश. वर्धमानेन शरावेण धवला छाया यस्य (with ०कलशे). वर्धमानः—म् saucer, a lid. Earthen pots marked with white lines are even now required in marriage ceremonies. The Com. remarks 'वर्धमानं शरावः...तद्धि मङ्गोललिप्तं विवाहे क्रियते इत्याचारः'. वधूवदनलावण्यमेव ज्योत्स्ना तया परिपीतं तमः यत्र (adj. of प्रदोषे). वृथो...वनेषु when the beds of night lotuses with their faces raised up (*i. e.* with expanding buds) as if laughed at the moon saying 'you have risen to no purpose.' The splendour of the moonlike face of the bride dispelled all the gloom of evening. As the gloom was dispelled by the beauty of the bride's face, the moon that rose in the sky had nothing left to dispel. The expanding of the buds of कुमुद is fancied to be the raising of faces by them. A person in ridiculing another also makes grimaces towards him. उल्लासित...चामरैः (*adj.* of पादातैः) that waved many flashing red chowries. उल्लासितानि स्फाराणि स्फुरितानि अरुणचामराणि यैः. उत्थितः (रागः अग्रपल्लव इव) रागाग्रपल्लवः येषाम् (with मनोरथैः); उत्थितः रागसदृशः अग्रपल्लवः येषाम् (with पादातैः). पुरो धावमानैः is common to both मनोरथैः and पादातैः. The idea is:—footmen waving red chowries ran before the bridegroom. The leaf-like red ends of the chowries were raised up. The desire of the bridegroom also ran before him. Desire had shooting from it passion (रागः). Connect पादातैः and वृन्दैः with आपूरितदिग्भागः (ग्रहवर्मा). उत्कर्णाः कटकहयाः तेषां प्रतिहेषितैः दीयमानं स्वागतं येभ्यः.

The idea is:—ग्रहवर्मा had with him troops of horses that neighed. The horses in the capital of प्रभाकरवर्धन neighed in response. This is represented as welcome offered to the horses of the son-in-law by the horses in the capital. चलानि कर्णचामराणि येषाम्. चामीकरं (सुवर्णं) तन्मयानि सर्वोपकरणानि येषाम् all whose trappings were made of gold. वर्णकलम्बिनाम्—C and T translate 'with gay housings.' वर्णकः painted cloth. करिणां...न्धकारम् with troops (घटा) of elephants, he (ग्रहवर्मा) as if made again darkness that was dissolved by the rise of the moon. Elephants are dark. नक्षत्रमालया मण्डितं मुखं यस्याः (with करिणीं and दिशम्). ग्रहवर्मा rode a female elephant whose head was decked with a necklace of 27 pearls. 'सैव नक्षत्रमाला स्यात्सप्तविंशतिमौक्तिकैः' इत्यमरः. निशा...रूढः as the moon had risen in the eastern quarter. पुरन्दर (इन्द्र) is the lord of the east, which also is decked with a line of stars (नक्षत्रमाला). See above p. 25. प्रकटितं विविधविहगानां विरुतं यैः (with ०चारणैः and उपवनैः). ताला...चारणैः क्रियमाणकोलाहलः the bards that danced to a particular time went before him and caused an uproar. बालः—ग्रहवर्मा was young. In वसन्त also the उपवनs resound with the chirping of various birds. गन्ध...लोकम् with the light of an array (चक्रवालं) of lamps, accompanied with the fragrance of perfumed oil poured on them (lamps), he rendered the whole world yellow, as if with a cloud of fragrant dust of saffron. उत्फुल्लानां मल्लिकानां (jasmine) मुण्डमाला (wreath) तस्याः मध्यं अध्यासितः कुसुमशेखरः यस्मिन् (with शिरसा). On his head he wore a wreath of jasmine, in the midst of which was a bunch of flowers. हसन्निव...प्रदोषम् he as if laughed at the moon-lit evening with its moon surrounded by a halo. सपरिवेशः क्षपाकरः यस्मिन्. The शेखर looked like the moon and the white wreath like halo. आत्मरूपेण निर्जितः (vanquished) मकरकेतुः (मदनः) तस्य करात् अपहृतेन. विरचितः वैकक्ष्यविलासः यस्य. वैकक्ष्यम् a garland worn over the left shoulder and under the right arm (like यज्ञोपवीत); hence a mantle. ग्रहवर्मा wore as an ornament a string of flowers on the left shoulder and under the other arm. He was more handsome than मदन. The bow of Cupid is flowery. A bow is also worn on the shoulder. By vanquishing मदन, ग्रहवर्मा took from his hand his flowery bow and wore it as a वैकक्ष्यक. The word कर suggests another meaning. One who is conquered has to offer tribute. कुसुमसौरभगर्वेण भ्रान्तं भ्रमरकुलं तस्य कलः प्रलापः तेन सुभगः (applies to both ग्रहवर्मा and पारिजात). As he had a garland of flowers bees hovered round him; they must have done so round पारिजात. पारिजात is one of the five trees of Paradise and was one of the 14 jewels churned out of the ocean. जातः श्रिया सह—ग्रहवर्मा had royal splendour from birth; पारिजात was produced (from the ocean) along with लक्ष्मी. पुन...मेदिनीम्—पारिजात was taken to Heaven when churned out and hence the words पुनः &c. नव...हृदयः—His heart was drawn by the curiosity to see the bride's face. One whose हृदय (*i. e.* the upper part of the body) is drawn forward may fall on his face. प्रत्यासन्नं (near) लग्नं यस्य. 'राशीनामुदयो लग्नम्' इत्यमरः.

P. 71 ll. 15-28 **राजा तु...प्रविवेश.** द्वारस्य समीपे उपद्वारम् (अव्ययीभाव). माधवः=वैशाखः (वसन्तः). यथाक्रमम्—ग्रहवर्मा embraced राज्यवर्धन first as the elder of the two. नृपतेः प्रणयी a favourite of the king. तात is often used as a term of address applied affectionately to any person, usually by a friend to a friend or by elderly persons to youngsters. राज्यश्रिया—(1) by राज्यश्री; (2) by royal glory. घटितौ goes with ०मुखरवंशौ. It was राज्यश्री who being married to ग्रहवर्मा brought about an alliance of the families of पुष्पभूति and मुखर. तेजोमयौ—applies to both सोम० and पुष्प०. सकलजगता गीयमानः बुधकर्णयोः आनन्दकारी गुणगणः ययोः—(1) whose many qualities, gratifying the ears of wise men, are sung by the whole world (with पुष्प०); (2) in which the many gratifying virtues of Mercury (बुध) and Karṇa are sung by the whole world (with सोम०). There is a further pun on the word गुण which also means 'threads, fibres' and वंश (bamboo). बुध was the son of the moon and कर्ण was the son of कुन्ती from the sun. सोम seduced तारा wife of बृहस्पति and did not give her back. Brahmâ returned Tārā to बृहस्पति. तारा was pregnant and at the command of बृ० discharged the गर्भ upon reeds. Both इन्दु and गुरु wanted the son. The gods asked तारा whose son he was, but she spoke nothing through shame. The new-born got angry, but ब्रह्मा intervened and drew from तारा the admission that he was the son of सोम, who said 'साधु साधु वत्स प्राज्ञोऽसीति बुध इति नाम चक्रे'. See विष्णु० IV. 6. The birth of कर्ण from कुन्ती when she was a maiden is well-known. आदिपर्व 64. 140 'सूर्याच्च कुन्तिकन्यायां जज्ञे कर्णो महाबलः। सहजं कवचं बिभ्रत्कुण्डलोद्द्योतिताननः॥' (Kumbha. ed). प्रथममेव...देवस्य—the qualities of ग्रहवर्मा had already made a great impression on the heart of प्रभाकरवर्धन. The कौस्तुभ, one of the fourteen jewels churned from the ocean, is worn on his chest (हृदय) by Vishṇu. 'कौस्तुभाख्यमभूद्रत्नं पद्मरागो महोदधेः। तस्मिन्हरिः स्पृहां चक्रे वक्षोऽलङ्करणे मणौ॥' भागवत VIII. The word is derived as 'कुं भुवं स्तुभ्नाति

व्याप्नोति इति कुस्तुभः समुद्रः तत्र भवः'. इदानीम्—now *i. e.* as a bridegroom. परमेश्वरेण = (1) शिवेन; (2) प्रभाकरवर्धनेन. Emperors had the titles परमेश्वर, महाराजाधिराज. See Introduction. S'iva has the moon on his head. A bridegroom is to be honoured by the father-in-law. समा...वेला the auspicious time (fixed for the marriage ceremony) approaches. कौतुकगृहम्—the house where the marriage thread (कौतुकं) is placed on the wrist of the bridegroom before the actual marriage ceremonies. Compare रघु० 8. 1. 'अथ तस्य विवाहकौतुकं ललितं बिभ्रत एव'. पतितानि—the eyes of women fell on him. The blue eyes resemble expanded blue lotuses. लङ्घयन् traversing, jumping over (the lotuses in the form of eyes).

P. 71 l. 29—**P. 72** l. 9 **अथ तत्र...पश्यत्.** The principal sentence is अथ तत्र...वधूमपश्यत्. कति...परिवाराम्—this and the following accusatives qualify वधूम्. कति...वाराम् who was attended by several relatives (आप्त), dear friends and her own people (*i. e.* servants), mostly women. अरुणं अंशुकं तेन अवगुण्ठितं मुखं यस्याः—whose face was veiled by a red silken cloth. The radiance of her face made the lamps pale before her. The radiant glow of morn also makes the lamps appear dim. अरुणः अंशुकमिव तेन अवगुण्ठितं मुखं यस्याः (प्रभातसन्ध्या)—the beginning of which is covered by Aruṇa that resembles a red silken garment. Or we may dissolve अरुणस्य अंशुकाः किरणाः &c. अति...गूढाम् The idea is that she was not a grown-up woman, but was almost a girl. A delicate substance if closely pressed may break. यौवन is fancied as afraid of hurting her by too close an embrace, as she was so delicate. साध्वसेन (भयेन) निरुध्यमानः (restrained) हृदयदेशः तस्मात् दुःखेन मुक्तैः—The sudden events of her marriage caused her heart to flutter and therefore she heaved sighs by way of relieving the pressure. निभृतायतैः secret and long. She tried to keep her emotion to herself. One who sorrows over anything heaves deep sighs. The sighs which she heaved for relief are fancied to be due to her lamenting her maidenhood that was leaving her. अत्युत्कम्पिनीं...धार्यमाणाम्—her heart was in a whirl of emotions; but she was kept motionless by bashfulness, as if through fear of her falling down. One who is trembling (in body) has to be supported (धार्यमाण) for fear of a fall. हस्तम् and शशिनम् are to be connected with अवलोकयन्तीम् (she was looking at her hand vacantly being absorbed in deep thought). ताम...पक्षं which was the rival of a red lotus *i. e.* her hand was red.

आसन्नं ग्रहणं यस्य the grasping of which (in marriage) was near ताम...पक्षम् (the moon) who is the enemy of red lotuses. आसन्नं ग्रहणं यस्य whose seizure (by Rāhu *i. e.* eclipse) was near. रोहिणी the favourite wife of the moon out of the 27 नक्षत्रs. भय...साम् —applies to both रोहिणी and वधू. रोहिणी would tremble at the approaching eclipse of her lord. चन्दनेन धवला तनुलता यस्याः. ज्योत्स्नादानेन सञ्चितं लावण्यं यस्य loveliness of which is accumulated by the gift of moonlight. कुमुद्s thrive in moonlight. The inside of the कुमुदिनी would be white. कुसु...हारिणीम्—she (वधू) was spreading about the perfume of flowers. वसन्त is the season of flowers. निःश्वासपरिमलेन आकृष्टं मधुकरकुलं यया. Her fragrant breath drew round her a swarm of bees. मलयमारुत- the breezes from the Malaya Mountain are charged with the perfume of sandal. कृत...सरणाम् (1) who did what Love dictated (with वधूम्); (2) who was followed by Cupid *i. e.* मदन acted as his wife रति dictated; कृतं कन्दर्पेण अनुसरणं यस्याः (with रतिम्). The bride was as handsome and loving as रति, the wife of मदन. C and T translate 'love followed in the train of one who seemed a reborn Rati.' This is not correct. प्रभा...माधुर्यैः—these five are to be connected respectively with the five *Ratnas* 'कौस्तुभ...मृत.' अपरा...श्रियम् she was as if another श्री (लक्ष्मी) formed by the ocean out of wrath against the gods and demons. The author here mentions six out of the fourteen रत्नs churned out of the ocean. There is an emphasis on the word श्री. राज्यश्री can naturally be called श्री. अपराम्—this word is used because there was one already produced at the churning. The ocean, being a mine of jewels, can produce fresh ones though fourteen were already taken away by the gods and demons. The anger of the ocean is due to his being deprived of the *Ratnas*. स्निग्धेन...तंसाम् affectionate young maids (बालिका + लोक) made for her an ear-ornament with the rays of pearls as if with clusters of white सिन्धुवार flowers. सिन्धु- (न्दु) वार is a plant called in Marathi निगडी. स्निग्धेन...लोकेन may also mean 'by the glossy soft light' (०आलोकेन). कर्णाभरणमरकतस्य प्रभा हरितशाद्वलं इव; ०मरकतप्रभासदृशं हरितशाद्वलम्. कर्णा...च्छायाम् who as if removed (*i. e.* rendered imperceptible) the lovely (हारिणी) beauty of her eyes by her broad cheeks on which there fell the lustre of the emerald of her ear-ornament, resembling a green meadow. स्थली means a plot of ground. हारिणीं =हरिणसम्बन्धिनीम्. So the words suggest another sense 'who entertained the eyes of deer with a plot of ground covered with green grass' (resembling emerald). अधोमुखीं—through bashfulness she hung her head. कृतः मुखोन्नमनप्रयत्नः येन—her friends tried to raise her face; in her heart also she wished to raise her face (to see the bridegroom). वर...कुलम् her friends were absorbed in looking at the wonderful bridegroom; her heart fluttered to look &c. हृदयं निर्भर्त्सयन्तीम् she censured her heart for its cowardice in not succeeding in raising her face to see the bridegroom, though she so much desired to raise it.

P. 72 ll. 10--23 **प्रविशन्त...विभावसुः.** वध्वा समर्पितम् handed over (to cupid) by the bride. जग्राह कन्दर्पः Cupid seized him *i. e.* he became enamoured of the bride. A thief is handed over to proper custody and is held fast by the custodian. परिहासेन स्मेराणि (smiling) मुखानि यासाम्. अतिपेशलम् very cleverly. कृतः परिणयस्य (विवाहस्य) अनुरूपः वेशपरिग्रहः यया. जगाम—connect this with वेदीम्. ०धवलाम् and the following clauses in the accusative qualify वेदीम्. नव...धवलाम् (1) brilliant with fresh white-wash; (2) white like fresh chunam (with उपत्यकाम्). सुधा may, in the latter case, also mean 'nectar', which is also white. तुषारशैलस्य हिमालयस्य उपत्यका a land at the foot of a mountain. 'उपाधिभ्यां त्यकन्नासन्नारूढयोः' पा. 5. 2. 34 (संज्ञायामित्यनुवर्तते । पर्वतस्यासन्नं स्थलमुपत्यका आरूढं स्थलमधित्यका । सि. कौ.). भूभृद्भिः (1) by kings; (2) by mountains. सेक...दन्तुरैः that bristled with barley shoots that looked soft on account of the sprinkling of water. पञ्चास्यैः with five mouths. कोम...चित्रैः variegated with soft colours. अमित्रमुखैः—C and T translate 'gleaming around it were earthen dolls, whose hands bore auspicious fruits, and which had five-mouthed cups bristling with dew-besprent blades of barley and enemies' faces painted with soft colours.' So they think that the कलशs were in the hands of dolls. But one fails to see how the sentence yields this sense. We must connect कलशैः with उद्भासितपर्यन्ताम्. अमित्रमुखैः should be taken as an adjective of कलशैः (अमित्राः शत्रवः मुखे येषाम्). The idea seems to be this:—there were कलशs with barley blades that resembled दन्तs, the कलशs had a lion's shape, they were painted in various colours; hence the whole presented an awful aspect, so that the कलशs seemed to have some terrible enemies in them. अञ्जलिकारिका—a clay doll. 'स्यात्सालभञ्जिका स्तम्भे लेप्येनाञ्जलिकारिका' इति क्षीरस्वामी. C reads अमत्रमुखैः which means 'that had the mouth of a goblet'. This seems to be a suspicious reading adopted to obviate the difficulties of अमित्रमुखैः. उपाध्यायेन उपधीयमानानि (heaped, placed) इन्धनानि तेन धूमायमानः अग्निः तस्य सन्धुक्षणे (kindling) अक्षणिका

उपद्रष्टृद्विजाः यस्याम् (adj. of वेदीम्). उपद्रष्टृ means 'one who supervises.' अक्षणिक not having leisure, busy. कृशानोः (अग्नेः) समीपे इति उपकृशानु निहिताः अनुपहताः (new, not used) हरितकुशाः यस्याम्. संनिहितः दृषदां अजिनानां आज्यस्य स्रुचां (ladles) समित्पूलीनां (bundles of fuel sticks) निवहः यस्याम्. C reads स्रक् (garland) for स्रुक्; but it is not very appropriate in the context. नूतनशूर्पे अर्पिताः श्यामलशमीपलाशमिश्रिताः लाजाः (fried grain) तैः हसतीति हासिनीम्. The लाजs being white are spoken of as the हास of the वेदी. शमी is a sacred tree. पलाशं leaf. See रघुवंश VII. 26 'हविःशमीपल्लवलाजगन्धी पुण्यः कृशानोरुदियाय धूमः।'. कात्यायन says 'शमीपल्लवमिश्राँल्लाजानञ्जलिना वपति'. शूर्पः—र्पम् winnowing basket (Marathi सूप). सज्योत्स्नः—राज्यश्री resembled the light of the moon. See धर्मसिन्धु 'वधूवरौ पूर्वोक्तलक्षणां वेदीं मन्त्रघोषेणारुह्य &c.' समुत्ससर्प—connect this with 'शिखिनः (अग्नेः) समीपम्.' वेल्लिता...ल्लवस्य the red leaf-like flames of which were tremulous (with fire); the red flame-like leaves of which were tremulous (with रक्ताशोक). शिखिनः also may be applied to रक्ताशोक (it had a tapering foliage). कुसुमायुधः (कुसुमानि आयुधानि यस्य) इव—ग्रहवर्मा was handsome like मदन and राज्यश्री was like रति. रक्ताशोक is an excitant of love. In this sentence as well as in the preceding (आरुरोह तां दिवमिव), the author perhaps intentionally indicates the untimely death of ग्रहवर्मा. दक्षि...वृत्ताभिः that moved round to the right. Flames moving to the right are a good omen. ज्वालाभिरेव समं—the idea is :—the flames moved about; he also moved round the fire. नखमयूखैः धवलिता तनुः यस्य. When the bride let fall the oblation of parched grain into the fire from her hands, her brilliant nails brightened the fire. अदृष्टपूर्वं वधूवरयोः रूपं तेन विस्मयः तेन स्मेरः. Smile is white according to the poets; the brilliance of the nails transferred to the fire is the smile and the white लाजs are the teeth shown in smiling. For going round the fire and लाजहोम, see कुमारसम्भव VII. 80 'तौ दम्पती त्रिः परिणीय वह्निमन्योन्यसंस्पर्शनिमीलिताक्षौ । स कारयामास वधूं पुरोधास्तस्मिन्समिद्धार्चिषि लाजमोक्षम् ॥.' The आश्वलायनगृह्यसूत्र says 'वध्वञ्जला उपस्तीर्य भ्राता भ्रातृस्थानीयो वा द्विर्लाजानावपति' (I. 701). मेधातिथि on मनु॰ VIII. 227 remarks 'लाजहोममभिनिर्वर्त्य त्रिः प्रदक्षिणमग्निमावर्त्य सप्त पदानि स्त्री प्रक्रम्यते'.

P. 72 l. 24—**P. 73** l. 2 **अत्रान्तरे...वासगृहम्**. रुरोद वधूः—the bride wept because she was soon to be separated from her parents. स्वच्छ...यन्ती as if quenching the image of fire reflected inside her bright cheeks. स्थूलमुक्ताफलवत् विमलाः बाष्पबिन्दवः तेषां सन्दोहः (assemblage) तेन दर्शितं दुर्दिनं यया. दुर्दिनम् a rainy day. 'मेघच्छन्नेऽह्नि दुर्दिनम्' इत्यमरः. निर्वेदनविकारम् without showing any emotion on her face. उदश्रु विलोचनं यासाम्. प्रविवेश—connect with वासगृहम्. द्वारपक्षे लिखितं रतिप्रीतिदैवतं यस्मिन् on the side of the door of which was painted Rati, the presiding spirit of Love. प्रणयि... कुलैः—the bees, drawn by the perfume of flowers, entered the वासगृह before ग्रहवर्मा and looked like his friends. अलि...काशितम्—the idea is:—the lamps began to flicker owing to the breezes set in motion by the bees; the poet fancies that they trembled because they were afraid of being struck with the कर्णोत्पल (by राज्यश्री in order to put them out). एकदेशे लिखितः स्तबकितः (having bunches of flowers) रक्ताशोकतरुः तस्य तलं भजतीति ०भाक् तेन ०भाजा. अधिज्यचापेन whose bow was strung. तिर्यक्कूणितः नेत्रत्रिभागः यस्य a third part of whose eye was obliquely contracted. Cupid is represented as having a squint eye to symbolize the fact that love is generally blind. काञ्चनाचामरुकेण is not quite clear. We should read 'काञ्चनाचामनकेन' (काञ्चन+आचामनकेन)—a golden spitting vessel. This latter is really the reading of B, as the MSS often confound च and व. Read दन्त० for दान्त०. इतर... सनाथेन (शयनेन) bed that had on the other side a golden figure holding an ivory box, like Lakshmī herself having in her hand a lotus with a long stalk. The white ivory box resembled the white lotus and the golden figure was like लक्ष्मी. सोपधानेन with a pillow. स्वास्तीर्ण well covered with coverlets. कृता कुमुदैः कुमुदानां वा शोभा यस्य येन वा (1) that was decked with white lilies; (2) that gave beauty to the कुमुदs (with शशिना). The moon is the friend of love. See कुमारसम्भव IV. 13. राजतेन made of silver (and hence compared to the moon). निद्राकलशेन—auspicious jars were placed near the bed to ward off evil and to induce sleep. Compare कादम्बरी 'क्रमेण चोद्गते गगनमहापयोधिपुलिने सप्तलोकमङ्गलनिद्राकलशे कुमुदबान्धवे' (p. 178 of P.)

P. 73 ll. 3–9 तत्र च...गमदिति. प्रथमा...गवाक्षकेषु as if they were the faces of the family goddesses, (seen) in the jewelled lattice-windows, that had come out of curiosity to overhear the first words (of the bride and bridegroom). क्षणदाम्=निशाम्. अपुनरुक्तानि that were not monotonous. दत्त्वा...रणरणकम्—A door-keeper is always in attendance in a राजकुल; when ग्रहवर्मा went away, he left behind regret (in the heart of the members of the palace) at his departure. यौतक...लोकस्य taking with him the hearts of all people as the provisions for his journey offered to him as marriage gift. For यौतक, see above p. 52. शम्बलः—लम् पथिव्ययः (पाथेयम्). इति—shows the end of the उच्छ्वास.

४

Uchchhvāsa V

P. 74 Verse 1 नियतिः fate. Construe तरला नियतिः (विधिः) प्रथमं पुंसां सुखं विधाय उपरि (afterwards) दारुणं दुःखं निपातयति तरला (चञ्चला) तडित् (विद्युत्) इव आलोकं (light, flash) कृत्वा वज्रं निपातयति. This and the following verse are in the Āryā metre, for which see above p. 49. Both verses are suggestive of the misfortunes narrated in this Uchchhvāsa. Compare for the idea 'सुहृदिव प्रकटय्य सुखप्रदः प्रथममेकरसामनुकूलताम् । पुनरकाण्डविवर्तनदारुणो विधिरहो विशिनष्टि मनोरुजम् ॥' उत्तरराम० IV. 15.

Verse 2 सममेव—at one and the same time. अनादरेणैव without any qualm or regard. परिवर्तमानः revolving. अनन्तः—Time is without end. शैलान् परिवर्तमानः अनन्त इव (पातयति) as the serpent Ananta, moving (his hoods), makes the mountains fall. 'नागाः काद्रवेयास्तदीश्वरः । **शेषोऽनन्तः**' इत्यमरः. शेष has one thousand hoods, on which the earth is supposed to rest. It was believed that earthquakes occurred when शेष moved its hoods through weariness. See विष्णु० II. 5. 28 'यदा विजृम्भतेऽनन्तो मदाघूर्णितलोचनः । तदा चलति भूरेषा साद्रितोया सकानना ॥'.

P. 74 ll. 5–26 **अथ...तस्थौ.** राजा = प्रभाकरवर्धनः. कवचहरम्—of an age when he was fit to wear armour. कवचं हरतीति (affix अच्), acccording to 'वयसि च' पा. 3. 2. 10 (कवचहरः कुमारः । सि. कौ.). हूणान्—see p. 4 (notes). हरिः = सिंहः. प्रभाकर० is compared to the lion, राज्यवर्धन to a whelp and the Hūṇas to deer. चिरं...सारम् making him attended by advisers of long standing and devoted feudatories. अभिसारः companion, follower. अभिसारेण सह सा०. उत्तरापथम्—to the north. This word is used in contradistinction to दक्षिणापथ. Here उत्तरापथ seems to stand for the Punjab and Kashmir, countries towards the north of Thanesar. But generally the word stands for northern India. *Vide* Introduction for the inscriptions of Pulikes'in, where हर्ष himself is styled the lord of उत्तरापथ. कतिचित्प्रयाणकानि for some marches *i. e.* stages. प्रविष्टे...भ्रातरि when his brother entered the region (ककुभ् *f.*) resplendent with the brilliance of कैलास. कैलास is one of the peaks of the Himālayas. निवर्तमानः (the reading of B) does not suit the words नवे वयसि that follow. विक्रम...रोधिनि (youth) that follows (acts according to) its liking for adventure. शरभ is a fabulous animal with eight legs and believed to be stronger than the lion. तुषारशैलस्य हिमाचलस्य उपकण्ठेषु

(confines, outskirts). उत्कण्ठमानाः वनदेवताः तासां कटाक्षाः तेषां अंशवः (किरणाः, प्रभा) तैः शारिता (variegated) शरीरकान्तिः यस्य. The nymphs of the forests were smitten by the handsome form of Harsha and cast glances at him. The dark pupils and the white of their eyes shed a dappled hue on his body. The word उत्कण्ठमान may also convey the idea that the वनदेवताs were anxious for the safety of the beasts of the forest. बहिरेव व्यलम्बत he tarried outside (the region of कैलास). C and T translate as 'away from camp'. आकर्णान्तं आकृष्टं कार्मुकं तस्मात् निर्गताः भासुराः (bright) भल्लाः तान् वर्षतीति ०वर्षी. कर्मणे प्रभवतीति कार्मुकम् according to 'कर्मण उकञ्' पा० 5. 1. 103. भल्लः a crescent-shaped arrow. वास... यामे in the fourth watch of the night. वासतेयी—'पथ्यतिथिवसतिस्वपतेर्ढञ्' पा. 4. 4. 104 (पथि साधु पाथेयम् । आतिथेयम् । वसनं वसतिस्तत्र साधुः वासतेयी रात्रिः । सि. कौ.). It is believed that dreams seen in the small hours of the morning come to be true. चटुलानां (flickering) ज्वालानां पुञ्जेन पिञ्जरीकृताः (reddened) सकलककुभः येन (*adj.* of ०हुतभुजा). दवहुतभुजा = दवदहनेन forest conflagration. The death of the lion and his mate suggest the death of Harsha's father and mother. यदाकृष्टाः—यत् refers to स्नेहमयाः ०पाशाः. तिर्यञ्चः अपि even lower animals. Compare for the idea 'दारुभेदनिपुणोऽपि षडङ्घ्रिर्निष्क्रियो भवति पङ्कजबद्धः । बन्धनानि किल सन्ति बहूनि स्नेहरज्जुकृतबन्धनमन्यत् ॥'. दक्षिणात् इतरत्. The throbbing of the left eye in the case of men portends misfortune. विपप्रथे spread over. निर्निमित्तम् without any cause. अन्त...हृदयम् his heart as if went adrift (*lit.* moved) from its internal fastenings. गरीयसी very great (*f.* comparative of गुरु). दुःखासिका poignant despondency (दुःखं असिका इव). समुत्पन्नाः विविधाः विकल्पाः (doubts) तैः विमथिता मतिः यस्य. अपगता धृतिः (steadiness, composure) यस्य. स्तिमिता fixed, motionless) तारका यस्य. समुद्भिद्यमानं (shooting up) कमलिनीवनं (lotus-bed) यस्याम् (*adj.* of क्षौणीम्). He bent his lotus-like face in anxiety and looked fixedly on the ground. The poet fancies that his face was a lotus shooting forth from the earth (क्षौणी). चकोरेक्षणः—The eyes of a चकोर are red. Note कादम्बरी 'जरच्चकोरलोचनपुटपाटलकान्तिना' (p. 140 of P). Redness of the (corner of the) eye in men and women is a sign of beauty. आ...ह्नो when the sun had ascended to midday. हरिताः (greenish yellow) हयाः यस्य. The sun is called हरिदश्व. संवाह्यमानं तनु (small) तालवृन्तं (fan) यस्य. विततम् spread. अतिशिशिरः मलयजस्य (चन्दनस्य) रसः तस्य लवेन लुलितं (touched) वपुः (frame) यस्याः (*adj.* of पट्टिकाम्). इन्दुवत् धवलं उपधानं (pillow) धारयतीति. वेत्रपट्टिका cane couch.

P. 74 l. 27—**P. 75** l. 8 **अथ...द्राक्षीत्.** The principal sentence is अथ दूरादेव...०दीर्घाध्वगं कुरङ्गकनामानं आयान्तं अद्राक्षीत्. लेखः गर्भे यस्याः. नीलीरागेण (indigo colour) मेचका (blue) रुक् (कान्तिः) यस्याः. चैल...मालकम् whose head was encircled by the hems of a garment. The messenger carried the letter in a piece of cloth which he wrapped round his head. This is the practice of illiterate messengers even now. The reading of A 'चीरचीरिकया' would suggest that he wore rags on his head. This would be too much for a royal messenger. C and T suggest that the colour symbolizes the bad news. This may be so; or it was probably his uniform. आरोप्यमाणः कायकालिमा यस्य. कालिमन् *m.* (काल + affix इमन्) is formed according to 'पृथ्वादिभ्य इमनिज्वा' 'वर्णदृढादिभ्यः ष्यञ्च' पा. 5. 1. 122–123 (चादिमनिच्। शौक्ल्यम्, शुक्लिमा। सि. कौ.). शोकः...नीयमानम्—the poet fancies that the darkness of body due to fatigue and exposure to the sun is due to the fact that he was being reduced to charcoal by the fire of sorrow. अति...गम्यमानम्—on his body there was dust raised by his rapid walking; the poet fancies that under the guise of dust it was the earth that followed him to learn the news about the king, her lord. अभिमुखः (beating on his face) पवनः तेन प्रेङ्खन् (waving about) प्रविततः (spread) उत्तरीयपटः तस्य प्रान्तेन (hems) वीज्यमानौ उभयपार्श्वौ यस्य. अति...पतन्तम् who approached quickly, having as if winged himself because he was in a great hurry. His upper garment waved about his flanks owing to the strong breeze blowing in his face and thus he looked as if he was winged. प्रेर्य...देशेन—The poet fancies that the quick pace of the messenger was due to the fact that he was urged from behind by his master's command. स्विद्यत् ललाटतटं तस्मिन् घटमानं (being formed) प्रतिबिम्बं यस्य (*adj.* of भास्वता). क may optionally be added at the end of all बहुव्रीहि compounds. कार्य...भास्वता whose letter was if snatched by the sun out of curiosity to know the business (on which he was sent). संभ्रम... शरीरम्—His senses were not working normally; his only thought was to walk quickly; the poet fancies that he left them behind in his haste to depart. गौरव (1) Importance; (2) weight. One who has a large weight on his head may stumble. समेऽपि वर्त्मनि on an even road (without ups and downs). काल... वज्रस्य—The idea is:—first a cloud rises in the sky and then the thunderbolt falls; so the messenger (who was also dark like the cloud owing to fatigue and exposure) appeared first and would afterwards disclose the bad news. धूम...ज्वलनस्य—Before fire is kindled, there is a cloud of smoke, which is dark; the messenger also was dark and was in a short time to kindle the fire of sorrow in हर्ष. बीज...शाले: he was as if the paddy seed of sin that was about to bear friut. There are some varieties of paddy seed that are dark. अनि...ध्वर्गम् a messenger that had become an evil omen.

P. 75 ll. 9–18 **दृष्ट्वा...प्रावर्तत.** पूर्वनिमित्तपरम्पराभिः आविर्भाविता भातः यस्य. The reference is to his dream narrated on p. 19 of the text. प्रथम...लेखम् he first presented the dejection reigning (*lit.* sticking to) in his looks and then the letter. The idea is that before he presented the letter, his face told the whole tale. लेखा...सन्तापम्—there is a pun on the word गृहीत्वा, the idea being that he understood the contents of the letter and at the same time his heart was seized by affliction. अवग्रहरूपः—who was drought incarnate. This is not a very appropriate word. The reading 'आविग्नरूपः' of one of the MSS of B is good. It means 'whose face was dejected.' किं मान्द्यम् what is the illness ? खञ्जाक्षरैः क्षरद्भिः with halting words that flowed from him. युगपत्—the idea is:—his eye, his tears, face and faltering voice, all conveyed the same tale. पफाल *perfect* of फल् to burst. कृतं आचमनं येन. Before beginning religious ceremonies, before and after meals and before and after doing many other acts, it was enjoined that a man should sip water. 'स्नात्वा पीत्वा क्षुते सुप्ते भुक्त्वा रथ्योपसर्पणे। आचान्तः पुनराचामेद्वासो विपरिधाय च ॥' याज्ञ. I. 196. जन...ष्कामः desiring the long life of his father. परिबर्हः royal insignia, property. 'परिच्छदे नृपार्हेऽर्थे परिबर्हः' इत्यमरः. अभुक्तः एव who had not taken food. दापय...र्याणम् put the saddle on the horses. शिरःकृपाणम् a sword against his own forehead (by way of saluting). This is the object of बिभ्राणं, which qualifies युवानम्. परिवर्धकः groom. प्रावर्तत he started to go.

P. 75 ll. 19–32 **अकाण्ड...निशाम्.** अकाण्ड...क्षुभितं excited (startled) by the sudden (blowing of the) conch, which was the signal for a march. उद्भूतः मुखरः खुररवः तेन भरितं सकलभुवनविवरं येन (*adj.* of अश्वीयम्)—that filled all the world with the resonant tramp of the horses' hoofs. अश्वीयम्—अश्वानां समूहः—(cavalry) according to 'केशाश्वाभ्यां यञ्छावन्यतरस्याम्' पा. 4. 2. 48 (पक्षे ठगणौ। कैश्यम्, कैशिकम्। अश्वीयम्, आश्वम्। सि. कौ.). ढौकृ *1st A* to approach. प्रद...यान्तः going in the direction opposite the right one. प्रदक्षिणं means 'towards the right side, so that the right side is always

ing the Vampire by being ready to bring an offering of a skull. द्रविड included the tract of the country from the Tungabhadrā to the Coromandel coast and had काञ्ची as its capital. On आमर्दक the Com. says 'आमर्दको वेतालो रौद्रदेवताभेद इत्यन्ये'. बाण refers to the offerings of skulls to चण्डिका, who was worshipped by an old द्रविडधार्मिक 'फलितामिव मुण्डमण्डलैरुपहारहिंसां दर्शयन्तीम्' (p. 224 of P). आन्ध्रेण उद्ध्रियमाणः बाहुवप्रः तेन उपयाच्यमाना चण्डिका (दुर्गा यत्र) where Chaṇḍikā was being promised a present with his rampart-like arm raised up by a person from the Andhra country. बाहुः वप्रः इव. अन्ध्र corresponds pretty closely with modern Telingana and lay between the mouths of the गोदावरी and the कृष्णा. उपयाचनं is the same as नवस (in Marathi). शिरसि विधृतः विलीयमानः (melting) गुग्गुलुः (a kind of fragrant gum resin, गुग्गुळ in Marathi) तेन विकलाः नवसेवकाः तैः अनुनीयमानः महाकालः यस्मिन्. महाकाल is a name of शिव in his character as destroyer of the world. There is an emphasis on the words विकल and नव. Old servants would have gone through anything for the king without showing the least sign of pain; but new servants felt distressed even when hot gum slightly scorched their heads. निशिता शस्त्री (knife) तया निकृत्तं (cut off) आत्ममांसं तस्य होमे प्रसक्तः (engaged in) आप्तवर्गः यस्मिन्. प्रकाशं (openly) नरपतिकुमारकैः क्रियमाणः महामांसविक्रयस्य प्रक्रमः (beginning) यत्र. महामांसं human flesh. The शाक्त rites prescribed the offering of such horrible things. 'अष्टम्यां रुधिरैर्मांसैर्महामांसैः सुगन्धिभिः। पूजयेद्बहुजातीयैर्बलिभिर्भोजनैः शिवाम्॥' शब्द०. It was believed that by resorting to such disgusting rites a person would attain miraculous powers or objects otherwise difficult to secure. महामांस was offered to पिशाचs also who, it was believed, would become the helpers of the man offering it in anything. See मालतीमाधव V. 12 and the comment of जगद्धर thereon. यातु...ध्वस्तम् as if rendered desolate by fiends. 'यातूनि यातनाः धीयन्ते अस्मिन्' क्षीरस्वामी on 'यातुधानः पुण्यजनो नैर्ऋतो यातुरक्षसी' इत्यमरः. कवलित devoured. अधर्म...लुण्ठितम् as if plundered by the movements of unrighteousness. अनित्यतया धिक्कारः. अनि...क्रान्तम् overpowered by the slights (heaped on it) by transitoriness. Everybody felt the transitoriness of human existence. नि...कृतम् that was subdued by the workings of fate. विलक्षितम् bewildered. छलितम् cheated. प्रविश...ददर्श—the principal sentence is प्रविशन् एव विपणिवर्त्मनि (on the market-street) परलोकव्यतिकरं कथयन्तं ०पट्टिकं ददर्श. कुतूहलेन आकुलाः बहलाः बालकाः तैः परिवृतम् (*adj.* of ०पट्टिकं). ऊर्ध्वे...तते stretched out on a support (विष्कम्भः) of upright rods.

प्रेतनाथः = यमः. व्यतिकरम् incidents. इतर...कलितेन held in the other hand. In the left hand was the painted canvas and in the right a reed. शरकाण्ड: reed-stalk. यमपट्टिकं—see above p. 45 (notes).

P. 76 l. 21—**P. 77** l. 10 **तेन...कक्ष्यान्तरम्.** तेन = श्लोकेन. प्रतिषिद्धः सकललोकप्रवेशः यस्मिन्. अप्रसन्नः मुखरागः यस्य who had a dejected look (*lit.* the colour of whose face was not clear). उन्मु...द्रियैः who was as if left by his senses. अस्ति...न वा does father feel better to-day or not? यदि भवेत् there may be. मन्दं...विवेश—the principal sentence is मन्दं मन्दं...राजकुलं विवेश. ०सर्वस्वम्—this and the following clauses qualify राजकुलम्. प्रारब्धा अमृतचरुपचनक्रिया यत्र. चरुः is an oblation of rice or barley boiled for presentation to the gods. अमृतचरु perhaps means that milk or ghee was poured over it. क्रियमाणः षडाहुतिहोमः यस्मिन्. The Com. explains "'प्रजापतये स्वाहा' इति षण्णां देवतानां नाम गृहीत्वा षण्णामेवाहुतीनां प्रक्षेपः षडाहुतिहोम उच्यते." The six देवताs appear to be प्रजापति, सोम, अग्नि, इन्द्र, द्यावापृथिवी and धन्वन्तरि. हूयमानाः पृषदाज्यलवेन लिप्ताः प्रचलाः दूर्वापल्लवाः यस्मिन्. पृषदाज्यम्—Ghee mixed with coagulated milk. 'पृषदाज्यं सदध्याज्ये' इत्यमरः (पृषद्भिः दधिबिन्दुभिः सहितमाज्यम्' क्षीरस्वामी). पठ्य...विधानम्—this is a curious compound. It contains three separate elements. पठ्यमाना महामायूरी यस्मिन्, प्रवर्त्यमाना (begun) गृहशान्तिः यस्मिन्, निर्वर्त्यमानं भूतरक्षाबलिविधानं यस्मिन् (where the offering of oblations for protection against evil spirits was being performed). What the author refers to as महामायूरी is not quite clear. From the context it seems to be a prayer. Among the Buddhists महामायूरी is the name of one of the five amulets and of one of the five tutelary goddesses. शान्ति means 'a propitiatory rite for averting calamity.' प्रयतैः पवित्रैः विप्रैः प्रस्तुतः (begun) संहिताजपः यस्मिन्—holy Brahmins had begun the recitation in a low voice of the Saṃhitā text of the Vedas. This is the practice even now. 'पवित्रः प्रयतः पूतः' इत्यमरः. जप्यमाना रुद्रैकादशी तया शब्दायमानं शिवगृहं यत्र where the temple of S'iva resounded with the low repetition of the hymn to Rudra. The reference seems to be to what is popularly known as रुद्र, which is a prayer in 11 अनुवाकs addressed to रुद्र. Great merit is supposed to result from repeating that prayer 11 times or 121 times. सायण in his comment on the रुद्रभाष्य quotes the वायुपुराण 'रोगवान्पापवांश्चैव रुद्रं जप्त्वा जितेन्द्रियः। रोगात्पापाद्विनिर्मुक्तो ह्यतुलं सुखमश्नुते॥'. अतिशुचिभिः शैवैः सम्पाद्यमानं विरूपाक्षस्य (शिवस्य) क्षीरकलशसहस्रैः स्नपनं यस्मिन् where the image of S'iva was being bathed with thousands of milk jars by very holy devotees of शिव. क्षीराभिषेक is even now resorted to to propitiate Rudra. शिव is called विरूपाक्ष because of his third eye. अजिरो०—connect this and the following instrumentals with नरपतिभिः below. अजिरं courtyard. अनासादितं (not obtained) स्वामिनः (प्रभाकरवर्धनस्य) दर्शनं तेन दूयमानानि मानसानि येषाम्. अभ्यन्तरात् निष्पतिताः (coming out) निकटवर्तिनः परिजनाः तैः निवेद्यमाना वार्ता (news of the king's condition) येभ्यः. वार्ता...शयनैः to whom bathing, eating and sleeping had become mere news *i. e.* 'who knew these only in name, who did not bathe, eat or sleep as the king was seriously ill. उज्झितः आत्मसंस्कारः तेन मलिनः वेशः येषाम् whose clothes were dirty because they had abandoned the toilet of their bodies. लिखितै...श्चलैः who were motionless as if drawn in pictures. नीयमाननक्तन्दिवम् where night and day were passed. दुःखेन दीनानि वदनानि यस्य—connect this word with बाह्यपरिजनेन (p. 22. l. 6). प्रघ...मण्डलेन who were sitting in a circle in the porches before the palace-gate. The servants, not being intimately connected with the royal household, were sitting outside. 'प्रघाणप्रघणालिन्दा बहिर्द्वारप्रकोष्ठके' इत्यमरः. 'अगारैकदेशे प्रघणः प्रघाणश्च' पा. 3. 3. 79. उपांशुव्याहृतैः in whispered conversations. The servants that were outside assigned various causes for the sad plight of the king. There is a touch of humour in this description. केन...वयता some one (among the servants sitting outside) laid bare the errors on the part of doctors. असाध्य...पठता one recited passages containing the symptoms of incurable diseases. Diseases are generally classified into three classes, साध्य, दुःसाध्य and असाध्य. केन ... वृण्वता one expounded the story of a demon (as being at the root of the king's ailment). कार्तान्तिकादेशान् the prognostications of astrologers. कृतान्तं (दैवं) वेद इति कार्तान्तिकः (कृतान्त + ठक्). उपलिङ्गानि portents. अनित्य... लभमानेन one was revolving in his mind the transitoriness of life, was condemning this (everchanging) world, censured the wantonness of the Kali age and found fault with fate. धर्माय कुप्यता—he was angry with धर्म, because the latter could not do anything for such a righteous king as प्रभाकर०. क्लिष्ट...गर्हयता one censured the ill-luck of the noble youths that were afflicted. कथ्यमाना कष्टा पार्थिवावस्था यस्मिन्. विविधौषधिद्रव्याणां द्रवः (juice, exudation) तस्य गन्धः गर्भे यस्य (adj. of कक्ष्यान्तरम्). उत्क्वथतां...जिघ्रन् smelling the odour of boiling decoctions, of butter and oils that were being heated. कक्ष्या inner court. The रामायण (अयोध्या 20. 11-12) shows that the third कक्ष्या was set apart for the queen and her confidential attendants.

P 77 l.11—**P. 78** l. 35 **तत्र...द्राक्षीत्.** The principal sentence is तत्र च...धवलगृहे स्थितं (p. 23 l. 1)...देव्या यशोमत्या शिरसि वक्षसि च स्पृश्यमानं पितरमद्राक्षीत्. अतिनिःशब्दे—this and the following clauses in the locative qualify धवलगृहे (p. 23 l. 1). गृहावग्रहणीग्राहिणः बहुवेत्रिणः यत्र where many door-keepers stood in the vestibule. 'गृहावग्रहणी देहली' इत्यमरः. गृहावग्रहणी the threshold. त्रिगुणया तिरस्करिण्या तिरोहितः सुवीथीपथः यस्मिन्—where the way to the inner part of the house was shut off (from view) by a triple screen. वीथी is गृहप्रान्त according to क्षीरस्वामी. पिहितानि पक्षद्वारकाणि यस्मिन् where the private entrances were shut. 'प्रच्छन्नमन्तर्द्वारं स्यात्पक्षद्वारं तु पक्षकः' इत्यमरः. पिहित *past p. p.* of धा with अपि with the initial अ dropped, according to 'वष्टि भागुरिरल्लोपमवाप्योरुपसर्गयोः।'. परिहृतं कपाटरटितं यस्मिन् where the creaking of the panels was avoided. घटितैः (united, closed) गवाक्षैः रक्षितः (prevented) मरुत् (gust of wind) यस्मिन्. चरणताडनेन स्वनत् (rattling, creaking) सोपानं (staircase) तेन प्रकुपिताः प्रतीहाराः यस्मिन्. When some one ascended the staircase in a noisy way, the doorkeepers got angry with him for fear that his action might disturb the ailing king. निभृताभिः (noiseless) संज्ञाभिः (signs) निर्दिश्यमानानि (indicated, ordered) सकलकर्माणि यस्मिन्. कञ्चुकिन् a person wearing armour. कञ्चुकः or कञ्चुकः breast-plate 'उरश्छदः कञ्चुको जगरः कवचोऽस्त्रियाम्' इत्यमरः. कोणस्थितः आह्वानैः चकितः आचमनवाही यस्मिन् in a corner of which stood a servant bearing the bowl for rinsing the mouth, who was bewildered by numerous calls. चन्द्रशालिकायां लीनः मूकः मौललोकः यस्मिन्. For चन्द्र० see p. 21 above. मौलः an old or hereditary minister. मूलं प्रतिष्ठा तदस्ति अस्य इति मौलः. महान् आधिः (distraction of mind) तेन विधुरः (helpless) बान्धवाङ्गनावर्गः तेन गृहीतं प्रच्छन्नप्रग्रीवकं यस्मिन्. प्रग्रीवं or-कं a painted turret, window. सञ्जवनम् quadrangle, court formed by four houses on four sides 'सभा सञ्जवनं त्विदम्। चतुःशालम्' इत्यमरः. प्र ... णयिनि to which only a few friends (or favourites had been admitted). दुर्मनायमान *pr. p.* of दुर्मनायते, denominative verb from दुर्मनस्. मन्दायमानः (languishing) पुरोधाः (पुरोहितः) यस्मिन्. सीदन्तः (sinking into despair) सुहृदः यत्र. विद्राणाः (kept awake, without sleep) विपश्चितः (पण्डिताः) यत्र. सन्तप्ताः आप्ताः (trusted) सामन्ताः यस्मिन्. विचित्ताः (vacant-minded) चामरग्राहिणः यस्मिन्. दुःखेन क्षामाः (emaciated) शिरोरक्षिणः (body-guard) यस्मिन्. क्षीयमाणा प्रसादवित्तानां मनोरथसम्पद् यस्मिन् where the fulfilment (सम्पद्) of the desires of those that were (the king's) favourites was vanishing. प्रसादैः वित्ताः ख्याताः. स्वामिभक्त्या परित्यक्तः आहारः यैः ते स्वामि...हाराः हीयमानबलाः विकलाः (faint) वल्लभभूभृतः यस्मिन्. क्षितितले पतिताः सकलरजन्यां जागरूकाः

राजपुत्रकुमारकाः यस्मिन् where the young Rajputs, that had watched during the whole night, were lying on the ground. कुलक्रमागतैः कुलपुत्रकैः उह्यमाना शुक् (शोकः) यस्मिन्. Separate ०शुचि and शोक०. निरानन्दाः (joyless) बन्दिनः (court bards) यस्मिन्. 'स्युर्मागधास्तु मगधा बन्दिनः स्तुतिपाठकाः' इत्यमरः. निःश्वसन्तः निराशाः आसन्नसेवकाः यस्मिन्. निःसृतं ताम्बूलं यस्मात् स निःसृतताम्बूलः अत एव धूसरः अधरः यासां ताः निःसृत... धराः, ०धराः वारयोषितः (dancing girls) यस्मिन्. विलक्षैः (bewildered) वैद्यैः उपदिश्यमानं पथ्यं (wholesome diet) तस्य आहरणे (fetching) अवहितः (attentive) पौरोगवः यस्मिन्. पौरोगवः superintendent of the royal kitchen. 'रसवत्यां तु पाकस्थानमहानसे। पौरोगवस्तदध्यक्षः' इत्यमरः (on which क्षीरस्वामी says 'पुरो गौर्मांसं वा जलं वास्याः सा पुरोगुस्तस्याः रसवत्याः अयं पौरोगवः). अनुजीविभिः पीयमानं उच्चषकं (उत्कृष्टः चषकः यस्मिन्) धारावारि तेन विनोद्यमाना आस्यशोषरुक् यस्मिन् where the pain due to dryness of mouth was removed by streaming water drunk by attendants without cups. The attendants were working hard and felt thirsty. It is common experience that thirst is allayed much more quickly if one pours a stream of water into the mouth than if one holds the cup to the lips. C and T translate 'attendants were drinking streams of water from uplifted cups in order to distract the pain of the king's dry mouth'. We cannot understand how the king's dry mouth would have been relieved if the servants drank water. So also the words of the Com. 'उच्चषकमपगतपानभाजनम्' do not mean 'empty cups'; but rather 'without a cup'. We think that the context requires that it was the king that was thirsty and *not* the servants. So we suggest that we should read पाय्यमान for पीयमान and then the meaning would be 'where the pain of the dry mouth (of the king) was removed by streams of water without cups which he was made to drink by the attendants'. The reading of B and C 'उच्चचषक' is not bad. It means that the water was poured from a cup held high up and not from a cup applied to the lips. राजाभिलाषेण (at the king's desire) भोज्यमानाः बहुभुजः (gluttons) यत्र. Or the meaning may be 'gluttons were fed with the food which the king desired but which he could not himself eat'. भेषजसामग्रीसम्पादने व्यग्राः समग्राः व्यवहारिणः (merchants) यस्मिन्. मुहुर्मुहुः आहूयमानः तोयकर्मान्तिकः (waterman) तेन अनुमिता घोरा आतुरस्य (रोगार्तस्य) तृट् यस्मिन्. कर्मान्तिकः a servant. तुषारेण परिकरितः करकः तस्मिन् शिशिरीक्रियमाणं उदश्वित् यस्मिन् where buttermilk was being cooled (frozen) in jars that were covered in ice. उदश्वित् *n* (उदकेन श्वयति) buttermilk that contains 50 per cent water. 'तक्रं ह्युदश्विन्मथितं पादाम्ब्वर्धाम्बु निर्जलम्' इत्यमरः on which क्षीरस्वामी says 'द्विगुणाम्बु श्वेतरसमर्धोदकमुदश्वितम्। तक्रं त्रिभागभिन्नाम्बु केवलं मथितं स्मृतमिति धन्वन्तरिः'. The frozen buttermilk was probably applied to the burning feet and head of the feverish king. श्वेतार्द्रे कर्पटे (piece of cloth) अर्पिताः कर्पूरस्य परागाः (रेणवः) तेन शीतलीकृता शलाका (a collyrium stick) यस्मिन्. The stick treated with camphor powder was to be applied to the eye to produce a cooling effect. नाश्यानेन (न + आश्यानेन) पङ्केन लिप्यमानं नवं भाण्डं (vessel) तद्गतं गण्डूषग्रहणाय मस्तु (sour cream, whey) यस्मिन्. We expect अनाश्यान; probably अ was elided in the MSS after ०शलाके. आश्यान means 'dried' and so नाश्यान would mean 'wet'. The cool whey was probably required for relieving the dryness of the mouth of the patient who used it as a gargle from time to time. 'मण्डं दधिभवं मस्तु' इत्यमरः. तिम्यन्ति (wet) कोमलानि कमलिनीपलाशानि (lotus-leaves) तैः प्रावृताः मृदुमृणालकाः यत्र. सनालानि नीलोत्पलानि तेषां पूली (bundle) तया सनाथा (possessed of) सलिलपानभाजनभूः यत्र. The lotus leaves, fibres and flowers were all intended to produce a cooling effect. धारानिपातैः निर्वाप्यमाणं क्वथिताम्भः यस्मिन्—boiling-water was being cooled by being poured in streams (from vessel to vessel). Water first boiled and then cooled is given to a patient for drinking. पटु (sharp) पाटलशर्करायाः आमोदः तं मुञ्चतीति ०मुच् तस्मिन् that emitted the sharp odour of pale-red sugar. मञ्चकाश्रिता (resting on a stand) सिकतिला (sandy) कर्करी (jar) तस्मिन् विश्रान्तं आन्तरचक्षुः यस्मिन्. It is difficult to explain what आन्तरचक्षुः means. We must read with the two MSS of B 'आतुरचक्षुः'. The eye of the ailing king rested upon a porous jar. The sight of water trickling from the porous jar had a soothing effect. For सिकतिल, see notes on सैकत p. 30. सरसेन शैवलेन वलयितं (अत एव) गलत् गोलयन्त्रकं यस्मिन् where there were globes dripping because they were surrounded by wet water-plants (moss). गल्वर्कशालाजिरे उल्लासिताः लाजसक्तवः यस्मिन्—where there were parched grain and barley-flour spread in a crystal platter. Separate ०सक्तूनि and पीत०. क्षीरस्वामी says 'गल्वर्कोऽपि स्फाटिके पात्रेऽयं रूढः'. For शालाजिर, see above p. 54. The fried grain was used as light food for patients. पीता (yellow) मसारपारी (emerald cup) तस्यां परिगृहीता कर्कशर्करा (white sugar) यत्र. It is better to omit पीत with some of the MSS of B. C and T translate 'a paste of flour and curds was held in a yellow emerald cup.' शिशिरैः औषधरसैः चूर्णैः च अवकीर्णः स्फटिकशुक्तिशङ्खसञ्चयः यस्मिन्. Crystal, mother-o'pearl and conches are all cool to the touch. प्राचीनामलक myrobalans.

सुश्रुत (सूत्रस्थान chap 46) gives a long list of the fruits usually eaten. प्राचीनामलक (also called वारिबदर) had the effect of removing the three दोषs (वात, पित्त, कफ) and poison 'गरदोषहरं नीपं प्राचीनामलकं तथा' सु० 46. 158. मातुलुङ्ग citron (Marathi महाळुंग). प्रतिग्राहितैः (that were made to accept presents) विप्रैः विप्रकीर्यमाणाः शान्त्युदकस्य विप्रुषः (बिन्दवः) यस्मिन्. विप्रुष् *f.* drop. शान्त्युदकम् soothing or propitiatory water. प्रेष्याभिः पेष्यमाणः (being pounded) कल्काटलेपः तेन उपदिग्धा दृषद् (stone) यस्मिन्. पर...ज्वलनेन (father) round whom lustration was performed by the fire of fever for the conquest of the next world. राज् with निस् 'to perform the ceremony called नीराजन'. नीराजन was a military and religious ceremony performed by kings and generals in the month of आश्विन before they took the field; mantras were repeated and lights waved. Here fever is the fire and the king was about to proceed to the next world. Compare 'तस्मै सम्यग्धुतो वह्निर्वाजिनीराजनाविधौ । प्रदक्षिणार्चिर्व्याजेन हस्तेनेव जयं ददौ ॥' रघु. 4. 25. अनव...चेष्टमानम् who tossed on a bed waving (*i. e.* uneven) with his ceaseless rollings like the serpent S'esha (rolling) on the Milky Ocean on account of the fever of poison. तरङ्गिणि (1) that has waves (with उदन्वति); (2) that has wavy curls (on the bed). The bed had white coverlets and so resembled क्षीरसागर. The king was suffering from a fever (ऊष्मन्); शेष has poison in his hoods. The king was pale through serious illness and resembled the white-yellow शेष. मुक्ता...धवलितम् (1) who was made white with the dust of pearl-powder (with the king); (2) that was white with pearls and the grains of sand (with जलधि). Pearls are supposed to have a cooling effect. Pearls are found in the ocean and on its shores there is white sand. क्षयकाले शुष्यन्तम् (1) who had become withered at the time of death; (2) that dries up at the time of universal destruction (with जलधि). क्षय = प्रलय. 'संवर्तः प्रलयः कल्पः क्षयः कल्पान्त इत्यपि' इत्यमरः. A कल्प is a period of 1000 महायुगs (कृत, त्रेता, द्वापर and कलि constitute one महायुग). It is equal to a day of ब्रह्मा, the night also being of the same duration. At the end of a कल्प the whole universe (including the ocean) is destroyed. Compare भगवद्गीता 'सहस्रयुगपर्यन्तमहर्यद् ब्रह्मणो विदुः । रात्रिं युगसहस्रान्तां तेऽहोरात्रविदो जनाः ॥ अव्यक्ताद् व्यक्तयः सर्वाः प्रभवन्त्यहरागमे । रात्र्यागमे प्रलीयन्ते तत्रैवाव्यक्तसंज्ञके ॥' VIII. 17-18. For a description of कल्पान्त see विष्णुपुराण VI. 3 and 4. 'उदकावरणं यत्तज्ज्योतिषा पीयते तु तत् । ज्योतिर्वायौ लयं याति यात्याकाशे समीरणः ॥' विष्णु० VI. 4. 31. कालेन (1) by death

(with the king); (2) by the dark-coloured (दशानन). All Rākshasas are represented as dark. The king had the pallor of death and resembled the snowy कैलास. On one occasion रावण when travelling in the पुष्पकविमान near कैलास was stopped by नन्दी saying that शिव wanted to be in privacy there. Thereupon रावण in arrogance caught hold of कैलास and shook it. When पार्वती became afraid by the motion of the mountain, शिव in anger pressed the mountain with his toe and रावण's arms were crushed underneath and he began to scream. See रामायण VII. 16 for the story. 'पुष्पकस्य गतिश्छिन्ना यत्कृते मम गच्छतः । तमिमं शैलमुन्मूलं करोमि तव गोपते ॥ 23...एवमुक्त्वा ततो राम भुजान्विक्षिप्य पर्वते । तोलयामास तं शीघ्रं स शैलः समकम्पत ॥' 25. Compare कादम्बरी 'कैलासश्रियमिव दशमुखोन्मूलनक्षोभनिपतिताम्' (p. 129 of P). अविरत...स्पृश्यमानम्—the palms of the hands of the attendants were white with the sandal-paste with which they smeared his body. The poet fancies that the palms were white because they were reduced to ashes by touching the burning limbs of the king. Ashes are white. अत्युष्णावयवस्पर्शेन भस्मीभूतं उदरं येषां (*adj.* of करैः). Take away the comma after ०प्रस्थितम् and place it after स्पृश्यमानम्. लोका ... पृच्छ्यमानम् — The king was about to depart this world. When a person goes on a journey those that stay bid him farewell. The poet fancies that under the guise of the white sandal ointment, it was his spotless fame that embraced him and bade him a last farewell. Both sandal and fame are white. स्थास्नु (1) that remains on the body (with अनुलेपन); (2) remaining on the earth (यशः). There is a further suggestion. His fame would be everlasting (स्थास्नु) and not evanescent. अविच्छिन्नं (ceaselessly) दीयमानानि कमलकुमुदेन्दीवरदलानि यस्मै. Lotus petals have a cooling effect. कमलs are rosy, कुमुदs are white and इन्दीवर is blue. His body when covered with petals of various colours looked variegated. काल...शबलम्—Death was approaching him. The pupil of the eye is dark, the corner is red and the rest of the eye is white. There is a similar idea above. निबिडेन (tight) दुकूलपट्टेन निपीडिताः केशान्ताः तैः कथ्यमानः कष्टवेदनानां अनुबन्धः (continuity) यस्य. His head was bound tight with silk cloth because he was suffering from ceaseless headache. दुर्धरवेदनाभिः उन्नमत् (standing up) नीलशिराजालकं तेन करालं तेन (*adj.* of ०फलकेन). A net-work of dark veins due to unbearable pain stood up on his forehead. These the poet fancies to be the lines drawn by the fingers of Death representing the days that remained to him on the earth. In counting we draw lines on a board (फलकं) with our fingers. कालाङ्गुलिभिः लिख्यमानाः लेखाः ताभिः आख्यातं मरणावधिदिवससंख्यानं येन. अन्तःप्रविष्टा तारका यस्य the pupil of his eye had become contracted and dim owing to failing strength. The poet fancies that it was due to his agitation at the sight of approaching death. A person who is frightened by a terrible sight closes his eyes. शुष्यन्ती दशनपङ्क्तिः तस्याः प्रसृताः धूसराः (grey) दीधितयः तैः तरङ्गिणीम्. He heaved hot breaths that were mixed with ripples of grey rays from his dry teeth. Mirage (मृगतृष्णिका) is also उष्णा (due to heat) and presents waves (तरङ्गिणी). निवेद्यमानः दारुणसन्निपातस्य आरम्भः यस्मिन्. He had a dark tongue, which indicated that he was in the stage of सन्निपात. सन्निपात is the combined derangement of the three humours of the body (वात, पित्त and कफ) and is fatal. The योगरत्नाकर (आनन्दाश्रम ed p. 98) gives the general symptoms of सन्निपातज्वर, one variety of which called तन्द्रिक is described as 'प्रभूता तन्द्रार्तिर्ज्वरकफपिपासाकुलतरो भवेच्छ्यामा जिह्वा पृथुलकठिना कण्टकवृता।'. The poet fancies that the tongue was dark because it was burnt up by his very hot breaths. उरः...कान्तं—मणि and the other things were placd on his chest to produce a cooling effect. When a person of position pays a visit, it is usual to appear in one's best dress and to put on jewels &c. Take away the comma after ०युगलम्. अङ्ग... युगलम् who tossed up his arms in putting his limbs into various contortions (through agony). When he tossed up his arms, rays flashed from his nails; the rays resemble streams of water. So the poet fancies that he constructed with the rays of his nails a showerbath for तापशान्ति. नेदिष्ठ—superlative of (अन्तिक) very near. His reflections fell in water, jewelled pavements, and mirrors, all of which are cool to the touch. The poet fancies that he entered inside them (as reflection) for their cooling effect. स्पृशन्तीं goes with मूर्च्छां and प्रणयिनीं. He welcomed a swoon when it came over (स्पृशन्ती) him, because it was a source of relief. मूर्च्छा is compared to प्रणयिनी (beloved wife), who touches her husband and is a source of comfort to him. The reading विश्राम० is much better than विश्वास०, as the latter cannot be well construed with मूर्च्छा. अरिष्टैराविष्टम् overwhelmed with very bad symptoms (of death). अरिष्ट also means 'crow'. The cawing of crows is an evil omen and may be looked upon as the summons of death. 'तक्रे मरणचिह्ने चारिष्टं वृक्षे च फेनिले । सुराणां च शुभेऽपि

स्यात्काके निम्बे च पुंस्ययम् ॥' quoted by क्षीरस्वामी. महाप्रस्थान—the great journey *i. e.* death. At his approaching death, anguish seized the hearts of relatives. The words प्रस्थान and सन्तान (1 continuity; 2 offspring) suggest another idea. When a man starts on a journey, he transfers (*i. e.* entrusts) to the care of his relatives his children. छायया मुच्यमानम् who was bereft of brilliance (of body). He was languid and had lost his bright complexion. The poet fancies that छाया had left him through jealousy, as he was wedded to अरति. अरतिः langour. उद्योग...द्रवाणाम् who was the effort of all (bad) symptoms, or supervenient diseases. The idea is that all bad symptoms had concentrated themselves on him. सर्वास्त्र...तया: Emaciation had let fall all her missiles on him. हस्तीकृतं=वशीकृतम्. विहस्ततया by helplessness. विगतः हस्तः यस्य स विहस्तः तस्य भाव ०ता तया. विषयी...क्षयेण misery had made him its province, wasting had made him its field. गोचरीकृतम्=विषयीकृतम्. दुःखासिका—दुःखमासते अस्यामिति or दुःखमसिका इव—dejection. अस्वास्थ्यम् restlessness, anxiety. विधेयीकृतं made a servant *i. e.* brought under control. क्रोडः the chest; क्रोडीकृतम् embraced. लक्ष्यीकृतं made a target. दक्षिणाशया—the south is presided over by Yama. जग्ध devoured (*past p. p.* of अद् to eat). निगीर्ण swallowed (*past* P. P. of गॄ with नि). वैवर्ण्यम् (विवर्णस्य भावः) loss of colour, paleness. गात्रभङ्गः *lit.* breaking of limbs *i. e.* stiffness of body. वण्ट् *1 P.* to divide. लुण्ठ्यमान being robbed. आदित्सितं (*past p. p.* of the desiderative base of दा with आ) desired to be seized. निरूपितं marked, observed carefully. अभाव death, destruction. परिकलितम् grasped all round. परासुता death. दत्तः अवकाशः येन who made room for. वैमनस्यम् (विमनसः भाव) mental depression. समीपे—connect this and the following locatives with वर्तमानम् below. अन्ति...च्छासस्य who was near the last breath. मुखे...प्रवासस्य at the beginning of the great journey *i. e.* dying. Compare महाप्रस्थान above. The reading महाप्रयासस्य is not so good. जीवितेशः=यमः. विरलं वाचि broken in words. चलितं चेतसि shaken in mind. प्रचुरं प्रलापे profuse in incoherent speech. अनु...बन्धिकाभिः constantly followed by pains in the joints. Com. 'अनुबन्धिका गात्रसन्धिपीडाः' According to the मेदिनी, अनुबन्धी means 'hiccough' 'अनुबन्धी तु हिक्कायां तृष्णायामपि योषिति.' This meaning is preferable. अनवरतरोदनेन उच्छूने (swollen) नयने यस्याः (*adj.* of यशोमत्या). गृहीता चामरिका यया. गृहीत...वीजयन्त्या who fanned the king with her sighs alone, though she held a chowrie in her hand.

P. 79 ll. 1–18 **दृष्ट्वा च...धेति.** प्रथम...मतिः whose mind was overwhelmed by the first shock of sorrow. आ...भवत् he became as if afraid of fate. भागधेयेभ्यः is ablative. निरा...सीत् for a moment he was as if given up by his mind *i. e.* he became dazed. अव...धैर्येण discarded by steadiness. रिक्ती...रत्या he was made empty by delight *i. e.* there was not the least trace of gayness left in him. विषमविष terrible poison. तमसा...विशेषयन् excelling even Pātāla in darkness. पाताल as the haunt of demons is supposed to be dark. शून्यत्वे...शयानः excelling even space in its vacancy. His mind became a void. For the शून्यत्व of आकाश, compare above (text p. 2 l. 1) 'आकाशमयः शून्यतायाम्'. नाविन्दत कर्तव्यम् he did not know what to do. पस्पर्श...गाम् his heart came in contact with terror and his head with the earth. The idea is that his heart became extremely apprehensive for his father's life and he bowed low before his father (as a son should do). सा अवस्था यस्य सः तदवस्थः who was in that (terrible) condition. निर्भरेण स्नेहेन आवर्जितः influenced by deep affection. प्रधावमानः मनसा—being enfeebled, his body could not run, though his mind ran towards his son. शरी...गात् he rose from the couch with the upper part of his body. विन...न्नमय्य having raised him who bent through dutifulness. विशन्निव...मध्यम् as if plunging into the midst of the moon's disc. At the sight of his darling son, the king felt as much relief as he would have if he had plunged &c. The following clauses also suggest the cooling or comforting effect which the sight of his son produced upon the king in his burning fever. स्नाप...प्रस्रवणे as if wetting himself in a stream of Harichandana juice. हरिचन्दनः is a kind of very fragrant and yellow sandal. 'तैलपर्णिकगोशीर्षे हरिचन्दनमस्त्रियाम्' इत्यमरः (on which क्षीरस्वामी says 'हरेरिन्द्रस्य चन्दनं, हरि कपिलं वा, तच्चातिशीतंल पीतमाहुः'). तुषाराद्रिः = हिमालयः. कपोलेन...घट्टयन् rubbing his cheek against the cheek (of हर्ष). निमील...लोचने closing his eyes that let fall incessant tears that formed on the tips of his eyelashes. पक्ष्माग्रे ग्रथितं अजस्रं अस्रं तत् विस्रवति इति ०स्राविन्. He closed his eyes and shed tears through joy. विस्मृतः ज्वरस्य सञ्ज्वरः सन्तापः येन. अप...स्कारम् who drew aside and then bowed low. प्रणता जननी येन. For क see above p. 31. विगतः निमेषः यस्मात् सः वि...मेषः, ०मेषश्चासौ निश्चलश्च. क्षयेण क्षामः कण्ठः यस्य whose throat was parched by exhaustion. कृच्छात् with difficulty. तृतीय... स्याह्न to-day is the third day since he took food.

P. 79 l. 19—**P. 80** l. 4 **तच्छ्रुत्वा ... करवाणीति.** बाष्पवेगेन गृह्यमाणानि अक्षराणि यथा स्युः the words being choked by the flow of tears. आयतं निःश्वस्य heaving a deep sigh. ईदृशेषु in such (times or calamities). विधुरयति—विधुरं करोति (denominative verb from विधुर)—renders helpless. सर्वप्रमाथी that overpowers everybody. यतः wherefore. नार्ह...दातुम् you will please not give yourself up to extreme sorrow. निशितं sharpened. तक्ष्णोति 5th conj. P. of तक्ष् to pierce. तनिमा emaciation (from तनु with the affix इमन्). See notes p. 68 on कालिमा. परलोकश्च—A son was supposed to free by his birth the father from a hell called Put. 'पुत्रेण लोकाञ्जयति पौत्रेणानन्त्यमश्नुते। ...पुन्नाम्नो नरकाद्यस्मात्त्रायते पितरं सुतः। तस्मात्पुत्र इति प्रोक्तः स्वयमेव स्वयम्भुवा ॥' मनु० 9. 137-138. A omits परलोकश्च and this seems better from one point of view. The next sentence is 'यथा...प्रजानाम्'. In this last, the word प्रजानां is well-connected with प्राणाः in the preceding (यथा मम प्राणाः त्वयि स्थिताः तथा सर्वासां प्रजानां प्राणाः त्वयि स्थिताः). The idea is that the subjects love you so much. With the reading परलोकश्च it is possible to say that Harsha would be a very righteous emperor and keep the people in the path of righteousness and enable them all to attain Heaven. But there is another difficulty. As सुखं and राज्यं are co-ordinated with प्राणाः, we expect स्थितानि. If however it be said that the predicate agrees with the last word, then we must have स्थितः (with the reading परलोकश्च). अकलुषस्य कर्मणः—of spotless actions *i. e.* meritorious actions. कर...लक्षणानि the marks on your body indicate that the sovereignty of the four oceans is as it were in your hand. For the लक्षणs of an emperor, see above p. 20. त्वज्ज...स्मि by your birth alone I attained all my ends. निर...जीवितव्ये I have no desire to live (longer). भिषजाम् अनुरोधः acting according to the wishes of the physicians. Mark the two accusatives माम् and औषधम् with पाययति (causal of पा to drink). सर्वप्रजापुण्यैः उत्पत्स्यमानानाम्—for the idea see above. उत्पत्स्यमान—future participle of पद् with उद् (meaning 'desiring to be born'). प्रजाभि...ज्ञातिभिः—in their subjects and not in their kindred do kings have their relatives. For a converse statement of this fine sentiment, compare शाकुन्तल VI 'येन येन वियुज्यन्ते प्रजाः स्निग्धेन बन्धुना। स स पापादृते तासां दुष्यन्त इति घुष्यताम् ॥'. कृता...पथ्यम् when you have taken your meal, I shall myself also take my diet. अस्य=हर्षस्य. धक्ष्यम् about to burn (future participle of दह्). सन्दुधुक्षे—*perfect* of धुक्ष् with सम् I A to be kindled. अकाण्डे *Adv.* all of a sudden. महाप्रलयः great destruction *i. e.* great calamity. व्यभ्रः इव वज्रपातः like a bolt from a cloudless sky. विगतं अभ्रं यस्मात्. For this idea, see above text p. 2. 'अनभ्रवृष्टिरिव वैदग्ध्यस्य'.

सामान्योपि शोकः even a common sorrow. The construction is 'सामान्योऽपि शोकः सोच्छ्वासं मरणं किमुत विशेषाश्रितः शोकः'. सोच्छ्वासं मरणम् (a common sorrow) is a living death. Sorrow is equal to death except that breathing continues in sorrow, while in death there is no breathing. अनु...व्याधिः (sorrow) is a serious disease without there being any medicine prescribed for it. अनुपदिष्टं औषधं यस्य. अ...प्रवेशः it is a leap into fire without being reduced to ashes. अनुपरत not dead. नरकवासः—a person abides in Hell after death. But sorrow causes the torments of Hell though a man be not dead. नि...वर्षम् it is a rain of charcoal without fire. Charcoal is produced by fire (*i. e.* by kindling wood). अश...दारणम् it is sawing with a saw without cutting into pieces. अन्न...पातः the stroke of a diamond needle without a (visible) wound. किमु...श्रितः (if a common sorrow is a living death &c.), then what words will describe a sorrow of a special sort (of a deeper kind)?

P. 80 ll. 5-19 **राज...आवेदयितास्मीति.** धूम...पातान्—this and the following clauses are to be connected with कवलान् (l.7). धूम... पातान् (mouthfuls) that made him shed tears as if they (कवल) were made of smoke. While partaking of food, he wept over them. Smoke causes tears in the eyes. So the mouthfuls are fancied to be धूममय. Explain the following clauses similarly. अग्नि...दाहान् that produced burning in his heart, as if they (mouthfuls) were made of fire. जनितः हृदयदाहः यैः. दत्तः मूर्च्छावेगः यैः That brought on swoon. Poison also produces a swoon. उत्पादिता घृणा (disgust) यैः. **'जुगुप्साकरुणे घृणे'** इत्यमरः. महापातकs are five. 'ब्रह्महत्या सुरापानं स्तेयं गुर्वङ्गनागमः। महान्ति पातकान्याहुः संसर्गश्चापि तैः सह ॥' मनु० 11. 54. क्षार...वेदनान् that caused pain as if they were made of corrosive substances. अगृहीतं ताम्बूलं येन without taking the betel. As he was in grief he discarded betel. उत्ताम्यता मनसा with a distressed (or faint heart). अस्ता...सवितरि when the sun was about to set (lit. was desirous of setting). उपह्वरे in private. 'रहोऽन्तिकमुपह्वरे' इत्यमरः. पुनः...पितरम् you will hear that your father is again restored to his original condition (प्रकृति). The physicians outwardly say that Harsha's father will be restored to health. But the words प्रकृति and श्रोष्यसि suggest another sense, which is 'your father will be merged in the supreme spirit from which he came or his body will be reduced to the five elements out of which it was created'. Death is natural to all beings and life is an accident. **'मरणं प्रकृतिः** शरी-

by his entering fire like gold. कल्याणा (blessed, lovely) प्रकृतिः यस्य (applies to कार्तस्वर and कौलपुत्र). Gold also by being heated in fire becomes more brilliant. कुलपुत्रस्य भावः कौलपुत्रम्. कृतस्वरः आकरः तत्र भवं कार्तस्वरं हेम. किमस्य...तातः was not my father his father? अन्य...लोके in this world even when other (*i. e.* ordinary) masters are taken away (*lit.* become rare), life that is sustained becomes a cause for shame (to the servant). अमृत...जीविनाम् who was like nectar to his dependents. निर्व्याजबान्धवे who was their kinsman without any cause (disinterested). अवन्ध्यः (fruitful) प्रसादः (favour) यस्य. सांप्रतम् *adv.* properly. किं वा...दह्यते or what is burnt of him who is full of glory and abides firmly to the end of the world? आकल्पम्—कल्पं मर्यादीकृत्य (अव्ययीभाव). For कल्प see above p. 78. स्थेयस् is the comparative of स्थिर. ममापि...प्रतिष्ठन्ते As for me, what is that very important work, what is that unperformed task, what is the preoccupation (व्यापृतता) of my life, so that it, cruel as it is, does not yet start off? कृतात् शेषः. अन्तरायः obstacle. उत्तरीय...गुण्ठ्य having wrapped himself together with the head by his upper garment.

P. 81 . l. 24—p. 27 l. 3 इत्थंभूते...महोत्पाताः. सर्वस्य लोकेस्य—these words are to be connected with all the locatives from कपोलेषु to हृदयेषु. सर्वस्य...कराः the hands of all people seemed as if rivetted (कीलित) to their cheeks. One who is in deep sorrow or thought sits resting his cheek upon his hand. Compare 'वामहस्तोपहितवदना' in शाकुन्तल IV. The people grieving for प्रभाकरवर्धन remained in that position so long that it seemed that their cheeks and hands were nailed together. लोचने...स्रुतयः streams of tears seemed as if plastered to their eyes. लेप्यं plaster or cement. Plaster or cement sticks to the object to which it is applied and cannot be easily removed. Tears were to be constantly seen in the eyes of the people. ग्रथिताः tied, fastened. उत्कीर्णाः engraved. Engravings are permanent. हाकष्टानि the words 'Oh! alas!!'. लपने...श्वसितानि sighs were twisting themselves like foliage on their mouths (लपनं). They incessantly sighed. परि...पदानि words of lamentation. निधानीकृतानि treasured or stored up. उष्णाश्रु...निद्रा sleep came not to the hollows of their eyes, as if afraid of being scorched by the hot tears. निःश्वास...हासाः—no one smiled; the poet fancies that smiles vanished being thrown away by the wind of sighs that the people constantly heaved. निर...वाणी speech did not go on (*i. e.* no one talked anything) as if burnt by सन्ताप without leaving any remainder. सन्तापः (1) heat, (2) sorrow. कथास्व...हासाः—Not only no body cracked jokes, but nobody even told a tale containing jokes. गीतगोष्ठ्यः people assembled to hear music. गोष्ठी an assembly. जन्मान्तरातीतानि—what was experienced in a former life, no one remembers. लास्यानि—see notes p. 28. प्रसाधनानि decorations of the person, such as flowers &c. ख...मण्डलानि convivial parties at taverns became like sky-flowers *i. e.* absolutely non-existent. खपुष्प is an emblem of what is absolutely non-existent. Such emblems are summarised in the following verse 'एष वन्ध्यासुतो याति खपुष्पकृतशेखरः । मृगतृष्णाम्भसि स्नातः शशशृङ्गधनुर्धरः ॥'. बन्दिवाचः the words of court bards. Mark the words 'विगतजयशब्दम्' (text p. 20 l. 33). युगान्त...वृत्तयः pleasures seemed to belong to another Yuga as it were. पुन...केतुः—Kāma was once burnt by S'iva; see p. 38 above. But now at the approach of the king's death, all love-making in the world came to an end through grief. महा...पिशुनाः indicative of the fall of a great man. 'पिशुनौ खलसूचकौ' इत्यमरः. भूपतेरभावाय—is to be connected with समुदभवन्. Mark the dative. The result indicated by a portent is put in the dative, according to the वार्तिक 'उत्पातेन ज्ञापिते च' (वाताय कपिला विद्युत् । सि. कौ.). We may construe भयमुत्पादयन्तो भूतानाम् (causing terror to all beings) or भयमुत्पादयन्तो भूतानां महोत्पाताः great portents of the five elements (पृथिव्यप्तेजोवाय्वाकाश) causing fear. The महाभारत divides portents into three classes *viz.* दिव्य, आन्तरिक्ष and भौम. 'उत्पातांस्त्रिविधान्प्राह नारदो भगवानृषिः । दिव्यांश्चैवान्तरीक्षांश्च पार्थिवांश्च पितामह ॥' सभापर्व 46. 7-8. See also बृहत्संहिता 46. 2.

P. 82 ll. 4–26 **तथाहि...निशाम्.** तथाहि for instance. In the Rāmâyaṇa (अरण्य० 23) and in the महाभारत (वनपर्व 179; विराट० chapters 39 and 46; उद्योग 84) there are long lists of उत्पातs. For want of space it is not possible to quote them. But they seem to have been the source of Bāṇa's inspiration. दोलायमानं (swinging) सकलकुलाचलचक्रवालं यस्याः. The कुलाचलs (principal mountains) are seven. See notes p. 39. अचलद्धरित्री the earth quaked. पत्या...कामेव as if पृथ्वी was desirous of going with her lord (king प्रभाकरवर्धन, who was dying). Earthquakes were looked upon as portending great calamities and as punishments sent by God to chastise mankind for its sins. The poet Cowper writes in this strain in his poem 'Time-piece'. परास्परास्फालनेन वाचालाः वीचयः येषाम् the waves of which were noisy because they struck against each other. विजुघूर्णिरे *perfect 3rd plural* of घूर्ण् 1 A with वि to roll. धन्व...स्मरन्तः as though remembering धन्वन्तरि in that interval. When the sea was churned by the gods and demons, धन्वन्तरि emerged bearing the jar of nectar in his hand. 'अथोदधेर्मथ्यमानात्काश्यपैरमृतार्थिभिः । उदतिष्ठन्महाराज पुरुषः परमाद्भुतः ॥ 31....अमृतापूर्णकलशं बिभ्रद्वलयभूषितः । स वै भगवतः साक्षाद्विष्णोरंशांशसम्भवः ॥ 34 धन्वन्तरिरिति ख्यात आयुर्वेददृगिज्यभाक् ।' 35. भागवत॰ VIII. 8. धन्वन्तरि is also the promulgator of the science of medicine, as we learn from सुश्रुतसंहिता I. 1. 'अथ खलु भगवन्तममरवरं काशिराजं दिवोदासं धन्वन्तरिं...सुश्रुतप्रभृतय ऊचुः'. For curing the dying king, the ocean as if wanted धन्वन्तरि and lashed itself into fury as at the time of churning. Mark the genitive धन्वन्तरेः with स्मरन्तः. 'अधीगर्थदयेशां कर्मणि' पा. 2. 3. 52 (verbs having the sense of 'to remember' and the roots दय् and ईश् govern the genitive of the object). ॰भीतानाम् goes with ककुभाम् (दिशाम्). भूभृ...ककुभाम् high rose up comets, appearing like the hair of the quarters, that were apprehensive of the death of the king, (hair) that was plentiful (विकट, or frightful) and curly with extended knots. The quarters are fancied to be the wives of the king and comets (that are long) as hair. Women whose husbands are dying would never think of decorating their hair by making a triple braid, but would tie it together in a knot. वितत... कुटिलाः may give two more meanings; (1) that are plentiful and curly like the peacock's outstretched tail; (2) that are terrible (विकट) and crooked with outstretching masses of flames. (शिखा). It is usual to compare the hair of beautiful women with the peacock's tail. See रघु॰ 9. 67. Comets have flashing tails. धूमकेतवः—compare 'उपप्लवाय लोकानां धूमकेतुरिवोत्थितः ॥' कुमार॰ II. 32. धूमकेतवः may also mean 'fires'. But as दिग्दाह is mentioned below, it is better to take the sense of 'comet.' धूमकेतुभिः (by comets, fires) करालितानि (rendered terrible) दिङ्मुखानि यस्मिन् (*adj.* of भुवनम्). दिक्पालैः आरब्धः आयुष्कामहोमः तस्य धूमेन धूम्रम्. The quarters had a dark (threatening) aspect on account of the comets. The poet fancies that this is due to the smoke of the sacrificial fire kindled by दिक्पालs for securing long life to the king. For the eight guardians of the quarters, see notes p. 25. भ्रष्टा भाः (lustre) यस्य (*adj.* of ॰मण्डले). तप्त...बभ्रूणि reddish brown like a red hot iron jar. भानु...जहार In the sun's disc someone desiring the (continuance of) the life of the (dying) king offered as it were a human offering under the guise of a horrible headless trunk. A spot appeared on the sun's disc resembling the headless trunk (कबन्धः-न्धम्) of a man. This the poet fancies to be a human offering. Compare रामायण अरण्यकाण्ड Chap 23. 11 'कबन्धः परिघाभासो दृश्यते भास्करान्तिके ।'. ज्वलितं परिवेशमण्डलं (circle of halo) तस्य आभोगः (expanse) तेन भास्वरः (*adj*. of श्वेतभानुः, the moon). जिघृक्षया (ग्रहीतुमिच्छया) जृम्भमाणः (yawning) स्वर्भानुः (राहुः) तस्मात् भयं तस्मात्. उपरचितः अग्निप्राकारः येन. The moon had a circle of blazing halo round it. The poet fancies that it was a wall of fire raised by the moon out of the fear of Rāhu that had opened its mouth wide to swallow the moon. अवनि...साधिताः (1) won over by the valour of the king; (2) decked by the brilliance of the king. अदह्यन्त...दिशः the reddened quarters were as if burnt. The quarters glowed red (this is called दिग्दाह). A loving (अनुरक्त) woman would enter fire before her husband dies (प्रथमतर &c.). A woman who wants to die by burning herself would be decked with all decorations (प्रसाधित). स्रुतः शोणितशीकराणां (रक्तबिन्दूनां) आसारः (shower) तेन अरुणिता (reddened) तनुः यस्याः. अनुमरणाय for following (her lord, the king प्रभाकर°) in death. प्रावृतः पाटलः (red) अंशुकपटः यया. The earth was wet with a shower of blood. The poet fancies that the earth was going to be a सती and had covered herself in a red garment as a सती did. नरा...भीतैः afraid of the tumult that would arise on the king's death. कालायस... दिग्द्वाराणि the doors of the quarters were blocked by masses of untimely dark clouds as if they were iron door-panels. Though it was not the rainy season, dark clouds rose in the sky. The poet fancies them to be the doors of the sky. प्रेत... रटन्तः like the shrill (पटु) sounding drums beaten at the march of the Lord of the dead (यम). When a king marches, drums are beaten. हृदयस्फोटनाः (applies to पटहाः and निर्घोषाः) making the heart to burst. पस्फायिरे *perfect* of स्फाय् 1 A to swell. निर्घा...घोषाः the terrific sounds of whirl-winds. निर्घातः— 'पवनः पवनाभिहतो गगनादवनौ यदा समापतति । भवति तदा निर्घातः स च पापो दीप्तविहगरुतः ॥' बृहत्संहिता 39. 1. निकटीभवन् यममहिषः तस्य खुरपुटैः उद्धूताः. As the king was dying, the buffalo of यम is fancied to be near. द्युमणिः सूर्यः तस्य धाम (brilliance). This is the object of धूसरीचक्रुः (rendered dim). क्रमेलक...वृष्टयः showers of dust brown like camel hair. विरसविराविणीनाम् that howled disagreeably (so as to produce disgust). The reading विसर° would mean 'that howled in groups'. It is not so good.

उन्मुखीनाम् that had uplifted their faces. शिखिनो...राजयः rows of female jackals howled, receiving (प्रतीच्छन्त्यः) the flames of fire like meteors falling from the sky. The words in the text as they stand cannot be well construed. इव should have been placed after पतन्तीः or उल्काः. The idea seems to be that the jackals had blazing firebrands in their mouths and howled; meteors also blaze and fall from the sky. C and T translate 'like firebrands catching fire from flames that fell from the sky.' But then the difficulty is: what are the points of resemblance between rows of jackals and firebrands. Instead of being compared to firebrands, jackals are described as carrying firebrands. Compare 'नदन्मुखोल्काविचितामिषाभिः स वाह्यते राजपथः शिवाभिः ॥' रघु० 16. 12. If we read ज्वालाभिः with three MSS of B, all the difficulties may be removed. Then the meaning will be '(jackals) that as if received in the shape of flames of fire the meteors falling from the sky.' उल्का also means 'a firebrand.' धूमायमानः कबरीविभागः (सीमन्तः) तेन विभावितः विकारः यासाम् whose distress was shown by the fact that the parting line of their hair emitted smoke. प्रकीर्णेन केशपाशेन प्रकाशितः शोकः याभिः that as if manifested their grief by their dishevelled hair. One who is in grief has dishevelled hair. It was believed that in times of misfortune the hair of the images of goddesses in the house emitted smoke. That smoke is fancied to be dishevelled hair (both being dark). सिंहासनस्य समीपे उप० (अव्ययीभाव). भ्रामरम् — भ्रमराणामिदम्. Read विधूयमान for विदूय०. कालरात्र्याः विधूयमानः वृजिनः (curved, curling) वेणीबन्धः तस्य विभ्रमं (object of बिभ्राणम्)—(bearing) the appearance of the braided hair of कालरात्रि, that (hair) is curly and dangling (about the neck). वेणी is the hair of women twisted into a single unornamented braid (when their husbands are absent or ill). The dark and hovering bees resemble the dark and dangling braid. कालरात्रिः night of destruction at the end of the world. As the king was dying the word is appropriately used here. अटताम् goes with वायसानाम्. व्याक्रोशी the cawing (of crows). For the cry of the crow as an evil omen, see text p. 20 ll. 22-23. Compare वनपर्व 179. 44 'पृष्ठतो वायसः कृष्णो याहि याहीति शंसति'. ० मध्यात्—connect this with उच्चखान. सरस...लोहितम् as red as a piece of juicy meat. चञ्चन्ती (moving about) चञ्चुः (beak) यस्य. उच्चैः may be connected with कूजन् or with उच्चखान (tore away on high).

P. 82 l. 27—p. 28 l. 11 **अन्य...देव्या इति.** The principal sentence is 'अन्यस्मिन्नहनि समीपं अस्य (हर्षस्य) राजकुलात्...वेलेति नाम्ना यशोमत्याः प्रतीहारी आजगाम. द्रुतगतिवशेन विशीर्यमाणाः (broken) अलङ्काराः तैः झाङ्कारिणी (causing a tinkling). विज...षादस्य (she) seemed to be the triumphal proclamation of despondency. आकुलयोः चरणयोः चलन्ती तुलाकोटिः तस्याः कणितेन वाचालिताभिः. उद्ग्रीवाभिः that raised their necks. The Haṃsîs began to cackle when they heard the jingling of anklets and followed it. The poet fancies that they did so in order to ask the news. 'पादाङ्गदे तुलाकोटिर्मञ्जीरो नूपुरोऽस्त्रियाम्' अमरः ('तुलाकृतेर्जङ्घायाः कोटिरिव' क्षीरस्वामी). स्खलिते विशालश्रोण्यां शिञ्जाना रशना तां अनुरौति इति॰ राविणी ताभिः—that screamed in response to the girdle jingling on her broad hip when she stumbled. बाष्पान्धा—she stumbled being blinded by tears; when she stumbled, the bells of her girdle rang and the domesticated cranes screeched. It was their screeching that guided her. अदृष्टं कवाटपट्टं तस्य संघट्टेन (striking against) स्फुटितं ललाटपट्टं तस्य रुधिरपटलं तेन—her face was covered with blood as her forehead struck against the panels of doors which she did not observe in her weeping. The blood resembled the fringe (पटान्त) of a red silken garment (with which also women may veil their face). सन्तापबलेन विलीनं कनकवलयं तस्य रसधाराम्. She was throwing aside her cane (which she was to carry as a doorkeeper). The poet fancies that it was the stream of her golden bracelet that melted because of her सन्ताप (sorrow, heat). Both cane and gold are yellow. मुख...पटीं स्फुरन्तीं आकर्षन्ती she drew (into position) her flashing silken shawl that was waved about by her breath. मुख॰ and स्फुरन्तीं apply also to निर्मोकमञ्जरीम्. फणिनीव...र्षन्ती as a female serpent may draw after her a slough. Both the shawl and slough are white. नम्रां...स्रंसिना (*adj.* of ॰सव्यपेन) that hung over her bent shoulders. तमाल...वरेणेव—her dark hair resembled a tattered garment of Tamāla leaves (which are dark). धम्मिल्ल...रहितेन that was not arranged into a braid. 'धम्मिल्लः संयताः कचाः' इत्यमरः. शिरो... कुचा her bosom was covered with a dangling mass of hair. कुच... पीडया—beating the breast is a sign of sorrow. The word पीडया suggests that her breasts were hard (which is a sign of youth and beauty). समुच्छून swollen. If one were to scald his hands with boiling water (hot tears), the hands would be dark-red. निर्झरः a stream, spring. शीर्यति—that was scattered into drops (*adj.* of ॰निर्झरे). स्नपयन्तीव...लोकम्—the idea is:—in her bright cheeks the people were reflected. Tears flowed from her eyes in streams on her cheeks and thus the reflections were bathed in water (tears). She was to tell the people sad news and thus plunge them into the fire of sorrow. One who kills himself by entering fire has first to perform a ceremonial bath. ०प्रवृत्तैः starting from her restless eyes. तारकांशुभिः by the rays of the pupils. श्यामा...दहन्तीव—her pupils were dark and she cast dark glances, whereby the day looked darkened. The poet fancies that the day looked dark because it was burnt by her grief. प्रत्युद्गता received, welcomed. कुट्टिमे न्यस्तं हस्तयुगलं यया she made her obeisance to the prince. गलन्तीभिः &c.—Her lip was dry through grief; when she bent her face, the rays of her gleaming teeth fell upon the lip. The rays resemble water. किमपि...देव्या the queen has resolved upon something (strange).

P. 83 ll. 12—34 **ततस्त...लापान्.** अपरम्—he was already grieving for his father and now he had to grieve for his mother. च्युत ... सत्त्वेन as if left by firmness of mind. द्रुतः melted. आचान्तः drunk. तुलितः weighed *i. e.* lifted up, made light of. अङ्कीकृतः branded. आतङ्केन by pain. अप्रतिपत्तिः (अविद्यमाना प्रतिपत्तिः यस्य) who did not know how to proceed. प्रतिपन्ना संज्ञा येन who regained his consciousness. Put the dash and quotation mark after this and not before. दुःखाभिषङ्गः impact or contact of griefs. कठिने qualifies both हृदये and अश्मनि. द्रुत...पयति gives rise to fire. When an iron hammer falls upon hard stones (flint), sparks issue forth. When many causes for grief arise, the heart is set ablaze. निरनुक्रोशस्य = निर्दयस्य. तत्र... लापान्—the principal sentence is तत्र च...राजमहिषीणाम् अशृणोत् दूरादेव...आलापान्. The queens, being about to burn themselves, bid a last farewell to their favourite attendants, trees, pets and things. चिन्तय...जननी take care of yourself; your mother is going abroad. जातीगुच्छः a clump of jasmine. मर्षणीयाः...हाराः—It was the convention of poets that the अशोक tree blossomed when kicked by young damsels. Such conventions are summarized in the verse 'स्त्रीणां स्पर्शात्प्रियङ्गुर्विकसति बकुलः सीधुगण्डूषसेकात् पादाघाता- दशोकस्तिलककुरबकौ वीक्षणालिङ्गनाभ्याम् । मन्दारो नर्मवाक्यात् पटुमृदुहसना- च्चम्पको वक्त्रवाताच्चूतो गीतान्नमेरुर्विकसति च पुरो नर्तनात्कर्णिकारः ॥' quoted by मल्लिनाथ on मेघदूत II. 17. Compare कादम्बरी 'अशोकतरुताडनारणितरमणी- मणिनूपुरझङ्कारसहस्रमुखरेषु' (p. 138 of P). कर्ण...राधाश्च and the fautl of plucking thy tender leaves for (making them into) ear-ornaments. वारुणी...ललित naughty on account of receiving mouthfuls of wine. The बकुल blossomed by the sprinkling of mouthfuls of wine. See the verse quoted above. दातव्यो...लिः you should offer to me the handful of water. निवापः libation of water offered to deceased parents &c. at a श्राद्ध ('पितृदानं निवापः स्यात्' इत्यमरः.). अपत्यमसि gives the reason. किं व्याहरसि—why do you call me ? स्वप्ने—she wishes that the *Mainá* may dream of her departed mistress. मार्गलग्नम्—who clings to my path. सम्भावित honoured, celebrated. गृहहरिणिके domesticated doe (vocative). सौविदल्लः chamberlain. 'सुविदन्तं विवाहं जानन्तं लान्ति सुविदल्लाः ऊढाः स्त्रियः तत्र भवाः सौविदल्लाः' क्षीरस्वामी. वल्लकी lute. 'वीणा तु वल्लकी' इत्यमरः. अयं जनः—refers to the person speaking (one of the queens). कात्यायनी or—निका means 'a widow of middle age who puts on red garments'. 'कात्यायन्यर्धवृद्धा या काषायवसनऽधवा' इत्यमरः. अलक्षणाम् who am unlucky (*lit.* not possessed of auspicious signs) धात्रेयी foster—sister. अपश्चिमाम्—अविद्यमानं पश्चिमं यस्याः—who can be seen no further hereafter. अय...लिः Here do I fold my hands by way of bidding (last) farewell. अवर...ध्वङ्गः embrace at the time of death.

P. 83 l. 35—**P. 84** l. 24 **दह्यमान...ददर्श** The principal sentence is तैः (आलापैः) दह्यमानश्रवणः प्रविशन्नेव...निर्यान्तीं मातरं ददर्श. दत्तं सर्वं स्वापतेयं (धनं) यया. स्वपतौ साधु स्वापतेयं according to 'पथ्यतिथिवसतिस्वपतेर्ढञ्' पा. 4. 4. 104. गृहीतं मरणप्रसाधनं यया who put on all the decorations of death (as सती). जानकी...वेक्ष्यन्तीम् who was about to enter fire before her husband like Sîtâ. सीता entered fire in the presence of (पुरः) her husband. For the incidents leading to the अग्निशुद्धि of सीता, see रामायण युद्धकाण्ड Chap. 115-118. After the defeat and death of रावण, राम received सीता rather coldly and said that he could not take her back as she had dwelt long in another's house. सीता then called upon लक्ष्मण to prepare the funeral pyre. Going round राम and calling upon fire not to harm her if she was chaste, she entered it. The fire assumed bodily form and handed over सीता to राम. प्रत्यग्रं (fresh) स्नान तेन आर्द्रः देहः यस्याः सा °देहा तस्याः भावः °देहता तया. लक्ष्मी when it rose out of the ocean at the time of churning must have been wet as the queen was. कुसुम्भ...दधानाम् who wore two garments reddish brown with safflower juice, as if she were the Heaven with two twillights. सान्ध्य *adj.* (from सन्ध्या). We must read अविधवामरण°. Her husband was yet living and therefore she was going to die like a सुवासिनी with all her decorations, with ताम्बूल in her mouth and so on. The author specifies below some of these, such as कण्ठसूत्र, हार, अङ्गराग &c. ताम्बूल...पाटलम् reddened by the mass of the brilliance of her lip that was dyed dark-red with betel. पट्टांशुकम् a silken cloth (shawl &c.). ०चिह्नम्—all the signs of a सुवासिनी that she wore on her body were tinged with the hue of her lip. कण्ठसूत्र- (Marathi मंगळसूत्र)—is an indispensable ornament always worn on the neck by all women whose husbands are living. The red कण्ठसूत्र hanging on her bosom looked like a stream of blood issuing from her broken heart. तिर्य...त्पीडयन्तीम् who pressed her throat with a necklace the threads of which were drawn aside by the thorn-like point of her ear-rings that were bent crosswise, as if it (necklace) was a halter of white silk rolled together. The idea of पाश is suggested by her approaching death. The necklace of pearls with its threads resembled a white silken rope with which one may hang oneself. सरसः (juicy, thick) कुङ्कुमाङ्गरागः (saffron unguent) यस्याः सा ०रागा तस्याः भावः ०रागता तया. कवलिता devoured. दिधक्षता—instru. of the desiderative base of दह्. Her body glowed with saffron paste and therefore appeared as if it were surrounded by flames of fire. चिता...पूरयन्तीम्—tears fell on her garment. Being white they looked like flowers which would be required as offerings to the funeral fire. गृह...विकिरन्तीम्- bracelets that she wore fell from her hands at each step; they resembled offerings presented to गृहदेवताs in bidding them a last farewell. आप्रपदीनां reaching to the feet. 'स्यात्रिष्वाप्रपदीनं तत्प्राप्नोत्याप्रपदं हि यत्' अमरः. The word is formed according to 'आप्रपदं प्राप्नोति' पा. 5. 2. 8 (पादस्याग्रं प्रपदं तन्मर्यादीकृत्य आप्रपदम्). गुण...मालाम् a wreath of flowers strung together. The wreath reaching her feet resembled a swing, which also has गुणs (ropes) resembling garlands. The swing is said to be that of यम, because she was going to die. अन्तर्गुञ्जन्तः मधुकराः तैः मुखरेण. आमन्त्र्य...कर्णोत्पलेन—the idea is:—she had a lotus on her ear as an ornament. In that lotus bees were humming. The humming of bees is fancied to be the words of farewell uttered by her कर्णोत्पल to the lotus of her eyes (that were about to perish along with her). Domestic हंसs are always represented as following the tinkling of the anklets of ladies. See above (text) p. 27 ll. 28–29. बद्धं मण्डलं यथा स्यात् तथा in a circle. संनिहितः प्राणसमः यस्मिन् (1) on which her husband dear to her as her own life was drawn; (2) in which her husband dwelt (with चित्तम्). She held fast (अविचलं) in her hand a board; her mind also was fixed fast on dying. Remove the comma after ॰दामकाम्. अर्चार्थं (पूजार्थं) बद्धं उद्धयमानं धवलपुष्पाणां दाम यस्याम् (with पताकाम् and यष्टिम्). She had held fast to her bosom the spear-haft of her husband and had tied round it in worship a garland of white flowers. The poet fancies the प्रासयष्टि to be the banner of a पतिव्रता. The pole of a banner also has garlands of flowers hanging from it. 'प्रासस्तु कुन्तः' इत्यमरः. A सती if her husband died abroad was allowed to burn herself with his पादुकाs. Here यशोमती being the wife of a warrior appropriately takes प्रासयष्टि. बन्धोरिव—When a person in grief sees a friend or relative, tears begin to flow. Compare for the idea 'सन्तानवाहीन्यपि मानुषाणां दुःखानि सद्बन्धुवियोगजानि । दृष्टे जने प्रेयसि दुःसहानि स्रोतःसहस्रैरिव संप्लवन्ते ॥' उत्तरराम॰ IV. 8.; 'स्वजनस्य हि दुःखमग्रतो विवृतद्वारमिवोपजायते ॥' कुमार IV. पत्युः—is to be connected with सचिवान्. पादपतने समुद्गमत् अभ्यधिकं बाष्पाम्भः तस्य प्रवाहेण उपरुद्धा दृक् येषाम् whose eyes were choked up by the torrent of tears that welled up when they fell at her feet. कथ...देशान् who with difficulty understood the instructions (she gave). अनुनयेन (courteously) निवर्तितः अत एव विधुरः (distracted) वृद्धबन्धुवर्गः तेन वर्धमानः ध्वनिः यस्य. There was wailing in the house, which was augmented by the group of old kinsmen, who, when they followed the queen, were courteously asked by her to return to the house. भर्तृ... हृदयाम् whose heart was captivated by the roar of caged lions, that resembled the voice of her lord. धात्र्या...साधिताम् who was adorned by her nurse and by her own devotion to her lord. Her nurse had helped in decorating her person. In each of the following clauses, words like प्रसाधिताम् bear a literal and also a metaphorical meaning. जरत्या...धार्यमाणाम् she was supported by an old woman and by swoon, both being familiar. Frequent swoons gave relief to her aching heart and supported her. व्यसनसङ्गतया (1) who accompanied her in her misfortune (with सखी); (2) that was connected with (*i. e.* arose from) her misfortune (with पीडा). गृहीतसर्वावयवेन—her servants clasped her limbs; anguish pervaded all her limbs. कुल...ष्ठिताम् she was preceded by great nobles and she was full of heavy sighs. अतिवृद्धैः—the chamberlains were very old, while her sorrows were very heavy (वृद्ध grown, increased). कौलेयक a dog. Everything that pertained to her husband was dear to her and she was sorry to part even from the favourite dogs of her husband.

'कौलेयकः सारमेयः कुक्कुरो मृगदंशकः' इत्यमरः. The word is formed from कुल according to 'कुलकुक्षिग्रीवाभ्यः श्वास्यलङ्कारेषु' पा. 4. 2. 96. (ढकञ्। कौलेयकः श्वा, कौलोऽन्यः । सि. कौ.). सपत्नी...पतन्तीम्—in the hour of death, she forgot all petty jealousies.

P. 84 l. 25—**P. 85** l. 10 दूरादेव...प्रारोदीत्. सस्नेह...चूडः the hair on the top of whose head was as if affectionately kissed by the rays of the jewels of the anklets (of his mother). When he fell at his mother's feet, the rays of the jewelled anklets naturally fell on his hair. The poet fancies that the rays did so out of love. देवी...त्पतनम्—the sentence is देवी यशोमती...बाष्पोत्पतनं निवारयितुं न शशाक. पादयोः निहितं शिरः येन (*adj.* of तनये). विमनसि whose mind was distracted. गुरुणा...ष्टभ्यमाना arrested or enveloped by the great force of grief as by a large mountain. उद्वेगस्य आवेगः तेन. The reading of A and C 'उद्वेगवेगेन' is also good. If a torrent be arrested by a large mountain, it runs past with great force. मूर्च्छा एव अन्धतमसं (blinding darkness). 'अवसमन्धेभ्यस्तमसः' पा. 5. 4. 79 (तमस् when preceded by अव, सम् and अन्ध has अ added on to it). रसातल is one of the seven पातालs (अतल, वितल, सुतल, तलातल, रसातल, महातल and पाताल). पाताल, as the haunt of demons, must be dark. There is also another suggestion. A torrent flows on the earth (रसातल). चिर...ण्डितेन formed into a mass by being pent up for a long time. स्नेह...भूयमाना she was overwhelmed by a tide of love that manifested itself in full strength. If a flow (of water) were pent up for a long time, it bursts forth in a flood; similarly if one checks tears for a long time, they will gush forth irresistibly. कृताः प्रयत्नाः यया सा ०यत्ना. उत्कटः (great) कुचयोः उत्कम्पः तेन प्रकटितं असह्यशोकस्य आकूतं (emotion) यया. गद्गदिकया गृह्यमाणः गलः तेन विकला who was in a distressing condition with her throat choked up (on account of tears). निःसामान्येन (unparalleled) मन्युना (grief) तरलीक्रियमाणः अधरोद्देशः (अधरप्रान्तः) यस्याः. पुनरुक्तेन (repeated) स्फुरणेन निबिडितं (tightened) नासापुटं यस्याः. We may perhaps explain differently. Her grief was so great that it could be inferred from the tremor of her lip. But her nose also was in tremor. This latter was superfluous (पुनरुक्त) so far as the inference of the grief by which she was shaken was concerned. सञ्छाद्य—connect this with ०पटान्तेन and वदनेन्दुम्. सञ्छाद्य...वदनेन्दुं she covered up her moon-like face, that was raised up a little, with the hem of her shawl (अंशुकपट) the body of which was inlaid with a row of the rays of her nails, as if with a flood of lucid tears issuing through the small interstices (of the shawl). As she held the fine shawl with her hands, the rays of her bright nails shot through the interstices of the fine texture of the shawl. The bright rays resembled tears. करनखमयूखमालया खचिता तनुः यस्य (*adj.* of ०पटान्तेन). तन्वन्तरेभ्यः निर्गच्छत् अच्छं अस्रं तस्य स्रोतसा इव. सरन्ती—governs शैशवम् as its object. अङ्कशायिनः अस्य (हर्षस्य) of him while he lay on her lap. ज्ञाति...हृदया as her heart thought of her parents' home. न पश्यतम् do not look at (me). विश्रान्तं भागधेयं यस्याः whose good luck has come to an end. असंनिहितं—राज्यवर्धन had been sent away on the expedition against the Hūṇas. श्वशुर०—we saw at the end of the fourth उच्छ्वास that राज्यश्री left the parental roof with her husband. किम...जनेन How have I offended you? अपराद्धं तव—the root राध् with अप meaning 'to offend' governs the genitive or locative of the person offended. मुषितास्मि I am robbed. कृतान्तं = दैवम्. मुक्तः कण्ठः यथा स्यात्तथा—lit. giving a free scope to her throat *i. e.* bitterly, loudly. प्राकृतप्रमदेव like an ordinary (or low) woman.

P. 85 l. 11—**P. 86** l. 11 **प्रशान्ते ... पतत्.** प्रशान्ते ... वेगे when the force of grief had ceased. प्ररुदितस्य—connect this with दृष्टिम्. पक्ष्मपालीषु पुञ्ज्यमानः नखकिरणनिवहः यस्याः. पक्ष्म...मार्ज she wiped his eye that as if melting only flowed the more, on the tips of the lashes of which clustered a mass of the rays of her nails. When she placed her hand on his eye the rays of her nails looked like tears. स्वयमपि connect this with लोचने...प्रमृज्य (after wiping her son's eyes, she wiped her own). कठोर...दरे the inside of which (eyes) was bereft of whiteness that was swallowed up by a deep red. On account of long weeping her eyes had grown red. धवलिम्ना instrumental of धवलिमन् (from धवल). See notes on कालिमा above p. 68. क्वथत् अस्रं तेन श्वयन् पर्यन्तः ययोः the corners of which had become swollen by hot (*lit.* boiling) tears. शुक्लशीकरेण तारं (bright) तारकितं पक्ष्म ययोः the bright eyelashes of which were starred with lucid drops (of tears). तारकित (having stars *i. e.* spotted)—तारकाः सञ्जाताः अस्य—according to 'तदस्य सञ्जातं तारकादिभ्य इतच्' पा. 5. 2. 36. The bright drops of tears on the eyelashes resembled stars. सूक्ष्मतराणां अश्रुबिन्दूनां परिपाटी (series) तस्याः पतनानुबन्धः (continuous falling) तेन विधुरे (लोचने). बाष्पार्द्र...लताम् then she placed on the top of her ear her tresses that were loosened in her sorrow and that stuck (गृहीता) to her cheek wet with tears. अधःस्रस्त...सटाम् she then pushed aside the mass of her hair that hung obliquely (on her shoulder) and that was entangled with her ear-ornament that had got loose and was dangling about. बालिका । बालायां वालुकापत्रकाइलाकर्णभूषणे ॥' मेदिनी (कान्त० 130). अश्रु...त्तरीयम्—she raised into its position the shawl covering her bosom that had slightly slipped aside. तरङ्गित...मुखकमलम्—the passage as it stands is difficult to construe. So read लावण्यं and कुब्जिकावर्जित०, as done by C and T. तरङ्गितमिव (connect with पयसा below)—the idea is:—when she washed her face, it seemed as if it were flooded with waves, as a lotus growing in a lake may be tossed by ripples. The reading of B नखांशुपटलेन yields a good sense. In washing her face, she again and again passed her hand over it. The rays of the bright nails of her hand were like water and hence her face over which the rays spread looked as if flooded with waves. मग्नः अंशुकपटान्तः तस्य तनवः ताम्राः लेखाः ताभिः लाञ्छितं लावण्यं यस्य (*adj.* of ०कमलम्). She had pressed the hem of her shawl against her face when she wiped off her tears. The red lines caused by the pressure of the hem marked her beautiful face. A lotus flower has also red lines on its petals which are small and deeply impressed like the hem of a shawl. (मग्नाः अंशुकपटान्तवत् तनवः ताम्राः &c.). कुब्जिकया आवर्जितं राजतं राजहंसास्यं तस्मात् समुद्गीर्णेन—(with water) that was emitted from a swan-mouthed vessel of silver inclined by a hunch-backed girl. The attendants of the harem always included hunch-backed persons, dwarfs, deaf-mutes and eunuchs. See कादम्बरी 'प्रनृत्तकलमूककुब्जकिरातवामनबधिरजडजनपुरःसरेण' (p. 74 of P); 'कुब्जकिरातबधिरवामनवर्षधरकलमूकानुगतेन परिजनेन' (p. 59 of P). A lotus may also be bent and be tossed with water emitted from the mouth of a swan that being white resembles silver. The swan may be attracted by a कुब्जिका (a fragrant flower plant). कल...धृते held by deaf-mutes. 'कलमूकोऽवाक्श्रुतिः' इति हलायुधः. वासःशकले on a piece of cloth, napkin. नासि...र्हो वा It is not that you are not loved, nor are you devoid of good qualities, nor do you deserve to be abandoned. स्तन्ये... हृदयम्—She means to say that her whole heart is with him, as if it had been drunk up by him. प्रभूताः प्रभोः (प्रभाकरवर्धनस्य) प्रसादाः तैः अन्तरिता—She means:—between you and me (that am to see you) intervene the numerous favours bestowed on me by my husband. My eye only sees them and not you. पुरुषान्तरविलोकने व्यसनं (attachment) अस्ति अस्याः. Both लक्ष्मी (sovereignty or Glory) and earth (क्ष्मा) pass from one brave

कुल...क्रियाम् and thinking that only that course of conduct befitting a lady of high family was better. क्रियां refers to her resolve to die. अभिनन्दति...रूपम्—the author assigns this as a reason why हर्ष acquiesced in the resolve of his mother. Noble birth, though made timorous by love, approves of what is proper to the time and place. पौरा...दिग्भिः who was as if obstructed by the quarters that were full of the echoes of the wailings of the citizens. सरस्वती—is a river on the banks of which the modern Thanesar (स्थाण्वीश्वर) in Karnal District, Panjab, is situated. It rises in the Sirmur state on the borders of the Ambala District and is lost in the sands in the great desert for several miles. स्त्री...पातैः she cast terrified glances as is natural to women. Her eyes had grown red by weeping. Therefore the glances resembled red lotus flowers. We have seen above (notes p. 13) that red lotuses were to be used in the worship of the sun. भानु...न्दवी as the form of the moon enters the sun (on the day of the अमावास्या). Note 'चन्द्रमा वा अमावास्यायामादित्यमनुप्रविशति सोऽन्तर्धीयते तं न निर्जानन्ति' ऐतरेय ब्राह्मण, 8th पञ्चिका chap. 5; compare विक्रमोर्वशीय III. 7 'रविमावसते&c'. चित्रभानुम्—अग्निम्. चित्रभानु also means 'the sun'. इतरोपि refers to हर्ष. स्वल्पः अवशेषः यस्याः सा ०शेषा प्राणवृत्तिः यस्य तम् which was almost ebbing away. परिवर्त्यमाना तारका यस्य (1) the pupil of whose eye was being revolved (with the king); (2) that makes the stars revolve (with the moon). अस्त...षन्तम् (1) about to die; (2) about to set. अस...द्रुतः assailed by an excess of intolerable sorrow. त्याजितः...धैर्यम् affection made him lose all steadiness. Mark the construction (हर्षः धैर्यं त्यजति primitive; स्नेहः हर्षं धैर्यं त्याजयति causal; हर्षः स्नेहेन धैर्यं त्याजितः passive causal). आश्लिष्य—governs पादपद्मौ. सकल...लालितौ fondled by the crests of all haughty kings. अन्तस्ता...भवन्तम् as if it were his moonlike face melting through an inner fire. This and the following clauses are to be connected with अश्रुस्रोतसां सन्तानं वर्षन्. दशन...पद्यमानम् as if it were the net-work of the light of his teeth reduced to water. His bright tears resembled bright water. His teeth were very white. अच्छाच्छम् very bright. अश्रु...वर्षन् showering a continuous stream of tears as if his eyes were made up of a large cloud. इतरवत् like a common man. विमुक्तः आरावः (cry) येन.

P. 86 l 28—**P. 87** l. 10 **राजा तु...लोचने.** उपरुध्यमाना दृष्टिः यस्य whose sight was obstructed (*i. e.* whose eyes could not see his son in the last moments). अविरतरुदितशब्देन आश्रितौ श्रवणौ

यस्य whose ears were affected by the incessant weeping (of हर्ष). Sight failed the dying king, but the incessant weeping arrested his ears and roused him to some consciousness. अविद्यमानं महासत्त्वं येषाम् that have no firm heart. महा...बीजिता Firmness of mind is the first (foremost) stay of the people and royal blood comes after it. People first betake themselves to the man of strong will. सर्वैः अतिशयैः आश्रितः the abode of all eminent things (or virtues). क्व—क्व—two क्वs denote great disparity or incongruity. कुल...करणमिव to call you the lamp of the family is to slight you whose majesty is like that of the sun. प्रदीप (1) lamp; (2) ornament. To call a man a lamp when he is like the sun would be really condemning him. शौर्येण पटुप्रज्ञया (sharp intellect) च उपबृंहितः (magnified) पराक्रमः यस्य. The lion has only physical strength (पराक्रम), but no keen intellect and no heroic heart. लक्षणैः आख्यातं (declared) चक्रवर्तिपदं यस्य. पुनरुक्त superfluous. गृह्यतां श्रीः accept royal dignity. स्वयमेव...गृहीतस्य—लक्ष्मी herself has come to you. Compare for a somewhat similar idea 'लभेत वा प्रार्थयिता न वा श्रियं श्रिया दुरापः कथमीप्सितो भवेत्' कुमार॰ V. उभय...गीषोः who are desirous of conquering this world and the next. अपुष्कलम् not sufficient, little. शशिनः कराणां निकरः समूहः तद्वत् निर्मलं यशः तस्य सञ्चये एकः केवलः अभिनिवेशः (fondness) अस्ति अस्य इति॰ वेशिनः. When हर्ष has set his heart in achieving spotless fame alone, it is useless to ask him to take the treasury. राजकम्—राज्ञां समूहः. गतार्थम् meaningless. अनुचितनियोगः an injunction that is unworthy. दीर्घाभ्यां दोर्दण्डाभ्यां अर्गलितानि (bolted, safeguarded) दिङ्मुखानि येन. अनुवादः repetition. It is a technical term in the पूर्वमीमांसा system. When a Vedic text lays down an injunction (विधि), other passages, that either reiterate, explain or illustrate the विधि, are called अनुवादs. विधिविहितस्य वचनमनुवादः. Harsha was already protecting the world. To call upon him to protect the world was simply superfluous, a mere repetition in words. आनुषङ्गिकम्—necessarily following; incidental (अनुषङ्गात् आगतः ठक्). हर्ष was like a लोकपाल. If he guarded the whole world it necessarily followed that he would protect his attendants. धनुर्गुणस्य किणः तस्य कलङ्कः तेन कालीकृतः प्रकोष्ठः यस्य whose forearm is blackened by the spot of the scar of the bow-string. निग्राह्यताम्—It would be better to have निगृह्यताम्. चापलम् rashness, levity. नूतन...वयसि in tender years. निरवकाशा has no room or scope. सहज...चिन्ता this is a thought for your inherent valour *i. e.* this is a matter which will be dealt with by your valour; I need not enjoin you to do this. The words are capable of yielding another sense. To ask you to annihilate your foes is casting a doubt (चिन्ता) on your inherent valour. C and T translate 'Annihilate your foes is a suggestion of your inborn valour'. This is not clear. अपुनरुन्मीलनाय never again to open them. The reading of B 'प्रत्यपद्यत पूषात्मजः' would mean 'the son of the sun (*i. e.* यम) came to him.'

P 87 l. 11—**P. 88** l. 2 **अस्मिन्नेवान्तरे...नीयत.** पूषापि—The force of अपि lies in this that, as the king lost his life, so even the sun lost his brilliance, which is the sun's essence. लज्जमान इव अधोमुखः the sun hung down as if ashamed. One who feels ashamed hangs down his head. The sun hung down on the western horizon. भूपालस्य अभावः (death) तेन शोकः स एव शिखी (अग्निः) तेन. A thing heated in the fire becomes red. मन्दं...दिवः slowly the sun descended from heaven as if for paying a visit of condolence, following the practice of worldly men. अप्रियप्रश्न is opposed to कुशलप्रश्न. दित्सुः desirous of giving. अपरजलनिधि western ocean. सद्यो दत्तः नृपाय जलाञ्जलिः येन. आलोहितम् slightly red. Water is to be offered with कर (hand, ray). In offering water, one would naturally feel sorrow. एवं च...नीयत—the principal sentence is नरेन्द्रः...सरस्वतीं नीत्वा...यशःशेषतामनीयत. निधनेन निधीयमानं विपुलं वैराग्यं यस्मिन्. शान्तं वपुः यस्य. An ascetic has distaste for the world (वैराग्य); the sun, a short time after the king's death, lost his radiance (विरागस्य भावः वैराग्यम्, विगतः रागः रक्तिमा यस्य). An ascetic must be शान्त (restrained); so also the sun's body became subdued (*i. e.* lost its colour). An ascetic enters the recesses of mountain caves; the sun set behind the western mountain. समुपोह्यमानं (increasing) महाजनस्य अश्रु तदेव दुर्दिनं (stormy or rainy day) तेन आर्द्रीकृते. निर्वाति (loc. sing. of *pr. p.* of वा with निर्) आतपे when the heat (of the sun) became extinguished (as if wet with &c.). Separate रुचा (कान्त्या) इव. लोहितायति—loc. sing. of *pr. p.* of the denominative verb from लोहित. The world was reddened by the glow of the setting sun; but the poet attributes the glow of the world to the tear-flushed eyes of the people. उष्णायमानाः (hot) अनेकनराणां निश्वासाः तैः सन्तापः तेन प्लुष्टं (scorched). नृपा...कमलिनीषु when the lotus beds were left by glory, as if the latter had started to follow the king (in death). Day lotuses fade in the evening *i. e.* their glory leaves them. That लक्ष्मी is identified with राज्यलक्ष्मी and is fancied as leaving them to perish after the king. पति...भुवि when the earth, having covered itself in shadows, became dark as if through grief for her husband. A king is poetically spoken of as the husband of the earth. The shades of evening were falling fast and so the earth seemed to be shrouded in them. श्यामायमाना (1) becoming dark; (2) behaving like a श्यामा (a handsome lady). A handsome woman would have all her brilliance (छाया) covered up (*i. e.* gone) through grief for her husband. परिवृता (concealed) छाया (कान्तिः) यस्याः; छायाभिः परिवृता परिवृतछाया (like the compound राजदन्त). C and T prefer the reading परिवृत्त for परिवृत and explain 'the shadows have retraced their course eastwards.' परित्यक्तानि कलत्राणि यैः (applies to both कुलपुत्र and चक्रवाक). The चक्रवाक becomes separate from its mate at the approach of night. See above p. 10 and 57. वनान्तान् (1) vicinity of woods (with कुलपुत्र); (2) the fringes of water (with चक्रवाक). The noble young men betook to woods out of grief; the चक्रवाकs to water. 'वने सलिलकानने' इत्यमरः. छत्र...शयेषु when the water-lilies closed their calyx, as if afraid of losing the umbrella-like expanse of their petals. कुशे जले शेते इति कुशेशयम्. 'सहस्रपत्रं कमलं शतपत्रं कुशेशयम्' इत्यमरः. The lotuses closed their buds at the departure of the sun. The poet fancies that the lotuses did so because they were afraid that their petals would fade and their umbrella-like appearance would disappear. There is another meaning. The lotuses are compared to devoted servants (lying on mere कुश grass in their grief and not on soft beds). They were terrified by the breaking of the royal umbrella (*i. e.* by the death of the king) and hide the treasure (कोश) in order to safeguard it for the rightful heir. C and T explain that lotuses are compared to queens, who hide the treasures. But कुशेशय is not feminine. Besides it is not in keeping with Indian sentiment to represent the widowed queens as hiding treasures when engrossed in grief. छत्रभङ्ग would be a very bad omen, foretelling the death of the king. Compare बृहत्संहिता 46. 74 'शक्रध्वजेन्द्रकीलस्तम्भद्वारप्रपातभङ्गेषु । तद्वत्कपाटतोरणकेतूनां नरपतेर्मरणम् ॥'. स्फुटित...तपे when the red glow (of evening) flowed away (gradually vanished) as if it were the flood of blood from the broken hearts of the quarter wives. अनु...धीशे when the lord of brilliance (the sun) remained only in अनुराग (red glow; love). The sun vanished and what he left behind was only the red glow of the western sky. The king, who also was

तेजसामधीश, had gone away, leaving behind only love. ०वितन्यमानः बहलः रागः तेन पाटलायाम्. प्रेतपताकायाम्—A banner flies in the sky. स्फुरन्तीषु...लेखासु when streaks of darkness appeared obstructing sight. The black chowries of the hearse resemble darkness and are an evil omen when seen (दर्शने प्रतिकूला). असिता...काष्ठायाम् (1) असितागुरुवत् कालाः काष्ठाः दिशः यस्याम्–in which the quarters are dark like black aloe wood (with रजनी); (2) which had the black beams of dark aloe wood (with चिता). असितागुरोः कालानि काष्ठानि यस्याम्. दन्तामल...लक्ष्मीषु—Here there are numerous puns. The principal idea is that the night lotuses (कुमुद) began to expand. The night lotuses are compared to *satîs* joyfully following their husbands in death. दन्तवत् (like ivory) अमलैः पत्रैः (petals) प्रसाधिता कर्णिका यासाम् (with कुमुदs); दन्तस्य (of ivory) अमलैः पत्रैः (thin plates) प्रसाधिता (manufactured) कर्णिका (ear-ring) यासाम् (with women). पत्र may also mean 'painting or figures' in the latter case. 'कर्णललाटात्कनलङ्कारे' पा. 4. 3. 65. Compare ललाटिका above. केसराणां (filaments) मालाभिः कल्पिता मुण्डमालिका यासाम् on whose top (मुण्ड) there were rows of filaments (with कुमुदs); (केसराणां बकुलानां &c.) whose heads were wreathed with garlands of बकुल (with Satîs). We saw above that a Sati was to die with all her ornaments &c. प्र... मुखीषु (1) with expanding buds (with कुमुदs); with smiling faces (with Satîs). A Satî was not to show that she regretted the step that she was taking. The निर्णयसिन्धु (परि० III) quotes a passage from the स्कन्दपुराण 'अनुव्रजति भर्तारं गृहात्पितृवनं मुदा। पदे पदेऽश्वमेधस्य फलं प्राप्नोत्यनुत्तमम् ॥'. अव...कूजिते when the twitter of groups of birds lying in their nests (कुलायः-यम्) at the top of trees was heard as if it were the tinkling of the bells of the descending car (विमानः-नम्) of the gods. It was believed that celestial cars were sent to take heroes and great souls to heaven. नाक...पत्रे इव–the round and bright orb of the moon resembles a white umbrella. The moon rose in the east, of which Indra (पुरुहूत) is the lord. The poet fancies that the rising moon was the umbrella of Indra, come forward to welcome the king (प्रभाकर०) who was travelling along the path of heaven. नरेन्द्रः refers to प्रभाकरवर्धन; connect the word with अनीयत. स्वयं...स्कन्धैः—the feudatories themselves took on their shoulders the bier (शवशिबिका). शिबिसमः—शिबि was a king and is referred to as an ideal of self-sacrifice. Once इन्द्र assumed the form of a श्येन (hawk) and pursued धर्म

as कपोत. The latter threw himself on the lap of शिबि for help. The श्येन asked the king to give his own flesh in return for the कपोत whom he wanted to save. When the कपोत was placed in a balance, its weight increased and शिबि had to offer his whole body. Thereupon the gods showed themselves to him. See कथासरित्सागर I. 7. 88 ff; रामायण II. 12. 43 'शैब्यः श्येनकपोतीये स्वमांसं पक्षिणे ददौ ।'. पुरोहितः पुरःसरः येषाम्—headed by the family priest. हुताश...नीयत by being honoured with fire, he was reduced (to ashes), so that nothing but his fame remained.

P. 88 ll. 3–24 **देवोऽपि ... यामिनी.** पुञ्जीभूतेन—goes with लोकेन. All the persons connected with the king formed a group and were huddled up there. They were so many that it seemed as if the whole world had gathered there in grief. अन्त... सिच्यमानः wet as if outside (in the form of tears) by the melting of affection, which though inside, was heated by the fire of sorrow. Affection is internal; tears are visible. The poet fancies that the tears he shed were melted affection. निर्व्यवधानायां धरण्याम् on bare earth. व्यवधानम् what comes between, what intercepts. Nothing came between हर्ष and the earth. उपविष्ट एव—he sat; he did not even lie down. भीमरथी—name of the 7th night in the 7th month of the 77th year of a man's life. This was believed to be a most critical point. If a man survived it, it was believed that he would live for 100 years. The Com. gives three explanations 'भीमरथी नरकनदी कालरात्रिर्वा अन्ये तु सप्तसप्तत्या वर्षैस्तत्संख्यैश्च मासैर्दिनैश्च तावद्भिर्गतैरेका रात्रिर्भीमरथी भवति तामतिक्रान्तो वर्षशतजीवी नरो भवतीति प्राहुः'. ताते...लोकः now that my father is removed, the world of mortals is only this much *i. e.* the world cannot reach hereafter a higher stage. लोकस्य...पन्थानः the ways of the people are broken *i. e.* their progress is arrested. मनो... स्थानानि the splendid goals of ambition are blocked up (or rendered impossible). खिलम् means 'barren or waste soil.' खिलीभू means 'to become barren or impossible.' स्थगितानि covered, veiled. लुप्ता...यात्रा the business of the world has come to an end. प्रोषिताः ...काराः various kinds of manly deeds (or sports) are exiled. पुरुषकारः manliness. विश्रान्ता...भूमयः places where trust could be reposed have ceased to exist. अप...दानानि noble deeds are without an abode. अपदानम् (seems to be another form of अवदानम्) a pure course of conduct; a noble deed. निर...रसता the single-minded devotion to valour has no support now. कथा...ज्ञता capacity to judge has now become a matter of legend. और्जित्यम्

17

(ऊर्जितस्य भावः) might, vigour. Might has ceased to exist and so people may offer water to it just as they do to the dead. प्रव्रज्या—the order of a religious mendicant. बध्नातु...मनुष्यता let excellent manhood bind the widow's single braid. The idea is:—as the king is dead, वरमनुष्यता has now nobody to resort to. We have seen above that widows used to tie their hair in a single knot. समा...पदम् (1) let royal glory resort to a hermitage; (2) let राजश्री go to a hermitage. By the great resemblance in sound between राजश्री and राज्यश्री the words suggest the misfortunes of राज्यश्री. धवले वाससी—a widow was to wear white garments. See धर्मसिन्धु (परि० III विधवाधर्म) 'वासो न विकृतं वसेत्।'. वहतु वल्कले—wearing bark garments is a sign of forest life. क्व...ज्ञतया where will gratitude go to find him? महा...माणून् atoms for the creation of great men. For atoms see above pp. 12 and 44. जगज्जा...धर्मस्य the world has become a darkness for righteousness. The idea is that righteousness cannot now find its way to anybody, as the whole world is enveloped in darkness. दिवसम् (acc. of time) for the whole day. वीरगोष्ठ्यः assemblies of heroes. असम...भित्तयः—असमः (unparalleled) समररसः (liking for fighting) तेन समारब्धाः कलहकथाः (रणकथाः) ताभिः कण्टकिताः (thrilled) सुभटानां कपोलभित्तयः यासु. दीर्घरक्ते नयने यस्य (1) whose eyes were long and red (with मुख); the roots of which are long and red (with सरोज). For this latter meaning of नयन, compare the use of नेत्र in 'दीर्घरक्तनालनेत्रामुत्पलिनीमिव सरसी' (text p. 10. l. 3). लोह...गर्भम्—लोहस्तम्भात् अभ्यधिकः गरिमा गर्भे यस्य—that possessed a massiveness greater than that of an iron pillar. लोका...श्रूयेत सा भारती might I hear that voice of his calling me 'son' even in another world? सुधा...रन्ती emitting nectar. The ocean when churned gave up सुधा (अमृत). The words of the king were sweet like nectar. मध्यमानः क्षीरसागरः तस्य उद्गारवत् गम्भीरा (deep like the roar &c.).

P. 88 l. 25—**P. 89** l. 13 **ततः...जगाम.** ततः...हर्षः (p. 34 l. 2)—the principal sentence is ततः...चचाल उपस्थानाय देवो हर्षः. The poet now gives a graphic description of day-break. कृकवाकुः cock. 'कृकवाकुस्ताम्रचूडः कुक्कुटश्च रणायुधः' इत्यमरः. गृह...मयूरेषु when the domesticated peacocks let themselves fall from the tops of the trees growing on pleasure hills. गृहगिरि artificial eminences near the mansions. The peacocks rested in the branches of trees during the night and came down when the day broke. पत्ररथः a bird (पत्राणि पक्षाः रथः अस्य). सद्य...तमसि the darkness suddenly grew less and became exhausted. मन्दीभूतः आत्मस्नेहः येषाम् (1) in which the oil was failing; (2) whose love for their self had grown dull. A person who has lost all attachment to his self longs for death. The lamps also, as very little oil was left, were about to be extinguished. स्फुरन्तः अरुणस्य (रविसारथेः) किरणाः वल्कलमिव तेन प्रावृतं वपुः यस्य—the sky was covered with the flashing bark-like rays of early morn and therefore seemed to have taken to the life of a religious mendicant. A परिव्राजक also wears bark-garments that are red. प्रभात...तारकासु when the stars that were grey like the neck of a sparrow (कलविङ्कः) were being taken across by the morning. The idea seems to be that the vault of the sky is like a lake over which the stars were ferried and by morning found themselves on the other side. The stars looked dim in the light of morn. The grey stars resembled the fragments of the king's bones. The burnt up bones of the dead are collected on the third or fourth day in the morning and are carried to holy rivers like the Ganges and are thrown in them. See कुल्लूक on मनु० V. 59; the धर्मं० (परि० III) says 'अस्थिसञ्चयनं तु दाहदिनादारभ्य प्रथमदिने द्वितीये तृतीये चतुर्थे सप्तमे नवमे वा गोत्रजैः सह स्वस्वसूत्रोक्तप्रकारेण कार्यम् । ...अस्थ्नां गङ्गाम्भसि तीर्थान्तरे वा प्रक्षेपः ।'. The reading समुच्चीयमानासु of some MSS. of B is rightly preferred by C and T. It means 'being gathered together.' Bones are first gathered and then placed in a jar (see next clause). But if we take the reading in the text, we have first a reference to the carrying of the bones and then to the jars, which inverts the natural order. भूभृ...धारिषु (1) possessing round foreheads that had on them mountain minerals (with elephants); (2) carrying jars that contained the remains (bones) of the king. भूभृतां पर्वतानां धातवः गैरिकादयः (red chalk &c.) तद्गर्भाः कुम्भाः तान् धारयन्तीति; भूभृतः राज्ञः धातवः (अस्थीनि) तद्गर्भाः कुम्भाः घटाः &c. 'कुम्भौ घटेभमूर्धांशौ' इत्यमरः. विविध...मुखेषु—applies to both the wild elephants and those that carried the ashes of the king. तीर्थम् a descent into a river (Marathi घाट); a place of pilgrimage. It is better to read शावे शुचि० with some MSS. of B. शावः (1) tawny; (2) funeral, relating to a dead body (शवसम्बन्धी). शावः शुचि... पाण्डुरश्च शाव...पाण्डुरः. शुचि...पाण्डुरः (1) pale as a ball of white wax; (2) pale with a mass of boiled rice. सिक्थः boiled rice; सिक्थम् bee's wax. The pale moon in the morning looked like a पिण्ड of boiled rice offered to the dead. *Pindas* are often offered on the sandy banks of sacred rivers and the ocean. The moon was going to dip into the western ocean. परिसर: vicinity. क्रमेण—connect this with अस्तमुपगते रजनिकरे. नृप...तेजसीव—the poet fancies that the dimness of the moon's disc in the morning is due to the mass (विसर:) of the smoke of the pyre on which the king was burnt. नरपतिशोकः एव पावकः तेन दाहः तेन किणः (scar) तस्य कलङ्केन कालीकृतं चेतः यस्य. On the dim disc of the moon was seen a dark spot, which the poet fancies to be his mind bu-nt to charcoal by the fire of sorrow for the king. प्रोषितानां (gone on a journey *i. e.* dead) समस्तानां अन्तःपुरपुरंध्रीणां मुखचंद्राः तेषां वृन्दं तस्य उद्वेगेन विद्राणं वपुः यस्य. We saw above that all the queens had prepared themselves to die (text p. 28 l. 17 तत्र च मर्तु-मुद्यतानां राजमहिषीणां &c). The poet fancies that on seeing the agony (उद्वेग) of the women of the harem, the moon (as if out of compassion for the other moons-faces) vanished bodily (*i. e.* set). विद्राण run away (past p. p. of द्रा with वि). C and T translate विद्राण as 'stupefied'. प्रथमं अस्तमिता रोहिणी तया रणरणकः (eagerness, anxiety) तेन विमनाः (distracted) तस्मिन्. रोहिणी is the favourite wife of the moon out of the 27 नक्षत्रs. राजतीव... सवितरि when the sun that had mounted the sky shone like the king (प्रभाकर०). The king also mounted heaven after dying. The reading राजनीव preferred by C and T would no doubt improve the sense, but is not supported by the MSS. used by B. परि...प्रबन्धे when the continuance (प्रबन्धः) of night was turned back, like the kingdom. The kingdom also had changed hands. परिवृत्तम् exchanged; turned back. प्रबुद्ध...कर इव like a bed of lotuses roused by the awakened flamingoes. हर्ष also was advised by the circle of wise (प्रबुद्ध) swan-like kings (to give up wailing). Read चापस्नानाय for चोप०. अपस्नानम् bathing on the death of a relative. Drop the comma after ०हंसेषु. नूपुररवस्य विरामेण (cessation) मूकाः मन्दाश्च मन्दिरहंसाः येषु (*adj.* of शुद्धा०). We saw above (p. 92) that हंसs followed the jingling of the anklets of young ladies. But as all the queens had perished on the death of the king, there were no young ladies left. पतितः यूथपः यस्य. कक्ष्या...जने his father's servants stood in the courts of the palace. कक्ष्या also signifies 'the girth rope of an elephant or horse'. विषादि...कुञ्जरे when the king's sad elephant reclined against its post, motionless and dull and having its rider weeping on its back. उपरि रुदन् निषादी (हस्तिपकः) यस्य (*adj.* of ०कुञ्जरे). 'आधोरणा हस्तिपका हस्त्यारोहा निषादिनः' इत्यमरः. मन्दुरापालकस्य (stable keeper) आक्रन्दैः कथिते. अजिरं (courtyard) भजते इति. विश्रान्तः जयशब्दकलकलःयस्मिन्.

आस्थानमण्डपः Hall of audience. अपस्नातः'—अपस्नातो मृतस्नातः' इत्यमरः—one who has bathed after the death of a relative. अनि...मौलिः without wringing his hair. उद्गम...वाससी two white silken robes. 'तत्स्यादुद्गमनीयं यद्धौतयोर्वस्त्रयोर्युगम्' इत्यमरः. निरातपत्रः without an umbrella (the insignia of royalty). निरुत्सारणः without anybody to remove people from his path. समुप...सप्तौ although a horse was brought near. चक्षुषा...उद्गिरन् as if emitting from his eye the fire of sorrow through fear of burning his father who now remained only in his (हर्ष's) heart. His eyes were extremely red. The poet fancies that the redness was the fire of sorrow in his heart. हर्ष emitted it from his eye, so that his father now enshrined in the heart might not be burnt by the fire. अताम्बू...क्षालितस्य—हर्ष had not taken betel for many days and had washed his lip a long time before (yet it was red by nature). कल्प...लयस्य—the tender leaves of any tree are reddish; much more therefore of कल्पतरु. The धर्म० (परि० III) says 'तत्राशौचमध्ये माषमांसापूपमधुरलवणदुग्धाभ्यङ्गताम्बूलक्षाराणि वर्ज्यानि.' अधर...मोक्षैः on account of the brilliance of his spraylike lip, he seemed to vomit, as he sent forth hot sighs, lumps of flesh and blood, because his heart was struck. If one were beaten in the region of the heart, he may vomit blood. When he heaved up deep sighs his red lips quivered and presented the appearance of blood being vomited.

P. 89 ll. 14–27 **राज...विचेरुः.** उद्बाष्पैः (उद्गतं बाष्पं येषाम्) full of tears. आत्मानम् mark the reflexive use of आत्मानम् with the plural केचित्. भृगु...बन्धुः some tied themselves to precipices *i. e.* killed themselves by falling from precipices. 'प्रपातस्त्वतटो भृगुः' इत्यमरः. अनशनैः शुचम् असमाम् अशमयन् they destroyed their unparalleled sorrow by fasting (*i. e.* they died fasting). शलभाः moths. गृहीतवाचः that took the vow of silence. तुषारशिखरिणं = हिमालयम्. उपत्यका—see p. 63. सेवाविमुखाः disgusted with service (*i. e.* with the life of a servant at the royal court). परि...जगृहुः resorted to untenanted spots in forests subsisting on a limited number of morsels. परिच्छिन्नैः पिण्डकैः may also mean 'with thin bodies.' धर्मः एव धनं येषाम्. धमन्त्यः धमनयः येषाम् with veins fully blown up (*i. e.* all the veins appeared prominent, they were emaciated). गृहीतं काषायं (red cloth) यैः. कषायेण रक्तं काषायम्, according to 'तेन रक्तं रागात्' पा. 4. 2. 1. कापिलं—कपिलस्य इदम्. कपिल is the founder of the सांख्य system, which enumerates 25 तत्त्वs. अधिजगिरे perfect of इ with अधि to study. It is to be noted that the wearing of

काषाय is here associated with कापिलमत; but याज्ञ० prescribes काषाय for all those that desire मोक्ष 'त्यागः परिग्रहाणां च जीर्णकाषायधारणम्' ॥ III. 157. आचोटिताः चूडामणयः यैः the crest-jewels of which were torn away. शरणीकृतः धूर्जटिः (शिवः) यैः. जटाः जघटिरे tied knots of matted hair. परिपाटलं प्रलम्बं चीवराम्बरं (tattered garment) तेन संवीताः enveloped. स्वाम्य...चक्रुः—they rendered glorious their devotion to their master. अनुराग also means 'redness'. By putting on red garments, they made redness appear brilliant. तपोवनहरिणानां जिह्वाञ्चलैः (tips of the tongues) उल्लिह्यमानाः (licked) मूर्तयः येषाम्. They became वानप्रस्थs and resorted to the forest. पाणि...मृष्टैः wiped (or scoured) with their spray-like hands. आताम्रः (slightly red) रागः (colour) येषाम्. नयन...वहन्तः they bore water in their eyes and in their jars. The idea is:—they shed tears, which they wiped with their hands and their eyes were red by weeping. They also rubbed their jars with their hands and carried water in them. The baked jars were red in colour. गृहीतं व्रतं यैः who took the vow of an ascetic (संन्यासी). See वसिष्ठस्मृति Chap. 10 for the धर्मs of a परिव्राजक. 'मुण्डोऽममोऽपरिग्रहः सप्तागाराण्यसङ्कल्पितानि चरेद्भैक्षं विधूमे सन्न—मुसले। 17...यज्ञोपवीती उदककमण्डलुहस्तः शुचिर्ब्राह्मणो वृषलान्नवर्जी न हीयते ब्रह्मलोकात्'। 24.

P. 89 l.28—**P. 90** l. 4 **देवमपि...वारयन्.** The principal sentence is देवमपि हर्षं...मुनयः...पौराणिकाः पर्यवारयन्. श्रियं शाप इति—supply मन्यमानम् (l. 32) after this pair and after each of the pairs in the following clauses. श्रियं शाप इति म० who regarded royal glory as a curse. It will be noticed that the poet is influenced in his choice of words in this passage by the jingling assonance of sounds. महीं महापातकम्—As we must shun महापातकs, he shunned the earth. For महापातकs, see above (p.84). भोगान् भुजङ्गाः—as the serpent, so charming to look at, is yet deadly, so the objects of worldly enjoyments he regarded as dangerous. निलयं निरय इति who looked upon home as Hell (because he suffered torments). जीवितमयशः—to have continued to live after the death of such a noble father was really infamy. कल्यता health. 'कल्यौ सज्जनिरामयौ' इत्यमरः. विषममृतमिति—poison he regarded as nectar, because the former, if taken by him, would have assuaged all his torments and united him by death with his father. कामं क्रकच इति—he looked upon desire as a saw *i. e.* to entertain desires for anything when his father was dead was as painful to him as sawing with a saw. पितृ...गताः

whose fathers and grand-fathers had enjoyed (court favour). कुलपुत्राः—This and the following words like गुरवः are to be connected with पर्यवारयन् below. वंशक्रमेण आहितं गौरवं येषु to whom respect was paid for generations. ग्राह्याः गिरः येषाम्—whose words were to be accepted (or acted upon)—qualifies गुरवः. श्रुति = वेद. स्मृति—like those of Manu, Yājnavalkya &c. इतिहास—this is often employed to denote the महाभारत. It is defined as 'आर्षादिबहुधाख्यानं देवर्षिचरिताश्रयम् । इतिहासमिति प्रोक्तं भविष्यद्भूतधर्मयुक् ॥'. श्रुता...शालिनः possessing learning, noble birth and character. मूर्धाभिषिक्ताः—crowned. We must connect the two adjectives ०शालिनः and ०षिक्ताः with अमात्याः and राजानः respectively. C and T connect मू० with अमात्याः and take राजानः as qualifying अमात्याः and translate 'anointed counsellors of royal rank endowed with learning &c.' But this is far-fetched. यथावत् अधिगतं आत्मतत्त्वं यैः that have correctly understood the truth about the self. संस्तुताः = परिचिताः. मस्करिणः = भिक्षवः 'भिक्षुः परिव्राट् कर्मन्दी पाराशर्यपि मस्करी' इत्यमरः. 'मस्करमस्करिणौ वेणुपरिव्राजकयोः' पा. 6. 1. 154. पतञ्जलि derives the word as 'मा कृत मा कृत कर्माणि शान्तिर्वः श्रेयसीति आहातो मस्करी परिव्राजकः' महाभाष्य ed. by Kielhorn Vol. III. p. 96 (from मा + कृ). सम...नाभयः Dependent kinsmen who shared his joys and sorrows. समे सुखदुःखे येषाम्. 'सपिण्डास्तु सनाभयः' इत्यमरः ('समानो नाभिर्मूलमेषां सनाभयः' क्षीर०). चित्तज्ञाः clever in reading the thoughts (of their master or of the people). निष्का...मुनयः sages that were disinterested friends. सं...वादिनः students of the Vedānta philosophy expert in expounding the unsubstantial character of the world. 'मीमांसको जैमिनीये वेदान्ती ब्रह्मवादिनि' क्षीर०. The position of the thorough-going Vedântin is summarized in a half-verse 'ब्रह्म सत्यं जगन्मिथ्या जीवो ब्रह्मैव नापरः ॥'. पौराणिकाः—पुराणानि अधीते वेद वा पौराणिकः (पुराण + ठक्). The Purāṇas are a class of works attributed to Vyāsa containing information principally on mythology, cosmogony, the legendary origin of royal families and their doings, the doctrines of various sects &c. Bāṇa in the third उच्छ्वास specifically refers to the वायुपुराण.

P. 90 ll. 5-19 **अस्व...तिष्ठदिति.** अ...तैः not being left to himself by them. तैः refers to the कुलपुत्रs, गुरुs and others referred to in the preceding paragraph. मनसापि...चरितुम् even in thought he had no opportunity to do as his grief dictated. If left to himself Harsha in his grief might have caused some harm to himself. But as he was always surrounded by numerous people who engaged his mind in various things, he could not even think of (much less actually do) any harm to himself. अपि नाम न गृह्णीयाद्वल्कले how much do I wish that he may not assume bark robes ! He is afraid that राज्यवर्धन would betake himself to a forest. We have to understand अपि नाम before अस्त्र...पृथिवीम् and the following clauses. अस्त्र...पृथिवीम्—would he whose lotus-like eyes are filled with tears see that the earth is helpless (without a lord)? One whose eyes are full of water cannot see clearly. The Com. seems to have read न in each clause 'अत्र च सर्वत्र नेत्याशङ्कायाम्'. Then the meaning would be 'I am afraid that he would not see &c'. But here the force of अपि नाम is gone and the sentences are not so striking as they are without न. प्रथम...विह्वलः overwhelmed by the terrible poison of this first calamity (father's death). पुरुषोत्तमः refers to राज्यवर्धन. It also means विष्णु, When the gods and demons churned the ocean for jewels, the first thing that came out was the poison हालाहल. See रामायण I. 44. and भागवतपु. VIII. प्रथमं व्यसनं एव विषमं विषं तेन विह्वलः. अभिषेकम् (1) coronation; (2) bath. One who is suffering from heat, would take a bath and find it very refreshing. राज...चरेत् (How do I wish) that he may not act the contrary when addressed by the princes (to assume sovereignty). पराचीनता = प्रातिकूल्यम्. पक्षपाती devoted to. तातश्लाघया by way of praising father. काञ्चन०— As प्रभाकर० was fair in complexion, the word काञ्चन is put before ताल. दिवसक...कसितम् that was upturned and expanded the whole day with love for the sun. A lotus blooms by day. The king प्रभा० was devoted to the sun (see text p. 3) and had a smiling (विकसित) face all day. हसितः मदेन अलसः हलधरः (बलरामः) तस्य इव विभ्रमः येषां (*adj*. of विलासाः)—that had the appearance of the grace of the laughing Balarāma lazy with drink. बलराम, the brother of कृष्ण, has the ploughshare as his weapon. He is described as fond of drink. See विष्णुपु० V. 25. वदान्य liberal.

sentence is अनन्तरं च...ज्येष्ठं भ्रातरमपश्यत्. द्वार...कथ्यमानम् who was announced by the lamentation of the doorkeeper, as if it (आक्रन्द) were an attendant that entered first. At the sight of राज्य० the doorkeepr wept. The द्वारपाल allows (मुक्त) high personages and their attendants to enter. The attendants precede the high personages to show them the way. दूर... बाहुल्येन—this and the following instrumentals qualify परिजनेन. दूरं द्रुतं आगमनं तेन मुषितं बाहुल्यं यस्य whose numbers were thinned (*lit.* robbed) by the long and quick march. विच्छिन्नः छत्रधारः यस्मिन् in which the umbrella-bearer was not to be found (he lagged behind). लम्बितः (lagged behind) अम्बरवाही (the man in charge of the wardrobe) यस्मिन्. भृङ्गारः a golden pitcher 'भद्रकुम्भः पूर्णकुम्भो भृङ्गारः कनकालुका' इत्यमरः. आचमनधारिन् spittoon-bearer. ताम्यन् (exhausted) ताम्बूलिकः (betel-bearer) यस्मिन्. खञ्जन् (limping) खड्गग्राही यस्मिन्. कति...प्रायेण mostly consisting of a few well-known (प्रकाश) servants. For दासेरक, see p. 28. बहुवासरान्तरितं स्नानभोजनशयनं तेन श्यामं क्षामं (emaciated) वपुः यस्य. अविरला मार्गधूलिः तया धूसरितं शरीरं यस्य सः ०शरीरः तस्य भावः ०शरीरता तया. अविद्यमानं शरणं यस्याः. The poet fancies that the earth in the form of dust resorted to him because it had become bereft of a protector by the death of प्रभाकर०. क्रमागतया (1) that was hereditary in his family ; (2) that came to him (stuck to his body) by his walking (with धूलि). हूणानां निर्जयाय समरे शरैः व्रणाः तेषु बद्धैः पट्टकैः (pieces of cloth) शबलीकृतः (spotted) कायः यस्य. The long and white bandages are fancied to be the glances of राज्यलक्ष्मी that was approaching him (he was the king after his father). Long eyes is a sign of beauty. The inside of the eye is white like the bandages. हुतं मांसं येषाम्. आवेद्यमानः दुःखभारः यस्य. He had lost flesh through grief. The poet fancies that the flesh so lost had been offered into the fire of grief for preserving his father's life. When a sacrifice is performed, offerings are given in fire. There is a striking contrast presented by the inference of a heavy weight from lean (कृश) limbs. Ordinarily lean limbs do not carry heavy weights. अपगतः चूडामणिः यस्मात्. मलिनाः आकुलाः (dishevelled) कुन्तलाः यस्य. शेखरः garland of flowers on the head. His head was not decorated through grief. The poet fancies that grief had mounted on it. आतपेन गलिता स्वेदराजिः यस्मात् (*adj* of ०पट्टेन). रुदतेव—Drops of perspiration stood out on his forehead owing to heat. The poet fancies that his forehead was eager to bow at the feet of his father and wept, as it could not do so owing to the death of प्रभा०. प्रथीयस् comparative of पृथु. One who faints has water sprinkled on his face. राज्य० shed tears which fell on the earth. The poet fancies that the tears were water poured over the earth that had swooned away owing to the death of her honoured lord. निम्नीकृत dug out, made hollow. His cheeks that were once round and fleshy had become hollow. Constant dripping of water wears away even stones. The poet fancies that the constant falling of tears on the cheeks wore away the cheeks and made them hollow. गलितः ताम्बूलरागः यस्मात्. राज्य० used no betel owing to grief. So his lip had not its usual redness. The poet fancies that the ताम्बूलराग came in the way of his very hot breaths, became melted and disappeared from his lip. पवित्रिकामात्रे अवशेषः यस्याः सा ०शेषा इन्द्रनीलिका &c. पवित्रि... द्दहन्तम्—the idea is:—in his यज्ञोपवीत there was a sapphire ring, the rays of which shot upwards and rendered his ear dark. The poet fancies that the darkness of the ear is due to its being burnt by the fire of the great grief at the recent news of his father's death. पवित्रकं = शणसूत्रजालं क्षत्रियस्य यज्ञोपवीतम्. The only इन्द्रनील he had was on the ring in his यज्ञोपवीत. C and T render 'his sapphire ornament of which only the amulet was left'. अस्फुटाभिव्यक्तं व्यञ्जनं (beard) यस्मिन्. '**व्यञ्जनं** लाञ्छनश्मश्रुनिष्ठानावयवेष्वपि' इत्यमरः. His face had only a slight growth of beard, which was rendered darker by the light of the dark pupils of his downcast and motionless eye. One who is in mourning has to allow his beard to grow. Though he had a slight growth of beard, he seemed to have a thick growth of it owing to the rays of his eye. महा...ह्वलम् (1) overwhelmed by the fall of a great mountain (with lion); (2) overwhelmed by the death of the great king (with राज्यवर्धन). निरवलम्बनम् without refuge or support. If a mountain falls on a lion, the latter will lose a place for prowling and will be stunned. तेजःपतिः (सूर्यः, नृपतिश्च) तस्य पतनेन परिम्लाना श्रीः यस्य. दिवसमिव श्यामीभूतम्—who (राज्य०) had become dark (in complexion) like the day. The day also turns into night when the sun dips down into the sea. श्यामीभूतं means रात्रीभूतं with दिवसम्. '**श्यामा** स्याच्छारिवा **निशा**' इत्यमरः. नन्दनम्—the garden of Indra. भग्नः कल्पपादपः यस्य. If the tree in the नन्दनवन be broken there will be no shade (छाया). राज्य० also had no छाया (splendour) left, as his father, who was a veritable कल्पवृक्ष to suppliants, was dead. प्रोषितः

दिक्कुञ्जरः (दिग्गजः) यस्मात्. If the दिग्गजs went away, the quarters would be empty (शून्य). राज्य० also was शून्य (vacant-minded). The eight quarters are guarded by eight दिग्गजs. 'ऐरावतः पुण्डरीको वामनः कुमुदोऽञ्जनः । पुष्पदन्तः सार्वभौमः सुप्रतीकश्च दिग्गजाः ॥' इत्यमरः. दिशां भावः दिग्भावः (the state of the quarters). गुरुः (heavy, crushing) वज्रपातः तेन दारितम् (with गिरि); गुरौ (पितरि) वज्रपातः (मृत्युः) तेन दारितम् (with राज्य०). The wings of mountains were clipped by Indra with his thunderbolt. See p. 19 above. किङ्क...रुण्येन enslaved by sorrow. दुर्मनसः भावः दौर्मनस्यम्—despondency. स्विन्न...पेन all perspiring through सन्ताप (heat, sorrow). उच्चितम् gathered, collected. लुप्तम् robbed. C and T would prefer वृतं the reading of two MSS. of B for धृतं for the sake of alliteration. प्रत्या...ख्यानेन discarded by reflection. Compare 'अवष्टम्भो ज्ञानं धैर्यं प्रतिसंख्यानमित्यस्तमितैषा कथा' कादम्बरी (p. 156 of P). दूरी...भवत्वेन cast aside by firmness (*lit.* the quality of being invincible). अबो...बुद्धीनाम् that was beyond the counsels of the aged. The instrumentals from अबोध्येन qualify शोकेन below. असा ... तानाम् that was not to be cured by the words of the good. अग...गिराम् that was inaccessible to the eloquence of elders. अशक्ये...शक्तीनाम् not within the reach of the power of scriptures. अ...यत्नानाम् that was beyond the way of the efforts of wisdom. The idea is that the efforts of wise men would not avail to lessen his sorrow. अभूमि...चयानाम् that was not a proper place for gradual healing up. उपचयः *lit.* increase, prosperity. आवेगेन उद्गताः कृत्स्नस्नेहस्य उत्कलिकाः ताभिः उत्क्षिप्यमाणः कायः यस्य—whose body was lifted up on the waves of the whole love that surged up through emotion. स्नेह is compared to the sea; emotion caused by the sight of राज्य० to the tide of the sea. The agitation (उत्कलिका) due to the emotion is compared to waves (उत्कलिका). A man swimming in the sea is borne on the crest of waves. Harsha's body was shaken by agitation.

P. 92 l. 20—**P. 93** l. 2 **अथ तं...स्थात्.** कलितं held in. ०सारितेन goes with ०द्वयेन. We must read संकलयन्निव (as if grasping). He stretched out his long arms to embrace हर्ष. The poet fancies that he did so in order to embrace all sorrows (*i. e.* he would thereby become full of all sorrows). सङ्कल्पयन् hardly yields any sense. पतितं क्षौमं यस्मात् from which the fine garment had fallen (or slipped away). सब...हृदयानि (their) hearts were as if uprooted together with their fastenings. A and C omit the sentence अश्रु...लोकेन. That sentence seems to mean 'the people let fall in their eyes a stream of tears resembling veins of blood'. The preceding sentence spoke of the uprooting of hearts. If that were actually done, blood would flow forth from the veins of the body. The stream of tears is fancied to be the veins of blood. स्मृतः नृपतिः (प्रभाकरवर्धनः) येन. When the princes wept, the king's favourite also wept. He seemed to be the echo of the princes. निर्वृष्टं नयनजलं येन. Rain ceases in autumn of its own accord; no one can stop it. So राज्यवर्धन stopped weeping after a long time. तोयेन—connect this with अक्षालयत्. तस्कर...लेखमिव (eye) that seemed to have a streak of foam produced by a big flood of water because of the pencils of the rays of his finger-nails. When he washed his face, he moved his hand over it. The rays of his bright nails resembled white foam and so his eye seemed to be covered with foam. पक्ष्माग्रे सङ्गलन्तः बिन्दवः तेषां वृन्दं तेन मन्दः उन्मेषः तेन मुषितं दर्शनं यस्य (his eye) the vision of which was robbed by the fact that its opening (उन्मेषः) was obstructed by the mass of tear-drops gathering on the tips of his eyelashes. वाससा...न्ममार्ज—he wiped his face with a white towel. The towel resembled moonlight in whiteness and in being cool. So the poet fancies that he wiped his face scorched by very hot tears with a piece of moonlight. विभूषं...ष्पीड्य having carelessly wrung his head (मौलिः) that was unadorned and the locks on which were disturbed and dishevelled. विगता भूषा यस्मात्. वित्रस्ताः व्यस्ताः (scattered about) कुन्तलाः यस्य. सावशेष...अधरेण—(connect this with कुर्वाणः)—by his lower lip that quivered on account of the remnants of sorrow, which (lip) therefore seemed as if desirous of living and as if desirous of kissing itself, as it was charming on account of its bath. The idea is:—when राज्य० bathed he washed his lip and eyes. As his grief had not all died out, his lip quivered. One who lives makes movements. So the quivering of the lip showed that in spite of grief it wanted to live. In kissing also the lips move. So the poet imagines that the lip quivered because it wanted to kiss itself on account of its own agreeableness due to the bath. अवशेषेण सह साव० (बहुव्रीहि), सावशेषः मन्युः तेन स्फुरितः. शारदः (शरदि भवः) शशी तस्य करैः विकसितानि विशदानि (shining) कुमुदवनानि तेषां दलावलिः एव बलिः तस्य विक्षेपैः (throwing). The कुमुद्s bloom in moon-light. The moon is at its best in शरद्. His quivering lip resembled the flashes of lightning become rare when शरद् comes; his washed face resembled the clear moon of शरद्. When राज्य० cast glances in various directions, the poet imagines that he did worship to the दिग्देवताs with the offerings of petals of कुमुदs. चतुःशालम् a quadrangle enclosed by four buildings. चतसृणां शालानां समाहारः चतुःशालम्. वितर्दिका—platform, terrace. See p. 53. नीचापाश्रये विनिहितः एकः उपबर्हः यस्याम्—on which a single cushion was placed beneath a low awning. For अपाश्रय, see p. 21. 'उपधानं तूपबर्हः' इत्यमरः. जोषम् *adv.* silently.

P. 93 ll. 3–15 **देवोऽपि...मण्डलम्.** ०कुथायां प्रसारिता मूर्तिः (शरीरं) येन. कुथा a blanket or carpet. औरस...शोकस्य for the sight of a very near relative is the youth of sorrow. औरसः—उरसा निर्मितः according to 'उरसोऽण् च' पा. 4. 4. 94. The word is primarily applied to a son and extended to any close blood relation like a brother. The idea is that at the sight of one's near relations grief increases in intensity. Compare notes p. 96. सः (l. 8) refers to दिवसः. प्रत्यग्र...तनुरिव as if his body had recently (प्रत्यग्र) been chopped by the chisel of त्वष्टृ. The sun at the time of setting looked red. One whose body is recently cut would be red with blood and flesh. वहद्बहलरुधिररसं (वहन् बहलः रुधिररसः यस्मिन् तत्) मांसं तस्य इव छविः (कान्तिः) यस्य that looked like flesh moistened by plentiful blood. प्रत्यग्रत्वष्टृ०—त्वष्टृ is the architect of the gods. He had a daughter named संज्ञा that was married to the sun. She could not bear the light of the sun. त्वष्टृ, wishing to reduce the superfluous lustre of the sun, placed him on his lathe and trimmed off some of his lustre. With the portion thus taken away त्वष्टृ manufactured the चक्र of विष्णु, the त्रिशूल of रुद्र and the other weapons of the gods. Vide विष्णुपु० III. 2. 9–12 and मार्कण्डेयपु० Chap. 77. 'भ्रमिमारोप्य सूर्यं तु तस्य तेजोविशातनात् । कृत्तवानष्टमं भागं न व्यशातयताव्ययम् ॥' विष्णु० III. 2. 9. Note रघु० VI. 32 'आरोप्य चक्रभ्रममुष्णतेजास्त्वष्ट्रेव यत्नोल्लिखितो विभाति ॥'. अपरः (western) पारावारः ocean. मञ्जिष्ठावत् अरुणः. मञ्जिष्ठा Bengal madder. It is used as a red dye. अरुणः सारथिः यस्य. मुकुलायमानाः (closing) कमलिनीकोषाः तेन विकलम् (distressed). चकाण perfect of कण् to cry in distress, hum. The कमल closes its petals at sunset. चञ्चरीकः = भ्रमरः. On this word क्षीरस्वामी remarks 'चञ्चरीकभसनेन्दिन्दिररोलम्बा देश्याम्'. सविधः (near, approaching) विरहव्याधिः तेन विधुरा वधूः तया बाध्यमानम् (*adj.* of चक्रवालम्). विबुद्धस्य (blooming) बन्धूकस्य इव भाः (तेजः) यस्य (*adj.* of भास्वति). बन्धूकम् is a kind of red flower.

अस्रैः सह सास्राम् tearful. चक्रवालम्—group. For the separation of the चक्रवाक from its mate at sunset, see pp. 10, 57. सञ्चरन्त्याः goes with श्रियः. श्री is said to be wandering because प्रभाकरवर्धन being dead there is yet no new king installed. मधुकररवेण सह स... रवं. कैरवाकरं must be taken as the object of सञ्चरन्त्याः. The कैरवs are white lotuses that expand at nightfall. The bees buzzed over them. The poet fancies that this buz ing was the jingling of the small bells on the girdle of लक्ष्मी. कल... रमणीयम् goes with ०करम्. The कलहंसीs were there near the कैरव beds and lent their grace to them. आण—perfect of अण् to sound. The bees were like bells, the कलहंसीs like माणिक्यकाञ्ची and the white lotuses like the fair complexion of लक्ष्मी. प्रकटः कलङ्कः यस्य (*adj.* of ०मण्डलम्). उदयमानम् (*pr. p.* of अय् 1 A with उद्) rising. विशङ्कटः (large) विषाणः (horn) तेन उत्कीर्णः (scattered) पङ्कः तस्य सङ्करः (contact) यस्य सः ०सङ्करः शङ्करस्य शकुरः (tame) शक्करः (bull) तस्य ककुदकूटः (conical hump) तत्सङ्काशं तत्सदृशम्. 'विशङ्कटं पृथु बृहत्' इत्यमरः. The moon was like the hump of the white bull of शिव and the horns of the moon resembled the horns of the bull and the spot on the moon was like the mud on the horn of the bull. This passage is full of suggestions, as C and T observe. The word शशाङ्कमण्डलम् indicates the rise of the गौड king (शशाङ्क as the com. says), who murdered राज्यवर्धन. The red sunset symbolizes bloody wars.

P. 93 ll. 16—**P. 94** l. 18 **अस्यां...धरण्याम्.** नास्ति अतिक्रमणं यस्य तत् अनतिक्रमणं वचनं येषाम् whose words could not be disregarded. भूमिः...योगानाम् ycu are a proper person for the injunctions of elders *i. e.* elders enjoin you to do something because they feel sure that you would not disobey. Or गुरु may mean 'father', the sense being 'our father used to give you instruction as you were the fittest person to receive it.' अग्राहि चित्तवृत्तिः you held the heart. A person may seize a banner that has ropes. The king's mind also was गुणवत्; or the king's mind was the banner of the virtuous (गुणवतां पताका) *i. e.* he was the foremost or preeminent among the virtuous (as a banner is). विधेयम् docile, obedient. विधेः विधानेन उपनतं नैर्घृण्यं (निर्घृणस्य निर्दयस्य भावः) यस्य (my heart) that has become callous by the decrees of fate. C and T translate 'विधि०' as 'my heart, softened to compliance with the decrees of fate.' This is wrong. बिभणिषति = भणितुमिच्छति. प्रेमविलोमा which runs counter to affection. Read ०विलोमा for ०विलोपा. वामता perverseness, refractory spirit. वैधेयः fool, dullard.

'अज्ञे मूढयथाजातमूर्खवैधेयबालिशाः' इत्यमरः (विधेयः एव वैधेयः स्वार्थेऽण्). लोकवृत्तम् ways of the world. मान्धान्तृ—see for his story p. 23. प्रभाकर० was a pre-eminent चक्रवर्ती as मान्धाता was. 'यौवनाश्वोऽथ मान्धाता चक्रवर्त्यवनीं प्रभुः। सप्तद्वीपवतीमेकः शशासाच्युत तेजसा ॥' भागवतपु० 9. 6. 34. पुरुकुत्स was the son of मान्धातृ and killed the मौनेयगन्धर्वs that had ousted the Nâgas and re-instated the latter. He married नर्मदा. See विष्णुपुराण IV. 3. भ्रूलतया आदिष्टानि अष्टादश द्वीपानि येन who issued commands to the eighteen worlds with his brow. दिलीपे मृते वा रघुणा (किं कृतम्)—Bâna seems to follow the रघुवंश here in making रघु the son of दिलीप. According to the रामायण (II. 110 and I. 70) दिलीप's son was भगीरथ, whose grandson was रघु. So according to the विष्णुपुराण (IV. 4) दिलीप's son was दीर्घबाहु whose son was रघु. महान् असुरसमरः तन्मध्ये अध्यासितः त्रिदशानां (देवानां) रथः येन. Compare for the idea that दशरथ helped the gods in battle रघु० 9. 19 'स किल संयुगमूर्ध्नि सहायतां मघवतः प्रतिपद्य महारथः।'. It was in this battle with the demon शम्बर that कैकेयी, who had helped दशरथ, got two वरs from him. See रामायण अयोध्याकाण्ड 2. गोष्पदीकृताः चतुर्णां उदन्वतां अन्ताः येन—who looked upon the confines of the four oceans as a puddle. गोष्पदम् (गो + पद)—स् is inserted according to 'गोष्पदं सेवितासेवितप्रमाणेषु' पा. 6. 1. 145. (गावः पद्यन्तेऽस्मिन्देशे स गोभिः सेवितो गोष्पदः। प्रमाणे, गोष्पदमात्रं क्षेत्रम्। सि. कौ.). The four oceans were as small to him as a puddle that is as deep as a cow's hoof. तिष्ठन्तु...देते let alone these. तातेन—refers to प्रभाकरवर्धन. शतात् समधिकाः (more than a hundred) अध्वराः तेषां धूमः तस्य विसरेण (mass) धूसरितं वासवस्य (इन्द्रस्य) वयः येन—who rendered the youth of Indra grey by &c. It was believed that whoever performed a hundred अश्वमेध sacrifices would displace Indra. Indra is therefore always represented as anxious to put obstacles in the performance of these sacrifices. Indra grew old through anxiety and jealousy when he learnt of the hundred and more sacrifices of प्रभा०. सुगृहीतं नाम यस्य—of blessed memory. This is a term used in respectfully addressing or speaking of a person (particularly a deceased person). कुत्सितः पुरुषः कापुरुषः, according to 'विभाषा पुरुषे' पा. 6. 3. 106 (कापुरुषः। कुपुरुषः). स्त्रैणं womanishness. आस्पदम् = स्थानम्. भू... र्यस्ते (1) the king being killed; (2) the mountain being shattered or laid low. If a mountain were shattered to pieces, all the torrents will be at once let loose; so the king being killed, all his tears flow in torrents. अस्त...तेजसि—refers to the setting of the sun and the death of the king. अन्धकारीभूताः दश आशाः (दिशः)

यस्य. प्र...लोकः the light of wisdom fails. When the sun sets, there is no light in the ten quarters. The king being dead, राज्य० cannot think wisely and looks on the whole world as dark. Remove the comma after हृदयं, which is the object of उपसर्पति. My heart is aflame with grief and therefore विवेक does not come to it, as if afraid of being burnt by the fire in the heart. सन्ताप (1) sorrow, (2) heat. जातुषम्—made of lac. जतुनो विकारः, according to 'त्रपुजतुनोः षुक्' पा. 4. 3. 138 (आभ्यामण् स्यात् विकारे एतयोः षुगागमश्च त्रापुषम् । जातुषम् । सि. कौ.). पदे पदे (1) at every word; (2) at every step. दिग्धः (poisoned) रोपः (arrow) तेन आहता. 'पत्री रोप इषुर्द्वयोः' इत्यमरः. 'विषाक्ते दिग्धलिप्तकौ' इत्यमरः. दूरेण भ्रमति (1) wanders far; (2) wanders at a distance (from the person hated). परिहरन्ती avoiding. अम्बा—refers to यशोमती. वार्धु...वित्तानि money that is employed by a moneylender or usurer. वार्धुषिक (from वृद्धि)—वृद्ध्यर्थं द्रव्यं वृद्धिः तां गर्ह्यां प्रयच्छति इति—according to वार्तिक 'वृद्धेर्वृधुषिभावो वक्तव्यः' on 'प्रयच्छति गर्ह्यम्' पा. 4. 4. 30. A very exacting moneylender would stipulate for interest to be calculated from day to day; and even without such stipulation, ordinarily every day adds to the interest that has to be paid. ०धूमसम्भारात् सम्भूतः अम्भोधरः (मेघः) तेन भरितमिव. पञ्चजनः—*lit.* people of the five races (*i. e.* the Aryans in the four quarters and the निषादs); hence, people in general. Compare ऋग्वेद III. 59. 8 'मित्राय पञ्च येमिरे जना अभिष्टिशवसे'. 'स्युः पुमांसः पञ्चजनाः पुरुषाः' इत्यमरः. पञ्चत्वं प्रयाति is dissolved into the five elements (पृथिव्यप्तेजोवाय्वाकाश). असाम्परायिकम् not warlike, cowardly. सम्परायः = युद्धम्. अवष्टभ्य having enveloped. शोकः—connect it with दहति and the following verbs. वाडव...राशिम्—this and the following three clauses are to be respectively connected with दहति and the three following verbs. वाडवः—is the submarine fire, otherwise called और्व. The sons of कार्तवीर्य, with the desire of destroying the descendants of भृगु, killed even the children in the womb. One of the women of the family secreted the child in her womb in her thigh (ऊरु) and preserved it. Hence the child was called और्व. At sight of him, the sons of कार्तवीर्य were struck blind and his wrath gave rise to a flame which was going to burn the whole world, when at the desire of his पितृs, the भार्गवs, he cast it into the ocean. Compare शाकुन्तल III. 3 'त्वयि ज्वलत्यौर्व इवाम्बुराशौ'. See आदिपर्व for the story. पविरिव पर्वतं (दारयति)—for the clipping of the wings of mountains, see p. 19. क्षय...करं (तनूकरोति)—for showing greater favour to रोहिणी than to his other wives, the नक्षत्रs, the moon was cursed by their father दक्ष to be a consumptive. Compare 'दर्शयन्निव चिरकाललग्नं दक्षशापानलदाहचिह्नं' कादम्बरी (p. 178 of P). सुमेरुकल्पस्य resembling Meru. For Meru, see p. 85. For कल्प, see notes on देशीय p. 38. कल्प...पुरुषस्य who was a noble spirit (to be found once) in a कल्प. For कल्प, see p. 78. Another meaning also may be suggested 'a noble spirit like a कल्पवृक्ष'. अतिवाहयितुम् to get through. विरक्तं (1) disgusted; (2) tinged redder. चकोरस्य—It was believed that the eyes of चकोरs became red at the sight of poison. अर्थशास्त्र of कौटिल्य says 'क्रौञ्चो विषाभ्याशे माद्यति। ग्लायति जीवञ्जीवकः। म्रियते मत्तकोकिलः। चकोरस्याक्षिणी विरज्येते' (pp. 40–41). काम० says 'चकोरस्य विरज्येते नयने विषदर्शनात्। सुव्यक्तं माद्यति क्रौञ्चो म्रियते कोकिलः किल ॥' VII. 12. बहवः मृतपटाः अवगुण्ठनं यस्याः that covers her face with many shrouds of the dead. The चाण्डालs were in the habit of taking the clothes in which corpses were shrouded. रञ्जितः रङ्गः (समाजः) यया that pleases the audience or sight-seers. People were diverted by the sight of the various shrouds worn by Chandāla females. जनङ्गमः=चण्डालः. राज्यवर्धन says he wants to give up राज्यलक्ष्मी, which he compares to the श्री of चण्डालs. 'चण्डालप्लवमातङ्गदिवाकीर्तिजनङ्गमाः' इत्यमरः. It would be better to read जनङ्गमाङ्गनाम् as C and T suggest. वंशबाह्याम्—(1)which is outside of (noble) family; (2) which is to be borne on bamboo-poles. बाह्य in the latter case is equal to वाह्य, as there is no difference between ब and व, र and ल, ड and ल in यमक, श्लेष and चित्र 'यमकश्लेषचित्रेषु बवयोर्डलयोर्न भित्। नानुस्वारविसर्गौ च चित्रभङ्गाय संमतौ ॥' वाग्भटालंकार I. 20. चण्डालs carry all their belongings on poles. अनार्याम् (1) disreputable; (2) not of Aryan lineage. The चण्डालs were outside the pale of Âryan society. दग्ध...कुलिरिव as a bird in a burnt dwelling. दग्धगृहे may also mean 'in this palace accursed' (by the king's death). स्नेहमल is to be connected with मनसि and वाससि. स्नेह (1) affection (2) oil. Affection clung to his heart and he wanted to get rid of it in a hermitage. An oily and dirty spot sticks to a garment which must be washed in water. अन्तरितानि यौवनसौख्यानि यस्याम् in which the pleasures of youth cannot be had (*adj*. of जरां and ०चिन्ताम्). The cares of the kingdom would not allow हर्ष to enjoy youth as otherwise he would have done. अनभिमताम् not esteemed or liked (with जराम् and चिन्ताम्). जरामिव पूरुः—ययाति married देवयानी daughter of शुक्र preceptor of the दैत्यs. शर्मिष्ठा, daughter of the king of

दैत्य, was her servant. ययाति fell in love with her and secretly married her. When देवयानी complained, her father शुक्र cursed him to be prematurely old. ययाति propitiated शुक्र and obtained permission to transfer his old age to any one that would accept it. He had two sons यदु and तुर्वसु from देवयानी and द्रुह्य, अनु and पूरु from शर्मिष्ठा. All his sons except पूरु refused to take up the decrepitude of their father. पूरु, the youngest, dutifully took it up and was placed on the throne by ययाति. See विष्णुपु. IV. 10; रामायण VII. 58–59; महाभारत आदिपर्व. गुरोः (1) of his father (with पूरु); (2) of me who am your elder (brother). त्यक्ताः सकलाः बालक्रीडाः येन (applies to हर्ष and हरि both). हरिणा = विष्णुना. दीयता...लक्ष्म्यै give your chest to लक्ष्मी. हर्ष is asked to accept sovereignty. विष्णु took लक्ष्मी as his wife. बालक्रीडा— these words suggest the doings of कृष्ण (the incarnation of विष्णु) in गोकुल. रुक्मिणी the wife of कृष्ण is looked upon as the incarnation of लक्ष्मी. 'राघवत्वेऽभवत्सीता रुक्मिणी कृष्णजन्मनि' विष्णु० I. 9. 141. निस्त्रिंशः—a sword—(निष्क्रान्तस्त्रिंशतोऽङ्गुलिभ्यः इति which is longer than 30 finger-breadths).

P. 94 l. 19—**P 95** l. 22 **अथ...तिष्ठत.** निशिता शिखा यस्य the point of which is very sharp. मामन्तरेण concerning me. It may also mean 'without me *i. e.* behind my back.' शोकात् जन्म यस्य (*adj.* of ०क्षेपः). चेतसः समाक्षेपः Distraction or aberration of mind. आहो...भवति ? Is it possible that he is not my brother ? The idea is that he speaks so unlike my brother that I am forced to doubt whether he is the same as my brother. विवक्षितं = वक्तुमिष्टम्. निपातनोपायः a means of decline or downfall. निखिलपुण्यस्य परिक्षयः तस्य उपक्षेपः (indication). कर्मणां is to be connected with निखिल०. The idea is :—do these unexpected words of my brother indicate that all the merit I gathered by my actions has now been exhausted ? अन...लसितं वा or is it the wanton act of the group of all unfavourable planets ? तातस्य विनाशेन निःशङ्कः (fearless) कलिकालः तस्य क्रीडितम् (prank, freak). The idea is that प्रभाकर० had held कलि in cheek. अयं—refers to राज्य० यःकश्चिदिव like a low person. यत्किंचनकारिणं माम्—connect with समादिष्टवान्. यत्किच...म्भूतमिव (he has ordered) me (thinking me) capable of doing anything, as if I were not born of the line of पुष्पभूति. अनात्मानुजमिव as if I were not his own younger brother. The reading अदृष्टदोषमपि breaks the symmetry of the clauses, all of which contain an इव; but yields a good sense. The reading दृष्टदोषमिव of A and C means 'as if I were one detected in committing a fault.' श्रोत्रियमिव—What Harsha says is this:—to ask me to assume sovereign power when my elder brother is quite competent to do it is as detestable as to ask a श्रोत्रिय to drink wine, to induce a faithful servant to prove treacherous to his master &c. सुरापान was one of the five महापातकs, for which see above p. 84. नीचोपसर्पणम् to approach or wait upon a mean person. तदे...यत् This much (out of what राज्य० does) is indeed befitting that &c. शौर्यस्य उन्मादः एव मदिरा तया मत्तं समस्तं सामन्तमण्डलं एव समुद्रः तस्य मथने मन्दरः तस्मिन्. The feudatories intoxicated by the pride of valour are compared to the ocean; as the ocean was churned with मन्दर as the churning handle, so प्रभाकर० was the churning handle of the kings (*i. e.* subdued them and made them yield tribute as the ocean had to yield jewels). For मन्दर, see above p. 42. For the technical meaning of मण्डल, see p. 42. The king प्रभा० was in the midst of the मण्डल as the handle मन्दर was in the midst of the ocean. The ocean also had मदिरा (वारुणी, one of the 14 jewels). या...वृष्टिः as for this command to me to assume sovereignty, it scorches me who am already burnt and is a shower of cinders on me who am like a desert parched by drought. अवग्रहेण (वृष्टेर्विघातेन) ग्लपितः (past p. p. of the causal of ग्लै). धन्वन् *m.* a barren or dry soil. 'समानौ मरुधन्वानौ' इत्यमरः. 'वृष्टिर्वर्षं तद्विघातेऽवग्राहावग्रहौ समौ' इत्यमरः. यद्यपि...मानः—supply जगति दुर्लभः after this and after every-one of the following clauses. विभु...मानः a person in power without pride. द्विजातिः = ब्राह्मणः. अविद्यमाना एषणा (greed, covetousness) यस्य. मुनिररोषणः a sage without anger. The Purâṇas illustrate only too well this *dictum*. वणि...रः a trader who is not a thief (knave). प्रिया जाया यस्य स० जानिः. जाया becomes जानि when it is the last member of a बहुव्रीहि compound. 'जायाया निङ्' पा. 5. 4. 134. प्रिय...हनः (it is rare to find) a husband fond of his wife who is also not jealous. कुहन *adj.* jealous. 'कुहना दम्भचर्यायामीर्ष्यालौ कुहनं त्रिषु' इति मेदिनी. कीना...गतः (it is rare to find) a poor man who is not an eyesore. 'कृतान्ते पुंसि कीनाशः क्षुद्रकर्षकयोर्निषु' इत्यमरः. मृगयुः a hunter. पारा...ब्राह्मण्यः (it is rare to find) a mendicant who possesses the qualities of a (good) ब्राह्मण. पाराशरिन् originally means 'one who studies the भिक्षुसूत्र promulgated by पाराशर्य'; hence any mendicant (whether learned in the Vedānta or not). 'पाराशर्य—शिलालिभ्यां भिक्षुनटसूत्रयोः' पा. 4. 3. 110 (पाराशर्येण प्रोक्तं भिक्षुसूत्रमधीयते पाराशरिणो भिक्षवः । सि. कौ.). कितवः a gambler. The reading of A and C is good. परि...क्षुः an ascetic who is not desirous of enjoying (life). गोप्यः a servant. राज...नीतः (it is rare to find) a king's son who is not wicked (or ill-educated). This last is the matter in hand. हर्ष means:—king's sons are generally badly educated; and so an ordinary prince would have done as राज्य० wants me to do. But I am the pupil of no less a person than राज्य० himself. को हि नाम—connect these words with चण्ड, कोऽपि. राज...कुञ्जरे who is a गन्धद्विप to the (elephants in the form of) kings (*i. e.* from fear of whom kings run away). For गन्धद्विप see p. 4 (notes). विफली...भुजे who has rendered useless his large thighs and arms resembling a stone pillar. Or we may take that the thighs resembled a slab of stone and the arms a pillar. सकल...पवित्रम्—people would shed tears when they would hear that राज्य० had abandoned the kingdom. मृद्गो...धानम् a sphere of mud called earth. वसुधा अभिधानं यस्य. मृद्गोलकं—is the object of कामयेत. धनमदेन खेलाः (playful) निखिलाः खलाः तेषां मुखविकारलक्षणैः आख्यायमानं नीचाचरणं यस्याः whose vile conduct is exposed by the indications offered by the changing features of the faces of the wicked &c. The idea is:—लक्ष्मी very often resorts to wicked men who become purse-proud and whose faces assume arrogant looks. Thus it is लक्ष्मी that is responsible for the arrogance and conceit of the wicked. कुम्भदासी a bawd, procuress. 'कुम्भो राश्यन्तरे हस्तिमूर्धांसे राक्षसान्तरे । कार्मुके वारनार्यां च' मेदिनी. लक्ष्मी goes about seeking the deeds of the valorous, and is therefore like a bawd. कथमि...र्येण how did my brother think this which is extremely improper to be possible (in me)? अनवदातम् Impure. चेतसः च्युतः passed from his mind. सौमित्रिः—लक्ष्मणः. लक्ष्मण is the Hindu ideal of a younger brother and so are भीम, अर्जुन, नकुल and सहदेव. It is to be noted that it is not a mere rhetorical touch that Bâṇa puts this sentiment in the mouth of Harsha. The inscriptions of हर्ष (for which see Introduction) show that हर्ष revered his brother as much as (or perhaps more than) his father. अनपेक्षितः भक्तजनः यया that cared not for those that loved him. प्रभविष्णुता—the position of being a lord. Harsha means that राज्य० was never before so heedless of the feelings of those that were devoted to him. कुलिशस्य (thunderbolt) शिखरवत् खरं (sharp) नखरं (claw) तस्य प्रचयः (mass, thickness.) तस्य प्रचण्डाचपेटा तया पाटितं मत्तमातङ्गस्य उत्तमाङ्गं (शिरः) तस्य मदच्छटा (mass or streak of ichor) तया छुरितः चारुकेसरभारः तेन भास्वरं मुखं यस्य.

निवासं...पृष्ठतः who protects behind his back the mountain cave—his dwelling? प्रतापः सहायः येषाम्. कश्चप...यैस्य what indeed is this considerate treatment (अनुरोधः) of my brother towards लक्ष्मी which is fickle? चीवरेण अन्तरितौ (covered) कुचौ यस्याः. हर्ष's idea is:—if राज्यवर्धन wants to go to तपोवन, why does he not take राज्यलक्ष्मी which is rightfully his with him to the forest and there make her follow the life of an ascetic? Why does he press me to accept her? जराजालिनी (1) that presents the appearance of old age (with लक्ष्मी); (2) that falls into a snare which resembles old age (with मृगी). A मृगी also carries कुश and leaves in its mouth (on which it subsists) and is often caught in a net. The word जराजालिनी further suggests the idea that लक्ष्मी should remain in the forest with राज्य० till old age and then it will be time for हर्ष to think of becoming a king. In olden times, Indian kings transferred their kingdoms when they grew old to their sons and went to a forest to practise austerities. Compare रघु० 7. 71 'तदुपहितकुटुम्बः शान्तिमार्गोत्सुकोऽभून्नहि सति कुलधुर्ये सूर्यवंश्या गृहाय ॥'.; उत्तरराम० I. 22. किल्बिषम् sin (object of आपास्यति, the subject being तपः). 'पापं किल्बिषकल्मषम्' इत्यमरः. मनसा...वनम् who in thought went to the forest before (his brother.).

P. 95 ll. 23–31 अत्रान्तरे...पातयत्. The principal sentence is अत्रान्तरे...सहसैव प्रविश्य...राज्यश्रियः परिचारकः संवादको नाम... सदसि आत्मानमपातयत्. We have a number of nouns in the locative (absolute). पूर्वादिष्टेन—who had been previously ordered (by राज्य०). वस्त्रकर्मान्तिक—keeper of the wardrobe. कर्मान्तिकः—कर्मणि अन्तिकः or कर्मान्ते नियुक्तः—a servant. Read ०ताडनभियेव for ०ताडनमिव. निर्दय...स्त्रैणे when the women in the palace were screaming as if their heart being afraid of the rough beating with their hands had disappeared somewhere. The women in grief at the departure of राज्य० to a forest beat their bosom (हृदय) and wept. The poet imagines that they screamed because they had lost their heart. When one loses a thing, one raises a hue and cry to find it. ब्रह्मणि साधु ब्रह्मण्यम्, न ब्र० अब्रह्मण्यम्—this is an exclamation used when some calamity befalls. It originally meant 'what is not good to a Brâhmaṇa;' hence 'any calamity or misfortune.' ऊर्ध्वौ दोषौ (arms, from दोस्) यस्य. दोषन् is optionally substituted for दोस् from the accu. plural. पाद...परे—the citizens fell at the feet of राज्य० to dissuade him from his resolve. विद्राति (*loc.* sing. of the *pr. p.* of द्रा with वि) running away.

सात्त्विकभावs; these two and रोमाञ्च are often described when lovers meet. Compare 'आसीद्वरः कण्टकितप्रकोष्ठः स्विन्नाङ्गुलिः संववृते कुमारी' रघु० 7. 22. पुनरपि—We saw above (text p. 39 l. 18) that राज्य० laid down his sword on the earth. शस्त्रग्रहणेन मुदिता राजलक्ष्मीः तया क्रियमाणा दिष्टवृद्धिः (congratulation) तस्यां विधुता सिन्दूरधूलिः. Even now at marriage celebrations and other festivities, red powder is sprinkled over people. For दिष्टवृद्धि see above p. 11. समासन्नाः सकलमहीपालाः तेषां चूडामणीनां चक्रं तस्य आक्रमणेन जातः अहङ्कारः यस्य. He sat in a posture peculiar to warriors of old. His upturned right foot he placed on his left thigh and the left foot was placed on the ground. निष्ठुरं अङ्गुष्ठेन कषणं (rubbing) तेन निष्ठ्यूता (emitted) धूमलेखा येन. निर्वी...शिख इव as if he had let loose the knot of hair on his head for making the earth void of (rival) heroes. He violently rubbed his toe against the pavement and a streak of smoke was thereby produced. This is dark and hence fancied to be a knot of hair (शिखा). An irascible person may take a vow not to tie up his hair until his enemies are uprooted, as चाणक्य did. Vide मुद्राराक्षस III. 29. 'शिखां मोक्तुं मुक्तामपि पुनरयं धावति करः'; VII. 17 'पूर्णप्रतिज्ञेन मया केवलं बध्यते शिखा ॥'. The word विमुक्तशिखः may suggest another meaning. He violently pressed his toe against the ground whereby a dark line of smoke was produced. That indicated that he was about to give out a flame (शिखा). Fire burns the earth and frees it of Arjuna trees. 'नदीसर्जो वीरतरुरिन्द्रद्रुः ककुभोर्जुनः' इत्यमरः. वीर also means 'reeds'. दर्पेण स्फुटिताः सरसाः व्रणाः तेभ्यः उच्छलितं (sent up, spurted) रुधिरं तस्य छटा तया अवसेकः. राज्यवर्धन's wounds were fresh and by his agitation they again cracked and blood began to flow. प्रबोधयन्निव—has two senses. When one faints through poison, water is sprinkled over to rouse him. The blood served to rouse his valour that had been inert owing to sorrow. राज्य० also wanted to give advice to हर्ष. इदं...प्रजाः—what he means is:—I leave these as they are; you must look after them; I cannot do it; I have only one task to discharge. भूपतिः (प्रभाकरवर्धनः) तस्य भुजौ परिघौ (bar, bolt) इव. अत्यन्तं अविनीतः (wicked, ill-mannered) अरिः तस्य निग्रहः. सोऽयं...वंशस्य च—The construction is यो मौखराणां मालवैः परिभवः...सोऽयं कुरङ्गकैः कचग्रहः केसरिणः—that the Mālavas should insult the Maukharas and the line of पुष्पभूति is like the seizure of the hair of the lion by deer. करपातः slapping. वत्सकै...ग्रहस्य the taking of the tiger as a captive by calves.

अलगर्दः a water-serpent. **गरुड** is the enemy of all serpents and shows no mercy to them. 'अलगर्दो जलव्यालः' इत्यमरः. अयुतं ten thousand.

P. 97 ll. 1–24 **तं च...मित्रम्.** जामिः sister. **'जामिः स्वसृकुलस्त्रियोः'** इत्यमरः. ०विज्ञानेन प्रकोपः तस्य आधानं (production) **तेन दूयमाने. दूरं प्ररूढा प्रणयपीडा यस्य. मनसि...पीड इव** when his mind had pain due to love (for राज्य०) much augmented by the plea that he (**हर्ष**) should return (remain behind). The reading **निवर्तनादेशेन** (by the order of राज्य० to stay behind) is much better. **कमिव...गमनेन** what possible harm does my lord see in my following (my lord)? **यदि...सि** if you raise the objection that I am a mere boy, that is a greater reason why I should not be left behind. **'बाल आ षोडशाद्वर्षात्'.** This passage may be looked upon as indicating that **हर्ष** was about sixteen at this time. **रक्षणीय...स्थानम्**—If you assign for my staying behind the reason that I need protection (and therefore should not be taken on a campaign), then your arms are a cage for me. What greater protection can there be than your own powerful arm? **सं...करोति**—if you say that I am not to be taken with you because I require to be carefully brought up, then separation from you will make me thin (whatever other care may be bestowed on me in your absence). **स्त्री...सि** then I am placed among women *i. e.* I am treated just as women (who are delicate and unable to bear hardships). **तत् (सुखं) प्रयाति**—all my happiness, being centred in you, marches with you. **विरहो...तरः** separation from you is more difficult to bear (than even the toils of the journey). **कलत्रं...वसति**—the idea seems to be :—you may say that you leave me behind because you want me to guard your harem; but then Glory (which is really the only wife you care to have) dwells in your sword *i. e.* Glory, the only wife you should have, is taken by you on your sword and not placed under protection. राज्य० was to secure Glory by his sword. C and T translate 'if you would have me watch over my wife &c.'; but this does not appear to be correct. There is no connection between **हर्ष**'s watching over his own wife and the fact of Glory residing in his brother's sword. **पृष्ठ...तापः** if you leave me behind (to guard your rear), that is unnecessary, as your valour remains behind (and will guard everything). **राज...गुणैः** if you say that the circle of princes will be without supervision, then (I say there is no need for it as) the princes are well secured by your virtues. A person is also bound (बद्ध) with ropes (गुण). न...गणयसि if you say that a great man (like yourself) does not require an outsider as a companion, then you count me as distinct from yourself. I regard myself and yourself as identical. प्रलघुः (very small) परिकरः (retinue, train). लघु also means light (in weight). पाद...भारः what great weight is there in the dust of your feet? हर्ष means that he is like the dust of his brother's feet and so there is no भार (weight, responsibility) in taking him on the expedition. द्वयो...श्या If you argue that it is not proper that both of us should go, then favour me by ordering *me* to go (and you may remain behind). सदृशो दोषः the idea is :—if you leave me behind because you are afraid out of your affection for me (of what may befall me) then I say I am afraid of what may befall you in my absence. So this fault of कातरत्व is common to both of us and should not be urged against me alone, according to the न्यायवैशेषिक maxim 'यत्रोभयोः समो दोषः परिहारोऽपि वा समः । नैकः पर्यनुयोक्तव्यस्तादृगर्थ विचारणे ॥' तर्कभाषा. आत्मम्भरिता selfishness, greed. 'फलेग्रहिरात्मम्भरिश्च' पा. 3. 2. 26 (आत्मानं बिभर्तीति). क्षीरोदफेनपटलवत् or–पटलेन पाण्डुरम्. Fame is poetically represented as white. The foam of the milky ocean must be very white. When अमृत was churned out of the ocean, it must have been white with the foam &c. अव...देषु I have never before been deceived (*i. e.* deprived) of favours *i. e.* you always granted whatever favours I asked. अति...हितः why should a very insignificant foe be given great importance by making too great a preparation? हरि...म्भारः a host of lions for (catching) a hare causes great shame. ह्रेपण—from ह्रेपयति, causal of ह्री 3rd *conj.* कवचयन्ति put on armour. आशुशुक्षणयः—fires. This is a word used more in the Vedas. अष्टादश द्वीपाः एव अष्टमङ्गलकं तस्य माला अस्ति अस्याः that is wreathed with the bracelet in the form of the eighteen द्वीपs. The com. says 'अष्टमङ्गलकं कङ्कणमित्यन्ये.' A horse is called अष्टमङ्गलक. कुल... वाहिनः blowing against the group of principal mountains. For the कुलपर्वतs, see p. 39. न संनह्यन्ति do not gird up their loins, do not put on armour. सुमेरोः वप्रः (slope) तस्मिन् प्रणयः (liking) तेन प्रगल्भाः (bold) or सुमेरौ वप्रः (butting) तस्मिन् &c. For सुमेरु, see pp. 8, 85. न परिणमन्ति do not stoop to strike with their tusks. Elephants and bulls are represented as butting against the slopes of hills and mounds of earth. सकलपृथ्वीपतीनां प्रलयस्य

उत्पाते धूमकेतुम् that (bow) is a comet portending the destruction of all kings. For धूमकेतु as an उत्पात, see above p. 89. मान्धाता इव—see p. 23 above. चारुः चामीकरपत्रलता एव अलङ्कारः स एव अङ्कः यस्य स०राङ्कः, ०राङ्कः कायः यस्य—the frame of which is marked with ornamental and charming figures in gold. 'चामीकरं जातरूपं महारजतकाञ्चने' इत्यमरः (चमीकरे आकरे भवम्). विं...तायाम् in the hunger for destroying my enemy that has been roused in me. एकाकिनः goes with मम. राज्य० says 'do not claim a share in killing मालवराज; let me alone secure him as my victim'. अयं कोपकवलः एकः this one morsel of my wrath. The morsel is the king of Mālvā. अभ्यमित्रम्—अमित्रस्य अभिमुखम् (अव्ययीभाव).

P. 97 l. 25—**P. 98** l. 13 **अथ...करोत्**. तथागते भ्रातरि his brother being in that condition (*i. e.* so occupied). There is another suggested meaning. तथागत is a name of बुद्ध. 'सर्वज्ञः सुगतो बुद्धो धर्मराजस्तथागतः' इत्यमरः. So the meaning is 'his brother having become a Buddha' (*i. e.* having died in the Buddhist faith). We learn from the Madhuban inscription (see Introduction) that राज्यवर्धन was a very devout Buddhist. दत्तः प्रजागरः यस्मै: who was kept awake. तृतीयो भागः त्रिभागः, त्रिभागः शेषः यस्याः. यामिकः watchman. द्वीपैः उपगीताः गुणाः (virtues, cables) यस्य. A ship also has गुणs (cables, ropes); a ship is laden with heaps of jewels or rich merchandise of every description. रत्नराशि may also mean 'the sea' (generally called रत्नाकर). Ships bring the essence of the sea *i. e.* the best things from beyond the seas. This verse is suggestive of the fall of राज्य०. अनि...वनया by the thought of the evanescent nature (of things). प्रक्षीणं भूयिष्ठं यस्याः when (night) had almost come to an end. Dreams seen in the early morning were believed to come to be true. अभ्रंलिहम् touching the clouds. This is another indication of the fall of the mighty राज्य०. अनुबध्नन्ति persistently follow. अकल्याणस्य आख्याने विचक्षणम् clever in announcing evil. The throbbing of the left eye and arm in the case of men portends evil. अक्षु...क्षाणाः declaring the downfall of no mean king. अविकलः कायबन्धः यस्य whose bodily frame is not maimed, is perfect. कबन्ध...बिम्बे in the disc of the sun that has a headless trunk. 'भास्कराहस्करब्रध्नप्रभाकरविभाकराः' इत्यमरः. राहु is a demon without trunk and is all head. In the disc of the sun a headless trunk was seen and thus राहु was as if provided with a complete body when it seized the sun. विभाव्यते is seen. See above text p. 27 l. 9. (भानुमण्डले भयङ्करकबन्धकायव्याजेन). The बृहत्संहिता says 'दण्डे नरेन्द्रमृत्युर्व्या-

धिभयं स्यात्कबन्धसंस्थाने ।' (III. 17.). सप्तर्षयः—the constellation of the Great Bear. The Great Bear emitted a dark smoke-like streak and thereby darkened all the planets. The poet fancies that the smoke emitted is what they had taken in while performing तपः. To inhale only smoke is a kind of तपः. The बृहत्संहिता (13. 7) says 'उल्काशनिधूमाद्यैर्हता विवर्णा विरश्मयो ह्रस्वाः । हन्युः स्वं स्वं वर्गं विपुलाः स्निग्धाश्च तद्वृद्ध्यै ॥'. दिशां दाहाः—Note बृहत्संहिता 'दाहो दिशां राजभयाय पीतो देशस्य नाशाय हुताशवर्णः ।' (31. 1.) and 'योऽतीव दीप्त्या कुरुते प्रकाशं छायामपि व्यञ्जयतेऽर्कवच्च । राज्ञो महद्वेदयते भयं सः' &c. (31. 2.). तारागणः—the falling stars appear like the particles of ashes due to दिग्दाह. The falling of stars is looked upon as an evil omen. See बृहत्संहिता (33. 11) 'अम्बरमध्याद्बह्व्यो निपतन्त्यो राजराष्ट्रनाशाय ।'. तारा…शुचेव—the moon is called तारानाथ or नक्षत्रेश; the poet fancies that the moon, the lord of stars, was grieved at their fall and therefore lost colour. The उल्काs appear like so many missiles in the battle of the planets. विलोलाः तारकाः यासां or यासु (1) the pupils of which are unsteady; (2) the stars in which fall down. The quarters are compared to ladies frightened at the sight of a battle. सञ्चारयतीव क्ष्मां as if carries the earth. वहत् बहलं रजःपटलं तेन कलिलः शर्कराशकलैः सत्कारी च whistling with bits of gravel and full of flying (वहत्) and thick clouds of dust. न … लग्नस्य I don't see that this hour is auspicious. For लग्न, see pp. 24, 60. असिन्न…पन्थी who will obstruct fate when it seizes even a delicate scion in our family as an elephant seizes the tender shoot of a bamboo (वंशः). The scion is राज्यवर्धन. करीरः—रम् shoot of a bamboo; shoot in general. 'वंशाङ्कुरे करीरोऽस्त्री' इत्यमरः. द्रवदिव—his heart melted or was wet with स्नेह (oil or affection). Another meaning is—his heart was broken inside and was as if running away (द्रवत्); but he somehow kept it firm. यथा…करोत् he performed all his various duties, as he was in the habit of doing them.

P. 98 ll. 14–23 आस्थान … श्रौषीत्. असह्यं दुःखं तेन उष्णाः निश्वासाः तेषां धूमः तेन रक्ताः (coloured) तन्तवः यस्य. His body was dressed in dirty clothes. The author fancies that the mud was the smoke of his hot breaths, which (smoke) coloured the threads. जीवित…लज्जया—he was ashamed that he should continue to live after his master's death. नासा…दृष्टिम् whose eye was fixed on the tip of his long nose. दुःखेन दूरप्ररूढानि रोमाणि यस्मिन् on which there was a long growth due to sorrow. His face, though mute, told the tale by the long growth of beard. बृहदश्ववारः a great horseman, an officer of cavalry. अभिजाततम of very noble birth.. चक्षुषि सलिलेन—supply अगृह्यत—water (tears) came to his eyes. उत्सङ्गे भुवा the earth came to his lap *i. e.* he lay on the bare earth (in grief). अगृह्यत लोकपालैः—वरुण (the lord of सलिल), the wind, the fire are among the eight लोकपाल्s 'सोमाग्न्यर्कानिलेन्द्राणां वित्ताप्पत्योर्यमस्य च। अष्टानां लोकपालानां वपुर्धारयते नृपः ॥' मनु 5. 96. तस्मात्—from कुन्तल. हेलया (easily) निर्जितं मालवानीकं येन. मिथ्योपचारैः उपचितः विश्वासः यस्मिन् in whom trust was increased by false civilities.

P. 98 l. 24—**P. 99** l. 4 **श्रुत्वा…यासीत्.** ०कोपः एव पावकः तस्य प्रसरेण परिचीयमानः (increased) शोकावेगः यस्य. The principal sentence is ततश्च…परां भीषणतां अयासीत्. अमर्षेण (क्रोधेन) विधुतं शिरः तस्मात् शीर्यमाणानि शिखामणीनां शकलानि तैः अङ्गारकितम्. Pieces of jewels from his crest were scattered about when he shook his head in wrath, which (pieces) looked like the live coals of the fire of wrath he sent forth. अङ्गारकित is formed from अङ्गारक on the analogy of तारकित, for which see p. 98. रोष…च्छेदेन with his lip that was curved through wrath. When a man drinks anything he moves his lips and makes them curved. लोहितायमाने (becoming red) लोचने तयोः आलोकः (light) तस्य विक्षेपैः (casting). He cast glances with his blood-shot eyes in all directions, which were thereby made lurid. For दिग्दाह, see above (text l. 5). रोषानलेनापि—connect with वितन्यमान. असह्यः सहजशौर्योष्मदहनः तेन दह्यमानेन. वितन्यमानं ०दुर्दिनं (स्वेदसलिलशीकराणां आसारः एव दुर्दिनं) यस्मिन्. His wrath made him perspire and drops of perspiration stood out like drops of rain on his body. When one is oppressed with heat, one sprinkles drops of water over one's body. The poet imagines that the perspiration was water sprinkled by the fire of his wrath over itself, being afraid of the hotter and unbearable fire of his inborn valour. पूर्वं अदृष्टः अदृष्टपूर्वः कोपः तस्मात् भीतैः. His limbs shook through wrath; the poet fancies that his limbs were afraid of his wrath which they had never seen before. A terror-stricken man trembles. हरः = शिवः. कृतः भैरवः भयङ्करः आकारः येन (with राज्य०); कृतः भैरवस्य आकारः येन (with हरः) who assumed the form of भैरव. भैरव is the name of a terrible form of शिव. हरिः = विष्णुः. प्रकटितं नरसिंहरूपं येन (1) who presented the appearance of a brave man; (2) who manifested the Man-Lion form. In the latter case the reference is to the नृसिंह incarnation of Vishnu, for which see above p. 39.

Words like सिंह are employed to denote pre-eminence, bravery &c.' 'स्युरुत्तरपदे व्याघ्रपुङ्गवर्षभकुञ्जराः। सिंहशार्दूलनागाद्याः पुंसि श्रेष्ठार्थगोचराः ॥' इत्यमरः. नरः सिंह इव (कर्म०). अपरस्य तेजःप्रसरः तस्य दर्शनेन प्रज्वलितः that burst forth into flame at the sight of the spread of another's brilliance. राज्य० was fired by the action of his foe (the गौड king); the सूर्यकान्त emits fire at the sight of the sun (a second source of light). Compare for the idea 'न तेजस्तेजस्वी प्रसृतमपरेषां प्रसहते स तस्य स्वो भावः प्रकृतिनियतत्वादकृतकः । मयूखैरश्रान्तं तपति यदि देवो दिनकरः किमाग्नेयग्रावा निकृत इव तेजांसि वमति ॥' उत्तरराम० VI. 14. क्षय—दिवसः = कल्पान्तदिवसः. उदिताः द्वादश दिनकराः तैः दुर्निरीक्ष्या मूर्तिः यस्य (with दिवसः). ०दिनकरवत् दुर्निरीक्ष्या मूर्तिः यस्य (with राज्य०). For कल्पान्त, see above p. 78. At the time of प्रलय, it is supposed that twelve suns simultaneously rise in the sky. Compare 'दग्धुं विश्वं दहनकिरणैर्नोदिता द्वादशार्काः' वेणीसंहार III; 'यावत्प्राणिमि तावदस्य कल्पान्तोदितद्वादशदिनकरकिरणातपतीव्रस्य' &c. कादम्बरी (p. 156 of P). महो...कारी who caused trembling to all भूभृत्s (kings, mountains) like a portentous hurricane. विवर्धमानः विग्रहस्य (शरीरस्य) उत्सेधः (sublimity, height) यस्य—(1) the grandeur of whose form increased (with राज्य०); (2) whose height increased (with विन्ध्य). The विन्ध्य wanted the sun to revolve round itself as it did round Meru. The sun refused, whereupon the विन्ध्य began to grow higher and higher in order to obstruct the sun's path. The gods in fear sent Agastya who came to the mountain and asked it to allow him to go to the south and to remain in its original state till he returned. अगस्त्य never returned and so विन्ध्य remained low in height. *Vide* महाभारत वनपर्व chap. 104. Compare रामायण 'मार्गं निरोद्धुं सततं भास्करस्याचलोत्तमः । सन्देशं पालयंस्तस्य विन्ध्यशैलो न वर्धते ॥' अरण्य० 11. 86. दुर्नरेन्द्रेण (by a wicked king; by a bad snake-charmer) अभिभवः (insult) तेन रोषितः. आशीविषः—आशीसु आशीःषु वा (तालुगतदंष्ट्रासु) विषं अस्य—a serpent. For नरेन्द्र see p. 33. पारीक्षितः = son of परीक्षित् *i. e.* जनमेजय. सर्वे...द्यतः who was bent upon burning all भोगिन्s (kings, serpents). परीक्षित्, the grandson of अर्जुन, died of snake-bite and जनमेजय made a resolve to extirpate the whole serpent race in revenge. He instituted a सर्पसत्र in which all serpents were burnt except तक्षक who was saved by the intercession of the sage आस्तीक, at whose request the sacrifice was closed. See महाभारत आदि० chap. 49-58. 'उरगः पन्नगो भोगी' इत्यमरः ('भोगः सर्पदेहः कुटिला गतिर्वास्यास्तीति' क्षीर०). 'भोगी भुजङ्गमेऽपिस्याद्ग्रासपात्रे नृपे पुमान्' मेदिनी. वृकोदरः = भीमः. He took a vow to kill दुःशासन when the latter dragged द्रौपदी by her hair and called the पाण्डवs 'गौगौं:' and killed and drank his blood. See कर्णपर्व chap. 83 'सत्यां चिकीर्षुर्मतिमान्प्रतिज्ञां भीमोऽपिबच्छोणितमस्य कोष्णम् ।' 29. सुरगजः=ऐरावतः. प्रतिपक्षस्य वारणाय प्रधावितः who ran to repel his foe (with राज्य०); प्रतिपक्षश्चासौ वारणश्च (गजश्च) तस्मिन् प्रधावितः who ran *i. e.* attacked a rival elephant. पूर्वा...षस्य who was the first advent of prowess. आगमः may also be taken in the sense of 'tradition, revealed scriptures, Veda.' It is believed that the Veda is eternal and that in each कल्प there is only a fresh manifestation. Hence the word पूर्व. उन्माद इव मदस्य—he was the fullest realization of मद. आवेग...लेपस्य the impetuous onrush of haughtiness. सर्वोद्योगः the full endeavour. यु...ष्मणः the inauguration of an era of youthful warmth. रणरसः passion for fighting. For नीराजन, see above p. 78. On the day of नीराजन, a king marches on an expedition. The idea is that he was the marching day of असहिष्णुता *i. e.* असहिष्णुता was to become active in his person from that day.

P. 99 l 5—**P. 102** l. 18 **अवादीच्च...व्यरंसीत्.** ०पुरुषं goes with आर्यम् (राज्यवर्धनम्). निर्व्याज...शस्त्रं who subdued all the kings by his valour that is free from stratagem and who had laid aside his weapon (this applies to both राज्य० and द्रोणाचार्य). कलशयोनिं=द्रोणं. As to the birth of द्रोण see आदिपर्व 63. 6 'भरद्वाजस्य च स्कन्नं द्रोण्यां शुक्रमवर्धत । महर्षेरुग्रतपसस्तस्माद्द्रोणो व्यजायत ॥'. In the great महाभारत war, once an elephant named अश्वत्थामा was killed and the report spread that अश्वत्थामा, the son of द्रोण, was killed. द्रोण asked धर्म, who replied 'हतः कुञ्जरः'. The last word was uttered in a low tone. The old man heard only the first word and in grief for his son laid aside his weapon when धृष्टद्युम्न killed him. See द्रोणपर्व chap. 190. कृष्णवर्त्मा (अग्निः) तस्मात् प्रसूतिः यस्य सः ०सूतिः धृष्टद्युम्नः. About the birth of धृष्टद्युम्नः see द्रोणपर्व chap. 191. 2 'य इद्धा मनुजेन्द्रेण द्रुपदेन महामखे । लब्धो द्रोणविनाशाय समिद्धाद्धव्यवाहनात् ।'. The word कृष्ण० further means 'who is the source of dark paths *i. e.* dark deeds' (as applied to गौडाधिप and also धृष्टद्युम्न). ईदृशेन मृत्युना—the reference is to the treachery practised by the गौड king. अनार्य...पातम्—the sentence is अनार्यं तं मुक्त्वा...केषां मनःसु आर्यशौर्यगुणाः पक्षपातं न कुर्युः—Excepting that vile wretch, in whose minds would not my lord's valour and other qualities produce a favourable impression ? भागीरथी...पाण्डुराः—The waters of the Ganges are white; the foam would be whiter still. Both राजहंस and the qualities are white like the foam. The राजहंसs cause

पक्षपात (movement with or flight on their wings) in the मानस lake (मनःसु सरःसु). पर...कृतः (1) that remind one of the valour of परशुराम (with ०गुणाः); (2) that remember the valour of परशुराम (with ०हंसाः). परशुराम, while he was learning धनुर्विद्या from शिव, being jealous of the power of स्कन्द who had once by his missile called शक्ति pierced the mountain क्रौञ्च, shot an arrow through that mountain and made a passage, through which it was believed the हंसs passed from the plains to the मानस lake. बाण perhaps derived his inspiration from the मेघदूत 'प्रालेयाद्रेरुपतटमतिक्रम्य तांस्तान्विशेषान् हंसद्वारं भृगुपतियशोवर्त्म यत्क्रौञ्चरन्ध्रम् ॥'. In the वनपर्व chap. 225. 33 'बिभेद स शरैः शैलं क्रौञ्चं हिमवतः सुतम् । तेन हंसाश्च गृध्राश्च मेरुं गच्छन्ति पर्वतम् ॥', it is स्कन्द who makes a hole for हंसs. अत्युग्रस्य— applies to गौडाधिप and निदाघरवि. कम...शोषणे in drying up the water of the bed of lotuses. The summer sun dries up the water in which lotuses grow. राज्यवर्धन is compared to कमलाकर, because he was also कमलाकर (the abode of लक्ष्मी) and सलिल to जीवित. अनपेक्षिता प्रीतिः यैः that paid no heed to his friendship (with the hands of गौडाधिप); that paid no heed to the bloom (*lit.* happiness) of the lotuses (with 'the rays of the summer sun'). गतिम् fate, state (after death). कस्मिन्नरके—In the विष्णुपु० (II. 6) a large number of hells such as रौरव is mentioned. So also in the मार्कण्डेयपु० chap. 10 and 12. श्वपाकः = चण्डालः. Construe पापकारिणः अस्य नामापि गृह्णतो मे जिह्वा &c. किं...कार्यम् *lit.* undertaking what object *i. e.* with what object in view. आर्यः— connect with तेन क्षयमुपनीतः. क्षुद्रेण goes with both तेन and घुणेन. अनुप्रविश्य who worked himself into favour with my lord; that bores inside (timber). विगता घृणा (दया) यस्य. घुणः—an insect that eats into timber and produces furrowed lines thereon resembling letters. Note the word घुणाक्षरन्याय. राज्य० is compared to a sandal pillar. मधुरसास्वाद (1) taste of honey; (2) taste of wine. भावी कष्ट...द्रवः the coming trouble of the fall of distressing शिलीमुखs (arrows, bees). One who takes away honey from the honeycomb is attacked by the bees. 'अलिबाणौ शिलीमुखौ' इत्यमरः (शिली शल्यं मुखे अस्य). निज...षणं (1) that is a blot on his own family (with अयशः); (2) that renders dirty one's house (with कज्जलं). जाल...केन (1) by one who lights up a path of deceit (with गौडाधमेन); with a lamp placed in a latticed window. Lampblack sticks to windows and mars the brightness of a house. 'जालं समूह आनायो गवाक्षक्षारकावपि' इत्यमरः. जालं deceit. Separate न तु आशु (quickly) अस्तम्. न वेधसादिष्टः शशी is there not the moon ordered by the creator? ग्रह...पः—ग्रहाणां षण्डे (समूहे) विहारः तस्मिन् एकः केवलः हरिणाधिपः सिंहः—who is the sole lion in roaming among the cluster of planets. The moon wanders in the midst of planets. It is compared to a lion, that also roams about in the midst of thickets. There are further suggestions due to paronomasia. विहार may mean 'reducing'. The moon puts into the shade the group of planets. The lion is called मृगाधिप (lord of beasts). The moon is हरिणाधिप because the spot on the moon is supposed to be a deer. 'अब्जादिकदम्बे षण्डमस्त्रियाम्' इत्यमरः. विनयविधायिनि that lays down (*i. e.* teaches) discipline or obedience. व्यालवारणः a wicked or unruly elephant. कुवैकटिकाः bad jewellers. 'मणिकारो वैकटिकः' क्षीर°. तेज...नाशकाः (1) those that destroy the best of spirited men (with तादृशाः); (2) those that destroy brilliant jewels. 'रत्नं स्वजातिश्रेष्ठेऽपि' इत्यमरः. इत्येतदभि (p. 44, l. 22)...विज्ञापितवान् (p. 45, l. 14). The principal sentence is इत्येतत् अभिदधतः एव अस्य (हर्षस्य) पितुः मित्रं सेनापतिः... सन्निधावेव समुपविष्टः सिंहनादनामा विज्ञापितवान्. सम...हरः foremost in all battles. हरितालं (yellow orpiment) तस्य शैलवत् अवदातः (polished, bright) देहः यस्य. परिणतः (full grown) प्रगुणः (straight) सालः (a tree) तस्य प्रकाण्डं (trunk) तत्प्रकाशः तत्सदृशः. अति...गतः that had reached maturity as if on account of the warmth of his great valour. Heat makes a thing ripe; or cooking (पाकः) is effected with heat. C and T translate 'tall as if ripened by valour's exceeding heat.' This is wrong. There is no connecttion whatever between tallness and ripening by heat. गतं भूयिष्ठं यस्य. °शयने आदौ सुप्तः पश्चादुत्थितः. The सेनापति very often lay wounded with arrows but always got over his wounds. There is another sense. सेनापति (*i. e.* सेनानी) is a name of स्कन्द, who also lay on a bed of शर (reeds). शरजन्मा is a name of स्कन्द. See for the story, रामायण I. 36 and 37. शान्तनवः=भीष्मः, son of शन्तनु and the Ganges. भीष्म also lay wounded on a bed of arrows, waiting for the उत्तरायण, after the advent of which he wanted to die. See भीष्मपर्व chap. 119. 'शरतल्पे महेश्वासं शयानं पुरुषर्षभम् । 92...तानब्रवीच्छान्तनवो नाहं गन्ता कथंचन । दक्षिणावर्ते आदित्ये एतन्मे मनसि स्थितम् ॥' 104. भीष्म was the grand-uncle of the पाण्डवs and yet was the most vigorous of the combatants in the महाभारत war. दु ... तया as his body was such that it could not be subdued (by old age). प्रकटितः प्रकम्पः यया (1) that manifested shaking (in him); (2) प्रकटितः प्रकम्पः यस्याम् (2) that had shaking. A person that is afraid trembles.

Through old age, his limbs shook. The poet fancies that it was जरा (not he) that was trembling, being afraid of touching him. परा...रुहेषु touched in his stiff hair. The idea is that his hair was turning grey. शशिनः कराः तेषां निकरः (समूहः) तद्वत् सिताः सरलाः शिरोरुहाः तैः सटालः (possessed of a mane). His grey hair looked like the lion's mane. He had the same straightforwardness and valour that the lion has. संक्रान्तो...जातिम्—the poet fancies that, even while he was alive, he was transformed into the class of lions. A man may become a lion *after death* (according to the theory of पुनर्जन्म); but he became a lion while living. परिजिहीर्षा desire to avoid. भ्रू...दृष्टिः his eye (or sight) was covered by brows the skin of which was wrinkled, loose and hanging down (over the eye). वलिन—(from वलि + affix न, according to 'लोमादिपामादिपिच्छादिभ्यः शनेलचः' 5. 2. 100 लोमशः । पामनः । पिच्छिलः)—वलयः सन्ति अस्य इति. धवल...मुखेन—in this clause we have first to take विक्रमकालं as qualifying शरदारम्भं and then take शरदारम्भं as qualifying विक्रमकालम्. धवला स्थूला गुञ्जा ('उत्तरोष्ठोपरि रोमराजिः' *com. i. e.* moustache) पिच्छमिव (like a feather) तेन प्रच्छादितः कपोलभागः तेन भास्वरं (bright) तेन (मुखेन). वि...शदं bright with blooming काश thickets. The काश flowers are seen in शरदृतु and are white. वमन्निव विक्रमकालं शरदारम्भं भीमेन मुखेन—The idea is:—The beginning of शरद् is the time to start on an expedition, as the rains are then over. In शरदृतु there are white काश flowers. On his face, he had white moustache resembling काश flowers. So the poet fancies that he vomited from his mouth शरदारम्भ, the time for expedition. अकालेऽपि—the force of this is:—in his old age, his moustache is white at all seasons. So he appears to vomit शरदृतु with its काश flowers at all seasons *i. e.* even when it is वसन्त or ग्रीष्म &c. Then there is a further suggestion. The विक्रमकाल (era so called) is used in the whole of northern India except Bengal and the year commences in चैत्र (except in Gujrat where it begins in कार्तिक). Hence the word अकालेऽपि is used. To Bāna, a विक्रम year beginning in शरद् would be अकाल. For a brief resume about the origin of the विक्रम era, see I. A. vol. 30 pp 3 and 4. शरदि आरम्भः यस्य सः विक्रमकालः. His white beard reaching his navel looked like a white chowrie, whereby he as if fanned the deceased king enshrined in his heart. परिणामेऽपि even in old age. विवृतं वदनं येषां (1) that were open, not yet healed (with व्रण०); (2) that open their mouth (with thirsty people). विषमितं (made rough or uneven) विशालं वक्षः यस्य. There were open gashes of wounds on his chest. The bright sword blade resembles water. A man suffering from thirst opens his lips when he wants to drink water. The poet fancies that the wounds were open because they wanted to drink water (sword blade) *i. e.* his chest would have welcomed more sword-cuts. निशितैः शस्त्रैः टङ्कानां (axe) कोटिभिश्च कुट्टिताः (impressed, engraved) बह्व्यः बृहद्व्रणाः एव अक्षरपङ्क्तयः ताभिः निरन्तरः (closely covered) तस्य भावः ०निरन्तरता तया. The many wounds on his chest resembled lines of letters engraved on a slab of stone. सकल...कुर्वन् as if making a calculation of the auspicious hours of victory in all battles. In calculating we have to draw lines on a board. He is compared to पूर्वपर्वत because the latter also has lines (furrows) made by chisels that are like sharp weapons (निशितशस्त्रसदृशैः टङ्ककोटिभिः &c.). The mountain also has पर्वन्s (joints, parts). पर्वन् means 'the day of new or full moon' and also 'the moment of the sun's entering a new sign.' C and T say that for calculating the ascensions of heavenly bodies the पूर्वपर्वत was used by astronomers. पादचारी (1) walking on foot (with सिंहनाद); (2) that is in the midst of the hills near it. 'पादाः प्रत्यन्तपर्वताः' इत्यमरः. वीररसः—the heroic sentiment. रामणीयकम् beauty. The महाभारत is full of warlike episodes. लघयन् (denominative verb from लघु)—casting into the shade. प्रति...निर्बन्धेन by his extreme persistence in destroying his enemies. परशुराममपि—see p. 38 above for his exploits. परशुराम killed the क्षत्रियs only 21 times; but सिंहनाद did so for times without number. अप्सु भ्रमणं तेन (1) in roving over seas (with सिंहनाद); (2) revolving in the water of the sea. अनादरात् श्रियः समाकर्षणं तस्य विभ्रमेण (लीलया)—by his ease in winning लक्ष्मी without effort. He without effort won several kingdoms for his master. The मन्दर mountain revolved in the sea at the time of the churning and helped in drawing out श्री. See notes p. 42 for मन्दर. वाहिनी...वर्तनेन (1) in acting according to the principles laid down for the commander of an army; (2) in not going beyond the limit prescribed for the lord of rivers. The sea is poetically spoken of as the husband of rivers (वाहिनी). स्थै...भिः in firmness, toughness, and elevation. अचलान् = पर्वतान्. ईश्वरभारस्य उद्वहनेन घृष्टं पृष्ठं यस्य सः ०पृष्ठः तस्य भावः ०पृष्ठता. He toiled very hard (*lit.* his back was abraded) to carry out the important tasks of his king. The back of the bull of शिव is also ground down under the weight of

ईश्वर (*i. e.* शिव). अरणि...ग्नि: who was the rubbing stick of the fire of wrath. The sacrificial fire was produced by the attrition of two pieces of S'amî wood. मदो मदस्य—the idea is that haughtiness found its fullest expression in him. विसर्प:—a dry spreading itch. In the choice of words here the poet is guided mainly by the assonance of sounds. उच्छ्वसितम् life. अङ्कुशो दुर्मदानाम् he was the goad of the unruly *i. e.* he subdued even the most unruly. नाग...भोगिनाम् he was a subduer of elephants (*i. e.* a goad) to wicked kings. There is a pun. नागदमन: means गरुड and भोगिन् means 'serpent' also. वि...ष्यताया: he was the end of the best manhood *i. e.* he was the acme, the perfection of &c. कुल...गोष्ठीनाम्—all assemblies of warriors took their lessons from him. तुला...शालिनाम् he assessed all warriors at their true value. शस्त्रग्राम: = शस्त्रसमूह:. A village (ग्राम:) has boundaries and officers supervise them. आघोष...र्थिनाम् the proclaiming drum of those that seek battle. The drum encourages the fighters. न...श्रयया—that does not stay (long) anywhere *i. e.* that is very fickle or unsteady. न चेतयन्ते do not know. लक्ष्मी deceives कापुरुषs. लक्ष्मी is fickle and मलिन (*i. e.* secured by dark deeds). The cuckoo is dark, but the crow is darker still. The cuckoo has no fixed abode and manages to deceive the crow by placing its eggs in the latter's nest for rearing. Compare 'प्रागन्तरिक्षगमनात् स्वमपत्यजातमन्यैर्द्विजै: परभृता: खलु पोषयन्ति' शाकुन्तल V. श्रियो...कारा: for लक्ष्मी possesses the faults pertaining to lotuses, *viz.* दोषान्धता. लक्ष्मी dwells in कमल; therefore the faults of कमल attach to her and consequently लक्ष्मी deceives other people. दोषान्धता—दोषेषु अन्धता or दोषायां अन्धता (1) being blind to error; (2) closing the buds at night. कमलs close their petals at night-fall. लक्ष्मी makes people blind to the errors they commit. Again कामलाविकारा: would mean 'the evil effects of jaundice' and दोषान्धता means:—a man suffering from jaundice (कामला) regards everything as yellow and may not detect his error; or he may become रात्र्यन्ध. छत्रछायया अन्तरित: रवि: येषाम्. छत्र is the symbol of राज्यलक्ष्मी. सर्वातिशायी शौर्यातिशय: तस्य श्वयथु: (increase, swelling) तेन कपिलौ (tawny) कपोलौ तयो: पुलक: तेन पल्लवित: कोपानल: येषु. The cheeks of warriors were tinged by their ardent passion for heroic deeds and were thrilled. The shooting hair on the cheek is represented as the पल्लव of कोपानल. A man always turns away his face from the brilliant sun (तेजस्विन्). A wretch dares not look at the

without securing all the oceans? The powerful do not rest till they have conquered the world. तेजस्विनः applies to वडवाग्नि also, which did not rest till it was submerged in the ocean. वृथा विततः विपुलफणानां भारः येन. शेष the lord of serpents has 1000 hoods and hence the word विपुल. बिभर्ति...केवलम् that supports merely a clod of earth on its hood. The idea is that शेष merely supports the earth (without the oceans); while the warrior supports all (earth and oceans together). भोग may also mean 'ruling over, government.' भुजङ्गानां भर्ता may mean 'the master of gallants.' The idea is:—'the master of gallants is a king in name, he merely rules over the earth but cannot protect it.' अप्रतिहतं शासनं तेन आक्रान्तिः तस्याः उपभोगः तस्य सुखं तस्य रसः तं (object of जानन्ति) the taste of the happiness of enjoying a suzerainty over the earth in which the edict (issued) is unresisted. Connect रसायाः (of the earth) with ०आक्रान्ति in the preceding compound. दिक्कुञ्जरकरभारवत् भास्वरः प्रकोष्ठः येषाम्. There may be another idea 'the forearm of which is glorious with the tribute levied from even दिग्गजs.' This sentence distinguishes वीरs from शेष; the latter only bears the earth on its भोग (it has no उपभोग); but the warrior enjoys the earth. उन्मुखाः पद्माकराः (lotus beds) तैः गृहीताः पादपल्लवाः (rays) यस्य (with रवि); उन्मुखा (that turns her face towards them, favourable) पद्मा ('लक्ष्मीः पद्मालया पद्मा' अमरः) तस्याः करेण गृहीतः पादपल्लवः (foot) यस्य (with शूरः). अखण्डितं तेजः यस्य (with शूरः); आखण्डितं (destroyed, reduced) तेजः यस्य (with रविः). The radiance of the sun becomes less in the evening. हरिणः हृदये यस्य--the spot in the moon is supposed to be a deer. हरिणस्येव हृदयं यस्य whose heart is (timid) like that of the deer (with कातरस्य). पाण्डुरं पृष्ठं यस्य. The moon is pale in hue; as to the coward 'पाण्डुरपृष्ठस्य देशभाषया निर्लज्जस्यापि' Com. लक्ष्मीः wealth or sovereignty; splendour (of the moon). द्विरात्रमपि— the moon is not the same even for two nights. पुरःप्रवृत्तः प्रतापः तेन प्रहताः. पुरः ... पौरुषस्य the paths of prowess are beaten (*i. e.* prepared) by valour that goes in front. People hear the प्रताप of a warrior and then his way is clear; there is no obstacle. शब्देन विद्रुताः द्विषन्तः येषु. At the word of a proud warrior enemies run away. Doors creak and then the panels fly asunder. शस्त्रस्य आलोकेन (1) by the light of weapons; (2) by the sight of weapons. शून्या दिशः—the world is open to him (*i. e.* nothing comes between him and the world); the world is empty (of enemies). रिपु...रज्यते—the earth is pleased by a shower (आसारः) of rain; लक्ष्मी becomes coloured (or loves) by the shower of blood. ०पतिमुकुटेषु मणिशिलाः शाणाः इव (touchstones) तेषां कोणेषु (points, edges) कषणेन. राजता royalty. Many kings bow at the feet of the overlord and thereby the latter's glory is brightened. The nails of his feet also are brightened by being rubbed against the jewels in the crowns of kings when they fall at his feet. राजता suggests also silver (रजतस्य इयं राजता) which when rubbed against a touchstone shows off brilliant. श्यामीभवन्ति (1) become dark (with hands); (2) become pale or terrified (with रिपुमुख). कव...पात्यमानाः dealt against the panel—like chests of enemies covered with coat of mail. Swords striking against armour produce sparks and also श्री (*i. e.* the successful warrior attains glory or royalty). अहितेन हतः स्वजनः यस्य. Remove the vertical line after ०दुःखम्, मनस्विजनः being the subject of कथयति, उच्छ्वसिति, रोदिति and ददाति. परु...सिति—whose sighs are the wind caused by the fall of the piercing sword-blade. निर्गतं उच्छ्वसितं (जीवितं) यस्मात् तत् ०सितं शत्रुशरीरं तस्मिन् अश्रुधारापातः तेन—the tears he sheds are those that are shed on the body of his lifeless enemy (by the latter's relatives and friends). It would be better if we could read ०शरीरास्रधारापातेन. अस्रम् means both 'tear' and 'blood.' विपक्ष...जलम्—Water is offered to the dead. The spirited offer water to their murdered relatives by the eyes of the wives of their enemies (who shed tears when their husbands are slain in revenge). स्वप्ने आदौ दृष्टाः पश्चान्नष्टाः तेषु. प्रबुद्धाः (1) the wise; (2) those that are awake. When awake we attach no value to things seen in dreams. The wise do not regard their evanescent bodies as their own (kinsmen). Compare for the idea in this and in स्थायिनि &c. 'किमप्यहिंस्यस्तव चेन्मतोऽहं यशः—शरीरे भव मे दयालुः। एकान्तविध्वंसिषु मद्विधानां पिण्डेष्वनास्था किल भौतिकेषु ॥' रघु०-II. 57. अनवरतं प्रज्वलितः तेजःप्रसरः यस्य स चासौ भास्वरस्वभावश्च तं. A jewelled lamp (a jewel shedding light) is naturally brilliant and shoots forth rays. Hence there is no कज्जल in its case. शोक also darkens (कलुषः) a man's face. प्रष्ठो...नाम् the foremost of the nobly born. 'पुरोगाग्रेसरप्रष्ठाग्रतःसरपुरःसराः' इत्यमरः. 'प्रष्ठोऽग्रगामिनि' पा. 8. 3. 92 (प्रतिष्ठते इति प्रष्ठो गौः। अग्रतो गच्छतीत्यर्थः। सि. कौ.). एताश्च—connect with ०भूमयः and भित्तयः. सततसन्निहिताः धूमायमानाः (giving out smoke) कोपाग्नयः यासाम् (*adj.* of ०भूमयः and ०भित्तयः). In cool retreats also fires are lighted which give out smoke. सुलभा असिधारातोयेन तृप्तिः यासु. Thirst is quenched in cool places by water. The bright sword-edge resembles water and is welcomed by these warriors. विकटाः (large) बाहवः एव वनच्छाया तया उपगूढाः—the retreats may be surrounded by the shade of trees. धीर...भूमयः cool places for the abode of courage. स्वायत्ताः = स्वाधीनाः. सिंहनाद means:—such warriors are at your service. धीरता dwells in comfortable (cool) lodgings the walls of which are the broad (panel-like) chests of warriors. यतः...भूयः whence (*i. e.* this being the case) what of the vile Gauḍa king? So act that no one else will again behave thus (treacherously). सर्वो...कामुकानाम् seeking the confidence of the whole earth; or the words may mean 'lovers of the whole earth believing that it will be theirs'. Compare 3rd उच्छ्वास 'भो विद्याधरीश्रद्धाकामुक'. ०विजि...श्वसितैः—the idea is:—kill these pretentious conquerors, so that their wives will weep and heave deep sighs. The sighs will fan them as chowries did before. रुधिरगन्धेन अन्धं गृध्रमण्डलं तेन आच्छादनं तैः. उच्छिन्धि...व्यसनानि remove their attachment to the shade of umbrellas (insignia of royalty) by the coverings made by the groups of vultures &c. Vultures hover over dead bodies and with their large wings appear like umbrellas. कदुष्णं (tepid) शोणितं उदकं इव तस्य स्वेदैः. कु + उष्ण = कदुष्ण; Vide. notes on कदर्थ p. 101 and 'कवं चोष्णे' पा. 6. 3. 107 (कवोष्णं कोष्णं कदुष्णम्। सि. कौ.). कुलक्ष्मीः एव कुलटा तस्याः कटाक्षैः चक्षूरागरोगाः (चक्षूरागाः एव रोगाः) तान्. This is a compound complicated by puns. The sinful sovereignty of other kings is compared to a harlot. A harlot casts glances by which people are enamoured. The wicked kings also are enamoured of कुलक्ष्मी. चक्षूराग (1) redness of the eye (due to some disease); (2) love as manifested by the exchange of glances. If a man is suffering from an eye disease, he is treated by the process of स्वेद (fomentation with tepid water). The idea briefly is:—kill rival kings and their tepid blood will come out and will extinguish their love for sovereignty obtained by unfair means (कुलक्ष्मी). For चक्षूराग, see उत्तररामः V —'भूयसा जीविधर्म एष यद्रसमयी कस्यचित् क्वचित् प्रीतिः, यत्र लौकिकानामुपचारस्तारामैत्रकं चक्षूराग इति'. ०शरैः शिरावेधः तैः. अकार्ये शौर्यमेव श्वयथुः. If a part is swollen, it has to be pierced with a lancet to let out foul matter. लोहनिगडः आपीडमाला इव तस्याः मलः (dark spot due to wearing iron chains) एव महौषधं तैः. पादपीठे (foot-stool) दोहदः (longing) तेन दुर्ललितः (wanton, fondled) पादः तस्य पट्टमान्द्यानि (sharp pains or stiffness). The idea is:—put iron fetters on the feet of kings that desire to rest their feet on foot-stools (which were attached to the throne of a king on which feudatories laid their heads). If a person has feet stiffened by some disease like paralysis or epilepsy, iron rings are placed round them. तीक्ष्णानि आज्ञाक्षराणि (words of command) एव क्षाराः तेषां पातैः. ०कण्डूः is accu. plural. Itch was cured by the application of क्षारs (caustic). ०मरीचयः एव चन्दनचर्चा तया ललाटलेपाः तैः. अनमितानि स्तिमितानि (stiff) मस्तकानि तेषां स्तम्भविकाराः (rigidity) तान्. If the head became rigid, some लेप had to be applied to it. Make the kings bow their unbending heads at your feet, so that the rays of your bright nails, resembling sandal paste, will be a salve to their foreheads. करदानस्य (payment of tribute) सन्देशः (message, order) एव सन्दंशः (forceps). द्रविणदर्पेण उष्णायमाणाः दुःशीललीलाः एव शल्यानि. For taking out शल्य (the point of a dart), forceps are required. Kings did all sorts of wicked and wanton deeds owing to the warmth of wealth. Send a message to them levying tribute and their pride of wealth will be gone. ०पीठस्य दीधितयः एव प्रदीपिकाः (torches or lamps). शुष्कः (vain) सुभटाटोपः (pride of being a great warriar) तेन भ्रुकुटिबन्धः एव अन्धकारः. Darkness is removed by torches. Make the vain and frowning kings bend on your jewelled पादपीठ. चरणलङ्घनं (insulting with the feet, kicking) तेन लाघवं तेन गलितं शिरोगौरवं (weight in the head) तस्मात् आरोग्यं तैः. मिथ्याभिमान is compared to सन्निपात, for which see p. 80. Remove the false pride of kings by kicking them, so that they will not hold their head high. In सन्निपात, there is a feeling of heaviness in the head, which is removed by लङ्घन (fasting). म्रदय denominative verb from मृदु. ०ञ्जलिषु मुकुलितः (closed, folded) करसम्पुटः तस्य ऊष्मभिः. इष्वसनं (इषवः अस्यन्ते अनेन) धनुः तस्य गुणः (string) तेन किणः तस्य कार्कश्यानि (hardness). If the hands be always folded together, heat is produced in the cavity. A hard callosity may become soft by fomentation. देवभूयं गते having reached the state of being a god *i. e.* having gone to heaven. 'स्याद् ब्रह्मभूयं ब्रह्मत्वं ब्रह्मसायुज्यमित्यपि । देवभूयादिकं तद्वत्' इत्यमरः. नरेन्द्रे = प्रभाकरवर्धने. वृत्ते...प्रलये when this great Pralaya (calamity) has taken place. धरणी...शेषः you alone are left to support the world. शेष also means the serpent शेष that supports the earth on its hoods. See p. 19. अविद्यमानं शरणं यासाम्. **'शरणं गृहरक्षित्रोः'** इत्यमरः. शरत्सवितेव like the sun in autumn. क्ष्मापतीनां (1) of kings; (2) of mountains. ललाटन्तप—burning the forehead. पादः foot, ray. आयाहि... ताम्—become one whose feet have a variegated hue (black and white). There is another sense 'become कल्माषपाद'. King मित्रसह son of सुदास came to be called कल्माषपाद. The king killed a tiger out of two. When killed it became a राक्षस. The other vowed revenge. The king performed a sacrifice at the end of which the राक्षस came disguised as वसिष्ठ and asked for a meal of flesh. Then the राक्षस assumed the form of a cook and served human flesh. The real वसिष्ठ came and knowing what was served cursed the king to be a cannibal. The king, knowing that he was innocent, took water to curse वसिष्ठ, when his queen मदयन्ती dissuaded him from cursing the sage. He threw the water taken for the curse on his own feet, which became spotted. See विष्णुपु० IV. 4; भागवत 9. 9. 20-25 and रामायण VII. 65 (where the king's name is वीर्यसह). रामायण I. 70 gives a different story. अभिनवा सेवादीक्षा तया दुःखं तेन सन्तप्ताः श्वासाः एव धूममण्डलानि तैः. दीक्षा means 'initiating a person into some rite or work.' The kings were to be subdued and made to attend upon हर्ष for the first time. Naturally they would heave hot sighs, which are compared to धूममण्डल. नखम्पचैः scorching the nails. 'मितनखे च' पा. 3. 2. 34 (मितंपचा ब्राह्मणी । नखंपचा यवागूः । सि. कौ.). The hot breaths of kings when they bowed at his feet would scorch his nails and the jewels in their crowns that moved when they bowed would emit rays resembling the mellow light of morn (बालातप). सहजं ब्राह्मण्यमार्दवं तेन सुकुमारं मनः यस्य. चण्डेन चापवनानां अटनिः (the notched extremity of a bow) तस्याः टाङ्कारनादेन निर्मदीकृताः दिग्गजाः येन (*adj.* of राज्यन्यकम्)—(the क्षत्रिय race) that had deprived the quarter elephants of their intoxication by the terrible twanging of the extremities of the forest of (*i. e.* group of) bows. The idea is that the क्षत्रियs had subdued the whole earth. गुञ्जत् ज्यानां जालं तेन जनितः जगतः ज्वरः येन (*adj.* of राजन्यकम्). उद्यतम् making an (united) effort. कृत्ताः वंशाः यस्य the families of which were cut off (by परशुराम). वंशs (bamboos) also are cut off, produce a sound and their thickets are burnt. Or कृत्तवंशं (कृत्ताः वंशाः यथा स्युः) may be taken as an adverb modifying उत्खातवान्. कृतवंशं (कृताः संस्कृताः वंशाः यस्य) is not a good reading. राजन्यकम्—the race of क्षत्रियs. 'अथ राजकम् । राज्यन्यकं च नृपतिक्षत्रियाणां गणे क्रमात् ॥' इत्यमरः. नैसर्गिकेण कायकार्कश्येन कुलिशायमानं मानसं यस्य whose mind acts like the thunder-bolt on account of the natural hardness of his body. मूर्धन्यः foremost (मूर्धनि भवः). ०ध्वस्तये for the destruction &c. जीवितानां सङ्कलने आकुलः कालः यमः तस्य अकाण्डे यात्रा तस्याः चिह्नध्वजं—(bow) which is the banner indicating the unexpected expedition of Yama eager to gather lives. The idea is :—your bow will do terrific carnage among your foes. A ध्वज is carried in front of an army. Harsha has to resolve on fighting all of a sudden. अरातिः शत्रुः तस्य रक्तमेव चन्दनचर्चा तया शिशिरोपचारः (cooling treatment) तमन्तरेण (without that). दुःखमेव दाहज्वरः. In दाहज्वर sandal paste is applied. Blood resembles रक्तचन्दनचर्चा. निकारेण (insult) सन्तापः तस्य शान्तिः तस्याः उपायानां परिक्षये--when no other means to allay the heat of insult could be found. रिपुरुधिरं एव अमृतं. For the reference, see above p. 139. पवनात्मजेन=भीमेन. अमन्दरोपायम् (न विद्यते मन्दरः उपायः यत्र)—for being able to drink अमृत, the gods required the mountain मन्दर; see p. 42. But भीम obtained रुधिरामृत without मन्दर. हिडिम्बा was a राक्षसी, wife of भीम. भीम drank the blood of दुःशासन with zest, as if it had first been touched by the lips of his wife हिडिम्बा. Being a राक्षसी, she is appropriately mentioned in connection with blood. See आदिपर्व 155 for the union of हिडिम्बा and भीम. As to the extirpation of the क्षत्रियs by परशुराम, see above p. 38. 'त्रिःसप्तकृत्वः पृथिवीं कृत्वा निःक्षत्रियां प्रभुः । समन्तपञ्चके पञ्च चकार रुधिरहृदान् ॥ स तेषु तर्पयामास भृगून् भृगुकुलोद्वहः ।' वनपर्व 117. 9–10; see also आदिपर्व 2. 3–5. जामदग्न्येन—परशुरामेण. शाम्यन् ०सञ्ज्वरः (मन्युः क्रोधः एव शिखी तस्य शिखानां ज्वालानां सञ्ज्वरः) तस्मिन् सुखायमानेषु स्पर्शशीतलेषु च &c. क्षत्रियाणां क्षतजं रुधिरं तस्य हृदेषु (lakes).

P. 102 l. 19—**P. 103** l. 13. **देवस्तु...भुवनस्य.** मान्येन refers to सिंहनाद. इतरथा—even otherwise *i. e.* even if this treachery of the Gauda king had not kindled my wrath. मे goes with भुजस्य. गृहीत...भुजस्य. दायमादत्ते दायादः—one who shares in the ancestral estate. The idea is:—my arm does not like the idea of sharing the burden of the earth with शेष. It wants the whole to itself. गच्छति qualifies ग्रहग्रणे. The idea is :—When the stars go up (reach the zenith), my brow wants to check their rise (*i. e.* I am so ambitious as to crave not only the control of this earth but also of heavenly bodies). Explain the following similarly. अनमत्सु...कचग्रहम्—one who does not bend may be made to bend by seizing his hair. दुर्विदग्ध conceited. चामराणि—I wish to make the rays of the sun my chowrie-bearers. Chowries are held in the hand (कर, also ray). राज...रुषा As I resent the title 'king' (applied to the lion). The lion is called मृगराज. I cannot bear that anyone else should bear the title of king in this world. Compare for the idea 'नूनं तेषामभ्यसूयापरोऽभूद्वीर्योदग्रे राजशब्दे मृगेषु' रघु० 9. 64. स्व...गृहीतानाम् (*adj.* of दिशाम्) that have been seized (occupied) at their sweet will by the self-willed (uncontrolled) लोकपालs. For लोकपालs, see above p. 137. The author seems to have used the word लोकपाल in the sense of दिक्पाल, but the two are slightly different, as will be seen from pp. 25, 137. आक्षेपादेशाय for giving the order of snatching them (quarters) away (from their hands). दुर्जातं—calamity. 'दुर्जातं व्यसने क्लीबेऽसम्यग्जातेऽन्यलिङ्गकम्' मेदिनी. The construction is इतरथा हि मे...भुजस्य...किं पुनरीदृशे...जाते. Put a vertical line after जाते. हृदय...शल्ये who is a painful thorn in my heart. मुसल्ये—मुसलेन वध्यः—deserving to be pounded with a pestle. The word is formed on the analogy of विष्य (विषेण वध्यः according to पा. 4. 4. 91 which is a very long सूत्र). पोटा—Hermaphrodite 'पोटा स्त्रीपुंसलक्षणा.' प्रतिकारशून्यम् (adverb) helplessly. शुष्कः अधरपुटः यस्य (with हृषे) whose lips are dry (through the fever of grief). With पोटा, the word cannot be explained for reasons of propriety. अधरं स्त्रीयोनिः. अकृतं रिपुबलस्य अबलानां (wives) विलोललोचनेषु उदकं (tears) एव दुर्दिनं येन. He says he cannot offer water to his deceased brother with ordinary water, but will do so with the tears &c. Supply कुतः before अदृष्ट०. धूम causes tears. शपामि...स्पर्शेन—the thing with which an oath is taken is put in the instrumental. परिगणितैः counted *i. e.* limited. सकलचापानां चापलेन (quickness, fickleness) दुर्ललिताः (naughty, spoilt) नरपतयः तेषां चरणेषु रणरणायमानाः (resounding) निगडाः यस्याम्. The kings of the earth are quick archers. Those who are fickle are spoilt. तनूनपाति = अग्नौ. पीतं सर्पिः घृतं येन—fed with ghee. पतङ्गः a moth flies against the flame of a lamp. महा...कृतम् the great minister for peace and war. सन्धिश्च विग्रहश्च तयोः अधिकृतः. महांश्चासौ ०कृतश्च. This officer is often spoken of as महासान्धिविग्रहिक (see I. A. Vol. 15 p. 304; E. I. Vol. III. p. 267, 270). Compare C. I. Vol. III. p. 35 'अन्वयप्राप्तसाचिव्यः व्यापृतसन्धिविग्रहः'. अन्तिके तिष्ठतीति ०स्थः. आ is a कर्मप्रवचनीय governing a noun in the ablative and means 'up to'. चारणः—a heavenly chorister, a semi-divine being. त्रिकूटकटके (capital) कुट्टाकटङ्कैः लिखितः काकुत्स्थेन (रामेण) लङ्कालुण्ठनव्यतिकरः यस्मिन्—where the incident of the devastation of लङ्का by Rāma was engraven with cutting axes on the capital situated on त्रिकूट. त्रिकूट was a hill on which the capital of रावण was situated. 'स सागरमनाधृष्यमतिक्रम्य महाबलः । त्रिकूटस्य तटे लङ्कां स्थितः स्वस्थो ददर्श ह ॥' अरण्यकाण्ड 2. 1. कुट्टाक *adj.* that cuts. सुवेल is a mountain identical with त्रिकूट according to हेमचन्द्र. See also अनर्घराघव VI. 17. वरुण is the lord of the ocean and of the West. परिमलैः सुगन्धयः पाषाणाः तैः वासितं गुह्यगृहं यस्मिन्. गुह्यकs are semi-divine beings that are the attendants of कुबेर and guardians of his treasures. The unguents they employ perfume the caves where they dwell. गन्धमादनः name of a mountain to the east of मेरु famous for its fragrant forests. There भीम had gone to bring सौगन्धिकपुष्प for द्रौपदी. See वनपर्व 152 ff. सज्जी...ग्रहणाय वा—In this and the following clauses he offers them a choice between submitting to him and offering battle. गृह्यन्तां...चामराणि वा either seize the quarters or chowries *i. e.* either be my chowrie-bearers or hold fast by your kingdoms and fight. गृह्यन्तां दिशः may also mean 'run away, fly from your kingdoms'. नमन्तु धनूंषि—bows are bent in discharging arrows. कर्णपूरः an ear-ornament. कर्ण... मौर्व्यः either honour my commands (by listening to them) or draw the strings (मौर्वी) of your bows to the ear (in discharging arrows). शेख...शिरस्त्राणि turn the dust of my feet into chaplets or don the helmet. शेखरः a chaplet worn on the head. घटन्तां करि...बन्धाः arrange the arrays (घटा) of elephants. समा...यष्टयः either take hold of canes or lances. Canes were held by chamberlains or doorkeepers. मच्चरणनखेषु &c. He asks them either to bow at his feet, on the bright nails of which they will be reflected or to take bright swords. परा...मिति because I am come. This gives the reason why the kings should make a choice. निवृत्तिः cessation, rest. सकल...मयः consisting of the jewels in the crowns &c. *i. e.* all kings must bow at my feet. A person maimed has to apply a लेप to his feet. स्वस्थवत् like one who is at ease (as if nothing had happened). श्रुता प्रतिज्ञा येन. शाम्यन् ऊष्मा यस्य (*adj*. of दिवसः). The idea is:—the day passed away together with its heat. The poet says that it was not the heat that faded away from the day of the worlds, but it was the pride that faded (at hearing the terrible प्रतिज्ञा of हर्ष).

P. 103 l. 14—P. 104 l. 4 **ततश्च...मिच्छामीति.** Read अहिमभासि, for अहिम. अहिमा भाः यस्य. निजा०—The setting of the sun is represented as due to the fear of the sun that the angered हर्ष may deprive him also of his sovereignty, just as he vowed that he would do in the case of the kings of the earth. निगूढाः शिलीमुखानां भ्रमराणां आलापाः येषु. The red lotuses closed their petals at sunset and the humming of bees was heard no more. The poet fancies that they did so through fear. One who is afraid remains silent and contracts himself (or hides). शिलीमुख also means 'arrow'. (निगूढः शिलीमुखानां आलापः twang येषु). Further a picturesque effect is produced by the words

मुख and आलाप and by reading इषुत्रासात्. समुपसंहृतः निजपक्षाणां (wings) विक्षेपः (tossing, movement) यैः ते ०क्षेपाः, ०क्षेपाश्च ते निश्चलाश्च. The birds lay in their nests and did not flap their wings. पक्ष also means 'side, partisans.' The suggested meaning is:—When the excitement of the partisans had died away and hence they were motionless. भुवनव्यापिनीम् (1) that spread over the whole world (with सन्ध्या); (2) that embraced or applied to the whole world (with प्रतिज्ञा). ०दिक्पालैः दीयमानानि अभ्रंलिहानि लोहप्राकारवलयानि यासु. Pitchy darkness began to envelope the sky and the quarters. Darkness is fancied to be iron ramparts (प्राकारः) touching the sky erected by दिक्पालs afraid of losing their position (as दिक्पालs) at the hands of हर्ष. प्रदोषास्थाने in the evening assembly. नमन् नृपलोकः तस्य लोलानि अंशुकानि तेषां पवनेन कम्पिताः शिखाः (flames) येषाम्. The lamps flickered owing to the wind set in motion by the upper garments of the kings when they bowed before departing. The poet says that the flickering was as if the bowing of lamps. उत्तानः stretched out, lying on the back. दीपः द्वितीयः यस्य He had no companion except the lamp. अभि...सरः जग्राह as an attendant (or servant) finding a proper opportunity wins (the mind of his master). 'अनुप्लवः सहायश्चानुचरोऽभिसरः समाः' इत्यमरः. C and T render 'finding its opportunity like a brigand.' तरसा (instru. of तरस् *n.*) quickly. उपर्यु...श्वासाः one after another his sighs went forth as if searching for his brother's life. धवलां...प्लवेन his bright tears resembled the hem of a white garment. परिणामः result, end. ०सङ्घातवत् or ०सङ्घातैः कर्कशः कायबन्धः यस्य (with तातात् and अचलात् respectively). इयं सा प्रीतिः this is my love for my brother (the idea intended to be conveyed being that he had no real love for his brother). अनुवृत्तिः acting according to, obedience. बालिशो...वितम् who even if a child (or fool) would think it possible that I would continue to live even after the death of my honoured brother ? ऐक्यम् Unity of hearts or thoughts. पृथक्कृतः separated. दग्धरोषेण अन्तरिता शुक् यस्य (*adj.* of मया) whose grief was intercepted (obscured) by accursed wrath (against the गौड king). गतघृणेन निर्दयेन. लूता...छिदुराः as brittle (easy to cut) as the webs of the spider (लूता). तन्तुच्छटा = तन्तुजालम्. तुच्छाः worthless. लोक...बान्धवता ties of kindred rest solely upon the conventions of the world. He means:—kinship is no reality, but is a mere conventional bond. लोकयात्रा एव ०मात्रं निबन्धनं (suppor.) यस्याः. परस्परप्रीतिबन्धेन निर्वृतं (blessed) हृदयं यस्य. विघटिते—being separated. चन्द्र...गुणाः—the idea is :—while राज्य० was alive his qualities delighted the world like the moon, but when he passed away, the same qualities burn the world, as if through contact with the funeral fire. लग्नः चिताग्निः येषां (*adj.* of गुणाः). पर्यदेवत he bewailed. अशेष...कृतम् commander of the whole elephant host. स्कन्दगुप्त is probably the same स्कन्दगुप्त that is mentioned as a great officer of Harsha in the Madhuban inscription (E. I. VII. p. 155). *Vide* Introduction.

P. 104 l. 5—**P. 105** l. 3 **अथ ... करोत्.** The principal sentence is अथ...हूयमानः स्वमन्दिरात्...स्कन्दगुप्तो विवेश राजकुलम्. अप्रति... रेणुः who did not wait for his own elephant. करेणुः an elephant in general, or a female elephant. के मूर्ध्नि रेणुरस्य or अस्याः. प्रणमतः... दिशम् bowing (to him) on every side. दिशि दिशि प्रति० (अव्ययी०). वर...पृच्छन् questioning as to the night's news concerning the best elephants. पृच्छन् governs two accusatives इभभिषग्वरान् and ०वार्ताः. उच्छ्रित०—The instrumentals in this and the following clauses are to be connected with क्रियमाणकोलाहलः (l. 19), which qualifies स्कन्दगुप्तः below. Various groups belonging to the camp raised noises about him. उच्छ्रितं शिखिपिच्छैः लाञ्छितं वंशलतावनगहनं तेन गृहीतः दिगायामः यैः that measured the expanse of the sky with tall thickets of bamboos that were decked with peacock's feathers. In the विन्ध्य forest grow high bamboos on which sit peacocks. The elephant-riders had tall bamboos in their hands on which were hung peacock's feathers. वारण...गतैः that had come to undertake the encounter for capturing elephants (or the encounter for securing elephants that had got loose). C and T translate ' come for the purpose of bursting the animals' fastenings.' This is not clear. The com. read अनायत्त० and explains 'अनायत्ता हस्तिपार्श्वरक्षिणः'. C and T translate 'throngs of unemployed persons'. We take अना० as an *adj.* of ०गणैः. अनायतानि मण्डलानि येषाम् whose groups were not restrained (*i. e.* that did not run in proper order). 'आधोरणाः हस्तिपका हस्त्यारोहा निषादिनः' अमरः. नवः ग्रहः येषां ते ०ग्रहाः गजपतयः elephants recently caught. आत्मीय...वेदयद्भिः that reported the advent of rut in the elephants entrusted to them. डिण्डि...यद्भिः that made a request that a drum be mounted (on the elephants in their charge). प्रमादेन पतितः अपराधः तेन अपहृतः द्विरदः तस्मात् दुःखं तेन धृतं दीर्घश्मश्रु यैः that had a long beard due to the grief caused by their being deprived of an elephant because they were guilty of an offence committed through carelessness. अभि...स्रुतैः that had recently come (for being engaged as servants). कर्पटिभिः that were clothed in rags (because they had not yet been engaged). गणिका—'गजानां प्रतिलोभनार्थां हस्तिनी' com. चिरात् लब्धं अन्तरं यैः that found an opportunity (to speak to स्कन्दगुप्त) after a long time. उच्छ्रितौ (uplifted) करौ येषाम्. Remove the comma after ०करैः. कर्मण्य...कुलैः busy in enumerating the female elephants that were clever in that act (in decoying wild elephants). कर्मणि साधुः कर्मण्यः. उल्लासितानि (tossed) पल्लवचिह्नानि यैः. Being foresters, it is but proper that their badges should be पल्लवs. Remove the comma after ०पङ्क्तिमिश्र. निष्पादितः (secured) नवग्रहाणां नागानां (गजानां) निवहः &c. उत्तम्भितं (raised up) तुङ्गं तोत्रवनं यैः. तोत्रम् (from तुद्) a goad. महामात्राः (महती मात्रा परिच्छदः येषाम्) प्रधानहस्त्यारोहाः (chiefs of elephant riders) तेषां पेटकैः समूहैः. प्रकटितं करिकर्मणे चर्मपुटं यैः. Figures of elephants made of leather were used for training elephants to fight. अभि...वृन्दैः by crowds of messengers sent by the keepers of elephant forests for conveying the news of the movements of fresh herds of elephants. प्रति...कूटैः that examined at each moment the heaps of fodder for elephants. Remove the comma after वृन्दैः. Being men from the forest, they were naturally led to examine every mouthful that they saw elephants eating before them. कट...वेदयमानैः that reported about the gleaning of corn (for elephants) in villages, towns and marts (निगमः). कटानां सस्यानां ओषधीनामिति यावत् हस्तेन भङ्गः छेदनम्. Three things combined to give an air of command to स्कन्दगुप्त even when he was indifferent (he did not intend to issue any order). ०सम्भृतेन added to, increased. महा...ष्कारेण by the appearance (outward signs *i. e.* dress &c.) of the high position he held. अव...भोगेन by the great majesty (of his form). अवष्टम्भस्य आभोगः (expanse). असंख्य...सम्पादनाय—C and T translate 'to provide a limitless supply of shells for elephants' ears.' We do not know what shells had to do with elephants' ears. असंख्यकरिणां कर्णाः शङ्खाश्च (parts between the tusks) तेषां सम्पत् (beauty) तस्याः सम्पादनाय. Conchshells are found on the sea-shore. So he as if ordered the seas to supply शङ्ख (*i. e.* beautiful temples to the elephants). कर्ण also means 'the rudder of a ship'. For the meanings of शङ्ख see p. 42. शृङ्गार...संग्रहाय for making a store of the unguents (अङ्गरागः), *viz.* red-chalk (गैरिकपङ्कः), for making marks (on the elephant's forehead). 'शृङ्गारः सुरते नाट्यरसे च गजमण्डने' मेदिनी. दिग्ग...हरैः Depriving the elephant (ऐरावत) of Indra of his authority as a दिग्गज over the quarters. स्कन्दगुप्त wielded power over the quarters with his elephants and so deprived even ऐरावत of his अधिकार, though ऐ० was patronised by the powerful इन्द्र. अपहरन् governs two accusatives, ०कारं and ऐरावतम्. C and T tranlsate 'to deprive Indra of his Airâvata's charge over the sky elephants.' This is not correct. It was *not* Indra that was deprived. For the meanings of हरि, see p. 40. हरपदभारेण नमितः कैलासगिरिः तद्वत् गुरुभिः (heavy). गुरुभार० heavy weight. गति...लम्बस्य—As he walked about, his arms moved to and fro and reached his knees. Arms reaching the knees indicated sovereignty or great position. 'करिकरसदृशौ वृत्तावाजान्ववलम्बनौ समौ पीनौ। बाहू पृथिवीशानाम्' बृहत्संहिता 67. 35. आलान...मालाम् a row of stone pillars for tying elephants. ई...लम्बेन slightly raised and pendulous. कवलेने...लोभयन्—the idea is:–a female elephant is allured by the sight of a mouthful of fresh sprays that are high up hanging from a tree. His lip was red and resembled tender leaves and so allured the करेणुका, *viz.* श्री (glory or prosperity). His lip was such as indicated the high position he had attained. The whole of chap. 67 of the बृहत्संहिता gives the सामुद्रिकलक्षणs of men. निज...दधानः having a straight (bamboo-like) nose as long as his master's pedigree. This is rather a strange simile. A long nose indicated beauty and prosperity 'दीर्घया तु सौभाग्यम्' बृहत्संहिता 67. 61. स्निग्ध glossy (with eyes); oily, sticky (with क्षीरोद). पिब...यामम् he as if drank the expanse of the quarters with the expanse of his two eyes. पीतः क्षीरोदः (क्षीरसागरः) येन. विकटं विपुलं च अलिकं (forehead) यस्य. He had a forehead that was broader than the slopes of Meru. There is a further suggestion. As मेरु is a mountain of gold, his forehead also was gold-coloured (fair). सतत...वशादिव—His hair was long, dark and soft like tendrils. The poet fancies that this was due to its growing under the shade of an umbrella (which was the sign of his authority). भङ्गुर curling. कुन्तलाः (tresses) एव बालवल्लरी तस्याः वेल्लितं (tossing) तेन विलासिना. बर्बरक (also written वर्वर or—क) means curly hair. A young creeper also may be long, green, soft and curling. लुन...करान्—His hair deprived by its darkness the rays of the sun of their light. लुप्तः आलोकः येषाम्. अरिपक्षस्य परिक्षयेण परित्यक्तं कार्मुककर्म येन सः. ०दिगन्तेषु श्रूयमाणः गुरुः गुणध्वनिः यस्य. If he had given up archery, how can the twang of his bowstring (गुण) be heard ? This विरोध is removed by taking गुण in the sense of 'virtue.' आत्मसं (under his control) सकल-

मत्तमातङ्गसाधनं यस्य. मदेन (1) by ichor; (2) by pride. भूति...मयः— though full of भूति (ashes), he was yet full of oili-ness. Ashes can never contain oil. So we must explain 'though full of prosperity, yet possessing a sweet manner'. पार्थिवो...मयः though made up of earthy substance, yet produced from गुण. पृथ्वी is a द्रव्य according to the न्यायवैशेषिक system. What is made of द्रव्य cannot at the same time be an effect of गुण (the 2nd पदार्थ of the above system). The विरोध is got over by translating 'though he was in rank a king, yet he was full of good qualities.' The com. says 'गुणास्तन्तवोऽपि। नहि घटः पटो भवतीति विरोधः' (*i. e.* पार्थिव means a घट and गुणमय a पट). This is another way of putting forward the विरोध, but is not so striking as the one we give. दानव...स्थितः standing at the head of the generous. दानवत् also means 'full of rut' and qualifies 'करिणाम्'. स्कन्दगुप्त was superintendent (उपरिस्थितः) of elephants. भृत्य...द्वहन्—the idea is:— though he was a servant, he had never borne any humiliation, just as if he were the master (or king). भर्तृ (1) master; (2) husband. अनन्यगम्याम् (1) not to be reached by anyone else (with प्रसादभूमि); (2) not approachable by anyone else (with कुलाङ्गना). विदग्ध learned. अभृत...भजताम् an unpaid servant of those that resorted to him (for protection). उभय...तलं he rested both his hands on the earth and touched it with his head.

P. 105 l. 4—**P. 106** l. 20 **उपविष्टं...निर्जगाम**. Read नाति°. अस्य...तस्य of what I desire to do. प्र...गतानि gone out to the pastures (प्रचारः). भर्तृभक्तेः from devotion to my master. पुष्प...जनस्य (worthy) of the race sprung from पुष्प°. आभिजात्यम् (अभिजातस्य भावः) nobility of birth. उपक्रान्तम् undertaken, begun. काकोदरः अभिधानं यस्य called a snake. 'काकोदरः फणी' इत्यमरः. (काकस्येव उदरं यस्य). निकारम् insult, injury. उदन्तः 'वार्ताप्रवृत्तिर्वृतान्त उदन्तः स्यात्' इत्यमरः. विषयः a district. From the inscriptions we shall find that विषय is a portion of राष्ट्र. आकाराः features. व्याहारः speech. व्यवहारः dealings, pursuit. प्र...देवः your Majesty has heard everyday many stories about the disasters due to the fault of carelessness. 'अभिषङ्गः पराभवे' इत्यमरः. श्रुताः बह्व्यः वार्ताः येन. यथा—the following passage contains numerous interesting stories of love and intrigue. They appear to have a historical basis; many of them occur in the अर्थशास्त्र of कौटिल्य; a few in the कामन्दकीयनीतिसार and in the बृहत्संहिता. नागकुले जन्म यस्य. सारिकया श्राविताः मन्त्रः यस्य— whose line of policy was published (to the world) by a सारिका bird. पद्मावती—What particular city is meant, we cannot say.

उत्सवः' अमरः. महा...वातूलम् whose head was turned by his belief in (the efficacy of) the sale of human flesh. For महामांस, see above p. 72. जघ...द्योतस्य the younger brother of प्रद्योत. रसायनरसे अभिनिवेशः अस्य ०वेशिनः (*adj.* of गणपतेः). That had set his heart upon the elixir of life. It was believed that mercury if properly treated would make men immortal. वैद्यव्यञ्जनाः persons professing to be doctors. सुबहुपुरुषान्तरैः प्रकाशिताः औषधगुणाः यैः that had advertised the virtues of their medicines through various people. विदेह was a country that comprised a part of modern Nepal, the district of Tirhut and Champaran. राजयक्ष्मन् *m.* consumption. ०श्वासिनः (*adj.* of भद्रसेनस्य). महा...भाक् who secretly found access into the wall of the chief queen's apartment. कालिङ्ग king of कलिङ्ग, which was a country between the mouths of the Godāvarī and the Mahānadî. तूलिका—a mattress filled with cotton. दध्रस्य—दध्र is the name of the king. करूष—seems to be a country near Jubbulpore. It is closely connected with Chedi. For this and the preceding, see काम० VII. 51. 'देवीगृहगतं भ्राता भद्रसेनममारयत् । मातुः शय्यान्तरालीनः कारूषं चौरसः सुतः ॥'. उत्सारके रुचिः (liking) यस्य. 'दण्डी दौवारिको वेत्री उत्सारकश्च' क्षीर०. चकोरनाथः king of चकोर. चकोर is the name of a mountain in the Purāṇas. गण्डकः a rhinoceros. उद्दण्डं high-stemmed. नड्वलं abounding in reeds. नलवन forest of reeds. चम्पा was the capital of अङ्ग or north Bengal. चमूं चरन्तीति ०चराः भटाः. चामुण्डी seems to have been the name of a city. बन्दि...परम् who was absorbed in his fondness for bards. परप्रयुक्ताः employed by his enemy. ०मुखरं मुखं येषाम्. मल्लाः bards. कामि...गुप्तः concealing his identity by the dress of a woman. अशातयत्—from the causal of शद्. 'चन्द्रगुप्तभ्रातृजायां ध्रुवदेवीं प्रार्थयमानश्चन्द्रगुप्तेन ध्रुवदेवीवेषधारिणा स्त्रीवेषजनपरिवृतेन रहसि व्यापादितः' Com. शकपति—the S'akes are identified with the Scythian hordes that invaded India before the beginning of the Christian era. मधुमोदितम् exhilarated with wine. मधुरकं = विषम्. Compare for the story काम० VII. 52. व्याज...दर्पा who pretended to be in a passion of love. क्षुरधारा पर्यन्ते यस्य that had the edge of a razor. परन्तप who subdued others. जारूथ—was the name of the king. Supply जघान here and in the following clauses. विषचूर्णेन चुम्बितः मकरन्दः यस्य. सौह्य—king of सुह्म, Western Bengal, the capital of which was ताम्रलिप्त. योगपरागः magic powder. वैरन्त्यं king of वैरन्ती or विरन्ती. In the whole of this passage the names are corrupt and there is no agreement between the MSS on the one hand and the authorities we have quoted. Some MSS read वैरन्त्या. वृष्णिम्—belonging to the वृष्णिs, a यादव clan. विदूरथम्—

'शस्त्रेण वेणीविनिगूहितेन विदूरथं स्वा महिषी जघान । विषप्रदिग्धेन च नूपुरेण देवी विरक्ता किल काशिराजम् ॥' बृहत्संहिता 78. 1; see काम० VII. 54. सौवीर—seems to have been a country west of Mount Abu. अदृश्या...वदना who smeared the inside of her mouth with an invisible antidote. ०पायनेन by making him drink &c. Note the following from the अर्थशास्त्र of कौटिल्य ' देवीगृहे हि लीनो भ्राता भद्रसेनं जघान । मातुश्शयान्तर्गतश्च पुत्रः कारूशम् । लाजान्मधुनेति विषेण पर्यस्य देवी काशिराजम् । विषदिग्धेन नूपुरेण वैरन्त्यं मेखलामणिना सौवीरं जालूथमादर्शेन वेण्यागूढं शस्त्रं कृत्वा देवी विदरथं जघान ।' (p. 41).

P. 106 l. 21—**P. 107** l. 12 **देवोऽपि...वात्येति.** राज्यस्थितीः—establishment of good order in his state; or, all the usual duties of a king. प्रतिसामन्तानां rival chiefs. उदवसितेषु = गृहेषु. उपलिङ्गानि portents. अविप्रकृष्टाः not far, approaching. चटुलाः moving about, restless. कृष्ण...श्रेणयः rows of black antelopes. The spotted antelopes resembled the dark glances of यमदूतs. See about the running of deer, p. 70 above. If we read प्रविष्ट० then the meaning is 'the glances of यमदूत that had entered (the chiefs' palaces)'. प्रचलि...प्रतिमाः resembling the jingling of the anklets of लक्ष्मी that had started away (in order to leave them). मधुसरघा honey bees. जहादिरे *perfect* of ह्राद् 1 A to sound. चिरम् for अजिरे is not a good reading. विवृतात् विकृतात् वदनविवरात् विसृतः वह्निविसरः यासाम् from whose wide-open and terrible mouths spread flames of fire. The reading 'उपशिबिरं शवार्थं' would mean ' near the royal camp for corpses '. For howling jackals, see p. 91. शवानां पिशिते (मांसे) प्ररूढः प्रसरः येषाम् whose expansion or growth (of body) had grown out of the flesh of corpses. The idea is:—as the vultures (काननकपोताः) fed on carrion, their wings also should have the colour of rotten flesh (dark-red). The reading of A and C 'प्ररूढप्रणयेव' seems to be a mistake for ०प्रणयाः इव, which latter C and T translate 'full well acquainted'. कपिपोतस्य कपोलवत् कपिला पक्षतिः (पक्षमूलं) येषाम्. आमन्त्रयमाणाः as if bidding farewell (to the kings who were to be defeated by हर्ष). सभाशालभञ्जिकाः the statues of females in the halls. आसन्नः कचग्रहः तस्मात् भयं तेन उद्भ्रान्तं उत्तमाङ्गं यस्य as if their heads had run away out of fear of the seizure of hair (in killing them) that was approaching. चक्रशङ्खकमलानि लक्ष्माणि (marks, चिह्नानि) येषाम्. According to the सामुद्रिकशास्त्र, चक्र, शङ्ख and कमल are some of the marks of an emperor's feet. What is indicated is that some emperor will humble their husbands. For the lines on the hands of an emperor, see above p. 20. व्यघटन्त were separated or broken. मधु...गोष्ठ्यः the honey-drinking bouts. ताम्यन्तः languid. स्तम्बकरि forming into sheaves or clusters (*i. e.* grown, ripe). स्तम्बं करोतीति. हरयः = अश्वाः. चल...लालिताः caressed (or coaxed) by the music of the clapping of the girls' hands resonant with the moving bracelets. रजनिकरः चन्द्रः तस्य हरिणः (*i. e.* the spot) तस्मिन् निहिते नयने येषाम्— the idea is—the dogs as if wanted to hunt down the deer in the moon. तोरणस्य समीपे उप० (अव्ययीभाव) near the outer gate (of the palace). कौलेयक—see above p. 97. Compare for a similar idea 'सूर्योदयेऽर्काभिमुखो विरौति ग्रामस्य मध्ये यदि सारमेयः । एको यदा वा बहवः समेताः शंसन्ति देशाधिपमन्यमाशु ॥' बृहत्संहिता 89. 2. गतायुषः—is the object of गणयन्ती—गतं आयुः येषां ते गता० तान्. तर्जन...तर्जन्या with her forefinger that was quickly moved for frightening. वाटकेषु in the gardens. कोटवी—'स्त्री नग्निका कोटवी स्यात्' इत्यमरः. दिवसम् (*accu.* of time) the whole day. कुटिल...तरङ्गिण्य wavy like the curling hair on the hoofs of deer. जनितः वेणीबन्धः येषु—in which the hair was tied in a single knot (as in the case of a widow). See above p. 108. निरञ्जनानि च तानि रोचनारोचींषि च (रोचनायाः इवरोचिः कान्तिः येषाम्) that had no collyrium (in the eyes) and had the colour of yellow pigment. A widow is not to put collyrium in the eye. The reflection appeared pale (as if through grief). If we read निरञ्जनलोचन० as C and T propose, the meaning would be 'having the appearance of eyes without collyrium.' चषकमधुनि in the wine in the goblets. समासन्ना०—the poet fancies that the earth quaked (trembled) because it was afraid of its seizure (by हर्ष from the hands of other kings) that was impending. वध्या...च्छटाः streaks of red sandal paste with which persons sentenced to be hanged were decked. विकसितं बन्धूककुसुमं तद्वत् शोणितं शोचिः (द्युतिः) यासाम्. Compare मृच्छकटिक X. 5 'सर्वगात्रेषु विन्यस्तै रक्तचन्दनहस्तकैः । पिष्टचूर्णावकीर्णश्च पुरुषोहं पशूकृतः ॥.' पर्यग्नी...श्रियम् as if carrying a torch round sovereignty that was to pass away (into the hands of हर्ष). A torch was carried round the animal to be offered in a sacrifice. श्री was going to be offered to हर्ष and the meteors served as torches for that purpose. अविरलं स्फुरन्तः स्फुलिङ्गाः तेषां अङ्गारोद्गारः तेन दग्धः तारागणः यैः that burnt the stars with the eruptions of fire due to the incessantly flashing sparks. गणशः in masses. उल्कादण्डाः—उल्काः दण्डाः इव. A torch has a staff. प्रतीहारीव—प्रतीहारी carries in her hands chowries, umbrellas, fans for the king. प्रतिभवनं (भवने भवने इति) at each house. वात्या a hurricane 'स्यात् वात्या वातमण्डली' त्रिकाण्डशेष. 'पाशादिभ्यो यः' पा. 4. 2. 49.

Uchchhvāsa VII

Verse 1 अङ्गनवेदी वसुधा—(to the hero that has taken a vow) the whole earth is a mere raised spot in his courtyard. वेदी is a quadrangular spot in a temple or courtyard. The idea is that just as one walks easily and fearlessly in his courtyard, so a hero has an easy walk-over in the case of the earth. कुल्या a canal. Verse 2. धृतं धनुः येन. We expect धृतधन्वनि, as धनुः becomes धन्वन् when it is the last member of a बहुव्रीहि. 'धनुषश्च' पा. 5. 4. 132 (धनुरन्तस्य बहुव्रीहेरनङादेशः स्यात्). कैव गणना of what account. Compare for the use of गणना, 'का वा गणना सचेतनेषु, अपगतचेतनान्यपि सङ्घट्टयितुमलं (मदनः)' काद० (p. 157 of P). रिपुः संज्ञा येषां. For क see above p. 36.

P. 108 ll. 5-22 अथ...जगाम. The principal sentence is अथ व्यतीतेषु केषुचिद्दिवसेषु...भवनान्निर्जगाम (हर्षः). शत...णिते well calculated a hundred times (*i. e.* again and again, so that no mistake may be committed). दत्ते...लग्ने when an hour for the expedition was given (*i. e.* settled) that was fit for the conquest of even the four quarters (east, south &c.). For लग्न, see above p. 24. दण्डः army. यात्रा expedition. सलिल...दैः (1) that were skilled in pouring water (with कुम्भैः); (2) that were clear by the dropping of water (with अम्भोधरैः). When a cloud is full of water, it is dark; when it has poured all the water it had (as after the rains) it becomes white. कालधौतैः (1) made of silver (with कुम्भैः); (2) washed or white by time *i. e.* by the passing away of the rains (with ०धरैः). कलधौतं silver. कालेन धौतैः. शातकौम्भैः made of gold. 'तपनीयं शातकौम्भं' इत्यमरः (शतकुम्भे गिरौ भवं शातकौम्भं सुवर्णम्). स्नात्वा—this refers to the bath of coronation. नीललोहितस्य शिवस्य अर्चां पूजाम्. 'कृशानुरेताः सर्वज्ञो धूर्जटिर्नीललोहितः' इत्यमरः ('नीलः कण्ठे लोहितश्चकेशेऽतो नीललोहित इति पुराणम्' क्षीर०). उद्गतानि अर्चींषि यस्य the flames of which went up. प्रदक्षिणावर्तः शिखाकलापः यस्य the mass of the flames of which curved towards the right. This was an auspicious sign; see p. 25. Compare रघु० IV. 25 'तस्मै सम्यग्घुतो वह्निर्वाजिनीराजनाविधौ। प्रदक्षिणार्चिर्व्याजेन हस्तेनेव जयं ददौ॥'. दत्त्वा—the objects are ०पात्राणि and गाः. See for तिलपात्रदान, चतुर्वर्ग० (दानखण्ड) p. 600. कनकपत्रलताभिः अलङ्कृतानि शफाः शृङ्गशिखराणि च यासाम्—the hoofs and tips of the horns of which were decked with figures of gold. अर्बुदशः—अर्बुदम् ten crores. विततं व्याघ्रचर्म यस्मिन्. भद्रासनम्—'नृपासनं तु यद्भद्रासनं सिंहासनं तु तत्' इत्यमरः. विलिप्य

—the object is शरीरम्. प्रथमं विलिप्तं आयुधं येन—before anointing his body with sandal, he first of all anointed his weapon (by way of doing worship to it). राज...लक्ष्मणी—०मिथुनं लक्ष्म (चिह्नं) ययोः—on the silken robes was drawn a pair of राजहंस. सदृशे suited to his position (as emperor). परमे...भूताम् (1) that is the special mark of शिव (with शशिकला); (2) that became the mark of an emperor (with ०मालिका). शशिकला also is white like flowers and is placed on the head by शिव. नीत्वा कर्णगोचरतां दूर्वा-पल्लवम् having placed in the region of the ear a Dūrvâ spray. The green दूर्वा resembles the rays of emerald, that also may be worn on the ear as an ear-ornament. गोरोचनया आच्छुरितम् (blended with). For गोरोचना, see p. 36. विन्यस्य...प्रकोष्ठे having placed on his forearm an amulet-ribbon auspicious for his march together with a seal bracelet. 'भवेत्प्रतिसरो मन्त्रभेदे माल्ये च कङ्कणे। ...आरक्षे करसूत्रे च' मेदिनी. ०पूजितः प्रहृष्टः पुरोहितः तस्य करेण प्रकीर्यमाणः ०निकरः तेन अभ्युक्षितं शिरः यस्य. For शान्तिसलिल, see p. 73. संप्रेष्य—connect with भूभुजाम्. महार्हाणि वाहनानि very valuable vehicles (horses, elephants &c.). बहलः रत्नानां आलोकः तेन लिप्ताः ककुभः दिशः यैः (*adj.* of भूषणानि). संविभज्य having distributed. संविभज्य ...दानैश्च—this cannot be well construed as it stands, as no persons among whom the distribution took place are mentioned. We must read, as C and T do, ०लोकम् उचितैः for लोकमोचितैः. क्लिष्ट...लोकम् among distressed pilgrims and well-born persons. क्लिष्ट may be construed with both कार्पटिक and कुलपुत्र. कार्पटिकः (from कर्पट) one who carries water from one sacred place to another. बन्धनानि prisoners. For letting loose prisoners, see above p. 25. नियुज्य connect with भुजस्तम्भम्. तत्काल...कारे that (arm) throbbed at that moment as if to remind that it was ready for the task of conquering the 18 द्वीपs. तत्काल...रणेन (1) that appears the moment it is remembered (with a person who offers his services); (2) that throbbed at the time in order to remind हर्ष of the task undertaken by him (with भुजस्तम्भ). तत्काले स्मरणं तस्मिन् स्फुरणम्; तत्काले स्मरणार्थं स्फुरणम्. The throbbing of the right arm is a good omen in the case of men. अहमहमिकया with emulation, with eagerness. 'अहमहमिका तु सा स्यात्परस्परं यो भवत्यहङ्कारः' अमरः. Servants pressed forward to do whatever was ordered. Good omens welcomed him as he went. हिरण्य...करणाय—as हिरण्यगर्भ (emerged) from the egg of Brahmâ to start an age of holiness. For हिरण्यगर्भ, see pp. 30, 37. कृत was the first युग after हिरण्य० was born. For कृतयुग see pp. 3, 40.

P. 108 l. 23—**P. 109** l. 9 **नातिदूरे...पटीयांसः.** सरस्वत्याः समीपे उप० (अव्ययीभाव). समुत्तम्भितानि तुङ्गानि तोरणानि यस्मिन् in which high outer gates had been erected. 'तोरणोऽस्त्री बहिर्द्वारम्' इत्यमरः. वेद्यां विनिहितः पल्लवललामः (पल्लवः ललामं चिह्नं भूषणं वा यस्य) हेमकलशः यस्मिन्. 'ललामं पुच्छपुण्ड्राश्वभूषाप्राधान्यकेतुषु' इत्यमरः. A jar with sprays at its top is an auspicious thing. Compare 'उभयपार्श्वस्थापितोत्पल्लवमुखपूर्णहेमकलशं (कायमानं)' काद० (p. 281 of P). 'वनमाला पुष्पपत्रप्रतियोजिता स्रक्' com. भ्रमन्तः शुक्लवाससः परिजनाः यस्मिन्. पठन्तः द्विजन्मानः (विप्राः) यस्मिन्. प्रस्थानम् = विजिगीषोः प्रयाणम्. ग्रामाक्षपटलिकः—the keeper of the records of the village. In the अर्थशास्त्र we have an interesting chapter headed 'अक्षपटले गाणनिक्याधिकारः'. From the description given it seems that the अक्षपटल was a record and accountant-general's office of modern times and that the ग्रामाक्षपटल was something like the modern *chavdi* in the villages of Mahārāshtra, where the village accounts were kept. 'अक्षपटलमध्यक्षः प्रत्यङ्मुखमुदङ्मुखं वा विभक्तोपस्थानं निबद्धपुस्तकस्थानं कारयेत्' (p. 62 of अर्थशास्त्र). In the Banskhera plate of Harsha we have a महाक्षपटलाधिकरणाधिकृत (E. I. IV. pp. 208, 211). सकलकरणिनः परिकरः यस्य. करणिन् or करणिक means 'a writer of documents, clerk.' करणम् a writing, document. See मनु० VIII. 52, 154. Com. 'करणिर्लेख्यं कायस्थ इत्यन्ये'. अवन्ध्यं शासनं यस्य whose edicts are never fruitless. करोतु...शासनानाम् let your Majesty this very day begin the day of your Majesty's orders (to us). He means that Harsha had come to the throne recently and that till then he had issued no royal edict and requests him to issue one that very day. वृषः अङ्कः यस्याः that had a bull as its emblem. On the Sonpat copper seal of हर्ष there is a नन्दी (see C. I. I. Vol. III p. 231 ff). अभि...निन्ये he presented a new-made golden seal. मुद्रा may also mean 'a coin' but that is not suitable here. मृत्पिण्डे—the ball of earth was presented in order that an impression with the new-made seal might be made upon it. मन्दाश्यानं पङ्कपटलं यस्मिन् on which there was mud that was nearly dry. अम...नि that thought it to be an evil omen (that the new-made seal should fall down from the king's hands). अ...दर्शिन्यः not able to see the truth. एकं (केवलं) शासनं तस्य मुद्रा अङ्कः यस्याः which will be marked with the seal of my single command. The only seal that will mark the earth will be mine. अन्य... ग्राम्याः the villagers understand it differently. This episode reminds one of what happened to William, the Norman Duke, when he first set foot on English soil. सीरसहस्रेण संमिता

सीमा येषाम् whose boundaries were measured (*i. e.* comprised) by a thousand ploughs. Each village comprised as much land as would be ploughed by a thousand ploughs. गलति...यामे when the third watch (of the night) had passed away. Time was measured by means of a water-clock and hence the word गलति. सुप्तानि समस्तानि सत्त्वानि यस्मिन् स चासौ निःशब्दश्च. दिक्कुञ्जरस्य इव जृम्भमाणः गम्भीरध्वनिः यस्य the deep sound of which swelled like the roar of the quarter elephant. प्र...पकाः that made (the people) count the क्रोशs of that day's march. The eight strokes indicated that that day eight *kros'as* were to be covered.

P. 109 l. 10—**P. 111** l. 2 **ततो...राजद्वारम्.** The principal sentence is ततः...प्रयाणसमये (p. 55 l. 14)...राजभिः आपुपूरे राजद्वारम्. रटन्तः पटहाः यस्मिन्. This and the following locatives qualify प्रयाणसमये. नन्दन्ती (joyous) नान्दी यस्मिन्. For नान्दी see p. 17. 'नान्दी मङ्गलपटहः' com. गुञ्जन्तः कुञ्जाः यस्मिन् in which the arbours resounded. कुञ्ज is out of place here. We must read गुञ्जद्गुञ्जे as some MSS. of B do. गुञ्जन्त्यः गुञ्जाः यस्मिन्. गुञ्जा a trumpet, according to the com. "गुञ्जासंज्ञः शङ्खभेदो यत्पृष्ठे जतु परिकलितं भवति । 'सन्ना' इति यस्य प्रसिद्धिः" or 'a drum' according to मेदिनी. **'गुञ्जा** तु काकचिञ्चायां पटहे च कलध्वनौ ।' मेदिनी. See भट्टिकाव्य XIV. 2. 'वेणून् पुपूरिरे **गुञ्जा जुगुञ्जुः** करघट्टिताः ॥'. कूजन्ती काहला (a large drum) यस्मिन्. 'काहला वाद्यभाण्डस्य भेदे चाप्सरसां भिदि' मे०. क्रमेण उपचीयमानः कटककलकलः यस्मिन्. परिजनोत्थापने व्यापृताः व्यवहारिणः (officers) यत्र. व्यवहारिन् ordinarily means 'a trader.' द्रुतः द्रुघनघातः तेन घट्यमानः (being joined or added) कोणिकाकीलकोलाहलः तेन कलिताः ककुभः यस्मिन्. द्रुघनः a wooden mallet for striking a thick plate of iron or bell-metal (for indicating time &c.). कोणिका drum. कीलः stick. बले अधिकृतैः (commanders) बध्यमानः (collected) पाटीपतीनां पेटकः (समूहः) यस्मिन्. पाटीपतिः—superintendent of barracks 'पाटी बहुपरिवारपुरुषगृहीतो निवासभूभागः कुलपुत्रकसमूह इत्यन्ये ।...'पाठीपति' इति पाठे...प्रतिनियतस्वस्थानपरिरक्षिणः ।'. पाठीपति would mean 'those that guard the place assigned to them.' जनैः ज्वलितं उल्कासहस्रं तस्य आलोकेन लुप्यमानं त्रियामातमः यस्मिन्. यामचेट्या चरणचलनेन उत्थाप्यमानं कामिमिथुनं यस्मिन्. यामचेटी a servant of the watch, a female watchman; compare यामाकेनी above p. 16. We must read कटुककटुनिर्देश० with some MSS of B. कटुकानां कटुनिर्देशेन नश्यन्ती निद्रा तस्याः उन्मिषन्तः निषादिनः यस्मिन् when the elephant riders woke up from sleep that was dispelled by the sharp commands of their superior officers. प्रबुद्धेन हास्तिकेन (हस्तिसमूहेन) शून्यीक्रियमाणं (vacated) शय्यागृहं यस्मिन्. 'हास्तिकं गजता वृन्दे' इत्यमरः, 'अचित्तहस्तिधेनोष्ठक्' पा. 4. 2. 47. आदौ

सुप्तं पश्चात् उत्थितं अश्वीयं तेन विधूयमानाः सटाः यस्मिन्. For अश्वीय, see p. 69. रटत् कटकं (camp) तेन मुखरैः खनित्रैः (spades) खन्यमानाः क्षोणीपाशाः यस्मिन्. The tents had been fastened by ropes twisted round pegs driven into the earth. These were dug up. समुत्कील्यमानाः कीलाः तैः शिञ्जानाः हिञ्जीराः यस्मिन् where the fetters (for tying elephants' feet to posts) were rattling because their pins were being taken away. As the army was to march, the fetters were to be removed. We must read अपनीय० for उपनीय०. The reading पनीयमान is equal to अपनीयमान, as the अवग्रह (here after हिञ्जीरे in the last clause) is very often omitted in MSS. As the fetters of elephants were removed, so also the chains with which horses' hoofs were tied for the night were removed when the army was about to march. अपनीयमानं निगडतालकं तस्य कलरवेण उत्तालाः (wild, shying) तुरङ्गाः तैः तरङ्ग्यमाणाः (curved) खुरपुटाः यस्मिन्. 'निगडार्थं तालकं तालपत्रं निगडतालकम् । लौह एवाश्वबन्धनविशेष इत्यन्ये' com. C and T take उपनीयमान. तालकं bolt, latch. लेशिकैः (हस्त्यारोहैः) मुच्यमानाः मदस्यन्दिनः दन्तिनः तेषां सन्दानशृङ्खलानां (chains for tying) खनखननिनादेन निर्भरं भरिताः दश दिशः यस्मिन्. घासपूलकप्रहारेण प्रमृष्टं पांसुलं (dusty) करिपृष्ठं तस्मिन् प्रसार्यमाणं प्रस्फोटितं (bursting) प्रमृष्टं (wiped *i. e.* clean) चर्म यस्मिन्. The dust from the backs of elephants was rubbed off with bundles of hay and then leather bags that burst because they were more than full were placed on the backs. संवेष्ट्यमानानि (being rolled up) पटकुटीनां ०मण्डपानां च परिवस्त्रा वितानकानि च यस्मिन्. गृहचिन्तकचेटकः a servant whose business was to look after the tents and lodgings of the soldiers. पटकुटी a small tent. काण्ड...मण्डपः a large tent subdivided into rooms by screens. परिवस्त्रा the screens that form the body of the tent. वितानकं the awning. कीलककलापेन आपूर्यमाणं चिपिट (flat) चर्मपुटं (leathern bag) यस्मिन्. सं... रिणि where the superintendent of the store-room was collecting the utensils (platters &c.). भाण्डागारवहने वाह्यमानाः बहवः नालीवाहीकाः यस्मिन् when many elephant attendants were made to work in carrying the stores. 'नालीवाहिकः करिणां घासग्रहणनियुक्तो हस्तिपको मेण्ठाख्यः' com. निषादिभिः निश्चलाः अनेकानीकपाः तेषु आरोप्यमाणाः कोशकलशपीडानां आपीडाः (समूहाः) तैः सङ्कटायमानानि सामन्तौकांसि यस्मिन् When the dwellings of chieftains were full of rows of boxes containing cups and jars that were being placed on numerous elephants that were held motionless by their riders. It is better to read अनेकानेकप. अनेकप means 'an elephant', as it drinks water by the trunk and mouth. अनीकप 'one that saves the army;' so by

लक्षणा an elephant. 'पिटकः पेटकः पीडा' इत्यमरः. दूरगतैः (that stood at a distance from the bad animals) दक्षैः दासेरकैः क्षिप्रं प्रक्षिप्यमाणः उपकरणसम्भारः तेन भ्रियमाणाः (filled, covered) दुष्टाः (restive, bad) दन्तिनः यस्मिन्. For दासेरक, see p. 28. तिर्यक् (side-ways) आनमन्तः (bending) जाघनिककराः तैः कृच्छ्रेण आकृष्टः (अत एव) लम्बमानः (lagging behind) परतन्त्रः चुन्दीजनः तेन जनितः जनहासः यस्मिन्. चुन्दी—a procuress. क्षीर० remarks that it is a देश्य word. The idea is:—the procuresses were very fat. Hence their legs (जाघनिक from जघन) were bent outwards (they were bandy-legged) and they could draw their bodies forward with difficulty. पीड्यमानः (tightened) शारशारिवरत्रागुणः तेन ग्राहितः (held fast, restrained) गात्रविहारः (free movement of limbs) तेन बृंहन्तः बहवः बृहन्तः मदकरिणः यस्मिन्. The root बृंह् is used for the cry of the elephant. शार of various colours. शारिः elephant's housings. वरत्रागुणः girth or strap. '**शारिर्ना**ऽक्षोपकरणे स्त्रियां शकुनिकान्तरे । **युद्धार्थगजपर्याणे,** मे०. करिघटासु (arrays of elephants) घटमानः &c. ०कण्ठालकैः (bags) कदर्थिताः (अत एव) कूजन्तः करभाः (camels) यस्मिन्. The camels disliked the placing of bags and so bellowed. अभिजातराजपुत्रैः प्रेष्यमाणाः कुप्रयुक्ताः (bad confidants) तैः आकुलानि (troubled, full of) कुलीनकुलपुत्रकलत्रवाहनानि यस्मिन्. गमनवेलाविप्रलब्धाः वारणाधोरणैः अन्विष्यमाणाः नवसेवकाः यस्मिन् where servants recently engaged, being in error as to the time of starting, were being sought out by elephant riders. C and T think that it was the elephant riders that were deceived as to the time of starting. But that is wrong. प्रसादवित्तैः पत्तिभिः (footmen) नीयमानाः नरपतिवल्लभाः वारवाजिनः यस्मिन्. प्रसादेन वित्ताः (प्रसिद्धाः) well-known as being high in the king's favour. '**प्रतीते** प्रथितख्यात**वित्त**विज्ञातविश्रुताः' इत्यमरः. पाणिनि uses the word in this sense in 'तेन वित्तश्चुञ्चुप्चणपौ' पा. V. 2. 26. वारवाजिन् *lit.* a horse for an (grand) occasion *i. e.* a show-horse. There is another reading वरवाजिनि. ०सैन्यैः न्यस्यमानाः नासीरेण (कर्पूरेण) मण्डलाडम्बरार्थाः स्थूलाः स्थासकाः यस्मिन् where gay warriors applied thick unguents of camphor to their persons for showing circular lines upon it. चारभटः warrior. मण्डल a circle. आडम्बरः show. For स्थासक see p. 55. The usual meaning of नासीर is 'the van of an army or the soldiers in the van.' नासीरं सेनामुखं नासीराः अग्रेसराः. The meaning then will be 'where gay warriors applied thick unguent paste to their body in order to show off that they formed the vanguard'. न्यस्यमानाः नासीरमण्डलाडम्बराय &c. स्थानपालानां (अश्वपालानां) पर्याणे (on the saddle) लम्बमानानि ०सनाथानि सङ्कलितानि (fastened) तलसारकाणि (martingales) यस्मिन्. The com. reads

लवणकालायी and explains 'मृगाकृतिः अश्वानां दारुमयी क्रियते' *i. e.* a wooden figure of a deer. नालीसनाथ together with hollow stalks (of reeds &c.). 'तलसारिको अश्वमुखपट्टिका ऊर्णादिसूत्रमयी । उरःपट्टिकेत्यन्ये' com. It is not clear for what purpose the wooden figure was required. कुण्डलीकृतैः (coiled) अवरक्षणीजालैः जटिलाः (confounded with, entangled in) वल्लभपालाः यासां ता० पालाः अश्वघटाः (rows of horses) तासु निवेश्यमानाः शाखामृगाः (कपयः) यस्मिन्. अवरक्षणी reins. वल्लभः 'a horse with auspicious marks' + पालः a groom. 'वल्लभपालोऽश्वपालः । अन्ये तु यो बलवान् महाकारो हयोपकरणं यवसतण्डुलादि वहति स वल्लभपालोऽश्वपाल इत्याहुः' com. According to the com. the monkeys were carried as auspicious. We think it not unlikely that they were carried by way of amusement, when the soldiers had nothing to do. परिवर्धकैः (grooms) आकृष्यमाणाः अर्धजग्धाः ०प्रारोहकाः यस्मिन्. प्रभाते भवा प्राभातिका योग्या (martial exercise) तस्यां अशनार्थं प्रारोहकाः. The grooms had thrown shoots in front of the horses before they were to be taken through some morning exercises. As the order to march was given early, the grooms took up the half-eaten shoots and started. The com. seems to have read प्रौढिके for प्रारोहके 'प्रौढिको योग्याशनार्थं प्रसेवको यो बुक्कण इति प्रसिद्धः'. प्रौढिक means 'bag'. व्याक्रोश्या (परस्पराह्वानेन) विजृम्भमाणः (growing) घासिकानां आघोषः (noise) यस्मिन्. घासिकः one who is in charge of the food of the horses. गमनसंभ्रमेण भ्रष्टाः (running away) भ्रमन्तः उत्तुण्डाः तरुणतुरङ्गमाः तैः तन्यमानः अनेकमन्दुराणां विमर्दः (breaking, devastation) यस्मिन्. उत्तुण्डाः (with their nostrils raised up, rearing). सज्जीकृता करेणुका तस्यां आरोहः तदर्थं आह्वानं तस्मिन् सत्वरं सुन्दरीभिः दीयमानं मुखालेपनं यस्मिन्. The unguents were to be applied to the face of the करेणुका. चलितेषु मातङ्गतुरङ्गेषु प्रधावितः प्राकृतः(low) प्रातिवेश्यकलोकः तेन लुण्ठ्यमानः(plundered) निर्घाससस्यसञ्चयः यस्मिन्. प्रातिवेश्यकः neighbour. The low people in the neighbourhood took away the loads of grass that were left when the army started. But no food had been left (निर्घास). The com. explains otherwise 'निर्घासो भुक्तशेषो घासः'. सञ्चरन्तः चेलचक्रेण आक्रान्ताः चक्रीवन्तः (गर्दभाः) यस्मिन्. The donkeys were laden with bundles of clothes. The com. says that चेल also means 'a boy,' the meaning being 'boys followed on donkeys.' 'चेलं वसनमंशुकम्' इत्यमरः. चेल = चेट according to the com. चक्रैः चीत्कारी गन्त्रीगणः तेन गृह्यमाणं प्रहतं (beaten) वर्त्म यस्मिन्. गन्त्री a cart drawn by oxen. अकाण्डे दीयमानैः भाण्डैः (utensils) भरिताः अनड्वाहः यस्मिन्. निकट...सौरभेये in which powerful oxen, driven in advance, tarried out of greed for fodder lying near (on their way). The com. takes differently 'लम्बमानो गर्दभदासो वणिजां कर्मकरो वा' *i. e.* oxen were driven by servants that tarried. 'अनड्वान् सौरभेयो गौः' इत्यमरः (सुरभेरपत्यं सौरभेयः). प्रमुखे (in front) प्रवर्त्यमानं etc. महानसं kitchen. पुरः प्रधावन्तः ध्वजवाहिनः यस्मिन्. ०शतैः उपलभ्यमानं आसङ्कट...रालेभ्यो निःसरणं यस्मिन् where the exit (of the soldiers) from the rather crowded inside of the huts was seen by hundreds of friends. सङ्कट crowded, full. करिचरणैः चलिता (shaken) मठिका (cell, cottage) तस्याः उत्थितेन लोकेन लोष्टैः हन्यमामाः मेण्ठाः (elephant keepers) तैः क्रियमाणाः आसन्नाः साक्षिणः यस्मिन् where the bystanders were made witnesses by &c. The reading दलित is much better. सङ्घट्टेन (collision) विघट्टमाना (crushed) व्याघ्रपल्ली तस्याः पलायमानानि क्षुद्रकुटुम्बकानि यस्मिन्. 'व्याघ्रपल्ली तृणकुटीभेदः' com. (a hut thatched with grass). कल ... वणिजि when the traders ran after their oxen laden with wealth that ran away owing to the fear of the tumult. For विद्राण see p. 75. The com. takes विद्राण in the sense of सशोक (*i. e.* that despaired). पुरःसरं... कदम्बकं यस्मिन् when the group of female elephants carrying the harem started when the crowd of people grew less owing to the light of torches that were carried in front. We may also translate 'owing to the light of torches carried by servants walking in front.' ०आहूयमानाः लम्बिताः (that tarried) श्वानः यस्मिन्. C and T 'dogs tied behind them.' But this is not proper. If they were *tied*, there was no necessity to call them up. सरभस... गणे when the groups of tall तङ्गण horses were being praised by men inured to a hard life who felt comfortable by the steady motion of the tramp of their quick feet. We must read तङ्गण and not तुङ्गण. तङ्गण is the name of a country; see बृह० X. 12 and XVI. 6. The com. says 'खक्खटाः वृद्धाः' but the meaning assigned to the word in lexicons is 'hard'. स्रस्ताः वेसरविसंवादिनः सीदन्तः दाक्षिणात्यसादिनः यस्मिन् where Deccan riders sitting on mules fell down, not being able to keep their bodies moving with the motion of the mules. There are no mules in the Deccan and the Deccan people not being accustomed to their ways and pace fell down from their backs. सीदन्तः may also mean 'dejected or sinking on the ground' (because they fell). विसंवादिन् not agreeing with. 'सादी तुरङ्गमातङ्गरथारोहेषु दृश्यते' मे०. C and T translate 'Deckhan riders disconsolately contended with fallen mules.' Our interpretation seems to be preferable. प्रति...च्छद्भिः coming from every direction. This and the following instrumentals qualify राजभिः (p. 56 l. 1) below. आधो...शार्ङ्गैः whose bows spotted (शार) with golden figures (पत्रभङ्गः) were held up by elephant riders. शाङ्गैः—र्ङ्गम् (शृङ्गस्य विकारः) 'शाङ्गैः कार्मुकमात्रेऽपि' मे०. अन्तरासने आसीनैः अन्तरङ्गैः (confidential persons) गृहीताः असयः येषाम्. पश्चिमासनिकेभ्यः अर्पिताः भस्त्राभरणाः (भस्त्रा आभरणं यासां) भिन्दिपालपूलिकाः यैः that had consigned to those occupying the back seats (on their elephants) bundles of javelins encased in quivers. 'भस्त्राभरणं तूणभेदः' com. आसनिक from आसन. भिन्दतः पालयति इति भिन्दि० हस्तक्षेप्यो लगुडः. पत्रलतावत् or पत्रलताभिः कुटिलाः कलधौतनलकाः तैः पल्लवितं पर्याणं येषाम् whose saddles bristled with silver arrows curved like (or with) paintings of figures. What नलक means is not clear. To us it seems the meaning is 'a cylinder, a case or quiver.' कलधौतं silver or gold. पर्याणपक्षकयोः परिक्षेपार्थं पट्टिका तया बन्धः तेन निश्चलं पट्टोपधानं तेन स्थिरं अवधानं येषाम् whose attention was fixed because the silk cushion (on which they sat) was motionless, being secured by a girth that confined both ends of the saddle. We must rather read स्थानैः for धानैः, the meaning being 'whose seat was firm &c.' प्रचला पादफलिका तस्याः आस्फालनेन (striking) स्फायमानः (increased) पदबन्धस्य (anklet) मणिशिलाशब्दः येषाम्. पादफलिका is the foot-rest on each side of the saddle. The com. reads पादबन्धः and C and T prefer it. उद्गतानि चित्राणि येषु तानि उच्चित्राणि नेत्राणि (अंशुकानि) तैः सुकुमाराणि (fine) स्वस्थाने (at the proper place) स्थगितानि (covered) जङ्घाकाण्डानि (shanks) येषाम्. उच्चित्र on which the pictures appeared prominently. For नेत्र, see pp. 37, 55. The com. says 'स्वस्थानं स्वस्थानिति यस्याः प्रसिद्धिः'. This is not clear. The other reading स्वस्थगनस्थगित conveys a good sense. The garments were so fine that they were not noticed on the body (स्व—स्थगन) and yet they covered the shanks &c. कार्दमिकपटेन कल्माषिता (variegated) पिशङ्गा (reddish brown) पिङ्गा (leg) येषाम्. कर्दमेन रक्तं का०—mud-stained. The com. says 'पिङ्गा जङ्घिका । अन्ये जङ्घालेत्याहुः' *i. e.* पिङ्गा means either 'leg' or 'trousers.' अलिवत् नीला मसृणा सतुला तया समुत्पादितः सितसमायोगस्य परभागः येषाम् whose white accoutrements were heightened by the breeches blue and glossy like bees. 'सतुला अर्धजङ्घिका, अन्ये अर्धजङ्घालेत्याहुः' com. *i. e.* सतुला either means 'the upper part of the leg' or 'breeches.' 'समायोगो व्यापृतकेषु प्रसिद्धः' com. For परभाग, see p. 54. 'परभागो वर्णस्य वर्णान्तरेण शोभातिशयः'. We must read '०मेचककञ्चुकैः'. ०वर्णे विराजमानाः राजावर्ताः तैः मेचकाः कञ्चुकाः येषां whose jackets looked dark-blue with black diamonds shining on their bright bodies. 'राजावर्ताः कृष्णपाषाणाः' com. राजावर्तः a kind of diamond or other gem of inferior quality regarded as a lucky possession, though not esteemed as an ornament.

It comes from the country of विराट. The बृह० (chap. 80. 4) speaks of a राजमणि. अपचिताः चीनचोलकाः यैः that wore China-made shawls. 'संव्यानमुत्तरीयं च चोलः कूर्पासकोऽस्त्रियाम्' इत्यमरः. Another meaning would be 'whose China-made shawls were very fine' or 'who highly thought of their shawls.' तारमुक्ताभिः स्तबकिताः स्तवरकवार— बाणाः येषां whose coats made of स्तवरक cloth showed clusters of bright (तार) pearls. 'मुक्ताशुद्धौ च **तारः** स्यात्'. For स्तवरक, see p. 56. 'कञ्चुको वारबाणोऽस्त्री' इत्यमरः. स्तबकित—स्तबकाः (bunches of flowers) सञ्जाताः अस्य; compare तारकित p. 98. नानाकषायैः कर्बुराः कूर्पासकाः येषां whose bodices were variegated with various decoctions. 'निर्यासेऽपि कषायोऽस्त्री' इत्यमरः. कर्बुर white-grey, variegated. 'चोलः कूर्पासकोऽस्त्रियाम्' इत्यमरः. शुकपिच्छस्येव छाया येषां तानि ०च्छायानि आच्छादनानि (upper garments, shawls) येषाम्. व्यायामेन उल्लुप्तः (made thin) पार्श्वप्रदेशः (sides) तस्मिन् प्रविष्टानि (fastened) चारुशस्त्राणि येषाम्. If we read शस्तैः the meaning is 'fine waist bands were twisted round their flanks &c.' 'शस्तं पट्टिकाठोरः कटिसूत्रमित्यर्थः' com. गतिवशेन वेल्लिताः (moving) हारलताः तासु गलत् (lit. dropping *i. e.* touching) लोलं (dangling) कुण्डलं तस्य उन्मोचनाय प्रधाविताः परिजनाः येषाम्. चामीकरपत्राङ्कुरैः कर्णपूरकः तेन विघट्टमानः वाचालः बालपाशः येषाम् Whose ear-ornaments resounded as they were struck by the ear-ring made up of golden wires. बालपाशः (or वाल०) seems to be the same ornament as वालपाश्या. 'वालपाश्या पारितथ्या पत्रपाश्या ललाटिका' इत्यमरः. उष्णीषपट्टेषु विष्टब्धं कर्णोत्पलस्य नालं येषां the stalk of whose ear-lotus was fixed in their turban-cloth. कुङ्कुमरागेण कोमलं उत्तरीयं तेन अन्तरितं (wrapped) उत्तमाङ्गं (शिरः) येषाम्. चूडामणिखण्डेन खचितः (inlaid) क्षौमः (linen) खोलः (helmet, turban) येषाम्. खोलः or खोलकः '**खोलकः** पाकवल्मीकपूगकोश**शिरस्त्रके**' इति विश्वकोशः. Compare 'क्षणमप्यमुक्तकालकम्बलखण्डखोलेन' काद० (p. 228 of P). The reading ०चोलैश्च is not good; we have already had a description of चोलक above. ०पत्रायमाणानि शेखरषट्पदपटलानि येषां the swarms of bees on whose chaplets looked like an umbrella of peacock feathers. मायूरं आतपत्रं तद्वत् आचरतीति मायूरातपत्रायते. The shining bees looked like peacock's tails and formed an umbrella over their heads. The reading मायूरपत्रायमाण is not so good; it simply means 'that resemble peacocks' feathers.' मार्गागताः (that covered a long distance) शारिकशारिवाह्याः वेगदण्डाः येषाम्. 'वेगदण्डस्तरुणो हस्ती' com. शा...ह्याः that carried housings rendered variegated (by a long march). For शारि, see above p. 170 पुरश्चलन्ति चामराणि येषां ते ०चामराः किर्मीरं कार्दरङ्गचर्ममण्डलं मण्डनं येषां ते ०मण्डनाः, उड्डीयमानाः चटुलाः (restless) डामराः (dreadful, riotous) चारभटाः तैः भरितं भुवनान्तरं यैः. '**चित्रकिर्मीर**—

the bones). अमरपतिः = इन्द्रः. अग्र...कुलः intent upon wiping off the stain of the slaughter of his elder brother. This applies to हर्ष as well as to इन्द्र, who wanted to get rid of the sin of killing a ब्राह्मण (अग्रज). इन्द्र killed वृत्र son of त्वष्टृ who was a ब्राह्मण. He became free from the sin of ब्रह्महत्या by performing an अश्वमेध sacrifice. See रामायण उत्तरकाण्ड 84 and 85. 'तमिन्द्रं ब्रह्महत्याशु गच्छन्तमनुगच्छति' 84. 16. पृथिव्याः परिशोधनस्य अवधानेन सङ्कलितान् सकलमहीभृतः समुत्सारयतीति (1) who urged forward all the assembled kings with the fixed purpose of cleansing the earth (of a कण्टक like गौड); who cast away all the gathered mountains with &c. See notes p. 1 for पृथु who levelled the earth. पुरः...कारकैः—Harsha was preceded by ushers (दण्डिभिः) that went in front and that uttered complimentary words like जय, जीव, आलोकय &c. 'आलोको जयशब्दः स्यात्' इति हलायुधः (quoted by मल्लिनाथ on रघु 17. 27). The com. explains it differently 'लोक इत्येवं ये वदन्ति ते आलोककारकाः' those who cry 'Ho! people'. This does not seem to be quite correct. The rays of the sun also go before him (before he is seen) and cause light (आलोकः). सहस्र...किरणैः—The sun is called सहस्ररश्मि; हर्ष also had thousands of servants. अधिकारचातुर्येण (cleverness in discharging their duties) चञ्चलाः चरणाः येषाम्. All the instrumentals qualify दण्डिभिः below. व्य...निष्ठुरैः rigorous in maintaining order. भय...ग्राहयद्भिः who as if made the people take to the ten quarters, that were screened (from Harsha's view) by the mass of people running through fear. They cleared the way for Harsha so well that people in fear ran far away from him. चलितानां कदलिकानां (banners) सम्पातेन (mass) पीतः प्रचारः (movement) यस्य. The wind was hemmed in by a number of waving banners and so could not blow fiercely. The poet represents this as teaching the wind discipline or humility. कदलिका also means the plantain tree, the long leaves of which might retard the motion of the wind and the leaves of which become yellow when dry. द्रुतचरणैः उद्धतं (raised up) धूलिपटलं तेन अवधूतान् (despised *i. e.* obscured). ०लतानां आलोकेन विक्षिप्यमाणं (dispersed). The light of the golden canes in the hands of the ushers cast daylight into the shade as it were and hence daylight is fancied to be removed by the ushers.

P. 111 l. 28—P. 112 l. 4 **अवनमति...राजकम्.** अवनमति connect with राजचक्रे (*loc. alcolute*). चलनेन शिथिलाः मणयः येषां तानि ०मणीनि कनकमुकुटानि तेषां किरणनिकरेण रुचिरं शिरः यस्य. विलुलितं

०शेखररजः यस्य the pollen in the chaplets on the head of which was shaken (or tossed about). It should be noticed that from अवनमति to ०कुसुम every letter is short. अवाञ्चः downwards. उदञ्चः upwards. चाष...चेलुः the rays moved like flocks of blue jays for effecting good omens. The flight of the चाष bird to the right of a person or the sight of the चाष when a man starts on a journey was an omen indicating prosperity. Compare बृहत्संहिता 'पूर्णाननः कृमिपतङ्गपिपीलिकाद्यैश्चाषः प्रदिक्षणमुपैति नरस्य यस्य।...तस्यार्थलाभमचिरात्सुमहत्करोति ॥' 88. 23 and 'सन्दर्शनं शुभदमस्य सदैव यातुः' 88. 25. मेघायमानः रेणुः तेन मेदुरं (thick with, full off)—*adj.* of खम्. The dust raised by the marching army was like a cloud. उड्डीयमानाः applies both to शिखण्डिनः and मरीचयः (from the preceding clause). The rays of the crest jewels shooting up into the sky looked like house peacocks. The peacocks fly up towards the cloud and dance when it appears. The feathers present numerous tints. The rays were of different hues. The cloud of dust represents दिग्द्वार. The shooting rays of jewels appear like the delicate पल्लव of कल्पवृक्ष. वन्दनमाला—is an auspicious garland fixed on the outer gate of a mansion 'मङ्गलस्रक्तोरणोर्ध्वे भवेद्वन्दनमालिका' क्षीर०. नेत्रत्रिभागैः—glances in which only a third part of the eye is open. समग्रेक्षितैः full glances. 'अवञ्चितैः अचलितैः' com. छेकालापः insinuation, *double entendre*. 'छेको विदग्धे' क्षीर०; 'छेको गृह्याश्रितमृगपक्षिणोर्नागरे त्रिषु' मे०. छेक means 'clever or polished'. आ...वीराणां who as if bought the souls of the heroes consisting in honour by gifts (tokens) of his favour. The glances, smiles and jests &c. were the price he paid for what they gave, *viz.* the honour they did him. यथा...राजकम् he distributed among the kings according to their worth (his favours).

P. 112 l. 5—**P. 114** l. 16 अथ...जगाम. तस्तार spread. तारतारः very loud. दिग्गजेभ्यः is dative, according to 'क्रुधद्रुहेर्ष्यासूयार्थानां यं प्रति कोपः' पा. 1. 4. 37. The elephants of Harsha were wroth with the दिग्गजs for the latter's pre-eminence and so wanted to establish their own superiority by the flow of their rut. त्रिप्रसृतानां that emitted a flow (of rut) from three places, the trunk, the eyes and the temples. मद...स्यन्दिरे with the tracks of the streams of ichor dark with swarms of bees, thousands of the windings of the Jumna as if began to flow. The waters of the Jumna are dark and so resembled the ichor with bees on it. The word त्रि in त्रिप्रसृतानां is suggestive. Ordinarily the braid of a woman whose husband is living is triple. Further there is a striking effect produced by laying emphasis on त्रि and सहस्र. सिन्दूर०—we saw above that red powder was sprinkled over people on festive or auspicious occasions. So much red powder was used that the sun appeared red and birds (like the चक्रवाक) feared that sunset was near (though really it was not). करिणां—connect with ०निस्वनैः. मांसलैः augmented by. कर्णतालः flapping of elephant's ears. दोधूयमान (frequentative of धू pass.) being again and again waved. अश्वीयं—See p. 69. शिश्विन्दे—*perfect* of श्विन्द् 1 A. to become white. पिण्डीभूतानि तगराणि तेषां स्तबकवत् पाण्डुराणि (white). परस्परसङ्घट्टेन नष्टाः अष्ट दिशः यस्मिन् (*adj.* of दिवसम्) where the eight quarters were not to be recognised on account of the close contact (of the umbrellas). The umbrellas were so many that no space was left uncovered by them. The sunlight paled before the golden handles and white sheen of the umbrellas. उच्चः चामीकरदण्डः येषाम्. रजः (dust) एव रजनी तया निमीलितः (closed, blinded). The day was dark with clouds of dust; but had the mellow light of morning with the jewels of the coronets. मण्डनक...कृताः rendered green (or tawney) by the clanging ornaments of horses (made of gold and silver). 'स्याद्भाण्डमश्वाभरणे' इत्यमरः. ह्राद् 1 A to sound. परिह्रादाः resounding. हरितः = दिशः. शिशीकरे *perfect* of शीक् 1 A to sprinkle. चक्षुषामुन्मेषं मुमुषुः robbed the eye of the power to open. The lightning also robs the eye of this power. विसिष्मिये *perfect* of स्मि with वि. It will be noticed that from तस्तार (at the beginning of the paragraph) to विसिष्मिये the author uses the perfect tense only. बलानां stands for बलैः—(the king wondered at his own vast army). आवासस्थान camping ground. अधोक्षजः (विष्णुः) तस्य कुक्षेः (उदरात्). युगादौ = कल्पादौ. The army starting from its encampment looked like the world rising from the belly of Vishṇu at the beginning of a कल्प. Compare (text) p. 10 ll. 1–2 'यशोमती गर्भेणाधत्त नारायणमूर्तिरिव वसुधां देवीं राज्यश्रियम्.' कुम्भभुवः = अगस्त्यस्य. प्लावितं (flooded) भुवनं येन. अगस्त्य was born from a कुम्भ in which the seed of मित्र and वरुण was placed. See for the story रामायण VII 56 and 57. He drank the ocean to help the gods against the Kāleyas who hid themselves in the sea. Compare 'भूतधात्री कलशयोनिपानपरिकलितसकलसलिलं सागरमवतीर्णा' काद० (p. 124 of P.). ०सहस्रेण आदौ सम्पिण्डितं पश्चाद् उन्मुक्तम् at first stemmed and then let loose. अर्जुन is सहस्रार्जुन कार्तवीर्य. 'योऽसौ भगवदंशमत्रिकुलप्रसूतं दत्तात्रेयाख्यमाराध्य बाहुसहस्रमधर्मसेवानिवारणं धर्मेण पृथिवीजयं धर्मतश्चानुपालनमरातिभ्योऽपराजयमखिलजगत्प्रख्यात-

पुरुषाच्च मृत्युमित्येतान्वरान् लेभे' विष्णुपु० IV. 11. See मार्कण्डेयपु. 18. While once bathing in the Narmadâ, he wanted to see the power of his thousand arms and stemmed the waters and then let them off in a flood. See रामायण VII. 32. सहस्रधा प्रवर्तमानं applies also to the army. प्रसर तात—In these and the following words (up to p. 58 l. 6) the author gives us what the soldiers and camp-followers talked among themselves. भाव—this is a word showing respect in addressing a person. 'मान्ये भावोऽपि वक्तव्यः' भरतः (quoted by क्षीर०). त्वङ्गति तुरङ्गमः—a horse is galloping. This gives the reason why the man tarried. He waited till the galloping horse passed. भग्न...पतन्ति you walk as if you were lame, while these men of the van come in furious speed upon you. वाह...ष्ट्रम् why do you drive the camel? निःशूक= निर्दय, 'शूकोऽस्त्री शुङ्गदययोः' मे०. Separate निःशूक शिशुम्. रजसि...भव be near me so that you may not be missed in the dust. गलति...वकः the sack of barley-meal leaks. प्रसेवः or—कः a sack or bag. इत्वर a traveller, one who walks. सौ...वरि leaving the track of oxen, you run in the midst of horses, O fish-woman! The track of oxen would be safer for pedestrians than that of horses. We may also translate 'Oh ox! why do you leave the proper track and run in the midst of horses? Oh! fishwoman, do you wish to come along'? On this latter interpretation, we must take सौरभेय as a vocative and connect धीवरि with विशसि. गन्तु...मार्गम् Oh female elephant! do you wish to enter the way of the male elephants? अङ्ग is a term of address applied to a friend &c. गलति...रटन्तम् the bag of peas is crosswise and leaks; you don't mind my bawling. We must read अतटेन for अवटेन. अव...तरसि you are descending into a pit from a precipice. 'गर्तावटौ भुवि श्वभ्रे' इत्यमरः. 'प्रपातस्त्वतटो भृगुः' इत्यमरः. The com. says 'अवटेन. अमार्गेण'. सुख...भग्नः 'you uncontrolled female, be quiet. The jar of sour barley-gruel is broken.' This is addressed to some woman who carried a jar and, stumbling in hurry, had it broken. Or it may have been addressed to a female elephant on the back of which the jar was placed. Or we may take 'सुख...णि' by itself and regard सौवीरक as a vocative (meaning 'a man from the सौवीर country' or 'a person carrying the sour gruel'). 'आरनालकसौवीरकुल्माषाभिषुतानि तु । अवन्तिसोमधान्याम्लकुञ्जलानि च काञ्जिके ॥' इत्यमरः (सुवीरेषु प्रायो भवं सौवीरकम्). मन्थ...क्षुम्—this is addressed to some one who lagged behind while sucking sugarcane. 'You will suck it when you have finished your journey.' उक्षाणं प्रसारय drive on your bull. This should be taken with the preceding. If we read प्रसादय, we must regard it as an independent sentence. प्रसादय make quiet. दूरं गन्तव्यम् we have to go a long way. कि...यात्रा Droṇaka! why do you run even to-day (the first day of the march)? The expedition is going to be for a very long time (so you will have plenty of time to run). वि...साकम् excepting that one cruel man, this is the belief (निष्ठा) of all of us (that the expedition is going to be very long). We must read निष्ठेयं for निष्क्रेयम्. C and T translate the words किमद्यैव...साकम् as 'why do you linger, Droṇaka, now? this long expedition is at a standstill for one rascal.' One fails to see how दण्डयात्रा is connected with निष्ठेयम्. अग्रतः...स्थालीम् the road in front is uneven; स्थावरक, see you don't break the jar of raw-sugar. स्थावरक may mean 'you mountain (of flesh).' 'स्थपुटं तु नतोन्नतम्' क्षीर०. 'मत्स्यण्डी फाणितं खण्डविकारे शर्करा सिता' इत्यमरः. Separate गण्डक तण्डुल०. न...दम्यः the bullock cannot carry it (to the end of the journey). माषीणम् a field of माष (beans), according to 'धान्यानां भवने क्षेत्रे खञ्' पा. 5. 2. 1 and 'विभाषा तिलमाषोमाभङ्गाणुभ्यः' पा. 5. 2. 4. (माषाणां भवनं क्षेत्रं माष्यं माषीणं वा). अमुतः from yonder. द्राक्...लुनीहि quickly cut with a knife a bundle of a mouthful of fodder. को...गतानाम् when we are gone, who will know what happened to his crop? Or better still 'who will detect the bundle lying in the midst of the fodder, when we are gone.' The idea is that they would keep the raw beans concealed in the fodder. धव...मिदम् O man, keep away your oxen, this field is guarded by barbarians. He calls the watchmen barbarians. The com. says 'वाहीकः काष्ठकः परिपालक इत्यन्ये गोरक्षक इति चान्ये'. लम्बिता...युङ्क्ष्व the cart has lagged behind; harness to the yoke an excellent (धवल) ox (शाकर) capable of bearing the burden (धुरन्धर). धुरं धायतीति ०धरः or धूर्धरः. यक्षपालित may be a proper name or it may mean 'one protected by यक्षs, a man possessed by a ghost.' दीव्य...दण्डे you are playing on the trunk of the elephant (instead of minding your business as a rider). समद is addressed to an elephant. न...स्खलसि you lose your footing in the mud due to the crowd (संमर्दः). माणवक is a name very frequeutly cited in the phrase 'अग्निर्माणवकः'. घनेभ...सरणिः in the thickness of the meeting of the array of elephants, there is no way to come out (if you once get entangled therein). If we read निस्तरणम् it would mean 'there is no getting out &c.' ०प्रवर्तमानाः अनेकसंलापाः यस्मिन् (*adj.* of स्कन्धावारम् above). All the following accusatives also qualify स्कन्धावारम्. In the following long passage Bāna uses many obscure words, the meanings of which are doubtful and which are rarely found in classical works. The commentary is our only authority in some cases. स्वेच्छया (at their will) मृदितानि उद्दामानि (plentiful) सस्यघासविघसात् सुखेन सम्पन्नानि (easily obtained) अन्नानि तैः पुष्टाः तैः. सस्य...घसात् from the leavings of the grain (for horses &c.). 'अमृतं **विघसो** यज्ञशेषभोजनशेषयोः' इत्यमरः. केलिकलैः that were noisy with jests. मेण्ठ...मण्डलैः by groups of elephant—keepers, bachelors (वण्ठ), dullards (वठर), donkey boys (लम्बन), elephant-riders (लेशिक), thieves, servants, rogues (चाटः) and grooms. '**वण्ठा** अकृतविवाहाः तरुणाः ये दण्डमादाय हस्तिनां दर्पमाकर्षयन्ति । पत्तय इत्यन्ये लम्बनाः गर्दभदासाः ।... शाटा धूर्ताः चण्डाला अश्वपालाः' Com. The com. seems to have read शाट for चाट. For लेशिक see above. चाट 'चाटाः प्रतारकाः विश्वास्य ये परधनमपहरन्ति' मिताक्षरा on याज्ञ० I. 336. आण्डीर bold, according to the com. It also suggests that the word may be राण्डीर (from रण्डा) 'harlot's sons.' असहायैः (helpless) goes with ०पुत्रकैः (l. 12). क्लेशेन आर्जिताः कुग्रामकुटुम्बिसम्पादिताः सीदन्तः (sinking, weak) सौरभेयाः तैः शम्बलस्य संवाहने आयासः तेन आवेगः तेन आगतः संयोगः येषाम् who gathered together on account of the excitement caused by the worry &c. The com. says 'आयासो योगस्तेन गतसंयोगैरुत्पन्नचित्तक्षोभैरिति समासः'. So it read आयासगतसंयोगैः. स्वयंगृहीतानि गृहोपस्करणानि यैः. As the oxen could not carry, they had to put their own shoulders to the work. We must change the punctuation. Read ०तलम् । तृष्णा...भवतु । शिवं सेवा करोतु ।. तृष्णा...भवतु let there be an end of this height of greed! न भवनं अभवनिः. 'आक्रोशे नञ्यनिः' पा. 3. 3. 112. (नञि उपपदे अनिः स्यादाक्रोशे । अजीवनिस्ते शठ भूयात् । सि. कौ.). 'अकरणिरित्यादयः शापे' अम०. शिवं०—May (this) service do us good !! भूतिः prosperity *i. e.* excess. दुःखकूटाय = दुःखराशये. 'निःस्वस्तु **दुर्विधो** दीनो **दरिद्रो** दुर्गतोऽपि सः' इत्यमरः. अति ... द्रवद्भिः by people that ran (द्रवत्) quickly in lines, as if they were tied together and as if they were on board a boat carried along by a very sharp current. जनैः goes with सर्वमेव...कारयद्भिः. कृष्णकठिनस्कन्धयोः गुरवः लगुडाः येषाम्. गृहीताः...हाः यैः. सौवर्णपादपीठी golden footstool. करङ्कः—betel-box. Compare ताम्बूलकरङ्कवाहिनी, which occurs very frequently in the कादम्बरी (*e. g.* p. 148 of P). पतद्ग्रहः a spittoon. 'प्रतिग्राहः पतद्ग्रहः' इत्यमरः. अवग्राहः = स्नानद्रोणी com. It seems that the correct reading as अवगाह and not अवग्राह.

प्रत्यास...दुर्वारैः that were hard to check in their pride for being in charge of the appurtenances (उपकरणं) of their king who was near by. सर्वे...द्भिः that pushed aside everybody. भूपति...वाहिभिश्च and by the porters (भारिक) engaged by the king, that carried the kitchen utensils. 'भारवाहस्तु भारिकः' इत्यमरः. बद्धः वराहवध्रेण वाध्रीणसः यैः that had tied a rhinoceros by straps (वध्रं) of pig-skin. 'खङ्गं शृङ्गमस्यास्तीति खङ्गी वाध्रीणसोऽपि' क्षीर. But the com. says 'वाध्रीणसा यज्ञियाश्छागविशेषाः.' लम्बमानाः हरिणानां चटुकाः ('पूर्वभागाः' com.) चटकानां (sparrows) जूटाश्च (mass) तैः जटिलाः तैः. चटु means उदर according to the मेदिनीकोश. शिशु...ग्राहिभिः that had a collection of young rabbits, vegetables (शाकः), leaves and shoots of bamboo. वेत्राग्राणि = 'वंशांकुराः' com. शुक्लकर्पटेन प्रावृतं मुखं यस्य तत् ०मुखं; एकदेशे दत्ता आर्द्रा मुद्रा (seal) तया गुप्तः गोरसः यस्मिन् तत् ०गोरसं; ०मुखानि ०गोरसानि भाण्डानि येषाम्. गोरसः may mean 'cow's milk or butter-milk.' '**दण्डाहतं कालशेय**मरिष्टमपि **गोरसः**' अम०. तलक...भारिकैः carrying loads of baskets full of तलक &c. 'तलकोऽग्निशाटिका । तापकोऽपूपादिकरणस्थानम् । तापिका काकपालिका यत्र तैलादिना भक्ष्याः पच्यन्ते । हस्तको शूलम्' com. तापकः oven. तापिका pan. हस्तकः spit. ताम्रचरुकः a copper vessel (in which rice or barley may be boiled). कटाहः a frying pan (Marathi कढई). फलकाले at the time of reward or payment. अन्य...स्थास्यन्ते other rogues will approach or be near. पदे...पततां falling at each step. The com. says 'स्खलने प्रेरणे.' This is a sense hardly ever met with. We would translate 'who were appointed to look after the tripping of the oxen.' The reading खेटच्चेटकैः will mean 'servants from the hamlets.' खेद्यमानः असंविभक्तः (not separated *i. e.* whole) कुलपुत्रलोकः यस्मिन् (*adj.* of स्कन्धावारम्). The noble youths were pestered by the servants with the words 'क्लेशो—स्थास्यन्ते'. प्रजविताः प्रधाविताः ग्रामेयकजनपदाः यस्मिन्. ग्रामेयक = ग्रामीण. आग्रहरिकजाल्मैः—connect this with ०धूलिपटलम् below—the rogues that had appropriated to themselves the अग्रहारs (endowments of lands conferred on Brāhmaṇas). The lands had been granted by former kings to Brāhmaṇas and some rogues enjoyed the lands free from tax when the families of the original grantees became extinct. Or आग्र...जाल्मैः may mean 'wretches from the अग्रहार villages.' पुरःसराः जरन्तः (old) महत्तराः (headmen of villages) तैः उत्तम्भिताः (raised up) अम्भःकुम्भाः येषु (*adj.* of ०जाल्मैः). The water jars are a good omen. महत्तर as the name of an officer occurs in numerous grants (Compare I. A. VIII, p. 20 and I. A. vol. XII p. 25). खण्डः candied sugar. धनेन घटिताः पेटकाः येषाम् that had boxes full of money (as

Nazaraṇa). प्र...द्रुतैः that fled being frightened by the angered and fierce staff-bearers. असतो...यद्भिः that laid bare the imaginary (असतः) faults of former provincial officers. असतः that did not exist. There is a touch of humour here and in many other places in this passage. भोग or भुक्ति frequently occurs as a sub-division of a country (see I. A. vol. 19 p. 303, 304). अति...शंसद्भिः praising hundreds of former (subordinate) officers (युक्तक). The reading आयुक्तक also is good. Both these occur in numerous grants. For आयुक्तक see I. A. vol. 16 p. 24; I. A. vol. 15 p. 187. As'oka's edicts mention certain officers called युता, who correspond to the युक्तकs (see the third edict in E. I. vol. II. p. 448 ff). चिरन्त... धानैः—the word चाट seems to have some technical sense. In grants of villages the word 'अचाटभटप्रवेश्यः' occurs very frequently. Dr Fleet renders it 'irregular troops' (C. I. I. III p. 98 n. 2). एकान्त...रक्षणम् in which protection of crops was sought against the coming Gauḍa king who was repeatedly thought of by a group of horsemen riding in a part (of the army). आदिष्ट...तुष्टैः who were pleased with the protecting officers to whom orders had been issued. लूयमानं निष्पन्नं (ripe) सस्यं तेन प्रकटितः विषादः यैः. Their crops had been taken for the army. क्षेत्रशुचा out of grief for (the state of) their fields. प्ररूढः प्राणच्छेदः येषाम् the destruction of whose lives had taken deep root *i. e.* whose lives were in imminent danger. Those who reviled the king were severely dealt with 'त्रैविद्यनृपदेवानां क्षेप उत्तमसाहसः' याज्ञ० II. 2 11.; राज्ञोऽनिष्टप्रवक्तारं तस्यैवाक्रोशकारिणम् । तन्मन्त्रस्य च भेत्तारं छित्वा जिह्वां प्रवासयेत् ॥' याज्ञ० II. 302. परितापेन (grief) त्याजितं भयं येषाम्. प्रारब्धा नरनाथस्य (हर्षस्य) निन्दा यस्मिन् (*adj.* of स्कन्धावारं). शशकैः—this is to be connected with कृतकलकलम् (p. 59 l. 4). प्रजः...बद्धैः (hares) pursued by swift crowds with formidable sticks in their hands. गिरिः...हन्यमानैः that were struck as if they were clods of earth (that also are struck with thick clubs in preparing the soil for crops). C and T translate 'struck like polo balls.' सञ्चरद्भिः goes with शशकैः. अपरः—take with शशकैः. युग...तित that came upon them all at once. अनेक...कुशलिभिः (hares) clever in escaping between the legs of many animals. कुटिलिकया (वक्रगमनेन) व्यंसिताः सादिनां बहवः श्वानः यैः that gave the slip to many dogs of riders by dodges. व्यंस् *10th conj.* to foil. पतन्त्यः...यष्टयः येषु. कुद्दालः spade. खनित्रं hoe. निःस...बलात् that escaped because they were to live longer (though on them fell clods &c.). सङ्घशः in groups. घासिकैः—connect with

०धूलिपटलम्. घासे नियुक्तः one in charge of fodder. बुसधूल्या धूसरितानि घासजालेन जालकितानि (covered) जघनानि येषाम्. बुसं chaff. पुराणपर्याणस्य एकदेशात् दोलायमानानि दात्राणि (knives) येषाम्. शीर्णोर्णाशकलैः (with bits of torn wool) शिथिलाः मलिनाः मलकुथाः (dirty blankets) येषाम्. 'मलकुथैरिति पाठः। मलकुथा मलपट्टी छविरित्यर्थः । अंसोपरि वास इत्यन्ये' com. प्रभुणा प्रसादीकृतः पाटितः पटच्चरे चलन् चोलकः तं धारयन्ति इति—that wore a jacket dangling on a tattered garment, that was (once) presented by their master, (but now) all torn. 'पटच्चरं जीर्णवस्त्रम्' इत्यमरः. एकान्त...विग्रहम्—A portion of this compound occurs above (text p. 58 l. 28). The copyist was probably misled by the occurrence of the word उद्धूयमानधूलिपटलम् which in both places precedes the sentence. The proper text in the former place seems to be '०धूलिपटलम्, विमृग्यमाणसंस्यसंरक्षणम्'. ०चक्रेण चर्व्यमाणः आगामी गौडविग्रहः यस्मिन् where the coming fight with the Gauḍa king was reflected upon by &c. If we read चर्च्यमाण, then the meaning is 'being discussed.' This is better. पङ्किलस्य (muddy) प्रदेशस्य पूरणाय आदेशः तेन आकुलैः सकललोकैः लूयमानाः तृणपूलकाः यस्मिन्. तलवर्तिनः (standing at the root of the trees) वेत्रिणः तेषां वेत्रैः वित्रास्यमानाः (being frightened) शाखिशिखरगताः विवादिनः ब्राह्मणाः यस्मिन्. कुलुण्ठकपाशे विवेष्ट्यमानाः (enveloped) ग्रामीणकानां (villagers) ग्रामेण समूहेन आकृष्टाः कौलेयकाः (dogs) यस्मिन्. For कौलेयक, see p. 97. 'कुलुण्ठकाः शुनां बन्धनलगुडाः' com. C and T prefer to read ग्रासाकृष्ट and translate 'village dogs, entrapped by bits of food, were being tied in leashes'. It is better to hold that powerful dogs (not village curs) were being led by villagers pressed into the service of the army. अन्योन्यविभवस्पर्धया उद्धुरैः राजपुत्रैः वाह्यमानाः वाजिनः तेषां संघट्टेन (collision, race) मण्डितम्. 'उन्नतमुद्धुरम्' क्षीर०. उद्धुर unchecked, bold. अनेक...जननम् that caused interest by its numerous incidents. जगतः ग्रासेन ग्रहणम्. The sea at the time of Pralaya engulfs (ग्रास) the world and makes it its own. The army wanted to seize the world and to hold it in its grasp. महा...गुप्तये (1) for the protection of the great serpents; (2) for the protection of great kings or rather headmen of villages. 'भोगी भुजङ्गमेऽपि स्याद् ग्रामपात्रे नृपे पुमान्' मे०. Pātāla is the abode of the Nâgas. कैलासम्—On कैलास, परमेश्वर (शिव) resides. See above p. 79. हर्ष was परमेश्वर (an emperor). दृश्यमानः सकलप्राणिनां पर्यायः यस्मिन् where all the animals were seen in succession (with ०कोशम्); in which all beings were seen to walk about (in military order). पर्यायः succession, rotation; regular order. प्रजापतीनाम्—see p. 55 for them. ब्रह्मा produced the ten प्रजापतिs, who in their turn produced the seven Manus, the Devas, demons, men, birds and beasts &c. See मनु I. 36 ff. For the four Yugas, see p. 3. For the creation of various beings see विष्णुपु. I. 5. चतु...कोशमिव like the collection (or store) of the creation of the four Yugas. There is another meaning. In a कोश (lexicon) there are seen synonyms (पर्यायः) for all beings. Perhaps Bâṇa alludes to some lexicon divided into four *sargas* (sections). चतुर्युग may itself mean कृतयुग (as कृत means four in the language of astronomers). When the world was first created, the कृतयुग began. क्लेशबहुलम् though abounding in troubles (applies to both 'army' and 'austerity'). क्रम...कल्याणानाम् The army would in the end achieve victory; तपःकरण (performance of austerities) leads gradually to happiness.

P. 114 l. 17—**P. 115** l. 2 **आसन्न...सिष्ट.** आसन्नवर्तिनाम् and तत्रभवताम् qualifiy पार्थिवकुमाराणां (l. 32). 'पूज्ये तत्रभवानत्रभवांश्च भगवानपि'. It would be better to read तत्रभवता as the com. does. तत्रभवता goes with मान्धात्रा. For मान्धातृ, see pp. 23, 123. अप्रतिहतं रथरंहः (रथवेगः) यस्य. प्रसादनम् purifying, making clear (of enemies); calming down. The reading प्रसाधनम् of some mss. would be much better, being quite in keeping with Bâṇa's style. प्रसाधनम् accomplishing (conquering); ornamenting. करद one who pays tribute. For the conquest of the world by रघु, see रघुवंश IV. करदीचकार made them pay tribute. चक्रम् goes with भूभुजाम्. क्रमागतानां भुजबलं अभिजनः (noble ancestry) धनं च तेषां मदेन अवलिप्तानाम् (haughty). सव्यसाची applies to अर्जुन only out of the five पाण्डवs. 'उभौ मे दक्षिणौ पाणी गाण्डीवस्य विकर्षणे । तेन देवमनुष्येषु सव्यसाचीति मां विदुः ॥' विराटपर्व 44. 19. चीनविषयं = चीनदेशम्. राज...दे for completing the राजसूय. राजसूय was a sacrifice performed by a universal monarch at the time of his coronation to mark his undisputed sovereignity. See सभापर्व 32 ff. for the incidents of the राजसूय performed by युधिष्ठिर. क्रुध्यन्तः गन्धर्वाः तेषां धनुष्कोटीनां टाङ्कारेण कूजिताः कुञ्जाः यस्य. हेमकूट was the abode of the गन्धर्वs. अर्जुन is said to have conquered the गन्धर्वs (सभापर्व 2. 58). पराजैष्ट *Aorist* of जि with परा. जि necessarily takes the Âtmanepada when preceded by वि and परा. 'विपराभ्यां जेः' पा. 1. 3. 19. सङ्कल्पेन अन्तरितः separated or screened by resolve. तरस्विन् strong. The idea is:—In the case of the strong, what comes between the conquest of the world and them is the wish or resolve. As long as they do not desire, conquest is far off. The moment they desire it, it is theirs. सहिमः हिमवान् तेन व्यवहितः—though screened by the हिमालय with its snows. बाहु...कातरः afraid of the clash of his prowess (against that of his enemy). अकृती not happy, wretched. द्रुमः—was a king of किंपुरुषs. 'द्रुमो किंपुरुषेशश्च उपास्ते धनदेश्वरम्' ॥ सभापर्व 10. 29. भगदत्त...प्रभृतयः—these are the names of various kings that were present in the great Mahâbhârata war. भगदत्त was king of प्राग्जोतिष and a partisan of दुर्योधन. He was killed by अर्जुन. दन्तवक्र was defeated by सहदेव in his दक्षिणदिग्विजय (सभापर्व 31, 3). क्राथ was a son of धृतराष्ट्र killed by भीम. शिशुपाल, कर्ण and जरासन्ध are well-known. शाल्व was a partisan of दुर्योधन and king of म्लेच्छ tribes. He was killed by सात्यकि (शल्यपर्व 20). सिन्धुराज is जयद्रथ. धनञ्जयजयेन जनितः जगत्कम्पः येन. समीप एव—The किंपुरुषs or किन्नरs are a race of semidivine beings with the face of a horse. Their country called किंपुरुषवर्ष was next to भारतवर्ष. The विष्णुपुराण (II. 2.) tells us that किंपुरुषवर्ष was next to भारतवर्ष between हिमवत् and हेमकूट. Compare 'इतश्च नातिदूरे तस्यासाद्भारतवर्षादुत्तरेणानन्तरे किंपुरुषनाम्नि वर्षे वर्षपर्वतो हेमकूटो नाम निवासः' काद० (p. 136 of P). अलसः dull, lazy. There is a picturesque contrast between अलस and the literal meaning of the name चण्डकोश. चण्ड means 'fierce, powerful.' स्त्रीराज्यम्—see above p. 27. There is an untranslateable pun on the word चण्डकोश in relation to women. Put a vertical line after ०मादनयोः. ह्रसी...मादनयोः very short is the distance between the Himālaya and the गन्धमादन. The idea is:—When even the distant countries of the Turks and the Persians are a mere span to the persevering hero, then surely the distance between the हिमालय and the गन्धमादन is small indeed. उत्सा...विषयः to the persevering the land of the Turushkas (Turks) is but a cubit. 'किष्कुर्हस्ते वितस्तौ च' इत्यमरः. Understand उत्साहिनः in each of the following clauses. It will be noticed that in the choice of words the poet is guided only by similarity of sounds. पारसीकदेशः Persia. प्रादेशः span. 'प्रादेशतालगोकर्णास्तर्जन्यादियुते तते ॥ अङ्गुष्ठे सकनिष्ठे स्याद्वितस्तिर्द्वादशाङ्गुलः ॥' इत्यमरः ('तर्जन्या युते तते प्रसारितेऽङ्गुष्ठे मध्यं, प्रादिश्यते प्रादेशः' क्षीर०). शकस्थानम् the country of the S'akas. The S'akas are identified with the Scythians, who migrated to India and established themselves at Taxila in Punjab, at Mathurā and in Kathiawad. अदृश्यमानः प्रतिप्रहारः यस्मिन् in which there is none to give a counter-stroke. पारियात्र is one of the seven principal mountains of India. From the बृहत्संहिता (69. 11-12) it seems that it was in Malva and corresponded to the western portion of the Vindhya and the Aravali Hills. यात्रैव शिथिला an expedition (against पारियात्र) is very easy. शौर्यं शुल्कं

यस्य—the price of which is valour *i. e.* by showing valour it can be won. शुल्कं originally meant the price of a bride taken by her parents. 'शुल्कं यद् गृहीत्वा कन्या दीयते' मिताक्षरा on याज्ञ० II. 144. दक्षिणापथ—the whole of the country south of the Narmadā up to Cape Comorin; sometimes, the country between the नर्मदा and the कृष्णा. 'सेतुनर्मदामध्यं सार्धसप्तलक्षं दक्षिणापथं पालयामास' E. I. Vol. IV. p. 305 Bāṇa seems to have used it in the latter sense, as the next sentence shows. दक्षिणार्णवस्य कल्लोलाः (waves) तेषां अनिलैः चलिताः चन्दनलताः तासां सौरभेण सुन्दरीकृतानि दरीमन्दिराणि यस्य. दर्दु...मलयः—मलय is very near to the mountain दर्दुर. नेदीयसि *loc. sing.* of the comparative of अन्तिक. For मलय, see above p. 39. दर्दुर is a mountain in the extreme south of India and closely associated with मलय. Compare रघु. IV. 51 'स निर्विश्य यथाकामं तटेष्वालीनचन्दनौ । स्तनाविव दिशस्तस्याः शैलौ मलयदर्दुरौ ॥.' महेन्द्र is one of the seven कुलाचलs and corresponds to the eastern Ghauts on the Coromandel coast. उद्योगद्योतकानाम् that manifested or encouraged energetic efforts. प्रास्तः समायोगः येन who dismissed the people round him.

P. 115 ll. 3—27 **अथ तत्र ... देवस्येति.** प्राग्ज्योतिष—corresponds with modern Assam. It was also called कामरूप. कुमार is the name of the king of Assam. C and T think that he was only the heir-apparent. But the word ०श्वरेण militates against that view. Besides see text p. 63 ll. 25–26. अन्तरङ्ग confidential. दक्षतया through cleverness, promptness. क्षिति...राच्च and on account of the regard shown by the king Harsha (for the messenger). नयनानन्दसम्पादनाय सुभगः आभोगः तेन भद्रया (form) that was agreeable on account of its charming fulness (आभोगः, proportions) that caused delight to the eye. आकृत्यैव समु...गरिमा whose very personal charms exceeded the greatness of his qualities. It is the convention of Sanskrit poets to say that a noble exterior is an indication of noble qualities of the head and the heart; compare 'आकारसदृशप्रज्ञः' रघु I. 15. The exterior of हंसवेग was in comparison grander than his qualities. प्राभृतं present, *Nazarana.* आरादेव = दूरादेव. पञ्चाङ्गैः आलिङ्गितं अङ्गनं येन who fell prostrate on the courtyard with five limbs (*i. e.* hands, feet and head). Read प्रधावितोपसृतः who approached the king running. पादपीठे लुठिता ललाटलेखा येन. न्यस्त...पार्थिवेन on whose back the king laid his hand. पार्थिवेन is to be connected with न्यस्त in the compound ०हस्तः. अविप्रकृष्टं not far (from the king). तिरश्चीं...दधानः slightly bending his body on one side. संमुखीनः having turned his face towards him (हंसवेग). सप्रश्रयम् *adv.* respectfully, politely. हंसवेग continues his speech from the words 'चतुरम्भोधि०'. चतु...भूतस्य who is the (worthy) abode of the prosperity (or grandeur) due to enjoying the four oceans. Construe देवस्य अन्यत् अनुरूपं प्राभृतमेव दुर्लभं लोके another present worthy of your Majesty is difficut to find in this world. सद्भावः गर्भे यस्य. सद्भा...मेकम् excepting one thing, *viz.* a heart full of goodness. He means:—an affectionate heart is the only present that can be worthy of your Majesty. सन्दे...नयता who wanted to make his message solid. अशून्य not empty, solid. वारुणातपत्रम् an umbrella derived from Varuṇa. See text p. 63 below. आभोगः आख्या यस्य. The umbrella is appropriately named आभोगः (expanse). अनु...तत् this has been made blessed by being deposited in a proper place. He means that Harsha is a proper person to whom the umbrella (emblem of sovereignty) may be entrusted. कुतूहलं कुर्वन्ति इति०कृन्ति. शैत्य... छायायाः for the purpose of giving coolness to its shade. प्रध्यानानन्तरम् after reflection *i. e.* after the person possessing it desires. दन्तवीणा chattering of the teeth due to cold. चन्द्रभासाम् चन्द्रस्येव भाः येषां (waters) that are as bright as the moon. मणिशलाकाभ्यः from the jewelled ribs. इच्छामनतिक्रम्य यावदिच्छं as long or as much as desired. प्रचेताः 'प्रचेता वरुणः पाशी' इत्यमरः. सप्तार्चिः—fire. पृषदश्वः wind 'पृषदश्वो गन्धवहः' इत्यमरः ('पृषन्मृगविशेषोऽश्वोऽस्य पृषदश्वः, पृषन्त्यम्बुकणाः सन्त्यश्वा अस्येत्येके' क्षीर०). विस्रब्धं confidentially. We must supply देवः as the subject of श्रोष्यति or read श्रोष्यसि as C and T suggest. विवृत्य having turned round (from वृत् with वि).

P. 115 l. 28—**P. 116** l. 21 स...महच्छत्रम्. तत् = आतपत्रम्. धौ...षीत् he took it out of its case made of white silk. 'निचोलः प्रच्छदपटः' इत्यमरः. अतिसितं महः (तेजः) यस्य. ०महसि goes with यस्मिन्. In the following clauses the author makes a very imaginative effort to convey the extreme whiteness and brilliance of the umbrella. सरभ...हरेण S'iva as if laughed wildly. S'iva's laugh is called अट्टहास. Smiles and laughs are spoken of as white. अहासि Aorist passive of हस्. There are many such Aorist forms in the following clauses. रसा...मण्डलेन—शेष, the king of Nâgas, dwells in पाताल and its 1000 hoods are pale in colour. चक्रीभूय having assumed the form of a circle. The umbrella was round. The poet says it looked like the milky ocean transformed into a circle. गगनमेव अङ्गनं तस्मिन्. The clouds (बलाहकः) in S'arad are white. A गोष्ठीबन्ध (an assembly of learned men) is held in one's अङ्गन. विश्रान्त that had taken rest. वितता पक्षतिः (पक्षमूलं)

long and resembles the long lotus stalk. प्रथिमन् *m.* breadth. समुच्छ्राय: height. स्तबक...स्तम्भस्य it was like a bunch of flowers on the trunk (tree) of Brahmâ *i. e.* it was the pick, the cream of the world. नाभि०—As the spokes start from the round nave (नाभि) of a wheel, so from it radiated light. कीर्ति is white.

P. 116 l. 22—**P. 117** l. 13 **च...छायाम्.** कार्मा: ='स कार्मः कर्मशीलो यः' इत्यमरः. 'कार्मस्ताच्छील्ये' पा. 6. 4. 172. परार्ध्यरत्नानां अंशुभिः शोणीकृताः दिग्भागाः यैः (*adj.* of अलङ्कारान्). Remove the comma after दिग्भागान्. For भगदत्त, see above p. 187 and text p. 63. परागत come, handed down. आहतलक्षणान् = प्रसिद्धान्, 'गुणैः प्रतीते तु कृतलक्षणाहतलक्षणौ' इत्यमरः (आहतानि उद्घोषितानि लक्षणानि यस्य). प्रभा... त्कर्षान् the best of crest jewels that covered (everything) with their sheen. अनेक...क्षौमाणि— silken cloth rolled up in charming variously coloured cane boxes and bright like the rays of the autumn moon and that were capable of purifying a person. उल्लिखित carved out. For गल्वर्क, see p. 77. निचोलकैः (cases) रक्षिता रुक् (कान्तिः) येषाम्. ०भङ्गेन भङ्गुराणां wavy with charming figures in gold. अतिबन्धुरः परिवेशः (fringe, hem) येषाम्. कार्दरङ्गचर्मणाम् of कार्दरङ्ग shields. कार्दरङ्ग seems to be the name of a country. जातीपट्टिकाः loin-cloths. 'जातीपट्टिकाः श्रेष्ठानि जघनग्रन्थनानि' com. चित्रपट cloth with paintings or figures. समूरुक is a kind of deer. उपधानम् pillow. '**समूरुश्चेति** हरिणा अमी अजिनयोनयः' इत्यमरः. प्रियङ्गुप्रसववत् पिङ्गला त्वक् येषाम्. प्रियङ्गुः millet. प्रसवः fruit. अगुरुवल्कलेन कल्पितः सञ्चयः येषाम् the leaves of which were made of अगुरु bark. परिणतं (अत एव) पाटलं पटोलं तस्येव त्विट् (कान्तिः) येषाम्. पटोल is called in Marathi पडवळ. तरुण...हरिन्ति as green as a young pigeon. Some of the betel nuts were green and some red. क्षीरक्षारीणि from which milky juice was oozing (being recently cut from the trees). ०कपोलवत् कपिलानि कापोतिकापलाशानि तेषां कोश्या कवचितं अङ्गं यासाम् that were covered with cases of the leaves of the कापोतिका plant as tawny as the cheeks &c. स्थवीयसी *f.* comparative of स्थूल. वैणवीर्नाडीः (object of प्रकाशयांचक्रुः) tubes of bamboo. पट्ट...र्पितान् (connect with राशीन्) placed in bags made of woven silk. For प्रसेवक, see p. 180. भिन्ना...गुरुणः of black aloe (कृष्णागुरु *n.*) as dark as pounded collyrium. This and the following genitives are to be connected with राशीन्. गोशीर्षम् is a kind of very fragrant sandal. 'तैलपर्णिकगोशीर्षे हरिचन्दनमस्त्रियाम्' इत्यमरः ('तैलपर्णगोशीर्षौ गिरी आकरौ अस्य' क्षीर०). कस्तू...कानां of bags of musk. कक्कोलं a fragrant berry (Marathi कंकोळ). जातीफलं nutmeg. अतिमधुरः मधुरसः

तस्य आमोदेन निर्हारिणीः redolent of the perfume of very sweet wine. The com. takes the word to be मधुरसा. 'मृद्वीका गोस्तनी द्राक्षा स्वाद्वी मधुरसेति च' इत्यमरः. उल्लककलशीः pitchers of उल्लक. 'उल्लकः सुगन्धिफलविशेषरस : । आसवभेद इत्यन्ये' com. अवलम्बमानानि तूलिकाः (brushes) अलाबुकानि च येभ्यः—अलाबुकम् vessel made of a gourd (to hold paints). आ...टान् boxes of boards for drawing pictures. कनकशृङ्खलया नियमिताः ग्रीवाः येषां or यासाम्. For किंनर, see above p. 187. C and T suggest that some species of ape may be meant here. वनमानुषी 'ourang—outang' C and T. जीवञ्जीवक is a bird, the चकोर according to अमरकोश. Compare 'पाणितलसंवर्धितं मे जीवञ्जीवमिथुनं क्रीडापर्वते यथा न विपद्यते तथा कर्तव्यम्' काद० p. 316. परिमलेन आमोदिताः ककुभः (दिशः) यैः. गेह... चमरीः chamarî deer accustomed to move about the house. चामीकर...गतान् placed in cages of cane painted with gold. बहुसुभाषितैः जल्पाका जिह्वा येषाम्. जल्पाक garrulous. 'स्याज्जल्पाकस्तु वाचालः' इत्यमरः. 'जल्पभिक्षकुट्टलुण्टवृङः षाकन्' पा. 3. 2. 155. प्रवालः—लम्—coral. जल...कुण्डलानि rings of the long tusks of hippopotamus, bristling (दन्तुर) with rows of large (उदग्र) pearls from their headfronts. It was believed that pearls were found in the temples of elephants. 'द्विपभुजगशुक्तिशङ्खाभ्रवेणुतिमिसूकरप्रसूतानि । मुक्ताफलानि तेषां बहु साधु च शुक्तिजं भवति ॥' बृह० 81. 1. Compare 'शशिकेसरिविदार्यमाणतमःकरिकुम्भसम्भवेन मुक्ताफलक्षोदेनेव धवलतामुपनीयमान्' काद० p. 160 of P. सकल...धाम्नः that is the abode of all precious things (applies both to महार्णव and कुमार). परमे...र्हस्य which is fit to be held on the head of a परमेश्वर (emperor); which is to be held on the head by परमेश्वर (शिव). शिव placed the moon on his head to lessen the fever of his body due to हालाहल. कुमुदबान्धवस्य = चन्द्रस्य. न विस्मयाय does not cause wonder *i. e.* does not make me wonder. बाल...कृतयः favours (bestowed on others) are the first lessons of the great. मङ्गलाकाङ्क्षी desiring an auspicious (conclusion to his expedition). प्राङ्मुखः with his face to the east. आभोगस्य—the umbrella was so called.

P. 117 l. 19—**P. 118** l. 9 **अथ विशत...वनानाम्.** अस्य = हर्षस्य. छायायाः जन्म यस्य (*adj.* of जडिम्ना). जडिम्ना...बिम्बम् by the coolness it seemed as if the disc of the moon had become his crest jewel *i. e.* under the shade of the umbrella he felt as much coolness as he would have if the moon had been placed on his crest. Explain the following similarly. Everyone of his limbs and his whole body felt the coolness. अम्बुबिन्दून् मुञ्चन्तीति ०मुचः (*adj.* of मणयः). It should be noted that all the objects mentioned are white and cool. चन्द्रकान्त—moonstone, that was believed to ooze when the rays of the moon fell upon it. कर्पू...युगले his eyes felt the coolness of camphor applied to them. गलन्तः तुहिनकणाः तेषां निकरेण कृतः नीहारः (frost, dew) येषाम्. हरि...मुरसि—हरिचन्दनम् is a kind of yellowish sandal. अन्त... दङ्गानि a concealed melting slab of ice as if smeared his limbs. अजर्यं सङ्गतम् undying or everlasting friendship 'अजर्यं सङ्गतम्' पा. 3. 1. 105 (नञ्पूर्वात् जीर्यतेः कर्तरि यत् सङ्गतं चेद्विशेष्यम् । सि. कौ.). प्रतिकौशलिका a present in return (from कुशलं). हंसवेगाय—connect with प्राहिणोत्. धवलकर्पटेन प्रावृतं धौतं (bright, polished) नालिकेरं (cocoanut shell used as a box) तस्मिन् परिगृहीतम् contained. विलिप्तशेषं चन्दनम् (object of प्राहिणोत्) sandal paste that remained after he (हर्ष) had anointed himself. This was deemed a mark of great favour and friendship. अङ्गस्पृष्टे—touched by his own person. शरदि तारकाः तेषां इव आकारः यासां ताः ०काराः ताराः (pure and bright) मुक्ताः तैः स्तबकितं पदं यस्य. The stars shine very brightly in the clear autumnal sky. कटिसूत्रम् belt. कटक...तरत्—the setting of the sun is represented as due to his desire to wash his body rendered dusky by dust. 'मलीमसं तु मलिनम्' इत्यमरः. वारुणीं दिशम्—वरुण presides over the West. अयासीत्—the subject is अंशुमाली. कमलs close their petals at sunset. प्रमुखे एव at the very beginning (of his expedition). The closing petals of the lotuses are represented as the folded hands of the earth. The earth as if submitted to him at the very start of his march. नृपा...मयः इव (the glow of twilight) was as if made up of the अनुराग (love, redness) for the king. The idea is:—the twilight made the whole world aglow; the poet fancies it was rather the अनुराग of the world that spread over it. निखिल...बन्धुः which is a kinsman (*i. e.* closely connected) with the folding of the hands of the people. People perform सन्ध्यावन्दन in the evening; people also fold their hands before a king. ०शङ्किनी afraid of. प्रचितः तिमिरस्य निवहः (समूहः) यस्याम्. निर्वाणः (extinguished) अन्यनृपप्रतापानलकलापः यस्याम्. When we quench fire, black charcoal is left. अवचकरुः *perfect 3rd plu.* of कृ with अव to spread. मेदिनी...ककुभः—clusters of stars resembling expanded *Tagara* flowers twinkled in the sky and seemed as if they were the bunches of flowers spread in the evening audience-hall of the lord of the earth. मार्गो...वतस्य the track of ऐरावत grey with dust shone in the sky. ऐरावत is the vehicle of इन्द्र, the lord of the east. The dust is represented to be raised by ऐरावत that fled from the गन्धगजs of Harsha. रजःपाण्डुः also means 'pale like or with the pollen of flowers'. The east became lit up with the rays of the moon that was about to rise. कुपितः नृपः (हर्षः) व्याघ्र इव तेन आघ्राताम् (smelt, touched). उपसृष्टामिव as if it were possessed by an evil spirit. पौरुहूतीम् = ऐन्द्रीम्. रोहिणीरमणः = चन्द्रः. For रोहिणी being the favourite wife of the moon, see pp. 9, 47, 62. The simple idea is that the moon rose up high in the sky. रोहिणीरमण also means 'a bull', that leaves a place where he smells the tiger. रोहिणी a tawny cow. 'अर्जुन्यघ्न्या रोहिणी स्यादुत्तमा गोषु नैचिकी' इत्यमरः. C and T see here a reference to the growing power of शशाङ्क the Gauḍa king. मानिनी...भेदिन्यः the rays of the moon melt the heart of proud women *i. e.* they become favourable to their husbands with whom they were displeased. प्रयाण ...भेदिन्यः as the news of the march (of Harsha's army) breaks the heart of proud women (because they are afraid of the death of their husbands when they oppose him). नवनृपस्य (हर्षस्य) दण्डयात्रा &c. चक्षुभु...हिनीनाम् the lords of rivers (oceans) became agitated *i. e.* after the rise of the moon the ocean has a full tide. This tidal agitation is fancied to be due to the fear of the expedition of हर्ष. वाहिनीनां पतयः also means 'commanders'. तरलिताः सत्त्वानां प्राणिनां वृत्तयः येषु the movements of the animals in which were made unsteady (with oceans). By the tide the aquatic animals were carried here and there. तरलिता सत्त्वस्य धैर्यस्य वृत्तिः येषाम् whose steadiness of mind was shaken. चिन्ता— anxiety entered the hearts of kings (भूभृत्). Darkness entered the caves of mountains (भूभृत्) *i. e.* only the caves were dark; the rest was lighted up by the moon. विमुक्ताः सर्वाः आशाः दिशः यया (*adj.* of सन्ततिः); विमुक्ता सर्वा आशा (hope) यस्यां (*adj.* of चिन्ता). निद्रा...वनानाम्—The कुमुद lotuses open in moon-light. प्रति...निद्रा sleep left the eyes of the rivals of हर्ष.

P. 118 l. 10—**P. 119** l. 12 अस्यां...स्वामिन इति. महावराहसम्पर्केण सम्भृतः गर्भः यस्याः. महावराह refers to the Boar incarnation of विष्णु. Compare 'यदाहमुद्धृता नाथ त्वया सूकरमूर्तिना । त्वत्स्पर्शसम्भवः पुत्रस्तदायं मय्यजायत ॥' विष्णुपु० 5. 29. 23. नरक was king of प्राग्ज्योतिष. कृष्ण killed him at the request of Indra. He deprived वरुण of his umbrella, took away मणिपर्वत from मन्दर, the ear-rings of अदिति &c. 'छत्रं यत्सलिलस्रावि तज्जहार प्रचेतसः ।' विष्णु० 5. 29. 10. त्रिभुवनं भुङ्क्ते इति ०भुक् तस्य. भुजयोः शौण्डः प्रवीणः. The construction is यस्य... आशया विना रविरस्तं न अव्राजीत्. ०वाकीभिः कोपकुटिलैः कटाक्षैः ईक्षितः. The चक्रवाकी is separated from her lord at sunset and so fearing it looks angrily at the sun. भयचकितेन अरुणेन परिवर्तितः (turned)

रथः यस्य. अरुण is the charioteer of the sun. बहि...यमिव as if it (छत्र) were his heart dwelling outside. The छत्र was as dear to वरुण as his own heart. Only the छत्र was outside his body. अन्वये in the line or family. भगदत्त was a contemporary of the Pâṇḍavas and took part in the great war. See above p. 187. वज्रदत्त was son of भगदत्त and was defeated by the Pāndavas in their अश्वमेध. See आश्वमेधिकपर्व chap. 76. कैलासस्य इव स्थिरा स्थितिः यस्य whose sense of duty was as firm as Kailâsa. अग्रजेन...कारेण who was born together with pride, as if the latter was the elder of the two. The idea is:—he and अहङ्कार were twin brothers; but अहङ्कार was the elder of the two *i. e.* he paid more regard to, subordinated everything to अहङ्कार. From his very birth he was proud. The reading अजेनेव does not yield a good sense. प्रतिग्रहान् (1) presents (with द्विजातीन्); (2) the rear of an army. अरातीन् प्रतिग्रहान् अग्राहयत् he made his enemies take to the rear of their armies *i. e.* to run from the battlefield. 'सैन्यपृष्ठे प्रतिग्रहः' इत्यमरः. यत्र परं...लक्ष्म्या in whom लक्ष्मी (royal glory) attained her greatest sweetness. There is a picturesque contradiction in saying that लक्ष्मी sprung from the *salt* ocean became *sweet*. Effects generally possess the properties of their causes. वाहिनीनाथानां (1) of commanders of armies; (2) of oceans. शङ्ख was an emblem of command. The great warriors in the महाभारत war had each a शङ्ख which they blew before beginning the fight. Both शङ्खs and jewels are found in the sea as well as with commanders. स्थैर्यः...करम् he took the steadiness of the earth, but did not levy tribute from it. He was as steady as the earth. अवनिभृतां = राज्ञां, पर्वतानां च. गौरव...नैष्ठुर्यम्—mountains have गौरव and नैष्ठुर्य both. He took the one (*i. e.* he was majestic) and not the other (*i. e.* he was not harsh). There is a suggested sense. He deprived the kings of their high position. C and T take भास्करद्युति as the name of the king. This does not seem to be correct. भास्करस्य इव द्युतिर्यस्य. The king's name was कुमार alias भास्करवर्मन्. See above text p. 60. l. 4. भास्करद्युति as the name of a king will probably be found nowhere (with the last word द्युति in the feminine gender). The word कुमार suggests another idea. भीष्म remained a कुमार (prince) all his life; he never became a king. सङ्कल्पः resolve. स्थेयान् *nom. sing. m.* of the comparative of स्थिर. प्रचण्डेन प्रतापज्वलनेन जनितः दिशां दाहः येन. जगत्येकवीरेण who is the only (unequalled) warrior in the world. मैत्री...भृताम् the friendship of kings generally is dependent upon some purpose *i. e.* it is never disinterested. य...दैवम् which when mentioned would make your Majesty a friend (of the king भास्करवर्मा). सञ्चिचीषतः desiring to collect. He now mentions several purposes which induce kings to form friendships and dismisses them all by saying that Harsha is in need of none of them. First he takes up wealth. बहिरङ्ग external *i. e.* not of the essence. बाहा...काशः As he relies solely upon his arm, the desire of even his other limbs to help him has no scope *i. e.* even his other limbs cannot offer him any help; what can a stranger do? चतुःसागराणां ग्रामः समूहः तस्य ग्रहणे घस्मरस्य (greedy). उपन्यासः proposal. The word ग्राम suggests that even the four oceans are but a small village to हर्ष. अभि...भनमपि अकिञ्चित्करम् even the allurement of the gift of a beautiful maiden is of no value. लक्ष्मीमुखारविन्ददर्शनेन दुर्ललिता (fondled) दृष्टिः यस्य. No maiden can be more alluring than लक्ष्मी. अघट...पदार्थेऽस्मिन् this being an object that is attainable by means which are all incapable of attaining it. प्रार्थनामात्रकमेव—connect with शृणोतु. अनुरुध्यमानः being favourably disposed. देवेन—connect with अजर्यं सङ्गतमिच्छति. एक...द्विषा like that of Kubera with the enemy of Cupid. He cast a glance at उमा and lost his left eye and the right became yellow. See रामायण VII. 13. 22–24. एकं पिङ्गं (नेत्रं) यस्य. The author instances five memorable friendships. For दशरथ and Indra, see p. 123. पुष्कराक्षः=पुण्डरीकाक्षः (कृष्णः). वैकर्तनः—son of विकर्तन (the sun) *i. e.* कर्ण. कर्ण was made king of अङ्ग by दुर्योधन. 'अस्य राज्यप्रदानस्य सदृशं किं ददानि ते।...अत्यन्तं सख्यमिच्छामीत्याह तं स सुयोधनः॥' आदिपर्व 136. 39–40. मलयानिल and माधव (वसन्त) are both excitants of love. मैत्रीयति—feels friendship. अवगच्छति...इति (and if your Majesty's) heart understands that friends discharge a slavery under another name. The idea is that friendship entails so many obligations that one has to work day and night for the other. तत...स्यते then why sit (silent)? अनुभवतु—the object is गाढोपगूढानि (close embraces). विष्णो...रिरिव as the mountain Mandara had the close embrace of विष्णु. मन्दर was the churning handle and विष्णु churned the ocean and the mountain rubbed against his body. विकट...मणीनां विघट्टनेन (striking against) क्वणितानि (jingling) कटकमणिशिलाशकलानि येषु. केयूरक is an ornament of the arm and कटक is a bracelet. In a close embrace these two ornaments will strike against each other. कटकः—कम् also means 'the slope of a hill'. 'कटकाऽस्त्री नितम्बोद्रेः' इत्यमरः. The केयूरक of विष्णु clashed against the slopes of मन्दर in churning. कामरूप is the same as प्राग्ज्योतिष. अस्मिन् goes with ०शशिनि. आ तृप्तेः till she (श्री) is satisfied. अन...ईरिणि that pours forth a constant spring of nectar in the form of spotless beauty and grandeur. लालयतु let her please or indulge. The simple idea is:—let the king of प्राग्ज्योतिष see your Majesty's face. But the words चिरात्, शशिनि and श्रीः suggest another sense. लक्ष्मी sprang from the ocean as the moon did and therefore लक्ष्मी is the sister of the moon. Let the sister separated from her brother see him after a long time. नाभि...प्रणयम् If your Majesty does not welcome his love or if your Majesty does not approve of his request.

P. 119 ll. 13–24 **विरत...त्कण्ठा इति.** पूर्वोपलब्धैः which he had heard of (by hearsay). आरोपितः बहुमानः यस्मिन् in whom great regard (for कुमार) had been produced. ०व्यतिकरेण by the incident of &c. महान् अभिजनः (family) यस्य. प्राग्रहरः foremost (प्रकृष्टं अग्रं हरति). परोक्षसुहृदि who is a friend without seeing me. शिशिरायन्ते become cool. कमलाकरे on a bed of lotuses. तिग्मं तीक्ष्णं तेजः यस्य = रवेः. The idea is that the कमलs do not feel that the rays of the sun are hot. सु...सख्यस्य being bought by his numerous qualities, who am I to (form) friendship? The idea is:—his qualities have already made me his. It is not in my hands to *form* a friendship which did not exist before. सज्जन...दिशः the ten quarters are the unhired slaves of the sweetness of the good. The good make the world theirs by their sweetness. एकान्तावदातः उत्तानः स्वभावः तेन सम्भृतं सादृश्यं येन. The कुमुद is extremely white; so is the moon. The कुमुद is उत्तान (has its petals turned up towards the moon); the moon also is उत्तान (open, straightforward). Thus the two resemble each other and form friendship without anybody's intercession. Compare 'समानशीलव्यसनेषु सख्यम्'. समालम्बितं शरासनं येन. अव...हृदयस्य the heart feels great regard for the proud lion, though a beast.

P. 119 l. 25—**P. 121** l. 16 **हंसवेगस्तु...निर्जगाम.** किमप...देवेन 'What else will now give pain (to both of you)? Your Majesty has spoken noble words.' He says that nothing else but the eagerness to see one another will hereafter pain the two kings. अहङ्कारः धनं यस्य. वैष्णवो वंशः—the family of भास्करवर्मा descended from नरक, the son of the earth and महावराह. पुरुषस्य हि—the principal sentence is पुरुषस्य हि सेवां प्रति...अभिमुखीक्रियमाणस्य...राजकुलं संप्रवेष्टुं कृतचित्तस्य (p. 64 l. 33)...किं प्रायश्चित्तम्...कीदृशं जीवितम् &c. (p. 66 ll. 1–3). सेवा...क्रियमाणस्य who is induced to (enter) service by his extremely wretched state, like a bad old mother. अतिवृद्धया very old; very much aggravated. 'निरयो दुर्गतिः स्त्रियाम्' अम०. वा— It will be noticed that in each clause up to अनुवर्त्यमानस्य there is वा. These are put forward as the various reasons which led a man to accept the service of a king. कुदु...प्रेर्यमाणस्य who is urged (towards service) by greed like a discontented wife. A discontented wife always urges her husband to earn more. तृष्णा also can never be gratified to the full. All genitives in this long passage are to be connected with पुरुषस्य. असत्सङ्कल्पैः by evil thoughts. यौव...षिभिः (apply both to bad children and ०सङ्कल्प) that are born of youth and that desire many things. जरत्कु...पश्यतः who sees (*i. e.* expects) a great position like an old maid (a daughter rather advanced in age for marriage). पर...योग्याम् that is commensurate with the solicitations he addresses to others (with अवस्थाम्); that is fit to be sought by others (with ०त्कुमारीम्). परेषां मार्गणं (याचनं) तस्य योग्याम्; परैः मार्गणं तस्य &c. स्वगृहे...योगम् who is compelled to make efforts by all badly placed planets in their houses like bad kinsmen. स्वगृहे—in his own house; in their 'houses' or 'mansions' (with ग्रहैः). The planets are believed to be very powerful when they are in 'mansions' (स्वगृह) *e. g.* सिंह is the स्वगृह of रवि, कर्क of the Moon, मेष and वृश्चिक of Mars and so on. दुःस्थितैः in distressed circumstances; in evil aspects with other planets. 'आभिमुख्येन उद्यमः अभियोगः' क्षीर०. पुरातनैः of long standing; done in former lives (with कर्मभिः). अतिदुस्त्यजैः—old servants cannot be easily got rid of; the fruits of evil deeds done in past lives cannot be avoided. मलिनैः dirty (servants); sinful. It is the sinful deeds in past lives that follow a man and make him take service. सकल...करम् goes with both कारीषाग्निम् and राजकुलम्. कारीषस्य अग्निः fire of dried cowdung. Its heat is more intense than that of fire fed with wood. करीषं शुष्कगोमयं तस्य समूहः कारीषम्. कृत...कुलम् who has made up his mind to enter the palace (*i. e.* the service of a king). दुष्कृतिनः one who is guilty of some deadly sin. He may be condemned to be burnt alive. उपहता सक...शक्तिः यस्य. मिथ्यैव...लाषस्य who has vain hopes of seizing the whole gamut of the sensual pleasures his heart desires. The servant vainly thinks that he would by entering service enjoy all विषयs; the old voluptuary also thinks the same. प्रथममेव शुष्यतो...रुद्धस्य first of all (before a man actually gets into royal service) he is obstructed by the doorkeepers and has to wither away at the portal for days. The वन्दनमाला also is tied to the portals and becomes dried by time. For वन्दनमाला see p. 178. करि...पुटस्य—see (text p. 49 l. 17) for ०पुट. प्रति...मानस्य—he is driven out by doorkeepers who beat him with their hands. The leather figure also is beaten by the कर (trunk of elephants) encased in a covering. 'प्रतिहारेण वेष्टनेन मण्डलं यस्य करस्य तत्प्रहारैश्च' com. अधो...भवतः who bends down his face (*i. e.* bows low) through greed of money. निधि...रोहस्य—it was believed that a tree with treasure beneath it had boughs bending in a peculiar way. See above text p. 4 'निधिस्तरुविकारेण'. अमार्गणस्यापि (1) though he is not a suppliant; (2) though not an arrow. अतिविप्रकृष्टैः आदौ विवृत्तः पश्चात् विसर्जितः he is made to turn back by very mean (servants at the court) and then dismissed. दूरं उद्वेगं व्रजतः he becomes extremely dejected. An arrow also is अति...व्रजतः. It is drawn (विवृत्त) very far (up to the ear) and then discharged. दूरं उद्वेगं व्रजतः (an arrow) reaches a long distance very swiftly (उत्कृष्टः वेगः यथा स्यात्तथा). विवृत also will yield a good meaning. He is first thoroughly examined by low people. The arrow (*i. e.* the bow) is opened very wide. अकण्टक...माणस्य he dogs the feet of persons about the court, who draw him and throw him out quickly, though he is not a thorn. कण्टक has also a technical meaning 'a troublesome person'. The अर्थशास्त्र has a section on कण्टकशोधन. क्षेपीयः used as an *adv.* (comparative of क्षिप्र). A thorn also pierces the sole of one's feet, is taken out and thrown away. अ...केतोः (1) though he is not Cupid; though he is innocent of love affairs (being engrossed in thoughts of service). अकालोपसर्पणेनः कुपितः ईश्वरः (राजा, शिवश्च) तस्य दृष्ट्या दग्धस्य. मदन tried to influence शिव when the latter was engaged in meditation and was burnt; see p. 38. The candidate for service approaches the king at an improper moment and angers him. प्रलय...तः (1) who is destroyed (with Cupid); (2) who disappears (with पुरुषस्य). अभिन्नः मुखरागः यस्य (applies both to कपि and पुरुष)—The redness of the ape's face remains as before. The servant shows no sign on his face though soundly rated. ब्रह्मघ्नः— the murderer of a ब्राह्मण. ब्रह्महत्या was a महापातक; see p. 84. प्रतिदिवसवन्दनेन उद्घृष्टं शिरःकपालं यस्य येन वा—the aspirant after service has to bow down every day and his head is thereby rubbed off. One that murders a ब्राह्मण has to bow by way of प्रायश्चित्त before a skull. Remove the comma after ०कपालस्य. स्पर्श...र्वहतः the servant is devoid of the pleasures of senses and has to carry out degrading duties. स्पर्शः means 'pleasant feelings, pleasure'. The slayer of a Brāhmaṇa had to avoid society and had to live by unworthy means. Note '**शिरःकपाली ध्वजवान्** भिक्षाशी कर्म वेदयन् । **ब्रह्महा** द्वादशाब्दानि मितभुक् शुद्धिमाप्नुयात् ॥' याज्ञ० III. 243 ('तच्च कपालं स्वव्यापादितब्राह्मणशिरःसम्बन्धि ग्राह्यम् । ... तदलाभे अन्यस्य ब्राह्मणस्यैव ग्राह्यम्' मिताक्षरा). See मनु 11. 78, which prescribes for him a forest dwelling. अर्वाक्शिरसः—with head downwards (*i. e.* bent). The servant has day and night to bow to his master. त्रिशङ्कुः—He was a king of the solar race and father of हरिश्चन्द्र. He wished to go to heaven with his mortal body by performing a यज्ञ. His family priest वसिष्ठ declared it impossible. He went to the sons of वसिष्ठ who rejected his proposal. त्रिशङ्कु told them that he would go to another preceptor, whereupon they cursed him to be a चण्डाल. विश्वामित्र, whose family त्रिशङ्कु had saved from starvation in a famine, took pity on him and raised त्रिशङ्कु towards heaven, when Indra refused to admit him and made him fall down headlong. Thereupon विश्वामित्र called upon him to stay where he was and began to create new worlds, नक्षत्रs &c. The gods intervened and made his creations as eternal as those of ब्रह्मा and त्रिशङ्कु blazed forth as a constellation, but with head downwards. See रामायण I. 57–60. Compare 'सुरलोकमारोहतस्त्रिशङ्कोरिव कुपितशतमखहुंकारनिपतिता राजलक्ष्मीः' काद० p. 8. सुखवाह्यम् easily driven (with वाजिनः); who is bereft of happiness (with पुरुषस्य). In the latter case वाह्य is equal to बाह्य; compare वंशबाह्याम् (text p. 39 l. 12, notes p. 125). अनशनशायिनः—One who has resolved upon dying by starvation. हृदये स्थापिता जीवनस्य (of livelihood) आशा येन the man has hopes in his heart of making a livelihood by service. हृदये स्थापितः जीवनाशः येन. निज...खस्य—being engrossed in his duties, the servant has no time to bestow on his wife. The application of निज...खस्य to a dog cannot be explained for the sake of decency. जघन्ये अधमे कर्मणि लग्नं सक्तम्. जघन्यं (जघने भवं) कर्म सुरतं तस्मिन् लग्नम्. अनु...पिण्डस्य—the servant has to take his food in some dirty place. अन्नपिण्ड is offered to the dead (प्रेत) in places (*viz.* river &c.) where the deceased was never accustomed to take food. बलिभुजः = काकस्य. जिह्वायाः लौल्येन उपयुक्तं पुरुषवर्चः येन who wasted his manly spirit for satisfying his fastidious tongue. जिह्वालौल्येन उपयुक्तं (भुक्तं) पुरुषस्य वर्चः (excrement) येन (with crow). 'तेजःपुरीषयोर्वर्चः' अम. वृथा...जीवतः who lives a life applied to no purpose (applies to both). The crow is supposed to live long. 'काकोऽपि जीवति चिरं च बलिं च भुङ्क्ते'. वृथा विहितं

आयुः यस्य. The com. separates 'विभ्यः पक्षिभ्यः हितमायुः यस्य' who has a life useful to birds (with crow). दग्ध...कृताम् rendered rugged by the ashes of persons burnt (with श्म॰); rendered harsh by their accursed prosperity (with ॰वल्लभान्). दग्धानां भूत्या; दग्धा चासौ भूतिः तया. पिशाचs were supposed to resort to the trees of the cemetery. विपरीतजिह्वया जनितं माधुर्यं येषाम् (1) who talk sweet words by a false tongue (with kings); who talk sweetly with a tongue that is turned backwards (with parrots). ओष्ठमात्रे (ओष्ठे एव) प्रकटितः रागः (प्रीतिः, रक्तत्वं च) येषाम्. The hearts of the kings know no affection; it is only their words that are full of affection. The beak of the parrot is red. राजानः शुकाः इव. राजशुकाः—a variety of parrots. मुग्ध...मानस्य who is fooled and allured. नरेन्द्र...विष्टस्य that takes possession of a person by the power of a wizard (with वेताल); who is overcome by the power of his king (with servant). For नरेन्द्र in the sense of wizard, see p. 33. न कि...तः there is nothing that he will not do (with both) वेताल and servant. चित्रधनुष इव like a painted bow. अलीकं गुणाध्यारोपणं एव एका क्रिया तस्यां नित्यनम्रस्य—the painted bow is always bent and has a false (*i. e.* unreal, painted) string placed upon it. The servant is also humble and solely engaged in ascribing false virtues to his master. निर्वाणं (extinguished) तेजः यस्य (with धनुषः and पुरुषस्य). The pictured bow has not the force of the real one. संमार्जन्या (broom-stick) समुपार्जितं रजः (dust) येन—the servant has to scour the dust off the floor by a broom-stick; dust is accumulated by a broom-stick and thrown on अवकरकूट. अवकरकूटः heep of sweepings. 'संमार्जनी शोधनी स्यात् सङ्करोऽवकरस्तया । क्षिप्ते' अम॰. निर्माल्यम् flowers used and cast off. These may be thrown on the heap of sweepings; the servant is often given what his master has worn. Besides the word may suggest that he wears no माल्य (flowers, which produce beauty and are a sign of happiness). C and T suggest that निर्माल्य may mean purity. We fail to see how; and even if it does, it cannot be made to fit in here. कटुकै...मानस्य—the servant is worried by the sharp words of his master; or कटुक has the same sense as on p. 54 l. 14 (text). A man suffering from कफ is treated with कटुक (bitters). See अष्टाङ्गहृदय I. 13. 10. 'श्लेष्मणो विधिना युक्तं तीक्ष्णं वमनरेचनम् । अन्नं रूक्षाल्पतीक्ष्णोष्णं कटुतिक्तकषायकम् ॥.' कटुकं also means 'Ginger, long and black pepper'. सौगतस्य—बौद्धस्य. सुगत is a name of बुद्ध and सौगत means a follower of बुद्ध. अर्थशून्या (धनविरहिता, बाह्यवस्तुशून्या) विज्ञप्तिः (प्रार्थना, विज्ञानं च)

तया जनितं वैराग्यं यस्य. The servant becomes despondent because his requests are not followed by the bestowal of wealth and wants to be a भिक्षु. It is the doctrine of one of the Buddhist schools, called विज्ञानवादिन्, that there is no positively existing entity in the world. All that exists is a train of momentary cognitions. Compare 'बौद्धबुद्धिमिव निरालम्बनाम्' काद० p. 131; 'न जिनस्येवार्थवादशून्यानि दर्शनानि' हर्षचरित 2nd उच्छ्वास. निशा...माणस्य—the servant is hurried off on various errands even at night. बलि is offered to the Mâtṛis at the advent of night; compare मृच्छकटिक I 'मातृभ्यो बलिमुपहर.' For the मातृs, see p. 26. कुशयनेन जनिता...दुःखवृत्तिः यस्य—the servant's worry is aggravated by having to lie down on bad beds or on the bare ground. कु=पृथ्वी. A person in mourning has very slight bedding. See above p. 116. तुलायन्त्रम् seems to mean 'the water-wheel.' पश्चात्कृतं गौरवं येन who leaves aside all ideas of self-respect (with servant). पश्चात्कृतं गौरवं (weight) यस्य. The wheel is turned by a man with his hands. In front of him are the empty pots; those that are filled are farther away from him. The servant has to bow; the wheel goes down to bring up water. अतिकृपण very wretched. शिरसा...स्पृशतः—the idea is:—the servant is not content with bowing his head at the feet of his superiors; with his words also he worships them (sings panegyrics of them). The words suggest another sense. A very miserly person may not be satisfied even with the head of his debtor. दैन्येन सङ्कोचितं (contracted, mean) हृदयं तेन हृतः अवकाशः यस्याः. आहोपुरुषिका—'आहोपुरुषिका दर्पाद्या स्यात्सम्भावनात्मनि' अम० ('अहो पुरुषोऽहमित्यस्य भावः आहो०' क्षीर०)—confident self-respect. He is bereft of self-respect because in his heart contracted through meanness there is no room for it. उन्नति elevation (of thought or mind). धन...र्जयतः thinking of amassing riches, he secures trouble. स्व...वर्धयतः thinking that he is making himself prosper, he merely increases his humiliation. स्वं means 'wealth' also. सत्यपि...रचयतः who folds his hands in greed though there are forests scented with the perfume of various flowers. The idea is that the servant at a court should rather take to a life in the forest. There is a striking effect produced by taking वन in the sense of water, 'though there is water, yet he folds his hands in thirst.' The com. suggests another idea. तृष्णा stands for मृगतृष्णा; 'the servant is after a mirage, though there is water fragrant with flowers.' कृतं आगः (अपराधः) येन.

दर्श...जन्मनः—the painted flower is charming to behold, but useless; so is the court attendant. For वैधेय see p. 122. अपशब्दं (अपगतशब्दं मूकं) मुखं यस्य; अपशब्दाः मुखे यस्य. The fool has in his mouth ungrammatical (or, vulgar) words. The courtier, though he knows, cannot speak out his mind and so is silent. There is a contradiction in विदुषः and वैधेयस्य (if he is a पण्डित, he cannot be a fool). श्वित्रिन् a leper, a person suffering from white leprosy. सङ्कोचितं करयुगलं यस्य. समानां तुल्यानां समुत्कर्षेषु. सम...पच्यमानस्य when his equals are raised to a higher position (than his own), he is boiled without fire. He suffers the same torments as boiling would inflict. नीच...म्रियमाणस्य when his inferiors are brought up to his level, he is dying without actually perishing. दुःखा...वृतेः on account of the wind of pain, he has no rest (he gets no happiness in service). The wind allows no rest (tranquility निर्वृति) to a lamp. ज्वलतो...भक्तस्य he is worried in attending court, he is devoted and yet not endowed (by his master with gifts). There is a suggestion of boiled rice (भक्त) also in which case अभक्त means 'without boiled rice'. निरूष्मणः०-he has no heat (pride) and yet he causes heat (pain) to his relatives (who feel for his low position). वि...कस्य though he is disrespected, yet he has no alternative (and remains where he is). There is another sense 'though a विमान (aerial car or chariot), yet he has no motion.' च्युतं गौरवं (respect, weight) यस्य. What has weight goes down. Though he is given no respect, yet he bends (in homage). निःसत्त्व spiritless; that has no being with him. महा...कुर्वतः he sells human flesh *i. e.* his own body (to his master). For महामांस, see p. 72. Without an animal, no मांस can be had and sold. नि...वृत्तेः though free from intoxication, yet not master of himself. मद also means 'pride.' The court servant is under the control of another. One intoxicated totters. ध्यानेन वशीकृतः आत्मा यस्य येन वा. The courtier's mind is absorbed in contemplating (ध्यान) how to acquire wealth. ध्यान is one of the eight *Angas* of योग. 'यमनियमासनप्राणायामप्रत्याहारधारणाध्यानसमाधयोऽष्टावङ्गानि (योगस्य)' योगसूत्र II. 29. A *Yogin* controls his mind (आत्मा). 'योगश्चित्तवृत्तिनिरोधः' योगसूत्र I. 2. अयोगिन् also means 'one that has no luck or armour.' योगः = दैवयोगः. 'योगः संनहनोपायध्यानसङ्गतियुक्तिषु' अम०. दग्धं मुण्डं यस्य—the servant's head is burnt by the heat of the sun, when going on errands. दग्धमुण्ड was the name of a sect of ascetics according to the com. शय्यायाः उत्थाय ०त्थायम्—gerund in अम् (णमुल)

दिवादनम्' अम०. कोणः fiddlestick; stick. वराक...भोगी if a wretched servant (is to be counted) among men, then even a राजिल will be a cobra. 'समौ राजिलडुण्डुभौ' अम० ('निर्विषो द्विमुखोऽहिः' क्षीर०). पुलाकः shrivelled grain 'स्यात्पुलाकस्तुच्छधान्ये' अम०. **'शालयः कलमाद्याश्च'** अम०. Put a vertical line after कलमः. वरं...मानवता It is better that manliness (मानवता) be shown even for a moment by the man that respects himself. मानवता *instru.* of मानवत्. The student will notice how the same letters are repeated with different senses, as in यमक. न मत...मनस्विनः. The highminded do not approve of even the enjoyment of the sovereignty of three worlds by one who bows down (for it). नमतः goes with ०भोगः and मतः with मनस्विनः. अभिनन्दितः (welcomed) अस्मदीयः प्रणयः (friendship or request). परागतः come, arrived.

P. 121 l. 17—P. 122 l. 4 **राजापि...पादयोः**. कुमारदर्शनौत्सुक्येन स्वीकृतं (seized, engrossed) हृदयं यस्य. आत्मा...करणम् to offer oneself heart and soul captivates the great without roots and spells. For वशीकरण (magic power over the minds of others), roots and spells were required. But the fact that Kumāra devoted himself heart and soul to Harsha captivated the mind of the latter. प्रतिप्राभृतम् gifts in return (for those received). ०दूतैः अधिष्ठितं (supervised by). आत्मनापि by himself, so far as he was concerned. अमित्रमभिलक्ष्य = अभ्य० (अव्ययीभाव)—towards his enemy (the गौड king). For साधन, see above p. 130. आवासितम् encamped. मूर्च्छा...विवेश he entered the darkness of a swoon. प्रतीहारस्य निवारणेन निभृतः निःशब्दः परिजनः यस्मिन् where attendants were motionless and speechless by the prohibition of the doorkeeper. The principal sentence is अथ भण्डिः एकेनैव वाजिना...राजद्वारमाजगाम. निखाताः बहवः लोहकीलकाः तेषां परिकरः (समूहः) तेन रक्षितं स्फुटनं यस्य the breaking of which was prevented by an array of numerous iron nails implanted in it. Nails prevent a tottering structure from giving way. The poet fancies that the numerous points of arrows on his chest were nails implanted to prevent his heart from breaking through grief (for राज्यवर्धन). Understand उपलक्षितः after हृदयेन. हृदयलग्नैः resting on or reaching his chest (with beard); deeply impressed on the heart (with ०सत्कृतैः). स्वामिसत्कृतैः the honours bestowed on him by his master. For the growing of the beard in sorrow, see p. 118. दूरीकृतः (given up) व्यायामः तेन शिथिलः भुजदण्डः तस्मिन् दोलायमानं मङ्गलवलयं एव एका केवला शेषालङ्कृतिः यस्य—The only ornament he wore was a single auspicious bracelet (on the left hand) that moved up and down owing to his arm being languid. For the wearing of bracelets by men see pp. 15, 46. अनादरेण (without particular care) उपयुक्तं (भुक्तं) ताम्बूलं तेन विरलः रागः (रक्तत्वं) यस्य. Supply उपलक्षितः after अधरेण. He was careless in taking betel; therefore his lip was faint in colour. The poet fancies that the lip was a coal from his heart burning with grief, which (coal) was pressed out by the force of his deep sighs. ०विरहे विधृतं जीवितं एव अपराधः तेन वैलक्ष्यं (विलक्षस्य भावः) तस्मात्—as if through embarrassment (or shame) at the fault of continuing to live though his master was dead. One abashed covers his face with his garment. His face was covered with tears. Tears (being bright) resemble the hem of a white garment. विशन्निव अपत्रयया स्वाङ्गं अङ्गैः Through shame his limbs appeared to be entering his own body (*i. e.* his body was shrunk). वमन्निव—he heaved deep and hot sighs, which, the poet fancies, were the warmth of his valour emitted by him because it was useless (as he could not save राज्यवर्धन). मुषितः robbed. छलितः cheated. वेग...णः a young elephant. For वेगदण्ड, see p. 174. सूर्या...करः—there is a suggested sense. सूर्य stands for राज्यवर्धन and कमला means लक्ष्मी. दुर्योधननिधनेन दुर्मनाः (sad). द्रौणिः son of द्रोण *i. e.* अश्वत्थामा. See शल्यपर्व 65 'वार्तिकाणां सकाशात्तु श्रुत्वा दुर्योधनं हतम्। हतशिष्टास्ततो राजन् कौरवाणां महारथाः। ... ततो द्रौणिर्महाराज बाष्पपूर्णेक्षणः श्वसन्।' 12. दुर्योधन...र्मनाः also means 'who (Bhandin) was sad on account of the death of (राज्यवर्धन) who was hard to fight with.' अपहृतं रत्नं (राज्यवर्धनरूपं) यस्य. अपहृतानि रत्नानि यस्य (with सागरः).

P. 122 ll. 5–34 **अवनि...कैस्ताम्.** उत्थाय...द्गम्य he got up and went out a few steps to receive him. For व्यतिकर, see pp. 72, 130. देवभूयं गते—see above p. 150. गुप्तः इति नाम यस्य तेन. See Introduction for the significance of this. कुशस्थलम्—seems to be the same as कान्यकुब्ज. In the रामायण (I. 32) we are told that कुश, son of ब्रह्मा, had four sons, one of whom कुशनाभ founded the city of महोदय, which is identified with कान्यकुब्ज. कुशनाभ's son was गाधि. कान्यकुब्ज is designated गाधिनगर in a grant of जयचन्द्र of Kanoj. See I. A. Vol. 15 p. 6, 7. किं...पदिभिः what is the use of other seekers (for राज्यश्री) ? अनुपदिन्—'अन्वेष्टानुपदी समौ' क्षीर०. परित्यक्तं अन्यक्लृप्तं येन. कारितं ०वपनकर्म येन who was made to shave &c. शारीरिक for the body; or rather the meaning is 'he sent flowers, unguents &c., which he had meant for himself'. सपरिबर्ह together with the equipage

(paraphernalia). 'परिच्छदे नृपार्हेऽर्थे **परिबर्हः**' अम०. करिणः, हरीन् and the following nouns in the accusative are governed by दर्शयाम्बभूव. ०गण्डान् qualifies करिणः. ०मदः मदिरा इव तस्याः आमोदेन मुखराणां मधुकराणां जूटः तेन जटिलः करटः (cheek) पट्टः इव तेन पङ्किलः गण्डः (face) येषाम्. गण्ड...क्रमान्—the elephants looked like moving rocks. '**गण्डशैलास्तु** च्युताः स्थूलोपला गिरेः' अमरः ('च्युताः भूकम्पादिना गलिताः' क्षीर०). गम्भीरः गर्जितरवः येषाम् (with जलधरान्); गम्भीरगर्जितवत् रवः येषाम् (with करिणः). Both clouds and elephants are dark. सप्तच्छद is the same as Marathi सातवीण. The odour of the ichor was like the scent of the सप्तच्छद, which blossoms in शरद्. चारु... हरीन् the horses had chowries with gold work on their heads. Note for the चामरs on horse's heads 'निष्कम्पचामरशिखा निभृतोर्ध्वकर्णाः' शाकुन्तल I. हरिणस्य इव रंहः (वेगः) येषाम्. बाला...वर्षिणाम् that shed a mass of light mellow like that of morn. किरणै...दिशाम् that covered the quarters with many rain-bows on account of their rays. ०कृतः (wonderful) qualifies हारान्. स्मरेण उन्मादिताः मालव्यः तेषां कुचपरिमलेन दुर्ललितान् (fondled, caressed). The necklaces had once rolled on the breasts of Malva females and rubbed off the sandal applied by them to their bosom. तारान् bright. There is a pun here. तारा means a star. A star has only a twinkling light. The हारs, though तार, flooded the world with their light. उडुपतिः चन्द्रः तस्य पादानां (किरणानां) सञ्चयवत् शुचीनि शुभ्राणि. निज० refers to Harsha. जातरूपमयं नालं यस्य the handle of which was made of gold. लक्ष्मी dwells in a white lotus. The white umbrella resembled पुण्डरीक and the handle resembled a lotus-stalk. वारविलासिनीः dancing girls. बहूनि समररसेण साहसानि तस्मिन् अनुरागः तेन अवतीर्णाः. The Apsarases are represented as fond of heroes and as welcoming them to heaven. See above p. 101. Here the damsels are represented as Apsarases come down on earth out of their fondness for gallant deeds. आसन्दी chair of state. 'आसन्दी पीठिका' क्षीर०. ससंख्यानि आलेख्यपत्राणि येषु which were accompanied with written records giving the number (in each chest). अलङ्काराणां आपीडस्य पीडा तया सह सा० that groaned under (the weight of) the wreaths of ornaments. If we read ०पेडापीडान् the meaning will be 'that were wreathed with small bags (पेडा) of ornaments.' यथा...कारम् according to their respective functions.

P. 123 l. 1—P. 124 l. 24 **अथ...वसदिति.** The principal sentence is अथ प्रविशन् दूरादेव...वनग्रामकं ददर्श तत्रैव च अवसत्. दह्यमान... दधानैः—this clause qualifies वनप्रदेशैः (l. 4)—that were rendered grey by the smoke of granaries (बीजधानी) of wild corn, in which (granaries) fire flared up on account of heaps of smouldering षष्टिक chaff. षष्टिकः a kind of rice ripening in sixty days from the day of sowing. 'षष्टिका. षष्टिरात्रेण पच्यन्ते' पा. 5. 1. 90. ०विसरैः विसारी विभावसुः (अग्निः) यासु (*adj.* of ०धानीनाम्). ०शाखासञ्चयेन रचितानि गोवाटानि (cowpens) तैः वेष्टिताः विकटाः (large) वटाः येषु.०रोषेण रचितानि व्याघ्रयन्त्राणि येषु—where tiger-traps had been placed in wrath at the slaughter of young calves. वत्सस्येव रूपं येषां ते वत्सरूपकाः that were like their own children. अयन्त्रितैः (uncontrolled) वनपालैः हठेन (forcibly) ह्रियमाणाः परग्रामीणानां काष्ठिकानां (wood-cutters) कुठाराः यस्मिन्. The reading यन्त्रित० is not suitable. C and T render it by 'zealous.' ०षण्डे निर्मितः चामुण्डामण्डपः येषु. चामुण्डामण्डप seems to mean 'a flimsy structure used as a temple of Durgā.' प्रकाश्यमानम् qualifies वनग्रामकं (text p. 69 l. 24). अटवीप्रायः प्रान्तः यस्य स ०प्रान्तः तस्य भावः. ०प्रान्तता तया—as the forest settlement was bordered on all sides by forest (the villagers found it hard to secure fields for cultivation). कुद्दालप्राया कृषिः येषाम् whose agriculture depended almost on spades *i. e.* they had no ploughs and no oxen. कृषीवलैः is to be connected with भज्यमान०. अविद्यमानाः बलीवर्दाः येषाम् (*adj.* of कृषी०). अवलद्भिः who did not hasten, who were slow. This does not yield a good sense. A and C omit अबलीवर्दैः and read अबलवद्भिः. It is probable that अवलद्भिः is a mistake for अबलवद्भिः. भज्यमानानि भूरीणि शालिखलक्षेत्राणां खण्डलकानि यस्मिन्. उच्च...खण्डलकम् where many small pieces of rice-fields and threshing grounds were being divided (by farmers) in high-pitched language. खलः—लम्—threshing floor. क्षेत्र is to be connected with शालि and खल. उच्चः भागः यस्य तत् ०भागं भाषितम्. भाग seems to be redundant. The reading भज्यमानभूरिखिलक्षेत्र० is better. The meaning would be 'where many pieces of waste land (खिलक्षेत्रं) were being broken by farmers accompanied with talk on higher ground or with loud talk.' अल्पावकाशैः—of small extent. This and the following instrumentals qualify केदारैः (l. 9). काशि...कठिनैः that abounded in काश grass and that were hard with black soil resembling iron. स्थानस्थानेषु स्थापिताः स्थाणवः तेभ्यः उत्थिताः स्थूलाः पल्लवाः येषु. Trees had been cut off from the fields, leaving only the trunks imbedded in the earth, which again put forth vigorous foliage. दुरुपगमा श्यामाकप्ररूढिः येषु in which the growth of श्यामाक was impenetrable. श्यामाक is a kind of grain. अल...क्षुपैः that abounded in अलम्बुस and were thick with कोकिलाक्ष bushes. 'ह्रस्वशाखाशिफः क्षुपः'

अम०. नातिप्रवृत्तं गतागतं (गतं च आगतं च तयोः समाहारः) तेन अप्रहता भूः यस्मिन् (*adj.* of वनग्रामकं)—where the earth was not trodden because there was not much coming and going. क्षेत्राणां समीपे उप० (अव्य०). मञ्चै...द्रुमम् where the (high) platforms (or scaffolds for watchmen to sleep on) suggested the depredations of wild beasts. The next clause is दिशि दिशि च...अटवीप्रवेशप्रपाणां शैत्येन त्याजयन्तमिव ग्रैष्ममुष्माणम् (l. 20). All the genitives in this clause qualify ०प्रपाणां. प्रति...कृतानाम् (प्रपाs) made of (or, under) trees growing about the roads. पथिक...छायानाम्—Travellers walking barefooted used leaves to wipe off (प्रस्फोटन) the dust off their feet and left the leaves at the प्रपा when they started. Compare 'विश्रान्तकार्पटिकप्रस्फोटितचरणधूलिधूसरकिसलयलाञ्छितोपकण्ठैः' काद० p. 223 l. 15. अटवीसुलभानि सालकुसुमानि तेषां स्तबकैः अञ्चिता (marked, decked) नवखाता (recently dug) कूपिका तस्याः उपकण्ठे (समीपे) प्रतिष्ठिताः नागस्फुटाः यासु. नागस्फुट or–टा seems to be some kind of bush. अच्छिद्रैः (closely woven) कटैः (straw mats) कल्पितं कुटीरकं (hut) यासु. कुटिला कीटानां (insects, flies) वेणी (row, line) तया वेष्ट्यमाना शक्तुशारा (spotted with barley meal) शरावश्रेणी (lines of platters) तया श्रितानाम् (०प्रपानाम्). अध्वगजनेन जग्धानि जम्बूफलानि तेषां अस्थिभिः (stones) शबलाः समीपभुवः यासाम्. जम्बूफल is Marathi जांभूळ. उद्धूलिता धूली येषां ते ०धूलीकाः कदम्बस्तबकाः तेषां प्रकरेण पुलकिनीनाम्. C and T take धूलीकदम्ब to be a tree, which also is good. Bunches of कदम्ब flowers the pollen of which was scattered about were lying near the प्रपाs and resembled hair (पुलकः) standing on end. रोमाञ्च is often compared to कदम्ब flowers. Compare 'अनिलैरपि कदम्बकेसरोत्करवाहिभिः कण्टकितैरिवानुगतम्' काद० p. 217; 'ततोऽपि घनजलधारासीकरपुलकितकाया कदम्बकलिकेव' काद० p. 254. See also उत्तरराम III. 'सस्वेदरोमाञ्चित' &c. कण्टकितं कर्करीचक्रं तेन आक्रान्ता काष्ठमञ्चिका (wooden stand) तया मुषिता तृट् (thirst) यासु. कर्करी a water jar. The idea expressed by कण्टकित is :—the porous jars had very small particles of water (due to cooled vapour) on their outside which resembled hair standing on end. C and T translate 'bristling' and suggest that the jars contained grass stalks. तिम्यत् (wet) तलं यासां ताः ०तलाः शीतलाः सिकतिलाः (porous) कलश्यः ताभिः शमितः श्रमः यासु. For सिकतिल, see p. 30. आश्यानेन (partially dry, moist) शैवलेन श्यामलितः अलिञ्जरः (a large pitcher) तेन जायमानः जलस्य जडिमा (coldness) यासु. उदकुम्भेभ्यः आकृष्टानि पाटलशर्कराशकलानि तैः शिशिरीकृता दिक् यासु. What पाटलशर्करा means is not clear. C and T translate 'pink gravel'. But compare 'पटुपाटलशर्करामोदमुचि' above (text p. 22 l. 30), where पाटलशर्करा is said to have a fragrance. It was probably 'a lump of red raw sugar.' घटमुखेषु घटितानि (formed) कटहारेण (by a rope of straw) पाटलापुष्पपुटानि यासु. पाटला is a plant with red flowers. If we read करहाट it will mean 'with the fibrous root of a lotus'. शीकरेण पुलकिताः (bristling) पल्लवाः तेषां पूल्या पाल्यमानाः (preserved) शोष्याः (liable to wither) सरसाः शिशवः सहकाराः (mangotrees) तेषां फलानां जूटी तया जटिलाः स्थाणवः (pillars) यासाम् (*adj.* of प्रपानाम्). This seems to be a description of the care taken to preserve young grafted mango plants. विश्राम्यन्तः कार्पटिकाः तेषां पेटकाः (समूहाः) तेषां परिपाट्यः (successive rows) ताभिः पीयमानं पयः यासु. For कार्पटिक, see p. 166. अटवी...ष्माणम् that was made to give up the heat of summer by the coolness of the water arbours at the entrances to the forest. त्याजयन्तम् qualifies वनग्रामकम् below. प्रपा पानीयशालिका—Marathi पाणपोई. ग्राहय...व्योकारैः—we have to understand ग्रैष्ममुष्माणम् with ग्राहयन्तम्—that was made to take up the heat of summer by blacksmiths that burnt heaps of wood for charcoal. 'व्योकारो लोहकारकः' अम०. The next clause is a very long one सर्वतश्च...व्याप्तदिगन्तरम् (text p. 69 l. 7). Read **०वासिना** for ०वासिनाम्. This and the following instrumentals are connected with ०लोकेन (l. 26). प्राति...वासिना that dwelt in the neighbouring district (विषयः). समासन्नेषु ग्रामगृहेषु स्थापितैः स्थविरैः परिपाल्यमानेन पाथेयेन (provisions) स्थगितः (covered, surrounded) तेन (*adj.* of ०लोकेन). पथि साधु पाथेयम्, according to 'पथ्यतिथिवसतिस्वपतेर्ढञ्' पा. 4. 4. 104. See p. 67 on वासतेयी. कृतः दारुण—दारुव्यायामयोग्यः अङ्गाभ्यङ्गः येन that had rubbed their body with oil befitting their hard toil in the forest. अभ्यङ्ग removes fatigue. स्कन्धं अध्यासितः कठोरकुठारः यस्य स ०कुठारः कण्ठे लम्बमानं प्रातराशपुटं यस्य स ०पुटः, ०कुठारश्चासौ ०पुटश्च तेन. प्रातराशः breakfast. पाटच्चराणां (चौराणां) प्रत्यवायेन (obstacle) प्रतिपन्नं पटच्चरं (rags) येन. 'पटच्चरं जीर्णवस्त्रं' अम०. कालवेत्रकस्य (black cane) त्रिगुणः (triple) व्रततिवलयपाशः तेन ग्रथिता (encircled) ग्रीवा तस्यां ग्रथितैः (fastened)–qualifies पीतकुटैः. पत्रवीटया (a bundle of leaves used as a cork) आवृतं मुखं येषाम्. We must read पीतकुटैः. Compare कुटहारिका above p. 28. ऊढं (carried) वारि येन (*adj.* of ०लोकेन). पुरःसरौ: वलन्तौ (moving, quick) बलीवर्दौ तयोः युगं (pair). तेन सरतीति ०सरेण. Or युगं may mean 'yoke'. For वलत् some read बलवत्. निकटे भवः नैकटिकः. कुटुम्बिन् a peasant. ०लोकेन is to be connected with व्याप्तदिगन्तरम् below (p. 69 l. 7). श्वापदानां व्यधनं (shooting) तदर्थं व्यवधानानि (screens) तेषां बहली तस्यां समारोपिताः कुटीकृताः (twisted) कूटपाशाः (traps) यैः (*adj.* of व्याधैः). बहली seems to mean 'heap'. गृहीतानि मृगतन्तवः तन्त्रयः जालवलयानि वागुराश्च यैः. The मृगतन्तुs (animal sinews) were for mending nets; the lutes (तन्त्रीs) for luring the deer. Or मृग...तन्त्री may mean 'strings made of animals' sinews.' बहिः विचरद्भिः व्याधैः (व्याप्तदिगन्तरम्). The hunters wandered outside the वनग्रामक. अंसे अवसक्तः (attached to, fixed) वीतंसः (aviary) तेन व्यालम्बमानाः (hanging about, loitering) बालपाशिकाः येषाम् (*adj.* of शाकुनिकैः). बालपाशिकः a boy hunter. सङ्गृहीताः ०जलादीनां पञ्जरकाः (cages) यैः. ग्राहकः falcon. ककरः partridge. शाकुनिक—शकुनान् हन्ति इति—according to 'पक्षिमत्स्यमृगान् हन्ति' पा. 4. 4. 35 च्युतः लासकलेशः तेन लिप्ता लता तस्यां वधूलट्वाः तासु लम्पटानाम् (eagerly following). लासकः soup, broth. लट्व means a भ्रमरक according to क्षीर०. C and T translate वधूलट्वा as 'female sparrows.' पैटकैः goes with व्याप्तदिगन्तरम्. पाशिक—a fowler. तृणस्तम्बेन अन्तरितः (concealed) तित्तिरिः तेन तरलायमानं (rendered restive) कौलेयककुलं तस्य चाटुकारैः that coaxed the dogs &c. ०मृगयां is the object of क्रीडद्भिः. मृगयुयुवभिः by youths that were hunting. परिणतः (fully grown) चक्रवाकः तस्य कण्ठवत् कषाया रुक् (colour) येषाम् (वल्कलानाम्). शीधव्यानाम्—what tree is meant is not clear. कलापान्—connect this and the following accusatives with आदाय (l. 5). धातोः इव त्विट् येषाम् the hue of which was like metallic ore (such as गैरिक). गोणीः अगणिताः countless bags. धातकीपुष्प is very red. पिचव्यानां च (गोणीः) and of cotton plants. अतसी...मूलकानां of cloth made from a quantity of flax and of radish. The reading अतसीशणपूलकानां is easier 'of bundles of flax and hemp.' मधुनो माक्षिकस्य of honey derived from bees. मयूराङ्गजस्य of peacock's tails. अक्लिष्टं (untouched by anyone else) मधूच्छिष्टं (wax) तस्य चक्रं (balls) तेषां मालानाम्. लम्बमाना लामज्जकजूटजटा येषाम् (*adj.* of ०काष्ठानाम्). लामज्जकम् is the root of a fragrant grass. अपगता त्वक् येषां (barkless). कुष्ठ—a kind of plant, with a fragrant adour. बभ्रु tawny. रोध्र a tree with white or red flowers. Construe भारकान् आदाय व्रजता लोकेन (व्याप्त०). प्रविचितैः (gathered) ०फलैः पूरिताः पिटकाः मस्तके यासाम्. अभ्य...गत्वरीभिः hastening to the neighbouring villages. The next clause is इतस्ततश्च...संस्कारम् (l. 9). युक्ताः (yoked) शूराः शकुराः (tame) शाकराः (oxen) यासु (*adj.* of श्रेणीनाम्). पुराण...हिनीनां carrying heaps of dry cowdung (करीषं) and old dust-heaps. उत्करः heap. धूर्गताः (sitting on the poles) धूलिधूसराः सैरिकाः तैः सरोषस्वरेण सार्यमाणानाम् that were being driven with angry voices by ploughmen &c. सैरिक—सीरं वहति इति—'हलसीराट्ठक्' पा. 4. 4. 81. सैरिभ would mean 'a buffalo.' संक्रीडन्ति (creaking) चटुलानि (loose) चक्राणि तैः चीत्कारिणीनाम् (noisy). सम्पातः multitude. संपाद्यमानः दुर्बलोर्व्या विरूक्षाणां क्षेत्राणां संस्कारः यस्मिन् where the fields parched up on account of the poor soil were being prepared. आरक्ष...वृतिभिः—*adj.* of वाटैः. आरक्षार्थं (for protection) क्षिप्तः क्षिप्रः

दान्तवाहकदण्डः तेन उड्डीयमानैः हरिणैः हेलया (लीलया) लङ्घिता तुङ्गा वैणवा वृतिः (hedge of bamboos) येषाम्. दान्तः (an ox broken to the yoke) +वाहकः driver. निखातः (implanted) गौरस्य (buffalo) करङ्कः (skeleton) यस्मिन् सः ०करङ्कः'. शङ्कुः (a dart, stake) तस्मात् शङ्कितैः शशकैः शकलिताः तुङ्गाः शुङ्गाः येषाम्. शुङ्गः the sheath or calyx of a bud. प्रयत्नेन प्रभृताः (nourished) विशङ्कटाः (large) विटपाः येषाम्. वाटैः ऐक्षवैः gardens of sugarcane. ऐक्षव—from इक्षु. ०कण्ठम् (*adj.* of वनग्रामकम्). अतिविप्रकृष्टं अन्तरं येषाम्. This and the following instrumentals qualify गृहैः below. स्नुहा the milk-hedge plant. कार्मुककर्मणि साधुः ०कर्मण्यः वंशः तस्य विटपैः सङ्कटानि (full of). ०गर्मुतां गुल्मैः गहना गृहवाटिका येषाम्. उरुबूकः = एरण्डः castor plant. वचा, वङ्कक and सुरस are various plants. सूरण—Marathi सुरण. शिग्रु—Marathi शेगवा or शेगट. ग्रन्थिपर्ण is a fragrant कन्द. गवेधुका a grass eaten by cattle. गर्मुत् a kind of grass. निखातानि (planted in the earth) उच्चानि काष्ठानि तेषु आरोपितः काष्ठालुकलताप्रतानः तेन विहिता छाया येषु. परिमण्डल circular. परि... रूपैः where calves were tied to pegs of Khadira &c. For वत्सरूप see above p. 210. संनिवेशः situation. अङ्गना...वापिकैः.Here the text is unsatisfactory. What क्षिप्र...पूपिका means is not clear. अङ्गनागस्ति–the अगस्ति plant in the courtyard. पूपिका a sweet cake. वापिका tank. Some MSS. read क्षिप्रपूपिका. May we read क्षिप्त for क्षिप्र (the meaning being 'where there were tanks constructed under the courtyard अगस्ति plants, on which (tanks) were thrown (क्षिप्त) cakes for birds'). विकीर्णानि बदराणां पाटलानि पटलानि (heaps) येषु. ०मयवृतिभि विहिताः भित्तयः येषु the walls of which were made of fences consisting of slips (पोटः) of bamboo, leaves (दलं), stalks and reeds (शरः). नलः means 'a kind of reed.' किंशुक...राशिभिः hardly yields a sense. So read ०रोचनाविरचितमण्डनैः बल्वज०. किंशुकैः रोचनया च रचितं मण्डनं येषाम्. किंशुक is a red flower without fragrance. बल्वजैः बद्धः अङ्गारराशिः येषु where a heap of charcoal was tied with बल्वज grass. संनिहिताः...तण्डुलाः येषु. नलशालिः rice from नल reeds (probably देवभात). शालूकं roots of waterlily. 'शालूकमेषां कन्दः स्यात्' अम०. खण्ड candied sugar. We must read with B ०हीततमालबीजैः. भस्ममलिनाः म्लानैः काश्मर्यकूटैः व्याधृताः कटाः येषु where mats were dusty with ashes and full of heaps of drying काश्मर्य plants. आश्यानानि (partially dry) ... फलानि तैः स्फीतैः abounding. 'राजादनः फलाध्यक्षः' अम०. मधूक a flower of the मधूक tree. आसवः extract or decoction. कुसुम्भकुम्भाः गण्डे यस्य सः ०गण्डः कुसूलः(granary) येषाम् the granaries of which were filled to the mouth with pots of safflower. अविरहितानि...बीजानि येषु. राजमाषः a kind of bean. त्रपुषं cucumber. कर्कटिका species of cucumber. मालुधानः a kind of serpent. 'मालुधानो मातुलाहिः' अम०. It is hard to say what शालिजात and जातक are. वनग्रामकम्-a village settlement in a forest.

Uchchhvāsa VIII

Verse 1. दैवेनापि...सेवेव Even Fate as if serves beforehand the fortunate. The idea is:–there is no wonder that people pay homage to the fortunate; even Fate serves them, which is an earnest of the good things that are to be theirs at a later stage of their career. 'फलकल्याणयोर्भव्यम्' क्षीर०. *Verse 2.* सम्पर्कः union, association. नष्टः इष्टः ज्ञातिः (बन्धुः, स्वजनः) तस्य दर्शनमेव अभ्युदयः. कस्य...भवति—the answer expected is सर्वस्यैव सुखाय भवति. It is better to read भुवने. भवने would mean 'in the house.' Both the verses are suggestive of the events narrated in this उच्छ्वास. हर्ष is to meet a sage in the person of दिवाकरमित्र, he further finds his sister and receives a wonderful necklace from दिवाकरमित्र.

P. 125 l. 5—**P. 126** l. 13 **अथापरे...गोचरमिति.** The principal sentence is एकदा तु भूपतेः भ्रमत एव...व्याघ्रकेतुर्नाम कुतोऽपि...शबरयुवानमादायाजगाम. भूप...एव while the king was wandering. आटविकसामन्तः a feudatory dwelling in the forest. अटव्यां भवः आटविकः. ललाटस्य उपरि अधिललाटम् (अव्ययीभाव). श्यामलता—is a creeper called 'गन्धप्रियङ्गु' according to क्षीर०. कृतः मौलिबन्धः यस्य—whose hair was tied. This and the following accusatives qualify शबरयुवानम् below. 'चूडाकिरीटकेशाश्च संयता मौलयस्त्रयः' अम०. अन्धकारिणीं dark (*adj.* of ललाटस्थलीं). अका...यामामिव which resembled night on account of the frown of his eyebrow divided into three branches, which (frown) was natural (not due to any particular cause). Emphasis is laid on the word त्रि. Night is divided into *three* watches; his brow was dark and naturally covered with *three* wrinkles. So it is like त्रियामा. Night causes darkness (अन्धकारिणी). तिस्रः शाखाः यस्य. साहस० applies to both. Night is the friend of adventures; his forehead was always with him in adventures. साहसानां or साहसेषु सहचारिणी. अवतंसितः (made into an ear-ornament) एकः शुकस्य पक्षकः (wing) तस्य प्रभया हरितायमानेन (looking green). पिनद्धा (tied) काचरा (glass-like) काचमणेः (crystal) कर्णिका (ear-ring) यस्मिन्. For कर्णिका, see p. 106. चुल्ल blear-eyed. 'स्युः क्लिन्नाक्षे चुल्ल—चिल्लपिल्लाः क्लिन्नेऽक्ष्णि चाप्यमी' अम. प्रविरलं पक्ष्म (eye-lashes) यस्य. सहजेन...क्षरन्तम् The blood of a hyena is employed as a medicine. His eyes were naturally red and therefore it appeared as if his eyes let fall the blood of a hyena useful in preparing Rasāyanas. रोचिः = दीप्तिः. 'तरक्षुस्तु मृगादनः'. तरक्षोः इदं तारक्षवम्. क्षतजम् = रुधिरम्. अवनाटा (नता low) नासिका यस्य.

'अवटीटोऽवनाटश्चावभ्रटो नतनासिके' अम०. चिपिटः (thick, large) अधरः यस्य. चिकिनं (flat) चिबुकं (chin) यस्य. अहीना (full) हनुः (chin) तस्यां उत्कटः (prominent) कपोलकूटास्थिपर्यन्तः यस्य—the tops of whose round cheek bones were prominent over a full chin. ईषत् अवाग्रः (अवनतः) ग्रीवाबन्धः यस्य whose neck was slightly bent. स्कन्नः (drooping) स्कन्धस्य अर्धभागः यस्य. अनवरतं कोदण्डस्य (धनुषः) कुण्डलीकरणं (bending) तेन कर्कशः (hard) व्यायामः तेन विस्तारितेन. अंसल strong 'बलवान्मांसलोंऽसलः' अम०. उरसा...गिरेः who as if laughed at the breadth of the rock on the slopes of the Vindhya by his chest that was &c. अजगरः a huge serpent said to swallow goats. लघयन्तम् ridiculing, casting into the shade. तुहिनशैलः हिमालयः तस्मिन् शालद्रुमाः तेषाम्. द्राघिमाणं (लघयन्तम्)—his arms were long like the शाल tree. वराह...प्रकोष्ठे on his forearm the back of which was thickly covered with a mass of the roots of the नागदमन plant which was fastened with the hair of a boar. ०बालैः वलितं बन्धनं यासाम्. 'नागदमनो विषहर ओषधिभेदः । जूटिका लघुमूलम् । वाटिका पूल्यः' com. गो... चित्रम् decorated with गोदन्त beads. According to the com. 'decked with the head gem of गोदन्त serpents.' गोदन्तं yellow orpiment, white fossil substance. त्रापुषं made of tin (from त्रपु, according to 'त्रपुजतुनोः षुक्' पा. 4. 3. 138). See जातुष p. 124. अतु...भम् though not fat, he had a prominent navel. 'वृद्धनाभौ तुण्डिलतुण्डिभौ' अम०. 'तुन्दिवलिवटेर्भः' पा. 5. 2 139 (वृद्धा नाभिस्तुन्दिः । सि. कौ.). तुण्डिभ also means 'fat' and hence the apparent contradiction. अहीरमणी (according to com.) a serpent with two heads. The other reading अहीरणि means the same thing. ०चर्मणा निर्मिते पट्टिके तयोः—inside (*i. e.* between) two strips of the skin of &c. चित्रा (variegated) चित्रकत्वक् तया तारकितः (spotted) परिवारः (scabbard) यस्याः (*adj.* of कृपाण्या). चित्रक seems to be a kind of serpent. सङ्कुब्जं अजिनं तेन जालकितया that was encased in a contracted deer skin. What सङ्कुब्ज means is not clear. C and T translate 'short'. शृङ्गमयः (made of horn) मसृणः (smooth, glossy) मुष्टिभागः (handle) तेन भास्वरया. मस्तकं end. कृपाण्या...प्रदेशम् whose broad loins were made formidable by a dagger. For विशङ्कट (written also as विसङ्कट), see p 122. प्रथमयौवनेन उल्लिख्यमानः (being pared or thinned) मध्यभागः (waist) तस्मात् भ्रष्टं मांसं तेन भरितौ. By exercise in youth his waist became thin and his thighs thick. The poet fancies that the flesh from the reduced waist went to the thighs. अच्छभल्लः bear. भल्ली... भृता—bearing numerous arrows most of which were crescent-shaped. All the instrumentals qualify भल्लाभरणेन. शबल...पीडितेन made fast with a broad spotted tiger skin. अलिकुलेन or कुलवत् कालानि कम्बललोमानि यस्य the blanket-like hair of which (bear's skin) was dark with (or like) &c. भस्त्रा...दर्शयन्तम् who exhibited a darkness as if blossoming with a quiver. भस्त्रा आभरणमिव. We must read कार्ष्ण्यं for कार्श्यम्. He was already dark enough and had a dark quiver and spotted tiger-skin &c., which looked like the पल्लव of darkness. उत्तर...शिखरे—this and the following locatives qualify दोषि. उत्तरत्रिभागे उत्तंसितं चाषपिच्छं तेन चारु शिखरं यस्य (arm) the top of which was charming with a blue jay's tail placed as an ornament on the upper third part of it (arm). 'पुंस्युत्तंसावतंसौ द्वौ कर्णपूरेऽपि शेखरे' अम०. खदिरजटानामिव निर्माणं यस्य the make or essence of which was (tough) like the fibres (or branches) of Khadira. The खदिर is a very tough tree. खरः प्राणः यस्य. 'शक्तिः पराक्रमः प्राणः' अम०. प्रचुरा मयूरपित्तेन पत्रलता (figures) तेन चित्रिता त्वक् यस्य. त्वचिसारः वंशः (bamboo) तद्वत् गुरुणि. वामस्कन्धे अध्यासितं धनुः यस्य. दोषि लम्बमानेन hanging from his arm. This and the following instrumentals qualify शशेन. अवाक् शिरः यस्य. शितशरेण कृतं एकं नलकविवरं तस्मिन् प्रवेशिता इतरा जङ्घा तेन जनितः स्वस्तिकबन्धः यस्य. स्वस्तिकबन्ध is a posture in योग in which the toes are placed in the inner hollow of the knee. 'जानूर्वोरन्तरे सम्यक् कृत्वा पादतले उभे। ऋजुकायो विशेन्मन्त्री स्वस्तिकं तत्प्रचक्षते ॥'. One leg of the hare was made to enter a cylindrical hole made in the other by a sharp arrow. For नलक, see above p. 173. बन्धूकवत् लोहिता रुधिरराजिः तया रञ्जितं (stained) घ्राणवर्त्म (nose) यस्य. वपुर्विततया व्यक्तं विभाव्यमानः कोमलक्रोडरोम्णां शुक्लिमा यस्य the whiteness of whose fine hair on the chest was clearly visible on account of its body being stretched out fully (as the hare hung from the arm of the forester). शितायां अटनीशिखायां (notched extremity of the bow) ग्रथिता (fastened) ग्रीवा यस्य—qualifies तित्तिरिणा. Separate च अपावृत &c. अपावृता (open) चञ्चुः तया उत्तानं ताम्रं तालु यस्य whose (of the partridge) red palate was displayed as its beak was wide open. वर्णकमुष्टि a handful of paints or unguents. वर्ण...दर्शयन्तम्—on his arm hung a partridge and a hare. These seemed to be unguents with which he had smeard his body when hunting. विषमेण (terrible, powerful) विषेण दूषितं वदनं यस्य (with विकर्णेन and ०हिना). विकर्ण- - a kind of arrow. मूलगृहीतेन held by the tail (with arrow); caught or subdued by some drug. व्यग्रं दक्षिणकराग्रं यस्य. तमाल has dark leaves and the शबर youth also was dark. यन्त्रो...भ्रमन्तम् he was like a moving pillar of solid stone cut out (chiselled) by a machine (from a mountain). अञ्जन...छेदम् a piece of collyrium slab. अयःसारः essence of iron. पाकलम्—He worked havoc among elephants, as fever does. For पाकल, see p. 5. कालपाशम् the noose of death. काल—he was also black. धूम...चक्राणाम् he was a comet (indicating the destruction of) to the multitude of lions. There is a pun on the word राजचक्र. A comet portends evil to kings. महानवमी—is the 9th of the bright half of आश्विन. The day is sacred to Durgā. See चतुर्वर्गचिन्तामणि व्रतखण्ड chap 13 p. 903 for महानवमी. 'अश्वयुक्शुक्लपक्षस्य अष्टमी मूलसंयुता । सा महानवमी नाम त्रैलोक्येऽपि सुदुर्लभा ॥...तस्यै ये ह्युपयुज्यन्ते प्राणिनो महिषादयः । सर्वे ते स्वर्गतिं यान्ति घ्नतां पापं न विद्यते ॥' p. 909. महः=उत्सवः. On this day goats and buffaloes were offered to the goddess Kālî or Durgā. हृदय...हिंसायाः in him one would have found the heart of destruction *i. e.* हिंसा at its highest. फलमिव—sin is represented as dark. He was the result of sin as it were. कलिकाल—Kali, the age of sin, is dark. कामु...रात्रेः the lover of the night of universal destruction. For कालरात्रि see p. 91. कालरात्रि—(also) dark night. He loved to start in pursuit of adventure on dark nights. सर्व...हरः the leader of all the chiefs of (forest) hamlets. स्वस्त्रीयः स्वसुरपत्यम्—sister's son. 'स्वसुश्छः' पा. 4. 1. 143. उप...यनम् he presented the present of the hare together with the partridge. उद्देशस्य=प्रदेशस्य. विहार...भवन्तः you are in the habit of wandering in the forest in these days. उदारं रूपं यस्याः of noble bearing or form.

P. 126 ll. 14–29 **निर्घातस्तु...गन्तुम्.** दर्शितः आदरः यथा स्यात्तथा. अपरिगताः without being known. अविद्यमानं अन्यत् कृत्यं येषाम्. इत...मात्रे एव only a *Kros'a* from this place. गव्यूति 'गव्यूतिः स्त्री क्रोशयुगम्' अम॰—from गो+यूति. मुनिमहिते honoured by sages. मही...षण्डे in a thicket of trees growing at the foot of a mountain chain. पिण्डपाती—पिण्डपातः अस्ति अस्य—living on alms. 'छात्रान्तेवासिनौ शिष्ये' अम॰. पाराशरी—see p. 127. स...वार्ताम् perhaps he may know some news. मैत्रायणीयः—belonging to the मैत्रायणीयशाखा of the Yajurveda. त्रयी—the three Vedas. 'स्त्रियामृक्सामयजुषी इति वेदास्त्रयस्त्रयी' अम॰. 'ब्राह्मणायनः द्विजवरिष्ठः' com. 'शुद्धसन्तानजो विप्रः' त्रिकाण्डशेष. उत्पन्ना समाधिः यस्य. उत्पन्न...मते who concentrated his mind on the doctrines of सुगत (बुद्ध) or who was reconciled to the doctrines of बुद्ध. काषायाणि—the red robes of a monk. इति is to be connected with श्रूयते. अभि...सर्वस्य good qualities (persons possessing) are fit to be approached by everyone. कस्य...मावः who would not look up to (with reverence) the position of an ascetic? धर्मगृहिणी the wife of धर्म *i. e.* intimately associated with धर्म. The idea is that even if a dullard takes to the life of an ascetic, respect is paid to him. ०मनांसि मुष्णातीति who wins the hearts &c. प्रास...कल्याणम् this is an accidental thing that has happened and that will be very auspicious to me. पश्यामः—governs जनम्. प्रयत्नेन प्रार्थितं दर्शनं यस्य.

P. 126 l. 30—**P. 127** l. 34 **अथ...गन्तुम्.** The principal sentence is अथ क्रमेण गच्छत एव तस्य...पुरस्ताद्दर्शनपथं अवतेरुः तरवः. तस्य =हर्षस्य. अ...नः full of fruits. 'वन्ध्योऽफलोऽवकेशी च' अम०. कुड्मलिताः कार्णिकाराः येषु. कर्णिकार has flowers of excellent colour but without fragrance. प्रचुराः (abundant) चम्पकाः येषु. स्फीताः फलेग्रहयः येषु in which some trees had abundant fruit. 'स्यादवन्ध्यः फलेग्रहिः'—फलानि गृह्णातीति—'फलेग्रहिरात्मम्भरिश्च' पा. 3. 2. 26. नमेरु is a kind of tree. नीलानि दलानि येषां ते ०दलाः नलदानां नारिकेलानां निकराः येषु. नलदं a kind of fragrant grass. हरिकेसरसरलाः परिकरे येषाम्. सरल is a tree. हरि yellowish. केसर 'चाम्पेयः केसरो नागकेसरः काञ्चनाह्वयः' अम०. कोरकनिकुरुम्बेण रोमाञ्चिताः कुरबकराजयः येषु in which rows of कुरबक trees bristled with heaps of buds. 'कलिका कोरकः पुमान्' अम०. 'निकुरम्बं कदम्बकम्' अम०. प्रविकसिताः केसराः तेषां रजोविसरेण बध्यमानः वासरधूसरिमा येषु. स्वरजसा सिकतिलं तिलकतलं येषु where the ground underneath तिलक trees was sandy with their own pollen. हिङ्गु assafoetida plant. पूग Betel nut. प्रसवानां (flowers) पूगेन (समूहेन) पिङ्गलाः प्रियङ्गवः येषु. परागेण पिञ्जरिताः मञ्जर्यः तासु पुञ्ज्यमानाः मधुपाः तेषां मञ्जुशिञ्जया जनिता जनमुद् (जनानन्दः) येषु. मदमलेन (by the stain of ichor) मेचकिताः ०स्कन्धाः (branches) काण्डं च (trunk) तैः कथिता निःशङ्कानां करिणां करटस्य कण्डूतिः येषु. The elephants rubbed their itching temples against मुचुकुन्द trees. उड्डीयमानाः निःशङ्काः चटुलाः कृष्णशारशावाः येषु तानि सकलानि शाद्वलानि (grassy plots) तैः सुभगाः भूमयः येषु. तमोवत् कालतमा (very dark) तमालमाला तया मीलितः (covered, obscured) आतपः येषु. स्तबकैः दन्तुरिताः देवदारवः येषु. दन्तुरित bristling with. तरलैः (moving to and fro) ताम्बूलीस्तम्बैः जालकिताः (entangled) जम्बूजम्बीरवीथयः येषु. जम्बीरः citron. कुसुमरजसा धवलाः धूलीकदम्बाः तेषां चक्रेण (समूहेन) चुम्बितं व्योम येषु. बहलमधुमोक्षेण उक्षिता (sprinkled) क्षितिः येषु. परिमलेन घटिता (effected) घ्राणस्य तृप्तिः यैः. ०कुक्कुट्या कुटीकृतः कुटजकोटरः (hollow of the कुटज tree) येषु. कुटीकृत used as a hut *i. e.* tenanted. चटकाभिः (sparrows) सञ्चार्यमाणाः (being taken from one tree to another) वाचाटाः चाटकेराः (young of sparrows) तैः क्रियमाणं चाटु (प्रियवाक्यं flattery) येषाम्. We must read चाटकैर 'चटका कलविङ्कः स्यात् तस्य स्त्री चटका तयोः । पुमपत्ये चाटकैरः' अम०. 'चटकाया

of the Jainas, a तीर्थङ्कर. The philosophy of the Jainas is called आर्हतदर्शन in the सर्वदर्शनसंग्रह. मस्करिभिः—see above p. 113. श्वेतपटः—this probably refers to the श्वेताम्बर sect among Jains. पाण्डुरभिक्षुभिः—the com. explains that these were ascetics that had abandoned the red robes peculiar to Buddhist monks. भागवत—a devotee of भगवत् *i. e.* वासुदेव or कृष्ण. वर्णिभिः—'**वर्णिनो ब्रह्मचारिणः**' **अम०**, from वर्ण + इन्—according to 'वर्णाद्ब्रह्मचारिणि' पा. 5. 2. 134. केशलुञ्चनैः that pulled out their hair. 'लुञ्चिताः पिच्छिकाहस्ताः पाणिपात्रा दिगम्बराः' सर्व० आर्हतदर्शन. कापिलैः followers of कपिल, the founder of the सांख्य system. जैनैः—the com. renders it by बौद्धैः. Though जिन is a name of बुद्ध, the word जैन does not popularly mean बौद्ध. The word आर्हत also would mean बौद्ध as अर्हत् is a name of बुद्ध. लोकायतिक—is a materialist, an atheist, a follower of चार्वाक, who held that there was no intelligent ruler of the universe, that there was no soul, that there was no पुनर्जन्म, that only प्रत्यक्षप्रमाण was to be accepted and that all beings were created from the *four* elements. Compare 'लोकायतिकविद्येवाधर्मरुचेः' काद० p. 150. लोकायतं शास्त्रमस्ति अस्य इति लो०. काणादैः followers of कणाद, who was the founder of the वैशेषिक system. औपनिषदैः that were students of the doctrines of the Upanishads. The Upanishads, often called वेदान्त, are works forming the last portions of the several Vedas and are concerned with philosophical problems, such as the orign of the Universe, the relation of the individual soul to the Supreme Spirit and so on. ऐश्वर...कैः who believed in ईश्वर as the cause (or creator) of the world. This probably applies to the माहेश्वरमत, according to which ईश्वर is only निमित्तकारण and which is refuted in the ब्रह्मसूत्र (II. 2. 37–41) or to the न्याय system founded by गौतम which regards ईश्वर as the निमित्तकारण. 'कारन्धमिभिः धातुवादिभिः' com. This probably refers to the school of alchemists (called रसेश्वरदर्शन) who believed that mercury, if properly treated, would make men immortal. *Vide* सर्वदर्शनसंग्रह for this दर्शन. '**कारन्धमी** कांस्यकारे धातुवादरतेऽपि च' मे०. धर्मशास्त्रिभिः those that studied the Smṛitis, like those of Âpastamba, Vasishṭha, Baudhāyana, Manu &c. पौराणिकैः—see p. 113. साप्ततन्तवैः those who studied the sacrifice. This probably stands for the students of the पूर्वमीमांसा system founded by जैमिनि, in which the most prominent place is assigned to sacrifice.'सप्ततन्तुर्मखः क्रतुः' अम० (सप्तभिश्छन्दोभिस्तन्यते इति क्षीर०). शाब्दैः = वैयाकरणैः, whose position was that the व्याकरणशास्त्र would lead to मोक्ष 'तद्द्वारमपवर्गस्य

वाङ्मलानां चिकित्सितम् । पवित्रं सर्वविद्यानामधिविद्यं प्रकाशते ॥' वाक्यपदीय I.; compare महाभाष्य 'एकः शब्दः सम्यग्ज्ञातः शास्त्रान्वितः सुप्रयुक्तः स्वर्गे लोके कामधुग्भवति' vol III p. 58. पाञ्चरात्रिकैः followers of the पञ्चरात्र doctrines. In the महाभारत we are told that नारद promulgated the पञ्चरात्र doctrines after receiving them from नारायण 'सांख्ययोगकृतं तेन पञ्चरात्रानुशब्दितम् । नारायणमुखोद्गीतं नारदोऽश्रावयत्पुनः ॥ शान्ति० 340–112. सिद्धान्तान् dogmas, established truths. अभि...शयानैः absorbed in (the pursuit of their special philosophy), pondering, repeating, doubting. व्युत्पादयद्भिः giving etymologies. व्याचक्षाणैः expounding. आवेद्यमानम् indicated, pointed out (qualifies दिवाकरमित्रम् below). कपिभिः—this and the following nouns in the instrumental are to be connected with उपास्यमानम्. कपिभि...परैः (waited upon) even by monkeys that had taken refuge with the 'three refuges' and that were engaged in doing the menial work about चैत्यs (or of चैत्य). त्रिसरणं (Pāli तिसरणं, Sanskrit त्रिशरणं)—the three Refuges are बुद्ध, धर्म (the Law) and सङ्घ (the assembly). The formula in which faith in these three is professed may be looked upon as the *credo* of Buddhism. It consists in repeating thrice the words 'बुद्धं सरणं गच्छामि धम्मं सरणं गच्छामि संघं सरणं गच्छामि'. परमो...दिशद्भिः by parrots, greatly devoted to Buddha and skilled in his teaching, giving instruction in the कोश. According to C and T कोश is the Buddhist dictionary by Vasubandhu. ०शालिनीभिः—शिक्षापदानां उपदेशेन दोषोपशमः तेन शालन्ते इति—that had secured the extinguishment of the दोषs (sins) by instruction in the शिक्षापदs. The शिक्षापदs (Pāli सिक्खापद) are ten and are the precepts regulating the life of a Buddhist monk. They are the same as the ten शीलs for which see below. धर्मदेशना instruction in the धर्म. अनवरतश्रवणेन गृहीतः आलोकः यैः that had attained light (enlightenment) by incessant listening to instruction. Owls (कौशिक) cannot see in daylight (आलोकः). बोधिसत्त्वजातकानि—the Jātakas are the stories of the former lives of बुद्ध before he had attained perfect knowledge. जातकं is the tenth book of the Khuddakanikāya and contains 550 *Jātakas* or birthstories. बोधिसत्त्व is a term applied to बुद्ध in his various births before he attained Buddhahood. शीलं (Pāli सीलं)—There are ten moral precepts laid down by Buddha, prohibiting the destruction of life, theft, impurity, lying, use of intoxicants, eating at forbidden hours, attending worldly amusements, use of unguents and ornaments, the use of a large or ornamented couch and receiving money. जातः सौगतशीलैः शीतलः स्वभावः येषाम्

whose natures became mild by the (practice of the) moral precepts enjoined by बुद्ध. आसनोपान्ते उपविष्टाः विस्रब्धाः अनेककेसरिशावकाः यस्य सः °शावकः तस्य भावः शावकता तया. मुनिपरमेश्वरम्—he was the foremost of sages. ⟨अकृत्रिम...निषण्णम्—A परमेश्वर (emperor) sits on a सिंहासन (throne) which is only artificial (*i. e.* it has the *shape* of a lion); while दिवाकर° sat on a real सिंहासन (lion–seat). There is another idea. बुद्ध is called मुनीन्द्र or मुनीश्वर. So दिवाकर° seemed to be बुद्ध himself. 'मुनीन्द्रः श्रीघनः शास्ता' अम°. उप...पल्लवम्—deer licked his feet. The poet fancies that they drank from his feet tranquility of mind. नीवाराः wild rice. 'तृणधान्यानि नीवाराः' अम°. प्रियां...यन्तम् who propitiated मैत्री that was dear to his heart. मत्री means 'good will towards the whole world'. 'अपकारिण्यभिप्रीतिः मैत्री' com. The young dove looked like a lotus placed on the ear. The word प्रियां suggests another sense. मैत्री was as if his wife and he propitiated her by °कर्णोत्पल (the पारावत). Remove the comma after व्यामोहम्. In this long passage and elsewhere Bāna shows considerable acquaintance with Buddhist dogma and technique. जनितः जनव्यामोहः येन–the people were infatuated by the rays of the nails of his right hand (as he poured water into the beak of a peacock). The shining and dark-green neck of the peacock resembled an emerald water pot. 'कमण्डलौ च करकः' अम°. The long neck of the peacock was like the neck of a jar. Take away the comma after संवीतम्. संवीत (*past p. p.* of व्ये with सम्)—'संवीतं रुद्धमावृतम्' अम°. पौरन्दर—पुरन्दरस्य इन्द्रस्य अयं पौरन्दरः. दिवाकर° was covered with a red robe and looked like the eastern quarter arrayed in the mellow light of morn. उल्लिखितः (polished, wrought) पद्मरागः तस्य प्रभा प्रतिमा यस्याः (*adj.* of देहप्रभया). रक्तावदातया red and bright (pure). The quarters were reddened by the glow of his body. The poet fancies that he taught the quarters to assume the red robes (peculiar to Buddhist monks). अनौद्धत्यम् freedom from insolence, modesty. मन्द...कारेण that resembled a night lotus slightly closed. The कुमुद is white; his eye was white. मन्द...मुदस्येव आकारः यस्य. जनेन क्षुण्णाः (trampled upon) क्षुद्रजन्तवः तेषां जीवनार्थम्. अमृत is स्निग्ध (glossy), धवल and प्रसन्न (transparent); while his eye was affectionate (स्निग्ध), धवल and प्रसन्न (quiet, unruffled). सर्व...र्मितम्—the idea is that he knew all the S'āstras. From परमाणुs the whole material world is produced. See above p. 12. परमसौगतः a very aealous or devout follower of Buddha. अवलोकितः ईश्वरः येन who saw (*i. e.* recognised) an ईश्वर. The Buddhists do not recognise an intelligent Supreme Ruler of the Universe. This contradiction is got over by taking अव० in another sense. अव० is a बोधिसत्त्व worshipped by the northern Buddhists. अस्ख...लग्नम् though he never faltered (in the path of धर्म), yet he clung to austerities. One who falters has to cling to something for support. आलोकः light. यथा...प्रकाशकम् he explained the proper worth of each thing; light shows objects as they are. दर्शनार्थिनाम् (1) those who want to see; (2) those who desire to have correct knowledge. सुगतस्य = बुद्धस्य. अभि...नीयम् fit to be approached. प्र...नीयमिव whose grace was to be prayed for even by Favour. आत्मनो...णीयम् who was to be longed for even by the Soul. जन्म जपस्य the source of जप (inaudible prayers). जन्म यमस्य would mean 'the source of यम.' यम is the first of the eight *Angas* of योग. 'अहिंसासत्यास्तेयब्रह्मचर्यापरिग्रहाः यमाः' योगसूत्र II. 30. नेमिं नियमस्य the circumference (*i. e.* the utmost limit or reach) of religious observances. नियम may also mean the seconed *Anga* of Yoga. 'शौच—सन्तोष—तपः—स्वाध्याय—ईश्वरप्रणिधानानि नियमाः' योगसूत्र II. 32. तत्त्वं essence. कोशं कुशलस्य the treasure of bliss or auspiciousness. सर्व...तायाः the all-in-all of good conduct. दाक्ष्यं दाक्षिण्यस्य the civility of courteousness *i. e.* the perfection of courteousness. पारं...याः the highest limit of compassion for others. निर्वृतिं सुखस्य—Happiness itself would find pleasure in him. ०गम्भीराकारेण आरोपितः बहुमानः यस्मिन् in whom high regard (for दिवा०) was produced by his &c. शिरसा...ववन्दे he uttered words of salutation and also bent his head.

P. 128 l. 33—**P. 129** l. 16 दिवाकर...विशत्. महानु...भाजा possessing the magnificence belonging to noble persons. This qualifies ०विशेषेण. अप्राकृतेन not belonging to common men. ०प्रकाशकेन goes with प्रश्रयेण. प्रश्रयेण = विनयेन. चक्षुषि...ग्रहीत् he took him (*i. e.* greeted him) by his eye and heart. We may also connect आह्लादितः with चक्षुषि and चेतसि. सम्पादितं ससम्भ्रमं अभ्युत्थानं येन who (दिवाकर०) rose up hurriedly (to receive हर्ष). सङ्कलय्य having held together. उद्ग...लोलं disordered by his rising up. उत्क्षिप्य having raised up (his hand). महा...प्रशस्तं हस्तं—see for these बृह० 67. 44–48, one of which is quoted on p. 20 above. गुरु...मानः highly thinking of हर्ष that had come as a guest, as if he were his *guru*. स्वेन आसनेन—this is the highest mark of respect that can be shown to a guest.

आध्वम् (*Imperative 2nd plural* of आस् to sit). अलोह...जातानाम् goodness is in the case of the noble a fetter for tying fast, though not made of iron. स्थाने it is quite proper. दर्शनमेव पुण्यं तेन अनुगृहीतस्य—the idea is:—your very sight adds to the store of my merit (पुण्य) and that is a great favour in itself. पुनरुक्तः superfluous. अनुग्रहः the favour (*viz.* hospitable treatment by आसनदान and पादोदक &c.). चक्षुः प्रमाणं यस्य सः ०माणः प्रसादः तेन स्वीकृतस्य (मम)—I was accepted by you as your own by bestowing on me a favour whose standard is the eye *i. e.* your very eye showed me the greatest favour possible. पर...चेष्टितम् the acts of civility (उपचारः), such as offering a seat &c., make me a stranger *i. e.* these civilities are to be shown to strangers only. अति...पुरः in your presence to have the bare ground as a seat is the highest pitch (of honour). There is another meaning also 'to sit even on bare ground in the presence of a person like you is an impropriety (a violation of proper limits).' Read ०वृत्ति and take away the vertical line after it. सम्भाषणमेव अमृतं तेन अभिषेकः तेन क्षालितं सकलं वपुः यस्य. प्रदेशे वृत्तिः यस्य. The idea is:—when my *whole* body has bathed in the nectar of speech with you, water for the feet, that will only wash a part (प्रदेश) of my body, is useless (अपार्थक). 'पाद्यं पादाय वारिणि' अम०. If we read अतिभूमिरेव भवादृशां...वृत्तिः the meaning will be 'when my *whole* body has been bathed &c., then my remaining here in a particular spot before you will be the height of impropriety.' This is not very happy.

P. 129 l. 17—**P. 130** l. 13 **अलङ्कारो...भाव्यते इति.** अल...शयः great politeness (प्रश्रयः) is really the true ornament of the powerful (and not jewels &c., which are mere stones). प्रभवत् one who rules, powerful. न प्रत्य...वचनम् when the king did not accede to the words (of the sage). ०निहितं ०युगलमेव निगडः (fetters) तेन निश्चलीकृतं हृदयं यस्य. कालकलाम् a portion of time. **'पापं किल्बिषकल्मषम्'** अम०. मूल...वनम्—the idea is:—he subsisted on fruits and roots only; consequently his breath was fragrant. When he opened his lips, he as if sent forth (in the form of his breath) a bower of creepers fragrant with white flowers. His white teeth were like flowers. अभ्यवहारः (food, eating) तस्मात् सम्भवः यस्य (*adj.* of ०वनम्). अद्य...संसारः—from this day this संसार (worldly life) is not only not to be blamed, but has become fit to be saluted (praised). प्रकाशितं सत्सारं येन that has manifested its excellent essence. संसार is often spoken of as

असार, but now it is सत्सार (सत् being opposed to असत् represented by अ in असार). Or प्रकाशितः सत्सु सारः श्रेष्ठः (हर्षः) यस्मिन्. 'सारो बले स्थिरांशे च न्याय्ये क्लीबं वरे त्रिषु' अम०. किं...ऋतं what wonders may not living beings see ? The meaning is:—your splendid form is the greatest wonder in this world. That being seen, a living person may be blessed to see many wonders, that are less marvellous. अचिन्ति...तम् presented unexpectedly. जन्मान्तरेषु अवस्थितानि सुकृतानि. दत्तमेव goes with फलम्. दर्शयता goes with तपःक्लेशेन. देवानां प्रियम् beloved of the gods. Bāṇa uses the word in the same way as As'oka does in his edicts. As'oka calls himself देवानां प्रिय. The महाभाष्य uses it in a good sense 'के पुनर्भवदादयः । भवान् दीर्घायुः देवानां प्रियः आयुष्मानिति' on पा. V. 3. 14 (Kielhorn vol. II p. 405). But later Sanskrit grammarians assign the meaning of 'fool' to this word. जातं...सुखस्य my mind has no longing for the happiness of final emancipation. We must read निर्वृति० with C. निवृत्ति० also may be made to yield (though rather in a far-fetched way) the same sense. निवृत्ति cessation of the round of births and deaths). But the com. says 'निवृत्तिश्चित्तविभ्रमः.' ०जीवितजनकम् who gives life *i. e.* who protects and supports. पुण्य...णाम: blessed even are those merits, of which thou art the fruit (the fulfilment). Compare the words of प्रभाकरवर्धन 'फलमस्यनेक... अकलुषस्य कर्मणः' (text p. 24). सुकृतं तपः यैः. परिगृहीताः सर्वावयवाः यैः. ये...वाः that constitute all your limbs. भव्यः...यः fortunate is manliness in that it has resorted to you. यत्सत्यं to say the truth. पुण्यभाजं = हर्षम्. पुनः...जन्मनि Once more faith in human birth has been generated in me. He means:—up till now I had looked upon human birth as an unmixed evil, a thing to fly from; but now I think it has some inherent good in it. नेच्छद्भिः—I don't desire to see the working of Cupid; but in your person I have seen Kāma (*i. e.* you are as handsome as काम). अमृत...कार्यमेव—the idea is:—that your words are so sweet is natural; you are yourself full of अमृत and so your words (the effect) must possess the quality (माधुर्य) of the cause (you). Compare वैशेषिकसूत्र II. 1. 24 'कारणगुणपूर्वकः कार्यगुणो दृष्टः.' There is a well-known न्याय (maxim) 'कारणगुणा हि कार्यगुणानारभन्ते'. उपाध्या... यामि even though I reflect deeply I cannot fancy who your teacher could have been (in this humility). गुणग्रामः—there is a suggested idea. A village also may become शून्य (tenantless) when nobody has a long life. वंशे family; bamboo. It was supposed that pearls were found in bamboos. See above p. 193.

मुक्तः आमयः येन free from disease or hurt. पारिप्लवं restless. 'चञ्चलं तरलं चैव पारिप्लवपरिप्लवे' अम०. के वयम्—who are we to offer (fruits and roots that we share in common with all the foresters)? The idea is:—there is nothing in this forest that I can call my own; fruits and roots belong to the foresters as well as to me. So I cannot offer them to you as something special. अपरो...साकम् this wretched body, that was never made useful to others, belongs to us. कलि is the age of sin; so कायकलि means 'sinful body'. C and T strangely enough translate 'But this wretched body of ours is only for another's service.' सर्वे...थ्याय all that has been left to us is for the welcome of our friend (इष्ट). He says:—All that I can call my own is my wretched body, but that was never made useful to anybody. But that is all that is left to me and I shall use it for welcoming you my friend. स्वायत्ताः...कतिचित्—he means:—besides my body, I possess a few drops of learning that are completely at my disposal. उप...यति but my affection for you does not stop to consider whether they (विद्याबिन्दवः) will be of any use to you. In my affection for you I place my learning at your disposal, whether useful to you or not does not matter. C and T translate 'our friendship cannot hesitate how to make use of them.' This is not correct. Read कञ्चित् for कश्चित्. यदि...लवम् He says that he would not press him to tell, if thereby he was likely to hinder even the smallest business of his (हर्ष's). अरक्षणीयानि अक्षराणि यस्य (*adj.* of कथनीयम्) the words of which are not to be kept secret. कियान् अवधिः यस्य. Separate वा अयम्. सन्तप्तरूपेव विभाव्यते is seen to be as if afflicted.

P. 130 ll. 14—P. 131 l.6 **राजा तु...कीदृशीति.** दर्शितः संभ्रमः यस्मिन् (*adj.* of वचसा) that shows the flurry (of your mind due to my arrival). हृदय...करम् that supports (*i. e.* encourages, gladdens) the heart. अभ्यर्हितम्=पूज्यम्. अनु...यमपि though I do not deserve to be treated with respect. विनष्टाः निखिलाः इष्टबन्धवः यस्य. जीवि...बन्धनम् the sole tie that keeps up my life. निबन्धनम् tie, suport. अनुबन्धः continuity. He means that he continues to live because of her. विन्ध्यवनम्—is the object of अविशत्. The student will notice that all the letters from ०वन...to ०शत् are short. ०बहुलम् abounding in &c. ०कुलैः कलिलम् full of 'कलिलं गहनं समे' अम०. ०शरभेभ्यः भयं यस्मिन्. For शरभ, see p. 66. ०महिषैः मुषितं पथिकगमनं यस्मिन् where the journeys of travellers are hindered by huge buffaloes. शर reed. कुश a kind of grass. अवटः

pit. तस्याः वार्ता तद्वार्ता. अभाजनं...भवताम् we are not fit (destined) to make such presents (उपायनं) of glad tidings to you. शमि...मानः of an age when passions are restrained. जाता करुणा यस्य. प्रक्षरितं चक्षुः यस्य whose eye was full of tears. महु...वर्तते there is a very pitiable occurrence. व्यसनं misfortune. पूर्वं भूता भूतपूर्वा. भूत...रूपा who seems to have seen prosperity in former days. सम्भा...भगवान् honour her before her life leaves her. अप्रोषिताः प्राणाः यस्याः. अभ्यु...श्वासनैः favour her with suitable comforting words. अनुपरतपूर्वं कृमि...मपि आर्यस्य गोचरगतम् even insects when once within your sight have never died before. जाता अनुजायाः आशङ्का यस्य who suspected that she was his sister. अन्तर्द्रुतः इव as if melting inside. For दोदूयमान, see p 42. गद्गदिकया गृहीतः कण्ठः यस्य whose throat was choked up. विकला वाक् यस्य whose accents were broken. जीवे...वन्तम् would she be still alive? आकारतो कीदृशी what sort of woman is she in appearance?

P. 131 l. 7—**P. 133** l. 26 **तथा...निवेदितवानिति.** रोधसा by the bank. यदृच्छया by chance. हिम...कातराणां frightened by the lotus beds withering through frost. रसितं humming. He compares the weeping of females to the hum of bees and the tones of lutes. सार्यमाण being touched gently with the fingers. अति...वर्तिनीनाम्—that were tuned to a high protracted tone. वीणातन्त्रीणाम् of the strings of lutes. एकः तानः यस्मिन् in which the note was one (and not complex). तान is defined in the सङ्गीतरत्नाकर I. 4. 27 as '**तानाः** स्युर्मूर्च्छनाः शुद्धाः षाडवौडवितीकृताः॥'. तान is a mode of मूर्छना, for which see above p. 206. With रुदितं, एकतानं means 'incessant.' अधृतिकरम् that caused loss of firmness *i. e.* that agitated me. The principal sentence is दृष्टवान् अस्मि च...अबलानां चक्रवालेन परिवृताम् (l. 25)...योषितम् (p. 77. l. 22). दृष...ल्लोहितेन—this and the following instrumentals qualify चक्रवालेन below. दृषत्खण्डैः खण्डिताः अङ्गुलयः ताभ्यः गलत् लोहितं यासाम् from whose toes shattered by pieces of stones blood was oozing. पार्ष्णिषु प्रविष्टानि शरशलाकाशल्यानि तैः शूलः तेन सङ्कोचितानि चक्षूंषि येषाम् whose eyes became contracted by the sharp pain of the points of the long *S'ara* grass that entered their heels (पार्ष्णि *m.*). अध्वनीनेन श्रमेण श्वयथुः तेन निश्चलौ चरणौ यस्य whose feet could not move owing to the swelling caused by the fatigue of the journey: अध्वनीन from अध्वन्. स्थाणवैः व्रणैः व्यथिताः गुल्फाः (ankles) तेषु बद्धा भूर्जत्वक् येन. स्थाणव due to stakes or posts (from स्थाणु). वातेन (inflammation) खुडानां (ankle-joints) खेदः (pain) तेन खञ्जा जङ्घा (leg) तया जातः ज्वरः यस्य. 'वातखुडो गतिप्रतिघातलक्षणो

वातव्याधिः' com. Or we may take वातखुड as the name of a disease like rheumatism or gout. The अष्टाङ्गहृदय describes the disease called खुड or वातशोणित as follows:—'प्रायेण सुकुमाराणामचङ्क्रमणशीलिनाम् । अभिघातादशुद्धेश्च नृणामसृजि दूषिते ॥...आढ्यरोगं खुडं वातबलासं वातशोणितम् । तदाहुर्नामभिस्तच्च पूर्वं पादौ प्रधावति ॥ विशेषाद्यानयानाद्यैः प्रलम्बौ तस्य लक्षणम् ॥' III. 16. 2, 4–5. पिण्डिका calf of the leg. ०जटया (by the twisted fibres of date-palms) जर्जरितं जानु यस्य. शतावर्या विदारितः ऊरुः यस्य. शतावरी is a plant otherwise called नारायणी. विदार्या दारितः (torn) तनुदुकूलपल्लवः यस्य. विदारी is a plant called in Marathi भुईकोहळा. उत्कटाः (prominent) वंशविटपानां कण्टकाः तेषां कोटिभिः पाटितं कञ्चुककर्पटं (bodice-cloth) यस्य. फललोभेन आलम्बितानि (held) आनम्राणि ०जालकानि उद्गताः कण्टकाः येषाम् (*adj.* of ०जालकैः). उल्लिखितं (scratched) सुकुमारं करोदरं यस्य. कदर्थिताः (teased, pained) बाहवः यस्य. With the pointed horns of deer they dug up roots &c. for their food and their arms were wearied by the exertions. For कदर्थित, see p. 101. ताम्बूलविरहेण (absence of betel) विरसं (dry) मुखं तेन खण्डितं कोमलं आमलकीफलं येन. Everyone knows how welcome an आमलक fruit is in one's childhood, when one is thirsty. कुशकुसुमानां आहत्या लोहितानां. The flowers of कुश grass struck their eyes, which became red and swollen. श्वयताम्—*gen. sing.* of *present p.* of श्वि 1 P. to swell. लेपीकृता मनःशिला येन. They applied red arsenic (Marathi मनशीळ) to their swollen eyes. The अष्टाङ्गसंग्रह (उत्तरस्थान chap. 16) prescribes red assenic for swollen eyes 'दाहोपदेहरागाश्रुशोफशान्त्यै विडालकम् । कुर्यात्सर्वत्र पत्रैलामरिचस्वर्णगैरिकैः ॥ 2...मनोह्वाफलिनीक्षौद्रैः कफे सर्वैस्तु सर्वजे ॥ 3.' कण्टकिनीभिः लताभिः लूनः अलकलेशः (small curls) यस्य. किसलयैः उपपादितं आतपत्रकृत्यं यस्य to whom tender foliage served as an umbrella (against the sun). ०पुटे गृहीतं अम्भः येन. पाथेयीकृता मृणालपूलिका येन that made a bundle of the fibrous roots of lotuses their provisions (in their wanderings). For पाथेय, see p. 212. ०शिक्ये निहिता नारिकेलकोशस्य कलशी तस्यां कलितं रसालतैलं येन that placed mango oil in a cup made of the outer (hard) covering of cocoanut fruit placed in a loop (शिक्यं) made of the hems (दशा) of their China-made garments. There is another reading ०सरलतैलेन (the oil of pine). कतिपयावशेषाः ०बर्बराः तैः अविरलेन full of deafmutes, hunch-backed persons, dwarfs, deaf men and barbarians, that were helpless through grief and of whom only a few remained. We must read कलमूक (for कलामूक) for which see p. 99. These are usually described as the attendants and guardians of the ladies of the harem. बर्बर: a low person, one not an Aryan. The com. says 'कलामूकाः पण्डकाः । एवमादयोऽन्तःपुररक्षिणः बर्बरा एतद्देशजाः'. So it takes कलामूक in the sense of 'eunuch.' आप...लावण्येन—her grace which covered every thing by its brilliance did not leave her even in misfortune. A person born of a noble family does not forsake his master or friend even in adversity. प्रति...कायाम्—the tender (and therefore reddish) shoots of creepers were reflected in her bright complexion. The poet fancies that her body was reddened by the bloody wounds of sorrow (and not by red shoots). सरसैः (किसलयैः) means 'juicy.' Read पाटली० for पटली०. ०ङ्कुरेण क्षतं तस्मात् क्षरतीति तेन ०क्षारिणा. Her feet were red with blood from wounds caused by sharp दर्भ grass. The poet fancies that it was Alaktaka dye which ladies usually applied to their feet. In the forest they had no अलक्तक; but blood took its place. अनुसरणं habit. कृता छाया यस्य that was shaded. विगता छाया यस्य that had lost its lustre. There is a pun on छाया. आका...शयानाम् that surpassed even आकाश in शून्यता (being vacant-minded, being a void). For आकाश and शून्यता, see above (text p. 2 ll. 1-2). निश्चेतनतया she was fainting; earth has no intelligence (चैतन्य) in it (it is जड). मरु...न्मदा she heaved so many sighs that she seemed to be all sighs (*i. e.* wind). Explain the following clauses similary. सन्तापः heat; grief. निर...तया—she had no support (*i. e.* she had nothing that could keep up her drooping spirits); आकाश is also without support; it rests on nothing. पारिप्लवतया—she was trembling (through grief); lightning flashes are tremulous. मुक्तानि मुक्ताः (pearls) अंशुकं (fine silken robes) रत्नानि कुसुमानि कनकं पत्राभरणानि (paintings on cheeks &c.) यया (with योषितम्). She had no ornaments &c. on her person, as she had escaped from imprisonment and she was in grief. The com. takes मुक्तांशुक as one word 'मुक्ताख्यमंशुकं मालवदेशजमुत्तरीयम्'. The कल्पलता is a mythical plant that was supposed to yield what was desired by its votary. It may also drop down मुक्ता, अंशुक &c. In this case we must take पत्रं as equal to वाहनं (vehicles) and take आभरणं (ornaments) by itself. महावने—the woman was in a great forest; कल्पवृक्ष is in the great garden of Indra. The com. takes वन in the sense of जल. Then we may explain that पारिजात, which is one of the कल्पवृक्षs, was produced from the sea (महावन) at the time of the churning. परमेश्वरस्य (शिवस्य) उत्तमाङ्गे

पातेन दुर्ललितं अङ्गं यस्याः (with गङ्गाम्) who is insolent by failing &c.; परमेश्वरस्य (of the great king ग्रहवर्मा, her husband) उत्तमाङ्गपातः तेन दुर्ललितानि अङ्गानि यस्याः (with योषितम्) whose limbs were wayward by the fall of the head of &c. गां गताम्—the Ganges came down to the earth from the matted hair of शिव; the woman was lying on the earth (through grief) or walking on the earth (as she had no vehicle). भगीरथ brought the Ganges from Heaven, which fell on the head of शिव and which thought that by its force it would crush शिव. 'विशाम्यहं हि पातालं स्रोतसा गृह्य शङ्करम्' रामायण बाल० 43. 6. ०पादपल्लवाम्—her feet (पाद) were grey with pollen; the rays of the moon also were grey. Remove the comma after पल्लवाम्. लोकान्तर०—she wished that death might take her away to her deceased husband; the moon also goes to another sphere in the morning. निजजलमोक्षेण कदर्थिता दर्शिता धवलायतयोर्नेत्रयोः शोभा यया her long and white eyes were wearied by shedding tears and became dim. If the water of the Ganges goes very low, then the lotus bed will show its long and white roots (नेत्र). For नेत्र, see pp. 37, 53. Remove the comma after शोभाम्. निमीलिताम् she was languid by the fierce heat of the sun; a कुमुदिनी closes its petals in the sun. दग्ध...दिताम् the woman was disappointed at her wretched state (दशा); the flame of the lamp at dawn is made to fail by the wick (दशा) being burnt. पाण्डु वपुः यस्याः her body was pale; the flame also becomes dimmer and dimmer. पार्श्ववर्तिनां वारणे अभियोगः तेन रक्ष्यमाणां who was saved by the perseverance of her attendants .in dissuading her. पार्श्ववर्ती वारणः तस्य अभियोगात् रक्ष्यमाणां being saved from the attack of an elephant near her (with करिणीम्). महा...ग्नाम् the woman had bathed in a lake before she burnt herself in grief; the करिणी plunged in a deep lake. प्रविष्टां ध्याने she was in deep thought. स्थितां मरणे she was resolved on dying. दूरीकृताम् separated from. वि...षा she was exhausted by wandering and was empty of life (as she had resolved on dying). आकुलाम्०— her hair was dishevelled; she was absorbed in finding the means of dying. धृत... मौनेन च she had placed her hand on her mouth (in deep thought) and her lips were also silent. मन्युना = शोकेन. भ्रष्टै... लासैश्च—here and with the following instrumentals we have to supply the word उपलक्षिताम्. भ्रष्टै...लासैश्च with her kindred and graceful gestures all gone. मुक्त...त्मना her ears were bereft (of ornaments) and her spirit was drooping. आरम्भः effort, undertaking. भग्नैः वलयैः—because she was a widow. चरण०—her attendants fell at her feet to dissuade her from dying; and points of grass pierced her feet. हृदय—her eye was down-cast; she had enshrined in her heart her husband. दीर्घैः केशैः her hair was loose and not tied into a braid. क्षीणेन...पुण्येन—She was so miserable that it seemed that the whole stock of her merit was exhausted. स्वल्पा०—she had only a few attendants left; she had not long to live. अलसामुन्मेषे she was careless (or lazy) in opening (her eyes). It will be noticed that the auther employs pairs of adjectives that are opposed in sense, such as अलसां and दक्षां, कृशां and स्थूलां, निश्चलां and चलिताम्. विच्छिन्नां आशासु broken in hopes (*i. e.* she had no hope left). रिक्तां सत्त्वेन she was empty of energy or vitality. अध्या...सेन she was full of worry (lit. tenanted by). शून्यां हृदयेन deserted by her heart. आधा...नाम् a receptacle of agonies. अव...नाम् the abode of vicissitudes. अधृतिः want of steadiness. अवसादः langour, fainting. अभियोगः effort. उद्वेगः—she was the highest pitch of despondency. पारं—the other side *i. e.* the highest point of helplessness. उपतापाः sorrows, distress. This is a favourite sentiment with Bāna; compare 'अहो दुर्निवारता व्यसनोपनिपातानां यदीदृशीमप्याकृतिमनभिभवनीयामात्मीयां कुर्वन्ति । सर्वथा न न कंचन स्पृशन्ति शरीरधर्माणमुपतापाः' काद० p. 135. सा अवस्था यस्याः सा तदवस्था. कथं...श्रये how shall I address this noble lady? Compare the end of the पूर्वभाग for a passage in a similar strain 'अतिप्रियोऽसीति पौनरुक्त्यम् &c.' काद० p. 237. वत्से...प्रणयः—He means that he is a perfect stranger and so cannot use the very affectionate mode of address 'वत्से,' which is only appropriate in parents &c. चाटु flattery. She was so young and he was comparatively so aged that there would have been no semblance of truth in calling her 'मातः.' आत्मसम्भावना honouring one's own self. He would be placing himself on an equality with her by calling her a sister. देवि...लापः—Only her attendants can call her 'your Majesty'; I am not one of them. अस्फुटम् not clear, very general (mode of address). उपासिका a lay female votary of बुद्ध as distinguished from a Bhikshuṇî. An उपासक is one that reveres the रत्नत्रय *viz.* बुद्ध, धर्म and सङ्घ and observes the first five शीलs for which see p. 223. मनोरथः—to call her 'उपासिका,' without knowing whether she is one already, would be only expressing my desire that she should be a follower of बुद्ध. भृत्य...गमः accepting the position of a servant of hers (which I am not). इतर...चितम् suitable to ordinary women

(and not to one so exalted as she seemed to be). अव...प्रियम्—to address her as 'longlived one' would be distasteful to her in her present condition (when she wanted to die). कल्या...रुद्धम्—to address her as 'fortunate one' would be opposed to her present state (when she was a widow). अमुनिमतम्—that mode of address is not approved of by ascetics. बाले...पेतम् to call her a girl would be disrespectful to her. जरारोपणम् attributing old age (which does not exist in her). आर्या is a suitable term for an elderly lady. फलविपरीतम् opposed to the result which she is experiencing. सर्वसाधारणम् common to all ladies (high or low). अनभिजातम् not well-bred, rude. मा...शोभते—as long as the cause of grief is not removed, so long one cannot ask her not to weep. समा...श्रित्य If I were to say 'be comforted', what is that on which she is to rely for consolation? स्वागतम्—these words are addressed to anybody and are very formal. यातयामम्—stale. 'जीर्णं च परिभुक्तं च यातयाममिदं द्वयम्' अम० ('याताः यामाः क्षपांशाः अस्य' क्षीर०). सुख...ते 'are you well or happy?' मिथ्या—because her very surroundings indicate that she is not. क्षौण—see p. 35. आर्यायाः इव रूपं यस्याः who had the appearance of a venerable lady. कति...शारं variegated with partially grey hair. अतिकृपणैः very pathetic. Connect हृदयं with दहन्ती. प्रतिपन्ना (accepted) परदुःखस्य क्षपणं तस्य दीक्षा तस्यां दक्षाः skilful (or assiduous) in their vow taken by them of removing the sorrows of others. सौगताः=बौद्धाः. करुणा...गृहं—a lady is honoured and made much of in her father's house. So is करुणा in the teaching (शासन) of बुद्ध. करुणा and मैत्री are two out of the four *Appamaññas* (अप्पमञ्ञा), the other two being मुदिता and उपेक्षा. सज्जनता जैनी—the saints that follow जिन (*i. e.* बुद्ध). 'समन्तभद्रो भगवान् मारजिल्लोकजिज्जिनः' अम०. पर...मुनीनाम् it is the duty of *munis* to strive to attain the next world. C and T translate 'the religion of the Munis is a means to attain the next world.' This is not correct. The argument is:—प्राणरक्षण is the highest पुण्य, पुण्य leads to परलोक and परलोकसाधन is the धर्म laid down for मुनिs. You, being a मुनि, must therefore save the life of our mistress. विप...भूताः overwhelmed by misfortunes. आर्तं वचः येषाम् those whose words are distressed (*i. e.* convey the distress they are in). सिद्धक्षेत्र is the land of the सिद्धs *i. e.* those that have attained wonderful powers (such as the eight सिद्धिs, अणिमा, लघिमा &c.). The idea is :—those that are distressed will find that good men are their land of promise and that

jests. अग्रामी...गिणि that lovest virtues not found among villagers (*i. e.* noble). अन्तरं room. आपृच्छते bids farewell. नाटक...धारी who managed dramatic performances for you. पश्चिमः last. कतिकृत्वः how many times? निर्माण...शः generally all creation comes to this (*i. e.* all created beings have to suffer these reverses of fortune). धीरयसि किम् why do you comfort (or encourage) me still? केय...नानाम् what has (my present) condition to do with consolations (*i. e.* I am past all consoling words). कृताः...रोधाः I have disregarded the wooing (of my mind) by my loving friends by falling at my feet. पृष्ठतः कृ— to turn the back towards, leave behind, disregard. ग्रहिणि— you who are persistent (in dissuading me by holding my feet). 'निर्बन्धोपरागार्कादयो ग्रहाः' अम०. महत्तरिका—chamberlain. दृष्टासि I have seen you (*i. e.* I am at least fortunate enough to have seen you when departing this life). कर्मणां विपाकाः the fruit or reward of actions. आर्यचरणानाम्—she probably refers to हर्ष her elder brother. परः...प्रणामः this is my last salutation at the time of departing to the next world. 'हलहलकः उत्कण्ठा' com. It seems to be a Des'ya word. It will be perceived that here there is a change from grief to joy, which suggests the coming of Harsha, according to the common belief of Sanskrit poets expressed in the words 'आवेदयन्ति प्रत्यासन्नमानन्दमग्रजातानि शुभानि निमित्तानि'. उच्चं रोमाञ्चं मुञ्चन्तीति ०मुञ्चि. किमङ्गीकृत्य relying upon what? वामेन—the throbbing of the left eye in the case of women is a good omen. वृथा विरमसि in vain dost thou stop or stay. रम् 1 A when preceded by वि, आ and परि takes the परस्मैपद only. 'व्याङ्परिभ्यो रमः' पा. 1. 3. 82. क्षीरिणि वृक्षे on a milky tree (like the figtree, or उदुम्बर &c.). The crow sitting on milky trees was a good omen. Note 'सुस्निग्धपत्रपल्लवकुसुमफलानम्रसुरभिमधुरेषु। सक्षीराव्रणसुस्थितमनोज्ञवृक्षेषु चार्थकरः॥' बृह० 95. 33; see also 95. 16 and 1. हेषितम् neighing. उत्तरतः to the north. आर्यस्य = हर्षस्य. उपससर्प— supply हर्षः.

P. 135 l. 27—**P. 136** l. 25 **अथ तेन...भुवमिति.** भ्रातुः is to be connected with हस्तसंस्पर्शेन (l. 31). प्रकोष्ठ...क्षरता (the touch of his hand) that as if dropped a flood of juice capable of restoring life from the herbs tied on his forearm. हर्ष had on his forearm some herbs by way of amulets. His touch revived राज्यश्री; the poet fancies that it was the juice of those herbs that revived her. वमते...भावम् (touch) that as if emitted the inconceivable power of the jewels in his bracelet. It was believed that various drugs and jewels had mysterious powers; compare 'लौकिकानामपि मणिमन्त्रौषधिप्रभृतीनां देशकालनिमित्तवैचित्र्यवशाच्छक्तयो विरुद्धानेककार्यविषया दृश्यन्ते।' शाङ्करभाष्य on वेदान्तसूत्र II. 1. 27. 'आवापकः पारिहार्यः कटको वलयोऽस्त्रियाम्' अम०. अमृत...द्गिरा—his bright nails resembled the moon's rays, which shower nectar (*i. e.* a sensation of coolness and pleasure). चन्द्रोदयेन च्युतः शिशिरः शीकरः यस्मात्. समुन्मिमील opened her eyes. असम्भावितं आगमनं यस्य whose arrival was not thought to be possible. स्वप्ने दृष्टं दर्शनं यस्य. तत्काले (हर्षस्य) आविर्भावः तेन निर्भरः तेन which was full on account of his sudden appearance. अभिभूतः सर्वात्मा येन. Connect ०सम्भारेण with उत्सृजन्ती०वारि. स्थूलः प्रवाहः यस्य (*adj.* of ०वारि). नदी...वारि—she shed such floods of tears from her two eyes that there seemed to be two river channels (प्रणाल:) at their mouth let loose. A river at its mouth is very full. ०मन्युना goes with भ्राता. समुद्भूतः भगिनीस्नेहसद्भावः तस्य भारः तेन भावितः मन्युः यस्य whose sorrow became manifested by the great feeling of affection for his sister that swept over him. करेण स्थगितं (covered) मुखं यस्याः. अग्रजः elder brother. विश्रम्य...तव्यम् stop and then weep again (after some time). चिरसम्भावितः अनेकदुःखनिवहः तस्य निर्वहणं तेन बाष्पोत्पीडः तेन पीड्यमानः कण्ठभागः यस्याः whose throat was choked by a flood of tears due to the completion (निर्वहणं) of the numerous griefs that she had suffered for a long time. काहलेन resembing that of a drum (काहलं). आक्षिप्य being led away. तथा in that way *i. e.* by the incidents that had happened. मुहूर्तं...वाह्य having allowed some time to pass. नि...नीतं brought by his pupil who was informed by a secret sign. चिरप्रवृत्तं अश्रुजलजालं यस्मिन्. Her eyes red with weeping resembled a red lotus. If we read जातं for जालं then the meaning is 'her eye red with weeping was like a red lotus sprung from the water of her long continued flow of tears.' पुनरानीतं नेत्राम्भः यस्याः. पति...म्भसि whose eyes again filled with tears by the shock of hearing that he was familiar with her husband. उद्घातः allusion; blow. प्रयत्नेन रक्षितः आगत...सम्भारः तेन भज्यमानं धैर्यं तेन आर्द्रे लोचने यस्य whose eyes moistened because his serenity was broken by the flood of rising tears that he checked with effort. परावृत्त turned aside. कल्याणराशे—this is addressed to हर्ष.

P. 136 l. 26—**P. 137** l. 27 **अथ भूपति···मन्दाकिनीम्.** अनु...चारम् obeying the observances of the world. तस्यां=भूमौ. आहितं अवधानं येन attentively. परवती शुचा beside herself through grief. पतिपिण्डे प्रदर्शितः प्रयत्नः तेन प्रतिपन्नं अभ्यवहारकरणं यया who consented to take food when Harsha had made efforts to offer oblations to her deceased husband *i. e.* she ate when she saw that Pindas had been offered to her husband. बन्धनात् प्रभृति—she had been imprisoned in Kanoj by the king of Malva that killed her husband (text p. 41). विस्तरतः—connect with सर्वमशृणोत्. ०सम्भ्रमं—is governed by अशृणोत्. गौडसंभ्रमम् the tumult of the Gauda king. What this was is not clear. The order in which the events are arranged here shows that the गौड king caused some tumult in Kanoj before राज्यवर्धन was treacherously murdered by him. But we know that the king of Malva took कान्यकुब्ज by killing ग्रहवर्मा. If we read संभ्रमगुप्तितः, the sense is not much improved. But if we read ०सम्भ्रमे, then the meaning is:—'he heard how his sister was sent away from Kanoj out of her prison by a noble named गुप्त at the time of the tumult caused by the गौड king.' With this reading it is easy to say that the tumult refers to the treachery of the Gauḍa king against राज्यवर्धन whose death राज्यश्री naturally heard after escaping from imprisonment. निराकरणम् despising, giving up. पराहता struck down, faint. उपक्रमणं undertaking, commencement. यावत् up to. विविक्तभुवि in a lonely spot. लेशतः little by little. अयं refers to ताराराजः (the moon). परिभूय... भार्याः—the moon has 27 wives, the नक्षत्रs. यौ...तारेण तरलतराः very brilliant by the advent of youth (*adj.* of भार्याः). रजनी...पूरः the ear-ornament of night. पुरुहूतः इन्द्रः तस्य पुराधाः (family priest) तस्य. धिषणस्य—'बृहस्पतिः सुराचार्यो गीष्पतिर्धिषणो गुरुः' अम०. पुरन्ध्री matron. पत्नीयन्—पत्नीं आत्मनः इच्छन्—Wishing to make her his wife. पत्नीयति is a denominative verb from पत्नी, according to 'सुप आत्मनः क्यच्' पा. 3. 1. 8. अतितरलः extremely fickle. तारा—for her seduction by the moon, see p. 60. चकितचकोरस्य इव लोचने यस्याः. अतिकामया whose love for him was excessive. सर्वाकारैः अभिरामया charming in every gesture. सर्व...गौरवात् out of respect for the words of all the gods. अविद्यमानानि इन्धनानि यथा स्युः (अव्ययी०). वरारोहा a beautiful woman (वरः आरोहः यस्याः). 'श्रोण्यामप्यारोहो वरस्त्रियाः' अम०. शै...मानः rising from the mountain in the east. 'अस्तस्तु चरमक्ष्माभृदुदयः पूर्वपर्वतः।' अम०. We often have the word उदयशैल as in 'उदयशैलो मित्रमण्डलस्य' काद०. वारुणालयस्य—सागरस्य. सस्मरः=समदनः. स्मेरं गण्डस्थलं यस्य the cheek of which was dimpled with a smile. Sanskrit poets compare the cheeks of beautiful women with the moon. Compare मृच्छकटिक I. 57. 'उदयति हि शशाङ्कः कामिनीगण्डपाण्डुः.' सस्मार मुखस्य—the genitive is used in accordance with the सूत्र 'अधीगर्थदयेशां कर्मणि' explained above. स्वःस्थोऽप्यस्वस्थः—स्वःस्थ means 'being in the heavens' and स्वस्थ which resembles स्वःस्थ in sound means 'at ease'. 'स्वरव्ययं स्वर्गनाक &c.' अम०. स्वीयसः qualifies ०बिन्दून्. पीतः ०प्रवाहः तेन धवला तारा (pupil) यस्य. आचेमुः मुक्ताशुक्तयः pearl oysters drank them. विषमुचाम् = सर्पाणाम्. तैः मुक्ताफलैः—तारागण is seen in the sky and not in पाताल. But the pearls were like stars and being taken to पाताल made the latter look like the sky. एकावली a necklace with a single string of pearls. The moon is said to be the lord of plants also. 'ओषधीशो निशापतिः' अम०. हिममेव अमृतं तस्मात्सम्भवः यस्याः सा ०सम्भवा तस्याः भावः ०वत्वं. Or we may dissolve as 'हिमं च अमृतं च ताभ्यां &c'. The moon is cool and has also nectar in it. पर्यधत्त wore. नागार्जुनो नाम भिक्षुः—नागार्जुन is a famous name among the Buddhists. The राजतरङ्गिणी (I. 172–173) refers to him as a king that lived 150 years after Buddha. In the बृहत्कथामञ्जरी (XIV. 392–407) he is represented as an adept in रसायनविद्या and as the minister of a king called चिरायु. The कथासरित्सागर tells us that he was a बोधिसत्त्व. त्रिसमुद्राधिपतये—*i. e.* the lord of the Deccan, the peninsula of India, with seas to the east, south and west. C and T think that सातवाहन ruled over जम्बुद्वीप, प्लक्षद्वीप and शाल्मलिद्वीप. But that is not correct. The kings of the Deccan were represented as lords of the three oceans, while universal kings were represented to be lords of the four oceans. Compare 'चतुरम्भोधिभोगभूति०' (text p. 60 l. 16 above) and the words 'देवस्य चतुःसमुद्राधिपतेः...हर्षस्य' in the 2nd उच्छ्वास; and the words 'तिसमुदतोयपीतवाहनस' applied to king 'सातकणि' (शातकर्णि) in the Nasik Inscription (No. 2); vide Bombay Gazetteer vol. 16 p. 550. King सातकणि is there styled 'सातवाहनकुलयसपतिठापनकरस.' सातवाहन is the name of a family of kings of whom many were named शातकर्णि. यद्यपि...चारः although entertaining persons like you by gifts seems to be an insult. ओषधिबुद्ध्या looking upon it as a medicine. सर्व...प्रवृत्तेन who has set about to protect all beings. रक्षणीयं शरीरं यस्य. विष...क्षया with the object of protection against poison. अभ्याशे समीपे वर्तते इति ०वर्ती तस्य.

P. 137 l. 28—**P. 138** l. 25 उन्मुच्य...कर्तव्यानामिति. उन्मुच्यमानायाः while it was being untied. लब्धः अवकाशः येन that found their opportunity (of illuminating the world). विशदं (brilliant) महः (तेजः) यस्य. युगपत्—all the quarters were simultaneously rendered bright. मुकुलि...तरुभिः the trees as if blossomed forth from their very roots, longing for their budding brides—the creepers. The idea is that the splendour of the एकावली was the same that would be seen if trees blossomed forth even from their roots. In this and the following clauses the author tries to convey the effect of the whiteness and brilliance produced by the unveiling of the bright necklace of pearls. अभि...यूथैः—As the rays of the एकावली spread all round, it seemed as if हंसs (that have white wings) were flying for lotus fibres. भर—by the very weight of the केतकी flowers, the pollen was scattered about. गर्भभेदेन सूचितः सूचीसञ्चयः तेन शुचिभिः bright with the numerous pointed leaves made manifest by the opening of the inside (of the bud, that was at one time closed). The केतकी flower is pale-white and bright. We should read उद्दलित for उद्गलित. उद्...दिनीभिः the night lotuses seemed to wake up, bristling with their opening petals. 'दन्तुरस्तून्नतरदे तथोन्नतनते त्रिषु' मे०. There is a suggestion. The petals of (white) कुमुदs resemble the teeth. When a handsome woman gets up from sleep and yawns, her gleaming teeth are seen. सितदशनानां अंशवः तेषां माला तस्याः आलोकेन लिप्यमानं बनं यथा स्यात् तथा. प्रहसितमिव—smiles and laughs are white. The teeth of बनदेवताs would send forth rays. काश flowers are white. शिथिलितः कुसुमकोशः तस्य केसराणां अट्टहासेन निरङ्कुशं यथा स्यात्तथा they bloomed forth smiling without restraint with the filaments of their loosened buds. चमरी deer have white tails. बालाः (hair) पल्लव इव तस्य परिवेशेन (circle) श्वेतायमानैः. स्फायमानाः (swelling) फेनिलाः (foamy) तरलतराः तरङ्गाः (ripples) तान् उद्गिरति इति ०द्गारी तेन. Foam is white. The light of the full moon resembled the light of the एकावली and the pearls resembled stars (which pearls are fancied to be अपरतारागण). ०चक्रेण आक्रान्ताः ककुभः येन. दावानलधूलिना धूसरितः दिगन्तः येन. The idea is:—the quarters were obscured by the ashes of the forest fires; but if water were poured over, then the bright day would shine forth. The एकावली was like the fair faces of the women (राजश्री and her attendants) that were washed after being tear-bedewed. मांसलैः thick. आकुली...चक्षुः again and again opening and closing his eye that was overpowered by the rays &c. सर्वा...रणीं filling all the quarters (with संहतिम्); fulfilling all desires (with एकावलीम्). पङ्क्ती...हतिम्—the row of pearls resembled the spray from the trunks of दिग्गजs, when it is collected in a row (पङ्क्ति). घनमुक्ताम् (घनाः मुक्ताः यस्याम्) having pearls thickly arranged; (घनेन

मुक्ताम्) free from cloud (with ज्योत्स्नाम्). लेखीकृताम् turned into a streak. The necklace was like autumnal moonlight. प्र...चिह्नाम् (प्रकटं पदकचिह्नं यस्याम्) which is clearly marked by the central jewel (with एकावली); which is marked with clear foot-prints. सञ्चारणवीथी road for moving about. The pearls looked like the stars of the Great Bear. Only the latter change their position in the sky from evening to morning. हस्तमुक्ताम् which fell from the hand (because of the round and glossy pearls); that were without हस्त, a constellation (with सप्तर्षि). अभिभूतः ०भूषणानां (कौस्तुभादीनां) भूतेः प्रभावः यया (एकावली) that cast into the shade the powerful magnificence of the ornaments in the whole world; अभिभूतः ०भूषणस्य (शिवस्य) भूतेः (ashes) प्रभावः यया that surpassed the glory of the ashes of शिव who is the ornament of the whole world. ऐशानीं belonging to ईशान (*i. e.* शिव). शिव placed the digit of the moon on his head. 'ईश्वरः शर्व ईशानः' अम०. धवल...हीताम् possessed of the quality of whiteness (with कान्तिम्); possessed of whiteness and thread (with एकावली). क्षीरसागर is white. The एकावली was as if the whiteness of क्षीरसागर come out of it. महीभृतः राजानः पर्वताश्च. The Ganges goes round several mountains. The एकावली had passed through the hands of many kings. The Ganges purifies a man and prevents his falling into hell (दुर्गति). The एकावली would remove poverty. अनवरतं स्फुरिताः तरलस्य (मध्यमणेः) अंशुकाः यस्याम् (with एकावली); अनवरतं स्फुरितं तरलं (moving) अंशुकं (fine silk cloth) यस्याः (with पताका). A banner is carried in front (पुरःसर) and its cloth is waving. महे...गमस्य of the approach (आगमः) of the position of a great emperor. एकावली announced like a पताका the great position that हर्ष was to occupy. A banner also indicates the existence of (a temple of) शिव (महेश्वर). घनसारवत् शुक्लाम् white like camphor (with एकावली). दन्तपङ्क्ति also is घन (thickset), strong and white; or it is white like camphor. ईश्वर is हर्ष who sat facing (अभिमुख) the necklace. ईश्वर means शिव also. Or a king (ईश्वर) when favourable (अभिमुख) smiles on the man with whom he is pleased. वर = श्रेष्ठ (with एकावली). वरः a bridegroom. The garland at the time of स्वयंवर gratifies the desire of the bridegroom when thrown round his neck. The एकावली fulfilled the highest ambitions and was white like flowers (स्रज्). The world-bride as if chose हर्ष as the bridegroom by the garland-necklace. निज...लेक्ष्याम्—the necklace could not be gazed at being surrounded by its own (dazzling) rays.

A laughing woman may cover her face with her own hands (निजकर) and then it would be difficult to see her smile. एकावली is fancied to be the smile (both being white) of the earth indicating its love for (हर्ष). विहसतिका gentle laughter. For चक्षूराग, see p. 149. The reading सुधायाः is not so good. सुधा is white. अक्षमाला rosary. It is राजधर्म to be absorbed in मन्त्र (state policy), कोष (treasury) and साधन (army); one who takes a rosary (*i. e.* becomes an ascetic) is intent upon mastering the numerous *Mantras* (hymns or spells). स...भूतां that (एकावली) was an ornament of the ocean (the pearls of it being found in the ocean). स...भूतां which was ornamented with the seal (of कुबेर). संख्या...काम् which was as if the board or fillet engraved with the calculations of the treasures of कुबेर. Each pearl of the necklace resembled a figure drawn in calculation. कुबेर is the lord of riches and treasures. बन्धुर high, raised 'बन्धुरं तून्नतानतम्' अम०. के...त्मनोऽपि who are we even to control our own selves? The idea is that he is not master even of his own self, that his soul has come to belong to the ascetic. किमुत...नस्य वा much more therefore have I no control in accepting or rejecting (the necklace). परवन्तः in the hands of others. अत्र...कर्तव्यानाम् you may do what you like with this (body). कामचारः acting according to one's will.

P. 138 l. 26—**P. 140** l. 12 समतिक्रान्ते...ज्यरंसीत्. लब्धःविश्रम्भः यया who took courage. उपांशु *adv.* in a whisper. शुचा...विनयम् the unbearableness of her sorrows impels her and lessens her modesty, being ordered by wretched fate. हतदैवेन दत्तः आदेशः यस्यै (with असह्यता). This passage is corrupt. Some MSS read व्यापारयति, which is a good reading; others read व्याहारयति (makes her speak). Another reading is हतदैवदत्ता च दशा, which is better than the text. अवलम्बनं support; compare मनु० 9. 3. 'पिता रक्षति कौमारे भर्ता रक्षति यौवने। रक्षन्ति स्थविरे पुत्रा न स्त्री स्वातन्त्र्यमर्हति ॥'; there is a similar passage in अनुशासनपर्व 20. 21. दुः...मानं serving as fuel to the fire of sorrow. प्राणित...केवलम् to continue to live is sheer immodesty. For शालीन, see p. 28. प्रतिहतः frustrated. काषा...श्रया by being allowed to assume the red robe. पर्यायः synonym. आक्षेपः epilepsy 'आक्षेपस्त्वापस्मारस्य' com. This is not the usual meaning of the word. तारुण्यं तमसः (sorrow) is the youth of darkness. Darkness reigns supreme when a person gives himself up to sorrows. विशेषणं विषस्य it is a kind of poison. Or the meaning may be 'sorrow is an epithet of poison.' अनन्तकः...यकः

it is the lord of the city of the dead, but without यम. अविद्यमानः अन्तकः यस्मिन्. यम is the lord of प्रेतनगर. The विरोध is got over by taking अनन्तक in the sense of 'never-ending'. अविद्यमानः अन्तः यस्य. For क, see p. 68. प्रेत...नायकः also means 'that leads to प्रेतनगर' *i. e.* that kills a man. Explain the following विरोधs in a similar way. अनिर्वृतिः धर्मः यस्य the characteristic of which is that it is not extinguished. But fire can be extinguished. So अ...धर्मः means 'the characteristic of which is that there is no happiness in it.' अक्षयः not consumption. But राजयक्ष्मन् is the same as consumption (क्षयः). So अक्षयः means 'endless'. अ...निवासः who is not the abode of लक्ष्मी; which is the abode of distress. लक्ष्मी dwells on the chest of विष्णु (जनार्दन); शोक is जनार्दन *i. e.* torments people (जनानर्दयतीति). अपु...त्तः that is not working for पुण्य; that is due to one's sins (in former lives). A Jaina mendicant (क्षपणकः) takes to the order of mendicancy for storing merit. क्षपणक also means 'that destroys' (life). अ...धः in which there is no waking up; in which there is no discrimination (in the mind). After sleep, one gets up. निद्राप्रकारः also means '(sorrow) that scatters about *i. e.* destroys sleep.' अन...धर्मा the characteristic of which is to be active (not dull or dazed); which resembles fire (अनलस-धर्मा and अनल-सधर्मा). In सन्निपातज्वर a man becomes अलस. For सन्निपात see p. 80. सन्निपात also means 'that pulls down people.' धर्म becomes धर्मन् at the end of a बहुव्रीहि when preceded by a single word 'धर्मादनिच्केवलात्' पा. 5. 4. 124. अ...चरः that is not in the company of शिव; that is ever associated with evil. विनायकः = गणेशः. Pictures of शिव are generally represented as having गणेश on his lap. विनायक also means 'an obstacle,' or 'one that leads a man astray.' 'विनायकस्तु हेरम्बे तार्क्ष्ये विघ्ने जिने गुरौ'. Compare 'अशिवमूर्तयो महाविनायकाधिष्ठिताः' काद० p. 287. There is another meaning also. A Jaina (*i. e.* sight of a जैन) is associated with evil; compare text p. 20 'अभिमुखमाजगाम...नग्नाटकः.' अ...वितः not attended upon by mercury; not resorted to by wise men. ग्रहवर्गः the group of planets; a number of eclipses or ghosts. 'निर्बन्धोपरागार्कादयो ग्रहाः' अम०. अ...समुत्थः not caused by योग; springing from bad luck or evil conjunctions of stars. For योग, see above p. 204. ज्योतिःप्रकारः a kind of light (*i. e.* highest knowledge); a kind of fire. Higher knowledge (about ब्रह्म) cannot be had without योग (चित्तवृत्तिनिरोध). स्नेहा...कोपः it is a delirium due to स्नेह (affection, oil). वायु is one of the three humours and प्रकोप

means its excess. Oil is prescribed against वायुप्रकोप as an outward application; so in स्नेहात्...पः there is a विरोध, which is removed by taking स्नेह to mean affection. मानसात् from the मानस lake; from the mind. There can be no fire in the lake. आर्द्रभावात् from moisture; from tender feelings. रजःक्षोभः agitation of passion; scattering of dust. Dust is *laid*, not *scattered* by moisture. रसात् out of juice (or fluid); out of affection. अभिशोषः dryness (of mouth); that makes a man wither. रागात् out of affection; out of redness. कालपरिणामः that ends in death; that is transformed into darkness. Out of redness one cannot make a dark thing. तदस्या०—The construction is तत् (तस्मात्) अस्य (शोकस्य)...विदुषामपि हृदयानि न अलं सोढुं आपातं...किमुत अबलानां हृदयम्. Read अजस्रास्रस्राविणः (that makes one shed tears continuously, that makes blood to ooze forth continually). हृदयमहाव्रणस्य—शोक is a great wound of the heart. Blood comes out from a wound. बहुलाः दोषाः अन्धकारः इव तेन लब्धः प्रवेशप्रसरः येन—sorrow enters the heart that is labouring under the darkness of many faults and robs the man of his life. A robber also enters in the darkness of night. बहुलस्य (कृष्णपक्षस्य) दोषा (रात्रिः) तस्याः अन्धकारे लब्धः प्रवेशप्रसरः येन. शून्यताहेतोः which is the cause of the mind being vacant; that causes depopulation. महाभूतग्रामः (प्राणिसमूहः) तस्य घातकः तस्य—sorrow kills many beings. महान्ति भूतानि यस्मिन् स महाभूतः ग्रामः (village) &c. One who destroys a village causes depopulation. महाभूतानि पृथिव्यप्तेजोवाय्वाकाशानि तेषां ग्रामः &c. If the five elements are destroyed nothing will be left. सकल...दक्षः expert in exhausting the whole body; expert in destroying all in battles. दोष...वर्तिनः pre-eminent among faults; a bad emperor. कार्श्यम् emaciation. श्वासः sighing, hard breathing. प्रलापः lamentation; delirium. उपद्रवः affliction; bad supervenient symptoms. असद्ग्रहस्य an evil planet; which is persistence in a bad thing. सकल...केतोः which indicates the destruction of the whole world; which is fire in destroying &c. शोक is a fire (धूमः केतुः चिह्नं यस्य). 'अग्न्युत्पातौ धूमकेतू' अम०. जीवि० applies to both शोक and वज्र in the same sense. अक्षणरुचेः न क्षणे (उत्सवे) रुचिः (liking) यस्मिन्. 'कालविशेषोत्सवयोः क्षणः' अम०. अविद्यमाना क्षणरुचिः (विद्युत्) यस्मिन्. विद्युत् flashes only for a moment (क्षणं रुचिः यस्याः). When a bolt falls in a cloudless sky, there is naturally no lightning. क्षणप्रभा is given by अमर as a synonym of विद्युत्. For ०वज्रपातस्य, see p. 25 (text) l. 1. Compare महा० उद्योगपर्व 84. 5. 'अनभ्रेऽशनिनिर्घोषः.' स्फुरन्त्यः अनवद्याः (blameless, pure) विद्याः एव विद्युतः ताभिः उद्द्योतमानानि illumined by flashing and pure lightning-like lores. The lores are either four or fourteen. 'पुराणन्यायमीमांसाधर्मशास्त्राङ्गमिश्रिताः । वेदाः स्थानानि विद्यानां धर्मस्य च चतुर्दश ॥' याज्ञ० I. 3. (*i. e.* the four Vedas, six वेदाङ्गs, पुराण, न्याय, मीमांसा and धर्मशास्त्र). The four (in the case of kings) are आन्वीक्षिकी, त्रयी (वेदत्रयी), वार्ता and दण्डनीति (अर्थशास्त्र p. 6). विद्युत् also is flashing (स्फुरत्) and bright. गहनाः ग्रन्थाः ग्रन्थयः इव तेषां गूढः गर्भः तस्य ग्रहणेन गम्भीराणि profound by grasping the hidden meanings lying in deep works. The interior of a fleshy knot is also deep. कठोर well-developed; hard. A swelling (ग्रन्थि) is hard; a गर्भ becomes developed (कठोर). बहु...बृहन्ति big with carrying many S'āstras. A swelling makes the part swollen look big and heavy. So a गर्भ also has to be borne (उद्वहन) by the mother. न अलं सोढुं आपातं are not able to bear the onset (of sorrow). नवमालिका jasmine. सरस juicy (with बिसतन्तु); affectionate (with हृदयम्). सत्यं व्रतं यस्याः who is true to her vow. उपालभ्यते rebuked. अमूढेन without being bewildered. मर्त्यधर्मणा = मनुजेन. पुरा...कर्तुम् who can change these ancient rules of conduct ? There is a suggested meaning:—these decrees of fate due to actions in former lives, who can gainsay. In this and the following there are laboured puns everywhere. जन्म...घटनानि (union, happening) एव ०रज्जवः. For पञ्चजन, see p. 124. All people have to undergo the long round of births, deaths and old age. The ropes of the water-wheel also are very long and revolve (संसरन्त्यः) night and day. पञ्चमहाभूतान्येव पञ्चकुलः तेन अधिष्ठितः अन्तःकरणव्यवहारः तस्य दर्शने निपुणाः; पञ्चमहाभूतेषु *i. e.* ०भूतात्मके शरीरे अधिष्ठितं अन्तःकरणं. The ideas here are rather complicated. The mind presides over the body (*i. e.* regulates its movements) that is made up of the five elements. यम notes what men do and what is passing in their minds. Compare the verse 'आदित्यचन्द्रावनिलोऽनलश्च द्यौर्भूमिरापो हृदयं यमश्च । अहश्च रात्रिश्च उभे च सन्ध्ये धर्मोऽपि जानाति नरस्य वृत्तम् ॥'. 'धर्मराजः पितृपतिः... यमः ॥' अम०. यम spares none (सर्वंकष) and is terrible. A king's ordinances (राजस्थितयः) are applicable to all (सर्वंकषा). The king sees into the transactions and documents (करणं) of the पञ्चकुल officers. They seem to be the same as modern Panchait. Compare the word पञ्चमण्डली in C. I. I. vol. III. p. 31, 32. For करण, see above p. 167. धर्मसदृशो राजा तस्य स्थितयः. We must read अक्षममाणाः. क्षण...माणाः not allowing even a moment to pass (every moment is calculated by the water-clock). कालनालिकाः the Ghaṭikâs of

Death (काल); the Ghaṭikās of time. नाडिका also means 'a water-clock'. आयुष्क...कुशलाः expert in calculating the span (कला, portion) of life (allotted to each individual); expert in calculating the कलाs. निलये निलये in each house; at the time of destruction (or in each Hell). निलय is equal to निरय; see above p. 125 for identity of र् and ल्. कला, क्षण and नाडिका are measures of time 18 or 15 निमेषs are equal to a काष्ठा, 30 काष्ठाs to a कला, 30 कलाs to a क्षण and 12 क्षणs to a मुहूर्त which is equal to two घटिकाs. See अमरकोश for this. For a different table and for a water-clock, see ब्रह्मपुराण 231. 6–9 'निमेषो मानुषो योऽयं मात्रामात्रप्रमाणतः। तैः पञ्चदशभिः काष्ठा त्रिंशत्काष्ठास्तथा कला॥ नाडिका तु प्रमाणेन कलाश्च दश पञ्च च। उन्मानेनाम्भसः सा तु पलान्यर्धत्रयोदश॥ हेममाषैः कृतच्छिद्रा चतुर्भिश्चतुरङ्गुलैः। मागधेन प्रमाणेन जलप्रस्थस्तु स स्मृतः॥ नाडिकाभ्यामथ द्वाभ्यां मुहूर्तो द्विजसत्तमाः।.' आयुष्कला is proper according to 'इदुदुपधस्य चाप्रत्ययस्य' पा. 8. 3. 41. चण्डिका fierce; the goddess Durgā. The command of Yama goes forth in the world. सर्व...पातिनी—at Yama's word, the lives of beings are offered at his feet; to Durgā all sorts of animals are offered. उपहारः=बलिः. प्रेतपतिः यमः तस्य पटहाः. Drums announce the march (प्रयाण) of a king's army. The drums of Yama announce the departure of the life of all beings. पेटकैः in groups. प्रतप्तलोहवत् लोहिते अक्षिणी येषाम् whose eyes are red like heated iron. कालकूटस्य इव कान्तिः यस्य सः ०कान्तिः कालः (dark) कायः येषाम्. कालपाशः पाणौ येषाम्. कालकूट is the same as हालाहल poison, which first came out at the churning and darkened the throat of शिव. There is an allusion to gamblers, whose eyes are red through late hours, envy and hatred and who have dark dice (पाशः) in their hands. भीषणकिङ्कराणां करैः घट्टितः (struck) यम...पुटः तस्य पटुना (sharp) टाङ्कारेण भयङ्कराः. Separate घोराः घातघोषणाः the terrible proclamation of death (with यमकिङ्कर); and read घोरा...षणाः as one word (with *servants*)—proclamations in which there is fierce beating (of the drum or bell). घोरः आघातः यस्यां सा ०घाता घोषणा. King's proclamations are announced by his servants that ring a bell and collect (संहरणं) all people to listen to them. The messengers of Death (किङ्कर) destroy (संहरणं) all beings. वहन्ति—is to be connected with वीथयः. बहुचितानां धूमैः धूसरिता ०पताका तस्यां पटुपतिता गृध्रदृष्टिः यासु—where the keen eye of vultures falls on the banners of Yama darkened by the smoke of numerous funeral pyres. शोकेन कृतः कोलाहलः याभि· ताः ०हलाः ०म्बिन्यः तासां विकीर्णाः (dishevelled) ०कलापाः तैः शबलं शववशिबिकासहस्रं येन सङ्कुलाः—

round the biers of their husbands widows scream and their hair sticks to them. किलकिलायमानाः श्मशानशिबिरे शिवाशावकाः यासु—there are howling young ones of female jackals in the cemetery. परलोकः आवसथः इव तस्य पथिकाः तेषां सार्थः तस्य प्रस्थाने विशिखाः तेषां वीथयः (rows, lines). 'रथ्या प्रतोली विशिखा' अम०. The roads lead the sojourners to the next world to their destination. There is another meaning. आवसथः a resting-place, an asylum for students and ascetics. Roads lead the intending travellers to an आवसथ (outside the town) whence they makes their प्रस्थान (start for the journey). There are heaps (चिता) of fuel and cowdung burning near it and a पताका too. Vultures hover over it in search of crumbs. Their wives scream round their palanquins (शिबिका) when they start and urchins are merry round the encampment (शिबिरं) of travellers. The student will note the chain of alliteration in the next clause. सकल...लम्पटा greedy to taste the mouthful *viz.* the whole world. He means the night of destruction (कालरात्री) threatens all and would spare no man. बहुला thick. 'वहंलिहा छिद्रान्वेषिणी' com—striking at a weak point. लोहितेन आचिता full of blood. चिताङ्गारैः काली dark with the charcoal of the pyre. The words suggest the tongue of a cow. The tongue is बहुला and वहंलिहा (licks the shoulder of the calf). 'स्कन्धप्रदेशस्तु वहः' अम०. The tongue licks mouthfuls of grass. It is red (लोहिता) and full (आचिता) and the cow may be dark like अङ्गार. तृप्ति...मृत्योः the hunger of Death that devours all beings never learns satiety. अति...वाहिनी flowing very quickly. महान् भूतग्रामः (भूतसङ्घः) तस्य गोष्ठ्यः (meetings). According to Buddhist philosophy everything is transitory (सर्वं क्षणिकं) and hence the group of five elements also must be so. रात्रि...देहिनाम् the sticks of the cage of the machine—like body of men are liable to break in the night. A cage set to catch wild animals may be shattered by them at night. रात्रिषु may refer to कालरात्रि. अशु...माणवः the atoms that create this body, being helpless against the oncoming (आवेशः) of good and evil, are liable to be shattered. विशरारु from शृ with वि. जीव...तन्तवः the threads of the strings that fasten the soul (in the body). The threads of पाश (snares) and the strings of lutes also are likely to break. सर्वं...नश्वरम् the whole world, which is perishable, is not independent (is not master of itself). तमसः...यातुम् to allow full scope to darkness (ignorance).तमः is the third गुण of out of the three (सत्त्व, रजस् and तमस्). मेधाविनि is addressed to राज्यश्री; it also goes with मनसि. एको...भूते: A single moment of discernment becomes the support of steadiness of mind *i. e.* makes the mind steady. For प्रतिसंख्यान see p. 119. अपेक्षणीय: to be cared for. पितृकल्प: almost like your father. For कल्प, see p. 38. काषायग्रहणं करोतीति तं. ज्याय:...व्रताम् this (प्रव्रज्या) is the best place for the wise (for the self-restrained). वत्सल: affectionate. सर्व...योगे by all means you must act according to his order.

P. 140 l. 13—**P. 141** l. 6 उपरत...जगाम. अन...मिता: created by Fate, though not requested to do so. विषम...स्तम्भा: pillars for support in serious calamities. Pillars support a house. स्नेहा...मूर्तय: who are full of affection; that are wet with oil. मोहा...ध्वंसिन: that destroy the darkness of error (delusion). धर्मप्रदीपा: that illuminate the law. A lamp also destroys darkness &c. प्रणय...लिता rendered naughty by the gift of affection; spoilt by giving what is asked for. A spoilt child may ask for what is दुर्लभ. धीर...वल्लभत्वम् the knowledge that one is loved emboldens even a steady man, the levity of his heart urging him to transgress proper limits. हृदयस्य लघिम्ना लङ्घितं (°ल्लभत्वम्). शालीन...गल्भ्यम् the desire to secure one's objects teaches even a modest man to be overbold. For शालीन, see p. 28. अभ्य...मार्या: the noble respect the limits of request, as the ocean does. The idea is:—the ocean, though so full, does not pass beyond the prescribed limits; so the noble, though galled by unreasonable requests, do not reject them but respect them. दत्तमेव च शरीरम्—See text p. 75 ll. 7-8. सर्व...लालनीया must be fondled for a while even in spite of the neglect of all my duties. °अवधीरणं (neglect) एव उपरोध: (obstacle). बाहोर्विधेयै: being the servants of (*i. e.* under the control of) our arm. दीय...मिदम् Give this your body to me who am your guest *i. e.* you must be my guest and accompany me. अयं जन: refers to हर्ष himself. यावत्...प्रजा: while I lessen the burden of my vow (*i. e.* fulfil my vow) and comfort the subjects distressed by the sorrow of my father's death. तावदिमां...अस...मेव प्रतिबोध्यमानामिच्छामि so long I desire that she should be enlightened, while still remaining by my side. The instrumentals कथाभि:, उपदेशै, &c., are to be connected with प्रतिबोध्यमानाम्. कथाभि: धर्म्याभि: by righteous discourses. कुशल...रजोभि: by advice free from passion, that brings about right knowledge. अविद्यमानं रज: (रजोगुण:) यस्मिन्. शीलो...नाभि: by instruction that produces quiescence by the practice of the

भिक्षादानं तस्मिन् शौण्डः पुरमथनः तेन मुक्तं मुण्डं तस्य शिरानाडीनां रुधिरं तेन पूरणं तेन कपिलः. We must read ०पूरणकपिलः. We may also take रुद्रभिक्षा in the sense of terrible alms. The story alluded to is the cutting off of the fifth head of Brahmā by S'iva. The Rudras are eleven, chief of whom is शङ्कर or शम्भु. शङ्कर is called त्रिपुरान्तक or पुरमथन because he burnt down the three cities of gold, silver and iron built by Maya for demons in the sky, air and earth. See द्रोणपर्व chap. 202. 64 'असुराणां पुराण्यासंस्त्रीणि वीर्यवतां दिवि। आयसं राजतं चैव सौवर्णं परमं महत् ॥'. पितृवधेन रुषितः रामः (परशुरामः) तेन रागेण रचितः. 'रागस्तु मात्सर्ये लोहितादिषु। क्लेशादावनुरागे च गान्धारादौ नृपेऽपि च ॥' मे०. With the sun, we may explain 'रामः तस्य रागः (redness) तेन रचितः' possessing the redness of परशुराम &c. पृथुः (broad) विकटः (formidable) कार्तवीर्यस्य अंसकूटः (the hump-like or peak-like shoulder) तस्य कुट्टाकः कुठारः तस्य तुण्डेन तष्टानि (chopped off) कण्ठकुहराणि तेषां रुधिरकुल्याप्रणालाः तेषां सहस्रेण पूरितः. दूररोधी stretching far and wide (applies to the lake and to the sun's rays also). रुधिरस्यायं रौधिरः. For the five lakes of blood and for the destruction of क्षत्रियs, see pp. 152, 38. भयेन निगूढानि (concealed) करचरणमुण्डानि यस्य स चासौ मण्डलाकृतिश्च that presented the shape of a sphere because the hands &c. were contracted through fear. The sun also is मण्डलाकृति. गुरुः गरुडस्य नखपञ्जरः तेन आक्षेपः तेन क्षपणं (smashing) तेन क्षिप्तं क्षतजं (blood) तेन उक्षितः (sprinkled). विगताः असवः यस्य (dead). Remove the comma after विभावसुः. कमठः tortoise. See महा० आदिपर्व chap 29–30. विभावसु and सुप्रतीक were brothers. सुप्रतीक the younger asked विभा० to give him his share. Thereupon विभावसु cursed him to be an elephant and सुप्रतीक cursed him to be a tortoise. They were always fighting in a lake. When गरुड set out for bringing nectar, he seized, carried into space and ate both of them. लोठ्यमानो नभसि—the sun also rolls in the sky. अरुणः गर्भः यस्य सः ०गर्भः मांसपिण्डाण्डः the egg containing a mass of flesh forming the embryo Aruṇa. The sun is also round (like an egg) and is like the red flesh of an embryo. खण्डिमानमानीतः broken into pieces (with egg); reduced in effulgence. ०पातेन दूयमाना दाक्षायणी तया क्षिप्तः thrown by विनता that was anxious by the passing away of the period fixed (for pregnancy). C and T following the com. take the clause 'नियत... क्षिप्तः' with धातुतटः. That construction does not yield a good sense. We do not know when Meru was tossed by दाक्षायणी (which com. renders by काली). कद्रू and विनता were two of the daughters of

दक्ष and wives of कश्यप. Her husband said that कद्रू would have a thousand sons and विनता only two. कद्रू gave birth to 1000 serpents. 'अण्डाभ्यां विनतायास्तु मिथुनं न व्यदृश्यत। ततः पुत्रार्थिनी देवी व्रीडिता च तपस्विनी ॥ अण्डं बिभेद विनता तत्र पुत्रमपश्यत। अप्यर्धकायसम्पन्नमितरेणाप्रकाशता।' आदिपर्व 16. 16-17. धातु...रोः like the slope of Meru containing metallic ores. Meru is a mountain of gold; the sky suffused with the glow of evening resembled it; and the disc of the sun looked like चरु. असुरवधाय अभिचारः तस्य चरुः तस्य पचनं तस्य पिशुनः (सूचकः) indicating the cooking of an oblation in some magic rites for the destruction of the demons. For अभिचार see p. 145. A चरु (oblation of rice) may be smeared with red powder. If the gods wanted to perform any rite for असुरवध, they would do so on Meru. We may also take असुर... पिशुनः with कटाहः. In that case we have to look upon धातु... मेरोः as an independent clause by itself (the disc of the sun being red like the slope of Meru). शोणितकाथेन कषायितः कुक्षिः यस्य the sides of which are red with the decoction of blood. For विसङ्कट see p. 122. कटाह...त्यः the cauldron of बृहस्पति. The sun looks like a cauldron. बृहस्पति is the priest of the gods. The poet fancies that he was engaged in boiling in a cauldron an oblation for the purpose of killing the असुरs. सद्यो गलितं गजदानवस्य (गजासुरस्य) लोहितं (blood) तस्य उपलेपेन (smearing) भीषणः. मुख... भोगः the expanse of the round face. महाभैरव is a form of शिव. गजासुर was a demon, son of महिषासुर, slain by S'iva. The sun was भीषण like the application (उपलेप) of the blood &c. ०जले प्रतिबिम्बिता रविबिम्बराजिः तेन भास्वरं अभ्रं (cloud) तदवलम्बते इति. गृहीतः आर्द्रमांसभारः यया. वासरा...निभा the evening resembled a वेताल (vampire). Flesh is offered to वेताल. The idea is:—in the evening the sky was overspread with clouds which were suffused red by the lustre of the reflections of the sun in the ocean. The clouds are like वेताल and their glow is like मांस. After night-fall, वेतालs begin to appear (वेतालाः नितरां भान्ति यस्याम्). ज्वलन् सन्ध्यारागः तेन रज्यमानः जलप्रवाहः यस्य. पुराणपुरुषः (विष्णुः) तस्य पीवरं ऊरुसम्पुटं तेन पिष्टौ मधुकैटभौ तयोः रुधिरपटलं (pool of blood) तेन पाटलं वपुः यस्य. अर्णसाम्=जलानाम्. मधु and कैटभ were two demons born from the ear of Vishṇu, when he was absorbed in Yogic sleep at the end of the *Kalpa*. They were about to devour Brahmā. The latter woke up Vishṇu, who asked them to choose a boon. They asked him to choose one, when विष्णु chose that they be killed by him. He killed them between his thighs 'स्वकावनावृतावूरू दृष्ट्वा देववरस्तदा । मधुकैटभयो राजन् शिरसी मधुसूदनः ॥ चक्रेण शितधारेण न्यकृन्तत महायशाः ॥' वनपर्व 203. 35. See मार्कण्डेयपुराण chap. 81. Compare 'अचिरमृदितमधुकैटभरुधिरारुणेन हरिमिवोरुयुगलेन विराजमानम्' काद० p. 9. अवसिते The sentence is अवसिते ०समये समनन्तरं...श्वेतभानुः उपानीयत निशया नरेन्द्राय when the time of evening ended, immediately afterwards the moon was presented to the king (Harsha) by night. अपरि...कीर्त्या as if it were a goblet made from a pearl slab (presented) by the Glory of his family to him who had a thirst for drinking boundless fame. The bright moon resembled a goblet of pearls. His family was already glorious, just as the night may be glorious with the twinkling stars. But Harsha was not satisfied with that. He thirsted for glory that would embrace the whole world like the moon's rays. कृत...ताय who was bent on starting the कृतयुग (*i. e.* an era of perfect righteousness). हर्ष wanted to bring back in कलियुग the pristine righteousness of कृतयुग. For कृतयुग and धर्म see pp. 3, 40. The bright moon resembled a round silver coin or edict stamped with the royal seal. आदिराजस्य राजतः ०निवेशः the stamp on silver of the primeval king's seal conferring authority (on Harsha). Night is compared to राज्यश्री (royal glory). राज्यश्री originally belonged to the first king (either Manu or Pṛithu) who reigned in the Kṛita age. His authority was transferred to Harsha. Authority is conferred by a शासन (copperplate or patent) impressed with the royal seal. Compare for आदिराज 'पृथुः प्रथमपुरुषकः परिभूतवान् पृथिवीम्' हर्षचरित (3rd उच्छ्वास). Probably there is a veiled allusion. राज्यश्री, Harsha's sister, called upon Harsha to assume the sovereignty of the world including her husband's realm. सकल...चलिताय that had set off on the conquest of all the continents. For श्वेतद्वीप, see above p. 190. The people from श्वेतद्वीप are all white; so the moon is aptly compared to a messenger from श्वेतद्वीप. निशा is compared to आयति (Future; or, Glory). A दूत is sent either to encourage a person or to make peace with him. इति shows that the chapter ends here. C and T suggest that the descriptions of sunset and of moonrise indicate bloody wars and the fall of Harsha's enemy, followed by the rise of Harsha's glory.

In the third Uchchhvāsa, Bāna promised to his cousins a narrative of Harsha's career and described it thus far. The narrative is suddenly brought to a close.

Appendix

A Brief Analysis of the Harshacharita.

Chap. I & II. After the usual invocation and sympathetic references to his great predecessors, Bāṇa gives us an account of his family and of himself which has been summarised in the Introduction (pp. II–IV) and need not be repeated here.

Chap. III. When Bāṇa returned from Harsha's court, he was pressed by his cousins with the request that he should entertain them with a narrative of the life and career of Harsha. Bāṇa expressed his inability to do even the slightest justice to the remarkable career of Harsha and said that he was ready to narrate to them only a portion of the brilliant career of Harsha. He then proceeded to narrate as follows. In the country of S'rîkaṇṭha, there is a district named Sthāṇvîs'vara. In ages long past there reigned a king named Pushpabhūti. He was a great devotee of S'iva. He formed friendship with a great S'aivite teacher from the Deccan named Bhairavāchārya. The latter made a present of a wonderful sword named Aṭṭahāsa to the king. Pushpabhūti offered to help the S'aiva ascetic in a magic rite. While engaged in his task, he had a vision of Lakshmî, who promised him that he would be the founder of a mighty line of kings, one of whom Harsha would have a most glorious career.

Chap. IV. In Pushpabhūti's line, as time rolled on, was born Prabhākaravardhana alias Pratāpas'îla, who fought successfully against the Hūṇas, the king of the Gūrjaras and the lords of Sindhu, Gāndhāra, Lāṭa and Mālava. His queen was Yas'omatî. The king was a great devotee of the sun. Rājyavardhana was the first child of the king and the queen. Then was born Harsha on the 12th of the dark half of the month of Jyeshtha. The birth of Harsha was heralded by auspicious signs prognosticating his future greatness. When Rājyavardhana was in his sixth year and Harsha was an infant just beginning to take a few steps with the help of his nurse and prattling a few indistinct words, a daughter named Rājyas'rî was born to the king and queen. About the time of the birth of Rājyas'rî, queen Yas'omatî's brother handed over to the king Prabhākaravardhana his son Bhaṇḍin about eight years old as a companion to the two princes, between whom and Bhaṇḍin sprang up a close and intimate friendship. The king in course of time brought, as companions for the growing princes, two brothers, sons of the king of Mālava, named Kumāragupta and Mādhavagupta, the elder Kumāragupta being about 18 years old at the time. These two followed the princes like their shadow. When Rājyas'rî grew up an accomplished princess she was married to Grahavarman, the eldest son of Avantivarman of the Maukhari family. Rājyas'rî went with her husband to his country of Kānyakubja.

Chap. V. When Rājyavardhana was old enough to bear arms, Prabhākaravardhana sent him accompanied by hereditary ministers and devoted feudatories to the north against the Hūṇas. Harsha accompanied him for some distance and when Rājyavardhana entered the Kailāsa range, Harsha remained behind and devoted some time to hunting. A courier from Prabhākaravardhana announced his serious illness. He started in hot haste and riding day and night reached the capital on the third day. He saw the whole city given up to performing rites of various sects and faiths for the sake of his father. On entering the palace he found the king lying in the clutches of death with queen Yas'omatî weeping over him. Two days afterwards when the king's condition became hopeless, Yas'omatî ascended the funeral pyre and the king died a short time afterwards. Harsha performed the funeral rites and anxiously waited for the arrival of his elder brother to whom he had already despatched swift messengers.

Chap. VI. About a fortnight after the death of Prabhākaravardhana, Rājyavaradhana arrived wounded in his successful war against the Hūṇas and with a thin growth of hair on his chin. The next day Rājyavardhana announced his intention of refusing the throne and of taking to a life in the forest. Harsha was taken aback by the strange resolve of his brother and had a mind to follow him, when one of Rājyas'rî's attendants, named Saṃvādaka, threw himself into the hall where the brothers sat and narrated a harrowing tale. He told Rājyavardhana that on the very day on which the news of Prabhākaravardhana's death reached Kānyakubja (Kanoj), Grahavarman, the husband of Rājyas'rî, was slain by the king of Mālava, that Rājyas'rî was put into prison at Kânyakubja with fetters on her feet like a brigand's wife and that the king of Mālava had designs even against Sthāṇvîs'vara. On that very day Rājyavardhana, who did not listen to Harsha's entreaties that, though a boy, he should be allowed to accompany him, started against the king of Mālava accompanied by Bhaṇḍin with ten thousand cavalry. After many days had elapsed, Harsha saw Kuntala, a high cavalry officer and a great favourite of Rājyavardhana, coming with sorrow written on his face. He brought the news that Rājyavardhana, though he subdued with ease the Mālava prince, was treacherously slain by the king of the Gauḍas, who had induced Rājyavardhana to go alone to the former's place. Siṃhanāda, the old and faithful commander-in-chief of Prabhākaravardhana, encouraged Harsha to avenge his brother's death. Harsha took the vow of destroying the Gauḍa king and dictated to his minister for foreign affairs named Avanti a proclamation to be sent to all kings either to submit to Harsha or to offer battle. The next morning, Harsha called Skandagupta, the chief of his elephant hosts, and asked him to get ready his whole army for an expedition. Skandagupta applauded Harsha's project but implored his master to learn the lesson of distrust from the fate of Rājyavardhana and narrated for his master's edification the stories of numerous former kings that fell victims to treachery and intrigue.

Chap. VII. A few days afterwards Harsha crowned himself and set out on an auspicious day, after worshipping S'iva. The first halt was made not far from the capital (Thanesar) on the banks of the Sarasvatî. There the chief accountant of the village waited upon him with a golden seal marked with the emblem of the bull and requested Harsha to issue a charter. The next day Harsha marched on with his vast army. When the day's march was over, he gave audience to Haṃsavega, a confidential messenger of Kumāra alias Bhāskaravarman, king of Prāgjyotisha (Assam). The messenger announced that the prince of Assam desired to form an undying friendship with Harsha and offered many wonderful presents, the chief of which was a miraculous parasol that originally belonged to Varuṇa. At night Haṃsavega informed Harsha how the parasol came into the possession of the kings of Assam. He traced the descent of Kumāra alias Bhāskaravarman from Naraka and mentioned that Kumāra was the great-great-grandson of Bhūtivarman, great-grandson of Chandramukhavarman, grandson of Sthitivarman and son of Susthiravarman alias Mṛigānka from his queen S'yāmādevî. Bhāskaravarman was a devotee of S'iva and desired the friendship of Harsha. Harsha was highly pleased with the king of Assam and sent back Haṃsavega with numerous presents. Harsha then proceeded for several days against his enemy (the king of Gauḍa). On the way he met Bhaṇḍin who brought with him the booty wrested from the Mālava king by Rājyavardhana. He brought news that after Kānyakubja was seized by Gupta, Rājyas'rî escaped from prison and had betaken herself to the Vindhya forest. Harsha then asked Bhaṇḍin to march against the Gauḍa king and himself entered the Vindhya forest in search of his unlucky sister.

Chap. VIII. After roaming about in the forest for several days, he met Vyāghraketu, son of the Bhil chieftain S'arabhaketu, who presented to Harsha a young Bhil by name Nirghāta, the commander-in-chief of the Bhils. He informed the king of an ascetic named Divākaramitra who was a convert from Brahmanism to Buddhism. Harsha remembered him as the friend of Grahavarman from the latter's childhood. Harsha resting his right hand on the shoulder of Mādhavagupta went to the hermitage of Divākaramitra, where he saw the latter surrounded by pupils and students of various sects. Just then a Bhikshu came unexpectedly and informed his teacher Divākaramitra that a woman of noble birth was about to burn herself for grief in the neighbourhood. Harsha hastened with the Bhikshu leading the way and saw his sister ready to perish in fire. From his sister he learnt how she was helped out of prison by a noble named Gupta at the time of the tumult of the Gauḍa king in Kānyakubja, how she then heard of the death of Rājyavardhana, how she gave up food on hearing it, how she came to the Vindhya forest and how in despair she prepared to burn herself. Divākaramitra then made to Harsha a present of a necklace named Mandākinî, brought by Nāgārjuna from the Nāgas in Pātāla and handed over to Sātavāhana, overlord of the Deccan. Rājyas'rī expressed to her brother her wish to put on the red robe. Harsha implored her to remain with him till he carried out his vow of destroying the Gauḍa king and requested Divākaramitra to be the spiritual adviser of his sister. He further said that after fulfilling his vow, he would himself assume the red robes along with his sister. When Divākaramitra acceded to the wishes of Harsha, the latter returned to his army encamped on the banks of the Ganges.

Here the narrative of Harsha's career comes to an end.

INDEX

THE HARSHACARITA OF BĀṆABHAṬṬA

THE HARSHACARITA OF BĀṆABHAṬṬA

(*Text of Uchchhvāsas I — VIII*)

Edited with an Introduction and Notes
by
MAHĀMAHOPĀDHYĀYA
P. V. KANE

MOTILAL BANARSIDASS PUBLISHERS PRIVATE LIMITED • DELHI

First Edition: Bombay, 1918
Reprint: Delhi, 1965, 1973, 1986, 1997

ISBN: 81-208-0032-x (Cloth)
ISBN: 81-208-0051-6 (Paper)

Also available at:

MOTILAL BANARSIDASS
41 U.A. Bungalow Road, Jawahar Nagar, Delhi 110 007
8, Mahalaxmi Chamber, Warden Road, Mumbai 400 026
120 Royapettah High Road, Mylapore, Madras 600 004
Sanas Plaza, Subhash Nagar, Pune 411 002
16 St. Mark's Road, Bangalore 560 001
8 Camac Street, Calcutta 700 017
Ashok Rajpath, Patna 800 004
Chowk, Varanasi 221 001

PRINTED IN INDIA
BY JAINENDRA PRAKASH JAIN AT SHRI JAINENDRA PRESS,
A-45 NARAINA, PHASE I, NEW DELHI 110 028
AND PUBLISHED BY NARENDRA PRAKASH JAIN FOR
MOTILAL BANARSIDASS PUBLISHERS PRIVATE LIMITED,
BUNGALOW ROAD, DELHI 110 007

PREFACE.

The present edition contains the whole of the text of he Harshacharita (Uchchhvāsas I–VIII). As there is at present no other annotated edition of the Harshacharita in the market, the present edition needs no apology. This edition will, it is hoped, meet all the requirements of the University student. No pains have been spared to make the book useful not only to the college student, but also to the general reader. As the work was published in two parts in two years, the paging of one part is independent of the other.

The commentary of S'aṃkara published by the Nirṇaya-sāgara Press has been highly useful to me. The elegant and spirited translation of the Harshacharita by Prof. Cowell and Mr. Thomas is a monument of skill and learning. Though I have unfortunately had frequent occasion to differ from them, my sincerest thanks are due to them, particularly for happy renderings of words and phrases. The Harshacharita is a difficult book and I am afraid that many passages have still remained obscure. I crave the indulgence of the reader and will most thankfully receive all suggestions and criticisms.

P. V. KANE.

A list of some of the abbreviations employed in the work.

अ०—The Nirṇaya-sāgara edition of the हर्षचरित.

अम०—अमरकोश.

अलं०—अलंकारसर्वस्व of रुय्यक.

उत्तरराम०—उत्तररामचरित of भवभूति.

क—The Calcutta edition of the Harshacharita by Īsvara-chandra Vidyāsāgara.

का० or **काम०**—कामन्दकीयनीतिसार.

काद०—कादम्बरी (Dr. Peterson's edition).

क्षीर०—क्षीरस्वामी, commentator of the अमरकोश.

चतु०—चतुर्वर्गचिन्तामणि of हेमाद्रि.

पा०—पाणिनि's अष्टाध्यायी.

ब—The edition of the Harshacharita in the Bombay Sanskrit Series.

बृह०—बृहत्संहिता of वराहमिहिर (edited by Prof. Kern).

भागवतपु०—भागवतपुराण. **महा०**—महाभारत (Bombay edition).

मनु०—मनुस्मृति. **मे०**—मेदिनीकोश.

याज्ञ० or **याज्ञवल्क्य०**—याज्ञवल्क्यस्मृति. **रघु०**—रघुवंश.

वायु०—वायुपुराण (Ānandās'rama ed.).

विष्णुपु० or **विष्णु०**—विष्णुपुराण. **शब्द०**—शब्दकल्पद्रुम.

सं०—संकेत, commentary on the हर्षचरित. **सि. कौ.**=सिद्धान्तकौमुदी.

A—The Nirṇaya-sāgara edition of the Harshacharita.

Anand. ed.—Ānandās'rama edition.

B—The edition of the Harshacharita in the Bombay Sanskrit Series.

B. R. W. W.—Beal's Buddhist records of the Western World.

C—Is'varachandra's edition of the Harshacharita.

C. I. or *C. I. I.*—Corpus Inscriptionum Indicarum.

C and *T.*—The translation of the Harshacharita by Prof. Cowell and Mr. Thomas.

E. I.—Epigraphia Indica.

I. A.—Indian Antiquary.

J. B. B. R. A. S.—Journal of the Bombay Branch of the Royal Asiatic Society.

J. R. A. S.—Journal of the Royal Asiatic Society.

P—Dr. Peterson's edition of the Kādambarī.

TABLE OF CONTENTS

Introduction.

I. Personal History of Bâṇa.

About the personal history of Sanskrit authors and especially poets, our knowledge is generally very meagre. In the case of many Sanskrit poets, we know next to nothing beyond their names. Around the names of some (*e. g.* Kâlidâsa), tradition has been busy in weaving such fanciful and bewildering stories that it is no easy task to separate the solid grain of truth from the chaff. In the case of some, the meagre account of themselves contained in their own works has to be eked out with information derived from contemporary or subsequent records in literature, grants and inscriptions. There are a few who have left to posterity a tolerably full account of themselves in their works*. Bâṇa perhaps stands at the head of such Sanskrit authors. To his Kâdambarî is prefixed a brief account of his family. But in his Harshacharita, we find a much fuller account of his ancestors and himself. The first two Uchchhvâsas of the Harshacharita are taken up with the history of Bâṇa's forefathers and Bâṇa himself. The personal narrative is continued even in the third Uchchhvâsa. Space does not permit us to give in detail a full account of Bâṇa as gathered from the Harshacharita. We propose to dwell upon only a few salient points of the narrative of Bâṇa's personal history.

The genealogical tree of Bâṇa's family as constructed

---

* In this connection we may mention Bilhaṇa and Mankha, who, in the Vikramânkadevacharita and the S'rîkanṭhacharita respectively, furnish a full account of their lives, their contemporaries &c.

from the Harshacharita* is given in the footnote below. In the introductory verses to the Kâdambarî the genealogy is given as follows. Kubera was a Brâhmaṇa of the Vâtsyâyana gotra and was honoured by many Gupta kings. His son was Arthapati, whose son was Chitrabhânu who was Bâṇa's father. The student will notice that in this narrative, Pâs'upata, who appears to have been the great-grand-father of Bâṇa, if we are to rely upon the Harshacharita, is omitted. It is strange that Bâṇa (or his son who is supposed by some to have written the introductory verses to the Kâdambarî) should have forgotten his own great-grand-father. The only explanation that we offer (of course with great hesitation) is that the verses containing the reference to Pâs'upata were not to be found in the Mss. used for preparing the printed editions of the Kâdambarî.

The progenitor of Bâṇa's family, Vatsa, lived in a place called Prîtikûṭa on the banks of the Hiraṇyabâhu, otherwise called S'oṇa. Bâṇa's mother, Râjadevî, died while he was yet a child. He was all the more dear to his father, who was a very mother to him. Bâṇa had the misfortune to lose his father when he was about fourteen years old. Bâṇa tells us that he thereafter led a wandering life. He mentions as the

* वत्स, cousin of सारस्वत who was the son of सरस्वती and दधीच.

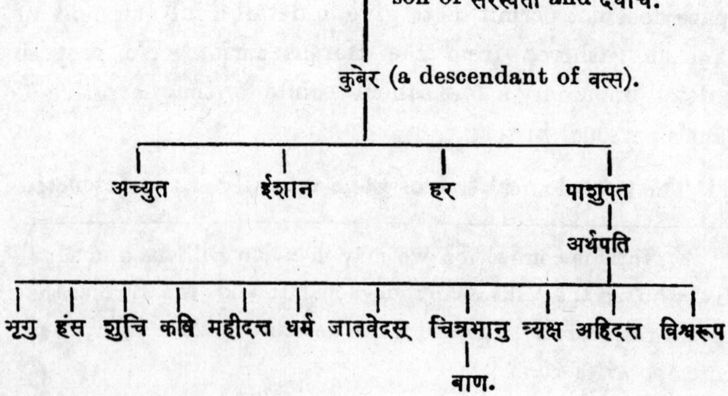

companions of his wanderings a number of persons*. Although Bâṇa had ancestral wealth sufficient to maintain him in ease and comfort, yet his strong curiosity to see differen' lands impelled him to wander from place to place and made him an object of ridicule in the eyes of his elderly contemporaries. After finishing his wanderings in which he gathered a rich harvest of wisdom and experience, he returned to his native place Brâhmaṇâdhivâsa (or Prîtikûṭa) with broadened sympathies and a widened outlook.

One day in the height of summer, when Bâṇa sat in his house after the midday meal his cousin (born of a S'ûdra woman) Chandrasena ushered in a courier who brought a letter from Kṛishṇa, a brother (cousin) of Emperor Harsha. In the letter Kṛishṇa referred Bâṇa to the messenger Mekhalaka and bade him lose no time in carrying out the wishes of the writer. The message was:—"Emperor Harsha's ears have been poisoned against you by some wicked people. But I knew the truth about you and interceded on your behalf with the king and told him that you (Bâṇa) must not have been guilty of anything beyond youthful rashness and folly. The king admits this and so you should come to the emperor's court without delay."

After a good deal of misgiving as to how he would be received at the court of Harsha, Bâṇa performed some auspicious rites and set out from his native place Prîtikûṭa. On the third day he reached the camp of Harsha which was then on the Ajirâvatî near the town Maṇitâra.

---

* "अभवंश्चास्य वयसा समानाः सुहृदः सहायाश्च । तथा च । भ्रातरौ पारशवौ चन्द्रसेनमातृषेणौ, भाषाकविरीशानः परं मित्रं, प्रणयिनौ रुद्रनारायणौ, विद्वांसौ वारबाणवासबाणौ, वर्णकविर्वेणीभारतः, प्राकृतकृत्कुलपुत्रो वायुविकारः, बन्दिनावनङ्गबाणसूचिबाणौ, कात्यायनिका चक्रवाकिका, जाङ्गुलिको मयूरकः, ताम्बूलदायकश्चण्डकः, भिषक्पुत्रो मन्दारकः, पुस्तकवाचकः सुदृष्टिः, कलादश्चामीकरः, हैरिकः सिन्धुषेणः, लेखको गोविन्दकः, चित्रकृद्वीरवर्मा, पुस्तकृत्कुमारदत्तः, मार्दङ्गिको जीमूतः, गायनौ सोमिलग्रहादित्यौ, सैरन्ध्री कुरङ्गिका, वांशिकौ मधुकरपारावतौ, गान्धर्वोपाध्यायो दर्दुरकः, संवाहिका केरलिका, लासकयुवा ताण्डविकः, आक्षिक आखण्डलः, कितवो भीमकः, शैलालियुवा शिखण्डकः, नर्तकी हरिणिका, पाराशरी सुमतिः, क्षपणको वीरदेवः, कथको जयसेनः, शैवो वक्रघोणः, मन्त्रसाधकः करालः, असुरविवरव्यसनी लोहिताक्षः, धातुवादविद्विहङ्गमः, दार्दुरिको दामोदरः, ऐन्द्रजालिकश्चकोराक्षः, मस्करी ताम्रचूडः ।"

When Bâṇa was presented to Harsha who had with him the son of the king of Mâlvâ, the emperor received him at first with mock signs of anger, but afterwards showed him much favour. After basking in the sunshine of royal favour, Bâṇa returned to his native place. He was greeted with a cordial welcome by his friends and relatives. The reader Sudṛishṭi entertained him with a recital of the Vâyupurâṇa. Then the bard Sûchîbâṇa recited two verses (Âryâs), which pointedly referred to the life of Harsha. All were charmed and Bâṇa's cousins (sons of his paternal uncles), Gaṇapati, Adhipaṭi, Târâpati and S'yâmala, looked at one another and the youngest of them, S'yâmala, made bold to ask Bâṇa to tell them from the beginning the wondrous story of Harsha's life. Bâṇa expressed his inability to do justice to the mighty deeds of the emperor and, as the day was far advanced, began the narrative the next morning.

Here ends the autobiographical part of the Harshacharita with which alone we are concerned at present.

As to the later stages of Bâṇa's life we have no account left. He died leaving his romance of Kâdambarî unfinished. Bâṇa's son tells us in the introduction to the Uttarabhâga that he finished the Kâdambarî as a work of filial duty and not out of pride*. Dr. Buhler says that the name of Bâṇa's son was Bhûshaṇabâṇa†. In some MSS. of the Kâdambarî, the son is called Pulinda‡ or Pulina. Dhanapâla, while praising Bâṇa in his introduction to the Tilakamanjarî, seems to suggest that Pulinda was the name of his son§.

---

* "याते दिवं पितरि तद्वचसैव सार्धं विच्छेदमाप भुवि यस्तु कथाप्रबन्धः । दुःखं सतां तदसमाप्तिकृतं विलोक्य प्रारब्ध एव स मया न कवित्वदर्पात् ॥"

† See Dr. Peterson's Introduction to Kâdambarî p. 40.

‡ *Vide* Prof. S. R. Bhandarkar's report on the search for MSS. 1904-5, 1905-6 p. 39; see also Dr. Stein's catalogue of Sanskrit MSS. at Jammu p. 299.

§ केवलोऽपि स्फुरन्बाणः करोति विमदान्कवीन् ।
किं पुनः क्लृप्तसन्धानपुलिन्ध्र (न्द?) कृतसन्निधिः ॥ verse 26.

(It will be noticed that the verse has two meanings).

It is said that the poet Mayûra was a contemporary and father-in-law of Bâṇa. Mayûra praised the sun in hundred verses, which make up the Sûryas'ataka and became free from leprosy. Bâṇa became jealous of him, maimed himself, composed the Chaṇḍîs'ataka in honour of Durgâ, who made him all right. The story of Mayûra's freedom from disease is alluded to in the Kâvyaprakâs'a*. There are Subhâshitas in which Bâṇa and Mayûra are spoken of as contemporaries and as patronized by king Harsha†. Verses from the Sûryas'ataka are quoted in the Dhvanyâloka (latter half of 9th century A. D.)‡. The Kavikaṇṭhâbharaṇa of Kshemendra mentions Mayûra by name and quotes a verse as his which is found in the Sûryas'ataka§. So it is not beyond the bounds of probability that Bâṇa and Mayûra were contemporaries. A Mayûraka is mentioned as one of the companions of Bâṇa in his wanderings (see the passage quoted above on p. III). But as he is mentioned there as a snake-doctor ('Jângulika' = Vishavaidya), it seems to us that he is not the same as the poet Mayûra. The commentators of the Bhaktâmarastotra of the Jain Mânatungâchârya say that Mânatunga lived at the court of Bhoja in Ujjayinî and was a contemporary of Bâṇa and Mayûra. They further narrate various stories about Bâṇa and Mayûra. We believe that those stories have no historic basis and are purely imaginary. We therefore refrain from reproducing them here.

II The date of Bâṇa.

As we are fortunate in possessing some account of Bâṇa from his own pen, so also we are lucky in being able to fix

---

* 'आदित्यादेर्मयूरादीनामिवानर्थनिवारणम्'

† 'अहो प्रभावो वाग्देव्या यन्मातङ्गदिवाकरः ।
श्रीहर्षस्याभवत्सभ्यः समो बाणमयूरयोः ॥'

This verse is ascribed to Râjas'ekhara and is quoted in the Subhâshitâvali and the S'ârngadharapaddhati.

'स चित्रवर्णविच्छित्तिहारिणोरवनीपतिः ।
श्रीहर्ष इव सङ्घट्टं चक्रे बाणमयूरयोः ॥'
नवसाहसाङ्कचरित II. 18.

‡ The verse 'दत्तानन्दाः' &c. (9th in the Nir. ed. of सूर्यशतक.)

§ In the fourth सन्धि of the कविकण्ठाभरण the verse 'अस्तव्यस्तत्वशून्यो' &c. is quoted as Mayūra's (verse 18 of the सूर्यशतक).

(6) Abhinanda wrote the Kâdambarîkathâsâra, in which he faithfully versifies the story of Bâṇa's Kâdambarî. Abhinanda tells us that his great-great-grand-father, S'akti-svâmin was a minister of Muktâpîḍa, a king of the Kꝛrkoṭa family*. Abhinanda is praised for the excellence of his Anushṭubh verses by Kshemendra in his Suvṛitta-tilaka†.

(7) The author of the Dhvanyâloka, Ânandavardhana, flourished in the reign of king Avantivarman (855-883 A. D.)‡ of Kashmir. In the Dhvanyâloka, Bâṇa and his two prose compositions are mentioned by name$. From this it follows that in the latter half of the 9th century Bâṇa's works had attained a pre-eminent position in the world of letters.

(8) Vâmana, in his Kâvyâlaṃkârasûtravṛitti seems to quote a few words from the Kâdambarî§. Vâmana flour-

---

* स **शक्तिस्वामिनं** पुत्रमवाप श्रुतशालिनम् । राज्ञः **कर्कोटवंशस्य मुक्ता-पीडस्य** मन्त्रिणम् ॥ verse 7 of कादम्बरीकथासार.

† 'अनुष्टुप्सततासक्ता साभिनन्दस्य नन्दिनी । विद्याधरस्य वदने गुलिकेव प्रभावभूः ॥'

We wish here to call the attention of the reader to a curious fact. Abhinava-gupta says in his Dhvanyâlokalochana that Bhaṭṭajayantaka wrote Kâdambarîkathâ-sâra; p. 142 "कथातात्पर्ये सर्गबन्धो यथा भट्टजयन्तकस्य कादम्बरीकथासारम्." The question arises whether this is a different work from that of Abhinanda or whether it is a slip on the part of the learned author of the Lochana or whether it is a mistake of the scribe's. We know that Abhinanda was the son of Bhaṭṭajayanta, called Vṛitti-kâra.

‡ 'मुक्ताकणः शिवस्वामी कविरानन्दवर्धनः । प्रथां रत्नाकरश्चागात्साम्राज्येऽव-न्तिवर्मणः ॥' राजतरङ्गिणी V. 34.

$ यथा स्थाण्वीश्वराख्यजनपदवर्णने **भट्टबाणस्य** 'यत्र च मत्तमातङ्गगामिन्यः' ध्वन्यालोक p. 100; यथा **हर्षचरिते** 'समवाय इव विरोधिनां पदार्थानाम्' p. 101; "यथा **हर्षचरिते** सिंहनादवाक्येषु—'वृत्तेऽस्मिन्महाप्रलये' p. 127; 'यथा **कादम्बर्यां** कादम्बरीदर्शनावसरे' p. 87. On p. 99 of the ध्वन्यालोक a passage is quoted from the Harshacharita (उच्छ्वास II) without naming it.
१

§ "'**अनुकरोति भगवतो नारायणस्य**' इत्यत्रापि, मन्ये, सशब्दः कविना प्रयुक्तो लेखकैस्तु प्रमादान्न लिखित इति" on 'आहेति भूतेऽन्यणलन्तभ्रमाद् ब्रुवो लटि' काव्यालंकारसूत्र V. 2. 44. For the words 'अनुकरोति भगवतो नारायणस्य' see कादम्बरी p. 6 of Dr. Peterson's edition.

ished in the latter half of the 8th century. We shall briefly indicate the data that enable us to arrive at this date for Vâmana. (a) Vâmana quotes from the Uttararâmacharita of Bhavabhûti a verse*. Bhavabhûti flourished before 700 A. D†. So Vâmana is later than 700 A. D. (b) He is often quoted by Pratîhârendurâja, the commentator of Udbhaṭa's Kavyâlaṃkâra‡. Pratîhârendurâja, who was a pupil of Mukula, son of Kallaṭa, flourished in the first half of the 10th century. Therefore Vâmana is earlier than 900 A. D. (c) Abhinavagupta says § that Ânandavardhana, bearing in mind the conflicting views of Vâmana and Bhâmaha as regards Samâsokti and Âkshepa, gave the verse 'Anurâgavatî sandhyâ' (p. 37 Dhvanyâloka) as an example. So according to Abhinavagupta, Vâmana flourished before Ânandavardhana *i. e.* before the latter half of 9th century A. D. (d) A Vâmana is mentioned as the minister ¶ of king Jayâpîḍa (745—776 A. D.) of Kashmir and is identified by Kashmirian Pandits with the author of the Kâvyâlaṃkârasûtra. These four lines of inquiry make it highly probable, if not certain, that Vâmana flourished in the latter half of the 8th century. Bâṇa's Kâdambarî was well-known, as shown above, in the latter half of the 8th century.

Thus from the 12th century backwards to the 8th, we have a host of writers who refer in unmistakable terms to Bâṇa and his works. Besides those mentioned by us above, there are writers of less note such as the authors of the Nalachampû and the Kîrtikaumudî that refer to Bâṇa. We refrain from quoting them for want of space.

The date of Bâṇa is of paramount importance for the chronology of Sanskrit writers. Bâṇa in the introduction to his Harshacharita mentions a number of Sanskrit works

---

* 'इयं गेहे लक्ष्मीरियममृतवर्तिर्नयनयोः' &c. on काव्यालंकारसूत्र IV. 3. 2. (रूपक).

† See Dr. Bhandarkar's preface to the Mâlatîmâdhava p. IX.

‡ See Folios 12, 55, 56, &c. of the Deccan College Ms. of Pratîhârendurâja's commentary.

§ 'वामनाभिप्रायेणायमाक्षेपः, भामहाभिप्रायेण तु समासोक्तिरित्यमुमाशयं हृदये गृहीत्वा समासोक्त्याक्षेपयोरिदमेकमेवोदाहरणं व्यतरद्ग्रन्थकृत्।' लोचन p. 37.

¶ 'मनोरथः शङ्खदत्तश्चटकः सन्धिमांस्तथा। बभूवुः कवयस्तस्य वामनाद्याश्च मन्त्रिणः॥' राजतरंगिणी IV. 497.

and poets*. The first half of the 7th century is the *terminus ad quem* of these poets. In this connection we strongly recommend that the student should read Dr. Peterson's valuable and instructive Introduction to his edition of the Kâdambarî. Although we have the misfortune to differ from the learned author of the Indroduction on a number of points, we feel confident that the Introduction will surely rouse the student's critical faculty†.

As one point (*viz.* the relative position of Subandhu and Bâṇa) on which we differ from Dr. Peterson is of great importance in connection with the date of Bâṇa, we shall discuss it here.

---

* The works and poets mentioned by name are:–Vyâsa, Vâsavadattâ, Bhaṭṭâra–Harichandra, Sâtavâhana, the Setu of Pravarasena, Bhâsa, Kâlidâsa, Bṛihatkathâ and Âḍhyarâja.

† The following are the most important among the points on which we differ from Dr. Peterson, though with the greatest diffidence:—(1) 'it is clear that by *Akhyâyikâ* in the present passage, Bâṇa refers *to metrical stories*, such as furnished him with the material of his own romance' (p. 70); (2) Bhâsa being the contemporary or immediate predecessor of Bâṇa (p. 71); (3) the Vâsavadattâ mentioned in the Harshacharita is not the one that was written by Subandhu; (4) the Nâṭakas, with a sûtradhâra in their beginning, were novelties in Bâṇa's day (p. 80); (5) Kâlidâsa was a contemporary of Bâṇa (p. 81); (6) Aḍhyarâja, mentioned in the Harshacharita, is not a proper noun (p. 96); (7) that Indian Astronomy, as taught by Âryabhaṭa and Varâhamihira and as known to Kâlidâsa and Bâṇa, is of Greek origin. About Âkhyâyikâ, we shall speak later on. It should be noted that in the Mâlavikâgnimitra, Kâlidâsa calls himself 'Vartamânakavi' and styles Bhâsa as of world-wide fame. So Bhâsa, who must have preceded Kâlidâsa by some generations, could not have been a contemporary or immediate predecessor of Bâṇa. We shall try to show that Subandhu preceded Bâṇa. That Âḍhyarâja was a name we know from a verse that occurs in the Sarasvatîkaṇṭhâbharaṇa (vol.I.p.136 Benares edition) 'केऽभूवन्नाढ्यराजस्य काले प्राकृतभाषिणः । काले श्रीसाहसाङ्कस्य के न संस्कृतभाषिणः ॥'. The commentary explains that आढ्यराज stands for शालिवाहन and साहसाङ्क for विक्रम. It is not possible to dismiss the other points briefly.

Dr. Peterson was inclined to place Subandhu, the author of the extant Vâsavadattâ, after Bâṇa. His reasons are given on pp. 71—73 of his introduction. 'For that after the graceless string of extravagant and indecent puns presented by the present Vâsavadattâ had been received with approval into the national literature, a reversion should have been possible to the chastity, alike of sentiment and of diction, of Bâṇa and Bhavabhûti would be a literary miracle almost incredible.' We have to strike here a note of caution. We should always beware of foisting our modern conceptions of literary style and beauty on authors and critics that flourished centuries before us. How are we to know that the skill of Subandhu in stringing together puns might not have kindled the admiration of Bâṇa who seems to have himself thought very highly of such puzzles as Prahelikâs? It is curious to note that Dr. Peterson, in his preface to the Subhâshitâvali of Vallabhadeva (p. 133), abandons the position taken up by him as to the relative position of Subandhu and Bâṇa in his introduction to the Kâdambarî.

We think that the Vâsavadattâ praised in the Harshacharita so* eloquently is the present work of that name written by Subandhu. Our reasons are:—

(1) In Vâmana's Kâvyâlamkârasûtravṛitti, a passage is quoted which is found in the Harshacharita and the extant Vâsavadattâ of Subandhu with very slight variations†.

* कवीनामगलद्दर्पो नूनं **वासवदत्तया** । शक्त्येव पाण्डुपुत्राणां गतया कर्णगोचरम् ॥. The महाभाष्य commenting on the वार्तिक 'अधिकृत्य कृते ग्रन्थे लुबाख्यायिकाभ्यो बहुलम्' mentions three works of the आख्यायिका class, *viz.* वासवदत्ता, सुमनोत्तरा and भैमरथी (Kielhorn vol. II p. 313). In another place he speaks of a person who studies the आख्यायिका वासवदत्ता (vol II p. 284). It is not probable that Bâṇa refers to this work. It is to be noted that the extant वासवदत्ता would have to be called a कथा and not an आख्यायिका as defined below.

† 'कुलिशशिखरखरनखरप्रचयप्रचण्डचपेटापाटितमत्तमातङ्गकुम्भस्थलगलन्मदच्छटाच्छुरितचारुकेसरभारभासुरमुखे केसरिणि' काव्यालंकारसूत्रवृत्ति I. 3. 25. See Vâsavadattâ (p. 331 of the S'rîrangam edition and p. 266 of Hall's). See हर्षचरित (उच्छ्वास VI) p. 40 of our text. In the वासवदत्ता the words are '०चपेटपाटितमत्तमातङ्गकुम्भस्थलरुधिरच्छटाच्छुरितचारुकेसरभारभासुरकेसरिकदम्बेन.' This correspondence between the वासवदत्ता and the हर्षचरित opens up the question whether Bâṇa

We have seen above that Vâmana probably flourished in the latter half of the 8th century and that he quotes the Kâdambarî also. It is difficult to say from what author Vâmana takes his quotation. But from the locative 'Kesariṇi' it seems that the Harshacharita is drawn upon.

(2) Kavirâja, the author of the Râghavapâṇḍavîya, mentions Subandhu, Bâṇa and himself as the masters of Vakrokti *. We think that the three are mentioned by the author in chronological order, placing himself last of all.

(3) Vākpatirâja, the author of Gauḍavaho, a Prakrit poem, refers to the composition of Subandhu †. No other poet bearing the name of Subandhu, except the author of the Vâsavadattâ, is known to us. Therefore we are justified in holding that Vâkpatirâja refers to the author of the extant Vâsavadattâ. Vâkpatirâja was a protégé of Yas'ovarman of Kânyakubja and an admirer (and perhaps friend and pupil) of Bhavabhûti. Pandit comes to the conclusion (Introduction to Gauḍavaho, p. 100) that Vâkpatirâja wrote his poem between 700-725 A. D. It is curious to note that while Vâkpatirâja mentions the work of Subandhu in the same breath with Bhâsa and Kâlidâsa, he is silent as regards Bâṇa who wrote a prose work similar to Subandhu's. What then is the probable conclusion ? It is that when Vâkpatirâja wrote Subandhu was a famous author while Bâṇa was yet unknown to fame.

From the foregoing it seems very probable that Subandhu, the author of the present Vâsavadattâ, preceded Bâṇa.

In Mankha's S'rikanṭhacharita we find a verse where both Bâṇa and Subandhu are praised together ‡.

---

actually borrowed the words of the वासवदत्ता. There are many passages where Bâṇa's words and ideas coincide with those of the Vâsavadattâ. For want of space we refrain from quoting them.

* 'सुबन्धुर्बाणभट्टश्च कविराज इति त्रयः । वक्रोक्तिमार्गनिपुणाश्चतुर्थो विद्यते न वा ॥' राघवपाण्डवीय I. 41.

† 'भासम्मि जलणमित्ते कन्तीदेवे अ जस्स रहुआरे । सोबन्धवे अ बन्धम्मि हारियन्दे अ आणन्दो ॥'

Pandit's Gaudavaho, verse 800.

‡ 'मेण्ठे स्वर्दिरदाधिरोहिणि वशं याते सुबन्धौ विधेः शान्ते हन्त च भारवौ विघटिते बाणे विषादस्पृशः ।' श्रीकण्ठचरित II. 53.

III Bâṇa's works.

Before proceeding with the subject of this section, a few remarks concerning the origin and development of Sanskrit Rhetoric and of Kathâ and Âkhyâyikâ in particular would not be out of place here.

The oldest writer who specifically mentions Âkhyâyikâs is Kâtyâyana*. Kâtyâyana seems to intimate that the Âkhyâyikâs he refers to were not the episodes contained in such books as the Mahâbhârata, but that they were independent and distinct works. Patanjali in his Mahâbhâshya, while commenting upon the above-mentioned Vârtika, gives the names of three Âkhyâyikâs, *viz.* Vâsavadattâ, Sumanottarâ and Bhaimarathî†. In another place Patanjali speaks of one who knows or studies the Âkhyâyikâ Vâsavadattâ or Sumanottarâ‡. Subandhu, who, we saw above, preceded Bâṇa, alludes to some canons of the art of poetry. In one place§ he says that the composition of a good poet should not contain superfluous words such as 'tu', 'hi' &c. In another place he says that the utterances of a good poet should be divided into Uchchhvâsas (chapters) and should contain fine puns and verses in the Vaktra metre¶. This seems to refer to what are called Âkhyâyikâs, as we shall see later on. Daṇḍin,|| who is gene-

---

* 'लुबाख्यायिकाभ्यो बहुलम्' a वार्तिक on 'अधिकृत्य कृते ग्रन्थे' पा॰IV.3. 87.; 'आख्यानाख्यायिकेतिहासपुराणेभ्यश्च' वार्तिक on पा॰ IV. 2. 60.

† "'अधिकृत्य कृते ग्रन्थे' बहुलं लुग्वक्तव्यः । वासवदत्ता सुमनोत्तरा । न च भवति । भैमरथी ।"

‡ Mahâbhāshya (Kielhorn) vol. II. p. 284 'वासवदत्तिकः सौमनोत्तरिकः'. Vide p. XI above.

§ 'सत्कविकाव्यबन्ध इवाबद्धतुहिनः' वासवदत्ता p. 134 (Hall).

¶ 'दीर्घोच्छ्वासरचनाकुलं सुश्लेषवक्त्रघटनापटु सत्कविवचनमिव' वासवदत्ता p. 184 (Hall).

|| A few scholars are inclined to place Daṇḍin later. This is not the place to discuss at length the question. Our reasons for placing him in the 6th century are briefly these:—(1) he is mentioned as an ancient writer along with Bhâmaha and Udbhaṭa (latter half of 8th century) by Jayaratha (p. 3. अलङ्कारसर्वस्व); (2) Namisâdhu speaks of Daṇḍin as follows:—'ननु दण्डि-मेधाविरुद्र-भामहादिकृतानि सन्त्येवालङ्कारशास्त्राणि' (p. 2 of रुद्रटकाव्यालङ्कार). We believe the authors are arranged chrono-

rally assigned to the 6th century A. D., refers to the distinction drawn between Kathâ and Âkhyâyikâ by certain writers, disapproves of it and finally says that both are different names for the same class of composition*. Daṇḍin further says that an Âkhyâyikâ should exhibit a profusion of compounds†. The lexicon of Amarasiṃha defines‡ Kathâ and Âkhyâyikâ, pointing out that the former is imaginary and has very little historical value, while the latter deals with matters of history. Bâṇa himself often alludes to the two classes of prose compositions§. Bâṇa offers a glowing tribute of praise to the writers of Âkhyâyikâs that preceded him¶. He refers to some peculiarities that distinguished the Âkhyâyikâ from other classes of compositions, *viz.* division into Uchchhvâsas and the occurrence of the Vaktra metre. Bâṇa himself clearly intimates that his Harshacharita is an Âkhyâyikâ‖. The introductory verses to the Pûrvabhâga clearly indicate that the Kâdambarî was intended to be a Kathâ ꠸ (technically so called). This makes it clear that Bâṇa *did not* strike out a new path in writing his two prose works, that he had before him certain works which went under the name of Âkhyâyikâ and that criticism had been busy in laying down canons for regulating the two classes of prose compositions.

---

logically, as मेधाविरुद्र is mentioned in Bhâmaha's work; (3) Daṇḍin's treatment appears crude and unscientific as compared with Bhâmaha's; (4) Bhâmaha in a few places refers to the opinions of some (अपरे, अन्ये &c.) and these are found in Daṇḍin's work. (5) Tamil and Canarese writers belonging to the 8th century refer to him.

* See Kâvyâdars'a I. 23–30.

† 'तद्गुरूणां लघूनां च बाहुल्यालपत्वमिश्रणैः । उच्चावचप्रकारं तद् दृश्यमाख्यायिकादिषु ॥' काव्यादर्श I. 81.

‡ 'आख्यायिकोपलब्धार्था' अमर० I. 6. 5; 'प्रबन्धकल्पना कथा'.

§ 'काव्यनाटकाख्यानकाख्यायिकालेख्यव्याख्यानादिक्रियानिपुणैः' p. 3 of कादम्बरी (Peterson); 'कथासु नाटकेषु आख्यायिकासु काव्येषु' p. 75 (Peterson).

¶ **उच्छ्वासान्ते**ऽप्यखिन्नास्ते येषां **वक्त्रे** सरस्वती । **कथमाख्यायिकाकारा** न ते वन्द्याः **कवीश्वराः** ॥' हर्षचरित.

‖ 'तथापि नृपतेर्भक्त्याभीतो निर्वहणाकुलः । **करोम्याख्यायिकाम्भोधौ** जिह्वाप्लवनचापलम् ॥' हर्षचरित.

꠸ 'द्विजेन तेनाक्षतकण्ठकौण्ठ्यया महामनोमोहमलीमसान्धया । अलब्धवैदग्ध्यविलासमुग्धया धिया निबद्धेयमतिद्वयी **कथा** ॥'

It is believed by some Sanskrit scholars that Bâṇa wrote before Sanskrit rhetoricians had done their best to degrade the sublime art of poetry to a pedantic enumeration of set similes and metaphors (*vide* Dr. Peterson's Introduction p. 43). We hold, with the greatest deference, that this is, to a great extent, fallacious. We possess ample evidence to establish that long before Bâṇa flourished, the science of Rhetoric had made great progress. We find that an inscription of Rudradâman (150 A. D.) exhibits a prose containing very long compounds, alliteration (Anuprâsa) and other figures*. In the same inscription reference is made to prose (Gadya) and poetry (Padya) that are ornate, fine on account of the (poetic) conventions observed in them and that contain perspicuous, short, sweet, striking and charming words†. An inscription of the time of Samudragupta (4th century A. D.) contains a prose that vies with that of Bâṇa himself‡. The Mandasor inscription dated in the Mâlava era 529 (*i. e.* 473 A. D.) contains verses that rival in diction and imagery the best efforts of Kâlidâsa, Bhavabhûti and other masters of classical Sanskrit. § Daṇḍin, who, as we said above, is not placed later than the 6th century A. D., gives a tolerably full treatment of Rhetoric. He says that he only improves upon what other Âchâryas that preceded him

---

* See Archaeological Survey, Western India. vol. II (about Kathiawad) p. 128.

† 'स्फुटलघुमधुरचित्रकान्तशब्दसमयोदारालङ्कृतंगद्यपद्य'

‡ Dr. Fleet's Corpus Inscriptionum Indicarum vol. III. p. 8. Mark the following 'कृपणदीनानाथातुरजनोद्धरणसमन्त्रदीक्षाद्युपगतमनसः समिद्धस्य विग्रहवतो लोकानुग्रहस्य धनदवरुणेन्द्रान्तकसमस्य स्वभुजबलविजितानेकनरपतिविभवप्रत्यर्पणनित्यव्यापृतायुक्तपुरुषस्य निशितविदग्धमतिगान्धर्वललितैर्व्रीडितत्रिदशपतिगुरुतुम्बुरुनारदादेर्विद्वज्जनोपजीव्यानेककाव्यक्रियाभिः प्रतिष्ठितकविराजशब्दस्य' &c.

§ See Dr. Fleet's Corpus Inscriptionum vol. III p. 76ff. We shall quote only two verses. 'चतुःसमुद्रान्तविलोलमेखलां सुमेरुकैलासबृहत्पयोधराम् । वनान्तवान्तस्फुटपुष्पहासिनीं कुमारगुप्ते पृथिवीं प्रशासति ॥ स्मरवशगतरुणजनवल्लभाङ्गनाविपुलकान्तपीनोरु–स्तनजघनघनालिङ्गननिर्भर्त्सिततुहिन–हिमपाते ॥' It will be noticed that the second verse (an Âryâ) forms a single compound.

had laid down*. Daṇḍin asserts that a profusion of compounds is the very life of prose†. This dictum has been followed by later prose-writers only too well. Bhaṭṭi devotes four *sargas* of his Bhaṭṭikâvya to the illustration of subjects that properly fall to be treated under Rhetoric. He exemplifies more than thirty figures of speech. He wrote in Valabhi under a king named Dharasena. Four kings of the Valabhi dynasty bore the name Dharasena. The dates of the four kings fall between about 500 A. D. and 651 A. D. So Bhaṭṭi was a predecessor or at least a contemporary of Bâṇa. In Subhandhu's Vâsavadattâ we meet with a number of allusions to Rhetoric. Subandhu boasts of his skill in composing a work full of paronomasia on each syllable‡. He refers to S'ṛinkhalâbandha (a peculiar arrangement of words) and mentions the figures of speech Utprekshâ and Âkshepa§. Bâṇa refers to such puzzles and conundrums as Prahelikâ and mentions in the introduction to the Harshacharita a few figures of speech such as Jâti (Svabhâvokti), Utprekshâ and S'lesha¶. In the Introduction to the Kâdambarî are mentioned the figures Dîpaka, Upamâ, S'lesha and Jâti.

In this brief *resume* we have shown that, before Bâṇa flourished, Rhetoric had made great progress, though it had not reached perfection.

The Harshacharita$ and the Kâdambarî are well-known as the works of Bâṇa. A third work, the Chaṇḍîs'ataka,

---

* 'किं तु बीजं विकल्पानां **पूर्वाचार्यैः** प्रकल्पितम् । तदेव परिसंस्कर्तुमयमस्तपरिश्रमः ॥' काव्यादर्श II. 2.

† 'ओजः समासभूयस्त्व**मेतद्गद्यस्य जीवितम्** ।' काव्यादर्श I. 80.

‡ सरस्वतीदत्तवरप्रसादश्चक्रे **सुबन्धुः** सुजनैकबन्धुः । प्रत्यक्षर**श्लेष**मयप्रबन्धविन्यासवैदग्ध्यनिधिर्निबन्धम् ॥

§ 'शृङ्खलाबन्धो वर्णग्रथनासु उत्प्रेक्षाक्षेपौ काव्यालङ्कारेषु' वासवदत्ता p. 126 (Hall).

¶ 'अक्षरच्युतकमात्राच्युतकबिन्दुमतीगूढचतुर्थपादप्रहेलिकाप्रदानादिभिः' p. 3 of कादम्बरी (Peterson); 'बिन्दुमतीं चिन्तयता प्रहेलिकां भावयता' p. 88 of कादम्बरी.

$ The learned translators of the Harshacharita intimate that the Harshacharita was forgotten by Indian writers, though rare copies existed unknown in libraries. They mention only the साहित्यदर्पण and the काव्यप्रकाश as referring to the हर्षचरित. We is ascribed to him. There is nothing improbable in Bâṇa's authorship of a century of verses in honour of Chaṇḍî. We know that he gives in the Kâdambarî a powerful and picturesque description of the temple of Chaṇḍikâ. Still many hesitate to assert that Bâṇa *was* the author of the Chaṇḍîs'ataka*. A drama styled Pârvatîpariṇaya is also ascribed to Bâṇa. In the prelude to the Pârvatîpariṇaya, we are told that the drama was composed by Bâṇa of the Vatsa Gotra†. The author of the Kâdambarî also was descended from Vatsa. The drama, though not of the highest order of merit, has some excellences of its own. The subject is the same as that of the Kumârasambhava of Kâlidâsa. There are remarkable coincidences, both of phrase and thought, between the two works. Hence it is said by some scholars that the Pârvatîpariṇaya is only the work of a plagiarist and not of an eminent author like Bâṇa. We think, however, that this argument does not possess much force. We know that the fine verses of Kâlidâsa were the delight of Bâṇa and had kindled his admiration‡. When the subject was the same, it was quite natural that Bâṇa should unconsciously imitate in thought and expression his favourite author. Even in Kâlidâsa we recognise the words of the Mahâbhârata and the Bhagvatgîtâ. It is further argued that the Pârvatîpariṇaya is, as compared with the Harshacharita and the Kâdambarî, quite common-place. We

---

have quoted above passages from आनन्दवर्धन, नमिसाधु and रुय्यक that mention the हर्षचरित by name. It is clear that, at all events in Kashmir, the Harshacharita was carefully preserved and studied. For Kalhaṇa's indebtedness to the Harshacharita, see Dr. Stein's Kalhaṇa vol. I p. 133.

* We may draw the attention of the reader to the fact that verses from the Chaṇḍîs'ataka occur in the सरस्वतीकण्ठाभरण, in the काव्यप्रकाश and in अर्जुनवर्मदेव's टीका on अमरुशतक. अर्जुनवर्मदेव (p. 3) expressly ascribes the authorship of the चण्डीशतक to बाण "उपनिबद्धं च भट्टबाणेनैवंविध एव संग्रामप्रस्तावे देव्यास्तद्भङ्गिभिर्भगवता भर्गेण सह प्रीतिप्रतिपादनाय बहुधा नर्म-यथा 'दृष्टावासक्तदृष्टिः' &c." (verse 37 of चण्डी०)

† 'अस्ति कविसार्वभौमो वत्सान्वयजलधिसम्भवो बाणः । नृत्यति यद्रसनायां वेधोमुखलासिका वाणी ॥' 4th verse, Act I.

‡ 'निर्गतासु न वा कस्य कालिदासस्य सूक्तिषु । प्रीतिर्मधुरसान्द्रासु मञ्जरीष्विव जायते ॥' Introduction to हर्षचरित.

think that this, even if entirely true, would not militate against Bâṇa's authorship of the work. The work might have been written before Bâṇa had attained the mastery of his mature years. In the Pârvatîpariṇaya we fiud that Bâṇa is feeling his way. His prose in the drama reminds us of the Kâdambarî and the Harshacharita. Many ideas and turns of expression are common to the drama and the two prose works of Bâṇa. We cite below only one of them for want of space*. Besides we must not forget that Bâṇa was handicapped in verse. We have quoted above a critic's opinion that Bâṇa does not excel so much in verse as in prose. That remark could not have been based on the few verses that occur in the two prose works of Bâṇa. They rather refer to some compositions in verse written by Bâṇa. We suggest that the Pârvatîpariṇaya may be one of them. Chanḍapâla and Guṇavinayagaṇi, the commentators of the Nalachampû of Trivikramabhaṭṭa, inform us that Bâna wrote a drama entitled Mukuṭatâḍitaka†. We know nothing about this drama from other sources. Kshemendra quotes a verse as Bâṇa's‡, in which the sad plight of Kâdambarî due to separation from her lover is described. It seems therefore that Bâṇa wrote, according to Kshemendra, the story of Kâdambarî in verse also.

In the Kâvyaprakâs'a we read that Bâṇa obtained money from king Harsha§. A few scholars relying upon Kashmir tradition are of opinion that the drama Ratnâvali was really

---

* Act I 'हिमवान्—देवि कन्यापितृत्वं खलु गृहमेधिनामधिकतरं दुःखमावहति ।...कुचयुगलं परिणद्धं यथा यथा वृद्धिमेति तन्वङ्गयाः । वरचिन्ताहृतमनसस्तथा तथा कार्श्यमेति मे गात्रम् ॥'. Compare this with the passage in the हर्षचरित (उच्छ्वास IV) 'हृदयमन्धकारयति मे दिवसमिव पयोधरोन्नतिरस्याः ।...सेयं सर्वाभिभाविनी शोकाग्नेर्दाह शक्तिर्यदपत्यत्वे समानेऽपि जातायां दुहितरि दूयन्ते सन्तः' (p. 13 of our text).

† "यदाह मुकुटताडितकनाटके बाणः 'आशाः प्रोषितदिग्गजा इव गुहाः प्रध्वस्तसिंहा इव द्रोण्यः कृत्तमहाद्रुमा इव भुवः प्रोत्खातशैला इव । बिभ्राणाः क्षयकालरिक्तसकलत्रैलोक्यकष्टां दशां जाताः क्षीणमहारथाः कुरुपतेर्देवस्य शून्याः सभाः ॥' "

‡ "यथा वा भट्टबाणस्य–'हारो जलार्द्रवसनं नलिनीदलानि प्रालेयशीकरमुचस्तुहिनांशुभासः । यस्येन्धनानि सरसानि च चन्दनानि निर्वाणमेष्यति कथं स मनोभवाग्निः ॥' अत्र विप्रलम्भभरभग्नधैर्यायाः कादम्बर्या विरहव्यथावर्णना &c." औचित्यविचारचर्चा.

§ 'श्रीहर्षादेर्बाणादीनामिव धनम्.' Many MSS. read धावकादीनाम्.

the work of Bâṇa, who, in return for the money bestowed by king Harsha upon him, published the work in his patron's name. This view seems to us to be entirely wrong. In the first pla~e, there are three dramas, the Ratnâvali, the Priyadars'ikâ and the Nâgânanda, the authorship of which is claimed by Harsha. The Prastâvanâs to all the three dramas are identical almost word for word. In the Prastâvanâ of each of the three dramas Harsha is said to be the author. No one ascribes the Priyadars'ikâ and the Nâgânanda to Bâṇa. Hence the Ratnāvali also is not the work of Bâṇa. The Ratnâvali is quoted by Damodaragupta in his Kuṭṭanîmata (8th century A. D.). The Ratnâvali and the Nâgânanda are quoted by name in the Dhvanyâloka (p. 150, p. 176 respectively). The Ratnâvali is quoted at least a score of times in the Das'arûpa. The Nâgânanda and the Priyadars'ikâ are also quoted in the Das'arûpa but not so frequently. But in none of these writings is there the slightest hint that the author of the Ratnâvali was Bâṇa and not Harsha. It is remarkable that Kshemendra, himself a very erudite Kashmirian scholar, quotes some verses from the Ratnāvali and attributes them to S'rîharsha*.

The introductory verses attached to the Kâdambarî are supposed by some scholars to be the composition not of Bâṇa, but of his son or some one else. We demur to this conclusion on the following grounds. (a) If the verses had been written by Bâṇa's son, he would have referred to his authorship of them, as he does in the case of the introductory verses prefixed to the Uttarabhâga. Moreover he would not have mentioned his father in the colourless way in which the last verse (of the Pûrvabhâga) speaks of Bâṇa as 'Dvijena tena &c.' (b) Kshemendra quotes in his works at least four verses of the Introduction and twice distinctly says that they are Bâṇa's (in Auchityavichâracharchâ†

* In the कविकण्ठाभरण (सन्धि V) "इन्द्रजालपरिचयो यथा श्रीहर्षस्य 'एष ब्रह्मा सरोजे' &c. (रत्नावलि IV. 11). In the औचित्यविचारचर्चा he quotes the following verses as श्रीहर्ष's:—'परिम्लानं &c.' (रत्ना० II. 12); 'विश्रान्तविग्रहकथः &c.' (रत्ना० I. 8); 'उद्दामोत्कलिकां &c.' (रत्ना० II. 4); भयानके यथा श्रीहर्षस्य 'कण्ठे कृत्तावशेषं &c.', अपि च 'नष्टं वर्षवरैः' (रत्ना० II. 2–3).

† न तु यथा भट्टबाणस्य 'जयत्युपेन्द्रः स चकार दूरतः' &c.; the कविकण्ठा-भरण quotes the verse 'कडु कणन्तो' &c. as Bāṇa's.

and the Kavikaṇṭhâbharaṇa). (c) It is next to impossible that Bâṇa, an orthodox writer, should have commenced his work without any kind of salutation at the beginning.

IV Kathâ and Âkhyâyikâ.

We shall now briefly indicate the characteristics of these two classes of writings as defined by Sankrit rhetoricians.

The earliest known writer. who puts down the points of difference between Kathâ and Âkhyâyikâ as defined by some rhetoricians (although he himself disapproves of them), is Daṇḍin. (1) In an Âkhyâyikâ, it is the hero himself who tells the whole story; while in a Kathâ, the story is told either by the hero or by someone else. (2) An Âkhyâyikâ is divided into sections named Uchchhvâsas and contains verses in the Vaktra and Aparavaktra metres, while in a Kathâ it is not so. (3) In a Kathâ, such topics as the kidnapping of a girl, battles, separation, the rise of the sun and the moon are described; in an Âkhyâyikâ it is not so. (4) A Kathâ is distinguished by possessing certain catchwords which the author intentionally puts in. Daṇḍin remarks that no hard and fast line of demarcation can be drawn between the two classes of works, and that the points mentioned above have not been invariably followed by writers and that hence Kathâ and Âkhyâyikâ are but two names for the same species of prose composition. Bhâmaha's definitions of Kathâ and Âkhyâyikâ are given below.* In Rudraṭa's Kâvyâlaṃkâra, Kathâ and Âkhyâyikâ are defined†. The author seems to have had in mind the Kâdambarî and the Harshacharita in defining the two species of prose composition. We have seen above that a profusion of compounds was said by Daṇḍin to constitute the very essence of prose and hence long compounds form the ruling characteristic of Kathâ and Âkhyâyikâ. But certain restrictions were laid

---

* प्रकृतानाकुलश्राव्यं शब्दार्थपदवृत्तिना । गद्येन युक्तोदात्तार्था सोच्छ्वासाऽऽख्यायिका मता ॥ वृत्तमाख्यायते तस्यां नायकेन स्वचेष्टितम् । वक्त्रं चापरवक्त्रं च काले भाव्यर्थशंसि च ॥ कवेरभिप्रायकृतैरङ्कनैः कैश्चिदङ्किता । कन्याहरणसंग्रामविप्रलम्भोदयान्विता ॥ न वक्त्रापरवक्त्राभ्यां युक्ता नोच्छ्वासवत्यपि । संस्कृतं संस्कृता चेष्टा कथाऽपभ्रंशभाक् तथा ॥ अन्यैः स्वचरितं तस्यां नायकेन तु नोच्यते । स्वगुणाविष्कृतिं कुर्यादभिजातः कथं जनः ॥ भामह I. 25–29.

† See Rudraṭa's Kâvyâlaṃkâra XVI. 20–30.

prose.* We give below a few verses containing appreciations of Bâṇa by various Sanskrit writers.†

We shall briefly point out some of the merits and defects of Bâṇa's writings. The student will do well to read Dr. Peterson's eloquent appreciation of Bâṇa in his Introduction to the Kâdambarî (pp. 36-43).

1. He shows great skill and discrimination in characterization. All the characters in the Kâdambarî are life-like and consistent. The gentle and youthful Hârîta; the generous and loving king Târâpîḍa; the trusted S'ukanâsa whose first thought was always for the king; the tender queen Vilâsavatî; the devoted Patralekhâ, who followed the prince Chandrâpîḍa like his shadow; the affectionate yet stern Kapinjala; Mahâs'vetâ, holy in mind as she was fair in body, who serves as the foil for the heroine; these are characters that are bound to make a deep impression on the heart of the reader. Bâṇa, however, lavished all his skill in depicting the hero and the heroine of his romance. We think that Bâṇa, as has been remarked in the case of Shakespeare, was more successful in delineating his heroine than his hero. 'On Kâdambarî in particular, Bâṇa has spent all his wealth of observation, fullness of imagery, and keenness of sympathy.' 'From the moment when for the first

* It was said by rhetoricians that prose was the touchstone of poets 'गद्यं कवीनां निकषं वदन्ति' quoted by वामन in his काव्यालङ्कार-सूत्रवृत्ति cn का. सू. I. 3. 21.

† शश्वद्बाणद्वितीयेन नमदाकारधारिणा ।
धनुषेव गुणाढ्येन निःशेषो रञ्जितो जनः ॥—नलचम्पू.
युक्तं कादम्बरीं श्रुत्वा कवयो मौनमाश्रिताः ।
बाणध्वनावनध्यायो भवतीति स्मृतिर्यतः ॥—कीर्तिकौमुदी I. 15.
जाता शिखण्डिनी प्राग्यथा शिखण्डी तथावगच्छामि ।
प्रागल्भ्यमधिकमाप्तुं वाणी बाणो बभूवेति ॥—आर्यासप्तशती of गोवर्धन.
केवलोपि स्फुरन्बाणः &c. quoted above from धनपाल's तिलकमञ्जरी.
सुबन्धुर्बाणभट्टश्च कविराज इति त्रयः ।
वक्रोक्तिमार्गनिपुणाश्चतुर्थो विद्यते न वा ॥—राघवपाण्डवीय I. 41.
श्लेषे केचन शब्दगुम्फविषये केचिद्रसे चापरेऽ-
लंकारे कतिचित्सदर्थविषये चान्ये कथावर्णने ।
आ सर्वत्र गभीरधीरकविताविन्ध्याटवीचातुरी-
सञ्चारी कविकुम्भिकुम्भभिदुरो बाणस्तु पञ्चाननः ॥—श्रीचन्द्रदेव,
(the last) quoted from Mr. Parakhi's work.

time her eye falls and rests on Chandrâpîḍa, this image of a maiden heart, torn by the conflicting emotions af love and virgin shame, of hope and despondency, of cherished filial duty and a new-born longing, of fear of the world's scorn and the knowledge that a world given in exchange for this will be a world well lost, takes full possession of the reader.

2. Though the Kâdambarî contains glowing descriptions of love, they are chaste and free from grossness of any kind. In this respect the Das akumâracharita contrasts most unfavourably with the Kâdambarî. In the former, the reader is disgusted with the filthy intrigues of the ruffian heroes of that book.

3. Although Bâṇa was fettered by the canons of Rhetoric which laid down that long compounds were of the essence of prose, he displays considerable variety of style. His diction is generally smooth and graceful and he could write with force and brevity when it suited his purpose to do so. In this connection we may refer to the stern advice of Kapinjala to Punḍarîka. Bâṇa's prose is generally ornate and full of poetic fancies. He revels in the jingling assonance of sounds. Upamâ, Rûpaka and Utprekshâ are met with at every step. Among the other figures of speech may be mentioned Dîpaka, Sahokti, Virodha, Nidars'anâ and Vishama.

4. He seems to have been a close observer not only of courts and kings, but even of the less bright aspects of human life. His description of the old Draviḍa ascetic, though somewhat long-drawn and tedious, shows that he had an eye for the ridiculous and the bizarre. His descriptions of court and life in cities present a vivid picture of the time in which he lived. The advice of S'ukanâsa to Chandrâpîḍa is a masterpiece. It sets out very clearly all the evils that beset not only the path of Chandrâpîḍa, but of all princes in all climes. The Harshacharita of Bâṇa possesses great interest for the antiquarian from the fact that it affords a vivid picture of Indian society in the 7th century and of the manners and customs of those far-off days.

5. Bâṇa seems to have been a great lover of Nature. He is never tired of using for poetic purposes the flora and fauna of India. His references to plants and flowers, though sometimes overdrawn and fanciful, are generally charming.

6. Although most of the characters of the Kâdambarî are shadowy and some of them are in their second or even third birth, the poet's genius is so superb and his power of developing love and pathos is so great that the reader soon forgets the unreal character of the work and his mind is enthralled by the engrossing interest of the woes and happiness of the characters. 'We find ourselves face to face with the story of human sorrow and divine consolation, of death and the passionate longing for a union after death that goes straight from the heart of one who had himself felt the pang and nursed the hope, to us who are of like frame with him'. In the Harshacharita the hero is a historic personage. The author's task is thereby rendered more difficult. Yet Bâṇa acquits himself most creditably. It will be seen later on that he has nowhere stretched any point in favour of his hero and that his version is generally corroborated by independent evidence.

His defects.

One of the greatest flaws of Bâṇa's writings is that they abound in puns on words and recondite allusions. The reader is often at a loss, amidst the array of double-meaning words, bold and fanciful allusions, to grasp the exact meaning of the author. Though this is a blemish according to modern ideas of criticism, ancient India thought otherwise. These by-ways of puns were called Vakrokti (crooked speech), which was raised to the position of an Alaṃkâra. Subandhu, we have seen above, boasts of his skill in puns on each letter.

Another serious blemish is that in the Kâdambarî we meet with a defect in constructive art, which is due to the device of weaving stories within stories. The reader is unable to carry in his head the bewildering turns and convolutions of the story and the confusion of curses and counter curses. The fact that the greater part of the story is put in the mouth of a parrot is a serious drawback to the verisimilitude of the work.

Bâṇa seems to have had very little sense of proportion. In his descriptions of Mahâs'vetā and the temple of Chaṇḍikâ he tires the reader by dwelling too much on every detail. The patience of the reader is exhausted by the overloading of single words with epithets and of the epithets to these epithets. It sometimes so seems that the poet cares only for the gorgeous description of the evening, morning, moonrise or the limbs of the heroine and leaves the plot to take care of itself.

It is necessary to say a few words about Bâṇa's son. It may be at once admitted that the highest praise is due to the dutiful son of Bâṇa for having creditably performed his self-imposed task. He possesses not a few of the excellences of his father. He has almost the same command over the Sanskrit language as his father. His style is as ornate and as full of figures of speech as his father's. But we must not forget that in the son's work the defects of his father are exaggerated and others peculiar to the son alone are added. We miss in the Uttarabhâga the bold and striking fancies of Bâṇa with which we become familiar in the Pûrvabhâga. The description of the love torment of Kâdambarī is insipid and drawn out to a tedious length. The references to mythological and other lore are few and far between in the Uttarabhâga. The different lines of the story are made to converge far more rapidly than Bâṇa would have done. The picturesque descriptions of flora and fauna in which Bâṇa is profuse are lacking in the Uttarabhâga. Such masterpieces of realism as the advice of S'ukanâsa to Chandrâpîḍa are conspicuous by their absence in the Uttarabhâga. The perusal of the Uttarabhâga leaves the reader under the impression that the author was only anxious to bring the story to a close somehow. The touch of genius that appeals to the mind and makes the characters live before the eyes of the reader is altogether wanting.

VI The Harshacharita.

A comparison of the Harshacharita with the Kādambarī is instructive and interesting. Both works are composed in the same ornate and elaborate style. Both exhibit, more or less, the same merits and defects. But the Harshacharita is very much inferior to the Kādambarī as a literary work In the Harshacharita the author cares more for the jingling repetition of the same letters than in the Kādambarī. The puns are generally more laboured in the Harshacharita.

The Kādambarī is much more free from the use of provincial expressions than the Harshacharita. In the Harshacharita the author seems to have consciously employed a very large number of words that are found only in the lexicons. In the Harshacharita we never come across that subtle analysis of human nature that we meet with at every step in the Kādambarī. The characters of the Kādambarī are all of them painted with a finer brush than those in the Harshacharita. In the ease and flow of speech, in the force and vigour of thought and expression, and in the happy description of impulses, emotions and sentiments that sway human conduct, the Kādambarî vastly excels the Harshacharita. In the whole of the Harshacharita there is hardly any passage that approaches, in elegance and grace of language, in the keen observation of human nature and the springs of human action, in apt and happy sentiments, the advice of S'ukanāsa to Chandrāpîḍa or the friendly exhortation of Kapinjala to Puṇḍarîka. But the Harshacharita enjoys certain advantages over the Kādambarī. The Harshacharita is of prime importance to the historian of ancient India. It contains a mass of information on the state of ancient Indian society, on social and religious observances and practices, on military organization, on the actualities of life in camp and city, on the progress of medicine and the various arts and industries.

There is one striking point in which both the Kādambarī and the Harshacharita are similar. The hand of Death prevented the former work from being completed. The latter also comes to an abrupt conclusion. We can only speculate as to the reason why Bāṇa left only a partial account of the career of Harsha. Probably the author never intended to offer to the world a complete account of his patron's life.* Perhaps Bāṇa was swayed by the consideration that the glorious career of his patron after he re-

* It should be noted that Bāṇa expressed his inability to do justice to the whole of the career of Harsha and promised his cousins that he would deal only with a portion of it. 'कः खलु पुरुषायुषशतेनापि शक्नुयादविकलमस्य चरितं वर्णयितुम् । एकदेशे तु यदि कुतूहलं वः, सज्जा वयम्' 3rd उच्छ्वास.

covered his sister Rājyas'rī was very fresh in the memory of the people when he wrote and needed no words of praise from him. Bāṇa wrote the Harshacharita rather as a literary work than as a history of Harsha's reign and was satisfied when his Muse had taken a sufficiently long flight. Whatever may have been the reason, the student of Indian antiquities cannot but express his regret and mortification that the work was left incomplete.

Besides the Harshacharita, the writings of Chinese authors, particularly of Hiuen Tsang, supply reliable information about Harsha and his times. Moreover there are several inscriptions of Harsha himself and his contemporaries that shed a flood of light on the topics which the Harshacharita deals with. All this information, when put together, gives us a fairly accurate and life-like picture of the times of Harsha. But several considerations, particularly of space and utility, prevent us from entering into a detailed examination of the data furnished by the authorities indicated above. To those that desire a full treatment of this subject, we would recommend the standard work of Mr. V. A. Smith on the early History of India. All that we can endeavour to do here is to dwell upon some of the salient features of the life and career of Harsha as delineated in the Harshacharita, to note the important points of divergence between the Harshacharita and our other authorities and to supplement the information furnished by the Harshacharita from the other materials mentioned above.

VII The predecessors of Harsha.

The Harshacharita tells us that the remote ancestor of Harsha was Pushpabhūti. Between him and Prabhākaravardhana, father of Harsha, intervened several unnamed kings. The Madhuban and Banskhera copper-plates* of Harsha furnish the following genealogy :—

---

* The following is the text of the Madhuban copper-plate inscription of Harsha (See E. I. vol VII. p. 155 and also E. I. vol. I p. 67). ओम् । स्वस्ति महानौहस्त्यश्वजयस्कन्धावारात् **कपित्थिकाया:** महाराजश्री**नरवर्धन**स्तस्य पुत्रस्तत्पादानुध्यातः श्री**वज्रिणीदेव्या**मुत्पन्नः परमादित्यभक्तो महाराजश्री**राज्यवर्धन**स्तस्य पुत्रस्तत्पादानुध्यातः श्री**अप्सरोदेव्या**मुत्पन्नः परमादित्यभक्तो महाराजश्रीम**दादित्यवर्धन**स्तस्य पुत्रस्तत्पादानुध्यातः श्री**महासेनगुप्तादे**व्यामुत्पन्नश्चतुःसमुद्रातिक्रान्तकीर्तिः प्रतापानुरागोपनतान्यराजो वर्णाश्रमव्यवस्थापनप्रवृत्तचक्र एकचक्ररथ इव प्रजानामार्तिहरः परमादित्यभक्तः परमभट्टारकमहाराजाधिराज-

श्री**प्रभाकरवर्धन**स्तस्य पुत्रस्तत्पादानुध्यातः सितयशःप्रतानविच्छुरितसकलभुवनमण्डलः परिगृहीतधनदवरुणेन्द्रप्रभृतिलोकपालतेजाः सत्पथोपार्जितानेकद्रविणभूमिप्रदानसंप्रीणितार्थिहृदयोऽतिशयितपूर्वराजचरितो देव्याममलयशोमत्यां श्री**यशोमत्या**मुत्पन्नः परमसौगतः सुगत इव परहितैकरतः परमभट्टारकमहाराजाधिराजश्री**राज्यवर्धनः**

राजानो युधि दुष्टवाजिन इव श्री**देवगुप्ता**दयः
कृत्वा येन कशाप्रहारविमुखाः सर्वे समं संयताः ।
उत्खाय द्विषतो विजित्य वसुधां कृत्वा प्रजानां प्रियं
प्राणानुज्झितवानरातिभवने सत्यानुरोधेन यः ॥

तस्यानुजस्तत्पादानुध्यातः परममाहेश्वरो महेश्वर इव सर्वसत्त्वानुकम्पी परमभट्टारकमहाराजाधिराजश्री**हर्षः** **श्रावस्तीभुक्तौ** **कुण्डधानी**वैषयिक**सोमकुण्डका**ग्रामे समुपगतान् महासामन्त—महाराज—दौःसाधसाधनिक—प्रमातार—राजस्थानीय—कुमारामात्योपरिक—विषयपति—भटचाटसेवकादीन् प्रतिवासिजनपदांश्च समाज्ञापयति । अस्तु वः संविदितम् । अयं **सोमकुण्डका**ग्रामो ब्राह्मणवामरथ्येन कूटशासनेन भुक्तक इति विचार्य यतस्तच्छासनं भङ्क्त्वा तस्मादाक्षिप्य च स्वसीमापर्यन्तः सोद्रङ्गः सर्वराजकुलाभाव्यप्रत्यायसमेतः सर्वपरिहृतपरिहारो विषयादुद्धृतपिण्डः पुत्रपौत्रानुगश्चन्द्रार्कक्षितिसमकालीनो भूमिच्छिद्रन्यायेन मया पितुः परमभट्टारकमहाराजाधिराजश्री**प्रभाकरवर्धनदेवस्य** मातुः परमभट्टारिकामहादेवीराज्ञीश्री**यशोमतीदेव्याः** ज्येष्ठभ्रातृपरमभट्टारकमहाराजाधिराजश्री**राज्यवर्धनदेव**पादानां च पुण्ययशोभिवृद्धये सावर्णिसगोत्रच्छन्दोगसब्रह्मचारिभट्टवातस्वामि—विष्णुवृद्धसगोत्रबह्वृचसब्रह्मचारि-भट्टशिवदेवस्वामिभ्यां प्रतिग्रहधर्मणाग्रहारत्वेन प्रतिपादितः । विदित्वा भवद्भिः समनुमन्तव्यः प्रतिवासिजनपदैरप्याज्ञाश्रवणविधेयैर्भूत्वा यथासमुचिततुल्यमेयभागभोगकरहिरण्यादिप्रत्याया अनयोरेवोपनेयाः सेवोपस्थानं च करणीयमिति । अपि च

असत्कुलक्रममुदारमुदाहरद्भिरन्यैश्च दानमिदमभ्यनुमोदनीयम् ।
लक्ष्म्यास्तडित्सलिलबुद्बुदचञ्चलाया दानं फलं परयशःपरिपालनं च ॥
कर्मणा मनसा वाचा कर्तव्यं प्राणिने हितम् ।
हर्षेणैतत्समाख्यातं धर्मार्जनमनुत्तमम् ॥

दूतकोऽत्र महाप्रमातार-महासामन्त-श्री**स्कन्दगुप्तः** महाक्षपटलाधिकरणाधिकृतसामन्तमहाराजेश्वरगुप्तसमादेशाच्चोत्कीर्णं गर्जरेण (गुर्जरेण?) । संवत् २० ५ मार्गशीर्ष वदि ६. The Banskhera plate of Harsha (see E. I. vol. IV p. 208 ff) contains the same details as above, except the following:—The charter is issued from Vardhamānakoṭî; the donees are Bālachandra, a Rigvedin of the Bharadvājagotra and Bhadrasvāmin, a Sāmavedin; the village granted is Markaṭasāgara, which was in the *Bhukti* of Ahichchhatrā and in the western *Pathaka* of the Angadîya *Vishaya;* the keeper of the records is one Bhāna or Bhānu and the concluding words are 'उत्कीर्णमीश्वरेणेदमिति संवत् २० २ कार्ति वदि १ स्वहस्तो मम महाराजाधिराजश्रीहर्षस्य ।'.

स्व ह स्तो म म म हा रा जा धि रा ज श्री ह र्ष स्य

Autograph of Harsha from the Banskhera plate.

Naravardhana=Vajriṇîdevî

|

Rājyavardhana=Apsarodevī

|

Âdityavardhana=Mahāsenaguptā

|

Prabhākaravardhana=Yas'omatī

|

Rājyavardhana | Harsha | Rājyas'rī

Hiuen Tsang begins with Prabhākaravardhana and informs us that Rājyavardhana was the elder brother of Harsha.* Bāṇa tells us that Harsha's ancestors ruled at Sthāṇvîs'vara (modern Thanesar), while Hiuen Tsang makes Kānyakubja the capital of Harsha.† The explanation probably lies in this fact that when Hiuen Tsang visited Harsha (which was about 643 A. D.), Kānyakubja was one of the capitals of Harsha's vast empire. When Rājyas'ri's husband Grahavarman was killed and she became a Buddhist nun, Harsha might have taken over the kingdom of Kanoj and made the latter his capital as being more in the centre of his dominions than Thanesar.

Hiuen Tsang tells us that the family of Harsha belonged to the Vais'ya caste. It has been rightly pointed out that the learned Chinese traveller confounds the third of the four principal castes with the Bais clan of Rajputs (who were Kshatriyas).‡ Bâṇa nowhere gives the slightest hint that the family of Harsha was not of Kshatriya descent. There are moreover indications to the contrary. Harsha's sister was married to Grahavarman, who came of the ancient Kshatriya family of the Maukharis (for whom see below). Prabhākaravardhana was the son of Mahāsenaguptā, who seems to have been the sister of Mahāsenagupta of Magadha. Unfortunately Bāṇa does not tell us the family from which

The Sonpat copper seal inscription of Harshavardhana (C. I. I. vol. III p. 231 ff), though much defaced, confirms the statements made in the two copperplates.

* See B. R. W. W. vol. I p. 210.

† B. R. W. W. vol. I p. 209.

‡ B. R. W. W. Vol. I p. 209 n. 12.

Harsha's mother came. Dr. Hoernle* thinks that her very name indicates that Yas'omatî must have been the daughter of the famous king of Mālava, Yas'odharma Vikramāditya. One fails to see how her very name shows that she was the daughter of Yas'odharman. Some support may be lent to the conjecture of Dr. Hoernle by the words of Yas'omatî that she was born in a family 'rendered glorious by Dharma'.† It further appears from certain words in the Harshacharita that Yas'omatî's father was a mighty warrior and that her parents were living at the time of her death.‡

The kingdom of Thanesar must not originally have been very large. It was surrounded on all sides by petty states, which waged constant wars among themselves. There is small wonder in this. Even Great Britain, which is such a small country, was divided only a few centuries ago into three kingdoms the rulers of which indulged in sanguinary feuds on the slightest pretexts. The inscriptions of Harsha style his ancestors (except Prabhākaravardhana) 'mahārāja'. It is only Prabhākaravardhana who is styled 'Mahārājādhirāja' which was one of the *birudas* of an aspirant for universal sovereignty. The Harshacharita informs us that Prabhākaravardhana fought successfully against the Hûṇas, the kings of Sindhu, Gurjara, Gāndhāra, Lāṭa (Broach) and Mālava. The conquest of the Hûṇas, if effected by Prabhâkaravardhana, must have been very perfunctory, as, a short time before his death, he had to send Râjyavardhana against them.

When Râjyavardhana came to the throne he must have been a very young man (about 19 or 20). We are told in the Harshacharita that the elder of the two Gupta princes named Kumāragupta, who was a companion of Rājyavardhana and Harsha, was about 18 years old. So Rājyavardhana was also of the same age at the time. Further we see that when Rājyavardhana returned after vanquishing

---

* See J. R. A. S. for 1903 p. 556.

† 'धर्मधवले कुले जाता' text p. 30 (5th उच्छ्वास).

‡ 'वीरजा वीरजाया &c.' text p. 30; 'अम्ब तात न पश्यतं पापां परलोकप्रस्थितां माम् &c.' same page.

the Hûṇas, there was a slight growth of hair on his chin. Harsha was the junior of Rājyavardhana by about four years and Rājyasrî was younger by about six years than her eldest brother. So Harsha and Rājyasrî were respectively about sixteen and fourteen years old when their father died. This is confirmed by the fact that Harsha is in several places* spoken of as '*Bāla*' and Rājyas'rî as 'Bālā.'† It seems that Prabhâkaravardhana died in 605 A. D. and therefore it follows that Harsha was born about 590 A. D. and ascended the throne in 606 A. D.‡ From the astronomical data furnished by Bāṇa about the birth of Harsha, Mr. C.V.Vaidya shows that Harsha was born on 4th June 590 A. D.§ Grahavarmā, the husband of Rājyas'rî, was killed by a king of Mālava. Who this Mālava king was is not quite clear. We are told in the Harshacharita that Rājyavardhana marched against this king with a small but picked force of cavalry under Bhaṇḍin and utterly routed him. In the inscriptions of Harsha we read that Rājyavardhana vanquished a certain king named Devagupta. As Rājyavardhana died very young he could not have waged many wars. Buhler conjectured with great probability that it was this Devagupta that had killed Grahavarman and was therefore chastised by Rājyavardhana. This conjecture is to some extent supported by the fact that the Harshacharita mentions a certain Gupta as having seized Kānyakubja.$ Dr Hoernle does not approve of the conjecture of Buhler. ¶ There are no doubt difficulties in the way of Buhler's guess. The two companions of Harsha and his elder brother are Mālava princes. Harsha is represented in the Harshacharita as very intimate with the younger of the two Mālava princes *viz.* Mâdhavagupta. || In another place we find Harsha talking to 'the son of the

* See text p. 42 'यदि बाल इति नितरां तर्हि न परित्याज्योऽसि'; p. 56 'बाल एवाखण्डलभूमिमारूढः'; p. 85 'इयं नः स्वसा बाला च बहुदुःखखेदिता च.'

† See V. A. Smith's Early History of India p. 312 (2nd edition).

‡ See above p. IV.

§ See J. B. B. R. A. S. vol. 24 pp. 252–254.

$ See text p. 67 'गुप्तनाम्ना गृहीते कुशस्थले'.

¶ J. R. A. S. 1903 p. 561.

|| See text p. 72 'अवलम्ब्य दक्षिणेन हस्तेन च माधवगुप्तमंसे'.

Mālava king that sat behind (Harsha)'.* So then it could not have been possible that these two princes were in any way related to the Mālava king that killed Grahavarmā. If they had been, they would naturally have been objects of suspicion rather than of trust. It is to be noted that Rājyas'rî is let off from imprisonment by a *certain noble* called Gupta.. † It is remarkable that he is not designated 'Rājaputra' or 'Rāja' but only 'Kulaputra.' So obviously he is not the king of Mālava that killed Grahavarmā nor can he be one of the two Gupta princes, the companions of Harsha, that were 'Rājaputras.' If it was Devagupta that killed Grahavarmā, he could not have been the same as the Mahārājādhirāja Devagupta of Magadha, whose approximate dates according to Dr. Fleet are 680–700 A. D. (see Deo Baranark Inscription pp. 213, 215) and who was the maternal grand-father of the Vākāṭaka king Pravarasena II (*vide* Chammak and Sivani copperplate inscriptions in C. I. vol. III pp. 240 and 247).

Rājyavardhana, young and confiding, was treacherously murdered, according to the Harshacharita, by a Gauḍa king. One MS. of the Harshacharita calls him Narendragupta. ‡ The commentator of the Harshacharita tells us that his name was S'as'ānka. He is corroborated by the statement of Hiuen Tsang that She-shang-kia (S'as'ānka) king of Karṇasuvarṇa (Bengal) murdered Rājyavardhana. § Bāṇa perhaps purposely omitted the express mention of the murderer of the reigning emperor's elder brother.$ But there are passages containing veiled allusions to the name S'as'ānka which we have pointed out in the notes (see *e. g.* text p. 38).

VIII The accession of Harsha and his relations with his contemporaries.

Bāṇa tells us that Harsha quietly ascended the throne

* 'पृष्ठतो निषण्णस्य मालवराजसूनोरकथयत्' 2nd उच्छ्वास.

† 'कान्यकुब्जाद्गौडसंभ्रमे गुप्तितो गुप्तनाम्ना कुलपुत्रेण निष्कासनम्' text p. 81.

‡ See E. I. vol. I. p. 70.

§ B. R. W. W. vol. I. p. 210.

$ Note the verse 'आत्मनाम गुरोर्नाम नामातिकृपणस्य च। श्रेयस्कामो न गृह्णीयाज्ज्येष्ठापत्यकलत्रयोः ॥'.

after the murder of his elder brother. But Hiuen Tsang has surrounded the accession of Harsha in an atmosphere of mystery and suspicion. We are told that the minister Bhaṇḍī asked the ministers to choose Harsha as king and that they accepted his advice; but Harsha had his own scruples and wanted to consult a statue of Avalokites'vara Bodhisattva on the Ganges before accepting the crown offered to him.* It is this account that leads Mr. V. A. Smith to remark that 'some unknown obstacle stood in the way of Harsha's accession and compelled him to rely for his title to the crown upon election by the nobles rather than upon his hereditary claims'.† We believe that the story was probably invented by the Buddhist admirers of Harsha to show that the latter was under the particular care of the Bodhisattva Avalokites'vara. We know from the Harshacharita that Bhaṇḍī, instead of being merely a great minister as Hiuen Tsang says, was a first cousin, being the mother's brother's son of Harsha and a very intimate friend. Bhaṇḍī was about eight years of age when Rājyas'rī was born and was thus slightly senior to Rājyavardhana. After ascending the throne Harsha started on his brilliant career of conquest and within a few years (about six) made himself the overlord of the whole of Northern India including Gujarat from the Himālayas to the Narmadā and from the bay of Bengal to Sindh. He had a long reign of about forty-two years and may fitly be styled the last Hindu Emperor of Northern India.

The Harshacharita contains a few references to these conquests. We are told in the third Uchchhvāsa that he vanquished the king of Sindhu and that he levied tribute from the Himālayan territory which is difficult of access.‡ On his relations with the Guptas we have already made a few remarks above. It seems that Harsha crowned Kumāragupta,§ the elder of the two Mālava princes, the companions

---

* See B. R. W. W. vol. I pp. 211-213.

† See Early History of India p. 312 (2nd edition).

‡ 'अत्र पुरुषोत्तमेन सिन्धुराजं प्रमथ्य लक्ष्मीरात्मीकृता ।...अत्र परमेश्वरेण तुषारशैलभुवो दुर्गाया गृहीतः करः'.

§ 'अत्र देवेनाभिषिक्तः कुमारः' 3rd उच्छ्वास and com. thereon.

of his boyhood. What became of this Kumāragupta we do not know. We saw above that the younger of the two Mālava princes, Mādhavagupta, was in high favour with Harsha. The Aphsad stone Inscription speaks of Mādhavagupta of Magadha who was anxious to meet the glorious Harsha.* The former was most probably the same as the favourite companion of Harsha's early years. Further particulars of the Guptas of Magadha may be learnt from Dr. Fleet's Gupta Inscriptions (pp. 200–218).† Another royal family with whom Harsha came in close contact was the Maukhari. His sister Rājyas'rî was married to Grahavarmā, son of Avantivarman. His capital was Kānyakubja. Bāṇa intimates that the Maukhari family was very ancient and highly honoured and that the Maukharis were great devotees of S'iva. ‡ Particulars of the Maukhari kings and their genealogy will be found in Dr. Fleet's Gupta Inscriptions pp. 219–230. The Maukharis and the Guptas of Magadha went often to war.§ The Harshacharita tells us that Kumāra alias Bhāskaravarman, king of Prāgjyotisha (Assam), formed a close friendship with Harsha on the eve of the latter's career of world conquest. Hiuen Tsang confirms this and tells us how once Harsha followed on the southern bank of the Ganges towards Kanoj while Kumāra-rāja kept pace with him on the northern. $

Harsha's glorious career of conquest suffered one memorable check. Pulakes'in II, the greatest of the

---

* See C. I. vol. III p. 200, 204 'श्रीहर्षदेवनिजसङ्गमवाञ्छया च.'

† Bāṇa says that one of his ancestors was honoured by several Guptas 'अनेकगुप्तार्चितपादपङ्कजः कुबेरनामांश इव स्वयम्भुवः' Introductory verses to the Kādambarî.

‡ The correct form seems to be मौखरि. Mark 'नमामि भर्वोश्चरणाम्बुजद्वयं सशेखरैर्मौखरिभिः कृतार्चनम् ।' Introductory verses to काद०. The Asirgad copper seal of S'arvavarman uses the words 'शर्ववर्मा मौखरिः' (C. I. vol. III. p. 220). But the Jaunpur stone inscription of ईश्वरवर्मन् sanctions the form मौखर 'मौखराणां भूभुजाम्' (C. I. vol. III p. 229).

§ See *e. g.* Aphsad Stone Inscription (C. I. vol. III p. 200, 203).

$ B. R. W. W. vol. I pp. 217–218; see also vol. II pp. 196–198, where Hiuen Tsang relates how he went to the court of Kāmarūpa.

religions in the times of Harsha, viz. Brahmanism, Buddhism and Jainism. Of these the last (particularly the Digambara sect of it) does not appear to have been popular in Northern India. The sight of a naked Jain ascetic is cited as a very bad omen.* The two other religions were in a flourishing state. It should not be supposed that ordinarily Buddhism was looked upon by orthodox Hindus as something to be abhorred. On the contrary Bāṇa everywhere speaks of things Buddhist with fairness and tolerance.† People passed from one persuasion to the other without much fear of persecution. So Divākaramitra is represented as originally being a student of the Maitrāyaṇîya recension of the Yajurveda and as passing over to Buddhism while still young. In spite of his Buddhistic predilections, he is waited upon by persons of various shades of opinions and beliefs, such as S'aivas, Bhāgavatas, Jainas, Paurāṇikas, Mîmāṇsakas, all intent upon arriving at the truth in the giddy whirlpool of opposing doctrines. Bāṇa, though himself an orthodox Brahmin writer, does not gloss over the fact that Rājyavardhana had strong leanings in favour of Buddhism. The companions of Rājyas'rî are represented as invoking the Buddha in their distress.‡ Bāṇa makes even Harsha say that he would don the red robes of the Buddhist order along with his sister after he had fulfilled his vow.§ Harsha describes in his inscription his brother Rājyavardhana as a very devout Buddhist (Paramasaugataḥ) and speaks of him more reverently than even his own father. The inscriptions of Harsha show that even in the royal family there was no strict adherence to a particular deity or form of faith. The three immediate ancestors of Harsha are described as great devotees of the sun (Paramādityabhaktaḥ). Bāṇa tells us that Pushpabhūti, the remote ancestor of Harsha, was a devout worshipper of S'iva.$ But Bāṇa himself describes how Prabhākara-

---

* *Vide* text p. 20 'अभिमुखमाजगाम शिखिपिच्छलाञ्छनो नग्नाटकः.'

† See *e. g.* text p. 78 ll 4–7.

‡ भगवन् भक्तजने सञ्चरिणि **सुगत** सुप्तोऽसि' text p. 79.

§ 'इयं तु ग्रहीष्यति मयैव समं समासक्तलेन काषायाणि' text p. 85.

$ 'तस्य...सहजैव...अन्यदेवताविमुखी...भगवति...भवे भूयसी भक्तिरभूत्' 3rd उच्छ्वास.

vardhana everyday devoutly worshipped the sun with red flowers. Harsha calls himself a devout worshipper of S'iva (Paramamāhes'varaḥ). The Sonpat seal of Harsha has the emblem of a Nandī. Bāṇa informs us that Harsha set out on his expedition after worshipping S'iva* and that the head accountant of the village where Harsha put up on the first day presented a golden seal with the crest of a bull. From these data one may say that between Brahmin and Buddhist and between the devotee of one deity and that of another there did not exist that great gulf which minds brought up in other environments are apt to suppose as having existed. There were certain root-ideas, certain habits of thought and modes of life, that were common to all. Coming to matters of detail, we find that Prabhākaravardhana celebrated many and elaborate sacrifices.† In describing the houses of his cousins, Bāṇa gives us an instructive picture of their surroundings in the 7th century A. D.‡ When Harsha made fun of Bāṇa by dwelling upon the wild years of his youth, Bāṇa in self-defence mentioned several things which entitled him to be better treated by the king.§ On his return from the court of Harsha, Bāṇa questions his kinsmen on matters that were vital to the Brahmins of his day, viz. the performances of sacrifices. the incessant study of the Vedas, of grammar, logic, the Mīmāṇsā and poetry. Bāṇa tells us that Paurāṇikas were as popular in those days as in these. His friend Sudṛishṭi treated him to a recital of the Vāyupurâṇa. We are told that Paurāṇikas clever in comforting those striken with grief surrounded Harsha after the death of his father. From the Kādambarī we learn that then as now the Mahābhārata was a favourite book with all, especially with women. The Harshacharita also dwells upon the popularity of the great

* 'विरचय्य परमया भक्त्या भगवतो नीललोहितस्यार्चाम्' text p. 53.

† Vide text pp. 2 and 38.

‡ Note the first paragraph of the 2nd उच्छ्वास.

§ 'ब्राह्मणोऽस्मि जातः सोमपायिनां वंशे वात्स्यायनानाम् । यथाकालमुपनयनादयः कृताः संस्काराः । सम्यक्पठितः साङ्गो वेदः । श्रुतानि यथाशक्ति शास्त्राणि । दारपरिग्रहादभ्यागारिकोऽस्मि ।...लोकद्वयाविरोधिभिस्तु चापलैः शैशवमशून्यमासीत् ' अत्रानपलापोऽस्मि ।' 2nd उच्छ्वास.

epic.* The description of the rites performed when Prabhâkaravardhana was on his deathbed, though somewhat weird, shows us what popular Hindu religious practices and observances were in the 7th century A. D.† When Bâṇa started on his visit to Harsha, he gives us a graphic and entertaining description of the way in which an orthodox Brahmin should make preparations to leave his home on an important undertaking. The long and rather curious list of the companions of Bâṇa in his youth (p. III above) shows us with what a strange medley of people an orthodox Brâhmaṇa could associate without running any serious risk of losing caste or position. It is to be noted that two of his most intimate associates were his cousins born of a S'ûdra mother. We may draw the attention of the student to the elaborate descriptions of the festivities on the birth of Harsha‡ and the marriage of Rājyas'rī. §

Hiuen Tsang dwells at great length on the condition of religion in the times of Harsha. He mentions that towards the end of his career Harsha became a very devout Buddhist and once in every five years he held a great assembly when he emptied his treasury to give away all in charity. $ We hope that the student of the Harshacharita will not fail to read the curious incidents and ancedotes that the Chinese traveller relates conecrning Harsha.

XI. The text of the Harshacharita.

The present edition is based on three editions of the Harshacharita, *viz.* the Nirṇayasāgara edition, that in the Bombay Sanskrit Series and the Calcutta edition of Is'varachandra. The first and third agree closely. The edition of Dr. Fuhrer contains in the footnotes very valuable material derived from eight MSS. We do not follow any particular edition. All important readings have been discussed in the notes. In a few cases the punctuation is wrong in the text, but has been corrected in the notes.

---

* 'महाभारतभावितात्मानः' 3rd उच्छ्वास; 'कस्य न द्वितीयमहाभारते भवे-दस्य चरिते कुतूहलम्' 3rd उच्छ्वास; 'विविधवीररसवृत्तान्तरामणीयकेन महाभारतमपि लघयन्निव' text p. 45.

† *Vide* text p. 21.

‡ Text pp. 7–9.

§ Text pp. 13–14.

$ B. R. W. W. Vol. I. pp. 214–215.

XII. Commentaries.

The only commentary available is the Sanketa written by S'ankara. The commentary so far as it goes is very valuable, particularly in the explanation of obscure words and puns. But it is very often meagre and passes over whole pages with scarcely a word of comment. So we did not include it in our edition. We know very little concerning the age or native place of the commentator. As the commentary has only been found in Kashmir, it is not unreasonable to suppose that S'ankara was a native of Kashmir. His father's name was Puṇyākara and he invokes Ganes'a at the beginning of his work. Among the authors and works named by him are:—Amarasiṃha, Kālidāsa, Kātyāyana author of the Vārtikas, Kṛishṇa (a Prakrit poet), Kauṭilya, Gāruḍas'āstra, Chāṇakya, Bharatamuni, Bhāmaha, Manu, Mahābhārata, Rājas'ekhara, Lāṭāchārya (an astronomical writer), Vātsyāyana (author of Kāmasūtra), Vyāḍi (author of the grammatical work Saṃgraha). Among the works from which quotations are taken without specifying the author are (besides those mentioned above):—Kāvyālaṃkâra of Udbhaṭa, Dhvanyâloka, Bhagavatgîtā, Meghadūta, Raghuvaṃs'a. The commentator very frequently refers to previous commentators in the words 'kechit', 'anye', 'apare' &c. At the end of his commentary S'ankara tells us that he follows tradition in explaining the difficult Harshacharita.* Hence it is clear that he was preceded by a number of commentaries.

As to the age of the commentator, we can give only an approximate result. As he either names or quotes from Rājas'ekhara, Udbhaṭa and the Dhvanyāloka, he is later than the 9th century A. D. But he is comparatively an early writer. One of the Mss of the commentary was, we are told by Dr. Fuhrer, dated Saṃvat 1520 i. e. 1464 A. D. if it is the Vikrama era to which the date refers, as is likely Besides the fact that, instead of quoting such eminent Âlaṃkārikas as Mammaṭa and Ruyyaka (both Kashmirians), he quotes the ancient Kashmirian rhetoricians Bhāmaha and

* 'दुर्बोधे हर्षचरिते संप्रदायानुरोधतः। गूढार्थोन्मुद्रणां चक्रे शङ्करो विदुषां कृते ॥'.

Udbhaṭa goes to strengthen the view that he was an early writer. He may therefore have flourished before the 12th century A. D.

It is to be noted that S'ankara cites a few vernacular words in explaining the Harshacharita. These may furnish some clue to his nationality.*

It appears that Ruyyaka, the famous author of the Alaṃkārasarvasva, wrote a commentary on the Harshacharita called Harshacharitavārtika.† The author of the commentary on the Vyaktiviveka of Mahimabhaṭṭa, who is generally regarded to be the same as Ruyyaka, also refers to his own commentary on the Harshacharita called Harshacharitavārtika.‡ It is a pity that this ancient commentary on the Harshacharita by so able and eminent a critic as Ruyyaka has not yet been brought to light. If it ever comes to light, it will be of great help in explaining many of the difficulties in the Harshacharita and in settling the text which is very corrupt in several places.

XIII The plan of the Notes.

The method adopted in the notes is as follows:—First of all a long passage is taken and is split up into clauses. Each difficult clause in then translated. In order to indicate clearly the meanings of words, Sanskrit words are often enclosed in brackets after their English equivalents. If a clause be difficult, the idea is expanded and clearly explained. Difficult compounds occurring in that clause are dissolved, quotations from kos'as such as that of Amarasiṃha are cited, references to mythology are dealt with at length and difficult words are traced to their origin. All grammatical peculiarities have been carefully noted. Parallel passages from the author's work or from the works of other authors

---

* *e. g.* on the word गुञ्जा he remarks 'सन्ना इति यस्य प्रसिद्धिः' notes p. 168; on प्रौढिक he says 'योग्याशनार्थं प्रसेवकः यो बुक्कण इति प्रसिद्धः'; on लम्बापटह्राः he says 'तमिला इति प्रसिद्धाः' notes p. 175.

† p. 61 of अलङ्कारसर्वस्व. *Vide* p. VI above.

‡ 'एतदस्माभिर्हर्षचरितवार्तिके विस्तृत्य प्रतिपादितं तत एवावसेयम्' p. 44 of the commentary of the व्यक्तिविवेक (Trivandrum Sanskrit series).

are given to further elucidate the meaning. Bold type has been employed in the notes to draw attention to important citations. Only easy passages have not been fully translated.

XIV The Appendices.

The first appendix contains an abstract of the Harsha-charita. The second appendix contains the Suprabhâta-stotra. The third appendix is a general index dealing with proper names, mythological references, information of general interest and other kindred matters occurring in the notes.

हर्षचरितम् ।

प्रथम उच्छ्वासः ।

[1]नमस्तुङ्गशिरश्चुम्बिचन्द्रचामरचारवे ।
त्रैलोक्यनगरारम्भमूलस्तम्भाय शम्भवे ॥ १ ॥
हरकण्ठग्रहानन्दमीलिताक्षीं नमाम्युमाम् ।
कालकूटविषस्पर्शजातमूर्छागमामिव ॥ २ ॥
नमः सर्वविदे तस्मै व्यासाय कविवेधसे ।
चक्रे पुण्यं सरस्वत्या यो वर्षमिव भारतम् ॥ ३ ॥
प्रायः कुकवयो लोके रागाधिष्ठितदृष्टयः ।
कोकिला इव जायन्ते वाचालाः कामकारिणः ॥ ४ ॥
सन्ति श्वान इवासंख्या जातिभाजो गृहे गृहे ।
उत्पादका न बहवः कवयः शरभा इव ॥ ५ ॥
अन्यवर्णपरावृत्त्या बन्धचिह्ननिगूहनैः ।
अनाख्यातः सतां मध्ये कविश्चौरो विभाव्यते ॥ ६ ॥
श्लेषप्रायमुदीच्येषु प्रतीच्येष्वर्थमात्रकम् ।
उत्प्रेक्षा दाक्षिणात्येषु गौडेष्वक्षरडम्बरः[2] ॥ ७ ॥
नवोऽर्थो जातिरग्राम्या श्लेषोऽक्लिष्टः स्फुटो रसः ।
विकटाक्षरबन्धश्च कृत्स्नमेकत्र दुष्करम् ॥ ८ ॥
किं कवेस्तस्य काव्येन सर्ववृत्तान्तगामिनी ।
कथेव भारती यस्य न [3]व्याप्नोति जगत्रयम् ॥ ९ ॥
उच्छ्वासान्तेऽप्यखिन्नास्ते येषां वक्त्रे सरस्वती ।
कथमाख्यायिकाकारा न ते वन्द्याः कवीश्वराः ॥ १० ॥
कवीनामगलद्दर्पो नूनं वासवदत्तया ।
शक्त्येव पाण्डुपुत्राणां गतया कर्णगोचरम् ॥ ११ ॥

---

१ अस्मात्प्राक् 'इच्छादिशक्तिनिचयप्रसरक्रमेण विश्वावभासनविधौ प्रथितप्रभावा। याध्यायिनां हृदयकोकनदप्रतिष्ठा रूपं प्रकाशयति नौमि सरस्वतीं ताम्' इत्ययं श्लोको ब-पुस्तके दृश्यते. २ 'डम्बरम्' ब. ३ 'प्राप्नोति दिगन्तरम्' क.

पदबन्धोज्ज्वलो हारी कृतवर्णक्रमस्थितिः ।
भट्टारहरिचन्द्रस्य गद्यबन्धो नृपायते ॥ १२ ॥
अविनाशिनमग्राम्यमकरोत्सातवाहनः ।
विशुद्धजातिभिः कोशं रत्नैरिव सुभाषितैः ॥ १३ ॥
कीर्तिः प्रवरसेनस्य प्रयाता कुमुदोज्ज्वला ।
सागरस्य परं पारं कपिसेनेव सेतुना ॥ १४ ॥
सूत्रधारकृतारम्भैर्नाटकैर्बहुभूमिकैः ।
सपताकैर्यशो लेभे भासो देवकुलैरिव ॥ १५ ॥
निर्गतासु न वा कस्य कालिदासस्य सूक्तिषु ।
प्रीतिर्मधुरसान्द्रासु[1] मञ्जरीष्विव जायते ॥ १६ ॥
समुद्दीपितकन्दर्पा कृतगौरीप्रसाधना ।
हरलीलेव नो कस्य विस्मयाय बृहत्कथा ॥ १७ ॥
आढ्यराजकृतोत्साहैर्हृदयस्थैः स्मृतैरपि ॥
जिह्वान्तः कृष्यमाणेव न कवित्वे प्रवर्तते ॥ १८ ॥
तथापि नृपतेर्भक्त्या भीतो निर्वहणाकुलः ।
करोम्याख्यायिकाम्भोधौ जिह्वाप्लवनचापलम् ॥ १९ ॥
सुखप्रबोधललिता सुवर्णघटनोज्ज्वलैः ।
शब्दैराख्यायिका भाति शय्येव प्रतिपादकैः ॥ २० ॥
जयति ज्वलत्प्रतापज्वलनप्राकारकृतजगद्रक्षः ।
सकलप्रणयिमनोरथसिद्धिश्रीपर्वतो हर्षः ॥ २१ ॥

एवमनुश्रूयते—पुरा किल भगवान्स्वलोकमधितिष्ठन्परमेष्ठी विकासिनि पद्मविष्टरे समुपविष्टः सुनासीरप्रमुखैर्गीर्वाणैः परिवृतो ब्रह्मोद्याः कथाः कुर्वन्नन्याश्च निरवद्या विद्यागोष्ठीर्भावयन्कदाचिदासाञ्चक्रे। तथासीनं च तं त्रिभुवनप्रतीक्ष्यं मनुदक्षचाक्षुषप्रभृतयः प्रजापतयः सर्वे च सप्तर्षिपुरःसरा महर्षयः सिषेविरे। केचिदृचः स्तुतिचतुराः समुदचारयन्। केचिदपचितिभाञ्जि यजूंष्यपठन्। केचित्प्रशंसासामानि जगुः। अपरे विवृतक्रतुक्रियातन्त्रान्मन्त्रान्व्याचचक्षिरे। विद्याविसंवादकृताश्च तत्र तेषामन्योन्यस्य विद्याविवादाः[2] प्रादुरभवन्।

अथातिरोषणः प्रकृत्या महातपा मुनिरत्रेस्तनयस्तारापतेर्भ्राता नाम्ना दुर्वासा द्वितीयेन[3] मन्दपालनाम्ना मुनिना सह कलहायमानः साम गायन्क्रोधान्धो विस्वरमकरोत्। सर्वेषु च शापभयप्रतिपन्नमौनेषु मुनिष्वन्यालापलीलयावधीरयति कमलसम्भवे भगवती कुमारी किञ्चिदुन्मुक्तबालभावे

१ '०सार्द्रासु' क–ब. २ 'अन्योन्यस्य विवादाः' ब. ३ 'द्वितीयेनोपमन्युनाम्ना' ब.

भूषितनवयौवने वयसि[1] वर्तमाना, गृहीतचामरप्रचलद्भुजलता पितामहमुपवीजयन्ती, निर्भर्त्सनताडनजातरागाभ्यामिव स्वभावारुणाभ्यां पादपल्लवाभ्यां समुद्भासमाना, शिष्यद्वयेनेव पदक्रममुखरेण नूपुरयुगलेन वाचालितचरणा, मदन[2]नगरतोरणस्तम्भविभ्रमं बिभ्राणा जङ्घाद्वितयम्, सलीलमुत्ककलहंसकुलकलालापप्रलापिनि मेखलादाम्नि[3] विन्यस्तवामहस्तकिसलया, विद्वन्मानसनिवासलग्नेन गुणकलापेनेवांसावलम्बिना ब्रह्मसूत्रेण पवित्रीकृतकाया, भास्वन्मध्यनायकमनेकमुक्तानुयातमपवर्गमार्गमिव हारमुद्वहन्ती, वदनप्रविष्टसर्वविद्या[4]चरणालक्तकरसेनेव पाटलेन स्फुरता दशनच्छदेन विराजमाना, संक्रान्तकमलासनकृष्णाजिनप्रतिमां साममधुरगीताकर्णनावतीर्णशशिहरिणामिव कपोलस्थलीं दधाना, तिर्यक्सावज्ञमुन्नमितैकभ्रूलता, श्रोत्रमेकं विस्वरश्रवणकलुषितं प्रक्षालयन्तीवापाङ्गनिर्गतेन लोचनाश्रुजलप्रवाहेणेतरश्रवणेन च विकसितसितसिन्धुवारमञ्जरीजुषा हसतेव प्रकटितविद्यामदा, श्रुतिप्रणयिभिः प्रणवैरिव कर्णावतंसकुसुममधुकरकुलैरुपास्यमाना, सूक्ष्मविमलेन प्रज्ञाप्रतानेनेवांशुकेनाच्छादितशरीरा, वाङ्मयमिव निर्मलं दिक्षु दशनज्योत्स्नालोकं विकिरन्ती देवी सरस्वती श्रुत्वा जहास।

दृष्ट्वा च तां तथा हसन्तीं स मुनिः 'आः पापकारिणि, दुर्गृहीतविद्यालवावलेपदुर्विदग्धे, मामुपहससि' इत्युक्त्वा शिरःकम्पशीर्यमाणबन्धविशरारोरुन्मिषत्पिङ्गलिम्नो जटाकलापस्य रोचिषा[5] सिञ्चन्निव रोषदहनद्रवेण दश दिशः, कृतकालसन्निधानामिवान्धकारितललाटपट्टाष्टापदामन्तः[6]पुरमण्डनपत्रभङ्गमकरिकां भ्रुकुटिमाबध्नन्, अतिलोहितेन चक्षुषामर्षदेवतायै स्वरुधिरोपहारमिव प्रयच्छन्, निर्दयदष्टदशनच्छदभयपलायमानामिव वाचं रुन्धन्दन्तांशुच्छलेन, अंसावस्रंसिनः शापशासनपट्टस्येव ग्रथ्नन्ग्रन्थिमन्यथा कृष्णाजिनस्य, स्वेदकणप्रतिबिम्बितैः शापशङ्काशरणागतैरिव सुरासुरमुनिभिः प्रतिपन्नसर्वावयवः, कोपकम्पतरलिताङ्गुलिना करेण प्रसादनलग्नामक्षरमालामिवाक्षमालामाक्षिप्य कामण्डलवेन वारिणा समुपस्पृश्य शापजलं जग्राह।

अत्रान्तरे स्वयम्भुवोऽभ्याशे समुपविष्टा देवी मूर्तिमती पीयूषफेनपटलपाण्डरं कल्पद्रुमदुकूलवल्कलं वसाना, बिसतन्तुमयेनांशुकेनोन्नतस्तनमध्यबद्धगात्रिकाग्रन्थिः, तपोबलनिर्जितत्रिभुवनजयपताकाभिरिव तिसृभिर्भस्मपुण्ड्रकराजिभिर्विराजितललाटाजिरा, स्कन्धावलम्बिना[7] सुधाफेनधवलेन तपःप्रभावकुण्डलीकृतेन गङ्गा[8]स्रोतसेव योगपट्टकेन विरचितवैकक्ष्यका, सव्येन ब्रह्मोत्पत्तिपुण्डरीकमुकुलमिव स्फटिककमण्डलुं करेण कलयन्ती, दक्षिणम-

---

१ '०यौवने नवे वयसि' अ-क. २ 'धर्मनगर' ब. ३ 'धाम्नि' ब. ४ '०विद्यालक्तक०' अ-क. ५ 'शोचिषा' ब-क्. ६ 'अन्तकमण्डन०' ब. ७ '०लम्बिनाफेन०' ब. ८ 'गगनगङ्गा०' ब.

क्षमालाकृतपरिक्षेपं कम्बुनिर्मितोर्मिकादन्तुरितं तर्जनतरङ्गिततर्जनीकमुत्क्षिपन्ती करम्, 'आः पाप, क्रोधोपहत, दुरात्मन्, अज्ञ, अनात्मज्ञ, ब्रह्मबन्धो, मुनिखेट, अपसद, निराकृत, कथमात्मस्खलितविलक्षः सुरासुरमुनिमनुजवृन्दवन्दनीयां त्रिभुवनमातरं भगवतीं सरस्वतीं शप्तुमभिलषसि' इत्यभिदधाना, रोषविमुक्तवेत्रासनैरोङ्कारमुखरितमुखैरुत्क्षेपदोलायमानजटाभारभरितदिग्भिः परिकरबन्धभ्रमितकृष्णाजिनाटोपच्छायाश्यामायमानदिवसैरमर्षनिःश्वासदोलाप्रेङ्खोलितब्रह्मलोकैः सोमरसमिव स्वेदविसरव्याजेन स्रवद्भिरग्निहोत्रपवित्रभस्मस्मेरललाटैः कुशतन्तुचारुचामरचीरचीवरिभिराषाढिभिः प्रहरणीकृतकमण्डलुमण्डलैर्मूर्तैश्चतुर्भिर्वेदैः सह वृषीमपहाय सावित्री समुत्तस्थौ।

ततो 'मर्षय भगवन्, अभूमिरेषा शापस्य' इत्यनुनाथ्यमानोऽपि विबुधैः, 'उपाध्याय, स्खलितमेकं क्षमस्व' इति बद्धाञ्जलिपुटैः प्रसाद्यमानोऽपि स्वशिष्यैः, 'पुत्र, मा कृथास्तपसः प्रत्यूहम्' इति निवार्यमाणोऽप्यत्रिणा, रोषावेशविवशो दुर्वासाः 'दुर्विनीते, व्यपनयामि ते विद्याजनितामुन्नतिमिमाम्, अधस्ताद्गच्छ मर्त्यलोकम्' इत्युक्त्वा तच्छापोदकं विससर्ज। प्रतिशापदानोद्यतां सावित्रीं 'सखि, संहर रोषम्, असंस्कृतमतयोऽपि जात्यैव द्विजन्मानो माननीयाः' इत्यभिदधाना सरस्वत्येव न्यवारयत्।

अथ तां तथा शप्तां सरस्वतीं दृष्ट्वा पितामहो भगवान्कमलोत्पत्तिलग्नमृणालसूत्रामिव धवलयज्ञोपवीतिनीं तनुमुद्वहन्, उद्गच्छदच्छाङ्गुलीयकमरकतमयूखलताकलापेन त्रिभुवनोपप्लवप्रशमकुशापीडधारिणेव दक्षिणेन करेण निवार्य शापकलकलम्, अतिविमलदीर्घैर्भाविकृतयुगारम्भसूत्रपातमिव दिक्षु पातयन् दशनकिरणैः, सरस्वतीप्रस्थानमङ्गलपटहेनेव पूरयन्नाशाः स्वरेण, सुधीरमुवाच—'ब्रह्मन्, न खलु साधुसेवितोऽयं पन्था येनासि प्रवृत्तः। निहन्त्येष परस्तात्। उद्दामप्रसृतेन्द्रियाश्वसमुत्थापितं हि रजः कलुषयति दृष्टिमनक्षजिताम्। कियद्दूरं वा चक्षुरीक्षते। विशुद्धया हि धिया पश्यन्ति कृतबुद्धयः सर्वानर्थानसतः सतो वा। निसर्गविरोधिनी चेयं पयःपावकयोरिव धर्मक्रोधयोरेकत्र वृत्तिः। आलोकमपहाय कथं तमसि निमज्जसि। क्षमा हि मूलं सर्वतपसाम्। परदोषदर्शनदक्षा दृष्टिरिव कुपिता बुद्धिर्न त आत्मरागदोषं पश्यति। क्व महातपोभारवैवधिकता, क्व पुरोभागित्वम्। अतिरोषणश्चक्षुष्मानन्ध एव जनः। नहि कोपकलुषिता विमृशति मतिः कर्तव्यमकर्तव्यं वा। कुपितस्य प्रथममन्धकारीभवति विद्या, ततो भ्रुकुटिः। आदाविन्द्रियाणि रागः समास्कन्दति, चरमं चक्षुः। आरम्भे तपो गलति, पश्चात्स्वेदसलिलम्। पूर्वमयशः स्फुरति, अनन्तरमधरः। कथं लोकविनाशाय

---

१ 'आक्षेप' ब. २ 'कृष्णाजिनपटच्छाया' क. ३ 'इन्द्रियाधिष्ठानं रागः' ब.

ते विषपादपस्येव जटावल्कलानि जातानि। अनुचिता खल्वस्य मुनिवेशस्य हारयष्टिरिव वृत्तमुक्ता चित्तवृत्तिः। शैलूष इव वृथा वहसि कृत्रिममुपशमशून्येन चेतसा तापसाकल्पम्। अल्पमपि न ते पश्यामि कुशलजातम्। अनेनातिलघिम्नाद्याप्युपर्येव प्लवसे ज्ञानोदन्वतः। न खल्वनेलमूका एडा[1] जडा वा सर्व एते महर्षयः। रोषदोषनिषद्ये स्वहृदये निग्राह्ये किमर्थमसि निगृहीतवाननागसं सरस्वतीम्। एतानि तान्यात्मप्रमाद[2]स्खलितवैलक्ष्याणि, यैर्याति[3] वाच्यतामविदग्धो जनः' इत्युक्त्वा पुनराह—'वत्से सरस्वति विषादं मा गाः। एषा त्वामनुयास्यति सावित्री विनोदयिष्यति चास्मद्विरहदुःखिताम्। आत्मजमुखकमलावलोकनावधिश्च ते शापोऽयं भविष्यति' इति। एतावदभिधाय विसर्जितसुरासुरमुनिमनुजमण्डलः ससंभ्रमोपगतनारदस्कन्धविन्यस्तहस्तः समुचिताह्निककरणायोदतिष्ठत्। सरस्वत्यपि शप्ता किञ्चिदधोमुखी धवलकृष्णशारां कृष्णाजिनलेखामिव[4] दृष्टिमुरसि पातयन्ती, सुरभिनिःश्वासपरिमललग्नैर्मूर्तैः शापाक्षरैरिव षट्चरणचक्रैराकृष्यमाणा, शापशोकशिथिलितहस्ता, अधोमुखीभूतेनोपदिश्यमानमर्त्यलोकावतरणमार्गेव नखमयूखजालकेन, नूपुरव्याहाराहूतैर्भवनकलहंसकुलैर्ब्रह्मलोकनिवासिहृदयैरिवानुगम्यमाना समं सावित्र्या गृहमगात्।

अत्रान्तरे सरस्वत्यवतरणवार्तामिव कथयितुं मध्यमं लोकमवततारांशुमाली। क्रमेण च मन्दायमाने मुकुलितबिसिनीविसरव्यसनविषण्णसरसि वासरे, मधुमदमुदितकामिनीकोपकुटिलकटाक्षक्षिप्यमाण इव क्षेपीयः क्षितिधरशिखरमवतरति तरुणतरकपिलपनलोहिते लोकैकचक्षुषि भगवति, प्रस्नुत[5]मुखमाहेयीयूथक्षरत्क्षीरधाराधवलितेष्वासन्नचन्द्रोदयोद्दामक्षीरोदलहरीक्षालितेष्विव दिव्याश्रमोपशल्येषु, अपराह्णप्रचारचलिते चामरिणि चामीकरतटताडना[6]रुणितरदने रदति सुरस्रवन्तीरोधांसि स्वैरमैरावते, प्रसृतानेकविद्याधराभिसारिकासहस्रचरणालक्तकरसानुलिप्त इव प्रकटयति च तारापथे पाटलताम्, तारापथप्रस्थितसिद्धदत्तदिनकरास्तमयार्घ्योवर्जिते रञ्जितककुभि कुसुम्भभासि स्रवति पिनाकिप्रणतिमुदितसंध्यास्वेदसलिल इव रक्तचन्दनद्रवे, वन्दारुमुनिवृन्दारकवृन्दबध्यमानसंध्याञ्जलिवने ब्रह्मोत्पत्तिकमलसेवागतसकलकमलाकर इव राजति ब्रह्मलोके, समुच्चारिततृतीयसवनं[7]ब्रह्मणि ब्रह्मणि, ज्वलितवैतानज्वलनज्वालाजटालाजिरेष्वारब्धधर्मसाधनशिबिरनीराजनेष्विव सप्तर्षिमन्दिरेषु, अघमर्षणमुषितकिल्बिषविषगदोल्लाघलघुषु यतिषु, संध्योपासनासीनतपस्विपङ्क्तिपूतपुलिने प्लवमाननलिनयोनियानहंसहासदन्तुरितोर्मिणि मन्दाकिनीजले, जलदेवतातपत्रे पत्त्ररथकुलकलत्रान्तःपुरसौधे

---

१ 'पण्डा जडा वा' क. २ 'प्रसाद' ब. ३ 'याप्यतां यात्यविदग्धो' अ–क. ४ अस्मात्परं 'तपसे' इत्यधिकं ब–पुस्तके. ५ 'प्रस्तुतमखमाहेयी' ब. ६ '०ताडनरणितरदने' अ–क. ७ 'सवनव्रतब्रह्मणि' ब.

निजमधुमधुरामोदिनि कृतमधुपमुदि मुमुदिषमाणे कुमुदवने, दिवसावसानताम्यत्तामरसमधुरमधुसपीतिप्रीते सुषुप्सति मृदुमृणालकाण्डकण्डूयनकुण्डलितकन्धरे धुतपक्षराजिवीजितराजीवसरसि[1] राजहंसयूथे, तटलताकुसुमधूलिधूसरितसरिति सरति[2] सिद्धपुरपुरंध्रिधम्मिल्लमल्लिकागन्धग्राहिणि सायन्तने तनीयसि निशानिःश्वासनिभे नभस्वति, सङ्कोचोदञ्चदुच्चकेसरकोटिसङ्कटकुशेशयकोशकोटरकुटीशायिनि[3] षट्चरणचक्रे, नृत्तोद्धूतधूर्जटिजटाटवीकुटजकुड्मलनिकरनिभे नभस्थलं स्तबकयति तारागणे, संध्यानुबन्धताम्रे परिणमत्तालफलत्वक्त्विषि कालमेवमेदुरे मेदिनीं मीलयति नववयसि तमसि, तरुणतरतिमिरपटलपाटनपटीयसि समुन्मिषति यामिनीकामिनीकर्णपूरचम्पककलिकाकदम्बके प्रदीपप्रकरे, प्रतनुतुहिनकिरणकिरणलावण्यालोकपाण्डुन्याश्यानलीनीरमुक्तकालिन्दीकूलवालुकापुलिनायमाने[4] शातक्रतवे कशयति[5] तिमिरमाशामुखे, खमुचि मेचकितविकचितकुवलयसरसि शशधरकरनिकरकचग्रहाविले विलीयमाने मानिनीमनसीव शर्वरीशबरीचिकुरचये चापपक्षत्विषि तमसि, उदिते भगवत्युदयगिरिशिखरकटककुहरहरिखरनखरनिवहहेतिनिहतनिजहरिणगलितरुधिरनिचयनिचितमिव लोहितं वपुरुदयरागधरमधरमिव विभावरीवध्वा धारयति श्वेतभानौ, अचलच्युतचन्द्रकान्तजलधाराधौत इव ध्वस्ते ध्वान्ते, गोलोकगलितदुग्धविसरवाहिनि दन्तमयमकरमुखमहाप्रणाल इवापूरयितुं प्रवृत्ते पयोधिमिन्दुमण्डले, स्पष्टे प्रदोषसमये सावित्री शून्यहृदयामिव किमपि ध्यायन्तीं सास्रां सरस्वतीमवादीत्—'सखि, त्रिभुवनोपदेशदानदक्षायास्तव पुरो जिह्वा जिह्रेति मे जल्पन्ती। जानास्येव यादृश्यो विसंस्थुला गुणवत्यपि जने दुर्जनवन्निर्दाक्षिण्याः क्षणभङ्गिन्यो दुरतिक्रमणीया[6] न रमणीया दैवस्य वामा वृत्तयः। निष्कारणा च निकारकणिकापि कलुषयति[7] मनस्विनोऽपि मानसमसदृशजनादापतन्ती। अनवरतनयनजलसिच्यमानश्च तरुरिव विपल्लवोऽपि सहस्रधा प्ररोहति शोकः। अतिसुकुमारं च जनं सन्तापपरमाणवो मालतीकुसुममिव म्लानिमानयन्ति। महतां चोपरि निपतन्नणुरपि सृणिरिव करिणां क्लेशः कदर्थनायालम्। सहजस्नेहपाशग्रन्थिबन्धनाश्च बान्धवभूता दुस्त्यजा जन्मभूमयः। दारयति दारुणः क्रकचपात इव हृदयं संस्तुतजनविरहः। सा नार्हस्येवं भवितुम्[8]। अभूमिः खल्वसि दुःखक्ष्वेडाङ्कुरप्रसवानाम्[9]। अपि च पुराकृते कर्मणि बलवति शुभेऽशुभे वा फलकृति तिष्ठत्यधिष्ठातरि प्रष्ठे पृष्ठतश्च कोऽ-

---

१ 'राजीवरजसि' ब. २ एतन्नास्ति अ-क-पुस्तकयोः. ३ 'कुशेशयकोटर०' क; 'कुटीकोटर०' ब. ४ 'बालपुलिना०' अ-क. ५ 'कृशयति' अ. ६ 'क्रमणीया दैवस्य' ब. ७ 'क्लेशयति' ब. ८ एतन्नास्ति अ-क-पुस्तकयोः. ९ 'प्रभावानाम्' ब-क.

णोत् । उपजातकुतूहला च निर्गत्य लतामण्डपाद्विलोकयन्ती विकचकेतकीगर्भपत्रपाण्डुरं रजःसङ्घातं नातिदवीयसि संमुखमापतन्तमपश्यत् । क्रमेण च सामीप्योपजायमानाभिव्यक्ति तस्मिन्महति शफरोदरधूसरे रजसि पयसीव मकरचक्रं प्लवमानं पुरः प्रधावमानेन, प्रलम्बकुटिलकचपल्लवघटितललाटजूटकेन, धवलदन्तपत्रिकाद्युतिहसितकपोलभित्तिना, पिनद्धकृष्णागुरुपङ्ककल्कच्छुरणकृष्णशबलकषायकञ्चुकेन, उत्तरीयकृतशिरोवेष्टनेन, वामप्रकोष्ठनिविष्टस्पष्टहाटककटकेन, द्विगुणपट्टपट्टिकागाढग्रन्थिग्रथितासिधेनुना, अनवरतव्यायामकृशकर्कशशरीरेण, वातहरिणयूथेनेव मुहुर्मुहुः खमुड्डीयमानेन, लङ्घितसमविषमावटविटपेन, कोणधारिणा, कृपाणपाणिना, सेवागृहीतविविधवनकुसुमफलमूलपर्णेन, 'चल चल, याहि याहि, अपसर्पापसर्प, पुरः प्रयच्छ पन्थानम्' इत्यनवरतकृतकलकलेन, युवप्रायेण, सहस्रमात्रेण पदातिबलेन सनाथमश्ववृन्दं सन्ददर्श ।

मध्ये च तस्य सार्धचन्द्रेण मुक्ताफलजालमालिना विविधरत्नखण्डखचितेन शङ्खक्षीरफेनपाण्डुरेण क्षीरोदेनेव स्वयं लक्ष्मीं दातुमागतेन गगनगतेनातपत्रेण कृतच्छायम्, अच्छाच्छेनाभरणद्युतीनां निवहेन दिशामिव दर्शनानुरागलग्नेन चक्रवालेनानुगम्यमानम्, आनितम्बविलम्बिन्या मालतीशेखरस्रजा सकलभुवनविजयार्जितया रूपपताकयेव विराजमानम्, उत्सर्पिभिः शिखण्डखण्डिका[1]पद्मरागमणेररुणैरंशुजालैरदृश्यमानवनदेवताविधृतैर्बालपल्लवैरिव प्रमृज्यमानमार्गरेणु[2]परुषवपुषम्, बकुलकुड्मलमण्डलीमुण्डमालामण्डनमनोहरेण कुटिलकुन्तलस्तबकमालिना मौलिना मीलितातपं पिबन्तमिव दिवसम्, पशुपतिजटामुकुटमृगाङ्कद्वितीयशकलघटितस्येव सहजलक्ष्मीसमालिङ्गितस्य ललाटपट्टस्य मनःशिलापङ्कपिङ्गलेन लावण्येन लिम्पन्तमिवान्तरिक्षम्, अभिनवयौवनारम्भावष्टम्भप्रगल्भदृष्टिपाततृणीकृतत्रिभुवनस्य चक्षुषः प्रथिम्ना विकचकुमुदकुवलयकमलसरःसहस्रसञ्छादितदशदिशं शरदमिव प्रवर्तयन्तम्, आयतनयननदीसीमान्तसेतुबन्धेन ललाटतटशशिमणिशिलातलगलितेन कान्तिसलिलस्रोतसेव द्राघीयसा घोणावंशेन शोभमानम्, अतिसुरभिसहकारकर्पूरकक्कोललवङ्गपारिजातकपरिमलमुचा मत्तमधुकरकुलकोलाहलमुखरेण मुखेन सनन्दनवनं वसन्तमिव [3]वमन्तम्, आसन्नसुहृत्परिहासभावनोत्तानितमुखमुग्धहसितैर्दशनज्योत्स्नास्नपितदिङ्मुखैः पुनःपुनर्नभसि सञ्चारिणं चन्द्रालोकमिव कल्पयन्तम्, कदम्बमुकुलस्थूलमुक्ताफलयुगलमध्याध्यासितमरकतस्य त्रिकण्टककर्णाभरणस्य प्रेङ्खतः प्रभया समुत्सर्पन्त्या कृतसकुसुमहरितकुन्दपल्लवकर्णावतंसमिवोपलक्ष्यमाणम्, आमोदितमृगमदपङ्कलिखितपत्रभङ्गभास्वरं भुजयुगलमुद्दाममकराक्रान्तशिखरमिव म-

---

१ 'गण्डिका' क–ब. २ 'रेणुरूषितपरुष' ब. ३ 'अवतारयन्तम्' ब.

करकेतुकेतुदण्डद्वयं दधानम्, धवलब्रह्मसूत्रसीमन्तितं सागरमथनसामर्षगङ्गास्रोतःसन्दानितमिव मन्दरं देहमुद्वहन्तम्, कर्पूरक्षोदमुष्टिच्छुरणपांशुलेनेव कान्तोच्चकुचचक्रवाकयुगलविपुलपुलिनेनोरःस्थलेन स्थूलभुजायामपुञ्जितं पुरो विस्तारयन्तमिव दिक्चक्रम्, पुरस्तादीपदधोनाभिनिहितैककोणकमनीयेन पृष्ठतः कक्ष्याधिकक्षिप्तपल्लवेनोभयतः संवलनप्रकटितोरुत्रिभागेन हारीतहरिता निबिडनिपीडितेनाधरवाससा विभज्यमानतनुतरमध्यभागम्, अनवरतश्रमोपचितमांसं[1]कठिनविकटमकरमुखसंलग्नजानुभ्यां विशालवक्षःस्थलोपलवेदिकोत्तम्भनशिलास्तम्भाभ्यां चारुचन्दनस्थासकस्थूलकान्तिभ्यामूरुदण्डाभ्यामुपहसन्तमिवैरावतकरायामम्, अतिभरितोरुभारवहनखेदेनेव तनुतरजङ्घाकाण्डम्, कल्पपादपपल्लवद्वयस्येव पाटलस्योभयपार्श्वावलम्बिनः पादद्वयस्य दोलायमानैर्नखमयूखैरश्वमण्डनचामरमालामिव रचयन्तम्, अभिमुखमुच्चैरुदञ्चद्भिरतिचिरमुपरि विश्राम्यद्भिरिव वलितविकटं पतद्भिः खुरैः खण्डितभुवि प्रतिक्षणदशनै[2]ग्रहमुक्तिखणखणायितखरखलीने दीर्घघ्राणै[3]लीनलालिकललाटलुलितचारुचामीकरचक्रके शिञ्जानशातै[4]कौम्भजयनशोभिनि मनोरंहसि गोलाङ्गूलकपोलकालकायलोम्नि नीलसिन्धुवारवर्णे वाजिनि महति समारूढम्, उभयतः पर्याणपट्टश्लिष्टहस्ताभ्यामासन्नपरिचारकाभ्यां दोधूयमानधवलचामरिकायुगलम्, अग्रतः पठतो बन्दिनः सुभाषितमुत्कण्टकितकपोलफलकेन लग्नकर्णोत्पलकेसरपक्ष्मशकलेनेव मुखशशिना भावयन्तम्, अनङ्गयुगावतारमिव दर्शयन्तम्, चन्द्रमयीमिव सृष्टिमुत्पादयन्तम्, विलासप्रायमिव जीवलोकं जनयन्तम्, अनुरागमयमिव सर्गान्तर[5]मारचयन्तम्, शृङ्गारमयमिव दिवसमापादयन्तम्, रागराज्यमिव प्रवर्तयन्तम्, आकर्षणाञ्जनमिव चक्षुषोः, वशीकरणमन्त्रमिव मनसः, स्वस्थावेशचूर्णमिवेन्द्रियाणाम्, असन्तोषमिव कौतुकस्य, सिद्धयोगमिव सौभाग्यस्य, पुनर्जन्मदिवसमिव मन्मथस्य, रसायनमिव यौवनस्य, एकराज्यमिव रामणीयकस्य कीर्तिस्तम्भमिव रूपस्य, मूलकोषमिव लावण्यस्य, पुण्यकर्मपरिणाममिव संसारस्य, प्रथमाङ्कुरमिव कान्तिलतायाः, सर्गाभ्यासफलमिव प्रजापतेः; प्रतापमिव विभ्रमस्य, यशःप्रवाहमिव वैदग्ध्यस्य, अष्टादशवर्षदेशीयं युवानमद्राक्षीत्। पार्श्वे च तस्य द्वितीयमपरसंश्लिष्टतुरङ्गम्, प्रांशुमुत्तप्ततपनीयस्तम्भाकारम्, परिणतवयसमपि व्यायामकठिनकायम्, नीचनखश्मश्रुकचम्, शुक्तिखलतिम्, ईषत्तुन्दिलम्, रोमशोरःस्थलम्, अनुल्बणोदारवेशतया जरामपि विनयमिव शिक्षयन्तम्, गुणानपि गरिमाणमिवानयन्तम्, महानुभावतामपि शिष्यतामिवानयन्तम्, आचारस्याचार्यकमिव कुर्वाणम्, धवलवारबाणधारिणम्, धौतदुकूलपट्टिकापरिवेष्टितमौलिं पुरुषम्।

---

१ 'मांसबन्धविकट' ब. २ 'दशनविमुक्त' अ–क. ३ 'घ्राणालीनलालिके ललाटपट्टलुठित' ब. ४ 'कुम्भायान' ब. ५ 'मार्गान्तरमानयन्तम्' अ–क.

अथ स युवा पुरोयायिनां यथादर्शनं प्रतिनिवृत्य[1] विस्मितमनसां कथयतां पदातीनां सकाशादुपलभ्य दिव्याकृति तत्कन्यायुगलमुपजातकुतूहलः प्रतूर्णतुरगो दिदृक्षुस्तं लतामण्डपोद्देशमाजगाम दूरादेव च तुरगादवततार। निवारितपरिजनश्च तेन द्वितीयेन साधुना सह चरणाभ्यामेव सविनयमुपससर्प। कृतोपसंग्रहणौ तौ सावित्री समं सरस्वत्या किसलयासनदानादिना सकुसुमफलार्घावसानेन वनवासोचितेनातिथ्येन यथाक्रममुपजग्राह। आसीनयोश्च तयोरासीना नातिचिरमिव स्थित्वा तं द्वितीयं प्रवयसमुद्दिश्यावादीत्—'आर्य, सहजलज्जाधनस्य प्रमदाजनस्य प्रथमाभिभाषणमशालीनता, विशेषतो वनमृगीमुग्धस्य कुलकुमारीजनस्य। केवलमियमालोकनकृतार्थाय चक्षुषे स्पृहयन्ती प्रेरयत्युदन्तश्रवणकुतूहलिनी श्रोत्रवृत्तिः। प्रथमदर्शने चोपायनमिवोपनयति[2] सज्जनः प्रणयम्। अप्रगल्भमपि जनं प्रभवता प्रश्रयेणार्पितं मनो मध्विव वाचालयति। अयत्नेनैव चातिनम्रे साधौ धनुषीव गुणः परां कोटिमारोपयति[3] विस्रम्भः। जनयन्ति च विस्मयमतिधीरधियामप्यदृष्टपूर्वा दृश्यमाना जगति स्रष्टुः सृष्ट्यतिशयाः, यतस्त्रिभुवनाभिभावि रूपमिदमस्य महानुभावस्य। सौजन्यपरतन्त्रा चेयं देवानांप्रियस्यातिभद्रता कारयति कथां न तु युवतिजने सहोत्था तरलता। तत्कथयागमनेनापुण्यभाक्तमो विजृम्भितविरहव्यथः शून्यतां नीतो देशः। क्व वा गन्तव्यम्। कस्य वायमपहृतहरहुङ्काराहङ्कारोऽपर इवानन्यजो युवा। किंनाम्नः समृद्धतपसः पितुरयममृतवर्षी कौस्तुभमणिरिव हरेर्हृदयमाह्लादयति। का चास्य त्रिभुवननमस्या प्रभातसंध्येव महतस्तेजसो जननी। कानि वास्य पुण्यभाञ्जि भजन्त्यभिख्यामक्षराणि। आर्यपरिज्ञानेऽप्ययमेव क्रमः कौतुकानुरोधिनो हृदयस्य'। इत्युक्तवत्यां तस्यां प्रकटितप्रश्रयोऽसौ प्रतिव्याजहार—'आयुष्मति, सतां हि प्रियंवदता कुलविद्या। न केवलमाननं हृदयमपि च ते चन्द्रमयमिव सुधाशीकरशीतलैरानन्दयति वचोभिः। सौजन्यजन्मभूमयो भूयसा शुभेन सज्जननिर्माणशिल्पकला[4] भवादृश्यो जायन्ते। दूरे तावदन्योन्यस्यालापनमभिजातैः सह दृशोऽपि मिश्रीभूता[5] महतीं भूमिमारोपयन्ति। श्रूयताम्—अयं खलु भूषणं भार्गववंशस्य भगवतो भूर्भुवःस्वस्त्रितयतिलकस्य, अदभ्रप्रभावस्तम्भितजम्भारिभुजस्तम्भस्य, सुरासुरमुकुटमणिशिलाशयनदुर्ललितपादपङ्केरुहस्य, निजतेजःप्रसरप्लुष्टपुलोम्नश्च्यवनस्य बहिर्वृत्ति जीवितं दधीचो नाम तनयः। जनन्यस्य जितजगतोऽनेकपार्थिवसहस्रानुयातस्य शर्यातस्य सुता राजपुत्री त्रिभुवनकन्यारत्नं सुकन्या नाम। तां खलु देवीमन्तर्वत्नीं विदित्वा वैजनने मासि प्रसवाय पिता पत्युः पार्श्वात्स्वगृहमानाययत्। असूत च सा तत्र देवी

---

१ 'प्रतीत्य' अ. २ '०नयन्ति सज्जनाः' क. ३ 'कटिमारोहन्ति' ब. ४ 'शिल्पकला इव' ब. ५ 'मिश्रीकृता महतीं...पयन्ति प्रणयम्' ब.

दीर्घायुषमेनम् । अनेहसावर्धत तत्रैवायमानन्दितज्ञातिवर्गो बालस्तारकाराज इव राजीवलोचनो राजगृहे । भर्तृभवनमागच्छन्त्यामपि दुहितरि नासेचनकदर्शनमिमममुञ्चन्मातामहो मनोविनोदनं नप्तारम् । अशिक्षतायं तत्रैव सर्वा विद्याः सकलाश्च कलाः । कालेन चोपारूढयौवनमिममालोक्याहमिवासावप्यनुभवतु मुखकमलावलोकनानन्दमस्येति मातामहः कथंकथमप्येनं पितुरन्तिकमधुना व्यसर्जयत् । मामपि तस्य देवस्य सुगृहीतनाम्नः शर्यातस्याज्ञाकारिणं विकुक्षिनामानं भृत्यपरमाणुमवधारयतु भवती । पितुः पादमूलमायान्तं मया साभिसारमकरोत्स्वामी । तद्धि नः कुलक्रमागतं राजकुलम् । उत्तमानां च चिरन्तनता जनयत्यनुजीविन्यपि जने कियन्मात्रमपि मन्दाक्षम् । अक्षीणः खलु दाक्षिण्यकोशो महताम् । इतश्च गव्यूतिमात्रमिव पारेशोणं तस्य भगवतश्च्यवनस्य स्वनाम्ना निर्मितव्यपदेशं च्यावनं नाम चैत्ररथकल्पं काननं निवासः । तदवधिश्चेयं नौ यात्रा । यदि च गृहीतक्षणं दाक्षिण्यमनवहेलं वा हृदयमस्माकमुपरि भूमिर्वा प्रसादानामयं जनः श्रवणार्हो वा, ततो न विमाननीयोऽयं नः प्रथमः प्रणयः कुतूहलस्य । वयमपि शुश्रूषवो वृत्तान्तमायुष्मत्योः । नेयमाकृतिर्दिव्यतां व्यभिचरति । गोत्रनामनी तु श्रोतुमभिलषति नौ हृदयम् । तत्कथय कतमो वंशः स्पृहणीयतां जन्मना नीतः । का चेयमत्रभवती भवत्याः समीपे समवाय इव विरोधिनां पदार्थानाम् । तथा हि । सन्निहितबालान्धकारा भास्वन्मूर्तिश्च, पुण्डरीकमुखी हरिणलोचना च, बालातपप्रभाधरा कुमुदहासिनी च, कलहंसस्वना समुन्नतपयोधरा च, कमलकोमलकरा हिमगिरिशिलापृथुनितम्बा च, करभोरुर्विलम्बितगमना च, अमुक्तकुमारभावा स्निग्धतारका च' इति । सा त्ववादीत्—'आर्य, श्रोष्यसि कालेन । भूयसो दिवसानत्र स्थातुमभिलषति नौ हृदयम् । अल्पीयांश्चायमध्वा । परिचय एव प्रकटीकरिष्यति । आर्येण न विस्मरणीयोऽयमनुषङ्गदृष्टो जनः' इत्यभिधाय तूष्णीमभूत् । दधीचस्तु नवाम्भोभरगम्भीराम्भोधरध्वाननिभया भारत्या नर्तयन्वनलताभवनभाजो भुजगभुजः सुधीरमुवाच—'आर्ये, करिष्यति प्रसादमार्याराध्यमाना । पश्यामस्तावत्तातम् । उत्तिष्ठ । व्रजामः' इति । तथेति च तेनाभ्यनुज्ञातः शनकैरुत्थाय कृतनमस्कृतिरुच्चचाल । तुरगारूढं च तं प्रयान्तं सरस्वती सुचिरमुत्तम्भितपक्ष्मणा निश्चलतारकेण लिखितेनेव चक्षुषा व्यलोकयत् । उत्तीर्य शोणमचिरेणैव कालेन दधीचः पितुराश्रमपदं जगाम । गते च तस्मिन्सा तामेव दिशमालोकयन्ती सुचिरमतिष्ठत् । कृच्छ्रादिव च सञ्जहार दृशम् ।

अथ मुहूर्तमिव स्थित्वा स्मृत्वा च तां तस्य रूपसम्पदं पुनः पुनर्व्यंसयतास्या हृदयम् । भूयोऽपि चक्षुराचकाङ्क्ष तद्दर्शनम् । अवशेव केनाप्य-

नीयत तामेव दिशं दृष्टिः। अप्रहितमपि मनस्तेनैव सार्धमगात्। अजायत च नवपल्लव इव बालवनलतायाः कुतोऽप्यस्या अनुरागश्चेतसि। ततः प्रभृति साऽलस्येव शून्येव सनिद्रेव दिवसमनयत्। अस्तमुपयाति च प्रत्यक्पर्यस्तमण्डले लाङ्गलिकास्तबकताम्रत्विषि कमलिनीकामुके कठोरसारसशिरःशोणशोचिषि सवित्रे त्रयीमये तेजसि, तरुणतरतमालश्यामले च मलिनयति व्योम व्योमव्यापिनि तिमिरसञ्चये, सञ्चरत्सिद्धसुन्दरीनूपुररवानुसारिणि च मन्दं मन्दं मन्दाकिनीहंस इव समुत्सर्पति शशिनि गगनतलम्, कृतसंध्याप्रणामा निशामुख एव निपत्य विमुक्ताङ्गी पल्लवशयने तस्थौ। सावित्र्यपि कृत्वा यथाक्रियमाणं सायन्तनं क्रियाकलापमुचिते शयनकाले किसलयशयनमभजत। जातनिद्रा च सुष्वाप।

इतरा तु मुहुर्मुहुरङ्गवलनैर्विलुलितकिसलयशयनतला निमीलितलोचनापि नाभजत निद्राम्। अचिन्तयच्च—'मर्त्यलोकः खलु सर्वलोकानामुपरि, यस्मिन्नेवंविधानि सम्भवन्ति त्रिभुवनभूषणानि सकलगुणग्रामगुरूणि रत्नानि। तथा हि। तस्य मुखलावण्यप्रवाहस्य निष्यन्दबिन्दुरिन्दुः। तस्य च चक्षुषो विक्षेपा विकचकुमुदकुवलयकमलाकराः। तस्य चाधरमणेर्दीधितयो विकसितबन्धूकवनराजयः। तस्य चाङ्गस्य परभागोपकरणमनङ्गः। पुण्यभाञ्जि तानि चक्षूंषि चेतांसि यौवनानि वा स्त्रैणानि, येषामसौ विषयो दर्शनस्य।[1] क्षणं नु दर्शयता च तमन्यजन्मजनितेनेव मे फलितमधर्मेण। का प्रतिपत्तिरिदानीम्' इति चिन्तयन्त्येव कथंकथमप्युपजातनिद्रा चिरात्क्षणमशेत। सुप्ता च तं दीर्घलोचनं स्वप्ने ददर्श। स्वप्नासादितद्वितीयदर्शना चाकर्णाकृष्टकार्मुकेण मनसि निर्दयमताड्यत प्रतिबुद्धा मकरकेतुना।[2] मदनशरताडितायाश्च तस्या वार्तामिवोपलब्धुमरतिराजगाम। तथा हि। ततः प्रभृति कुसुमधूलिधवलाभिर्वनलताभिरताडितापि वेदनामधत्त। मन्दमन्दमारुतविधुतैः कुसुमरजोभिरदूषितलोचनाप्यश्रुजलं मुमोच। हंसपक्षतालवृन्तैवा[3]न्तवातवर्तितैः शोणशीकरैरसिक्ताप्यार्द्रतामगात्। प्रेङ्खत्कादम्बमिथुनैरनूढा[4]प्यघूर्णत वनकमलिनीकल्लोलदोलाभिः। विघटमानचक्रवाकयुगलविसृष्टैरस्पृष्टापि श्यामतामाससाद विरहनिःश्वासधूमैः। पुष्पधूलिधूसरैरदष्टापि व्यचेष्टत मधुकरकुलैः।

अथ गणरात्रापगमे निवर्तमानस्तेनैव वर्त्मना तं देशमागत्य तथैव निवारितपरिजनश्छत्रधारद्वितीयो विकुक्षिर्डुढौके। सरस्वती तु तं दूरादेव संमुखमागच्छन्तं प्रीत्या ससंभ्रममुत्थाय वनमृगीवोद्ग्रीवा विलोकयन्ती मार्गपरिश्रान्तमस्नपयदिव धवलितदशदिशा दृशा। कृतासनपरिग्रहं तु तं प्रीत्या सावित्री पप्रच्छ—'आर्य, कच्चित्कुशली कुमारः' इति। सोऽब्रवीत्—

१ 'येषामसावविषयः' ब. २ 'अताड्यत मकरकेतुना प्रतिबुद्धाया मदन०' अ–क.
३ '०वृन्तव्रात' अ–क. ४ 'मिथुनाभिरनूढा' अ–ब.

'आयुष्मति, कुशली । स्मरति च भवत्योः । केवलममीषु दिवसेषु तनीयसीमिव तनुं बिभर्ति । अविज्ञायमानां चानिमित्तां शून्यतामिवाधत्ते । अपि च । अन्वे[1]क्षमागमिष्यत्येव मालतीति नाम्ना वाणिनी वार्तां वो विज्ञातुम् । उच्छ्वसितं सा कुमारस्य' इति । तच्छ्रुत्वा पुनरपि सावित्री समभाषत—'अतिमहानुभावः खलु कुमारो यदेवमविज्ञायमाने क्षणदृष्टेऽपि जने परिचितिमनुबध्नाति । तस्य हि गच्छतो यदृच्छया कथमप्यंशुकमिव मार्गलतासु मानसमस्मासु मुहूर्तमासक्तमासीत् । अशून्यं हि सौजन्यमाभिजात्येन वः स्वामिसूनोः । अलसः खलु लोको यदेवं सुलभसौहार्दानि येनकेनचिन्न क्रीणाति महतां मनांसि । सोऽयमौदार्यातिशयः कोऽपि महात्मनामितरजनदुर्लभो येनोपकरणीकुर्वन्ति त्रिभुवनम्' इति । विकुक्षिरुच्चावचैरालापैः सुचिरमिव स्थित्वा यथाभिलषितं देशमयासीत् ।

अपरेद्युरुद्यति भगवति द्युमणावुद्दामद्युतावभिद्रुततारके तिरस्कृततमसि तामरसव्या[2]सव्यसनिनि सहस्ररश्मौ शोणमुत्तीर्यायान्ती, तरलदेहप्रभावितानच्छलेनात्यच्छं सकलं शोणसलिलमिवानयन्ती, स्फुटितातिमुक्तककुसुमस्तबकसमत्विषि सटाले महति मृगपताविव गौरी तुरङ्गमे स्थिता, सलीलमुरोब[3]न्धारोपितस्य तिर्यगुत्कर्णतुरगाकर्ण्यमाननूपुरपटुरणितस्यातिबहलेन पिण्डालक्तकेन पल्लवितस्य कुङ्कुमपिञ्जरितपृष्ठस्य चरणयुगलस्य प्रसरद्भिरतिलोहितैः प्रभाप्रवाहैरुभयतस्ताडनदोहदलोभागतानि किसलयितानि रक्ताशोकवनानीवाकर्षयन्ती, सकलजीवलोकहृदयहठहरणाघोषणयेव रशनया शिञ्जानजघनस्थला, धौतधवलनेत्रनिर्मितेन निर्मोकलघुतरेणाप्रपदीनेन कञ्चुकेन तिरोहिततनुलता, छातकञ्चुकान्तरदृश्यमानैराश्यानचन्दनधवलैरवयवैः स्वच्छसलिलाभ्यन्तरविभाव्यमानमृणालकाण्डेव सरसी, कुसुम्भरागपाटलं पुलकबन्धचित्रं चण्डातकमन्तः[4]स्फुटं स्फटिकभूमिरिव रत्ननिधानमादधाना, हारेणामलकीफलनिस्तु[5]लमुक्ताफलेन स्फुरितस्थूलग्रहगणशारा शारदीव श्वेतविरलजलधरपटलावृता द्यौः, कुचपूर्णकलशयोरुपरि रत्नप्रालम्बमालिकामरुणहरितकिरणकिसलयिनीं कस्यापि पुण्यवतो हृदयप्रवेशव[6]नमालिकामिव बद्धां धारयन्ती, प्रकोष्ठनिविष्टस्यैकैकस्य हाटककटकस्य मरकतमकरवेदिकासनाथस्य हरितीकृतदिगन्ताभिर्मयूखसन्ततिभिः स्थलकमलिनीभिरिव लक्ष्मीशङ्कयानुगम्यमाना, बहलताम्बूलकृष्णिकान्धकारितेनाधरसम्पुटेन मुखशशिपीतं ससंध्यारागं तिमिरमिव वमन्ती, विकचनयनकुवलयकुतूहलालीनयालिकुलसंहत्या नीलांशुकजालिकयेव निरुद्धार्धवदना, नीलीरागनिहितनीलिम्ना शिखिगलशितिना वामश्रवणाश्रयिणा दन्तपत्रेण कालमेघपल्लवेन विद्यु-

१ 'अन्वक्षसमागमिष्यत्येव' क. २ 'तामरसव्याकोश०' क. ३ 'उरोबन्धारोपित०' ब. ४ 'अन्तःस्फुरस्फटिक' ब. ५ 'निस्तुल०' अ. ६ 'वन्दनमालिका०' ब. ७ 'प्रबाल०' ब. ८ 'शिति' अ–क.

दिव द्योतमाना, बकुलफलानुकारिणीभिस्त्रिसृभिर्मुक्ताभिः कल्पितेन बालिकायुगलेनाधोमुखेनालोकजलवर्षिणा सिञ्चन्तीवातिकोमले भुजलते, दक्षिणकर्णावतंसितया केतकीगर्भपलाशलेखया रजनिकरजिह्वालतयेव लावण्यलोभेन लिह्यमानकपोलतला, तमालश्यामलेन मृगमदामोदनिष्यन्दिना तिलकबिन्दुना मुद्रितमिव मनोभवसर्वस्वं वदनमुद्वहन्ती, ललाटलासकस्य सीमन्तचुम्बिनश्चटुल[1]तिलकमणेरुदञ्चता चटुलेनांशुजालेन रक्तांशुकेनेव कृतशिरोवगुण्ठना, पृष्ठप्रेङ्खदनादरसंयमनशिथिलजूटिकाबन्धा नीलचामरावचूलिनीव चूडामणिमकरिकासनाथा मकरकेतुकेतुपताका, कुलदेवतेव चन्द्रमसः, पुनःसञ्जीवनौषधिरिव पुष्पधनुषः, वेलेव रागसागरस्य, ज्योत्स्नेव यौवनचन्द्रोदयस्य, महानदीव रतिरसामृतस्य, कुसुमोद्गतिरिव सुरतरोः, बालविद्येव वैदग्ध्यस्य, कौमुदीव कान्तेः, धृतिरिव धैर्यस्य, गुरुशालेव गौरवस्य, बीजभूमिरिव विनयस्य, गोष्ठीव गुणानाम्, मनस्वितेव महानुभावतायाः, तृप्तिरिव तारुण्यस्य, कुवलयदलदामदीर्घलोचनया पाटलाधरया कुन्दकुड्मलस्फुटदशनया शिरीषमालासुकुमारभुजयुगलया कमलकोमलकरया बकुलसुरभिनिःश्वसितया चम्पकावदातया कुसुममय्येव ताम्बूलकरङ्कवाहिन्या महाप्रमाणाश्वतरारूढयानुगम्यमाना, कतिपयपरिचारकपरिकरा मालती समदृश्यत। दूरादेव च दधीचप्रेम्णा सरस्वत्या लुण्ठितेव मनोरथैः, आकृष्टेव कुतूहलेन, प्रत्युद्गतेवोत्कलिकाभिः, आलिङ्गितेवोत्कण्ठया, अन्तःप्रवेशितेव हृदयेन, स्नपितेवानन्दाश्रुभिः, विलुप्तेव स्मितेन, वीजितेवोच्छ्वसितैः, आच्छादितेव चक्षुषा, अभ्यर्चितेव वदनपुण्डरीकेण, सखीकृतेवाशया सविधमुपययौ। अवतीर्य च तुरगाद्दूरादेवावनतेन मूर्ध्ना प्रणाममकरोत्। आलिङ्गिता च ताभ्यां सविनयमुपाविशत्। सप्रश्रयं ताभ्यां सम्भाषिता च पुण्यभाजमात्मानममन्यत। अकथयच्च दधीचसन्दिष्टं शिरसि विनिहितेनाञ्जलिना नमस्कारम्। अगृह्णाच्चाकारतः प्रभृत्यग्राम्यतया तैस्तैरपि पेशलैरालापैः सावित्रीसरस्वत्योर्मनसी।

क्रमेण चातीते मध्यन्दिनसमये शोणमवतीर्णायां सावित्र्यां स्नातुमुत्सारितपरिजना साकूता मालती कुसुमप्रस्तरशायिनीं समुपसृत्य सरस्वतीमाबभाषे—'देवि, विज्ञप्यं नः किञ्चिदस्ति रहसि। अतो मुहूर्तमवधानदानेन प्रसादं क्रियमाणमिच्छामि' इति। सरस्वती तु दधीचसन्देशाशङ्किनी किं वक्ष्यतीति स्तनविनिहितवामकरनखकिरणदन्तुरितमुद्भिद्यमानकुतूहलाङ्कुरनिकरमिव हृदयमुत्तरीयदुकूलवल्कलैकदेशेन सञ्छादयन्ती, गलतावतंसपल्लवेन श्रोतुं श्रवणेनेव धावमानेनानवरतश्वाससन्दोहदोलायितां जीविताशामिव समासन्नलतामवलम्बमाना, समुत्फुल्लस्य मुखशशिनो लावण्यप्रवाहेण शृङ्गाररसेनेव प्लावयन्ती जीवलोकम्, शयनकुसुमपरिमललग्नैर्मधुकरकदम्बकैर्मि-

---

१ 'चटुलातिलक' अ-क.

दनानलदाहश्यामलैर्मनोरथैरिव निर्गत्य मूर्तैरुत्क्षिप्यमाणा, कुसुमशयनीयात्स्मरशरसंज्वरिणी मन्दं मन्दमुदगात्। 'उपांशु कथय' इति कपोलतलप्रतिबिम्बितां लज्जयेव कर्णमूलं मालतीं प्रवेशयन्ती मधुरया गिरा सुधीरमुवाच—'सखि मालति किमर्थमेवममिदधासि। काहमवधानदानस्य शरीरस्य प्राणानां वा। सर्वस्यां[1]प्रार्थितोऽपि प्रभवत्येवा[2]तिवेलं चक्षुष्यो जनः। सा न काचिद्या न भवसि मे स्वसा सखी प्रणयिनी प्राणसमा च। नियुज्यतां यावतः कार्यस्य क्षमं क्षोदीयसो गरीयसो वा शरीरकमिदम्। अनवस्करमाश्रवं मे त्वयि हृदयम्। प्रीत्या प्रतिसे[3]रा विधेयास्मि ते। व्यावृणु वरवर्णिनि विवक्षितम्' इति। सा त्ववादीत्—'देवि, जानास्येव माधुर्यं विषयाणाम्, लोलुपतां चेन्द्रियग्रामस्य, उन्मादितां च नवयौवनस्य, पारिप्लवतां च मनसः। प्रख्यातैव मन्मथस्य दुर्निवारता। अतो न मामुपालम्भेनोपस्थातुमर्हसि। न च बालिशता चपलता चारणता वा वाचालतायाः कारणम्। न किंचिन्न कारयत्यसाधारणा स्वामिभक्तिः। सा त्वं देवि यदैव दृष्टासि देवेन तत एवारभ्यास्य कामो गुरुः, चन्द्रमा जीवितेशः, मलयमरुदुच्छ्वासहेतुः, आधयोऽन्तरङ्गस्थानेषु, सन्तापः परमसुहृत्, प्रजागर आप्तः, मनोरथाः सर्वगताः, निःश्वासा विग्रहाग्रेसराः, मृत्युः पार्श्ववर्ती, रणरणकः सञ्चारकः, सङ्कल्पा बुद्ध्युपदेशवृद्धाः। किं वा विज्ञापयामि। अनुरूपो दे[4]व्या इत्यात्मसम्भावना, शीलवानिति प्रक्रमविरुद्धम्, धीर इत्यवस्थाविपरीतम्, सुभग इति त्वदायत्तम्, स्थिरप्रीतिरिति निपुणोपक्षेपः, जानाति सेवितुमित्यस्वामिभावोचितम्, इच्छति दासभावमामरणात्कर्तुमिति धूर्तालापः, भवनस्वामिनी भवसीत्युपप्रलोभनम्, पुण्यभागिनी भजति भर्तारं तादृशमिति स्वामिपक्षपातः, त्वं तस्य मृत्युरित्यप्रियम्, अगुणज्ञासीत्यधिक्षेपः, स्वप्नेऽस्य बहुशः कृतप्रसादासीत्यसाक्षिकम्, प्राणरक्षार्थमर्थयत इति कातरता, तत्रागम्यतामित्याज्ञा, वारितोऽपि बलादागच्छतीति परिभवः। तदेवमगोचरे गिरामसीति श्रुत्वा देवी प्रमाणम्' इत्यभिधाय तूष्णीमभूत्।

अथ सरस्वती प्रीतिविस्फारितेन चक्षुषा प्रत्यवादीत्—'अयि, न शक्नोमि बहु भाषितुम्। एषास्मि ते स्मितवादिनि वचसि स्थिता। गृह्यन्ताममी प्राणाः' इति। मालती तु 'यदाज्ञाप[5]यस्यतिप्रसादः' इति व्याहृत्य प्रहर्षपरवशा प्रणम्य प्रजविना तुरगेण ततार शोणम्। अगाच्च दधीचमानेतुं च्यवनाश्रमपदम्। इतरा तु सखीस्नेहेन सावित्रीमपि विदितवृत्तान्तामकरोत्। उत्कण्ठाभारभृता च ताम्यता चेतसा कल्पायितं कथंकथमपि दिवसशेषमनैषीत्। अस्तमुपगतवति भगवति गभस्तिमति, स्तिमिततरमवतरति तमसि, प्रहसितामिव सितां दिशं पौरन्दरीं दरीमिव केसरिणि मुञ्चति चन्द्रमसि,

---

१ 'प्रार्थितेऽपि' ब. २ 'प्रभवत्येवातिपेशलः' क–ब. ३ 'प्रतिसरास्मि ते' ब. ४ 'देव' ब. ५ 'यथाज्ञापयिष्यसि प्रसादः' ब.

सरस्वती शुचिनि चीनांशुकसुकुमारे तरङ्गिणि दुकूलकोमले शयन इव शोण-सैकते समुपविष्टा स्वप्नकृतप्रार्थनापादपतनलग्नां दधीचचरणनखचन्द्रिकामिव ललाटिकां दधाना, गण्डस्थलादर्शप्रतिबिम्बितेन 'चारुहासिनि, अयमसावाहृतो हृदयदयितो जनः' इति श्रवणसमीपवर्तिना निवेद्यमानमदनसन्देशेवेन्दुना, विकीर्यमाणनखकिरणचक्रवालेन बालव्यजनीकृ[1]तचन्द्रकलाकलापेनेव करेण वीजयन्ती स्वेदिनं स्पष्टकपोलपट्टम्, 'अत्र दधीचादृते न केनचित्प्रवेष्टव्यम्' इति तिरश्चीनं चित्तभुवा पातितां विलासवेत्रलतामिव बालमृणालिकामधिस्तनं स्तनयन्[2]ती कथमपि हृदयेन वहन्ती प्रतिपालयामास। आसीच्चास्या मनसि—'अहमपि नाम सरस्वती यत्रामुना मनोजन्मना जघ[3]न्येव परवशीकृता। तत्र का गणनेतरासु तपस्विनीष्वतितरलासु तरुणीषु' इति।

आजगाम च मधुमास इव सुरभिगन्धवहः, हंस इव कृतमृणालधृ[4]तिः, शिखण्डीव घनप्रीत्युन्मुखः, मलयानिल इवाहितसरसचन्दनधवलतनुलतोत्कम्पः, कृष्यमाण इव कृतकरकचग्रहेण ग्रहपतिना, प्रेर्यमाण इव कन्दर्पोद्दीपनदक्षेण दक्षिणानिलेन, उह्यमान इवोत्कलिकाबहलेन रतिरसेन, परिमलसम्पातिना मधुपपटलेन पटेनेव नीलेनाच्छादिताङ्गयष्टिः, अन्तःस्फुरत मत्तमदनकरिकर्णशङ्कायमानेन प्रतिमेन्दुना प्रथमसमागमविलासविलक्षस्मितेनेव धवलीक्रियमाणैककपोलोदरो मालतीद्वितीयो दधीचः। आगत्य च हृदयगतदयितानूपुररवमिश्रयेव हंसगद्गदया गिरा कृतसम्भाषणो यथा मन्मथः समाज्ञापयति, यथा यौवनमुपदिशति, यथानुरागः शिक्षयति, यथा विदग्धताध्यापयति, तथा तामभिरामां रामामरमयत्। उपजातविस्रम्भा चात्मानमकथयदस्य सरस्वती। तेन[5] तु सार्धमेकं दिवसमिवानयत्संवत्सरमधिकम्।

अथ दैवयोगात्सरस्वती बभार गर्भम्। असूत चानेहसा सर्वलक्षणाभिरामं तनयम्। तस्मै च जातमात्रायैव 'सम्यक्सरहस्याः सर्वे वेदाः सर्वाणि च शास्त्राणि सकलाश्च कलाः मत्प्रसादात्स्वयमाविर्भविष्यन्ति' इति वरमदात्। सञ्जर्तृश्लाघया दर्शयितुमिव हृदयेनादाय दधीचं पितामहादेशात्समं सावित्र्या ब्रह्मलोकमारुरोह। गतायां च तस्यां दधीचोऽपि हृदये ह्रादिन्येवाभिहतो भार्गववंशसम्भूतस्य भ्रातुर्ब्राह्मणस्य जायामक्षमालाभिधानां मुनिकन्यकामात्मसूनोः संवर्धनाय नियुज्य विरहातुरस्तपसे वनमगात्। यस्मिन्नेवावसरे सरस्वत्यसूत तनयं तस्मिन्नेवाक्षमालापि सुतं प्रसूतवती। तौ तु सा निर्विशेषं सामान्यस्तन्या शनैः शनैः शिशू समवर्धयत्। एकस्तयोः सारस्वताख्य

---

१ 'कृतचन्द्रकरेणेव करेण' ब. २ 'स्तनयन्तीम्' क; 'स्तनन्ती' ब. ३ 'जानत्येव' ब. ४ 'वृत्तिः' ब. ५ 'तया' अ—क.

एवाभवत्, द्वितीयोऽपि वत्सनामाभवत् । आसीच्च तयोः सोदर्ययोरिव स्पृहणीया प्रीतिः ।

अथ सारस्वतो मातुर्महिम्ना यौवनारम्भ एवाविर्भूताशेषविद्यासम्भारस्तस्मिन्सवयसि भ्रातरि प्रेयसि प्राणसमे सुहृदि वत्से वाङ्मयं समस्तमेव सञ्चारयामास । चकार च कृतदारपरिग्रहस्यास्य तस्मिन्नेव प्रदेशे प्रीत्या प्रीतिकूटनामानं निवासम् । आत्मनाप्याषाढी, कृष्णाजिनी, वल्कली, अक्षवलयी, मेखली, जटी च भूत्वा तपस्यतो जनयितुरेव जगामान्तिकम् ।

अथ तस्मात्[1]प्रवर्धमानादिपुरुषजनितात्मचरणोद्धतिनिर्गतप्रघोषः, परमेश्वरशिरोधृतः, सकलकलागमगम्भीरः, महामुनिमान्यः, विपक्षक्षोभक्षमः, क्षितितललब्धायतिः, अस्खलितप्रवृत्तो भागीरथीप्रवाह इव पावनः प्रावर्तत विपुलो[2] वंशः । यस्मादजायन्त वात्स्यायना नाम गृहमुनयः, आश्रितश्रौता अप्यनालम्बितालीकबककाकवः, कृतकुक्कुटवृत्ता अप्यबैडालवृत्तयः, विवर्जितजनपङ्क्तयः, परिहृतकपटकीर[3]कुचीकूर्चाकृताः, अगृहीतगह्वराः, न्यक्कृतनिकृतयः, प्रसन्नप्रकृतयः, विगतविकृतयः, परपरिवादपराचीनचेतसः, वर्णत्रयव्यावृत्तिविशुद्धान्धसः, धीरधिषणो[4]वधूताध्येषणाः, असङ्कसुकस्वभावाः, प्रणतप्रणयिनः, शमितसमस्तशाखान्तरसंशीतयः, उद्घाटितसमग्रग्रन्थार्थग्रन्थयः, कवयः, वाग्मिनः, विमत्सराः, सरसै[5]भाषितव्यसनिनः, विदग्धपरिहासवेदिनः, परिचयपेशलाः, नृत्यगीतवादित्रेष्वबाह्याः, ऐतिह्यस्यावितृष्णाः, सानुक्रोशाः, सत्यशुचयः, साधुसंमताः, सर्वसत्त्वसौहार्दद्रवार्द्रहृदयाः, तथा सर्वगुणोपेता राजसेनानभिभूताः, क्षमाभाज आश्रितनन्दनाः, अनिस्त्रिंशा विद्याधराः, अजडाः कलावन्तः, अदोषास्तारकाः, अपरोपतापिनो भास्वन्तः, अनुष्माणो हुतभुजः, अकुसृतयो भोगिनः, अस्तम्भाः पुण्यालयाः, अलुप्तक्रतुक्रिया दक्षाः, अव्यालाः कामजितः, असाधारणा द्विजातयः ।

तेषु चैवमुत्पद्यमानेषु, संसरति संसारे, यात्सु युगेषु, अवतीर्णे कलौ, वहत्सु वत्सरेषु, व्रजत्सु वासरेषु, अतिक्रामति च काले, प्रसवपरम्पराभिरनवरतमापतति विकाशिनि वात्स्यायनकुले, क्रमेण कुबेरनामा वैनतेय इव गुरुपक्षपाती द्विजो जन्म लेभे । तस्याभवन्नच्युत ईशानो हरः पाशुपतश्चेति चत्वारो युगारम्भा इव ब्रह्मतेजोजन्यमानप्रजाविस्तारा नारायणबाहुदण्डा इव सच्चक्रनन्दकास्तनयाः । तत्र पाशुपतस्यैक एवाभवद्भूभार इवाचलकुलस्थितिश्चतुरुदधिगम्भीरोऽर्थपतिरिति नाम्ना समग्राग्रजन्मचक्रचूडामणिर्महात्मा सूनुः । सोऽजनयद्भृगुं हंसं शुचिं कविं महीदत्तं धर्मं जातवेदसं

१ 'वत्साद्'ब. २ 'विमलः' ब. ३ 'कौर' क; 'कौर' ब. ४ '०धिषणा विधूताध्येषणा' ब. ५ 'परसुभाषित०' ब.

चित्रभानुं [1]त्र्यक्षमहिदत्तं विश्वरूपं चेत्येकादश रुद्रानिव सोमामृतरसशीकरच्छुरितमुखान्पवित्रान्पुत्रान् । अलभत च चित्रभानुस्तेषां मध्ये राजदेव्यभिधानायां ब्राह्मण्यां बाणमात्मजम् । स बाल एव विधेर्बलवतो वशादुपसम्पन्नया व्ययुज्यत जनन्या । जातस्नेहस्तु नितरां पितैवास्य मातृतामकरोत् । अवर्धत च तेनाधिकतरमे[2]धीयमानधृतिर्धाम्नि निजे ।

कृतोपनयनादिक्रियाकलापस्य समावृत्तस्य चतुर्दशवर्षदेशीयस्य पितापि श्रुतिस्मृतिविहितं कृत्वा द्विजजनोचितं निखिलं पुण्यजातं कालेनादशमीस्थ एवास्तमगात् । संस्थिते च पितरि महता शोकेनाभीलमनुप्राप्तो दिवानिशं दह्यमानहृदयः कथंकथमपि कतिपयान्दिवसानात्मगृह एवानैषीत् । गते च विरलतां शोके शनैः शनैरविनयनिदानतया स्वातन्त्र्यस्य, कुतूहलबहलतया च बालभावस्य, धैर्यप्रतिपक्षतया च यौवनारम्भस्य, शैशवोचितान्यनेकानि चापलान्याचरन्नित्वरो बभूव । अभवंश्चास्य व[3]यसा समानाः सुहृदः सहायाश्च । तथा च । भ्रातरौ पारशवौ चन्द्रसेनमातृषेणौ, भा[4]षाकविरीशानः परं मित्रम्, प्रणयिनौ रुद्रनारायणौ, विद्वांसौ वारबाणवासबा[5]णौ, वर्णकविर्वेणीभारतः, प्राकृतकृत्कुलपुत्रो वायुविकारः, बन्दिनावनङ्गबाणसूचीबाणौ, कात्यायनिका चक्रवाकिका, जाङ्गुलिको [6]मयूरकः, ताम्बूलदायकश्चण्डकः, भिषक्पुत्रो मन्दारकः, पुस्तकवाचकः सुदृष्टिः, कलादश्चामीकरः, हैरिकः सिन्धुषेणः, लेखको गोविन्दकः, चित्रकृद्वीरवर्मा, पुस्तकृत्कुमारदत्तः, मार्दङ्गिको जीमूतः, गायनौ सोमिलग्रहादित्यौ, सैरन्ध्री कुरङ्गिका, वांशिकौ मधुकरपारावतौ, गान्धर्वोपाध्यायो दर्दुरकः, संवाहिका केरलिका, लासकयुवा ताण्डविकः, आक्षिक आखण्डलः, कितवो भीमकः, शैलालियुवा शिखण्डकः, नर्तकी हरिणिका, पाराशरी सुमतिः, क्षपणको वीरदेवः, कथको जयसेनः[7], शैवो वक्रघोणः, मन्त्रसाधकः करालः, असुरविवरव्यसनी लोहिताक्षः, धातुवादविद्विहङ्गमः, दा[8]र्दुरिको दामोदरः, ऐन्द्रजालिकश्चकोराक्षः, मस्करी ताम्रचूडः । स एतैश्चान्यैश्चानुगम्यमानो बालतया निघ्नतामुपगतो देशान्तरालोकनकौतुकाक्षिप्तहृदयः सत्स्वपि पितृपितामहोपात्तेषु ब्राह्मणजनोचितेषु विभवेषु सति चाविच्छिन्ने विद्याप्रसङ्गे गृहान्निरगात् । अगाच्च निरवग्रहो ग्रहवानिव नव[9]यौवनेन स्वैरिणा मनसा महतामुपहास्यताम् ।

अथ शनैः शनैरत्युदारव्यवहृतिर्मनोहन्ति बृहन्ति राजकुलानि वीक्षमाणः, निरवद्यविद्याविद्योतितानि च गुरुकुलानि सेवमानः, महार्हालापगम्भीरगुणवद्गोष्ठीश्चोपतिष्ठमानः, स्वभावगम्भीर[10]धीधनानि विदग्धमण्ड-

१ 'त्र्यक्षं महिदत्तम्' ब. २ 'आधीयमान०' ब. ३ 'सवयसः समानाः' ब. ४ 'कविरीशानः' ब. ५ 'वासधारौ ब. ६ 'मायूरकः' ब. ७ 'सिद्धसेनः' ब. ८ 'दार्दरिकः' ब. ९ 'यौवनस्वैरिणा' ब. १० '०धीर्धनानि' ब–अ.

क्तानि च गाहमानः, पुनरपि तामेव वैपश्चितीमात्मवंशोचितां प्रकृतिमभजत्। महतश्च कालात्तामेव भूयो वात्स्यायनवंशाश्रयामात्मनो जन्मभुवं ब्राह्मणाधिवासमगमत्। तत्र च चिरदर्शनादभिनवीभूतस्नेहसद्भावैः ससंस्तवप्रकटितज्ञातेयैराप्तैरुत्सवदिवस इवाभिनन्दितागमनो बालमित्रमण्डलस्य मध्यगतो मोक्षसुखमिवान्वभवदिति।

इति श्रीबाणभट्टकृतौ हर्षचरिते वात्स्यायनवंशवर्णनं नाम प्रथम उच्छ्वासः।

१ 'ससंभ्रम०' क; 'संस्तवप्रकटित' ब. २ 'इति श्रीमहाकविचक्रचूडामणिश्रीबाणभट्टविरचिते हर्षचरिते महाकाव्ये वात्स्यायनवंशवर्णनं नाम प्रथम उच्छ्वासः सम्पूर्णः' ब.

द्वितीय उच्छ्वासः।

अतिगम्भीरे भूपे कूप इव जनस्य निरवतारस्य।
दधति समीहितसिद्धिं गुणवन्तः पार्थिवा घटकाः ॥ १ ॥

रागिणि नलिने लक्ष्मीं दिवसो निदधाति दिनकरप्रभवाम्।
अनपेक्षितगुणदोषः परोपकारः सतां व्यसनम् ॥ २ ॥

अथ तत्रानवरताध्ययनध्वनिमुखराणि, भस्मपुण्ड्रकपाण्डुरललाटैः कपिलशिखाजालजटिलैः कृशानुभिरिव क्रतुलोभागतैर्बटुभिरध्यास्यमानानि, सेकसुकुमारसोमकेदारिकाहरितायमानप्रघनानि, कृष्णाजिनविकीर्णशुष्यत्पुरोडाशीयश्यामाकतण्डुलानि, बालिकाविकीर्यमाणनीवारबलीनि, शुचिशिष्यशतानीयमानहरितकुशपूलीपलाशसमिन्धि, इन्धनगोमयपिण्डकूटसङ्कटानि, आमिक्षीयक्षीरक्षारिणीनामग्निहोत्रधेनूनां खुरवलयैर्विलिखिताजिरवितर्दिकानि, [1]कमण्डलव्यमृत्पिण्डमर्दनव्यग्रयतिजनानि, वैतानवेदीशङ्कव्यानामौदुम्बरीणां शाखानां राशिभिः पवित्रितपर्यन्तानि, वैश्वदेवपि[2]ण्डपङ्क्तिपाण्डुरितप्रदेशानि, हविर्धूमधूसरिताङ्गनविटपिकिसलयानि, [3]वत्सीयवत्सपालकलालितललत्तरलतर्णकानि, क्रीडत्कृष्णशारच्छागशावकप्रकटितपशुबन्धप्रबन्धानि, शुकसारिकारब्धाध्ययनदीयमानोपाध्यायविश्रान्तिसुखानि, साक्षात्त्रयीतपोवनानीव चिरदृष्टानां बान्धवानां प्रीयमाणो भ्रमन्भवनानि सुखमतिष्ठत्।

तत्रस्थस्य चास्य कदाचित्कुसुमसमययुगमुपसंहरन्नजृम्भत ग्रीष्माभिधानः सम्फुल्लमल्लिकाधवलाट्टहासो महाकालः। प्रत्यग्रनिर्जितस्यास्तमुपगतवतो वसन्तसामन्तस्य बालापत्येष्विव पयःपायिषु नवोद्यानेषु दर्शितस्नेहो मृदुरभूत्। अभिनवोदितश्च सर्वस्यां पृथिव्यां सकलकुसुमबन्धनमोक्षमकरोत्प्रतपत्तुष्णसमयः। स्वयमृतुराजस्याभिषेका[4]र्द्रा[5]श्चामरकलापा इवागृह्यन्त कामिनीनां चिकुरचयाः कुसुमायुधेन। हिमदग्धसकलकमलिनीकोपेनेव हिमालयाभिमुखीं यात्रामदादंशुमाली।

अथ ललाटन्तपे तपति तपने लिखि[5]तललाटिकापुण्ड्रकैरल[6]कचीरचीवरसंवीतैः स्वेदोदबिन्दुमुक्ताक्षवलयवाहिभिर्दिनकराराधननियमा इवागृह्यन्त ललनाललाटेन्दु[7]भिः। चन्दनधूसराभिरसूर्यम्पश्याभिः कुमुदिनीभिरिव दिवसमसुप्यत सुन्दरीभिः। निद्रालसा रत्नालोकमपि नासहन्त दृशः, किमुत जरठमातपम्। अशिशिरसमयेन चक्रवाकमिथुनाभिनन्दिताः सरित इव

---

१ 'कामण्डलव्य०' अ–क. २ '०पिण्डपाण्डुरित०' ब. ३ 'वत्सीयबालकलालित०' अ–क. ४ '०राजस्यागृह्यन्ताभिषेका०' ब. ५ 'चन्दनलिखित०' ब. ६ 'अलकचीवर०' ब. ७ '०ललाटेन्दुद्युतिभिः' ब.

समूर्धानम्, प्रविशन्तं लेखहारकमद्राक्षीत् । अप्राक्षीच्च दूरादेव—'भद्र, भद्रमशेषभुवननिष्कारणबन्धोस्तत्रभवतः कृष्णस्य' इति । सः 'भद्रम्' इत्युक्त्वा प्रणम्य नातिदूरे समुपाविशत् । विश्रान्तश्चाब्रवीत्—'एष खलु स्वामिनो माननीयस्य लेखः प्रहितः' इति विमुच्य चार्पयत् । अथ बाणः सादरं गृहीत्वा स्वयमेवावाचयत्—'मेखलकात्सन्दिष्टमवधार्य फलप्रतिबन्धी धीमन्निरपहरणीयः कालातिपात इत्येतावदत्रार्थजातम् । इतरद्वार्तासंवादनमात्रकम्' । अवधृतलेखार्थश्च समुत्सारितपरिजनः सन्देशं पृष्टवान् । मेखलकस्त्ववादीत्—'एवमाह मेधाविनं स्वामी—जानात्येव मान्यो यथैकगोत्रता वा, [1]समानजातिता वा, समं संवर्धनं वा, एकदेशनिवासो वा, दर्शनाभ्यासो वा, परस्परानुरागश्रवणं वा, परोक्षोपकारकरणं वा, समानशीलता वा, स्नेहस्य हेतवः । त्वयि तु विना कारणेनादृष्टेऽपि प्रत्यासन्ने बन्धाविव बद्धपक्षपातं किमपि स्निह्यति मे हृदयं दूरस्थेऽपीन्दोरिव कुमुदाकरे । भवन्तमन्तरेणान्यथा चान्यथा चायं चक्रवर्ती दुर्जनैर्ग्राहित आसीत् । न च तत्तथा । न सन्त्येव ते येषां सतामपि सतां न विद्यन्ते मित्रोदासीनशत्रवः । शिशुचापलपराचीनचेतोवृत्तितया च भवतः केनचिदसहिष्णुना यत्किञ्चिदसदृशमुदीरितमितरो लोकस्तथैव तद्गृह्णाति वक्ति च । सलिलानीव खलु गतानुगति[2]कानि लोलानि भवन्त्यविवेकिनां मनांसि बहुमुखश्रवणनिश्चलीकृतनिश्चयः किं करोतु पृथिवीपतिः । तत्त्वान्वेषिभिश्चास्माभिर्दूरस्थितोऽपि प्रत्यक्षीकृतोऽसि । विज्ञपश्चक्रवर्ती त्वदर्थं यथा—प्रायेण प्रथमे वयसि सर्वस्यैव चापलैः शैशवमपराधीति । तथेति च प्रतिपन्नं स्वामिना । अतो भवता राजकुलमकृतकालक्षेपमागन्तव्यम् । अवकोशीवादृष्टपरमेश्वरो बन्धुमध्यमधिवसन्नासि मे बहुमतः । न च सेवावैषम्यविषादिना वा परमेश्वरोपसर्पणभीरुणा वा भवता भवितव्यम् । यतो यद्यपि—

स्वेच्छोपजातविषयोऽपि न याति वक्तुं
देहीति मार्गणशतैश्च ददाति दुःखम् ।
मोहात्समाक्षिपति जीवनमप्यकाण्डे
कष्टं मनोभव इवेश्वरदुर्विदग्धः ॥ ३ ॥

तथाप्यन्ये ते भूपतयः, अन्य एवायं न्यक्कृतनृगनलनिषधनहुषाम्बरीषदशरथदिलीपनाभागभरतभगीरथययातिरमृतमयः स्वामी । नास्याहङ्कारकालकूटविषदिग्धदुष्टा दृष्टयः, न गर्वगुरुगरगलग्रहगद्गदा गिरः, नातिस्मयोष्मापस्मारविस्मृतस्थैर्याणि स्थानकानि, नोद्दामदर्पदाहज्वरवेगविक्लवा विकाराः, नाभिमानमहासंनिपातनिर्मिताङ्गभङ्गानि गतानि, न मदार्दितवक्रीकृतौष्ठनिष्ठ्यूतनिष्ठुराक्षराणि जल्पितानि । तथा च, अस्य विमलेषु साधुषु रत्नबुद्धिः, न शिलाशकलेषु । मुक्ताधवलेषु प्रसाधनधीः, नाभरणभारेषु ।

---

१ 'समानज्ञानता वा' इत्येतदधिकं ब-पुस्तके. २ 'गतागतिकानि' अ-क.

दानवत्सु कर्मसु साधनश्रद्धा, न करिकीटेषु। सर्वाग्रेसरे[1] यशसि महाप्रीतिः, न जीवितजरत्तृणे। गृहीतकरास्वाशासु प्रसाधनेताभियोगः[2], न निजकलत्रधर्मे[3]-मैपुत्रिकासु। गुणवति धनुषि सहायबुद्धिः, न पिण्डोपजीविनि सेवकजने। अपि च। अस्य मित्रोपकरणमात्मा, भृत्योपकरणं प्रभुत्वम्, पण्डितोपकरणं वैदग्ध्यम्, बान्धवोपकरणं लक्ष्मीः, कृपणोपकरणमैश्वर्यम्, द्विजोपकरणं सर्वस्वम्, सुकृतसंस्मरणोपकरणं हृदयम्, धर्मोपकरणमायुः, साहसोपकरणं शरीरम्, असिलतोपकरणं पृथिवी, विनोदोपकरणं राजकम्, प्रतापोपकरणं प्रतिपक्षः। नास्याल्पपुण्यैरवाप्येत सर्वातिशायिसुखरसप्रसूतिः पादपल्लवच्छाया' इति। श्रुत्वा च तमेव चन्द्रसेनं समादिशत्—'कृतकशिपुं विश्रान्तसुखिनमेनं कारय' इति।

अथ गते च तस्मिन्, पर्यस्ते च वासरे, सङ्घट्ट[4]मानरक्तपङ्कजसम्पुटपीयमान इव क्षयिणि क्षामतां व्रजति बालवायसास्यारुणेऽपराह्णातपे, शिथिलितनिजवाजिजवे जपापीडपाटले[5]ऽस्ताचलशिखरस्खलिते खञ्जतीव कमलिनीकण्टकक्षतपादपल्लवे पतङ्गे, पुरः परापतति प्रेङ्खदन्धकारलेश[6]लम्बालके शशिविरहशोकश्याम इव श्यामामुखे, कृतसंध्योपासनः शयनीयमगात्। अचिन्तयच्चैकाकी—'किं करोमि। अन्यथा सम्भावितोऽस्मि राज्ञा। निर्निमित्तबन्धुना च सन्दिष्टमेवं कृष्णेन। कष्टा च सेवा। विषमं च भृत्यत्वम्। अतिगम्भीरं महद्राजकुलम्। न च तत्र मे पूर्वजप्रवर्तिता प्रीतिः, न कुलक्रमागता गतिः, नोपकारस्मरणानुरोधः, न बालसेवास्नेहः, न गोत्रगौरवम्[7], न पूर्वदर्शनदाक्षिण्यम्, न प्रज्ञासंविभागोपप्रलोभनम्, न विद्यातिशयकुतूहलम्, नाकारसौन्दर्यादरः, न सेवाकाकुकौशलम्, न विद्वद्गोष्ठीबन्धवैदग्ध्यम्, न वित्तव्ययवशीकरणम्, न राजवल्लभपरिचयः। अवश्यं गन्तव्यम्। सर्वथा भगवान्पुरारातिर्भुवनगुरुर्गतस्य[8] मे[9] सर्वं सांप्रतमाचरिष्यति' इत्यवधार्य गमनाय मतिमकरोत्।

अथान्यस्मिन्नहन्युत्थाय, प्रातरेव स्नात्वा, धृतधौतधवलदुकूलवासाः, गृहीताक्षमालः, प्रास्थानिकानि सूक्तानि मन्त्रपदानि च बहुशः समावर्त्य, देवदेवस्य विरूपाक्षस्य क्षीरस्नपनपुरःसरां सुरभिकुसुमधूपगन्धध्वजबलिविलेपनप्रदीपकबहुलां विधाय पूजां परमया भक्त्या, प्रथमहुततरलतिलत्वग्विघट्टन[10]चटुलमुखरशिखाशेखरं प्राज्याज्याहुतिप्रवर्धितदक्षिणार्चिषं भगवन्तमाशुशुक्षणिं हुत्वा, दत्वा द्युम्नं यथाविद्यमानं द्विजेभ्यः, प्रदक्षिणीकृत्य प्राङ्मुखीं नैचिकीम्, शुक्लाङ्गरागः, शुक्लमाल्यः, शुक्लवासाः, रोचनाचित्रदूर्वाग्रपल्लवग्रथितगिरिकर्णिकाकुसुमकृतकर्णपूरः, शिखासक्तसिद्धार्थकः, पितुः कनीयस्या

१ 'सर्वाशाग्रेसरे' ब. २ 'दिक्षु प्रसाधनाभियोगः' ब. ३ 'धर्मे' ब. ४ 'संघटमान' ब. ५ 'पाटलिम्नि' ब. ६ 'लेखा' ब. ७ 'तन्त्रगौरवम्' ब. ८ 'भवानीपतिर्भुवनपतिः' ब. ९ 'मे शरणं सर्वं' ब. १० 'विचटन' अ—क.

स्वस्त्रा मात्रेव स्नेहार्द्रहृदयया श्वेतवाससा साक्षादिव भगवत्या महाश्वेतया मालत्याख्यया कृतसकलगमनमङ्गलः, दत्ताशीर्वादो बान्धववृद्धाभिः, अभिनन्दितः परिजनजरन्तीभिः, वन्दितचरणैरभ्यनुज्ञातो गुरुभिः, अभिवादितैराघ्रातः शिरसि कुलवृद्धैः, वर्धितगमनोत्साहः शकुनैः, मौहूर्तिकमतेन कृतनक्षत्रदोहदः, शोभने मुहूर्ते हरितगोमयोपलिप्ताजिरस्थण्डिलस्थापितमसितेतरकुसुममालापरिक्षिप्तकण्ठं पिष्ट[1]पञ्चाङ्गुलपाण्डुरं मुखनिहितनवचूतपल्लवं पूर्णकलशमुदीक्षमाणः, प्रणम्य कुलदेवताभ्यः, कुसुमफलपाणिभिरप्रतिरथं जपद्भिर्निजद्विजैरनुगम्यमानः, प्रथमचलितदक्षिणचरणः, प्रीतिकूटान्निरगात् ।

प्रथमेऽहनि घर्मकालकष्टं निरुदकं निष्पत्रपादपविषमं पथिकजननमस्क्रियमाणप्रवेशपादपोत्कीर्णकात्यायनीप्रतियातनं शुष्कमपि पल्लवितमिव तृषितश्वापदकुललम्बितलोलजिह्वालतासहस्रैः पुलकितमिवाच्छभल्लगोला[2]ङ्गूललिह्यमानमधुगोलचलितसरघासङ्घातै रोमाञ्चितमिव दग्धस्थलीरूढस्थूलाभीरुकन्दलशतैः शनैश्चण्डिकाका[3]ननमतिक्रम्य मल्लकूटनामानं ग्राममगात् । तत्र च हृदयनिर्विशेषेण भ्रात्रा सुहृदा च जगत्पतिनाम्ना सम्पादितसपर्यः सुखमवसत् । अथापरेद्युरुत्तीर्य भगवतीं भागीरथीं यष्टिग्र[4]हकनाम्नि वनग्रामके निशामनयत् । अन्यस्मिन्दिवसे स्कन्धावारमुपमणिता[5]रमन्वजिरवति कृतसंनिवेशमाससाद । अतिष्ठच्च नातिदूरे राजभवनस्य ।

निर्वर्तितस्नानाशनव्यतिकरो विश्रान्तश्च मेखलकेन सह याममात्रावशेषे दिवसे भुक्तवति भूभुजि प्रख्यातानां क्षितिभुजां बहून्शिबिरसंनिवेशान्वीक्षमाणः शनैः शनैः पट्टबन्धार्थमुपस्थापितैश्च डिण्डिमाधिरोहणायाहृतैश्चाभिनवबद्धैश्च विक्षेपोपार्जितैश्च कौशलिकागतैश्च नागवीथीपालप्रेषितैश्च प्रथमदर्शनकुतूहलोपनीतैश्च दूतसंप्रेषणप्रेषितैश्च पल्लीपरिवृढढौकितैश्च स्वेच्छायुद्धक्रीडाकौतुककारितैश्च दीयमानैश्चाच्छिद्यमानैश्च मुच्यमानैश्च यामस्था[6]पितैश्च सर्वद्वीपविजिगीषया गिरिभिरिव सागरसेतुबन्धार्थमेकीकृतैर्ध्वजपटपटुपटहशङ्खचामराङ्गरागरमणीयैः पुष्याभिषेकदिवसैरिव कल्पितैर्वारणेन्द्रैः श्यामायमानम्, अनवरतचलितखुरपुटप्रहतमृदङ्गैर्नर्तयद्भिरिव राजलक्ष्मीमुपहसद्भिरिव सृक्किपुटप्रसृतफेनाट्टहासेन जवजडजङ्घां हरिणजातिमाकारयद्भिरिव सङ्कट्टहेतोर्हर्षहेषिते[7]नोच्चैःश्रवसमुत्पतद्भिरिव दिवसकररथतुरगरुषा पक्षायमाणमण्डनचामरमालैर्गगनतलं तुरङ्गैस्तरङ्गायमानम्, अन्यत्र प्रेषितैश्च प्रेष्यमाणैश्च प्रेषितप्रतिनिर्वृ[8]त्तैश्च बहुयोजनग-

१ 'दत्तपिष्ट०' ब. २ 'शुष्कगलगो०' ब. ३ 'चण्डिकायतनकानन०' ब. ४ 'यष्टिगृहक०' ब. ५ 'मणिपुरमन्व०' ब. ६ 'यामावस्थितैश्च' ब. ७ 'हेषितेनोच्चैरुच्चैःश्रवस०' ब. ८ 'प्रतीपनिवृत्तै०' अ-क.

मनगणनसंख्याक्षरावलीमिरिव वराटिकावलीमिर्घटितमुखमण्डनकैस्तारकितै-रिव संध्यातपच्छेदैररुणचामरिकारचितकर्णपूरैः सरक्तोत्पलैरिव रक्तशालि-शालेयैरन्तरतक्षणक्षणायमानचारुचामीकरघुरुघुरुकमालिकैर्जरत्करञ्जवनैरिव रणितशुष्कबीजकोशीशतैः श्रवणोपान्तप्रेङ्खत्पद्मरागवर्णोर्णाचित्रसूत्रजूटज-टालैः कपिकपोलकपिलैः क्रमेलककुलैः कपिलायमानम्, अन्यत्र शरज्जल-धैररिव सद्यःसुतपयःपटलधवलतनुभिः कल्पपादपैरिव मुक्ताफलजाल-कजायमानालोकलुसच्छायामण्डलैर्नारायणनाभिपुण्डरीकैरिवाश्लिष्टगरुडपक्षैः क्षीरोदोद्देशैरिव द्योतमानविकटविद्रुमदण्डैः शेषफणाफलकैरिवोपरिस्फुरत्स्फी-तमाणिक्यखण्डैः श्वेतगङ्गापुलिनैरिव राजहंसोपसेवितैरभिभवद्भिरिव निदा-घसमयमुपहसद्भिरिव विवस्वतः प्रतापमापिबद्भिरिवातपं चन्द्रलोकमयमिव जीवलोकं जनयद्भिः कुमुदमयमिव कालं कुर्वद्भिर्ज्योत्स्नामयमिव वासरं विरचयद्भिः फेनमयीमिव दिवं दर्शयद्भिरकालकौमुदीसहस्राणीव सृजद्भिरु-पहसद्भिरिव शातक्रतवीं श्रियं श्वेतायमानैरातपत्रखण्डैः श्वे[1]तायमानम्, क्षण-दृष्टनष्टाष्टदिङ्मुखं च मुष्णद्भिरिव भुवनमाक्षेपोत्क्षेपदोलायितं दिनं गतागता-नीव कारयद्भिरिव कुनृपतिसम्पर्ककलङ्ककालीं कालेयीं स्थितिं विकचविश-दकाशवनपाण्डुरदिशं शरत्समयमिवोपपादयद्भिर्बिसतन्तुमयमिवान्तरिक्षमा-विर्भावयद्भिः शशिकरशुचीनां चलतां चामराणां सहस्रैर्दोलायमानम्, अपि च हंसयूथायमानं करिकर्णशङ्खैः, कल्पलतावनायमानं कदलिकाभिः, माणि-क्यवृक्षकवनायमानं मायूरातपत्रैः, मन्दाकिनीप्रवाहायमानमंशुकैः, क्षीरो-दायमानं क्षौमैः, कदलीवनायमानं मरकतमयूखैः, जन्यमानान्यदिवसमिव पद्मरागबालातपैः, उत्प[2]द्यमानापराम्बरमिवेन्द्रनीलप्रभापटलैः, आरभ्यमा-णापूर्वनिशमिव महानीलमयूखान्धकारैः, स्यन्दमानानेककालिन्दीसहस्रमिव गरुडमणिप्रभाप्रतानैः, अङ्गारकितमिव पुष्परागरश्मिभिः, कैश्चित्प्रवेशमल-भमानैरधोमुखैश्चरणनखपतितवदनप्रतिबिम्बनिभेन लज्जया स्वाङ्गानीव वि-शद्भिः कैश्चिदङ्गुलीलिखितायाः क्षितेर्विकीर्यमाणकरनखकिरणकदम्बकव्याजेन सेवाचामराणीवार्पयद्भिः कैश्चिदुरःस्थलदोलायमानेन्द्रनीलतरलप्रभापट्टैः स्वा-मिप्रकोपप्रशमनाय कण्ठबद्धकृपाणपट्टैरिव, कैश्चिदुच्छ्वाससौरभभ्राम्यद्भ्रमर-पटलान्धकारितमुखैरपहृतलक्ष्मीशोकधृतलम्बश्मश्रुभिरिवान्यैः शेखरोड्डीय-मानमधुपमण्डलैः प्रणामविडम्बनाभयपलायमानमौलिभिरिव निर्जितैरपि संमानितैरिवानन्यशरणैरन्तरान्तरा निष्पततां प्रविशतां चान्तरप्रतीहाराणा-मनुमार्गप्रधावितानेकार्थिजनसहस्राणामनुयायिनः पुरुषानश्रान्तैः पुनः पुनः पृच्छद्भिः 'भद्र, अद्य भविष्यति भुक्त्[3]वास्थानं दास्यति दर्शनं परमेश्वरः, निष्पतिष्यति वा बाह्यां कक्ष्याम्' इति दर्शनाशया दिवसं नयद्भिर्भुजनि-र्जितैः शत्रुमहासामन्तैः समन्तादासेव्यमानम्, अन्यैश्च प्रतापानुरागागतै-

१ 'श्वेतद्वीपायमानम्' ब—क. २ 'उत्पाद्यमाना०' ब. ३ 'भुक्त्वा स्थाने' अ—क.

नानादेशजैर्महीपालैः प्रतिपालयद्भिर्नरपतिदर्शनकालमध्यास्यमानम्, एकान्तोपविष्टैश्च जैनैरार्हतैः पाशुपतैः पाराशरिभिर्वर्णिभिश्च सर्वदेशजन्मभिश्च जनपदैः सर्वाम्भोधिवेलावनवलयवासिभिश्च म्लेच्छजातिभिः सर्वद्वीपान्तरागतैश्च दूतमण्डलैरुपास्यमानम्, सर्वप्रजानिर्माणभूमिमिव प्रजापतीनां लोकत्रयसारोच्चयरचितं चतुर्थमिव लोकम्, महाभारतशतैरप्यकथनीयसमृद्धिसम्भारम्, कृतयुगसहस्रैरिव कल्पितसंनिवेशम्, स्वर्गार्बुदैरिव विहितरामणीयकम्, राजलक्ष्मीकोटिभिरिव कृतपरिग्रहं राजद्वारमगमत्।

अभवच्चास्य जातविस्मयस्य मनसि—'कथमिवेदमियत्प्रमाणं प्राणिजातं जनयतां प्रजासृजां नासीत्[1]परिश्रमो महाभूतानां वा परिक्षयः, परमाणूनां वा परि[2]च्छेदः, कालस्य वान्तः, आयुषो वा व्युपरमः, आकृतीनां वा परिसमाप्तिः' इति। मेखलकस्तु दूरादेव द्वारपाललोकेन प्रत्यभिज्ञायमानः 'तिष्ठतु तावत्क्षणमात्रमत्रैव पुण्यभागी' इति तमभिधायाप्रतिहतः पुरः प्राविशत्।

अथ स मुहूर्तादिव प्रांशुना, कर्णिकारगौरेण, वीध्रककञ्चुकच्छन्नवपुषा, समुन्मिषन्माणिक्यपदकबन्धबन्धुरशस्त्र[3]बन्धकृशावलग्नेन, हिमशैलशिलाविशालवक्षसा, हरवृषककुदकूटविकटांसतटेन, उरसा चपलहृषीकहरिणकुलसंयमनपाशमिव हारं बिभ्रता, 'कथयतं यदि सोमवंशसम्भवः सूर्यवंशसम्भवो वा भूपतिरभूदेवंविधः' इति प्रष्टुमानीताभ्यां सोमसूर्याभ्यामिव श्रवणगताभ्यां मणिकुण्डलाभ्यां समुद्भासमानेन, वहद्[4]वदनलावण्यविसरवेणिकाक्षिप्यमाणैरधिकारगौरवाद्दीयमानमार्गेणेव दिनकृतः किरणैः, प्रसादलब्धया विकचपुण्डरीकमुण्डमालिकयेव दीर्घया दृष्ट्या दूरादेवानन्दयता, नैष्ठुर्याधिष्ठानेऽपि प्रतिष्ठितेन पदे प्रश्रयमिवावनम्रेण मौलिना पाण्डुरमुष्णीषमुद्वहता, वामेन स्थूलमुक्ताफलच्छुरणदन्तुरत्सरुं करकिसलयेन कलयता कृपाणम्, इतरेणापनीततरलतां ताडितीमिव लतां शातकौम्भीं वेत्रयष्टिमुन्मृष्टां धारयता पुरुषेणानुगम्यमानो निर्गत्यावोचत्—'एष खलु महाप्रतीहाराणामनन्तरश्चक्षुष्यो देवस्य पारियात्रनामा दौवारिकः। समनुगृह्णात्वेनमनुरूपया प्रतिपत्त्या कल्याणाभिनिवेशी' इति। दौवारिकः समुपसृत्य कृतप्रणामो मधुरया गिरा सविनयमभाषत—'आगच्छत। प्रविशत दर्शनाय। कृतप्रसादो देवः' इति। बाणस्तु 'धन्योऽस्मि, यदेवमनुग्राह्यं मां देवो मन्यते' इत्युक्त्वा तेनोपदिश्यमानमार्गः प्राविशदभ्यन्तरम्।

अथ वनायुजैः, आरट्टजैः, काम्बोजैः, भारद्वाजैः, सिन्धुदेशजैः, पारसीकैश्च, शोणैश्च, श्यामैश्च, श्वेतैश्च, पिञ्जरैश्च, हरिद्भिश्च, तित्तिरिकल्माषैश्च, पञ्चभद्रैश्च, मल्लिकाक्षैश्च, कृत्तिकापिञ्जरैश्च, आयतनिर्मांसमुखैः, अनुत्कटक-

---

१ 'नासीन्महाभूतानां' अ–क. २ 'विच्छेदः' ब. ३ 'वस्तबन्धलुलाव०' ब.
४ 'बृहद्वदन०' अ.

र्णकोशैः, सुवृत्तश्लक्ष्णसुघटितघण्टिकाबन्धैः, यूपानुपूर्वीवक्रायतोदग्रग्रीवैः, उपचयश्वयत्स्कन्धसन्धिभिः, निर्भुग्नोरःस्थलैः, अस्थूलप्रगुणप्रसृतैर्लोहपीठककठिनखुरमण्डलैः, अतिजवत्रुटनभयादनिर्मितान्त्राणीवोदराणि वृत्तानि धारयद्भिः, उद्यद्द्रोणीविभज्यमानपृथुजघनैः, जगतीदोलायमानबालपल्लवैः, कथमप्युभयतो निखातदृढभूरि[1]पाशसंयमननियन्त्रितैः, आयतैरपि पश्चात्पाशबन्धप्रसारितैकाङ्घ्रिभिरायततरैरिवोपलक्ष्यमाणैः, बहुगुणसूत्रग्रथितग्रीवागण्डकैरामीलितलोचनैः, दूर्वारसश्यामलफेनलवशबलान्दशनगृहीतमुक्तान्फरफरितत्वचः कण्डूजुषः प्रतीका[2]न्प्रचालयद्भिः, सालसवलितवालधिभिः, एकशफविश्रान्तिस्रस्तशिथिलितजघनार्धैः, निद्रया प्रध्यायद्भिश्च, स्खलितहुङ्कारमन्दमन्दशब्दायमानैश्च ताडितखुरधरणीरणितमुखरशिखरखुरलिखितक्ष्मातलैर्घासमभिलषद्भिश्च, प्रकीर्यमाणयवसग्रासरसमत्सरोद्भूतक्षोभैश्च, प्रकुपितचण्डचण्डालहुङ्कारकातरतरतरलतारकैश्च, कुङ्कुमप्रमृष्टिपिञ्जराङ्गतया सततसंनिहितनीराज[3]नानलैरिव लक्ष्यमाणैरुपरिविततवितानैः, पुरः पूजिताभिमतदैवतैः, भूपालवल्लभैस्तुरङ्गैरारचितां मन्दुरां विलोकयन्, कुतूहलाक्षिप्तहृदयः किञ्चिदन्तरमतिक्रान्तो हस्तवामेनात्युच्चतया निरवकाशमिवाकाशं कुर्वाणम्, महता कदलीवनेन परिवृतपर्यन्तं सर्वतो मधुकरमयीभिर्मदस्रुतिभिर्नदीभिरिवापतन्तीभिरापूर्यमाणम्, आशामुखविसर्पिणा बकुलवनानामिव विकसतामामोदेन लिम्पन्तं घ्राणेन्द्रियं दूरादव्यक्तमिभधिष्[4]ण्यागारमपश्यत्। अपृच्छच्च—'अत्र देवः किं करोति' इति। असावकथयत्—'एष खलु देवस्यौपवाह्यो बाह्यं हृदयं जात्यन्तरित आत्मा बहिश्चराः प्राणा विक्रमक्रीडासुहृद्दर्पशात इति यथार्थनामा वारणपतिः। तस्यावस्थानमण्डपोऽयं महान्दृश्यते' इति। स तमवादीत्—'भद्र, श्रूयते दर्पशातः। यद्येवमदोषो वा पश्यामि तावद्वारणेन्द्रमेव। अतोऽर्हसि मामत्र प्रापयितुम्। अतिपरवानस्मि कुतूहलेन' इति। सोऽभाषत—'भवत्वेवम्। आगच्छतु भवान्। को दोषः। पश्यतु तावद्वारणेन्द्रम्' इति।

गत्वा च तं प्रदेशं दूरादेव गम्भीरगलगर्जि[5]तैर्वियति चातककदम्बकैर्भुवि च भवननीलकण्ठकुलैः कलकेकाकलकलमुखरमुखैः क्रियमाण[6]कलकोलाहलम्, विकचकदम्बसंवादिमदसुरासौरभभरितभुवनम्, कायवन्तमिवा[7]कालमेघकालम्, अविरलमधुबिन्दुपिङ्गलपद्मजालकितां सरसीमिवाभ्यवगाढां दशां चतुर्थीमुत्सृजन्तम्, अनवरतमवतंसशङ्खैरामन्द्रकर्णतालदुन्दुभिध्वनिभिः पञ्चमीप्रवेशमङ्गलारम्भमिव गा[8]यन्तम्, अविरतचलनचित्रत्रिपदीललितलास्य-

---

१ 'भूमिपाश' ब. २ 'प्रदेशान्' ब. ३ '°नलरक्ष्यमाणैरिवो०' अ–क. ४ '०दव्यक्तमिव धिष्ण्याकार०' ब; 'धृष्ण्या०' अ. ५ 'गर्जितोर्जितैः' अ–क. ६ 'क्रियमाणाकाल०' ब. ७ 'कायवन्तमिव काल०' ब. ८ 'सूचयन्तम्' ब.

लघैर्दोलायमानदीर्घदेहाभोगतया[1] मेदिनीविदलनभयेन भारमिव लघयन्तं दिग्भित्तितटेषु कायमिव कण्डूयमानम्, आह्वायोदस्तहस्ततया दिग्वारणानिवाह्वयमानम्, अन्धस्तम्भमिव स्थूलनिशितदन्तेन करपत्रेण पाटयन्तम्, अमान्तं भुवनाभ्यन्तरे बहिरिव निर्गन्तुमीहमानम्, सर्वतः सरसकिशलयलतालासिभिर्लेशिकैश्चिरपरिचयोपचितैर्वनैरिव[2] विक्षिप्तसशैवलबिसविसरशबलसलिलैः सरोभिरिव चाधोरणैराधीयमाननिदाघसमयसमुचितोपचारानन्दम्, अपि च प्रतिगजदानपवनादानदूरोत्क्षिप्तेनानेकसमरविजयगणनालेखाभिरिव वलिवलयराजिभिस्तनीयसीभिस्तरङ्गितोदरेणातिस्थवीयसा हस्तार्गलदण्डेनार्गलयन्तमिव सकलं सकुलशैलसमुद्रद्वीपकाननं ककुभां चक्रवालम्, एकं करान्तरार्पितेनोत्पलाशेन कदलीदण्डेनान्तर्गतशीकरसिच्यमानमूलं मुक्तपल्लवमिवापरं लीलावलम्बिना मृणालजालकेन समररसोच्चरोमाञ्चकण्टकितमिव दन्तकाण्डं वहन्तम्, विसर्पन्त्या च दन्तकाण्डयुगलकस्य कान्त्या सरःक्रीडास्वादितानीव कुमुदवनानि बहुधा वमन्तं निजयशोराशिमिव दिशामपर्यन्तं कुकरिकीटपाटनदुर्ललितान्सिंहानिवोपहसन्तं कल्पद्रुमदुकूलमुखपटमिव चात्मनः [3]कल्पयन्तम्, हस्तकाण्डदण्डोद्धरणलीलासु च लक्ष्यमाणेन रक्तांशुकसुकुमारतलेन[4] तालुना कवलितानि रक्तपद्मवनानीव वर्षन्तमभिनवकिसलयराशिमिवोद्गिरन्तम्, कमलकवलपीतं मधुरसमिव स्वभावपिङ्गलेन [5]वमन्तं चक्षुषा, चूतचम्पकलवलीलवङ्गकक्कोलवन्त्येलालतामिश्रितानि ससहकाराणि कर्पूरपूरपूरितानि पारिजातकवनानीवोपभुक्तानि[6] पुनः पुनः करटाभ्यां बहलमदामोदव्याजेन विसृजन्तम्, अहर्निशं विभ्रमकृतहस्तस्थितिभिरर्धखण्डितपुण्ड्रेक्षुकाण्डकण्डूयनलिखितैरलिकुलवाचालितैर्दानपट्टकैर्विलभमानमिव सर्वकाननानि करिपतीनाम्, अविरलोदबिन्दुस्यन्दिना हिमशिलाशकलमयेन विभ्रमनक्षत्रमालागुणेन शिशिरीक्रियमाणम्, सकलवारणेन्द्राधिपत्यपट्टबन्धबन्धुरमिवोच्चैस्तरां शिरो दधानम्, मुहुर्मुहुः स्थगितापावृतदिङ्मुखाभ्यां कर्णतालवृन्ताभ्यां वीजयन्तमिव भर्तृभक्त्या दन्तपर्यङ्किकास्थितां राजलक्ष्मीम्, आयतवंशक्रमागतेन गजाधिपत्यचिह्नेन चामरेणेव चलता वालधिना विराजमानम्, स्वच्छशिशिरशीकरच्छलेन दिग्विजयपीताः सरित इव पुनः पुनर्मुखेन मुञ्चन्तम्, क्षणमवधानदाननिस्पन्दीकृतसकलावयवानामन्यद्विरदडिण्डिमाकर्णनाङ्कवलनानामन्ते दीर्घफूत्कारैः परिभवदुःखमिवावेदयन्तम्, अलब्धयुद्धमिवात्मानमनुशोचन्तम्, आरोहाधिरूढिपरिभवेन लज्जमानमिवाङ्गुलीलिखितमहीतलं मदं मुञ्चन्तम्, अवज्ञागृहीतमुक्तकवलकुपितारोहारटनानुरोधेन मदतन्द्रीनिमीलितनेत्रत्रिभागं कथं कथमपि मन्दमन्दमनादरादाददानं कवलान्, अवजग्धतमालपल्लवस्नुतश्यामलरसेन प्रभूततया मद-

---

१ '०भोगवत्तया' ब. २ '०चितैर्घनै०' अ-क. ३ 'कलयन्तम्' अ-क. ४ '०सुकुमारतरेण' ब. ५ 'गलन्तम्' ब. ६ '०भुक्तानि पुरः करटाभ्याम्' अ-क.

प्रवाहमिव मुखेनाप्युत्सृजन्तम्, दलन्तमिव[1] दर्पेण, श्वसन्तमिव शौर्येण, मूर्च्छन्तमिव मदेन, गृध्यन्तमिव तारुण्येन, द्रवन्तमिव दानेन, वल्गन्तमिव बलेन, म.द्यन्तमिव मानेन, उद्यन्तमिवोत्साहेन, ताम्यन्तमिव तेजसा, लिम्पन्तमिव लावण्येन, सिञ्चन्तमिव सौभाग्येन, स्निग्धं नखेषु, परुषं रोमविषये, गुरुं मुखे, सच्छिष्यं विनये, मृदुं शिरसि, दृढं परिचयेषु, ह्रस्वं स्कन्धबन्धे, दीर्घमायुषि, दरिद्रमुदरे, सततप्रवृत्तं दाने, बलभद्रं मदलीलासु, कुलकलत्रमायत्ततासु, जिनं क्षमासु, वह्निवर्षं क्रोधमोक्षेषु, गरुडं नागोद्धृतिषु, नारदं कलहकुतूहलेषु, शुष्काशनिपातमवस्कन्देषु, मकरं वाहिनीक्षोभेषु, आशीविषं दशनकर्मसु, वरुणं हस्तपाशाकृष्टिषु, यमवागुरामरातिसंवेष्टनेषु, कालं परिणतिषु, राहुं तीक्ष्णकरग्रहणेषु, लोहिताङ्गं वक्रचारेषु, अलातचक्रं मण्डलभ्रान्तिविज्ञानेषु, मनोरथसम्पादकं चिन्तामणिपर्वतं विक्रमस्य, दन्तमुक्ताशैलस्तम्भनिवासप्रासादमभिमानस्य, घण्टाचामरमण्डनमनोहरमिच्छासञ्चरणविमानं मनस्वितायाः, मदधारादुर्दिनान्धकारं गन्धोदकधारागृहं क्रोधस्य, सकाञ्चनप्रतिमं महानिकेतनमहङ्कारस्य, सगण्डशैलप्रस्रवणं क्रीडापर्वतमवलेपस्य, सदन्ततोरणं वज्रमन्दिरं दर्पस्य, उच्चकुम्भकूटाट्टालकविकटं सञ्चारि गिरिदुर्गं राज्यस्य, कृतानेकबाणविवरसहस्रं लोहप्राकारं पृथिव्याः, शिलीमुखशतझाङ्कारितं पारिजातपादपं भूनन्दनस्य, तथा च सङ्गीतगृहं[2] कर्णतालताण्डवानाम्, आपानमण्डपं मधुपमण्डलानाम्, अन्तःपुरं शृङ्गाराभरणानाम्, मदनोत्सवं मदलीलालास्यानाम्, अक्षुण्णप्रदोषं नक्षत्रमालामण्डलानाम्, अकाल[3]प्रावृट्कालं मदमहानदीपूरप्लवानाम्, अलीकशरत्समयं सप्तच्छदवनपरिमलानाम्, अपूर्वहिमागमं शीकरनीहाराणाम्, मिथ्याजलधरं गर्जिताडम्बराणाम्, दर्पशातमपश्यत्।

आसीच्चास्य चेतसि—'नूनमस्य निर्माणे गिरयो ग्राहिताः परमाणुताम्। कुतोऽन्यथा गौरवमिदम्। आश्चर्यमेतत्। विन्ध्यस्य दन्तावादिवराहस्य करः' इति विस्मयमानमेव[4] तं दौवारिकोऽब्रवीत्—'पश्य।

मिथ्यैवालिखितां मनोरथशतैर्निःशेषनष्टां श्रियं
चिन्तासाधनकल्पनाकुलधियां भूयो वने विद्विषाम्।
आयातः कथमप्ययं स्मृतिपथं शून्यीभवच्चेतसां
नागेन्द्रः सहते न मानसगतानाशागजेन्द्रानपि ॥ ४ ॥

तदेहि। पुनरप्येनं द्रक्ष्यसि। पश्य तावद्देवम्' इत्यभिधीयमानश्च तेन मदजलपङ्किल[5]कपोलपट्टपतितां मत्तामिव मदपरिमलेन मुकुलितां कथमपि तस्माद्दृष्टिमाकृष्य तेनैव दौवारिकेणोपदिश्यमानवर्त्मा समतिक्रम्य भूपालसहस्रसङ्कुलानि त्रीणि कक्ष्यान्तराणि चतुर्थे भुक्तास्थानमण्डपस्य पुरस्तादजिरे

---

१ 'चलन्तमिव' अ. २ 'गृहकं' ब. ३ 'अकाण्ड' ब. ४ '०मानमेतं' अ—क. ५ '०जलकज्जलकालकपोल०' ब.

स्थितम्, दूरादूर्ध्वस्थितेन प्रांशुना कर्णिकारगौरेण व्यायामव्यायतवपुषा शस्त्रिणा मौलेन शरीरपरिचारकलोकेन पङ्क्तिस्थितेन कार्तस्वरस्तम्भमण्डलेनेव परिवृतम्, आसन्नोपविष्टविशिष्टे[1]ष्टलोकम्, हरिचन्दनरसप्रक्षालिते तुषारशीकरशीतलतले दन्तपाण्डुरपादे शशिमय इव मुक्ताशैलशिलापट्टशयने समुपविष्टम्, शयनीयपर्यन्तविन्यस्ते समर्पितसकलविग्रहभारं भुजे, दिङ्मुखविसर्पिणि देहप्रभाविताने विततमणिमयूखे घर्मसमयसुभगे सरसीव मृदुमृणालजालजटिलजले सराजकं रममाणम्, तेजसः परमाणुभिरिव केवलैर्निर्मितम्, अनि[2]च्छन्तमपि बलादारोपयितुमिव सिंहासनं सर्वावयवेषु सर्वलक्षणैर्गृहीतम्, गृहीतब्रह्मचर्यमालिङ्गितं राजलक्ष्म्या, प्रतिपन्नासिधाराधारणव्रतमविसंवादिनं राजर्षिम्, विषमराजमार्गविनिहितपदस्खलनभियेव सुलग्नं धर्मे, सकलभूपालपरित्यक्तेन भीतेनेव लब्धवाचा सर्वात्मना सत्येन सेव्यमानम्, आसन्नवारविलासिनीप्रतियातनाभिश्चरणनखपातिनीभिर्दिग्भिरिव दश[3]भिः प्रणम्यमानम्, दीर्घैर्दिगन्तपातिभिर्दृष्टिपातैर्लोकपालानां कृताकृतमिव प्रत्यवेक्षमाणम्, मणिपादपीठपृष्ठप्रतिष्ठितकरेणोपरिगमनाभ्यनुज्ञां मृग्यमाणमिव दिवसकरेण, भूषणप्रभासमुत्सारणबद्धपर्यन्तमण्डलेन प्रदक्षिणीक्रियमाणमिव[4] दिवसेन, अप्रणमद्भिर्गिरिभि[5]रपि दूयमानं शौर्योष्मणा, फेनायमानमिव चन्दनधवलं लावण्यजलधिमुद्वहन्तम्, एकराज्यौ[6]र्जित्येन निजप्रतिबिम्बान्यपि नृपचक्रचूडामणिधृतान्यसहमानमिव, दर्पदुःखासिकया चामरानिलनिभेन बहुधेव श्वसन्तीं राजलक्ष्मीं दधानम्, सकलमिव चतुःसमुद्रलावण्यमादायोत्थितया श्रिया समुपश्लिष्टम्, आभरणप्रभाजालजायमानानीन्द्रधनुःसहस्राणीन्द्रप्राभृतप्रहितानि विलभमानमिव राज्ञाम्, सम्भाषणेषु परित्यक्तमपि मधु वर्षन्तम्, काव्यकथास्वपीतमप्यमृतमुद्वमन्तम्, विस्रम्भभाषितेष्वनाकृष्टमपि हृदयं दर्शयन्तम्, प्रसादेषु निश्चलामपि श्रियं स्थाने स्थाने स्थापयन्तम्, वीरगोष्ठीषु पुलकितेन कपोलस्थलेनानुरागसन्देशमिवोपांशु रणश्रियः शृण्वन्तम्, अतिक्रान्तसुभटकलहालापेषु स्नेहवृष्टिमिव दृष्टिमिष्टे कृपाणे पातयन्तम्, परिहासस्मितेषु गुरुप्रतापभीतस्य राजकस्य स्वच्छमाशयमिव दशनांशुभिः कथयन्तम्, सकललोकहृदयस्थितमपि न्याये तिष्ठन्तम्, अगोचरे गुणानामभूमौ सौभाग्यानामविषये वरप्रदानानामशक्ये आशिषाममार्गे मनोरथानामतिदूरे दैवस्यादिश्युपमानानामसाध्ये धर्मस्यादृष्टपूर्वे लक्ष्म्या महत्त्वे स्थितम्, अरुणपादपल्लवेन सुगतमन्थरोरुणा वज्रायुधनिष्ठुरप्रकोष्ठपृष्ठेन वृषस्कन्धेन भास्वद्बिम्बाधरेण प्रसन्नावलोकितेन चन्द्रमुखेन कृष्णकेशेन वपुषा सर्वदेवतावतारमिवैकत्र दर्शयन्तम्, अपि च मांस-

---

१ '०विष्टेष्टविशिष्टलोकम्' ब. २ 'अनिच्छन्तं बला०' अ–क. ३ अस्मात्परं 'विग्रहावर्जिताभिः' इत्यधिकं ब–पुस्तके. ४ अस्मात्परं 'गलितोष्मणा' इत्यधिकं ब–पुस्तके. ५ 'गिरिभिरपि भूभृद्भिः' ब. ६ '०राज्योर्जितेन' ब.

लमयूखमालामलिनितमहीतले महति महार्हे माणिक्यमालामण्डितमेखले महानीलमये पादपीठे कलिकालशिरसीव सलीलं विन्यस्तवामचरणमाक्रान्तकालिर.फणाचक्रवालं बालमिव पुण्डरीकाक्षम्, क्षौमपाण्डुरेण चरणनखदीधितिप्रतानेन प्रसरता महीं महादेवीपट्टबन्धेनेव महिमानमारोपयन्तम्, अप्रणतलोकपालकोपेनेवातिलोहितौ सकलनृपतिमौलिमालास्वतिपीतं पद्मरागरत्नातपमिव वमन्तौ सर्वतेजस्विमण्डलास्तमयसंध्यामिव धारयन्तावशेषराजकशेखरकुसुममधुरसस्रोतांसीव स्रवन्तौ समस्तसामन्तसीमन्तोत्तंसस्रक्सौरभभ्रान्तैर्भ्रमरमण्डलैरमित्रोत्तमाङ्गैरिव मुहूर्तमप्यविरहितौ संवाहनतत्परायाः श्रियो विकचरक्तपङ्कजवनवासभवनानीव कल्पयन्तौ जलजशङ्खमीनमकरसनाथतलतया कथितचतुरम्भोधिभोगचिह्नाविव चरणौ दधानम्, दिङ्नागदन्तमुसलाभ्यामिव विकटमकरमुखप्रतिबन्धबन्धुराभ्यामुद्वेललावण्यपयोनिधिप्रवाहाभ्यामिव फेनाहितशोभाभ्यां चन्दनद्रुमाभ्यामिव[1] भोगिमण्डलशिरोरत्नरश्मिरज्यमानमूलाभ्यां हृदयारोपितभूभारधारणमाणिक्यस्तम्भाभ्यामूरुदण्डाभ्यां विराजमानम्, अमृतफेनपिण्डपाण्डुना मेखलामणिमयूखखचितेन नितम्बबिम्बव्यासङ्गिना विमलपयोधौतेन नेत्रसूत्रनिवेशशोभिनाधरवाससा वासुकिनिर्मोकेणेव मन्दरं द्योतमानम्, अघनेन सतारागणेनोपरिकृतेन द्वितीयाम्बरेण भुवनाभोगमिव भासमानम्, इभपतिदशनमुसलसहस्रोल्लेखकठिनमसृणेनापर्याप्ताम्बरप्रथिम्ना विविधवाहिनीसंक्षोभकलकलसंमर्दसहिष्णुना कैलासमिव महता स्फटिकतटेनोरुणोरःकवाटेन राजमानम्, श्रीसरस्वत्योरुरोवदनोपभोगविभागसूत्रेणेव पातितेन शेषेणेव च तद्भुजस्तम्भविन्यस्तसमस्तभूभारलब्धविश्रान्तिसुखप्रसुप्तेन हारदण्डेन परिवेष्टित[2]कन्धरम्, जीवितावधिगृहीतसर्वस्वमहादानदीक्षाचीरेणेव हारमुक्ताफलानां किरणनिकरेण प्रावृतवक्षःस्थलम्, अजजिगीषया बालैर्भुजैरिवापरैः प्ररोहद्भिर्बाहूपधानशायिन्याः श्रियः कर्णोत्पलमधुरसधारासन्तानैरिव गलद्भिर्भुजजन्मनः प्रतापस्य निर्गमनमार्गैरिवाविर्भवद्भिररुणैः केयूररत्नकिरणदण्डैरुभयतः प्रसारितमणिमयपक्षवितानमिव माणिक्यमहीधरम्, सकललोकालोकमार्गार्गलेन चतुरुदधिपरिक्षेपखातशिलाप्राकारेण[3] सर्वराजहंसबन्धवज्रपञ्जरेण भुवनलक्ष्मीप्रवेशमङ्गलमहामणितोरणेनातिदीर्घदोर्दण्डयुगलेन दिशां दिक्पालानां च युगपदायतिमपहरन्तम्, सोदर्यलक्ष्मीचुम्बनलोभेन[4] कौस्तुभमणेरिव मुखावयवतां गतस्याधरस्य गलता रागेण पारिजातपल्लवरसेनेव सिञ्चन्तं दिङ्मुखानि, अन्तरान्तरा सुहृत्परिहासस्मितैः प्रकीर्यमाणविमलदशनशिखाप्रतानैः प्रकृतिमूढाया राजश्रियाः प्रज्ञालोकमिव दर्शयन्तम्, मुखजनितेन्दुसन्देहागतानि कुमुदिनीवनानीव प्रेषयन्तम्, स्फुटस्फटिकधवलदशन-

---

१ 'कल्पचन्दन०' ब. २ 'परिवलित०' अ. ३ 'खातशातकुम्भशिला' ब.
४ 'सौन्दर्य०' ब.

पङ्क्तिकृतकुमुदवनशङ्काप्रविष्टां शरज्ज्योत्स्नामिव विसर्जयन्तम्, मदिरामृतपारिजातगन्धगर्भेण भरितसकलककुभा मुखामोदेनामृतमथनदिवसमिव सृजन्तम्, विकचमुखकमलकर्णिकाकोशेनानवरतमापीयमानश्वाससौरभमिवाधोमुखेन नासावंशेन, चक्षुषः क्षीरस्निग्धस्य धवलिम्ना दिङ्मुखान्यपूर्ववदनचन्द्रोदयोद्वेलक्षीरोदप्लावितानीव कुर्वाणम्, विमलकपोलफलकप्रतिबिम्बितां चामरग्राहिणीं विग्रहिणीमिव मुखनिवासिनीं सरस्वतीं दधानम्, अरुणेन चूडामणिशोचिषा सरस्वतीर्ष्याकुपितलक्ष्मीप्रसादनलग्नेन चरणालक्तकेनेव लोहि[1]तायितललाटतटम्, आपाटलांशुतन्त्री[2]सन्तानवलयिनीं कुण्डलमणिकुटिलकोटिबालवीणामनवरतचलितचरणानां वादयतामुपवीणयतामिव स्वरव्याकरणविवेकविशारदं श्रवणावतंसमधुकरकुलानां कलक्वणितमाकर्णयन्तम्, उत्फुल्लमालतीमयेन राजलक्ष्म्याः कचग्रहलीलालग्नेन नखज्योत्स्नावलयेनेव मुखशशिपरिवेशमण्डलेन मुण्डमालागुणेन परिकलितकेशान्तम्, शिखण्डाभरणभुवा मुक्ताफलालोकेन मरकतमणिकिरणकलापेन चान्योन्यसंवलनवृजिनेन प्रयागप्रवाहवेणिकावारिणेवागत्य स्वयमभिषिच्यमानम्, श्रमजलविलीनबहलकृष्णागुरुपङ्कतिलककलङ्ककल्पितेन कालिम्ना प्रार्थनाचाटुचतुरचरणपतनशतश्यामिकाकिणेनेव नीलायमानललाटेन्दु[3]लेखाभिः क्षुभितमानसोद्गतैरुत्कलिकाकलापैरिव हारैरुल्लसद्भिरवष्टभ्यमानाभिर्विलासवल्गनचटुलैर्भ्रूलताकल्पैरीर्ष्यया श्रियमिव तर्जयन्तीभिरायामिभिः श्वसितैरविरलपरिमलैर्मलयमारुतमयैः पाशैरिवाकर्षन्तीभिर्विकटबकुलावलीवराटकवेष्टितमुखैर्बृहद्भिः स्तनकलशैः स्वदारसन्तोषरसमिवाशेषमुद्धरन्तीभिः कुचोत्कम्पिकाविकारप्रेङ्खितानां हारतरलमणीनां रश्मिभिराकृष्य हृदयमिव हठात्प्रवेशयन्तीभिः प्रभामुचामाभरणमणीनां मयूखैः प्रसारितैर्बहुभिरिव बाहुभिरालिङ्गन्तीभिर्जृम्भानुबन्धबन्धुरवदनारविन्दावरणीकृतैरुत्तानैः करकिसलयैः सरभसप्रधावितानि मानसानीव निरुन्धतीभिर्मदान्धमधुकरकुलकीर्यमाणकर्णकुसुमरजःकणकूणितकोणानि कुसुमशरशरनिकरप्रहारमूर्च्छामुकुलितानीव लोचनानि चतुरं सञ्चारयन्तीभिरन्योन्यमत्सरादाविर्भवद्भङ्गुरभ्रुकुटिविभ्रमक्षिप्तैः कटाक्षैः कर्णेन्दीवराणीव ताडयन्तीभिरनिमेषदर्शनसुखरसराशिं मन्थरितपक्ष्मणा चक्षुषा पीतमिव कोमलकपोलपालीप्रतिबिम्बितं वहन्तीभिरभिलाषलीलानिर्निमित्तस्मितैश्चन्द्रोदयानिव मदनसाहायकाय सम्पादयन्तीभिरङ्गभङ्गवलनान्योन्यघटितोत्तानकरवेणिकाभिः स्फुटनमुखराङ्गुलीकाण्डकुण्डलीक्रियमाणनखदीधितिनिवहनिभेनाकिञ्चित्करकामकार्मुकाणीव रुषा भञ्जतीभिर्वारविलासिनीभिर्विलुप्यमानसौभाग्यमिव सर्वतः, स्पर्शस्विन्नवेपमानकरकिसलयगलितचरणारविन्दां चरणग्राहिणीं विहस्य कोणेन लीलालसं शिरसि ताडयन्तम्, अनवरतकरकलितकोणतया चात्मनः प्रियां वीणामिव श्रिय-

१ 'लोहितायत' अ—क. २ 'तनुतन्त्री०' ब. ३ 'ललाटलेखाभिः' अ—क.

मपि शिक्षयन्तम्, निःस्नेह इति धनैरनाश्रयणीय इति दोषैर्निग्रहरुचिरितीन्द्रियैर्दुरुपसर्प इति कलिना नीरस इति व्यसनैर्भीरुरित्ययशसा दुर्ग्रहचित्तवृत्तिरिति चित्तभुवा स्त्रीपर इति सरस्वत्या षण्ढ इति परकलत्रैः काष्ठामुनिरिति यतिभिर्धूर्त इति वेश्याभिर्नेय इति सुहृद्भिः कर्मकर इति विप्रैः सुसहाय इति शत्रुयोधैरेकमप्यनेकधा गृह्यमाणम्, शन्तनोर्महावाहिनीपतिम्, भीष्माजितकाशिनम्, द्रोणाच्चापलालसम्, गुरुपुत्रादमोघमार्गणम्, कर्णान्मित्रप्रियम्, युधिष्ठिराद्बहु[1]क्षमम्, भीमादनेकनागायुतबलम्, धनञ्जयान्महाभारतरणयोग्यम्, कारणमिव कृतयुगस्य, बीजमिव विबुधसर्गस्य, उत्पत्तिद्वीपमिव दर्पस्य, एकागारमिव करुणायाः, प्रातिवेशिकमिव पुरुषोत्तमस्य, खनिपर्वतमिव पराक्रमस्य, सर्वविद्यासङ्गीतकगृहमिव सरस्वत्याः, द्वितीयामृतमथनदिवसमिव लक्ष्मीसमुत्थानस्य, बलदर्शनमिव वैदग्ध्यस्य, एकस्थानमिव स्थितीनाम्, सर्वस्वकथनमिव कान्तेः, अपवर्गमिव रूपपरमाणुसर्गस्य, सकलदुश्चरितप्रायश्चित्तमिव राज्यस्य, सर्वबलसन्दोहावस्कन्दमिव कन्दर्पस्य, उपायमिव पुरन्दरदर्शनस्य, आवर्तनमिव धर्मस्य, कन्यान्तःपुरमिव कलानाम्, परमप्रमाणमिव सौभाग्यस्य, राजसर्गसमाप्त्यवभृथस्नानदिवसमिव सर्वप्रजापतीनाम्, गम्भीरं च प्रसन्नं च त्रासजननं च रमणीयं च कौतुकजननं च पुण्यं च चक्रवर्तिनं हर्षमद्राक्षीत्।

दृष्ट्वा चानुगृहीत इव निगृहीत इव साभिलाष इ[2]व तृप्त इव रोमाञ्चमुचा मुखेन मुञ्चन्नानन्दबाष्पवारिबिन्दून्दूरादेव विस्मयस्मेरः समचिन्तयत्—'सोऽयं सुजन्मा सुगृहीतनामा तेजसां राशिः चतुरुदधिकेदारकुटुम्बी भोक्ता ब्रह्मस्तम्भफलस्य सकलादिराजचरितजयज्येष्ठमल्लो देवः परमेश्वरो हर्षः। एतेन च खलु राजन्वती पृथ्वी, नास्य हरेरिव वृषविरोधीनि बालचरितानि, न पशुपतेरिव दक्षोद्वेगकारीण्यैश्वर्यविलसितानि, न शतक्रतोरिव गोत्रविनाशपिशुनाः प्रवादाः, न यमस्येवातिवल्लभानि दण्डग्रहणानि, न वरुणस्येव निस्त्रिंशग्राहसहस्ररक्षिता रत्नालयाः, न धनदस्येव निष्फलाः सन्निधिलाभाः, न जिनस्येवार्थवादशून्यानि दर्शना[3]नि, न चन्द्रमस इव बहुलदोषोपहताः श्रियः। चित्रमिदमत्यमरं राजत्वम्। अपि चास्य त्यागस्यार्थिनः, प्रज्ञायाः शास्त्राणि, कवित्वस्य वाचः, सत्त्वस्य साहसस्थानानि, उत्साहस्य व्यापाराः, कीर्तेर्दिङ्मुखानि, अनुरागस्य लोकहृदयानि, गुणगणस्य संख्या, कौशलस्य कला, न पर्याप्तो विषयः। [4]अस्मिंश्च राजनि यतीनां योगपट्टकाः, पुस्तकर्मणां पार्थिवविग्रहाः, षट्पदानां दानग्रहणकलहाः, वृत्तानां पादच्छेदाः, अष्टापदानां चतुरङ्गकल्पना, पन्नगानां द्विजगुरुद्वेषाः, वाक्यविदामधिकरणविचाराः' इति। समुपसृत्य चोपवीती स्वस्तिशब्दमकरोत्।

---

१ 'बाहुक्षमम्' ब. २ 'इवातृप्त इव' ब. ३ 'विज्ञानदर्शनानि' ब. ४ 'यस्मिंश्च' ब.

अथोत्तरेण[1] नातिदूरे राजधिष्ण्यस्य गजपरिचारको मधुरमपरवक्त्रमुच्चै-रगायत्—

'करिकलभ विमुञ्च लोलतां चर विनयव्रतमानताननः ।
मृगपतिनखकोटिभङ्गुरो गुरुरुपरि क्षमते न तेऽङ्कुशः' ॥ ५ ॥

राजा तु तच्छ्रुत्वा दृष्ट्वा च तं गिरिगुहागतसिंहबृंहितगम्भीरेण स्वरेण पूरयन्निव नभोभागमपृच्छत्—'एष स बाणः' इति । 'यथाज्ञापयति देवः । सोऽयम्' इति विज्ञापितो दौवारिकेण । 'न तावदेनमकृतप्रसादैः[2] पश्यामि' इति तिर्यङ्नीलधवलांशुकशारां तिरस्करिणीमिव भ्रमयन्नपाङ्गनीयमानतरलतारकस्यायामिनीं चक्षुषः प्रभां परिवृत्य प्रेष्ठस्य पृष्ठतो निषण्णस्य मालवराजसूनोरकथयत्—'महानयं भुजङ्गः' इति । तूष्णीम्भावेन त्वगमितनरेन्द्रवचसि तस्मिन्मूके च राजलोके मुहूर्तमिव तूष्णीं स्थित्वा बाणो व्यज्ञापयत्—'देव अविज्ञाततत्त्व इव, अश्रद्दधान इव, नेय इव, अविदितलोकवृत्तान्त इव च कस्मादेवमाज्ञापयसि । स्वैरिणो विचित्राश्च लोकस्य स्वभावाः प्रवादाश्च । महद्भिस्तु यथार्थदर्शिभिर्भवितव्यम् । नार्हसि मामन्यथा सम्भावयितुमविशिष्टमिव । ब्राह्मणोऽस्मि जातः सोमपायिनां वंशे वात्स्यायनानाम् । यथाकालमुपनयनादयः कृताः संस्काराः । सम्यक्पठितः साङ्गो वेदः । श्रुतानि यथाशक्ति शास्त्राणि । दारपरिग्रहादभ्यगारिकोऽस्मि । कामे भुजङ्गता । लोकद्वयाविरोधिभिस्तु चापलैः शैशवमशून्यमासीत् । अत्रानपलापोऽस्मि । अनेनैव च गृहीतविप्रतीसारमिव मे हृदयम् । इदानीं तु सुगत इव शान्तमनसि मनाविव कर्तरि वर्णाश्रमव्यवस्थानां समवर्तिनीव च साक्षाद्दण्डभृति देवे शासति ससाम्बुराशिरशनामशेषद्वीपमालिनीं महीं क इवाविशङ्कः सर्वव्यसनबन्धोरविनयस्य मनसाप्यभिनयं कल्पयिष्यति । आसतां तावन्मानुष्यकोपेताः । त्वत्प्रभावादलयोऽपि भीता इव मधु पिबन्ति, रथाङ्गनामानोऽपि लज्जन्त इवाभ्यनुवृत्तिव्यसनैः प्रियाणाम्, कपयोपि चकिता इव चपलायन्ते, शरारवोऽपि सानुक्रोशा इव श्वापदगणाः पिशितानि भुञ्जते । सर्वथा कालेन मां ज्ञास्यति स्वामी स्वयमेव । अनपाचीनचित्तवृत्तिग्राहिण्यो हि भवन्ति प्रज्ञावतां प्रकृतयः' इत्यभिधाय तूष्णीमभूत् ।

भूपतिरपि 'एवमस्माभिः श्रुतम्' इत्यभिधाय तूष्णीमेवाभवत् । सम्भाषणासनदानादिना तु प्रसादेन नैनमन्वग्रहीत् । केवलममृतवृष्टिभिः स्नपयन्निव स्नेहगर्भेण दृष्टिपातमात्रेणान्तर्गतां प्रीतिमकथयत् । अस्ताभिलाषिणि च लम्बमाने सवितरि विसर्जितराजलोकोऽभ्यन्तरं प्राविशत् । बाणोपि निर्गत्य धौतारकूटकोमलातपत्विषि निर्वाति वासरे, अस्ताचलकूटकिरीटे निचुलमञ्जरीभांसि तेजांसि मुञ्चति वियन्मुचि मरीचिमति[3], रोमन्थमन्थरकुरङ्गकुटुम्बकाध्यास्यमानप्रदिष्टगोष्ठीनपृष्ठास्वरण्यस्थलीषु, शोकाकुलकोककामिनीकूजितक-

---

१ 'अथोत्तरे' अ. २ '०प्रसादं' ब. ३ 'मरीचिमालिनि, अतिरोमन्थ०' अ.

अथ ते तमूचुः—'तात, सन्तोषजुषां सततसन्निहितविद्याविनोदानां वैतानवह्निमात्रसहायानां कियन्मात्रं नः कृत्यं सुखितया सकलभुवनभुजि भुजङ्गराजदेहदीर्घे रक्षति क्षितिं क्षिति[१]भुजो भुजे । सर्वथा[२] सुखिन एव वयम्, विशेषेण तु त्वयि विमुक्तकौसीद्ये परमेश्वरपार्श्ववर्तिनि वेत्रासनमधितिष्ठति । सर्वे च यथाशक्ति यथाविभवं यथाकालं च सम्पाद्यन्ते विप्रजनोचिताः क्रियाकलापाः' इति । एवमादिभिरालापैः स्कन्धावारवार्ताभिश्च शैशवातिक्रान्तक्रीडानुस्मरणैः पूर्वजकथाभिश्च विनोदितमनास्तैः सह सुचिरमतिष्ठत् । उत्थाय च मध्यन्दिने यथाक्रियमाणाः स्थितीरकरोत् । भुक्तवन्तं च तं सर्वे ज्ञातयः पर्यवारयन् ।

अत्रान्तरे दुकूलपट्टप्रभवे शिखण्ड्यपाङ्गपाण्डुनी पौण्ड्रे वाससी वसानः, स्नानावसानसमये बन्दितया तीर्थमृदा गोरोचनया च रचिततिलकः, तैलामलकमसृणितमौलिः, अनुच्चचूडाचुम्बिना निबिडेन कुसुमापीडकेन समुद्भासमानः, [३]सकृदुपयुक्तताम्बूलविमलाधरकान्तिः, एकशलाकाञ्जनजनितलोचनरुचिः, अचिरभुक्तः, विनीतमार्यं च वेषं दधानः, पुस्तकवाचकः सुदृष्टिराजगाम । नातिदूरवर्तिन्यां चासन्द्यां निषसाद । स्थित्वा च मुहूर्तमिव तत्कालापनीतसूत्रवेष्टनमपि नखकिरणैर्मृदुमृणालसूत्रैरिव वेष्टितं पुस्तकं पुरोनिहितशरशलाकायन्त्रके निधाय, पृष्ठतः सनीडसन्निविष्टाभ्यां मधुकरपारावताभ्यां[४] दत्ते स्थानके, प्राभातिकप्रपाठकच्छेदचिह्नीकृतमन्तरं[५]पत्रमुत्क्षिप्य, गृहीत्वा च कतिपयपत्रलघ्वीं क[६]र्पाटिकाम्, क्षालयन्निव मषीमलिनान्यक्षराणि दन्तकान्तिभिः, अर्चयन्निव सितकुसुममुक्तिभिर्ग्रन्थम्, मुखसन्निहितसरस्वतीनूपुररवैरिव गमकैर्मधुरैराक्षिपन्मनांसि श्रोतॄणां गीत्या पवमानप्रोक्तं पुराणं पपाठ ।

तस्मिंश्च तथा श्रुतिसुभगगीतिगर्भं पठति सुदृष्टौ नातिदूरवर्ती बन्दी सूचीबाणस्तारमधुरेण गीतिध्वनिमनुवर्तमानः स्वरेणेदमार्यायुगलमपठत्[७]—

'तदपि मुनिगीतमतिपृथु तदपि जगद्व्यापि पावनं तदपि ।
हर्षचरितादभिन्नं प्रतिभाति हि मे पुराणमिदम् ॥ ३ ॥
वंशानुगमविवादि स्फुटकरणं भरतमार्गभजनगुरु ।
श्रीकण्ठविनिर्यातं गीतमिदं हर्षराज्यमिव ॥ ४ ॥'

तच्छ्रुत्वा बाणस्य चत्वारः पितामहमुखपद्मा इव वेदाभ्यासपवित्रितमूर्तयः, उपाया इव सामप्रयोगललितमुखाः, गणपतिरधिपतिस्तारापतिः श्यामल इति पितृव्यपुत्रा भ्रातरः, प्रसन्नवृत्तयो गृहीतवाक्याः कृतगुरुपदन्यासा न्यायवेदिनः[८] सुकृतसंग्रहाभ्यासगुरवो लब्धसाधुशब्दा लोक इव व्याकरणे-

१ 'क्षितिपो भुजे' ब. २ 'सर्वदा' ब. ३ 'असकृदुप०' अ–क. ४ अस्मात्परं 'वांशिकाभ्याम्' इत्यधिकं ब–पुस्तके. ५ 'अन्तरं पत्रं' ब. ६ 'कापालिकाम्' ब. ७ 'अगायत्' ब. ८ 'न्यायवादिनः' अ–क.

ऽपि, सकलपुराणराजर्षिचरिताभिज्ञाः, महाभारतभावितात्मानः, विदितसकलेतिहासाः, महाविद्वांसः, महाकवयः, महापुरुषवृत्तान्तकुतूहलिनः, सुभाषितश्रवणरसरसायनावितृष्णाः[1], वयसि वचसि यशसि तपसि महसि वपुषि यजुषि च प्रथमाः, पूर्वमेव कृतसङ्गराः, विवक्षवः स्मितसुधाधवलितकपोलोदराः, परस्परस्य मुखानि व्यलोकयन्।

अथ तेषां कनीयान्कमलदलदीर्घलोचनः श्यामलो नाम बाणस्य प्रेयान्प्राणानामपि वशयिता दत्तसंज्ञस्तैः सप्रणयं दशनज्योत्स्नास्नपितककुभा मुखेन्दुना बभाषे—'तात बाण, द्विजानां राजा गुरुदारग्रहणमकार्षीत्। पुरूरवा ब्राह्मणधनतृष्णया दयितेनायुषा व्ययुज्यत। नहुषः परकलत्राभिलाषी महाभुजङ्ग आसीत्। ययातिराहितब्राह्मणीपाणिग्रहणः पपात। सुद्युम्नः स्त्रीमय एवाभवत्। सोमकस्य प्रख्याता[2] जन्तुवधनिर्घृणता। मान्धाता मार्गणव्यसनेन सपुत्रपौत्रो रसातलमगात्। पुरुकुत्सः कुत्सितं कर्म तपस्यन्नपि मेकलकन्यकायामकरोत्। कुवलयाश्वो भुजङ्गलोकपरिग्रहादश्वतरकन्यामपि न परिजहार। पृथुः प्रथमपुरुषकः परिभूतवान्पृथिवीम्। नृगस्य कृकलासभावे[3] वर्णसङ्करः समदृश्यत। सौदासेन नरक्षिता पर्याकुलीकृता क्षितिः। नलमवशाक्षहृदयं कलिरभिभूतवान्। संवरणो मित्रदुहितरि विक्लवतामगात्। दशरथ इष्टरामोन्मादेन मृत्युमवाप। कार्तवीर्यो गोब्राह्मणातिपीडनेन निधनमयासीत्[4]। मरुत्त इष्टबहुसुवर्णकोऽपि देवद्विजबहुमतो न बभूव। शन्तनुरतिव्यसनादेकाकी वियुक्तो वाहिन्या विपिने विललाप। पाण्डुर्वनमध्यगतो मत्स्य इव मदनरसाविष्टः प्राणान्मुमोच। युधिष्ठिरो गुरुभयविषण्णहृदयः समरशिरसि सत्यमुत्सृष्टवान्। इत्थं नास्ति राजत्वमपकलङ्कमृते देवदेवादमुतः सर्वद्वीपभुजो हर्षात्। अस्य हि बहून्याश्चर्याणि श्रूयन्ते। तथा हि—अत्र बलजिता निश्चलीकृताश्चलन्तः कृतपक्षाः क्षितिभृतः। अत्र प्रजापतिना शेषभोगिमण्डलस्योपरि क्षमा कृता। अत्र पुरुषोत्तमेन सिन्धुराजं प्रमथ्य लक्ष्मीरात्मीकृता[5]। अत्र बलिना मोचितभूभृद्वेष्टनो मुक्तो महानागः। अत्र देवेनाभिषिक्तः कुमारः। अत्र स्वामिनैकप्रहारपातितारातिना प्रख्यापिता शक्तिः। अत्र नरसिंहेन स्वहस्तविशसितारातिना प्रकटीकृतो विक्रमः। अत्र परमेश्वरेण तुषारशैलभुवो दुर्गाया गृहीतः करः। अत्र लोकनाथेन दिशां मुखेषु परिकल्पिता लोकपालाः सकलभुवनकोशश्चाग्रजन्मनां विभक्त इति। एवमादयः प्रथमकृतयुगस्येव दृश्यन्ते महासमारम्भाः। अतोऽस्य[6] सुगृहीतनाम्नः पुण्यराशेः पूर्वपुरुषवंशानुक्रमेणादितः प्रभृति चरितमिच्छामः श्रोतुम्। सुमहान्कालो नः शुश्रूषमाणानाम्। अयस्कान्तमणय इव लोहानि नीरसनि-

---

१ '०रसायनाः, वितृष्णाः,' अ. २ अस्मात्परं 'जगति' इत्यधिकं ब–पुस्तके. ३ '०भावेऽपि' ब. ४ अस्मात्परं 'रामो मनोभवभ्रान्तहृदयो जनकतनयामपि न परिहृतवान्' इत्यधिकं ब–पुस्तके. ५ 'आत्मीया कृता' ब. ६ 'यतो यस्य' ब.

क्षुराणि क्षुल्लकानामप्याकर्षन्ति मनांसि महतां गुणाः, किमुत स्वभावसरसमृदूनीतरेषाम्। कस्य न द्वितीयमहाभारते भवेदस्य चरिते कुतूहलम्। आचष्टां भवान्। भवतु भार्गवोऽयं वंशः शुचिरानेन राजर्षिचरितश्रवणेन सुतरां शुचितरः' इत्येवमभिधाय तूष्णीमभूत्।

बाणस्तु विहस्याब्रवीत्—'आर्य, न युक्तयनुरूपमभिहितम्। अघटमानमनोरथमिव भवतां कुतूहलमवकल्पयामि। शक्याशक्यपरिसंख्यानशून्याः प्रायेण स्वार्थतृषः। परगुणानुरागिणी प्रियजनकथाश्रवणरसरभसमोहिता च मन्ये महतामपि मतिरपहरति प्रविवेकम्। पश्यत्वार्यः क्व परमाणुपरिमाणं बटुहृदयम्, क्व समस्तब्रह्मस्तम्भव्यापि देवस्य चरितम्, क्व परिमितवर्णवृत्तयः कतिपये शब्दाः, क्व संख्यातिगास्तद्गुणाः। सर्वज्ञस्याप्ययमविषयः, वाचस्पतेरप्यगोचरः, सरस्वत्या अप्यतिभारः, किमुतास्मद्विधस्य। कः खलु पुरुषायुषशतेनापि शक्नुयादविकलमस्य चरितं वर्णयितुम्। एकदेशे तु यदि कुतूहलं वः, सज्जा वयम्। इयमधिगतकतिपयाक्षरलवलघीयसी जिह्वा क्वोपयोगं गमिष्यति। भवन्तः श्रोतारः। वर्ण्यते हर्षचरितम्। किमन्यत्। अद्य तु परिणतप्रायो दिवसः। पश्चाल्लम्बमानकपिलकिरणजटाभारभास्वरो भगवान्भार्गवो राम इव समन्तपञ्चकरुधिरमहाह्रदे निमज्जति संध्यारागपटले पूषा। श्वो निवेदयितास्मि' इति। सर्वे च ते 'तथा' इति प्रत्यपद्यन्त। नातिचिरादुत्थाय संध्यामुपासितुं शोणमयासीत्।

अथ मधुमदपल्लवितमालवीकपोलकोमलातपे मुकुलितेऽह्नि कमलिनीमीलनादिव लोहिततमे तमोलिहि रवौ लम्बमाने, रविरथतुरगमार्गानुसारेण यममहिष इव धावति नभसि तमसि, क्रमेण च गृहतापसकुटीरकपटलावलम्बिषु रक्तातपच्छेदैः सह संहृतेषु वल्कलेषु, कलिकल्मषमुषि पुण्णति[1] गगनमग्निहोत्रधामधूमे, सनियमे यजमानजने मौनव्रतिनि, विहारवेलाविलोले पर्यटति पल्लीजने, विकीर्यमाणहरितश्यामाकशालिपूलिकासु दुग्धासु होमकपिलासु, हूयमाने वैतानतनूनपाति, पूतविष्टरोपविष्टे कृष्णाजिनजटिले जटिनि, जपति बटुजने, ब्रह्मासनाध्यासिनि ध्यायति योगिगणे, तालध्वनिधावमानानन्तान्तेवासिनि अलसवृद्धश्रोत्रियानुमतेन गलद्ग्रन्थदण्डकोद्गारिणि संध्यां समवधारयति[2] वठरविटबटुसमाजे, समुन्मज्जति च ज्योतिषि तारकाख्ये खे, प्राप्ते प्रदोषारम्भे भवनमागत्योपविष्टः स्निग्धैर्बन्धुभिश्च सार्धं तयैव गोष्ठ्या तस्थौ। नीतप्रथमयामश्च गणपतेर्भवने परिकल्पितं शयनीयमसेवत। इतरेषां तु सर्वेषां निमीलितदशामप्यनुपजातनिद्राणां कमलवनानामिव सूर्योदयं प्रतिपालयतां कुतूहलेन कथमपि सा क्षपा क्षयमगच्छत्।

अथ यामिन्यास्तुर्ये यामे प्रतिबुद्धः स एव बन्दी श्लोकद्वयमगायत्—

---

१ 'मुष्णाति' ब. २ 'समवधीरयति' ब.

'पश्चादङ्घ्रिं प्रसार्य त्रिकनतिविततं द्राघयित्वाङ्गमुच्चै-
रासज्याभुग्नकण्ठो मुखमुरसि सटां धूलिधूम्रां विधूय।
घासग्रासाभिलाषादनवरतचलत्प्रोथतुण्डस्तुरङ्गो
मन्दं शब्दायमानो विलिखति शयनादुत्थितः क्ष्मां खुरेण ॥ ५ ॥
कुर्वन्नाभुग्नपृष्ठो मुखनिकटकटिः कन्धरामातिरश्चीं
लोलेनाहन्यमानं तुहिनकणमुचा चञ्चता केसरेण।
निद्राकण्डूकषायं कषति निबिडितश्रोत्रशुक्तिस्तुरङ्ग-
स्त्वङ्गत्पक्ष्माग्रलग्नप्रतनुबुसकणं कोणमक्ष्णः खुरेण ॥ ६ ॥'

बाणस्तु तच्छ्रुत्वा समुत्सृज्य निद्रामुत्थाय प्रक्षाल्य वदनमुपास्य भगवतीं संध्यामुदिते भगवति सवितरि गृहीतताम्बूलस्तत्रैवातिष्ठत्। अत्रान्तरे सर्वेऽस्य ज्ञातयः समाजग्मुः परिवार्य चासाञ्चक्रुः। असावपि पूर्वोद्धातेन विदिताभिप्रायस्तेषां पुरो हर्षचरितं कथयितुमारेभे—

श्रूयताम्—अस्ति पुण्यकृतामधिवासो वासवावास इव वसुधामवतीर्णः, सततमसङ्कीर्णवर्णव्यवहारस्थितिः कृतयुगव्यवस्थः, स्थलकमलबहलतया पोत्रोन्मूल्यमानमृणालैरुद्गीतमेदिनीसारगुणैरिव कृतमधुकरकोलाहलैर्हलैरुल्लिख्यमानक्षेत्रः, क्षीरोदपयःपायिपयोदसिक्ताभिरिव पुण्ड्रेक्षुवाटसन्ततिभिर्निरन्तरः, प्रतिदिशमपूर्वपर्वतकैरिव खलधानधामभिर्विभज्यमानैः सस्यकूटैः सङ्कटसीमान्तः, समन्तादुद्धातघटीसिच्यमानैर्जीरकजूटैर्जटिलितभूमिः, उर्वरावरीयोभिः शालेयै[1]रलङ्कृतः, पाकविशरारुराजमाषनिकरकिर्मीरितैश्च स्फुटितमुद्गफलकोशीकपिशितैर्गोधूमधामभिः स्थलीपृष्ठैरधिष्ठितः, महिषपृष्ठप्रतिष्ठितगायद्गोपालपालितैश्च कीटपटलल्म्पटचटकानुसृतैरवटुघटितघण्टाघटीरटितरमणीयैरटद्भिरटवीं हरवृषभपीतमामयाशङ्कया बहुधा विभक्तं क्षीरोदमिव क्षीरं क्षरद्भिर्बाष्पच्छेद्यतृणतृप्तैर्गोधनैर्धवलितविपिनः, विविधमखहोमधूमान्धशतमन्युमुक्तै[2]र्लोचनैरिव सहस्रसंख्यैः कृष्णशारैः शारीकृतोद्देशः, धवलधूलीमुचां केतकीवनानां रजोभिः पाण्डुरीकृतैः प्रमथनाथो[3]द्धूलनभस्मधूसरैः शिवपुरस्येव प्रवेशैः प्रदेशैरुपशोभितः, शाककन्दलश्यामलितग्रामोपकण्ठकाश्यपीपृष्ठः, पदे पदे करभपालीभिः पीलुपल्लवप्रस्फोटितैः करपुटपीडितमातुलुङ्गीदलरसोपलिप्तैः स्वेच्छाविचितकुङ्कुमकेसरकृतपुष्पप्रकरैः प्रत्यग्रफलरसपानसुखसुप्तपथिकैर्वनदेवतादीयमानामृतरसप्रपागृहैरिव द्राक्षामण्डपैः स्फुटत्[4]फलानां च बीजलग्नशुकचञ्चुरागाणामिव समारूढकपिकुलकपोलसन्दिह्यमानकुसुमानां दाडिमीनां वनैर्विलोभनीयोपनिर्गमः, वनपालपीयमाननारिकेलरसासवैश्च पथिकलोकलुप्यमानपिण्डखर्जूरैर्गोलाङ्गूललिह्यमानमधुरामोदपिण्डीरसैश्चकोरचञ्चुजर्जरितारुकैरुपवनैरभिरामः, तुङ्गार्जुनपालीपरिवृतैश्च गोकुलावतारकलु-

---

१ 'शालीयैः' अ—क. २ 'सक्तैः' ब. ३ 'प्रमथोद्धूलनधूसरैः' अ—क. ४ 'स्फुरत्फलानां' अ—क.

पितकूलकीलालैरध्वगशतशरण्यैररण्य[1]धराबन्धैरवन्ध्यवनरन्ध्रः, करभीयकुमारकपाल्यमानैरौष्ट्रकैरौरभ्रकैश्च कृतसम्बाधः, दिशि दिशि रविरथतुरगविलोभनायेव विलोठनमृदितकुङ्कुमस्थलीरससमालब्धानामुत्प्रोथपुटैरुन्मुखैरुदरशायिकिशोरकजवजननाय प्रभञ्जनमिव चापिबन्तीनां वातहरिणीनामिव स्वच्छन्दचारिणीनां वडवानां वृन्दैर्विचरद्भिराचितः, अनवरतक्रतुधूमान्धकारप्रवृत्तैर्हंसयूथैरिव [2]बाणैर्धवलितभुवनः, सङ्गीतगतमुरजरवमत्तैर्मयूरैरिव विभवैर्मुखरितजीवलोकः, शशिकरावदातवृत्तैर्मुक्ताफलैरिव गुणिभिः प्रसाधितः, पथिकशतविलुप्यमानस्फीतफलैर्महातरुभिरिव सर्वातिथिभिरभिगमनीयः, मृगमदपरिमलवाहिमृगरोमाच्छादितैर्हिमवत्पादैरिव महत्तरैः स्थिरीकृतः, प्रोद्दण्डसहस्रपत्रोपविष्टद्विजोत्तमैर्नारायणनाभिमण्डलैरिव तोयाशयैर्मण्डितः, मथितपयःप्रवाहप्रक्षालितक्षितिभिः क्षीरोदमथनारम्भैरिव महाघोषैः पूरिताशः श्रीकण्ठो नाम जनपदः ।

यत्र त्रेताग्निधूमाश्रुपातजलक्षालिता इवाक्षीयन्त कुदृष्टयः । पच्यमानचयनेष्टकादहनदग्धानीव नादृश्यन्त दुरितानि । छिद्यमानयूपदारुपरशुपाटित इव व्यदीर्यताधर्मः । मखशिखिधूमजलधरधाराधौत इव ननाश वर्णसङ्करः । दीयमानानेकगोसहस्रशृङ्गखण्ड्यमान इवापलायत कलिः । सुरालयशिलाघट्टनटङ्कनिकरनिकृत्ता इव व्यदीर्यन्त विपदः । महादानविधानकलकलाभिद्रुता इव प्राद्रवन्नुपद्रवाः । दीप्यमानसत्त्रमहानससहस्रसन्तापिता इव व्यलीयन्त व्याधयः । वृषविवाहप्रहतपुण्यपटहपटुरवत्रासिता इव नोपासर्पन्नपमृत्यवः । सन्ततब्रह्मघोषबधिरीकृता इवापजग्मुरीतयः । धर्माधिकारपरिभूतमिव न प्राभवद्दुर्दैवम् ।

तत्र चैवंविधे नानारामाभिरामकुसुमगन्धपरिमलसुभगो यौवनारम्भ इव भुवनस्य, कुङ्कुममलनपि[3]ञ्जरितबहुमहिषीसहस्रशोभितोऽन्तःपुरनिवेश इव धर्मस्य, मरुदुद्धूयमानचमरीबालव्यज[4]नशतधवलितप्रान्त एकदेश इव सुरराज्यस्य, ज्वलन्मखशिखिसहस्रदीप्यमानदशदिगन्तः शिबिरसन्निवेश इव कृतयुगस्य, पद्मासनस्थितब्रह्मर्षिध्यानाधीयमानसकलाकुशलप्रशमः प्रथमोऽवतार इव ब्रह्मलोकस्य, कलकलमुखरमहावाहिनीशतसङ्कुलो वि[5]पक्ष इवोत्तरकुरूणाम्, ईश्वरमार्गणसन्तापानभिज्ञसकलजनो विजिगीषुरिव त्रिपुरस्य, सुधारससिक्तधवलगृहपङ्क्तिपाण्डुरः प्रतिनिधिरिव चन्द्रलोकस्य, मधुमत्त[6]मत्तकाशिनीभूषणरवभरितभुवनो नामाभिहार इव कुबेरनगरस्य, स्थाण्वीश्वराख्यो जनपदविशेषः ।

यस्तपोवनमिति मुनिभिः, कामायतनमिति वेश्याभिः, सङ्गीतशालेति लासकैः; यमनगरमिति शत्रुभिः, चिन्तामणिभूमिरित्यर्थिभिः, वीरक्षेत्रमिति

१ 'अरण्यवरुणधरा०' ब. २ 'गुणैः' ब. ३ '०मलनापञ्जरित०' ब. ४ 'व्यजनधवलित०' अ–क. ५ 'विक्षेपः' ब–क. ६ 'मधुमदमत्तकासिनी' ब.

शस्त्रोपजीविभिः, गुरुकुलमिति विद्यार्थिभिः, गन्धर्वनगरमिति गाथनैः, विश्वकर्ममन्दिरमिति विज्ञानिभिः, लाभभूमिरिति वैदेहकैः, द्यूतस्थानमिति बन्दिभिः, साधुसमागम इति सद्भिः, वज्रपञ्जरमिति शरणागतैः विटगोष्ठीति विदग्धैः, सुकृतपरिणाम इति पथिकैः, असुरविवरमिति वातिकैः, शाक्याश्रम इति शमिभिः, अप्सरःपुरमिति कामिभिः, महोत्सवसमाज इति चारणैः, वसुधारेति च विप्रैरगृह्यत ।

यत्र च मातङ्गगामिन्यः शीलवत्यश्च, गौर्यो विभवरताश्च, श्यामाः पद्मरागिण्यश्च, धवलद्विजशुचिवदना मदिरामोदिश्वसनाश्च, चन्द्रकान्तवपुषः शिरीषकोमलाङ्ग्यश्च, अभुजङ्गगम्याः कञ्चुकिन्यश्च, पृथुकलत्रश्रियो दरिद्रमध्यकलिताश्च, लावण्यवत्यो मधुरभाषिण्यश्च, अप्रमत्ताः प्रसन्नोज्ज्वलरागाश्च,[1] अकौतुकाः प्रौढाश्च प्रमदाः ।

यत्र च प्रमदानां चक्षुरेव सहजं मुण्डमालामण्डनं भारः कुवलयदलदामानि । अलकप्रतिबिम्बान्येव कपोलतलगतान्यक्लिष्टाः श्रवणावतंसाः पुनरुक्तानि तमालकिसलयानि । प्रियकथा एव सुभगाः कर्णालङ्कारा आडम्बरः कुण्डलानि[2] । कपोला एव सततमालोककारका विभवो[3] निशासु मणिप्रदीपाः। निःश्वासाकृष्टमधुकरकुलान्येव रमणीयं मुखावरणं कुलस्त्रीजनाचारो जालिका। वाण्येव मधुरा वीणा बाह्यविज्ञानं तन्त्रीताडनम् । हासा एवातिशयसुरभयः पटवासा निरर्थकाः कर्पूरपांसवः । अधरकान्तिविसर एवोज्ज्वलतरोऽङ्गरागो निर्गुणो लावण्यकलङ्कः कुङ्कुमपङ्कः । बाहव एव कोमलतमाः परिहासप्रहारवेत्रलता निष्प्रयोजनानि मृणालानि । यौवनोष्मस्वेदबिन्दव एव विदग्धाः कुचालङ्कृतयो हारास्तु भाराः । श्रोण्य एव विशालस्फाटिकशिलातलचतुरस्रा रागिणां विश्रमकारणमनिमित्तं भवनमणिवेदिकाः । कमललोभनिलीनान्यलिकुलान्येव मुखराणि पदाभरणकानि निष्फलानीन्द्रनीलनूपुराणि। नूपुररवा[4]हूता भवनकलहंसा एव समुचिताः सञ्चरणसहाया ऐश्वर्यप्रपञ्चाः परिजनाः।

तत्र च साक्षात्सहस्राक्ष इव सर्ववर्णधरं धनुर्दधानः, मेरुमय इव कल्याणप्रकृतित्वे, मन्दरमय इव लक्ष्मीसमाकर्षणे, जलनिधिमय इव मर्यादायाम्, आकाशमय इव शब्दप्रादुर्भावे, शशिमय इव कलासंग्रहे, वेदमय इवाकृत्रिमालापत्वे, धरणिमय इव लोकधृतिकरणे, पवनमय इव सर्वपार्थिवरजोविकारहरणे, गुरुर्वचसि, पृथुरुरसि, विशालो मनसि, जनकस्तपसि, सुयात्रस्तेजसि, सुमन्त्रो रहसि, बुधः सदसि, अर्जुनो यशसि, भीष्मो धनुषि, निषधो वपुषि, शत्रुघ्नः समरे, शूरः शूरसेनाक्रमणे, दक्षः प्रजाकर्मणि, सर्वादिराजतेजःपुञ्जनिर्मित इव राजा पुष्पभूतिरिति नाम्ना बभूव ।

---

१ '०मुखरागाश्च' ब. २ 'कुण्डलादिः' अ–क. ३ 'विभवो निश्वासमणि०' ब.
४ 'रवोहृताः' ब.

पृथुना गौरियं[1] कृतेति यः स्पर्धमान इव महीं महिषीं चकार । निसर्गस्वैरिणी स्वरुच्यनुरोधिनी च भवति हि महतां मतिः । यतस्तस्य केनचिदनुपदिष्टा सहजैव शैशवादारभ्यान्यदेवताविमुखी[2] भगवति भक्तिसुलभे भुवनभृति भूतभावने भवच्छिदि भवे भूयसी भक्तिरभूत् । अकृतवृषभध्वजपूजाविधिर्न स्वप्नेऽप्याहारमकरोत् । अजम्, अजरम्, अमरगुरुम्, असुरपुररिपुम्, अपरिमितगणपतिम्, अचलदुहितृपतिम्, अखिलभुवनकृतचरणनतिम्, पशुपतिं प्रपन्नोऽन्यदेवताशून्यममन्यत त्रैलोक्यम् । भर्तृचित्तानुवर्तिन्यश्चानुजीविनां प्रकृतयः । तथा हि । गृहे गृहे भगवानपूज्यत खण्डपरशुः । ववुरस्य होमालवाल[3]विलीयमानबहलगुग्गुलुगन्धगर्भाः स्नपनक्षीरशीकरक्षोदक्षारिणो बिल्वपल्लवदामदलोद्वाहिनः पुण्य[4]विषयेषु वायवः । शिवसपर्यासमुचितैरुपायनैः प्राभृतैश्च पौराः पादोपजीविनः सचिवा भुजबलनिर्जिताश्च करदीकृता महासामन्तास्तं सिषेविरे । तथा हि । कैलासकूटधवलैः कनकपत्रलतालङ्कृतविषाणकोटिभिर्महाप्रमाणैः संध्याबलिवृषैः सौवर्णैश्च स्नपनकलशैरर्घभाजनैश्च धूपपात्रैश्च पुष्पपट्टैश्च मणियष्टिप्रदीपैश्च ब्रह्मसूत्रैश्च महार्हमाणिक्यखण्डखचितैश्च मुखकोषैः परितोषमस्य मनसि चक्रुः । अन्तःपुराण्यपि स्वयमारब्धबालेयतण्डुलकण्डनानि[5] देवगृहोपलेपनलोहिततरकरकिसलयानि कुसुमग्रथनव्यग्रसमस्तपरिजनानि तस्याभिलषितमन्ववर्तन्त । तथा च । परममाहेश्वरः स भूपालो लोकतः शुश्राव भुवि भगवन्तमपरमिव साक्षाद्दक्षमखमथनं दाक्षिणात्यं बहुविधविद्याप्रभावप्रख्यातैर्गुणैः शिष्यैरिवानेकसहस्रसंख्यैर्व्याप्तमर्त्यलोकं भैरवाचार्यनामानं महाशैवम् । उपनयन्ति हि हृदयमदृष्टमपि जनं शीतलसंवादाः । यतः स राजा श्रवणसमकालमेव तस्मिन्भैरवाचार्ये भगवति द्वितीय इव कपर्दिनि दूरगतेऽपि गरीयसीं बबन्ध भक्तिम् । आचकाङ्क्ष च मनोरथैरप्यस्य सर्वथा दर्शनम् ।

अथ कदाचित्पर्यस्तेऽस्ताचलचुम्बिनि वासरेऽन्तःपुरवर्तिनं राजानमुपसृत्य प्रतीहारी विज्ञापितवती—'देव, द्वारि परिव्राडास्ते कथयति च भैरवाचार्यवचनाद्देवमनुप्राप्तोऽस्मि' इति । राजा तु तच्छ्रुत्वा सादरम्—'क्वासौ आनयाशु । प्रवेशयैनम्' इति चाब्रवीत् । तथा चाकरोत्प्रतीहारी । न चिराच्च प्रविशन्तं प्रांशुमाजानुभुजम्, भैक्षक्षाममपि स्थूलास्थिभिरवयवैः पीवरमिवोपलक्ष्यमाणम्, पृथूत्त[6]माङ्गमुत्तुङ्गवलिभङ्गस्थपुटललाटम्, निर्मांसगण्डकूपकम्, मधुबिन्दुपिङ्गलपरिमण्डलाक्षम्, ईषदावक्रघोणम्, अतिप्रलम्बैककर्णपाशम्, अलाबुबीजविकटोन्नतदन्तपङ्क्तिम्, तुरगानुकश्लथाधरलेखम्, लम्बचिबुकायततरलपनम्, अंसावलम्बिना काषायेण योगपट्टकेन विरचितवैकक्षकम्, हृदयमध्यनिबद्धग्रन्थिना च रागेणेव खण्डशः कृतेन धातुरसारुणेन

१ 'गौरिवेयं' ब. २ 'अनन्यदेवता भगवति' ब. ३ 'होमालवालानलविलीय०' ब. ४ 'पुण्याविषयेषु' ब. ५ 'खण्डनानि' ब. ६ 'पृथुत्तमाङ्गम्' ब.

कर्पटेन कृतोत्तरासङ्गम्, पुनरुक्तबालप्रग्रहवेष्टननिश्चलमूलेन बद्धमृत्परिशोधनवंशत्वक्तितउना कौपीनसनाथशिखरेण खर्जूरपुटसंपुटकगर्भीकृतभिक्षाकपालकेन दारवफलकत्रयत्रिकोणत्रियष्टिनिविष्टकमण्डलुना बहिरुपपादितपादुकावस्थानेन स्थूलदशासूत्रनियन्त्रितपुस्तिकापूलिकेन वामकरधृतेन योगभारकेणाध्यासितस्कन्धम्, इतरकरगृहीतवेत्रासनं मस्करिणमद्राक्षीत्। क्षितिपतिरप्युपगतमुचितेन चैनमादरेणान्वग्रहीत्। आसीनं च पप्रच्छ—'क्क भैरवाचार्यः' इति। सादरनरपतिवचनमुदितमनास्तु परिव्राट् तमुपनगरं सरस्वतीतटवनावलम्बिनि शून्यायतने स्थितमाचचक्षे। भूयश्चाबभाषे—'अर्चयति हि महाभागं भगवानाशीर्वचसा' इत्युक्त्वा चोपनिन्ये योगभारकादाकृष्य भैरवाचार्यप्रहितानि रत्नवन्ति बहलालोकलिप्तान्तःपुराणि पञ्च राजतानि पुण्डरीकाणि।

नरपतिस्तु प्रियजनप्रणयभङ्गकातरो[1] दाक्षिण्यमनुरुध्यमानो ग्रहणलाघवं च लङ्घयितुमसमर्थो दोलायमानेन मनसा स्थित्वा कथं कथमप्यतिसौजन्यनिघ्नस्तानि जग्राह। जगाद च—'सर्वफलप्रसवहेतुः शिवभक्तिरियं नो मनोरथदुर्लभानि फलति फलानि। येनैवमस्मासु प्रीयते तत्रभगवान्भुवनगुरुर्भैरवाचार्यः। श्वो द्रष्टास्मि भगवन्तम्' इत्युक्त्वा च मस्करिणं व्यसर्जयत्। अनया च वार्तया परां मुदमवाप। अपरेद्युश्च प्रातरेवोत्थाय[2] वाजिनमधिरुह्य समुच्छ्रितश्वेतातपत्रः समुद्धूयमानधवलचामरयुगलः कतिपयैरेव राजपुत्रैः परिवृतो भैरवाचार्यं सवितारमिव शशी द्रष्टुं प्रतस्थे। गत्वा च किञ्चिदन्तरं तदीयमेवाभिमुखमापतन्तमन्यतमं शिष्यमद्राक्षीत्। अप्राक्षीच्च—'क्क भगवानास्ते' इति। सोऽकथयत्—'अस्य जीर्णमातृगृहस्योत्तरेण बिल्ववाटिकामध्यास्ते' इति। गत्वा च तं प्रदेशमवततार तुरगात्। प्रविवेश च बिल्ववाटिकाम्।

अथ महतः कार्पटिकवृन्दस्य मध्ये प्रातरेव स्नातम्, दत्ताष्टपुष्पिकम्, अनुष्ठिताग्निकार्यम्, कृतभस्मरेखापरिहारपरिकरे हरितगोमयोपलिप्तक्षितितलवितते व्याघ्रचर्मण्युपविष्टम्, कृष्णकम्बलप्रावरणनिभेनासुरविवरप्रवेशाशङ्कया पातालान्धकारावासमिवाभ्यस्यन्तम्, उन्मिषता विद्युत्कपिलेनात्मतेजसा महामांसविक्रयक्रीतेन मनःशिलापङ्केनेव शिष्यलोकं लिम्पन्तम्, जटीकृतैकदेशलम्बमानरुद्राक्षशङ्खगुटिकेनोर्ध्वबद्धेन शिखापाशेन बध्नन्तमिव विद्यावलेपदुर्विदग्धानुपरि सञ्चरतः सिद्धान्, धवलकतिपयशिरोरुहेण वयसा पञ्चपञ्चाशतं वर्षाण्यतिक्रामन्तम्, खालित्यक्षीयमाणशङ्खलोमलेखम्, लोमशकर्णशष्कुलीप्रदेशम्, पृथुललाटतटम्, तिरश्च्या भस्मललाटिकया बहुशः शिरोर्ध्वधृतदग्धगुग्गुलुसन्तापस्फुटितकपालास्थिपाण्डुरराजिशङ्कामिव जनयन्तम्, सहजललाटवलिभङ्गसङ्कोचितकूर्चभागां बभ्रुभासं भ्रूसङ्गत्या

१ 'कातरम्' ब. २ अस्मात्परं 'कृतकृत्यः' इत्यधिकं ब-पुस्तके.

निरन्तरामायामिनीमेकामिव[1] भ्रूलेखां बिभ्राणम्, ईषत्काचकाचरकनीनिकेन[2] रक्तापाङ्गनिर्गतांशुप्रतानेन मध्यधवलभासेन्द्रायुधेनेवातिदीर्घेण लोचनयुगलेन परितो महामण्डलमिवानेकवर्णरागमालिखन्तं सितपीतलोहितपताकावलीशबलं शिवबलिमिव दिक्षु विक्षिपन्तम्, तार्क्ष्यतुण्डकोटिकुब्जाग्रघोणम्, दूरविदीर्णसृक्किसंक्षिप्तकपोलम्, किञ्चिद्दन्तुरतया सदाहृदयसन्निहितहरमौलिचन्द्रातपेनेव निर्गच्छता दन्तालोकेन धवलयन्तं दिशां जालकम्, जिह्वाग्रस्थितसर्वशैवसंहितातिभारेणेव मनाक्प्रलम्बितौष्ठम्, प्रलम्बश्रवणपालीप्रेङ्खिताभ्यां स्फाटिककुण्डलाभ्यां शुक्रबृहस्पतिभ्यामिव सुरासुरविजयविद्यासिद्धिश्रद्धयानुबध्यमानम्, बद्धविविधौषधिमन्त्रसूत्रपङ्क्तिना सलोहवलयेनैकप्रकोष्ठेन शङ्खखण्डं पूष्णो दन्तमिव भगवता भवेन भग्नं भक्त्या भूषणीकृतं कलयन्तम्, अखिलरसकूपोदञ्चनघटीयन्त्रमालामिव रुद्राक्षमालां दक्षिणेन पाणिना भ्रमयन्तम्, उरसि दोलायमानेनापिङ्गलाग्रेण कूर्चकलापेन संमार्जयन्तमिवान्तर्गतं निजरजोनिकरम्, अतिनिबिडनीललोममण्डलनिचितं च ध्यानलब्धेन ज्योतिषा दग्धमिव हृदयदेशं दधानम्, ईषत्प्रशिथिलवलिवलयबध्यमानतुन्दम्, उपचीयमानस्फिञ्मांसपिण्डकम्, पाण्डुरपवित्रक्षौमावृतकौपीनम्, सावष्टम्भपर्यङ्कबन्धमण्डलितेनामृतफेनश्वेतरुचा योगपट्टकेन वासुकिनेवाप्रतिहतानेकमन्त्रप्रभावाविर्भूतेन प्रदक्षिणीक्रियमाणम्, अरुणतामरससुकुमारतलस्य पादयुगलस्य निर्मलैर्नखमयूखजालकैर्जर्जरयन्तमिव महानिधानोद्धरणरसेन रसातलम्, तोयक्षालितशुचिना धौतपादुकायुगलेन हंसमिथुनेनेव भागीरथीतीर्थयात्रापरिचयागतेनामुच्यमानचरणान्तिकम्, शिखरनिखातकुब्जकालायसकण्टकेन वैणवेन विशाखिकादण्डेन सर्वविद्यासिद्धिविघ्नविनायकापनयनाङ्कुशेनेव सततपार्श्ववर्तिना विराजमानम्, अबहुभाषिणम्, मन्दहासिनम्, सर्वोपकारिणम्, कुमारब्रह्मचारिणम्, अतितपस्विनम्, महामनस्विनम्, कृशक्रोधम्, अकृशानुरोधम्, महानगरमिवादीनप्रकृतिशोभितम्, मेरुमिव कल्पतरुपल्लवराशिसुकुमारच्छायम्, कैलासमिव पशुपतिचरणरजःपवित्रितशिरसम्, शिवलोकमिव माहेश्वरगणानुयातम्, जलनिधिमिवानेकनदनदीसहस्रप्रक्षालितशरीरम्, जाह्नवीप्रवाहमिव बहुपुण्यतीर्थस्थानशुचिम्, धाम धर्मस्य, तीर्थं तथ्यस्य, कोशं कुशलस्य, पत्तनं पूततायाः, शालां शीलस्य, क्षेत्रं क्षमायाः, शालेयं शालीनतायाः, स्थानं स्थितेः, आधारं धृतेः, आकरं करुणायाः, निकेतनं कौतुकस्य, आरामं रामणीयकस्य, प्रासादं प्रसादस्य, अगारं गौरवस्य, समाजं सौजन्यस्य, सम्भवं सद्भावस्य, कालं कलेः, भगवन्तं साक्षादिव विरूपाक्षं भैरवाचार्यं ददर्श। भैरवाचार्यस्तु दूरादेव राजानं दृष्ट्वा शशिनमिव जलनिधिश्चचाल। प्रथमतरोत्थितशिष्यलोकश्चोत्थाय प्रत्युज्जगाम

---

१ 'एकामेव' ब. २ 'ईषत्काचर०' ब.

समर्पितश्रीफलोपायनश्च जह्नुकर्णसमुद्गीर्यमाणगङ्गाप्रवाहह्रादगम्भीरया गिरा स्वस्तिशब्दमकरोत्।

नरपतिरपि प्रीतिविस्तार्यमाणधवलिम्ना चक्षुषा प्रत्यर्पयन्निव बहुतराणि पुण्डरीकवनानि ललाटपट्टपर्यस्तेन चोदंशुना शिखामणिना महेश्वरप्रसादमिव तृतीयनयनोद्गमेन प्रकाशयन्नावर्जितकर्णपल्लवपलायमानमधुकरः शिवसेवासमुन्मूलिताशेषपापलवमुच्यमान[1] इव दूरावनतः प्रणाममभिनवं चकार। आचार्योऽपि—'आगच्छ। अत्रोपविश' इति शार्दूलचर्मात्मीयमदर्शयत्। उपदर्शितप्रश्रयस्तु राजा मत्तहंसकलगद्गदस्वरसुभगां मधुरसमर्यी महानदीमिव प्रवर्तयन्वाचं व्याजहार—'भगवन्, नार्हसि मामन्यनृपस्खलितैः खलीकर्तुम्। अशेषराजकोपेक्षितताया हतलक्ष्म्याः खल्वयं शीलापराधो द्रविणदौरात्म्यं वा यदेवमाचरति मयि गुरुः। अभूमिरयमुपचाराणाम्। अलमतियन्त्रणया। दूरस्थितोऽपि मनोरथशिष्योऽयं जनो भवताम्। माननीयं च गुरुवन्नोल्लङ्घनमर्हति गुरोरासनम्। आसतां च भवन्त एवात्र' इति व्याहृत्य परिजनोपनीते वाससि निषसाद। भैरवाचार्योऽपि प्रीत्यानतिक्रमणीयं नृपवचनमनुवर्तमानः पूर्ववत्तदेव व्याघ्राजिनमभजत।

आसीने च सराजके परिजने शिष्यजने च समुचितमर्घ्यादिकं चक्रे। क्रमेण च नृपमाधुर्यहृतान्तःकरणः शशिकरनिकरविमला दशनदीधितीः स्फुरन्तीः शिवभक्तीरिव साक्षाद्दर्शयन्नुवाच—'तात, अतिनम्रतैव ते कथयति गुणानां गौरवम्। सकलसम्पत्पात्रमसि। विभवानुरूपास्तु प्रतिपत्तयः। जन्मनः प्रभृत्यदत्तदृष्टिरस्मि स्वापतेयेषु। यतः सकलदोषकलापानलेन्धनैर्धनैरविक्रीतं क्वचिच्छरीरकमस्ति। भैक्षरक्षिताः सन्ति प्राणाः। दुर्गृहीतानि कतिचिद्विद्यन्ते विद्याक्षराणि। भगवच्छिवभट्टारकपादसेवया समुपार्जिता[2] कियत्यपि सन्निहिता पुण्यकणिका। स्वीक्रियतां यदत्रोपयोगार्हम्। प्रतनुगुणग्राह्याणि कुसुमानीव हि भवन्ति सतां मनांसि। अपि च। विद्वत्संमताः श्रूयमाणा अपि सुखयन्ति[3] साधवः शब्दा इव, सुधीरेऽपि हि मनसि यशांसि कुर्वन्ति विवरं, विशतः कुतूहलस्य फेनधवलैः स्रोतोभिरिवापह्रियमाणो गुणगणैरानीतोऽस्मि कल्याणिना' इति।

राजा तु तं प्रत्यवादीत्—'भगवन्, अनुरक्तेष्वपि शरीरादिषु साधूनां स्वामिन एव प्रणयिनः। युष्मद्दर्शनादुपार्जितमेव चापरिमितं कुशलजातम्। अनेनैवागमनेन[4] स्पृहणीयं पदमारोपितोऽस्मि गुरुणा।' इति विविधाभिश्च कथाभिश्चिरं स्थित्वा गृहमगात्।

अन्यस्मिन्दिवसे भैरवाचार्योऽपि राजानं द्रष्टुं ययौ। तस्मै च राजा सान्तःपुरं सपरिजनं सकोषमात्मानं निवेदितवान्। स च विहस्योवाच—

१ 'पापमललव०' ब. २ 'समुपार्जिताः कियत्योपि सन्निहिताः पुण्यकणिकाः' ब ३ 'सुखयन्ति' इति नास्ति अ-क—पुस्तकयोः. ४ 'कृतमनेनैवानुगमनेन' ब.

'तात, क्व विभवः, क्व च वयं वनवर्धिताः। धनोष्मणा म्लायत्यलं लतेव मनस्विता। खद्योतानामिवास्माकमियमपरोपतापिनी राजते तेजस्विता। भवादृशा एव भाजनं भूतेः' इति स्थित्वा च कञ्चित्कालं जगाम।

परिव्राट् तेनैव क्रमेण पञ्च पञ्च राजतानि पुण्डरीकाण्युपायनीचकार। एकदा तु श्वेतकर्पटावृतं किमप्यादाय प्राविशत्। उपविश्य च पूर्ववत्स्थित्वा मुहूर्तमब्रवीत्—'महाभाग, भवन्तमाह भगवान्यथास्मच्छिष्यः पातालस्वामिनामा ब्राह्मणः। तेन ब्रह्मराक्षसहस्तादपहृतो महासिरट्टहासनामा। सोऽयं भवद्भुजयोग्यो गृह्यताम्'। इत्यभिधायापहृतकर्पटावच्छादनात्परिवारादाचकर्ष शरद्गगनमिव पिण्डतां नीतम्, कालिन्दीप्रवाहमिव स्तम्भितजलम्, नन्दकजिगीषया कृष्णकोपितं कालियमिव कृपाणतां गतम्, लोकविनाशाय प्रकाशितधारासारं प्रलयकालमेघखण्डमिव नभस्तलात्पतितम्, दृश्यमानविकटदन्तमण्डलं हासमिव हिंसायाः, हरिबाहुदण्डमिव कृतदृढमुष्टिग्रहम्, सकलभुवनजीवितापहरणक्षमेण कालकूटेनेव निर्मितम्, कृतान्तकोपानलतप्तेनेवायसा घटितम्, अतितीक्ष्णतया पवनस्पर्शेनापि रुषेव क्वणन्तम्, मणिसभाकुट्टिमपतत्प्रतिबिम्बच्छद्मनात्मानमपि द्विधेव पाटयन्तम्, अरिशिरश्छेदलग्नैः कचैरिव किरणैः करालितधारम्, मुहुर्मुहुस्तडिदुन्मेषतरलैः प्रभाचक्रच्छुरितैर्जर्जरितातपम्, खण्डशश्छिन्दन्तमिव दिवसम्, कटाक्षमिव कालरात्रेः, कर्णोत्पलमिव कालस्य, ओङ्कारमिव क्रौर्यस्य, अलङ्कारमहङ्कारस्य, कुलमित्रं कोपस्य, देहं दर्पस्य, सुसहायं साहसस्य, अपत्यं मृत्योः, आगमनमार्गं लक्ष्म्याः, निर्गमनमार्गं कीर्तेः, कृपाणम्।

अवनिपतिस्तु तं गृहीत्वा करेणायुधप्रीत्या प्रतिमानिभेनालिङ्गन्निव सुचिरं ददर्श। सन्दिदेश च—'वक्तव्यो भगवान्परद्रव्यग्रहणावज्ञादुर्विदग्धमपि हि मे मनो युष्मद्विषये न शक्नोति वचनव्यतिक्रमव्यभिचारमाचरितुम्' इति। परिव्राट् तु गृहीते तस्मिन्परितुष्टः 'स्वस्ति भवते, साधयामः' इत्युक्त्वा निरयासीत्। नृपश्च प्रकृत्या वीररसानुरागी तेन कृपाणेनामन्यत करतलवर्तिनीं मेदिनीम्।

अथ व्रजत्सु दिवसेष्वेकदा भैरवाचार्यो राजानमुपह्वरे सोपग्रहमवादीत्—'तात, स्वार्थालसाः[1] परोपकारदक्षाश्च प्रकृतयो भवन्ति भव्यानाम्। भवादृशां चार्थिदर्शनं महोत्सवः प्रणयनमाराधनमर्थग्रहणमुपकारः। भूमिरसि सर्वलोकमनोरथानां येनाभिधीयसे। श्रूयताम्। भगवतो महाकालहृदयनाम्नो महामन्त्रस्य कृष्णस्रगम्बरानुलेपेनाकल्पेन कल्पकथितेन महाश्मशाने जपकोट्या कृतपूर्वसेवोऽस्मि। तस्य वेतालसाधनावसाना सिद्धिः। असहायैश्च सा दुरवापा। त्वं चालमस्मै कर्मणे। त्वयि च गृहीतभरे भविष्यन्त्यपरे

१ 'स्वार्थलालसाः' ब.

विलासविक्षिप्तेन धवलव्यायामफालीपटान्तेन धरणितलगेन धार्यमाण इव पृष्ठतः शेषेण, स्थिरस्थूलोरुदण्डः, भूमिभङ्गभयेनेव मन्थराणि स्थापयन्पदानि, निर्भरगर्वगुरु कथमपि शैलमिव गात्रमुद्वहन्दर्पेण, मुहुर्मुहुरुरसि द्विगुणिते दोष्णि वामे तिर्यगुत्क्षिप्ते च दक्षिणे जङ्घाकाण्डे कुण्डलिते चण्डस्फोटनटाङ्कारैः कर्मविघ्ननिर्घातानिव पातयन्नेकेन्द्रियविकलमिव जीवलोकं कुर्वन्कुवलयश्यामलः पुरुष उज्जगाम। जगाद च विहस्य नरसिंहनादनिर्घोषघोरया भारत्या—'भो विद्याधरीश्रद्धाकामुक किमयं विद्यालवावलेपः सहायमदो वा यदस्मै जनायाविधाय बलिं बालिश इव सिद्धिमभिलषसि। का ते दुर्बुद्धिरियम्। एतावता कालेन क्षेत्राधिपतिरस्य मन्त्राङ्गैव लब्धव्यपदेशस्य देशस्य नागतस्ते श्रोत्रोपकण्ठं श्रीकण्ठनामा नागोऽहम्। अनिच्छति मयि का शक्तिर्ग्रहगणस्यापि गन्तुं गगने। भूनाथोऽप्ययमनाथस्तपस्वी यस्त्वादृशैः शैवापसदैरुपकरणीक्रियते। सहस्वेदानीं सहामुना दुर्नरेन्द्रेण दुर्नरेन्द्रदुर्नयस्य फलम्' इत्यभिधाय च निष्ठुरैः प्रकोष्ठप्रहारैस्त्रीनपि टीटिभप्रभृतीनभिमुखं प्रधावितान्सशरीरावरणकृपाणानपातयत्।

अथापूर्वाधिक्षेपश्रवणादशस्त्रव्रणैरप्यमर्षस्वेदच्छलेनानेकसमरपीतमसितमसिधाराजलमिव वमद्भिरवयवैरपि रोमाञ्चनिभेन मुक्तशरशतशल्यनिकरभरलघुमिवात्मानं रणाय कुर्वद्भिरट्टहासेनापि प्रतिबिम्बिततारागणेन स्पष्टदृष्टधवलदन्तमालमवज्ञया हसतेव कथ्यमानसत्त्वावष्टम्भः परिकरबन्धविभ्रमभ्रमितकरनखकिरणचक्रवालेन व्यपगमनाशङ्कया नागदमनमन्त्रमण्डलबन्धेनेव रुन्धन्दश दिशो नरनाथः सावज्ञमवादीत्—'अरे काकोदर काक, मयि स्थिते राजहंसे न जिह्रेषि बलिं याचितुम्। अमीभिः किं वा परुषभाषितैः। भुजे वीर्यं निवसति सताम्[2], न वाचि। प्रतिपद्यस्व शस्त्रम्। अयं न भवसि। अगृहीतहेतिष्वशिक्षितो मे भुजः प्रहर्तुम्' इति। नागस्तु—'अनादृततरमेहि। किं शस्त्रेण। भुजाभ्यामेव भनज्मि भवतो दर्पम्' इत्यभिधायास्फोटयामास। नरपतिरपि निरायुधमायुधेन युधि लज्जमानो जेतुमुत्सृज्य सचर्मफलकमट्टहासमसिमर्धोरुकस्योपरि बबन्ध बाहुयुद्धाय कक्ष्याम्। युयुधाते च निर्दयास्फोटनस्फुटितभुजरुधिरशीकरसिच्यमानौ शिलास्तम्भैरिव पतद्भिर्बाहुदण्डैः शब्दमयमिव कुर्वाणौ भुवनं तौ। नचिराच्च पातयामास भूतले भुजङ्गं भूपतिः। जग्राह च केशेषु। उच्चखान च शिरश्छेत्तुमट्टहासम्। अपश्यच्च वैकक्षकमालान्तरेणास्य यज्ञोपवीतम्। उपसंहृतशस्त्रव्यापारश्चावादीत्—'दुर्विनीत, अस्ति ते दुर्नयनिर्वाहबीजमिदम्। यतो विश्रब्धमेवाचरसि चापलानि' इत्युक्त्वोत्ससर्ज तम्। अनन्तरं च सहसैवातिबहलां ज्योत्स्नां

---

१ 'दुर्नरेन्द्रेण दुर्नयस्य' अ-क. २ एतन्नास्ति अ-क-पुस्तकयोः.

ददर्श शरदि विकसतां कमलवनानामिव च घ्राणावलेपिनमामोदमजिघ्रत्। झटिति च नूपुरशब्दमश्रृणोत्। व्यापारयामास च शब्दानुसारेण दृष्टिम्।

अथ करतलस्थितस्याट्टहासस्य[1] मध्ये तडितमिव नीलजलधरोदरे स्फुरन्तीम्, प्रभया पिबन्तीमिव त्रियामाम्, तामरसहस्ताम्, कोमलाङ्गुलिरागराजिजालकानि च चरणलग्नानि वेलाबालविद्रुमलतावनानीवाकर्षन्तीम्, करपङ्कजसङ्कोचाशङ्कया शशाङ्कमण्डलमिव खण्डशः कृतं निर्मलचरणनखनिवहनिभेन बिभ्रतीम्, गुल्फावलम्बिनूपुरपुटतया स्थितनिबिडकटकावलिबन्धनादिव परिभ्रश्यागताम्, बहुविधकुसुमशकुनिशतशोभितात्पवनचलिततनुतरङ्गादतिस्वच्छादंशुकादुदधिसलिलादिवोत्तरन्तीम्, उदधिजन्मप्रेम्णा त्रिवलिच्छलेन त्रिपथगयेव परिष्वक्तमध्याम्, अत्युन्नतस्तनमण्डलाम्, दृश्यमानदिङ्नागकुम्भामिव ककुभम्, मदेलग्नैरावतकरशीकरनिकरमिव[2] शरत्तारागणतारं हारमुरसा दधानाम्, धवलचामरैरिव च मन्दमन्दनिःश्वासदोलायितैर्हारकिरणैरुपवीज्यमानाम्, स्वभावलोहितेन मदान्धगन्धेभकुम्भास्फालनसंक्रान्तसिन्दूरेणेव करद्वयेन द्योतमानाम्, हरशिखण्डेन्दुद्वितीयखण्डेनेव कुण्डलीकृतेन ज्योत्स्नामुचा दन्तपत्रेण विभ्राजमानाम्, कौस्तुभगभस्तिस्तबकेनेव च श्रवणलग्नेनाशोककिसलयेनालङ्कृताम्, महता मातङ्गमदमयेन तिलकेनादृश्यच्छत्रच्छायामण्डलेनेवाविरहितललाटाम्, आपादतलादासीमन्ताच्च चन्द्रातपधवलेन चन्दनेनादिराजयशसेव धवलीकृताम्, धरणितलचुम्बिनीभिः कण्ठकुसुममालाभिः सरिद्भिरिव सागराधिष्ठाभिरधिष्ठिताम्[3], मृणालकोमलैरवयवैः कमलसम्भवत्वमनक्षरमाचक्षाणां स्त्रियमपश्यत्। असंभ्रान्तश्च पप्रच्छ—'भद्रे, कासि कस्यासि[4]। किमर्थं वा दर्शनपथमागतासि' इति। सा तु स्त्रीजनविरुद्धेनावष्टम्भेनाभिभवन्तीवाभाषत तम्—'वीर, विद्धि मां नारायणोरःस्थलीलीलाविहारहरिणीम्, पृथुभरतभगीरथादिराजवंशपताकाम्[5], सुभटभुजजयस्तम्भविलासशालभञ्जिकाम्, रणरुधिरतरङ्गिणीतरङ्गक्रीडादोहददुर्ललितराजहंसीम्, सितनृपच्छत्रषण्डशिखण्डिनीम्, अतिनिशितशस्त्रधारावनभ्रमणविभ्रमसिंहीम्, असिधाराजलकमलिनीं श्रियम्। अपहृतास्मि तवामुना शौर्यरसेन। याचस्व। ददामि ते वरमभिलषितम्' इति।

वीराणां त्वपुनरुक्ताः परोपकाराः। यतो राजा तां प्रणम्य स्वार्थविमुखो भैरवाचार्यस्य सिद्धिं ययाचे। लक्ष्मीस्तु देवी प्रीततरहृदया विस्तीर्यमाणेन चक्षुषा क्षीरोदेनेवोपरि पर्यस्तेनाभिषिञ्चन्ती भूपालम् 'एवमस्तु' इत्यब्रवीत्। अवादीच्च पुनः—'अनेन सत्त्वोत्कर्षेण भगवच्छिवभट्टारकभक्त्या चासाधार-

---

१ '०स्थितस्यैवाट्ट' ब. २ 'मध्यलग्नैरा०' ब. ३ 'सागराद्दृष्टाभिः' ब. ४ एतन्नास्ति अ–क–पुस्तकयोः. ५ '०राजपृथुवंश०' ब.

णया भवान्भुवि सूर्याचन्द्रमसोस्तृतीय इवाविच्छिन्नस्य प्रतिदिनमुपचीयमानवृद्धेः शुचिसुभगसत्यत्यागधैर्यशौण्डपुरुषप्रकाण्डप्रायस्य[1] महतो राजवंशस्य कर्ता भविष्यति। यस्मिन्नुत्पत्स्यते सर्वद्वीपानां भोक्ता हरिश्चन्द्र इव हर्षनामा चक्रवर्ती त्रिभुवनविजिगीषुर्द्वितीयो मान्धातेव। यस्यायं करः स्वयमेव कमलमपहाय ग्रहीष्यति चामरम्' इति वचसोऽन्ते तिरोबभूव।

भूमिपालस्तु तदाकर्ण्य हृदयेनातिमात्रमप्रीयत। भैरवाचार्योऽपि तस्या देव्यास्तेन वचसा कर्मणा च सम्यगुपपादितेन सद्य एव कुन्तली किरीटी हारी केयूरी मेखली मुद्गरी खड्गी[2] च भूत्वावाप विद्याधरत्वम्। प्रोवाच च—'राजन्, अदूरव्यापिनः फल्गुचेतसामलसानां मनोरथाः। सतां तु भुवि विस्तारवत्यः स्वभावेनैवोपकृतयः। स्वप्नेऽप्यसम्भावितां दातुमिमां दक्षिणां क्षमः कोऽन्यो भवन्तमपहाय। सम्पत्कणिकामपि प्राप्य तुलेव लघुप्रकृतिरुन्नतिमायाति। त्वदीयैर्गुणैरुपकरणीकृतस्य त्वत्त एव च लब्धात्मलाभस्य निर्लज्जतेयमस्य मूढहृदयस्य यदिच्छामि[3] येन केनचित्कार्यलवोपपादनोपयोगेन स्मरयितुमात्मानम्' इति। प्रत्युपकारदुष्प्रवेशास्तु भवन्ति धीराणां हृदयावष्टम्भाः। यतस्तं राजा 'भवत्सिद्ध्यैव परिसमाप्तकृत्योऽस्मि। साधयतु मान्यो यथासमीहितं स्थानम्' इति प्रत्याचचक्षे।

तथोक्तश्च भूभुजा जिगमिषुः सुदृढं समालिङ्ग्य टीटिभादीन्कुवलयवनेनेवावश्यायशीकरस्राविणा सास्रेण चक्षुषा वीक्षमाणः क्षितिपतिं पुनरुवाच—'तात, ब्रवीमि—यामीति न स्नेहसदृशम्। त्वदीयाः प्राणा इति पुनरुक्तम्। गृह्यतामिदं शरीरकमिति व्यतिरेकेणार्थकरणम्। तिलशः क्रीता वयमिति नोपकारानुरूपम्। बान्धवोऽसीति दूरीकरणमिव। त्वयि स्थितं हृदयमित्यप्रत्यक्षम्। त्वद्विरहकारिणी[4] कारणेयं नः सिद्धिरित्यश्रद्धेयम्। निष्कारणस्तवोपकार इत्यनुवादः। स्मर्तव्या वयमित्याज्ञा। सर्वथा कृतघ्नालापेष्वसज्जनकथासु च चेतसि कर्तव्योऽयं स्वार्थनिष्ठुरो जनः' इत्यभिधाय वेगच्छिन्नहारोच्छलितमुक्ताफलनिकरताडिततारागणं गगनतलमुत्पपात। ययौ च सीमन्तितग्रहग्रामः सिद्धचुचितं धाम। श्रीकण्ठोऽपि—'राजन्, पराक्रमक्रीतः कर्तव्येषु नियोगेनानुग्राह्यो ग्राहितविनयोऽयं जनः[5]' इत्यभिधाय राजानुमोदितस्तदेव भूयो भूविवरं विवेश।

नरपतिस्तु क्षीणभूयिष्ठायां क्षपायां, प्रवातुमारब्धे प्रबुध्यमानकमलिनीनिःश्वाससुरभौ वनदेवताकुचांशुकापहरणपरिहासस्वेदिनीव सावश्यायशी-

---

१ '०सुभगमान्यसत्यत्यागशौर्यशौण्डि०' ब. २ अस्मात्परं 'कवची' इत्यधिकं ब-पुस्तके. ३ 'तदिच्छामि' अ-क. ४ '०रहानुकारिणी' ब. ५ 'परिजनः' ब.

करे परिमलाकृष्टमधुकृति कुमुदनिद्रावाहिनि निशापरिणतिजडे तुषारलेशि[1]नि वनानिले, विरहविधुरचक्रवाकचक्रनिःश्वसितसन्तापितायामिवापरजलनिधिमवतरन्त्यां त्रियामायां, साक्षादागतलक्ष्मीविलोकनकुतूहलिनीष्विव समुन्मीलन्तीषु नलिनीषु, उन्निद्रपक्षिणि क्षरति कुसुमविसरमिव तुहिनकणनिकरं मृदुपवनलासितलते कानने, कमललक्ष्मीप्रबोधमङ्गलशङ्खेष्विव रसत्स्वन्तर्बद्धध्वनन्मधुकरेषु मुकुलायमानेषु कुमुदेषु, उज्जिहानरविरथवाजिविसृष्टैः प्रोथपवनैः प्रोत्सार्यमाणास्विव वारुण्यां ककुभि पुञ्जीभवन्तीषु श्यामालताकलिकासु तारकासु, मन्दरशिखराश्रयिणि मन्दानिललुलितकल्पलतावनकुसुमधूलिविच्छुरित इव धूसरीभवति सप्तर्षिमण्डले, सुरवारणाङ्कुश इव च्युते गलति तारामये मृगे, त्रीनपि टीटिभादीन्गृहीत्वा नागयुद्धव्यतिकरमलीमसानि शुचिनि वनवापीपयसि प्रक्षाल्याङ्गानि नगरं विवेश । अन्यस्मिन्नहनि तेषामात्मशरीरान[2]न्तरस्नानभोजनाच्छादनादिना प्रीतिमकरोत् ।

कतिपयदिवसापगमे च परिव्राट् भूभुजा वार्यमाणोऽपि वनं ययौ। पातालस्वामिकर्णतालौ तु शौर्यानुरक्तो तमेव सिषेवाते । सम्पादितमनोरथातिरिक्तविभवौ च सुभटमण्डलमध्ये निष्कृष्टमण्डलाग्रौ समरमुखेषु प्रथममुपयुज्यमानौ कथान्तरेषु चान्तरान्तरा राज्ञा समादिष्टौ विचित्राणि भैरवाचार्यचरितानि शैशववृत्तान्तांश्च कथयन्तौ तेनैव सार्धं जरामाजग्मतुरिति ।

इति श्री[3]बाणभट्टकृते हर्षचरिते राजवंशवर्णनं नाम
तृतीय उच्छ्वासः ।

---

१ 'तुषारलेखिनि' ब. २ 'शरीरानन्तरं स्नान' ब. ३ 'इति श्रीमहाकविचक्रचूडामणि–श्रीबाणभट्टविरचिते हर्षचरिते महाकाव्ये राजवंशवर्णनं नाम तृतीय उच्छ्वासः सम्पूर्णः' ब.

चतुर्थ उच्छ्वासः।

योगं स्वप्नेऽपि नेच्छन्ति कुर्वते न करग्रहम्।
महान्तो नाममात्रेण भवन्ति पतयो भुवः॥ १॥

सकलमहीभृत्कम्पकृदुत्पद्यत एक एव नृपवंशे।
विपुलेऽपि पृथुप्रतिमो दन्त इव गणाधिपस्य मुखे॥ २॥

अथ तस्मात्पुष्पभूतेः[1] द्विजवरस्वेच्छागृहीतकोषो नाभिपद्म इव पुण्डरीकेक्षणात्, लक्ष्मीपुरःसरो रत्नसञ्चय इव रत्नाकरात्, गुरुबुधकविकलावत्[2]तेजस्विभूनन्दनप्रायो ग्रहगण इवोदयस्थानात्, महाभारवाहनयोग्यः सागर इव सगरप्रभावात्, दुर्जयबलसनाथो हरिवंश इव शूरान्निर्जगाम राजवंशः। यस्मादविनष्टधर्मधवलाः प्रजासर्गा इव कृतमुखात्, प्रतापाक्रान्तभुवनाः किरणा इव तेजोनिधेः, विग्रहव्याप्तदिङ्मुखा गिरय इव भूभृत्प्रभवात्[3], धरणिधारणक्षमा दिग्गजा इव ब्रह्मकरात्, उदधीन्पातुमुद्यता जलधरा इव घनागमात्, इच्छाफलदायिनः कल्पतरव इव नन्दनात्, सर्वभूताश्रया विश्वरूपप्रकारा इव श्रीधरादजायन्त राजानः।

तेषु चैवमुत्पद्यमानेषु क्रमेणोदपादि हूण[4]हरिणकेसरी सिन्धुराजज्वरो गुर्जरप्रजागरो गान्धाराधिपगन्धद्विपकूट[5]पाकलो लाटपाटव[6]पाटच्चरो मालवलक्ष्मीलतापरशुः प्रतापशील इति प्रथितापरनामा प्रभाकरवर्धनो नाम राजाधिराजः। यो राज्याङ्गसङ्गीन्यभिषिच्यमान एव मलानीव मुमोच धनानि। यः परकीयेणापि कातरवल्लभेन रणमुखे तृणेनेव धृतेनालज्जत जीवितेन। यः करधृतधौतासिप्रतिबिम्बितेनात्मनाप्यदूयत समितिषु सहायेन रिपूणां पुरः प्रश्नेषु धनुषापि नमता। यो मानी मानसेनाखिद्यत। यश्चान्तर्गता[7]परिमितरिपुशल्यशङ्कुकीलितामिव निश्चलामुवाह राजलक्ष्मीम्। यश्च सर्वासु दिक्षु समीकृत[8]सरित्तटावटविटपाटवीतरु[9]तृणगुल्मवल्मीकगिरिगहनैर्दण्डयात्रापथैः पृथुभिर्भृत्योपयोगाय व्यभजतेव वसुधां बहुधा। यं चालब्धयुद्धदोहदमात्मीयोऽपि सकलरिपुसं[10]मुत्सारकः परकीय इव ततापं प्रतापः। यस्य च वह्निमयो हृदये-

---

१ 'पुष्यभूतेः' ब. २ 'कलाभृत्' ब. ३ 'भूभृत्प्रवरात्' ब. ४ 'हून॰' ब. ५ '॰कूटहस्तिज्वरः पाकलो' ब. ६ 'पाटज्वरः' ब. ७ 'अन्तर्गतामपरि॰' ब. ८ 'समीकृततटावट' अ. ९ 'तरुकण्टकतृण' ब. १० 'रिपुसमूहसमु॰' ब.

षु जलमयो लोचनपुटेषु मारुतमयो निःश्वसितेषु क्षमामयोऽङ्गेषु आकाशमयः शून्यतायां पञ्चमहाभूतमयो मूर्त इवादृश्यत निहतप्रतिसामन्तान्तःपुरेषु प्रतापः। यस्य चासन्नेषु भृत्यरत्नेषु प्रतिबिम्बितेव तुल्यरूपा समलक्ष्यत लक्ष्मीः। तथा च यस्य प्रतापाग्निना भूतिः शौर्योष्मणा सिद्धिरसिधाराजलेन वंशवृद्धिः शस्त्रव्रणमुखैः पुरुषकारोक्तिर्धनुर्गुणकिणेन करगृहीतिरभवत्। यश्च वैरमुपायनं विग्रहमनुग्रहं समरागमं महोत्सवं शत्रुं निधिदर्शनमरिबाहुल्यमभ्युदयमाहवाह्वानं वरप्रदानमवस्कन्दपातं दिष्टवृद्धिं शस्त्रप्रहारपतनं वसुधारा[1]ममन्यत। यस्मिंश्च राजनि निरन्तरैर्यूपनिकरैरङ्कुरितमिव कृतयुगेन, दिङ्मुखविसर्पिभिरध्वरधूमैः पलायितमिव कलिना, ससुधैः सुरालयैरवतीर्णमिव स्वर्गेण, सुरालयशिखरोद्धूयमानैर्धवलध्वजैः पल्लवितमिव धर्मेण, बहिरुपरचितविकटसभासत्त्रप्रपाप्राग्वंशमण्डपैः प्रसूत[2]मिव ग्रामैः, काञ्चनमयसर्वोपकरणैर्विभवैर्विशीर्णमिव मेरुणा, द्विजदीयमानैरर्थकलशैः फलितमिव भाग्यसम्पदा।

तस्य च जन्मान्तरेऽपि सती पार्वतीव शङ्करस्य, गृहीतपर[3]हृदया लक्ष्मीरिव लोकगुरोः, स्फुरत्तरलतारका रोहिणीव कलावतः, सर्वजनजननी बुद्धिरिव प्रजापतेः, महाभूभृत्कुलोद्गता गङ्गेव वाहिनीनायकस्य, मानसानुवर्तनचतुरा हंसीव राजहंसस्य, सकललोकार्चितचरणा त्रयीव धर्मस्य, दिवानिशममुक्तपार्श्वस्थितिररुन्धतीव महामुनेः, हंसमयीव गतिषु, परपुष्टमयीवालापेषु, चक्रवाकमयीव पतिप्रेम्णि, प्रावृण्मयीव पयोधरोन्नतौ, मदिरामयीव विलासेषु, निधिमयीवार्थसञ्चयेषु, वसुधारामयीव प्रसादेषु, कमलमयीव कोषसंग्रहेषु, कुसुममयीव फलदानेषु, संध्यामयीव वन्द्यत्वे, चन्द्रमयीव निरूष्मत्वे, दर्पणमयीव प्रतिप्राणिग्रहणेषु, सामुद्रमयीव परचित्तज्ञानेषु, परमात्ममयीव व्याप्तिषु, स्मृतिमयीव पुण्यवृत्तिषु, मधुमयीव सम्भाषणेषु, अमृतमयीव तृष्यत्सु, वृष्टिमयीव भृत्येषु, निर्वृतिमयीव सखीषु, वेतसमयीव गुरुषु, गोत्रवृद्धिरिव विलासानाम्, प्रायश्चित्तशुद्धिरिव स्त्रीत्वस्य, आज्ञासिद्धिरिव मकरध्वजस्य, व्युत्थानबुद्धिरिव रूपस्य, दिष्टवृद्धिरिव रतेः, मनोरथसिद्धिरिव रामणीयकस्य, दैवसम्पत्तिरिव लावण्यस्य, वंशोत्पत्तिरिवानुरागस्य, वरप्राप्तिरि[4]व कान्तेः, सर्गसमाप्तिरिव सौन्दर्यस्य, आयतिरिव यौवनस्य, अनभ्रवृष्टिरिव वैदग्ध्यस्य, अयशःप्रमृष्टिरिव लक्ष्म्याः, यशःपुष्टिरिव चारित्रस्य, हृदयतुष्टिरिव धर्मस्य, सौभाग्य[5]परमाणुसृष्टिरिव प्रजापतेः, शमस्यापि शान्तिरिव, विनयस्यापि विनीतिरिव, आभिजात्यस्याप्यभिजातिरिव, संयमस्यापि संयतिरिव, धैर्यस्यापि धृतिरिव, विभ्रमस्यापि विभ्रान्तिरिव यशोमती नाम महा-

---

१ '०धारारसममन्यत' अ. २ 'प्रसुतमिव' ब. ३ 'गृहीतहृदया' ब. ४ 'वरप्राप्तिरिव सौभाग्यस्य, उत्पत्तिभूमिरिव कान्तेः' ब. ५ 'सौहार्दस्य भाग्यरूपपरमाणु०' ब.

देवी प्राणानां प्रणयस्य विस्रम्भस्य धर्मस्य सुखस्य च भूमिरभूत्। यास्य वक्षसि नरकजितो लक्ष्मीरिव ललास।

निसर्गत एव च स नृपतिरादित्यभक्तो बभूव। प्रतिदिनमुदये दिनकृतः स्नातः सितदुकूलधारी धवलकर्पटप्रावृतशिराः प्राङ्मुखः क्षितौ जानुभ्यां स्थित्वा कुङ्कुमपङ्कानुलिप्ते मण्डलके पवित्रपद्मरागपात्रीनिहितेन स्वहृदयेनेव सूर्यानुरक्तेन रक्तकमलषण्डेनार्चां[1] ददौ। अजपच्च जप्यं सुचरितः प्रत्युषसि मध्यन्दिने दिनान्ते चापत्यहेतोः प्राध्वं प्रयतेन मनसा जञ्जपूको मन्त्रमादित्यहृदयम्।

भक्तजनानुरोधविधेयानि तु भवन्ति देवतानां मनांसि। यतः स राजा कदाचिद्ग्रीष्मसमये यदृच्छया सितकरकरसितसुधाधवलस्य हर्म्यस्य पृष्ठे सुष्वाप। पार्श्वे चास्य द्वितीयशयने देवी यशोमती शिश्ये। परिणतप्रायायां तु श्यामायाम्, आसन्नप्रभातवेलाविलुप्यमानलावण्ये लिलम्बिषमाणे सीदत्तेजसि तारकेश्वरे, कराग्रस्पृष्टकुमुदिनीप्रमोदजन्मनि शशधरस्वेद इव गलत्यतिशीतलेऽवश्यायपयसि, मधुमदमत्तप्रसुप्तसीमन्तिनीनिःश्वासाहतेषु संक्रान्तमदेष्विव घूर्णमानेष्वन्तःपुरप्रदीपेषु, राजनि च विमलनखप्रतिबिम्बिताभिः संवाह्यमानचरण इव तारकाभिर्विस्रब्धप्रसारितैर्दिगङ्गनानामिवार्पितैरङ्गैर्मधुसुगन्धिभिः स्वहस्तकमलतालवृन्तवातैरिव श्वसितैर्मुखश्रिया वीज्यमाने विमलकपोलस्थलस्थितेन सितकुसुमशेखरेणेव रतिकेलिकचग्रहलम्बितेन प्रतिमाशशिबिम्बेन विराजिते स्वपति देवी यशोमती सहसैव 'आर्यपुत्र, परित्रायस्व परित्रायस्व' इति भाषमाणा भूषणरवेण व्याहरन्तीव परिजनमुत्कम्पमानाङ्गयष्टिरुदतिष्ठत्।

अथ तेन सर्वस्यामपि पृथिव्यामश्रुतपूर्वेण किमुत देवीमुखे परित्रायस्वेति ध्वनिना दग्ध इव श्रवणयोरेकपद एव निद्रां तत्याज राजा। शिरोभागाच्च कोपकम्पमानदक्षिणकराकृष्टेन कर्णोत्पलेनेव निर्गच्छताच्छधारेण धौतासिना सीमन्तयन्निव निशामन्तरालव्यवधायकमाकाशमिवोत्तरीयांशुकं विक्षिपन्वामकरपल्लवेन करविक्षेपवेगगलितेन हृदयेनेव भयनिमित्तान्वेषिणा भ्रमता दिक्षु कनकवलयेन विराजमानः, सत्वरावतारितवामचरणाक्रान्तिकम्पितप्रासादः, पुरःपतितेनासिधारागोचरगतेन शशिमयूखखण्डेनेव खण्डितेन हारेण राजमानः, लक्ष्मीचुम्बनलग्नताम्बूलरसरञ्जिताभ्यामिव निद्रया कोपेन चातिलोहिताभ्यां लोचनाभ्यां पाटलयन्[2]पर्यन्तानाशानाम्, बद्धान्धकारया त्रिपताकया भ्रुकुट्या पुनरिव त्रियामां परिवर्तयन् 'देवि, न भेतव्यम्, न भेतव्यम्' इत्यभिदधानो वेगेनोत्पपात। सर्वासु च दिक्षु विक्षिप्तचक्षुर्यदा नाद्राक्षीत्किंचिदपि तदा पप्रच्छ तां भयकारणम्।

---

१ 'अर्घं' ब. २ 'पटलयन्' ब.

अथ गृहदेवतास्विव प्रधावितासु यामिकिनीषु, प्रबुद्धे च समीपशायिनि परिजने, शान्ते च हृदयोत्कम्पकारिणि साध्वसे सा समभाषत—'आर्यपुत्र, जानामि स्वप्ने भगवतः सवितुर्मण्डलान्निर्गत्य द्वौ कुमारकौ तेजोमयौ बालातपेनेव पूरयन्तौ दिग्भागान् वैद्युतमिव जीवलोकं कुर्वाणौ मुकुटिनौ कुण्डलिनौ अङ्गदिनौ कवचिनौ गृहीतशस्त्रौ इन्द्रगोपकरुचा रुधिरेण[1] स्नातौ उन्मुखेनोत्तमाङ्गघटमानाञ्जलिना जगता निखिलेन प्रणम्यमानौ कन्ययैकया च चन्द्रमूर्त्येव सुषुम्णरश्मिनिर्गतयानुगम्यमानौ क्षितितलमवतीर्णौ। तौ च मे विलपन्त्याः शस्त्रेणोदरं विदार्य प्रवेष्टुमारब्धौ । प्रतिबुद्धास्मि चार्यपुत्रं विक्रोशयन्ती वेपमानहृदया' इति।

एतस्मिन्नेव च कालक्रमे राजलक्ष्म्याः प्रथमालापः प्रथयन्निव स्वप्नफलमुपतोरणं रराण प्रभातशङ्खः । भाविनीं भूतिमिवाभिदधाना दध्वनुरमन्दं दुन्दुभयः। चकाण कोणाहतानन्दादिव[2] प्रत्यूषनान्दी । जय जयेति प्रबोधमङ्गलपाठकानामुच्चैर्वाचोऽश्रूयन्त। पुरुषश्च वल्लभतुरङ्गमन्दुरामन्दिरे मन्दमन्दं सुप्तोत्थितः सक्षीनां कृतमधुरहेषारवाणां पुरश्च्योतत्तुषारसलिलशीकरं किरन्मरकतहरितं यवसं वक्त्रापरवक्त्रे पपाठ—

'निधिस्तरुविकारेण सन्मणिः स्फुरता धाम्ना।
शुभागमो निमित्तेन स्पष्टमाख्यायते लोके ॥ ३ ॥
अरुण इव पुरःसरो रविं पवन इवातिजवो जलागमम्।
शुभमशुभमथापि वा नृणां कथयति पूर्वनिदर्शनोदयः' ॥ ४ ॥

नरपतिस्तु तच्छ्रुत्वा प्रीयमाणेनान्तःकरणेन तामवादीत्—'देवि, मुदोऽवसरे विषीदसि। सम्वृद्धास्ते गुरुजनाशिषः पूर्णा नो मनोरथाः परिगृहीतासि कुलदेवताभिः प्रसन्नस्ते भगवानंशुमाली नचिरेणैवातिगुणवदपत्यत्रयलाभेनानन्दयिष्यति भवतीम्' इति । अवतीर्य च यथाक्रियमाणाः क्रियाश्चकार। यशोमत्यपि[3] तुतोष तेन पत्युर्भाषितेन।

ततः समतिक्रान्ते कस्मिंश्चित्कालांशे देव्यां च यशोमत्यां देवो राज्यवर्धनः प्रथममेव सम्बभूव गर्भे। गर्भस्थितस्यैव च यस्य यशसेव पाण्डुतामादत्त जननी। गुणगौरवक्रान्तेव गात्रमुद्वोढुं न शशाक। कान्तिविसरामृतरसतृप्तेवाहारं प्रति पराङ्मुखीबभूव । शनैः शनैरुपचीयमानगर्भभरालसा च गुरुभिर्वारितापि वन्दनाय कथमपि सखीभिर्हस्तावलम्बेनानीयत। विश्राम्यन्ती सालभञ्जिकेव समीपगतस्तम्भभित्तिष्वलक्ष्यत । कमललोभनिलीनैरलिभिरिव वृतावुद्धर्तुं नाशकच्चरणौ। मृणाललोभेन च चरणनखमयूखलग्नैर्भवनहंसैरिव सञ्चार्यमाणा मन्दमन्दं बभ्राम। मणिभित्तिपातिनीषु प्रतिमास्वपि हस्तावलम्बनलोभेन प्रसारयामास करकमलम्, किमुत सखीषु।

---

१ 'रुधिरेण धाम्ना स्नातौ' ब. २ 'कोणाभिहता०' ब. ३ 'यशोवत्यपि' अ.

माणिक्यस्तम्भदीधितीरप्यालम्बितुमाचकाङ्क्ष, किं पुनर्भवनलताः। समादेष्टुमप्यसमर्थासीद्गृहकार्याणि कैव कथा कर्तुम्। आस्तां नूपुरभारखेदितं चरणयुगलं मनसापि नोदसहत सौधमारोढुम्। अङ्गान्यपि नाशक्नोद्धारयितुं दूरे भूषणानि। चिन्तयित्वापि क्रीडापर्वताधिरोहणमुत्कम्पितस्तनी तस्तान। प्रत्युत्थानेषूभयजानुशिखरविनिहितकरकिसलयापि गर्वादिव गर्भेणाधार्यत। दिवसं चाधोमुखी स्तनपृष्ठसंक्रान्तेनापत्यदर्शनौत्सुक्यादन्तःप्रविष्टेनेव मुखकमलेनैवं प्रीयमाणा ददर्श गर्भम्। उदरे तनयेन हृदये च भर्त्रा तिष्ठता द्विगुणितामिव लक्ष्मीमुवाह। सख्युत्सङ्गमुक्तशरीरा च शरीरपरिचारिकाणामङ्केषु सपत्नीनां तु शिरःसु पादौ चकार। अवतीर्णे च दशमे मासि सर्वोर्वीभृत्पक्षपाताय वज्रपरमाणुभिरिव निर्मितम्, त्रिभुवनभारधारणसमर्थं शेषफणामण्डलोपकरणैरिव कल्पितम्, सकलभूभृत्कम्पकारिणं दिग्गजावयवैरिव विहितमसूत देवं राज्यवर्धनम्। यस्मिञ्जाते जातप्रमोदा नृत्यमय्य इवाजायन्त प्रजाः। पूरितासंख्यशङ्खशब्दमुखरं प्रहतपटहशतपटुरवं गम्भीरभेरीनिनादनिर्भरभरितभुवनं प्रमोदोन्मत्तमर्त्यलोकमनोहरं मासमेकं दिवसमिव महोत्सवमकरोन्नरपतिः।

अथान्यस्मिन्नतिक्रान्ते कस्मिंश्चित्काले कन्दलिनि कुड्मलितकदम्बतरौ रूढ[1]तोक्मतृणस्तम्बे स्तम्भिततामरसे विकसितचातकचेतसि मूकमानसौकसि नभसि मासि[2] देव्या देवक्या इव चक्रपाणिर्यशोमत्या हृदये गर्भे च सममेव सम्बभूव हर्षः। शनैः शनैश्चास्याः सर्वप्रजापुण्यैरिव परिगृहीता भूयोऽप्यापाण्डुतामङ्गयष्टिर्जगाम। गर्भारम्भेण श्यामायमानचारुचूचुकचूलिकौ चक्रवर्तिनः पातुं मुद्रिताविव[3] पयोधरकलशौ बभार[4]। स्तन्यार्थमाननिहिता दुग्धनदीव दीर्घस्निग्धधवला माधुर्यमधत्त दृष्टिः। सकलमङ्गलगणाधिष्ठितगात्रगरिम्णेव गतिरमन्दायत। मन्दं मन्दं सञ्चरन्त्या निर्मलमणिकुट्टिमनिमग्नप्रतिबिम्बनिभेन गृहीतपादपल्लवा पूर्वसेवामिवारेभे पृथिव्यस्याः। दिवसमधिशयानायाः शयनीयगपाश्रयपत्रभङ्गपुत्रिकाप्रतिमा विमलकपोलोदरगता प्रसवसमयं प्रतिपालयन्ती लक्ष्मीरिवालक्ष्यत। क्षपासु सौधशिखराग्रगताया गर्भोन्माथमुक्तांशुके स्तनमण्डले संक्रान्तमुडुपतिमण्डलमुपरि गर्भस्य श्वेतातपत्रमिव केनापि धार्यमाणमदृश्यत। सुप्ताया वासभवने चित्रभित्तिचामरग्राहिण्योऽपि चामराणि चालयांचक्रुः। स्वप्नेषु करविधृतकमलिनीपलाशपुटसलिलैश्चतुर्भिरपि दिक्करिभिरक्रियताभिषेकः। प्रतिबुध्यमानायाश्च चन्द्रशालिकासालभञ्जिकापरिजनोऽपि जयशब्दमसकृदजनयत्। परिजनाह्वानेष्वादिशेत्यशरीरा वाचो निश्चेरुः। क्रीडायामपि नासहताज्ञाभङ्गम्। अपि च चतुर्णामपि महार्णवानामेकीकृतेनाम्भसा स्नातुं वाञ्छा बभूव। वेला-

---

१ अ omits रूढ. २ अ omits मासि. ३ 'मुद्रिताविव जतुना' ब.
४ 'बभारोरुस्थलम्' ब.

वनलतागृहोदरपुलिनपरिसरेषु पर्यटितुं हृदयमभिललाष । आत्ययिकेष्वपि कार्येषु सविभ्रमं भ्रूलता चचाल । सन्निहितेष्वपि मणिदर्पणेषु मुखमुत्खाते खड्गपट्टे वीक्षितुं व्यसनमासीत् । उत्सारितवीणाः स्त्रीजनविरुद्धा ''नुर्ध्वनयः श्रुतावसुखायन्त । पञ्जरकेसरिषु चक्षुररमत । गुरुप्रणामेष्वपि स्तम्भितमिव शिरः कथमपि ननाम । सख्यश्चास्याः प्रमोदविस्फारितैर्लोचनपुटैरासन्नप्रसवमहोत्सवधियेव धवलयन्त्यो भवनं विकचकुमुदकमलकुवलयपलाशवृष्टिमयं रक्षाबलिविधिमिवानवरतं विदधाना दिक्षु क्षणमपि न मुमुचुः पार्श्वम् । आत्मोचितस्थाननिषण्णाश्च महान्तो विविधौषधिधरा भिषजो भूधरा इव भुवो धृतिं चक्रुः । पयोनिधीनां हृदयानीव लक्ष्म्या सहागतानि ग्रीवासूत्रग्रन्थिषु प्रशस्तरत्नान्यबध्यन्त ।

ततश्च प्राप्ते ज्येष्ठामूलीये मासि बहुलासु बहुलपक्षद्वादश्यां व्यतीते प्रदोषसमये समारुरुक्षति क्षपायौवने सहसैवान्तःपुरे समुदपादि कोलाहलः स्त्रीजनस्य । निर्गत्य च ससंभ्रमं यशोमत्याः स्वयमेव हृदयनिर्विशेषा धात्र्याः सुता सुयात्रेति[1] नाम्ना राज्ञः पादयोर्निपत्य 'देव, दिष्ट्या वर्धसे द्वितीयसुतजन्मना' इति व्याहरन्ती पूर्णपात्रं जहार ।

अस्मिन्नेव च काले राज्ञः परमसंमतः शतशः संवादितातीन्द्रियादेशो दर्शितप्रभावः सङ्कलिती[2] ज्योतिषि सर्वासां ग्रहसंहितानां पारदृश्वा सकलगणकमध्ये महितो हितश्च त्रिकालज्ञानभाग्भोजकस्तारको नाम गणकः समुपसृत्य विज्ञापितवान्—'देव, श्रूयताम्[3] । मान्धाता किलैवंविधे व्यतीपातादिसर्वदोषाभिषङ्गरहितेऽहनि सर्वेषूच्चस्थानस्थितेष्वेवं ग्रहेष्वीदृशि लग्ने भेजे जन्म । अर्वाक्ततोऽस्मिन्नन्तराले पुनरेवंविधे योगे चक्रवर्तिजनने नाजनि जगति कश्चिदपरः । सप्तानां चक्रवर्तिनामग्रणीश्चक्रवर्तिचिह्नानां महारत्नानां च भाजनं सप्तानां सागराणां पालयिता सप्ततन्तूनां सर्वेषां प्रवर्तयिता सप्तसप्तिसमः सुतोऽयं देवस्य जातः' इति ।

अत्रान्तरे स्वयमेवानाध्माता अपि तारमधुरं शङ्खा विरेसुः । अताडितोऽपि क्षुभितजलनिधिजलध्वनिधीरं जुगुञ्जाभिषेकदुन्दुभिः । अनाहतान्यपि मङ्गलतूर्याणि रेणुः । सर्वभुवनाभयघोषणापटह इव दिगन्तरेषु बभ्राम तूर्यप्रतिशब्दः । विधुतकेसरसटाश्च साटोपगृहीतहरितदूर्वापल्लवकवलप्रशस्तैर्मुखपुटैः समहेषन्त हृष्टा वाजिनः । सलीलमुत्क्षिप्तैर्हस्तपल्लवैर्नृत्यन्त इव श्रवणसुभगं जगर्जुर्गजाः । ववौ चाचिराच्चक्रायुधमुत्सृजन्त्या लक्ष्म्या निःश्वास इव सुरामोदसुरभिर्दिव्यानिलः । यज्वनां मन्दिरेषु प्रदक्षिणशिखाकलापकथितकल्याणागमाः प्रजज्वलुरनिन्धना वैतानवह्नयः । भुवस्तलात्तपनीयशृङ्खलाबन्धबन्धुरकलशीकोशाः समुदगुर्महानिधयः । प्रहतमङ्गलतूर्यप्रतिशब्दनिभेन दिक्षु दिक्पालैरपि प्रमोदादक्रियतेव दिष्टवृद्धिकलकलः । तत्क्षण एव च शुक्लवाससो

---

१ 'सुपात्रेति' ब. २ 'सङ्कलितो' ब. ३ 'श्रूयते' ब.

ब्रह्ममुखाः कृतयुगप्रजापतय इव प्रजावृद्धये समुपतस्थिरे द्विजातयः। साक्षाद्धर्म इव शान्त्युदकफलहस्तस्तस्थौ पुरः पुरोधाः। पुरातन्यः स्थितय इवादृश्यन्त्यागता बान्धववृद्धाः। प्रलम्बश्मश्रुजालजटिलाननानि बहलमलपङ्ककलङ्ककालकायानि नश्यतः कलिकालस्य बान्धवकुलानीवाकुलान्यधावन्त मुक्तानि बन्धनवृन्दानि। तत्कालापक्रान्तस्याधर्मस्य शिबिरश्रेणय इवालक्ष्यन्त लोकविलुण्ठिता विपणिवीथ्यः। विलसदुन्मुखवामनकबधिरवृन्दवेष्टिताः साक्षाज्जातमातृदेवता इव बहुबालकव्याकुला ननृतुर्वृद्धधात्र्यः। प्रावर्तत च विगतराजकुलस्थितिरधःकृतप्रतीहाराकृतिरपनीतवेत्रिवेत्रो निर्दोषान्तःपुरप्रवेशः समस्वामिपरिजनो निर्विशेषबालवृद्धः समानशिष्टाशिष्टजनो दुर्ज्ञेयमत्तामत्तप्रविभागस्तुल्यकुलयुवतिवेश्यालापविलासः प्रनृत्तसकलकटकलोकः पुत्रजन्मोत्सवो महान्।

अपरेद्युरारभ्य सर्वाभ्यो दिग्भ्यः स्त्रीराज्यानीवावर्जितानि, असुरविवराणीवापावृतानि, नारायणावरोधानीव प्रचलितानि, अप्सरसामिव महीमवतीर्णानि कुलानि, परिजनेन पृथुकरण्डपरिगृहीताः स्नानीयचूर्णावकीर्णकुसुमाः सुमनःस्रजः, स्फटिकशिलाशकलशुक्लकर्पूरखण्डपूरिताः पात्रीः, कुङ्कुमाधिवासभाञ्जि भाजनानि च मणिमयानि, सहकारतैलतिम्यत्तनुखदिरकेसरजालजटिलानि चन्दनधवलपूगफलफालीदन्तुरदन्तशफरुकाणि, गुञ्जन्मधुकरकुलपीयमानपारिजातपरिमलानि पाटल[1]कानि च, सिन्दूरपात्राणि च पिष्टातकपात्राणि च बाललतालम्बमानविटकवीटकांश्च ताम्बूलवृक्षकान्बिभ्राणेनानुगम्यमानानि चरण[2]निकुट्टनरणितमणिनूपुरमुखरितदिङ्मुखानि नृत्यन्ति राजकुलमागच्छन्ति समन्तात्सामन्तान्तःपुरसहस्राण्यदृश्यन्त।

शनैः शनैर्व्यजृम्भत च क्वचिन्नृत्तानुचितचिरन्तनशालीनकुलपुत्रकलोकलास्यप्रथितपार्थिवानुरागः क्वचिदन्तःस्मितक्षितिपालापेक्षितक्षीबक्षुद्रदासीसमाकृष्यमाणराजवल्लभः क्वचिन्मत्तकटककुट्टनीकण्ठलग्नवृद्धार्यसामन्तनृत्तनिर्भरहसितनरपतिः क्वचित्क्षितिपाक्षिसंज्ञादिष्टदुष्टदासेरकगीतसूच्यमानसचिवचौर्यरतप्रपञ्चः क्वचिन्मदोत्कटकुटहारिकापरिष्वज्यमानजरत्प्रव्रजितजनितजनहासः क्वचिदन्योन्यनिर्भरस्पर्धोद्धुरविटचेट[3]कारब्धावाच्यवचनयुद्धः क्वचिन्नृपाबलाबलात्कारनर्त्यमाननृत्यानभिज्ञान्तःपुरपालभावितभुजिष्यः, सपर्वत इव कुसुमराशिभिः, सधारागृह इव सीधुप्रपाभिः, सनन्दनवन इव पारिजातकामोदैः, सनीहार इव कर्पूररेणुभिः, साट्टहास इव पटहरवैः, सामृतमथन इव कलकलैः, सावर्त इव रासकमण्डलैः, सरोमाञ्च इव भूषणमणिकिरणैः, सपट्टबन्ध इव चन्दनललाटिकाभिः, सप्रसव इव प्रतिशब्दकैः, सप्ररोह इव प्रसाददानैरुत्सवामोदः।

---

१ 'पाटलानि पोटलकानि च सिन्दूर०' अ. २ 'चरणानि कुट्टन० ब. ३ 'चेटकपेटकारब्ध॰ ब.

स्कन्धावलम्बमानकेसरमालाः काम्बोजवाजिन इवास्कन्दन्तस्तरलतारका हरिणा इवोड्डीयमानाः सगरसुता इव खनित्रैर्निर्दयैश्चरणाभिघातैर्दारयन्तो भुवमनेकसहस्रसंख्याश्चिक्रीडुर्युवानः। कथमपि तालावचरचारणचरणक्षोभं चक्षमे क्षमा। क्षितिपालकुमारकाणां खेलतामन्योन्यास्फालैराभरणेषु मुक्ताफलानि फेलुः। सिन्दूररेणुना पुनरुत्पन्नहिरण्यगर्भगर्भशोणितशोणाशमिव ब्रह्माण्डकपालमभवत्। पटवासपांशुपटलेन प्रकटितमन्दाकिनीसैकतसहस्रमिव शुशुभे नभस्तलम्। विप्रकीर्यमाणपिष्टातकपरागपिञ्जरितातपा भुवनक्षोभविशीर्णपितामहकमलकिञ्जल्करजोराजिरञ्जिता इव रेजुर्दिवसाः। सङ्घट्टविघटितहारपतितमुक्ताफलपटलेषु चस्खाल लोकः।

स्थानस्थानेषु च मन्दमन्दमास्फाल्यमानालिङ्ग्यकेन[1] शिञ्जानमञ्जुवेणुना झणझणायमानझल्लरीकेण ताड्यमानतन्त्रीपटहिकेन वाद्यमानानुत्तानालाबु[2]वीणेन कलकांस्यकोशीक्वणितकाहलेन समकालदीयमानानुत्तालतानकेनातो[3]द्यवाद्येनानुगम्यमानाः, पदेपदे झणझणितभूषणरवैरपि सहृदयैरिवानुवर्त[4]मानताललयाः, कोकिला इव मदकलकाकलीकोमलालापिन्यो विटानां कर्णामृतान्यश्लीलरासकपदानि गायन्त्यः, समुण्डमालिकाः, सकर्णपल्लवाः, सचन्दनतिलकाः, समुच्छ्रिताभिर्वलयावलीवाचालाभिर्बाहुलतिकाभिः सवितारमिवालिङ्गयन्त्यः, कुङ्कुमप्रमृष्टिरुचिरकायाः काश्मीरकिशोर्य इव वल्गन्त्यः, नितम्बबिम्बलम्बिविकटकुरण्टकशेखराः प्रदीप्ता इव रागाग्निना, सिन्दूरच्छटाच्छुरितमुखमुद्राः शासनपट्टपङ्क्तय इवाप्रतिहतशासनस्य कन्दर्पस्य, मुष्टिप्रकीर्यमाणकर्पूरपटवासपांसुलमनोरथसञ्चरणरथ्या इव यौवनस्योद्दामकुसुमदामताडिततरुणजनाः प्रतीहार्य इव तरुणमहोत्सवस्य, प्रचलत्पत्रकुण्डला लसन्त्यो लता इव मदनचन्दनद्रुमस्य, ललितपदहंसकरवमुखराः समुल्लसन्त्यो वीचय इव शृङ्गाररस[5]सागरस्य, वाच्यावाच्यविवेकशून्या बालक्रीडा इव सौभाग्यस्य, घनपटहरवोत्कण्टकितगात्रयष्टयः केतक्य इव कुसुमधूलिमुद्गिरन्त्यः, कमलिन्य इव दिवसमुत्फुल्लाननाः, कुमुदिन्य इव रात्रावनुपजातनिद्राः, आविष्टा इव नरेन्द्रवृन्दपरिवृताः, प्रीतय इव हृदयमपहरन्त्यः, गीतय इव रागमुद्दीपयन्त्यः, पुष्टय इवानन्दमुत्पादयन्त्यः, मदमपि मदयन्त्य इव, रागमपि रञ्जयन्त्य इव, आनन्दमपि आनन्दयन्त्य इव, नृत्यमपि नर्तयमाना इव, उत्सवमप्युत्सुकयन्त्य[6] इव, कटाक्षेक्षितेषु पिबन्त्य इवापाङ्गशुक्तिभिः, तर्जनेषु संयमयन्त्य इव नखमयूखपाशैः, कोपाभिनयेषु ताडयन्त्य इव भ्रूलताविभागैः, प्रणयसम्भाषणेषु वर्षन्त्य इव सर्वरसान्, चतुरचङ्क्रमणेषु विकिरन्त्य इव विकारान्, पण्यविलासिन्यः प्रानृत्यन्।

---

१ '०मानलिङ्गकेन' ब. २ 'अनुत्तालालाबु०' ब. ३ ०'तालिकेन' ब. ४ 'अनुवर्त्यमान०' ब. ५ 'शृङ्गाररसस्य' अ. ६ 'उत्सवयन्त्यः' ब.

अन्यत्र वेत्रिवेत्रवित्रासितजनदत्तान्तरालाः, ध्रियमाणधवलातपत्रवना वनदेवता इव कल्पतरुतलविचारिण्यः, काश्चित्स्कन्धोभयपालीलम्बमानलम्बोत्तरीयलग्नहस्ता[1] लीलादोलाधिरूढा इव प्रेङ्खन्त्यः, काश्चित्कनककेयूरकोटिपाट्यमानपट्टांशुकोत्तरङ्गास्तरङ्गिण्य इव तरच्चक्रवाकसीमन्त्यमानस्रोतसः, काश्चिदुद्धूयमानधवलचामरसटालग्नत्रिकण्टकवलितविकटकटाक्षाः सरस्य इव हंसाकृष्यमाणनीलोत्पलवनाः, काश्चिच्चलच्चरणच्युतालक्तकारुणस्वेदशीकरसिच्यमानभवनहंसाः संध्यारागरज्यमानेन्दुबिम्बा इव कौमुदीरजन्यः, काश्चित्कण्ठनिहितकाञ्चनकाञ्चीगुणाञ्चितकञ्चुकिविकारा[2]कुञ्चितभ्रुवः कामवागुरा इव प्रसारितबाहुपाशा राजमहिष्यः प्रारब्धनृत्या विलेसुः[3]।

सर्वतश्च नृत्यतः स्त्रैणस्य गलद्भिः पदालक्तकैररुणिता रागमयीव शुशोण क्षोणी। समुल्लसद्भिः स्तनमण्डलैर्मङ्गलकलशमय इव बभूव महोत्सवः। भुजलताविक्षेपैर्मृणालवलयमय इव रराज जीवलोकः। समुल्लसद्भिर्विलासस्मितैस्तडिन्मय इवाक्रियत कालः। चञ्चलानां चक्षुषामंशुभिः कृष्णसा[4]रमया इवासन्वासराः। समुल्लसद्भिः शिरीषकुसुमस्तबककर्णपूरैः शुकपिच्छमय इव हरितच्छायोऽभूदातपः। विस्रंसमानैर्धम्मिल्लतमालपल्लवैः कज्जलमयमिवालक्ष्यतान्तरिक्षम्। उत्क्षिप्तैर्हस्तकिशलयैः कमलिनीमय्य इव बभासिरे सृष्टयः। माणिक्येन्द्रायुधानामर्चिषा चाषपत्रमया इव चकाशिरे रविमरीचयः। रणतामाभरणगणानां प्रतिशब्दकैः किङ्किणीमय्य इव शिशिञ्जिरे दिशः। जरत्योऽप्युन्मादिन्य इव रमण्यो रेणुः। वर्षीयांसोऽपि ग्रहगृहीता इव नापत्रेपिरे। विद्वांसोऽपि मत्ता इवात्मानं विसस्मरुः। निनर्तिषया मुनीनामपि मनांसि विपुस्फुलुः। सर्वस्वं च ददौ नरपतिः। दिशि दिशि कुबेरकोषा इवालुप्यन्त लोकेन द्रविणराशयः।

एवं च वृत्ते तस्मिन्महोत्सवे शनैः शनैः पुनरप्यतिक्रामति काले, देवे चोत्तमाङ्गनिहितरक्षासर्षपे[5], समुन्मिषत्प्रतापाग्निस्फुलिङ्ग इव गोरोचनापिञ्जरितवपुषि, समभिव्यज्यमानसहजक्षात्रतेजसीव हाटकबद्धविकटव्याघ्रनखपङ्क्तिमण्डितग्रीवके, हृदयोद्भिद्यमानदर्पाङ्कुर इव प्रथमाव्यक्तजल्पितेन सत्यस्य शनैः शनैरोंकारमिव कुर्वाणे, मुग्धस्मितैः कुसुमैरिव मधुकरकुलानि बन्धुहृदयान्याकर्षति, जननीपयोधरकलशपयःशीकरसेकादिव जायमानैर्विलासहसिताङ्कुरैर्दशनकैरलंक्रियमाणमुखकमलके, चारित्र इवान्तःपुरस्त्रीकदम्बकेन पाल्यमाने, मन्त्र इव सचिवमण्डलेन रक्ष्यमाणे, वृत्त इव कुलपुत्रकलोकेनामुच्यमाने, यशसीवात्म[6]वंशेन संवर्ध्यमाने, मृगपतिपोत इव रक्षिपुरुषशस्त्रपञ्जरमध्यगते, धात्रीकराङ्गुलिलग्ने पञ्चषाणि पदानि प्रयच्छति हर्षे, षष्ठं

---

१ '०लग्ना लीला०' अ. २ 'विकारकुञ्चितभुवः' ब. ३ 'विरेसुः' ब. ४ 'कृष्णशार०' अ. ५ '०सर्षपकणे' ब. ६ 'आत्मवशेन' ब.

त्रभङ्गपुत्रिकाप्रतिविम्बगर्भकपोलं मुखं चन्द्रमसमिव हृदयस्थितरोहिणीक-मुद्वहन्तम्, अचपलस्तिमिततारकेणाधोमुखेन चक्षुषा शिक्षयन्तमिव लक्ष्मी-लाभोत्तानितमुखानि पङ्कजवनानि विनयम्, स्वाम्यनुरागमिव म्लातकमु-त्तंसीकृतं शिरसा धारयन्तम्, निर्दयया कङ्कणभङ्गभीतसकलकार्मुकार्पि-तामिव नम्रतां प्रकाशयन्तम्, शैशव एव निर्जितैरिन्द्रियैररिभिरिव संयतैः शो-भमानम्, प्रणयिनीमिव विश्वासभूमिं कुलपुत्रतामनुवर्तमानम्, तेजस्विनमपि शीलेनाह्लादकेन सवितारमिव शशिनान्तर्गतेन विराजमानम्, अचलानामपि कायकार्कश्येन गन्धनमिवाचरन्तम्, दर्शनक्रीतमानन्दहस्ते विक्रीणानमिव जनं सौभाग्येन कुमारगुप्तम्, पृष्ठतस्तस्य कनीयांसमतिप्रांशुतया गौरतया च मनःशिलाशैलमिव सञ्चरन्तम्, अम्लानमालतीकुसुमशेखरनिभेन निर्जि-गमिषता गुरुणा शिरसि चुम्बितमिव यशसा, परस्परविरुद्धयोर्विनययौवन-योश्चिरात्प्रथमसङ्गमचिह्नमिव भ्रूसङ्गतकेन कथयन्तम्, अतिधीरतया हृदय-निहितां स्वामिभक्तिमिव निश्चलां दृष्टिं धारयन्तम्, अच्छाच्छचन्दनरसानु-लेपशीतलं सन्निहितहारोपधानं वक्षःस्थलमनन्तसामन्तसंक्रान्तिश्रान्तायाः श्रियो विशालं शशिमणिशिलापट्टशयनमिव बिभ्राणम्, चक्षुः कुरङ्गैर्घोणा-वंशं वराहैः स्कन्धपीठं महिषैः प्रकोष्ठबन्धं व्याघ्रैः पराक्रमं केसरिभिर्गमनं मतङ्गजैर्मृगयाक्षपितशेषैर्भीतैरुत्कोचमिव दत्तं दर्शयन्तं माधवगुप्तं ददृशतुः।

प्रविश्य च तौ दूरादेव चतुर्भिरङ्गैरुत्तमाङ्गेन च गां स्पृशन्तौ नमश्चक्रतुः। स्निग्धनरेन्द्रदृष्टिनिर्दिष्टामुचितां भूमिं भेजाते। मुहूर्तं च स्थित्वा भूपतिरा-दिदेश तौ—'अद्यप्रभृति भवद्भ्यां कुमारावनुवर्तनीयौ। [1]अहर्निशमस्तापर-व्यापाराभ्यां प्रतिबिम्बकाभ्यामिवाङ्गभूताभ्यामनयोः कुमारयोश्चरतोस्तिष्ठतोः स्वपतोर्जाग्रतोश्चान्तिकं क्षणमपि न मोक्तव्यम्। एवं वामचिरात्सकलाः सङ्कल्पाः कल्पतरव इवाभिमतफलसम्पदुत्कर्षविशेषप्रदा भविष्यन्ति' इत्या-कर्ण्य 'यथाज्ञापयति देवः' इति मेदिनीदोलायमान[2]मौलिभ्यां युगपदभिहिते ताभ्यामुत्थाय राज्यवर्धनहर्षौ पितरं प्रणेमतुः। आदाय च तौ निर्जग्मतुः। ततश्चारभ्य क्षणमपि निमेषोन्मेषाविव चक्षुर्गोचरादनपयान्तावुच्छ्वासनिःश्वा-साविव नक्तन्दिवमभिमुखं स्थितौ भुजाविव सततं पार्श्ववर्तिनौ कुमारयोस्तौ बभूवतुः।

अथ राज्यश्रीरपि नृत्यगीतादिषु विदग्धासु सखीषु सकलासु कलासु च प्रतिदिवसमुपचीयमानपरिचया शनैः शनैरवर्धत परिमितैरेव च दिवसैर्यौवन-मारुरोह। निपेतुरेकस्यां तस्यां शरा इव लक्ष्यभुवि भूभुजां सर्वेषां दृष्टयः। दूतप्रेषणादिभिश्च तां ययाचिरे राजानः। कदाचित्तु राजान्तःपुरप्रासादस्थितो बाह्यकक्ष्यावस्थितेन पुरुषेण स्वप्रस्तावागतां गीयमानामार्यामशृणोत्—

---

१ 'अहर्निश...भविष्यन्ति' इति नास्ति अ-पुस्तके. २ 'मौलिभ्यामुत्थाय राज्यवर्ध-नहर्षौ प्रणेमतुः। तौ च पितरम्' अ.

'उद्वेगमहावर्ते पातयति पयोधरोन्नमनकाले[1]।
सरिदिव तटमनुवर्षं विवर्धमाना सुता पितरम् ॥ ५ ॥'

तां च श्रुत्वा पार्श्वस्थितां महादेवीमुत्सारितपरिजनो जगाद—

'देवि, तरुणीभूता वत्सा राज्यश्रीः। एतदीया गुणवत्तेव[2] क्षणमपि हृदयान्नापयाति मे चिन्ता। यौवनारम्भ एव च कन्यकानामिन्धनीभवन्ति पितरः सन्तापानलस्य। हृदयमन्धकारयति मे दिवसमिव पयोधरोन्नतिरस्याः। केनापि कृता धर्म्या नाभिमता मे स्थितिरियं यदङ्गसम्भूतान्यङ्कलालितान्यपरित्याज्यान्यपत्यकान्यकाण्ड एवागत्यासंस्तुतैर्नीयन्ते। एतानि तानि खल्वङ्कनस्थानानि संसारस्य। सेयं सर्वाभिभाविनी शोकाग्नेर्दाहशक्तिर्यदपत्यत्वे समानेऽपि जातायां दुहितरि दूयन्ते सन्तः। एतदर्थं जन्मकाल एव कन्यकाभ्यः प्रयच्छन्ति सलिलमश्रुभिः साधवः। एतद्भयादकृतदारपरिग्रहाः परिहृतगृहवसतयः शून्यान्यरण्यान्यधिशेरते मुनयः। को हि नाम सहेत[3] सचेतनो विरहमपत्यानाम्। यथा यथा समापतन्ति दूता वराणां वराकी लज्जमानेव चिन्ता तथा तथा नितरां प्रविशति मे हृदयम्। किं क्रियते। तथापि गृहगतैरनुगन्तव्या एव लोकवृत्तयः। प्रायेण च सत्स्वप्यन्येषु वरगुणेष्वभिजनमेवानुरुध्यन्ते धीमन्तः। धरणीधराणां च मूर्ध्नि स्थितो माहेश्वरः पादन्यास इव सकलभुवननमस्कृतो मौखरिवंशः[4]। तत्रापि तिलकभूतस्यावन्तिवर्मणः सूनुरग्रजो ग्रहवर्मा नाम ग्रहपतिरिव गां गतः पितुरन्यूनो गुणैरेनां प्रार्थयते। यदि भवत्या अपि मतिरनुमन्यते ततस्तस्मै दातुमिच्छामि' इत्युक्तवति भर्तरि दुहितृस्नेहकातरतरहृदया साश्रुलोचना महादेवी प्रत्युवाच—'आर्यपुत्र, संवर्धनमात्रोपयोगिन्यो धात्रीनिर्विशेषा भवन्ति खलु मातरः कन्यकानाम्। प्रदाने तु प्रमाणमासां पितरः। केवलं कृपाकृतविशेषः सुदूरेण तनयस्नेहादतिरिच्यते दुहितृस्नेहः। यथा[5] नेयं यावज्जीवमावयोरार्तिता प्रतिपद्यते तथार्यपुत्र एव जानाति' इति।

राजा तु जातनिश्चयो दुहितृदानं प्रति समाहूय सुतावपि विदितार्थावकार्षीत्। शोभने च दिवसे ग्रहवर्मणा कन्यां प्रार्थयितुं प्रेषितस्य पूर्वागतस्यैव प्रधानदूतपुरुषस्य करे सर्वराजकुलसमक्षं दुहितृदानजलमपातयत्। जातमुदि कृतार्थे गते च तस्मिन्नासन्नेषु च विवाहदिवसेषूद्दामदीयमानताम्बूलपटवासकुसुमप्रसाधितसर्वलोकम्, सकलदेशादिश्यमानशिल्पिसार्थागमनम्, अवनिपालपुरुषगृहीतसमग्रग्रामीणानीयमानोपकरणसम्भारम्, राजदौवारिकोपनीयमानानेकनृपोपायनम्, उपनिमन्त्रितागतबन्धुवर्गसंवर्गणव्यग्रराजवल्लभम्, लब्धमधुमदप्रचण्डचर्मकारकरपुटोल्लालितकोणपटुविघट्टनरणन्मङ्गलपटहम्, पिष्टपञ्चाङ्गुलमण्ड्यमानोलूखलमुसलशिलाद्युपकरणम्, अशेषाशा-

१ '०कालः' ब. २ 'गुणवृत्तेव' ब. ३ 'सहते विरह०' अ. ४ 'मौखरी' ब. ५ 'यथा यावज्जीव०' अ.

मुखाविर्भूतचारणपरम्परापूर्यमाण[1]प्रकोष्ठं प्रतिष्ठाप्यमानेन्द्राणीदैवतम्, सितकुसुमविलेपनवसनसत्कृतैः सूत्रधारैरादीयमानविवाहवेदीसूत्रपातम्, उत्कूर्चककरैश्च सुधाकर्परस्कन्धैरधिरोहिणीसमारूढैर्धवलीक्रियमाणप्रासादप्रतोलीप्राकारशिखरम्, क्षुण्णक्षाल्यमानकुसुम्भकसम्भाराम्भःप्लवपूररज्यमानजनपादपल्लवम्, निरूप्यमाणयौतकयोग्यमातङ्गतुरङ्गतरङ्गिताङ्गनम्, गणनाभियुक्तगणकगणगृह्यमाणलग्नगुणम्, गन्धोदकवाहिमकरमुखप्रणालीपूर्यमाणक्रीडावापीसमूहम्, हेमकारचक्रप्रक्रान्तहाटकघटनटाङ्कारवाचालितालिन्दकम्, उत्थापिताभिनवभित्तिपात्यमानबहलवालुकाकण्ठकालेपाकुलालेपकलोकम्, चतुरचित्रकरचक्रवाललिख्यमानमङ्गल्यालेख्यम्, लेप्यकारकदम्बकक्रियमाणमृण्मयमीनकूर्ममकरनारिकेलकदलीपूगवृक्षकम्, क्षितिपालैश्च स्वयमाबद्धकक्ष्यैः स्वाम्यर्पितकर्मशोभासम्पादनाकुलैः सिन्दूरकुट्टिमभूमीश्च मसृणयद्भिर्विनिहितसरसातर्पणहस्तान्विन्यस्तालक्तकपाटलांश्च चूताशोकपल्लवलाञ्छितशिखरानुद्वाहवितर्दिकास्तम्भानुत्तम्भयद्भिः प्रारब्धविविधव्यापारम्, आसूर्योदयाच्च प्रविष्टाभिः सतीभिः सुभगाभिः सुरूपाभिः सुवेशाभिरविधवाभिः सिन्दूररजोराजिराजितललाटाभिर्वधूवरगोत्रग्रहणगर्भाणि श्रुतिसुभगानि मङ्गलानि गायन्तीभिर्बहुविधवर्णकादिग्धाङ्गुलीभिर्ग्रीवासूत्राणि च चित्रयन्तीभिश्चित्रपत्त्रलतालेख्यकुशलाभिः कलशांश्च धवलिताञ्शीतलशाराजिरश्रेणीश्च मण्डयन्तीभिरभिन्नपुटकर्पासतूलपल्लवांश्च वैवाहिककङ्कणोर्णासूत्रसंनाहांश्च रञ्जयन्तीभिर्बलाशनाघृतघनीकृतकुङ्कुमकल्कमिश्रितांश्चाङ्गरागांल्लावण्यविशेषकृन्ति च मुखालेपनानि कल्पयन्तीभिः कक्कोलमिश्राः सजातीफलाः स्फुरत्स्फीतस्फाटिककर्पूरशकलखचितान्तराला लवङ्गमाला रचयन्तीभिः समन्तात्सामन्तसीमन्तिनीभिर्व्याप्तम्, बहुविधभक्तिनिर्माणनिपुणपुराणपौरपुरंध्रिबध्यमानैर्बद्धैश्चाचारचतुरान्तःपुरजरतीजनितपूजाराजमानर[2]जकरज्यमानै रक्तैश्चोभयपटान्तलग्नपरिजनप्रेङ्खोलितैश्छायासु शोष्यमाणैः शुष्कैश्च कुटिलक्रमरूपक्रियमाणपल्लवपरभागैरपरैरारब्धकुङ्कुमपङ्कस्थासकच्छुरणैरपरैरुद्धुजभुजिष्याभज्यमानभङ्गुरोत्तरीयैः क्षौमैश्च बादरैश्च दुकूलैश्च लालातन्तुजैश्चांशुकैश्च नेत्रैश्च निर्मोकनिभैरकठोररम्भागर्भकोमलैर्निःश्वासहार्यैः स्पर्शानुमेयैर्वासोभिः सर्वतः स्फुरद्भिरिन्द्रायुधसहस्रैरिव सञ्छादितम्, उज्ज्वलनिचोलकावगुण्ठ्यमानहंसकुलैश्च शयनीयैस्तारामुक्ताफलोपचीयमानैश्च कञ्चुकैरनेकोपयोगपाठ्यमानैश्चापरिमितैः पट्टपटीसहस्रैरभिनवरागकोमलै[3]र्दुकूलराजमानैश्च पटवितानैः स्तवरकनिवहनिरन्तरच्छाद्यमानसमस्तपटलैश्च मण्डपैरुल्बिणनेत्रपटवेष्ट्यमानैश्च स्तम्भैरुज्ज्वलं रमणीयं चौत्सुक्यदं च मङ्गल्यं चासीद्राजकुलम्।

१ 'प्रकोष्ठप्रतिष्ठाप्य०' अ. २ 'रजकमहादारजतरज्यमानैः' ब. ३ '०कोमलैर्दुकूल०' ब.

देवी तु यशोमती विवाहोत्सवपर्याकुलहृदया हृदयेन भर्तरि कुतूहलेन जामातरि स्नेहेन दुहितरि उपचारेण निमन्त्रितस्त्रीषु आदेशेन परिजने शरीरेण सञ्चरणे चक्षुषा कृताकृतप्रत्यवेक्षणेषु आनन्देन महोत्सवे एकापि बहुधा विभक्तेवाभवत्। भूपतिरप्युपर्युपरि विसर्जितोष्ट्रवामीजनितजामातृजोषः सत्यप्याज्ञासम्पादनदक्षे मुखेक्षणपरे परिजने समं पुत्राभ्यां दुहितृस्नेहविक्लवः सर्वं स्वयमकरोत्।

एवं च तस्मिन्नविधवामय[1] इव भवति राजकुले, मङ्गलमय इव जायमाने जीवलोके, चारणमयेष्विव लक्ष्यमाणेषु दिङ्मुखेषु, पटहमय इव कृतेऽन्तरिक्षे, भूषणमय इव भ्रमति परिजने, बान्धवमय इव दृश्यमाने सर्गे, निर्वृत्तिमय इवोपलक्ष्यमाणे काले, लक्ष्मीमय इव विजृम्भमाणे महोत्सवे, निधान इव सुखस्य फल इव जन्मनः परिणाम इव पुण्यस्य यौवन इव विभूतेर्यौवराज्य इव प्रीतेः सिद्धिकाल इव मनोरथस्य वर्तमाने, गण्यमान इव जनाङ्गुलीभिः, आलोक्यमान इव मार्गध्वजैः, प्रत्युद्गम्यमान इव मङ्गल्यवाद्यप्रतिशब्दकैः, आहूयमान इव मौहूर्तिकैः, आकृष्यमाण इव मनोरथैः, परिष्वज्यमान इव वधूसखीहृदयैराजगाम विवाहदिवसः। प्रातरेव प्रतीहारैः समुत्सारितनिखिलानिबद्धलोकं विविक्तमक्रियत राजकुलम्।

अथ महाप्रतीहारः प्रविश्य नृपसमीपम् 'देव, जामातुरन्तिकात्ताम्बूलदायकः पारिजातकनामा संप्राप्तः' इत्यभिधाय स्वाकारं युवानमदर्शयत्। राजा तु तं दूरादेव जामातृबहुमानाद्दर्शितादरः 'बालक, कच्चित्कुशली ग्रहवर्मा' इति पप्रच्छ। असौ तु समाकर्णितनराधिपध्वनिर्धावमानः कतिचित्पदान्युपसृत्य प्रसार्य च बाहू सेवाचतुरश्चिरं वसुन्धरायां निधाय मूर्धानमुत्थाय 'देव, कुशली यथाज्ञापयस्यर्चयति च देवं नमस्कारेण' इति व्यज्ञापयत्। आगतजामातृनिवेदनागतं च तं ज्ञात्वा कृतसत्कारं राजा 'यामिन्याः प्रथमे यामे विवाहकालात्ययकृतो यथा न भवति दोषः[2]' इति सन्दिश्य प्रतीपं प्राहिणोत्।

अथ सकलकमलवनलक्ष्मीं वधूमुख इव सञ्चार्य समवसिते वासरे, विवाहदिवसश्रियः पादपल्लव इव रज्यमाने सवितरि, वधूवरानुरागलघूकृतप्रेमलज्जितेष्विव विघटमानेषु चक्रवाकमिथुनेषु, सौभाग्यध्वज इव रक्तांशुकसुकुमारवपुषि नभसि स्फुरति संध्यारागे, कपोतकण्ठकर्बुरे वरयात्रागमनरजसीव कलुषयति दिङ्मुखानि तिमिरे, लग्नसम्पादनसज्ज इवोज्जिहाने ज्योतिर्गणे, विवाहमङ्गलकलश इवोदयशिखरिणा समुत्क्षिप्यमाणे वर्धमानधवलच्छाये ताराधिपमण्डले वधूवदनलावण्यज्योत्स्नापरिपीततमसि प्रदीपे वृथोदितमुपहसत्स्विव रजनिकरमुत्तानितमुखेषु कुमुदवनेष्वाजगाम मुहुर्मुहु-

१ 'अविधवाधन्ये' ब. २ 'दोषस्तथा विधीयतामिति' ब.

रुल्लासितस्फारस्फुरितारुणचामरैर्मनोरथैरिवोत्थितरागाग्रपल्लवैः पुरो धावमानैः पादातैरुत्कर्णकटकहयप्रतिहेषितदीयमानस्वागतैरिव वाजिनां वृन्दैश्चापूरितदिग्भागश्चलकर्णचामराणां चामीकरमयसर्वोपकरणानां वर्ण्कलम्बिनां बलिनां घण्टाटाङ्कारिणां करिणां घटाभिः घटयन्निव पुनरिन्दूदयविलीनमन्धकारं नक्षत्रमालामण्डितमुखीं करिणीं निशाकर इव पौरन्दरीं दिशमारूढः प्रकटितविविधविहगविरुतैस्तालावचरचारणैः पुरःसरैर्बालो वसन्त इवोपवनैः क्रियमाणकोलाहलो गन्धतैलावसेकसुगन्धिना दीपिकाचक्रवालस्यालोकेन कुङ्कुमपटवासधूलिपटलेनेव पिञ्जरीकुर्वन्सकलं लोकमुत्फुल्लमल्लिकामुण्डमालामध्याध्यासितकुसुमशेखरेण शिरसा हसन्निव सपरिवेशक्षपाकरं कौमुदीप्रदोषमात्मरूपनिर्जितमकरकेतुकरापहृतेन कार्मुकेणेव कौसुमेन दाम्ना विरचितवैकक्ष्यकविलासः कुसुमसौरभगर्वभ्रान्तभ्रमरकुलकलप्रलापसुभगः पारिजात इव जातः श्रिया सह पुनरवतारितो मेदिनीं नववधूवदनावलोकनकुतूहलेनेव कृष्यमाणहृदयः पतन्निव मुखेन प्रत्यासन्नलग्नो ग्रहवर्मा ।

राजा तु तमुपद्वारमागतं चरणाभ्यामेव राजचक्रानुगम्यमानः ससुतः प्रत्युज्जगाम । अवतीर्णं च तं कृतनमस्कारं मन्मथमिव माधवः प्रसारितभुजो गाढमालिलिङ्ग । यथाक्रमं परिष्वक्तराज्यवर्धनहर्षं च हस्ते गृहीत्वाभ्यन्तरं निन्ये । स्वनिर्विशेषासनदानादिना चैनमुपचारेणोपचचार ।

नचिराच्च गम्भीरनामा नृपतेः प्रणयी विद्वान्द्विजन्मा ग्रहवर्माणमुवाच—'तात, त्वां प्राप्य चिरात्खलु राज्यश्रिया घटितौ तेजोमयौ सकलजगद्गीयमानबुधकर्णानन्दकारिगुणगणौ सोमसूर्यवंशाविव पुष्पभूतिमुखरवंशौ । प्रथममेव कौस्तुभमणिरिव गुणैः स्थितोऽसि हृदये देवस्य । इदानीं तु शशीव शिरसा परमेश्वरेणासि वोढव्यो जातः' इति । एवं वदत्येव तस्मिन्नृपमुपसृत्य मौहूर्तिकाः 'देव, समासीदति लग्नवेला व्रजतु जामाता कौतुकगृहम्' इत्यूचुः । अथ नरेन्द्रेण 'उत्तिष्ठ गच्छ' इति गदितो ग्रहवर्मा प्रविश्यान्तःपुरं जामातृदर्शनकुतूहलिनीनां स्त्रीणां पतितानि लोचनसहस्राणि विकचनीलकुवलयवनानीव लङ्घयन्नाससाद कौतुकगृहद्वारम् । निवारितपरिजनश्च प्रविवेश ।

अथ तत्र कतिपयाप्तप्रियसखीस्वजनप्रमदाप्रायपरिवाराम्, अरुणांशुकावगुण्ठितमुखीं प्रभातसंध्यामिव स्वप्रभया निष्प्रभान्प्रदीपकान्कुर्वाणाम्, अतिसौकुमार्यशङ्कितेनेव यौवनेन नातिनिर्भरमुपगूढाम्, साध्वसनिरुध्यमानहृदयदेशदुःखमुक्तैर्निभृतायतैः श्वसितैरपर्यान्तं कुमारभावमिवानुशोचन्तीम्, अत्युत्कम्पिनीं पतनभियेव त्रपया निष्पन्दं धार्यमाणाम्, हस्तं तामरसप्रतिपक्षमासन्नग्रहणं शशिनमिव रोहिणीं भयवेपमानमानसामवलोकयन्तीम्,

चन्दनधवलतनुलतां ज्योत्स्नादानसञ्चितलावण्यात्कुमुदिनीगर्भादिव प्रसूताम्, कुसुमामोदनिर्हारिणीं वसन्तहृदयादिव निर्गताम्, निःश्वासपरिमलाकृष्टमधुकरकुलां मलयमारुतादिवोत्पन्नाम्, कृतकन्दर्पानुसरणां रतिमिव पुनर्जाताम्, प्रभालावण्यमदसौरभमाधुर्यैः कौस्तुभशशिमदिरापारिजातामृतप्रभवैः सर्वैरत्नगुणैरपरामिव सुरासुररुषा रत्नाकरेण कल्पितां श्रियम्, स्निग्धेन बालिकालोकेन सितसिन्धुवारकुसुममञ्जरीभिरिव मुक्तादीधितिभिः कल्पितकर्णावतंसाम्, कर्णाभरणमरकतप्रभाहरितशाद्वलेन कपोलस्थलीतलेन विनोदयन्तीमिव हारिणीं लोचनच्छायाम्, अधोमुखीं वरकौतुकालोकनाकुलं मुहुर्मुहुः कृतमुखोन्नमनप्रयत्नं सखीजनं हृदयं च निर्भर्त्सयन्तीं वधूमपश्यत्।

प्रविशन्तमेव तं हृदयचौरं वध्वा समर्पितं जग्राह कन्दर्पः। परिहासस्मेरमुखीभिश्च नारीभिः कौतुकगृहे यद्यत्कार्यते जामाता तत्तत्सर्वमतिपेशलं चकार। कृतपरिणयानुरूपवेशपरिग्रहां गृहीत्वा करे वधूं निर्जगाम। जगाम च नवसुधाधवलां निमन्त्रितागतैस्तुषारशैलोपत्यकामिव त्र्यम्बकाम्बिकाविवाहाहूतैर्भूभृद्भिः परिवृताम्, सेकसुकुमारयवाङ्कुरदन्तुरैः पञ्चास्यैः कलशैः कोमलवर्णिकाविचित्रैरमित्रमुखैश्च मङ्गल्यफलहस्ताभिरञ्जलिकारिकाभिरुद्भासितपर्यन्ताम्, उपाध्यायोपश्रीयमानेन्धनधूमायमानाभिसन्धुक्षणाक्षणिकोपद्रष्टृद्विजाम्, उपकृशानुनिहितानुपहतहरितकुशाम्, संनिहितदृषदजिनाज्यस्रुक्समित्पूलीनिवहाम्, नूतनशूर्पार्पितश्यामलशमीपलाशमिश्रलाजहासिनीं वेदीम्। आरुरोह च तां दिवमिव सज्योत्स्नः शशी। समुत्ससर्प च वेल्लितारुणशिखापल्लवस्य शिखिनः कुसुमायुध इव रतिद्वितीयो रक्ताशोकस्य समीपम्। हुते च हुतभुजि दक्षिणावर्तप्रवृत्ताभिर्वधूवदनविलोकनकुतूहलिनीभिरिव ज्वालाभिरेव सह प्रदक्षिणं बभ्राम। पात्यमाने च लाजाञ्जलौ नखमयूखधवलिततनुरदृष्टपूर्ववधूवररूपविस्मयस्मेर इवादृश्यत विभावसुः।

अत्रान्तरे स्वच्छकपोलोदरसंक्रान्तमनलप्रतिबिम्बमिव निर्वापयन्ती स्थूलमुक्ताफलविमलबाष्पबिन्दुसन्दोहदर्शितदुर्दिना निर्वेदनविकारं रुरोद वधूः। उदश्रुविलोचनानां च बान्धववधूनामुदपादि महानाक्रन्दः। परिसमापितवैवाहिकक्रियाकलापस्तु जामाता वध्वा समं प्रणनाम श्वशुरौ। प्रविवेश च द्वारपक्षलिखितरतिप्रीतिदैवतं प्रणयिभिरिव प्रथमप्रविष्टैरलिकुलैः कृतकोलाहलम्, अलिकुलपक्षपवनप्रेङ्खोलितैः कर्णोत्पलप्रहारभयप्रकम्पितैरिव मङ्गलप्रदीपैः प्रकाशितम्, एकदेशलिखितस्तबकितरक्ताशोकतरुतलभाजाधिज्यचापेन तिर्यक्कूणितनेत्रत्रिभागेण शरमृजूकुर्वता कामदेवेनाधिष्ठितम्, एकपार्श्वन्यस्तेन काञ्चनाचामरुकेणेतरपार्श्ववर्तिन्या च दान्तशफरुकधारिण्या कनकपुत्रिकया साक्षाल्लक्ष्म्येवोद्दण्डपुण्डरीकहस्तया सनाथेन सोपधानेन स्वास्तीर्णेन

१ 'प्रदक्षिणा०' ब. २ 'काञ्चनावामनकेन' ब.

शयनेन शोभमानम्, शयनशिरोभागस्थितेन च कृतकुमुदशोभेन कुसुमायुधसाहायकायागतेन शशिनेव निद्राकलशेन राजतेन विराजमानं वासगृहम्।

तत्र च ह्रीताया नववधूकायाः पराङ्मुखप्रसुप्तायाः मणिभित्तिदर्पणेषु मुखप्रतिबिम्बानि प्रथमालापाकर्णनकौतुकागतगृहदेवताननानीव मणिगवाक्षकेषु वीक्षमाणः क्षणदां निन्ये। स्थित्वा च श्वशुरकुले शीलेनामृतमिव श्वश्रूहृदये वर्षन्नभिनवाभिनवोपचारैरपुनरुक्तान्यानन्दमयानि दश दिनानि स्थित्वा दत्त्वा राजदौवारिकमिव राजकुले रणरणकं यौतकनिवेदितानीव शम्बलान्यादाय हृदयानि सर्वलोकस्य कथं कथमपि विसर्जितो नृपेण वध्वा सह स्वदेशमगमदिति।

इति श्रीबाणभट्टकृतौ हर्षचरिते चक्रवर्तिजन्मवर्णनं नाम चतुर्थ उच्छ्वासः।

पञ्चम उच्छ्वासः ।

नियतिर्विधाय पुंसां प्रथमं सुखमुपरि दारुणं दुःखम् ।
कृत्वालोकं तरला तडिदिव वज्रं निपातयति ॥ १ ॥

पातयति महापुरुषान्सममेव बहूननादरेणैव ।
परिवर्तमान एकः कालः शैलानिवानन्तः ॥ २ ॥

अथ कदाचिद्राजा राज्यवर्धनं कवचहरमाहूय हूणान्[1] हन्तुं हरिणानिव हरिर्हरिणेशकिशोरकमपरिमितबलानुयातं चिरन्तनैरमात्यैरनुरक्तैश्च महासामन्तैः कृत्वा साभिसरमुत्तरापथं प्राहिणोत् ।

प्रयान्तं च तं देवो हर्षः कतिचित्प्रयाणकानि तुरङ्गमैरनुवव्राज । प्रविष्टे च कैलासप्रभाभासिनीं ककुभं भ्रातरि वर्तमानो[2] नवे वयसि विक्रमरसानुरोधिनि केसरिशरभशार्दूलवराहबहुलेषु तुषारशैलोपकण्ठेषूत्कण्ठमानवनदेवताकटाक्षांशुशारितशरीरकान्तिः क्रीडन्मृगयां मृगलोचनः कतिपयान्यहानि बहिरेव व्यलम्बत । चकार चाकर्णान्ताकृष्टकार्मुकनिर्गतभासुरभल्लवर्षी स्वल्पीयोभिरेव दिवसैर्निःश्वापदान्यरण्यानि[3] । एकदा तु वासतेय्यास्तुरीये यामे प्रत्युषस्येव स्वप्ने चटुलज्वालापुञ्जपिञ्जरीकृतसकलककुभा दुर्निवारेण दवहुतभुजा दह्यमानं केसरिणमद्राक्षीत् । तस्मिन्नेव च दावदहने समुत्सृज्य शावकानुप्लुत्य चात्मानं पातयन्तीं सिंहीमपश्यत् । आसीच्चास्य चेतसि—'लोके हि लोहेभ्यः कठिनतराः खलु स्नेहमया बन्धनपाशाः, यदाकृष्टास्तिर्यञ्चोऽप्येवमाचरन्ति' इति । प्रबुद्धस्य चास्य मुहुर्मुहुर्दक्षिणेतरमक्षि पस्पन्दे । गात्रेषु चाकस्मादेव वेपथुर्विपप्रथे । निर्निमित्तमेवान्तर्बन्धनस्थानाच्चचालेव हृदयम् । अकारणादेव चाजायत गरीयसी दुःखासिका । किमिदमिति च समुत्पन्नविविधविकल्पविमथितमतिरपगतधृतिश्चिन्तावनमितवदनः स्तिमिततारकेण चक्षुषा समुद्भिद्यमानस्थलकमलिनीवनामिव चकार चकोरेक्षणः क्षणं क्षौणीम् । अह्नि च तस्मिञ्शून्येनैव च चेतसा चिक्रीड मृगयाम् । आरोहति च हरितहये मध्यमह्नो भवनमागत्योभयतो मन्दमन्दं संवाह्यमानतनुतालवृन्तः क्षितितलवितताममतिशिशिरमलयजरसलवलुलितवपुषमिन्दुधवलोपधानधारिणीं वेत्रपट्टिकामधिशयानः साशङ्क एव तस्थौ ।

अथ दूरादेव लेखगर्भया नीलीरागमेचकरुचा चैलचीरिकया[4] रचितमुण्डमालकम्, श्रमातपाभ्यामारोप्यमाणकायकालिमानमन्तर्गतेन शोकशिखिनाङ्गारतामिव नीयमानम्, अतित्वरागमनद्रुततरपदोद्धूयमानधूलिराजिव्याजेन राजवार्ताश्रवणकुतूहलिन्या मेदिन्येवानुगम्यमानम्, अभिमुखपवन-

१ 'हूनान्' ब. २ 'निवर्तमानो' ब. ३ 'निःश्वासप्रदानि' ब. ४ 'चीरचीरिकया' अ.

प्रेङ्खत्प्रविततोत्तरीयपटप्रान्तवीज्यमानोभयपार्श्वमतित्वरया कृतपक्षमिवाशु परापतन्तम्, प्रेर्यमाणमिव पृष्ठतः स्वाम्यादेशेन, कृष्यमाणमिव पुरस्तादायतैः श्रमश्वासमोक्षैः, स्विद्यल्ललाटतटघटमानप्रतिबिम्बकेन कार्यकौतुकादपह्रियमाणलेखमिव भास्वता, संभ्रमभ्रष्टैरिवेन्द्रियैः शून्यीकृतशरीरम्, लेखार्पितप्रयोजनगौरवादिव समेऽपि वर्त्मनि शून्यहृदयतया स्खलन्तम्, कालमेघशकलमिव पतिष्यतो दुर्वार्तावज्रस्य, धूमपल्लवमिव ज्वलिष्यतः शोकज्वलनस्य, बीजमिव फलिष्यतो दुष्कृतशालेरनिमित्तभूतदीर्घाध्वगं कुरङ्गकनामानमायान्तमद्राक्षीत् ।

दृष्ट्वा च पूर्वनिमित्तपरम्पराविर्भावितभीतिरभिद्यत हृदयेन । कुरङ्गकस्तु कृतप्रणामः समुपसृत्य प्रथममाननलग्नं विषादमुपनिन्ये, पश्चाल्लेखम् । तं च देवो हर्षः स्वयमेवादायावाचयत् । लेखार्थेनैव च समं गृहीत्वा हृदयेन सन्तापमवग्रहरूपोऽभ्यधात्—'कुरङ्गक, किं मान्द्यं तातस्य' इति । स चक्षुषा बाष्पजलबिन्दुभिर्मुखेन च खञ्जाक्षरैः क्षरद्भिर्युगपदाचचक्षे—'देव दाहज्वरो महान्' इति । तच्चाकर्ण्य सहसा सहस्रधेवास्य हृदयं पफाल । कृताचमनश्च जनयितुरायुष्कामोऽपरिमितमणिकनकरजतजातमात्मपरिबर्हमशेषं ब्राह्मणसादकरोत् । अभुक्त एवोच्चचाल । 'दापय वाजिनः पर्याणम्' इति च पुरःस्थितं शिरःकृपाणं बिभ्राणं बभाण युवानम् । वेपमानहृदयश्च संभ्रमप्रधावितपरिवर्धकोपनीतमारुह्य तुरङ्गमेकाक्येव प्रावर्तत ।

अकाण्डप्रयाणसंज्ञाशङ्खक्षुभितं तु संभ्रमात्सज्जीभूतमुद्धूतमुखरखुररवभरितसकलभुवनविवरमागत्यागत्य सर्वाभ्यो दिग्भ्यो धावमानमश्वीयमढौकत । प्रस्थितस्य चास्य प्रदक्षिणेतरं प्रयान्तो विनाशमुपस्थितं राजसिंहस्य हरिणाः प्रकटयांबभूवुः । अशिशिररश्मिमण्डलाभिमुखश्च हृदयमवदारयन्निव दावशुष्के दारुणि दारुणं रराण वायसः । कज्जलमय इव बहुदिवसमुपचितबहलमलपटलमलिनिततनुरभिमुखमाजगाम शिखिपिच्छालाञ्छनो नग्नाटकः । दुर्निमित्तैरनभिनन्द्यमानगमनश्च नितरामशङ्कत हृदयेन पितृस्नेहाहितप्रदिम्ना च तत्तदुपेक्षमाणस्तुरङ्गमस्कन्धबद्धलक्ष्यं चक्षुरविचलं दधानो दुःसमवसितहसितसङ्कथस्तूष्णींभूतेन भूपाललोकेनानुगम्यमानो बहुयोजनसम्पिण्डितमध्वानमेकेनैवाह्ना समलङ्घयत् ।

उपलब्धनरेन्द्रमान्द्यवार्ताविषण्ण इव नष्टतेजस्यधोमुखीभवति भगवति भानुमति भण्डिप्रमुखेन प्रणयिना राजपुत्रलोकेन बहुशो विज्ञाप्यमानोऽपि नाहारमकरोत् । पुरःप्रवृत्तप्रतीहारगृह्यमाणग्रामीणपरम्पराप्रकटितप्रगुणवर्त्मा च वहन्नेव निन्ये निशाम् ।

अन्यस्मिन्नहनि मध्यन्दिने विगतजयशब्दम्, अस्तमिततूर्यनादम्, उपसंहृतगीतम्, उत्सारितोत्सवम्, अप्रगीतचारणम्, अप्रसारितापणपण्यम्,

१ 'उत्तरीयकर्पट' ब.

स्थानस्थानेषु पवनबलकुटिलाभिः कोटिहोमधूमलेखाभिरुल्लसन्तीभिर्यममहिषविषाणकोटिभिरिवोल्लिख्यमानम्, कृतान्तपाशवागुराभिरिवावेष्ट्यमानम्, उपरि कालमहिषालङ्कारकालायसकिङ्किणीभिरिव कटु क्वणन्तीभिर्दिवसं वायसमण्डलीभिर्भ्रमन्तीभिरावेद्यमानप्रत्यासन्नाशुभम्, क्वचित्प्रतिशायितस्निग्धबान्धवाराध्यमानाहिर्बुध्नम्, क्वचिद्दीपिकादह्यमानकुलपुत्रकप्रसाद्यमानमातृमण्डलम्, क्वचिन्मुण्डोपहाराहरणोद्यतद्रविडप्रार्थ्यमानामर्दकम्, क्वचिदान्ध्रोद्क्रियमाणबाहुवप्रोपयाच्यमानचण्डिकम्, अन्यत्र शिरोविधृतविलीयमानगुग्गुलुविकलनवसेवकानुनीयमानमहाकालम्, अपरत्र निशितशस्त्रीनिकृत्तात्ममांसहोमप्रसक्तासवर्गम्, अपरत्र प्रकाशनरपतिकुमारकक्रियमाणमहामांसविक्रयप्रक्रमम्, उपहतमिव श्मशानपांशुभिरमङ्गलैरिव परिगृहीतम्, यातुधानैरिव विध्वस्तम्, कलिकालेनेव कवलितम्, पापपटलैरिव सञ्छादितम्, अधर्मविक्षेपैरिव लुण्ठितम्, अनित्यताधिकारैरिवाक्रान्तम्, नियतिविलासैरिवात्मीकृतम्, शून्यमिव सुप्तमिव मुषितमिव विलक्षितमिव छलितमिव मूर्छितमिव स्कन्धावारं समाससाद ।

प्रविशन्नेव च विपणिवर्त्मनि कुतूहलाकुलबहलबालकपरिवृतमूर्ध्वयष्टिविष्कम्भवितते वामहस्तवर्तिनि भीषणमहिषाधिरूढप्रेतनाथसनाथे चित्रवति पटे परलोकव्यतिकरमितरकरकलितेन शरकाण्डेन कथयन्तं यमपट्टिकं ददर्श । तेनैव च गीयमानं श्लोकमशृणोत्—

'मातापितृसहस्राणि पुत्रदारशतानि च ।
युगे युगे व्यतीतानि कस्य ते कस्य वा भवान् ॥ ३ ॥' इति

तेन चाधिकतरमवदीर्यमाणहृदयः क्रमेण राजद्वारं प्रतिषिद्धसकललोकप्रवेशं ययौ । तुरगादवतीर्णश्चाभ्यन्तरान्निष्क्रामन्तमप्रसन्नमुखरागमुन्मुक्तमिवेन्द्रियैः सुषेणनामानं वैद्यकुमारकमद्राक्षीत् । कृतनमस्कारं चाप्राक्षीत्—'सुषेण, अस्ति तातस्य विशेषो न वा' इति । सोऽब्रवीत्—'नास्तीदानीं यदि भवेत्कुमारं दृष्ट्वा' इति । मन्दं मन्दं द्वारपालैः प्रणम्यमानश्च दीयमानसर्वस्वम्, पूज्यमानकुलदेवतम्, प्रारब्धामृतचरुपचनक्रियम्, क्रियमाणषडाहुतिहोमम्, हूयमानपृषदाज्यलवलिप्तप्रचलद्दूर्वापल्लवम्, पठ्यमानमहामायूरीप्रवर्त्यमानगृहशान्तिनिर्वर्त्यमानभूतरक्षाबलिविधानम्, प्रयतविप्रप्रस्तुतसंहिताजपम्, जप्यमानरुद्रैकादशीशब्दायमानशिवगृहम्, अतिशुचिशैवसम्पाद्यमानविरूपाक्षक्षीरकलशसहस्रस्नपनम्, अजिरोपविष्टैश्चानासादितस्वामिदर्शनदूयमानमानसैरभ्यन्तरनिष्पतितनिकटवर्तिपरिजननिवेद्यमानवार्तैर्वार्तीभूतस्नानभोजनशयनैरुज्झितात्मसंस्कारमलिनवेशैर्लिखितैरिव निश्चलैर्नरपतिभिर्नीयमाननक्तन्दिवं दुःखदीनवदनेन च प्रघनेषु बद्धमण्डलेनोपांशुव्याहृतैः

१ 'दीपिकादहनदह्यमान०' ब. २ 'विलीयमानबहलगलद्गुग्गुलु०' ब. ३ 'अनित्यताधिकारैः' ब. ४ '०वान्तैः' ब.

केनचिच्चिकित्सकदोषानुद्भावयता, केनचिदसाध्यव्याधिलक्षणपदानि पठता, केनचिद्दुःस्वप्नानावेदयता, केनचित्पिशाचवार्तां विवृण्वता, केनचित्कार्तान्तिकादेशान्प्रकाशयता, केनचिदुपलिङ्गानि गायता, अन्येनानित्यतां भावयता संसारं चापवदता कलिकालविलसितानि च निन्दता दैवं चोपालभमानेनापरेण धर्माय कुप्यता राजकुलदेवताश्चाधिक्षिपता, अपरेण क्लिष्टकुलपुत्रकभाग्यानि गर्हयता, बाह्यपरिजनेन कथ्यमानकष्टपार्थिवावस्थं राजकुलं विवेश ।

अविरलबाष्पपयःपरिप्लुतलोचनेन पितृपरिजनेन वीक्ष्यमाणो विविधौषधिद्रव्यद्रवगन्धगर्भमुत्क्वथतां क्वाथानां सर्पिषां तैलानां च पच्यमानानां गन्धमाजिघ्रन्नवाप तृतीयं कक्ष्यान्तरम् ।

तत्र चातिनिःशब्दे गृहावग्रहणीग्राहिबहुवेत्रिणि, त्रिगुणतिरस्करिणीतिरोहितसुवीथीपथे, पिहितपक्षद्वारके, परिहृतकपाटरटिते, घटितगवाक्षरक्षितमरुति, दूयमानपरिचारके, चरणताडनस्वनत्सोपानप्रकुपितप्रतीहारे, निभृतसंज्ञानिर्दिश्यमानसकलकर्मणि, नातिनिकटोपविष्टकञ्चुकिनि,कोणस्थिताह्वानचकिताचमनवाहिनि, चन्द्रशालिकालीनमूकमौललोके, महाधिविधुरबान्धवाङ्गनावर्गगृहीतप्रच्छन्नप्रग्रीवके, सञ्जवनपुञ्जितोद्विग्नपरिजने, प्रविष्टकतिपयप्रणयिनि, गम्भीरज्वरारम्भभीतभिषजि, दुर्मनायमानमन्त्रिणि, मन्दायमानपुरोधसि, सीदत्सुहृदि, विद्राणविपश्चिति, सन्तप्तासमसामन्ते, विचित्तचामरग्राहिणि, दुःखक्षामशिरोरक्षिणि, क्षीयमाणप्रसादवित्तमनोरथसम्पदि, स्वामिभक्तिपरित्यक्ताहारहीयमानबलविकलवल्लभभूभृति, क्षितितलपतितसकलरजनीजागरूकराजपुत्रकुमारके, कुलक्रमागतकुलपुत्रकनिवहोह्यमानशुचिशोकसङ्कुचितकञ्चुकिनि, निरानन्दवन्दिनि, निःश्वसन्निराशासन्नसेवके, निःसृतताम्बूलधूसराधरवारयोषिति, विलक्षवैद्योपदिश्यमानपथ्याहरणावहितपौरोगवे, अनुजीविपीयमानोच्चंपकधारावारिविनोद्यमानास्यशोषरुजि, राजाभिलापभोज्यमानबहुभुजि, भेषजसामग्रीसम्पादनव्यग्रसमग्रव्यवहारिणि, मुहुर्मुहुराहूयमानतोयकर्मान्तिकानुमितघोरातुरतृषि, तुषारपरिकरितकरकशिशिरीक्रियमाणोदश्विति, श्वेतार्द्रकर्पटार्पितकर्पूरपरागशीतलीकृतशलाके, नाश्यानपङ्कलिप्यमाननवभाण्डगतगण्डूषग्रहणमस्तुनि, निम्यत्कोमलकमलिनीपलाशप्रावृतमृदुमृणालके, सनालनीलोत्पलपूलीसनाथसलिलपानभाजनभुवि, धारानिपातनिर्वाप्यमाणक्वथिताम्भसि, पटुपाटलशर्करामोदमुच्चि, मञ्चकाश्रितसिकतिलकर्करीनिश्रान्तान्तरचक्षुषि, सरसशैवलवलयितगलद्गोलयन्त्रके, गल्वर्कशालाजिरोल्लासितलाजसक्तुनिपीतमसारपारीपरिगृहीतकर्कशर्करे, शिशिरौपधरसचूर्णावकीर्णस्फटिकशुक्तिशङ्खसञ्चये, सञ्चितप्रचुरप्राचीनामलकमातुलुङ्गद्राक्षादाडिमादिफले, प्रतिग्राहितविप्रविप्रकीर्यमाणशान्त्युदकविप्रुषि, प्रेष्यापेष्यमाणल-

१ 'पीयमानोच्चचपक' ब. २ '°श्विनि' ब. ३ 'सरल' अ.

ललाटलेपोपदिग्धद्वपदि धवलगृहे स्थितम्, परलोकविजयाय नीराज्यमानमिव ज्वरज्वलनेनानवरतपरिवर्तनैस्तरङ्गिणि शयनीये शेषमिव विषोष्मणा क्षीरोदन्वति विचेष्टमानम्, मुक्ताफलवालुकाधूलिधवलितं जलधिमिव क्षयकाले शुष्यन्तम्, कालेन कैलासमिव दशाननेनोद्ध्रियमाणम्, अविरतचन्दनचर्चापराणां परिचारकाणामत्युष्णावयवस्पर्शभस्मीभूतोदरैरिव धवलैः करैः स्पृश्यमानं लोकान्तरप्रस्थितम्, स्थास्नुना स्वयशसैव चन्दनानुलेपनच्छलेनापृच्छ्यमानम्, अविच्छिन्नदीयमानकमलकुमुदेन्दीवरदलं कालकटाक्षपतनशबलमिव शरीरमुद्वहन्तम्, निबिडदुकूलपट्टनिपीडितकेशान्तकथ्यमानकष्टवेदनानुबन्धं मूर्धानं धारयन्तम्, दुर्धरवेदनोन्नमन्नीलशिराजालककरालेन च कालाङ्गुलिलिख्यमानलेखाख्यातमरणावधिदिवससंख्यानेनेव ललाटफलकेन भयमुपजनयन्तम्, आसन्नयमदर्शनोद्वेगादिव च किंचिदन्तःप्रविष्टतारकं चक्षुर्दधानम्, शुष्यद्दशनपङ्क्तिप्रसूतधूसरदीधितितरङ्गिणीं मृगतृष्णिकामिवोष्णां निश्वासपरम्परामुद्वहन्तम्, अत्युष्णनिश्वासदग्धयेव श्यामायमानया रसनया निवेद्यमानदारुणसन्निपातारम्भम्, उरःस्थलस्थापितमणिमौक्तिकहारचन्दनचन्द्रकान्तं कृतान्तदूतदर्शनयोग्यमिवात्मानं कुर्वाणम्, अङ्गभङ्गवलनोत्क्षिप्तभुजयुगलम्, पर्यस्तहस्तनखमयूखैर्धारागृहमिव तापशान्तये रचयन्तम्, नेदिष्ठसलिलमणिकुट्टिमादर्शोदरेषु निपतद्भिः प्रतिबिम्बैरपि सन्तापातिशयमिव कथयन्तम्, स्पृशन्तीं प्रणयिनीमिव विश्रामभूमिं मूर्छामपि बहु मन्यमानम्, अन्तकाह्वानाक्षरैरिव सभयभिषग्दष्टैररिष्टैराविष्टम्, महाप्रस्थानकाले स्वसन्तापसन्तानमाप्तहृदयेषु सञ्चारयन्तम्, अरतिपरिगृहीतमीर्ष्ययेव छायया मुच्यमानम्, उद्योगमिवोपद्रवाणाम्, सर्वास्त्रमोक्षमिव क्षामतायाः, हस्तीकृतं विहस्ततया, विषयीकृतं वैषम्येण, क्षेत्रीकृतं क्षयेण, गोचरीकृतं ग्लान्या, दष्टं दुःखासिकया, आत्मीकृतमस्वास्थ्येन, विधेयीकृतं व्याधिना, क्रोडीकृतं कालेन, लक्ष्यीकृतं दक्षिणाशया, पीतमिव पीडाभिः, जग्धमिव जागरेण, निगीर्णमिव वैवर्ण्येन, ग्रासीकृतं गात्रभङ्गेन, ह्रियमाणमिव विपद्भिः, वण्ट्यमानमिव वेदनाभिः, लुण्ठ्यमानमिव दुःखैः, आदिष्टितं दैवेन, निरूपितं नियत्या, घ्रातमनित्यत्वेन, अभिभूयमानमभावेन, परिकलितं परासुतया, दत्तावकाशं क्लेशस्य, निवासं वैमनस्यस्य, समीपे कालस्य, अन्तिकेऽन्त्योच्छ्वासस्य[1], मुखे महाप्रवासस्य[2], द्वारि दीर्घनिद्रायाः, जिह्वाग्रे जीवितेशस्य वर्तमानम्, विरलं वाचि, चलितं चेतसि, विह्वलं वपुषि, क्षीणमायुषि, प्रचुरं प्रलापे, सन्ततं श्वसिते, जितं जृम्भिकाभिः, पराधीनमाधिभिः, अनुबद्धमनुबन्धिकाभिः, पार्श्वोपविष्टयानवरतरोदनोच्छूननयनया गृहीतचामरिकयापि निश्वसितैरेव वीजयन्त्या विविधौषधिधूलिधूसरितशरीरया मुहुर्मुहुः 'आर्यपुत्र स्वपिषि' इति व्याहरन्त्या देव्या यशोमत्या शिरसि वक्षसि च स्पृश्यमानं पितरमद्राक्षीत्।

---

१ 'विश्वास०' अ. २ '०प्रयासस्य' अ.

दृष्ट्वा च प्रथमदुःखसम्पातमथ्यमानमतिराशङ्कित इव भागधेयेभ्यः समभवत्। अन्तकपुरवर्तिनमेव च पितरममन्यत। निराकृत इव चान्तःकरणेन क्षणमासीत्। अवधूतश्च धैर्येण, क्षेत्रीकृतः क्षोभेण, रिक्तीकृतो रत्या, विषयीकृतो विषादेन, पावकमयमिव हृदयमुद्वहन्, विषमविषदूषितानीव मुह्यन्तीन्द्रियाणि बिभ्राणः, तमसा रसातलमपि विशेषयन्, शून्यत्वेनाकाशमप्यतिशयानो नाविन्दत कर्तव्यम्। पस्पर्श च हृदयेन भियमुत्तमाङ्गेन च गाम्।

अवनिपतिस्तु दूरादेव दृष्ट्वातिदयितं तनयं तदवस्थोऽपि निर्भरस्नेहावर्जितः प्रधावमानो मनसा प्रसार्य भुजौ 'एह्येहि' इत्याह्वयञ्शरीरार्धेन शयनादुदगात्। ससंभ्रममुपसृतं चैनं विनयावनम्रमुन्नमय्य बलादुरसि निवेश्य विशन्निव प्रेम्णा निशाकरमण्डलमध्यम्, मज्जन्निवामृतमये महासरसि, स्नापयन्निव[1] महति हरिचन्दनरसप्रस्रवणे, अभिषिच्यमान इव तुषाराद्रिद्रवेण, पीडयन्नङ्गैरङ्गानि, कपोलेन कपोलमवघट्टयन्, निमीलयन्पक्ष्माग्रग्रथिताजस्रास्रविस्राविणी विलोचने विस्मृतज्वरसंज्वरः सुचिरमालिलिङ्ग कथं कथमपि चिराद्विमुक्तमपसृत्य[2] कृतनमस्कारं प्रणतजननीकमुपागतमासीनं च शयनान्तिके पिबन्निव विगतनिमेषनिश्चलेन चक्षुषा व्यलोकयत्। पस्पर्श च पुनः पुनर्वेपथुमता पाणितलेन क्षयक्षामकण्ठश्च कृच्छ्रादिवावादीत्—'वत्स, कृशोऽसि' इति। भण्डिस्त्वकथयत्—'देव, तृतीयमहः कृताहारस्यास्याद्य' इति।

तच्छ्रुत्वा बाष्पवेगगृह्यमाणाक्षरं कथं कथमप्यायतं निःश्वस्योवाच—'वत्स, जानामि त्वां पितृप्रियमतिमृदुहृदयम्। ईदृशेषु विधुरयति धीमतोऽपि धियमतिदुर्धरो बान्धवस्नेहः सर्वप्रमाथी यतो[3] नार्हस्यतिमात्रमात्मानं शुचे दातुम्। उद्दामदाहज्वरदग्धोऽपि दह्ये खल्वहमधिकतरमनेनायुष्मदाधिना। निशितमिव शस्त्रं तक्ष्णोति मां त्वदीयस्तनिमा। सुखं च राज्यं च वंशश्च प्राणाश्च परलोकश्च त्वयि मे स्थिताः। यथा मम तथा सर्वासां प्रजानाम्। त्वद्विधानां पीडाः पीडयन्ति सकलमेव भुवनतलम्। न ह्यल्पपुण्यभाजां वंशमलङ्कुर्वन्ति भवादृशाः। फलमस्यनेकजन्मान्तरोपार्जितस्याकलुषस्य कर्मणः। करतलगतमिव कथयन्ति चतुर्णामप्यर्णवानामाधिपत्यं ते लक्षणानि। त्वज्जन्मनैव कृतार्थोऽस्मि। निरभिलाषोऽस्मि जीवितव्ये। भिषगनुरोधः पाययति मामौषधम्। अपि च सर्वप्रजापुण्यैः सकलभुवनतलपरिपालनार्थमुत्पत्स्यमानानां भवादृशां जन्मग्रहणोपायः पितरौ। प्रजाभिस्तु बन्धुमन्तो राजानः, न ज्ञातिभिः। तदुत्तिष्ठ। कुरु पुनरेव सर्वाः क्रियाः। कृताहारे च त्वय्यहनपि स्वयमुपयोक्ष्ये पथ्यम्' इत्येवमभिहितस्य चास्य धक्ष्यन्निव हृदयमतितरां शोकानलः सन्दुधुक्षे। क्षणमात्रं च स्थित्वा पित्रा पुनराहारार्थमादिश्यमानो धवलगृहादवततार। चकार च चेतसि—'अकाण्डे खल्वयं समु-

१ 'स्नानिव' अ. २ 'उपसृत्य' अ. ३ 'अतो नार्हस्यात्मानम्' अ. ४ A omits this.

दिवापि नामुच्यन्त शयनानि । शनैः शनैश्च महापुरुषविनिपातपिशुनाः समं समन्तात्समुदभवन्भुवने भूयांसो भूपतेरभावाय भयमुत्पादयन्तो भूतानां महोत्पाताः ।

तथा हि । दोलायमानसकलकुलाचलचक्रवाला पत्या सार्धं गन्तुकामेव प्रथममचलद्धरित्री । धन्वन्तरेरिवान्तरे तस्मिन्स्मरन्तः परस्परास्फालनवाचालवीचयो विजुघूर्णिरेऽर्णवाः । भूभृदभावभीतानां विततशिखाकलापविकटकुटिलाः केशपाशा इवोर्ध्वीबभूवुर्धूमकेतवः ककुभाम् । धूमकेतुकरालितदिङ्मुखं दिक्पालारब्धायुष्कामहोमधूमधूम्रमिवाभवद्भुवनम् । भ्रष्टभासि तप्तकालायसकुम्भबभ्रुणि भानुमण्डले भयङ्करकबन्धकायव्याजेन कोऽपि पार्थिवप्राणितार्थी पुरुषोपहारमिवोपजहार । ज्वलितपरिवेशमण्डलाभोगभास्वरो जिघृक्षाजृम्भमाणस्वर्भानुभयादुपरचिताग्निप्राकार इव प्रत्यदृश्यत श्वेतभानुः । अवनिपतिप्रतापप्रसाधिताः प्रथमतरकृतपावकप्रवेशा इवादह्यन्तानुरक्ता दिशः । स्रुतशोणितशीकरासारारुणिततनुरनुमरणाय प्रावृतपाटलांशुकपटेवादृश्यत वसुधावधूः । नराधिपविनाशसंभ्रमभीतैर्लोकपालैरिव कालायसकवाटपुटैरकालकालमेघपटलैररुध्यन्त दिग्द्वाराणि । प्रेतपतिप्रयाणप्रहताः पटवः पटहा इवारटन्तो हृदयस्फोटनाः पस्फायिरे निर्घातानां घोरा निर्घोषाः । निकटीभवद्यममहिषखुरपुटोद्धूता इव द्युमणिधाम धूसरीचक्रुः क्रमेलककचकपिलाः पांशुवृष्टयः । विरसविराविणीनामुन्मुखीनां शिखिनो ज्वालाः प्रतीच्छन्त्य इव पतन्तीरुल्का नभसो ववाशिरे शिवानां राजयः । राजधामनि धूमायमानकबरीविभागविभावितविकाराः प्रकीर्णकेशपाशप्रकाशितशोका इव प्राकाशन्त प्रतिमाः कुलदेवतानाम् । उपसिंहासनमाकुलं कालरात्रिविदूयमानवृजिनवेणीबन्धविभ्रमं बिभ्राणं बभ्राम भ्रामरं पटलम् । अटतामन्तःपुरस्योपरि क्षणमपि न शशाम व्याक्रोशी वायसानाम् । श्वेतातपत्रमण्डलमध्याजीवितमिव राज्यस्य सरसपिशितपिण्डलोहितं चञ्चच्चञ्चुरुच्चैरुच्चखान खण्डं माणिक्यस्य कूजञ्जरद्गृध्रः । महोत्पातदूयमानश्च कथमपि निनाय निशाम् ।

अन्यस्मिन्नहनि समीपमस्य राजकुलाद्द्रुतगतिवशविशीर्यमाणालङ्कारझङ्कारिणी विजयघोषणेव विषादस्याकुलचरणचलत्तुलाकोटिक्वणितवाचालिताभिरुद्ग्रीवाभिः किं किमिति पृच्छ्यमानेव दूरादेव भवनहंसीभिः, स्खलितविशालश्रोणिशिञ्जानरशनानुराविणीभिश्च बाष्पान्धा समुपदिश्यमानमार्गेव गृहसारसीभिः, अदृष्टकवाटपट्टसङ्घट्टस्फुटितललाटपट्टरुधिरपटलेन पटान्तेनेव रक्तांशुकस्य मुखमाच्छाद्य प्ररुदती, सन्तापबलविलीनकनकवलयरसधारामिव वेत्रलतामुत्सृजन्ती, मुखमरुत्तरङ्गितामुत्तरीयांशुकपटीं स्फुरन्तीं फणिनीव

---

१ 'विततशिखी०' अ. २ 'भयङ्करं कबन्ध०' ब. ३ 'पस्फायिरे निपततां' ब. ४ 'विसर०' अ. ५ 'पदान्तेनेव' ब.

निर्मोकमञ्जरीमाकर्षन्तीं, नम्रांसस्रंसिनानिलविलोलेन नीलतमेन तमालपल्लवचीरचीवरेणेव शोकोचितेन धम्मिल्लरचनारहितेन शिरोरुहसञ्चयेन चञ्चता प्रावृतकुचा, कुचताडनपीडया समुच्छूनाताम्रश्यामतलं मुहुर्मुहुरत्युष्णाश्रुप्रमार्जनप्रदग्धमिव करकिशलयं धुनाना, चक्षुर्निर्झरे शीर्यति स्नपयन्तीव शोकाग्निप्रवेशाय स्वकपोलतलप्रतिबिम्बितमासन्नलोकं, लोललोचनप्रवृत्तैस्तरलैस्तारकांशुभिः श्यामायमानमात्मदुःखेन दिवसमपि दहन्तीव 'क्व कुमारः, क्व कुमारः' इति प्रतिपुरुषं पृच्छन्ती वेलेति नाम्ना यशोमत्याः प्रतीहार्याजगाम । विषण्णलोकलोचनप्रत्युद्गता चोपसृत्य कुट्टिमन्यस्तहस्तयुगला गलन्तीभिः सिञ्चतीव शुष्यन्तं दशनदीधितिधाराभिराधूसरमधरमधोमुखी विज्ञापितवती—'देव, परित्रायस्व परित्रायस्व । जीवत्येव भर्तरि किमप्यध्यवसितं देव्या' इति ।

ततस्तदपरमाकर्ण्य च्युत इव सत्त्वेन, द्रुत इव दुःखेन, आचान्त इव चिन्तया, तुलित इव तापेन, अङ्कीकृत इवातङ्केनाप्रतिपत्तिरासीत् । आसीच्चास्य चेतसि—'प्रतिपन्नसंज्ञस्य बहुशोऽपि हृदये दुःखाभिषङ्गो निपतन्नश्मनीव लोहप्रहारः कठिने हुतभुजमुत्थापयति न तु भस्मसात्करोति मे निरनुक्रोशस्य कायम्' इति । उत्थाय च त्वरमाणोऽन्तःपुरमगात् । तत्र च मर्तुमुद्यतानां राजमहिषीणामश्रृणोद्दूरादेव 'तात चूत, चिन्तयात्मानं प्रवसति ते जननी । वत्स जातीगुच्छ, गच्छाम्यापृच्छस्व माम् । मया विनाद्यानाथा भवसि भगिनि भवनदाडिमलते । रक्ताशोक, मर्षणीयाः पादप्रहाराः कर्णपूरपल्लवभङ्गापराधाश्च । पुत्रक अन्तःपुरबालबकुलक वारुणीगण्डूषग्रहणदुर्ललित, दृष्टोऽसि । वत्से प्रियङ्गुलतिके, गाढमालिङ्ग मां दुर्लभा भवामि ते । भद्र भवनद्वारसहकारक, दातव्यो निवापतोयाञ्जलिरपत्यमसि । भ्रातः पञ्जरशुक, यथा न विस्मरसि माम्, किं व्याहरसि दूरीभूतास्मि ते । शारिके, स्वप्ने नः समागमः पुनर्भूयात् । मातः, मार्गलग्नं कस्य समर्पयामि गृहमयूरकम् । अम्ब, सुतवल्लालनीयमिदं हंसमिथुनं मन्दपुण्यया मया न सम्भावितोऽस्य चक्रवाकयुगलस्य विवाहोत्सवः । मातृवत्सले, निवर्तस्व गृहहरिणिके । समुपनय सौविदल्ल वल्लभवल्लकीं परिष्वजे तावदेनाम् । चन्द्रसेने, सुदृष्टः क्रियतामयं जनः । बिन्दुमति, इयं तेऽन्त्या वन्दना । चेटि, मुञ्च चरणौ । आर्ये कात्यायनिके, किं रोदिषि नीतास्मि दैवेन । तात कञ्चुकिन्, किं मामलक्षणां प्रदक्षिणीकरोषि । धात्रेयि, धारयात्मानं किं पादयोः पतसि । भगिनि, गृहाण मामपश्चिमां कण्ठे । कष्टं न दृष्टा प्रियसखी मलयवती । कुरङ्गवति, अयमामन्त्रणाञ्जलिः । सानुमति, अयमन्त्यः प्रणामः । कुवलयवति, एष तेऽवसानपरिष्वङ्गः । सख्यः, क्षन्तव्याः प्रणयकलहाः' इत्येवंप्रायानालापान् ।

दह्यमानश्रवणश्च तैः प्रविशन्नेव निर्यान्तीं दत्तसर्वस्वापतेयां गृहीतमरणप्रसाधनाम्, जानकीमिव जातवेदसं पत्युः पुरः प्रवेक्ष्यन्तीम्, प्रत्यग्रस्ना-

नार्द्रदेहतया श्रियमिव भगवतीं सद्यः समुद्रादुत्थिताम्, कुसुम्भबभ्रुणी वाससी दिवमिव तेजसी सांध्ये दधानाम्, ताम्बूलदिग्धरागान्धकाराधरप्रभापटलपाटलं पट्टांशुकमिव विधवामरणचिह्नमङ्गलग्नमुद्वहन्तीम्, रक्तकण्ठसूत्रेण कुचान्तरावलम्बिना स्फुटितहृदयविगलितरुधिरधाराशङ्कां कुर्वतीम्, तिर्यक्कुटिलकुण्डलकोटिकण्टकाकृष्टतन्तुना हारेण वलितेन सितांशुकपाशेनेव कण्ठमुत्पीडयन्तीम्, सरसकुङ्कुमाङ्गरागतया कवलितामिव दिधक्षता चितार्चिष्मता, चितानलार्चनकुसुमैरिव धवलधवलैरश्रुविन्दुभिरंशुकोत्सङ्गमापूरयन्तीम्, गृहदेवतामन्त्रणबलिमिव वलयैर्विगलद्भिः पदे पदे विकिरन्तीम्, आप्रपदीनां कण्ठे गुणकुसुममालां यमदोलामिवारूढाम्, अन्तर्गुञ्जन्मधुकरमुखरेणामन्त्र्यमाणलोचनोत्पलामिव कर्णोत्पलेन, प्रदक्षिणीक्रियमाणामिव मणिनूपुरबन्धुभिर्बद्धमण्डलं भ्रमद्भिर्भवनहंसैः, संनिहितप्राणसमं मरणाय चित्तमिव चित्रफलकमविचलं धारयन्तीम्, अर्चाबद्धोद्धूयमानधवलपुष्पदामकाम्, पतिव्रतापताकामिव पतिप्रासयष्टिमिष्टामुपगूहमानाम्, बन्धोरिव निजचारित्रधवलस्य नृपातपत्रस्य पुरो नेत्रोदकमुत्सृजन्तीम्, पत्युः पादपतनसमुद्गमदभ्यधिकबाष्पाम्भःप्रवाहप्रतिरुद्धदृशः कथमपि प्रतिपन्नादेशान्सचिवान्सन्दिशन्तीम्, अनुनयनिवर्तितविधुरवृद्धबन्धुवर्गवर्धमानध्वनिभिर्गृहाक्रन्दैराकृष्यमाणश्रवणाम्, भर्तृभाषितनिभैः पञ्जरसिंहबृंहितैर्ह्रियमाणहृदयाम्, धात्र्या भर्तृभक्त्या च निजया प्रसाधिताम्, जरत्या मूर्च्छया च संस्तुतया धार्यमाणाम्, सख्या पीडया च व्यसनसङ्गतया समालिङ्गिताम्, परिजनेन सन्तापेन च गृहीतसर्वावयवेन परीताम्, कुलपुत्रैरुच्छ्वसितैश्च[1] महत्तरैरधिष्ठिताम्, कञ्चुकिभिर्दुःखैश्चातिवृद्धैरनुगताम्, भूपालवल्लभान्कौलेयकानपि सास्रमालोकयन्तीम्, सपत्नीनामपि पादयोः पतन्तीम्, चित्रपुत्रिका अप्यामन्त्रयमाणाम्, गृहपतत्रिणामप्यञ्जलिं पुरस्तादुपरचयन्तीम्, पशूनप्यापृच्छयमानाम्, भवनपादपानपि परिष्वजमानां मातरं ददर्श ।

दूरादेव च बाष्पायमाणदृष्टिरभ्यधात्—'अम्ब, त्वमपि मां मन्दपुण्यं त्यजसि । प्रसीद । निवर्तस्व' इत्यभिदधान एव च सस्नेहमिव नूपुरमणिमरीचिभिश्चुम्ब्यमानचूडश्चरणयोर्न्यपतत् । देवी तु यशोमती तथा तिष्ठति पादनिहितशिरसि विमनसि कनीयसि प्रेयसि तनये गुरुणा गिरिणेवोद्वेगावेगेनावष्टभ्यमाना, मूर्च्छान्धतमसं रसातलमिव प्रविशन्ती, बाष्पप्रवाहेणेव चिरनिरोधसम्पिण्डितेन स्नेहसम्भारेण निर्भराविर्भूतेनाभिभूयमाना, कृतप्रयत्नापि निवारयितुं न शशाक बाष्पोत्पतनम् । उत्कटकुचोत्कम्पप्रकटितासह्यशोकाकूता च गद्गदिकागृह्यमाणगलविकला निःसामान्यमन्युतरलीक्रियमाणाधरोद्देशा पुनरुक्तस्फुरणनिबिडितनासापुटा निमील्य नयने नयनाम्भःसेकप्लवेन प्लावयन्ती विमलौ कपोलौ सम्छाद्य करनखमयूखमालाखचिततनुना

---

१ 'कुलपुत्रोच्छ्वसितैश्च' ब.

तन्वन्तरनिर्गच्छदच्छास्रस्रोतसेवांशुकपटान्तेन किंचिदुत्तानितं वदनेन्दुं दूयमानमानसा स्मरन्ती प्रस्नुतस्तनी प्रसवदिवसादारभ्य सकलमङ्कशायिनः शैशवमस्य ज्ञातिगृहगतहृदया 'अम्ब, तात, न पश्यतं पापां परलोकप्रस्थितां मामेवमतिदुःखिताम्' इति मुहुर्मुहुराक्रन्दन्ती पितरौ, 'हा वत्स, विश्रान्तभागधेयया न दृष्टोऽसि' इति प्रेष्ठं ज्येष्ठं तनयमसंनिहितं क्रोशन्ती, 'अनाथा जाता' इति श्वशुरकुलवर्तिनीं दुहितरमनुशोचन्ती, 'निष्करुण, किमपराद्धं तवामुना जनेन' इति दैवमुपालभमाना, 'नास्ति मत्समा सीमन्तिनी दुःखभागिनी' इति निन्दन्ती बहुविधमात्मानम्, 'मुषितास्मि नृशंस त्वया' इत्यकाण्डे कृतान्तं गर्हमाणा मुक्तकण्ठमतिचिरं प्राकृतप्रमदेव प्रारोदीत्।

प्रशान्ते च मन्युवेगे सस्नेहमुत्थापयामास सुतम्। हस्तेन चास्य प्ररुदितस्य पक्ष्मपालीपुञ्ज्यमाननखकिरणनिवहां द्रुतामिवाधिकतरं क्षरन्तीं दृष्टिमुन्ममार्ज। स्वयमपि कठोररागपरिपीयमानेन धवलिम्ना मुच्यमानोदरे क्वथदस्रश्वयत्पर्यन्ते शुक्लशीकरतारतारकितपक्ष्मणी सूक्ष्मतराश्रुबिन्दुपरिपाटीपतनानुबन्धविधुरे लोचने पुनः पुनरापूर्यमाणे प्रमृज्य बाष्पार्द्रगण्डगृहीतां च श्रवणशिखरमारोप्य शोकलम्बामलकलतामधःस्रस्तविलोलबालिकाव्याकुलितां च समुत्सार्य तिरश्चीं चिकुरसटामश्रुप्रवाहपूरितमार्द्रं च किंचिच्च्युतमुत्क्षिप्य हस्तेन स्तनोत्तरीयं तरङ्गितमिव[1] मग्नांशुकपटान्ततनुताम्रलेखालाञ्छितलावण्यकुब्जिका[2]वर्जितराजतराजहंसास्यसमुद्गीर्णेन पयसा प्रक्षाल्य मुखकमलं कलमूकलोकविधृते वासःशकले शुचिनि समुन्मृज्य पाणौ सुतवदनविनिहितनिभृतनयनयुगला चिरं स्थित्वा पुनः पुनरायतं निश्वस्यावादीत्—'वत्स, नासि न प्रियो निर्गुणो वा परित्यागार्हो वा। स्तन्येनैव सह त्वया पीतं मे हृदयम्। अस्मिंश्च समये प्रभूतप्रभुप्रसादान्तरिता त्वां न पश्यति दृष्टिः। अपि च पुत्रक, पुरुषान्तरविलोकनव्यसनिनी राज्योपकरणमकरुणा वा नास्मि लक्ष्मीः क्षमा वा। कुलकलत्रमस्मि चारित्रमात्रधना धर्मधवले कुले जाता। किं विस्मृतोऽसि मां समरशतशौण्डस्य पुरुषप्रकाण्डस्य केशरिण इव केशरिणीं गृहिणीम्। वीरजा वीरजाया वीरजननी च मादृशी पराक्रमक्रीता कथमन्यथा कुर्यात्। एवंविधेन पित्रा ते भरतभगीरथनाभागनिभेन नरेन्द्रवृन्दारकेण गृहीतः पाणिः। आसेवितः सेवासंभ्रान्तानन्तसामन्तसीमन्तिनीसमावर्जितजाम्बूनदघटाभिषेकः शिरसा। लब्धो मनोरथदुर्लभो महादेवीपट्टबन्धसत्कारलाभो ललाटेन। आपीतौ युष्मद्विधैः पुत्रैरमित्रकलत्रबन्दीवृन्दविधूयमानचामरमरुच्चलचीनांशुकधरौ पयोधरौ। सपत्नीनां शिरःसु निहितं नमन्निखिलकटककुटुम्बिनीकिरीटमाणिक्यमालार्चितं चरणयुगलकम्। एवं कृतार्थसर्वावयवा किमपरमपेक्षे क्षीणपुण्या। मर्तुमविधवैव

---

१ 'तरङ्गितमिव नखांशुपटलेन' ब. २ 'कुब्जिका' ब.

वाञ्छामि। न च शक्नोमि दग्धस्य भर्तुरार्यपुत्रविरहिता रतिरिव निरर्थकान्प्रलापान्कर्तुम्। पितुश्च ते पादधूलिरिव प्रथमं गगनगमनमावेदयन्ती बहुमता भविष्यामि शूरानुरागिणीनां सुराङ्गनानाम्। प्रत्यग्रदृष्टदारुणदुःखदग्धायाश्च मे किं धक्ष्यति धूमध्वजः। मरणाच्च मे जीवितमेवास्मिन्समये साहसम्। अतिशीतलः पतिशोकानलादक्षयस्नेहेन्धनादस्मादनलः। कैलासकल्पे प्रवसति जीवेश्वरे जरत्तृणकणिकालघीयसि जीविते लोभ इति क्व घटते। अपि च जीवन्तीमपि मां नरपतिमरणावधीरणमहापातकिनीं न स्प्रक्ष्यन्ति पुत्र पुत्रराज्यसुखानि। दुःखदग्धानां च भूतिरमङ्गला चाप्रशस्ता च निरुपयोगा च भवति। वत्स, विश्वस्तानां यशसा स्थातुमिच्छामि लोके न वपुषा। तदहमेव त्वां तावत्तात प्रसादयामि न पुनर्मनोरथप्रातिकूल्येन कदर्थनीयास्मि।' इत्युक्त्वा पादयोरपतत्।

स तु ससंभ्रममपनीय चरणयुगलमवनमिततनुरुभयकरविधृतवपुषमवनितलगतशिरसमुदनमयन्मातरम्। दुर्निवारतां च शुचः समवधार्य कुलयोषिदुचितां च तामेव श्रेयसीं मन्यमानः क्रियां कृतनिश्चयां च तां ज्ञात्वा तूष्णीमधोमुखोऽभवत्।

अभिनन्दति हि स्नेहकातरापि कुलीनता देशकालानुरूपम्। देव्यपि यशोमती परिष्वज्य समाघ्राय च शिरसि निर्गत्य चरणाभ्यामेव चान्तःपुरात्पौराक्रन्द[1]प्रतिशब्दनिर्भराभिरुपरुध्यमानेव दिग्भिः सरस्वतीतीरं ययौ। तत्र च स्त्रीस्वभावकातरैर्दृष्टिपातैः प्रविकसितरक्तपङ्कजपुञ्जैरिवार्चयित्वा भगवन्तं भानुमन्तमिव मूर्तिरैन्दवी चित्रभानुं प्राविशत्। इतरोऽपि मातृमरणविह्वलो बन्धुवर्गपरिवृतः पितुः पार्श्वं प्रायात्। अपश्यच्च स्वल्पावशेषप्राणवृत्तिं परिवर्त्यमानतारकं तारकराजमिवास्तमभिलषन्तं जनयितारम्। असह्यशोकोद्रेकाभिद्रुतश्च त्याजितः स्नेहेन धैर्यम्। आश्लिष्यास्य सकलदुर्मदमहीपालमौलिमालालालितौ पादपद्मावन्तस्तापान्मुखचन्द्रमिव द्रवीभवन्तं दशनज्योत्स्नाजालमिव जलतामापद्यमानं लोचनलावण्यमिव विलीयमानं मुखसुधारसमिव स्यन्दमानमच्छाच्छमश्रुस्रोतसां सन्तानं महामेघमयविलोचन इव वर्षन्नितरवद्विमुक्तारावश्चिरं रुरोद।

राजा तु तमुपरुध्यमानदृष्टिरविरतरुदितशब्दाश्रितश्रवणः प्रत्यभिज्ञाय शनैः शनैरवादीत्—'पुत्र, नार्हस्येवं भवितुम्। भवद्विधा न ह्यमहासत्त्वाः। महासत्त्वता हि प्रथममवलम्बनं लोकस्य पश्चाद्राजबीजिता। सत्त्ववतां चाग्रणीः सर्वातिशयाश्रितः क्व भवान्, क्व वैक्लव्यम्। 'कुलप्रदीपोऽसि' इति दिवसकरसदृशतेजसस्ते लघूकरणमिव। 'पुरुषसिंहोऽसि' इति शौर्यपटुप्रज्ञोपबृंहितपराक्रमस्य निन्देव। 'क्षितिरियं तव' इति लक्षणाख्यातचक्रवर्तिपदस्य पुनरुक्तमिव। 'गृह्यतां श्रीः' इति स्वयमेव श्रिया गृहीतस्य विपरीतमिव।

१ 'पौराक्रन्दनिर्भराभिः' अ.

'अध्यास्यतामयं लोकः' इत्युभयलोकविजिगीषोरपुष्कलमिव। 'स्वीक्रियतां कोषः' इति शशिकरनिकरनिर्मलयशःसञ्चयैकाभिनिवेशिनो निरुपयोगमिव। 'आत्मीक्रियतां राजकम्' इति गुणगणात्मीकृत[1]जगतो गतार्थमिव। 'उह्यतां राज्यभारः' इति भुवनत्रयभारोचितस्यानुचितनियोग इव। 'प्रजाः परिरक्ष्यन्ताम्' इति दीर्घदोर्दण्डार्गलितदिङ्मुखस्यानुवाद इव। 'परिजनः परिपाल्यताम्' इति लोकपालोपमस्यानुषङ्गिकमिव। 'शस्त्राभ्यासः कार्यः' इति धनुर्गुणकिणकलङ्ककालीकृतप्रकोष्ठस्य किमादिश्यते। 'निग्राह्यतां चापलम्' इति नूतनतरवयसि निगृहीतेन्द्रियस्य निरवकाशेव मे वाणी। 'निरवशेषतां शत्रवो नेयाः' इति सहजस्य तेजस एवेयं चिन्ता।' इत्येवं वदन्नेवापुनरुन्मीलनाय निमिमील राजसिंहो लोचने[2]।

अस्मिन्नेवान्तरे पूषाप्यायुषेव तेजसा व्ययुज्यत। ततश्च लज्जमान इव नरपतिजीवितापहरणजनितादात्मापराधादधोमुखः समभवत्। भूपालाभावशोकशिखिनेव चान्तस्ताप्यमानस्ताम्रतां प्रपेदे। मन्दं मन्दमप्रियप्रश्नार्थमिव स्थितिमनुवर्तमानो लौकिकीमवातरद्दिवः। दित्सुरिव जनेशाय जलाञ्जलिमपरजलनिधिसमीपमुपससर्प। सद्योद[3]त्तनृपजलाञ्जलिर्दुःखदहनदग्धमिव करसहस्रमालोहितमधत्त।

एवं च महानराधिपनिधननिधीयमानविपुलवैराग्य इव शान्तवपुषि विशति गिरिगुहागह्वरं गभस्तिमालिनि, समुपोह्यमानमहाजनाश्रुदुर्दिनार्द्रीकृत इव निर्वात्यातपे, रोदनताम्रसकललोकलोचनरुचेव लोहितायति जगति, उष्णायमानानेकनरनिश्वाससन्तापप्लुष्ट इव च नीलायमाने दिवसे, नृपानुगमनप्रचलितयेव लक्ष्म्या मुच्यमानासु कमलिनीषु, पतिशुचेव परिवृतच्छायायां श्यामायमानायां भुवि, कुलपुत्रेष्विव परित्यक्तकलत्रेषु कृतकरुणप्रलापेषु वनान्तानाश्रयत्सु दुःखितेषु चक्रवाकेषु, छत्रभङ्गभीतेष्विव निगूढकोशेषु कुशेशयेषु, स्फुटितदिग्वधूहृदयरुधिरप्लव इव गलिते रक्तातपे, क्रमेण च लोकान्तरमुपगतवत्यनुरागशेषे जाते तेजसामधीशे, गगनतलवितन्यमानबहलरागपाट[4]लायां प्रेतपताकायामिव प्रवृत्तायां संध्यायाम्, शवशिबिकालङ्काकृष्णचामरमालास्विव स्फुरन्तीषु दर्शनप्रतिकूलासु तिमिरलेखासु, असितागुरुकालकाष्ठायां केनापि चितायामिव रचितायां रजन्याम्, दन्तामलपत्रप्रसाधितकर्णिकासु केसरमालाकल्पितमुण्डमालिकासु अनुमर्तुमिवोद्यतासु प्रहसितमुखीषु कुमुदलक्ष्मीषु, अवतरत्त्रिदशविमानकिङ्किणीक्वणित इव श्रूयमाणे शाखिशिखरकुलायलीयमानशकुनिकुलकूजिते, नाकपथप्रस्थितपार्थिवप्रत्युद्गतपुरुहूतातपत्र इव पूर्वस्यां दिशि दृश्यमाने चन्द्रमसि, नरेन्द्रः स्वयं समर्पितस्कन्धैर्गृहीत्वा शवशिबिकां शिबिसमः सामन्तैः पौरैश्च पुरोहितपुरःसरैः सरितं

---

१ '०गणात्मीकृतं जगतो' ब. २ 'प्रत्यपद्यत च पूषात्मजः' इत्यधिकं ब-पुस्तके. ३ '०दत्तजला०' अ. ४ '०पटलायाम्' अ.

सरस्वतीं नीत्वा नरपतिसमुचितायां चितायां हुताशसत्क्रियया यशः-शेषतामनीयत।

देवोऽपि हर्षः पुञ्जीभूतेन सकलेनेव जीवलोकेन लोकेन राजकुलसम्बद्धे-नाशेषेण शोकमूकेन परिवृतोऽन्तर्वर्तिनापि शोकानलतप्तेन स्नेहद्रवेण बहि-रिव सिच्यमानो निर्व्यवधानायां धरण्यामुपविष्ट एव तां निशीथिनीं भीमर-थीभीमामखिलां सराजको जजागार। अजनि चास्य चेतसि। 'ताते दूरी-भूते संप्रत्येतावान्खलु जीवलोकः, लोकस्य भग्नाः पन्थानः, मनोरथानां खिलीभूतानि भूतिस्थानानि, स्थगितान्यानन्दस्य द्वाराणि, सुप्ता सत्यवा-दिता, लुप्ता लोकयात्रा, विलीना बाहुशालिता, प्रलीना प्रियालापिता, प्रोषिताः पुरुषकारविहारविकाराः, समाप्ता समरशौण्डता, ध्वस्ता परगुण-प्रीतिः, विश्रान्ता विश्वासभूमयः, अपदान्यपदानानि, निरुपयोगानि शा-स्त्राणि, निरवलम्बना विक्रमैकरसता, कथावशेषा विशेषज्ञता, ददातु जनो जलाञ्जलिमौर्जित्याय, प्रतिपद्यतां प्रव्रज्यां प्रजापालता, बध्नातु वैधव्यवेणीं वरमनुष्यता, समाश्रयतु राजश्रीराश्रमपदम्, परिधत्तां धवले वाससी वसुमती, वहतु वल्कले विलासिता, तपस्यतु तपोवनेषु तेजस्विता, प्रावृणोतु चीवरे वीरता, क्व गम्यतां पुनस्तस्य कृते कृतज्ञतया, क्व पुनः प्राप्स्यति तादृ-शान्महापुरुषनिर्माणपरमाणून्परमेष्ठी, शून्याः संवृत्ता दश दिशो गुणानाम्, जगज्जातमन्धकारं धर्मस्य, निष्फलमधुना जन्म शस्त्रोपजीविनाम्। तातेन विना कुतस्त्यास्तादृश्यो दिवसमसमसमररससमारब्धकलहकथाकण्टकितसु-भटकपोलभित्तयो वीरगोष्ठ्यः। अपि नाम स्वप्नेऽपि दृश्येत दीर्घरक्तनयनं पुनस्तन्मुखसरोजम्, जन्मान्तरेऽपि पुनः परिष्वज्येत तल्लोहस्तम्भाभ्यधिक-गरिमगर्वं भुजयुगलम्। लोकान्तरेऽपि पुत्रेत्यालपतः श्रूयेत सा सुधारसमु-द्गिरन्ती मथ्यमानक्षीरसागरोद्गारगम्भीरा भारती' इति। एतानि चान्यानि च चिन्तयत एवास्य कथमपि सा क्षयमियाय यामिनी।

ततः शुचेव मुक्तकण्ठमारटत्सु कृकवाकुकुलेषु, गृहगिरितरुशिखरेभ्यः पातयत्स्वात्मानं मन्दिरमयूरेषु परित्यक्तनिवासेषु च वनाय प्रस्थितेषु पत्र-रथेषु, सद्यस्तनूभूते ताम्यति तमसि, मन्दीभूतात्मस्नेहेष्वभावमभिलषत्सु प्रदीपेषु, स्फुरदरुणकिरणवल्कलप्रावृतवपुषि प्रव्रज्यामिव प्रतिपन्ने नभसि, प्रभातसमयेन समुत्तीर्यमाणासु पार्थिवास्थिशकलकलास्विव कलविङ्ककन्ध-राधूसरासु तारकासु, भूभृद्धातुगर्भकुम्भधारिषु विविधसरःसरित्तीर्थाभिमुखेषु प्रस्थितेषु वनकरिकुलेषु, शावशुचिसिक्थपटलपाण्डुरे पिण्ड इवापरपयोनिधि-पुलिनपरिसरे पात्यमाने शशिनि, क्रमेण नृपचितानलधूमविसरधूसरीकृत-तेजसीव नरपतिशोकपावकदाहकिणकलङ्ककालीकृतचेतसीव प्रोषितसमस्ता-न्तःपुरपुरंध्रिमुखचन्द्रवृन्दोद्वेगविद्राणवपुषीव प्रथमास्तमितरोहिणीरणरणकवि-मनसीव चास्तमुपगते रजनिकरे, राजतीव देवे दिवमारूढे सवितरि, परिवृत्ते

राज्य इव रजनीप्रबन्धे प्रबुद्धराजहंसमण्डलप्रबोध्यमानः पङ्कजाकर इव चचाल[1] चोपस्नानाय देवो हर्षः। ततश्च नूपुररवविराममूकमन्दमन्दिरहंसेषु, शोकाकुलकतिपयकञ्चुकिमात्रावशेषेषु शुद्धान्तेषु, पतितयूथप इव वनगजयूथे कक्ष्यान्तरवर्तिनि पितृपरिजने, विषादिन्युपरिरुदन्निषादिनि च स्तम्भनिषण्णे निष्पन्दमन्दे राजकुञ्जरे, मन्दुरापालकाक्रन्दकथिते चाजिरभाजि राजवाजिनि, विश्रान्तजयशब्दकलकले च शून्ये च महास्थानमण्डपे दह्यमानदृष्टिर्निर्जगाम राजकुलात्। अगाच्च सरस्वतीतीरं तस्यां स्नात्वा पित्रे ददावुदकम्। अपस्नातश्चानिष्पीडितमौलिरेव परिधायोद्गमनीयदुकूलवाससी निश्वासपरो निरातपत्रो निरुत्सारणः समुपनीतेऽपि सप्तौ चरणाभ्यामेव नासाग्रासक्तेन रक्ततामरसताम्रेण चक्षुषा हृदयावशेषस्यापि पितुर्दाहशङ्कया शोकाग्निमिव उद्गिरन्नताम्बूलस्यापि सुचिरप्रक्षालितस्य कल्पतरुकिसलयस्येव[2] स्वभावपाटलस्याधरपल्लवस्य प्रभया मांसरुधिरकवलानिव हृदयाभिघातादुद्वमन्नुष्णनिश्वासमोक्षैर्भवनमाजगाम।

राजवल्लभास्तु भृत्याः सुहृदः सचिवाश्च तस्मिन्नेवाहनि निर्गत्य प्रियं पुत्रदारमुत्सृज्योद्बाष्पैर्बन्धुभिर्वार्यमाणा अपि बहुनृपगुणगणहृतहृदयाः केचिदात्मानं भृगुषु बबन्धुः, केचित्तत्रैव तीर्थेषु तस्थुः, केचिदनशनैरास्तीर्णतृणकुशा व्यथमानमानसाः शुचमसमामशमयन्, केचिच्छलभा इव वैश्वानरं शोकावेगविवशा विविशुः, केचिद्दारुणदुःखदहनदह्यमानहृदया. गृहीतवाचस्तुषारशिखरिणं शरणमुपययुः, केचिद्विन्ध्योपत्यकासु वनकरिकुलकरशीकरासारसिच्यमानतनवः पल्लवशयनशयिनः सन्तापमशमयन्, केचित्संनिहितानपि विषयानुत्सृज्य सेवाविमुखाः परिच्छिन्नैः पिण्डकैरटवीभुवः शून्या जगृहुः, केचित्पवनाशना धर्मधना धमद्धमनयो मुनयो बभूवुः, केचिद्गृहीतकाषायाः कापिलं मतमधिजगिरे गिरिषु, केचिदाचोटितचूडामणिषु शिरःसु शरणीकृतधूर्जटयो जटा जघटिरे। अपरे परिपाटलप्रलम्बचीवराम्बरसंवीताः स्वाम्यनुरागमुज्वलं चक्रुः। अन्ये तपोवनहरिणजिह्वाञ्चलोलिह्यमानमूर्तयो जरां ययुः। अपरे पुनः पाणिपल्लवप्रमृष्टैराताम्रलोचनैर्नयनपुटैः कमण्डलुभिश्च वारि वहन्तो गृहीतव्रता मुण्डा विचेरुः।

देवमपि हर्षं तदवस्थं पितृशोकविह्वलीकृतम्, श्रियं शाप इति महीं महापातकमिति राज्यं रोग इति भोगान्भुजङ्गा इति निलयं निरय इति बन्धुं बन्धनमिति जीवितमयश इति देहं द्रोह इति कल्यतां कलङ्क इति आयुरपुण्यफलमिति आहारं विषमिति विषममृतमिति चन्दनं दहन इति कामं क्रकच इति हृदयस्फोटनमभ्युदय इति च मन्यमानम्, सर्वासु क्रियासु विमुखम्, पितृपितामहपरिग्रहागताश्चिरन्तनाः कुलपुत्राः वंशक्रमाहितगौरवाश्च ग्राह्यगिरो गुरवः श्रुतिस्मृतीतिहासविशारदाश्च जरद्द्विजातयः श्रुताभि-

---

१ 'चचाल देवो हर्षः' अ. २ 'किसलयकोमलस्येव' ब.

जनशीलशालिनो मूर्धाभिषिक्ताश्चामात्या राजानो यथावदधिगतात्मतत्त्वाश्च संस्तुता मस्करिणः समदुःखसुखाश्च[1] समाश्रिताः सनाभयश्चित्तज्ञाश्च प्रधाना सचिवाः निष्कारणबान्धवाश्च मुनयः संसारासारत्वकथनकुशला ब्रह्मवादिनः शोकापनयननिपुणाश्च पौराणिकाः पर्यवारयन् ।

अस्वतन्त्रीकृतश्च तैर्मनसापि नालभत शोकानुप्रवणमाचरितुम् । अनुनीयमानश्च कथं कथमप्याहारादिकासु क्रियास्वाभिमुख्यमभजत । भ्रातृगतहृदयश्चाचिन्तयत्—अपि नाम तातस्य मरणं महाप्रलयसदृशमिदमुपश्रुत्य आर्यो बाष्पजलस्नातो न गृह्णीयाद्वल्कले, नाश्रयेद्वा राजर्षिराश्रमपदम्, न विशेद्वा पुरुषसिंहो गिरिगुहाम्, अस्रसलिलनिर्भरभरितनयननलिनयुगलो वा पश्येदनाथां पृथिवीम्, प्रथमव्यसनविषमविषविह्वलः स्मरेदात्मानं वा पुरुषोत्तमः, अनित्यतया जनितवैराग्यो वा न निराकुर्यादुपसर्पन्तीं राज्यलक्ष्मीम्, दारुणदुःखदहनप्रज्वलितदेहो वा प्रतिपद्येताभिषेकम्, इहागतो वा राजभिरभिधीयमानो न पराचीनतामाचरेत् । अतिपितृपक्षपाती खल्वार्यः । सर्वदा तातश्लाघया[2] मामभिधत्ते—'तात हर्ष, कस्यचिदभून्नभविष्यति वा पुनः काञ्चनतालतरुप्रांशु कायप्रमाणमिदम्[3] । ईदृक्च दिवसकरप्रीत्या दिवसमुन्मुखविकसितं मुखमहाकमलम् । एतौ च वज्रस्तम्भभास्वरौ भुजकाण्डौ । एते च हसितमदालसहलधरविभ्रमा विलासाः । कोऽन्यो मानी विक्रान्तो वदान्यो वा' इति । एतानि चान्यानि च चिन्तयन्दर्शनोत्सुकहृदयो भ्रातुरागमनमुदीक्षमाणः कथं कथमप्यतिष्ठदिति ।

इति श्रीबाणभट्टकृतौ हर्षचरिते महाराजमरणवर्णनं नाम पञ्चम उच्छ्वासः ।

---

१ '०सुखाश्च मुनयः' अ. २ 'तातश्लाघायाम्' ब. ३ '०प्रांशु प्रमाण०' ब.

षष्ठ उच्छ्वासः।

उच्छिद्योच्छिद्य भुवि प्रहितनिगूढात्मदूतनीतानाम्।
विजिगीषुरिव कृतान्तः शूराणां संग्रहं कुरुते ॥१॥
विस्रब्धघातदोषः स्ववधाय खलस्य वीरकोपकरः।
नवतरुभङ्गध्वनिरिव हरिनिद्रातस्करः करिणः ॥२॥

अथ प्रथमप्रेतपिण्डभुजि भुक्ते द्विजन्मनि, गतेषूद्वेजनीयेष्वशौचदिवसेषु, चक्षुर्दाहदायिनि दीयमाने द्विजेभ्यः शयनासनचामरातपत्रामत्रपत्रशस्त्रादिके नृपनिकटोपकरणकलापे, नीतेषु तीर्थस्थानानि सह जनहृदयैः कीकसेषु, कल्पितशोकशल्ये सुधानिचयचिते चिताचैत्यचिह्ने, वनाय विसर्जिते महाजिजिति राजगजेन्द्रे, क्रमेण च मन्देष्वाक्रन्देषु, विरलीभवत्सु च विलापेषु, विश्राम्यत्यश्रुणि, शिथिलीभवत्सु श्वसितेषु, अविस्पष्टेषु हाकष्टाक्षरेषु, उत्सार्यमाणासु च व्यसनशय्यासु, उपदेशश्रवणक्षमेषु श्रोत्रेषु, अनुरोधावधानयोग्येषु हृदयेषु, गणनीयेषु नृपगुणेषु, प्रदेशवृत्तितामाश्रयति शोके, कृतेषु कविरुदितकेषु, जाते च स्वप्नावशेषदर्शने हृदयावशेषावस्थाने, चित्रावशेषाकृतौ काव्यावशेषनाम्नि नरनाथे देवो हर्षः कदाचिदुत्सृष्टव्यापारः पुञ्जीभूतवृद्धबन्धुवर्गाग्रेसरेणावनतमूकमुखेन महाजनेन मौलेनाकाल आत्मानं वेष्ट्यमानमद्राक्षीत्। दृष्ट्वा चाकरोन्मनसि—'किमन्यदार्यमागतमावेदयत्ययं शोकपराभूतो लोकाकरः' इति। वेपमानहृदयश्च पप्रच्छ प्रविशन्तमधिकतरप्रचारमन्यतमं पुरुषम् 'अङ्ग, कथय किमार्यः प्राप्तः' इति। स मन्दमब्रवीत्—'देव, यथादिशसि द्वारि' इति श्रुत्वा च सोदर्यस्नेहनिहितनिरतिशयमन्युमृदूकृतमनाः कथमपि न ववाम बाष्पवारिप्रवाहोत्पीडेन सह जीवितम्।

अनन्तरं च द्वारपालमुक्तेन प्रथमप्रविष्टेन परिजनेनेवाक्रन्देन कथ्यमानम्, दूरद्रुतागमनमुषितबाहुल्येन विच्छिन्नच्छत्रधारेण लम्बिताम्बरवाहिना भ्रष्टभृङ्गारग्राहिणा च्युताचमनधारिणा ताम्यत्ताम्बूलिकेन खञ्जत्खड्गग्राहिणा कतिपयप्रकाशदासेरकप्रायेण बहुवासरान्तरितस्नानभोजनशयनश्यामक्षामवपुषा परिजनेन परिवृतम्, अविरलमार्गधूलिधूसरितशरीरतया शरणीकृतमिवाशरणया क्रमागतया वसुन्धरया, हूणनिर्जयसमरशरव्रणबद्धपट्टैर्दीर्घधवलैः समासन्नराज्यलक्ष्मीकटाक्षपातैरिव शबलीकृतकायम्, अवनिपतिप्राणपरित्राणार्थमिव च शोकहुतभुजि हुतमांसैरतिकृशैरवयवैरावेद्यमानदुःखभारम्, अपगतचूडामणिनि मलिनाकुलकुन्तले शेखरशून्ये शिरसि शुचमारूढां मूर्तिमतीमिव दधानम्, आतपगलितस्वेदराजिना रुदतेव पितृपादपतनोत्कण्ठितेन ललाटपट्टेन लक्ष्यमाणम्, प्रथीयसा बाष्पपयःप्रवाहेनाभिमतपतिमरणमूर्च्छि-

तामिव महीमनवरतं सिञ्चन्तम्, अनन्तसन्तताश्रुप्रवाहनिपतननिम्नीकृताविव दुःखक्षामौ कपोलावुद्वहन्तम्, अत्युष्णमुखमारुतमार्गगतेन द्रवतेव गलित-ताम्बूलरागेणाधरबिम्बेनोपलक्षितम्, पवित्रिकामात्रावशेषेन्द्रनीलिकांशुश्यामायमानमचिरश्रुतपितृमरणमहाशोकाग्निदग्धमिव श्रवणप्रदेशमुद्वहन्तम्, अस्फुटाभिव्यक्तव्यञ्जनेनाप्यधोमुखस्तिमितनयननीलतारकामयूखमालाखचितेन शोकप्ररूढश्मश्रुश्यामलेनेव मुखशशिना लक्ष्यमाणम्, केशरिणमिव महाभूभृद्विनिपातविह्वलं निरवलम्बनम्, दिवसमिव तेजःपतिपतनपरिम्लानश्रियं श्यामीभूतम्, नन्दनमिव भग्नकल्पपादपं विच्छायम्, दिग्भावमिव प्रोषितदिक्कुञ्जरं शून्यम्, गिरिमिव गुरुवज्रपातदारितं कम्पमानम्, क्रीतमिव कृशिम्ना, किङ्करीकृतमिव कारुण्येन, दासीकृतमिव दौर्मनस्येन, शिष्यीकृतमिव शोचितव्येन, आत्मीकृतमिवाधिना,[1] मूकीकृतमिव मौनेन, पिष्टमिव पीडया, स्विन्नमिव सन्तापेन, उच्चितमिव चिन्तया, लुप्तमिव विलापेन, धृतमिव वैराग्येण, प्रत्याख्यातमिव प्रतिसंख्यानेन, अवज्ञातमिव प्रज्ञया, दूरीकृतमिव दुरभिभवत्वेन, अबोध्येन वृद्धबुद्धीनाम्, असाध्येन साधुभाषितानाम्, अगम्येन गुरुगिराम्, अशक्येन शास्त्रशक्तीनाम्, अपथेन प्रज्ञाप्रयत्नानाम्, अगोचरेण सुहृदनुरोधानाम्, अविषयेण विषयोपभोगानाम्, अभूमिभूतेन कालक्रमोपचयानां शोकेन कवलीकृतं ज्येष्ठं भ्रातरमपश्यत्। आवेगोद्गतकृत्स्नस्नेहोत्कलिकाकलापोत्क्षिप्यमाणकाय इव च परवशः समुदगात्।

अथ तं दूरादेव दृष्ट्वा देवो राज्यवर्धनश्चिरकालकलितं बाष्पवेगं मुमुक्षुः सुदूरप्रसारितेन सङ्कल्पयन्निव सर्वदुःखानि दीर्घेण दोर्दण्डद्वयेन गृहीत्वा कण्ठे मुक्तकण्ठं पुनः पतितक्षौमे क्षामे वक्षसि पुनः कण्ठे पुनः स्कन्धभागे पुनः कपोलोदरे निधाय तथा तथा रुरोद यथा सबन्धनानीवोदपाट्यन्त हृदयानि। अश्रुस्रोतः शिरा इव अमुच्यत लोचनेषु लोकेन।[2] स्मृतनृपतिना राजवल्लभेनापि प्रतिशब्दनिभेन निर्भरमिवारुद्यत। सुचिराच्च कथं कथमपि निर्वृष्टनयनजलः पर्जन्य इव शरदि स्वयमेवोपशशाम। उपविष्टश्च परिजनोपनीतेन तोयेन तत्कर[3]नखमयूखपुञ्जतया महाजलप्लवजायमानफेनलेखमिव पुनः पुनः प्रमृष्टमपि पक्ष्माग्रसङ्गलद्बिन्दुवृन्दमन्दोन्मेषमुषितदर्शनं कथं कथमपि चक्षुरक्षालयत्। ताम्बूलिकोपस्थापितेन च वाससा चन्द्रातपशकलेनेवोष्णोष्णबाष्पदग्धं वदनमुन्ममार्ज। तूष्णीमेव च चिरं स्थित्वोत्थाय स्नानभूमिमगात्। तस्यां च स्थित्वा विभूषं विलस्तव्यस्तकुन्तलं मौलिमनादरान्निष्पीड्य सावशेषमन्युस्फुरितेन जिजीविषतेव जलधौतसुभगमात्मानमपि चुचुम्बिषतेवाधरेण क्षालितस्य चक्षुषः श्वेतिम्ना च शारदशशिकरविकसित-

---

१ 'अन्धीकृत०' ब. २ एतद्वाक्यं नास्ति अ-पुस्तके. ३ 'तरत्कर०' ब.

विशदकुमुदवनदलावलिबलिविक्षेपैरिव दिग्देवतार्चनकर्म कुर्वाणश्चतुःशालवितर्दिकायां[1] नीचापाश्रयविनिहितैकोपबर्हायां पर्यङ्किकायां निपत्य जोषमस्थात्।

देवोऽपि हर्षस्तथैव स्नात्वा धरणितलनिहितकुथाप्रसारितमूर्तिरदूर एवास्य तूष्णीमेव समवातिष्ठत। दृष्ट्वा दृष्ट्वा दूयमानमानसमग्रजन्मानं समस्फुटदिवास्य सहस्रधा हृदयम्। औरसदर्शनं हि यौवनं शोकस्य। लोकस्य तु नरपतिमरणदिवसादपि दारुणः स बभूव दिवसः। सर्वस्मिन्नेव नगरे न केनचिदपाचि न केनचिदस्नायि नाभोजि सर्वस्य सर्वेणारोदि। केवलमनेन क्रमेणातिचक्राम दिवसः। स च प्रत्यग्रत्वष्टृटङ्कतष्टतनुरिव वहद्बहलरुधिररसमांसच्छविरपरपारावारपयसि ममज्ज मञ्जिष्ठारुणोऽरुणसारथिः। मुकुलायमानकमलिनीकोषविकलं चकाण चञ्चरीककुलं कमलसरसि। सविधविरहव्याधिविधुरवधूवाध्यमानं बबन्ध बन्धाविव विबुद्धबन्धूकभासि भास्वति सास्रां दृशं चक्रवाकचक्रवालम्। सञ्चरन्त्याः समधुकररवं कैरवाकरं कलहंसरमणीरमणीयं माणिक्यकाञ्चीकिङ्किणीजालमिवोण[2] श्रियः। प्रकटकलङ्कमुदयमानं विशङ्कटविषाणोत्कीर्णपङ्कसङ्करशङ्करशर्कुर[3]शक्करककुदकूटसङ्काशमकाशताकाशे शशाङ्कमण्डलम्।

अस्यां च वेलायामनतिक्रमणवचनैरुपसृत्य प्रधानसामन्तैर्विज्ञाप्यमानः कथं कथमप्यभुक्त। प्रभातायां च शर्वर्यां सर्वेषु प्रविष्टेषु राजसु समीपस्थितं हर्षदेवमुवाच—'तात, भूमिरसि गुरुनियोगानाम्। शैशव एवाग्राहि गुणवत्पताकेव भवता तातस्य चित्तवृत्तिः। यतो भवन्तमेवंविधं विधेयं विधिविधानोपनतनैर्घृण्यमिदं किमपि विभणिषति मे हृदयम्। नावलम्बनीया बालभावसुलभा प्रेमविलोपा वामता। वैधेय इव मा कृथाः प्रत्यूहमीहितेऽस्मिन्। शृणु। न खलु न जानासि लोकवृत्तम्। लोकत्रयत्रातरि मान्धातरि मृते किं कृतं पुरुकुत्सेन भ्रूलतादिष्टाष्टादशद्वीपे दिलीपे वा रघुणा महासुरसमरमध्याध्यासितत्रिदशरथे दशरथे वा रामेण गोष्पदीकृतचतुरुदन्वदन्ते दुष्यन्ते वा भरतेन। तिष्ठन्तु तावदेते तातेनैव शतसमधिकाध्वरधूमविसरधूसरितवासववयसि सुगृहीतनाम्नि तत्रभवति परासुतां गते पितरि किं नाकारि राज्यम्। यं च किल शोकः समभिभवति तं कापुरुषमाचक्षते शास्त्रविदः। स्त्रियो हि विषयः शुचाम्। तथापि किं करोमि। स्वभावस्य सेयं कापुरुषता वा स्त्रैणं वा यदेवमास्पदं[4] पितृशोकहुतभुजो जातोस्मि। मम हि भूभृति पर्यस्ते निरवशेषतः प्रस्रवणानीव स्रुतान्यश्रूण्यस्तमिते महति तेजस्यन्धकारीभूतदशाशस्य प्रणष्टः प्रज्ञालोकः[5] प्रज्वलितं हृदयम्, आत्मदाहभीत इव स्वप्नेऽपि नोपसर्पति विवेकः, बली-

---

१ 'वितर्दिकाविनिवेशितायामप्रतिपादिकायां चापाश्रय०' ब. २ 'जालमिवाचकाण' अ. ३ 'बर्कुरशक्कर' ब. ४ 'यदेवमसादपि' ब. ५ 'प्रज्ञानलोकः' अ.

यस्य सन्तापेन जातुषमिव विलीनमखिलं धैर्यम्, पदे पदे दिग्धरोपाहतेव हरिणी मुह्यति मतिः, पुरुषद्वेषिणीव दूरेण[1] भ्रमति परिहरन्ती स्मृतिः, अम्बेव तातेनैव सह गता धृतिः, वार्द्धुषिकप्रयुक्तानीव वित्तानि प्रतिदिवसं वर्धन्ते दुःखानि, शोकानलधूमसम्भारसम्भूताम्भोधरभरितमिव वर्षति नयनवारिधाराविसरं शरीरम्। सर्वः पञ्चजनः पञ्चत्वमुपरतः[2] प्रयाति वितथमेतद्वदति बालो लोकः। तातो हुताशनतामेव केवलामापन्नो[3] येनैवं दहति माम्। इदमसाम्परायिकमिव हृदयमवष्टभ्य व्युत्थितः शोको दुर्निवारः वाडव इव वारिराशिम्, पविरिव पर्वतम्, क्षय इव क्षपाकरम्, राहुरिव रविम्, दहति दारयति तनूकरोति कवलयति च माम्। न शक्नोति मे हृदयं तादृशस्य सुमेरुकल्पस्य कल्पमहापुरुषस्य विनिपातमश्रुभिरेव केवलैरतिवाहयितुम्। राज्ये विष इव चकोरस्य मे विरक्तं चक्षुः। बहुमृतपटावगुण्ठनां रञ्जितरङ्गां जनङ्गमानामिव वंशबाह्यामनार्यां श्रियं त्यक्तुमभिलषति मे मनः। क्षणमपि दग्धगृहे शकुलिरिव न पारयामि स्थातुम्। सोऽहमिच्छामि मनसि वाससीव सुलग्नं स्नेहमलमिदममलैः शिखरिशिखरप्रस्रवणस्वच्छस्रोतोऽम्बुभिः क्षालयितुमाश्रमपदे। यतस्त्वमन्तरितयौवनसुखामनभिमतामपि जरामिव पूरुराज्ञया गुरोर्गृहाण मे राज्यचिन्ताम्। त्यक्तसकलबालक्रीडेन हरिणेव दीयतामुरो लक्ष्म्यै। परित्यक्तं मया शस्त्रम्।' इत्येवमभिधाय खड्गग्राहिणो हस्तादादाय निजं निस्त्रिंशमुत्ससर्ज धरण्याम्।

अथ तच्छ्रुत्वा निशितशिखेन शूलेनेवाहतः प्रविदीर्णहृदयो देवो हर्षः समचिन्तयत्—किं नु खलु मामन्तरेणार्यः केनचिदसहिष्णुना किंचिद्ग्राहितः कुपितः स्यात्। उतानया दिशा परीक्षितुकामो माम्। उत शोकजन्मा चेतसः समाक्षेपोऽयमस्य। आहोस्विदार्य एवायं न भवति। किं वार्येणान्यदेवाभिहितमन्यदेवाश्रावि मया शोकशून्येन श्रवणेन्द्रियेण। आर्यस्य वान्यदेव विवक्षितमन्यदेवापतितं मुखेन। अथवा सकलवंशविनाशाय निपातनोपायोऽयं विधेः, मम वा निखिलपुण्यपरिक्षयोपक्षेपः कर्मणामननुकूलसमग्रग्रहचक्रवालविलसितं वा, अथवा तातविनाशनिःशङ्ककलिकालक्रीडितं येनायं यः कश्चिदिव यत्किंचनकारिणं मामपुष्पभूतिवंशसम्भूतमिव, अतातनयमिव, अनात्मानुजमिव, अभक्तमिव, अदृष्टदोषमपि[4] श्रोत्रियमिव सुरापाने सद्भृत्यमिव स्वामिद्रोहे सज्जनमिव नीचोपसर्पणे सुकलत्रमिव व्यभिचारे, अतिदुष्करे कर्मणि समादिष्टवान्। तदेतत्तावदनुरूपं यच्छौर्योन्मादमदिरोन्मत्तसमस्तसामन्तमण्डलसमुद्रमथनमन्दरे[5] तादृशि पितरि मृते तपोवनं वा गम्यते वल्कलानि वा गृह्यन्ते तपांसि वा सेव्यन्ते। या तु मयि राज्याज्ञा सा दग्धेऽपि दाहकारिणी मय्यवग्रहग्लपिते धन्वनीवाङ्गार-

१ 'दूरत एव भ्रमन्ती परिहरति' अ. २ 'उपरतः' इति नास्ति ब-पुस्तके. ३ 'आपन्नोऽपि नैवं मां दहति.' ब. ४ 'दृष्टदोषमिव' अ. ५ 'मन्दिरे' ब.

तं च तथा समादिशन्तमाकर्ण्य जामिजामातृवृत्तान्तविज्ञानप्रकोपाधानदूयमाने मनसि निवर्तनापदेशेन[1] दूरप्ररूढप्रणयपीड इव प्रोवाच देवो हर्षः—'कमिव दोषं पश्यत्यार्यो ममानुगमनेन । यदि बाल इति नितरां तर्हि न परित्याज्योऽस्मि, रक्षणीय इति भवद्भुजपञ्जरं रक्षास्थानम्, अशक्त इति क्व परीक्षितोऽस्मि, संवर्धनीय इति वियोगस्तनूकरोति, अक्लेशसह इति स्त्रीपक्षे निक्षिप्तोऽस्मि, सुखमनुभवत्विति त्वयैव सह तत्प्रयाति, महानध्वनः क्लेश इति विरहोऽविषह्यतरः, कलत्रं रक्षत्विति श्रीस्ते निस्त्रिंशेऽधिवसति, पृष्ठतस्तिष्ठत्विति[2] तिष्ठत्येव ते प्रतापः, राजकमनधिष्ठितमिति तत्सुबद्धमार्यगुणैः, न बाह्यः सहायो महत इति व्यतिरिक्तमेव मां गणयसि, प्रलघुपरिकरः प्रयामीति पादरजसि कोऽतिभारः, द्वयोर्गमनमसांप्रतमिति मामनुगृहाण गमनाज्ञया, कातरो भ्रातृस्नेह इति सदृशो दोषः । का चेयमात्मम्भरिता भुजस्य ते यदेकाकी क्षीरोदफेनपटलपाण्डुरममृतमिव यशः पिपासति । अवञ्चितपूर्वोऽस्मि प्रसादेषु[3] । तत्प्रसीदत्वार्यो नयतु मामपि' इत्यभिधाय क्षितितलविनिहितमौलिः पादयोरपतत् ।

तमुत्थाप्य पुनरग्रजो जगाद—'तात किमेवमतिमहारम्भपरिग्रहणेन गरिमाणमारोप्यते बलादतिलघीयानप्यहितः । हरिणार्थमतिक्षेपणः सिंहसम्भारः । तृणानामुपरि कति कवचयन्त्याशुशुक्षणयः । अपि च तवाष्टादशद्वीपाष्टमङ्गलकमालिनी मेदिन्यस्त्येव विक्रमस्य विषयः । नहि कुलशैलनिवहवाहिनो वायवः संनह्यन्त्यतितरले तूलराशौ । न सुमेरुवप्रप्रणयप्रगल्भा वा दिक्करिणः परिणमन्त्यणीयसि वल्मीके । ग्रहीष्यसि सकलपृथ्वीपतिप्रलयोत्पातमहाधूमकेतुं मान्धातेव चारुचामीकरपत्रलतालङ्काराङ्कायं कार्मुकं ककुभां विजये । मम तु दुर्निवारायामस्यां विपक्षक्षपणक्षुधि क्षुभितायां क्षम्यतामयमेकाकिनः कोपकवल एकः । तिष्ठतु भवान् ।' इत्यभिधाय च तस्मिन्नेव वासरे निर्जगामाभ्यमित्रम् ।

अथ तथागते भ्रातरि, उपरते च पितरि, प्रोषितजीविते च जामातरि, मृतायां च मातरि, संयतायां च स्वसरि, स्वयूथभ्रष्ट इव वन्यः करी देवो हर्षः कथं कथमप्येकाकी कालं तमनैषीत् । अतिक्रान्तेषु बहुषु वासरेषु कदाचित्तयैव भ्रातृगमनदुःखासिकया दत्तप्रजागरस्त्रिभागशेषायां त्रियामायां यामिकेन गीयमानामिमामार्यां शुश्राव—

'द्वीपोपगीतगुणमपि समुपार्जितरत्नराशिसारमपि ।
पोतं पवन इव विधिः पुरुषमकाण्डे निपातयति ॥ ३ ॥'

तां च श्रुत्वा सुतरामनित्यताभावनया दूयमानहृदयः प्रक्षीणभूयिष्ठायां क्षपायां क्षणमिव निद्रामलभत स्वप्ने चाभ्रंलिहं लोहस्तम्भं भज्यमानमपश्यत् । उत्कम्पमानहृदयश्च पुनः प्रत्यबुध्यत । अचिन्तयच्च—'किं नु खलु

१'निवर्तनादेशेन' अ. २ 'पृष्ठतः शून्य'-ब. ३ 'विप्रप्रसादेषु' ब.

मामेवममी सततमनुबध्नन्ति दुःस्वप्नाः। स्फुरति च दिवानिशमकल्याणाख्यानविचक्षणमदक्षिणमक्षि। सुदारुणाश्चाक्षुद्रक्षितिपक्षयमाचक्षाणाः क्षणमपि न शाम्यन्ति पुनरुत्पाताः। प्रत्यहं राहुरविकलकायबन्ध इव कबन्धवति ब्रध्नबिम्बे घटमानो विभाव्यते। तपःकरणकालकवलितानिव धूसरितसमग्रग्रहानुद्गिरन्ति धूमोद्गारान्सप्तर्षयः। दिने दिने दारुणा दिशां दाहा दृश्यन्ते। दिग्दाहभस्मकणनिकर इव निपतति नभस्तलात्तारागणः। तारापातशुचेव निष्प्रभः शशी। निशि निशि इतस्ततः प्रज्वलिताभिरुल्काभिरुग्रं ग्रहयुद्धमिव वियति विलोकयन्ति विलोलतारकाः ककुभः। राज्यसञ्चारसूचकः सञ्चारयतीव क्ष्मां क्वापि वहद्बहलरजःपटलकलिलशर्कराशकलसूत्कारी मारुतः। न कुशलमिव पश्यामि लग्नस्य। अस्मिन्नस्मद्वंशे करिण इव करीरं कोमलमपि कलयतः कृतान्तस्य कः परिपन्थी। सर्वथा स्वस्ति भवत्वार्याय।' इति चिन्तयित्वा च अन्तर्भिन्नं भ्रातृस्नेहकातरं द्रवदिव हृदयं कथं कथमपि संस्तभ्योत्थाय यथाक्रियमाणं क्रियाकलापमकरोत्।

आस्थानगतश्च सहसैव प्रविशन्तम्, अनुप्रविशता विषण्णवदनेन लोकेनानुगम्यमानम्, असह्यदुःखोष्णनिश्वासधूमरक्ततन्तुनेव मलिनेन पटेन प्रावृतवपुषम्, जीवितधारणलज्जयेवावनतमुखम्, नासावंशस्याग्रे ग्रथितदृष्टिम्, दुःखदूरप्ररूढरोम्णा मूकेनापि मुखेन स्वामिव्यसनमविच्छिन्नैरश्रुबिन्दुभिर्विज्ञापयन्तं कुन्तलं नाम बृहदश्ववारम्, राज्यवर्धनस्य प्रसादभूमिमभिजा[1]ततमं ददर्श। दृष्ट्वा च जाताशङ्कश्चक्षुषि सलिलेन, मुखशशिनि श्वसितेन, हृदये हुताशेन, उत्सङ्गे भुवा, दारुणाप्रियश्रवणसमये सममिव सर्वेष्वङ्गेष्वगृह्यत लोकपालैः। तस्माच्च हेलानिर्जितमालवानीकमपि गौडाधिपेन मिथ्योपचारोपचितविश्वासं मुक्तशस्त्रमेकाकिनं विश्रब्धं स्वभवन एव भ्रातरं व्यापादितमश्रौषीत्।

श्रुत्वा च महातेजस्वी प्रचण्डकोपपावकप्रसरपरिचीयमानशोकावेगः सहसैव प्रजज्वाल। ततश्चामर्षविधुतशिरःशीर्यमाणशिखामणिशकलाङ्गारकि[2]र्तमिव रोषाग्निमुद्वमन्, अनवरतस्फुरितेन पिबन्निव सर्वतेजस्विनामायूंषि रोषनिर्भुग्नेन दशनच्छदेन, लोहितायमानलोचनालोकविक्षेपैर्दिग्दाहानिव दर्शयन्, रोषानलेनाप्यसह्यसहजशौर्योष्मदहनदह्यमानेनेव वितन्यमानस्वेदसलिलशीकरासारदुर्दिनः, स्वावयवैरप्यदृष्टपूर्वप्रकोपभीतैरिव कम्पमानैरुपेतः, हर इव कृतभैरवाकारः, हरिरिव प्रकटितनरसिंहरूपः, सूर्यकान्तशैल इवापरतेजःप्रसरदर्शनप्रज्वलितः, क्षयदिवस इवोदितद्वादशदिनकरदुर्निरीक्ष्यमूर्तिः, महोत्पातमारुत इव सकलभूभृत्कम्पकारी, विन्ध्य इव विवर्धमानविग्रहोत्सेधः, महाशीविष इव दुर्नरेन्द्राभिभवरोषितः, पारीक्षित इव सर्वभोगिदहनोद्यतः, वृकोदर इव रिपुरुधिरतृषितः, सुरगज इव प्रतिपक्षवारणप्र-

---

१ 'अभिज्ञात०' ब. २ 'शकलाङ्गारकिताङ्गमिव' ब.

धावितः, पूर्वागम इव पौरुषस्य, उन्माद इव मदस्य, आवेग इवावलेपस्य, तारुण्यावतार इव तेजसः, सर्वोद्योग इव दर्पस्य, युगागम इव यौवनोष्मणः, राज्याभिषेक इव रणरसस्य, नीराजनदिवस इवासहिष्णुतायाः, परां भीषणतामयासीत् ।

अवादीच्च । 'गौडाधिपाधममपहाय कस्तादृशं महापुरुषं तत्क्षण एव निर्व्याजभुजवीर्यनिर्जितसमस्तराजकं मुक्तशस्त्रं कलशयोनिमिव कृष्णवर्त्मप्रसूतिरीदृशेन सर्ववीरलोकविगर्हितेन मृत्युना शमयेदार्यम् । अनार्यं च तं मुक्त्वा भागीरथीफेनपटलपाण्डुराः केषां मनःसु सरःसु राजहंसा इव परशुरामपराक्रमस्मृतिकृतो न कुर्युरार्यशौर्यगुणाः पक्षपातम् । कथमिवात्युग्रस्यास्यार्यजीवितहरणे निदाघरवेरिव कमलाकरसलिलशोषणेऽनपेक्षितप्रीतयः प्रसृताः कराः । कां नु गतिं गमिष्यति, कां वा योनिं प्रवेक्ष्यति, कस्मिन्वा नरके निपतिष्यति । श्वपाकोऽपि क इदमाचरेत् । नामापि गृह्णतोऽस्य पापकारिणः पापमलेन लिप्यत इव मे जिह्वा । किं वाङ्गीकृत्य कार्यमार्यस्तेन क्षुद्रेणानुप्रविश्य विगतघृणेन घुणेनेव सकलभुवनाह्लादनचतुरश्चन्दनस्तम्भः क्षयमुपनीतः । नूनं नानेन मूढेन मधुरसास्वादलुब्धेन मध्विवार्यजीवितमाकर्षता भावी दृष्टः[१] कष्टशिलीमुखसम्पातोपद्रवः । निजगृहदूषणं जालमार्गप्रदीपकेन कज्जलमिवातिमलिनं केवलमयशः सञ्चितं[२] गौडाधमेन । न त्वाश्वेवास्तमुपगतवत्यपि त्रिभुवनचूडामणौ सवितरि वेधसादिष्टः[३] सत्पथशत्रोरन्धकारस्य निग्रहाय ग्रहषण्डविहारैकहरिणाधिपः शशी । विनयविधायिनि भग्नेऽपि चाङ्कुशे विद्यत एव व्यालवारणस्य विनयाय सकलमत्तमातङ्गकुम्भस्थलस्थिरशिरोभागभिदुरः खरतरः केसरिनखरः । तादृशाः कुवैकटिका इव तेजस्विरत्नविनाशकाः कस्य न वध्याः । क्वेदानीं यास्यति दुर्बुद्धिः ।' इत्येतदभिदधत एवास्य पितुरपि मित्रं सेनापतिः समग्रविग्रहप्राग्रहरो हरितालशैलावदातदेहः, परिणतप्रगुणसालप्रकाण्डप्रकाशः, प्रांशुरतिशौर्योष्मणेव परिपाकमागतो गतभूयिष्ठे वयसि वर्तमानः, बहुशरशयनसुप्तोत्थितोऽपि हसन्निव शान्तनवमतिदीर्घेणायुषा, दुरभिभवशरीरतया जरयापि भीतभीतयेव प्रकटितप्रकम्पया परामृष्टः कथमपि सारमयेषु शिरोरुहेषु, शशिकरनिकरसितसरलशिरोरुहसटालः[४] सैंहीमिव निष्कपटपराक्रमरसरचितां संक्रान्तो जीवन्नेव जातिम्, अपरस्वामिमुखदर्शनमहापातकपरिजिहीर्षयेव भ्रूयुगलेन वलिन[५]शिथिलप्रलम्बचर्मणा स्थगितदृष्टिः, धवलस्थूलगुञ्जापिच्छप्रच्छादितकपोलभागभास्वरेण वमन्निव विक्रमकालमकालेऽपि विकाशिकाशकाननविशदं शरदारम्भं भीमेन मुखेन, मृतमपि हृदयस्थितं स्वामिनमिव सितचामरेण वीजयन्नाभिलम्बेन कूर्चकलापेन, परिणामेऽपि धौतासिधाराजलपानतृषितैरिव विवृतवदनैर्बृहद्भिर्व्रणविदारैर्विषमितविशालवक्षाः, निशितशस्त्रटङ्ककोटि-

---

१ 'दृष्टः शिली'-अ. २ 'सञ्चितं नत्वाश्वेवास्त' ब. ३ 'वेधसादिसृष्टः' ब.
४ 'सटालम्' अ. ५ 'वलित' अ.

कुट्टितबहुबृहद्व्रणाक्षरपङ्क्तिनिरन्तरतया च सकलसमरविजयपर्वगणनामिव कुर्वन्पूर्वपर्वत इव[1] पादचारी, विविधवीररसवृत्तान्तरामणीयकेन महाभारतमपि लघयन्निव, प्रतिपक्षक्षपणातिनिर्बन्धेन परशुराममपि शिक्षयन्निव, अभ्रमणेनानादरश्रीसमाकर्षणविभ्रमेण मन्दरमपि मन्दयन्निव, वाहिनीनायकमर्यादानुवर्तनेनाम्भोधिमप्यभिभवन्निव, स्थैर्यकार्कश्योन्नतिभिरचलानपि ह्रेपयन्निव, सहजप्रचण्डतेजःप्रसरपरिस्फुरणेन सवितारमपि तृणीकुर्वन्निव, ईश्वरभारोद्वहनघृष्टपृष्ठतया हरवृषभमपि हसन्निव, अरणिरमर्षाग्नेः, ऐश्वर्यं शौर्यस्य, मदो मदस्य, विसर्पो दर्पस्य, हृदयं हठस्य, जीवितं जिगीषुतायाः, उच्छ्वसितमुत्साहस्य, अङ्कुशो दुर्मदानाम्, नागदमनो दुष्टभोगिनाम्, विरामो वरमनुष्यतायाः, कुलगुरुर्वीरगोष्ठीनाम्, तुला शौर्यशालिनाम्, सीमान्तदृश्वा शस्त्रग्रामस्य, निर्वोढा प्रौढवादानाम्, संस्तम्भयिता भग्नानाम्, पारगः प्रतिज्ञायाः, मर्मज्ञो महाविग्रहाणाम्, आघोषणापटहः समरार्थिनाम्, सन्निधावेव समुपविष्टः सिंहनादनामा स्वरेणैव दुन्दुभिनिर्घोषगम्भीरेण सुभटानां समररसमानयन्विज्ञापितवान्—'देव, न क्वचित्कृताश्रयया मलिनया मलिनतराः कोकिलया काका इव कापुरुषा हतलक्ष्म्या विप्रलभ्यमानमात्मानं न चेतयन्ते। श्रियो हि दोषान्धतादयः कामला विकाराः। छत्रच्छायान्तरितरवयो विस्मरन्त्यन्यं तेजस्विनं जडधियः। किं वा करोतु वराकः येनातिभीरुतया नित्यपराङ्मुखेन न तु दृष्टान्येव सर्वातिशायिशौर्यातिशयश्वयथुकपिलकपोलपुलकपल्लवितकोपानलानि कुपितानां तेजस्विनां मुखानि। नासौ तपस्वी जानात्येवं यथाभिचारा इव विप्रकृताः सद्यः सकलकुलप्रलयमुपाहरन्ति मनस्विनः। जलेऽपि ज्वलन्ति ताडितास्तेजस्विनः। सकलवीरगोष्ठीबाह्यस्य तस्यैवेदमुचितमनुत्तारनिरयनिपातनिपुणं कर्म। मनस्विनां हि प्रधनप्रधानधने धनुषि ध्रियमाणे सति च कमलाकलहंसीकेलिकुवलयकानने कृपाणे कृपणोपायाः पयोधिमथनप्रभृतयोऽपि श्रीसमुत्थानस्य किं पुनरीदृशाः। येषां च धात्रा धरित्रीं त्रातुं नियुक्ताः स्वयमसमर्था इव कुलिशकर्कशभुजपरिघप्रहरणहेतोरुद्गिरन्ति गिरयोऽपि लोहानि ते कथमिव बाहुशालिनो मनसापि विमलयशोबान्धवा ध्यायेयुरकार्यम्। सर्वग्रहाभिभवभास्वराणां हि सुभटकराणामग्रतो दिग्ग्रहणे पङ्गवः पतङ्गकराः। महामहिषशृङ्गतरङ्गभङ्गभङ्गुर[2]भीषणान्तराला लोकप्रवादमात्रेण दक्षिणाशा परमार्थतो भटभ्रुकुटिरधिवासो यमस्य। चित्रं च यदुन्मुक्तसिंहनादानां सहसासाहसरसरोमाञ्चकण्टकनिकरेण सह न निर्यान्ति सटाः शूराणां रणेषु। द्वयमेव च चतुःसागरसम्भूत[3]स्य भूतिसम्भारस्य भाजनं प्रतिपक्षदाहि दारुणं वडवामुखं वा महापुरुषहृदयं वा। तेजस्विनः सकलाननवाप्य पयोराशीन्सहजस्य कुतो निवृत्तिरूष्मणः। वृथावितत विपुलफणाभारो भुजङ्गानां भर्ता

---

१ 'पर्वपूर्वपर्वत इव' ब. २ 'भङ्गुरभङ्गिभीषणा—' ब. ३ 'सम्भृतस्य' ब.

बिभर्ति यो भोगीन मृत्पिण्डमेव केवलम् । अप्रतिहतशासनाक्रान्त्युपभोग-
सुखरसं तु रसाया दिक्कुञ्जरकरभारभास्वरप्रकोष्ठा वीरबाहव एव जानन्ति ।
रविरिवोन्मुखपद्माकरगृहीतपादपल्लवः सुखेनाखण्डिततेजा दिवसान्नयति
शूरः । कातरस्य तु शशिन इव हरिणहृदयस्य पाण्डुरपृष्ठस्य कुतो द्विरात्रमपि
निश्चला लक्ष्मीः । अपरिमितयशःप्रकरवर्षी विकासी वीररसः । पुरःप्रवृत्तप्र-
तापप्रहताः पन्थानः पौरुषस्य । शब्दविद्रुतद्विषन्ति भवन्ति द्वाराणि दर्पस्य ।
शस्त्रालोकप्रकाशिताः शून्या दिशः शौर्यस्य । रिपुरुधिरशीकरासारेण भूरिव
श्रीरप्यनुरज्यते । बहुनरपतिमुकुटमणिशिलाशाणकोणकषणेन चरणनखराजि-
रिव राजताप्युज्वलीभवति । अनवरतशस्त्राभ्यासेन करतलानीव रिपुमुखानि
श्यामीभवन्ति । विविधव्रणबद्ध[1]पट्टकशतैः शरीरमिव यशोऽपि धवली-
भवति । कवचिषु रिपूरःकपाटेषु पात्यमानाः पावकशिखामिव श्रियमपि
वमन्ति निष्ठुरा निस्त्रिंशप्रहाराः । यश्चाहितहतस्वजनो मनस्विजनो द्विषद्यो-
षिदुरस्ताडनेन कथयति हृदयदुःखम् । परुषा[2]सिलतानिपातप[3]वनेनोच्छ्वसिति
निरुच्छ्वसितशत्रुशरीराश्रुधारापातेन रोदिति विपक्षवनिताचक्षुषा ददाति
जलं स श्रेयान्नेतरः । न च स्वप्नदृष्टनष्टेष्विव क्षणिकेषु शरीरेषु निबध्नन्ति
बन्धुबुद्धिं प्रबुद्धाः । स्थायिनि यशसि शरीरधीर्वीराणाम् । अनवरतप्रज्वलि-
ततेजःप्रसरभास्वरस्वभावं च मणिप्रदीपमिव कलुषः कज्जलमलो न स्पृश-
त्येव तेजस्विनं शोकः । स त्वं सत्त्ववतामग्रणीः प्राग्रहरः प्राज्ञानां प्रथमः
समर्थानां प्रष्ठोऽभिजातानामग्रेसरस्तेजस्विनामादिरसहिष्णूनाम् । एताश्च स-
ततसन्निहितधूमायमानकोपाग्नयः सुलभासिधारातोयतृप्तयो विकटबाहुवन-
च्छायोपगूढा धीरताया निवासशिशिरभूमयः स्वायत्ताः सुभटानामुरःकवा-
टभित्तयः । यतः किं गौडाधिपाधमेनैकेन । तथा कुरु यथा नान्योऽपि
कश्चिदाचरत्येवं भूयः । सर्वोर्वीश्रद्धाकामुकानामलीकविजिगीषूणां सञ्चारय
चामराण्यन्तःपुरपुरंध्रिनिश्वसितैः । उच्छिन्धि रुधिरगन्धान्धगृध्रमण्डलाच्छा-
दनैश्छत्रच्छायाव्यसनानि । अपाकुरु कदुष्णशोणितोदकस्वेदैः कुलक्ष्मीकुल-
टाकटाक्षचक्षूरागरोगान् । उपशमय निशितशरशिरावेधै[4]र्वैकार्यशौर्यश्वयथून् ।
उन्मूलय लोहनिगडापीडमालामलै[5]र्महौषधैः पादपीठदोहददुर्ललितपादपटु-
माम्द्यानि । क्षपय तीक्ष्णाज्ञाक्षरक्षारपातैर्जयशब्दश्रवणकर्णकण्डूः । अपनय
चरणनखमरीचिचन्दनचर्चाललाटलेपैरनमितस्तिमितमस्तकस्तम्भविकारान् ।
उद्धर करदानसन्देशसन्दंशैर्द्रविणदर्पोष्मायमाणदुःशीललीलाशल्यानि ।
भिन्धि मणिपादपीठदीधितिप्रदीपिकाभिः शुष्कसुभटाटोपभ्रुकुटिबन्धान्धका-
रान् । जय चरणलङ्घनलाघवगलितशिरोगौरवारोग्यैर्मिथ्याभिमानमहासन्नि-
पातान् । म्रदय सततसेवाञ्जलिमुकुलितकरसम्पुटोष्मभिरिष्वसनगुणकिण-

---

१ 'बन्ध' ब. २ 'परुषानसि' ब. ३ 'निपातवनेन' अ. ४ 'वेधैर्वीरकार्य'- ब.
५ 'मालामलयमहौषधैः' ब.

कार्कश्यानि। येनैव ते गतः पिता पितामहः प्रपितामहो वा तमेव मा हासीस्त्रिभुवनस्पृहणीयं पन्थानम्। अपहाय कुपुरुषोचितां शुचं प्रतिपद्यस्व कुलक्रमागतां केसरीव कुरङ्गीं राजलक्ष्मीम्। देव, देवभूयं गते नरेन्द्रे दुष्टगौडभुजङ्गजग्धजीविते च राज्यवर्धने वृत्तेऽस्मिन्महाप्रलये धरणीधारणायाधुना त्वं शेषः। समाश्वासय अशरणाः प्रजाः क्ष्मापतीनां शिरःसु शरत्सवितेव ललाटंतपान्प्रयच्छ पादन्यासान्। अहितानामभिनवसेवादीक्षादुःखसन्तप्तश्वासधूममण्डलैर्नखम्पचैः प्रचलितचूडामणिचक्रवालबालातपैश्चायाहि कल्माषपादताम्। अपि च हते पितर्येकाकी तपस्वी मृगैः सह संवर्धितः सहजब्राह्मण्यमार्दवसुकुमारमनाः कृतनिश्चयश्चण्डचापवनाटनिटांकारनादनिर्मदीकृतदिग्गजं गुञ्जज्ज्याजालजनितजगज्ज्वरं समग्रमुद्यतमेकविंशतिकृत्वः कृत्तवंशमुत्खातवान्राजन्यकं परशुरामः। किं पुनर्नैसर्गिककायकार्कश्यकुलिशायमानमानसो मानिनां मूर्धन्यो देवः। तदद्यैव कृतप्रतिज्ञो गृहाण गौडाधमजीवितध्वस्तये जीवितसङ्कलनाकुलकालाकाण्डयात्राचिह्नध्वजं धनुः। न ह्ययमरातिरक्तचन्दनचर्चाशिशिरोपचारमन्तरेण शाम्यति परिभवानलपच्यमानदेहस्य देवस्य दुःखदाहज्वरः सुदारुणः। निकारसन्तापशान्त्युपायपरिक्षये हि हिडिम्बाचुम्बनास्वादितमिव रिपुरुधिरामृतममन्दरोपायमपायि पवनात्मजेन। जामदग्न्येन च शाम्यन्मन्युशिखिशिखासंज्वरसुखायमानस्पर्शशीतलेपु क्षत्रियक्षतजह्रदेष्वस्नायि।' इत्युक्त्वा व्यरंसीत्।

देवस्तु हर्षस्तं प्रत्यवादीत्—'करणीयमेवेदमभिहितं मान्येन। इतरथा हि मे गृहीतभुवि भोगिनाथेऽपि दायादद्दृष्टिरीर्ष्यालोर्भुजस्य। उपरि गच्छतीच्छति निग्रहाय ग्रहगणेऽपि भ्रूलता चलितुम्। अनमत्सु शैलेष्वपि कचग्रहमभिलषति दातुं करः। तेजोदुर्विदग्धानर्ककरानपि चामराणि ग्राहयितुमीहते हृदयम्। राजशब्दरुषा मृगराजानामपि शिरांसि वाञ्छति पादः पादपीठीकर्तुम्। स्वच्छन्दलोकपालस्वेच्छागृहीतानामाक्षेपादेशाय दिशामपि स्फुरत्यधरः। किं पुनरीदृशे दुर्जाते जाते जातामर्षनिर्भरे च मनसि नास्त्येवावकाशः शोकक्रियाकरणस्य। अपि च हृदयविषमशल्ये मुसल्ये जीवति जाल्मे जगद्विगर्हिते गौडाधिपाधमचण्डाले जिह्रेमि शुष्काधरपुटः पोटेव प्रतिकारशून्यं शुचा सूत्कर्तुम्। अकृतरिपुबलाबलाविलोललोचनोदकदुर्दिनस्य मे कुतः करयुगलस्य जलाञ्जलिदानम्। अदृष्टगौडाधमचिताधूममण्डलस्य वा चक्षुषः स्वल्पमप्यश्रुसलिलम्। श्रूयतां मे प्रतिज्ञा। शपाम्यार्यस्यैव पादपांशुस्पर्शेन यदि परिगणितैरेव वासरैः सकलचापचापलदुर्ललितनरपतिचरणरणरणायमाननिगडां निर्गौडां न करोमि मेदिनीं ततस्तनूनपाति पीतसर्पिषि पतङ्ग इव पातकी पातयाम्यात्मानम्।' इत्युक्त्वा च महासन्धिविग्रहाधिकृतमवन्तिमन्तिकस्थमादिदेश—'लिख्यताम्। आ रविरथच-

---

१ 'कृतवंशं' ब.

क्रचीत्कारचकितचारणमिथुनमुक्तसानोरुदयाचलात्, आ त्रिकूटकटककुट्टाकटङ्कलिखितकाकुत्स्थलङ्कालुण्ठनव्यतिकरात्सुवेलात्, आ वारुणीमदस्खलितवरुणवरनारीनूपुररवमुखरकुहरकुक्षेरस्तगिरेः, आ गुह्यकगेहिनीपरिमलसुगन्धिगन्धपाषाणवासितगुहागृहाच्च गन्धमादनात्, सर्वेषां राज्ञां सज्जीक्रियन्तां कराः करदानाय शस्त्रग्रहणाय वा, गृह्यन्तां दिशश्चामराणि वा, नमन्तु शिरांसि धनूंषि वा, कर्णपूरीक्रियन्तामाज्ञा मौर्व्यो वा, शेखरीभवन्तु पादरजांसि शिरस्त्राणि वा, घटन्तामञ्जलयः करिघटाबन्धा वा, मुच्यन्तां भूमय इषवो वा, समालम्ब्यन्तां वेत्रयष्टयः कुन्तयष्टयो वा, सुदृष्टः क्रियतामात्मा मच्चरणनखेषु कृपाण[1]दर्पणेषु वा परागतोऽहमिति। पङ्गोरिव मे कुतो निवृत्तिस्तावद्यावन्न कृतः सर्वद्वीपान्तरसञ्चारी सकलनरपतिमुकुटमणिशिलालोकमयः पादलेपः।' इति कृतनिश्चयश्च मुक्तास्थानो विसर्जितराजलोकः स्नानारम्भाकाङ्क्षी सभामत्याक्षीत्। उत्थाय च स्वस्थवन्निःशेषमाह्निकमकार्षीत्। अगलच्च दर्पप्रसर इव श्रुतप्रतिज्ञस्य शाम्यदूष्मा दिवसस्त्रिभुवनस्य।

ततश्च निजाधिकारापहारभीत इव भगवत्यपि क्वापि गते गततेजस्यहिमतामरसवनेष्वपि निगूढशिलीमुखालापेषु त्रासादिव सङ्कुचत्सु, विहगगणेष्वपि समुपसंहृतनिजपक्षविक्षेपनिश्चलेषु भियेवाप्रकटीभवत्सु, भुवनव्यापिनीं संध्यां प्रतिज्ञामिव मानयति नतशिरसि घटिताञ्जलिवने जने सकले, स्वपदच्युतिचकितदिक्पालदीयमानाभ्रंलिहलोहप्राकारवलया[2]स्विव बहलतिमिरमालातिरोधीयमानासु दिक्षु प्रदोषास्थाने नातिचिरं तस्थौ। नमन्नृपलोकलोलांशुकपवनकम्पितशिखैर्दीपिकाचक्रवालैरपि प्रणम्यमान इव प्राहिणोल्लोकं प्रतिषिद्धपरिजनप्रवेशश्च शयनगृहं प्राविशत्। उत्तानश्च मुमोचाङ्गानि शयनतले। दीपद्वितीयं च तमभिसर इव लब्धावसरस्तरसा भ्रातृशोको जग्राह। जीवन्तमिव हृदये निमीलितलोचनो ददर्शाग्रजम्। उपर्युपरि भ्रातृजीवितान्वेषिण इव प्रसस्रुः श्वासाः। धवलांशुकपटान्तेनेव चाश्रुजलप्लवेन मुखमाच्छाद्य निःशब्दमतिचिरं रुरोद। चकार च चेतसि। कथं नामाकृतेस्तादृश्या युक्तः परिणामोऽयमीदृशः। पृथुशिलासङ्घातकर्कशकायबन्धात्तातादचलादिव लोहधातुः कठिनतर आसीदार्यः। कथं चास्य मे हतहृदयस्यार्यविरहे सकृदपि युक्तमुच्छ्वसितुम्। इयं सा प्रीतिर्भक्तिरनुवृत्तिर्वा। बालिशोऽपि कः सम्भावयेदार्यमरणे मज्जीवितम्। तत्तादृशमैक्यमेकपद एव क्वापि गतम्। अयत्नेनैव हतविधिना पृथक्कृतोऽस्मि। दग्धरोषान्तरितशुचा सुचिरं रुदितमपि न मुक्तकण्ठं गतघृणेन मया। सर्वथा लूतातन्तुच्छटाच्छिद्रुरास्तुच्छाः प्रीतयः प्राणिनाम्। लोकयात्रामात्रनिबन्धना बान्धवता यतोऽहमपि नाम पर इवार्ये स्वर्गस्थे स्वस्थ इवासे। किं च दैवहतकेन फलमासादितमीदृशि परस्परप्रीतिबन्धनिर्वृतहृदये सुखभाजि भ्रातृमिथुने विघटिते। तथा

---

१ 'मणिदर्पणेषु' ब. २ 'वलयकंलितास्विव' ब.

चन्द्रमया इव जगदाह्लादिनो लोकान्तरीभूतस्य लग्नचिताग्नय इवार्यस्य त एव दहन्ति गुणाः। इत्येतानि चान्यानि च हृदयेन पर्यदेवत। प्रभातायां च शर्वर्यां प्रातरेव प्रतीहारमादिदेशाशेषगजसाधनाधिकृतं स्कन्दगुप्तं द्रष्टुमिच्छामीति।

अथ युगपत्प्रधावितबहुपुरुषपरम्पराहूयमानः, स्वमन्दिरादप्रतिपालितकरेणुश्चरणाभ्यामेव संभ्रान्तः, ससंभ्रमैर्दण्डिभिरुत्सार्यमाणजनपदः, पदे पदे प्रणमतः प्रतिदिशमिभभिषग्वरान्वरवारणानां विभावरीवार्ताः पृच्छन् उच्छ्रितशिखिपिच्छलाञ्छितवंशलतावनगहनगृहीतदिगायामैर्विन्ध्यवनैरिव वारणबन्धविमर्दोद्योगागतैः पुरःप्रधावद्भिरनायतमण्डलैराधोरणगणैश्च मरकतहरितघासमुष्टीश्च दर्शयद्भिर्नवग्रहगजपतींश्च प्रार्थयमानैश्च लब्धाभिमतमत्तमातङ्गमुदितमानसैश्च सुदूरमुपसृत्य नमस्यद्भिरात्मीयमातङ्गमदागमांश्च निवेदयद्भिः, डिण्डिमाधिरोहणाय च विज्ञापयद्भिः, प्रमादपतितापराधापहृतद्विरददुःखधृतदीर्घश्मश्रुभिरग्रतो गच्छद्भिः, अभिनवोपसृतैश्च कर्पटिभिर्वारणाप्तिसुखप्रत्याशया धावमानैः, गणिकाधिकारिगणैश्चिरलब्धान्तरैरुच्छ्रितकरैः, कर्मण्यकरेणुकासङ्कथनाकुलैरुल्लासितपल्लवचिह्नाभिररण्यपालपङ्क्तिभिश्च, निष्पादितनवग्रहनागनिवहनिवेदनोद्यताभिरुत्तम्भिततुङ्गतोत्रवनाभिर्महामात्रपेटकैश्च प्रकटितकरिकर्मचर्मपुटैः, अभिनवगजसाधनसञ्चरणवार्तानिवेदनविसर्जितैश्च नागवनवीथीपालदूतवृन्दैः, प्रतिक्षणप्रत्यवेक्षितकरिकवलकूटैः, कटभङ्गसंग्रहं ग्रामनगरनिगमेषु निवेदयमानैः, कटककदम्बकैः क्रियमाणकोलाहलः, स्वामिप्रसादसम्भृतेन महाधिकाराविष्कारेण स्वाभाविकेन चावष्टम्भाभोगेनोदासीनोऽप्यादिशन्निव, असंख्यकरिकर्णशङ्खसम्पत्सम्पादनाय समुद्रानाज्ञापयन्निव, शृङ्गारगैरिकपङ्काङ्गरागसंग्रहाय गिरीन्मुष्णन्निव, दिग्गजाधिकारं ककुभामैरावतमिवापहरन्हरेर्हरपदभारनमितकैलासगिरिगुरुभिः पादन्यासैर्गुरुभारग्रहणगर्वमुर्व्याः संहरन्निव, गतिवशविलोलस्य चाजानुलम्बस्य बाहुदण्डद्वयस्य विक्षेपैरालानशिलास्तम्भमालामिवोभयतो निखनन्, ईषदुत्तुङ्गलम्बेनाधरबिम्बेनामृतरसस्वादुना नवपल्लवकोमलेन कवलेनेव श्रीकरेणुकां विलोभयन्, निजनृपवंशदीर्घं नासावंशं दधानः, अतिस्निग्धमधुरधवलविशालतया पीतक्षीरोदेनेव पिबन्नीक्षणयुग्मायामेन दिशामायामम्, मेरुतटादपि विकटविपुलालिकः, सततमविच्छिन्नच्छत्रच्छायाप्ररूढिवशादिव नितान्तायतनीलकोमलच्छविसुभगेन स्वभावभङ्गुरेण कुन्तलबालवल्लरीवेल्लितविलासिना लुनन्निव लुप्तालोकान्कर्कराञ्बर्बरकेण, अरिपक्षपरिक्षयपरित्यक्तकार्मुककर्मापि सकलदिगन्तश्रूयमाणगुरुगुणध्वनिः, आत्मस्थसमस्तमत्तमातङ्गसाधनोऽप्यस्पृष्टो मदेन, भूतिमानपि स्नेहमयः, पार्थिवोऽपि गुणमयः, करिणामिव दानवतामुपरि स्थितः, स्वामितामिव स्पृहणीयां भृत्यतामप्यपरिभूतामुद्वहन्नेकभर्तृभक्तिनिश्चलां कुलाङ्गनामिवान-

१ 'प्रमादापतित' ब.

न्यगम्यां प्रभुप्रसादभूमिमारूढः, निष्कारणबान्धवो विदग्धानाम्, अभृतभृत्यो भजताम्, अक्रीतदासो विदुषाम्, स्कन्दगुप्तो विवेश राजकुलम्। दूरादेव चोभयकरकमलावलम्बितं स्पृशन्मौलिना महीतलं नमस्कारमकरोत्।

उपविष्टं नतिनिकटे तं तदा जगाद देवो हर्षः—'श्रुतो विस्तर एवास्यार्यव्यतिकरस्यास्मच्चिकीर्षितस्य च। अतः शीघ्रं प्रवेश्यन्तां प्रचारनिर्गतानि गजसाधनानि। न क्षाम्यत्यतिस्वल्पमप्यार्यपरिभवपीडापावकः प्रयाणविलम्बम्।'[1] इत्येवमभिहितश्च प्रणम्य व्यज्ञापयत्—'कृतमवधारयतु स्वामी समादिष्टं किंतु स्वल्पं विज्ञाप्यमस्ति भर्तृभक्तेः। तदाकर्णयतु देवः। देवेन हि पुष्पभूतिवंशसम्भूतस्याभिजनस्याभिजात्यस्य[2] सहजस्य तेजसो दिक्करिकरप्रलम्बस्य बाहुयुगलस्यासाधारणस्य च सोदरस्नेहस्य सर्वं सदृशमुपक्रान्तम्। काकोदराभिधानाः कृपणाः कृमयोऽपि न मृष्यन्ति निकारं[3] किमुत भवादृशास्तेजसां राशयः। केवलं देवराज्यवर्धनोदन्तेन कियदपि दृष्टमेव देवेन दुर्जनदौरात्म्यम्। ईदृशाः खलु लोकस्वभावाः प्रतिग्रामं प्रतिनगरं प्रतिविषयं प्रतिदेशं प्रतिद्वीपं प्रतिदिशं च भिन्ना वेशाश्चाकाराश्चाहाराश्च व्याहाराश्च व्यवहाराश्च जनपदानाम्। तदियमात्मदेशाचारोचिता स्वभावसरलहृदयजा त्यज्यतां सर्वविश्वासिता। प्रमाददोषाभिषङ्गेषु श्रुतबहुवार्त एव प्रतिदिनं देवः। यथा नागकुलजन्मनः सारिकाश्रावितमन्त्रस्या[4]सीन्नाशो नागसेनस्य पद्मावत्याम्। शुकश्रुतरहस्यस्य च श्रीरशीर्यत श्रुतवर्मणः श्रावस्त्याम्। स्वप्नायमानस्य च मन्त्रभेदोऽभून्मृत्यवे मृत्तिकावत्यां सुवर्णचूडस्य। चूडामणिलग्नलेखप्रतिबिम्बवाचिताक्षरा च चारुचामीकरचामरग्राहिणी यमतां ययौ यवनेश्वरस्य। लोभबहुलं च बहुलनिशि निधानमुत्खनन्तमुत्खातखङ्गप्रमाथिनी ममन्थ माथुरं बृहद्रथं विदूरथवरूथिनी। नागवनविहारशीलं च मायामातङ्गाङ्गान्निर्गता महासेनसैनिका वत्सपतिं न्ययंसिषुः। अतिदयितलास्यस्य च शैलूषमध्यमध्यास्य मूर्धानमसिलतया मृणालमिवालुनादग्निमित्रात्मजस्य सुमित्रस्य मित्रदेवः। प्रियतन्त्रीवाद्यस्यालाबूवीणाभ्यन्तरशुषिरनिहितनिशिततरवारयो गान्धर्वच्छात्रच्छद्मानः चिच्छिदुरश्मकेश्वरस्य शरभस्य शिरो रिपुपुरुषाः। प्रज्ञादुर्बलं च बलदर्शनव्यपदेशदर्शिताशेषसैन्यः सेनानीरनार्यो मौर्यं बृहद्रथं पिपेष पुष्यमित्रः स्वामिनम्। आश्चर्यकुतूहली च चण्डीपतिर्दण्डोपनतयवननिर्मितेन नभस्तलयायिना यन्त्रयानेनानीयत क्वापि। काकवर्णः शैशुनागिश्च नगरोपकण्ठे कण्ठे निचकृते निस्त्रिंशेन। अतिस्त्रीसङ्गरतमनङ्गपरवशं शुङ्गममात्यो वसुदेवो देवभूतिदासीदुहित्रा देवीव्यञ्जनया वीतजीवितमकारयत्। असुरविवरव्यसनिनं चापजहुरपरिमितरमणीमणिनूपुरझणझणाहादरम्यया मागधं गोधनगिरिसुरुङ्गया स्वविषयं मेकलाधिपमन्त्रिणः। महाकालमहे च महा-

---

१ 'प्रणयविलम्बम्' ब. २ 'सम्भूतस्याजात्यस्य' अ-क. ३ 'विकारम्' अ-क. ४ 'प्लावितमन्त्रस्य' ब.

मांसविक्रयवादवातूलं वेतालस्तालजङ्घो जघान जघन्यजं प्रद्योतस्य पौणकिं कुमारं कुमारसेनम्। रसायनरसाभिनिवेशिनश्च वैद्यव्यञ्जनाः सुबहुपुरुषान्तरप्रकाशितौषधगुणा गणपतेर्विदेहराजसुतस्य राजयक्ष्माणमजनयन्। स्त्रीविश्वासिनश्च महादेवीगृहगूढभित्तिभागभ्राता भद्रसेनस्याभवन्मृत्यवे कालिङ्गस्य वीरसेनः। मातृशयनीयतूलिकातलनिषण्णश्च तनयोन्यं तनयमभिषेक्तुकामस्य दध्रस्य करूषाधिपतेरभवन्मृत्यवे। उत्सारकरुचिं च रहसि ससचिवमेव दूरीचकार चकोरनाथं शूद्रकदूतश्चन्द्रकेतुं जीवितात्। मृगयासक्तस्य च मध्नतो गण्डकानुद्दण्डनड्वलनलवननिलीनाश्च चम्पाधिपचमूचरभटाश्चामुण्डीपतेराचेमुः प्राणान्पुष्करस्य। बन्दिरागपरं च परप्रयुक्ता जयशब्दमुखरमुखा मङ्घा मौखरिं मूर्खं क्षत्रवर्माणमुदखनन्। अरिपुरे च परकलत्रकामुकं कामिनीवेशगुप्तश्च चन्द्रगुप्तः शकपतिमशातयदिति। प्रमत्तानां प्रमदाकृताः प्रमादाः श्रुतिविषयमागता एव देवस्य। यथा मधुमोदितं मधुरकसंलिप्तैर्लाजैः सुप्रभा पुत्रराज्यार्थं महासेनं काशिराजं जघान। व्याजजनितकन्दर्पदर्पा च दर्पणेन क्षुरधारापर्यन्तेनायोध्याधिपतिं परन्तपं रत्नवती जारूथम्, विषचूर्णचुम्बितमकरन्देन च कर्णेन्दीवरेण देवकी देवरानुरक्ता देवसेनं सौह्मयम्, योगपरागविसरवर्षिणा च मणिनूपुरेण वल्लभा सपत्नीरुषा वैर[1]न्त्यं रन्तिदेवम्, वेणीनिगूढेन च शस्त्रेण बिन्दुमती वृष्णिं विदूरथम्, रसदिग्धमध्येन च मेखलामणिना हंसवती सौवीरं वीरसेनम्, अदृश्यागदलिप्तवदना च विषवारुणीगण्डूषपायनेन पौरवी पौरवेश्वरं सोमकम्।' इत्युक्त्वा विरराम स्वाम्यादेशसम्पादनाय च निर्जगाम।

देवोऽपि हर्षः सकलराज्यस्थितीश्चकार। ततश्च तथा कृतप्रतिज्ञे प्रयाणं विजयाय दिशां सम[2]ादिशति देवे हर्षे गतायुषां प्रतिसामन्तानामुदवसितेषु बहुरूपाण्युपलिङ्गानि वितेनिरे। तथा ह्यविप्र[3]कृष्टाः कालदूतदृष्टय इवेतस्ततश्चेरुश्चटुलाः कृष्णशारश्रेणयः। प्रचलितलक्ष्मीनूपुरप्रणादप्रतिमा मधुसरघासंघातझंकारा जह[4]ादिरेऽजिरे। विवृतविकृतवदनविवरविसृतवह्निविसरा वासरेऽपि विरसं विरेसुश्रिर[5]मशिवार्थमशिवाः शिवाः। शवपिशितप्ररूढ[6]प्रसरा इव कपिपोतकपोलकपिलपक्षतयः काननकपोताः पेतुः। आमन्त्र्यमाणा इव दधुरकालकुसुमानि सममुपवनतरवः। तरलकरतलप्रहारप्रहतपयोधरा रुरुदुः प्रसभं सभाशालभञ्जिकाः। ददृशुरासन्नकचग्रहभयोद्भ्रान्तोत्तमाङ्गमिवात्मानं कबन्धमादर्शोदरेषु योधाः। चूडामणिषु चक्रशङ्खकमललक्ष्माणः प्रादुरभवन्पादन्यासा राजमहिषीणाम्। चेटीचामराण्यकस्मादधावन्त पाणिपल्लवात्। प्रणयकलहेऽपि दत्तपृष्ठाश्चिरमभवन्भटाः पराङ्मुखा मानिनीनाम्। करि[7]कपोलेषु व्यघटन्त मधुलिहां मधुमदिरापानगोष्ठ्यः। समाघ्रातयममहिषगन्धा

---

१ 'वैरन्त्या' ब. २ 'दित्सति' ब. ३ 'प्रविष्टकाल०' ब. ४ 'जहादिरे। चिरम्' ब. ५ 'विरेसुरुपशिबिरं शवार्थम्' ब. ६ 'प्ररूढप्रणयेव' अ-क. ७ '०करिणीकपोलेषु' ब.

इव ताम्यन्तः स्तम्बकरिमपि हरयो हरितं नवयवसं न चेरुः। चलवलयावलीवाचालबालिकातालिकातोद्यलालिता अपि न ननृतुर्मन्दा मन्दिरमयूराः। निशि निशि रजनिकरहरिणनिहितनयन इवोन्मुखस्तारमुपतोरणमकारणमकाणीत्कौलेयकगणः। गणयन्तीव गतायुषस्तर्जनतरलया तर्जन्या दिवसमाट वाटकेषु कोटवी। कुट्टिमेषु कुटिलहरिणखुरवेणीतरङ्गिण्यः शष्पराजयोऽजायन्त। जनितवेणीबन्धानि निरञ्जनरोचनारोचींषि चषकमधुनि मुखकमलप्रतिबिम्बान्यदृश्यन्त भटीनाम्। समासन्नात्मापहारचकिता इव चकम्पिरे भूमयः। वध्यालङ्काररक्तचन्दनरसच्छटा इवालक्ष्यन्त शूराणां पतिताः शरीरेषु विकसितबन्धूककुसुमशोणितशोचिषः शोणितवृष्टयः। पर्यग्नीकुर्वाणा इव विनश्वरीं श्रियमविरलस्फुरत्स्फुलिङ्गाङ्गारोद्गारदग्धतारागणा गणशः पतन्तः प्रज्वलन्तो न व्यरंसिषुरुल्कादण्डाः। प्रथममेव प्रतीहारीवापहरन्ती प्रतिभवनं चामरातपत्रव्यजनानि परुषा बभ्राम वात्येति।

इति श्रीबाणभट्टकृतौ[1] हर्षचरिते राजप्रतिज्ञावर्णनं नाम षष्ठ उच्छ्वासः।

---

१ '०कृते हर्षचरिते षष्ठ' क; 'इति श्रीमहाकविचक्रचूडामणिश्रीबाणभट्टविरचिते हर्षचरिते महाकाव्ये राजप्रतिष्ठा नाम षष्ठ उच्छ्वासः सम्पूर्णः' ब.

सप्तम उच्छ्वासः।

अङ्गनवेदी वसुधा कुल्या जलधिः स्थली च पातालम्।
वल्मीकश्च सुमेरुः कृतप्रतिज्ञस्य वीरस्य ॥ १ ॥

धृतधनुषि बाहुशालिनि शैला न नमन्ति यत्तदाश्चर्यम्।
रिपुसंज्ञकेषु गणना कैव वराकेषु काकेषु ॥ २ ॥

अथ व्यतीतेषु च केषुचिद्दिवसेषु मौहूर्तिकमण्डलेन शतशः सुगणिते सुप्रशस्तेऽहनि दत्ते चतसृणामपि दिशां विजययोग्ये दण्डयात्रालग्ने सलिलमोक्षविशारदैः शारदैरिवाम्भोधरैः कालधौतैः शातकौम्भैश्च[1] कुम्भैः स्नात्वा विरचय्य परमया भक्त्या भगवतो नीललोहितस्यार्चामुदर्चिषं हुत्वा प्रदक्षिणावर्तशिखाकलापमाशुशुक्षणिं दत्त्वा द्विजेभ्यो रत्नवन्ति राजतानि जातरूपमयानि च सहस्रशस्तिलपात्राणि कनकपत्रलतालङ्कृतशफश्रृङ्गशिखरा गाश्चार्बुदशः समुपविश्य विततव्याघ्रचर्मणि भद्रासने विलिप्य प्रथमविलिप्तायुधो निजयशोधवलेनाचरणतश्चन्दनेन शरीरं परिधाय राजहंसमिथुनलक्ष्मणी सदृशे दुकूले परमेश्वरचिह्नभूतां शशिकलामिव कल्पयित्वा सितकुसुममुण्डमालिकां शिरसि नीत्वा कर्णाभरणमरकतमयूखमिव कर्णगोचरतां[2] गोरोचनाच्छुरितमभिनवं दूर्वापल्लवं विन्यस्य सह शासनवलयेन गमनमङ्गलप्रतिसरं प्रकोष्ठे परिपूजितप्रहृष्टपुरोहितकरप्रकीर्यमाणशान्तिसलिलसीकरनिकराभ्युक्षितशिराः संप्रेष्य महार्हाणि वाहनानि बहलरत्नालोकलिप्तककुम्भि च भूषणानि भूभुजां संविभज्य क्लिष्टकार्पटिककुलपुत्रलोकमोचितैः प्रसाददानैश्च विमुच्य बन्धनानि नियुज्य तत्कालस्मरणस्फुरणेन कथितात्मानमिव चाष्टादशद्वीपजेतव्याधिकारे दक्षिणं भुजस्तम्भमहमहमिकया सेवकैरिव सुनिमित्तैरपि समग्रैरग्रतो भवद्भिः प्रमुदितप्रजाजन्यमानजयशब्दकोलाहलो हिरण्यगर्भ इव ब्रह्माण्डात्कृतयुगकरणाय भवनान्निर्जगाम।

नातिदूरे च नगरादुपसरस्वति निर्मिते महति तृणमये, समुत्तम्भिततुङ्गतोरणे, वेदीविनिहितपल्लवललामहेमकलशे, बद्धवनमालादाम्नि[3], धवलध्वजमालिनि, भ्रमच्छुक्लवाससि, पठद्द्विजन्मनि, मन्दिरे प्रस्थानमकरोत्। तत्रस्थस्य चास्य ग्रामाक्षपटलिकः सकलकरणिपरिकरः 'करोतु देवो दिवसग्रहणमद्यैवावन्ध्यशासनः शासनानाम्' इत्यभिधाय वृषाङ्कामभिनवघटितां हाटकमयीं मुद्रामुपनिन्ये। जग्राह च तां राजा। समुपस्थापिते च प्रथमत एव मृत्पिण्डे परिभ्रश्य करकमलादधोमुखी महीतले पपात मुद्रा। मन्दाश्यानपङ्कपटले मृदुमृदि सरस्वतीतीरे स्फुटं व्यराजन्त राजयो वर्णानाम्।

---

१ 'शातकुम्भैश्च' क. २ 'कर्णपूरगोचरताम्' ब. ३ 'धाम्नि' ब.

अमङ्गलाशङ्किनि च विषीदति परिजने नरपतिरकरोन्मनस्येतत्—'अतत्त्व[1]-दर्शिन्यो हि भवन्त्यविदग्धानां धियः। तथाहि एकशासनमुद्राङ्का भूर्भवतो भविष्यतीति निवेदितमपि निमित्तेनान्यथा गृह्णन्ति ग्राम्याः।' इत्यभिनन्द्य मनसा महानिमित्तं तत्सीरसहस्रसंमितसीम्नां ग्रामाणां शतमदाद्द्विजेभ्यः। निनाय च तत्र तं दिवसम्। प्रतिपन्नायां शर्वर्यां संमानितसर्वराजलोकः सुष्वाप।

अथ गलति तृतीये यामे सुप्तसमस्तसत्त्वनिःशब्दे दिक्कुञ्जरजृम्भमाणगम्भीरध्वनिरताड्यत प्रयाणपटहः। अग्रतः स्थित्वा च मुहूर्तमिव पुनः प्रयाणक्रोशसंख्यापकाः स्पष्टमष्टावदीयन्त प्रहाराः पटहे पटीयांसः।

ततो रटत्पटहे, नन्दन्नान्दीके, गुञ्जत्कुञ्जे, कूजत्काहले, शब्दायमानशङ्खे, क्रमोपचीयमानकटककलकले, परिजनोत्थापनव्यापृतव्यवहारिणि, द्रुतद्रुघनघातघट्यमानकोणिकाकीलकोलाहलकलितककुभि, बलाधिकृतबध्यमानपाटीपतिपेटके, जनज्वलितोल्कासहस्रालोकलुप्यमानत्रियामातमसि, यामचेटीचरणचलनोत्थाप्यमानकामिमिथुने, कटुकटुक[2]निर्देशनश्यन्निद्रोन्मिषन्निषादिनि, प्रबुद्धहास्तिकशून्यीक्रियमाणशय्यागृहे, सुप्तोत्थिताश्वीयविधूयमानसटे, रटत्कटकमुखरखनित्रखन्यमानक्षोणीपाशे, समुत्कील्यमानकीलशिञ्जानहिञ्जीरे, उप[3]नीयमाननिगडतालककलरवोत्तालतुरङ्गतरङ्ग्यमाणखुरपुटे, लेशिकमुच्यमानमदस्यन्दिदन्तिसन्दानशृङ्खलाखनखननिनादनिर्भरभरितदशदिशि, घासपूलक[4]प्रहारप्रमृष्टपांसुलकरिपृष्ठप्रसार्यमाणप्रस्फोटित[5]प्रमृष्टचर्मणि, गृहचिन्तकचेटकसंवेष्ट्यमानपटकुटीकाण्डपटमण्डपपरिवस्त्रावितानके, कीलककलापापूर्यमाणचिपिटचर्मपुटे, सम्भाण्डायमानभाण्डागारिणि, भाण्डागारवहनवाह्यमानबहुनालीवाहिके, निषादिनिश्चलानेकानीक[6]पारोप्यमाणकोशकलशपीडापीडसङ्कटायमानसामन्तौकसि, दूरगतदक्षदासेरकक्षिप्रप्रक्षिप्यमाणोपकरणसम्भारभ्रियमाणदुष्टदन्तिनि, तिर्यगानमज्जाघ[7]निककरकृच्छ्राकृष्टलम्बमानपरतन्त्रतुन्दिलचुन्दीजनजनितजनहासे, पीड्यमानशारशारिवरत्रागुणग्राहितगात्रविहारबृंहद्बहुबृहदुन्मदकरिणि, करिघटाघटमानघण्टाटांकारक्रियमाणकर्णज्वरे, पृष्ठप्रतिष्ठाप्यमानकण्ठालककदर्थितकूजत्करभे, अभिजातराजपुत्रप्रेष्यमाणकुप्रयुक्ताकुलकुलीनकुलपुत्रकलत्रवाहने, गमनवेलाविप्रलब्धवारणाधोरणान्विष्यमाणनवसेवके, प्रसादवित्तपत्तिनीयमाननरपतिवल्लभवारवाजिनि, चारुचारभटसैन्यन्यस्यमाननासीरमण्डलाडम्बरस्थूलस्थासके, स्थानपालपर्याणलम्बमानलवणकला[8]यीकिङ्किणीनालीसनाथसङ्कलिततलसारके, कुण्डलीकृतावरक्षणीजालजटिलवल्लभपालाश्वघटानिवेश्यमानशाखामृगे, परिव-

---

१ 'तत्त्व-' अ. २ 'कटुककटुक-' अ-क. ३ 'पनीयमान' ब. ४ 'पूलिक' ब. ५ 'प्रस्फोटितचर्मणि' अ-क. ६ 'अनेकानेकपा-' अ-क. ७ 'घनिकर' अ. ८ 'कलापि' क.

दिक्पालैः प्रणम्यमानश्च नेत्रत्रिभागैश्च कटाक्षैश्च समप्रेक्षितैर्भ्रूवक्षितैश्चार्धस्मितैश्च परिहासैश्च छेकालापैश्च कुशलप्रश्नैश्च प्रतिप्रणामैश्चोन्मत्तभ्रूवीक्षितैश्चाज्ञादानैश्चाक्रीणन्निव[1] मानमयान्प्राणान्प्रणयदानैः प्रवीराणां वीरो यथानुरूपं विबभाज राजकम्।

अथ प्रस्थिते राजनि कलकलत्रस्तदिङ्नागशूत्काररव इवेतस्ततस्तस्तार तारतरस्तूर्याणां प्रतिध्वनिराशातटेषु। दिग्गजेभ्यः प्रकुपितानां त्रिप्रस्रुतानां करिणां मदप्रस्रवणवीथीभिरलिकुलकालीभिः कालिन्दीवेणिकासहस्राणीव सस्यन्दिरे। सिन्दूररेणुराशिभिररुणायमानबिम्बे रवावस्तमयसमयं शशङ्किरे शकुनयः। करिणां षट्पदकोलाहलमांसलैः कर्णतालनिस्वनैस्तिरोदधिरे दुन्दुभिध्वनयः। दोधूयमानश्च सचराचरमाचचाम चामरसङ्घातो विश्वम्। अश्वीयश्वासनिक्षिप्तैः शिश्विन्दे सिन्धुवारदामशुचिभिर्निरन्तरमन्तरिक्षं फेनपिण्डैः। पिण्डीभूततगरस्तबकपाण्डुराणि पपुरिव परस्परसङ्घट्टनष्टाष्टदिशं[2] दिवसमुच्चचामीकरदण्डान्यातपत्रवनानि। रजोरजनीनिमीलितोपि मुकुटमणिशिलावलीबालातपेन विचकास वासरः। राजतैर्हिरण्मयैश्च मण्डनकभाण्डमण्डलैर्ह्लादमानैर्हरितीकृताः[3] परिह्लादा हरितो बधिरतां दधुः। अरिप्रतापानलनिर्मूलनायेव मदोष्मशीकरैः शिशीकिरे[4] करिणः ककुभां चक्रम्। चक्षुषामुन्मेषं मुमुषुस्तडिच्चञ्चलानि चूडामणीनामर्चींषि। स्वयमपि विसिष्मिये बलानां भूपालः सर्वतो विक्षिप्तचक्षुश्चाद्राक्षीदावासस्थानसकाशात्प्रतिष्ठमानं स्कन्धावारम्, अधोक्षजकुक्षेरिव युगादौ निष्पतन्तं जीवलोकम्, अम्भोनिधिमिव कुम्भभुवो वदनात्प्लावितभुवनमुद्गच्छन्तम्, अर्जुनबाहुदण्डसहस्रसंपिण्डितोन्मुक्तमिव सहस्रधा प्रवर्तमानं प्रवाहं नर्मदायाः। 'प्रसर तात। भाव, किं विलम्बसे। त्वङ्गति[5] तुरङ्गमः। भद्र, भग्नचरण इव सञ्चरसि यावदमी पुरःसराः सरभसमुपरि पतन्ति। वाहयसि किमुष्ट्रम्। न पश्यसि निर्दय निःशूकशिशुं शयानम्। वत्स रामिल, रजसि यथा न नश्यसि[6] तथा समीपे भव। किं न पश्यसि गलति सक्तुप्रसेवकः। किमेवमित्वर त्वरसे। सौरभेयसरणिमपहाय हयमध्यं धावसि धीवरि। विशसि गन्तुकामा मातङ्गि मातङ्गमार्गम्। अङ्ग, गलति तिरश्चीना चणकगोणी गणयसि न मामारटन्तम्। अवटमेवटेनावतरसि[7]। सुखमास्स्व स्वैरिणि सौवीरककुम्भो भग्नः। मन्थरक, खादिष्यसि गतः सन्निक्षुम्। उक्षाणं प्रसारय[8]। कियच्चिरं चिनोषि चेट बदराणि दूरं गन्तव्यम्। किमद्यैव विद्रासि द्रोणक द्राघीयसी दण्डयात्रा। विनैकेन निष्ठुरकेण निष्क्रेयमस्माकम्। अग्रतः पन्थाः स्थपुटकः[9]। स्थावरक, यथा न भनक्षि फाणितस्थालीम्। गरीयान्गण्डकतण्डुलभारको न निर्वहति दम्यः। दासक, मोषीणा-[10]

---

१ '०क्रीडन्निव' अ. २ 'दिशि' ब. ३ '०कृतापराह्लादा' ब. ४ 'शिशेकिरे' अ-क. ५ 'लङ्घति' ब. ६ 'नश्यसि न पश्यसि' अ; 'नश्यसि नो पयसि' क. ७ 'अतटेन' अ-क. ८ 'प्रसादय' अ-क. ९ 'स्थपुटक' अ-क. १० 'माषीणाममुतो' अ.

दमुतो द्रागदात्रेण मुखघासपूलकं लुनीहि। को जानाति यवसगतं गतानाम्। धव, वारय बलीवर्दान्, वाहीकरक्षितं क्षेत्रमिदम्। लम्बिता शकटी, शाक्करं धुरन्धरं धुरि धवलं नियुङ्क्ष्व। यक्षपालित, प्रमदाः पिनक्षि। अक्षिणी किं ते स्फुटिते। हत हस्तिपक[1] रे, दीव्यसि करिकरदण्डे। समद, संमर्दकर्दमे स्खलसि। भ्रातर्भाव विधुरबन्धो[2], उद्धर पङ्कादनड्वाहम्। इत एहि माणवक, घनेभघटासङ्घट्टसङ्कटे नास्ति निस्सरणसरणिः[3]।' इत्येवमादिप्रवर्तमानानेकसंलापं क्वचित्स्वेच्छामृदितोद्दामसस्यघासविघससुखसम्पन्नान्नपुष्टैः केलिकलैः किलकिलायमानैर्मेण्ठवण्ठवठरलम्बनलेशिकलुण्ठकचेटचाट[4]चण्डालमण्डलैराण्डीरैः स्तूयमानम्, क्वचिदसहायैः क्लेशार्जितकुग्रामकुटुम्बिसम्पादितसीदत्सौरभेयशम्बलसंवाहनायासावेगागतसंयोगैः स्वयंगृहीतगृहोपस्करणैः 'इयमेका कथंचिद्दण्डयात्रा यातु। यातु पातालतलं तृष्णाभूतेरभवनिः। भवतु शिवम्। सेवा करोतु। स्वस्ति सर्वदुःखकूटाय कटकाय' इति दुर्विधकुलपुत्रकैर्निन्द्यमानम्, क्वचिदतितीक्ष्णसलिलस्रोतःपातिनौगतैरिव ग्रथितैरिव पङ्क्तिभूतैर्जनैरतिद्रुतं द्रवद्भिः कृष्णकठिनस्कन्धगुरुलगुडैर्गृहीतसौवर्णपादपीठीपर्यङ्क[5]करङ्ककलशपतद्ग्रहावग्राहैः[6] प्रत्यासन्नपार्थिवोपकरणग्रहणगर्वदुर्वारैः सर्वमेव बहिः कारयद्भिर्भूपतिभृतकभारिकैर्महानसोपकरणवाहिभिश्च बद्धवराहवध्रवाध्रीणसैर्लम्बमानहरिणचटुकचटकजूटजटिलैः शिशुशशकशाकपत्रवेत्राग्रसंग्रहसंग्राहिभिः शुक्लकर्पटप्रावृतमुखैकदेशदत्तार्द्रमुद्रागुप्तगोरसभाण्डैस्तलकतापकतापिकाहस्तकताम्रचरुककटाहसङ्कटपिटकभारिकैः समुत्सार्यमाणपुरोवर्तिजनम्, क्वचित् 'क्लेशोऽस्माकम्। फलकालेऽन्य एव विटाः समुपस्थास्यन्ते' इति मुखरैः पदे पदे पततां दुर्बलबलीवर्दानां नियुक्तैः[7] स्खलने खलचेटकैः खेद्यमानासंविभक्तकुलपुत्रलोकम्, क्वचिन्नरपतिदर्शनकुतूहलादुभयतः प्रजवितप्रधावितग्रामेयकजनपदम्, मार्गग्रामनिर्गतैराग्रहारिकजाल्मैः पुरःसरजरन्महत्तरोत्तम्भिताम्भःकुम्भैरुपायनीकृतदधिगुडखण्डकुसुमकरण्डैर्धनघटितपेटकैः सरभसं समुत्सर्पद्भिः प्रकुपितप्रचण्डदण्डिवित्रासनविद्रुतैर्दूरगतैरपि स्खलद्भिरपि पतद्भिरपि नरेन्द्रनिहितदृष्टिभिरसतोऽपि पूर्वभोगपतिदोषानुद्भावयद्भिरतिक्रान्तयुक्तकशतानि च शंसद्भिश्चिरन्तनचाटापराधांश्चाभिदधानैरुद्धूयमानधूलिपटलम्, क्वचिदेकान्तप्रवृत्ताश्ववारचर्क्रैचर्व्यमाणा[8]गामिगौडविमृग्यमाणसस्यसंरक्षणम्, अपरैरादिष्टपरिपालकपुरुषपरितुष्टैः 'धर्मः प्रत्यक्षो देवः' इति स्तुतीरातन्वद्भिरपरैर्लूयमाननिष्पन्नसस्यप्रकटितविषादैः क्षेत्रशुचा सकुटुम्बैरेव निर्गतैः प्ररूढप्राणच्छेदैः परितापत्याजितभयैः 'क्व राजा कुतो राजा कीदृशो वा राजा' इति प्रारब्धनरनाथनिन्दम्, शशकैश्च पदे पदे प्रजविप्र-

---

१ 'हस्तिपको नेदीयसि करीकरदण्डे समदः' ब. २ 'विधुरे बन्धुरुद्धर' ब. ३ 'निस्तरणम्' अ-क. ४ 'शाट' ब. ५ 'पीठीकरङ्क' अ-क. ६ 'पतद्ग्राहावगाहैः' अ-क. ७ 'नियुक्तैः खेटने खेटचेटकैः' अ-क. ८ 'चर्च्यमाण' ब.

चण्डदण्डपाणिपेटकानुबद्धैर्गिरिगुडकैरिव हन्यमानैरितस्ततः सञ्चरद्भिरपरैर्युगपत्परापतितमहाजनग्रस्तैस्तिलशो विलुप्यमानैरनेकजन्तुजङ्घान्तरालनिःसरणकुशलिभिः कुटिलिकाव्यंसितसादिबहुश्वभिः पतल्लोष्टलगुडकोणकुठारकीलकुद्दालखनित्रदात्रयष्टिभिरपि[1] निःसरद्भिरायुषो बलात्कृतकलकलम्, अन्यत्र सङ्घशो घासिकैर्बुसधूलीधूसरितघासजालजालकितजघनैश्च पुराणपर्याणैकदेशदोलायमानदात्रैश्च शीर्णोर्णांशकलशिथिलमलिनमलकुथैश्च प्रभुप्रसादीकृतपाटितपटच्चरचलच्चोलकधारिभिश्च धावमानैरुद्धूयमानधूलिपटलम्, क्वचिदेकान्तप्रवृत्ताश्ववारचक्रचर्व्यमाणागामिगौडविग्रहम्, क्वचित्पङ्किलप्रदेशपूरणादेशाकुलसकललोकलूयमानतृणपूलकम्, क्वचित्तलवर्तिवेत्रिवेत्रवित्रास्यमानशाखिशिखरगतविक्रोशद्विवादिब्राह्मणम्, क्वचित्कुलुण्ठकपाशविवेष्ट्यमानग्रासीणकग्रा[2]माकृष्टकौलेयकम्, क्वचिदन्योन्यविभवस्पर्धोद्धुरराजपुत्रवाह्यमानवाजिसङ्घट्टम[3]ण्डितम्, अनेकवृत्तान्ततया कौतुकजननम्, प्रलयजलधिमिव जगद्ग्रासग्रहणाय प्रवृत्तम्, पातालमिव महाभोगिनां गुप्तये समुत्पादितम्, कैलासमिव परमेश्वरवसतये सृष्टम्, दृश्यमानसकलप्राणिपर्यायं चतुर्युगसर्गकोशमिव प्रजापतीनाम्, क्लेशबहुलमपि तपःकरणमिव क्रमकारणं[4] कल्याणानाम्, एवं च वीक्षमाणः कटकं जगाम।

आसन्नवर्तिनां च तत्रभवताम्, 'मान्धात्रा प्रवर्तिताः पन्थानो दिग्विजयाय। अप्रतिहतरथरंहसा रघुणा लघुनैव कालेनाकारि ककुभां प्रसादनम्। शरासनद्वितीयः करदीचकार चक्रं क्रमागतभुजबलाभिजनधनमदावलिप्तानां भूभुजां पाण्डुः। पाण्डवः सव्यसाची चीनविषयमतिक्रम्य राजसूयसम्पदे क्रुध्यद्गन्धर्वधनुष्कोटिटांकारकूजितकुञ्जं हेमकूटपर्वतं पराजैष्ट। सङ्कल्पान्तरितो विजयस्तरस्विनाम्। सहिमहिमवद्व्यवहितोऽप्युवाह बाहुबलव्यतिकरकातरः करं कौरवेश्वरस्य किङ्कर इवाकृती द्रुमः। नातिजिगीषवः खलु पूर्वे येनाल्प एव भूभागे भूयांसो भगदत्तदन्तवक्त्रक्राथकर्णकौरवशिशुपालसाल्वजरासन्धसिन्धुराजप्रभृतयोऽभवन्भूपतयः। सन्तुष्टो राजा युधिष्ठिरो यो ह्यसहत समीप एव धनञ्जयजयजनितजगत्कम्पः किंपुरुषाणां राज्यम्। अलसश्चण्डकोशो यो न प्राविक्षत्क्ष्मां जित्वा स्त्रीराज्यम्। हसीय एवान्तरं तुषारगिरिगन्धमादनयोः उत्साहिनः किष्कुस्तुरुष्कविषयः, पारसीकदेशः प्रादेशः, शशपदं शकस्थानम्, अदृश्यमानप्रतिप्रह्वारे पारियात्रे यात्रैव शिथिला, शौर्यशुल्कः सुलभो दक्षिणापथः, दक्षिणार्णवकल्लोलानिलचलितचन्दनलतासौरभसुन्दरीकृतदरीमन्दिराद्दर्दुरादद्रेर्नेदीयसि मलयो मलयलग्न एव च महेन्द्रः।' इत्येवंप्रायानुयोगद्योतकानामालापान्पार्थिवकुमाराणां बाहुशालिनां शृण्वन्नेवाससादावासम्। मन्दिरद्वारि चोभयतः सबहुमानं भ्रूलताभ्यां विसर्जितराजलोकः

१ 'यष्टिवृष्टिभिरपि' ब. २ 'कुलुण्डकपाशविवेद्य' क. ३ 'विभाव' ब. ४ 'कारिणम्' क.

प्रविश्य चावततार बाह्यास्थानमण्डपस्थापितमासनमाचक्राम । प्रास्तसमायोगश्च क्षणमासिष्ट ।

अथ तत्र प्रतीहारः पृथ्वीपृष्ठप्रतिष्ठापितपाणिपल्लवो विज्ञापितवान्—'देव, प्राग्ज्योतिषेश्वरेण कुमारेण प्रहितो हंसवेगनामा दूतोऽन्तरङ्गस्तोरणमध्यास्ते' इति । राजा तु 'तमाशु प्रवेशय' इति सादरमादिदेश । अथ दक्षतया क्षितिपालादराच्च प्रतीहारः स्वयमेव निरगात् । अनन्तरं च हंसवेगः सविनयमाकृत्यैव नयनानन्दसम्पादनसुभगाभोगभद्रया समुल्लङ्घ्यमानगुणगरिमा प्रभूतप्राभृतभृतां पुरुषाणां समूहेन महतानुगम्यमानः प्रविवेश राजमन्दिरम् । आरादेव पञ्चाङ्गालिङ्गिताङ्गनः प्रणाममकरोत् । 'एह्येहि' इति सबहुमानमाहूतश्च प्रधावितोऽपसृतः पादपीठलुठितललाटलेखो न्यस्तहस्तः पृष्ठे पार्थिवेनोपसृत्य भूयो नमश्चक्रे । स्निग्धनरेन्द्रदृष्ट्या निर्दिष्टमविप्रकृष्टं स प्रदेशमध्यास्त । ततो राजा तिरश्चीं तनुमीषदिव दधानश्चामरग्राहिणीमन्तरालवर्तिनीं समुत्सार्य संमुखीनस्तं सप्रश्रयं पप्रच्छ—'हंसवेग, श्रीमान्कच्चित्कुशली कुमारः' इति । स तमन्ववादीत्—'अद्य कुशली येनैवं स्नेहस्नपितया सौहार्दद्रवार्द्रया सगौरवं गिरा पृच्छति देवः' इति ।

स्थित्वा च मुहूर्तमिव पुनः स चतुरम्भोधिभोगभूतिभाजनभूतस्य देवस्य सद्भावगर्भमपहाय हृदयमेकमन्यदनुरूपं प्राभृतमेव दुर्लभं लोके तथाप्यस्मत्स्वामिना सन्देशमशून्यतां नयता पूर्वजोपार्जितं वारुणातपत्रमाभोगाख्यमनुरूपस्थानन्यासेन कृतार्थीकृतमेतत् । अस्य च कुतूहलकृन्ति बहूनि आश्चर्याणि दृश्यन्ते । तथाहि प्रतिदिवसं प्रविशति शैत्यहेतोश्छायायाः किरणसहस्रादेकैकः सोमस्य रश्मिरस्मिन् । यस्मिन्प्रविष्टे प्रध्यानानन्तरं स्वादवो दन्तवीणोपदेशाचार्याश्च्योतन्ति चन्द्रभासामम्भसां मणिशलाकाभ्यो यावदिच्छमच्छा धाराः । प्रचेता इव यश्चतुर्णामर्णवानामधिपतिर्भूतो भावी वा तमिदमनुगृह्णाति च्छायया नेतरम् । इदं च न सप्तार्चिर्दहति, न पृषदश्वो हरति, नोदकमार्द्रयति, न रजांसि मलिनयन्ति, न जरा जर्जरयति । एतत्तावदनुगृह्णातु दृशा देवः सन्देशमपि विस्रब्धं श्रोष्यति ।' इत्येवमभिधाय विवृत्यात्मीयं पुरुषमभ्यधात्—'उत्तिष्ठ दर्शय देवस्य' इति ।

स वचनानन्तरमुत्थाय पुमानूर्ध्वीचकार तद्धौतदुकूलकल्पिताच्च निचोलकादकोषीत् । आकृष्यमाण एव च यस्मिन्नतिसितमहसि सरभसमहासीव हरेण, रसातलादुदलासीव शेषफणिफणाफलकमण्डलेन, अस्थायीव चक्रीभूयान्तरिक्षे क्षीरोदेन, अघटीव गगनाङ्गने गोष्ठीबन्धः शारदेन बलाहकव्यूहेन, विश्रान्तमिव विततपक्षतिना वियति पितामहविमानहंसयूथेन, अत्रिनेत्रनिर्गतस्य धवलधाममण्डलमनोहरो दृष्ट इव जनेन जन्मदिवसः कुमुदबन्धोः, प्रत्यक्षीकृत इवोद्गमनक्षणो नारायणनाभिपुण्डरीकस्य, आहितेव कौमुदीप्रदोषदर्शनानन्दतृप्तिरक्षणाम्, उदमाङ्क्षीदिव मन्दाकिनीपुलिनमण्डलं

महदम्बरोदरे, परिवर्तित इव दिवसः पौर्णमासीनिशया, मन्दमन्दमिन्दूदयसन्देहदूयमानमानसैर्विघटितं विघटमानचञ्चुच्युतमृणालकोटिभिरासन्नकमलिनीचक्रवाकमिथुनैः, शरज्जलधरपटलाशङ्कासङ्कोचितकेकारवमूकमुखपुटैः पराङ्मुखीभूतं भवनशिखण्डिमण्डलैः, प्रबुद्धमाबद्धचन्द्रानन्दोद्दामोद्दलद्दलपुटाट्टहासविशदं कुमुदषण्डैः ।

चित्रीयमाणचेताश्च सराजको राजा दण्डानुसाराधिरोहिण्या दृष्ट्या सादरमैक्षिष्ट तत्तिलकमिव त्रिभुवनस्य, शैशवमिव श्वेतद्वीपस्य, अंशावतारमिव शरदिन्दोः, हृदयमिव धर्मस्य, निवेशमिव शशिलोकस्य, दन्तमण्डलकद्युतिधवलं मुखमिव चक्रवर्तित्वस्य, मौक्तिकजालपरिकरसितं सीमन्तचक्रमिव दिवः, बहलज्योत्स्नाशुक्लोदरमैन्दवमिव परिवेशवलयम्, शौक्ल्यापहसितशङ्खश्रीकं श्रवणमण्डलमिव निश्चलतां गतमैरावतस्य, श्वेतगङ्गावर्तपाण्डुरं पदमिव त्रिभुवनवन्दनीयं त्रिविक्रमस्य, प्रचेतसश्चूडामणिमरीचिशिखाभिरिव श्लिष्टाभिर्मानसबिसतन्तुमयीभिश्चामरिकावलीभिर्विरचितपरिवेशम्, उपरि चक्रवर्तिलक्ष्मीनूपुरस्वनश्रवणदोहदनिश्चलेनेव लक्ष्मणा विततपत्रेण हंसेन सनाथीकृतशिखरम्, स्पर्शवता च प्रभावस्तम्भितेन मन्दाकिनीमृणालेन मुकुलितफणेन वासुकिनेव नीतेन दण्डतां द्योतमानम्, धवलिम्ना क्षालयदिव नक्षत्रपथम्, प्रभाप्रवाहप्रथिम्ना प्रावृण्वदिव दिवसम्, समुच्छ्रायेणाधःकुर्वदिव दिवम्, उपरिस्थितमिव सर्वमङ्गलानाम्, श्वेतमण्डपमिव श्रियः, स्तबकमिव ब्रह्मस्तम्भस्य, नाभिमण्डलमिव ज्योत्स्नायाः, विशदहासमिव कीर्तेः, फेनराशिमिव खड्गधाराजलानाम्, यशःपटलमिव शौर्यशालितायाः, त्रैलोक्याद्भुतं महच्छत्रम् ।

दृष्टे च तस्मिन्राज्ञा प्रथमं शेषमपि प्राभृतं प्रकाशयांचक्रुः क्रमेण कार्माः । तद्यथा परार्ध्यरत्नांशुशोणीकृतदिग्भागान्, भगदत्तप्रभृतिख्यातपार्थिवपरागतानाहतलक्षणानलङ्कारान्, प्रभालेपिनां च चूडामणीनां समुत्कर्षान्, क्षीरोदधेर्धवलताहेतूनिव हारान्, अनेकरागरुचिरवेत्रकरण्डकुण्डलीकृतानि शरच्चन्द्रमरीचिरुञ्चि शौचक्षमाणि क्षौमाणि कुशलशिल्पिलोकोल्लिखितानां च शुक्तिशङ्खगल्वर्कप्रमुखानां पानभाजनानां निचयान्, निचोलकरक्षितरुचां च रुचिरकाञ्चनपत्रभङ्गभङ्गुराणामतिबन्धुरपरिवेशानां कार्दरङ्गचर्मणां सम्भारान्, भूर्जत्वक्कोमलाः स्पर्शवतीः जातीपट्टिकाः, चित्रपटानां च म्रदीयसां समूरुकोपधानादीन्विकारान्, प्रियङ्गुप्रसवपिङ्गलत्वञ्चि चासनानि वेत्रमयान्यगुरुवल्कलकल्पितसञ्चयानि च सुभाषितभाञ्जि पुस्तकानि, परिणतपाटलपटोलत्विषि च तरुणहारीतहरिन्ति क्षीरक्षारीणि च पूगानां पल्लवलम्बीनि सरसानि फलानि, सहकारलतारसानां च कृष्णागुरुतैलस्य च कुपितकपिकपोलकपिलकापोतिकापलाशकोशीकवचिताङ्गीः स्थवीयसीर्वैणवीर्नाडीश्च, पट्टसूत्रप्रसेव-

१ 'दूयमान' अ-क. २ 'मण्डलधवलं' अ-क. ३ '०तैलस्य च कपोतकपिल०' ब.

कार्पितांश्च भिन्नाञ्जनकृष्णस्य कृष्णागुरुणो गुरुपरितापमुषश्च गोशीर्षचन्दनस्य तुषारशिलाशकलशिशिरस्वच्छसितस्य च कर्पूरस्य कस्तूरिकाकोशकानां च पक्वफलजूटजटिलानां च कक्कोलपल्लवानां लवङ्गपुष्पमञ्जरीणां जातीफलस्तबकानां च राशीन्, अतिमधुरमधुरसामोदनिर्हारिणीश्चोल्लककलशीः सितासितस्य च चामरजातस्य निचयान्, अवलम्बमानतूलिकालाबुकांश्च लिखितानालेख्यफलकसम्पुटान्, कुतूहलकृन्ति कनकशृङ्खलानियमितग्रीवाणां किंनराणां च वनमानुषीणां च जीवञ्जीवकानां च जलमानुषाणां च मिथुनानि, परिमलामोदितककुभश्च कस्तूरिकाकुरङ्गान्, गेहपरिसरणपरिचिताश्च चमरीः, चामीकररसचित्रवेत्रपञ्जरान्तर्गतांश्च बहुसुभाषितजल्पाकजिह्वांश्च शुकशारिकाप्रभृतीन्पक्षिणः प्रवालपञ्जरगतांश्च चकोरान्, जलहस्तिनामुदग्रकुम्भमुक्ताफलदामदन्तुराणि च दन्तकाण्डकुण्डलानि।

राजा तु छत्रदर्शनात्प्रहृष्टहृदयः प्रथमप्रयाणे शोभननिमित्तमिति मनसा जग्राह। हंसवेगं च प्रीयमाणो बभाषे—'भद्र, सकलरत्नधाम्नः परमेश्वरशिरोधारणार्हस्यास्य महातपत्रस्य महार्णवादिव कुमुदबान्धवस्य कुमाराल्लाभो न विस्मयाय। बालविद्याः खलु महतामुपकृतयः' इति। अपनीते च तस्मात्प्रदेशात्प्राभृतसम्भारे क्षणमिव स्थित्वा 'हंसवेग, विश्रम्यताम्' इति प्रतीहारभवनं विसर्जयांबभूव। स्वयमप्युत्थाय स्नात्वा मङ्गलाकाङ्क्षी प्राङ्मुखः प्राविशदाभोगस्य छायाम्।

अथ विशत एवास्य छायाजन्मना जडिम्ना चूडामणितामनीयतेव शशिबिम्बमम्बुबिन्दुमुचश्चुम्बुरिव चन्द्रकान्तमणयो ललाटतटं कर्पूररेणव इव व्यलीयन्त लोचनयुगले गलत्तुहिनकणनिकरकृतनीहारा हारा इवाबध्यन्त हरिचन्दनरसासारेणेवापाति सन्ततमुरसि कुमुदमयमिव हृदयमभवदतिशिशिरमन्तर्हितहिमशिलेव विलीयमाना व्यलिम्पदङ्गानि। जातविस्मयश्चाकरोन्मनसि एकमजर्यं सङ्गतमपहाय कास्त्यन्या प्रतिकौशलिकेति। आहारकाले च हंसवेगाय धवलकर्पटप्रावृतधौतनालिकेरपरिगृहीतं विलिप्तशेषं चन्दनमङ्गस्पृष्टे च वाससी शरत्तारकाकारतारमुक्तास्तबकितपदं परिवेशं नाम कटिसूत्रमतिमहार्हपद्मरागालोकलोहितीकृतदिवसं च तरङ्गकं नाम कर्णाभरणं प्रभूतं च भोज्यजातं प्राहिणोत्। एवंप्रायेण च क्रमेण जगाम दिवसः।

ततः कटकस्थबलबहलधूलिधूसरितवपुरंशुमाली मलीमसमङ्गमिव क्षालयितुमपरजलनिधिमवातरत्। आभोगातपत्रप्रदानवार्तामिव निवेदयितुं वरुणाय वारुणीं दिशमयासीत्। मुकुलायमानसकलकमलवना प्रमुख एव बद्धसेवाञ्जलिपुटेव सद्वीपा भूरभूद्भूपतेः। नृपानुरागमय इव निखिलजीवलोकलोकाञ्जलिबन्धबन्धुर्जगज्जग्राह संध्यारागः। गौडापराधशङ्किनीव श्या-

---

१ 'वर्णस्य' ब. २ 'लिखितानेकलेख्य०' ब. ३ '०जिह्वांश्च जातीः कौशिकशुक०' ब. ४ 'अजर्ये' ब. ५ 'भूपालानुरागराशिमय' ब. ६ 'बद्ध' ब.

मतां प्रपेदे दिक्प्राची। प्रचिततिमिरनिर्वहा[1] निर्वाणान्यनृपप्रतापानलकलापेव कालिमानमतानीन्मेदिनी। मेदिनीशप्रदोषास्थानपुष्पनिकरमिव विकचतगैर[2]-रुचिरमवचकरुडुनिकरमविरलं ककुभः। स्कन्धावारगन्धगजमदामोदधावितस्येव मार्गो वियति विरराज रजःपाण्डुरैरावतस्य। कुपितनृपव्याघ्राघ्रातामुपसृष्टामिव पौरुहूतीं विहाय विहायस्तलमारुरोह रोहिणीरमणः। प्रयाणवार्ता इव मानिनीनां हृदयभेदिन्यो ययुरिन्दुदीधितयो दश दिशः। नवनृपदण्डयात्रात्रासातुरा इव तरलितसत्त्ववृत्तयश्चक्षुभुः पतयो वाहिनीनाम्। चिन्तेव भूभृतां हृदयानि विवेश गुहाविवराणि विमुक्तसर्वाशा तिमिरसन्ततिः। प्रतिसामन्तचक्षुषामिव ननाश निद्रा कुमुदवनानाम्।

अस्यां च वेलायां विततवितानतलवर्ती नरेन्द्रो 'यात तावत्' इति विसर्ज्यानुजीविनो हंसवेगमादिष्टवान्--'कथय सन्देशम्' इति। प्रणम्य स कथयितुं प्रास्तावीत्—'देव, पुरा महावराहसम्पर्कसम्भृतगर्भया भगवत्या भुवा नरको नाम सूनुरसावि रसातले। वीरस्य यस्याभवन्बाल्य एव पादप्रणामप्रणयिनश्चूडामणयो लोकपालानाम्। यस्य च त्रिभुवनभुजो भुजशौण्डस्य भवनकमलिनीचक्रवाकीकोपकुटिलकटाक्षेक्षितोऽपि भयचकितारुणपरिवर्तितरथो नाज्ञया विना रविरस्तमव्राजीत्। यश्च वरुणस्य बहिर्वृत्ति हृदयमिदमातपत्रमहार्षीत्। महात्मनस्तस्यान्वये भगदत्तपुष्पदत्तवज्रदत्तप्रभृतिषु व्यतीतेषु बहुषु मेरूपमेषु महत्सु महीपालेषु प्रपौत्रो महाराजभूतिवर्मणः पौत्रश्चन्द्रमुखवर्मणः पुत्रो देवस्य कैलासस्थिरस्थितेः स्थितिवर्मणः सुस्थिरवर्मा नाम महाराजाधिराजो जज्ञे तेजसां राशिर्मृगाङ्क इति [3]यं जना जगुः। योऽयमर्ज[4]जेनेवाजायत सहैवाहंकारेण। यश्च बाल एव प्रीत्या द्विजातीनप्रीत्या चारातीन्समग्रान्प्रतिग्रहानग्राहयत्। यत्र चातिदुर्लभं लवणालयसम्भूतायाः परं माधुर्यमभूल्लक्ष्म्याः। तथा च यो वाहिनीनाथानां शङ्खानहार न रत्नानि, पृथिव्याः स्थैर्यं जग्राह न करम्, अवनिभृतां गौरवमादत्त न नैष्ठुर्यम्। तस्य च सुगृहीतनाम्नो देवस्य देव्यां श्यामादेव्यां भास्करद्युतिर्भास्करवर्मापरनामा तनयः शन्तनोर्भागीरथ्यां भीष्म इव कुमारः समभवत्। अयमस्य च शैशवादारभ्य सङ्कल्पः स्थेयान्स्थाणुपादारविन्दद्वयादृते नाहमन्यं नमस्कुर्यामिति। ईदृशश्चायं मनोरथस्त्रिभुवनदुर्लभस्त्रयाणामन्यतमेन सम्पद्यते सकलभुवनविजयेन वा मृत्युना वा यदि वा प्रचण्डप्रतापज्वलनं[5]जनितदिग्दाहेन जगत्येकवीरेण देवोपमेन मित्रेण। मैत्री च प्रायः कार्यव्यपेक्षिणी क्षोणीभृताम्। कार्यं च कीदृशं नाम तद्भवेद्यदुपन्यस्यमानमुपनयेन्मित्रतां देवम्। देवस्य हि यशांसि सञ्चिचीषतो बहिरङ्गभूतानि धनानि। बाहावेव च केवले निषण्णस्य शेषावयवानामपि साहायकसम्पादनमनोरथो निरवकाशः किमुत बाह्यजन-

१ 'निर्वाहा' ब. २ 'तवर' ब. ३ 'प्रियं जना' ब. ४ 'योऽयमजेनेवा०' अ-क.
५ 'ज्वलनदिग्दाहेन' अ-क.

स्य। चतुःसागरग्रामग्रहणघस्मरस्य पृथिव्येकदेशदानोपन्यासेनापि का तुष्टिः। अभिरूपकन्याविश्राणनविलोभनमपि लक्ष्मीमुखारविन्ददर्शनदुर्ललितदृष्टेरकिंचित्करम्। एवमघटमानसकलोपायसम्पादितपदार्थेऽस्मिन्प्रार्थनामात्रकमेव केवलमनुरुध्यमानः शृणोतु देवः। प्राग्ज्योतिषेश्वरो हि देवेनैकपिङ्ग इवानङ्गद्विषा, दशरथ इव गोत्रभिदा, धनञ्जय इव पुष्कराक्षेण, वैकर्तन इव दुर्योधनेन, मलयानिल इव माधवेन, अजर्यं सङ्गतमिच्छति। यदि च देवस्यापि मैत्रीयति हृदयमवगच्छति च पर्यायान्तरितं दास्यमनुतिष्ठन्ति सुहृद इति ततः किमास्यते समाज्ञाप्यतामनुभवतु विष्णोर्मन्दरगिरिरिव विकटकेयूरकोटिमणिविघट्टनक्वणितकटकमणिशिलाशकलानि गाढोपगूढानि देवस्य कामरूपाधिपतिः। अस्मिन्नातृप्तेरनवरतविमललावण्यसौभाग्यसुधानिर्झरिणि मुखशशिनि चिराच्चक्षुषी लालयतु प्राग्ज्योतिषेश्वरश्रीः। नाभिनन्दति चेद्देवः प्रणयमाज्ञापयतु किं कथनीयं मया स्वामिनः' इति।

विरतवचसि तस्मिन्भूपालः पूर्वोपलब्धैरेव गुरुभिर्गुणैरारोपितबहुमानः कुमारे सुदूरमाभोगातपत्रव्यतिकरेण तु परां कोटिमारोपिते प्रेम्णि लज्जमान इव सादरं जगाद—'हंसवेग, कथमिव तादृशि महात्मनि महाभिजने पुण्यराशौ गुणिनां प्राग्रहरे परोक्षसुहृदि स्निह्यति मद्विधस्यान्यथा स्वप्नेऽपि प्रवर्तेत मनः। सकलजगदुत्तापनपटवोऽपि शिशिरायन्ते त्रिभुवननयनानन्दकरे कमलाकरे करास्तिग्मतेजसः। सुबहुगुणगणक्रीताश्च के वयं सख्यस्य। सज्जनमाधुर्याणामभृतदास्यो दश दिशः। एकान्तावदातोत्तानस्वभावसम्भृतसादृश्यस्य कुमुदस्य कृते केनाभिहितः शिशिररश्मिः। श्रेयांश्च सङ्कल्पः कुमारस्य। स्वयं बाहुशाली मयि च समालम्बितशरासने सुहृदि हरादृते कमन्यं नमस्यति। संवर्धिता मे प्रीतिरमुना सङ्कल्पेन। अवलेपिनि पशावपि केसरिणि बहुमानो हृदयस्य किं पुनः सुहृदि। तत्तथा यतेथा यथा न चिरमियमस्मान्क्लेशयति कुमारदर्शनोत्कण्ठा' इति।

हंसवेगस्तु विज्ञापयाम्बभूव—'देव, किमपरमिदानीं क्लेशयत्यभिजातमभिहितं देवेन। सेवाभीरवो हि सन्तः, तत्रापि विशेषेणायमहङ्कारधनो वैष्णवो वंशः। आस्तां तावदस्मत्स्वामिवंशः। पश्यतु देवः पुरुषस्य हि सेवां प्रति दुर्जनन्येवातिवृद्धया दुर्गत्या वाभिमुखीक्रियमाणस्य, कुटुम्बिन्येवासन्तुष्टया तृष्णया वा प्रेर्यमाणस्य, दुरपत्यैरिव यौवनजनितैर्नानाभिलाषिभिरसत्सङ्कल्पैर्वाकुलीक्रियमाणस्य, जरत्कुमारीमिव परमार्गणयोग्यामतिमहतीं वा अवस्थां पश्यतः, स्वगृहे दुर्बन्धुभिरिव दुःस्थितैः समग्रैर्ग्रहैर्वा ग्राह्यमाणस्याभियोगं, पुरातनैरतिदुस्त्यजैर्भृत्यैरिव मलिनैः कर्मभिर्वानुवर्त्यमानस्य, सकलशरीरसन्तापकरं कारीषाग्निमिव दुष्कृतिनः कृतचित्तस्य संप्रवेष्टुं राजकुलम्, उपहतसकलेन्द्रियशक्तेरिव मिथ्यैव हृदयगतविषयग्रामग्रहणाभिलाषस्य, प्रथममेव तोरणतले वन्दनमालाकिशलयस्येव शुष्यतो द्वाररक्षिभिर्निरुद्धस्य, पीडितस्य

प्रविशतो द्वारे हरिणस्येवापरैर्हन्यमानस्य, करिकर्मचर्मपुटस्येव मुहुर्मुहुः प्रतिहारमण्डलकरप्रहारैर्निरस्यमानस्य, निधिपादपप्ररोहस्येव[1] द्रविणाभिलाषादधोमुखीभवतः, दूरममार्गणस्याप्यतिविप्रकृष्टविवृत्त[2]विसर्जितस्योद्वेगं व्रजतः, अकण्टकस्यापि चरणतललग्नस्याकृष्य क्षेपीयः क्षिप्यमाणस्य, अमकरकेतोरप्यकालोपसर्पणप्रकुपितेश्वरदृष्टिदग्धस्य प्रलयमुपगच्छतः, कपेरिव कोपनिर्भर्त्सितस्याप्यभिन्नमुखरागस्य, ब्रह्मघ्न इव प्रतिदिवसवन्दनोद्घृष्टशिरःकपालस्य, स्पर्शरहितस्याशुभकर्माणि निर्वहतः, त्रिशङ्कोरिवोभयलोकभ्रष्टस्य नक्तन्दिनमर्वाक्शिरसस्तिष्ठतः, वाजिन इव कवलवशेन सुखवाह्यमात्मानं विदधानस्य, अनशनशायिन इव हृदयस्थापितजीवनाशस्य शरीरं क्षपयतः, शुन इव निजदारपराङ्मुखस्य जघन्यकर्मलग्नमात्मानं ताडयतः, प्रेतस्येवानुचितभूमिदीयमानान्नपिण्डस्य, बलिभुज इव जिह्वालौल्योपयुक्तपुरुषवर्चसो वृथा विहितायुषो जीवतः, श्मशानपादपानिव पिशाचस्य दग्धभूत्या परुषीकृताम्राजवल्लभानुपसर्पतः, विपरीतजिह्वाजनितमाधुर्यैरोष्ठमात्रप्रकटितरागै राजशुकालापैः शिशोरिव मुग्धविलोभ्यमानस्य, वेतालस्येव नरेन्द्रप्रभावाविष्टस्य न किंचिन्नाचरतः, चित्रधनुष इवालीकगुणाध्यारोपणैकक्रियानित्यनम्रस्य निर्वाणतेजसः, संमार्जनीसमुपार्जितरजसोऽवकरकूटस्येव निर्माल्यवाहिनः, कफविकारिण इव दिने दिने कटुकैरुद्वेज्यमानस्य, सौगतस्येवार्थशून्यविज्ञप्तिजनितवैराग्यस्य काषायाण्यभिलषतः, निशास्वपि मातृबलिपिण्डस्येव दिक्षु विक्षिप्यमाणस्य, अशौचगतस्येव कुशयनजनितसमधिकतरदुःखवृत्तेः, तुलायन्त्रस्येव पश्चात्कृतगौरवस्य तोयार्थमपि नमतः, अतिकृपणस्य शिरसा केवलेनासन्तुष्टस्य वचसापि पादौ स्पृशतः, निर्दयवेत्रिवेत्रताडनत्रस्तयेव त्रपया त्यक्तस्य, दैन्यसङ्कोचितहृदयहृतावकाशयेवाहोपुरुषिकया परिवर्जितस्य, कुत्सितकर्माङ्गीकरणकुपितयेवोन्नत्या वियुक्तस्य, धनश्रद्धया क्लेशानुपार्जयतः, स्ववृद्धिबुद्ध्यावमानं वर्धयतो मूढस्य, सत्यपि विविधकुसुमाधिवाससुरभिणि वने तृष्णाञ्जलिमुपरचयतः, कुलपुत्रस्यापि कृतागस इव भीतभीतस्य समीपमुपसर्पतः, दर्शनीयस्याप्यालेख्यकुसुमस्येव निष्फलजन्मनः, विदुषोऽपि वैधेयस्येवापशब्दमुखस्य, शक्तिमतोऽपि श्वित्रिण इव सङ्कोचितकरयुगलस्य, समसमुत्कर्षेषु निरग्निपच्यमानस्य, नीचसमीकरणेषु निरुच्छ्वासं म्रियमाणस्य, परिभवैस्तृणीकृतस्य, दुःखानिलेनानिर्वृतेः, ज्वलतो भक्तस्याप्यभक्तस्य, निरूष्मणः सन्तापयतो बन्धूनविमानस्याप्यगतिकस्य, च्युतगौरवस्याप्यधस्ताद्गच्छतः, निःसत्त्वस्यापि महामांसविक्रयं कुर्वतः, निर्मदस्याप्यस्वतन्त्रवृत्तेरयोगिनोऽपि ध्यानवशीकृतात्मनः शय्योत्थायं प्रणमतो दग्धमुण्डस्य गोत्रविदूषकस्य नक्तंदिनं नृत्यतो मनस्विजनं हासयतः, कुलाङ्गारस्य वंशं दहतः, नृपशोः तृणेऽपि लब्धे कन्धरामवनमयतः, जठरपरिपूरणमात्रप्रयोजनजन्मनो मांसपिण्डस्य गर्भरोगस्य

---

१ '०प्ररोठदारुमयदेहस्येव द्रविणा–' ब. २ 'विवृत' ब.

मातुः, अपुण्यानां कर्मणामाचरणाद्भृतकस्य किं प्रायश्चित्तम्, का प्रतिपत्तिक्रिया, क्व गतस्य शान्तिः, कीदृशं जीवितम्, कः पुरुषाभिमानः, किंनामानो विलासाः, कीदृशी भोगश्रद्धा, प्रबलपङ्क इव सर्वमधस्तान्नयति दारुणो दासशब्दः। धिक्तदुच्छ्वसितमुपयातु[1] तद्धनं निधनमभवनिर्भूतेरस्तु तस्याः नमो भगवद्भ्यस्तेभ्यः सुखेभ्यस्तस्यायमञ्जलिरैश्वर्यस्य तिष्ठतु दूर एव सा श्रीः शिवं स परिच्छदः करोतु यदर्थमुत्तमाङ्गं गां गमिष्यति[2] मुखप्रियरतः क्लीबः पूतिमांसमयः कृमिरगण्यमानो नरकः, पादरजोधूसरोत्तमाङ्गो जङ्गमः पादपीठः, पुंस्कोकिलः काकुक्वणितेषु, शिखी सुखकरकेकासु, स्थूलकूर्मः क्रोडकषणेषु, श्वा नीचचाटुकरणेषु, वेणुर्मूर्च्छनासु, वेश्याकायः करणबन्धक्लेशेषु, पलालं सत्त्वशालिषु, कृकलासः[3] शिरोविडम्बनासु, जाहक आत्मसङ्कोचनेषु, प्रतिपादकः पादसंवाहनासु, कन्दुकः करतलताडनेषु, वीणादण्डः कोणाभिघातेषु, वराकः सेवकोऽपि मर्त्यमध्ये राजिलोऽपि वा भोगी पुलाकोऽपि वा कलमः वरं क्षणमपि कृता मानवता[4] मानवता न मतो नमतस्त्रैलोक्याधिराज्योपभोगोऽपि मनस्विनः। तदेवमभिनन्दितास्मदीयप्रणयो देवोऽपि दिवसैः कतिपयैरेव परागतः प्राग्ज्योतिषेश्वर इति करोतु चेतसि' इत्युक्त्वा तूष्णीमभूदचिराच्च नमस्कृत्य निर्जगाम।

राजापि रजनीं तां कुमारदर्शनौत्सुक्यस्वीकृतहृदयः समनैषीत्। आत्मार्पणं हि महताममूलमन्त्रमयं वशीकरणम्। प्रभाते च प्रभूतं प्रतिप्राभृतं प्रधानप्रतिदूताधिष्ठितं दत्त्वा हंसवेगं प्राहिणोत्। आत्मनापि ततः प्रभृति प्रयाणकैरनवरतैरभ्यमित्रं प्रावर्तत। कदाचित्तु राज्यवर्धनभुजबलोपार्जितमशेषं मालवराजसाधनमादायागतं समीप एवावासितं लेखहारकाद्भण्डिमश्रृणोत्। श्रुत्वा चाभिनवीभूतभ्रातृशोकहुताशनः कातरहृदयो बभूव मूर्च्छान्धकारमिव विवेशातिष्ठच्च समुत्सृष्टसकलव्यापारः प्रतीहारनिवारणनिभृतनिःशब्दपरिजने निजमन्दिरे सराजकपरिवारस्तदागमनमुदीक्षमाणो मुहूर्तम्।

अथ भण्डिरेकेनैव वाजिना कतिपयकुलपुत्रपरिवृतो मलिनवासा रिपुशरशल्यपूरितेन निखातबहुलोहकीलकपरिकररक्षितस्फुटनेनेव हृदयेन, हृदयलग्नैः स्वामिसत्कृतैरिव श्मश्रुभिः शुचं समुपदर्शयन्, दूरीकृतव्यायामशिथिलभुजदण्डदोलायमानमङ्गलवलयैकशेषालङ्कृतिः, अनादरोपयुक्तताम्बूलविरलरागेण शोकदहनदह्यमानस्य हृदयस्याङ्गारेणेव दीर्घनिश्वासवेगनिर्गतेनाधरेण शुष्यता, स्वामिविरहविधृतजीवितापराधवैलक्ष्यादिव बाष्पवारिपटलेन पटेनेव प्रावृतवदनः, विशन्निव दुर्बलीभूतैः स्वाङ्गमपत्रपयाङ्गैः, वमन्निव च व्यर्थीभूतभुजोष्माणमायतैर्निश्वसितैः, पातकीव, अपराधीव, द्रोहीव, मुषित

---

१ 'उपयातु निधनं धनम्' ब. २ 'गमिष्यत्यशापानुग्रहक्षमस्तपस्वी मुख–' ब.
३ 'कृकलासः⋯सङ्कोचनेषु' इत्येतत् 'नीचचाटुकरणेषु' इत्यस्यानन्तरं ब–पुस्तके.
४ 'मानवताम्' ब.

इव, छलित इव, यूथपतिपतनविषण्ण इव वेगदण्डवारणः, सूर्यास्तमयनिःश्रीक इव कमलाकरः, दुर्योधननिधनदुर्मना इव द्रौणिः, अपहृतरत्न इव सागरो राजद्वारमाजगाम। अवतीर्य च तुरङ्गमादवनतमुखो विवेश राजमन्दिरम्। दूरादेव च विमुक्ताक्रन्दः पपात पादयोः।

अवनिपतिरपि दृष्ट्वा तमुत्थाय विरलैः पदैः प्रत्युद्गम्योत्थाप्य च गाढमुपगुह्य कण्ठे करुणमतिचिरं रुरोद। शिथिलीभूतमन्युवेगश्च पुरेव पुनरागत्य निजासने निषसाद। प्रथमप्रक्षालितमुखे च भण्डौ मुखमक्षालयत्। समतिक्रान्ते च कियत्यपि काले भ्रातृमरणवृत्तान्तमप्राक्षीत्। अथाकथयच्च यथावृत्तमखिलं भण्डिः। अथ नरपतिस्तमुवाच—'राज्यश्रीव्यतिकरः कः' इति। स पुनरवादीत्—'देव,देवभूयं गते देवे राज्यवर्धने गुप्तनाम्ना च गृहीते कुशस्थले देवी राज्यश्रीः परिभ्रश्य बन्धनाद्विन्ध्याटवीं सपरिवारा प्रविष्टेति लोकतो वार्तामश्रृणवम्। अन्वेष्टारस्तु तां प्रति प्रभूताः प्रहिता जना नाद्यापि निवर्तन्ते' इति। तच्चाकर्ण्य भूपतिरब्रवीत्—'किमन्यैरनुपदिभिः यत्र सा तत्र परित्यक्तान्यकृत्यः स्वयमहं यास्यामि। भवानपि कटकमादाय प्रवर्ततां गौडाभिमुखम्।' इत्युक्त्वा चोत्थाय स्नानभुवमगात्। कारितशोकश्मश्रुवपनकर्मणा च महाप्रतीहारभवनस्नातेन शारीरिकवसनकुसुमाङ्गरागालङ्कारप्रेषणप्रकटितप्रसादेन भण्डिना सार्धमभुक्त निनाय च तेनैव सह वासरम्।

अथापरेद्युरुषस्येव भण्डिर्भूपालमुपसृत्य व्यज्ञापयत्—'पश्यतु देवः श्रीराज्यवर्धनभुजबलार्जितं साधनं सपरिबर्हं मालवराजस्य' इति। नरपतिना स 'एवं क्रियताम्' इत्यभ्यनुज्ञातो दर्शयाम्बभूव। तद्यथा—अनवरतगलितमदमदिरामोदमुखरमधुकरजूटजटिलकरटपट्टपङ्क्लिगण्डान् गण्डशैलानिव जङ्गमान् गम्भीरगर्जितरवाञ्जलधरानिव महीमवतीर्णानुत्फुल्लसप्तच्छदवनामोदमुचः शरद्दिवसानिव पुञ्जीभूताननेकसहस्रसंख्यान्करिणः, चारुचामीकरचित्रचामरमण्डलमनोहरांश्च हरिणरंहसो हरीन्, बालातपविसरवर्षिणां च किरणैरनेकेन्द्रायुधीकृतदशदिशामलङ्काराणां विशेषान्, विस्मयकृतः स्मरोन्मादितमालवीकुचपरिमलदुर्ललितांश्च निजज्योत्स्नापूरप्लावितदिगन्तानपि तारान्हारान्, उडुपतिपादसञ्चयशुचीनि निजयशांसीव बालव्यजनानि, जातरूपमयनालं च निवासपुण्डरीकमिव श्रियः श्वेतातपत्रम्, अप्सरस इव बहुसमररससाहसानुरागावतीर्णा वारविलासिनीः, सिंहासनशयनासन्दीप्रभृतीनि राज्योपकरणानि, कालायसनिगडनिश्चलीकृतचरणयुगलं च सकलं मालवराजलोकमशेषांश्च ससंख्यालेख्यपत्रान् सालङ्कारापीडपीडान्[2] कोषकलशान्। अथालोच्य तत्सर्वमवनिपालः स्वीकर्तुं यथाधिकारमादिक्षदध्यक्षान्। अन्यस्मिंश्चाहनि हयैः स्वसारमन्वेष्टुमुच्चचाल विन्ध्याटवीमवाप च परिमितैरेव प्रयाणकैस्ताम्।

---

१ 'कालकलाकलापे' ब. २ सालङ्कारपेडापीडान्' ब.

अथ प्रविशन्दूरादेव दह्यमानषष्टिकबुसविसरविसारिविभावसूनां वन्यधान्यबीजधानीनां धूमेन धूसरिमाणमादधानैः, शुष्कशाखासञ्चयरचितगोवाटवेष्टितविकटवटैः, व्यापादितवत्सरूपकरोषरचितै[1]र्व्याघ्रयन्त्रैः, [2]अयन्त्रितवनपालहठह्रियमाणपरग्रामीणकाष्ठिककुठारैः, गहनतरुषण्डनिर्मितचामुण्डामण्डपैर्वनप्रदेशैः प्रकाश्यमानम्, अटवीप्रायप्रान्ततया कुटुम्बभरणाकुलैः कुद्दालप्रायकृषिभिः कृषीवलैरबलीवर्दैरवलद्भिरुच्चभागभाषितेन भज्यमानभूरि[3]शालिखलक्षेत्रखण्डलकम्, अल्पावकाशैश्च [4]कापिलैः कालायसैरिव कृष्णमृत्तिकाकठिनैः स्थानस्थानस्थापितस्थाणूत्थितस्थूलपल्लवैः दुरुपगमश्यामाकप्ररूढिभिरलम्बुसबहुलैरविरहितकोकिलाक्षक्षुपैर्विरलविरलैः केदारैः कृच्छ्रकृष्यमाणैर्नातिप्रभूतप्रवृत्तगतागताप्रहतभुवमुपक्षेत्रमुपरचितैरुच्चैर्मञ्चैश्च सूच्यमानश्वापदोपद्रवम्, दिशि दिशि च प्रतिमार्गद्रुमकृतानां पथिकपादप्रस्फोटनधूलिधूसरैर्नव[5]पल्लवैर्लाञ्छितच्छायानाम्, अटवीसुलभसालकुसुमस्तबकाञ्चितनवखातकूपिकोपकण्ठप्रतिष्ठितनागस्फुटानामच्छिद्रकटकल्पितकुटीरकाणाम्, कुटिलकीटवेणीवेष्ट्यमानशक्तुशारशरावश्रेणीश्रितानामध्वगजनजग्धजम्बूफलास्थिशबलसमीपभुवामुद्धूलितधूलीकदम्बस्तबकप्रकरपुलकिनीनाम्, कण्टकितकर्करीचक्राक्रान्तकाष्ठमञ्चिकामुषिततृषाम्, तिम्यत्तलशीतलसिकतिलकलशीशमितश्रमाणामाश्यानशैवलश्यामलितालिञ्जरजायमानजलजडिम्नामुदकुम्भाकृष्टपाटलशर्कराशकलशिशिरीकृतदिशाम्, घटमुखघटितकटहारपाटलापुष्पपुटानाम्, शीकरपुलकितपल्लवपूलीपाल्यमानशोष्यसरसशिशुसहकारफलजूटीजटिलै[6]स्थाणूनाम्, विश्राम्यत्कार्पटिकपेटकपरिपाटीपीयमानपयसामटवीप्रवेशप्रपाणां शैत्येन त्याजयन्तमिव ग्रैष्ममुष्माणं क्वचिदन्यत्र ग्राहयन्तमिवाङ्गारीयदारुसंग्रहदाहिभिः व्योकारैः, सर्वतश्च प्रातिवेश्यविषयवासिनां समासन्नग्राम[7]गृहस्थापितस्थविरपरिपाल्यमानपाथेयस्थगितेन कृतदारुणदारुव्यायामयोग्याङ्गाभ्यङ्गेन स्कन्धाध्यासितकठोरकुठारकण्ठलम्बमानप्रातराशपुटेन पाटच्चरप्रत्यवायप्रतिपक्षपटच्चरेण कालवेत्रकत्रिगुणव्रततिवलयपाशग्रथितग्रीवाग्रथितैः पत्रवीटावृतमुखैः पीतकूटैरूढवारिणा पुरःसरवलद्बलीवर्दयुगसरेण नैकटिककुटुम्बिकलोकेन काष्ठसंग्रहार्थमटवीं प्रविशता, श्वापदव्यधनव्यवधानबहलीसमारोपितकुटीकृतकूटपाशैश्च गृहीतमृगतन्तुतन्त्रीजालवलयवागुरैः बहिर्व्याधैर्विचरद्भिः, अंसावसक्तवीतंसव्यालम्बमानबालपाशिकैश्च संगृहीतग्राहकक्रकरकपिञ्जलादिपञ्जरकैः शाकुनिकैः सञ्चरद्भिः, च्युतलासकलेशलिप्तलतावधूलट्वालम्पटानां च पेटकैः पाशिकशिशूनामटद्भिः, तृणस्तम्बान्तरिततित्तिरितरलायमानकौलेयककुलचाटुकारैश्च विहगमृगयां मृगयुयुवभिः क्रीडद्भिः, परिणतचक्रवाककण्ठकषायरुचां शीधव्यानां वल्कलानां

---

१ 'रोषाविष्टगोपालकल्पितव्याघ्र–' ब. २ 'यन्त्रित' अ–क. ३ 'भूरिखिलक्षेत्र०' ब.
४ 'कापिलैः' अ. ५ 'वनपल्लवैः' ब. ६ 'स्थूणानाम्.' ब. ७ 'ग्रामगृहस्थगृह०' ब.
८ 'संचरद्भिश्चतच्युत' ब.

कलापान्, नातिचिरोद्धृतानां च धातुत्विषां धातकीकुसुमानां गोणीरगणिताः पिचव्यानां चातसीगणपट्टमूलकानां पुष्कलान्सम्भारान्, भारांश्च मधुनो माक्षिकस्य मयूराङ्गजस्याक्लिष्टमधूच्छिष्टचक्रमालानां लम्बमानलामज्जक[1]जूटजटानामपत्वचां खदिरकाष्ठानां कुष्ठस्य कठोरकेशरिसटाभारबभ्रुणश्च रोध्रस्य भूयसो भारकान् लोकेनादाय व्रजता प्रविचितविविधवनफलपूरितपिटकमस्तकाभिश्चाभ्यर्णग्रामगत्वरीभिस्त्वरमाणाभिर्विक्रयचिन्ताव्यग्राभिर्ग्रामेयिकाभिर्व्याप्तदिगन्तरम्, इतस्ततश्च युक्तशूरशकुरशाक्कराणां पुराणपांसूत्किरकरीषकूटवाहिनीनां धूर्गतधूलिधूसरसैरिकं[2]सरोषस्वरसार्यमाणानां संक्रीडच्चटुलचक्रचीत्कारिणीनां शकटश्रेणीनां सम्पातैः सम्पाद्यमानदुर्बलोर्वीविरूक्षक्षेत्रसंस्कारम्, आरक्षक्षिप्तक्षिप्रदान्तवाहकदण्डोड्डीयमानहरिणहेलालङ्घिततुङ्गवैणववृतिभिश्च निखातगौरकरङ्कशङ्कुशङ्कितशशकशकलितत‍ुङ्गशुङ्गैः प्रयत्नप्रभृतविशङ्कटविटपैर्वाटैरैक्षवैर्बहुभिः श्यामायमानोपकण्ठम्, अतिविप्रकृष्टान्तरैर्मरकतस्निग्धस्नुहावाटवेष्टितैः कार्मुककर्मण्यवंशविटपसङ्कटैः कण्टकितकरञ्जराजिदुष्प्रवेश्यैः उरुबूकवचावङ्ककसुरससूरणशिग्रुग्रन्थिपर्णगवेधुकागर्मुद्गुल्मगहनगृहवाटिकैः, निखातोच्चकाष्ठारोपितकाष्ठालुकलताप्रतानविहितच्छायैः, परिमण्डलबदरीमण्डपकतलनिखातखादिरकीलबद्धवत्सरूपैः; कथमपि कुक्कुटरटितानुमीयमानसंनिवेशैरङ्ग[3]नागस्तिस्तम्बसलविरचितक्षिप्रपक्षिपूपिकावापिकैर्विकीर्णबदरपाटलपटलैः, वेणु[4]पोटदलनलशरमयवृतिविहितभित्तिभिः, किंशुकरोचनारचितमण्डलमण्डपबल्वजबद्धाङ्गारराशिभिः, शाल्मलिफलतूलसञ्चयबहुलैः, संनिहितनलशालिशालूकखण्डकुमुदबीजवेणुतण्डुलैः, सङ्गृहीतमालबीजैः, भस्मलिनम्लानकाश्मर्यकूटव्याधतकटैराश्यानराजादनमदनफलस्फीतैर्मधूकासवमद्यप्रायैः, कुसुम्भकुम्भगण्डकुसूलैरविरहितराजमाषत्रपुषकर्कटिकाकूष्माण्डालाबुबीजैः, पोष्यमाणवनबिडालमालुधाननकुलशालिजातजातकादिभिरटवीकुटुम्बिनां गृहैरुपेतं वनग्रामकं ददर्श तत्रैवं[5] चावसदिति ।

इति श्रीबाणभट्टकृतौ हर्ष[6]चरिते छत्रलब्धिर्नाम

सप्तम उच्छ्वासः ।

---

१ 'लामज्जकमुञ्जजूटक' ब. २ 'सैरिभ' अ-क. ३ 'अङ्गनाशस्तिस्तम्भ...क्षिप्रपूपिका अ-क. ४ 'पोटपटलनलकलितशरमय' ब. ५ 'तत्रैव च तं दिवसमत्यवाहयत्' ब. ६ '०कृते हर्षचरिते सप्तम' क; 'इति श्रीमहाकविचक्रचूडामणिश्रीबाणभट्टविरचिते श्रीहर्षचरिते महाकाव्ये छत्रलब्धिर्नाम सप्तम उच्छ्वासः सम्पूर्णः' ब.

प्रचुरपूगफलाः, प्रसवपूगपिङ्गलप्रियङ्गवः, परागपिञ्जरितमञ्जरीपुञ्ज्यमानमधुपमञ्जुशिञ्जाजनितजनमुदः, मदमलमेचकितमुचुकुन्दस्कन्धकाण्डकथ्यमाननिःशङ्ककरिकरटकण्डूतयः, उड्डीयमाननिःशङ्कचटुलकृष्णशारशावसकलशाड्वलसुभगभूमयः, तमःकालतमतमालमालामीलितातपाः, स्तबकदन्तुरितदेवदारवः, तरलताम्बूलीस्तम्बजालकितजम्बूजम्बीरवीथयः, कुसुमरजोधवलधूलीकदम्बचक्रचुम्बितव्योमानः, बहलमधुमोक्षोक्षितक्षितयः, परिमलघटितघ्राणतृप्तयः, कतिपयदिवसप्रसूतकुक्कुटीकुटीकृतकुटजकोटराः, चटकासञ्चार्यमाणवाचाटचाटकेरक्रियमाणचाटवः, सहचरीचारणचञ्चुरचकोरचञ्चवः, निर्भयभूरिभुरुण्डभुज्यमानपाककपिलपीलवः, सदाफलकटुफलफलविशसननिःशूकशुकशकुन्तशातितशलाटवः, शैलेयसुकुमारशिलातलसुखशयितशशशिशवः, शेफालिकाशिफाविवरविस्रब्धविवर्तमानगौधेरराशयः, निरातङ्करङ्कवः, निराकुलनकुलकुलकेलयः, कलकोकिलकुलकवलितकलिकोद्गमाः, सहकारारामरोमन्थायमानचमूरयूथाः, यथासुखनिषण्णनीलाण्डजमण्डलाः, निर्विकारवृकविलोक्यमानपोतपीतगवयधेनवः, श्रवणहारिसनीडगिरिनितम्बनिर्झरनिनादनिद्रानन्दमन्दायमानकरिकुलकर्णतालदुन्दुभयः, समासन्नकिन्नरीगीतरवरसमानरुरवः, प्रमुदिततरतरक्षवः क्षतहरितहरिद्राद्रवरज्यमाननववराहपोतपोत्रवलयः, गुञ्जाकुञ्जगुञ्जज्जाहकाः, जातीफलकसुप्तशालिजातकवलयः, दशनकुपितकपिपोतपेटकपाटितपाटलमुखकीटपुटकाः, लकुचलम्पटगोलाङ्गूललङ्घ्यमानलवलयः, बद्धवालुकालवालवलयाः, कुटिलकुटावलिवलितवेगगिरिनदिकास्रोतसः, निबिडशाखाकाण्डलम्बमानकमण्डलवः, सूत्रशिक्यासक्तरिक्तभिक्षाकपालपल्लवितलतामण्डपाः, निकटकुटीकृतपाटलमुद्राचैत्यकमूर्तयः, चीवराम्बररागकषायोदकदूषितोद्देशाः, मेघमया इव कृतशिखण्डिकुलकोलाहलाः, वेदमया इवापरिमितशाखाभेदगहनाः, माणिक्यमया इव महानीलतनवः, तिमिरमया इव सकलजननयनमुषः, यामुना इवोर्ध्वीकृतमहाह्रदाः, मरकतमणिश्यामलाः क्रीडापर्वतका इव वसन्तस्य, अञ्जनाचला[1] इव पल्लविताः, तनया इवाटवीजाता विन्ध्यस्य, पातालान्धकारराशय इव भित्त्वा भुवमुत्थिताः, प्रतिप्रवेशका[2] इव वर्षावासराणाम्, अंशावतारा इव कृष्णरात्रीणाम्[3], इन्द्रनीलमयाः प्रासादा इव वनदेवतानाम्, पुरस्ताद्दर्शनपथमवतेरुस्तरवः।

ततो नरपतेरभवन्मनस्यदूरवर्तिना खलु भवितव्यं भदन्तेनेति। अवतीर्य च गिरिसरिति समुपस्पृश्य युगपद्विश्रामसमयसमुन्मुक्तहेषाघोषवधिरीकृताटवीगहनामस्मिन्नेव प्रदेशे स्थापयित्वा वाजिसेनामवलम्ब्य च तपस्विजनदर्शनोचितं विनयं हृदयेन दक्षिणेन च हस्तेन माधवगुप्तमंसे विरलैरेव राजभिरनुगम्यमानश्चरणाभ्यामेव प्रावर्तत गन्तुम्।

---

१ 'अञ्जनाचलमया इव' ब. २ 'प्रतिवेशिका' अ. ३ 'कृष्णार्घरात्रीणाम्' ब.

अथ तेषां तरूणां मध्ये नानादेशीयैः स्थानस्थानेषु स्थाणूनाश्रितैः शिलातलेषूपविष्टैर्लताभवनान्यध्यावसद्भिररण्यानीनिकुञ्जेषु निलीनैर्विटपच्छायासु निषण्णैस्तरुमूलानि निषेवमाणैर्वीतरागैरार्हतैर्मस्करिभिः श्वेतपटैः पाण्डुरभिक्षुभिर्भागवतैर्वर्णिभिः केशलुञ्चनैः कापिलैर्जैनैर्लोकायतिकैः काणादैरौपनिषदैरैश्वरकारणिकैः कारन्धमिभिर्धर्मशास्त्रिभिः पौराणिकैः साप्ततन्तवैः शैवैः शाब्दैः पाञ्चरात्रिकैरन्यैश्च स्वान्स्वान्सिद्धान्ताञ्शृण्वद्भिरभियुक्तैश्चिन्तयद्भिश्च प्रत्युच्चरद्भिश्च संशयानैश्च निश्चिन्वद्भिश्च व्युत्पादयद्भिश्च विवदमानैश्चाभ्यस्यद्भिश्च व्याचक्षाणैश्च शिष्यतां प्रतिपन्नैर्दूरादेवावेद्यमानम्, अतिविनीतैः कपिभिरपि चैत्यकर्म कुर्वाणैस्त्रिसरणपरैः परमोपासकैः शुकैरपि शाक्यशासनकुशलैः कोशं समुपदिशद्भिः शिक्षापदोपदेशदोषोपशमशालिनीभिः शारिकाभिरपि धर्मदेशनां दर्शयन्तीभिरनवरतश्रवणगृहीतालोकैः कौशिकैरपि बोधिसत्त्वजातकानि जपद्भिर्जातसौगतशीलशीतलस्वभावैः शार्दूलैरप्यमांसाशिभिरुपास्यमानम्, आसनोपान्तोपविष्टविस्रब्धानेककेसरिशावकतया मुनिपरमेश्वरमकृत्रिम इव सिंहासने निषण्णम्, उपशममिव पिबद्भिर्वनहरिणैर्जिह्वालताभिरुपलिह्यमानपादपल्लवम्, वामकरतलनिविष्टेन नीवारमश्नता पारावतपोतेन कर्णोत्पलेनेव प्रियां मैत्रीं प्रसादयन्तम्, इतरकरकिसलयनखमयूखलेखाभिर्जनितजनव्यामोहम्, उद्ग्रीवं मयूरं मरकतमणिकरकमिव वारिधाराभिः पूरयन्तम्, इतस्ततः पिपीलकश्रेणीनां श्यामाकतण्डुलकणान्स्वयमेव किरन्तम्, अरुणेन चीवरपटलेन म्रदीयसा संवीतम्, बहलबालातपानुलिप्तमिव पौरन्दरं दिग्भागमुल्लिखितपद्मरागप्रभाप्रतिमया रक्तावदातया देहप्रभया पाटलीकृतानां काषायग्रहणमिव दिशामप्युपदिशन्तम्, अनौद्धत्यादधोमुखेन मन्दमुकुलितकुमुदाकारेण स्निग्धधवलप्रसन्नेन चक्षुषा जनक्षुण्णक्षुद्रजन्तुजीवनार्थममृतमिव वर्षन्तम्, सर्वशास्त्राक्षरपरमाणुभिरिव निर्मितं परमसौगतमप्यवलोकितेश्वरम्, अस्खलितमपि तपसि लग्नम्, आलोकमिव यथावस्थितसकलपदार्थप्रकाशकं दर्शनार्थिनाम्, सुगतस्याप्यभिगमनीयमिव, धर्मस्याप्याराधनीयमिव, प्रसादस्यापि प्रसादनीयमिव, मानस्यापि माननीयमिव, वन्द्यत्वस्यापि वन्दनीयमिव, [1]आत्मनोऽपि स्पृहणीयमिव, ध्यानस्यापि ध्येयमिव, ज्ञानस्यापि ज्ञेयमिव, जन्म[2] जपस्य, नेमिं नियमस्य, तत्त्वं तपसः, शरीरं शौचस्य, कोशं कुशलस्य, वेश्म विश्वासस्य, [3]सर्वस्वं सद्वृत्तता[4]याः, दाक्ष्यं दाक्षिण्यस्य, पारं परानुकम्पायाः, निर्वृतिं सुखस्य, मध्यमे वयसि वर्तमानं दिवाकरमित्रमद्राक्षीत्। अतिप्रशान्तगम्भीराकारारोपितबहुमानश्च सादरं दूरादेव समं शिरसा मनसा वचसा च ववन्दे।

दिवाकरमित्रस्तु मैत्रीमयः प्रकृत्या विशेषतस्तेनापरेणादृष्टपूर्वेणामानुष-

१ 'आत्मनोऽपि...ज्ञेयमिव' इत्येतन्नास्ति अ-क पुस्तकयोः. २ 'जन्म यमस्य' अ-क. ३ 'सद्वृत्तम्' अ-क. ४ 'सद्वृत्ततायाः, सर्वस्वं सर्वज्ञतायाः' अ-क.

लोकोचितेन सर्वाभिभाविना महानुभावाभोगभाजा भ्राजिष्णुना भूपतेरप्राकृतेनाकारविशेषेण तेन चाभिजात्यप्रकाशकेन गरीयसा प्रश्रयेण चाह्लादितश्चक्षुषि च चेतसि च युगपदग्रहीत् । वीरस्वभावोऽपि च सम्पादितससंभ्रमाभ्युत्थानः सङ्कलय्य किंचिदुद्गमनकेन विलोलं विलम्बमानं वामांसाच्चीवरपटान्तमुत्क्षिप्यानेकाभयदानदीक्षादक्षिणो दक्षिणं महापुरुषलक्षणलेखाप्रशस्तं हस्तं स्निग्धमधुरया वाचा सगौरवमारोग्यदानेन राजानमन्वग्रहीत् । अभ्यनन्दच्च स्वागतगिरा गुरुमिवाभ्यागतं बहु मन्यमानः स्वेनासनेनाध्वमत्रेति निमन्त्रयांचक्रे । पार्श्वे स्थितं च शिष्यमब्रवीत्—'आयुष्मन्, उपानय कमण्डलुना पादोदकम्' इति । राजा त्वचिन्तयत्—'अलोहः खलु संयमनपाशः सौजन्यमभिजातानाम् । स्थाने खलु तत्रभवान्गुणानुरागी ग्रहवर्मा बहुशो वर्णितवानस्य गुणान्' इति । प्रकाशं चाबभाषे—'भगवन्, दर्शनपुण्यानुगृहीतस्य मम पुनरुक्त इवायमार्यप्रयुक्तः प्रतिभात्यनुग्रहः । चक्षुष्प्रमाणप्रसादस्वीकृतस्य च परकरणमिवासनादिदानोपचारचेष्टितम् । अतिभूमिर्भूमिरेवासनं[1] भवादृशां पुरः सम्भाषणामृताभिषेकप्रक्षालितसकलवपुषश्च मे प्रदेशवृत्तिः । पाद्यमप्यपार्थकम् । आसतां भवन्तो यथासुखम् । आसीनोऽहम्' इत्यभिधाय क्षितावेवोपाविशत् ।

'अलंकारो हि परमार्थतः प्रभवतां प्रश्रयातिशयः, रत्नादिकस्तु शिलाभारः' इत्याकलय्य पुनः पुनरभ्यर्थ्यमानोऽपि यदा न प्रत्यपद्यत पार्थिवो वचनं तदा स्वमेवासनं पुनरपि भेजे भदन्तः । भूपतिमुखनलिननिहितनिभृतनयनयुगलनिगडनिश्चलीकृतहृदयश्च स्थित्वा कांचित्कालकलां[2] कलिकालकल्मषकालुष्यमिव क्षालयन्नमलाभिर्दन्तमयूखमालाभिर्मूलफलाभ्यवहारसम्भवमुद्गमन्निव च परिमलसुभगं विकचकुसुमपटलपाण्डुरं लतावनमवादीत्—'अद्यप्रभृति न केवलमयमनिन्द्यो वन्द्योऽपि प्रकाशितसत्सारः संसारः । किं नाम नालोक्यते जीवद्भिरद्भुतं येन रूपमचिन्तितोपनतमिदं दृक्पथमुपगतम् । एवंविधैरनुमीयन्ते जन्मान्तरावस्थितसुकृतानि हृदयोत्सवैः । इहापि जन्मनि दत्तमेवास्माकममुना तपःक्लेशेन फलमसुलभदर्शनं दर्शयता देवानां प्रियम् । आ तृप्तेः पीतममृतमीक्षणाभ्याम् । जातं निरुत्कण्ठं मानसं निवृत्तिसुखस्य । महद्भिः पुण्यैर्विना न विश्राम्यन्ति सज्जने त्वादृशि दृशः । सुदिवसः स यस्मिञ्जातोऽसि । सा सुजाता जननी या सकलजीवलोकजीवितजनकमजनयदायुष्मन्तम् । पुण्यवन्ति पुण्यान्यपि तानि येषामसि परिणामः । सुकृततपसस्ते परमाणवो ये तव परिगृहीतसर्वावयवाः । तत्सुभगं सौभाग्यमाश्रितोऽसि येन । भव्यः स पुरुषभावो भवत्यवस्थितो यः । यत्सत्यं मुमुक्षोरपि मे पुण्यभाजमालोक्य पुनः श्रद्धा जाता मनुजजन्मनि । नेच्छद्भिरप्यस्माभिर्दृष्टः कुसुमायुधः । कृतार्थमद्य चक्षुर्वनदेव-

---

१ 'अतिभूमिरेव भवादृशाम्' अ-क. २ 'कालकक्ष्याम्' ब.

तानाम् । अद्य सफलं जन्म वनपादपानां येषामसि गतो गोचरम् । अमृतमयस्य भवतो वचसां माधुर्यं कार्यमेव । अस्य त्वीदृशे शैशवे विनयस्योपाध्यायं ध्यायन्नपि न सम्भावयामि । भुवि सर्वथा शून्य आसीदजाते दीर्घायुषि गुणग्रामः । धन्यः स भूभृद्यस्य वंशे मणिरिव मुक्तामयः सम्भूतोऽसि । एवंविधस्य च पुण्यवतः कथंचित्प्राप्तस्य केन प्रियं समाचराम इति पारिप्लवं चेतो नः । सकलवनचरसार्थसाधारणस्य[1] कन्दमूलफलस्य गिरिसरिदम्भसो वा के वयम् । अपरोपकरणीकृतस्तु कायकलिरयमस्माकम् । सर्वस्वमवशिष्टमिष्टातिथ्याय । स्वायत्ताश्च विद्यन्ते विद्याबिन्दवः कतिचित् । उपयोगं तु न प्रीतिर्विचारयति । यदि च नोपरुणद्धि कश्चित्कार्यलवमरक्षणीयाक्षरं वा कथनीयं तत्कथयतु भवाञ्श्रोतुमभिलषति हृदयं सर्वमिदं नः । केन कृत्यातिभारेण भव्यो भूषितवान्भूमिमेतामभ्रमणयोग्याम् । कियदवधिर्वायं शून्याटवीपर्यटनक्लेशः कल्याणराशेः । कस्माच्च सन्तप्तरूपेव ते तनुरियमसन्तापार्हा विभाव्यते' इति ।

राजा तु सादरतरमब्रवीत्—'आर्य, दर्शितसंभ्रमेणानेन मधुरसविसरमसृतमिव[2] हृदयध्रतिकरमनवरतं वर्षता वचसैव ते सर्वमनुष्ठितम् । धन्योऽस्मि यदेवमभ्यर्हितमनुपचरणीयमपि मान्यो मन्यते माम् । अस्य च महावनभ्रमणपरिक्लेशस्य कारणमवधारयतु मतिमान् । मम हि विनष्टनिखिलेष्टबन्धोर्जीवितानुबन्धस्य निबन्धनमेकैव यवीयसी स्वसावशेषा[3] । सापि भर्तुर्वियोगाद्वैरिपरिभवभयाक्रमन्ती कथमपि विन्ध्यवनमिदम्, अशुभशबरबलबहुलम्, अगणितगजकुलकलिलम्, अपरिमितमृगपतिशरभभयम्, उरुमहिषमुषितपथिकगमनम्, अतिनिशितशरकुशपरुषम्, अवटशतविषममविशत् । अतस्तामन्वेष्टुं[4] वयमनिशं निशिनिशि च सततमिमामटवीमटामः । न चैनामासादयामः । कथयतु च गुरुरपि यदि कदाचित्कुतश्चिद्वने चरतः श्रुतिपथमुपगता तद्वार्ता' इति ।

अथ तच्छ्रुत्वा जातोद्वेग इव भदन्तः पुनरभ्यधात्—'धीमन्, न खलु कश्चिदेवंरूपो वृत्तान्तोऽस्मानभ्युपगतवान् । अभाजनं हि वयमीदृशानां प्रियाख्यानोपायनानां भवताम्[5] ।' इत्येवं भाषमाण एव तस्मिन्नकस्मादागत्यापरः शमिनि वयसि वर्तमानः संभ्रान्तरूप इव पुरस्तादुपरचिताञ्जलिर्जातकरुणः प्रक्षरितचक्षुर्भिक्षुरभाषत—'भगवन्भदन्त, महत्करुणं वर्तते । बालैव बलवद्व्यसनाभिभूता भूतपूर्वापि कल्याणरूपा स्त्री शोकवेगविवशा वैश्वानरं विशति । सम्भावयतु तामप्रोषितप्राणां भगवान् । अभ्युपपद्यतां समुचितैः समाश्वासनैः । अनुपरतपूर्वं कृमिकीटमपि दुःखितं दयाराशेरार्यस्य गोचरगतम्' इति ।

---

१ 'सार्थासाधारणस्य' ब. २ 'विसरं धृतमिव हृदय-' ब. ३ 'अवशेषात्' ब. ४ 'अयोगादतस्ताम्' ब. ५ 'भवतम्' ब.

राजा तु जातानुजाशङ्कः सोदर्यास्नेहाक्रान्तद्रुत इव दुःखेन दोदूयमानहृदयः कथमपि गद्गदिकागृहीतकण्ठो विकलवाग्बाष्पायमाणदृष्टिः पप्रच्छ—"पाराशरिन्, कियद्दूरे सा योषिदेवंजातीया जीवेद्वा कालमेतावन्तमिति। पृष्टा वा त्वया 'कासि, कस्यासि, कुतोऽसि, किमर्थं वनमिदमभ्युपगतासि, विशसि च किंनिमित्तमनलम्' इत्यादितः प्रभृति कात्स्न्र्येन कथ्यमानमिच्छामि श्रोतुं कथमार्यस्य गता गोचरमाकारतो वा कीदृशी" इति।

तथाभिहितस्तु भूभुजा भिक्षुराचचक्षे—'महाभाग, श्रूयताम्। अहं हि प्रत्यूषस्येवाद्य वन्दित्वा भगवन्तमनेनैव गिरिनदीरोधसा सैकतसुकुमारेण यदृच्छया विहृतवानतिदूरम्। एकस्मिंश्च वनलतागहने गिरिनदीसमीपभाजि भ्रमरीणामिव हिमहतकमलाकरकातराणां रसितं सार्यमाणानामतितारतानवर्तिनीनां वीणांतन्त्रीणामिव[1] झांकारमेकतानं नारीणां रुदितमध्वतिकरमतिकरुणमाकर्णितवानस्मि। समुपजातकृपश्च गतोऽस्मि तं प्रदेशम्। दृष्टवानस्मि च दृषत्खण्डखण्डिताङ्गुलिगलल्लोहितेन च पार्ष्णिप्रविष्टशरशलाकाशल्यशूलसङ्कोचितचक्षुषा चाध्वनीनश्रमश्वयथुनिश्चलचरणेन च स्थाणवव्रणव्यथितगुल्फबद्धभूर्जत्वचा च वातखुडखेदखञ्जजङ्घाजातज्वरेण च पांसुपाण्डुरपिण्डिकेन च खर्जूरजूटजटाजर्जरितजानुना च शतावरीविदारितोरुणा च विदारीदारिततनुदुकूलपल्लवेन चोत्कटवंशविटपकण्टककोटिपाटितकञ्चुककर्पटेन च फललोभालम्बितानम्रबदरीलताजालकैरुत्कण्टकैरुल्लिखितसुकुमारकरोदरेण च कुरङ्गशृङ्गोत्खातैः कन्दमूलफलैः कदर्थितबाहुना च ताम्बूलविरहविरसमुखखण्डितकोमलामलकीफलेन च कुशकुसुमाहतिलोहितानां श्वयतामक्ष्णां[2] लेपीकृतमनःशिलेन च कण्टकिलताल्लूनालकलेशेन च केनचित्किसलयोपपादितातपत्रकृत्येन केनचित्कदलीदलव्यजनवाहिना केनचित्कमलिनीपलाशपुटगृहीताम्भसा केनचित्पाथेयीकृतमृणालपूलिकेन केनचिच्चीनांशुकदशाशिक्यनिहितनालिकेरकोशकलशीकलितरसालतैलेन[3], कतिपयावशेषशोकविक्लवकलामूक[4]कुब्जवामनबधिरबर्बराविरलेनाबलानां चक्रवालेन परिवृताम्, आपत्कालेऽपि कुलोद्गतेनेवामुच्यमानां प्रभालेपिना लावण्येन, प्रतिबिम्बितैरासन्नवनलताकिसलयैः सरसैर्दुःखक्षतैरिवान्तःपटलीक्रियमाणकायाम्, कठोरदर्भाङ्कुरक्षतक्षारिणा क्षतजेनानुसरणालक्तकेनेव रक्तचरणाम्, उष्मालेनान्यतरनारीधृतेनारविन्दिनीदलेन कृतच्छायमपि विच्छायं मुखमुद्वहन्तीम्, आकाशमपि शून्यतयातिशयानाम्, मृण्मयीमिव निश्चेतनतया, मरुन्मयीमिव निश्वाससम्पदा, पावकमयीमिव सन्तापसन्तानेन, सलिलमयीमिवास्रप्रस्रवणेन, वियन्मयीमिव निरवलम्बनतया, तडिन्मयीमिव पारिप्लवतया, शब्दमयीमिव

---

१ 'वर्णांतन्त्रीणाम्' ब. २ 'श्वयथ्युमता-' ब. ३ 'कलितसरलतैलेन' ब. ४ 'विक्लमूक' अ-क.

परिदेवितवाणीबाहुल्येन, मुक्तमुक्तांशुकरत्नकुसुमकनकपत्त्राभरणां कल्पलतामिव महावने पतिताम्, परमेश्वरोत्तमाङ्गपातदुर्ललिताङ्गीं गङ्गामिव गां गताम्, वनकुसुमधूलिधूसरितपादपल्लवाम्, प्रभातचन्द्रमूर्तिमिव लोकान्तरमभिलषन्तीम्, निजजलमोक्षकदर्थितदर्शितधवला[1]यतनेत्रशोभाम्, मन्दाकिनीमृणालिनीमिव परिम्लायमानाम्, दुःसहरविकिरणसंस्पर्शखेदनिमीलितां कुमुदिनीमिव दुःखेन दिवसं नयन्तीम्, दग्धदशाविसंवादितां प्रत्यूषप्रदीपशिखामिव क्षामक्षामां पाण्डुवपुषम्, पार्श्ववर्तिवारणाभियोगरक्ष्यमाणां वनकरिणीमिव महाह्रदे निमग्नाम्, प्रविष्टां वनगह[2]ने ध्याने च, स्थितां तरुतले मरणे च, पतितां धात्र्युत्सङ्गे महानर्थे च, दूरीकृतां भर्त्रा सुखेन च, विरेचितां श्रमणेनायुषा च, आकुलां केशकलापेन मरणोपायेन च, विवर्णितामध्वधूलिभिरङ्गवेदनाभिश्च, दग्धां चण्डातपेन वैधव्येन च, धृतमुखीं पाणिना मौनेन च, गृहीतां प्रियसखीजनेन मन्युना च, तथा च भ्रष्टैर्बन्धुभिर्विलासैश्च, मुक्तेन श्रवणयुगलेनात्मना च, परित्यक्तैर्भूषणैः सर्वारम्भैश्च, भग्नैर्वलयैर्मनोरथैश्च, चरणलग्नाभिः परिचारिकाभिर्दर्भाङ्कुरसूचीभिश्च, हृदयविनिहितेन चक्षुषा प्रियेण च, दीर्घैः शोकश्वसितैः केशैश्च, क्षीणेन वपुषा पुण्येन च, पादयोः पतन्तीभिर्वृद्धाभिरश्रुधाराभिश्च, स्वल्पावशेषेण परिजनेन जीवितेन च, अलसामुन्मेषे, दक्षामश्रुमोक्षे, सन्ततां चिन्तासु, विच्छिन्नामाशासु, कृशां काये, स्थूलां श्वसिते, पूरितां दुःखेन, रिक्तां सत्त्वेन, अध्यासितामायासेन, शून्यां हृदयेन, निश्चलां निश्चयेन, चलितां धैर्यात्, अपि च वसतिं व्यसनानाम्, आधानमाधीनाम्, अवस्थानमनवस्थानाम्, आधारमधृतीनाम्, आवासमवसादानाम्, आस्पदमापदाम्, अभियोगमभाग्यानाम्, उद्वेगमुद्वेगानाम्, कारणं करुणायाः, [3]पारं परायत्तताया योषितम्। चिन्तितवानस्मि च चित्रमीदृशीमप्याकृतिमुपतापाः स्पृशन्तीति। सा तु समीपगते मयि तदवस्थापि सबहुमानमानतमौलिः प्रणतवती। अहं तु प्रबलकरुणाप्रेर्यमाणस्तामालपितुकामः पुनः कृतवान्मनसि—कथमिव महानुभावामेनामामन्त्रये। 'वत्से' इत्यतिप्रणयः, 'मातः' इति चाटु, 'भगिनि' इत्यात्मसम्भावना, 'देवि' इति परिजनालापः, 'राजपुत्रि' इत्यस्फुटम्, 'उपासिके' इति मनोरथः, 'स्वामिनि' इति भृत्यभावाभ्युपगमः, 'भद्रे' इतीतरस्त्रीसमुचितम्, 'आयुष्मति' इत्यवस्थायामप्रियम्, 'कल्याणिनि' इति दशायां विरुद्धम्, 'चन्द्रमुखि' इत्यमुनिमतम्, 'बाले' इत्यगौरवोपेतम्, 'आर्ये' इति जरारोपणम्, 'पुण्यवति' इति फलविपरीतम्, 'भवति' इति सर्वसाधारणम्। अपि च 'कासि' इत्यनभिजातम्, 'किमर्थं रोदिषि' इति दुःखकारणस्मरणकारि, 'मा रोदीः' इति शोकहेतुमनपनीय न शोभते, 'समाश्वसिहि' इति किमाश्रित्य, 'स्वागतम्' इति यातयामम्, 'सुखमास्यते' इति मिथ्या। इत्येवं

---

१ '०धवलायित०' ब. २ 'गहनं ध्यानं च' अ–क. ३ 'पदं परायत्ततताया' ब.

चिन्तयत्येव मयि तस्मात्क्षणादुत्थायान्यतरा योषिदार्यरूपेव शोकविक्लवा समुपसृत्य कतिपयपलितशारं शिरो नीत्वा महीतलमतुलहृदयसन्तापसूचकैरश्रुबिन्दुभिश्चरणयुगलं दहन्ती ममातिकृपणैरक्षरैश्च हृदयमभिहितवती—'भगवन्, सर्वसत्त्वानुकम्पिनी प्रायः प्रव्रज्या। प्रतिपन्नपरदुःखक्षपणदीक्षादक्षाश्च भवन्ति सौगताः। करुणाकुलगृहं च भगवतः शाक्यमुनेः शासनम्। सकलजनोपकारसज्जा सज्जनता जैनी। परलोकसाधनं च धर्मो मुनीनाम्। प्राणरक्षणाच्च न परं पुण्यजातं जगति गीयते जनेन। अनुकम्पाभूमयः प्रकृत्यैव युवतयः किं पुनर्विपदभिभूताः। साधुजनश्च सिद्धक्षेत्रमार्तवचसाम्[1]। यत इयं नः स्वामिनी मरणेन[2] पितुरभावेन भर्तुः प्रवासेन च भ्रातुः भ्रंशेन च शेषस्य बान्धववर्गस्यातिमृदुहृदयतयानपत्यतया च निरवलम्बना, परिभवेन च नीचारातिकृतेन प्रकृतिमनस्विनी, अमुना च महाटवीपर्यटनक्लेशेन कदर्थितसौकुमार्या, दग्धदैवदत्तैरेवंविधैर्बहुभिरुपर्युपरि व्यसनैर्विक्लवीकृतहृदया, दारुणं दुःखमपारयन्ती सोढुं निवारयन्तमनतिक्रान्तपूर्वं स्वप्नेऽप्यवगणय्य गुरुजनमनुनयन्तीरखण्डितप्रणया नर्मस्वपि समवधीर्य प्रियसखीर्विज्ञापयन्तमशरणमश्रुव्याकुलनयनमपरिभूतपूर्वं मनसापि परिभूय भृत्यवर्गमग्निं प्रविशति। परित्रायताम्। आर्योऽपि तावदसह्यशोकापनयनोपायोपदेशनिपुणां व्यापारयतु वाणीमस्याम्' इति चातिकृपणं व्याहरन्तीमहमुत्थाप्योद्विग्नतरः शनैरभिहितवान्—'आर्ये, यथा कथयसि तथा अस्मद्गिरामगोचरोऽयमस्याः पुण्याशयायाः शोकः। शक्यते चेन्मुहूर्तमात्रमपि त्रातुमुपरिष्टान्न व्यर्थेयमभ्यर्थना भविष्यति। मम हि गुरुरपर इव भगवान्सुगतः समीपगत एव। कथिते मयास्मिन्नुदन्ते नियतमागमिष्यति परमदयालुः। दुःखान्धकारपटलभिदुरैश्च सौगतैः सुभाषितैः स्वकैश्च दर्शितनिदर्शनैर्नानागमगुरुभिर्गिरां कौशलैः कुशलशीलामेनां प्रबोधपदवीमारोपयिष्यति' इति। तच्च श्रुत्वा 'त्वरतामार्यः' इत्यभिदधाना सा पुनरपि पादयोः पतितवती। सोऽहमुपगत्य त्वरमाणो व्यतिकरमिममधतिकरमशरण[3]कृपणबहुयुवतिमरणमतिकरुणमत्रभवते गुरवे निवेदितवान्' इति।

अथ भूभृद्भिक्षवं समवधार्य तद्भाषितमश्रुमिश्रितमश्रुतेऽपि स्वसुर्नाम्नि निम्नीकृतमना मन्युना सर्वाकारसंवादिन्या दशयैव दूरीकृतसन्देहो दग्ध इव सोदर्यावस्थाश्रवणेन श्रवणयोः श्रमणाचार्यमुवाच—'आर्य, नियतं सैवेयमनार्यस्यास्य जनस्यातिकठिनहृदयस्यातिनृशंसस्य मन्दभाग्यस्य भगिनी भागधेयैरेतामवस्थां नीता निष्कारणवैरिभिर्वराकी विदीर्यमाणं मे हृदयमेवं निवेदयति' इत्युक्त्वा तमपि श्रमणमभ्यधात्—'आर्य, उत्तिष्ठ। दर्शय क्वासौ।

---

१ 'आर्यवचसाम्' ब. २ 'मरणेन च मातुः प्रवसनेन च पितुरभावेन च भर्तुः परलोकगमनेन च भ्रातुर्भ्रंशेन च' ब. ३ 'अशरणम्' ब.

यतस्व प्रभूतप्राणिपरित्राणपुण्योपार्जनाय । यामः । यदि कथंचिज्जीवन्तीं सम्भावयामः' इति भाषमाण एवोत्तस्थौ।

अथ समग्रशिष्यवर्गानुगतेनाचार्येण तुरगेभ्यश्चावतीर्य समस्तेन सामन्तलोकेन पश्चादाकृष्यमाणाश्चीयेनानुगम्यमानः पुरस्ताच्च तेन शाक्यपुत्रीयेण प्रदिश्यमानवर्त्मा पद्भ्यामेव तं प्रदेशमविरलैः पदैः पिबन्निव प्रावर्तत। क्रमेण च समुपगतः शुश्राव लतावनान्तरितस्य मुमूर्षोर्महतः स्त्रैणस्य तत्कालोचितानेनकप्रकारानालापान्—'भगवन्धर्म, धाव शीघ्रम्। क्वासि कुलदेवते। देवि धरणि, धीरयसि न दुःखितां दुहितरम्। क्व नु खलु प्रोषिता पुष्पभूतिकुटुम्बिनी लक्ष्मीः। अनाथां नाथ मुखरवंश्य विविधाधिविधुरां वधूं विधवां विबोधयसि किमिति नेमाम्। भगवन्, भक्तजने संज्वरिणि सुगत सुप्तोऽसि। राजधर्म पुष्पभूतिभवनपक्षपातिन्, उदासीनीभूतोऽसि कथम्। त्वय्यपि विपद्बान्धव विन्ध्य वन्ध्योऽयमञ्जलिबन्धः। मातर्महाटवि, रटन्तीं न शृणोषीमा[2]मापत्पतिताम्। पतङ्ग, प्रसीद पाहि पतिव्रतामशरणाम्। प्रयत्नरक्षित कृतघ्न चारित्रचण्डाल, न रक्षसि राजपुत्रीम्। किमवधृतं लक्षणैः। हा देवि दुहितृस्नेहमयि यशोमति, मुषितासि दग्धदैवदस्युना। देव, दुहितरि दह्यमानायां नापतसि प्रतापशील, शिथिलीभूतमपत्यप्रेम। महाराज राज्यवर्धन, न धावसि मन्दीभूता भगिनीप्रीतिः। अहो निष्ठुरः प्रेतभावः। व्यपेहि पाप पावक स्त्रीघातनिर्घृण, ज्वलन्न लज्जसे। आर्तवार्त, दासी तवास्मि। संवादय द्रुतं देवीदाहं देवाय दुःखितजनार्तिहराय हर्षाय। नितान्तनिःशूक शोकश्वपाक, सकामोऽसि। दुःखदायिन्वियोगराक्षस, तुष्टोसि। विजने वने कमाक्रन्दामि, कस्मै कथयामि, कमुपयामि शरणम्, कां दिशं प्रतिपद्ये, करोमि किमभागधेया। गान्धारि, गृहीतोऽयं लतापाशः। पिशाचि मोचनिके, मुञ्च शाखाग्रहणकलहम्। कलहंसि, हंसि किमतः[3]परमुत्तमाङ्गम्। मङ्गलिके, मुक्तगलं किमद्यापि रुद्यते। सुन्दरि, दूरीभवति सखीसार्थः। स्थास्यसि कथमिवाशिवे शवशिबिरे शबरिके। सुतनु, तनूनपाति पतिष्यसि त्वमपि। मृणालकोमले मालावति, म्लानासि। मातर्मातङ्गिके, अङ्गीकृतस्त्वयापि मृत्युः। वत्से वत्सिके, वत्स्यसि [4]कथमनभिप्रेते प्रेतनगरे। नागरिके, गरिमाणमागतास्यनया स्वामिभक्त्या। विराजिके, विराजितासि राजपुत्रीविपदि जीवितव्ययव्यवसायेन। भृगुपतनाभ्युद्यमभागाभिज्ञे भृङ्गारधारिणि, धन्यासि। केतकि, कुतः पुनरीदृशी [5]सुस्वामिनी। मेनके, जन्मनि जन्मनि देवीदास्यमेव ददातु देवो देहं दहन्दहनः। विजये वीजय कृशानुम्। सानुमति, नमतीन्दीवरिका दिवं गन्तुकामा। कामदासि, देहि दहनप्रदक्षिणावकाशम्। विचरिके, विरचय वह्निम्। विकिर किरातिके कुसुमप्रकरम्। कुररिके, कुरु

---

१ 'यतः सुप्रभूतप्राण०' अ–क. २ 'शृणोषि मामापत्०' ब. ३ 'किमपरमुत्त०' ब. ४ 'कथनमभि–' अ–ब. ५ 'स्वस्वामिनी' ब.

कुरुबककोरकाचितां चिताम्। चामरं चामरग्राहिणि गृहाण। पुनरपि कण्ठे मर्षयितव्यानि नर्मदे नर्मनिर्मितानि निर्मर्यादहसितानि। भद्रे सुभद्रे, भद्रमस्तु ते परलोकगमनम्। अग्रामीणगुणानुरागिणि ग्रामेयिके, गच्छ सुगतिम्। वसन्तिके, अन्तरं प्रयच्छ। आपृच्छते छत्रधारी देवि देहि दृष्टिम्। दृष्टा तव जहाति जीवितं विजयसेना। सेयं मुक्तिका मुक्तकण्ठमारटति निकटे नाटकसूत्रधारी। पादयोः पतति ते ताम्बूलवाहिनी बहुमता राजपुत्रि पत्रलता। कलिङ्गसेने, अयं पश्चिमः परिष्वङ्गः पीडय निर्भरमुरसा माम्। असवः प्रवसन्ति वसन्तसेने। मञ्जुलिके, मार्जयसि कतिकृत्वः सुदुःसहदुःखसहस्रास्रदिग्धं दग्धचक्षुरिदं रोदिषि कियदाश्लिष्य च माम्। निर्माणमीदृशं प्रायशो यशोधने। धीरयस्यद्यापि किं मां माधविके। केयमवस्था संस्थापनानाम्। गतः कालः कालिन्दि सखीजनानुनयाञ्जलीनाम्। उन्मत्तिके मत्तपालिके, कृताः पृष्ठतः प्रणयिनीप्रणिपातानुरोधाः। शिथिलय चकोरवति चरणग्रहणं ग्रहिणि। कमलिनि, किमनेन पुनः पुनर्दैवोपालम्भेन। न प्राप्तं चिरं सखीजनसङ्गमसुखम्। आर्ये महत्तरिके तरङ्गसेने नमस्कारः। सखि सौदामिनि, दृष्टासि। समुपनय हव्यवाहनार्चनकुसुमानि कुमुदिके। देहि चितारोहणाय रोहिणि हस्तावलम्बनम्। अम्ब धात्रि, धीरा भव। भवन्त्येवंविधा एव कर्मणां विपाकाः पापकारिणीनाम्। आर्यचरणानामयमञ्जलिः। परः परलोकप्रयाणप्रणामोऽयं मातः। मरणसमये कस्माल्लवलिके हलहलको बलीयानानन्दमयो हृदयस्य मे। हृष्यन्त्युच्चरोमाञ्चमुच्चि किमङ्गीकृत्याङ्गानि। वामनिके, वामेन मे स्फुरितमक्ष्णा। वृथा विरमसि वयस्य वायस वृक्षे क्षीरिणि क्षणे क्षणे क्षीणपुण्यायाः पुरः। हरिणि, हेषितमिव हयानामुत्तरतः। कस्येदमातपत्रमुच्चमत्र पादपान्तरेण प्रभावति विभाव्यते। कुरङ्गिके, केन सुगृहीतनाम्नो नाम गृहीतममृतमयमार्यस्य। देवि, दिष्ट्या वर्धसे देवस्य हर्षस्यागमनमहोत्सवेन।' इत्येतच्च श्रुत्वा सत्वरमुपससर्प। ददर्श च मुह्यन्तीमग्निप्रवेशायोद्यतां राजा राज्यश्रियम्। आललम्बे च मूर्च्छामीलितलोचनाया ललाटं हस्तेन तस्याः ससंभ्रमम्।

अथ तेन भ्रातुः प्रेयसः प्रकोष्ठबद्धानामोषधीनां रसविसरमिव प्रत्युज्जीवनक्षमं क्षरता वमतेव पारिहार्यमणीनामचिन्त्यं प्रभावममृतमिव नखचन्द्ररश्मिभिरुद्गिरता बध्नतेव चन्द्रोदयच्युतशिशिरशीकरं चन्द्रकान्तचूडामणिं मूर्धनि मृणालमयाङ्गुलिनेवातिशीतलेन निर्वापयता दह्यमानं हृदयं प्रत्यानयतेव कुतोऽपि जीवितमाह्लादकेन हस्तसंस्पर्शेन सहसैव समुन्मिमील राज्यश्रीः। तथा चासम्भावितागमनस्याचिन्तितदर्शनस्य सहसा प्राप्तस्य भ्रातुः स्वप्नदृष्टदर्शनस्येव कण्ठे समाश्लिष्य तत्कालाविर्भावनिर्भरेणाभिभूतसर्वात्मना दुःखसम्भारेण निर्दयं नदीमुखप्रणालाभ्यामिव मुक्ताभ्यां स्थूलप्रवाहमुत्सृजन्ती

---

१ 'प्लक्षवृक्षे' ब.

बाष्पवारि विलोचनाभ्याम् 'हा तात, हा अम्ब, हा सख्यः' इति व्याहरन्ती मुहुर्मुहुरुच्चैस्तरां च, समुद्भूतभगिनीस्नेहसद्भावभारभावितमन्युना मुक्तकण्ठमतिचिरं विक्रुश्य 'वत्से, स्थिरा भव त्वम्' इति भ्रात्रा करस्थगितमुखी समाश्वास्यमानापि, 'कल्याणिनि, कुरु वचनमग्रजस्य गुरोः' इत्याचार्येण याच्यमानापि, 'देवि, न पश्यसि देवस्यावस्थाम् । अलमतिरुदितेन' इति राजलोकेनाभ्यर्थ्यमानापि, 'स्वामिनि, भ्रातरमवेक्षस्व' इति परिजनेन विज्ञाप्यमानापि, 'दुहितः, विश्रम्य पुनरारटितव्यम्' इति निवार्यमाणापि बान्धववृद्धाभिः, 'प्रियसखि, कियद्रोदिषि । तूष्णीमास्स्व । दृढं दूयते देवः' इति सखीभिरनुनीयमानापि, चिरसम्भावितानेकदुःखनिवहनिर्वहणबाष्पोत्पीडपीड्यमानकण्ठभागा, प्रभूतमन्युभारभरितान्तःकरणा करुणं [1]काहलेन स्वरेण कालमतिदीर्घं रुरोद । विगते च मन्युवेगे वह्नेः समीपादाक्षिप्य भ्रात्रा नीता निकटवर्तिनि तरुतले निषसाद ।

शनैराचार्यस्तु तथा हर्ष इति विज्ञाय विवर्धितादरः सुतरां मुहूर्तमिवातिवाह्य निभृतसंज्ञाज्ञापितेन शिष्येणोपनीतं नलिनीदलैः स्वयमादाय नम्रो मुखप्रक्षालनायोदकमुपनिन्ये । नरेन्द्रोऽपि सादरं गृहीत्वा प्रथममनवरतरोदनाताम्रं चिरप्रवृत्ताश्रुजलजालं रक्तपङ्कजमिव स्वसुश्चक्षुरक्षालयत्पश्चादात्मनः । प्रक्षालितमुखशशिनि च महीपाले सर्वतो निःशब्दः सम्बभूव सकलो लिखित इव लोकः । ततो नरेन्द्रो मन्दमन्दमब्रवीत्स्वसारम्—'वत्से, वन्दस्वात्रभवन्तं भदन्तम् । एष ते भर्तुर्हृदयं द्वितीयमस्माकं च गुरुः' इति । राजवचनात्तु राजदुहितरि पतिपरिचयश्रवणोद्धातेन पुनरानीतनेत्राम्भसि नमन्त्यामाचार्यः प्रयत्नरक्षितागतबाष्पाम्भःसम्भारभज्यमानधैर्यार्द्रलोचनः किंचित्परावृत्तनयनो दीर्घं निशश्वास । स्थित्वा च क्षणमेकं प्रदर्शितप्रश्रयो मृदुवादी मधुरया वाचा व्याजहार—'कल्याणराशे, अलं रुदित्वातिचिरम् । राजलोको नाद्यापि रोदनान्निवर्तते । क्रियतामवश्यकरणीयः स्नानविधिः । स्नात्वा च गम्यतां तामेव भूयो भुवम्' इति ।

अथ भूपतिरनुवर्तमानो लौकिकमाचारमाचार्यवचनं चोत्थाय स्नात्वा गिरिसरिति सह स्वस्रा तामेव भूमिमयासीत् । तस्यां च सपरिजनां प्रथममाहितावधानः पार्श्ववर्ती परवर्ती शुचा पतिपिण्डप्रदर्शितप्रयत्नप्रतिपन्नाभ्यव[2]हारकरणां भगिनीमभोजयत् । अनन्तरं च स्वयमाहारस्थितिमकरोत् । भुक्तवांश्च बन्धनात्प्रभृति विस्तरतः स्वसुः कान्यकुब्जाद्गौडसंभ्रमं गुप्तितो गुप्तनाम्ना कुलपुत्रेण निष्कासनं निर्गतायाश्च राज्यवर्धनमरणश्रवणं श्रुत्वा चाहारनिराकरणमनाहारपराहतायाश्च विन्ध्याटवीपर्यटनखेदं जातनिर्वेदायाः पावकप्रवेशोपक्रमणं यावत्सर्वमश्रृणोद्व्यतिकरं परिजनतः । ततः सुखासीनमेकत्र तरुतले विविक्तभुवि भगिनीद्वितीयं दूरस्थितानुजीविजनं राजान-

१ 'करुणकाहलेन' अ-क. २ '०हारकारणाम्' ब.

माचार्यः समुपसृत्य शनैरासांचक्रे। स्थित्वा च कंचित्कालांशं लेशतो वक्तुमुपचक्रमे—'श्रीमन्, आकर्ण्यताम्। आख्येयमस्ति नः किंचित्—

अयं हि यौवनोन्मादात्परिभूय भूयसीर्भार्या यौवनावतारतरलतरास्ताराराजो रजनीकर्णपूरः पुरुहूतपुरोधसो धिषणस्य पुरंध्रीं धर्मपत्नीं पत्नीयन्नतितरलस्तारां नामापजहार। नाकतश्च पलायांचक्रे। चकितचकोरलोचनया तया सहातिकामया सर्वाकाराभिरामया रममाणो रमणीयेषु देशेषु चचार। चिराच्च कथंचित्सर्वगीर्वाणवाणीगौरवाद्गिरां पत्युः पुनरपि प्रत्यर्पयामास ताम्। हृदये त्वनिन्धनमदह्यत विरहाद्वरारोहायास्तस्याः सततम्।

एकदा तु शैलादुदयादुदयमानो विमले वारिणि वारुणालयस्य संक्रान्तमात्मनः प्रतिबिम्बं विलोकितवान्। दृष्ट्वा च तदा सस्मार स्मरः स्मेरगण्डस्थलस्य ताराया मुखस्य। मुमोच च मन्मथोन्मादमथ्यमानमानसः स्वःस्थोऽप्यस्वस्थः स्थवीयसः पीतसकलकुमुदवनप्रभाप्रवाहधवलताराभ्यामिव लोचनाभ्यां बाष्पवारिबिन्दून्। अथ पततस्तानुदन्वति समस्तानेवाचेमुर्मुक्ताशुक्तयः। तासां च कुक्षिकोषेषु मुक्ताफलीभूतानवाप तान्कथमपि रसातलनिवासी वासुकिर्नाम विषमुचामीशः। स च तैर्मुक्ताफलैः पातालतलेऽपि तारागणमिव दर्शयद्भिरेकावलीमकल्पयत्। चकार च मन्दाकिनीति नाम तस्याः। सा च भगवतः सोमस्य सर्वासामोषधीनामधिपतेः प्रभावादत्यन्तविषघ्नी हिमामृतसम्भवत्वाच्च स्पर्शेन सर्वसत्त्वसन्तापहारिणी बभूव। यतः स तां सर्वदा विषोष्मशान्तये वासुकिः पर्यधत्त।

समतिक्रामति च कियत्यपि काले कदाचित्तामेकावलीं तस्मान्नागराजान्नागार्जुनो नाम नागैरेवानीतः पातालतलं भिक्षुरभिक्षत लेभे च। निर्गत्य रसातलात्त्रिसमुद्राधिपतये सातवाहननाम्ने नरेन्द्राय सुहृदे स ददौ ताम्। सा चास्माकं कालेन शिष्यपरम्परया कथमपि हस्तमुपगता। यद्यपि च परिभव इव भवति भवादृशां दत्त्रिम उपचारस्तथाप्योषधिबुद्ध्या बुद्धिमता सर्वसत्त्वराशिरक्षाप्रवृत्तेन रक्षणीयशरीरेणायुष्मता विषरक्षापेक्षया गृह्यताम्। इत्यभिधाय भिक्षोरभ्याशवर्तिनश्चीवरपटान्तसंयतां मुमोच तामेकावलीं मन्दाकिनीम्।

उन्मुच्यमानाया एव यस्याः प्रभालेपिनि लब्धावकाशे विशदमहसि[1] महीयसि विसर्पति रश्मिमण्डले युगपद्धवलायमानेषु दिङ्मुखेषु मुकुलितलतावधूत्कण्ठितैरामूलाद्विकसितमिव तरुभिः, अभिनवमृणाललुब्धैर्धावितमिव धुतपक्षपुटपटलधवलितगगनं वनसरसीहंसयूथैः, स्फुटितमिव भरवशविशीर्यमाणधूलिधवलैर्गर्भभेदसूचितसूचीसञ्चयशुचिभिः केतकीवाटैः, उद्दलितदलदन्तुराभिः[2] प्रबुद्धमिव कुमुदिनीभिः, विधुतसितसटाभारभरितदिक्चक्रैश्च-

१ 'विषद' अ-क. २ 'उद्दलित-' ब.

लितमिव केसरिकुलैः, प्रहसितमिव सितदशनांशुमालालोकलिप्यमानवनं वनदेवताभिः, विकसितमिव शिथिलितकुसुमकोशकेसराट्टहासनिरङ्कुशं काशकाननैः, भ्रान्तमिव संभ्रमभ्रमितबालपल्लवपरिवेशश्वेतायमानैश्चमरीकदम्बकैः, प्रसृतमिव स्फायमानफेनिलतरलतरतरङ्गोद्गारिणा गिरिनदीपूरेण, अपरतारागणलाभमुदितेनोदितमिव विकचमरीचिचक्राक्रान्तककुभा पूर्णचन्द्रेण, प्रक्षालित इव दावानलधूलिधूसरितदिगन्तो दिवसः, पुनरिव धौतान्यश्रुजलक्लिष्टानि नारीणां मुखानि।

राजा तु मांसलैस्तस्याः संमुखैर्मयूखैराकुलीक्रियमाणं मुहुर्मुहुरुन्मीलयन्निमीलयंश्च चक्षुः कथमपि प्रयत्नेन ददर्श सर्वाशापूरणीं पङ्क्तीकृतामिव दिङ्नागकरशीकरसंहतिम्, घनमुक्तां शारदीमिव लेखीकृतां ज्योत्स्नाम्, प्रकटपदकचिह्नां सञ्चारणवीथीमिव बालेन्दोर्निश्चलीभूतां सप्तर्षिमालामिव हस्तमुक्ताम्, अभिभूतसकलभुवनभूषणभूतिप्रभावाम[2]ैशानीमिव शशिकलाम्, धवलतागुणपरिगृहीतां कान्तिमिव निर्गतां क्षीरराशेः, अनेकमहामहीभृत्परम्परागतां गङ्गामिव दुर्गतिहराम्, अनवरतस्फुरिततरलांशुकां पुरःसरपताकामिव महेश्वरभावागमस्य, घनसारशुक्लां दन्तपङ्क्तिमिवाभिमुखस्येश्वरस्य, वरमनोरथपूरणसमर्थां स्वयंवरस्रजमिव भुवनश्रियः, निजकरपल्लवावरणदुर्लक्ष्यां चक्षूरागविहसतिकामिव वसुधायाः, मन्त्रकोषसाधनप्रवृत्तस्याक्षमालामिव राजधर्मस्य, समुद्रालङ्कारभूतां संख्यालेख्यपट्टिकामिव कुबेरकोशस्य। पश्यंश्चैतां विस्मयमाजगाम मनसा सुचिरम्। आचार्यस्तु तामुद्धृत्य बबन्ध बन्धुरे स्कन्धभागे भूपतेः। अथ नरपतिरपि प्रीतिमुपदर्शयन्प्रत्यवादीत्—'आर्य, रत्नानामीदृशानामनर्हाः प्रायेण पुरुषाः। तपःसिद्धिरियमार्यस्य देवताप्रसादो वा। के च वयमिदानीमात्मनोऽपि किमुत ग्रहणस्य प्रत्याख्यानस्य वा। दर्शनात्प्रभृति प्रभूतगुरुगुणगणहृतेन हृदयेन परवन्तो वयम्। सङ्कल्पितमिदमा मरणादार्योपयोगाय शरीरम्। अत्र कामचारो वः कर्तव्यानाम्' इति।

समतिक्रान्ते च कियत्यपि काले गते चैकावलीवर्णनालापे लोकस्यानन्तरं लब्धविश्रम्भा राज्यश्रीस्ताम्बूलवाहिनीं पत्रलतामाहूयोपांशु किमपि कर्णमूले शनैरादिदेश। दर्शितविनया च पत्रलता पार्थिवं व्यज्ञापयत्—देव, देवी विज्ञापयति न स्मराम्यार्यस्य पुरः कदाचिदुच्चैर्वचनमपि। कुतो विज्ञापनम्। इयं हि शुचामसह्यता[3] व्यापारयन्ती हतदैव[4]दत्तादेशा शिथिलयति विनयम्। अबलानां हि पतिरपत्यं वावलम्बनम्। उभयविकलानां तु दुःखानलेन्धनायमानं प्राणितमशालीनत्वमेव केवलम्। आर्यागमनेन च

---

१ 'लोभ' ब. २ 'प्रभावामिवैशानीम्' ब. ३ 'असह्यतां...हतदैवदत्ता च दशा' ब. ४ 'देव०' अ.

कृतोऽपि प्रतिहतो मरणप्रयत्नः । अतः काषायग्रहणाभ्यनुज्ञयानुगृह्यतामयमपुण्यभाजनं जनः' इति । जनाधिपस्तु तदाकर्ण्य तूष्णीमेवावातिष्ठत ।

अथाचार्यः सुधीरमभ्यधात्—'आयुष्मति, शोको हि नाम पर्यायः पिशाचस्य रूपान्तरमाक्षेपस्य तारुण्यं तमसो विशेषणं विषस्यानन्तकः प्रेतनगरनायकः । अयमनिर्वृतिधर्मा दहनः । अयमक्षयो राजयक्ष्मा । अयमलक्ष्मीनिवासो जनार्दनः । अयमपुण्यप्रवृत्तः क्षपणकः । अयमप्रतिबोधो निद्राप्रकारः । अयमनलसधर्मा सन्निपातः । अयमशिवसहचरो विनायकः । अयमबुधसेवितो ग्रहवर्गः । अयमयोगसमुत्थो ज्योतिःप्रकारः । अयं स्नेहाद्वायुप्रकोपः, मानसादग्निसम्भवः, आर्द्रभावाद्रजःक्षोभः, रसादभि[1]शोषः, रागात्कालपरिणामः । तदस्याजस्रस्राविणो हृदयमहाव्रणस्य बहुलदोषान्धकारलब्धप्रवेशप्रसरस्य प्राणतस्करस्य शून्यताहेतोर्महाभूतग्रामघातकस्य सकलविग्रहक्षपणदक्षस्य दोषचक्रवर्तिनः कार्श्यश्वासप्रलापोपद्रवबहलस्य दीर्घरोगस्यासह्यस्य सकललोकक्षयधूमकेतोर्जीवितापहारदक्षस्याक्षणरुचेरनभ्रवज्रपातस्य स्फुरदनवद्यविद्याविद्युदुद्द्योतमानानि गहनग्रन्थग्रन्थिगूढगर्भग्रहणगम्भीराणि भूरिकाव्यकथाकठोराणि बहुशास्त्रोद्वहनबृहन्ति विदुषामपि हृदयानि नालं सोढुमापातं किमुत नवनवमालिकाकुसुमकोमलानां सरसबिसतन्तुदुर्बलकमबलानां हृदयम् ।

एवं सति सत्यव्रते, वद किमत्र क्रियते, कतम उपालभ्यते, कस्य पुर उच्चैराक्रन्द्यते, हृदयदाहि दुःखं वा ख्याप्यते । सर्वमक्षिणी निमील्य सोढव्यममूढेन मर्त्यधर्मणा । पुण्यवति, पुरातन्यः स्थितय एताः केन शक्यन्तेऽन्यथाकर्तुम् । संसरन्त्यो नक्तंदिवं द्राघीयस्यो जन्मजरामरणघटनघटीयन्त्रराजिरजवः पञ्चजनानाम् । पञ्चमहाभूतपञ्चकुलाधिष्ठितान्तःकरणव्यवहारदर्शननिपुणाः सर्वंकषा विषमा धर्मराजस्थितयः । क्षणमपि क्षममाणा गलन्त्यायुष्कलाकलनकुशला निलये निलये कालनालिकाः । जगति सर्वजन्तुजीवितोपहारपातिनी सञ्चरति झटिति चण्डिका यमाज्ञा । रटन्त्यनवरतमखिलप्राणिप्रयाणप्रकटनपटवः प्रेतपतिपटहाः । प्रतिदिशं पर्यटन्ति पेटकैः प्रतिपुरं प्रतप्तलोहलोहिताक्षाः कालकूटकान्तिकालकायाः कालपाशपाणयः कालपुरुषाः । प्रतिभवनं भ्रमन्ति भीषणकिङ्करकरघट्टितयमघण्टापुटपटुटांकारभयङ्कराः सर्वसत्त्वसङ्घसंहरणाय घोराघातघोषणाः । दिशि दिशि वहन्ति बहुचिताधूमधूसरितप्रेतपतिपताकापटुपतितगृध्रदृष्टयः शोककृतकोलाहलाकुलकुटुम्बिनीविकीर्णकेशकलापशबलशवशिबिकासहस्रसङ्कुलाः किलकिलायमानश्मशानशिबिरशिवाशावकाः परलोकावसथपथिकसार्थप्रस्थानविशिखावीथयः । सकललोककवलावलेहलम्पटा बहला वहंलिहा लेढि लोहिताचिता चिताङ्गारकाली कालरात्रीजिह्वा जीवितानि जीविनाम् । तृप्तिमशिक्षिता च

---

१ 'अतिशोषः' ब.

NOTES

Uchchhvāsa I

हर्षस्य चरितमधिकृत्य कृतो ग्रन्थः हर्षचरितम्. The affixes अण् (अ) and छ (ईय) are added to words to denote works, according to the Sûtra 'अधिकृत्य कृते ग्रन्थे' पा. IV. 3. 87. But, according to the Vārtika 'लुबाख्यायिकाभ्यो बहुलम्', these affixes are generally omitted in the case of works called आख्यायिकाs. The हर्षचरित is an आख्यायिका, for a definition of which see Intro. p. XX. उच्छ्वासः means 'a chapter of a book.' It is a division peculiarly associated with works of the आख्यायिका class. Note verse 10 below.

In some Mss. the first verse is इच्छादि०, which contains a salutation to सरस्वती. इच्छादि...प्रभावा the power of which, in presenting the whole (world) by the successive working (प्रसरः) of the several faculties beginning with volition, is well-known. निचयः collection. Ideas are conveyed by words over which सरस्वती presides. Words are made up of letters (sounds) the production of which is explained by the following from the शिक्षा 'आत्मा बुद्ध्या समेत्यार्थान् मनो युङ्क्ते विवक्षया। मनः कायाग्निमाहन्ति स प्रेरयति मारुतम्। मारुतस्तूरसि चरन् मन्द्रं जनयति स्वरम्।... सोदीर्णो मूर्ध्न्यभिहतो वक्त्रमापद्य मारुतः। वर्णाञ्जनयते &c.' It will be noticed that according to this quotation it is the *desire* to speak (विवक्षा = वक्तुमिच्छा) that is the first step in the evolution of वर्णs. Separate या (सरस्वती) आध्यायिनाम् (of those who reflect). आध्यायिनां may be connected with हृदय in the compound हृदय० or with रूप. The poet perhaps intends both. हृदयमेव कोकनदं तस्मिन् प्रतिष्ठा यस्याः which is installed in the lotus of the heart (of reflecting men). The heart is fitly compared to कोकनद which is a red lotus. 'रक्तोत्पलं कोकनदम्' इत्यमरः. In the Upanishads the heart is often spoken of as a lotus in which the supreme soul dwells. 'अथ यदिदमस्मिन् ब्रह्मपुरे दहरं पुण्डरीकं वेश्म दहरोऽस्मिन्नन्तराकाशस्तस्मिन्यदन्तस्तदन्वेष्टव्यम्' छान्दोग्य 8.1.1. सरस्वती is but a शक्ति of the Supreme Soul. रूपं प्रकाशयति—It is speech that manifests (conveys) objects (रूपं) to the mind. The meaning may also be 'that manifests her real nature (to those who are contemplative).' वाक् is said to be fourfold, परा, पश्यन्ती, मध्यमा and वैखरी. This is a description of परा वाक्. The metre is वसन्ततिलका. We may also read या ध्यायिनां or separate as या अध्यायिनां (from इ with अधि).

Verse 1. Connect नमः with शम्भवे. It is usual for Sanskrit authors to begin their works with an invocation to some deity. तुङ्गं शिरः चुम्बते इति ०चुम्बी चन्द्रः एव चामरं तेन चारुः तस्मै. The head of शिव never bows down to any one else; hence it is तुङ्ग. Both the moon and चामर are white. त्रैलोक्यमेव नगरं तस्य आरम्भे मूलस्तम्भः तस्मै—who is the first pillar in constructing the city in the form of the three worlds. The author looks upon शिव as the supreme deity, the cause of the creation, maintenance and absorption of the Universe. It is well-known that in constructing a house the first pillar (whether of wood or stone) is erected on an auspicious day and with great ceremony. चामरs may be tied on to it for the sake of beauty and auspiciousness. 'नगरारम्भे हि मूलस्तम्भो भवति। तत्र च पट्टबन्धादिवदुत्क्षेपणानन्तरमुन्नते पृष्ठदेशे चन्द्रतुल्यं श्वेतं चामरं क्रियते इति स्थितिः' सं. शङ्कर notes that other commentators construe the word शम्भु as referring also to विष्णु and ब्रह्मा. " 'स्वयम्भूः शम्भुरादित्यः' इति नामसहस्रे दृष्टत्वाद्धरेः, 'शम्भू ब्रह्मत्रिलोचनौ' इत्यभिधाकोशदर्शनाच्च ब्रह्मणोऽपि नमस्कारोऽयमित्यन्ये वदन्ति। व्याकुर्वते च हरिपक्षे त्रैलोक्याक्रमणकाले यद्वा 'यस्याग्निरास्यं द्यौर्मूर्धा खं नाभिश्चरणौ मही' इत्यभिप्रायेण तुङ्गमुच्छ्रितं शुलक्षणं यच्छिरस्तच्चुम्बि चन्द्र एव चामरं तेन चारवे। ब्रह्मपक्षे चन्द्रः स्वर्णं तन्मयं चामरमिव चामरं केशकलापः। हिरण्यकेशो हि ब्रह्मा त्रैलोक्यादीनि सर्वत्र तुल्यमिति." From this verse and from indications in the 2nd उच्छ्वास (देवदेवस्य विरूपाक्षस्य...विधाय पूजां परमया भक्त्या) we can say that Bāṇa was specially devoted to शिव. C and T note that this verse occurs entire in an inscription (vide Indian Antiquary vol. XIII. p. 92) of the western चालुक्य king त्रिभुवनमल्ल II dated S'ake 1006.

Verse 2. हरस्य कण्ठः तस्य ग्रहः तेन आनन्दः तेन मीलिते (closed) अक्षिणी यस्याः—Whose eyes were closed by the joy of clasping the neck of S'iva. कालकूटविषस्य स्पर्शेन जातः मूर्च्छायाः आगमः (advent, beginning) यस्याः. When the gods and demons churned the ocean for jewels, the first thing that came out was the poison हालाहल. शिव drank it to save the universe from destruction. The poison showed its strength by making S'iva's throat dark. See रामायण I. 45 (निर्णयसागर ed.) and भागवतपुराण VIII. Compare 'अमृतमथनसमयमिव तीरावस्थितशितिकण्ठपीयमानविषम्' कादम्बरी (p. 123 of P). Umā (पार्वती) clasped the neck of S'iva and closed her eyes in the ecstasy of love. The poet fancies that the closing of the eyes was due to the fainting fit caused by touching the poison in the throat of शिव. It is well-known that poison causes fainting. For the derivation of उमा see कुमार० I. 26. 'उ मेति मात्रा तपसो निषिद्धा पश्चादुमाख्यां सुमुखी जगाम.'

Verse 3. The poet in this verse after invoking deities salutes Vyāsa the author of the महाभारत and thereby shows his great reverence for him. सर्वं वेत्तीति सर्वविद् तस्मै. कविवेधसे—who is Brahmā among poets. Brahmā is called सुरज्येष्ठ; so व्यास is the best of poets. The word may also mean 'who is the creator of (the effusions of) poets.' The idea is that later poets derive their inspiration from his work. The महाभारत itself gives expression to this idea. 'इतिहासोत्तमादस्माज्जायन्ते कविबुद्धयः' आदिपर्व 2. 385; 'इदं कविवरैः सर्वैराख्यानमुपजीव्यते' आदि० 2. 389; 'यदिहास्ति तदन्यत्र यन्नेहास्ति न तत्क्वचित्'. यः सरस्वत्याः वर्षमिव पुण्यं भारतं चक्रे who composed the sacred (work called) Bhārata which is as it were a shower of speech. The भारत contains the choicest speech in abundance. The poet conveys another idea. यः सरस्वत्या (वाचा) भारतं पुण्यं चक्रे सरस्वत्या (नद्या) भारतं वर्षमिव. Vyāsa by his holy words sanctified भारतवर्ष (India) as the sacred river सरस्वती sanctifies भारतवर्ष. According to ancient ideas of Geography, the earth was divided into seven द्वीपs (जम्बु, प्लक्ष, शाल्मल, कुश, क्रौञ्च, शाक and पुष्कर). Each of these द्वीपs was subdivided into 9 वर्षs, had its own mountains and was surrounded by a sea. जम्बुद्वीप had 9 वर्षs (कुरु, हिरण्मय, रम्यक, इलावृत, हरि, केतुमाल, भद्राश्व, किन्नर and भारत). Vide विष्णुपुराण II. 1-3 and मार्कण्डेय chap. 54 ff. भारतवर्ष is defined as 'उत्तरं यत्समुद्रस्य हिमाद्रेश्चैव दक्षिणम् । वर्षं तद्भारतं नाम भारती यत्र सन्ततिः ॥'. सरस्वती was a sacred river in the Panjab now lost in the sands of the great desert of India. We may also interpret 'who sanctified the line descended from भरत by his speech.' The महाभारत narrates the story of the Kauravas and Pāṇḍavas who were descendants of भरत, son of दुष्यन्त and शकुन्तला. Vide आदिपर्व chap. 74. 'भरताद्भारती कीर्तिर्येनेदं भारतं कुलम् ॥' verse 131. The word कविवेधसे may also mean 'who is a creator in the form of a poet.' A poet is often spoken of as a creator (of high thoughts and aspirations). Compare the first verse of काव्यप्रकाश and 'अपारे काव्यसंसारे **कविरेव प्रजापतिः** । यथास्मै रोचते विश्वं तथेदं परिवर्तते' ॥ ध्वन्यालोक III. p. 222 and also अग्निपुराण chap. 339. 10.

Verse 4. कुकवयः bad poets, poetasters. रागेण अधिष्ठिता दृष्टिः येषाम्—whose vision (intellect) is dominated by (evil) passions (with कुकवयः); whose eye is dominated by redness (with कोकिलाः). Poetasters are not inspired by noble ideals and thoughts; but their effusions are due to the envy of good poets and such other evil tendencies. The three words रागा०,

वाचालाः and °कारिणः apply equally to bad poets and cuckoos and so the author compares bad poets with cuckoos. वाचालाः loquacious (with poets); making a noise (with cuckoos). कामकारिणः doing just as they please; that excite passion (with कोकिलाः). Poetasters compose poems throwing to the winds all canons of good taste and sound criticism. The notes of the cuckoo are an excitant of love. According to the terminology of Sanskrit rhetoricians रति is the स्थायिभाव of शृङ्गाररस; the नायक and नायिका are the आलम्बनविभाव; वसन्त, the moon, the notes of the cuckoo are the उद्दीपनविभाव; external indications such as स्वेद are the अनुभावs and चिन्ता, जडता &c. are व्यभिचारिभावs. Bāṇa in this verse finds fault with poetasters and says that the voice of a true poet is very rarely heard amidst the din of poetasters. The com. suggests another meaning; 'such is the natural charm of poetry; even bad poets give pleasure; how much more will those who are specially gifted ?' But this is rather strained and not in keeping with the next verse. सं० gives another sense of कुकवयः 'कुकन्ति गृह्णन्ति चेतांसि इति कुकाः ते च वयो मयूरप्रवराः पक्षिणः'.

Verse 5. This verse is full of puns. The plain meaning is 'Innumerable are the poets to be found in each house that can write only plain and matter of fact descriptions, like dogs (that are also numberless). Poets that possess creative genius are not many, like शरभs'. जाति is another name for स्वभावोक्ति. It consists in describing objects (particularly the doings of children, lower animals &c.) as they are in their various positions. 'नानावस्थं पदार्थानां रूपं साक्षाद्विवृण्वती । स्वभावोक्तिश्च जातिश्चेत्याद्या सालङ्कृतिर्यथा ॥' काव्यादर्श II. 8. See also भोज's सरस्वतीकण्ठाभरण III and रुद्रट's काव्यालंकार 7. 30–31. जाति (or स्वभावोक्ति) is opposed to वक्रोक्ति, which latter was often looked upon as the soul of poetry and as something which a poet should strive for. Note 'सैषा सर्वत्र वक्रोक्तिरनयार्थो विभाव्यते । यत्नोऽस्यां कविना कार्यः कोऽलङ्कारोऽनया विना ॥' भामह II. जातिभाजः also means 'possessed of the common characteristic' (श्वत्व or कवित्व). The idea is:—the most wretched cur and the best hound are both dogs *i. e.* they possess the जाति (species) श्वत्व in common; but there is great disparity in their worth; so poetasters (कुकवयः) possess the जाति कवित्व in common with poets of genius. असंख्याः also means 'of no account, useless (with poets); that do not fight' (with dogs). 'मृधमास्कन्दनं संख्यं समीकं सांपरायिकम्' इत्यमरः. उत्पादकाः उद्गताः पादकाः (पादाः)

येषां that have feet upwards (growing on their backs). शरभाः—शरभ is a fabulous animal with eight legs and stronger than a lion. See वनपर्व chap. 119 for the story of a dog that was successively turned into a leopard, a tiger, an elephant, a lion and lastly into a शरभ 'अष्टपादूर्ध्वनयनः शरभो वनगोचरः। स सिंहं हन्तुमागच्छन्मुनेस्तस्य निवेशनम् ॥' verse 13.

Verse 6. In this verse Bāṇa speaks of so-called poets that are merely plagiarists. अन्य—वृत्त्या by (merely) changing the words of other (poets). बन्ध...गूहनैः by concealing the distinctive marks of their compositions. अना...भाव्यते a poet without being (expressly) declared (to be so) is revealed to be a thief (a plagiarist) in the midst of the good. The idea is:—the composition of a plagiarist is seen in its true light by the good, though there is no express declaration that it is merely a patchwork. The words अना...मध्ये may also mean 'who is not esteemed among the good.' This meaning also suits the word चौरः. We can also separate as अ-ना आख्यातः 'he (the plagiarist or the thief) is not counted a man'. ना is the nom. sing. of नृ. बन्ध...गूहनैः—the idea (according to the com.) is:—great poets compose works containing particular words like श्री, लक्ष्मी in particular verses or in some particular order. The plagiarist in copying suppresses such indications. बन्धः also means the arrangements of the letters of a stanza in a particular way, such as खड्गबन्ध, शृङ्खलाबन्ध, सर्वतोभद्र. Or बन्धचिह्न may be used in a general sense *viz.* 'the characteristic style of a good composition.' 'बन्धः पदरचना' वामन's काव्यालंकारसूत्रवृत्ति 3. 1. 4. A thief also changes colour *i. e.* his face becomes pale (when challenged in the midst of the good). He also tries to conceal the marks left (in his flesh) by the chains (with which he was bound when caught). Although a thief conceals these marks and so is not declared to be a thief (अनाख्यात), yet by the pallor that comes over his face when challenged he is revealed in his true light.

Verse 7. The author in this verse points out that the poets of particular countries exhibit only a few poetic excellences in their works and not all. श्लेष...च्येषु Among the northern (poets), a work most exhibits puns. श्लेष is of two kinds, शब्दश्लेष and अर्थश्लेष. In the first a particular word when used gives rise to different senses; but if that word be omitted and a synonym substituted, then the double meaning vanishes *e. g.* बालेवोद्यानमालेयं **सालकाननशोभिनी.** Here take the word साल० as meaning सालकं (अलकैः सह) आननं तेन शोभिनी (with बाला) and सालानां काननं तेन शोभिनी (with उद्यानमाला). If for सालक we substitute सकुन्तल then the श्लेष vanishes. In अर्थश्लेष, even if we change the words, there are two meanings; *e. g.* 'उदयमयते दिङ्मालिन्यं निराकुरुतेतरां नयति निधनं निद्रामुद्रां प्रवर्तयति क्रियाः । रचयतितरां स्वैराचारप्रवर्तनकर्तनं बत बत लसत्तेजःपुञ्जो विभाति विभाकरः ॥' काव्यप्रकाश X. (Here a king called विभाकर and the Sun are both praised). अर्थमात्रकम्—The poets of the west care only for the meaning (they do not exhibit charm of style or figures of speech). उत्प्रेक्षा is a figure of speech. To explain it briefly, it consists in representing (poetically, not through mistake) one thing as another thing or in representing a particular effect as due to some cause other than the real one or representing something done with one motive as due to another. It is generally introduced by such words as मन्ये, शङ्के, ध्रुवं or इव (as it were). Bāṇa's works bristle at every step with this figure. The verse 'हरकण्ठ' is a good example of उत्प्रेक्षा. गौडे...डम्बरः among Gauḍa poets there is only show of words (high-flown language). Their works do not contain charming thoughts or such qualities as perspicuity &c. Daṇḍin, who was at least a contemporary of Bāṇa, if he was not earlier still, speaks of two literary styles. (रीति), *viz.*, वैदर्भी and गौडी. He says that ten Guṇas (such as प्रसाद, माधुर्य and ओजः) are the essence of the Vaidarbhî style, while the Gauḍî style is the reverse of the Vaidarbhî (काव्यादर्श I. 41–42). He tells us that the Gauḍas were very fond of अनुप्रास (काव्यादर्श I. 54) and that even in verse they employed long compounds (काव्यादर्श I. 80). वामन says in his काव्यालङ्कारसूत्रवृत्ति (I. 2. 12.) 'समस्तात्युद्भटपदामोजःकान्तिगुणान्विताम् । गौडीयामपि गायन्ति रीतिं रीतिविचक्षणाः ॥'. गौड is the district of Gaur, central part of Bengal; formerly it extended from वङ्ग to the borders of Orissa.

Verse 8. नवोर्थः—a new topic (*i. e.* a subject not dealt with by former writers) or a striking subject or meaning. This refers to the imaginative side of a poet's mind, called प्रतिभा by Sanskrit rhetoricians. 'प्रज्ञा नवनवोन्मेषशालिनी **प्रतिभा** मता'. जातिरग्राम्या description of nature or objects that is not vulgar. For जाति, see above p. 4. दण्डी gives the following as examples of ग्राम्य and अग्राम्य ways of description respectively, although the meaning is the same. 'कन्ये कामयमानं मां न त्वं कामयसे कथम्। इति ग्राम्योऽयमर्थात्मा वैरस्याय प्रकल्पते ॥ कामं कन्दर्पचाण्डालो मयि वामाक्षि निर्दयः । त्वयि निर्मत्सरो दिष्ट्येत्यग्राम्योऽर्थो रसावहः ॥' (काव्या० I. 63-64). जाति also means a particular class of metres regulated by Mātrās, such as आर्या. Compare 'पद्यं चतुष्पदी तच्च वृत्तं जातिरिति द्विधा' काव्या० I. 11. जाति also means 'a composition or verse in which the same words represent Sanskrit or Prakrit.' Both these meanings are not suitable here. श्लेषः—for explanation, see the preceding verse. अक्लिष्टः not laboured. 'व्यवहितार्थप्रत्ययं क्लिष्टम्' काव्यालङ्कारसूत्र II. 1. 21. स्फुटो रसः A sentiment (which is the subject matter of a poem) that is easily understood. रस is the soul of Kāvya. It is that sentiment which rules a composition and which is the object of the poem to present to the mind of the reader. Rasas are eight शृङ्गार, वीर, करुण, हास्य, रौद्र, भयानक, बीभत्स, अद्भुत. Some add a ninth रस *viz.* शान्त. विक...बन्धः—The Com. says 'उदारतालक्षणबन्धगुणयुक्तः यत्र सति नृत्यन्तीव पदानि प्रतिभासन्ते.' In this he follows वामन's काव्यालङ्कारसूत्र III. 1. 22 'विकटत्वमुदारता'—वृत्ति "बन्धस्य विकटत्वं यदसौ उदारता । यस्मिन्सति नृत्यन्तीव पदानीति जनस्य वर्णभावना भवति तत् विकटत्वं लीलायमानत्वमित्यर्थः । यथा 'स्वचरणविनिविष्टैर्नूपुरैर्नर्तकीनां झणिति रणितमासीत्तत्र चित्रं कलं च' । न पुनः 'चरणकमलकलग्नैर्नूपुरैर्नर्तकीनां झटिति रणितमासीन्मञ्जु चित्रं च तत्र.'" This means that in विकटत्व the sound must be an echo to the sense. C and T translate 'language rich in sonorous words.' The author in our opinion rather refers to ओजोगुण about which दण्डी says 'ओजः समासभूयस्त्वमेतद्गद्यस्य जीवितम् । पद्येऽप्यदाक्षिणात्यानामिदमेकं परायणम् ॥' काव्या. I. 80. कृत्स्न...ष्करम् all this it is difficult to find in one composition.

Verse 9. किं...काव्येन what is the use of the poetry of that poet? C and T translate 'what has that poet to do with poetry?' This does not yield a good sense. Construe यस्य सर्ववृत्तान्तगामिनी भारती जगत्त्रयं न व्याप्नोति सर्ववृत्तान्तगामिनी भारती कथेव (सा यथा जगत्त्रयं व्याप्नोति)—whose Muse comprehending the furthest limit of metrics does not cover the three worlds (*i. e.* does not become well-known in the world) like the Bhārata story. सर्वेषां वृत्तानां (metres) अन्तं गच्छति इति (with Muse); सर्वान् वृत्तान्तान् (इतिहासान्) गमयतीति that conveys all sorts of narratives (with भारती कथा). The Mahābhārata contains numerous episodes.

Verse 10. Here Bāṇa offers his meed of praise to the authors of आख्यायिकाs that preceded him. आख्यायिकाs were composed from very ancient times. Vide Introduction p. XIII.

For a definition of आख्यायिका given by भामह, see Introduction p. XX. The salient points are that it is in prose, has a high topic, is divided into sections called उच्छ्वासs, contains verses in the वक्त्र and अपरवक्त्र metres which suggest coming events. The साहित्यदर्पण (परिच्छेद VI) calls the sections आश्वासs. कथ...श्वराः how are those princes among poets, *viz.* the authors of आख्यायिकाs, not to be praised ? (*i. e.* they deserve the highest praise). उच्छ्वा...न्नाः unwearied even at the end of an उच्छ्वास *i. e.* who are able to compose another उच्छ्वास equal in merit to its predecessor. येषां...स्वती in whose verses (in the वक्त्र metre) the goddess of speech dwells. In the वक्त्र metre, there are eight syllables in each पाद as in अनुष्टुभ्. It is defined as 'नाद्यान्नसौ स्यातामब्धेर्योऽनुष्टुभि ख्यातम्'. After the first letter in each पाद there should be no नगण nor सगण and after the first four letters there should be a यगण. उच्छ्वा...खिन्नाः—conveys another idea. A man who is tired heaves out a deep breath. There is an apparent विरोध in saying that they are not exhausted even when they are breathing hard. कवीश्वराः may also mean 'the omniscient gods' *i. e.* the creator (the plural being used for श्लेष or to show respect). The supreme spirit is often called कवि in the Upanishads and the Gîtā. 'कविं पुराणमनुशासितारं' &c. गीता 8. 9; 'कविर्मनीषी परिभूः स्वयम्भूः' ईशावास्योपनिषद् 8. उच्छ्वा...खिन्नाः would mean 'not exhausted or afflicted even at the end of the Universe.' In the Upanishads the Universe containing the Vedas, the Heavens, the earth &c. is said to be the निःश्वसित of the Supreme. 'अस्य महतो भूतस्य निःश्वसितमेतद्यदृग्वेदो... अस्यैवैतानि निःश्वसितानि' बृहदारण्यकोपनिषद् II. 4. 10. वक्त्रे...सरस्वती The goddess of speech is often poetically described as dwelling in the mouth of Brahmā. Compare 'चतुर्मुखमुखाम्भोजवनहंसवधूर्मम । मानसे रमतां नित्यं सर्वशुक्ला सरस्वती ॥' काव्यादर्श I. 1.

Verse 11. Construe कर्णगोचरं गतया वासवदत्तया नूनं कवीनां दर्पः अगलत् कर्णगोचरं गतया पाण्डुपुत्राणां शक्त्या इव कवीनां (दर्पः अगलत्). The pride of poets indeed melted away on account of वासवदत्ता when it reached their ears, just as the pride of Droṇa vanished when the missile of the sons of Pāṇḍu given by Vāsava (Indra) came near Karṇa. वासवदत्ता—This seems to be the work of Subandhu. It is a कथा technically so called. Vide Introduction p. XX. It cannot be the आख्यायिका वासवदत्ता mentioned by Patañjali (Introduction p. XIII). The authors of आख्यायिकाs came in for high praise in the preceding verse. We naturally expect that in this verse the author should refer to another class of works. In this Introduction Bāṇa assigns only one verse to each of the poets or works mentioned below. There is no reason why he should depart from that rule in the case of आख्यायिका. A कथा is very much like an आख्यायिका and so it is but proper that the वासवदत्ता of सुबन्धु (being a कथा) should receive encomiums after the authors of आख्यायिकाs, if सुबन्धु preceded Bāṇa, as we hold. कवि also means द्रोण. The plural कवीनां may be explained as due to the exigencies of श्लेष or as expressing respect. द्रोण was the son of भरद्वाज 'भरद्वाजस्य च स्कन्नं द्रोण्यां शुक्रमवर्धत । महर्षेरुग्रतपसस्तस्माद् द्रोणो व्यजायत ॥' आदिपर्व 63. 6. कवि is a name for शुक्र and so indicates द्रोण. The story of कर्ण, the son of कुन्ती, is well-known. The reference seems to be to the defeat of कर्ण by भीम (vide द्रोणपर्व chap 129, 131, 133). We may also construe कवीनां पाण्डुपुत्राणां (दर्पः) कर्णगोचरं गतया वासवदत्तया शक्त्या इव (अगलत्) 'as the pride of the wise sons of Pâṇḍu melted away through the javelin that was given by इन्द्र and that came to the hands of Karṇa. Karṇa was a generous man. Once Indra who was interested in Arjuna came to Karṇa as a Brāhmaṇa and begged of him his divine armour and ear-rings. Karṇa true to his word gave Indra what he wanted. Indra being pleased with Karṇa gave him a शक्ति that would kill one महारथी whoever he might be. See आदिपर्व chap. 111. 'ददौ शक्तिं सुरपतिर्वाक्यं चेदमुवाच ह ॥ देवासुरमनुष्याणां गन्धर्वोरगरक्षसाम् । यमेकं जेतुमिच्छेथाः सोऽनया न भविष्यति ॥' verses 29–30.

Verse 12. भट्टार...यते the prose composition of the revered हरिचन्द्र acts like a king *i. e.* is pre-eminent like a king. भट्टारः or भट्टारकः is a term of respect applied to kings in dramas and inscriptions. 'राजा भट्टारको देवः' इत्यमरः. It was also applied by Jain writers to those who abandoned the worldly life. नृप इव आचरति नृपायते according to 'कर्तुः क्यङ् सलोपश्च' पा. 3. 1. 11. पद...ज्ज्वलः charming or brilliant on account of the arrangement of words (with गद्यबन्ध); splendid on account of the firmness of his position (with नृप). पदानां शब्दानां बन्धेन (रचनया) उज्ज्वलः; पदस्य बन्धेन &c. हारी charming (with गद्यबन्ध); wearing a necklace (with नृप). We may also separate as ०ज्ज्वलो अहारी (with गद्यबन्ध). अहारी not stealing (from the works of others). कृत...स्थितिः—कृता वर्णानां क्रमेण (अलङ्कारशास्त्रानुसारेण) स्थितिः यस्मिन्; कृता वर्णानां ब्राह्मणादीनां क्रमेण (शास्त्रक्रमेण) स्थितिः येन—In which letters are employed in accordance with the rules of poetics (with गद्यबन्ध); who makes the four Varṇas follow the rules prescribed for each (with नृप). It was the canon of rhetoricians that माधुर्यगुण was most appropriate in शृङ्गार and करुण, and ओजः in वीररस. माधुर्य consists in employing letters from क् to म्, except टवर्ग, preceded by the nasals of their class, and that in ओजः one should employ conjunct consonants joining the first and second or third and fourth letters of each class, टवर्ग, श् and ष्. 'टवर्गवर्जिताः स्पर्शाः स्वस्ववर्गान्तशेखराः । लघुरेफलकारौ च कोमलाः परिकीर्तिताः ॥ रेफेन यस्य कस्यापि योग आद्यतृतीययोः । स्वोत्तराभ्यां तुल्ययोर्वा परुषाष्टगणः शषौ ॥' रत्नापण on प्रतापरुद्र. भट्टारहरिचन्द्र is no more than a mere name to us. His prose composition has not yet been discovered. There is a *poem* called धर्मशर्माभ्युदय written by a Jain writer हरिचन्द्र. A verse of the Gauḍavaho (Vide Intro. p. XII) speaks of a हारियन्द (Prakrit for हारिचन्द्र) बन्ध. Is this a reference to this हरिचन्द्र ?

Verse 13. The principal sentence is सातवाहनः सुभाषितैः रत्नैरिव कोशमकरोत्—सातवाहन made a treasure with fine sayings as with jewels. अविनाशिनम् Immortal (as applied to the collection of सुभाषित); inexhaustible (with the treasure of jewels). अग्राम्यम्—not vulgar or indecent *i. e.* refined (with सुभाषितकोश); not produced in villages (with रत्नकोश). Jewels are found in the sea or in mines (not in villages). विशुद्धा जातिः स्वभावोक्तिः येषु (with सुभाषितैः); विशुद्धा जातिः येषां (with रत्नैः) of purest character. विशुद्धजातिभिः means the same thing as 'जातिरग्राम्या' above. कोशं–a collection of verses that are unconnected with one another *i. e.* the same subject does not run through them all. It also means 'a treasure.' 'कोशः श्लोकसमूहस्तु स्यादन्योन्यानपेक्षकः' साहित्यदर्पण VI. See also काव्यादर्श I. 13. "मुक्तकं कुलकं कोशः सङ्घात इति तादृशः । सर्गबन्धाङ्गरूपत्वादनुक्तः पद्यविस्तरः ॥'. In this verse the author seems to praise the गाथासप्तशती of हाल. That work consists of 700 Prakrit verses. It is a collection of verses composed by हाल (सप्तशती I. 3) in the Āryā metre (which is a subdivision of जाति for which see p. 7). 'मात्राभिर्गणना यत्र सा जातिरिति काश्यप ।' अग्निपुराण chap. 337. 22. सातवाहन (Prakrit सालाहण) is identified by हेमचन्द्र with हाल 'सालाहणम्मि हालो' देशीनाममाला VIII. 66. In the अभिधानचिन्तामणि we have 'हालः स्यात्सातवाहनः'. हाल seems to us to be an abbreviated form of the Prakrit सालाहण (स् and ह् being often interchanged even in modern vernaculars like the Gujarati). क्षीरस्वामी quotes several verses enumerating the names of famous emperors of old among whom occurs हाल 'हालः स्याच्छालिवाहनः'. A king सातवाहन is connected with गुणाढ्य the author of the बृहत्कथा, for which see verse 17. सुभाषित is defined as 'पुराणेष्वितिहासेषु तथा रामायणादिषु । वचनं सारभूतं यत्तत्सुभाषितमुच्यते ॥'.

Verse 14. प्रवरसेनस्य कुमुदोज्ज्वला (कुमुदवत् उज्ज्वला) कीर्तिः सेतुना सागरस्य परं पारं प्रयाता कुमुदोज्ज्वला (कुमुदेन तदाख्येन वानरसेनापतिना) उज्ज्वला कपिसेना सेतुना सागरस्य परं पारमिव प्रयाता. The author here praises the Prakrit poem called सेतुबन्ध or रावणवध. Bāṇa is engaged in this Introduction in celebrating the names of *authors* and their works. Hence it follows that प्रवरसेन was the author of सेतुबन्ध. There is a tradition that the सेतुबन्ध was composed by कालिदास and that प्रवरसेन was only the patron of that great poet. Bāṇa's words at least do not lend any support to this tradition. The Rājataranginī speaks of several kings of Kashmir that bore the name प्रवरसेन. At the command of हर्ष-विक्रमादित्य of उज्जयिनी the kingdom of काश्मीर was offered to a poet मातृगुप्त who is often identified with कालिदास without any reason beyond the fact that both names mean the same thing. When at Harsha's death मातृगुप्त abdicated the throne, प्रवरसेन (II) ascended it and generously treated मातृगुप्त; vide राजतरङ्गिणी III. 125-323. Daṇḍin says that the language of the country of Mahārāshṭra is Prakrit *par excellence* and that the सेतुबन्ध is composed in (महाराष्ट्री) प्राकृत. 'महाराष्ट्राश्रयां भाषां प्रकृष्टं प्राकृतं विदुः । सागरः सूक्तिरत्नानां सेतुबन्धादि यन्मयम् ॥' काव्यादर्श I. 34. If, as tradition says, the author of the सेतुबन्ध was a king, may we hazard a conjecture that he may have been one of the Vākāṭaka kings? In the Chammak and Sivani copperplate grants (C. I. I. III pp. 235, 243) we have two प्रवरसेनs of the Vakāṭaka family. In the army of the monkeys कुमुद was a commander. 'शरभः कुमुदो वह्निर्वानरो रम्भ एव च ॥ एते चान्ये च बहवो वानराः कामरूपिणः ।' रामायण किष्किन्धा 39. 37-38. The monkeys under the supervision of their leader नल, son of विश्वकर्मा, constructed the bridge by means of which they crossed over to लङ्का. See युद्धकाण्ड chapter 22. 74-75 'तानि कोटिसहस्राणि वानराणां महौजसाम् ॥ बध्नन्तः सागरे सेतुं जग्मुः पारं महोदधेः ।'. The Com. construes प्रवरसेनस्य also with कपिसेना 'प्रवे प्लुते रसो येषां ते प्रवरसाः वानरास्तेषामिनः स्वामी, प्रवरा च सेना यस्य स सुग्रीवश्च'. According to this प्रवरसेन is सुग्रीव (प्रव-रस-इन), because he was the master of monkeys who have a liking for leaping or because he had an excellent army. कुमुद is a white lotus and कीर्ति is poetically represented as white.

Verse 15. Bāṇa here eulogises the dramatist Bhāsa. Kālidāsa speaks of him in his मालविकाग्निमित्र as very famous. For a reference to him in the Gauḍavaho see p. XII of the Introduction. The सरस्वतीकण्ठाभरण quotes the verse 'भासवत्यपि भासादी कविवर्गे जगत्त्रयीम् । के न यान्ति निबन्धारः कालिदासस्य दासताम् ॥'. The सूक्तिमुक्तावलि quotes a verse of राजशेखर about भास 'भासनाटकचक्रेऽपि छेकैः क्षिप्ते परीक्षितुम् । स्वप्नवासवदत्तस्य दाहकोऽभून्न पावकः ॥' Peterson's Intro. to सुभाषितावलि pp. 80-81. Until very recently it was believed by all that Bhāsa's dramas were lost. Mr. T. Ganapatisastri of Trivandrum has published about thirteen plays the authorship of which he ascribes to Bhāsa on several grounds. We have our own doubts as to whether the plays now put forward are the genuine works of Bhāsa. But obvious considerations prevent us from entering into that question here. The principal sentence is भासः नाटकैः देवकुलैरिव यशो लेभे. सूत्र...रम्भैः—सूत्रधारेण कृतः आरम्भः येषाम्—that had an introduction spoken by the manager of the stage (with नाटकैः); that were constructed by architects (with देवकुलैः). बहवो भूमिकाः येषु; बहवः भूमयः येषु—in which there are numerous characters (with नाटकैः); in which there are several stories. The affix क is optionally added to all बहुव्रीहि compounds. सपताकैः containing पताकाs (with नाटकैः); possessed of banners (with देवकुलैः). पताका is a term in dramaturgy. There are five अर्थप्रकृतिs (the leading sources of the principal object in a drama) *viz.*, बीज, बिन्दु, पताका, प्रकरी and कार्य. पताका is defined by भरत 'यद्वृत्तं हि परार्थं स्यात्प्रधानस्योपकारकम् । प्रधानवच्च कल्प्येत सा पताकेति कीर्तिता ॥' नाट्यशास्त्र. 19. 23. It is an episode which has no purpose in itself, but is put in by the author for serving as a foil to the principal theme; *e. g.* the representation of the career of सुग्रीव when the principal theme is रामचरित. The दशरूप says 'प्रासङ्गिकं परार्थस्य स्वार्थो यस्य प्रसङ्गतः। सानुबन्धं पताकाख्यं प्रकरी च प्रदेशभाक् ॥' I. 13. On this धनिक's comment is 'दूरं यदनुवर्तते प्रासङ्गिकं सा पताका । सुग्रीवादिवृत्तान्तवत् । पताकेवासाधारणनायकचिह्नवत्तदुपकारित्वात् । यदल्पं सा प्रकरी श्रवणादिवृत्तान्तवत्.' The साहित्यदर्पण defines पताका as 'व्यापि प्रासङ्गिकं वृत्तं पताकेत्यभिधीयते.' This is quite different from पताकास्थानक, which is of four kinds. See साहित्यदर्पण VI. for it. It is not to be supposed that Bhāsa alone among the dramatists before Bāṇa wrote plays that were commenced by सूत्रधारs or that contained varied dramatis personae or पताकाs. Bāṇa's only object is to show, by taking three paronomastic clauses, similarity between temples and dramas.

Verse 16. In this verse Bāṇa offers a very glowing tribute of praise to the prince of Sanskrit poets. Translate 'who indeed does not feel delight the moment the fine sayings of Kālidāsa are uttered, sayings which are sweet and agreeable (सान्द्र) like sprays of flowers?' The idea is that even men of ordinary intelligence are delighted with Kālidāsa's sayings, much more therefore will those possessed of high critical faculty find delight in them. वा does not mean 'or' here. It is to be connected with कस्य (कस्य वा न प्रीतिर्जायते), the meaning being 'I should like to know who is not &c.' Compare for this use of वा 'परिवर्तिनि संसारे मृतः को वा न जायते.' Note also the use of इव in a similar way 'परैस्त्वदन्यः क इवापहारयेन्मनोरमामात्मवधूमिव श्रियम् ॥' किरातार्जुनीय I. 31. निर्गतासु when uttered by anyone (with सूक्तिषु); come out (मञ्जरीषु). The मञ्जरी also is fragrant and thick or glossy (सान्द्र). The reading मधुरसार्द्रासु (wet with sweet juice) is not so good, as it cannot be well construed with सूक्तिषु. This verse indicates, in our humble opinion, that Kālidāsa was an household word in the days of Bāṇa and that therefore the former preceded the latter by a long interval of time.

Verse 17. The principal sentence here is—बृहत्कथा हरलीला इव कस्य विस्मयाय नो (भवेत्)—In whom would the बृहत्कथा not cause marvel, as the sportive action of S'iva does? The बृहत्कथा here spoken of is a work in a Prakrit dialect called पैशाची ascribed to गुणाढ्य. The original work in पैशाची is not now extant. But it is certain that in the 11th and 12th centuries of the Christian era it was available. We have abridgments of the work in Sanskrit compiled by two Kashmirian Pandits, Kshemendra (11th century) and Somadeva (12th century). सोमदेव tells us in the कथासरित्सागर 'यथामूलं तथैवैतन्न मनागप्यतिक्रमः । ग्रन्थविस्तरसंक्षेपमात्रं भाषा च भिद्यते ॥' I. 1. 10. A third redaction of the ancient बृहत्कथा was issued by a French Scholar M. Lacôte. See J. R. A. S. for 1906 p. 689 for a Tamil work based upon the बृहत्कथा. Why the book was written in पैशाची is explained in the 6th and 7th chapters (तरङ्ग) of the first लम्बक of the कथासरित्सागर. The story resembles that of the sibylline books. गुणाढ्य was originally a minister of शातवाहन king of the Deccan. Being defeated in a wager he went to the विन्ध्य forest, learnt पैशाची, wrote a work in his own blood containing seven lakhs of verses. When the king would not receive a strange

seems to be an emendation due to the difficulty of explaining आढ्यराज. One edition reads 'कृतोच्छ्वासैः' which also seems to be an unauthorised emendation. Pischel held that आढ्यराज was Harsha himself (J. R. A. S. for 1903 p. 830). But it is not clear why Harsha should be called आढ्यराज. Some take the verse in a sarcastic sense. If आढ्यराज is शालिवाहन (or सातवाहन), we know how he discouraged (the opposite of उत्साह) गुणाढ्य when the latter brought his strange work of seven lakhs of verses. But several objections can be urged against this way of explaining the verses. There is no reason why Bâṇa should indulge in sarcasm against a famous king that died several centuries before him. Besides this sense does not fall in well with the next verse. Mr. F. W. Thomas is troubled by the word अपि in स्मृतैरपि and thinks that the reference may be to some psychological doctrine according to which memory does not reside in the heart (J. R. A. S. 1903 p. 830).

Verse 19. तथापि although I am afraid of the ridicule that may be poured upon me in striving to reach the position of a poet of the eminence of आढ्यराज. नृपते... चापलम् through my devotion to my king (Harsha), I, being undismayed and eager to carry out (my undertaking), make bold to plunge with my tongue in the ocean of Âkhyâyikâ. He means that he is going to write an आख्यायिका about हर्ष and sing his praises with his tongue. That is a rash undertaking (चापलं) for one like him. Separate भक्त्या अभीतः. अभीतः may also mean 'being surrounded *i. e.* protected all round' (अभि + इतः). प्लवनं Swimming. प्लवनं एव चापलम्. It is a rash act to plunge in the deep ocean. निर्वहणे आकुलः would also mean 'anxious to go across to the other side' (with one who plunges into the ocean).

Verse 20. Here आख्यायिका is compared to a bed (शय्या). सुख...लिता (सुखेन प्रबोधः ज्ञानं तेन ललिता) charming on account of conveying knowledge with ease or charming on account of its being easy to understand. The Vedas and S'āstras contain injunctions laying down how one should act. Poetry like a bitter pill coated with sugar inculcates good conduct and abstinence from sin in a sweet persuasive manner. Compare 'स्वादुकाव्यरसोन्मिश्रं शास्त्रार्थमपि भुञ्जते। प्रथमालीढमधवः पिबन्ति कटु भेषजम् ॥'; compare also 'कटुकौषधवच्छास्त्रमविद्याव्याधिनाशनम् । आह्लाद्यमृतवत्काव्यमविवेकगदापहम् ॥' काव्यालङ्कारकामधेनु. सुख...ललिता that is agreeable because one rises from it in a happy mood (with शय्या). सुखः प्रबोधः (waking up from sleep) तेन ललिता. शोभनानां वर्णानां घटना (arrangement) तेन उज्ज्वलैः (शब्दैः). See above p. 10 as to the employment of particular letters for a particular purpose. सुवर्ण...ज्ज्वलैः brilliant on account of being overlaid with gold or on account of the combination of agreeable colours (with प्रतिपादकैः). प्रतिपादकैः that convey sense (with शब्दैः); with the feet (of the bed). शय्या is used in another sense also. It means 'such a collocation of words in a poem that no word can be substituted by another without marring the beauty of the poem. 'या पदानां परान्योन्यमैत्री शय्येति कथ्यते ।' प्रतापरुद्र (वृत्ति—पदविनिमयासहिष्णुत्वाद्बन्धस्य पदानुगुण्यरूपा शय्या). बाण employs the word in this sense in the कादम्बरी 'स्फुरत्कलालापविलासकोमला करोति रागं हृदि कौतुकाधिकम् । रसेन **शय्यां** स्वयमभ्युपागता कथा जनस्याभिनवा वधूरिव ॥' (Intro. 8th verse). The words सुख०, सुवर्ण० and प्रति० mean the same thing with शय्या in this sense as with आख्यायिका. The अग्निपुराण says that शय्या is the same as मुद्रा 'अभिप्रायविशेषेण कविशक्ति विवृण्वती । मुत्प्रदायिनीति सा मुद्रा सैव शय्यापि नो मते ॥' 342.26.

Verse 21. ज्वलन् प्रतापज्वलनः एव प्राकारः तेन कृता जगतः रक्षा येन who protects the world by the rampart-wall (प्राकारः) of the fire of his glorious valour. सकलानां प्रणयिनां मनोरथाः तेषां सिद्धौ श्रीपर्वतः Who is a श्रीपर्वत in fulfilling the desires of all suppliants. प्रणयिन् a friend, or one who comes with a request. श्रीपर्वत is a mountain in Telingana sacred to शिव. 'श्रीपर्वते महादेवो देव्या सह महाद्युतिः । न्यवसत्परमप्रीतो ब्रह्मा च त्रिदशैः सह ॥' वनपर्व 85. 19-20. The story runs that लक्ष्मी practised penance there and secured the boon of always reclining on the chest of Vishṇu. Compare 'श्रीपर्वताश्चर्यवार्तासहस्राभिज्ञेन जरद्द्रविडधार्मिकेण (p. 227 of कादम्बरी Peterson's ed.).

P. 2 ll. 20—28 **एव... प्रादुरभवन्.** अनुश्रूयते *lit.* it is heard *i. e.* it is handed down by tradition. किल indicates 'as the story goes.' '**वार्तासम्भाव्ययोः किल**' इत्यमरः. स्व...तिष्ठन् presiding over (or dwelling in) his world (*i. e.* ब्रह्मलोक or सत्यलोक). परमेष्ठी = ब्रह्मा (परमे पदे तिष्ठतीति). It is the subject of आसाञ्चक्रे. विका... विष्टः occupying his lotus seat that was fully expanded. इन् (in विकासिन्) is affixed in the sense of नित्ययोग (the lotus on which ब्रह्मा reclines is always expanded). 'भूमनिन्दाप्रशंसासु **नित्ययोगे**ऽतिशायने । सम्बन्धेऽस्तिविवक्षायां च भवन्ति मतुबादयः ॥'. पद्मं एव विष्टरः (विस्तीर्यते इति). '**विष्टरो** विटपी दर्भमुष्टिः **पीठाद्यमासनम्**' इत्यमरः. ब्रह्मा is called कमलासन. सुनासीरः (इन्द्रः) प्रमुखः येषाम्. The word is also written as शुनासीर; क्षीरस्वामी derives as 'शोभना नासीरा अग्रेसरा अस्य शुनासीरयोरपत्यमित्येके'. गीर्वाणैः = देवैः. गीः (वाक्) एव वाणः (बवयोरभेदात्) बाणः येषाम्. सं. also explains as 'गिरः स्तुतिरूपा वणन्ति भजन्तीति'. ब्रह्मो...कुर्वन् engaged in philosophical discussion about ब्रह्म. ब्रह्मोद्यं = ब्रह्मणः वदनं उक्तिः. ब्रह्मोद्य is generally used as a noun in the neuter, but here it is an adjective of कथाः. ब्रह्म means either Veda or the supreme all-pervading apirit which is the subject–matter of the Upanishads. 'वदः सुपि क्यप् च' पा. 3.1.106 (वदेर्भावे क्यप् स्यात् चात् यत् अनुपसर्गे सुपि उपपदे । ब्रह्मोद्यम् । ब्रह्मवद्यम् । सि. कौ.). सं० explains 'ब्रह्मोद्या सा कथा यस्यामुच्यते ब्रह्म शाश्वतम्.' See मनुस्मृति 3.231 'यद्यद्रोचेत विप्रेभ्यस्तत्तद्दद्यादमत्सरः । ब्रह्मोद्याश्च कथाः कुर्यात्पितृणामेतदीप्सितम् ॥'. मेधातिथि on मनु० explains 'ब्रह्मोद्या ब्रह्मणि वेदे या उद्यन्ते कथ्यन्ते ता ब्रह्मोद्याः देवासुरयुद्धं वृत्रवधः सरमादूत्यमित्याद्याः । अथवा कः स्विदेकाकी चरतीत्यादि'. अन्याश्च...भावयन् engaged in (*lit.* causing to be, putting forward) other blameless (निरवद्य) discussions on various lores. विद्याs were either four or fourteen. The four are आन्वीक्षिकी (metaphysics), त्रयी (the three Vedas), वार्ता (agriculture and trade), दण्डनीति (science of Government). See चाणक्य's अर्थशास्त्र p. 6. 'पुराणन्यायमीमांसाधर्मशास्त्राङ्गमिश्रिताः । वेदाः स्थानानि विद्यानां धर्मस्य च चतुर्दश ॥' याज्ञ० I. 3 (*i. e.* four Vedas, six वेदाङ्गs, पुराण, न्याय, मीमांसा and धर्मशास्त्र). These are the fourteen Vidyâs. गोष्ठी an assembly or discourse. In ancient times गोष्ठी was somewhat like a modern club. 'समानविद्यावित्तशीलबुद्धिवयसामनुरूपैरालापैरेकत्रासनबन्धो गोष्ठी' सं. If we read निरवद्याविद्या as one word, then we shall have to separate as निरवद्य अविद्या०, which does not yield a good sense. If we read निरवद्यविद्या० the meaning will be the same or we may interpret as 'discussion about the knowledge of the Blameless One' (*i. e.* ब्रह्म). निरवद्य is an epithet of ब्रह्म. Compare 'निष्कलं निष्क्रियं शान्तं निरवद्यं निरञ्जनम्' श्वेताश्वतरोपनिषद् 6.19. Note the words 'निरवद्यविद्याविद्योतितानि' in the last para. of the first उच्छ्वास (p. 19 text). Separate तथा आसीनं (sitting). त्रिभुवनेन प्रतीक्ष्यं पूज्यम् (from ईक्ष् with प्रति). प्रजापतयः—In the मनुस्मृति the ten प्रजापतिs enumerated do not include मनु, दक्ष and चाक्षुष. 'पतीन्प्रजानामसृजं महर्षीनादितो दश ॥ मरीचिमत्र्यङ्गिरसौ पुलस्त्यं पुलहं क्रतुम् । प्रचेतसं वसिष्ठं च भृगुं नारदमेव च ॥' मनु० I. 34-35. In the मनुस्मृति (I. 36) we are told that these ten प्रजापतिs created seven Manus of whom चाक्षुष is the sixth (मनु० I. 62). The रामायण gives a slightly different list (अरण्यकाण्ड 14.7-9). दक्ष is a well-known प्रजापति. He was born from the right अङ्गुष्ठ of ब्रह्मा (*vide* आदिपर्व 66.10). Probably the author uses the word प्रजापति not in a technical sense, but in a general sense 'progenitors.' सप्तर्षयः पुरःसराः (मुख्याः) येषाम्. The seven sages are मरीचि, अत्रि, अङ्गिरस्, पुलस्त्य, पुलह, क्रतु, वसिष्ठ. के...चारयन् some uttered with proper accents hymns from the Rigveda that are appropriate for praising (God). The Rigveda mostly consists of verses praising various deities, describing their wondrous works and soliciting the gods for various boons. केचि... पठन् some recited the Yajus formula containing worship. 'क्षयार्चयोरपचितिः' इत्यमरः. अपचितिं पूजां भजन्ते इति. प्रशंसासामानि Sāman hymns containing praise. साम verses are to be sung. Almost the whole of the सामवेद is taken from the Rigveda. A Yajus is in prose, while a ऋक् is in a metrical form. Bāṇa uses appropriate verbs and descriptive words with reference to the ऋग्वेद, the यजुर्वेद and the सामवेद. विवृतं क्रतुक्रियातन्त्रं यैः that explained (*lit.* laid bare) the doctrines (or dogmas) of the performance of sacrifice. 'तन्त्रं प्रधाने सिद्धान्ते' इत्यमरः. व्याचचक्षिरे expounded (3rd plu. Perfect of चक्ष् with वि and आ). विद्यानां विसंवादः (difference) तेन कृताः due to the difference of the lores they had studied. It is better to read with B 'अन्योन्यस्य विवादाः.' प्रादुरभवन्—(naturally or spontaneously) arose. What the author means is:—The sages had each of them made a profound study of some particular विद्या and so disputes arose among them not out of envy or pride, but because each was specially devoted to a particular विद्या and so gave expression to his views without meaning any offence to other personages present.

P. 2 l. 29–p. 3 l. 15 **अथाति...जहास.** अति...प्रकृत्या by nature extremely irritable. अत्रेस्तनयः-अत्रि's wife was अनसूया a daughter of दक्ष. अत्रि had three sons सोम, दुर्वासस् and दत्तात्रेय. See विष्णुपुराण I. 10. तारापतेः (चन्द्रमसः) भ्राता. The moon is said to have sprung from the lustre of Atri's eye. See हरिवंश 25 'नेत्राभ्यां वारि सुस्राव दशधा द्योतयद्दिशः। तं गर्भं विधिना हृष्टा दश देव्यो दधुस्तदा॥ समेत्य धारयामासुर्न च ताः समशक्नुवन्॥ स ताभ्यः सहसैवाथ दिग्भ्यो गर्भः प्रभान्वितः। पपात भासयँल्लोकाञ्शीतांशुः सर्वभावनः॥' verses 6–8. Note 'अत्रिनेत्रनिर्गतस्य... दृष्ट इव जनेन जन्मदिवसः कुमुदबन्धोः' हर्षचरित 7th उच्छ्वास. मन्दपालः नाम यस्य सः मन्दपालनामा तेन. कलहं करोति इति कलहायते according to 'शब्दवैरकलहाभ्रकण्वमेघेभ्यः करणे' पा. 3.1.17 (एभ्यः कर्मभ्यः करोत्यर्थे क्यङ् स्यात्। सि. कौ.). विस्वरमकरोत् he struck a discordant note. विस्वरम् may be taken as an adjective of साम or as an adverb. सर्वेषु goes with मुनिषु. शापभयात् प्रतिपन्नं मौनं यैः that took to silence through fear of a curse. दुर्वासस् was well-known for cursing persons at the slightest offence. अन्या...सम्भवे while Brahmâ paid no heed (to the lapse of दुर्वासस्) being engaged in conversing with some one else. ब्रह्मा is supposed to have sprung from the lotus in the navel of Vishṇu. Compare first para of the 4th उच्छ्वास 'द्विजवरस्वेच्छागृहीतकोषो नाभिपद्म इव पुण्डरीकेक्षणात्.' भगवती कुमारी—connect these with देवी सरस्वती below. The principal sentence is भगवती कुमारी देवी सरस्वती श्रुत्वा जहास. किञ्चित् उन्मुक्तः बालभावः यस्मिन् or येन (*adj.* of वयसि) which had just cast aside childhood *i. e.* which had just passed the stage of being a mere girl. भूषितं नवयौवनं येन—The idea is:—she was so charming at that age that youth itself had its charms heightened by claiming her as one of its owners. गृहीतचामरा प्रचलन्ती भुजलता यस्याः whose creeperlike hand held a chowrie and was waving. पितामहं = ब्रह्माणम्. उपवीजयन्ती fanning. निर्भर्त्सनार्थं ताडनं तेन जातः रागः (रक्तवर्णः) ययोः. निर्भर्त्सन... समाना brilliant with her spray-like feet naturally red, that as if seemed to have grown red by stamping (on the ground) for censuring (दुर्वासस्). Her feet were naturally red; the poet fancies that they grew red because she stamped with her feet on the ground by way of finding fault with दुर्वासस् who had committed a mistake in singing a साम verse. शिष्य... चरणा whose feet were musical with two anklets that jingled in accordance with the movements (क्रमः) of her steps, as if they (नूपुरयुगल) were two pupils. वाचालितौ चरणौ यस्याः. As she moved about, the anklets on the feet jingled. The words पद० and वाचा० yield another sense with शिष्यद्वय. The पदपाठ of the Rigveda is ascribed to शाकल्य in the निरुक्त. क्रम, जटा and घन are certain arrangements of the verses of the Rigveda intended to preserve the purity of the text. The क्रमपाठ is ascribed to पाञ्चाल बाभ्रव्य. See शान्तिपर्व 343.103. The अनुशासनपर्व (85.90) mentions both पद and क्रम. The क्रमपाठ of the verse 'इदं विष्णुर्विचक्रमे त्रेधा निदधे पदम्' would be 'इदं विष्णुः । विष्णुर्वि । वि चक्रमे । चक्रमे त्रेधा । त्रेधा नि । नि दधे । दधे पदम् । पदमिति पदम् ।'. शिष्यs would be noisy (मुखर) by repeating the पदपाठ and the क्रमपाठ. The words चरण and शाखा are sometimes used as synonyms; चरण means 'शाखाध्येतृ' *i. e.* 'those who study a particular शाखा of the Veda, an ideal succession of teachers and pupils.' This latter sense is required here (with शिष्य०). मदन... द्वितयम् who (सरस्वती) had legs appearing like the pillars of the arched portal of the city of love. मदननगरस्य तोरणं तस्य स्तम्भयोः इव विभ्रमः यस्य (*adj.* of °द्वितयम्). Her legs were straight and delicately proportioned. Therefore they as if supported (*i. e.* excited) love, as pillars support the portal of a city. This is not a very elegant way of describing सरस्वती. The reading धर्मनगर० would make सरस्वती the support of धर्म. This is somewhat better. सलीलं is to be connected with विन्यस्त०. उत्काः कलहंसाः तेषां कुलं तस्य कलः आलापः तद्वत् प्रलपति इति °प्रलापिनि. सलील...किसलया who had sportively placed her sprout-like left hand on the string of her girdle that jingled like the sweet murmur of the swarms of love-sick कलहंसs. उत्कः= उत्कण्ठितः. 'उत्क उन्मनाः' पा. 5.2.80. Small bells were attached to girdles. विन्यस्तं वामहस्त एव किसलयं यया. विद्व... काया whose body was rendered pure by the Brahmanical thread hanging down from her shoulder, as if it (ब्रह्मसूत्र) were a coil of virtues that stuck to her on account of dwelling in the heart of the wise. ब्रह्मसूत्रं=यज्ञोपवीतम् (ब्रह्मणि वेदग्रहणकाले धृतं सूत्रम्). सरस्वती dwells in the mind of the wise; गुणs (virtues) also occupy the heart of the wise. The मानस lake was created by ब्रह्मा whose daughter was सरस्वती; so she may be said to be dwelling on the मानस lake. ब्रह्मसूत्र is a coil of गुणs (threads). 'कैलासशिखरे राम मनसा निर्मितं सरः। ब्रह्मणा प्रागिदं यस्मात्तदभून्मानसं सरः॥' रामायण. Compare the description of महाश्वेता 'मण्डलीकृतेन ब्रह्मसूत्रेण पवित्रीकृतकायाम्' कादम्बरी p. 130 of P. भास्वान् मध्यनायकः (मध्यरत्नं) यस्य—the central gem of which is brilliant. अने... यातं inlaid with many pearls (अनेकमुक्ताभिः अनुयातम्). अपवर्गमार्गम्=मोक्षमार्गम्. हार is fancied to be मोक्षमार्ग because the two epithets भास्व० and अनेक० apply to both. भास्वतः सूर्यस्य मध्यं नयतीति ०नायकः—the path of final beatitude leads through the sun. The Upanishads speak of two paths, देवयान and पितृयाण. Those who follow the doctrine of works, reach by various stages the moon and after enjoying the fruits of their good works there, they have to be born again. Those who follow the path of knowledge were supposed to reach by various stages the sun and thence to attain to मोक्ष. When there is मोक्ष, the cycle of births and deaths ceases. 'ते य एवमेतद्विदुर्ये चामी अरण्ये श्रद्धां सत्यमुपासते तेऽर्चिरभिसम्भवन्ति, अर्चिषोऽहः, अह्न आपूर्यमाणपक्षमापूर्यमाणपक्षाद्यान्षण्मासानुदङ्ङादित्य एति मासेभ्यो देवलोकं देवलोकादादित्यमादित्याद्वैद्युतं तान्वैद्युतान्पुरुषोऽमानव एत्य ब्रह्मलोकान् गमयति तेषु ब्रह्मलोकेषु पराः परावतो वसन्ति तेषां न पुनरावृत्तिः' बृहदारण्यकोपनिषद् XI. 2. 14. In the गीता, they are called शुक्लगति and कृष्णगति. 'शुक्लकृष्णे गती ह्येते जगतः शाश्वते मते। एकया यात्यनावृत्तिमन्ययावर्तते पुनः॥' VIII. 26. The com. quotes the verse 'परिव्राड् योगयुक्तश्च शूरश्चाभिमुखं हतः। द्वाविमौ पुरुषौ लोके सूर्यमण्डलभेदिनौ॥' which is महा० उद्योगपर्व

33. 61 with slight variations. वदन...राजमाना resplendent with her quivering lip that was red as if with the Alaktaka dye from the feet of all the Vidyās that had entered her mouth. Alaktaka dye was applied to the feet by young ladies. Her lip was naturally red. The poet fancies that the redness was due to the fact that Vidyâs (ladies) in entering her mouth left some lac sticking to her lip. A very learned person is often spoken of as one on the tip of whose tongue dance Vidyâs. Compare 'अमुष्य विद्या रसनाग्रनर्तकी.' सरस्वती, as presiding over all Vidyâs, would naturally have them at the tip of her tongue. 'ओष्ठाधरौ तु रदनच्छदौ दशनवाससी' इत्यमरः. सं... प्रतिमाम् (her cheek) on which was reflected (संक्रान्त) an image of the black antelope skin of Brahmâ. साम... हरिणामिव as if the deer in the moon had got down on it for listening to her singing sweet with Sâman (hymns). सामभिः or साम्नां मधुरं गीतं तस्य आकर्णनाय अवतीर्णः शशिहरणः यस्याम् (*adj.* of कपोलस्थलीम्). Deer are very found of music. The spots on the moon were supposed to be either a deer or hare. Compare the verse 'अङ्कं केऽपि शशङ्किरे जलनिधेः पङ्कं परे मेनिरे सारङ्गं कतिचिच्च सञ्जगदिरे भूच्छायमैच्छन्परे ॥ इन्दौ यद्दलितेन्द्रनीलशकलश्यामं दरीदृश्यते तत्सान्द्रं निशि पीतमन्धतमसं कुक्षिस्थमाचक्ष्महे ॥.' The reflection of the deerskin of Brahmâ on her bright cheek is fancied as being the deer in the moon. The bright cheek was like the moon. As the goddess was in heaven, it is appropriate that the deer in the moon is spoken of (and not an ordinary one). ति... लता One of whose creeper—like eyebrows was raised in a curve (तिर्यक्) and with contempt (सावज्ञम्). अवज्ञया सह यथा स्यात्तथा. She felt contempt for दुर्वासस् when the latter committed a mistake through wrath. श्रोत्र... प्रवाहेण as if washing one ear that was soiled by hearing the discordant note (of दुर्वासस्) with a stream of tears issuing out of the corner (अपाङ्गः) of her eye. The poet fancies that, her ear being soiled, she wanted to wash it clean with water. The curved eyebrow looked like a stream of water issuing from the corner of the eye and proceeding towards its neighbour the ear to free it of its taint. It is not to be supposed that she had tears in her eyes. इतर... मदा who, with the other ear that had on it a white full-blown सिन्धुवार bunch and that looked as if it were smiling, manifested her pride of knowledge. Smiles are poetically represented as white. The सिन्धुवार flower on her ear is fancied as the smile of सरस्वती. We smile at the fall

of others. सरस्वती under the garb of the white flower smiled at the lapse of दुर्वासस्. श्रुति...समाना who was attended upon by swarms of bees in the flowers of her ear-ornament that (bees) besought her ear, as if they (bees) were Oṁkâras. The bees hovering round the flowers on her ear seemed to be making requests (प्रणय) to her ear. प्रणव *(i. e.* the syllable Om) also is श्रुतिप्रणयि *(i. e.* the friend or constant attendant of Veda). The mystic syllable ओम् precedes the study of the Veda or a Vedic text. Compare 'ओङ्कारः स्वर्गद्वारं तस्माद् ब्रह्म अध्येष्यमाणः एतदादि प्रतिपद्येत' आपस्तम्बधर्मसूत्र I. 13.6; 'आसीन्महीक्षितामाद्यः प्रणवश्छन्दसामिव' रघु. I. 11. श्रुतिं वेदं प्रणयन्ति that lead forth *i. e.* introduce Veda. सूक्ष्म...शरीरा whose figure was covered with a spotless silken robe of fine texture (सूक्ष्म) as if with a flash of intellect. प्रतानः shoot or tendril. सूक्ष्म subtle (with प्रज्ञा). विमल pure (and not wicked or sinful), with प्रज्ञा. Her fine robe was like the subtle flashes of intellect. वाङ्मयं...किरन्ती spreading in all directions the pure moon-light of her teeth, as if it were literature. ज्योत्स्नायाः आलोकः तम्. The bright teeth of सरस्वती gleamed forth when she laughed at दुर्वासस्. The teeth, as they belonged to सरस्वती, were really वाङ्मय (वाचः सरस्वत्याः विकारः). वाङ्मयं also means 'literature.' Pure literature spreads enlightenment in the world.

P. 3 ll. 16-25 **दृष्ट्वा...जग्राह.** The principal sentence is दृष्ट्वा च तां तथा हसन्तीं स मुनिः...वारिणा समुपस्पृश्य शापजलं जग्राह. दुर्गृहीतः विद्यालवः तेन अवलेपः तेन दुर्विदग्धे (vocative) that are puffed up with vanity at the (acquisition of) particle of ill-understood knowledge. शिरः...शरारोः *(adj.* of ०कलापस्य) that fell dishevelled as the knot was unloosened when he shook his head. शिरःकम्पेन शीर्यमाणः बन्धः तेन विशरारुः (from शॄ with वि) तस्य. 'शॄवन्द्योरारुः' पा. 3.2.173 (शरारुः, वन्दारुः). उन्मिषन् पिङ्गलिमा यस्य the yellow colour of which flashed forth. पिङ्गलिमन् *m.* from पिङ्गल with affix इमन्. 'पृथ्वादिभ्य इमनिज्वा' पा. 5.1.122. रोचिषा = तेजसा कान्त्या वा. सिञ्च...दिशः as if sprinkling the ten quarters with the fluid of the fire of his wrath. The reddish—yellow gleam of his matted hair is fancied to be a fluid spreading over the world. Fire has a reddish flame. The reddish जटा is like a flame of fire (here identified with wrath). कृत...बध्नन्—This clause contains a complicated pun. The plain sense is that Durvāsas knit his eyebrow into a terrific curve whereby his broad forehead was contracted into wrinkles. These wrinkles looked like the lines on a chessboard (अष्टापदम्). अन्धकारितं ललाटपट्टमेव अष्टापदं यया (*adj.* of भ्रुकुटिम्). This is one of the earliest allusions to the game of chess, which was invented in India. 'अष्टापदं शारिफलम्' इत्यमरः (अष्टौ पदान्यस्य). It is a board divided into eight rows, each row having eight squares. It is a question with some whether अष्टापद is a chess board or only a draught board (Marathi सोंगट्यांचा पट). We incline to the former view. Bâṇa at all events associates it with the game of chess. Compare 'अष्टापदानां चतुरङ्गकल्पना' हर्षचरित 2nd उच्छ्वास. चतुरङ्ग refers to the four arms of the ancient Indian army *viz.* infantry, cavalry, elephant riders and chariots. Pâṇini was aware of the word अष्टापद being used in a technical sense 'अष्टनः संज्ञायाम्' पा. 6.3.125 (उत्तरपदे दीर्घः । अष्टापदम् । सि. कौ.). Moreover Pâṇini refers to a particular position of S'āras (chessmen) in 'अनुपद-सर्वान्न-अयानयं बद्धा-भक्षयति-नेयेषु' पा. 5.2.9 (अयानयः स्थलविशेषः तं नेयः आयानयीनः शारः । सि. कौ.). पतञ्जलि comments on this सूत्र and explains the technical meaning of अय and अनय (see Kielhorn's महाभाष्य vol. II. p. 373). In कादम्बरी we have 'अष्टापदपरिचयचतुराभिः' (p. 196 of P.). कृत...धानाम् has three senses· (1) कृतं कालस्य कृष्णवर्णस्य सन्निधानं यया that had blackness near it (with भ्रुकुटि, which was dark); (2) कृतं कालस्य कृष्णवर्णशारस्य सन्निधानं येन (with अष्टापद)—That had black chessmen on it. Chessmen were grouped into black and white or red to mark the opposing sides. कृतं कालस्य यमस्य सन्निधानं यया (with अन्तःपुर... मकरिका) that was near यम or that took persons in the presence of यम. दुर्वासस् by his curses made people perish and so brought them before यम. So his भ्रुकुटि is properly spoken of as driving people into the presence of यम. अन्तः...मकरिकाम् that (frowning eyebrow) was the crocodile ornament painted on the (faces of the) wives (of यम). पत्रभङ्ग–drawings of ornamental figures on the face, bosom etc. The knit brow resembled the figure of a crocodile drawn on the cheeks of Yama's wives. A crocodile is an emblem of death and so is an appropriate decoration for Yama s wives. अति... प्रयच्छन् with his extremely red eye offering as it were the oblation (उपहारः) of his own blood to the goddess of wrath (अमर्षः). His eyes were suffused red with wrath and seemed to drop down blood. So the poet fancies that he was going to offer an oblation of blood to अमर्षदेवता. निर्दयं दष्टः दशनच्छदः तस्मात् भयं तेन पलायमानाम्. निर्दय...च्छलेन under the guise of the rays of his teeth, confining his speech that was as if fleeing through fear at the merciless biting of his lip. The idea is:–दुर्वासस् being enraged bit his lips and when he did so his bright teeth gleamed forth. The poet fancies that his speech was afraid of being mercilessly dealt with as his lip was and so wanted to run away, but was confined inside by the rays of his gleaming teeth. अंसा...जिनस्य tying in another way the knot of his deerskin that slipped from his shoulder, as if it were an edict (giving him authority) for cursing. As the skin slipped from his shoulder he tied it in another way so as not to allow it to drop down. The deerskin had a brownish surface with dark spots. A शासनपट्ट is a grant (generally on copperplate or silk cloth) of land or it is a proclamation announcing the orders of a king. The brown deerskin resembled a copperplate or silken charter and the dark spots resembled the letters. In the case of दुर्वासस् it is fancied to be a charter giving him the authority to curse others. स्वेद...यव: held in all limbs by gods, demons and sages that were reflected in the drops of perspiration (on his body) and that had as if come in refuge to him out of fear of the curse (that he might pronounce). प्रतिपन्नाः सर्वे अवयवाः यस्य. दुर्वासस् perspired on account of his intense rage and the assembly of gods was reflected in the bright drops. The poet fancies that they out of fear of a curse came beseeching him to be merciful. कोपात् कम्पः तेन तरलिताः (tremulous) अङ्गुलयः यस्य (*adj.* of करेण). करेण... क्षिप्य tossing aside his rosary (अक्षमाला) as if it were a string of letters that stuck (to his hand) for propitiating (प्रसादनं) him. He had his rosary in his hand, but, when he began to shake with wrath, he threw it away. The poet fancies that it was not the अक्षमाला that was thrown away, but the letters of the alphabet. The letters of the alphabet are here represented as the partisans of सरस्वती and as interceding with दुर्वासस् for सरस्वती (who presides over all learning and therefore also over letters). The sage as if intimated that he would listen to no intercession. अक्षरमाला suggests अक्षमाला for two reasons. Letters constitute a string as beads do. Besides अक्ष may be used as an abbreviated way of indicating all the letters from अ to क्ष. कामण्डलव (from कमण्डलु with the affix अण्) contained in his water pot. समुपस्पृश्य having sipped water and ejected it. A curse was generally pronounced with the pouring of water.

3

P. 3 l. 26—**P. 4.** l. 10 **अत्रान्तरे…समुत्तस्थौ.** The principal sentence is अत्रान्तरे स्वयम्भुवोऽभ्याशे समुपविष्टा देवी सावित्री चतुर्भिर्वेदैः सह समुत्तस्थौ. स्वयम्भुवः ब्रह्मणः अभ्याशे समीपे. मूर्तिमती in a corporeal form. पीयूष…वसाना wearing a fine bark robe of the tree of paradise that (robe) was as white as the mass of the foam of nectar. This and the following clauses in the nominative qualify सावित्री. बिस…ग्रन्थिः that had tied between her high breasts a knot with an upper garment (a shawl) made of lotus filaments. उन्नतस्तनयोर्मध्ये बद्धा गात्रिक ग्रन्थिः यया. सं० remarks 'गात्रिकाग्रन्थिर्ग्रन्थिविशेषः स्वस्तिकाकारः स्त्रीणामुत्तरीयस्य स्तनोद्देशे भवति.' She had tied the knot of her shawl in the form of a स्वस्तिक on her bosom. तपोबलेन निर्जितं त्रिभुवनं तस्य जयः तस्य पताकाभिः. भस…राजिभिः with lines of the marks of ashes. पुण्ड्रकः a mark on the forehead made with sandal &c., showing the particular sect to which the votary belongs. विराजितं ललाटाजिरं (ललाटं अजिरमिव) यस्याः Her forehead being broad is compared to a court-yard. The three lines of ashes on her forehead are compared to banners indicating her conquest of the worlds by the power of her austere penance. The worlds are three and पताकाs may be fluttering on an open space (अजिरं). 'वक्रा ललाटगास्तिस्रो भस्मरेखास्त्रिपुण्ड्रकम् ॥' हारावली. 'ऊर्ध्वपुण्ड्रं मृदा कुर्यात् त्रिपुण्ड्रं भसना सदा । तिलकं वै द्विजः कुर्याच्चन्दनेन यदृच्छया ॥'. योग…कक्ष्यका whose वैकक्ष्यक scarf was made up of an ascetic's wrap. वैकक्ष्यकम् or वैकक्षकम् (विकक्षायां भवं) is primaring a garland (and secondarily an ornamental robe) worn over one shoulder and under the other like a यज्ञोपवीत. 'वैकक्षकं तु तत् । यत्तिर्यक् क्षिप्तमुरसि' इत्यमरः. योगपट्टकं a cloth thrown over the back and knees of an ascetic during contemplation. 'पृष्ठजान्वोः समायोगे वस्त्रं वलयवद् दृढम् । परिवेष्टय यदूर्ध्वज्ञुस्तिष्ठेत्तद्योगपट्टकम् ॥'. स्कन्धा … ना hanging down from her shoulder (with पट्टकेन); that supports itself on a section of the wind (with ०स्रोतसा). The wind (वायु) is believed to be divided in-to seven स्कन्धs, one of which called परिवह supports the Ganges. Compare शाकुन्तल VII '**त्रिस्रोतसं** वहति यो गगनप्रतिष्ठां…वायोरिमं परिवहस्य वदन्ति मार्गम् ॥'. See विष्णुपु. II. 12. 28 also. सुधाफेनवत् धवलेन (with both पट्टकेन and स्रोतसा). तपः…स्रोतसेव—The idea is :—The white योगपट्टक passing over her shoulder and underneath is fancied to be the stream of the Ganges (both being white and both being ०लम्बिन्) that had been coiled round her body by the power of her austerities. सव्येन goes with करेण. कलयन्ती holding. ब्रह्मो… कमण्डलुं—the crystal vessel resembled the white lotus bud from which Brahmā was supposed to spring. दक्षिणं goes with करं

(p. 4 l. 2) which is the object of उत्क्षिपन्ती. अक्षमालया कृतः परिक्षेपः यस्य—that (कर) was encircled by a rosary. कम्बुनिर्मिताः (made of conch-shell) ऊर्मिकाः (rings) ताभिः दन्तुरितं (bristling). On her right hand she had bright rings of conch-shell (instead of glass bangles as at present). 'कम्बुर्ना वलये शङ्खे' इति, 'अङ्गुलीयकमूर्मिका' इति चामरः. तर्जने तरङ्गिता तर्जनी यस्य the fore-finger of which was waved in chiding (दुर्वासस्). For क see above p. 12. उत्क्षिपन्ती raising or tossing up. क्रोधोपहत overwhelmed by wrath. अनात्मज्ञ not knowing thyself. ब्रह्मबन्धु is a term of reproach meaning 'a ब्राह्मण only by caste or in name and not in deeds.' 'ब्रह्मबन्धुरधिक्षेपः' इत्यमरः (ब्राह्मणस्य बन्धुः परमनुष्ठानाभावाज्जातिब्राह्मणः—क्षीरस्वामी). मुनिखेट miserable or villainous sage. खेट added to words gives the sense of 'अधम.' अपसदः = नीचः. निराकृत an abandoned wretch (lit. expelled). The com. explains 'निराकृतोऽस्वाध्यायः' *i. e.* one who does not study the Vedas. आत्मनः स्खलितेन (mistake) विलक्षः (dismayed or ashamed). 'विलक्षो विस्मयान्विते' इत्यमरः. रोषात् विमुक्तं वेत्रासनं यैः. This and the following words in the instrumental qualify वेदैः (l. 9). ओङ्कारेण मुखरितं (noisy) मुखं येषाम्. The Vedas are represented as repeating loudly the sacred syllable ओम्. उत्क्षेपेण (by their rapid rising up) दोलायमानः (waving to and fro) जटाभारः तेन भरिताः दिशः यैः. The reading आक्षेप० (snatching) does not yield a good sense. परिकरबन्धे भ्रमितं कृष्णाजिनं तस्य आटोपः (expanse) तस्या छाया तया श्यामायमानः दिवसः येषाम् who made the day look dark with the colour of their expanded deer skins that were flung round (their body) in girding up their loins. They girt up their loins out of impatience at Durvāsas' conduct. The reading कृष्णाजिनपटच्छाया० is not bad. It means 'the colour of their deer skin garments.' अमर्षात् क्रोधात् निःश्वासाः एव दोलाः (swings) तासु प्रेङ्खोलितः (tossed, swung) ब्रह्मलोकः यैः—the whole ब्रह्मलोक vibrated with their rapid breaths. सोम...स्रवद्भिः—They perspired through wrath. The poet fancies that it was सोमरस that oozed from their body and not perspiration. विसरः = समूहः. अग्निहोत्रस्य पवित्रं भस्म तेन स्मेरं ललाटं येषाम् whose forehead was bright with the holy ashes of oblations offered into fire. कुश...वरिभिः—कुशतन्तूनां चारु चामरं चीरचीवरं च ते ०चीवरे स्तः एषां—who had a charming chowrie of Kus'a threads (*i. e.* slender कुश grass) and were clad in bark garments. The affix इन् is added to the द्वन्द्व compound ०चीवरे. आषाढिभिः bearing a staff of the पलाश wood. 'पालाशो दण्ड आषाढः' इत्यमरः (आषाढासु जातः—क्षीर०). 'विशाखाषाढादण् मन्थदण्डयोः' पा. 5. 1. 110 (वैशाखो मन्थः, आषाढो दण्डः). A ब्रह्मचारी of each of the three Varṇas was to carry a staff of a particular tree 'ब्राह्मणो बैल्वपालाशौ क्षत्रियो वाटखादिरौ । पैलवौदुम्बरौ वैश्यो दण्डानर्हन्ति धर्मतः ॥' मनुस्मृति II. 45. प्रहरणीकृतं कमण्डलुमण्डलं यैः. They seized their water vessels in their hands as their weapons. मूर्तैः in a corporeal form. वृषीमपहाय abandoning their seats. बृषी or वृषी ('व्रतिनामासनं वृषी' इत्यमरः) a seat of कुश grass for ascetics.

P. 4 ll. 11–17 **ततो...न्यवारयत्.** मर्षय forgive. अभू...शापस्य she is not a fit person for a curse. अनु...बुधैः though besought by the gods. नाथ् 1 P to solicit, but A when it means 'to bless'. बद्धं अञ्जलिपुटं यैः that folded their hands. मा...हृम् Do not cause loss to your austerities. **'विघ्नोऽन्तरायः प्रत्यूहः'** इत्यमरः. It was supposed that by pronouncing a curse a person lost his merit. रोषस्य आवेशेन विवशः beside himself with the emotion of wrath. दुर्विनीत impudent, ill-mannered. व्यपनयामि I shall remove. उन्नतिम्—is used in two senses; (1) going up, (2) exalted or proud position. The first meaning contrasts well with the words 'अधस्ताद्गच्छ.' प्रति...द्यतां who was ready to give a curse in return. सावित्रीम्—is the object of न्यवारयत्. असं...माननीयाः Brāhmaṇas, though their minds are not well disciplined, deserve respect solely for their very birth (caste). Compare वनपर्व 200. 89 'यथा श्मशाने दीप्तौजाः पावको न प्रदुष्यति । एवं विद्वानविद्वान्वा ब्राह्मणो दैवतं महत् ॥'.

P. 4 l. 18—**P. 5** l. 16 **अथ तां...मगात्.** पितामहः is the subject of उवाच (l. 23). कम...द्वहन् having a body wearing a white sacrificial thread as if lotus fibres stuck to it when it (body) sprang from the lotus. कमलात् उत्पत्तौ लग्नानि मृणालसूत्राणि यस्याः. For the birth of ब्रह्मा from the lotus in the navel of Vishṇu, see above p. 20. The fibres and यज्ञोपवीत are both white. The poet fancies that lotus fibres stuck to the body of Brahmā when he sprang from a lotus. उद्ग...कलम् having stopped the tumult consequent upon the curse with his right hand, from which shot up a pencil of the rays of the clear emerald on his ring and which therefore seemed to hold a bundle of Kus'a grass for warding off the calamity of the three worlds. उद्गच्छन् अच्छस्य अङ्गुलीयकमरकतस्य मयूखलताकलापः यस्मिन्. त्रिभुवनस्य उपप्लवः (calamity, injury) तस्य प्रशमाय कुशानां आपीडः समूहः तं धारयतीति. The rays of the emerald resemble green blades of कुश grass. कुश grass was supposed to ward off evil. It was a calamity for the three worlds that सरस्वती was cursed. C and T refer to अथर्ववेद 19. 30. 4 and 6. 43. 1 (where दर्भ is called मन्युशमन) for showing that कुश grass originated from a

understand the mistake you committed. So you should rather feel ashamed in their presence than select सरस्वती for cursing. The reading षण्ढाः means 'eunuch'. The idea would be 'these sages are not impotent, they also can curse you in return, but they have restrained themselves.' रोषः एव दोषः तेन निषद्ये that is fit to be inhabited by the sin of wrath; or रोषदोषस्य निषद्या (market) यस्मिन्. 'आपणस्तु निषद्यायाम्' इत्यमरः. स्व...ग्राह्ये when your own heart should have been checked. अनागस् *adj.* innocent. आत्मनः प्रमादः तेन स्खलितं तस्मात् वैलक्ष्याणि (विलक्षस्य भावः) occasions of shame arising from mistakes due to one's own carelessness (प्रमादः). यै...जनः whereby a person not properly educated incurs blame. The reading याप्यतां conveys the same sense. याप्य = गर्ह्य. विनोदयिष्यति will divert or comfort. आत्मजस्य मुखकमलं तस्य अवलोकनं अवधिः यस्य—that will end at the sight &c. विसर्जितं (dismissed, dissolved) ०मण्डलं येन. ससंभ्रमं (hastily) उपगतः नारदः तस्य स्कन्धे विन्यस्तः हस्तः येन (*adj.* of पितामहः above). देवर्षि नारद was one of the ten mind-born sons of ब्रह्मा. See मनु० I. 35 quoted above p. 18. समु...तिष्ठत् got up for the performance of his usual daily rites. 'आह्निकं स्यात्पुनरहर्निर्वर्त्ये नित्यकर्मणि' हेमचन्द्र. सरस्वत्यपि—connect this with गृहमगात् (l. 16). धवल...पातयन्ती who let fall on her bosom her glance that was white, dark and variegated, as if it (दृष्टि) were a strip of deer-skin. The white of the eye and the dark pupil together make the glance variegated and make it resemble a deer-skin with dark spots thereon. The word धवलः further suggests a bold contradiction. धवलः कृष्णशारः (spotted antelope) यस्मिन्. A कृष्णशार cannot be धवल. षट्...माणा The dark bees are fancied to be the incarnate letters of the curse. A curse being an evil thing would be dark. शापशोकेन शिथिलितौ (without energy) हस्तौ यस्याः. उपदिश्यमानः मर्त्यलोकावतरणमार्गः यस्यै. अधो...जालकेन—the idea is:—The rays of her nails naturally spread downwards; the poet fancies that in spreading downwards from heaven they pointed out to her the way to descend to the world of mortals. अधोमुखीभूतेन—one who tells another unpleasant news hangs down his face. नूपुराणां व्याहारः (utterance, noise) तेन आहूतैः. Domestic हंसs are always represented as following the tinkling of the anklets of ladies. Compare 'प्रदक्षिणीक्रियमाणामिव मणिनूपुरबन्धुभिर्बद्धमण्डलं भ्रमद्भिर्भवनहंसैः' हर्षचरित 5th उच्छ्वास. The कलहंसs are compared to the hearts of the inhabitants of ब्रह्मलोक who, out of their affection for सरस्वती, followed her mentally.

P. 5 l. 17—p. 7 l. 10 **अत्रान्तरे...इति.** मध्यमं लोकम्—the earth (which is between the Heavens and the पाताल). अंशुमाली = सूर्यः. सरस्वती...माली—the idea is:—the sun descended from his position in mid heavens to the western horizon (the earth) in the evening. This is fancied to be due to the fact that the sun wanted to announce that सरस्वती was coming down to the earth. मुकुलितानां बिसिनीनां (कमलिनीनां) विसरः समूहः तस्य व्यसनं (calamity) तेन विषण्णानि (dejected) सरांसि यस्मिन्. Lotuses close their petals in the evening. The day looked gloomy when they did so. मन्दायमाने वासरे when the day waned. This and the following clauses up to स्पष्टे प्रदोषसमये (p. 6 l. 18) are locatives absolute, the principal sentence being सावित्री सरस्वतीमवादीत् (p. 6 l. 19). मधुमद...भगवति when the holy (sun), the sole eye of the world, as red as the face (लपनं) of a very young monkey, quickly (क्षेपीयः) descended on to the peak of (the western) mountain, as if he (the sun) was tossed down by the angrily bent glances of loving women exhilarated by the intoxication of wine. The beauties flushed with wine were eager for the night. The natural descent of the sun to the western horizon is fancied as being due to his being thrown by the angry glances of the beauties. क्षेपीयः (comparative of क्षिप्र) is here used as an adverb. सं० explains the propriety of some words 'सम्भोगान्तरायकारी कथमयमद्यापि नास्तमेतीत्यतः कोपः। क्षिप्यमाणश्चातित्वरितं पतति...लोकेत्यादिना सम्भोगविघ्नकारित्वमेव प्रकाश्यते'. प्रस्तुतानि मुखानि (nipples of udders) यासां ताः ०मुखाः माहेय्यः तासां यूथस्य क्षरन्त्यः क्षीरधाराः ताभिःधवलितेषु that were white with the flowing streams of milk of the herds of cows the udders of which began to drip. 'माहेयी सौरभेयी गौः' इत्यमरः (मह्यते पूज्यते महा तस्या अपत्यं माहेयी—क्षीरस्वामी). आसन्नेन चन्द्रोदयेन उद्दामः (tumultuous) क्षीरोदः (क्षीरसागरः) तस्य लहरीभिः क्षालितेषु. उपशल्य out-skirts. 'ग्रामान्त उपशल्यं स्यात्' इत्यमरः. It is well-known that the waters of the ocean rise up at moonrise. The oceans are said to be seven surrounding the seven द्वीपs. 'एते द्वीपाः समुद्रैस्तु सप्त सप्तभिरावृताः। लवणेक्षुसुरासर्पिर्दधिदुग्धजलैः समम्॥' विष्णुपुराण II. 2. 6. The reading प्रस्तुतमखमाहेयी० would mean 'cows that are useful for the sacrifices that were begun'. अपरा...रावते when ऐरावत starting on his afternoon stroll (प्रचारः) and having a chowric (on his head) was rending at his will (स्वैरं) the banks of the river (स्रवन्ती) of the gods, his tusks being reddened by striking against the golden sides (of the river). चामरिणि—chowries were placed on the heads of elephants and horses. चामीकरतटे (सुवर्णतटे) ताडनेन अरुणिताः रदनाः (दन्ताः) यस्य. रदति pr. p. of रद् 1 P to split. सुरस्रवन्ती the Ganges. ऐरावत is the elephant of Indra. His tusks became red because some of the gold stuck to them after the impact. Elephants are represented as fond of butting against banks and mounds. The reading ०ताडनरणितरदने would mean 'whose tusks resounded by striking etc.' प्रस्...पाटलताम् when the sky (तारापथः) presented a rosy colour, as if it (sky) were besmeared (अनुलिप्त) with the Alaktaka dye of the feet of the several thousands of विद्याधर damsels that were moving about (towards their rendezvous). The sky was suffused red in the evening; the poet fancies that the rosy colour was due to the अलक्तक etc. विद्याधर is a class of semi-divine beings. अभिसारिका a young woman who goes out to meet her lover or keeps on appointment made by him. 'कान्तार्थिनी तु या याति सङ्केतं साऽभिसारिका' इत्यमरः. तारापथ...द्रवे when red sandal juice, poured out (आवर्जित) in the sun-set worship offered by the Siddhas journeying in the sky, flowed colouring the quarters and possessing the hue of safflower (कुसुम्भं) as though it (juice) were the perspiration of the Evening delighted at her obeisance to S'iva. तारापथे प्रस्थिताः सिद्धाः (semidivine beings) तैः दत्तं दिनकरस्य अस्तमये अर्घ्यं तस्मिन् आवर्जिते (*adj.* of द्रवे). अर्घ्यम्--materials of worship, such as water, sandal &c. रञ्जिताः ककुभः (दिशः) येन (*adj.* of ०द्रवे). कुसुम्भस्य इव भाः यस्य. Connect स्रवति (pr.p. loc. sing.) with ०द्रवे. पिनाकिने प्रणतिः तया मुदिता &c. As सन्ध्या is red, her perspiration also would look red. The red sandal juice is fancied to be the perspiration of Evening. वन्दारु...लोके when the world of ब्रह्मा, where crowds of the best of worshipping sages folded their hands in evening adoration, seemed as though all the lotus beds had come to wait upon that from which Brahmā sprang. For वन्दारु see शरारु above p. 23. वन्दारूणां (bowing) मुनीनां वृन्दारकाः (श्रेष्ठाः) तेषां वृन्दं तेन बध्यमानं सन्ध्याञ्जलिवनं यस्मिन्. ब्रह्मणः उत्पत्तिः यस्मात् तत् ब्रह्मोत्पत्ति कमलं तस्य सेवायै आगतः सकलानां कमलानां आकरः यस्मिन्. The hands folded in सन्ध्या adoration look like lotus buds; hence the उत्प्रेक्षा in ब्रह्मोत्पत्ति०. समुच्चा...ब्रह्मणि when Brahmā had uttered the Vedic hymns of the third Savana. समुच्चारितं तृतीयसवनस्य ब्रह्म (वेदः) येन. There were three सवन (sacrifices at which libations of सोम were offered) प्रातःसवन, माध्यन्दिनसवन and तृतीयसवन. The meaning may also be 'when Brāhmaṇas had uttered &c.' Here the singular ब्रह्मणि is used for the whole class. Some taken सवन in the sense of स्नान.

ज्वलित...मन्दिरेषु when the houses of the seven sages had their courts full (जटाल) of the flames of blazing sacrificial (वैतान) fires, as if in them (houses) was begun the lustration of the camp that was a means of securing the performance of one's duties. ज्वलिताः वैतानाः ज्वलनाः तेषां ज्वालाः ताभिः जटालानि अजिराणि येषाम्. आरब्धं धर्मसाधनस्य शिबिरस्य नीराजनं येषु or आरब्धं धर्मसाधनाय शिबिरस्य &c. नीराजन was a religious and military ceremony, performed by kings and generals before they took the field; it consisted in waving lights before the components of an army. As sacrificial fires blazed in the houses, the poet fancies that नीराजन was being performed over the houses (which looked like camps), the object for which the houses were erected being धर्मसाधन and not जयसाधन or अर्थसाधन. Another sense also is suggested. साधन means 'army'. An army is housed in a camp (शिबिर) over which नीराजन may be performed. For सप्तर्षि see above p. 19. C and T translate 'as though a camp lustration had commenced in an army devoted to Dharma'. This is not correct and does not bring out the उत्प्रेक्षा properly. अघमर्षणेन मुषितः किल्बिषविषगदः (किल्बिषं पापं एव विषगदः) येषां ते ०गदाः उल्लाघाः लघवश्च. अघ...यतिषु when the hermits had light hearts, being free from the poison disease of sin that was removed by the अघमर्षण hymn. उल्लाघ convalescent. 'उल्लाघो निर्गतो गदात्' इत्यमरः. A person who has been taking medicines against poison becomes convalescent and light—hearted. अघमर्षण is a term applied to the hymn (of three verses) beginning with 'ऋतं च सत्यं चाभीद्धात्तपसोऽध्यजायत' (ऋग्वेद X. 190). 'सर्वैनसामपध्वंसि जप्यं त्रिष्वघमर्षणम्' इत्यमरः. सन्ध्योपासनाय आसीनानां तपस्विनां पङ्क्त्या (row, line) पूतं पुलिनं (sandy bed) यस्य (*adj.* of ०जले). प्लवमानाः नलिनयोनियानहंसाः एव हासः तेन दन्तुरिताः ऊर्मयः यस्य the waves of which were furrowed by the smile-like हंसs, the vehicles of ब्रह्मा, floating thereon. हंस is the वाहन of ब्रह्मा. हंसs are white and so resemble हास which is poetically described as white. One who smiles shows his teeth. The हंसs sailing on the waves divide them into crests that look like teeth. जल...वने when the beds of कुमुदs (night-lotuses) were about to expand, causing delight to bees and sweetly perfumed with their own honey, that (beds) were the umbrellas of water nymphs and were the private mansions of the wives of the tribes of birds. Water nymphs dwelt under the shelter of कुमुदs and birds also made them their haunts. कृता मधुपानां मुत् येन. There is another sense also. When Kumudas open (*i. e.* at night) those who drink wine (मधुप) are exhilarated. मुमुदिषमाणे *pr. p.* of the desiderative of मुद् to delight or expand with joy. दिवसा...यूथे when the crowds of flamingoes, delighted by their drinking bout on the sweet honey of the day-lotuses that were going to languish as the day closed, were about to sleep, fanning the blue-lotus (राजीवं) lakes with rows of their flapping (धुत) wings and turning their necks into coils in order to be scratched by the soft lotus stalks. दिवसस्य अवसाने ताम्यतां तामरसानां मधुरं मधु तस्य सपीतिः (सहपानं) तया प्रीते. 'सपीतिः स्त्री तुल्यपानम्' इत्यमरः. सुषुप्सति *pr. p.* loc. sing. of the desiderative base of स्वप्. ०काण्डेन कण्डूयनं तदर्थं कुण्डलिता कन्धरा येन. The flamingoes bent their neck in a circle round the lotus stalks in order to get it scratched. धुतानां पक्षाणां राज्या वीजितं राजीवसरः येन. तट...नभस्वति when a slight (तनीयस्) evening breeze, resembling the sigh of Night, began to blow, making the river grey with the pollen of the flowers of creepers growing on the bank, and bearing the perfume of the jasmine flowers in the braids (धम्मिल्लः) of the matrous (पुरन्ध्रि) of the city of Siddhas. ०धूलिभिः धूसरिता सरित् येन (qualifies नभस्वति). सरति *pr. p. loc. sing.* of सृ. ०पुरन्ध्रीणां धम्मिल्लेषु मल्लिकाः तासां गन्धं गृह्णन्ति इति. मल्लिका is a flower that opens in the evening. सङ्कोचेन उदञ्चन्तः (erected) उच्चाः (stiff) केसराः तेषां कोटिभिः सङ्कटः कुशेशयानां कमलानां कोशः तस्य कोटरः एव कुटी तस्यां शेते इति—that lay in the hut in the form of the cavity of the lotuses that were full of the tips of filaments high and stiff by the closing (of the petals). As the lotuses contracted at sunset, their filaments that were loose became straightened up and barred the way of escape out of the lotuses, the bees being confined inside as in a hut. नृत्तो...गणे the constellations of stars, presenting the appearance of the bunches of कुटज buds in the forest of the matted hair of S'iva tossed up in dance, were scattered in clusters in the sky. स्तबकयति a denominative verb from स्तबक. The clusters of stars looked like कुटज buds, which are white. कुटज is a wild flower and hence the word अटवी is put in. The stars appeared scattered about. शिव is represented as fond of dancing. When शिव danced, the flowers in his hair would be scattered about. सन्ध्या...तमसि darkness, that was not yet full grown, that was reddish with the continuance of twilight, that had the colour of the skin of a ripe Tāla fruit and that was thick (मेदुर) like a dark cloud, closed round the earth. सन्ध्यायाः अनुबन्धः तेन ताम्रे—twilight had not yet completely vanished and so a slight rosy hue still persisted and was mixed up with the darkness. परिणमत् तालफलं तस्य त्वचः इव त्विट् (कान्तिः) यस्य. कालमेघ also means 'the clouds at the end of the world.' नवं वयः यस्य. तरुण...प्रकरे when numerous lamps, capable of piercing (पाटनं) the veil of fresh (not yet fullgrown *i. e.* not deep or pitchy) darkness, began to blaze forth, being a cluster of champaka buds serving as the ear-ornaments of the lady of Night. The flame of a lamp is like a चम्पक bud. Therefore the lamps lit at night are said to be the कर्णपूरs of the lady (Night). प्रतनु...मुखे when the region of Indra (*i. e.* the east), pale with the lovely light of the few rays of the moon and appearing like the sandy islet of the Jumna slightly dry and free from its blue waters, reduced the darkness. In the east the moon was about to rise. The first rays of the moon lessened the darkness and the east lookd grey (white-dark). The east therefore resembled the sandy bed of the Jumna from which the waters had just receded, the sand being white, but the remnants of water being dark. The water of the Jumna is dark as compared with the Ganges. प्रतनु (slight) तुहिनकिरणस्य शीतरश्मेः किरणाः तेषां लावण्यं तस्य आलोकेन पाण्डुनि. आश्यानं (partially dried) नीलनीरेण मुक्तं कालिन्दीकूलं तस्य वालुकायुक्तं पुलिनं, पुलिनं इव आचरति पुलिनायते. The reading बालपुलिनायमाने for वालुका० is better, as in कूलवालुका० there are too many words. बालपुलिनं would mean 'a sandy spot just raised out of water.' शतक्रतोः (इन्द्रस्य) इदं शातक्रतवम्. कृशयति *pr. p. loc.* sing. of कृशयति denominative verb from कृश. खमुचि...तमसि when darkness that had blackened (मेचकित) the lake of expanded blue lotuses, that (तमः) was a veritable cluster of the tresses of the S'abarî in the form of the night, that (तमः) had the colour of the wings of a jay (चाषः), was leaving the sky and was being dissolved, being disturbed by having its hair seized by the rays of the moon, like the mind of a proud beauty. खं आकाशं मुञ्चति इति ख०. At the approaching rise of the moon darkness left the sky and was massed on the earth. मेचकितं ०सरः येन. शश...विले and विलीयमाने apply both to तमसि and ०मनसि. शशधरस्य कराणां (किरणानां) निकरेण कचग्रहः तेन आविले. When a person is seized by the hair, he is harshly and forcibly dealt with. The moon's rays forcibly drove away darkness. आविल turbid, muddy. शशधर...मनसि—the idea here is:—a proud young lady, being offended with her husband, resolved upon accepting no reconciliation. When the moon caressed her hair with its rays, her resolve began to waver and at last her proud mind gave way (विलीयमान) and she was quickly reconciled. The word कर also means 'hand' and the clause suggests 'when her tresses were stroked by the gentle hand of her husband by way of reconciliation, she wavered'. शर्वरी (निशा) एवं शबरी तस्याः चिकुरचयः कुन्तलभारः. शबरी is a woman of an aboriginal tribe, such as the Bhils. Both शर्वरी and शबरी are dark and further the two words are almost the same in sound. चाषपक्षस्य इव त्विट् यस्य. उदिते...श्वेतभानौ when the moon (श्वेतभानुः), now risen, assumed a red form (वपुः) as though covered (निचित) with the mass of blood dropping from his own deer slain by the weapon (हेति) of the sharp paw of the lion (हरिः) in the cave of the slopes (कटकं) of the peaks of the Rising Mountain, a red form that was as though the lower lip of the damsel of Night possessed of glow at the rise (of the moon). The disc of the moon was red when it rose. There are two उत्प्रेक्षाs in this clause. The first up to निचितमिव is concerned with redness and the second (in उदय...धरमिव) is concerned with the red orb of the moon. The poet fancies that the natural redness of the disc at moon-rise is due to the blood &c. For the deer in the moon see notes p. 22. उदयगिरि a fabulous mountain in the east from behind which the sun and the moon were supposed to come up. The red and round orb of the moon appears like the red and full lip of a young lady. So the poet fancies it to be the lip of the lady of Night. The word उदयरागधरम् conveys two ideas. The lip of a fair woman possesses the same redness (रागः) as is seen (in the moon) at moon-rise. The night also possesses rosy hue (राग) at moon-rise (on the eastern horizon). C and T translate 'the form of the Lord of white splendour... assumed the glow of the Udaya mountain, resembling the lip of the nymph of night'. This does not appear to us to be correct. वपुः is the object of धारयति and ०धरमधरम् is in apposition to वपुः. अचलात् (पर्वतात् अर्थात् उदयगिरेः) च्युताः चन्द्रकान्तस्य जलधाराः ताभिः धौते. From the चन्द्रकान्त stone water oozes at the rise of the moon. ध्वान्ते = तमसि. गो...मण्डले when the orb of the moon had begun to fill the ocean, as though it (orb) were a great ivory conduit with the shape of a crocodile's mouth bearing a stream of milk dropping from the world of cows. The bright rays of the moon fell on the ocean which rose in a high tide. The streaming rays of the moon looked like a stream of milk. The pale white moon looked like ivory (hence दन्तमय). The orb of the moon presented the appearance of the end of a conduit pipe (प्रणाल:) as large as the mouth of a crocodile. गो also means 'rays'. दन्तमय: मकरमुख: (मकरस्य इव मुखं यस्य) महाप्रणाल: तस्मिन्. स्पष्टे... समये when the evening time was clear *i. e.* when the night had advanced beyond the stage of dusk or twilight. त्रि...जल्पन्ती my tongue prattling to thee feels shame before thee that are clever enough to instruct the three worlds. यादृश्य:—connect with दैवस्य वामा: वृत्तय:. जानास्येव...वृत्तय: thou knowest already what the crooked actions (वृत्तय:, ways) of Fate are, actions that are unsteady (विसंस्थुल), that are unkind like the wicked even to worthy men, changing in a moment, not to be resisted and unpleasant. The word वामा: also means 'handsome women, or women in general'. Women also, according to the estimation of many people, are unsteady, changeful to a degree, heartless hard to be resisted (when once they set their heart on achieving an object). Compare 'विमुक्तधर्माश्चपलास्तीक्ष्णा भेदकरा: स्त्रिय:॥' अरण्यकाण्ड 45.30. 'पौंश्चल्याच्चलचित्ताच्च नैस्नेह्याच्च स्वभावत: ।' मनुस्मृति 9.15. न रमणीया: does not well apply to women. Hence the words should have been omitted in the text (as B does). निष्कारणा...पतन्ती even the slightest insult, when without cause, coming from an inferior person, disturbs the mind even of a high-souled person. निकार: insult or wrong. कणिका a particle. Here सरस्वती is the high-souled person and दुर्वासस the inferior man. मानस means also 'the मानस lake.' It may become turbid by a particle (of dust) falling in it. अन...सिच्यमान:—sprinkled with ceaseless tears (with शोक:); अनवरतं नयनं यस्य एतादृशं जलं तेन सिच्यमान: sprinkled with water that is carried incessantly (with तरु:). विपल्लव:—विपद: (of adversity) लव: यस्मिन् in which there is a slight misfortune *i. e.* caused by slight misfortune (with शोक:); विपल्लव: void of foliage (with तरु:). प्ररोहति increases (with शोक:); puts forth shoots. The more one dwells on one's misfortune and sheds tears, the greater the pangs of it. अतिसुकुमारं applies both to जनं and ०कुसुमम्. सन्तापपरमाणव: atoms of affliction *i. e.* slight affliction (with जनम्); atoms of heat *i. e.* slight heat (with ०कुसुमम्). महतां on the great; of large size (elephants). अणु: small (with क्लेश:); with a fine edge (with सृणि:). अणुरपि...लम् even a slight affliction is sufficient to torment them (the great) as the piercing goad is sufficient to humble (the big elephants). कदर्थनम् is a noun from the denominative verb कदर्थयति, which is formed from कदर्थ.

'कोः कत्तत्पुरुषेऽचि' पा. 6. 3. 101 (कु when followed in a तत्पुरुष by a word beginning with a vowel becomes कत्). कुत्सितः अर्थः कदर्थः. अलम् in the sense of 'sufficient or able' governs the dative. सहजः स्नेहपाशः (स्नेहः पाशः इव) तस्य ग्रन्थिना बन्धनं येषां or यासाम्. सहज...भूमयः our native home, which is linked to us like a kinsman by fast (*lit.* knotted) ties of natural affection, is hard to give up. जन्मभूमिः also means 'mother'. दारुणः terrible (with ०विरहः); of wood (with ०पातः). Construe दारुणः ०विरहः हृदयं दारयति ०पातः दारुणः हृदयं (central part) इव. क्रकचपातः the stroke of a saw. संस्तुत familiar, dear. अभूमि...सवानाम् you are not the soil for the shoots of the poison plant of sorrow. The idea is that sorrow should not take a footing in you. **'क्ष्वेडस्तु** गरलं **विषम्'** इत्यमरः. अपि च...शुचाम् what occasion have the wise for grief, when in front of and behind us stand our powerful deeds, whether good or bad, that rule us and yield fruit to us? It is our own actions, good or bad, that produce the vicissitudes of our lives. If adversities assail us, that is due to the bad actions of our former lives. If we were put into trouble without any fault on our part, then there would be room for sorrow. But we know that under the inexorable law of *Karma* there is no such thing as chance. The idea of तिष्ठ...पृष्ठतश्च is:—It is our own *Karma* that determines the rewards that we are to enjoy and *Karma* encompasses us on all sides. शुचाम् is genitive plural of शुच्. प्रष्ठ=पुरःसर. 'प्रष्ठोऽग्रगामिनि' पा. 8. 3. 92 (प्रतिष्ठते इति प्रष्ठो गौः । अग्रतो गच्छतीत्यर्थः । सि. कौ.). Compare for the idea 'यादृशं कुरुते कर्म तादृशं फलमश्नुते' रामायण उत्तरकाण्ड 15. 23. त्रिभुवनस्य मङ्गलं तदर्थं एकं (केवलं) कमलम्. अपवित्रं कुर्वन्ति अपवित्रयन्ति. तदलम् therefore enough (of this weeping). अवतितीर्षति desires to descend. पुण्यभाजि—that will be blest (by your descent thereon). तपोवनधामसु=तपोवनस्थानेषु. तपस्यन्ती performing austerities. अयं सखीजनः means सावित्री herself. उप...पेशलः skilful in serving you and agreeable (पेशल) on account of familiarity with you (commencing from) playing in the dust together. The idea is they were intimate playmates since early childhood. न अन्यत् शरणं (रक्षितृ) यस्याः सा ०शरणा who seeks no other refuge (than S'iva). प्रतिपद्यस्व resort to (the object being त्र्यम्बकम्). सर्व...तारम् the author of all lores. धातारम् the supporter of all. **स्वश्रेयसे** for your own welfare. Connect this with प्रतिपद्यस्व. स्वचरणरजसा पवित्रिताः त्रिदशाः असुराश्च येन (adj. of त्र्यम्बकम्). सुधासूतिः (सुधायाः अमृतस्य सूतिः यस्मात्) चन्द्रः एव कलिका तया कल्पितः कर्णावतंसः यस्य (**adj. of** त्र्यम्बकम्)—whose ear-ornament is formed by the crescent (*lit.* bud) of the moon. त्रिभुवनगुरुम् to be honoured by the three worlds. त्र्यम्बकं = शिवम्. The reading of A and C दातारं श्वःश्रेयसस्य means 'who bestowes future happiness'. श्वः tomorrow *i. e.* future. From Bāṇa's usual style we can infer that he wrote as in the text (repeating धातारम्). श्वः-श्रेयसस्य is rather an unusual combination and ungrammatical. ते = तुभ्यम्. शापेन शोकः तस्य विरतिम् (cessation). वितरिष्यति दास्यति. ब्रह्मा had already declared (text p. 5 l. 9) that the curse would end with the birth of a son. By S'iva's favour that happy event would follow in a very short time.

P. 7 ll. 11-27 **एवमुक्ता...निर्जगाम.** मुक्ताः मुक्ताफलवत् धवलाः लोचनजललवाः यया that shed tears bright like pearls. केवलं...हृदयम् it is only the happiness of serving Brahmā (to which I shall be a stranger till the curse lasts) that makes my heart soft (*i. e.* makes my heart wistful and sad). भुवि...धामानि the places on the earth where Dharma can be performed. समाधि-साधनानि means of abstract meditation; or the word may be taken as in apposition to स्थानानि, meaning 'places that will help in abstract meditation'. समाधि is the eighth and last अङ्ग of योग. 'यमनियमासनप्राणायामप्रत्याहारधारणाध्यानसमाधयोऽष्टावङ्गानि' योगसूत्र II. 29. योग is defined as 'योगश्चित्तवृत्तिनिरोधः' योगसूत्र. I. 2. रणरणकेन उपनीतः प्रजागरः यस्यै who was kept awake by agitation. अनिमीलिते (not closed) लोचने यस्याः. त्रिभुवनशेखरे head jewel of the three worlds. खण...वपुषि whose form was red, as though with the blood (क्षतजम्) scattered from the mouths of his (the sun's) own horses pierced by the rough (खर) and clanking bit (खलीनः-नम्). The redness of the morning sun is fancied to be due to the blood &c. Vide a similar conceit above in the case of the moon (text p. 6 l. 15). उद...मणौ—the resplendent sun appeared like a crest jewel of the eastern mountain. जरन् कृकवाकुः (कुक्कुटः) तस्य चूडा तद्वत् अरुणः अरुणः पुरःसरः यस्य who is ushered by Aruṇa rosy like an old cock's comb. Aruṇa is a personification of the ruddy sky before sunrise. He is the charioteer of the sun. 'कृकवाकुस्ताम्रचूडः कुक्कुटश्चरणायुधः' इत्यमरः (कृकेण शीरोग्रीवेण वक्ति—क्षीर०). विरोचने = सूर्ये. नाति...र्ती not being far away (from the place where सरस्वती passed a sleepless night). विविच्य having reflected. पिता...पालः the keeper of the tribe of Haṁsas that are the conveyances (विमानः-नम्) of Brahmā. अपरवक्त्र is a metre defined as 'अयुजि ननरला गुरुः समे तदपर-

वक्त्रमिदं नजौ जरौ' (in the first and third pādas there are eleven letters *i. e.* two तगणs, a रगण, one लघु letter and one गुरु letter and in the 2nd and 4th पादs there are twelve letters, the गणs being न, ज, ज, र). An आख्यायिका must contain verses in the वक्त्र and अपरवक्त्र metres. Vide Intro. XX. तर...त्सुकाम् why do you make thy anxious eye tremulous ? अक...लालिते (vocative) you that are fondled by dwelling with Brahmā whose mind is pure (with सरस्वती); that are fondled by dwelling in the pure मानस lake (with कलहंसी). अकलुषं मानसं यस्य स ०मानसः ब्रह्मा तेन वासः &c. अकलुषं मानसं (सरः) तस्मिन् वासः &c. अवतर वापिकाम् descend into the well (with कलहंसी). The word वापिका suggests the world of mortals where we have to reap as we sow (वप्). The कलहंसी finds it hard to descend into a pond after being long familiar with the pure मानस lake; so सरस्वती found it hard to descend to earth after enjoying the pure atmosphere of Heaven. पङ्कजालयम् the abode of lotuses *i. e.* the lake (with ०हंसी); Brahmā (with सरस्वती). पङ्कजं आलयः यस्य. Brahmā sprang from a lotus. अह...युक्ता it was as if I that was asked by him (or censured by him). कृतः महीतलावतरणस्य सङ्कल्पः (resolve) यया. वियोगेन विक्लवम् (distressed). परित्यज्य—the object is ०परिजनम्. ज्ञाति...गणस्य not minding her kindred. अवगणा (*adj.* of सरस्वती) separated from her companions (अवयुक्ता गणात्). कथमपि with great difficulty. अनुनयेन निवर्तितः अनुयायिव्रतिव्रातः यया—who sent back with courteous words the crowd of devotees that followed her.

P. 7 l. 28—**P. 8** l. 30 **ततः क्रमेण...वाहयत्.** The first sentence is ततः क्रमेण...मन्दाकिनीमनुसरन्ती मर्त्यलोकमवततार (P. 8 l. 12). ध्रुव...धराम्—this and the following clauses qualify मन्दाकिनीम् below. ध्रुवप्रवृत्ताम् (1) that springs from Vishṇu or that flows from the firmament or from the ध्रुव constellation; that starts from a post. The Ganges is said to have sprung from the toe of Vishṇu. See 'श्वेतगङ्गावर्तपाण्डुरं पदमिव त्रिविक्रमस्य' हर्ष० 7th उच्छ्वास. Compare 'वामपादाम्बुजाङ्गुष्ठे नखस्रोतोविनिर्गता । विष्णोर्बिभर्ति यां भक्त्या शिरसाहर्निशं ध्रुवः ॥' विष्णुपु० II. 8. 10; see also मार्कण्डेयपु० 56. 1. ध्रुव is a name of विष्णु. Vide विष्णुसहस्रनाम in अनुशासनपर्व 149. 'स्थविष्ठः स्थविरो ध्रुवः' verse 19. विष्णु's third step is ध्रुव (constellation) and as the Ganges springs from the foot of विष्णु, it may be said to be ध्रुवप्रवृत्त. 'ऊर्ध्वोत्तरमृषिभ्यस्तु ध्रुवो यत्र व्यवस्थितः । एतद्विष्णुपदं दिव्यं तृतीयं व्योम्नि भास्वरम् ॥' विष्णुपुराण 2. 8. 99. आकाश is ध्रुव (*i. e.* नित्य) according to the नैयायिकs. A cow also starts from a post (ध्रुवः) to which it is tied. 'स्थाणुर्वा ना ध्रुवः शङ्कुः' इत्यमरः. अधो धावमानाः

धवलाः पयोधराः (मेघाः यस्याः) the clouds from which (celestial Ganges) are white and stream downwards (towards the earth). The water of the Ganges being white, the clouds are supposed to be white. अधो...धराम् (with धेनु) the white udders of which stream downwards. The Ganges is called धर्मधेनु because it enables one to secure holiness and merit. उद्धुरः (unchecked, loud) ध्वनिः यस्याः. अन्धकमथनः शिवः तस्य मौलिः (शिरः) तस्मिन् मालतीमालिकाम्. The celestial Ganges fell on the head of शिव in its descent to the earth to purify the sons of सगर reduced to ashes by Kapila. Both the Ganges and a wreath of Mālatī are white. The demon अन्धक was slain by S'iva when the former attempted to carry off पारिजात from heaven. See रामायण III. 30. 27 'रुद्रेणेव विनिर्दग्धः श्वेतारण्ये यथान्धकः.' आलीयमानैः वालखिल्यैः रुद्धं रोधः यस्याः the banks of which were covered (or obstructed) by the वालखिल्यs that settled down upon it. The वालखिल्यs were 60000 diminutive sages born of the प्रजापति क्रतु and his wife सन्नति as large as a man's thumb. 'षष्टियानि सहस्राणि मुनीनामूर्ध्वरेतसाम् । अङ्गुष्ठपर्वमात्राणां ज्वलद्भास्करतेजसाम् ॥' विष्णुपुराण I. 10. 12. Vide मार्कण्डेयपुराण 52. 24-25. Compare 'अनेकशो वालखिल्यकदम्बककृतसन्ध्योपासनं (सरः)' कादम्बरी p. 123 (of P.). अरुन्धत्या धौता तारवी (तरोः इयं) त्वक् यस्याम्. तारवत्वक् bark of a tree (used as a garment). अरुन्धती, the wife of वसिष्ठ, is a type of holiness and conjugal fidelity. Note the high praise of her in the उत्तररामचरित IV. 10. 'यया पूतंमन्यो निधिरपि पवित्रस्य महसः &c'. Read त्वङ्गत्तुङ्ग for त्वङ्गत्तङ्ग. त्वङ्गन्तः तुङ्गाः तरङ्गाः तेषु तरन्तः तरलतराः ताराः तारकाः यस्याम्—that had the tremulous bright (तार) stars crossing over high surging (त्वङ्गत्) waves. It should be remembered that it is the celestial Ganges that is being described. तापसैः विकीर्णं (scattered) विरलं तिलोदकं तेन पुलकितानि (bristling) पुलिनानि यस्याः. तिलाश्च उदकं च तिलोदकं तेषां समाहारः (समाहारद्वन्द्व). पुलकित—from पुलक (=रोमाञ्च) with the affix इत according to 'तदस्य सञ्जातं तारकादिभ्य इतच्' पा. 5. 2. 36. Sesame and water were offered to the dead. वितीर्ण (given) is also a good reading. Note मनुस्मृति III 207 and 210. 'अवकाशेषु चोक्षेषु नदीतीरेषु चैव हि । विविक्तेषु च तुष्यन्ति दत्तेन पितरः सदा ॥ तेषामुदकमानीय सपवित्रांस्तिलानपि । अग्नौ कुर्यादनुज्ञातो ब्राह्मणो ब्राह्मणैः सह ॥'. आप्लवनेन (स्नानेन) पूतः पितामहः (ब्रह्मा) तेन पातिताः पितृपिण्डाः (पितृभ्यो दत्ताः पिण्डाः) तैः पाण्डुरितः पारः यस्याः. पितृ here must be taken in the sense of 'a particular class of divine beings' and not in the sense of 'father' or 'dead ancestors'. There is some incongruity in ascribing to Brahmā human actions such as पितृपिण्डदान. The balls of rice are white and hence the word पाण्डुरित is used. 'अक्रोधनाः शौचपराः सततं ब्रह्मचारिणः। न्यस्तशस्त्रा महाभागाः पितरः **पूर्वदेवताः** ॥' मनु० III. 192. See the following verses for various classes of Pitṛis. पर्यन्ते सुप्ताः सप्तर्षयः तेषां कुशशयनेन सूचितः सूर्यग्रहसूतके उपवासः यस्याम्—on which the fast due to the impurity (सूतकं) caused by a solar eclipse was indicated by the Kus'a bed of the seven sages sleeping nearby. An eclipse causes impurity and people observe a fast before it and on the day of eclipse. Compare धर्मसिन्धु (परिच्छेद I) 'त्रिरात्रमेकरात्रं वा समुपोष्य ग्रहणे स्नानदानाद्यनुष्ठाने महाफलम्, एकरात्रपक्षे ग्रहणदिनात्पूर्वदिने उपवास इति केचित् ग्रहणसम्बन्धाहोरात्र उपवास इत्यपरे'. So निर्णयसिन्धु (परिच्छेद I) says 'सर्वेषामेव वर्णानां **सूतकं** राहुदर्शने। स्नात्वा कर्माणि कुर्वीत शृतमन्नं विवर्जयेदिति हेमाद्रौ षट्त्रिंशन्मतात्'. A person in impurity was to sleep on a spare bed of mats, grass &c. Note धर्मसिन्धु (परिच्छेद III) 'तृणकटास्तीर्णभूमौ पृथक्शयीरन्कम्बलाद्यास्तीर्णभूमौ.' आचमनेन शुचिः शचीपतिः (इन्द्रः) तेन मुच्यमानः अर्चनकुसुमानां निकरः (समूहः) तेन शाराम्. The flowers being of various colours, the river looked variegated. The voluptuous Indra did not care to bathe, as Brahmā did. शिवपुरात् आपतितं निर्माल्यमन्दारदाम यस्याम् in which was dropped from the city of S'iva a garland of मन्दार flowers that had been already offered in worship. For क, see above p. 12. निर्माल्यं remains of flowers and other things offered to deities, flowers that are used and cast off. मन्दार is one of the five trees of Paradise. 'पञ्चैते देवतरवो **मन्दारः** पारिजातकः। सन्तानः कल्पवृक्षश्च पुंसि वा हरिचन्दनम् ॥' इत्यमरः. अना...दृषदम् that cleft with ease the stones in the caves of Mandara. The celestial Ganges had such a powerful stream that it cleft stones. मन्दर is a mountain to the east of Meru. Compare मार्क० 56. 3-5 'मेरुकूटतटान्तेभ्यो निपतन्ती विवर्तिता ॥ विकीर्यमाणसलिला निरालम्बा पपात सा। **मन्दराद्येषु पादेषु** प्रविभक्तोदका समम् ॥ चतुर्ष्वपि **पपाताम्बु**विभिन्नाद्रिशिलोच्चया ॥.' अनेकनाकनायकानां निकायाः तेषां कामिन्यः तासां कुचकलशैः विलुलितः विग्रहः (शरीरं) यस्याः which was tremulous with the jar-like bosoms of the beautiful wives of the hosts (निकायः) of the chief leaders of heaven. The beauties bathed in the Ganges and caused ripples. ग्राहाणां ग्राव्णां च ग्रामः (समूहः) तस्मिन् स्खलनं तेन मुखरितं स्रोतः यस्याः the stream of which resounded as it stumbled over numerous crocodiles and stones. सुषुम्णास्रुता शशिनः सुधा तस्याः शीकराणां स्तबकेन तारकितं तीरं यस्याः—the banks of which were spotted with clusters of the spray of the nectar of the moon flowing from the सुषुम्णा ray. It was believed that the waxing of the moon was due to a ray of the sun called सुषुम्ण. We should read सुषुम्ण०,

music of a lute. मन्दीकृता मन्दाकिनीद्युतिः येन that obscured the lustre of the Ganges. उपकण्ठभूमयः places in the neighbourhood. पक्ष...मे my heart has taken a liking to stay here. अभिनन्दितं (approved) वचनं यस्याः (*adj*. of सरस्वती). तथेति is to be connected with अभिनन्दित. सावित्री approved of सरस्वती's choice. तया = सावित्र्या (सह). ०मण्डपे...बबन्ध she fixed upon a bower as her house. उच्चितानि (gathered) अर्चनाय कुसुमानि यया. पुलिनपृष्ठे प्रतिष्ठापितं सैकतं शिवलिङ्गं यया. पञ्चब्रह्माणि पुरःसराणि यस्याः (*adj*. of पुष्पिकाम्) that was preceded by the पञ्चब्रह्म prayer. This is a prayer recited by the Brahmaṇas at the time of smearing the body with sacred ashes. The prayer is addressed to सद्योजात, वामदेव, तत्पुरुष, अघोर and ईशान. See ऋग्वेदि-ब्रह्मकर्म (भस्मधारणविधि). Compare शिवस्तुति 3rd verse '**महेश** महितोसि **तत्पुरुष** पूरुषाग्र्यो भवा**नघोर** रिपुघोर तेऽनवम **वामदेवा**ञ्जलिः । नमः **सपदिजात** ते त्वमिति **पञ्चरूपो**चित प्रपञ्चचयपञ्चवृन्मम मनस्तमस्ताडय ॥'. सम्यङ् मुद्राबन्धः तेन विहितः परिकरः यस्याः (*adj*. of ०पुष्पिकाम्) which was preceded by the ceremony of properly intertwining the fingers and hands in worship. परिकरः 'beginning'. On मुद्राबन्ध note 'मुद्राविमुक्तहस्तेन क्रियते कर्म दैविकम् । यदि तन्निष्फलं तस्मात्कर्म मुद्रान्वितश्चरेत् ॥'. ध्रुवा गीतिः गर्भे यस्याः (*adj*. of ०पुष्पिकाम्) between the intervals of which she sang the ध्रुवा song. 'गीतिस्रुग्भेदयोर्ध्रुवा' शाश्वतः 4. The song was probably in the ध्रुवताल. अवनि...ध्यायन्ती contemplating all the eight forms *viz*. the earth, the wind, water (वनं), the sky, the fire, the sun (तपनः), the moon and the sacrificer. These are said to be the eight forms of शिव. Vide the first verse of the शाकुन्तल. अष्टपुष्पिका a bunch of eight flowers (with referene to the eight forms). Compare कादम्बरी 'अतिरोषणतया कदाचिद्दुर्न्यस्ताष्टपुष्पिकापातोत्पादितक्रोधेन' p. 227 of P. The commentators on the कादम्बरी say 'बकं द्रोणं च दुर्धूरं सुमना पाटला तथा । पद्ममुत्पलगोसूर्यमष्टौ पुष्पाणि शङ्करे ॥'. सं० also explains that अष्टपुष्पिका refers to the eight acts of worship each of which may be metaphorically called पुष्प. They are:—पार्थिवपुष्प *i. e.* smearing the deity with some fragrant substance, because गन्ध is the special quality of पृथ्वी; आप्यपुष्प *i.e.* bathing with water or milk, as रस is the special quality of अप्; तैजस० *i. e.* waving lights; वायवीय *i. e.* applying cooling unguents, as स्पर्श is the special quality of वायु; आकाशीय *i. e.* playing on musical instruments and singing, as शब्द is the special गुण of आकाश; मानस *i. e.* contemplation of the god S'iva; बौद्ध *i. e.* a firm idea that S'iva is all pervading, as the विषय of बुद्धि is निश्चय; आहङ्कारिक *i. e.* the knowledge of the non-difference of the soul from the Supreme, expressed by the Upanishads in the words

'अहं ब्रह्मास्मि'. अय...तेन that was obtained without effort. अमृत... स्वादिम्ना that tended (*lit.* desired) to surpass even nectar by its sweetness. अति...माणेन *pr. p.* of the desiderative base of शी with अति. स्वादिम्ना *Instru. sing.* of स्वादिमन् which is formed like पिङ्गलिमन् (notes p. 23). शरीर...रोत् she sustained her body. अतिवाहितः (passed) दिवसः यया. कल्पितं पल्लवानां शयनं यया.

P. 8 l. 31—**P. 9** l. 12 **एव...सन्ददर्श.** याम ... रवौ when the sun had gone up (in the sky) only for one watch. यामः means a period of three hours. 'द्वौ यामप्रहरौ समौ' इत्यमरः. ककुभि = दिशि. प्रतिशब्दैः (by the echoes) पूरितं वनगह्वरं (वनगुहा) येन. तुरङ्ग... ह्रादम् the sound (ह्रादः) of the neighing of horses. विकच...सङ्घातं mass of dust grey like the inner leaves of the blossoming Ketakî. नातिदवीयसि (*loc. sing.* of दवीयस् which is the comparative form of दूर) not very far from her. क्रमेण च—the principal sentence is क्रमेण च...पदातिबलेन सनाथमश्ववृन्दं सन्ददर्श. सामीप्येन उपजायमाना अभिव्यक्तिः यस्य that became distinctly visible the nearer it came. This qualifies अश्ववृन्दम्. शफरो...प्लवमानं floating in the dust grey like the belly of a fish, as though it were a school of crocodiles floating in water. शफ...सरे (with पयसि) means 'grey with the bellies of fishes'. प्लवमानं goes with ०वृन्दं below. पुरः प्रधावमानेन—this and the following clauses in the instrumental qualify ०बलेन below. प्रलम्बैः कुटिलैः कचपल्लवैः घटितं ललाटे जूटकं येन that had on their foreheads a mass of long curling hair. सं० says 'घटितललाटजूटा दाक्षिणात्येषु वेशः.' धवल...भित्तिना whose ample cheeks were smiling (*i. e.* bright) with the lustre of the white ear-ornaments (दन्तपत्रिका). पिनद्धाः कृष्णागुरुपङ्ककल्कस्य च्छुरणेन कृष्णशबलकषायाः कञ्चुकाः येन that had girt themselves in jackets dark, variegated and fragrant (कषाय) by being smeared with the paste (कल्कः-म्) of black aloe-wood. पिनद्ध is *past p. p.* of नह् with अपि, अ being elided in accordance with 'वष्टि भागुरिरल्लोपमवाप्योरुपसर्गयोः'. उत्तरीयेण कृतं शिरोवेष्टनं यस्य that had made their upper garments into turbans. वाम...कटकेन that had bright (स्पष्ट) golden bracelets (कटकः-कम्) placed on their left fore-arms (प्रकोष्ठः). Even now rich men sometimes wear golden bracelets on their left forearms. द्वि...धेनुना whose daggers (असिधेनुः) were fastened in firm knots of their sashes (पट्टिका) of double folded cloth. 'छुरिका चासिधेनुका' इत्यमरः. The daggers were fixed fast by having their handles wrapped in bandages of fine cloth which were doubled. अनवरतः व्यायामः (physical exercise) तेन कृशं कर्कशं (hard) शरीरं यस्य. वात...मानेन that leapt high again and again as if they were a herd of swift deer. वातहरिण is a very swift deer (called also वातप्रमी). लङ्घित...विटपेन that jumped over even and uneven ground, pits (अवटः) and bushes (विटपः). कोणः a stick, club. सेवायै (for worship) गृहीतानि विविधानि वन... पर्णानि येन. अनवरतं कृतः कलकलः येन. युवप्रायेण consisting mostly of young men. सनाथम् accompanied by.

P. 9 l. 13—**P. 10** l. 33 **मध्ये च...पुरुषम्.** The sentence is मध्ये च तस्य (अश्ववृन्दस्य) अष्टादशवर्षदेशीयं युवानमद्राक्षीत् (p.10 l. 27). ०चन्द्रेण, ०मालिना, ०खचितेन and ०पाण्डुरेण qualify both क्षीरोदेन and आतपत्रेण. सार्धचन्द्रेण—the umbrella had the figure of a crescent-shaped moon on it; the sea is सार्धचन्द्र, as the moon sprang from it at the time of the churning. मुक्ता...मालिना that (umbrella) was encircled by a heap of pearls. अर्धचन्द्र also means 'the semi-circular marks on a peacock's tail.' The umbrella might have such marks by way of ornament. The sea also has in it heaps of pearls. रत्न...खचितेन—the umbrella was inlaid with precious stones; the sea also is called रत्नाकर. शङ्ख...पाण्डुरेण white like a conch, milk and foam (with umbrella); white with conches, milk and foam (with क्षीरोदेन). क्षीरोदेनेव—The umbrella being सार्धचन्द्र, मुक्ता...मालिन् &c., the poet fancies it to be क्षीरसागर. स्वयं...तेन—the umbrella lent a charm (लक्ष्मी) to the youth over whom it was held. The force of स्वयं in the case of क्षीरोद is this:—when the three worlds became devoid of श्री by the curse of दुर्वासस् pronounced against Indra, the gods had to churn the ocean to find out the jewels including लक्ष्मी. The ocean did not of his own accord yield up लक्ष्मी. But the umbrella fancied to be क्षीरोद lent a लक्ष्मी (charm) to the young man without the latter making any effort to acquire it. गगनगतेन raised high in the air. आतपत्रेण—an umbrella is among the insignia of royalty. कृता छाया यस्य. कृतच्छायम्—this and the following clauses in the accusative qualify युवानं below (p. 10 l. 27). अच्छाच्छेन...गम्यमानम्—the idea is:—the youth was surrounded by a bright circle of the rays of the brilliant ornaments he wore. The poet fancies that it was a ring (चक्रवालं) of the quarters that stuck very close round him, because the quarters were very fond of seeing him (who was so young and handsome). Ordinarily चक्रवाल (horizon) is far from a person. आनितम्ब... राजमानम् who was decked with a wreath of Mālatī flowers on his head that hung down to his hips, as if it (wreath) were the banner of his beauty won by the conquest of the whole world. He surpassed by his beauty everyone in the world. A conqueror triumphantly carries away the banner from his vanquished rivals. The long wreath looked like a waving pennon. उत्सर्पिभिः...वपुषम् whose body rendered dirty by the dust on the road was being rubbed by the red up-shooting (उत्सर्पिभिः) rays of the ruby in his crest, as if with tender leaves held by invisible nymphs of the forest. 'शिखण्डखण्डिका चूडाभरणम्' com. The red rays resemble slender and reddish fresh leaves. प्रमृज्यमानं मार्गरेणुना परुषं वपुः यस्य. Dust may be rubbed off with पल्लवs. The reading रूषित would mean 'covered or soiled'. बकुल...दिवसम् with his head lovely by being decked with a wreath (मुण्डमाला) of Bakula buds and having a profusion of curling hair, he seemed as though drinking the day, the light of which was contracted. मीलितः आतपः यस्य (*adj.* of दिवसम्). The brilliance of the day is lessened by the approach of night. The white Bakula is like the light of day and his dark hair in contact with the white Bakula buds is like night. With his dark hair he as though lessened the light of day, which remained only in a scattered form in the shape of Bakula buds. पशु रिक्षम् with the brilliance, yellowish red like arsenic paste, of his broad forehead that was possessed of natural (सहज) loveliness (लक्ष्मी), he as though smeared the sky as if it (the forehead) were composed of the second portion of the moon that is the crown of the matted hair of S'iva. He had a bright and naturally lovely forehead. It was bright like the moon and so the poet fancies that it was made of the moon. The propriety of द्वितीय° is this:—शिव placed the crescent of the moon on his head. So if his ललाट was made of the moon, it could not have been that (part of the) moon that was placed by शिव on his head and so the forehead must have been made of the remaining portion of the moon (the second piece). The forehead being thus fancied to be मृगाङ्कघटित, it would be naturally embraced by लक्ष्मी that was born of the ocean along with the moon (सहज). For the churning of the ocean, see विष्णुपुराण I. 9 and रामायण I. 44. अभिनवं यौवनं तस्य आरम्भेण अवष्टम्भः (pride) तेन प्रगल्भाः दृष्टिपाताः तैः तृणीकृतं त्रिभुवनं येन. He was proud and his eye seemed to look upon the world as of no account. Compare 'दृष्टिस्तृणीकृतजगत्त्रयसत्त्वसारा' उत्तररामचरित VI. 19. प्रथिम्ना (instru. sing. of प्रथिमन् from पृथु)—vide notes on पिङ्गलिमा p. 23. °सहस्रैः सञ्छादिताः दश दिशः यया (*adj.* of शरदम्). In शरद् lotuses of various sorts abound. कुमुद is a white lotus, while कुवलय is dark and कमल is red. When he cast glances from his large eyes, the white of his eyes looked like कुमुद्s and the dark pupils like कुवलयs and the red corners looked like कमलs. शर...तैयन्तम् who as though caused the season of autumn. आयत...शोभमानम्—the idea is:—his long nose is deemed to be a dam (सेतुबन्धः) over the borders (सीमान्त) of the two rivers *viz.*, the two eyes. His nose separated the two eyes, as a dam would separate a river in two. Further the nose is fancied to be a stream of the water of beauty dropping from the slab of moonstone in the form of the forehead. His bright forehead resembled चन्द्रकान्त, from which water oozes when the moon rises. The nose also rises up after there is a depression from the forehead. His nose was charming and so is fancied to be the stream of the water of loveliness. अति...वमन्तम् with his mouth emitting the perfume of very fragrant mango, camphor, *kakkola*, cloves and Pârijātaka and resounding with the hum of the swarms of intoxicated bees, he vomited as if the season of spring together with the Nandana garden. Even now camphor, कक्कोल (Marathi कंकोळ) and cloves are taken with ताम्बूल. सहकार and पारिजातक are explained by the com. as certain fragrant substances, 'सहकारः सुगन्धद्रव्यभेदः सहकारफलेनैव क्रियते पारिजातकोऽनेकद्रव्यसंस्कृतो मुखवासविशेषः'. The youth had partaken of कर्पूर, कक्कोल &c. with his ताम्बूल and emitted their fragrance with his breath. In वसन्त also, there is the fragrance of mango blossoms and of other flowers and the humming of bees. नन्दन is the garden of Indra. पारिजातक is one of the five trees of Paradise. *Vide* notes p. 43. Hence the poet says 'सनन्दनवनं'. The reading अवतारयन्तम् is more striking than वमन्तम्, but is probably an emendation. It means 'he made वसन्त descend to the earth together with नन्दनवन'. The critics had laid down that the use of words like वान्त (*past p. p.* of वम्) and उद्गीर्ण in their literal sense was against good taste (ग्राम्य) and so the copyists thinking that the word वमन्तं was so used here probably changed it to अवतारयन्तम्. But it is to be noted that Bāna uses it only in a figurative sense. 'निष्ठ्यूतोद्गीर्णवान्तादि गौणवृत्तिव्यपाश्रयम्। अतिसुन्दरमन्यत्र ग्राम्यकक्षां विगाहते॥' काव्या॰ I. 95. आसन्नाः सुहृदः तेषां परिहासाः (jests) तेषां भावनया (appreciation, understanding) उत्तानितं मुखं तस्य मुग्धैः हसितैः. दशनज्योत्स्नया स्नपितानि दिङ्मुखानि यैः that bathed the quarters in the moonlight of his teeth. Whenever he smiled at the jests of his friends, his bright teeth gleamed forth and cast their lustre all round. That lustre resembled moonlight. पुनः पुनः...कल्पयन्तम् who again and again created the light of the moon moving about in the sky. As he smiled now and then (and not continuously), he seemed to create moonlight at different times and so the poet uses the word पुनःपुनः. There is a pun on the word नभसि (in the sky; in the month of श्रावण). In श्रावण, the moon is seen now and then on account of the clouds and not continuously (just like his bright smiles). कदम्बमुकुलवत् स्थूलं मुक्ताफलयुगलं तस्य मध्ये अध्यासितं (placed) मरकतं यस्मिन् (*adj.* of ०भरणस्य). त्रि... भरणस्य three-pointed ear-ornament. His ear-ornament was made of two big pearls between which was inserted an emerald. This ornament seems to be somewhat like the भिकबाळी worn by men in Mahārāshṭra. त्रिकण्टक 'त्रिकण्टकस्तु त्र्यश्रः स्यात्रिभी रत्नैश्च भूषणम्'. Compare 'काश्चिदुद्धूयमानधवलचामरसटालग्नत्रिकण्टकवलितवि कटकटाक्षाः' हर्ष० 4th उच्छ्वास. प्रेङ्खतः (*adj.* of ०भरणस्य) dangling. प्रभया... लक्ष्यमाणम् by the up-spreading lustre (of the ear-ornament) it seemed as though he had an ear-ornament made of green *Kunda* leaves together with their flowers. *Kunda* flowers, being white, are like pearls and the leaves are green like emerald. कृतः सकुसुमेन हरितकुन्दपल्लवेन कर्णावतंसः यस्य. आमोदितः (आमोदः सञ्जातः अस्य) मृगमदपङ्कः तेन लिखितः पत्रभङ्गः तेन भास्वरम् adorned with ornamental lines drawn with very fragrant musk paste. 'मृगनाभिर्मृगमदः कस्तूरी च' इत्यमरः. For पत्रभङ्ग see notes p. 24. भुजयुगलम्—object of दधानम्. उद्दाम...दधानम् possessing (arms) that seemed to be the two poles of the banner of Cupid (मकरकेतुः), that (poles) had on their tops (the figure of) a formidable crocodile. उद्दामेन मकरेण आक्रान्तं शिखरं यस्य. This may apply to भुजयुगलं also, meaning '(arms) the tops of which had on them a loose (or formidable) crocodile-shaped ornament'. Long arms are a sign of good fortune and high position. As he was handsome like Cupid and had long arms, they (arms) are said to be poles. The marks of the black musk on the arms looked like the dark crocodile, which is the emblem on the banner of Cupid. सीमन्तितं parted (*adj.* of देहम्). सीमन्त is the parting line of the hair of women. It is white. His ब्रह्मसूत्र also was white and was placed across his body like a line. He had a formidable body which was encircled by the white यज्ञोपवीत. The white यज्ञोपवीत is like the fair Ganges. So the poet fancies that his body was the मन्दर mountain chained (encircled) by the stream of the Ganges indignant at the churning of the ocean. When the ocean was churned for jewels, मन्दर was made the churning handle. The ocean is poetically spoken of as the husband of the Ganges (and also of all other rivers). The Ganges (ब्रह्मसूत्र) was as if angry at the harassment of her husband and bound down मन्दर (his body) in order to stay the churning. **'मन्थानं मन्दरं** कृत्वा नेत्रं कृत्वा तु वासुकिम् । मथ्यताममृतं देवाः साह्याय्ये मय्यवस्थिते ॥' विष्णुपु० I. 9. 76. 'बद्धे सन्दानितम्' इत्यमरः. कर्पूर... पांशुलेन rendered dusty, being smeared with a handful of camphor powder (क्षोदः). कान्तायाः उच्चौ कुचौ एव चक्रवाकौ तयोः युगलं तस्य विपुलं पुलिनं तेन. His broad chest was like a vast sandy beach for the चक्रवाकs—*viz.*, the high breasts of his (future) wife. His wife would rest on his broad chest, as the चक्रवाक does on a पुलिन. A beach also is dusty (पांशुल) with white sand (resembling camphor). उरःस्थलेन...क्रम्—the idea is:—He had a very broad chest and stout long arms. The poet fancies that by his long arms he embraced the distant quarters and brought them together in a heap (पुञ्जित). The heaped up quarters were allowed expansion on his broad chest. आयामः length. पुरस्ता...भागम्—the author describes here the under-garment (something like modern मांडचोळणा) of the youth. पुरस्ता...कमनीयेन that was charming because one end (कोणः) of it was set in front a little below his navel. पृष्ठत...पल्लवेन the hem of which hung behind over his girdle (कक्ष्या). पल्लव (Marathi गोंडा) the hem of the strings with which the garment was made fast. उभय...भागेन that was so wound on both sides as to display a third part of his thighs. हारीत...वाससा by his lower garment that was green like the हारीत (pigeon) bird and that tightly (निबिड) pressed (his waist). विभ...भागम् whose very slender waist was divided (from the upper part of his body). अनवरतव्यायामेन उपचितमांसे कठिने विकटे मकरमुखसंलग्ने जानुनी ययोः (*adj.* of ऊरुदण्डाभ्याम्) the knees of which had flesh accumulated by incessant exercise, were hard, formidable and firmly knit to the parts above them. 'मकरमुखं जानुनोरुपरिभागः' सं०. We may also explain मकरमुखसंलग्न as 'knees that had a crocodile shape and that were thick-set (and not loose or flabby)'. विशाल... स्तम्भाभ्याम् (thighs) that were stone pillars for supporting (उत्तम्भन) the stone platform of his broad chest. The image here is taken from architecture. His long and tapering thighs were like stone columns. His broad chest was like the entablature (constituting the architrave, frieze and cornice) resting on slender pillars. चारु...कान्तिभ्याम् the beauty of which was rendered patent by the lovely marks of sandal thereon. Sandal paste had been applied to that part of the thighs that was not covered. स्थासकः perfuming the body with unguents. 'चर्चा तु चार्चिक्यं स्थासकः' इत्यमरः. ऊरु...यामम् with his long thighs, he as if laughed in scorn at the length of the trunk of ऐरावत. The trunk of an elephant is long and tapering downwards like the thigh. ऐरावत is white and the youth's thigh also was besmeared with white sandal paste. अति...काण्डम् his shanks (जङ्घा) were very slender, as though through the fatigue (खेदः) caused by bearing the burden of his very stout (भरित) thighs (ऊरु). One who carries burdens is slim (and not fat). कल्प...पाटलस्य—his feet were red like the fresh shoots of the tree of Paradise. The shoots of a tree are red; much more of a कल्पवृक्ष. उभय...लम्बिनः His feet hung on both sides (of the horse he was riding). दोला...रचयन्तम्—the idea is:—the motion of the horse caused the rays from his toe-nails to move about. The bright rays of the nails resemble a white chowrie. As he was riding the nails appeared to be a chowrie placed on the horse. Chowries were placed on horses and elephants. Compare शाकुन्तल I 'निष्कम्पचामरशिखा निभृतोर्ध्वकर्णाः । ...धावन्त्यमी मृगजवाक्षमयेव रथ्याः ॥'. अभि...भुवि that (horse) tore the earth with its hoofs that were raised (उदञ्चत्) aloft in front, that seemed as though to rest long in the air and that fell forcibly on account of their curvetting (वलितं). The high spirited steed pranced, remained standing on its hind legs for a long time as if it wanted to give them rest and then came down on the earth with force with its front legs, thereby raising dust from the earth. वलितेन विकटं यथा स्यात्तथा (अव्ययीभाव)—to be taken with पतद्भिः. ०भुवि and the following locatives qualify वाजिनि (l. 15). प्रतिक्षणं दशनैः (आदौ) ग्रहः (पश्चात्) मुक्तिश्च ताभ्यां खणखणायितं खरं खलीनं (खे तालुनि लीनम्) येन. The hard bridle-bit made a sound when the horse bit it between its teeth and then let it off. The reading दशनविमुक्त conveys almost the same sense. दीर्घघ्राणे लीना लालिका यस्य सः ०लालिकः स चासौ ललाट...चक्रकश्च. ललाटे लुलितानि (tossed, waving) चारूणि चामीकरस्य (सुवर्णस्य) चक्रकाणि (rings) यस्य. लालिका is explained by सं० as 'the end of the bit'. It is better to read with B 'दीर्घ...लालिके ललाट०,' as then it is easier to dissolve the compounds. शिञ्जान...शोभिनि

adorned with tinkling (शिञ्जान) golden trappings. 'तपनीयं शातकौम्भम्' इत्यमरः ('शतकुम्भे गिरौ भवं शातकौम्भम्, अनुशतिकादित्वादुभयपदवृद्धिः, शातकुम्भमित्येके' क्षीर०). शातकौम्भम् (or—कुम्भम् according to some) gold. 'जयनं हयमण्डनमाला' सं०. 'अश्वादीनां च सन्नाहे जये च जयनं मतम्' शाश्वत 515. मनसः इव रंहः (वेगः) यस्य. गोलाङ्गूलस्य कपोलवत् कालानि (dark) कायलोमानि यस्य. गोलाङ्गूलः an ape with a dark face and a tail like a cow's. 'कृष्णमुखो गोलाङ्गूलः' क्षीर०. उभय...हस्ताभ्याम् whose hands gripped the saddle (पर्याणं) cloth on both sides. आसन्नपरिचारकः body-guard. दोधूयमानं (*pr. p.* of the frequentative base of धू to shake) चामरिकायुगलं यस्य. बन्दिनः of the bard. 'बन्दिनः स्तुतिपाठकाः' इत्यमरः. सुभाषितम्—object of भावयन्तम्. उत्कण्टकितः (रोमाञ्चितः) कपोलफलकः यस्य. लग्न...कलेनेव—the idea is:—his cheek had hair standing on end on account of emotion roused by the song of the bard; the poet fancies the रोमाञ्च to be pieces of the fine hairy growth (पक्ष्म) on the filaments (केसरम्) of the lotus on his ear. भावयन्तम् reflecting over, appreciating. अनङ्ग...दर्शयन्तम् who as if showed (in his person) the advent of the *yuga* (the era) of Cupid. He was charming like Cupid. सं० says 'अनङ्गजन्मना यदुपलक्षितं युगं कालविशेषः, तस्य नूतनमदनसादृश्यात्, यद्वा अनङ्गयोर्युगं तदवतारमिव । द्वित्वसंख्यापूर्वकत्वात्'. This and the following clauses lay stress on the extreme loveliness of the youth in various ways and the effects he produced on others. चन्द्र...यन्तम् who as though created a world full of moonlight. He was bright like the moon and shed his lustre over the whole world. विलासप्रायम्—his youthful smiles and gestures were to be seen everywhere. अन्यः सर्गः (सृष्टिः) सर्गान्तरम्. अनु...रचयन्तम्—this world is full of love and hatred; but he was the centre of the affection of all; no one hated him. So he brought about another world as it were, where there was nothing but affection. The student will note Bāṇa's command over language. He uses different words like उत्पादयन्तं, जनयन्तं &c., to convey the same sense. शृङ्गारमयम्—full of love. He was the cynosure of all eyes the whole day. राग...यन्तम् inaugurating a reign of affection. आक...चक्षुषोः he was to the eyes as though the infatuating collyrium. It was supposed that some magical collyrium when applied to the eye by a person made that person attractive to every spectator. He by his beauty fascinated the eyes of all. वशी०—certain incantations were supposed to have the power of subduing the will of others. Note the following मन्त्र credited with great power. 'ॐ

गणपतये स्वाहेति । अयं गणपतेर्मन्त्रो धनविद्याप्रदायकः । इममष्टसहस्रं च जप्त्वा बद्ध्वा शिखां ततः । व्यवहारे जयः स्याच्च शतजाप्यान्नृणां प्रियः ॥.' स्वस्था...णाम् he was as though a powder that influences the senses to be comfortable. The idea is:—in his presence, the senses of the spectators were lulled into pleasure. C and T translate to the senses a powder able to affect the healthiest'. This is not so good as the meaning we suggest. अस...कस्य—the curiosity to see him is never satiated. सिद्ध...ग्यस्य he was as though the never-failing remedy of blessedness. The moment he was seen, everyone felt blessed. पुनर्ज॰—Cupid was once burnt by S'iva; but on seeing that handsome youth, hearts fell under the sway of Love (*i. e.* love was born again). रसायनमिव यौवनस्य—रसायनम् (रसः mercury + अयनम्) a medical preparation containing mercury. In ancient India, it was believed, as in many other countries, that mercury, if properly prepared, would make men immortal and free from old age. Note the passages 'संसारस्य परं पारं दत्तेऽसौ पारदः स्मृतः'; 'एकोऽसौ रसराजः शरीरमजरामरं कुरुते'. The सर्वदर्शनसंग्रह devotes a chapter to रसेश्वरदर्शन 'the philosophy of Mercury' (रस being identified with शिव). As रसायन produces perfect health, so youth attained perfection in the young man. एक...रामणीयकस्य—रामणीयक shared the youth with nothing else *i. e.* loveliness reigned supreme in him. कीर्ति...रूपस्य.—He was so charming that he seemed to be a pillar set up for all time to commemorate the triumph of beauty. मूल...लावण्यस्य as the principal amount of loveliness. The loveliness in others is like interest *i. e.* it is subsidiary (inferior) to the principal (the youth's charms). पुण्य...संसारस्य—the good deeds of the world bore fruit in the splendid form of the youth. कान्तिः (beauty) एव लता तस्याः प्रथमाङ्कुरम्—none as handsome as the youth had preceded him. सर्गा...पतेः—Brahmā had created the world several times. By practice one acquires great skill and perfection. So the beauty of the youth was the result of the skill acquired by Brahmā. प्रतापः glory, greatness. विभ्रमः amorous or sportive movements. यशः...नध्यस्य—learning had attained the highest pitch of excellence in him. अष्टा...देशीयम् about 18 years old. The affixes कल्प, देश्य and देशीय are added in the sense ef 'a little less than, about'. 'ईषदसमाप्तौ कल्पब्देश्यदेशीयरः' पा. 5. 3. 67. (ईषदूनो विद्वान् विद्वत्कल्पः विद्वद्देशीयः । सि. कौ.). द्वितीयम्—This and the following clauses in the accusative qualify पुरुषम् (l. 33). अपर...तुरङ्गम्—न परेण संश्लिष्टः तुरङ्गः यस्य whose horse was not touched by another. This may mean that his saddle was not held by any attendants as that of the youth was or that his horse was not closely followed by another *i. e.* other riders kept at a respectful distance. We prefer the former meaning. From the fact that the young man was cracking jokes with his companions, it seems that they were close to him (and so to the old man also). उत्तप्त...कारम् whose form was like a pillar of heated (molten) gold (तपनीयं) *i. e.* he was bright and red in complexion. परिणतं वयः यस्य—old. नीच...कचम् who had short nails, beard and hair. He did not allow these to grow. शुक्तिखलतिम् bald-headed as a shell. His head had no hair and the skin was white and glossy like mother-o'-pearl. रोमशं उरःस्थलं यस्य. 'लोमादिपामादि—पिच्छादिभ्यः श-न-इलचः' पा. 5. 2. 100 (लोमादिभ्यः शः । लोमशः । रोमवान् । पामादिभ्यो नः । पामनः । सि. कौ.). र् and ल् are often interchanged as in रोमन् and लोमन्. अनु...शिक्षयन्तम् who, being dressed elegantly but not gaudily, seemed as though to teach even old age decorousness. It is old age that makes men decorous. He was old and such an embodiment of decorum that old age might have taken lessons from him. उल्बण showy, gaudy. गुणा...नयन्तम् who seemed as though lending weight (importance or greatness) even to virtues. He was so virtuous that he seemed to heighten the worth of the virtues themselves. गरिमा—from गुरु. Vide notes on पिङ्गलिमा p. 23. महानुभावता dignity or nobility. He was so noble or dignified that even Dignity may have something to learn from him. आचारः correct deportment. आचार्यकम् teaching, instruction. आचार्यस्य भावः कर्म वा—according to 'योपधाद्गुरूपोत्तमाद्वुञ्' पा. V. 1. 132 (रामणीयकम् । आभिधानीयकम् । सि. कौ.). वारबाणः or–वाणः a coat of mail, jacket. 'कञ्चुको वारवाणोऽस्त्री' इत्यमरः (वारं आच्छादकं वानमस्य इति वारवाणः—क्षीर०). ०पट्टिकया परिवेष्टितः मौलिः यस्य. पुरुषम्—is to be connected with अद्राक्षीत् (l. 27) above.

P. 11 l. 1—**P. 12** l. 32 **अथ स...दशम्.** पुरोयायिनाम् soldiers that had gone ahead, vanguard. यथा...कथयताम् who, having come back, narrated all as they saw with astonished minds. The vanguard was deep in wonder at the superhuman beauty of the two maidens. The reading प्रतीत्य may mean प्रतिनिवृत्य and also 'having approached'. उपलभ्य having learnt. दिव्या आकृतिः यस्य (*adj.* of ०युगलम्). ०युगलम्—object of उपलभ्य. प्रतूर्णतुरगः whose horse began to gallop (*i. e.* he urged his horse to greater speed). निवारितः परिजनः येन who prohibited his servants (to follow him).

तेन—refers to the old companion of the youth described above. कृतं उपसङ्ग्रहणं याभ्याम् who made a respectful salutation. तौ—object of उपजग्राह. किस...जग्राह received them according to their precedence with hospitality usual in forest life beginning with the offering of a seat of tender foliage and ending with the present of fruit and flowers. सकुसुमैः फलैः अर्घः (पूजाविधिः) अवसानं (अन्तः) यस्य (*adj.* of आतिथ्येन). आसीनयोश्च तयोः when they sat. प्रवयस् an old man. प्रगतं वयः यस्य. 'प्रवयाः स्थविरो वृद्धः' इत्यमरः. सहजा (inborn) लज्जा धनं यस्य. सहज...जनस्य to address (another man) first (*i. e.* before he addresses) is (seems) an immodest act in the case of young women to whom innate bashfulness is all-in-all, particularly in the case of highborn maidens that are simple like the does of the forest. शालीन—bashful, shy–from शाला with the affix ख (ईन). 'शालीनकौपीने अधृष्टाकार्ययोः' पा. 5. 2. 20 (शालाप्रवेशमर्हति शालीनः अधृष्टः। सि. कौ.। अप्रागल्भ्यादन्यत्र गन्तुमशक्तः शालामेव प्रवेष्टुमर्हतीत्यर्थः। तत्त्वबोधिनी). The propriety of the word वन is this. A doe, by contact with human beings, may become bold; but one brought up in the forest far from human habitation will retain its original shyness and innocence. केवल...वृत्तिः But this (my) sense of hearing, envious of (my) eye that is blest (कृतार्थ) by seeing you, urges me, being eager to hear the news (of you). What सावित्री means is:—on seeing this extremely handsome young man, our eyes have been rewarded and gratified; but our ears have not yet heard anything concerning him and are therefore envious of the eye. चक्षुषे स्पृहयन्ती (०वृत्तिः)—स्पृह् governs the dative of the object of desire or envy. 'स्पृहेरीप्सितः' पा. 1. 4. 36. 'वार्ता प्रवृत्तिर्वृत्तान्त उदन्तः स्यात्' इत्यमरः. प्रथम...प्रणयम् a good man at first sight offers his affection (प्रणयः) as though it were a present. She means that both the men, being good, have given their good will to the two maidens even at the first meeting. अप्र...वाचालयति *lit.* the heart offered by the great (प्रभवत्) with courtesy (प्रश्रयः) makes even a timid person talkative, as wine does. She means:—we are timid. You are great and courteously offered your heart (*i. e.* your regard) to us. This your regard for us makes us bold enough to address you. Wine also makes even a timid person garrulous, when he gets drunk. प्रभ...र्पितं (with मधु) means 'proffered with over-powering courtesy' or 'proffered by a great man with courtesy'. अति...विस्रम्भः confidence easily reaches its highest pitch in the case of a very yielding good man, as the bowstring on the bow. She means:—you are very good and yielding. So we treat you with the greatest confidence. The words नम्र and कोटि are श्लिष्ट. The bow-string easily reaches the furthest tip (कोटि) when the bow is extremely bent (नम्र). It is better to read आरोहति with B. With आरोपयति (causal of रुह् with आ) we naturally expect one more noun in the accusative (besides कोटिम्). आरोपयति will yield a very good sense, if we could read विस्रम्भम् and in that case गुणः (virtue, string) will be श्लिष्ट and will be construed with both साधौ and धनुषि. अति... धियाम् in those whose minds are steady or who are very wise. स्रष्टुः...शयाः master-pieces of creation from the Creator's hands. त्रि...भावि surpassing (everything) in the three worlds. अस्य— refers to the young man. सौजन्य...तरलता it is not fickleness that is natural to young women that causes me to speak, but it is the great beauty of this one dear to the gods, which (भद्रता) is under the control of kindness (that makes me talk). She means:—this young man is extremely handsome and yet very considerate (and not capricious in the vanity of his charms). It is this that urges me to know something more about him. सावित्री very much desired that सरस्वती should be married to such a young man if otherwise eligible. सह उत्तिष्ठति इति सहोत्था. The word देवानां प्रिय is used by Bâṇa in a good sense *i. e.* as meaning 'worthy, honourable'. Compare 'इहापि जन्मनि दत्तमेवासाकममुना तपःक्लेशेन फलमसुलभदर्शनं दर्शयता देवानां प्रियम्' हर्षचरित 8th उच्छ्वास. As'oka in his edicts calls himself देवानां प्रिय. The महाभाष्य uses it in a good sense 'के पुनर्भवदादयः । भवान् दीर्घायुः देवानां प्रियः आयुष्मानिति' on पा. 5. 3. 14 (Kielhorn vol. II. p. 405). But later Sanskrit grammarians assign the meaning of 'fool' to this Aluk compound. Mr. R. R. Kale takes देवानां प्रिय in this sense and applies it to सावित्री, but that is not correct. Besides the sense becomes involved. We may also take देवानां प्रियस्य as referring to the old courtier. आगमनेन—connect with शून्यतां नीतः. अपुण्यभाक् unhappy. विजृम्भिता विरहव्यथा यस्य in which the pain of separation is growing. अपहृतः हरस्य हुङ्काराहङ्कारः येन who humbles the pride of the defiant roar of S'iva. A wrathful man makes the sound हुम्. शिव in wrath burnt मदन by the fire from his third eye. Vide p. 14 (notes). But the youth, who was as handsome as Cupid, humbled S'iva's pride by his very existence. This passage is reminiscent of the verse 'असह्यहुङ्कारनिवर्तितः पुरा पुरारिमप्राप्तमुखः शिलीमुखः । इमां हृदि व्यायतपातमक्षिणोद्विशीर्णमूर्तेरपि पुष्पधन्वनः ॥

(आसेचनकं दर्शनं यस्य) whose sight never satiated him *i. e.* though he saw him continuously, he wanted to see him more still. 'तदासेचनकं तृप्तेर्नास्त्यन्तो यस्य दर्शनात्' इत्यमरः (आसिच्यते आप्यायते दृगनेन आसेचनकं यस्य दर्शनात् दृग्न तृप्यति—क्षीर०). मातामहः—refers to शर्यात. मनोविनोदनम् that diverted or gave solace to his mind. विद्याः—see above p. 18. कलाः—The Kalās were said to be 64, such as नृत्त, गीत, आलेख्य. They are enumerated in वात्स्यायन's कामसूत्र (I. 3.). उपारूढं यौवनं यस्मिन्. अहमिव refers to शर्यात and असौ to च्यवन. सुगृहीतं नाम यस्य whose name is auspicious. भृत्यपरमाणुम् an atom of a servant *i. e.* an insignificant servant. अवधारयतु understand. आयान्तम्—refers to दधीच. मया...स्वामी my master made me his attendant. अभिसारः companion. अभिसारेण सह साभि० (बहुव्रीहि). Compare 'महासामन्तैः कृत्वा साभिसारम्' first para 5th उच्छ्वास. तद्धि... कुलम् that (of शर्यात) is a royal family to which we (*i. e.* I) have been hereditarily attached. C and T translate 'our royal house follows the rule of heredity'. This inverts the sequence of ideas. उत्तमानां...मन्दाक्षम् length (of service) produces in the good (in good masters) a certain amount of kindly (or partial) feeling even towards dependents. मन्दाक्षम्—partiality, connivance. मन्दं अक्षि इव यत्र मन्दाक्षम्, according to 'अक्ष्णोऽदर्शनात्' पा. 5. 4. 76. (अचक्षुःपर्यायादक्ष्णोऽच् स्यात्समासान्तः। गवामक्षीव गवाक्षः। सि. कौ.). He puts down this and the following sentences for showing that, though he is unworthy to be the confidential companion of the noble prince, yet his master favoured him for his long and faithful service. अ...महताम् inexhaustible indeed is the treasure of kindness in the great. इत...मात्रमिव only at the distance of about two kros'as from this place. This is accusative of distance. 'गव्यूतिः स्त्री क्रोशयुगम्' इत्यमरः (from गो + यूति according to the Vārtikas 'गोर्यूतौ छन्दस्युपसंख्यानम्' and 'अध्वपरिमाणे च' on 'वान्तो यि प्रत्यये' पा. 6. 1. 79.). पारेशोणम्—beyond the S'oṇa. शोणस्य पारे पारे०, according to 'पारे मध्ये षष्ठ्या वा' (पारमध्यशब्दौ षष्ठ्यन्तेन सह वा समस्येते। एदन्तत्वं चानयोर्निपात्यते। पक्षे षष्ठीतत्पुरुषः। पारेगङ्गादानय। गङ्गापारात्।...सि. कौ.). स्व...देशम् the appellation of which was derived from his own name. निर्मितः व्यपदेशः यस्य. चैत्र...कल्पम् almost like चैत्ररथ. For the affix कल्प, *vide* notes on अष्टादशवर्षदेशीय above p. 55. चैत्ररथम् name of the garden of कुबेर, the lord of riches. 'अलकायाः बहिश्चान्यद्वनं चैत्ररथं प्रिये। योजनायुतविस्तीर्णं सर्वं कल्पद्रुमाकुलम्॥'. तत् (काननं) अवधिः यस्याः. तद...यात्रा this our journey is to end there. यदि...परि if your courteousness accepts or seizes this moment (to do us a favour) or your heart entertains regard for us. गृहीतः क्षणः येन. अविद्यमाना अवहेला (disdain or contempt) यस्मिन्. भूमि...र्हो वा or if this person (*i. e.* I) is an object of favour (with you) or worthy of being listened to (by you). प्रथमः...हलस्य first request of curiosity (*i. e.* due to or out of curiosity). शुश्रूषवः desirous to hear. शुश्रूषु—from the desiderative base of श्रु with the affix उ, according to सनाशंस-भिक्ष उः' पा 3. 2. 168. ने...चरति this your (noble) form cannot fail to be (*i. e.* must be) divine. The idea is that there is an invariable concomitance between such nobility of form and दिव्यता. गोत्रनामनी family and name. स्पृहणीयतां नीतः was made an object of envy. सम...र्थानाम् who is a combination of mutually conflicting things. तथा हि for instance, to explain. It will be noticed that in the following four lines, the विरोध is only verbal, the words being श्लिष्ट and that in each case the incongruity is explained away by taking different senses of the same words. सन्नि...र्तिश्च-(1) सन्निहितः बालः अन्धकारः यस्याम् in whom fresh darkness was present; (2) सन्निहितः बालेषु अन्धकारः यस्याम् who had darkness (*i. e.* dark colour) present in her locks. (1) भास्वतः (सूर्यस्य) मूर्तिः यस्याम् in whom the sun was present; (2) भास्वती मूर्तिः यस्याः whose form was brilliant. Here if the first sense of the two words be taken, there is विरोध, but there is none if the second sense of each clause be taken. पुण्ड...मुखी (1) with a tiger in her face (पुण्डरीकः व्याघ्रः मुखे यस्याः); (2) with a face resembling a lotus. हरिणलोचना (1) having deer in her eye; (2) who had the eyes of a deer. 'व्याघ्रेऽपि पुण्डरीको ना' इत्यमरः. C and T following the com. take पुण्डरीक as 'lion'. बाला...धरा (1) possessing the lustre of the young sun; (2) bright like the lustre of the morning sun or having a lower lip lustrous like the morning sun. बालातपप्रभः अधरः यस्याः. कु...सिनी (1) possessing laughing night-lotuses; (2) whose smile is bright like कुमुदs. कुमुदs are white lotuses that open by night. There is विरोध in saying that she possessed the morning sunlight and also opening कुमुदs. But the विरोध vanishes if we say that her complexion was rosy like fresh morn and her smile was bright like कुमुदs. Smiles are poetically said to be white. कल...स्वना (1) that possessed the cackling of कलहंसs (कलहंसानां स्वनः यस्याम्); (2) whose voice was like that of a कलहंस (कलहंसस्य इव स्वनः यस्याः). स...धरा (1) that had clouds rising (समुन्नताः पयोधराः मेघाः यस्याम्); (2) whose bosom was high-swelling (समुन्नतौ पयोधरौ यस्याः). When there are clouds, the sound of कलहंसs cannot be heard, because at the approach of the rains हंस were supposed to migrate to the मानस lake. Or the विरोध may be this:—if there is thunder in her, how can she have the low cackling of कलहंस ? कमल...करा (1) possessing the delicate lustre of lotuses; (2) whose hand is delicate like a lotus. हिम...तम्बा (1) whose hips are broad with slabs of the Himālaya mountain; (2) whose hips are broad like &c. Lotuses and slabs of snow cannot exist together, as snow blights lotuses. Compare 'हिमसेकविपत्तिरत्र मे नलिनी पूर्वनिदर्शनं मता' रघु० VIII. 45. करभोरुः (1) having the thigh of a camel; (2) having a thigh round and tapering like the trunk of an elephant. करभः a young camel; also ' the back portion of the hand from the wrist to the root of the fingers.' वि...मना (1) whose gait is slow; (2) whose gait is languidly sportive. A camel is well-known to be a fast animal. One who has the camel's thigh cannot be slow. अमु...भावा (1) who has not given up devotion to Kumāra *i. e.* कार्तिकेय; (2) who has not yet passed the stage of girlhood. अमुक्तः कुमारे स्कन्दे भावः भक्तिः यया. अमुक्तः कुमारभावः यया. स्निग्धः (affectionate) तारकः (तदाख्यः असुरः) यस्याम्. स्निग्धा (charming) तारका (pupil of the eye) यस्याः. The demon तारक was killed by स्कन्द. One who is devoted to स्कन्द cannot secure the affection of तारक. अध्वा the road *i. e.* the distance. परि...रिष्यति Familiarity (with us) will surely make (everything) clear. अनुषङ्गे दृष्टः seen by chance. अनुषङ्गः incidental connection. नवः अम्भसां भरः (burden) तेन गम्भीरः अम्भोधराणां (मेघानां) ध्वानः (ध्वनिः) तन्निभया तत्सदृश्या. भारत्या in a voice. नर्तयन् भुजगभुजः making the peacocks dance. Peacocks subsist on reptiles and dance when clouds thunder. The voice of दधीच was mistaken by the peacocks to be the thunder of clouds. भुजगभुजः (with दधीच) would mean 'whose arms were (long and lithe) like snakes.' Separate प्रसादम् आर्या आराध्य०. कृता नमस्कृतिः येन. उच्चचाल started away. उत्तम्भितं पक्ष्म यस्य the eyelashes of which were raised up. निश्चला तारका यस्य. लिखितेनेव चक्षुषा with an eye that was as though drawn in a picture (*i. e.* that was quite motionless). कृच्छ्रा...दृशम् with difficulty she withdrew her eye (from that direction).

P. 12 l. 33—**P. 13** l. 10. अथ...सुष्वाप. तस्य = दधीचस्य. रूपसम्पदम् perfection of beauty. अवशेव as though helpless. अप्रहितमपि though not sent. कुतोऽपि (1) from some indescribable cause; (2) from the earth. The creeper with its shoots springs from the earth. सालस्या इव—आलस्येन सह (बहुव्रीहि). शून्या vacant in mind.

सनिद्रा sleepy, dreamy. अस्तमुपयाति—connect with तेजसि. प्रत्यक् पर्यस्तं मण्डलं यस्य whose orb was thrown westward. लाङ्ग...त्विषि the brilliance of which was rosy like a bunch of लाङ्गलिका. कमलिनीकामुक the lover of lotuses plants. कमलिनी plants bloom at the advent of the sun. कठोर...शोचिषि the lustre (शोचिः) of which was red like the head of a fully developed (कठोर) crane. सावित्रं सवितुः इदं सावित्रम्. त्रयीमये—त्रयीमय is an appellation of the sun. त्रयी means 'the three Vedas'. As the sun is worshipped with the Veda or as the most sacred verse of the Rigveda, the गायत्री, is addressed to the sun, the latter is called त्रयीमय or त्रयीतनु. Compare भागवतपुराण 5. 20. 4. **'त्रय्या विद्यया** भगवन्तं **त्रयीमयं** सूर्यमात्मानं यजन्ते'. तमाल is a tree the leaves of which are dark. मलिनयति *loc. sing.* of the *pr. p.* of the denominative verb मलिनयति from मलिन. व्योम is the object of मलिनयति. सञ्च...तलम् when the moon very slowly crept up the sky, like a swan of the Ganges following the tinkling of the anklets of the roaming Siddha damsels. For सिद्ध, see above (text p. 5 l. 25). सिद्ध does not mean 'saint' here as C and T think. A हंस is white and hence the moon is compared to हंस. The moon sailed in the Milky Way, which is white and resembles the मन्दाकिनी. कृतः सन्ध्यायै प्रणामः यया. निशामुखे at the very beginning of night. She was languid and tired and so took the first opportunity to lie down. This contrasts with उचिते शयनकाले below. विमुक्तानि अङ्गानि यस्याः whose limbs were drooping or languid. कृत्वा...कलापम् having gone through her evening ritual as it was being usually performed by her. कलापः = समूहः. This shows that she was unaffected, while सरस्वती was perturbed by the wave of passion.

P. 13 ll. 11—28 इतरा...कुलैः. अङ्ग...तला whose bed of tender leaves was disarranged (विलुलित) by the tossing of her limbs. निमीलित closed. मर्त्य...परि the world of mortals is surely above (*i. e.* superior to) all worlds. एवंविधानि—refers to दधीच. सक...गुरूणि (1) worthy of respect on account of (the possession of) all virtues (with दधीच); (2) heavy even to the collection of all threads (with रत्नानि). Even numerous threads may not bear the burden of a big jewel; what of a single thread? ग्रामः = समूहः. She explains in the following clauses how he possesses all the qualities and is an ornament to त्रिभुवन. तस्य...न्दुः—the moon is but a drop oozing from the stream of the beauty of his face. The moon is round and bright like a drop. His face is so much more charming than the moon, that the latter seems but a drop as compared with the stream of his beauty. Explain the following clauses similarly. विक्षेपाः glances. For विकच...कराः, compare above 'चक्षुषः प्रथिम्ना विकचकुमुदकुवलयकमलसरःसहस्रसञ्छादितदशदिशं' (text p. 9. ll. 23–24 and notes p. 50). आकरः = समूहः. अधरमणेः of. his jewel-like lip. His red lip is like a red jewel. दीधितयः = किरणाः. बन्धूकम् is a red flower. The word विकसित is put in to indicate deep red. तस्य...नङ्गः The disembodied one (Cupid) is only a means (उपकरणं) of enhancing the beauty of his body. There is a picturesque effect in saying that his अङ्ग has its beauty enhanced by अनङ्ग (one who is without body). 'परभागो गुणोत्कर्षः' क्षीरस्वामी. बाण is fond of this word. Compare 'उपहितकान्तिपतिपरभागा लक्ष्मच्छायेव चन्द्रमसः' कादम्बरी p. 267 of P; "कुटिलक्रमरूपक्रियमाणपल्लवपरभागैरपरैः' हर्षचरित 1st उच्छ्वास. Connect स्त्रैणानि with the three, चक्षूंषि, चेतांसि and यौवनानि. स्त्रैणानि of women (from स्त्री). 'स्त्रीपुंसाभ्यां नञ्स्नञौ भवनात्' पा. 4. 1. 87. येषा...दर्शनस्य within whose vision be comes. The reading अविषयः is explicable. The meaning then would be 'the eyes, minds and youths of those women are blessed who do not see him', the idea perhaps being that it is better that he be not seen at all rather than suffer for his sake an insatiable longing. क्षणं...धर्मेण in showing him to me only for a moment, my evil deeds of former lives have as though borne their fruit. She means that if he could be seen continuously, there would then be no distress, but only bliss. This sentence has been explained differently. 'My misconduct (in laughing at दुर्वासस्), though done in this very life, has borne fruit, as though it were done in a previous life, by showing that rare young man to me, though for a moment'. It is generally the actions of past lives that bear fruit in this life. But this is not a very happy explanation. We think that the mere fact of laughing at a mistake would hardly be called an अधर्म even by सरस्वती. It will be noticed that from the words अजायत च नवपल्लव &c. (p. 13 l. 1 ff), Bāṇa describes the various stages of Love in strict accordance with writers on Rhetoric. 'अभिलाषश्चिन्ता–स्मृति–गुणकथनोद्वेगसम्प्रलापश्च । उन्मादोऽथ व्याधिर्जडता मृतिरिति दशाऽत्र कामदशाः ॥' साहित्यदर्पण III. 190. The sentence अजायत० shows अभिलाष; the next shows चिन्ता. The sentence 'कृतसन्ध्याप्रणामा...तस्थौ' indicates स्मृति and in 'मर्त्यलोकः खलु' we have the fourth अवस्था 'गुणकथन.' In the sentence 'मदनशर०' (l. 21) we have the 5th stage of उद्वेग. प्रतिपत्तिः course of action; means. का...दानीम् what should I do now? स्वप्ने आसादितं द्वितीयं दर्शनं यया. आकर्णं आकृष्टं

कार्मुकं (धनुः) येन. Cupid smote her with all his power. प्रतिबुद्धा when she awoke. At his very first sight she fell in love with him. But when she saw him again in her dreams, she was hopelessly smitten by love. मदन...जगाम unrest came to her who was struck by the arrows of Cupid, as though to learn the news (of her state). The plain meaning is:—being smitten by love, she became restless. When a person falls ill or is beaten or meets with an accident, people call on him to express their sympathy or regard. So here अरति is fancied to have made a call on her. अरतिः—'स्वाभीष्टवस्त्वलाभेन चेतसो याऽनवस्थितिः । अरतिः सा'. Another sense also is hinted. रति is the wife of मदन. As मदन struck her (सरस्वती), अरति (one who is opposed to रति, the wife of the offending मदन) made a call on her. The meanings of नञ् (अ) are six 'तत्सादृश्यमभावश्च तदन्यत्वं तदल्पता । अप्राशस्त्यं **विरोध**श्च नञर्थाः षट् प्रकीर्तिताः ॥'. कुसुम...धत्त—one who is beaten feels pain. But she felt pain though not beaten. The cause of pain was really her love-sick condition. In this and the following five sentences Bāṇa describes her condition by employing the figure of speech called विभावना. It consists in stating that an effect follows though its cause is non—existent. 'क्रियायाः प्रतिषेधेऽपि फलव्यक्तिर्विभावना' काव्यप्रकाश X. In such cases only the well-known cause is absent; while some other cause works to bring about the effect. Compare for this and the last clause 'कुसुमितलताभिरहताप्यधत्त रुजमलिकुलैरदष्टाऽपि ।' परिवर्तते स नलिनीलहरीभिरलोलिताप्यघूर्णत सा ॥'. मन्द... मुमोच when dust (रजः) enters one's eyes, tears fall. She shed tears through love-pangs, though the pollen (रजः) of flowers did not soil her eyes. हंसपक्षाः एव तालवृन्तानि (fans) तै वान्ताः (emitted) वाताः तैः विततः (spread) तैः. शोणशीकरैः the spray of the S'oṇa river. आर्द्रता (1) becoming wet; (2) becoming full of soft feeling. प्रेङ्ख...दोलाभिः though not borne on the pairs of roving (प्रेङ्खत्) Kādambas she rolled on the swinging waves of the sylvan lotus ponds. 'कादम्बः कलहंसः स्यात्' इत्यमरः. कमलिनी—a place abounding in कमलs. 'पुष्करादिभ्यो देशे' पा. 5. 2. 135 (पुष्करिणी । पद्मिनी । सि. कौ.). The ripples of the pond wafting the scent of lotuses excited her and made her roll on her bed. विघटमानानि (separating) चक्रवाकयुगलानि तैः विसृष्टैः (*adj.* of धूमैः). श्यामतामाससाद she became dark (*i. e.* lost the colour of her complexion as she was love-sick). One is darkened by smoke. The sighs heaved by the separated चक्रवाकs are like धूम. The चक्रवाक male was poetically supposed to become separated from its mate at the approach of night. व्यचेष्टत she wriggled. A man stung by bees would fling his body about.

P. 13 l. 29—**P. 14** l. 11 **अथ...यासीत्.** गण...गमे after the lapse of many nights. 'गणरात्रं निशा बह्वयः' इत्यमरः. निवर्तमानः— विकुक्षि returned after accompanying दधीच to his father's place. तथैव—as before (when दधीच left his attendants behind). छत्रधारः (umbrella-bearer) द्वितीयः यस्य. डुढौके Perfect of ढौक् 1 A to approach. वन...द्रीवा stretching her neck like a woodland doe. मार्ग...दृशा she as though bathed him who was tired by the journey with her glance that whitened the ten quarters. One's fatigue is lessened by a bath. She steadfastly looked at him. The glances of her bright eye were like water. कृतः आसनपरिग्रहः येन. कच्चि...कुमारः is the prince well? कच्चित् *(ind.)* indicates 'I hope'. स्मरति भवत्योः—the genitive is used in accordance with 'अधीगर्थदयेशां कर्मणि' पा. 2. 3. 52 (words having the sense of इ with अधि 'to remember' and दय् and ईश् govern the genitive of the object). केव...बिभर्ति only he is somewhat emaciated in body in these days. अवि...धत्ते he has a certain vacantness (of mind) which is inexplicable and without any (apparent) cause. अन्वक्षम् *adv.* immediately, forthwith. अक्षस्य (रथस्य इन्द्रियस्य वा) पश्चात् अन्वक्षम् (अव्ययीभाव). The reading अन्वक् means the same thing. 'अन्वगन्वक्षमनुगेऽनुपदं क्लीबमव्ययम्' इत्यमरः. The meaning प्रत्यक्षं assigned by the com. does not suit the context. वाणिनी = दूती. 'वाणिन्यौ नर्तकीदूत्यौ' इत्यमरः. उच्छ्वसितं—the breath or life *(i. e.* she is a great confidante of the prince). महानुभावः magnanimous, noble. यदे...बध्नाति that he thus keeps up familiarity with a person not known to him and seen only for a moment. तस्य...मासीत् his mind was somehow by chance fixed on us (caught by us) while he passed (on his way), as a shawl may be caught by wayside creepers (in the case of a traveller). अशून्यं...सूनोः the nobility of your prince is not devoid of high birth *i. e.* in the prince high birth and nobility of character are combined. अशून्यम् not devoid of, full. स्वामिसूनु must mean prince here. विकुक्षि was the servant of शर्यात, whose *grandson* (and not son) दधीच was. Or सूनु may be used in the sense of 'offspring in general'. A daughter's son was in ancient times like a son of the body. 'औरसो धर्मपत्नीजस्तत्समः पुत्रिकासुतः ।' याज्ञ॰ II. 128. अलसः...मनांसि people are indeed lazy that they do not make their own *(lit.* buy) the hearts of the great that are easily befriended by offering something or other. सुलभं सौहार्दं (मैत्री) येषाम्. She means:—she and her friend did very little for the prince; but he being great and noble offered his affection to them in return for what little they did. If the world will also offer something ever so little to the great, the latter will befriend them. सो... भुवनम् it is this excess of magnanimity in the great, not found in ordinary people, that makes the three worlds the instruments (of the great). The three worlds come under the control (are willing to abide by the orders) of the great on account of the latter's औदार्य. उच्चावचैः high and low, various. 'उच्चावचैः प्रकृतवस्त्वसंस्पर्शिभिः, विचित्रैरिति वा' सं॰. 'उदक् च अवाक् च उच्चावचं उन्नतं चावनतं च वा' क्षीरस्वामी. It is a compound of the मयूरव्यंसकादि class (पा. II. 1. 72.).

P. 14 l. 12—**P. 15** l. 25. **अपरे...र्मनसी.** The first sentence is अपरेद्युः मालती समदृश्यत (p. 15. l. 17). उद्यति loc. sing. of *pr. p.* of इ with उद्. द्युमणौ—the jewel of the heavens. उद्दामा द्युतिः यस्य. अभिद्रुताः (attacked) तारकाः येन. तामरसानां व्यासः (विकासः) तस्य व्यसनं (intent application) अस्ति अस्य इति व्यसनिन् तस्मिन्. Red lotuses open at sunrise. आयान्ती this and the following adjectives (in the *nom. sing. f.*) qualify मालती (p. 15. l. 17). तरल...नयन्ती under the guise (छलं) of the covering of the sparkling (तरल) complexion of her body, she seemed to bring all the very clear water of the S'oṇa. The poet fancies that her sparkling complexion was really the transparent water of the शोण which she brought with her when crossing it. वितानः—म् canopy. Here the figure is अपह्नुति, which consists in the poetic denial of the real character of a thing and establishing in its place something else resembling it. 'प्रकृतं यन्निषिध्यान्यत्स्थाप्यते सा त्वपह्नुतिः' काव्यप्रकाश X. स्फुटितानां (opened, expanded) अतिमुक्तककुसुमानां स्तबकेन समा त्विट् (कान्तिः) यस्य—*adj.* of तुरङ्गमे and मृगपतौ. सटाल having a mane (*adj.* of both मृगपतौ and तुरङ्गमे). मृगपतौ इव गौरी as पार्वती rides a lion. गौरी also means 'fair' (as applied to मालती). सिंह is the वाहन of दुर्गा. सली...तस्य (*adj.* of ॰युगलस्य) that were gracefully placed on the girth of the horse. उरोबन्धम्—the leathern strap passing round the horse's chest. तिर्य...रणितस्य (*adj.* of ॰युगलस्य) the sharp jingle (रणितं) of the anklets on which was listened to by the horse with slantingly upraised ears. अति... वितस्य that were decked with very thick Alaktaka dye. 'पिण्डालक्तकः कथितोऽलक्तकरसः' सं॰. पल्लवितस्य—पल्लवाः सञ्जाताः अस्य सः पल्लवितः—the soles of the feet were so dyed with Alaktaka as to look like the new leaves (which are reddish) of trees. कु...पृष्ठस्य the upper surface of which (feet) was reddened with saffron. उभयतः—as she rode astride, her feet were on both sides of the horse. ताडन...गतानि come out of their craving for her kicks. It was a convention among Sanskrit poets that the red As'oka tree put forth blossoms when kicked by handsome young ladies. Such conventions are summarised in the following verse 'स्त्रीणां स्पर्शात् प्रियङ्गुर्विकसति बकुलः सीधुगण्डूषसेकात् पादाघातादशोकस्तिलककुरबकौ वीक्षणालिङ्गनाभ्याम् । मन्दारो नर्मवाक्यात्पटुमृदुहसनाच्चम्पको वक्त्रवाताच्चूतो गीतान्नमेरुर्विकसति च पुरो नर्तनात्कर्णिकारः ॥' quoted by मल्लिनाथ on मेघदूत' II. 17. 'रक्ताशोकश्चलकिसलयः'. दोहदम् longing. 'अथ दोहदम् । इच्छाकाङ्क्षा स्पृहेहा तृट्' इत्यमरः. Her feet being dyed red both beneath and above and being on both sides of the horse, the poet fancies that she as if drew along with her forests of red As'oka trees that had put forth foliage (किसलयित) and that accompanied her in the desire of being kicked by her. The lines (पल्लवs) of अलक्तक dye on her soles correspond to the किसलयs of the रक्ताशोक. सकल...स्थला on whose hips jingled a girdle as though it were a proclamation (आघोषणा) for forcibly seizing the hearts of the whole mortal world. She was so handsome that she forcibly captivated the hearts of all. The jingling रशना was the proclamation announcing this pillage of the hearts. C and T translate 'a proclamation devoting to murder and rapine the hearts'. It is difficult to see how 'murder' comes in here. धौत...लता whose creeper-like form was covered by a gown (कञ्चुकः) made of washed and white silk and reaching up to her toes and lighter than even serpent's slough (निर्मोकः). नेत्रम्—silk cloth. 'स्याज्जटांशुकयोर्नेत्रम्' इत्यमरः. निर्मोकात् लघुतरेण. आप्रपदीन—from आप्रपद with the affix ख (ईन), according to 'आप्रपदं प्राप्नोति' पा. 5. 2. 8. (पादस्याग्रं प्रपदं तन्मर्यादीकृत्य आप्रपदम्). छात...सरसी who, with her limbs white with slightly dried (आश्यान) sandal and visible through the fine (छात) gown, seemed as though she were a lotus plant, the stalks of which were clearly visible (विभाव्यमान) in the transparent water. 'अमांसो दुर्बलश्छातः' इत्यमरः. छात lean, thin (from छो to cut). अवयवैः—understand उपलक्षिता after it. The instrumental is used in accordance with 'इत्थम्भूतलक्षणे' पा. 2. 3. 21 (जटाभिस्तापसः । सि. कौ.). कुसुम्भ...दधाना wearing a petticoat (चण्डातकं) red with safflower dye, variegated with spots (पुलकः) of different colours and gleaming inside (the gown), as thoush she were a crystal spot bearing a treasure (निधानं) of jewels. Her gown was white and glossy like crystal. Inside it was the red चण्डातक as inside the crystal ground red gems may be found. Jewels are red like safflower dye (कुसुम्भरागवत् पाटलं). The spots of various colours on the petticoat looked like precious stones called पुलक. पुलक also means 'yellow orpiment.' "नानावर्णबिन्दुविन्यासः पुलकबन्धः, मणिविशेषाश्च पुलकाः' सं°. 'कृमिप्रभेदे रोमाञ्चे पुलकं प्रस्तरे विदुः' शाश्वत 373. चण्डातकं—a petticoat reaching to the middle of the thighs. 'अर्धोरुकं वरस्त्रीणां स्याच्चण्डातकमंशुकम्' इत्यमरः. हारेणा...चौः with a necklace having pearls round like Āmalakī fruit, she seemed to be the autumnal sky variegated (शार) with bright (स्फुरित) and large clusters of stars and overcast with a veil of thin white clouds. She was like the autumnal sky; her white silken कञ्चुक like the white thin clouds of शरद् and the large and round pearls like the stars in the sky. आमलकीफलवत् निस्तलानि (without a bottom *i. e.* round) मुक्ताफलानि यस्य. The reading निस्तुल (incomparable) is not good. कुच...धारयन्ती over her breasts resembling full jars, she had tied a jewelled necklace shooting forth red and green rays, as though it (necklace) were a garland of wild flowers (indicating) the entrance into her heart of some (indescribable) happy man. कुचौ पूर्णकलशौ इव. प्रालम्बमालिका is a garland or necklace reaching from the neck to the chest. 'प्रालम्बमृजुलम्बि स्यात्कण्ठात्' इत्यमरः. The jewels were red and green (emerald) and so resembled red and green leaves (किसलय). Jars full of water were placed at the entrance of houses as auspicious. पल्लवs were placed on the tops of such jars and garlands were tied round the necks of jars and on gates. Hence the poet fancies that her breasts on which rolled a necklace were jars with leaves and flowers indicating the auspicious entrance of some one in her heart. He whoever swayed her heart with love must be called blessed (पुण्यवत्). 'वनमाला विधातव्या पल्लवैः कुसुमैः फलैः' विष्णुरहस्य. Compare for the ideas 'उभयपार्श्वस्थापितोत्पल्लवमुखपूर्णहेमकलशं (कायमानं)' कादम्बरी p. 281 of P; 'वेदीविनिहितपल्लवललामहेमकलशे बद्धवनमालादाम्नि ...मन्दिरे' हर्षचरित 7th उच्छ्वास (2nd para); 'समुल्लसद्भिः स्तनमण्डलैर्मङ्गलकलशमय इव बभूव लोकः' हर्षचरित IV. एकैकस्य of each one (out of the many she wore). हाटककटकस्य of the golden bracelet. मर...नाथस्य—the golden bracelets were inlaid with emerald stones cut into the shape of a crocodile. वेदिका—level ground (on which the stone was set). स्थल...माना who was as though followed by land lotus plants under the belief that she was लक्ष्मी. The emeralds on her bracelets emitted pencils (सन्तति) of green rays in all directions, which (pencils) the poet fancies to be स्थलकमलिनीs that are also green (with leaves). Lotus plants are ordinarily in water. As she moved on land the मयूखसन्तति is fancied to be स्थलकमलिनी. लक्ष्मी dwells in lotus beds. मालती resembled लक्ष्मी in her beauty. बहल...वमन्ती from her lips darkened by the dark streak (कृष्णिका) of plenty of betel, she as though emitted darkness mixed with the glow of evening that was drunk by the moon of her face. The moon swallows darkness. Her face was like the moon. The dark-red tint of ताम्बूल taken by her in abundance resembled darkness mingled with evening radiance. मुखमेव शशी तेन पीतम्. विकचं नयनकुवलयं तस्मिन् कुतूहलेन आलीनया (settling or sitting upon). संहत्या = समूहेन. निरुद्धं अर्धवदनं यस्याः. Bees followed her dark eyes, thinking them to be lotuses and covered the upper part of her face, as though with a veil (जालिका) of blue silk. नीलीरागेण निहितः नीलिमा यस्मिन् (*adj.* of दन्तपत्रेण) which was made blue with indigo-colour. नीलिमा is formed from नील like पिङ्गलिमा (p. 23). शिखि...शितिना as blue as the throat of a peacock. The reading शितिगल० would mean 'as blue as (the throat of) शिव.' शिव is called शितिकण्ठ, as his throat grew dark when he drank कालकूट. See notes p. 2. दन्तपत्रं an ear-ornament. काल...माना— she was fair and bright like lightning and the dark दन्तपत्र was like a streak of dark (काल) cloud. पल्लवs also are placed on the ear as ornament. कल्पितेन made. बालिका—an ear-ornament dangling from the lobe of the ear. '**बालिका** । बालायां वालुकापत्रकाह्वला-**कर्णभूषणे** ॥' मेदिनी (कान्तवर्ग 130). आलोकः (light) एव जलं or जलमिव तत् वर्षतीति. The bright light of the pearl pendants hanging downwards (अधोमुख) fell on her creeperlike arms. Tender creepers may be watered by two girls (बालिकायुगल) bending down. The bright light resembles clear water. दक्षिण...तला with the inner leaf of Ketakī flower placed on her right ear as an ear-ornament, she seemed to have her cheek licked through greed for beauty by the creeperlike tongue of the moon. The long and white केतकी leaf dangling on her cheek is fancied to be the tongue of the moon. The moon desired more grace and licked her cheek, which was very bright and fair. मृग...ष्यन्दिना that emitted the perfume of musk. तिलक... दहन्ती with the round mark on her forehead she bore a face which seemed to be the all-in-all of Cupid kept under a seal. The dark round तिलक of कस्तूरी resembled the mark of a seal.

One keeps one's treasure under seal. Her beautiful face was the सर्वस्व of Cupid *i. e.* she was calculated to inspire love in anyone. लला...चुम्बिनः dancing on her forehead and touching the parting line of her hair. The com. reads 'चटुलातिलक' and explains 'सुवर्णशृङ्खलाबद्धो नानारत्नौघमण्डितः । ललाटलम्ब्यलङ्कारश्चटुलातिलको मतः ॥'. चटुलतिलकमणि may mean 'a jewel dangling on the forehead' (where the तिलक mark is made). उदञ्चता shooting up. कृतं शिरोऽवगुण्ठनं यस्याः. The red rays of the jewel on the forehead shooting round her head are fancied to be a red veil of silk. पृष्ठे प्रेङ्खन् अनादरसंयमनेन शिथिलश्च जूटिकाबन्धः यस्याः—whose thick hair dangled on her back, being loose as she tied it carelessly. नील... पताका as though she, who had a crocodile-like crest jewel (in her hair), was the banner of Cupid, with the ornament of a blue chowrie. Her loose and dangling hai was like a dark chowrie, which is placed as an ornament on banners; chowries are generally white, but her hair being dark, we have नीलचामर here. On the banner of Cupid (who is called मकरकेतु) there would be figures of crocodiles. Her चूडामणि was of the shape of a crocodile. A banner indicates the approach of a conquering general. She would help Cupid to subdue anybody by her charms. 'अवचूलं चिह्नम्' सं०. अवचूलः—a pendant tuft or garland, an ornament hanging from the top of a banner. मल्लिनाथ on शिशुपालवध 5. 13. says '"अस्योच्चूडावचूडाख्यावूर्ध्वाधोमुखचूडकौ' इति ध्वजाङ्गेषु हलायुधः'. बाण is very fond of this word. Compare 'दिवसकरवारणस्यावचूलचामरकलाप इवोपलक्ष्यमाणे...किरणजाले' का० p. 26; 'समदगजघटावचूलसहस्रसंरुद्धम्' p. 114. 'बहलरजोधूसरितमशिशिरकिरणबिम्बमवचूलचामरमिव निष्प्रभमभवत्' का० p. 116; **केशकलापकान्तिना च कृष्णचामरावचूलेन**... छपरचितदण्डं (ध्वजम्)' का० p. 224. कुल...मसः—As one worships one's कुलदेवता everyday and on every important undertaking, so the moon, by honouring her, would obtain her charms (in which the moon falls far short of her). पुनः०—Cupid was once burnt by S'iva; but she would revive him again (*i. e.* she inspires love in anyone). सञ्जीवनौषधि brings a person back to life. 'पुष्पधन्वा रतिपतिः' इत्यमरः. वेले...गरस्य As the ocean cannot go beyond the shore, so love reaches its high water-mark in her. Or the meaning is 'As the ocean beats with the greatest fury on the shore, so she creates the most furious passion by her charm.' ज्योत्स्ने...दयस्य as at moonrise, moonlight covers everything, so her charming youth brings under its sway everything. रतिरसः एव अमृतं तस्य—A great river has plenty of water

('पयः कीलालममृतम्' इत्यमरः). She was full of ambrosial (*i. e.* delightful) love. कु...तरोः a tree reaches its perfection by putting forth flowers. बाल...ग्ध्यस्य what one learns in boyhood, one hardly forgets. So she was never left by cleverness. कौमुदीव कान्तेः—even Grace may derive charms from her, as the mellow moonlight lends beauty to everything. धृ...र्यस्य she was the strength of firmness *i. e.* she was so firm of resolve that even Firmness may draw upon her to add to itself. सं० gives another curious explanation 'यद्वा धृतिः प्रवेशरक्षणम् । यथा प्रविशन्कश्चिद्राजनिकटं ध्रियते केनचित्तथा धैर्यं तावत्प्रसरति यावदेषा न दृष्टा । एतस्यां दृष्टायां सर्वे धैर्यशून्या इति.' गुरु...वस्य she is as though the teacher's hall for reverence. Even Reverence would respect her or even reverence would learn from her as one learns in a teacher's house. बीज...नयस्य modesty would be nursed in her *i. e.* she would be the source of all modesty. गोष्ठी०—all virtues met in her, as persons meet at an assembly or in a club. मन...भावतायाः—Those who are noble are always spirited and yet they would have to take lessons from her in मनस्विता. मनस्विता high-spirited nature. तृप्ति...ण्यस्य—तारुण्य after reaching her was satisfied *i. e.* did not find another, who could surpass her in charms. ०दामवत् दीर्घे लोचने यस्याः. This and the following words in the instru. qualify ०करङ्कवाहिन्या. पाटलः (red) अधरः यस्याः. पाटल is also a kind of flower. कुन्दकुड्मलवत् स्फुटाः (bright) दशनाः यस्याः. कुन्द buds are white. शिरीष is one of the most delicate of flowers. चम्पकवत् अवदातया who was bright and fair (in complexion) like the *champaka*. 'अवदातः सिते पीते' इत्यमरः. कुंसुममय्या इव—It will be noticed that her limbs, body and breath are compared to various flowers and hence the poet fancies that she was made of flowers. ताम्बूलकरङ्कवाहिनी the bearer of betel-box. महाप्रमाणः अश्वतरः (mule) तमारूढया. कतिपये परिचारकाः (attendants) परिकरः (retinue) यस्याः. दधीचप्रेम्णा on account of the love she bore for दधीच (whose confidante मालती was). This is to be connected with the words लुण्ठिता, आकृष्टा &c. लुण्ठि...रथैः she (मालती) was plundered by सरस्वती with her desires. Although मालती was far away, from her face सरस्वती's longing and loving heart understood what मालती had to say. So the poet says that मनोरथs of सरस्वती looted from मालती what she came to convey. प्रत्युद्र...काभिः she (मालती) was received with welcome by her (सरस्वती's) longings. 'उत्कण्ठोत्कलिके समे' इत्यमरः. Though she was far off, on seeing her सरस्वती became eager to know her message and her eager heart went

'प्रतिसरश्चमूपृष्ठे नियोज्यकरसूत्रयोः' हेमचन्द्रः. विधेय controlled by, at the disposal of. प्रीत्या...ते Through my affection I am dependent on you and at your disposal. व्या...क्षितम् lay open, fair lady, what you desire to say. विवक्षित *past p. p.* of the desiderative base of वच्. वर: वर्णः (complexion) अस्याः इति वर०. That word also suggests another sense 'one who describes the bridegroom I have chosen'. लोलु...ग्रामस्य (you know well) that the array of senses ardently hankers (after gratification). पारिप्लवता = चञ्चलता. अतो...मर्हसि hence you will please not blame me (*lit.* wait upon me with censure). न च...कारणम् my talkativeness is not due to my foolishness or fickleness or trickery. A चारण is a wandering actor, who has to change his appearance as occasion demands. Hence चारणता means धूर्तता. न...भक्तिः there is nothing that great devotion to one's master would not induce a person to do (*i. e.* a devoted servant would do anything for his master). अस्य कामो गुरुः Cupid is his teacher (*i. e.* he is learning the lore of Love). अस्य (दधीचस्य) is to be connected with each of the following clauses. Another sense is 'his Love (for you) is great (गुरु).' चन्द्र...शः the moon is the lord of his life (*i. e.* cools down his torment by its ambrosial rays). जीवितेशः also means 'Death'. The moon increases the excitement of those who are love-sick and thus may cause their death. Compare शाकुन्तल III. 'तव कुसुमशरत्वं शीतरश्मित्वमिन्दोर्द्वयमिदमयथार्थं दृश्यते मद्विधेषु।'. The com. gives a third sense. As दधीच is called देव (king) above, he requires a पुरोहित. जीवितेश means पुरोहित. पुरोहित was the first of the ten ministers that constituted a king's council according to the S'ukranīti (See Sacred Books of the Hindus vol. 13 p. 68). So the meaning would be 'the moon is his first councillor.' मलय...हेतुः the wind from the मलय mountain (in the south) is support to him. उच्छ्वासहेतु means 'a source of consolation *i. e.* a friend'. It also means 'a cause of sighs.' The southern wind is an excitant of love and causes a love-sick person to heave deep sighs (उच्छ्वास). Compare 'तस्याश्चन्दनपरिमल इव दक्षिणानिलेन सह समागच्छति मोहः' का० p. 255 of P. मलय is one of the seven principal mountains of India 'महेन्द्रो मलयः सह्यः शुक्तिमानृक्षपर्वतः। विन्ध्यश्च पारियात्रश्च सप्तैते कुलपर्वताः॥' वायुपुराण 45. 88. आध...स्थानेषु mental torments are in place of (*i. e.* occupy the position of) confidential persons. Another meaning is 'mental distress pervades his inside parts (*i. e.* his heart).' स...हृत् pain is his great friend. Another meaning is 'pain greatly harasses his life' (separate परम् + असु + हृत्) Or we may take 'परम् + अ—सुहृत्' (pre-eminently an enemy). प्र...प्तः wakefulness is his relative or friend. आप्त also means 'obtained,' the idea being 'he has secured wakefulness.' मनो...गताः yearnings are his spies. Another meaning is 'desires (for union with you) pervade him all round.' निः...सराः sighs are his vanguard (also 'sighs go in front of his body'). विग्रहः battle, body. मृत्यु...वर्ती Death is his personal attendant; also 'death stands near him' *i. e.* he will die if he be not united with you. He, being a prince, has death attending him (*i. e.* he condemns offenders to death). Compare 'यस्य प्रसादे पद्मा श्रीर्विजयश्च पराक्रमे। मृत्युश्च वसति क्रोधे सर्वतेजोमयो हि सः॥' मनु० VII. 11. रण...रकः Disquiet is his emissary; also 'his unrest makes him wander about.' सं० says 'द्विविधा हि चाराः संस्थाः सञ्चारकाश्च' (*i. e.* spies are of two kinds, those who stay in one place and those who move about from place to place). In सर्वगताः above we had the first kind of spies. सङ्क...वृद्धाः his fancies are the elders that instruct his intellect; also 'his fancies have increased, being incited by his intellect.' The idea is he listens to his fancies, as one would listen to the advice of elders. अनु..वना If I were to say 'he is a good match for your ladyship', then it would be highly honouring oneself. In this and the following sentences, she puts forward several sentiments and finds fault with each as not being suited to adequately express her master's feeling towards सरस्वती. In saying 'अनुरूपो' &c., she would be regarded as only honouring her master, as being partial to him. That must be said by others and by सरस्वती. The words आत्म० also mean 'that is purely my own supposition' (not necessarily shared by सरस्वती and others). Bâṇa is very fond of passages in this strain. Compare हर्षचरित 3rd उच्छ्वास 'यामीति न स्नेहसदृशम् &c.' (text p. 54); 'अतिप्रियोऽसीति पौनरुक्त्यम् &c.' कादम्बरी p. 237 of P. शील...रुद्धम् If I were to say 'he is possessed of a noble character,' that would be in conflict with what he has now begun. A man of high character would not be over head and ears in love with a maiden seen only casually and would not send a दूती to her. धीर...रीतम् If I say 'he is firm or wise,' that would be inconsistent with his state (described by me already). सु...यत्तम् If I say 'he is blessed', that is in your hands. It is in your hands to make him happy by accepting him as your husband. सुभग means 'a person fortunate in securing the love of the woman he loves.' स्थिर...क्षेप: If I say 'he is constant in his affection,' that would be a clever hint or statement. Those words would insinuate that other handsome young men are not constant in their affections. जानाति...चितम् If I say 'he knows how to serve (his fiancee),' that would not be appropriate to his position as a prince. A prince does not ordinarily know how to serve; he only knows how to command. इच्छति...लाप: to say 'he desires to be your slave till death' would be the words of a rogue (*i. e.* all false). Being a prince, he cannot be a *slave*. भवन...लोभनम् 'you would be the mistress of his home' would be offering an allurement. A noble lady like you would not be tempted by the allurements of pomp and wealth and palaces. You would accept him only for his intrinsic worth. पुण्य...पात: 'blessed is she who secures such a husband' would be (sheer) partiality for one's master. त्वं...प्रियम् 'you are his death' is unpleasant (speech). अगु...क्षेप: 'you do not know his worth' would be a censure (of you). स्वप्ने...क्षिकम् 'you have often shown him favours in his dreams' would be without a witness. She means:—he is so deep in love with you, that he often sees you in his dreams. But that statement cannot be corroborated by producing any witness, as no one saw him dreaming of you. अविद्यमानः साक्षी यस्य. For क, see above p. 12. प्राण...तरता 'he solicits you for his life' would be cowardliness. A prince like him should not beg even for his life. She intimates by this how deep his love is. तत्रा...ज्ञा 'come there' would be a command. She means she has no authority nor right to command her (सरस्वती). वारि...भव: 'even though forbidden (by you), he will perforce come' would be an insult to you. तदे...मसि you are thus beyond the range of words. She means that she (मालती) has not words that would appropriately describe what दधीच feels for her and what she (सरस्वती) should do for him. The words she may employ are defective in some way or other.

P. 16 l. 26—**P. 17** l. 11 **अथ सरस्वती...इति.** विस्फारित wide, expanded. सितेन वदतीति ०वादिनी. ०वादिनि O lady of smiling speech. यदा...साद: what you order is a great favour (*i. e.* even your orders are &c.). प्र...वशा beside herself with joy. विदितः वृत्तान्तः यया. उत्कण्ठायाः भारं बिभर्ति इति ०भृत् तेन—that laboured under the burden of longing. ताम्यता languishing. One carrying a burden feels fatigue. कल्पायितम्—*past p. p.* of कल्पायते

denominative verb from कल्प (कल्प इव आचरति). The rest of the day seemed to her as long as a कल्प on account of her longing. कल्प is a day of Brahmā, and is a period of 1000 महायुगs (कृत, त्रेता, द्वापर and कलि being one महायुग). Each महायुग has 4320000 human years. गभस्तिमति = रवौ. The sentence here is सरस्वती (p. 17 l. 1) प्रतिपालयामास (l. 8). स्तिमिततरम् noiselessly. प्रहसि... चन्द्रमसि when the moon came up from the eastern quarter that was now bright as if smiling, as a lion comes out of a cave. The east gleamed with moonlight and hence is said to be प्रहसिता (smiles being described as white). पुरन्दरः इन्द्रः तस्य इयं पौरन्दरी. इन्द्र is the lord of the East. *Vide p.* 36. above. The words शुचिनि...कोमले may apply to both शयने and ०सैकते. But there would be repetition in ची...मारे and ०कोमले. So it is better to take the first three words with सैकते and ०कोमले alone with शयने as the com. does. शुचिनि white; pure. ची...मारे (1) soft with china silk; (2) soft like &c. तरङ्गिणि (1) that has waves *i. e.* is crumpled up or has a shining coverlet; (2) that has ripples (marks left by receding ripples). स्वप्न...दधाना having an ornamental mark on her forehead that (mark) seemed to be the lustre (चन्द्रिका) of the toe-nails of दधीच, that (चन्द्रिका) stuck (to her forehead) when she in her dream fell at his feet in supplication. स्वप्ने कृता प्रार्थना तस्यां पादपतनं तस्मिन् लग्नाम्. The white mark of sandal on her forehead is fancied to be the light of दधीच's toes sticking to her forehead &c. गण्डस्थलमेवादर्शः तस्मिन् प्रति० *(adj.* of इन्दुना). अय...जनः Here have I brought the person (दधीच) dear to you. निवेद्यमानः मदनसन्देशः यस्मै—The moon was reflected in her bright cheek. The poet fancies that that moon as if whispered in her ear this message of Love 'अयमसौ &c.' विकीर्य...पट्टम् fanning her perspiring bright (स्पष्ट) cheek with her hand that scattered pencils (चक्रवालं) of the rays of her nails, as though it (hand) had turned into a yak-tail fan the digits of the moon. She had no fan; therefore she fanned her cheek with her hand. Her cheek perspired on account of the deep emotion agitating her heart. स्वेद is one of the eight सात्त्विकभावs that are indicative of deep feeling. 'स्तम्भः स्वेदोऽथ रोमाञ्चः स्वरभङ्गोऽथ वेपथुः । वैवर्ण्यमश्रु प्रलय इत्यष्टौ सात्त्विकाः स्मृताः ॥'. When she moved her hand to and fro, the rays of her bright nails were tossed about. Those rays resemble the digits of the moon. A yak's tail is also white. बालव्यजनीकृतः चन्द्रकलाकलापः येन. Connect ०मृणालिकां with वहन्ती. She had placed across her breasts a fresh lotus-stalk to allay the fever of love. She placed the stalk across the breasts as they were plump and not between them. सं० explains 'स्तनमध्ये प्रवेशाभावात्तिरश्चीनमित्युक्तम्.' स्तनयोरधि अधिस्तनम् (अव्ययीभाव). The white lotus-stalk resembled a cane. The poet fancies that the lotus-stalk was a cane sportively let fall on her bosom by Cupid (चित्तभू) intimating that no one but दधीच was to enter her heart (*i. e.* only दधीच was to be her lover). A doorkeeper also uses his cane and prevents people from entering the royal gate. स्तनयन्ती murmuring (to herself). If we read स्तनयन्तीम्, the meaning is 'the lotus-stalk on her bosom made a sound'. मनोजन्मना=कामेन. जघन्या इव like a low woman. 'जघन्योन्त्येऽधमेपि च' इत्यमरः. का…तरुणीषु of what account are other poor (तपस्विनी) extremely excitable young women?

P. 17 ll. 12—23 **आजगाम…धिकम्.** The sentence is आजगाम च…मालतीद्वितीयो दधीचः (l. 18.). मधुमासः—the month of चैत्र, the first month of वसन्त. **'स्याच्चैत्रे** चैत्रिको **मधुः'** इत्यमरः. In this and the following clauses, the poet compares दधीच, who was accompanied by मालती, to several things by paronomastic words. मधुमास is an excitant of love. The poet hints by reference to मधुमास, मलयानिल &c., that the love of both दधीच and सरस्वती had reached the highest pitch through exciting surroundings. सु…वहः which has sweet breezes (with मधुमासः); who bore (on his body) sweet perfumes (with दधीच). Spring is the season of flowers and hence the breezes are charged with fragrance. सुरभिः गन्धवहः (वायुः) यस्मिन्; सुरभिं गन्धं वहतीति. कृता मृणालानां धृतिः (धारणं) येन—who bore lotus-stalks; कृता मृणालैः धृतिः (प्राणधारणं) येन that subsists on lotus-stalks. दधीच bore lotus-stalks to alleviate the burning torment of love. Hamsas subsist on lotus-stalks. Compare 'मृणाललोभेन च चरणनखमयूखलग्नैर्भवनहंसैरिव सञ्चार्यमाणा मन्दमन्दं बभ्राम' हर्षचरित 4 उच्छ्वास. शिखण्डी peacock. घनप्रीत्या उन्मुखः—that uplifts its face in joy at (seeing) a cloud (with शिखण्डी); whose face was upturned (in expectation) on account of his deep (घन) love (with दधीच). आहितः सरसायाः चन्दनस्य धवलायाः तनुलतायाः उत्कम्पः येन that shakes a juicy tender white creeper (growing) on a sandal tree (with मलयानिल). Or we may explain as the com. does. 'सरसान् चन्दनान् धवांश्च लान्ति इति सरस…लाः तनुलताः' *i. e.* tender creepers that hang upon juicy sandal and धव trees. आहितः सरसेन चन्दनेन धवलायाः तनुलतायाः उत्कम्पः यस्मिन् whose delicate body white with viscous sandal had a tremor (with दधीच). We may also dissolve as आहितः…उत्कम्पः येन who caused the delicate body (of

सरस्वती) to shake (through love for him). But this is rather far-fetched. The poet is describing the personal appearance of दधीच and not of सरस्वती. दधीच's body shook with the emotion of love. कम्प is one of the eight सात्त्विकभावs, for which see above p. 79. कृष्य...पतिना as if drawn forward by the lord of planets (the moon) that as though seized his hair by his करs (rays, hands). When we want to drag a man, we may do so by seizing his hair with our hands. The moon's rays fell on his head. The moon is an excitant of love and urged him forward. कृतः करैः (रश्मिभिः) करेण (हस्तेन) वा कचग्रहः येन. कन्दर्पस्य उद्दीपने (exciting) दक्षेण. उह्यमान...रसेन as though he was borne by the रस (sentiment, water *i. e.* flood) of love abounding in उत्कलिकाs (agitation, waves). The student will notice the appropriate words कृष्यमाण, प्रेर्यमाण, उह्यमान used by the author in each clause. परि...यष्टिः whose body was covered with a swarm of bees that crowded (over him) on account of the perfumes (his body bore), as though it (swarm) was a blue piece of cloth. अन्तः...दरः one of whose cheeks was whitened by the reflection of the moon gleaming inside it, which (reflected moon) appeared like the temporal bone over the ear of the intoxicated cupid—elephant, as though by the graceful embarrassed smile of the first union (of a loving couple). 'शङ्खो निधौ ललाटास्थि' इत्यमरः. मत्तः मदनकरी (मदनः एव करी) तस्य कर्णशङ्खवत् आचरति ०शङ्खायते तेन. His bright cheek had a reflection of the moon. The bright image of the moon on his cheek looked like the temporal bone over the ears of an elephant. Bones are white. An intoxicated elephant, from whose temples मद flows, might expose the temporal bone to view. The moon is a friend and excitant of Love. Hence the poet says मत्तमदनकरी. Or we may explain in another way. The reflection of the moon was like the temporal bone and her broad cheek was like the broad ear of an elephant. Smiles are bright and so resemble the image of the moon. The poet probably puts in the word एक in एककपोलोदरः by way of a picturesque contrast to मालतीद्वितीयः. Or perhaps the idea is that only one of his cheeks was turned towards the rising moon. हृदय...गिरा in a voice broken like that of Haṁsas, as though mingled with the tinkling of the anklets of his beloved enshrined in his heart. His voice was broken by emotion. The poet fancies that it was interrupted by the tinkling &c. कृतं सम्भाषणं येन. यथा...ज्ञापयति—connect this and the following clauses with तथा तां...रामाम् अरमयत्. उपजातः विस्रम्भः (confidence) यस्याम्. आत्मानमकथयत्—she declared to him who she really was (*i. e.* she told him that she was सरस्वती). संवत्सरमधिकम् a year or more. It will be noticed how Bāṇa very appropriately draws the veil of silence over the amorous sports of the meeting of सरस्वती and दधीच. It is a canon of rhetoricians that the love sports of divinities are not to be dwelt upon in a poem. In this respect Bāṇa offers a pleasing contrast to Kālidāsa who could not resist the temptation of describing the S'ṛingāra of S'iva and Pārvatī in the कुमारसम्भव (VIII). Vide ध्वन्यालोक (उद्द्योत III under verse 14) 'तस्मादभिनेयार्थे च काव्ये यदुत्तमप्रकृते राजादेरुत्तमप्रकृतिभिर्नायिकाभिः सह ग्राम्यसम्भोगवर्णनं तत्पित्रोः सम्भोगवर्णनमिव सुतरामसभ्यम्। तथैवोत्तमदेवताविषयम्। **न च सम्भोगशृङ्गारस्य सुरतलक्षण एवैकः प्रकारः**, यावदन्येऽपि प्रभेदाः परस्परप्रेमदर्शनादयः सम्भवन्ति। ते कस्मादुत्तमप्रकृतिविषये न वर्ण्यन्ते।...**यत्त्वेवंविधे विषये महाकवीनामप्यसमीक्ष्यकारिता लक्ष्ये दृश्यते स दोष एव।**'.

P. 17 l. 24—**P. 18** l. 8 **अथ दैव...मान्तिकम्.** सर्व...रामम् lovely on account of possessing all (auspicious) characteristics. The following verse summarises most of them 'त्रिषु विपुलो गम्भीरस्त्रिष्वेव षडुन्नतश्चतुर्ह्रस्वः। सप्तसु रक्तो राजा पञ्चसु दीर्घश्च सूक्ष्मश्च॥' बृहत्संहिता 68. 84. जातमात्रायैव the moment he was born. सरहस्याः together with the esoteric or mystical meaning. Or सरहस्याः may mean 'together with the esoteric portion *viz.* the Upanishads.' वेद is often defined as 'मन्त्रब्राह्मणात्मकः'. Compare 'वेदः कृत्स्नोऽधिगन्तव्यः सरहस्यो द्विजन्मना॥' मनु II. 165, where मेधातिथि says 'रहस्यमुपनिषदः'. स्वय...ध्यन्ति will spontaneously manifest themselves. सद्भर्तृ...दधीचम् The idea is:—when सरस्वती left the mortal world at the bidding of ब्रह्मा, she started, enshrining her husband दधीच in her heart. The poet fancies that she carried him in her heart for the purpose of boastfully displaying to the heavenly assembly that she had secured an ideal husband. श्लाघा boast. पिता...देशात्—her curse was to end, according to Brahmā, when she bore a son. Vide text p. 5. l. 9. हृदये...हतः struck in the heart as though by a thunderbolt or by a lightning flash. 'ह्रादिन्यौ वज्रतडितौ' इत्यमरः. भ्रातुः of his cousin (as दधीच had no brother). C and T think that भ्रातृ was a proper name, as it would be unnecessary to describe दधीच's brother or cousin as a Brāhmaṇa. In our opinion ब्राह्मणस्य is purposely put in. दधीच was the son of च्यवन and सुकन्या (the daughter of a क्षत्रिय) and so was only ब्राह्मणसदृश. Vide मनु० 10. 6 'स्त्रीष्वनन्तरजातासु द्विजैरुत्पादितान्सुतान्। सदृशानेव तानाहुर्मातृदोषविगर्हितान्॥'. बाण wants to intimate that

दधीच's cousin was the offspring of Brâhmaṇa parents. अक्षमाला अभिधानं यस्याः. निर्विशेषम् *adv.* without making any difference (connect with समवर्धयत्). सामान्यं स्तन्यं ययोः who were fed alike with the same milk. सारस्वतः (सरस्वत्याः अपत्यं पुमान्) आख्या यस्य. सोदर्ययोरिव like that of brothers. समानोदरे शयितः सोदर्यः according to 'विभाषोदरे' पा. 6. 3. 88 and 'सोदराद्यः' पा. 4. 4. 109. आविर्भूतः अशेषाणां (सकलानां) विद्यानां सम्भारः (समूहः) यस्मिन्. सवयसि—of the same age. समानं वयः अस्य सवयाः. वाङ्मयं...यामास imparted the whole literature. प्राचुर्येण प्रस्तुता वाक् अत्र इति वाङ्मयम् according to 'तत्प्रकृतवचने मयट्' पा. 5. 4. 21. कृतः दाराणां परिग्रहः येन who took a wife. अस्य...वासम् he out of affection made for him in that very place a dwelling named प्रीतिकूट. प्रीतिकूट seems to be the name given to the house of Bāṇa's ancestors. It was so called because सारस्वत built it out of love (प्रीति) for his cousin. आत्मनाऽपि as for himself. आषाढी—see above p. 27. कृष्णाजिनं अस्ति अस्य. These and the following words show that he remained a ब्रह्मचारी. मेखला is a girdle made of grass (मुञ्ज &c). तपस्यतः—*geni. sing.* of the *pr. p.* of तपस्यति denominative verb from तपस् (तपः आचरति).

P. 18 ll. 9--25 **अथ तस्मात्...द्विजातयः.** The first sentence is अथ तस्मात् (वत्सात्)...प्रावर्तत विपुलो वंशः. All the adjectives apply to भागीरथीप्रवाह and वंश. The reading वत्सात् is good. प्रवर्धमानः आदिपुरुषैः (भार्गवादिभिः) जनिता या आत्मचरणस्य उन्नतिः तया निर्गतः प्रघोषः यस्य whose noisy fame went on increasing on account of the eminence of the school (चरणः) established by the first founders (with वंश). वत्स belonged to भार्गवगोत्र. For चरण see above p. 20. Or प्रवर्धमान may be connected with आदिपुरुष, meaning 'who increased *i. e.* had progeny'. प्रवर्धमानः आदिपुरुषः (विष्णुः) तेन जनिता आत्मचरणात् उन्नतिः यस्य ०न्नतिः स चासौ निर्गतप्रघोषश्च (with ०प्रवाहः)—that emitted a loud uproar, issuing from the foot of Vishṇu. The com. sees here (in प्रवर्धमान) a reference to the वामनावतार, when विष्णु, first coming to बलि as a dwarf, assumed a huge form and covered the worlds. 'किल त्रैलोक्याक्रान्तिकाले ब्रह्मलोकप्राप्ताद्विष्णुपदाद् ब्रह्मणा कमण्डलुजलक्षालितात् गङ्गा समभवदिति वार्ता'. For the Ganges rising from the foot of विष्णु, see above p. 41. परमेश्वरेण (शिवेन) शिरसि धृतः (०प्रवाहः); परमेश्वरैः (नृपैः) शिरसि धृतः honoured by kings (with वंश). The Ganges in her descent at भगीरथ's request to purify his ancestors fell on S'iva's head. सकलकलः (कलकलेन सह) आगमः (आगमनं) तेन गम्भीरः—deep (in stream) on account of its coming (from heaven) with an uproar (with ०प्रवाहः); सकलानां कलानां (नृत्यादीनां) आगमेन (by the acquisition) गम्भीरः deep *i. e.* well versed (with

वंशः). महा...मान्यः applies in the same sense to both. Or महामुनि may refer to जह्नु, whose daughter the Ganges became by being let off from his ear. Note रामायण I. 43. 'ततो हि यजमानस्य जह्नोरद्भुतकर्मणः। गङ्गा संप्लावयामास यज्ञवाटं महात्मनः॥ 35 तस्यावलेपनं ज्ञात्वा क्रुद्धो जह्नुश्च राघव। अपिबत्तु जलं सर्वं गङ्गायाः परमाद्भुतम् ॥ 36...गङ्गां चापि नयन्ति स्म दुहितृत्वे महात्मनः। ततस्तुष्टो महातेजाः श्रोत्राभ्यामसृजत्प्रभुः ॥ 38.' विपक्षाणां शत्रूणां क्षोभः तस्य क्षमः (with वंशः); विपक्षाणां (विगताः पक्षाः येषां ते विपक्षाः पर्वताः तेषां) क्षोभः &c. The Ganges wears out mountains by its flood. Mountains had once wings and harassed the earth by flying anywhere. Indra cut off their wings. Compare 'उदधिमिव भयान्तःप्रविष्टसपक्षभूमिभृत्सहस्रसङ्कुलम्' काम्दबरी p. 90 of P; also रघु० 13. 7. क्षितितले लब्धा आयतिः (दैर्घ्यं प्रभावश्च) येन. The Ganges stretches for a long distance over the earth. The family attained dignity (आयति). अस्ख...त्तः that proceeded without stumbling *i. e.* without minding any obstacle (with गङ्गा); that conducted itself without deviating (from the path of right). The sentence is यस्माद् अजायन्त वात्स्यायना नाम...द्विजातयः. गृहमुनयः who were sages dwelling in houses (and not in forests). A मुनि is a sage or a recluse, who has given up worldly life. The ancestors of Bāṇa were householders but their conduct was so pure that they might be as well styled *munis*. Compare भगवद्गीता 2. 56 for a description of a मुनि. आश्रितं श्रौतं यैः that had recourse to ritual prescribed by the Vedas. अनालम्बिता अलीका बककाकुः यैः (1) that did not resort to the crane-like disagreeable (अलीक) tones; (2) that did not assume false hypocritical tones. There is an apparent contradiction between आश्रितश्रौताः and अना...काकवः in the first sense. Those who studiously perform the ritual of the Vedas have to recite in disagreeable tones the Vedic texts. This विरोध is got over by taking the second sense of अना०. A बक is a symbol of hypocrisy, as it stands on one leg as though deep in meditation and then pounces down upon a fish. काकुः is a change of voice due to fear, sorrow &c. 'काकुः स्त्रियां विकारो यः शोकभीत्यादिभिर्ध्वनेः' इत्यमरः. For बकवृत्ति, note मनु० 'बकवच्चिन्तयेदर्थान्' VII. 106. Explain the विरोध in the following clauses similarly. Read ०व्रता for ०वृता. कृतं कुक्कुटव्रतं यैः (1) that observed the vow of fasting called कुक्कुटव्रत; (2) that devoured cocks. अबैडाला वृत्तिः येषाम् (1) whose conduct was not ferocious, (2) whose conduct was not cat-like. Cats (बिडाल) pounce upon cocks. There is विरोध in the second senses of both compounds; but none if the first sense of each be taken. In कुक्कुटव्रत, one is to subsist on a lump of food not bigger than the egg of a hen. विवर्जिता जनपङ्क्तिः यैः (1) that avoided the cooking of (ordinary or low) people *i. e.* who did not take food cooked by common people; (2) that avoided the company of their castemen at dinner (*i. e.* that avoided a life of bustle and luxury). C and T translate 'averse to worldly pretence.' We cannot understand how this sense is arrived at. परि...कूताः that were free from thoughts (आकूतं) of fraud, bragging and hypocrisy (कूर्चं). It is difficult to say what the words कीर and कुची mean. कीर means a parrot and so might stand for 'uttering words without understanding the meaning, bragging.' अगृहीतं गह्वरं यैः (1) that did not resort to caves (*i. e.* remained householders and did not become recluses); (2) that were not hypocrites. 'गुहादम्भौ गह्वरे द्वे' इत्यमरः. न्यक्कृता निकृतिः (शाठ्यं) यैः that disdained dishonesty. प्रसन्ना (tranquil) प्रकृतिः (स्वभावः) येषाम्. We may also dissolve प्रसन्नाः प्रकृतयः (राजामात्याः) येषु. 'अमात्याद्याश्च पौराश्च सद्भिः प्रकृतयः स्मृताः' क्षीर० quoting कात्य. विगताः विकृतयः (changes of mind) येभ्यः. परेषां परिवादः (निन्दा) तस्मात् पराचीनं (पराङ्मुखं) चेतः येषाम्. वर्णत्रयस्य व्यावृत्त्या विशुद्धं अन्धः (अन्नं) येषाम् whose food was pure, the three Varnas being excluded *i. e.* they did not take food with people of the three Varṇas other than that to which they belonged. व्यावृत्तिः exclusion. C and T suggest another sense. 'Whose darkness *i.e.* delusion was corrected by sublating the three colours'. In the श्वेताश्वतरोपनिषद्, (IV. 5. अजामेकां लोहितशुक्लकृष्णां &c.) the three colours शुक्ल, लोहित and कृष्ण represent सत्त्व, रजः and तमः and stand for the material world as opposed to the spirit. Having excluded the material world, their error was at an end and they properly understood the Reality underlying the material world. धीरया धिषणया (बुद्ध्या) अवधूताः अध्येषणाः यैः—who disregarded desires by their firm intellect. 'सनिस्त्वध्येषणा याच्ञा' इत्यमरः. The reference is probably to बृहदारण्यकोपनिषद् 4. 4. 22 'ते ह स्म पुत्रैषणायाश्च वित्तैषणायाश्च लोकैषणायाश्च व्युत्थायाथ भिक्षाचर्यं चरन्ति' or to desires in general. असङ्कसुकः—स्थिरः. 'सङ्कसुकोऽस्थिरे' इत्यमरः (from कस् 10 'to move' with सम्). प्रणत०—who befriended those that came seeking their help (*lit.* that bowed to them). शमिताः समस्तानां शाखान्तराणां संशीतयः (संशयाः) यैः that removed (explained) all the doubts of other schools. शाखा is a traditional recension of a particular Veda, as शाकल of the ऋग्वेद. Here it seems to be used in the sense of शाखाध्येतृ. उद्घाटिताः (opened *i. e.* expounded) समग्राः

ग्रन्थार्थानां ग्रन्थयः (knotty or difficult points) यैः. वाग्मिनः eloquent. वाग्मिन् is used in a good sense, while वाचाल and वाचाट (derived from the same word वाच्) are used in a bad sense. स...निनः fond of clever speech. If we read परसुभा० then the meaning is 'fond of the good sayings of others'. विद...वेदिनः appreciating clever jokes. They did not *themselves crack* jokes, but could appreciate them; they, though वेदाभ्यासरत, were not devoid of a sense of wit and humour. परि...बाह्याः they were charming in their intercourse (with others) and not strangers to dancing, singing and music. They knew a little of नृत्य and other arts, but were not solely devoted to them. ऐति...तृष्णाः who were never surfeited with traditional tales. 'पारम्पर्योपदेशे स्यादैतिह्यमितिहाव्ययम्' इत्यमरः. ऐतिह्यम् from इति ह with the affix ञ्य (य), according to 'अनन्तावसथेतिहभेषजाञ्ञ्यः' पा. 5. 4.23. (आनन्त्यम्, ऐतिह्यम्). सानुक्रोशाः = सदयाः. सत्येन शुचयः pure on account of truthfulness. सर्वसत्त्वेषु सौहार्दं (good will, friendship) एव द्रवः तेन आर्द्रं हृदयं येषाम्. तथा सर्व० the clauses from this downwards are to be taken singly and also in pairs. Taken singly each is construable by itself; if they are taken in pairs, there is an apparent विरोध. सर्व...पेताः possessed of all virtues. सर्व...भूताः possessed of all Guṇas (सत्त्व, रजः and तमः) and (yet) not overwhelmed by the quality of रजस्. राजसेन (गुणेन) अनभिभूताः. राजस is from रजस्. राज...भूताः is construable by itself; but in avoiding the विरोध with सर्व...पेताः, we may explain it as राजसेनया अनभिभूताः—not treated with dishonour by the royal army (०सेना अनभि०). Explain the following clauses similarly. क्षमाभाजः who are forbearing. क्षमा...नन्दनाः who resort to the earth and have recourse to the Nandana garden. नन्दन is the garden of Indra. Those who resort to it cannot be on the earth. आ...नन्दनाः also means 'who delight their dependents'. अनिस्त्रिंशाः = अक्रूराः. विद्याधराः—those that possess Vidyās. अनि...धराः—that are without swords and (yet) विद्याधरs. निस्त्रिंशः a sword. निष्क्रान्तस्त्रिंशतोङ्गुलिभ्यः—that which is longer than 30 finger-breadths. विद्याधरs are semi-divine beings that are always armed with swords. 'मालाखड्गगुलिकाञ्जनादिना भेदेन भिन्नानामपि विद्याधराणां खड्गहस्तत्वं न व्यभिचरति' सं०. अज...वन्तः not dull and well-versed in the arts. अज...वन्तः not cold and (yet) moons. 'शिशिरो जडः' इत्यमरः. अदो...काः free from faults (sins) and helping others (against difficulties or sins). तारयन्तीति तारकाः. अदो...काः without nights (दोषा) and yet constellations. Stars cannot be seen without night. अप...

स्वन्तः not causing distress to others and brilliant (in appearance); not heating others and yet suns. अनु...भुजः without pride (ऊष्मन् *m.*) and sacrificers; without heat and (yet) fires. हुतं भुञ्जते those who enjoy (the fruit of) what they offer as an oblation. अकु...गिनः who had no deceit and were not addicted to pleasure; who did not creep on the earth and (yet) were serpents. अविद्यमाना कुसृतिः शाठ्यं येषाम्. 'कुसृतिर्निकृतिः शाठ्यम्' इत्यमरः. अविद्यमाना कौ (पृथिव्यां) सृतिः (सरणं) येषाम्. भोगिन् *m.* 'a serpent' (from भोगः hood + इन्). अस्त...लयाः who were free from stiffness (arrogance) and were abodes of good deeds; without pillars and (yet) holy places (temples &c.) A house cannot be without a pillar. अलुप्त...दक्षाः who never ceased in the performance of sacrifices and were skilful; the performance of their sacrifice was not disturbed and (yet) they were दक्षs. दक्ष was a famous प्रजापति. He once celebrated a sacrifice at which he did not invite his own daughter सती and her husband शिव. She went uninvited, was insulted and threw herself into fire. S'iva destroyed the sacrifice of दक्ष, pursued the latter and killed him. Compare 'न पशुपतेरिव दक्षोद्वेगकारीण्यैश्वर्यविलसितानि' हर्षचरित II;'दक्षाध्वरक्रियामिवोद्धतगणकचग्रहभयोपसेवितत्र्यम्बकाम्' कादम्बरी p. 128 of P. and कुमारसम्भव I. 21. अ...जितः who were not deceitful and had restrained desires; without serpents and vanquishers of Cupid (*i. e.* S'ivas). S'iva has serpents encircling his body. कामान् जयन्तीति or कामं कन्दर्पं जयन्तीति. 'भेद्यलिङ्गे **शठे व्यालः** पुंसि श्वापद**सर्प**योः' इत्यमरः. असा...जातयः who were pre-eminent and Brāhmaṇas; who had nothing in common (with others) and (yet) had two jātis. A जाति (genus) is defined as 'नित्यमेकमनेकानुगतम्'. A जाति like गोत्व is common to all cows. So if they had two जातिs they must have certain characteristics in common with others and so could not be असाधारण.

P. 18 l. 26–**P. 19** l. 5 **तेषु...निजे.** संसरति संसारे the world went on or revolved. वहत्सु वत्सरेषु as years rolled. प्रसवः... कुले as the वात्स्यायन family incessantly went on growing in an unbroken chain of progeny. वैनतेयः = गरुडः. गुरु...पाती (1) who was devoted to (had a liking for) his teachers or parents (with कुबेरनामा); that flies on his big wings (with गरुड). द्विजः (1) a Brāhmaṇa; a bird. गरुड was the son of विनता one of the wives of कश्यप. विनता lost a wager with her co-wife कद्रू and had to be the latter's slave. She was released from slavery by Garuda who gave nectar as a ransom after vanquishing Indra. युगा...विस्तारः (1) whose progeny expanded by their Brāhmanical lustre (*i. e.* by their knowledge of the Vedas); (2) which have a vast creation of beings produced from Brahmā's lustre (with युगारम्भाः.). In the beginning of the कृतयुग, ब्रह्मा was alone and from him sprang the creation. चत्वारः may be connected also with युगारम्भाः as there are four Yugas. स...नन्दकाः— (1) that delighted the assembly of the good (with sons); that have the discuss and the नन्दक sword (with नारायणबाहु०). सतां (साधूनां) चक्रं नन्दयन्तीति; सतौ चक्रनन्दकौ येषाम्. चक्र is one of the weapons of नारायण, who also has four arms. नन्दक is the sword of विष्णु. भूभारः इव like the heavy earth. अचल...स्थितिः (1) who never swerved from the usages of his family (with सूनुः); (2) that obtained steadiness by the group of mountains. अचला कुलस्थितिः यस्य; अचलकुले (पर्वतसमूहे) स्थितिः यस्य. It was believed that the earth, which was at first unsteady, was made steady by the mountains. Compare 'भिषजो भूधरा इव भुवो धृतिं चक्रुः' हर्षचरित IV; 'अनुजीविभूभृच्छतसहस्रकल्पिताष्टम्भं सञ्चारिणं द्वितीयमिव मेदिनीसंनिवेशम्' कादम्बरी. Each वर्ष has its कुलपर्वतs; for the seven कुलपर्वतs of भरतवर्ष, see above p. 76. In अचलकुल, the author refers to the कुलपर्वतs. चतुरुदधिवत् गम्भीरः (सूनुः), चतुरुदधिभिः गम्भीरः (भूभारः). समग्राणां अग्रजन्मनां (ब्राह्मणानां) चक्रं समूहः तस्य चूडामणिः. एकादश—the eleven sons are compared to the Rudras that are also eleven. They are manifestations of शिव. सोमा...मुखान् (1) whose mouths were full of the spray of the nectar-like Soma juice (with पुत्रान्); whose faces are covered with the spray of the nectar from the moon (with रुद्रान्). सोम juice was drunk in sacrifices. सोमः अमृतरस इव तस्य शीकरैः च्छुरितानि मुखानि येषाम्; सोमस्य (चन्द्रमसः) अमृतरसः तस्य शीकरः तेन &c. शिव has the moon on his head and, as the moon was full of nectar, शिव's face would be covered with nectar spray. राजदेवी अभिधानं यस्याः. उपसम्पन्नया who died (connect with विधेर्वशात्). एधीयमाना (increasing) धृतिः (energy, steadiness) यस्य. धाम्नि = गृहे.

P. 19 ll. 6–28 **कृतोप...हास्यताम्.** कृतः उपनयनादिक्रियाकलापः यस्य. समावृत्त *lit.* 'returned' *i. e.* one who returns from his teacher's house to his home after finishing his study. Compare मनु० III. 4. 'गुरुणानुमतः स्नात्वा समावृत्तो यथाविधि। उद्वहेत द्विजो भार्यां सवर्णां लक्षणान्विताम्॥.' समावर्तन is what is now symbolised in सोडमुंज (in Marathi). For देशीय, see above (notes p. 55). चतुर्दश०–fourteen was rather an early age for समावर्तन, but it contrasts most favourably with the unseemly haste with which समावर्तन is now performed. श्रुति means the Vedas and Smṛitis are woks like the मनुस्मृति, which contain

the धातुवाद *i. e.* the transmutation of metals into gold, an alchemist. Vide notes above p. 55 as to mercury. दार्दुरिकः a potter, according to 'शब्ददर्दुरं करोति' पा. 4.4.34 (शब्दं करोति शाब्दिकः। दर्दुरं करोति दार्दुरिकः कुलालः). दर्दुर was a musical instrument like a drum. The word probably means 'a player on दर्दुर' like मार्दङ्गिक above. ऐन्द्रजालिकः juggler, illusionist. मस्करी = परिव्राजकः A Sannyāsin. 'भिक्षुः परिव्राट् कर्मन्दी पाराशर्यपि मस्करी' इत्यमरः. पतञ्जलि derives the word from मा and कृ. 'मा कृत मा कृत कर्माणि शान्तिर्वः श्रेयसीति आहातो मस्करी परिव्राजकः' महाभाष्य (Kielhorn Vol. III. p. 96). The word occurs in the 5th उच्छ्वास also. बाल...गतः being easily guided (led away) on account of his youth. निघ्न dependent, in the hands of others. 'अधीनो निघ्न आयत्तः' इत्यमरः. ०कौतुकेन आक्षिप्तं (drawn) हृदयं यस्य. उपात्त obtained. सति...सङ्गे in spite of the fact that his attachment to learning was unbroken. His self-willed action in wasting his valuable youth in wanderings made him a butt of ridicule to the great. अगाच्च—connect with उपहास्यताम्. निरवग्रहः being without any check. 'स्वच्छन्दो निरवग्रहः' इत्यमरः. ग्रह...यौवनेन as if possessed by his fresh youth. One possessed by a ghost does strange things. स्वैरिन् doing just as it pleases.

P. 19 l. 29–**P. 20** l. 5. **अथ...भवद्विति**. अत्युदारा व्यवहृतिः यस्य whose conduct or dealing was very charming or noble. This would be an adjective of बाण. Some MSS. read ०हृतिमनोहन्ति 'charming on account of noble practices.' राजकुलानि courts. निर...द्योतितानि made illustrious by blameless lores. Vide notes p. 18 on निरवद्यविद्या. गुरुकुलानि schools. Mark the contrast between वीक्षमाणः and सेवमानः. महार्हैः आलापैः गम्भीराः (deep *i. e.* full) गुणवतां गोष्ठ्यः. महा...मानः attending the meetings of the meritorious that were full of valuable discussions. स्वभावेन गम्भीरा धीः धनं येषाम्. पुनर...भाजन् he again recovered that same scholarly attitude of mind which was appropriate to his family. विपश्चितः इयं वैपश्चिती. 'विद्वान् विपश्चिद्दोषज्ञः' इत्यमरः. ब्राह्मणाधिवास may be the name of Bāṇa's village, as प्रीतिकूट was the name of his home. ब्राह्मणाधिवास would also mean 'the resort of Brāhmaṇas.' अभिनवीभूतौ स्नेहसद्भावौ येषाम् whose affection and amiability were renewed. संस्तवेन प्रकटितं ज्ञातेयं (बन्धुता) यैः that manifested their relationship by being very intimate with him. 'संस्तवः स्यात्परिचयः' इत्यमरः. ज्ञातेय—from ज्ञाति, according to 'कपिज्ञात्योर्ढक्' पा० 5. 1. 127 (कापेयम्, ज्ञातेयम्)–ज्ञातेर्भावः कर्म वा ज्ञातेयम्. अभिनन्दितं अभिगमनं यस्य. आप्तैः relatives; those whose words are always true (Seers).

बाल...गत: being in the midst of the friends of his boyhood. The words may also mean 'going through the midst of the disc of the sun (मित्र) that has become mild.' The liberated soul was supposed to proceed through the sun on the path of liberation. Vide notes p. 21 on देवयान. The com. says that the sun's lustre is reduced at sight of a Yogin. "उक्तं च—'तपस्यन्तं रविं दृष्ट्वा निस्तेजा जायते रविः। मोक्षमार्गप्रयत्ने तु तेजो नैवास्य विद्यते ॥.'" इति— This is added to show that the chapter has come to an end.

Uchchhvāsa II

Verse 1. The verse contains many श्लिष्ट words. The sentence is अतिगम्भीरे भूपे निरवतारस्य जनस्य समीहितसिद्धिं गुणवन्तः घटकाः पार्थिवाः दधति कूपे इव--with a very profound king it is the virtuous and energetic princes that bring about the fulfilment of what is desired by people who have no entrance (to the king), as with a well. The idea is that good princes that are about the person of an emperor intercede with the latter for bestowing favours on people. This and the next verse suggest how कृष्ण the cousin of हर्ष introduced बाण to the favour of हर्ष. गम्भीर means one whose feelings of anger &c. are not indicated by his gestures or appearance. अवतारः entrance or access. घटकाः those that accomplish. अतिगम्भीरे कूपे निरवतारस्य जनस्य गुणवन्तः पार्थिवाः घटकाः ०सिद्धिं दधति in the case of a deep well, small earthen (पार्थिव) jars to which strings (गुण) are attached bring about the fulfilment of the desires of people who have no means of descending (into the well). अवतारः a flight of steps. The metre is Âryā. From the definition of आख्यायिका (Intro. p. XX) it will be seen that the verses occurring therein were to suggest future events.

Verse 2. रागि...भवाम्—the day plants in the red lotus beauty that is due to the sun. रागिन् also means 'affectionate, devoted.' लक्ष्मी wealth. This suggests how कृष्ण (who was like दिवस) planted wealth in Bāṇa who was devoted to the king हर्ष (who corresponds to the sun), the wealth being the gift of हर्ष and he (कृष्ण) being only the intercessor. अनपेक्षिताः गुणदोषाः यस्मिन् in which no regard is paid to merits or faults. The good are passionately devoted to the task of helping others, irrespective of their merits or faults. Here there is a veiled reference to the चापल of Bāṇa's youth.

P. 21 ll. 5-16 **अथ...तिष्ठत्.** The principal sentence is अथ तत्र...बान्धवानां भवनानि भ्रमन् सुखमतिष्ठत्. भस्मपुण्ड्रकैः पाण्डुराणि ललाटानि येषाम् (*adj.* of बटुभिः). For पुण्ड्रक, see notes p. 26. कपि... टिलैः that had tawny hair (with बटुभिः); that were full of tawny flames (with कृशानुभिः). कृशानुभिः = अग्निभिः. क्रतु०—The boys had come to see the sacrifices and partake of the दक्षिणा. They are fancied to be fires coming with the desire that sacrifices may be offered to them. अध्यास्यमानानि inhabited. This and the following nouns in the accusative qualify भवनानि below. सेकेन सुकुमारा सोमकेदारिका तया हरितायमानाः प्रघनाः येषाम् the porches in front of the doors of which were green with the small beds of Soma plants that looked fine (fresh) on account of being (recently) watered. केदारिका small field. 'प्रघाणप्रघणालिन्दा बहिर्द्वारप्रकोष्ठके' इत्यमरः. The juice of Soma plants was required in sacrifices. कृष्णाजिनेषु विकीर्यमाणाः (spread) शुष्यन्तः पुरोडाशीयाः श्यामाकतण्डुलाः येषु. पुरोडाशीय (from पुरोडाश with the affix छ *i. e.* ईय) useful for पुरोडाश, which means 'a sacrificial oblation made of ground rice and offered in vessels.' 'विभाषा हविरपूपादिभ्यः' पा. 5. 1. 4. (पुरोडाश्याः तण्डुलाः, पुरोडाशीयाः वा). श्यामाकः a kind of grain (called सांवे in Marathi). बालिकाभिः विकीर्यमाणाः नीवार—बलयः येषु. नीवार is a kind of wild rice growing without cultivation. The girls offered the grain to the birds and their pets. ०शतैः आनीयमानाः ०समिधः येषु. पूली a bundle. पलाशम् a leaf. समिध् *f.* fuel. They brought green Kus'a grass, leaves and fuel. Or we make take पलाशसमिधः as meaning 'small twigs of the पलाश tree' that were required for being thrown into the fire. इन्ध... कूटानि full of heaps (कूटः) of fuel (इन्धनं) and cowdung cakes. आमिक्षा a mixture of curds and boiled milk, offered in the वैश्वदेव oblation. 'पक्के पयसि दध्यानयति सा वैश्वदेव्यामिक्षा' quoted by क्षीर० as a श्रुति. For आमिक्षीय (आमिक्षायै हित) see पुरोडाशीय above. खुर...र्दिकानि the covered platforms (वितर्दिः) in the court-yards of which were rubbed by the round hoofs. 'स्याद्वितर्दिस्तु वेदिका' इत्यमरः (दारुपरिष्कृता चतुरस्रा विश्रान्तिभूः' क्षीर०). कमण्डलव्य useful or fit for making pots (कमण्डलु). 'उ—गवादिभ्यो यत्' पा. 5. 1. 2. मर्दनम् pounding. वै...व्यानाम् useful for making pegs for measuring the sacrificial (वैतान) altar. शङ्कव्य from शङ्कु with affix यत्, according to 'तस्मै हितम्' पा. 5. 1. 5. (शङ्कवे हितं शङ्कव्यम्). Pegs of the branches of उदुम्बर trees were used in measuring altars. पवित्रिताः पर्यन्ताः (borders, outskirts) येषाम्. वैश्वदेवपिण्ड—the offerings of boiled rice made to all the deities (विश्वेदेवाः) before taking one's dinner. हवि...लयानि the tender leaves of the trees (विटपिन् *m.*) in the courts of which were darkened with the smoke of the oblations. वत्सीय...तर्णकानि where the newly born calves, being caressed (लालित) by the cowherds (वत्सपालकः) that were fond of them, frisked about. वत्सीयः (वत्सेभ्यो हितः) is formed like शङ्कव्य. From the numerous words formed with the affixes छ (ईय) and यत् it seems as though बाण wanted to illustrate the first Pāda of the 5th अध्याय of the अष्टाध्यायी. 'सद्योजातस्तु तर्णकः' इत्यमरः. ०पालकैः लालिताः ललन्तः (sportive) तरलाः (चञ्चलाः) तर्णकाः येषु. क्रीडद्भिः कृष्णशारच्छागशावकैः प्रकटितः पशुबन्धानां (यज्ञानां) प्रबन्धः (सन्ततिः) येषु where the continuous performance of animal sacrifices was indicated by the young goats, dark and variegated (शार), playing about. This shows that in Bāṇa's day animal sacrifices were frequently performed. शुक...सुखानि where the teachers were given rest by the fact that parrots and *mainas* (सारिका) commenced to repeat (the Vedas). The idea is:—the parrots and सारिकाs, having repeatedly heard the teachers reciting the Vedas, themselves correctly repeated them and the students could take lessons from them, instead of from the teachers, who thus got rest. Compare 'स्वतःप्रमाणं परतःप्रमाणं कीराङ्गना यत्र गिरं गिरन्ति । द्वारस्थनीडान्तरसंनिरुद्धा जानीहि तन्मण्डनपण्डितौकः ॥' माधवाचार्य's शङ्करदिग्विजय VIII. 6. सा...नीव as though they were the penance groves of the three Vedas incarnate. भवनानि—is the object of भ्रमन्.

P. 27 ll. 17–23 **तत्र...माली.** Bāṇa now describes the advent of summer in highly paronomastic sentences, the season (कालः) being identified with शिव in his terrific form (महाकाल). तत्रस्थस्य while staying in the houses of his kinsmen. कुसुमसमयः (वसन्तः) एव युगम्. उपसंहरन् bringing to an end. ग्रीष्म brings to an end the season of spring. शिव when destroying the world brings the युग to an end. अजृम्भत *lit.* yawned *i. e.* increased. ग्रीष्मः अभिधानं यस्य. सम्फुल्लमल्लिकाभिः धवलाः अट्टाः (market stalls) एव हासाः यस्य where the stalls smiled with white full blown jasmine flowers. The मल्लिका is a flower of the hot season. ०मल्लिकावत् धवलः अट्टहासः यस्य. The loud laugh of शिव is called अट्टहास. महाकालः the great season (of summer); S'iva. प्रत्य...तस्य recently conquered. The poet now changes the metaphor. ग्रीष्म is a conqueror that subdues the prince वसन्त, but at first treats kindly the children of his vanquished rival. वसन्तः एव सामन्तः तस्य. पयः पायिषु that drink milk (with बालापल्लवेषु); that drink water *i. e.* are thirsty (with नवोद्यानेषु). दर्शितः स्नेहः येन. स्नेहः affection; moisture. नवोद्यानेषु (with ०पल्लवेषु) would also mean 'who have just begun to walk.' मृदुरभूत्—summer did not at once scorch the gardens, but was mild at first. सकल...रोत् made the stalks of all flowers loose *i. e.* summer scorched the flowers of spring which easily dropped down from the stem.

A king at his accession (अभिनवोदितः) lets loose prisoners from his jails. It was usual to set prisoners free on the accession of a king or at the birth of a prince or on other great occasions. Compare हर्षं॰ 4th उच्छ्वास 'अधावन्त मुक्तानि बन्धनवृन्दानि' and notes thereon. प्रतपन् showing his valour; very hot. ऋतुः एव राजा तस्य. अभिषेकार्द्राः wet after a bath (with कामिनीनां ॰चयाः); wet at the time of the coronation (with चामरकलापाः). At a king's coronation, holy water is poured over him. Chowries are a symbol of royalty; they may become wet at a coronation. In ग्रीष्म, young women bathe their heads with water; their hair looks very charming after the bath and excites love. In वसन्त, love is excited spontaneously, but in the scorching heat of ग्रीष्म, such extraneous aids as charming tresses are required. This is spoken of as कामिनीनां ॰चयाः कुसुमायुधेन स्वयमगृह्यन्त. The hair of the women is fancied to be the chowrie of the king-summer, that is held in his own hand by Cupid. Bāṇa seems to follow the रघुवंश in this description as suggested by the com. Compare 'स्नानार्द्रमुक्तेष्वनुधूपवासं विन्यस्तसायन्तनमल्लिकेषु । कामो वसन्तात्ययमन्दवीर्यः केशेषु लेभे रतिमङ्गनानाम् ॥' रघु॰ 16. 50. हिमा...माली the sun made his expedition towards the Himālaya (*i. e.* towards the north). यात्रा journey, expedition. It is in ग्रीष्म that the sun reaches the northernmost point in his apparent yearly motion. This natural phenomenon is fancied to be due to the wrath which the sun feels at the fact that the lotuses (that open by day-light) are blighted by snow. For the effect of हिम on कमलिनी, see notes p. 63.

P. 21 l. 24—**P. 22** l. 2 **अथ...सन्तापात्.** ललाटं तपतीति ललाटन्तपः scorching the brow (*lit.* forehead), according to 'असूर्यललाटयोर्दृशितपोः' पा. 3. 2. 36 (असूर्यंपश्या राजदाराः, ललाटन्तपः सूर्यः । सि. कौ.), a nasal being inserted after ललाट in accordance with 'अरुर्द्विषदजन्तस्य मुम्' पा. 6. 3. 67. तपने = सूर्ये. लिखितः ललाटिका एव पुण्ड्रकः यैः. For ललाटिका, see p. 44 and for पुण्ड्रक, see p. 26. अलकाः (curls) एव चीरचीवरं (ragged dress of a mendicant) तेन संवीतैः (covered). दिन...न्दुभिः the foreheads of ladies as though undertook vows (नियमाः) for propitiating the sun. One who observes a व्रत has a पुण्ड्रक on his forehead, wears ragged garments and a rosary; ladies (on account of the fierce heat) had sandal mark on their foreheads, allowed their curls to play about their foreheads and had drops of perspiration (resembling pearls in their brightness). चन्दनेन धूसराभिः (with सुन्दरीभिः); चन्दनवत् धू० (with कुमुदिनीभिः). असूर्यम्पश्या—see notes above on ललाटन्तप. The women did not come out in the sun; the कुमुद plants close their buds in the day. कुमुदs are white and so the plants are called चन्दनधू०. दिवसमसुप्यत—the ladies slept the whole day; the कुमुद plants closed their petals in the day. निद्रा...तपम् the eyes, heavy with sleep, could not bear even the light of the jewels; what of the fully grown heat? अशि...शर्वर्यः In the season of summer the moonlit nights became shorter and shorter, being esteemed by pairs of चक्रवाकs, like rivers. चक्रवाक is separated from its mate at night and so they welcome the shortness of the nights. सोडुपाः possessed of the moon (with शर्वर्यः); with rafts (with सरितः). There are boats on rivers, which are welcomed by चक्रवाकs, as they live near them. उडुपः lord of stars (उडु *f. n.*) *i. e.* the moon. उडुपः–पम् raft. अभिनवः पटुः (strong) पाटलानां आमोदः तेन सुरभिः परिमलः यस्य (*adj.* of जलं and पवनं also). पाटल (trumpet flower) is a kind of fragrant summer flower. Compare शाकुन्तल I 'सुलभसलिलावगाहाः पाटलसंसर्गसुरभिवनवाताः ।'.

P. 22 l. 3–**P. 23** l. 5. **क्रमेण......मातरिश्वानः.** The sentence is क्रमेण च ...प्रावर्तन्त...मातरिश्वानः. खराः (fierce) खगस्य (सूर्यस्य) मयूखाः यस्मिन्. 'शरार्कविहगाः खगाः' इत्यमरः. This and the following clauses in the locative qualify निदाघकाले (l. 12). खण्डितं शैशवं यस्य whose childhood was gone *i. e.* when the season had far advanced. सीदन्ति स्रोतांसि यस्मिन् when the streams sank low *i. e.* had hardly any water left in them. झिल्लि...रिणि resounding with the cries of crickets. कातर...विश्वे when the world was deafened by the continued cooing of the distressed doves. वि...त्रिणि when the birds breathed very heavily. करीषङ्कषः मरुत् यस्मिन् when the wind swept dried cowdung. 'सर्वकूलाभ्रकरीषेषु कषः' पा. 3–2–42. (सर्वङ्कषः खलः । कूलङ्कषा नदी । करीषङ्कषा वात्या । सि. कौ). 'गोविड् **गोमय**मस्त्रियाम् । तत्तु **शुष्कं करीषो**ऽस्त्री' इत्यमरः. विरलाः वीरुधः (लताः) यस्मिन्. As the leaves fell off through heat, the creepers grew less dense. रुधिर...स्तबके when the bunches of fullgrown (कठोर) धातकी flowers were licked by the young of lions in their greed for blood. धातकी flowers are very red. ताम्यत् स्तम्बेरमानां यूथं तस्य वमथुः तेन तिम्यन्तः महामहीधराणां नितम्बाः यस्मिन् where the slopes (नितम्बः) of large mountains became wet with the spray spouted from the trunks of languid elephants. स्तम्बेरमः हस्ती

स्तम्बे (तृणे) रमते इति (अलुक्समास) according to 'स्तम्बकर्णयो रमिजपोः' पा. 3-2-13. (स्तम्बेरमः कर्णेजपः). 'वमथुः करशीकरः' इत्यमरः. दिनकरेण दूयमानाः द्विरदाः तेषां दीनेषु (distressed) वदनेषु आश्याना (partially dried) दानस्य (ichor) श्यामिका (dark streak) तस्यां आलीनाः मूकाः मधुलिहः (bees) यस्मिन्. The thirsty bees stuck to whatever was left of the ichor. लोहितायमानाः मन्दारैः सिन्दूरिताः सीमानः यस्मिन् when the boundaries (of villages) looked red, being as though smeared with vermilion by the मन्दार flowers. मन्दार trees were planted on the boundaries. Their red flowers looked like सिन्दूर. Even now boundary stones are smeared with सिन्दूर. स्यन्दः stream, trickling line. सन्दोहः mass. ०सन्दोहस्य सन्देहेन मुह्यन्तः महामहिषाः तेषां विषाणकोटिभिः विलिख्यमानाः (scratched) स्फुटन्त्यः स्फाटिकदृषदः यस्मिन्—The crystal slabs looked like trickling water; so the buffaloes in hopes of getting more water vehemently struck them with their horns. घर्मेण (by heat) मर्मरिताः (rustled) गर्मुतः (creepers) यस्मिन्. The leaves being dry, the creepers produced a rustle. त...किरे when the scratching cocks were afraid of scratching (for food) in husk-fire due to the heated dust. कुकूलः-लम् fire burning in chaff. Cocks ordinarily scratch for food in chaff, which is heaped up in dust. The dust being heated set fire to a portion of the chaff and so cocks became afraid to scratch near it. विकिरः a bird, particularly, a cock (from कॄ with वि). 'विष्किरः शकुनिर्विकिरो वा' पा. 6. 1. 150. विवरशरणाः (विवरं शरणं येषां) श्वाविधाः (porcupines) यस्मिन्. Generally the word is श्वाविध्, but Bāṇa uses the form श्वाविध. तटा...म्भसि when the waters of the ponds (being dried up) left only mud and were coloured by the fish rolling (विवर्तमान) on their backs, the fish being distressed by the cries (कूजा) of the ospreys (कुरराः) on the Arjuna trees on the banks of the ponds. The com. reads कूटज्वर० and explains 'कूटः शब्द एव सन्तापकारित्वात् ज्वरः.' ०वर्तमानाः उत्तानाः शफराः तै शारं पङ्कशेषं (पङ्कः शेषः यस्य) पल्वलाम्भः यस्मिन्. On the connection between the cries of ospreys and the distress of fishes, the com. remarks 'कुररास्तटस्था यदा कूजन्ति तदा मत्स्याः पीडिताः सन्तः उत्प्लवन्तीति वस्तुधर्मोऽयम्.' दावेन जनितं जगन्नीराजनं यस्मिन्. The forest conflagration as though performed the नीराजन rite of the world. For नीराजन, see above p. 34. रज...यक्ष्मणि which was the (cause of) the consumption of night. In summer night slowly dwindles, as a man gradually becomes emaciated in consumption. Compare 'घर्मवृद्धिरपां प्रस्थः क्षपाह्रास उदग्गतौ' वेदाङ्गज्योतिष. कठो...काले when the season of summer was far advanced. प्रति...लुण्ठका: that openly carried off in desert places the roofs (पटलं) of water-sheds (प्रपा), garden enclosures (वाट:) and huts, as though they were leaping in all directions. This and the following nouns in the nominative qualify उन्मत्ता मातरिश्वान: below. A mad man (उन्मत्त) also wanders (आटीकमान) everywhere. ऊषर: a desert. प्रपा is Marathi पाणपोई. लुण्ठक: robber. प्रपक...स्थली: rubbing against sandy (शर्करिल) hard (कर्कर) places, as though they (the winds) were all of a sudden itching on account of their rashness in cracking (आच्छोटनं) the lines of the bushes of ripe कपिकच्छू. A person whose skin is itching rubs it against a hard substance. The wind broke the bushes of the prickly कपिकच्छू plant (that causes itch) and also dragged the sand off hard stony places. 'स्त्री शर्करा शर्करिल: शार्कर: शर्करावति । देश एवादिमौ' इत्यमर:. Vide notes on सैकत above p. 44. A mad man also may break the bush of the prickly कपिकच्छू, have itch thereby and rub his hands against stones. कपीनामपि कच्छू: यस्या: सा कपिकच्छू:. स्थूल...मुच:—The strong winds carried off gravel of comparatively large size. मुचु...दन्तुरा: bristling with the shoots (कन्दल:-लम्) of मुचुकुन्द broken by them. दलनं breaking. The broken shoots looked like teeth. A mad man also shows his teeth. In most of the following clauses reference is made to a mad man's appearance and actions. We shall not explain all of them, as almost all can be easily understood. समन्त...तनव: that were moistened by the spray from the mouths of the noisy tribes of crickets (चीरी) flying all round. 'भृङ्गारी चीरुका चीरी झिल्लिका च स्त्रियामिमा:' इत्यमर:. ०शीकरे शीक्यमाना तनु: येषाम्. शीक् 10th *conj.* to moisten. तरुणतर: तरणि: (सूर्य:) तस्य तापेन तरले चञ्चले (*adj.* of ०वारिणि). तरुण...वारिणि as though floating on the illusory and tremulous waters of the mirage, as they (waters) trembled with the heat of the fierce (*lit.* young) sun. The heat of the sun produced the appearance of a mirage on sandy deserts. The air being set in motion by the heat produced the appearance of waves. As the winds swept over the desert while the mirage lasted, they are fancied to be floating in the false water &c. तरङ्गिणी a stream. A mad man also may lie on a sandy bank and pretend to be swimming though there be no water. शुष्य...जङ्घाला: (winds) that blew with velocity easily crossing the desert tracks rustling (मर्मर) with dry S'amī trees. The winds swept with violence over deserts. मारव from मरु with the affix अ. मरो: अयं मारव: मार्ग: तस्य लङ्घने लाघवं (नैपुणं) तेन

जवः तेन जङ्घालाः (rapid). A mad man also runs rapidly. 'जङ्घालोऽतिजवस्तुल्यौ' इत्यमरः. रैणवः (रेणूनां अयं) आवर्तः (circular motion, eddy) तेषां मण्डली (समूहः) तस्याः रेचकं रासे रसेन रभसारब्धं नर्तनं तस्य आरम्भे आरभटीनटाः (winds) that were wild actors in beginning a dance commenced with violence through liking (रसः) for the circular dance (रासः), that (नर्तनं) purged (swept away) whirling columns of dust. The idea is that whirl-winds arose, raised moving columns of dust and carried the dust columns from place to place. This clause contains several technical words pertaining to the science of dramaturgy. आरभटी is one of the four styles (वृत्ति) in dramatic compositions, the other three being भारती, सात्वती and कैशिकी. It is defined in Bharata's नाट्यशास्त्र as follows:—'आरभटप्रायगुणा तथैव बहुकपटवञ्चनोपेता। दम्भानृतवचनवती त्वारभटी नाम विज्ञेया ॥ प्रस्तावपातप्लुतलङ्घितानि छेद्यानि मायाकृतमिन्द्रजालम्। चित्राणि युद्धानि च यत्र नित्यं तां तादृशीमारभटीं वदन्ति ॥' chap 20. 25–26. The साहित्यदर्पण (VI. 132–133) says 'मायेन्द्रजालसंग्रामक्रोधोद्भ्रान्तादिचेष्टितैः ॥ संयुक्ता वधबन्धाद्यैरुद्धतारभटी मता ।.' This style consists in representing intrigues, deceits, falsehoods, illusions, fight, imprisonments &c. The com. derives as 'इरयन्तीति (*v. l.* इयरतीति) अरा अराश्च ते भटाश्च अरभटास्तेषामियमारभटी.' रास is a dance in a circle in which men and women join, holding one another's hands. It is frequently mentioned in connection with कृष्ण and the Gopīs. See भागवतपुराण X. 33. 'तत्रारभत गोविन्दो रासक्रीडामनुव्रतैः । स्त्रीरत्नैरन्वितः प्रीतैरन्योन्याबद्धबाहुभिः ॥' 2. The com. quotes 'अष्टौ षोडश द्वात्रिंशद्यत्र नृत्यन्ति नायकाः । पिण्डीबन्धानुसारेण तन्नृत्तं रासकं स्मृतम् ॥.' In a रास, there is आवर्तमण्डली *i. e.* a ring of dancers that moves round and round. Compare 'सावर्त इव रासकमण्डलैः' हर्ष० 4th उच्छ्वास. रेचक means 'movements of the eye, brows &c. which indicate love'. 'तत्राक्षिभ्रूविकाराश्च शृङ्गाराकारसूचकाः । सग्रीवा रेचका ज्ञेयो हावश्चित्तसमुत्थितः ॥' नाट्यशास्त्र chap. 22. 10. As to रेचक, the com. says that they are three कटीरेचक, हस्तरेचक and ग्रीवारेचक. Mad men also dance. मलनं crushing. Mad men also are मलिन. We may connect this clause with the next. A क्षपणक remained as मलिन as soot. Compare 'कज्जलमय इव बहुदिवसमुपचितबहलमलपटलमलिनिततनुरभिमुखमाजगाम शिखिपिच्छलाञ्छनो नग्नाटकः' हर्ष० 5th उच्छ्वास. Note the आचाराङ्गसूत्र (Sacred Books of the East Vol. XXII. p. 124) II. 2. 2. 1. 'Some householders are of clean habits and the mendicants, because they never bathe, are covered with uncleanliness.' शिक्षित...चिन्वतः that (winds) gathered up the feathers of the forest peacocks, as though they had learnt the ways of Jain ascetics. Jain ascetics (Digambara) carry peacock's feathers to sweep insects from their path. 'लुञ्चिताः पिच्छिकाहस्ताः पाणिपात्रा दिगम्बराः' सर्वदर्शनसंग्रह (आर्हतदर्शन). सप्र...जालकैः—करञ्ज is a wild tree so called even in Marathi. The dried seeds in its pods (मञ्जरी) rattle when the wind violently blows against them. That rattling resembles the noise of drums (गुञ्जा) beaten to announce the march of a prince &c. 'गुञ्जा तु काकचिञ्चायां पटहे च कलध्वनौ' मेदिनी. See भट्टिकाव्य XIV. 2. 'वेणून् पुपूरिरे गुञ्जा जुगुञ्जुः करघट्टिताः.' आतपेन आतुराः (distressed) वनमहिषाः तेषां नासाः निकुञ्जाः (bowers) इव तेषां स्थूलनिश्वासैः—the buffaloes heavily snorted. Their noses being compared to bowers, their deep breaths are properly fancied to be shoots (प्ररोहः). वातहरिण very swift deer. परिपाटी row, line. पेटकैः=समूहैः. The very swift deer springing up in the air seemed to be the children of the winds, as they equalled the wind in velocity. सभ्रु...कोटिभिः with the curling (कुटिल) lines of the smoke of the burning heaps of chaff (बुसं) on the threshing floor (खलधानं), they (winds) as though seemed to knit their brows. The curved lines of smoke resemble dark and curved eyebrows. सा...मुक्तिभिः by the emission of great heat, they (winds) seemed as though possessed of the waves of the अवीचि hell. Hell is a place of torments. अवीचि is one of the numerous hells mentioned in the Purāṇas. 'स्यान्नारकस्तु नरको... । तद्भेदास्तपनावीचिमहारौरवरौरवाः' इत्यमरः. अवीचिवीचिभिः सह सावीचि० (*adj.* of मातरिश्वानः). The waves are of fire burning in them. मनुस्मृति (IV. 87-90) enumerates 21 hells of which महावीचि is one. लोम...तन्तुभिः with the threads of the cotton of the silk-cotton pods that were cleft (by the heat), they (winds) seemed as though they were shaggy. Mad men do not shave and so are लोमश. दद्रुणा...ष्टिभिः by the carrying of the heaps of dried leaves, they seemed as though suffering from leprosy or cutaneous eruptions. The dry leaves present the appearance of दद्रू. Or we may explain that those who suffer from दद्रू cover the skin with leaves to ward off flies. दद्रुण is formed from दद्रू with the affix न like पामन from पामन्, according to 'रोमादिपामादिपिच्छादिभ्यः शनेलचः' पा. 5. 2. 100. दद्रू is one of the eleven क्षुद्रकुष्ठकs. It is a name for skin diseases such as Eczema, Erysipelas. 'सकण्डुरागपिटिकं दद्रुमण्डलमुद्गतम्.' सिरा... करणैः by scattering the long lines of grass, they seemed to have exposed their veins. वेणी and veins are both dark. Mad men, being underfed, may expose their veins. उच्छम...शङ्कुभिः with the shaking points (शङ्कुः) of the pieces of barley awns (शूकः—

कम्), they seemed to have long beards. उद्गतं श्मश्रु येषाम्. दंष्ट्रा... शतैः—The pointed quills (शललं) of porcupines resemble teeth. जिह्वा...खाभिः—the flames of fire resemble tongues. उत्स...लाः possessed of crests in the serpents' sloughs that were whirled up by them. ब्रह्म...स्यन्तः that, with the hot honey of lotuses, practised the taking of mouthfuls for the purpose of swallowing up the moisture in the whole universe. The winds carried away the hot honey of lotuses. They made a mouthful of it. The poet fancies that the winds were only practising in order to be able to swallow the fluid (*i. e.* to dry up) of the whole universe. अभ्यवहरणं भोजनम्. Another sense is suggested. There are six *rasas* मधुर, अम्ल, लवण, कटु, कषाय and तिक्त. The winds took the sweet (मधुर) honey, the first रस, in order gradually to be able to taste all the six. ब्रह्मस्तम्भः the universe. The word is usually written as ०स्तम्ब. 'स्तम्बशब्देनोर्ध्वत्वादिसादृश्याद्द्रौण्या भुवनाण्डान्युच्यन्ते' वीरराघव on महावीरचरित 3. 48. For ब्रह्मस्तम्भ, see text p. 30 l. 3. सकल... यन्तः producing an alarm (विभीषिका) for the three worlds by the sharp sounds of the cracking of dried bamboo forests, as though they (sounds) were drums announcing the (might) of heat (घर्मः) that dries up all water. ०च्छोषणः घर्मः तस्य घोषणा तदर्थं पटहैः. Read त्रिभुवनविभीषिका०. च्युत...सृतयः that made the roads (सृतिः) variegated by the rows of the falling feathers of moving jays. The feathers of चाष are dark. त्विषि...ताङ्गाः that (winds) were marked with sparks (स्फुलिङ्गः) and cold cinders in the bursting Gunjā berries, as though their bodies were dark-red by being scorched with the firebrand of the rays of the sun. Small round Gunjā berries are red with a patch of black. The red represents sparks and the dark stands for charcoal (अङ्गारः). A firebrand (अलातं) is red and the scorched skin is dark. त्विषिमान् सूर्यः तस्य मयूखलता एव अलातं तेन प्लोषः (burning) तेन कल्माषं (variegated) वपुः येषाम्. By the sun's rays the Gunjā berries were split up. The bursting berries look like patches of skin scorched by contact with firebrands. गिरिगुहासु गम्भीराः झाङ्काराः तैः भीषणा भ्रान्तिः (भ्रमणं) येषाम् the movements of which were terrible as they roused echoes in the mountain caves (by their fierce velocity). Mad men also wander among mountains. भुवनभस्मीकरणार्थं अभिचारः तस्य चरुः तस्य पचने चतुराः. अभिचारः a magical spell for securing some malevolent purpose. चरुः an oblation of rice. One who wants to effect some evil object offers a चरु with red powder sprinkled thereon or offers even blood. The bunches of the पारिभद्र flowers, being red, resemble oblations of blood. तारवः—तरोः अयम्. तर्पय... वसून् propitiating the forest fires (feeding) on trees. Oblations are thrown into fire. The winds carried the red पारिभद्र flowers and there were forest fires also. The poet fancies that the winds propitiated fires with oblations of blood. पारिभद्र is निम्बतरु. Compare हर्ष० 8th उच्छ्वास last para. 'असुरवधाभिचारचरुपिशुनः शोणितकाथकषायितकुक्षिः...कटाह इव च बार्हस्पत्यः.' अशि...रंहसः the velocity (the path) of which was bestarred with hot sand. शिलाजतुः bitumen. It is used as a medicine. ०रसलवैः लिप्ताः दिशः यैः. दावदहनेन पच्यमानानि चटकाण्डानि तेषां खण्डैः खचितानि तरुकोटरकीटपटलानि तेषां पुटपाकः तेन गन्धः तेन कटवः. The forest fires made the sparrow's eggs burst open. The shells of the eggs fell all round the insects in the hollows of trees and covered them as in a vessel of leaves. Inside them the insects were baked. That produced a strong smell. पुटपाक is a particular method of preparing drugs. The ingredients are wrapped up in leaves and then plastered over with clay. The whole is then roasted in the fire of cowdung cakes. मातरिश्वानः =वायवः. मातरि आकाशे श्वयति or श्वसिति or मातरि शु (आशु) अनिति.

P. 23 ll. 6–22. **सर्वतश्च...दावाग्नयः.** The sentence is सर्वतश्च... प्रत्यदृश्यन्त दावाग्नयः. भूरि...वायुभिः with the breaths blowing from the deep cavern-like jaws of old huge serpents, they (forest fires) seemed to be as though kindled by being fanned with thousands of bellows (भस्त्रा). क्वचि...हरिणाः—fires are yellowish (हरिण) and burn grass. Deer (हरिणाः) also subsist on grass. 'हरिणः पाण्डुरः पाण्डुः' इत्यमरः. In this and the following clauses up to ०स्थितयः (l. 14) there are pairs of words that serve to qualify दावाग्नयः and also serve another purpose. The latter in each pair of words is a noun with which the former can be construed as an adjective. क्वचित्—क्वचित् in some places—in other places. ०विवर्तिनः rolling. बभ्रवः yellowish-red; ichneumons. 'विपुले नकुले विष्णौ बभ्रुः स्यात्पिङ्गले त्रिषु' इत्यमरः जटा...कपिलाः resting on fibrous roots and tawny. जटा also means 'matted hair.' कपिलाः the sage Kapila, the founder of the सांख्य system, the plural being used to show respect. Or कपिलाः may stand for 'followers of कपिल'. शकु...श्येनाः that make the nests (कुलायः) of birds fall and are white (श्येन). Hawks (श्येनाः) bring down the nests of smaller birds. विलीनलाक्षारसवत् लोहिता छविः (कान्तिः) येषाम्. अधराः that could not be controlled. The lips of ladies are red like melting lac and also red with lac. आसा...

would be disgusted with the smell of fat and would avoid sacrificing the tortoises. 'विस्रं स्यादामगन्धि यत्' इत्यमरः. अघृणाः also means 'pitiless.' स्व...भक्षयन्तः that swallowed up their own smoke as though through the fear of the rise of clouds. Clouds are dark like smoke. The poet fancies that the fires thought that smoke might form into clouds which bring rain and extinguish them. So the fires consumed their own smoke. Or we may explain differently. Smoke itself was supposed to form clouds. Compare 'धूमज्योतिःसलिलमरुतां सन्निपातः क मेघः' मेघदूत. सति...कक्षेषु—The fires burnt up the small insects on grass and-thereby produced a crackling sound. Sesame also are small and produce a crackling sound when thrown into fire. 'कक्षौ च तृणवीरुधौ' इत्यमरः. प्लोषेण विचटन्तः वल्कलवत् धवलाः शम्बूकशुक्तयः येषु. श्वित्रिण...सरःसु that made the bi-valvular shells white like barks burst open by heat in dried-up lakes, like leprous persons. 'शम्बूका जलशुक्तयः' इत्यमरः. The shells in the beds of lakes were split by the heat and made a crackling noise. श्वित्रिणः persons suffering from white leprosy (श्वित्रम्). The skin (वल्कलं) of lepers is white like shells and cracks up owing to the burning sensation (प्लोषः) they feel. स्वेदि...काननेषु in forests they had showers of bees'-wax dropping from bee-hives that began to melt, as though they had perspiration. The drops of wax look like drops of perspiration. विलीयमानः मधुपटलगोलः तस्मात् गलितं मधूच्छिष्टं तस्य वृष्टिः येषां ते ०वृष्टयः. खल...षरेषु. ऊषरः-रम् barren saline soil. As nothing grew on the barren soil, the flames (शिखा) of the fires lost their thickness *i. e.* became gradually extinguished. A bald man (खलतिः) also has very scanty hair (शिखा) on his head. ज्वलितानि सूर्यमणिशकलानि येषु (*adj.* of शिलोच्चयेषु). गृहीत...च्चयेषु—The सूर्यकान्त emits fire when the sun blazes forth. In summer these stones began to blaze forth and their blaze mingled with the forest fires, which thus seemed to be devouring pieces of stones.

P. 23 ll. 23–29 **तथाभूते...इति.** अपराह्णसमये—connect with प्रविश्य and not with भुक्तवतः as C and T do. For पारशव, see above p. 89. चतुः...पतेः—this was a title applied to universal kings that ruled over the whole (known) world. Vide Intro. p. XV (last footnote). The earth was often spoken of as bounded by four oceans in the (principal) directions. Compare 'चतुरम्भोधिभोगभूतिभाजनस्य देवस्य' हर्ष० 7th उच्छ्वास. सकलं राजचक्रं

(राजसमूहः) तस्य चूडामणीनां श्रेणी (row) सा एव शाणः (touch-stone) तस्य कोणैः (corners) कषणं तेन निर्मलीकृताः चरणनखमणयः यस्य सः ०मणिः तस्य. Diamonds are made bright by being rubbed against शाणs. हर्ष's toe-nails were bright like jewels. When the feudatory kings bowed their crowned heads at the feet of हर्ष, the jewels in their crowns rubbed his toes and made his nails look brighter. धौरेयस्य =मुख्यस्य. 'धुरो यड्ढकौ' पा. 4. 4. 77. धुरं वहतीति धुर्यः धौरेयः. महा...श्वर०—these were the titles assumed by paramount kings. Compare the inscription of Harsha, Intro. p. XXVIII. and the 2nd footnote on p. XXXVI. of the Intro. भ्रात्रा—must mean here 'cousin.' प्रज्ञाततमः most famous. दीर्घाध्वगः *lit.* that goes a long distance *i. e.* a messenger.

P. 23 l. 30—**P. 25** l. 10 **अथ तेना...इति.** The first sentence is अथ तेन (भ्रात्रा) आनीयमानं...लेखहारकमद्राक्षीत् (p. 24. l. 1). अतिदूरागमनेन गुर्वी (heavy) जडा (slow) जङ्घा (leg) यस्य. कार्दमिकं चेलं (वस्त्रं) तस्य चीरिका (strip) तया नियमितं (bound, girt) उच्चण्डं (gaudy) चण्डातकं (tunic) यस्य. For चण्डातक, see above p. 69. कर्दमेन रक्तं कार्दमिकं (stained with mud). पृष्ठे प्रेङ्खन् (rolling) पटच्चरकर्पटघटितः गलितः ग्रन्थिः यस्य—who had a loose knot made of a strip (कर्पटः-टम्) of ragged cloth rolling on his back. The knot contained probably some coin. It was loose by long travel. 'पटच्चरं जीर्णवस्त्रम्' इत्यमरः. If we read गलग्रन्थिम्, then the meaning is:—he had round his throat a portion of a ragged garment, the rest being allowed to roll on his back. अतिनिबिडसूत्रबन्धे निम्नितं अन्तरालं तेन कृतः व्यवच्छेदः यस्याः. The letters he carried were tied in the middle by a thick thread. Thereby the middle part was much depressed (निम्नित) and the bundle of letters was thus divided into two distinct portions. व्यवच्छेदः division. लेखमालिकया—there were many letters, sent with him by other people also. Or it is possible that because the letter was placed on the head, the author compares it to a chaplet. परिकलितः (occupied) मूर्धा यस्य. तत्रभवतः पूज्यस्य. 'पूज्ये तत्रभवानत्र भवांश्च भगवानपि.' तत्रभवत् is applied to a person who is not present. विमुच्य having unloosened it. मेखलक was the name of the messenger. सन्दिष्टमवधार्य having understood the message. फल...पातः loss of time should be avoided by the wise, as it hinders the (desired) object. धीमद्भिः—refers to Bāṇa. एता...मात्रकम् this is the only substantial thing in this letter; all else is merely communication of (ordinary) news. मेखलक was to deliver the real message orally. The letter contained only one important sentence *viz.* that Bāṇa should start at once. All else in the letter was of a complimentary character. अवधृतः (understood) लेखार्थः येन. समुत्सारितः (sent away) परिजनः येन. मेधाविनं refers to बाण. स्वामी refers to कृष्ण. एकगोत्रता belonging to the same family. In this sentence are collected most of the circumstances that give rise to friendship and affection. समानजातिता belonging to the same caste. The words समानज्ञानता in B would mean 'pursuing the same subject of study'. दर्शनाभ्यासः repeatedly seeing each other. परो...करणं conferring benefits in one's absence. प्रत्यासन्न near. बद्धः पक्षपातः (liking) येन. किमपि in an indescribable way. कुमुदानाम् आकरे. भवन्त...आसीत् with reference to you, this (our) emperor had been informed by bad men in various ways *i. e.* he had been prejudiced by them against you. न...था but that is not so *i. e.* there is no truth in what the wicked said about you. न...शत्रवः there exist no persons who, even though they may be good, will not have friends, neutrals and enemies. सतामपि सताम्—this has a picturesque effect. The first सताम् means 'साधूनाम्.' शिशु...भवतः as your mind was not averse to boyish follies. Read चापलापराचीन. ०चापलेभ्यो अपराचीना चित्तवृत्तिः यस्य सः ०वृत्तिः तस्य भावः ०वृत्तिता तया. 'पराङ्मुखः पराचीनः' इत्यमरः. असदृशम् not worthy of or deserved by you. इतरो...वक्ति च other people take it up and repeat it. सलि...मनांसि the minds of the unreflecting (public) are blind and fickle, like water. गतस्य अनुगतिर्यस्य. The unreflecting people blindly follow what others say. Water also rushes in a continuous stream. Put a vertical line after मनांसि. बहु...श्चयः who arrives at a firm conclusion after listening to many people. A king has to form his opinion as best as he can after listening to the various opinions of other people about things and individuals. पृथिवीपतिः refers to हर्ष. तत्त्वान्वेषिभिः who seek to know the truth. दूर...कृतोऽसि though you are far off, I know you as well as if you were before me. सर्वे...राधि the youth of every one is guilty of follies. It is unfortunate that Bāṇa nowhere specifies clearly the follies he was guilty of. He merely makes a vague reference to 'चापल.' In the penultimate paragraph of the first उच्छ्वास also, he vaguely alludes to 'चापलानि'. Again in the last para of this chapter, he speaks of 'बालचरितचापल'. Later on हर्ष accuses him of being a भुजङ्ग (a gallant, a dissolute person) but he repudiates that charge. तथे...मिना and the king accepted it to be so *i. e.* he accepted that proposition or excuse (about बाण). अकृतः कालस्य क्षेपः यथा स्यात्तथा

(अव्ययीभाव) without loss of time. Read अवकेशी &c. अवके...मतः I do not approve of your dwelling in the midst of your kindred without seeing the great king (हर्ष), like a tree without fruit. अवकेशी इव. 'वन्ध्योऽफलोऽवकेशी च' इत्यमरः (अवके शून्ये ईष्टे इति—क्षीर०). A tree without fruits is not liked by anybody. अदृष्टः परमेश्वरः येन that does not see the god (sun). बन्धु...वसन् being in the midst of (*i. e.* in the shade of) other trees. न च...भवितव्यम् you should not be despondent (विषादिन्) by the difficulties of attendance in court nor should you be afraid of waiting upon the lord. यतो०–There is one sentence from यतो to स्वामी (including the verse). The words in the verse are capable of three meanings, one applying to Cupid (मनोभव), the second to a vain master and the third to S'iva (ईश्वर). The first and second are those principally intended. स्वस्य इच्छया सङ्कल्पेन उपजातः उत्पन्नः विषयः यस्य the realm of which (Cupid) springs from one's own fancy. काम is called सङ्कल्पज. Compare दशकुमारचरित 'कः कामः सङ्कल्पः'. स्वेच्छोपजाताः विषयाः यस्य (with a bad king) that has under his rule as many countries as he desires. स्वेच्छायाः उपजाताः विषयाः यस्य from whose mere will, this world of objects springs up (with शिव). न...देहीति who cannot be described as possessing a body (with काम). काम is अनङ्ग and so he cannot be called देही. न...देहि इति who cannot be addressed with the words 'give' (with a bad king). A bad king, though possessed of vast territory, cannot be thus addressed for fear of his punishing the suppliant. शिव cannot be described as देही, because thereby one would detract from his all-pervading nature. मार्ग...दुःखम् he causes pain with numerous darts (with काम). मार्गणाः बाणाः. मार्गण also means याचक (with bad king). मार्गण will mean 'search for truth' or begging (with शिव). One has to pray to शिव with hundreds of requests; or one has to search for truth about God in various ways. This causes trouble. मोहा...काण्डे all of a sudden he snatches life (of lovers) by producing infatuation (with काम). मोहा...काण्डे (a bad king) takes away livelihood (such as grants of villages &c.) through his folly. मोहात्...काण्डे—शिव, who typifies the principle of destruction, takes away the lives of all, when मोह (*i. e.* तमोगुण) predominates. कष्टं alas. ईश्वरदुर्विदग्धः (with काम) badly burnt by शिव. ईश्वरश्चासौ दुर्विदग्धश्च a conceited king. C and T understand the verse differently. They take ईश्वर...ग्ध as 'one who is unskilled in waiting upon a king' (ईश्वरे दुर्विदग्धः). This sense may possibly be extracted from the

10

words, but to regard that sense as the principal one (as C and T do) is wrong. The subject matter of discussion is the conduct of kings and not the want of skill of courtiers. न्यक्कृता:... ०ययातयः येन who humbles, puts into the shade Yayāti &c. Here is a long list of famous ancient emperors. The story of नृग who was cursed for making delay in deciding a disputed claim is narrated in रामायण उत्तरकाण्ड chap. 53. नल is well-known. नल was king of निषध. What king is meant by निषध is not clear. It is probably निषध the great-grandson of राम. Vide रघु० 18. 1 and हरिवंश 15. 26. नहुष son of आयुः and father of ययाति. He was cursed to be अजगर. See विष्णुपुराण IV. 10. अम्बरीष is referred to in कौटिल्य's अर्थशास्त्र as a king that had conquered the six enemies (काम &c.). दिलीप was an ancestor of Rāma. नाभाग—See विष्णुपु० IV. 1. and मार्कण्डेय chap. 113. ff. भरत—the son of दुष्यन्त and शकुन्तला. भगीरथ who brought down the Ganges is well-known. ययाति, son of नहुष, transferred his old age to पूरु. अहङ्कारः एव कालकूटविषं तेन दिग्धाः अत एव दुष्टाः. ना...दृष्टयः. his eyes are not polluted and stained with the deadly poison of conceit. As he is called अमृतमय, कालकूट, which is the opposite of अमृत, is naturally suggested and अहङ्कार is compared to it. न...गिरः his speech is not choked by the disease of the throat due to the terrible poison (गरः) of pride *i. e.* he does not speak proudly. गर्वः गुरुगरः तेन गलग्रहगदः तेन गद्गदाः. गलग्रहः inflammation of the throat due to various causes. अतिस्मयेन ऊष्मा एव अपस्मारः तेन विस्मृतं स्थैर्यं येषु. नाति...स्थानकानि his postures are not such that he will forget his serenity by the epilepsy of puffed up pride. स्मयः pride. ऊष्मा stiffness. In epilepsy there is loss of consciousness (विस्मृतं) and the body becomes stiff (*i. e.* the man falls down in a fit). उद्दामः (overbearing) दर्पः एव दाहज्वरः (burning fever) तस्य वेगेन (operation) विक्लवाः (distressed, overwhelmed). अभिमानः एव महासन्निपातः तेन निर्मितः अङ्गभङ्गः यस्मिन्. गतानि movements. सन्निपात is a fatal fever in which there is a combined derangement of the three humours वात, पित्त and कफ. The योगरत्नाकर (आनन्दाश्रम ed. p. 98) gives the general symptoms. In it there is अङ्गभङ्ग (the limbs become stiff and painful). मदः एव अर्दितं तेन वक्रीकृतः ओष्ठः तस्मात् निष्ठ्यूतानि (emitted) निष्ठुराणि अक्षराणि येषु. A haughty man may curl up his lips and utter harsh words. अर्दित is a वातव्याधि, which may affect the lips. 'उच्चैर्व्याहरतोऽत्यर्थं खादतः कठिनानि च। हसतो जृम्भतो भाराद्विषमाच्छयनासनात्॥ शिरोनासौष्ठचिबुकललाटेक्षणसन्धिषु। अर्दयत्यनिलो वक्त्रमर्दितं जनयेत्ततः॥'. अस्य...

शकलेषु he looks upon good men of unblemished character as jewels and not on pieces of stone. He cares for नररत्नs and not for ordinary jewels. In this and the following clauses बाण employs the figure of speech called परिसंख्या, of which he is very fond. It occurs where an express specification of one thing, either made in answer to a question or not, tends to exclude either expressly or impliedly other similar things; *i. e.* किं भूषणं सुदृढमत्र यशो न रत्नं किं कार्यमार्यचरितं सुकृतं न दोषाः।. In the text, the figure occurs without a preceding question. 'किंचित्पृष्टमपृष्टं वा कथितं यत्प्रकल्पते। तादृगन्यव्यपोहाय परिसंख्या तु सा स्मृता॥' काव्यप्रकाश X. Read ०धवलेषु गुणेषु. मुक्ता...भारेषु He looks upon virtues pure like pearls as decorations and not on loads of ornaments white with pearls. दान...कीटेषु he believes in deeds of liberality as साधन and not in the worms of elephants that are दानवत्. दानवत् endowed with gifts; possessed of ichor. 'मदो दानम्' इत्यमरः. साधनम् a means of accomplishing one's object; army. Elephants were one of the four component parts of the ancient Indian army. सर्वाग्रेसरे that is the foremost of all. He wanted such fame as would make him the most pre-eminent man. जीवितं एव जरत्तृणम्—to him life was like rotten grass; glory was everything. Life (with ordinary men) is the foremost of all (things). If we read सर्वाशा० then आशा means 'quarters, hopes'. It is a good reading. गृहीतः करः (tribute) याभ्यः; गृहीतः करः (पाणिः) यासाम् (with ०पुत्रिकासु). गृहीत...योगः he exerts himself to subdue (*lit.* to accomplish) the quarters from which he levies tribute. अभियोगः exertion, perseverance. He makes no प्रसा...योगः (effort to adorn) the dolls *viz.* his wives whose hand he took (in marriage). चर्मपुत्रिका dolls of leather. गुणवति strung (with धनुषि); possessed of good qualities (with ०जने). पिण्डो० that live on the crumbs that he gives. अस्य...मात्मा His soul is for serving his friends *i. e.* he is devoted heart and soul to his friends. उपकरणम् what helps; an instrument, means *i. e.* something subservient or subsidiary. भृत्यो...भुत्वम् his sovereignty is for helping his servants. पण्डित...ग्ध्यम्—his learning enables him to understand the worth of learned men and to help them. कृपण wretched. सु...हृदयम् his heart is to him a means to remember the good deeds of others or to gratefully remember the benefits received from others. साह...शरीरम्—the one use that he makes of his body is to plunge in bold undertakings. असि...थिवी the earth enables him to show his skill in sword-play *i. e.* he vanquishes everyone in the world with his sword. वि...जकम् he requires the circle of kings (attending on him) for amusing himself (he does not require their help in battle). 'अथ **राजकम्** । राजन्यकं च **नृपतिक्षत्रियाणां गणे** क्रमात् ॥' इत्यमरः. प्र...पक्षः his enemies only serve to show his valour (or glory). सर्वम् अतिशेते ०शायि सुखमेव रसः तस्य प्रसूतिः यस्याः from which flows happiness that excels other pleasures. As his feet are compared to पल्लव, the happiness of serving him is compared to रस. पल्लवs give shade. His feet afford protection. पाद...च्छाया may also mean the brilliance of his sprout-like (*i. e.* red) feet. कृतं कशिपु (food and clothing) यस्य. 'कशिपु त्वन्नमाच्छादनं द्वयम्' इत्यमरः. विश्रान्तश्चासौ सुखी च that has taken rest and feels refreshed.

P. 25 ll. 11-24. **अथ गते...मकरोत्**. पर्यस्ते वासरे when the day was scattered about (was drawing to a close). सङ्घट्ट...तपे when the afternoon sunlight, red like a young crow's mouth, was growing fainter and fainter (क्षाम *lit.* emaciated), as though drunk by the cavities (सम्पुटः) of the closing red lotuses. सङ्घट्ट् or सङ्घट् 1 A to unite or join. क्षयिणि decreasing; consumptive. A consumptive also becomes emaciated. Red lotuses close their cups in the evening. The poet fancies that the sunlight grew faint because it was drunk the whole day by the red lotuses that were fully expanded. One may drink water with हस्तसम्पुट. शिथिलितः (lessened) निजवाजिजवः येन (*adj.* of पतङ्ग) The sun is represented as drawn by seven horses. जपा...ले as rosy as a bunch (आपीडः) of china roses. अस्ता...पतङ्गे when the sun stumbled (स्खलित) on to the top of the setting mountain, as though he was limping, having tender feet pierced by the thorns of lotus plants. The hairy growth on the stems of lotus plants is like thorns. One whose feet are pierced by thorns limps and may stumble if he has to ascend to the tops of mountains. ०कण्टकैः क्षतः पादपल्लवः यस्य. पुरः...मुखे when the first part (मुखं) of the night (श्यामा) came hurrying in the east (पुरः), having her long tresses of slight darkness dangling about, and being dark through grief at the absence of the moon. अन्धकारलेशः एव लम्बालकाः, प्रेङ्खन्तः ०लकाः यस्मिन्. The idea is that it was a moonless night and the east began to look dark. श्यामा also 'a handsome young woman.' खञ्जति *loc. sing.* of *pr. p.* of खञ्ज् 1 P to limp. A lady's face (मुखं) also may lose its brightness through separation and she might have her hair rolling on her back, because not tied up. A woman, whose husband had gone on a journey, was not to decorate her body &c. 'हास्यं परगृहे यानं समाजोत्सवदर्शनम् । क्रीडां शरीरसंस्कारं त्यजेत्प्रोषितभर्तृका ॥.' कृतं सन्ध्योपासनं येन. अन्य...राज्ञा I have been misunderstood by the king. निर्निमित्त = निष्कारण. कष्टा distressing. विषमम् full of difficulties. तत्र = राजकुले. न...गतिः I cannot claim to have affection for the royal family first started by my ancestors, nor have I access to it from their time. In these and the following clauses he intimates that neither his ancestors nor himself had ever before visited the court and so he is diffident as to how he might acquit himself when once there. नो...रोधः nor do I possess that regard (of the king) which comes of remembering (former) benefits. अनुरोधः consideration. बाल...स्नेहः affection that springs from serving (the king) from one's childhood. गोत्रगौरवम् family position or importance. पूर्व...ण्यम् the courtesy due to old acquaintance. न प्रज्ञा...लोभनम् nor can I offer the allurement of the exchange of thoughts. विद्या...हलम् nor can I claim the admiration due to vast learning. आ...दरः—regard paid to fine appearance. सेवा...लम् skill in the changes of tones necessary in service. A servant has to assume tones of humility even when exasperated. For काकु, see above p. 84. वि...ग्ध्यम् the cleverness requisite in the meeting of the learned. वित्तव्ययेन वशीकरणम् winning over (people about the court) by expenditure of money. अवश्यं गन्तव्यम्—In spite of all these drawbacks I must go. पुरारातिः 'enemy of the cities' *i. e.* शिव. He was so called because he burnt down the three cities of gold, silver and iron built by Maya for demons in the sky, air and earth. 'असुराणां पुराण्यासंस्त्रीणि वीर्यवतां दिवि । आयसं राजतं चैव सौवर्णं परमं महत् ॥' द्रोणपर्व chap. 202. 64. भुवनगुरुः the object of worship to the world. गतस्य...ष्यति will do everything that is proper (सांप्रत) when I go there.

P. 25 l. 25—**P. 26** l. 9 **अथान्य...रगात्.** The sentence is अथ अन्यस्मिन्नहनि...प्रीतिकूटात् निरगात्. In this paragraph we have a very interesting and instructive account of how an orthodox Brāhmaṇa left his home on an important undertaking. धृतं धौतं धवलं दुकूलवासः येन. गृहीता अक्षमाला (rosary) येन. प्रास्था...वर्त्य having many times recited the Vedic hymns and portions of *mantras* suited to one starting on a journey. प्रस्थाने भवं or प्रस्थानं प्रयोजनमस्य इति प्रास्थानिकम्, according to 'प्रयोजनम्' पा. 5. 1. 109. विरूपाक्षः शिवः. He is so called because he has three eyes. क्षीरस्नपनं पुरःसरं यस्याः

(*adj.* of पूजा) preceded by a bath of milk. The image of शिव was washed with milk by Bāṇa. क्षीराभिषेक is even now resorted to to propitiate Rudra. Compare 'अतिशुचिशैवसम्पाद्यमानविरूपाक्षक्षीरकलश-सहस्रस्नपनं (राजकुलं)' हर्ष० 5th उच्छ्वास. सुर...बहुलां mostly consisting of or abounding in sweet flowers &c. विलेपनं sandal ointment. प्रथमहुताः तरलाः तिलाः तेषां त्वचः विघटनं तेन चटुलाः मुखराः शिखा एव शेखरः यस्य—whose crest was formed by the rolling and crackling flames that split open the husks of the sesame that were offered first of all and hurled about (being heated by the fire). प्राज्यं (plentiful) आज्यं (ghee) तस्य आहुत्या प्रवर्धिता दक्षिणार्चिः यस्य whose right flame was kindled &c. Flames of fire curving to the right were regarded as indicating good luck. Compare 'तस्मै सम्यग्घुतो वह्निर्वाजिनीराजनाविधौ । प्रदक्षिणार्चिर्व्याजेन हस्तेनेव जयं ददौ ॥' रघु० IV. 25; 'प्रदक्षिणार्चिर्हविरग्निराददे । बभूव सर्वं शुभशंसि तत्क्षणं' रघु० III. 14; 'उदर्चिषं हुत्वा प्रदक्षिणावर्तशिखाकलापमाशुशुक्षणिं' हर्ष० 7th उ० 1st para. आशुशुक्षणिं = अग्निम्. This is a Vedic word rarely used in classcial literature. It is variously derived from शुच् or शुष्. द्युम्नं = धनम् This is again a word very frequently used in the Vedas. यथाविद्यमानं according to his means. प्राङ्मुखीं facing the east. नैचिकी an excellent cow or a sacrificial cow. 'उत्तमा गोषु नैचिकी' इत्यमरः. शुक्लः अङ्गरागः (ointment) यस्य. शुक्लं माल्यं (garland) यस्य. रोचनया चित्राः दूर्वाग्रपल्लवाः तैः ग्रथितानि ०कुसुमानि तैः कृतः कर्णपूरः यस्य whose ear was adorned with गिरिकर्णिका flowers that were interwoven with the tips of दूर्वा grass that was smeared with रोचना. रोचना—bright yellow pigment prepared from the urine or bile of a cow or found in its head. All the three रोचना, दूर्वा and गिरिकर्णिका (a kind of white flower) are auspicious. रोचना was used to ward off evil spirits and the evil eye. शिखायां आसक्ताः सिद्धार्थकाः (white mustard) येन. The white mustard was believed to protect against evil spirits. सिद्धः अर्थः यस्मात्. मात्रे...यया whose heart overflowed with affection, as if she were his mother. श्वेतं वासः यस्याः. कनीयस्या स्वस्रा this is a personal matter mentioned only casually by the author. महाश्वेतया—it is difficult to say what goddess is alluded to. Both दुर्गा and सरस्वती are fair and may be called महाश्वेता. We believe it is दुर्गा that is meant. दुर्गा is also named गौरी and सर्वमङ्गला. Here the chief point is the auspicious rites performed when Bāṇa started. The देवीभागवत says 'श्वेतं शुक्लं शिवस्थानं यस्माच्चेह समागता । महाभावसमुत्पन्ना महाश्वेता ततः स्मृता ॥'. सं० says 'महाश्वेता देवताविशेषः रविस्थदेवतेत्यन्ये'. महाश्वेतया would also mean 'who (मालती) was very fair'. अभि...जरन्तीभिः congratulated or applauded by the old female servants. वन्दितौ चरणौ येषाम्. अभि... वृद्धैः kissed on the head by the elders in the family at whose feet he fell. वर्धितः गमनोत्साहः यस्य. मौहू...हृदः having made, in accordance with the opinions of astrologers, offerings to the lunar mansions to satisfy their desires *i. e.* he offered such things as were calculated to propitiate the नक्षत्र on which he started. मुहूर्तं वेद मौहूर्तिकः (with affix ठक्), according to 'तदधीते तद्वेद' पा. 4. 2. 59. कृतं नक्षत्रदोहदं येन. हरितगोमयेन उपलिप्तं (plastered) अजिरं तस्मिन् स्थण्डिलं (a raised plot for sacrifice) तस्मिन् स्थापितम् (*adj.* of ०कलशं). असितेतराणां (धवलानां) कुसुमानां मालया परिक्षिप्तः (encircled) कण्ठः यस्य (*adj.* of ०कलशं). पिष्ट...पाण्डुरं white with five finger marks of flour. The five fingers were dipped in some powder (or flour) mixed with milk and the jar was smeared with the finger—marks by way of मङ्गल. Compare 'पिष्टपञ्चाङ्गुल--मण्ड्यमानोलूखलमुसलशिलाद्युपकरणम्' हर्ष० 4th उ० below. मुख...पल्लवम् even now आम्रपल्लवs are placed in the mouth of jars as auspicious. For पूर्णकलश as being auspicious, *vide* notes above p. 70. कुसुमानि फलानि च पाणिषु येषाम्. अप्र...पङ्क्तिः that recited the *apratiratha* hymn. It is ऋग्वेद X. 103. अप्रतिरथ is the name of the sage who composed the hymn. निजद्विजैः by the Brāhmaṇas that were his dependents. प्रथम...चरणः putting forward his right foot first. The right foot, eye, hand in the case of males and the left foot, eye, hand in the case of females are auspicious.

P. 26 ll 10–18 **प्रथमे...भवनस्य.** घर्म...कष्टं very distressing owing to summer. This and the clauses up to रोमाञ्चितमिव qualify ०काननम् (l. 14). निष्प...षमं terrible on account of the leafless trees. पथिकजनेन नमस्क्रियमाणाः प्रवेशपादपे उत्कीर्णाः कात्यायनीप्रतियातनाः यस्मिन् in which the images of Durgā carved under (or on) the trees at the entrance (of the forest) were paid homage by travellers. '**प्रतिमा प्रतियातना** प्रतिच्छाया' इत्यमरः. शुष्क...सहस्रैः though dried up, it (forest) seemed as though full of sprouts with thousands of tremulous long tongues that hung from (the mouths of) thirsty beasts. The red and tremulous tongues resemble red and restless पल्लवs. पुलकित...सङ्घातैः seemed to be spotted with the swarms of bees (सरघा) flying from the honey combs (मधुगोलः) that were licked by bears and monkeys. अच्छाः निर्मलाः भल्लाः शस्त्राणि नखानि यस्य. For पुलक in the sense of 'spots,' see above notes pp. 69–70. As रोमाञ्चित follows immediately afterwards, we cannot take पुलकित in the sense of रोमाञ्चित. For गोलाङ्गूल see p. 54. 'सरघा मधुमक्षिका' इत्यमरः.

रोमा... शतैः bristling with horripilation with the hundreds of the stout shouts of asparagus (अभीरु) that grew on the soil burnt (by forest fires). दग्धस्थलीषु रूढा अभीरुः तस्याः कन्दलशतैः. अभीरु is a plant called शतावरी or नारायणी. When soil is burnt, it becomes more fertile; hence the word स्थूल. Seeds that are lying deep down in the debris spring up vigorously after the burning of forest trees by conflagration. हृदयनिर्विशेषेण not different from (*i. e.* as dear as) his own heart. The com. takes भ्रात्रा to refer to चन्द्रसेन. सुहृदा is to be connected with जगत्पतिनाम्ना. We may possibly take भ्रात्रा (cousin) also with जगत्पति. We are not told anywhere that चन्द्रसेन accompanied Bāṇa. सम्पादिता सपर्या (पूजा) यस्य. स्कन्धावारम् (object of आससाद) army. मणितारस्य समीपे उप० (अव्ययीभाव). मणितार was a town. अजिरवतीमन्वायतम् अन्व० (अव्ययीभाव) along the river अजिरवती. कृतः सन्निवेशः येन encamped.

P. 26 l. 19—**P. 28** l. 7. **निर्वर्तित...गमत्.** The principal sentence is निर्वर्तित...करः मेखलकेन सह...राजद्वारमगमत्. निर्वर्तितः ०करः येन who carried out the usual incidents of bathing and taking his meals. याममात्रं अवशेषः यस्य when only one watch (of three hours) remained. पट्ट...पितैः that were brought (near the royal gate) for tying on their heads the fillets of honour. This and the following nouns in the instrumental qualify वारणेन्द्रैः (p. 26. l. 27). A पट्टबन्ध was a mark of great honour. Compare 'लब्धो मनोरथदुर्लभो महादेवीपट्टबन्धसत्कारलाभो ललाटेन' हर्ष० 5th उ०. डिण्डि...हृतैश्च (some) brought for mounting drums (डिण्डिमः) on their backs. विक्षे...प्रेषितैः some acquired by way of tribute, some received as presents and some sent by the rangers of the elephant depots. सं० says 'विक्षेपः करः;' we may translate 'वि०...र्जितैः' as 'collected for being despatched to various places'. कौशलिकं or–का a present (from कुशलम्). नागवीथी rows of elephants or place where elephants were caught and trained. प्रथम...ढौकितैः that were brought near for being seen with curiosity (or admiration) for the first time, that were sent at the time of despatching an envoy, and that were presented (ढौकित) by the chiefs of small villages (in forests). पल्ली a small village or settlement. परिवृढः Head. 'प्रभुः परिवृढोऽधिपः' इत्यमरः. स्वेच्छा...कारितैः that were called for the pleasure. (कौतुक) of a mimic fight at will. दीय...मानैश्च that were given (*i. e.* put together for a sham fight), that were separated (when they had faught for some time) and were led off. यामस्थापितैः that were placed at the watch (at the place where the hours of the watch were marked). सर्व...कृतैः that were collected together, as though they were mountains, for constructing a dam across the ocean in order to conquer all continents. The elephants were dark and big like mountains. The king wanted to conquer the continents beyond the sea. He would cast the hills of elephants into the sea and would thereby cross over to the other side. In the Purāṇas, the द्वीps are seven (जम्बु, प्लक्ष, शाल्मल, कुश, क्रौञ्च, शाक and पुष्कर). See विष्णुपु. II. 1. 11. *ff.* Sometimes they are spoken of as eighteen. 'अष्टादशद्वीपनिखातयूपः' रघु० 6. 38; 'भ्रूलतादिष्टाष्टादशद्वीपे दिलीपे' and 'अष्टादशद्वीपाष्टमङ्गलकमालिनी मेदिनी' हर्ष० 6th उ०. ध्वज...कल्पितैः that were made like so many festive days of पुष्याभिषेक, charming with banner-cloths, sharp drums, conches, chowries and unguents. पुष्याभिषेक is the day when the king takes a ceremonial bath, the moon being in the Pushya asterism. On these days the king is accompanied by ध्वज &c., which are the insignia of royalty. The elephants also had these on their body. श्यामायमानम्—this qualifies राजद्वारम् (p. 28. l. 7). The dark elephants made the gate look dark. There is another sense suggested. 'The day looked like night on account of the dark elephants.' अनवरतचलितैः खुरपुटैः प्रहतं मृदः (पृथिव्याः) अङ्गं यैः—that struck the earth with their hoofs that pranced ceaselessly. ०पुटैः प्रहतः मृदङ्गः यैः the sound of the hoofs resembled the beating of a tabor to the accompaniment of dancing. Hence the poet says 'न...लक्ष्मीम्'—that made Royal Glory to dance (while they themselves beat the drum). उप...जातिम् with the laugh-like foam spreading over the the corners of their lips, they seemed as though mocking the tribe of deer that (compared with the horses) had slow legs. The idea is that the horses were swifter than deer. Both फेन and हास are white. सृक्किन् *n.* corner of the lip. आका...श्रवसम् that challenged with their joyous neighing the horse of Indra to a combat (सङ्घट्टः). उच्चैःश्रवस् is the horse of Indra, one of the 14 jewels churned from the ocean. उत्पत...तलं that as though flew up into the sky in anger against the horses of the sun, their ornamental chowries serving them as wings. पक्षायमाणा मण्डनचामरमाला येषाम्. पक्षः इव आचरति पक्षायते. तुरङ्गै...मानम् (राजद्वारम्) that was as though in waves with horses. प्रे...वृत्तैः returning after being sent. From प्रेषितैश्च to ०कपिलैः (p. 27 l. 5) we have words qualifying क्रमेलककुलैः. बहु...मण्डनकैः their mouths were ornamented with rows of cowries (वराटिका) as though they (cowries) were rows of numerical figures in counting the distance of many *yojanas* they had travelled. तार...च्छेदैः that looked as though they were patches (छेद) of evening light marked with stars. The white cowries on the mouths of the camels looked like stars and their tawny skins like the yellow glow of sunlight in the evening. अरुण...लेयैः that, having their ears ornamented with red chowries, looked as though they were fields of red rice covered with red lotuses. The अरुणचामरिका looked like red chowrie and the tawny skin like a field of red rice. 'क्षेत्रं व्रैहेयशालेयं व्रीहिशाल्युद्भवोचितम्' इत्यमरः. 'व्रीहिशाल्योर्ढक्' पा. 5. 2. 2. (शालीनां भवनं क्षेत्रम् । ढक्). अनव...शतैः having strings of charming golden bells tinkling incessantly, they seemed to be groves of old *karanja* trees with hundreds of dry pods of seed rattling on them. घुरुघुरुक a small bell (Marathi घुंगुर). For करञ्जबीज see text p. 22 l. 20. श्रव...जटालैः that were full of beautiful (चित्र) tufts of woollen threads of five colours, dangling near their ears. The next clause is अन्यत्र...आतपत्रखण्डैः श्वेतायमानम् (l. 13). शर...तनुभिः (umbrellas) that were white like milk freshly flowing, as though they were autumnal clouds. Autumnal clouds are white when a mass of water (पयःपटल) drops from them. कल्प...मण्डलैः the circular shadow of which was annihilated by the light (आलोकः) due to a mass of pearls (which encircled the umbrellas), as though they were trees of paradise. A कल्पपादप yields whatever one desires and so it may yield pearls. नारा...पक्षैः had jewels (emeralds) sticking to them, as though they (आतपत्र) were the lotuses in the navel of Vishṇu. पुण्डरीकs and the umbrellas are white. The lotus in Vishṇu's navel may touch the wings of गरुड who is the वाहन of विष्णु. आश्लिष्टाः गरुडपक्षाः येषु. गरुडपक्ष is a kind of gem, otherwise called गारुत्मत. 'गारुत्मतं मरकतम्' इत्यमरः. क्षीरो...दण्डैः that had brilliant and large rods of coral, as though they were regions (उद्देशः) of the milky ocean. The umbrellas were white like milk. Coral is found in the sea. शेष...खण्डैः that had large (स्फीत) rubies sparkling on them, as though they were the board-like (*i. e.* broad) hoods of शेष. It was supposed that serpents had red gems in their hoods. शेष has a 1000 hoods and is as white as the umbrellas. श्वेत...सेवितैः that were resorted to by swanlike kings, as though they were the islands of the heavenly Ganges.

The blue topaz would look like charcoal. If it was reddish, then it would look like a live piece of coal or like Mars (अङ्गारक). The next sentence is कैश्चि...शश्रुमहासामन्तैः समन्तादासेव्यमानम् (l. 34). कैश्चि...विशद्भिः some did not get admission, hung down their heads (on that account) and seemed, under the guise (निभः) of the image of faces reflected in the nails of their feet, to enter their own bodies through shame. 'निभस्तु कथितो व्याजे पुल्लिङ्गः सदृशे त्रिषु' मेदिनी. As they hung down their faces, the latter were reflected in the bright toe-nails. The poet fancies that through shame they entered their own bodies in the shape of reflections. कैश्चि...र्पयद्भिः under the guise (व्याजः) of the pencil of the rays of the nails of their hands that were scattered about, some (kings) seemed to hand over chowries for service to the earth which they scratched with their fingers. To scratch the earth is inauspicious. The vanquished kings, being deeply engrossed in sad thoughts and having nothing to do, drew lines on the ground with their nails. The rays of the bright nails resemble chowries. The poet fancies that chowries were handed over to the earth (poetically represented as the queen of a king) that the latter might thereafter serve king Harsha with the chowrie. 'रेषानिर्माणमुर्व्यां च्छदतृणलवनं पादयोश्चाप्यपूजा दन्तानामप्यशौचं वसनमलिनता रूक्षता मूर्धजानाम्। सन्ध्यायुग्मे च निद्रा विवसनशयनं ग्रासहास्यातिरेकः स्वाङ्गे वाद्यं च पुंसां निधनमुपनयेत्केशवस्यापि लक्ष्मीम् ॥'. उरःस्थले दोलायमानः इन्द्रनीलतरलप्रभापट्टः येषाम्. तरल is the central gem in a necklace. 'तरलो हारमध्यगः' इत्यमरः. कैश्चि...पट्टैः—the rays of the blue sapphire resemble a sword blade. The poet fancies that the kings had suspended from their necks swords (instead of carrying them in their hands) in order to propitiate their lord (हर्ष). तरल (=चञ्चल) suggests that the swords flashed like sapphires. कैश्चि...श्मश्रुभिरिव—the bees hovering round their faces are fancied to be the beard allowed to grow through grief at the loss of their kingdoms. One who is in mourning for the death of a relative does not shave himself. शेखरे (chaplet) उड्डीयमानं मधुपमण्डलं येषाम्. ०भयेन पलायमानः मौलिः (crown of the head) येषाम्. The bees on the white chaplet are fancied to be their heads (with the dark hair growing on them) running away for fear of having to submit to the humiliation of bowing at Harsha's feet. अविद्यमानं (हर्षात्) अन्यत् शरणं येषाम् that have no protector other than हर्ष. Another sense is (अविद्यमानं अन्यस्मात् शरणं रक्षणं येषाम्) 'who are not protected by any one else'; with

11

this latter sense we have to construe संमानितैरिव—they were as though honoured because they did not require another to protect them. 'शरणं रक्षणे गेहे बधरक्षकयोरपि' हेमचन्द्रः. अन्तरान्तरा from time to time. निष्पतताम् coming out. आन्तर...पृच्छद्भिः that ceaselessly (अश्रान्त) asked again and again the servants that accompanied inner doorkeepers after whose track ran thousands of suppliants. अद्य भविष्यति will it be to-day ? भुक्तं आस्थानं यस्मिन्. भुक्ता...कक्ष्याम् will the emperor grant an interview after sitting in the audience-hall ? Will he come out into the outer court ? भुक्तं आस्थानं यथा स्यात्तथा or भुक्तं आस्थानं यस्मिन्. We may take 'अद्य...स्थानं' as one sentence and translate 'will there be an audience hall (*i. e.* will he hold his court) after taking his dinner ?' If we read भुक्त्वास्थाने, the meaning is 'will he, after taking his dinner, grant an interview in the audience-hall ?' The king was to enter the hall of justice after taking his dinner. 'भुक्तवान् विहरेच्चैव स्त्रीभिरन्तः-पुरे सह । विहृत्य तु यथाकालं पुनः कार्याणि चिन्तयेत् ॥' मनु० VII. 221. आसेव्यमानम्—qualifies राजद्वारम्. Connect महीपालैः with अध्यास्यमानम् (occupied). प्रति...कालम् that waited for the time when the emperor would be seen. एका...विष्टैः sitting in a spot by themselves. जैनैः आर्हतैः—we must understand the Bauddhas by जैनैः as आर्हतैः follows. जिन and अर्हत् are epithets that are applied to the founders of both Jainism and Buddhism by their followers. But in the usage of Brahmanical writers आर्हत stands for the system of महावीर (as in आर्हतदर्शन in the सर्वदर्शनसंग्रह). So जैनैः is equal to बौद्धैः. Compare 'न जिनस्येवार्थवादशून्यानि दर्शनानि' below (text p. 35. ll. 25-26). पाशुपतैः—The पाशुपतs are a sect of माहेश्वरs. For a brief statement and refutation of the पाशुपत system see शारीरकभाष्य on वेदान्तसूत्र II. 2. 37. *ff.* According to them शिव is called पशुपति (the lord of पशुs *viz.* the जीवs) and is only the निमित्तकारण of the world. पाराशरिभिः—for the meaning, see above p. 90. वर्णिभिः—वर्णिन् means 'ब्रह्मचारिन्' (from वर्ण + इन्) 'वर्णिनो ब्रह्मचारिणः'-according to 'वर्णाद्ब्रह्मचारिणि' पा. 5. 2. 134. For a longer list of the followers of various sects, see हर्ष० 8th उ० 5th para. सर्वदेशेषु जन्म येषाम्. सर्व...दूतमण्डलैः we know that ambassadors used to be sent to Indian courts by kings of Persia, Greece, Rome &c. In the frescoes in the caves of Ajanta there is a representation of a Persian embassy. सर्व...पतीनाम्—there were so many people of various tribes and nations that it seemed as though it was the place where the primeval sages created beings of various kinds. For प्रजापतिs, see above p. 18. It was these ten

प्रजापतिs that created everything. *Vide* मनु I. 36-41. लोक...रचितं made by gathering together the essence of the three worlds. अकथनीयः समृद्धिसम्भारः यस्य. The महाभारत is the biggest work in the Sanskrit language and yet a work of that vast extent would have fallen far short of adequately describing the glory of Harsha's gate. कृत...वेशम् the position of which was effected by a thousand कृतयुगs. Various meanings are possible. The royal gate was so gorgeous that it would seem to an observer to have been the work of long ages. Or the royal gate conveyed an atmosphere of so much purity and righteousness that as though a thousand कृतयुगs had combined to form it. For कृतयुग as an era of unmixed virtue, *vide* p. 45. स्वर्गाणां अर्बुदैः. अर्बुद is equal to 10 कोटिs. 'लक्षं च नियुतं चैव कोटिरर्बुदमेव च । वृन्दः खर्वो निखर्वश्च शङ्खपद्मौ च सागरः । अन्त्यं मध्यं परार्धं च दशवृद्ध्या यथाक्रमम् ॥'. विहितं रामणीयकं यस्य. राज...ग्रहं that was surrounded or resorted to (*lit.* accepted) by crores of royal glories.

P. 28 ll. 8-13 **अभव...प्राविशत्.** जातः विस्मयः यस्मिन्. इयत् प्रमाणं यस्य (*adj.* of ०जातं) of this (vast) extent. प्रजासृजां of those (प्रजापतिs) that created beings. महा...क्षयः how is it that the great elements were not exhausted (in creating these numerous beings) ? महाभूतs are the five gross elements *viz.* पृथिवी, अप्, तेजः, वायु and आकाश, from which the bodies of all beings are created. परिच्छेदः limit. The idea is that in creating so many beings, the furthest limit of the number of atoms must have been reached and exhausted. विच्छेदः is a better reading, but is probably an emendation. परमाणूनां परिच्छेदः is more in accordance with the style of Bāṇa who cares for अनुप्रास more than for anything else. व्युपरमः cessation, end. आकृ...ति: the exhaustion of all forms. पुण्यभागी (refers to बाण)—because he was soon to be ushered into the presence of the glorious हर्ष. तम् = बाणम्. अप्रतिहतः without being obstructed.

P. 28 ll. 14-30 **अथ स...भ्यन्तरम्.** The first sentence is अथ स मुहूर्तादिव...पुरुषेणानुगम्यमानः निर्गत्य अवोचत्. सः = मेखलकः. The instrumentals from प्रांशुना qualify पुरुषेण. कर्णिकारवत् गौरेण. वीध्रकेन (विमलेन) कञ्चुकेन छन्नं वपुः यस्य. समु...लग्नेन whose waist (अवलग्नं) was small, being bound by a belt (शस्तं) that was studded (बन्धुर) with ornaments of flashing rubies. पदकं metal plate studded with stones. ०पदकबन्धेन बन्धुरं शस्तं तस्य बन्धेन कृशं अवलग्नं यस्य. In the lexicons the meaning assigned to शस्त is 'finger-guard'

'अङ्गुलित्रं शस्तकं च तथा चाङ्गुष्ठरक्षकम्'. But that meaning will not do here. If we read वस्तबन्ध, the meaning is 'by a strap of goat-skin.' ०शिलावत् विशालं वक्षः यस्य. हरस्य (शिवस्य) वृषः तस्य ककुदं (hump) तस्य कूटो (राशिः) तद्वत् विकटः (formidable) अंसतटः. He was fair and formidable like हरवृष. उरसा...बिभ्रता wearing on his chest a necklace as though it (हार) were a rope to restrain the tribe of deer in the form of restless organs of sense. हृषीकं = इन्द्रियम्. इति... समानेन—the jewelled rings in his ear are fancied to be the sun and the moon brought there to inquire of them whether there existed any one in their families equal to हर्ष. वह...किरणैः for whom room was as though made by the rays of the sun out of regard for his (पुरुष's) position, the rays being eclipsed (*lit.* pulled away) by the flowing (वहत्) stream (वेणिका) of the beauty of his face. विसरः = समूहः. When there is a crowd and a way has to be made for a great man, people have to be dragged out (आक्षिप्यमाण). The bright lustre of his face surpassed the sun's rays. प्रसादेन लब्धया obtained through the favour of his master (with ०मालिकया); serene (with दृष्ट्या). लब्धः प्रसादः (serenity) यया सा लब्धप्रसादा or प्रसादलब्धा, according to 'वाहिताग्न्यादिषु' पा. 2. 2. 37 (आहिताग्निः । अग्न्याहितः). आहिताग्नि is an आकृतिगण (illustrative list only and not exhaustive). मुण्डमालिका a chaplet. नैष्ठु...इता bearing on his bent head a white turban as if it (turban) were courtesy itself, though he occupied a position that was the centre (अधिष्ठानं) of sternness. As the chief of all doorkeepers his position required him to be stern in keeping discipline; yet he was courteous and had bent his head when approaching Bāṇa. C and T translate 'lifting his white turban as a token of respect'. This is quite wrong. No one in India would lift his turban *as a token of respect*. The learned authors are misled by western notions. वामेन goes with ०लयेन and ०त्सरुं with कृपाणम्, which latter is the object of कलयता. स्थूलमुक्ताफलानां छुरणेन (inlaying) दन्तुरः (uneven, jagged) त्सरुः (handle) यस्य. कलयता (goes with पुरुषेण) holding. 'त्सरुः खड्गादिमुष्टौ स्यात्' इत्यमरः. इतरे...धारयता holding in the other (*i. e.* right) hand a polished (उन्मृष्टां) golden staff, as though it (staff) were a streak of lightning without its unsteadiness. अपनीता तरलता यस्याः. For शातकौम्भ see above p. 54. ताडिती is from तडित्. अप...रलतां (with वेत्रयष्टिम्) also means 'that prevents wanton actions' (of the crowd at the door). अपनीता तरलता यया. अनन्तरः = मुख्यः. चक्षुष्यः = प्रियः. See above p. 75. द्वारे नियुक्तः

दौवारिकः. सम...वेशी let your honour (Bāṇa) who is intent on welfare treat him with befitting behaviour. प्रतिपत्तिः respectful behaviour, course of conduct. कल्याणे अभिनिवेशः अस्य ०शिन्. The word means the same thing as कल्याणिन्. Compare 'आलोकयतु तावत्कल्याणाभिनिवेशी लक्ष्मीमेव प्रथमाम्' का० p. 104 of P; 'एतत्प्रायेण कल्याणाभिनिवेशिनः श्रुतिविषयमापतितमेव' का० p. 136 (P). आगच्छत—the plural shows the respect he paid to बाण. एव...ग्राह्यं worthy to be thus favoured.

P. 28 l. 31—**P. 29** l. 25. **अथ...इति.** The first sentence is अथ...तुरङ्गैः आरचितां मन्दुरां विलोकयन् (l. 14)...अव्यक्तं इभधिष्ण्यागारमपश्यत् (l. 19). वनायुजैः born in the country of वनायु. The words in the instrumental from वनायुजैः qualify तुरङ्गैः below (l. 14). From वनायुजैः to पारसीकैः we have the breeds of horses from various countries. हलायुध and विश्व give वनायुज and पारसीक as synonyms. But that will not do here as पारसीक follows. आरट्ट—'पञ्च नद्यो वहन्त्येता यत्र निःसृत्य पर्वतात् । आरट्टा नाम वाहीका न तेष्वार्यो द्व्यहं वसेत् ॥'. The country of कम्बोज was beyond the Hindookush mountains (probably eastern Persia) and was known in very ancient times. It produced one of the best breeds of horses. See रघु० IV. 69-70. यास्क refers to the country 'शवतिर्गतिकर्मा कम्बोजेष्वेव भाष्यते विकारमस्यार्येषु भाषन्ते शव इति' निरुक्त. See पाणिनि IV. 1. 75. पारसीक is Persia. From शोणैः, we have horses of various colours. ति...षैः dappled like partridges. In this para, the author shows his familiarity with शालिहोत्र, the science of horses. पञ्चभद्रः-horse having on the head and four hoofs five auspicious marks. According to सं०, it is a horse whose face together with the head and four hoofs is white.' 'सिताश्च यस्य वाजिनः शफाः समस्तकं मुखं स पञ्चभद्रनामको नृपस्य राज्यसौख्यदः ।' 'पञ्चभद्रस्तु हृत्पृष्ठमुखपार्श्वेषु पुष्पितः' हेमचन्द्र. On मल्लिकाक्षैः, सं० says "शुक्लपर्यन्ते असिततारके नयने येषां ते मल्लिकाक्षाः । उक्तं च 'पृथुस्निग्धाः समा चैव मल्लिकाकुसुमप्रभा । राजी यस्य तु पर्यन्ते परिक्षिप्ये तु लोचने । स हयो मल्लिकाक्षस्तु दृष्टिपर्यन्ततारकः ॥' इति." They are horses on the corners of whose eyes there are spots of white hair. कृत्तिकापिञ्जरैः—सं० 'तारकाकदम्बककल्पानेकबिन्दुकल्माषितत्वचः'—horses the coat of which is marked with numerous starlike spots. कृत्तिका is a cluster of six stars. आयतं (long) निर्मांसं मुखं येषाम्. अनुत्कटः (ह्रस्वः) कर्णकोशः येषाम्. सुवृत्तः (well rounded) श्लक्ष्णः (soft or delicate) सुघटितः (well proportioned) घण्टिकाबन्धः येषाम्. घण्टिकाबन्ध-that part of the neck where bells are tied. The com. says "शिरसो ग्रीवायाश्च यन्मध्यं स घण्टिकाबन्धः यो निगाल इत्युच्यते । तस्य सुवृत्तादि शस्यते । यदाह 'ग्रीवाशिरोन्तर-

श्लिष्टो दीर्घवृत्तः समाहितः । नोद्वर्तो नार्धितो नातिदुर्नाह्योऽतिविधानतः । सुदिग्धोनुपदिग्धश्च निगालो गदितः शुभः ॥' इति". यूपानुपूर्व्या वक्रा आयता उदग्रा ग्रीवा येषाम् with curved, long and up-turned necks resembling a sacrificial post in their contour. आनुपूर्वी order, regular succession of parts. पूर्वानुक्रमेण अनुपूर्वं तस्य भावः आनुपूर्वी or °पूर्व्यम्. उपचयेन श्वयन्तः स्कन्धसन्धयः येषाम् whose shoulder joints were stout (swelling) on account of the accumulation (of flesh). निर्भुग्नं (projecting, convex) उरःस्थलं येषाम्. The com. says 'स्थूलास्थि महदच्छिद्रं पृथुलं यच्च निर्वलि । उर ईदृक्प्रशंसन्ति स्थूलक्रोडं महत्तरम् ॥'. अस्थूलाः (not thick) slender प्रगुणाः (straight) प्रसृताः (legs) येषाम्. लोहपीठवत् कठिनं खुरमण्डलं येषाम्. अति...धारयद्भिः that had bellies round and as though without entrails through fear of their being broken through great speed. अनिर्मिताणि अन्त्राणि येषु. अन्त्राणि suggests the idea of interstices or ups and downs. What is वृत्त (well rounded) cannot have ups and downs. उद्यन्त्या (large) द्रोण्या विभज्यमानं पृथुजघनं येषाम् whose broad flanks were divided by a large depression. द्रोणी is a feature of beauty in a horse. It is a depression on the chest, back and flanks of a horse. The com. quotes 'पृष्ठोरःकटिपार्श्वस्य मांसोत्कर्षणनिर्मिता । द्रोणिकेति प्रशंसन्ति शोभा वाजिनि पञ्चमी ॥'. जगती...पल्लवैः whose leaf-like tails rolled on the ground (जगती). C and T translate 'with the hairs like new shoots swaying about in the wind'. कष्ट...यन्त्रितैः that were restrained with difficulty by the numerous firm ropes fixed (in the earth) on both sides. The ropes held their necks. If we read भूमिपाश°, then the meaning is 'ropes in the ground firmly fixed &c'. We then expect the order to be भूमिनिरवात &c. आय...माणैः although already long enough, they (horses) seemed to be longer still as one of their hinder legs was stretched because it was tied with a rope. पाशबन्ध is Marathi पायबन्द. बहुगुणेन सूत्रेण ग्रथितः ग्रीवागण्डकः येषाम् the neck-ornament of which was suspended with a cord of many strings. आमीलिते (closed) लोचने येषाम्. दूर्वा...चालयद्भिः that kept moving their limbs that were itching, the skin of which twitched, that were held between the teeth and then let go, that were spotted with bits of foam darkened by Dūrvā juice. दशनैः आदौ गृहीताः पश्चात् मुक्ताः. फरफरिता पुनः पुनः ईषत्कम्पिता त्वक् येषाम्. When their limbs had itch, the skin twitched and they held the itching skin between their teeth to ease the itching sensation. This caused the foam and the juice of the Dūrvās they were grazing upon to stick to their bodies. 'प्रतीकोऽवयवेऽपि स्यात्' मेदिनी.

C and T take the word as meaning 'mouths'. But we cannot then construe ०मुक्तान् with प्रतीकान्, as mouths cannot be bitten by teeth. सालसं वलितः वालधिः (पुच्छं) यैः that lazily moved their tails. बाला धीयन्ते अस्मिन् इति बालधिः (वालधिः also). एक...घनार्धैः half of whose flanks was drooping (स्रस्त) and relaxed as they rested on one hoof. निद्र...यद्भिः that seemed to ponder when they slept. स्खलित...यमानैः that emitted low rumbling neighing when they stumbled. ताडिता खुरधरणी तस्याः रणितेन मुखरं शिखरं येषां ते ०शिखराः खुराः तैः लिखितं क्ष्मातलं यैः. खुरधरणी is a wooden foot-rest. The object may be to allow the urine to pass through a hole in the foot-rest into a gutter underneath over which the plank is placed. प्रकीर्यमाणाः यवसग्रासाः तेषु रसः (liking) तेन or तस्मात् मत्सरः तेन उद्भूतः क्षोभः येषाम्. When fodder was scattered before other horses, they became enraged and jealous. प्रकुपिताः चण्डाः चण्डालाः (अश्वपालाः) तेषां हुङ्कारैः (threatening words) कातरतराः तरलाः तारकाः (pupils) येषाम्. कुङ्कुम...लक्ष्यमाणैः As their bodies were yellowish red because saffron was rubbed over them, they seemed to have always near them the lustration-fires. Both कुङ्कुम and fire are red. For नीराजन, see above p. 34. उपरिविततं वितानं (canopy) येषाम्. पुरः पूजितं अभिमतदैवतं येषाम्. The अभिमत-दैवत according to the com. is गोविन्द. आरचितां filled. मन्दुरा stable. 'वाजिशाला तु मन्दुरा' इत्यमरः. हस्तवामेन to the left of his hand. अत्युच्च...कुर्वाणम्—this and the following clauses qualify ०गारम्. अत्युच्च०—which, on account of its great height, as though left the sky no room. The elephant stable was very high and crowded the whole sky. कदली plantain tree; banner. परिवृताः पर्यन्ताः यस्य the outskirts of which were surrounded. सर्व...पूर्यमाणम् that was filled on all sides with streams (स्रुति) of ichor full of bees, as though with rivers. आशा...न्द्रियं that filled the nostrils with the odour, as though of blooming Bakula trees, spreading in all directions. The odour of the ichor of the best elephants was said to be like that of Bakula. Separate विकसताम् + आमोदेन. The com. says "तदुक्तम् । 'मालतीमुक्तपुन्नागबकुलोपमसौरभम् । दानं पि(मि?)ष्टाम्बुसदृशं मुञ्चच्छ्रेष्ठं तु शीतलम् ॥.' दूरादव्यक्तम् not quite distinct owing to distance. इभ...गारम् a stable where elephants were housed. 'धिष्ण्यं स्थाने गृहे' इत्यमरः. अत्र...करोति—the elephant—stable looked from a distance like a palace. So बाण asked this question. औपवाह्यः—'राजवाह्यस्त्वौपवाह्यः सन्नाह्यः समरोचितः' क्षीरस्वामी—a king's elephant meant for riding only (and not for fighting). जात्यन्तरितः आत्मा his very soul separated from him by another species. The king's soul was in a human body, while in दर्पशात it was in an elephantine body. दर्पशातः—literally means 'one who destroys the pride' (of other elephants). दर्पं शातयति इति. C and T strangely enough explain it as 'keen (or perhaps attenuated and lacking) in pride'. श्रूयते—I have only *heard*, but never seen. यद्ये...न्द्रमेव If it be so (*i. e.* if दर्पशात is housed here) and if there be no objection (in seeing it), then I shall first of all see the great elephant. अतिपरवान् overcome.

P. 29 l. 26—**P. 31** l. 22. **गत्वा च...पश्यत्.** The principal sentence is गत्वा च दूरादेव...दर्पशातमपश्यत्. गम्भीर...गर्जितैः—by the deep sounds issuing from his throat. कल low, sweet. गम्भीर...हलम्—the idea is :—The big elephant trumpeted in deep grunts (as is usual with these animals); that sound resembled the rumbling of a cloud. So the चातक and the peacock welcomed the sound (thinking that a cloud was near) with vociferous notes. A चातक was supposed not to be able to drink the water flowing on the earth; it had to rest content with a few drops from the cloud falling direct into its mouth. Hence the word वियति with चातककदम्बकैः and भुवि with peacocks (नीलकण्ठ). Compare 'चातका इव तृष्णावन्तो न शक्यन्ते ग्रहीतुमकुलीनाः' हर्ष० 4th उ०. See for peacocks dancing when it thunders, p. 63. क्रियमाणः कलः कोलाहलः यस्य. This and the following words in the accusative singular qualify दर्पशातं below. विकचानि कदम्बानि संवदति (resembling) इति ०संवादी मदः सुरा इव तस्याः सौरभेण भरितं भुवनं येन. काय...कालम् that seemed as though he were the premature season of clouds wearing an embodied form. Both the elephant and clouds are dark. In the season of clouds (rains) one sees चातकs, peacocks dancing and the कदम्ब tree putting forth buds. Therefore the elephant (whose ichor resembled the odour of *Kadamba* buds) is fancied to be the season of clouds incarnate. It was then the middle of ग्रीष्म and not वर्षा. So the word अकाल is put in. अविरल...त्सृजन्तम् leaving (about to leave) the fourth stage of life that had reached its perfection by his skin being marked with spots brown like thick drops of honey as though it were a lake. अभ्यवगाढाम् full developed (with दशाम्); deep (with सरसीम्). अविरलमधुबिन्दुवत् पिङ्गलानि पद्मजालकानि सञ्जातानि अस्याः इति ०जालकिताम् (with दशाम्). *Vide* notes on तारकित p. 42. पद्मजालकम्—marks of reddish spots on the elephant's skin. 'पद्मकं बिन्दुजालकम्' इत्यमरः (पद्मप्रतिकृति

रक्तत्वात्पद्मकम् तारुण्ये हि हस्तिनां देहे रक्तबिन्दवः स्युः। क्षीर०). 'चतुर्थ्यामवगाढायां लेखाबिन्दुभिराचितः' सं०. ०बिन्दुभिः पिङ्गलानि पद्मानि (कमलानि) तैः जालकितामु (with सरसीम्). There is brown honey in lotuses. सरसीम्—'दक्षिणापथे हि महान्ति सरांसि सरस इत्युच्यन्ते' महाभाष्य (Kielhorn Vol I, p. 73.). चतुर्थीदशा means 'the age between 30 and 40'; compare कौटिल्य's अर्थशास्त्र 'That which is seven अरत्नि in height, nine in length, ten in circumference and is 40 years old is the best' (translation p. 207). आमन्द्रः कर्णताल एव दुन्दुभिध्वनिः येषु (*adj.* of शंखैः). अन...गायन्तम् that chanted (the tune suited to) the beginning of his auspicious entrance into the fifth stage with the conch-shell ornaments on his ears that were blended with the low drum-like rumbling of the flapping of his ears. For शङ्ख on elephant's ears, see above text p. 27 l. 18. At an auspicious ceremony such as the first entrance in a new house, there is the music of drums (दुन्दुभि) and conches may be blown. पञ्चमी stands for पञ्चमीदशा. अविरतचलने चित्रा (charming) त्रिपदी एव ललितं (fine) लास्यं (dancing) तस्य लयैः (harmony). त्रिपदी standing on three legs, while one is lifted up. This is a characteristic action with the elephant. 'गानगेययोरन्यूनाधिक्ये श्लिष्टता लयो द्रुतादिः वाद्यादीनामन्योन्यं समत्वमिति यावत्' क्षीरस्वामी. The elephant moved incessantly and he rested his body on three legs. So he seemed to be engaged in dancing and there was a certain rhythmical method in his movements. दोलायमानः दीर्घदेहस्य आभोगः (expanse) यस्य सः ०भोगः तस्य भावः ०भोगता तया. मेदिनी...यमानम्—the idea is:—by his incessantly standing on three legs, he seemed to be lessoning his weight on the earth for fear of (otherwise) breaking it (विदलन). His incessant movements to and fro looked like rubbing the itching body against the quarters. Buffaloes and elephants may rub their bodies against walls. लघयन्तम् *pr. p.* of लघयति denominative verb from लघु. आहवः fight. उदस्तहस्ततया because he threw up his trunk (into space). उदस्त *past p. p.* of अस् to throw with उद्. There are eight guardian elephants of the eight quarters. 'ऐरावतः पुण्डरीको वामनः कुमुदोऽञ्जनः। पुष्पदन्तः सार्वभौमः सुप्रतीकश्च दिग्गजाः॥' इत्यमरः. ह्वे with आ in the sense of 'to challenge to a fight' takes the आत्मनेपद only. 'स्पर्धायामाङः' पा. 1. 3. 31. (कृष्णश्चाणूरमाह्वयते). करपत्रम् saw (Marathi करवत); saw-like trunk (करः पत्रमिव). स्थूलाः निशिताः दन्ताः यस्य. A saw has teeth and cleaves pillars (स्तम्भः). स्थूलौ निशितौ दन्तौ यस्मिन् (with trunk). He moved his trunk armed with sharp tusks and seemed to cleave the world (ब्रह्मस्तम्भः). See above

p. 102 for ब्रह्मस्तम्भ. अमा...मानम् he seemed to desire to go out, as though the world could not contain him. His incessant movements and large body give rise to this conceit. The next clause is सर्वतः...नन्दम्, the chief portion of which is सर्वतः लेशिकैः आधोरणैः च आधीय...नन्दम्—to whom delight was caused by riders (लेशिक) and keepers (आधोरण) who treated him with remedies (उपचारः) appropriate to summer. आधीयमानः ०समयसमुपचितोपचारैः आनन्दः यस्मिन्. 'आधोरणा हस्तिपकाः' इत्यमरः. सरस...वनैरिव by riders who tossed (over the elephants) creepers full of juice and sprouts and who seemed as though they were forests gathered together through long familiarity. In forests also there are dancing creepers full of juice &c. The elephant roamed in forests which as though came there in crowds (उपचित) to alleviate his torment. If we read घनैः, the words चिर...चितैः cannot be well-explained; clouds also cause creepers to dance when they pour water over them. विक्षिप्त...धोरणैः keepers that threw water mixed with juicy moss and bundles (विसरः) of lotus stalks (on them) looked like lakes. In lakes also there are waters, moss and lotus stalks. The chief words in the next clause are अपि च अतिस्थवीयसा ०दण्डेन अर्गलयन्तमिव सकलं ककुभां चक्रवालम्-and who seemed to chain the circle of the quarters by his very stout bolt-like trunk. स्थवीयस् comparative of स्थूल. प्रति...क्षिप्तेन (*adj.* of ०दण्डेन) that was tossed aloft as though he smelt (*lit.* took the wind) the ichor of some rival elephants. प्रतिगजदानपवनस्य आदानेन दूरक्षिप्तः तेन. अनेक...दरेण which was wavy with small lines of wrinkles (वलिः) round it as though with marks (lines) to reckon his victories in many battles. Ignorant persons reckon by drawing lines on the earth or wall &c. The wrinkles on the trunk are fancied to be such lines. Compare 'बहुयोजनगमनगणनसंख्याक्षरावलीभिरिव' &c. (text p. 27 l. 1). कुलशैलाः समुद्राः द्वीपाः काननानि च तैः सह (बहुव्रीहि)—*adj.* of चक्रवालम्. For the कुलपर्वतs, see above p. 76, for the seven seas p. 32 and the seven continents p. 3. एकं and अपरं qualify दन्तकाण्डम्. करा...पल्लवमिव—When a plant is watered it puts forth पल्लवs. The leaves of the कदली held in the trunk seemed to be the पल्लवs of his tusk, the tusk being watered by the juice oozing from the कदली stem. करान्तरे अर्पितेन. उद्गतानि पलाशानि यस्य. मुक्ताः पल्लवाः येन. It is not correct to understand मुक्तपल्लव as 'a shooting twig of pearls.' In that case मुक्तपल्लव cannot be properly dissolved and the उत्प्रेक्षा is not properly worked out. अपर...दन्तकाण्डं—From the other tusk hung down lotus fibres, which resembled रोमाञ्च due to his great zest for fighting. 'विसर्पन्त्या…कान्त्या'-these words are to be connected with वमन्तं, अर्पयन्तं, ०हसन्तं and कल्पयन्तम्. सर…वमन्तम्—His tusks were very white. कुमुदs also are white. When the brilliance of the tusks spread all round, the poet fancies that he vomitted the कुमुद bed that he had eaten when he sported in the lakes. On the use of वान्त in poetry, *vide* p. 50. निज… र्पयन्तम्—the brilliance of tusks spreading in the world is fancied to be his fame (which is white) spreading in all directions. कु…हसन्तम्—he seemed to laugh at lions that were naughty (दुर्ललित) because they had broken down some wretched worms of elephants. हास is white. कल्प…कल्पयन्तम् he seemed to make for himself a silken veil manufactured from the heavenly tree. The brilliance of his tusks spreading round his face looked like a fine white silken veil. हस्त…लक्ष्यमाणेन which (palate) was seen when he gracefully lifted up his trunk. रक्ता…वर्षन्तम् when he showed his red palate, be seemed to vomit the red lotuses he had devoured. His तालु was red like रक्तांशुक and fresh किसलय. A red तालु showed an excellent elephant and so did a brown (पिङ्गल) eye. Compare बृहत्संहिता 'ताम्रोष्ठतालुवदनाः' 67. 6. चूत…विसृजन्तम्—the plain idea is that the ichor flowing from his cheeks (करटः) was as fragrant as चूत, पारिजातक &c. 'काकेभगण्डौ करटौ' इत्यमरः. अहर्निशं… पतीनाम् that seemed to bestow on the elephants all the forests by दानपट्टकs, on which he gracefully placed his trunk, that were rubbed with a half-cut sugarcane reed, and that resounded with a swarm of bees. विभ्रमेण (लीलया) कृता हस्तस्य शुण्डायाः स्थितिः येषु. अर्धखण्डितं पुण्ड्रेक्षुकाण्डं तेन कण्डूयनं तस्मिन् लिखितैः. पुण्ड्र is a kind of very sweet red sugarcane. करिपतीनाम्—the genitive is used in the sense of the dative. दानपट्टकैः is used in two senses; (1) streams of ichor; (2) royal grants declaring a gift. All the clauses have an application to royal grants. विभ्रम…स्थितिभिः on which (royal copperplates or other edicts) the hand (royal signature) is gracefully (or hastily) made. Mark the use of the word हस्त in inscriptions as in 'स्वहस्तो मम &c'. Intro. p. XXIX footnote. लिखितैः suggests that royal orders are written with a pen (लेखनी) of reed (resembling इक्षुकाण्ड). वाचालितैः— royal grants are loudly read by the donees (who resemble bees that seek the दान). Take away the comma after क्रियमाणम्. शिशिरी० qualifies शिरः. अविरल…दधानम्—the idea is:—As the heat was intense, his high head was cooled with a garland made of pieces of ice. His head on which the white pieces of ice were placed seemed to be covered with a पट्टबन्ध (fillet) studded with bright jewels. The jewels resemble stars, as do the pieces of ice. A पट्टबन्ध indicated authority. *Vide* notes p. 116. 'बन्धुरं तून्नतानतम्' इत्यमरः. 'सैव नक्षत्रमाला स्यात्सप्तविंशतिमौक्तिकैः' इत्यमरः. As there were no pearls, but only icy pieces, the author says विभ्रमन० &c. आदौ स्थगितानि (covered, concealed) पश्चात् अपावृतानि (opened, laid bare) दिङ्मुखानि याभ्यां. कर्णौ तालवृन्ते (fans) इव. As he flapped his large ears, he screened from view for sometime the worlds and then again allowed them to be seen. Compare for a similar conceit 'क्षणदृष्टनष्टाष्टदिङ्मुखं' &c. (text p. 27 l. 13). कर्ण...क्ष्मीम् out of devotion to his master, he, as though fanned Royal glory resting on the couch of his tusks. A lady resting on a couch of ivory (in summer) may be fanned by a servant. The elephant is a symbol of लक्ष्मी. Further the elephant helped the king to secure राजलक्ष्मी. The flapping ears would fan his tusks. आ...गतेन (1) that descended in a well-proportioned shape from the backbone (with वालधिना); that was handed down through a long family in succession (with चामरेण). A chowrie was one of the signs of royalty (आधिपत्यचिह्न) and may be handed down from father to son. चलता waving (applies to both चामर and वालधि). वंशः family; back-bone. आयत long. On आयत-वंश०, सं० remarks "आयतवंशः, वक्रवंशः, शरवंशः, बालवंशश्चेति चत्वारो वंशाः। तेषु वालवंश आयत एव शास्त्रकृतामभिप्रेतः। तथा च 'यावत्पूरितपाशश्च वंशश्चापलता-कृतिः। शुभो श्रेयो गजेन्द्राणामायतः कुरुते सुखम् ॥' इति तैरुक्तम्। आयताद्वंशात्तत्क्र-मेण गोपुच्छवदायत इति विग्रहः। समानार्हो हि वालधिः शोकं करोति। यदुक्तम् 'वक्रं स्थूलं च ह्रस्वं च पुच्छं कचविवर्जितम्। समानार्हं हि नागस्य भर्तुः शोककरं स्मृतम् ॥.' शीकर the spray from the elephant's trunk. दिग्विजयपीताः—he had drunk the waters of several rivers when he accompanied his master Harsha on the latter's दिग्विजय. अवधानदानेन निस्पन्दीकृताः (made motionless) सकलावयवाः येषु (*adj.* of वलनानां). अन्य...वलनानाम् of the twistings of his body when he heard the sound of the drum borne by other elephants. क्षण...शोचन्तम्–the idea is:—When he heard the sound of drums on other elephants, he attentively listened for a moment and then again became restless and trumpeted. A person, when insulted, heaves deep sighs. The author fancies that the elephant trumpeted because it wanted to convey that it was insulted by there being other elephants carrying drums and that it bewailed its own lot that it could not fight with those elephants. आरो...मुञ्चन्तम्—the elephant scratched the ground and dropped ichor (मद). The poet fancies that the elephant did these actions through shame at the humiliation of having to bear on his back the riders (आरोहाः). A person who feels ashamed scratches the ground and gives up pride (मद). अवज्ञया (आदौ) गृहीताः (पश्चात्) मुक्ताः कवलाः तैः कुपिताः आरोहाः तेषां आरटनस्य अनुरोधेन in obedience to the shouts of the riders &c. The riders shouted angrily when the elephant took up mouthfuls and then dropped them. मदस्य तन्द्रा (drowsiness) निमीलितः नेत्रत्रिभागः यथा स्यात्तथा. अनादरात् unwillingly. अवजग्धेभ्यः (eaten) तमालपल्लवेभ्यः स्रुतः श्यामलः रसः यस्मिन् (*adj.* of मुखेन). As the juice of तमाल leaves was dark, it resembled मद. मुखेनापि—it is from the temples that ichor flows. दल...र्पेण he seemed as though splitting with pride. It will be noticed that from these words up to सिञ्चन्तमिव सौभाग्येन, there are pairs of words, each of which begins with the same letter. So the reading दलन्तं is better than चलन्तम्. श्व...मदेन who breathed heavily as though through bravery (that finds no outlet), who swelled as though through pride. मूर्च्छन्तम् also means 'fainting.' मदेन through intoxication. त्र्यु...दानेन breaking through youth, flowing with ichor. He was so full of youthful energy that it, not being contained within him, as though split him up. वल्गन्तम् prancing. माद्य...त्साहेन he was as though intoxicated through arrogance and seemed to rise aloft through his energy. ताम्य...सौभाग्येन he gasped on account of his own brilliance, he smeared (everything) with his grace, he sprinkled (the world) with his loveliness. Heat (तेजस्) makes one languid (ताम्यत्). स्निग्धं smooth; affectionate. Smooth nails in elephants were highly thought of. "उक्तं च 'नखाः स्निग्धाः सिताः शस्ताः' इति" सं०. परुष rough; unkind. It will be noticed that the first words in each pair of clauses are contradictory as in स्निग्धं परुषं and गुरुं सच्छिष्यम्. गुरुम् large; teacher. सच्छिष्यं विनये a good disciple in modesty or discipline. मृदुं soft; affectionate. दृढं hard; firm (in friendship). ह्रस्वं...बन्धे short of neck. दरिद्रं slender; poverty-stricken. सत...दाने ceaselessly flowing with ichor; ceaselessly giving gifts. बलभद्र is बलराम, the elder brother of कृष्ण. मदलीलासु in pranks due to being in rut; pranks due to drink. भद्र is an elephant of the best type. *Vide* चाणक्य's अर्थशास्त्र II. chap. 31 for भद्र and मन्द्र elephants and बृहत्सं-

gate of ivory. सदन्तः तोरणः यस्य. 'तोरणोऽस्त्री बहिर्द्वारम्' इत्यमरः. दन्तौ च तोरणं च तैः सह. A गिरिदुर्ग (hill-fort) is stationary. The elephant is like a difficult (दुर्ग) hill or affords protection like a hill-fort, but is moving (सञ्चारि). उच्चौ कुम्भकूटौ अट्टालकौ इव ताभ्यां विकटम् formidable with his tower-like high temple bones (कुम्भकूट) (with दर्पशात); a hill fort is formidable with कूटs and towers. 'अट्टालकः प्राकाराग्रे रणगृहमिति कौटिल्यः' क्षीर०. 'कूटं पूर्द्वारि यद्धस्तिनखस्तस्मिन्' इत्यमरः ('दुर्गद्वारावतरणार्थः क्रमनिम्नो हस्तिनखाभो मृत्कूटः' क्षीर०) *i. e.* it is a sloping earthen mound at the gate of a fort. The elephant was dark and strong like an iron rampart (प्राकारः) and served to protect the earth as a rampart does. कृतानि अनेकबाणैः विवरसहस्राणि यस्मिन्—the elephant was pierced in battle by arrows. कृतानि अनेकबाणविवरसहस्राणि यस्मिन् in the fort-wall, there were loopholes for discharging arrows. The com. says this is called इन्द्रकोश in चाणक्य's work. 'Between the tower and the broad street there shall be constructed an Indrakosha which is made up of covering pieces of wooden planks affording seats for three archers' अर्थशास्त्र (English Translation) p. 58. दर्पशात is called पारिजातपादप for two reasons. He belonged to the king (भूनन्दनः) and had bees humming (over his ichor). नन्दन, the garden of इन्द्र, has पारिजात which is pursued by bees (शिलीमुखः). भूः एव नन्दनं or भुवः नन्दनः. For भूनन्दन (prince), see 4th उच्छ्वास first para. In a music hall, there is dancing. The loud flapping of दर्पशात's ears resembled ताण्डव. आपा...ण्डलानाम् a drinking saloon for the swarms of bees. मधुप also means 'drunkards.' Amorous sports (शृङ्गार) and ornaments are seen in the ladies of the harem. दर्पशात also had ornaments and शृङ्गार (marks with vermilion on the head and trunk). 'शृङ्गारं चूर्णसिन्दूरलवङ्गकुसुमेषु च' विश्वः. In the festival of Cupid (which is now celebrated in फाल्गुन) there is dancing through intoxication of youth (or drink). दर्पशात was full of graceful movements (लीलालास्य) due to being in ichor. अक्षुण्णप्रदोषम्—on a clear (*lit.* untrodden) night, the stars are visible. दर्पशात had the नक्षत्रमाला ornament, for which see text p. 30 l. 23. मदः एव महानदीपूरः तेन प्लवः (flooding). दर्पशात emitted floods of ichor even without the proper season of rain. सप्तच्छद—The tree सप्तच्छद (Marathi सातवीण) blossoms in शरद् and ichor has an odour resembling its flowers. *Vide.* रघु० IV. 23. 'प्रसवैः सप्तपर्णानां मदगन्धिभिराहताः। असूययेव तन्नागाः सप्तधैव प्रसुस्रुवुः ॥' Dew (नीहारः) is found only in the cold season; but dewy spray (from the trunk) was emitted by him at all times. A cloud thunders. The elephant produced thunder-like trumpetings. 'आडम्बरस्तूर्यरवे गजेन्द्राणां च गर्जिते' इत्यमरः.

P. 31 l. 23—**P. 35** l. 17 **आसी...द्राक्षीत्.** नून...णुताम् surely in creating this elephant, hills were used as atoms. Ordinarily the size of atoms from which all things are produced is atomic. But the elephant was so vast that it seemed impossible that atoms could make his huge body. So hills must have been taken as the smallest constituents which went to make up his body. विन्ध्य...करः—this is a hyperbolical description. The idea is:—बाण saw the firm and stout tusks and the formidable trunk. The elephant was massive and strong like the विन्ध्य mountain. The strikingness consists in assigning tusks to a mountain. दन्त suggests 'peak'. दर्पशात was powerful like the primeval Boar. The Boar had no कर (hand); but दर्पशात had a कर (trunk). **Verse 4**. Read 'लिखतां' for लिखिताम्. This verse is full of puns and is applicable to दर्पशात (the best of elephants) and also to the king. The principal portion is विद्विषां कथमपि स्मृतिपथं आयातः नागेन्द्रः मान...नपि न सहते—When this big elephant is somehow remembered by the enemies (of the king हर्ष), he (दर्पशात) does not brook even the hope-elephants in their minds *i. e.* the high hopes (of regaining their kingdoms) crumble to nothing the moment they remember the prowess of दर्पशात. The words मान... गजेन्द्रानपि also mean 'he does not brook the (presence of) दि-ग्गजs residing on the मानस lake'. आशा = दिशा. शून्यीभवत् चेतः येषाम्—whose minds are vacant and who therefore are totally at a loss what to do. आलिखताम् (*adj.* of विद्विषाम्). मि...श्रियम् who vainly paint in their desires their royalty which is totally lost to them. They build high hopes of regaining what they have lost. चिन्ता... धियाम् (1) whose intellect is distracted by thoughts that are simply a source of anxiety; (2) whose minds are overwhelmed with thoughts (चिन्ता) and imaginings as to the means (of regaining their lost kingdoms). वने that were banished in the forests. King Harsha also does not brook the hopes they entertain, the moment he is remembered. The metre is शार्दूलविक्रीडित. तेन = दौवारिकेण. ०जलेन पङ्किलः (dirty, soiled) कपोलपट्टः तस्मिन् पतिताम् (*adj.* of दृष्टिम्). दृष्टिमाकृष्य—बाण took away his eyes with difficulty from the elephant. One who is मत्त may fall in dirt and has half-closed (मुकुलित) eyes, and has to be dragged out of mire by his friends. सङ्कुलानि crowded. क-

क्ष्यान्तराणि courts (object of समतिक्रम्य). भुक्ते आस्थानमण्डपः तस्य पुरस्तात् in front of an audience-pavilion after he had taken his meal. For भुक्तास्थान, see above text p. 27. l. 32. स्थितम्—the principal sentence is स्थितं...चक्रवर्तिनं हर्षमद्राक्षीत् (p. 35. l. 17). The next clause is दूरा...वृतम्. दूरात् (surrounded) at a distance. ऊर्ध्व-स्थितेन standing erect. All the adjectives qualify ०लोकेन ard ०स्तम्भमण्डलेन. प्रांशुना tall; the rays of which spread all round. प्रकृष्टाः or प्रसृताः अंशवः यस्य. व्यायामेन व्यायतं (firm, powerful) वपुः यस्य (with ०लोकेन); व्यायामव्यायतं वपुः यस्य that were as long (व्यायत) as the distance between the outstretched hands (about six feet). शस्त्रिणा armed; on which weapons were tied or that were shaped with instruments (with स्तम्भमण्डलेन). व्यायाम is the same as व्याम (Marathi वांव). 'व्यामो बाह्वोः सकरयोस्ततयोर्तिर्यगन्तरम्' इत्यमरः. मौलेन hereditary (मूलं वेत्ति मूलादागतो मूले भवो वा); placed on a base or pedestal. As the attendants were of ruddy complexion they are compared to golden pillars. आ...लोकम् near whom were sitting his distinguished (विशिष्ट) favourites. हरिचन्दन is a kind of very fragrant sandal. तुषारः ice. दन्त...पादे the feet of which (bedstead) were white being made of ivory; the rays of which are white like ivory. The words ०तले and ०पादे furnish the reason why the bedstead of pearl-stone is fancied to be made of the moon. शय...भुजे who rested the whole weight of his body on his arm that was placed on the end of the bedstead. दिङ्मुख...रममाणम्—the idea is:—The lustre of his body spread all round like a canopy (वितानं), being blended with the rays of jewels. As the Emperor with his vassal kings was bathed in the brilliance, he seemed to be bathing in a lake, the lustre being the water and the rays of jewels lotus fibres. A bath is very agreeable (सुभग) in summer. वितताः मणिमयूखाः यस्मिन् (*adj.* of ०विताने). राजकेन सह. For राजक, see p. 112. तेजसः...र्मितम्—Ordinarily every being is पञ्चमहाभूतात्मक. But he, being all brilliance, seemed to be created from the atoms of तेजस् alone. अनि...गृहीतम् he was seized by all auspicious marks in all limbs as though in order to place him on the throne, though he was unwilling to occupy it. The idea is—all his limbs had the auspicious signs as required by the सामुद्रिकशास्त्र. One who has such signs becomes a king. If a person be unwilling to sit in a place, he has to be made to occupy the place by being seized. The word गृहीत has two senses 'seized, accepted.' C and T think that in this clause there is probably a reference to the facts underlying Hiuen Tsang's story that Harsha at the advice of a Bodhisattva refrained from mounting the '*siṃhāsana.*' We do not think there is any such reference. The author indulges in an उत्प्रेक्षा on seeing the king occupying the throne and his great brilliance. Compare 'लक्षणैरपि रागाविष्टैरिवाधिष्ठितसर्वाङ्गाम्' (कादम्बरीम्) का॰ p. 186 of P. गृहीतं ब्रह्मचर्यं येन who was observing the vow of celibacy. There is विरोध between गृही...चर्यम् and आ...क्ष्म्या. Compare 'द्यूतं च जनवादं च परिवादं तथानृतम् । स्त्रीणां च प्रेक्षणालम्भमुपघातं परस्य च ॥' मनु॰ 2. 179 (ब्रह्मचारी वर्जयेत्). The विरोध can be got over by taking आ...क्ष्म्या as meaning 'who was possessed of royal glory.' गृ॰ may be explained in this way. According to Manu, a householder who was devoted solely to his wife and observed certain rules about cohabitation was as good as a ब्रह्मचारी. 'ऋतुकालाभिगामी स्यात्स्वदारनिरतः सदा । पर्ववर्जं व्रजेच्चैनां तद्व्रतो रतिकाम्यया ॥ निन्द्यास्वष्टासु चान्यासु स्त्रियो रात्रिषु वर्जयन् । ब्रह्मचार्येव भवति यत्र तत्राश्रमे वसन् ॥' मनु॰ III. 45 and 50. The com. refers to a curious tradition "था त्वेवमनुश्रूयते 'यावन्मया न सकला जिता भूमिस्तावन्मे ब्रह्मचर्यम्' इति श्रीहर्षः प्रतिज्ञातवान् । द्वादशभिश्च वर्षैर्जित्वा तां महिषीमब्रवीत् 'प्रतिज्ञा मे निर्व्यूढा' इति । ततो रोषात् 'अहमपि द्वादशवर्षं ब्रह्मचर्यं चरामि' इति सा प्रतिज्ञामकरोत् । इति ब्रह्मचर्येणाज्ञाकालोऽतिवाहितः." We may expllain गृहीत॰ as गृहीता ब्रह्मणः वेदस्य चर्या येन 'who practised the study of the Veda.' In the next clause also there is an apparent विरोध. प्रतिपन्नं (accepted) असिधाराधारणव्रतं येन. A ऋषि has nothing to do with wielding a sword. So he could not be called a consistent (अविसंवादिन्) ऋषि, as he wielded a sword. But there is no inconsistency in his wielding the sword for protecting the good and the distressed and in being a saintly king (राजर्षि). प्रति॰ suggests another sense 'who wields the sword against those that come to him for protection'. प्रतिपन्नेषु असिधाराधारणं व्रतं यस्य. If he does so, how can he be called a राजर्षि (whose first duty is to protect)? Compare मनु I. 89 and 10. 80. प्रति॰ also means 'who observes the vow called असिधाराव्रत.' A ऋषि would observe such a व्रत. It is explained as 'यत्रैकशयनस्थापि प्रमदा नोपभुज्यते । असिधाराव्रतं नाम वदन्ति मुनिपुङ्गवाः ॥.' *Vide* मल्लिनाथ on रघु 13. 67. विषम...धर्मे who firmly clung to धर्म as though through fear of stumbling in his steps placed on the uneven path of kings. विषमः (uneven, difficult to carry out) राजमार्गः (royal road, the duties of kings) तस्मिन् विनिहितं पदं (foot, position) तस्य स्खलनं (stumbling, deviating)

तस्य भिया (भीत्या). One who is afraid of stumbling on a public road supports himself (तुलय) on a stick. भीते...सेव्यमानम् who was attended whole-heartedly by Truth that had obtained his word, as though it (truth) were afraid. The idea is:– all kings had given up truth; हर्ष alone stuck to it whole-heartedly. One who is abandoned by others becomes afraid and goes to another who would promise to protect him. लब्धा वाक् (रक्षणरूपा येन). Truth resorts to speech *i. e.* it is word that must be kept. वारविलासिनी nautch girl. प्रतियातना reflection. In the ten toe-nails of his feet the girls were reflected. The poet fancies that the ten quarters (the ten reflections) were bowing to him. दीर्घै...वेक्षमाणम् with his long glances that reached the ends of the quarters he seemed as though to examine what the regents of the worlds had done or left undone. Bāṇa seems to use the word लोकपाल in the sense of दिक्पाल. The दिक्पालs and लोकपालs are eight, but slightly differ. 'इन्द्रो वह्निः पितृपतिर्नैर्ऋतो वरुणो मरुत् । कुबेर ईशः पतयः पूर्वादीनां दिशां क्रमात् ॥' इत्यमरः. 'सोमाग्न्यर्कानिलेन्द्राणां वित्ताप्पत्योर्यमस्य च । अष्टानां लोकपालानां वपुर्धारयते नृपः ॥' मनु 5. 96. मणि...करेण—मणि...पृष्ठे प्रतिष्ठिताः कराः (किरणाः, हस्ताः) यस्य. The sun's rays were reflected in his footstool (पादपीठ). One who makes a request may fold his hands at the feet of the king. भूषणप्रभया समुत्सारणं (driving away) तेन बद्धं पर्यन्ते मण्डलं (circle, ring) येन. The idea is:—daylight was eclipsed by the brilliance of his ornaments up to a certain distance from the king on all sides; beyond that he was surrounded by daylight as in a circle. So the poet fancies that daylight performed प्रदक्षिणा round him. The reading गलितोष्मणा would mean 'whose pride (or heat) was gone.' शौर्यमेव ऊष्मा तेन. He was so brave that he could not endure that the mountains should remain stiff before him. Heat (ऊष्मा) causes distress. फेना...इन्तम्—his personal grace being compared to the ocean, the white sandalwood paste applied to his body to alleviate heat is compared to the foam of the ocean. The reading भूभृद्भिः would mean 'that support the earth; kings.' The com. connects शौर्योष्मणा with फेनायमानम् 'जलं सन्तापेन सफेनं भवति'. This is not bad. एक...र्जित्येन on account of his greatness in wielding the sole sovereignty of the world. ऊर्जितस्य भावः और्जित्यम्. When the vassal kings fell at his feet, his image was reflected in their crest jewels. He could not endure that the kings should honour anyone else (even though his own reflection). Compare 'यः करधृतधौतासिप्रतिबिम्बितेनात्मनाप्यदूयत समितिषु सहायेन' हर्ष० 4th उ० 2nd para. दर्प...दधानम् who bore royal glory that, under the guise of the breezes of chowries, as though heaved many sighs through the pain of pride. He had snatched the राजलक्ष्मी of other kings. This rankled in her heart and she heaved deep sighs—the breezes set in motion by chowries. दुःखमासते अस्यामिति or दुःखं असिका इव poignant pain or grief. सकल...श्लिष्टम्—At the time of the churning, लक्ष्मी (the wife of विष्णु) rose from the *single ocean;* but he was embraced by लक्ष्मी that came to him bringing the *entire* लावण्य (beauty, salt) of the *four* oceans. This shows his superiority over विष्णु. In the case of विष्णु, लक्ष्मी did not bring all लावण्य (as the sea is still very salt).लवणस्य भावः लावण्यम्. In his case, लक्ष्मी brought all the लावण्य (beauty). आभरण...राज्ञाम् he as though distributed among the vassal kings thousands of rainbows produced from the radiance of his ornaments, as though they were sent by Indra as a present to him (हर्ष). The rays of his jewels presented rainbow colours and spread over his vassals. The poet insinuates that even Indra sent presents (इन्द्रधनुः) to हर्ष. प्राभृतम् present. 'प्रकर्षेण आराधनार्थं आभ्रियते ढौक्यते स प्राभृतम् ' क्षीर०. For वि...राज्ञाम् compare above 'विलभमानमिव सर्वकाननानि करिपतीनाम्' text p. 30 ll. 21–22. मधु honey, wine. सम्भा...वर्षन्तम्—There is विरोध in his showering मधु when he had given it up. But he had given up (drinking) wine and he was very sweet in conversation. परित्यक्तमपि (as an *adj.* of the king) would mean 'though he was so poor, (still he showered मधु)'. The words अमृतं, हृदयं and श्रियम् in the three following clauses are similarly श्लिष्ट. काव्य...मन्तम्—One vomits what one has eaten or drunk. In discussion about poetry he poured out sweet words that were all his own (which he had not copied from anyone else). He had not drunk अमृत (only the gods did so) and yet he poured it out. विश्रम्भ०—In confidential conversations, he exhibited his हृदय though he did not draw it out (of his body). What is meant is he showed his real thoughts, though the persons speaking with him did not draw him out. प्रसादेषु...पयन्तम्—लक्ष्मी is निश्चल in him (and not चञ्चल as in other kings) and yet in showing favours he distributed it in various places (that is made लक्ष्मी leave himself). What is meant is that he distributed श्री (wealth) among worthy objects (स्थाने). वीरगोष्ठीषु in meetings of heroes. When he heard about the heroic deeds of his soldiers that had secured a victory his cheek became thrilled. The poet fancies that the thrill (रोमाञ्च) was due to the message of love whispered in his ear by रणश्री (victory). Love causes रोमाञ्च, which is one of the eight सात्त्विकभावs. *Vide* p. 79. उपांशु *adv.* secretly. अति...पातयन्तम् in talking about his past fights with warriors, he cast his glance at his favourite sword, as though it (दृष्टि) were a shower of स्नेह (affection, oil). He lovingly looked at his sword as his trusty companion in battles. When fighting is over (अतिक्रान्त) oil is applied to swords in order that they may not get rusty. परिहास...यन्तम्—when he smiled at jests, the rays of his teeth spread round the kings. The pure rays of teeth are fancied to be his good will (pure meaning) towards them. One who is afraid of great heat (प्रताप) will gain confidence, if a clear reservoir (of water) be shown to him. सकल...तिष्ठन्तम्—there is विरोध in saying that he was सकल० and yet stood in न्याय alone. न्याये तिष्ठन्तम् means (in a secondary sense) 'he held fast to the path of right'. The words अगोचरे, अभूमौ, अविषये, अमार्गे, अतिदूरे, अदिशि all mean the same thing and all the clauses are to be explained similarly, connecting स्थितम् with each. अगोचरे गुणानाम् (स्थितम्) who stood beyond the reach of गुणs. The idea is:—he was perfect in virtues; he was wanting in none and so there was no scope for any गुण to come to him and make him perfect. अवि...नाम् boons could not make him more prosperous than he already was. अदि...धर्मस्य he was beyond all comparison and there was nothing which धर्म could accomplish for him. अदृष्ट...स्थितम् he had an unprecedented vastness of glory (or wealth). All the words from अरुण to कृष्णकेशेन have two meanings, one referring to his body and the other to some देवता. अरुणाः (red) पादपल्लवाः यस्य. All the instrumentals qualify वपुषा. अरुणः (the charioteer of the sun) पादपल्लवे यस्य. सुगतौ (of graceful gait) मन्थरौ (slow) ऊरू (thighs) यस्य; सुगतः (बुद्धः) मन्थरयोः ऊर्वोः यस्य. वज्रायुधवत् (like the weapon thunderbolt) निष्ठुरं (hard) प्रकोष्ठस्य (forearm) पृष्ठं यस्य; वज्रायुधः इन्द्रः (वज्रं आयुधं यस्य) निष्ठुरे प्रकोष्ठपृष्ठे यस्य. वृषस्य इव स्कन्धः यस्य whose shoulder was stout like that of a bull; वृषः (धर्मः) स्कन्धे यस्य. 'वृषो हि भगवान्धर्मः' मनु० VIII. 16. भास्वान् (bright) बिम्बवत् अधरः (lip resembling the ripe *bimba* fruit) यस्य. भास्वान् (रविः) तस्य बिम्बं अधरे यस्य. प्रसन्नं (mild, gracious) अवलोकितं (glance) यस्य; प्रसन्नः अवलोकितः (अवलोकितेश्वरः) यस्य. अवलोकितेश्वर is a बोधिसत्त्व specially worshipped in northern Buddhism. Compare 'परमसौगतमप्यवलोकितेश्वरम्' हर्ष० 8th उ० 4th para. There is another possible explanation. प्रसन्ना अवलोकिते यस्य. This explanation keeps the symmetry of the passage. The first word in each clause is a देवता. That will be departed from if we take अवलोकित as the देवता. प्रसन्ना means 'wine', which is generally personified as वारुणी देवता. 'बभूव वारुणी देवी मदाघूर्णितलोचना ।' विष्णुपु० I. 9, 92. 'गन्धोत्तमा प्रसन्नेरा' इत्यमरः. The only objection is that वारुणी is not a देवता to which any honour would be paid by बाण and who would hardly be enumerated along with धर्म, कृष्ण &c. कृष्णाः केशाः यस्य; कृष्णः केशेषु यस्य. **P. 33.** मांसलाभिः (thick) मयूखमालाभिः मलिनितं (darkened) महीतलं येन (*adj.* of ०पीठे). माणिक्यमालया मण्डिता मेखला (girdle, centre) यस्य. महानील was a kind of blue gem. कलि...चरणम्—to plant one's left foot on another's head is symbolical of utterly humiliating him. कलि, being an age of sin, is dark. The poet fancies that the blue footstool on which the king's foot rested was the head of कलि, the idea being that Harsha's reign ousted the evil age of sin. आक्रान्त...क्षम्—who looked like the child Krishna (पुण्डरीकाक्ष) that trod on the line of the hoods of कालिय. The foot-stool of blue gems looked like the dark hoods of कालिय. हर्ष was lotus-eyed (पुण्डरीकाक्ष). The serpent कालिय was in the waters of the Jumna and rendered it poisonous. No tree except a कदम्ब grew on its banks. कृष्ण threw himself from the कदम्ब into the river and trampled upon the hoods of the serpent. The serpent and its wives begged कृष्ण to be merciful. कृष्ण said 'नात्र स्थेयं त्वया सर्प कदाचिद्यमुनाजले । सभृत्यपरिवारस्त्वं समुद्रसलिलं व्रज ॥ मत्पदानि च ते सर्प दृष्ट्वा मूर्धनि सागरे । गरुडः पन्नगरिपुस्त्वयि न प्रहरिष्यति ॥' विष्णुपु० V. 7. 75-76. क्षौमवत् पाण्डुरेण pale like fine linen (with प्रतानेन); क्षौमेण पाण्डुरः तेन pale-white with fine linen (with ०बन्धेन). ०प्रतानेन...यन्तम्—The bright rays of the toe-nails spread over the earth; the poet fancies that they were the पट्टबन्ध, which he conferred on the earth and thus raised her to high rank. The earth is often spoken of as the wife of a king. A crowned queen wears a पट्टबन्ध (tiara) of fine silk or linen. *Vide* notes on पट्टबन्ध p. 116. All the words from ०लोहितौ to ०चिह्नौ qualify चरणौ. अप्र...लोहितौ–his feet were naturally red. The poet fancies that they became red because the लोकपालs did not bow to them. For लोकपाल see above p. 140. सकल...धारयन्तौ—the idea is:—when the vassal chiefs bowed their heads at his feet, the yellowish (अतिपीत) brilliance of his feet resembling the पद्मराग (rubies) spread over them; the rosy light of his feet resembled the rosy hues of evening, when the disc of the luminary (the sun) sets. His feet also deprived all powerful persons (तेजस्विन्) of their might. His feet as though drank (पीत) the light of rubies अशेष...स्रवन्तौ—the hue of his feet was like that of the honey in the flowers of the chaplets on the heads of kings (which heads were placed on his feet). समस्त...रहितौ—his feet were never left by bees because they were attracted by the fragrance of the chaplets (उत्तंस) of the chieftains who bowed their heads. The dark bees looked like the heads of his enemies covered with hair (their crowns being wrested from them). पुंस्युत्तंसावतंसौ द्वौ कर्णपूरेऽपि शेखरे' इत्यमरः. संवाहनं shampooing. श्रियो...कल्पयन्तौ—his red feet resembled red lotuses and were charming (*i. e.* लक्ष्मी waited on them to shampoo them). लक्ष्मी is represented as dwelling in a red lotus. Mark the name पद्मालया given to लक्ष्मी. Compare 'अधोमुखेन चक्षुषा शिक्षयन्तमिव लक्ष्मीलाभोत्तानितमुखानि पङ्कजवनानि विनयम्' हर्ष० 4th उ०. जलजशङ्खमीनमकराः तैः सनाथं तलं ययोः तयोः भावः ०तलता तया. जलजं कमलम्. The soles of his feet were marked with lines that resembled a lotus, conch &c. These are looked upon as very auspicious signs and as indicative of greatness. कथित... चिह्नौ इव that had marks announcing his sovereignty of the four oceans. There were four marks जलज, शङ्ख, मीन and मकर and these four indicated that he would rule over the four oceans (*i. e.* the whole world). ०मुसलाभ्याम् and the following instrumentals are to be connected with ऊरुदण्डाभ्याम्. ०मुसलाभ्याम् his thighs were like huge (pestle-like) tusks of दिग्गज. विकट... बन्धुराभ्याम् that were uneven (or charming) on account of the obstruction caused by the block of flesh over the knees. For मकरमुख see notes p. 52. The evenness of his thigh was broken by the protuberant (fleshy) part above the knee. उद्वेलः (going beyond the usual water line) लावण्यपयोनिधिः. फेनेन आहिता शोभा ययोः. His thighs that were charming looked more beautiful by being rubbed over with the polishing powder of white cuttle-fish bone (फेनः). The ocean also looks charming with foam. चन्दन...मूलाभ्याम्—at the foot of sandal trees, serpents (भोगिन्) dwell, in whose hoods jewels were supposed to exist. The roots of his thighs were coloured by the head jewels of kings (भोगिन्) that bowed ot his feet. ०रश्मिभिः रज्यमानं मूलं ययोः. 'भोगी भुजङ्गमेऽपि स्यादाममात्रे नृपे पुमान्' मेदिनी. हृदये आरोपितः भूभारः तस्य धारणाय माणिक्यस्तम्भौ. His fair thighs were like ruby pillars. Pillars support weight. His thighs supported his broad chest (हृदय) on which rested the earth. His mind cared for the government of his kingdom. Compare for a similar conceit 'विशालवक्षःस्थलोपलवेदिकोत्तम्भनशिलास्तम्भाभ्यां...ऊरुदण्डाभ्याम्' (text p. 10 ll. 7-8). The words from अमृत...पाण्डुना to ०शोभिना qualify both अधरवाससा (lower garment) and ०निर्मोकेण (slough of the serpent वासुकि). For mountain मन्दर as the churning handle and the serpent वासुकि as the rope (नेत्रम्), see notes p. 52. The king looked like मन्दर and his lower garment like slough. ०पिण्डवत् पाण्डुना (०वाससा); ०पिण्डेन पाण्डुना (with ०निर्मोकेण). As अमृत was churned out of the ocean, its foam might have stuck to मन्दर. मेखला girdle; the central part of a mountain. The garment was covered with the jewels of the girdle she wore. The slough had the rays of the jewels on the centre of मन्दर. नितम्बः hips; slopes. व्यासङ्गिन् in contact with, clinging. पयः water, milk. It was the क्षीरसागर that was churned. नेत्र...शोभिना charming by the texture of the silken (नेत्रं) threads; charming on account of being placed on the rope. 'स्याज्जटांशुकयोर्नेत्रम्' इत्यमरः, 'नेत्रं मन्थगुणे वस्त्रभेदे मूले द्रुमस्य च' मेदिनी. अघनेन...मानम्—the king looked like the expanse (आभोगः) of the world. He had a second garment (upper one). The world also has अम्बर (the sky). अघनेन not thick (*i. e.* fine); without clouds. स...गणेन spotted with stars of various colours; full of stars (sky). उपरिकृतेन that he wore on the upper part of his body; that is overhead. इभ...राजमानम्—his broad (उरु) chest (उरःकवाटं panel-like chest) is compared to स्फटिकतट and he himself is compared to कैलास. इभ...मसृणेन (applies both to ०कवाटेन and ०तटेन in the same sense) glossy though hardened by being struck with the tusks of elephants. The king was struck in battles and elephants are found in the कैलास range. अपर्याप्तः अम्बरप्रथिमा यस्य which was not contained within the limits of his dress (coat); which was not contained within the limits of the sky. वाहिनी army; river. संक्षोभः shock; agitation. कैलास is white and very high and so is chosen for comparison. श्री...पातितेन (हारदण्डेन)—his long neklace looked like a dividing line for separating the respective realms of glory and learning. The proper sphere of सरस्वती is the mouth and of राज्यश्री the chest (on which it is represented as resting). So the necklace at the neck serves to separate these two. शेषेणेव—the necklace resembled in colour the शेष serpent. तस्य (हर्षस्य) भुजस्तम्भे विन्यस्तः समस्तः भूभारः तेन लब्धं विश्रान्तिसुखं तेन प्रसुप्तेन. शेष is supposed to support the earth. Compare 'त्रिभुवनभारधारणसमर्थ शेषफणामण्डलोपकरणैरिव कल्पितम्' हर्ष० 4th उ० and notes thereon. The poet fancies that the necklace lying on his chest is the serpent शेष gone to sleep because it has no longer to support the earth. परिवेष्टिता कन्धरा यस्य. जीविता...स्थलम्—His chest was covered with the pure rays of the pearls of the necklace. They looked like a bark garment (चीरं) which is worn when a person carries out the vow (दीक्षा) of making a gift of all he possessed as long as he lived. In this one may see a reference to the practice of Harsha, as narrated by Hiouen Tsang, of giving everything in charity once every five years. *Vide* Intro. XL. In the विश्वजित् sacrifice, everything was given away. **'स विश्वजितमाजह्रे यज्ञं सर्वस्वदक्षिणम्।'** रघु० IV. 86. अज...महीधरम्—In this clause, the principal part is अरुणै:...धरम्—with the reddish rays of the jewels of the armlets (he wore on the upper arms) he seemed to be a mountain of rubies having as though outstretched canopy-like wings of jewels. Formerly Mountains had wings; *vide* p. 84. प्रसारितं मणिमयं पक्षवितानं यस्मिन्. In अज...भैवद्भिः there are three उत्प्रेक्षाs suggested by the spreading rays of the jewels on the armlets. अज...रोहद्भिः as if they (rays) were other arms freshly growing with the desire of vanquishing Vishṇu. Vishṇu has four arms; so the king in order to rival him had as if growing on his arms others in the form of the rays. **'अजा विष्णुहरच्छागाः'** इत्यमरः. बाहुरेव उपधानं (pillow) तस्मिन् शेते इति ०शायिनी. बाहू...गलद्भिः-लक्ष्मी is poetically represented as resting on the arm of a king. Women used to place a lotus as an ornament on the ear. The rays of the jewels resembled the honey in a lotus (which is yellowish red). भुज...भैवद्भिः—the pencils of rays looked like long avenues that served as the outlets for the प्रताप (prowess; bright light) of his arms. भुजात् जन्म यस्य. In the next clause the principal part is अति...हरन्तम्—with his very long arms he simultaneously deprived the regions and their guardians of their आयति (length; might or greatness). 'स्यात्प्रभावेऽपि चायतिः' इत्यमरः. Long arms were looked upon as a sign of greatness. For दिक्पाल, see above p. 140. सकल...र्गलेन which (arms) were the bolts to all the paths of लोकालोक. A bolt blockades the path leading to a destination beyond the door. लोकालोक is a mythical mountain in पुष्करद्वीप, the last of the seven द्वीपs. On the other side of the mountain there was complete darkness and on this side, the sun and light. See विष्णु पु० II. 4. 'लोकालोकस्ततः शैलो योजनायुतविस्तृतः। ततस्तमः समावृत्य तं शैलं सर्वतः स्थितम्। तमश्चाण्डकटाहेन समन्तात् परिवेष्टितम्॥' 95-96. Note 'लोकालोकजूंषि...पूषा पुनरपि

सञ्जहार जालकानि रोचिषाम्' हर्ष० 8th उ० last para. His arms protected the world up to लोकालोक. सकल...गेलेम also means 'that were the bolts to the vision of all people *i. e.* that arrested the sight of all people by their prowess'. चतु...कारेण that were the stone wall to the ditch (खातं) of the circle of the four oceans. He ruled over (*i. e.* protected the earth girt by) the four oceans. Ordinarily it is the ditch that surrounds the wall. But his wall-like arms protected (surrounded) the ditch-like oceans. सर्व...पञ्जरेण—He had vanquished all great kings by the adamantine power of his arms. A राजहंस (swan) may be confined in a cage (पञ्जरं). भुवन...तोरणेन—The लक्ष्मी (*i. e.* the dominion) of the worlds came to him (*lit.* entered him) by the power of his arms. A person makes an entrance under an auspicious तोरण (arch). His arms were decked with jewels and so are said to be मणितोरण. सोदर्य...दिङ्मुखानि—the idea is:—his red lip cast its red lustre in all directions. The poet fancies that the red lip was कौस्तुभमणि that had become a part of his mouth with the desire of kissing लक्ष्मी, its sister, (that dwelt with the king). Both लक्ष्मी and कौस्तुभ were born of the ocean, when the fourteen jewels were churned out and so are here said to be सोदर्य. दिङ्मुखानि is the object of सिञ्चन्तम्, which qualifies हर्षम् below. The redness (राग) of the lips spreading all round is fancied to be the exudation of the पल्लवs (that are red) of पारिजात. अन्तरान्तरा at intervals. प्रकीर्यमाणः विमलानां दशनशिखानां प्रतानः येषु (*adj.* of स्मितैः). शिखा ray of light. अन्तरा...दर्शयन्तम्—the idea is:—when he smiled at the jests of his friends, bright rays from his white teeth shot forth. The poet fancies that the king displayed the light of intelligence to लक्ष्मी that is by nature dull. The two clauses ending with प्रेषयन्तम् and विसर्जयन्तम् are to be connected with सुहृ...स्मितैः. मुखेन जनितः इन्दुसन्देहः तेन आगतानि. His face was like the moon. कुमुदs are white like स्मित and open at night. The poet fancies that कुमुद lotus plants in the form of smiles had come mistaking his face to be the moon. He sent them away in the form of the spreading rays of his teeth. स्फटिकवत् धवलाः दशनाः तेषां पङ्क्तिः तया कृता कुमुदवनशङ्का तया प्रविष्टाम्. His smile was like autumnal moonlight, which rests on कुमुदs blooming at night. मदिरा...जातानां गन्धः गर्भे यस्य. भरिताः सकलाः ककुभः दिशः येन. His mouth (that had partaken of ताम्बूल) emitted a fragrance like that of wine, अमृत and पारिजात. मदिरा, अमृत and पारिजात were among the jewels churned out of the ocean, when their combined fragrance must have spread over the world. मदिरा...गर्भेण may also mean '(his mouth) that had the fragrance of ambrosial wine and पारिजात (a fragrant powder).' For पारिजात in this sense, see text p. 9. l. 27 'अतिसुरभि...पारिजातकपरिमलमुचा...मुखेन... वसन्तमिव वमन्तम्.' विकच...वंशेन—the fragrance of his breath was as though continuously inhaled by his high overhanging nose which was the pericarp cup of his lotus-like face. चक्षुषः... कुर्वाणम्—the brilliance of the white of his eye spread all round. It seemed as though the world was flooded by the Milky Ocean rising high (उद्वेल) at the rise of the moon of his unsurpassed face. अपूर्वः वदनमेव चन्द्रः तस्य उदयेन उद्वेलः क्षीरोदः तेन प्लावितानि. विग्रहिणी = शरीरिणी. The female chowrie-bearer was reflected in his bright cheek. The poet fancies that in the form of reflection he bore the embodied सरस्वती in his mouth. सरस्वती is described as मुखनिवासिनी or रसनाग्रनर्तकी. ०शोचिषा = कान्त्या. लोहितायितः ललाटतटः यस्य. लोहितायित *past p. p.* of लोहितायति (or-ते) denominative verb from लोहित, according to 'लोहितादि-डाज्भ्यः क्यष्' पा. 3. 1. 13 and 'वा क्यषः' पा. 1. 3. 90. सरस्वतीर्ष्याकुपिता लक्ष्मीः तस्याः प्रसादने लग्नेन. The idea is:—The red rays of his crest jewel rendered his forehead red. The poet fancies that the redness of the forehead was due to the अलक्तक dye of the feet of लक्ष्मी sticking to his forehead when he bowed at her feet to appease her. लक्ष्मी was angry because he showed preference to सरस्वती. Sanskrit poets delight in dwelling upon the feud between लक्ष्मी and सरस्वती. आ...यन्तम् the principal idea is 'he was listening to the sweet (कल) song of bees that served as an ornament (अवतंसः) to his ear.' The author indulges in a metaphor derived from playing on a lute. आपाट...वादयताम् (of bees) that played on the small lute made up by the curved ends (कोटिः) of the jewel in his ear-ring and which (lute) was surrounded (वलयिनी) by a web of strings (तन्त्री) in the form of slightly red rays (of the jewels). The reddish rays resemble the copper strings of a वीणा. अन...चरणानाम् the bees constantly moved their feet (*i. e.* they hovered round the कुण्डलमणि). One playing on a lute has constantly to move his fingers. उप...मिव—as if they worshipped him by playing on a lute. It is from उपवीणयति a denominative verb. स्वर...शारदं (may be construed both with the king and with क्वणित) who was proficient in the understanding of the analysis of notes (with हर्ष); that (क्वणित) was emineut by its judicious evolution

with knit brows through mutual jealousy. The dark pupils of their eyes resembled the इन्दीवर on the ears and so grew jealous of them and shot glances at them. अनिमेषं दर्शनं तस्य सुखरसः तस्य राशिम् (हर्षम्). मन्थरितं (made motionless) पक्ष्म यस्य. अनिमेष... वहन्तीभिः-the idea is:—they looked with a steadfast eye at him, whereby they derived immense pleasure. He was also reflected in their bright cheeks. The poet fancies that his reflection on the cheeks was due to his being drunk by them with their eyes. A रसराशि (mass of water) may be reflected in a bright-surface like that of a jewel. If we read ०राशिमन्थरित०, that yields a good sense. ०सुखराशिना मन्थरितं पक्ष्म यस्य. We need not in this case take ०राशि as referring to हर्ष. अभि...स्मितैः with their causeless (*i. e.* spontaneous, natural) smiles in their playful longings. Smiles are bright like moonlight. The moon is a friend (an excitant) of Love. *Vide* p. 81. साहायकं (from सहायः) assistance. So far the author described the various charms of the dancing girls and the various tricks they employed to captivate the king's mind. But they failed in their object. अङ्गभङ्गवलने अन्योन्यघटिताः उत्तानाः करवेणिकाः ताभिः—they bent their limbs in various modes (while dancing); in doing so they intertwined the fingers of their hands and opened them towards the king. Their fingers cracked. When we want to crack our finger-joints, we intertwine our fingers and push the palms out. The intertwined hands look like वेणिका (braid). स्फुटनेन मुखराणि अङ्गुलीकाण्डानि तेषु कुण्डलीक्रियमाणः नखदीधितिनिवहः तस्य निभेन (under the guise). अकिञ्चित्कर of no use. The idea is:—When their fingers cracked the rays of the bright nails formed a curve over them. That curve looked like a bent bow. The poet says that it was not their fingers that they cracked, but that it was the bow of Cupid that was snapped by them in anger, as it was of no avail against हर्ष. वार...सर्वतः—If his सौभाग्य was eclipsed by them, they must have been very handsome indeed. स्पर्शेन स्विन्नं (perspiring) वेपमानं करकिसलयं तस्मात् गलितं चरणारविन्दं यस्याः. चरणग्राहिणी the woman that shampooed his feet. The woman on touching his feet became thrilled with emotion and perspired and his feet slipped from her hands. स्वेद and वेपथु are among the eight सात्त्विकभावs. Vide p. 79. कोणेन with the bow (of a lute) or fiddle-stick. 'कोणो वीणादिवादनम्' इत्यमरः. विहस्य he laughed because he understood why she let slip his foot fpom her hand and struck her with the कोण by way of a mild chastisement. लीलया अलसं (slowly) यथा स्यात्तथा. अनवरतं करे कलितः (held) कोणः येन सः ०कोणः तस्य भावः ०कोणता तया. प्रियां—both the lute and श्री were dear to him. शिक्षयन्तम् teaching. कोण also means 'a point of the compass' *i. e.* a region. The meaning (with श्री) is 'who held all the regions and thus taught the राजश्री of the whole world (to attend on him).' निःस्नेह...गृह्यमाणम्—the idea in this clause is that though हर्ष was good and virtuous, yet various persons and things found fault with him, as he could not make them his own. Though one he looked different to different eyes. Understand गृह्यमाणम् after each sub-clause. निःस्नेह...धनैः Riches took him to be wanting in affection *i. e.* he had no regard for lucre. अना...दोषैः—sins found him inaccessible. निग्रहे रुचिः (liking) यस्य who was bent upon curbing (the senses). निग्रहः also means 'punishment or imprisonment'. दुरु...कलिना—the age of sin and discord found him difficult to approach. नीरस...व्यसनैः vices found him to be नीरस (dry, passionless) *i. e.* he had no vice in him. भीरु...शसा *i. e.* he was afraid of infamy. दुर्ग्राहा चित्तवृत्तिः यस्य—whose mind was difficult to seize or understand. चित्तभुवा = मदनेन. Cupid could not sway his mind. स्त्रीपर...सरस्वत्या—To be स्त्रीपर (*i. e.* स्त्रीलम्पट) is ordinarily a blemish. सरस्वती found that he was solely devoted to woman, *viz.* herself *i. e.* he was a single-minded votary of learning. C and T suggest that स्त्री refers to लक्ष्मी but that is not good. षण्ढः impotent. काष्ठा...यतिभिः the ascetics found him to be a काष्ठामुनि. We see that all the words in this clause convey some apparent defect, which, on being properly understood, turns out to be a merit. So काष्ठामुनि should be taken to mean 'an ascetic only for a moment'. काष्ठा is $\frac{1}{30}$ th of a कला. 'अष्टादशनिमेषास्तु काष्ठा त्रिंशत्तु ताः कलाः' इत्यमरः. काष्ठा also means दिशा. So काष्ठामुनि would mean the same thing as राजर्षि. The com. assigns another meaning 'काष्ठा परा धारा (highest limit) तत्प्रधानो मुनिः काष्ठामुनिरतिशयवांस्तपस्वी'. धूर्तः clever, gambler. He does not fall a victim to the wiles of वेश्याs. नेयः easily led (*i. e.* misled); doing as his friends desire. कर्मकरः a mere servant; who performs the proper rites. Read शत्रुयोधैः. सु...योधैः the warriors opposed to him found that he was सुसहाय. शोभनाः सहायाः यस्य who has good allies or councillors. This is good; but the apparent defect that is suggested is 'he has no intrinsic worth; he has only good allies'. शन्त...पतिम्—he was more truly a महावाहिनीपति than शन्तनु. महावाहिनी great army; the great river *i. e.* the Ganges. In this and the following clauses, the poet establishes by श्लिष्ट words that Harsha deserved certain epithets far better than many heroes of old to whom they were applied. शन्तनु married the Ganges. Their son was भीष्म. Vide महाभारत आदिपर्व chap. 98–99. गङ्गा married for the sake of the eight Vasus who were cursed by वसिष्ठ. She plunged in water each son as he was born. When the 8th was born, she spared him at the pressing request of शन्तनु and left him. The ablative शन्तनोः is used in accordance with 'पञ्चमी विभक्ते' पा. 2. 3. 42 (विभागो विभक्तम् । निर्धार्यमाणस्य यत्र भेद एव तत्र पञ्चमी स्यात् । माथुराः पाटलिपुत्रकेभ्य आढ्यतराः । सि. कौ.). जितकाशिनम्—has several senses. भीष्म vanquished काशिराज and married his daughters अम्बिका and अम्बालिका to विचित्रवीर्य, son of शन्तनु and सत्यवती. See आदिपर्व chap 102. जितः काशी (काशिराजः) येन. जितकाशी also means 'जितेन्द्रिय.' शन्तनु fell in love with सत्यवती, the daughter of a fisherman. Out of fear of Bhīshma, he would not allow शन्तनु to marry her. भीष्म promised to resign the kingdom in favour of the son of सत्यवती. Then the fisherman said that he feared that भीष्म's sons would contest the claims of सत्यवती's son. Thereupon भीष्म promised to remain a celibate all his life and carried out the promise. See महाभारत आदिपर्व chap 103. जितकाशी also means 'proud of victories' (जितेन जयेन काशते शोभते इति जययुक्तः). द्रोण was the teacher of the कौरव and पाण्डव princes in धनुर्वेद. See p. 9 for the story of his birth. चापे लालसम् fond of the bow. We may also explain चापले अलसम् (with the king) 'who was averse to follies'. We may separate as च अपलालसम् (अपगता लालसा यस्मात्) 'who was free from desires'. गुरुपुत्र is a term applied to अश्वत्थामा, the son of द्रोण, who was the गुरु of the कौरवs and पाण्डवs. अमोघाः (unerring, reaching the mark) मार्गणाः बाणाः यस्य. अमोघं मार्गणं (याचनं) यस्मिन् requests made to whom were never fruitless. The point of the allusion in the case of अश्वत्थामा is this:–When भीमसेन ran after अश्वत्थामा to kill the latter for his night attack, he discharged a terrible missile called ब्रह्मशिरः for the destruction of all the पाण्डवs. अर्जुन discharged an equally terrible अस्त्र, but only for the purpose of nullifying the effect of अश्वत्थामा's missile and not for killing अश्वत्थामा. Later on अर्जुन withdrew his अस्त्र, but अश्वत्थामा could not do so. The अस्त्र, being अमोघ, deprived अश्वत्थामा of his jewel on the head and killed the गर्भ of उत्तरा by way of a compromise at the desire of Vyāsa. *Vide* सौप्तिकपर्व chap. 13-15. 'गर्भेषु पाण्डवेयानाममोघं चैतदुत्तमम् । न च शक्तोऽसि भगवन्संहर्तुं पुनरुद्यतम् ॥'

chap. 15. 32. कर्ण was the son of कुन्ती, born mysteriously from repeating a Mantra sacred to the Sun. See आदिपर्व chap. 111. So he is represented as the son of the Sun who took special interest in him. मित्रप्रियम् dear to his friends (with the king). कर्ण also was dear to his friend दुर्योधन. बह्वी क्षमा (forbearance, patience) यस्य (with युधिष्ठिर). बहुक्षमम् who ruled over plenty of land (with हर्ष). क्षमा earth. युधिष्ठिर was very patient even under the gravest of provocations (*viz.* द्रौपदीवस्त्रहरण). अनेकनागायुतानां बलं यस्य who had the strength of several thousands of Nāgas (with भीम); who had an army consisting of several thousands of elephants (with हर्ष). अयुतम् ten thousand. भीम was poisoned by दुर्योधन and thrown into water. He was taken to नागलोक, where through the favour of वासुकि he became endowed with the strength of thousands of नागs. *Vide* आदिपर्व chap. 128–129. 'यत्ते पीतो महाबाहो रसोऽयं वीर्यसम्भृतः । तस्मान्नागायुतबलो रणेऽधृष्यो भविष्यसि ॥' chap. 129. 22. धनञ्जय is अर्जुन, the greatest warrior in the great Bhārata war. महाभारत-रण-योग्यम् fit to figure in the great war of the महाभारत. महा-भार-तरण-योग्यम् worthy of wielding (*lit.* crossing) great responsibility (of governing the world). कारण...युगस्य—कृतयुग is an age of complete virtue and righteousness. Under Harsha also these reigned supreme. विबुधसर्गस्य (1) of the creation of gods (विबुधः); of the creation of wise men. He encouraged learned men. उत्पत्ति... दर्पस्य he was the first among the proud or confident. एकागारम् the only house. प्रातिवेशिकः a next door neighbour *i. e.* a very intimate friend; also 'closely resembling.' पुरुषोत्तमस्य of the best of men; of विष्णु. हर्ष befriended good men and resembled विष्णु. खनिपर्वत—a mountain where mines are opened (for jewels &c). सर्व...त्याः the music hall where all lores meet for सरस्वती. सरस्वती was delighted with him as one is delighted in a सङ्गीतगृह. He was the meeting place of all विद्याs. लक्ष्मीसमुत्थान (1) the rising of लक्ष्मी (out of the ocean); increase of royal glory. As there was already one लक्ष्मीसमुत्थान at the time of churning, the author uses the word द्वितीया°. बल...ध्यस्य it was in him that cleverness exhibited its utmost strength. एक... तीनाम् in him all rules of good conduct were to be found in one place. सर्व...कान्तेः Beauty announced in his person her all-in-all *i. e.* he was the *beau ideal*, the *ne plus ultra* of loveliness. अप... सर्गस्य who was the perfection of the creation of the atoms of beauty. अपवर्गः completion, highest point. 'स्यादपवर्गस्त्यागे मोक्षे

कार्यावसानसाफल्ये' मेदिनी. There is another sense hinted at. Where there is अपवर्ग (*i. e.* मोक्ष), सर्ग (birth) comes to an end (अपवर्ग). सकल...राज्यस्य—the idea is:—he was so holy and pure that all the misdeeds of the kings (of all ages in securing kingdoms) were altogether got rid of by expiation. It is not proper to explain that his merit was sufficient to expiate all the sins of subjects put together (as Mr Kale does). सर्व...पैस्य he was as though the surprise attack of Cupid with all his forces *i. e.* he was irresistible in his charms. उपा...र्शनस्य he was a means of seeing पुरन्दर *i. e.* in him one saw पुरन्दर. पुरन्दर—Indra; one who storms cities. आवर्तनम् fusing together; practising. धर्म was as though put into a crucible and moulded into his form. He practised धर्म incessantly. कन्या...लानाम् as women confined in the अन्तःपुर move about freely there, so the कलाs were to be found only in him and to the fullest extent. परमप्रमाणं highest authority. राज...पतीनाम्—For प्रजापतिs, see above p. 18. When a sacrifice was finished, the sacrificer took a ceremonial bath called अवभृथस्नान. The प्रजापतिs, to whom was entrusted the task of creation, produced Harsha as the highest point (समाप्ति) of perfection in the creation of kings. गम्भीरं च प्रसन्नं च. There are three pairs of adjectives in each of which there is an apparent विरोध. गम्भीरम् (deep; serene). प्रसन्न transparent; gracious. When water is deep, we cannot see the bottom (it is not transparent). त्रासजननं—he produced fear in the irreverent or sinful. The com. refers to रघु I. 16. 'भीमकान्तैर्नृपगुणैः स बभूवोपजीविनाम् । अधृष्यश्चाभिगम्यश्च यादोरत्नैरिवार्णवः ॥'. कौतुकम् curiosity; admiration. What rouses one's curiosity may be sinful.

P. 35 ll. 18—33 **दृष्ट्वा...करोत्.** अनुगृहीत इव as though blessed (by the sight of such a holy king). निगृहीत इव as though checked (by the august appearance of the king). साभि...तृप्त इव eager (to see him more) and yet satisfied (by feeling blessed on seeing him). रोमाञ्चं मुञ्चतीति ०मुच् तेन. विस्मयेन स्मेरः (smiling). शोभनं जन्म यस्य. सुगृहीतं नाम यस्य whose name is honoured. चत्वारः उदधयः एव केदारं तेन कुटुम्बी who is a house-holder of the field in the form of the four oceans *i. e.* who looks upon the whole world as his family. Compare 'उदारचरितानां तु वसुधैव कुटुम्बकम् ।'. For ब्रह्मस्तम्ब, see above p. 102. हर्ष enjoyed the best the universe could yield. A केदारकुटुम्बी (*i. e.* an humble farmer) enjoys the standing crops. सकलानां आदिराजानां चरितं तस्य जये ज्येष्ठः (प्रधानः) मल्लः the foremost protagonist in vanquishing (*i. e.*

eclipsing) the deeds of the primeval kings (like मनु, पृथु). राजन्वती ruled by a good king. राजवती ruled by a king. 'सुराज्ञि देशे राजन्वान् स्यात्ततोऽन्यत्र राजवान्' इत्यमरः. 'राजन्वान् सौराज्ये' पा. 8. 2. 14. नास्य...चरितानि his youthful actions are not opposed to वृष (धर्म), as those of Krishṇa were. Even as a boy he did not do any rash act. कृष्ण killed a demon अरिष्ट that had assumed the form of a bull (वृष). *Vide* विष्णुपु० V. 14. In these and the following clauses up to न...श्रियः, the author shows by श्लिष्ट words the superiority of हर्ष to various deities. न...लसितानि the manifestations of his ऐश्वर्य (greatness, prosperity) do not cause sorrow to दक्ष (clever men), as those of शिव did. The king, though prosperous, does not offend the clever. ऐश्वर्य also means 'ईश्वरस्य शिवस्य भावः'. For दक्ष whose sacrifice was destroyed by शिव, *vide* p. 87. There is an emphasis on the word पशुपति. शिव acted very brutally in destroying his own father-in-law. न...वादाः There are no प्रवादs (rumours) about him indicating (पिशुन) the ruin of his गोत्र (family), as in the case of Indra. प्रवादाः also 'myths.' गोत्राः mountains (गां पृथ्वीं त्रायन्ते इति). There are myths relating that Indra destroyed the wings of mountains. Indra is therefore called गोत्रभिद्. *Vide* p. 84. 'पिशुनौ खलसूचकौ' इत्यमरः. दण्डग्रहणानि (1) taking of fines (as punishment); (2) holding the rod. दण्डधर is one of the names of यम. The king did not like to be too severe in exacting fines. नि...रक्षिताः guarded by thousands of pitiless (निस्त्रिंश)sea-monsters (ग्राहः). रत्नालयाः treasure-houses; the seas. In the sea we have cruel ग्राहs. वरुण is the lord of the sea. निस्त्रिंशग्राह would mean 'swordsman.' धनदः = कुबेरः. न निष्फला...लाभाः obtaining his presence (*i. e.* an interview with him) is never fruitless *i. e.* he bestows gifts on those who come near him. In the case of कुबेर, the excellent निधिs (treasures) that he has secured are lying idle (he does not make a gift of anything). कुबेर is the lord of the nine निधिs. 'महापद्मश्च पद्मश्च शङ्खो मकरकच्छपौ । मुकुन्दकुन्दनीलाश्च खर्वश्च निधयो नव ॥'. न अर्थ...दर्शनानि the sight of him (हर्ष) is never bereft of solid gain *i. e.* when anyone sees him, one gets अर्थ (wealth) and people talk (वाद) about it. जिन must mean here बुद्ध. दर्शनानि means 'systems of philosophy'. अर्थ...शून्यानि not recognising the doctrine of the existence of (material) objects. There are four Buddhistic schools, सौत्रान्तिक, वैभाषिक (both of which maintained that thoughts as well objects are real), योगाचार and माध्यमिक (that maintained the unreality of thoughts, as well as objects). What is common to all these schools is the idea of क्षणिकत्व. The author here refers to the योगाचार school. That school holds that the only reality is विज्ञान (thought); there are no real entities (अर्थ or बाह्यार्थ) in the external world corresponding to the thoughts that a person is conscious of. This theory is called विज्ञानवाद. *Vide* वेदान्तसूत्र II. 2. 28 and S'aṅkara's Bhāshya thereon. Compare 'बौद्धबुद्धिमिव निरालम्बनाम्' कादम्बरी p. 131 of P. बहुलैः दोषैः उपहताः marred by many sins. श्रियः = लक्ष्म्यः. बहुलस्य कृष्णपक्षस्य दोषा (रात्रिः) तस्यां उपहताः (reduced). श्रियः—beauty. चित्रम् wonderful. अत्यमरम् surpassing the gods. अमरान् अतिक्रान्तं अत्यमरम्. 'अत्यादयः क्रान्ताद्यर्थे द्वितीयया' वार्तिक on पा. I. 4. 79. अपि...र्थिनः (न पर्याप्तो विषयः) and moreover suppliants do not afford a sufficient (पर्याप्त) scope for his liberality *i. e.* there is not a sufficient number of suppliants to enable him to exercise his liberality to the fullest. Understand 'न पर्याप्तो विषयः' in each of the following clauses and explain similarly. प्रज्ञायाः शास्त्राणि all the शास्त्रs do not give sufficient employment to his intellect. कवित्वस्य वाचः language fails to give adequate expression to his poetic gifts. सत्त्वं spirit, courage. उत्साह (energy) is one of the three शक्तिs of a king *viz.* प्रभुशक्ति, उत्साहशक्ति and मन्त्रशक्ति. व्यापाराः undertakings. कीर्तेर्दिङ्मुखानि the ten regions are not sufficient to contain his fame. गुण...संख्या—*i. e.* his virtues were beyond enumeration. कौशलस्य कला the 64 *kalās* did not exhaust his skill. अस्मिंश्च राजनि while this king rules. यती...ट्टकाः—योगपट्टक was to be seen only with यतिs and nowhere else (in another sense). For the योगपट्टक of ascetics, see p. 26 above. योगपट्टकाः—योगेन कूटकर्मणा युक्ताः पट्टकाः false or forged grants. For योग in the sense of 'deceit', *vide* the first verse of the 4th उच्छ्वास. There are numerous examples of परिसंख्यालङ्कार here. पुस्त...ग्रहाः—पार्थिवविग्रहs (earthen bodies; fights among princes) were to be seen in पुस्तकर्म only (in the manufacture of dolls). *Vide* notes on पुस्तकृत् above p. 90. षट्पदः = भ्रमरः. दान...लहाः the quarrels over receiving ichor; quarrels about the recovery of debts. As nobody incurred debts there were no quarrels about the recovery of money lent. वृत्तानां of metres. पादच्छेदाः division into four parts; the cutting off of feet. अष्टापदानाम्—*Vide* notes p. 24. चतु...ल्पना arrangement of the four members (*i. e.* chess); the cutting off of the four limbs (hands and feet). No one committed grave offences for which hacking of limbs was prescribed by the Smṛitis. द्विज...द्वेषाः hatred of the chief of birds (*i. e.* गरुड); hatred of Brāhmaṇas and teachers. वाक्यविदाम् those who know the rules of the interpretation of Vedic sentences *i. e.* मीमांसकs. अधिकरणविचाराः examination of अधिकरणs (cases for discussion); considerations in a court of justice. No one resorted to the courts of justice, as there were no disputes. Or we may separate as अधिक–रण–विचाराः (thoughts of great fights). The पूर्वमीमांसा of जैमिनि and the उत्तरमीमांसा of बादरायण are divided into अध्यायs, each अध्याय into पादs and each पाद into अधिकरणs, each अधिकरण containing one or more सूत्रs and completely treating of one topic. अधिकरण has five members. 'विषयो विशयश्चैव पूर्वपक्षस्तथोत्तरम् । निर्णयश्चेति सिद्धान्तः शास्त्रेऽधिकरणं स्मृतम् ॥'. According to others the five members are विषय, सन्देह (or विशय), सङ्गति, पूर्वपक्ष and सिद्धान्त. उपवीती—'प्रोद्धृते दक्षिणे पाणावुपवीत्युच्यते द्विजः'—क्षीरस्वामी quoting from मनु–wearing the sacred cord in the usual manner (over the left shoulder and under the right arm). 'उपवीतं यज्ञसूत्रं प्रोद्धृते दक्षिणे करे' इत्यमरः.

P. 36 ll. 1–27. **अथोत्तरेण...मभूत्.** उत्तरेण...धिष्ण्यस्य not far to the north of the royal seat. Words ending in एन like दक्षिणेन and उत्तरेण govern the accusative or genitive. अपरवक्त्रम्—*Vide* notes p. 40. **Verse 5.** करिकलभ (vocative) young elephant ! लोलता = चञ्चलता. चर...व्रतम् observe the vow of discipline (humility). आनतं आननं यस्य whose head is bent (not held high in pride). मृगपतिनखवत् भङ्गुरः (curved). गुरुः formidable. उपरि held above (the elephant's head). क्षमते...शः the hook would not tolerate your लोलता. The अङ्कुश brought round the elephant when it became restless and disobedient. This verse contains a veiled rebuke of Bāṇa for his लोलता in his youth, when he was like करिकलभ. The words मृगपति and गुरुः (who teaches or chastises) refer to the king. The verse reminds the king of the presence of बाण, about whose चापल he had heard reports. Mr. R. R. Kale sees a veiled allusion to the king even in the words करिकलभ &c., but that does not seem to us to be proper. He takes गुरु as referring to the preceptor of the king. तं = बाणम्. गिरि...गम्भीरेण as deep as the roar (बृंहितं) of a lion in a mountain cave. एष... बाणः is he that बाण ? न...पश्यामि I shall not see him without showing him favour. Bāṇa conveys that the very way in which the king addressed him (महानयं भुजङ्गः) showed that the king had favoured him. The king spoke the words to the मालव

prince and then looked बाण in the face. The reading अकृतप्रसादम् (अकृतः प्रसादः यस्मिन्) would convey the same sense. नीलैः धवलैः अंशुकैः (किरणैः, वस्त्रैः) शाराम् (variegated) *adj.* of प्रभाम् and तिरस्करिणीम्. भ्रमयन्—the object is प्रभाम्. अपाङ्गे नीयमाना तरला तारका (pupil) यस्य. आयामिनीं long *i. e.* spreading. परिवृत्य having turned (his body). In order to look at the मालव prince, he turned his eye sideways (तिर्यक्). The rays of the dark pupil became mixed with the lustre of the white eye and so the lustre of the whole eye looked शार. The rays of the eye resembled a curtain made of white and dark silk. His pupil was moved towards the corner of the eye. A curtain may have stars on the borders (अपाङ्ग). प्रेष्ठ superlative of प्रिय. मालवराजसूनोः—(*Vid.* Intro. p. XXXII) this seems to have been माधवगुप्त the younger of the two princes that were the companions of Harsha and his elder brother. भुजङ्गः a gallant, a man of dissolute habits. 'भुजङ्गः सर्पषिङ्गयोः' हेमचन्द्रः. तूष्णी...तस्मिन् when that (मालव prince) showed by his silence that he had not understood the king's words. अगमितं नरेन्द्रवचः येन. अविज्ञातं तत्त्वं येन who does not know the truth. अश्रद्दधान इव as if you do not believe me (in my real character). नेय इव like one led (by others). आज्ञापयसि—this and the correlative विज्ञापयामि or विज्ञापयति are employed by ordinary persons in addressing a person very much superior in the sense of वदसि, कथयामि &c. स्वैरिणः capricious, unrestrained. विचित्राः various, strange. प्रवादाः rumours. महद्भि...तव्यम् but the great ought to see things as they are. नार्ह...शिष्टमिव you will please not misunderstand me, as if I were an ordinary man. अविशिष्टम् without anything to distinguish him. सोमपायिनाम् that drink सोम *i. e.* that performed the सोमयागs. संस्काराः the purificatory ceremonies performed in the case of a द्विज from conception to death, such as जातकर्म, नामकरण, उपनयन &c. साङ्गः—the अङ्गs (auxiliary branches of study) of the वेद are six, *viz.* शिक्षा (phonetics), कल्प (ritual of sacrifices), व्याकरण (grammar), निरुक्त (etymology and exegesis), छन्दः (metrics) and ज्योतिष (astronomy). In these three sentences बाण seems to have in view the well-known verse 'जन्मना ब्राह्मणो ज्ञेयः संस्कारैर्द्विज उच्यते। विद्यया याति विप्रत्वं त्रिभिः श्रोत्रिय उच्यते॥'. शास्त्राणि—such as अलङ्कार, न्याय, वेदान्त &c. दार...रिकोऽस्मि since my marriage I have been a diligent householder. 'कुटुम्बव्यापृतस्तु यः। स्यादभ्यागारिकः' इत्यमरः. 'अभितोऽगारे भवः अभ्यागारिकः' क्षीर०. कामे भुजङ्गता—this sentence is capable of three senses, two of which are principally intended. (1) Wherein consists my भुजङ्गता (being a lewd person)? What is there in all my life which deserves to be referred to in the words 'महानयं भुजङ्गः?' (2) भुजङ्गता is to be found only in काम (Cupid) and not in me. (3) What woman was embraced by me? (का मे भुजं गता). लोक...मासीत् but (I must admit) that my youth was not without those follies which are not inconsistent with the two worlds (*i. e.* this world and the next). He says he was guilty of trifling follies that would not be very much censured in this world or would not come in the way of his attaining heaven. अविद्यमानः अपलापः (concealment, denial) यस्य. अत्रा...स्मि I do not deny this much. अनेनै...हृदयम् my heart does feel repentance (विप्रतीसारः) for this. सुगतः=बुद्धः. शान्तमनसि—this, कर्तरि and दण्डभृति are to be connected with देवे. मना...स्थानाम् who carries out all the rules of the (four) Varṇas and the (four) *ās'ramas*, like Manu. Bāṇa refers probably to the मनुस्मृति wherein are laid down the rules of वर्णs and आश्रमs that were supposed to have been promulgated by Manu. *Vide* मनुस्मृति I. 2 and 107. सम...भृति when you wield the rod of punishment like यम. 'धर्मराजः पितृपतिः समवर्ती परेतराट्' इत्यमरः. Death deals equally with all; यम is also called दण्डधर. The king also is दण्डधर (he punishes wrongdoers). सप्त...रशनाम् whose girdle is formed of the seven oceans. For the seven oceans, see p. 32. For the द्वीपs, see p. 3. अविशङ्कः without fear. क इव सर्वे...कल्पयिष्यति what man possibly will act the part of improper conduct even in his mind, improper conduct which is closely related to all calamities. From अविनय spring all calamities. Even the *acting* of improper conduct is impossible; much more actual performance. आसतां...पेताः let alone human beings. मनुष्यस्य भावः मनुष्याणां समूहो वा मानुष्यकम्. त्वत्प्र...पिबन्ति In consequence of your power, even bees drink honey in fear. To drink मधु (wine) was a महापातक. So the bees are as though afraid of the punishment that may be meted out to them. 'ब्रह्महत्या सुरापानं स्तेयं गुर्वङ्गनागमः। महान्ति पातकान्याहुः संसर्गश्चापि तैः सह ॥' मनु० 11. 54. रथाङ्गं (चक्रं) नाम येषाम् (चक्रवाकाः). लज्जन्ते...प्रियाणाम् are ashamed of their great attachment to their mates. अभ्यनुवृत्तिः (pleasing, following) एव व्यसनं (vice; attachment). A चक्रवाक is a type of love. चपलायन्ते play their tricks. शरारवः destructive, ferocious. For शरारु see p. 23. सानुक्रोशा इव as though compassionate. पिशितानि=मांसानि. अन...ग्राहिण्यः understanding the minds of others as they are. अनपाचीन not opposite (to the real state of things).

P. 36 l. 28—**P. 37.** l. 32. **भूपति...णेति.** केवल...कथयत् he only revealed his inward pleasure by merely casting at him an affectionate glance which seemed to bathe him in a shower of nectar. The king did not show him any *outward* marks of favour such as सम्भाषण; but बाण understood from the king's look that *inwardly* the king was pleased with him. लम्बमाने hanging (on the western horizon). The next sentence is बाणोऽपि... निवासस्थानमगात् (l. 21). धौतः (washed, polished) आरकूटः (brass) तस्य इव कोमला आतपत्विट् यस्मिन् (*adj.* of वासरे). The light of the sun in the evening (on trees and mountains) looked like polished brass. निर्वाति *loc. sing.* of *pr. p.* of वा with निर्—to be extinguished. अस्ता...मति when the sun (मरीचिमत्), leaving the sky, the diadem (किरीटं) of the crest of the setting mountain, let fall his rays like the sprays of *Nichula* trees. 'कूटोऽस्त्री शिखरं शृङ्गं' इत्यमरः. निचुलमञ्जरीणामिव भाः येषाम्. निचुल is a tree with scarlet flowers. 'निचुलो हिज्जलोऽम्बुजः' इत्यमरः. रोमन्थेन मन्थराणि कुरङ्गकुटुम्बकानि तैः अध्यास्यमानं म्रदिष्ठं गोष्ठीनपृष्ठं यासु. रोमन्थ... स्थलीषु when the soft surfaces of deserted cowpens in the forests had families of deer sitting on them lazily ruminating. म्रदिष्ठ—superlative of मृदु. We must read गौष्ठीन. गोष्ठः भूतपूर्वः (that was formerly a cow-pen) गौष्ठीनं, according to 'गोष्ठात् खञ् भूतपूर्वे' पा. 5. 2. 18. शोका...तटीषु when the banks of rivers were plaintive with the cries (कूजितं) of the female चक्रवाक birds overwhelmed with sorrow. At the approach of night the चक्रवाकs were supposed to be separated from their mates. वासविटपेषु (on branches where they had made their nests) उपविष्टानि वाचाटानि चटकानां चक्रवालानि येषु. आलवालेषु (basins round trees) आवर्जिताः (emptied) सेकार्थे जलकुटाः (water pots) येषु—*adj.* of निष्कुटेषु (pleasure groves). 'घटः कुटनिपावस्त्री' इत्यमरः. 'गृहारामास्तु निष्कुटाः' इत्यमरः (कुटात् गृहात् निष्क्रान्ताः निष्कुटाः). दिवस...व्राते when herds of hungry calves (तर्णकः) began to suck the flowing udders of cows that returned after wandering (विहृतिः) the whole day. प्रस्नुताः स्तनाः यस्य (*adj.* of वर्गम्). स्तनन्धय—from स्तन and the root धे 1 P. to suck (स्तनं धयतीति), a nasal being inserted according to 'नासिकास्तनयोर्ध्माधेटोः' पा 3. 2. 29. उद्धृतं क्षीरं यस्मात्. Read चास्तधराधर॰. अस्त...मण्डले when the disc of the sun, the boat in the ocean of evening (twilight), with red hue, sank (below the horizon), as though it were plunged into the flood of the stream (धुनी) of the minerals (धातुः) on the western mountain. गैरिक (red chalk) is particularly known as धातु (in the case of mountains). 'धातुर्मनःशिलाद्यद्रेर्गैरिकं तु विशेषतः' इत्यमरः. पतङ्गस्य इदं पातङ्गम्. The sun's disc became extremely red when about to dip into the ocean. The poet fancies that it was swept into the stream of red chalk. The disc resembles a small boat and the rosy hues of the evening sky resemble the sea. पानपात्रे is not so good as यानपात्रे. It will mean 'the disc of the sun looked like a goblet for drinking the ocean of evening.' The evening being red, the goblet containing it would also look red. ०जलेन शुचयः शयच्चरणाः येषाम्. 'पञ्चशाखः शयः पाणिः' इत्यमरः. Brāhmanical ascetics washed their hands and feet before worshipping in the shrine. चैत्यः a sanctuary; a temple; a holy tree (growing by the side of a road). 'चैत्यामायतनं तुल्ये' इत्यमरः ('चित्यायामिदं चैत्यं देवकुलमहावृक्षाद्युपाश्रयः' क्षीर०). पाराशरिषु—see above p. 90. यज्ञपात्रैः पवित्राः पाणयः येषाम् (*adj.* of ०जने). प्रकीर्णाः (spread round) बर्हिषः (कुशाः) यस्य (*adj.* of ०वेदसि). उद्गतं तेजः यस्य the flames of which leapt up (when oblations were thrown into it). वषट्कृ to offer (an oblation) with the cry वषट्. वषट् is an exclamation on offering an oblation (the name of the deity being put in the dative) *e. g.* इन्द्राय वषट्. यायजूकः—one who frequently performs sacrifices—from यज् with affix ऊक, according to 'यजजपदशां यङः' पा. 3. 2. 166 (यायजूकः, जञ्जपूकः, दन्दशूकः). निद्राविद्राणानि द्रोणकुलानि तैः कलिलाः (full of) कुलायाः येषु. द्रोणाः काकाः. The com. explains निद्राविद्राण as 'dull with sleep'. But elsewhere विद्राण is used in the sense of 'awake'. Compare 'विद्राणविपश्चिति' हर्ष० 5th उ० 11th para. So we take 'निद्राविद्राण' as 'not yet gone to sleep' (though crowding in their nests). Or we may separate as निद्रा-अविद्राण meaning 'not awake through sleep'. कापेयविकलानि (free from their pranks) कपिकुलानि येषु. At night the monkeys desist from their pranks. 'कापेयं चापलादिकम्' क्षीर० (कपेः भावः कर्म वा). आरामतरुषु on the trees in the gardens. निर्जि...कुले when the swarms of owls (कौशिकः), settled (*lit.* householders) in their huts *viz.* the hollows of old trees, were about to go out. मुनि...रम्बे—The clusters of bright stars looked like the bright drops of water scattered about in सन्ध्यावन्दन by the sages. दन्तुरयति *loc. sing.* of *pr. p.* of दन्तुरयति (make indented or serrated) denominative verb from दन्तुर. The clusters also looked like the bright teeth (of a lady *viz.* the sky). As drops are scattered on the ground (स्थली), so the stars were scattered in the sky. स्थवीयस्—comparative of स्थूल. 'निकुरम्बं कदम्बकम्' इत्यमरः. अम्बरा...शिखण्डे when the topknot of the S'abarî of night rose in the sky *i. e.* when the sky was overcast with darkness. For शर्वरीशबरी compare 'शर्वरीशबरीचिकुरचये...तमसि' text p. 6. l. 13. अम्बरा०—The topknot of a शबरी may be dangling on her garment (अम्बरं). खण्डपरशुः (शिवः) तस्य कण्ठवत् काले (dark)-goes with ०तारे. For S'iva's dark throat, see notes p. 2. कव...तारे when the young (fresh, recent) *avatara* (advent) of darkness swallowed all that remained of the evening light. सान्ध्यम्-सन्ध्यायाः अयं सान्ध्यः (०शेषः) तम्. तिमिर... र्गतासु (०तर्जनाय निर्गतासु) that came forth as if to chide darkness. दहनं प्रविष्टः दिनकरः तस्य करशाखासु (fingers; branch-like rays). The blazing lamps are fancied to be the fingers of the sun. Fingers start from the hand and one of them (called तर्जनी) is employed in threatening or chiding a person. Flames are tapering like fingers. It was believed that the sun, when setting, entered fire. Compare रघु० IV. 1. 'स राज्यं गुरुणा दत्तं प्रतिपद्याधिकं बभौ । दिनान्ते निहितं तेजः सवित्रेव हुताशनः ॥'. अररसम्पुटसंक्रीडनेन कथिता आवृत्तिः यैः. अररं panel. 'कवाटमररं तुल्ये' इत्यमरः. 'पुरद्वारं तु गोपुरम्' इत्यमरः. अरर...पुरेषु when the city gates as though announced their clo sing (आवृत्ति) by the creaking of their folding panels. It would be better if we could read ०वृतिषु. आवृति means 'shutting', while आवृत्ति usually means 'revolving.' शय...जुषि enjoying the pleasure (उपजोषः) of lying on their beds. They first lay on their beds for some time and then went to sleep. जरतीभिः कथिताः कथाः यस्यै. शिशयिषमाणे (*pr. p.* of the desiderative of शी) was about to sleep. जरन् महिषः मषी (lamp-black, ink) च तद्वत् मलीमसं (dark) तमः यस्य. जनितः पुण्यजनानां (goblins) प्रजागरः येन. 'यातुधानाः पुण्यजनाः' अमरः. Goblins stalk abroad at night. पुण्यजन also means 'यक्ष'. They are guardians of कुबेर's treasures and as such must be awake at night. विजृम्भमाणे (growing, yawning). तमीमुखे the mouth (or first part) of Night. 'रजनी यामिनी तमी' अमरः मुखरितं (twanging) विततज्यं (वितता ज्या यस्य) धनुः यस्य (*adj.* of ०ध्वजे). अशेषस्य संसारस्य शेमुषीं (मतिं) मुष्णाति इति ०मुष् तस्मिन्—Cupid blinds the intellect of every one in the world. रतस्य आकल्पः (dress) तस्य आरम्भेण शोभते इति. शम्भलीनां (procuress) भाषितं भजते इति. 'कुट्टनी शम्भली समे' अमरः. भूषा ornaments, decoration. भुजिष्या a maid harlot. सैरन्ध्या बध्यमानं रशनाजालं तेन जल्पाकं (noisy, jingling) जघनं (loins) यासाम्. 'स्याज्जल्पाकस्तु वाचालः' अमरः. For सैरन्ध्री, see notes p. 90. जनीषु young ladies. 'समाः स्नुषा जनी वध्वः' अमरः. वशिकासु (empty) विशिखासु (roads) विहरन्तीति विहारिण्यः (wandering) तासु. 'वशिकं तुच्छरिक्तके' अमरः. 'रथ्या प्रतोली विशिखा' अमरः (विगतशिखा मुण्डितेव, समन्ताद्विशीर्यंते जनसंमर्देन वा' क्षीर०). अनन्यजः (कामः) अनुप्लवः

the tribe of हंसs as guests by offering them clear water. धौतासिनिभं (०सदृशं) नभः यस्मिन्. In शरद् the sky is blue and clear. भास्वरः भास्वान् (सूर्यः) यस्मिन्. शुचिः शशी यस्मिन्. In the rains the moon is obscured by clouds. तरुणः (young, bright) तारागणः यस्मिन्. गलत् (disappearing) सुनासीरस्य (इन्द्रस्य) शरासनं (धनुः) यस्मिन्. Rain-bows are seen when there are clouds. For सुनासीर, see pp. 17–18. सीदत् (vanishing, sinking) सौदामन्याः (विद्युतः) दाम (streak, girdle) यस्मिन्. दामोदरनिद्रायै दुह्यति इति that (शरद्) was an enemy to the sleep of विष्णु. दाम उदरे यस्य (दाम्ना उदरे बद्धः). *Vide* विष्णुपु० V. 6.20 for derivation. विष्णु was supposed to fall asleep in आषाढ for the four months of the rainy season and to get up in कार्तिक. Compare 'शापान्तो मे भुजगशयनादुत्थिते शार्ङ्गपाणौ' मेघदूत; 'जलधरसमयमिव वनगहनमध्यसुखसुप्तहरिम्' कादम्बरी p. 40 of P; 'न खलु सांप्रतमाचरति जलशयनदोहदं देवो रथाङ्गपाणिः' कादम्बरी p. 124 of P. द्रुतं (running, flowing) वैदूर्यवर्णं (of the colour of *lapis lazuli*) अर्णः (water) यस्मिन्. घूर्णमानाः (rolling about) मिहिकावत् लघवः मेघाः तैः मोघः (idle) मघवा (इन्द्रः) यस्मिन् मिहिका fog, dew. The clouds, if at all seen, are very light in autumn and hardly any rain falls. So इन्द्र, the lord of rain, is then idle. निमीलन्तः (closing) नीपाः यस्मिन्. नीप is कदम्ब. A कदम्ब tree puts forth buds in the rainy season. Compare 'मरुन्नवाम्भःप्रविधूतसिक्ता कदम्बयष्टिः स्फुटकोरकेव ॥' उत्तररामचरित III. 42; 'कुड्मलितकदम्बतरौ...नभसि मासि' हर्ष० 4th उ०, 11th para. नि...कुटजे—कुटज trees blossom in the rains. निर्मु...कन्दले when the plantain puts forth no buds. मधुस्यन्दि इन्दीवरं (blue lotus) यस्मिन्. कह्लारैः (water-lilies) आह्लादिनि. शेफालिकया शीतलीकृता निट् (रात्रिः) यस्मिन्. यूथिकाभिः (jasmine) आमोदिनि. मोदमानैः कुमुदैः (white night lotuses) अवदाताः (सिताः) दश दिशः यस्मिन्. सप्तच्छदानां धूलिभिः (pollen) धूसरः समीरः (wind) यस्मिन्. For सप्तच्छद, see above p. 136. स्तबकितैः (formed into bunches) बन्धुरैः (lovely) बन्धूकैः आबध्यमाना अकाण्डसन्ध्या (sudden evening hues) यस्मिन्. बन्धूक is a red flower. नीराजिताः वाजिनः यस्मिन्. The नीराजन ceremony was performed in शरद्. For नीराजन, see p. 34. *Vide.* रघु० IV. 24–25. उद्दामाः (wild, unchecked) दन्तिनः यस्मिन्. दर्पेण क्षीबं (intoxicated) औक्षकं यस्मिन्. औक्षकम् multitude of oxen. 'उक्ष्णां संहतिरौक्षकम्' अमरः. It is derived from उक्षन् *(m)* with affix वुञ् according to 'गोत्रोक्षोष्ट्रोरभ्रराजराजन्यराजपुत्रवत्समनुष्याद्वुञ्' पा. 4. 2. 39. (एभ्यः समूहे वुञ् स्यात्). क्षीयमाणं पङ्कस्य (mud) चक्रवालं (समूहः) यस्मिन्. बालपुलिनैः (small islands) पल्लवितानि सिन्धूनां (नदीनां) रोधांसि (banks) यस्मिन्. The waters having receded, small islands are formed in the rivers in शरद्. परिणामेन (by being ripe) आश्यानाः (partially dry)

श्यामाकाः यस्मिन्. जनितं प्रियङ्गुमञ्जरीषु रजः (pollen) यस्मिन्. कठोरा त्रपुसत्वक् यस्मिन्. त्रपुसं cucumber. कुसुमैः स्मेराः शराः (reeds) यस्मिन्.

P. 38 ll. 17—30 **समुप...इति.** समुपलब्धः भूपालात् (हर्षात्) संमानातिशयः तेन परितुष्टाः. ज्ञातयः kinsmen. श्लाघमानाः applauding. कांश्चि...मानः—he bowed to those that were older than himself and was saluted by those that were younger. Explain each of the following pairs similarly. सम्भ्रान्तेन (excited, flurried) परिजनेन उपनीतं (brought). आसनं...भेजे he took his seat after his elders had taken theirs. भज...त्कारं accepting the hospitality consisting of flower offerings &c. कच्चि...यूयम् have you been happy all these days? (I hope you have &c.). अप्रत्यूहा = अविघ्ना. सम्यक्करणेन परितोषितं द्विजचक्रं यस्याम्. अप्र...क्रिया does the performance of sacrifice proceed without obstacles, gratifying the groups of Brāhmaṇas by its proper procedure? क्रतोः इयं क्रातवी. यथा...भुजः do the fires consume the oblations accompanied by faultless mantras as prescribed (in works on ritual)? अविकलान् मन्त्रान् भजन्ते इति भाञ्जि (हवींषि). A मन्त्र is अविकल (perfect, entire) when it is recited with correct accent and without slurring over any letter. Compare '**मन्त्रो हीनः स्वरतो वर्णतो** वा मिथ्याप्रयुक्तो न तमर्थमाह। स वाग्वज्रो यजमानं हिनस्ति यथेन्द्रशत्रुः स्वरतोऽपराधात्॥' शिक्षा. अविच्छिन्नः unbroken, continuous. कच्चि...योगः. Is there (I hope there is) the same intent application as in years long past to the practice of यज्ञविद्या (the lore of sacrifice)? अभियोगः—'आभिमुख्येन उद्यमः' क्षीर°. परस्परस्पर्धानुबन्धेन अवन्ध्यः (not useless, fruitful) दिवसः तेन दर्शितः आदरः येषु. The words सः, तानि, सा are used in the sense of प्रसिद्ध. तान्येव...मण्डलानि are there the same assemblies for the exposition of grammar, showing their regard (to the study of व्याकरण) by days rendered fruitful by continuous emulation of each other? Each one of the assembly tried to excel the others in the exposition of knotty points of grammar. On व्याख्यान, the महाभाष्य says 'न केवलं चर्चापदानि व्याख्यानं वृद्धिः आत् ऐजिति। किं तर्हि। उदाहरणं प्रत्युदाहरणं वाक्याध्याहार इत्येतत्समुदितं व्याख्यानं भवति' (Kielhorn Vol. I. p. 11). परित्यक्तं अन्यकर्तव्यं यस्याम् which disregarded all other occupations. प्रमाणगोष्ठी assembly or society for the discussion of the means of knowledge. This refers to logic. The very first topic for treatment mentioned in the first Sūtra of the न्यायसूत्र is प्रमाण. Generally four प्रमाणs are mentioned *viz.* प्रत्यक्ष, अनुमान, उपमान and शब्द. मन्दीकृतः इतरशास्त्रेषु रसः (liking) येन. मीमांसा—refers to the पूर्वमीमांसा of जैमिनि and to the उत्तरमीमांसा of बादरायण. In these three clauses बाण suggests that his cousins were पदवाक्यप्रमाणज्ञ, पद standing for grammar, वाक्य for मीमांसा and प्रमाण for न्यायशास्त्र. अभिनवं सुभाषितं एव सुधा तां वर्षन्तीति. For सुभाषित see p. 11.

P. 39 ll. 1–9 **अथ...वारयन्.** तात a term of endearment applied even by elders to youngsters and by friends to friends. Compare 'नहि कल्याणकृत्कश्चिद्दुर्गतिं तात गच्छति' गीता. 6. 40. सन्तोषजुषां who are contented (*adj.* of नः). सततं सन्निहितः विद्याविनोदः (intellectual diversion) येषाम्. वैतानः वह्निः एव ०वह्निमात्रं सहायः येषाम्. किय...तया what have we to do with being happy (we have but little concern with being happy)? It should be noticed that the first question asked by बाण was 'कच्चित्...सुखिनो यूयम्.' They reply by saying that they have all those things that make for happiness *viz.* friends (वैतानवह्नि), amusements and contentment and that they need not bother themselves further, as king हर्ष will look to the rest (to their protection &c.). सकलभुवनानि भुनक्ति (protects). भुजङ्गराजः शेषः तस्य देहवत् दीर्घे. शेष also supports (protects) the earth. क्षितिभुजः = हर्षस्य. विमुक्तं कौसीद्यं येन. कौसीद्य— from कुसीद (कुत्सितं सीदति अस्मिन्) with affix ष्यञ्. The kinsmen of बाण administer him a delicate rebuke. यथाविभवं as our wealth permits. शैश...कथाभिः remembrances of past boyish sports and stories of their ancestors. यथा...करोत् he performed the usual observances.

P. 39 ll. 10—22 **अत्रान्तरे...पपाठ.** दुकू...वसानः wearing a pair of silken Pauṇḍra garments, as white as the corner of the peacock's eye, and cut off from a long piece of silk cloth. पट्ट here stands for what is called तागा in Marathi. He had cut off two pieces from a long roll of silk cloth. पौण्ड्र–Manufactured in the Puṇḍra country. पुण्ड्र would correspond to modern Bengal and Bihar. शिखण्डिनः अपाङ्गवत् पाण्डुनी. अवसानं end. बन्दितया because he was a bard. The bards formed a distinct class, sprung from क्षत्रिय father and S'ūdra mother. तीर्थे...तिलकः whose *tilaka* (on the forehead) was made of *gorochanā* and clay from a sacred spot (river &c.). Various substances were prescribed as affording fit material for making a तिलक. 'तीर्थमृद्यज्ञकाष्ठं च बिल्वो मलयसम्भवम् । जाह्नवीमृन्महानिम्बतुलसीकाष्ठमेव च । ...गोरोचना गन्धकुष्ठं जलं चागुरुगोमयम् ।...स्नानान्ते सर्ववर्णानामाश्रमाणां तथैव च । एतानि तिलकान्याहुः सन्ध्यादिसर्वकर्मसु ॥.' तैलामलकाभ्या मसृणितः (made smooth and glossy) मौलिः (केशाः) यस्य. अनु...चुम्बिना kissing his short topknot. निबिडेन dense with flowers. सकृ...कान्तिः the colour of his lip was bright because he had chewed betel only once. If he had taken betel very often, his lip would have been dark-red and not विमल. So the reading असकृदुपयुक्त is not good. एक...रुचिः the lustre of whose eye was heightened by the application of an eye-salve with a pin. विनी...दधानः wearing a simple (not gaudy) and respectable dress. आसन्दी = पीठिका—a chair. तत्कालं अपनीतं सूत्रवेष्टनं यस्य (*adj.* of पुस्तकं). तत्काल...निधाय having laid, on a stand (यन्त्रकं) made of reedstalks placed in front, his book which seemed as if bound with soft lotus fibres on account of the rays of his nails, although its band was removed at that very moment. His nails were bright and the rays from them resembled lotus-fibres. When he passed his hand round the book in unloosening the string in which it was wrapped, he as though seemed to be tying it up again. पृष्ठतः... स्थानके when a place was assigned behind him to मधुकर and पारावत that sat near (सनीड). The two seem to have been persons that played upon flutes by way of accompaniment. So the reading of B 'वांशिकाभ्यां' is good. C and T translate मधुकर and पारावत as bee and dove. What purpose these served is not clear. Perhaps they were pets. वांशिक-वंशवादनं शिल्पमस्य (from वंश + ठक्) according to 'शिल्पम्' पा. 4. 4. 55. It would mean 'that served as flute-players.' प्राभातिक...क्षिप्य having taken out the leaf inserted inside as a mark to indicate the portion read in the morning. प्राभातिकः प्रपाठकः (section) तस्य छेदः (end) तस्य चिह्नीकृतम्. प्रपाठक also means 'reader', the meaning being 'made as a mark to denote the portion read by the morning reader.' गृहीत्वा...पाटिकां he took a small block (*lit.* panel) light (not heavy) because there were a few leaves only. क्षालय...ग्रन्थम्—the idea is:—the bright rays of his teeth when he recited the verses looked like bright water and like white flowers. मुख...श्रोतृणाम् captivating the hearts of his hearers by the sweet intonations of his voice, as though they were the jinglings of the anklets of सरस्वती residing in his mouth (tongue). सरस्वती is spoken of as dwelling in the mouth of a learned man. On गमक the com. says 'गमयन्ति रागस्वरूपमिति गमकाः असाधारणानि स्वराणां निमीलनानि यानि लक्ष्येष्वान्तरमार्गे इति प्रसिद्धास्तैर्गमकैः स्वरयतिविशेषैः.' गमक is thus defined 'गमकः स्वश्रुतिस्थानच्छायां श्रुत्यन्तराश्रयाम् । स्वरो यो मूर्छनामेति गमकः स इहोच्यते ॥ कम्पितः स्फुरितो नीलो भिन्नः स्थविर एव च । आहतान्दोलितौ चेति गमकाः सप्त कीर्तिताः ॥.' According to the सङ्गीतरत्नाकर, गमक

is a certain कम्प of the voice; it enumerates 15 kinds of it 'स्वरस्य कम्पो गमकः श्रोतृचित्तसुखावहः ।' 3rd chap. 45. गीत्या पपाठ he sang or chanted. पवमानप्रोक्तं पुराणं the Purāṇa promulgated by Vāyu *i. e.* the वायुपुराण. सूत says in the वायुपुराण I. 47–48. 'पुराणं संप्रवक्ष्यामि यदुक्तं मातरिश्वना ॥ पृष्टेन मुनिभिः पूर्वं नैमिषीयैर्महात्मभिः ।'. सूत had learnt it from व्यास (verse 46). The वायुपुराण is one of the most ancient of Purāṇas. The topics generally treated of in a पुराण are summarised in the following verse 'सर्गश्च प्रतिसर्गश्च वंशो मन्वन्तराणि च । वंशानुचरितं चैव पुराणं पंचलक्षणम् ॥'.

P. 39 l. 23—**P. 40** l. 5 **तस्मिंश्च...लोकयन्.** श्रुतिभिः सुभगा गीतिः गर्भे यथा स्यात् तथा. श्रुति is a technical term in music. It means 'a particular division of the octave, a quarter tone or interval.' They are 22 in number. श्रुतिs are those elementary नादs from which the seven स्वरs (सरिगमपधनि) are evolved. 'हृद्यूर्ध्वनाडिकास्य-द्वाविंशत्यणुतिरोजनाडीषु । तावन्तः श्रुतिसंज्ञाः स्युर्नादाः परपरोच्चोच्चाः ॥ एवं गले च शीर्षे ताभ्यः सप्त स्वराः श्रुतिभ्यः स्युः ।' रागविबोध verses 13–14. तार...स्वरेण accompanying the note of the chant in a voice loud (तार) and sweet. **Verse 3.** The first half contains words that apply both to हर्षचरित and पुराण. तदपि that also. मुनिगीतम् sung by sages. अतिपृथु very large. The वायुपुराण contains several thousand verses. अतिपृथु surpassing पृथु, the first king (पृथुमतिक्रान्तं). For पृथु vide notes on the 2nd verse in the 4th उ०. पावनं holy (applies to both). पावनं also means 'composed by पवन *i. e.* by वायु'. हर्ष...मिदम् this Purāṇa does not seem to me to differ from the career of Harsha. **Verse 4.** The four adjectives qualify both गीत and हर्षराज्य. वंशा...वादि that is chanted in notes that are in harmony with the flute (with गीत); where disputants follow their family *i. e.* where there are no disputes among members of the same family. वंशस्य (flute) अनुगमः ययोः तौ ०गमौ विवादिनौ (स्वरौ) यत्र; वंशस्य (family) अनुगमः येषां ते ०गमाः विवादिनः यस्मिन्. The seven स्वरs are gruped into four classes in भरत's नाट्यशास्त्र (Chap. 28. 23.) 'चतुर्विधत्वमेतेषां विज्ञेयं श्रुतियोगतः । वादी चैवाथ संवादी ह्यनुवादी विवाद्यपि ॥'. Then he says 'विवादिनस्तु ये तेषां स्याद्विंशतिकमन्तरम् । तद्यथा ऋषभगान्धारौ धैवतनिषादौ'. Those are विवादिस्वरs (*viz.* ऋषभ and गान्धार, धैवत and निषध) between which there is a difference of 20 श्रुतिs. The रागविबोध (verse 38) puts the matter differently 'एकश्रुत्यन्तरितौ विवादिनौ वैरिणौ मिथो भवतः ।'. Those are विवादिs that are separated by one श्रुति (*i. e.* ultimately 20 श्रुतिs, as there are only 22 श्रुतिs) and are destructive of the harmony of each other. स्फुटकरणं which is clearly pronounced or the rhythmie pauses of which are clear

(with गीत). स्फुटं करणं (pronunciation) यस्मिन् or स्फुटानि करणानि यस्मिन्. करणं means 'the beating of the hands to indicate the proper ताल'. मल्लिनाथ on कुमारसम्भव 6. 40 says "करणैस्तालव्यवस्थापकैस्ताडनविशेषैः । तदुक्तं राजकन्दर्पेण 'नृत्यवादित्रगीतानां प्रयोगवशभेदिनाम् । संस्थानं ताडनं रोधः करणानि प्रचक्षते ॥' इति". स्फुटानि करणानि यस्मिन् (with ०राज्यम्) in which the documents (of sale &c.) were clear (and not ambiguous). For this meaning of करण see मनु० VIII. 145. भरत... गुरु weighty (important) because of its conforming to the path of Bharata (with गीत). भरत is the reputed author of the science of dancing and music. The extant नाट्यशास्त्र claims to be his work. The chant of सुदृष्टि conformed to the rules laid down by भरत. भरत...गुरु (with राज्यं) 'that was wide because it embraced the path (the region) of Bharata.' Here there is a reference to भरतवर्ष (India) which was so named according to the वायुपुराण (chap. 33. 50–52) and the भागवतपुराण (V. 4. 9. and XI. 2. 15–17) after भरत, son of ऋषभ. According to ब्रह्मपुराण (13. 57) भरतवर्ष was named after भरत son of दुष्यन्त and शकुन्तला. श्री... यतिम्—(1) issuing from a sweet throat (with गीत); issuing from श्रीकण्ठ. श्रीकण्ठ was the name of the country where हर्ष's ancestors ruled. श्रीयुक्तः कण्ठः श्रीकण्ठः. Or श्रीकण्ठ means शिव. Then गीत would refer to the वायुपुराण and not the chanting of it by सुदृष्टि. As all learning springs from शिव, the पुराण may also be called श्री०. हर्षराज्यम् (with गीतम्) would mean 'which is the realm of joy'. These verses serve to introduce the request made by Bāṇa's cousins. चत्वारः qualifies ०पद्माः and भ्रातरः. पितामहमुखानि एव पद्माः. Brahmā has four mouths. वेदाभ्यासेन पवित्रिताः मूर्तयः येषाम् (applies to both ०पद्माः and भ्रातरः). Each of the four Vedas was promulgated by a special mouth of Brahmā. *Vide* विष्णुपुराण I. 5. ऋग्वेद, यजुर्वेद, सामवेद and अथर्ववेद were respectively created from his four mouths beginning with the eastern. उपायाः—these are the four methods of policy in politics *viz.* साम (reconciliation), दान (bribery), भेद (internal dissensions) and दण्ड (open attack). साम...मुखाः whose mouths are charming by the repeating of the सामवेद or by adopting the policy of conciliation (with भ्रातरः); the commencement of which is charming by the employment of reconciliation (with उपायाः). साम is the first उपाय. गणपति—These are the names of बाण's cousins. भ्रातरः—connect this with परस्परस्य मुखानि व्यलोकयन्. प्रसन्न...व्याकरणेऽपि—In the world as well as in grammar they were प्रसन्नवृत्तयः &c. The words in this clause have two meanings throughout. प्रसन्ना वृत्तिः येषाम् whose conduct is gracious or mild (with लोके); whose exposition (of पाणिनि's सूत्रs) is clear (with व्याकरणे). It is not posssible to suppose that the काशिकावृत्ति of वामन and जयादित्य is referred to here. According to Itsing's statement, the काशिकावृत्ति was composed about 660 A. D. But Itsing's statements are rather confused and in our humble opinion not entitled to the weight given to them by western scholars. *Vide* Dr. Takakusu's translation of Itsing's work (Oxford 1896 pp. 175–176 for what is called वृत्तिसूत्र there). गृहीतं वाक्यं (गुरुवाक्यं आप्तवाक्यं वा) यैः that listened to the words of relatives or elders (with लोके); that had understood the Vārtikas of कात्यायन (according to the com.). वाक्य may refer also to the वाक्यपदीय of भर्तृहरि. कृतः गुरुपदे न्यासः यैः that followed in the footsteps of their teachers or that had planted their feet on (*i. e.* had attained) an eminent position (with लोके); कृतः (अभ्यस्तः) गुरुपदेषु न्यासः यैः that studied the न्यास on difficult words (in the Sūtras of पाणिनि). न्यास is a name applied to the commentary of जिनेन्द्रबुद्धि on the काशिकावृत्ति. But it is hardly possible that Bāṇa refers to it. न्यास was a name given to several grammatical works. Bhāmaha (8th century A. D.) mentions a न्यास, which seems to be जिनेन्द्रबुद्धि's work. 'शिष्टप्रयोगमात्रेण न्यासकारमतेन वा। तृचा समस्तषष्ठीकं न कथञ्चिदुदाहरेत् ॥'. माघ in शिशु० II. 112. refers to a न्यास, वृत्ति and निबन्धन (*i. e.* महाभाष्य). न्यायवेदिनः who knew what was proper; who knew the maxims of grammar. The महाभाष्य mentions many न्यायs like the कूपखानकन्याय (vol I. p. 11), कुम्भीधान्यन्याय (vol I p. 265), अर्धजरतीयन्याय (vol II p. 231), अविरविकन्याय (vol. III. p. 124). Or न्याय means 'rules for the interpretation of the Sūtras', such as 'असिद्धं बहिरङ्गमन्तरङ्गे' (vol I. p. 26) or 'छंदोवत्सूत्राणि भवन्ति' (vol I. p. 37). सु...गुरवः (सुकृतं पुण्यं तस्य संग्रहः (सञ्चयः) तस्य अभ्यासे गुरवः) that were great in the repeated accumulation of merit; सुकृतः संग्रहस्य अभ्यासः तेन गुरवः who became teachers (of grammar) because they had well studied the संग्रह (a work of व्याडि). In the महाभाष्य, the work called संग्रह is frequently referred to 'संग्रहे एतत्प्राधान्येन परीक्षितं नित्यो वा स्यात्कार्यो वेति' (vol I. p. 6). In the days of भर्तृहरि, author of the वाक्यपदीय, the work was lost. 'प्रायेण संक्षेपरुचीनल्पविद्यापरिग्रहान्। सम्प्राप्य वैयाकरणान् संग्रहेऽस्तमुपागते ॥' वाक्यपदीय II. 484. Therefore it seems unlikely that बाण is serious when he says that his cousins had studied the संग्रह. His sole aim is to bring out similarity between लोक and व्याकरण by puns. लब्ध...शब्दाः that were called 'good' by the people ; that employed only grammatically correct words. महाभारतेन भाविताः (purified) आत्मानः येषाम्. 'आर्षादिबहुधाख्यानं देवर्षिचरिताश्रयम् । इतिहासमिति प्रोक्तं भविष्यद्भूतधर्मयुक् ॥.' महा...हलिनः eager to know the stories of heroes. सुभाषितश्रवणे रसः एव रसायनं तस्मिन् अवितृष्णाः not free from desire as to the elixir *viz.* pleasure of listening to सुभाषितs. For रसायन, see p. 55. They had no desires except this. वयसि प्रथमाः foremost in years. वचसि in eloquence. महसि in (Brahmanical) lustre. यजुषि in sacrificial prayers, or in the (study of) the यजुर्वेद. पूर्व...ङ्गराः who had already made an agreement (सङ्गरः) (to request बाण to tell the story of Harsha's life). विवक्षवः = वक्तुम् इच्छवः. सितं एव सुधा तया धवलितं कपोलोदरं येषाम्

P. 40 l. 6–**P. 41** l. 4. **अथ...मभूत्.** कमलदलवत् दीर्घे लोचने यस्य. दत्ता संज्ञा यस्मै to whom a signal was given. दशनानां ज्योत्स्नया स्नपिताः ककुभः येन. The rays of his white teeth resembled moonlight. द्विजानां...कार्षीत् The moon, lord of *dvijas*, carried off the wife of his preceptor. In this and the following sentences, the author finds various faults in the kings and heroes of old to show that only Harsha is spotless. Some of the blemishes, however, are merely verbal. 'द्विजराजः शशधरः नक्षत्रेशः क्षपाकरः' इत्यमरः. गुरुदारग्रहण is a महापातक. *Vide* notes p. 160. It is to be noted that this passage up to युधिष्ठिरः &c. corresponds almost *verbatim* with a passage in the वासवदत्ता of सुबन्धु, where however there is no reference to मान्धाता, सौदास, मरुत्त, पाण्डु and पृथु. Our humble opinion is that examples had already been collected in works that preceded सुबन्धु and बाण and that both derived their inspiration from them. If there is any borrowing between the two, then it is बाण that borrows. बाण adds to the list and also to the phraseology employed in the वासवदत्ता, as we shall show later on. *Vide* Hall's Vāsavadattā pp. 273-276 and pp. 337–340 of the Srīrangam edition. सोम performed राजसूय and became conceited. He carried away तारा, the wife of बृहस्पति, and did not give her back though asked by Brahmā to do so. He had a son from her named बुध. *Vide* विष्णुपु० IV. 6. See 'सकलजगद्गीयमानबुधकर्णानन्दकारिणौ सोमसूर्यवंशाविव' हर्ष० 4th उ० and notes thereon. दयिते...त was separated from Āyus, dear to him. आयुस् means 'life' also. आयुस् was the son of पुरूरवस् and उर्वशी. The com. gives the story alluded to here as follows:—'पुरूरवाः पूर्वां दिशं जेतुं गच्छन्केनाप्याहृतप्रभूतधनेन विप्रेण यज्ञे निमन्त्रितो लोभाक्षिप्तस्तद्धनं जिहीर्षुस्तच्छापान्नष्टः। तस्मिन्मृते स विप्रो नृपं विना प्रजा

निवर्तते इति ज्ञात्वा तदायुषा राजर्षिमायुर्नामानमजीजनदिति'. In the वासवदत्ता we have 'पुरूरवा ब्राह्मणधनतृष्णया विननाश.' नहुष...आसीत्—नहुष, desiring another's wife, became a great serpent. Note that भुजङ्ग also means 'a lewd or dissolute person'. नहुष was the eldest son of आयुः. When Indra ran away through fear of the sin of ब्रह्महत्या in killing वृत्र, नहुष, who had performed numerous sacrifices, was appointed इन्द्र by the gods. In his vanity he cast lustful eyes on शची, the wife of इन्द्र. At the advice of बृहस्पति, she agreed to yield to his wishes if he would come to her in a palanquin carried by sages. While coming in that way, he struck अगस्त्य, who was slow, with his foot urging him to greater speed with the words 'सर्प सर्प'. Then अगस्त्य cursed him to be a सर्प. *Vide* महाभारत वनपर्व Chapter 181. Compare रघु० 13. 36. 'भ्रूभेदमात्रेण पदान्मघोनः प्रभ्रंशयां यो नहुषं चकार ।'. ययाति was the second son of नहुष and married देवयानी, the daughter of शुक्र, who was a ब्राह्मण. आहितं ब्राह्मण्याः पाणिग्रहणं येन—Who took the hand of a Brāhmaṇa girl (*i. e.* married her); who held a ब्राह्मणी (देवयानी) in his hand (when rescuing her from a well). पपात fell off from caste usages; perished (*i. e.* became prematurely old). A male belonging to any one of the four Varṇas could marry a girl of the same Varṇa as himself or of a lower Varṇa; but was forbidden to marry one of a higher वर्ण. Compare what ययाति himself says 'अविवाह्या हि राजानो देवयानि पितुस्तव ।' आदि० 81. 18. ययाति being a क्षत्रिय, there could be no marriage between him and देवयानी, who was a ब्राह्मणी, according to caste usages. Therefore he incurred sin. शुक्र was the preceptor of वृषपर्वा, king of the असुरs. The latter's daughter शर्मिष्ठा quarrelled with देवयानी and threw her in a well. ययाति, while hunting, found her there and took her out with his hand. वृषपर्वा, afraid of शुक्र's curse, wanted to please her. She demanded that his daughter शर्मिष्ठा should be her slave. शुक्र, seeing that his daughter loved ययाति, consented to their marriage. Seeing शर्मिष्ठा in her service, he secretly married her also. When देवयानी complained to her father of ययाति's faithlessness he cursed him to be prematurely old. It will be seen from the above that marrying a ब्राह्मणी was not the *cause* of ययाति's premature old age; but that the latter was only an incident that occurred later on. बाण of course presses it in his service to find fault with ययाति. *Vide* महाभारत आदिपर्व chap. 78–83. Note 'तामथो ब्राह्मणीं राजा विज्ञाय नहुषा-

त्मजः । गृहीत्वा दक्षिणे पाणावुज्जहार ततोऽवटात् ॥ chap. 78. 22. स्त्रीमय एवाभवत्—there are three senses; (1) he was born a woman; (2) he became a woman; (3) he could think of nothing but women *i. e.* he was extremely lascivious. The last is the fault found in him. The first two are matters of mythology. See the following from विष्णुपुराण IV. 1. 8. *ff.* 'इष्टिं च मित्रावरुणयोर्मनुः पुत्रकामश्चकार । तत्रापहृते होतुरपचारादिला नाम कन्या बभूव ॥ सैव मित्रावरुणप्रसादात्सुद्युम्नो नाम मनोः पुत्रो मैत्रेयासीत्पुनश्चेश्वरकोपात् स्त्री सती सोमसूनोर्बुधस्याश्रमसमीपे बभ्राम ।' *Vide* also मार्कण्डेयपु० chap. 111. सुद्युम्न, when hunting, trespassed upon a grove sacred to पार्वती who was promised by शिव that whoever trespassed on the spot where it was would become a female. सुद्युम्न then again became a female. See भागवत पुराण 9.1. जन्तु...निर्घृणता cruelty of killing living beings; cruelty in killing (his own son) जन्तु. सोमक had 100 wives and only one son in old age. The son जन्तु was once bitten by an ant and the whole royal family was very much distressed and therefore he wanted a hundred sons. 'धिगस्त्विहैकपुत्रत्वमपुत्रत्वं वरं भवेत् ।' वनपर्व chap. 127. 12. He sacrificed his only son and after smelling the smoke of his fat his queens gave birth to a 100 sons. The com. gives the story "सोमकस्य राज्ञो जन्तुर्नाम एकः पुत्रोऽभूत् । स च एकपुत्रत्वादपुत्रत्वं वरमिति जानन्नुद्विग्नः पुरोधसा अभ्यधायि 'बहून्पुत्रांश्चेदिच्छसि तदस्य सुतस्य वपया होमः क्रियताम् । ततो यावत्यो धूममाजिघ्रन्ति ताः पुत्रैर्युज्यन्ते' इति । स चापि घृणामपहाय तथा कारितवानिति ।" See वनपर्व chap. 127-128. मार्गणव्यसनेन—by his great liking for arrows (*i. e.* for fighting); by his vice of begging. रसातलमगात्—went to पाताल; perished. रसातल is one of the seven पातालs, अतल, वितल, सुतल, महीतल, रसातल, तलातल and पाताल. मान्धाता, son of युवनाश्व, conquered the earth and wanted to vanquish इन्द्र. Indra offered to hand over his kingdom when he would conquer the demon लवण. So मान्धाता attacked लवण, who had secured a शूल of miraculous powers from शिव. मान्धाता perished with all his army in the fight against लवण. *Vide* रामायण उत्तरकाण्ड chap. 67. The रामायण does not mention that the son and grandson of मान्धाता accompanied him in the fight. पुरुकुत्सः...करोत्—पुरुकुत्स, though practising penance, committed a bad deed on the daughter of मेकल (the suggestion being that he had intercourse with a कन्यका a maiden). मेकलकन्यका means the river नर्मदा. पुरुकुत्स was guilty of bad conduct while practising penance on the Narmadâ. The com. says 'पुरुकुत्सः पुरा तपश्चरन्नर्मदायां स्नानं कुर्वन्कामप्यङ्गनामालोक्य कामाविष्टो नीतिमुत्ससर्ज'. The वासदत्ता has 'पुरुकुत्सः

कुत्सित एवाभवत्.' कुवलयाश्वः—According to the मार्कण्डेयपुराण (chap. 20 ff.) the king ऋतध्वज had secured a horse named कुवलय. He pursued a demon that had disturbed the sage गालव in his austerities and went to पाताल. After various incidents which need not be detailed here, he married मदालसा, daughter of a नाग अश्वतर. भुज...ग्रहात् by resorting to the world of नागs (*viz.* पाताल); by associating with भुजङ्गs (rakes). अश्वतरकन्या means 'the daughter of a mule'. न परिजहार did not omit. The com. gives the story differently 'कुवलयाश्वो राजा मृगयाक्रीडनप्रसङ्गेन घर्मातुरो मज्जनरभसेन सरसीमवतीर्णो रसातलं प्राप्तोऽश्वतराभिधां नागकन्यामूढवानिति'. The वासदत्ता has 'कुवलयाश्वो अश्वतरकन्यामपि जगाम.' प्रथमपुरुषकः the first man; foremost of bad men. क is added according to 'कुत्सिते' पा. 5. 3. 74. कुत्सितः पुरुषः पुरुषकः. परि... पृथिवीम् violated पृथिवी; humbled the earth. पृथु was the first king. During his reign, on account of a draught, people were dying of hunger and the earth yielded nothing. People came to him. He took his bow, when the earth assumed the form of a cow and ran away. Then पृथु pursued her and got from her whatever he desired. *Vide* विष्णुपु० I. 13. कृकलासभावे in being a chameleon (Marathi सरडा). वर्णसङ्करः—a combination of colours; confusion of castes (by intermarriage). It is well-known that the chameleon changes the colours of its skin. वर्णसङ्कर was looked upon as sinful. Compare गीता I. 42. 'सङ्करो नरकायैव.' नृग gave by mistake the cow belonging to one ब्राह्मण to another. The real owner and the donee had a dispute and came to the king's palace to get it settled. नृग, being absorbed in pleasures, did not see them for many days. They cursed him. 'अर्थिनां कार्यसिद्ध्यर्थं यस्मात्त्वं नैषि दर्शनम्। अदृश्यः सर्वभूतानां कृकलासो भविष्यसि ॥' रामायण उत्तरकाण्ड Chap. 53. 18. The वासदत्ता says 'नृगः कृकलासतामगमत्.' सौदा...क्षितिः by सौदास the earth was not protected but (only) disturbed or agitated. न रक्षिता (goes with क्षितिः). नरक्षिता (instru. sing. of नरक्षित्) will also mean 'who killed human beings' (with सौदासेन). To protect the earth is the first duty of a king. 'क्षत्रियस्य परो धर्मः प्रजानामेव पालनम्' मनु० 7. 144. King सौदास also called कल्माषपाद, when tired by hunting, asked a sage named शक्ति the eldest son of वसिष्ठ to make way for him on a road. When he did not move the king whipped him, whereupon the sage cursed him to be a राक्षस subsisting on human flesh. नरान् क्षिणोति इति नरक्षित्. See महाभारत आदिपर्व chap. 176. नलम्—the story of नल is well-known. अवशं अक्षहृदयं यस्य who was not master of the secret of managing dice. गृहीत्वा चाश्वहृदयं राजन्भाङ्गासुरिर्नृपः ॥ निषधाधिपतेश्चापि दत्वाक्षहृदयं नृपः।' वनपर्व Chap. 77. 18–19. अवशानि अक्षाणि हृदयं च यस्य whose heart and senses were not under his control. This is the fault found in him and also that कलि overcame him (while हर्ष had controlled his senses and his reign was an era of righteousness). दमयन्ती chose नल, though even gods like इन्द्र had attended the स्वयंवर. कलि enraged at this entered the body of नल. नल became addicted to gambling, lost his kingdom in favour of his brother who was an expert in gambling, and had to leave his country. After various vicissitudes, he learnt अक्षहृदय from ऋतुपर्ण and regained his wife, kingdom &c. *Vide* वनपर्व Chap. 53–77. The वासवदत्ता has 'नलः कलिनाभिभूतः.' मित्र ...गात् had his mind disturbed in regard to the daughter of मित्र; had a weakness for his friend's daughter. The last is the fault found in him. One's friend's daughter should be like one's own daughter. संवरण—सूर्य had a daughter named तपती, who was married by king संवरण who was a devotee of the sun. *Vide* आदिपर्व Chap. 171–173. इष्टः (प्रियः) रामः तस्य उन्मादेन (intense love); इष्टा रामा (a handsome woman) तस्याः उन्मादेन (by his mad love for). The latter is the fault found in दशरथ. दशरथ died when राम left for the forest to keep his father's promise given to कैकेयी. कार्तवीर्यः refers to सहस्रार्जुन. A king, according to ancient ideas, should be गोब्राह्मणप्रतिपालक and not ०पीडक. गो...पीडनेन also means 'by troubling a ब्राह्मण for a cow'. कार्तवीर्य, a king of माहिष्मती on the नर्मदा, took away the calf of the कामधेनु of जमदग्नि, father of परशुराम. परशुराम killed him. His sons killed जमदग्नि when परशुराम in revenge took the vow of destroying the क्षत्रिय race. *Vide* वनपर्व chap. 115–117. इष्टं बहु सुवर्णं यस्य to whom plenty of gold was dear. इष्टः बहुसुवर्णकः येन who performed a sacrifice called बहुसुवर्णक (in which there was gold and nothing else. *i. e.* in which the utensils were of gold and gold was distributed like water). देवानां द्विजः बृहस्पतिः तस्य बहुमतः (liked); देवानां द्विजानां च बहुमतः. The fault found in him is that he was not देव...मतः (while हर्ष was देवद्विजबहुमत). *Vide* विष्णुपु० IV. 1. 'मरुत्तस्य यथा यज्ञस्तथा कस्याभवद्भुवि। सर्वं हिरण्मयं यस्य यज्ञवस्त्वतिशोभितम् ॥ अमाद्यदिन्द्रः सोमेन दक्षिणाभिर्द्विजातयः। मरुतः परिवेष्टारः सदस्याश्च दिवौकसः ॥ 18–19. The verse मरुतः परिवेष्टारो मरुत्तस्या &c. is well-known to every Brāhmaṇa. मरुत्त desiring to rival इन्द्र asked बृहस्पति to officiate at his sacrifice, but the latter refused. So he had it performed by बृहस्पति's brother संवर्त. बृहस्पति was very much pained at the prosperity of मरुत्त. *Vide* chap. 8. 36. *Vide* महाभारत आश्वमेधिकपर्व chap. 6–10. For शन्तनु see above p. 153. अतिव्यसनात् through extreme attachment. वियुक्तो वाहिन्या separated from the river (Ganges); separated from his army. One who is separated from an army is left all alone (एकाकी). To cry because he was left alone does not become a great king. The वासवदत्ता has 'शन्तनुरतिव्यसनाद्वने विललाप.' वन—means 'forest' (with पाण्डु) and 'water' (with मत्स्य). मदनरसेन आविष्ट: overwhelmed by the passion of love; that has tasted the fruit of the मदन tree. For this story see आदिपर्व chap. 125. He had been cursed by sage किन्दम that he would die when he had intercourse with his wife. गुरु...हृदय: whose heart was despondent through fear (of the prowess) of his teacher (द्रोणाचार्य). गुरुभय also means 'great fear'. It does behove a king to give up truth through fear, however great it may be. When द्रोण made a terrible havoc in the Pāṇḍava hosts, a rumour spread that अश्वत्थामा (son of द्रोण) was killed. द्रोण who believed implicitly in the truthfulness of युधिष्ठिर asked him what the truth was. यु०, who knew that it was only an elephant named अश्वत्थामा that was killed, said 'हत: कुञ्जर:,' the latter word being uttered in a very low tone. The old man heard only the first word, laid aside his weapon in grief, when धृष्टद्युम्न killed him. *Vide* द्रोणपर्व chap. 190. Compare 'मुक्तशस्त्रं कलशयोनिमिव कृष्णवर्त्मप्रसूति:' हर्ष० 6thउ०. The वासवदत्ता omits 'गुरु...हृदय:'. इत्थ...कलङ्कम् thus there has been no king without (some) stain. अपगत: कलङ्क: यस्मात्. ऋते except (governs the ablative). तथाहि—Here follow several sentences in which बाण shows by श्लिष्ट words how हर्ष emulates the deeds of gods and heroes of old. बल...भृत: (1) by Indra, the moving mountains possessed of wings (पक्ष:) were made steady; by Harsha who subdues armies, fickle kings, that had formed coalitions, were paralysed. In this sentence the king is shown as doing what इन्द्र did. For the cutting off of the wings of mountains, see p. 84. अत्र...कृता (1) By Brahmā (प्रजापति) the earth (क्ष्मा) was placed over the hoods of the serpent (भोगिन्) शेष; by (हर्ष) the lord of the people, forgiveness was shown to the circle of the remaining kings. For शेष, see above p. 145. अत्र पुरु...कृता (1) Vishṇu, having churned the ocean-king (*viz.* क्षीरसागर), made लक्ष्मी his own (wife); by (हर्ष) the best of men, glory was made his by vanquishing the king of सिन्धु. सिन्धु—country on the Sindhu river. There is a reference to the conquests of हर्ष

that of an atom. बटुहृदयम्—refers to Bāṇa. For ब्रह्मस्तम्भ, see above p. 102. परिमितेषु वर्णेषु वृत्तिः (वर्तनं, जीवनं) येषाम् that are produced by a small number of letters; that subsist upon &c. The letters of the alphabet which go to make up words are very few. संख्यामतिगच्छन्ति numberless. वाचस्पतेः=बृहस्पतेः. अगोचरः=अविषयः. सरस्व...भारः even the goddess of speech will find this (narration of हर्षचरित) a very heavy burden. अविकलम् entire. एक...वयम् if your curiosity will be satisfied with a part, then I am ready. अधिगताः कतिपयाक्षरलवाः तैः लघीयसी which is light by having acquired a few drops of letters. जिह्वा was originally जड (when बाण was a child), but later on it acquired agility. What is nimble can turn in any direction. किमन्यत्—what more (can be desired)? This is the best combination to induce a person to wax eloquent. परि...दिवसः the day is almost ended. पश्चाल्लम्बमानाः कपिलकिरणाः एव जटाभारः तेन भास्वरः—(1) brilliant with the tawny rays, resembling matted hair, that hang down in the west (with पूषा); brilliant with matted hair hanging behind resembling the tawny rays of the evening sun (with रामः). भगवान् goes with रामः and पूषा. भार्गवो रामः—Rāma of the भृगु race *viz.* परशुराम. महाह्रदे in the great lake. निमज्जति sinks; bathes. पूषा the sun. समन्त...ह्रदे—As to the extirpation of the क्षत्रियs by परशुराम, see 'परशुराममिव क्षत्रक्षपणक्षीणपरशुपाशचिह्नितं' हर्ष०4th उ० and notes thereon. परशुराम accumulated the blood of the slaughtered क्षत्रियs in five lakes. 'त्रिःसप्तकृत्वा पृथिवीं कृत्वा निःक्षत्रियां प्रभुः। समन्तपञ्चके पञ्च चकार रुधिरह्रदान्॥ स तेषु तर्पयामास भृगून् भृगुकुलोद्वहः।' वनपर्व 117. 9-10; see also आदिपर्व 2. 3-5. Bāṇa very frequently refers to the story of परशुराम. समन्तपञ्चक was in कुरुक्षेत्र. Compare 'जामदग्न्येन च शाम्यन्मन्युशिखिशिखासज्वरसुखायमानस्पर्शशीतलेषु क्षत्रियक्षतजह्रदेष्वस्नायि' हर्ष० 6th उ०. तथा...पद्यन्त they assented with the words 'let it be so'.

P. 41 ll. 19—32 **अथ...गच्छत्.** The first sentence is 'अथ...प्रदोषारम्भे...बन्धुभिश्च सार्धं तयैव गोष्ठया तस्थौ (बाणः). मधुमदेन (by the intoxication of wine) पल्लविताः (reddish) मालवीकपोलाः तद्वत् कोमलः आतपः (glow) यस्य. मालवी a lady from Malva. मुकुलितेऽह्नि when the day had closed (*lit.* folded itself like a bud). कम...लम्बमाने when the sun hung down kissing darkness, being very red as though through the closing of the lotus plants. The idea is:—when the sun was about to set, the day lotuses closed their petals. The poet fancies that the sun, on finding that the कमलिनीs did not respond to his feelings, became angry (red) and began to kiss darkness instead (in revenge against the कमलिनीs). रवि...तमसि when darkness came hurrying on in the sky following the track of the horses of the Sun, as though it (तमः) were Yama's buffalo. The simple idea is that the east first became dark and that darkness gradually spread over the whole sky up to the western horizon. A buffalo is dark and Yama's buffalo must be particularly so. गृह...वल्कलेषु when the bark garments hanging from the roofs (पटलं) of the huts (कुटीरकः) of house ascetics were removed along with the patches (च्छेदः) of the red sunglow. Ascetics may wander from place to place or may have a fixed abode. They had exposed the garments for drying and removed them at nightfall. The lingering red glow also vanished. कलेः कल्मषं (पापं) मुष्णाति इति ०मुष् तस्मिन्. पुष्णाति *loc. sing* of *pr. p.* of पुष् 9th con. गगनं object of पुष्णाति. कलि...धूमे when the smoke issuing from the places where the sacred fire was kindled filled (*lit.* nourished) the sky, the smoke that removed the sins of the Kali age. सनियमे that had undertaken the performance of some vow. 'नियमस्तु स यत्कर्मानित्यमागन्तुसाधनम्' इत्यमरः. मौनव्रतं अस्ति अस्य इति ०व्रतिन्. वि...लोले restless because it was the time for amusing themselves (by moving about here and there). Just when the sun went down, the house-wives had some time which they spent in strolling about. विकीर्यमाणाः हरिताः श्यामाकशालिपूलिकाः यासाम् before whom were spread green bundles of the hay of श्यामाक corn. दुग्धासु that had been milked. कपिला a cow (from its tawny colour). वैतान sacrificial (from वितान). 'क्रतुविस्तारयोरस्त्री वितानम्' इत्यमरः. तनूनपात् = अग्निः (तनूं देहं न पातयति इति). पूते विष्टरे (आसने) उपविष्टे. कृष्णाजिनेन जटिले looking hairy with antelope skin. जटिन् ascetic wearing matted hair. ब्रह्मासनं अध्यास्ते इति ०सिन्. ब्रह्मासन means a posture of the body for profound meditation. It seems that ब्रह्मासन was a generic name applicable to any आसन, such as पद्मासन. 'ध्यानयोगासने ब्रह्मासनम्' अमरः (ब्रह्मणः सम्बन्धि आसनं ब्रह्मासनम्; ध्यानस्य योगः उपायः ध्यानमेव योगः इति वा तस्यासनम्). Some define it as 'एकपादमुरौ दत्त्वा तिष्ठेद्दण्डाकृतिर्भवेत्'. तालध्वनिभिः धावमानाः अन्तेवासिनः शिष्याः यस्मिन्. The meaning is that the disciples came running and clapping their hands (as boys would do) or that the disciples came running, being called by the clapping of their preceptors' hands. अलस...मतेन under the supervision (*lit.* with the permission) of languid and old teachers of the Veda. गलन्तः ग्रन्थदण्डकाः तान् उद्गिरति इति or गलन्तः ग्रन्थदण्डकाः यथा

स्युः तथा उद्गिरति इति that recited (*lit.* emitted) disconnected lines (दण्डकः) of the text or that recited the texts in such a way that many lines were dropped (in the effort to recite). The idea seems to be this:—naughty and dull boys were called upon by their wearied old teachers to perform सन्ध्यावन्दन either by repeating what the teacher would himself first pronounce or by repeating what they had been taught before. In this process the careless boys omitted certain portions and loudly repeated the rest. The old and wearied preceptors did not seem to notice the lapses of the students. सन्ध्यां...यति that listened to the evening prayer. The reading समवधीरयति is in one way better, meaning 'that treated with contempt the evening prayer.' वठरः dullard; compare 'मुनिनाथोऽपि...कृपावानात्मानं वठरसत्त्वेभ्यः कतिकृत्वो न दत्तवान्' हर्ष० 8th उ०. विटः sensualist, dandy. तारका आख्या (name) यस्य (*adj.* of ज्योतिषि). समुन्म...खे (*lit.*) when in the sky (खं) emerged the lights called stars *i. e.* when the stars began to twinkle. तयै...तस्थौ he stood in the same company (as before). नीतः प्रथमः यामः (प्रहरः) येन who passed the first part of the night. गणपतेः—गणपति was one of the four cousins of बाण mentioned above (text p. 39 l. 30). निमीलिता (closed) दृक् (eye) येषां. अनुपजाता निद्रा येषाम्—They could not sleep (through expectant curiosity) though they closed their eyes. सूर्यो...लयताम् that waited for the rise of the sun. कमलs also close their buds at night and wait for सूर्योदय when they bloom.

P. 41 l. 33—**P. 42** l. 12 अथ...रेभे. तुर्ये चतुर्थे. प्रतिबुद्धः waking up. **Verse 5.** This is cited by the काव्यप्रकाश as an instance of the figure स्वभावोक्ति. For जाति or स्वभावोक्ति *vide* notes p. 4. The principal sentence is तुरङ्गः क्ष्मां (पृथ्वीं) खुरेण विलिखति (paws, scratches). पश्चा...सार्यं having stretched his foot behind. त्रिक...मुच्चैः having lengthened out upwards his body that was stretched (to full length) by bending the lower part of the spine. 'पृष्ठवंशाधरे त्रिकम्' अमरः (पृष्ठास्थ्नोऽध ऊर्वोः सन्धौ त्रिसङ्घट्टस्त्रिकम्—क्षीर०). विततं *adj.* of अङ्गम् or we may take it as an अव्ययीभाव. त्रिकस्य नत्या विततं यथा स्यात्तथा. द्राघयति is a denominative verb from दीर्घ. आस...रसि with bent (आभुग्न) neck having rested his mouth on his chest. सटां...धूय having tossed his mane grey with dust. घासः fodder. अनवरतं चलत् प्रोथं यस्य तत् अ...प्रोथं ०त्प्रोथं तुण्डं यस्य सः ०तुण्डः (nostril). 'घोणा तु प्रोथमस्त्रियाम्' अमरः. मन्दं शब्दायमानः gently neighing. शब्दं करोति इति शब्दायते, according to 'शब्दवैरकलहाभ्रकण्वमेघेभ्यः करणे' पा. 3. 1. 17. The metre is स्रग्धरा. **Verse 6.**

कुर्वन् (तुरङ्गः)—the object is कन्धराम् (neck). आभुग्नं पृष्ठं यस्य. मुख...कटिः bringing his loins near his mouth. आतिरश्चीम् curved sideways. लोलेना...केसरेण that (कोण) was struck with his restless and waving mane that dropped down particles of dew (तुहिनं). केसर is that part of the mane which is on the forehead. निद्रा...कषायम् that was reddish through the itch after sleep (or through sleep and itch). कषति—the subject is तुरङ्गः and the object is कोणम्. निबिडिता श्रोत्रशुक्तिः येन that closed his shell-like ears (with his mane). त्वङ्गन्ति पक्ष्माग्राणि तेषु लग्नाः प्रतनुबुसकणाः यस्मिन् (the corner of the eye) on the restless lashes of which stuck small particles of chaff. खुरेण—is to be connected with कषति. The metre is स्रग्धरा. ज्ञातयः=बान्धवाः. पूर्वो...प्रायः who understood their intention by the discussion that had already taken place. उद्धातः allusion, reference.

P. 42 l. 13—**P. 43** l. 12. **श्रूयताम्...जनपदः.** The principal sentence is अस्ति...श्रीकण्ठो नाम जनपदः. पुण्य...तीर्णः which was inhabited by the meritorious, as though it were the abode (आवासः) of Indra descended upon the earth. पुण्यकृत् also means 'gods'. It was believed that those who accumulated merit by the performance of sacrifices went to Indra's heaven and returned to the earth when their merit was exhausted. Compare 'त्रैविद्या मां सोमपाः पूतपापा यज्ञैरिष्ट्वा स्वर्गतिं प्रार्थयन्ते । ते **पुण्यमासाद्य सुरेन्द्रलोक**मश्नन्ति दिव्यान्दिवि देवभोगान् ॥ ते तं भुक्त्वा स्वर्गलोकं विशालं क्षीणे पुण्ये मर्त्यलोकं विशन्ति ।' भगवद्गीता Chap. IX. 20–21. असङ्कीर्णे वर्णानां व्यवहारस्थिती (व्यवहारः स्थितिश्च) यस्मिन् where the practices and usages of the (four) Varṇas were not confused. कृतयुगस्येव व्यवस्था यस्मिन्. In कृतयुग there was no वर्णसङ्कर, nor was there any in the country of श्रीकण्ठ. If we read कृतकृत०, then we dissolve as कृता कृतयुगस्य व्यवस्था यस्मिन्. स्थल...क्षेत्रः abounding as it did in land lotuses, its fields were broken by ploughs (हलम्) the points (पोत्रं) of which uprooted lotus fibres and which caused a humming of bees, as though they (हल) sang the excellent (सार) qualities of the soil. स्थलकमल—distinguish them from water-lotuses, that are simply कमलs. पोत्रैः उन्मूल्यमानानि मृणालानि येषाम्. **'मुखाग्रे क्रोडहलयोः** पोत्रम्' अमरः. उद्गीताः मेदिन्याः साराः गुणाः यैः. There is a श्लेष on the word गुण (quality, string). The मृणालs are गुणs. The poet fancies that the hum of bees on the lotuses that were uprooted is a song declaring the fertility of the soil. उल्लिख्यमानानि क्षेत्राणि यस्य. क्षीरो...न्तरः that was dense with rows of plantations (वाटः–टम्) of Puṇḍra sugarcane, as though they

(rows) were watered by clouds that had drunk the waters of the milky ocean. पुण्ड्र is a very sweet variety of sugar-cane. The poet fancies that the sweetness must be due to their being watered by clouds from क्षीरसागर (and not from the salt ocean). It is a general rule that the qualities of effects arise from similar qualities in their causes. Compare 'कारणगुणपूर्वकः कार्यगुणो दृष्टः' वैशेषिकसूत्र II. 1. 24 or the न्याय 'कारणगुणा हि कार्यगुणानारभन्ते.' प्रति...सीमान्तः the borders of which were in every direction crowded (सङ्कट) with heaps of corn, as though they were strange hills, separated (from each other) by threshing floors. खलधानं threshing floor. धामन् *n.* place. The heaps were big like hills. The com. says 'खलधानधामभिः खलपालैः' *i. e.* it takes it to mean 'by the owners or watchmen of the threshing floors.' (खलधानं धाम येषाम्). This is not good. सम...भूमिः the ground of which was thickly covered (जटिलित) with beds of cumin seed (जीरकः) being watered by the pots of the water-wheel. क्षीर० says that, according to कौटिल्य, उद्घातन means 'घटीयन्त्र.' We must ascribe the same sense to उद्घात. 'उद्घाटनं घटीयन्त्रम्' अमरः. उर्वरा...कृतः adorned with rice fields extending (beyond their proper limits) on account of the very fertile soil. 'उर्वरा सर्वसस्याढ्या' अमरः. For शालेय see p. 118. वरीयः is the comparative of उरु. The idea is:—the land surrounding the rice fields also was fertile and so beyond the fields proper grew ricecrops due to the fact that some grains were carried away by the birds or by the ants and grew luxuriantly there. पाक...छितः that had stretches of wheat fields (गोधूमधामन्) variegated (किर्मीरित) by heaps of *Rājamāsha* beans bursting as they were ripe and rendered brown (कपिशित) by the split pods of *mudga.* मुद्ग is Marathi मूग. पाकेन विशरारवः राजमाषाः तेषां निकरैः किर्मीरितानि तैः. The next clause is महिष...विपिनः. महिषपृष्ठे प्रतिष्ठिताः (mounted) गायन्तः गोपालाः तैः पालितानि तैः *(adj.* of गोधनैः). कीट...सृतैः (गोधनैः) that were followed by sparrows greedy (लम्पट) for the swarms of insects. The insects (probably flies) pursued the cows (as they had ulcers on their backs or feet &c.) and were in their turn pursued by चटकाs. अवटुः (ग्रीवा) तस्यां घटिताः घण्टाः एव घट्यः तासां रटितेन रमणीयैः charming with the tinkling of jar-like bells bound round their necks. 'कम्बुग्रीवा त्रिरेखा सावटुर्घाटा कृकाटिका' अमरः. अटद्भिरटवीं that wandered over the forest. क्षर...क्षरद्भिः that dropped milk (from their udders), as though it (milk) were the milky ocean drunk by the bull of S'iva and then distributed in many places (*viz.* the cows) for fear of disease (*i. e.* indigestion). बाष्प...तृणैः that were fed on very tender grass. बाष्प...तृण means 'grass that can be cut with tears' *i. e.* very soft and tender. Note 'कृत्यैरधिकार्थवचने' पा. 2. 1. 33. (स्तुतिनिन्दाफलकमर्थवादवचनमधिकार्थवचनं तत्र कर्तरि करणे च तृतीया कृत्यैः सह प्राग्वत् । वातच्छेद्यं तृणम् । काकपेया नदी । सि. कौ.). कृत्य means potential participles. 'गोधनं स्याद्गवां व्रजे' अमरः. धवलितानि विपिनानि यस्य. The cows were white. विविध...देशः the districts (उद्देशः) of which were variegated with black antelopes in thousands, as though they were the eyes let fall (from heaven on earth) by Indra (शतमन्युः) blinded by the smoke of the offerings of various sacrifices. शतं मन्यवः क्रतवः अस्य इति शतमन्युः. Indra also has a 1000 eyes; eyes are कृष्णशार (dark and variegated). The pupil is dark, while the corners of the eye are reddish and the other part is white; hence the word कृष्णशार. For the 1000 eyes of इन्द्र *vide* 'सहस्रनेत्रदर्शनयोग्यां जयन्तीमिव शची' हर्ष० 4th उ० and notes thereon. धवल...शोभितः adorned with regions whitened with the pollen of *Ketakī* groves that scattered about white dust, as though they (regions) were the entrances of the city of S'iva grey with the ashes sprinkled over the lord of प्रमथs. प्रमथs are the attendants of शिव. उद्धूलनम् smearing the body with ashes. शिव is represented as fond of this. शाककन्दलैः श्यामलितानि ग्रामाणां उपकण्ठे (समीपे) काश्यपीपृष्ठानि यस्मिन्. शाककन्दलैः with the shoots of vegetables; or 'with vegetables and plantains.' काश्यपी—the earth, so called because परशुराम, after vanquishing the क्षत्रियs, made a gift of it to कश्यप. 'क्षोणी ज्या काश्यपी क्षितिः' अमरः. करभपालीभिः with rows of young camels. Understand उपलक्षितः after this, in accordance with the Sūtra 'इत्थम्भूतलक्षणे' पा. 2. 3. 21. For करभ, mark the Sūtra 'शृङ्खलमस्य बन्धनं करभे' पा. 5. 2. 79. (शृङ्खलकः करभः). The instrumentals from ०प्रस्फोटितैः to ०पथिकैः qualify द्राक्षामण्डपैः. पीलुपल्लवैः प्रस्फोटितं येषु—where (the dust on the feet of travellers) was rubbed off with the tender leaves of the Pīlu tree. For this use of प्रस्फोटित compare 'पथिकपादप्रस्फोटनधूलिधूसरैर्नवपल्लवैर्लाञ्छितच्छायानाम् (अटवीप्रवेशप्रपाणां)' हर्ष० 7th उ० last para; 'विश्रान्तकार्पटिकप्रस्फोटितचरणधूलिधूसरकिसलयलाञ्छितोपकण्ठैः' कादम्बरी p. 223 of P. प्रस्फोटित may also mean 'pierced.' The com. says 'प्रस्फोटितैर्नीराजनीकृतैः.' करपुटैः पीडितानि (squeezed) मातुलुङ्गीदलानि (citron leaves) तेषां रसेन उपलिप्तैः besmeared. मातुलुङ्गी is Marathi महाळुंग. स्वेच्छया विचिताः कुङ्कुमकेसराः तैः कृतः पुष्पप्रकरः येषु—where the saffron filaments gathered at their pleasure (by the travellers) served as the offering of flowers. प्रत्यग्राणां (fresh) फलानां रसः तस्य पानेन सुखसुप्ताः पथिकाः येषु. वन...गृहैरिव—the poet fancies that the vine arbours under which the travellers rested were as though the water-hostels where nectar was given by wood nymphs. The juice of the sweet grapes that the travellers eat is like nectar. The words from ०प्रस्फोटितैः to ०पथिकैः suggest certain characteristics of a प्रपागृह (Marathi पाणपोई). The dust in a प्रपा may be cleared away with पल्लवs; it may be उपलिप्त with cowdung as green as मातुलुङ्गीदलरस. Offerings of flowers (पुष्पप्रकरः) are made on the floor of प्रपाs. Travellers take rest after drinking water (रसपान) there. द्राक्षामण्डपैः—is to be connected with विलो... र्गमः. स्फुटन्ति (bursting open) फलानि यासाम्—*adj.* of दाडिमीनां. बीजलग्नः शुकचञ्चुरागः यासाम्. The reddish grains of the pomegranate look like the red beaks of parrots. The poet fancies that the redness of beaks stuck to the seeds, when parrots pecked the फलs. समारूढं कपिकुलं तस्य कपोलैः सन्दिह्यमानानि कुसुमानि यासाम्. The flowers of the pomegranate trees looked like the cheeks of the monkeys that had climbed them, so that one had difficulty in distinguishing them. विलोभनीयाः उपनिर्गमाः यस्य the approaches to which (country of श्रीकण्ठ) were fascinating. वनपालैः पीयमानः नारिकेलरसासवः (the wine of cocoanut juice) येषु— *adj.* of उपवनैः. पथिकलोकेन लुप्यमानाः (pillaged) पिण्डखर्जूराः (datetrees) येषु *adj.* of उपवनैः. गोलाङ्गूलैर्लिह्यमानः मधुरामोदः (मधुरः आमोदः यस्य) पिण्डीरसः येषु. पिण्डी is a kind of palm tree. For गोलाङ्गूल, see p. 54. ०चञ्चुभिः जर्जरिताः आरुकाः येषु. आरुकः a plant growing in the हिमालय with cooling properties. ०वृतैः—*adj.* of ०बन्धैः. अर्जुन is a kind of tree. गोकुलानां अवतारेण कलुषितं कूलकीलालं येषाम्—the water on the edges of which was rendered turbid by the descent of herds of kine. अध्वगः a traveller. शरण्य that afforded refuge. शरणे साधुः शरण्यः, according to 'तत्र साधुः' पा. 4. 4. 98. अरण्यधराबन्धैः forest pools. अवन्ध्यानि वनरन्ध्राणि यस्मिन् the hollows (or valleys) in the forests of which are not barren (on account of pools). करभेभ्यो हितः करभीयः; *vide* notes on शङ्कव्य and वत्सीय p. 94. उष्ट्राणां (camels) समूहः औष्ट्रकम्, उरभ्राणां (rams) समूहः औरभ्रकम्, according to 'गोत्रोक्षोष्ट्रोरभ्रराजराजन्यराजपुत्रवत्समनुष्याजाद्वुञ्' पा. 4. 2. 39 (एभ्यः समूहे वुञ् स्यात्). *Vide* औक्षक p. 166. कृतः सम्बाधः (crowd) यस्मिन्. In the next clause दिशि...चितः, the principal part is वडवानां...चितः full of the wandering droves of mares (वडवा). विलो...लब्धानाम् that were smeared with the juice of saffron plots that were crushed

(मृदित) by their rolling (विलोठनं) on them. समालब्ध 'smeared with unguents'. For the rolling of horses on saffron spots, compare रघु. 4. 67. विनीताध्वश्रमास्तस्य सिन्धुतीरविचेष्टनैः । दुधुवुर्वाजिनः स्कन्धाँल्लग्नकुङ्कुमकेसरान् ॥.' The poet fancies that the mares were smeared with saffron and wandered about (as अभिसारिकाs would do) for seducing the horses (seven) of the Sun. उत्प्रोथपुटैः and उन्मुखैः are equivalent to उद्गतप्रोथ॰ and उद्गतमुखैः—with their up-turned nostrils and mouths. उदर...पिबन्तीनाम्—the poet fancies that the mares turned up their noses because they wanted to take in the wind (प्रभञ्जनः) for the purpose of producing speed in the young lying in their wombs. वातहरिणीनामिव–This word has several senses. वातहरिण is a very swift kind of deer. The wind-gods (Maruts) are supposed to be drawn by deer. पृषदश्व is a synonym of वात. The word may also suggest the sense 'that surpass the wind (in speed)'. अनवरतानां क्रतूनां धूमः तेन अन्धकारः तस्मिन् प्रवृत्तैः that were produced (kindled) in the darkness of the smoke of &c. बाणैः—fires. हंसs have white wings and hence the fires are fancied to be हंसयूथs. हंसs move about in the dark (अन्धकार) resembling the smoke &c. There is an apparent विरोध between अन्धकारप्रवृत्तैः and धवलितभुवनः. What springs from darkness cannot whiten the world. If we read गुणैः for बाणैः, then the meaning is similar. By the performance of क्रतुs, merit is produced. पुण्य and यशः are poetically said to be white. सङ्गीत...लोकः with the vast resources (prosperity) of which the mortal world resounded, as though with peacocks intoxicated by the sound of drums. ॰मुरजः a drum beaten in a concert. Peacocks are overjoyed when it thunders. They mistook मुरजरव for thunder. Another sense is suggested by सङ्गीत...मत्तैः—the wealth of the people was so vast that they were mad after singing &c. शशि...वृत्तैः whose conduct was as pure (अवदात) as the rays of the moon (with virtuous men); that were round (वृत्त) and bright like the rays of the moon (with pearls). गुणिभिः (with pearls) would also mean 'that were strung together.' प्रसाधितः adorned. पथिकशतैः विलुप्यमानानि (pillaged) स्फीतानि (abundant) फलानि येषाम् (with trees); ॰विलुप्यमानं स्फीतं फलं (ऐश्वर्यं येषाम्)—the guests obtained plenty of money in that country, which (money) was distributed by them among other travellers. अभिगमनीयः sought for (by all guests); inviting (with big trees). मृग...कृतः that was steadied (protected) by the headmen of villages (महत्तरः) clad in garments of deer-skin bearing the fragrance of musk, as though they were the hills at the foot of the हिमालय. For मृगमद, see p. 51. मृग...दितैः (with ०पादैः) means 'covered with the hair of the deer scented with' &c. The musk-deer is found in the Himālaya range. महत्तरैः with ०पादैः means 'very large.' 'पादाः प्रत्यन्तपर्वताः' अमरः. महत्तर as the name of an officer occurs in numerous grants (compare I. A. vol. VIII p. 20 and vol. XII p. 25). The word occurs in the 7th उच्छ्वास also. प्रोद्दण्ड...त्तमैः on the lotuses of which with upraised stalks were seatd the best of birds (with reservoirs of water); on the lotus of which with upraised stalk was seated Brahmā (with the navel of Vishṇu). 'सहस्रपत्रं कमलम्' इत्यमरः. For नारायणनाभि, see notes pp. 20 and 28 above. For द्विजोत्तम as meaning ब्रह्मा, see 'द्विजवरस्वेच्छागृहीतकोषो नाभिपद्म इव' हर्ष० 4th उ० first para. प्रोद्दण्ड...मण्डितः also conveys another sense. The best of Brāhmanas in thousands sat on thousands of leaves near the lakes in that country for perfoming सन्ध्यावन्दन &c. मथितः...क्षितिभिः where the ground (or earth) was washed with streams of churned milk (with महाघोषैः aud ०रम्भैः). मथितं also means 'buttermilk.' 'तक्रं ह्युदश्विन्मथितं पादाम्बर्धाम्बु निर्जलम्' अमरः. महाघोषः a big hamlet of cowherds. महान् घोषः (uproar) येषु (*adj.* of रम्भैः). At the time when the gods and demons began to churn there must have been a great uproar. पूरिताशः the regions of which were filled (with जनपदः). The directions were filled with great uproar at the time of churning or the effort of churning satisfied the hopes (of the gods and demons). जनपदः a country.

P. 43 ll. 13—21. **यत्र...दैवम्.** यत्र...दृष्टयः where wrong doctrines faded away, as though washed by the water of the tears due to the smoke of the three fires. 'दक्षिणाग्निर्गार्हपत्याहवनीयौ त्रयोऽग्नयः। अग्नित्रयमिदं त्रेता' अमरः. As the people stuck to Vedic rites, heresies departing from the Veda ceased to exist. कुदृष्टयः also 'weak eyesight.' Weak eyesight may be cured by medicines applied to the eye, which cause the eye to drop tears. पच्य...दुरितानि sins were not seen (*i. e.* vanished) as though burnt by the fire of the bricks (इष्टका) that were being baked for constructing altars. As the people were virtuous, no sins were committed. The poet fancies that sins vanished because they were consumed &c. Explain the following उत्प्रेक्षाs similarly. छिद्यमानं यूपाय दारु येन सः ०दारुः परशुः तेन पाटितः cleft. मख...धौत इव as though washed by the streams of the clouds made up of the smoke of sacrificial fires (शिखिन् *m.*). For clouds being formed of smoke, see notes p. 106. वर्णसङ्कर: (a combination of colours) may be washed with water and then no colour would remain. सुरा...इव as though cut up by numerous chisels (टङ्क:) for shaping (घट्टनं) the stones of the temples. 'टङ्क: पाषाणदारण:' अमर:. महा...द्रवा: calamities ran away, as though routed by the tumult of the making of महादानs. महादान is a name of certain very munificent gifts (16 in number), the first being तुलापुरुषदान. उपद्रव: a misfortune or national calamity (such as a famine). दीप्य...पिता इव as though heated by thousands of blazing kitchens in the great sacrifices. 'सत्रमाच्छादने यज्ञे' अमर:. वृष...त्रासिता: इव as though frightened by the sharp sound of the holy drums beaten at the marriages of bulls. On the eleventh day after the death of a person, a bull is let loose along with cows, which is called वृषोत्सर्ग or वृषविवाह. 'एकादशाहे प्रेतस्य यस्य चोत्सृज्यते वृष: । प्रेतलोकं परित्यज्य स्वर्गलोकं स गच्छति ॥.' अपमृत्यव: untimely deaths. ब्रह्मघोष = वेदघोष. 'वेदस्तत्त्वं तपो ब्रह्म' अमर:. ईतय:—Distress or calamity. ईतिs are usually said to be six. 'अतिवृष्टिरनावृष्टिर्मूषिका: शलभा: शुका: । अत्यासन्नाश्च राजान: षडेता ईतय: स्मृता: ॥.' क्षीर०. शलभा: locusts. अत्यासन्ना: राजान: extreme proximity of kings (*i. e.* encampment of soldiers, whether hostile or friendly). धर्मा... दैवम् As the sole अधिकार (power) rested with धर्म, दुर्दैव could not become a प्रभु (lord) in that country.

P. 43 ll. 22—31. तत्र...विशेष:. The principal sentence is तत्र च एवंविधे...स्थाण्वीश्वराख्यो जनपदविशेष:. नाना आरामा: (gardens) तेषां अभिराम: ०परिमल: तेन सुभग: (with ०विशेष:). नाना रामा: (beautiful women) अभिरामा: ०परिमलाश्च तै: सुभग: (with यौवनारम्भ:). As youth is the most charming period of one's life, so the country was the most charming in the world. कुङ्कुम...शोभित: decked with many thousands of buffaloes reddened (पिञ्जरित) by crushing (*i. e.* rolling in) saffron (with country); decked with many thousands of crowned queens (महिषी) reddened with saffron unguents (with अन्त:पुरनिवेश:). अन्त:...धर्मस्य—As the अन्त:पुर is a spot loved by a king, where he moves about freely and confidently, so in that country धर्म reached its highest pitch. मरुता (वातेन) उद्धूयमानानि ०व्यजनानि तेषां शतै: धवलिता: प्रान्ता: यस्य (with the country); मरुत्सु (देवेषु) उद्धूयमानानि (being waved) ०व्यजनानि &c. In the country roamed चमरी deer the tails of which were shaken by the wind. In heaven (सुरराज्य) chowries are waved before gods. ज्वलन्त: मखशिखिन: तेषां सहस्रै: दीप्यमाना: दश दिगन्ता:

यस्मिन्. As thousands of sacrifices were performed, a vast store of merit was accumulated. In कृतयुग also there was vast merit. So the country is fancied to be an encampment. In a camp also fires blaze forth at night. Or the reference may be to the fires in the नीराजन ceremony of the camp. *Vide* p. 34. The com. shows that कृतयुग also means 'king'. 'कृतं प्रतिसमाहितं युगं द्वयं स्वपक्षपरपक्षरूपं येन स राजोच्यते.' पद्ममेव आसनं तस्मिन् स्थितः ब्रह्मर्षिः(ब्रह्मा चासौ ऋषिश्च) तस्य ध्यानेन आधीयमानः (brought about) सकलस्य अकुशलस्य (evil, calamity) प्रशमः यस्मिन् (with अवतारः); पद्मासनं आसनभेदः तस्मिन् स्थिताः ब्रह्मर्षयः तेषां ध्यानेन &c. Brahmā sits on the lotus in the navel of विष्णु. For ब्रह्मा warding off evil, compare 'त्रिभुवनोपप्लवप्रशमकुशापीडधारिणेव दक्षिणेन करेण' (text) p. 4. l. 20. In the country there were ब्रह्मर्षिs (saintly Brāhmaṇas) sitting in the *yogic* posture called पद्मासन. In this आसन the right foot is placed on the left thigh and the left foot on the right thigh; the toes are to be firmly held by the hands; the chin is to be on the heart and one has to look at the tip of the nose. 'वामोरूपरि दक्षिणं च चरणं संस्थाप्य वामं तथा दक्षोरूपरि पश्चिमेन विधिना धृत्वा कराभ्यां दृढम् । अङ्गुष्ठौ हृदये निधाय चिबुकं नासाग्रमालोकयेदेतद्व्याधिविनाशकारि यमिनां पद्मासनं प्रोच्यते ॥ हठयोगप्रदीपिका. महावाहिनी great river; great army. विपक्ष...कुरूणाम् that was as though the enemy (*i. e.* the rival) of the country of उत्तरकुरु. An enemy (विपक्ष) has large armies. In the country described there were both large armies and large rivers. उत्तरकुरु is one of the four द्वीपs near मेरु (भीष्मपर्व 6. 13). The great river there is the Ganges. 'दक्षिणेन तु नीलस्य मेरोः पार्श्वे तथोत्तरे । उत्तराः कुरवो राजन् पुण्याः सिद्धनिषेविताः॥' भीष्मपर्व 7. 2. If we read विक्षेपः the meaning is 'that throws off (into the background) *i. e.* surpasses.' वि...पुरस्य like the conqueror of the three cities *i. e.* like S'iva; that desired to conquer (*i. e.* that equalled in splendour) the three cities of the Asuras (with the country). For त्रिपुरदाह, see p. 113 above. ईश्वरः शिवः तस्य मार्गणाः बाणाः तैः सन्तापः तस्य अनभिज्ञाः सकलजनाः यस्मिन्; ईश्वरस्य नृपस्य मार्गणं तस्य &c. The idea in the latter case is either that the people of that country did not know the harassment due to the exacting demands of the king or that they did not know how to solicit favours from the king. सुधारसेन (by *chunam* or whitewash) सिक्तानि धवलगृहाणि तेषां पङ्क्त्या पाण्डुरः. The country had whitewashed houses and so resembled moonlight. In चन्द्रलोक there must be houses sprinkled with nectar (as the moon is full of सुधा). मधुमत्ताः (intoxicated by drink) मत्तकाशिन्यः (handsome and fascinating women) तेषां भूषणरवेण भरितं भुवनं यस्मिन्. मत्तकाशिनी—मत्ता क्षीबा इव काशते भाति इति मत्तकाशिनी. The com. says that मत्तकाशिनी also means 'यक्षिणी'. यक्षs are the servants of कुबेर. नामाभिहारः carrying away the name (and depositing it in another place) *i. e.* a synonym. As there was the jingling of the ornaments of मत्तकाशिनीs, the country was a synonym of कुबेरनगर. स्थाण्वीश्वरः—the modern Thanesar. जन...शेषः—श्रीकण्ठ was a large country of which स्थाण्वीश्वर was a part.

P. 43 l. 32—**P. 44** l. 6. **यस्तपो...गृह्यत.** The principal sentence is यः...अगृह्यत. We have to supply अगृह्यत in each clause. कामायतनम् abode of Cupid or the temple of Cupid. लासकैः = नटैः. यम...शुभिः—the country was so well guarded that enemies were as much afraid of it as of Death. For चिन्तामणि, see above p. 135. वीरक्षेत्रम् It was the home of heroes. गन्धर्वनगरम्–गन्धर्वs are the musicians of the gods. गायनैः by singers. विश्वकर्मा—is the architect of the gods and presides over all arts. विज्ञानिभिः by artisans, by those skilled in the 64 arts. 'मोक्षे धीर्ज्ञानमन्यत्र विज्ञानं शिल्पशास्त्रयोः' अमरः. वैदेहकैः = वणिग्भिः. 'वैदेहकः सार्थवाहो नैगमो वाणिजो वणिक्' अमरः. द्यूत...बन्दिभिः—bards looked upon it as a gambling house. In a gambling house fortunes are made (and also lost) in a day. Bards were richly rewarded in that country. विट...दग्धैः by sharpwitted men (or crafty) it was looked upon as a club of clever voluptuaries. सुकृतपरिणामः as the fulfilment (ripening) of their good deeds. Travellers got there everything they desired. It is only through one's good deeds in former lives that one is so fortunate as to secure whatever one desires. असुरविवरम्—*vide* notes p. 90. वातिकैः—com. paraphrases as 'विवरव्यसनिभिराचार्यैः.' Probably there is a pun on the word वातिक which means 'mad' and 'those whose heads are turned by the thought of amassing money.' Mad men are confined in dark places. That country gave as much money to fortune-hunters as असुरविवर was supposed to yield. शा...भिः it was looked upon as a Buddhist monastery by those who wanted tranquility of mind. महोत्सवसमाजः concourse of people on a great festival. चारणैः wandering actors (देशान्तरभ्रमणाज्जीवति इति चारणः). वसुधारा stream of wealth. Munificent gifts were made to Brāhmaṇas in that country.

P. 44 ll.7—11 **यत्र च...प्रमदाः.** In this paragraph, each adjective independently qualifies प्रमदाः. Further in each pair of adjectives there is an apparent contradiction due to श्लेष. मातङ्गगामिन्यः possessing the gait of elephants; having sexual intercourse with chaṇḍālas. 'चण्डालप्लवमातङ्गदिवाकीर्तिजनङ्गमाः ।' अमरः. If they were मातङ्ग० (in the 2nd sense), they could not be शीलवत्यः (of pure conduct). गौर्यः fair; Gaurîs (पार्वती). विभवरताः attached to pomp and luxury; attached to a place where no शिव existed. विगतः भवः यस्मात् तस्मिन् रताः. If they were पार्वती, they must be भवरत (and not विभवरत). श्यामाः handsome; dark. श्यामा is a handsome lady described as 'शीते सुखोष्णसर्वाङ्गी ग्रीष्मे या सुखशीतला । तप्तकाञ्चनवर्णाभा सा स्त्री श्यामेति कथ्यते ॥'. पद्म० decked with rubies; having the colour of (red) lotus. What is dark cannot be red. श्यामाः also means 'nights' and पद्मरागिण्यः would mean 'loving lotuses.' Nights cannot love day lotuses. धवल... वदनाः whose faces are bright with white teeth; whose mouths are pure like those of pure Brāhmaṇas. मदि...सनाः whose breath is fragrant like wine; whose breath...with wine. If they drank wine, their mouths could not be pure. Wine-drinking was forbidden to all, particularly to Brāhmaṇas. *Vide* notes above p. 160. चन्द्र...वपुषः whose bodies are charming like the moon; whose bodies are (hard) like the चन्द्रकान्त stone. शिरीष is a very delicate flower. अ...गम्याः not to be approched by gallants; not to be approached by serpents. कञ्चुकिन्यः wearing a bodice; female serpents (*lit.* possessed of slough). कञ्चुकिन्यः also means 'libidinous.' पृथु...श्रियः whose glory as wives spread far and wide (also 'whose beautiful hips are broad'); whose retinue of women is large. 'कलत्रं श्रोणिभार्ययोः' अमरः. दरिद्र...लिताः possessed of a slender waist; counted among the poor. लावण्यवत्यः possessed of beauty; possessed of salt. अप्रमत्ताः not rash or careless; not intoxicated. प्रसन्नः (clear) उज्ज्वलः रागः (colour) यासाम्; प्रसन्नावत् उज्ज्वलः रागः येषाम्. प्रसन्ना means 'wine.' *Vide* notes p. 143 on प्रसन्ना. अकौतुकाः that did not wear the marriage thread; that were free from (girlish) curiosity. For the meaning of कौतुक compare रघु० 8. 1 'अथ तस्य विवाहकौतुकं ललितं बिभ्रत एव पार्थिवः'. Being grown up (प्रौढ) they must once have worn the marriage thread.

P. 44 l. 12—24 **यत्र च...परिजनाः.** In this passage the poet describes that the women possessed naturally those things which they had added by way of decoration and so the latter were really superfluous. चक्षु...दामानि their very eyes are a natural wreath for the head, the garlands of lotus petals are

प्रजापति. *Vide* notes p. 18. The प्रजापतिs were entrusted with the task of creating all sorts of beings. सर्वादि०—It will be noticed that in this passage famous primeval kings like पृथु are associated with the limbs and qualities of the king पुष्पभूति.

P. 45 ll. 1–23 **पृथुना...दर्शनम्.** पृथुना...कृता—for this legend, *vide* notes p. 176. इति therefore. स्पर्धमान इव as if vying with (पृथु). महिषी crowned queen; she-buffalo. निसर्ग...मतिः the minds of the great are by nature unrestrained and follow their own likings. अनुपदिष्टा (*adj.* of भक्तिः) untaught. भुवनभृति (*adj.* of भवे) who upholds the worlds. भूतभावने who creates all beings. भवच्छिदि that destroys the cycle of births and deaths. भवे = शिवे. 'जन्महरौ भवौ' अमरः. अकृतः वृषभध्वजस्य (शिवस्य) पूजाविधिः येन. अजरम् free from old age, never aging. अमरगुरुम् venerated by the gods. अपरिमितानां गणानां पतिम् the lord of innumerable attendants called गणs. अचलदुहितृ = पार्वती. ०नैः कृता चरणयोः नतिः यस्य. The student will notice that all the letters from अजम् to ०नतिम् are short, when the सन्धि rules are observed. पशुपतिं = शिवम्. प्रपन्नः devoted. भर्तृ...प्रकृतयः the dispositions of dependents follow the mind of their master. खण्डपरशुः = शिवः. ववुः अस्य... पुण्यविषयेषु वायवः in his holy country winds blew. ०गर्भः and the two following words qualify वायवः. होमालवाले (अग्निकुण्डे) विलीयमानः (melting) बहलः गुग्गुलुः तस्य गन्धः गर्भे येषाम्. For गुग्गुलु being burnt in the temples of शिव, *vide* notes p. 105. स्नपन... क्षारिणः that dropped particles (क्षोदः) of the spray of the milk for bathing (the images of शिव). For क्षीरस्नपन, *vide* notes p. 114. बिल्व...हिनः that carried along petals from the wreaths of *Bilva* leaves. शिव...चितैः proper in the worship of शिव. उपायनं a present (made personally). प्राभृतम् a present (sent with a messenger or servant). प्रकर्षेण आराधनार्थं आभ्रियते ढौक्यते स्म. पादोपजीविनः his dependents. करदीकृताः that were made to pay tribute (from करद one who pays tribute). तथाहि for instance. कैलास...वृषैः with huge bulls that were to be let loose in the evening worship (of शिव), white like the peaks of कैलास, the tips of whose horns were decked with golden figure-work. For पत्रलता, see notes on पत्रभङ्ग p. 24. Mr. R. R. Kale takes ०वृषैः to be stone or clay images of the bull of शिव; but there is very little warrant for this supposition. सन्ध्याबलिवृषैः bulls that were intended to be let loose as offerings in the evening worship of शिव. स्नपनकलश pitchers (for hoiding milk) for bathing (the image of शिव). अर्घभाजन vessels useful in worship. 'मूल्ये

पूजाविधावर्घः' अमरः. पुष्पपट्टैः cloths on which there were ornamental flowers woven in (with threads). मणि...प्रदीपैः lamps on jewelled sticks (stands). ब्रह्मसूत्रं = यज्ञोपवीतम्. महा... कोषैः cases (for covering शिवलिङ्ग) inlaid with pieces of very costly gems. 'मुखयुक्ताः कोषाः मुखकोषाः ये लिङ्गोपरि दीयन्ते' सं०. अन्तः पुराण्यपि...तस्य अभिलषितमन्ववर्तन्त his queens also complied with his desire. स्वयमारब्धं बालेयतण्डुलकण्डनं यैः that themselves threshed the rice used for making oblations (to शिव). बलये हिताः बालेयाः तण्डुलाः, according to 'छदिरुपधिबलेर्ढञ्' पा. 5. 1. 13. देवगृहस्य उपलेपनं (plastering with cowdung) तेन लोहिततराणि करकिसलयानि येषाम्. Their hands were already red; but the manual labour, to which the queens were not accustomed, made their palms redder. कुसुमग्रथने (in making wreaths) व्यग्रः समस्तः परिजनः येषाम्. परममाहेश्वरः a great devotee of शिव. हर्ष himself is called परममाहेश्वर; *vide* Intro. p. XXIX footnote. शुश्राव—the object is महाशैवम्. अपर... मथनम्—For the destruction of दक्ष's sacrifice *vide* notes p. 87. According to the भागवतपुराण (4th स्कन्ध 5th chap.) शिव produced from his जटा a terrific being called वीरभद्र that destroyed दक्ष's sacrifice. भैरव was the name of the S'aiva ascetic and भैरव is also one of the terrific forms of शिव. So the author says 'अपरमिव...मथनम्'. दाक्षिणात्य (from दक्षिणा with the affix त्यक्), according to 'दक्षिणापश्चात्पुरसस्त्यक्' पा. 4. 2. 98 (दक्षिणेत्याजन्तमव्ययम्). बहु...लोकम् who covered the world with thousands of good qualities, as though with pupils, that became far-famed by the mastery of various sciences. Read शीलसंवादाः. उप...वादाः Resemblance in character draws a person, though unseen, to one's heart (*i. e.* affection for him springs up even without seeing him). कपर्दिन्—कपर्दः जटाजूटः विद्यते अस्य इति कपर्दी शिवः. आच...दर्शनम् he desired even in his wishes to see him by all means. The emphasis lies on the word मनोरथैः. If we want to see a person, we may use a chariot (रथ) for that purpose. He employed even मनोरथ for that purpose.

P. 45 l. 24—**P. 46** l. 11. **अथ...पुण्डरीकाणि.** पर्यस्ते scattered about, fading. वासरे the day, the sun. नचिराच्च—the sentence here is नचिराच्च...मस्करिणमद्राक्षीत् (p. 46. l. 5). All the words in the accusative singular from प्रविशन्तं qualify मस्करिणम्. आजानुभुजम् whose arms reached his knees. Arms reaching the knees were looked upon as a sign of greatness. भैक्ष...लक्ष्यमाणम् though emaciated (क्षाम) by living on alms, he appeared to be fat (पीवर) on account of his limbs having stout bones. भैक्षम्—भिक्षाणां समूहो भैक्षम्, according to 'भिक्षादिभ्योऽण्' पा. 4. 2. 38. पृथु

उत्तमाङ्गं (शिरः) यस्य. If we read पृथुतमाङ्गम्, then dissolve as पृथुतमं अङ्गं (शरीरं) यस्य. उत्तुङ्गेन वलिभङ्गेन स्थपुटं ललाटं यस्य—whose forehead was undulating with prominent folds of wrinkles. 'स्थपुटं तु नतोन्नतम्' क्षीरस्वामी. निर्मांसः गण्डकूपकः यस्य. गण्डकूपक is the hollow beneath the eye and above the cheek. मधु...क्षम् whose eyes were round and brown like drops of honey. ई...घोणम whose nose (घोणा) was slightly curved. अतिप्रलम्बः एकः कर्णपाशः (प्रशस्तः कर्णः) यस्य one of whose ears hung down very much. अलाबु... पङ्क्तिम् the row of whose teeth was prominent and formidable (विकट) like the seeds of bottle-gourd. These seeds are white and long. तुरगानूकवत् श्लथा अधरलेखा यस्य whose lip was loose like the अनूक of a horse. According to the com. अनूक is the lower lip of a horse. अनूकः-कम् means 'backbone or spine.' लम्बेन चिबुकेन आयततरं लपनं (मुखं) यस्य whose mouth looked elongated on account of a hanging chin. काषाय red. For योगपट्टक, see p. 26 above. विरचितः वैकक्षकः यस्य. For वैकक्षक see p. 26. हृदयमध्ये निबद्धः ग्रन्थिः (knot) यस्य. धातुरसारुणेन red because dyed with red chalk. *Vide* notes p. 161 for धातु. रागेणेव...कृतेन—the poet fancies that the red piece of cloth was राग (passion, redness) which he had cut into pieces. The ascetic had uprooted passions (राग) which sway the human heart (हृदय) and had as though tied into a knot on the chest the pieces of passion as red garment. कर्पटः a ragged garment. कृतः उत्तरासङ्गः यस्य. उत्तरासङ्गः upper garment (उत्तरे ऊर्ध्वाङ्गे आसज्यते उत्तरासङ्गः). पुन...मूलेन—this and the following instrumentals qualify योगभारकेण. What a योगभारक means is not quite clear. It seems to have been something like an 'hold-all,' a bag tied to a pole. C and T render it as 'yoke pole'. पुनरुक्तं ०वेष्टनं तेन निश्चलं मूलं यस्य the root of which was made firm with fastenings (प्रग्रहः) of hair tied over and over again. The bag was tied to the pole by hair ropes. दृढः मृत्परिशोधनाय वंशत्वचः तितउः यस्मिन् on which was tied a sieve (तितउः) of bamboo bark for straining earth. 'चालनी तितउः पुमान्' अमरः. कौपीनेन सनाथं शिखरं यस्य. कौपीनम्—loin-cloth (from कूप) according to 'शालीनकौपीने अधृष्टाकार्ययोः' पा. 5. 2. 20 (कूपपतनमर्हति कौपीनं पापं तत्साधनत्वात्तद्वद्गोप्यत्वात्पुरुषलिङ्गमपि । तत्सम्बन्धात्तदाच्छादनमपि । सि. कौ.). खर्जूर...कपालके whose alms bowl was placed inside a box (समुद्गकः) made of date leaves. दारव...कमण्डलुना that had his water pot placed on a stool of three sticks inserted into the corners of three wooden planks. दारव-from दारु. Three planks were joined together to make a triangular base. In their corners a stick was fixed.

बहिरुपपादितं ०स्थानं यस्मिन् outside which a place was found for his slippers (of wood). स्थूलेन दशासूत्रेण नियन्त्रिता पुस्तिकापूलिका यस्मिन्— that had his bundle of manuscripts tied by a stout rope made of the hems of garments. अध्यासितः स्कन्धः यस्य. इतरकरेण (दक्षिणेन करेण) गृहीतं वेत्रासनं (caneseat) येन. मस्करिणम्—*vide* notes p. 91. This clause gives a vivid and picturesque description of an ascetic and reminds us of modern *Gosavis* and *Sādhus.* उपगतम् when he came near. नगरस्य समीपे उपनगरम् (अव्ययीभाव). शून्यायतने in a deserted house or temple. उपनिन्ये presented. बहलेन आलोकेन लिप्तं अन्तःपुरं यैः. राजतानि made of silver.

P. 46 ll. 12—23 **नरपति...वाटिकाम्.** प्रिय...कातरः afraid to go contrary to the request or love of a person dear to him. दाक्षिण्यमनुरुध्यमानः following the dictates of courtesy. ग्रहण...समर्थः not able to get free from the (charge of) mean-mindedness if he accepted them. दोलायमानेन—vacillating. The king was afraid that if he refused the present, he would offend the ascetic for whom he had high regard; but the king also felt that if he being a king accepted from a poor mendicant a gift, that would be an act deserving to be censured by the people. अति...निघ्नः yielding to his own extreme goodness. सर्व...हेतुः the cause of the production of all rewards (goes with ०भक्तिः).शिव... फलानि It is our devotion to शिव that yields rewards that could not (otherwise) have been secured even in desires. येन since. समुच्छ्रितं श्वेतातपत्रं यस्य whose white umbrella was held high over him. समुद्धूयमानं (being waved) धवलं चामरयुगलं यस्य. The white umbrella and two chowries were indispensable insignia of royalty in ancient India. Compare 'अदेयमासीत् त्रयमेव भूपतेः **शशिप्रभं छत्रमुभे च चामरे**' रघु० 3. 16. राजपुत्रैः nobles. अन्तरं distance. अभि...शिष्यं another pupil coming towards (the king). He was other than the one that had come before with the five silver lotuses. अस्य...त्तरेण to the north of this dilapidated temple of the Mātṛis. The Mātris are eight (or seven, according to others) divinities said to be the attendants of शिव. 'ब्राह्मी माहेश्वरी चैन्द्री वाराही वैष्णवी तथा। कौमारी चर्ममुण्डा च कालसङ्कर्षणीति च ॥'. *Vide* 'साक्षाज्जातमातृदेवता इव बहुबालकन्याकुला ननृतुर्वृद्धधात्र्यः' हर्ष० 4th उ० and notes thereon. For उत्तरेण, *vide* notes p. 158.

P. 46 l. 24—**P. 48** l. 2 **अथ महतः...मकरोत्.** The first sentence is अथ...भगवन्तं...भैरवाचार्यं ददर्श (p. 47 l. 32). महत...मध्ये in the midst of a large crowd of pilgrims. कार्पटिक is derived from कर्पट with the affix ठक् (कर्पटेन चरति). स्नातम्—this and the following adjectives in the accusative singular qualify भैरवाचार्यं below. दत्ता अष्टपुष्पिका येन. For अष्टपुष्पिका, *vide* notes p. 46. पुष्पाणामष्टकमष्टपुष्पिका. अनुष्ठितं अग्निकार्यं येन. कृतः भस्मरेखापरिहारेण परिकरः यस्य that was surrounded by a circle of ashes. परिहारः a tract of common land round a village; hence, here 'a tract or circle'. Compare 'धनुःशतं परीहारो ग्रामस्य स्यात्समन्ततः ।' मनु० 8. 237. The com. says 'परिहारोऽत्र मर्यादा'. हरितेन गोमयेन उपलिप्तं ०तलं तस्मिन् वितते (spread). कृष्ण...भ्यस्यन्तम् under the guise (निभः) of wrapping himself in a dark woollen blanket, he as though was practising residence (आवासः) in the darkness of *pātāla* in the apprehension that he might have to enter into an *Asura* cavern. For असुरविवर, *vide* notes p. 90. Pātāla as the haunt of demons and sinners is supposed to be dark. An असुरविवर must also be very dark, if our explanation of it be correct. He did not want to enter असुरविवर; but the poet fancies that he was familiarising himself with darkness because he feared that he might one day have do so. उन्मिषता...लिम्पन्तम् who covered his disciples with the flashing lustre of his body as tawny as lightning, as though with red arsenic paste purchased by the sale of human flesh. मनःशिला is red and therefore would be like the glow of his body. मनःशिला costs money and so the question arises how the poor ascetic got it. The words महा...क्रीतेन explain this. They suggest that भैरवाचार्य was a शाक्त, had offered human flesh to शक्ति and the पिशाचs and thereby secured super-human powers. Compare 'अपरत्र प्रकाशनरपतिकुमारकक्रियमाणमहामांसविक्रयप्रक्रमम्' हर्ष० 4th उ० 7th para. The शाक्तs say 'अष्टम्यां रुधिरैर्मांसैर्महामांसैः सुगन्धिभिः । पूजयेद्बहुजातीयैर्बलिभिर्भोजनैः शिवाम् ॥.' जटी...सिद्धान् with his hair tied in a lump so as to peep upwards from a portion of which that was matted hung down the round globes of conch-shell and his rosary beads, he seemed to be imprisoning the Siddhas conceited by the pride of knowledge and roaming overhead (in the sky). जटीकृतः एकदेशः तस्मात् लम्बमानाः रुद्राक्षाणां शंखानां च गुटिकाः यस्मिन्. प्रशस्ता शिखा शिखापाशः. The शिखा was long (like a cord) and ऊर्ध्वबद्ध hence the उत्प्रेक्षा 'बध्नन्तमिव &c.' For सिद्धs, see above p. 83. The poet wants to suggest that he had secured superhuman powers (सिद्धिs) which enabled him even to imprison the सिद्धs. धवलाः कतिपये शिरोरुहाः (hair) यस्मिन् (*adj* of वयसा). वयसा...क्रामन्तम् in age he had passed beyond 55 years. खालित्येन क्षीयमाणा शङ्खलोम्नां लेखा यस्य the line of the hair on the front part of his head was faint owing to baldness. We expect खाल्य (from खलति) for खालित्य. **'शङ्खो निधौ ललाटास्थि'** अमरः. लोमशः (hairy) कर्णशष्कुलिप्रदेशः (the outer part of the ear) यस्य. तिरश्च्या...जनयन्तम् with his slanting forehead mark made with ashes, he led one to think that it was the white line of his skull-bone burst by the heat of the burnt *guggulu* repeatedly held over his head. It is better to read शिरोविधृत with some MSS. For ललाटिका, see p. 44. For the burning of गुग्गुलु in the temple of शिव and on the head, *vide* notes p. 105. Bones are white. The line of white ashes on the forehead is fancied to be the skull bone split up by heat. सहज...बिभ्राणम् who had as though a single, long (आयामिनी) and unbroken (निरन्तरा) brow by the meeting together of his brows, as the part between the brows was contracted by the natural folds of the wrinkles on his forehead, the brow being tawny in colour. ०भङ्गैः सङ्कोचितः कूर्चभागः यस्याः. 'कूर्चमस्त्री भ्रुवोर्मध्यम्' अमरः. बभ्रुः भाः यस्याः. Between the brows there is ordinarily a part of the head. But as his forehead was deeply wrinkled, the two brows presented a continuous line. निरन्तराम् leaving no intervening space. ईषत् काचवत् काचरा कनीनिका यस्य the pupil of which was greenish like glass. रक्तापाङ्गाभ्यां निर्गतः अंशुप्रतानः यस्य from the red corners of which shot forth rays. मध्ये धवला भाः यस्य तेन ०भासा. These three qualify ०युगलेन. इन्द्रायुधेनेव—The rainbow also presents red and green colours and so his eyes are fancied to be इन्द्रायुध. Then there are two more उत्प्रेक्षाs. लोचन...लिखन्तम्—the idea is:—when he cast glances all round from his eyes that were white, red (in the corners) and greenish-yellow (in the pupil), he seemed to draw all round a large circle tinged with various colours. A मण्डल is drawn on the ground in worshipping a deity. Compare 'कुङ्कुमपङ्कानुलिप्ते मण्डलके...रक्तकमलषण्डेनार्चां ददौ' हर्ष० 4th उ०, 4th para. सित...क्षिपन्तम् he seemed to scatter in all directions an oblation to शिव variegated with rows of white, yellow and red flags (or marks). That flags were used in the worship of शिव we see from the 2nd उ० 'सुरभिकुसुमधूपगन्धध्वजबलिविलेपनप्रदीपकबहुलां विधाय पूजाम्' (text p. 25). If we take पताका as meaning 'mark' (in a secondary sense), then there is a reference to an oblation of rice (which is white) smeared with red powder and yellow turmeric. Such oblations are even now placed where four roads meet. ताक्ष्यतुण्डकोटिवत् कुब्जा अग्रघोणा (घोणायाः अग्रं or rather अग्रं चासौ घोणा च) यस्य the tip of whose nose was curved like the end of Garuḍa's beak. 'गरुत्मान्गरुडस्तार्क्ष्यः' अमरः. For the form अग्रघोणा, mark वामन's काव्यालङ्कारसूत्र 5. 2. 20 'हस्ताग्राग्रहस्तादयो गुणगुणिनोर्भेदाभेदात्'. दूर...कपोलम् whose cheeks looked narrow on account of the corners of his mouth being very far gashed. दूरविदीर्णे सृक्किणी ताभ्यां संक्षिप्तौ कपोलौ यस्य. किञ्चिद्दन्तुरतया because he had slightly prominent teeth. सदा हृदये सन्निहितः हरः तस्य मौलौ चन्द्रः तस्य आतपेन इव. He had white and prominent teeth, the brilliance of which brightened the circle of the quarters. The poet fancies that it was the light of S'iva's crescent issuing out of his mouth, शिव being always present in his heart. जिह्वाग्र...तौष्ठम्—his lip naturally hung down a little. He knew by heart (जिह्वाग्रस्थित) all the canonical works (संहिता) of the S'aivite sect. The poet fancies that his lip hung down as though on account of the weight of the संहिताs that were on the tip of the tongue. प्रलम्ब...बध्यमानम् with his crystal ear-rings dangling from his pendulous (प्रलम्ब) ear-lobes, he seemed as though pursued by Venus and Jupiter in the belief of acquiring (from him) a lore which would enable them to conquer the gods and demons (respectively). शुक्र and गुरु were respectively the preceptors of the असुरs and देवs. Venus and Jupiter, with which the two are identified, are the brightest of the planets. So the crystal ear-rings are fancied to be शुक्र and गुरु. बद्ध... कलयन्तम् wearing, on one of his forearms (प्रकोष्ठः) that had an iron bracelet and on which was tied a bundle of magic threads with various herbs, a piece of conchshell, as though it were the tooth of Pūshan broken by S'iva and turned by him (भैरवाचार्य) into an ornament out of devotion to शिव. The piece of शङ्ख was white like teeth. विविधौषधिभिः मन्त्रैः च युक्ता सूत्रपङ्क्तिः, बद्धा ०पङ्क्तिः यस्मिन्. Even now people wear dark thread on their forearms supposed to have magical properties. पूष्णो दन्तमिव— When वीरभद्र produced from S'iva's matted hair destroyed the sacrifice of दक्ष, some of the gods were severely dealt with. भग lost his eye, while one of the teeth of पूषन् was broken. *Vide* for the story भागवतपुराण 4. 5. 'भगस्य नेत्रं भगवान्पातितस्य रुषा भुवि। उज्जहार सदःस्थोऽक्ष्णो यः शपन्तमसूसुचत् ॥ पूष्णश्चापातयद्दन्तान् कालिङ्गस्य यथा बलः। शप्यमाने गरिमणि योऽहसद्दर्शयन्दतः ॥' verses 20–21. As the दन्त became holy by the touch of वीरभद्र, the ascetic is fancied as wearing it with भक्ति. There seems to be some faint reference even in the Rigveda to the story about the loss of the tooth of पूषन्. Compare 'वामं पूषा वामं भगो वामं देवः करूळती' (which last is explained as कृत्तदन्त) Rigveda IV. 30. 24. अखिल...मालामिव—The beads of the rosary looked like the pots for throwing up (उदञ्चन) the water (रस) in a well and the string of the rosary like the rope on which the pots are placed at intervals. He revolved the rosary in his right hand. A water-wheel also is turned with the right hand. अखिलस्य रसस्य कूपात् उदञ्चनं तदर्थं घटीयन्त्रमाला. The रुद्राक्षमाला also threw out all pleasures (रस) from his heart (which was concentrated solely on शिव). आ (ईषत्) पिङ्गलानि अग्राणि यस्य. कूर्चकलापेन by his thick beard. संमार्जे...निकरम्—the idea is:—a कूर्च (brush, peacock's feathers) is used in sweeping off a heap (निकरः) of dust (रजः); his beard that rubbed his chest. is fancied as sweeping off रजः (passion) contained in the heart. रजः is one of the three Guṇas according to the सांख्यs. It is रजोगुण that gives rise to काम and क्रोध and leads a person into sin. 'सत्त्वं लघु प्रकाशकमिष्टमुपष्टम्भकं चलं च रजः। गुरु वरणकमेव तमः' सांख्यकारिका; 'अथ केन प्रयुक्तोऽयं पापं चरति पूरुषः। अनिच्छन्नपि वार्ष्णेय बलादिव नियोजितः॥ काम एष क्रोध एष **रजोगुणसमुद्भवः।'** गीता chap. 3. 36–37. निचितं full of (*adj.* of ०देशं). ध्यान...दधानम्—the idea is:—By meditation he had acquired the illumination (ज्योतिः) of knowledge. Light (ज्योतिः) such as that of fire or the sun burns; what is burnt up becomes dark. The dark hair on his chest is fancied to be the effect of ज्योतिः which illumines his heart. ईषत्प्रशिथिलेन वलिवलयेन बध्यमानं तुन्दं (उदरं) यस्य. उपचीयमानः (protuberant) स्फिङ्मांसपिण्डकः यस्य. स्फिच् *f.* buttocks, hips. 'स्त्रियां **स्फिचौ कटिप्रोथौ'** अमरः. पाण्डुरेण पवित्रेण क्षौमेण (linen cloth) आवृतं कौपीनं (private parts) यस्य. For कौपीन see above notes p. 198. सा...मण्डलितेन that was passed round (his body) while he sat in a dignified पर्यङ्क posture. When a person sits on his hams with legs cross-wise and a piece of cloth is firmly tied round his knees, loins and back, it is called पर्यङ्कबन्ध (Marathi जेठा मारून बसणें). बाण's description leaves no doubt about the meaning of पर्यङ्कबन्ध. But मल्लिनाथ commenting on the words 'पर्यङ्कबन्धस्थिरपूर्वकायम्' (कुमारसम्भव 3. 45) explains it as वीरासन and quotes two definitions of the latter, which do not agree with our explanation. *Vide* मल्लिनाथ's comment. अमृतफेनवत् श्वेता रुक् (कान्तिः) यस्य (with योगपट्टकेन); ०फेनेन श्वेता रुक् यस्य (with वासुकिना). For योगपट्टक, see p. 26. For वासुकि being the rope in churning, *vide* p. 52. वासुकि must have been sprinkled with the foam of अमृत as it came out of the churned ocean. अप्रतिहतः (irresistible) अनेकमन्त्राणां प्रभावः तेन आविर्भूतः तेन. The poet fancies that the योगपट्टक encircling his body was वासुकि manifesting itself through the irresistible might of the ascetic's incantations and then performing a प्रदक्षिणा round him. Even now it is believed that a मान्त्रिक can call out a serpent from its hiding place by the power of मन्त्रs. The suggested meaning is that, as वासुकि is the king of serpents, the ascetic must have been a great magician indeed. Compare for the conceit 'सुधाफेनधवलेन तपःप्रभावकुण्डलीकृतेन गङ्गास्रोतसेव योगपट्टकेन विरचितवैकक्ष्यका' (text p. 3 ll. 29-30 above). अरुणतामरसवत् सुकुमारं तलं यस्य. जर्जरयन्त...तलम्—the idea is:—the bright rays of his reddish soles spread on the surface (तल) of the earth (रसा). The poet fancies that he crushed the earth (with the rays) in his passion or zeal (रसः) for bringing out the great treasures (supposed to be lying in the earth). The person who is believed to be able to see treasures hidden in the earth is called (in Marathi) पायाळु. तोयेन क्षालितं अत एव शुचि तेन (applies to both युगलेन and ०मिथुनेन). हंस...गतेन as though they were two हंसs that had come there in order to become familiar with the pilgrimage to holy places on the Ganges. He had often been to the holy Ganges and would again go there. Therefore हंसs (in the form of the wooden slippers) never left his feet. In the next clause the principal part is वैणवेन विशाखिकादण्डेन सततपार्श्ववर्तिना विराजमानम्—who had constantly at his side a bamboo विशाखिका staff. What विशाखिका means is not quite clear. Probably it is a staff the upper part of which branches off into two and forms a loop. Compare 'विशाखिकाशिखरनिबद्धनालिकेरीफलवल्कलमयधौतोपानद्युगोपेताम्' कादम्बरी p. 133 of P. The commentators of the कादम्बरी explain it variously as 'विशाखिका भूमिशुद्ध्यर्थमाद्रियमाणा लोहयष्टिरूपा शिक्यभेदो वा;' 'विशाखिका रुद्राङ्कुशः; विशाखिका विशाखा सा तरोरवयवान्तरम्'. शिखरे निखाताः (imbedded) कुब्जाः (curved) कालायसकण्टकाः (iron hooks) यस्य. Even now people in the Konkan use a staff that has a few iron hooks fixed at the top, which rattle when a man walks and frighten away reptiles. ०कण्टकेन applies to ०ङ्कुशेन also. An अङ्कुश (goad) also has an iron barb imbedded in it. सर्व...ङ्कुशेनेव as though it were a goad for driving away Ganes'a who causes obstacles in the mastery of all the lores. It should be remembered that an elephant is controlled by a goad and that गणेश has the head of an elephant. विनायक is called विघ्नराज (he controls as well as causes obstacles). विनायक also presides over learning. The suggestion is:—the ascetic had mastered all विद्याs; he had the goad-like staff always with him by way of a threat to गणेश if the latter wanted to cause any obstacle. बाण often uses विनायक for श्लेष. Compare 'अयमशिवसहचरो विनायकः' हर्ष० 8th उ०; 'अशिवमूर्तयो महाविनायकाधिष्ठिताः' कादम्बरी p. 287 of P. The words सर्व० would also mean 'with a goad that drives away the chief (विनायक) obstacles &c.' or 'with a goad that subdues (विनायक) and drives away the obstacles &c.' कुमारब्रह्मचारिणम् who had observed the vow of celibacy all his life from boyhood (*i. e.* he was a नैष्ठिकब्रह्मचारी 'a perpetual student' and not उपकुर्वाण). कृशः (thin *i. e.* restrained) क्रोधः यस्य. अकृशः (not thin *i. e.* great) अनुरोधः (complying with another's request, kindness) यस्य. 'अनुरोधोऽनुवर्तनम्' अमरः. अदीना (not wretched *i. e.* noble) प्रकृतिः (nature) तया शोभितम्. अदीन...शोभितम् (with महानगर 'capital') means 'adorned by noble ministers &c. or rich guilds'. प्रकृति means 'the constituent elements of a kingdom' or 'guilds of citizens.' 'स्वाम्यमात्यसुहृत्कोशराष्ट्रदुर्गबलानि च । राज्याङ्गानि प्रकृतयः पौराणां श्रेणयोऽपि च ॥' अमरः. क्षीर० quotes कात्य as "यत्कात्यः 'अमात्याद्याश्च पौराश्च सद्भिः प्रकृतयः स्मृताः.'" There is another sense possible. प्रकृति means 'the base' or 'the original accent of a word.' Each word (whether single or compounded with another word) has generally only one उदात्त accent. If a word be compounded with another, it may lose its accent and take the accent for the whole compound as determined by the rules. There is a rule that 'when नगर is the second member of a समास, the first letter of the first member has the उदात्त accent, except when the first word is महत् or नवन्.' 'अमहन्नवन्नगरेऽनुदीचाम्' पा. 6. 2. 89. In महानगर, the first word is महत्; therefore नगर retains its original accent (प्रकृतिस्वर) and the first letter has not the उदात्त accent. Thus in महानगर the प्रकृति (स्वर) is अदीन (not low-pitched; but is high-pitched, as उदात्त is). 'उच्चैरुदात्तः' and 'नीचैरनुदात्तः' पा. 1. 2. 29–30. कल्प...च्छायम्—०राशिवत् सुकुमारा छाया (कान्तिः) यस्य (with भैरवाचार्य); ०राशिभिः सुकुमारा छाया (shade) यस्य (with मेरु). मेरु is shaded with the delicate leaves of the trees of paradise. ०रजसा पवित्रितं शिरः (head, top) यस्य. On the top of कैलास dwells शिव. He had bowed his head at the feet of the image of शिव. मा...यातम् followed by a crowd (गणः) of S aivas (with भैरवाचार्य); peopled with the attendants (गणाः) of शिव. महेश्वरस्य इमे माहेश्वराः गणाः (प्रमथाः). 'सङ्घाते प्रमथे गणः' अमरः. ०सहस्रे प्रक्षालितं शरीरं येन; ०स्रेण प्रक्षालितं शरीरं यस्य (with जलनिधि). The ascetic had bathed in numerous rivers. Numerous rivers fall into the ocean. बहु...शुचिम् pure by residing in many holy spots (with भैरवाचार्य); pure with many holy तीर्थs situated on it (with ०प्रवाहम्). धाम place, dwelling. तीर्थं तथ्यस्य the sacred place of truth. कुशलस्य of welfare or prosperity. पूतता holiness. शालेयं शालीनतायाः the ricefield of modesty. For शालेय, see p. 118 and for शालीन p. 57. स्थानं स्थितेः abode of all propriety or decorum. आधारं धृतेः support of steadiness. आकरः mine. निकेतनं कौतुकस्य the house of admiration. All admired him. आरामं रामणीयकस्य the garden of loveliness. प्रासादं प्रसादस्य the palace of good-will (towards all). अगारं गौरवस्य house of respect. All respected him. समाजं सौजन्यस्य the conference of goodness. सम्भवं सद्भावस्य the source of amiability. कालं कलेः the death of Kali. He nullified the effects of Kali, the age of sin and discord. विरूपाक्षम् = शिवम्. शशि...चाल he got up, as the ocean rises up on seeing the moon. At moonrise, the waters of the ocean begin to rise in a tide. प्रथमतरं उत्थितः शिष्यलोकः यस्य. प्रत्युज्जगाम went forward to receive. समर्पितं श्रीफलोपायनं येन who gave him the present of Bilva fruit. **'बिल्वे** शाण्डिल्यशैलूषौ मालूरश्री**फलावपि'** अमरः. The बिल्व tree is sacred to शिव. जह्नुकर्णात् समुद्गीर्यमाणः (emitted) गङ्गाप्रवाहः तस्य ह्रादः (roar) तद्वत् गम्भीरया. For Jahnu, see p. 84.

P. 48 ll. 3-15 **नरपति...भजत.** प्रीत्या विस्तार्यमाणः धवलिमा यस्य the whiteness of which increased through the joy he felt. प्रत्यर्प...वनानि—When he bowed, he cast glances from the whites of his eyes. These resembled the silver lotuses that भैरवाचार्य had sent. The poet fancies that he returned in the form of his glances the lotuses that he had received. The only difference was that he returned many (as he cast many glances), while he had received only five. ललाट...प्रकाशयन् with his crest-jewel dangling about on his forehead and having its rays shooting up he as though manifested the favour of S'iva by the appearance of a third eye. उद्गताः अंशवः यस्य. शिव has a third eye on the forehead. The red jewel dangling on the forehead of the king, when he bowed to भैरव, is fancied to be the third eye that appeared (उद्गमः) just at that moment. शिव favoured the king so much that he made him त्रिनेत्र like himself. आवर्जितः (bent down) कर्णपल्लवः तस्मात् पलायमानाः मधुकराः यस्य. When he bent down to bow, the bees ran away from his ear-ornament of flowers. शिवसेवया समुन्मूलिताः अशेषपापलवाः तैः मुच्यमानः. The dark bees look like sins (which are supposed to be dark). दूरावनतः bending very low. अभिनवम्—his bow is called अभिनव (a new or unique one), because it is accompanied by all the wonderful results described above. शार्दूल...दर्शयत्—the ascetic desired the king to be seated on his own tiger skin. To seat a person on one's आसन is a mark of great respect and friendship. It shows that the person so treated is at least the equal, if not the superior, of the person so treating. उपदर्शितः प्रश्रयः (humility) येन. मत्तहंसस्य कलः गद्गदः स्वरः तेन सुभगां (with नदीम्); तद्वत् सुभगां (with वाचम्). मधुरसमयीम् full of sweetness (with वाचम्); full of sweet water (with नदीम्). प्रवर्तयन् making flow; uttering. नार्हसि...कर्तुम् you will please not ill-treat me on account of the misdeeds of other kings. His meaning is:—Other kings might not have reverence for holy ascetics like you and might sit on the seat occupied by you. But I cannot occupy that seat honouring you as I do; and I do not like such formal treatment from you. अशेष...गुरुः that the teacher (your reverence) so deals with me is the fault of the character of that wretched Lakshmî (royalty) that is looked up to by all kings or is the ill-natured-ness of lucre. All kings care too much for लक्ष्मी and become wicked through wealth. You think that I am also one of those kings and would take umbrage if you did not offer me your own seat. The usual meaning of उपेक्षित is 'neglected, slighted.' But that meaning does not suit the context. अभूमि...चाराणाम् this person (*i. e.* I) is not a fit subject for ceremonious behaviour (उपचारः). अल...णया enough of great restraint (*i. e.* formality). मनोरथशिष्यः a pupil in wishes (*i. e.* I desired to be your disciple). नोल्लङ्घनमर्हति does not deserve to be trodden. परिजनेन उपनीते (brought). वाससि on a garment. अनतिक्रमणीय irresistible. अनुवर्तमानः acceding to, complying with.

P. 48 ll. 16—31 आसीने...मगात्. राजकेन सह सराजके (*adj.* of परिजने). अर्घ्यम् respectful offering of flowers, water &c. अर्घः पूजाविधिः तदर्थं द्रव्यं अर्घ्यम्. 'पादार्घाभ्यां च' पा. 5. 4. 25 (यत्). नृपमाधुर्येण हृतं (captivated) अन्तःकरणं यस्य. शशि...मलाः pure like the rays of the moon (with दशनदीधितीः); pure with the rays of the moon (with ०भक्तीः). शिवभक्तीः (*accu. plu.* of ०भक्ति)—if one were to worship शिव, then one's devotion would be illumined by the light of the moon that is on the head of शिव. अति...गौरवम् your very modesty declares the greatness (vast extent) of your qualities. The more the virtues that a man possesses, the more modest does he become, as he comes to know of his defects. It is only those that are shallow that become puffed up. गौरव also means 'weight'. What is heavy makes the carrier bend down. सकल...मसि you are a fit receptacle for all prosperity. विभ...पत्तयः your conduct (or undertakings) is quite in keeping with your greatness. जन्मनः...तेयेषु since my birth I never cast my eyes on wealth (*i. e.* I never paid any regard to it). स्वापतेयं wealth, from स्वपति, according to 'पथ्यतिथिवसतिस्वपतेर्ढञ्' पा. 4. 4. 104 (पथि साधु पाथेयम्।...स्वापतेयं धनम्। सि. कौ.). यतः...मस्ति since I possess this poor body not sold for money that is the fuel to the fire of all sins. He says that he is master of his own body, poor though it be. All persons sell their bodies to others for amassing money. As fuel feeds fire, so money feeds sins. So he never cared for money. क is added to शरीर to indicate that he does not care much even for that body. कुत्सितं शरीरं शरीरकम्. दुर्गृ...क्षराणि I have a few ill-understood syllables of knowledge. This he speaks in great humility. भट्टारक *adj.* venerable; *m.* god. पुण्यकणिका particle of merit. अत्र—out of the things enumerated (by him) *viz.* body, प्राणाः, विद्या and पुण्य. प्र...ग्राह्याणि to be captivated by a few virtues (with मनांसि); to be bound by a fine (प्रतनु) thread (with कुसुमानि). The comparison shows that the minds of the good are tender like flowers. विद्वत्संमताः highly thought of by the learned (with साधवः); approved by the learned (with शब्दाः). श्रूयमाणा अपि even when merely heard (though not actually seen). साधवः the good; grammatically pure (with words). सुधीरे...विवरम् fame makes a hole (*i. e.* an impression) in a mind even though it be very steady. A hole (विवर) cannot be easily made on what is firm. विशतः...कल्याणिना I, who was being borne away by the currents, white with foam, of curiosity that entered my heart, am now brought back by your auspicious self with your virtues. The idea is:—so long, not having seen you, my heart overflowed with curiosity to see you; but now that I see you, *you* occupy my heart and not *mere curiosity* about you. A stream becomes white with foam. गुणगण is white like foam. A person who is borne away by a flood is brought back by ropes (गुणगण). If we omit सुखयन्ति, then this passage becomes involved and difficult to explain. Then we must stop at कुर्वन्ति and take विवरं with विशतः. अनु...प्रणयिनः In the case of the bodies &c. of the good, though they be dear to them, friends are the masters

is dark. *Vide* p. 2. कृतान्त...घटितम् as though manufactured of steel heated by the fire of the wrath of Yama. It was not ordinary fire that heated the steel going to make up the sword. In order to make it most destructive, it was heated in the fire of Yama's wrath. अति...क्वणन्तम्—A very irritable (तीक्ष्ण) man may fly into a rage even when merely touched by the wind. A very irritable person is popularly said to be one who quarrels with the wind. The sword having a very fine blade sounded when the wind blew upon it. मणि...पाटयन्तम् under the guise of its reflection falling on the jewelled pavement (कुट्टिमः-मम्) of the hall, it (sword) as though cleft itself in two. 'कुट्टिमोऽस्त्री निबद्धा भूः.' अरि...धारम् the edge of which looked indented (करालित) with the rays (shooting from it) as though they (rays) were hair sticking to it at the time of cutting off enemies' heads. कराल means दन्तुर. The rays look like so many दन्तs of the sword. 'करालो दन्तुरे तुङ्गे' अमरः. करालिता (uneven, jagged) धारा यस्य. मुहु...दिवसम् that as if cut into pieces daylight that was crushed by overspreading (छुरित) it with the circle of its radiance flickering again and again like flashes (उन्मेषः) of lightning. जर्जरितः आतपः यस्य (*adj.* of दिवसम्). The flashing light of the sword blade spread through and through over daylight and thus seemed to cleave it asunder into portions. Remove the comma after ॰तपम्. कटा...रात्रेः a glance as though of the night of destruction. रात्रि is dark and so the sword is said to be its कटाक्ष. काल also means 'dark'. This and the following clauses are intended to convey the terrific aspect of the sword. उत्पल is a blue lotus. Hence the sword is said to be the ear lotus of Death. ओङ्कारमिव॰—The syllable *om* precedes the study of the Veda. It is a mystic syllable credited with supernatural powers and is symbolical of Brahma itself. So the sword was the essence or centre of cruelty. Compare 'सत्यस्य शनैः शनैरोङ्कारमिव कुर्वाणे' हर्ष॰ 4th उ॰ and the notes thereon. Note 'एकाक्षरं परं ब्रह्म' मनु॰ 2.83. अलङ्का...कारस्य—It was an ornament to arrogance *i. e.* whoever had the sword could afford to be arrogant. कुलमित्रं family friend *i. e.* friend of long standing. देहं दर्पस्य—it was pride incarnate. अपत्यं मृत्योः—it possessed the qualities of Death, as a child is endowed with the qualities of its parent. आग...लक्ष्म्याः it was the way by which लक्ष्मी came *i. e.* it helped in securing wealth (and kingdom). निर्ग...कीर्तेः—it was the way by which fame went out into the world *i. e.* the sword would enable one to do heroic deeds whereby one's fame would spread in the world.

P. 49 ll. 21—26 **अवनि...मेदिनीम्.** आयुध...लिङ्गन्निव he seemed, under the guise of his reflection, as though embracing it out of affection for it (or out of his love for weapons of all kinds). The king was reflected in the bright sword-blade. The poet fancies that the king embraced it out of love for it. पर...विदग्धमपि though it is ill-mannered (or proud) enough to scorn accepting another's property. The words may also mean 'ignorant of the humiliation *viz.* accepting another's property.' But as here the emphasis is laid upon the word व्यतिक्रम, so अवज्ञा also must be understood in the sense of 'disregarding.' युष्मद्विषये in your case. वचन...रितुम् to commit (to be guilty of) the crime of disregarding your words (request). The words referred to are 'भवद्भुजयोग्यो गृह्यताम्'. साधयामः is used in the sense of 'गच्छामः,' which latter is not used, as it was believed to be an inauspicious word indicating 'perishing.' प्रकृत्या...रागी by nature loving the heroic temper.

P. 49 l. 27—**P. 50** l. 10 **अथ...इति.** उपह्वरे in secret. उपह्वरः a lonely place. उपग्रहेण यथा स्यात्तथा सोपग्रहम् in a conciliatory tone; with a request. स्वार्थ...भव्यानाम् The dispositions of the good are careless of their own interests but vigilant in obliging others. For भव्य, compare the first verse of the 8th उच्छ्वास 'दैवेनापि क्रियते **भव्यानां** पूर्वसेवेव.' भवादृशां...कारः to such as you the sight of suppliants is a great festival, requests (preferred by the needy) are a means of giving pleasure, acceptance of gifts (by others) is an obligation. The idea is that great persons like पुष्पभूति are pleased (आराधन) when requests are made to them; great persons feel obliged when the gifts they offer are accepted by others. भैरवाचार्य wants the king's help in a perilous undertaking and so makes this highly flattering introduction. भूमि...धीयसे you are the centre of all men's hopes; therefore you are addressed (by me). He means that all men hope to fulfil their desires through your help. महाकालहृदयं नाम यस्य. महाकाल is शिव. As to the wonderful power ascribed to *mantras*, *vide* pp. 54–55. कृष्णाः स्रगम्बरानुलेपाः यस्मिन् (*adj* of आकल्पेन)—in which the garland, garment and unguents were all dark. आकल्पः decoration, equipment. कल्पकथितेन as declared in the ritualistic works (of the S'aiva sect). 'इतिकर्तव्यकलापोपदेशको ग्रन्थः कल्पः' सं०. जपकोट्या by muttering (the *mantra*) a crore of times. पूर्वं कृता कृतपूर्वा, कृतपूर्वा सेवा येन सः ०सेवः. वेतालसाधनं अवसाने (अन्ते) यस्य. तस्य...सिद्धिः complete attainment of that *mantra* ends with the subduing of a goblin. वेतालः ghost occupying a dead body. त्वं...कर्मणे you are quite a match for that deed (*i. e.* you will be able to achieve this). अलं in the sense of 'being sufficient for a thing or able to do a thing' governs the dative. 'नमः—स्वस्तिस्वाहास्वधाऽलंवषड्योगाच्च' पा. 2. 3. 16 (अलमिति पर्याप्त्यर्थग्रहणम् । दैत्येभ्यो हरिरलम् । सि. कौ.). गृहीतः भरः येन. त्वयि...भरे when you undertake the responsibility. भवन्तमुपतिष्ठते who waits upon you (who brought the silver lotuses). The Ātmanepada is in accordance with the वार्तिक 'उपाद्देवपूजासङ्गतिकरणमित्रकरणपथिष्विति वाच्यम्' (on 'उपान्मन्त्रकरणे' पा. 1. 3. 25). द्राविडः inhabitant of the द्रविड country. द्रविड was roughly between the कृष्णा and the कावेरी. Its capital was काञ्ची. यदि...मन्यसे If you approve. दिङ्नागः दिग्गजः तस्य हस्तवत् दीर्घः. गृहीतः अट्टहासः येन. नीयतामयं निशा...बाहुः let this arm (of yours) be made a bolt of one of the quarters for one night *i. e.* you must guard one of the (four) quarters on one night (that I shall appoint). The student will find that the king and the three others mentioned here guarded the four quarters while भैरवाचार्य was engaged in grim rites. कृतं वचः येन—when he had finished his words. अन्ध...प्रकाशः (delighted) like one in darkness that sees a light. प्राप्तः उपकारस्य अवकाशः (opportunity) येन—The king had been obliged by the ascetic who had made him a present of the sword called अट्टहास and of several silver lotuses. The king desired to oblige the ascetic in return. And this was the first opportunity he found to do so. अनेन...वैमि I look upon myself as accepted by you (as yours) by this task (निदेशः) which is shared by me in common with your pupils. कृतः परिग्रहः (स्वीकारः) यस्य. निदेशः order; appointed task. व्याहृतं utterance. सङ्केतः an appointment; a place of meeting. असितपक्ष dark fortnight. The 14th day of the dark fortnight (particularly of माघ) is sacred to शिव. इयत्यां वेलायां at this hour or at such an hour.

P. 50 ll. 11–23. **अथाति...तमुद्देशम्.** शैवेन...दीक्षितः being initiated into the S'aiva ritual. नियमवान्—observing a fast (or other rules of a दीक्षा). कृतः अधिवासः यस्य—on which purificatory ceremonies were performed. अधिवासः or अधिवासनम् application of scents and perfumes 'संस्कारो गन्धमाल्याद्यैर्यः स्यात्तदधिवासनम्' अमरः. But बाण immediately afterwards says 'समाहित...पूजम्.' So अधिवास must be taken in the sense of 'preliminary consecration of an object of worship with suitable *mantras* before the commencement of a sacrifice.' 'अधिवासो नियमदिवसादाद्येऽहनि यथाशास्त्रं विधिना

मन्त्रन्यासादिः' सं०. सम्पादिता गन्ध...माल्यादिना पूजा यस्य. The next sentence is ततः परिणते दिवसे...एकाकी नगरान्निरगात्. परिणते दिवसे when the day came to a close. केनापि...दिक्षु when the regions put on a rosy hue as though someone had made offerings of blood for the purpose of securing success in his undertaking. कृतं रुधिरबलिविधानं यासु. The natural redness of the regions in the evening is fancied to be due to the offerings of blood. रुधिर... दीधितिषु when the rays of the sun hung down as though they were the tongues of goblins greedy (लम्पट) for the offering of blood. Blood is scattered about to propitiate वेतालs. लम्बमानासु applies to 'tongues' also, as they also loll out when greedy. रुधिर...लम्पटासु may apply to the rays of the sun. 'That are greedy (*i. e.* that fall upon) for red offerings' (smeared with red powder). Such offerings are placed on roads in the evening. नरेन्द्रा... सवितरि when the sun, that resorted to the west, as though himself desired to do duty as a guardian of the quarters out of affection for the king. The king had been asked to guard one direction. The sun set in the west. The poet fancies that the sun, seeing that his friend (the king) was to be दिक्पाल, himself wanted to be दिक्पाल and so resorted to the west. गृहीता अपरदिक् (west) येन; गृहीता अपरा (another, other than the one the king would accept) दिक् येन. यातुधानी = राक्षसी. The long and dark shadows of trees looked like demons. पाताल...मण्डलेषु—It was believed that demons infested पाताल, stalked abroad at night and caused obstacles to यज्ञ. पाताल is also supposed to be a region of darkness. पाताल०—this applies both to दानवेषु and ०मण्डलेषु. नभसि...गणे when the clusters of stars formed groups in the sky, as though they desired to witness the terrible rite. On कृष्णचतुर्दशी the night is very dark and so the clusters of stars appear very clear. Sight-seers gather together in small groups. रौद्रं कर्म may also mean 'rite of which the देवता is रुद्र (*i. e.* शिव).' विगाढा dense, deep. विगाढायां शर्वर्याम् in the depth of night *i. e.* when the night had advanced a great deal. सुप्ताः जनाः यस्मिन् (*adj.* of निशीथे). निःशब्दस्तिमिते noiseless and motionless. निशीथे at midnight. 'अर्धरात्रनिशीथौ द्वौ' अमरः. वञ्चयित्वा deceiving *i. e.* eluding. वामकरे स्फुरन् त्सरुः (hilt) यस्य (*adj.* of राजा). उत्खात drawn. विसर्पता...यष्टिः by the spreading radiance of the sword, his whole body was concealed as in a blue silken robe for fear that he might be seen. The king wanted to go unobserved. The dark hue of his sword surrounded his body as in a dark robe and effected his object. अनादिष्टया अपि although not ordered by him. पृष्ठतः...कर्षन् in the shape of the rows (*lit.* braids) of bees pursuing him on account of the fragrance (of his body) he dragged behind him by the hair success in the rite. The dark bees resemble the dark braid of a woman. The bees came behind him. The poet fancies that he seized by the hair कर्मसिद्धि and dragged her behind him (made her follow him), the suggestion being that it was a foregone conclusion that the undertaking was to be successful. उद्देशः spot.

P. 50 l. 24—**P. 51** l. 6. **अथ...भूमिम्.** The first sentence is अथ प्रत्युज्जग्मुस्ते त्रयः...टीटिभ...स्वामिनः (p. 51 l. 1) निवेदितवन्तश्चात्मानम्. द्रौणि...सौप्तिके like the son of द्रोण (*i. e.* अश्वत्थामा), कृप and कृतवर्मन् in the night attack. सुप्तेषु भवं सौप्तिकम्. The reference is to the सौप्तिकपर्व of the महाभारत. While कृप and कृतवर्मा lay under a न्यग्रोध tree at night towards the close of the great war, अश्वत्थामा saw an owl killing crows at night when they were asleep in their nests. This suggested to him a night attack on the Pāṇḍava camp. कृप and कृतवर्मा followed him. अश्वत्थामा entered into the camp and stationed the other two at the door. He killed almost all and those that ran towards the door were killed by कृप and कृतवर्मा. सन्नद्धाः wearing armour. गृहीतः विकटः (frightful, gaudy) वेशः यैः. क्रियमाणः मन्त्रैः शिखाबन्धः येषाम्. कुसुम... चरणैः—bees hovered over the flowers they wore in their top-knot and hummed. The poet fancies that the humming was the reciting of *mantras* and the dark bees were themselves the knot of their hair that was being tied to the accompaniment of mystic *mantras* (in order that they may come unscathed out of the perilous undertaking). उष्णीष...मूर्धभिः on their heads they wore turban wraps that were tied in a knot in the form of a large *svastika* on the middle part of their forehead, as though they were sectarial marks (on the forehead). ललाटमध्ये घटितः (formed) विकटः स्वस्तिकाग्रन्थिः यैः. We rather expect स्वस्तिकग्रन्थीन्. स्वस्तिक is a mystical figure and so the author indulges in the उत्प्रेक्षा 'महामुद्राबन्धानिव.' The *svastika*-like knot of the turban on the forehead seemed to be some mystic मुद्रा on the forehead. For another meaning of मुद्रा (which also may be applicable here) see p. 46. The figure of स्वस्तिक due to wrapping of the turban looks like the intertwining of the hands and figures practised in worship. 'अन्योन्यग्रथिताङ्गुष्ठा प्रसारितपराङ्गुली । महामुद्रेयमुदिता परमीकरणे बुधैः ॥'. एकश्रवणविवरे विततं

(spread, stretching) विमलं दन्तपत्रं (ear-ring) तस्य प्रभालोकलेपेन धवलितः कपोलः येषाम् (*adj.* of मुखैः). आपिबन्तः—governs अन्धकारम् as its object. निशा...षैया from the desire to thin the (numbers of) goblins. निशाचराणां अपचयः (reducing) शर्वर्याः इदं शार्वरम्. If they swallowed up the darkness of night, the goblins would vanish. अच्छाच्छया रुचा by the very clear brilliance. गो...लब्धाः anointed as though with *gorochanā* (yellow pigment) over which *mantras* were muttered. For गोरोचना *vide* notes on रोचना p. 114. स्व...स्त्रिशान् brandishing sharp swords in which their images were reflected, they seemed to make offerings of human beings for the success of their undertaking. The images reflected in the bright sword-blade are fancied to be human beings killed by the sword-blade for ensuring success. निस्त्रिंशस्य अंशवः तेषां सन्तानेन सीमन्तितं तिमिरं यस्याः (*adj.* of त्रियामाम्). निस्त्रिंशांशु...पाटयन्तः—the idea is:—by the rays of their swords they (being three) parted (सीमन्तित) the darkness of night into three parts. The poet fancies that they cut up the night into three parts in order to guard their several regions. Read खण्डैः for खड्गैः. सार्ध...घटयन्तः with their shields that had crescents on them and had flashing on them star-like silver knobs, which (shields) looked like pieces of night sheared (निकृत्त) by the sharp edge of their swords, they seemed to create another night all of a sudden. In a night there is generally the moon; on that particular night there could be no moon as it was कृष्णचतुर्दशी. Their shields had bright crescent-shaped figures. कलधौतं gold or silver 'कलधौतं रूप्यहेम्नोः' अमरः. ०वलिः एव तरलः तारागणः येषाम्. Stars twinkle in the night; on the shields there were star-like silver patches. The shields were dark. For these three reasons the poet fancies them to be pieces of night. They walked in a line holding their dark shields; and so the author fancies that they created another night. For बुद्बुद (a sphere or knob) compare 'परिणतवराटकघटितबुद्बुदार्धचन्द्रखण्डखचितं (ध्वजं)' काद० p. 224. काञ्चनशृङ्खलाकलापेन नियमितं (fastened) निबिडं (thick or close-fitting) निष्प्रवाणि (new unbleached cloth) येषाम्. 'अनाहतं निष्प्रवाणि' अमरः (छेदः क्षालनं भोगश्च आहननं तद्रहितमनाहतम्-क्षीर०). 'निष्प्रवाणिश्च' पा. 2. 2. 160 (कबभावोऽत्र निपात्यते। प्रवाणी तन्तुवाय-शलाका। निर्गता प्रवाणी अस्य निष्प्रवाणिः पटः। समाप्तवानः नवः इत्यर्थः। सि.कौ.). बद्धा असिधेनुः यैः that had daggers fixed (in their waist-belt). निवे...त्मानम् they announced themselves. ताम्—this and the following adjectives in the accu. sing. (*f.*) qualify ०भूमिम्. बलि...

दिग्भागतया the regions being filled with the smoke of *guggulu* and incense that was overspread with the light of the lamps (that were lit in worship). विक्षिप्य...निशामिव—the idea is:—white mustard was being scattered in all directions for protection from evil spirits. The poet fancies that the smoke of गुग्गुलु and धूप looking glossy on account of बलिदीप was really the night running away, having its darkness half burnt by the mustard seeds. One whose limbs are half burnt runs away (not one who is completely burnt). For white mustard, see p. 114. समुपकल्पितानि (got ready) सर्वाणि उपकरणानि यस्याम्. साधनभूमिः place of accomplishing an object by magic *i. e.* cemetery.

P. 51 ll. 7—22 **तस्यां च...कृतवान्.** The first sentence is तस्यां च...भैरवाचार्यमपश्यत् (l. 18). कुमु...धवलेन as white as the pollen of कुमुद्s (white night lotus). दीप्ततरः तेजःप्रसरः यस्य whose radiance was very much aglow. Remove the comma after ०प्रसरम्. पृथु...सवितारम् like the sun in autumn surrounded by a broad halo (परिवेशः). In शरद्, the sun's disc is clear and not clouded (as it often is in summer). भैरवाचार्य looked like the sun and the circle of ashes like the halo. मध्य...मन्दरम्—भैरवाचार्य looked like the मन्दर mountain and the circle of ashes like the whirlpool of the milky ocean. For मन्दर as the churning handle, *vide* p. 52. रक्तानि स्रक् अम्बरं आभरणानि च यस्य (*adj.* of शवस्य). उत्तानशयस्य lying on its back. जातः जातवेदाः अग्निः यस्मिन् (*adj.* of मुखकुहरे). प्रारब्धं अग्निकार्यं येन. भैरवाचार्य sat on the chest of a corpse and offered oblations to fire kindled (by magic power) in the mouth of the corpse. कृष्णः अङ्गरागः (unguents) यस्य. कृष्णः प्रतिसरः (amulet) यस्य. 'भवेत्**प्रतिसरो** मन्त्रभेदे माल्ये च कङ्कणे ।...**आरक्षे करसूत्रे** च' मेदिनी. कृष्ण...नयन्तम् under the guise of the oblation of black sesame, he seemed as though annihilating the defiled atoms that were the cause of his being born a man, with the desire of becoming a विद्याधर. The black sesame are fancied to be the atoms that go to make up the human body. They are supposed to be कलुषित (defiled) as compared with the constituents of the body of विद्याधरs. The तिलs being कृष्ण, the atoms are said to be कालुष्यपरमाणुs. आहुति...दीधितिभिः with the rays of his nails that were scattered about when he offered the oblations, he seemed to cleanse the fire that was polluted by contact with the mouth of a corpse. The bright rays resemble water used for cleansing. धूमेन आलोहितः (slightly red) तेन. क्षतजं blood.

The glances of his red eyes are fancied to be offerings of blood. ईषत् विवृतं (open) अधरपुटं तेन प्रकटितानि सितानि दशनशिखराणि यस्मिन् (*adj.* of मुखेन). दृश्य...पङ्क्तिना इव–the white tips of his teeth are fancied to be the lines of the syllables of the *mantras* he was muttering. होम...यवान्—the lamps that were lighted near him were reflected in the perspiration due to his efforts in offering oblations. The poet fancies that he burnt his body with those lamps to ensure success. बहुगुणेन consisting of many threads (with ब्रह्मसूत्रेण); of great efficacy (with विद्याराजेन). विद्याराज is a particular *mantra.* बहुगुणेन may also mean 'repeated many times' (with विद्याराजेन). There is another sense suggested. ब्रह्मसूत्र is the work of बादरायण dealing with the Vedānta philosophy. ब्रह्मविद्या is the king of विद्याs (विद्याराज). Compare गीता 9. 2 '**राजविद्या** राजगुह्यं पवित्रमिदमुत्तमम्'. शातक्रतवीमाशाम् the quarter of Indra (*i. e.* the east). For the guardians of the eight quarters, see p. 140. कौबेरीम् the north presided over by कुबेर. प्राचेतसीम् west presided over by प्रचेतस् (*i. e.* वरुण). त्रै...ककुभम् the quarter marked with the constellation of त्रिशङ्कु *i. e.* the south. त्रिशङ्कु was father of हरिश्चन्द्र. He wished to go to heaven with his mortal body. He went to his family priest वसिष्ठ who declared it to be impossible. He then went to वसिष्ठ's sons who also rejected his proposal. त्रिशङ्कु then went to विश्वामित्र who raised him towards heaven, when Indra refused to admit him and made him fall headlong. Then विश्वामित्र called upon him to stay where he was and created new worlds, नक्षत्रs &c. The gods intervened and made विश्वामित्र's creations as eternal as those of ब्रह्मा and त्रिशङ्कु blazed forth as a constellation. *Vide* रामायण बालकाण्ड 57–60. Compare 'त्रिशङ्कोरिवोभयलोकभ्रष्टस्य नक्तन्दिवमर्वाक्शिरसस्तिष्ठतः' हर्ष० 7th उ०; 'सुरलोकमारोहतस्त्रिशङ्कोरिव कुपितशतमखहुङ्कारनिपतिता राजलक्ष्मीः' कादम्बरी p. 8 of P. The author avoids the use of the words दक्षिणां दिशम्, as they are inauspicious.

P. 51 l. 23—**P. 52** l. 14. **एवं...पातयत्.** दिक्पाल...चार्ये while भैर० fearlessly performed his terrific work, being inside the cage of the arms of the four guardians of the quarters (*viz.* the king and the three others). अति...कौणपेषु when the demons causing obstacles, after making much noise for a long time and after having found that their efforts (to frighten the guardians and cause obstacles) proved futile, became quiet (*i. e.* vanished). '**राक्षसः कौणपः** क्रव्यात्' अमरः (कुणपमत्ति कौणपः). गल...समये when midnight had just passed. मण्डल...रेण not far to the north of the circle (of ashes in which भैर० was sitting). प्रलय...दीर्यत the earth was rent open, as though exhibiting a chasm of the jaws of the Great Boar at the time of *pralaya.* For प्रलय see above p. 210. The demon हिरण्याक्ष, on the strength of a boon from Bramhā, became insolent and carried the earth into the ocean. Vishṇu assumed the form of a boar and brought it up. See भागवतपुराण 3rd स्कन्ध chap. 13–19. Compare 'येन **प्रलयवराह**घोणाभिघातभीता भूतधात्री... सागरमवतीर्णा' कादम्बरी p. 124 of P; 'वसति दशनशिखरे धरणी तव लग्ना । शशिनि कलङ्ककलेव निमग्ना । केशव धृतसूकररूप जय जगदीश हरे ॥' गीतगोविन्द. The next sentence is सहसैव...तस्मात् विवरात्...कुवलयश्यामलः पुरुष उज्जगाम (p. 52 l. 6). आशावारणैः (दिग्गजैः) उत्क्षिप्तः (tossed up, uprooted). आ...स्तम्भः इव as though he were the iron post for tying elephants. 'आलानं बन्धस्तम्भे' अमरः. The post is fixed in the earth. As the पुरुष was dark-coloured, formidable and suddenly rose up from the earth, he is fancied to be आ...स्तम्भ. महावराहस्य इव पीवरं स्कन्धपीठं यस्य (*adj.* of पुरुषः) whose square shoulders were stout like those of the Great Boar. नर...द्भूतः—By the contact of महावराह with the earth at the time of raising it up out of the ocean, a demon was born of the earth, named नरक. He was very powerful and deprived वरुण of his umbrella, took away the ear-rings of अदिति. 'यदाहमुद्धृता नाथ त्वया सूकरमूर्तिना । त्वत्स्पर्शसम्भवः पुत्रस्तदायं मय्यजायत ॥' विष्णुपुराण 5. 59. 23. The पुरुष also rose from the bowels (गर्भात्) of the earth. Compare 'पुरा महावराहसम्पर्कसम्भृतगर्भया भगवत्या भुवा नरको नाम सूनुरसावि रसातले' हर्ष० 7th उ०. बलि...पातालम् he seemed to be the demon Bali rising up after cleaving asunder *Pātāla.* When Bali became very powerful, Vishṇu assumed the form of a Brāhmaṇa boy and begged of him land measuring his three steps. Then Vishṇu assumed a universal form, covered heaven and earth in two steps and placed the third on Bali's head and sent him down to पाताल where he is supposed to reign even now, as he is one of the seven चिरजीविन्s. *Vide* भागवतपुराण 8th स्कन्ध chap. 20–23. Note 'तावत्सुतलमध्यास्तां विश्वकर्मविनिर्मितम् ।' chap. 22. 32. उपरि ज्वलितः रत्नप्रदीप यस्य. Remove the comma after ०प्रदीपः. As his body and hair were dark, he is said to be a mansion of sapphire. As he had a brilliant मालती wreath on his head we have the words उपरि... दीपः. Jewelled lamps are lighted in palaces. स्निग्ध...मौलिः the top (मौलिः) of whose head was charming with glossy, dark, thick and curling hair. उन्मीलन्ती (gleaming) मालतीमुण्डमाला यस्य. गद्गद... मदेन by his gurgling (faltering) voice and his naturally red eye, he seemed as though drunk by the pride (or 'intoxication') of youth. One who has drunk wine has a red eye and hoarse voice. **'मत्ते शौण्डोत्कटक्षीबाः'** अमरः. वल्गत् गलदाम यस्य whose necklace dangled about his throat. For क 'added to बहुव्रीहि compounds, *vide* p. 12. कर...पङ्कयन् with the mud crushed in his clenched hands he again and again smeared his big shoulders resembling the foreheads of the elephants of the quarters. ०कुम्भस्य इव आभा ययोः. कुम्भः frontal globe on the temple of an elephant. This action is characteristic of our wrestlers even now. सान्द्र... देशः with the irregularly made marks of moist-(सान्द्र) sandal paste, he seemed to be a part of the autumnal sky variegated (शारित) with pieces of very white clouds. 'अविद्यमाना व्यवस्था येषु ते अव्यवस्थाः स्थासकाः तैः. For स्थासक, see p. 53 above. He had applied white sandal paste to his body in various places without any order. His body was dark like the clear blue sky of शरद्. In the sky also irregular patches of clouds are seen in शरद्. शारदं (शरदः इदं) आकाशं तस्य एकदेशः. For चण्डातक, see above p. 69. क्षामतरीकृतः कुक्षिः यस्य whose flanks looked small (by his waist being tightly bound). कक्ष्या...शेषेण after having tightly girt his waist, he gracefully let loose on the ground the fringe of his white cotton cloth used at exercise time and thereby he appeared as though supported from behind by शेष. The idea is:—over his चण्डातक, he had firmly tied his waist with the coils of a long white piece of cotton cloth which he used at the time of taking exercise. A portion of that cloth remained, which he allowed to reach the ground behind him. Being white, it resembled the serpent शेष that is also white. शेष also is धरणितलग *i. e.* it supports the earth. 'फाली कक्ष्याबन्धः' सं०. **'फालः** पुंसि महादेवे कालिन्दीभेदनेपि च। क्लीबं सीरोपकरणे **त्रिषु कार्पासवाससि** ॥' मेदिनी. स्थिरौ स्थूलौ ऊरुदण्डौ यस्य. भूमि...पदानि he planted his steps slowly as though he feared that the earth would break (if he walked faster). निर्भर...गुरु heavy with great pride. A शैल (mountain) also is heavy (गुरु). मुहुर्मुहुः... टाङ्कारैः by the terrible and twanging slapping (with his hand) of his left arm that was doubled (द्विगुणित) on his chest and of his right thigh, put forward slantingly and thus appearing to be coiled up. टाङ्कार is an onomatopoetic word. It is better to read चण्डास्फोटन. The पुरुष smote loudly his left arm doubled on his chest and his right thigh with his hand. This is a characteristic action for wrestless and is a sort of challenge. कर्म...कुर्वन्—The noise made by the slapping was so terrific that it seemed as though the पुरुष sent down निर्घातs for hindering the rite on which भै० was embarked and as though depriving the mortal world of one organ (*i. e.* of the sense of hearing). The noise of the आस्फोटन was deafening. निर्घातः 'noise of contending winds in the sky; a whirlwind.' 'पवनः पवनाभिहतो गगनादवनौ यदा समापतति । भवति तदा निर्घातः स च पापो दीप्तविहगरुतः ॥' बृहत्संहिता 39. 1. कुवलय is a blue lotus. नर...भारत्या in a voice as terrific as the echo (निर्घोषः) of the roar of the Man-lion. This is a reference to the 5th incarnation of Vishṇu when the latter tore off with his nails the chest of हिरण्यकशिपु विद्या...कामुक confident lover of विद्याधरीs. This is said in derision भैर० wanted to be a विद्याधर and believed that he would become one by the successful performance of the rite he was engaged in The emphasis is on the word श्रद्धा, the idea being 'you are sure that you would be a विद्याधर, but I shall show that your belief is worthless.' किम...लषसि Is this pride due to (the possession of) a little knowledge or the arrogance due to being helped by friends that without making an offering to this person (*i. e.* myself) you desire success (in this rite) like a fool? एतावता कालेन during all this time. क्षेत्राधिपतिः lord or tutelary deity of a place. अस्य... देशस्य (to be connected with ०पतिः) of this country that is styled (श्रीकण्ठ) after me. लब्धः व्यपदेशः (नाम) येन. नागोहम्—even now the belief in the existence of guardian नागs presiding over various places is very common. अनि...गगने what power have the planets to move in the sky against my will? Even the planets cannot act against his wishes. What of भै० who wanted to go to heaven as विद्याधर? भूनाथो...क्रियते Though a king, he is no king and is wretched since he is made a tool by vile S'aivas like you. 'निहीनोऽपसदो जाल्मः' अमरः. The word अपसद is generally used at the end of compounds as a term of abuse. The contrast is between भूनाथः and अनाथः (no king; helpless in the hands of भै०). सहस्वे...फलम् now receive along with this bad king the fruit of the bad conduct of a bad snake-charmer. नरेन्द्र means 'a snake-doctor.' भैरवाचार्य was a bad नरेन्द्र in that he did not propitiate the नाग. A and C read दुर्नरेन्द्रेण दुर्नयस्य, but the reading in the text is preferable, as it is more in keeping with Bāṇa's style. नरेन्द्र—compare 'आविष्टा इव नरेन्द्रवृन्दपरिवृताः' हर्ष० 4th उ० and notes thereon; compare also 'महाशीविष इव दुर्नरेन्द्राभिभवरोषितः' हर्ष० 6th उ०. प्रकोष्ठप्रहारैः by the strokes of his forearms. स... कृपाणान् together with their armours and swords.

P. 52 l. 15—**P. 53** l. 2 **अथापूर्व...द्दष्टिम्.** अपू...श्रवणात् on hearing the unprecedented insult. This was the first time that the king heard such insulting language. अविद्यमानः शस्त्रव्रणः येषाम् (*adj.* of अवयवैः). अशस्त्र...वमद्भिः that (limbs), though unwounded (then), as though vomitted, under the guise of the sweat due to wrath, the dark water of sword-edges drunk in many battles. The idea is:—He was sorely pained at heart by the insulting words of the नाग, though he was not physically wounded. Sweat due to fury appeared on his body. The poet fancies that the sweat was the 'water' of the sword edges (of his enemies) which had struck him in former battles. अवय...कुर्वद्भिः with his limbs, that under the guise of horripilation, made him light for battle by shooting out an array of arrow-points. His body had रोमाञ्च due to rage. The hair looked like arrow-points. The poet fancies that the hair were arrowheads, planted in his body in former battles but now taken out in order to make his body fit for combat. प्रतिबिम्बितः तारागणः यस्मिन् (*adj.* of अट्टहासेन). स्पष्टं दृष्टा धवला दन्तमाला यथा स्यात्तथा. अवज्ञया in contempt. हसता इव—The stars reflected in the blade looked like white teeth seen when one laughs. कथ्यमानः सत्त्वस्य (courage, spirit) अवष्टम्भः (pride, majesty) यस्य. The three clauses ०वमद्भिः, ०कुर्वद्भिः and ०हसता इव are to be connected with कथ्यमान. These three indicated the greatness of his courage, in spite of the fact that his three companions had been brought to the ground in no time. परिकरबन्धे विभ्रमेण भ्रमितः करः तस्य नखानां किरणचक्रवालेन. व्यप...दिशः—the idea is:—the king girded up his loins as a preparation for the impending fight. The rays of his hand gracefully girding up spread round. The poet fancies that the circle of rays was a charmed circle which the king drew for imprisoning the नाग and preventing it from running in the ten directions (which the king thought the नाग would do). For परिकरबन्ध, see text p. 4. l. 6 and notes thereon. नागदमनाय मन्त्रैः मण्डलबन्धः तेन. The com. says 'मण्डलं गारुडशास्त्रप्रसिद्धमैन्द्रादिकम्.' 'कुण्डली गूढपाचक्षुःश्रवाः **काकोदरः फणी'** अमरः (काकस्येव उदरमस्य). The king addressed the नाग as काक out of contempt. It is only a crow that asks for a बलि (as the नाग did above). Further the word is in contrast with the word राजहंस below. राजहंसे swan-like king; a राजहंस. A crow is a nonentity before राजहंसs. अमी...भाषितैः what is the use of these harsh words? अ‌ं न भवसि you will be no more *i. e.* I shall kill you. अगृहीता हेतिः (weapon) यैः. अगृही...हर्तुम्

my arm has not been taught to strike the unarmed. It is better to take अनादृततरं outside the quotation marks. Connect अनादृततरम् (with great unconcern or disdain) with अभिधाय. आस्फोटयामास he slapped (his arm and thigh). निरायुधम्—object of जेतुम्. चर्मफलकेन सह स...फलकम् (*adj.* of असिम्) together with the shield. अर्धो...कक्ष्याम् above his cloak he girt up his loins for a fight with fists. अर्धोरुक is the same as चण्डातक. **'अर्धोरुकं वरस्त्रीणां स्याच्चण्डातकमंशुकम्'** अमरः (ऊर्वोरर्धाच्छादकमंशुकमर्धोरुकं—क्षीर०). कक्ष्या girdle, waist. निर्दयेन आस्फोटनेन स्फुटितौ भुजौ तयोः रुधिरं तस्य शीकरेण सिच्यमानौ. The furious slapping of their arms caused blood to come out of them. शब्द...भुवनम्—the incessant slapping of their arms filled the world with the sound. उच्चखान drew out (of the sheath). अपश्य...वीतम् the king saw inside the wreath his sacred thread. For वैकक्षक, see p. 26. It is worn like the यज्ञोपवीत and hence the king did not notice it before. उपसंहृतः (stopped) शस्त्रव्यापारः येन. दुर्विनीत impudent. अस्ति... मिदम् you possess this seed (*i. e.* means) which (safely) carries you over your bad deeds. विश्रब्धम् *adv.* confidently. The यज्ञोपवीत showed that the नाग was a ब्राह्मण. A ब्राह्मण was never to be killed, however great his offence might be. ब्रह्महत्या was a महापातक; *vide* p. 160 above. Hence the king laid aside his weapon. घ्राणावलेपिनम् smearing his nose (*i. e.* overpowering it).

P. 53 ll. 3-28. **अथ...इति.** The first sentence is **अथ...** अट्टहासस्य मध्ये...स्फुरन्तीं...स्त्रियमपश्यत् (l. 20). तडि...स्फुरन्तीम्—the lady was fair like a flash of lightning and the sword was like a dark cloud. प्रभया...यामाम् that as though swallowed up the night by her radiance. तामरसं (red lotus) हस्ते यस्याः. The woman of whom the king had a vision was लक्ष्मी. So she was तामरसहस्ता. कोमला...कर्षन्तीम् that drew the webs of the glow of her delicate toes, as though they were the coral creepers on the seaside sticking to her feet. Her toes were red like coral. कर...बिभ्रतीम्—पद्म closes its petals in moonlight. Her toe-nails were bright like moonlight. Therefore the poet fancies that लक्ष्मी desiring to have the lotus in her hand always blooming carried the moon cut into pieces (*viz.* her toe-nails). To explain (as C and T and Mr. Kale do) that it was a night lotus and that therefore she carried the pieces of the moon is not happy. गुल्फा...गताम् as her anklets lay about her ankles (गुल्फः) she appeared to have escaped from fetters (or imprisonment) in which there were many thick links. कटकं a link. स्थिता निबिडा

figure) is carved on stone pillars. रण...हंसीम् the female flamingo spoilt (दुर्ललित) by the yearning (दोहदं) for playing on the ripples of the rivers of blood in battles. लक्ष्मी cannot be had without bloodshed. A राजहंसी plays on the ripples of rivers. सित...ण्डिनीम् the female peacock in the forest (षण्ड:-ण्डम्) of white umbrellas of kings. A peacock dwells in thickets. White umbrellas are insignia of royalty. So लक्ष्मी may be said to dwell in them. 'अब्जादिकदम्बे **षण्ड**मस्त्रियाम्' अमरः. अति...सिंहीम् the lioness that sportively wanders in the forest of the edges of very sharp weapons. असि...कमलिनीम्—the idea is:—A lotus plant grows in water, so लक्ष्मी grows on the 'water' of swords' edges (*i. e.* it is the sharpest sword that wins लक्ष्मी). अप...रसेन I am captivated by this your love (रसः) for bravery. A fluid or stream (रसः) may carry away a person.

P. 53 l. 29—**P. 54** l. 5 **वीराणां...बभूव.** वीराणां...काराः In the case of heroes conferring of obligations on others is never wearisome *i. e.* heroes love to confer numerous obligations on others. पुनरुक्त repeated, superfluous; hence 'wearisome.' प्रीततरं हृदयं यस्याः. She was pleased to see that the king cared more for the success of भैरवाचार्य's undertaking than for any personal gain. विस्तीर्य...भूपालम्—the idea is—with an eye dilated through pleasure she looked at the king. The white of her eye was like the waters of क्षीरसागर. The poet fancies that the king was bathed in क्षीरसागर poured (पर्यस्त) over his head. At the time of coronation (अभिषेक), a king's head is bathed with holy water. सत्त्वोत्कर्षेण by the excess of courage or spirit. सूर्याचन्द्रमसोः—for the lengthening of सूर्य in this द्वन्द्व compound, note the Sūtra 'देवताद्वन्द्वे च' पा. 6. 3. 26 (इहोत्तरपदे परे आनङ् । मित्रावरुणौ । सि. कौ.). Two वंशs, that of the sun and the moon, were already well-known. लक्ष्मी promises him that he would be the founder of a third वंश as famous as the other two. अविच्छिन्नस्य unbroken. उपचीयमाना (growing) वृद्धिः यस्य. शुचीनि सुभगानि (handsome) सत्यत्यागधैर्यशौण्डानि पुरुषप्रकाण्डानि तत्प्रायस्य—mostly consisting of eminent men fond of truthfulness, liberality and courage. प्रकाण्ड at the end of compounds means 'pre-eminent.' 'मतल्लिकामचर्चिका**प्रकाण्ड**मुद्धतल्लजौ । प्रशस्तवाचकान्यमूनि' अमरः. हरिश्चन्द्रः—the story of हरिश्चन्द्र and his persecution by विश्वामित्र are well-known. *Vide* मार्कण्डेपु० chap. 7-8 for details. हरिश्चन्द्र was lord of all the earth except काशी, which was under the protection of शिव himself. Hence the words सर्वद्वीपानां भोक्ता.

मान्धाता was a great चक्रवर्ती and was desirous of conquering heaven after he had conquered the earth. Compare 'मान्धाता किलैवंविधे...हनि भेजे जन्म । अर्वाक्ततोऽस्मिन्नन्तराले पुनरेवंविधे योगे चक्रवर्तिजनने नाजनि जगति कश्चिदपरः' हर्ष० 4th उ० and *vide* notes thereon. यस्यायं...चामरम् over whom this hand (of mine) will itself wave the chowrie, abandoning the lotus. लक्ष्मी says she will throw away the lotus in her hand and hold a chowrie in it for waving it over that gret king. तिरोबभूव became invisible.

P. 54 ll. 6–16. **भूमि...चचक्षे.** देव्या...वचसा—लक्ष्मी had said 'एवमस्तु' when the king solicited her to crown the undertaking of भै० with success. कर्मणा...पादितेन because the rite was properly performed (to its finish). सद्य एव at once. केयूरी wearing an armlet. मेखली with a girdle. मुद्गरी with a mallet or club. खड्गी—with a sword. विद्याधरs always carry swords. Compare 'अनिस्त्रिंशा विद्याधराः' above (text p. 18. l. 22). अदूर...रथाः the ambitions of indolent and weak-minded people never soar high. फल्गु चेतः येषाम्. 'असारं फल्गु' अमरः. फल्गु unsubstantial, worthless, feeble. सतां...कृतयः but the favours of the good are naturally far-reaching. स्वप्नेऽप्यसम्भावितां not imagined even in dreams. दक्षिणाम् gift. सम्प...याति a man light by nature goes up (becomes puffed up) like a balance even after obtaining a particle of prosperity. In the case of a delicate balance, the equilibrium is disturbed even by a particle. त्वदीयैः...कृतस्य that is already made an instrument by your qualities. He says:—my heart is already captivated by your qualities. There is also another sense suggested. Threads (गुणs) are employed in binding a thing. लब्धः आत्मलाभः येन. त्वत्त...लाभस्य that has obtained its present position through you. He says that he owes his विद्याधरत्व to the king and to no one else. भै० wanted to do some good turn to the king out of gratitude. निर्ल...त्मानम् this my foolish heart is shameless in that I desire to keep myself in your memory by serving you in accomplishing some small affair of yours. प्रत्युप...दृम्भाः the dignity of the hearts of the wise is inaccessible to (the receiving of a) favour in return *i. e.* the wise never receive something in return for what they have done for others. प्रत्याचचक्षे he refused (the offer of भै०).

P. 54 ll. 17—28 **तथोक्त...विवेश.** कुवलय...स्राविणा as though it were a grove of blue lotuses dropping the spray of dew (अवश्यायः). The pupil of his eye resembled कुवलय and the bright tears dew-drops. ब्रवीमि...सदृशम् if I say 'I am going', that would not be suitable to the affection I bear to you. The roots या and गम् were inauspicious and would not be used by a person parting from his friend. In these and the following clauses, भैरवाचार्य puts forward various sentences and dismisses each of them as not suited to adequately express his sentiments when parting from his friend, the king. त्वदीयाः...सक्तम् If I say 'my life is at thy disposal,' that is merely superfluous. His meaning is 'without my saying so, my life is already at your service; so those words need not be uttered.' गृह्यता...करणम् 'take this wretched body' would be to keep things distinct (which are not so). You and I are one. Therefore what is mine is already yours. To ask you to receive my body would be to make a distinction (व्यतिरेकः) between you and me which does not exist. तिल...रूपम् 'I am purchased by you bit by bit' would not be appropriate to your obligations. Your obligations are so many and so great, that even if I were cut up into small particles the number of those particles would be too small as compared with them. बान्ध...करणमिव 'you are my kinsman' would be placing you at a distance. One is not necessarily very friendly and affectionate to one's kinsman. त्वयि...प्रत्यक्षम् 'my heart remains with you' cannot be directly perceived. I cannot show by प्रत्यक्षप्रमाण (by the testimony of the eye) that my heart is bound to yours. त्व...श्रद्धेयम् 'this my success (or attainment of superhuman power) that causes separation from you is a veritable torment (कारणा)' cannot be believed. As I aspired to be विद्याधर and worked hard to secure my object, no one will believe me if I say that my सिद्धि is a torment to me. **'कारणा तु यातना** तीव्रवेदना' अमरः. निष्का...वादः 'your kindness was disinterested' is a mere repetition (or praise). निष्कारणः would also mean 'without any merit in me (to deserve such kindness).' He means:—if I say 'निष्का...कारः,' I do not say anything new; it is your nature to do kind deeds without any merit in those whom you so benefit. So my words will repeat what already exists and I may be looked upon as simply praising you. Vedic sentences are divided into विधि and अर्थवाद. A विधि is that which lays down a rule or injunction or a religious commandment such as स्वर्गकामो ज्योतिष्टोमेन यजेत. An अर्थवाद is a sentence which recommends a विधि, which illustrates it, praises those that followed the विधि and points out the evils of not following a विधि. अनुवाद is one of the three kinds of अर्थवादs. अनुवाद is explained as 'सिद्धस्य उपन्यासः' or as 'विधिविहितस्य अनुवचनमनुवादः.' स्मर्तव्या...ज्ञा 'I should be remembered' sounds as a command. He says—'you are so great that it would be presumptuous on my part to command you.' सर्वथा...जनः At all events this person (*i. e.* I), remorseless in pursuing his own selfish purpose, should be kept in mind in talking about ungrateful persons and in narrating the accounts of bad men. He requests the king to remember him at least among ungrateful and bad men. वेगेन छिन्नः हारः तस्मात् उच्छलितः (shaken, tossed about) मुक्ताफलनिकरः तेन ताडितः तारागणः यस्मिन् (*adj.* of ०तलम्) or we may take it as an adverb (ताडितः तारागणः यथा स्यात्तथा). As he rose up with violent speed, his necklace was rent asunder and he struck the stars with the falling pearls. सीमन्तितः (parted) ग्रहग्रामः ग्रहसमूहः येन. As the white line parts the hair of women so he parted the planets while going through them. ग्राहितः विनयः येन who was taught modesty. श्रीकण्ठ had been humbled by the king. कर्तव्येषु...ग्राह्यः अयं जनः I should be favoured with a command whenever necessary.

P. 54 l. 29—**P. 55** l. 12 **नरपति...करोत्**. The principal sentence is नरपतिः...नगरं विवेश. क्षीण...क्षपायाम् when the night had almost run out. प्रवातुमारब्धे (connect with वनानिले) began to blow. प्रबुध्य...सुरभौ fragrant with the exhalations of the opening lotus plants; fragrant like the breaths of waking handsome women. कमलिनी = पद्मिनी. Writers on erotics divide women into four classes पद्मिनी, चित्रिणी, हस्तिनी and शङ्खिनी, the first being the best. ०परिहासेन स्वेदिनि इव. अवश्यायशीकरेण सह सावः (बहुव्रीहि). वन...शीकरे—the idea is:—the wind was charged with the dew of dawn; the poet fancies that the wind was a lover who was covered with sweat (in the form of dew drops) at the joke of removing the shawls from the bosoms of forest nymphs. परिमलेन आकृष्टाः मधुकृतः (मधुकराः) येन. कुमुद...वाहिनि that brought sleep to moon-lotuses. At the advent of morn कुमुदs close their petals. निशा...जडे chilled by the end of night; void of the warmth (of love) on account of the old age of Night. तुषारलेशिनि having particles of frost or snow. विरहेण विधुरं (helpless) चक्रवाकचक्रं तस्य निःश्वसितैः सन्तापितायाम् इव. विरह...त्रियामायाम्—the idea is:—चक्रवाक pairs are separated at night. Throughout the night they heaved hot sighs. The poet fancies that the night was corched by those hot sighs and entered the western ocean to allay the heat. One that is heated enters into water. As a matter of fact there is a glow of light in the east at dawn, while the west is still dark. Hence the words 'अपरजल०.' For चक्रवाक, *vide* notes pp. 67, 97. साक्षा... नलिनीषु when the lotus plants began to open (their eyes) as though curious to see Lakshmī that was bodily present. लक्ष्मी had showed herself to the king. As night was drawing to a close, the lotuses began to open. The poet fancies that they were curious to see the bodily presence of लक्ष्मी. उन्निद्राः पक्षिणः यस्मिन् (*adj.* of कानने) the birds in which awoke from sleep. क्षरति...कानने when the forests, the creepers in which were made to dance by a soft breeze, dropped down a mass of particles of frost as though it were a heap of flowers. Both flowers and particles of frost are bright. मृदुपवनेन लासिताः लताः यस्मिन्. कमल...कुमुदेषु when the closing *kumudas* (night lotuses) inside which were imprisoned buzzing bees hummed forth, as though they were auspicious conches (blown) to awaken the glory of day lotuses. Kings and great persons are aroused from sleep in the morning by the blowing of conches, by the lays of bards &c. अन्तर्बद्धाः ध्वनन्तः मधुकराः येषु. कुमुदs began to close in the morning and the bees were confined in them and made a noise inside. This noise is fancied to be the blowing of a conch. उज्जिहानाः (getting up from their beds) रविरथवाजिनः तैः विसृष्टैः. प्रोथपवनैः the breaths of their nostrils. प्रोत्सार्य...तारकासु when the stars, the buds of the creeper of Night, clustered together in the west, as though they were driven away (by the breaths of the sun's horses). श्यामा (रात्रिः) एव लता तस्याः कलिकासु or श्यामालता प्रियङ्गुलता तस्याः कलिकासु. The stars were like buds. In the east no stars were visible on account of the glow of day-break. The poet fancies that on the breaths of the sun's horses, stars were wafted towards the west and there clustered together. वारुण्यां ककुभि—वरुण is the lord of the west. मन्दानिलेन लुलितानि (shaken) ०कुसुमानि तेषां धूल्या विच्छुरिते (inlaid, covered). मन्दानिल... मण्डले—the constellation of the Great Bear looked grey in the light of morn. The poet fancies that it looked grey being covered with pollen &c. मन्दर...श्रयिणि—मन्दर is a mountain to the east of Meru. *Vide* notes above p. 43. The Sun, the Moon and the stars were supposed to revolve round Meru. Compare भागवतपुराण 5. 22. 'यथा कुलालचक्रेण भ्रमता सह भ्रमतां तदाश्रयाणां पिपीलिकादीनां गतिरन्यैव प्रदेशान्तरेष्वप्युपलभ्यमानत्वादेवं **नक्षत्रराशिभिरुपलक्षितेन कालचक्रेण ध्रुवं मेरुं च प्रदक्षिणेन** परिधावता सह &c.' सुर...मृगे when the starry deer sank (towards the west) as though it were the fallen goad of the elephant of the gods (*i. e.* of ऐरावत). The reference is to the constellation of मृगशीर्ष, particularly to the three stars (constituting the belt of Orion) that look like a dart. Those dart-like stars seemed to be the goad of ऐरावत fallen from the rider's hand. नाग...मलीमसानि (*adj.* of अङ्गानि) soiled by the incident (व्यतिकरः) of the fight with the Nāga. शुचिनि *adj.* of ०पयसि. आत्म...करोत् pleased all the three with bath, food and clothing that did not differ from his own. आत्मशरीरात् अनन्तरं (अविद्यमानं अन्तरं विशेषः यस्य) स्नान...च्छादनादि तेन. He gave them the same food that he partook of, the same rich clothing that he wore &c. The com. explains differently. The king made them bathe, take food &c. before himself and then took his bath, food &c. 'आत्मशरीरमनन्तरं यस्य तादृशेन स्नानभोजनाच्छादिना। तेषु कृत्वा पश्चादात्मनः करोतीत्यर्थः' सं०. C and T translate 'with unguents, food and clothing immediately after his own person.'

P. 55 ll. 13-17 **कतिपय...जग्मतुरिति.** परिव्राट् refers to टीटिभ. शौर्यानुरक्तौ devoted to the king on account of his bravery. सम्पादितः मनोरथात् अतिरिक्तः विभवः ययोः on whom was bestowed wealth exceeding even their desires. सुभ...मण्डलाग्रौ who drew out their swords in the midst of the guard of warriors. They were allowed, on account of their rank and devotion to the king, to walk with drawn swords in the midst of the king's guard or in the midst of the king's warlike courtiers. 'कौक्षेयको मण्डलाग्रः करवालः कृपाणवत्' अमरः (मण्डलाकृति अग्रमस्य). समर... युज्यमानौ they occupied the foremost rank in battle. अन्तरान्तरा now and then. राज्ञा समादिष्टौ when ordered by the king. शैशववृत्तान्तान् the incidents of their boyhood.

Uchchhvāsa IV

For a brief analysis of the contents of the first three Uchchhvāsas, see Appendix A. In the third Uchchhvāsa Bāṇa narrated how Pushpabhûti, king of Sthāṇvîs'vara (modern Thanesar) and the ancestor of Emperor Harsha, made the friendship of a S'aiva ascetic Bhairavāchārya, how the latter presented a miraculous sword to the king, and how the king helped the ascetic in the practice of magic for attaining a divine form.

P. 56 Verse 1 The words योग and करग्रह have two meanings. The great even in dreams do not desire to employ deceitful tricks (योग) nor do they take कर (tribute). In these two respects they are distinguishable from others who become *Pati.* Husbands desire union with their wives and take the hand of their wives (at the time of marriage). Without these two (योग and करग्रहण) the great become the masters (पति) of the world by their mere name *i. e.* their very name is sufficient to bring to them the devoted allegiance of the world.

Verse 2 Construe विपुलेऽपि नृपवंशे सकल...कृत् पृथुप्रतिमः एक एव उत्पद्यते विपुलेऽपि गणाधिपस्य मुखे पृथुप्रतिमः एक एव दन्त इव. सकल...कृत् One who strikes terror in (the heart of) all kings. पृथुप्रतिमः— resembling the (ancient king) Pṛithu. Pṛithu was the son of वेन. Formerly the mountains were rebellious and covered the earth just as they pleased. As no corn grew, people became famished and prayed to Pṛithu for deliverance. He levelled the earth by casting away the mountains with his bow and made it fertile. So पृथु also was सकल...कृत् (as महीभृत् means 'mountain' also). See विष्णुपुराण I. 13 'तत उत्सारयामास शैलान् शतसहस्रशः। धनुष्कोट्या तदा वैन्यस्तेन शैलविवर्धिताः' ॥ 82. Compare कादम्बरी (p. 5 of P) 'वैन्य इव चापकोटिसमुत्सारितसकलारातिकुलाचलः'. गणाधिप is the god गणेश, one of whose names is एकदन्त. 'सुमुखश्चैकदन्तश्च कपिलो गजकर्णकः। लम्बोदरश्च विकटो विघ्ननाशो गणाधिपः ॥ धूम्रकेतुर्गणाध्यक्षो भालचंद्रो गजाननः ॥' गणेशपुराण I chap. 92. पृथुः प्रतिमा यस्य (with दन्त) the size of which is great. प्रतिमा also means 'the part of an elephant's head between the tusks'. How Ganes'a became

एकदन्त is explained by the ब्रह्मवैवर्तपुराण. The story is:—एकदा रहसि स्थितयोः पार्वतीपरमेश्वरयोर्द्वारपालत्वमङ्गीकृतं गजाननेन। एतस्मिन्नन्तरे परशुरामः शिवं द्रष्टुमागतः। शिवदर्शनोत्सुकस्यान्तर्जिगमिषोर्द्वाररोधे कृते गणपतिना सह तस्य तुमुलं युद्धमभवत्। परशुरामक्षिप्तेन परशुना च गजाननस्य एको दन्तो भग्नः'.

In these two verses the poet suggests the greatness of Harsha whose birth forms the principal topic of the fourth Uchchhvāsa.

अथ...राजवंशः The principal sentence is अथ तस्मात् पुष्पभूतेः राजवंशः निर्जगाम. There are five dependent clauses containing comparisons. It is to be noted that all the words in these five clauses except the उपमानपदs apply also to राजवंश and पुष्पभूति (according to their respective cases). द्विज...क्षणात् as the navel lotus, the calix of which was resorted to of his own will by Brahmā, (springs) from विष्णु (पुण्डरीकेक्षण). द्विजवरेण ब्रह्मणा स्वेच्छया गृहीतः कोषः (कर्णिका) यस्य (स नाभिपद्मः). 'वा पुंसि पद्मं नलिनम्' इत्यमरः. In the Purāṇas Brahmā is represented as being born in a lotus which springs from the navel of विष्णु. Being स्वयम्भू, his birth must be said to be due to his own will. राजवंश also was द्विज... कोषः (द्विजवरैः ब्राह्मणश्रेष्ठैः स्वेच्छया गृहीतः कोषः यस्य). The kings of पुष्पभूति's line allowed learned Brahmins to take from their treasury as much as they liked. पुष्पभूति was पुण्डरीकेक्षण (कमलनयन). Dr. Buhler (E. I. I. p. 68) says that पुष्यभूति must have been the name of the king (after the constellation of पुष्य) and that the Mss. make little distinction between य and प. लक्ष्मी...रत्नाकरात् as the series of (14) jewels, chief of which was लक्ष्मी, (sprang) from the ocean. लक्ष्मीः पुरःसरा यस्य. This refers to the churning of the ocean, for which see विष्णुपुराण I. 9 and रामायण I. 44. राजवंश was favoured by लक्ष्मी (prosperity) and पुष्पभूति was रत्नाकर (रत्नानां आकरः mine of jewels, *i. e.* possessed all the best things in the world). गुरु...स्थानात् as the assembly of planets mostly consisting of Jupiter (गुरु), mercury (बुध), Venus (कवि), the moon (कलावत्), the sun (तेजस्विन्) and Mars (भूनन्दन) comes up from the mount in the east. गुरु...प्रायः (with राजवंशः) means 'mostly consisting of teachers, wise men, poets, artists (कलावत्), brave men and princes' (भूनन्दन). According to ancient Hindu astronomy there were nine ग्रहs (including the sun). उदयस्थानात् the sun, the moon and the planets were supposed to rise from a mountain in the east, more often called उदयगिरि. But for श्लेष, the word उदयस्थान is used here. कला 'digits of the moon'; 'the 64 arts, such as painting, dancing &c.' पुष्पभूति was the source of prosperity (उदयस्थान) to गुरुबुध०. महा...प्रभावात् as the ocean fit for bearing the great burden sprang from the might of the Sagaras (sons of सगर). By महाभार may be meant विष्णु who sleeps on the ocean or the reference may be to the ocean's keeping the earth inviolate. When the sacrificial horse of सगर was stolen away by इन्द्र, his sixty thousand sons dug the whole earth. The void thus created was filled by the rush of the Ganges brought from heaven by भगीरथ, descendant of सगर. राजवंश was महा...योग्यः (fit to bear the great responsibility of protecting the world). पुष्पभूति was सगरप्रभाव (सगरस्य इव प्रभावः यस्य). दुर्जय...शूरात् as the हरिवंश which comprises Vishṇu (दुर्जय) and Balarāma (sprang) from शूर. दुर्जयः बलश्च ताभ्यां सनाथः. दुर्जय is given as one of the thousand names of विष्णु in the अनुशासनपर्व (महाभारत 13.149.96 समावर्तो निवृत्तात्मा दुर्जयो दुरतिक्रमः). शूर was a descendant of यदु and grandfather of कृष्ण. राजवंशः दुर्जयेन बलेन सैन्येन सनाथः. पुष्पभूति was brave (शूर).

P. 56 यस्मा...राजानः The principal sentence is यस्मात् अजायन्त राजानः. Syntax requires that यस्मात् must be taken with राजवंशः. But it would be better to take it with पुष्पभूतेः, if the sense of what follows be carefully considered. Here again there are numerous dependent clauses containing comparisons. अविनष्ट...मुखात् As the creations of beings, rendered glorious by (the existence of) धर्म in its unimpaired state, are produced in the beginning of the Kṛita age. अविनष्टः (सकलः) धर्मः तेन धवलाः. According to ancient Hindu ideas, in the कृतयुग धर्म existed in its fullest splendour and there was not a trace of अधर्म. In each of the other three युगs (त्रेता, द्वापर and कलि) धर्म decreased by one quarter, and अधर्म increased by one quarter in an ascending scale. 'चतुष्पात्सकलो धर्मः सत्यं चैव कृते युगे। नाधर्मेणागमः कश्चिन्मनुष्यान्प्रति वर्तते ॥ इतरेष्वागमाद्धर्मः पादशस्त्ववरोपितः। चौरिकानृतमायाभिर्धर्मश्चापैति पादशः ॥' मनु० I. 81-82. The kings (राजानः) were also rendered glorious by the fact that in their regime धर्म was never on the wane. कृतं संस्कृतं मुखं यस्य (goes with यस्मात्). प्रतापेन (by light; by valour) आक्रान्तं भुवनं यैः. तेजोनिधेः (from the sun; from the राजवंश that is the centre of bravery). विग्रहेण व्याप्तानि दिङ्मुखानि यैः that covered the quarters with their bodies (with गिरयः); that filled the world with their battles (with राजानः). भूभृत्प्रभवात् from ब्रह्मा who is the creator of mountains (with गिरयः); from that which is the source of kings. Mountains had at first wings and they went where they pleased. The reading भूभृत्प्रवरात् would mean 'from the best of mountains (हिमकर); from the best of kings'. The latter meaning is unsuitable if we take यस्मात् as referring to राजवंश. धर...क्षमा capable of bearing the earth (applies to both दिग्गजाः and राजानः). There are eight guardian elephants of the quarters. They are supposed to support the earth. 'कमठकुलाचलदिग्गजफणिपतिविधृतापि चलति वसुधेयम्' भर्तृहरि. On the birth of the दिग्गजs from ब्रह्मकर, the हस्त्यायुर्वेद of पालकाप्य tells us 'सूर्यस्याण्डकपाले द्वे समानीय प्रजापतिः। हस्ताभ्यां परिगृह्यादौ सप्त सामान्यगायत॥ गायतो ब्रह्मणस्तस्य समुत्पन्ना मतङ्गजाः। chap I. 218–219 (Anand. ed). ब्रह्मकरात् from that which produces ब्रह्म *i. e.* learning (with यस्मात्). 'वेदस्तत्त्वं तपो ब्रह्म' इत्यमरः. पातुम् to drink (with जलधराः); to protect (with राजानः). घनागमः वर्षाकालः तस्मात्. घनः (दृढः) आगमः (sacred knowledge) यस्य or यस्मिन् (with यस्मात्). इच्छा...यिनः applies to both तरवः and राजानः. कल्पतरु was one of the five trees of Paradise. 'पञ्चैते देवतरवो मन्दारः पारिजातकः। सन्तानः **कल्पवृक्षश्च** पुंसि वा हरिचन्दनम्॥'. नन्दनात् from the garden of Indra; from that which gladdened. सर्व...धरात् as the various forms in the universe having for their substrata all the beings spring from Hari. सर्वभूतानि आश्रयाः येषाम् (with प्रकाराः); सर्वभूतानामाश्रयाः that gave shelter to all beings (with राजानः). विश्वस्य रूपाणि तेषां प्रकाराः. श्रीधरात् (with यस्मात्) that was possessed of prosperity.

P. 56 l. 16—**P. 2** l. 13 **तेषु...सम्पदा.** तेषु—supply राजसु. उदपादि 3rd sing. Aorist of पद् with उद्. हूण...केसरी a very lion to the deer in the form of the Hûṇas. हूणाः एव हरिणाः तेषां केसरी. Huns—This is a name given to several peoples:—(1) the Huns who invaded the Roman Empire between 372–453 A. D. and were most formidable under Attila; (2) the White Huns or Ephthalites who troubled Persia from 420 to 557 A. D.; they are probably the सितहूणs mentioned by वराहमिहिर (बृहत्संहिता 11.61); (3) the Hûṇas who invaded India about the same period. See the Mandasor stone inscription of यशोधर्मन् (C. I. III p. 146) and the Bhitari stone pillar inscription of स्कन्दगुप्त (C. I. III p. 54) of whom it is said, 'हूणैर्यस्य समागतस्य समरे दोर्भ्यां धरा कम्पिता'. गुर्जरप्रजागरः—who caused loss of sleep (through fear) to the Gurjara king (*i. e.* king of Bhinmal in Rajputana). गान्धाराधिपः एव गन्धद्विपः तस्य कूटपाकलः. गान्धार was the country round modern Kandahar. गन्धद्विपः an elephant of the best type. यस्य गन्धं समाघ्राय न तिष्ठन्ति प्रतिद्विपाः। स वै गन्धगजो नाम नृपतेर्विजयावहः॥. कूटपाकलः

is a fever which attacks elephants. The reading in the text is better than 'कूटहस्तिज्वरः पाकलः'. The हस्त्यायुर्वेद of पालकाप्य tells us that all the fevers of elephants are called पाकल and that there are ten varieties of them. See अध्याय 9, which is styled पाकलाध्याय. कूट is one of the varieties and it is the deadliest of all. पालकाप्य says that it is called कूट because it kills elephants at once. 'तत्र गजस्यामीक्ष्णशो रूक्षान्नयवसकवलकुवलतिक्तकटुकषायलघुविषमरूक्षबह्वन्नभोजनात्, अथवातिगुरुभारहरणतरणविलङ्घनात्कुप्यति अनिलः । तदात्मकश्च कूटः । कूटो नामाशुघातनम् आशुघातनाद् द्विरदानाम् । तस्मात्कूटपाकलमाचक्ष्महे । तत्र श्लोकः । यथा हि हन्यात्कूटेन मृगशावं वनेचरः । तथा वातात्मको नागं हन्ति वै कूटपाकलः ॥'. The other reading would mean 'who was पाकल, that is a fever of elephants, working secretly'. This does not bring out the force and terror of the king's attack upon his enemies. Every fever (पाकल) is not equally dangerous to elephants. Compare 'अचिरेण वैकृतविवर्तदारुणः कलभं कठोर इव कूटपाकलः ॥' (मालतीमाधव I). लाट...चरः who steals (*i. e.* removes, renders nugatory) the skill of the king of Lāṭa (country about Broach *i. e.* Southern Gujerat). C and T translate 'a looter to the lawlessness of the Lāts.' This does not seem to be correct. मालवलक्ष्मीः एव लता तस्याः परशुः. मालव is modern Malva. प्रथितं (well-known) अपरनाम यस्य. The author means to say that प्रभाकरवर्धन had conquered the Huns, the Gurjaras &c. See Introduction. यो... धनानि who, the moment he was crowned, gave up wealth that sticks to the राज्याङ्गs (constituent elements of a state), as if it were dirt. One who bathes removes the dirt (मल m. n.) from his body (अङ्ग). In a coronation a king is bathed with the waters of sacred rivers and in commemoration of it money is distributed among Brahmins. राज्याङ्गानि सप्त 'स्वाम्यमात्यसुहृत्कोशराष्ट्रदुर्गबलानि च । राज्याङ्गानि' इत्यमरः. यः...जीवितेन who felt ashamed even when others clung to life in the first rush of battle, life which is dear to the cowardly, as if it were grass held in the mouth. To hold grass in the mouth is a sign of defeat and abject submission. Note the Marathi proverb 'दांतीं तृण धरून'. It is only the chickenhearted that will cling to life and save it at the cost of self-respect. When the king's enemies submitted to him in battle, he felt ashamed at *their* abject submission to save life, which to the brave is as तृण. कातरवल्लभेन goes with both तृणेन and जीवितेन. करे धृतः धौतः असिः तस्मिन् प्रतिबिम्बितेन. समितिषु सहायेन that (reflection of self) was his (only) companion in battles. प्रधनेषु in battles. The idea is this:—When the king fought with his enemies, he bent his bow for discharging arrows. In his bright sword-blade appeared the reflection of the king bending his bow. It appeared as if the king was helped by his reflection and even this made him uneasy (with the thought of having to receive another's help in battle). Further he was pained by the fact that his bow bent before his foes (though only for killing them). यो...खिद्यत there seems to be a pun, giving two opposite senses. यो मानी (proud) मानसेन अखिद्यत (was troubled by mind *i. e.* by the high soaring desires of his mind); यो मानी मानसे न अखिद्यत—who, proud as he was, was never troubled in mind (by difficulties). अन्तर्गताः अपरिमिताः रिपवः एव शल्यानि शङ्कवश्च तैः कीलिताम् nailed with the inserted (अन्तर्गत) points of darts in the form of numberless enemies in his empire. लक्ष्मी is said to be चंचल. But in his case it was निश्चल *i. e.* never left him. What is nailed becomes fixed. His sovereignty extended over many kings—his enemies whom he had subdued; so though they were like so many thorns in his side, yet they served the purpose of nails and made his sovereignty निश्चल. The reading in the text seems better than अन्तर्गताम्. Nails are inside; so the subdued kings were inside his empire. C and T take अन्तर्गत to mean 'dead' (with foes). यश्च...बहुधा who, by the numerous (पृथु) roads for the march (यात्रा) of his troops (दण्डः) as it were cut up the earth in many parts in all directions for the benefit of his servants, (roads) by which (*i. e.* in making which) the river-banks, pits, trees with luxuriant branches, clumps of grass, anthills and forests were levelled up. समीकृतानि सरित्तटाः अवटाः, विटपानामटवी (समूहः) तया युक्ताः तरवः, तृणानां गुल्माः (समूहाः), वल्मीकगिरयः, गहनानि (वनानि) च—यैः (०पथैः). The king's victorious armies marched in various directions and so roads had to be prepared for them or were made by the very fact of marching in large numbers. Rivers, banks, clumps of trees and grass, and hills and forests-these serve as boundaries to demarcate one province from another. But these were all removed by his armies. It was only the broad roads that separated the several provinces which the king apportioned among his own servants. See मनु० 8. 246—47 '**सीमावृक्षांश्च** कुर्वीत न्यग्रोधाश्वत्थकिंशुकान् । गुल्मान्वेणूंश्च विविधाञ्छमीवल्लीस्थलानि च । शरान् कुब्जकगुल्मांश्च तथा सीमा न नश्यति ॥.' याज्ञवल्क्य II. 151 '**नयेयुरेते** सीमानं स्थला—ङ्गारतुषद्रुमैः । **सेतुवल्मीक**निम्नास्थिचैत्याद्यैरुपलक्षिताम् ॥'. **अलब्धं युद्धस्य दोहदं येन** whose longing or thirst for battle was not gratified. यं चा...

प्रताप: the idea is—his prowess was so great that nobody dared oppose him; the result was that his desire to fight was never gratified and his own prowess in this way caused him uneasiness, as if it were the prowess of another. If anyone else had great prowess that would have been a source of trouble to him. **P. 57** यस्य च...प्रताप:—the principal sentence is यस्य प्रताप: निहत... पुरेषु पञ्च...मयो मूर्त इवादृश्यत—whose prowess appeared as if it had an embodied existence made up of the five great elements in the wives of the chieftains that were slain in opposing him. निहता: प्रतिसामन्ता: तेषां अन्त:पुराणि तेषु. By his prowess the princes that opposed him were killed and their wives' hearts burnt through anguish, their eyes shed tears, they waved deep sighs, they had earth on their bodies because they rolled on the ground through grief, they felt the world a void (शून्य), as their husbands were dead. The author fancies that प्रताप was identical with the effects it produced on the widows of the princes that were killed. As these effects were perceptible, he says प्रताप was मूर्त. The word क्ष्मा means 'the earth'. All visible bodies are made up of the five elements पृथ्वी (here the word क्ष्मा is used for a pun), अप्, तेज:, वायु and आकाश. क्ष्मा also means 'patience'. The women had to suffer. यस्य...लक्ष्मी:—The idea is:—The best of his servants that were near him (*i. e.* high officers of state) were endowed by him with so much wealth and splendour that they appeared like him. A reflection is generally seen in objects that are near (आसन्न) and bright like jewels &c. 'जातौ जातौ यदुत्कृष्टं तद्रत्नमभिधीयते.' यस्य...भवत् Here the words भूति, सिद्धि, वंश, उक्ति, कर have double meanings. प्रताप: अग्निरिव तेन; also प्रतापसदृश: अग्नि: तेन. Dissolve शौर्योष्मणा and असिधाराजलेन similarly. यस्य प्रता...भूति: अभवत् who had भूति (prosperity, ashes) by the fire of his prowess. He became prosperous by his prowess; fire produces भूति (ashes). Explain the following similarly. शौर्योष्मणा सिद्धि: he attained his objects by the heat of his bravery. सिद्धि also means 'cooking', which is effected by ऊष्मन् (heat). असि...वृद्धि: his family (वंश) prospered by the water of his sword—blade. वंश (bamboo) when watered grows. शस्त्र...रोक्ति: his manliness (पुरुषकार:) was proclaimed by the mouths of the wounds received by him from weapons. उक्ति (utterance) can be made only by the mouth (मुख). धनु...गृहीति:—he levied tribute by the scar made by the string of his bow *i. e.* fought his enemies with the bow, vanqu-

ing (the राजहंस) to the मानस lake. The मानस lake is said to be the native place of swans, where they are said to flock at the beginning of the monsoon. The king was a राजहंस (a swan among kings *i. e.* the best), while यशोमती was clever in acting according to the wishes of the king. सकल... धर्मस्य—त्रयी means वेदत्रयी (ऋग्वेद, यजुर्वेद and सामवेद). सकललोकैः अर्चिताः चरणाः यस्याः—(the three Vedas) the various schools of which are honoured by the people. The words चरण and शाखा are sometimes used as synonyms; sometimes चरण means 'शाखाध्येतृ' *i. e.* those who study a particular शाखा of the Veda, an ideal succession of teachers and pupils. This latter is the sense here. The king was धर्म incarnate and यशोमती was सकल ... चरणा (सकललोकेन वन्दितौ चरणौ यस्याः). दिवा ... महामुनेः—The great sage is वसिष्ठ here whose wife is अरुन्धती. अमुक्ता पार्श्वे स्थितिः यया—who always remains by his side. The star of अरुन्धती is always seen by the side of वसिष्ठ in the constellation of the Great Bear. अरुन्धती is regarded by the Indians as the type of conjugal fidelity and constancy and is pointed out to the bride by the bridegroom in marriage ceremonies. Note the high praise put by भवभूति in the mouth of जनक as regards अरुन्धती 'यया पूतंमन्यो निधिरपि पवित्रस्य महसः' (उत्तररामo IV). The king was महामुनि (a राजर्षि) and the queen never left his side day and night. हंसमयी...प्रेम्णि (literally) in her gait she was mostly a swan, in her tones a cuckoo, in love for her husband a ruddy goose (चक्रवाक) *i. e.* she had the gait of a हंस, the sweet high—pitched tone of a cuckoo &c. परपुष्ट=कोकिल (also called परभृत्). It was believed that cuckoos place their eggs in the nest of crows and thus have their young ones looked after by others. 'प्रागन्तरिक्षगमनात्स्वमपत्यजातमन्यैर्द्विजैः परभृताः खलु पोषयन्ति ॥' शाकुन्तल V. The चक्रवाक bird is supposed to be separated from its mate at the advent of night and is a type of abiding love. Even though separated merely by a lotus leaf it cries for its mate. मय is affixed in the sense of प्राचुर्य or विकार. 'तत्प्रकृतवचने मयट्' पा. 5. 4. 21 and 'मयड्वैतयोर्भाषामभक्ष्याच्छादनयोः' पा. 4. 3. 143. प्रावृण्म...विलासेषु In the fulness of पयोधर (breast, cloud) she was as if the rainy season, in playfulness she was as if wine. निधि...प्रसादेषु in the collection of wealth, she was a treasure, in (bestowing) favours she was a stream of wealth. कोषसंग्रह (1) amassing a rich treasure (2) having a calix (with कमल). फलदानेषु—the queen gave what was desired by suppliants; flowers give rise to fruits. सन्ध्या०—people perform adoration (called सन्ध्यावन्दन) in the morning and evening; the queen was honoured by all people. चन्द्र...ष्मत्वे the moon and the queen had no ऊष्मन् (heat, pride of wealth). दर्पण...ग्रहणेषु a mirror takes in (*i. e.* reflects) every being; she drew (*i. e.* influenced by her goodness) all beings. सामुद्र...ज्ञानेषु In the knowledge of the character of others, she was the science of palmistry. समुद्र is supposed to be the author of the सामुद्रिकशास्त्र. परमा...व्याप्तिषु—The supreme spirit pervades everything; the queen could comprehend everything. According to the Vedānta, परमात्मन् (ब्रह्म) is everywhere and everything. Compare भगवद्गीता 'मया ततमिदं सर्वं जगदव्यक्तमूर्तिना.' स्मृति...वृत्तिषु Smṛitis, like that of मनु, lay down what is pure conduct (वृत्ति); her thoughts (वृत्ति) were pure or holy. अमृत...तृष्यत्सु she was full of अमृत (nectar, water) to the thirsty. निर्वृतिः bliss, happiness. वेतस... गुरुषु towards her elders, she was a वेतस (*i. e.* she was humble). वेतस is a symbol of humility. It bends when a flood sweeps down upon it. गोत्र...विलासानाम् she was the prosperity of the family of elegant gestures *i. e.* in her one could find the acme of fine gestures and dalliances. प्राय...स्त्रीत्वस्य she was as if the penance purity of womanhood. Penance purifies a sinful person. She had inherently the purity that comes of प्रायश्चित्त. आज्ञा... ध्वजस्य she was as if the fruition of the mandate of काम. She could have bewitched any one by her charms. व्युत्थान...रूपस्य she was as if the post-concentration consciousness of beauty. The idea is:—रूप had as if been in a समाधि (*i. e.* had given up moving about in the world); then रूप gave up its state of समाधि as a Yogin does and became conscious in the person of the queen. व्युत्थान means समाधिनिवृत्ति (cessation of the state of Yogic trance). For the meaning of व्युत्थान, note योगसूत्र III. 36 'ते समाधावुपसर्गा व्युत्थाने सिद्धयः' on which व्यासभाष्य says 'ते प्रतिभादयः समाहितचित्तस्योत्पद्यमाना उपसर्गास्तद्दर्शनप्रत्यनीकत्वात् । व्युत्थितचित्तस्योत्पद्यमानाः सिद्धयः'. C and T render the words as 'the Eureka of loveliness.' दिष्ट...रतेः she was as if the ovation of passion. दिष्टम् means 'fortune' (good or bad); here, good fortune. वृद्धि means congratulation; compare the use of the root वृध् in 'दिष्ट्या पुत्रमुखदर्शनेन भवान् वर्धते'. मनो...णीयकस्य she was the attainment of the desires of beauty. Beauty had been longing for a proper person to represent her and found the fulfilment of that longing in the person of the queen. वंशो...रागस्य she was the root of the ancestry of love. As a family traces its ancestry back to some founder, so true love started with her and was then propagated through succeeding generations of loving women. The readings of B also make good sense. सर्ग...सौन्दर्यस्य she was the utmost limit of the creation of loveliness. In her loveliness found its perfection. आयति...यौवनस्य she was as if the majesty of youth. 'प्रभावेपि चायतिः' इत्यमरः. अनभ्र...वैदग्ध्यस्य she was the cloudless rain of intelligence. Rainfall requires clouds; hence rain without clouds is looked upon as an extraordinary thing, a wonder. Her intelligence was wonderful. अयशः...लक्ष्म्याः. लक्ष्मी is said to be चञ्चल. This bad name that लक्ष्मी had acquired was wiped off by the queen, in whom लक्ष्मी was स्थिर. Compare 'येन श्रियः संश्रयदोषरूढं स्वभावलोलेत्ययशः प्रमृष्टम्' रघु० VI. 41. यशः... चारित्रस्य she was the fulness of the fame of chastity. C and T translate 'goodness' bloom of beauty', which is not correct. सौभाग्य...पतेः she was Brahmā's creation of the atoms of beauty. The idea seems to be this :—By creating her, Brahmā created the परमाणुs of beauty ; whenever he wants to create another lovely form he would draw upon her beauty (the परमाणुs). According to the Vais'eshika philosophy, from atoms the whole world is produced. शम...शान्तिरिव the quietude of quiescence. शमः is restraint of passions or of the mind. The idea is that even शम would derive शान्ति from her. Explain the remaining clauses similarly. आभिजात्यम् (अभिजातस्य भावः) high birth. संयमः restraint. धैर्यम्—steadiness (of mind). विभ्रमः sportive or amorous action. यशोमती—From the Sonpat seal we see that the name of हर्ष's mother was यशोमती and not यशोवती. See Introduction. प्राणानां भूमिः she was the centre of the life of the king, she was the very life of the king. विश्रामस्य भूमिः—the king confided everything to her. धर्मस्य भूमिः she was the source of the righteousness of the king. A wife is the source of धर्माचरण, as said by आपस्तम्ब 'धर्मप्रजासम्पत्तिः प्रयोजनं दारसंग्रहस्य.' No यज्ञ could be performed without her. See तैत्तिरीय ब्राह्मण III. 3. 3. 1 'अयज्ञो वा एष योऽपत्नीकः'. The महाभारत says that the wife is the source of त्रिवर्ग (धर्म, अर्थ and काम) 'अर्धं भार्या मनुष्यस्य भार्या श्रेष्ठतमः सखा । भार्या मूलं त्रिवर्गस्य भार्या मूलं तरिष्यतः ॥' आदिपर्व 74.40. C and T render 'the centre of all creatures' love, confidence, duty and felicity'. This is not correct. अस्य = राज्ञः प्रभाकरवर्धनस्य. नरकजितः (1) of the conqueror of the demon नरक (*i. e.* of

विष्णु); (2) of the vanquisher of Hell. The king by his धर्माचरण had removed the possibility of going to Hell. लक्ष्मी is represented as resting on the bosom of Vishṇu. कृष्ण killed नरक who was the son of भूमि (the earth) and was king of प्राग्ज्योतिष; see विष्णुपुराण V. 29.

P. 58 ll. 3–8 निसर्गत...हृदयम्. उदये...कृतः at the rise of the sun (दिनकृत्). धवलेन कर्पटेन (piece of cloth) प्रावृतं शिरः यस्य. प्राङ्मुखः with his face towards the east. कुङ्कुममण्डलके in a circle that was smeared with saffron paste. C and T translate 'kneeling eastward upon the ground in a circle.' This is wrong. The king did not *kneel in a circle.* He had drawn up a circle with saffron paste on to which he put his offerings. पद्मराग—ruby (which is red in colour). स्व...ददौ he offered worship (अर्चा) with a bunch (षण्ड *m. n.*) of red lotuses that were reddened (अनुरक्त) by the sun, as if it (bunch) were his own heart devoted to the sun. सूर्ये अनुरक्तम् (हृदयम्); सूर्येण अनुरक्तम् (षण्डम्). The heart and the bunch of lotuses are both red and ०नुरक्त. जप्यम्—muttered prayer. शोभनं चरितं यस्य स सुचरितः· अपत्यहेतोः for the purpose of (securing) issue. प्राध्वम् *ind.* favourably, suitably. 'आनुकूल्यार्थके प्राध्वम्' इत्यमरः. Here it may be taken as an adjective of मन्त्रम् meaning 'favourable.' प्रयत restrained, devout. जञ्जपूकः one who mutters prayers. 'यजजपदशां यङः' पा. 3. 2. 166 (The affix ऊक is applied to the frequentative base of यज्, जप् and दश्. यायजूक, दन्दशूक, जञ्जपूक). मन्त्रमादित्यहृदयम्—आदित्यः हृदयं (रहस्यं) यस्य. The आदित्यहृदय is a well-known स्तोत्र declared by कृष्ण to अर्जुन (see बृहत्स्तोत्ररत्नाकर Nir. ed.). For some of the details given in the text, note the following from the स्तोत्र. 'वृत्तं वा चतुरस्रं वा लिप्तभूमौ न्यसेच्छुचिः । त्रिधा तत्र लिखेत्पद्ममष्टपत्रं सकर्णिकम् ॥ 99...सकेसराणि पद्मानि करवीराणि चार्जुन । रक्तचन्दनमिश्राणि कृत्वा वै ताम्रभाजने । धृत्वा शिरसि तत्पात्रं जानुभ्यां धरणीं स्पृशेत् ॥ 104–5.

P. 58 ll. 9–21 भक्त...तिष्ठत्. भक्तजनानां अनुरोधः (entreaty) तेन विधेयानि—influenced by the entreaties of their devotees. सितकरस्य (चन्द्रमसः) कराः तद्वत् सिता (शुभ्रा) सुधा *(chunam)* तया धवलस्य. द्वितीयशयने on a second couch. On the propriety of this, see the com. 'द्वितीयेत्यादिनास्य सदाचारनिष्ठोक्ता । उक्तं हि नाश्नीयाद्भार्यया साकं न च सुप्यात्तया समम् ॥'. See मनु० 'समानशयने चैव न शयीत तया सह ॥' IV. 40. शिश्ये—Perfect 3rd sing. of शी. परिणत...तिष्ठत्—the principal sentence is देवी यशोमती सहसैव 'आर्यपुत्र परित्रायस्व' इति भाषमाणा उदतिष्ठत्. परिण...श्यामायाम् when the night had reached its close. आसन्ना

(approaching) प्रभातवेला तया विलुप्यमानं लावण्यं यस्य. लिलम्बिषमाणे (*loc. pr. p.* of the desiderative of लम्ब्) when (the moon) was declining (*lit.* about to hang down). सीदत् (sinking, waning) तेजः यस्य. तारकाणां ईश्वरः चन्द्रः. कराग्रैः स्पृष्टा कुमुदिनी तया प्रमोदः तस्मात् जन्म यस्य (with ०स्वेदे). कराग्र...पयसि when very cool drops of dew (अवश्यायः) were falling as if they were the perspiration of the moon (शशधरः) evoked by the joy of touching the night lotuses with the tips of his कर s (rays, hands). The poets represent that when a young person intensely in love touches his sweetheart, he perspires. स्वेद is one of the eight सात्त्विकभावs. मधु... प्रदीपेषु when the lamps in the harem, being smitten (आहत *lit.* struck) by the breath of the sleeping beauties that were intoxicated by wine, flickered as if intoxication had been transferred to them. The lamps flickered owing to the breaths of sleeping women. The author represents this flickering as the staggering of intoxication. The lamps caught intoxication from the breath of women wafting the smell of wine. संक्रान्तः मदः येषु. राजनि—construe this with स्वपिति below. विमल...तारकाभिः whose feet were as if shampooed by the stars that were reflected in his white nails. संवाह्यमानौ चरणौ यस्य तस्मिन् (राजनि). It should be remembered that the king is represented as sleeping on the roof of his palace in the summer. Hence the stars were reflected in his nails. विस्रब्ध...अङ्गैः he had his limbs spread carelessly as if they were consigned to the women in the form of the quarters. Understand लक्षिते after अङ्गैः, the instrumental being used in accordance with the Sûtra 'इत्थंभूतलक्षणे' पा. 2. 3. 21. (जटाभिस्तापसः). दिश एव अङ्गनाः. मधु...वीज्यमाने who was fanned by the beauty (श्री) of his face with breath that was scented with मधु (wine, honey), as if the (breaths) were the breezes of the fan *viz.* the lotus in her hand. The king had drunk wine and his breath was charged with its odour. The poet fancies that he was fanned by the लक्ष्मी of his face with the breath. लक्ष्मी is represented as having a lotus in her hand. कमल would have मधु (honey in it). If the lotus were used as a fan the breeze would be charged with the scent of honey. ०गन्धिभिः goes with ०वातैः as well as श्वसितैः. स्वहस्ते यत्कमलं तदेव तालवृन्तं तस्य वातैः. विमल...विराजिते who was adorned by the image of the moon's disc reflected on his bright (विमल) cheek which (image) looked like a chaplet (शेखरः) of white flowers displaced by the seizing of hair in amorous sports. The reflection of the white moon looked like a white garland. A शेखर (which is worn on the head) may be displaced and dangle on the cheek when seized in रतिकेलि. रतिकेल्यां कचग्रहः तेन लम्बितः तेन. भूषण...जनम् as if calling on her attendants by the tinkling of her ornaments. उत्कम्पमाना (trembling) अङ्गयष्टिः यस्याः.

P. 58 ll. 22–33 अथ तेन...कारणम्. तेन—connect this with ध्वनिना. सर्वस्या...मुखे which (cry) was never heard before even in the whole world, much less in the queen's mouth. The king protected the world so well that not even the meanest had ever to cry 'help.' एकपदे *ind.* at once. शिरो...निशाम् who as if drew a parting line in the night with his bright (धौत) sword having a glittering edge, which (sword) was snatched from that part of his bed on which his head rested with his right hand that quivered with wrath, as if it (sword) were the white lotus in his ear coming out. सीमन्त the parting line in the hair on the head of women. सीमन्तयन् is the *pr. p.* of the denominative verb from सीमन्त. Night is dark as hair. The flash of the bright sword made a सीमन्त in the hair of the woman (night) *i. e.* darkness was parted by the white streak. The sword was kept below his pillow to be taken out in case of necessity. Being taken from under his head, the bright sword resembled a white lotus which is often placed on the ear as an ornament. अच्छा धारा यस्य. C and T translate 'whose glittering edge drew a line like a prolongation of his ear-wreath across the night.' This is obscure and does not bring out the sense. अन्तराल...पल्लवेन tossing aside with his left hand his upper garment, as if it were the ether that intervened in space. The garment was very fine and thin and hence is compared to आकाश. The fine garment screened his limbs. आकाश also screens from our view the things in space (अन्तराल). कर...राजमानः—his golden bracelet (worn on the left hand with which he tossed aside his upper garment) dropped down (from his hand) by the violent tossing of his hand and went rolling in all directions on the ground. The poet fancies that the वलय was his heart which wandered about in search of the cause of the alarm (of the queen). Some rich men even now wear golden वलयs on their left hand. सत्वरं अवतारितः (brought down) वामचरणः तस्य आक्रान्तिः (placing) तया कम्पितः प्रासादः येन. पुरः...मानः—his necklace was torn asunder by his violent movements, fell down before him and was reflected in the edge of his sword and looked like a piece of the rays of the moon. लक्ष्मी...आशानाम् he made the ends (पर्यन्त *m.*) of the quarters ruddy with his eyes that were red owing to sleep and rage, as if they (eyes) were coloured with betel juice when kissed by Lakshmî. The poet fancies that लक्ष्मी (sovereignty) had chewed betel and then out of love kissed his eyes. पाटलयन् is *pr. p.* of the denonimative verb from पाटल (red). The reading पटलयन् means 'veiling or covering' and does not yield a good sense. बद्धा...वर्तयन् as if again bringing back the night (त्रियामा) by his frowning brow that was trident—shaped and that caused darkness. बद्धः अन्धकारः यया. तिस्रः पताकाः (रेखा) यस्याः. His forehead was wrinkled into three lines by rage and his brows were dark. The author lays emphasis on त्रि in त्रिपताकया and त्रियामां. विक्षिप्तं चक्षुः येन.

P. 59 ll. 1–9 **अथ...इति.** यामिकिनी—a woman of the night watch (from यामिका meaning night). 'साध्वसं भयम्' इत्यमरः. बाला ...भागान् filling the different quarters as if with the glory of morn. कुण्डलिनौ...कवचिनौ wearing earrings, armlets and coat of mail. इन्द्र...स्नातौ bathed in saffron (juice) of the hue of the इन्द्रगोपक insect. The इन्द्रगोपकs are red insects that are seen at the beginning of the rainy season. इन्द्रगोपकस्येव रुक् (कान्तिः) यस्य. Saffron is auspicious and women used to apply saffron तिलक on their forehead as a mark of auspiciousness. C and T translate 'bathed in blood cochineal red'. This is bad. To see in a dream a person bathed in blood is not a good omen. The author intends the whole description to indicate good fortune. 'अथ कुङ्कुमम् ॥...रक्तसङ्कोचपिशुनं वीरलोहितचन्दनम् ॥' इत्यमरः (on which क्षीरस्वामी says 'रञ्जनाद्रक्तम् । अत एवासृक्संज्ञम्'). On the two meanings of रुधिर, note रघु 11. 20 'राममन्मथशरेण ताडिता दुःसहेन हृदये निशाचरी । गन्धवद्रुधिरचन्दनोक्षिता जीवितेशवसतिं जगाम सा ॥'. उत्तमाङ्गे (शिरसि) घटमानः अञ्जलिः यस्य that folded their hands on their heads (in token of submission and adoration). चन्द्रं...निर्गतया as if she were the moon issuing out from the सुपुम्ण ray. It was believed that the waxing of the moon was due to a ray of the sun called सुषुम्ण and that the waning was due to the digits of the moon being drunk by the gods. 'सूर्यरश्मिः सुषुम्नो यस्तर्पितस्तेन चन्द्रमाः । कृष्णपक्षेऽमरैः शश्वत्पीयते वै सुधामयः॥' विष्णु० II. 11. 22. यास्क has a very interesting note on this "अथाप्यस्यैको रश्मिश्चन्द्रमसं प्रति दीप्यते तदेतेनोपेक्षितव्यमादित्यतोऽस्य दीप्तिर्भवतीति । 'सुषुम्णः सूर्यरश्मिश्चन्द्रमा गन्धर्वः' इत्यपि निगमो भवति ।" निरुक्त II. 2. 2. Bāṇa frequently refers to this belief. See कादम्बरी 'अलीकं चेदं यथा किल सकलाः कलाः कलावतो बहुलपक्षे क्षीयमाणस्य

सुषुम्णनाम्ना रश्मिना रविरापिबतीति;' हर्षचरित 'सुषुम्णास्रुतिश्चशिसुधाशीकरस्तबकतारकिततीराम्' (मन्दाकिनीम्). It should be noted that in the passage from कादम्बरी Bāṇa attributes the waning of the moon to सुषुम्णरश्मि. मे विलपन्त्याः In spite of the fact that I was weeping.

P. 59 ll. 10–24 **एतस्मिन्नेव...पत्युर्भाषितेन.** तोरणस्य समीपे उपतोरणम् (अव्ययीभाव)—near the royal porch. रराण *perfect 3rd. p. sing.* of रण् to sound. राज...फलम् as if it were the first utterance of royal splendour (personified) proclaiming the result of (*i. e.* indicated by) the dream. भाविनीं भूतिम् future prosperity. अमन्दम् violently. चकाण *perfect* of कण् *1. P.* to sound. कोणेन (drum-stick) आहता. Separate हता आनन्दात्. नान्दी—This has been explained as 'the symphony of twelve drums beaten simultaneously' ('एकदा द्वादशमृदङ्गघोषो नान्दी' रङ्गराज on उत्तररामचरित). प्रबोध...पाठकानाम् of (minstrels) that recited auspicious (verses or words) that rouse from sleep. वल्लभाः तुरङ्गाः तेषां मन्दुरामन्दिरम् (stables). आदौ सुप्तः पश्चादुत्थितः सुप्तोत्थितः. सप्ति...पुरः in front of the horses (सप्ति *m*) that neighed sweetly (कृतः मधुरहेषारवः यैः). च्योतन्तः तुषारसलिलस्य शीकराः यस्मात् (*adj.* of यवसम्) from which oozed out the spray of frost—water. किरन् *nom. sing. m.* of *pr. parti.* of कॄ (qualifies पुरुषः and has यवसं for its object). वक्त्रा ...वक्त्रे two verses in the वक्त्र and अपरवक्त्र metres respectively. According to some writers the species of composition called आख्यायिका (the हर्षचरित is one) should be divided into sections called उच्छ्वासs and should contain verses in the वक्त्र and अपरवक्त्र metres foreshadowing coming events. See the quotation from भामह in the Introduction. अपरवक्त्र is an अर्धसमवृत्त having eleven letters (न, न, र, ल, ग) in the 1st and 3rd Pāda and twelve letters (न, ज, ज, र) in the 2nd and 4th. 'अयुजि ननरला गुरुः समे तदपरवक्त्रमिदं नजौ जरौ ॥'. It is also called वैतालीय, as said by the वृत्तरत्नाकर 'वदन्त्यपरवक्त्राख्यं वैतालीयं विपश्चितः'. वक्त्र is defined as 'नाद्यान्नसौ स्यातामब्धेर्योऽनुष्टुभि ख्यातम्.' Like the अनुष्टुभ् it has eight letters in a पाद. After the first four letters in each पाद there is a यगण. C and T take वक्त्रा and अपरवक्त्रा to be the names of the metres. निधिस्तरुविकारेण स्पष्टमाख्यायते a hidden treasure is clearly indicated by the change in a tree (*i. e.* by some singular or remarkable thing about a tree). The com. says 'यत्राधो निधिस्तत्र परिणाहोद्गताधोमुखशाखामूलादिभाजो वृक्षा भवन्ति.' शुभस्य आगमः the advent of luck. अरुण is the charioteer of the sun in mythology and is a personification of the radiant sky at daybreak; compare 'यावत्प्रतापनिधिराक्रमते न भानुरह्नाय तावदरुणेन तमो निरस्तम्.' अतिजवः very rapid. पूर्व...दयः the previous appearance of an omen. मुदो...षीदसि you feel dejected when it is a time of joy. परिगृहीतासि thou art accepted (*i. e.* favoured). अंशुमाली = सूर्यः. अवतीर्य descending (from the roof where the king had slept).

P. 59 l. 25—**P. 60** l. 15 ततः समति...पतिः. गर्भ...जननी his mother took upon herself pallor as if on account of his glory though he was only in the womb yet. Being pregnant, she became pale. यशः is represented by poets as white. The poet fancies that her pallor (really) due to pregnency was due to the glory the son in the womb was to attain in future. गुण...क्लान्तेव as if exhausted by the weight of his virtues. कान्ति...बभूव she became averse to food as if she were satiated with the nectar of the expanding brilliance. On account of pregnancy, she became more brilliant in complexion and lovely. This the poet compares to अमृत. One who has taken अमृत would have no appetite for ordinary food. उपचीयमानः (increasing) गर्भः तस्य भरः तेन अलसा. गुरुभिर्वारितापि although dissuaded by her elders. C and T translate गुरु as parents. This is not necessary. She would have to bow to all elderly persons including her parents. Further it seems questionable whether her parents would be at her husband's palace ordinarily. वन्दनाय...अनीयत she was taken by her friends for saluting (her elders) with difficulty by supporting her with their hands. सालभञ्जिकेव The queen would support herself against walls and pillars and would look like a doll. कमल...रणौ she could not lift up her feet as if they were surrounded by bees that had sat upon them out of their greed for a lotus. Her feet were radiant like lotuses. She could not walk swiftly because she was गर्भभरालसा. The poet represents that this was due to the weight of bees. The rays from her bright toenails resembled the delicate fibres of lotus plants. हंसs subsist upon मृणालs. मणि...कमलम्—the idea is that she was so eager for support that she would stretch out her hand expecting support even from her own images reflected in the jewelled walls. समा...कर्तुम् she was unable even to issue commands for the performance of household duties, much less to do them herself. आस्तां...रोढुम्—The idea is:—she could not bear to mount to the roof of the palace even in thought, much less with her feet that were oppressed by the weight of the anklets. उत्कम्पितौ स्तनौ यस्याः (on account of hard breathing). तस्तान (perfect of स्तन्) she groaned, breathed hard. प्रत्युत्थानेषु at times of rising to receive (some person worthy of honour). उभयजानुशिखरविनिहितौ करकिसलयौ यस्याः. गर्वा...थेत she was held up by the child in the womb as if through pride. The idea is:—she wanted to rise to receive and tried to get up by placing her hands upon her knees. But she did not after all get up. The poet fancies that the child in the womb, being proud, did not like to bow to any body, as it would have to do if its mother bowed and so prevented her from rising. दिवसं all day long (accu. of time). The sentence is दिवसं अधोमुखी ददर्श गर्भम्. Her face was reflected in her bright bosom. The poet fancies that her face had entered inside her body (in the form of the reflection) because it was anxious to see the child. सखीनामुत्सङ्गेषु मुक्तं शरीरं यया. निर्मितं, कल्पितं and विहितं qualify राज्यवर्धनम् . सर्वोर्वी...र्मितम् composed as if with the atoms of वज्र for destroying the alliances of all kings. सर्वेषां उर्वीभृतां (राज्ञां) पक्षः (समूहः) तस्य पाताय (with राज्यवर्धन); सर्वेषां उर्वीभृतां पर्वतानां पक्षाः (wings) तेषां पाताय (with इन्द्र understood). The mountains had once wings and troubled the earth by flying anywhere. Indra cut off their wings with his वज्र. बाण refers to this story very often. कादम्बरी 'अशनिभयपुञ्जितकुलशैलमध्यगतमिव कनकशिखरिणम्'; 'मैनाकेनेवाविदितपक्षपातेन'. शेष...कल्पितम् as if made with the means, *viz.* the numerous hoods of शेष. It is supposed that the earth is borne by the serpent शेष on its hoods. Compare 'किं शेषस्य भरव्यथा न वपुषि क्ष्मां न क्षिपत्येष यत्' भर्तृहरि. राज्यवर्धन also would be able to bear the responsibility of the world. सकल...विहितम् (she gave birth to रा०) who caused tremor to all भूभृत्s (kings, mountains) and who was as if made with the limbs of the elephants of the quarters. ०मुखरं, ०रवं, ०भुवनं and मनोहरं qualify महोत्सवम्. पूरिताः असंख्याः शङ्खाः तेषां शब्दैः मुखरम् (resounding). प्रहतानि पटहशतानि तैः पटुः रवः यस्मिन्. गम्भीरेण भेरीनिनादेन निर्भरं भरितं भुवनं यस्मिन्. प्रमोदेन उन्मत्तः मर्त्यलोकः तेन मनोहरम्. मास...दिवसमिव for one month as if it were a single day.

P. 60 l. 16—**P. 61** l. 10 **अथान्य...बध्यन्त.** The locatives from कन्दलिनि to ०कसि qualify नभसि (*i. e.* the month of श्रावण). कन्दलिनि abounding in plantain trees. Wild plantain plants grow up spontaneously in the rainy season. कुड्मलिताः कदम्बतरवः यस्मिन् in which the *Kadamba* trees have put forth buds. The कदम्ब tree is said to put forth buds at the advent of thunder and rain;

compare 'मरुन्नवाम्भःप्रविधूतसिक्ता कदम्बयष्टिः स्फुटकोरकेव' उत्तरराम० III. कुड्मलाः सञ्जाताः अस्य इति कुड्मलितः according to 'तदस्य सञ्जातं तारकादिभ्य इतच्' पा. 5. 2. 36. रूढाः तोक्मतृणस्तम्बाः यस्मिन् in which the clusters (स्तम्बः) of barley blades had taken firm root. 'शितशूकयवौ समौ ॥ तोक्मस्तु तत्र हरिते' इत्यमरः. स्तम्भितानि तामरसानि यस्मिन् in which the red lotuses were supported (*i. e.* stood firm and erect, being nourished with plenty of water). विकसितं (delighted) चातकचेतः यस्मिन्. It was believed that the चातक could not drink water on the earth, but subsisted on a few drops from the clouds. मूकाः मानसौकसः (हंसाः, मानसे ओकः सद्म येषां) यस्मिन्. हंसs are said to migrate to the मानस lake at the commencement of the rainy season and so on the plains the cackling of हंसs was not heard. नभसि मासि—कृष्ण was born in श्रावण; while the poet says that हर्ष was conceived in श्रावण. चक्रं पाणौ यस्य = विष्णु (*i. e.* कृष्ण). हर्ष also was चक्रपाणि *i. e.* on his hand there were lines resembling a चक्र, which was looked upon as one of the चक्रवर्तिलक्षणs. See बृहत्संहिता 67. 47 'चक्रासिपरशुतोमरशक्तिधनुःकुन्तसन्निभा रेखाः। कुर्वन्ति चमूनाथं' &c. सममेव at the same time. हृदये हर्षः—यशोमती was delighted at heart and conceived the future हर्ष. सर्व...गृहीता as if accepted (*i. e.* endowed with) by all the merits of her subjects. पुण्य is represented as white. The queen's body became slightly pallid (आपाण्डु) on account of pregnancy; the poet fancies that it was the पुण्य of the subjects that had assumed shape and come to her in the form of her गर्भ, the idea being that the birth of a good Emperor like हर्ष is due to the पुण्य of the subjects. गर्भारम्भेण as pregnancy came on. श्यामायमाने चारुचूचुकचूलिके ययोः (also श्यामायमाना चारुचूचुकसदृशी चूलिका ययोः) चूचुक nipple. चूलिका crest. पयोधरौ कलशौ इव (also पयोधरसदृशौ कलशौ or पयसः धरौ पयोधरौ कलशौ). The queen's breasts had nipples growing dark on account of pregnancy. They would be sucked by an emperor (चक्रवर्तिन् *i. e.* हर्ष). Drinking *water* was brought for emperors in sealed (मुद्रित) jars in order to prevent poisoning. The dark crest of the seal resembled the crest of the nipple. स्तन्यार्थे...दृष्टिः her eye, long, glossy (स्निग्ध) and white became sweeter as if it were a stream of milk placed in her face for (supplying) milk (to her breast). दुग्धनदी also would be दीर्घ, स्निग्ध (viscous) and धवल. See for the same simile 'स्नपयति हृदयेशं स्नेहनिष्यन्दिनी ते धवलमधुरमुग्धा दुग्धकुल्येव दृष्टिः॥' उत्तरराम III. 23. सकलमङ्गलानां गणेन अधिष्ठितं (occupied) गात्रं (body) तस्य गरिम्णा (by the weight). अमन्दायत became slow (from the denominative verb मन्दायते). Her gait became slow owing to pregnancy. The poet fancies that the slowness was due to the weight of the numerous auspicious signs due to the conception of a चक्रवर्तिन्. निर्मलं मणिकुट्टिमं (floor inlaid with gems) तस्मिन् निमग्नं प्रतिबिम्बं (reflection of the queen) तस्य निभेन (under the guise). गृहीतौ पादपल्लवौ यया. पूर्वं ... पृथिवी अस्याः (यशोमत्याः)—The queen was reflected in the brilliant pavement. The poet fancies that the earth was worshipping her feet by way of a prelude to what would follow when her son became the emperor of the world. दिवसम् *accu.* of time. शयनीयं is the object of अधिशयानायाः (यशोमत्याः). अपाश्रयः awning. पत्रभङ्गः drawing of lines or figures. ०प्रतिमा image of a figure drawn on the awning. विमलकपोलोदरे गता reflected in the bright cheek (of the queen). गर्भो...संक्रान्तम् reflected in her round bosom from which the garment had been taken away on account of the agitation (उन्माथः) of pregnancy. गर्भस्य उन्माथेन मुक्तं अंशुकं यस्मात्. उडुपतिः the moon. The reflection of the moon in the bosom appeared like a white umbrella held over the गर्भ. A white umbrella is an emblem of चक्रवर्तित्व; compare रघुवंश 3. 16. 'अदेयमासीत्रयमेव भूपतेः शशिप्रभं छत्रमुभे च चामरे.' चित्र...ग्राहिण्योपि even the women holding chowries on the painted walls (*i. e.* even pictures moved chowries). चामरs are among the insignia of royalty. करे (by the trunk) विधृतं कमलिन्याः पलाशानां (पत्राणां) पुटं तस्मिन् सलिलानि तैः. She dreamt that the four दिग्गजs bathed her with water. This was a precursor of the future sovereignty of her son. प्रतिबुध्यमानायाश्च and when she woke up. चन्द्रशालिका—a chamber on the roof. 'चन्द्रशाला शिरोगृहम्' क्षीरस्वामी. Even the puppets cried 'victory.' परिज...निश्चेरुः When she called out to her attendants, incorporeal voices issued forth saying 'command.' क्रीडा...भङ्गम्—This sentence and the following give expression to the popular notion that the mother's mind is influenced by the potential thoughts of the child in the womb, as said by the com. 'गर्भस्थजनचित्तवृत्त्यनुसारेण गर्भिण्या अपि चित्तवृत्तिर्भवति'. चतुर्णामपि—This indicates that हर्ष's empire would extend up to the four oceans. The oceans are sometimes spoken of as four or as seven. वेला...सरेषु in the vicinity (परिसरः) of sandy banks (पुलिनं, 'तोयोत्थितं तत्पुलिनम्' इत्यमरः) inside the bowers of creepers on the seashore. आत्य...चचाल Even as regards business of extreme importance, her eyebrow moved playfully. The idea is that she felt no concern or anxiety even as regards serious matters; so calm and collected she was. आत्ययिक—अत्ययः प्रयोजनं अस्य 'प्रयोजनम्' पा. 5. 1. 109 (प्रयोजनं फलं कारणं च). सन्नि...सीत though jewelled mirrors were near her, she had a strong liking (व्यसनम्) for seeing her face in a drawn (उत्खात) sword blade. उत्सारिता वीणा यैः. श्रुतौ असुखायन्त gave pleasure to her ear. स्तम्भितम् stiffened. सख्यश्चास्याः &c.—construe सख्यश्च अस्याः पार्श्वे क्षणमपि न मुमुचुः. विस्फारित stretched wide. आसन्न...भवनम् brightening the house as if with the idea of celebrating the festival of her delivery that was approaching. At जन्ममहोत्सव houses are washed with chunam. The friends whitened the house with their eyes expanded wide. विकच...विदधाना—The friends cast glances in all directions from their widely expanded eyes (that were white). The author fancies that the glances were so many white and blue flowers of various kinds of lotuses, offered in worship to protect the queen from evil. कुमुद is a white night lotus. कुवलय is a blue lotus. कमल is pale red. The white of the eye was mixed with the blue of the pupil and the white—red of the corners. आत्मो...चक्रुः eminent physicians holding various drugs and sitting in their proper places supported the queen like high mountains (occupying their proper places and having various plants growing on them and that made the earth steady). It was believed that the earth, which was formerly unsteady, was made steady by the mountains. Compare कादम्बरी 'अनुजीविभूभृच्छतसहस्रकल्पितावष्टम्भं सञ्चारिणं द्वितीयमिव मेदिनीसंनिवेशम्.' ग्रीवा...बध्यन्त in the knots of her necklace cord were tied excellent jewells. लक्ष्म्या...गतानि that had come with लक्ष्मी (*i. e.* royal splendour). She being a queen could command jewels. There is a pun on these words. Jewels were also produced from the oceans (पयोनिधि) at the time of the churning along with लक्ष्मी who was one of them. See above for सागरमन्थन.

P. 61 ll. 11–15 **ततश्च...जहार.** ज्येष्ठामूलीये मासि in the month of ज्येष्ठ. ज्येष्ठा मूलं च ज्येष्ठामूले. 'द्वन्द्वाच्छः' पा. 4. 2. 6 नक्षत्रद्वन्द्वाद्युक्ते काले छः स्यात्. बहुलासु = कृत्तिकासु—when the moon was in the कृत्तिका constellation. बहुलपक्ष = कृष्णपक्ष. समा...यौवने when the youth of the night was about to climb up (*i. e.* when night was just beginning). समारुरुक्षति *loc. sing.* of the *desiderative part.* of रुह् with सम् and आ. हृदयनिर्विशेषा not different from her own heart *i. e.* who was as dear to यशोमती as her own self. दिष्ट्या... जन्मना you are to be congratulated on the birth of a second son.

world. Even now proclamations are made known to the people by beat of drum. विधुताः केसरसटाः यैः that tossed the hair of their manes. Both केसर and सटा mean 'mane'. साटोपं (in a stately manner) गृहीतः हरितानां (green) दूर्वापल्लवानां कवलः (mouthful) तेन प्रशस्तैः (graced). हस्तपल्लवैः—has two senses. Those who dance make graceful movements with their hands (हस्त). The elephants tossed about their trunks (हस्त) in a graceful manner. सुरायाः आमोदः तद्वत् सुरभिः (with दिव्यानिलः); सुरायाः आमोदः तेन सुरभिः (निःश्वासः). Breezes redolent of the perfume of wine blew at the birth of हर्ष. This is fancied to be the sigh of लक्ष्मी leaving विष्णु. The idea suggested is—at the birth of हर्ष, लक्ष्मी left विष्णु and came to हर्ष. When leaving her husband विष्णु she sighed. चक्रं आयुधं यस्य. Compare for दिव्यानिल 'दिशः प्रसेदुर्मरुतो ववुः सुखाः प्रदक्षिणार्चिर्हविरग्निराददे । बभूव सर्वं शुभशंसि तत्क्षणं भवो हि लोकाभ्युदयाय तादृशाम् ॥' रघु० III. 14. प्रदक्षिणशिखानां कलापः तेन कथितः कल्याणागमः यैः that told of the forthcoming good luck by the mass of their flames curving to the right. अविद्यमानं इन्धनं (fuel) येषाम्. वैतानवह्नयः sacrificial fires. तपनीयस्य (सुवर्णस्य) शृङ्खला तया बन्धः तेन बन्धुरः (charming) कलशीकोशः येषाम्. कलशी a jar. कोश means 'the cuplike head or upper part of a jar'. Round the neck of the jar were tied chains of gold. समुदगुः aorist of इ with सम् and उद्. प्रहत...निभेन under the guise of the echo of the auspicious tabors that were beaten. दिक्पाल—these are eight 'इन्द्रो वह्निः पितृपतिर्नैर्ऋतो वरुणो मरुत् । कुबेर ईशः पतयः पूर्वादीनां दिशां क्रमात् ॥' इत्यमरः. दिष्टवृद्धिकलकलः—clamour of congratulation. The idea is—दिक्पालs were overjoyed at the birth of हर्ष. The echo of the tabors is fancied to be the clamour of congratulations from the दिक्पालs. शुक्लं वासः येषाम् (*adj.* of द्विजातयः). ब्रह्म वेदः मुखे येषाम् (with द्विजातयः); ब्रह्मा (the god ब्रह्मा) मुखं येषाम्—who had ब्रह्मा at their head (०पतयः). The Vedas being eternal, it may be said that the primeval प्रजापतिs also had the Veda on their lips. प्रजावृद्धये (1) for the well-being of the child (with ०जातयः); (2) for the propagation of the human race (with ०पतयः). कृतयुगप्रजापतयः—see मनुस्मृति I. 34-35 'अहं प्रजाः सिसृक्षुस्तु तपस्तप्त्वा सुदुश्चरम् । पतीन्प्रजानामसृजं महर्षीनादितो दश ॥ मरीचिमत्र्यङ्गिरसौ पुलस्त्यं पुलहं क्रतुम् । प्रचेतसं वसिष्ठं च भृगुं नारदमेव च ॥'. शान्त्युदकं फलं च हस्ते यस्य. पुरोधाः = पुरोहितः. पुरातन्यः स्थितयः as if they were the ancient rules (of conduct). प्रलम्बं (long) श्मश्रुजालं (beards) तेन जटिलानि आननानि येषाम्. It was usual to set prisoners free on the birth of a son or other great occasions. Note the अर्थशास्त्र of कौटिल्य 'बन्धनागारे च बालवृद्धव्याधितानाथानां च जातनक्षत्रपौर्णमासीषु विसर्गः' p. 146. बहलः मलपङ्ककलङ्कः तेन कालः (dark)

कायः (शरीरं) येषाम्. नश्यतः...कुलानीव as if they were the kindred of the Kali age that was vanishing. कलि (the age of sin) is fancied as dark. By the advent of हर्ष, an era of धर्म would be started and अधर्म would have to run away. The prisoners besmeared with dirt (and so dark) and running disorderly (आकुल) when freed are represented as the kindred of कलिकाल. बन्धनवृन्दानि crowds of prisoners. तत्कालापक्रान्तस्य that ran away at that moment (*viz.* at हर्ष's birth). शिबिरश्रेणयः rows of camps or tents. लोक...वीथ्यः the rows of stalls (विपणिः) that were plundered by the people. It seems that the stalls were looted by the permission of the king who compensated the traders for their loss. The stalls that were looted (and were therefore empty) looked like the camp lines from which अधर्म had run away, leaving them empty. विलसन्तः (making graceful movements) उन्मुखाः वामनकाः (dwarfs) बधिराश्च तेषां वृन्दं तेन वेष्टिताः (*adj.* of ०धात्र्यः). Dwarfs are often spoken of as the attendants of the harem 'निषेवितो वर्षवरैः कञ्चुकोष्णीषधारिभिः । अन्तःपुरेषु विचरेत् कुब्जकैरातवामनैः ॥' काम० 7. 41. जात...व्याकुलाः—the com. explains that 'in the lying-in-chamber a figure with a cat's face and surrounded by a crowd of children is set up' (probably to ward off evil). 'जातमातृदेवता मार्जारानना बहुपुत्रपरिवारा सूतिकागृहे स्थाप्यते.' Or we may take साक्षा...देवताः in another sense 'as if they were the divine Mātṛis become visible.' The Mātṛis, divine mothers, are said to attend on शिव and are seven cr eight. 'ब्राह्मी माहेश्वरी चैन्द्री वाराही वैष्णवी तथा । कौबेरीत्यपि कौमारी सप्तैव मातरः स्मृताः ॥' हलायुधः. प्रावर्तत—the subject is पुत्रजन्मोत्सवः. The lines that follow contain clauses qualifying ०त्सवः. विगता राजकुलस्य स्थितिः यस्मिन् in which the rules of etiquette to be observed in the palace were (for the moment) gone. अधःकृता प्रतीहारस्य आकृतिः यस्मिन् in which the figure of the doorkeeper was disregarded *i. e.* anybody entered without minding the प्रतीहार. अपनीतः वेत्रिणां वेत्रः यस्मिन् in which the cane of the warders was taken away. निर्दोषः अन्तःपुरे प्रवेशः यस्मिन्. Ordinarily no one could have entered the seraglio. समौ स्वामिपरिजनौ यस्मिन् in which master and servant were brought to the same level. निर्विशेषौ बालवृद्धौ यस्मिन् in which there was no distinction between young and old. दुर्ज्ञेयः मत्तामत्तयोः प्रविभागः यस्मिन् in which no distinction was perceptible between drunk and sober persons (*i. e.* both acted in the same way). तुल्यौ कुलयुवतिवेश्ययोः आलापविलासौ यस्मिन् in which the words and gestures of noble ladies and harlots were the same. प्रनृत्तः सकलकटकलोकः यस्मिन्. कटकं—capital.

P. 62 ll. 12–21 **अपरेद्यु...दृश्यन्त.** The principal sentence is अपरेद्युः...बिभ्राणेन परिजनेन अनुगम्यमानानि...समन्तात् सामन्तान्तःपुरसहस्राणि अदृश्यन्त. अपरेद्युरारभ्य beginning from the next day. स्त्रीरा...तानि as if they (*i. e.* the wives of the सामन्तs) were the kingdoms of amazons brought together or poured forth (आवर्जित). The idea is that the women were so many. In the महाभारत, we read of प्रमीला, who fought with Arjuna, as being at the head of a स्त्रीराज्य. असुर...वृतानि as if they were the mines opened wide. For असुरविवर, see the description of स्थाण्वीश्वर in the 3rd उच्छ्वास, where we have 'असुरविवरमिति वार्तिकैः.' नारा...लितानि as if they were the wives of Vishṇu (*i. e.* Kṛishṇa) moving onwards. अवरोध is m., while अवरोधन is *n;* we should therefore read०रोधनानि. In the विष्णुपुराण, कृष्ण is said to have had 16101 wives 'षोडशसहस्राण्येकोत्तरशताधिकानि स्त्रीणामभवन्' विष्णु० 4. 15; 'षोडशात्र सहस्राणि स्त्रीणामन्यानि चक्रिणः।...निशासु जगतः स्रष्टा तासां गेहेषु केशवः। उवास विप्र सर्वासां विश्वरूपधरो हरिः॥' विष्णु० 5. 28. 5 and 18. Besides these, रुक्मिणी and seven others were his chief wives. The भागवतपु० gives the number of 16000 in various places (see X. 59. 33; X. 69. 8 and 44). अप्स...कुलानि—The Apsarases are the damsels of heaven and have fourteen कुलs as described by बाण himself in कादम्बरी 'एतत्प्रायेण कल्याणाभिनिवेशिनः श्रुतिविषयमापतितमेव यथा विबुधसद्मन्यप्सरसो नाम कन्यकाः सन्ति। तासां चतुर्दश कुलानि.' This clause shows that the wives of सामन्तs were very handsome. परिजनेन—this word is to be read with बिभ्राणेन below. स्रजः, पात्रीः and others are the objects of बिभ्राणेन. पृथु...स्रजः (carrying garlands of flowers (सुमनस् *f n*) contained in a large bamboo box (करण्डः) and which were sprinkled over (अवकीर्ण) with bath powder. स्नानीयं (स्नानाय हितं चूर्णं) तेन अवकीर्णानि कुसुमानि यासाम्. स्फटिकशिलायाः शकलवत् शुक्लं कर्पूरखण्डं तेन पूरिताः. पात्रीः dishes. कुङ्कुमा...मयानि jewelled pots containing the fragrant powder (अधिवासः) of saffron. सह...रुकाणि ivory boxes (दन्तशफरुकम्) jagged (दन्तुर) with rows (फाली) of arecanuts white like sandalwood and tufted (जटिल) with masses of small खदिर fibres wet (तिम्यत्) with mango-oil. सहकारतैलेन तिम्यत् तनुखदिरकेसरजालं तेन जटिलानि चन्दनवत् धवलानि पूगफलानि (the dry areca nut with the upper coating peeled off is white) तेषां फाली तेन दन्तुराणि दन्तशफरुकाणि. तिम् 4th P. to become wet. The solid extract of खदिर called खदिरसार (catechu) is now used for ताम्बूल. It seems that tender and small fibres of खदिर were so used in Bāṇa's time. गुञ्जन्तः मधुकराः तेषां कुलं तेन पीयमानः पारिजातपरिमलः येषाम्. पाटलकानि च—take away the comma after this. पाटलकानि pink red (*adj.* of ०पात्राणि). सिन्दूर...पात्राणि boxes of vermilion and fragrant powder (for perfuming garments). 'पिष्टातः पटवासकः' इत्यमरः. The reading of B, पोटलकानि, does not make much sense. पोटलक means 'bundle, packet.' बाल...बिभ्राणेन carrying betel trees with bundles of rolls of betel leaves hanging from young creepers. We must read वीटिकावीटकांश्च as suggested by C and T. विटक makes no sense. वीटिका is the same as Marathi विडा. बाललताभ्यः लम्बमानाः वीटिकावीटकाः येषु. The com. remarks 'विटकवीटकं पञ्चाशत्ताम्बूलपत्रैः क्रियते.' चरणनिकुट्टनेन रणिताः मणिनूपुराः तैः मुखरितानि दिङ्मुखानि यैः—that made the quarters to resound with the jewelled anklets that jingled when they stamped the earth with their feet (in dancing). The reading of B makes no sense.

P. 62 ll. 22–33 शनैः...मोदः. The principal sentence is शनैः शनैः व्यजृम्भत...उत्सवामोदः. क्वचित्—क्वचित् in one place, in another place. नृत्तस्य अनुचितः (not accustomed) चिरन्तनः (of ancient families) शालीनः (high born) कुलपुत्रकलोकः तस्य लास्यं तेन प्रथितः (shown) पार्थिवे अनुरागः यस्मिन्. This and the following nominatives qualify ०मोदः. शालीन not bold, bashful (usually applied to high born ladies) 'स्यादधृष्टे तु शालीनः' इत्यमरः. शालीन formed from शाला with the affix ख (ईन) according to 'शालीनकौपीने अधृष्टाकार्ययोः' पा. 5. 2. 20 (शालाप्रवेशमर्हति शालीनः अधृष्टः । सि. कौ. । अप्रागल्भ्यादन्यत्र गन्तुमशक्तः शालामेव प्रवेष्टुमर्हतीत्यर्थः । तत्वबोधिनी). कुलपुत्रकः a nobly born young man. लास्यम् is a peculiar kind of dance 'ललिताङ्गहाराभिनयं कैशिकीवृत्तिप्रधानं वासकसज्जादिनायिकाचरितं डोंचिल्लिकादिनिबद्धं श्लिष्टत्वाल्लास्यम् । नृत्तं त्वङ्गविक्षेपमात्रं विवाहाभ्युदयादौ' क्षीरस्वामी. अन्तः स्मितं यस्य तेन क्षितिपालेन (प्रभाकरवर्धनेन) अपेक्षिताः क्षीबाभिः (drunk) क्षुद्रदासीभिः समाकृष्यमाणाः राजवल्लभाः यस्मिन्. The king smiled to himself when the drunken maids caught hold of his favourites. We expect अवेक्षिताः for अपेक्षिताः. The reading of two MSS. of B, उपेक्षित, would be also good. मत्ता कटककुट्टनी (bawd of the capital) तस्याः कण्ठे लग्नः वृद्धः आर्यः (noble, respectable) सामन्तः (chieftain, feudatory) तस्य नृत्तेन निर्भरं (much, loudly) हसितः नरपतिः यस्मिन्. क्षितिपस्य (प्रभाकरवर्धनस्य) अक्षिसंज्ञा (sign or hint given by the eye or glance) तया आदिष्टाः (ordered, instigated) दुष्टाः दासेरकाः (भृत्याः) तेषां गीतैः सूच्यमानः सचिवानां चौर्यरतप्रपञ्चः (numerous secret amours) यस्मिन्. दासेरक son of a दासी. दासेर is formed from दासी according to 'क्षुद्राभ्यो वा' पा. 4. 1. 131 (अङ्गहीनाः शीलहीनाश्च क्षुद्रास्ताभ्यो वा ढ्रक् । पक्षे ढक् । दासेरः दासेयः । सि. कौ.). मदोत्कटा कुटहारिका (water-girl) तया परिष्वज्यमानः जरन् (old) प्रव्रजितः (ascetic, संन्यासिन्) तेन जनितः जन-

हासः यस्मिन्. कुटः—टम् a water-jar + हारिका carrier. 'घटः कुटनिपावस्त्री' इत्यमरः. अन्योन्यस्य निर्भरा (excessive) स्पर्धा तया उद्धुराः (unrestrained, उद्धता धूः येभ्यः) विटचेटकाः तैः आरब्धं अवाच्यवचनयुद्धं यस्मिन्. विटः is a voluptuary and companion of a dissolute young man or courtezan. See the मृच्छकटिक for a specimen. चेटकः a servant. अवाच्यं वचनम् words that should not be uttered *i. e.* foul words. The servants engaged in a war of choice Billingsgate. नृपाबलाभिः (royal ladies) बलात्कारेण (by force) नर्त्यमानाः (made to dance) नृत्ये अनभिज्ञाः अन्तःपुरपालाः (chamberlains) तैः भाविताः (enlivened, entertained) भुजिष्याः परिचारिकाः यस्मिन्. 'नियोज्यकिङ्करप्रैष्यभुजिष्यपरिचारकाः' इत्यमरः ('भुङ्क्ते स्वाम्युच्छिष्टं भुजिष्यः' क्षीरस्वामी). स...राशिभिः with heaps of flowers it looked as if it were a mountain. Mountains have trees full of flowers. In the festival also heaps of flowers were used. स...प्रपाभिः with rum-booths it looked as if it had a showerbath. धारागृहम् is a showerbath or house furnished with jets of water. सीधुः rum. प्रपा lit. a place where water is distributed to travellers. In the festival rum flowed like water. पारि...मोदैः with the fragrance of पारिजातक. The पारिजातक is one of the five trees of Indra's garden (नन्दनवन). नीहारः frost. The dust of camphor spread in the उत्सव looked like frost. अट्टहासः the laugh of शिव in his ताण्डव dance. The sounds of drums beaten in the birth festival resembled the अट्टहास of शिव. अमृतमथनेन सह सा० (बहुव्रीहि). The uproar was so great that it resembled the noise made by the gods and demons at the time of the churning of the ocean as the रत्नs came out of the ocean. रास or—क is a dance (in a ring) practised by कृष्ण and गोपीs. See भागवतपुराण X. 33 'तत्रारभत गोविन्दो रासक्रीडामनुव्रतैः। स्त्रीरत्नैरन्वितः प्रीतैरन्योन्याबद्धबाहुभिः ॥ 2'. आवर्तः a whirlpool 'स्यादावर्तोऽम्भसां भ्रमः' इत्यमरः. The ring of dancers resembled a vortex. सरो...किरणैः—the rays shooting from the jewelled ornaments resembled hair standing on end. पट्टबन्धः tying of a piece of cloth on the head (a tiara, turban &c.). चन्दनललाटिका sandal marks on the forehead. Sandal is white and is compared to white cloth tied round the head. 'कर्णललाटात्कनलङ्कारे' पा. 4. 3. 65 (कर्णिका, ललाटिका). प्रसवः progeny, offspring. The echoes were as if the progeny of the original sounds. प्ररोहः sprout, leaf. The gifts of favour were given and appeared to spring forth like so many sprouts shooting forward in all directions.

P. 63 ll. 1–9 **स्कन्धा...लोकः.** स्कन्धा...मालाः—स्कन्धे अवलम्बमानाः केसरमालाः (बकुलपुष्पमालाः) येषाम् (युवानः); स्कन्धे अवलम्बमानाः केसरमालाः

(केसराः माला इव) येषाम् (with ०वाजिनः). The manes of the horses are compared to garlands. काम्बोजवाजिनः horses from the country of Kamboja. This country was looked upon as producing one of the best breeds of horses. See रघुवंश IV. 69-70 '**काम्बोजाः समरे सोढुं तस्य वीर्यमनीश्वराः।...तेषां सदश्वभूयिष्ठास्तुङ्गा द्रविणराशयः।**'. 'वनायुजाः पारसीकाः काम्बोजा वाह्लिका हयाः।' इत्यमरः. The country of कम्बोज was beyond the Hindookush mountain (probably eastern Persia) and it was known from very ancient times. See पाणिनि IV. 1. 75. Yāska refers to it 'शवतिर्गतिकर्मा कम्बोजेष्वेव भाष्यते... विकारमस्यार्येषु भाषन्ते शव इति' (निरुक्त II). आस्कन्दन्तः—treading the ground (with youths); leaping (with horses). तरलाः (unsteady) तारकाः (pupil of the eye) येषाम्—applies to both the youths and deer. सगर...भुवम्—who rent the earth with the violent stamping (अभिघातः) of their feet, as the sons of सगर did with spades. See p. 3 for the story of the sons of सगर. See विष्णुपुराण IV. 4 and रामायण I. 38-44. अनेक...संख्याः may apply also to the sons of सगर (who were 60000). कथमपि...क्षमा the earth bore with difficulty the agitation caused by the feet of the bards (चारणाः) dancing to time. तालः keeping time (in music) + अवचरः one who moves. अन्योन्यास्फालैः striking each other (in play). आभ... फेलुः the pearls in the ornaments were cleft asunder. फेलुः *perfect* of फल् 1 P. ब्रह्माण्डकपालम्—the world. पुनः उत्पन्नः हिरण्यगर्भस्य गर्भः तस्य शोणितेन शोणाः (रक्ताः) आशाः (दिशः) यस्मिन्. स्वयम्भू first of all produced waters and cast the seed in them. That seed became an egg and in it हिरण्यगर्भ remained for a year and then the egg was split into two parts. See मनुस्मृति 'सोभिध्याय शरीरात्स्वात्सिसृक्षुर्विविधाः प्रजाः। अप एव ससर्जादौ तासु बीजमवासृजत्॥ तदण्डमभवद्धैमं सहस्रांशुसमप्रभम्। तस्मिञ्जज्ञे स्वयं ब्रह्मा सर्वलोकपितामहः॥ तस्मिन्नण्डे स भगवानुषित्वा परिवत्सरम्। स्वयमेवात्मनो ध्यानात्तदण्डमकरोद्द्विधा॥' मनुस्मृति I. 8-9, 12. The world was reddened by the vermilion powder. Blood is red. The poet fancies that हिरण्यगर्भ was again being born in ब्रह्माण्डकपाल. पट...पटलेन by the cloud of the fragrant powder (used in perfuming garments). The fragrant powder resembled the sandy banks of the celestial Ganges. प्रकटितं मन्दाकिन्याः (वियद्गङ्गायाः) सैकतसहस्रं यस्मिन्. सैकतम् (from सिकता) according to 'सिकताशर्कराभ्यां च' and 'देशे लुबिलचौ च' पा. 5. 2. 104-5 (सिकताः सन्त्यस्मिन् देशे इति सिकताः। सिकतिलः। सैकतिलः। सि. कौ.). विप्रकीर्यमाणः पिष्टातकः (पटवासकः) तस्य परागः (pollen) तेन पिञ्जरितः (rendered yellow) आतपः (light) येषाम् (with दिवसाः). भुवनस्य क्षोभः तेन विशीर्णं पितामहस्य (ब्रह्मणः) कमलं तस्य किञ्जल्काः (filaments) तेषां रजोराजिः तया रञ्जिताः

इव. The world was disturbed by the riotous festival days. The poet fancies that the lotus on which ब्रह्मा sits was shattered by the भुवनs being shaken by the birth festivities. सङ्घट्ट...लोकः people tripped over masses of pearls that had fallen from necklaces rent asunder (विघटित) in collision (when people running in haste jostled against each other).

P. 63 ll. 10–33 **स्थान...प्रानृत्यन्.** The principal sentence is स्थानस्थानेषु च...वाद्येन अनुगम्यमानाः...पण्यविलासिन्यः प्रानृत्यन्. The instrumentals from ०लिङ्ग्यकेन to तानकेन qualify ०वाद्येन. मन्द...लिङ्ग्यकेन in which tambourines were struck gently. आलिङ्ग्यकः a drum having the shape of a barley-corn. According to the अमरकोश, it is a kind of मृदङ्ग 'मृदङ्गा मुरजा भेदास्त्वङ्क्यालिङ्ग्योर्ध्वकास्त्रयः'. 'चतुरङ्गुलहीनोऽङ्क्यान्मुखे चैकाङ्गुलेन यः। यवाकृतिः स आलिङ्ग्य आलिङ्ग्य स हि वाद्यते॥' शब्दार्णवः. शिञ्जानः (jingling) मञ्जुः (sweet) वेणुः (flute) यस्मिन्. झणझणायमाना झल्लरी यस्मिन् in which cymbals tinkled. झणझणायमाना pr. p. of the onomatopoetic verb ०णायते. क (in ०झल्लरीक) is affixed to बहुव्रीहि compounds having as the last member a feminine noun ending ई, ऊ, ॠ or a noun ending in ऋ. 'नद्यृतश्च' पा. 5. 4. 153. ताड्यमाना तन्त्रीपटहिका यस्मिन्—in which a stringed drum was played upon. वाद्यमाना अनुत्ताना अलाबुवीणा यस्मिन् in which the gourd lute that had its mouth turned downwards (अनुत्तान) was being played. This seems to have been some instrument like the बीन of these days. The reading of B 'अनुत्ताल०' makes a good sense. अनुत्ताल means 'low-pitched.' कलकांस्यकोश्या क्वणिताः काहलाः (बृहड्ढक्काः) यस्मिन् in which there were kāhalas booming sweetly and indistinctly on account of the sounding boxes of bell-metal. समकाले दीयमानः अनुत्तालः तानकः यस्मिन् in which a protracted tone was indulged in at the interval called सम. The reading of B is better and should have been kept in the text. ०दीयमाना अनुत्ताला तालिका यस्मिन् in which the hands were clapped gently at the interval called सम. सम is the principal interval in a ताल. C and T translate 'while all the time a subdued clapping proceeded.' आतोद्यवाद्येन by instrumental music. 'ततं चैवावनद्धं च घनं सुषिरमेव। चतुर्विधं तु विज्ञेयमातोद्यं लक्षणान्वितम्॥' नाट्यशास्त्र 28. 1. According to अमरकोश, आतोद्य and वाद्य are synonyms. अनुगम्यमानाः adj. of पण्यविलासिन्यः (harlots). अनुवर्तमानौताललयौ यासाम्. तालः keeping time. लयः harmony. Even the ornaments of the *naikins* kept time and jingled in harmony with their singing and thus looked as if they were intelligent beings (सहृदय).

There is another idea. Those who are masters in singing (सहृदय = मार्मिक) will unconsciously keep time when another person is singing. मदेन कला काकली तथा कोमलः आलापः अस्ति आसां इति० लापिन्यः—who sang delicate tunes in a voice sweet but low on account of passion. 'काकली तु कले सूक्ष्मे ध्वनौ तु मधुरास्फुटे' इत्यमरः. विटानां...गायन्त्यः who sang the vulgar words of रासकs that were the nectar of the ear of dissolute young men. रासक here means either (1) a particular kind of dance (for which see above p. 29); or (2) a species of dramatic composition. See for a definition of the latter the साहित्यदर्पण VI. It has only five characters, it is in various dialects; there is no सूत्रधार; there is a single Act; the hero is a fool, while the heroine is famous. स... मालिकाः they had wreaths on their heads. समुच्छ्रित raised up (past p. p. of श्रि with सम् and उद्). कुङ्कुम...वल्गन्त्यः like Kashmir fillies they pranced, having bodies radiant with the stains of saffron. कुङ्कुमेन प्रमृष्टिः (rubbing the body) तया रुचिरः कायः येषाम् (with ०विलासिन्यः); कुङ्कुमे प्रमृष्टिः (rolling in) तया &c. (with किशोर्यः). नितम्बबिम्बे लम्बमानाः विकटाः (large) कुरण्टकशेखराः यासाम्. कुरण्टकः Amaranth. The glow cast on their bodies by the flowers is fancied to be due to the fire of राग (passion). सिन्दूरस्य छटाभिः (streaks) छुरिता (overspread) मुखमुद्रा (colour of their face) यासाम्. The women had marked their faces with vermilion streaks. These are fancied to be the lines of the plates (पट्टः) of the edict (शासन) of cupid. The plates were smeared with सिन्दूर in order that the letters of the seal might look prominent. सिन्दू...छुरिता मुखे मुद्रा (seal) यासाम् (with ०पङ्क्तयः). अप्रतिहतं शासनं यस्य whose command is irresistible. मुष्ट्या प्रकीर्यमाणौ कर्पूरपटवासौ ताभ्यां पांसुलाः. Read ०पांसुला मनो०. मनो...यौवनस्य they were as if the roads for the wandering of the desires of youth *i. e.* the desires of young men converged in them. There is a pun. A रथ (in मनोरथ) requires a road for सञ्चरण and the road may be पांसुल (dusty.) प्रतीहार्य इव—It is the business of door-keepers in any festival to use their canes when people make a rush. The women are fancied to be प्रतीहारीs of तरुणमहोत्सव. All young men would flock to them. Hence the propriety of the word तरुण. C and T translate तरुण० as 'of a children's festival'. This is wrong. प्रचलन्ति पत्रसदृशानि कुण्डलानि यासां—whose ear-rings resembling leaves dangled about (when they danced); प्रचलन्ति पत्राणि कुण्डलानीव यासाम् (with लताः) whose leaves resembling ear-rings tossed about. लसन्त्यः dancing;

moving (with लताः). मदनः चन्दनद्रुम इव; मदनसदृशः चन्दनद्रुमः. The harlots danced out of passion. The creeper clinging to a sandal tree would also move about when tossed by the wind. ललिते पदे हंसकः (पादकटकः anklet) तस्य रवेण मुखराः (with ०विलासिन्यः); ललितं पदं (gait) येषां ते ललितपदाः हंसकाः (हंसाः) तेषां रवेण मुखराः (with वीचयः). शृङ्गाररसः सागर इव. The harlots were the ripples of the ocean of passion. हंसs may be cackling near the waves of a lake. वाच्या...शून्याः void of discrimination as to what was to be said or not said (applies to both ०विलासिन्यः and ०क्रीडाः). घनः (deep) पटहरवः तेन उत्कण्टकिताः (thrilled) गात्रयष्टयः यासाम् (with ०विलासिन्यः); घनः मेघः पटहः इव तस्य रवः तेन उत्कण्टकिताः (सञ्जातकण्टकाः) गात्रयष्टयः यासाम् (with केतक्यः). The pollen from the flowers worn by the women was carried about. The केतकी flower also has pollen. The केतक blossoms forth when the cloud thunders (in the rainy season (and there are कण्टकs on the केतक petals). दिवसम् (acc. of time) the whole day. उत्फुल्लं आननं यासाम्. The कविसमय is that the कमल expands in the day and the कुमुद at night. अनुपजाता निद्रा यासाम्. The women had no sleep at night. The कुमुद plants open their buds at night. आविष्टाः इव like persons possessed. नरेन्द्र...वृताः surrounded by a host of princes; surrounded by a host of magicians. नरेन्द्रः means generally a विषवैद्य and not one who exorcises evil spirits. See शिशुपालवध II. 88. 'सुनिग्रहा नरेन्द्रेण फणीन्द्रा इव शत्रवः' (where also there is a pun). रागमुद्दीपयन्त्यः kindling passion (with women); heightening the melody. The principal रागs are six. पुष्टयः fatness. मदमपि मदयन्त्य इव who as if intoxicated intoxication itself. Even मद could draw upon them for adding to itself. The reading उत्सवयन्त्यः would be more in keeping with what precedes. कटाक्षे...शुक्तिभिः in casting sidelong eyes, they seemed to be drinking with the shells (शुक्ति) of the corners of their eyes. The idea is:—when they cast glances, they took the pupil of the eye far away and exposed only the white portion of the eye. The white of the eye resembles mother-o'-pearl which is used in drinking (particularly milk &c.). तर्जनेषु in frightening a person they seemed as if to fetter him with the chains of the rays of their nails. They used the forefinger (तर्जनी) in chiding people. Naturally their nails flashed. The rays are fancied to be पाशs with which to bind the person chid. कोपाभिनयेषु—when a person is angry or wants to convey that he is angry, he knits his brows. चतुर...विकारान् in their clever movements they seemed to scatter about emotions. Their various movements caused the spectators to be roused to various emotions.

P. 64 ll. 1–9 **अन्यत्र…विलेसुः.** The principal sentence is अन्यत्र…राजमहिष्यः…विलेसुः. वेत्रिणां वेत्रेण वित्रासिताः जनाः तैः दत्तं अन्तरालं यासाम् for whom room was made by people that had been terrified away by the cane of the warders or chamberlains. A cane is the symbol of the authority of a कञ्चुकिन्. Note 'आचार इत्यवहितेन मया गृहीता या वेत्रयष्टिरवरोधगृहेषु राज्ञः' शाकुन्तल II. This and the following adjectival clauses qualify राजमहिष्यः. ध्रियमाणं धवलातपत्राणां वनं (समूहः) यासु over whom was held a forest of white parasols. कल्प…रिण्यः wandering under the tree of paradise. The queens resembled the nymphs of the woods. स्कन्धयोः उभयपालीभ्यां लम्बमानं लम्बं उत्तरीयं तस्मिन् लग्नौ हस्तौ यासाम् whose hands clung to the waving upper garment hanging down from both sides of their shoulders. लीला…प्रेङ्खन्त्यः who swung as if mounted on a swing in play. The shawls of the queens when they danced fluttered on their shoulders and they tried to hold them with both their hands. This looked as if they held the ropes of a swing with their hands. कनककेयूर-कोट्या पाट्यमानं पट्टांशुकं तेन उत्तरङ्गाः that were waving because the fine cloth they wore was torn by the ends of the golden armlets. तरन्तः चक्रवाकाः तैः सीमन्त्यमानं स्रोतः यासाम् (rivers) the water of which was separated into two by the चक्रवाक birds that floated in them. सीमन्त्यमान (from the noun सीमन्तः) *pr. p.* of the passive of the denominative verb सीमन्तयति. The golden armlet was like चक्रवाक, the fine cloth was like the stream and the queens therefore resembled rivers. उद्धूयमाना (being waved) धवला चामरसटा तस्यां लग्नः त्रिकण्टकः तस्मिन् वलिताः (turned) विकटाः कटाक्षाः यासाम्. हंसैः आकृष्यमाणं नीलोत्पलवनं यासु. सरस्यः lakes. त्रिकण्टकः an ear-ornament containing three gems 'त्रिकण्टकस्तु त्र्यश्रः स्यात्रिभी रत्नैश्च भूषणम्' quoted by the com. Their chowries stuck to their ear-ornament. When this happened they looked at the ornament to disentangle them. Their dark eyes resembled blue lotuses and the ornament with three gems resembled हंसs with their two feet and long beak; and the white chowries resembled the white body of the swans. The resemblance may also be due to the red colour of the gems and the redness of the feet and beak of राजहंसs. 'राजहंसास्तु ते चञ्चुचरणैर्लोहितैः सिताः' इत्यमरः. चलन्तौ चरणौ ताभ्यां च्युतः अलक्तकः तेन अरुणाः स्वेदशीकराः तैः सिच्यमानाः भवनहंसाः याभिः. सन्ध्यारागेण रज्यमानमिन्दुबिम्बं यासु. कौमुदीरजन्यः nights of the full moon in कार्तिक (which is in शरद्दतु). In शरद्दतु moonlight is at its best. The fair queens are like कौमुदी nights, the white हंसs like the moon's disc and the sweat reddened by lac-dye like the glow of evening. कण्ठे निहितः काञ्चनकाञ्चीगुणः तेन अञ्चितः (bent) कञ्चुकी तस्य विकाराः तै आकुञ्चिताः भ्रुवः यासाम्. The queens put their golden girdles round the neck of the chamberlain and bent him. The कञ्चुकिन् made contortions when so treated, at which the women knit their brows (in derision). वागुरा net. प्रसारितौ बाहुपाशौ याभिः. The out-stretched arms resemble the cords of the net (of love).

P. 64 ll. 10–22 **सर्वतश्च…राशयः.** स्त्रैणम् bevy of women. 'स्त्रीपुंसाभ्यां नञ्स्नञौ भवनात्' पा. 4. 1. 87. रागमयी full of राग (redness, love). शुशोण perfect of शोण् I P to become red. मङ्गलकलशमयः—jars full of water are looked upon as a good omen. विक्षेपः tossing. Their tender arms resembled the filaments of lotuses. विलासस्मितैः—Their flashing smiles appeared like the flashes of lightning. The word कालः means 'time (such as day &c.) or dark.' With the last meaning there is a विरोध in saying that काल became तडिन्मय (bright). Both smiles and lightning are bright. अंशुभिः = किरणैः. कृष्ण…वासराः the days seemed as if dappled. कृष्णसारः (1) spotted antelope; (2) dark and variegated. शिरीष…पुरैः by the bunches of शिरीष flowers used as ornaments of the ear. The शिरीष is a very delicate flower and used as ear-ornament. See शाकुन्तल I 'अवतंसयन्ति प्रमदा दयमानाः शिरीषकुसुमानि'. हरिता (green) छाया (कान्तिः) यस्य. आतपः daylight. विस्रंस…रिक्षम् the sky seemed as if full of collyrium by the sprays of तमाल in the braided hair becoming loose (by dancing). The तमाल leaf is dark and was used as decoration for the hair. 'धम्मिल्लः संयताः कचाः' इत्यमरः. हस्तकिशलयैः—their hands were delicate like tender leaves. माणिक्ये…षा by the radiance of the rain-bow in the gems. चाषपत्रमयाः full of the wings of चाष (blue jay). The sun's rays falling upon the gems of the women gave rise to rain-bow colours. ग्रहगृहीताः seized by a ghost. निनर्तिषया with the desire to dance (निनर्तिषा noun from the desiderative base of नृत्). विपुस्फुलुः *perfect* of स्फुल् 6 P with वि to throb, to vibrate. कुवेरकोषाः the treasures of कुबेर. कुबेर is the lord of riches and treasures. अलुप्यन्त were plundered.

P. 64 l. 23—**P. 65** l. 2 **एवं च…श्रियम्.** The principal sentence is देवी यशोमती गर्भेणाधत्त…राज्यश्रियम्. वृत्ते concluded. देवे—

this is to be connected with हर्षे below (last line of p. 9). उत्तमाङ्गे निहिताः रक्षासर्षपाः यस्य on whose head were placed mustard seeds to ward off (evil). This and the following words in the locative qualify हर्षे. समुन्मिषन्तः प्रतापः एव अग्निः तस्य स्फुलिङ्गाः यस्मिन् In whom the sparks of the fire of prowess were as if bursting forth. The idea is that the सर्षपs on the head were so many sparks of fire &c. The punctuation in the text is wrong. Take away the comma after सर्षपे, वपुषि and ग्रीवके and put it after स्फुलिङ्ग इव, तेजसीव, दर्पाङ्कुर इव. The सर्षपs employed were probably red. The white सर्षप is usually called सिद्धार्थ and is used as a protection against evil spirits. गोरोचनया पिञ्जरितं वपुः यस्य whose body was rendered yellow with गोरोचना. गोरोचना is a bright yellow pigment prepared from the urine or bile of a cow or found in the head of a cow; it is used as a medicine and to ward off the evil eye and evil spirits. समभिव्यज्यमानं सहजं क्षात्रतेजः यस्य. The yellow गोरोचना resembles तेजः. हाटके (सुवर्णे) बद्धा विकटा (large) व्याघ्रनखपङ्क्तिः तया मण्डिता ग्रीवा यस्य स °ग्रीवकः तस्मिन्. Even now the same ornament is tied round the necks of children. When क is added at the end of बहुव्रीहि compounds, the preceding vowel, if long, is shortened. 'केऽणः' पा. 7. 4. 13. (के परे अणो ह्रस्वः स्यात्). हृदयात् उद्भिद्यमानाः दर्पाङ्कुराः यस्मिन्. The poet fancies that the tiger's claws worn on the chest were the buds of pride bursting out of his heart. प्रथ...कुर्वाणे by his first indistinct prattle he seemed to make a beginning of truth. ओंकारं कृ (lit.) to utter Om *i. e.* to make a beginning. The syllables ओम् and अथ are very auspicious and are therefore uttered at the beginning of many things. A child even now is first taught the words 'ओं नमः सिद्धम्'. प्रणव or ओंकार precedes the study of the Veda. 'ओङ्कारः स्वर्गद्वारं तस्माद् ब्रह्माध्येष्यमाण एतदादि प्रतिपद्येत' आपस्तम्ब I. 13. 6. Compare रघु० I. 11 'आसीन्महीक्षितामाद्यः प्रणवश्छन्दसामिव'. Connect मुग्धस्मितैः with आकर्षति, which qualifies हर्षे. Smiles and flowers are both white. जनन्याः पयोधरौ कलशौ इव तयोः पयः दुग्धं तस्य शीकरः तस्य सेकः. वदन is compared to कमल, small teeth to अङ्कुर. पयोधर also means मेघ and पयः means 'water.' The child smiled a happy smile when nursed at the breast and showed its teeth, which looked like buds. चारित्र...पाल्यमाने—he was as much guarded by the women in the seraglio as their own chastity. मन्त्रः state policy determined upon by a king in consultation with his ministers. 'मन्त्रो विजयमूलं हि राज्ञो भवति राघव' अयोध्याकाण्ड 100. 16; 'विजयो मन्त्रमूलो हि राज्ञो भवति भारत' सभापर्व 5. 27. The मनुस्मृति says

'यस्य मन्त्रं न जानन्ति समागम्य पृथग्जनाः । स कृत्स्नां पृथ्वीं भुङ्क्ते कोशहीनोऽपि पार्थिवः ॥' VII. 148. 'मन्त्रमूलं यतो राज्यं तस्मान्मन्त्रं सुरक्षितम् । कुर्याद्यथास्य न विदुः कर्मणामा फलोदयात् ॥ याज्ञ० I. 344. वृत्तम् good conduct. यश...वर्ध्यमाने who was cherished by his kindred like their own good name. पञ्च वा षड् वा पञ्चषाणि (बहुव्रीहि). गर्भेणाधत्त राज्यश्रियम् became pregnant with राज्यश्री. Read वसुधां for वसुधा. गर्भे...वसुधाम् as the form of नारायण produced the earth through गर्भ (*i. e.* हिरण्यगर्भ). We have seen above (p. 30) that स्वयम्भू cast seed in the water, which became an egg in which हिरण्यगर्भ was produced. This हिरण्यगर्भ in his turn created heaven and earth. 'ताभ्यां स शकलाभ्यां च दिवं भूमिं च निर्ममे ।' मनु० I. 13. नारायण is identified in the मनुस्मृति with ब्रह्मा (see I. 10). If we take गर्भेणाधत्त in its ordinary sense (*viz.* 'conceived') it is difficult to point out the particular story to which Bāṇa alludes. We may explain thus:—the whole universe at the time of प्रलय lies in नारायणोदर and comes out of it at the time of creation; so पृथिवी is in the गर्भ (उदर) of नारायण.

P 65 ll. 3–8 **पूर्णेषु...राजत.** The principal sentence is (देवी यशोमती) प्रसूतवती दुहितरम्. दीर्घ...सरसी as the lake gives birth to a lotus plant that has long and red stalks and roots. दीर्घाणि रक्तानि नालानि नेत्राणि (मूलानि) च यस्याः (with उत्पलिनी). This and the adjectives in the following clauses apply to दुहितरं also. दीर्घरक्ते नालवत् नेत्रे यस्याः whose eyes are red and long like a lotus-stalk. Redness of the corner of the eye was looked upon as a sign of beauty. हंसैः मधुरः स्वरः यस्याम् (with शरदम्); हंसवत् मधुरः स्वरः यस्याः (with दुहितरम्). कुसुमैः सुकुमाराः अवयवाः भागाः यस्याः (वनराजिम्); कुसुमवत् सुकुमाराः अवयवाः हस्तादयः यस्याः (दुहितरम्). मधुश्रीः vernal beauty. महाकनकेन (grains of gold) अवदाता (resplendent); महाकनकवत् अवदाता. The com. says 'महाकनकं तिलसुवर्णं वसुधारा धनवृष्टिः । इयं च महाभ्युदयसूचनाय दिवा पतति ।'. वेला the shore of the sea. The sea is called रत्नाकर. सहस्रनेत्रः इन्द्रः तेन दर्शनं तस्य योग्याम्; सहस्रनेत्रैः दर्शनस्य योग्याम्. शची is the wife of इन्द्र. अहल्या the wife of the sage गौतम was seduced by इन्द्र who assumed the form of the sage. For this the sage cursed अहल्या to be a stone and इन्द्र had a thousand marks on his body, which were afterwards turned into eyes. See रामायण I. 48 and VII. 30 for the story. The कथासरित्सागर contains the story 'वराङ्गलुब्धस्याङ्गे ते तत्सहस्रं भविष्यति । दिव्यस्त्रीं विश्वकर्मा यां निर्मास्यति तिलोत्तमाम् ॥ तां विलोक्य तदैवाक्ष्णां सहस्रं भविता च ते ।' III. 3. 144–145. कुमारिलभट्ट in his तन्त्रवार्तिक explains this story along with others in a rationalistic manner. सर्वैः भूभृद्भिः

प्रांशुः (tall) सालः (rampart) तद्वत् अभिरामौ (charming); प्रांशुसालेन अभिरामौ (with संनिवेशौ). 'प्राकारो वरणः सालः' इत्यमरः. साल is also a tree. महा...वेशः the site of a large city. सर्व...क्षमौ capable of giving shelter to all people (applies to both).

P 65 l. 23--**P. 66** l. 9 **अथ चन्द्र...जग्मतुः.** The principal sentence is अथ...राज्यवर्धन इति हर्ष इति सर्वस्यामेव पृथिव्यां...द्वीपान्तरेष्वपि प्रकाशतां जग्मतुः. चन्द्र...निरीक्ष्यौ—they (the princes) were charming and not to be gazed at. They overpowered the world by their valour and their fame resembling flashing moonlight and therefore were like the sun and the moon. स्फुरन्ती ज्योत्स्ना तत्सदृशं यशः (द्वयोरपि धवलत्वात्) प्रतापश्च ताभ्यां आक्रान्तं भुवनं याभ्याम्. The moon is अभिराम, while the sun is दुर्निरीक्ष्य. स्फुरन्ती ज्योत्स्ना यशः इव प्रतापश्च (heat) ताभ्यां &c. The भुवन्s are either three or fourteen. अग्नि...भूतौ the princes were like fire and wind acting in unison and manifesting there effulgence and force. If fire and wind combined, the devastation wrought by them would be appalling. शिलाभिः कठिनः कायबन्धः ययोः (with हिमवत् and विन्ध्य); शिलावत् कठिनः (with princes). अचलौ—never wavering; mountains. महा...योग्यौ like two big bulls, they were fit for कृतयुग. The two princes were so righteous that they were fit to live in कृतयुग (the age of virtue, see above p. 3 notes). Bulls are fit to carry the yoke (युगं). There is another suggestion. वृष also means 'धर्म.' 'शुक्रले मूषिके श्रेष्ठे सुकृते वृषभे वृषः' इत्यमरः. धर्म is fit to live in its entirety in कृतयुग only. हरिः (अश्वः) वाहनं ययोः तौ हरिवाहनौ; विभक्तं शरीरं ययोः तौ ०शरीरौ—who rode horses and had well-proportioned bodies. हरि means सूर्य and विष्णु also. Mark the numerous senses of हरि 'यमानिलेन्द्रचन्द्रार्कविष्णुसिंहांशुवाजिषु। शुकाहिकपिभेकेषु हरिर्ना कपिले त्रिषु' इत्यमरः. हरिवाहने विभक्तं शरीरं ययोः (अरुणगरुडौ) whose bodies are assigned for carrying the sun and Vishṇu. अरुण is the charioteer of the sun and गरुड is the vehicle of विष्णु. उपेन्द्रः विष्णुः. नागेन्द्रगतौ—the princes rode the best of elephants. Or their gait was like that of the best of elephants (नागेन्द्रस्य इव गतं ययोः). Both इन्द्र and विष्णु are नागेन्द्रगत. इन्द्र rides the best of elephants (ऐरावत); विष्णु sleeps on शेष (the best of serpents). 'गजेऽपि नागमातङ्गौ' इत्यमरः. कुण्डल...धरौ the princes wore ear-rings and diadem. कर्ण, who had a कुण्डल and कवच given to him by the sun from his very birth, is a type of charity. Indra (who was careful to guard his son अर्जुन) came to Karṇa disguised as a ब्राह्मण and begged of him his कुण्डल and कवच and got them. इन्द्र being pleased with his liberality gave him a शक्ति. See वनपर्व Chap. 310-311

(Kumbakonam ed.). अर्जुन was called किरीटिन्. See विराटपर्व 43 'किरीटं सूर्यसंकाशं भ्राजते मे शिरोगतं 129...इन्द्रदत्तमनाहार्यं तेनाहुर्मां किरीटिनम्।' 130. सर्वतेजस्विनाम् of all luminaries; of all spirited persons. उदयास्तमयौ rising and setting; prosperity and decline. अमान्ता...कुटीरके who on account of their great pride could not contain themselves in the hut of the earth hemmed in (सङ्कट) by the restraint of the bolt in the shape of the shores that are near it. अमान्तौ *pr. p.* of मा with the negative particle. आसन्ना वेला एव अर्गलः तेन निरोधः तेन सङ्कटः. कुः पृथ्वी एव कुटीरकः. The earth is bounded by the shores of the sea; and therefore it fell short of their ambitions. मान also means 'size.' कुकुटीरक also means 'wretched hut.' In a wretched hut even an ordinary man cannot contain himself. तेजः...मानौ who disliked even their shadow falling away from light. The shadow of an object naturally falls in the direction opposite to that from which a light comes. They being तेजस्विन् desired that everything that was theirs (even a shadow) should be तेजःसंमुख and not ०पराङ्मुख. जुगुप्समानौ—*pr. p.* of the desirative base of गुप् (though there is no sense of desire). 'गुप्तिज्किद्भ्यः सन्' पा० 3. 1. 5. (गुपेर्निन्दायाम्। जुगुप्सते). स्वात्म...लज्जमानौ. The idea is that they could not bear even this that their image should be reflected in the toe-nails of others (and thus it might appear that they were bowing at the feet of others). The idea is similar to 'यः करधौतासिप्रतिबिम्बितेनात्मनापि &c.' (p. 1 text). भङ्गेन (1) by the curling; (2) defeat or running away. चूडा...माणौ—the idea is:—when the umbrella (one of the insignia of sovereignty) was held over them it was reflected in their crest jewel and thus a second umbrella seemed to exist. They could not tolerate the existence of a second umbrella (a rival emperor) and therefore felt ashamed even when a second umbrella existed in reflection only. षण्मुखः कार्तिकेयः the son of शिव. स्वामिन् is one of the names of कार्तिकेय. असुखायमानौ श्रवणौ ययोः. The idea is that they wanted the term स्वामि (lord) to be applied to themselves alone and could not bear that any one else (even the God स्कन्द) should be so called. कार्तिकेय or स्कन्द is the Mars or god of war of Indian mythology. Most of his epithets have reference to the circumstances of his birth. शिव cast his seed in Agni, who unable to bear it, cast it into the Ganges. It was then transferred to the six कृत्तिकाs, each of whom bore a son. The six sons were then mysteriously combined into one with six mouths. He was the commander of the gods against the demon तारक whom he slew. See रामायण बालकाण्ड 36 and 37, कथासरित्सागर III. 6. and बृहत्कथामञ्जरी III. 1. 142. ff. प्रतिपुरुष (1) reflection; (2) rival. सन्ध्या...माङ्गौ Even in folding their hands at the morning and evening adoration, their heads ached. शूलायमानं उत्तमाङ्गं (शिरः) येषाम्. To fold the hands is a sign of humility and submission. They had to fold hands in सन्ध्यावन्दन. Even this caused them मस्तकशूल. जल...हृदयौ their hearts were pained even by the bow borne by the cloud. They could not tolerate any one wielding a bow and hence were distressed when they saw the rain-bow in the cloud. दोदूयमान *pr. p.* of the intensive base of दू. The reading दोधूयमान is not so good as दोदूयमान. It would mean 'whose hearts were shaken.' आले... पतिभिः by the kings painted in pictures. They were accustomed to the fact that ordinary rulers bowed at their feet. परिमितं मण्डलं (disc) तेन सन्तुष्टम्. The sun has only a limited मण्डल (disc); they wanted an unlimited मण्डल (sphere of influence extending over numerous neighbouring and distant kings). The कामन्दकीयनीतिसार (in the 8th Sarga) gives the views of several authors on the number of kings constituting a मण्डल. Ordinarily मण्डल comprises twelve near and distant kings. 'इतिप्रकारं बहुधा मण्डलं परिचक्षते । सर्वलोकप्रतीतं हि स्फुटं द्वादशराजकम् ॥' का. 8. 41. See the मिताक्षरा on याज्ञवल्क्य० I. 345 'अरिर्मित्रमुदासीनोऽनन्तरस्तत्परः परः । क्रमशो मण्डलं चिन्त्यं सामादिभिरुपक्रमैः ॥'. भूभृता (पर्वतेन मन्दरेण) अपहृता लक्ष्मीः यस्य. In churning the ocean the gods made मन्दर the churning handle. 'मन्थानं मन्दरं कृत्वा नेत्रं कृत्वा तु वासुकिम् । मथ्यतामममृतं देवाः साहाय्ये मय्यवस्थिते ॥' विष्णु० I. 9. 76. लक्ष्मी was one of the 14 jewels churned out. The princes (हर्ष and राज्य०) never allowed any भूभृत् (king) to carry off their लक्ष्मी (glory) and therefore laughed at the ocean that allowed its लक्ष्मी (the goddess) to be carried off by a भूभृत् (mountain). For क in ०लक्ष्मीकं see above p. 31. अकृतः विग्रहः (शरीरं) येन. A powerful person would offer विग्रह (battle); the wind though powerful offered no विग्रह (it had no body). चमरीणां बालव्यजनेन वीजितं तेन. चमरी deer, of the tails of which chowries are made, are to be found in the Himālayas. The चामर is an emblem of sovereignty. Therefore they could not bear that the mountain should be fanned by the tails of चमरीs. जल... खिद्यमानौ—conches are found on the seashore. Conches were blown by great warriors only. There is perhaps another idea. शङ्ख is one of the nine निधिs. They could not allow शङ्ख (treasure) to remain with जलधि. The author perhaps intends also a picturesque effect. शङ्कु and जलधि are words meaning enormous numbers. 'लक्षं च नियुतं चैव कोटिरर्बुदमेव च । वृन्दः खर्वो निखर्वश्च शङ्कुपद्मौ च सागरः । अन्त्यं मध्यं परार्धं च दशवृद्ध्या यथाक्रमम् ॥'. चतु...सहमानौ. वरुण (प्रचेतस्) is the lord of the ocean in mythology. हर्ष's sovereignty extended over the earth bounded by the four oceans. अनपहृतानि छत्राणि येषाम्. विगता छाया (shade; splendour) येषाम्. Parasols shade one from the sun. Though they did not carry away the parasols of kings whom they vanquished, they made them विच्छाय (*i. e.* void of splendour; void of shade against the sun). There is an apparent contradiction which is removed by taking the other sense of छाया. साधु...क्षरन्तौ they were pleased with (*i. e.* they bestowed favours upon) the good, though not courted by them (the good), and poured nectar (sweet words) with their lips on them. There is another meaning due to श्लेष, which gives rise to विरोधाभास. प्रसन्न means 'transparent, clear' (as applied to wine). मधु means 'wine'. 'Even on good (*i. e.* teetotallers) people they poured wine with their lips, they being प्रसन्न without having taken (wine)'. Remove the comma after ०प्रसन्नौ. वंशः (1) family; (2) bamboo. ऊष्मणा (1) by their pride; (2) by heat. म्लानि (1) decline; (2) withering. दूरस्थितानपि. The force of अपि lies in this—if bamboos were to be destroyed fire would have to be brought near them; but the two princes brought about the decline of even *distant* kings. दिवसे दिवसे अनुदिवसं (अव्ययीभाव). Read शस्त्राभ्यास० for शास्त्राभ्यास०. शस्त्राभ्यासेन श्यामिका (darkness) तया कलङ्कितम्. अशेषं राजकं (राज्ञां समूहः) तस्य प्रतापः एव अग्निः तस्य निर्वापणं तेन मलिनम्. 'अथ राजकम् ॥ राजन्यकं च नृपतिक्षत्रियाणां गणे क्रमात् ।' इत्यमरः. Their hands were darkened by the practice of sword play. That darkness is fancied to be due to the extinguishing of the fire of the prowess of kings. योग्याकालेषु at the times of (martial) exercise. धीर deep. अभ्यर्णोपभोगात् after enjoyment that was near (*i. e.* that occurred a short while before). दिग्...लपन्तौ—the twang of their bows spread in all directions. The author fancies that the twang was the talk of the princes with the damsels (the quarters). आविर्भूतः शब्दस्य प्रादुर्भावः ययोः—whose names became known. द्वीपान्तरेषु—The द्वीपs are either spoken of as seven (जम्बु, प्लक्ष, शाल्मल, कुश, क्रौञ्च, शाक and पुष्कर) or eighteen. See विष्णुपुराण II. 1. 11 ff. and व्यासभाष्य on योगसूत्र III. 25 (for सप्तद्वीपा वसुमती) and रघुवंश for 'अष्टादशद्वीपनिखातयूपः' 6. 38.

P. 66 ll. 10–22 **एकदा...दिदेश.** भुक्तवान् that had taken his dinner. प्रथमं...भृत्याः good servants, the first essential of sovereignty, are difficult to obtain. For the seven Angas of राज्य see above p. 5. प्रायेण...क्षुद्राः generally mean persons, being agreeable in company, make the king their wealth, like atoms. The idea is that mean persons are agreeable to whatever the king says when they are in his company and thus by flattery make him the source of wealth to themselves. There are double meanings. It is the atoms that produce the पार्थिव द्रव्य (earthy substance). द्रव्य and समवाय are technical words in the न्यायवैशेषिक philosophy. The द्रव्यs are 'पृथिव्यप्तेजोवाय्वाकाशकालदिगात्ममनांसि नवैव.' समवाय is one of the seven categories of the न्यायवैशेषिक system 'द्रव्यगुणकर्मसामान्यविशेषसमवायाभावाः सप्त पदार्थाः'. समवाय is defined as 'नित्यसम्बन्धः समवायोऽयुतसिद्धवृत्तिः' *i. e.* it is an inseparable connection of such things as the whole and its parts, qualities and actions and their abode &c. Action is produced in the atoms by the will of God; two परमाणुs give rise to a द्व्यणुक and three द्व्यणुकs to a चतुरणुक and so on, when the earthy and other substances are ultimately evolved. The परमाणुs are the causes of द्व्यणुक &c. and between these latter and the परमाणुs there is समवाय. So सम...भूय means (in the case of atoms) 'being favourable to समवाय (*i. e.* entering into समवाय relation with their effects, the द्व्यणुक &c.). क्रीडारसेन on account of their liking for play. नर्तयन्तः making to dance. बालिशाः (1) children (2) triflers. Children in play make the peacock dance. Rogues, in whose hands the king becomes a puppet, make him dance (act) as they please. The com. gives another sense of मयूर 'धूर्तजनयोग्यो हासः'. But this is not absolutely necessary. दर्पण...पल्लविकाः rogues having entered into the heart (*i. e.* having secured influence over the prince's mind) transfer their disposition to him, as in a mirror. In a mirror also tendrils transfer bodies (*i. e.* the forms of tendrils are reflected). 'पल्लविको विटः' क्षीरस्वामी. The शब्दकल्पद्रुम gives वेश्यापति as the meaning of पल्लवक and कामुक as the meaning of पल्लविक. विप्रलम्भकाः deceivers, impostors. मिथ्यादर्शनैः (1) by false sights; (2) by false doctrines. असद्बुद्धि (1) ideas about things that have no existence (असतः अविद्यमानस्य बुद्धिः, with स्वप्नः); (2) false notions. Impostors warp the mind of the prince with false doctrines; dreams delude us by presenting things to our vision that do not exist. गीत...वातिकाः rogues, not being watched, bring about intoxication by singing, dancing and laughter. उपेक्षिताः वातिकाः विकाराः—as diseases of wind when neglected bring on madness. वात is one of the three humours of the body (वात, पित्त and कफ).

A mad man sings, dances and laughs. तृष्णावन्तः (1) thirsty; (2) greedy (for wealth). अकुलीनाः (1) not lying on the earth; (2) low-born. न शक्यन्ते ग्रहीतुम्—(1) cannot be seized; (2) cannot be reconciled. The चातक bird always feels thirst because it cannot drink the water on the earth, but subsists on a few drops from the cloud. Sailing as it does through the sky (कौ पृथिव्यां लीनो न भवति इति अकुलीनः) it cannot be seized. मानसे (1) in the मानस lake; (2) in the mind. स्फुरन्तम् (1) moving about; (2) appearing. जालिकाः (1) fishermen; (2) cheats. जालेन चरतीति जालिकः. Fishermen catch fish in the मानस lake. Cheats are so clever that they grasp the thought (of the prince) the moment it rises in his mind. Ordinarily one's thoughts are understood by their effects. यमपट्टिकाः—those who exhibit canvas on which are drawn the torments of Hell inflicted by Yama on sinners. See मुद्राराक्षस Act I where we have a person showing यमपट. अम्बरे (1) on canvas ; (2) in the sky. उद्गीतकाः who sing loudly. Rogues draw paintings in the sky *i. e.* build castles in the air, represent to the king as possible what is impossible. शल्यम् (1) the point of an arrow, barb ; (2) pain. अतिमार्गणाः (1) very keen arrows; (2) importunate in their demands. Read अभिषङ्गैः for ०ष्वङ्गैः. अभिषङ्गः contact. उपधाभिः परीक्षितौ tested by trials of honesty. 'उपधा धर्माद्यैर्यत्परीक्षणम्' इत्यमरः. The अर्थशास्त्र of कौटिल्य contains a chapter styled 'उपधाभिः शौचाशौचज्ञानममात्यानाम्' (I. 6.) and details four kinds of उपधा called धर्मोपधा, अर्थो०, कामो० and भयोपधा. विक्रान्तौ valiant. अभिरूपौ handsome or learned. मालव...पुत्रौ sons of the king of Malva, or Rajputs from Malva. भुजा...रिक्तौ not separable from my body like my two arms (*i. e.* I regard them as my own body). कुमारगुप्त०—for these see Introduction. भव ... भवितव्यम्—You two should not behave towards them on the same footing as other attendants.

P 66 l. 22—**P. 67** l. 17 **नचिरात्...ददृशतुः.** The principal sentence is नचिरात्...राज्यवर्धनहर्षौ प्रतीहारेण सह प्रविशन्तं अग्रतो ज्येष्ठं...कुमारगुप्तं (p. 12 l. 9) पृष्ठतस्तस्य कनीयांसं ... माधवगुप्तं ददृशतुः. प्रविशन्तम्—this and the following adjectives in the accusative qualify कुमारगुप्तं below. अग्रतो ज्येष्ठम्—the eldest of the two brothers was in front, as was proper. अष्टादशवर्षाणि वयः यस्य. अतिखर्वम् very low in stature. अति...र्वीम् who, with very heavy steps, as if steadied the earth that was unsteady on account of being transferred to numerous kings. The earth has passed through the hands of several kings and so is चञ्चल like लक्ष्मी. ०नृपतिषु सञ्चरणं तेन चला. C and T translate 'which trembled with the movements of numerous kings.' This is not so striking as the sense given by us. अनवरताभ्यस्तं लङ्घनं (leaping) तेन घनः उपचयः (growth or mass) यस्य एतादृशं मांसं तेन मेदुरात् (fat). अन... भासमानम् endowed with a pair of very thin shanks (जङ्घा) issuing from the knee joints that were not prominent and that (therefore) appeared as if to fall down from a pair of thighs that were plump with hard flesh of tough growth due to leaping constantly practised. His thighs were muscular and round, while the knee bones were not prominent (as they would be n the case of one who was not muscular) and his legs were thin. The shanks therefore appeared to jump out of his rounded thighs. उल्लिखिताभ्यां पार्श्वाभ्यां (sides) प्रकाशितः कृशिमा यस्य तेन (with मध्येन). सुरासुरैः रभसेन (with force) भ्रमितः वासुकिः तेन कषणं (rubbing) तेन क्षीणेन. कुमारगुप्त had a waist the smallness of which was laid bare by his sides that were hollowed (being void of fatty layers). At the time of churning the ocean for the 14 jewels, मन्दर became the handle and वासुकि was the rope. See above (notes) p. 42. The sides of मन्दर were scratched off by the violent rubbing of the rope Vāsuki and so its मध्य became slight. स्वामि...यच्छन्तम् giving room to innumerable (tokens of) regard received from his master. Even now it is usual to wear on the chest medals awarded to a person for excelling in anything. C and T render 'offered room for unbounded feelings of respect for his master.' This is not good. The poet is giving the good points in the physique of कुमारगुप्त and not the largeness of his heart. The plural सम्भावनानाम् is also against the latter interpretation. निभृत...क्षेपैः by the quiet and graceful movements. One who swims has to move his arms backwards and forwards as in walking. Youth is a period that can scarcely be crossed without pit-falls. वामकरे कटकं (वलयं) तस्य माणिक्यं तस्य. मरीचीनां मञ्जरी तस्याः जालमस्याः अस्तीति ०जालिन्या (with ०लेखया). समुद्भिद्यमानः प्रतापानलस्य शिखापल्लवः यस्याः (with ०लेखया). अङ्कितः पीवरः प्रकोष्ठः यस्य वामकर...प्रकोष्ठम् whose round fore-arm was marked by the line of the scar of the bow-string, the scar that had a pencil of rays from the ruby in the bracelet of the left hand and from which (therefore) the budlike flame of the fire of valour seemed to shoot forward. As to the wearing of वलय on the left forearm, see notes above p. 15. His forearm had a scar made by the bowstring and on the scar rays from the jewelled bracelet fell, which appeared like flames of fire. आलोहिनीम् slightly red. उच्चं अंसतटं अवलम्बते इति that hung down from his high shoulder. On his shoulder fell the reddish light of the jewel in his ear-ornament. It resembled the skin of the Ruru deer, which is worn across the chest and shoulder by a क्षत्रियब्रह्मचारिन्. Hence the word अस्त्रग्रहणव्रतविधृताम्. See बौधायनस्मृति I. 2. 14 'कृष्णरुरुबस्ताजिनान्यजिनानि.' For a graphic description of the equipment of a क्षत्रियब्रह्मचारिन्, see उत्तररामचरित IV. 20. उद्गता कोटिः यस्य सः उत्कोटिः केयूरः तस्य पत्रभङ्गे पुत्रिका तस्याः प्रतिबिम्बं गर्भे यस्य सः ०गर्भः, ०गर्भः कपोलः यस्य. हृदये स्थिता रोहिणी यस्य. ०कपोलं मुखं—a face on the cheeks of which there was a reflection of a female figure drawn in lines on the armlets that had projecting points. His face was like the moon. रोहिणी is said to be the special favourite of the moon. On his cheek there was the reflection of a पुत्रिका. The moon's heart thinks of रोहिणी. The star रोहिणी has flashing light, as the points of the केयूर flash light. For क at the end of बहुव्रीहि compounds, see above. p. 31. अचपला स्तिमिता च तारका (pupil) यस्य. लक्ष्म्याः लाभः तदर्थं उत्तानितानि मुखानि येषाम्. He had a downcast eye (by way of showing his humility) and therefore taught humility to lotus beds. लक्ष्मी is represented as standing in an expanded lotus. He, though desirous of लक्ष्मी (glory), had a downcast look and not an uplifted face like the lotuses. उत्तंसः crest, ornament worn on the crown of the head. अम्लातक is a kind of red flower. स्वाम्यनुरागः loyalty. रागः means 'redness' also. नम्रता (1) humility; (2) capacity to bend, flexibility. कङ्कणभङ्गात् भीतानि सकलानि कार्मुकाणि तैः अर्पिताम्—presented by all the bows that were afraid of being broken in their rings (*i. e.* their crests). Connect निर्दयया with भङ्ग. But to connect separate words with part of a समास is rather unusual. The reading of some of the MSS of B 'निर्दयाकर्षणभङ्ग' is much better, but seems to be a conscious improvement. Bows have नम्रता (they bend) and transferred it to him. संयतैः confined, restrained. प्रण...वर्तमानम् who acted according to the status of a nobly born youth, that (status) is the seat of trust, as if it were his sweet-heart. तेजस्विन् (1) brilliant; (2) high-spirited. आह्लादक applies to both शीलेन and शशिना. He was high-spirited and had a winning disposition and therefore resembled the sun, having a moon inside it. गन्धनम्—hurting, rubbing. दर्शन...सौभाग्येन who by the charm of his person purchased the people at sight and sold them into the hands of joy. The moment the people saw him, they gave their allegiance to him and were further delighted. What one buys, one may sell to another. कुमारगुप्तम्—connect with ददृशतुः. प्रांशु tall. गौर fair, white-red. मनःशिला (Mar. मनशीळ) red arsenic. अनुल्बण...निभेन under the guise of a crest of मालती flowers, that (crest) was not very prominent. This shows his विनय. निर्जिगमिषता = गन्तुमिच्छता. The white मालती crest resembled his great (गुरु) यशः which is poetically represented to be white. His यशः wanted to go out (*i. e.* spread in the world) and therefore kissed him on the head (as मालती flower) as a father (गुरु) when leaving the house on a journey may kiss his son on the head. भ्रूसङ्गतकेन by the meeting of his eyebrows. विनय and यौवन were united in him for the first time after a long interval. यौवन and विनय are rarely found together. His eyebrows that met were as it were the first sign of this union. हृदयनिहिता (1) placed in the heart (with ०भक्ति); (2) fixed on his chest (with ०दृष्टि). अच्छाच्छस्य अतिशुभ्रस्य चन्दनरसस्य अनुलेपेन शीतलम् (वक्षःस्थलं, which is the object of बिभ्राणम्). संनिहितं हारः एव उपधानं (pillow) यस्य. अनन्त...श्रान्तायाः tired by passing to innumerable chieftains. शशि...शयनम् a bed of the slabs of चद्रकान्त stones. His chest was smeared with cool चन्दन paste and therefore resembled the चन्द्रकान्त stone, which is also white and शीतल. His chest had a necklace of pearls which resembled a white pillow. His chest was broad like a slab. लक्ष्मी rested on his chest after being tired &c. चक्षुः and the other words in the accusative up to गमनं are governed by दर्शयन्तम्. चक्षुः कुरङ्गकैः भीतैरुत्कोचमिव दत्तं—eye which was given to him as a bribe (उत्कोचः) by the terrified deer. The same words are to be understood after वराहैः &c. The idea is that his eye was beautiful like that of the deer; the rest to be construed similarly. घोणावंशं bamboo-like (*i. e.* high) nose. स्कन्धपीठं broad shoulders. मृगया...शेषैः that remained out of those that were left after being hunt down in chase.

P. 67 ll. 18–28 **प्रविश्य...बभूवतुः.** चतुर्भिः अङ्गैः with four limbs *i. e.* hands and knees. गाम् the earth. स्निग्धा (affectionate) नरेन्द्रस्य दृष्टिः तया निर्दिष्टाम् (indicated). अस्तः (cast aside) अपरः व्यापारः याभ्याम्. सङ्कल्पाः...भविष्यन्ति your desires will give you this special distinction that the result will follow in all its fulness, like the trees of Paradise. मेदिन्यां दोलायमानः मौलिः ययोः whose head hung on the earth *i. e.* who prostrated themselves. युगपत् at the same time. ताभ्याम् by कुमारगुप्त and माधवगुप्त. उत्थाय—रा० and हर्ष got up. The reading of A 'उत्थाय राज्यवर्धनहर्षौ प्रणेमतुः तौ च पितरम्' means they (कुमारगुप्त and माधवगुप्त) got up and bowed to रा० and हर्ष and these two latter bowed to their father. It is better to suppose that राज्यवर्धन and हर्ष did not allow the young men any time to bow to themselves. निमेषो...यान्तौ not going away from the range of the (prince's) eye, like the opening and shutting of the eye. निमेष and उन्मेष are always present in the eye. The two princes always stood before हर्ष and राज्यवर्धन. उच्छ्वास (exhalation) and निश्वास (inhalation) are also अभिमुख (done through the mouth). भुजाविव पार्श्ववर्तिनौ our hands are constantly at our side.

P. 67 l. 29—**P. 68** l. 24 **अथ राज्यश्री...जानातीति.** विदग्धासु (applies to both सखीषु and कलासु)—clever; fine. कलासु—The कामसूत्र of वात्स्यायन (I. 3.) enumerates the 64 arts such as गीत, वाद्य, नृत्य, आलेख्य &c. उपचीयमानः परिचयः यस्याः whose familiarity (with सखीs and कलाs) was on the increase. शरा...भुवि as arrows on the target. बाह्य...स्थितेन occupying the outer court. स्व...गताम् that came (*i. e.* occurred to him) in its own context. The man was thinking on some topic or story and in connection with it he remembered a verse which he sang loudly. आर्या—'यस्याः प्रथमे पादे द्वादश मात्रास्तथा तृतीयेऽपि। अष्टादश द्वितीये चतुर्थके पञ्चदश साऽऽर्या ॥'. *Verse 5*. The sentence is विवर्धमाना सुता पितरं उद्वेगमहावर्ते पातयति सरित् तटमिव—a growing daughter casts her father in the whirlpool of gloom, as a rising river casts its bank in a whirlpool. उद्वेगः महावर्तः इव (with सुता); उद्वेगसदृशः महावर्तः (with सरित्). पयोधराणां (मेघानां) उन्नमनं तस्य काले at the time of the impending clouds; पयोधरयोः स्तनयोः उन्नमनं (elevation) तस्य काले. अनुवर्षम्—(वर्षे वर्षे इति अव्ययीभाव) each year (with सुता). वर्षमनु after rainfall. अनु as a कर्मप्रवचनीय governs वर्ष in the accusative. Or we may also take अनुवर्षम् in the sense of 'at each rainy season.' It should be noted that the verse fits in with the topic of the youth of राज्यश्री and the seeking of her hand by various kings. उत्सारितः परिजनः येन. गुणवत्ता possession of good qualities. चिन्ता—anxiety (as to finding a proper husband for her) never left his heart, just as her गुणवत्ता never left him (*i. e.* he was always dwelling upon her good qualities). The reading गुणवृत्तेव makes no sense. C and T say in the appendix that गुणवृत्ता is an easier reading. We fail to see how. They render गुणवृत्ता as 'as if become an attribute' and therefore take it as an adjective of चिन्ता इन्धनीभवन्ति become the fuel (of the fire of torment). अस्याः पयोधरोन्नतिः (पयोधरयोः स्तनयोः उन्नतिः) मे हृदयमन्धकारयति. पयोधराणां मेघानां उन्नतिः दिवसमन्धकारयति. केना...रियं this rule of conduct (regarded as) right, by whomsoever it may have been made, is not approved of by me. धर्म्या—धर्मादनपेता—according to 'धर्मपथ्यर्थ—न्यायादनपेते' पा. 4. 4. 92. अङ्कलालितानि fondled on our knees. अकाण्ड एव...नीयन्ते are taken away by strangers (असंस्तुत) who come all of a sudden. एतानि...संसारस्य these indeed are the branded spots of this worldly existence *i. e.* these are the most painful of the events of this संसार. सर्वाभिभाविनी overwhelming all. अपत्य...सन्तः good men are grieved at the birth of a daughter though both (son and daughter) are equally (their) offspring. जन्मकाल...साधवः good men offer water by their tears to their daughters even at the time of their birth. Emphasis is laid on the word जन्मकाले, because water is offered to the dead. Good men shed tears when a daughter is born. अकृतः दाराणां परिग्रहः (acceptance) यैः. परिहृता (avoided) गृहे वसतिः यैः. अरण्यानि is the object of अधिशेरते. The roots शी, स्था, and आस्, when preceded by अधि, govern the accusative of the abode (आधार). 'अधिशीङ्—स्थासां कर्म' पा. 1. 4. 46. यथा...हृदयम् the more do the envoys of the suitors come in, the more does wretched anxiety enter deep into my heart, like a woman abashed. लज्जमानेव—a woman that feels abashed will run inside the house. गृहगतैः=गृहस्थैः. लोकवृत्तयः–the ways of the world. वरगुणेषु qualities in a bridegroom (or 'excellent qualities'). अभि...धीमन्तः the wise follow (*i. e.* pay great regard to) noble birth alone. Mark the verse 'कन्या वरयते रूपं माता वित्तं पिता श्रुतम् । बान्धवाः कुलमिच्छन्ति मृष्टान्नमितरे जनाः ॥' quoted by commentators on कुमारसम्भव V. 72. धर...स्थितः standing at the head of all kings. धरणीधराणां= पर्वतानाम्. माहेश्वरः पादन्यासः the foot-print of महेश्वर (शिव). शिव is said to reside on the top (मूर्धन्) of the कैलास mountain. माहेश्वरः with मौखरिवंशः would mean 'that was devoted to महेश्वर (*i. e.* शिव)'. मौखरिवंशः—for the Maukharis, see Introduction. From the inscriptions it appears that the correct form is either मौखरि or मौखर. The reading of A 'मौखरीवंशः' is therefore bad. Bāṇa in his introduction to the कादम्बरी has 'नमामि भर्वोश्चरणाम्बुजद्वयं सशेखरैर्मौखरिभिः कृतार्चनम् ।'. ग्रह...गतः as if he were the sun (ग्रहपति) come to the earth. पितु...गुणै. not inferior to his father in his virtues. एनाम्—refers to राज्यश्री. दुहितृस्नेहेन कातरतरं हृदयं यस्याः.

संवर्धन...गिन्य: useful only in nursing them (and not in determining such delicate questions as their disposal in marriage). धात्रीनिर्विशेषा: not different from (*i. e.* no better than) their nurses. प्रदाने...पितर: in bestowing them (in marriage) their fathers are the (sole) authority. कृपया कृतः विशेषः यस्मिन्—the difference being made by pity. कृपा...स्नेहः—यशोमती gives expression to the general feeling of Indian mothers that they love their daughters more than their sons and assigns the reason for this. The position of the daughter in society excites the pity of the mother more than that of the sons. Read आर्तितां for आर्तिता. यथा...जानाति my lord knows how to act so that she (राज्यश्री) will not become a lifelong (source of) anxiety to us. The reading of A 'यथा यावज्जीवमावयोरार्तिता' is not good. The meaning then would be ' my lord knows how lifelong anxiety would be caused to us '. C reads 'आवयोर्नाधितां प्रतिपद्यते', which yields the same sense as the text (न + आधिताम्).

P. 68 l. 25—**P. 69** l. 32 **राजा तु ... कुलम्.** प्रति governs the accusative according to the वार्तिक 'अभितःपरितःसमयानिकषाहाप्रतियोगेऽपि' on 'उपान्वध्याङ्वसः' I. 4. 48. विदितः अर्थः याभ्याम्. जाता मुद् (delight) यस्य—qualifies तस्मिन्, which refers to प्रधानदूतपुरुष. The principal sentence is जातमुदि...गते तस्मिन् आसन्नेषु विवाहदिवसेषु... ०लोकम्...आसीत् राजकुलम्. The author now gives a graphic description of the preparations of a marriage in a royal family. उद्दामं दीयमानानि ताम्बूलपटवासकुसुमानि तैः प्रसाधितः सर्वलोकः यस्मिन् all the people in which were decked by the betel, fragrant powders and flowers that were being given with an unrestrained hand. सकलदेशेभ्यः आदिश्यमानं शिल्पिनां सार्थस्य (समूहस्य) आगमनं यस्मिन्. Skilled artisans were invited from all countries. अवनिपालपुरुषैः (king's officers) गृहीतः समग्रैः ग्रामीणैः (villagers) आनीयमानानां उपकरणानां (useful materials) सम्भारः (collection) यस्मिन्. ग्रामे भवः ग्रामीणः. राजदौवारिकैः उपनीयमानानि अनेकनृपाणां उपायनानि यस्मिन् where the presents sent by numerous chiefs were brought (to the royal presence) by the doorkeepers of the king (प्रभाकरवर्धन). दौवारिकः—द्वारे नियुक्तः according to 'तत्र नियुक्तः' पा. 4. 4. 69. उपनिमन्त्रिताः (invited) आगताः बन्धुवर्गाः तेषां संवर्गणं (attracting, winning) तस्मिन् व्यग्राः राजवल्लभाः यस्मिन्. लब्धं मधु (wine) तस्य मदेन प्रचण्डाः (wild) चर्मकाराः तेषां करपुटैः उल्लालिताः (shaken, moved) कोणाः (drumsticks) तैः पटु (sharp) विघट्टनं (striking) तेन रणन्तः मङ्गलपटहाः यस्मिन्. Leather workers had been summoned to make drums and were plied with wine. In their intoxication they struck the drums lustily. पिष्टपञ्चाङ्गुलेन मण्ड्यमानानि उलूखलमुसलशिलाद्युपकरणानि यस्मिन् in which such utensils as mortar, pestle and grinding stones were decked with five finger-prints of powder (of turmeric probably). The five fingers were dipped in turmeric mixed with water and the mortar &c. were smeared with the finger-marks by way of मङ्गल. In the 2nd उच्छ्वास we read 'पिष्टपञ्चाङ्गुलपाण्डुरं मुखनिहितनवचूतपल्लवं पूर्णकलशमुदीक्षमाणः...प्रीतिकूटान्निरगात्' on which the Com. says 'पिष्टपञ्चाङ्गुलमाजकोक्ताभिः पंचभिरङ्गुलिभिर्मङ्गल्याय दीयते'. Even now the pestle and grinding stones are so marked. अशेषेभ्यः आशामुखेभ्यः आविर्भूता चारणानां (bards) परम्परा तया आपूर्यमाणाः प्रकोष्ठाः (quadrangles) यस्मिन्. प्रतिष्ठाप्यमानं इन्द्राणीदैवतं यस्मिन् where images of इन्द्राणी (wife of इन्द्र) were being set up. A reads ०प्रकोष्ठप्रतिष्ठाप्य०, which would mean that 'images of इन्द्राणी were being set up in quadrangles.' The works on marriage ritual lay down that शची should be worshipped. "विवाहे शचीपूजनं नारदीयसंहितायाम् 'सम्पूज्य प्रार्थयित्वा तां शचीदेवीं गुणाश्रयाम्' इति । तथा च प्रयोगरत्नाकरे । ततो दाता पात्रस्थसिततण्डुलपुञ्जे शचीमावाह्य षोडशोपचारैः पूजयेत्तां च कन्यैवं प्रार्थयेत् 'देवेन्द्राणि नमस्तुभ्यं देवेन्द्र-प्रियभामिनि । विवाहं भाग्यमारोग्यं पुत्रलाभं च देहि मे ।' " quoted from Mr. Nardurgikar's notes on रघु० VII. 3. The धर्मसिन्धु says 'अन्योन्यालिङ्गितगौरीहरयोः प्रतिमां सुवर्णरौप्यादिनिर्मितां कात्यायनीमहालक्ष्मीशचीभिः सह पूजयेत् ।'. सूत्रधारैः (carpenters) आदीयमानः विवाहवेद्याः सूत्रपातः यस्मिन् where carpenters began to measure with their measuring line the marriage altar. सित...सत्कृतैः—the carpenters were honoured for their trouble by presents of white flowers, unguents and clothes. उत्कूर्चकः (उद्गतः कूर्चकः यस्मिन्) करः येषाम्—whose hands had brushes held up (in whitewashing). सुधायाः *(chunam)* कर्परः (pail) स्कन्धे येषाम्. अधि...रूढैः mounted on ladders. धवैः = पुरुषैः. धवलीक्रियमाणं प्रासादस्य प्रतोलीप्राकारशिखरं यस्मिन् where the top of the palace wall (प्राकारः) on the street (प्रतोली) was being whitened. आदौ क्षुण्णं पश्चात् क्षाल्यमानं कुसुम्भकं तस्य सम्भारः तस्य अम्भः—प्लवपूरेण रज्यमानाः जनपादपल्लवाः यस्मिन् where the feet of the people were coloured by the flood of the torrents of water from the heap (सम्भारः) of safflower that was powdered (क्षुण्ण) and then washed. निरूप्यमाणाः यौतकयोग्याः मातङ्गाः (गजाः) तुरङ्गाश्च तैः तरङ्गितं अङ्गनं यस्मिन् where the courtyard was surging with horses and elephants that were being examined as suitable bridal gifts. यौतक (n) is a kind of स्त्रीधन. यौतक means the gifts that are given to a woman at the time of marriage when she is seated with her husband. 'यौतकं विवाहादिकाले पत्या सहैकासने प्राप्तं युतयोर्यौतकमिति निघण्टूक्तेरिति मदनः' व्यवहारमयूख. गणने अभियुक्तः (engaged in)

on the inside of the cloth and hence they were done in the reverse order of nature (कुटिलक्रम), so that the outside (that would be visible to others) would show the beautiful पल्लवs in their natural form. C and T translate 'some, now dry, were having all the charm of sprays reproduced in their twisted shapes.' This is obscure. अपरैः—अपरैः some—others. आरब्धं कुङ्कुमपङ्कस्थासकानां छुरणं येषु in which the spotting with saffron paste had commenced *i. e.* some of the textures were being marked with spots of saffron paste. स्थासकः perfuming the body with unguents. 'स्नानं चर्चा तु चार्चिक्यं स्थासकोऽथ प्रबोधनम्' इत्यमरः. उद्भुजाः भुजिष्याः परिचारिकाः ताभिः भज्यमानानि भङ्गुराणि उत्तरीयाणि येषु the fragile upper garments among which were torn by the maids that had lifted up their arms. The idea is not quite clear. The meaning seems to be :—The maids raised their hands to gather together the textures as they became ready. In doing so they tore away their own fragile upper garments. क्षौमैश्च...नेत्रैश्च—these words indicate the material of which the garments were made. क्षौमैः made of flax, linen. क्षुमायाः विकारः क्षौमम्. बादरैः mad्e of cotten. बदरायाः बदराफलस्य वा विकारः बादरम्. 'कर्पासी बदरेति च' इति; 'वाल्कं क्षौमादि फालं तु कार्पासं बादरं च तत्' इति च अमरः. दुकूलैः—The अमरकोश treats क्षौम and दुकूल as synonyms. C and T translate दुकूल as 'bark silk.' लालातन्तुजैः lit. 'made of the threads of saliva' *i. e.* made of spider's thread. This is otherwise called पत्रोर्णम् on which क्षीरस्वामी remarks 'लकुचवटादिपत्रेषु कृमिलालोर्णाकृतं पत्रोर्णम्'. अंशुक is used in the sense of 'वस्त्र' in general. It must here mean a वस्त्र made from a particular material. C and T translate 'muslin'. नेत्रैश्च—silk garments. The अमरकोश gives it as a synonym of अंशुक. 'स्याज्जटांशुकयोर्नेत्रम्'. निर्मोकनिभैः resembling the slough of serpents. अकठोरा रम्भा तस्याः गर्भवत् कोमलैः as delicate (or fine) as the inside of a plantain plant not fully developed. C and T translate 'soft as the unripe plaintain's fruit.' This is not correct. रम्भा means the plant and not its fruit. No one in India need be told how fine and delicate the *inside* of the plantain *plant* is. The inside of the *fruit*, however unripe, is not soft. निश्वासहार्यैः The clothes were so fine and light that even the breath of a person made them move on the body of the wearer. स्पर्शानुमेयैः—the garments were of such fine texture that they were not visible to the eye, but were only determined to be on the body by touch. इन्द्रायुधसहस्रैः—the garments being variously tinted presented the hues of the rainbow. संछादितम् qualifies राजकुलम्. उज्ज्वलाः निचोलकाः तैः अवगुण्ठ्यमानानि हंसकुलानि यैः (*adj.* of शयनीयैः)—by the brilliant coverlets of which (beds) the swarms of Hamsas were veiled (*i. e.* were cast into the shade). हंसs are white 'हंसास्तु श्वेतगरुतः' इत्यमरः. 'निचोलः प्रच्छदपटः' इत्यमरः. शयनीयैः, कञ्चुकैः, ०सहस्रैः and other nouns in the instrumental are to be connected with उज्ज्वलं and the following adjectives. तारा...कञ्चुकैः with bodices that were added to (*i. e.* overlaid) with brilliant pearls. अने...सहस्रैः with thousands of pieces of fine cloth rent asunder for various uses. अभि...तानैः with canopies of cloth that were glowing with fine silk garments freshly dyed. अभिनवः रागः येषाम् तानि ०रागाणि अत एव कोमलानि दुकूलानि तैः राजमानैः. स्तवरकनिवहेन निरन्तरं छाद्यमानानि समस्तानि पटलानि येषाम्. स्तवरक... मण्डपैः with *pandals* all the thatches (पटलं) of which were covered with masses of clothes. The word स्तवरक is unusual. उच्चित्राः (having paintings prominent on them) नेत्रपटाः (fine silk cloth) तैः वेष्ट्यमानैः. औत्सुक्यं ददातीति ०दम् causing eagerness or excitement.

P. 70 ll. 1–16 **देवी तु...राजकुलम्.** हृदयेन भर्तरि—connect each instrumental with the following locative. The principal sentence is देवी यशोमती एका अपि बहुधा विभक्ता इव अभवत्—she, though one, seemed to be divided in manifold ways. हृदयेन...जामातरि—her heart was with her husband, her curiosity was with the bridegroom. These clauses explain how she was विभक्त. She was curious to know what the bridegroom looked like. उपचारः respectful behaviour, courtesy. शरीरेण सञ्चरणे her body was engaged in moving about. चक्षुषा...वेक्षणेषु her eye was occupied in seeing things done and left undone. उपर्युपरि now and then, again and again. विसर्जिताभिः (despatched) उष्ट्रवामीभिः (camels and mares) जनितः जामातुः जोषः (pleasure) येन. एवं च—The principal sentence is एवं च तस्मिन्नविधवामये इव भवति राजकुले...आजगाम विवाहदिवसः. अवि...राजकुले—In marriage ceremonies only those women whose husbands are living take any prominent part. चारण...दिङ्मुखेषु—So many minstrels had come there that it seemed that the quarters contained nothing else but them. Explain the following clauses similarly. भूषण...जने—Even the domestics were loaded with so many ornaments that they seemed to be nothing but ornaments. सर्गः creation, world. Read निर्वृति० for निर्वृत्ति०. लक्ष्मी...महोत्सवे when the festival seemed to grow as if it were made of Lakshmî, *i. e.* everything in the festival was so gorgeous and splendid. निधाने (treasure)—connect this and the following locatives with वर्तमाने below. यौवने...प्रीतेः it seemed as if there was a youth of prosperity and as if there was a new regime of pleasure (प्रीति). यौवराज्यम्—from युवराज—the heir-apparent. The installation of an heir-apparent is a very important function, as will appear from the रामायण. गण्यमानः—one counts with the aid of one's fingers. आलो...ध्वजैः—the unfurled banners seemed to be looking out for the arrival (of the marriage day), as a person stretches his neck and tries to descry a person coming from a distance. प्रत्यु...शब्दकैः the echoes of the drums beaten in the palace spread far and wide. The echoes went so far, the poet fancies, to receive the coming विवाहदिवस. मौहूर्तिकैः—मुहूर्तं वेद मौहूर्तिकः (astrologer). समुत्सारितः निखिलः अनिबद्धलोकः यस्मात्. अनिबद्ध—unconnected *i. e.* strangers. विविक्तम् lonely.

P. 70 ll. 16–25 **अथ...प्राहिणोत्.** शोभनः आकारः यस्य सः स्वाकारः तम्. त—object of पप्रच्छ. दर्शितः आदरः येन. कच्चित्—this is a particle indicating 'I hope.' यथाज्ञापयसि—servants were to use the verb आज्ञापय् with reference to whatever the king said or asked. आगत...ज्ञात्वा knowing him to have come to intimate the arrival of the bridegroom. यामे = प्रहरे. विवाह...दोषः (so act) that there will be no defect due to the passing away of the hour fixed for marriage. The reading of B is better, but seems to be an emendation purposely mode. प्रतीपं प्राहिणोत् sent him back.

P. 70 l. 26—**P. 71** l. 14 **अथ...ग्रहवर्मा.** The principal sentence is अथ...समवसिते वासरे...आजगाम (p. 15 l. 33)...ग्रहवर्मा. सकल...वासरे—कमलs fade in the evening. The bride's face glowed with expectation of the hour of marriage. The poet fancies that the glory of the fading कमलs was transferred to the beaming face of the bride. समवसित ended (*past. p. p.* of सो with सम् and अव). विवाह...सवितरि when the sun looked radiant like the tender feet of the Glory of the bridal day. The sun looks red when setting. The feet of handsome young ladies are red. वधूवरयोः अनुरागः तेन लघूकृतं प्रेम तेन लज्जितेषु. विघटमानेषु separating. The ruddy goose becomes separate from its mate at the close of day and is a type of abiding love. See notes p. 10. This separation is fancied to be due to the shame felt at the fact that the चक्रवाक pairs were eclipsed in love by the bride and bridegroom. सौभाग्य...रागे when the radiance of the evening looking as delicate as a red silken garment flashed in the sky as if it were the banner of marital felicity. A banner also waves in the sky and may be of red silk. रक्तांशुकस्य इव सुकुमारं वपुः यस्य; रक्तांशुकेन &c. कपोत...तिमिरे when darkness variegated like the pigeon's throat began to obscure the faces of the quarters as if it were the dust (raised) by the arrival of the bridegroom's procession. Both तिमिर and dust are dark and obscure the face. कपोत...कबुरे should be construed with तिमिर and *not* with सन्ध्यारागे, as C and T do. कर्बुर according to अमरसिंह is a synonym of कल्माष, शबल &c., 'चित्रं किर्मीरकल्माषशबलैताश्च कर्बुरे'. कर्बुर means 'dark-white' and not 'yellow'. See उत्तरराम VI. 4 'अवदग्धकर्बुरितकेतुचामरैः &c.' लग्न... सज्जे ready to effect the लग्न (the auspicious aspect of the heavenly bodies). This applies to both the stars and the astrologers. उज्जिहान *pr. p.* of हा 3 A with उद् going up, rising. ज्योतिर्गणे (1) galaxy of luminaries; (2) astrologers. A person who is सज्ज gets up. वर्धमाना धवला छाया यस्य. The round disc of the moon resembles a round मङ्गलकलश. वर्धमानेन शरावेण धवला छाया यस्य (with ०कलशे). वर्धमानः—म् saucer, a lid. Earthen pots marked with white lines are even now required in marriage ceremonies. The Com. remarks 'वर्धमानं शरावः...तद्धि मक्कोललिप्तं विवाहे क्रियते इत्याचारः'. वधूवदनलावण्यमेव ज्योत्स्ना तया परिपीतं तमः यत्र (adj. of प्रदोषे). वृथो...वनेषु when the beds of night lotuses with their faces raised up (*i. e.* with expanding buds) as if laughed at the moon saying 'you have risen to no purpose.' The splendour of the moonlike face of the bride dispelled all the gloom of evening. As the gloom was dispelled by the beauty of the bride's face, the moon that rose in the sky had nothing left to dispel. The expanding of the buds of कुमुद is fancied to be the raising of faces by them. A person in ridiculing another also makes grimaces towards him. उल्लासित...चामरैः (*adj.* of पादातैः) that waved many flashing red chowries. उल्लासितानि स्फाराणि स्फुरितानि अरुणचामराणि यैः. उत्थितः (रागः अग्रपल्लव इव) रागाग्रपल्लवः येषाम् (with मनोरथैः); उत्थितः रागसदृशः अग्रपल्लवः येषाम् (with पादातैः). पुरो धावमानैः is common to both मनोरथैः and पादातैः. The idea is:— footmen waving red chowries ran before the bridegroom. The leaf-like red ends of the chowries were raised up. The desire of the bridegroom also ran before him. Desire had shooting from it passion (रागः). Connect पादातैः and वृन्दैः with आपूरितदिग्भागः (ग्रहवर्मा). उत्कर्णाः कटकहयाः तेषां प्रतिहेषितैः दीयमानं स्वागतं येभ्यः.

The idea is:—ग्रहवर्मा had with him troops of horses that neighed. The horses in the capital of प्रभाकरवर्धन neighed in response. This is represented as welcome offered to the horses of the son-in-law by the horses in the capital. चलानि कर्णचामराणि येषाम्. चामीकरं (सुवर्णं) तन्मयानि सर्वोपकरणानि येषाम् all whose trappings were made of gold. वर्णकलम्बिनाम्—C and T translate 'with gay housings.' वर्णकः painted cloth. करिणां...न्धकारम् with troops (घटा) of elephants, he (ग्रहवर्मा) as if made again darkness that was dissolved by the rise of the moon. Elephants are dark. नक्षत्रमालया मण्डितं मुखं यस्याः (with करिणीं and दिशम्). ग्रहवर्मा rode a female elephant whose head was decked with a necklace of 27 pearls. 'सैव नक्षत्रमाला स्यात्सप्तविंशतिमौक्तिकैः' इत्यमरः. निशा...रूढः as the moon had risen in the eastern quarter. पुरन्दर (इन्द्र) is the lord of the east, which also is decked with a line of stars (नक्षत्रमाला). See above p. 25. प्रकटितं विविधविहगानां विरुतं यैः (with ०चारणैः and उपवनैः). ताला...चारणैः क्रियमाणकोलाहलः the bards that danced to a particular time went before him and caused an uproar. बालः—ग्रहवर्मा was young. In वसन्त also the उपवनs resound with the chirping of various birds. गन्ध...लोकम् with the light of an array (चक्रवालं) of lamps, accompanied with the fragrance of perfumed oil poured on them (lamps), he rendered the whole world yellow, as if with a cloud of fragrant dust of saffron. उत्फुल्लानां मल्लिकानां (jasmine) मुण्डमाला (wreath) तस्याः मध्यं अध्यासितः कुसुमशेखरः यस्मिन् (with शिरसा). On his head he wore a wreath of jasmine, in the midst of which was a bunch of flowers. हसन्निव...प्रदोषम् he as if laughed at the moon-lit evening with its moon surrounded by a halo. सपरिवेशः क्षपाकरः यस्मिन्. The शेखर looked like the moon and the white wreath like halo. आत्मरूपेण निर्जितः (vanquished) मकरकेतुः (मदनः) तस्य करात् अपहृतेन. विरचितः वैकक्ष्यविलासः यस्य. वैकक्ष्यम् a garland worn over the left shoulder and under the right arm (like यज्ञोपवीत); hence a mantle. ग्रहवर्मा wore as an ornament a string of flowers on the left shoulder and under the other arm. He was more handsome than मदन. The bow of Cupid is flowery. A bow is also worn on the shoulder. By vanquishing मदन, ग्रहवर्मा took from his hand his flowery bow and wore it as a वैकक्ष्यक. The word कर suggests another meaning. One who is conquered has to offer tribute. कुसुमसौरभगर्वेण भ्रान्तं भ्रमरकुलं तस्य कलः प्रलापः तेन सुभगः (applies to both ग्रहवर्मा and पारिजात). As he had a garland of flowers bees hovered round him; they must have done so round पारिजात. पारिजात is one of the five trees of Paradise and was one of the 14 jewels churned out of the ocean. जातः श्रिया सह—ग्रहवर्मा had royal splendour from birth; पारिजात was produced (from the ocean) along with लक्ष्मी. पुन...मेदिनीम्—पारिजात was taken to Heaven when churned out and hence the words पुनः &c. नव...हृदयः—His heart was drawn by the curiosity to see the bride's face. One whose हृदय (*i. e.* the upper part of the body) is drawn forward may fall on his face. प्रत्यासन्नं (near) लग्नं यस्य. 'राशीनामुदयो लग्नम्' इत्यमरः.

P. 71 ll. 15–28 **राजा तु...प्रविवेश.** द्वारस्य समीपे उपद्वारम् (अव्ययीभाव). माधवः=वैशाखः (वसन्तः). यथाक्रमम्—ग्रहवर्मा embraced राज्यवर्धन first as the elder of the two. नृपतेः प्रणयी a favourite of the king. तात is often used as a term of address applied affectionately to any person, usually by a friend to a friend or by elderly persons to youngsters. राज्यश्रिया—(1) by राज्यश्री; (2) by royal glory. घटितौ goes with ०मुखरवंशौ. It was राज्यश्री who being married to ग्रहवर्मा brought about an alliance of the families of पुष्पभूति and मुखर. तेजोमयौ—applies to both सोम० and पुष्प०. सकलजगता गीयमानः बुधकर्णयोः आनन्दकारी गुणगणः ययोः—(1) whose many qualities, gratifying the ears of wise men, are sung by the whole world (with पुष्प०); (2) in which the many gratifying virtues of Mercury (बुध) and Karṇa are sung by the whole world (with सोम०). There is a further pun on the word गुण which also means 'threads, fibres' and वंश (bamboo). बुध was the son of the moon and कर्ण was the son of कुन्ती from the sun. सोम seduced तारा wife of बृहस्पति and did not give her back. Brahmâ returned Tārā to बृहस्पति. तारा was pregnant and at the command of बृ० discharged the गर्भ upon reeds. Both इन्दु and गुरु wanted the son. The gods asked तारा whose son he was, but she spoke nothing through shame. The new-born got angry, but ब्रह्मा intervened and drew from तारा the admission that he was the son of सोम, who said 'साधु साधु वत्स प्राज्ञोऽसीति बुध इति नाम चक्रे'. See विष्णु० IV. 6. The birth of कर्ण from कुन्ती when she was a maiden is well-known. आदिपर्व 64. 140 'सूर्याच्च कुन्तिकन्यायां जज्ञे कर्णो महाबलः। सहजं कवचं बिभ्रत्कुण्डलोद्द्योतिताननः॥' (Kumbha. ed). प्रथममेव...देवस्य—the qualities of ग्रहवर्मा had already made a great impression on the heart of प्रभाकरवर्धन. The कौस्तुभ, one of the fourteen jewels churned from the ocean, is worn on his chest (हृदय) by Vishṇu. 'कौस्तुभाख्यमभूद्रत्नं पद्मरागो महोदधेः। तस्मिन्हरिः स्पृहां चक्रे वक्षोऽलङ्करणे मणौ॥' भागवत VIII. The word is derived as 'कुं भुवं स्तुभ्नाति

व्याप्नोति इति कुस्तुभः समुद्रः तत्र भवः'. इदानीम्—now *i. e.* as a bridegroom. परमेश्वरेण = (1) शिवेन; (2) प्रभाकरवर्धनेन. Emperors had the titles परमेश्वर, महाराजाधिराज. See Introduction. S'iva has the moon on his head. A bridegroom is to be honoured by the father-in-law. समा...वेला the auspicious time (fixed for the marriage ceremony) approaches. कौतुकगृहम्—the house where the marriage thread (कौतुकं) is placed on the wrist of the bridegroom before the actual marriage ceremonies. Compare रघु० 8. 1. 'अथ तस्य विवाहकौतुकं ललितं बिभ्रत एव'. पतितानि—the eyes of women fell on him. The blue eyes resemble expanded blue lotuses. लङ्घयन् traversing, jumping over (the lotuses in the form of eyes).

P. 71 l. 29—**P. 72** l. 9 **अथ तत्र...पश्यत्.** The principal sentence is अथ तत्र...वधूमपश्यत्. कति...परिवाराम्—this and the following accusatives qualify **वधूम्.** कति...वाराम् who was attended by several relatives (आप्त), dear friends and her own people (*i. e.* servants), mostly women. अरुणं अंशुकं तेन अवगुण्ठितं मुखं यस्याः—whose face was veiled by a red silken cloth. The radiance of her face made the lamps pale before her. The radiant glow of morn also makes the lamps appear dim. अरुणः अंशुकमिव तेन अवगुण्ठितं मुखं यस्याः (प्रभातसन्ध्या)—the beginning of which is covered by Aruṇa that resembles a red silken garment. Or we may dissolve अरुणस्य अंशुकाः किरणाः &c. अति...गूढाम् The idea is that she was not a grown-up woman, but was almost a girl. A delicate substance if closely pressed may break. यौवन is fancied as afraid of hurting her by too close an embrace, as she was so delicate. साध्वसेन (भयेन) निरुध्यमानः (restrained) हृदयदेशः तस्मात् दुःखेन मुक्तैः—The sudden events of her marriage caused her heart to flutter and therefore she heaved sighs by way of relieving the pressure. निभृतायतैः secret and long. She tried to keep her emotion to herself. One who sorrows over anything heaves deep sighs. The sighs which she heaved for relief are fancied to be due to her lamenting her maidenhood that was leaving her. अत्युत्कम्पिनीं...धार्यमाणाम्—her heart was in a whirl of emotions; but she was kept motionless by bashfulness, as if through fear of her falling down. One who is trembling (in body) has to be supported (धार्यमाण) for fear of a fall. हस्तम् and शशिनम् are to be connected with अवलोकयन्तीम् (she was looking at her hand vacantly being absorbed in deep thought). ताम...पक्षं which was the rival of a red lotus *i. e.* her hand was red.

आसन्नं ग्रहणं यस्य the grasping of which (in marriage) was near ताम...पक्ष्म् (the moon) who is the enemy of red lotuses. आसन्नं ग्रहणं यस्य whose seizure (by Rāhu *i. e.* eclipse) was near. रोहिणी the favourite wife of the moon out of the 27 नक्षत्रs. भय...साम् —applies to both रोहिणी and वधू. रोहिणी would tremble at the approaching eclipse of her lord. चन्दनेन धवला तनुलता यस्याः. ज्योत्स्नादानेन सञ्चितं लावण्यं यस्य loveliness of which is accumulated by the gift of moonlight. कुमुद्s thrive in moonlight. The inside of the कुमुदिनी would be white. कुसु...हारिणीम्—she (वधू) was spreading about the perfume of flowers. वसन्त is the season of flowers. निःश्वासपरिमलेन आकृष्टं मधुकरकुलं यया. Her fragrant breath drew round her a swarm of bees. मलयमारुत- the breezes from the Malaya Mountain are charged with the perfume of sandal. कृत...सरणाम् (1) who did what Love dictated (with वधूम्); (2) who was followed by Cupid *i. e.* मदन acted as his wife रति dictated; कृतं कन्दर्पेण अनुसरणं यस्याः (with रतिम्). The bride was as handsome and loving as रति, the wife of मदन. C and T translate 'love followed in the train of one who seemed a reborn Rati.' This is not correct. प्रभा...माधुर्यैः—these five are to be connected respectively with the five *Ratnas* 'कौस्तुभ...मृत.' अपरा...श्रियम् she was as if another श्री (लक्ष्मी) formed by the ocean out of wrath against the gods and demons. The author here mentions six out of the fourteen रत्नs churned out of the ocean. There is an emphasis on the word श्री. राज्यश्री can naturally be called श्री. अपराम्—this word is used because there was one already produced at the churning. The ocean, being a mine of jewels, can produce fresh ones though fourteen were already taken away by the gods and demons. The anger of the ocean is due to his being deprived of the *Ratnas*. स्निग्धेन...तंसाम् affectionate young maids (बालिका + लोक) made for her an ear-ornament with the rays of pearls as if with clusters of white सिन्धुवार flowers. सिन्धु-(न्दु) बार is a plant called in Marathi निगडी. स्निग्धेन...लोकेन may also mean 'by the glossy soft light' (०आलोकेन). कर्णाभरणमरकतस्य प्रभा हरितशाद्वलं इव; ०मरकतप्रभासदृशं हरितशाद्वलम्. कर्णा...च्छायाम् who as if removed (*i. e.* rendered imperceptible) the lovely (हारिणी) beauty of her eyes by her broad cheeks on which there fell the lustre of the emerald of her ear-ornament, resembling a green meadow. स्थली means a plot of ground. हारिणीं = हरिणसम्बन्धिनीम्. So the words suggest another sense 'who entertained the eyes of deer with a plot of ground covered with green grass' (resembling emerald). अधोमुखीं—through bashfulness she hung her head. कृतः मुखोन्नमनप्रयत्नः येन—her friends tried to raise her face; in her heart also she wished to raise her face (to see the bridegroom). वर...कुलम् her friends were absorbed in looking at the wonderful bridegroom; her heart fluttered to look &c. हृदयं निर्भर्त्सयन्तीम् she censured her heart for its cowardice in not succeeding in raising her face to see the bridegroom, though she so much desired to raise it.

P. 72 ll. 10-23 **प्रविशन्त...विभावसुः.** वध्वा समर्पितम् handed over (to cupid) by the bride. जग्राह कन्दर्पः Cupid seized him *i. e.* he became enamoured of the bride. A thief is handed over to proper custody and is held fast by the custodian. परिहासेन स्मेराणि (smiling) मुखानि यासाम्. अतिपेशलम् very cleverly. कृतः परिणयस्य (विवाहस्य) अनुरूपः वेशपरिग्रहः यया. जगाम—connect this with वेदीम्. ०धवलाम् and the following clauses in the accusative qualify वेदीम्. नव...धवलाम् (1) brilliant with fresh white-wash; (2) white like fresh chunam (with उपत्यकाम्). सुधा may, in the latter case, also mean 'nectar', which is also white. तुषारशैलस्य हिमालयस्य उपत्यका a land at the foot of a mountain. 'उपाधिभ्यां त्यकन्नासन्नारूढयोः' पा. 5. 2. 34 (संज्ञायामित्यनुवर्तते । पर्वतस्यासन्नं स्थलमुपत्यका आरूढं स्थलमधित्यका । सि. कौ.). भूभृद्भिः (1) by kings; (2) by mountains. सेक...दन्तुरैः that bristled with barley shoots that looked soft on account of the sprinkling of water. पञ्चास्यैः with five mouths. कोम...चित्रैः variegated with soft colours. अमित्रमुखैः—C and T translate 'gleaming around it were earthen dolls, whose hands bore auspicious fruits, and which had five-mouthed cups bristling with dew-besprent blades of barley and enemies' faces painted with soft colours.' So they think that the कलशs were in the hands of dolls. But one fails to see how the sentence yields this sense. We must connect कलशैः with उद्भासितपर्यन्ताम्. अमित्रमुखैः should be taken as an adjective of कलशैः (अमित्राः शत्रवः मुखे येषाम्). The idea seems to be this :— there were कलशs with barley blades that resembled दन्तs, the कलशs had a lion's shape, they were painted in various colours; hence the whole presented an awful aspect, so that the कलशs seemed to have some terrible enemies in them. अञ्जलिकारिका—a clay doll. 'स्यात्सालभञ्जिका स्तम्भे लेप्येनाञ्जलिकारिका' इति क्षीरस्वामी. C reads अमत्रमुखैः which means 'that had the mouth of a goblet'. This seems to be a suspicious reading adopted to obviate the difficulties of अमित्रमुखैः. उपाध्यायेन उपधीयमानानि (heaped, placed) इन्धनानि तेन धूमायमानः अग्निः तस्य सन्धुक्षणे (kindling) अक्षणिका

उपद्रष्टृद्विजाः यस्याम् (adj. of वेदीम्). उपद्रष्टृ means 'one who supervises.' अक्षणिक not having leisure, busy. कृशानोः (अग्नेः) समीपे इति उपकृशानु निहिताः अनुपहताः (new, not used) हरितकुशाः यस्याम्. संनिहितः दृषदां अजिनानां आज्यस्य स्रुचां (ladles) समित्पूलीनां (bundles of fuel sticks) निवहः यस्याम्. C reads स्रक् (garland) for स्रुक्; but it is not very appropriate in the context. नूतनशूर्पे अर्पिताः श्यामलशमीपलाशमिश्रिताः लाजाः (fried grain) तैः हसतीति हासिनीम्. The लाजs being white are spoken of as the हास of the वेदी. शमी is a sacred tree. पलाशं leaf. See रघुवंश VII. 26 'हविःशमीपल्लवलाजगन्धी पुण्यः कृशानोरुदियाय धूमः।'. कात्यायन says 'शमीपल्लवमिश्राँल्लाजानञ्जलिना वपति'. शूर्पः—र्पम् winnowing basket (Marathi सूप). सज्योत्स्नः—राज्यश्री resembled the light of the moon. See धर्मसिन्धु 'वधूवरौ पूर्वोक्तलक्षणां वेदीं मन्त्रघोषेणारुह्य &c.' समुत्ससर्प—connect this with 'शिखिनः (अग्नेः) समीपम्.' वेल्लिता...ल्लवस्य the red leaf-like flames of which were tremulous (with fire); the red flame-like leaves of which were tremulous (with रक्ताशोक). शिखिनः also may be applied to रक्ताशोक (it had a tapering foliage). कुसुमायुधः (कुसुमानि आयुधानि यस्य) इव—ग्रहवर्मा was handsome like मदन and राज्यश्री was like रति. रक्ताशोक is an excitant of love. In this sentence as well as in the preceding (आरुरोह तां दिवमिव), the author perhaps intentionally indicates the untimely death of ग्रहवर्मा. दक्षि...वृत्ताभिः that moved round to the right. Flames moving to the right are a good omen. ज्वालाभिरेव समं—the idea is :—the flames moved about; he also moved round the fire. नखमयूखैः धवलिता तनुः यस्य. When the bride let fall the oblation of parched grain into the fire from her hands, her brilliant nails brightened the fire. अदृष्टपूर्वं वधूवरयोः रूपं तेन विस्मयः तेन स्मेरः. Smile is white according to the poets; the brilliance of the nails transferred to the fire is the smile and the white लाजs are the teeth shown in smiling. For going round the fire and लाजहोम, see कुमारसम्भव VII. 80 'तौ दम्पती त्रिः परिणीय वह्निमन्योन्यसंस्पर्शनिमीलिताक्षौ । स कारयामास वधूं पुरोधास्तस्मिन्समिद्धार्चिषि लाजमोक्षम् ॥.' The आश्वलायनगृह्यसूत्र says 'वध्वञ्जला उपस्तीर्य भ्राता भ्रातृस्थानीयो वा द्विर्लाजानावपति' (I. 701). मेधातिथि on मनु० VIII. 227 remarks 'लाजहोममभिनिर्वर्त्य त्रिः प्रदक्षिणमग्निमावर्त्य सप्त पदानि स्त्री प्रक्रम्यते'.

P. 72 l. 24—**P. 73** l. 2 **अत्रान्तरे...वासगृहम्.** रुरोद वधूः—the bride wept because she was soon to be separated from her parents. स्वच्छ...यन्ती as if quenching the image of fire reflected inside her bright cheeks. स्थूलमुक्ताफलवत् विमलाः बाष्पबिन्दवः तेषां सन्दोहः (assemblage) तेन दर्शितं दुर्दिनं यया. दुर्दिनम् a rainy day. 'मेघच्छन्नेऽह्नि दुर्दिनम्' इत्यमरः. निर्वेदनविकारम् without showing any emotion on her face. उदश्रु विलोचनं यासाम्. प्रविवेश—connect with वासगृहम्. द्वारपक्षे लिखितं रतिप्रीतिदैवतं यस्मिन् on the side of the door of which was painted Rati, the presiding spirit of Love. प्रणयि... कुलैः—the bees, drawn by the perfume of flowers, entered the वासगृह before ग्रहवर्मा and looked like his friends. अलि...काशितम्—the idea is:—the lamps began to flicker owing to the breezes set in motion by the bees; the poet fancies that they trembled because they were afraid of being struck with the कर्णोत्पल (by राज्यश्री in order to put them out). एकदेशे लिखितः स्तबकितः (having bunches of flowers) रक्ताशोकतरुः तस्य तलं भजतीति ०भाक् तेन ०भाजा. अधिज्यचापेन whose bow was strung. तिर्यक्कूणितः नेत्रत्रिभागः यस्य a third part of whose eye was obliquely contracted. Cupid is represented as having a squint eye to symbolize the fact that love is generally blind. काञ्चनाचामरुकेण is not quite clear. We should read 'काञ्चनाचामनकेन' (काञ्चन + आचामनकेन)—a golden spitting vessel. This latter is really the reading of B, as the MSS often confound च and व. Read दन्त० for दान्त०. इतर... सनाथेन (शयनेन) bed that had on the other side a golden figure holding an ivory box, like Lakshmī herself having in her hand a lotus with a long stalk. The white ivory box resembled the white lotus and the golden figure was like लक्ष्मी. सोपधानेन with a pillow. स्वास्तीर्ण well covered with coverlets. कृता कुमुदैः कुमुदानां वा शोभा यस्य येन वा (1) that was decked with white lilies; (2) that gave beauty to the कुमुदs (with शशिना). The moon is the friend of love. See कुमारसम्भव IV. 13. राजतेन made of silver (and hence compared to the moon). निद्राकलशेन—auspicious jars were placed near the bed to ward off evil and to induce sleep. Compare कादम्बरी 'क्रमेण चोद्गते गगनमहापयोधिपुलिने सप्तलोकमङ्गलनिद्राकलशे कुमुदबान्धवे' (p. 178 of P.)

P. 73 ll. 3–9 तत्र च...गमदिति. प्रथमा...गवाक्षकेषु as if they were the faces of the family goddesses, (seen) in the jewelled lattice-windows, that had come out of curiosity to overhear the first words (of the bride and bridegroom). क्षणदाम् = निशाम्. अपुनरुक्तानि that were not monotonous. दत्त्वा...रणरणकम्—A door-keeper is always in attendance in a राजकुल; when ग्रहवर्मा went away, he left behind regret (in the heart of the members of the palace) at his departure. यौतक...लोकस्य taking with him the hearts of all people as the provisions for his journey offered to him as marriage gift. For यौतक, see above p. 52. शम्बलः—लम् पथिव्ययः (पाथेयम्). इति—shows the end of the उच्छ्वास.

Uchchhvāsa V

P. 74 Verse 1 नियतिः fate. Construe तरला नियतिः (विधिः) प्रथमं पुंसां सुखं विधाय उपरि (afterwards) दारुणं दुःखं निपातयति तरला (चञ्चला) तडित् (विद्युत्) इव आलोकं (light, flash) कृत्वा वज्रं निपातयति. This and the following verse are in the Āryā metre, for which see above p. 49. Both verses are suggestive of the misfortunes narrated in this Uchchhvāsa. Compare for the idea 'सुहृदिव प्रकटय्य सुखप्रदः प्रथममेकरसामनुकूलताम् । पुनरकाण्डविवर्तनदारुणो विधिरहो विशिनष्टि मनोरुजम् ॥' उत्तरराम० IV. 15.

Verse 2 सममेव—at one and the same time. अनादरेणैव without any qualm or regard. परिवर्तमानः revolving. अनन्तः—Time is without end. शैलान् परिवर्तमानः अनन्त इव (पातयति) as the serpent Ananta, moving (his hoods), makes the mountains fall. 'नागाः काद्रवेयास्तदीश्वरः । शेषोऽनन्तः' इत्यमरः. शेष has one thousand hoods, on which the earth is supposed to rest. It was believed that earthquakes occurred when शेष moved its hoods through weariness. See विष्णु० II. 5. 28 'यदा विजृम्भतेऽनन्तो मदाघूर्णितलोचनः । तदा चलति भूरेषा साद्रितोया सकानना ॥'.

P. 74 ll. 5–26 **अथ...तस्थौ.** राजा = प्रभाकरवर्धनः. कवचहरम्—of an age when he was fit to wear armour. कवचं हरतीति (affix अच्), acccording to 'वयसि च' पा. 3. 2. 10 (कवचहरः कुमारः । सि. कौ.). हूणान्—see p. 4 (notes). हरिः = सिंहः. प्रभाकर० is compared to the lion, राज्यवर्धन to a whelp and the Hūṇas to deer. चिरं...सारम् making him attended by advisers of long standing and devoted feudatories. अभिसारः companion, follower. अभिसारेण सह सा०. उत्तरापथम्—to the north. This word is used in contradistinction to दक्षिणापथ. Here उत्तरापथ seems to stand for the Punjab and Kashmir, countries towards the north of Thanesar. But generally the word stands for northern India. *Vide* Introduction for the inscriptions of Pulikes'in, where हर्ष himself is styled the lord of उत्तरापथ. कतिचित्प्रयाणकानि for some marches *i. e.* stages. प्रविष्टे...भ्रातरि when his brother entered the region (ककुभ् *f.*) resplendent with the brilliance of कैलास. कैलास is one of the peaks of the Himālayas. निवर्तमानः (the reading of B) does not suit the words नवे वयसि that follow. विक्रम...रोधिनि (youth) that follows (acts according to) its liking for adventure. शरभ is a fabulous animal with eight legs and believed to be stronger than the lion. तुषारशैलस्य हिमाचलस्य उपकण्ठेषु

(confines, outskirts). उत्कण्ठमानाः वनदेवताः तासां कटाक्षाः तेषां अंशवः (किरणाः, प्रभा) तैः शारिता (variegated) शरीरकान्तिः यस्य. The nymphs of the forests were smitten by the handsome form of Harsha and cast glances at him. The dark pupils and the white of their eyes shed a dappled hue on his body. The word उत्कण्ठमान may also convey the idea that the वनदेवताs were anxious for the safety of the beasts of the forest. बहिरेव व्यलम्बत he tarried outside (the region of कैलास). C and T translate as 'away from camp'. आकर्णान्तं आकृष्टं कार्मुकं तस्मात् निर्गताः भासुराः (bright) भल्लाः तान् वर्षतीति ०वर्षी. कर्मणे प्रभवतीति कार्मुकम् according to 'कर्मण उकञ्' पा० 5. 1. 103. भल्लः a crescent-shaped arrow. वास... यामे in the fourth watch of the night. वासतेयी—'पथ्यतिथिवसतिस्वपतेर्ढञ्' पा. 4. 4. 104 (पथि साधु पाथेयम् । आतिथेयम् । वसनं वसतिस्तत्र साधुः वासतेयी रात्रिः । सि. कौ.). It is believed that dreams seen in the small hours of the morning come to be true. चटुलानां (flickering) ज्वालानां पुञ्जेन पिञ्जरीकृताः (reddened) सकलककुभः येन (*adj.* of ०हुतभुजा). दवहुतभुजा = दवदहनेन forest conflagration. The death of the lion and his mate suggest the death of Harsha's father and mother. यदाकृष्टाः—यत् refers to स्नेहमयाः ०पाशाः. तिर्यञ्चः अपि even lower animals. Compare for the idea 'दारुभेदनिपुणोऽपि षडङ्घ्रिर्निष्क्रियो भवति पङ्कजबद्धः । बन्धनानि किल सन्ति बहूनि स्नेहरज्जुकृतबन्धनमन्यत् ॥'. दक्षिणात् इतरत्. The throbbing of the left eye in the case of men portends misfortune. विपप्रथे spread over. निर्निमित्तम् without any cause. अन्त...हृदयम् his heart as if went adrift (*lit.* moved) from its internal fastenings. गरीयसी very great (*f.* comparative of गुरु). दुःखासिका poignant despondency (दुःखं असिका इव). समुत्पन्नाः विविधाः विकल्पाः (doubts) तैः विमथिता मतिः यस्य. अपगता धृतिः (steadiness, composure) यस्य. स्तिमिता fixed, motionless) तारका यस्य. समुद्भिद्यमानं (shooting up) कमलिनीवनं (lotus-bed) यस्याम् (*adj.* of क्षौणीम्). He bent his lotus-like face in anxiety and looked fixedly on the ground. The poet fancies that his face was a lotus shooting forth from the earth (क्षौणी). चकोरेक्षणः—The eyes of a चकोर are red. Note कादम्बरी 'जरच्चकोरलोचनपुटपाटलकान्तिना' (p. 140 of P). Redness of the (corner of the) eye in men and women is a sign of beauty. आ...ह्नो when the sun had ascended to midday. हरिताः (greenish yellow) हयाः यस्य. The sun is called हरिदश्व. संवाह्यमानं तनु (small) तालवृन्तं (fan) यस्य. वितताम् spread. अतिशिशिरः मलयजस्य (चन्दनस्य) रसः तस्य लवेन लुलितं (touched) वपुः (frame) यस्याः (*adj.* of पट्टिकाम्). इन्दुवत् धवलं उपधानं (pillow) धारयतीति. वेत्रपट्टिका cane couch.

turned towards the object that is circumambulated'. उपस्थितं that had approached. राजसिंहस्य—the poet says that the passing of the deer to the left of हर्ष (who was a lion among kings) was a precursor of misfortune. If deer pass the lion without circumambulating him (*i. e.* without showing respect to him), that indicates that the lion's fall is near. In the कादम्बरी we read that the passing of the deer to the right of women is an ill omen 'प्रस्थितामिवानभीष्टदक्षिणवातमृगागमनाम्' (p. 218 of P). In the case of men it must be the left and so we have 'प्रदक्षिणेतरम्' (adverb). Similarly in the गाथासप्तशती we read 'एक्को वि कालसारो ण देइ गन्तुं पहाइणवलन्तो' I. 25. अशिशिररश्मिः सूर्यः. हृदयम्—supply हर्षस्य. The cry of the crow is an evil omen. See बृहत्संहिता 95.19 'ऐन्द्यादिदिगवलोकी सूर्याभिमुखो रुवन् गृहे गृहिणः। राजभयचोरबन्धनकलहाः स्युः पशुभयं चेति॥' and also 'एकचरणोर्कमीक्षन् विरुवंश्च पुरो रुधिरहेतुः' 30. For female jackals howling towards the sun, see रघु. II. 61. बहुदिवसम् (*acc.* of time) is to be connected with उपचित in the following समास. शिखिपिच्छा (tail of the peacock) लाञ्छनं (characteristic mark) यस्य. The Jain ascetics carry peacock feathers to sweep insects out of their path. नग्नाटकः a naked Jain ascetic (दिगम्बर). क्षीरस्वामी says 'भिक्षुः श्वेतः श्वेतपटः क्षपणर्षिर्दिगम्बरः। नग्नाटः श्रावकोऽह्रीको निर्ग्रन्थो जीवजीवकौ॥'. In the मुद्राराक्षस Act IV the sight of a क्षपणक is said by अमात्यराक्षस to be an evil omen. 'लुञ्चिताः पिच्छिकाहस्ताः पाणिपात्रा दिगम्बराः' सर्वदर्शनसंग्रह (आर्हतदर्शन). पितृस्नेहेन आहितः म्रदिमा यस्मिन् (*adj.* of हृदयेन). For म्रदिमा (from मृदु) see notes above p. 68. on कालिमन्. तत्तदुपेक्षमाणः thinking about this and that. The reading उत्प्रेक्षमाणः of some MSS of B is much better. तुरङ्गमस्कन्धे बद्धं लक्ष्यं यस्य (*adj.* of चक्षुः). दुःसमवसिते हसितं सङ्कथा च येन who painfully brought to an end all laughter and talk. बहु...ध्वानम् a journey that was made up of many योजनs. What particular distance was covered by a योजन is a point on which there has been much divergence of opinion. Various scholars have taken it to be from 4½ miles to ten miles. उपलब्धा नरेन्द्रमान्द्यस्य वार्ता तेन विषण्णे (dejected). One who is dejected loses all spirit (तेजः) and bends down his face. In the evening the sun also lost its lustre (तेजः) and hung down on the western horizon. This is fancied to be due to sorrow at the news of the king's illness. पुरः प्रवृत्ताः प्रतीहाराः तैः गृह्यमाणा ग्रामीणपरम्परा तया प्रकटितं प्रगुणं वर्त्म यस्य to whom the best way (to reach the capital) was shown by troops of villagers that were secured by waiters who marched ahead. वहन्ने निशाम् he passed the night riding.

P. 75 l. 33—**P 76** l. 20 **अन्य...इति.** The principal sentence is अन्यासन्नहानं मध्यन्दिने...स्कन्धावारं समाससाद. विगताः जयशब्दाः यस्मात्—bards were in the habit of uttering the words 'जय जीव' &c. in the presence of the king. See text p. 4. l. 12. But as the king was on his death-bed all this was stopped. This and the following words in the accusative qualify स्कन्धावारम् (capital). अस्त...नादम् not a drum was heard. अप्रसारितानि आपणे पण्यानि यस्मिन् in which merchandise was not exhibited (for sale) in the market. पवन...लिख्यमानम् that (capital) was rubbed by the waving streaks of the smoke of कोटिहोम, that (streaks) were twisted into curls by the force of the wind and which were as if the tips of the horns of Yama's buffalo. The curly smoke of the *Homa* performed for the welfare of the king is fancied to be the twisted horn of the buffalo of यम. यम rides a buffalo. As the king was on his death-bed, Yama comes in here very appropriately. कोटिहोम was a kind of offering into fire. वराहमिहिर prescribes it against दिव्योत्पातs. 'दिव्यमपि शममुपैति प्रभूतकनकान्नगोमहीदानैः । रुद्रायतने भूमौ गोदोहात् कोटिहोमाच्च ॥' बृह॰ 46. 6. कृतान्त...वेष्ट्यमानम्—As the city was lying under a cloud of smoke, the poet further fancies that it was encircled by the cords of Yama's net. उपरि...शुभम्—troops of crows roamed about and cawed. This portended approaching evil *i. e.* death here. The black crows resembled small bells of iron (कालायसं). It is usual to tie bells round the necks of buffalos and bulls. क्वचित्—क्वचित् and अन्यत्र—अपरत्र mean 'in one place—in another place.' प्रतिशायिताः स्निग्धबान्धवाः तैः आराध्यमानः अहिर्बुध्नः (शिवः) यस्मिन्. अहिब्रध्न also means the same. प्रतिशायित is one who lies down before a deity without food in order to secure some desired object. See कादम्बरी 'कृष्णाजिनप्रावृताङ्गैः कुरङ्गैरपि **प्रतिशयितै**रिव ... आराध्यमानाम्' (p. 226 of P). दीपिकाभिः दह्यमानाः कुलपुत्रकाः तैः प्रसाद्यमानं मातृमण्डलं यस्मिन्. For the divine Mothers, see above p. 26. The idea seems to be this:—the young nobles did not burn their limbs with lamps; they rather kept lamps on their heads to propitiate the Mothers and now and then had their skin burnt by accident. Even now worshippers of अम्बिका are in the habit of placing lamps on their heads and reverently going round the idol. Compare कादम्बरी 'ज्वलितलोहितमूर्धरत्नरश्मिभिः कृष्णसर्पैरपि शिरोधृतमणिदीपकैरिवाराध्यमानाम्' (p. 226 of P). मुण्डोण्हाराहरणे उद्यतः द्रविडः तेन प्रार्थ्यमानः आमर्दकः यस्मिन्—where a man from the द्रविड country was soliciting the Vampire by being ready to bring an offering of a skull. द्रविड included the tract of the country from the Tungabhadrā to the Coromandel coast and had काञ्ची as its capital. On आमर्दक the Com. says 'आमर्दको वेतालो रौद्रदेवताभेद इत्यन्ये'. बाण refers to the offerings of skulls to चण्डिका, who was worshipped by an old द्रविडधार्मिक 'फलितामिव मुण्डमण्डलैरुपहारहिंसां दर्शयन्तीम्' (p. 224 of P). आन्ध्रेण उद्ध्रियमाणः बाहुवप्रः तेन उपयाच्यमाना चण्डिका (दुर्गा यत्र) where Chaṇḍikā was being promised a present with his rampart-like arm raised up by a person from the Andhra country. बाहुः वप्रः इव. अन्ध्र corresponds pretty closely with modern Telingana and lay between the mouths of the गोदावरी and the कृष्णा. उपयाचनं is the same as नवस (in Marathi). शिरसि विधृतः विलीयमानः (melting) गुग्गुलुः (a kind of fragrant gum resin, गुग्गुळ in Marathi) तेन विकलाः नवसेवकाः तैः अनुनीयमानः महाकालः यस्मिन्. महाकाल is a name of शिव in his character as destroyer of the world. There is an emphasis on the words विकल and नव. Old servants would have gone through anything for the king without showing the least sign of pain; but new servants felt distressed even when hot gum slightly scorched their heads. निशिता शस्त्री (knife) तया निकृत्तं (cut off) आत्ममांसं तस्य होमे प्रसक्तः (engaged in) आप्तवर्गः यस्मिन्. प्रकाशं (openly) नरपतिकुमारकैः क्रियमाणः महामांसविक्रयस्य प्रक्रमः (beginning) यत्र. महामांसं human flesh. The शाक्त rites prescribed the offering of such horrible things. 'अष्टम्यां रुधिरैर्मांसैर्महामांसैः सुगन्धिभिः। पूजयेद्बहुजातीयैर्बलिभिर्भोजनैः शिवाम् ॥' शब्द०. It was believed that by resorting to such disgusting rites a person would attain miraculous powers or objects otherwise difficult to secure. महामांस was offered to पिशाचs also who, it was believed, would become the helpers of the man offering it in anything. See मालतीमाधव V. 12 and the comment of जगद्धर thereon. यातु... ध्वस्तम् as if rendered desolate by fiends. 'यातूनि यातनाः धीयन्ते अस्मिन्' क्षीरस्वामी on 'यातुधानः पुण्यजनो नैर्ऋतो यातुरक्षसी' इत्यमरः. कवलित devoured. अधर्म...लुण्ठितम् as if plundered by the movements of unrighteousness. अनित्यतया धिक्कारः. अनि...क्रान्तम् overpowered by the slights (heaped on it) by transitoriness. Everybody felt the transitoriness of human existence. नि...कृतम् that was subdued by the workings of fate. विलक्षितम् bewildered. छलितम् cheated. प्रविश...ददर्श—the principal sentence is प्रविशन् एव विपणिवर्त्मनि (on the market-street) परलोकव्यतिकरं कथयन्तं ०पट्टिकं ददर्श. कुतूहलेन आकुलाः बहलाः बालकाः तैः परिवृतम् (*adj.* of ०पट्टिकं). ऊर्ध्व... तते stretched out on a support (विष्कम्भः) of upright rods.

प्रेतनाथः = यमः. व्यतिकरम् incidents. इतर...कलितेन held in the other hand. In the left hand was the painted canvas and in the right a reed. शरकाण्डः reed-stalk. यमपट्टिकं—see above p. 45 (notes).

P. 76 l. 21—**P. 77** l. 10 **तेन...कक्ष्यान्तरम्.** तेन = श्लोकेन. प्रतिषिद्धः सकललोकप्रवेशः यस्मिन्. अप्रसन्नः मुखरागः यस्य who had a dejected look (*lit.* the colour of whose face was not clear). उन्मु... द्रियैः who was as if left by his senses. अपि...न वा does father feel better to-day or not? यदि भवेत् there may be. मन्दं...विवेश—the principal sentence is मन्दं मन्दं...राजकुलं विवेश. °सर्वस्वम्—this and the following clauses qualify राजकुलम्. प्रारब्धा अमृतचरुपचनक्रिया यत्र. चरुः is an oblation of rice or barley boiled for presentation to the gods. अमृतचरु perhaps means that milk or ghee was poured over it. क्रियमाणः षडाहुतिहोमः यस्मिन्. The Com. explains "'प्रजापतये स्वाहा' इति षण्णां देवतानां नाम गृहीत्वा षण्णामेवाहुतीनां प्रक्षेपः षडाहुतिहोम उच्यते." The six देवताs appear to be प्रजापति, सोम, अग्नि, इन्द्र, द्यावापृथिवी and धन्वन्तरि. हूयमानाः पृषदाज्यलवेन लिप्ताः प्रचलाः दूर्वापल्लवाः यस्मिन्. पृषदाज्यम्—Ghee mixed with coagulated milk. 'पृषदाज्यं सदध्याज्ये' इत्यमरः (पृषद्भिः दधिबिन्दुभिः सहितमाज्यम्' क्षीरस्वामी). पठ्य... विधानम्—this is a curious compound. It contains three separate elements. पठ्यमाना महामायूरी यस्मिन्, प्रवर्त्यमाना (begun) गृहशान्तिः यस्मिन्, निर्वर्त्यमानं भूतरक्षाबलिविधानं यस्मिन् (where the offering of oblations for protection against evil spirits was being performed). What the author refers to as महामायूरी is not quite clear. From the context it seems to be a prayer. Among the Buddhists महामायूरी is the name of one of the five amulets and of one of the five tutelary goddesses. शान्ति means 'a propitiatory rite for averting calamity.' प्रयतैः पवित्रैः विप्रैः प्रस्तुतः (begun) संहिताजपः यस्मिन्—holy Brahmins had begun the recitation in a low voice of the Saṃhitā text of the Vedas. This is the practice even now. 'पवित्रः प्रयतः पूतः' इत्यमरः. जप्यमाना रुद्रैकादशी तया शब्दायमानं शिवगृहं यत्र where the temple of S'iva resounded with the low repetition of the hymn to Rudra. The reference seems to be to what is popularly known as रुद्र, which is a prayer in 11 अनुवाकs addressed to रुद्र. Great merit is supposed to result from repeating that prayer 11 times or 121 times. सायण in his comment on the रुद्रभाष्य quotes the वायुपुराण 'रोगवान्पापवांश्चैव रुद्रं जप्त्वा जितेन्द्रियः । रोगात्पापाद्विनिर्मुक्तो ह्यतुलं सुखमश्नुते ॥'. अतिशुचिशैवैः सम्पाद्यमानं विरूपाक्षस्य (शिवस्य) क्षीरकलशसहस्रैः स्नपनं यस्मिन् where the image of S'iva was being bathed with thousands of milk jars by very holy devotees of शिव. क्षीराभिषेक is even now resorted to to propitiate Rudra. शिव is called विरूपाक्ष because of his third eye. अजिरो०—connect this and the following instrumentals with नरपतिभिः below. अजिरं courtyard. अनासादितं (not obtained) स्वामिनः (प्रभाकरवर्धनस्य) दर्शनं तेन दूयमानानि मानसानि येषाम्. अभ्यन्तरात् निष्पतिताः (coming out) निकटवर्तिनः परिजनाः तैः निवेद्यमाना वार्ता (news of the king's condition) येभ्यः. वार्ता...शयनैः to whom bathing, eating and sleeping had become mere news *i. e.* 'who knew these only in name, who did not bathe, eat or sleep as the king was seriously ill. उज्झितः आत्मसंस्कारः तेन मलिनः वेशः येषाम् whose clothes were dirty because they had abandoned the toilet of their bodies. लिखितै...श्चलैः who were motionless as if drawn in pictures. नीयमाननक्तन्दिवम् where night and day were passed. दुःखेन दीनानि वदनानि यस्य—connect this word with बाह्यपरिजनेन (p. 22. l. 6). प्रघ...मण्डलेन who were sitting in a circle in the porches before the palace-gate. The servants, not being intimately connected with the royal household, were sitting outside. 'प्रघाणप्रघणालिन्दा बहिर्द्वारप्रकोष्ठके' इत्यमरः. 'अगारैकदेशे प्रघणः प्रघाणश्च' पा. 3. 3. 79. उपांशुव्याहृतैः in whispered conversations. The servants that were outside assigned various causes for the sad plight of the king. There is a touch of humour in this description. केन...वयता some one (among the servants sitting outside) laid bare the errors on the part of doctors. असाध्य... पठता one recited passages containing the symptoms of incurable diseases. Diseases are generally classified into three classes, साध्य, दुःसाध्य and असाध्य. केन ... वृण्वता one expounded the story of a demon (as being at the root of the king's ailment). कार्तान्तिकादेशान् the prognostications of astrologers. कृतान्तं (दैवं) वेद इति कार्तान्तिकः (कृतान्त + ठक्). उपलिङ्गानि portents. अनित्य... लभमानेन one was revolving in his mind the transitoriness of life, was condemning this (everchanging) world, censured the wantonness of the Kali age and found fault with fate. धर्माय कुप्यता—he was angry with धर्म, because the latter could not do anything for such a righteous king as प्रभाकर०. क्लिष्ट...गर्हयता one censured the ill-luck of the noble youths that were afflicted. कथ्यमाना कष्टा पार्थिवावस्था यस्मिन्. विविधौषधिद्रव्याणां द्रवः (juice, exudation) तस्य गन्धः गर्भे यस्य (adj. of कक्ष्यान्तरम्). उत्क्वथतां...जिघ्रन् smelling the odour of boiling decoctions, of butter and oils that were being heated. कक्ष्या inner court. The रामायण (अयोध्या 20. 11-12) shows that the third कक्ष्या was set apart for the queen and her confidential attendants.

P 77 l.11—**P. 78** l. 35 **तत्र…द्राक्षीत्.** The principal sentence is तत्र च…धवलगृहे स्थितं (p. 23 l. 1)…देव्या यशोमत्या शिरसि वक्षसि च स्पृश्यमानं पितरमद्राक्षीत्. अतिनिःशब्दे—this and the following clauses in the locative qualify धवलगृहे (p. 23 l. 1). गृहावग्रहणीग्राहिणः बहुवेत्रिणः यत्र where many door-keepers stood in the vestibule. 'गृहावग्रहणी देहली' इत्यमरः. गृहावग्रहणी the threshold. त्रिगुणया तिरस्करिण्या तिरोहितः सुवीथीपथः यस्मिन्—where the way to the inner part of the house was shut off (from view) by a triple screen. वीथी is गृहप्रान्त according to क्षीरस्वामी. पिहितानि पक्षद्वारकाणि यस्मिन् where the private entrances were shut. 'प्रच्छन्नमन्तर्द्वारं स्यात्पक्षद्वारं तु पक्षकः' इत्यमरः. पिहित *past p. p.* of धा with अपि with the initial अ dropped, according to 'वष्टि भागुरिरल्लोपमवाप्योरुपसर्गयोः।'. परिहृतं कपाटरटितं यस्मिन् where the creaking of the panels was avoided. घटितैः (united, closed) गवाक्षैः रक्षितः (prevented) मरुत् (gust of wind) यस्मिन्. चरणताडनेन स्वनत् (rattling, creaking) सोपानं (staircase) तेन प्रकुपिताः प्रतीहाराः यस्मिन्. When some one ascended the staircase in a noisy way, the doorkeepers got angry with him for fear that his action might disturb the ailing king. निभृताभिः (noiseless) संज्ञाभिः (signs) निर्दिश्यमानानि (indicated, ordered) सकलकर्माणि यस्मिन्. कञ्चुकिन् a person wearing armour. कङ्कटः or कङ्कटकः breast-plate 'उरश्छदः कङ्कटको जगरः कवचोऽस्त्रियाम्' इत्यमरः. कोणस्थितः आह्वानैः चकितः आचमनवाही यस्मिन् in a corner of which stood a servant bearing the bowl for rinsing the mouth, who was bewildered by numerous calls. चन्द्रशालिकायां लीनः मूकः मौललोकः यस्मिन्. For चन्द्र० see p. 21 above. मौलः an old or hereditary minister. मूलं प्रतिष्ठा तदस्ति अस्य इति मौलः. महान् आधिः (distraction of mind) तेन विधुरः (helpless) बान्धवाङ्गनावर्गः तेन गृहीतं प्रच्छन्नप्रग्रीवकं यस्मिन्. प्रग्रीवं or-कं a painted turret, window. सञ्जवनम् quadrangle, court formed by four houses on four sides 'सभा सञ्जवनं त्विदम्। चतुःशालम्' इत्यमरः. प्र … णयिनि to which only a few friends (or favourites had been admitted). दुर्मनायमान *pr. p.* of दुर्मनायते, denominative verb from दुर्मनस्. मन्दायमानः (languishing) पुरोधाः (पुरोहितः) यस्मिन्. सीदन्तः (sinking into despair) सुहृदः यत्र. विद्राणाः (kept awake, without sleep) विपश्चितः (पण्डिताः) यत्र. सन्तप्ताः आप्ताः (trusted) सामन्ताः यस्मिन्. विचित्ताः (vacant-minded) चामरग्राहिणः यस्मिन्. दुःखेन क्षामाः (emaciated) शिरोरक्षिणः (body-guard) यस्मिन्. क्षीयमाणा प्रसादवित्तानां मनोरथसम्पद् यस्मिन् where the fulfilment (सम्पद्) of the desires of those that were (the king's) favourites was vanishing. प्रसादैः वित्तः ख्यातः. स्वामिभक्त्या परित्यक्तः आहारः यैः ते स्वामि…हाराः हीयमानबलाः विकलाः (faint) वल्लभभूभृतः यस्मिन्. क्षितितले पतिताः सकलरजन्यां जागरूकाः

राजपुत्रकुमारकाः यस्मिन् where the young Rajputs, that had watched during the whole night, were lying on the ground. कुलक्रमागतैः कुलपुत्रकैः उह्यमाना शुक् (शोकः) यस्मिन्. Separate ०शुचि and शोक०. निरानन्दाः (joyless) बन्दिनः (court bards) यस्मिन्. 'स्युर्मागधास्तु मगधा बन्दिनः स्तुतिपाठकाः' इत्यमरः. निःश्वसन्तः निराशाः आसन्नसेवकाः यस्मिन्. निःसृतं ताम्बूलं यस्मात् स निःसृतताम्बूलः अत एव धूसरः अधरः यासां ताः निःसृत... धराः, ०धराः वारयोषितः (dancing girls) यस्मिन्. विलक्षैः (bewildered) वैद्यैः उपदिश्यमानं पथ्यं (wholesome diet) तस्य आहरणे (fetching) अवहितः (attentive) पौरोगवः यस्मिन्. पौरोगवः superintendent of the royal kitchen. 'रसवत्यां तु पाकस्थानमहानसे । पौरोगवस्तदध्यक्षः' इत्यमरः (on which क्षीरस्वामी says 'पुरो गौर्मांसं वा जलं वास्याः सा पुरोगुस्तस्याः रसवत्याः अयं पौरोगवः). अनुजीविभिः पीयमानं उच्चषकं (उत्कृष्टः चषकः यस्मिन्) धारावारि तेन विनोधमाना आस्यशोषरुक् यस्मिन् where the pain due to dryness of mouth was removed by streaming water drunk by attendants without cups. The attendants were working hard and felt thirsty. It is common experience that thirst is allayed much more quickly if one pours a stream of water into the mouth than if one holds the cup to the lips. C and T translate 'attendants were drinking streams of water from uplifted cups in order to distract the pain of the king's dry mouth'. We cannot understand how the king's dry mouth would have been relieved if the servants drank water. So also the words of the Com. 'उच्चषकमपगतपानभाजनम्' do not mean 'empty cups'; but rather 'without a cup'. We think that the context requires that it was the king that was thirsty and *not* the servants. So we suggest that we should read पाय्यमान for पीयमान and then the meaning would be 'where the pain of the dry mouth (of the king) was removed by streams of water without cups which he was made to drink by the attendants'. The reading of B and C 'उच्चचषक' is not bad. It means that the water was poured from a cup held high up and not from a cup applied to the lips. राजाभिलाषेण (at the king's desire) भोज्यमानाः बहुभुजः (gluttons) यत्र. Or the meaning may be 'gluttons were fed with the food which the king desired but which he could not himself eat'. भेषजसामग्रीसम्पादने व्यग्राः समग्राः व्यवहारिणः (merchants) यस्मिन्. मुहुर्मुहुः आहूयमानः तोयकर्मान्तिकः (waterman) तेन अनुमिता घोरा आतुरस्य (रोगार्तस्य) तृट् यस्मिन्. कर्मान्तिकः a servant. तुषारेण परिकरितः करकः तस्मिन् शिशिरीक्रियमाणं उदश्वित् यस्मिन् where buttermilk was being cooled (frozen) in jars that were covered in ice. उदश्वित् *n* (उदकेन श्वयति) buttermilk that contains 50 per cent water. 'तक्रं ह्युदश्विन्मथितं पादाम्ब्वर्धाम्बु निर्जलम्' इत्यमरः on which क्षीरस्वामी says 'द्विगुणाम्बु श्वेतरसमर्धोदकमुदश्वितम्। तक्रं त्रिभागभिन्नाम्बु केवलं मथितं स्मृतमिति धन्वन्तरिः'. The frozen buttermilk was probably applied to the burning feet and head of the feverish king. श्वेतार्द्रे कर्पटे (piece of cloth) अर्पिताः कर्पूरस्य परागाः (रेणवः) तेन शीतलीकृता शलाका (a collyrium stick) यस्मिन्. The stick treated with camphor powder was to be applied to the eye to produce a cooling effect. नाश्यानेन (न + आश्यानेन) पङ्केन लिप्यमानं नवं भाण्डं (vessel) तद्गतं गण्डूषग्रहणाय मस्तु (sour cream, whey) यस्मिन्. We expect अनाश्यान; probably अ was elided in the MSS after ॰शलाके. आश्यान means 'dried' and so नाश्यान would mean 'wet'. The cool whey was probably required for relieving the dryness of the mouth of the patient who used it as a gargle from time to time. 'मण्डं दधिभवं मस्तु' इत्यमरः. तिम्यन्ति (wet) कोमलानि कमलिनीपलाशानि (lotus-leaves) तैः प्रावृताः मृदुमृणालकाः यत्र. सनालानि नीलोत्पलानि तेषां पूली (bundle) तया सनाथा (possessed of) सलिलपानभाजनभूः यत्र. The lotus leaves, fibres and flowers were all intended to produce a cooling effect. धारानिपातैः निर्वाप्यमाणं क्वथिताम्भः यस्मिन्—boiling-water was being cooled by being poured in streams (from vessel to vessel). Water first boiled and then cooled is given to a patient for drinking. पटु (sharp) पाटलशर्करायाः आमोदः तं मुञ्चतीति ॰मुच् तस्मिन् that emitted the sharp odour of pale-red sugar. मञ्चकाश्रिता (resting on a stand) सिकतिला (sandy) कर्करी (jar) तस्मिन् विश्रान्तं आन्तरचक्षुः यस्मिन्. It is difficult to explain what आन्तरचक्षुः means. We must read with the two MSS of B 'आतुरचक्षुः'. The eye of the ailing king rested upon a porous jar. The sight of water trickling from the porous jar had a soothing effect. For सिकतिल, see notes on सैकत p. 30. सरसेन शैवलेन वलयितं (अत एव) गलत् गोलयन्त्रकं यस्मिन् where there were globes dripping because they were surrounded by wet water-plants (moss). गल्वर्कशालाजिरे उल्लासिताः लाजसक्तवः यस्मिन्—where there were parched grain and barley-flour spread in a crystal platter. Separate ॰सक्तुनि and पीत॰. क्षीरस्वामी says 'गल्वर्कोऽपि स्फाटिके पात्रेऽयं रूढः'. For शालाजिर, see above p. 54. The fried grain was used as light food for patients. पीता (yellow) मसारपारी (emerald cup) तस्यां परिगृहीता कर्कशर्करा (white sugar) यत्र. It is better to omit पीत with some of the MSS of B. C and T translate 'a paste of flour and curds was held in a yellow emerald cup.' शिशिरैः औषधरसैः चूर्णैः च अवकीर्णः स्फटिकशुक्तिशङ्खसञ्चयः यस्मिन्. Crystal, mother-o'pearl and conches are all cool to the touch. प्राचीनामलक myrobalans.

सुश्रुत (सूत्रस्थान chap 46) gives a long list of the fruits usually eaten. प्राचीनामलक (also called वारिबदर) had the effect of removing the three दोषs (वात, पित्त, कफ) and poison 'गरदोषहरं नीपं प्राचीनामलकं तथा' सु० 46. 158. मातुलुङ्ग citron (Marathi महाळुंग). प्रतिग्राहितैः (that were made to accept presents) विप्रैः विप्रकीर्यमाणाः शान्त्युदकस्य विप्रुषः (बिन्दवः) यस्मिन्. विप्रुष् *f.* drop. शान्त्युदकम् soothing or propitiatory water. प्रेष्यासिः पेष्यमाणः (being pounded) कलाटलेपः तेन उपदिग्धा दृषद् (stone) यस्मिन्. पर...ज्वलनेन (father) round whom lustration was performed by the fire of fever for the conquest of the next world. राज् with निस् 'to perform the ceremony called नीराजन'. नीराजन was a military and religious ceremony performed by kings and generals in the month of आश्विन before they took the field; mantras were repeated and lights waved. Here fever is the fire and the king was about to proceed to the next world. Compare 'तस्मै सम्यग्घुतो वह्निर्वाजिनीराजनाविधौ । प्रदक्षिणार्चिर्व्याजेन हस्तेनेव जयं ददौ ॥' रघु. 4. 25. अनव...चेष्टमानम् who tossed on a bed waving (*i. e.* uneven) with his ceaseless rollings like the serpent S'esha (rolling) on the Milky Ocean on account of the fever of poison. तरङ्गिणि (1) that has waves (with उदन्वति); (2) that has wavy curls (on the bed). The bed had white coverlets and so resembled क्षीरसागर. The king was suffering from a fever (ऊष्मन्); शेष has poison in his hoods. The king was pale through serious illness and resembled the white-yellow शेष. मुक्ता...धवलितम् (1) who was made white with the dust of pearl-powder (with the king); (2) that was white with pearls and the grains of sand (with जलधि). Pearls are supposed to have a cooling effect. Pearls are found in the ocean and on its shores there is white sand. क्षयकाले शुष्यन्तम् (1) who had become withered at the time of death; (2) that dries up at the time of universal destruction (with जलधि). क्षय = प्रलय. 'संवर्तः प्रलयः कल्पः क्षयः कल्पान्त इत्यपि' इत्यमरः. A कल्प is a period of 1000 महायुगs (कृत, त्रेता, द्वापर and कलि constitute one महायुग). It is equal to a day of ब्रह्मा, the night also being of the same duration. At the end of a कल्प the whole universe (including the ocean) is destroyed. Compare भगवद्गीता 'सहस्रयुगपर्यन्तमहर्यद् ब्रह्मणो विदुः । रात्रिं युगसहस्रान्तां तेऽहोरात्रविदो जनाः ॥ अव्यक्ताद् व्यक्तयः सर्वाः प्रभवन्त्यहरागमे । रात्र्यागमे प्रलीयन्ते तत्रैवाव्यक्तसंज्ञके ॥' VIII. 17-18. For a description of कल्पान्त see विष्णुपुराण VI. 3 and 4. 'उदकावरणं यत्तज्ज्योतिषा पीयते तु तत् । ज्योतिर्वायौ लयं याति यात्याकाशे समीरणः ॥' विष्णु० VI. 4. 31. कालेन (1) by death

(with the king); (2) by the dark-coloured (दशानन). All Rākshasas are represented as dark. The king had the pallor of death and resembled the snowy कैलास. On one occasion रावण when travelling in the पुष्पकविमान near कैलास was stopped by नन्दी saying that शिव wanted to be in privacy there. Thereupon रावण in arrogance caught hold of कैलास and shook it. When पार्वती became afraid by the motion of the mountain, शिव in anger pressed the mountain with his toe and रावण's arms were crushed underneath and he began to scream. See रामायण VII. 16 for the story. 'पुष्पकस्य गतिश्छिन्ना यत्कृते मम गच्छतः । तमिमं शैलमुन्मूलं करोमि तव गोपते ॥ 23...एवमुक्त्वा ततो राम भुजान्विक्षिप्य पर्वते । तोलयामास तं शीघ्रं स शैलः समकम्पत ॥' 25. Compare कादम्बरी 'कैलासश्रियमिव दशमुखोन्मूलनक्षोभनिपतिताम्' (p. 129 of P). अविरत...स्पृश्यमानम्— the palms of the hands of the attendants were white with the sandal-paste with which they smeared his body. The poet fancies that the palms were white because they were reduced to ashes by touching the burning limbs of the king. Ashes are white. अत्युष्णावयवस्पर्शेन भस्मीभूतं उदरं येषां (*adj.* of करैः). Take away the comma after ०प्रस्थितम् and place it after स्पृश्यमानम्. लोका ... पृच्छ्यमानम् — The king was about to depart this world. When a person goes on a journey those that stay bid him farewell. The poet fancies that under the guise of the white sandal ointment, it was his spotless fame that embraced him and bade him a last farewell. Both sandal and fame are white. स्थासु (1) that remains on the body (with अनुलेपन); (2) remaining on the earth (यशः). There is a further suggestion. His fame would be everlasting (स्थासु) and not evanescent. अविच्छिन्नं (ceaselessly) दीयमानानि कमलकुमुदेन्दीवरदलानि यस्मै. Lotus petals have a cooling effect. कमलs are rosy, कुमुदs are white and इन्दीवर is blue. His body when covered with petals of various colours looked variegated. काल...शबलम्— Death was approaching him. The pupil of the eye is dark, the corner is red and the rest of the eye is white. There is a similar idea above. निबिडेन (tight) दुकूलपट्टेन निपीडिताः केशान्ताः तैः कथ्यमानः कष्टवेदनानां अनुबन्धः (continuity) यस्य. His head was bound tight with silk cloth because he was suffering from ceaseless headache. दुर्धरवेदनाभिः उन्नमत् (standing up) नीलशिराजालकं तेन करालं तेन (*adj.* of ०फलकेन). A net-work of dark veins due to unbearable pain stood up on his forehead. These the poet fancies to be the lines drawn by the fingers of Death representing the days that remained to him on the earth. In counting we draw lines on a board (फलकं) with our fingers. कालाङ्गुलिभिः लिख्यमानाः लेखाः ताभिः आख्यातं मरणावधिदिवससंख्यानं येन. अन्तःप्रविष्टा तारका यस्य the pupil of his eye had become contracted and dim owing to failing strength. The poet fancies that it was due to his agitation at the sight of approaching death. A person who is frightened by a terrible sight closes his eyes. शुष्यन्ती दशनपङ्क्तिः तस्याः प्रसृताः धूसराः (grey) दीधितयः तैः तरङ्गिणीम्. He heaved hot breaths that were mixed with ripples of grey rays from his dry teeth. Mirage (मृगतृष्णिका) is also उष्णा (due to heat) and presents waves (तरङ्गिणी). निवेद्यमानः दारुणसन्निपातस्य आरम्भः यस्मिन्. He had a dark tongue, which indicated that he was in the stage of सन्निपात. सन्निपात is the combined derangement of the three humours of the body (वात, पित्त and कफ) and is fatal. The योगरत्नाकर (आनन्दाश्रम ed p. 98) gives the general symptoms of सन्निपातज्वर, one variety of which called तन्द्रिक is described as 'प्रभूता तन्द्रार्तिर्ज्वरकफपिपासाकुलतरो भवेच्छ्यामा जिह्वा पृथुलकठिना कण्टकवृता ।'. The poet fancies that the tongue was dark because it was burnt up by his very hot breaths. उरः...कान्तं—मणि and the other things were placd on his chest to produce a cooling effect. When a person of position pays a visit, it is usual to appear in one's best dress and to put on jewels &c. Take away the comma after ०युगलम्. अङ्ग... युगलम् who tossed up his arms in putting his limbs into various contortions (through agony). When he tossed up his arms, rays flashed from his nails; the rays resemble streams of water. So the poet fancies that he constructed with the rays of his nails a showerbath for तापशान्ति. नेदिष्ठ—superlative of (अन्तिक) very near. His reflections fell in water, jewelled pavements, and mirrors, all of which are cool to the touch. The poet fancies that he entered inside them (as reflection) for their cooling effect. स्पृशन्तीं goes with मूर्च्छां and प्रणयिनीं. He welcomed a swoon when it came over (स्पृशन्ती) him, because it was a source of relief. मूर्च्छा is compared to प्रणयिनी (beloved wife), who touches her husband and is a source of comfort to him. The reading विश्राम० is much better than विश्वास०, as the latter cannot be well construed with मूर्च्छा. अरिष्टैराविष्टम् overwhelmed with very bad symptoms (of death). अरिष्ट also means 'crow'. The cawing of crows is an evil omen and may be looked upon as the summons of death. 'तक्रे मरणचिह्ने चारिष्टं वृक्षे च फेनिले । सुराणां च शुभेऽपि

स्यात्काके निम्बे च पुंस्ययम् ॥' quoted by क्षीरस्वामी. महाप्रस्थान—the great journey *i. e.* death. At his approaching death, anguish seized the hearts of relatives. The words प्रस्थान and सन्तान (1 continuity; 2 offspring) suggest another idea. When a man starts on a journey, he transfers (*i. e.* entrusts) to the care of his relatives his children. छायया मुच्यमानम् who was bereft of brilliance (of body). He was languid and had lost his bright complexion. The poet fancies that छाया had left him through jealousy, as he was wedded to अरति. अरतिः langour. उद्योग...द्रवाणाम् who was the effort of all (bad) symptoms, or supervenient diseases. The idea is that all bad symptoms had concentrated themselves on him. सर्वास्त्र...तयाः Emaciation had let fall all her missiles on him. हस्तीकृतं=वशीकृतम्. विहस्ततया by helplessness. विगतः हस्तः यस्य स विहस्तः तस्य भाव ०ता तया. विषयी...क्षयेण misery had made him its province, wasting had made him its field. गोचरीकृतम्=विषयीकृतम्. दुःखासिका—दुःखमासते अस्यामिति or दुःखमसिका इव—dejection. अस्वास्थ्यम् restlessness, anxiety. विधेयीकृतं made a servant *i. e.* brought under control. क्रोडः the chest; क्रोडीकृतम् embraced. लक्ष्यीकृतं made a target. दक्षिणाशया—the south is presided over by Yama. जग्ध devoured (*past p. p.* of अद् to eat). निगीर्ण swallowed (*past* P. P. of गृ with नि). वैवर्ण्यम् (विवर्णस्य भावः) loss of colour, paleness. गात्रभङ्गः *lit.* breaking of limbs *i. e.* stiffness of body. वण्ट् *1 P.* to divide. लुण्ठ्यमान being robbed. आदित्सितं (*past p. p.* of the desiderative base of दा with आ) desired to be seized. निरूपितं marked, observed carefully. अभाव death, destruction. परिकलितम् grasped all round. परासुता death. दत्तः अवकाशः येन who made room for. वैमनस्यम् (विमनसः भाव) mental depression. समीपे—connect this and the following locatives with वर्तमानम् below. अन्ति...च्छासस्य who was near the last breath. मुखे...प्रवासस्य at the beginning of the great journey *i. e.* dying. Compare महाप्रस्थान above. The reading महाप्रयासस्य is not so good. जीवितेशः=यमः. विरलं वाचि broken in words. चलितं चेतसि shaken in mind. प्रचुरं प्रलापे profuse in incoherent speech. अनु...बन्धिकाभिः constantly followed by pains in the joints. Com. 'अनुबन्धिका गात्रसन्धिपीडाः' According to the मेदिनी, अनुबन्धी means 'hiccough' 'अनुबन्धी तु हिक्कायां तृष्णायामपि योषिति.' This meaning is preferable. अनवरतरोदनेन उच्छूने (swollen) नयने यस्याः (*adj.* of यशोमत्या). गृहीता चामरिका यया. गृहीत...वीजयन्त्या who fanned the king with her sighs alone, though she held a chowrie in her hand.

P. 79 ll. 1–18 **दृष्ट्वा च...धेति.** प्रथम...मतिः whose mind was overwhelmed by the first shock of sorrow. आ...मवत् he became as if afraid of fate. भागधेयेभ्यः is ablative. निरा...सीत् for a moment he was as if given up by his mind *i. e.* he became dazed. अव...धैर्येण discarded by steadiness. रिक्ती...रत्या he was made empty by delight *i. e.* there was not the least trace of gayness left in him. विषमविष terrible poison. तमसा...विशेषयन् excelling even Pātāla in darkness. पाताल as the haunt of demons is supposed to be dark. शून्यत्वे...शयानः excelling even space in its vacancy. His mind became a void. For the शून्यत्व of आकाश, compare above (text p. 2 l. 1) 'आकाशमयः शून्यतायाम्'. नाविन्दत कर्तव्यम् he did not know what to do. पस्पर्श...गाम् his heart came in contact with terror and his head with the earth. The idea is that his heart became extremely apprehensive for his father's life and he bowed low before his father (as a son should do). सा अवस्था यस्य सः तदवस्थः who was in that (terrible) condition. निर्भरेण स्नेहेन आवर्जितः influenced by deep affection. प्रधावमानः मनसा—being enfeebled, his body could not run, though his mind ran towards his son. शरी...गात् he rose from the couch with the upper part of his body. विन...न्नमय्य having raised him who bent through dutifulness. विशन्निव...मध्यम् as if plunging into the midst of the moon's disc. At the sight of his darling son, the king felt as much relief as he would have if he had plunged &c. The following clauses also suggest the cooling or comforting effect which the sight of his son produced upon the king in his burning fever. स्नाप...प्रस्रवणे as if wetting himself in a stream of Harichandana juice. हरिचन्दनः is a kind of very fragrant and yellow sandal. 'तैलपर्णिकगोशीर्षे हरिचन्दनमस्त्रियाम्' इत्यमरः (on which क्षीरस्वामी says 'हरेरिन्द्रस्य चन्दनं, हरि कपिलं वा, तच्चातिशीतंल पीतमाहुः'). तुषाराद्रिः = हिमालयः. कपोलेन...घट्टयन् rubbing his cheek against the cheek (of हर्ष). निमील...लोचने closing his eyes that let fall incessant tears that formed on the tips of his eyelashes. पक्ष्माग्रे ग्रथितं अजस्रं अस्रं तत् विस्रवति इति ०स्राविन्. He closed his eyes and shed tears through joy. विस्मृतः ज्वरस्य सञ्ज्वरः सन्तापः येन. अप...स्कारम् who drew aside and then bowed low. प्रणता जननी येन. For क see above p. 31. विगतः निमेषः यस्मात् सः वि...मेषः, ०मेषश्चासौ निश्चलश्च. क्षयेण क्षामः कण्ठः यस्य whose throat was parched by exhaustion. कृच्छ्रात् with difficulty. तृतीय...स्याद्य to-day is the third day since he took food.

P. 79 l. 19—**P. 80** l. 4 **तच्छ्रुत्वा ... करवाणीति.** बाष्पवेगेन गृह्यमाणानि अक्षराणि यथा स्युः the words being choked by the flow of

रिणां विकृतिर्जीवितमुच्यते बुधैः' रघु॰ 8. 87. The five भूतs (पृथ्वी, अप्, तेजस्, वायु and आकाश) are the प्रकृति of all bodies. पौनर्वसवः a descendant of पुनर्वसु or one who studies the science of medicine promulgated by पुनर्वसु. According to the चरकसंहिता (सूत्रस्थान I) Indra taught आयुर्वेद to भरद्वाज who instructed several sages of whom पुनर्वसु was one. पुनर्वसु imparted it to his pupils, अग्निवेश and five others, each of whom composed a work on आयुर्वेद. चरक edited what अग्निवेश had composed. 'अथ मैत्रीपरः पुण्यमायुर्वेदं पुनर्वसुः। शिष्येभ्यो दत्तवान् षड्भ्यः सर्वभूतानुकम्पया ॥' verse 29. अष्टा...देशीयः—for देशीय see notes p. 38. अष्टाङ्गस्य—The science of medicine is said by सुश्रुत to have eight parts *viz.* (1) शल्य (surgery), (2) शालाक्य (diseases of the eye, ear and other parts of the head), (3) कायचिकित्सा, (4) भूतविद्या, (5) कौमारभृत्यं (rearing up of children), (6) अगदतन्त्रं (antidotes), (7) रसायनतन्त्रं, (8) वाजीकरणतन्त्रम्. See सुश्रुत सूत्रस्थान Chap. I. 6–7. आयुर्वेद is an उपवेद of the अथर्ववेद. 'आयुरस्मिन् विद्यते अनेन वा आयुर्विन्दतीत्यायुर्वेदः' सुश्रुत सूत्रस्थान I. 14. सुत...लालितः cherished on the same footing as a son. पटीयसी *f.* comparative of पटु. सास्रः (अस्रेण सह, बहुव्रीहि) shedding tears. कथय...पश्यसि tell me the truth, if you perceive any thing evil (about the king's illness). यथा...यितास्मि I shall inform you (of the facts) as they are. Mark the first future आवेदयितास्मि. The young man by his profound study of the science of medicine understood that the king would not live for more than day.

P. 80 ll. 20–34 अत्रैव...नैषीत्. भवन...पालः the keeper of the palace lotus beds. कोकमाश्वासयन् encouraging or comforting a ruddy goose. 'कोकश्चक्रश्चक्रवाको रथाङ्गाह्वयनामकः' इत्यमरः. It should he remembered that Harsha called together the doctors in the evening (text p. 25 l. 10). In the evening the चक्रवाक becomes separated from its mate. For अपरवक्त्र, see notes p. 17. C and T read 'अपरवक्त्रा.' आस्व...वर्त्मनि remain in the path of discernment. सह...विरोचनः the sun mounts (resorts to) the top of Meru together with the glory of the beds of lotuses. सरोजिनी may mean 'bed' or 'lake' (compare the use of पुष्करिणी). 'पुष्करादिभ्यो देशे' पा. 5. 2. 135 (पुष्करिणी। पद्मिनी। सि. कौ.). कमल fades (*i. e.* its glory departs) when the sun sets. 'मेरुः सुमेरुर्हेमाद्री रत्नसानुः सुरालयः' इत्यमरः. All the planets were supposed to revolve round the fabulous mountain Meru. See व्यासभाष्य on योगसूत्र III. 25 'सप्तद्वीपा वसुमती यस्याः सुमेरुर्मध्ये पर्वतराजः...तस्य सूर्यप्रचाराद्रात्रिन्दिवं लग्नमिव वर्तते'. See also रघु॰ VII. 24. The verse suggests that the king (who was resplendent,

विरोचन) was going to Meru (heaven) together with his fair wife (the mother of Harsha). वा...ज्ञः who was proficient in the prognostications of words. क्षता (destroyed) धृतिः (courage) यस्य. तत्र च...नैषीत्—the principal sentence is तत्र च...एवंप्रायान् पितुरालापान् अनवरतं (ceaselessly) आकर्णयन्...निशां अनैषीत्. हारान्—pearl necklaces are cool. Notice that in this and the following clauses there is a charming resemblance of sounds between the names of the ladies addressed and the words in which they are called upon to do something for the king. मणि...वैदेहि—Vaidehî! place jewelled mirrors on my body. घन...क्षि Dhavalākshî! place (on me) the dust of the powder (क्षोदः) of camphor (घनसारः). 'अथ कर्पूरमस्त्रियाम्। घनसारश्चन्द्रसंज्ञः सिताभ्रो हिमवालुका' इत्यमरः ('घनस्येव सारोऽस्य शैत्यात् सिताभ्रत्वाच्च' क्षीरस्वामी). चन्दनचर्चा smearing the body with sandal. पाटय...मारुतम् cleave asunder (*i. e.* cause movement) the wind with a cloth. He wants her to cause a breeze with a piece of cloth. The Com. remarks 'पाटय पटुं कुरु'. But this it not necessary. Remove the comma after इन्दुमति and place it after अरविन्दैः. जलार्द्रा a fan wetted with water. मल्लिनाथ on शिशुपालवध I. 65 paraphrases जलार्द्राणां as 'जलोक्षिततालवृन्तानाम्'. But the अभिधानचिन्तामणि says 'जलार्द्रा क्लिन्नवाससि'. Compare कादम्बरी 'जलदेवताभिरिव सद्यःस्नातार्द्रचिकुरहस्ताभिरुपगृहीतसुरभिकोमलजलार्द्रिकाभिः' (p. 283 of P). Hence the meaning 'wet cloth' is preferable. तरलय make unsteady *i. e.* move. मूर्धानं...बधान bind my giddy (*lit.* running) head. उरसि...कुरु place on my chest the hand with spray. 'शीकरोऽम्बुकणाः स्मृताः' इत्यमरः. नैति निद्रा sleep does not come (to my eyes). अनैषीत् *Aorist* of नी.

P. 81 ll. 1–23 **उषसि ... तिष्ठत्.** आतुरागमनार्थम्—It should be remembered that राज्यवर्धन had gone to vanquish the Hūṇas. उपर्युपरि one after another. क्षिप्र...ध्वगान् couriers that ran quickly. प्रज...पालान् swift camel-riders. परिजनेन उपनीतम् (brought, presented). प्रतिकर्म personal decoration, toilet. 'प्रतिकर्म प्रसाधनम्' इत्यमरः. विगतं मनः येषाम् (bewildered). अव्यक्तम् indistinct. किं रसायनः what about र०? अनुबध्यमानाः pressed, importuned. प्लुष्ट...स्तापेन as if scorched by an inner fire. उत्पाट्यमानम् torn up by the roots. कामं...जनः A high-born (अभिजातः) person would indeed cease to exist himself rather than convey like an ordinary (इतरः) man words that are unwelcome and distressing (अरतिकर). कृच्छ्रे in a calamity. उज्ज्वली...मस्य his noble birth naturally blessed has been rendered more brilliant by his entering fire like gold. कल्याणा (blessed, lovely) प्रकृतिः यस्य (applies to कार्तस्वर and कौलपुत्र). Gold also by being heated in fire becomes more brilliant. कुलपुत्रस्य भावः कौलपुत्रम्. कृतस्वरः आकरः तत्र भवं कार्तस्वरं हेम. किमस्य...तातः was not my father his father? अन्यं...लोके in this world even when other (*i. e.* ordinary) masters are taken away (*lit.* become rare), life that is sustained becomes a cause for shame (to the servant). अमृत...जीविनाम् who was like nectar to his dependents. निर्व्याजबान्धवे who was their kinsman without any cause (disinterested). अवन्ध्यः (fruitful) प्रसादः (favour) यस्य. सांप्रतम् *adv.* properly. किं वा...दह्यते or what is burnt of him who is full of glory and abides firmly to the end of the world? आकल्पम्—कल्पं मर्यादीकृत्य (अव्ययीभाव). For कल्प see above p. 78. स्थेयस् is the comparative of स्थिर. ममापि...प्रतिष्ठन्ते As for me, what is that very important work, what is that unperformed task, what is the preoccupation (व्यापृतता) of my life, so that it, cruel as it is, does not yet start off? कृतात् शेषः. अन्तरायः obstacle. उत्तरीय...गुण्ठ्य having wrapped himself together with the head by his upper garment.

P. 81 . l. 24—p. 27 l. 3 इत्थंभूते...महोत्पाताः. सर्वस्य लोकेस्य—these words are to be connected with all the locatives from कपोलेषु to हृदयेषु. सर्वस्य...कराः the hands of all people seemed as if rivetted (कीलित) to their cheeks. One who is in deep sorrow or thought sits resting his cheek upon his hand. Compare 'वामहस्तोपहितवदना' in शाकुन्तल IV. The people grieving for प्रभाकरवर्धन remained in that position so long that it seemed that their cheeks and hands were nailed together. लोचने...स्रुतयः streams of tears seemed as if plastered to their eyes. लेप्यं plaster or cement. Plaster or cement sticks to the object to which it is applied and cannot be easily removed. Tears were to be constantly seen in the eyes of the people. ग्रथिताः tied, fastened. उत्कीर्णाः engraved. Engravings are permanent. हाकष्टानि the words 'Oh! alas!!'. लपने...श्वसितानि sighs were twisting themselves like foliage on their mouths (लपनं). They incessantly sighed. परि...पदानि words of lamentation. निधानीकृतानि treasured or stored up. उष्णाश्रु...निद्रा sleep came not to the hollows of their eyes, as if afraid of being scorched by the hot tears. निःश्वास...हासाः—no one smiled; the poet fancies that smiles vanished being thrown away by the wind of sighs that the people constantly heaved. निर...वाणी speech did not go on (*i. e.* no one talked anything) as if burnt by सन्ताप without leaving any remainder. सन्तापः (1) heat, (2) sorrow. कथास्व... हासाः—Not only no body cracked jokes, but nobody even told a tale containing jokes. गीतगोष्ठ्यः people assembled to hear music. गोष्ठी an assembly. जन्मान्तरातीतानि—what was experienced in a former life, no one remembers. लास्यानि—see notes p. 28. प्रसाधनानि decorations of the person, such as flowers &c. ख...मण्डलानि convivial parties at taverns became like sky—flowers *i. e.* absolutely non-existent. खपुष्प is an emblem of what is absolutely non-existent. Such emblems are summarised in the following verse 'एष वन्ध्यासुतो याति खपुष्पकृतशेखरः । मृगतृष्णाम्भसि स्नातः शशशृङ्गधनुर्धरः ॥'. बन्दिवाचः the words of court bards. Mark the words 'विगतजयशब्दम्' (text p. 20 l. 33). युगान्त...वृतयः pleasures seemed to belong to another Yuga as it were. पुन...केतुः—Kāma was once burnt by S'iva; see p. 38 above. But now at the approach of the king's death, all love-making in the world came to an end through grief. महा... पिशुनाः indicative of the fall of a great man. 'पिशुनौ खलसूचकौ' इत्यमरः. भूपतेरभावाय—is to be connected with समुद्भवन्. Mark the dative. The result indicated by a portent is put in the dative, according to the वार्तिक 'उत्पातेन ज्ञापिते च' (वाताय कपिला विद्युत् । सि. कौ.). We may construe भयमुत्पादयन्तो भूतानाम् (causing terror to all beings) or भयमुत्पादयन्तो भूतानां महोत्पाताः great portents of the five elements (पृथिव्यप्तेजोवाय्वाकाश) causing fear. The महाभारत divides portents into three classes *viz.* दिव्य, आन्तरिक्ष and भौम. 'उत्पातांस्त्रिविधान्प्राह नारदो भगवानृषिः । दिव्यांश्चैवान्तरीक्षांश्च पार्थिवांश्च पितामह ॥' सभापर्व 46. 7-8. See also बृहत्संहिता 46. 2.

P. 82 ll. 4–26 **तथाहि...निशाम्.** तथाहि for instance. In the Rāmâyaṇa (अरण्य॰ 23) and in the महाभारत (वनपर्व 179; विराट॰ chapters 39 and 46; उद्योग 84) there are long lists of उत्पातs. For want of space it is not possible to quote them. But they seem to have been the source of Bāṇa's inspiration. दोलायमानं (swinging) सकलकुलाचलचक्रवालं यस्याः. The कुलाचलs (principal mountains) are seven. See notes p. 39. अचलद्धरित्री the earth quaked. पत्या...कामेव as if पृथ्वी was desirous of going with her lord (king प्रभाकरवर्धन, who was dying). Earthquakes were looked upon as portending great calamities and as punishments sent by God to chastise mankind for its sins. The poet Cowper writes in this strain in his poem 'Time-piece'. परास्परास्फालनेन वाचालाः वीचयः येषाम् the waves of which were noisy because they struck against each other. विजुघूर्णिरे *perfect 3rd plural* of घूर्ण् 1 A with वि to roll. धन्व...स्मरन्तः as though remembering धन्वन्तरि in that interval. When the sea was churned by the gods and demons, धन्वन्तरि emerged bearing the jar of nectar in his hand. 'अथोदधेर्मथ्यमानात्काश्यपैरमृतार्थिभिः । उदतिष्ठन्महाराज पुरुषः परमाद्भुतः ॥ 31....अमृतापूर्णकलशं बिभ्रद्वलयभूषितः । स वै भगवतः साक्षाद्विष्णोरंशांशसम्भवः ॥ 34 धन्वन्तरिरिति ख्यात आयुर्वेददृगिज्यभाक् ।' 35. भागवत० VIII. 8. धन्वन्तरि is also the promulgator of the science of medicine, as we learn from सुश्रुतसंहिता I. 1. 'अथ खलु भगवन्तममरवरं काशिराजं दिवोदासं धन्वन्तरिं...सुश्रुतप्रभृतय ऊचुः'. For curing the dying king, the ocean as if wanted धन्वन्तरि and lashed itself into fury as at the time of churning. Mark the genitive धन्वन्तरेः with स्मरन्तः. 'अधीगर्थदयेशां कर्मणि' पा. 2. 3. 52 (verbs having the sense of 'to remember' and the roots दय् and ईश् govern the genitive of the object). ०भीतानाम् goes with ककुभाम् (दिशाम्). भूभृ...ककुभाम् high rose up comets, appearing like the hair of the quarters, that were apprehensive of the death of the king, (hair) that was plentiful (विकट, or frightful) and curly with extended knots. The quarters are fancied to be the wives of the king and comets (that are long) as hair. Women whose husbands are dying would never think of decorating their hair by making a triple braid, but would tie it together in a knot. वितत...कुटिलाः may give two more meanings; (1) that are plentiful and curly like the peacock's outstretched tail; (2) that are terrible (विकट) and crooked with outstretching masses of flames. (शिखा). It is usual to compare the hair of beautiful women with the peacock's tail. See रघु० 9. 67. Comets have flashing tails. धूमकेतवः—compare 'उपप्लवाय लोकानां धूमकेतुरिवोत्थितः ॥' कुमार० II. 32. धूमकेतवः may also mean 'fires'. But as दिग्दाह is mentioned below, it is better to take the sense of 'comet.' धूमकेतुभिः (by comets, fires) करालितानि (rendered terrible) दिङ्मुखानि यस्मिन् (*adj.* of भुवनम्). दिक्पालैः आरब्धः आयुष्कामहोमः तस्य धूमेन धूम्रम्. The quarters had a dark (threatening) aspect on account of the comets. The poet fancies that this is due to the smoke of the sacrificial fire kindled by दिक्पालs for securing long life to the king. For the eight guardians of the quarters, see notes p. 25. भ्रष्टा भाः (lustre) यस्य (*adj.* of ०मण्डले). तप्त...बभ्रुणि reddish brown like a red hot iron jar. भानु...जहार In the sun's disc someone desiring the (continuance of) the life of the (dying) king offered as it were a human offering under the guise of a horrible headless trunk. A spot appeared on the sun's disc resembling the headless trunk (कबन्धः-न्धम्) of a man. This the poet fancies to be a human offering. Compare रामायण अरण्यकाण्ड Chap 23. 11 'कबन्धः परिघाभासो दृश्यते भास्करान्तिके ।'. ज्वलितं परिवेशमण्डलं (circle of halo) तस्य आभोगः (expanse) तेन भास्वरः (*adj.* of श्वेतभानुः, the moon). जिघृक्षया (ग्रहीतुमिच्छया) जृम्भमाणः (yawning) स्वर्भानुः (राहुः) तस्मात् भयं तस्मात्. उपरचितः अग्निप्राकारः येन. The moon had a circle of blazing halo round it. The poet fancies that it was a wall of fire raised by the moon out of the fear of Rāhu that had opened its mouth wide to swallow the moon. अवनि...साधिताः (1) won over by the valour of the king; (2) decked by the brilliance of the king. अदह्यन्त...दिशः the reddened quarters were as if burnt. The quarters glowed red (this is called दिग्दाह). A loving (अनुरक्त) woman would enter fire before her husband dies (प्रथमतर &c.). A woman who wants to die by burning herself would be decked with all decorations (प्रसाधित). स्रुतः शोणितशीकराणां (रक्तबिन्दूनां) आसारः (shower) तेन अरुणिता (reddened) तनुः यस्याः. अनुमरणाय for following (her lord, the king प्रभाकर॰) in death. प्रावृतः पाटलः (red) अंशुकपटः यया. The earth was wet with a shower of blood. The poet fancies that the earth was going to be a सती and had covered herself in a red garment as a सती did. नरा...भीतैः afraid of the tumult that would arise on the king's death. कालायस... दिग्द्वाराणि the doors of the quarters were blocked by masses of untimely dark clouds as if they were iron door-panels. Though it was not the rainy season, dark clouds rose in the sky. The poet fancies them to be the doors of the sky. प्रेत... रटन्तः like the shrill (पटु) sounding drums beaten at the march of the Lord of the dead (यम). When a king marches, drums are beaten. हृदयस्फोटनाः (applies to पटहाः and निर्घोषाः) making the heart to burst. पस्फायिरे *perfect* of स्फाय् 1 A to swell. निर्घा...घोषाः the terrific sounds of whirl-winds. निर्घातः— 'पवनः पवनाभिहतो गगनादवनौ यदा समापतति । भवति तदा निर्घातः स च पापो दीप्तविहगरुतः ॥' बृहत्संहिता 39. 1. निकटीभवन् यममहिषः तस्य खुरपुटैः उद्धूताः. As the king was dying, the buffalo of यम is fancied to be near. द्युमणिः सूर्यः तस्य धाम (brilliance). This is the object of धूसरीचक्रुः (rendered dim). क्रमेलक...वृष्टयः showers of dust brown like camel hair. विरसविराविणीनाम् that howled disagreeably (so as to produce disgust). The reading विसर॰ would mean 'that howled in groups'. It is not so good.

उन्मुखीनाम् that had uplifted their faces. शिखिनो...राजयः rows of female jackals howled, receiving (प्रतीच्छन्त्यः) the flames of fire like meteors falling from the sky. The words in the text as they stand cannot be well construed. इव should have been placed after पतन्तीः or उल्काः. The idea seems to be that the jackals had blazing firebrands in their mouths and howled; meteors also blaze and fall from the sky. C and T translate 'like firebrands catching fire from flames that fell from the sky.' But then the difficulty is: what are the points of resemblance between rows of jackals and firebrands. Instead of being compared to firebrands, jackals are described as carrying firebrands. Compare 'नदन्मुखोल्काविचिताभिषाभिः स वाह्यते राजपथः शिवाभिः ॥' रघु० 16. 12. If we read ज्वालाभिः with three MSS of B, all the difficulties may be removed. Then the meaning will be '(jackals) that as if received in the shape of flames of fire the meteors falling from the sky.' उल्का also means 'a firebrand.' धूमायमानः कबरीविभागः (सीमन्तः) तेन विभावितः विकारः यासाम् whose distress was shown by the fact that the parting line of their hair emitted smoke. प्रकीर्णेन केशपाशेन प्रकाशितः शोकः याभिः that as if manifested their grief by their dishevelled hair. One who is in grief has dishevelled hair. It was believed that in times of misfortune the hair of the images of goddesses in the house emitted smoke. That smoke is fancied to be dishevelled hair (both being dark). सिंहासनस्य समीपे उप० (अव्ययीभाव). भ्रामरम् — भ्रमराणामिदम्. Read विधूयमान for विदूय०. कालरात्र्याः विधूयमानः वृजिनः (curved, curling) वेणीबन्धः तस्य विभ्रमं (object of बिभ्राणम्)—(bearing) the appearance of the braided hair of कालरात्रि, that (hair) is curly and dangling (about the neck). वेणी is the hair of women twisted into a single unornamented braid (when their husbands are absent or ill). The dark and hovering bees resemble the dark and dangling braid. कालरात्रिः night of destruction at the end of the world. As the king was dying the word is appropriately used here. अटताम् goes with वायसानाम्. व्याक्रोशी the cawing (of crows). For the cry of the crow as an evil omen, see text p. 20 ll. 22-23. Compare वनपर्व 179. 44 'पृष्ठतो वायसः कृष्णो याहि याहीति शंसति'. ० मध्यात्—connect this with उच्चखान. सरस...लोहितम् as red as a piece of juicy meat. चञ्चन्ती (moving about) चञ्चुः (beak) यस्य. उच्चैः may be connected with कूजन् or with उच्चखान (tore away on high).

P. 82 l. 27—p. 28 l. 11 **अन्य...देव्या इति.** The principal sentence is 'अन्यस्मिन्नहनि समीपं अस्य (हर्षस्य) राजकुलात्...वेलेति नाम्ना यशोमत्याः प्रतीहारी आजगाम. द्रुतगतिवशेन विशीर्यमाणाः (broken) अलङ्काराः तैः झाङ्कारिणी (causing a tinkling). विज...षादस्य (she) seemed to be the triumphal proclamation of despondency. आकुलयोः चरणयोः चलन्ती तुलाकोटिः तस्याः क्वणितेन वाचालिताभिः. उद्ग्रीवाभिः that raised their necks. The Haṃsîs began to cackle when they heard the jingling of anklets and followed it. The poet fancies that they did so in order to ask the news. 'पादाङ्गदे तुलाकोटिर्मञ्जीरो नूपुरोऽस्त्रियाम्' अमरः ('तुलाकृतेर्जङ्घायाः कोटिरिव' क्षीरस्वामी). स्खलिते विशालश्रोण्यां शिञ्जाना रशना तां अनुरौति इति॰ राविणी ताभिः—that screamed in response to the girdle jingling on her broad hip when she stumbled. बाष्पान्धा—she stumbled being blinded by tears; when she stumbled, the bells of her girdle rang and the domesticated cranes screeched. It was their screeching that guided her. अदृष्टं कवाटपट्टं तस्य संघट्टेन (striking against) स्फुटितं ललाटपट्टं तस्य रुधिरपटलं तेन—her face was covered with blood as her forehead struck against the panels of doors which she did not observe in her weeping. The blood resembled the fringe (पटान्त) of a red silken garment (with which also women may veil their face). सन्तापबलेन विलीनं कनकवलयं तस्य रसधाराम्. She was throwing aside her cane (which she was to carry as a doorkeeper). The poet fancies that it was the stream of her golden bracelet that melted because of her सन्ताप (sorrow, heat). Both cane and gold are yellow. मुख...पटीं स्फुरन्तीं आकर्षन्ती she drew (into position) her flashing silken shawl that was waved about by her breath. मुख॰ and स्फुरन्तीं apply also to निर्मोकमञ्जरीम्. फणिनीव...र्षन्ती as a female serpent may draw after her a slough. Both the shawl and slough are white. नम्रां...स्रंसिना (*adj.* of ॰सञ्चयेन) that hung over her bent shoulders. तमाल...वरेणेव—her dark hair resembled a tattered garment of Tamāla leaves (which are dark). धम्मिल्ल...रहितेन that was not arranged into a braid. 'धम्मिल्लः संयताः कचाः' इत्यमरः. शिरो... कुचा her bosom was covered with a dangling mass of hair. कुच... पीडया—beating the breast is a sign of sorrow. The word पीडया suggests that her breasts were hard (which is a sign of youth and beauty). समुच्छून swollen. If one were to scald his hands with boiling water (hot tears), the hands would be dark-red. निर्झरः a stream, spring. शीर्यति—that was scattered into drops (*adj.* of ॰निर्झरे). स्नपयन्तीव...लोकम्—the idea is:—in her bright cheeks the people were reflected. Tears flowed from her eyes in streams on her cheeks and thus the reflections were bathed in water (tears). She was to tell the people sad news and thus plunge them into the fire of sorrow. One who kills himself by entering fire has first to perform a ceremonial bath. ०प्रवृत्तैः starting from her restless eyes. तारकांशुभिः by the rays of the pupils. श्यामा...दहन्तीव—her pupils were dark and she cast dark glances, whereby the day looked darkened. The poet fancies that the day looked dark because it was burnt by her grief. प्रत्युद्गता received, welcomed. कुट्टिमे न्यस्तं हस्तयुगलं यया she made her obeisance to the prince. गलन्तीभिः &c.—Her lip was dry through grief; when she bent her face, the rays of her gleaming teeth fell upon the lip. The rays resemble water. किमपि...देव्या the queen has resolved upon something (strange).

P. 83 ll. 12--34 **ततस्त...लापान्.** अपरम्—he was already grieving for his father and now he had to grieve for his mother. च्युत ... सत्त्वेन as if left by firmness of mind. द्रुतः melted. आचान्तः drunk. तुलितः weighed *i. e.* lifted up, made light of. अङ्कीकृतः branded. आतङ्केन by pain. अप्रतिपत्तिः (अविद्यमाना प्रतिपत्तिः यस्य) who did not know how to proceed. प्रतिपन्ना संज्ञा येन who regained his consciousness. Put the dash and quotation mark after this and not before. दुःखाभिषङ्गः impact or contact of griefs. कठिने qualifies both हृदये and अश्मनि. हुत...पयति gives rise to fire. When an iron hammer falls upon hard stones (flint), sparks issue forth. When many causes for grief arise, the heart is set ablaze. निरनुक्रोशस्य = निर्दयस्य. तत्र... लापान्—the principal sentence is तत्र च...राजमहिषीणाम् अशृणोत् दूरादेव...आलापान्. The queens, being about to burn themselves, bid a last farewell to their favourite attendants, trees, pets and things. चिन्तय...जननी take care of yourself; your mother is going abroad. जातीगुच्छः a clump of jasmine. मर्षणीयाः...हाराः—It was the convention of poets that the अशोक tree blossomed when kicked by young damsels. Such conventions are summarized in the verse 'स्त्रीणां स्पर्शात्प्रियङ्गुर्विकसति बकुलः सीधुगण्डूषसेकात् पादाघाता- दशोकस्तिलककुरबकौ वीक्षणालिङ्गनाभ्याम् । मन्दारो नर्मवाक्यात् पटुमृदुहसना- च्चम्पको वक्त्रवाताच्चूतो गीतान्नमेरुर्विकसति च पुरो नर्तनात्कर्णिकारः ॥' quoted by मल्लिनाथ on मेघदूत II. 17. Compare कादम्बरी 'अशोकतरुताडनारणितरमणी- मणिनूपुरझङ्कारसहस्रमुखरेषु' (p. 138 of P). कर्ण...राधाश्च and the fautl of plucking thy tender leaves for (making them into) ear-ornaments. वारुणी...ललित naughty on account of receiving mouthfuls of wine. The बकुल blossomed by the sprinkling of mouthfuls of wine. See the verse quoted above. दातव्यो...लिः you should offer to me the handful of water. निवापः libation of water offered to deceased parents &c. at a श्राद्ध ('पितृदानं निवापः स्यात्' इत्यमरः.). अपत्यमसि gives the reason. किं व्याहरसि—why do you call me ? स्वप्ने—she wishes that the *Mainâ* may dream of her departed mistress. मार्गलग्नम्—who clings to my path. सम्भावित honoured, celebrated. गृहहरिणिके domesticated doe (vocative). सौविदल्लः chamberlain. 'सुविदन्तं विवाहं जानन्तं लान्ति सुविदल्लाः ऊढाः स्त्रियः तत्र भवाः सौविदल्लाः' क्षीरस्वामी. वल्लकी lute. 'वीणा तु वल्लकी' इत्यमरः. अयं जनः—refers to the person speaking (one of the queens). कात्यायनी or—निका means 'a widow of middle age who puts on red garments'. 'कात्यायन्यर्धवृद्धा या काषायवसनाऽधवा' इत्यमरः. अलक्षणाम् who am unlucky (*lit.* not possessed of auspicious signs) धात्रेयी foster—sister. अपश्चिमाम्—अविद्यमानं पश्चिमं यस्याः—who can be seen no further hereafter. अय...लिः Here do I fold my hands by way of bidding (last) farewell. अवर...ष्वङ्गः embrace at the time of death.

P. 83 l. 35—**P. 84** l. 24 **दह्यमान...ददर्श** The principal sentence is तैः (आलापैः) दह्यमानश्रवणः प्रविशन्नेव...निर्यान्तीं मातरं ददर्श. दत्तं सर्वं स्वापतेयं (धनं) यया. स्वपतौ साधु स्वापतेयं according to 'पथ्यतिथिवसतिस्वपतेर्ढञ्' पा. 4. 4. 104. गृहीतं मरणप्रसाधनं यया who put on all the decorations of death (as सती). जानकी...वेक्ष्यन्तीम् who was about to enter fire before her husband like Sîtâ. सीता entered fire in the presence of (पुरः) her husband. For the incidents leading to the अग्निशुद्धि of सीता, see रामायण युद्धकाण्ड Chap. 115–118. After the defeat and death of रावण, राम received सीता rather coldly and said that he could not take her back as she had dwelt long in another's house. सीता then called upon लक्ष्मण to prepare the funeral pyre. Going round राम and calling upon fire not to harm her if she was chaste, she entered it. The fire assumed bodily form and handed over सीता to राम. प्रत्यग्रं (fresh) स्नान तेन आर्द्रः देहः यस्याः सा ०देहा तस्याः भावः ०देहता तया. लक्ष्मी when it rose out of the ocean at the time of churning must have been wet as the queen was. कुसुम्भ...दधानाम् who wore two garments reddish brown with safflower juice, as if she were the Heaven with two twillights. सान्ध्य *adj.* (from सन्ध्या). We must read अविधवामरण०. Her husband was yet living and therefore she was going to die like a सुवासिनी with all her decorations, with ताम्बूल in her mouth and so on. The author specifies below some of these, such as कण्ठसूत्र, हार, अङ्गराग &c. ताम्बूल...पाटलम् reddened by the mass of the brilliance of her lip that was dyed dark-red with betel. पट्टांशुकम् a silken cloth (shawl &c.). ०चिह्नम्—all the signs of a सुवासिनी that she wore on her body were tinged with the hue of her lip. कण्ठसूत्र- (Marathi मंगळसूत्र)—is an indispensable ornament always worn on the neck by all women whose husbands are living. The red कण्ठसूत्र hanging on her bosom looked like a stream of blood issuing from her broken heart. तिर्य...त्पीडयन्तीम् who pressed her throat with a necklace the threads of which were drawn aside by the thorn-like point of her ear-rings that were bent crosswise, as if it (necklace) was a halter of white silk rolled together. The idea of पाश is suggested by her approaching death. The necklace of pearls with its threads resembled a white silken rope with which one may hang oneself. सरसः (juicy, thick) कुङ्कुमाङ्गरागः (saffron unguent) यस्याः सा ०रागा तस्याः भावः ०रागता तया. कवलिता devoured. दिधक्षता—instru. of the desiderative base of दह्. Her body glowed with saffron paste and therefore appeared as if it were surrounded by flames of fire. चिता...पूरयन्तीम्—tears fell on her garment. Being white they looked like flowers which would be required as offerings to the funeral fire. गृह...विकिरन्तीम्- bracelets that she wore fell from her hands at each step; they resembled offerings presented to गृहदेवताs in bidding them a last farewell. आप्रपदीनां reaching to the feet. 'स्यात्रिष्वाप्रपदीनं तत्प्राप्नो- त्याप्रपदं हि यत्' अमरः. The word is formed according to 'आप्रपदं प्राप्नोति' पा. 5. 2. 8 (पादस्याग्रं प्रपदं तन्मर्यादीकृत्य आप्रपदम्). गुण...मालाम् a wreath of flowers strung together. The wreath reaching her feet resembled a swing, which also has गुणs (ropes) resembling garlands. The swing is said to be that of यम, because she was going to die. अन्तर्गुञ्जन्तः मधुकराः तैः मुखरेण. आमन्त्र्य...कर्णोत्पलेन—the idea is:—she had a lotus on her ear as an ornament. In that lotus bees were humming. The humming of bees is fancied to be the words of farewell uttered by her कर्णोत्पल to the lotus of her eyes (that were about to perish along with her). Domestic हंसs are always represented as following the tinkling of the anklets of ladies. See above (text) p. 27 ll. 28–29. बद्धं मण्डलं यथा स्यात् तथा in a circle. संनिहितः प्राणसमः यस्मिन् (1) on which her husband dear to her as her own life was drawn; (2) in which her husband dwelt (with चित्तम्). She held fast (अविचलं) in her hand a board; her mind also was fixed fast on dying. Remove the comma after ०दामकाम्. अर्चार्थे (पूजार्थे) बद्धं उद्धूयमानं धवलपुष्पाणां दाम यस्याम् (with पताकाम् and यष्टिम्). She had held fast to her bosom the spear-haft of her husband and had tied round it in worship a garland of white flowers. The poet fancies the प्रासयष्टि to be the banner of a पतिव्रता. The pole of a banner also has garlands of flowers hanging from it. 'प्रासस्तु कुन्तः' इत्यमरः. A सती if her husband died abroad was allowed to burn herself with his पादुकाs. Here यशोमती being the wife of a warrior appropriately takes प्रासयष्टि. बन्धोरिव—When a person in grief sees a friend or relative, tears begin to flow. Compare for the idea 'सन्तानवाहीन्यपि मानुषाणां दुःखानि सद्बन्धुवियोगजानि । दृष्टे जने प्रेयसि दुःसहानि स्रोतःसहस्रैरिव संप्लवन्ते ॥' उत्तरराम० IV. 8.; 'स्वजनस्य हि दुःखमग्रतो विवृतद्वारमिवोपजायते ॥' कुमार IV. पत्युः—is to be connected with सचिवान्. पादपतने समुद्गमत् अभ्यधिकं बाष्पाम्भः तस्य प्रवाहेण उपरुद्धा दृक् येषाम् whose eyes were choked up by the torrent of tears that welled up when they fell at her feet. कथ...देशान् who with difficulty understood the instructions (she gave). अनुनयेन (courteously) निवर्तितः अत एव विधुरः (distracted) वृद्धबन्धुवर्गः तेन वर्धमानः ध्वनिः यस्य. There was wailing in the house, which was augmented by the group of old kinsmen, who, when they followed the queen, were courteously asked by her to return to the house. भर्तृ... हृदयाम् whose heart was captivated by the roar of caged lions, that resembled the voice of her lord. धात्र्या...साधिताम् who was adorned by her nurse and by her own devotion to her lord. Her nurse had helped in decorating her person. In each of the following clauses, words like प्रसाधिताम् bear a literal and also a metaphorical meaning. जरत्या...धार्यमाणाम् she was supported by an old woman and by swoon, both being familiar. Frequent swoons gave relief to her aching heart and supported her. व्यसनसङ्गतया (1) who accompanied her in her misfortune (with सखी); (2) that was connected with (*i. e.* arose from) her misfortune (with पीडा). गृहीतसर्वावयवेन—her servants clasped her limbs; anguish pervaded all her limbs. कुल...ष्ठिताम् she was preceded by great nobles and she was full of heavy sighs. अतिवृद्धैः—the chamberlains were very old, while her sorrows were very heavy (वृद्ध grown, increased). कौलेयक a dog. Everything that pertained to her husband was dear to her and she was sorry to part even from the favourite dogs of her husband.

'कौलेयकः सारमेयः कुक्कुरो मृगदंशकः' इत्यमरः. The word is formed from कुल according to 'कुलकुक्षिग्रीवाभ्यः श्वास्यलङ्कारेषु' पा. 4. 2. 96. (ढकञ्। कौलेयकः श्वा, कौलोऽन्यः । सि. कौ.). सपत्नी...पतन्तीम्—in the hour of death, she forgot all petty jealousies.

P. 84 l. 25—**P. 85** l. 10 दूरादेव...प्रारोदीत्. सस्नेह...चूडः the hair on the top of whose head was as if affectionately kissed by the rays of the jewels of the anklets (of his mother). When he fell at his mother's feet, the rays of the jewelled anklets naturally fell on his hair. The poet fancies that the rays did so out of love. देवी...त्पतनम्—the sentence is देवी यशोमती...बाष्पोत्पतनं निवारयितुं न शशाक. पादयोः निहितं शिरः येन (*adj.* of तनये). विमनसि whose mind was distracted. गुरुणा...ष्टभ्यमाना arrested or enveloped by the great force of grief as by a large mountain. उद्वेगस्य आवेगः तेन. The reading of A and C 'उद्वेगवेगेन' is also good. If a torrent be arrested by a large mountain, it runs past with great force. मूर्च्छा एव अन्धतमसं (blinding darkness). 'अवसमन्धेभ्यस्तमसः' पा. 5. 4. 79 (तमस् when preceded by अव, सम् and अन्ध has अ added on to it). रसातल is one of the seven पातालs (अतल, वितल, सुतल, तलातल, रसातल, महातल and पाताल). पाताल, as the haunt of demons, must be dark. There is also another suggestion. A torrent flows on the earth (रसातल). चिर...ण्डितेन formed into a mass by being pent up for a long time. स्नेह...भूयमाना she was overwhelmed by a tide of love that manifested itself in full strength. If a flow (of water) were pent up for a long time, it bursts forth in a flood; similarly if one checks tears for a long time, they will gush forth irresistibly. कृताः प्रयत्नाः यया सा °यत्ना. उत्कटः (great) कुचयोः उत्कम्पः तेन प्रकटितं असह्यशोकस्य आकूतं (emotion) यया. गद्गदिकया गृह्यमाणः गलः तेन विकला who was in a distressing condition with her throat choked up (on account of tears). निःसामान्येन (unparalleled) मन्युना (grief) तरलीक्रियमाणः अधरोद्देशः (अधरप्रान्तः) यस्याः. पुनरुक्तेन (repeated) स्फुरणेन निबिडितं (tightened) नासापुटं यस्याः. We may perhaps explain differently. Her grief was so great that it could be inferred from the tremor of her lip. But her nose also was in tremor. This latter was superfluous (पुनरुक्त) so far as the inference of the grief by which she was shaken was concerned. सञ्छाद्य—connect this with °पटान्तेन and वदनेन्दुम्. सञ्छाद्य...वदनेन्दुं she covered up her moon-like face, that was raised up a little, with the hem of her shawl (अंशुकपट) the body of which was inlaid with a row of the rays of her nails, as if with a flood of lucid tears

man to another and feel no pang in leaving one to go to another. कुलकलत्रम्—I am a lady of a noble house. चारित्रमात्रं धनं यस्याः. धर्मेण धवले spotless on account of its righteousness. प्रशस्तः पुरुषः पुरुषप्रकाण्डम्. 'मतल्लिका मचर्चिका प्रकाण्डमुद्धतल्लजौ । प्रशस्तवाचकान्यमूनि' इत्यमरः. वीरजा—Unfortunately Bāṇa does not give us the name of the family in which यशोमती was born. पराक्रमक्रीता bought by valour *i. e.* who cares only for valour or whose heart is won by valour. भरत—The reference is probably to भरत, the son of दुष्यन्त and शकुन्तला. There was another भरत, son of ऋषभ and grandson of नाभि after whom India came to be called भारतवर्ष. See for his story विष्णुपुराण II. 1 and 13 and मार्कण्डेय पु. 53. 40. भगीरथ—son of दिलीप and descendant of सगर—brought down the Ganges from Heaven. नाभाग—For the story of नाभाग, see विष्णुपु० IV. 1. and मार्कण्डेयपु० 113. There is a great deal of confusion about नाभाग. The रामायण makes him the son of नहुष and grandson of अम्बरीष (अयोध्याकाण्ड 110. 33); while in the विष्णु० he is represented to be the son of नेदिष्ट and father of अम्बरीष. In the अर्थशास्त्र of कौटिल्य (p. 12) we find that अम्बरीष was the son of नाभाग. वृन्दारक best; *m.* god. सेवायां संभ्रान्ताः (flurried) अनन्तसामन्तसीमन्तिन्यः ताभिः समावर्जितैः (poured) जाम्बूनदघटैः अभिषेकः. जाम्बूनदम् gold ('जम्बूद्वीपे जम्बूफलरसोत्थनद्यां जातं जाम्बूनदम्' क्षीरस्वामी). महादेवी...ललाटेन—My forehead secured the honour of having the fillet of chief queen tied round it. पट्ट is the broad band which runs round the crown immediately above the forehead. The बृहत्संहिता (chap. 49) gives some directions about पट्टs to be worn on the crowns of kings, queens &c. अमित्राणां कलत्राणि एव बन्दीवृन्दं (troop of captives) तेन. विधूयमानं चामरं तस्य मरुता चलं चीनांशुकं (silken cloth from China) तस्य धरौ. शिरःसु निहितं चरणयुगलम्—we need not take these words literally. What she means is that she completely humbled her co-wives. नमन्त्यः निखिलकटककुटुम्बिन्यः (the matrons of the whole capital) तासां किरीटेषु (diadems) माणिक्यानि तेषां मालाभिः अर्चितम्. All the matrons of the capital bowed at her feet, as she was the Mahādevî. एवं... यवा all whose limbs have thus been blessed. किमपरमपेक्षे what else should I expect (or hanker after)? आर्यपुत्रविरहिता bereft of husband (applies to both रति and यशोमती). दग्धस्य भर्तुः—काम, the husband of रति, was burnt by शिव; the king's body also would be burnt after his death. निरर्थकान्प्रलापान्—the author seems to have in mind particularly the fourth Sarga of the कुमारसम्भव of कालिदास, where we have रतिविलाप. We know from the Introduction to the हर्षचरित that बाण was a great admirer of कालिदास. पितुश्च...धूलिः I am like the dust of the feet of thy father *i. e.* I am very much inferior to your father. There is another idea. Dust raised up by the feet of a person goes up into the sky. She says that like dust she will go to heaven before her husband to announce the arrival of a hero like him to the Apsarases, who will therefore be pleased with her as the harbinger of good news. It was a poetic convention that the Apsarases were ready to welcome to heaven the heroes that died gloriously on the battle-field. प्रत्यग्र—fresh. धूमः ध्वजः यस्य—fire. मरणा...साहसम्—not to die, but to live at this time would be a cruel thing in me. अक्षयं—स्नेहेन्धनं (स्नेहः एव इन्धनं) यस्य. The fire of sorrow for my husband is fed up by the fuel of imperishable love; while ordinary fire is fed with fuel that may be exhausted. स्नेहः also means 'oil'. कैलासात् ईषत् न्यूनः कैलासकल्पः; see notes on the affixes कल्प, देश्य and देशीय p. 38. प्रवसति...श्वरे when the lord of my life is departing on a journey (*i. e.* is dying). जरत् तृणं तस्य कणिकावत् लघीयः (जीवितं) light like a bit of old (*i. e.* rotten) grass. जीविते...घटते *lit.* where can it be possible (or proper) that one should be covetous of life ? नर...पातकिनीम् that am guilty of the deadly sin of disregarding the death of the king. She means that to continue to live after the king's death would be a great sin in her. न स्प्रक्ष्यन्ति will not touch (*i. e.* I cannot enjoy the pleasures of your rule). दुःख...मवति prosperity (or grandeur) in those that are consumed by sorrow is inauspicious, accursed and useless. भूतिः means 'ashes' also. Ashes, except of the sacrificial fire, are अमङ्गल. 'भूतिर्भस्मनि सम्पदि' इत्यमरः. विश्व...वपुषा I wish to abide in this world not in flesh and blood, but in the glory of widows. The glory of widows was to burn themselves on the funeral pyre of their husbands. प्रसादयामि I beseech you. न...कदर्थनीयास्मि I should not be slighted by opposing my desire (to burn myself). कदर्थनीय *potential pass. p.* of the denominative verb from कदर्थ. कुत्सितः अर्थः कदर्थः, according to 'कोः कत्तत्पुरुषेऽचि' पा. 6. 3. 101 (when कु being the first member of a तत्पुरुष compound is followed by a word beginning with a vowel, it is changed to कत्).

P. 86 ll. 12–27 स तु...रुरोद. उभयकराभ्यां विधृतं वपुः यस्याः holding her body in both his arms. अवनितलगतं शिरः यस्याः. दुर्नि...धार्य concluding that her grief was impossible of being checked.

कुल...क्रियाम् and thinking that only that course of conduct befitting a lady of high family was better. क्रियां refers to her resolve to die. अभिनन्दति...रूपम्—the author assigns this as a reason why हर्ष acquiesced in the resolve of his mother. Noble birth, though made timorous by love, approves of what is proper to the time and place. पौरा...दिग्भिः who was as if obstructed by the quarters that were full of the echoes of the wailings of the citizens. सरस्वती—is a river on the banks of which the modern Thanesar (स्थाण्वीश्वर) in Karnal District, Panjab, is situated. It rises in the Sirmur state on the borders of the Ambala District and is lost in the sands in the great desert for several miles. स्त्री...पातैः she cast terrified glances as is natural to women. Her eyes had grown red by weeping. Therefore the glances resembled red lotus flowers. We have seen above (notes p. 13) that red lotuses were to be used in the worship of the sun. भानु...न्दवी as the form of the moon enters the sun (on the day of the अमावास्या). Note 'चन्द्रमा वा अमावास्यायामादित्यमनुप्रविशति सोऽन्तर्धीयते तं न निर्जानन्ति' ऐतरेय ब्राह्मण, 8th पञ्चिका chap. 5; compare विक्रमोर्वशीय III. 7 'रविमावसते&c'. चित्रभानुम्—अग्निम्. चित्रभानु also means 'the sun'. इतरोपि refers to हर्ष. स्वल्पः अवशेषः यस्याः सा ०शेषा प्राणवृत्तिः यस्य तम् which was almost ebbing away. परिवर्त्यमाना तारका यस्य (1) the pupil of whose eye was being revolved (with the king); (2) that makes the stars revolve (with the moon). अस्त...षन्तम् (1) about to die; (2) about to set. अस...द्रुतः assailed by an excess of intolerable sorrow. त्याजितः...धैर्यम् affection made him lose all steadiness. Mark the construction (हर्षः धैर्यं त्यजति primitive; स्नेहः हर्षं धैर्यं त्याजयति causal; हर्षः स्नेहेन धैर्यं त्याजितः passive causal). आश्लिष्य—governs पादपद्मौ. सकल...लालितौ fondled by the crests of all haughty kings. अन्तस्ता...भवन्तम् as if it were his moonlike face melting through an inner fire. This and the following clauses are to be connected with अश्रुस्रोतसां सन्तानं वर्षन्. दशन...पद्यमानम् as if it were the net-work of the light of his teeth reduced to water. His bright tears resembled bright water. His teeth were very white. अच्छाच्छम् very bright. अश्रु...वर्षन् showering a continuous stream of tears as if his eyes were made up of a large cloud. इतरवत् like a common man. विमुक्तः आरावः (cry) येन.

P. 86 l 28—**P. 87** l. 10 **राजा तु...लोचने.** उपरुध्यमाना दृष्टिः यस्य whose sight was obstructed (*i. e.* whose eyes could not see his son in the last moments). अविरतरुदितशब्देन आश्रितौ श्रवणौ

यस्य whose ears were affected by the incessant weeping (of हर्ष). Sight failed the dying king, but the incessant weeping arrested his ears and roused him to some consciousness. अविद्यमानं महासत्त्वं येषाम् that have no firm heart. महा...बीजिता Firmness of mind is the first (foremost) stay of the people and royal blood comes after it. People first betake themselves to the man of strong will. सर्वैः अतिशयैः आश्रितः the abode of all eminent things (or virtues). क—क—two कs denote great disparity or incongruity. कुल...करणमिव to call you the lamp of the family is to slight you whose majesty is like that of the sun. प्रदीप (1) lamp; (2) ornament. To call a man a lamp when he is like the sun would be really condemning him. शौर्येण पटुप्रज्ञया (sharp intellect) च उपबृंहितः (magnified) पराक्रमः यस्य. The lion has only physical strength (पराक्रम), but no keen intellect and no heroic heart. लक्षणैः आख्यातं (declared) चक्रवर्तिपदं यस्य. पुनरुक्त superfluous. गृह्यतां श्रीः accept royal dignity. स्वयमेव...गृहीतस्य—लक्ष्मी herself has come to you. Compare for a somewhat similar idea 'लभेत वा प्रार्थयिता न वा श्रियं श्रिया दुरापः कथमीप्सितो भवेत्' कुमार॰ V. उभय...गीषोः who are desirous of conquering this world and the next. अपुष्कलम् not sufficient, little. शशिनः कराणां निकरः समूहः तद्वत् निर्मलं यशः तस्य सञ्चये एकः केवलः अभिनिवेशः (fondness) अस्ति अस्य इति॰ वेशिनः. When हर्ष has set his heart in achieving spotless fame alone, it is useless to ask him to take the treasury. राजकम्—राज्ञां समूहः. गतार्थम् meaningless. अनुचितनियोगः an injunction that is unworthy. दीर्घाभ्यां दोर्दण्डाभ्यां अर्गलितानि (bolted, safeguarded) दिङ्मुखानि येन. अनुवादः repetition. It is a technical term in the पूर्वमीमांसा system. When a Vedic text lays down an injunction (विधि), other passages, that either reiterate, explain or illustrate the विधि, are called अनुवादs. विधिविहितस्य वचनमनुवादः. Harsha was already protecting the world. To call upon him to protect the world was simply superfluous, a mere repetition in words. आनुषङ्गिकम्—necessarily following; incidental (अनुषङ्गात् आगतः ठक्). हर्ष was like a लोकपाल. If he guarded the whole world it necessarily followed that he would protect his attendants. धनुर्गुणस्य किणः तस्य कलङ्कः तेन कालीकृतः प्रकोष्ठः यस्य whose forearm is blackened by the spot of the scar of the bow-string. निग्राह्यताम्—It would be better to have निगृह्यताम्. चापलम् rashness, levity. नूतन...वयसि in tender years. निरवकाशा has no room or scope. सहज...चिन्ता this is a thought for your inherent valour *i. e.* this is a matter which will be dealt with by your valour; I need not enjoin you to do this. The words are capable of yielding another sense. To ask you to annihilate your foes is casting a doubt (चिन्ता) on your inherent valour. C and T translate 'Annihilate your foes is a suggestion of your inborn valour'. This is not clear. अपुनरुन्मीलनाय never again to open them. The reading of B 'प्रत्यपद्यत पूषात्मजः' would mean 'the son of the sun (*i. e.* यम) came to him.'

P 87 l. 11—**P. 88** l. 2 **अस्मिन्नेवान्तरे...नीयत.** पूषापि—The force of अपि lies in this that, as the king lost his life, so even the sun lost his brilliance, which is the sun's essence. लज्जमान इव अधोमुखः the sun hung down as if ashamed. One who feels ashamed hangs down his head. The sun hung down on the western horizon. भूपालस्य अभावः (death) तेन शोकः स एव शिखी (अग्निः) तेन. A thing heated in the fire becomes red. मन्दं...दिवः slowly the sun descended from heaven as if for paying a visit of condolence, following the practice of worldly men. अप्रियप्रश्न is opposed to कुशलप्रश्न. दित्सुः desirous of giving. अपरजलनिधि western ocean. सद्यो दत्तः नृपाय जलाञ्जलिः येन. आलोहितम् slightly red. Water is to be offered with कर (hand, ray). In offering water, one would naturally feel sorrow. एवं च...नीयत—the principal sentence is नरेन्द्रः...सरस्वतीं नीत्वा...यशःशेषतामनीयत. निधनेन निधीयमानं विपुलं वैराग्यं यस्मिन्. शान्तं वपुः यस्य. An ascetic has distaste for the world (वैराग्य); the sun, a short time after the king's death, lost his radiance (विरागस्य भावः वैराग्यम्, विगतः रागः रक्तिमा यस्य). An ascetic must be शान्त (restrained); so also the sun's body became subdued (*i. e.* lost its colour). An ascetic enters the recesses of mountain caves; the sun set behind the western mountain. समुपोह्यमानं (increasing) महाजनस्य अश्रु तदेव दुर्दिनं (stormy or rainy day) तेन आर्द्रीकृते. निर्वाति (loc. sing. of *pr. p.* of वा with निर्) आतपे when the heat (of the sun) became extinguished (as if wet with &c.). Separate रुचा (कान्त्या) इव. लोहितायति—loc. sing. of *pr. p.* of the denominative verb from लोहित. The world was reddened by the glow of the setting sun; but the poet attributes the glow of the world to the tear-flushed eyes of the people. उष्णायमानाः (hot) अनेकनराणां निश्वासाः तैः सन्तापः तेन प्लुष्टं (scorched). नृपा...कमलिनीषु when the lotus beds were left by glory, as if the latter had started to follow the king (in death). Day lotuses fade in the evening *i. e.* their glory leaves them. That लक्ष्मी is identified with राज्यलक्ष्मी and is fancied as leaving them to perish after the king. पति...भुवि when the earth, having covered itself in shadows, became dark as if through grief for her husband. A king is poetically spoken of as the husband of the earth. The shades of evening were falling fast and so the earth seemed to be shrouded in them. श्यामायमाना (1) becoming dark; (2) behaving like a श्यामा (a handsome lady). A handsome woman would have all her brilliance (छाया) covered up (*i. e.* gone) through grief for her husband. परिवृता (concealed) छाया (कान्तिः) यस्याः; छायाभिः परिवृता परिवृतछाया (like the compound राजदन्त). C and T prefer the reading परिवृत्त for परिवृत and explain 'the shadows have retraced their course eastwards.' परित्यक्तानि कलत्राणि यैः (applies to both कुलपुत्र and चक्रवाक). The चक्रवाक becomes separate from its mate at the approach of night. See above p. 10 and 57. वनान्तान् (1) vicinity of woods (with कुलपुत्र); (2) the fringes of water (with चक्रवाक). The noble young men betook to woods out of grief; the चक्रवाकs to water. 'वने सलिलकानने' इत्यमरः. छत्र...शयेषु when the water-lilies closed their calyx, as if afraid of losing the umbrella-like expanse of their petals. कुशे जले शेते इति कुशेशयम्. 'सहस्रपत्रं कमलं शतपत्रं कुशेशयम्' इत्यमरः. The lotuses closed their buds at the departure of the sun. The poet fancies that the lotuses did so because they were afraid that their petals would fade and their umbrella-like appearance would disappear. There is another meaning. The lotuses are compared to devoted servants (lying on mere कुश grass in their grief and not on soft beds). They were terrified by the breaking of the royal umbrella (*i. e.* by the death of the king) and hide the treasure (कोश) in order to safeguard it for the rightful heir. C and T explain that lotuses are compared to queens, who hide the treasures. But कुशेशय is not feminine. Besides it is not in keeping with Indian sentiment to represent the widowed queens as hiding treasures when engrossed in grief. छत्रभङ्ग would be a very bad omen, foretelling the death of the king. Compare बृहत्संहिता 46. 74 'शक्रध्वजेन्द्रकीलस्तम्भद्वारप्रपातभङ्गेषु । तद्वत्कपाटतोरणकेतूनां नरपतेर्मरणम् ॥'. स्फुटित...तपे when the red glow (of evening) flowed away (gradually vanished) as if it were the flood of blood from the broken hearts of the quarter wives. अनु...धीशे when the lord of brilliance (the sun) remained only in अनुराग (red glow; love). The sun vanished and what he left behind was only the red glow of the western sky. The king, who also was

तेजसामधीश, had gone away, leaving behind only love. ०वितन्यमानः बहलः रागः तेन पाटलायाम्. प्रेतपताकायाम्—A banner flies in the sky. स्फुरन्तीषु...लेखासु when streaks of darkness appeared obstructing sight. The black chowries of the hearse resemble darkness and are an evil omen when seen (दर्शने प्रतिकूला). असिता...काष्ठायाम् (1) असितागुरुवत् कालाः काष्ठाः दिशः यस्याम्–in which the quarters are dark like black aloe wood (with रजनी); (2) which had the black beams of dark aloe wood (with चिता). असितागुरोः कालानि काष्ठानि यस्याम्. दन्तामल...लक्ष्मीषु—Here there are numerous puns. The principal idea is that the night lotuses (कुमुद) began to expand. The night lotuses are compared to *satîs* joyfully following their husbands in death. दन्तवत् (like ivory) अमलैः पत्रैः (petals) प्रसाधिता कर्णिका यासाम् (with कुमुदs); दन्तस्य (of ivory) अमलैः पत्रैः (thin plates) प्रसाधिता (manufactured) कर्णिका (ear-ring) यासाम् (with women). पत्र may also mean 'painting or figures' in the latter case. 'कर्णललाटात्कनलङ्कारे' पा. 4. 3. 65. Compare ललाटिका above. केसराणां (filaments) मालाभिः कल्पिता मुण्डमालिका यासाम् on whose top (मुण्ड) there were rows of filaments (with कुमुदs); (केसराणां बकुलानां &c.) whose heads were wreathed with garlands of बकुल (with Satîs). We saw above that a Satı was to die with all her ornaments &c. प्र... मुखीषु (1) with expanding buds (with कुमुदs); with smiling faces (with Satîs). A Satî was not to show that she regretted the step that she was taking. The निर्णयसिन्धु (परि० III) quotes a passage from the स्कन्दपुराण 'अनुव्रजति भर्तारं गृहात्पितृवनं मुदा। पदे पदेऽश्वमेधस्य फलं प्राप्नोत्यनुत्तमम् ॥'. अव...कूजिते when the twitter of groups of birds lying in their nests (कुलायः-यम्) at the top of trees was heard as if it were the tinkling of the bells of the descending car (विमानः-नम्) of the gods. It was believed that celestial cars were sent to take heroes and great souls to heaven. नाक...पत्रे इव–the round and bright orb of the moon resembles a white umbrella. The moon rose in the east, of which Indra (पुरुहूत) is the lord. The poet fancies that the rising moon was the umbrella of Indra, come forward to welcome the king (प्रभाकर०) who was travelling along the path of heaven. नरेन्द्रः refers to प्रभाकरवर्धन; connect the word with अनीयत. स्वयं...स्कन्धैः—the feudatories themselves took on their shoulders the bier (शवशिबिका). शिबिसमः—शिबि was a king and is referred to as an ideal of self-sacrifice. Once इन्द्र assumed the form of a श्येन (hawk) and pursued धर्म

as कपोत. The latter threw himself on the lap of शिबि for help. The श्येन asked the king to give his own flesh in return for the कपोत whom he wanted to save. When the कपोत was placed in a balance, its weight increased and शिबि had to offer his whole body. Thereupon the gods showed themselves to him. See कथासरित्सागर I. 7. 88 ff; रामायण II. 12. 43 'शैब्यः श्येनकपोतीये स्वमांसं पक्षिणे ददौ ।'. पुरोहितः पुरःसरः येषाम्—headed by the family priest. हुताश...नीयत by being honoured with fire, he was reduced (to ashes), so that nothing but his fame remained.

P. 88 ll. 3–24 देवोऽपि ... यामिनी. पुञ्जीभूतेन—goes with लोकेन. All the persons connected with the king formed a group and were huddled up there. They were so many that it seemed as if the whole world had gathered there in grief. अन्त... सिच्यमानः wet as if outside (in the form of tears) by the melting of affection, which though inside, was heated by the fire of sorrow. Affection is internal; tears are visible. The poet fancies that the tears he shed were melted affection. निर्व्यवधानायां धरण्याम् on bare earth. व्यवधानम् what comes between, what intercepts. Nothing came between हर्ष and the earth. उपविष्ट एव—he sat; he did not even lie down. भीमरथी—name of the 7th night in the 7th month of the 77th year of a man's life. This was believed to be a most critical point. If a man survived it, it was believed that he would live for 100 years. The Com. gives three explanations 'भीमरथी नरकनदी कालरात्रिर्वा अन्ये तु सप्तसप्तत्या वर्षैस्तत्संख्यैश्च मासैर्दिनैश्च तावद्भिर्गतैरेका रात्रिर्भीमरथी भवति तामतिक्रान्तो वर्षशतजीवी नरो भवतीति प्राहुः'. ताते...लोकः now that my father is removed, the world of mortals is only this much *i. e.* the world cannot reach hereafter a higher stage. लोकस्य...पन्थानः the ways of the people are broken *i. e.* their progress is arrested. मनो... स्थानानि the splendid goals of ambition are blocked up (or rendered impossible). खिलम् means 'barren or waste soil.' खिलीभू means 'to become barren or impossible.' स्थगितानि covered, veiled. लुप्ता...यात्रा the business of the world has come to an end. प्रोषिताः ...काराः various kinds of manly deeds (or sports) are exiled. पुरुषकारः manliness. विश्रान्ता...भूमयः places where trust could be reposed have ceased to exist. अप...दानानि noble deeds are without an abode. अपदानम् (seems to be another form of अवदानम्) a pure course of conduct; a noble deed. निर...रसता the single-minded devotion to valour has no support now. कथा...ज्ञता capacity to judge has now become a matter of legend. और्जित्यम्

(ऊर्जितस्य भावः) might, vigour. Might has ceased to exist and so people may offer water to it just as they do to the dead. प्रव्रज्या—the order of a religious mendicant. बध्नातु...मनुष्यता let excellent manhood bind the widow's single braid. The idea is:—as the king is dead, वरमनुष्यता has now nobody to resort to. We have seen above that widows used to tie their hair in a single knot. समा...पदम् (1) let royal glory resort to a hermitage; (2) let राजश्री go to a hermitage. By the great resemblance in sound between राजश्री and राज्यश्री the words suggest the misfortunes of राज्यश्री. धवले वाससी—a widow was to wear white garments. See धर्मसिन्धु (परि० III विधवाधर्म) 'वासो न विकृतं वसेत् ।'. वहतु वल्कले—wearing bark garments is a sign of forest life. क...ज्ञतया where will gratitude go to find him? महा...माणून् atoms for the creation of great men. For atoms see above pp. 12 and 44. जगज्जा...धर्मस्य the world has become a darkness for righteousness. The idea is that righteousness cannot now find its way to anybody, as the whole world is enveloped in darkness. दिवसम् (acc. of time) for the whole day. वीरगोष्ठ्यः assemblies of heroes. असम...भित्तयः—असमः (unparalleled) समररसः (liking for fighting) तेन समारब्धाः कलहकथाः (रणकथाः) ताभिः कण्टकिताः (thrilled) सुभटानां कपोलभित्तयः यासु. दीर्घरक्ते नयने यस्य (1) whose eyes were long and red (with मुख); the roots of which are long and red (with सरोज). For this latter meaning of नयन, compare the use of नेत्र in 'दीर्घरक्तनालनेत्रामुत्पलिनीमिव सरसी' (text p. 10. l. 3). लोह...गर्भम्—लोहस्तम्भात् अभ्यधिकः गरिमा गर्भे यस्य—that possessed a massiveness greater than that of an iron pillar. लोका...श्रूयेत सा भारती might I hear that voice of his calling me 'son' even in another world? सुधा...रन्ती emitting nectar. The ocean when churned gave up सुधा (अमृत). The words of the king were sweet like nectar. मथ्यमानः क्षीरसागरः तस्य उद्गारवत् गम्भीरा (deep like the roar &c.).

P. 88 l. 25—**P. 89** l. 13 **ततः...जगाम.** ततः...हर्षः (p. 34 l. 2)—the principal sentence is ततः...चचाल उपस्थानाय देवो हर्षः. The poet now gives a graphic description of day-break. कृकवाकुः cock. 'कृकवाकुस्ताम्रचूडः कुक्कुटश्च रणायुधः' इत्यमरः. गृह...मयूरेषु when the domesticated peacocks let themselves fall from the tops of the trees growing on pleasure hills. गृहगिरि artificial eminences near the mansions. The peacocks rested in the branches of trees during the night and came down when the day broke. पत्ररथः a bird (पत्राणि पक्षाः रथः अस्य). सद्य...तमसि the darkness suddenly grew less and became exhausted. मन्दीभूतः आत्मस्नेहः येषाम् (1) in which the oil was failing; (2) whose love for their self had grown dull. A person who has lost all attachment to his self longs for death. The lamps also, as very little oil was left, were about to be extinguished. स्फुरन्तः अरुणस्य (रविसारथेः) किरणाः वल्कलमिव तेन प्रावृतं वपुः यस्य—the sky was covered with the flashing bark-like rays of early morn and therefore seemed to have taken to the life of a religious mendicant. A परिव्राजक also wears bark-garments that are red. प्रभात...तारकासु when the stars that were grey like the neck of a sparrow (कलविङ्कः) were being taken across by the morning. The idea seems to be that the vault of the sky is like a lake over which the stars were ferried and by morning found themselves on the other side. The stars looked dim in the light of morn. The grey stars resembled the fragments of the king's bones. The burnt up bones of the dead are collected on the third or fourth day in the morning and are carried to holy rivers like the Ganges and are thrown in them. See कुल्लूक on मनु० V. 59; the धर्म० (परि० III) says 'अस्थिसञ्चयनं तु दाहदिनादारभ्य प्रथमदिने द्वितीये तृतीये चतुर्थे सप्तमे नवमे वा गोत्रजैः सह स्वस्वसूत्रोक्तप्रकारेण कार्यम् ।...अस्थ्नां गङ्गाम्भसि तीर्थान्तरे वा प्रक्षेपः ।'. The reading समुच्चीयमानासु of some MSS. of B is rightly preferred by C and T. It means 'being gathered together.' Bones are first gathered and then placed in a jar (see next clause). But if we take the reading in the text, we have first a reference to the carrying of the bones and then to the jars, which inverts the natural order. भूभृ...धारिषु (1) possessing round foreheads that had on them mountain minerals (with elephants); (2) carrying jars that contained the remains (bones) of the king. भूभृतां पर्वतानां धातवः गैरिकादयः (red chalk &c.) तद्गर्भाः कुम्भाः तान् धारयन्तीति; भूभृतः राज्ञः धातवः (अस्थीनि) तद्गर्भाः कुम्भाः घटाः &c. 'कुम्भौ घटेभमूर्धांशौ' इत्यमरः. विविध...मुखेषु—applies to both the wild elephants and those that carried the ashes of the king. तीर्थम् a descent into a river (Marathi घाट); a place of pilgrimage. It is better to read शावे शुचि० with some MSS. of B. शावः (1) tawny; (2) funeral, relating to a dead body (शवसम्बन्धी). शावः शुचि... पाण्डुरश्च शाव...पाण्डुरः. शुचि...पाण्डुरः (1) pale as a ball of white wax; (2) pale with a mass of boiled rice. सिक्थः boiled rice; सिक्थम् bee's wax. The pale moon in the morning looked like a पिण्ड of boiled rice offered to the dead. *Piṇḍas* are often offered on the sandy banks of sacred rivers and the ocean. The moon was going to dip into the western ocean. परिसरः vicinity. क्रमेण—connect this with अस्तमुपगते रजनिकरे. नृप...तेजसीव—the poet fancies that the dimness of the moon's disc in the morning is due to the mass (विसरः) of the smoke of the pyre on which the king was burnt. नरपतिशोकः एव पावकः तेन दाहः तेन किणः (scar) तस्य कलङ्केन कालीकृतं चेतः यस्य. On the dim disc of the moon was seen a dark spot, which the poet fancies to be his mind burnt to charcoal by the fire of sorrow for the king. प्रोषितानां (gone on a journey *i. e.* dead) समस्तानां अन्तःपुरपुरंध्रीणां मुखचंद्राः तेषां वृन्दं तस्य उद्वेगेन विद्राणं वपुः यस्य. We saw above that all the queens had prepared themselves to die (text p. 28 l. 17 तत्र च मर्तुमुद्यतानां राजमहिषीणां &c). The poet fancies that on seeing the agony (उद्वेग) of the women of the harem, the moon (as if out of compassion for the other moons-faces) vanished bodily (*i. e.* set). विद्राण run away (past p. p. of द्रा with वि). C and T translate विद्राण as 'stupefied'. प्रथमं अस्तमिता रोहिणी तया रणरणकः (eagerness, anxiety) तेन विमनाः (distracted) तस्मिन्. रोहिणी is the favourite wife of the moon out of the 27 नक्षत्रs. राजतीव... सवितरि when the sun that had mounted the sky shone like the king (प्रभाकर०). The king also mounted heaven after dying. The reading राजनीव preferred by C and T would no doubt improve the sense, but is not supported by the MSS. used by B. परि...प्रबन्धे when the continuance (प्रबन्धः) of night was turned back, like the kingdom. The kingdom also had changed hands. परिवृत्तम् exchanged; turned back. प्रबुद्ध...कर इव like a bed of lotuses roused by the awakened flamingoes. हर्ष also was advised by the circle of wise (प्रबुद्ध) swan-like kings (to give up wailing). Read न्चापस्नानाय for चोप०. अपस्नानम् bathing on the death of a relative. Drop the comma after ०हंसेषु. नूपुररवस्य विरामेण (cessation) मूकाः मन्दाश्च मन्दिरहंसाः येषु (*adj.* of शुद्धा०). We saw above (p. 92) that हंसs followed the jingling of the anklets of young ladies. But as all the queens had perished on the death of the king, there were no young ladies left. पतितः यूथपः यस्य. कक्ष्या...जने his father's servants stood in the courts of the palace. कक्ष्या also signifies 'the girth rope of an elephant or horse'. विषादि...कुञ्जरे when the king's sad elephant reclined against its post, motionless and dull and having its rider weeping on its back. उपरि रुदन् निषादी (हस्तिपकः) यस्य (*adj.* of ०कुञ्जरे). 'आधोरणा हस्तिपका हस्त्यारोहा निषादिनः' इत्यमरः. मन्दुरापालकस्य (stable keeper) आक्रन्दैः कथिते. अजिरं (courtyard) भजते इति. विश्रान्तः जयशब्दकलकलःयस्मिन्.

आस्थानमण्डपः Hall of audience. अपस्नातः'—अपस्नातो मृतस्नातः' इत्यमरः—one who has bathed after the death of a relative. अनि...मौलिः without wringing his hair. उद्गम...वाससी two white silken robes. 'तत्स्यादुद्गमनीयं यद्धौतयोर्वस्त्रयोर्युगम्' इत्यमरः. निरातपत्रः without an umbrella (the insignia of royalty). निरुत्सारणः without anybody to remove people from his path. समुप...सप्तौ although a horse was brought near. चक्षुषा...उद्गिरन् as if emitting from his eye the fire of sorrow through fear of burning his father who now remained only in his (हर्ष's) heart. His eyes were extremely red. The poet fancies that the redness was the fire of sorrow in his heart. हर्ष emitted it from his eye, so that his father now enshrined in the heart might not be burnt by the fire. अताम्बू...क्षालितस्य—हर्ष had not taken betel for many days and had washed his lip a long time before (yet it was red by nature). कल्प...लयस्य—the tender leaves of any tree are reddish; much more therefore of कल्पतरु. The धर्म० (परि० III) says 'तत्राशौचमध्ये माषमांसापूपमधुरलवणदुग्धाभ्यङ्गताम्बूलक्षाराणि वर्ज्यानि.' अधर...मोक्षैः on account of the brilliance of his spraylike lip, he seemed to vomit, as he sent forth hot sighs, lumps of flesh and blood, because his heart was struck. If one were beaten in the region of the heart, he may vomit blood. When he heaved up deep sighs his red lips quivered and presented the appearance of blood being vomited.

P. 89 ll. 14–27 **राज...विचेरुः.** उद्बाष्पैः (उद्गतं बाष्पं येषाम्) full of tears. आत्मानम् mark the reflexive use of आत्मानम् with the plural केचित्. भृगु...बन्धुः some tied themselves to precipices *i. e.* killed themselves by falling from precipices. 'प्रपातस्त्वतटो भृगुः' इत्यमरः. अनशनैः शुचम् असमाम् अशमयन् they destroyed their unparalleled sorrow by fasting (*i. e.* they died fasting). शलभाः moths. गृहीतवाचः that took the vow of silence. तुषारशिखरिणं = हिमालयम्. उपत्यका—see p. 63. सेवाविमुखाः disgusted with service (*i. e.* with the life of a servant at the royal court). परि...जगृहुः resorted to untenanted spots in forests subsisting on a limited number of morsels. परिच्छिन्नैः पिण्डकैः may also mean 'with thin bodies.' धर्मः एव धनं येषाम्. धमन्यः धमनयः येषाम् with veins fully blown up (*i. e.* all the veins appeared prominent, they were emaciated). गृहीतं काषायं (red cloth) यैः. कषायेण रक्तं काषायम्, according to 'तेन रक्तं रागात्' पा. 4. 2. 1. कापिलं—कपिलस्य इदम्. कपिल is the founder of the सांख्य system, which enumerates 25 तत्त्वs. अधिजगिरे perfect of इ with अधि to study. It is to be noted that the wearing of

काषाय is here associated with कापिलमत; but याज्ञ० prescribes काषाय for all those that desire मोक्ष 'त्यागः परिग्रहाणां च जीर्णकाषायधारणम्' ॥ III. 157. आचोटिताः चूडामणयः यैः the crest-jewels of which were torn away. शरणीकृतः धूर्जटिः (शिवः) यैः. जटाः जघटिरे tied knots of matted hair. परिपाटलं प्रलम्बं चीवराम्बरं (tattered garment) तेन संवीताः enveloped. स्वाम्य...चक्रुः—they rendered glorious their devotion to their master. अनुराग also means 'redness'. By putting on red garments, they made redness appear brilliant. तपोवनहरिणानां जिह्वाञ्चलैः (tips of the tongues) उल्लिह्यमानाः (licked) मूर्तयः येषाम्. They became वानप्रस्थs and resorted to the forest. पाणि...मृष्टैः wiped (or scoured) with their spray-like hands. आताम्रः (slightly red) रागः (colour) येषाम्. नयन...वहन्तः they bore water in their eyes and in their jars. The idea is:—they shed tears, which they wiped with their hands and their eyes were red by weeping. They also rubbed their jars with their hands and carried water in them. The baked jars were red in colour. गृहीतं व्रतं यैः who took the vow of an ascetic (संन्यासी). See वसिष्ठस्मृति Chap. 10 for the धर्मs of a परिव्राजक. 'मुण्डोऽममोऽपरिग्रहः सप्तागाराण्यसङ्कल्पितानि चरेद्भैक्षं विधूमे सन्नमुसले। 17...यज्ञोपवीती उदककमण्डलुहस्तः शुचिर्ब्राह्मणो वृषलान्नवर्जी न हीयते ब्रह्मलोकात्' । 24.

P. 89 l.28—**P. 90** l. 4 **देवमपि...वारयन्.** The principal sentence is देवमपि हर्षं...मुनयः...पौराणिकाः पर्यवारयन्. श्रियं शाप इति—supply मन्यमानम् (l. 32) after this pair and after each of the pairs in the following clauses. श्रियं शाप इति म० who regarded royal glory as a curse. It will be noticed that the poet is influenced in his choice of words in this passage by the jingling assonance of sounds. महीं महापातकम्—As we must shun महापातकs, he shunned the earth. For महापातकs, see above (p.84). भोगान् भुजङ्गाः—as the serpent, so charming to look at, is yet deadly, so the objects of worldly enjoyments he regarded as dangerous. निलयं निरय इति who looked upon home as Hell (because he suffered torments). जीवितमयशः—to have continued to live after the death of such a noble father was really infamy. कल्यता health. 'कल्यौ सज्जनिरामयौ' इत्यमरः. विषममृतमिति—poison he regarded as nectar, because the former, if taken by him, would have assuaged all his torments and united him by death with his father. कामं क्रकच इति—he looked upon desire as a saw *i. e.* to entertain desires for anything when his father was dead was as painful to him as sawing with a saw. पितृ...गताः

Uchchhvāsa VI

P. 91 Verse 1 The metre of this verse and the next is आर्या, for which see p. 49. उच्चित्य having collected or gathered. प्रहिताः निगूढाः आत्मदूताः तैः नीतानाम्. The king sends his spies to find out valiant men; यम also sends his दूतs. विजिगीषुः (from the desiderative base of जि with वि) a conqueror. 'सनाशंसभिक्ष उः' पा. 3. 2. 168 (the affix उ is applied to desiderative bases, to the roots शंस् with आ and भिक्ष्). This verse contains a suggestion of the fate of राज्यवर्धन who was treacherously murdered by the गौड king, whose name the com. gives as शशाङ्क 'अनेनोच्छ्वासार्थः सङ्गृहीतः। तथाहि कृतोऽन्तो विनाशो येन स शशाङ्कनामा गौडाधिपतिः शूराणां राज्यवर्धनानुचराणां तत्सहितानां संग्रहमकरोत्। ...तथाहि तेन शशाङ्केन विश्वासार्थं दूतमुखेन कन्याप्रदानमुक्त्वा प्रलोभितो राज्यवर्धनः स्वगेहे सानुचरो भुञ्जान एव छद्मना व्यापादितः।'.

Verse 2 Construe खलस्य विस्रब्धघातदोषः वीरकोपकरः स्ववधाय (भवति). वि...करः the sin of murdering the confiding produces resentment in the mighty and brings about the death (of the murderer himself). नव...करिणः—the elephant wantonly breaks a young tree, but the noise of breaking robs the sleep of the lion that kills the elephant. Here खल refers to the गौड king who killed the young राज्य०. राज्यवर्धन's death by treachery roused हर्ष (वीर) to wrath and led to the destruction of the गौड king.

P. 91 ll. 5–20 **अथ...जीवितम्.** अथ...द्राक्षीत्—the sentence is अथ...देवो हर्षः...महाजनेन...अकाले आत्मानं वेष्ट्यमानं अद्राक्षीत्. प्रथमं प्रेतपिण्डं भुङ्क्ते इति० भुक् तस्मिन्. प्रथम...जन्मनि when the ब्राह्मण, that takes the first oblation offered for the dead, had been fed. गतेषु अशौचदिवसेषु—the impurity due to the death of a सपिण्ड lasts for ten days. 'दशाहं शावमाशौचं सपिण्डेषु विधीयते।' मनु० V. 59. दीयमा...कलापे—even now the bed and other things of the dead are given to ब्राह्मणs. The धर्मसिन्धु (परि० III) says 'एकादशाहे शय्यादाने एष विधिः स्मृतः। तेनोपभुक्तं यत्किंचिद्वस्त्रवाहनभाजनम्॥ यद्यदिष्टं च तस्यासीत्तत्सर्वं परिकल्पयेत् ।'; and 'अश्वं रथं गजं धेनुं महिषीं शिबिकादिकम्। शालग्रामं पुस्तकं च कस्तूरी कुङ्कुमादिकम्॥ दासीं रत्नं भूषणादि शय्यां छत्रं च चामरम्। दद्याद्वित्तानुसारेण प्रेतस्तत्तत्सुखं लभेत्॥.' अमत्रम् a goblet, vessel. पत्रम् vehicles. 'पत्रं वाहनपक्षयोः' इत्यमरः. C and T read 'नृपतिकट' and translate 'the various appurtenances of the royal bier.' This is not good. The personal property, as it were, of the deceased king was distributed, as, if retained, it would have reminded the survivors every now and then of the use which the departed made of those articles. कीकसम् bone. The bones of the deceased king were taken to holy places. The people's hearts also, when they heard that the bones were being taken to तीर्थs, ran thither out of devotion to the king. कल्पित...चिह्ने when the tomb on the spot of the funeral pyre had been covered with a plaster of *chunam*, which (tomb) became a dart of sorrow. कल्पितं शोकशल्यं येन—the tomb remained there to remind people of their loss, as the point of a dart may permanently remain in the body. चैत्यचिह्नम् monument, tombstone. B reads कल्पित...शल्येषु; and C and T connect it with कीकसेषु. This is not bad. The meaning would be 'the bones had been like the points of darts' (in the hearts of the people). महाजिजिति the victor in great battles (आजिः). विसर्जिते—even now on the 11th or 12th day after death a bull is let loose for the dead. As the deceased was a king, an elephant was let loose. उत्सार्य... शय्यासु when the beds used in misfortune were being cast aside. The धर्मसिन्धु says that in mourning one should lie down on a bed of mats 'तृणकटास्तीर्णभूमौ पृथक्शयीरन् न कम्बलाद्यास्तीर्णभूमौ' (परि० III). उप...क्षमेषु capable of listening to advice. अनु...योग्येषु fit to pay attention to requests (अनुरोधः). गण...गुणेषु—when everybody had become so far composed as to be able to recount the virtues of the king. प्रदेश...शोके—C and T translate 'Grief was becoming a moral theme'. It is not clear how this meaning is arrived at. The meaning seems to us to be 'when grief came to have a limited scope' *i. e.* when शोक was not to be found at all seasons and places, but only at particular times and places. कृतेषु...तकेषु when the poets had sung their dirges. Take away the comma after ०स्थाने. स्वप्नावशेषं दर्शनं यस्य—For some days after his death, the people felt as if the king was among them. उत्सृष्टः व्यापारः येन who was doing nothing. महाजनेन by a great company. मौलेन hereditary. किमन्यत् what else (can it be)? लोकानां आकरः समूहः. अधिकतरः प्रचारः यस्य who moved about more (than the others). C and T translate 'a man of distinguished bearing'. सोदर्यस्नेहे निहितः (*lit.* placed in *i. e.* added to) निरतिशयः मन्युः शोकः तेन मृदूकृतं मनः यस्य. What is p aced in स्नेह (oil) may become soft. उत्पीडः mass, flood.

P. 91 l. 21—**P. 92** l. 19 **अनन्तरं...गात्.** The principal sentence is अनन्तरं च...ज्येष्ठं भ्रातरमपश्यत्. द्वार...कथ्यमानम् who was announced by the lamentation of the doorkeeper, as if it (आक्रन्द) were an attendant that entered first. At the sight of राज्य° the doorkeepr wept. The द्वारपाल allows (मुक्त) high personages and their attendants to enter. The attendants precede the high personages to show them the way. दूर... बाहुल्येन—this and the following instrumentals qualify परिजनेन. दूरं द्रुतं आगमनं तेन मुषितं बाहुल्यं यस्य whose numbers were thinned (*lit.* robbed) by the long and quick march. विच्छिन्नः छत्रधारः यस्मिन् in which the umbrella-bearer was not to be found (he lagged behind). लम्बितः (lagged behind) अम्बरवाही (the man in charge of the wardrobe) यस्मिन्. भृङ्गारः a golden pitcher 'भद्रकुम्भः पूर्णकुम्भो भृङ्गारः कनकालुका' इत्यमरः. आचमनधारिन् spittoon-bearer. ताम्यन् (exhausted) ताम्बूलिकः (betel-bearer) यस्मिन्. खञ्जन् (limping) खड्गग्राही यस्मिन्. कति...प्रायेण mostly consisting of a few well-known (प्रकाश) servants. For दासेरक, see p. 28. बहुवासरान्तरितं स्नानभोजनशयनं तेन श्यामं क्षामं (emaciated) वपुः यस्य. अविरला मार्गधूलिः तया धूसरितं शरीरं यस्य सः °शरीरः तस्य भावः °शरीरता तया. अविद्यमानं शरणं यस्याः. The poet fancies that the earth in the form of dust resorted to him because it had become bereft of a protector by the death of प्रभाकर°. क्रमागतया (1) that was hereditary in his family; (2) that came to him (stuck to his body) by his walking (with धूलि). हूणानां निर्जयाय समरे शरैः व्रणाः तेपु बद्धैः पट्टकैः (pieces of cloth) शबलीकृतः (spotted) कायः यस्य. The long and white bandages are fancied to be the glances of राज्यलक्ष्मी that was approaching him (he was the king after his father). Long eyes is a sign of beauty. The inside of the eye is white like the bandages. हुतं मांसं येषाम्. आवेद्यमानः दुःखभारः यस्य. He had lost flesh through grief. The poet fancies that the flesh so lost had been offered into the fire of grief for preserving his father's life. When a sacrifice is performed, offerings are given in fire. There is a striking contrast presented by the inference of a heavy weight from lean (कृश) limbs. Ordinarily lean limbs do not carry heavy weights. अपगतः चूडामणिः यस्मात्. मलिनाः आकुलाः (dishevelled) कुन्तलाः यस्य. शेखरः garland of flowers on the head. His head was not decorated through grief. The poet fancies that grief had mounted on it. आतपेन गलिता स्वेदराजिः यस्मात् (*adj* of °पट्टेन). रुदतेव—Drops of perspiration stood out on his forehead owing to heat. The poet fancies that his forehead was eager to bow at the feet of his father and wept, as it could not do so owing to the death of प्रभा०. प्रथीयस् comparative of पृथु. One who faints has water sprinkled on his face. राज्य० shed tears which fell on the earth. The poet fancies that the tears were water poured over the earth that had swooned away owing to the death of her honoured lord. निम्नीकृत dug out, made hollow. His cheeks that were once round and fleshy had become hollow. Constant dripping of water wears away even stones. The poet fancies that the constant falling of tears on the cheeks wore away the cheeks and made them hollow. गलितः ताम्बूलरागः यस्मात्. राज्य० used no betel owing to grief. So his lip had not its usual redness. The poet fancies that the ताम्बूलराग came in the way of his very hot breaths, became melted and disappeared from his lip. पवित्रिकामात्रे अवशेषः यस्याः सा ०शेषा इन्द्रनीलिका &c. पवित्रि... द्दहन्तम्—the idea is:—in his यज्ञोपवीत there was a sapphire ring, the rays of which shot upwards and rendered his ear dark. The poet fancies that the darkness of the ear is due to its being burnt by the fire of the great grief at the recent news of his father's death. पवित्रकं = शणसूत्रजालं क्षत्रियस्य यज्ञोपवीतम्. The only इन्द्रनील he had was on the ring in his यज्ञोपवीत. C and T render 'his sapphire ornament of which only the amulet was left'. अस्फुटाभिव्यक्तं व्यञ्जनं (beard) यस्मिन्. 'व्यञ्जनं लाञ्छनश्मश्रुनिष्ठानावयवेष्वपि' इत्यमरः. His face had only a slight growth of beard, which was rendered darker by the light of the dark pupils of his downcast and motionless eye. One who is in mourning has to allow his beard to grow. Though he had a slight growth of beard, he seemed to have a thick growth of it owing to the rays of his eye. महा...ह्वलम् (1) overwhelmed by the fall of a great mountain (with lion); (2) overwhelmed by the death of the great king (with राज्यवर्धन). निरवलम्बनम् without refuge or support. If a mountain falls on a lion, the latter will lose a place for prowling and will be stunned. तेजःपतिः (सूर्यः, नृपतिश्च) तस्य पतनेन परिम्लाना श्रीः यस्य. दिवसमिव श्यामीभूतम्—who (राज्य०) had become dark (in complexion) like the day. The day also turns into night when the sun dips down into the sea. श्यामीभूतं means रात्रीभूतं with दिवसम्. 'श्यामा स्याच्छारिवा निशा' इत्यमरः. नन्दनम्—the garden of Indra. भग्नः कल्पपादपः यस्य. If the tree in the नन्दनवन be broken there will be no shade (छाया). राज्य० also had no छाया (splendour) left, as his father, who was a veritable कल्पवृक्ष to suppliants, was dead. प्रोषितः

दिक्कुञ्जरः (दिग्गजः) यस्मात्. If the दिग्गजs went away, the quarters would be empty (शून्य). राज्य० also was शून्य (vacant-minded). The eight quarters are guarded by eight दिग्गजs. 'ऐरावतः पुण्डरीको वामनः कुमुदोऽञ्जनः। पुष्पदन्तः सार्वभौमः सुप्रतीकश्च दिग्गजाः॥' इत्यमरः. दिशां भावः दिग्भावः (the state of the quarters). गुरुः (heavy, crushing) वज्रपातः तेन दारितम् (with गिरि); गुरौ (पितरि) वज्रपातः (मृत्युः) तेन दारितम् (with राज्य०). The wings of mountains were clipped by Indra with his thunderbolt. See p. 19 above. किङ्क...रुण्येन enslaved by sorrow. दुर्मनसः भावः दौर्मनस्यम्—despondency. स्विन्न...पेन all perspiring through सन्ताप (heat, sorrow). उच्चितम् gathered, collected. लुप्तम् robbed. C and T would prefer वृतं the reading of two MSS. of B for धृतं for the sake of alliteration. प्रत्या...ख्यानेन discarded by reflection. Compare 'अवष्टम्भो ज्ञानं धैर्यं **प्रतिसंख्यान**मित्यस्तमितैषा कथा' कादम्बरी (p. 156 of P). दूरी...भवत्वेन cast aside by firmness (*lit.* the quality of being invincible). अबो...वृद्धीनाम् that was beyond the counsels of the aged. The instrumentals from अबोध्येन qualify शोकेन below. असा ... तानाम् that was not to be cured by the words of the good. अग...गिराम् that was inaccessible to the eloquence of elders. अशक्ये...शक्तीनाम् not within the reach of the power of scriptures. अ...यत्नानाम् that was beyond the way of the efforts of wisdom. The idea is that the efforts of wise men would not avail to lessen his sorrow. अभूमि...चयानाम् that was not a proper place for gradual healing up. उपचयः *lit.* increase, prosperity. आवेगेन उद्गताः कृत्स्नस्नेहस्य उत्कलिकाः ताभिः उत्क्षिप्यमाणः कायः यस्य—whose body was lifted up on the waves of the whole love that surged up through emotion. स्नेह is compared to the sea; emotion caused by the sight of राज्य० to the tide of the sea. The agitation (उत्कलिका) due to the emotion is compared to waves (उत्कलिका). A man swimming in the sea is borne on the crest of waves. Harsha's body was shaken by agitation.

P. 92 l. 20—**P. 93** l. 2 **अथ तं...स्थात्.** कलितं held in. ०सारितेन goes with ०द्वयेन. We must read संकलयन्निव (as if grasping). He stretched out his long arms to embrace हर्ष. The poet fancies that he did so in order to embrace all sorrows (*i. e.* he would thereby become full of all sorrows). सङ्कलपयन् hardly yields any sense. पतितं क्षौमं यस्मात् from which the fine garment had fallen (or slipped away). सब...हृदयानि (their) hearts were as if uprooted together with their fastenings. A and C omit the sentence अश्रु...लोकेन. That sentence seems to mean 'the people let fall in their eyes a stream of tears resembling veins of blood'. The preceding sentence spoke of the uprooting of hearts. If that were actually done, blood would flow forth from the veins of the body. The stream of tears is fancied to be the veins of blood. स्मृतः नृपतिः (प्रभाकरवर्धनः) येन. When the princes wept, the king's favourite also wept. He seemed to be the echo of the princes. निर्वृष्टं नयनजलं येन. Rain ceases in autumn of its own accord; no one can stop it. So राज्यवर्धन stopped weeping after a long time. तोयेन—connect this with अक्षालयत्. तस्कर...लेखमिव (eye) that seemed to have a streak of foam produced by a big flood of water because of the pencils of the rays of his finger-nails. When he washed his face, he moved his hand over it. The rays of his bright nails resembled white foam and so his eye seemed to be covered with foam. पक्ष्माग्रे सङ्गलन्तः बिन्दवः तेषां वृन्दं तेन मन्दः उन्मेषः तेन मुषितं दर्शनं यस्य (his eye) the vision of which was robbed by the fact that its opening (उन्मेषः) was obstructed by the mass of tear-drops gathering on the tips of his eyelashes. वाससा...न्ममार्ज—he wiped his face with a white towel. The towel resembled moonlight in whiteness and in being cool. So the poet fancies that he wiped his face scorched by very hot tears with a piece of moonlight. विभूषं...ष्पीड्य having carelessly wrung his head (मौलिः) that was unadorned and the locks on which were disturbed and dishevelled. विगता भूषा यस्मात्. वित्रस्ताः व्यस्ताः (scattered about) कुन्तलाः यस्य. सावशेष...अधरेण—(connect this with कुर्वाणः)—by his lower lip that quivered on account of the remnants of sorrow, which (lip) therefore seemed as if desirous of living and as if desirous of kissing itself, as it was charming on account of its bath. The idea is:—when राज्य० bathed he washed his lip and eyes. As his grief had not all died out, his lip quivered. One who lives makes movements. So the quivering of the lip showed that in spite of grief it wanted to live. In kissing also the lips move. So the poet imagines that the lip quivered because it wanted to kiss itself on account of its own agreeableness due to the bath. अवशेषेण सह साव० (बहुव्रीहि), सावशेषः मन्युः तेन स्फुरितः. शारदः (शरदि भवः) शशी तस्य करैः विकसितानि विशदानि (shining) कुमुदवनानि तेषां दलावलिः एव बलिः तस्य विक्षेपैः (throwing). The कुमुद्s bloom in moon-light. The moon is at its best in शरद्. His quivering lip resembled the flashes of lightning become rare when शरद् comes; his washed face resembled the clear moon of शरद्. When राज्य० cast glances in various directions, the poet imagines that he did worship to the दिग्देवताs with the offerings of petals of कुमुदs. चतुःशालम् a quadrangle enclosed by four buildings. चतसृणां शालानां समाहारः चतुःशालम्. वितर्दिका—platform, terrace. See p. 53. नीचापाश्रये विनिहितः एकः उपबर्हः यस्याम्—on which a single cushion was placed beneath a low awning. For अपाश्रय, see p. 21. 'उपधानं तूपबर्हः' इत्यमरः. जोषम् *adv.* silently.

P. 93 ll. 3–15 **देवोऽपि...मण्डलम्.** ०कुथायां प्रसारिता मूर्तिः (शरीरं) येन. कुथा a blanket or carpet. औरस...शोकस्य for the sight of a very near relative is the youth of sorrow. औरसः—उरसा निर्मितः according to 'उरसोऽण् च' पा. 4. 4. 94. The word is primarily applied to a son and extended to any close blood relation like a brother. The idea is that at the sight of one's near relations grief increases in intensity. Compare notes p. 96. सः (l. 8) refers to दिवसः. प्रत्यग्र...तनुरिव as if his body had recently (प्रत्यग्र) been chopped by the chisel of त्वष्टृ. The sun at the time of setting looked red. One whose body is recently cut would be red with blood and flesh. वहद्बहलरुधिररसं (वहन् बहलः रुधिररसः यस्मिन् तत्) मांसं तस्य इव छविः (कान्तिः) यस्य that looked like flesh moistened by plentiful blood. प्रत्यग्रत्वष्टृ०—त्वष्टृ is the architect of the gods. He had a daughter named संज्ञा that was married to the sun. She could not bear the light of the sun. त्वष्टृ, wishing to reduce the superfluous lustre of the sun, placed him on his lathe and trimmed off some of his lustre. With the portion thus taken away त्वष्टृ manufactured the चक्र of विष्णु, the त्रिशूल of रुद्र and the other weapons of the gods. Vide विष्णुपु० III. 2. 9–12 and मार्कण्डेयपु० Chap. 77. 'भ्रमिमारोप्य सूर्यं तु तस्य तेजोविशातनात्। कृत्तवानष्टमं भागं न व्यशातयताव्ययम् ॥' विष्णु० III. 2. 9. Note रघु० VI. 32 'आरोप्य चक्रभ्रममुष्णतेजास्त्वष्टेव यत्नोल्लिखितो विभाति ॥'. अपरः (western) पारावारः ocean. मञ्जिष्ठावत् अरुणः. मञ्जिष्ठा Bengal madder. It is used as a red dye. अरुणः सारथिः यस्य. मुकुलायमानाः (closing) कमलिनीकोषाः तेन विकलम् (distressed). चकाण perfect of कण् to cry in distress, hum. The कमल closes its petals at sunset. चञ्चरीकः = भ्रमरः. On this word क्षीरस्वामी remarks 'चञ्चरीकभसनेन्दिन्दिररोलम्बा देश्याम्'. सविधः (near, approaching) विरहव्याधिः तेन विधुरा वधूः तया बाध्यमानम् (*adj.* of चक्रवालम्). विबुद्धस्य (blooming) बन्धूकस्य इव भाः (तेजः) यस्य (*adj.* of भास्वति). बन्धूकम् is a kind of red flower.

अस्रैः सह सास्राम् tearful. चक्रवालम्—group. For the separation of the चक्रवाक from its mate at sunset, see pp. 10, 57. सञ्चरन्त्याः goes with श्रियः. श्री is said to be wandering because प्रभाकरवर्धन being dead there is yet no new king installed. मधुकररवेण सह स... रवं. कैरवाकरं must be taken as the object of सञ्चरन्त्याः. The कैरवs are white lotuses that expand at nightfall. The bees buzzed over them. The poet fancies that this buz ing was the jingling of the small bells on the girdle of लक्ष्मी. कल... रमणीयम् goes with ०करम्. The कलहंसीs were there near the कैरव beds and lent their grace to them. आण—perfect of अण् to sound. The bees were like bells, the कलहंसीs like माणिक्यकाञ्ची and the white lotuses like the fair complexion of लक्ष्मी. प्रकटः कलङ्कः यस्य (*adj.* of ०मण्डलम्). उदयमानम् (*pr. p.* of अय् 1 A with उद्) rising. विशङ्कटः (large) विषाणः (horn) तेन उत्कीर्णः (scattered) पङ्कः तस्य सङ्करः (contact) यस्य सः ०सङ्करः शङ्करस्य शकुरः (tame) शक्करः (bull) तस्य ककुदकूटः (conical hump) तत्सङ्काशं तत्सदृशम्. 'विशङ्कटं पृथु बृहत्' इत्यमरः. The moon was like the hump of the white bull of शिव and the horns of the moon resembled the horns of the bull and the spot on the moon was like the mud on the horn of the bull. This passage is full of suggestions, as C and T observe. The word शशाङ्कमण्डलम् indicates the rise of the गौड king (शशाङ्क as the com. says), who murdered राज्यवर्धन. The red sunset symbolizes bloody wars.

P. 93 ll. 16—**P. 94** l. 18 **अस्यां...धरण्याम्.** नास्ति अतिक्रमणं यस्य तत् अनतिक्रमणं वचनं येषाम् whose words could not be disregarded. भूमिः...योगानाम् you are a proper person for the injunctions of elders *i. e.* elders enjoin you to do something because they feel sure that you would not disobey. Or गुरु may mean 'father', the sense being 'our father used to give you instruction as you were the fittest person to receive it.' अग्राहि चित्तवृत्तिः you held the heart. A person may seize a banner that has ropes. The king's mind also was गुणवत्; or the king's mind was the banner of the virtuous (गुणवतां पताका) *i. e.* he was the foremost or preeminent among the virtuous (as a banner is). विधेयम् docile, obedient. विधेः विधानेन उपनतं नैर्घृण्यं (निर्घृणस्य निर्दयस्य भावः) यस्य (my heart) that has become callous by the decrees of fate. C and T translate 'विधि०' as 'my heart, softened to compliance with the decrees of fate.' This is wrong. बिभणिषति = भणितुमिच्छति. प्रेमविलोमा which runs counter to affection. Read ०विलोमा for ०विलोपा. वामता perverseness, refractory spirit. वैधेयः fool, dullard.

'अज्ञे मूढयथाजातमूर्खवैधेयबालिशाः' इत्यमरः (विधेयः एव वैधेयः स्वार्थेऽण्). लोकवृत्तम् ways of the world. मान्धान्तृ—see for his story p. 23. प्रभाकर० was a pre-eminent चक्रवर्ती as मान्धाता was. 'यौवनाश्वोऽथ मान्धाता चक्रवर्त्यवनीं प्रभुः । सप्तद्वीपवतीमेकः शशासाच्युत तेजसा ॥' भागवतपु० 9. 6. 34. पुरुकुत्स was the son of मान्धातृ and killed the मौनेयगन्धर्वs that had ousted the Nâgas and re-instated the latter. He married नर्मदा. See विष्णुपुराण IV. 3. भ्रूलतया आदिष्टानि अष्टादश द्वीपानि येन who issued commands to the eighteen worlds with his brow. दिलीपे मृते वा रघुणा (किं कृतम्)—Bâna seems to follow the रघुवंश here in making रघु the son of दिलीप. According to the रामायण (II. 110 and I. 70) दिलीप's son was भगीरथ, whose grandson was रघु. So according to the विष्णुपुराण (IV. 4) दिलीप's son was दीर्घबाहु whose son was रघु. महान् असुरसमरः तन्मध्ये अध्यासितः त्रिदशानां (देवानां) रथः येन. Compare for the idea that दशरथ helped the gods in battle रघु० 9. 19 'स किल संयुगमूर्ध्नि सहायतां मघवतः प्रतिपद्य महारथः।'. It was in this battle with the demon शम्बर that कैकेयी, who had helped दशरथ, got two वरs from him. See रामायण अयोध्याकाण्ड 2. गोष्पदीकृताः चतुर्णां उदन्वतां अन्ताः येन—who looked upon the confines of the four oceans as a puddle. गोष्पदम् (गो + पद)—स् is inserted according to 'गोष्पदं सेवितासेवितप्रमाणेषु' पा. 6. 1. 145. (गावः पद्यन्तेऽस्मिन्देशे स गोभिः सेवितो गोष्पदः । प्रमाणे, गोष्पदमात्रं क्षेत्रम् । सि. कौ.). The four oceans were as small to him as a puddle that is as deep as a cow's hoof. तिष्ठन्तु...देते let alone these. तातेन—refers to प्रभाकरवर्धन. शतात् समधिकाः (more than a hundred) अध्वराः तेषां धूमः तस्य विसरेण (mass) धूसरितं वासवस्य (इन्द्रस्य) वयः येन—who rendered the youth of Indra grey by &c. It was believed that whoever performed a hundred अश्वमेध sacrifices would displace Indra. Indra is therefore always represented as anxious to put obstacles in the performance of these sacrifices. Indra grew old through anxiety and jealousy when he learnt of the hundred and more sacrifices of प्रभा०. सुगृहीतं नाम यस्य—of blessed memory. This is a term used in respectfully addressing or speaking of a person (particularly a deceased person). कुत्सितः पुरुषः कापुरुषः, according to 'विभाषा पुरुषे' पा. 6. 3. 106 (कापुरुषः । कुपुरुषः). स्त्रैणं womanishness. आस्पदम् = स्थानम्. भू... र्ध्वस्ते (1) the king being killed; (2) the mountain being shattered or laid low. If a mountain were shattered to pieces, all the torrents will be at once let loose; so the king being killed, all his tears flow in torrents. अस्त...तेजसि—refers to the setting of the sun and the death of the king. अन्धकारीभूताः दश आशाः (दिशः)

यस्य. प्र...लोकः the light of wisdom fails. When the sun sets, there is no light in the ten quarters. The king being dead, राज्य० cannot think wisely and looks on the whole world as dark. Remove the comma after हृदयं, which is the object of उपसर्पति. My heart is aflame with grief and therefore विवेक does not come to it, as if afraid of being burnt by the fire in the heart. सन्ताप (1) sorrow, (2) heat. जातुषम्—made of lac. जतुनो विकारः, according to 'त्रपुजतुनोः षुक्' पा. 4. 3. 138 (आभ्यामण् स्यात् विकारे एतयोः षुगागमश्च त्रापुषम् । जातुषम् । सि. कौ.). पदे पदे (1) at every word; (2) at every step. दिग्धः (poisoned) रोपः (arrow) तेन आहता. 'पत्री **रोप इषुर्द्वयोः**' इत्यमरः. '**विषाक्ते दिग्ध**लिप्तकौ' इत्यमरः. दूरेण भ्रमति (1) wanders far; (2) wanders at a distance (from the person hated). परिहरन्ती avoiding. अम्बा—refers to यशोमती. वार्धु...वित्तानि money that is employed by a moneylender or usurer. वार्धुषिक (from वृद्धि)—वृद्ध्यर्थं द्रव्यं वृद्धिः तां गर्ह्यां प्रयच्छति इति—according to वार्तिक 'वृद्धेर्वृधुषिभावो वक्तव्यः' on 'प्रयच्छति गर्ह्यम्' पा. 4. 4. 30. A very exacting moneylender would stipulate for interest to be calculated from day to day; and even without such stipulation, ordinarily every day adds to the interest that has to be paid. ०धूमसम्भारात् सम्भूतः अम्भोधरः (मेघः) तेन भरितमिव. पञ्चजनः—*lit.* people of the five races (*i. e.* the Aryans in the four quarters and the निषादs); hence, people in general. Compare ऋग्वेद III. 59. 8 'मित्राय **पञ्च** येमिरे **जना** अभिष्टिशवसे'. 'स्युः पुमांसः पञ्चजनाः पुरुषाः' इत्यमरः. पञ्चत्वं प्रयाति is dissolved into the five elements (पृथिव्यप्तेजोवाय्वाकाश). असाम्परायिकम् not warlike, cowardly. सम्परायः=युद्धम्. अवष्टभ्य having enveloped. शोकः—connect it with दहति and the following verbs. वाडव...राशिम्—this and the following three clauses are to be respectively connected with दहति and the three following verbs. वाडवः—is the submarine fire, otherwise called और्व. The sons of कार्तवीर्य, with the desire of destroying the descendants of भृगु, killed even the children in the womb. One of the women of the family secreted the child in her womb in her thigh (ऊरु) and preserved it. Hence the child was called और्व. At sight of him, the sons of कार्तवीर्य were struck blind and his wrath gave rise to a flame which was going to burn the whole world, when at the desire of his पितृs, the भार्गवs, he cast it into the ocean. Compare शाकुन्तल III. 3 'त्वयि ज्वलत्यौर्व इवाम्बुराशौ'. See आदिपर्व for the story. पविरिव पर्वतं (दारयति)—for the clipping of the wings of mountains, see p. 19. क्षय...करं (तनूकरोति)—for showing greater favour to रोहिणी than to his other wives, the नक्षत्रs, the moon was cursed by their father दक्ष to be a consumptive. Compare 'दर्शयन्निव चिरकाललग्नं दक्षशापानलदाहचिह्नं' कादम्बरी (p. 178 of P). सुमेरुकल्पस्य resembling Meru. For Meru, see p. 85. For कल्प, see notes on देशीय p. 38. कल्प...पुरुषस्य who was a noble spirit (to be found once) in a कल्प. For कल्प, see p. 78. Another meaning also may be suggested 'a noble spirit like a कल्पवृक्ष'. अतिवाहयितुम् to get through. विरक्तं (1) disgusted; (2) tinged redder. चकोरस्य—It was believed that the eyes of चकोरs became red at the sight of poison. अर्थशास्त्र of कौटिल्य says 'क्रौञ्चो विषाभ्याशे माद्यति। ग्लायति जीवञ्जीवकः। म्रियते मत्तकोकिलः। चकोरस्याक्षिणी विरज्येते' (pp. 40–41). काम० says 'चकोरस्य विरज्येते नयने विषदर्शनात्। सुव्यक्तं माद्यति क्रौञ्चो म्रियते कोकिलः किल ॥' VII. 12. बहवः मृतपटाः अवगुण्ठनं यस्याः that covers her face with many shrouds of the dead. The चाण्डालs were in the habit of taking the clothes in which corpses were shrouded. रञ्जितः रङ्गः (समाजः) यया that pleases the audience or sight-seers. People were diverted by the sight of the various shrouds worn by Chandāla females. जनङ्गमः=चण्डालः. राज्यवर्धन says he wants to give up राज्यलक्ष्मी, which he compares to the श्री of चण्डालs. 'चण्डालप्लवमातङ्गदिवाकीर्तिजनङ्गमाः' इत्यमरः. It would be better to read जनङ्गमाङ्गनाम् as C and T suggest. वंशबाह्याम्—(1) which is outside of (noble) family; (2) which is to be borne on bamboo-poles. बाह्य in the latter case is equal to वाह्य, as there is no difference between ब and व, र and ल, ड and ल in यमक, श्लेष and चित्र 'यमकश्लेषचित्रेषु बवयोर्डलयोर्न भित्। नानुस्वारविसर्गौ च चित्रभङ्गाय संमतौ ॥' वाग्भटालंकार I. 20. चण्डालs carry all their belongings on poles. अनार्याम् (1) disreputable; (2) not of Aryan lineage. The चण्डालs were outside the pale of Âryan society. दग्ध...कुलिरिव as a bird in a burnt dwelling. दग्धगृहे may also mean 'in this palace accursed' (by the king's death). स्नेहमल is to be connected with मनसि and वाससि. स्नेह (1) affection (2) oil. Affection clung to his heart and he wanted to get rid of it in a hermitage. An oily and dirty spot sticks to a garment which must be washed in water. अन्तरितानि यौवनसौख्यानि यस्याम् in which the pleasures of youth cannot be had (*adj.* of जरां and ०चिन्ताम्). The cares of the kingdom would not allow हर्ष to enjoy youth as otherwise he would have done. अनभिमताम् not esteemed or liked (with जराम् and चिन्ताम्). जरामिव पूरुः—ययाति married देवयानी daughter of शुक्र preceptor of the दैत्यs. शर्मिष्ठा, daughter of the king of

दैत्यs, was her servant. ययाति fell in love with her and secretly married her. When देवयानी complained, her father शुक्र cursed him to be prematurely old. ययाति propitiated शुक्र and obtained permission to transfer his old age to any one that would accept it. He had two sons यदु and तुर्वसु from देवयानी and द्रुह्य, अनु and पूरु from शर्मिष्ठा. All his sons except पूरु refused to take up the decrepitude of their father. पूरु, the youngest, dutifully took it up and was placed on the throne by ययाति. See विष्णुपु. IV. 10; रामायण VII. 58–59; महाभारत आदिपर्व. गुरोः (1) of his father (with पूरु); (2) of me who am your elder (brother). त्यक्ताः सकलाः बालक्रीडाः येन (applies to हर्ष and हरि both). हरिणा = विष्णुना. दीयता...लक्ष्म्यै give your chest to लक्ष्मी. हर्ष is asked to accept sovereignty. विष्णु took लक्ष्मी as his wife. बालक्रीडा—these words suggest the doings of कृष्ण (the incarnation of विष्णु) in गोकुल. रुक्मिणी the wife of कृष्ण is looked upon as the incarnation of लक्ष्मी. 'राघवत्वेऽभवत्सीता रुक्मिणी कृष्णजन्मनि' विष्णु० I. 9. 141. निस्त्रिंशः—a sword—(निष्क्रान्तस्त्रिंशतोऽङ्गुलिभ्यः इति which is longer than 30 finger-breadths).

P. 94 l. 19—**P 95** l. 22 **अथ...तिष्ठत.** निशिता शिखा यस्य the point of which is very sharp. मामन्तरेण concerning me. It may also mean 'without me *i. e.* behind my back.' शोकात् जन्म यस्य (*adj.* of ०क्षेपः). चेतसः समाक्षेपः Distraction or aberration of mind. आहो...भवति ? Is it possible that he is not my brother ? The idea is that he speaks so unlike my brother that I am forced to doubt whether he is the same as my brother. विवक्षितं = वक्तुमिष्टम्. निपातनोपायः a means of decline or downfall. निखिलपुण्यस्य परिक्षयः तस्य उपक्षेपः (indication). कर्मणां is to be connected with निखिल०. The idea is :—do these unexpected words of my brother indicate that all the merit I gathered by my actions has now been exhausted ? अन...लसितं वा or is it the wanton act of the group of all unfavourable planets ? तातस्य विनाशेन निःशङ्कः (fearless) कलिकालः तस्य क्रीडितम् (prank, freak). The idea is that प्रभाकर० had held कलि in cheek. अयं—refers to राज्य० यःकश्चिदिव like a low person. यत्किंचनकारिणं माम्—connect with समादिष्टवान्. यत्किंच...म्भूतमिव (he has ordered) me (thinking me) capable of doing anything, as if I were not born of the line of पुष्पभूति. अनात्मानुजमिव as if I were not his own younger brother. The reading अदृष्टदोषमपि breaks the symmetry of the clauses, all of which contain an इव; but yields a good sense. The reading दृष्टदोषमिव of A and C means 'as if I were one detected in committing a fault.' श्रोत्रियमिव—What Harsha says is this:—to ask me to assume sovereign power when my elder brother is quite competent to do it is as detestable as to ask a श्रोत्रिय to drink wine, to induce a faithful servant to prove treacherous to his master &c. सुरापान was one of the five महापातकs, for which see above p. 84. नीचोपसर्पणम् to approach or wait upon a nean person. तदे...यत् This much (out of what राज्य० does) is indeed befitting that &c. शौर्यस्य उन्मादः एव मदिरा तया मत्तं समस्तं सामन्तमण्डलं एव समुद्रः तस्य मथने मन्दरः तस्मिन्. The feudatories intoxicated by the pride of valour are compared to the ocean; as the ocean was churned with मन्दर as the churning handle, so प्रभाकर० was the churning handle of the kings (*i. e.* subdued them and made them yield tribute as the ocean had to yield jewels). For मन्दर, see above p. 42. For the technical meaning of मण्डल, see p. 42. The king प्रभा० was in the midst of the मण्डल as the handle मन्दर was in the midst of the ocean. The ocean also had मदिरा (वारुणी, one of the 14 jewels). या...वृष्टिः as for this command to me to assume sovereignty, it scorches me who am already burnt and is a shower of cinders on me who am like a desert parched by drought. अवग्रहेण (वृष्टेर्विघातेन) ग्लपितः (past p. p. of the causal of ग्लै). धन्वन् *m.* a barren or dry soil. 'समानौ मरुधन्वानौ' इत्यमरः. 'वृष्टिर्वर्षं तद्विघातेऽवग्राहावग्रहौ समौ' इत्यमरः. यद्यपि...मानः—supply जगति दुर्लभः after this and after every-one of the following clauses. विभु...मानः a person in power without pride. द्विजातिः = ब्राह्मणः. अविद्यमाना एषणा (greed, covetousness) यस्य. मुनिररोषणः a sage without anger. The Purâṇas illustrate only too well this *dictum*. वणि...रः a trader who is not a thief (knave). प्रिया जाया यस्य स० जानिः. जाया becomes जानि when it is the last member of a बहुव्रीहि compound. 'जायाया निङ्' पा. 5. 4. 134. प्रिय...हनः (it is rare to find) a husband fond of his wife who is also not jealous. कुहन *adj.* jealous. 'कुहना दम्भचर्यायामीर्ष्यालौ कुहनं त्रिपु' इति मेदिनी. कीना...गतः (it is rare to find) a poor man who is not an eyesore. 'कृतान्ते पुंसि कीनाशः क्षुद्रकर्षकयोस्त्रिषु' इत्यमरः. मृगयुः a hunter. पारा...ब्राह्मण्यः (it is rare to find) a mendicant who possesses the qualities of a (good) ब्राह्मण. पाराशरिन् originally means 'one who studies the भिक्षुसूत्र promulgated by पाराशर्य'; hence any mendicant (whether learned in the Vedānta or not). 'पाराशर्यशिलालिभ्यां भिक्षुनटसूत्रयोः' पा. 4. 3. 110 (पाराशर्येण प्रोक्तं भिक्षुसूत्रमधीयते पाराशरिणो भिक्षवः । सि. कौ.). कितवः a gambler. The reading of A

विद्रुतं चेतः यस्य whose heart was melted or agitated. पर्याकुलं वासः यस्य whose dress was disorderly. निवारणे उद्यतं मनः यस्य. नखेन लिखितं मणिकुट्टिमं (jewelled pavement) यैः—when a person is in reverie, he often scratches the pavement with his nails. प्रज्ञाततमः extremely well-known. विमुक्तः आक्रन्दः येन.

P. 95 l. 32—**P. 41** l. 8 **अथ...इति.** अस्माकं व्यसनं तस्मिन् व्यवसायः तस्य वर्धनं तस्मिन् बद्धा धृतिः येन (*adj.* of विधिः) that is fi·m in increasing its efforts (व्यवसाय) to bring down calamities on us. अधृतिकरम् causing loss of steadiness of mind. The sentence is विधिः इतः अधिकतरं अधृतिकरं किं अपरं दुःखातिशयं समुपनयति. छिद्रेषु प्रहर्तुं शीलं एषां इति छिद्र० that strike at a weak point. अवनिपतिः = प्रभाकरवर्धनः. ग्रहवर्मा मालवराजेन जीवलोकं त्याजितः—ग्रह० was made to leave this world (*i. e.* was killed) by the king of Mālvā. Dr. Buhler suggested that देवगुप्त was the name of the Mālava king and that मालव is not Mālvā in Central India, but the Mālvā in Punjab near Thanesar (E. I. Vol. I. p. 70). Vide Introduction. आत्मनः...त्याजितः—(the मालव king) in killing ग्रहवर्मा made his own (मालवराज's) merit to leave himself. The idea is that he by that act became bereft of all पुण्य if he had any. This is a fine example of the figure सहोक्ति. कालायसनिगडयुगलेन चुम्बितौ चरणौ यस्याः. निगडः chains. कान्यकुब्जे—the modern Kanoj, which seems to have been the capital of the Maukhari ग्रहवर्मा. किंवदन्ती rumour. अ...मत्वा thinking that the army is without a leader. The reference is to the army of Thanesar. **'साधनं** मृतसंस्कारे **सैन्ये** सिद्धौषधे गतौ' इति मेदिनी. जिघृक्षुः desirous of seizing (this kingdom).

P.96 ll. 9–34 **ततश्च...दिदेश.** अनुपेक्षणीय—not fit to be treated with indifference. व्यतिकरः occurrence, calamity. **'अथ व्यतिकरः** पुंसि **व्यसन**व्यतिषङ्गयोः' मेदिनी. अश्रुत...भवस्य humiliation not having been even heard of before (by राज्य०). The author assigns reasons why the deep-seated affliction of राज्य० at once disappeared. परिभव refers to the treatment meted out to राज्यश्री, the sister of राज्य०. वीर...जन्मनः because his birth was in a family of heroes. कृपा...भूतायाः who now became an object for compassion (because she was widowed and imprisoned). बद्धं मूलं येन that had taken deep root. ललाट...भिद्यत on his forehead a frightful frown of the eyebrow appeared. The frowning brow is compared to यमुना, the sister of यम, the waters of which are dark (श्यामायमाना). The brow also is dark. केशिनिषूदनः (कृष्णः) तस्मात् शङ्का (fear) तया आकुलं कालियकुलं तस्य भङ्गुरा भ्रूः तस्याः

भङ्गैः तरङ्गिणी—The river had ripples owing to the knitting of the brows of the family of the serpent कालिय that was afraid of कृष्ण. The eyebrow of राज्य० also presented a wavy appearance on account of the frowns it had. केशिन् was a दैत्य in the form of a horse sent by कंस to kill कृष्ण in वृन्दावन. कृष्ण put his hand in its mouth, when it increased. Kes'in was cut in two. See विष्णु पु० V. 16. कालिय—the reference is to कालियमर्दन. The serpent was in the waters of the यमुना and rendered it poisonous. No tree except a कदम्ब grew on its banks. कृष्ण threw himself from the कदम्ब into the Jumna and trod upon the hoods of the serpent. The serpent and its wives begged कृष्ण to show mercy. कृष्ण said 'नात्र स्थेयं त्वया सर्प कदाचिद्यमुनाजले। सभृत्यपरिवारस्त्वं समुद्रसलिलं व्रज ॥ मत्पदानि च ते सर्प दृष्ट्वा मूर्धनि सागरे। गरुडः पन्नगरिपुस्त्वयि न प्रहरिष्यति ॥'. विष्णुपु. V. 7. 75-76. यमुना was the daughter of सूर्य and संज्ञा and sister of यम. See मार्कण्डेयपु० 77. परामृशन् (*adj.* of ०पल्लवः) rubbing or striking. दिङ्नागस्य (दिग्गजस्य) कुम्भकूटवत् विकटः तस्य—that was as broad (or formidable) as the conical head front of a दिग्गज. For कुम्भ, see p. 109. बाहु...पल्लवः—with his left hand he stroked the upper part of his (right) arm, as wrestlers do when they get ready for a wrestling match. The word कोष is used because the upper part looked like a bud. नख...षेकमिव चकार—When he stroked his arm with his hand, the rays of the nails, which looked like water, brightened it. Hence the poet fancies that the arm was bathed in the water (rays of nails) in order to honour it preparatory to undertaking the responsibility of a fight. The com. says that कोष is an ordeal. With this sense all the words cannot be explained. But it is possible to explain some. Before the ordeal, the person charged had to bathe (अभिषेक). The कोश ordeal is described as follows in the व्यवहारमयूख 'तमाहूयाभिशस्तं तु मण्डलाभ्यन्तरे स्थितम्। आदित्याभिमुखं कृत्वा पाययेत्प्रसृतित्रयम् ॥ पूर्वोक्तेन विधानेन स्नातमार्द्राम्बरं शुचिम्। अर्चयित्वा तु तं देवं प्रक्षाल्य सलिलेन तु। एनश्च श्रावयित्वा तु पाययेत्प्रसृतित्रयम् ॥'. सङ्गलत् स्वेदसलिलं तेन पूरितं उदरं यस्य (*adj.* of पाणिरपरः). निर्मूलं...केश इव as if he had seized the hair (of the Mālava king) in order to tear him up by the roots. His wrath made him perspire and quiver and made his right hand seize his sword. The dark sword resembles केश. So the poet fancies he seized not the sword but the hair of मालवराज. दुर्मद...ण्ठयेव as if eager to seize the hair of the haughty Glory (in amorous sport). स्वेद and कम्प are two of the eight

सात्त्विकभावs; these two and रोमाञ्च are often described when lovers meet. Compare 'आसीद्वरः कण्टकितप्रकोष्ठः स्विन्नाङ्गुलिः संववृते कुमारी' रघु० 7. 22. पुनरपि—We saw above (text p. 39 l. 18) that राज्य० laid down his sword on the earth. शस्त्रग्रहणेन मुदिता राजलक्ष्मीः तया क्रियमाणा दिष्टवृद्धिः (congratulation) तस्यां विधुता सिन्दूरधूलिः. Even now at marriage celebrations and other festivities, red powder is sprinkled over people. For दिष्टवृद्धि see above p. 11. समासन्नाः सकलमहीपालाः तेषां चूडामणीनां चक्रं तस्य आक्रमणेन जातः अहङ्कारः यस्य. He sat in a posture peculiar to warriors of old. His upturned right foot he placed on his left thigh and the left foot was placed on the ground. निष्ठुरं अङ्गुष्ठेन कषणं (rubbing) तेन निष्ठ्यूता (emitted) धूमलेखा येन. निर्वी...शिख इव as if he had let loose the knot of hair on his head for making the earth void of (rival) heroes. He violently rubbed his toe against the pavement and a streak of smoke was thereby produced. This is dark and hence fancied to be a knot of hair (शिखा). An irascible person may take a vow not to tie up his hair until his enemies are uprooted, as चाणक्य did. Vide मुद्राराक्षस III. 29. 'शिखां मोक्तुं मुक्तामपि पुनरयं धावति करः'; VII. 17 'पूर्णप्रतिज्ञेन मया केवलं बध्यते शिखा ॥'. The word विमुक्तशिखः may suggest another meaning. He violently pressed his toe against the ground whereby a dark line of smoke was produced. That indicated that he was about to give out a flame (शिखा). Fire burns the earth and frees it of Arjuna trees. 'नदीसर्जो वीरतरुरिन्द्रद्रुः ककुभोऽर्जुनः' इत्यमरः. वीर also means 'reeds'. दर्पेण स्फुटिताः सरसाः व्रणाः तेभ्यः उच्छलितं (sent up, spurted) रुधिरं तस्य छटा तया अवसेकः. राज्यवर्धन's wounds were fresh and by his agitation they again cracked and blood began to flow. प्रबोधयन्निव—has two senses. When one faints through poison, water is sprinkled over to rouse him. The blood served to rouse his valour that had been inert owing to sorrow. राज्य० also wanted to give advice to हर्ष. इदं...प्रजाः—what he means is :—I leave these as they are; you must look after them; I cannot do it; I have only one task to discharge. भूपतिः (प्रभाकरवर्धनः) तस्य भुजौ परिघौ (bar, bolt) इव. अत्यन्तं अविनीतः (wicked, ill-mannered) अरिः तस्य निग्रहः. सोऽयं...वंशस्य च—The construction is यो मौखराणां मालवैः परिभवः...सोऽयं कुरङ्गकैः कचग्रहः केसरिणः—that the Mālavas should insult the Maukharas and the line of पुष्पभूति is like the seizure of the hair of the lion by deer. करपातः slapping. वत्सकै...ग्रस्य the taking of the tiger as a captive by calves.

अलगर्दे: a water-serpent. गरुड is the enemy of all serpents and shows no mercy to them. 'अलगर्दो जलव्यालः' इत्यमरः. अयुतं ten thousand.

P. 97 ll. 1–24 **तं च...मित्रम्.** जामि: sister. 'जामिः स्वसृकुलस्त्रियोः' इत्यमरः. ०विज्ञानेन प्रकोपः तस्य आधानं (production) तेन दूयमाने. दूरं प्ररूढा प्रणयपीडा यस्य. मनसि...पीड इव when his mind had pain due to love (for राज्य०) much augmented by the plea that he (हर्ष) should return (remain behind). The reading निवर्तनादेशेन (by the order of राज्य० to stay behind) is much better. कमिव...गमनेन what possible harm does my lord see in my following (my lord)? यदि...सि if you raise the objection that I am a mere boy, that is a greater reason why I should not be left behind. 'बाल आ षोडशाद्वर्षात्'. This passage may be looked upon as indicating that हर्ष was about sixteen at this time. रक्षणीय...स्थानम्—If you assign for my staying behind the reason that I need protection (and therefore should not be taken on a campaign), then your arms are a cage for me. What greater protection can there be than your own powerful arm? सं...करोति—if you say that I am not to be taken with you because I require to be carefully brought up, then separation from you will make me thin (whatever other care may be bestowed on me in your absence). स्त्री...सि then I am placed among women *i. e.* I am treated just as women (who are delicate and unable to bear hardships). तत् (सुखं) प्रयाति—all my happiness, being centred in you, marches with you. विरहो...तरः separation from you is more difficult to bear (than even the toils of the journey). कलत्रं...वसति—the idea seems to be :—you may say that you leave me behind because you want me to guard your harem; but then Glory (which is really the only wife you care to have) dwells in your sword *i. e.* Glory, the only wife you should have, is taken by you on your sword and not placed under protection. राज्य० was to secure Glory by his sword. C and T translate 'if you would have me watch over my wife &c.'; but this does not appear to be correct. There is no connection between हर्ष's watching over his own wife and the fact of Glory residing in his brother's sword. पृष्ठ...ताप: if you leave me behind (to guard your rear), that is unnecessary, as your valour remains behind (and will guard everything). राज...गुणे: if you say that the circle of princes will be without supervision, then (I say there is no need for it as) the princes are well secured by your virtues. A person is also bound (बद्ध) with ropes (गुण). न...गणयसि if you say that a great man (like yourself) does not require an outsider as a companion, then you count me as distinct from yourself. I regard myself and yourself as identical. प्रलघुः (very small) परिकरः (retinue, train). लघु also means light (in weight). पाद...भारः what great weight is there in the dust of your feet? हर्ष means that he is like the dust of his brother's feet and so there is no भार (weight, responsibility) in taking him on the expedition. द्वयो...श्रया If you argue that it is not proper that both of us should go, then favour me by ordering *me* to go (and you may remain behind). सदृशो दोषः the idea is :—if you leave me behind because you are afraid out of your affection for me (of what may befall me) then I say I am afraid of what may befall you in my absence. So this fault of कातरत्व is common to both of us and should not be urged against me alone, according to the न्यायवैशेषिक maxim 'यत्रोभयोः समो दोषः परिहारोऽपि वा समः । नैकः पर्यनुयोक्तव्यस्तादृगर्थ विचारणे ॥' तर्कभाषा. आत्मम्भरिता selfishness, greed. 'फलेग्रहिरात्मम्भरिश्च' पा. 3. 2. 26 (आत्मानं बिभर्तीति). क्षीरोदफेनपटलवत् or–पटलेन पाण्डुरम्. Fame is poetically represented as white. The foam of the milky ocean must be very white. When अमृत was churned out of the ocean, it must have been white with the foam &c. अव...देषु I have never before been deceived (*i. e.* deprived) of favours *i. e.* you always granted whatever favours I asked. अति...हितः why should a very insignificant foe be given great importance by making too great a preparation? हरि...म्भारः a host of lions for (catching) a hare causes great shame. ह्रेपण—from ह्रेपयति, causal of ह्री 3rd *conj.* कवचयन्ति put on armour. आशुशुक्षणयः—fires. This is a word used more in the Vedas. अष्टादश द्वीपाः एव अष्टमङ्गलकं तस्य माला अस्ति अस्याः that is wreathed with the bracelet in the form of the eighteen द्वीपs. The com. says 'अष्टमङ्गलकं कङ्कणमित्यन्ये.' A horse is called अष्टमङ्गलक. कुल...वाहिनः blowing against the group of principal mountains. For the कुलपर्वतs, see p. 39. न संनह्यन्ति do not gird up their loins, do not put on armour. सुमेरोः वप्रः (slope) तस्मिन् प्रणयः (liking) तेन प्रगल्भाः (bold) or सुमेरौ वप्रः (butting) तस्मिन् &c. For सुमेरु, see pp. 8, 85. न परिणमन्ति do not stoop to strike with their tusks. Elephants and bulls are represented as butting against the slopes of hills and mounds of earth. सकलपृथ्वीपतीनां प्रलयस्व

उत्पाते धूमकेतुम् that (bow) is a comet portending the destruction of all kings. For धूमकेतु as an उत्पात, see above p. 89. मान्धाता इव—see p. 23 above. चारुः चामीकरपत्रलता एव अलङ्कारः स एव अङ्कः यस्य स०राङ्कः, ०राङ्कः कायः यस्य—the frame of which is marked with ornamental and charming figures in gold. 'चामीकरं जातरूपं महारजतकाञ्चने' इत्यमरः (चमीकरे आकरे भवम्). विं...तायाम् in the hunger for destroying my enemy that has been roused in me. एकाकिनः goes with मम. राज्य० says 'do not claim a share in killing मालवराज; let me alone secure him as my victim'. अयं कोपकवलः एकः this one morsel of my wrath. The morsel is the king of Mālvā. अभ्यमित्रम्—अमित्रस्य अभिमुखम् (अव्ययीभाव).

P. 97 l. 25—**P. 98** l. 13 **अथ...करोत्.** तथागते भ्रातरि his brother being in that condition (*i. e.* so occupied). There is another suggested meaning. तथागत is a name of बुद्ध. 'सर्वज्ञः सुगतो बुद्धो धर्मराजस्तथागतः' इत्यमरः. So the meaning is 'his brother having become a Buddha' (*i. e.* having died in the Buddhist faith). We learn from the Madhuban inscription (see Introduction) that राज्यवर्धन was a very devout Buddhist. दत्तः प्रजागरः यस्मै: who was kept awake. तृतीयो भागः त्रिमागः, त्रिभागः शेषः यस्याः. यामिकः watchman. द्वीपैः उपगीताः गुणाः (virtues, cables) यस्य. A ship also has गुणs (cables, ropes); a ship is laden with heaps of jewels or rich merchandise of every description. रत्नराशि may also mean 'the sea' (generally called रत्नाकर). Ships bring the essence of the sea *i. e.* the best things from beyond the seas. This verse is suggestive of the fall of राज्य०. अनि...वनया by the thought of the evanescent nature (of things). प्रक्षीणं भूयिष्ठं यस्याः when (night) had almost come to an end. Dreams seen in the early morning were believed to come to be true. अभ्रंलिहम् touching the clouds. This is another indication of the fall of the mighty राज्य०. अनुबध्नन्ति persistently follow. अकल्याणस्य आख्याने विचक्षणम् clever in announcing evil. The throbbing of the left eye and arm in the case of men portends evil. अक्षु...क्षाणाः declaring the downfall of no mean king. अविकलः कायबन्धः यस्य whose bodily frame is not maimed, is perfect. कबन्ध...बिम्बे in the disc of the sun that has a headless trunk. 'भास्कराहस्करब्रध्नप्रभाकरविभाकराः' इत्यमरः. राहु is a demon without trunk and is all head. In the disc of the sun a headless trunk was seen and thus राहु was as if provided with a complete body when it seized the sun. विभाव्यते is seen. See above text p. 27 l. 9. (भानुमण्डले भयङ्करकबन्धकायव्याजेन). The बृहत्संहिता says 'दण्डे नरेन्द्रमृत्युर्व्या-

धिभयं स्यात्कबन्धसंस्थाने ।' (III. 17.). सप्तर्षयः—the constellation of the Great Bear. The Great Bear emitted a dark smoke-like streak and thereby darkened all the planets. The poet fancies that the smoke emitted is what they had taken in while performing तपः. To inhale only smoke is a kind of तपः. The बृहत्संहिता (13. 7) says 'उल्काशनिधूमाद्यैर्हता विवर्णा विरश्मयो ह्रस्वाः । हन्युः स्वं स्वं वर्गं विपुलाः स्निग्धाश्च तद्वृद्ध्यै ॥'. दिशां दाहाः—Note बृहत्संहिता 'दाहो दिशां राजभयाय पीतो देशस्य नाशाय हुताशवर्णः ।' (31. 1.) and 'योऽतीव दीप्त्या कुरुते प्रकाशं छायामपि व्यञ्जयतेऽर्कवच्चः । राज्ञो महद्वेदयते भयं सः' &c. (31. 2.). तारागणः—the falling stars appear like the particles of ashes due to दिग्दाह. The falling of stars is looked upon as an evil omen. See बृहत्संहिता (33. 11) 'अम्बरमध्याद्बह्व्यो निपतन्त्यो राजराष्ट्रनाशाय ।'. तारा…शुचेव—the moon is called तारानाथ or नक्षत्रेश; the poet fancies that the moon, the lord of stars, was grieved at their fall and therefore lost colour. The उल्काs appear like so many missiles in the battle of the planets. विलोलाः तारकाः यासां or यासु (1) the pupils of which are unsteady; (2) the stars in which fall down. The quarters are compared to ladies frightened at the sight of a battle. सञ्चारयतीव क्ष्मां as if carries the earth. वहत् बहलं रजःपटलं तेन कलिलः शर्कराशकलैः सूत्कारी च whistling with bits of gravel and full of flying (वहत्) and thick clouds of dust. न … लग्नस्य I don't see that this hour is auspicious. For लग्न, see pp. 24, 60. असिन्न…पन्थी who will obstruct fate when it seizes even a delicate scion in our family as an elephant seizes the tender shoot of a bamboo (वंशः). The scion is राज्यवर्धन. करीरः—रम् shoot of a bamboo; shoot in general. 'वंशाङ्कुरे करीरोऽस्त्री' इत्यमरः. द्रवदिव—his heart melted or was wet with स्नेह (oil or affection). Another meaning is—his heart was broken inside and was as if running away (द्रवत्); but he somehow kept it firm. यथा…करोत् he performed all his various duties, as he was in the habit of doing them.

P. 98 ll. 14–23 **आस्थान … श्रौषीत्.** असह्यं दुःखं तेन उष्णाः निश्वासाः तेषां धूमः तेन रक्ताः (coloured) तन्तवः यस्य. His body was dressed in dirty clothes. The author fancies that the mud was the smoke of his hot breaths, which (smoke) coloured the threads. जीवित…लज्जया—he was ashamed that he should continue to live after his master's death. नासा…दृष्टिम् whose eye was fixed on the tip of his long nose. दुःखेन दूरप्ररूढानि रोमाणि यस्मिन् on which there was a long growth due to sorrow. His face, though mute, told the tale by the long growth of beard. बृहदश्ववार: a great horseman, an officer of cavalry. अभिजाततम of very noble birth.. चक्षुषि सलिलेन—supply अगृह्यत—water (tears) came to his eyes. उत्सङ्गे भुवा the earth came to his lap *i. e.* he lay on the bare earth (in grief). अगृह्यत लोकपालैः—वरुण (the lord of सलिल), the wind, the fire are among the eight लोकपाल्स 'सोमाग्न्यर्कानिलेन्द्राणां वित्ताप्पत्योर्यमस्य च। अष्टानां लोकपालानां वपुर्धारयते नृपः ॥' मनु 5. 96. तस्मात्—from कुन्तल. हेलया (easily) निर्जितं मालवानीकं येन. मिथ्योपचारैः उपचितः विश्वासः यस्मिन् in whom trust was increased by false civilities.

P. 98 l. 24—**P. 99** l. 4 श्रुत्वा...यासीत्. ०कोपः एव पावकः तस्य प्रसरेण परिचीयमानः (increased) शोकावेगः यस्य. The principal sentence is ततश्च...परां भीषणतां अयासीत्. अमर्षेण (क्रोधेन) विधुतं शिरः तस्मात् शीर्यमाणानि शिखामणीनां शकलानि तैः अङ्गारकितम्. Pieces of jewels from his crest were scattered about when he shook his head in wrath, which (pieces) looked like the live coals of the fire of wrath he sent forth. अङ्गारकित is formed from अङ्गारक on the analogy of तारकित, for which see p. 98. रोष...च्छेदन with his lip that was curved through wrath. When a man drinks anything he moves his lips and makes them curved. लोहितायमाने (becoming red) लोचने तयोः आलोकः (light) तस्य विक्षेपैः (casting). He cast glances with his blood-shot eyes in all directions, which were thereby made lurid. For दिग्दाह, see above (text l. 5). रोषानलेनापि—connect with वितन्यमान. असह्यः सहजशौर्योष्मदहनः तेन दह्यमानेन. वितन्यमानं ०दुर्दिनं (स्वेदसलिलशीकराणां आसारः एव दुर्दिनं) यस्मिन्. His wrath made him perspire and drops of perspiration stood out like drops of rain on his body. When one is oppressed with heat, one sprinkles drops of water over one's body. The poet imagines that the perspiration was water sprinkled by the fire of his wrath over itself, being afraid of the hotter and unbearable fire of his inborn valour. पूर्वं अदृष्टः अदृष्टपूर्वः कोपः तस्मात् भीतैः. His limbs shook through wrath; the poet fancies that his limbs were afraid of his wrath which they had never seen before. A terror-stricken man trembles. हरः=शिवः. कृतः भैरवः भयङ्करः आकारः येन (with राज्य०); कृतः भैरवस्य आकारः येन (with हरः) who assumed the form of भैरव. भैरव is the name of a terrible form of शिव. हरिः=विष्णुः. प्रकटितं नरसिंहरूपं येन (1) who presented the appearance of a brave man; (2) who manifested the Man-Lion form. In the latter case the reference is to the नृसिंह incarnation of Vishnu, for which see above p. 39.

Words like सिंह are employed to denote pre-eminence, bravery &c.' 'स्युरुत्तरपदे व्याघ्रपुङ्गवर्षभकुञ्जराः। सिंहशार्दूलनागाद्याः पुंसि श्रेष्ठार्थगोचराः॥' इत्यमरः. नरः सिंह इव (कर्म०). अपरस्य तेजःप्रसरः तस्य दर्शनेन प्रज्वलितः that burst forth into flame at the sight of the spread of another's brilliance. राज्य० was fired by the action of his foe (the गौड king); the सूर्यकान्त emits fire at the sight of the sun (a second source of light). Compare for the idea 'न तेजस्तेजस्वी प्रसृतमपरेषां प्रसहते स तस्य स्वो भावः प्रकृतिनियत्वादकृतकः। मयूखैरश्रान्तं तपति यदि देवो दिनकरः किमाग्नेयग्रावा निकृत इव तेजांसि वमति॥' उत्तरराम० VI. 14. क्षय—दिवसः = कल्पान्तदिवसः. उदिताः द्वादश दिनकराः तैः दुर्निरीक्ष्या मूर्तिः यस्य (with दिवसः). ०दिनकरवत् दुर्निरीक्ष्या मूर्तिः यस्य (with राज्य०). For कल्पान्त, see above p. 78. At the time of प्रलय, it is supposed that twelve suns simultaneously rise in the sky. Compare 'दग्धुं विश्वं दहनकिरणैर्नोदिता द्वादशार्काः' वेणीसंहार III; 'यावत्प्राणिमि तावदस्य कल्पान्तोदितद्वादशदिनकरकिरणातपतीव्रस्य' &c. कादम्बरी (p. 156 of P). महो...कारी who caused trembling to all भूभृत्s (kings, mountains) like a portentous hurricane. विवर्धमानः विग्रहस्य (शरीरस्य) उत्सेधः (sublimity, height) यस्य—(1) the grandeur of whose form increased (with राज्य०); (2) whose height increased (with विन्ध्य). The विन्ध्य wanted the sun to revolve round itself as it did round Meru. The sun refused, whereupon the विन्ध्य began to grow higher and higher in order to obstruct the sun's path. The gods in fear sent Agastya who came to the mountain and asked it to allow him to go to the south and to remain in its original state till he returned. अगस्त्य never returned and so विन्ध्य remained low in height. *Vide* महाभारत वनपर्व chap. 104. Compare रामायण 'मार्गं निरोद्धुं सततं भास्करस्याचलोत्तमः। सन्देशं पालयंस्तस्य विन्ध्यशैलो न वर्धते॥' अरण्य० 11. 86. दुर्नरेन्द्रेण (by a wicked king; by a bad snake-charmer) अभिभवः (insult) तेन रोषितः. आशीविषः—आशीसु आशीःषु वा (तालुगतदंष्ट्रासु) विषं अस्य—a serpent. For नरेन्द्र see p. 33. पारीक्षितः = son of परीक्षित् *i. e.* जनमेजय. सर्व...द्यतः who was bent upon burning all भोगिन्s (kings, serpents). परीक्षित्, the grandson of अर्जुन, died of snake-bite and जनमेजय made a resolve to extirpate the whole serpent race in revenge. He instituted a सर्पसत्र in which all serpents were burnt except तक्षक who was saved by the intercession of the sage आस्तीक, at whose request the sacrifice was closed. See महाभारत आदि० chap. 49-58. 'उरगः पन्नगो भोगी' इत्यमरः ('भोगः सर्पदेहः कुटिला गतिर्वास्यास्तीति' क्षीर०). 'भोगी भुजङ्गमेऽपिस्याद्ग्रासपात्रे नृपे पुमान्' मेदिनी. वृकोदरः = भीमः. He took a vow to kill दुःशासन when the latter dragged द्रौपदी by her hair and called the पाण्डवs 'गौगौं:' and killed and drank his blood. See कर्णपर्व chap. 83 'सत्यां चिकीर्षुर्मतिमान्प्रतिज्ञां भीमोऽपिबच्छोणितमस्य कोष्णम् ।' 29. सुरगजः = ऐरावतः. प्रतिपक्षस्य वारणाय प्रधावितः who ran to repel his foe (with राज्य०); प्रतिपक्षश्चासौ वारणश्च (गजश्च) तस्मिन् प्रधावितः who ran *i. e.* attacked a rival elephant. पूर्वा...षस्य who was the first advent of prowess. आगमः may also be taken in the sense of 'tradition, revealed scriptures, Veda.' It is believed that the Veda is eternal and that in each कल्प there is only a fresh manifestation. Hence the word पूर्व. उन्माद इव मदस्य—he was the fullest realization of मद. आवेग...लेपस्य the impetuous onrush of haughtiness. सर्वोद्योगः the full endeavour. यु...ष्मणः the inauguration of an era of youthful warmth. रणरसः passion for fighting. For नीराजन, see above p. 78. On the day of नीराजन, a king marches on an expedition. The idea is that he was the marching day of असहिष्णुता *i. e.* असहिष्णुता was to become active in his person from that day.

P. 99 l 5—**P. 102** l. 18 **अवादीच...व्यरंसीत्.** ०पुरुषं goes with आर्यम् (राज्यवर्धनम्). निर्व्याज...शस्त्रं who subdued all the kings by his valour that is free from stratagem and who had laid aside his weapon (this applies to both राज्य० and द्रोणाचार्य). कलशयोर्नि = द्रोणं. As to the birth of द्रोण see आदिपर्व 63. 6 'भरद्वाजस्य च स्कन्नं द्रोण्यां शुक्रमवर्धत । महर्षेरुग्रतपसस्तस्माद्द्रोणो व्यजायत ॥'. In the great महाभारत war, once an elephant named अश्वत्थामा was killed and the report spread that अश्वत्थामा, the son of द्रोण, was killed. द्रोण asked धर्म, who replied 'हतः कुञ्जरः'. The last word was uttered in a low tone. The old man heard only the first word and in grief for his son laid aside his weapon when धृष्टद्युम्न killed him. See द्रोणपर्व chap. 190. कृष्णवर्त्मा (अग्निः) तस्मात् प्रसूतिः यस्य सः ०सूतिः धृष्टद्युम्नः. About the birth of धृष्टद्युम्नः see द्रोणपर्व chap. 191. 2 'य इष्ट्वा मनुजेन्द्रेण द्रुपदेन महामखे । लब्धो द्रोणविनाशाय समिद्धाद्धव्यवाहनात् ।'. The word कृष्ण० further means 'who is the source of dark paths *i. e.* dark deeds' (as applied to गौडाधिप and also धृष्टद्युम्न). इंद्दशेन मृत्युना—the reference is to the treachery practised by the गौड king. अनार्य...पातम्—the sentence is अनार्यं तं मुक्त्वा...केषां मनःसु आर्यशौर्यगुणाः पक्षपातं न कुर्युः—Excepting that vile wretch, in whose minds would not my lord's valour and other qualities produce a favourable impression ? भागिरथी...पाण्डुराः—The waters of the Ganges are white; the foam would be whiter still. Both राजहंस and the qualities are white like the foam. The राजहंसs cause

पक्षपात (movement with or flight on their wings) in the मानस lake (मनःसु सरःसु). पर...कृतः (1) that remind one of the valour of परशुराम (with ०गुणाः); (2) that remember the valour of परशुराम (with ०हंसाः). परशुराम, while he was learning धनुर्विद्या from शिव, being jealous of the power of स्कन्द who had once by his missile called शक्ति pierced the mountain क्रौञ्च, shot an arrow through that mountain and made a passage, through which it was believed the हंसs passed from the plains to the मानस lake. बाण perhaps derived his inspiration from the मेघदूत 'प्रालेयाद्रेरुपतटमतिक्रम्य तांस्तान्विशेषान् हंसद्वारं भृगुपतियशोवर्त्म यत्क्रौञ्चरन्ध्रम् ॥'. In the वनपर्व chap. 225. 33 'बिभेद स शरैः शैलं क्रौञ्चं हिमवतः सुतम् । तेन हंसाश्च गृध्राश्च मेरुं गच्छन्ति पर्वतम् ॥', it is स्कन्द who makes a hole for हंसs. अत्युग्रस्य— applies to गौडाधिप and निदाघरवि. कम...शोषणे in drying up the water of the bed of lotuses. The summer sun dries up the water in which lotuses grow. राज्यवर्धन is compared to कमलाकर, because he was also कमलाकर (the abode of लक्ष्मी) and सलिल to जीवित. अनपेक्षिता प्रीतिः यैः that paid no heed to his friendship (with the hands of गौडाधिप); that paid no heed to the bloom (*lit.* happiness) of the lotuses (with 'the rays of the summer sun'). गतिम् fate, state (after death). कस्मिन्नरके—In the विष्णुपु० (II. 6) a large number of hells such as रौरव is mentioned. So also in the मार्कण्डेयपु० chap. 10 and 12. श्वपाकः = चण्डालः. Construe पापकारिणः अस्य नामापि गृह्णतो मे जिह्वा &c. किं...कार्यम् *lit.* undertaking what object *i. e.* with what object in view. आर्यः— connect with तेन क्षयमुपनीतः. क्षुद्रेण goes with both तेन and घुणेन. अनुप्रविश्य who worked himself into favour with my lord; that bores inside (timber). विगता घृणा (दया) यस्य. घुणः—an insect that eats into timber and produces furrowed lines thereon resembling letters. Note the word घुणाक्षरन्याय. राज्य० is compared to a sandal pillar. मधुरसास्वाद (1) taste of honey; (2) taste of wine. भावी कष्ट...द्रवः the coming trouble of the fall of distressing शिलीमुखs (arrows, bees). One who takes away honey from the honeycomb is attacked by the bees. 'अलिबाणौ शिलीमुखौ' इत्यमरः (शिली शल्यं मुखे अस्य). निज...षणं (1) that is a blot on his own family (with अयशः); (2) that renders dirty one's house (with कज्जलं). जाल...केन (1) by one who lights up a path of deceit (with गौडाधमेन); with a lamp placed in a latticed window. Lampblack sticks to windows and mars the brightness of a house. 'जालं समूह आनायो गवाक्षक्षारकावपि' इत्यमरः. जालं deceit. Separate न तु आशु (quickly) अस्तम्. न वेधसादिष्टः शशी is there not the moon ordered by the creator? ग्रह...पः—ग्रहाणां षण्डे (समूहे) विहारः तस्मिन् एकः केवलः हरिणाधिपः सिंहः—who is the sole lion in roaming among the cluster of planets. The moon wanders in the midst of planets. It is compared to a lion, that also roams about in the midst of thickets. There are further suggestions due to paronomasia. विहार may mean 'reducing'. The moon puts into the shade the group of planets. The lion is called मृगाधिप (lord of beasts). The moon is हरिणाधिप because the spot on the moon is supposed to be a deer. 'अब्जादिकदम्बे षण्डमस्त्रियाम्' इत्यमरः. विनयविधायिनि that lays down (*i. e.* teaches) discipline or obedience. व्यालवारणः a wicked or unruly elephant. कुवैकटिकाः bad jewellers. 'मणिकारो वैकटिकः' क्षीर०. तेज...नाशकाः (1) those that destroy the best of spirited men (with तादृशाः); (2) those that destroy brilliant jewels. 'रत्नं स्वजातिश्रेष्ठेऽपि' इत्यमरः. इत्येतदभि (p. 44, l. 22)...विज्ञापितवान् (p. 45, l. 14). The principal sentence is इत्येतत् अभिदधतः एव अस्य (हर्षस्य) पितुः मित्रं सेनापतिः... सन्निधावेव समुपविष्टः सिंहनादनामा विज्ञापितवान्. सम...हरः foremost in all battles. हरितालं (yellow orpiment) तस्य शैलवत् अवदातः (polished, bright) देहः यस्य. परिणतः (full grown) प्रगुणः (straight) सालः (a tree) तस्य प्रकाण्डं (trunk) तत्प्रकाशः तत्सदृशः. अति...गतः that had reached maturity as if on account of the warmth of his great valour. Heat makes a thing ripe; or cooking (पाकः) is effected with heat. C and T translate 'tall as if ripened by valour's exceeding heat.' This is wrong. There is no connecttion whatever between tallness and ripening by heat. गतं भूयिष्ठं यस्य. ०शयने आदौ सुप्तः पश्चादुत्थितः. The सेनापति very often lay wounded with arrows but always got over his wounds. There is another sense. सेनापति (*i. e.* सेनानी) is a name of स्कन्द, who also lay on a bed of शर (reeds). शरजन्मा is a name of स्कन्द. See for the story, रामायण I. 36 and 37. शान्तनवः = भीष्मः, son of शन्तनु and the Ganges. भीष्म also lay wounded on a bed of arrows, waiting for the उत्तरायण, after the advent of which he wanted to die. See भीष्मपर्व chap. 119. 'शरतल्पे महेश्वासं शयानं पुरुषर्षभम् । 92...तानब्रवीच्छान्तनवो नाहं गन्ता कथंचन । दक्षिणावर्ते आदित्ये एतन्मे मनसि स्थितम् ॥' 104. भीष्म was the grand-uncle of the पाण्डवs and yet was the most vigorous of the combatants in the महाभारत war. दु ... तया as his body was such that it could not be subdued (by old age). प्रकटितः प्रकम्पः यया (1) that manifested shaking (in him); (2) प्रकटितः प्रकम्पः यस्याम् (2) that had shaking. A person that is afraid trembles.

Through old age, his limbs shook. The poet fancies that it was जरा (not he) that was trembling, being afraid of touching him. परा...रुहेषु touched in his stiff hair. The idea is that his hair was turning grey. शशिनः कराः तेषां निकरः (समूहः) तद्वत् सिताः सरलाः शिरोरुहाः तैः सटालः (possessed of a mane). His grey hair looked like the lion's mane. He had the same straightforwardness and valour that the lion has. संक्रान्तो...जातिम्—the poet fancies that, even while he was alive, he was transformed into the class of lions. A man may become a lion *after death* (according to the theory of पुनर्जन्म); but he became a lion while living. परिजिहीर्षा desire to avoid. भ्रू...दृष्टिः his eye (or sight) was covered by brows the skin of which was wrinkled, loose and hanging down (over the eye). वलिन—(from वलि + affix न, according to 'लोमादिपामादिपिच्छादिभ्यः शनेलचः' 5. 2. 100 लोमशः। पामनः। पिच्छिलः)—वलयः सन्ति अस्य इति. धवल...मुखेन—in this clause we have first to take विक्रमकालं as qualifying शरदारम्भं and then take शरदारम्भं as qualifying विक्रमकालम्. धवला स्थूला गुञ्जा ('उत्तरोष्ठोपरि रोमराजिः' *com. i. e.* moustache) पिच्छमिव (like a feather) तेन प्रच्छादितः कपोलभागः तेन भास्वरं (bright) तेन (मुखेन). वि...शदं bright with blooming काश thickets. The काश flowers are seen in शरदृतु and are white. वमन्निव विक्रमकालं शरदारम्भं भीमेन मुखेन—The idea is:—The beginning of शरद् is the time to start on an expedition, as the rains are then over. In शरदृतु there are white काश flowers. On his face, he had white moustache resembling काश flowers. So the poet fancies that he vomited from his mouth शरदारम्भ, the time for expedition. अकालेऽपि—the force of this is:—in his old age, his moustache is white at all seasons. So he appears to vomit शरदृतु with its काश flowers at all seasons *i. e.* even when it is वसन्त or ग्रीष्म &c. Then there is a further suggestion. The विक्रमकाल (era so called) is used in the whole of northern India except Bengal and the year commences in चैत्र (except in Gujrat where it begins in कार्तिक). Hence the word अकालेऽपि is used. To Bāna, a विक्रम year beginning in शरद् would be अकाल. For a brief resume about the origin of the विक्रम era, see I. A. vol. 30 pp 3 and 4. शरदि आरम्भः यस्य सः विक्रमकालः. His white beard reaching his navel looked like a white chowrie, whereby he as if fanned the deceased king enshrined in his heart. परिणामेऽपि even in old age. विवृतं वदनं येषां (1) that were open, not yet healed (with व्रण०); (2) that open their mouth (with thirsty people). विषमितं (made rough

face of enraged heroes. तपस्वी miserable or helpless man. अभिचारः magical spell for securing some malevolent purpose. विप्रकृताः (1) insulted, injured (with मनस्विनः); (2) worked by Brāhmaṇas (with अभिचाराः). When high-souled (or spirited) persons are insulted they at once bring about the ruin of the whole family, as spells employed by Brāhmaṇas do. जले...तेजस्विनः—every word has double meanings here. जडेऽपि...स्विनः the mighty, when struck, become inflamed even against a dullard. Because it is a fool that strikes, they would not tolerate it. In श्लेष, ड् and ल् are identical. See above p. 125. जले...स्विनः the bright (flashes) of lightning blaze forth even in water. तडित् (विद्युत्) तस्याः इमे ताडिताः. सकल...बाह्यस्य who is outside the pale of all assemblies of heroes. He has rendered himself an outcast by this deed. Or we may also explain that he, never frequenting वीरगोष्ठी, does not know the code of chivalry. अविद्यमानः उत्तारः (crossing) यस्य स अनुत्तारः निरयः (hell) तस्मिन् पातः तत्र निपुणम्. This action will hurl him into hell from which there will be no return. प्रधने (युद्धे) प्रधानं धनं. The bow is the chief wealth in battle to the powerful. कमला (लक्ष्मीः) एव कलहंसी तस्याः केलिः (sport) तदर्थं कुवलयकाननम् (in apposition with कृपाणे) The sword being dark is compared to कुवलयकानन (as कुवलय is a blue lotus). The कलहंसी plays among lotuses. लक्ष्मी plays among swords *i. e.* it goes over to the stronger sword. मनस्विनां कृपणो...त्थानस्य to the strong the churning of the sea &c. are but vile expedients to raise Lakshmî up. We may also say 'कृपणानां देवासुराणां उपायाः' (means to be employed only by wretched persons). लक्ष्मी rose up (समुत्थान) from the sea after मथन. लक्ष्मी (fame) rises up (*i. e.* spreads) in the case of the strong, who employ only their bow and sword for achieving it. ईदृशाः—refers to the treachery of the Gauḍa king. त्रातुं नियुक्ताः गिरयः—It was believed that the mountains made the earth steady. See p. 6. ll. 8–9 (text) 'भिषजो भूधरा इव भुवो धृतिं चक्रुः'. कुलिशं (वज्रं) तद्वत् कर्कशः भुजः परिघः इव तस्मिन् प्रहरणं (शस्त्रं) तस्य हेतोः तदर्थम्. स्वयम...लोहानि the idea is :—mountains yield iron from which weapons are made. The poet fancies that mountains yield iron, because they are themselves unable to discharge the task of protecting the earth and desire that others should do their work with the weapons made of iron. येषाम्—connect with उद्गिरन्ति गिरयो लोहानि—'for whom.' ०हेतोः (उद्गिरन्ति)—when the word हेतु is used for denoting 'object or purpose,' it is put in the genitive 'षष्ठी हेतुप्रयोगे' पा. 2. 3. 36 (अन्नस्य हेतोर्वसति । सि. कौ.). वि...न्धवाः friends of spotless fame. कथं ध्यायेयुः अकार्यम् how will they even think of doing an evil deed? सर्व...स्वराणाम् (1) glorious by the overwhelming strength in seizing everything (सर्वस्य ग्रहः तेन अभिभवः तेन भास्वराः); (2) brilliant by overshadowing all the planets (सर्वेषां ग्रहाणां अभिभवः तेन &c.). सु...तः in front of (*i. e.* as compared with) the hands of great warriors. दि...कराः the करs (hands, rays) of the sun are crippled in grasping the quarters (as compared with &c.). The idea is:—the sun's rays take time in occupying all the directions; but the warriors seize the world by a single stroke. दिग्ग्रहणे—here there is also an allusion to पाणिग्रहण in marriage. लोक...यमस्य merely in popular report is the south the abode of Yama, but in reality it is the frowning brow of a warrior (that is the abode of यम) *i. e.* it is the wrath of the warrior that deals death. महा...ला (1) the spaces of which are rendered terrible and curling with the wavy lines of the horns of the great Buffalo (महामहिषशृङ्गस्य तरङ्गवत् भङ्गाः तैः भङ्गुराणि भीषणानि अन्तरालानि यस्याः); (2) the intervening space between which (eyebrows) is terrible and wavy like the curling lines of the horns &c. (with भ्रुकुटिः, ०भङ्गवत् भङ्गुरं भीषणं च अन्तरालं यस्याः). The Com. seems to have read तरङ्गभङ्गुरभङ्गभीष०, which is good (तरङ्गवत् भङ्गुरः भङ्गः तेन तद्वत् वा &c.). For यम and his buffalo, see pp. 71, 81. चित्रम् *adv.* it is wonderful. उन्मुक्तः सिंहनादः यैः (1) who raise a war-cry; (2) who let loose सिंहनाद (the commander-in-chief of हर्ष). Separate सहसा साहस०. साहसरसेन रोमाञ्चाः एव कण्टकाः तेषां निकरेण. The idea is:—warriors raise war-cries in battle and their bodies are thrilled. When they raise सिंहनाद, the रोमाञ्च comes out (निर्यान्ति); then it is but natural to expect that manes should come out on their bodies by सिंहनाद along with रोमाञ्च. But this does not happen and hence the word चित्रम्. द्वयमेव...भाजनम् only two are (the proper) receptacles for the mass of wealth that springs from the four oceans. प्रति...दाहि that burns its enemies (applies to both ०मुखं and ०हृदयं). वडवामुख the submarine fire. See for वाडव or और्व, p. 124. The submarine fire is supposed to have the face of a horse (वडवा a mare). See महाभारत आदिपर्व 180. 'ततस्तं क्रोधजं तात और्वोऽग्निं वरुणालये । उत्ससर्ज स चैवाप उपयुङ्क्ते महोदधौ ॥ महद्धयशिरो भूत्वा यत्तद्वेदविदो विदुः । तमग्निमुद्गिरद्वक्त्रात्पिबत्यापो महोदधौ ॥' 21–22. The word भूति also means 'ashes'. Ashes are collected in a vessel (भाजनम्). तेजस्विनः...निवृत्तिः how can the inborn fire of the powerful rest without securing all the oceans? The powerful do not rest till they have conquered the world. तेजस्विन: applies to वडवाग्नि also, which did not rest till it was submerged in the ocean. वृथा विततः विपुलफणानां भारः येन. शेष the lord of serpents has 1000 hoods and hence the word विपुल. बिभर्ति...केवलम् that supports merely a clod of earth on its hood. The idea is that शेष merely supports the earth (without the oceans); while the warrior supports all (earth and oceans together). भोग may also mean 'ruling over, government.' भुजङ्गानां भर्ता may mean 'the master of gallants.' The idea is:—'the master of gallants is a king in name, he merely rules over the earth but cannot protect it.' अप्रतिहतं शासनं तेन आक्रान्तिः तस्याः उपभोगः तस्य सुखं तस्य रसः तं (object of जानन्ति) the taste of the happiness of enjoying a suzerainty over the earth in which the edict (issued) is unresisted. Connect रसायाः (of the earth) with ०आक्रान्ति in the preceding compound. दिक्कुञ्जरकरभारवत् भास्वरः प्रकोष्ठः येषाम्. There may be another idea 'the forearm of which is glorious with the tribute levied from even दिग्गजs.' This sentence distinguishes वीरs from शेष; the latter only bears the earth on its भोग (it has no उपभोग); but the warrior enjoys the earth. उन्मुखाः पद्माकराः (lotus beds) तैः गृहीताः पादपल्लवाः (rays) यस्य (with रवि); उन्मुखा (that turns her face towards them, favourable) पद्मा ('लक्ष्मीः पद्मालया पद्मा' अमरः) तस्याः करेण गृहीतः पादपल्लवः (foot) यस्य (with शूरः). अखण्डितं तेजः यस्य (with शूरः); आखण्डितं (destroyed, reduced) तेजः यस्य (with रविः). The radiance of the sun becomes less in the evening. हरिणः हृदये यस्य—the spot in the moon is supposed to be a deer. हरिणस्येव हृदयं यस्य whose heart is (timid) like that of the deer (with कातरस्य). पाण्डुरं पृष्ठं यस्य. The moon is pale in hue; as to the coward 'पाण्डुरपृष्ठस्य देशभाषया निर्लज्जस्यापि' Com. लक्ष्मीः wealth or sovereignty; splendour (of the moon). द्विरात्रमपि— the moon is not the same even for two nights. पुरःप्रवृत्तः प्रतापः तेन प्रहताः. पुरः ... पौरुषस्य the paths of prowess are beaten (*i. e.* prepared) by valour that goes in front. People hear the प्रताप of a warrior and then his way is clear; there is no obstacle. शब्देन विद्रुताः द्विषन्तः येषु. At the word of a proud warrior enemies run away. Doors creak and then the panels fly asunder. शस्त्रस्य आलोकेन (1) by the light of weapons; (2) by the sight of weapons. शून्या दिशः—the world is open to him (*i. e.* nothing comes between him and the world); the world is empty (of enemies). रिपु...रज्यते—the earth is pleased by a shower (आसारः) of rain; लक्ष्मी becomes coloured (or loves) by the shower of blood. ०पतिमुकुटेषु मणिशिलाः शाणाः इव (touchstones) तेषां कोणेषु (points, edges) कषणेन. राजता royalty. Many kings bow at the feet of the overlord and thereby the latter's glory is brightened. The nails of his feet also are brightened by being rubbed against the jewels in the crowns of kings when they fall at his feet. राजता suggests also silver (रजतस्य इयं राजता) which when rubbed against a touchstone shows off brilliant. श्यामीभवन्ति (1) become dark (with hands); (2) become pale or terrified (with रिपुमुख). कव...पात्यमानाः dealt against the panel—like chests of enemies covered with coat of mail. Swords striking against armour produce sparks and also श्री (*i. e.* the successful warrior attains glory or royalty). अहितेन हतः स्वजनः यस्य. Remove the vertical line after ०दुःखम्, मनस्विजनः being the subject of कथयति, उच्छ्वसिति, रोदिति and ददाति. परु...सिति—whose sighs are the wind caused by the fall of the piercing sword-blade. निर्गतं उच्छ्वसितं (जीवितं) यस्मात् तत् ०सितं शत्रुशरीरं तस्मिन् अश्रुधारापातः तेन—the tears he sheds are those that are shed on the body of his lifeless enemy (by the latter's relatives and friends). It would be better if we could read ०शरीरास्रधारापातेन. अस्रम् means both 'tear' and 'blood.' विपक्ष...जलम्—Water is offered to the dead. The spirited offer water to their murdered relatives by the eyes of the wives of their enemies (who shed tears when their husbands are slain in revenge). स्वप्ने आदौ दृष्टाः पश्चान्नष्टाः तेषु. प्रबुद्धाः (1) the wise; (2) those that are awake. When awake we attach no value to things seen in dreams. The wise do not regard their evanescent bodies as their own (kinsmen). Compare for the idea in this and in स्थायिनि &c. 'किमप्यहिंस्यस्तव चेन्मतोऽहं यशः—शरीरे भव मे दयालुः। एकान्तविध्वंसिषु मद्विधानां पिण्डेष्वनास्था किल भौतिकेषु ॥' रघु०-II. 57. अनवरतं प्रज्वलितः तेजःप्रसरः यस्य स चासौ भास्वरस्वभावश्च तं. A jewelled lamp (a jewel shedding light) is naturally brilliant and shoots forth rays. Hence there is no कज्जल in its case. शोक also darkens (कलुषः) a man's face. प्रष्ठो...नाम् the foremost of the nobly born. 'पुरोगाग्रेसरप्रष्ठाग्रतःसरपुरःसराः' इत्यमरः. 'प्रष्ठोऽग्रगामिनि' पा. 8. 3. 92 (प्रतिष्ठते इति प्रष्ठो गौः। अग्रतो गच्छतीत्यर्थः। सि. कौ.). एताश्च—connect with ०भूमयः and भित्तयः. सततसन्निहिताः धूमायमानाः (giving out smoke) कोपाग्नयः यासाम् (*adj.* of ०भूमयः and ०भित्तयः). In cool retreats also fires are lighted which give out smoke. सुलभा असिधारातोयेन तृप्तिः यासु. Thirst is quenched in cool places by water. The bright sword-edge resembles water and is welcomed by these warriors. विकटाः (large) बाहवः एव वनच्छाया तया उपगूढाः—the retreats may be surrounded by the shade of trees. धीर...भूमयः cool places for the abode of courage. स्वायत्ताः = स्वाधीनाः. सिंहनाद means:—such warriors are at your service. धीरता dwells in comfortable (cool) lodgings the walls of which are the broad (panel-like) chests of warriors. यतः...भूयः wLence (*i. e.* this being the case) what of the vile Gauḍa king? So act that no one else will again behave thus (treacherously). सर्वो...कामुकानाम् seeking the confidence of the whole earth; or the words may mean 'lovers of the whole earth believing that it will be theirs'. Compare 3rd उच्छ्वास 'भो विद्याधरीश्रद्धाकामुक'. ०विजि...श्वसितैः—the idea is:—kill these pretentious conquerors, so that their wives will weep and heave deep sighs. The sighs will fan them as chowries did before. रुधिरगन्धेन अन्धं गृध्रमण्डलं तेन आच्छादनं तैः. उच्छिन्धि...व्यसनानि remove their attachment to the shade of umbrellas (insignia of royalty) by the coverings made by the groups of vultures &c. Vultures hover over dead bodies and with their large wings appear like umbrellas. कदुष्णं (tepid) शोणितं उदकं इव तस्य स्वेदैः. कु + उष्ण = कदुष्ण; Vide. notes on कदर्थं p. 101 and 'कवं चोष्णे' पा. 6. 3. 107 (कवोष्णं कोष्णं कदुष्णम् । सि. कौ.). कुलक्ष्मीः एव कुलटा तस्याः कटाक्षैः चक्षूरागरोगाः (चक्षूरागाः एव रोगाः) तान्. This is a compound complicated by puns. The sinful sovereignty of other kings is compared to a harlot. A harlot casts glances by which people are enamoured. The wicked kings also are enamoured of कुलक्ष्मी. चक्षूराग (1) redness of the eye (due to some disease); (2) love as manifested by the exchange of glances. If a man is suffering from an eye disease, he is treated by the process of स्वेद (fomentation with tepid water). The idea briefly is:—kill rival kings and their tepid blood will come out and will extinguish their love for sovereignty obtained by unfair means (कुलक्ष्मी). For चक्षूराग, see उत्तरराम० V —'भूयसा जीविधर्म एष यद्रसमयी कस्यचित् कचित् प्रीतिः, यत्र लौकिकानामुपचारस्तारामैत्रकं चक्षूराग इति'. ०शरैः शिरावेधः तैः. अकार्ये शौर्यमेव श्वयथुः. If a part is swollen, it has to be pierced with a lancet to let out foul matter. लोहनिगडः आपीडमाला इव तस्याः मलः (dark spot due to wearing iron chains) एव महौषधं तैः. पादपीठे (foot-stool) दोहदः (longing) तेन दुर्ललितः (wanton, fondled) पादः तस्य पटुमान्द्यानि (sharp pains or stiffness). The idea is :—put iron fetters on the feet of kings that desire to rest their feet on foot-stools (which were attached to the throne of a king on which feudatories laid their heads). If a person has feet stiffened by some disease like paralysis or epilepsy, iron rings are placed round them. तीक्ष्णानि आज्ञाक्षराणि (words of command) एव क्षाराः तेषां पातैः. ०कण्डूः is accu. plural. Itch was cured by the application of क्षारs (caustic). ०मरीचयः एव चन्दनचर्चा तया ललाटलेपाः तैः. अनमितानि स्तिमितानि (stiff) मस्तकानि तेषां स्तम्भविकाराः (rigidity) तान्. If the head became rigid, some लेप had to be applied to it. Make the kings bow their unbending heads at your feet, so that the rays of your bright nails, resembling sandal paste, will be a salve to their foreheads. करदानस्य (payment of tribute) सन्देशः (message, order) एव सन्दंशः (forceps). द्रविणदर्पेण उष्णायमाणाः दुःशीललीलाः एव शल्यानि. For taking out शल्य (the point of a dart), forceps are required. Kings did all sorts of wicked and wanton deeds owing to the warmth of wealth. Send a message to them levying tribute and their pride of wealth will be gone. ०पीठस्य दीधितयः एव प्रदीपिकाः (torches or lamps). शुष्कः (vain) सुभटाटोपः (pride of being a great warriar) तेन भ्रुकुटिबन्धः एव अन्धकारः. Darkness is removed by torches. Make the vain and frowning kings bend on your jewelled पादपीठ. चरणलङ्घनं (insulting with the feet, kicking) तेन लाघवं तेन गलितं शिरोगौरवं (weight in the head) तस्मात् आरोग्यं तैः. मिथ्याभिमान is compared to सन्निपात, for which see p. 80. Remove the false pride of kings by kicking them, so that they will not hold their head high. In सन्निपात, there is a feeling of heaviness in the head, which is removed by लङ्घन (fasting). म्रदय denominative verb from मृदु. ०ञ्जलिषु मुकुलितः (closed, folded) करसम्पुटः तस्य ऊष्मभिः. इष्वसनं (इषवः अस्यन्ते अनेन) धनुः तस्य गुणः (string) तेन किणः तस्य कार्कश्यानि (hardness). If the hands be always folded together, heat is produced in the cavity. A hard callosity may become soft by fomentation. देवभूयं गते having reached the state of being a god *i. e.* having gone to heaven. 'स्याद् ब्रह्मभूयं ब्रह्मत्वं ब्रह्मसायुज्यमित्यपि । देवभूयादिकं तद्वत्' इत्यमरः. नरेन्द्रे = प्रभाकरवर्धने. वृत्ते...प्रलये when this great Pralaya (calamity) has taken place. धरणी...शेषः you alone are left to support the world. शेष also means the serpent शेष that supports the earth on its hoods. See p. 19. अविद्यमानं शरणं यासाम्. **'शरणं गृहरक्षित्रोः'** इत्यमरः. शरत्सवितेव like the sun in autumn. क्ष्मापतीनां (1) of kings; (2) of mountains. ललाटन्तप—burning the forehead. पादः foot, ray. आयाहि... ताम्—become one whose feet have a variegated hue (black and white). There is another sense 'become कल्माषपाद'. King मित्रसह son of सुदास came to be called कल्माषपाद. The king killed a tiger out of two. When killed it became a राक्षस. The other vowed revenge. The king performed a sacrifice at the end of which the राक्षस came disguised as वसिष्ठ and asked for a meal of flesh. Then the राक्षस assumed the form of a cook and served human flesh. The real वसिष्ठ came and knowing what was served cursed the king to be a cannibal. The king, knowing that he was innocent, took water to curse वसिष्ठ, when his queen मदयन्ती dissuaded him from cursing the sage. He threw the water taken for the curse on his own feet, which became spotted. See विष्णुपु० IV. 4; भागवत 9. 9. 20-25 and रामायण VII. 65 (where the king's name is वीर्यसह). रामायण I. 70 gives a different story. अभिनवा सेवादीक्षा तया दुःखं तेन सन्तप्ताः श्वासाः एव धूममण्डलानि तैः. दीक्षा means 'initiating a person into some rite or work.' The kings were to be subdued and made to attend upon हर्ष for the first time. Naturally they would heave hot sighs, which are compared to धूममण्डल. नखम्पचैः scorching the nails. 'मितनखे च' पा. 3. 2. 34 (मितंपचा ब्राह्मणी । नखंपचा यवागूः । सि. कौ.). The hot breaths of kings when they bowed at his feet would scorch his nails and the jewels in their crowns that moved when they bowed would emit rays resembling the mellow light of morn (बालातप). सहजं ब्राह्मण्यमार्दवं तेन सुकुमारं मनः यस्य. चण्डेन चापवनानां अटनिः (the notched extremity of a bow) तस्याः टाङ्कारनादेन निर्मदीकृताः दिग्गजाः येन (*adj.* of राज्यन्यकम्)—(the क्षत्रिय race) that had deprived the quarter elephants of their intoxication by the terrible twanging of the extremities of the forest of (*i. e.* group of) bows. The idea is that the क्षत्रियs had subdued the whole earth. गुञ्जत् ज्यानां जालं तेन जनितः जगतः ज्वरः येन (*adj.* of राजन्यकम्). उद्यतम् making an (united) effort. कृत्ताः वंशाः यस्य the families of which were cut off (by परशुराम). वंशs (bamboos) also are cut off, produce a sound and their thickets are burnt. Or कृत्तवंशं (कृत्ताः वंशाः यथा स्युः) may be taken as an adverb modifying उत्खातवान्. कृतवंशं (कृताः संस्कृताः वंशाः यस्य) is not a good reading. राजन्यकम्—the race of क्षत्रियs. 'अथ राजकम् । राज्यन्यकं च नृपतिक्षत्रियाणां गणे क्रमात् ॥' इत्यमरः. नैसर्गिकेण कायकार्कश्येन कुलिशायमानं मानसं यस्य whose mind acts like the thunder-bolt on account of the natural hardness of his body. मूर्धन्यः foremost (मूर्धनि भवः). ०ध्वस्तये for the destruction &c. जीवितानां सङ्कलने आकुलः कालः यमः तस्य अकाण्डे यात्रा तस्याः चिह्नध्वजं—(bow) which is the banner indicating the unexpected expedition of Yama eager to gather lives. The idea is:—your bow will do terrific carnage among your foes. A ध्वज is carried in front of an army. Harsha has to resolve on fighting all of a sudden. अरातिः शत्रुः तस्य रक्तमेव चन्दनचर्चा तया शिशिरोपचारः (cooling treatment) तमन्तरेण (without that). दुःखमेव दाहज्वरः. In दाहज्वर sandal paste is applied. Blood resembles रक्तचन्दनचर्चा. निकारेण (insult) सन्तापः तस्य शान्तिः तस्याः उपायानां परिक्षये--when no other means to allay the heat of insult could be found. रिपुरुधिरं एव अमृतं. For the reference, see above p. 139. पवनात्मजेन=भीमेन. अमन्दरोपायम् (न विद्यते मन्दरः उपायः यत्र)—for being able to drink अमृत, the gods required the mountain मन्दर; see p. 42. But भीम obtained रुधिरामृत without मन्दर. हिडिम्बा was a राक्षसी, wife of भीम. भीम drank the blood of दुःशासन with zest, as if it had first been touched by the lips of his wife हिडिम्बा. Being a राक्षसी, she is appropriately mentioned in connection with blood. See आदिपर्व 155 for the union of हिडिम्बा and भीम. As to the extirpation of the क्षत्रियs by परशुराम, see above p. 38. 'त्रिःसप्तकृत्वः पृथिवीं कृत्वा निःक्षत्रियां प्रभुः। समन्तपञ्चके पञ्च चकार रुधिरह्रदान्॥ स तेषु तर्पयामास भृगून् भृगुकुलोद्वहः।' वनपर्व 117. 9–10; see also आदिपर्व 2. 3–5. जामदग्न्येन—परशुरामेण. शाम्यन् ०सञ्ज्वरः (मन्युः क्रोधः एव शिखी तस्य शिखानां ज्वालानां सञ्ज्वरः) तस्मिन् सुखायमानेषु स्पर्शशीतलेषु च &c. क्षत्रियाणां क्षतजं रुधिरं तस्य ह्रदेषु (lakes).

P. 102 l. 19—**P. 103** l. 13. **देवस्तु...भुवनस्य.** मान्येन refers to सिंहनाद. इतरथा—even otherwise *i. e.* even if this treachery of the Gauda king had not kindled my wrath. मे goes with भुजस्य. गृहीत...भुंजस्य. दायमादत्ते दायादः—one who shares in the ancestral estate. The idea is:—my arm does not like the idea of sharing the burden of the earth with शेष. It wants the whole to itself. गच्छति qualifies ग्रहग्रणे. The idea is :—When the stars go up (reach the zenith), my brow wants to check their rise (*i. e.* I am so ambitious as to crave not only the control of this earth but also of heavenly bodies). Explain the following similarly. अनमत्सु...कचग्रहम्—one who does not bend may be made to bend by seizing his hair. दुर्विदग्ध conceited. चामराणि—I wish to make the rays of the sun my chowrie-bearers. Chowries are held in the hand (कर, also ray). राज...रुषा As I resent the title 'king' (applied to the lion). The lion is called मृगराज. I cannot bear that anyone else should bear the title of king in this world. Compare for the idea 'नूनं तेषामभ्यसूयापरोऽभूद्वीर्योदग्रे राजशब्दे मृगेषु' रघु० 9. 64. स्व...गृहीतानाम् (*adj.* of दिशाम्) that have been seized (occupied) at their sweet will by the self-willed (uncontrolled) लोकपालs. For लोकपालs, see above p. 137. The author seems to have used the word लोकपाल in the sense of दिक्पाल, but the two are slightly different, as will be seen from pp. 25, 137. आक्षेपादेशाय for giving the order of snatching them (quarters) away (from their hands). दुर्जातं—calamity. 'दुर्जातं व्यसने क्लीबेऽसम्यग्जातेऽन्यलिङ्गकम्' मेदिनी. The construction is इतरथा हि मे...भुजस्य...किं पुनरीदृशे...जाते. Put a vertical line after जाते. हृदय...शल्ये who is a painful thorn in my heart. मुसल्ये—मुसलेन वध्यः—deserving to be pounded with a pestle. The word is formed on the analogy of विष्य (विषेण वध्यः according to पा. 4. 4. 91 which is a very long सूत्र). पोटा—Hermaphrodite 'पोटा स्त्रीपुंसलक्षणा.' प्रतिकारशून्यम् (adverb) helplessly. शुष्कः अधरपुटः यस्य (with हर्ष) whose lips are dry (through the fever of grief). With पोटा, the word cannot be explained for reasons of propriety. अधरं स्त्रीयोनिः. अकृतं रिपुबलस्य अबलानां (wives) विलोललोचनेषु उदकं (tears) एव दुर्दिनं येन. He says he cannot offer water to his deceased brother with ordinary water, but will do so with the tears &c. Supply कुतः before अदृष्ट०. धूम causes tears. शपामि...स्पर्शेन—the thing with which an oath is taken is put in the instrumental. परिगणितैः counted *i. e.* limited. सकलचापानां चापलेन (quickness, fickleness) दुर्ललिताः (naughty, spoilt) नरपतयः तेषां चरणेषु रणरणायमानाः (resounding) निगडाः यस्याम्. The kings of the earth are quick archers. Those who are fickle are spoilt. तनूनपाति=अग्नौ. पीतं सर्पिः घृतं येन—fed with ghee. पतङ्गः a moth flies against the flame of a lamp. महा...कृतम् the great minister for peace and war. सन्धिश्च विग्रहश्च तयोः अधिकृतः. महांश्चासौ ०कृतश्च. This officer is often spoken of as महासान्धिविग्रहिक (see I. A. Vol. 15 p. 304; E. I. Vol. III. p. 267, 270). Compare C. I. Vol. III. p. 35 'अन्वयप्राप्तसाचिव्यः व्यापृतसन्धिविग्रहः'. अन्तिके तिष्ठतीति ०स्थः. आ is a कर्मप्रवचनीय governing a noun in the ablative and means 'up to'. चारणः—a heavenly chorister, a semi-divine being. त्रिकूटकटके (capital) कुट्टाकटङ्कैः लिखितः काकुत्स्थेन (रामेण) लङ्कालुण्ठनव्यतिकरः यस्मिन्—where the incident of the devastation of लङ्का by Rāma was engraven with cutting axes on the capital situated on त्रिकूट. त्रिकूट was a hill on which the capital of रावण was situated. 'स सागरमनाधृष्यमतिक्रम्य महाबलः । त्रिकूटस्य तटे लङ्कां स्थितः स्वस्थो ददर्श ह ॥' अरण्यकाण्ड 2. 1. कुट्टाक *adj.* that cuts. सुवेल is a mountain identical with त्रिकूट according to हेमचन्द्र. See also अनर्घराघव VI. 17. वरुण is the lord of the ocean and of the West. परिमलैः सुगन्धयः पाषाणाः तैः वासितं गुहागृहं यस्मिन्. गुह्यकs are semi-divine beings that are the attendants of कुबेर and guardians of his treasures. The unguents they employ perfume the caves where they dwell. गन्धमादनः name of a mountain to the east of मेरु famous for its fragrant forests. There भीम had gone to bring सौगन्धिकपुष्प for द्रौपदी. See वनपर्व 152 ff. सज्जी...ग्रहणाय वा—In this and the following clauses he offers them a choice between submitting to him and offering battle. गृह्यन्तां...चामराणि वा either seize the quarters or chowries *i. e.* either be my chowrie-bearers or hold fast by your kingdoms and fight. गृह्यन्तां दिशः may also mean 'run away, fly from your kingdoms'. नमन्तु धनूंषि—bows are bent in discharging arrows. कर्णपूरः an ear-ornament. कर्ण... मौर्व्यः either honour my commands (by listening to them) or draw the strings (मौर्वी) of your bows to the ear (in discharging arrows). शेख...शिरस्त्राणि turn the dust of my feet into chaplets or don the helmet. शेखरः a chaplet worn on the head. घटन्तां करि...बन्धाः arrange the arrays (घटा) of elephants. समा...यष्टयः either take hold of canes or lances. Canes were held by chamberlains or doorkeepers. मच्चरणनखेषु &c. He asks them either to bow at his feet, on the bright nails of which they will be reflected or to take bright swords. परा...मिति because I am come. This gives the reason why the kings should make a choice. निवृत्तिः cessation, rest. सकल...मयः consisting of the jewels in the crowns &c. *i. e.* all kings must bow at my feet. A person maimed has to apply a लेप to his feet. स्वस्थवत् like one who is at ease (as if nothing had happened). श्रुता प्रतिज्ञा येन. शाम्यन् ऊष्मा यस्य (*adj.* of दिवसः). The idea is:—the day passed away together with its heat. The poet says that it was not the heat that faded away from the day of the worlds, but it was the pride that faded (at hearing the terrible प्रतिज्ञा of हर्ष).

P. 103 l. 14—**P. 104** l. 4 **ततश्च...मिच्छामीति.** Read अहिमभासि, for अहिम. अहिमा भाः यस्य. निजा०—The setting of the sun is represented as due to the fear of the sun that the angered हर्ष may deprive him also of his sovereignty, just as he vowed that he would do in the case of the kings of the earth. निगूढाः शिलीमुखानां भ्रमराणां आलापाः येषु. The red lotuses closed their petals at sunset and the humming of bees was heard no more. The poet fancies that they did so through fear. One who is afraid remains silent and contracts himself (or hides). शिलीमुख also means 'arrow'. (निगूढः शिलीमुखानां आलापः twang येषु). Further a picturesque effect is produced by the words

मुख and आलाप and by reading इषुत्रासात्. समुपसंहृतः निजपक्षाणां (wings) विक्षेपः (tossing, movement) यैः ते ०क्षेपाः, ०क्षेपाश्च ते निश्चलाश्च. The birds lay in their nests and did not flap their wings. पक्ष also means 'side, partisans.' The suggested meaning is:—When the excitement of the partisans had died away and hence they were motionless. भुवनव्यापिनीम् (1) that spread over the whole world (with सन्ध्या); (2) that embraced or applied to the whole world (with प्रतिज्ञा). ०दिक्पालैः दीयमानानि अभ्रंलिहानि लोहप्राकारवलयानि यासु. Pitchy darkness began to envelope the sky and the quarters. Darkness is fancied to be iron ramparts (प्राकारः) touching the sky erected by दिक्पालs afraid of losing their position (as दिक्पालs) at the hands of हर्ष. प्रदोषास्थाने in the evening assembly. नमन् नृपलोकः तस्य लोलानि अंशुकानि तेषां पवनेन कम्पिताः शिखाः (flames) येषाम्. The lamps flickered owing to the wind set in motion by the upper garments of the kings when they bowed before departing. The poet says that the flickering was as if the bowing of lamps. उत्तानः stretched out, lying on the back. दीपः द्वितीयः यस्य He had no companion except the lamp. अभि...सरः जग्राह as an attendant (or servant) finding a proper opportunity wins (the mind of his master). 'अनुप्लवः सहायश्चानुचरोऽभिसरः समाः' इत्यमरः. C and T render 'finding its opportunity like a brigand.' तरसा (instru. of तरस् *n.*) quickly. उपर्यु...श्वासाः one after another his sighs went forth as if searching for his brother's life. धवलां...प्लवेन his bright tears resembled the hem of a white garment. परिणामः result, end. ०सङ्घातवत् or ०सङ्घातैः कर्कशः कायबन्धः यस्य (with तातात् and अचलात् respectively). इयं सा प्रीतिः this is my love for my brother (the idea intended to be conveyed being that he had no real love for his brother). अनुवृत्तिः acting according to, obedience. बालिशो...वितम् who even if a child (or fool) would think it possible that I would continue to live even after the death of my honoured brother ? ऐक्यम् Unity of hearts or thoughts. पृथक्कृतः separated. दग्धरोषेण अन्तरिता शुक् यस्य (*adj.* of मया) whose grief was intercepted (obscured) by accursed wrath (against the गौड king). गतघृणेन निर्दयेन. लूता...छिदुराः as brittle (easy to cut) as the webs of the spider (लूता). तन्तुच्छटा = तन्तुजालम्. तुच्छाः worthless. लोक...बान्धवता ties of kindred rest solely upon the conventions of the world. He means:—kinship is no reality, but is a mere conventional bond. लोकयात्रा एव ०मात्रं निबन्धनं (suppor.) यस्याः. परस्परप्रीतिबन्धेन निर्वृतं (blessed) हृदयं यस्य. विघटिते—being separated. चन्द्र...गुणाः—the idea is :—while राज्य० was alive his qualities delighted the world like the moon, but when he passed away, the same qualities burn the world, as if through contact with the funeral fire. लग्नः चिताग्निः येषां (*adj.* of गुणाः). पर्यदेवत he bewailed. अशेष...कृतम् commander of the whole elephant host. स्कन्दगुप्त is probably the same स्कन्दगुप्त that is mentioned as a great officer of Harsha in the Madhuban inscription (E. I. VII. p. 155). *Vide* Introduction.

P. 104 l. 5—**P. 105** l. 3 **अथ ... करोत्.** The principal sentence is अथ...हूयमानः स्वमन्दिरात्...स्कन्दगुप्तो विवेश राजकुलम्. अप्रति... रेणुः who did not wait for his own elephant. करेणुः an elephant in general, or a female elephant. के मूर्ध्नि रेणुरस्य or अस्याः. प्रणमतः... दिशम् bowing (to him) on every side. दिशि दिशि प्रति० (अव्ययी०). वर...पृच्छन् questioning as to the night's news concerning the best elephants. पृच्छन् governs two accusatives इभभिषग्वरान् and ०वार्ताः. उच्छ्रित०—The instrumentals in this and the following clauses are to be connected with क्रियमाणकोलाहलः (l. 19), which qualifies स्कन्दगुप्तः below. Various groups belonging to the camp raised noises about him. उच्छ्रितं शिखिपिच्छैः लाञ्छितं वंशलतावनगहनं तेन गृहीतः दिगायामः यैः that measured the expanse of the sky with tall thickets of bamboos that were decked with peacock's feathers. In the विन्ध्य forest grow high bamboos on which sit peacocks. The elephant-riders had tall bamboos in their hands on which were hung peacock's feathers. वारण...गतैः that had come to undertake the encounter for capturing elephants (or the encounter for securing elephants that had got loose). C and T translate ' come for the purpose of bursting the animals' fastenings.' This is not clear. The com. read अनायत्त० and explains 'अनायत्ता हस्तिपार्श्वरक्षिणः'. C and T translate 'throngs of unemployed persons'. We take अना० as an *adj.* of ०गणैः. अनायतानि मण्डलानि येषाम् whose groups were not restrained (*i. e.* that did not run in proper order). 'आधोरणाः हस्तिपका हस्त्यारोहा निषादिनः' अमरः. नवः ग्रहः येषां ते ०ग्रहाः गजपतयः elephants recently caught. आत्मीय...वेदयद्भिः that reported the advent of rut in the elephants entrusted to them. डिण्डि...यद्भिः that made a request that a drum be mounted (on the elephants in their charge). प्रमादेन पतितः अपराधः तेन अपहृतः द्विरदः तस्मात् दुःखं तेन धृतं दीर्घश्मश्रु यैः that had a long beard due to the grief caused by their being deprived of an elephant because they were guilty of an offence committed through carelessness. अभि...सुतैः that had recently come (for being engaged as servants). कर्पटिभिः that were clothed in rags (because they had not yet been engaged). गणिका—'गजानां प्रतिलोभनार्था हस्तिनी' com. चिरात् लब्धं अन्तरं यैः that found an opportunity (to speak to स्कन्दगुप्त) after a long time. उच्छ्रितौ (uplifted) करौ येषाम्. Remove the comma after ०करैः. कर्मण्य...कुलैः busy in enumerating the female elephants that were clever in that act (in decoying wild elephants). कर्मणि साधुः कर्मण्यः. उल्लासितानि (tossed) पल्लवचिह्नानि यैः. Being foresters, it is but proper that their badges should be पल्लवs. Remove the comma after ०पङ्क्तिभिश्च. निष्पादितः (secured) नवग्रहाणां नागानां (गजानां) निवहः &c. उत्तम्भितं (raised up) तुङ्गं तोत्रवनं यैः. तोत्रम् (from तुद्) a goad. महामात्राः (महती मात्रा परिच्छदः येषाम्) प्रधानहस्त्यारोहाः (chiefs of elephant riders) तेषां पेटकैः समूहैः. प्रकटितं करिकर्मणे चर्मपुटं यैः. Figures of elephants made of leather were used for training elephants to fight. अभि...वृन्दैः by crowds of messengers sent by the keepers of elephant forests for conveying the news of the movements of fresh herds of elephants. प्रति...कूटैः that examined at each moment the heaps of fodder for elephants. Remove the comma after वृन्दैः. Being men from the forest, they were naturally led to examine every mouthful that they saw elephants eating before them. कट...वेदयमानैः that reported about the gleaning of corn (for elephants) in villages, towns and marts (निगमः). कटानां सस्यानां ओषधीनामिति यावत् हस्तेन भङ्गः छेदनम्. Three things combined to give an air of command to स्कन्दगुप्त even when he was indifferent (he did not intend to issue any order). ०सम्भृतेन added to, increased. महा...ष्कारेण by the appearance (outward signs *i. e.* dress &c.) of the high position he held. अव...भोगेन by the great majesty (of his form). अवष्टम्भस्य आभोगः (expanse). असंख्य...सम्पादनाय—C and T translate 'to provide a limitless supply of shells for elephants' ears.' We do not know what shells had to do with elephants' ears. असंख्यकरिणां कर्णाः शङ्खाश्च (parts between the tusks) तेषां सम्पत् (beauty) तस्याः सम्पादनाय. Conchshells are found on the sea-shore. So he as if ordered the seas to supply शङ्ख (*i. e.* beautiful temples to the elephants). कर्ण also means 'the rudder of a ship'. For the meanings of शङ्ख see p. 42. शृङ्गार...संग्रहाय for making a store of the unguents (अङ्गरागः), *viz.* red-chalk (गैरिकपङ्कः), for making marks (on the elephant's forehead). 'शृङ्गारः सुरते नाट्यरसे च गजमण्डने' मेदिनी. दिग...रैः Depriving the elephant (ऐरावत) of Indra of his authority as a दिग्गज over the

The scene of the मालतीमाधव is laid in पद्मावती, which seems to have been in Malva. As to the secrecy to be observed in the case of मन्त्र, see above p. 37. The Com. says 'नागसेननामा...राजा मन्त्रिणमर्धराज्यहरमपाकर्तुं शारिकासमक्षं मन्त्रमकरोत् । स चापि मन्त्री शारिकामुखाद्विज्ञाय विस्रम्भपूर्वकं तं दण्डेनावधीत्'. शुकात् श्रुतं रहस्यं यस्य. श्रावस्त्याम्—श्रावस्ती was a famous city in the ancient kingdom of अयोध्या north of the Ganges, identified with the ruins at Sahet-Mahet. स्वप्नायमानस्य speaking in a dream. चूडामणौ लग्नं लेखप्रतिबिम्बं तस्मिन् वाचितानि अक्षराणि यया. What the king had written was reflected in his crest jewel, which the chowrie-bearer standing by his side read. यमतां ययौ became यम *i. e.* caused his death. यवनेश्वर—A Yavana king. The word यवन primarily meant the Greeks, but was subsequently applied to any non-Indian people. लोभबहुलं full of greed. बहुलनिशि on a night of कृष्णपक्ष. निधानम् a treasure. उत्खा...थिनी pounding with drawn swords. माथुरम् of मथुरा (on the Jumna). माया...गैताः issuing from the body of a sham elephant. वत्सपति king of the वत्स country. न्ययंसिषुः—*Aorist* of यम् with नि—imprisoned. उदयन, king of वत्स, the capital of which was कौशाम्बी (modern Kosam about 30 miles above Allahabad) is a famous king in ancient legendary lore. चण्डमहासेन, king of उज्जयिनी, wanted to conquer him. उदयन was fond of catching elephants. So चण्डमहासेन prepared a wooden elephant, had warriors concealed in it and placed it in the विन्ध्य forest. उदयन was captured and brought to उज्जयिनी, but spared at the request of the citizens. उदयन taught music to वासवदत्ता, daughter of चण्ड°, and after several adventures escaped with her from prison and married her. See for a full account बृहत्कथामञ्जरी II. 2. कालिदास refers to it in the मेघदूत 'प्रद्योतस्य प्रियदुहितरं वत्सराजोऽत्र जह्रे'. अतिदयितं लास्यं यस्य. For लास्य, see p. 28. शैलूषः an actor, 'शैलालिनस्ते शैलूषा जायाजीवाः कृशाश्विनः । भरता इत्यपि नटाः' अमरः ('शिलूषस्य ऋषेरपत्यं शैलूषः' क्षीर°). The Com. says: 'सुमित्रो राजा...स्त्रीजनपरिवारे इव नटजने विस्रब्धो मित्रदेवेन नटत्वमाश्रित्य हतः । स च योगचूर्णावचूर्णितस्तिरोहितो बभूवेति । अतो व्यसनिभिः प्रकृतलोकविश्वसिभिर्न भाव्यमित्युक्तम्'. प्रियाणि तन्त्रीवाद्यानि (stringed instruments, lutes) यस्य. अलाबूः (gourd) वीणा च तयोः अभ्यन्तरे सुषिरं (cavity) तस्मिन् निहिताः निशिताः तरवारयः (swords) यैः. गान्धर्व...छद्मानः who had disguised themselves as students of music. गान्धर्वम्—the art of the गन्धर्वs *i. e.* music. अश्मक is the name of the country about the Ajanta caves. See J. B. B. R. A. S. Vol. VII p. 62. प्रज्ञादुर्बलम् weak in intelligence, foolish. बल...सैन्यः who displayed his whole army on the pretext of showing his power (to his master). मौर्यम् of the famous Maurya dynasty of Magadha, to which the great चंद्रगुप्त and अशोक belonged. In this case we are on firmer ground. According to the Purāṇas, बृहद्रथ was the last of the Mauryas. पुष्यमित्र was the founder of the S'unga dynasty. The महाभाष्य also refers to him as a contemporary (Kielhorn's ed. Vol. II pp. 34 and 123). See the विष्णुपु० IV. 24 and भागवतपु. XII. 1. for the S'ungas, where numerous dynasties of kings are mentioned. आश्च...ली being curious to know or see marvels. चण्डीपतिः seems to be the name of some king; or means 'king of चण्डी.' दण्डे उपनतः यवनः तेन निर्मितेन prepared by a यवन that had been imprisoned or that had approached for punishment. The idea seems to be that चण्डीपति had taken some यवन as captive who prepared an aerial car moving by some machinery. C and T translate 'by a यवन condemned to death' and connect काकवर्णः with अनीयत in this sentence. काकवर्णः शैशुनारिः—we must read शैशुनागिः with three MSS. of B. The विष्णुपु० (IV. 24) mentions a शैशुनागवंश of ten kings, the founder of which was शिशुनाग and the second of whom was काकवर्ण. शुङ्गम् belonging to the शुङ्ग dynasty. The name of the last शुङ्ग king was देवभूति according to the विष्णुपु०. वसुदेवः—he was the founder of the कण्व dynasty. देवीव्यञ्जनया disguised as his queen. असु...सनिनं (*adj.* of मागधं) who was very fond of mines (of treasure). The word असुरविवर is used very frequently by बाण. It is not easy to give the exact sense. In the 3rd उच्छ्वास we have 'यः...असुरविवरमिति वार्तिकैः (अगृह्यत)'; on p. 7 (text, 4th उच्छ्वास) we have 'असुरविवराणीवापावृतानि'; 'लब्धासुरविवरप्रवेशपिशाचेन' कादम्बरी (p. 227 of P.). One of the companions of Bâṇa's youth was 'असुरविवरव्यसनी'. We think that असुरविवर was a term applied to mines worked up in bygone days. They were believed to have been the work of असुरs and to lead to the treasures of Pātāla in hopes of reaching which many people might have endangered their lives. The Com. remarks "वार्तिकछद्मभिः 'अहिविवरं साधितं तपसास्माभिः' इत्युक्त्वा मागधो गुहाद्वारप्रतिद्वारैर्बद्धोऽभूत्". सुरुङ्गा or सुरङ्गा—a subterranean passage or tunnel. In the passage many women had been placed, whose jingling anklets allured the king onwards. मागधम् king of मगध, modern Bihar. 'गोधनः सूर्याख्यः पर्वतः' Com. The ब्रह्मपुराण mentions a mountain गोधन (27. 22). मेकल is that mountain from which the नर्मदा springs. महाकालमहे in the festival of महाकाल. महाकाल is a form of शिव. There is a celebrated shrine of महाकाल at उज्जयिनी. 'मह उद्धव

उत्सवः' अमरः. महा...वातूलम् whose head was turned by his belief in (the efficacy of) the sale of human flesh. For महामांस, see above p. 72. जघ...द्योतस्य the younger brother of प्रद्योत. रसायनरसे अभिनिवेशः अस्य °वेशिनः (*adj.* of गणपतेः). That had set his heart upon the elixir of life. It was believed that mercury if properly treated would make men immortal. वैद्यव्यञ्जनाः persons professing to be doctors. सुबहुपुरुषान्तरैः प्रकाशिताः औषधगुणाः यैः that had advertised the virtues of their medicines through various people. विदेह was a country that comprised a part of modern Nepal, the district of Tirhut and Champaran. राजयक्ष्मन् *m.* consumption. °श्वासिनः (*adj.* of भद्रसेनस्य). महा...भाक् who secretly found access into the wall of the chief queen's apartment. कालिङ्ग king of कलिङ्ग, which was a country between the mouths of the Godāvarī and the Mahānadî. तूलिका—a mattress filled with cotton. दध्रस्य—दध्र is the name of the king. करूष—seems to be a country near Jubbulpore. It is closely connected with Chedi. For this and the preceding, see काम० VII. 51. 'देवीगृहगतं भ्राता भद्रसेनममारयत् । मातुः शय्यान्तरालीनः कारूषं चौरसः सुतः ॥'. उत्सारके रुचिः (liking) यस्य. 'दण्डी दौवारिको वेत्री उत्सारकश्च' क्षीर०. चकोरनाथः king of चकोर. चकोर is the name of a mountain in the Purāṇas. गण्डकः a rhinoceros. उद्दण्डं high-stemmed. नड्वलं abounding in reeds. नलवन forest of reeds. चम्पा was the capital of अङ्ग or north Bengal. चमूं चरन्तीति °चराः भटाः. चामुण्डी seems to have been the name of a city. बन्दि...परम् who was absorbed in his fondness for bards. परप्रयुक्ताः employed by his enemy. °मुखरं मुखं येषाम्. मल्लाः bards. कामि...गुप्तः concealing his identity by the dress of a woman. अशातयत्—from the causal of शद्. 'चन्द्रगुप्तभ्रातृजायां ध्रुवदेवीं प्रार्थयमानश्चन्द्रगुप्तेन ध्रुवदेवीवेषधारिणा स्त्रीवेषजनपरिवृतेन रहसि व्यापादितः' Com. शकपति—the S'akes are identified with the Scythian hordes that invaded India before the beginning of the Christian era. मधुमोदितम् exhilarated with wine. मधुरकं = विषम्. Compare for the story काम० VII. 52. व्याज...दर्पो who pretended to be in a passion of love. क्षुरधारा पर्यन्ते यस्य that had the edge of a razor. परन्तप who subdued others. जारूथ—was the name of the king Supply जघान here and in the following clauses. विषचूर्णेन चुम्बितः मकरन्दः यस्य. सौह्य—king of सुह्म, Western Bengal, the capital of which was ताम्रलिप्त. योगपरागः magic powder. वैरन्त्यं king of वैरन्ती or विरन्ती. In the whole of this passage the names are corrupt and there is no agreement between the MSS on the one hand and the authorities we have quoted. Some MSS read वैरन्त्या. वृष्णिम्—belonging to the वृष्णिs, a यादव clan. विदूरथम्—

'शस्त्रेण वेणीविनिगूहितेन विदूरथं स्वा महिषी जघान । विषप्रदिग्धेन च नूपुरेण देवी विरक्ता किल काशिराजम् ॥' बृहत्संहिता 78. 1; see काम० VII. 54. सौवीर—seems to have been a country west of Mount Abu. अदृश्या...वदना who smeared the inside of her mouth with an invisible antidote. ०पायनेन by making him drink &c. Note the following from the अर्थशास्त्र of कौटिल्य 'देवीगृहे हि लीनो भ्राता भद्रसेनं जघान । मातुश्शयान्तर्गतश्च पुत्रः कारूशम् । लाजान्मधुनेति विषेण पर्यस्य देवी काशिराजम् । विषदिग्धेन नूपुरेण वैरन्त्यं मेखलामणिना सौत्रीरं जालूथमादर्शेन वेण्यागूढं शस्त्रं कृत्वा देवी विदरथं जघान ।' (p. 41).

P. 106 l. 21—**P. 107** l. 12 **देवोऽपि...वात्येति.** राज्यस्थितीः—establishment of good order in his state; or, all the usual duties of a king. प्रतिसामन्तानां rival chiefs. उदवसितेषु = गृहेषु. उपलिङ्गानि portents. अविप्रकृष्टाः not far, approaching. चटुलाः moving about, restless. कृष्ण...श्रेणयः rows of black antelopes. The spotted antelopes resembled the dark glances of यमदूत s. See about the running of deer, p. 70 above. If we read प्रविष्ट० then the meaning is 'the glances of यमदूत that had entered (the chiefs' palaces)'. प्रचलि...प्रतिमाः resembling the jingling of the anklets of लक्ष्मी that had started away (in order to leave them). मधुसरघा honey bees. जहादिरे *perfect* of ह्राद् 1 A to sound. चिरम् for अजिरे is not a good reading. विवृतात् विकृतात् वदनविवरात् विसृतः वह्निविसरः यासाम् from whose wide-open and terrible mouths spread flames of fire. The reading 'उपशिबिरं शवार्थं' would mean 'near the royal camp for corpses'. For howling jackals, see p. 91. शवानां पिशिते (मांसे) प्ररूढः प्रसरः येषाम् whose expansion or growth (of body) had grown out of the flesh of corpses. The idea is:—as the vultures (काननकपोताः) fed on carrion, their wings also should have the colour of rotten flesh (dark-red). The reading of A and C 'प्ररूढप्रणयेव' seems to be a mistake for ०प्रणयाः इव, which latter C and T translate 'full well acquainted'. कपिपोतस्य कपोलवत् कपिला पक्षतिः (पक्षमूलं) येषाम्. आमन्त्रयमाणाः as if bidding farewell (to the kings who were to be defeated by हर्ष). सभाशालभञ्जिकाः the statues of females in the halls. आसन्नः कचग्रहः तस्मात् भयं तेन उद्भ्रान्तं उत्तमाङ्गं यस्य as if their heads had run away out of fear of the seizure of hair (in killing them) that was approaching. चक्रशङ्खकमलानि लक्ष्माणि (marks, चिह्नानि) येषाम्. According to the सामुद्रिकशास्त्र, चक्र, शङ्ख and कमल are some of the marks of an emperor's feet. What is indicated is that some emperor will humble their husbands. For the lines on the hands of an emperor, see above p. 20. व्यघटन्त were separated or broken. मधु...गोष्ठयः the honey-drinking bouts. ताम्यन्तः languid. स्तम्बकारि forming into sheaves or clusters (*i. e.* grown, ripe). स्तम्बं करोतीति. हरयः =अश्वाः. चल...लालिताः caressed (or coaxed) by the music of the clapping of the girls' hands resonant with the moving bracelets. रजनिकरः चन्द्रः तस्य हरिणः (*i. e.* the spot) तस्मिन् निहिते नयने येषाम्—the idea is—the dogs as if wanted to hunt down the deer in the moon. तोरणस्य समीपे उप० (अव्ययीभाव) near the outer gate (of the palace). कौलेयक—see above p. 97. Compare for a similar idea 'सूर्योदयेऽर्काभिमुखो विरौति ग्रामस्य मध्ये यदि सारमेयः । एको यदा वा बहवः समेताः शंसन्ति देशाधिपमन्यमाशु ॥' बृहत्संहिता 89. 2. गतायुषः—is the object of गणयन्ती—गतं आयुः येषां ते गता० तान्. तर्जन...तर्जन्या with her forefinger that was quickly moved for frightening. वाटकेषु in the gardens. कोटवी—'स्त्री नग्निका कोटवी स्यात्' इत्यमरः. दिवसम् (*accu.* of time) the whole day. कुटिल...तरङ्गिण्य wavy like the curling hair on the hoofs of deer. जनितः वेणीबन्धः येषु—in which the hair was tied in a single knot (as in the case of a widow). See above p. 108. निरञ्जनानि च तानि रोचनारोचींषि च (रोचनायाः इवरोचिः कान्तिः येषाम्) that had no collyrium (in the eyes) and had the colour of yellow pigment. A widow is not to put collyrium in the eye. The reflection appeared pale (as if through grief). If we read निरञ्जनलोचन० as C and T propose, the meaning would be 'having the appearance of eyes without collyrium.' चषकमधुनि in the wine in the goblets. समासन्ना०—the poet fancies that the earth quaked (trembled) because it was afraid of its seizure (by हर्ष from the hands of other kings) that was impending. वध्या...च्छटाः streaks of red sandal paste with which persons sentenced to be hanged were decked. विकसितं बन्धूककुसुमं तद्वत् शोणितं शोचिः (द्युतिः) यासाम्. Compare मृच्छकटिक X. 5 'सर्वगात्रेषु विन्यस्तै रक्तचन्दनहस्तकैः । पिष्टचूर्णावकीर्णश्च पुरुषोहं पशूकृतः ॥.' पर्यग्नी...श्रियम् as if carrying a torch round sovereignty that was to pass away (into the hands of हर्ष). A torch was carried round the animal to be offered in a sacrifice. श्री was going to be offered to हर्ष and the meteors served as torches for that purpose. अविरलं स्फुरन्तः स्फुलिङ्गाः तेषां अङ्गारोद्गारः तेन दग्धः तारागणः यैः that burnt the stars with the eruptions of fire due to the incessantly flashing sparks. गणशः in masses. उल्कादण्डाः—उल्काः दण्डाः इव. A torch has a staff. प्रतीहारीव—प्रतीहारी carries in her hands chowries, umbrellas, fans for the king. प्रतिभवनं (भवने भवने इति) at each house. वात्या a hurricane 'स्यात् वात्या वातमण्डली' त्रिकाण्डशेष. 'पाशादिभ्यो यः' पा. 4. 2. 49.

Uchchhvāsa VII

Verse 1 अङ्गनवेदी वसुधा—(to the hero that has taken a vow) the whole earth is a mere raised spot in his courtyard. वेदी is a quadrangular spot in a temple or courtyard. The idea is that just as one walks easily and fearlessly in his courtyard, so a hero has an easy walk-over in the case of the earth. कुल्या a canal. Verse 2. धृतं धनुः येन. We expect धृतधन्वनि, as धनुः becomes धन्वन् when it is the last member of a बहुव्रीहि. 'धनुषश्च' पा. 5. 4. 132 (धनुरन्तस्य बहुव्रीहेरनङादेशः स्यात्). कैव गणना of what account. Compare for the use of गणना, 'का वा गणना सचेतनेषु, अपगतचेतनान्यपि सङ्घट्टयितुमलं (मदनः)' काद० (p. 157 of P). रिपुः संज्ञा येषां. For क see above p. 36.

P. 108 ll. 5-22 **अथ...जंगाम.** The principal sentence is अथ व्यतीतेषु केषुचिद्दिवसेषु...भवनान्निर्जगाम (हर्षः). शत...णिते well calculated a hundred times (*i. e.* again and again, so that no mistake may be committed). दत्ते...लग्ने when an hour for the expedition was given (*i. e.* settled) that was fit for the conquest of even the four quarters (east, south &c.). For लग्न, see above p. 24. दण्डः army. यात्रा expedition. सलिल...दैः (1) that were skilled in pouring water (with कुम्भैः); (2) that were clear by the dropping of water (with अम्भोधरैः). When a cloud is full of water, it is dark; when it has poured all the water it had (as after the rains) it becomes white. कालधौतैः (1) made of silver (with कुम्भैः); (2) washed or white by time *i. e.* by the passing away of the rains (with ०धरैः). कलधौतं silver. कालेन धौतैः. शातकौम्भैः made of gold. 'तपनीयं शातकौम्भं' इत्यमरः (शतकुम्भे गिरौ भवं शातकौम्भं सुवर्णम्). स्नात्वा—this refers to the bath of coronation. नीललोहितस्य शिवस्य अर्चां पूजाम्. 'कृशानुरेताः सर्वज्ञो धूर्जटिर्नीललोहितः' इत्यमरः ('नीलः कण्ठे लोहितश्चकेशेऽतो नीललोहित इति पुराणम्' क्षीर०). उद्गतानि अर्चींषि यस्य the flames of which went up. प्रदक्षिणावर्तः शिखाकलापः यस्य the mass of the flames of which curved towards the right. This was an auspicious sign; see p. 25. Compare रघु० IV. 25 'तस्मै सम्यग्घुतो वह्निर्वाजिनीराजनाविधौ। प्रदक्षिणार्चिर्व्याजेन हस्तेनेव जयं ददौ॥'. दत्त्वा—the objects are ०पात्राणि and गाः. See for तिलपात्रदान, चतुर्वर्ग० (दानखण्ड) p. 600. कनकपत्रलताभिः अलङ्कृतानि शफाः शृङ्गशिखराणि च यासाम्—the hoofs and tips of the horns of which were decked with figures of gold. अर्बुदशः—अर्बुदम् ten crores. विततं व्याघ्रचर्म यस्मिन्. भद्रासनम्—'नृपासनं तु यद्भद्रासनं सिंहासनं तु तत्' इत्यमरः. विलिप्य

—the object is शरीरम्. प्रथमं विलिप्तं आयुधं येन—before anointing his body with sandal, he first of all anointed his weapon (by way of doing worship to it). राज...लक्ष्मणी—०मिथुनं लक्ष्म (चिह्नं) ययोः—on the silken robes was drawn a pair of राजहंस. सदृशे suited to his position (as emperor). परमे...भूताम् (1) that is the special mark of शिव (with शशिकला); (2) that became the mark of an emperor (with ०मालिका). शशिकला also is white like flowers and is placed on the head by शिव. नीत्वा कर्णगोचरतां दूर्वापल्लवम् having placed in the region of the ear a Dūrvâ spray. The green दूर्वा resembles the rays of emerald, that also may be worn on the ear as an ear-ornament. गोरोचनया आच्छुरितम् (blended with). For गोरोचना, see p. 36. विन्यस्य...प्रकोष्ठे having placed on his forearm an amulet-ribbon auspicious for his march together with a seal bracelet. 'भवेत्प्रतिसरो मन्त्रभेदे माल्ये च कङ्कणे । ...आरक्षे करसूत्रे च' मेदिनी. ०पूजितः प्रहृष्टः पुरोहितः तस्य करेण प्रकीर्यमाणः ०निकरः तेन अभ्युक्षितं शिरः यस्य. For शान्तिसलिल, see p. 73. संप्रेष्य—connect with भूभुजाम्. महार्हाणि वाहनानि very valuable vehicles (horses, elephants &c.). बहलः रत्नानां आलोकः तेन लिप्ताः ककुभः दिशः यैः (*adj.* of भूषणानि). संविभज्य having distributed. संविभज्य ...दानैश्च—this cannot be well construed as it stands, as no persons among whom the distribution took place are mentioned. We must read, as C and T do, ०लोकम् उचितैः for लोकमोचितैः. क्लिष्ट...लोकम् among distressed pilgrims and well-born persons. क्लिष्ट may be construed with both कार्पटिक and कुलपुत्र. कार्पटिकः (from कर्पट) one who carries water from one sacred place to another. बन्धनानि prisoners. For letting loose prisoners, see above p. 25. नियुज्य connect with भुजस्तम्भम्. तत्काल...कारे that (arm) throbbed at that moment as if to remind that it was ready for the task of conquering the 18 द्वीपs. तत्काल...रणेन (1) that appears the moment it is remembered (with a person who offers his services); (2) that throbbed at the time in order to remind हर्ष of the task undertaken by him (with भुजस्तम्भ). तत्काले स्मरणं तस्मिन् स्फुरणम्; तत्काले स्मरणार्थं स्फुरणम्. The throbbing of the right arm is a good omen in the case of men. अहमहमिकया with emulation, with eagerness. 'अहमहमिका तु सा स्यात्परस्परं यो भवत्यहङ्कारः' अमरः. Servants pressed forward to do whatever was ordered. Good omens welcomed him as he went. हिरण्य...करणाय—as हिरण्यगर्भ (emerged) from the egg of Brahmâ to start an age of holiness. For हिरण्यगर्भ, see pp. 30, 37. कृत was the frst युग after हिरण्य० was born. For कृतयुग see pp. 3, 40.

P. 108 l. 23—**P. 109** l. 9 **नातिदूरे…पटीयांसः.** सरस्वत्याः समीपे उप० (अव्ययीभाव). समुत्तम्भितानि तुङ्गानि तोरणानि यस्मिन् in which high outer gates had been erected. 'तोरणोऽस्त्री बहिर्द्वारम्' इत्यमरः. वेद्यां विनिहितः पल्लवललामः (पल्लवः ललामं चिह्नं भूषणं वा यस्य) हेमकलशः यस्मिन्. 'ललामं पुच्छपुण्ड्राश्वभूषाप्राधान्यकेतुपु' इत्यमरः. A jar with sprays at its top is an auspicious thing. Compare 'उभयपार्श्वस्थापितोत्पल्लवमुखपूर्णहेमकलशं (कायमानं)' काद० (p. 281 of P). 'वनमाला पुष्पपत्रप्रतियोजिता स्रक्' com. भ्रमन्तः शुक्लवाससः परिजनाः यस्मिन्. पठन्तः द्विजन्मानः (विप्राः) यस्मिन्. प्रस्थानम्=विजिगीषोः प्रयाणम्. ग्रामाक्षपटलिकः—the keeper of the records of the village. In the अर्थशास्त्र we have an interesting chapter headed 'अक्षपटले गाणनिक्याधिकारः'. From the description given it seems that the अक्षपटल was a record and accountant-general's office of modern times and that the ग्रामाक्षपटल was something like the modern *chavdi* in the villages of Mahārāshtra, where the village accounts were kept. 'अक्षपटलमध्यक्षः प्रत्यङ्मुखमुदङ्मुखं वा विभक्तोपस्थानं निबद्धपुस्तकस्थानं कारयेत्' (p. 62 of अर्थशास्त्र). In the Banskhera plate of Harsha we have a महाक्षपटालाधिकरणाधिकृत (E. I. IV. pp. 208, 211). सकलकरणिनः परिकरः यस्य. करणिन् or करणिक means 'a writer of documents, clerk.' करणम् a writing, document. See मनु० VIII. 52, 154. Com. 'करणिर्लेख्यं कायस्थ इत्यन्ये'. अवन्ध्यं शासनं यस्य whose edicts are never fruitless. करोतु…शासनानाम् let your Majesty this very day begin the day of your Majesty's orders (to us). He means that Harsha had come to the throne recently and that till then he had issued no royal edict and requests him to issue one that very day. वृषः अङ्कः यस्याः that had a bull as its emblem. On the Sonpat copper seal of हर्ष there is a नन्दी (see C. I. I. Vol. III p. 231 ff). अभि…निन्ये he presented a new-made golden seal. मुद्रा may also mean 'a coin' but that is not suitable here. मृत्पिण्डे—the ball of earth was presented in order that an impression with the new-made seal might be made upon it. मन्दाश्यानं पङ्कपटलं यस्मिन् on which there was mud that was nearly dry. अम…नि that thought it to be an evil omen (that the new-made seal should fall down from the king's hands). अ…दर्शिन्यः not able to see the truth. एकं (केवलं) शासनं तस्य मुद्रा अङ्कः यस्याः which will be marked with the seal of my single command. The only seal that will mark the earth will be mine. अन्य…ग्राम्याः the villagers understand it differently. This episode reminds one of what happened to William, the Norman Duke, when he first set foot on English soil. सीरसहस्रेण संमिता

सीमा येषाम् whose boundaries were measured (*i. e.* comprised) by a thousand ploughs. Each village comprised as much land as would be ploughed by a thousand ploughs. गलति...यामे when the third watch (of the night) had passed away. Time was measured by means of a water-clock and hence the word गलति. सुप्तानि समस्तानि सत्त्वानि यस्मिन् स चासौ निःशब्दश्च. दिक्कुञ्जरस्य इव जृम्भमाणः गम्भीरध्वनिः यस्य the deep sound of which swelled like the roar of the quarter elephant. प्र...पकाः that made (the people) count the क्रोशs of that day's march. The eight strokes indicated that that day eight *kros'as* were to be covered.

P. 109 l. 10—**P. 111** l. 2 **ततो...राजद्वारम्.** The principal sentence is ततः...प्रयाणसमये (p. 55 l. 14)...राजभिः आपुपूरे राजद्वारम्. रटन्तः पटहाः यस्मिन्. This and the following locatives qualify प्रयाणसमये. नन्दन्ती (joyous) नान्दी यस्मिन्. For नान्दी see p. 17. 'नान्दी मङ्गलपटहः' com. गुञ्जन्तः कुञ्जाः यस्मिन् in which the arbours resounded. कुञ्ज is out of place here. We must read गुञ्जद्गुञ्जे as some MSS. of B do. गुञ्जन्त्यः गुञ्जाः यस्मिन्. गुञ्जा a trumpet, according to the com. "गुञ्जासंज्ञः शङ्खभेदो यत्पृष्ठे जतु परिकलितं भवति । 'सन्ना' इति यस्य प्रसिद्धिः" or 'a drum' according to मेदिनी. **'गुञ्जा** तु काकचिञ्चायां पटहे च कलध्वनौ ।' मेदिनी. See भट्टिकाव्य XIV. 2. 'वेणून् पुपूरिरे **गुञ्जा जुगुञ्जुः** करघट्टिताः ॥'. कूजन्ती काहला (a large drum) यस्मिन्. 'काहला वाद्यभाण्डस्य भेदे चाप्सरसां भिदि' मे०. क्रमेण उपचीयमानः कटककलकलः यस्मिन्. दरिजनोत्थापने व्यापृताः व्यवहारिणः (officers) यत्र. व्यवहारिन् ordinarily means 'a trader.' द्रुतः द्रुघनघातः तेन घट्यमानः (being joined or added) कोणिकाकीलकोलाहलः तेन कलिताः ककुभः यस्मिन्. द्रुघनः a wooden mallet for striking a thick plate of iron or bell-metal (for indicating time &c.). कोणिका drum. कीलः stick. बले अधिकृतैः (commanders) बध्यमानः (collected) पाटीपतीनां पेटकः (समूहः) यस्मिन्. पाटीपतिः—superintendent of barracks 'पाटी बहुपरिवारपुरुषगृहीतो निवासभूभागः कुलपुत्रकसमूह इत्यन्ये ।...'पाठीपति' इति पाठे...प्रतिनियतस्वस्थानपरिरक्षिणः ।'. पाठीपति would mean 'those that guard the place assigned to them.' जनैः ज्वलितं उल्कासहस्रं तस्य आलोकेन लुप्यमानं त्रियामातमः यस्मिन्. यामचेट्या चरणचलनेन उत्थाप्यमानं कामिमिथुनं यस्मिन्. यामचेटी a servant of the watch, a female watchman; compare यामाकेनी above p. 16. We must read कटुककटुनिर्देश० with some MSS of B. कटुकानां कटुनिर्देशेन नश्यन्ती निद्रा तस्याः उन्मिषन्तः निषादिनः यस्मिन् when the elephant riders woke up from sleep that was dispelled by the sharp commands of their superior officers. प्रबुद्धेन हास्तिकेन (हस्तिसमूहेन) शून्यीक्रियमाणं (vacated) शय्यागृहं यस्मिन्. 'हास्तिकं गजता वृन्दे' इत्यमरः, 'अचित्तहस्तिधेनोष्ठक्' पा. 4. 2. 47. आदौ

सुप्तं पश्चात् उत्थितं अश्वीयं तेन विधूयमानाः सटाः यस्मिन्. For अश्वीय, see p. 69. रटत् कटकं (camp) तेन मुखरैः खनित्रैः (spades) खन्यमानाः क्षोणीपाशाः यस्मिन्. The tents had been fastened by ropes twisted round pegs driven into the earth. These were dug up. समुत्कील्यमानाः कीलाः तैः शिञ्जानाः हिञ्जीराः यस्मिन् where the fetters (for tying elephants' feet to posts) were rattling because their pins were being taken away. As the army was to march, the fetters were to be removed. We must read अपनीय० for उपनीय०. The reading पनीयमान is equal to अपनीयमान, as the अवग्रह (here after हिञ्जीरे in the last clause) is very often omitted in MSS. As the fetters of elephants were removed, so also the chains with which horses' hoofs were tied for the night were removed when the army was about to march. अपनीयमानं निगडतालकं तस्य कलरवेण उत्तालाः (wild, shying) तुरङ्गाः तैः तरङ्ग्यमाणाः (curved) खुरपुटाः यस्मिन्. 'निगडार्थं तालकं तालपत्रं निगडतालकम् । लौह एवाश्वबन्धनविशेष इत्यन्ये' com. C and T take उपनीयमान. तालकं bolt, latch. लेशिकैः (हस्त्यारोहैः) मुच्यमानाः मदस्यन्दिनः दन्तिनः तेषां सन्दानशृङ्खलानां (chains for tying) खनखननिनादेन निर्भरं भरिताः दश दिशः यस्मिन्. घासपूलकप्रहारेण प्रमृष्टं पांसुलं (dusty) करिपृष्ठं तस्मिन् प्रसार्यमाणं प्रस्फोटितं (bursting) प्रमृष्टं (wiped *i. e.* clean) चर्म यस्मिन्. The dust from the backs of elephants was rubbed off with bundles of hay and then leather bags that burst because they were more than full were placed on the backs. संवेष्ट्यमानानि (being rolled up) पटकुटीनां ०मण्डपानां च परिवस्त्रा वितानकानि च यस्मिन्. गृहचिन्तकचेटकः a servant whose business was to look after the tents and lodgings of the soldiers. पटकुटी a small tent. काण्ड...मण्डपः a large tent subdivided into rooms by screens. परिवस्त्रा the screens that form the body of the tent. वितानकं the awning. कीलककलापेन आपूर्यमाणं चिपिट (flat) चर्मपुटं (leathern bag) यस्मिन्. सं... रिणि where the superintendent of the store-room was collecting the utensils (platters &c.). भाण्डागारवहने वाह्यमानाः बहवः नालीवाहीकाः यस्मिन् when many elephant attendants were made to work in carrying the stores. 'नालीवाहिकः करिणां घासग्रहणनियुक्तो हस्तिपको मेण्ठाख्यः' com. निषादिभिः निश्चलाः अनेकानीकपाः तेषु आरोप्यमाणाः कोशकलशपीडानां आपीडाः (समूहाः) तैः सङ्कटायमानानि सामन्तौकांसि यस्मिन् When the dwellings of chieftains were full of rows of boxes containing cups and jars that were being placed on numerous elephants that were held motionless by their riders. It is better to read अनेकानेकप. अनेकप means 'an elephant', as it drinks water by the trunk and mouth. अनीकप 'one that saves the army;' so by

लक्षणा an elephant. 'पिटकः पेटकः पीडा' इत्यमरः. दूरगतैः (that stood at a distance from the bad animals) दक्षैः दासेरकैः क्षिप्रं प्रक्षिप्यमाणः उपकरणसम्भारः तेन भ्रियमाणाः (filled, covered) दुष्टाः (restive, bad) दन्तिनः यस्मिन्. For दासेरक, see p. 28. तिर्यक् (side-ways) आनमन्तः (bending) जाघनिककराः तैः कृच्छ्रेण आकृष्टः (अत एव) लम्बमानः (lagging behind) परतन्त्रः चुन्दीजनः तेन जनितः जनहासः यस्मिन्. चुन्दी—a procuress. क्षीर० remarks that it is a देश्य word. The idea is:—the procuresses were very fat. Hence their legs (जाघनिक from जघन) were bent outwards (they were bandy-legged) and they could draw their bodies forward with difficulty. पीड्यमानः (tightened) शारशारिवरत्रागुणः तेन ग्राहितः (held fast, restrained) गात्रविहारः (free movement of limbs) तेन बृंहन्तः बहवः बृहन्तः मदकरिणः यस्मिन्. The root बृंह् is used for the cry of the elephant. शार of various colours. शारिः elephant's housings. वरत्रागुणः girth or strap. '**शारिर्ना**ऽक्षोपकरणे स्त्रियां शकुनिकान्तरे । **युद्धार्थगजपर्याणे,** मे०. करिघटासु (arrays of elephants) घटमानः &c. ०कण्ठालकैः (bags) कदर्थिताः (अत एव) कूजन्तः करभाः (camels) यस्मिन्. The camels disliked the placing of bags and so bellowed. अभिजातराजपुत्रैः प्रेष्यमाणाः कुप्रयुक्ताः (bad confidants) तैः आकुलानि (troubled, full of) कुलीनकुलपुत्रकलत्रवाहनानि यस्मिन्. गमनवेलाविप्रलब्धाः वारणाधोरणैः अन्विष्यमाणाः नवसेवकाः यस्मिन् where servants recently engaged, being in error as to the time of starting, were being sought out by elephant riders. C and T think that it was the elephant riders that were deceived as to the time of starting. But that is wrong. प्रसादवित्तैः पत्तिभिः (footmen) नीयमानाः नरपतिवल्लभाः वारवाजिनः यस्मिन्. प्रसादेन वित्ताः (प्रसिद्धाः) well-known as being high in the king's favour. '**प्रतीते** प्रथितख्यात**वित्त**विज्ञातविश्रुताः' इत्यमरः. पाणिनि uses the word in this sense in 'तेन वित्तश्चुञ्चुप्चणपौ' पा. V. 2. 26. वारवाजिन् *lit.* a horse for an (grand) occasion *i. e.* a show-horse. There is another reading वरवाजिनि. ०सैन्यैः न्यस्यमानाः नासीरेण (कर्पूरेण) मण्डलाडम्बरार्थाः स्थूलाः स्थासकाः यस्मिन् where gay warriors applied thick unguents of camphor to their persons for showing circular lines upon it. चारभटः warrior. मण्डल a circle. आडम्बरः show. For स्थासक see p. 55. The usual meaning of नासीर is 'the van of an army or the soldiers in the van.' नासीरं सेनामुखं नासीराः अग्रेसराः. The meaning then will be 'where gay warriors applied thick unguent paste to their body in order to show off that they formed the vanguard'. न्यस्यमानाः नासीरमण्डलाडम्बराय &c. स्थानपालानां (अश्वपालानां) पर्याणे (on the saddle) लम्बमानानि ०सनाथानि सङ्कलितानि (fastened) तलसारकाणि (martingales) यस्मिन्. The com. reads

लवणकालायी and explains 'मृगाकृतिः अश्वानां दारुमयी क्रियते' *i. e.* a wooden figure of a deer. नालीसनाथ together with hollow stalks (of reeds &c.). 'तलसारिको अश्वमुखपट्टिका ऊर्णादिसूत्रमयी। उरःपट्टिकेत्यन्ये' com. It is not clear for what purpose the wooden figure was required. कुण्डलीकृतैः (coiled) अवरक्षणीजालैः जटिलाः (confounded with, entangled in) वल्लभपालाः यासां ता० पालाः अश्वघटाः (rows of horses) तासु निवेश्यमानाः शाखामृगाः (कपयः) यस्मिन्. अवरक्षणी reins. वल्लभः 'a horse with auspicious marks' + पालः a groom. 'वल्लभपालोऽश्वपालः। अन्ये तु यो बलवान् महाकारो हयोपकरणं यवसतण्डुलादि वहति स वल्लभपालोऽश्वपाल इत्याहुः' com. According to the com. the monkeys were carried as auspicious. We think it not unlikely that they were carried by way of amusement, when the soldiers had nothing to do. परिवर्धकैः (grooms) आकृष्यमाणाः अर्धजग्धाः ०प्रारोहकाः यस्मिन्. प्रभाते भवा प्राभातिका योग्या (martial exercise) तस्यां अशनार्थं प्रारोहकाः. The grooms had thrown shoots in front of the horses before they were to be taken through some morning exercises. As the order to march was given early, the grooms took up the half-eaten shoots and started. The com. seems to have read प्रौढिके for प्रारोहके 'प्रौढिको योग्याशनार्थं प्रसेवको यो बुक्कण इति प्रसिद्धः'. प्रौढिक means 'bag'. व्याक्रोश्या (परस्पराह्वानेन) विजृम्भमाणः (growing) घासिकानां आघोषः (noise) यस्मिन्. घासिकः one who is in charge of the food of the horses. गमनसंभ्रमेण भ्रष्टाः (running away) भ्रमन्तः उत्तुण्डाः तरुणतुरङ्गमाः तैः तन्यमानः अनेकमन्दुराणां विमर्दः (breaking, devastation) यस्मिन्. उत्तुण्डाः (with their nostrils raised up, rearing). सज्जीकृता करेणुका तस्यां आरोहः तदर्थं आह्वानं तस्मिन् सत्वरं सुन्दरीभिः दीयमानं मुखालेपनं यस्मिन्. The unguents were to be applied to the face of the करेणुका. चलितेषु मातङ्गतुरङ्गेषु प्रधावितः प्राकृतः(low) प्रातिवेश्यकलोकः तेन लुण्ठ्यमानः(plundered) निर्घाससस्यसञ्चयः यस्मिन्. प्रातिवेश्यकः neighbour. The low people in the neighbourhood took away the loads of grass that were left when the army started. But no food had been left (निर्घास). The com. explains otherwise 'निर्घासो भुक्तशेषो घासः'. सञ्चरन्तः चेलचक्रेण आक्रान्ताः चक्रीवन्तः (गर्दभाः) यस्मिन्. The donkeys were laden with bundles of clothes. The com. says that चेल also means 'a boy,' the meaning being 'boys followed on donkeys.' 'चेलं वसनमंशुकम्' इत्यमरः. चेल = चेट according to the com. चक्रैः चीत्कारी गन्त्रीगणः तेन गृह्यमाणं प्रहतं (beaten) वर्त्म यस्मिन्. गन्त्री a cart drawn by oxen. अकाण्डे दीयमानैः भाण्डैः (utensils) भरिताः अनड्वाहः यस्मिन्. निकट...सौरभेये in which powerful oxen, driven in advance, tarried out of greed for fodder lying near (on their way). The com. takes differently 'लम्बमानो गर्दभदासो वणिजां कर्मकरो वा' *i. e.* oxen were driven by servants that tarried. 'अनड्वान् सौरमेयो गौः' इत्यमरः (सुरभेरपत्यं सौरमेयः). प्रमुखे (in front) प्रवर्त्यमानं etc. महानसं kitchen. पुरः प्रधावन्तः ध्वजवाहिनः यस्मिन्. ०शतैः उपलभ्यमानं आसङ्कट...रालेभ्यो निःसरणं यस्मिन् where the exit (of the soldiers) from the rather crowded inside of the huts was seen by hundreds of friends. सङ्कट crowded, full. करिचरणैः चलिता (shaken) मठिका (cell, cottage) तस्याः उत्थितेन लोकेन लोष्टैः हन्यमामाः मेण्ठाः (elephant keepers) तैः क्रियमाणाः आसन्नाः साक्षिणः यस्मिन् where the bystanders were made witnesses by &c. The reading दलित is much better. सङ्घट्टेन (collision) विघट्टमाना (crushed) व्याघ्रपल्ली तस्याः पलायमानानि क्षुद्रकुटुम्बकानि यस्मिन्. 'व्याघ्रपल्ली तृणकुटीभेदः' com. (a hut thatched with grass). कल ... वणिजि when the traders ran after their oxen laden with wealth that ran away owing to the fear of the tumult. For विद्राण see p. 75. The com. takes विद्राण in the sense of सशोक (*i. e.* that despaired). पुरःसरं... कदम्बकं यस्मिन् when the group of female elephants carrying the harem started when the crowd of people grew less owing to the light of torches that were carried in front. We may also translate 'owing to the light of torches carried by servants walking in front.' ०आहूयमानाः लम्बिताः (that tarried) श्वानः यस्मिन्. C and T 'dogs tied behind them.' But this is not proper. If they were *tied*, there was no necessity to call them up. सरभस... गणे when the groups of tall तङ्गण horses were being praised by men inured to a hard life who felt comfortable by the steady motion of the tramp of their quick feet. We must read तङ्गण and not तुङ्गण. तङ्गण is the name of a country; see बृह० X. 12 and XVI. 6. The com. says 'खक्खटाः वृद्धाः' but the meaning assigned to the word in lexicons is 'hard'. त्रस्ताः वेसरविसंवादिनः सीदन्तः दाक्षिणात्यसादिनः यस्मिन् where Deccan riders sitting on mules fell down, not being able to keep their bodies moving with the motion of the mules. There are no mules in the Deccan and the Deccan people not being accustomed to their ways and pace fell down from their backs. सीदन्तः may also mean 'dejected or sinking on the ground' (because they fell). विसंवादिन् not agreeing with. 'सादी तुरङ्गमातङ्गरथारोहेषु दृश्यते' मे०. C and T translate 'Deckhan riders disconsolately contended with fallen mules.' Our interpretation seems to be preferable. प्रति...च्छद्भिः coming from every direction. This and the following instrumentals qualify राजभिः (p. 56 l. 1) below. आधो...शार्ङ्गैः whose bows spotted (शार) with golden

कल्माषशबलैताश्च **कर्बुरे'** इत्यमरः. चर्ममण्डलं round shield. On कार्दरङ्गक (the reading of the com.), it says 'कार्दरङ्गकानि कार्दरङ्गदेशोद्भवानि बहुसुवर्णसूत्ररचितानि चर्माणि .स्फोटकाः स्निग्धवर्णमांसस्फारणि कार्दरङ्गचर्माणि'. आस्कन्दन्तः (careering) काम्बोजवाजिनः तेषां शतं तस्य शिञ्जानं जातरूपायानं (golden ornament) तस्य रवेण मुखरितानि दिङ्मुखानि यैः. As to the breed of काम्बोज horses, see above p. 30. 'आयानमश्वभूषणम्' com. **'लम्बापटहाः** पटहभेदाः तमिलाः इति प्रसिद्धाः' com. उन्मुखैः पादातैः प्रतिपाल्यमानः आज्ञापातः येषाम् whose commands were awaited by footmen with upturned (*i. e.* expectant) faces.

P. 111 ll. 2–27 **उदिते...नरपतिः.** समा...शंसी declaring the time of the king's arranging his army. **'समायोगस्तु** संयोगे **समवाये** प्रयोजने' मे०. The principal sentence is अथ नचिरादिव प्रथमप्रयाणे एव दिग्विजयाय...निर्जगाम नरपतिः. प्रथम०—the idea is:—many kings start on दिग्विजय after several less ambitious expeditions; but in the case of हर्ष his very first march was for दिग्विजय. दिग्गज...कुर्वाणया that as if brought the king into the company of the *diggajas* by the graceful play of the movements of its ears waving to and fro as it went on. The flapping of ears produced a sound which caused echoes in the sky and reached the दिग्गजs who thus came in contact with हर्ष. Or समागम may mean 'assemblage' (of दिग्गजs). सिद्धयात्रया (सिद्धा यात्रा यस्याः) auspicious for expedition. वैदू...कटेन that looked formidable with its rod of *lapis lazuli*. विदूरात् प्रभवति वैदूर्यम् according to 'विदूराञ्ञ्यः' पा. 4. 8. 84. उपरि goes with ध्रियमाणेन. प्रत्युप्ताः (inlaid) पद्मरागखण्डाः तैः खचितं तस्य भावः ०खचितता तया. सूर्योदय०—The idea is:—the umbrella was inlaid with rubies; hence it looked dark-red. The poet fancies that it was angry at the sight of the red rising sun. It could not brook another round object like itself. A person's face, when angry, becomes red. Supply उपलक्षितः after मङ्गलातपत्रेण, according to 'इत्थंभूतलक्षणे' पा. 2. 3. 21. कदलीगर्भात् अभ्यधिकः म्रदिमा यस्य (*adj.* of कञ्चुकेन). See p.14 (text) 'अकठोररम्भागर्भकोमलै':. भोगिनां अधिपतिः = शेषः. भोगिनाम् also means 'of kings'. कञ्चुकेन—हर्ष wore a tunic, which resembled the slough (कञ्चुक) of a serpent, which also is अङ्गलग्न. क्षीरोद...वाही—हर्ष wore clothes (अम्बरं) as white as the foam of the Milky Ocean. The day of churning had a sky (अम्बरं) white with the clouds of foam. So the king is compared to मथनदिवस. His white umbrella was like the sky white with foam and his fine robes were like the fine slough of Vāsuki, who served as the rope in the churning. 'शेषोऽनन्तो

वासुकिस्तु सर्पराजोऽथ गोनसे इत्यमरः. For वासुकि and अमृतमथन, see p. 46. बाल...रूढः who attained to the position of Indra, while still young (with हर्ष); which grew in the land of Indra (heaven) while still young (with पारिजात tree). The पारिजात tree, the moment it was churned out, was taken by Indra. विधूयमानेन चामरेण यः मरुत् तेन विधूता कर्णपूर—कुसममञ्जरी तस्याः रजसा (with the pollen). दिशः छुरयन् overspreading the quarters. The pollen spread on the earth; the poet fancies that it was the magic powder for subduing the world. अभिमुखे (turned towards the sun, or worn in front) चूडामणौ घटमानं (formed) पाटलं (reddish) प्रतिबिम्बं यस्य. As the morning sun was red, its reflection also was red. The poet fancies that हर्ष as if drank with his own lustre the sun (in the form of the reflection in his crest-jewel). बहलं ताम्बूलं सिन्दूरमिव तेन छुरितया (०मुद्रया) that was overspread with thick vermilion-like betel. ओष्ठमुद्रया by his closed lips. विलभ...रागस्य as if making a gift of the various continents to अनुराग (redness, devotion or loyalty). His lips red with betel made the world red (*lit.* gave up the world to redness). A devoted servant receives gifts which are confirmed with the stamp of the royal seal (मुद्रा) in virmilion. Vide above p. 32. स्फुरन्ति महाहारमरीचीनां चक्रवालानि. स्फुर...ग्राहयन् the idea is:—the rays of the large necklace worn by Harsha spread in all directions. The rays were white like chowries. So the poet fancies that he made the quarters hold chowries for him. राजकस्य ईक्षणे उत्क्षिप्तः त्रिभागः (तृतीयो भागः) यस्याः (*adj.* of भ्रूलतया). A command may be given by the movement of the brow. बाहुप्राकारेण by the rampart of his arms. परि...खातान् as if surrounding even the seven ocean ponds with the desire of protecting them. There is a picturesque effect. Ordinarily it is a ditch (खातं) that protects a wall (प्राकारः) against an attack. Here the seven oceans are so many ponds in the eye of Harsha, who protects them with his arms, the walls. लक्ष्म्या...गूढः he was embraced by लक्ष्मी (sovereignty; लक्ष्मी that sprang out of the ocean). The eyes of the people of the camp were fixed on him (drank him). The poet says they did so because he had become अमृतमय as लक्ष्मी embraced him taking with her all the sweetness of the ocean. हृदयेषु...मज्जन्निव he plunged into the hearts (of the kings) by the greatness of his qualities. Every thing that has गौरव (heavinsss) also goes deep in a fluid. स्नेहार्द्र affectionate; fluid with oil. मज्जामपि even the marrow (of the bones). अमरपतिः = इन्द्रः. अग्र...कुलः intent upon wiping off the stain of the slaughter of his elder brother. This applies to हर्ष as well as to इन्द्र, who wanted to get rid of the sin of killing a ब्राह्मण (अग्रज). इन्द्र killed वृत्र son of त्वष्टृ who was a ब्राह्मण. He became free from the sin of ब्रह्महत्या by performing an अश्वमेध sacrifice. See रामायण उत्तरकाण्ड 84 and 85. 'तमिन्द्रं ब्रह्महत्याशु गच्छन्तमनुगच्छति' 84. 16. पृथिव्याः परिशोधनस्य अवधानेन सङ्कलितान् सकलमहीभृतः समुत्सारयतीति (1) who urged forward all the assembled kings with the fixed purpose of cleansing the earth (of a कण्टक like गौड); who cast away all the gathered mountains with &c. See notes p. 1 for पृथु who levelled the earth. पुरः...कारकैः—Harsha was preceded by ushers (दण्डिभिः) that went in front and that uttered complimentary words like जय, जीव, आलोकय &c. 'आलोको जयशब्दः स्यात्' इति हलायुधः (quoted by मल्लिनाथ on रघु 17. 27). The com. explains it differently 'लोक इत्येवं ये वदन्ति ते आलोककारकाः' those who cry 'Ho! people'. This does not seem to be quite correct. The rays of the sun also go before him (before he is seen) and cause light (आलोकः). सहस्र...किरणैः—The sun is called सहस्ररश्मि; हर्ष also had thousands of servants. अधिकारचातुर्येण (cleverness in discharging their duties) चञ्चलाः चरणाः येषाम्. All the instrumentals qualify दण्डिभिः below. व्य...निष्ठुरैः rigorous in maintaining order. भय...ग्राहयद्भिः who as if made the people take to the ten quarters, that were screened (from Harsha's view) by the mass of people running through fear. They cleared the way for Harsha so well that people in fear ran far away from him. चलितानां कदलिकानां (banners) सम्पातेन (mass) पीतः प्रचारः (movement) यस्य. The wind was hemmed in by a number of waving banners and so could not blow fiercely. The poet represents this as teaching the wind discipline or humility. कदलिका also means the plantain tree, the long leaves of which might retard the motion of the wind and the leaves of which become yellow when dry. द्रुतचरणैः उद्धतं (raised up) धूलिपटलं तेन अवधूतान् (despised *i. e.* obscured). ०लतानां आलोकेन विक्षिप्यमाणं (dispersed). The light of the golden canes in the hands of the ushers cast daylight into the shade as it were and hence daylight is fancied to be removed by the ushers.

P. 111 l. 28—**P. 112** l. 4 **अवनमति...राजकम्.** अवनमति connect with राजचक्रे (*loc. absolute*). चलनेन शिथिलाः मणयः येषां तानि ०मणीनि कनकमुकुटानि तेषां किरणनिकरेण रुचिरं शिरः यस्य. विलुलितं

०शेखररजः यस्य the pollen in the chaplets on the head of which was shaken (or tossed about). It should be noticed that from अवनमति to ०कुसुम every letter is short. अवाञ्चः downwards. उदञ्चः upwards. चाष...चेलुः the rays moved like flocks of blue jays for effecting good omens. The flight of the चाष bird to the right of a person or the sight of the चाष when a man starts on a journey was an omen indicating prosperity. Compare बृहत्संहिता 'पूर्णाननः कृमिपतङ्गपिपीलिकार्थैश्चाषः प्रदिक्षणमुपैति नरस्य यस्य।...तस्यार्थलाभमचिरात्सुमहत्करोति॥' 88. 23 and 'सन्दर्शनं शुभदमस्य सदैव यातुः' 88. 25. मेघायमानः रेणुः तेन मेदुरं (thick with, full off)—*adj.* of खम्. The dust raised by the marching army was like a cloud. उड्डीयमानाः applies both to शिखण्डिनः and मरीचयः (from the preceding clause). The rays of the crest jewels shooting up into the sky looked like house peacocks. The peacocks fly up towards the cloud and dance when it appears. The feathers present numerous tints. The rays were of different hues. The cloud of dust represents दिग्द्वार. The shooting rays of jewels appear like the delicate पल्लव of कल्पवृक्ष. वन्दनमाला—is an auspicious garland fixed on the outer gate of a mansion 'मङ्गलस्त्रक्तोरणोर्ध्वे भवेद्वन्दनमालिका' क्षीर०. नेत्रत्रिभागैः—glances in which only a third part of the eye is open. समग्रेक्षितैः full glances. 'भ्रूवञ्चितैः भ्रूचलितैः' com. छेकालापः insinuation, *double entendre.* 'छेको विदग्धे' क्षीर०; 'छेको गृहाश्रितमृगपक्षिणोर्नागरे त्रिषु' मे०. छेक means 'clever or polished'. आ...वीराणां who as if bought the souls of the heroes consisting in honour by gifts (tokens) of his favour. The glances, smiles and jests &c. were the price he paid for what they gave, *viz.* the honour they did him. यथा...राजकम् he distributed among the kings according to their worth (his favours).

P. 112 l. 5—**P. 114** l. 16 **अथ...जगाम.** तस्तार spread. तारतारः very loud. दिग्गजेभ्यः is dative, according to 'क्रुधद्रुहेर्ष्यासूयार्थानां यं प्रति कोपः' पा. 1. 4. 37. The elephants of Harsha were wroth with the दिग्गजs for the latter's pre-eminence and so wanted to establish their own superiority by the flow of their rut. त्रिप्रसृतानां that emitted a flow (of rut) from three places, the trunk, the eyes and the temples. मद...स्यन्दिरे with the tracks of the streams of ichor dark with swarms of bees, thousands of the windings of the Jumna as if began to flow. The waters of the Jumna are dark and so resembled the ichor with bees on it. The word त्रि in त्रिप्रसृतानां is suggestive. Ordinarily the braid of a woman whose husband is living is triple. Further there is a striking effect produced by laying emphasis on त्रि and सहस्र. सिन्दूर०–we saw above that red powder was sprinkled over people on festive or auspicious occasions. So much red powder was used that the sun appeared red and birds (like the चक्रवाक) feared that sunset was near (though really it was not). करिणां—connect with ०निस्वनैः. मांसलैः augmented by. कर्णतालः flapping of elephant's ears. दोधूयमान (frequentative of धू pass.) being again and again waved. अश्वीयं—See p. 69. शिश्विन्दे—*perfect* of श्विन्द् 1 A. to become white. पिण्डीभूतानि तगराणि तेषां स्तबकवत् पाण्डुराणि (white). परस्परसङ्घट्टेन नष्टाः अष्ट दिशः यस्मिन् (*adj.* of दिवसम्) where the eight quarters were not to be recognised on account of the close contact (of the umbrellas). The umbrellas were so many that no space was left uncovered by them. The sunlight paled before the golden handles and white sheen of the umbrellas. उच्चः चामीकरदण्डः येषाम्. रजः (dust) एव रजनी तया निमीलितः (closed, blinded). The day was dark with clouds of dust; but had the mellow light of morning with the jewels of the coronets. मण्डनक...कृताः render-ed green (or tawney) by the clanging ornaments of horses (made of gold and silver). 'स्याद्भाण्डमश्वाभरणे' इत्यमरः. ह्राद् 1 A to sound. परिह्रादाः resounding. हरितः = दिशः. शिशीकरे *perfect* of शीक् 1 A to sprinkle. चक्षुषामुन्मेषं मुमुषुः robbed the eye of the power to open. The lightning also robs the eye of this power. विसिष्मिये *perfect* of स्मि with वि. It will be noticed that from तस्तार (at the beginning of the paragraph) to विसिष्मिये the author uses the perfect tense only. बलानां stands for बलैः—(the king wondered at his own vast army). आवासस्थान camping ground. अधोक्षजः (विष्णुः) तस्य कुक्षेः (उदरात्). युगादौ = कल्पादौ. The army starting from its encampment looked like the world rising from the belly of Vishṇu at the beginning of a कल्प. Compare (text) p. 10 ll. 1–2 'यशोमती गर्भेणाधत्त नारायणमूर्तिरिव वसुधां देवीं राज्यश्रियम्.' कुम्भभुवः = अगस्त्यस्य. प्लावितं (flooded) भुवनं येन. अगस्त्य was born from a कुम्भ in which the seed of मित्र and वरुण was placed. See for the story रामायण VII 56 and 57. He drank the ocean to help the gods against the Kāleyas who hid them-selves in the sea. Compare 'भूतधात्री कलशयोनिपानपरिकलितसकलसलिलं सागरमवतीर्णा' काद० (p. 124 of P.). ०सहस्रेण आदौ सम्पिण्डितं पश्चात् उन्मुक्तम् at first stemmed and then let loose. अर्जुन is सहस्रार्जुन कार्तवीर्य. 'योऽसौ भगवदंशमत्रिकुलप्रसूतं दत्तात्रेयाख्यमाराध्य बाहुसहस्रमधर्म-सेवानिवारणं धर्मेण पृथिवीजयं धर्मतश्चानुपालनमरातिभ्योऽपराजयमखिलजगत्प्रख्यात-

पुरुषाच्च मृत्युमित्येतान्वरान् लेभे' विष्णुपु० IV. 11. See मार्कण्डेयपु. 18. While once bathing in the Narmadâ, he wanted to see the power of his thousand arms and stemmed the waters and then let them off in a flood. See रामायण VII. 32. सहस्त्रधा प्रवर्तमानं applies also to the army. प्रसर तात—In these and the following words (up to p. 58 l. 6) the author gives us what the soldiers and camp-followers talked among themselves. भाव—this is a word showing respect in addressing a person. 'मान्ये भावोऽपि वक्तव्यः' भरतः (quoted by क्षीर०). त्वङ्गति तुरङ्गमः—a horse is galloping. This gives the reason why the man tarried. He waited till the galloping horse passed. भग्न...पतन्ति you walk as if you were lame, while these men of the van come in furious speed upon you. वाह...ङ्कम् why do you drive the camel? निःशूक= निर्दय, 'शूकोऽस्त्री शुक्रदययोः' मे०. Separate निःशूक शिशुम्. रजसि...भव be near me so that you may not be missed in the dust. गलति...वकः the sack of barley-meal leaks. प्रसेवः or—कः a sack or bag. इत्वर a traveller, one who walks. सौ...वरि leaving the track of oxen, you run in the midst of horses, O fish-woman! The track of oxen would be safer for pedestrians than that of horses. We may also translate 'Oh ox! why do you leave the proper track and run in the midst of horses? Oh! fishwoman, do you wish to come along'? On this latter interpretation, we must take सौरभेय as a vocative and connect धीवरि with विशसि. गन्तु...मार्गम् Oh female elephant! do you wish to enter the way of the male elephants? अङ्ग is a term of address applied to a friend &c. गलति...रटन्तम् the bag of peas is crosswise and leaks; you don't mind my bawling. We must read अतटेन for अवटेन. अव...तरसि you are descending into a pit from a precipice. 'गर्तावटौ भुवि श्वभ्रे' इत्यमरः. 'प्रपातस्त्वतटो भृगुः' इत्यमरः. The com. says 'अवटेन. अमार्गेण'. सुख...भग्नः 'you uncontrolled female, be quiet. The jar of sour barley-gruel is broken.' This is addressed to some woman who carried a jar and, stumbling in hurry, had it broken. Or it may have been addressed to a female elephant on the back of which the jar was placed. Or we may take 'सुख...णि' by itself and regard सौवीरक as a vocative (meaning 'a man from the सौवीर country' or 'a person carrying the sour gruel'). 'आरनालकसौवीरकुल्माषाभिषुतानि तु । अवन्तिसोमधान्याम्लकुञ्जलानि च काञ्जिके ॥' इत्यमरः (सुवीरेषु प्रायो भवं सौवीरकम्). मन्थ...क्षुम्—this is addressed to some one who lagged behind while sucking sugarcane. 'You will suck it when you have finished your journey.' उक्षाणं प्रसारय drive on your bull. This should be taken with the preceding. If we read प्रसादय, we must regard it as an independent sentence. प्रसादय make quiet. दूरं गन्तव्यम् we have to go a long way. कि...यात्रा Droṇaka! why do you run even to-day (the first day of the march)? The expedition is going to be for a very long time (so you will have plenty of time to run). वि...साकम् excepting that one cruel man, this is the belief (निष्ठा) of all of us (that the expedition is going to be very long). We must read निष्ठेयं for निष्क्रेयम्. C and T translate the words किमद्यैव...साकम् as 'why do you linger, Droṇaka, now? this long expedition is at a standstill for one rascal.' One fails to see how दण्डयात्रा is connected with निष्ठेयम्. अग्रतः...स्थालीम् the road in front is uneven; स्थावरक, see you don't break the jar of raw-sugar. स्थावरक may mean 'you mountain (of flesh).' 'स्थपुटं तु नतोन्नतम्' क्षीर°. 'मत्स्यण्डी फाणितं खण्डविकारे शर्करा सिता' इत्यमरः. Separate गण्डक तण्डुल°. न...दम्यः the bullock cannot carry it (to the end of the journey). माषीणम् a field of माष (beans), according to 'धान्यानां भवने क्षेत्रे खञ्' पा. 5. 2. 1 and 'विभाषा तिलमाषोमाभङ्गाणुभ्यः' पा. 5. 2. 4. (माषाणां भवनं क्षेत्रं माष्यं माषीणं वा). अमुतः from yonder. द्राक्...लुनीहि quickly cut with a knife a bundle of a mouthful of fodder. को...गतानाम् when we are gone, who will know what happened to his crop? Or better still 'who will detect the bundle lying in the midst of the fodder, when we are gone.' The idea is that they would keep the raw beans concealed in the fodder. धव...मिदम् O man, keep away your oxen, this field is guarded by barbarians. He calls the watchmen barbarians. The com. says 'वाहीकः काष्ठकः परिपालक इत्यन्ये गोरक्षक इति चान्ये'. लम्बिता...युङ्क्ष्व the cart has lagged behind; harness to the yoke an excellent (धवल) ox (शाक्कर) capable of bearing the burden (धुरन्धर). धुरं धायतीति °धरः or धूर्धरः. यक्षपालित may be a proper name or it may mean 'one protected by यक्षs, a man possessed by a ghost.' दीव्य...दण्डे you are playing on the trunk of the elephant (instead of minding your business as a rider). समद is addressed to an elephant. सं...स्खलसि you lose your footing in the mud due to the crowd (संमर्दः). माणवक is a name very frequeutly cited in the phrase 'अग्निर्माणवकः'. घनेभ...सरणिः in the thickness of the meeting of the array of elephants, there is no way to come out (if you once get entangled therein). If we read निस्तरणम् it would mean 'there is no getting out &c.' ०प्रवर्तमानाः अनेकसंलापाः यस्मिन् (*adj.* of स्कन्धावारम् above). All the following accusatives also qualify स्कन्धावारम्. In the following long passage Bāna uses many obscure words, the meanings of which are doubtful and which are rarely found in classical works. The commentary is our only authority in some cases. स्वेच्छया (at their will) मृदितानि उद्दामानि (plentiful) सस्यघासविघसात् सुखेन सम्पन्नानि (easily obtained) अन्नानि तैः पुष्टाः तैः. सस्य...घसात् from the leavings of the grain (for horses &c.). 'अमृतं **विघसो** यज्ञशेषभोजनशेषयोः' इत्यमरः. केलिकलैः that were noisy with jests. मेण्ठ...मण्डलैः by groups of elephant—keepers, bachelors (वण्ठ), dullards (वठर), donkey boys (लम्बन), elephant-riders (लेशिक), thieves, servants, rogues (चाटः) and grooms. '**वण्ठा** अकृतविवाहाः तरुणाः ये दण्डमादाय हस्तिनां दर्पमाकर्षयन्ति । पत्तय इत्यन्ये लम्बनाः गर्दभदासाः ।... शाटा धूर्ताः चण्डाला अश्वपालाः' Com. The com. seems to have read शाट for चाट. For लेशिक see above. चाट 'चाटाः प्रतारकाः विश्वास्य ये परधनमपहरन्ति' मिताक्षरा on याज्ञ० I. 336. आण्डीर bold, according to the com. It also suggests that the word may be राण्डीर (from रण्डा) 'harlot's sons.' असहायैः (helpless) goes with ०पुत्रकैः (l. 12). क्लेशेन आर्जिताः कुग्रामकुटुम्बिसम्पादिताः सीदन्तः (sinking, weak) सौरभेयाः तैः शम्बलस्य संवाहने आयासः तेन आवेगः तेन आगतः संयोगः येषाम् who gathered together on account of the excitement caused by the worry &c. The com. says 'आयासो योगस्तेन गतसंयोगैरुत्पन्नचित्तक्षोभैरिति समासः'. So it read आयासगतसंयोगैः. स्वयंगृहीतानि गृहोपस्करणानि यैः. As the oxen could not carry, they had to put their own shoulders to the work. We must change the punctuation. Read ०तलम् । तृष्णा...भवतु । शिवं सेवा करोतु ।. तृष्णा...भवतु let there be an end of this height of greed! न भवनं अभवनिः. 'आक्रोशे नञ्यनिः' पा. 3. 3. 112. (नञि उपपदे अनिः स्यादाक्रोशे । अजीवनिस्ते शठ भूयात् । सि. कौ.). 'अकरणिरित्यादयः शापे' अम०. शिवं०—May (this) service do us good !! भूतिः prosperity *i. e.* excess. दुःखकूटाय = दुःखराशये. 'निःस्वस्तु **दुर्विधो** दीनो **दरिद्रो** दुर्गतोऽपि सः' इत्यमरः. अति ... द्रवद्भिः by people that ran (द्रवत्) quickly in lines, as if they were tied together and as if they were on board a boat carried along by a very sharp current. जनैः goes with सर्वमेव...कारयद्भिः. कृष्णकठिनस्कन्धयोः गुरवः लगुडाः येषाम्. गृहीताः...हाः यैः. सौवर्णपादपीठी golden footstool. करङ्कः—betel-box. Compare ताम्बूलकरङ्कवाहिनी, which occurs very frequently in the कादम्बरी (*e. g.* p. 148 of P). पतद्ग्रहः a spittoon. 'प्रतिग्राहः पतद्ग्रहः' इत्यमरः. अवग्राहः = स्नानद्रोणी com. It seems that the correct reading as अवगाह and not अवग्राह.

प्रत्यास...दुर्वारै: that were hard to check in their pride for being in charge of the appurtenances (उपकरणं) of their king who was near by. सर्व...द्भि: that pushed aside everybody. भूपति...वाहिभिश्च and by the porters (भारिक) engaged by the king, that carried the kitchen utensils. 'भारवाहस्तु भारिक:' इत्यमर:. बद्ध: वराहवध्रेण वाध्रीणस: यै: that had tied a rhinoceros by straps (वध्रं) of pig-skin. 'खङ्गं शृङ्गमस्यास्तीति खङ्गी वाध्रीणसोऽपि' क्षीर. But the com. says 'वाध्रीणसा यज्ञियाश्छागविशेषा:.' लम्बमाना: हरिणानां चटुका: ('पूर्वभागा:' com.) चटकानां (sparrows) जूटाश्च (mass) तै: जटिला: तै:. चटु means उदर according to the मेदिनीकोश. शिशु...ग्राहिभि: that had a collection of young rabbits, vegetables (शाक:), leaves and shoots of bamboo. वेत्राग्राणि = 'वंशांकुरा:' com. शुष्ककर्पटेन प्रावृतं मुखं यस्य तत् ०मुखं; एकदेशे दत्ता आर्द्रा मुद्रा (seal) तया गुप्त: गोरस: यस्मिन् तत् ०गोरसं; ०मुखानि ०गोरसानि भाण्डानि येषाम्. गोरस: may mean 'cow's milk or butter-milk.' '**दण्डाहतं कालशेय**मरिष्टमपि **गोरस:**' अम०. तलक...भारिकै: carrying loads of baskets full of तलक &c. 'तलकोऽग्निशाटिका। तापकोऽपूपादिकरणस्थानम्। तापिका काकपालिका यत्र तैलादिना भक्ष्या: पच्यन्ते। हस्तको शूलम्' com. तापक: oven. तापिका pan. हस्तक: spit. ताम्रचरुक: a copper vessel (in which rice or barley may be boiled). कटाह: a frying pan (Marathi कढई). फलकाले at the time of reward or payment. अन्य...स्यास्यन्ते other rogues will approach or be near. पदे...पतता falling at each step. The com. says 'स्खलने प्रेरणे.' This is a sense hardly ever met with. We would translate 'who were appointed to look after the tripping of the oxen.' The reading खेटचेटकै: will mean 'servants from the hamlets.' खेद्यमान: असंविभक्त: (not separated *i. e.* whole) कुलपुत्रलोक: यस्मिन् (*adj.* of स्कन्धावारम्). The noble youths were pestered by the servants with the words 'क्लेशो—स्थास्यन्ते'. प्रजविता: प्रधाविता: ग्रामेयकजनपदा: यस्मिन्. ग्रामेयक = ग्रामीण. आग्रहरिकजाल्मै:—connect this with ०धूलिपटलम् below—the rogues that had appropriated to themselves the अग्रहारs (endowments of lands conferred on Brāhmaṇas). The lands had been granted by former kings to Brāhmaṇas and some rogues enjoyed the lands free from tax when the families of the original grantees became extinct. Or आग्र...जाल्मै: may mean 'wretches from the अग्रहार villages.' पुर:सरा: जरन्त: (old) महत्तरा: (headmen of villages) तै: उत्तम्भिता: (raised up) अम्भ:कुम्भा: येषु (*adj.* of ०जाल्मै:). The water jars are a good omen. महत्तर as the name of an officer occurs in numerous grants (Compare I. A. VIII, p. 20 and I. A. vol. XII p. 25). खण्ड: candied sugar. धनेन घटिता: पेटका: येषाम् that had boxes full of money (as

Nazarana). प्र...द्रुतैः that fled being frightened by the angered and fierce staff-bearers. असतो...यद्भिः that laid bare the imaginary (असतः) faults of former provincial officers. असतः that did not exist. There is a touch of humour here and in many other places in this passage. भोग or भुक्ति frequently occurs as a sub-division of a country (see I. A. vol. 19 p. 303, 304). अति...शंसद्भिः praising hundreds of former (subordinate) officers (युक्तक). The reading आयुक्तक also is good. Both these occur in numerous grants. For आयुक्तक see I. A. vol. 16 p. 24; I. A. vol. 15 p. 187. As'oka's edicts mention certain officers called युता, who correspond to the युक्तकs (see the third edict in E. I. vol. II. p. 448 ff). चिरन्त...धानैः—the word चाट seems to have some technical sense. In grants of villages the word 'अचाटभटप्रवेश्यः' occurs very frequently. Dr Fleet renders it 'irregular troops' (C. I. I. III p. 98 n. 2). एकान्त...रक्षणम् in which protection of crops was sought against the coming Gauḍa king who was repeatedly thought of by a group of horsemen riding in a part (of the army). आदिष्ट...तुष्टैः who were pleased with the protecting officers to whom orders had been issued. लूयमानं निष्पन्नं (ripe) सस्यं तेन प्रकटितः विषादः यैः. Their crops had been taken for the army. क्षेत्रशुचा out of grief for (the state of) their fields. प्ररूढः प्राणच्छेदः येषाम् the destruction of whose lives had taken deep root *i. e.* whose lives were in imminent danger. Those who reviled the king were severely dealt with 'त्रैविद्यनृपदेवानां क्षेप उत्तमसाहसः' याज्ञ० II. 2 11.; राज्ञोऽनिष्टप्रवक्तारं तस्यैवाक्रोशकारिणम् । तन्मन्त्रस्य च भेत्तारं छित्वा जिह्वां प्रवासयेत् ॥' याज्ञ० II. 302. परितापेन (grief) त्याजितं भयं येषाम्. प्रारब्धा नरनाथस्य (हर्षस्य) निन्दा यस्मिन् (*adj.* of स्कन्धावारं). शशकैः—this is to be connected with कृतकलकलम् (p. 59 l. 4). प्रजः...बद्धैः (hares) pursued by swift crowds with formidable sticks in their hands. गिरिः...हन्यमानैः that were struck as if they were clods of earth (that also are struck with thick clubs in preparing the soil for crops). C and T translate 'struck like polo balls.' सञ्चरद्भिः goes with शशकैः. अपरैः—take with शशकैः. युग...तित that came upon them all at once. अनेक...कुशलिभिः (hares) clever in escaping between the legs of many animals. कुटिलिकया (वक्रगमनेन) व्यंसिताः सादिनां बहवः श्वानः यैः that gave the slip to many dogs of riders by dodges. व्यंस् *10th conj.* to foil. पतन्त्यः...यष्टयः येषु. कुद्दालः spade. खनित्रं hoe. निःस...बलात् that escaped because they were to live longer (though on them fell clods &c.). सङ्घशः in groups. घासिकैः—connect with

०धूलिपटलम्. घासे नियुक्तः one in charge of fodder. बुसधूल्या धूसरितानि घासजालेन जालकितानि (covered) जघनानि येषाम्. बुसं chaff. पुराणपर्याणस्य एकदेशात् दोलायमानानि दात्राणि (knives) येषाम्. शीर्णोर्णाशकलैः (with bits of torn wool) शिथिलाः मलिनाः मलकुथाः (dirty blankets) येषाम्. 'मलकुथैरिति पाठः । मलकुथा मलपट्टी छविरित्यर्थः । अंसोपरि वास इत्यन्ये' com. प्रभुणा प्रसादीकृतः पाटितः पटच्चरे चलन् चोलकः तं धारयन्ति इति—that wore a jacket dangling on a tattered garment, that was (once) presented by their master, (but now) all torn. 'पटच्चरं जीर्णवस्त्रम्' इत्यमरः. एकान्त...विग्रहम्—A portion of this compound occurs above (text p. 58 l. 28). The copyist was probably misled by the occurrence of the word उद्धूयमानधूलिपटलम् which in both places precedes the sentence. The proper text in the former place seems to be '०धूलिपटलम्, विमृग्यमाणसस्यसंरक्षणम्'. ०चक्रेण चर्व्यमाणः आगामी गौडविग्रहः यस्मिन् where the coming fight with the Gauḍa king was reflected upon by &c. If we read चर्च्यमाण, then the meaning is 'being discussed.' This is better. पङ्किलस्य (muddy) प्रदेशस्य पूरणाय आदेशः तेन आकुलैः सकललोकैः लूयमानाः तृणपूलकाः यस्मिन्. तलवर्तिनः (standing at the root of the trees) वेत्रिणः तेषां वेत्रैः वित्रास्यमानाः (being frightened) शाखिशिखरगताः विवादिनः ब्राह्मणाः यस्मिन्. कुलुण्ठकपाशे विवेष्ट्यमानाः (enveloped) ग्रामीणकानां (villagers) ग्रामेण समूहेन आकृष्टाः कौलेयकाः (dogs) यस्मिन्. For कौलेयक, see p. 97. 'कुलुण्ठकाः शुनां बन्धनलगुडाः' com. C and T prefer to read ग्रासाकृष्ट and translate 'village dogs, entrapped by bits of food, were being tied in leashes'. It is better to hold that powerful dogs (not village curs) were being led by villagers pressed into the service of the army. अन्योन्यविभवस्पर्धया उद्धुरैः राजपुत्रैः वाह्यमानाः वाजिनः तेषां संघट्टेन (collision, race) मण्डितम्. 'उन्नतमुद्धुरम्' क्षीर०. उद्धुर unchecked, bold. अनेक...जननम् that caused interest by its numerous incidents. जगतः ग्रासेन ग्रहणम्. The sea at the time of Pralaya engulfs (ग्रास) the world and makes it its own. The army wanted to seize the world and to hold it in its grasp. महा...गुप्तये (1) for the protection of the great serpents; (2) for the protection of great kings or rather headmen of villages. 'भोगी भुजङ्गमेऽपि स्याद् ग्रामपात्रे नृपे पुमान्' मे०. Pātāla is the abode of the Nâgas. कैलासम्—On कैलास, परमेश्वर (शिव) resides. See above p. 79. हर्ष was परमेश्वर (an emperor). दृश्यमानः सकलप्राणिनां पर्यायः यस्मिन् where all the animals were seen in succession (with ०कोशम्); in which all beings were seen to walk about (in military order). पर्यायः succession, rotation; regular order. प्रजापतीनाम्—see p. 55 for them. ब्रह्मा produced the ten प्रजापतिs, who in their turn produced the seven Manus, the Devas, demons, men, birds and beasts &c. See मनु I. 36 ff. For the four Yugas, see p. 3. For the creation of various beings see विष्णुपु. I. 5. चतु...कोशमिव like the collection (or store) of the creation of the four Yugas. There is another meaning. In a कोश (lexicon) there are seen synonyms (पर्यायः) for all beings. Perhaps Bâṇa alludes to some lexicon divided into four *sargas* (sections). चतुर्युग may itself mean कृतयुग (as कृत means four in the language of astronomers). When the world was first created, the कृतयुग began. क्लेशबहुलम् though abounding in troubles (applies to both 'army' and 'austerity'). क्रम...कल्याणानाम् The army would in the end achieve victory; तपःकरण (performance of austerities) leads gradually to happiness.

P. 114 l. 17—**P. 115** l.2 **आसन्न...सिष्ट.** आसन्नवर्तिनाम् and तत्रभवताम् qualifiy पार्थिवकुमाराणां (l. 32). 'पूज्ये तत्रभवानत्रभवांश्च भगवानपि'. It would be better to read तत्रभवता as the com. does. तत्रभवता goes with मान्धात्रा. For मान्धातृ, see pp. 23, 123. अप्रतिहतं रथरंहः (रथवेगः) यस्य. प्रसादनम् purifying, making clear (of enemies); calming down. The reading प्रसाधनम् of some mss. would be much better, being quite in keeping with Bâṇa's style. प्रसाधनम् accomplishing (conquering); ornamenting. करद one who pays tribute. For the conquest of the world by रघु, see रघुवंश IV. करदीचकार made them pay tribute. चक्रम् goes with भूभुजाम्. क्रमागतानां भुजबलं अभिजनः (noble ancestry) धनं च तेषां मदेन अवलिप्तानाम् (haughty). सव्यसाची applies to अर्जुन only out of the five पाण्डवs. 'उभौ मे दक्षिणौ पाणी गाण्डीवस्य विकर्षणे । तेन देवमनुष्येषु सव्यसाचीति मां विदुः ॥' विराटपर्व 44. 19. चीनविषयं = चीनदेशम्. राज...दे for completing the राजसूय. राजसूय was a sacrifice performed by a universal monarch at the time of his coronation to mark his undisputed sovereignity. See सभापर्व 32 ff. for the incidents of the राजसूय performed by युधिष्ठिर. क्रुध्यन्तः गन्धर्वाः तेषां धनुष्कोटीनां टाङ्कारेण कूजिताः कुञ्जाः यस्य. हेमकूट was the abode of the गन्धर्वs. अर्जुन is said to have conquered the गन्धर्वs (सभापर्व 2. 58). पराजैष्ट *Aorist* of जि with परा. जि necessarily takes the Âtmanepada when preceded by वि and परा. 'विपराभ्यां जेः' पा. 1. 3. 19. सङ्कल्पेन अन्तरितः separated or screened by resolve. तरस्विन् strong. The idea is :—In the case of the strong, what comes between the conquest of the world and them is the wish or resolve. As long as they do not desire, conquest is far off. The moment they desire it, it is theirs. सहिमः हिमवान् तेन व्यवहितः—though screened by the हिमालय with its snows. बाहु...कातरः afraid of the clash of his prowess (against that of his enemy). अकृती not happy, wretched. द्रुमः—was a king of किंपुरुष. 'द्रुमो किंपुरुषेशश्च उपास्ते धनदेश्वरम्' ॥ सभापर्व 10. 29. भगदत्त...प्रभृतयः—these are the names of various kings that were present in the great Mahâbhârata war. भगदत्त was king of प्राग्जोतिष and a partisan of दुर्योधन. He was killed by अर्जुन. दन्तवक्र was defeated by सहदेव in his दक्षिणदिग्विजय (सभापर्व 31. 3). क्राथ was a son of धृतराष्ट्र killed by भीम. शिशुपाल, कर्ण and जरासन्ध are well-known. शाल्व was a partisan of दुर्योधन and king of म्लेच्छ tribes. He was killed by सात्यकि (शल्यपर्व 20). सिन्धुराज is जयद्रथ. धनञ्जयजयेन जनितः जगत्कम्पः येन. समीप एव—The किंपुरुषs or किन्नरs are a race of semidivine beings with the face of a horse. Their country called किंपुरुषवर्ष was next to भारतवर्ष. The विष्णुपुराण (II. 2.) tells us that किंपुरुषवर्ष was next to भारतवर्ष between हिमवत् and हेमकूट. Compare 'इतश्च नातिदूरे तस्यास्माद्भारतवर्षादुत्तरेणानन्तरे किंपुरुषनाम्नि वर्षे वर्षपर्वतो हेमकूटो नाम निवासः' काद० (p. 136 of P). अलसः dull, lazy. There is a picturesque contrast between अलस and the literal meaning of the name चण्डकोश. चण्ड means 'fierce, powerful.' स्त्रीराज्यम्—see above p. 27. There is an untranslateable pun on the word चण्डकोश in relation to women. Put a vertical line after ०मादनयोः. हसी...मादनयोः very short is the distance between the Himālaya and the गन्धमादन. The idea is:—When even the distant countries of the Turks and the Persians are a mere span to the persevering hero, then surely the distance between the हिमालय and the गन्धमादन is small indeed. उत्सा...विषयः to the persevering the land of the Turushkas (Turks) is but a cubit. 'किष्कुर्हस्ते वितस्तौ च' इत्यमरः. Understand उत्साहिनः in each of the following clauses. It will be noticed that in the choice of words the poet is guided only by similarity of sounds. पारसीकदेशः Persia. प्रादेशः span. 'प्रादेशतालगोकर्णास्तर्जन्यादियुते तते ॥ अङ्गुष्ठे सकनिष्ठे स्याद्वितस्तिर्द्वादशाङ्गुलः ॥' इत्यमरः ('तर्जन्या युते तते प्रसारितेऽङ्गुष्ठे मध्यं, प्रादिश्यते प्रादेशः' क्षीर०). शकस्थानम् the country of the S'akas. The S'akas are identified with the Scythians, who migrated to India and established themselves at Taxila in Punjab, at Mathurā and in Kathiawad. अदृश्यमानः प्रतिप्रहारः यस्मिन् in which there is none to give a counter-stroke. पारियात्र is one of the seven principal mountains of India. From the बृहत्संहिता (69. 11-12) it seems that it was in Malva and corresponded to the western portion of the Vindhya and the Aravali Hills. यात्रैव शिथिला an expedition (against पारियात्र) is very easy. शौर्यं शुल्कं

यस्य. पिता...यूथेन the swarm of swans that are the conveyance of Brahmâ. हस्तs have white wings 'हंसास्तु श्वेतगरुतः' इत्यमरः. अत्रिनेत्रनिर्गतस्य—The moon is said to have sprung from the lustre of Atri's eye. See हरिवंश 25 'नेत्राभ्यां वारि सुस्राव दशधा द्योतयद्दिशः। तं गर्भं विधिना हृष्टा दश देव्यो दधुस्तदा ॥ समेत्य धारयामासुर्न च ताः समशक्नुवन् । स ताभ्यः सहसैवाथ दिग्भ्यो गर्भः प्रभान्वितः । पपात भासयंल्लोकाञ्शीतांशुः सर्वभावनः ।' verses 6–8. Compare 'अथ नयनसमुत्थं ज्योतिरत्रेरिव द्यौः' रघु. II. 75. कुमुद्s bloom in moonlight. उद्गमनक्षणः the moment of the emergence. पुण्डरीक has a long stalk like the handle of an umbrella and is white. आहिते...क्षणाम् as if the eyes (of people) had been satiated with the delight of seeing a moonlit evening. उदमांक्षीत्—Aorist of मस्ज् with उद्—emerged. मन्दाकिनी is the celestial Ganges and hence the word अम्बरोदरे (in the sky). महत् goes with ०मण्डलम्. The umbrella also was covered with an अम्बर (cloth). परि...निशया as if the day had been exchanged for a full moon night. The umbrella was raised up in space. But its mellow white light made the day look like night lit up by the full moon. The full moon also is white and round. इन्दूदयसन्देहेन दूयमानं मानसं येषाम् (*adj.* of मिथुनैः). As the umbrella looked like the moon, the चक्रवाकs thought that the time for separation had come. See p. 57 for चक्रवाक. विघटितं connect with ०मिथुनैः. विघटमानाभ्यः (that separated or opened) चञ्चुभ्यः च्युताः मृणालकोटयः येषाम्. The चक्रवाकs opened their beaks from grief and let fall from them the ends of fibres. आसन्नकमलिनी neighbouring lotus lake. ०पटलाशङ्कया सङ्कोचितं केकारवमूकं मुखपुटं येषाम्. The peacock is in its glory before the advent of the rains and its feathers begin to drop after the rains. The white umbrella they took to be an autumnal cloud. प्रबुद्धं कुमुदषण्डैः the beds of कुमुदs awoke (opened). आबद्धः चन्द्रात् (चन्द्रदर्शनात्) आनन्दः तेन उद्दामं उद्दलत् (opening) दलपुटं तस्य अट्टहासः तेन विशदं यथा स्यात् तथा. चित्रीयमाणं (विस्मयमानं) चेतः यस्य. चित्रीयते is a denominative verb from चित्र according to 'नमोवरिवश्चित्रङः क्यच्' पा. 3. 1. 19. The principal sentence is ०चेता...राजा दृष्टया सादरं ऐक्षिष्ट तत्...महच्छत्रम्. दण्डस्य अनुसारेण अधिरोहतीति—(eye) that mounted up following the track of the handle (of the umbrella). शैश...द्वीपस्य as if it were the babyhood of the white continent. A person, when a baby, is much fairer than when grown up. श्वेतद्वीप—In श्वेतद्वीप everything was supposed to be white; compare श्वेत द्वीपनिवासमिव...अनुभवति जने' का.द० (p. 162). For a description of श्वेतद्वीप see शान्तिपर्व chap. 336. 'आलोकयन्नुत्तरपश्चिमेन ददर्श चाप्यद्भुत-

मुक्तरूपम् । क्षीरोदधेर्योत्तरतो हि द्वीपः श्वेतः स नाम्ना प्रथितो विशालः ।।' 8 'श्वेताः पुमांसो गतसर्वपापाः' 10. अंशावतार—partial incarnation. When a portion of a deity appears in flesh and blood, that is अंशावतार, as opposed to पूर्णावतार. धर्म must be white (pure); its heart will be whiter. दन्ताः मण्डलकमिव तस्य द्युतिः तेन धवलं. A face (मुख) is illuminated by the lustre of white teeth. The commencement (मुखं) of the regime of an emperor (चक्रवर्तिन्) is marked by a मण्डल. For मण्डल (with reference to चक्रवर्ति) see p. 42. Further the umbrella was white and round and resembled ivory (दन्त) in its whiteness; or perhaps its ribs were made of ivory. मौक्तिक... दिवः—०परिकरेण or परिकरवत् वा सितम्. The idea is:—The umbrella was white, being surrounded by a band of bunches of pearls. It resembled the parting line of the hair of the damsel (Heaven). In the सीमन्त of a woman there may be a pearl ornament. The heaven has the ring (चक्र) of the Milky Way which is white and is like a सीमन्त and the stars therein resemble pearls. बहलज्योत्स्नया शुक्लं उदरं यस्य. The fully expanded umbrella was like the halo of the moon and its centre was like the orb of the moon. शौक्ल्येन अपहसिता शङ्खश्रीः यस्य येन वा. The umbrella was whiter than a conch. It was also whiter than the head front (शङ्खः) of ऐरावत. ऐरावत is white; compare 'ऐरावतदेहच्छविमिव (महाश्वेताम्)' काद० p. 129. An elephant's ear is always flapping and hence the umbrella is compared to the motionless ear of ऐ०. आवर्तः whirlpool. त्रिविक्रमस्य = विष्णोः. The Ganges is said to have sprung from the foot of Vishṇu. Compare 'वामपादाम्बुजाङ्गुष्ठे नखस्रोतोविनर्गता । विष्णोर्बिभर्ति यां भक्त्या शिरसाहर्निशं ध्रुवः ।।' विष्णुपु० II. 8. 110. See also मार्कण्डेय 56. प्रचेतसः = वरुणस्य. मानस...वेशम् which (umbrella) was surrounded by rows of chowries made of lotus fibres from the मानस lake. The white fibres resemble the bright rays of the crest jewel of वरुण. श्लिष्ट closely stuck. उपरि लक्ष्मणा... शिखरम्—on the top of the umbrella there was the emblem (लक्ष्मन् *n*) of a हंस with wings spread out. वितते पत्रे (पक्षौ) यस्य. चक्र...निश्चलेनेव—the figure of the हंस on the umbrella was naturally motionless. The poet fancies that it was a living हंस motionless because it was intent upon listening to the jingle of the anklets of the Glory of an emperor. For हंसs listening to anklets, see p. 95. स्पर्शवता = सुखस्पर्शेन or मृदुस्पर्शेन. प्रभाव...मृणालेन नीतेन दण्डताम्— its handle was made of a lotus stalk from the मन्दाकिनी, which (stalk) was made stiff by the power (of वरुण). मुकुलिता (contracted) फणा यस्य. वासुकि the lord of serpents is pale and long and resembles the long lotus stalk. प्रथिमन् *m.* breadth. समुच्छाय: height. स्तबक...स्तम्भस्य it was like a bunch of flowers on the trunk (tree) of Brahmâ *i. e.* it was the pick, the cream of the world. नाभि०—As the spokes start from the round nave (नाभि) of a wheel, so from it radiated light. कीर्ति is white.

P. 116 l. 22—**P. 117** l. 13 **च...छायाम्.** कार्मा: = 'स कार्मः कर्मशीलो यः' इत्यमरः. 'कार्मस्ताच्छील्ये' पा. 6. 4. 172. परार्ध्यरत्नानां अंशुभिः शोणीकृताः दिग्भागाः यैः (*adj.* of अलङ्कारान्). Remove the comma after दिग्भागान्. For भगदत्त, see above p. 187 and text p. 63. परागत come, handed down. आहतलक्षणान् = प्रसिद्धान्, 'गुणैः प्रतीते तु कृतलक्षणाहतलक्षणौ' इत्यमरः (आहतानि उद्घोषितानि लक्षणानि यस्य). प्रभा...त्कर्षान् the best of crest jewels that covered (everything) with their sheen. अनेक...क्षौमाणि— silken cloth rolled up in charming variously coloured cane boxes and bright like the rays of the autumn moon and that were capable of purifying a person. उल्लिखित carved out. For गल्वर्क, see p. 77. निचोलकैः (cases) रक्षिता रुक् (कान्तिः) येषाम्. ०भङ्गेन भङ्गुराणां wavy with charming figures in gold. अतिबन्धुरः परिवेशः (fringe, hem) येषाम्. कार्दरङ्गचर्मणाम् of कार्दरङ्ग shields. कार्दरङ्ग seems to be the name of a country. जातीपट्टिकाः loin-cloths. 'जातीपट्टिकाः श्रेष्ठानि जघनग्रन्थनानि' com. चित्रपट cloth with paintings or figures. समूरुक is a kind of deer. उपधानम् pillow. 'समूरुश्चेति हरिणा अमी अजिनयोनयः' इत्यमरः. प्रियङ्गुप्रसववत् पिङ्गला त्वक् येषाम्. प्रियङ्गुः millet. प्रसवः fruit. अगुरुवल्कलेन कल्पितः सञ्चयः येषाम् the leaves of which were made of अगुरु bark. परिणतं (अत एव) पाटलं पटोलं तस्येव त्विट् (कान्तिः) येषाम्. पटोल is called in Marathi पडवळ. तरुण...हरिन्ति as green as a young pigeon. Some of the betel nuts were green and some red. क्षीरक्षारीणि from which milky juice was oozing (being recently cut from the trees). ०कपोलवत् कपिलानि कापोतिकापलाशानि तेषां कोश्या कवचितं अङ्गं यासाम् that were covered with cases of the leaves of the कापोतिका plant as tawny as the cheeks &c. स्थवीयसी *f.* comparative of स्थूल. वैणवीर्नाडीः (object of प्रकाशयांचक्रुः) tubes of bamboo. पट्ट...र्पितान् (connect with राशीन्) placed in bags made of woven silk. For प्रसेवक, see p. 180. भिन्ना...गुरुणः of black aloe (कृष्णागुरु *n.*) as dark as pounded collyrium. This and the following genitives are to be connected with राशीन्. गोशीर्षम् is a kind of very fragrant sandal. 'तैलपर्णिकगोशीर्षे हरिचन्दनमस्त्रियाम्' इत्यमरः ('तैलपर्णगोशीर्षौ गिरी आकरौ अस्य' क्षीर०). कस्तू...कानां of bags of musk. कक्कोलं a fragrant berry (Marathi कंकोळ). जातीफलं nutmeg. अतिमधुरः मधुरसः

तस्य आमोदेन निर्हारिणीः redolent of the perfume of very sweet wine. The com. takes the word to be मधुरसा. 'मृद्वीका गोस्तनी द्राक्षा स्वाद्वी मधुरसेति च' इत्यमरः. उल्लककलशीः pitchers of उल्लक. 'उल्लकः सुगन्धिफलविशेषरस: । आसवभेद इत्यन्ये' com. अवलम्बमानानि तूलिकाः (brushes) अलाबुकानि च येभ्यः—अलाबुकम् vessel made of a gourd (to hold paints). आ...टान् boxes of boards for drawing pictures. कनकशृङ्खलया नियमिताः ग्रीवाः येषां or यासाम्. For किंनर, see above p. 187. C and T suggest that some species of ape may be meant here. वनमानुषी 'ourang—outang' C and T. जीवञ्जीवक is a bird, the चकोर according to अमरकोश. Compare 'पाणितलसंवर्धितं मे जीवञ्जीवमिथुनं क्रीडापर्वते यथा न विपद्यते तथा कर्तव्यम्' काद० p. 316. परिमलेन आमोदिताः ककुभः (दिशः) यैः. गेह... चमरीः chamarî deer accustomed to move about the house. चामीकर...गतान् placed in cages of cane painted with gold. बहुसुभाषितैः जल्पाका जिह्वा येषाम्. जल्पाक garrulous. 'स्याज्जल्पाकस्तु वाचालः' इत्यमरः. 'जल्पभिक्षकुट्टलुण्टवृङः षाकन्' पा. 3. 2. 155. प्रवालः—लम्—coral. जल...कुण्डलानि rings of the long tusks of hippopotamus, bristling (दन्तुर) with rows of large (उदग्र) pearls from their headfronts. It was believed that pearls were found in the temples of elephants. 'द्विपभुजगशुक्तिशङ्खाभ्रवेणुतिमिसूकरप्रसूतानि । मुक्ताफलानि तेषां बहु साधु च शुक्तिजं भवति ॥' बृह० 81. 1. Compare 'शशिकेसरिविदार्यमाणतमःकरिकुम्भसम्भवेन मुक्ताफलक्षोदेनेव धवलतामुपनीयमान्' काद० p. 160 of P. सकल...धाम्नः that is the abode of all precious things (applies both to महार्णव and कुमार). परमे...हंस्य which is fit to be held on the head of a परमेश्वर (emperor); which is to be held on the head by परमेश्वर (शिव). शिव placed the moon on his head to lessen the fever of his body due to हालाहल. कुमुदबान्धवस्य = चन्द्रस्य. न विसयाय does not cause wonder *i. e.* does not make me wonder. बाल...कृतयः favours (bestowed on others) are the first lessons of the great. मङ्गलाकाङ्क्षी desiring an auspicious (conclusion to his expedition). प्राङ्मुखः with his face to the east. आभोगस्य—the umbrella was so called.

P. 117 l. 19—**P. 118** l. 9 **अथ विशत...वनानाम्.** अस्य = हर्षस्य. छायायाः जन्म यस्य (*adj.* of जडिम्ना). जडिम्ना...बिम्बम् by the coolness it seemed as if the disc of the moon had become his crest jewel *i. e.* under the shade of the umbrella he felt as much coolness as he would have if the moon had been placed on his crest. Explain the following similarly. Everyone of his limbs and his whole body felt the coolness. अम्बुबिन्दून् मुञ्चन्तीति ०मुचः (*adj.* of मणयः). It should be noted that all the objects mentioned are white and cool. चन्द्रकान्त—moonstone, that was believed to ooze when the rays of the moon fell upon it. कर्पू...युगले his eyes felt the coolness of camphor applied to them. गलन्तः तुहिनकणाः तेषां निकरेण कृतः नीहारः (frost, dew) येषाम्. हरि...मुरसि—हरिचन्दनम् is a kind of yellowish sandal. अन्त... दङ्गानि a concealed melting slab of ice as if smeared his limbs. अजर्यं सङ्गतम् undying or everlasting friendship 'अजर्यं सङ्गतम्' पा. 3. 1. 105 (नञ्पूर्वात् जीर्यतेः कर्तरि यत् सङ्गतं चेद्विशेष्यम् । सि. कौ.). प्रतिकौशलिका a present in return (from कुशलं). हंसवेगाय—connect with प्राहिणोत्. धवलकर्पटेन प्रावृतं धौतं (bright, polished) नालिकेरं (cocoanut shell used as a box) तस्मिन् परिगृहीतम् contained. विलिप्तशेषं चन्दनम् (object of प्राहिणोत्) sandal paste that remained after he (हर्ष) had anointed himself. This was deemed a mark of great favour and friendship. अङ्गस्पृष्टे—touched by his own person. शरदि तारकाः तेषां इव आकारः यासां ताः ०काराः ताराः (pure and bright) मुक्ताः तैः स्तबकितं पदं यस्य. The stars shine very brightly in the clear autumnal sky. कटिसूत्रम् belt. कटक...तरत्— the setting of the sun is represented as due to his desire to wash his body rendered dusky by dust. 'मलीमसं तु मलिनम्' इत्यमरः. वारुणीं दिशम्—वरुण presides over the West. अयासीत्—the subject is अंशुमाली. कमलs close their petals at sunset. प्रमुखे एव at the very beginning (of his expedition). The closing petals of the lotuses are represented as the folded hands of the earth. The earth as if submitted to him at the very start of his march. नृपा...मयः इव (the glow of twilight) was as if made up of the अनुराग (love, redness) for the king. The idea is:—the twilight made the whole world aglow; the poet fancies it was rather the अनुराग of the world that spread over it. निखिल...बन्धुः which is a kinsman (*i. e.* closely connected) with the folding of the hands of the people. People perform सन्ध्यावन्दन in the evening; people also fold their hands before a king. ०शङ्किनी afraid of. प्रचितः तिमिरस्य निवहः (समूहः) यस्याम्. निर्वाणः (extinguished) अन्यनृपप्रतापानलकलापः यस्याम्. When we quench fire, black charcoal is left. अवचकरुः *perfect 3rd plu.* of कृ with अव to spread. मेदिनी...ककुभः—clusters of stars resembling expanded *Tagara* flowers twinkled in the sky and seemed as if they were the bunches of flowers spread in the evening audience-hall of the lord of the earth. मार्गो...वतस्य the track of ऐरावत grey with dust shone in the sky. ऐरावत is the vehicle of इन्द्र, the lord of the east. The dust is represented to be raised by ऐरावत that fled from the गन्धगजs of Harsha. रजःपाण्डुः also means 'pale like or with the pollen of flowers'. The east became lit up with the rays of the moon that was about to rise. कुपितः नृपः (हर्षः) व्याघ्र इव तेन आघ्राताम् (smelt, touched). उपसृष्टामिव as if it were possessed by an evil spirit. पौरुहूतीम् = ऐन्द्रीम्. रोहिणीरमणः = चन्द्रः. For रोहिणी being the favourite wife of the moon, see pp. 9, 47, 62. The simple idea is that the moon rose up high in the sky. रोहिणीरमण also means 'a bull', that leaves a place where he smells the tiger. रोहिणी a tawny cow. 'अर्जुन्यघ्न्या रोहिणी स्यादुत्तमा गोषु नैचिकी' इत्यमरः. C and T see here a reference to the growing power of शशाङ्क the Gauḍa king. मानिनी...भेदिन्यः the rays of the moon melt the heart of proud women *i. e.* they become favourable to their husbands with whom they were displeased. प्रयाण ...भेदिन्यः as the news of the march (of Harsha's army) breaks the heart of proud women (because they are afraid of the death of their husbands when they oppose him). नवनृपस्य (हर्षस्य) दण्डयात्रा &c. चक्षुभु...हिनीनाम् the lords of rivers (oceans) became agitated *i. e.* after the rise of the moon the ocean has a full tide. This tidal agitation is fancied to be due to the fear of the expedition of हर्ष. वाहिनीनां पतयः also means 'commanders'. तरलिताः सत्त्वानां प्राणिनां वृत्तयः येषु the movements of the animals in which were made unsteady (with oceans). By the tide the aquatic animals were carried here and there. तरलिता सत्त्वस्य धैर्यस्य वृत्तिः येषाम् whose steadiness of mind was shaken. चिन्ता— anxiety entered the hearts of kings (भूभृत्). Darkness entered the caves of mountains (भूभृत्) *i. e.* only the caves were dark; the rest was lighted up by the moon. विमुक्ताः सर्वाः आशाः दिशः यया (*adj.* of सन्ततिः); विमुक्ता सर्वा आशा (hope) यस्यां (*adj.* of चिन्ता). निद्रा...वनानाम्—The कुमुद lotuses open in moon-light. प्रति...निद्रा sleep left the eyes of the rivals of हर्ष.

P. 118 l. 10—**P. 119** l. 12 **अस्यां...स्वामिन इति.** महावराहसम्पर्केण सम्भृतः गर्भः यस्याः. महावराह refers to the Boar incarnation of विष्णु. Compare 'यदाहमुद्धृता नाथ त्वया सूकरमूर्तिना । त्वत्स्पर्शसम्भवः पुत्रस्तदायं मय्यजायत ॥' विष्णुपु० 5. 29. 23. नरक was king of प्राग्ज्योतिष. कृष्ण killed him at the request of Indra. He deprived वरुण of his umbrella, took away मणिपर्वत from मन्दर, the ear-rings of अदिति &c. 'छत्रं यत्सलिलस्रावि तज्जहार प्रचेतसः ।' विष्णु० 5. 29. 10. त्रिभुवनं भुङ्क्ते इति ०भुक् तस्य. भुजयोः शौण्डः प्रवीणः. The construction is यस्य... आज्ञया विना रविरस्तं न अव्राजीत्. ०वाकीभिः कोपकुटिलैः कटाक्षैः ईक्षितः. The चक्रवाकी is separated from her lord at sunset and so fearing it looks angrily at the sun. भयचकितेन अरुणेन परिवर्तितः (turned)

रथः यस्य. अरुण is the charioteer of the sun. बहि...यमिव as if it (छत्र) were his heart dwelling outside. The छत्र was as dear to वरुण as his own heart. Only the छत्र was outside his body. अन्वये in the line or family. भगदत्त was a contemporary of the Pâṇḍavas and took part in the great war. See above p. 187. वज्रदत्त was son of भगदत्त and was defeated by the Pāndavas in their अश्वमेध. See आश्वमेधिकपर्व chap. 76. कैलासस्य इव स्थिरा स्थितिः यस्य whose sense of duty was as firm as Kailâsa. अग्रजेन... कारेण who was born together with pride, as if the latter was the elder of the two. The idea is:—he and अहङ्कार were twin brothers; but अहङ्कार was the elder of the two *i. e.* he paid more regard to, subordinated everything to अहङ्कार. From his very birth he was proud. The reading अजेनेव does not yield a good sense. प्रतिग्रहान् (1) presents (with द्विजातीन्); (2) the rear of an army. अरातीन् प्रतिग्रहान् अग्राहयत् he made his enemies take to the rear of their armies *i. e.* to run from the battlefield. 'सैन्यपृष्ठे प्रतिग्रहः' इत्यमरः. यत्र परं...लक्ष्म्या in whom लक्ष्मी (royal glory) attained her greatest sweetness. There is a picturesque contradiction in saying that लक्ष्मी sprung from the *salt* ocean became *sweet.* Effects generally possess the properties of their causes. वाहिनीनाथानां (1) of commanders of armies; (2) of oceans. शङ्ख was an emblem of command. The great warriors in the महाभारत war had each a शङ्ख which they blew before beginning the fight. Both शङ्खs and jewels are found in the sea as well as with commanders. स्थैर्यः...करम् he took the steadiness of the earth, but did not levy tribute from it. He was as steady as the earth. अवनिभृतां = राज्ञां, पर्वतानां च. गौरव...नैष्ठुर्यम्—mountains have गौरव and नैष्ठुर्य both. He took the one (*i. e.* he was majestic) and not the other (*i. e.* he was not harsh). There is a suggested sense. He deprived the kings of their high position. C and T take भास्करद्युति as the name of the king. This does not seem to be correct. भास्करस्य इव द्युतिर्यस्य. The king's name was कुमार alias भास्करवर्मन्. See above text p. 60. l. 4. भास्करद्युति as the name of a king will probably be found nowhere (with the last word द्युति in the feminine gender). The word कुमार suggests another idea. भीष्म remained a कुमार (prince) all his life; he never became a king. सङ्कल्पः resolve. स्थेयान् *nom. sing. m.* of the comparative of स्थिर. प्रचण्डेन प्रतापज्वलनेन जनितः दिशां दाहः येन. जगत्येकवीरेण who is the only (unequalled) warrior in the world. मैत्री...भृताम् the friendship of kings generally is dependent upon some purpose *i. e.* it is never disinterested. य...देवम् which when mentioned would make your Majesty a friend (of the king भास्करवर्मा). सञ्चिचीषतः desiring to collect. He now mentions several purposes which induce kings to form friendships and dismisses them all by saying that Harsha is in need of none of them. First he takes up wealth. बहिरङ्ग external *i. e.* not of the essence. बाहा...काशः As he relies solely upon his arm, the desire of even his other limbs to help him has no scope *i. e.* even his other limbs cannot offer him any help; what can a stranger do? चतुःसागराणां ग्रामः समूहः तस्य ग्रहणे घस्मरस्य (greedy). उपन्यासः proposal. The word ग्राम suggests that even the four oceans are but a small village to हर्ष. अभि...भनमपि अकिञ्चित्करम् even the allurement of the gift of a beautiful maiden is of no value. लक्ष्मीमुखारविन्ददर्शनेन दुर्ललिता (fondled) दृष्टिः यस्य. No maiden can be more alluring than लक्ष्मी. अघट...पदार्थेऽस्मिन् this being an object that is attainable by means which are all incapable of attaining it. प्रार्थनामात्रकमेव—connect with शृणोतु. अनुरुध्यमानः being favourably disposed. देवेन—connect with अजर्यं सङ्गतमिच्छति. एक...द्विषा like that of Kubera with the enemy of Cupid. He cast a glance at उमा and lost his left eye and the right became yellow. See रामायण VII. 13. 22–24. एकं पिङ्गं (नेत्रं) यस्य. The author instances five memorable friendships. For दशरथ and Indra, see p. 123. पुष्कराक्षः = पुण्डरीकाक्षः (कृष्णः). वैकर्तनः—son of विकर्तन (the sun) *i. e.* कर्ण. कर्ण was made king of अङ्ग by दुर्योधन. 'अस्य राज्यप्रदानस्य सदृशं किं ददानि ते।...अत्यन्तं सख्यमिच्छामीत्याह तं स सुयोधनः॥' आदिपर्व 136. 39–40. मलयानिल and माधव (वसन्त) are both excitants of love. मैत्रीयति—feels friendship. अवगच्छति...इति (and if your Majesty's) heart understands that friends discharge a slavery under another name. The idea is that friendship entails so many obligations that one has to work day and night for the other. तत...स्यते then why sit (silent)? अनुभवतु—the object is गाढोपगूढानि (close embraces). विष्णो...रिरिव as the mountain Mandara had the close embrace of विष्णु. मन्दर was the churning handle and विष्णु churned the ocean and the mountain rubbed against his body. विकट...मणीनां विघट्टनेन (striking against) कणितानि (jingling) कटकमणिशिलाशकलानि येषु. केयूरक is an ornament of the arm and कटक is a bracelet. In a close embrace these two ornaments will strike against each other. कटकः—कम् also means 'the slope of a hill'. 'कटकोऽस्त्री नितम्बोद्रेः' इत्यमरः. The केयूरक of विष्णु clashed against the slopes of मन्दर in churning. कामरूप is the same as प्राग्ज्योतिष. अस्मिन् goes with ०शशिनि. आ तृप्तेः till she (श्री) is satisfied. अन...र्झरिणि that pours forth a constant spring of nectar in the form of spotless beauty and grandeur. लालयतु let her please or indulge. The simple idea is:—let the king of प्राग्ज्योतिष see your Majesty's face. But the words चिरात्, शशिनि and श्रीः suggest another sense. लक्ष्मी sprang from the ocean as the moon did and therefore लक्ष्मी is the sister of the moon. Let the sister separated from her brother see him after a long time. नाभि...प्रणयम् If your Majesty does not welcome his love or if your Majesty does not approve of his request.

P. 119 ll. 13–24 **विरत...त्कण्ठा इति.** पूर्वोपलब्धैः which he had heard of (by hearsay). आरोपितः बहुमानः यस्मिन् in whom great regard (for कुमार) had been produced. ०व्यतिकरेण by the incident of &c. महान् अभिजनः (family) यस्य. प्राग्रहरः foremost (प्रकृष्टं अग्रं हरति). परोक्षसुहृदि who is a friend without seeing me. शिशिरायन्ते become cool. कमलाकरे on a bed of lotuses. तिग्मं तीक्ष्णं तेजः यस्य = रवेः. The idea is that the कमलs do not feel that the rays of the sun are hot. सु...सख्यस्य being bought by his numerous qualities, who am I to (form) friendship? The idea is:—his qualities have already made me his. It is not in my hands to *form* a friendship which did not exist before. सज्जन...दिशः the ten quarters are the unhired slaves of the sweetness of the good. The good make the world theirs by their sweetness. एकान्तावदातः उत्तानः स्वभावः तेन सम्भृतं सादृश्यं येन. The कुमुद is extremely white; so is the moon. The कुमुद is उत्तान (has its petals turned up towards the moon); the moon also is उत्तान (open, straightforward). Thus the two resemble each other and form friendship without anybody's intercession. Compare 'समानशीलव्यसनेषु सख्यम्'. समालम्बितं शरासनं येन. अव...हृदयस्य the heart feels great regard for the proud lion, though a beast.

P. 119 l. 25—**P. 121** l. 16 **हंसवेगस्तु...निर्जगाम.** किमप...देवेन 'What else will now give pain (to both of you)? Your Majesty has spoken noble words.' He says that nothing else but the eagerness to see one another will hereafter pain the two kings. अहङ्कारः धनं यस्य. वैष्णवो वंशः—the family of भास्करवर्मा descended from नरक, the son of the earth and महावराह. पुरुषस्य हि—the principal sentence is पुरुषस्य हि सेवां प्रति...अभिमुखीक्रियमाणस्य...राजकुलं संप्रवेष्टुं कृतचित्तस्य (p. 64 l. 33)...किं प्रायश्चित्तम्...कीदृशं जीवितम् &c. (p. 66 ll. 1–3). सेवा...क्रियमाणस्य who is induced to (enter) service by his extremely wretched state, like a bad old mother. अतिवृद्धया very old; very much aggravated. 'निरयो दुर्गतिः स्त्रियाम्' अम०. वा—It will be noticed that in each clause up to अनुवर्त्यमानस्य there is वा. These are put forward as the various reasons which led a man to accept the service of a king. कुट...प्रेर्यमाणस्य who is urged (towards service) by greed like a discontented wife. A discontented wife always urges her husband to earn more. तृष्णा also can never be gratified to the full. All genitives in this long passage are to be connected with पुरुषस्य. असत्सङ्कल्पैः by evil thoughts. यौव...षिभिः (apply both to bad children and ०सङ्कल्प) that are born of youth and that desire many things. जरत्कु...पश्यतः who sees (*i. e.* expects) a great position like an old maid (a daughter rather advanced in age for marriage). पर...योग्याम् that is commensurate with the solicitations he addresses to others (with अवस्थाम्); that is fit to be sought by others (with ०कुमारीम्). परेषां मार्गणं (याचनं) तस्य योग्याम्; परैः मार्गणं तस्य &c. स्वगृहे...योगम् who is compelled to make efforts by all badly placed planets in their houses like bad kinsmen. स्वगृहे—in his own house; in their 'houses' or 'mansions' (with ग्रहैः). The planets are believed to be very powerful when they are in 'mansions' (स्वगृह) *e. g.* सिंह is the स्वगृह of रवि, कर्क of the Moon, मेष and वृश्चिक of Mars and so on. दुःस्थितैः in distressed circumstances; in evil aspects with other planets. 'आभिमुख्येन उद्यमः अभियोगः' क्षीर०. पुरातनैः of long standing; done in former lives (with कर्मभिः). अतिदुस्त्यजैः—old servants cannot be easily got rid of; the fruits of evil deeds done in past lives cannot be avoided. मलिनैः dirty (servants); sinful. It is the sinful deeds in past lives that follow a man and make him take service. सकल...करम् goes with both कारीषाग्निम् and राजकुलम्. कारीषस्य अग्निः fire of dried cowdung. Its heat is more intense than that of fire fed with wood. करीषं शुष्कगोमयं तस्य समूहः कारीषम्. कृत...कुलम् who has made up his mind to enter the palace (*i. e.* the service of a king). दुष्कृतिनः one who is guilty of some deadly sin. He may be condemned to be burnt alive. उपहता सक...शक्तिः यस्य. मिथ्यैव...लाषस्य who has vain hopes of seizing the whole gamut of the sensual pleasures his heart desires. The servant vainly thinks that he would by entering service enjoy all विषयs; the old voluptuary also thinks the same. प्रथममेव शुष्यतो...रुद्धस्य first of all (before a man actually gets into royal service) he is obstructed by the doorkeepers and has to wither away at the portal for days. The वन्दनमाला also is tied to the portals and becomes dried by time. For वन्दनमाला see p. 178. करि...पुटस्य—see (text p. 49 l. 17) for ०पुट. प्रति...मानस्य—he is driven out by doorkeepers who beat him with their hands. The leather figure also is beaten by the कर (trunk of elephants) encased in a covering. 'प्रतिहारेण वेष्टनेन मण्डलं यस्य करस्य तत्प्रहारैश्च' com. अधो...भवतः who bends down his face (*i. e.* bows low) through greed of money. निधि...रोहस्य—it was believed that a tree with treasure beneath it had boughs bending in a peculiar way. See above text p. 4 'निधिस्तरुविकारेण'. अमार्गणस्यापि (1) though he is not a suppliant; (2) though not an arrow. अतिविप्रकृष्टैः आदौ विवृत्तः पश्चात् विसर्जितः he is made to turn back by very mean (servants at the court) and then dismissed. दूरं उद्वेगं व्रजतः he becomes extremely dejected. An arrow also is अति...व्रजतः. It is drawn (विवृत्त) very far (up to the ear) and then discharged. दूरं उद्वेगं व्रजतः (an arrow) reaches a long distance very swiftly (उत्कृष्टः वेगः यथा स्यात्तथा). विवृत also will yield a good meaning. He is first thoroughly examined by low people. The arrow (*i. e.* the bow) is opened very wide. अकण्टक...माणस्य he dogs the feet of persons about the court, who draw him and throw him out quickly, though he is not a thorn. कण्टक has also a technical meaning 'a troublesome person'. The अर्थशास्त्र has a section on कण्टकशोधन. क्षेपीयः used as an *adv.* (comparative of क्षिप्र). A thorn also pierces the sole of one's feet, is taken out and thrown away. अ...केतोः (1) though he is not Cupid; though he is innocent of love affairs (being engrossed in thoughts of service). अकालोपसर्पणेनः कुपितः ईश्वरः (राजा, शिवश्च) तस्य दृष्ट्या दग्धस्य. मदन tried to influence शिव when the latter was engaged in meditation and was burnt; see p. 38. The candidate for service approaches the king at an improper moment and angers him. प्रलय...तः (1) who is destroyed (with Cupid); (2) who disappears (with पुरुषस्य). अभिन्नः मुखरागः यस्य (applies both to कपि and पुरुष)—The redness of the ape's face remains as before. The servant shows no sign on his face though soundly rated. ब्रह्मघ्नः— the murderer of a ब्राह्मण. ब्रह्महत्या was a महापातक; see p. 84. प्रतिदिवसवन्दनेन उदघृष्टं शिरःकपालं यस्य येन वा—the aspirant after service has to bow down every day and his head is thereby rubbed off. One that murders a ब्राह्मण has to bow by way of प्रायश्चित्त before a skull. Remove the comma after ०कपालस्य. स्पर्श...र्वहतः the servant is devoid of the pleasures of senses and has to carry out degrading duties. स्पर्शः means 'pleasant feelings, pleasure'. The slayer of a Brāhmaṇa had to avoid society and had to live by unworthy means. Note '**शिरःकपाली ध्वजवान्** भिक्षाशी कर्म वेदयन् । **ब्रह्महा** द्वादशाब्दानि मितभुक् शुद्धिमाप्नुयात् ॥' याज्ञ० III. 243 ('तच्च कपालं स्वव्यापादितब्राह्मणशिरःसम्बन्धि ग्राह्यम् । ... तदलाभे अन्यस्य ब्राह्मणस्यैव ग्राह्यम्' मिताक्षरा). See मनु 11. 78, which prescribes for him a forest dwelling. अर्वाक्शिरसः—with head downwards (*i. e.* bent). The servant has day and night to bow to his master. त्रिशङ्कुः—He was a king of the solar race and father of हरिश्चन्द्र. He wished to go to heaven with his mortal body by performing a यज्ञ. His family priest वसिष्ठ declared it impossible. He went to the sons of वसिष्ठ who rejected his proposal. त्रिशङ्कु told them that he would go to another preceptor, whereupon they cursed him to be a चण्डाल. विश्वामित्र, whose family त्रिशङ्कु had saved from starvation in a famine, took pity on him and raised त्रिशङ्कु towards heaven, when Indra refused to admit him and made him fall down headlong. Thereupon विश्वामित्र called upon him to stay where he was and began to create new worlds, नक्षत्रs &c. The gods intervened and made his creations as eternal as those of ब्रह्मा and त्रिशङ्कु blazed forth as a constellation, but with head downwards. See रामायण I. 57–60. Compare 'सुरलोकमारोहतस्त्रिशङ्कोरिव कुपितशतमखहुंकारनिपतिता राजलक्ष्मीः' काद० p. 8. सुखवाह्यम् easily driven (with वाजिनः); who is bereft of happiness (with पुरुषस्य). In the latter case वाह्य is equal to बाह्य; compare वंशबाह्याम् (text p. 39 l. 12, notes p. 125). अनशनशायिनः—One who has resolved upon dying by starvation. हृदये स्थापिता जीवनस्य (of livelihood) आशा येन the man has hopes in his heart of making a livelihood by service. हृदये स्थापितः जीवनाशः येन. निज...खस्य—being engrossed in his duties, the servant has no time to bestow on his wife. The application of निज...खस्य to a dog cannot be explained for the sake of decency. जघन्ये अधमे कर्मणि लग्नं सक्तम्. जघन्यं (जघने भवं) कर्म सुरतं तस्मिन् लग्नम्. अनु...पिण्डस्य—the servant has to take his food in some dirty place. अन्नपिण्ड is offered to the dead (प्रेत) in places (*viz.* river &c.) where the deceased was never accustomed to take food. बलिभुजः = काकस्य. जिह्वायाः लौल्येन उपयुक्तं पुरुषवर्चः येन who wasted his manly spirit for satisfying his fastidious tongue. जिह्वालौल्येन उपयुक्तं (भुक्तं) पुरुषस्य वर्चः (excrement) येन (with crow). 'तेजःपुरीषयोर्वर्चः' अम. वृथा...जीवतः who lives a life applied to no purpose (applies to both). The crow is supposed to live long. 'काकोऽपि जीवति चिरं च बलिं च भुङ्क्ते'. वृथा विहितं

आयुः यस्य. The com. separates 'विभ्यः पक्षिभ्यः हितमायुः यस्य' who has a life useful to birds (with crow). दग्ध...कृताम् rendered rugged by the ashes of persons burnt (with श्म०); rendered harsh by their accursed prosperity (with ०वल्लभान्). दग्धानां भूत्या; दग्धा चासौ भूतिः तया. पिशाचs were supposed to resort to the trees of the cemetery. विपरीतजिह्वया जनितं माधुर्यं येषाम् (1) who talk sweet words by a false tongue (with kings); who talk sweetly with a tongue that is turned backwards (with parrots). ओष्ठमात्रे (ओष्ठे एव) प्रकटितः रागः (प्रीतिः, रक्तत्वं च) येषाम्. The hearts of the kings know no affection; it is only their words that are full of affection. The beak of the parrot is red. राजानः शुकाः इव. राजशुकाः—a variety of parrots. मुग्ध...मानस्य who is fooled and allured. नरेन्द्र...विष्टस्य that takes possession of a person by the power of a wizard (with वेताल); who is overcome by the power of his king (with servant). For नरेन्द्र in the sense of wizard, see p. 33. न कि...तः there is nothing that he will not do (with both) वेताल and servant. चित्रधनुष इव like a painted bow. अलीकं गुणाध्यारोपणं एव एका क्रिया तस्यां नित्यनम्रस्य—the painted bow is always bent and has a false (*i. e.* unreal, painted) string placed upon it. The servant is also humble and solely engaged in ascribing false virtues to his master. निर्वाणं (extinguished) तेजः यस्य (with धनुषः and पुरुषस्य). The pictured bow has not the force of the real one. संमार्जन्या (broom-stick) समुपार्जितं रजः (dust) येन—the servant has to scour the dust off the floor by a broom-stick; dust is accumulated by a broom-stick and thrown on अवकरकूट. अवकरकूटः heep of sweepings. 'संमार्जनी शोधनी स्यात् सङ्करोऽवकरस्तया । क्षिप्ते' अम०. निर्माल्यम् flowers used and cast off. These may be thrown on the heap of sweepings; the servant is often given what his master has worn. Besides the word may suggest that he wears no माल्य (flowers, which produce beauty and are a sign of happiness). C and T suggest that निर्माल्य may mean purity. We fail to see how; and even if it does, it cannot be made to fit in here. कटुकै...मानस्य—the servant is worried by the sharp words of his master; or कटुक has the same sense as on p. 54 l. 14 (text). A man suffering from कफ is treated with कटुक (bitters). See अष्टाङ्गहृदय I. 13. 10. 'श्लेष्मणो विधिना युक्तं तीक्ष्णं वमनरेचनम् । अन्नं रूक्षाल्पतीक्ष्णोष्णं कटुतिक्तकषायकम् ॥.' कटुकं also means 'Ginger, long and black pepper'. सौगतस्य—बौद्धस्य. सुगत is a name of बुद्ध and सौगत means a follower of बुद्ध. अर्थशून्या (धनविरहिता, बाह्यवस्तुशून्या) विज्ञप्तिः (प्रार्थना, विज्ञानं च)

from स्था with उद्. This gerund here conveys the idea of haste. 'अपादाने परीप्सायाम्' पा. 3. 4. 52. (परीप्सा त्वरा। शय्योत्थायं धावति ॥ सि. कौ). The courtier is in a hurry to bow to his master, the moment he leaves his bed. The ascetic also performs obeisance. The courtier degrades his family (गोत्र॰). The विदूषक (the buffoon of the Indian stage) remains in the family of the hero, makes grimaces and makes his master laugh. The courtier dances (attendance) on his master. The servant is a blot on the fair name of his family (कु॰). वंशं दहतः bamboos also are burnt by अङ्गार (live coal). नृपशोः...नमयतः a beast such as a bull bends its neck when grass is seen by it. The courtier bows even when a trifle is given by his master. The courtier is a mere mass of flesh (with no spirit or brains) who is born solely for the purpose of filling his belly. मांस also fills one's belly when eaten. गर्भरोगस्य मातुः—he is a diseased growth in the womb of his mother. There are certain diseases of the womb (*e. g.* mole) characterized by fleshy growths or knots. अपु...भृतस्य who becomes a servant because he committed sinful deeds (in past lives). प्रतिपत्तये क्रिया what action should bring exaltation (or honour) to him ? क... शान्तिः whither shall he go to secure rest. कः...मानः what manly pride can he entertain ? किं...श्रद्धा what sort of pleasures can he have ? What means his belief that he will enjoy (life) ? प्रबल...यति if once a man's feet stick in deep mud, the more he struggles to extricate himself, the deeper does he go. अभ... तस्याः may that advancement (of the courtier) come to an end ! For अभवनिः see above p. 182. तस्या....र्थस्य here do I fold my hands to such grandeur (*i. e.* I bid farewell to it). परिच्छदः paraphernalia, pomp. यदर्थे...ष्यति for the sake of which the head must prostrate itself on the earth. He says that if for securing wealth, rank and pomp, one has to bow his head, then it is not worth the trouble. Put a vertical line after गमिष्यति. मुख...कलमः—the construction is (यदि) मुख...रतः क्लीबः...सेवकोऽपि मर्त्यमध्ये (गण्यते) (तदा) राजिलोऽपि वा भोगी पुलाकोऽपि वा कलमः (भवेत्). The reading of B 'अशापा॰' gives a good sense. तपस्वी ascetic; wretched. तपस्वी was capable of cursing or bestowing a boon. क्लीबः coward, mean; impotent. मुखप्रियं रतं यस्य—whose affection is pleasing only in his mouth *i. e.* who expresses only lip loyalty (and his heart feels no affection for his master). With क्लीब (impotent) the meaning cannot be explained in English. मुखे प्रियं रतं (सुरतं) यस्य. See सुश्रुत शारीरस्थान chap. 2. 38. 'पित्रोरत्यल्प-

बीजत्वादासेक्यः पुरुषो भवेत् । स शुक्रं प्राश्य लभते ध्वजोच्छ्रायमसंशयम् ॥'. पूति... मयः springing from (or consisting of) rotten flesh. पूति Putrid, foul smelling. Worms are found in rotten flesh. The courtier is a despicable creature (कृमि) emitting foul smell from his body (because he has no time to bathe). अगण्यमानः—of no account; of vast dimensions (अगण्यं मानं यस्य). नरकः an insignificant man; a hell. कुत्सितः नरः नरकः, कुत्सार्थे कन्. 'कुत्सिते' पा. 5. 3. 74. पादरजसा धूसरं उत्तमाङ्गं यस्य. A courtier's head is rendered dusty by bowing at the feet of his master. A foot-stool has its top dusty because the feet rest upon it. पुंस्कोकिलः a male cuckoo; a man like a cuckoo (पुमान् कोकिल इव). काकुः *f.* is the change of voice due to different feelings such a joy, sorrow &c. 'काकुः स्त्रियां विकारो यः शोकभीत्यादिभिर्ध्वनेः' अम०. The courtier can change his voice to suit the occasion. The cuckoo cries sweetly expressing its feeling of joy (in spring). C and T read स्थलकूर्मः which is preferable. क्रोडकषणेषु in rubbing the chest. 'न ना क्रोडं भुजान्तरम्' अम०. The courtier has to toil hard; the tortoise has its chest rubbed against the earth when moving. नीच...करणेषु in mean flattery, 'अस्त्री चाटु चटु श्लाघा प्रेम्णा मिथ्या विकत्थनम्' क्षीर०. मूर्च्छना—a duly regulated rise and fall of sounds due to the letting out of the air in a particular way; modulation of voice 'क्रमात्स्वराणां सप्तानामारोहश्चावरोहणम् । सा मूर्च्छेत्युच्यते' सङ्गीतरत्नाकर I. 4. 9. मूर्च्छना also means 'fainting or delusion.' करण...शेषु in the trouble of tying the limbs of the body. The servant has his various limbs tied to work of various kinds. करणं also means 'a posture of the body; a kind of dance.' 'करणं हेतुकर्मणोः । वणिजादौ हस्तलेपे नृत्यगीतप्रभेदयोः । क्रियाभेदेन्द्रियक्षेत्रकायसंवेशनेषु च' मे०. 'कामशास्त्रोदितकरणानि' com. पलालम् husk or straw (*i. e.* as worthless). सत्त्वशालिषु among those that are possessed of manliness. शालि suggests rice. कृकलासः lizard, chameleon. 'सरटः कृकलासः स्यात्' अम० (कृकं शिरोग्रीवं लासयति). The lizard now and again raises its head. The courtier has to nod his head to whatever his master speaks. जाहकः a polecat. आत्म...नेषु in contracting the body (with जाहक); in making his mind have a narrow vision (with servant). 'जाहको गात्रसङ्कोची' क्षीर०. 'आखुर्जाहकः प्राणिभेदः; कूर्म इत्यन्ये.' प्रतिपादकः 'footstool' C and T. पाद...सु in shampooing the feet (of his master); in bearing the feet. Compare verse 20 in the introduction to हर्षचरित ' शब्दैराख्यायिका भाति शय्येव प्रतिपादकैः '. प्रतिपादक seems to mean a block on which the leg of a couch rests. कर...ताडनेषु—the servant is slapped by his master. 'कोणो वीणा-

दिवादनम्' अम०. कोण: fiddlestick; stick. वराक...भोगी if a wretched servant (is to be counted) among men, then even a राजिल will be a cobra. 'समौ राजिलडुण्डुभौ' अम० ('निर्विषो द्विमुखोऽहिः' क्षीर०). पुलाक: shrivelled grain 'स्यात्पुलाकस्तुच्छधान्ये' अम०. 'शालयः कलमाद्याश्च' अम०. Put a vertical line after कलमः. वरं...मानवता It is better that manliness (मानवता) be shown even for a moment by the man that respects himself. मानवता *instru.* of मानवत्. The student will notice how the same letters are repeated with different senses, as in यमक. न मत...मनस्विनः. The highminded do not approve of even the enjoyment of the sovereignty of three worlds by one who bows down (for it). नमतः goes with ०भोगः and मतः with मनस्विनः. अभिनन्दितः (welcomed) अस्मदीयः प्रणयः (friendship or request). परागतः come, arrived.

P. 121 l. 17—P. 122 l. 4 **राजापि...पादयोः**. कुमारदर्शनौत्सुक्येन स्वीकृतं (seized, engrossed) हृदयं यस्य. आत्मा...करणम् to offer oneself heart and soul captivates the great without roots and spells. For वशीकरण (magic power over the minds of others), roots and spells were required. But the fact that Kumāra devoted himself heart and soul to Harsha captivated the mind of the latter. प्रतिप्राभृतम् gifts in return (for those received). ०दूतैः अधिष्ठितं (supervised by). आत्मनापि by himself, so far as he was concerned. अमित्रमभिलक्ष्य = अभ्य० (अव्ययीभाव)—towards his enemy (the गौड king). For साधन, see above p. 130. आवासितम् encamped. मूर्च्छा...विवेश he entered the darkness of a swoon. प्रतीहारस्य निवारणेन निभृतः निःशब्दः परिजनः यस्मिन् where attendants were motionless and speechless by the prohibition of the doorkeeper. The principal sentence is अथ भण्डिः एकेनैव वाजिना...राजद्वारमाजगाम. निखाताः बहवः लोहकीलकाः तेषां परिकरः (समूहः) तेन रक्षितं स्फुटनं यस्य the breaking of which was prevented by an array of numerous iron nails implanted in it. Nails prevent a tottering structure from giving way. The poet fancies that the numerous points of arrows on his chest were nails implanted to prevent his heart from breaking through grief (for राज्यवर्धन). Understand उपलक्षितः after हृदयेन. हृदयलग्नैः resting on or reaching his chest (with beard); deeply impressed on the heart (with ०सत्कृतैः). स्वामिसत्कृतैः the honours bestowed on him by his master. For the growing of the beard in sorrow, see p. 118. दूरीकृतः (given up) व्यायामः तेन शिथिलः भुजदण्डः तस्मिन् दोलायमानं मङ्गलवलयं एव एका केवला शेषालङ्कृतिः यस्य—The only ornament he wore was a single auspicious bracelet (on the left hand) that moved up and down owing to his arm being languid. For the wearing of bracelets by men see pp. 15, 46. अनादरेण (without particular care) उपयुक्तं (भुक्तं) ताम्बूलं तेन विरलः रागः (रक्तत्वं) यस्य. Supply उपलक्षितः after अधरेण. He was careless in taking betel; therefore his lip was faint in colour. The poet fancies that the lip was a coal from his heart burning with grief, which (coal) was pressed out by the force of his deep sighs. ०विरहे विधृतं जीवितं एव अपराधः तेन वैलक्ष्यं (विलक्षस्य भावः) तस्मात्—as if through embarrassment (or shame) at the fault of continuing to live though his master was dead. One abashed covers his face with his garment. His face was covered with tears. Tears (being bright) resemble the hem of a white garment. विशन्निव अपत्रयया स्वाङ्गं अङ्गैः Through shame his limbs appeared to be entering his own body (*i. e.* his body was shrunk). वमन्निव—he heaved deep and hot sighs, which, the poet fancies, were the warmth of his valour emitted by him because it was useless (as he could not save राज्यवर्धन). मुषितः robbed. छलितः cheated. वेग...णः a young elephant. For वेगदण्ड, see p. 174. सूर्या...करः—there is a suggested sense. सूर्य stands for राज्यवर्धन and कमला means लक्ष्मी. दुर्योधननिधनेन दुर्मनाः (sad). द्रौणिः son of द्रोण *i. e.* अश्वत्थामा. See शल्यपर्व 65 'वार्तिकाणां सकाशात्तु श्रुत्वा दुर्योधनं हतम् । हतशिष्टास्ततो राजन् कौरवाणां महारथाः । ... ततो द्रौणिर्महाराज बाष्पपूर्णेक्षणः श्वसन् ।' 12. दुर्योधन...मनाः also means 'who (Bhandin) was sad on account of the death of (राज्यवर्धन) who was hard to fight with.' अपहृतं रत्नं (राज्यवर्धनरूपं) यस्य. अपहृतानि रत्नानि यस्य (with सागरः).

P. 122 ll. 5–34 **अवनि...कैस्ताम्.** उत्थाय...द्रम्य he got up and went out a few steps to receive him. For व्यतिकर, see pp. 72, 130. देवभूयं गते—see above p. 150. गुप्तः इति नाम यस्य तेन. See Introduction for the significance of this. कुशस्थलम्—seems to be the same as कान्यकुब्ज. In the रामायण (I. 32) we are told that कुश, son of ब्रह्मा, had four sons, one of whom कुशनाभ founded the city of महोदय, which is identified with कान्यकुब्ज. कुशनाभ's son was गाधि. कान्यकुब्ज is designated गाधिनगर in a grant of जयचन्द्र of Kanoj. See I. A. Vol. 15 p. 6, 7. किं...पदिभिः what is the use of other seekers (for राज्यश्री)? अनुपदिन्—'अन्वेष्टानुपदी समौ' क्षीर०. परित्यक्तं अन्यकृत्यं येन. कारितं ०वपनकर्म येन who was made to shave &c. शारीरिक for the body; or rather the meaning is 'he sent flowers, unguents &c., which he had meant for himself'. सपरिबर्ह together with the equipage

(paraphernalia). 'परिच्छदे नृपार्हेऽर्थे **परिबर्हः**' अम०. करिणः, हरीन् and the following nouns in the accusative are governed by दर्शयाम्बभूव. ०गण्डान् qualifies करिणः. ०मदः मदिरा इव तस्याः आमोदेन मुखराणां मधुकराणां जूटः तेन जटिलः करटः (cheek) पट्टः इव तेन पङ्किलः गण्डः (face) येषाम्. गण्ड...क्रमान्—the elephants looked like moving rocks. '**गण्डशैलास्तु** च्युताः स्थूलोपला गिरेः' अमरः ('च्युताः भूकम्पादिना गलिताः' क्षीर०). गम्भीरः गर्जितरवः येषाम् (with जलधरान्); गम्भीरगर्जितवत् रवः येषाम् (with करिणः). Both clouds and elephants are dark. **सप्तच्छद** is the same as Marathi सातवीण. The odour of the ichor was like the scent of the सप्तच्छद, which blossoms in शरद्. चारु... **हरीन्** the horses had chowries with gold work on their heads. Note for the चामरs on horse's heads 'निष्कम्पचामरशिखा निभृतोर्ध्वकर्णाः' **शाकुन्तल** I. हरिणस्य इव रंहः (वेगः) येषाम्. बाला...वर्षिणाम् that shed a mass of light mellow like that of morn. किरणै...दिशाम् that covered the quarters with many rain-bows on account of their rays. ०कृतः (wonderful) qualifies हारान्. स्मरेण उन्मादिताः मालव्यः तेषां कुचपरिमलेन दुर्ललितान् (fondled, caressed). The necklaces had once rolled on the breasts of Malva females and rubbed off the sandal applied by them to their bosom. तारान् bright. There is a pun here. तारा means a star. A star has only a twinkling light. The हारs, though तार, flooded the world with their light. उडुपतिः चन्द्रः तस्य पादानां (किरणानां) सञ्चयवत् शुचीनि शुभ्राणि. **निज०** refers to Harsha. जातरूपमयं नालं यस्य the handle of which was made of gold. लक्ष्मी dwells in a white lotus. The white umbrella resembled पुण्डरीक and the handle resembled a lotus-stalk. वारविलासिनीः dancing girls. बहूनि समररसेण साहसानि तस्मिन् अनुरागः तेन अवतीर्णाः. The Apsarases are represented as fond of heroes and as welcoming them to heaven. See above p. 101. Here the damsels are represented as Apsarases come down on earth out of their fondness for gallant deeds. आसन्दी chair of state. 'आसन्दी पीठिका' क्षीर०. ससंख्यानि आलेख्यपत्राणि येषु which were accompanied with written records giving the number (in each chest). अलङ्काराणां आपीडस्य पीडा तया सह सा० that groaned under (the weight of) the wreaths of ornaments. If we read ०पेडापीडान् the meaning will be 'that were wreathed with small bags (पेडा) of ornaments.' **यथा...कारम्** according to their respective functions.

P. 123 l. 1—**P. 124** l. 24 **अथ...वसदिति**. The principal sentence is अथ प्रविशन् दूरादेव...वनग्रामकं ददर्श तत्रैव च अवसत्. दह्यमान... दधानैः—this clause qualifies वनप्रदेशैः (l. 4)—that were rendered grey by the smoke of granaries (बीजधानी) of wild corn, in which (granaries) fire flared up on account of heaps of smouldering षष्टिक chaff. षष्टिकः a kind of rice ripening in sixty days from the day of sowing. 'षष्टिका· षष्टिरात्रेण पच्यन्ते' पा. 5. 1. 90. ०विसरैः विसारी विभावसुः (अग्निः) यासु (*adj.* of ०धानीनाम्). ०शाखासञ्चयेन रचितानि गोवाटानि (cowpens) तैः वेष्टिताः विकटाः (large) वटाः येषु.०रोषेण रचितानि व्याघ्रयन्त्राणि येषु—where tiger-traps had been placed in wrath at the slaughter of young calves. वत्सस्येव रूपं येषां ते वत्सरूपकाः that were like their own children. अयन्त्रितैः (uncontrolled) वनपालैः हठेन (forcibly) ह्रियमाणाः परग्रामीणानां काष्ठिकानां (wood-cutters) कुठाराः यस्मिन्. The reading यन्त्रित० is not suitable. C and T render it by 'zealous.' ०षण्डे निर्मितः चामुण्डामण्डपः येषु. चामुण्डामण्डप seems to mean 'a flimsy structure used as a temple of Durgā.' प्रकाश्यमानम् qualifies वनग्रामकं (text p. 69 l. 24). अटवीप्रायः प्रान्तः यस्य स ०प्रान्तः तस्य भावः. ०प्रान्तता तया—as the forest settlement was bordered on all sides by forest (the villagers found it hard to secure fields for cultivation). कुद्दालप्राया कृषिः येषाम् whose agriculture depended almost on spades *i. e.* they had no ploughs and no oxen. कृषीवलैः is to be connected with भज्यमान०. अविद्यमानाः बलीवर्दाः येषाम् (*adj.* of कृषी०). अवलम्बिः who did not hasten, who were slow. This does not yield a good sense. A and C omit अबलीवर्दैः and read अबलवद्भिः. It is probable that अवलम्बिः is a mistake for अबलवद्भिः. भज्यमानानि भूरीणि शालिखलक्षेत्राणां खण्डलकानि यस्मिन्. उच्च...खण्डलकम् where many small pieces of rice-fields and threshing grounds were being divided (by farmers) in high-pitched language. खलः—लम्—threshing floor. क्षेत्र is to be connected with शालि and खल. उच्चः भागः यस्य तत् ०भागं भाषितम्. भाग seems to be redundant. The reading भज्यमानभूरिखिलक्षेत्र० is better. The meaning would be 'where many pieces of waste land (खिलक्षेत्रं) were being broken by farmers accompanied with talk on higher ground or with loud talk.' अल्पावकाशैः—of small extent. This and the following instrumentals qualify केदारैः (l. 9). काशि...कठिनैः that abounded in काश grass and that were hard with black soil resembling iron. स्थानस्थानेषु स्थापिताः स्थाणवः तेभ्यः उत्थिताः स्थूलाः पल्लवाः येषु. Trees had been cut off from the fields, leaving only the trunks imbedded in the earth, which again put forth vigorous foliage. दुरुपगमा श्यामाकप्ररूढिः येषु in which the growth of श्यामाकs was impenetrable. श्यामाक is a kind of grain. अल...क्षुपैः that abounded in अलम्बुस and were thick with कोकिलाक्ष bushes. 'ह्रस्वशाखाशिफः क्षुपः'

अम०. नातिप्रवृत्तं गतागतं (गतं च आगतं च तयोः समाहारः) तेन अप्रहता भूः यस्मिन् (*adj.* of वनग्रामकं)—where the earth was not trodden because there was not much coming and going. क्षेत्राणां समीपे उप० (अव्य०). मञ्चै...द्रमम् where the (high) platforms (or scaffolds for watchmen to sleep on) suggested the depredations of wild beasts. The next clause is दिशि दिशि च...अटवीप्रवेशप्रपाणां शैत्येन त्याजयन्तमिव ग्रैष्ममुष्माणम् (l. 20). All the genitives in this clause qualify ०प्रपाणां. प्रति...कृतानाम् (प्रपाs) made of (or, under) trees growing about the roads. पथिक...छायानाम्—Travellers walking barefooted used leaves to wipe off (प्रस्फोटन) the dust off their feet and left the leaves at the प्रपा when they started. Compare 'विश्रान्तकार्पटिकप्रस्फोटितचरणधूलिधूसरकिसलयलाञ्छितोपकण्ठैः' काद० p. 223 l. 15. अटवीसुलभानि सालकुसुमानि तेषां स्तबकैः अञ्चिता (marked, decked) नवखाता (recently dug) कूपिका तस्याः उपकण्ठे (समीपे) प्रतिष्ठिताः नागस्फुटाः यासु. नागस्फुट or–टा seems to be some kind of bush. अच्छिद्रैः (closely woven) कटैः (straw mats) कल्पितं कुटीरकं (hut) यासु. कुटिला कीटानां (insects, flies) वेणी (row, line) तया वेष्ट्यमाना शक्तुशारा (spotted with barley meal) शरावश्रेणी (lines of platters) तया श्रितानाम् (०प्रपानाम्). अध्वगजनेन जग्धानि जम्बूफलानि तेषां अस्थिभिः (stones) शबलाः समीपभुवः यासाम्. जम्बूफल is Marathi जांभूळ. उद्धूलिता धूली येषां ते ०धूलीकाः कदम्बस्तबकाः तेषां प्रकरेण पुलकिनीनाम्. C and T take धूलीकदम्ब to be a tree, which also is good. Bunches of कदम्ब flowers the pollen of which was scattered about were lying near the प्रपाs and resembled hair (पुलकः) standing on end. रोमाञ्च is often compared to कदम्ब flowers. Compare 'अनिलैरपि कदम्बकेसरोत्करवाहिभिः कण्टकितैरिवानुगतम्' काद० p. 217; 'ततोऽपि घनजलधारासीकरपुलकितकाया कदम्बकलिकेव' काद० p. 254. See also उत्तरराम III. 'सस्वेदरोमाञ्चित' &c. कण्टकितं कर्करीचक्रं तेन आक्रान्ता काष्ठमञ्चिका (wooden stand) तया मुषिता तृट् (thirst) यासु. कर्करी a water jar. The idea expressed by कण्टकित is :—the porous jars had very small particles of water (due to cooled vapour) on their outside which resembled hair standing on end. C and T translate 'bristling' and suggest that the jars contained grass stalks. तिम्यत् (wet) तलं यासां ताः ०त्तलाः शीतलाः सिकतिलाः (porous) कलश्यः ताभिः शमितः श्रमः यासु. For सिकतिल, see p. 30. आश्यानेन (partially dry, moist) शैवलेन श्यामलितः अलिञ्जरः (a large pitcher) तेन जायमानः जलस्य जडिमा (coldness) यासु. उदकुम्भेभ्यः आकृष्टानि पाटलशर्कराशकलानि तैः शिशिरीकृता दिक् यासु. What पाटलशर्करा means is not clear. C and T translate 'pink gravel'. But compare 'पटुपाटलशर्करामोदमुचि' above (text p. 22 l. 30), where पाटलशर्करा is said to have a fragrance. It was probably 'a lump of red raw sugar.' घटमुखेषु घटितानि (formed) कटहारेण (by a rope of straw) पाटलापुष्पपुटानि यासु. पाटला is a plant with red flowers. If we read करहाट it will mean 'with the fibrous root of a lotus'. शीकरेण पुलकिताः (bristling) पल्लवाः तेषां पूल्या पाल्यमानाः (preserved) शोष्याः (liable to wither) सरसाः शिशवः सहकाराः (mangotrees) तेषां फलानां जूटी तया जटिलाः स्थाणवः (pillars) यासाम् (*adj.* of प्रपानाम्). This seems to be a description of the care taken to preserve young grafted mango plants. विश्राम्यन्तः कार्पटिकाः तेषां पेटकाः (समूहाः) तेषां परिपाट्यः (successive rows) ताभिः पीयमानं पयः यासु. For कार्पटिक, see p. 166. अटवी...ष्माणम् that was made to give up the heat of summer by the coolness of the water arbours at the entrances to the forest. त्याजयन्तम् qualifies वनग्रामकम् below. प्रपा पानीयशालिका—Marathi पाणपोई. ग्राहय...व्योकारैः—we have to understand ग्रैष्ममुष्माणम् with ग्राहयन्तम्—that was made to take up the heat of summer by blacksmiths that burnt heaps of wood for charcoal. 'व्योकारो लोहकारकः' अम०. The next clause is a very long one सर्वतश्च...व्याप्तदिगन्तरम् (text p. 69 l. 7). Read **०वासिना** for ०वासिनाम्. This and the following instrumentals are connected with ०लोकेन (l. 26). प्राति...वासिना that dwelt in the neighbouring district (विषयः). समासन्नेषु ग्रामगृहेषु स्थापितैः स्थविरैः परिपाल्यमानेन पाथेयेन (provisions) स्थगितः (covered, surrounded) तेन (*adj.* of ०लोकेन). पथि साधु पाथेयम्, according to 'पथ्यतिथिवसतिस्वपतेर्ढञ्' पा. 4. 4. 104. See p. 67 on वासतेयी. कृतः दारुण—दारुव्यायामयोग्यः अङ्गाभ्यङ्गः येन that had rubbed their body with oil befitting their hard toil in the forest. अभ्यङ्ग removes fatigue. स्कन्धं अध्यासितः कठोरकुठारः यस्य स ०कुठारः कण्ठे लम्बमानं प्रातराशपुटं यस्य स ०पुटः, ०कुठारश्चासौ ०पुटश्च तेन. प्रातराशः breakfast. पाटच्चराणां (चौराणां) प्रत्यवायेन (obstacle) प्रतिपन्नं पटच्चरं (rags) येन. 'पटच्चरं जीर्णवस्त्रं' अम०. कालवेत्रकस्य (black cane) त्रिगुणः (triple) व्रततिवलयपाशः तेन ग्रथिता (encircled) ग्रीवा तस्यां ग्रथितैः (fastened)–qualifies पीतकुटैः. पत्रवीटया (a bundle of leaves used as a cork) आवृतं मुखं येषाम्. We must read पीतकुटैः. Compare कुटहारिका above p. 28. ऊढं (carried) वारि येन (*adj.* of ०लोकेन). पुरःसरौ वलन्तौ (moving, quick) बलीवर्दौ तयोः युगं (pair). तेन सरतीति ०सरेण. Or युगं may mean 'yoke'. For वलत् some read बलवत्. निकटे भवः नैकटिकः. कुटुम्बिन् a peasant. ०लोकेन is to be connected with व्याप्तदिगन्तरम् below (p. 69 l. 7). श्वापदानां व्यधनं (shooting) तदर्थं व्यवधानानि (screens) तेषां बहली तस्यां समारोपिताः कुटीकृताः (twisted) कूटपाशाः (traps) यैः (*adj.* of व्याधैः). बहली seems to mean 'heap'. गृहीतानि मृगतन्तवः तन्त्र्यः जालवलयानि वागुराश्च यैः. The मृगतन्तुs (animal sinews) were for mending nets; the lutes (तन्त्रीs) for luring the deer. Or मृग...तन्त्री may mean 'strings made of animals' sinews.' बहिः विचरद्भिः व्याधैः (व्याप्त-दिगन्तरम्). The hunters wandered outside the वनग्रामक. अंसे अवसक्तः (attached to, fixed) वीतंसः (aviary) तेन व्यालम्बमानाः (hanging about, loitering) बालपाशिकाः येषाम् (*adj.* of शाकुनिकैः). बालपाशिकः a boy hunter. सङ्गृहीताः ०ञ्जलादीनां पञ्जरकाः (cages) यैः. ग्राहकः falcon. क्रकरः partridge. शाकुनिक—शकुनान् हन्ति इति—according to 'पक्षिमत्स्यमृगान् हन्ति' पा. 4. 4. 35 च्युतः लासकलेशः तेन लिप्ता लता तस्यां वधूलट्वाः तासु लम्पटानाम् (eagerly following). लासकः soup, broth. लट्व means a भ्रमरक according to क्षीर०. C and T translate वधूलट्वा as ' female sparrows.' पैटकैः goes with व्याप्तदिगन्तरम्. पाशिक—a fowler. तृणस्तम्बेन अन्तरितः (concealed) तित्तिरिः तेन तरलायमानं (rendered restive) कौलेयककुलं तस्य चाटुकारैः that coaxed the dogs &c. ०मृगयां is the object of क्रीडद्भिः. मृगयुयुवभिः by youths that were hunting. परिणतः (fully grown) चक्रवाकः तस्य कण्ठवत् कषाया रुक् (colour) येषाम् (वल्कलानाम्). शीध-०ग्यानाम्—what tree is meant is not clear. कलापान्—connect this and the following accusatives with आदाय (l. 5). धातोः इव त्विट् येषाम् the hue of which was like metallic ore (such as गैरिक). गोणीः अगणिताः countless bags. धातकीपुष्प is very red. पिचव्यानां च (गोणीः) and of cotton plants. अतसी...मूलकानां of cloth made from a quantity of flax and of radish. The reading अतसीशणपूलकानां is easier 'of bundles of flax and hemp.' मधुनो माक्षिकस्य of honey derived from bees. मयूराङ्गजस्य of peacock's tails. अक्लिष्टं (untouched by anyone else) मधूच्छिष्टं (wax) तस्य चक्रं (balls) तेषां मालानाम्. लम्बमाना लामज्जकजूटजटा येषाम् (*adj.* of ०काष्ठानाम्). लामज्जकम् is the root of a fragrant grass. अपगता त्वक् येषां (barkless). कुष्ठ—a kind of plant, with a fragrant adour. बभ्रु tawny. रोध्र a tree with white or red flowers. Construe भारकान् आदाय व्रजता लोकेन (व्याप्त०). प्रविचितैः (gathered) ०फलैः पूरिताः पिटकाः मस्तके यासाम्. अभ्य...गत्वरीभिः hastening to the neighbouring villages. The next clause is इतस्ततश्च...संस्कारम् (l. 9). युक्ताः (yoked) शूराः शकुराः (tame) शाक्कराः (oxen) यासु (*adj.* of श्रेणीनाम्). पुराण...हिनीनां carrying heaps of dry cowdung (करीषं) and old dust-heaps. उत्किरः heap. धूर्गताः (sitting on the poles) धूलिधूसराः सैरिकाः तैः सरोषस्वरेण सार्यमाणानाम् that were being driven with angry voices by ploughmen &c. सैरिक—सीरं वहति इति—'हलसीराट्ठक्' पा. 4. 4. 81. सैरिभ would mean 'a buffalo.' संक्रीडन्ति (creaking) चटुलानि (loose) चक्राणि तैः चीत्कारिणीनाम् (noisy). सम्पातः multitude. संपाद्यमानः दुर्बलोर्व्या विरूक्षाणां क्षेत्राणां संस्कारः यस्मिन् where the fields parched up on account of the poor soil were being prepared. आरक्ष...वृतिभिः—*adj.* of वाटैः. आरक्षार्थे (for protection) क्षिप्तः क्षिप्रः

दान्तवाहकदण्डः तेन उड्डीयमानैः हरिणैः हेलया (लीलया) लङ्घिता तुङ्गा वैणवा वृतिः (hedge of bamboos) येषाम्. दान्तः (an ox broken to the yoke) +वाहकः driver. निखातः (implanted) गौरस्य (buffalo) करङ्कः (skeleton) यस्मिन् सः ०करङ्कः'. शङ्कुः (a dart, stake) तस्मात् शङ्कितैः शशकैः शकलिताः तुङ्गाः शुङ्गाः येषाम्. शुङ्गः the sheath or calyx of a bud. प्रयत्नेन प्रभृताः (nourished) विशङ्कटाः (large) विटपाः येषाम्. वाटैः ऐक्षवैः gardens of sugarcane. ऐक्षव—from इक्षु. ०कण्ठम् (*adj.* of वनग्रामकम्). अतिविप्रकष्टं अन्तरं येषाम्. This and the following instrumentals qualify गृहैः below. स्नुहा the milk-hedge plant. कार्मुककर्मणि साधुः ०कर्मण्यः वंशः तस्य विटपैः सङ्कटानि (full of). ०गर्मुतां गुल्मैः गहना गृहवाटिका येषाम्. उरुबूकः = एरण्डः castor plant. वचा, वङ्कक and सुरस are various plants. सूरण—Marathi सुरण. शिग्रु—Marathi शेगवा or शेगट. ग्रन्थिपर्ण is a fragrant कन्द. गवेधुका a grass eaten by cattle. गर्मुत् a kind of grass. निखातानि (planted in the earth) उच्चानि काष्ठानि तेषु आरोपितः काष्ठालुकलताप्रतानः तेन विहिता छाया येषु. परिमण्डल circular. परि... रूपैः where calves were tied to pegs of Khadira &c. For वत्सरूप see above p. 210. संनिवेशः situation. अङ्गना...वापिकैः.Here the text is unsatisfactory. What क्षिप्र...पूपिका means is not clear. अङ्गनागस्ति–the अगस्ति plant in the courtyard. पूपिका a sweet cake. वापिका tank. Some MSS. read क्षिप्रपूपिका. May we read क्षिप्त for क्षिप्र (the meaning being 'where there were tanks constructed under the courtyard अगस्ति plants, on which (tanks) were thrown (क्षिप्त) cakes for birds'). विकीर्णानि बदराणां पाटलानि पटलानि (heaps) येषु. ०मयवृतिभि विहिताः भित्तयः येषु the walls of which were made of fences consisting of slips (पोटः) of bamboo, leaves (दलं), stalks and reeds (शरः). नलः means 'a kind of reed.' किंशुक...राशिभिः hardly yields a sense. So read ०रोचनाविरचितमण्डनैः बल्वज०. किंशुकैः रोचनया च रचितं मण्डनं येषाम्. किंशुक is a red flower without fragrance. बल्वजैः बद्धः अङ्गारराशिः येषु where a heap of charcoal was tied with बल्वज grass. संनिहिताः...तण्डुलाः येषु. नलशालिः rice from नल reeds (probably देवभात). शालूकं roots of waterlily. 'शालूकमेषां कन्दः स्यात्' अम०. खण्ड candied sugar. We must read with B ०हीततमालबीजैः. भस्ममलिनाः म्लानैः काश्मर्यकूटैः व्याधृताः कटाः येषु where mats were dusty with ashes and full of heaps of drying काश्मर्य plants. आश्यानानि (partially dry) ... फलानि तैः स्फीतैः abounding. 'राजादनः फलाध्यक्षः' अम०. मधूक a flower of the मधूक tree. आसवः extract or decoction. कुसुम्भकुम्भाः गण्डे यस्य सः ०गण्डः कुसूलः(granary) येषाम् the granaries of which were filled to the mouth with pots of safflower. अविरहितानि...बीजानि येषु. राजमाषः a kind of bean. त्रपुषं cucumber. कर्कटिका species of cucumber. मालुधानः a kind of serpent. 'मालुधानो मातुलाहिः' अम०. It is hard to say what शालिजात and जातक are. वनग्रामकम्-a village settlement in a forest.

Uchchhvāsa VIII

Verse 1. दैवेनापि...सेवेव Even Fate as if serves beforehand the fortunate. The idea is:-there is no wonder that people pay homage to the fortunate; even Fate serves them, which is an earnest of the good things that are to be theirs at a later stage of their career. 'फलकल्याणयोर्भव्यम्' क्षीर०. *Verse 2.* सम्पर्कः union, association. नष्टः इष्टः ज्ञातिः (बन्धुः, स्वजनः) तस्य दर्शनमेव अभ्युदयः. कस्य...भवति—the answer expected is सर्वस्यैव सुखाय भवति. It is better to read भुवने. भवने would mean 'in the house.' Both the verses are suggestive of the events narrated in this उच्छ्वास. हर्ष is to meet a sage in the person of दिवाकरमित्र, he further finds his sister and receives a wonderful necklace from दिवाकरमित्र.

P. 125 l. 5—**P. 126** l. 13 अथापरे...गोचरमिति. The principal sentence is एकदा तु भूपतेः भ्रमत एव...व्याघ्रकेतुर्नाम कुतोऽपि...शबरयुवानमादायाजगाम. भूप...एव while the king was wandering. आटविकसामन्तः a feudatory dwelling in the forest. अटव्यां भवः आटविकः. ललाटस्य उपरि अधिललाटम् (अव्ययीभाव). श्यामलता—is a creeper called 'गन्धप्रियङ्गु' according to क्षीर०. कृतः मौलिबन्धः यस्य—whose hair was tied. This and the following accusatives qualify शबरयुवानम् below. 'चूडाकिरीटकेशाश्च संयता मौलयस्त्रयः' अम०. अन्धकारिणीं dark (*adj.* of ललाटस्थलीं). अका...यामामिव which resembled night on account of the frown of his eyebrow divided into three branches, which (frown) was natural (not due to any particular cause). Emphasis is laid on the word त्रि. Night is divided into *three* watches; his brow was dark and naturally covered with *three* wrinkles. So it is like त्रियामा. Night causes darkness (अन्धकारिणी). तिस्रः शाखाः यस्य. साहस० applies to both. Night is the friend of adventures; his forehead was always with him in adventures. साहसानां or साहसेषु सहचारिणी. अवतंसितः (made into an ear-ornament) एकः शुकस्य पक्षकः (wing) तस्य प्रभया हरितायमानेन (looking green). पिनद्धा (tied) काचरा (glass-like) काचमणेः (crystal) कर्णिका (ear-ring) यस्मिन्. For कर्णिका, see p. 106. चुल्ल blear-eyed. 'स्युः क्लिन्नाक्षे चुल्ल—चिल्लपिल्लाः क्लिन्नेऽक्ष्णि चाप्यमी' अम. प्रविरलं पक्ष्म (eye-lashes) यस्य. सहजेन...क्षरन्तम् The blood of a hyena is employed as a medicine. His eyes were naturally red and therefore it appeared as if his eyes let fall the blood of a hyena useful in preparing Rasāyanas. रोचिः = दीप्तिः. 'तरक्षुस्तु मृगादनः'. तरक्षोः इदं तारक्षवम्. क्षतजम् = रुधिरम्. अवनाटा (नता low) नासिका यस्य.

'अवटीटोऽवनाटश्चावभ्रटो नतनासिके' अम०. चिपिटः (thick, large) अधरः यस्य. चिकिनं (flat) चिबुकं (chin) यस्य. अहीना (full) हनुः (chin) तस्यां उत्कटः (prominent) कपोलकूटास्थिपर्यन्तः यस्य—the tops of whose round cheek bones were prominent over a full chin. ईषत् अवाग्रः (अवनतः) ग्रीवाबन्धः यस्य whose neck was slightly bent. स्कन्नः (drooping) स्कन्धस्य अर्धभागः यस्य. अनवरतं कोदण्डस्य (धनुषः) कुण्डलीकरणं (bending) तेन कर्कशः (hard) व्यायामः तेन विस्तारितेन. अंसल strong **'बलवान्मांसलोंऽसलः'** अम०. उरसा...गिरेः who as if laughed at the breadth of the rock on the slopes of the Vindhya by his chest that was &c. अजगरः a huge serpent said to swallow goats. लघयन्तम् ridiculing, casting into the shade. तुहिनशैलः हिमालयः तस्मिन् शालद्रुमाः तेषाम्. द्राघिमाणं (लघयन्तम्)—his arms were long like the शाल tree. वराह...प्रकोष्ठ on his forearm the back of which was thickly covered with a mass of the roots of the नागदमन plant which was fastened with the hair of a boar. ०बालैः वलितं बन्धनं यासाम्. 'नागदमनो विषहर ओषधिभेदः। जूटिका लघुमूलम्। वाटिका पूल्यः' com. गो... चित्रम् decorated with गोदन्त beads. According to the com. 'decked with the head gem of गोदन्त serpents.' गोदन्तं yellow orpiment, white fossil substance. त्रापुषं made of tin (from त्रपु, according to 'त्रपुजतुनोः षुक्' पा. 4. 3. 138). See जातुष p. 124. अतु...भम् though not fat, he had a prominent navel. **'वृद्धनाभौ तुण्डिलतुण्डिभौ'** अम०. 'तुन्दिवलिवटेर्भः' पा. 5.'2 139 (वृद्धा नाभिस्तुन्दिः। सि. कौ.). तुण्डिभ also means 'fat' and hence the apparent contradiction. अहीरमणी (according to com.) a serpent with two heads. The other reading अहीरणि means the same thing. ०चर्मणा निर्मिते पट्टिके तयोः—inside (*i. e.* between) two strips of the skin of &c. चित्रा (variegated) चित्रकत्वक् तया तारकितः (spotted) परिवारः (scabbard) यस्याः (*adj.* of कृपाण्या). चित्रक seems to be a kind of serpent. सङ्कुब्जं अजिनं तेन जालकितया that was encased in a contracted deer skin. What सङ्कुब्ज means is not clear. C and T translate 'short'. शृङ्गमयः (made of horn) मसृणः (smooth, glossy) मुष्टिभागः (handle) तेन भास्वरया. मस्तकं end. कृपाण्या...प्रदेशम् whose broad loins were made formidable by a dagger. For विशङ्कट (written also as विसङ्कट), see p 122. प्रथमयौवनेन उल्लिख्यमानः (being pared or thinned) मध्यभागः (waist) तस्मात् भ्रष्टं मांसं तेन भरितौ. By exercise in youth his waist became thin and his thighs thick. The poet fancies that the flesh from the reduced waist went to the thighs. अच्छभल्लः bear. भल्ली... भृता—bearing numerous arrows most of which were crescent-shaped. All the instrumentals qualify भल्लाभरणेन. शबल...पीडितेन made fast with a broad spotted tiger skin. अलिकुलेन or कुलवत् कालानि कम्बललोमानि यस्य the blanket-like hair of which (bear's skin) was dark with (or like) &c. भस्त्रा...दर्शयन्तम् who exhibited a darkness as if blossoming with a quiver. भस्त्रा आभरणमिव. We must read कार्ष्ण्यं for कार्श्यम्. He was already dark enough and had a dark quiver and spotted tiger-skin &c., which looked like the पल्लव of darkness. उत्तर...शिखरे—this and the following locatives qualify दोषि. उत्तरत्रिभागे उत्तंसितं चाषपिच्छं तेन चारु शिखरं यस्य (arm) the top of which was charming with a blue jay's tail placed as an ornament on the upper third part of it (arm). 'पुंस्युत्तंसावतंसौ द्वौ कर्णपूरेऽपि शेखरे' अम०. खदिरजटानामिव निर्माणं यस्य the make or essence of which was (tough) like the fibres (or branches) of Khadira. The खदिर is a very tough tree. खरः प्राणः यस्य. 'शक्तिः पराक्रमः प्राणः' अम०. प्रचुरा मयूरपित्तेन पत्रलता (figures) तेन चित्रिता त्वक् यस्य. त्वचिसारः वंशः (bamboo) तद्वत् गुरुणि. वामस्कन्धे अध्यासितं धनुः यस्य. दोषि लम्बमानेन hanging from his arm. This and the following instrumentals qualify शशेन. अवाक् शिरः यस्य. शितशरेण कृतं एकं नलकविवरं तस्मिन् प्रवेशिता इतरा जङ्घा तेन जनितः स्वस्तिकबन्धः यस्य. स्वस्तिकबन्ध is a posture in योग in which the toes are placed in the inner hollow of the knee. 'जानूर्वोरन्तरे सम्यक् कृत्वा पादतले उभे। ऋजुकायो विशेन्मन्त्री स्वस्तिकं तत्प्रचक्षते ॥'. One leg of the hare was made to enter a cylindrical hole made in the other by a sharp arrow. For नलक, see above p. 173. बन्धूकवत् लोहिता रुधिरराजिः तया रञ्जितं (stained) घ्राणवर्त्म (nose) यस्य. वपुर्विततया व्यक्तं विभाव्यमानः कोमलक्रोडरोम्णां शुक्लिमा यस्य the whiteness of whose fine hair on the chest was clearly visible on account of its body being stretched out fully (as the hare hung from the arm of the forester). शितायां अटनीशिखायां (notched extremity of the bow) ग्रथिता (fastened) ग्रीवा यस्य—qualifies तित्तिरिणा. Separate च अपावृत &c. अपावृता (open) चञ्चूः तया उत्तानं ताम्रं तालु यस्य whose (of the partridge) red palate was displayed as its beak was wide open. वर्णकमुष्टि a handful of paints or unguents. वर्ण...दर्शयन्तम्—on his arm hung a partridge and a hare. These seemed to be unguents with which he had smeard his body when hunting. विषमेण (terrible, powerful) विषेण दूषितं वदनं यस्य (with विकर्णेन and ०हिना). विकर्ण- - a kind of arrow. मूलगृहीतेन held by the tail (with arrow); caught or subdued by some drug. व्यग्रं दक्षिणकराग्रं यस्य. तमाल has dark leaves and the शबर youth also was dark. यन्त्रो...भ्रमन्तम् he was like a moving pillar of solid stone cut out (chiselled) by a machine (from a mountain). अञ्जन...छेदम् a piece of collyrium

ऐरक्' पा. 4. 1. 128. सहचरीणां चारणे (feeding) चञ्चुराः (expert) चकोरचञ्चवः येषु. ०भुरुण्डैः भुज्यमानानि पाकेन (ripening) कपिलानि पीलूनि येषु. भुरुण्डः a kind of bird. पीलु a kind of fruit. ०फलानां विशसने (destruction) निःशूकाः (निर्दयाः) शुकशकुन्ताः तैः शातितानि शलाटूनि येषु. सदाफल a kind of tree. कट्फल—Marathi कायफळ. शलाटु raw fruit. 'आमे फले शलाटुः स्यात्' अम०. शैलेय belonging to a mountain. शिफा fibrous root. ०विवरेषु विस्रब्धं (fearlessly) विवर्तमानाः (rolling about) गौधेरराशयः येषु. गौधेर young lizard. 'त्रयो गौधेरगौधार—गौधेया गोधिकात्मजे' अम०. निरातङ्काः (fearless) रङ्कवः (deer) येषु. निराकुलाः ०कुलस्य केलयः (play) येषु. आरामः garden, grove. ०रामेषु रोमन्थायमानं (ruminating) चमूरयूथं येषु. We must read चमूरु (a kind of deer). 'नीलाण्डजा मृगभेदाः' com. C and T suggest that by नीलाण्डज a bird is meant. निर्विकारैः (motionless) वृकैः (wolves) विलोक्यमानाः पोतैः (calves) पीताः गवयधेनवः येषु. गवयः an animal resembling an ox, Gayal. श्रवणहारी (charming to the ear) सनीडस्य (निकटस्य) गिरिनितम्बनिर्झरस्य निनादः तेन निद्रा तया आनन्दः तेन मन्दायमानाः ०दुन्दुभयः येषु. The elephants became drowsy by the murmur of the stream and stopped the flapping of their ears. ०रवं रसमानाः रुरवः येषु. We expect रसयमाणाः (tasting *i. e.* listening with appreciation). रुरु is a kind of deer. प्रमुदिततराः (very much delighted) तरक्षवः येषु. क्षता (pierced by boars) हरिता (yellowish) हरिद्रा (turmeric) तस्याः द्रवेण रज्यमानं नववराहपोतानां पोत्रवलयं येषु. पोतः young. पोत्रं snout—'मुखाग्रे क्रोडहलयोः पोत्रम्' अम०. ०कुञ्जेषु गुञ्जन्तः जाहकाः (polecat) येषु. जातीफलकेषु (nutmeg trees) सुप्तं शालिजातकवलयं येषु. For शालिजात as a pet, see text p. 69 l. 23. दशनेन कुपिताः ०पोतानां पेटकाः समूहाः तैः पाटितः पाटलमुखानां कीटानां पुटकः (hollow, nest) येषु. Some insects with red mouths bit the apes, which in anger crushed their nests. लकुचलम्पटाः गोलाङ्गूलाः तैः लङ्घ्यमानाः लवलयः येषु. लकुच the bread fruit tree. गोलाङ्गूल is a kind of monkey with a dark body and a tail like a cow's. लवली a kind of creeper. बद्धानि वालुकया आलवालवलयानि येषाम्. कुटिलाभिः कुटावलिभिः (rows of water-jars) वलितः (turned or checked) वेगः येषां तानि ०वेगानि गिरिनदिकास्रोतांसि येषु. ०काण्डेषु लम्बमानाः कमण्डलवः येषु. सूत्रशिक्येषु आसक्तानि रिक्तानि भिक्षाकपालानि तैः पल्लविताः लतामण्डपाः येषु. सूत्रशिक्यम् a loop made of threads. Compare Marathi शिंकें. निकटासु कुटीषु (huts) कृताः पाटलाः मुद्रया (by a stamp or seal) चैत्यकमूर्तयः येषु. The models of small चैत्यs were pink-red (पाटल) either because the mud used was red or because the stamp was impressed on vermilion. For the latter, compare p. 32. चैत्यः a monument, pyramidal column containing the ashes of deceased persons; or a sacred tree *(e. g. figtree)* growing on a mound; hall or temple. चीवराम्बरस्य रागेण (redness) कषायं उदकं तेन दूषितः उद्देशः (प्रदेशः) येषाम्. 'चीवरं मुनि-वासः' क्षीर०. मेघ…हलाः—peacocks ran wild in the forest and emitted loud notes. When a cloud is seen peacocks dance and cackle. Hence the trees are said to be मेघमय. वेद…गहनाः—the trees were full of numerous branches (शाखा); the वेद्s are subdivided into numerous schools; *e. g.* the ऋग्वेद् had 21 शाखाs of which शाकल and बाष्कल were the two principal ones. Note 'एकशतमध्वर्युशाखाः, सहस्रवर्त्मा सामवेदः, एकविंशतिधा बाह्वृच्यं, नवधाथर्वणो वेदः' महाभाष्य (Kielhorn) vol. I p. 9. महानीला (very dark) तनुः येषाम्. महानीलः is also a kind of sapphire or emerald. तिमिर…मुषः—the trees attracted the eyes of all people; darkness obscures people's eyes. तिमिर is also an eye disease. ऊर्ध्वीकृताः महाह्रदाः (great lakes) यैः—There were lakes in the forest; there are deep spots in the यमुना also. ०मणिवत् श्यामलाः—the trees were green like emerald, particularly in Spring. Hence they are said to be the pleasure—hill of वसन्त, dark with emerald. अञ्जनाचलाः—as the trees were dark with shade, they are represented to be hills of collyrium. For the same reason they are fancied to be the darkness of पाताल. As पाताल is supposed to be below the earth, the author says 'भित्त्वा भुवमुत्थिताः.' What प्रतिप्रवेशकाः means is difficult to say. A and C read प्रतिवेशिकाः (neighbours). The com. reads 'प्रतिप्रसवकाः प्रतिच्छन्दकाः' *i. e.* reflections, images. प्रति…शकाः may mean 'the ushers, those that introduce.' अंशावतार—see p. 191. कृष्णरात्रीणाम् of the nights of the dark half. The trees were dark like इन्द्रनील. अदूर…भदन्तेन the venerable sage must not be far off. भदन्तः a term of respect applied to a Buddhist. समुपस्पृश्य having sipped and ejected water as a religious act. युगपद्विश्रामेण (sudden rest) समुन्मुक्तः हेषाघोषः तेन बधिरीकृतं अटवीगहनं यया *(adj.* of वाजिसेनाम्). अवलम्ब्य…विनयं हृदयेन…मंसे having assumed in his heart humility and having leant with his right hand on the shoulder of माधवगुप्त. माधवगुप्त was the younger of the two princes from Mālava, who were the companions of Harsha in his boyhood. See text p. 12 l. 17.

P. 128 ll. 1–32 **अथ तेषां…ववन्दे.** The principal sentence is अथ तेषां तरूणां मध्ये…दिवाकरमित्रमद्राक्षीत्. The instrumentals from नानादेशीयैः are connected with आवेद्यमानम् (l. 8). स्थाणूनाश्रितैः sitting on or reclining against posts. अरण्यानी–'महारण्यमरण्यानी' अम०. निकुञ्जः bower. निलीन hidden. वीतः (विगतः) रागः (passion) येषाम्. This may be an *adj.* of आर्हतैः or may be taken independently. आर्हतैः by Jain philosophers. अर्हत्—a sanctified teacher of the Jainas, a तीर्थङ्कर. The philosophy of the Jainas is called आर्हतदर्शन in the सर्वदर्शनसंग्रह. मस्करिभिः—see above p. 113. श्वेतपटः—this probably refers to the श्वेताम्बर sect among Jains. पाण्डुरभिक्षुभिः—the com. explains that these were ascetics that had abandoned the red robes peculiar to Buddhist monks. भागवत—a devotee of भगवत् *i. e.* वासुदेव or कृष्ण. वर्णिभिः—'वर्णिनो ब्रह्मचारिणः' अम०, from वर्ण+इन्—according to 'वर्णाद्ब्रह्मचारिणि' पा. 5. 2. 134. केशलुञ्चनैः that pulled out their hair. 'लुञ्चिताः पिच्छिकाहस्ताः पाणिपात्रा दिगम्बराः' सर्व० आर्हतदर्शन. कापिलैः followers of कपिल, the founder of the सांख्य system. जैनैः—the com. renders it by बौद्धैः. Though जिन is a name of बुद्ध, the word जैन does not popularly mean बौद्ध. The word आर्हत also would mean बौद्ध as अर्हत् is a name of बुद्ध. लोकायतिक—is a materialist, an atheist, a follower of चार्वाक, who held that there was no intelligent ruler of the universe, that there was no soul, that there was no पुनर्जन्म, that only प्रत्यक्षप्रमाण was to be accepted and that all beings were created from the *four* elements. Compare 'लोकायतिकविद्ययेवाधर्मरुचेः' काद० p. 150. लोकायतं शास्त्रमस्ति अस्य इति लो०. काणादैः followers of कणाद, who was the founder of the वैशेषिक system. औपनिषदैः that were students of the doctrines of the Upanishads. The Upanishads, often called वेदान्त, are works forming the last portions of the several Vedas and are concerned with philosophical problems, such as the orign of the Universe, the relation of the individual soul to the Supreme Spirit and so on. ऐश्वर...कैः who believed in ईश्वर as the cause (or creator) of the world. This probably applies to the माहेश्वरमत, according to which ईश्वर is only निमित्तकारण and which is refuted in the ब्रह्मसूत्र (II. 2. 37–41) or to the न्याय system founded by गौतम which regards ईश्वर as the निमित्तकारण. 'कारन्धमिभिः धातुवादिभिः' com. This probably refers to the school of alchemists (called रसेश्वरदर्शन) who believed that mercury, if properly treated, would make men immortal. *Vide* सर्वदर्शनसंग्रह for this दर्शन. 'कारन्धमी कांस्यकारे धातुवादरतेऽपि च' मे०. धर्मशास्त्रिभिः those that studied the Smṛitis, like those of Âpastamba, Vasishṭha, Baudhāyana, Manu &c. पौराणिकैः—see p. 113. साप्ततन्तवैः those who studied the sacrifice. This probably stands for the students of the पूर्वमीमांसा system founded by जैमिनि, in which the most prominent place is assigned to sacrifice.'सप्ततन्तुर्मखः क्रतुः' अम० (सप्तभिश्छन्दोभिस्तन्यते इति क्षीर०). शाब्दैः = वैयाकरणैः, whose position was that the व्याकरणशास्त्र would lead to मोक्ष 'तद्द्वारमपवर्गस्य

वाङ्मलानां चिकित्सितम् । पवित्रं सर्वविद्यानामधिविद्यं प्रकाशते ॥' वाक्यपदीय I.; compare महाभाष्य 'एकः शब्दः सम्यग्ज्ञातः शास्त्रान्वितः सुप्रयुक्तः स्वर्गे लोके कामधुग्भवति' vol III p. 58. पाञ्चरात्रिकैः followers of the पञ्चरात्र doctrines. In the महाभारत we are told that नारद promulgated the पञ्चरात्र doctrines after receiving them from नारायण 'सांख्ययोगकृतं तेन पञ्चरात्रानुशब्दितम् । नारायणमुखोद्गीतं नारदोऽश्रावयत्पुनः ॥ शान्ति० 340-112. सिद्धान्तान् dogmas, established truths. अभि...शयानैः absorbed in (the pursuit of their special philosophy), pondering, repeating, doubting. व्युत्पादयद्भिः giving etymologies. व्याचक्षाणैः expounding. आवेद्यमानम् indicated, pointed out (qualifies दिवाकरमित्रम् below). कपिभिः—this and the following nouns in the instrumental are to be connected with उपास्यमानम्. कपिभि...परैः (waited upon) even by monkeys that had taken refuge with the 'three refuges' and that were engaged in doing the menial work about चैत्यs (or of चैत्य). त्रिसरणं (Pāli तिसरणं, Sanskrit त्रिशरणं)—the three Refuges are बुद्ध, धर्म (the Law) and सङ्घ (the assembly). The formula in which faith in these three is professed may be looked upon as the *credo* of Buddhism. It consists in repeating thrice the words 'बुद्धं सरणं गच्छामि धम्मं सरणं गच्छामि संघं सरणं गच्छामि'. परमो...दिशद्भिः by parrots, greatly devoted to Buddha and skilled in his teaching, giving instruction in the कोश. According to C and T कोश is the Buddhist dictionary by Vasubandhu. ०शालिनीभिः—शिक्षापदानां उपदेशेन दोषोपशमः तेन शालन्ते इति—that had secured the extinguishment of the दोषs (sins) by instruction in the शिक्षापदs. The शिक्षापदs (Pāli सिक्खापद) are ten and are the precepts regulating the life of a Buddhist monk. They are the same as the ten शीलs for which see below. धर्मदेशना instruction in the धर्म. अनवरतश्रवणेन गृहीतः आलोकः यैः that had attained light (enlightenment) by incessant listening to instruction. Owls (कौशिक) cannot see in daylight (आलोकः). बोधिसत्त्वजातकानि—the Jātakas are the stories of the former lives of बुद्ध before he had attained perfect knowledge. जातकं is the tenth book of the Khuddakanikāya and contains 550 *Jātakas* or birthstories. बोधिसत्त्व is a term applied to बुद्ध in his various births before he attained Buddhahood. शीलं (Pāli सीलं)—There are ten moral precepts laid down by Buddha, prohibiting the destruction of life, theft, impurity, lying, use of intoxicants, eating at forbidden hours, attending worldly amusements, use of unguents and ornaments, the use of a large or ornamented couch and receiving money. जातः सौगतशीलैः शीतलः स्वभावः येषाम्

whose natures became mild by the (practice of the) moral precepts enjoined by बुद्ध. आसनोपान्ते उपविष्टाः विस्रब्धाः अनेककेसरिशावकाः यस्य सः ०शावकः तस्य भावः शावकता तया. मुनिपरमेश्वरम्—he was the foremost of sages. अकृत्रिम...निषण्णम्—A परमेश्वर (emperor) sits on a सिंहासन (throne) which is only artificial (*i. e.* it has the *shape* of a lion); while दिवाकर० sat on a real सिंहासन (lion-seat). There is another idea. बुद्ध is called मुनीन्द्र or मुनीश्वर. So दिवाकर० seemed to be बुद्ध himself. 'मुनीन्द्रः श्रीघनः शास्ता' अम०. उप...पल्लवम्—deer licked his feet. The poet fancies that they drank from his feet tranquility of mind. नीवाराः wild rice. 'तृणधान्यानि नीवाराः' अम०. प्रियां...यन्तम् who propitiated मैत्री that was dear to his heart. मत्री means 'good will towards the whole world'. 'अपकारिण्यभिप्रीतिः मैत्री' com. The young dove looked like a lotus placed on the ear. The word प्रियां suggests another sense. मैत्री was as if his wife and he propitiated her by ०कर्णोत्पल (the पारावत). Remove the comma after व्यामोहम्. In this long passage and elsewhere Bāna shows considerable acquaintance with Buddhist dogma and technique. जनितः जनव्यामोहः येन–the people were infatuated by the rays of the nails of his right hand (as he poured water into the beak of a peacock). The shining and dark-green neck of the peacock resembled an emerald water pot. 'कमण्डलौ च करकः' अम०. The long neck of the peacock was like the neck of a jar. Take away the comma after संवीतम्. संवीत (*past p. p.* of व्ये with सम्)—'संवीतं रुद्धमावृतम्' अम०. पौरन्दर—पुरन्दरस्य इन्द्रस्य अयं पौरन्दरः. दिवाकर० was covered with a red robe and looked like the eastern quarter arrayed in the mellow light of morn. उल्लिखितः (polished, wrought) पद्मरागः तस्य प्रभा प्रतिमा यस्याः (*adj.* of देहप्रभया). रक्तावदातया red and bright (pure). The quarters were reddened by the glow of his body. The poet fancies that he taught the quarters to assume the red robes (peculiar to Buddhist monks). अनौद्धत्यम् freedom from insolence, modesty. मन्द...कारेण that resembled a night lotus slightly closed. The कुमुद is white; his eye was white. मन्द...मुदस्येव आकारः यस्य. जनेन क्षुण्णाः (trampled upon) क्षुद्रजन्तवः तेषां जीवनार्थम्. अमृत is स्निग्ध (glossy), धवल and प्रसन्न (transparent); while his eye was affectionate (स्निग्ध), धवल and प्रसन्न (quiet, unruffled). सर्व...मितम्—the idea is that he knew all the S'āstras. From परमाणुs the whole material world is produced. See above p. 12. परमसौगतः a very aealous or devout follower of Buddha. अवलोकितः ईश्वरः येन who saw (*i. e.* recognised) an ईश्वर. The Buddhists do not recognise an intelligent Supreme Ruler of the Universe. This contradiction is got over by taking अव० in another sense. अव० is a बोधिसत्त्व worshipped by the northern Buddhists. अस्ख...लग्नम् though he never faltered (in the path of धर्म), yet he clung to austerities. One who falters has to cling to something for support. आलोक: light. यथा...प्रकाशकम् he explained the proper worth of each thing; light shows objects as they are. दर्शनार्थिनाम् (1) those who want to see; (2) those who desire to have correct knowledge. सुगतस्य=बुद्धस्य. अभि...नीयम् fit to be approached. प्र...नीयमिव whose grace was to be prayed for even by Favour. आत्मनो...णीयम् who was to be longed for even by the Soul. जन्म जपस्य the source of जप (inaudible prayers). जन्म यमस्य would mean 'the source of यम.' यम is the first of the eight *Angas* of योग. 'अहिंसासत्यास्तेयब्रह्मचर्यापरिग्रहाः यमाः' योगसूत्र II. 30. नेमिं नियमस्य the circumference (*i. e.* the utmost limit or reach) of religious observances. नियम may also mean the seconed *Anga* of Yoga. 'शौच—सन्तोष—तपः—स्वाध्याय—ईश्वरप्रणिधानानि नियमाः' योगसूत्र II. 32. तत्त्वं essence. कोशं कुशलस्य the treasure of bliss or auspiciousness. सर्व...तायाः the all-in-all of good conduct. दाक्ष्यं दाक्षिण्यस्य the civility of courteousness *i. e.* the perfection of courteousness. पारं...याः the highest limit of compassion for others. निर्वृतिं सुखस्य—Happiness itself would find pleasure in him. ०गम्भीराकारेण आरोपितः बहुमानः यस्मिन् in whom high regard (for दिवा०) was produced by his &c. शिरसा...ववन्दे he uttered words of salutation and also bent his head.

P. 128 l. 33—**P. 129** l. 16 दिवाकर...विशत्. महानु...भाजा possessing the magnificence belonging to noble persons. This qualifies ०विशेषेण. अप्राकृतेन not belonging to common men. ०प्रकाशकेन goes with प्रश्रयेण. प्रश्रयेण=विनयेन. चक्षुषि...ग्रहीत् he took him (*i. e.* greeted him) by his eye and heart. We may also connect आह्लादितः with चक्षुषि and चेतसि. सम्पादितं ससम्भ्रमं अभ्युत्थानं येन who (दिवाकर०) rose up hurriedly (to receive हर्ष). सङ्कलय्य having held together. उद्ग...लोलं disordered by his rising up. उत्क्षिप्य having raised up (his hand). महा...प्रशस्तं हस्तं—see for these बृह० 67. 44–48, one of which is quoted on p. 20 above. गुरु...मानः highly thinking of हर्ष that had come as a guest, as if he were his *guru*. स्वेन आसनेन—this is the highest mark of respect that can be shown to a guest.

आध्वम् (*Imperative 2nd plural* of आस् to sit). अलोह...जातानाम् goodness is in the case of the noble a fetter for tying fast, though not made of iron. स्थाने it is quite proper. दर्शनमेव पुण्यं तेन अनुगृहीतस्य—the idea is:—your very sight adds to the store of my merit (पुण्य) and that is a great favour in itself. पुनरुक्तः superfluous. अनुग्रहः the favour (*viz.* hospitable treatment by आसनदान and पादोदक &c.). चक्षुः प्रमाणं यस्य सः ०माणः प्रसादः तेन स्वीकृतस्य (मम)—I was accepted by you as your own by bestowing on me a favour whose standard is the eye *i. e.* your very eye showed me the greatest favour possible. पर...चेष्टितम् the acts of civility (उपचारः), such as offering a seat &c., make me a stranger *i. e.* these civilities are to be shown to strangers only. अति...पुरः in your presence to have the bare ground as a seat is the highest pitch (of honour). There is another meaning also 'to sit even on bare ground in the presence of a person like you is an impropriety (a violation of proper limits).' Read ०वृत्ति and take away the vertical line after it. सम्भाषणमेव अमृतं तेन अभिषेकः तेन क्षालितं सकलं वपुः यस्य. प्रदेशे वृत्तिः यस्य. The idea is:—when my *whole* body has bathed in the nectar of speech with you, water for the feet, that will only wash a part (प्रदेश) of my body, is useless (अपार्थक). 'पाद्यं पादाय वारिणि' अम०. If we read अतिभूमिरेव भवादृशां...वृत्तिः the meaning will be 'when my *whole* body has been bathed &c., then my remaining here in a particular spot before you will be the height of impropriety.' This is not very happy.

P. 129 l. 17—**P. 130** l. 13 **अलङ्कारो...भाव्यते इति.** अल...श्रयः great politeness (प्रश्रयः) is really the true ornament of the powerful (and not jewels &c., which are mere stones). प्रभवत् one who rules, powerful. न प्रत्य...वचनम् when the king did not accede to the words (of the sage). ०निहितं ०युगलमेव निगडः (fetters) तेन निश्चलीकृतं हृदयं यस्य. कालकलाम् a portion of time. **'पापं किल्बिषकल्मषम्'** अम०. मूल...वनम्—the idea is:—he subsisted on fruits and roots only; consequently his breath was fragrant. When he opened his lips, he as if sent forth (in the form of his breath) a bower of creepers fragrant with white flowers. His white teeth were like flowers. अभ्यवहारः (food, eating) तस्मात् सम्भवः यस्य (*adj.* of ०वनम्). अद्य...संसारः—from this day this संसार (worldly life) is not only not to be blamed, but has become fit to be saluted (praised). प्रकाशितं सत्सारं येन that has manifested its excellent essence. संसार is often spoken of as

असार, but now it is सत्सार (सत् being opposed to असत् represented by अ in असार). Or प्रकाशितः सत्सु सारः श्रेष्ठः (हर्षः) यस्मिन्. 'सारो बले स्थिरांशे च न्याय्ये क्लीबं वरे त्रिषु' अम०. किं...द्भुतं what wonders may not living beings see? The meaning is:—your splendid form is the greatest wonder in this world. That being seen, a living person may be blessed to see many wonders, that are less marvellous. अचिन्ति...तम् presented unexpectedly. जन्मान्तरेषु अवस्थितानि सुकृतानि. दत्तमेव goes with फलम्. दर्शयता goes with तपःक्लेशेन. देवानां प्रियम् beloved of the gods. Bāṇa uses the word in the same way as As'oka does in his edicts. As'oka calls himself देवानां प्रिय. The महाभाष्य uses it in a good sense 'के पुनर्भवदादयः । भवान् दीर्घायुः देवानां प्रियः आयुष्मानिति' on पा. V. 3. 14 (Kielhorn vol. II p. 405). But later Sanskrit grammarians assign the meaning of 'fool' to this word. जातं...सुखस्य my mind has no longing for the happiness of final emancipation. We must read निर्वृति० with C. निवृत्ति० also may be made to yield (though rather in a far-fetched way) the same sense. निवृत्ति cessation of the round of births and deaths). But the com. says 'निवृत्तिश्चित्तविभ्रमः.' ०जीवितजनकम् who gives life *i. e.* who protects and supports. पुण्य...णामः blessed even are those merits, of which thou art the fruit (the fulfilment). Compare the words of प्रभाकरवर्धन 'फलमस्यनेक... अकलुषस्य कर्मणः' (text p. 24). सुकृतं तपः यैः. परिगृहीताः सर्वावयवाः यैः. ये...वाः that constitute all your limbs. भव्यः...यः fortunate is manliness in that it has resorted to you. यत्सत्यं to say the truth. पुण्यभाजं = हर्षम्. पुनः...जन्मनि Once more faith in human birth has been generated in me. He means:—up till now I had looked upon human birth as an unmixed evil, a thing to fly from; but now I think it has some inherent good in it. नेच्छद्भिः—I don't desire to see the working of Cupid; but in your person I have seen Kāma (*i. e.* you are as handsome as काम). अमृत...कार्यमेव—the idea is:—that your words are so sweet is natural; you are yourself full of अमृत and so your words (the effect) must possess the quality (माधुर्य) of the cause (you). Compare वैशेषिकसूत्र II. 1. 24 'कारणगुणपूर्वकः कार्यगुणो दृष्टः.' There is a well-known न्याय (maxim) 'कारणगुणा हि कार्यगुणानारभन्ते'. उपाध्या... यामि even though I reflect deeply I cannot fancy who your teacher could have been (in this humility). गुणग्रामः—there is a suggested idea. A village also may become शून्य (tenantless) when nobody has a long life. वंशे family; bamboo. It was supposed that pearls were found in bamboos. See above p. 193.

मुक्तः आमयः येन free from disease or hurt. पारिप्लवं restless. 'चञ्चलं तरलं चैव पारिप्लवपरिप्लवे' अम०. के वयम्—who are we to offer (fruits and roots that we share in common with all the foresters)? The idea is:—there is nothing in this forest that I can call my own; fruits and roots belong to the foresters as well as to me. So I cannot offer them to you as something special. अपरो...साकम् this wretched body, that was never made useful to others, belongs to us. कलि is the age of sin; so कायकलि means 'sinful body'. C and T strangely enough translate 'But this wretched body of ours is only for another's service.' सर्वे...थ्याय all that has been left to us is for the welcome of our friend (इष्ट). He says:—All that I can call my own is my wretched body, but that was never made useful to anybody. But that is all that is left to me and I shall use it for welcoming you my friend. स्वायत्ताः...कतिचित्—he means:—besides my body, I possess a few drops of learning that are completely at my disposal. उप...यति but my affection for you does not stop to consider whether they (विद्याबिन्दवः) will be of any use to you. In my affection for you I place my learning at your disposal, whether useful to you or not does not matter. C and T translate 'our friendship cannot hesitate how to make use of them.' This is not correct. Read कश्चित् for कश्चित्. यदि...लवम् He says that he would not press him to tell, if thereby he was likely to hinder even the smallest business of his (हर्ष's). अरक्षणीयानि अक्षराणि यस्य (*adj.* of कथनीयम्) the words of which are not to be kept secret. कियान् अवधिः यस्य. Separate वा अयम्. सन्तप्तरूपेव विभाव्यते is seen to be as if afflicted.

P. 130 ll. 14—**P. 131** l.6 राजा तु...कीदृशीति. दर्शितः संभ्रमः यस्मिन् (*adj.* of वचसा) that shows the flurry (of your mind due to my arrival). हृदय...करम् that supports (*i. e.* encourages, gladdens) the heart. अभ्यर्हितम्=पूज्यम्. अनु...यमपि though I do not deserve to be treated with respect. विनष्टाः निखिलाः इष्टबन्धवः यस्य. जीवि...बन्धनम् the sole tie that keeps up my life. निबन्धनम् tie, suport. अनुबन्धः continuity. He means that he continues to live because of her. विन्ध्यवनम्—is the object of अविशत्. The student will notice that all the letters from ०वन...to ०शत् are short. ०बहुलम् abounding in &c. ०कुलैः कलिलम् full of 'कलिलं गहनं समे' अम०. ०शरभेभ्यः भयं यस्मिन्. For शरभ, see p. 66. ०महिषैः मुषितं पथिकगमनं यस्मिन् where the journeys of travellers are hindered by huge buffaloes. शर reed. कुश a kind of grass. अवटः

pit. तस्याः वार्ता तद्वार्ता. अभाजनं...भवताम् we are not fit (destined) to make such presents (उपायनं) of glad tidings to you. शमि...मानः of an age when passions are restrained. जाता करुणा यस्य. प्रक्षरितं चक्षुः यस्य whose eye was full of tears. मह...वर्तते there is a very pitiable occurrence. व्यसनं misfortune. पूर्वं भूता भूतपूर्वा. भूत...रूपा who seems to have seen prosperity in former days. सम्भा...भगवान् honour her before her life leaves her. अप्रोषिताः प्राणाः यस्याः. अभ्यु...श्वासनैः favour her with suitable comforting words. अनुपरतपूर्वं कृमि...मपि आर्यस्य गोचरगतम् even insects when once within your sight have never died before. जाता अनुजायाः आशङ्का यस्य who suspected that she was his sister. अन्तर्द्रुतः इव as if melting inside. For दोदूयमान, see p 42. गद्गदिकया गृहीतः कण्ठः यस्य whose throat was choked up. विकला वाक् यस्य whose accents were broken. जीवे...वन्तम् would she be still alive? आकारतो कीदृशी what sort of woman is she in appearance?

P. 131 l. 7—**P. 133** l. 26 **तथा...निवेदितवानिति.** रोधसा by the bank. यदृच्छया by chance. हिम...कातराणां frightened by the lotus beds withering through frost. रसितं humming. He compares the weeping of females to the hum of bees and the tones of lutes. सार्यमाण being touched gently with the fingers. अति...वर्तिनीनाम्—that were tuned to a high protracted tone. वीणातन्त्रीणाम् of the strings of lutes. एकः तानः यस्मिन् in which the note was one (and not complex). तान is defined in the सङ्गीतरत्नाकर I. 4. 27 as '**तानाः** स्युर्मूर्च्छनाः शुद्धाः षाडवौडवितीकृताः॥'. तान is a mode of मूर्छना, for which see above p. 206. With रुदितं, एकतानं means 'incessant.' अधृतिकरम् that caused loss of firmness *i. e.* that agitated me. The principal sentence is दृष्टवान् असि च...अबलानां चक्रवालेन परिवृताम् (l. 25)...योषितम् (p. 77. l. 22). दृष...ल्लोहितेन—this and the following instrumentals qualify चक्रवालेन below. दृषत्खण्डैः खण्डिताः अङ्गुलयः ताभ्यः गलत् लोहितं यासाम् from whose toes shattered by pieces of stones blood was oozing. पार्ष्णिषु प्रविष्टानि शरशलाकाशल्यानि तैः शूलः तेन सङ्कोचितानि चक्षूंषि येषाम् whose eyes became contracted by the sharp pain of the points of the long *S'ara* grass that entered their heels (पार्ष्णि *m.*). अध्वनीनेन श्रमेण श्वयथुः तेन निश्चलौ चरणौ यस्य whose feet could not move owing to the swelling caused by the fatigue of the journey. अध्वनीन from अध्वन्. स्थाणवैः व्रणैः व्यथिताः गुल्फाः (ankles) तेषु बद्धा भूर्जत्वक् येन. स्थाणव due to stakes or posts (from स्थाणु). वातेन (inflammation) खुडानां (ankle-joints) खेदः (pain) तेन खञ्जा जङ्घा (leg) तया जातः ज्वरः यस्य. 'वातखुडो गतिप्रतिघातलक्षणो

वातव्याधिः' com. Or we may take वातखुड as the name of a disease like rheumatism or gout. The अष्टाङ्गहृदय describes the disease called खुड or वातशोणित as follows:—'प्रायेण सुकुमाराणामचङ्क्रमणशीलिनाम् । अभिघातादशुद्धेश्च नृणामसृजि दूषिते ॥...आढ्यरोगं खुडं वातबलासं वातशोणितम् । तदाहुर्नामभिस्तच्च पूर्वं पादौ प्रधावति ॥ विशेषाद्यानयानाद्यैः प्रलम्बौ तस्य लक्षणम् ॥' III. 16. 2, 4–5. पिण्डिका calf of the leg. ०जटया (by the twisted fibres of date-palms) जर्जरितं जानु यस्य. शतावर्या विदारितः ऊरुः यस्य. शतावरी is a plant otherwise called नारायणी. विदार्या दारितः (torn) तनुदुकूलपल्लवः यस्य. विदारी is a plant called in Marathi भुईकोहळा. उत्कटाः (prominent) वंशविटपानां कण्टकाः तेषां कोटिभिः पाटितं कञ्चुककर्पटं (bodice-cloth) यस्य. फललोभेन आलम्बितानि (held) आनम्राणि ०जालकानि उद्गताः कण्टकाः येषाम् (*adj.* of ०जालकैः). उल्लिखितं (scratched) सुकुमारं करोदरं यस्य. कदर्थिताः (teased, pained) बाहवः यस्य. With the pointed horns of deer they dug up roots &c. for their food and their arms were wearied by the exertions. For कदर्थित, see p. 101. ताम्बूलविरहेण (absence of betel) विरसं (dry) मुखं तेन खण्डितं कोमलं आमलकीफलं येन. Everyone knows how welcome an आमलक fruit is in one's childhood, when one is thirsty. कुशकुसुमानां आहत्या लोहितानां. The flowers of कुश grass struck their eyes, which became red and swollen. श्वयताम्—*gen. sing.* of *present p.* of श्वि 1 P. to swell. लेपीकृता मनःशिला येन. They applied red arsenic (Marathi मनशीळ) to their swollen eyes. The अष्टाङ्गसंग्रह (उत्तरस्थान chap. 16) prescribes red assenic for swollen eyes 'दाहोपदेहरागाश्रुशोफशान्त्यै विडालकम् । कुर्यात्सर्वत्र पत्रैलामरिचस्वर्णगैरिकैः ॥ 2...मनोह्वाफलिनीक्षौद्रैः कफे सर्वैस्तु सर्वजे ॥ 3.' कण्टकिनीभिः लताभिः लूनः अलकलेशः (small curls) यस्य. किसलयैः उपपादितं आतपत्रकृत्यं यस्य to whom tender foliage served as an umbrella (against the sun). ०पुटे गृहीतं अम्भः येन. पाथेयीकृता मृणालपूलिका येन that made a bundle of the fibrous roots of lotuses their provisions (in their wanderings). For पाथेय, see p. 212. ०शिक्ये निहिता नारिकेलकोशस्य कलशी तस्यां कलितं रसालतैलं येन that placed mango oil in a cup made of the outer (hard) covering of cocoanut fruit placed in a loop (शिक्यं) made of the hems (दशा) of their China-made garments. There is another reading ०सरलतैलेन (the oil of pine). कतिपयावशेषाः ०वर्बराः तैः अविरलेन full of deafmutes, hunch-backed persons, dwarfs, deaf men and barbarians, that were helpless through grief and of whom only a few remained. We must read कलमूक (for कलामूक) for which see p. 99. These are usually described as the attendants and guardians of the ladies of the harem. बर्बरः a low person, one not an Aryan. The com. says 'कलामूकाः पण्डकाः । एवमादयोऽन्तःपुररक्षिणः बर्बरा एतद्देशजाः'. So it takes कलामूक in the sense of 'eunuch.' आप...लावण्येन—her grace which covered every thing by its brilliance did not leave her even in misfortune. A person born of a noble family does not forsake his master or friend even in adversity. प्रति...कायाम्—the tender (and therefore reddish) shoots of creepers were reflected in her bright complexion. The poet fancies that her body was reddened by the bloody wounds of sorrow (and not by red shoots). सरसैः (किसलयैः) means 'juicy.' Read पाटली० for पटली०. ०ङ्कुरेण क्षतं तस्मात् क्षरतीति तेन ०क्षारिणा. Her feet were red with blood from wounds caused by sharp दर्भ grass. The poet fancies that it was Alaktaka dye which ladies usually applied to their feet. In the forest they had no अलक्तक; but blood took its place. अनुसरणं habit. कृता छाया यस्य that was shaded. विगता छाया यस्य that had lost its lustre. There is a pun on छाया. आका...शयानाम् that surpassed even आकाश in शून्यता (being vacant-minded, being a void). For आकाश and शून्यता, see above (text p. 2 ll. 1-2). निश्चेतनतया she was fainting; earth has no intelligence (चैतन्य) in it (it is जड). मरु...म्पदा she heaved so many sighs that she seemed to be all sighs (*i. e.* wind). Explain the following clauses similary. सन्तापः heat; grief. निर...तया—she had no support (*i. e.* she had nothing that could keep up her drooping spirits); आकाश is also without support; it rests on nothing. पारिप्लवतया—she was trembling (through grief); lightning flashes are tremulous. मुक्तानि मुक्ताः (pearls) अंशुकं (fine silken robes) रत्नानि कुसुमानि कनकं पत्राभरणानि (paintings on cheeks &c.) यया (with योषितम्). She had no ornaments &c. on her person, as she had escaped from imprisonment and she was in grief. The com. takes मुक्तांशुक as one word 'मुक्ताख्यमंशुकं मालवदेशजमुत्तरीयम्'. The कल्पलता is a mythical plant that was supposed to yield what was desired by its votary. It may also drop down मुक्ता, अंशुक &c. In this case we must take पत्रं as equal to वाहनं (vehicles) and take आभरणं (ornaments) by itself. महावने—the woman was in a great forest; कल्पवृक्ष is in the great garden of Indra. The com. takes वन in the sense of जल. Then we may explain that पारिजात, which is one of the कल्पवृक्षs, was produced from the sea (महावन) at the time of the churning. परमेश्वरस्य (शिवस्य) उत्तमाङ्गे

पातेन दुर्ललितं अङ्गं यस्याः (with गङ्गाम्) who is insolent by falling &c.; परमेश्वरस्य (of the great king ग्रहवर्मा, her husband) उत्तमाङ्गपातः तेन दुर्ललितानि अङ्गानि यस्याः (with योषितम्) whose limbs were wayward by the fall of the head of &c. गां गताम्—the Ganges came down to the earth from the matted hair of शिव; the woman was lying on the earth (through grief) or walking on the earth (as she had no vehicle). भगीरथ brought the Ganges from Heaven, which fell on the head of शिव and which thought that by its force it would crush शिव. 'विशाम्यहं हि पातालं स्रोतसा गृह्य शङ्करम्' रामायण बाल० 43. 6. ०पादपल्लवाम्—her feet (पाद) were grey with pollen; the rays of the moon also were grey. Remove the comma after पल्लवाम्. लोकान्तर०—she wished that death might take her away to her deceased husband; the moon also goes to another sphere in the morning. निजजलमोक्षेण कदर्थिता दर्शिता धवलायतयोर्नेत्रयोः शोभा यया her long and white eyes were wearied by shedding tears and became dim. If the water of the Ganges goes very low, then the lotus bed will show its long and white roots (नेत्र). For नेत्र, see pp. 37, 53. Remove the comma after शोभाम्. निमीलिताम् she was languid by the fierce heat of the sun; a कुमुदिनी closes its petals in the sun. दग्ध...दिताम् the woman was disappointed at her wretched state (दशा); the flame of the lamp at dawn is made to fail by the wick (दशा) being burnt. पाण्डु वपुः यस्याः her body was pale; the flame also becomes dimmer and dimmer. पार्श्ववर्तिनां वारणे अभियोगः तेन रक्ष्यमाणां who was saved by the perseverance of her attendants in dissuading her. पार्श्ववर्ती वारणः तस्य अभियोगात् रक्ष्यमाणां being saved from the attack of an elephant near her (with करिणीम्). महा...न्नाम् the woman had bathed in a lake before she burnt herself in grief; the करिणी plunged in a deep lake. प्रविष्टां ध्याने she was in deep thought. स्थितां मरणे she was resolved on dying. दूरीकृताम् separated from. वि...षा she was exhausted by wandering and was empty of life (as she had resolved on dying). आकुलाम्०— her hair was dishevelled; she was absorbed in finding the means of dying. धृत... मौनेन च she had placed her hand on her mouth (in deep thought) and her lips were also silent. मन्युना = शोकेन. भ्रष्टै... लासैश्च—here and with the following instrumentals we have to supply the word उपलक्षिताम्. भ्रष्टै...लासैश्च with her kindred and graceful gestures all gone. मुक्तेन...त्मना her ears were bereft (of ornaments) and her spirit was drooping. आरम्भः effort,

the good will remove their distress. The construction is यत इयं नः स्वामिनी...अग्निं प्रविशति...आर्योऽपि तावत् व्यापारयतु वाणीमस्याम्. पितुः refers to प्रभाकरवर्धन. भर्तुः refers to her husband ग्रहवर्मा. प्रवासेन by the journey (of हर्ष). The reading of B supplies a gap. The text does not refer to her mother nor to राज्यवर्धन. निरवलम्बना without support. नीचाराति refers to the king of Malva who killed ग्रहवर्मा. प्रकृतिमनस्विनी spirited by nature. कदर्थितं सौकुमार्यं यस्याः. उपर्युपरि व्यसनैः by calamities (befalling her) one after another. निवा...जनम् not minding her elders that dissuade her and whom she never disobeyed before even in dream. अख...स्वपि whose requests were not violated even in play. अविद्यमानं शरणं यस्य helpless. यथा...स्याः शोकः from what you say (I gather that) her sorrow is beyond the reach of my words. पुण्यः आशयः (अभिप्रायः) यस्याः whose thoughts are holy. उपरिष्टात् afterwards (after that moment). अभ्यर्थना request. दुःखमेव अन्धकारपटलं तस्य भिदुरैः capable of piercing &c. सौ...दर्शनैः by the sayings of बुद्ध and his own illustrated by examples. स्वकैः सुभाषितैः. दर्शितानि निदर्शनानि येषु. नाना...कौशलैः by his eloquent words weighty with various texts. कुशलं (पुण्यं) शीलं यस्याः. प्रबो...यिष्यति will place her on the path of enlightenment. अशरणानां कृपणानां (distressed) बहुयुवतीनां मरणं यस्मिन्.

P. 133 l. 27—**P. 135** l. 26 अथ...संभ्रमम्. भिक्षोरिदं भैक्षवम् (भाषितम्). निम्नीकृतं मनः यस्य—whose mind was depressed (by sorrow). सर्वैः आकारैः संवदति इति तया. सर्वा...सन्देहः whose doubts were dispelled by the very condition (of that woman) that agreed in all features with (that of his sister). श्रमणः a Buddhist ascetic. निष्कारणवैरिभिः goes with भागधेयैः. यदि...यामः if we can honour her somehow while she is alive *i. e.* if we can reach the place and find her alive. तेन शाक्यपुत्रीयेण refers to the pupil of दिवाकर॰ who had seen राज्यश्री. प्रदिश्यमानं वर्त्म यस्य. पद्भ्यामेव—connect with प्रावर्तत (started). तं...पिबन्निव as if drinking the distance by his rapid steps. मुमूर्षोः (from the desiderative base of मृ) desirous of dying. Read धारयसि. The root in धरणी is the same as in धारयसि. If the earth is धरणी (supporter), it must support even राज्यश्री. प्रभाकरवर्धन was धरणीनाथ. His daughter therefore is the daughter of the earth. पुष्पभूति was the ancestor of हर्ष. See p. 1 (text, 4th उच्छ्वास). मुखरवंश्य refers to ग्रहवर्मा, husband of राज्यश्री. विवि...धुराम् overwhelmed with various agonies (आधिः). न विबोधयसि why dost thou not enlighten (also why dost thou not bring to consciousness)? भक्त...सुप्तोऽसि thou art asleep when your devotees are suffering torments. पुष्प...पातिन् partial to the house of पुष्प०. राजधर्म was always associated with पुष्पभूति's line. The foremost duty of a king is to protect. The com. says 'राजधर्मो बुद्धः' पतङ्गः the sun. चारित्र is called ungrateful चण्डाल, because it does not help राज्यश्री, though she guarded it jealously. Many women are described as rising superior to all difficulties by their चारित्र (chastity). कि...लक्षणैः what have her auspicious marks settled for her? The idea is:—is this the end that the auspicious marks on her body indicated would be hers? प्रतापशील was an *alias* of प्रभाकरवर्धन (see p. 1 text). निष्ठुरः...भावः the world of the dead is cruel. संवादय declare. नितान्तनिःशूक extremely cruel. श्वपाकः = चण्डालः. सकामोऽसि thou hast secured thy desire. गान्धारि—This (गान्धारी) and the following are the names of the attendants of राज्यश्री, who are making ready to kill themselves along with their mistress. गृही...पाशः this creeper has already been taken by me. The idea is:—take another creeper for using it as a halter to kill yourself. पिशाचि—She is called पिशाची because पिशाचs are supposed to dwell on boughs. हंसि...ऽङ्गम् why do you still beat your head? The idea is there will be an end of grief soon. So don't beat your head now. मुक्तगलं = मुक्तकण्ठम्. दूरी...सार्थः your friends are going far off *i. e.* they are all going to a land whence there is no return and where you and they may never meet. शवशिबिरे in this camp of corpses (after the women have killed themselves). शबरिके—this is addressed to some *Bhil* woman of the forest who befriended them. तनूनपाति in fire. त्वमपि— there is a question here and in मातर्मातङ्गिके &c. वत्स्य... नगरे how will you dwell in the city of the dead which is hateful? विरा...सायेन you are illumined (*i. e.* made famous) by your resolve to sacrifice your life in the princess' misfortune. भृगु... भिज्ञे who know your lot *viz.* preparing to fall from a precipice. For भृङ्गार see p. 117. वीजय fan. Separate नमति इन्दीवरिका. देहि... काशम् give me room to go round the fire. कुरबककोरकैः (buds of कु०) आचिताम् (filled with). Remove the line after गृहाण. चामरं... कण्ठे Oh ! chowriebearer ! again hold the chowrie to the neck. This hardly makes any sense. So we must read चरमं for चामरम् the meaning being 'clasp me by the neck for the last time.' मर्ष...हसितानि you must forgive my unchecked laughs due to jests. अग्रामी...गिणि that lovest virtues not found among villagers (*i. e.* noble). अन्तरं room. आपृच्छते bids farewell. नाटक...धारी who managed dramatic performances for you. पश्चिमः last. कतिकृत्वः how many times? निर्माण...शः generally all creation comes to this (*i. e.* all created beings have to suffer these reverses of fortune). धीरयसि किम् why do you comfort (or encourage) me still? केय...नानाम् what has (my present) condition to do with consolations (*i. e.* I am past all consoling words). कृताः...रोधाः I have disregarded the wooing (of my mind) by my loving friends by falling at my feet. पृष्ठतः कृ— to turn the back towards, leave behind, disregard. ग्रहिणि— you who are persistent (in dissuading me by holding my feet). 'निर्बन्धोपरागार्कादयो ग्रहाः' अम०. महत्तरिका—chamberlain. दृष्टासि I have seen you (*i. e.* I am at least fortunate enough to have seen you when departing this life). कर्मणां विपाकाः the fruit or reward of actions. आर्यचरणानाम्—she probably refers to हर्ष her elder brother. परः...प्रणामः this is my last salutation at the time of departing to the next world. 'हलहलकः उत्कण्ठा' com. It seems to be a Des'ya word. It will be perceived that here there is a change from grief to joy, which suggests the coming of Harsha, according to the common belief of Sanskrit poets expressed in the words 'आवेदयन्ति प्रत्यासन्नमानन्दमग्रजातानि शुभानि निमित्तानि'. उच्चं रोमाञ्चं मुञ्चन्तीति ०मुञ्चि. किमङ्गीकृत्य relying upon what? वामेन—the throbbing of the left eye in the case of women is a good omen. वृथा विरमसि in vain dost thou stop or stay. रम् 1 A when preceded by वि, आ and परि takes the परस्मैपद only. 'व्याङ्परिभ्यो रमः' पा. 1. 3. 82. क्षीरिणि वृक्षे on a milky tree (like the figtree, or उदुम्बर &c.). The crow sitting on milky trees was a good omen. Note 'सुस्निग्धपत्रपल्लवकुसुमफलानम्रसुरभिमधुरेषु। सक्षीराव्रणसुस्थितमनोज्ञवृक्षेषु चार्थकरः॥' बृह० 95. 33; see also 95. 16 and 1. हेषितम् neighing. उत्तरतः to the north. आर्यस्य = हर्षस्य. उपसर्प— supply हर्षः.

P. 135 l. 27—**P. 136** l. 25 **अथ तेन...भुवमिति.** भ्रातुः is to be connected with हस्तसंस्पर्शेन (l. 31). प्रकोष्ठ...क्षरता (the touch of his hand) that as if dropped a flood of juice capable of restoring life from the herbs tied on his forearm. हर्ष had on his forearm some herbs by way of amulets. His touch revived राज्यश्री; the poet fancies that it was the juice of those herbs that revived her. वमते...भावम् (touch) that as if emitted the inconceivable power of the jewels in his bracelet. It was believed that various drugs and jewels had mysterious powers; compare 'लौकिकानामपि मणिमन्त्रौषधिप्रभृतीनां देशकालनिमित्तवैचित्र्यवशाच्छक्तयो विरुद्धानेककार्यविषया दृश्यन्ते।' शाङ्करभाष्य on वेदान्तसूत्र II. 1. 27. 'आवापकः पारिहार्यः कटको वलयोऽस्त्रियाम्' अम०. अमृत...द्गिरा—his bright nails resembled the moon's rays, which shower nectar (*i. e.* a sensation of coolness and pleasure). चन्द्रोदयेन च्युतः शिशिरः शीकरः यस्मात्. समुन्मिमील opened her eyes. असम्भावितं आगमनं यस्य whose arrival was not thought to be possible. स्वप्ने दृष्टं दर्शनं यस्य. तत्काले (हर्षस्य) आविर्भावः तेन निर्भरः तेन which was full on account of his sudden appearance. अभिभूतः सर्वात्मा येन. Connect ०सम्भारेण with उत्सृजन्ती०वारि. स्थूलः प्रवाहः यस्य (*adj.* of ०वारि). नदी...वारि—she shed such floods of tears from her two eyes that there seemed to be two river channels (प्रणालः) at their mouth let loose. A river at its mouth is very full. ०मन्युना goes with भ्राता. समुद्भूतः भगिनीस्नेहसद्भावः तस्य भारः तेन भावितः मन्युः यस्य whose sorrow became manifested by the great feeling of affection for his sister that swept over him. करेण स्थगितं (covered) मुखं यस्याः. अग्रजः elder brother. विश्रम्य...तव्यम् stop and then weep again (after some time). चिरसम्भावितः अनेकदुःखनिवहः तस्य निर्वहणं तेन बाष्पोत्पीडः तेन पीड्यमानः कण्ठभागः यस्याः whose throat was choked by a flood of tears due to the completion (निर्वहणं) of the numerous griefs that she had suffered for a long time. काहलेन resembing that of a drum (काहलं). आक्षिप्य being led away. तथा in that way *i. e.* by the incidents that had happened. मुहूर्त...वाह्य having allowed some time to pass. नि...नीतं brought by his pupil who was informed by a secret sign. चिरप्रवृत्तं अश्रुजलजालं यस्मिन्. Her eyes red with weeping resembled a red lotus. If we read जातं for जालं then the meaning is 'her eye red with weeping was like a red lotus sprung from the water of her long continued flow of tears.' पुनरानीतं नेत्राम्भः यस्याः. पति...म्भसि whose eyes again filled with tears by the shock of hearing that he was familiar with her husband. उद्घातः allusion; blow. प्रयत्नेन रक्षितः आगत...सम्भारः तेन भज्यमानं धैर्यं तेन आर्द्रे लोचने यस्य whose eyes moistened because his serenity was broken by the flood of rising tears that he checked with effort. परावृत्त turned aside. कल्याणराशे—this is addressed to हर्ष.

P. 136 l. 26—**P. 137** l. 27 अथ भूपति...मन्दाकिनीम्. अनु...चारम् obeying the observances of the world. तस्यां=भूमौ. आहितं अवधानं येन attentively. परवती शुचा beside herself through grief. पतिपिण्डे प्रदर्शितः प्रयत्नः तेन प्रतिपन्नं अभ्यवहारकरणं यया who consented to take food when Harsha had made efforts to offer oblations to her deceased husband *i. e.* she ate when she saw that Pindas had been offered to her husband. बन्धनात् प्रभृति—she had been imprisoned in Kanoj by the king of Malva that killed her husband (text p. 41). विस्तरतः—connect with सर्वमशृणोत्. ०सम्भ्रमं—is governed by अशृणोत्. गौडसंभ्रमम् the tumult of the Gauda king. What this was is not clear. The order in which the events are arranged here shows that the गौड king caused some tumult in Kanoj before राज्यवर्धन was treacherously murdered by him. But we know that the king of Malva took कान्यकुब्ज by killing ग्रहवर्मा. If we read संभ्रमगुप्तितः, the sense is not much improved. But if we read ०सम्भ्रमे, then the meaning is:—'he heard how his sister was sent away from Kanoj out of her prison by a noble named गुप्त at the time of the tumult caused by the गौड king.' With this reading it is easy to say that the tumult refers to the treachery of the Gauḍa king against राज्यवर्धन whose death राज्यश्री naturally heard after escaping from imprisonment. निराकरणम् despising, giving up. पराहता struck down, faint. उपक्रमणं undertaking, commencement. यावत् up to. विविक्तभुवि in a lonely spot. लेशतः little by little. अयं refers to ताराराजः (the moon). परिभूय... भार्याः—the moon has 27 wives, the नक्षत्रs. यौ...तारेण तरलतराः very brilliant by the advent of youth (*adj.* of भार्याः). रजनी... पूरः the ear-ornament of night. पुरुहूतः इन्द्रः तस्य पुराधाः (family priest) तस्य. धिषणस्य—'बृहस्पतिः सुराचार्यो गीष्पतिर्धिषणो गुरुः' अम०. पुरन्ध्री matron. पत्नीयन्—पत्नीं आत्मनः इच्छन्—Wishing to make her his wife. पत्नीयति is a denominative verb from पत्नी, according to 'सुप आत्मनः क्यच्' पा. 3. 1. 8. अतितरलः extremely fickle. तारा—for her seduction by the moon, see p. 60. चकितचकोरस्य इव लोचने यस्याः. अतिकामया whose love for him was excessive. सर्वाकारैः अभिरामया charming in every gesture. सर्वं...गौरवात् out of respect for the words of all the gods. अविद्यमानानि इन्धनानि यथा स्युः (अव्ययी०). वरारोहा a beautiful woman (वरः आरोहः यस्याः). 'श्रोण्यामप्यारोहो वरस्त्रियाः' अम०. शै...मानः rising from the mountain in the east. 'अस्तस्तु चरमक्ष्माभृदुदयः पूर्वपर्वतः।' अम०. We often have the word उदयशैल as in 'उदयशैलो मित्रमण्डलस्य' काद०. वारुणालयस्य—सागरस्य. सस्मरः=समदनः. स्मेरं गण्डस्थलं यस्य the cheek of which was dimpled with a smile. Sanskrit poets compare the cheeks of beautiful women with the moon. Compare मृच्छकटिक I. 57. 'उदयति हि शशाङ्कः कामिनीगण्डपाण्डुः.' सस्मार मुखस्य—the genitive is used in accordance with the सूत्र 'अधीगर्थदयेशां कर्मणि' explained above. स्वःस्थोऽप्यस्वस्थः—स्वःस्थ means 'being in the heavens' and स्वस्थ which resembles स्वःस्थ in sound means 'at ease'. 'स्वरव्ययं स्वर्गनाक &c.' अम०. स्ववीयसः qualifies ०बिन्दून्. पीतः ०प्रवाहः तेन धवला तारा (pupil) यस्य. आचेमुः मुक्ताशुक्तयः pearl oysters drank them. विषमुचाम् = सर्पाणाम्. तैः मुक्ताफलैः—तारागण is seen in the sky and not in पाताल. But the pearls were like stars and being taken to पाताल made the latter look like the sky. एकावली a necklace with a single string of pearls. The moon is said to be the lord of plants also. 'ओषधीशो निशापतिः' अम०. हिममेव अमृतं तस्मात्सम्भवः यस्याः सा ०सम्भवा तस्याः भावः ०वत्वं. Or we may dissolve as 'हिमं च अमृतं च ताभ्यां &c'. The moon is cool and has also nectar in it. पर्यधत्त wore. नागार्जुनो नाम भिक्षुः—नागार्जुन is a famous name among the Buddhists. The राजतरङ्गिणी (I. 172–173) refers to him as a king that lived 150 years after Buddha. In the बृहत्कथामञ्जरी (XIV. 392–407) he is represented as an adept in रसायनविद्या and as the minister of a king called चिरायु. The कथासरित्सागर tells us that he was a बोधिसत्त्व. त्रिसमुद्राधिपतये—*i. e.* the lord of the Deccan, the peninsula of India, with seas to the east, south and west. C and T think that सातवाहन ruled over जम्बुद्वीप, प्लक्षद्वीप and शाल्मलिद्वीप. But that is not correct. The kings of the Deccan were represented as lords of the three oceans, while universal kings were represented to be lords of the four oceans. Compare 'चतुरम्भोधिभोगभूति०' (text p. 60 l. 16 above) and the words 'देवस्य चतुःसमुद्राधिपतेः...हर्षस्य' in the 2nd उच्छ्वास; and the words 'तिसमुदतोयपीतवाहनस' applied to king 'सातकणि' (शातकर्णि) in the Nasik Inscription (No. 2); vide Bombay Gazetteer vol. 16 p. 550. King सातकणि is there styled 'सातवाहनकुलयसपतिठापनकरस.' सातवाहन is the name of a family of kings of whom many were named शातकर्णि. यद्यपि...चारः although entertaining persons like you by gifts seems to be an insult. ओषधिबुद्ध्या looking upon it as a medicine. सर्व...प्रवृत्तेन who has set about to protect all beings. रक्षणीयं शरीरं यस्य. विष...क्षया with the object of protection against poison. अभ्याशे समीपे वर्तते इति ०वर्ती तस्य.

P. 137 l. 28—**P. 138** l. 25 उन्मुच्य...कर्तव्यानामिति. उन्मुच्यमानायाः while it was being untied. लब्धः अवकाशः येन that found their opportunity (of illuminating the world). विशदं (brilliant) महः (तेजः) यस्य. युगपत्—all the quarters were simultaneously rendered bright. मुकुलि...तरुभिः the trees as if blossomed forth from their very roots, longing for their budding brides—the creepers. The idea is that the splendour of the एकावली was the same that would be seen if trees blossomed forth even from their roots. In this and the following clauses the author tries to convey the effect of the whiteness and brilliance produced by the unveiling of the bright necklace of pearls. अभि...यूथैः—As the rays of the एकावली spread all round, it seemed as if हंसs (that have white wings) were flying for lotus fibres. भर—by the very weight of the केतकी flowers, the pollen was scattered about. गर्भभेदेन सूचितः सूचीसञ्चयः तेन शुचिभिः bright with the numerous pointed leaves made manifest by the opening of the inside (of the bud, that was at one time closed). The केतकी flower is pale-white and bright. We should read उद्दलित for उद्गलित. उद्...दिनीभिः the night lotuses seemed to wake up, bristling with their opening petals. 'दन्तुरस्तून्नतरदे तथोन्नतनते त्रिषु' मे०. There is a suggestion. The petals of (white) कुमुदs resemble the teeth. When a handsome woman gets up from sleep and yawns, her gleaming teeth are seen. सितदशनानां अंशवः तेषां माला तस्याः आलोकेन लिप्यमानं वनं यथा स्यात् तथा. प्रहसितमिव—smiles and laughs are white. The teeth of वनदेवताs would send forth rays. काश flowers are white. शिथिलितः कुसुमकोशः तस्य केसराणां अट्टहासेन निरङ्कुशं यथा स्यात्तथा they bloomed forth smiling without restraint with the filaments of their loosened buds. चमरी deer have white tails. वालाः (hair) पल्लव इव तस्य परिवेशेन (circle) श्वेतायमानैः. स्फायमानाः (swelling) फेनिलाः (foamy) तरलतराः तरङ्गाः (ripples) तान् उद्गिरति इति ०द्गारी तेन. Foam is white. The light of the full moon resembled the light of the एकावली and the pearls resembled stars (which pearls are fancied to be अपरतारागण). ०चक्रेण आक्रान्ताः ककुभः येन. दावानलधूलिना धूसरितः दिगन्तः येन. The idea is:—the quarters were obscured by the ashes of the forest fires; but if water were poured over, then the bright day would shine forth. The एकावली was like the fair faces of the women (राजश्री and her attendants) that were washed after being tear-bedewed. मांसलैः thick. आकुली...चक्षुः again and again opening and closing his eye that was overpowered by the rays &c. सर्वा...रणीं filling all the quarters (with संहतिम्); fulfilling all desires (with एकावलीम्). पङ्क्ती...हतिम्—the row of pearls resembled the spray from the trunks of दिग्गजs, when it is collected in a row (पङ्क्ति). घनमुक्ताम् (घनाः मुक्ताः यस्याम्) having pearls thickly arranged; (घनेन

मुक्ताम्) free from cloud (with ज्योत्स्नाम्). लेखीकृताम् turned into a streak. The necklace was like autumnal moonlight. प्र...चिह्नाम् (प्रकटं पदकचिह्नं यस्याम्) which is clearly marked by the central jewel (with एकावली); which is marked with clear foot-prints. सञ्चारणवीथी road for moving about. The pearls looked like the stars of the Great Bear. Only the latter change their position in the sky from evening to morning. हस्तमुक्ताम् which fell from the hand (because of the round and glossy pearls); that were without हस्त, a constellation (with सप्तर्षि). अभिभूतः ०भूषणानां (कौस्तुभादीनां) भूतेः प्रभावः यया (एकावली) that cast into the shade the powerful magnificence of the ornaments in the whole world; अभिभूतः ०भूषणस्य (शिवस्य) भूतेः (ashes) प्रभावः यया that surpassed the glory of the ashes of शिव who is the ornament of the whole world. ऐशानीं belonging to ईशान (*i. e.* शिव). शिव placed the digit of the moon on his head. 'ईश्वरः शर्व ईशानः' अम०. धवल...हीताम् possessed of the quality of whiteness (with कान्तिम्); possessed of whiteness and thread (with एकावली). क्षीरसागर is white. The एकावली was as if the whiteness of क्षीरसागर come out of it. महीभृतः राजानः पर्वताश्च. The Ganges goes round several mountains. The एकावली had passed through the hands of many kings. The Ganges purifies a man and prevents his falling into hell (दुर्गति). The एकावली would remove poverty. अनवरतं स्फुरिताः तरलस्य (मध्यमणेः) अंशुकाः यस्याम् (with एकावली); अनवरतं स्फुरितं तरलं (moving) अंशुकं (fine silk cloth) यस्याः (with पताका). A banner is carried in front (पुरःसर) and its cloth is waving. महे...गमस्य of the approach (आगमः) of the position of a great emperor. एकावली announced like a पताका the great position that हर्ष was to occupy. A banner also indicates the existence of (a temple of) शिव (महेश्वर). घनसारवत् शुक्लाम् white like camphor (with एकावली). दन्तपङ्क्ति also is घन (thickset), strong and white; or it is white like camphor. ईश्वर is हर्ष who sat facing (अभिमुख) the necklace. ईश्वर means शिव also. Or a king (ईश्वर) when favourable (अभिमुख) smiles on the man with whom he is pleased. वर=श्रेष्ठ (with एकावली). वरः a bridegroom. The garland at the time of स्वयंवर gratifies the desire of the bridegroom when thrown round his neck. The एकावली fulfilled the highest ambitions and was white like flowers (स्रज्). The world-bride as if chose हर्ष as the bridegroom by the garland-necklace. निज...लंक्ष्याम्—the necklace could not be gazed at being surrounded by its own (dazzling) rays.

A laughing woman may cover her face with her own hands (निजकर) and then it would be difficult to see her smile. एकावली is fancied to be the smile (both being white) of the earth indicating its love for (हर्ष). विहसतिका gentle laughter. For चक्षूराग, see p. 149. The reading सुधाया: is not so good. सुधा is white. अक्षमाला rosary. It is राजधर्म to be absorbed in मन्त्र (state policy), कोष (treasury) and साधन (army); one who takes a rosary (*i. e.* becomes an ascetic) is intent upon mastering the numerous *Mantras* (hymns or spells). स...भूतां that (एकावली) was an ornament of the ocean (the pearls of it being found in the ocean). स...भूतां which was ornamented with the seal (of कुबेर). संख्या... काम् which was as if the board or fillet engraved with the calculations of the treasures of कुबेर. Each pearl of the necklace resembled a figure drawn in calculation. कुबेर is the lord of riches and treasures. बन्धुर high, raised 'बन्धुरं तून्नतानतम्' अम०. के...त्मनोऽपि who are we even to control our own selves? The idea is that he is not master even of his own self, that his soul has come to belong to the ascetic. किमुत...नस्य वा much more therefore have I no control in accepting or rejecting (the necklace). परवन्तः in the hands of others. अत्र...कर्तव्यानाम् you may do what you like with this (body). कामचारः acting according to one's will.

P. 138 l. 26—**P. 140** l. 12 **समतिक्रान्ते...व्यरंसीत्.** लब्धःविश्रम्भः यया who took courage. उपांशु *adv.* in a whisper. शुचा...विनयम् the unbearableness of her sorrows impels her and lessens her modesty, being ordered by wretched fate. हतदैवेन दत्तः आदेशः यस्यै (with असह्यता). This passage is corrupt. Some MSS read व्यापारयति, which is a good reading; others read व्याहारयति (makes her speak). Another reading is हतदैवदत्ता च दशा, which is better than the text. अवलम्बनं support; compare मनु० 9. 3. 'पिता रक्षति कौमारे भर्ता रक्षति यौवने। रक्षन्ति स्थविरे पुत्रा न स्त्री स्वातन्त्र्यमर्हति ॥'; there is a similar passage in अनुशासनपर्व 20. 21. दुः...मानं serving as fuel to the fire of sorrow. प्राणित...केवलम् to continue to live is sheer immodesty. For शालीन, see p. 28. प्रतिहतः frustrated. काषा... श्रया by being allowed to assume the red robe. पर्यायः synonym. आक्षेपः epilepsy 'आक्षेपस्यापस्मारस्य' com. This is not the usual meaning of the word. तारुण्यं तमसः (sorrow) is the youth of darkness. Darkness reigns supreme when a person gives himself up to sorrows. विश्लेषणं विषस्य it is a kind of poison. Or the meaning may be 'sorrow is an epithet of poison.' अनन्तकः...यकः

it is the lord of the city of the dead, but without यम. अविद्यमानः अन्तकः यस्मिन्. यम is the lord of प्रेतनगर. The विरोध is got over by taking अनन्तक in the sense of 'never-ending'. अविद्यमानः अन्तः यस्य. For क, see p. 68. प्रेत...नायकः also means 'that leads to प्रेतनगर' *i. e.* that kills a man. Explain the following विरोधs in a similar way. अनिर्वृतिः धर्मः यस्य the characteristic of which is that it is not extinguished. But fire can be extinguished. So अ...धर्मः means 'the characteristic of which is that there is no happiness in it.' अक्षयः not consumption. But राजयक्ष्मन् is the same as consumption (क्षयः). So अक्षयः means 'endless'. अ...निवासः who is not the abode of लक्ष्मी; which is the abode of distress. लक्ष्मी dwells on the chest of विष्णु (जनार्दन); शोक is जनार्दन *i. e.* torments people (जनानर्दयतीति). अपु...त्तः that is not working for पुण्य; that is due to one's sins (in former lives). A Jaina mendicant (क्षपणकः) takes to the order of mendicancy for storing merit. क्षपणक also means 'that destroys' (life). अ...धः in which there is no waking up; in which there is no discrimination (in the mind). After sleep, one gets up. निद्राप्रकारः also means '(sorrow) that scatters about *i. e.* destroys sleep.' अन...धर्मा the characteristic of which is to be active (not dull or dazed); which resembles fire (अनलस-धर्मा and अनल-सधर्मा). In सन्निपातज्वर a man becomes अलस. For सन्निपात see p. 80. सन्निपात also means 'that pulls down people.' धर्म becomes धर्मन् at the end of a बहुव्रीहि when preceded by a single word 'धर्मादनिच्केवलात्' पा. 5. 4. 124. अ...चरः that is not in the company of शिव; that is ever associated with evil. विनायकः = गणेशः. Pictures of शिव are generally represented as having गणेश on his lap. विनायक also means 'an obstacle,' or 'one that leads a man astray.' '**विनायकस्तु हेरम्बे** ताक्ष्र्ये **विघ्ने जिने** गुरौ'. Compare 'अशिवमूर्तयो महाविनायकाधिष्ठिताः' काद० p. 287. There is another meaning also. A Jaina (*i. e.* sight of a जैन) is associated with evil; compare text p. 20 'अभिमुखमाजगाम...नग्नाटकः.' अ...वितः not attended upon by mercury; not resorted to by wise men. ग्रहवर्गः the group of planets; a number of eclipses or ghosts. '**निर्बन्धोपरागार्कादयो ग्रहाः**' अम०. अ...समुत्थः not caused by योग; springing from bad luck or evil conjunctions of stars. For योग, see above p. 204. ज्योतिःप्रकारः a kind of light (*i. e.* highest knowledge); a kind of fire. Higher knowledge (about ब्रह्म) cannot be had without योग (चित्तवृत्तिनिरोध). स्नेहा...कोपः it is a delirium due to स्नेह (affection, oil). वायु is one of the three humours and प्रकोप

means its excess. Oil is prescribed against वायुप्रकोप as an outward application; so in स्नेहात्...पः there is a विरोध, which is removed by taking स्नेह to mean affection. मानसात् from the मानस lake; from the mind. There can be no fire in the lake. आर्द्रभावात् from moisture; from tender feelings. रजःक्षोभः agitation of passion; scattering of dust. Dust is *laid*, not *scattered* by moisture. रसात् out of juice (or fluid); out of affection. अभिशोषः dryness (of mouth); that makes a man wither. रागात् out of affection; out of redness. कालपरिणामः that ends in death; that is transformed into darkness. Out of redness one cannot make a dark thing. तदस्या०—The construction is तत् (तस्मात्) अस्य (शोकस्य)...विदुषामपि हृदयानि न अलं सोढुं आपातं...किमुत अबलानां हृदयम्. Read अजस्रास्रस्राविणः (that makes one shed tears continuously, that makes blood to ooze forth continually). हृदयमहाव्रणस्य—शोक is a great wound of the heart. Blood comes out from a wound. बहुलाः दोषाः अन्धकारः इव तेन लब्धः प्रवेशप्रसरः येन—sorrow enters the heart that is labouring under the darkness of many faults and robs the man of his life. A robber also enters in the darkness of night. बहुलस्य (कृष्णपक्षस्य) दोषा (रात्रिः) तस्याः अन्धकारे लब्धः प्रवेशप्रसरः येन. शून्यताहेतोः which is the cause of the mind being vacant; that causes depopulation. महाभूतग्रामः (प्राणिसमूहः) तस्य घातकः तस्य—sorrow kills many beings. महान्ति भूतानि यस्मिन् स महाभूतः ग्रामः (village) &c. One who destroys a village causes depopulation. महाभूतानि पृथिव्यप्तेजोवाय्वाकाशानि तेषां ग्रामः &c. If the five elements are destroyed nothing will be left. सकल...दक्षः expert in exhausting the whole body; expert in destroying all in battles. दोष...वर्तिनः pre-eminent among faults; a bad emperor. कार्श्यम् emaciation. श्वासः sighing, hard breathing. प्रलापः lamentation; delirium. उपद्रवः affliction; bad supervenient symptoms. असद्ग्रहस्य an evil planet; which is persistence in a bad thing. सकल...केतोः which indicates the destruction of the whole world; which is fire in destroying &c. शोक is a fire (धूमः केतुः चिह्नं यस्य). 'अग्न्युत्पातौ धूमकेतू' अम०. जीवि० applies to both शोक and वज्र in the same sense. अक्षणरुचेः न क्षणे (उत्सवे) रुचिः (liking) यस्मिन्. 'कालविशेषोत्सवयोः क्षणः' अम०. अविद्यमाना क्षणरुचिः (विद्युत्) यस्मिन्. विद्युत् flashes only for a moment (क्षणं रुचिः यस्याः). When a bolt falls in a cloudless sky, there is naturally no lightning. क्षणप्रभा is given by अमर as a synonym of विद्युत्. For ०वज्रपातस्य, see p. 25 (text) l. 1. Compare महा० उद्योगपर्व 84. 5. 'अनभ्रेऽशनिनिर्घोषः.' स्फुरन्त्यः अनवद्याः (blameless, pure) विद्याः एव विद्युतः ताभिः उद्द्योतमानानि illumined by flashing and pure lightning-like lores. The lores are either four or fourteen. 'पुराणन्यायमीमांसाधर्मशास्त्राङ्गमिश्रिताः । वेदाः स्थानानि विद्यानां धर्मस्य च चतुर्दश ॥' याज्ञ० I. 3. (*i. e.* the four Vedas, six वेदाङ्गs, पुराण, न्याय, मीमांसा and धर्मशास्त्र). The four (in the case of kings) are आन्वीक्षिकी, त्रयी (वेदत्रयी), वार्ता and दण्डनीति (अर्थशास्त्र p. 6). विद्युत् also is flashing (स्फुरत्) and bright. गहनाः ग्रन्थाः ग्रन्थयः इव तेषां गूढः गर्भः तस्य ग्रहणेन गम्भीराणि profound by grasping the hidden meanings lying in deep works. The interior of a fleshy knot is also deep. कठोर well-developed; hard. A swelling (ग्रन्थि) is hard; a गर्भ becomes developed (कठोर). बहु...बृहन्ति big with carrying many S'āstras. A swelling makes the part swollen look big and heavy. So a गर्भ also has to be borne (उद्वहन) by the mother. न अलं सोढुं आपातं are not able to bear the onset (of sorrow). नवमालिका jasmine. सरस juicy (with बिसतन्तु); affectionate (with हृदयम्). सत्यं व्रतं यस्याः who is true to her vow. उपालभ्यते rebuked. अमूढेन without being bewildered. मर्त्यधर्मणा = मनुजेन. पुरा...कर्तुम् who can change these ancient rules of conduct ? There is a suggested meaning:—these decrees of fate due to actions in former lives, who can gainsay. In this and the following there are laboured puns everywhere. जन्म...घटनानि (union, happening) एव ०रज्जवः. For पञ्चजन, see p. 124. All people have to undergo the long round of births, deaths and old age. The ropes of the water-wheel also are very long and revolve (संसरन्त्यः) night and day. पञ्चमहाभूतान्येव पञ्चकुलः तेन अधिष्ठितः अन्तःकरणव्यवहारः तस्य दर्शने निपुणाः; पञ्चमहाभूतेषु *i. e.* ०भूतात्मके शरीरे अधिष्ठितं अन्तःकरणं. The ideas here are rather complicated. The mind presides over the body (*i. e.* regulates its movements) that is made up of the five elements. यम notes what men do and what is passing in their minds. Compare the verse 'आदित्यचन्द्रावनिलोऽनलश्च द्यौर्भूमिरापो हृदयं यमश्च । अहश्च रात्रिश्च उभे च सन्ध्ये धर्मोऽपि जानाति नरस्य वृत्तम् ॥'. 'धर्मराजः पितृपतिः... यमः ॥' अम०. यम spares none (सर्वंकष) and is terrible. A king's ordinances (राजस्थितयः) are applicable to all (सर्वंकषा). The king sees into the transactions and documents (करणं) of the पञ्चकुल officers. They seem to be the same as modern Panchait. Compare the word पञ्चमण्डली in C. I. I. vol. III. p. 31, 32. For करण, see above p. 167. धर्मसदृशो राजा तस्य स्थितयः. We must read अक्षममाणाः. क्षण...माणाः not allowing even a moment to pass (every moment is calculated by the water-clock). कालनालिकाः the Ghaṭikâs of

Death (काल); the Ghaṭikās of time. नाडिका also means 'a water-clock'. आयुष्क...कुशलाः expert in calculating the span (कला, portion) of life (allotted to each individual); expert in calculating the कलाs. निलये निलये in each house; at the time of destruction (or in each Hell). निलय is equal to निरय; see above p. 125 for identity of र् and ल्. कला, क्षण and नाडिका are measures of time 18 or 15 निमेषs are equal to a काष्ठा, 30 काष्ठाs to a कला, 30 कलाs to a क्षण and 12 क्षणs to a मुहूर्त which is equal to two घटिकाs. See अमरकोश for this. For a different table and for a water-clock, see ब्रह्मपुराण 231. 6–9 'निमेषो मानुषो योऽयं मात्रामात्रप्रमाणतः। तैः पञ्चदशभिः काष्ठा त्रिंशत्काष्ठास्तथा कला॥ नाडिका तु प्रमाणेन कलाश्च दश पञ्च च। उन्मानेनाम्भसः सा तु पलान्यर्धत्रयोदश॥ हेममाषैः कृतच्छिद्रा चतुर्भिश्चतुरङ्गुलैः। मागधेन प्रमाणेन जलप्रस्थस्तु स स्मृतः॥ नाडिकाभ्यामथ द्वाभ्यां मुहूर्तो द्विजसत्तमाः।.' आयुष्कला is proper according to 'इदुदुपधस्य चाप्रत्ययस्य' पा. 8. 3. 41. चण्डिका fierce; the goddess Durgā. The command of Yama goes forth in the world. सर्व...पातिनी—at Yama's word, the lives of beings are offered at his feet; to Durgā all sorts of animals are offered. उपहारः = बलिः. प्रेतपतिः यमः तस्य पटहाः. Drums announce the march (प्रयाण) of a king's army. The drums of Yama announce the departure of the life of all beings. पेटकैः in groups. प्रतप्तलोहवत् लोहिते अक्षिणी येषाम् whose eyes are red like heated iron. कालकूटस्य इव कान्तिः यस्य सः °कान्तिः कालः (dark) कायः येषाम्. कालपाशः पाणौ येषाम्. कालकूट is the same as हालाहल poison, which first came out at the churning and darkened the throat of शिव. There is an allusion to gamblers, whose eyes are red through late hours, envy and hatred and who have dark dice (पाशः) in their hands. भीषणकिङ्कराणां करैः घट्टितः (struck) यम...पुटः तस्य पटुना (sharp) टाङ्कारेण भयङ्कराः. Separate घोराः घातघोषणाः the terrible proclamation of death (with यमकिङ्कर); and read घोरा...षणाः as one word (with *servants*)—proclamations in which there is fierce beating (of the drum or bell). घोरः आघातः यस्यां सा °घाता घोषणा. King's proclamations are announced by his servants that ring a bell and collect (संहरणं) all people to listen to them. The messengers of Death (किङ्कर) destroy (संहरणं) all beings. वहन्ति—is to be connected with वीथयः. बहुचितानां धूमैः धूसरिता °पताका तस्यां पटुपतिता गृध्रदृष्टिः यासु—where the keen eye of vultures falls on the banners of Yama darkened by the smoke of numerous funeral pyres. शोकेन कृतः कोलाहलः यामि- ताः °हलाः °भिन्यः तासां विकीर्णाः (dishevelled) °कलापाः तैः शबलं शवशिबिकासहस्रं तेन सङ्कुलाः—

Sīlas. For शील, see above p. 223. क्लेश...भूतैः that are the cause of the abandonment of the क्लेशs. क्लेश means 'evil passions'. They are ten such as लोभ, मोह, मान, दृष्टि (heresy), विचिकित्सा, (doubt), स्त्यानं (sloth), औद्धत्यम् &c. क्लेशs are the causes of sinful actions and therefore of rebirth. तथागतैर्दर्शनैः by the doctrines of बुद्ध. समासं कृत्स्नं येन (*adj.* of मया). अतिसृजन्ति grant. सुरनाथम् = इन्द्रम्. दधीचः—the gods requested दधीच for his bones which were to be turned into a वज्र for killing वृत्र. See वनपर्व chap. 100. मुनिनाथः = बुद्धः. 'मुनीन्द्रः श्रीघनः शास्ता' अम०. अनपेक्षिता आत्मस्थितिः येन who cared not for the continuance of his life. अनु...कृत्वा thinking that it was an act of compassion. जठरसत्त्वेभ्यः to animals that are dull *i. e.* to beasts like the lion. The com. refers to the story of Buddha's offering himself in a former life to a hungry lioness that was about to devour its own young. This story occurs in the जातकमाला (Harward series) where it is a व्याघ्री and not a lioness. भव्याः the good or worthy. Read इमं for इमाम्. Remove the line after इमं. Mark the construction (गुणाः बलिं गृह्णन्ति primitive; असौ जनः गुणान् बलिं ग्राहयति causal; गुणाः अमुना जनेन बलिं ग्राहिताः passive causal). चेतसा...जनेन this person (*i. e.* I) already made in his mind an offer of this body to your virtues. If we read कायकलि that will be in keeping with the words on p. 75 l. 7 (कायकलित्रसाकम्). उपयोगस्तु गुणवदायत्तः the use of it is in the hands of you, a virtuous man. तस्मिन् refers to दिवाकरमित्र. अभिनन्दितः प्रणयः येन who welcomed his request or friendship. निर्घात is the शबर who gave intelligence about दिवाकर०. अनुजाह्नवि along the banks of the Ganges. जाह्नव्याः अन्वायतम् (अव्ययीभाव).

P. 141 ll. 7—29 तत्र च...नरेन्द्रायेति. प्रणयिभ्यः to his friends. ततार crossed over *i. e.* set. बहल...पिङ्गलः tawny with thick and plentiful honey (with पङ्क०); tawny like thick &c. (with दिवस). पङ्कजानां आकरः (समूहः) bed. Both the lotuses and the day are dear to the चक्रवाक. See pp. 10, 57. The sentence is पूषा रोचिषां जालकानि पुनरपि निजवपुषि सञ्जहार—the sun again withdrew in his own body the masses of his rays. प्रकीर्णानि dispersed (with rays); published or promulgated, or scattered (with यजूंषि). नवरुधिररसवत् अरुणः वर्णः येषाम् (with जालकानि) or ०रसेन अरुणाः वर्णाः (letters) येषाम् (with यजूंषि). कुपित...वान्तानि vomited from the mouth of the angered याज्ञवल्क्य. याज्ञवल्क्य was the pupil of वैशम्पायन, who was the pupil of व्यास. वैशम्पायन incurred the sin of ब्रह्महत्या. He asked his pupil to perform some sacrifice whereby he might be purified. याज्ञवल्क्य said that the Brāhmaṇas to be invited for the sacrifice had no holiness in them. At this expression of disrespert for Brāhmaṇas his teacher got angry and said 'मुच्यतां यत्त्वयाधीतं मत्तो विप्रावमन्यक ॥ निस्तेजसो वदस्येतान्यस्त्वं ब्राह्मणपुङ्गवान् ।' Thereupon याज्ञवल्क्य vomited the Yajus hymns, which the other pupils took in the form of partridges (तित्तिरि). Those hymns came to be called कृष्णयजुर्वेद; while याज्ञवल्क्य promulgated a separate recension, which he received from the sun, called शुक्लयजुर्वेद. 'मयाप्यलं त्वयाधीतं यन्मया तदिदं द्विज ॥ इत्युक्त्वा रुधिराक्तानि सरूपाणि यजूंषि सः । छर्दयित्वा ददौ तस्मै स्वेच्छया चाययौ मुनिः ॥ यजूंष्यथ विसृष्टानि याज्ञवल्क्येन वै द्विज । जगृहुस्तित्तिरा भूत्वा तैत्तिरीयास्तु ते स्मृताः ॥' विष्णुपु. III. 5. 10–12. The com. makes याज्ञवल्क्य a pupil of शाकल्य. लोका...जूंषि—लोकस्य आलोकं जुषन्ते—that like to illumine the world (with rays). लोकालोकः पर्वतः तं जुषन्ते that visit or go to the mountain लो०. लोकालोक is a mythical mountain in पुष्करद्वीप, the last of the seven द्वीपs. Beyond लोकालोक there is complete darkness and on this side of it there is light. See विष्णुपु० II. 4. 'लोकालोकस्ततः शैलो योजनायुतविस्तृतः ।...ततस्तमः समावृत्य तं शैलं सर्वतः स्थितम् । तमश्चाण्डकटाहेन समन्तात्परिवेष्टितम् ॥' 95–96. पापं मुष्णन्ति इति पाप०—applies to both. क्रमेण च—the principal sentence is क्रमेण च उष्णांशुः (सूर्यः)...मुहूर्तमदृश्यत. समुपोह्यमानः (increasing) मांसलः (thick, deepened) रागः (red colour) तेन रोचिष्णुः. The poet now puts forward many similes to convey the idea of the redness of the disc of the setting sun. It resembled the congenital crest jewel (चूडामणि) of अश्वत्थामन् (son of द्रोण) placed in his turban. उष्णीषबन्धे (उष्णीषस्य बन्धः यत्र तत्र शिरसि) सहजः. 'उष्णीषं शिरोवेष्टकिरीटयोः' अम०. वृकोदरः भीमः तस्य करेण उत्पाटितः (snatched off). प्रत्यग्रं शोणितं तेन शोणः अङ्गरागः तेन रौद्रः (looking) terrible with the red unguent of his own fresh blood. When the jewel that was on his head from birth was snatched away, blood spurted on his body. The colour of the sun's body (अङ्गरागः) was red like fresh blood. For the story see महा० सौप्तिकपर्व chap. 14 and 15. अश्वत्थामा discharged ब्रह्मास्त्र and अर्जुन in return did the same; when नारद and व्यास intervened, अर्जुन took it back, but अश्वत्थामा could not and so he had to give the jewel on his head in exchange for his life. कपाल...पैतामहः (the sun looked) like the begging skull-vessel of Brahmā (पितामह) reddish by being filled with blood from the veins and arteries of the head, that was hurled down by S'iva who is skilled (or fond of) in giving alms to the Rudras. रुद्रेभ्यो

भिक्षादानं तस्मिन् शौण्डः पुरमथनः तेन मुक्तं मुण्डं तस्य शिरानाडीनां रुधिरं तेन पूरणं तेन कपिलः. We must read ०पूरणकपिलः. We may also take रुद्रभिक्षा in the sense of terrible alms. The story alluded to is the cutting off of the fifth head of Brahmā by S'iva. The Rudras are eleven, chief of whom is शङ्कर or शम्भु. शङ्कर is called त्रिपुरान्तक or पुरमथन because he burnt down the three cities of gold, silver and iron built by Maya for demons in the sky, air and earth. See द्रोणपर्व chap. 202. 64 'असुराणां पुराण्यासंस्त्रीणि वीर्यवतां दिवि। आयसं राजतं चैव सौवर्णं परमं महत् ॥'. पितृवधेन रुषितः रामः (परशुरामः) तेन रागेण रचितः. 'रागस्तु मात्सर्ये लोहितादिषु। क्लेशादावनुरागे च गान्धारादौ नृपेऽपि च ॥' मे०. With the sun, we may explain 'रामः तस्य रागः (redness) तेन रचितः' possessing the redness of परशुराम &c. पृथुः (broad) विकटः (formidable) कार्तवीर्यस्य अंसकूटः (the hump-like or peak-like shoulder) तस्य कुट्टाकः कुठारः तस्य तुण्डेन तष्टानि (chopped off) कण्ठकुहराणि तेषां रुधिरकुल्याप्रणालाः तेषां सहस्रेण पूरितः. दूररोधी stretching far and wide (applies to the lake and to the sun's rays also). रुधिरस्यायं रौधिरः. For the five lakes of blood and for the destruction of क्षत्रियs, see pp. 152, 38. भयेन निगूढानि (concealed) करचरणमुण्डानि यस्य स चासौ मण्डलाकृतिश्च that presented the shape of a sphere because the hands &c. were contracted through fear. The sun also is मण्डलाकृति. गुरुः गरुडस्य नखपञ्जरः तेन आक्षेपः तेन क्षपणं (smashing) तेन क्षिप्तं क्षतजं (blood) तेन उक्षितः (sprinkled). विगताः असवः यस्य (dead). Remove the comma after विभावसुः. कमठः tortoise. See महा० आदिपर्व chap 29–30. विभावसु and सुप्रतीक were brothers. सुप्रतीक the younger asked विभा० to give him his share. Thereupon विभावसु cursed him to be an elephant and सुप्रतीक cursed him to be a tortoise. They were always fighting in a lake. When गरुड set out for bringing nectar, he seized, carried into space and ate both of them. लोठ्यमानो नभसि—the sun also rolls in the sky. अरुणः गर्भः यस्य सः ०गर्भः मांसपिण्डाण्डः the egg containing a mass of flesh forming the embryo Aruṇa. The sun is also round (like an egg) and is like the red flesh of an embryo. खण्डिमानमानीतः broken into pieces (with egg); reduced in effulgence. ०पातेन दूयमाना दाक्षायणी तया क्षिप्तः thrown by विनता that was anxious by the passing away of the period fixed (for pregnancy). C and T following the com. take the clause 'नियत... क्षिप्तः' with धातुतटः. That construction does not yield a good sense. We do not know when Meru was tossed by दाक्षायणी (which com. renders by काली). कद्रू and विनता were two of the daughters of

दक्ष and wives of कश्यप. Her husband said that कद्रू would have a thousand sons and विनता only two. कद्रू gave birth to 1000 serpents. 'अण्डाभ्यां विनतायास्तु मिथुनं न व्यदृश्यत। ततः पुत्रार्थिनी देवी व्रीडिता च तपस्विनी ॥ अण्डं बिभेद विनता तत्र पुत्रमपश्यत। अप्यर्धकायसम्पन्नमितरेणाप्रकाशता।' आदिपर्व 16. 16–17. धातु...रोः like the slope of Meru containing metallic ores. Meru is a mountain of gold; the sky suffused with the glow of evening resembled it; and the disc of the sun looked like चरु. असुरवधाय अभिचारः तस्य चरुः तस्य पचनं तस्य पिशुनः (सूचकः) indicating the cooking of an oblation in some magic rites for the destruction of the demons. For अभिचार see p. 145. A चरु (oblation of rice) may be smeared with red powder. If the gods wanted to perform any rite for असुरवध, they would do so on Meru. We may also take असुर... पिशुनः with कटाहः. In that case we have to look upon धातु... मेरोः as an independent clause by itself (the disc of the sun being red like the slope of Meru). शोणितक्वाथेन कषायितः कुक्षिः यस्य the sides of which are red with the decoction of blood. For विसङ्कट see p. 122. कटाह...त्यः the cauldron of बृहस्पति. The sun looks like a cauldron. बृहस्पति is the priest of the gods. The poet fancies that he was engaged in boiling in a cauldron an oblation for the purpose of killing the असुरs. सद्यो गलितं गजदानवस्य (गजासुरस्य) लोहितं (blood) तस्य उपलेपेन (smearing) भीषणः. मुख... भोगः the expanse of the round face. महाभैरव is a form of शिव. गजासुर was a demon, son of महिषासुर, slain by S'iva. The sun was भीषण like the application (उपलेप) of the blood &c. ०जले प्रतिबिम्बिता रविबिम्बराजिः तेन भास्वरं अभ्रं (cloud) तदवलम्बते इति. गृहीतः आर्द्रमांसभारः यया. वासरा...निभा the evening resembled a वेताल (vampire). Flesh is offered to वेताल. The idea is:—in the evening the sky was overspread with clouds which were suffused red by the lustre of the reflections of the sun in the ocean. The clouds are like वेताल and their glow is like मांस. After night-fall, वेतालs begin to appear (वेतालाः नितरां भान्ति यस्याम्). ज्वलन् सन्ध्यारागः तेन रज्यमानः जलप्रवाहः यस्य. पुराणपुरुषः (विष्णुः) तस्य पीवरं ऊरुसम्पुटं तेन पिष्टौ मधुकैटभौ तयोः रुधिरपटलं (pool of blood) तेन पाटलं वपुः यस्य. अर्णसाम् = जलानाम्. मधु and कैटभ were two demons born from the ear of Vishṇu, when he was absorbed in Yogic sleep at the end of the *Kalpa*. They were about to devour Brahmā. The latter woke up Vishṇu, who asked them to choose a boon. They asked him to choose one, when विष्णु chose that they be killed by him. He killed them between his thighs 'स्वकावनावृतावूरू दृष्ट्वा देववरस्तदा । मधुकैटभयो राजन् शिरसी मधुसूदनः ॥ चक्रेण शितधारेण न्यकृन्तत महायशाः ॥' वनपर्व 203. 35. See मार्कण्डेयपुराण chap. 81. Compare 'अचिरमृदितमधुकैटभरुधिरारुणेन हरिमिवोरुयुगलेन विराजमानम्' काद० p. 9. अवसिते The sentence is अवसिते ०समये समनन्तरं...श्वेतभानुः उपानीयत निशया नरेन्द्राय when the time of evening ended, immediately afterwards the moon was presented to the king (Harsha) by night. अपरि...कीर्त्या as if it were a goblet made from a pearl slab (presented) by the Glory of his family to him who had a thirst for drinking boundless fame. The bright moon resembled a goblet of pearls. His family was already glorious, just as the night may be glorious with the twinkling stars. But Harsha was not satisfied with that. He thirsted for glory that would embrace the whole world like the moon's rays. कृत...ताय who was bent on starting the कृतयुग (*i. e.* an era of perfect righteousness). हर्ष wanted to bring back in कलियुग the pristine righteousness of कृतयुग. For कृतयुग and धर्म see pp. 3, 40. The bright moon resembled a round silver coin or edict stamped with the royal seal. आदिराजस्य राजतः ०निवेशः the stamp on silver of the primeval king's seal conferring authority (on Harsha). Night is compared to राज्यश्री (royal glory). राज्यश्री originally belonged to the first king (either Manu or Pṛithu) who reigned in the Kṛita age. His authority was transferred to Harsha. Authority is conferred by a शासन (copperplate or patent) impressed with the royal seal. Compare for आदिराज 'पृथुः प्रथमपुरुषकः परिभूतवान् पृथिवीम्' हर्षचरित (3rd उच्छ्वास). Probably there is a veiled allusion. राज्यश्री, Harsha's sister, called upon Harsha to assume the sovereignty of the world including her husband's realm. सकल...चलिताय that had set off on the conquest of all the continents. For श्वेतद्वीप, see above p. 190. The people from श्वेतद्वीप are all white; so the moon is aptly compared to a messenger from श्वेतद्वीप. निशा is compared to आयति (Future; or, Glory). A दूत is sent either to encourage a person or to make peace with him. इति shows that the chapter ends here. C and T suggest that the descriptions of sunset and of moonrise indicate bloody wars and the fall of Harsha's enemy, followed by the rise of Harsha's glory.

In the third Uchchhvāsa, Bāna promised to his cousins a narrative of Harsha's career and described it thus far. The narrative is suddenly brought to a close.

Appendix

A Brief Analysis of the Harshacharita.

Chap. I & II. After the usual invocation and sympathetic references to his great predecessors, Bāṇa gives us an account of his family and of himself which has been summarised in the Introduction (pp. II–IV) and need not be repeated here.

Chap. III. When Bāṇa returned from Harsha's court, he was pressed by his cousins with the request that he should entertain them with a narrative of the life and career of Harsha. Bāṇa expressed his inability to do even the slightest justice to the remarkable career of Harsha and said that he was ready to narrate to them only a portion of the brilliant career of Harsha. He then proceeded to narrate as follows. In the country of S'rîkaṇṭha, there is a district named Sthāṇvîs'vara. In ages long past there reigned a king named Pushpabhūti. He was a great devotee of S'iva. He formed friendship with a great S'aivite teacher from the Deccan named Bhairavāchārya. The latter made a present of a wonderful sword named Aṭṭahāsa to the king. Pushpabhūti offered to help the S'aiva ascetic in a magic rite. While engaged in his task, he had a vision of Lakshmî, who promised him that he would be the founder of a mighty line of kings, one of whom Harsha would have a most glorious career.

Chap. IV. In Pushpabhūti's line, as time rolled on, was born Prabhākaravardhana alias Pratāpas'îla, who fought successfully against the Hūṇas, the king of the Gūrjaras and the lords of Sindhu, Gāndhāra, Lāṭa and Mālava. His queen was Yas'omatî. The king was a great devotee of the sun. Rājyavardhana was the first child of the king and the queen. Then was born Harsha on the 12th of the dark half of the month of Jyeshtha. The birth of Harsha was heralded by auspicious signs prognosticating his future greatness. When Rājyavardhana was in his sixth year and Harsha was an infant just beginning to take a few steps with the help of his nurse and prattling a few indistinct words, a daughter named Rājyas'rî was born to the king and queen. About the time of the birth of Rājyas'rî, queen Yas'omatî's brother handed over to the king Prabhākaravardhana his son Bhaṇḍin about eight years old as a companion to the two princes, between whom and Bhaṇḍin sprang up a close and intimate friendship. The king in course of time brought, as companions for the growing princes, two brothers, sons of the king of Mālava, named Kumāragupta and Mādhavagupta, the elder Kumāragupta being about 18 years old at the time. These two followed the princes like their shadow. When Rājyas'rî grew up an accomplished princess she was married to Grahavarman, the eldest son of Avantivarman of the Maukhari family. Rājyas'rî went with her husband to his country of Kānyakubja.

Chap. V. When Rājyavardhana was old enough to bear arms, Prabhākaravardhana sent him accompanied by hereditary ministers and devoted feudatories to the north against the Hūṇas. Harsha accompanied him for some distance and when Rājyavardhana entered the Kailāsa range, Harsha remained behind and devoted some time to hunting. A courier from Prabhākaravardhana announced his serious illness. He started in hot haste and riding day and night reached the capital on the third day. He saw the whole city given up to performing rites of various sects and faiths for the sake of his father. On entering the palace he found the king lying in the clutches of death with queen Yas'omatî weeping over him. Two days afterwards when the king's condition became hopeless, Yas'omatî ascended the funeral pyre and the king died a short time afterwards. Harsha performed the funeral rites and anxiously waited for the arrival of his elder brother to whom he had already despatched swift messengers.

Chap. VI. About a fortnight after the death of Prabhākaravardhana, Rājyavaradhana arrived wounded in his successful war against the Hūṇas and with a thin growth of hair on his chin. The next day Rājyavardhana announced his intention of refusing the throne and of taking to a life in the forest. Harsha was taken aback by the strange resolve of his brother and had a mind to follow him, when one of Rājyas'rî's attendants, named Saṃvādaka, threw himself into the hall where the brothers sat and narrated a harrowing tale. He told Rājyavardhana that on the very day on which the news of Prabhākaravardhana's death reached Kānyakubja (Kanoj), Grahavarman, the husband of Rājyas'rî, was slain by the king of Mālava, that Rājyas'rî was put into prison at Kânyakubja with fetters on her feet like a brigand's wife and that the king of Mālava had designs even against Sthāṇvîs'vara. On that very day Rājyavardhana, who did not listen to Harsha's entreaties that, though a boy, he should be allowed to accompany him, started against the king of Mālava accompanied by Bhaṇḍin with ten thousand cavalry. After many days had elapsed, Harsha saw Kuntala, a high cavalry officer and a great favourite of Rājyavardhana, coming with sorrow written on his face. He brought the news that Rājyavardhana, though he subdued with ease the Mālava prince, was treacherously slain by the king of the Gauḍas, who had induced Rājyavardhana to go alone to the former's place. Siṃhanāda, the old and faithful commander-in-chief of Prabhākaravardhana, encouraged Harsha to avenge his brother's death. Harsha took the vow of destroying the Gauḍa king and dictated to his minister for foreign affairs named Avanti a proclamation to be sent to all kings either to submit to Harsha or to offer battle. The next morning, Harsha called Skandagupta, the chief of his elephant hosts, and asked him to get ready his whole army for an expedition. Skandagupta applauded Harsha's project but implored his master to learn the lesson of distrust from the fate of Rājyavardhana and narrated for his master's edification the stories of numerous former kings that fell victims to treachery and intrigue.

Chap. VII. A few days afterwards Harsha crowned himself and set out on an auspicious day, after worshipping S'iva. The first halt was made not far from the capital (Thanesar) on the banks of the Sarasvatî. There the chief accountant of the village waited upon him with a golden seal marked with the emblem of the bull and requested Harsha to issue a charter. The next day Harsha marched on with his vast army. When the day's march was over, he gave audience to Haṃsavega, a confidential messenger of Kumāra alias Bhāskaravarman, king of Prāgjyotisha (Assam). The messenger announced that the prince of Assam desired to form an undying friendship with Harsha and offered many wonderful presents, the chief of which was a miraculous parasol that originally belonged to Varuṇa. At night Haṃsavega informed Harsha how the parasol came into the possession of the kings of Assam. He traced the descent of Kumāra alias Bhāskaravarman from Naraka and mentioned that Kumāra was the great-great-grandson of Bhūtivarman, great-grandson of Chandramukhavarman, grandson of Sthitivarman and son of Susthiravarman alias Mṛigānka from his queen S'yāmādevî. Bhāskaravarman was a devotee of S'iva and desired the friendship of Harsha. Harsha was highly pleased with the king of Assam and sent back Haṃsavega with numerous presents. Harsha then proceeded for several days against his enemy (the king of Gauḍa). On the way he met Bhaṇḍin who brought with him the booty wrested from the Mālava king by Rājyavardhana. He brought news that after Kānyakubja was seized by Gupta, Rājyas'rî escaped from prison and had betaken herself to the Vindhya forest. Harsha then asked Bhaṇḍin to march against the Gauḍa king and himself entered the Vindhya forest in search of his unlucky sister.

Chap. VIII. After roaming about in the forest for several days, he met Vyāghraketu, son of the Bhil chieftain S'arabhaketu, who presented to Harsha a young Bhil by name Nirghāta, the commander-in-chief of the Bhils. He informed the king of an ascetic named Divākaramitra who was a convert from Brahmanism to Buddhism. Harsha remembered him as the friend of Grahavarman from the latter's childhood. Harsha resting his right hand on the shoulder of Mādhavagupta went to the hermitage of Divākaramitra, where he saw the latter surrounded by pupils and students of various sects. Just then a Bhikshu came unexpectedly and informed his teacher Divākaramitra that a woman of noble birth was about to burn herself for grief in the neighbourhood. Harsha hastened with the Bhikshu leading the way and saw his sister ready to perish in fire. From his sister he learnt how she was helped out of prison by a noble named Gupta at the time of the tumult of the Gauḍa king in Kānyakubja, how she then heard of the death of Rājyavardhana, how she gave up food on hearing it, how she came to the Vindhya forest and how in despair she prepared to burn herself. Divākaramitra then made to Harsha a present of a necklace named Mandākinî, brought by Nāgārjuna from the Nāgas in Pātāla and handed over to Sātavāhana, overlord of the Deccan. Rājyas'rī expressed to her brother her wish to put on the red robe. Harsha implored her to remain with him till he carried out his vow of destroying the Gauḍa king and requested Divākaramitra to be the spiritual adviser of his sister. He further said that after fulfilling his vow, he would himself assume the red robes along with his sister. When Divākaramitra acceded to the wishes of Harsha, the latter returned to his army encamped on the banks of the Ganges.

Here the narrative of Harsha's career comes to an end.

INDEX

XIII

CHRONOLOGICAL TABLE

BOOK FOUR

1812.	Battles of Smolensk, Borodino,
	Vittoria, Moscow.
	December, Return to Paris.
1813.	April, Battles of Lützen and Bautzen.
	July, Battle of Dresden.
	October 16th to 18th, battle of Leipzig.
1814.	Battles of Brienne, La Rothière,
	Champaubert, Montereau,
	Bas-sur-Aube, Laon, Arcis-sur-Aube.
	April 6th, Abdication in Fontainebleau.
	April 20th, Embarkation for Elba.
1815.	February 26th, Sails from Elba.
	March 13th, Outlawed.
	March 20th, Paris.
	June, Battles of Ligny and Waterloo.
	June 23rd, Second abdication.
	July 13th, Letter to the Prince Regent.
	July 31st, Declared a prisoner.

BOOK FIVE

1815.	October 17th, Arrival in St. Helena.
1821.	May 5th, Death.

Away from these fellows, who are Frenchmen! His gaze is still fixed upon his native isle, and it is to the advantage of Corsica that he twists the new sociological outlooks. We read in one of the essays: "How absurd to declare that divine laws forbid us to shake off a usurper's yoke! Were that so, then every regicide who has clambered into the vacant throne would be under God's protection, whereas in case of failure he would have lost his head. With how much better right, then, can a people drive out a usurping prince! Does not this speak for Corsicans?... Thus we can shake off the yoke of France, just as we shook off the yoke of Genoa. Amen."

Meanwhile, the fledgling genius wished to try its wings, and this urge led Napoleon to draft a novel on Corsica, and also some short stories. All were animated by hatred of France, but none of them was ever finished. Still he was learning his trade, spurred on by poverty, passion and sentiment. Imagination rules the world, but cannons are the instrument where by imagination realises its purposes. "I have no refuge but my work. I only change my linen once a week. Since I was ill, I have slept very little.... I eat only once a day."

He studies ordnance and munitions of war, always thinking in figures, so that every one says that he is a born mathematician. Now, side by side with the drafts of works of imagination, he draws up specifications of all the localities in the island where he would place batteries, dig trenches, station troops—if he had but the power! Beneath the network of poetical thoughts with which he has covered the island, he spreads over his maps a second network, wherein crosses denote big guns. Maps, maps! In his room beside the noisy cafe, he restudies everything conceivable, copies whole speeches out of the report of the parliamentary proceedings at Westminster, and sketches the remotest parts of the earth. At the end of the last of his copy-books, the final entry runs: "St. Helena, a small island in the Atlantic Ocean. English colony."

At this juncture he received a letter from his mother. Her powerful patron, the marshal, was dead; the house had lost its main prop; the mulberry orchard was no longer to be a means of coast. Now then, Paoli, for our last duel!

But the old man, enjoying the full tide of popular favour, has also the best of it as a soldier. He holds the citadel. When Napoleon, acting this time as a Frenchman, makes his second attempt to storm that stronghold, he succeeds no better that before. A last endeavour is made to take the fortress from the islands. It is fruitless!

There is no longer a place for him and his Corsica. They are banished by popular decree, and declared outlaws. The mother, so proud of her descent; her two sons, her two daughters, and her brother—all have been rendered shelterless by Napoleon's unsuccessful attack on Paoli. They must escape from the island at a few hours' notice. Through the silent woods, in whose recesses twenty-four years earlier she had found safety from the French, Letizia has now to flee towards the coast under the protection of the French. All her possessions are in the hands of her enemies. Nothing is left to her beyond the clothes she wears.

The artillery officer, twenty-three years of age, stands on the deck of the sailing ship that is bearing him to Toulon. Throughout the long June evening, he watches the coast recede; every cape, every ridge, is familiar to him. Thrice he has tried to conquer the island, as its liberator. Now he has been driven out by the Corsicans as a Frenchman. He is full of rage and of a thirst for revenge. The victories of France will strengthen him, and in days to come he will, after all, be master of Corsica!

But as he sails westward, and as the French coast draws near, our adventurer enjoys the sense of freedom that comes to him who is everywhere at home. Such is a happy lot of the man who has no country.

X

"How shabby their dresses are!", thinks Letizia , when her two half-grown girls come home from the market with their poor purchases. The refugees are living on the fourth floor of a confiscated house in Marseilles (the owner, a nobleman, has been which in earlier and subsequent letters consists of nothing but the name, includes, today, the writer's military title. Everything is calculated for effect. But his feelings break through, and in the postcript he discloses to his brother the two things he has most at heart; Luck and Woman.

At a later date he said: "I have two men within me, the man of the head and the man of the heart."

XIV

On the tribune of the Convention stands Buonaparte with his officers, hailed by the acclamations of the assembly, to whom the youthful saviour is being presented. He scarcely notices the applause, for such triumphs of the moment seem of little value to him. Coldly surveying the hall, he thinks: "So you are the leaders of the nation. You trembled with fear when you heard the thunder of the guns! You shall not forget how to tremble! I have become your protector. I shall go on protecting you until you have become my humble servants."

As a matter of course, he is appointed to the command of the Army of the Interior. He now has a great following: cashiered officers, who hope to climb in the footsteps of the cashiered general; officials who have dreaded the reaction; all who feel that they have been rescued. But the crowd must be learning to hate him, for, in that darkling hour, hundreds of unarmed citizens, ideal spectators, women have perished. What is that to him? It is not his aim to be loved.

Now, when he suddenly has money and servants and carriages at his disposal, he wants nothing for himself, everything for his kin. His younger brothers are given good positions; his mother can once more live a life after her own heart, and gratify her taste for saving; Joseph has the offer of several posts; there are places for the most distant relatives. But the letters become rarer, and the very first of them sounds a new note: "I shall do everything I can to revolution. Indeed, the people's army is an expression of the revolution. The soldiers on the Austrian side must be used thriftily, for they are drawn from a larger number of nationalities than the German emperor himself rules. Six different languages are spoken in the army, and the French are fighting as a united nation of thirty millions, and their army will be capable of perpetual regeneration for twenty years to come.

What is the French army fighting for? The new freedom of the republic, and to spread throughout the world the few and simple ideas which animate it! The French are fighting for the world revolution, and nothing short of that. But the army is not in pursuit of purely ideal aims. It has to defend liberty against the environing forces of legitimate monarchy, against the legitimists who are more concerned with self-defence than with the cause of the fallen Bourbons. The French cannot achieve their end by simply defending their own frontiers. They are surrounded by kings and emperors who wish to keep their peoples from any attempt to imitate the French revolution, and are therefore trying to destroy the very focus of the new ideas. Thus France is forced to assume the offensive as a means of self-defence. Those who in such a fashion become conquerors in spite of themselves, are surely entitled to declare that their conquests are achieved in the name of liberty.

This brings us to the third factor of Napoleon's success. While the commander is engaged in the attempt to conquer Lombardy, and then Italy, for France, he issues a series of manifestoes to tell the inhabitants of the territories he is invading that he comes to free them from the Habsburgs and the Sardinians, from dukes and patrician senates. Will not all who have been discontented with the old order be roused to action by the torrential force of such appeals? Have not the oppressed masses long had it in mind to rid themselves of their rulers? Have not the ideas of the revolution crossed the frontiers years ago, rousing, in many of the towns, students and burghers to revolt? Here in Italy were young people who longed for freedom: leaders who had been vainly clamouring shots; Muiron covers the general with his own body, is hit, and falls. Bonaparte saves himself on horseback.

That evening in camp, he is greatly depressed. Second day's fighting, and a vain attempt to storm the enemy's position. This abominable river. Seems impossible to get across it. For a long time, the fortunes of the third day, are no better than those of the first two.

At the eleventh hour, he has recourse to cunning. While the fight on the river rages uncertainly, he sends all the trumpeters and drummers he can get together, with part of the guard, in a wide half-circle to reach a position in the enemy's rear. There the charge is sounded. The wearied Austrians are panic stricken, and one of their divisions draws back. The French, encouraged by the rout of part of the foe, assume that all the opposing army is retreating, and act accordingly. Courage and ruse have snatched victory out of a morass of despair. The name of another village becomes famous. Arcola medals are struck in Paris. A picture is painted, showing the commander on the bridge of Arcola, waving imaginary colours.

The danger is over for a time. The enemy supports are withdrawn from Mantua, and soon the town must fall. Bonaparte makes a fresh disposition of his troops, and hastens to Milan. At length he will be able to administer the province from the capital, and have Josephine and hold her fast.

But Josephine is harder to catch than Wurmser. "I reach Milan, reach to your house, having thrown aside everything in order to clasp you in my arms. You are not there! You are gadding about somewhere, running away when I come to seek you. You care nothing about your Napoleon. A whim led you to give me your love, and now fickleness has made you indifferent. Inured to dangers, I know how to meet reverse of fortune.... Don't put yourself about, amuse yourself, happiness is made for you, all the world is happy to have the chance of pleasing you, your husband alone is most unhappy."

taller. Only the page continues to loll on the couch, for Eugene knows that his mother is unchallenged mistress of the house.

We are at Montebello, the huge castle near Milan, where Bonaparte is passing the summer. He is almost wholly the statesman now, for the war has been ended by the arrangement entered into at Leoben, and nothing more is needed than a formal ratification. He might be in Paris, receiving the adulation of which he dreamed in youth; but he prefers to stay in Italy. He will not return to Paris until the political consequences of his victories have assumed a concrete form, until the new States are consolidated and the Italian business over and done with. Meanwhile, during the many months he spends at Montebello, the life there is not so much that of a military headquarters, as that of a minor court.

But in no respect does he behave like an upstart. There are no pretences. In everything he will make his influence felt as one who is a child of the revolution that established a regime of equality. He has appointed sons of the people to the leading positions in his army; but he has no fear of what his noble guests, the dukes and princes of Italy, may think of it, should one of his valiant generals commit a solecism. He sees to reason for hiding his origin like a parvenu, although his adoption of French nationality might well incline him to conceal his Corsican birth. In actual fact, he had summoned the whole family to Milan. Now, with lavish oriental hospitality, he has invited them all to Montebello, and those who seek his favour must show his relatives due honor. Half Italy pays court to him, for his name is already acquiring the mythical power of that of a man of destiny. Besides the numerous persons who wish to harness their fortunes to his chariot, not a few come from afar to ask the sage's advice concerning family matters and private affairs.

He has found it hard to persuade his mother, proud and a woman of strict principles, to make friends with Josephine, whose reputation is an offence to her. Josephine reciprocates Madame Letizia's dislike; but Napoleon, though he idolises his wife and can refuse her nothing, compels her to observe the outward forms of respect. Now, the friction between the two women has become

JAICO GREAT LIVES SERIES

NAPOLEON

JAICO GREAT LIVES SERIES

NAPOLEON

A GREAT SOLDIER, POLITICIAN, LOVER AND FIRST MODERN EUROPEAN

THE DEFINITIVE BIOGRAPHY

EMIL LUDWIG

TRANSLATED BY
EDEN & CEDAR PAUL

JAICO PUBLISHING HOUSE

Ahmedabad Bangalore Chennai
Delhi Hyderabad Kolkata Mumbai

Published by Jaico Publishing House
A-2 Jash Chambers, 7-A Sir Phirozshah Mehta Road
Fort, Mumbai - 400 001
jaicopub@jaicobooks.com
www.jaicobooks.com

NAPOLEON
ISBN 81-7224-279-4

First Jaico Impression: 1957
40th Jaico Impression: 2025

Printed by
Pashupati Printers, Delhi

Napoleon went forth to seek Virtue but,
since she was not to be found, he got Power.

—**GOETHE.**

To

ELGA LUDWIG

TABLE OF CONTENTS

AUTHOR'S ACKNOWLEDGMENTS

The author wishes to make due acknowledgments to Professor Pariset of Strasburg and Herr Kurt Wildhagen of Heidelberg for advice during the preparation of the book.

XI

CHRONOLOGICAL TABLE

BOOK ONE

1769. August 15th, Napoleon born.
1779. At School in Brienne.
1784. At the military academy.
1785. Sub-Lieutenant of artillery.
1789. To Corsica.
1791. April, Lieutenant in Valence,
October, To Corsica.
1792. Putsch in Ajaccio, Banishment.
1793. Captain. Siege of Toulon.
1794. February, Brigadier General.
August, Arrested.
1795. June, at the Ministry for War.
October, Suppression of the Paris rising.
Commander of the Army of the Interior.
1796. March 2nd, Commander of the Army of Italy,
March 6th, Married to Josephine Beauharnais.

BOOK TWO

1796-7. Battles of Millesimo, Castiglione, Arcola,
Rivoli, Mantua.
1797. At the castle of Montebello.
Peace of Campo Formio.
1798. In Paris till May.
May 19th, Embarkation for Egypt.
Battle of the Pyramids.
1799. Jaffa, Acre, Aboukir.
October 7th, Landing in France.
November 9th, coup d'état of the
eighteenth Brumaire.
December 24th First Consul.

XII

CHRONOLOGICAL TABLE

BOOK THREE

1800.	June 14th, Battle of Marengo.
	December 24th, Attempted assassination.
1801.	Peace of Lunéville.
	Concordat with Pius VII.
1802.	Peace with England.
	Consul for life. Legion of Honour.
1804.	March 21st, Duke of Erghien shot.
	May 18th, Assumption of Imperial Title.
	December 2nd, Coronation.
1805.	October, Trafalgar.
	November, Vienna taken.
	December 2nd, Battle of Austerlitz.
	Peace of Pressburg.
1806.	Confederation of the Rhine. Joseph, King of Naples.
	Louis, King of Holland.
	October 14th, Battle of Jena.
	Berlin. Continental System.
1807.	Battles of Preussisch-Eylau and Friedland.
	June 7th, Treaty of Tilsit.
	Jerome, King of Westphalia.
1808.	Rome. Madrid. Bayonne. Joseph, King of Spain.
	Murat, King of Naples.
1809.	Excommunication. Battles of Aspern-Essling. Wagram, and Vienna.
1810.	January, Divorce.
	April, Married to Marie Louise.
1811.	March 20th, Birth of his son.

NAPOLEON

I

BOOK ONE
THE ISLAND

The story of Napoleon produces on me an impression like that produced by the Revelation of Saint John the Divine. We all feel there must be something more in it, but we do not know what.

—GOETHE

I

A YOUNG woman is sitting in a tent. Wrapped in a shawl, she is suckling her baby, and listening to a distant rumbling and roaring. Are they still shooting, though night has fallen? Maybe it is only the sound of one of those autumn thunderstorms whose echoes reverberate from the mountains; or perhaps it is nothing more than the murmur from the surrounding forest of pines and evergreen oaks, where foxes and wild swine have their lairs. She looks like a gypsy, sitting there with her white breast half covered by the shawl, brooding within the murky tent, uncertain what the fate of the day may have been. Now she hears the sound of hoof-beats. Is it he? He promised to come; but it is a long way from the fighting line, and the mists are rising.

The flap of the tent is thrown open, letting in a breath of night air. A man enters. An officer in a coloured tunic and wearing a plumed head-dress; a slim fellow, nimble of movement; a young patrician, in the middle twenties. He greets the woman ardently. Springing to her feet, she gives the nursling to her maid. Wine is brought. Taking the kerchief from her head, she stands before him, showing chestnut ringlets astray on a smooth, white brow. An eager question is on her well-shaped lips. Add to the picture that she has a long chin, a sign of energy; that her aquiline nose is thrown into relief by the firelight; and that on her hip there gleams the dagger which in this mountain land she never lays aside. We see a lovely amazon, daughter of an ancient race, sprung from men of action and resolution. The woman's forebears, like the man's, have for centuries been leaders and warriors; first across the water in Italy, and then in this craggy island.

But now, when all have gathered together against the hated enemy, have joined forces in the attempt to drive out the French, here, in the wildest part of the mountains, whither the brave girl of nineteen has followed the husband fighting for their fatherland; who, now, could recognise in her the brilliant patrician, the magnet of all eyes? Here, nothing but pride and courage show that she is of noble birth.

The man, full of life and vigour, ever in movement, tells her all his news. The enemy has been beaten, driven back towards the coast. There is no escape. Envoys have been sent to Paoli.

"There will be a true tomorrow. Letizia, we are winning! Corsica will be free!"

Every Corsican longs for many children. It is a land where an affront is instantly avenged by a dagger thrust; where the vendetta is sacred; where family feuds last from decade to decade and from century to century. The man before us wants many children, to ensure that his race shall persist; and the woman has learned from mother and grandmother that children are tokens of honour. She had become a mother at fifteen; but the baby she has just been nursing was her first boy.

The thought of freedom glows afresh, for the officer is adjutant to Paoli, the leader of the people. "No longer shall our children be the slaves of France!"

II

With the coming of spring, despondency prevails. The enemy has landed reinforcements; the children of the island take up arms once more; again the young wife accompanies her husband to the war; this time she carries a child beneath her heart, the child conceived during the storms of the previous autumn.

"Often, in search of news, I would steal forth from our mountain nook to the battlefield; I heard the bullets whistling, but I put my trust in Our Lady"-so she would tell the story in later years.

great men as sketched by Plutarch, especially the Roman heroes. Of these, he is always dreaming. No one tells us that he ever saw this boy laugh.

To his schoolfellows he seems half a savage, or at best a queer foreigner. He knows scarcely a word of French, and has little inclination to learn the language of the foe. What a tiny little chap he is, and what a ridiculous name! His coat is too long. No pocket-money, nothing to spend, and yet he claims to be of noble birth! The scions of the French nobility laugh. Who cares about Corsican noblemen?

"If you Corsicans are such brave fellows, why did you let yourselves be beaten by our unconquerable troops?"

"We were one to ten," the lad angrily exclaims. "You just wait till I'm grown up, and I will pay you Frenchmen out!"

"Your father is nothing more than a sergeant, after all!"

An outburst of wrath from the boy, who challenges his tormentor. The young Napoleon is "kept in." He writes to his father: "I am tired of explaining my poverty; of having to endure the mockery of these foreign boys, whose only superiority is in respect of money, for in nobility of feeling they are far beneath me. Must I really humble myself before these purse-proud fellows?" The answer from the island is: "We have no money. You must stay where you are."

He stays five years; and, just as his revolutionary feeling is intensified by every slight, so does his self-confidence grow proportionally with the growth of his contempt for his fellows. The masters, indeed, monks one and all, have a good opinion of him, although he does not make much headway except in mathematics, history, and geography-subjects which appeal to a precise mind, a seeing eye, and also to the bitterness of spirit characteristic of one who belongs to a conquered race.

For always his thoughts turn back to his native island. In secret, he is angry with his father for having come to terms with the French. He has made up his own mind. He will get all he can out of the king at whose cost he now pursues his studies, so that in due time he may use the knowledge against his patron. He has a presentiment that some day he will set Corsica free. As yet all the lad of fourteen can do is to pore over books about his homeland, for he who would make history must first study history. He devours, too, all that Voltaire, Rousseau, and the great king of Prussia shortly before his death, have written on behalf of the liberation of Corsica.

Such a boy as this–solitary, suspicious, questing and rebellious, brooding rancorously over vast designs–what is he likely to become? Precociously thoughtful; endowed with a knowledge of men that is beyond his years. When Joseph, his elder brother, wishes to abandon the priestly career and to adopt the profession of arms, the youngster writes of him: "1. He lacks courage to brave the perils of the battlefield. —He will be a good garrison officer: well-grown and handsome, quick-witted and therefore inclined to pay frivolous compliments, with his talents he will always make a good impression in society. But in battle? 2. 'Tis too late to make a change. He might have got a rich benefice, and what an advantage that would have been to the family! 3. What branch of the service will he enter? The navy? (a) He knows nothing of mathematics; (b) his health could never endure life at sea. He is too light-minded for the sustained work that will be needed if he is to be an artillery officer." These are the reflections of a fifteen-year-old observer, who sees in himself the qualities that his brother lacks; and it is a perfect description of Joseph, who was, indeed, his father's son.

From this same father, Napoleon had inherited versatility and a vigorous imagination; from his mother came pride, courage, and accuracy; from both was derived his strong family feeling.

IV

"Only the sword-belt belongs to France; the edge is my own" thinks the youth, as he first buckles on his sword. At sixteen he has become a sub-lieutenant–and he will don uniform a good many more times before he dies. He has qualified for this rank by a year in the Paris Cadets' School, where he spent his time as he had spent it at Brienne, poring over books. A lad of Spartan tastes, he finds the prodigal expenditure of the sprigs of the French nobility (by whom he is utterly outshone) extremely distasteful. Since, however, nature sets him, even more than most young men, in the centre of his own world, he makes a virtue of necessity, and pens a memorial to the effect that luxurious living is unsuitable for budding soldiers. He must not get into debt, for he knows how poor they are at home. Now, when his father dies, the family affection of this Italian becomes intensified. Though little more than a boy, he begins to save money in order to help his mother.

After his examination, passed with fair credit, his superiors wrote of him: "Reserved and diligent, he prefers study to any kind of conversation, and nourishes his mind upon good authors... He is taciturn, with a love for solitude; is moody, overbearing, and extremely egotistical. Though he speaks little, his answers are decisive and to the point, and he excels in argument. Much self-love, and overweening ambition."

Clad in his new uniform, the little sub-lieutenant goes to join his regiment at Valence, compelled by his poverty to walk a great part of the way. Three impulses stir his youthful heart; to despise and make use of his fellow-creatures, most of whom are empty-headed and pretentious; to extricate himself from the clutches of poverty; to learn much in order that he may rule others. The means and the goal are one. He is to be a leader in the struggle on the island, and then to make himself master of Corsica.

How dull life is in this garrison town! Of course, a young man should learn to dance, should taste the pleasures of lively society. He tries this, but soon abandons the attempt, for his teeming pride makes him want to hide his poverty. However, any one who holds converse with members of the burgher class, lawyers and shopkeepers, hears strange talk, gets wind of things that the young viscounts in Paris never dream of. Is it really true? Has the spirit of Voltaire's and Montesquieu's and Raynal's writings actually climbed down so soon, to stalk among the provincial petty bourgeois? Is the movement which these prophets were conjuring up now seriously afoot? Can it be that the revolution is at hand?

Books clamour it abroad. Reading is free as breathing; and when a man has read all the books in the lending library, he can spare a franc or two now and again to buy a new book. True, the youth lodges in a cafe, and the clicking of the billiard balls in the next room is tiresome. But it would be still more tiresome to more. In personal habits, he is conservative.

What about his sentiments? Judge for yourselves. Like every young man of his generation, he is keenly in interested in the State and society. There he sits in the room next to the billiard room; pale, lonely, in a hot and stuffy atmosphere. While his comrades, after their short hours of duty, scatter to seek distraction in gaming or the pursuit of women, the impoverished lieutenant bends over his books, reading with sure instinct about the things (and those only) that will be of use to him in days to come: artillery, its principles and its history; the art of siege; Plato's Republic; the constitution of the Persian, the Athenian, the Spartan states; the history of England; the campaigns of Frederick the Great; French finances; the Tartars and the Turks, their manners and customs, and the topography of their countries; the history of Egypt and the history of Carthage; descriptions of India; English accounts of contemporary France; Mirabeau, Buffon, and Machiavelli; the history and the constitution of Switzerland; the history and constitution of China, India, the Inca State; the history of the nobility and the story of patrician misdeeds; astronomy, geology, and meteorology; the laws of the growth of population; statistics of mortality.

He did not simply flutter the pages of his books, but was an attentive reader. There is extant a whole series of copy-books containing Napoleon's notes, penned in an almost illegible handwriting. The contents of these, reprinted, occupies four hundred pages. Here we find a map of a Saxon heptarchy with a list of the kings for three centuries; item, the varieties of foot-races in ancient Crete; item, the dates of twenty-seven caliphs, with a not of the strength of their cavalry, and an account of the misconduct of their wives.

Especially frequent are memoranda concerning Egypt and India, including even the measurements of the Great Pyramid and a catalogue of Brahminical sects. He copies a passage from Raynal: "In view of the position of Egypt, lying betwixt two seas, and in a fact betwixt the East and the West, Alexander the Great conceived the design of establishing the capital of his world-wide empire in that country, and of making Egypt the centre of world commerce. This most enlightened of the conquerors had realised that if there was any practicable way of amalgamating his conquests into one consolidated State, it was by this use of Egypt, created as a point of union between Africa, Asia, and Europe." Thirty years later, he still had the words by heart. He had read them so often.

At this date, too, he begins original composition, drafting more than a dozen essays and projects: the placing of artillery; suicide; monarchical authority; the inequality of men; and Corsica, above all, Corsica–each were the topics, Rousseau, the most popular author of those days, is pulverised by Napoleon's realism. The young officer is epitomising Rousseau's views on the origin of the human race (in the *Discours sur l' origine et less fondements de l'inégalité parmi les hommes*), but abruptly he breaks of the epitome with the comment: "I don't believe a word of this." Then come a couple of pages filled with his own counterstatement. Human beings were not, to begin with, solitary; nor were they nomadic. They were happy, and lived apart, because they were not numerous enough to be forced into close contact. When the population grew more thick upon the ground, "then imagination came forth from the cave in which for so long it had been prisoned: self-confidence, passion, and pride reared their heads; there arose ambitious men with pale features, who took control of affairs, and mastered the multicoloured young popinjays, the Lotharios and lady-killers."

Do not we already hear him rattling his chains, in the dark cavern where he himself is prisoned with his titanic imagination? Do not we see the fancy portrait of the young author, pale of visage, full of hatred for the brilliant lady-killers who are his messmates?

livelihood; Joseph had no paid occupation; could the second son give any help? Shortly after this appeal reached him, he went home on furlough. Are we to consider him, an unacknowledged conqueror, returning to the island of his plans and dreams? Read what he wrote in his diary:

"Always alone, though in the midst of men, I go back home that I may give myself up to my lonely dreams and to the waves of my melancholy. Whither, now, do my gloomy thoughts tend? Towards death. Yet I stand on the threshold of life, and may reasonably expect to draw breath for many, many years. For the last six or seven years I have been far away from my country. How great the joy–to see my own people once more! What demon, then, is it that tempts me to self-destruction?–Since misfortune dogs my footsteps, and nothing gives me pleasure, why should I go on bearing a life in which, for me, everything goes awry?–What a tragedy in the homeland! My fellow-countrymen, in chains, kiss the hand that beats them.–Proud, buoyed up by a sense of his own worth, so lived of yore the happy Corsican, giving his days to the service of the State, and spending his nights in the arms of his beloved wife–the nights which nature and affection made divine for him. With the disappearance of freedom, those happy times have vanished like a dream. Frenchmen, not only have you stolen from us our greatest good, by now you are corrupting our morals! That is how I see my country, and yet I am powerless to help. Are there not reasons enough for quitting a world in which I must glorify those whom I hate?–If it were but the life of one individual which stood between us and our liberties, I should not be slow to act–Life has become a burden to me, I have no enjoyment, nothing but pain,–and because I cannot live after my own fashion, everything is loathsome to me."

V

After a year spent in Corsica, a year rendered gloomy by money troubles and family cares, he was still in this mood of despair when his furlough expired. He returned not to Valence, but to Auxonne. What did the change matter?

But, at last, recognition comes. His new general, who sees that this subaltern of nineteen is well informed, puts into his hands the task of carrying out some works upon the parade ground. "Difficult calculations are involved; and so, for the last ten days, I have been busied from morning till night at the head of two hundred men. This unusual preferment has given some of my superiors a spite against me. They are furious that so important a job should have been taken out of their hands and given to a lieutenant."

The old depression recurs. Promotion will be desperately slow, and when he becomes a captain he will be retired on half pay. He will return home, to be despised because he is a pensioner of the French. At long last, he will be buried in his native soil. Of that privilege, at least, the French cannot rob him! Were they, then, nothing but froth, the dreams of liberty revealed in the books he had read? If mighty France herself was unable to shake off the yoke of the nobility, to rid herself of venality and nepotism, how was poor little Corsica to shake off the French tyranny?

The young author fills his diary with new schemes. He would have had to pay heavily for it if the book had fallen into the hands of his superiors. "Draft for a memorial concerning monarchical authority. Set forth details as to the usurped power which kings enjoy today in the twelve monarchies of Europe. There are few of them who have not merited dethronement." Thus does he vent his spleen in the faithful diary, whilst in public on every royal birthday, dressed in gala uniform, he must join in the cry: Long live the king!

Another year of his youth is spent in the dull routine of such service, while Napoleon holds his peace and waits, dividing his energies between imaginative writing and mathematics.

The year of destiny has opened. Into the most out-of-the-way regions of the slumbering province comes the presage of the trumpets that are about to sound. We are in the month of June 1789. The melancholy lieutenant feels that the day of vengeance draws near. Is the arrogance of those who have so long humiliated him, to bring destruction upon their own heads? May it not be that the call of the myriads is also the battle-cry of the island? He takes his *Letters on Corsica;* sends them to his admired exemplar Paoli, in exile, and writes: "General! I came into the world when my country was perishing. My cradle was surrounded by men with the death-rattle in their throats, and by those whom despair had driven to tears.... With them, hope vanished. Slavery was the reward of our subjugation. To justify themselves, the traitors have heaped calumnies upon you.... When I read this, my blood boiled, and I resolved to scatter the mists. Now I shall blacken with the brush of shame all who have betrayed the common cause.... If I lived in the capital, I should find other means.... Owing to my youth, this undertaking may be fruitless; but I shall be helped by my passion for truth, my love for my country, and my enthusiasm. If you, General, will encourage in this work a young man whose coming into the world you saw, I shall gain confidence.... My mother, Madame Letizia, has charged me to remind you of the old days in Corte."

We notice a new tone, a symphony of new tones: the soaring emotion of the epoch; the gesture of the tyrannicide; the whole equipment of scintillating words, not an uprush of feeling (as in the pages of his dairy), but deliberately chosen with an eye to their effect. Only one thing is alarmingly original quite peculiar to the writer: the decisive "I" at the opening of the letter, this "I" as a great thesis, fronting the world. Immeasurable self-confidence is breaking a trail; for now the drum-taps of a new era are sounding; an era which will give the palm, not to birth but to action, thus sweeping away the only hindrance that has hitherto been insuperable. An unprecedented claim is voiced, a claim which henceforward will never cease to be heard. But at the close of the letter, with a courteous turn of phrase, he slips back into the familiar, implying that he looks to Paoli for protection. What adroitness, what good manners, we find in all the letters of this adolescent who in person is still rough and enigmatical!

Paoli, the survival from an earlier day, is annoyed by such

arrogance, and answers with civil irony that young people should not try to write history.

Four weeks after the sending of the letter, young people begin to write history, for the first time in the eighteenth century. They storm the Bastille; the great signal has been given: and France leaps to arms. Even in the garrison town of our young lieutenant, the masses riot and loot, until the propertied classes join forces with the troops. Buonaparte is at his post with his battery in the streets, and helps to shoot down the people. This is the first time he has fired a gun in real earnest. He acts under orders from the king's officers; but there can be no doubt that he acts whole-heartedly against the mob, which he despises no less than he despises the nobility.

In the depths of his soul, he regards this as nothing more than a dispute among foreigners. What does he care about Frenchmen who raise their hands against other Frenchmen? His brain is fired by a single thought: "Corsica's hour has come!" Madness or enthusiasm, an ideal or merely a catchword? What matter? Let us carry the message to our island. Apply for leave; and, in the turmoil of the new movement, be the first to reach home!

VI

Lieutenant Buonaparte landed on his island like a prophet carrying a new doctrine to a foreign cost. He was the first to bring the red cockade; to promise liberty, equality, and fraternity. Was not this a race of free mountaineers, who of old had been self-governing, but for twenty years had groaned under the heel of the oppressor—a conqueror who ruled through the instrumentality of the nobles and the Church, but did not understand the people?

What did it matter to the young Jacobin that until yesterday he had lived upon his patrician birth, that solely because of his rank he had been educated at the king's cost? What was the king to him? At length the peoples were to be free to rule themselves. If the new France, just awakened, had proclaimed the right of self-government, Corsica, which the old France had loaded with chains, must proclaim its own freedom. Citizens, the hour has struck! To arms! Let every one wear the red cockade of the new era; let us form a National Guard, as they have done in Paris! Let us wrest the means of power from the king's troops. I am an artillerist, and I will be your leader!

Twenty years of age, pale of countenance, with cold, blue-grey eyes, but with a mouth full of glowing phrases, such is the aspect of young Buonaparte as he hastens through the streets of Ajaccio. Everyone in the little town knows him, and he is followed by a growing number of persons, some eager for liberty, and others in search of a change of any kind. To the crowd in the square, he seems a man bringing passionate hopes; his figure is that of a tribune of the people. In this half-oriental atmosphere, and among these quarrelsome families (so he says later), "a man soon learns to study the human heart."

But there is a set-back. No reinforcements come from the mountains; and, when the regular troops put, in an appearance, they scatter the revolutionists. Within a few hours, all have been disarmed, though, for prudence, no arrests are made. This is a further source of disillusionment. He is not even a martyr, but only a would-be popular leader who has been defeated; his position borders on the ludicrous. Yet the fever is still burning in his veins, and at all costs he must do something to cool himself. A statement of grievances to the National Assembly in Paris! First of all, in the florid style of the day, an ode to the new freedom, and then a spate of complaints and adjurations. To the gallows with the king's servants! Arm the citizens of the island! –A committee promptly joins him in signing the document.

Weeks of waiting. What answer will come from Paris? Here is the courier at last. The island, is to be a French province, having the same rights as the other provinces; in accordance with Mirabeau's proposal, Paoli and all the champions of liberty are free to return home. The Lieutenant is taken aback. A province? In spite of the new idea, and indeed because of them, the Corsicans are to remain Frenchmen? A strange form of liberty! But there, already, is the procession, headed by the authorities, on its way to the cathedral, where the decree from Paris is to receive a blessing. Buonaparte is prompt to seize the rope which all are seizing. He pens fiery manifestoes to his fellow-citizens, seeks supporters in the new political club, and engineers his elder brother's election to the town council. Meanwhile he continues to work at his history of Corsica, and reads to his mother choice passages of what he is writing.

"Can this be the great Paoli? That is the question Buonaparte asks himself, when, after twenty years' exile, the hero of his youthful enthusiasms returns amid popular acclamations. "His talk and his appearance are so humdrum, so politic, so unsoldierly." But it was expedient to keep on good terms with Paoli, for he was to be the commander of the National Guard. In the mountains, the young artillery officer was for some time closely associated with the man who had been his father's chief just before his own coming into the world.

When they were sitting together or riding together–the tried veteran and the darkly aspiring young Corsican,–the latter would eagerly expound to the former his plans for an armed rising, and even for the forcible severance of the island from the new France. On these occasions, Paoli would look at Buonaparte with mingled pride and alarm. He could not but feel that the author of the*Letters on Corsica* really had a claim upon him. But the young fellow had the devil in his body; and (which was worse) in his brain, for in the man's brain was the image of the world throne in solitary splendour. Shaking his head, Paoli would exclaim:

"There is nothing modern about you, Napolione. You come from the age of Plutarch!"

For the first time in his life young Napoleon felt that he was understood. The Roman heroes of Plutarch were alone adequate to his aspirations. Paoli was the first to recognise the Roman in Buonaparte.

At length he has a phrase upon which his self-esteem can luxuriate. Now, from his country retreat, when at Paoli's instigation he writes a manifesto, the superscription penned by his fevered imagination runs as follows: "23rd day of January in the 2nd year, from my study at Midilli." Ridiculous or sublime? However this may be, as soon as he has issued the dictatorial pronunciamento the young man has to hasten back to his military duties in France, for, his furlough, though renewed again and again, has finally expired. Is he to sacrifice this last firm standing-ground? To what end? Why should he stay in the island any longer? The first place is occupied!

VII

"I am in a peasant's hut writing to you, after a long talk with the good folk.... It is four in the afternoon; the weather is fresh but mild; I thoroughly enjoyed walking. No snow yet, but there is snow in the air–Everywhere I have found the peasants staunch;...they are all ready to die for the constitutions–The women are royalists almost without exception. No wonder for that, seeing that Liberty is fairer than they, and eclipses them. In Dauphiné, the priests have taken the oath of fealty to the constitution; they laugh at the bishops. –'Good society,' as it is called (three out of four are aristocrats), affects admiration for the British constitution. It is true that Peretti threatened Mirabeau with a dagger. This is little to our credit. The Patriotic Society must make Mirabeau a present of our national costume: biretta, vest, knee-breeches and hose, cartridge pouch, stiletto, pistol, and musket. It will certainly have a good effect."

Everything in this letter to Napoleon's maternal uncle, the Abbé Joseph Fesch, bears witness to observation and calculation, the elements upon which the politician's influence is based: the weather, the State, travelling on foot, the conciliation of a man in high position, men's motives–all have been the objects of careful consideration. Vanity and avarice, these are the weaknesses to which an appeal can be successfully directed. We see deep into his soul when, in a bluntly-worded letter dating from those weeks, he arraigns an opponent thus: "Tour study of human nature has taught you the price of every man's enthusiasm; for you, the difference between people's characters was summed up in a few gold pieces more or less!"

Gold pieces! Where were they to be had? Louis, the brother of thirteen, had come back to France with him. When Lieutenant Buonaparte (he had the full rank now) and his brother got back to Valence, they had no more between them than eighty-five francs, to provide for food, clothing, and the boy's education. They had to brush their own clothes.

Money! Not for enjoyment (he despises trivial pleasures), but to help him make his way in the world! Lyons Academy has offered a prize for an essay. Twelve hundred francs; one could for that sum equip half Corsica with weapons. "What truths and sentiments are most important to inculcate upon men for their happiness?" The lieutenant smiles. The subject suits him very well. First of all, so to say, he leaves his card on the academicians who have chosen the theme. They are disciples of Rousseau. Our essayist opens by extolling the joys of nature, friendship, ardent idleness–three things which he neither knew nor prized. Suddenly the argument takes a political turn, against kings, and on behalf of the universalisation of the free enjoyment of possessions and right. Then comes a sinister tone, as if the writer were contemplating in a mirror his own image as the pallid student of a few years before: "The ambitious man, pale of countenance, laughing sardonically, plays with crime, and intrigue is his chosen instrument.... If, at length, he gets his hand on the rudder of power, he soon wearies of the adulation of the crowd.... Men of great ambition have sought happiness, and have found fame."

Sublime forebodings, worthy of any of the characters in Plutarch. Soon the author expresses himself more plainly. His ideal is Sparta; courage and strength are the outstanding virtues. A Spartan moved through life as a man moves in the plenitude of his powers. "He was happy because he lived in accordance with the nature. Only the strong man is good; the weakling is evil." Another presage glows in the following utterance: "Men who are truly great are like meteors: they shine and consume themselves, that they may lighten the darkness of the earth."

between the townsfolk of Ajaccio and the Guard; must fan the flames, so that, amid the general confusion, he may assume the role of saviour! Is not the citadel, now occupied by the king's regular forces, a standing menace? Did not Frederick and Caesar always begin by storming citadels? Seize the commander of the regulars, drive out this well-born booby, and thus, at one stroke, free the island! France, now involved in wars, will be unable to reconquer Corsica. The liberator will become a popular hero, and old Paoli will be no more than a legend.

On Easter Sunday, 1792, an open struggle occurred. Was the National Guard provocative; were the townsfolk playing double? Who began the affray? An everlasting problem! This much is certain, that Buonaparte, at the head of his battalion, tried to seize the fortress. But the garrison was not to be intimidated. Guns were trained on his men, and he had to withdraw. A complaint against the young officer was lodged in Paris; he was accused of armed rebellion, and a trial for high treason was impending. His exculpatory phrases deceived no one. Paoli, who had from the outset been somewhat alarmed at the zeal of his turbulent fellow-islander, hastened to proclaim his own loyalty to France, and to cashier the son of his old friend.

"If you turn against me, Paoli; I will turn against you," thought Buonaparte. "You had better be careful what you are about! To Paris, post-haste. Not for nothing is there a revolution there!"

Through the streets of the French capital, these hot summer days, strolls our adventurer, fro whom everything has gone awry. He has neither money nor position. In France, he is a lieutenant, but regarded, more or less as a deserter; in Corsica, he is a cashiered lieutenant colonel. The gravest charges are likely to be brought against him, and tomorrow he may be actually starving. The Jacobins are his last hope, and he joins Robespierre's faction, for nothing can save him but the fall of the dynasty. To him, complete breakup of the old order has become essential.

Life in Paris is costly. He pawns his watch, and, in spite of this, gets into debt—a thing he has hitherto been sedulous to avoid.

Fifteen francs due to a wine dealer! He proposes to his friend Bourrienne that the pair shall become house agents. Does he envy those who sit in high places? No, he merely despises them. "Any one who sees at short range all that is going on, must admit that the peoples are hardly worth wooing for their favours. Here, human beings are perhaps even more base and calumniatory. Enthusiasm is merely enthusiasm, and the French nation is outworn. No one seeks anything but his won advantage, and everyone's family, that is the only lot worth having, with a fixed income of four or five thousand francs—if imagination would but cease to torment one, would quiet down!"

Woe to his who is thus plagued by a lively imagination! What colossal possibilities may be cooling in this Parisian cauldron, may arise out of the chaos of this titanic time! Being an Italian, a foreigner, he can contemplate with equanimity the destinies of these Frenchmen, and, as a cold-blooded adventurer, can seek to turn their fortunes to his own account. The Jacobins are already coming to the front.

When the sansculottes storm the Tuileries, Buonaparte is among the onlookers. What are the thoughts of the man under the harrow? "Thank God, we are free once more." But what does the army officer say? "I saw soldiers threatened by civilians, and was terribly shocked. Had the king shown himself on horseback, he would have gained the victory; such was the mood that morning." A few days earlier, when the king had been masquerading in the red cap of liberty, Napoleon had written: "What a fool! Why didn't he use grape shot? If a few hundred of the mob had been shot down, the others would have run away!"

Still, his main feeling was one of liberation. His opponents had been overthrown. The day after the storming of the Tuileries, he wrote to his uncle: "You needn't worry about your nephews. They will know how to look after themselves." The new government does the handsome thing by Napoleon. Not merely is the deserter taken back into the service, but he is promptly raised to the rank of captain. He has, however, no inclination to hasten to his regiment. What does it matter to him that the king of Prussia is on the Moselle? What does he care about the wars of France? "I am a Corsican! Back to the island!"

IX

Is it possible! Has not the fresh wind from the sea, has not even the pure breeze from the mountains, been able to dispel that partisan spirit into which, everywhere, the struggle of ideas tends to degenerate? Calumny, corruption, anarchy: these are the forms which the strife has assumed in the island. Saliceti, the Corsican delegate to the Convention in Paris, is Paoli's mortal enemy, and is therefore friendly to the Buonapartes now that they have turned against Paoli. The Jacobin Club in Ajaccio is divided, but revolutionary feeling is in the ascendant; and Paoli, the only honest man in the island, is stigmatised as a traitor because he is a moderate.

Who holds the reins of power? Everyone and no one. Mutual suspicion is ripe, for in Paris the guillotine has been set up, the king has passed by that red road, and no one knows who will be the ruler there tomorrow. In Corsica, all go armed, and not the mountaineers alone; but orders from the coastland break unavailingly against the crags of the interior. Everyone, here, is his own king; everyone, his own avenger. Can there be a better field for this adventurer, who has nothing more to lose? He makes a third attempt to become master of the island.

Brother Joseph, Brother Lucien, and Uncle Fesch, all have adherents, but Napoleon is the first to gather the scattered forces. He has the confidence of the deputy, who needs a skilled artillerist to help him in the next faction fight. For the same reason, the Club is inclined to court his favour. Might it not be a good move to accuse Paoli of treason against France? We know that he has been influenced by his twenty years' enjoyment of British hospitality, and is not in his mind to sell us to England? If Lucien were to go to Marseilles, and whisper the suspicion in the commissary's ears. Saliceti would soon be shouting it in the Convention. A little island like Corsica is a hotbed of intrigue. Since public life is controlled by two or three families, family life becomes merged in public life.

Ere long the Convention sends representatives to Corsica. Officers are appointed and dismissed without Paoli's leave or advice. Buonaparte, now a captain in the French service, regains in the island his position as commander. Before this, his abilities and the affection of his soldiers have enabled him to usurp the command once more, and the official appointment is no more than an endorsement of an accomplished fact. His chances are improving.

Then comes a terrible order from Paris. Paoli is to be arrested. But his opponents have overreached themselves. The hearts of the islanders warm towards the veteran hero. All rally to his support, and he defies the order.

Young Buonaparte is at a loss. Always he has had his ear at the heart of the people, not in the spirit of a lover, but in the investigatory mood of a physician. He tries to gain time, seeks a middle course, publicly proclaims himself on the side of the maligned Paoli; but also explains that he is a supporter of the sagacious Convention. Yet the Convention mistrusts this supporter, and now issues a warrant for his arrest also. Paoli likewise suspects him of wanting to have a foot in both camps. In a Paolist manifesto we read: "Since the brothers Buonaparte have supported the slander, and have sided with the commission, it would be beneath the dignity of the Corsican nation to have anything more to do with them. Enough to abandon them to remorse and public execration."

The enemies of the family raided the Buonaparte mansion, looted the place, and would have made short work of the inmates had not these already taken refuge with the commission.

Perhaps Buonaparte had wanted events to take this course. He had given the authorities in Paris plain proof that he was a staunch revolutionist. Certainly, they were now ready to show their trust in him. He, who a year before had led the Corsican volunteers against the French governmental artillery, was now made commander of this same artillery against the Corsican volunteers. Big guns! True, the other occupy the best positions, but at length he has power, ample power, with orders to protect the guillotined). The mother is in the early forties. The three children with her are earning bread for the family as best they can; the two youngest are still in Corsica, cared for by relatives. Since the Buonapartes are "persecuted patriots," they receive a part of their rations from the commandant. Letizia, who is proud as ever, makes no complaints.

Soon Napoleon, who is travelling, has the chance of putting some lucrative opportunities in his brother's way, affairs connected with the supply of munitions of war. Maternal Uncle Fesch lays aside the priestly habit and becomes a man of business, in the silk trade. Then Joseph, who is of fashionable exterior, resembling his father in appearance, and, as the eldest, following the father's example in styling himself Count Buonaparte,–wins the hand of one of the two heiresses of a Marseilles silk merchant. Napoleon entertains thoughts of marrying his sister-in-law Desiree, the late silk merchant's other daughter.

He is on the move throughout this summer; now at Nice, with his regiment; now on the Rhone; now at Toulon. All the time, his soldier's eyes are on the look-out; his artillerist's brain is noting the actual and the potential fortifications along this strip of coast. Soon he will make good use of the knowledge now acquired. Meanwhile he writes political dialogues. One of them, in conversation form, appears as a pamphlet, printed at the public expense.

In this conversation, the manufacturer is of a familiar type. The well-to-do folk of Toulon, like their brethren in Marseilles, are, in fact, under Robespierre's rule, afraid of losing their heads or even their property. Concern for their money-bags tends to make them ever more solicitous for the welfare of the sometime royal house, now on exile. At length, in the hope of saving their capital, they call the enemies of France to their aid, handing over the remnants of the navy to the English, who in return promise them protection.

This is a fearful blow for the young republic. On all fronts, France is at grips with the forces of reaction. Belgium has been lost; the Spaniards are advancing over the mountains; in Vendée, the Bourbon cause is gaining ground. Then comes the crowning disaster of Toulon. The republic calls up its last man for active service, enlists women, transforms the whole of France into an armed camp. Experts are doubly welcome.

Before Toulon, preparations are being made to drive out the English. As to how this is to be done, the Convention leaves that to the commander of the forces, originally a painter of pictures, in whom revolutionary enthusiasm is to make up for the lack of technical knowledge of the art of war.

Then it came to pass that young Captain Buonaparte, returning from Avignon whither he had been sent for a consignment of gunpowder, paid a visit to his fellow-countryman Saliceti, who introduced the young artillerist to the painter-general. After dinner, the dilettantes went for a stroll, and happened upon a 24-pounder, several miles from the sea. They began to boast of all that the gun would do. The expert assured them that, in its present position, it would be useless. He fired four shots to show them that the sea was quite out of range. Dumbfounded, they kept Buonaparte at Toulon, and set him to work.

"At last, one end of the rope is in my hands. Grip and hold fast!", thinks the lonely man with the strong will. With amazing activity, our captain has heavy guns brought from all possible places along the coast. In six weeks, he has more than a hundred pieces of ordnance at his disposal.

Now he will give a display of his talents as military commander. What is his plan? He will mount batteries on the tongue of land which divides the bay into twin harbours, and will thus cut off the hostile fleet from access to the sea. The British commander will not stay to be shot at in a mousehole with no outlet. He will set light to the arsenal and withdraw his forces from the town.

"Fantastical nonsense!", say the amateurs, mockingly. But Buonaparte, who has friends in the Convention, has a complaint lodged there against his chief. He also sends to Paris his scheme for the bombardment of Toulon, many pages of manuscript, containing, in addition, counsel of a more general nature: "Our fire must always be concentrated. If we can breach the wall, the balance will incline to our side, resistance will be fruitless, the place will be won. To live, we must divide; to strike, we must unite. Victory is impossible without unity of command. Time is everything!" Thus does a captain of twenty-four write to the central authorities

He has a powerful ally in Paris, the younger Robespierre, who has the reputation of a man of talent, and is not completely overshadowed by his all-powerful brother. "Should you ever need a man of iron for street fighting," said Joseph Robespierre to Maximilian, "a young man, a new man—then it must be this Buonaparte." Indeed, the Corsican adventurer had already been asked whether he would become military guardian of the terrorists, but considerations of caution had led him to decline. Now his plan was approved, and the painter-general was recalled. Who would replace him?

Buonaparte gnashes his teeth. Another dilettante! The new general is a medical man. He spends his time nosing out conspiracies hatched by the nobility—and meanwhile the enemy occupies the precious tongue of land. From Paris there had come State carriages filled with "men of genius," clad in brilliant uniforms, and resolved to end the siege of Toulon, to take the place out of hand. Buonaparte led them to an unprotected battery. When the enemy opened fire, and they looked round vainly for cover, their guide said gravely: "We do without cover, nowadays; we have patriotism instead." This young man with blue-grey eyes is more interested in actions than in intentions. Further complaints, and a new change in command. This time the chief is a tried warrior, who is prompt to appoint Napoleon battalion commander, and to adopt the young artillerist's plan for driving the enemy from the tongue of land.

When, finally, Toulon is stormed (still in accordance with Buonaparte's designs), his horse is shot under him; and he is wounded in the calf by an English lance—this being his first and almost his last wound. Moreover, it is his first victory, although he is not the official commander; and it is a victory over England. The enemy retreats to the ships, fires the arsenal, and withdraws, all in one night, just as Napoleon had foretold.

Conflagration and death, battle and the terrors of a naval port in which thousands of treasonable burghers are trying to escape the avengers; amid all the fierce passions of this December night, through the reek and the cries, across heaps of corpses, and to the accompaniment of the agonised curses of drowning civilians and the exultant shouts of looting soldiers, a new star rises in the firmament—Napoleon's fame.

XI

The popular festival held in Paris to celebrate the liberation of Toulon and fresh victories on the northern and eastern fronts, spreads Napoleon's name among the masses. He is raised to the rank of brigadier general, and his chief, sending in a report in which the subordinate is given due credit as the originator of the plan of siege, adds (betwixt fear and admiration) the amazing sentence: "Even though the Convention were to slight him, he would still force his way to the front." But five other young officers are likewise mentioned in dispatches, and when for the first time Napoleon sees his own name in the "Moniteur" there can be no doubt that he is vexed at being merely one among so many. How hard it is to climb!

Already, however, there are some young fellows who have noted the rising of the new star. Marmont and Junot, unknown officers, want to join their fortunes to his. He appoints them his adjutants; Brother Louis, too, now sixteen years of age. He has a group!

Big guns! The Convention commissions him to fortify the whole stretch of coast from Toulon to Nice. Is not Genoa, Corsica's ancient enemy, farther along the coast? He who takes Genoa has the island in his hands. Is not Genoa full of diplomats and agents? This is the place for weather-breeding among the neutrals; here, anyone with sharp eyes and keen ears can learn a great deal, and keep his information to himself. He gets himself appointed people's commissary, which gives him precedence over the chiefs in Genoa.

Ostensibly the appointment is made that he may help in the settlement of frontier questions.

In reality, this is the first step of Buonaparte the diplomatist. He intrigues with agents of various kinds, while taking note whether the representatives of France in that part of the world are genuinely revolutionary or only making a pretence of revolutionary fervour. At the same time, he keeps his eyes open to see where the cannons are. He comes back to Nice to write his report, and, without warning, he is arrested.

For, meanwhile, Robespierre had fallen, and had perished by the guillotine. There is a general movement of repudiation. Everyone wishes to make out that only under compulsion did he hold converse with the tyrant. Those who wish to prove themselves guiltless, look round for victims. The best victims will be those who are not in Paris to make a fight for it. Quick, quick, lest we should be suspected of having belonged to Robespierre's faction! General Buonaparte! He has just been on a secret mission to hostile Genoa. Lay the traitor by the heels! He was colloguing with Robespierre to bring about the destruction of our southern army. Hale him to Paris for trial!

Napoleon is in Fort Carrée near Nice. All his papers have been seized. It is his birthday. "Today I am twenty-five" he thinks, as he glances seaward through the grating. If he could lean out of the window, he would catch a glimpse of Corsica. How many attempts he has made there, only to be defeated! Was the destiny of a young aspiring soul ever before built upon such a series of catastrophes? What has Plutarch to say on this matter? Cashiered, banished, outlawed—as far as Corsica is concerned. Now, after all his plans, he is a prisoner of France. Next week, perhaps, he will be standing in the barrack yard, with his back against the wall, awaiting a score of bullets. What is to be done?

His faithful followers advise him to flee. He answers in an impassioned tone such as we rarely encounter in the sixty thousand of Napoleon's letters. He thanks them for their friendly counsel, but says: "Men may treat me unjustly; no matter, so long as I am innocent. My conscience is the tribunal before which I judge my own conduct, and my conscience is untroubled. Do nothing, for you would only compromise me." The one genuine phrase in this letter wherein he poses as a martyr, is the last. To Junot, the enthusiastic admirer, he speaks of motives which Junot, will understand. In reality, since he knows that there is not a lot of evidence of complicity with Robespierre, he does not wish to compromise himself. Flight would be an admission of guilt.

Writing from prison to an influential diplomat, he says: "I am somewhat affected by the tragical death of the younger Robespierre, for I loved the man and believed him genuine. Nevertheless, had he been my own father I would have stabbed him had he wished to become a tyrant." Is not that spoken like a true Roman? With even more circumspection, he writes to the Convention: "Although innocent of the charge, I shall never make any complaint against the committee, whatever it may decide.... But now hear me! Strike off my chains, and restore to me the respect of patriots! An hour afterwards, if the wicked clamour for my corpse, I shall be ready. I hold my life at little account, for I have risked it in the trenches too often. Nothing but the thought that I can serve my country enable me to endure my burdens cheerfully."

A week later, he is free. Saliceti, his fellow-countryman in the Convention, had been his accuser. Now, when the Corsican deputy has got over his first fright and feels that his own neck is safe, he pledged his word that Buonaparte is innocent. But at the close of his statement, he adds a phrase which is an unconscious prediction of the young officer's triumphs: "Besides, we need him in the army."

XII

How he is shunned! Powerful friends, to whom he sends letter after letter, long epistles, make no answer. He writes beseechingly for little things, such as "a good surveying outfit for the army," when he wishes to force an influential comrade to reply. All at once comes a signal from the island. Old Paoli has summoned the English to his aid. Corsica must be saved for France!

Back to Paris, in order to fan the flames. The expedition is actually decided on, and he eagerly hopes to secure the command. In a fortnight the fleet is back at Toulon, having sustained a reverse. Fresh disappointment! Why did they not put him in charge? Had he not conquered Toulon, fortified the coast—all with an eye towards the campaign against Corsica?

Reaction is in full swing. Napoleon is suspect. The authorities offer him high command in Vendée, for this will separate him from his adherents. At the same time he is transferred to the infantry, as a "supernumerary." How mortifying to a highly skilled artillerist!

The pale young man grew paler than ever, for he had made up his mind to refuse. He expostulated with the People's Commissary for War, who, in reply, twitted him with his youth. Napoleon looked the commissary, who knew little of active service, straight in the eyes, and said: "A man matures quickly on the battlefield, and it is from the battlefield that I come." Refusal to obey orders; expectation of dire consequences; just as it had been three years before.

What had I better do? Report sick? Apply for leave? The out-of-work general turns the possibilities over in his mind. Better stay where I am. Paris is the world's navel. True, Marmont and Junot, who have joined him without leave, are also penniless. What's Bourrienne doing? Speculating? Well, I can try that too, but assignats are falling. How badly you staged the last affair. Did you think you could make a coup d'état without cannon? But to Saliceti, who in his turn has had serious charges brought against him, and is being sheltered by a fellow-countrywoman, he writes: "You see, I might have paid you back in your own coin.... Who has played the better part, you or I? I might have taken vengeance on you, but have not done so.... Go in peace, to seek a refuge where you can, and meditate upon your country to better advantage. My lips will always be sealed about you. Take counsel with yourself, appreciate my motives ... they are noble and magnanimous."

During these summer weeks, the flood of life is obscurely murmuring, is heavily pulsing against the shores. He is profoundly moved by *Ossian*, the book of melancholy passion; and he is stirred by the tragical end of plays he witnesses, hastening from the theatre that his mood may not be jarred by the subsequent farce. "How preposterous, in this new opera, to give a happy ending to *Paul and Virginie* by having the girl rescued!" - "But what is happiness?", asks the lady to whom he says this.

"Happiness?", answers Buonaparte. "The highest possible development of my talents."

Just now they are lying fallow, that is what troubles him. He is a prey to increasing dejection and dumb rancour. When a comedy is being played (the wife of one of his friends reports this), every one else is laughing, but Buonaparte sits there in frozen silence. Sometimes he vanishes, to reappear with gloomy aspect at the other side of the stalls. Often enough his lips are twisted in an unsuccessful attempt to smile. He is an irresistible raconteur of campaign stories, but his laughter on these occasions is rough. He is often to be seen wandering through the streets, short in the leg, thin, sallow, sickly, irritable of mien, "awkward, hesitant, wearing an old round hat, from beneath which two badly powdered 'dog's ears' project, scurf upon his collar, his ungloved hands are long and lean and dark, ill-fitting boots."

He now plans a book traffic with foreign lands; but his first attempt, with a consignment to Basle, miscarries.

Sometimes he visits drawing rooms, for, as he writes to his brother, everyone here seeks distraction.... There are women all over the place, at the theatre, in the Bois, at the Library. The prettiest of girls are to be found in the studies of the learned. Indeed, it is right that women should rule here, for the men are infatuated, living only through and for women.

When Buonaparte is in the salon of Barras, the tribune (who outdoes himself in splendour and extravagance, so that all Paris talks; who can never have enough women round him), when he stands there among women famous for their beauty like Tallien and Récamier, he, who is small and gloomy and angular, can only make an impression by cleverness and caprice. Even then he seems a freak.

Always the solitary, he only "let himself go" in his long letters to his brothers. He is educating Louis, and writes: "The lad is a good soldier. What especially pleases me is that he combines so many excellent qualities: ardour, spirit, health, talent, trustworthiness, good nature.... He will certainly be the best of us four. Of course, none of us have enjoyed his advantages in the matter of education." He is thinking of having Jerome, the youngest, sent to Paris. He is at odds with Lucien. This talented brother is his rival. Indeed, Lucien vies with Napoleon in his knowledge of men, was the first to understand Napoleon, did so already when he was seventeen while his brother was twenty-three. In Napoleon," wrote young Lucien to Joseph, "I detect an ambition which is not wholly selfish, but is greater than his love for the public welfare. In a free State he would certainly be a dangerous man. He seems to me inclined to become a despot. I think he would become one, were he king. At any rate, his name would be a terror to posterity and to sensitive patriots." In Lucien's mouth, such grandiose vaticination is no mere playing with words. His own ambition is so intense that in this age and country he regards a development of the kind as quite possible for his brother, and he is mortified at the prospect that Napoleon is likely to outshine him.

For the nonce, Napoleon is in low spirits. He envies Joseph, whom money and happiness have made independent. He offers Joseph support in the way of introduction and papers; advises him to use the depreciated currency for the economical purchase of an estate. Yet we find him already writing to his elder brother, apropos of a letter on political questions: "Your letter was too dry; you must learn to write better than that."

A home! He wants a home of his own like Joseph. More eagerly in each successive letter he urges Joseph to make sure for him of the wealthy sister-in-law, with whom he has been in affectionate correspondence for more than a year. When she is slow to make up her mind, he presses for a decision. His brother and one of his intimate friends have married well; comrades of his against the Russians and the Austrians. In fancy, he already sees himself conversing with the sultan, beyond reach of the eyes of these everlasting republicans, in an obscure and closed country into which the doctrine of liberty has never made its way–a land where a man can still do whatever he pleases. Twelve days after his entry into the ministry, he asks to be transferred to Turkey.

The application is refused. Powerful opponents are already beginning to be afraid of this man. They want to get him out of the War Officer to send him to the front. His protest takes a new tone. As if he were foreseeing all the successes that are still hidden in his own heart, he begins to dictate. General Buonaparte, who commands the artillery under the most critical circumstances and has contributed to the greatest successes, expects from the justice of the members of the Committee that they shall reinstate him in his functions, and shall spare him the distress of seeing his position usurped by men who have always kept themselves in the background,... but who now press forward to snatch the fruits of victories whose dangers they well knew how to avoid."

In the third person, in the iron style of the historian Roman.

It avails nothing. Once more insubordinate officer's name in struck from the lists, and for a second time he has to yield. But he feels that his hour draws nigh; nothing, now, can seriously shake his position. A fresh change of government is at hand. Announcing to his brother the impending transformation, he says that he himself is in the good graces of all the party leaders who will have military posts at their disposal. "The prospect is rosy. Even were it otherwise, a man must live in the present. He who has courage, despises the future."

Because he despises it, it serves him. Henceforward men will serve him for the same reason.

A fortnight after this letter had been written, a conflict broke out between the government and the moderates, who were backed by the royalists. Once more, there was fighting on the boulevards, as there had been three years earlier. The National Guard is four times as strong as the governmental forces. Either from caution or from cowardice, the General of the Convention parleys with the leaders of the Guard. He is declared a traitor, and placed under arrest. The Convention meets in a panic. It is defenceless, intimidated by the left-wing and right-wing revolutionaries, who, for various reasons, have joined forces.

In the evening, Buonaparte hastens to the Convention, for a successor to the arrested general is needed, and he learns that the name of one of his rivals has been proposed. The heart of the silent onlooker beats furiously. Will his name now be mentioned? If he is asked to take command, shall he accept a task which he had refused in the days when Robespierre was supreme? Does not every one who leads soldiers against the people make himself hated, precisely because of his success? "Appoint Buonaparte!" Yes, his name has come up. "I turned the matter over in my mind for nearly half an hour." Such a mission will not bring renown, but it will bring power. He presents himself before the committee. It is past midnight the tumult is expected to begin early next morning; everything must be ready within a few hours.

In this situation, he demands that he shall be absolutely free from civilian supervision. This seems a monstrous request to make of the revolution, one of whose new principles it is to lay especial stress upon supervision of the dreaded military arm. "If you appoint me, I shall be responsible, and must have a free hand. To-day, it was the fault of the people's commissaries that the general found himself in so precarious a position. Do you expect that the people will give us permission to open fire upon the people?" The only man he will share the command with is Barras, who is the most powerful among the leaders, but is in his hands. The minutes are passing. There is no choice—Buonaparte was entrusted with the defence of the list of general officers.

For seven years the Parisian populace, when roused to action, has had to encounter nothing more than extemporised opposition. That is why the revolution has always made headway. Buonaparte is the first to prepare for the struggle. In one night, he transforms the Convention into a fortress. Even the alarmed deputies are supplied with weapons. They are still more frightened when they hear talk of cannon.

A young cavalry officer, Murat by name, undertakes to bring forty big guns from the suburbs. Murat thus opens a great career on the same day as his chief. Out in the streets he finds the masses, who are likewise on the prowl for artillery. Buonaparte cannot protect the Convention without ordnance. There are hours of tension, during which he must tranquilly devote himself to the disposition of his slender forces. At length, at five in the morning, he hears the rattling wheels of his old friends the big guns. Murat's men were mounted, and they have won the prize. Forward! Within two hours, everything must be ready.

In well-armed companies, the crowd advances threateningly. The lawyers in the Convention are shaking in their shoes. Speech after speech is made from the tribune, urging a parley, advocating the withdrawal of the troops. In the day light, the situation is so menacing that the civilians utterly lose heart. They weaken; towards noon, some of the troops want to fraternise with the people. Night is falling. Now or never! Is the commander to allow the mob to triumph? In like circumstances, he had laughed at the weakness of King Louis. Shall he himself play the weakling, when he is in command of the guns?

It is probable that Buonaparte ordered the firing of the first shot, or perhaps extorted the order from Barras, although in his report, and subsequently, he declared that his opponents had this "crime against the French people" on their consciences. Anyhow, the firing begins. The big guns win the day; blood besprinkles the pavements; the crowd scatters; in two hours the streets are clear. That night, Napoleon writes to his brother: "At length it is over; my first wish is to send you the Tuileries. We killed a lot of them, our own casualties being thirty killed and sixty wounded. We have disarmed the companies of the National Guard, and everything is quiet. As usual, I have escaped without a scratch. Brigadier General Buonaparte. Postscript. Luck is on my side. My compliments to Desirée and Julie."

This is Napoleon's first bulletin of victory. The enemy are Frenchmen; the battlefield is Paris; the offenders are revolutionists; most of the fatalities are on the opposing side; the signature, help you, shall spare no effort which can contribute to your happiness." From brother, he has become protector, head of the family.

During these weeks, when he is tasting the joys of fulfilment, he becomes involved in the only passion of his life.

Desirée has missed her chance. Only a few weeks before, writing from the office of the general staff, he had implored Joseph to interven on his behalf, to demand a prompt answer. "I am burning with desire to have a home of my own." At the same time, in several of his letters, we find more frequent references to charming women, allusions which betray a happy prospect of success. He has come to know la femme de trente ans, in her power and her beauty. He has made advances to two such women, in quick succession: once of them a Corsican of noble birth, a friend of his mother's; the other, a pretty cocotte, Chenier's mistress. Both of them are considerable older than he, and neither of them favours his suit. But the atmosphere surrounding these practitioners of the art of love, the electric atmosphere of the new salon, has exercised its influence on him: "A kiss for the two ladies: for the first, on the lips; for the second, on the cheek." Since he has hitherto known almost nothing of women, his lonely heart is susceptible.

Immediately after his appointment, the new generalissimo issues a decree against bearing arms. A search is made, and all weapons in civilian hands are confiscated. Now a boy of twelve, with engaging manners, turns up at the general's office with a plea for the return of his dead father's sword, which has been taken away from his mother. Napoleon conceded the point and shortly afterwards the mother comes to thank him. What an elegant woman—wayward, gracious, captivating. Thirty or more; who can say? Not so much beautiful, as enthralling; slender; distinguished, but with a slightly foreign air; the dark skin of the Creole, for she was born in Martinique, though brought up in Paris; and during the days of the Terror she has learned to conquer by he charms.

When the general pays her a visit at the little house in an out-of-the-way suburb, his eyes, sharpened by his own experience of poverty, detect evidence of an endeavour to put a good face upon poor circumstances. This does not trouble him. An army officer, who now, at the age of twenty-seven, can for the first time dispose of means which enable him to live as he pleases, he prizes money, but he does not prize rich people. Just as in the life of affairs, men can only move him by their capacity, by what they can do, so women can only please him by their capacity—by their personal appearance, their nature, and what they can make of these.

Josephine makes a great deal, as she needs to do. From Martinique, her tropical home, she was able to save nothing when she lost her husband, Vicomte de Beauharnais. For years she was separated from him, but was reunited with him after her return to Paris from a prolonged visit to her native island. During the Terror, he was executed as a royalist; and she spent three terrible months in gaol to be liberated after Robespierre's fall on the very day when Buonaparte was imprisoned. Friends came to her assistance in her difficulties; but her position and that of her two lovely young children, Horiense and Eugene, was precarious.

In this genteel poverty, its is expedient for her to make the best use of her charms. In any case, she is a born coquette, and is urged towards amorous adventures by the spur of her own love of pleasure. At this time, she is Barras' mistress, her handsome friend Tallien having taken up with a wealthy banker, handing over the man of might to Josephine. However, the two women hold Barras in joint control. The Committee of Public Safety supplies them with horses and carriages. But Beauharnais, being of gentle birth, knows how to give attractive dinner parties, and associates with members of both factions, although the counts and marquises who frequent her house leave their wives at home. She has become an adventure of the revolution.

Well, what about Buonaparte himself? Any change in the political situation may cost him his position. What more is he, as yet, than an adventurer of the revolution? If Murat had failed to shark up those guns the other night, the general would have been shot. Life is insecure, both for him and for Josephine.

What can be easier than to befool this misanthropic and misogynistic man in whose dumb soul the schoolmaster at Brienne had long ago discovered the hidden volcano? For the first time in his life he is in the toils of a woman, an expert in love; he is consumed by his passion for the Creole beauty. To Josephine, it seems a stroke of luck, and in cold blood she decides on marriage.

"You have seen General Buonaparte at my house. He is to become a father to my orphaned children, a husband to my widowed self.... I admire the General's courage, and I wonder how much he knows.... But, I must confess, I am alarmed at the energy which animates all his doings. In his questing glance there is something inexplicable, which intimidates even our Directors. What ought to please me most, the passionate ardour he displays, is the very thing which makes me hesitate. Now that I am past my first youth, can I hope that I shall be able to keep alive in him an affection so stormy, that it borders on madness?"

This lady of refinement does not dully understand what threatens her, and yet in the depths of her soul she shudders at the foreboding that she is to become the play of elemental force. For, if this man who covets all or nothing and cannot rest until he has all, this man who has never given himself up to any one person or any one thing because it has been his unceasing wish to gain everyone and everything, if Napoleon now gives himself for the first and only woman whom he clasps in his arms, first time in his life, he will shake his whole being, and will fetter it to the personality of the woman whom he clasps in his arms.

"I am waiting for you; I am wholly filled with you: your picture and the intoxicating evening leave my senses no peace. Sweet, incomparable Josephine, what have you done to my heart? Are you angry with me? Do you look sad? Are you ill at ease?.... But I find calm when I give myself up to my passion, that on your lips, at your heart, I may fan the flames which burn me. How plain it was to me last night that your picture can never replace the real you. At noon you will start; in three hours I shall see you; till then, mio dolce amor, a thousand kisses! But you must not give me kisses, for they burn my blood!"

He does not tell her his plans, and yet he tells her something more. "These Directors fancy that I need their protection. They will consider themselves happy, some day, to secure mine. I shall make my way with the sword."—"What do you think," writes Josephine, "of this faith in success? Can such self-confidence be based on anything else than immeasurable conceit? A brigadier general is to protect the heads of the government! I don't know what to make of it; and yet, often enough, this ludicrous self-assurance makes me believe that anything is possible which the strange man wants to achieve."

We feel as if we were standing in front of the iron door which guards a glowing human heart, and looking through the keyhole into the fiery furnace of a soul.

But this woman, whom he possesses, why does he take her to wife? That he may possess her for himself alone? His egotism is against, it, and, besides, he would be deluding himself. To gain advantages? In respect of money, and in respect influence with the powerful, she can offer him nothing that he does not already enjoy. Of course she might prove useful to him; he is certainly flattered that she is of noble birth; and beyond doubt he has taken into consideration the fact that if she, who had a place in the days of the old regime, becomes his wife this will put an end to the whispers that he is "only a Corsican." Yet it is as a Corsican, with the family feeling of an Italian (a feeling that has come down to him through the generations, and masters even him), that he desires marriage with a woman of birth. Finally, is it not obvious that this man who is so utterly self-centred must passionately long for a perpetuation of his own ego?

The one thing in the world which Napoleon cannot make without another's aid is an heir, and this heir must be made out of good materials. He is no man of the people. He has come into being amid the struggles of old families, and beneath a coat-of-arms bearing two stars which he now wishes to fuse into one. If he has helped to break down the prejudices against the masses, he has been moved along this course by delight in the elemental energy of action, and never by humanist feelings. Why should he wish to mix his blood with that of the people? When he marries the woman who long ere this has granted him all, he does so because, in both branches of her ancestry, she is the offspring of a long line of noble forebears. It is her birth, in addition to her charms, which makes her a welcome figure in a drawing-room, despite her reputation and her position. Since the Thirteenth Vendémiaire, Barras, the most powerful of the Directors, has regarded Buonaparte as his main prop—and he wishes to bind the general to his service by handing over Josephine. In this realm of erotic freedoms, a man who should wish, of a sudden, to insist on points of honour would simply make himself ridiculous. There are no knights and ladies now, but only citizens and citizenesses, who pair and separate as they please.

Barras has long since decided that Napoleon shall command the Army of Italy; and when Josephine, womanlike, is unable to make up her mind, Barras gives her a definite pledge to this effect. There are good reasons, too, why he should send the dangerous man to the most difficult front. Napoleon's great plan, the one which has procured him his position on the general staff, is now sent to Nice, and comes back with annotations by the commander-in-chief there. The man who has drafted the plan, says that worthy, must have been a lunatic. He had better come and try his own hand at the job. That is exactly what the Directory has been angling for. The writer of the criticism is recalled, and the "lunatic" is sent to take his place.

The position is assured; the prudent Josephine hesitates no longer. A legal friend has to certify that no birth certificate is now obtainable from the blockaded island in the West Indies, and that the authorities must therefore take the lady's word for the statement that she is twenty-eight. Since this knocks five years off her age, the bridegroom is gallant enough to add a year to his own. Thus the marriage begins with a twofold falsification of dates. A marriage settlement arranging for the division of property is signed, although the vicomtesse owns nothing but debts, and the warrior declares that his only possessions are his clothes, his uniform.

In the wedding ring, the words "To Destiny"! are engraved.

Two days later, he leaves Paris. Eleven crazy love letters are sent to her from eleven halting places. In Nice he joins his army, and takes over a command which will lead him beyond the frontiers of Europe.

It is the season of the equinoctial gales. From a turret he looks across at the enemy coast, and thinks: "This is the place I have always coveted as a starting-point. Behind me lies Paris and her bedchamber, hung with mirrors. That is happiness. It is mine, Over there, across the mountains, in that hostile land, is fame. The goal of my desire."

As he turns away, he catches sight of a familiar line of mountains shimmering in the distant blue. No longer does this hold his attention.

It is his lost homeland. The island.

BOOK TWO

THE TORRENT

So divine an illumination is always linked with youth and productivity; and, in very truth, Napoleon was one of the most productive men that ever lived.

—GOETHE

I

The towering peaks form a white, serrated ridge that thrusts upward into the blue of morning. Gleaming with perpetual snows, dangerous as the adventure he has undertaken, the Alps look down threateningly upon the bay, and mock the teeming crowds of men. Invincibly does nature, in symbolic fashion, here call a halt to the commander; here she has interposed a barrier between the land of his fathers and his new fatherland.

But he, who never trusts in force alone, who always outbid force with prudence, has to good purpose been pondering the old problem. Hannibal crossed the Alps; he, Napoleon, will go round them. If we come to grips with the enemy at the weakest point, where the Apennines press close to the Alps and a slight depression facilitates an entry, we need not wait for the summer. The earlier in the year, the firmer the snows, and the less danger from avalanches. Forward, into the land of my fathers!

Delay will be fatal. Not that the enemy is a danger to him. His foes are asleep in winter quarters: the Austrians in the east of Lombardy; the Sardinians in the west of the Lombard plain; and the numerous petty republics and duchies, the fragments of Italy, are not expecting an attack until the thaw has come. But the French soldiers are hungry. Paris, on the verge of ruin, through depreciation of the currency, can send them nothing but almost valueless assignats; and all of these disappear into the greedy maw of the army contractors. "France would tremble," said one of the generals in his letters home just before Buonaparte's arrival. "could every one know how many are dying here of famine and disease." What will the new commander do if he brings neither money nor bread with him?

"Soldiers, you are half starved and half naked. The Government owes you much, but can do nothing for you. Your patience, your courage, do you honour, but give you no glory, no advantage. I will lead you into the most fertile plains of the world. There you will find flourishing cities, teeming provinces. There you will reap honour, glory, and wealth. Soldiers of the Army of Italy, will you be wanting in courage and firmness?"

A faint cheer from the ranks answered the new commander when, at the first parade, he addressed his men in the foregoing words. But when they were all back in camp, one said to another: "General doesn't look very weatherproof, with his yellow hide. Fine talk, that, about the fertile plains. He'd better let us have some boots first, so that we can march there!" The people of Israel must have grumbled in much the same fashion when Moses spoke of the Promised Land. The new commander encounters nothing but opposition.

Who knows him among the soldiers of this army, which has now been encamped for three years on the crests of the hills? Those of them who remain, that is to say: for a fourth of the men are in hospital; and an equal number have been killed, or taken prisoner, or have deserted! The officers? Will not they, like those captains in Auxonne seven years ago, be inclined to encounter this wonderful young man's orders with passive resistance rather than ready obedience? Look at him as he sits there writing and calculating; his powdered hair is cut in a fringe over his forehead, but lengthens towards the back of the head to hand down over his shoulders; his coat is simple and scantily embroidered; he walks up and down and issues dictatorial orders, this foreigner whose French is still faulty. Not an officer in his staff is well-disposed towards him, except the three or four faithful followers whom he has brought with him. One of these latter tells us: "They looked upon him as a mathematician or a visionary."

What if he be both at once, and for this very reason a man of genius?

At first, he seems to be nothing but a calculator. Consider one of his early letters to the Directors-for he promptly opens an use of overwhelming forces, which he did not possess, and, indeed, could not have used, pressed as he was on both sides. The soldiers are amazed; their general is a man of his word! Literally, in a fortnight, he has fulfilled his promise.

Henceforward, the, men under his command put their trust in Bonaparte. It is as Bonaparte that he begins to sign himself from the outset of the campaign. Since Italy is the enemy, he will have nothing more to do with an Italian name.

Ere long, he will change his name again.

II

Why was he victorious? How can we explain that during the next few weeks he was able to deliver blow after blow? What is the solution of this riddle?

First of all, he owes his success to youth and health. A body that can endure interminable riding without fatigue; the power to sleep at any moment, and to wake whenever he pleases a stomach which can digest anything, and makes no complaint at being put on short commons; eyes that see and arrange everything.

But it is to the revolution that he is indebted for the fact that at the age of twenty-seven, when his splendid powers are in their first vigour, he has risen to a leading place, and can wield unrestricted dictatorship. Only, thanks to the new ideas of equality, in a world which prizes a man for what he does and not for his birth, can anyone become a leader in the prime of youth and after so rough an apprenticeship.

Look at the men who are in the field against him. Archduke Charles, with his delicately shaped and decadent Habsburg nose, how can he, with his education, vie with the Corsican in indifference to hardships, rival Bonaparte in knowledge of men? How can Beaulieu, the Austrian commander, cope with the French general? The former is seventy-two; the latter, twenty-seven. General Colli suffers from gout, and has to be carried throughout the campaign. Alvintzy is in the middle sixties. The King of Sardinia is an old man. What can the excellent General Wurmser, who is deaf, and a slow, elderly gentleman, cautious in his movements, do against a Commander who thinks nothing of changing his headquarters everyday, who surrounds himself with young men, and who takes "Time is everything." For his motto?

The oldest man in Napoleon's circle is the faithful Berthier, now forty-two, whom the new commander has taken over from his predecessor because Berthier has a good knowledge of the country. For two decades he is to be Bonaparte's slavishly devoted chief of general staff. Next to be mentioned comes Massena, a man of ardent temperament, who had been a cabin boy and a vagrant, and had served fourteen years under the Bourbons without rising to the rank of sergeant major; now, within a few weeks, he was to become a general. Augereau, too, a deserter from three armies, boaster, adventurer, and great thief. Such were the men drawn from the dregs of society out of whom their commander, the youngest of them all, was soon to make heroes and generalissimos, and subsequently princes and dukes.

In every dispatch, he recommends for promotion those, and only those, who have displayed courage. Thus, after three battles, a grenadier rises to the rank of colonel, and will climb yet higher. On the other hand, many of the generals who he has taken over with his command are dismissed with blunt censure: "Good enough for office work, knows nothing of war." His subordinates do not necessarily incur his displeasure because they are beaten: "The fortune of war, dear Massena, changes from day to day. Tomorrow, or later, we shall win back what you have just lost." But a division which has done badly is paraded to hear a rating. He says that he will have a mocking inscription worked upon its colours. Then the soldiers cry to him from the ranks: "Tomorrow we will lead the van." Next day, he has a thousand more enthusiasts among the troops. When they are victorious, in the orders of the day be calls them comrades and friends. Thus does he lead the sons of the people.

For it is a people's army that he is leading; that is the second great factor of his success. This, too, he owes to the for "Italia unità." The revolt, though still in chains, was rattling its chains outside the king's palace doors. The malcontents were ready to welcome the invading army, and to believe in its mission.

The commander, a man of Italian blood, bearing an Italian name, and speaking Italian as his mother tongue, was not for them a French warrior. He was the herald of liberty and equality, and the two great words headed all his letters. How terrible would be the disillusionment, should the invader prove, after all, a foreign oppressor! The commander is well aware how much turns upon this. Will he be able to keep his famished army within bounds? Can he make his soldiers behave as well as if they were fresh from a well-provisioned garrison town?

"Looting is on the wane," he writes home. "The thirst of an army which lacked everything has been quenched. There is an excuse for the poor devils. They have spent three years in the marches of the Alps. and now I have led them into the Promised Land! A famished soldier perpetrates excesses which make one ashamed of being a man.... I intend to restore order, for I will not remain in command of a robber band.... Tomorrow I am going to have several privates and a corporal shot, for having looted the plate from a church. Discipline will be re-established within a day or two. Italy has been amazed at the valour of our soldiers, and shall be amazed at their good behaviour. There have been terrible moments; things have happened which have made me shudder. Thank God, the retreating enemy behaved even worse!"

He puts his men on their honour. "Swear to me"–thus runs one of his early manifestoes- "to spare the peoples you are liberating; otherwise you will be the scourges of the people! Your victories, your courage, the blood of our fallen brothers, will be lost; honour and glory, too! I and my generals would blush at leading an undisciplined army!" Hard to carry out, despite his adjurations. Throughout the campaign, he is hampered by this, problem of looting. Again and again he issues orders to his generals telling them they are to shoot any one who fails to hand over his plunder within twenty-four hours, even if the stolen goods be horses and mules.

There are revolts and counter-attacks. Priests and nobles, agents of the princes, incite a town to resist. He is pitiless in his shootings, ruthless in his reprisals, whenever, in the conquered territory, anyone raises a hand against the new master. But this becomes increasingly rare, for in the towns he is skilful in enlisting the civil sense on the side of a new order which assumes imposing lineaments. He understands (and this is an additional factor of success) the Italian temperament; knows how to appeal to the sense of historic veneration: "Peoples of Italy, the army of France comes to break your chains. It is a friend to all the peoples. Have confidence! Your property, your customs, your religion, shall be respected." He goes on to speak to them of Athens, Sparta, classical Rome.

History inspires him. While with rapid strokes he is making history, history gives his spirit wings. In boyhood, he had studied Plutarch; as lieutenant, he had read the history of all times; now; from moment to moment, he turns the knowledge to account. Knowing who has ruled in every part of these territories, understanding how the governments he has overthrown came into being, he has appropriate measures for each area. Time-honoured figures are ever present in his imagination; he wants to resemble them, to outdo them. Thus, whatever he does is conceived in a historic setting; and he compels his army, the country with which he is dealing, and, soon, Europe as a whole, to breathe the same atmosphere. These first victories, which in reality nothing more than big skirmishes, are by the magic of his words transformed into battles, and the battles are magnified into history. In this way, half of what he achieves is achieved by the power of words. To the lands he is freeing, to his soldiers, he invariably suggests that they have done the whole thing themselves. Read his proclamation to the army in Milan.

"Soldiers, like a torrent you have rushed down from the heights of the Apennines.... Milan is yours.... We are the friends of all the peoples; but, above all, we are the friends of the offspring of Brutus and Scipio and the other great men who are our models. To re-establish the Capitol, to set up there the status of the heroes, to awaken the Roman people which for centuries has been paralysed by servitude—that is the fruit of your victories, that will amaze posterity. It is your title to immortal fame that you have given a new visage to the most beautiful land in Europe.... Then you will return to your homes, and your neighbours will point you out to one another, saying: "He was with the army in Italy!"

Did a commander ever before make such alluring appeals to soldiers, and peoples, to friends and foes? Who understood so well as Napoleon how to influence people through their imaginations instead of through a sense of obedience? At Arcola he shouts to his men: "Are you cowards, or are you the victors of Lodi?" In a month or two, he will be urging them onward by reminding them that they are the victors of Arcola. "We have crossed the Po, and have opened the second campaign," he writes to the Directors. All his reports to Paris are penned with consummate art. What he writes is the truth, but it is so skilfully adorned that it develops a life of its own as soon as the government communicates it to the press, and when from France it makes its way into foreign lands.

With the pen, Bonaparte rounds off the victories he has won with the sword.

III

"I have received your peace treaty with Sardinia. The army has approved it."

The Directors quake as they read the words. The arrival of this dispatch cancels the joy they had felt at the coming of so many captured colours. When, before, had a general in the field dared to write in such a fashion to his government? "For this letter, the young hero ought to be stood up before a firing squad, cry his opponents. But the fame of his victories, the glory of his conquest of Lombardy", have already secured him so strong a position in the hearts of the people that no one dares attack him. Recently, when the governmental commissary, his fellow-Corsican, Saliceti, came to his camp, Bonaparte ignored the official's authority, and himself signed the truce with Sardinia. These negotiations were the first in which he proved his mettle as diplomatist. When the other side wanted to bargain, he took out his watch, named the hour at which he had decided to attack, and said they had better make up their minds quickly. "I may lose battles," he said, "but no one will ever see me lose minutes either by over-confidence or by sloth." With this truce, he for the first time dispossessed a king. Without asking for instructions, he entered into negotiations with the dukes, with Tuscany. Was he not, before long, to do the same thing with the pope? What was the best way of dealing with this dangerous conqueror?

"We will send him a partner," thought the Directors, with a smile. "Let him share the supreme command with Kellermann, while Saliceti decides upon political issues." Orders to this effect reached him at Lodi, on the day of battle.

That was the first real battle he had won. A colossal bluff and a bold movement enabled him to storm the bridge over the Adda and to defeat the alarmed Austrians. There were to be much greater victories in days to come; but, in history of the man's spiritual development, not one of them was to equal this in importance.

For now, after a battle which decided the first part of his campaigns, having made himself master of a territory opened to him by an hour's struggle on the bridge,—this evening, Bonaparte feels for the first time how obscure plans and brilliant exploits of war, dream are reality, are interconnected. The consciousness of his own powers makes him realise that boundless possibilities lie before him. That was the first time on which a word concerning such aims crossed his lips. To his friend Marmont he said: "I feel that deeds await me of which the present generation has no inkling." Long afterwards, in retrospect, he declared: "That evening, after the Battle of Lodi, I first became aware that I was an exceptional man; from then I date the awakening of an ambition to do the great things which hitherto had existed for me only as the fantasies of a dream."

Such was his mood when the new orders came from Paris, What? The conquest of two or three continents was looming before his imagination—and he was to go halves with Kellermann? He strode up and down the room, pursing his lips, and then he issued his fiat to the government:

"If you put hindrances in my path, if you make my actions dependent upon the commissary's decision,.... you must not expect any more good results from me.... Here it is indispensable that you should have absolute confidence in your commander. If I do not enjoy that confidence, I shall without complaint endeavour to win your approval in some other post. Everyone has his own way of making war. General Kellermann has more experience, and would doubtless do it better; but, together, we should do it badly. I cannot serve the country unless I have your complete and undivided trust. Much courage, I know, is needed to write you this report, for it would be easy to charge me with ambition and pride! But you are responsible for my having to express my feelings.... I cannot serve jointly with a man who regards himself as the best commander in Europe. For the rest, one bad general is better that two good generals. With war, as with governance, it is a question of tact."

The general does not seem inclined to yield up his place to anyone. If the authorities in Paris insist on a divided command, is it not likely that he will march ahead on his own initiative, gain further victories with his unaided talents, then turn back to threaten France, and, as a condottiere, overthrow the government? The Directors think it will be better not to insist; with a smile, a wry one this time, they give way. After his first, noiseless victory over the government, Bonaparte feels he is master. Henceforward he behaves, substantially, as a king who is his own commander-in-chief, but who can only secure reinforcements and other requisites by reiterated adjurations. For months and years, therefore, his dispatches are still written in the tone of a subordinate; of one who does not threaten, but advises. Yet in reality he acts all the time as if he were already in the land of the sultan, towards which his masterful character draws him.

The Paris courier has been sent off. Bonaparte's first "No" is on its way. Another restless night in camp, and then to Milan!

In everything, he imitates the Roman general celebrating a triumph. As of old, the prisoners lead the way, the only difference being that nowadays they are not in chains. They are followed by five hundred cavalrymen. The citizens, who are used to seeing brilliant uniforms, are astonished at the tattered tunics, the sorry screws, the jaded appearance of the riders; and they are still more amazed when they see the thin little man on the inconspicuous white nag, at the head of his weary-looking suite. How grey the whole procession looks in the light of this brilliant spring day. At the gate the venerable archbishop, with a train of counts and dukes, bids him welcome. He dismounts, but does not draw near to the reception committee; he merely listens with forced politeness to the words of greeting. The onlookers are wondering what answer he will make. For a few seconds he keeps his lips tightly pressed together, and then contents himself with a single sentence, to the effect that France wishes the Lombards well. Remounting, he salutes, and rides on.

Leaders and crowd are deeply impressed; no enthusiasm, only astonishment. Not a sign of arrogance about this conqueror; nothing but resolution, and a force of will before which all must bend. Was his conduct deliberately planned to produce such an impression, though never before had he experienced anything of the kind? Was he "play-acting"? If so, all the more remarkable his knowledge of men; all the more plain that he was a master of the ruler's art!

Nevertheless, he is absent-minded today, for he has not all that he wants.

Now, the streets echo to the shouts of the crowd, who cannot restrain their expressions of astonishment as they watch the men who follow the commander—marching in a slack and almost disorderly fashion, clad in scarecrow uniforms patched with many colours. These Frenchmen seem in almost a sorrier case than the prisoners!

The commander is taking his ease in the archbishop's palace. He is having a bath. Hot baths are his one luxury, a luxury that he will continue to indulge in down to the day of his death, taking them hotter and hotter, staying in them longer and longer, as time goes on. Nothing can break him of the habit, for a hot bath is the only thing which really refreshes him, soothes his nerves. In the evening there is a reception. "You will be free, and in a safer position than the French. Milan will be the capital of this new republic, which has a population of five million. You shall have five hundred pieces of ordnance, and the friendship of France. From among you I will choose fifty men, who shall rule the country in the name of France. Adopt our laws, modifying them to suit your own customs.... Be sagacious and united, and all will go well . Such is my will. If Habsburg should again seize Lombardy, I swear to you that I will take up your cause, that I will never desert you. If your land perishes, I shall be no more. Athens and Sparta did not last for ever!"

Never since the days of Plutarch's heroes did a commander talk like this. It was the conqueror's first speech from the throne, and was compounded of all the elements with which, in his speeches and letters, he was to work upon the mind of Europe for twenty years to come. Everything is single and definite; there is so much fixity of purpose that every one wishes to comply. You are vassals, but freed. I am your master, but I will protect you. Five hundred pieces of ordnance and the friendship of France. "Such is my will." Then it is all over.

Through the May night, the wealthy town blazed with fireworks and resounded with music. The young commander-in-chief has moved on to the Palazzo Serbelloni; the banquet is over, and he stands at the window. The triumphal entry of which he dreamed in youth, towards which his virginal fancy strained, has now been accomplished. Does he look forward or back? With what is his mind busied?

"What do you imagine the Parisians are thinking of us?" he asks his adjutant. "Do you expect they are satisfied?" When Marmont makes the conventional reply, Napoleon goes on: "But Paris has seen nothing, so far. The future hides much great victories. The goddess of fortune has not smiled on me that I may scorn her. The more she favours me, the greater shall be my demands. In a few days we shall reach the Adige; then Italy will be at our feet. Perhaps we shall cross the river, and press onward. Our age has produced nothing great. I want to set an example."

IV

A royal couch in the Serbelloni Palace; never has he lain so soft before. But it is far too wide for one! Where is Josephine? What are triumphal entries and victories worth, without her? Fireworks and flags! Why has she not come? Is she really ill? Has she a lover?–He lies awake for hours.

From the very first this man, who inspired respect even in the veterans among the generals, imperilled that respect by his way of showing his wife's picture to all and sundry, and when he was in the middle of a conversation about service matters. "You will come soon, won't you?" So he wrote in one of his almost daily letters. "You must come to me. I want you on my heart, in my arms! Quick! Fly, fly!" He knows her frivolous disposition; that her senses are easily aroused; that she is always ready to give herself up to new impressions, new admirers. But now, now! What can be keeping her? He had expected her to come to Milan. His ambition had been to escape thither from the savagery of the campaign, that in one of the palaces of that city he might give her capricious charms a splendid setting worthy of her and himself.

But there is something which our great calculator has left out of his calculations. By his very feats of arms, he has kept her away from his side. For years in Paris she has been living in the half-world. Now, in this city which she loves, she wishes to shine forth in an assured position, as wife of the great commander whose name is in every newspaper, on everyone's lips. Does the little general really think she married him for love? When the first captured colours are exhibited, she drives out among the people, and, while she is loudly cheered, she thinks to herself how much more gratifying this is than to rough it in foreign towns surrounded by unmannerly soldiers. She seldom writes to him. His own words grow ever more urgent. "Have you a lover, have you taken up with some stripling of nineteen? If so, you have reason to dread Othello's fist!" She laughs, and says to Tallien: "A queer fellow, this Bonaparte!"

Another day, in the middle of a letter to Carnot dealing with urgent affairs, he writes: "I am in despair. My wife won't come here. I am sure she must have a lover, and that is what keeps her in Paris. I loathe women, one and all!" Then comes a letter in which she grasps at an expedient. Since there is no other way of avoiding the dangers and the dirt of camp life, she writes to him that she has hopes....

Thunder and lightning! Have all the spirits of good fortune united to shower blessings on him? Among his successes, that was the only thing he lacked to complete his happiness. For, if destiny is to carry him to the lofty altitudes he foresees, to the heights he has resolved to scale, then his greatest need is to have heirs. But this battle is only planned, not yet won; new dangers are impending. He shudders. Is it true? Is it his child?

"I am sorry!" –the words are penned in his almost illegible handwriting on the commander-in-chief's official stationery. "I have been pestering you with complaints, and you are ill. Love had robbed me of reason. Forgive me, but I think I shall never be reasonable again. My life is an unending dream; gloomy forebodings make it hard for me to breathe; I have lost all hope. Write me ten pages, for nothing else can console me. You are ill, you love me, you are with child, and I never see you. Who takes care of you? Hortense? I love the sweet girl more than ever when I think of her as taking care of you.... Soon you are to have in your arms a child as fascinating as yourself. If I could only spend a whole day with you. You know if I saw a lover with you, I should instantly tear the man to pieces!"

But who is to help her through her time of trouble? There is no friendship in the world, only the ties of blood. "I am in despair," he writes to Joseph under the same date. "My wife is ailing: I do not know whether I am standing on my head or my heels; dreadful forebodings rack my heart. Write to me, I implore you. Since early childhood, we have been bound together by kinship and affection. Do for her what I would so eagerly do for you.... You know how much I love her; know her ardent nature; know that I have never loved so passionately, that Josephine is the first woman whom I have adored. Her condition drives me crazy. But as soon as she is well again, well enough to travel, she must come to me. I must have her in my arms; I love her to distraction, and cannot live without her. If she no longer loves me, there is nothing more for me in the world. Oh, mon ami, do not keep the courier more than six hours in Paris; send him back to me with an answer which will give me new life. Be happy! For myself, nature has doomed me to win none but outward victories!"

On the same day, he dictates, inter alia: Order to Berthier to occupy Alessandria; dispatch to the Directors concerning urgently needed reinforcements; ultimatum to the Genoese Senate anent the murder of soldiers; letter introducing Murat to the same Senate; plan to sell some cannon which are still left on the Riviera; order to Masséna to procure ammunition from the arsenal in Venice; order to Lannes to advance no farther; order to send all suspects to Tortona; order to send a division to Toulon; report to Kellermann that money and troops are on the way.

His letter has an effect. Joseph asks Josephine to come with him to Milan. What pretext can she find for refusing? She sighs, packs her trunks, sheds tears at a farewell festival in the Luxembourg, gets into the carriage. After all, tomorrow is the thirtieth of June, the season is at an end, and she has good company for the journey. Of course Joseph, her vis-à-vis, is a homely fellow, but Junot is a dapper young man; Fortuné, her lap-dog, is a darling, as ever. Then there is Charles, another younger officer whose acquaintance she has recently made, and who has danced attendance on her ever since. Is he on the look-out for a career, or a conquest? What a choice Christian name, Hippolyte! How fine he looks in his chasseur uniform. He tells such amusing stories, has an expert knowledge of the latest shawls and wigs, and his legs are so well turned!

Milan, Bonaparte is away? More battles near Verona? No matter, this is a lovely place! Such a splendid palace; they all flock to pay their respects. But Hippolyte is hors concours; no one can rival the grace with which, sword clanking, he strides up and down the Corso. What a pity one has to be circumspect in one's behaviour under so many prying eyes. But Hippolyte knows his way about, and has found a discreet staircase.

Suddenly there is a stir of excitement. The commander-in-chief is coming from Verona. For two days and two nights, the lava of this volcano overwhelms her.

V

Thrice do the soldiers of Emperor Francis try to relieve Mantua, which Bonaparte is besieging. Mantua is the key position. Old Wurmser, marching down beside Lake Garda with fresh troops, drives back the opposing forces. If Bonaparte is to make front against him, Mantua must be abandoned for a time. Meanwhile, however, the enemy has blocked the line of retreat upon Milan. A terrible reverse, and the French army is in the utmost danger. Bonaparte, hastening from Milan, rides under the hot July sun across the plain, busily inspecting one division of the army after the other, gathering all his strength, for the fate of the whole campaign is at stake. A period of the utmost activity, and of extreme tension.

Since I left you," he writes on one of these evening, "I have been sad. I can only be happy when I am near you. I spend my whole time thinking of your kisses, your tears, your bewitching jealousy. The charm of the incomparable Josephine is perpetually rekindling the flames of my heart and my senses. When shall I be free, at length, free from cares and duties, free to devote all my time to you with nothing in world but to love you.... Since I have known you, I have come to respect you more day by day, which shows how wrong La Bruyere was when he said that love comes suddenly. Everything in nature runs its course, and increases by of despair that he writes to her in the evening, his pen storming over the paper: "I no longer love you, I hate you. You are hateful, stupid, inept. You do not write to me, do not love your husband. What are you doing all day, Madame? What important business makes it impossible for you to write to the man who loves you?.... Who is the fairy prince that claims all your time, so that you cannot write to your husband? Take care, Josephine: some fine night, the door will burst open, and I shall be there! Quite seriously, I am uneasy, my pretty one. Do write me four pages full of sweet words which will warm my heart with joy and happiness. In a few days I hope to clasp you in my arms, and to cover you with a million kisses, hot as the equator."

How his heart flutters, uncertain whether she is still to be trusted, miserable if she be unworthy of trust. There is a crisis in his own soul as well as out there on the battle-field. Responsibility, uncertainty, storm in the heart of this man who has perhaps already been dishonoured in his private life, and tomorrow may be dishonoured as a military commander—the man who still hopes to rule the world. During these days, when a suicide occurs among the troops, he issues an order: "The soldier must conquer the pain and the melancholy of the passions."

Two days after the date of the letter last quoted, he is standing near Arcola on a bridge spanning the Adige. The enemy is bombarding this bridge. The French troops shrink back; there seems no way of forcing a passage across the river. At length, after repeated summonses, the soldiers advance once more, but there are calls from the ranks to Napoleon: "Do not go any farther, General. You will be killed, and then we shall be lost!" Marmont is a little in the van. Turning round to see if his men are following, he notices that the commander is in the arms of Muiron, the adjutant, apparently wounded. Around them a group of motionless figures. Now that the movement of the vanguard is arrested, the troops seek the shelter of the embankment. Bonaparte, who has recovered, stumbles and falls into the ditch at the foot of the dyke. His brother Louis and Marmont drag him out. A horse! Confusion

Next morning. "You have no reason to trouble yourself about the happiness or unhappiness of a man whom you do not love. But it is my fate to love you.... Take no part in the unhappiness of your husband, who lives only for you. It would be unjust if I were to ask you to love me as I love you. Who can expect delicate lace to weigh as heavy as gold.... My fault is that nature has denied me the charms which might bind you to me. What I do deserve is nothing more than this, that Josephine should show me a little consideration, a little respect, for I love her to the verge of madness, her and her alone. Farewell, adorable woman.... If I were certain that she could no longer love me, I would hide my pain, and would content myself with being useful to her whenever I could.... I open the letter once more, to send you a kiss. Ah, Josephine! Josephine!"

What a confession! With ardour and ambition he pushes forward to the goal, but the enemy has escaped, and what is to be done? Resignation must be the first aim after a failure, not raging and cursing. A man must retain his self-respect, and act prudently. A little mockery, embellished with courtesy, will have its due effect. Next day, he has turned things over in his mind. I must have her. How shall I lure her back? To extol my exploits does not move her in the least. What does influence her? Flattery and service. Such is his calculation. A miscalculation: for he, who is masterful with kings, fails to see that the charming Josephine would fear a master, even though she would not worship him; that nothing makes her more secure in her own position than his confessed passion.

Napoleon's mistake is the outcome of his pride. His pride will lead him to the limits of what is humanly possible, but will in the long run mislead him into the greatest of his blunders. Now, it is pride that prevents his veiling a passion which he does not master because he does not wish to do so. After all his carefully planned phrases to the effect that he wishes to be of use to her, the foolish human heart drives him, with the gesture of a lovesick youth, to tear open his letter that he may "send a kiss."

VI

What is Paris saying?

Paris is radiant, for, after long years, it once more has a hero to worship. Bonaparte's picture is in all the shops; rhymed comparisons of him with the heroes of antiquity are in everyone's mouth; the actors speak of him when instructions are sent to announce a new victory; the colours he has taken from the enemy are on show at the Luxembourg; his reports, put about by the Directors, appear in the "Moniteur." Songs, medals, caricatures (a recent importation from across the Channel), enliven the boulevards.

He knows all this, he knows, likewise, that the rapid growth of his popularity is alarming the Directors, who feel that he has long ceased to be their creature. "The fellow's perpetual victories will be the death of us" they think, and put their heads together. A people's army is invincible, but it is dangerous unless its officers are genuinely devoted to the government. For the last seven years, it has been the rulers' way to threaten with the guillotine any general who has dared to meddle in politics on his own account. "A commander who does not comply with our orders, who makes light of the commissaries we send to his camp, must be dismissed, even if his name be Napoleon Bonaparte. Saliceti is too much under his thumb, being a fellow-Corsican, and having an uneasy conscience because he betrayed Bonaparte not very long ago. Let us send another commissary, Clarke, who is both prudent and ambitious."

Elegant and high-spirited, himself a general, Clarke, while on the journey to Milan, looks forward to twisting Bonaparte, round his fingers. That gawky little fellow in the threadbare uniform whom he had often met at Barras' should be easy enough to deal with. But in the Palazzo Serbelloni, the envoy is abashed before the commander. Napoleon has not grown any taller, certainly; but the manner of his entries and exits, while, all wait for his coming or make way for his going, suggests the ruler rather than the simple warrior. The commissary has a courteous reception, but he is far from being able to penetrate Bonaparte's secret plans and report them to his masters. On the contrary, within a couple of days the commander-in-chief has full knowledge of the Directors' private designs, about which Clarke ought to have kept his mouth shut. The commissary has bowed before the higher authority. "Here is the man of the future," says he to himself; and promptly changes sides. Napoleon's suspicions are now confirmed. He knows that the Directors are using his conquests as mere pawns in the game they are playing to secure peace with the Austrians. They have no intention of keeping Italy, and still less do they think of revolutionising it. Now that he is forewarned, he will make all his preparations to thwart the government's plans.

But he still has need of the Directors. "Reinforcements! Reinforcements! No in name only, not on paper merely, but armed men in the flesh.... My best soldiers are wounded none of my staff officers and generals are fit for active service. The new levies are raw and unsteady. The army is reduced to a handful of exhausted warriors. We are forsaken in the middle of Italy. The few brave fellows left to me, are marked out for death unless you send ample reinforcements. Soon may strike the hour of the valiant Augereau, the indomitable Masséna, Berthier, myself. What will happen then to the lads in the ranks? This thought makes me cautious. I no longer dare to defy death, for if I were to fall it would demoralise those who are the object of all my care."

Could anything be more artfully phrased?

Yes, he has another string to his bow. When he does not threaten imminent destruction, he cajoles with gifts. Month after month, to this government whose only resources have for sometime been piles of almost worthless paper currency, he sends a consignment of hard cash, gold extorted from princes and republics by the terms of truce. He is the first commander to send money home, instead of continually demanding money. And in addition he has little presents to spare for the Directors. "I am sending a hundred of the finest horses I can lay my hands on, to replace any you may have that are not really good enough to draw your carriages."

He asks for the troops quartered in the southern provinces of France, and is told that they are needed for home service. "It is better," he rejoins, "that there should be broils in Lyons, while we keep Italy, than conversely." When told to leave all diplomatic negotiations to the commissaries, his answer runs: "For such matters, you do not merely need a one and only general; you must see to it that no one and nothing interfere with him in his work.... My advance is no less precise than my thought process.... We have to do everything with a weak army; thrust back the German troops; lay siege to fortresses; keep our lines of communication open; threaten Genoa, Venice, Tuscany, Rome, and Naples; show our strength here, there, and everywhere. For this, absolute unity of the military, political, and financial command is indispensable.... Unless the general remains the great centre, you will be exposed to incessant danger. I hope this language will not be ascribed to personal ambition. For my own part, I am unfortunately overburdened with honours, and my health has been so seriously undermined that I may soon have to ask you to appoint my successor. I can no longer mount a horse; nothing is left to me but courage.... I am continuing the negotiations. Troops! troops!—if you want to keep Italy. Bonaparte."

The more popular he becomes, the more often does he tender his resignation, though his health is in truth excellent, and day after day he rides until his horse stumbles from fatigue. Woe to the Parisian lawyers if they run counter to his wishes. While he strengthens France's power in Italy, he is consolidating his own influence in Paris; this is his new idea. Although he neither champions popular freedom nor believes Italy ripe for it, he insists upon the formation of the "Cisalpine Republic," against the wishes of the Directors-among whom Carnot, at least, is a convinced democrat, though he wants to use Italy as a pawn in the French game.

This is the first occasion on which Bonaparte builds up an organism out of centrifugal forces. In days to come, he will repeat the process again, on an even grander scale of creation, his aim being to establish a United Europe. He now welds together the half dozen petty States of northern Italy, prescribes their constitution, appoints and dismisses their officials. Throughout, he is the dictator, and yet all the time he acts on rational principles and allows for elasticity in matters of detail. He issues brilliant proclamations, announcing that these States are to be free whether they like it or not, and that they are to pay him promptly in hard cash for the privilege.

"The French Republic has sworn hatred of the tyrants, brotherhood with the peoples. This principle of the constitution is the principle of the army as well. The despot who has so long kept Lombardy enslaved, has done great injury to France.... The victorious army of an insolent monarch was compelled to spread terror among the conquered. But the republican army, while waging war to the finish against its enemies, the kings, gives a pledge of friendship to the peoples it has set free. Respect for property, humanity, and religion—this is our animating principle. But the Lombards owe us, who are their brothers, a fair return.... Lombardy must support us with all her resources. We need provisions, for France is so far away that we cannot supply our requirements thence. We are entitled to them by the right of conquest; friendship must hasten to offer them to us. We have to requisition twenty million francs from the provinces. They are so rich that this will not be a serious burden."

Then he takes whatever he wants out of the taxes, the countryside, the camps, the arsenals, and the domains. In the articles of every truce, he demands money, oxen, and pictures. If he sends picture and statues to Paris, this will not, of course, stabilise the currency but it will tickle the vanity of the Parisians, and win him popular favour. In a period of intense financial stringency, Bonaparte, with Italy as his source of supply, stocks the Louvre with precious works of art, contributing far more than the most resplendent of kings.

But all the time, while he is ruthlessly extorting money from the Italians, he is not less ruthless with Frenchmen who are trying to feather their own nests. In one of his early dispatches, he writes: "The army consumes five times as much as it should, because the commissariat officers are falsifying their accounts.... Prodigality, venality, and peculation are rife. There is only one thing to do: a committee of three must be appointed, with power, during from three to five days, to shoot every dishonest administrator." When the deliveries of hay are found to be short weight, he declares: "It is of the utmost importance that not one of these rascals shall escape. Too long have the army and the country been the victims of cupidity." Innumerable are the documents bearing his signature which are directed against these plunderers. When the influx of women camp-followers exceeds all bounds, he issues the following order: "Any woman found among the troops without a permit twenty-four hours after the posting of this notice, will be blackwashed and publicly exposed for two hours."

On the other hand, this strict disciplinarian was humane in his desire to put an end to some of the barbarities which still characterised war in those days: "The infamous practice of flogging men to make them disclose secrets, must come to an end. The only result of torturing people in this way is that the poor wretches say whatever they think will please their captors. I forbid the use of means that are equally repugnant to humanity and reason."

VII

As a diplomat, he strengthens all the instruments of diplomacy; flattery and threats; lying and frankness-or sometimes, even in diplomatic negotiations, he will play the bluff soldier. He is especially shrewd in his dealings with the Vatican.

As thorough-going revolutionists, the Directors wish to put an end to the temporal power of the Pope; for the Papal States are the focus of the religion which revolutionary France has rejected. The prospect of this moral success, to be gilded by the wealth of the Vatican, charms them more than all Bonaparte's activities in the formation of border States. They insist upon his advancing against Rome. Now he will be able to see it close at hand, this city with which, from childhood onwards, his imagination has associated power, greatness, and fame. Like Caesar, he will be able to pluck laurels from the Capitol, for the papal troops cannot stand against him for a moment.

But he holds his hand. For him, the Pope is the only ruler who cannot be dethroned by big guns. He sees the idea behind the papacy, with its millennial influence on France and Europe; he knows the moral repercussions of martyrdom, and he has determined not to wage war upon the Pope, unless it be a make-believe. "The influence of Rome is incalculable. It was a serious error to break with this power, which will profit by our mistake."

He moves southward, and, literally, crosses the Rubicon, but there he stops. Because he is the stronger, he offers a truce; henceforward this will be his technique. The aged Pope accepts the offer, for Bonaparte is wise enough to leave all ecelesiastical questions open. Pius VI promises to pay France several millions; to hand over one hundred pictures, busts, vases, or statues as the French commissioners shall determine. There are only two articles for which the commander-in-chief makes a specific demand: He wants the busts of Junius Brutus and Marcus Brutus from the Capitol. He is a Roman from Corsica; he crosses the Rubicon, spares Rome, and does not enter the city; but he requisitions the busts of the two heroes of antiquity.

When the Pope fails to pay up, and makes difficulties, Napoleon sets out towards Rome a second time, but does not go to the city. After a trifling skirmish, he is willing to make peace. He will soon want to use his soldiers in the north. A Pope on the run would carry his treasures with him, and what would there be left then for the poor Directors in Paris? On his own initiative, he actually pardons the French priests who have refused to take the oath of allegiance to the constitution and have sought refuge in Rome. He makes friends everywhere among the clergy, compares a "citizen archbishop" to one of the apostles, and writes as follows in several of his letters to high ecclesiastics: "The teaching of the

Gospels is based on equality, and is therefore the most suitable for any Republic." What will they say to that in Paris, where Christ has been done away with?

Finally, he sends to the Pope, who is on the point of taking to flight, an assurance that there is nothing to be afraid of. "Tell the Holy Father that I am not an Attila; and that even if I were, the Holy Father should not forget that he is a successor of Leo." He thus dresses himself in historical trappings when he is dealing with the oldest of the thrones. But when the nuncio is slow to sign the new agreement, the polished man of the world is suddenly metamorphosed into a soldier, who tears up the draft and throws it into the fire. "We are not discussing terms of peace, Monsignore; there is merely a suspension of hostilities." The other side is alarmed. He doubles his demands, and this time he gets what he wants. Thereupon, the Pope writes his "dear son" a letter, and gives the child of the revolution his blessing.

He never wraps up his doings in mystery, as the diplomats of those days were wont to do. An hour after his first truce has been arranged, he discussed recent happenings with the freedom of a historian in the next generation. Talking to the conquered Piedmontese over the dinner table, he says: "My attack on the castle of Cossaria was needless; but your movement of the 17th was a sound tactical manœuvre."

At the end of the second campaign, he again shows himself a master in respect of both self-confidence and moderation. He has moved forward out of Lombardy in the beginning of March, and by the end of the month he is already in Styria, a few days' march from Vienna. If the Army of the Rhine follows up his blow by similar victories, they will be able to dictate peace to Emperor Francis. Yet he chooses to halt, and to offer peace to the vanquished. True, the Army of the Rhine is still a good way off, whilst Austria and Hungary are arming themselves in frenzied haste. To stay where he is as a menace, this is the conqueror's logic.

Bonaparte, however, is a statesman. The Directors want peace before the elections, and he still has need of the Directors. How would it be if he, he alone, the soldier, were to bring France the peace for which she has been waiting five years? Is he to share to glory of this achievements with his rivals in the Army of the Rhine? The fortune of war is uncertain, and none but the foolhardy will tempt it unless they must. Once more he has broken the troops of the Empire, cut off as they are from the Rhenish armies. For a year, Europe has been afraid of the new commander; it will become him now to make a gesture of peace, so that people may learn to revere the new statesman. Without courtly periphrases, and as an equal, he writes to the defeated Austrian leader, Emperor Francis' brother

"Commander-in-Chief, Sir! Our valiant soldiers are waging war and want peace. Has not the war lasted six years? Have we not killed enough people; have we not brought enough suffering upon mankind? Everywhere there is a reaction towards humaneness, and almost everywhere the enemies of France have laid down their arms. Your nation is the only exception. The omens of this new campaign are sinister. However it may end, each of us will slay a few thousands of the other's soldiers; and yet, in the end, we shall make peace, for everything comes to an end, even the fiercest hatred.... You, who stand so near to the throne, uplifted above the petty emotions of statesmen and governments, are not you disposed to win for yourself the title of benefactor of mankind, saviour of Germany? I regard it as quite possible for you to save your country by force of arms. But, even then, Germany will be laid waste. If these lines could save the life of but one man, I should pride myself more upon my civic crown than upon the melancholy renown of the battle-field."

This letter makes a strong appeal to Archduke Charles. A highly cultured man, declared enemy of all wars, and only acting as commander-in-chief from a sense of duty, with this document in his hand he will be able to make headway against the war party in Vienna and to influence the emperor. For what would happen should they refuse? Bonaparte would certainly publish his letter and their reply. He would have another chance of parading before Europe the humanist ideals of the republic, and contrasting with them the feudal militarism of the empire. He would lay the country waste with fire and sword, while censuring us before the world for our truculence. He is following up his letter by advancing his troops, and he has already occupied Leoben.

The emperor's envoys arrive, The French commander meets them at the foot of the stairs, speaks of the emperor and the Archduke with respect. When they beg for ten days' truce (during which Vienna will be able to continue preparations for war), he answers by inviting them to supper. After the meal, he agrees to a five days' suspension of hostilities.

While comparative calm now reigns in Vienna, The Directors in Paris are much perturbed. Is this general of ours going to make the Great Peace all by himself? If he can do that, he will have to come to Paris afterwards, and with one hand he will be able to push us from our seats. Most politely, therefore, they instruct him to await the coming of the envoy they are sending. All the more does Bonaparte press the other side for a decision. He knows what reports concerning him are current in Paris, and he cracks his whip over the Directors' heads: "I should like to have a rest. I have justified your confidence in me; in all my undertakings I have hazarded my life; I have covered myself with more glory than the most fortunate man could wish; now I have advanced upon Vienna, leaving Italy's lovely plains behind me, as I advanced once before in search of bread for the army which the republic could no longer feed. Calumny vainly attempts to discredit my intentions. My civic career, like my military career, will be unique and simple."

Ironies, beneath whose mask the writer is moving towards unnamed goals.

Endless negotiations. But why should the matter drag on? Give us Belgium and Lombardy. You can compensate the dispossessed princes with possessions in the Holy Roman Empire! Habsburg accepts this principle, for neither the emperor nor any one of the German princes is concerned any longer about the Holy Roman Empire. It is very old, in poor health, and will soon be laid in the tomb. This plain will given France a finger in the pie across the Rhine. But how Habsburg is to be compensated for the loss of Lombardy, remains uncertain.

Opportune is the arrival of letters from Venice reporting insurrections against the French and the murder of a number of French soldiers. At length the day of vengeance has come! Venice, too, is outworn, and ripe for destruction. "Since the discovery of the Cape route to the Indies and the rise of Trieste and Ancona, Venice has been on the decline," he writes to the Directors, to soothe their conscientious scruples-i.e., for use in a justificatory campaign. "It will hardly survive the blow. This wretched and cowardly population, unfitted for freedom, without land or water, must, of course, be handed over to those to whom the hinterland is allotted. First of all, we shall take the ships, empty the arsenal, carry off the big guns, and close the banks; we shall also keep Corfu and Ancona." Thus weakened, the Lagoons were to pass to Habsburg.

Bonaparte dealt in summary fashion with the old lords of the region, with the few partrician families which, as the successors of strong men, had ruled Venice for centuries, and made of it one of the most reactionary States in the world. "You have stirred up the peasants against us," he wrote to the doge while the negotiations with the Austrians were in progress. "Thanks to you, every one is shouting: 'Death to the French!' Hundreds of our soldiers have already perished through your machinations. Do not lie to me! You incited these disturbances. Do you imagine that because I am in the heart of Germany I shall be unable to enforce respect for the greatest nation in the world? I shall take vengeance for the blood of my companions-in-arms. War or peace! Unless you instantly band over the ringleaders, I shall declare war."

This is his tone when he wished to terrify a dozen tottering old patricians. When the envoys from the Senate come to his camp, he pretends to fly into a passion: "I shall have no more constitution and no more Senate. For Venice, I shall be a second Attila. Make me no more proposals. I will be your lawgiver." When the city is being handed over, the doge, a man of ninety, falls dead-the last doge of Venice. Bonaparte never forgot this scene.

Has he done with Italy now? Has not he got all he wants; has not he reached his end?

There is no end, for every step forward opens a new vista. Venice is merely a springboard, whence he can start his swim into the open sea. The islands first; then the Adriatic; and now he contemplates a more distant horizon. When he was in Ancona a while back, forcing his terms of peace upon Rome, he stood on the shore, looking seaward. There were the Ionian Islands, and beyond them lay Turkey. He wrote: "From this point, we could reach Macedonia in twenty-four hours; the place would be invaluable for our influence upon the destinies of the Turkish Empire." As brigadier on the general staff he had thought of engulfing himself in Turkey. From Ancona he sends agents to open up relationships with powerful pashas in Janina, Scutari, and Bosnia.

Now, when he is in Leoben, he makes sure of the island possessions of Venice, arranges for the occupation of Corfu and Zante, "to control simultaneously the Adriatic and the East. No one will be able to save the Turkish Empire. We shall watch its death agony. The occupation of the Ionian Islands leaves us the choice between supporting Turkey and making sure of our own share of the spoils."

The political reality underlying this is an attack on England. France has long looked forward to the acquisition of strongholds in the Mediterranean, and to thus imposing a barrier between England and India. In Bonaparte, this general aim acquires the impulsive energy of a personal ambition. He does not want the East that he may inflict a mortal wound on England as his arch enemy; he is in search of means to injure England that thereby he may win the East. Since his imagination always runs far ahead of his achievements, Europe, of which but yesterday he first seized a corner, is already beginning to seem too small for him. He says to Bourrienne:

"Only in the East have there been great empires and mighty changes; in the East, where six hundred million people dwell. Europe is a mole hill!"

even greater than at first. "This Creole says soft nothings to every man, and kisses every woman, instead of attending to her business of bearing children." The Corsican mother has given birth to thirteen. Josephine's barrenness dishonours Napoleon and his family. Letizia fancies that in the eyes of many of his adversaries she can read satisfaction and mockery because the great man cannot procreate a child. But it is not his fault. Josephine has led, and still leads, too loose a life. That is what is amiss.

When Letizia first met Napoleon again, after his battles and victories, she embraced him and said:

"You are thinner than ever! You are wearing yourself out!"

"Not a bit of it. I am really living, now!"

"Yes, for posterity...."

"Well, do you call that dying?"

When he leaves her, he says to her: "Do take good care of yourself, Mother. If you die, there will be no one left with any authority over me." His Corsican clannishness is almost as strong as his cosmopolitan self-confidence.

Three sisters, three brothers, and Uncle Fesch are, in their various ways, enjoying themselves at Montebello. The fascinating Pauline, sixteen years of age, cannot forgive Josephine, who, in deference to Napoleon's wishes, has interfered with her plans for a love marriage. She weds Leclerc in the castle chapel, and at the same time Elise and Bacciochi have to resolemnise their union in church, for the chief is eager to keep in the good graces of the Vatican. After the ceremony Letizia, who has no interest in these intrigues, returns to Corsica.

"This island, this province," as Bonaparte now calls it, as if it were an island or a province like any other, has now been regained from the English, who had occupied it in response to Paoli's call for aid. Bonaparte managed the affair from a distance, while busied in his campaign on the mainland. One foggy night, a couple of dozen Frenchmen, taking with them plenty of money and an abundance of weapons, landed in Corsica "to encourage the patriots," circulate pamphlets, and so on. Napoleon also sent Saliceti, his friend and his opponent of earlier days. Thus, by proxy and from afar, he was able to achieve what he had thrice failed to do in person.

"Can it really be only four years?" thinks Signora Letizia, when those who had driven her and hers into exile receive her with acclamations. Is this the very citadel which was for so long the centre of Napoleon's thoughts and feelings? Now, simply because he orders it, Elise's husband is to be commandant there. For a long while, already, Lucien has been intendant of the forces. To Napoleon, in Italy, his native island now seems an ancient family seat, a romantic and medieval spot where his kindred can dwell when convenient. With a contemptuous smile, not long ago, he had read a letter from the Bourbon pretender, in which Louis offered him the title of duke, or even hereditary viceroy, of Corsica, if he would espouse the royalist cause.

In Montebello, Bonaparte first learns how to separate his private life from his public life—a lesson which those born in the purple learn from childhood upwards.

The guardianship of the castle, strangely enough, is entrusted, not to French soldiers, but to three hundred Polish legionaries. In several of his battles, there had been danger that he would be taken prisoner, so he has formed a bodyguard, forty strong. They are called guides, are chosen from among the tallest and best of his soldiers, and have a dare-devil for their leader.

The castle is thronged with orderlies and couriers. Envoys are flocking from all quarters. The lion of St. Mark and the keys of St. Peter gleam on foreign epaulettes; Vienna, Leghorn, and Genoa are also represented at Montebello. Napoleon lives in state. Following the custom of the country, he keeps open house. Interested spectators are admitted to the gallery of the banqueting hall; and he drops a hint, lest they should forget to spread the news when they return home, that like them he drinks the wine of the country.

The reports of those who come to see him on service matters or other official business express astonishment that this young commander-in-chief is never embarrassed. He is dignified and yet perfectly natural; always the most simply dressed man in the company. None the less, he knows quite well how to keep people at a distance. Though nearly everyone who comes to see him towers over him in stature, he never tries to appear taller than he is. Instead, those conversing with him are inclined to stoop a little, and thus seem to be paying court to him. Henceforward, throughout life, he is able from his natural defect to derive an advantage whose ultimate psychical consequences are incalculable. One of the visitors to Montebello wrote: "Should this man have the luck to escape death in battle, within four years he will be in exile or seated on a throne." The writer was only three years out in his reckoning.

A student of his epoch, one who knows how fame is manufactured, he has in attendance an able journalist, the first publicity agent in history, whose business it is to blow Napoleon's trumpet in Paris and subtly to discredit the Directors. Being a disciple of Plutarch, Bonaparte knows through whose agency the story of great men's deeds is handed down to posterity; that is why the faces of poets, historians, artists, and men of science are so often seen at his Italian castle. A year before, a few days after the triumphal entry into Milan, and when overwhelmed with urgent business, he had found time to pen the following remarkable lines to a great astronomer:

"The sciences which are the glory of the human mind, the arts which beautify the world and bequeath great deeds to our offspring, must be cherished with especial care in free States, All men of genius, all those who are famous in the world of learning, are Frenchmen, no matter to what country they may belong." Hitherto, such men have had to lead a retired life. Now, freedom of thought prevails; intolerance is a thing of the past, there are no despots left. The talented can foregather under his patronage, and fearlessly tell him all their wishes. Any such person who wants to go to France may be sure of a cordial reception, "for the French people would rather win a great mathematician, painter, or other man of note, than win the wealthiest of provinces. That is why,

Citizen, I ask you to make these sentiments widely known among the great men of Milan!"

He commissions an attache, who, like most of his tribe, has little to think about and nothing to do, to make register of the art treasures in the possession of the petty States of Italy. In subsequent treaties, he demands the best of these for Paris.

For the Paris Conservatories, he instructs experts to make copies of the best Italian music. Writing on this topic, he says: "Of all the arts, music has the strongest influence on the passions, and for that reason the legislator must make it one of his chief concerns, An inspired symphony composed by a master cannot fail to stir our feelings, and has far more influence than a treatise on morality, which convinces our reason without affecting our conduct." When he becomes a member of the Institute, he flaunts this title at the head of all the letters he writes as commander-in-chief, and declares: "The soldier must, above all, regard his commander as wiser and more cultured than himself; and the soldier will regard this title with respect for the very reason that its meaning is obscure to him."

Such actions disclose, not the statesman alone, but the man born to rule, the prince who regulates every gesture, every word that he says or writes, with an eye to the legend as to his personality which he wishes to inculcate upon his people. But when the door is closed, and he is among intimates, he opens his heart.

Here is a description of Napoleon as he was in those days, penned by an exceptionally shrewd observer: "The power of the man impressed everyone with whom he came in contact... His demeanour was still rather ungainly at times; but there was something imperious in his nature, his glance, and his speech. Everyone obeyed his orders. In public, he deliberately tried to heighten this impression. In private life, on the other hand, he was unconstrained, genial, and even confidential; with a taste for witticisms, which were never ill-natured but were merry and discreet. Frequently, he shared in our amusements. He did not take his work too strenuously, not finding it necessary at that time to measure out his hours; and in leisure moments he was always accessible.

But when he had withdrawn to his workroom, his door was closed to every unauthorised intruder, without distinction of rank. —He needed a great deal of sleep, like all people of nervous temperament and very active mind. I have often known him to stay in bed for ten or eleven hours at a stretch; but if it was necessary to wake him up, he was unperturbed, and could easily make up for the lost hours afterwards—or could store up reserves of sleep in expectation of a strenuous time. He had the precious faculty of being able to go to sleep wherever and as often as he pleased. Fond of vigorous exercise, he rode very often, and at a great pace, though he had an exceedingly bad seat."

He has a taste for talking, and chooses politics or general questions of life as his theme if the conversation flags, he suggests the telling of stories; should this be followed by a general silence, he spins a yarn of his own, pregnant and humorous.

The loveliest women set their caps at him in vain; he is wholly devoted to Josephine. Not, indeed, so frenzied in his adoration as he was a year back, when she betrayed or disillusioned him; it is she, and she alone, who has trifled away this passion for self-surrender. Now there is a moving note in his tone towards her; a fervent courtship, a smile, a petition: "You are sad," he wrote to her while still in the field. "You do not write; are you longing to get back to Paris? Have you ceased to care for me? The thought makes me wretched. My life has become unbearable since I have known that you are not happy. Perhaps I shall soon make peace with the Pope; then I shall join you at once." Three days later: "The peace with Rome has just been signed. Bologna, Ferrara, and Romagna are ceded to us. –But there is not a word from you! Good God, how have I offended you?–I fear you know only too well how absolute is your power over me! For life, wholly yours."

Now, at Montebello, he is for the first time tasting the joys of uninterrupted connubiality, while he is delighted to watch Josephine's winning charm in social intercourse. Occassionally he steals time for a brief love festival. Thcy drive across to Lake Maggiore; and when, among the rhododendron bushes beneath the baroque stone edifices on Isola Bella, Grassini, the heroine of La Scala, uplifts her thrilling voice and sings an appassionata by Monteverde, Napoleon sits wrapped in thought, his companion's hand clasped in his own.

"In the carriage"–so his adjutant relates–"he would take marital liberties which were apt to be rather embarrassing to Berthier and me. But it was all so simple and natural, that there was no ground for offence."

IX

What is Paris saying?

Since yesterday, there has been a watchman on duty there: Hitherto, the cabinet ministers had all been nothing more than lawyers; now, a statesman was at work in that innermost circle. Sprung from the old nobility of France, a bishop, then as a Republican placed under the ban of the Church by the Pope, Talleyrand had recently spent years of waiting in the United States. Now he was back in Paris, and had grasped a share of power. The recently elected Chambers were predominantly "right", and had been railing against the Directors; the commander-in-chief in Italy wanted to revolutionise Europe; he wished to perpetuate the war; the rape of Venice was an infamy. Perhaps many of the accusations were only too true, but when the echoes of what was being said in the place of words made their way into the place of deeds, they could not fail to arouse the contempt of the man of might. He sent the Chambers a memorial, or, rather, a memento: "Speaking in the name of eighty thousand men, I warn you that the days when cowardly lawyers and pitiful chatterers could allow valiant soldiers to be butchered are over and done with!"

At this date Bonaparte had dispatched Augereau to defend the Directors, as he himself had defended them a year or two before; for the growing power of royalists and priests was becoming an even greater menace to the new constitution of the republic. If either of the Bourbon brothers should venture to set foot on

French soil, all the malcontents would flock to his standard, and in a hand's turn he would win his way to the throne. But the Bourbons stayed in their safe retreats, and the Directors could risk a little coup d'état. Now , they were five instead of three, and felt more self-confident.

Called to office after this coup, an expert was for the first time in charge of the Ministry for Foreign Affairs. From afar, he measured the strength of his only rival. Though he had never seen Bonaparte face to face, he knew him for the coming man. To begin with, at any rate, he was willing to play second fiddle, and set to work that he might win the confidence of one great than himself.

In all respects, Talleyrand was Napoleon's counterpart. Not a born negotiator; passionless, except for his avarice; cold and crafty, never natural and frank; always adapting himself to the mood of those he wished to use as his tools. His cynic's head, his long, pointed, praying nose, now surmounted the gold braided collar of the republic; they would surmount the imperial and the royal uniform; and then, for a fourth time in the service of the ruler of the French, he would don the livery of the bourgeois king. For forty years he served the man who happened to be in power; but never unreservedly, and therefore he was never tied to any ruler's fortunes. Lamed by an accident in childhood, he was unable to enter the army, and became a priest, remembering that, in this guise, the great Richelieu had been master of France. Talleyrand was the only man in the country able to measure his strength against that of Bonaparte. Never would the man of destiny be able to shake off Talleyrand even when he had come to hate the subtle diplomat; and when the final breach between the two men occurred, it was at the very time when Talleyrand, with a smile, could limp across the body of the master he had cast down and enter the cabinet of the enemy. Talleyrand was the man who overthrew Napoleon; but, if we think of elemental forces, Napoleon was felled by his own hand.

Tallleyrand's breadth of view and utter lack of principle make their due impression on the distant Bonaparte. These September days, the commander has gone to Udine, to sign the peace whose preliminaries had been arranged in the spring. In this spring of the old nobility, in this connoisseur of the rococo, in this cold nihilist, Napoleon sees the tool he will need. Hitherto, he wanted none but soldiers. Now, when he has become a statesman, he wants and finds a statesman. While he is discussing matters with the Austrians, he sends the new Minister for Foreign Affairs a long letter (a letter of betrothal, we might call it), disclosing his whole political programme:

"The organisation of French power has only just begun- Despite our good opinion of ourselves, –we Frenchmen are still tyros in political matters. As yet we do not even understand the difference between executive, legislature, and judiciary, In such a State as ours, where all authority issues from the nation, where the people is sovereign–governmental power, in the full comprehensiveness I ascribe to it, must be regarded as the true representative of the nation, who rules in accordance with the constitution."

"Does your heart express itself so openly, Bonaparte?" thinks the inscrutable recipient, smiling to himself as he reads.

"It is an immeasurable misfortune that, in the eighteenth century, a nation of thirty million persons should still be compelled to take up arms in order to save the country. These forcible means are a burden upon the legislator, seeing that a constitution for human beings must take human beings into account."

"Is your aim so high?" muses the reader, with astonishment. "He is already sated with martial fame, and aspires, under the new constitution, to become dictator!" Talleyrand reads on:

"Why should we not make sure of Malta?–I had good reason for confiscating the estates of the Knights of Malta.–With Malta and Corfu in our hands, we should be masters of the Mediterranean. If we cannot dislodge England from the Cape, we must take Egypt. With twenty-five thousand men and eight to ten ships of the line, the expedition could be risked. Egypt does not belong to the sultan. I wish you could find out what impression an Egyptian expedition would make upon the Porte. –The break-up of the huge Turkish Empire, day by day more imminent, must lead us to think of our trade in the East."

As he sits in the Foreign Office, reading this, the diplomat raises his eyebrows yet higher. He feels that the writer is a man of genius, if not the very devil. A week or two later, comes another letter.

"If our doings are guided by a sound policy, which is nothing else than the calculation of combinations and chances, we shall for a long time to come be the Great Nation and the arbiter of Europe. The scales are in our hands, and, should fate be propitious, within a few years there may be great happenings. Today, these may seem the vague anticipations of a visionary enthusiast; but a cold, pertinacious, and far-sighted man will be able to make them a reality."

X

How slow these German diplomats are to make up their minds. For weeks we have been at it, discussing matters far on into the night, and still the titles negotiators hesitate to sign the document, though any reasonable man would come to a decision in an hour or two! Throughout, the Austrians are looking over their shoulders at the emperor in Vienna. In the room where the conversations take place, there is an empty throne on which the shadowy Francis is supposed to be sitting beneath the canopy. "Better carry that chair away before we begin," says the commander. "I have never been able to see a raised seat without wanting to sit in it."

His letters to the enigmatical Minister for Foreign Affairs, those fervid preludes, had been nothing more than the soliloquies of a man chafing at idleness, to whom weeks spent in thinking about peace seem wasted, even though the peace be one for which Europe has been longing for years. His patience is exhausted, and he assumes a menacing tone: "I have been too lenient with you," he growls to the Austrians. "I might have made the conditions much harsher! You are frittering away my time. I stand before you as equal in rank of any of your princes. Don't talk to me about congresses.... With the means at our disposal, in a couple of years we Frenchmen can conquer the whole of Europe. Not that we want to do so. Our wish is to give our citizens peace, and quickly.... You tell me that this, that, and the other are your instructions. If, when the sun is shining, your instructions said that night had fallen, would you insist that it was dark?"

At last, to give them a salutary fright, he bursts into a rage, dashes a vase to the ground, and thus forces them to sign the peace in which every one gets what Napoleon had promised six months before in Leoben.

When Europe learns the news, there will be a sigh of relief But what is going on in Bonaparte's mind? The day after he has signed at Campo Formio the peace which ends a six years' war, the peace he has fought for and won, he writes to the Directors, in the most matter-of-fact way: "It is absolutely indispensable to our government that we should speedily overthrow the English monarchy. Unless we succeed in doing this, we can be sure that the corruption and the intrigues of these active islanders will ruin us. The moment is favourable. Let us concentrate our energies upon increasing our navy, so that we may crush England. Then Europe will be at our feet." He issues a manifesto to the navy: "Comrades! Now that we have established peace on land, let us conquer the freedom of the seas. Without your aid, the glory of the Continent. With your help, we shall cross the ocean, and the fame of our nation will reach the most distant lands!"

His mind is full of titanic schemes. As he gallops along the causeways of his great deeds, fame vanishes behind him in the dust raised by his charger's thundering hoofs, but fame ever looms in front of him, beckoning from the mirage of his fresh designs. In this spirit he hastens back to Milan, to Montebello, whence he is to give Italy her final orders; for now, carrying the peace treaty, he will go to Paris. In the tone of a prince speaking to his people, Bonaparte issues a proclamation to the newly formed Cisalpine Republic:

"Yours is the first nation in history to win freedom without partisan struggles, without a revolution, and without a blow. We have given you liberty, and you will know how to keep it! .Let your minds be full of the sense of your own strength, and of the self-respect proper to the free man.... Had the Romans of old used their powers as the French are using their powers today, the Roman eagles would still wave above the Capitol, and the human race would have escaped being dishonoured by eighteen centuries of slavery! To consolidate your liberties, and with the sole end of bringing you happiness, I have completed a task such as hitherto has only been performed by ambition and the will-to-power.... In a few days I shall leave you.... Your happiness and the glory of your republic will always be matters very dear to my heart."

Is this is a warrior blowing a trumpet? Is it a poet, into whose mouth the ecstasy of life puts words that are to arouse popular enthusiasm? During these very days, in the company of a diplomat belonging to this very country, he is strolling to and fro in the park of Montebello. His whole nature is straining towards Paris; his companion is a good listener, and a man of ability. Napoleon, in one of those burst of frankness which genius sometimes allows itself, delivers himself as follows:

"Do you fancy that I have won my triumphs in Italy that I may help the lawyers of the Directory... to achieve greatness? Or can you imagine that I want to stabilise the republic? What a ridiculous notion, a republic with thirty million inhabitants! With our customs! With our failings! France will soon forget these whims. The French need glory and the gratification of their vanity, by they do not understand the elements of freedom. Look at the army! Our victories have restored the French soldiers. If the Directors, for instance, were to try to withdraw my commission, they would soon see who is master of the army.

"The people need a chief, made resplendent by fame and victory; it does not want theories and governments, the phrases and the oratory of the ideologues. Give the masses a toy! They will play with it, and allow themselves to be led–provided always that the leader is adroit enough to hide his true aims! Here in Italy, it is not necessary for me to be so circumspect.... Still, the time is not yet ripe. For the present, it is necessary to yield to the fervour of the moment, so here we shall have two or three republics after the French model.... Peace is opposed to my interests.... If peace were firmly established, and if I were no longer at the head of the army, I should have to renounce the power and position I have gained, and should have to pay homage to the lawyers in the Luxembourg. If I leave Italy, it is only that I may play the same part in France. But that fruit, likewise, is not yet ripe. Paris is divided. There is a Bourbon party, and I cannot fight on its side. In due time I shall weaken the republicans, but I shall not do so to the advantage of the old dynasty!"

Such are Bonaparte's real plans. What he says is true: "Everything has happened as I foresaw; and I believe that I am the only person in the world who is not suprised. So will it be in the future; I shall make my way whithersoever I will."

A stream of confessions is forcing a way for itself. The words have come down to us in the memoirs of the man who heard them; of course the speaker would have denied them, had the hearer then ventured to repeat them. But it is true that he is far from being satisfied with what he has hitherto achieved. Seated beside Bourrienne in the carriage in which he is driving away from Italy after a stay of nearly two years, he says: "A few more campaigns like this, and we shall have made a fairly great name for ourselves, a name that will go down to posterity." When his friend interposes that Bonaparte has already secured a notable reputation, the Commander laughs him to scorn:

"You flatter me, Bourrienne! If I die today, ten centuries hence my record will not occupy more than half a page in universal history!"

XI

The Luxembourg palace has been transformed into an amphitheatre. Weapons and colours, the latest trophies, are displayed, side by side with the gold-blazoned slogans of the revolution, on the venerable walls within which of old, the satellite peers used to circle round their central luminary, the King of France. Paris has assembled, and all are dressed in gala attire, as if for a May day festival-though it is chill December. The front seats are filled with pretty women, friends of the men in power, for they want to get a close view of the little Commander with the leathery yellow skin, the hero of the occasion.

"He has already been a week in Paris, and not a soul has set eyes on him. Why does he modestly shun the acclamations of his people?"

"There is the signal for the entry! Look, the five Directors are coming onto the platform!"

The chorus sings the anthem of liberty, the crowd joining in the refrain. A pause. The sound of clanking sabres and clinking spurs is heard upon the perron without. People crane from the windows, look down from the roofs. He is coming! He is coming!

Napoleon wears a field uniform, for this looks less pretentious. His mien is grave and unassuming, as with firm step he strides along the gangway to the dais. He carries a roll of paper, and three adjutants follow in his train. But, as well as these, hard upon the heels of the plainly uniformed little figure with the martial gait, comes a man wearing silk stockings, and resplendent in gold lace; he walks with a limp. At this moment, a cannon shot is heard, the first shot of a salute; the sometime lieutenant of artillery is being honoured in appropriate fashion. Thunders of applause shake the building, and are echoed outside by the thousands who are waiting to greet Napoleon on his departure. Quiet once more. Talleyrand is speaking. Brilliantly, smoothly, with undercurrents of meaning which few can understand, he praises the classical simplicity of their great general, the saviour of his country, who scorns pomp, and is a servant of the things of the spirit. The minister closes with the words: "All France will be free; save only him, perhaps—that is his destiny."

graceful as ever. Unless he is fixing his gaze upon some object he particularly wishes to examine, he is generally looking upwards. It was always a delight to me to contemplate his beautiful, deep, sensitive eyes, at once severe and kindly, like those of our own Frederick."

XII

On the way to Paris, Napoleon had had to spend a few days in Rastatt, to discuss with the imperial envoys certain details connected with the carrying out of the peace treaty and the evacuation of Mainz. Here, expected with mingled curiosity and scepticism, he had assumed royal airs. He had alternately scolded and made much of the envoys, as best suited his plans at the moment, giving one of these Austrian counts a watch and the other a jewelled hat-buckle. "The two poor envoys were amazed that I had so much money to spend, for they were as poor as church mice."

This oriental lavishness in present-giving, the outcome of kindliness quite as much as of arrogance, will be a persistent characteristic. He will become known as a caliph who loves to shower gifts, displaying a, mingled disdain and generosity which throw a searching light upon his own spiritual make-up. But if he has to acknowledge some genuine service, then this same man (who from underlings exposed to danger demands scrupulous exactitude in the fulfilment of duty) will express his thanks in the most courtly fashion, as if he were one of Arthur's knights, and the world a jousting place. The warrior who has captured so many of the enemy colours is given one of the flags from Arcola, as a keepsake. He passes it on to General Lannes, writing.

"At Arcola, there was a moment when the fortune of the day was so uncertain that nothing but the utmost bravery on the part of the leaders could have saved the situation. Thereupon, bleeding from three terrible wounds, you left the field hospital, resolved to conquer or die. Again and again I saw you in the foremost ranks of the brave. You were the first.... to cross the Adda. Yours must be the honour of owning and guarding this glorious flag."

He knows exactly how his words will affect the people of Paris. If he makes a public display of such expressions of approval, he is just as sedulous to draw near to the footlights when he has to censure or to condemn. That is one of the tricks of his trade.

Now, he is careful to behave in such a way that all Paris, everyone of his opponents, the whole press, shall exclaim: "The modesty of true greatness!" Twice more, during these days, he makes ceremonial appearances, one of them being at a festival held in his honour by Talleyrand. He had hastened to pay his respects to the Minister for Foreign Affairs on the day after his return to Paris. Neither of them had as yet disclosed his ultimate plans, but Bonaparte, in his dealings with this scion of the old nobility, had not forgotten to speak of his own exalted antecedents. "You are the nephew of the Archbishop of Rheims," he had said in the first half hour. "One of my uncles, who helped in my education, is an archdeacon—in Corsica, you know, that means much the same as being a bishop in France." In this way Napoleon implied that he was no parvenu whom a man of ancient lineage was, in his heart, entitled to despise. From the first, he looked upon Talleyrand as a possible antagonist.

He has bought the little house in which Josephine used to live. Here he leads a retired life, with his wife, who has at length arrived in Paris. His circle is small, consisting of his brothers and a few friends who come and go. He often wears mufti, drives out alone, avoids parties, is easy of access. When he is cheered at the theatre, he draws back into the recesses of his box. This is the man who, a little while ago at Montebello, was keeping up a princely state. "If I am seen three or four times at the theatre, people will cease to notice me," he says to an intimate. "You except me to be pleased by such public demonstrations? There would be quite as big a crowd to see me guillotined!"

He invites men of learning to his house; attends most of the sittings of the Institute, and is willing to read a paper there now and again; discusses mathematics after dinner with Laplace, and shows the astronomer new Italian methods of calculating orbits; argues with Chénier about poetry, and even metaphysics (if he can't help himself!).

But he silently follows, all this time, every move made by the Directors, whose power is continually on the wane. Knowing them to be his secret enemies, he keeps out of their path, and to the relative strength of the various parties, and ponders his own course. "Paris has no memory. A new reputation drives out an old one; and if I linger here inactive, I shall be lost, I must not stay here." Often he walks to and fro in the garden arms locked behind, thinking.

"Too soon, Better wait until they have made a complete mess of things. Become their colleague, a member of the Directory, just when the pillars are cracking? A good thing that I am not yet forty, as the law demands. Meanwhile, I must capture the fancy of the crowd! How? There is peace throughout the Continent. Hardly a rival left to dread. Hoche, the most dangerous of them, is dead, thanks be! One of Josephine's lovers; a handsome fellow, certainly. His passing troubled her little; she is inconstant by nature. Carnot thrust aside, Moreau defeated. Augereau, in command of the Army of the Rhine, is jealous of me; I must put a spoke in his wheel. The Corsican stalwarts have little influence now; but that woman who came to warn me against the risk of poisoning was stabbed next day; there are conspiracies. Too soon. I must leave Paris once more."

"Get to work against England That would be the best plan, if only these idiots had not allowed the navy to get into so wretched a condition! I've been worrying them about the matter ever since the siege of Toulon. During the naval war of the last five years, we've lost half a dozen sea-fights. What about invasion? If only that were possible! Anyone who could defeat England would be master of the world. Sail along the coast, study the possibilities, and then, if there seems no chance of a successful landing on the other side of the Channel, back to the Mediterranean! Only there, in the East, can I throw off all restraint, and keep France a-quiver with curiosity and excitement. Egypt's the place, in the footsteps of Alexander; and there we can strike England a shrewd blow!"

After long preparations, the general visits Dunkirk and the Flemish coast. He asks questions wherever he goes, not forgetting to cross-examine fishermen and smugglers. Returning unexpectedly, he gives Josephine a fright, but it escapes his notice that she hastens to pen a few lines to the secretary of an old flame. In his campaigns, hundreds of spies have brought him secret missives; what would he say if he could read this one? "Bonaparte has come back this evening. Please tell Barras how sorry I am that I cannot come to supper after all. Say that he is not to forget me. You know better than anyone what my position is. –La Pagerie Bonaparte."

Thus undermined is the marriage in which he still puts his trust. Thus equivocal is the position of Barras, the impotent Director, who hates and mistrusts the mighty commander of the forces. Thus nonchalant is Josephine, as with carefree heart she makes her way through society, passing her time in women's boudiors and men's bedrooms-and, among the men, she has to put up with Bonaparte, although when she signs her married name she prefixes to it her maiden name, as though she were still mistress of her own destinies and free to choose her lover.

No doubt Barras is cursing Bonaparte this evening, but next day the general writes to him and the other Directors a long report, which begins as follows: "Even with our best efforts, it will take us several years to get the upper hand at sea. The invasion of England would be a desperate venture; it will only be possible if we take the islanders by surprise.... We shall need long nights, so it must be in winter. Consequently we cannot make the attempt till next year. Before then, it is likely enough that hindrances will have arisen on the Continent. Perhaps the great moment has been lost forever."

After this amazingly perspicacious renunciation of his scheme for the invasion of England, he goes on to formulate a yet more amazing plan for achieving the same end by other means, Substantially, he proposes eight naval campaigns, ranging from Spain to Holland, all the political conditions and consequences being carefully considered. If, however, ships and money are not forthcoming, the next best expedient will be to attack English commerce, beginning in Egypt, whence Bonaparte could get back to direct further operations against England.

Enough for the Directors to hear the word Egypt, and they

are ready to agree to this last plan. He shall have the command there, and all the help they can give. So dangerous a man as this—the farther away he is, the better! Best of all would be, to make an end of him!

The Egyptian plan is not new; it has been mooted at intervals for years. Talleyrand had brought it forward in connection with Bonaparte's letter, though his comment had been: "The leader of this campaign would not need to be a man of exceptional military talent." Was this remark prompted by a wish to keep Bonaparte in France, or was it nothing more than a spiteful innuendo? However that may be, the talented commander, when he read the words at a much later date, wrote in the margin: "Crazy!" But we anticipate. He drafted the terms of his own nomination as chief of the Army in the East: plenipotentiary powers; a commission to take Malta and Egypt, to drive the English from the Red Sea, to cut a canal through the Isthmus of Suez in order that France may be secure in the possession of the Red Sea.

With feverish energy he now devotes himself to preparations for the new undertaking. He has long been familiar with all the essentials of the problem. The Mediterranean is his home, in childhood, he was wont to contemplate the Moor's head on the scutcheon of Corsica, sailing ships from Africa often visited the island; not long ago, he had deprived Genoa and Venice of their fleets, he was already in touch with Tunisians and Greeks, with Albanians and Bosnians. Over all these machinations brooded the spirit of Alexander, who had chosen Egypt as the centre of his world empire.

For the first time, during these weeks of waiting, do the elements of Bonaparte's nature become formally compacted within him. What has been no more than a scheme of the unbridled imagination, the plan of one who aspires to resemble the most splendid exemplars of the ancient world, is now dissected, pondered, weighed in the calculating brain; it is refashioned, reconsidered; by degrees it is adapted to the actual possibilities of the situation. When preparing his Egyptian campaign, Bonaparte attempts, in the grand style, to unite the calculator with the dreamer, while it escapes his notice that there is an incalculable residue. His imagination, nourished upon dreams of the heroic age, blinds him to the fact that we are no longer living in the days of classical antiquity, that caliph and conqueror can no longer command millions of unthinking slaves, that even in distant Africa the peoples are awakening. Bonaparte is making ready for a titanic and insoluble conflict; and the more deeply he becomes involved in it, the more defiantly will he continue his vain attempts to solve it.

This man of genius, born two thousand years too late, is already spinning the threads of his own doom. With the hand of a demigod, he is sketching the outlines of his own fate.

XIII

"I am going to the East," he writes to his brother, "with all the means to ensure success. Should France need me, ... Should war break out and take an unfavourable turn, I shall come home, and public opinion will be more solidly on my side than it is now. But if the fortune of war should favour the republic, if another commander like myself should appear upon the scene, I shall, perhaps, by staying in the East, do the world more service than he can." When Bourrienne asks how long they are to be away, Bonaparte answers: "Six months or six years."

At the last moment, fate wants to give him another warning. In Rastatt, Austria refuses to cede the left bank of the Rhine; in Vienna, Benadotte, who is French envoy there, is so provocative that a new war already seems imminent. Would it not be better to stay in Europe? But the Directors speed the departure, saying that matters have now gone too far to withdraw. In May, exactly two years after Napoleon's entry into Milan, four hundred ships set sail from Toulon. Josephine waves farewell to her husband, and (doubtless with more concern) to Eugene. Not until the whole mighty apparatus has been set in motion at the master's nod, does he disclose to his subordinates the goal of the voyage. All are on deck, watching the gradual disappearance of the European coast; but Napoleon, on the "Orient," standing beside the main mast among the eight-pounders, is not, like the others, looking back at Europe. His gaze is directed towards the south-east.

At the same hour, Nelson and three other British admirals, standing on the decks of their ships, are searching the seas with telescopes for a sign of the hated enemy, who is, it is supposed, about to sail for Sicily. Where is he to be found? Yesterday, Nelson's fleet was scattered by a storm. Days pass before the ships can get together again, and the very storm which had detained Bonaparte for twenty-four hours in Toulon, saves the French. They reach Malta before the English fleet, and seize the important island by a coup de main. By the time the cat arrives, the mouse is gone. Under all sail, Nelson presses on to Egypt, but finds no one there, for he has outstripped the enemy. He tries the Syrian coast. Nothing! Back to Sicily. No one! "The Devil has the devil's own luck," says Nelson, cursing himself and the foe.

The French fleet is four weeks on the voyage, and Napoleon, who is a bad sailor, spends most of the time in bed. Is not this symbolic? Will the seasick general ever win the command of the sea? He is restless lying down, and, to pass the weary hours, he makes Bourrienne read aloud to him.

For on board this fleet there are not only two thousand guns. A whole university is sailing to the East. Astronomers, geometricians, mineralogists, chemists, antiquarians, bridge builders, road engineers, orientalists, political economists, painters, poets—one hundred and seventy-five learned civilians, with hundreds of boxes full of apparatus and books. Everything in this land of ancient story is to be meticulously studied. For France, Bonaparte is to win a colony, and for himself an African reputation. The soldiers have bluntly nicknamed these learned passengers, collectively, "the donkeys." But Bonaparte prizes them, and his wrath breaks loose on any of his officers who grumble at the presence of so many "idlers." He has chosen his experts with the utmost care, and has thought out every detail of what they are to do. He has brought a font of Arabic type, extracted with great difficulty from the State printing house. He has taken especial pains in the choice of books for the library with which the flagship is freighted for the voyage to Egypt. Novels are good for officers; and when he finds them reading novels, he laughs good humouredly. For himself, he has only *Werther and Ossian*, works of passion, his inseparable companions. On this journey, however, he seldom reads them.

What does Bourrienne read aloud to the chief? Travels in Egypt, which have been collected from various quarters, from Rome and elsewhere; Plutarch; Homer; Arrian's account of Alexander's campaigns; the Koran, which, logically enough, is housed among the political works, beside the Bible and Montesquieu.

After dinner, he is fond of holding sessions of "the Institute." He uses the name jestingly, and yet in the discussions he takes it seriously enough. He propounds a subject for debate, and nominates the champions. Mathematics and religion are his favourite topics on these occasions, for he has always been both calculator and dreamer. There sits the famous Monge, a man with a crooked nose, a receding forehead, and a massive chin; Napoleon has admired him for years, and thinks more of him than of any of the others. Beside Monge is Desaix, whom Bonaparte has just summoned from the Army of the Rhine; he has a thick nose and thick lips, a somewhat negroid but kindly face, and the strategist rivals the mathematician in the shrewdness of his eyes. Look at Kléber, a man of fearless countenance, full of courage and resolution; beside him, Laplace who peers earnestly at the company from beneath his eye-shade; next is Berthollet, with a head like a ram. Klébér runs atilt at geometry; but when one of the professors wishes to take up the cudgels on behalf of the things of the spirit, Bonaparte signs to him not to waste breath, and points with a smile to Berthier, who has fallen asleep in the corner over the *Sorrows of Werther*.

The weather is getting much warmer. Napoleon, wishing to breathe the night air, lies on deck till a late hour. His intimates are sitting round him in a circle, and discussion turns on the planets, on the question whether they are inhabited. Pros and cons are voiced by the disputants. This leads to the problem of the creation.

The sons of the revolution, disciples of Voltaire, be they generals or be they professors, are agreed upon one point, that the universe and its origin are rationally explicable in terms of natural science, without reference to the idea of God, Napoleon lies there, listening in silence. Then, pointing to the stars, he interjects:

"You may say what you like, but who made all those ?"

XIV

Bonaparte rides slowly across the desert sands to look upon the face of the Sphinx. The eyes of stone and the eyes of steel meet. Like the Sphinx, he knows how to be silent, but we can guess his thoughts.

"Alexander stood here. Cæsar stood here, They lived two thousand years after this image was sculptured, as I live two thousand years after them. Immeasurable empires, consecrated to the sun, extended around the Nile. Millions obeyed the will of one. What the ruler dreamed, was fashioned by his slaves with their myriad hands. Everything was possible to him. The king was the son of the the gods. All obeyed him as the descendant of the original conqueror. Because that first conqueror named himself king, and song of the gods, all believed him. Here, in the East, it is possible to say to human beings, 'I am your god,' and all believe Europe is a molehill,"

Soon, not many miles away, Napoleon makes ready for battle. Eight thousand Mamelukes, the best cavalry in the world, are ready to crush the invader. He rides up and down in front of his troops, points to the pyramids in the distance, and exclaims: "Soldiers, forty centuries are looking down on you." The Mamelukes charge the French, but are driven back by artillery fire; their camp is soon in Bonaparte's hands; they flee to the Nile, crossing the river in boats and by swimming; since it is notorious that they always have gold with them, the fight continues for hours on the bank and in the water until the victors have secured some of the treasure.

In Cairo, he knows how to win the support of the pashas and the sheikhs. He gives out that he loves and venerates the Turks and the Sultan. He is only attacking Mamelukes, who are their enemies likewise. Periphrases, bowings and scrapings, elaborate metaphors–these come natural to him, the man of the Mediterranean who is half an oriental. They are devices for lying even more circumstantially than do the diplomats of Europe with their speedier and more direct methods. Here he is following the oriental custom. While still on board the "Orient," he had dictated to his interpreter a letter to the Pasha of Egypt. It began as follows:

"Thou who shouldst be supreme over all the beys, but hast, as I know, neither power nor prestige in Cairo, thou wilt welcome my coming. Assuredly thou knowest that I have it not in mind to do anything against the Koran or against the Sultan. Come, therefore, to my help, and join with me in cursing the godless race of beys!"

To approximate his own creed to the faith of Allah, he begins, like a conjuror, to juggle with the Trinity. First of all he explains that he has conquered the Pope and the Maltese, and that for him the Koran is the word of God just as much as the Bible. But, at a later date, when the forces sent to dislodge his own are being disembarked, he argues as follows: "Allah is Allah, and Mohammed is his prophet. To the divan of Cairo, chosen from among the ablest, most learned, and most enlightened of men! The blessing of the Prophet be upon you!" He goes on to say that he has allowed these men to be landed in order that he may kill them all at one blow, "which will be a glorious sight for Cairo." There were Russians on board the invader's ships. "The Russians hate all who, like you and myself, believe in one God, for, in their own legends, they speak of three gods. They will learn, soon enough, that there is but one God, the father of Victory, who graciously fights on the side of the good."

Out of this potpourri of the religious, which ends on a more pagan note than he seems to be aware, he subsequently extracts unchristian France as a political instrument, saying that the religion of France is especially akin to Mohammedanism, He is continually appealing to the Koran as the basis of his thought. The holy book which he has included in the political section of his travelling library, shall be made to do him good service. When he dismisses a dangerous cadi in Cairo, he finds a justification for his action in the Koran: "All that is good comes from God; he gives us victory.... Whatever I undertake must succeed. All those whom I call my friends, thrive. But any one who helps my enemies, perishes."

If he had but had the luck to have been born here in Egypt four thousand years ago, he would have gained the victory by the power of suggestion alone. But nowadays even these brown fellows are sceptical! He despises them, while showering them with superlatives; but, at the same time, he threatens to punish with the utmost rigour any of his soldiers who injures a native. The first order of the day to the Army in the East runs: "The peoples with whom we are now in contact do not treat their women as we treat ours. Nevertheless, any one who harms a woman is looked upon as a monster here as in Europe. Looting enriches very few, dishonours all, destroys the sources of aid, and makes us hated by those with whom is it to our interest that we should be friends." No one is to enter a mosque, and groups must not even assemble around the doors. By cajolery and threats, by tolerance and intrigue, by Allah and the sword, by all the methods of the oriental, Bonaparte secures an authoritative position within a few weeks.

At length he can regard himself as master in the East. Is he any the happier for that?

Junot has received a letter about Josephine. If only this letter, like hundreds more, had been intercepted by the English! Then, at least, Napoleon could still have enjoyed the bliss of ignorance! For Junot feels it his duty to tell his commander and old friend all about the matter. It concerns Hippolyte Charles, as well as Josephine. Napoleon had cashiered the young man. Josephine and found him a job with an army contractor, and had lost sight of him for a time. But she has met him again, has come across him at a fashionable dancing school. Her old passion has revived. He has such graceful hips! He makes such elegant sallies! Now he has the added charm of wealth. Meanwhile, Josephine has bought a fine estate near Paris (though it is not yet paid for); the young dandy is living with her at Malmainson as master of the house....

Bonaparte walks up and down as he talks things over with Junot. He grows paler and paler; his face twitches; twice or thrice he strikes his forehead despairingly with his fist. Suddenly, turning upon Bourrienne, who is sitting in front of the tent, he says: "You are not a true friend! These women! Josephine! You ought to have told me. Junot, he is really my friend. Josephine and I am more than two thousand miles away! How can she betray me like this? Damn these puppies and coxcombs! I'll make short work of the lot of them. I will divorce her. Yes, a public, sensational divorce! I will write instantly. I know everything. If she is guilty, farewell! I will not be a mock for the flâneurs on the boulevards."

Bourrienne tries to pacify him; tells him that fame is more important than family happiness. "Fame! What is that worth? I would give everything in the world, so much do I love her, if only Junot's news were false."

But the English may intercept and publish anything he writes, so in his letter to his brother Joseph he can do no more than hint at this private calamity. The missive has a peculiar charm, which is perhaps given to it by the writer's enforced restraint, by the need for using veiled expressions. Tædium vitae of genius at its climax. This private letter is penned the day after a victorious and virile dispatch:

"No other country in the world is so rich as Egypt in maize, rice, vegetables, and meat. Barbarism reaches it highest level here. There is no money, not even for paying the troops. In two months I can be back in France. Look after my interests, I beseech you; I have a great deal of trouble at home; the veil has been torn off once for all–I have no one left in the world but you. Your affection is precious to me. Only one thing could increase my bitterness–if I were to lose you, if you also were to play the traitor. How terrible that all my affections should be concentrated upon one personality. You understand me? Make arrangements that as soon as I return home I shall have at my disposal a country house near Paris or in Burgundy, a place where I can spend the winter in absolute seclusion. Mankind has become loathsome to me,. I need rest and solitude. Greatness bores me to death. The fount of feeling is dried up. At twenty-nine years of age, I find that fame is vanity. I've got to the end of everything. Only one resource is left to me, to become an absolute egoist. I shall keep my house in Paris, and not hand it over to any one! I have nothing more than what I brought into the world with me. I have never been unjust to you, that you must admit, though I have often wanted to be. You will understand. Kiss your wife for me, and Jerome. Bonaparte."

This cynicism and misanthropy, the desire for vengeance and the demand for satisfaction, have at length, and for the first time, become merged in a symphony of melancholy. The melancholy note had been sounded twelve years before in his diary, but since then it has been silent. A heart that desired to give itself wholly, in which trust had been ever renewed despite many disillusionments, now seems to have been pierced through and through. Victory, glory, to be a second Alexander—all dust and ashes. If a man is deceived where he least deserves it, and where he has trusted with all the ardency of youth, what is greatness to him? He begins his letter with rice and vegetables, and ends with solitude and utter disheartenment. What is left for him in the world besides his brother? "I have got to the end of everything."

XV

A blow quickened him back to life.

Returning from a ride in the desert, he entered Marmont's tent to find that all his associates were greatly perturbed. What had happened? The French fleet had been destroyed. The day before, there had been a sea-fight in Aboukir Bay, and only four ships had escaped. All the rest had been sunk or captured by Nelson.

The officers stood in gloomy silence. The grenadier on sentry duty in front of the tent understood, everyone understood, the meaning of this reverse. Napoleon's face paled, but he recovered his composure instantly, realising that it was his business to

play an active part in the world; but he believes no less strongly in legitimacy. The hereditary succession of kingship is over and done with. The hereditary succession of efficiency is the new doctrine. Such is the fallacy by which his mind is enslaved.

After a while, he says savagely to one of his confidants: "The silly fool of a woman does not even know how to make children!" The gibe is retailed to her, and she exclaims mockingly: "It's not my fault, you know!" Bonaparte hears of the rejoinder, and his face is shadowed. He has no proof to the contrary. Nothing but the inner consciousness of a productivity such as no mortal has ever had before.

His spirit embraces the whole world in its grasp. But if nature has denied him the capacity for reproduction, the foundation of all activity has been shattered. His self-confidence would collapse.

XVI

In the Institute, the commander-in-chief sits as an equal among equals. He never tries, in argument there, to gain a victory by rank instead of reason. Yet many of the questions that are discussed relate to army matters of immediate practical importance, such as the filtering of Nile water, the erection of windmills, the search for ingredients needed to make gunpowder. On one occasion, Napoleon grew heated. Berthollet said quietly: "You are wrong, my friend, for you have lost your temper." A naval surgeon supported Berthollet. "You men of science are as thick as thieves," exclaimed Bonaparte. "Chemistry plays the cook for medicine, and plays the assassin for science!" The surgeon's answer came pat: "But how, Citizen-General, would you define the conqueror's art?" Within the republic of learning, this equality pleased the dictator, whom elsewhere hardly anyone now ventured to contradict.

For weeks in succession, the orders of the day ended with the words: "No news from France." Everything was at a standstill;

widespread uncertainty prevailed. Amid the general inertia, the travelling university was an exception; the savants were hard at work, studying, advising, ever ready to help in the second line. As far as they were concerned, this time of waiting was a great opportunity for research. A thorough investigation of the country and its resources was in progress; the fishes of the Nile and the minerals of the Red Sea, the flora of the Delta and the constituents of the desert sand–all were now for the first time being elaborately scrutinised. The exploitation of the natron lakes and the Nile mud was under consideration. The physicians of the expedition were enquiring into the causes of oriental plague; and of trachoma, the terrible form of ophthalmia which is so frequent a cause of blindness in Egypt. A dictionary and a grammar were printed; some of the buried temples of Upper Egypt were disinterred; the Wells of Moses were discovered. One day, an engineer officer came back from Rosetta bringing with him a granite slab on which there was a polyglot inscription, chiselled in Greek and in two variants of the ancient Egyptian picture-writing. The riddle of the hieroglyphs had been unriddled.

What especially interested the commander, however, was the possibility of cutting a canal through the Isthmus of Suez. He made long journeys in the desert, always exposed to the danger of Bedouin raids; traced the line of the ancient canal; planned the course of a new channel. All his speculations were confirmed half a century later by Lesseps. Not like an adventurer whose schemes have miscarried, but in the spirit of a conqueror, he designed to separate the continents and link the seas.

Now at length! Some merchants on small vessels have managed to slip through the English lines. From them, Napoleon learns that the destruction of the French fleet off Aboukir has brought about a general transformation. The Sultan has entered into an alliance with Russia, and the two powers have declared war on France. Achmed, the Turkish commander, is marching on Egypt through Syria. The malcontents in Cairo, encouraged by these tidings, rise in revolt. The insurrection is quelled by artillery fire, and the heads of the rebels are exposed on pikes as a warning.

"This will have a salutary effect. Clemency is no good here."

On the whole, the commander is more relieved than alarmed. If the Turks are marching southwards, so much the better; at length he will have a chance of beating them in open fight.

From most of his close associates he conceals his deeper cause for anxiety. When he left France to occupy Egypt, his aim was to secure a position that would help him in his scheme for the conquest of India. "With, ships, we can cross the seas; with camels we can cross the desert." He had allowed fifteen months for the conquest of Egypt and the consolidation of his power there, and for the preparation and equipment of his forces for the Indian campaign. That would need forty thousand men, and many camels, and one hundred and twenty field-guns. He had asked for extensive reinforcement; ships, guns, and men. These were to support his land army by sea.

The battle of the Nile and frustrated his fine schemes. The English were blockading the coast; the Sultan had become his enemy; Egyptian sentiment was now hostile. But it was Napoleon's way to adapt his plans to changing circumstances, and it seemed to him that he could derive advantage from the turn of events. The Turks and the English are going to make a joint landing? That threatens our very existence here? Well, then, let us attack to escape destruction! Seize all the magazines and ports from the Turks, arm the Syrian Christians, stir up the Druses! If we were to take the fortress of Acre, opinion in Cairo would veer round to our side. By June, we shall be in Damascus; shall thrust outposts forward into the Taurus; march eastward with 26,000 Frenchmen, 6,000 Mamelukes, and 18,000 Druses. Desaix will come direct from Egypt. The Sultan will find it expedient to keep quiet. The Shah of Persia has already agreed to our marching by way of Bassora and Shiraz. By March, if Allah favours us, we shall reach the Indus.

Once more, Bonaparte fashions a splendid dream out of pressing embarrassments. He sets out for Syria.

There are practically no roads. Sometimes he rides as many as forty-five miles in fifteen hours, invariably by night, without water, and almost always with the vanguard. When Jaffa falls, three thousand Turkish soldiers surrender. What on earth is he to do with them? Keep them prisoner? His own men are on short commons; and, besides, he would then have to spare thousands of Frenchmen to guard the Turks. Send them home? He has no ships. Exchange them? The Turks have no prisoners. Set them free? Then they will reinforce Acre, the next stronghold. What on earth is he to do? Council of war!

All are in favour of killing the prisoners. Only a few days before, the Turks killed one of our envoys! Our own troops would be infuriated if they were to go hungrier still because of these fellows. Bonaparte wavers, thinks matters over for three days, and finally agrees. The prisoners are marched down to the sea and slaughtered. Subsequent military critics, especially the Germans, have agreed that there was no choice.

Acre lies before us. There we shall find stores of new weapons. Then onwards toward the north! The great dream renews itself during these weeks. Now that Turkey has declared war, he is completely isolated, and forced into a life-and-death struggle. Everything is possible, for needs must when the devil drives. But he is not quite easy in his mind about the Indian scheme, for he mentions an alternative plan to one of his officers: "After I have seized Acre, I shall march upon Damascus and Aleppo, augmenting my army as I go, for I shall announce to the people the overthrow of the tyrannous pashas. Then, with overwhelming forces. I shall take Constantinople, make an end of Turkey, and found a new and great empire. This will bring me immortal fame. Perhaps I shall then make my way home through Adrianople or Vienna, after annihilating the house of Habsburg,"

Always the same visions, magnified now, when the situation grows desperate.

He reaches Acre, Not a big fortress, but well supplied with modern weapons, and defended by English officers and artillerists. Three successive attempts to storm the place are fruitless. English battleships arrive to support the besieged, and threaten the besiegers.

At last, after eight months, he has direct news from Paris! It is little to his taste. Talleyrand has not gone to Constantinople to treat with the Sultan. Is the rogue hedging? The French Republic is at war with Naples and Sardinia. Moreau and Augereau, Bonaparte's rivals, have high command. Why, in God's name, do we squat here on the burning sands, inactive? Storm the place! Are our schemes to be wrecked against these miserable walls?

Who is in charge of the defence? Phélippeaux is there, a skilled engineer, one of Napoleon's old comrades at the Cadets' School in Paris, afterwards an emigre who had entered the English service!

Why can they not take the place by storm? Bonaparte has no patience for a slow siege, for starving his enemy into surrender. The whole idea is foreign to his impetuous temperament. A fortress, like a woman, must be taken by storm, or not at all. He cannot beg, serve, or woo; and he cannot wait. Now time presses, and to wait is out of the question. Storm! The soldiers begin to murmur. Even among the officers there are mutterings which are the heralds of mutiny. "Let us have Kléber for our leader; he is humane and gentle."

Bonaparte sits in his tent, thinking matters over. A terrible hour! Is England to be ever invincible, even on land, even here in the East? Is the siege to drag on for months? Impossible! Europe is full of the clash of arms. Turn back, without having won a victory? An unprecedented experience, an entirely new feeling; but there is no choice. The enterprise must be abandoned. Back to Egypt! It is only half the truth to say that Acre barred his march upon India. Who can tell whether, if the fortress had been taken, he would have pressed on towards the Indus notwithstanding the ominous news from Paris. We should have to reckon with incalculable feelings here. Every coincidence is symbolical. Before Acre and on the Po, France is at war with the same monarchical coalition. None but the son of the revolution can save the situation. Contrary to his usual custom, he does not ride in the van, but for hours after the columns have started southward, till nightfall indeed, he stays behind on an elevation to contemplate the stubborn fortress, his mind filled with a sort of ferocious melancholy.

A ghastly retreat. No roads, no water, the plague as rearguard. Is Bonaparte's career to be ruined by the desert and the black death? Calm of aspect, he visits the sick in hospital, and encourages them wherever possible. The doctor points to fifty cases as hopeless. They must be put out of their misery, thinks Bonaparte; their path to death must be smoothed. With a royal assumption of responsibility, he orders a lethal does of opium. The doctor demurs. It remains uncertain whether someone else carried out the order. "In such circumstances," he says later, "I would have had my own son poisoned."

Two thousand sick men and six thousand who are still in health make their way slowly through the desert. Every four of the healthy have to carry a comrade who is too ill to walk, for there are not enough horses to bear the sick and the maimed. The staff officers are all marching with the rest. This is by Napoleon's command. An equerry asks him which horse he will ride. "Did you not hear the order?" retorts the commander, striking the man with his whip. "Everyone on foot!"

At length the retreating army reaches Cairo. By entering with a triumphal display of captured colours, and by proclamations and marches, he makes a vain attempt to delude the people of Egypt.

What is Paris saying? What shall he tell Paris? We did not occupy Acre, because the plague was raging there! That was why we withdrew from the siege! In the Institute, a committee is appointed to substantiate this tale. A doctor stands up, and, in the presence of a hundred savants, refuses to attach his name to this fiction. The commander yields with a wry face, but bears no grudge against the stalwart, whom he promotes more than once in years to come.

The Turks now arrive by sea, intending to make an end of the French. Once more, the whole existence of the expeditionary force is at stake. The enemy is to land in Aboukir Bay, just a year after the battle on the Nile. He lets them land, and then inflicts a crushing defeat on them, though their army outnumbers his by two to one. After the battle, Murat meets him, and embracing him, says: "General, you are as great as the world, but the world is too small for you!" Bonaparte writes to Cairo: You will have heard of the battle on the shores of Aboukir Bay, one of the finest I have ever seen! Of the army the enemy had landed, not a man escaped."

At this time he notices among the Mamelukes who have entered his service a tall, handsome fellow with blue eyes, a Georgian named Rustam, who has five times been sold as a slave. Fidelity is written on his countenance. Napoleon gives him a sword with an encased hilt and scabbard, and makes him his body-servant. For fifteen years, Rustam sleeps outside his master's door.

After the victory at Aboukir, Napoleon enters into a parley with the admiral of the blockading fleet. Ostensibly he wishes to discuss an exchange of prisoners with the English. Really he is hungering for news; newspapers are worth more than king's crowns. Some one manages to get hold of what he covets, and an adjutant brings them into his tent. The commander is asleep. "Here are newspapers, General. Bad news." He sits up. "What's happened?"

"Scherer has been beaten. We have lost nearly the whole of Italy." Napoleon jumps out of bed, seizes the papers, and goes on reading them all through the night, with an occasional pause for an outburst of wrath. At dawn, he sends for his admiral-in-chief, is closeted with the seaman for a couple of hours, and then sets out for Cairo.

"I have made up my mind to return to France," he says behind shut doors to the faithful Marmont. "You will come with me. Our armies in Europe have been defeated. God knows where the enemy will have got to by now. Italy is lost. What are they about, these incompetent idiots at the head of affairs? Stupidity and corruption! I have borne the whole burden single-handed, and by my victories have propped up a government which could never have maintained itself but for me. As soon as I leave, everything collapses. If I start at once, I shall get to Paris almost as soon as the news of my latest victory. My presence will restore confidence to the troops, and will reanimate the citizens with hope for a happier future."

"My future," he thinks, as soon as Marmont has gone. "People will say I have abandoned the army in Egypt. It will get along all right under Kléber. I came here to found a colony. It is founded, and the Turks have been beaten. Help can only come from France, and no one but myself can send it. I have nothing more to gain here, but everything to win on the battle-fields of Europe. Thirty years! How many days before I can get away? The admiral says it is a bad wind for Toulon, and that English warships swarm in the Mediterranean. I'm afraid I can't get to Paris in an air-balloon! But Paris is the heart of the world. I must risk the sea passage."

XVII

They show no lights, the two small frigates which had once flown Venetian colours. The vessel freighted with the commander is the "Muiron," thus rechristened in memory of the lieutenant who had died to save him at Arcola. Fifteen years later he is to do still more honour to this name. Here, off Cape Bon, is the most dangerous point. Literally, they sail through the English fleet, for they know the ships by their lights. An August night, but cold, for the mistral is blowing. They sit on deck in the starlight, feeling dull and rather depressed. Let's liven things up with a game of cards; there's just light enough to play! Bonaparte cheats, and is delighted that no one notices. Next morning, with mischievous glee, he owns up, and restores his ill-gotten gains.

What a different voyage from that of fifteen months ago! Only two ships now, and then there were four hundred. Half of the army is dead bones. True, France still holds the land of ancient story—but for how long? The hopes of striking an effective blow against England have been dashed. What has become of the plan for a landing at Dover? Gone to join the scheme for the invasion of India! He has had to steal away furtively from Egypt, for there might have been a mutiny had his impending departure become generally known among the soldiers of the army of occupation. Kléber was not appointed commander-in-chief until Napoleon had gone. The last order of the day had been dry and brief. The civilians had been sent to Upper Egypt, for Monge and Berthollet, who were in the know, and were now on board, might have blabbed the news to their colleagues. But poets were a nuisance! One of the fellows, keen-witted, had guessed what was in the wind, and had stolen aboard the frigate, whose destination was still undisclosed. Oh, well, let the beggar come along. He and his tribe are the brokers of fame, so we can't do without them. After the last victory, Paris will be on our side.

For weeks, the two frigates are in continual danger. "What would you do, if the English fleet were to heave in sight? Fright? Impossible! Surrender? You would none of you like that any better than I should. The only other alternative is to blow up the ship." A general silence. Monge, who is sitting beside the commander, grows pale. "That shall be your charge," adds Napoleon, turning to him with a mischievous smile. A few days later, a ship is sighted, and is wrongly supposed to be an English man-of-war. The mathematician vanishes, and is found afterwards at the door of the powder magazine.

This incident gives us the measure of Bonaparte's authority.

After a six weeks' cruise in the Mediterranean, an island is sighted on a fine October morning, a familiar ridge of mountains is seen on the horizon. The captain of the frigate consults his chart. "That is Corsica," says Bonaparte unhesitatingly. Does he order the seamen to slap on all sail and make for the island? No, they must find out, first, whether the place is still French. But a strong wind is blowing shoreward, and, even under light canvas, progress is rapid. His thoughts run swiftly, too.

"'Still French?' My question used to be, 'French yet? Only

six years ago. I was twenty-four then, and to be master of this island seemed to me the greatest thing in the world. Since then, I have had Italy at my feet; Egypt has been conquered; Paris smiles. All has happened as if by natural sequence. The wind is freshening. What will be the answer from the shore?" The signal shows that the harbour is open to a French ship. The native island of the man without a country is home to him once more.

They land, and all Ajaccio crowds to the harbour; thousands who once cursed the name of Bonaparte are now eager to welcome him. He regards the throng cynically. Many address him with the familiar "thou"; and hundreds wish to shake hands with him. He accepts these demonstrations unmoved. But suddenly he hears a voice: "Figlio? Caro figlio!" Camilla is speaking, his old nurse, a vigorous peasantwoman, hardly fifty years of age. The sight of her is the only thing that stirs his emotions.

Napoleon makes for his ancestral home, which his mother has had set in order once more, though she is away just now. He summons those best fitted to give him the news he craves. There, beside the family hearth, he learns what has, during the last three months, happened to his creations. Mantua and Milan have gone, and with them most of Italy, won by his feats of arms three short years ago. Genoa is still French, though hard to keep. Massena has been forced back through Switzerland! The English have landed in Holland! What is the first thing to do? Make for Nice! Instantly take the lead! Win back all in a storm of victories. "What's that you say?" Two of the Directors forcibly removed! Only by such tricks can the shaky government still keep in power? General Moulin is one of the Directors? Moulin, who the devil is he? The other substitute? Sieyés, you say? Another coup must be impending—perhaps a forcible change of government. We must make all speed for Paris. On board! On board! Take a big rowing boat in tow!

Two days' sail towards Toulon. Twilight when the coast is sighted. The look-out man reports English ships. "Put about!" orders the admiral. "Forward!" thunders Bonaparte. In case of need, we can make the shore in the big rowing boat! Once more his star blinds the enemy; once more he escapes capture by the English. Night falls. Impossible to land at Toulon? Let us make for Fréjus, then. Uncharted rocks there? Rocks everywhere! In sight of the French coast after a seven weeks' voyage, we must run all risks to land!

Does this Italian love the country on which he now sets his foot? To him it is nothing more than the fiddle on which he can play a better tune than on any other instrument.

Next day, in the little town of Fréjus, Bonaparte's name is on everyone's lips. Why is the harbour full of rowing boats, laden with sightseers? Why this popular rejoicing? What has the man done in Africa, that the inhabitants of the provincial town should greet him as if he were a Roman imperator celebrating a triumph? An official says something about quarantine. "We prefer the plague to the Austrians, and the Austrians are almost at our gates!" shouts the crowd, escorting him through the streets as a deliverer.

"France seems to be in a bad way," thinks the man in the carriage, as he acknowledges the vociferations. "It looks as if everyone had been waiting for me. A while back would have been too soon. Tomorrow would have been too late. I have come at the right moment."

He drives westward from Fréjus, and stays for a time in Aix, questioning everyone he meets. At Aix, a copy of a letter comes into his hands, an old letter that had miscarried: "The Directory is waiting for you, General; for you and your brave companions!" This was written in the panic of rulers who are at their wits' end for a saviour! What had he better do? Stay where he is for a time, and write before going to Paris "Egypt is wholly ours, and safe from invasion—I was cut off from newspapers till end of July, but when I heard of your troubles I instantly set out for home. I had to take all risks, for my place was the spot where I could be of most use. Had there been no frigate, I should have wrapped myself in my cloak and should have sailed in the first cockle-shell I could find. With Kléber in command, Egypt is in good hands. When I left, the whole country was under water—the best Nile for fifty years."

This carefully worded epistle goes as a herald to Paris. The people there must be told who is on the way. His northward journey is a via triumphalis; salutes are fired everywhere. Passing through Valence, he recognises among the onlookers the good woman who keeps the café where he used to lodge, the place with the billiard room; he gives her a keepsake from the East. In Lyons, he waits two or three hours to see the performance of a hastily extemporised drama, "The Hero's Return." Everything shows the powerful spell already exercised by his name. Perhaps the most signal instance is the sensational end of Baudin, one of the best of the deputies, who utters a shout of joy on hearing the news of Napoleon's return, and drops dead from surcharge of emotion. The light that radiates from the commander is so strong that it kills.

Paris draws near. He is still gathering news. But about private affairs, about Josephine, he can ask no questions. Is he already a divorcé? Where are his brothers? The news of his coming has been noised abroad; why has no one come to meet him? She, where is she? Will she, after all, be waiting for him in the mirrored room, ready to welcome him with a smile? In the grey dawn he passes the octroi, drives along the outer boulevards, turns into his own little street. There is the house. A woman stands alone at the door. Who is it?

His mother.

XVIII

"Bonaparte's landing is one of those events which at first we hesitate to believe. The news spread over night at theatres and in social gatherings. In the most obscure pot-houses, people were drinking to celebrate his return...." "Everyone hails him with delight, for he brings us new hope...." "Glory, peace, and happiness follow in his train."

which his relatives have told him all the scandal. True, some of his intimates warn him against applying for a divorce. In Paris, a cuckold is always a figure of fun. He is resolute, however: "I have done with her. What do I care about the chatter? It will only last for a day or two." He has her trunks packed, and carried down to the porter's lodge, so that she shall not enter the house. Could he give plainer proof that he dreads his own weakness?

She comes, breaks through the first life of defence, enters the fortress. He has locked himself in. She calls to him and pleads with him through the door. During her journey, the more she has come to realise that his name is in everyone's mouth, the more has her pride been humbled. But the citadel holds out. At length she decides to call up reinforcements for a final assault. Hortense and Eugene must come to her aid. They clamour, beseech, shed tears. Thus a night passes.

No dispassionate observer can fail to understand Josephine's motives in making this ridiculous scene. What of Bonaparte himself, the man with so profound a knowledge of the human soul? We he duped by a woman?

There he lies, returned after a long absence, with his head full of schemes for the conquest of a nation. Let us try to follow his thoughts. "They have deceived me one and all. The government, the political parties, my own companions-in-arms, were all endeavouring, during my absence, to exclude me from power, for they regarded me as a danger to themselves. As long as I was out of range, no one wanted me back; my brothers no more than the rest. This capricious woman, whose pretty whims I have never tried to restrain–would it be reasonable for me to expect that she should have spent a year and more thinking of no one but her absent husband, whose return seemed ever more unlikely as the days went by? When I am there, she is fascinating. If I make truce with her now, when the game is in my hands, she will agree to all my conditions, and I can exact guarantees for the future. What a lovely voice she has. There cannot have been any falling off in her adventurer! Mufti; green coat; round hat; Mameluke sword. The man wants to dazzle Paris into believing him a pasha. Did you notice that he has had his hair cut short? Wants to win people by an affectation of simplicity! Yet today he comes to call in great style. General on horseback, with all his aides. Brilliant uniforms. Paris agog. Very sinister, this change of aspect. Look at the way he sits and questions the five of us, as if he were a monarch holding audience.

"Why do you let the man impose on you?" say his enemies angrily to the Directors. He made a frightful mess of the Egyptian campaign. Your proper course is plain enough. Have him arrested for deserting the army under his command! He's got something up his sleeve, you may be sure!"

Bonaparte, meanwhile, receives visits from Jacobin leaders and Bourbon agents; gives advice to all and sundry, but tells no one what he really thinks; behaves like a man of family who has just returned from a long journey, and, with an air of good-natured boredom, allows his relatives to tell him all about their squabbles while he has been away. He has been home for two weeks now. The tension is increasing. Affairs of State are at the standstill, or nearly so; for the Five, who should be carrying on the work of government, are busied in intrigue. Amid the general confusion, the Councils have utterly lost prestige. The new constitution is rocking in the blast, but no one seems to know from which quarter the wind is blowing. Who is the real holder of power in the State? Who controls the army? General Moulin? General Bonaparte?

While no one can tell from day to day how the relationships between Napoleon and the government are likely to shape themselves, he goes to the Institute to deliver a lecture on the vestiges of the ancient Suez canal, and describes the Rossetta stone. On November 1st, there is a State banquet in honour of a victory won by Masséna. Where is Bonaparte? No doubt it is not to his taste to celebrate the triumphs of a brother-in-arms!

That evening he is closeted with Lucien and Abbé Sieyés. Talleyrand has at length brought him in touch with the ablest of the Directors. Sieyés and Bonaparte, the man who has rediscovered the constitution and the man who has rediscovered the secret of power, sit face to face; they vie with one another in ambition and in intellectual ability. "I have made the Great Nation," says the general. "You could not have done so, had we not first made the Nation," counters the abbé.

They discuss the details of the proposed coup d'état. On the critical day, they will spread the report that a Jacobin conspiracy is afoot. The Councils, in alarm, will transfer their sessions from Central Paris to Saint-Cloud. "As a measure of precaution," Bonaparte will be entrusted with the command of the Paris garrison. Sieyés has come to an understanding with Ducos. Persuasion, threats, or money, will induce the other three Directors to resign. Barras will take money. But what about Gohier? "Make short work of it," says Lucien. "Dissolve the Councils by force." But at night Napoleon, when he is alone, turns matters over in his mind:

"Force! How silly it was to use force four years ago! We see where it has led! The supreme art is to maintain the appearance of legality. Without cannon or bloodshed, without arrests and parties, that is the secret of the ideal coup d'état. Otherwise you set up something that may last a year before it wears out. After ten years of revolution, the republic is heartily sick of it all. She is an amazon who has borne arms till she is tired, and now asks nothing better than to be led by a strong man. She is ready for me."

"Can I depend upon Sieyés? Behind that receding forehead of his he thinks too much. For ten years he has been building constitutions, but he is nothing more than the ideologue whom a vigorous general can use before casting aside. Had I not arrived in the nick of time, he would have joined forces with Moreau. I shall turn the pair of them to account. I know I can trust Berthïer, Bourrienne, Murat, Marmont, and Leclerc. Is Lucien faithful? For the time being. Bernadotte? His spiteful look betrayed his true feelings. Still, he will not come into the field against me. What about Talleyrand? A dangerous man, and for that very reason I must have him on my side. Moulin? No time to waste; there are too many generals in Paris. Watch out!"

Next evening he went to Talleyrand's, for a private talk with that intriguer. They sat late, discussing plans. Suddenly there was a noise in the street. Trotting horses, which stop in front of the door. The patrol? "Bonaparte turned pale, and I fancy I must have done the same," wrote Talleyrand in his memoirs. Both men believe that they are about to be arrested. Lights out, and on tiptoe to the balcony. False alarm! An ordinary street scene, nocturnal revellers and police, nothing more. The conspirators breathe again. But why do not the Directors have them arrested on suspicion? The answer is simple. Bonaparte is already too commanding a figure to be touched!

On the 6th, there is a banquet at the Luxembourg. Bonaparte and Moreau are the guests, but the latter has the place of honour, and the hosts eye Bonaparte askance. He reciprocates his entertainers' suspicions, and eats nothing but bread and eggs, handed him by a trusty servant. After half an hour, he makes his excuses, and goes back to his confederates, to talk over the plan for bringing about the downfall of the men with whom he has just been dining. Next evening. Talleyrand, Roederer, and Sieyés, dine with Bonaparte; Jourdan and Bernadotte, who are to be won over, have also been invited. After dinner, he asks Jourdan what is to happen. This simple question is evidence enough of the prevailing crisis. Two generals who have never before exchanged a word except about commonplaces, meet, and look one another in the face. "What is going to happen?" enquires one. The other significantly grips his sword-hilt. The plotters agree to take action in forty-eight hours. The parts to be played by members of the inner ring are assigned. Murat, Lannes, and Marmont are to inform the officers of the three branches of the service; Berthier will acquaint the general staff.

Lucien undertakes to manage affairs in the Council of Five Hundred. He is President for the month, having been elected in honour of his brother's return. The President of the Council of Ancients is also a party to the conspiracy. The bedells will be told to overlook certain names when notice of the sitting are sent out. As soon as Bonaparte has been appointed commander of the Paris garrison, he will hand over the Tuileries to Lannes and the Palais Bourbon to Murat. Gohier and his wife will be invited to breakfast by Josephine—eight o'clock. Bonaparte will offer himself to Barras for luncheon, in order to put Barras off his guard. Joseph will persuade his brother-in-in-law Bernadotte to keep quiet, if Bernadotte will not actively participate. Roéderer writes the proclamation. His son knows a friendly printer who will set it up and machine it–on the quiet.

"Was Brutus' mood so paltry?" thinks Bonaparte. "But, in truth, we too wish to slay someone-Anarchy! A new era, a new century, to be ushered in by such petty and distasteful means! Camp life is cleaner!"

XIX

November 9th, a foggy autumn morning; the Eighteenth Brumaire is dawning. A bustle in the street opposite Bonaparte's house; officers arriving on horseback and in carriages. Is the blow to be struck at last? Most of those present were with him in Italy. The house is too small for such a concourse. They stroll up and down in the garden, discussing their chances; lively and cheerful and if they were on the Rhine. Appearances must be kept up. No one must be able to say that uniformed officers were about so early. All goes well. Messengers come to confirm the carrying out of the programme; both Councils were summoned at seven o'clock, but undesirable members have not received notice. The initiates were the first comers, and, as soon as, there was a quorum, Lucien in the Council of Five Hundred and his colleague in the Council. of Ancients had proposed Bonaparte's appointment to the command of the Paris garrison.

Here is the messenger with the commission, duly sealed! The formalities are being strictly observed. The general joins his faithful followers. Everything goes on as if they were in camp. With a great suite, he rides through the town, to the amazement of a huge crowd, which does not, however, show any political interest. A dragoon regiment which had been through the Italian campaign with Napoleon turns up on the Boulevard Madeleine without awaiting the orders of its colonel. Other officers follow with Ducos and Marmont. The latter summoned them at an early hour. When they said they could not come for lack of horses, he borrowed some from a riding-school.

The Tuileries garden is crowded. Many remain on horse-back; but Bonaparte dismounts and enters the Council of Ancients. Is he going to make a speech to people whom he despises, in this dark and unfamiliar hall? Why does he not take the oath to the constitution, the constitution he is about to destroy? The law directs that a general appointed to a new command should take this oath. Evading the formality, he speaks for the rostrum:

"The republic is in danger.... Recognising this, you have passed a law that will save it. Do not search history for examples that may give reason for restraining your activities. No epoch in history is like the end of the eighteenth century, and in that end there is nothing like this moment.... We want republic based on liberty and equality. We shall have it. With the aid of all the friends of liberty, I shall save the republic. In my own name and in that of my companions-in-arms, I swear it to you!"

"We swear it!" comes like an echo through the open doors of the hall. The Ancients move uneasily in their seats. "Companions-in-arms?" But Bonaparte has left the hall, drawing a breath of relief. These lawyers' eyes; bespectacled eyes! Effete pygmies! Has he noticed that he spoke to them as if he were on the parade ground, and that they did not like his tone?

His words and his voice have a very different ring outside, when, having remounted his charger, he summons his troops to save the republic. Then comes a report from Lucien, who has meanwhile adjourned to the following day the sitting of the Council of Five Hundred. What is that you say? The Directors' guard is on the way hither? Do they comes as friends or foes? "Is Sieyés sending them?" Their colonel says no. The two men laugh.

In fact, Sieyés, pale of countenance, is still at the gate of the

Luxembourg. For the last fortnight, our clever abbé has been taking riding lessons. It had been his design to ride at the head of his guard to join his new comrades. Before all the world, he would show his equality with these comrades by leaning from his saddle and embracing them. But the guard has started without his orders; their colonel has brought them to the Tuileries, riding hell-for-leather, too hot a pace for the abbé. Almost unnoticed, and much crestfallen, Sieyés drives after them in a carriage, with Ducos, who is pliable, by his side. Everyone in the know is aware by this time what will happen to the other three Directors.

Moulin looks at the matter from a soldier's standpoint. He estimates the opposing force at the Tuileries to be eight thousand strong, and his adjutants report to him that all the important points of the town are in Bonaparte's hands. He writes, therefore, saying: "At your service."

Honest Gohier is at home, blustering ineffectually. He had not thought it advisable to accept the strange invitation to an eight o'clock breakfast, and had been content to send his wife. Now, a sort of hostage, she is drinking tea with Josephine, while Bonaparte is betraying her husband—not, indeed, stealing his mistress, but stealing France. When the first news comes, Gohier sends for his colleagues, summoning them to a meeting of the Directory. No one turns up. Moulin has joined Sieyés and Ducos. Barras says he is in his bath.

When Talleyrand, the messenger of fate, visits Barras, the Director is shaving; he seems to be devoting the day to the arts of the toilet! But, at a glance or two from the other augur, he throws up the game, being content to ask for a safe-conduct. When his secretary brings this demand to Bonaparte, the general harangues the man publicly in the Tuileries garden "What have you done with France, that I should let you off so easily? I gave you peace, and I find war.... What have you done with the hundred thousand Frenchmen who were the companions of my glory? They are dead! We can go no farther along that road, for in three years it leads to despotism! We want a republic based on equality and liberty, toleration and morality!"

Thus berated, the little secretary shakes in his shoes. In reality. Bonaparte is perfectly calm, but it suits him to simulate wrath in the presence of so many witnesses. In a couple of hours, all Paris will hear of it.

Here comes Gohier. He does not lack courage, anyhow. Bearding the man of power surrounded by his troops, Gohier reminds him of his duty to the Directory.

"The Directory no longer exists!" storms Bonaparte. "The republic is in danger, and I intend to save it. Sieyés, Ducos, and Barras have resigned." As he speaks, a letter from Moulin is brought to him. "Are not you in league with Moulin? No? Well, here is his resignation too. You are the last. Do you intend to hold out all by yourself?"

Gohier is a stickler for the law, and refuses to give way. He goes back to the Luxembourg, and there he and his friends are kept under guard by five hundred men until all is over. Barras is waiting at home, uneasy till he has the answer to his message. What if Bonaparte were now to take vengeance? Who can depend on Josephine's moods? Here is Talleyrand back again, with the safe-conduct and a bag of gold. As to this last, no one knows whether Barras had the fingering of the money, or whether Talleyrand kept it as messenger's fee.

Thus the five heads of the republic were rendered powerless by General Bonaparte, But this was only the first day. Tomorrow, at Saint-Cloud, greater difficulties may have to be faced, Lucien, who has been all over the place, and is fully informed, exclaims with well-grounded anger: "The whole job ought to have been finished in one day! You have left them too much time! The Five Hundred are already crying out that they have been tricked! Tomorrow all will be in the melting-pot once more! The only thing to do is to send soldiers to clear out the Chambers, and to put the most dangerous members of the Councils under arrest."

Certainly there may be complications tomorrow. Bernadotte had wanted the Jacobin Club to appoint him general of the opposing forces. "But the fellows were in too great a funk!" The generals unsympathetic to the coup d'état must be put under lock and key. Bonaparte's associates urge this again and again, but in vain. He is resolute to maintain the semblance of legality.

"People would say I was afraid of the generals. No one shall have a right to accuse us of illegality, No parties; no force! The whole people must be associated with the decision through the votes of its deputies! No civil war! What begins with the shedding of civilian blood, will come to a shameful end!"

But at night, prepared for all eventualities, he has loaded pistols handy to his bedside.

XX

Next morning, an endless string of carriages and carts, an endless succession of riders and pedestrians, makes it's way to Saint-Cloud, as if to see a great military review. Bonaparte, too, drives instead of going on horseback attended by a bevy of mounted officers. That might be provocative. He has made up his mind to observe constitutional formalities to the very last moment. Could anyone say that there had been a breach of law the day before? Are not the Council entitled to remove their sittings to a spot beyond the precincts of the town, if they think that this would be safer? Is it not within their competence to appoint a new commander for the Paris garrison? Had not the Directors the right to resign? Will any one pretend that the Jacobin peril, which is the occasion for these happenings, is imaginary? Today, at public sittings, the Councils will alter the constitution. Three rulers will be provisionally appointed. Borrowing a title from ancient Rome.

They can be called Triumvirs, or, perhaps better, Consuls. Then the Councils will be prorogued, everything being done in due form of law.

But the deputies hold other views. Like cloud-drifts hanging low, they flit through the valleys of this forsaken palace, discussing the situation, and giving vent to their protests. Since the hall that is being furbished up for the sitting will not be ready before one o'clock, they have plenty of time to foment their wrath.

In a small room fronting on the park, sit the three men who will be Consul tomorrow. At least Sieyés and Ducos remain seated most of the time, but the third walks up and down impatiently, as his adherents come and go to report. He thinks: "How infernally slow civilians are! They have needed a whole morning to arrange a few benches. Then they must take an oath one by one, a thing which our recruits do in chorus, and get through it all in a couple of minutes! Why should I have to wait in a back room while these lawyers are deliberating in the council chamber?"

The Ancients meet upstairs in the Salle Apollo; the Five Hundred, downstairs in the Orangerie. Spectators, safe people, throng the hall of the Five Hundred. When, after the swearing-in, the discussions at length begin (Lucien is in the chair), the protests of the opposition gain weight from the circumstances. Speakers point to the threatening force of soldiery outside. When some of the orators exclaim: "No dictatorship! This Cromwell wants to bind us in chains!" almost all the delegates applaud. The reports that come to the back room are more and more unfavourable. The officers grow restive: "Chase the beggars out! What else have we got our men here for?"

Bonaparte's only answer is a cold glance. Buckling on his sword, he silently mounts the stairs to the hall of the Ancients. Two or three of the stalwarts follow him, shaking their heads. Is he going to talk once more, as he did yesterday, instead of shooting? Amazed but curious, the president allows him to speak. Will he put up a better case than yesterday, speaking to the point, and not simply haranguing them about himself?

"Yesterday, I was sitting quietly at home when you summoned me.... Today, I am overwhelmed with calumnies.... Since my return, all parties have been busied with my name.... The Council of Ancients must decide quickly. I am no intriguer. You know me. Have I not given proof and to spare, of my devotion to the country? ....Am I, a man whom even the great coalition could not conquer, to tremble before a few rioters? If I am a crafty schemer, you may well be all Brutuses!"

Uneasy stirrings: smiles. Why does he speak, instead of acting? He is not sure of his ground, for he goes on to day: "All France shall know what we have lived through. —Everyone of the parties wishes to turn this crisis to its own account, and everyone of them would like to me to side with it. But I have come to the Councils. If you hesitate, and if liberty is overthrown, you will be answerable to the world and to posterity!" His periods grow ever more confused. The Ancients surround the rostrum, interrupting him, demanding names. Suddenly he turns, and waves his hand towards the doors, as if pointing to the soldiers who are out of sight. He seems to be looking for an exit. He apostrophises the invisible soldiers:

"You, comrades, whom I see united in this circle, raise your bayonets with which we fought our way to victory together, raise them against my breast! But if an orator in foreign pay dares to call your general an outlaw, smite the wretch with the thunderbolts of battle! The god of battles and the goddess of good fortune are on my side..."

Will not a burst of laughter sweep the speaker away, and his coup d'état along with him? At length Bourrienne comes up to him from behind, takes him by the arm, and whispers in his ear: "Do stop, General. You really don't know what you're saying!" He turns, and follows Bourrienne from the hall. A deputy devoted to his interest takes the floor promptly, and does his best to put a good face upon the matter.

Outside, he draws a breath of relief. What could have been the matter with him? Why had his brain been clouded? Amid all the turmoil of battle, he is calm, fully master of himself; his decisions are well-rounded, brilliant, and cool, like polished marble spheres. Why is he unequal to the occasion on this day of days, when his whole future is at stake?

Because he is a man who knows how to command, but does not know how to beg. He can cajole, threaten, feign hesitation, lie; outdoing in these arts all the diplomatists with whom he negotiates treaties. He meets them as equals, but is always sustained by the feeling that, if he does not get his way by diplomacy, he can enforce his wishes by artillery fire. He can endure everything except having to ask favours, and except having to submit to a law which is not of his own making. He wants order and legality, but not such as existed before he established them!

With titanic energy, as he already foresees, he will head this country towards order, will found an orderly State after a decade of chaos. No one will be the worse for humble birth or for poverty, since all will have equal opportunities. But in these halls today sit lawyers, ridden by the spirit of faction, corrupt, outworn, besoiled by the grime of party politics. He is to implore them to be good enough to give him (and others) a power which has long been his, and which stands outside there, impatient to get to work!

He, who in the Institute could sit quietly among the savants, learning and questioning, is so little able to understand the mood of these legislative assemblies that he actually fancies the day already won. He sends a message to Josephine to tell her that all is going well; says a few encouraging words to his followers, and goes quickly downstairs to play a similar part before the Council of Five Hundred. It is just as well that his friends take the precaution to send into the hall with him four stalwart grenadiers, whose-strength and loyality can be thoroughly depended on.

No matter that this escort is quite out of keeping with his determination to be strict in the observance of parliamentary forms! Followed by his grenadiers, carrying hat and riding whip in his hand, he enters the hall of the Five Hundred. "Bonaparte!" All turn towards the door. The Jacobins shout: "Down with the tyrant! Down with the dictator! Outlaw him!" A few of the more hefty among the Five Hundred hurl themselves upon him; the grenadiers rally to his protection, encircling him, and sheltering him with their big bodies from the angry Jacobins' blows. The combat sways to and fro for a while, a knot of struggling and shouting people. Then, step by step, the five force their way backwards towards the door. Outside, surrounded by his own supporters, he is for a moment too much discomposed to speak; but, rallying were not sufficiently moved, were not yet ripe for action. Night was falling, and all were waiting on events. Lucien came out, leapt into the saddle, and the two brothers rode up and down the front. Outside the railings were Sieyés and Ducos in a carriage, ready for flight today or to become rulers tomorrow, as events might decide. The movement seemed to be without a head.

Then Lucien grasped the opportunity. He could make a better job of speaking to the soldiers than Napoleon had made of speaking to the deputies:

"Soldiers, as president of the Five Hundred I tell you that in the hall there the majority is being terrorised by a handful of armed Jacobins. These rascals are in English pay. They have dared to outlaw your general, who was appointed by the Councils. They actually tried to assassinate him. Look at the wounds! Use your bayonets to guard him against their daggers, so that the deliberations concerning the welfare of the country can be conducted in peace! Rocognise as deputies none but those who come with me into the midst of your ranks. Drive out the rest, all who would stay in the hall!"

Napoleon listens with pinched lips. When Lucien has finished, he speaks in his turn, shouting: "Kill any one who resists, Follow me! I am the god of battles!" Lucien, who is afraid of another speech, hisses: "For God's sake, hold your tongue!"

"Long live Bonaparte!" should the soldiers, who regard the brothers as military and civil authority conjoined. But not a man moves. All is lost, if they will not march now. Lucien grasps at the last expedient. With a theatrical flourish, he snatches an officer's sword and points it at Napoleon's breast: "I swear that I will run my brother through, should he ever dare to threaten the liberties of France!"

The phrase has the desired effect. Murat orders the sounding of a general advance, summons a troop of soldiers to follow him, and shouts: "Lads, chuck the whole rabble of them out of the hall!" At length he has raised a laugh. With bayonets at the charge, but good-humouredly and without hurting anyone, they thrust from the hall any of the deputies that are valiant enough to offer resistance. In the failing light, there is a confused scene in which red togas, birettas, and the caps of the guardsmen are intermingled. The last of the fleeing deputies escape through the windows.

The priceless Lucien now hastened upstairs to the Council of Ancients. Grossly exaggerating the injuries sustained by his brother at the hands of the Jacobin deputies, he induced the Ancients, in a panic, to appoint the three Consuls, and to adjourn their sitting until a late hour that night. Then the leaders foregathered in a small cafe for a meal, being all much in need of food.

That night, the most trustworthy among the deputies reasonable in the deserted hall at Saint-Cloud. By the light of a pair of candles, the thirty who were left to represent the people of France voted whatever they were told. While a hundred or so people of fashion, pretty women and their gallants, mockingly watched the midnight ceremony—while all went smoothly, society-at-large being quite undisturbed and the proletariat unruffled—the indefatigable Lucien insisted that the political mass should be worthily celebrated. At two in the morning, to the sound of drums, the three Consuls took the oath. "Long live the republic!" called a few weary voices.

At three o'clock, Consul Bonaparte drives back to Paris with Bourrienne. He looks straight in front of them, saying never a word. Not until he is at home, and Josephine is present, does he open his mouth:

"I say, Bourrienne, did I talk a frightful lot of nonsense today?"

"A fair amount, General."

"Those idiots drove me crazy. I'm no good at speaking in public assemblies."

Then, instead of going on to talk about the coup d'état, or to congratulate himself upon its amazing success (for from tomorrow onwards he will rule France) he alludes to personal enmities. Bernadotte's conduct is what rankles!

"That fellow Bernadotte! He wanted to betray me! His wife

I

ABOUT twenty men are seated round a large oval table. Some are quite young, some middle-aged, some elderly. They are plainly dressed, in accordance with the fashion of 1800, when wigs were no longer worn, and lace was out of date; those of them that are in uniform are not resplendent with gold braid, and they wear no orders. Some have the bold, self-confident look of the man of action; others, the thoughtful mien of the savant. From town and from countryside, from office and from laboratory, they come, but are unified by a common experience and a common aim. For ten years, they have been living through a revolutionary epoch; they meet to bring that epoch to a close. Around them is the chill splendour of the Tuileries, the palace of the last Bourbon kings. The golds and the reds of the rich carpets and the silken hangings are out of keeping with their bourgeois circumstantiality; the silvery sheen of the candles, reflected in rainbow tins from the myriad facets of the candelabra, recalls an era that scintillated with light and glowed with colour.

The Directors before them had been wont to entertain their lady friends in royal halls, but that was in the Luxembourg, the former meeting-place of the peers of France. The Tuileries seemed full of ghosts. Did not a curse lie upon the place? The dictator had broken the spell. Two months after the coup d'état, he had come with this fellow Consuls to take possession of the palace, which exerted a magical lure upon his imagination. Yet when, seven years after the arrest of the last scion of the royal line, the first of the bourgeois rulers made his formal entry, the affair had a strong flavour of burlesque. The Parisians could not but laugh to see the numbers of the hackney carriages peeping out from beneath the slips of paper which had been carelessly pasted over them. This seemed to symbolise the ludicrous aspect of time's revenges.

The Consul's own mood was no less haphazard as he looked round with childlike curiosity. "Well, here we are in the Tuileries," he said to one of his friends; "Let's see to it that we stay here!"

Several of those now seated at the oval table, had waited here of old—wearing powdered wigs, lace jabots, and pumps-tremulous with eagerness to learn whether His Majesty would receive them, and when. Some of them had sat at a similar table in the Luxembourg. There had been no stability about those deliberations. Laws had come and gone, urgency orders and exceptional provisions; transitional decrees had pushed foregoing decrees out of the way; three constitutions had risen and set, had shot up into the air swiftly and brilliantly like rockets, to vanish like these and to fall like rocket-sticks. The whole decade during which the new ideas had been trying to realise themselves in the concrete, had passed swiftly over Paris like a single night, amid a confusion of flashing lights and rumbling drums. The city had been like an armed camp with no fighting fronts and no battles, but perturbed by the to-and-fro march of armed political parties, deafened by the noisy wrangling between the old order and the new wishes, dazzled by the glare of venturesome ideas, confused by the clamour of disappointed hopes and the clash of warring ambitions—a titanic bacchanal of liberty, equality, and cozenage. Surveying the medley, looking down from the skies, were the shades of the two men whose books had set the whole in motion: Rousseau, with eyes of disgust; Voltaire, with a mocking smile.

But suddenly the tumult had been stilled. That little man at the head of the table had stilled it, the little general in the well-worn green uniform. Not that he, presiding over the Council of State, is in fact presiding over the State; the parties have withdrawn into their caves, satisfied or rancorous, but at any rate silenced, France, weakened by clubs and corruption, by the Terror and the demagogues, is turning back (like an adventuress weary of errant amours) to the arms of a strong man who can master her.

Enough, now, for Bonaparte that he should aspire to fulfil this masterful lover's role. No longer did he need to fight for the position. The man for whom France was longing, must be a man of order; must be one who had never before held power, who belonged to no party, and who none the less enjoyed popular favour. He must, therefore, be a soldier and a conqueror. Moreau lacked the self-confidence and adroitness needed to make him a successful rival; the other great generals were dead or overshadowed; there were no civilian competitors. After Bonaparte's outstanding military successes, it was easy for him to win supreme power in the State. He would have won it without a struggle had he not been so stubborn in his desire to observe constitutional formalities.

The attempt to be strictly constitutional had been a ludicrous failure, and had imposed artificial obstacles in his path. Yet this very fact was a token and a guarantee of his political talents. He was a man with a firm grip on the sword-hilt, but he was also a man who clearly understood the limits of the power of the sword. "Do you know," he said in those days, "What amazes me more than all else? The impotence of force to organise anything. There are only two powers in the world: the spirit and the sword. In the long run, the sword will always be conquered by the spirit ." Napoleon was the greatest military commander of his day, but neither now nor later was it his habit to strike the table with mailed fist, neither the Paris at this juncture nor elsewhere when negotiating a truce or a peace or an alliance. He was a political genius, who prized the sword, indeed, but prized it only as one of the two powers. His ear was never deafened by the clash of arms. As now, so for fifteen years to come, he is ever on the watch for indications of public opinion: always listening to the voice of the people, a voice which defies calculation; a voice which Napoleon, a man of figures, vainly tries to calculate. Precisely because of his failure to do this, the attempt to reckon with public opinion is always alluring to the imaginative side of his nature.

Because Bonaparte believes in the power of the spirit more than in the power of the sword, he strives for order and peace more resolutely than for war and conquest. The history of the next ten years will prove it.

For him, order denotes equality, but not liberty. He adopts into his dictatorship the former of these two gods of the revolution. Except for a few vacillations, he will cherish equality to the end, despite appearances to the contrary. But liberty? What liberty? "Both the savage and the civilised man need a lord and master, a magician, who will hold the imagination in check, impose strict discipline, bind man in chains, so that he may not bite out of season; one who will thrash him, and lead him to the chase. Obedience is man's destiny; he deserves nothing better, and he has no rights!" These threatening words of the misanthropist disclose no more than half of his secret thoughts. Through all the phases of his rule, he is ever in search of the efficient man, and to such a man he grants power over thousands, just as he himself, through energy and diligence, through natural and acquired superiority, has won to power over millions. In spite of all, he is the son of the revolution; and in this sense he will remain the son of the revolution, whatever forms his power may assume.

In part, that is the explanation of the mysterious influence he wields. The wider his domain extends, the more plainly do all realise that they are living in a system which promises to every efficient man place and power and wealth; which does these things because the Master has himself risen out of the crowd. He shows this, now, in his very first step. Sieyés has drafted a constitution, There is to be a grand elector, a president who can only represent and sign his name, With soldierly curtness, Bonaparte puts his pen through the item. "Away with this fat hog!" Instead, there is to be a First Consul, with plenary powers, and plenty of work. He is to be war lord and also director of foreign policy; he is to appoint all ministers and envoys, councillors of State and prefects, officers and judges. Thirty nominated senators are to elect their colleagues; but neither the Senate not the Legislative Assembly not the Tribunate is to have any power to initiate legislation. These bodies are merely brought into existence to give politicians a platform for their orations, and to provide senators with high salaries and opportunities for a resplendent life.

Although everything was dependent upon the will of one man, that one man insisted that those dependent on him should themselves be men, and not mere names. Neither birth nor pretentiousness nor prominence in a political party could lead to the front in the army or in civil life. Nothing but energy and capacity could ensure promotion. Such was the principle upon which Napoleon chose the members of the Council of State.

This last was a round table of experts, selected by the dictator on his own initiative. Among them was Laplace, whom, to honour the Institute, Napoleon had also appointed Minister for Home Affairs-an appointment the great mathematician held for a time, until he turned back from the mechanics of the State to the mechanics of the heavens. There, too, was Roéderer, official and journalist, the most independent man to be encountered by Napoleon during twenty years and the most valuable recorder of conversations. Tronchet, also, one of the finest jurists of the age, was there. In the council chamber all alike were citizens, and addressed one another by that plain title. Royalists and Jacobins sat there side by side, under a regime of equality, since reason was enthroned.

When the minutes of the sittings are shown to the citizen-consul, he says: "It is essential to give a full and accurate report of the opinions expressed by legal luminaries, for their words are weighty; but what we soldiers and moneyed men think is of little account. In the heat of the moment I have often said things which an instant afterwards I saw to have been unjust. I do not wish to seem better than I am." When he noticed that the councillors were simply echoing whatever he said, he was quick to call them to order: "You are not here, gentlemen, to agree with me, but to express your own views. If you do that, I can compare them with mine, and decide which is better."

The sittings, often enough, do not begin before nine in the evening, for up till then the Consul has been dealing with the urgent affairs of the day. They may last till five o'clock in the morning. The councillors get very tired during the small hours. Perhaps the Minister for War goes to sleep. Napoleon shakes them up, exclaiming: "Do let's keep awake, citizens. It's only two o'clock. We must earn our salaries." He, who presides, is indeed one of the youngest of the company, being now thirty. But in three campaigns he has learned how to watch over the interests of hundreds of thousand. Was not the management of an army which set out from the Alps, crossed the sea, and marched far into the desert—was not this the best school for the study of State administration? There, too, he had to think of money and bread, of rights and laws, or rewards and punishments, of rest and obedience and order.

During the very first night after the coup d'état, he had appointed two committees to draft a legal code; this was the first act of his dictatorship! The prevailing chaos had been the outcome of a lack of law. Down to the outbreak of the revolution, there had been no unified legal system; but even now, after eleven years, the promise was unfulfilled. That first summer, three great lawyers were set to work; four months later a draft of the Civil Code, subsequently rechristened the Code Napoleon, was ready; then the draft was discussed in the Council of State. In eighteen months the laws were voted. They passed into effect in 1804.

After more than a century, this Code is still the law of France; it was adopted in many of the lands conquered by Napoleon, having great influence on the legislation of Central and Southern Germany, Prussia, Switzerland, and Spain; and its influence spread still farther afield, to Central America and South America. All that is new and morally decisive in the Code Napoleon is revolutionary law. The law-book which the Dictator discussed in all its details for many months, the law-book, many of whose most contentious points were the direct outcome of his decisions, borrowed the fixed principles of reason that had been sketched in the first days of the revolution. Experienced and dispassionate minds, under Napoleon's guidance, worked them up, purified them, and made them into a new system of the rights of man. In this system, there was no longer a hereditary nobility; all children had an equal share in inheritance; all parents became legally responsible for the maintenance of their children; Jews became equal with Christians before the law; civil marriage was open to all, and was dissoluble.

Concerning this matter, as concerning all matters of family law, his Corsican family feeling persistently influenced his judgments; "We know that adultery is not a rare occurrence, but an ordinary one; that it can happen on any convenient sofa.... Some sort of restraint must be imposed upon these women who commit adultery for trinkets or verses, for Apollo and the nine Muses."

His sense of order leads him to be a thoroughgoing supporter of marriage. He even sees to it that women shall follow their husbands into transportation, "for how can we forbid a woman to do so when she is convinced of her husband's innocence? Or is this conviction of hers to deprive her of her rights as a married woman; is she to lose the title of wife, and to become the man's concubine? Many men have only become criminals owing to their wives. Are we to forbid those who have been the cause of the misfortune from sharing that misfortune?" He also thinks highly of the custom of old Roman days, when, at marriage, the woman was formally described as passing from her father's guardianship into that of her husband. "That would be excellent in Paris, where women do as they please. It would influence some of them, though not all."

Therefore, though he favours divorce, it must not be too easy: "What would happen to the most intimate of natural ties if people were suddenly to become estranged? Unless we make divorce difficult, a young woman will be ready to marry a quite unsuitable man, for fashion, convenience, simply to get a roof over her head. The law must warn her against this.... In truth, there are only three valid grounds for divorce: attempted murder, adultery, and impotence."

Such are the plastic thoughts of this expert in human nature, whose mathematical talents still leave him free to subsume facts under ideas; one who has an intelligence well fitted for the consideration of laws, seeing that it is equally swayed by theory and practice, by energetic activity and sceptical suspense. The conflict of trends within the legislator's mind is obvious, and it was intensified by his thoughts concerning Josephine's former infidelity and present faithfulness. (We know that she manifested a lively interest in the drafting of those sections of the Code that related to divorce! Napoleon at this time was already wondering whether, if his wife remained childless, he would not have to divorce her for reasons of State. Her own dread of this possibility led her to use her influence in favour of strengthening the marriage tie, whereas he was driven by self-interest to insist that marriage must not be indissoluble.)

It is a personal feeling, too, which drives him to avoid scandal, to save the honour of marriage. He opposes the interference of the law courts in conjugal questions; prefers that such matters should be settled by mutual understanding. So that the veil shall not be stripped off. "The desire of both parties for divorce is an indication that divorce is necessary. It is not the business of the court to establish the fact that this mutual desire exists; the court has simply to pronounce the divorce when the desire exists." His strong family feeling leads him to add that maltreatment, perversion, and adultery should be concealed beneath the formula of mutual desire; the need for divorce is to be settled at a family council, and the judge has merely to confirm this decision.

For the same reason, he introduces a semi-divorce, a judicial separation from bed and board. This is always to be arranged after a mutual private understanding, for it will be a barrier to the possibility of reconciliation if the grounds for the separation have been made public. His aim in all these matters is to maintain family life; he is a champion of order, an anti-revolutionist. His social sense is so strong that he maintains it would be necessary to punish an adulterous woman by criminal procedure unless she were punished by being divorced. Similar considerations regarding the sanctity of marriage lead him to raise the age at which marriage becomes permissible. At the revolution it had been lowered to thirteen for women and fifteen of men; he insists upon fifteen and twenty-one respectively.

For children, the Code promises all the things which the ensuing century is slowly to build up. Under the fatherhood of the man to whom they are born in lawful marriage, they have a secure position even before they enter the world. True, "the father cannot recognise the child as his own if he has been absent for fifteen months"–the figure is specified by Napoleon- "and has fought at Marengo." But, a man of position as well as a man of the world, he concludes by sayings "I will sacrifice honour to truth, but why should I sacrifice the wife's honour when no one will gain thereby? If the husband is not sure of his dates, he had better hold his tongue; the child's interest is paramount."

When someone proposes to restrict the elder children's right to maintenance, he rejoins: "Is a father to have the right to drive his fifteen-year-old daughter out of the house? Let us suppose him to have an income of sixty thousand francs, can we allow him to say to his son: "You are old enough to tend for yourself; be off with you to work!" If we limit this duty, we shall tend to make children entertain thoughts of putting their father out of the way." The suggestion is made that adoption shall be feasible by simple declaration before a notary, with revolutionary speed. He opposes the plan:

"We are not concerned here with a trivial formality. Human beings are controlled through their imaginations: that is what distinguishes them from animals. The main defect of the newer legislation is that it makes no appeal to men's imaginations. A soldier does not face death in order to earn a few pence a day, or to win some paltry order of merit. None but the man who touches his heart, can stir his enthusiasm! A notary cannot touch our hearts merely because we pay him a fee of twelve francs; that is why we need a legislative act. What is adoption? An imitation of nature, a sort of sacrament. By the will of society, the offspring of one human being's flesh and blood is supposed to become the offspring of another's flesh and blood. Could any action be more sublime? Thanks to it, two creatures between whom there is no tie of blood become inspired by a natural mutual affection. Whence must this action come? Like the lightning, from on high!"

By slow degrees, the huge machine (which for ten years has been standing still or moving backwards) is set in regular motion once more. Throughout the last decade, all the reports from the provinces have been full of complaints regarding the lack of public safety, sanitation, and order; the louis-d'or used to exchange for twenty-four francs, but now the ratio is one to eight thousand; the Directory's attempt to stabilise the franc has been an utter failure; the newly enriched have bought up the State domains, the Church lands, and the seignorial estates. No one is paying taxes. What is the new dictator going to do about it all?

Within a fortnight after the coup d'état, he had arranged for the establishment of tax-collecting offices in all the departments, for, as he put it: "Security and property are only to be found in a country which is not subject to yearly changes in the rate of taxation." Two months later, the Bank of France came into being; next year, there were new boards to supervise taxation, the registration of landed property, and forestry. Whereas his predecessors had simply squandered the State domains, he used what was left of them to defray repayment of national debt. The funds rose from 7 to 17; he continued the process of debt cancellation, renovated the Chambers of Commerce, regulated the Stock Exchange, put an end to speculation in the depreciated currency, stopped the frauds of the army contractors and other war profiteers, and by these and similar measures restored manufacturing industry whose productivity had sunk to a quarter or half of its former level.

What was his magical spell?

At the head of affairs was himself, a man of indomitable energy, and incorruptible. Men of the same stamp, energetic, diligent, and bold, were put in charge of the ministries, the departments, and the prefectures. Favouritism was done away with; sinecures were abolished. Preferment was obtainable only by the efficient, and to them it came regardless of birth or party. All officials, down to the mayors, were appointed from above, and paid from above- "a hierarchy, all First Consuls in miniature," to quote his own words.

There was no political opposition. "No reaction is possible," he prophesied. "I have not relied upon the credit or upon the strength of a party, and am therefore indebted to no one.-The men of intelligence who, a little while ago, were perpetrating crimes, are now being used by me to upbuild a new social edifice. There are excellent workmen among them, but the trouble is that they would all like to be master builders. Typically French, that trait; everyone thinks himself competent to rule the country!" Being careful to satisfy all parties, he gives the two most coveted portfolios to two rogues, mutually hostile, but both men of remarkable ability. Having done this, he is able to say: "What revolutionist can fail to have confidence in the social system when Fouché, the Jacobin, is Minister of Police. What nobleman would be unwilling to live under Talleyrand as Minister for Foreign Affairs? I have one of them on my right, and the other on my left. I open a wide road, in which all can find room."

To all the prefects and all the generals the order went forth: "No more clubs: no more parties. Tell the National Guardsmen and the citizens whenever you can, if a few ambitious fellows still feel the need to hate, that the rudder of State is now in strong hands, accustomed to overcome obstacles." A few weeks after the coup d'état, he issued a great proclamation, commending the new constitution to the people. It closed with the simple and lofty words: "Citizens, the revolution has returned to the principles with which it began. It is at an end."

II

It is not war.

"Returning to Europe after eighteen months' absence, I find that war has broken out once more between the French Republic and Your Majesty. The French people summons me to the first position in the State." In these terms, shortly after the coup d'état, he addresses the German emperor, just before marching against him. Napoleon writes as proudly as any monarch, as if before the journey he had already been the first man in the State; and he writes with the natural dignity to which, in large measure, he owes his success. That is his way. In this manner he puts his adversary in the wrong. But the emperor is unmoved. Well, Bonaparte's plans were made long since; he has only to carry them out.

First of all he surrounds himself with a guard, every member of which must have been through four campaigns-as many as the commander, but no more. Then, while he sends Moreau to fight on the Rhine, he makes his own preparations for an adventure in Italy. If he were to come along the coast, as he did four years ago, they would be ready for him. He must find a new plan! At Dijon, in full view of the Austrian spies, he collects from the rawest levies a pitiful reserve corps, and smiles as he reads the mocking comments in the Viennese papers. Meanwhile, he prepares a force of 32,000 men, no more, but the finest soldiers under his command. They are for a bold venture of which no one dreams, any more than they dreamed of his Egyptians campaign. Did not Hannibal cross the Alps, bidding the mountains make way for him? But nowadays a general must get cannon through the passes! Cut down trees, then, and make huge sleighs on which to drag the ordnance over the snows!

Thus in the spring after the coup d'état an army climbs the great St. Bernard, for the first time in two thousand years. The old monks in the hospice can hardly believe their eyes. The herdsman who guides the commander's mule, prattling the while about his wishes and his troubles, will soon afterwards learn that he has been talking to a fairy godmother, will be enriched by the gift of a house and a farm. Even the common soldiers seem to realise the epic character of this campaign, and vie with one another in their zeal to drag the guns. They are following their tried and trusted leader; they are returning to that Lombardy whither, four years ago, he had led them as to the Promised Land; these reflections, and the urgency of the occasion, increase the mysterious suggestiveness of the expedition. So little do the Austrians realise what is impending, that their chief, writing to a lady friend in Pavla, tells her she is quite safe there; no need to lcave. Twelve hours later, Bonapartc enters the town.

He knows, too, that, while France is always eager for glory, an even greater need at the moment is tranquillity. Above all, the country has need of him, personally; but he has enemies in his rear. Before, it mattered little that he should be away for a year or two at a time; but now, when he is dictator, so long an absence would be fatal. These multiple considerations explain his letter to Emperor Francis-surely an unparalleled dispatch from a conqueror on the battle-field. As soon as he has written it, he hastens to Milan.

What is Paris saying?

Is the capital satisfied at length? Is it not like Josephine, before whom one can pour out all the—treasures of the world—to find only that she takes them as a matter of course, and holds out her hand for more? Paris is by no means enthusiastic about the new master. "For eleven years," writes Roéderer in his diary, "the Parisian's first thought on waking in the morning had been: 'When shall we be able to rid ourselves of tyrants?' Now, the Parisians were saying: `Everything seems to be going on well. But these enterprises that are being started, this capital that is being invested, these houses that they are building, these trees that they are planting—what will happen to the lot of them, if the Man should perish?'-His victories, indeed, had made him the cynosure of all eyes; but it was his talent for statecraft that has raised men's hopes." Thus the Parisians are uneasy, but wellwishing. One among them, however, foresees the future, and writs to Napoleon at the theatre of war:

"General, I have just returned from the Tuileries, and shall not attempt to describe either the enthusiasm of the French or the amazement of foreigners.... Will posterity believe the miracle of this campaign? Favourable, indeed, are the auspices that preside over your homecoming! Never has there been an empire that was not founded upon miracle. In this instance, miracle has become reality."

Napoleon smiles, thinking: "In truth, Talleyrand is more than a flatterer; he is a soothsayer! But why does he give a name to my secret thoughts? Would he play the part of the Roman of old, who tempted Caesar with a crown?"

Here is another missive from Paris. A police report from Fouché, who tells how Talleyrand had recently summoned a few intimates to discuss what had better be done should the Consul have a misadventure, or perchance be defeated. The news of Marengo had come while they were at supper! "So he was alarmed!" thinks Bonaparte. "There were stirrings of what remained of a conscience. Good friends! Fine confidants! Their alleged concern for my safety, is but the mask for their secret longing to rid themselves of their master!"

Is it a mocking smile or is it an expression of pensive anxiety that purses Napoleon's lips? Certainly, he must be back in Paris as soon as possible! But this evening he goes to the Scala, where the heroine is the lovely Grassini-whose advances he had scorned a year or two back. Now she sings for his ear, has eyes for him alone; and though she may be piqued that his beckoning nod comes so late, the handsome Italian prima donna gives herself to the conqueror of Italy for the asking. She shall go to the Paris opera. As star, or as his mistress? Time will show!

Since in Germany, too, the enemy has been defeated, the subsequent peace of Lunéville is extremely favourable to France, the Rhine frontier being conceded, and the re-establishment of the Cisalpine Republic agreed to. Could more have possibly been achieved by a few weeks' campaign? His colleagues and other false friends make ready to receive him as hero of the hour; they write to him about plans for a triumph. "I shall make an unlooked-for entry into Paris," he rejoins, with malicious double meaning; "and I have no desire for triumphal arches or any kind of ceremonial. I have a sufficiently good conceit of myself to scorn such flummery. The only genuine triumph is public content."

A little later, he writes in a vein that is equally modest, or equally proud: "I accept the offer to erect a monument in my honour and should like a site to be chosen. But I would rather leave the actual building of the monument to future centuries, should these confirm your good opinion of me." It is as if he could sense the coming storm of iconoclasm, could foresee that in less than twenty years his idolators of today will be rolling his eagles in the dust!

After his return, the dictator devotes all his energies to the consolidation of peace. He outsoars himself: for whereas formerly, by forced marches and crashing blows, he has imposed his will on one country after another, now, by shrewd negotiations, he cements peace with his sometimes foes. Withing two years of his seizure of power, France is at peace with Austria, Prussia, Bavaria, Russia, Naples, Spain, Portugal and even with England.

Nine legitimate and therefore ardently legitimist rulers now recognise the republic which they had been fighting for a decade. France which two years before had been threatened by disruption from within and by dangerous impacts from without, had become to leading power on the Continent.

It is as First Consul, not as general and not as emperor, that Bonaparte leads the revolution to victory. In a Europe all the rest of which (except for Switzerland) is ruled by kings and princes, he not only establishes peace between the new ideas and the old forces, but also, unchallenged, compels his border States, Holland and northern Italy, to adopt the consular constitution. Neither Austria nor England attempts to interfere when, with a turn of the hand, he extends his grip over Piedmont, Genoa, Lucca and Elba. At the same time, when the compensation of the princes on the left bank of the Rhine is in question, the members of the oldest reigning houses of Germany throng around the great huckster, the man who has robbed them of their lands—thus teaching him to despise birth and heritage, nobles and crowns.

Only one chasm gapes in the structure he is building, but he will be able to close it.

At the opening of the revolution, reason took the palace of Christ. Indeed, this anti-Christian notion became extremely popular. Bonaparte stood almost alone in his rejection of it. Four years earlier, in Italy, he had granted the Pope all kinds of things which Paris wished to refuse; and, for reasons of his own, he had always been chivalrous in his attitude towards the clergy. Now he wished to heal the breach that had existed for ten years between France and the Church. He did not do this because he was a believer. "Among the Turks, I was a Mohammedan; now I shall become a

Catholic." He knew that this oldest of the powers could not be conquered either by the sword or by the spirit. He must come to terms with it in order to make use of it. "Catholicism kept the pope in being for me," he said later: "and, in view of my grip upon Italy, I continued to hope that sooner or later I should be able to bend him to my will. What immense influence I should then wield! What a means to have at my disposal in my dealings with Europe!"

It will be difficult to make Paris accept the rehabilitation of the Church! As a preliminary step, he is actually willing to present himself before the bishops in the guise of philosopher: "I am aware that in no State can a man be truly virtuous and upright unless he knows whence he comes and whither he is going. Unaided reason cannot tell us these things. Without religion, we grope in the dark. But the Catholic faith throws a clear light upon the origin and the destiny of human beings." Rome is dumbfounded for a time, when this and similar speeches are reported; but the shrewdest of worldly sages can find his master in the Vatican. When Cardinal Consalvi comes to Paris in order to discuss matters with Napoleon, and, at the first official audience, the consul wishes to browbeat him, the price of the Church smilingly stands his ground. What a spectacle for Talleyrand, who looks on in silence! Still agreement is reached on various important points, such as the celibacy of priests, the choice of bishops by Rome, and the re-establishment of the old canon law. But though these concessions are made to the Church, the payment of stipends by the State, which gives the latter decisive influence, is to remain.

A great ceremony in Notre Dame seals the agreement. The Consul, with the other State dignitaries, had wanted only to come for the TeDeum; but he found it expedient, after all, to attend Mass, stipulating that he was not to be expected to take the sacrament, "or to participate in all the rest of the hocus-pocus that makes a man ridiculous." To his brother, he said on this occasion: "We're going to Mass today. What will Paris say about it?"

"The audience will look on at the play, and will hiss if it does not please."

"Then I shall have the church cleared by the guards!"

"But what if the grenadiers join in the hissing?"

"They won't. My old war-dogs will be just as respectful in Notre Dame as they were in the Cairo mosques. They will keep their eyes on me, and when they see that their general is serious and well-behaved, they will follow his example, saying to themselves, "Those are the orders of the day!'"

III

The ground is still unsteady beneath his feet. His consulship is for ten years only, and there are but eight years more to run. Then a rival may take his place. He is dependent on popular favour, which he must court, and which he despises. What sort of a position is that for the head of a State in his dealings with foreign potentates? They will not take him seriously, any more than if he were an American president. Turning these thoughts over in his mind, he makes a sign to the Senate.

Always compliant (being dependent on his good graces), the Senate now proposes to ensure that the First Consul shall hold office for an additional term of ten years after the expiry of the present term. Put out of humour by this suggestion, he jogs the senators' thoughts and induces them to propose a lifelong tenure of the consulship. But, prudent as Caesar, he says that the matter must be referred to the "people," the source of all power. A plebiscite is taken, and there are nearly four million ayes against a handful of courageous noes. His powers are enlarged, He now has sole authority to sign treaties with foreign States; he alone appoints the senators, who arc themselves entitled to dissolve the Chambers; and he is granted the right to appoint his successor, When he compares his position with that of other European rulers, and notices that they all wear crowns, he consoles himself with the naive sophism: "Henceforward, I am as good as the other sovereigns, for they, likewise, rule for life only!"

By no means all among the millions who have voted for him are his whole-hearted adherents. Even in Paris, when he makes a triumphal entry into the Luxembourg, there is so little public applause that he says afterwards to his Minister of Police: "Why did you not work up opinion beforehand?"

Said Fouché: "We are still the children of the ancient Gauls, of whom it was said that they could neither endure liberty nor tolerate oppression."

"What do you mean?"

"I mean, Citizen Consul, that, in you last steps, the Parisians fancy the see the loss of liberty, and a tendency towards absolutism."

"I should not care to rule for six weeks, if I had but the shadow of power, and could not be master!"

"You have only to be humane, strong, and just, at one and the same time," rejoins the fox (who never showed any of these qualities himself, "and soon you will win all hearts once again."

"Public opinion is capricious. I shall know how to mend it," said Bonaparte, turning his back on his interlocutor.

A two-minutes' talk like this, and Napoleon has made up his mind. He dismisses Fouché, but not because he is afraid of the ex-cleric (whom he despises, rather). He abolishes the Ministry of Police, and transfers its functions to the Ministry of Justice, "for I wish to show Europe that my policy is peaceful, and that the French love me sincerely." We must get used to such phrasemongering, in which he cloaks his policy. To keep Fouché quiet, he makes the ex-minister a senator. When, on leaving office, Fouché discloses to the Consul a reserve fund of two and a half million francs, Bonaparte is amazed, and tells him to keep half the sum "as a token of personal regard." In the anteroom, the departing Fouché grins over his mental arithmetic, adding the undisclosed residue of the reserve to the amount of the First Consul's gift.

Such are Bonaparte's methods with a dangerous man who knows too much. As for public opinion, he can take his measures to get that on his side. It is because he is determined not to be indebted to any party or any individual, that he demands a popular ratification of his appointment as Consul for life, just as he had asked for popular approval after the coup d'état. The result gives him assurance that the revolution is over. "This consultation of the people has a twofold advantage. Besides confirming the prolongation of the consular term, it throws light on the sources of my power, which otherwise might have seemed ambiguous." The phrasing shows that he is aware of his dangerous position betwixt revolution and legitimacy. To the very last, he will be worried by this problem.

Like a Roman imperator, Bonaparte wishes to concentrate all the power of State in his own hands; but whereas the Roman's title to power was the commandership of the armies, Napoleon is supreme because of his supreme efficiency. That is why he bases his power, not upon the army, which loves him, but upon the people, to which he is hostile. He wants to be "tyrant," in the classical sense of the term; but he wishes to be tyrant on a democratic footing, as the outcome of a free popular decision. The people, the source of power, is to transfer power to Napoleon. None knows better than he the weakness of any such fiction, but it is imposed on him by the spirit of age. After all, Bonaparte can fearlessly quote in his own favour the revolutionary principle that power must go to talent instead of to birth, for where can a more talented man that himself be found? But instead of contenting himself with talent as the source of his power (the talent that has brought him victory in war and in peace, the talent that has enabled him to grasp the reins), he muddies this splendid source by a popular vote, feels morally compelled to do so, and even fancies that he is clarifying the waters by his action. If Bonaparte saves the revolution, he certainly kills the republic.

These ideas are not the outcome of calculating policy, but of the mood which seeks its stimulus in classical life. It is the same mood as that which draws him towards the East; the same mood as that which, on the day of the coup d'état, led him to make a fool of himself before the Councils. "Your place is among the men of Plutarch," said the first who really understood Bonaparte in early youth. The Consul was not a democrat in the sense that he believed in popular sovereignty. What he lacked was such days as those of classical antiquity, when genius did not need to entrench itself behind representative assemblies, but held sway on its own initiative; or Asia, where, even in modern times, there are monarchs in the literal sense. In his work-room at Saint-Cloud there are two busts, Scipio's and that of Hannibal. No other position than that of Roman emperor or that of caliph was suited to his temperament.

Immediately after the coup d'état, the Bourbons, with a childlike frankness, had made advances to him. The brother of the executed king, now Count of Provence, and in future days to reign as Louis XVIII, asked the son of the revolution to help him to the Throne. The demand was thrice repeated, and a handsome reward was offered. The Consul made no answer to the first two applications. To the third he replied as follows:

"Sir, I have received your letter, and thank you for what you are so kind as to say about myself. You cannot seriously wish to come back, for your return would cost a hundred thousand lives. You must sacrifice your personal interests to the peace and happiness of France, and history will thank you for the sacrifice. I am not insensitive to the misfortunes of your family... I shall be happy to do all in my power to contribute to the welfare and tranquility of your retirement. Bonaparte."

Very different is Napoleon's reception of the Vendée royalists, for he hopes to win them over to his side. At first they fail to understand him when, after a long time of waiting, the man of destiny, searing his old green coat, and with untidy hair, makes advances to them.

"Come over to my side. Mine will be the government of youth and enthusiasm! .... You struck shrewd blows for your princes.... But your princes have by no means covered themselves with glory. Why were they not in Vendée to lead the fight? Was not that their place?"

"They were kept in London by political considerations," answered the nobles.

"They should have crossed the Channel in the first fishing

smack they could get hold of," he answered passionately, and, so the report runs, "in a voice that seems to come from the depths of his stomach." Yes, my fine nobleman, from the depths of his stomach! The phrase carries with it the implications of an incident in universal history which was still recent, still vivid in Napoleon's memory. That was the tone proper to the bold adventurer who, in a tiny frigate, had made his way across the storm-tossed Mediterranean, through the enemy fleet, to reach the coast where power was his for the seizing. Hear how he mingles flattery and threats, the young wizard who has turned the whole continent upside down!

"What would you like to be? General or prefect? You and yours can have whatever you please, if you will come over to my side. Nothing? Would you think it a disgrace to wear the coat that Bonaparte wears?.... Unless you will make peace, I will march against you with a hundred thousand men, and burn your towns to ashes!"

"If you do," answers the count firmly, "we shall annihilate your columns."

"You dare to threaten me?" he exclaims—this time 'with a terrible voice.' But upon receiving a matter-of-fact answer, he is calm once more. The noble emissaries retire in disgust, having achieved nothing, having been perplexed by his foreign accent, and by the impetuous imagination, which leads him to complicate the issues to such an extent that it is often hard to follow his meaning.

None the less, the Consul induces a great many of the emigrés to return, disarming their hostility by making suitable provision for them. Forty thousand families promptly come back. At the same time, he negotiates with the Jacobins, although these, "With their metaphysics, are enough to ruin twenty governments." He feels sure of the support of those who follow the middle courses of democracy, for the democratic masses feel safe under his rule, now that Paris is no longer as sort of civilian camp, and now that (a benevolent despot) he is doing all in his power to bring better times.

Consider these instructions issued to various authorities:

persons. Within three years, there are 4,500 elementary schools, 750 middle schools, and 45 lycées. He honours the Institute by choosing a third of his first senators from among its members. The Ministry for Home Affairs is instructed to draw up lists "of the ten best painters sculptors, composers, musicians, architects, and other artists whose talents make them worthy of support." He orders great frescoes to be painted, which shall depict striking incidents in his battles. He gives his reasons for this State regulation of art, saying: "People complain that we have no literature. That is the fault of the Minister for Home Affairs!"

But if he tranquillizes persons of all occupations by bringing them prosperity, what opening will be left, in this nation of the ambitious, for the pursuit of fame? If there is to be no war and no court life, where will the French find an outlet for their vanity? He answers this question by founding the Legion of Honour.

The Legion will form a group of stalwart supporters, for those who have taken a solemn oath to resist any attempt, at the restoration of the feudalist regime will not be so likely to side against Bonaparte. Besides, it is not to be merely an officers' club, inasmuch as the aim is to provide distinctions for all who do good service. He therefore appoints a natural philosopher to the office of arch-chancellor; and when, in the Council of State, a warning reference is made to the kinship between these orders of distinction and the abuses which have been swept away, he answers with perfect seriousness:

"I doubt if there has ever been a republic without such distinctions. You declare that they are toys for children. Well, grown men are led by toys. I would not say that from a rostrum, but in a council of sages and statesmen I can speak my mind. I do not think that the French love liberty and equality; they have not been changed by ten years of revolution; they are what the Gauls were, fierce and fickle. They are accessible to only one sentiment, the love of honour. That is why we must have distinctions....Soldiers must be allured by fame and pay.... Here is a new kind of money assessed at a different valuation from current coin. Its source is inexhaustible. With no other kind of money is it possible to reward actions which are so sublime that they cannot be valued in current coin." In these notable words, we hear the rippling of the three fountains of his soul: contempt for mankind, understanding of the masses, and the critical aloofness of the foreigner who has chosen a new fatherland.

IV

On Christmas Eve, 1800, the Consul was driving to the opera. Josephine and her daughter were following in another carriage. In a narrow street an empty cart partially blocked the way, and caused a halt. The cart was pushed aside, and the coachman whipped up his horses. The instant after the carriage had passed, an infernal machine hidden in the cart exploded. About twenty persons were killed, but no one in either Napoleon's or Josephine's carriage was hurt. On reaching the opera, Napoleon went straight to his box. When his wife arrived, he said calmly: "Josephine, those rascals wanted to blow me up; send for a copy of the music." Outwardly unmoved, he listened to the performance of Haydn's recent work, *Creation.*

Ordinarily, good music made him forget all his schemes; but this evening his brain was busily at work, pondering the causes and foreseeing the consequences of the attempt on his life. It mattered little who "the rascals" were, revolutionaries of the left or revolutionaries of the right. He knew well enough that he had plenty of enemies on both sides. The question was, whether it would suit him best to assume that his would-be assassins belonged to the right or to the left. His mind was soon made up on this point. Had the attempt been successful, the consequences for France would have been immeasurably great. Well, the consequences of the unsuccessful attempt should be no less momentous. It was a lucky chance, and he would make it solve the problem of personal power.

Next morning, when people came to offer congratulations on his escape, and when all were agreed in the opinion that the outrage must have been planned by the royalists, with assumed heat Napoleon declared they were absolutely mistaken. "This was the work of Septembrists, intellectuals, the non-commissioned officers of the revolution—persons with a bolder imagination and more culture than the masses, but in close touch with them, and always ready to spur on the workers!" When, in the Council of State, a proposal was made to institute special proceedings, Bonaparte objected on the ground that the method would be too slow. His speech was impassioned:

"Either we must do nothing at all, and, like Augustus, forgive the sinners; or else we must act promptly, take far-reaching steps which will guarantee social order once for all.... No ordinary criminal procedure will suffice; this is a matter of statesmanship.... Blood must flow. As many of the guilty must be shot as there perished innocent persons in the streets. Two hundred of these raging wolves must be seized and transported. They are always watching and waiting for their prey. All our troubles are due to these metaphysicians!"

Old Tronchet shakes his head. The attempt had been the work of émigrés and Englishmen.

"Are you proposing that I should transport noblemen or priests?" asked Napoleon angrily. "Vendée is quiet, and I do not want to banish the servants of the most widely spread religion in the world. I shall have to dismiss all the members of the Council of State, for, with two or three exceptions, everyone of you believe in this fable of a royalist plot.... Do you think me a child? Am I to say that the country is in danger? Has France ever been in better case since the revolution, the army more victorious, the country more peaceful? A pretty thing that men who have never been among the true friends of liberty, should now display so much concern for liberty! Do not think to excuse yourselves by saying: 'I defended the patriots in the Council of State.' That might go down in a drawing-room, but it will not go down here, among the most enlightened men in France!" He abruptly close the sitting. Do the councillors understand his drift?

These alarums and excursions are not the outcome of any sense of personal danger, for if that were his motive, if his own alarmed will-to-live were at work, he would seek out the real offenders as object for vengeance. The whole scene was statecraft. Whom can we frighten here at home? Whom can we pacify across the frontier? That is what the Consul is asking himself. Those are the considerations that guide his actions. Of course, these is a personal motive as well. He thinks that his own safety can best be guarded by draconian measures. "I did not sleep well o' night," he said at a later date, "until I had had these leaders of the great towns sent across the seas. I was not afraid of the sort of conspirator who gets up at nine o'clock in the morning and puts on a clean shirt!"

At the same time, he is infuriated by an anonymous pamphlet, "Caesar, Cromwell, and Bonaparte," in which the writer advocates the establishment of a hereditary monarchy. Who is daring to disclose his own secret thoughts even though the indiscreet pamphleteer is a sympathiser? When one of his confidants says that the only thing wrong with the pamphlet is that the disclosure is premature, Bonaparte lets the observation pass. But these two attempts, the attack on his body and the attack on his mind, have terrible consequences as far as freedom is concerned. The Tribunate and the Chambers are purged of a fifth of their numbers, Constant, Chénier, and other noted democrats being excluded; sixty-one out of seventy-three newspapers are suppressed; pamphlets and plays are subjected to a censorship. When the Council of State reminds him of the freedom of the press, he answers: "Do you think that, in such a situation, we can allow public meetings? ... And is not every journalist an orator? Do not the subscribers to his newspaper really form a club? Calumny is like an oil spot, which always leaves traces.... In England it is different; there the Government is old-established; here it is new. People would write worse things about me day by day; saying, for instance, that I am so afraid of being poisoned that I dare not eat!... The only way of keeping the political parties in check is to deprive them of their battle-ground."

Jerome, the youngest, good-natured and frivolous, is brought up by his brother with paternal strictness. "I send you Citizen Jerome Bonaparte, who is to serve as a midshipman. As you know, he must be kept under strict discipline. See to it that he fulfils all his duties."

His sisters, again; he has loaded them with money and honours, but they give him little thanks, and are incessant in their demands for more. There is Elise! She and Lucien, her favourite brother, vie with one another in escapades that are the talk of Paris. At amateur theatricals, they disport themselves in pink tights, and the Consul thunders: "Disgraceful behaviour! While I am wearing myself out trying to make people moral and respectable once more my brother and my sister appear before the footlights almost naked!" But as soon as his back is turned, they laugh merrily, and follow their own bent.

Caroline, who has married General Murat, is already involving her husband and Bernadotte in intrigues against the Consul. The public learns nothing of these matters, but they come to Napoleon's ears, and he says angrily that Murat deserves to be shot.

Pauline loses her husband in a colonial campaign. She does no regret the loss. By her second marriage, she becomes Princess Borghese in Rome. Her innocence is no more than a cynical pose, but her brother remains fonder of her than of any of the others. Even when the looseness of her life imperils his reputation, and he thinks it necessary to remonstrate, he words his remonstrances cautiously.

Uncle Fesch, at first a priest, and then an army contractor, now enters political life and resumes the clerical habit. Napoleon secures his appointment as archbishop and then as cardinal. All the Bonapartes exploit the man of power, that they may win money and position, lead a splendid life, and enjoy themselves, whereas in his life of superhuman toil there is little scope for pleasure.

Only his mother continues to hold aloof. Although she is not better pleased with Josephine now than formerly, although she is still the woman of Corsica and continues to talk an island dialect, he invites her, immediately after the coup d'état, to come and live with him in the Tuileries. She refuses, prefers to stay with Joseph. At the first great parade he holds in the courtyard of the palace, when she appears on the balcony among the highest State officials, she is very simply dressed, all in black, and yet looks prouder than Josephine, hard by, decked out in peacock array. Letizia mistrusts all this splendour, being now inured to the vicissitudes of life. When anyone tries to flatter her by speaking of her son's greatness and power, she sagely answers, in her Italian French: "Pourvou que cela doure."

What is the source of these family dramas, some of which will end in farce, others in tragedy?

In Napoleon's heart, had he been nothing more than a parvenu of the familiar type, he would, when pressed by his nearest and dearest for a share in his good fortune, graciously or ungraciously, but infallibly, have kept this dozen or so of men and women far from his circle of influence, for he would have been fain to conceal an origin which conflicted with his affectation of French nationalism. He is dictator of France, and yet every time his mother opens her mouth she reminds all the nationalists of his foreign birth. Here is the sister of a man who ranks with kings, and she plays the maddest pranks before the eyes of the monarchs of Europe, who naturally delight in pointing the finger of scorn at the ill-breeding of the upstart's relatives. His brothers wallow in the practice of corrupt methods which it was a primary aim of the revolution to abolish. All this occurs in Paris, where irony has ever been the fundamental tone of criticism!

Yet he does not merely tolerate these embarrassing kinsfolk; he is continually showering honours on them, promoting them to high office, making them his representatives abroad.

Herein we see the working of his Italian blood, and, above all, of his island upbringing. Every Corsican family, patriarchal by tradition, is clannish to the core, while filled with sentiments of hatred and vengefulness towards the rival house of the puny isle. Such traditions are older than those of many of the royal families, and as a result of them the urge towards the gratification of pride and towards the vindication of honour is more powerful than the desire for wealth. With this inborn clannishness is associated and intertwined the intense longing of a conqueror to preserve for the heirs of his body all that he has snatched for himself by the strength of his genious and through the favour of fortune. Nevertheless, destiny (tragical in its working, being conditioned by his innermost sentiments, and therefore inexorable) has made this man childless. The wife, into whose arms he has been driven by all the passion of love, the wife who has borne two healthy children in previous marriage, remains barren in her second union; and the infirmity of barrenness, but for which the history of Europe would have taken a different turn, is obviously a consequence of her devotion to the art of love, of the facile amorousness with which she won Bonaparte's affection and held him for a time in thrall. For, when she first met him, she was little over thirty; and, as for him, in subsequent relationships with other women, he was able to procreate three sons. He urgently needs a legitimate heir. Even an heiress would serve his turn. There can be no doubt that Josephine's failure to satisfy him in his crucial instance had a decisive affect on his plans.

In view of the plenitude of his powers, how could it be otherwise? During the first years of his rise, Roéderer propounds the great theme: "The royalists are saying: 'Who will be Bonaparte's successor?' If you die tomorrow, what will happen to us? You must nominate your successor."

"What you suggest would not be a strong policy."

"France would be more at ease if she knew who was to succeed you."

"I have no children."

"You could adopt one."

"That would not meet the difficulties of the moment. I can see no other way out than that the Senate should appoint my successor. Only there of the senators and myself should know his name. But who is it to be?"

"They had better choose a lad of twelve."

"Why do you want him to be a child?"

"A boy who can grow up in your school; one whom you can train and love."

At length the Consul, driven into a corner, explains: "My natural heir is the French people."

The man who speaks is not old. He is little more than thirty. Though he is appointed dictator for ten years only, he plainly foresees that he will be monarch. But he is already alarmed by the dangers of the position. When he looks round in search of an heir, his only hope is in his brothers. The best return they can make for the gifts he showers on them is that they should raise up heirs to his name, heirs who will at least have the advantage of Bonapartist blood. That is why Napoleon is so furious with Lucien, not because he has taken a wife with a bad name, but because he has taken a wife with no name. Lucien must get a divorce, and thus win freedom to marry a woman of royal blood.

Lucien refuses, quite as much owing to spite for his all-powerful brother as owing to affection for his wife. He is, indeed, fond of her, but he is so ambitious that he would sacrifice anything in the world for the sake of supreme power. After a stormy scene between the pair, Bonaparte comes into Josephine's room, and his voice is shaken with emotion as he says: "It is all over! I have given Lucien his dismissal."

Similar considerations explain the long-lasting quarrel with Louis, to whom Josephine looks for the salvation of her own line. He cannot endure Josephine's daughter Hortense, who reciprocates the dislike and loves another man. Josephine, however, forces her to marry Louis, and the son of this ill assorted union becomes Napoleon's darling, and is looked upon as likely to be the heir. Thereupon, his sisters begin to intrigue, spreading abroad the report that Napoleon is really the father. Through these disputes, the unity of the family is shattered, at the very time when Europe envies it for its good fortune. Letizia sides with the young people who have been forced into a marriage; and also espouses the cause of the ostracised Lucien, whom she follows to Rome. There she can live happily, far from the glowing star that has sprung from her womb. There she can live as an Italian, a wealthy and respected associate of Rome's leading families, and treated by the pope with all the honours due to a woman of royal blood.

What if Bonaparte were to divorce Josephine? His sisters, who hate "the old woman," do what they can, and trot attractive beauties up and down in full view. As Josephine grows older, Napoleon's relations with her become more tranquil, but he needs her friendship. He has ceased to be fastidious and has transient love affairs with one pretty actress after another, or makes this or that companion of his sisters the mistress of a few evenings or a night or two.

Georges, who, like all the rest, is afraid of him, describes him as "an amiable and considerate man," who plays hide-and-seek with her, helps her to undress, and bends to her "childish caprices." Since her Christian name is Josephine, refuses to call her by it, and invents for her an Italian name. She is Giorgina. He asks her to tell him her own story, listens attentively, and nods approvingly–for he has taken care to learn all about her, and is pleased that she tells him the truth.

Sometimes the Consul's servants catch sight of him in the evening, as, in his stockinged feet, he steals up a secret winding staircase to visit the lovely Duchatel. She is gentle, slender, and blonde—the type he prefers. Duchatel is one of Josephine's ladies-in-waiting. He likes to play cards with her, sometimes, talking to her in an undertone about matters of love, while the uneasy Josephine, at another card table, strains her ears to catch what he is saying. The lady-in-waiting retires. Napoleon follows, to find her in the place of assignation. His wife, beside herself, pursues them, rattles the door-handle. Napoleon comes to the door in a rage. Next day he threatens her with divorce, but he is softened by her tears.

These amours are but occasional. He is always up to the eyes in work. Besides, he has made up his mind to avoid what has proved disastrous to so many kings. He will not squander his resources on inamoratas, and he will not allow them to interfere in matters of State. As regards affairs of love, he is prematurely old. It is with a sense of shock that we find this man of thirty writing in a letter to a friend: "My old heart, which now knows human beings for what they are..."

Josephine is racked with anxiety about his conduct, just as formerly he was racked with anxiety about hers. She relies on dresses, hats, the arts of the toilet; spends more than the late queen of France; and has still so little reticence that, though she is the first lady in the land, she cannot refrain from telling her maid when the Consul has spent the night with her. He forgives her much. Sometimes she sits at the weary man's bedside, reading to him in her lovely alto voice. He thanks her with his eyes. He is conservatively inclined, this man of the revolution. Rarely does he part with a general, dismiss an official. How, then, shall he divorce this woman whom he loves, despite her faults?

In the pleasant gardens at Malmaison, where during his year's absence in Egypt she lived with her light-of-love, Hippolyte, he runs races with Bourrienne, Rapp, and a few men of letters, while Eugene and Hortense look on. When he trips and falls he joins merrily in the others' laughter. Then he gets into his carriage for the drive to Paris, saying:

"Now I can put my head in the collar once more."

VI

"Bonaparte very seldom writes with his own hand. He dictates everything, while walking up and down his study; dictates to a young man of twenty named Méneval, the only one who has the entry to this study and three other rooms of the private suite. No use approaching Méneval; nothing to hope in that quarter; indeed, no one would dare to try. But the First Consul himself jots down the memoranda that relate to his most important plans. This... very special map, he locks up with his own hand, and always carries the key about with him. If he leaves his study,

Méneval has to put the map away in a cupboard screwed to the floor. Of course the map might be stolen, but it would instantly be missed. Suspicion would at once fall upon Méneval and the underling, who cleans the study and lights the fire, so the underling would have to make a bolt for it.... All the secret memoranda concerning his military operations must be in it, and since the only way of overthrowing his power would be to destroy his plans, the theft of this map would bring everything to naught."

Who writes the foregoing? A Bourbon spy? Or is it a traitor among the Consul's intimates?

Neither the one nor the other. The young man of twenty named Méneval writes it; and it is dictated to him by his chief, the First Consul, who is walking up and down the study. Acting on Bonaparte's orders, the Minister for Justice is sending a provocative agent to Munich, were the man is to get in touch with English agents of the Bourbons. The letter is to be part of the outfit. Many other details are given. We are told more about the royalist menial who cleans the study and lights the fire; what this fellow will get if he brings off the coup successfully; where he will spend the night during his escape. The commander is drafting the plan of a little campaign directed against himself.

He has good reason to be on his guard. Uneasy winter weeks are these, during which he collates the data sent in by a hundred spies in London, Vendée, and Paris itself. "Has the time come to strike?" his agents are continually asking. "Wait," he replies, and quietly goes on gathering information. At length he has all the proofs in his hands. His deadly enemies of the extreme right and the extreme left, the royalists and the Jacobians, have jointed forces for the destruction of their great enemy. Pichegru, the friend of the Bourbons, and Moreau, the champion of the republicans who are opposed to the dictatorship, are working together. Both the generals are his rivals. Now is the time to strike.

When the plot became public property, alarm spread across Europe. The legitimate rulers were amazed at Napoleon's perspicacity, 'but put their trust in his enemies, whose number must be great than the "Moniteur" was willing to admit. The English ambassador compromised! The great Moreau in jail! —Bonaparte hesitates a long time before arresting Moreau, having high esteem for the man who had shared his laurels. On the day of the arrest, the Consul sends repeatedly for news. Is his memory at work? Less than four years ago, he himself had a scare that night in Talleyrand's house when he believed his own arrest to be imminent! The trial is distressing; Moreau's complicity is clearly proved; but Napoleon thinks it better to pardon the victor of Hohenlinden on condition of withdrawal to the United States. Pichegru is found strangled in prison. Thirteen of the conspirators are executed. A man named Querelle, personally involved in the conspiracy, reveals that one of the Bourbon princes has been privy to the plot.

The Consul lends an eager ear. A Bourbon prince! Talleyrand draws attention to the fact that for a long time the Duke of Enghien has been living close to the Rhine frontier-presumably in order to watch through a telescope what is going on in France. Would a man spend his time thus inertly in Baden, simply in order to make love to a cardinal's niece? The Duke of Enghien is a scion of the house of Condé; he is a Bourbon, and is in English pay. Most likely he is a Bourbon price incriminated in the affair. At any rate, he is in touch with the agents who swarm in South Germany. An example must be made of this suspect of the blood royal. That will put an end to the reiterated attempts on the part of the exiled Bourbons to disturb the peace of France and to trouble the sleep of its master!

In a lengthy dispatch, the Consul orders an attack on the little Badenese town of Ettenheim, just across the Rhine. The number of boats and the soldiers' rations are prescribed with as much care as if the expedition were the siege of Mantua. Three hundred dragoons make a raid into Baden and carry off the duke. Four days later, he is brought in secret to the fortress of Vincennes.

Two of Napoleon's confidants warn the dictator that no compromising document have been found among the Duke of Enghien's belongings. But Talleyrand, who has ever an eye to his reservation regarding the French raid into Baden, of course absolutely indefensible, the condemnation was technically just.

Nevertheless, as Talleyrand subsequently said of the affair, it was worse than a crime-it was a blunder. In time of revolution, hundreds are put to death who are more innocent than was this prince. Even though he may not have been privy to the plot, he would have hailed with delight assassination of the usurper, and would, sword in hand (to quote his own words), have joined in the march on Paris to take vengeance on any of the regicides who remained alive. There would have been very little said about the court martialling and shooting of this young officer, had he not been a Bourbon, had he not been a symbol of that prince-ridden Europe whose system had been ended on French soil by the revolution. The shooting of the Duke of Enghien was a challenge to dozen thrones, and to the many millions of Europeans who believed in rule by divine right. It gave the signal for a rallying of forces against the dictator who had had neither part nor lot in the reign of terror, and who during his seven years as military commander and as statesman had never committed an outrage.

The day after the execution, a few tongue-tied and crestfallen guests were seated at his board. Josephine was doing her best to hide her fear, and Napoleon had been taciturn despite his tumultuous thought. Then, suddenly, he broke out: "At any rate, they will know now what we can do. Henceforward. I hope, they will leave us in peace." After dinner, he walked up and down the room, explaining to the silent listeners his reasons and what he thought of it all. Continuing to pace the room, he went on to speak movingly of genius, of statesmanship, and above all of Frederick the Great, for whom he had so profound an admiration:

"Ought a statesman to indulge in feelings? Is he not an isolated individual, always alone though always in company? Policy is his telescope, which must neither reduce things in size nor magnify them. Even while he is attentively watching the course of events, he must be pulling the strings which move them. Often enough, ill-matched horses are harnessed to his chariot. Do you think he can allow himself to heed some of those feelings which may in other respects be of great importance to the welfare of society?.... How often he will have to do things which seem quite out of keeping with the whole?... Try to get outside the limitations of your own epoch, enlarge your imagination instead of being content merely to blame, and you will see that those great personalities you had regarded as violent and cruel, are nothing but statesmen! They know themselves better than others know them; they are the best judges of their own conduct; if they have true ability, they will even know how to control their passions, for they will be competent to calculate the precise effect of these."

Suddenly breaking off this monologue, which discloses some of the deepest recesses of his soul, he sends for the documents bearing on the conspiracy and has them read over to him.

"You see," he says, "we have incontrovertible proot that the conspirators wanted to spread disorder in France, and hoped, through killing me, to slay the revolution! It was my business to defend the revolution, to avenge it! The Duke was a conspirator just like another, and had to be treated in the same way as the others... The madmen seek to kill me, though they would gain nothing by it, for a gang of fanatical Jacobins would take my place.... These Bourbons! If they ever do regain power, I will wager that their first concern will be with etiquette. If they were prepared to share in the rough and tumble of the battle-field, with its blood and its grime! ... But how can they expect to win back a kingdom with a letter dated from London and signed Louis? All the same, letters like that will incriminate incautious recipients ... I have shed blood; I had to. Perhaps I shall shed more in the future. But always without passion, quite simply, because blood-letting is indicated, I am a statesman: I am the French revolution, and shall know how to protect it!" Abruptly he dismisses his guests.

Such is his mood; such are his motives, his views, the undercurrents of his feelings. But his notable inferences are not yet disclosed.

VII

A week after the court martialling of the duke of Enghien a committee of the Senate comes to see the Consul, with a very remarkable twofold request; for the establishment of a State tribunal and the foundation of a monarchy. This is a cautious improvisation, to test the current of popular opinion. Can anything be more logical, or simpler? To scare the terrorists, to safeguard the head of the State, two things are requisite, a State tribunal and an heir!

As with all the decisions of his life, so also this premature resolve to become an emperor is an outgrowth of circumstance. In none of the decisive moments of his career, do we find evidence that he had a definite scheme of life, which he systematically endeavoured to realise. When he first invaded Italy, it was not in search of the crown of Milan, and still less in search of the crown of France. But, as he winged his soaring flight, the natural sequence was that wider and ever wider vistas of land and sea should unfold themselves before his eyes. What happened, was a fulfilment of his own guiding principle: "He will not go far who knows from the first whither he is going." Improvisation, which, in amazing fashion, characterizes so much of his activity, merely deprives him of the nebular glory of the mystical hero. As far as details are concerned, it leaves him free to make exact preparations, while restoring to him, as a whole, a liberty and a guilelessness which strengthen his genius.

Was the desire to become emperor a mistake? What urged him towards the adoption of such a role?

First of all, the imaginative side of his nature, which for the second time is blinding the cold reason of the calculator. Thus was it in Egypt, and thus was it to be for a third time in Russia. His ideal drives him to take this step. He had grown to manhood amid dreams of the antique world; classical imagery had filled his mind; his dictatorial nature necessarily craved for the forms of Roman imperialism. A poetical temperament which makes him look upon the successive occurrences in his life as phases in the unrolling of a saga, and makes him feel, on the very evening after a battle has been won, that the battle has already passed into the realm of history; this engine, driven by the power of fantasy; this eye that looks upward and beyond to see how posterity will crown his deeds with fame—they need a symbol which no one has today, but which shone over Europe two thousand years ago.

Yet the mathematician in his also needs this symbol; the statesman needs it, that he may safeguard his country without perpetual wars. Lastly, and perhaps most passionately of all, the man with strong family attachments needs it; the man who feels he has won nothing, if what he has won be no more than an adventurer's prize that will perish with the winner.

"The name of king is outworn. It carries with it a trail of obsolete ideas, and would make me nothing more than the heir of dead men's glories. I do not wish to be dependent upon any predecessor. The title of emperor is greater than that of king. Its significance is not wholly explicable, and therefore it stimulates the imagination." Here, in two or three sentences, are compendiously disclosed the impetuous and the hot, the cunning and the cold, motives of his soul.

Does he see the dangers, or does he overlook them? What are his antitoxins? "What is a throne? A piece of wood covered with satin!" When he has become emperor he will ask the question and answer it thus, more than once. But with this satin-covered piece of wood, as he knows, he can influence grown men, just as he could influence them with the toys of the Legion of Honour. Indeed, the glamour of the throne is stronger, and therefore he will take the establishment of his throne more seriously than he took the foundation of the Legion of Honour. It is an instrument of policy, a means for the familiar spirits to his aid, the private person, the poet or the philosopher, can raise his head heavenward without bearing the burden of a crown; but the statesman needs the insignia of power, for the dull populace cannot believe in the reality of power, unless he who wields power wears the insignia.

Are we to suppose that he, who can calculate all eventualities, does not see the danger that lurks in the symbol of the crown? Down he not know that for thousands of years people have regarded the monarch as akin to God? If he is aware of this, how without disaster will he be able to harmonise the illusion with his political cynicism? If the crown is the gift of his genius, how can be bequeath it without bequeathing the genius?

Nevertheless, all his endeavours, like those of the emperors of ancient Rome, are now concentrated upon the bequest of power. He, whose own genius has taught him that genius is always aboriginal and primary; he who with his own eyes has seen hereditary power perish amid blood and grime, and whose inmost heart said aye to the act of regicide; he, who today reproaches the Bourbons, not with their origin, but with the cowardice that keeps them trembling in their mouse-holes; he, Napoleon Bonaparte, who feels himself to be the man of a millennium; he, a principle of whose rule it is to grant honour and wealth only to merit and courage and talent; he, who is the symbol of revolt incorporated in human flesh—believes that in the place he has fought and won for himself through the storms of eight years, he will be able to perpetuate his blood for the sole reason that it is his own!

He knows Plutarch and the story of the Cæsars. He has studied the history of the great kings of France and England and Prussia, and has learned to look with contempt upon their decadence. And yet he is ready and eager to restore the hereditary principle for the succession to this, the highest office in the State! Here, and here only, he wishes to combine the newest of the new with the old, so that, as he says later in a phrase both profound and tragical: "I might achieve that harmony which I regarded as essential for the tranquillity of the world, a solitary man, driven forward by the impetus of my own personality. That is why I dropped sheet-anchors everywhere."

But side by side with these heroic words, which sufficed to class him with the heroes of Plutarch, were housed the simplest feelings of domestic life. For, when his confidant Roedérer urged him to seek a new wife, who would bear him a son, Napoleon answered in great excitement:

always being bridled; the strictness of the republic would have bored you to death.... Liberty is no more than a pretext; equality is your hobby horse; the people are content to be ruled by a prince who comes from the army .... Today, soldiers and people are on my side. A man who could not rule under such conditions would be an idiot."

He broke off, resumed a formal demeanour, and gave Madame de Rémusat an order of no importance whatever in the dry tone of the absolute master.

These moments of confession; these quarters of an hour in which we stand opposite him, silently listening and watching, while he lounges on his chair, this newly made emperor of thirty-four in his well-worn green coat, looking askance up and down the room, rising to walk restlessly to and fro, pouring out his most intimate thoughts and then with a brusque transition cutting of all the springs of familiarity; when we see him in such movingly close proximity, in scenes full of nature and purpose, full of surrender to destiny and animus against the present—we can see and hear for ourselves even more than he frankly discloses in simulated self-forgetfulness. We become aware of his easy contempt for persons of noble birth, which is none the less conjoined with a secret wish to make a good impression on them; we discern programmes which he is always willing to adapt to changing circumstances; we observe the robust cynicism aroused in him by the folly of mankind, and see that it exists side by side with the foreign character traits of this Corsican, the very traits which enable him to rule the lovely Marianne with such gallant rigour.

Of course he discloses no more than half his motives, for he is here confining himself to political issues. Still, at the outset of the imperial epoch these political issues exert a predominant influence. It seems as if, to begin with, he regards the change of title with the utmost sobriety: "My brother will not bear a word of his new title," writes Napoleon to Madame de Staël. "He says he is just the same man he was before, and at the same time he puts on great airs. The truly great man is the one who fully realises that such empty names, which only the system of society compels us to assume, make no difference to friendship, to family life, or to social relationships. I am certain that since I have been 'Your Majesty,' not one of those who live with me will have been able to detect any difference in me."

Yet it is an event that now for the third time he takes leave of his name. It may be nothing that the leading persons in the country who appear at the first court reception address him and Josephine as "Sire" and "Madame," and that the members of the noblesse, who on this same polished floor fifteen or twenty years earlier had said "Sire and "Madame," should feel their hearts revive as they bandy courtiers' compliments. That may be nothing. Certainly, as regards essential nature, clothing, and deportment, the Emperor of today is no different from the Consul of Yesterday.

But the proclamation, the thousand and one letters, memoranda, and decrees, will henceforward be signed with a new name. For eight years they have been signed with the rudiments of a "Bonaparte." Now he signs with a name which he himself has never written since he was a child, and which his nervous hand will speedily compress into an initial N. and a flourish. Josephine has always addressed him as "General." His brothers and his sisters have for a long time past spoken to him with the ceremonial "you" instead of the familiar "thou" (the change was initiated, not by the Consul himself, but by Joseph). Only his mother in rare moments of expansion has occasionally used her son's Christian name; and she utters it in her own dialect as "Napolione."

There is a profound significance in the newness of this name when, adding to it a brand new title, he writes for the first time in his life:

Napoleon I, Emperor of the French.

VIII

With the first steps, the dilemma begins. The new coins he issues bear the legend: "Emperor according to the Constitution of the Republic"–this paradox will dog him for another four years. When the anniversary of the taking of the Bastille and the outbreak of the revolution comes round once more, he celebrates it with imperial pomp. The gesture many look sublime, but it is nothing more than a measure of political expediency. Even on this very first occasion, the anniversary of the day of liberation is postponed to a Sunday. A year or two later, the commemoration is completely ignored. With it vanishes the revolutionary calendar, for the old one is restored by degrees.

All flock to his standard. Ere long, one hundred and thirty of those who twelve years earlier had voted for the king's execution, hold office under the Emperor. This is the revolutionary picture caricatured in France, while Europe looks on watching how first the forms, and then by slow stages the content, for whose sake so much blood has been shed, are laid aside in the museum of history. What can Europe do but smile?

Still more broadly smiles the old noblesse. In the Faubourg Saint-Germain, which the emperor watches as closely as he watched the working-class quarter of Saint Antoine, anecdotes are rife concerning the new master in the old Tuileries. Now that he is called "Sire", just like the last of the Bourbons, all the lorgnettes are turned on him, and he has become the focus of criticism. As far as his own personality is concerned, so great is his native dignity that he is practically above criticism; In Milan, already, when no more than general of the French Republic, he ruled simply because he was there. But his relatives, with their childish curiosity and jealousy, and with their gossip about everything that goes on in the palace, soon become the targets of mockery. Magnified by rumour, and carried across the frontiers, this ridicule besmirches the master.

Henceforeward England keeps in Paris, in addition to ordinary spies, a horde of quilldrivers, whose tales find credence whenever they are enlivened with wit. Caricatures pass from hand to hand, showing the little lieutenant being taught by the great Talma how to walk like an emperor–Napoleon, who has often taught Talma the best way of playing the royal roles in Corneille!

How otherwise could old Europe defend herself against this saga which has become reality? The only resource was to degrade to farce what was being staged with all the crude seriousness of tragicomedy.

For the Emperor needs a court! It is his way to do everything with due attention to detail; but the details of court life are beyond the range of his studies, and he has to call in the experts of the old regime. The sometime chamberlain at the court of the late king must lay aside his pen (literature had been the resource of his retirement), to resume his staff of office. Josephine, who at first is attended by no more than a few of the ladies of the former court, is at a loss as to the management of an empress' train. What has become of Marie Antoinette's lady-in-waiting? She is still alive, and keeps a school in Paris. Bring her forth from her obscurity! She comes, and in the same rooms, before the same mirrors, arranges the folds of the train round these Creole feet which know very different dances from those of the poor dead queen.

The Emperor organises his court with the same seriousness and the same precision as if he were organising the general staff of a new army. No one knows better than Napoleon the vanity of these things: "I am well aware that plenty of people are writing unfavourably about them. Even you, Monsieur Roéderer, are not complaisant enough to suppose that I have a little common sense! You ought to understand without my telling you why I have given my new marshals, plain republicans though they be, the title of 'Monseigneur'; it is only to safeguard my own imperial title of 'Majesty'! The marshals having grand titles of their own, cannot make fun of mine." His very first undertakings as Emperor involve him in the toils of such contradictions.

The two ex-consuls (these are the only offices suppressed by the Emperor) become respectively arch-treasurer of the Empire. Talleyrand, as grand chamberlain, brings back the old arts and graces into the old house. How easy it would be for the Emperor to appoint none but gentlemen and ladies of the old regime to the leading offices at court! Instead, he chooses the scions of the proletariat and the bourgeoisie, the men who have risen with him: Berthier, Murat, Lannes, Ney, and Devoust. Fourteen generals, who in youth had been bakehouse lads, stable boys, waiters, cabin boys, or vagrants, must now exchange their campaigners' uniforms for the gold-braided coats of the marshals of France, must double their military duties with offices at court, must wear lace ruffs and buckled shoes; their wives must learn how to curtsey in the grand manner, how to stand and sit properly, how to scratch at the door instead of knocking – all that Europe may see how the Emperor, who was himself a lieutenant, promotes his lieutenants according to merit. Marmont is there, still wearing his arm in a sling; he is decked out in silk and satin and gold; but the slit sleeve, with its reminiscence of martial glory, seems to mock the splendour of his breeches. The Emperor tactfully drops out of the ceremonial two details that were degrading to the dignity of the courtiers: the presentation of the shirt at the king's levee, and the kissing of the ruler's hand.

But how is the charm of the rococo court to be revived, now that a soldier sits upon the throne? True, that, after hours of deliberation, it is possible to decide what colours the empress and the highnesses (Napoleon's relatives) must wear when they go out hunting. When, however, the time has come to bring down the stag, and the Emperor's thoughts are wandering in other fields, no one else ventures to shoot, with the result that the stag escapes because the chief sportsman has so much else on his mind. The ceremonial "was conducted as if to the sound of drums; everything seemed to happen at the storming pace; and the dread which he inspired in all, drove away grace and ease.... Court life was cold and dull, was gloomy rather than dignified. Since we were following a prescribed ritual, our inner feeling was that we were only machines which someone had placed upon the new gilded couches."

The Emperor is bored by ladies' society. With blunt circumstantiality, he asks how many children they have had, and whether they suckle their own babies. He tries to make himself agreeable, but often fails, when his thoughts range to other matters. At Saint-Cloud, in a room full of ladies, he can find nothing to say but, again and again: "How hot it is here!"

All the same, everyone attached to the court grows rich. He gives princely salaries to the court officials, and only shows thrift in his payments to some of the members of the old noblesse, maliciously implying that such work is nothing more than their duty. In general, he pays munificently, for "ambition is the mainspring of action. People work so long as they are aspiring upwards.... I have made senators and princes in order to promote ambition, and to make them dependent on me." He thus uses both honours and money to attach people to his cause, making, not friends, but dependents.

He knows the value of money; and though at all the critical moments of his career he surprises us by improvisation, we are, in general, just as much astonished by the way in which he continually displays a bourgeois rationality and foresight. His own demands are moderate. The Emperor's personal salary is fixed at twenty-five millions, the amount paid to the late king; but whereas Louis had spent forty-five millions, Napoleon saves twelve. The whole court, resplendent though it is, does not cost a fourth as much as the Bourbon court. France, which has to foot the bill, owes this economy to the care and knowledge of the master, who once had to live on ninety francs a month, and even now declares that he could get along well enough with twelve hundred francs a year and a horse.

Three was no change in his routine of life. The Emperor was called at seven, and held his reception at nine. Most of the day, his secretaries were engaged in taking down from dictation. This dictation was at the speed of ordinary conversation, and must be transcribed with perfect accuracy. At night, when he had some difficulty in sleeping. Méneval must come to record his master's night thoughts. His dinner took twenty minutes, and he hardly noticed what he was eating. He was much more plainly clad than his gaily bedecked courtiers; and when, on State occasions, he had to dress ceremoniously, he was always in a bad temper while being arrayed, and greatly relieved when he could doff his finery. When he entered Saint-Cloud after the place had been done up, he regarded it with disfavour, saying: "Rooms like this are suitable for a kept woman; they lack seriousness."

He does not allow himself to be enslaved by anything, and never insists that his bed or his meals or the lighting shall be just so and not otherwise. Even the snuff-box that he always carries is no more than a toy. The only things which the Emperor finds indispensable are open fires, hot baths, eau-de-cologne, Chambertin, and clean linen twice a day.

Josephine is extravagant. Her seven hundred dresses and two hundred and fifty hats, her jewels, her shawls, and her hair-dressing, cost millions; and although the Emperor wants her to shine in the splendours which he scorns for himself, he often grumbles at the preposterous totals of the bills.

His brothers and sisters squander money too. He gives them everything, and they are never satisfied. There is an absurd rivalry between the five couples (Lucien is still banished) and Josephine, whom all the others detest. Of the six grand dignitaries who draw fabulous salaries, four are his near relatives, by blood or by marriage. Joseph is grand elector; Louis, constable; Eugene, arch-chancellor of State; and Murat, high admiral. Since the brothers are to be styled imperial Highnesses, the sisters have their noses put out of joint, and make a collective demand, complaining that Hortense, as the wife of Louis, has become Imperial Highness, while they are "nothing." He eyes them for a moment, and replies with a witticism which deserves a place in universal history: "When I listen to you, I can almost believe that His Majesty our father of blessed memory must have bequeathed us crown and realm!"

Indeed, one could almost believe it. For when he complies with their demand, with a good nature he is not apt to show towards others, and when for then years to come he showers honours and wealth, crowns and territories, upon these brothers and sisters who show no gratitude, who never obey him and never cease to trouble him — we cannot but ask ourselves once more what can be the prejudice which blinds his eyes where they are concerned. His pride is great; he is lonely in his self-confidence;

step would be opposed to his interest; it would give Louis' children a better position than his, because they would be the grandsons of an empress! He had the impudence to talk to me about his rights and his interests! He wanted to touch me on the raw! He might almost as well have boasted he had slept with my mistress! I will allow no one to rob me of her, or to share her with me!"

Thus does the volcano suddenly spout forth great rocks, in the midst of a conversation about trifles. But the rest of the conversation does not turn wholly on trifles. He speaks bitterly of his brothers and sisters, comparing them with Eugene and Hortense. "My stepchildren always side with me. If their mother is put out because I take a fancy for a pretty girl, they say to her; 'Oh, well, he's still quite young, you know. You mustn't make a fuss. No doubt he has faults, but you must not forget how much he has done for us all."

But nothing will keep him from pushing his brothers' advancement. When Joseph refuses all other occupations, Napoleon forces him into the army. "He must have military rank, get a nice wound, and win a good reputation for himself. I shall only give him easy jobs. Then he can win a battle, and I shall be able to promote him to a higher rank than all the other commanders." It sounds like the education of a degenerate son by a great father.

Louis has an enthusiasm for poetry; he becomes chief of the imperial guard, so that he may have a dignified position; but he can stay at home when the guns begin to shoot.

Murat and Caroline are frightfully extravagant; their table service is of gold. "As for Caroline, my own sister, if I have to discuss anything with her, I must make longer speeches than at the council of States....

"The whole lot of them are always thinking about my death. It's rather nasty of them to be continually bringing that into my mind.... Were it not that I find some happiness in my home life, I should be miserable! Why are they always so suspicious of my wife? What has she more than they? Diamonds and debts!... She's a good wife to me, and does them no harm! She's rather fond of playing the empress, with her jewels, her dresses, and the whimsies natural to her age. I have never been blinded by love. But I am just. She shall be crowned, even if it costs me two hundred thousand men!"

Thus he is continually bickering with a family which he could reduce to nonentity in a moment, but from which he is unable to cut adrift.

Only one of them is incorruptible, asks for nothing, and holds aloof. Lucien writes from Rome:

"Mother thinks that the First Consul is wrong to take the Bourbons' crown. She has uneasy presentiments which she will not confide to me. Her dread is that a gang of fanatics will assassinate the Emperor." - While this dignified mother of the family, still a beautiful woman though well over fifty, is led by her knowledge of the world and her gloomy forebodings to keep herself to herself, while she holds her tongue and only mentions her anxieties to a few intimates, in the Tuileries her children are quarrelling about titles and precedence, disputing who is to sit at the Emperor's right, debating whether they are entitled to walk out of the room in front of a sovereign price!

Then Napoleon summons Madame Mere to Paris. But here is one who will not obey him. At first she makes excuses. When more urgent commands are sent, she sets out on the journey, but takes her time, and does not reach Paris for the most splendid festival that a mortal mother can ever have witnessed. She hears and reads all that a gaping world says and writes about the affair. Her only comment is: "Pourvou que cela doure!"

IX

Meanwhile, Letizia's protector the Pope has become more compliant, and is already on the way to Paris. What else could the Holy Father do? The man of might had summoned him, and the Emperor must be kept in a good humour. Besides, he who is to be crowned is an Italian. As one of the cardinals had put it, in the decisive conclave: "After all, we have this satisfaction, that we are taking vengeance on the Gauls by setting an Italian family to rule over these barbarians." Napoleon is still regarded as a foreigner in France! But why does he not go to Rome for his coronation? Why is he not content to be anointed in Rome, as Charlemagne had been and all the emperors of the West since Charlemagne's day? What does he want a Pope for at all?

In this matter, once more, he is trying to harmonise the new with the old. At first he is silent about details, and merely asks the Pope "to give the highest religious consecration to the anointing and crowning of the first Emperor of the French." For weeks, letters have been exchanged between Rome and Paris, but the exact nature of the ceremony still remains obscure. Pius VII is in an uneasy frame of mind as he draws near to Paris, and his spirit is by no means one of benediction. Never before has a Pope been summoned . When the Emperor meets the Pope at the gate of the city, the Holy Father does not fail to note that Napoleon neither kneels to receive a blessing nor kisses hands in token of fealty. Paris is a town where people's faith is unstable and where popes are held in little honour. The visitor is chilled.

But Josephine is different. All devotion, she confides to him that she and her husband were not married in church, and that therefore from the Pope's point of view they are not married at all. She is eager to grasp the opportunity of consolidating her union, which seems to her frail in view of her barrenness. Taking the hint, Pius insists upon a religious celebration of the marriage before he will crown her as empress. In the palace chapel, two days before the festival, Uncle Fesch, clad in purple, solemnises the union of the pair who eight years before had needed the intervention neither of priests not civilian officials before coming together. There are no witnesses, not one who could laugh over this comedy in which cheating is still the order of the day–for even the Corsican uncle, is not aware what is about to happen.

On December 2, 1804, in Notre Dame, an abundance of precious stones reflects the light of a myriad candles, so that the place looks more like banqueting hall than a church. Everything has been prepared for weeks beforehand. A skilful museum director has even produced a colourable imitation of Charlemagne's sceptre. Ancient parchments from the days of the Roi Soleil had been consulted, to ensure that the crowning of this revolutionist should vie in every respect with that of the legitimate monarchs of France. Ségur had studied the etiquette of the occasion with the utmost care; Isabey had rehearsed the whole affair with an array of dolls; the old palace, Paris, France, were in a fever.

The Emperor is in a pleasant humour. Early in the morning he makes sure that Josephine's crown is a good fit. The great procession drives to the cathedral. Napoleon, robed in an antique imperial mantle, strides to the high altar leading the empress by the hand. Josephine's charm helps to divest the great moment of a certain sense of embarrassment. Surrounded by attendant cardinals, the Pope is seated, waiting. The organ peals forth.

Then, when the appointed instant has come, and all are expecting this man who has never bowed the knee to any one, to kneel before the Holy Father, Napoleon, to the amazement of the congregation, seizes the crown, turns his back on the Pope and the altar, and standing upright as always, crowns himself in the sight of France. Then he crowns his kneeling wife.

None but the Pope had known his intentions. Informed at the eleventh hour, Pius had lacked courage to threaten immediate departure. Now, all he could do was to anoint and bless the two sinners. Moreover, the crown on the Emperor's head is not a Christian crown at all, but a small pagan circlet of golden laurel leaves. All who describe the occasion agree in saying that the Emperor was pale but handsome. He resembled Emperor Augustus; and from now onwards, as if by some mystical power, his features grew more and more like those of the first emperor of Rome.

Thus, in this symbolical hour, Napoleon reduces to mockery the legitimate formalities he is affecting to copy. Furthermore, he makes a laughing-stock of the Pope, who will not forget the slight. In an instant the cloud of Bourbon reminiscence has been scattered; the flavour of imitation and parody has vanished; and on the steps of a temple there stands a soldier, a Roman imperator, whom a dozen years before this day no one had ever heard of, who since then has performed no miracles but only done deeds, and has now crowned himself with the golden laurels of these deeds. But his mantle is embroidered with golden bees, the emblem of activity.

Several incidents show that he has not, throughout this day of his coronation, wholly surrendered to the mood of a man who has made his own destiny.

When he was seated on the throne, crown on head, with the Pope in front of him, he said a low aside to his brother; "Joseph, if only Father could see this!" The remark, poignant at such an hour in the mouth of a man who was never wont to speak of his father, is fundamentally natural. The perfect simplicity, the unsophisticated innocence, of his course of action, lead his mind back to his origin. Memories of family feuds on the island, of the pride and ambition of the Corsican clans, direct his thought towards the stock from which he has sprung.

Semblance never holds his attention, which always reaches out to the core of reality. Thus he is not bewildered even in this amazing hour. When he wants to whisper something to his uncle, who stands just in front of him during Mass, he gives the cardinal a gentle dig in the back with his sceptre. As soon as all is over, and, alone with Josephine, he goes in to dinner, he says with a sigh of relief: "Thank God we're through with it! A day on the battle-field would have pleasured me better!" At their little dinner he tells her to keep on her crown, as if he and she were poet and actress, for, he says, she is charming, his little Creole woman as empress. Thus, in the most natural way in the world, he unmasks the whole masquerade, and we are at ease once more as we see the son of the revolution laughing his own empire to scorn.

The freedom of spirit shown by the foregoing petty details is splendidly illuminated by a admission he made the same evening, when, to a confidant, he summed up the whole matter with sceptical emotion: "No, Decrés, I have come into the world too late. There is nothing great left for me to do. I do not deny that I have had a fine career, but what a difference between me and the heroes of antiquity. Look at Alexander, for instance. After he has conquered Asia, he declares himself to be the son of Jupiter, and the whole East believes him, save only his mother and Aristotle and a handful of Athenian pedants. But if, I nowadays, were to declare myself the son of the Father Eternal, every fishwife would laugh in my face, There is nothing great left for me to do."

This was said a few hours after he had crowned himself emperor; said quite simply and quite truthfully. Is it not plain why the East has always allured him, and will continue to allure him? By nature he is endowed with immense powers, and is overburdened by their incredible weight. Nothing can be adequate to his aspirations, now that he has learned how readily people obey the man who can command obedience by his skill and by his deeds. He is strong in his own strength; what does Voltaire's enlightenment, what does Rousseau, matter to him? How can he wish to establish democracy, to install popular government, when he knows the weakness of the popular instincts, and all the corruptness of the leaders of the people? To expand his sway, to spread his name widely and even more widely, to leave more record of himself in the book of universal history than that half page of which he spoke a few years ago, to sacrifice life itself to the little golden circlet on his head, to do these things without enjoyment and without leisure and without pause—this is all that life now offers.

When, during these days, the sketch for an imperial seal is, laid before him, and the sees a lion couchant, he draws his pen across the picture, and writes in the margin: "An eagle volant".

X

But with a sinister energy the dangerous fluid of divide right radiates from the golden circlet, and slowly spreads its waves through the brain of the wearer, the chosen man. Vainly he endeavours to master and transform the millennial force that has been stored up in this crown, or to make light of it; it masters him, and from time to time forces him to quit the realm of his self-

Thus, a year after a coronation, the war with England is resumed, and will not end until Napoleon's star sets. There is no campaigning, at first; simply a state of war, in which this great military commander cannot force a decision, and which therefore, he cannot bring to a close. England has two notable advantages over her continental rivals, and over France in particular. It is an island realm; and it spreads athwart the world. Napoleon's historical sense, growing ever more alert, shows England to him as a new empire of Alexander, extending like Alexander's from homeland isles and peninsulas to Asia and to Africa, invincible so long as it remains a united whole. The dream of our new oriental splits upon this rock.

On this rock, too, are wrecked the mathematician's calculations. The day after Aboukir, he had said that a decade would be needed for the rebuilding of France's fleet. Half that time has elapsed, and England's naval predominance has steadily grown. During the brief peace, the soldiers of the unsuccessful Egyptian campaign are brought back to France in English bottoms; England is confirmed in the possession of the Cape and other overseas colonies; and France has more urgent claims on her energies than the building of the new fleet.

Fundamentally, what was a ship to the Emperor? He was competent to design a big gun, to cast it, to place every screw; and to repair every wheel and every shaft of an ammunition wagon. He knew when every horse in a cavalry squadron would have to be re-shod, and how must it would cost; and he knew exactly how many loaves a field bakery could turn out a day. This far-reaching knowledge was one of the secrets of his predominance; made his subordinates zealous in their terror of his incessant control, whether in peace time or in war time; aroused respect for the all-embracing intelligence of the chief; and ensured the exact carrying out of his military ideas.

But one who would know a ship, must have passed his youth among big guns. Even though his admirals were astonished to find how quickly he made himself at home in naval matters, how shrewd were his questions, and how sensible were his orders, still their commendation of Napoleon was no more than the praise of a kindly expert who, tacitly, is criticising a talented amateur. Napoleon knew this well enough. Since he lacked a great admiral quite as much as a great fleet, and had never been willing to entrust the conduct of a campaign to any subordinate, he invented a new kind of war which was to enable him, after all, to get the better of England. The European ports from Hamburg to Taranto were to be closed to English ships, and thus the nations of traders was to be vanquished in a trade war. At the same time, re revived his plans of invasion; for, could he but set foot on the island, he would be the military commander, and in his own element.

Just as he had done before the Egyptian campaign, so now in Boulogne, he studies the possibilities of embarkation and disembarkation. On land, his fantasy has found satisfaction and his mathematical powers have gained conquests in ardent imaginings; and yet, all the time, his battles have been realities, have realised these imaginings. But here, at sea, he is an arnateur, not an expert; is, for the first time, the onlooker instead of the man of action. In none other of his private letters do we find sentences akin to those which he writes from the coast to Josephine after a stormy night in which a gunboat has broken away from her moorings: "A wonderful sight! The minute-guns were firing; watch-fires were lighted along the coast. A ranging, foaming sea; uncertainty and anxiety throughout the night. But a kindly spirit brooded over the ocean and the night. No lives were lost, and I lay down to sleep with the feeling that I had been witnessing a romantic and epic vision-so that I could almost believe that I had been looking on quite alone."

A wonderful sight; but, alas, only a sight! The Ossianic note is sounded again, for the first time after fifteen years. Napoleon waxes romantic. How moving and how significant are the closing words of this artist, who suddenly feels that he has been robbed of the human material with which he works, and who is even a little alarmed (we cannot help but read this through the lines) at the unwonted sensation of being quite alone.

The unfamiliar element leads him astray. When a storm is threatening, he orders a naval review. Admiral Bruix does not carry out the order. The Emperor finds that no preparations are bring made, and sends for the admiral. A terrible scene.

"Why did you not obey my orders?"

"Your Majesty can see that for yourself. You would not needlessly risk brave men's lives in such weather!"

The Emperor, surrounded by his rigid officers, turns pale with wrath, and says: "Sir, I have given you an order. The consequences are no concern of yours. Do what you are told!"

"Sire, I cannot obey."

An ominous pause. Napoleon strides towards Bruix, riding-switch in hand, threateningly, though the switch is not raised. The admiral draws back a step, and lays his hand on his sword-hilt. A petrified group.

"You will leave Boulogne within twenty-four hours, and betake yourself to Holland. Rear-Admiral Magon, carry out my orders."

A naval review is held in a raging storm. A number of chaloupes are capsized, and their crews struggle in the water. The Emperor, to save himself, jumps into the first boat; all who can, follow his example. Two hundred bodies are washed ashore next day.

This incident, unique in Napoleon's career, a blunder, an act of cruelty, a direct disobedience on the part of a subordinate is a warning symptom. But there is a third indication.

A year before, an American inventor had come to Paris, and had offered the French admiralty two new inventions; one of them a ship to be propelled by steam power instead of by the wind; the other, a submarine boat which was to sink ships by the discharge of a kind of torpedo. "The man is a charlatan," was Napoleon's comment on Fulton, after an experiment in which the inventor's "plunging boat" had secured a partial success; and brought him models of a machine gun and a field telegraph, he would have opened his purse.

Napoleon failed to conquer England because this was the one matter in which he was not confident of victory. Failure was inevitable because here, and here only, his self-confidence was at fault; because his belief in his own powers was weakened by his want of expert knowledge and by the inaccessibility of a foe. By land! Yes, if he could only get at this island by land! The thought brings back to his mind the scheme of five years ago, when he had planned an attack on India by way of Herat. But for such a scheme, quiet and time are needed.

His first aim is to keep peace, to bring about which he has worked with his best powers for years. Immediately after the coronation, he writes in this sense to six monarchs, addressing each in a style appropriate to his correspondent's character, thinking out the effect of every detail, and considering even the exact working of his signature. Note, for instance, how he writes to the Shah:

"My reputation reaches so far, that you cannot fail to know who I am and what I have done; how I have made France supreme among the nations of the West; and how great an interest I take in the rulers of the East.... Orientals are full of courage and spirit, but their ignorance of certain arts and their neglect of military discipline put them at a disadvantage in war when they are faced by soldiers from the North.... Write me your wishes, and we will renew friendly and, commercial relationships.... Written in my Imperial Palace of the Tuileries ... in the first year of my reign. Napoleon" But, in the heading, the document sets forth a title which never existed, a title which Napoleon obviously uses to show the ruler of Persia that the writer is the general who made himself famous in the Egyptian compaign. The document purports to come from "Bonaparte, Emperor of the French."

On his table, as he signs the letter to the Shah, lies a letter to George III, though England and France are at war. It is penned with wonderful art, and is both moving and politic: "Does not all the blood that is being shed without apparent advantage to anyone, touch the consciences of the governments? I am not ashamed to take the first step. It seems to me I have shown the world that I have no dread of war and its caprices. My heart, indeed, longs for peace; but war has never dimmed my fame. I implore Your

Majesty not to deprive yourself of the good fortune of restoring peace to the world! Do not leave this precious task to your children. Never was there a more favourable opportunity of stilling angry passions. If this chance be missed, what will be the outcome of the war? During the last ten years, Your Majesty has won more territory and more treasure than all Europe possesses. What further could you expect from the war?"

How could the writer fail to smile at the realisation that the last argument could with equal force be turned against himself? The appeal is fruitless, for neither England nor the rulers on the mainland will tolerate the new power of France or its upstart emperor. A fourth coalition of the princes against the republic is imminent.

During the years of peace, he has been tolerably well content. His intimates at Malmaison have often described him as cheerful. Now he must take up arms once more, and resign himself to the knowledge that "it lies in the nature of things to continue this struggle between the past and the future, for the enduring coalition of our enemies makes it essential to attack them if we are to escape annihilation." There is the simple truth, spoken without exaggeration and without bitterness. If he did not create this nature of things, at any rate he stabilised it. Even though the first wars of France in the revolutionary epoch were purely defensive, the subsequent campaigns became offensive, and were transformed into wars of conquest by the impetus of the people's army and the outstanding genius of its commander.

Nevertheless, when he is thus challenged by opponents whom he has twice defeated, can we wonder that concrete plans which have hitherto followed his soaring imagination at a respectful distance, should now, likewise, begin to outsoar the boundaries of reason? In the opening years of the nineteenth century and here in the West, the Emperor might have kept the peace for another decade, that in the end he might measure his strength against England's in Asia. But when Europe's persistent desire for revenge upon revolutionary France spurs him into action, he conceives the great plan of the unified European realm. Now for the second time (and for the last time down to our own days) a great and saving work will be attempted, and the attempt will fail.

Thus it is that Napoleon's crowning political thought issues out of a personal defensive. Now, when a new coalition is being formed, and formed against him, his ideal takes a fresh shape. For years his inward gaze has been concentrated on Alexander; now, instead, he sees the figure of Charlemagne. He goes to Aix-la-Chapelle, for a ceremonial visit to the tomb of the great Frankish emperor. "There will be no peace in Europe," he says at this time to his trusted companions, "until the whole continent is under one suzerain, an emperor whose chief officers are kings, whose generals have become monarchs. ... Would you tell me that this plan is but an imitation of the old imperial constitution? Well, there is nothing new under the sun!"

This gradual transformation of his ideal, and the sustenance of the new ideal by the historical imagination, has immeasurable consequences. Precisely because the adoption of the Carlovingian scheme involves for him a renunciation, he storms forward in pursuit of it as if he were fighting for a province. The haste with which he tries to reconstruct the empire of Charlemagne is new, is symptomatic of a fever which will drive him towards new goals before he has reached the old ones.

XI

Since the spring, his army has been assembled in Boulogne in readiness for the repeatedly postponed landing in England. But in the autumn, when the menace of a fresh Austrian attack becomes a certainty, with a change of plans which is decided on in a couple of days and is carried out in a fortnight, he directs all his forces eastward, and is across the Rhine in advance of the news of his first movement. Just before leaving the coast, he dictates to Daru the whole scheme of the attack on Austria, "the order and length of the marches, the meeting places of the columns, the attacks by storm, the movements and the blunder of the enemy—

condition of peace, that you should give me guarantees against a fourth coalition with England.... Nothing would make me happier than to combine the tranquillity of my people with your friendship, upon which I venture to make a claim, despite the number and strength of my enemies in your entourage." At the same time, he marches on Vienna.

Then, while he is advancing at topmost speed, comes a blow. He learns that two days after his victory on land had come the sea-fight at Trafalgar, when England had almost annihilated the French fleet. Eighteen ships have been lost; Nelson is dead; the French admiral is a prisoner. Is this another disastrous hour, like the one when the news of Aboukir reached him in the desert? Courage! Then the situation was a hundredfold more difficult. We are not now cut off from Paris by the sea; we need no ships. With redoubled speed he marches on Vienna, which the enemy surrenders without a blow.

But the tidings of Trafalgar have renewed Francis, fixity of purpose, and have made Alexander firmer than ever. Both try to win over Prussia, which hesitates, and protracts negotiations. Napoleon vainly tempts the tsar with the promise of Turkey. In Brünn there is a great game of hide-and-seek, in which each power tries to keep the others in suspense and is disavowed by its own plenipotentiaries. The Emperor is the only ruler who improvises a political idea. Two days before the decisive battle, for which preparations are already being made, he writes to Talleyrand, who is negotiating in Brünn:

"I should have no serious objection to handing over Venice to the elector of Salzburg, and Salzburg to the house of Austria. I shall take Verona ... for the kingdom of Italy.... The elector can call himself King of Venice if he has a fancy that way.

"The electorate of Bavaria would become a monarchy.... I will give back the artillery, the magazines, and the fortresses, and they must pay me five millions .... Tomorrow, I think we shall have a pretty big battle with the Russians. I have done my utmost to avoid it, for it is only useless bloodshed. I have exchanged a few letters with the tsar, and learn from what he writes that he is a good fellow, with bad counsellors ... Write to Paris, but don't say anything about the battle, for that would make my wife anxious. You don't need to worry I am in a very strong position here, and my only regret is for the almost needless bloodshed which the battle will cost.... You write home for me; I have been in camp among my grenadiers for the last four days, and have to write on my knees, so I can't manage many letters."

Such is the Emperor's mood just before the most famous of his victories. While he is studying his maps, noting the name of every Moravian village, the width of every stream, and the condition of every road, and while he does his best to keep himself warm by the camp-fire, he is thinking of the ministers in Paris who are awaiting his commands, and of his wife who may be anxious. In the same half hour, he drafts a new programme for the partition of four or five States, talks of new crowns, of war indemnities, and of handing over fortresses. Twice his laments for the useless bloodshed light up the written page like the rising sun of one of these December days. Need we be surprised that such a man conquers the legitimate prices, who at this moment are dining in their palaces?

In the evening, when he learned the enemy's movements, he clapped his hands, and, "trembling with joy" (the words are his adjutant's), said: "They are walking into the trap! They are delivering themselves into my hands! By tomorrow evening their army will be annihilated!"

Then he sits down with his staff to supper in a peasant's hut, and, an unusual thing with him, remains at table for some time after his meal, emotioned and musing. He goes on to speak at considerable length concerning the nature of tragedy. From this, he passes to Egypt: "If I had taken Acre, I should have donned a turban, have clad my soldiers in wide Turkish trousers. But only in the utmost need should I have exposed my Frenchmen to serious danger; I should have made of them a corps of immortals, the Holy Battalion. I should have fought the war with the Turks to a finish by the use of Arab, Greek, and Armenian levies. I should have become Emperor of the East, and should have made my way back to Paris through Constantinople." The concluding words, so one who heard the soliloquy tells us, were accompanied with a smile, as if to show his awareness that he was being carried away by a rapturous dream.

But is not the scene we are describing a dream? Must we really and truly believe that little more than a century ago, a mortal man, the understudy of a demigod, stormed across modern Europe and remoulded it in accordance with his will? Did it not all happen in the Homeric age, when two princes in single combat would settle the fate of generations? Or, perhaps, he is a character in a fairy-tale, this man in the middle thirties, a little fellow, seated in a wattle-and-dab hut, on an unknown plain. He wears a greasy coat, a clammy shirt; stuffs potatoes and onions in his hungry mouth. Next day, by this one battle, he will renew the glories of Charlemagne, dead a thousand years since. Now, overnight, his unbridled imagination runs across Asiatic deserts, where a stone-heap successfully resisted him; dwells on that old frustrated plan; while his errant thoughts follow the wraith of the Macedonian to the Ganges.

Day dawns: A year ago, on the altar steps in Notre Dame, he had crowned himself with the circlet of golden laurels. In a fervent proclamation, he reminds his soldiers of that day, and concludes with the promise that for this once he will keep out of the firings line.

Never before has history recorded such words uttered by a commander. They have always been eager to declare their determination to defy death in the forefront of the battle. Napoleon, whose grenadiers have seen him in twenty fights and regard him as a heavenborn leader, can venture to tell his men that he will reward their valour by being careful of his own safety.

Then the Emperor defeats both his enemies, and makes famous for a thousand years an out-of the-way spot of which no one had ever heard before— the plain of Austerlitz.

"Soldiers," he says next day to the victors, "I am pleased

with you.... Name your children after me, and if one of them should prove worthy of us, I will make him my own son and appoint him my successor!" That is the emotional note he keeps for the army. To his wife, he writes as simply as possible: "I have beaten the Russian and Austrian armies. Rather tired, after a week in the open, when the nights have been chilly, tonight I shall sleep in a bed, in Prince Kaunitz, fine castle. I'm wearing a clean shirt, the first time for a week .... I hope to get two or three hours' sleep."

Quite a simple matter, these momentous happenings! It is but a new song in the rhapsody when, a day later, Emperor Francis comes to Count Kaunitz, castle, to beg for an interview with the little Corsican lieutenant. But the bird has flown. When the two men meet at length, it is in a windmill. Napoleon greets his brother emperor courteously, saying: "I regret, Sire, that I must receive you here, in the only place I have entered for two months." What self-confidence in the soldier interviewing the man born in the purple; what subtle mockery in the mouth of one who knows that in his distant capital, at news of his splendid victory, flags will soon wave and songs resound.

But the distinguished guest, a man of sound sense and good breeding, knows how to parry the trust; "Your present quarters are so profitable to you, Sire, that I think they cannot fail to please you." Both smile; and unobtrusively they eye one another up and down, for, though they have fought for a decade, they have never met. Of the same age, they had both reached power at twenty-six or thereabouts, though in such different ways; and neither of them can foresee how close Napoleon's will-to-peace is one day to bring them, or how widely Francis' will-to-revenge will ultimately sever them.

"Yesterday I had the German emperor in camp with me and we had two hours' talk .... He threw himself on my generosity. But I took good care of myself, as I am used to doing .... We have agreed to make peace promptly.... The battle of Austerlitz is the finest of all I have fought. We have taken forty-five regimental colours, more than one hundred and fifty guns, the flag of the

Russian guard, twenty generals, and thirty thousand prisoners in all. More than twenty thousand killed—a ghastly sight!" Did the jubilant outburst of a conqueror ever come to a stranger close? He luxuriates in the figures of his gains, and then, suddenly, the corpses of the dead rise before his eyes! Henceforward, such references become frequent; he writes in simple and heartfelt words about bloodshed.

In the peace negotiations, the minister has a contest with the master. The day after Austerlitz, Talleyrand writes to the Emperor: "How easy would it be, now, to destroy the Habsburgs once for all. But it would suit our book better to strengthen them, to give them a fixed place in France's system!" Napoleon, however, enforces the peace of Pressburg, in which the old German empire is shattered into fragments, while Austria vanishes from Germany and Italy. What is in the conqueror's mind?

Europe! A league of States under French hegemony. Russia is Asia; England is detached, an island. The Continent must be unified, must consist of middle-sized and small powers overshadowed by the eagles of France, and democratically ranged side by side. Now, after Austerlitz, the new thought takes shape. The victory has put it within his power to realise the greatest aim of a European, the unification of Europe.

He did not set out towards this goal. It was a gradual growth, the fruit of circumstances. He did not deliberately provoke the wars that were fought when the new idea was in its inception. Since Marengo, his chief wish has been for peace. At that time, Austria had been loath to make peace. The Austrian renewal of the attack was a logical outcome of legitimist theory, for Hubsburg and the revolution could not jointly rule Europe. Austerlitz had settled the dispute once more. Now it had become possible to reunite Charlemagne's resurrected Europe. But neither the kings and emperors (who were only beaten, not convinced), nor he himself (who had gained all by the sword and not by persuasion) could march along the way of the spirit towards the unification of Europe. The determinisms of his own past left Napoleon no option but to create his United States of Europe by force. Not till ten years later did he come to see that he had been seeking to achieve a great end by false means.

When he came to understand this, it was too late; he was impotent, in the great epilogue of his exile.

XII

"Tell the Pope that I am keeping my eyes open; tell him that I am Charlemagne, the Sword of the Church, his Emperor, and as such I expect to be treated."

Thus treateningly he writes to Rome. If he must bow before this mole-hill, at least he will enforce obedience. His demeanour is infused with a new tone since Austerlitz and Pressburg. From conquered Austria, he writes in a dictatorial style which neither he nor Europe has hitherto known. The Queen of Naples, despite his yearlong warnings, has permitted English ships to anchor in the bay. An army order is issued: "The Bourbon dynasty has ceased to reign in Naples." Simultaneously, he writes to Brother Joseph: "I think I have already told you that I intend the kingdom of Naples to accrue to my family, so that, like Switzerland, Holland, Italy, and the three German kingdoms, it may belong to my federated States, or, rather, to the French Empire."

Henceforward he endeavours to make the plan a reality, the plan whereby Europe shall be governed by one emperor with kings as vassals. Paris, which now acclaims the conqueror, shall be the capital city of the Continent. The Emperor has, in the best sense of the term, "come home again." He exclaims, "This campaign has made me fat! I believe that if all the princes of Europe were to ally themselves against me, I should develop an absurdly wide paunch!" In such a mood does he hurl himself from recent events into new adventures and allow them to run their course.

During the next few months he organises, from Paris, the following realms; Joseph becomes king of Naples; the princes of Bavaria and Wiirttemberg are turned into kings; Baden is changed into a grand duchy; Eugene weds a daughter of the House of Wittelsbach; a Bedenese hereditary prince marries a niece of Josephine's; a Württemberg princess is reserved for his youngest brother; sixteen states of southern and western Germany are jointed together to form the Confederation of the Rhine, vassals of the Emperor, liable for the payment of tribute and the provision of troops, and the sixteen German princes hasten to Paris to vow allegiance, hoping to get a share for themselves in the great mart; a dozen small principalities are wiped out; imperial fiefs are established for Talleyrand, Berthier, and Bernadotte.

Meanwhile Napoleon announces, curtly and conclusively: "Holland has no executive. She must have one. I will give her Prince Louis. We will frame a treaty.... For me the whole matter is settled: either thus, or annexation to France.... Not a minute must be lost." Why "not a minute"? Holland has been dependent for years; she only needs a crowned vassal; her dependence is to be made clear by the phrasing, "Napoleon bestows his brother on Holland." The Dutch object? Then they shall be gobbled up; the choice is quickly made. Louis does not care for the honour; climate bad; health weak? "It is better to die sitting on a throne, than to live a mere prince in France." Hortense must become a queen, Josephine is aglow for the consummation; the Dutch must present a solemn petition, and must be graciously received by the Emmperor in the Tuileries. But Napoleon is so overcome by the irony of the situation, he is so contemptuous, that after the audience he cannot resist telling his little nephew (son of the new king of Holland), in front of the ladies of the court, the fable of the frogs who wanted a king.

What next? His sisters are complaining and intriguing. Are there no more kingdoms available? The pity of it. Oh well, a few grand duchies must be vacated! Through Murat's promotion, Caroline becomes grand duchess of Cleves; Elise is made grand duchess of Tuscany; and the lovely Pauline Borghese weeps because she is nothing more than princess of Guastalla. "Why, it's no more than a village! And I'm to be princess of that?" Still, she soon finds consolation in an ocean of diamonds and lovers.

son will allow. She is watchful and conciliatory. He has installed her in the Trianon; gives her one million a year. No one understands why she is so thrifty. Some use the word "miserly." But she maintains that "we Corsicans have experienced many revolutions; All this may come to an end; what will then happen to my children? It is better that they should come to their mother, than go to strangers who might leave them in the lurch." From time to time she holds a reception, where she carries herself with natural dignity, and far more regally than many of her children who wear the royal crown. If any one haggles as to the price of the beads with which she works, she smiles and says: "No, you can't impose upon me, I do not play the princess as my daughters do." Though she is the mother of the Emperor, and of kings and princes, she laments that not a single trustworthy person is in her immediate entourage. She only unbends over a game of reversi with old friends of hers; or when she chats of an evening with her faithful servant, discussing "the happy days gone by.... They all say that I am the happiest of mothers. In truth I am always full of worry. Every news item makes me tremble lest the Emperor lie dead upon the battle-field."

On Sundays, following the tradition of her patrician ancestors, she dines with her children at the Tuileries. She does not invariably obey the Emperor; and when he constrains her, she is resentful. No doubt he is aware that she is too proud to accept the relationship which circumstances have established between them; and whenever he looks in the mirror, he cannot fail to see his increasing personal resemblance to his mother, in forehead, mouth, eyes, and hands. Sometimes he teases her:

"Do you find life at court tedious? Look at your daughters! Why do you hoard your money? You ought to spend freely!"

"You'd better allow me two millions instead of one, if that is what you want. But it's my nature to be thrifty."

She has as keen an eye for the detection of flatterers as Napoleon himself, and gently warns him against them from time to time. Though she never asks anything for herself, she will often enough beg him to help the numerous Corsicans who come to visit her, and thus does her best for whilom family friends. Once, indeed, and late in the day, she puts in a plea for something she has much at heart. She would like Ajaccio to become the capital of Corsica, instead of Corte. A stirring of family pride! The Emperor issues a decree to this effect, understanding perfectly well what moves her, and says: "My mother was born to reign over a kingdom,"

But she cannot get him to do anything for Lucien. "I love him more than all the others," she says, "because he's not been so lucky." The Emperor is adamant: "No feelings of affection can weigh against reasons of State. I will only accept as relatives, those who serve me. He who does not soar with me, ceases to belong to my family.

XIII

At Paris, in his study, Napoleon has a silent witness of his activities; a bronze bust of Frederick the Great.

He had grown up in the days when the renown of the last of the famous commanders was still fresh; and, indeed, he had become lieutenant before the king died. Like all the generals of the day, in the art of war he was a disciple of Frederick. He had not yet come into personal contact with the Prussian army, but he still had considerable respect for it, although Frederick's immediate successor had won no laurels against the soldiers of France. He knew Frederick William III to be foolish and weak; and if, none the less, he tried to induce the Prussian ruler to enter into an alliance, and hoped to turn Prussia's antagonism towards Austria and Russia to his own uses, it was because he continued to entertain an unavowed respect for the only foreign army in Europe which had covered itself with glory during the eighteenth century. But when Prussia showed him, not her strongest side, the military, but her weakest, the political, his respect waned.

In the previous year, before Austerlitz, he had offered Frederick William an alliance. After Trafalgar, when Francis and Alexander were courting Prussia, and after Austerlitz, when the indications were in favour of France, the weakling monarch continued to vacillate, always hoping to better his position by neutrality. Then, when the Emperor was stronger than ever before, the Prussian ruler seized the first pretext for making warlike preparations against France. Had not Napoleon violated Prussian neutrality last year by marching through Ansbach?

What has really decided the king's attitude is a mood of the democrats, in conjunction with this dread of mortified national pride, and, in especial, with his uncertainty as to the loyalty of some of his bellicose generals. In Nuremberg, a bookseller had been tried by court martial and shot for publishing a lampoon against the French army and circulating it in places which, in accordance with the terms of the treaty, were legitimately occupied by French troops. The decision of the court was formally just; but the indignation it aroused, being moral, was juster. The Emperor realised this, and wanted to avoid war. He proposed a mutual withdrawal of troops. Through the mouth of his envoy, he explained that Frederick William had only to say whether the presence of French soldiers in Westphalia annoyed him. Then he wrote personally to the king. "I hold unalterably to our alliance.... But if you answer shows me that on your side you repudiate this alliance, and put your trust solely in the power of arms, then indeed I shall be compelled to make war. Nevertheless, battles and victories notwithstanding my feelings will remain unchanged. Since I regard this war as a wicked one, I shall even then, propose peace."

In private, however, with mingled feelings of anger and contempt, he says hard things about Prussia. He cannot believe that country to be so mad as it seems. "Its cabinet is despicable; its sovereign a weakling; its court ruled by young officers who will risk anything."

A fortnight before the outbreak of war, he still finds it impossible to believe in its coming.

He is mistaken. The men of noble birth who officer the Prussian army, the men who, under Frederick the Great, defeated France, and were subsequently defeated by France, want to rehabilitate themselves. The middle classes are inspired with ardent nationalist sentiments. The Prussians are ready to "risk anything"; their eyes are fixed on a protectress in whom they trust. The Queen of Prussia is a passionate advocate of war, for the Tsar is now allied with Prussia, and during his stay in Berlin she has recognised in him the manliness that is lacking in her husband. After Austerlitz, Alexander had promptly withdrawn into his own realm, to await a more favourable opportunity. Now the opportunity had come. We learn from Talleyrand that Napoleon was full of secret disquietude at having to draw the sword once more. He had been dazzled by the feats of the great Frederick's soldiers. Never before had he fought against an army famous in story. "I fancy we shall find them tougher metal than the Austrians." All the more reason for getting quickly across the Rhine! A week after the beginning of the advance, he gains his first victory. At Saalfeld, the best of the Prussians fell, Prince Louis Ferdinand, the first and finest blossom shattered in the first storm.

Confusion prevails among the Prussians, and the king contributes to its spread. General Scharnhorst had advised him to attack two weeks earlier, but the irresolute ruler had waited for the French offensive. The Duke of Brunswick is commander-in-chief; but instead of leaving the managements of the campaign to this officer, at the last moment the king comes to the fighting frort "We don't know whether the headquarters should be called royal or ducal." The duke obeys the king when he ought to command. Questions of precedence necessitate the division of the forces into three army corps, for Prince Hohenlohe, who is a reigning prince, cannot possibly fight under a duke. Once more the enemy holds out the hand of friendship. Two days before the main battle, and while confident of victory, Napoleon writes:

"I do not wish to derive any advantage from the folly of your advisers, whose blunders in statesmanship amaze Europe, ... Well, we are at war .... But why should we lead our subjects to slaughter one another? I care nothing for a victory that is bought with the lives of many of my children. If I were at the beginning of my career, and had reason to dread misadventure in battle, I should have no right to use such language. But, Sire, you will be defeated. You will sacrifice the quiet of your days, and the lives of your subjects without the smallest justification.... I have nothing to gain from Your Majesty; I do not want and never have wanted anything from you. This war is unwise! I know that my letter may wound your sensibilities, but the circumstances make bluntness essential. I am telling you what I really think.... Restore peace to yourself and your territories. Even if I could never be your ally, you will always find in me a man, ... whose greatest wish it is never to shed blood by making war with princes who are not the adversaries of his industry, his commerce, and his policy."

Louise, who has followed her husband to the front, is a woman with more peaceful instincts than is pleasing to the ambition of the generals on the headquarters staff. When the letter is read, however, she agrees with their scornful view that Napoleon writes as he does because he is afraid of a catastrophe to himself. Is she, then, unable to realise that destiny has placed her among these men today, that she may influence her weak-willed husband in the direction of a humane settlement of the dispute? She cannot see it! Napoleon is nothing but "an infernal monster risen out of the mire," and tomorrow he must fall!

"My affairs march very well," writes this monster, meanwhile, to his wife. "Everything is going just as I should like. The king and the queen are in Erfurt. If they want to see a battle, they will have this gruesome delight. I feel splendid. Although I am travelling from eighty to a hundred miles a day, I have put on weight. I go to bed at eight in the evening, get up at midnight, and remember when I do so that you have not yet retired to rest." The last night before the battle he refuses to go to bed. At three in the morning, one of his officers urges him to take a nap, but he exclaims: "Impossible! I have my plans here" (he touches his forehead), "but nothing yet in my maps!" Then he quickly explains the whole plan. "Do you understand? ... To horse with you and

Because this woman has never interfered in politics, has not now affected a knowledge she does not possess, but in simple camaraderie has spoken on behalf of her absent husband, and with princely demeanour has pleaded for her country. She has made use neither of cajolery nor anger, but has kept the golden mean between pride and deference becoming to a conquered monarch. Years afterwards, the Emperor remembered this woman who by her noble bearing had saved her country and her dynasty.

In Berlin, he meets another woman. Count Hatzfeld, who has been negotiating with the conqueror on behalf of Berlin, writes indiscreetly to one of the discredited generals, and gives him details concerning the strength of the French troops. His letter is intercepted. The Emperor, in a rage, declares he is to be shot as a spy. Berthier is depressed by the command; Rapp endeavours to soften Napoleon. Countess Hatzfeld is brought to see him; she falls at his feet. He invites her to Potsdam: "When I showed her the count's letter she answered me guilelessly, with a sob, and with deep emotion: "Yes, that is certainly his handwriting.' As she read the document the tone of her voice moved me to my innermost being. I pitied her. You see," he concludes his report to Josephine, "I love good, simple, and gentle women."

Love? There stands the man of might; the countess in naught to him as far as her womanhood goes; hardly has he noticed her figure or her dress. But these natural passions, womanly, tears, and silences, move him deeply. He throws the letter into the fire: "The proof I had has been burned. Your husband is safe."

Thus does Napoleon the Conqueror deal with two German women whose husbands have fought against him. He deals leniently with them because their conduct appeals to his heart.

He dislikes Queen Louise. A politician, that woman, who has driven her country and her consort into a disastrous enterprise, who has egged this quiet-loving man into war when he could have had peace with honour. Napoleon execrates such a woman. Since she seizes every opportunity to spit fire at him, he determines to strip her of all her womanly dignity. He jeers at her in official bulletins: "She is a woman with beautiful features but little brain.... She must be terribly tortured by pangs of consciences for all the suffering she has brought upon her country. Her husband is a man of honour who desired happiness and peace for his people."

He has made a triumphal entry into Berlin. His suite is brilliantly dressed, but he is as simply clad as ever, and his hat is adorned with a cockade worth about a penny. Nothing interests him so keenly as Sans Souci. He holds the sword of the great Frederick in his hands, and takes it away as a trophy more priceless than any other he could ever find in his whole life. He would not exchange it for the throne of Prussia. But he heartily despises Frederick's descendants, and publicly attacks, the Queen:

"In the Queen's rooms was found the Tsar's picture, which he himself had given her. Also there was her correspondence with the King.... These documents go to prove how unhappy those princes can be who permit their wives to interfere in affairs of State. Notes and State papers reeked of musk, and lay beneath ribbons and laces and other fal-lals of the toilet."

An unworthy tone! He seems to have forgotten the patriotic impulse of the queen. If, however, we compare these taunts with what the best and greatest of contemporary Prussian statesmen, the non-Prussian Baron vom Stein, wrote about Queen Louise, we can understand the Emperor's humour, though hardly excuse it.

Serious considerations restrain him from destroying the house of Hohenzollern, though he had already drafted a decree to dethrone the king. Napoleon has to bear the tsar is mind. In Berlin he thinks in terms of Europe as a whole: "On the Elbe and on the Oder we have won our India, our Spanish colonies, and our Cape of Good Hope." The grandiose words as yet only announce the start of the voyage; but with mighty strokes of the oar he is now to round the cape of his hopes. In the castle at Charlottenburg he dictates the greatest, most unbloody, and most dangerous of all his declarations of war: Charlemagne closes all the harbours of Europe against English ships. If the island cannot be reached by his sword? Well, henceforward, Europe shall be placed out of her reach! All merchandise, parcels, postal communications, etc., from and to England and her colonies are to be held up; every Englishman at large on the Continent is now a prisoner of war.

How is the carrying-out of the scheme to be supervised? Hitherto, action has always followed close upon the heels of thought. Now, he has to make treaties with various States, and, first of all, with Russia and Austria. Austria has fragments of the sometimes realm of Poland within her frontiers, but Russia wants them for herself; Poland, tossed between the two, pays allegiance to neither. As to a god, the Poles turn to the Emperor. He, the champion of the freedom of the peoples, must come to their aid and free them. What is to be done? How does Napoleon solve the Polish problem?

"Shall I set up the throne of Poland anew, and thus restore a great nation to life? God alone, who has the fashioning of all things in his hands, can solve this riddle." Words of Delphic cunning, which he sends forth throughout Poland. God alone sees the smiles with which he signs the proclamation! In addition he takes three measures. He demands that the Poles shall provide troops, for "not until you have an army of forty thousand men will you be worthy of the name of Nation." Next he proposes to the Austrians an exchange of Galicia for Prussian Silesia. But the real key to the Polish problem he fishes out of the Bosphorus, for he tells the sultan to drive the Russians out of Moldavia, and to meet him, the Emperor, on the Dniester; thereby he hopes to bind, not only Russia, but also the trembling Austria, to the lower Danube.

There he sits in Sans Souci, the ancient candelabra in Frederick's study scintillate over his head, Voltaire's picture smiles sideways, through the wraith, at his great fellow-countryman. He sits alone at his games of chess, calculates the moves of his unseen opponent, his glance takes in wider and wider circles; suddenly the traits of his new ancestor suffer a change, the big blond beard vanishes, the nose is flatter, the eyes lose some of their confident glance, then become bolder again: instead of the great Charles, he is facing the great Alexander. Yes, now, indeed, he will conquer England in India! World dominion hovers before his eyes.

A new opponent leaps on to the board. Couriers bring the news of a revolt in Spain. He pales. The whole game is imperilled. Once more Napoleon sees clearly that he who would vanquish England must gain Russia's friendship. But in order to conquer Russia or to win her over to his side, he needs a fulcrum. He has one ready to hand: Poland in revolt. Napoleon journeys to Warsaw.

While in imagination he had, during these weeks, been weighing the fate of continents, his heart had felt lonely. Yet he did not trouble himself about women. Only to his wife did he write gallant things: "I love you, and long for you.... These Polish women [in Posen] are all Frenchwomen in their hearts. But for me there is only one woman. Do you know who she is? I would tell you what she is like, only I should have to flatter her too much, so that you could recognise yourself in the description. Seriously, my heart can say naught but good of her. Oh, these long nights, all alone!"

Josephine, with the keenness of a foxhound, senses a rival under these cajoleries. But she has no reason, as yet, to be jealous, or to make so long a journey. He answers her that "the agitation of your letter tells me that you beautiful women know of no limits to your powers. What you wish must come to pass. I, on the other hand, recognise that I am the most enslaved of men. My master has no mercy on me, for my master is the nature of things."

Hardly has he finished touching upon these airy trifles in weighty words, when a courier brings him tidings of the great consequences of a trifling affair: the beauty to whom Caroline had introduced him in the previous winter, and who was expecting a child before he went away, has been confined. At last! It is then proved that he does not lack the power which Dame Nature grants to other men! A great gift from above. A boy. He turns to his intimate and exclaims with the ingenuous delight of a youth: "Duroc! I've got a son!"

XIV

The brilliantly lighted ballroom forms a background where Poland displays her greatest beauty and her most precious jewels. This is the evening of evenings. In the old palace of Poland's kings at Warsaw, the Emperor of the French is to be shown the calibre of the nation that has been suffering so long. Will he admire the national dance, its music and its figures? Will the eyes of the ladies ravish him, those eyes which are pools of Slavic melancholy? Will the flattery of the speeches or the idolising comparisons appearing in the newspapers make his heart as wax? Such, according to the sanguine, are the questions upon which hang the fate of the nation. The procession has passed by; he has spoken to many in cheerful vein; now he is standing in a recess, dividing his attention between his interlocutor and the dancers. He is thinking of Paris, where, for seven years, he has never failed to be in January.

Suddenly his gaze is focused on a special point, and he forgets to carry on the conversation. A hundred watchful eyes follow the glance of the huntsman. Who is the quarry? A little later he approaches a group, asks for the names of those composing it, and smilingly, with a courtliness of manner rarely shown by him on public occasions, he draws the lady of his choice out of the circle of her companions. She is a gentle, fair-haired beauty, dainty and small, has blue eyes, appears to be of a yielding disposition, and is eighteen years of age. She is simpler in her dress than any of the others, and her behaviour is correspondingly quiet and without display or the lures of coquetry. The Emperor chooses her as partner in a contradance, delights in her grace and her lovely voice, finds her broken French bewitching. While she smiles and is covered with confusion, her name is whispered from room to room throughout the palace: Countess Walewska.

"Who is she?" asks Napoleon later of his friend Duroc. She is the daughter of an ancient line, the family so impoverished that the lady has been married off to a wealthy old count whose youngest grandchild is ten years older than the new wife.

"I had eyes only for you," he writes to the countess nest day. "I admired only you, and longed to be with you alone. Send me an answer quickly, in order that the fire which is consuming me may be appeased. N." But the messenger, Duroc, returns with neither answer nor tidings of any sort. The Emperor is nonplussed. Something quite new. Twelve years ago the brigadier general had had such a rebuff. But Napoleon, never. Have not all women. Whether princesses or actresses, have not all the beauties, invariably come to him at his slightest nod of invitation? The more enchanting, therefore, is this lady who shrinks back so virginally from the unveiled desire of a man.

"Have I displeased you? I hoped the opposite. Or has your first feeling vanished? My passion grows. You rob me of my rest. Vouchsafe a little joy, a little happiness, to the poor heart that would fain worship you! Is so hard to give me answer? You now owe me two." This second letter is unsigned. Suppose an amateur of such matters to come across it in a collection of love letters, would he dream of ascribing its authorship to Napoleon? Neither heavy nor dictatorial, neither emotional nor stilted, but romantic rather is the tone. Nevertheless, since worldly convention demands that she should pay no heed to his suit, again his missive remains unanswered. Terrible the position of the adjutant who for the second time has failed in the carrying out a movement ordered by his chief. The Emperor, controlling his passion, thinks:

"If neither my pleading nor my rank has any effect on this tender creature, I must try to gain my end by a half-promise, which I need not regard as binding." He writes: "There are moments in life when high position is a heavy burden. That is borne in on me at this moment.... If only you would! None but you can overcome the obstacles which separate us. My friend Duroc will do what he can to make it easy for you, Oh, come, come! All your wishes shall be fulfilled! Your country will be even dearer to me, if you have compassion on my heart. N."

Now we should recognise his wonted style, even without the capital N. Nevertheless, how amazingly the loneliness of the man of might breathes from these lines. The third love-letter is intelligently composed, and therefore achieves its purpose—but it discloses to us the tragical mask of destiny, the destiny of one who wishes to walk along the course he had planned for himself, and who is sacrificing his human happiness to this heroical monomania. He roams through the splendid palace, arms locked behind. For weeks his mood has been one of yearning, but always he has been alone. For months he has hardly been near a woman. Now, having fallen passionately, in love, storm-tossed, he dismisses his secretaries, will not discuss matters with his generals, refuses to admit deputations, will not go out riding. The whole mechanism he has constructed is stationary. The palace, the army, Paris, Europe–let them wait. He, more a slave than any other, refuses today to obey the nature of things; a man of thirty-seven whose wife, well past forty, no longer stirs his passion. Profoundly moved by a girl, twice rebuffed, he must devise lures from his other realms, must tempt her with the freedom of her country, in order that, after nearly a decade of quiescent feeling, he may spread upon the shoulders of a young woman the mantle of his yearning for tranquillity.

She, alarmed at the assault of this virile will, sits the same afternoon among her friends and relatives who are urging the sacrifice upon her, for Poland's sake. In this mood, she at length goes to see him. The three evening hours she spends with him are spent in tears. By gentle arts he restores her to calm, and to her astonishment she finds that this dreaded man of iron is a tender wooer.

"Marie, sweet Marie, my first thought is yours!" she reads next morning. "I shall see you at dinner. I pledge you my word. Please wear the nosegay that I send; it will be a secret messenger of our feelings amid the crowd; thus we shall understand one another. If I lay my hand on my heart, you will know that it is wholly yours; for answer, press your flowers to your bosom. Love me, my charming Marie; do not take your hand away from the flowers."

Not until three days later does she become his. Then she comes to see him every evening. But, as well as this, she must be present at every reception, for otherwise he stays away. What is she to him? The second creature in the world who asks nothing from him; his mother was the first. Never has he known another woman who did not expect his magician's palaces, crowns, money. This women wants nothing from him, and gives him everything. Countess Walewska is the quiet and loving companion whom Napoleon's stormy soul has sought. It will be long before he will be willing to part from her. "She is an angel. It may justly be said that her spirit is as lovely as her features."

Josephine wants to come? Now? He smiles. Since the Cairo days, Bonaparte has never had a mistress while campaigning, whereas his generals have had plenty of love-affairs. There can be no doubt that the story of this intrigue, distorted of course, will quickly be carried to Paris, and in veiled form will find a way to Josephine's ears. She is waiting there, waiting to be summoned to his side. Now, in the most graceful way in the world, he deceived the wife who had deceived him for years. The weather, the roads, the public insecurity, made it impossible. "How gladly should I be spending the long winter nights at your side.... If you are always weeping, then you lack courage and character. I cannot endure cowardly people. An empress must have courage!"

Now he betrays her, "I laughed when you wrote to me that you had taken a husband in order to be with him. In my simplicity, I had believed that woman was made for man; man for country, family, fame. Forgive my ignorance. One can always learn something from lovely women.... Besides, I could not think of any lady with whom I was exchanging letters. If there really were one, I can assure you she would have to be as beautiful as a newly opened rose. Does that apply to the lady of whom you speak?"

See how this ambiguous trifling amuses him. His heart is so light sometimes. He can play the gallant as if there had never been a revolution in the world. When, after a few weeks, he resumes a but the desire to remain hidden from the world, a wordless wish in the eyes of this sweet girl of eighteen who has learned to love him.

"I know," he says to her, "you would rather live without me. Yes, yes, don't protest; I know it! But you are good and gentle; your heart is pure. You don't want to rob me of the few hours of happiness which you can give me everyday? To think that people regard me as the happiest of men!"

A dispatch comes to tell him that his nephew and heir, the son of King Louis, is dead. How the news affects him is shown by his moving words to Josephine; but he cannot tell his wife all the thoughts that now enter his mind at Finckenstein. That little cocotte in Cairo, what he had really hoped from her was a son. How if this beautiful woman, this noblewomen whom he loves, were to give him an heir? Would he then make her his empress? Why not? He looks at Walewska, but keeps his own counsel.

What is Paris saying?

With ear attent, he listens to the rumours that reach him across the Polish steppe. The funds are falling. Malicious jests are current on the boulevards. "Where are our brave lads?" ask the Parisians. Caution is needed! What begins as a gentle shower, may turn into a raging storm; and the man who knows how to control the thunder is far away. He offers the beaten Prussians a separate peace, and even proposes a conference, but Queen Louise holds firmly to the alliance with the Tsar. Austria, too, is deaf to his voice.

Despite all, here and now, with enemies to right and to left of him, and without any firm standing-ground, he begins to dream once more of the conquests of Alexander. Messengers of Finckenstein; strangers bringing dispatches arrive from remote lands and make their way to him across distant mountains. To this northern headquarters comes a Persian envoy, and the messenger of the King of Kings reverently bows his head to greet the sublime Emperor of the West. Next day, Napoleon and the Persian emissary come to an understanding. The Emperor will force the Tsar to give back Georgia to the Shah. In return, the Shah will spur on the

Afghans and the tribes of Kandahar to attack the English in India; he will equip an army for the invasion of Hindustan. If the Emperor wishes to send an army against India, his men shall have free passage across Persia.

Hardly has the Persian departed, when a gorgeously attired Turk rides in past the astonished sentries, bringing golden gifts and a dispatch. A bespectacled oriental expert translates it. Standing in front of the fire, the Emperor, having reduced the eastern bombast to sober proportions, dictates a letter to the Sultan: "I regret very much that you ask for no more than five hundred men instead of several thousand.... State your demands clearly, and whatever you want shall be instantly done. Get into communication with the Shah of Persia, for he, too, is an enemy of the Russians.... I offered your envoy the artillerymen and other soldiers you need, but he would not accept them, being afraid of hurting Mohammedan susceptibilities. I am so powerful, and I am so desirous for your victory (I wish this because of my friendship for you and not on political grounds alone), that I can deny you nothing."

The same day, he writes to Brother Louis, who has been sending urgent appeals from his new kingdom, a letter which may be regarded as a sort of general instruction for kings, and which occupies five pages of print. He also sends orders to Joseph as to the latter's conduct in Naples. To Jerome, who in Breslau is commanding a corps of pretty actresses instead of his soldiers, Napoleon writes to ask why his brother never sends complete reports, and why he has left six hundred men in Schweidnitz, four hundred in Brieg. "Let me know your exact plans, down to the smallest details, so that I can form an accurate picture of your situation." He likewise sends a missive to all the bishops in France. They are to institute a public thanksgiving for the Emperor's victories; but he aims; also, at exercising personal influence on each of his episcopal correspondents, for he has learned that the dispute between himself and the Pope is making the ecclesiastics more and more uneasy in their consciences. Meanwhile he sends a dozen orders to Fouché: concerning Madame de Staël, and the extent of her influence; concerning the salons of the aristocratic quarter; and so on. He enquires about the two leading Parisian theatres; their condition, their finances, and their repertoire. "What has become of my librarian?" he asks in another letter "Is he dead, or enjoying himself in the country?" That would be a fine way of fulfilling his duties! I ordered him to send me all newly published books, and to let me have the publishers' announcement lists, but I have not had a word from him." Draft for a new historical university, where young people may learn about modern happenings as well as the story of ancient days. To the Minister for Home Affairs" "Literature needs encouragement. Let me hear your proposals for livening up the various forms of belles lettres." Enquiries as to the building of a new Stock Exchange and of the Madeleine. How can six millions be best applied for the encouragement of manufactures, and what will be the best way of raising the Money? Two millions are to be spent in renovating his palaces. Arrangements must be made for the Paris newspapers to publish articles ostensibly based on information from Bucharest and Tiflis, and describing Russia's desperate situation.

He smiles, glancing at his demure little friend. "You marvel at my manifold activities? I have to keep watch on all my posts. Before, I was only an acorn. Now I am an oak, the ruler of nations. All eyes are fixed on me because I am in so outstanding a position. A man must play his part and cannot always be natural. But, for you, I will become the acorn once more." Simple words, tranquilly uttered. One more evening with her, and then he must take the field again, for May has come, and the idyll ends with the leaving of winter quarters and the extinction of the fires at Finckenstein. He will see her again. They are both sure of this. But were he to forget her, he could read the posy in the ring she gives him:

"If you cease to love me, forget not that I love you."

XV

On the Memel, where it flows past Tilsit, a huge raft is anchored in mid-stream. The tree trunks and the planks are covered with carpets, and in the centre a tent gleams in the June sunlight, with the colours of France and of Russia flying above it. On the western and the eastern banks are ranged the guards of the two emperors. Boats set out from either shore. Napoleon and the Tsar enter the peace-tent simultaneously. The soldiers, who were shooting one another only ten days back, cheer lustily, and those in front, who can see, pass the word to the thousands in the rear. The foes of yesterday have embraced, their masters have made friends.

Immediately after the great victory of Friedland, Napoleon, as was his way, had offered his hand to the vanquished. At the opening parleys, since the appropriate response had not been made by the Sultan, he had given a hint that the Tsar might well hope, some day, to establish the cross once more on the dome of St. Sophia. The words were carefully chosen, for he knew that the man to whom they would be reported next day, a romanticist and a mystic, would be amenable to their influence. Alexander had been prompt to take the proffered hand of friendship. Now the enemies of Austerlitz and Friedland stood face to face in amicable converse. Napoleon coldly scrutinised his only serious rival on the Continent, a young man with feminine lineaments, compact, delicately moulded, rosy; hearing and eyesight rather weak. In an instant he felt assured that the tsar was a man who he could win over.

By the end of a fortnight, the sometime adversaries have not merely entered into an alliance, but have made friends. How has this come about?

"He is an amiable and pleasant fellow, a hero of romance," says Napoleon of him at this time. Inasmuch as the Emperor is bored by novels, and has no use for heroes of romance in the practical world of his calculations, there is an undercurrent of and drives together. Napoleon's handling of Alexander is masterly. At first, the Emperor assumes the role of the cavalier, who cannot sufficiently extol the heroism of the Russians; then he conveys the implication that ere long he must surround himself with a bodyguard of his ministers, lest he should be carried away by the tsar's charm. At table, in order to dazzle Alexander, he talks of his good luck—a thing to which the man of destiny rarely alludes. He tells an anecdote, for which this is the only warrant, of an incident that had happened in Egypt. He had fallen asleep beneath an ancient wall, which had suddenly crumbled to pieces without injuring him. Awaking, he found in his hand something which at first he believed to be a stone, but which, on examination, he saw to be a wonderfully beautiful cameo of Augustus. Could any playwright invent a more marvellous scene than this one invented by the Emperor, in an after-dinner hour, to stir the imagination of the mystical idealist, his companion?

Enthralled, the tsar listens to the man of wonders. If he could only know all that Napoleon knows! "I feel that I am not really emperor as you are, for I am dependent on my generals." He asks a hundred questions about the art of war. Naively, when the two men are not walking together, the tsar asks: "What sort of position is this? How would you defend it, and how would you attack it?" - "I explained matters to him; and I told him that, if I were ever again at war with Austria, he should lead an army corps of thirty thousand men under my order, so that he could learn the art of war."

Was ever woman in such humour wooed? Soon an offensive and defensive alliance is concluded.

"The lands between the Elbe and the Memel" (this is a secret note to the treaty), "are to form the barrier between the two great empires, a barrier to render harmless all the pinpricks which, in disputes between nations, are apt to precede the firing of the guns." In this treaty, each party to the alliance gives only in order to take; and in a couple of words the tsar sacrifices Prussia, the Emperor Poland, although each of the two rulers has pledged a woman to maintain the integrity of her country. Almost grotesque is the calm with which, seated in a small room in an out-of-the-way and little known town hard by the shores of the Baltic, the two men pour over the map and cut pieces out of countries like Hotspur and Owen Glendower in the play. The Emperor gives Coburg, Mecklenburg, and Oldenburg, whose rules have ties with the tsar, receiving the Ionian islands and Cattaro in return. Only when the tsar asks for the Bosphorus, does the Emperor demur. "Costantinople? That carries world dominion with it!" In the thorny thicket of these negotiations, we have stumbled upon the decisive word that slumbers beneath the treaties and notes. It is plain that when two men are dividing the world between them, they will in the long run come to blows.

The king of Prussia joins their company; and, since he lacks dignity and intelligence, he is ignored by both the emperors. Napoleon privately considers him a dullard, possessing neither talent nor character, and adversely criticiscs everything connected with him; even his dress, which is the uniform of a hussar, headgear and all complete. Since the king is anxious about the very existence of Prussia, he leaves no stone unturned to secure the safety of his State, and summons the queen to Tilsit, the Emperor, curious to see his beautiful foe, intimates that he would be pleased to received the lady there. He uses the neutral zone as a pretext for not setting out to meet her; but he has a charming residence prepared for her reception. Then, with a brilliant suite, though himself dressed in the simplest attire, he rides forth to visit her, and is received by the queen, who stands at the head of the flight of steps to welcome him.

She is clad in white silk, adorned with ancient jewels, beautiful and bitter. With seemingly innocent words, Louise breaks down the unbearable constraint

"Sire, I hope you will excuse these narrow steps."

"What would one not excuse to reach such a goal," he answers. But when he continues to speak in this complimentary tone, she says with dignity:

"Sire, have we come here to speak of trifles?"

Then she pleads as spouse and mother, and appeals to his "magnanimous heart."

"You will be glad to be back in Berlin?"

"Not in all circumstances. It depends upon you whether we return home without sorrow in our hearts."

"Madame, I should be only too pleased...."

When she moved to speak, he interjected:

"Madame, how came Prussia to venture upon this war?"

"The fame of Frederick the Great deceived us as to our strength."

"How many times have I offered peace? Austria showed more wisdom after Austerlitz."

"Today. I beg you to establish a claim upon our gratitude."

"Have you not yourself, destroyed my friendship for Prussia?"

"Your heart is noble; it unites with other fine qualities, the possession of a great character."

"Unfortunately, general considerations often stand in the way of special wishes."

"I do not understand questions of high politics; yet I do not feel that I am forgoing any of my dignity as a woman if I assure you ...."

He listens to her with growing interest. She notices "a kindly smile trembling at the corners of his mouth, which seemed to guarantee success, —when, at that moment, the king entered the room."

The conversation has no political consequences, but the human appeal has been very great. "It was just as well that the king put in an appearance when he did," the Emperor says to the tsar with a spice of coquetry. "I might have made her promises.... An exquisite woman. Instead of depriving her of a crown, one is tempted to lay one at her feet." After another talk with Queen Louise, Napoleon writes to Josephine: "She is a bewitching woman, and is most amiable in her behaviour towards me. But have no cause for jealousy.... I should have to pay dearly for it were I to play the gallant here.... She has been punished for her love of domination; but she has displayed much character in the midst of her misfortunes.... One has to concede that she said many sensible things."

Even more amazing is his effect upon her, who had once called him an infernal monster. She writes: "His head is shapely, his lineaments are those of a thinker, his whole appearsnce reminds one of a Roman emperor. When he smiles, his mouth assumes a kindly expression...."

This Napoleon's greatest victory. What other woman has, after a few weeks' acquaintance, been able to portray him more charmingly? And yet she has reasons enough to detest him, for, in spite of the humility of her attitude, he is an unyielding as iron. Soon, however, she arouses his irritability. When, at last, everything has been signed, and the Emperor, "in consideration of his friendship for the tsar," has secured the kingdom of Prussia against dissolution (though monstrous cantles have been sliced off!), she cannot refrain from making renewed attempts to soften him. Finally, he sees her into her carriage, and she seizes this opportunity to ask him, for the last time, why so mighty a man should have forgone the chances of earning her eternal gratitude. He throws courtesy to the winds, and answers with ironical bitterness:

"What will you, Madame? I am to be pitied, for this is obviously the work of my evil star!"

XVI

What is Paris saying?

"Even were I ten thousand miles away from my homeland, I could not leave the field free for bad citizens to stir up my capital to stir up my capital to strife!" He has now been ten months absent—longer away than ever before or afterwards.

He tightens up the home government all the more rigorously since he fears that his censorious Parisians are slipping out of his hands. This city, renowned for its biting wit, is not only venting its feelings is song and jokes that are the delight of the boulevards; it is now assuming a sceptical tone, and is more amused than impressed by his expeditions. Yes, he is right these Parisians need to be ruled by "an iron hand in a velvet glove." Now they are to experience both again, only the velvet seems to have worn rather thin. Indeed, the whole tone of the capital has become lax and disorderly. Do they want to return to Directory days, when every one said and printed exactly what he pleased?

A new more rigid censorship of newspapers and plays is introduced. Historical drama must deal only with matters of the remote past; and even Corneille, his ideal, is pruned of certain passages. Before every opera he must be consulted, not merely as to the general question of acceptance after it is written, but earlier, as to the choice of topic; religious subjects are forbidden, and mythology is recommended. With lavish means, on the imperial scale, a university is founded, modelled after the Jesuit schools he detests; the professors are exempt from military service, but to some extent celibacy is insisted on. Chateaubriand is attacked, and his "Mercure de France" is suppressed, because in opposition salons he has criticised the Emperor, and has quoted Tacitus the historian as having taken vengeance on Nero the tyrant.

Madame de Staël's new requests for permission to return to Paris are rejected , "for she is able to make people think." To the arch-chancellor he writes: "Summon Count R., and let him know that his wife's boudoir is the talk of Paris." To Fouché: "You are not policing Paris properly. Malicious gossip is rife. Keep watch on the speeches that are being made at Citerni's restaurant and in the Café Foy." That young people may learn who pleases God, every child in France patters the following catechism: "We owe our Emperor Napoleon I, love, respect, obedience, loyalty, military service, ... ardent prayers for his welfare, ... because God has showed gifts on him in peace and war, and has made him God's image on earth."

He has moved a long way. When the heir of countless generations believes such things of himself, others (or some of them) can believe them of him. But it is only three years since the Emperor, on the day of his coronation, had said that every fishwife laugh in his face were he to declare himself the son of God....

Is he no longer the same man! As of old, in personal matters he renounces display. He will not have money lavished on his study. Here, apart from the great writing table, there are only a small settee (on which he lounges when he is dictating, unless he wanders about the room), two tall bookcases, a couple of chandeliers, and the bust of Frederick the Great; in another simply furnished study, he has a bust of Cæsar. Looking through some bills, he says: "I was charged much less when I was lieutenant. Why should I pay more than anyone else?" When the private theatre of the palace is to be done up, he remarks: "There must still be a lot of upholstered benches and candelabras that were supplied at great expense for my coronation. No doubt they are stored away somewhere."

When Rémusat exceeds the Emperor's wardrobe allowance of twenty thousand francs, he is dismissed, and his successor is handed a long inventory of requirements, a list personally drafted by the Emperor: "I think we can make a few more savings even than this. See to it that the tailor does his work properly. Lay the new clothes out for my inspection and approval on the day of delivery, and then put them away at once in my drawers." In the case of uniform coats which are to be delivered every quarter, he remarks: "This coat must last three years.... In addition, forty-eight pairs of white breeches and waistcoats, at eighty francs a suit=frs. 3840. One pair of breeches and one waistcoat must be delivered every week, and they must last three years.... Also twenty-four pairs of shoes, to be delivered a pair every fortnight, must last two years=frs. 312." Shirts are the only things he orders in large quantities, to be delivered a dozen every week, must last six years.

Here, in his intimate life, he is the same man as before; just as, when he is campaigning, he is the old Bonaparte—a man of few enjoyments. But upon the formalities of majesty, upon court ceremonial, upon all the outworn display of the world whose power he has broken, he will squander, not money alone, but more precious, time, and, more precious still, human dignity and his own freedom.

He no longer laughs sarcastically when those who dwell in the aristocratic quarter frequent his court; he is genuinely pleased. His mood is difficult to understand. The men of birth who had mortified him in his cadet days by making fun of his poverty, now throng the court of this same Corsican, and their shadows on the shining parquet floor seem to mock the humility of their gestures. They are all back in the Tuileries now, the Montmorencys, the Montesquieus, the Radziwills, the Noailles, the Narbonnes, the Turennes, who for years had sworn the death of the upstart. The Princes of the Confederation of the Rhine clank through the halls in their German uniforms; the Mecklenburger pays his court to the empress; the heirs apparent of Baden and Bavaria are privileged to hear the discussions at the Council of State. To the old nobility this was a pastime; to the Emperor it was policy, for he wished to make sure of the allegiance of their class.

But now there happens something which should never have happened. Napoleon, the man who counts his coats as he counts his soldiers; the man who in the army gives promotion only for good service, and will never make an inefficient soldier a lieutenant merely because he is someone's son or nephew; the man who sits contentedly in a barn among his officers, or by the camp-fire among his grenadiers; the man who has expunged the privileges of birth from his legal code; the man who has contraposed the new idea of individual ability to the old idea of hereditary dignity, and has thus turned a whole continent upside down—this same Bonaparte, in the autumn of the year 1807, founds a new nobility, "because it is a part of human nature that a man should wish to hand down to his children, not property alone, but also tokens of esteem." Counts and princes, dukes and majorats, were created, not, as before, in order to bestow a supreme dignity upon the bravest marshals, the ablest senators and ministers, but that the sons and grandsons of these new nobles, ne'er-do-wells, wealthy Persian idlers, and degenerates, might enjoy the privileges which the men of a whole decade had fought and bled to abolish!

Even the Legion of Honour was now desecrated by its own creator, for these appointed knights, every one of whom had done good service to his country, were to be entitled to bequeath the semblance of this service as well as their property; and the great dignitaries were to bequeath their princely rank and appellation. Certainly, the bequest did not carry with it any special civic privileges, but none the less the new institution conflicted with the spirit of the Code Napoleon. "Liberty," he wrote with too much truth in a private letter at the time of the issue of this decree, "liberty is only the need of the few whom nature has endowed with exceptional talent; and there is no danger in restricting it. The crowd loves equality. I do not injure the many when I distribute titles without raising the old question of birth; they are bourgeois crowns, which anyone can win. Clever men impart their own movement to those whom they rule. My movement is an upward one, and therefore the nation must move upwards.... I know that these dukes whom I am endowing so richly that I make them independent of me, will endeavour to elude me, and that they are relying on what they call the caste spirit. But I can run quicker than they, and shall soon overtake them."

Rarely has a great error had so grand a foundation. Not many months before, in his letters, he had positively cudgelled his brother for having founded a nobility in Holland; and, speaking of his own intention to do the same thing, had excused himself by saying that the Dutch were a trading people, and that in the militarist French Empire matters were on an altogether different footing. But in the very fact that he himself had transformed France into a militarist State, lay the first danger; and the second danger was the imperial crown, which, with inexorable logic, was now diffusing its ancient symbolical power athwart his realm.

Before, when he had been Consul, he could with impunity bestow civic crowns, gather honour and glory into a Legion and transmit the stupendous momentum of his flywheel to the strongest of the lesser wheels in his country. But when he granted estates to the best among his followers, he had to supply titles to go with their estates, titles which were necessarily inheritable; and when to the second and third best he now gave titles without lands, the recipients naturally begged that the titles, too, should be hereditary. Thus in a generation, several thousand, and in three generations, as many as twenty thousand, would bear these new titles, not for services rendered, not for deeds splendidly performed, but with the semblance of superiority, and, if not with the political privileges attaching of old to birth and title, still with the social privileges which in former days had aroused revolt in the masses.

The treason and ingratitude which he is here laying up in store will in due time open his eyes to his mistake. In truth, the death sentence he passes on equality will prove to have been a more grievous blunder than the execution of the Duke of Enghien. Then he was destroying a scion of the past; now he is creating forebears who will resuscitate that past.

The resolve issues from a moody mind; for this is a dark year in Napoleon's soul, although nothing seems to be going awry. "You do not understand the nature of human motives," he said at this period to an honest democrat. "You democrats are unable to draw distinctions between one another, whereas personal interest plays its part in what everyone does. Look at Masséna. He has won an abundance of fame; but what he wants now is to become a prince, like Murat and Bernadotte. Soon he will get himself killed in the forefront of the battle, thanks to his eagerness to win this distinction. Ambition is what spurs the French!"

He grows colder in his manner, forbids his brothers to speak to him uninvited, is less regular in the arrangement of his work, needlessly extends sittings far into the night. Even at Fontainebleau, in the interludes between hunting and festivities, he will have nothing but tragedies staged; rises from his bed at midnight, and dictates to his secretaries till morning; can only soothe the increasing irritability of his nerves by spending hours in a hot bath. The cramps in his stomach trouble him more frequently and grow more severe.

has his belief in his unconquerable sword become, that he has lost sight of the moral canons which, ten years earlier, he (then a mere military commander with no experience in political matters) had with clear insight defended against the hectoring Directors, and had subsequently, though at considerable risk to his popularity, incorporated in the Concordat. Now he writes to Eugene that one of the cardinals has died leaving a history of the popes. "If it represents an attempt to set forth all the harm the popes have done to the Church and to Christendom, let it published forthwith."

Because the Pope refused to exclude English ships from his ports, the Emperor occupied Ancona, relying "upon the protection of God, who crowns all my enterprises with his glory— If your Holiness would like to give my envoy his papers, you are at liberty to do so. I should even prefer that you should receive the English, or the Caliph of the Constantinople.–In conclusion I pray to God that he may keep you for many years more at the head of our Holy Mother the Church. Your pious son, the Emperor of the French and the King of Italy, Napoleon."

The year before, simultaneously with these burlesque menaces, he had sent warnings through Uncle Fesch that his own role resembled that of Constantine, and had touched upon the old struggle of the Middle Ages about investiture: "For the Pope, I am Charlemagne, seeing that I have joined the crowns of France and Lombardy, and that my dominions border on the East.... On condition of good behaviour, I shall make no change in the outward semblance of things, but if the Pope thwarts me I shall degrade him to the status of a Roman bishop, ... and shall introduce the Concordat into Italy: for whatever can make people happy in France, can make them happy in Italy as well; and what does not contribute to the happiness of life in one land, cannot do so in the other."

This is truly Lutheran terminology! The man who lets his imagination riot when his temporal affairs are merged in historical mysticism, becomes circumstantially clear when religious mysticism is a cloak for worldly concerns. Napoleon's reasoning inclined him towards Protestantism throughout life, and it was only on grounds of policy that he resisted the inclination to impose Lutheranism on France. Having determined to make short work of it with the Head Shepherd (since the Pope hesitated to give England the go-by), he proposes to sweep away the hindrance that severs the North Italian and the South Italian kingdoms, that he may at length have all Italy for his own–the Italy of which he wrongfully calls himself king.

Now he writes to Eugene, the viceroy, in the style of his military decrees: "The present Pope has too much power. Priests are not made to rule. Why will he not render unto Cæsar's, and refrain from troubling my States? Perhaps the time is not far distant when I ... shall summon the Churches of France, Germany, Italy, and Poland to a council, and settle matters without the Pope." He wants to secure a majority among the cardinals by the appointment of French cardinals, but the Pope will not allow their number to be increased, and proposes to make up for this refusal by agreeing to crown Napoleon Emperor of the West. Now, however, what he had vainly asked for a year earlier has ceased to charm his imagination. Since it has become possible, he regards it as already achieved; and when the Pope shows himself pliable in money matters, Napoleon Emperor of the West. Now however, what he had vainly asked for a year earlier has he regards it as already achieved; and when the Pope shows himself pliable in money matters, Napoleon makes this an occasion for further exactions. He threatens "to reunite this group of my crown lands with the Empire at once, and to revoke the gift of Charlemagne."

In a word, having a large appetite, he will make one mouthful of all the Papal States. Thereupon the enraged Pope breaks off the negotiations, the Emperor has Rome occupied, and in April the Papal States become a province.

Napoleon, who has ranged from Cairo to Vienna, and will range from Madrid to Moscow, Napoelon, who has often been in Italy, hesitates to set foot in Rome; caution or circumstance always keeps him away. He never confirms by actual inspection the image he has carried in his mind from boyhood upwards. Now for the second time his generals take possession of what he had been wont to regard as the Eternal City. No member of his entourage protests against the occupation. But his mother feels it to be a mistake, and her distress affects her health, Whereas formerly she had been content to say sceptically of her son's great fortune: "If only it lasts!" now, with a presage of destruction, she confides her misgivings to her intimates:

"I foresee that he will bring disaster on himself and all his family. He should be content with what he has. He tries to grasp too much, and will lose all!"

XVII

"What the German peoples ardently desire is that persons who are not of noble birth but are talented shall have equal rights to your consideration and to office, so that there may be an end, once and for all, to any kind of subordination, and to all intermediaries between the ruler and the lowest classes of the population. The advantages brought by the Code Napoleon, publicity of legal procedure, and trial by jury, will be characteristics of your monarchy. To lay my whole thought before you: for the consolidation of this monarchy, I look more to the effects just named than to the results of the greatest victories. Your people must have a liberty, an equality, and a prosperity hitherto unknown in Germany. This way of ruling will be a stronger barrier between you and Prussia than the Elbe, than fortresses, than the protection of France. What nation would ever wish to go back to Prussian rule when it had once experienced the advantages of a liberal government?"

In these sentences (which are written as a private lesson, and are not penned with an eye to public effect), The Emperor expounds to his youngest brother the great mission that is being entrusted to the latter when he takes charge of the new kingdom of Westphalia. Jerome's task was to plant the fundamental ideas of the revolution on German soil, a pioneer work, this introduction of the first glimmer of self-government in a part of western Europe where hitherto the inhabitants have known only how to obey. In

When Jerome went to war, he took his whole court with him–not the queen, indeed, but all the prettiest of her ladies. He issued proclamations in the style of the Roi Soleil. But he was not mortified to receive the following imperial admonition:

"I have read an order of the day issued by you, in which you make yourself ridiculous. You are king, and the Emperor's brother! Fine qualities in war! In war, a man must be a soldier before everything. When I am in camp, I need neither ministers nor luxury. You must camp with the advance guard, be in the saddle day and night, march with the advance guard, so that you may get all the news without delay. If you don't like that, you had better stay at home in your palace! You make war like a satrap! God in heaven, you never learned that from me! I ride in front of the skirmishers, and do not allow even my minister for foreign affairs to follow me. ... You make vast claims; you have a certain amount of talent and a few good qualities, but these are put quite in the shade by your follies. Furthermore, you are insufferably conceited, and know absolutely nothing of public affairs."

The king sticks the letter into his jabot with a laugh. But the Emperor? Cannot he realise, while he talks to his brother like a father, that everyone to whom he gives unmerited power endangers the very essence of power? That these golden crowns and the extemporised coats-of-arms he provides for them create very unstable kings and princes? That homunculus escapes from the phial and makes fun of his master? This perennial weakness where his relatives are concerned leads him, at times, to assume what is a very unusual role for him, that of the good-natured man; for, though he begins by issuing orders to his brothers, he very often gives way to them in the end. "My brother, enclosed you will find the construction in matters of high politics, with a sentence that might have been taken out of a comic opera. When he is in a friendly humour, he will end a letter full of reproaches with a paternal smile: "Mon ami, I love you but you are so frightfully young!"

Napoleon is no longer young. Inevitably, as his plans grow, there must be an increase in that harshness which, in him, is mainly the outcome of overwork. When, twelve years earlier, he had come down from the Alps as a conqueror and his fame had spread before him across the plain of Lombardy, his youth had endowed the novelty of this campaign with a sort of romantic innocence which carried his contemporaries off their feet. Now, when the mountain torrent has long since widened into a river, bearing on its broad bosom ships freighted with the treasures of the world, and when the river is drawing near to the ocean in which its waters will soon mingle with all the waters of the earth; now, the gravity of this labour of Atlas has stamped its imprint upon his features, has written its message in his moments of merriment and sportive humour; and the heroical cynicism of his mission moulds him before the eyes of the world into a statue of bronze.

True, he had sent for his Polish countess, She was installed in the very street where Josephine had first charmed him, and where, again and again, a quaint superstition led him to house his lady friends. Walewska is munificently provided for, and Napoleon's physician visits her everyday. But, though there is no secret about the matter, she leads a retired life, does not use the box at the opera he has reserved for her, and seldom sees him now that she has come to Paris. This is an interlude between one idyll and the next. He had made up his mind that the child she is to bear him will be a son; and the event may have still greater consequences today than it would have had yesterday.

For the first of his illegitimate children, the one of whose birth he had received tidings in Berlin (when he had been reassured to learn that there was no justification for the common belief that he was sterile), has been put out of court by the mother's unwise importunity. Shortly after his return to Paris, she had called. He would not see her, sending a message to say that he received no one whom he had not summoned. He provided her with a house and an income, and would have nothing more to do with her. But he had the boy brought to him, and playfully teased the little chap. For a moment, he even thought of adopting him. All had to be done secretly. The invisible master, whom he called the "nature of things" and on rare occasions "fate," forbade him the unconcealed enjoyment of this most natural of scenes in our human life, one in which Napoleon could not play his part until he was nearly forty. At length he had a son of his body, who might become his heir. Yet he, Emperor of the West, could not step forward and say: "This is my son!" Wishing to give the boy at least half his own name, he called him Leon.

But the mother had become completely estranged from him, and Napoleon soon ceased to have any serious thought of making the child his successor. Perhaps he thought that the boy came of a bad stock; maybe he had a foreboding that this half Napoleon would become a half criminal and an outright ne'er-do-well.

All the more vigorously does his advance in years urge him towards a new marriage. There are long conversations between Napoleon and Josephine, between reason and sorrow; and after them it is not Josephine alone in whom the servants note the trace of tears. "How terrible to die childless!" he says on one occasion. Nevertheless his fondness for his helpmate increases. We know how difficult he found it to break with any of his collaborators; and his temperamental conservatism makes him cling to this first companion of his rise. "If I were to divorce her," he says to Talleyrand who advises him to take this step, "the witchery of my home would be gone. I should have to go to schools again in order to understand the ways and fancies of a young wife. The empress adapts herself to me perfectly, and understands me so well. Besides, it would be very ungrateful to divorce a woman who has done so much for me." Such are the motives, tender and reasonable, respectable and convenient—in a word, thoroughly middle class–which make the man cleave to his wife.

But the difficulties grow in number, and the need for a decisive step becomes more urgent. While he ponders the moral impression which his divorcing Josephine will make in France (where she inspires far more personal affection than he does), he, as his manner is, lays his plans deliberately, that, at last he may make an advance which no one anticipates, and will enable him to fulfil two wishes at once. He arranges for an interview with a man whom he has long needed, and whom he may now need more than ever. His mother is always interceding with him on Lucien's behalf; now, Napoleon, who is travelling in Italy, sends for Lucien.

The conversation between the brothers is the most interesting of all Napoleon's recorded conversations, and has been reported by Lucien with fidelity and picturesqueness. Napoleon is there portrayed to the life.

XVIII

Lucien was now just thirty-two. It was on a December evening when he had reached the castle of Mantua, after a journey during which the dread of imprisonment, aroused by his brother's summons, had been continually present to his mind. On entering a room extravagantly lighted by numerous candelabra, he was blinded for a moment by the glare. Then he heard Rustam's voice announcing him: "Sire, your brother Lucien!"

The man to whom the announcement is made does not stir. He is seated at a large, round table, which is covered by a huge map of Europe, the biggest Lucien has even seen. Supporting his head on his left hand, with the other hand he is thrusting coloured pins into the map, pins which presumably represent army corps or whole armies. It is so many years since Lucien has seen his brother, and Napoleon has changed so much, that the visitor is not quite sure whether he is looking at the Emperor, and he remains motionless for several minutes. At length the man sits up, yawns, rubs his back against the chair, takes up a small bell from the table, and rings it with one strong movement. The visitor advances a step or two:

"Sire, I am Lucien."

The Emperor jumps up from his chair, dismisses the servant, and takes his brother by the hand affectionately, though with a certain amount of reserve. Lucien feels called upon to embrace Napoleon, who does not repel the advance, but accepts it with a passive coldness, as if no longer used to such intimacies. Then taking the visitor by the hand once more, he pushes Lucien gently away to scrutinise him the better:

"So it's you, is it? How are you? How is your family? When did you leave Rome? Have you had a pleasant journey? What about the Pope? How is he? Does he like you?"

Lucien notes the nervousness masked by this flood of questions, turns them off lightly, and says he is glad to find his brother in good health.

"Yes, I'm very well." He pats his waistcoat, and adds: "I'm getting fat, and I'm afraid I shall get fatter still." He looks keenly at Lucien, takes a pinch of snuff, and says: "As for you! Do you know that you are looking uncommonly well? You used to be rather too thin. Now, you are almost handsome."

"Your Majesty is good enough to make fun of me."

"No, no, it's quite true. But let's sit down and have a talk." They seat themselves opposite the huge map, the Emperor fidgets with the pins, and Lucien waits for him to begin. But, since Napoleon does not open the ball, the younger man says, hesitatingly: "Sire ..." At this moment, the Emperor sweeps all the pins flat, and says abruptly: "Well, what have you to say to me?"

Lucien replies that he hopes his brother has forgiven him.

"You can have my pardon soon enough. It depends entirely on yourself."

Lucien expresses his willingness to do anything compatible with his honour.

"Well and good, but what sort of things will square with your honour?"

Lucien speaks of nature and religion.

"But politics; do politics mean nothing to you?"

Lucien demurs, saying that he has retired into private life.

"It rested entirely with yourself. You could have been a king just as well as your brothers."

"Sire, my wife's honour, my children's position ..."

"You keep on speaking of your wife, my children's position ..."

"You keep on speaking of your wife, when you know perfectly well that she has never been your wife. Is not, and never will be, for I shall never recognise her"

"Ah, Sire!"

"No, never, though the heavens should fall! Since you are my brother, I can forgive the wrong you have done me. But upon her my curse will rest!" There is a long tirade, until at length Lucien intervenes, laughing nervously, and saying:

"Moderate your words, Sire. There is a proverb: 'La processione torna, dove esce,'" and Lucien thinks it expedient to add a French translation. When Napoleon continues to talk of his brother's wife as a woman of bad reputation, and Lucien shows signs of taking offence, the Emperor tries to mollify him by admitting that these reports may be calumnious, but adds that nothing will induce him to recognise her. Besides, it is now a fundamental law, as firmly fixed as the Salic law, that no marriage in the Emperor's family is valid without the Emperor's consent. Lucien reminds him of the date of the marriage, and Napoleon answers: "Yes, but the law was passed because of what you had done!" This Napoleonic logic makes Lucien smile.

"What are you laughing at? I don't see anything laughable in it! I know what you and your wife and my enemies say about the matter. You choose your friends from among my enemies. But no good Frenchman approves of what you have done. The only way in which you can regain popular esteem is by espousing my cause, like Jerome."

Lucien, who is in the Emperor's hands, has absolutely determined to let nothing affront him. But he is spurred into opposition, springs to his feet, and does not sit down again:

"Your Majesty is mistaken! When your courtiers approve your attitude towards me as thanks for the service I was so happy to render you, they are only acting after their kind. On my side, too, my servants tell me that I am right!" –At these words,

Napoleon's brow is furrowed, his eyes flash, and his nostrils work, "an unmistakable sign of rage in members of our family." But Lucien has taken the bit between his teeth and goes on: "What ought the nation to do for me? What gratitude does it owe me? It ought to look upon me as the saviour of the man who saved it.... I am proud to think that it will rather be inclined to compare me with you than with Jerome. No, Sire, public opinion, which is mightier by far than all kings in the world, assigns everyone to his true place, whatever courtiers may say."

Napoleon grows calmer. Instead of flying into a passion, as Lucien dreaded for a moment, he controls himself, and says quietly:

"Talleyrand is right. You speak of the affair with an ardour worthy of a political club. Such eloquence, Citoyen, is, believe me, long since out of fashion. I am well aware that you did me good service on the Nineteenth Brumaire; but as for having been my 'saviour,' of that proof is lacking. This much I remember clearly, that you disputed with me the unity of power which I needed for the saving of France, and that I and Joseph spent half a night before we could get you to pledge yourself to silence when these questions should be touched upon.... Finally, after the victory, you were inclined to oppose my personal elevation, and this conduct on your part releases me from all obligation to show gratitude.

"But you, do you owe me no gratitude? When you 'saved' me at Saint-Cloud, were not yourself in mortal peril? I sent my grenadiers to save you from the hands of assassins. And if you, a bad brother, and unnatural brother, had really allowed that vote of my outlawry to be taken, do you imagine that I should have been such a fool as to accept the decree unresistingly? Had I not adherents enough, with God's aid, to defend this head that was destined to wear so many crowns?" He goes on to speak for a whole hour of those days, and of Corsican compatriots who had helped him; suddenly gives the conversation an intimate turn; speaks of his generals and the extent of their devotion; refers to political conflicts in which the brothers had held divergent views, and shows how his view had been right. Then he changes the subject, saying abruptly:

"Enough. That is all ancient history, like your great day of the Nineteenth Brumaire. I did not summon you that we might deliver lectures to one another." A long pause.

"Listen to me, Lucien, and weigh my words carefully, for, above all, let us avoid getting.... I am too powerful to have any desire to lose my temper. You have come to me trustfully, Corsican hospitality shall never be violated by the Emperor of the French. This virtue of our forefathers and fellow-countrymen is a guarantee for your absolute safety." The Emperor strides up and down the hall for a long time, pulling himself together, and then turns to Lucien, whose hand he takes and presses:

"We are alone here. You see? We are alone. No one can overhear us. I am wrong about your marriage.... Knowing your willfulness as I did, knowing your self-love–for everything, you know, depends on self-love, which regards itself as a virtue, just as we princes dignify by the name of policy everything which turns on our passions–I ought not to have interfered with your union. People slandered your wife to me, though some ventured to speak well of her, especially Mamma, who loves her, saying she makes you happy and is a good mother.... Lebrun, indeed, has sung her praises so often that Josephine once told the good fellow he must be in love with her himself. I am very much amused at my wife, who has more of a temper than people fancy. Still, I must say that Josephine never shows her claws to me! Well, I have no disrespect for your wife, but I detest her because this passion of yours for her has robbed me of the most capable of my brothers. However, her beauty will pass; you will be disillusioned; then, returning to political life, you will oppose my policy and I shall have to take measures against you whether I like it or not, for–let me say this to you–unless you are on my side, Europe is too small for the pair of us!"

"You are making fun of me."

"No, I'm in earnest; friend or foe! It is easier for you today than ever before. You need not be surprised; there has been a change in my family policy. You will see soon enough. Your children, which hitherto I have wanted to exclude, can now be of great use to me, but they must be dynastically recognised. The offspring of a marriage I do not recognise can have no right to the throne. Tell me, then, what would you do in my place?"

Lucien advises him to make the Senate pass a simple resolution to the effect that the children come within the right of succession.

"Of course I know that I can do that, but I must not. As you said just now, public opinion has to be conciliated. What would the family, the court, France, which all watch my slightest movements, say about such a step? A recantation of that kind would do me more harm than the loss of a battle."

Lucien points out that he cannot possibly ask pardon for a marriage which had been entered into long before Napoleon's accession to the throne. "Grant my request, Sire. You will have no more faithful servant than I. All the rest of my life will be an expression of my gratitude."

The younger man goes on talking for a long time, and throughout his speech Napoleon is incessantly taking snuff, but spilling most of the tobacco, so nervous is he, growing more and more anxious; in his perplexity exclaiming at length; "Good God, you press me hard, and I am weak. But I shall not be so weak as to move the Senate to pass the resolution you ask for. I cannot recognise your wife!"

Thereupon Lucien, who is now almost beside himself, says: "Well then, Sire, what do you really want of me?"

"What do I want? Simply that you should divorce your wife."

"But you have always maintained that we are not married, so how can we get a divorce?"

"I expected you to say that: What do you think I can mean by asking you to procure a divorce? Obviously, thereby I recognise your marriage, but not your wife. The divorce will be the best thing for your children, just like all that you have hitherto refused to do, all that I have so much wanted you to do: to annul the marriage and divorce her."

"That would be a dishonour for me and my children, and I will never do it!"

"Why is it, that with all your mother wit, you cannot see the difference between my earlier proposals and my present ones. In the former case, if your marriage had been declared null, your children would have become bastards!"

Lucien points out the difference between his children's dynastic rights and their civic rights. "You can bestow your thrones upon whom you will, Sire, for you won them at the point of the sword. But no one shall cheat my children out of their share in the modest heritage of Carlo Bonaparte, for they are as legitimate as anyone else's both by canon law and by State law. The Pope has even given one of my daughter the name of his mother!"

"Calm Yourself! .... Of course the divorce I ask for implies the recognition of your marriage. Nor do I wish to force an actual separation from your wife. She shall be honoured in accordance with her merits if she will make this sacrifice to my policy and to the future interests of France. I would even pay her a visit. But if she refuses, you and she will both be blamed for having sacrificed the true greatness of your children to your own egoism, and your children will curse your memory!"

Lucien answers mournfully.

"You are really incorrigible," rejoins Napoleon. "You take everything so tragically. I am not asking for any tragedies! Think it over."

After Lucien has again and again insisted upon his point of honour, and has several times wished to take leave, the Emperor once more brings up the distribution of the thrones. Eugene's position in Italy is merely provisional, and he would much rather see Lucien installed there. Napoleon complains about Hortense, too. None of them is satisfied. "Pauline is naturally the most reasonable in the matter of ambition, for she is the queen of at your disposal, if only you will divorce your wife before I divorce mine!"

Lucien is spellbound for a time by the feverish haste with which Napoleon speaks. At last he says: "Not even your lovely France, Sire, would bribe me to this divorce: and besides..." He hesitates; but the Emperor guesses his thoughts, and says dryly, with an imperious air such as Lucien has never before seen him assume:

"Do you think that you, as a private individual, are in a more secure position that I upon my throne? ... Do you believe that your friend the Pope is strong enough to protect you against me if I should seriously propose to take measures against you?" After reiterating arguments and enticements, he says in a formal tone: "You may be quite sure of this: everything for the divorced Lucien; nothing for the undivorced!"

Lucien glances at the door, as a hint to the Emperor that he would be glad to be given his dismissal; but Napoleon takes him by the hand, and says "in a vague tone, and with a demeanour which might mean anything":

"If I get a divorce, you will not be the only other one, Joseph is merely waiting for my divorce to arrange for his own. Madame Julie has been good for nothing but to bring girls into the world, whereas I urgently need boys. The only use of girls is to marry them off in advantageous alliances. Besides, your eldest girl is nearly fourteen, so you tell me; just the right age. Won't you send her to Mamma? If you do what I want, I will get Mamma to arrange something good for her.... You are not afraid that we shall do any harm to your spoiled darling? Tell her we shall be good friends, and that I will not pull her ears as if she were a child.... I need more nephews and nieces! The divorced Josephine, the grandmother of Hortense's children, will always be the enemy of my legitimate and my adopted son." Then, murmuring as if to himself, "It must be done. I have no other way of undermining the power of Louis' and Hortense's children."

He comes back to the subject of his own illegitimate children, says he intends to adopt them, enters into details, and suddenly exclaims: "You cannot suppose that I have not the power to legitimise my natural children, just as Louis XIV declared his bastards, the fruit of a twofold adultery, to be within the right of succession to the throne." Again he speaks of Joseph's intention to procure a divorce, and, when Lucien is sceptical, he rubs his hands delightedly, saying:

"Yes, yes! Joseph and you will both divorce your wives! We will all three get divorces, then marry again, all of us, on the very same day!" He adds a number of quips in the like merry vain. Then, suddenly: "But why have you become so serious? One might think you a sage of classical antiquity! You must stay with me for three days. I'll have a bed made ready for you in the next room to mine!"

He presses this invitation. Lucien, who dreads his brother's blandishments, has to invent an excuse, and says that one of his children is ill.

His wife, he goes on to say, has suffered because of the Emperor's dislike; so much so, that he had been afraid at one time her anxiety and distress about the matter would be too much for her.

"Is that really so? I'm sorry. You must take care of her! Whatever happens, she must not die before you get your divorce, for if she did I should not be able to legitimize her children!"

Lucien pretends that he will think the matter over.

"That's all right. Well, well, go if you must! But be sure to keep your word!" Napoleon takes Lucien by the hand, and at the same time presents his cheek for a kiss, which is not as brotherly as it might be. Lucien departs, and when he is in the anteroom he hears the Emperor calling: "Méneval!"

Lucien quickens his steps, for again the dread of imprisonment has seized him.

No one, no historian and no imaginative writer, has ever given a more brilliant description of Napoleon than the foregoing, penned by his brother with obvious fidelity. This evening, the because he does not wish to bow before the force of his brother's genius. For there is a secret contest between the pair, not about love or divorce, not about honour or crowns. Today, just as seven years before, when the younger man could not bring himself to obey the elder, the contest is between the innermost self-esteem of one rival and of the other. After all these years, in the privacy of his own thoughts Lucien is still convinced that he could have managed everything much better than Napoleon.

And yet, all the time, he loves him after his own fashion. Every word of his report betrays the obscure enmity between the brothers, the enmity that lives side by side with love. That is why he concedes nothing. The memory of the Nineteenth Brumaire has to be revived, and once more each of them is confident he was right. While these expert realists are talking, with the old phrases on their lips, the old verbiage about the greatness and the safety of France, they are really moved by nothing but their own passions. We seem to see to them posturing before the crowd (a doubt seizes them –"We are alone here. You see. We are alone. No one can overhear us"); but in truth they are alone, in a strange and foreign castle, beneath huge candelabra, on which the candles are burning low.

Nevertheless, despite Napoleon's wealth and all his crowns, despite his stupendous powers of intellect and imagination how poor a man he is, entangled in the threads of destiny, the threads which he has spun, but which are now spinning themselves in defiance of his wishes! For all his omnipotence, he is the slave of an incalculable, much-courted power, public opinion, which will not allow him to effect a reconciliation with his brother, to recognise his own children, or to marry the woman he loves. The importance of the man of might is displayed in his own exclamations. He asseverates his power to do anything and everything–and yet he dare not do what he wants. How pleased he is with his brother, whose affairs he could manage so beautifully now that they have met after many years of separation. If Lucien would only stay with him, were it but for three days, they would certainly be able to come to an understanding. "Good God, you press me hard, and I am weak."

During this night when an emperor was offering his brother a choice among the thrones of Europe, was there not talk of the heritage of Carlo Bonaparte, a poor nobleman, on a small out-of-the-way island? Did the Emperor of the French, conjure up the shade of the Corsican; was it he who evoked the penates of his birthplace for the protection of Brother Lucien, a negotiator in a hostile camp? Surely what we are recounting is a saga, told at midnight beside the fireplace in Mantua? Yes, it is the saga which the little Corsican lieutenant has woven out of the threads of his life: first a narrow band; but as he trails it after him, twists it and loops it, mixes colours and patterns, by degrees a carpet is formed; greater and more varied become the pictures produced out of the one thread, pictures of lands and thrones of seas and men.

The whole has been woven in the most natural way in the world. Not by a miracle, but only through the working of his talents, has the man become master of men. Tonight he wants to add yet another to the long list of his subjects. He has not enough time, even though he hopes to live till he is ninety. He cannot allow his brothers to have girl children, or to live with the women of their choice. But if these undesired nieces throng his stage, he must set up new nephews against them. If a wife is in danger of dying of grief, she must at least be good enough to wait until she is divorced. When the men of the family have at length forsaken the wives who are barren or can only bear daughters, then, on the same day, they will take new wives unto themselves–and all will go happily ever after. Look at him, when the conversation is drawing to a close, rubbing his hands in his satisfaction, a little magician who stands in front of his immense map. By the time he has impaled all the countries with his coloured pins, impaled them like butterflies to put away in his collection–well, by that time the candles have burned out and a large slice of tomorrow has already been devoured.

XIX

The Spanish dynasty seemed about to fall. Immediately after the conversation recorded above, war was declared. Had not the Emperor already predicted it? A king who had degenerated into being his wife's souteneur; a queen who only lacked courage to be a Messalina; a faithless minister; hatred between father and son; rascality, bribery, and corruption–to such a pass had sunk the house of Bourbon! He who wished to dethrone those who represented it, must use the same means as were used by the Spanish royal house itself. Never before had Napoleon's actions been more fiercely unscrupulous; never before had the degeneracy of his opponent been a more useful weapon to his hand. He had always adapted his methods to his adversary; and, in the case of this decayed dynasty, he had recourse to the wiles and trickery similar to those which the Spanish house availed itself of in a last effort to preserve its integrity. Absorbed in his schemes, he forgot the Spanish people, which was in no way responsible for such princes, and which in no way resembled the royal rulers: in days to come the Emperor was bitterly to rue his forgetfulness.

He who is for England, is against me! In support of this principle, Napoleon had already chased the Portuguese royal family from the throne. Now, since Spain, too, is on the side of England, in a prolonged intrigue he turns to his own advantage the struggle between the king and the crown prince; brings the latter to the front; then orders him to withdraw in favour of the father; and, finally, at a meeting of all parties in Bayonne, is able, by threats and cunning, to ensure that the Spanish crown shall be his own. The Mediterranean must belong to him; the coasts at any rate from Gibraltar to Cattaro. This is an essential part of the war on England.

At first his generals have an easy task in their work of conquest. "Do you know why I am invading Spain?" says Napoleon to Metternich. "I must feel safe at may back." Alas for him when he is no longer safe in that quarter!

On the critical day when he has settled matters with the Spanish princes, and has arranged that they shall be kept in a mild imprisonment, he is in a condition of moderate intoxication. The new crown gives him fresh impetus. He no longer sees Spain; his eyes are turned to contemplate the worldwide empire of Spain in the days of her vanished glory. On this occasion, a witness tells us, "the Emperor spoke, or rather dictated, at great length, in the Ossianic vein,... like one whose heart was uplifted.... In his picturesque, metaphorical style, he referred to the powerful kingdoms of Mexico and Peru, describing the might of their rule and their influence. Never have I heard him display such a wealth of imagery as on this day. He was sublime."

The one thing he lacks is an occupant for the vacant throne, since Lucien has not accepted the bribe. The only way out of the difficulty will be a general post, like that which occurs when a vacancy is filled in the upper ranks of the officialdom and every one is promoted a step. Let us do away with the kingdom of Holland, made it into a province, and discrown Louis The victim protests: "It does not suit me to be governor of a province. A king must rule by divine right.... How could I demand loyalty from my people if I myself were false to the oath I swore when I ascended the throne?" Napoleon is troubled once more by the consequence of having founded a dynasty. This modern Roman should have put his provinces in charge of generals and regents, whom he could recall whenever he pleased. But the ermine in which he dressed his puppets all the apparatus of coronation and Mass and anointing, awaken ideas which were being laid to rest, and fully justify little King Louis in his refusal. Joseph is more accommodating. Till yesterday, he was king in Naples: why should he not be king in Madrid tomorrow? Shortly after the Bayonne intrigue, King Joseph I enters his new capital, acclaimed, not indeed by the hearts of the people, but by the proper number of salute guns and all the ceremonial suitable to the occasion. Murat, whose wife has long been pestering her brother for a crown, Murat the son of the proletariat, becomes king of Naples, and thus the imposing couple gain a statelier field for their intrigues, and in due time for their treason.

But this Spanish affair is a great adventure, and has serious consequences. There is muttering "at the Emperor's back," for the Spaniards are proud, will not endure the conquest without a struggle, In front, across the Rhine, all the Prussians and all the Austrians who hate the Emperor have now reason to dread that Prussia and Austria may share the fate of Spain, have good grounds for yet another renewal of their offensive. In Berlin, Napoleon had declared that on the Elbe he had conquered the Ganges. Now he fails to see that in his dealings on the Tagus he is raising up new enemies on the Danube. But he knows that he cannot do as he pleases in Spain unless the tsar holds Austria in check for him. The tsar is man of unstable character. The only way to win over Alexander is by suggestion, as two years before, in Tilsit, and for this a personal interview will be necessary. The Emperor thereupon proposes to meet the tsar in central Germany, half way between their respective empires, thus initiating a form of policy new to him, a conference. Always before, when he has left France, it has been sword in hand, and he has invariably paved the way for negotiations by fighting. Now, to avoid a fight, a conference table is established in Erfurt.

Napoleon prepares for this new sort of campaign with as much care as if he had been preparing for a military expedition. Day after day he summons court officials and other dignitaries. "My journey must be extremely imposing. I want great names for the headquarters, ... and I wish to amaze Germany by the splendour of the occasion." For others are coming besides the tsar. The great double stars are attracting all the lesser stars, How can he best influence this assembly? The play's the thing wherein he'll catch the conscience of the kings! He stage-manages his theatre elaborately, devotes much thought to the cast, amends passages, and gives Talma (for whom he feels something akin to friendship) hints as to what requires to be emphasised–all with an eye to the royal audience "You are going to play your parts in a theatre where the stalls will be filled with kings."

In actual fact, the evenings at the theatre form the climax of the Erfurt weeks Among the audience are four kings and thirty-four princes, rivalling one another in the splendour of their retinues. The Emperor of the West and the Emperor of the East occupy the royal box. Almost every evening, this distinguished audience sees and hears what the kings of saga or the kings of history proclaim, what they struggle for, what they suffer. Talma, as Orestes, thunders forth.

The gods are the rulers of our times,
And yet fame is created by our own deeds.
Why should the heart allow the heavens to threaten?
Resolve to become immortal
And you will be as gods upon the earth!

The next evening they see Voltaire's *Mahomet*, of which the Emperor is especially fond, were it only because the hero so seldom quits the stage. The prophet's disciple exclaims:

All men are equal; it is not birth,
But virtue alone which makes them different.
There are certain mortals favoured by the gods
Who achieve everything by their own merits.
Who owe nothing to their forefathers.
Such a one is he whom I have chosen as master;
He alone, in all the world, has deserved his position.

Is there any one among the audience whose heart does not beat faster as he glances at the man up there in the royal box–though the passion may be a passionate antagonism? The princes by right of birth may dread to look at the Emperor, but at least their eyes will seek one another as if to secure a common understanding. They do not dare to smile. They tremble before the man who sits there in a plain green coat, the man who is revolt incorporated in human form. He knows what the German princes in the stalls do not yet know, that a new and stronger utterance will soon be made by Mahomet:

See, the Roman Empire falling into ruins,
That great torn body, whose scattered limbs
Lie spread about the earth dishonoured and lifeless:
On these fragments of a world we shall upbuild the far-flung East,

A new god reveals himself to the blind world!

Finally, the Emperor's policy of today and tomorrow is voiced in the words:

Who was it made the master a king?
Victory alone has crowned him! But now
To the name of Conqueror he will add
The name of Peacemaker.

At this instant, when all glance at him questioningly, Napoleon makes a slight movement as a sign that such is actually his intention, and for a political instant the illusion of the theatre is dispelled. But when, next evening, Oedipus proclaims: "A strong man's friendship is a gift of the gods!" the two emperors rise and clasp hands.

Napoleon knows well enough that Alexander is not a strong man, that his friendship is not a gift of the gods. He tries, therefore, by suggestion, to win over this vacillating personality. If the tsar is to be influenced to move along the lines laid down in the letter previously quoted, if he is to agree to divide with Napoleon the empire of the world, he will require a course of psychomagnetism, renewed from day-to-day, Napoleon rarely leaves the tsar to his own thoughts, but treats him like a woman who is to be wooed and won. The only person who is allowed to help the Emperor in this matter is Talleyrand.

The diplomat still limps after Napoleon as the Emperor strides forward, though recently the differences between the two men had found vent.

Talleyrand's shrewdness had led him–sooner than Napoleon, sooner than anyone–to detect the first cracks in his master's system. A year before, after the drawn game of Eylau he had foreseen the possibility of his master's failure in Russia. This had come to him as the vision of a great statesman, and he had promptly deduced therefrom the mission of a great and statesman-like traitor. Matters had been privately arranged between Napoleon and Alexander; the Emperor was relying on the tsar (to the exclusion of Talleyrand); Napoleon was cherishing a Carlovingian dream, interpenetrated with thought of Cæsarism: the fantastical elements in Napoleon's schemes for world conquest had estranged Talleyrand from his master's policy But instead of cutting adrift from Napoleon, he had been content, on specious pretexts, to resign his ministerial post, receiving instead a lucrative position among the dignitaries of the empire. Both men hoped to gain by the change; Napoleon thinking that he would be able to keep better watch on Talleyrand, and Talleyrand fancying that he would be able to keep better watch on the Emperor's secret thoughts. He was still grand chamberlain; and Champagny, his successor as minister, was a butt for Napoleon's shafts of ridicule. Thus, even after the divorce from his master, Talleyrand remained the sultan's favourite, and his power was redoubled by his shift as a trickster no longer hampered by official responsibility.

His doubts as to the stability of Napoleon's position were confirmed by the progress of events in Spain. Directly he saw that the Emperor's mind was set on this act of plunder, he realised that its upshot would be disastrous, and for that very reason encouraged his master to the venture. Since the days of Louis XIV, said Talleyrand, the Spanish crown had always been an apanage of the rulers of France. Napoleon, when his mind had been rendered effervescent by this and similar pseudo-arguments, decided upon the occupation of Catalonia "for the duration of the war with England." Now the intriguer promptly returned to a critical attitude, and laughed to himself when the Emperor gave him the ignominious task of entertaining the infantes of Spain in their durance at his mansion near Valençay.

He wants privacy, that he may keep watch on the kidnapped princes, and, through their instrumentality, not only spy upon England, but also keep England informed. Thence it is but a step to open betrayal, and that step Talleyrand now takes. This is in keeping with his whole career as a statesman. Henceforward he sends Tolstoy and Metternich (the envoys of Tsar Alexander and Emperor Francis in Paris) private information. How can he make his duplicity square with his duties to the master, to whose service he is pledged as imperial official, court official, and confidential adviser?

There is a scene about the matter.

"Well, you see," says the Emperor on his return from Spain,

"they all walked into the net I spread for them!"

"I think, Sire, you have lost more than you have won by what has happened at Bayonne."

"What do you mean?"

"Something quite simple. Let me explain my meaning by an example. If a man of standing commits follies, keeps mistresses, treats his wife and his friends badly, he will be blamed; but his wealth and his power will enable him to regain the good opinion of society. But if the same man cheats at cards, he is expelled from good society, which will never forgive him.

The Emperor turns pale–so Talleyrand reports–and will not speak to him for the rest of the day. Why does he not drive the plain speaker out of his circle? Why does he not banish Talleyrand to the West Indies? Napoleon receives a moral castigation from a scion of the old nobility, and still keeps the man in his entourage! Or was Talleyrand lying? We may have all the more confidence in the diplomat's memoirs, seeing that they were written twenty years later, after the Restoration; were written to show how he had always played double, and (of course, owing to his respect for the claims of the legitimate rulers!) had served his imperial master only by halves. We can assume that the words were actually spoken, and to a man to whom hardly anyone now spoke the truth, to a man whom even fewer now ventured to affront. Why does Napoleon keep Talleyrand in his service?

"He is the only one who understands me," said the Emperor of Talleyrand again and again. That accounts for much Talleyrand's unscrupulous way of thinking, his freedom from all qualms of conscience, furnished a tilting-ground on which the Emperor could joust freely when running a political course. The others had principles or considerations which must first be leapt over. Because Talleyrand was exempt from all prejudice of class and time, and also lacked the ordering ideas with which Napoleon fashioned his realm out of the chaos of chances, the wily opportunist, whose only passion was for money; was the best adviser of the other realist, who could only assuage his stormy imagination in a perpetual succession of new plans.

That is why they understood one another, though only the superficial regions of their respective characters. Napoleon never plumbed the depths of the treason that Talleyrand was preparing.

Here, in Erfurt, the great day for the double-dealer has at last dawned. When the German princes gather round him and listen as he talks of the Emperor, he gives little heed to these pygmies, for there is someone else who will pay a far higher price for information, will pay both in political advantages and in ready cash.

Alexander is prompt to seize the opportunity! The Russian has been well informed by his representative in Paris, and is almost as inquisitive concerning this Frenchman as he is concerning the Emperor. Talleyrand soon meets the tsar in the reception room of the Princess of Thurn and Taxis, who keeps open house every evening after the play. Talleyrand's report of the encounter, written several decades later, reads like the utterance of a Mephistopheles. "The arts which I had prepared for the capture of the tsar were quite unneeded. At my first word he understood me, just as I had wished him to understand."

The play of their eyes conveyed a meaning which was not manifest in the words, for on the first day Talleyrand had said to the tsar: "Sire, what are you thinking of doing here? It lies with you to save Europe. But you will not succeed in your task unless you become a match for the Emperor. The French people is civilised: their ruler is not. The ruler of Russia is civilised: his people is not. Thus, the ruler of Russia should be the ally of the French people.... Your Majesty should not ally yourself to be inveigled into any disciplinary measure against Austria, but should consent to undertake the same duties towards that country as those my master has undertaken."

During the long evening, over a glass of punch or a dish of tea, Talleyrand (who, like Napoleon, knows the manifold arts of the seducer) instils into the Tsar's brain all the truths and the hopes he wishes to bring to life within this suggestible spirit. The tsar shows his appreciation of the diplomat's indiscretions at France's expense by bestowing his favour upon the Emperor's confidential adviser. He promises the hand of a Russian princess to one of Talleyrand's nephews; she is the richest heiress in the eastern realm.

Alexander, who in any case had come to Erfurt in a cautious frame of mind (for his relatives had succeeded in arousing suspicions before he started), is now for the first time able to resist Napoleon. In their private interviews, each is always trying to humbug the other; the honeymoon atmosphere of Tilsit has vanished, and the tsar's enthusiasm for the Emperor is a thing of the past.

Napoleon is taken aback. He makes Talleyrand draft the new treaty of alliance. Then, with great labour, he transcribes it, inserting his own emendations, and takes it to Alexander, who has to promise that no one shall hear a word of what is written in this secret document. The tsar gives the required pledge; but the very same evening he hands Talleyrand the amended treaty, so that the author of the draft learns what alterations his master has made. In the end, this treaty is not signed.

At night, the Emperor summons Talleyrand, who plays the part of Iago admirably. The Emperor says: "I can make no headway with him; he takes such short views."

"But he is completely under your spell, Sire."

"He makes you think so, and you are taken in by him. If he is really fond of me, why won't he sign?"

"He is a man of knightly faith," answers Talleyrand. "His simple word and his inclinations will bind him more strongly than a treaty."

"I shall not talk to him about this matter any more; for if I do, he will think I have it very much at heart. Our private interviews will be enough to make Austria believe that there is a secret treaty.... I cannot understand your fondness for Austria, a country whose whole policy recalls that of our old regime!"

alliance between Austria and Russia can save the vestiges of Europe's independence." The Austrian diplomat writes exultantly in his report: "At length we have entered a new epoch, in which allies offer themselves to us from within the French Empire."

Farewells are taken. The Emperor, watched by the princes, exchanges a brotherly kiss with Alexander. All the onlookers are profoundly impressed by this token of friendship in the pair who rule the world. But Talleyrand, hat in hand, smiles inwardly, for over the teacups at the German princess' he has been able to undermine the foundations of this friendship.

In four years his labours will bear fruit, and the fruit will poison Napoleon.

XX

Brightly, against this dull background of German princelets, shines the torch of the German Spirit. "I have gained only one thing here to take back with me to Paris: that you will have a pleasant memory of me." To the Weimar circle, the Emperor says these words on the evening of his departure, for here and in Erfurt he has spent several evenings among those who are the true princes of Germany–princes who have no ancestors, but only genius. Himself a genius without ancestors, it is solely among them that he feels at home; though, during this fortnight, he experiences so much that increases his misanthropic contempt for his fellow-men, a contempt which has its counterpart in respect he feels for the German spirit. The words of the masters of German literature, are, indeed, unknown to him; but the knows their reputation, he knows the position they occupy in the invisible German and the imperial French Republic. That is why he seeks them out.

Two years before, in Potsdam, he had summoned Johannes von Müller to his presence, and nothing throws a stronger light upon the significance of their conversation than the reserve with which the Prussianised Swiss historian treats the incident. With all the precision of a mind that knew so well how to classify its and nowhere else? In the end they come to believe that virtue itself is nothing more than a fable."

Napoleon turns back to Tacitus, for he always keeps a sharp eye on this Roman historian, as if the man, like Madame de Stael today, might still work mischief in Parisian drawing-rooms. As a development of this criticism, speaking in a modern ball-room, Napoleon utters great things concerning the activities of men: "Tacitus has not sufficiently studied the causes and the inner motives of events. His enquiries into the mystery of actions and states of mind have not been sufficiently profound to enable him to hand down an uprejudiced judgement to posterity. A historian should take men and nations as they are, should appraise them as their time and their circumstances have made them..... I have heard him extolled because he would fain make tyrants dread the people, but that would be very unfortunate for the people! Perhaps I am boring you? We did not come here to talk about Tacitus. Look how beautifully Emperor Alexander dances!"

Wieland has been waiting for this moment. In a carefully prepared speech, he defends the old Roman against the new, so that, at the end, the Weimarian dignitaries and any others who are listening cannot restrain their jubiliation.

The Emperor has listened attentively. All now look at him, wondering what he will say. Will he politely withdraw from the discussion? Napoleon, as if on the battle-field, has been wondering upon what private information his adversary's unexpected attack can have been based, and how the onslaught can best be parried. Unquestionably, the speech was not improvised. But how on earth had it entered Wieland's mind to get up that particular topic? Suddenly the Emperor, who in the interim has talked to hundreds upon hundreds of persons, recalls his conversation with Johannes von Müller two years back.

"I certainly have a strong opponent," he says, when the old gentleman has finished the harangue. "You make full use of your advantages. Do you happen to be in correspondence with Herr Müller, whom I met in Potsdam?"

Everyone in the audience smiles, including Wieland, who is fonder of wit than of himself, and frankly rejoins:

"Yes, Sire, it was he who told me that you do not like Tacitus."

"Well, I do not admit defeat," says the Emperor. He returns to his Greek and Christian ideas, develops them further and more boldly, for he sees that the clever old Wieland is a sceptic: "Furthermore," he says in low tones, shading his mouth with his hand, and coming close to his interlocutor, "it remains an open question whether Christ ever lived."

Conqueror and poet. One of them is still in his prime, a ruler who has re-established the Christian faith upon the ruins of the revolutionary cult of reason, but is now more or less at odds with the Church. The other is a venerable poet, a pagan whom Napoleon has just coupled with Voltaire, a man who has maintained the cause of reason against the cause of Christ, a member of a conquered nation, and physically so frail that again and again he has to lean on the back of a chair. The former whispers to the latter that it is probable Christ never lived. But the old man has for half a century been justly regarded as the wittiest among the Germans. He will show the Emperor that, in the intellectual world at any rate, a German can courteously exchange thrusts with a Frenchman, and he hastens to reply: "I know that there are foolish people who doubt that Christ lived. But it would be just as absurd to doubt that Julius Cæsar lived; or that you, Sire, are alive today!"

Thus with a sally in the French manner Wieland upholds both German courtesy and wit, and the historicity of Christ. The Emperor, without committing himself, is content to drop the subject, and to clap the poet on the shoulder, saying: "Excellent, excellent, Herr Wieland!" Then raising his voice, talks to his ballroom audience about the value of Christianity as one of the buttresses of the State. But although he was obviously eager to continue his talk with Wieland, the latter showed plainly that he was too tired to stand any longer, and thus the old man's fatigue put a premature end to a scene which the aid of a couple of chairs might have made even more valuable.

One of the silent witnesses of this conversation was Goethe.

A few days earlier, in Erfurt, the Emperor had had an hour's talk with Goethe. They were together in a room where, as was Napoleon's custom when on a journey, he breakfasted, received, commanded, philosophised, and signed documents. Their conversation was a union of two minds, the balancing of counterpoised electrical forces. It was a process of mutual accommodation in which the two greatest men of their day contemplated the world together; a duologue in which most of their thoughts were never uttered, and in which the best elements were an expression of the homage the two paid one another. Goethe, who learned everything from nature, though in the reality of the world of men he could find only the confirmation of his previous imaginings, felt that this conversation was one of the greatest events in his life, and he described it as such. To the Emperor it was less significant.

For Goethe had followed the Emperor's course for a decade, marvelling all the while; and in his old age he said such profound things about Napoleon that a century after their utterance they have not been excelled. Napoleon, on the other hand, knew almost nothing about Goethe; in especial, he never surmised the poet's personal admiration for himself, since the German had hitherto confided his feelings only to his intimates and even now kept his own counsel. Though the Emperor had read *Werther* several times, the mood that work had aroused was as completely a thing of the past as those youthful feelings which are merely compensatory derivatives for an unoccupied imagination. What this grey-headed poet now signified, was at that time not realized by more than a hundred Germans, and hardly one Frenchman; and, since his name in his own country was little known (and, where known, was unpopular and evoked no enthusiasm), it was natural that the Emperor should know nothing of his save that he had written some wonderful things which were unknown to any except the poet's immediate circle, and that Goethe, at the time of the Battle of Jena, was minister to that Saxon prince who had incurred the Emperor's displeasure. When Napoleon summoned Goethe to an audience, he had less to expect from the poet than he had expected from Müller and from Wieland.

But such as Napoleon and Goethe need but look in a man's eyes to know all about him. Napoleon sits breakfasting at a large, round table; on his right is Talleyrand; on his left, Daru. Now he looks up, and, seeing the poet framed in the doorway, invites Goethe to approach. The Emperor is silent, amazed. There stands the sexagenarian, the most beautiful, the halest of old men, Goethe in the calm of his age, at the pinnacle of a strenuously wrought harmony of spirit, a harmony he had never possessed before and was so soon to lose. Napoleon is too full of admiration to speak. Then, more to himself than to his companions, he says:

"Voilà un homme!"

That is the golden shaft which pierces the heart and illuminates the scene: the word of a seer, deeply felt, an impression rather than a judgement–and it is meet that such it should be. For, precisely because the world ruler does not know that a world ruler is now before him, this utterance, the like of which he had never made to or of anyone in the past and which he is never to make in the future, shows the godlike kinship of a genius with his brother genius. It is as if two elemental forces hovering on high had recognised each other through a rift in the clouds, and had, despite themselves, stretched out arms to one another until the tips of their forefingers had met; then the mists of time once more rose between them. A fleeting moment in the course of a thousand years; there has been nothing to compare with it since the meeting between Diogenes and Alexander.

Goethe's discretion prevented him from recording the conversation for many a year, and even then the record was incomplete. Other memoirs provide us with fragments only.

Napoleon praises *Werther*, and adds: "I do not like the end of your romance."

"I can well believe that, Sire. You would rather that a romance had no end."

The Emperor calmly accepts this well nigh threatening epigram. He then continues to criticise the story, saying that Werther's love was likewise at work. The poet laughs (in two letters Goethe mentions this–a freedom rarely indulged in when the Emperor was present), and admits that the criticism is sound; but he adds that surely an artist may be forgiven for using an artifice which few readers will detect.

The Emperor is well content with his little victory in the other man's domain. Turning now to drama, he makes "very remarkable observations, like one who had studied tragedy with the closest attention, in the spirit of a judge presiding over a criminal trail, and of one who keenly regretted the departure of the French theatre from nature and truth." He spole unfavourably of the drama of destiny, saying that it was a relic of less enlightened days:

"What have we to do with destiny now! Politics are destiny!"

As he utters these words, he gives an object lesson in his own fashion, turning to Daru to discuss requisitions, and then speaking to Soult who has just entered. Turning back to Goethe, he manœuvres to get the poet to himself, and asks personal questions. Then he assumes the offensive:

"Does it please you here, Herr Goethe?"

But Goethe, too, knows how to seize political opportunities, and rejoins: "very much; and I hope these days will also prove advantageous to our little country.'

"Is your people happy?" asks the Emperor, not noticing that he has phrased the question as if he were talking to a sovereign prince–for he must often have used such words in conversation with rulers. Really, he has no interest now in Saxony, and is thinking: "How can this man of genius be useful to me? What a pity he does not write history. But as a novelist he might describe this congress, or he might write a play. – He would certainly do either much better than our fold; and, besides, this would have redoubled value coming from a foreigner." He therefore says:

"You would do well to stay here for the whole period of the conference, that you may write your impressions of this great drama. What does Herr Goethe think of the suggestion?"

Napoleon ends with this question (so unconsonant with his customary dictatorial manner) almost all his advances to the poet who is so hard to lure out of his reticence. Goethe says cautiously:

"I have not the pen of a classical author."

"That's in the political vein," thinks the Emperor. But what he says is:

"Your duke has invited me to Weimar. For a time he was sulky, but now he is in a better humour."

"If he was sulky, Sire, the punishment was certainly rather sharp; but perhaps I ought not to express an opinion on these matters. At any rate, we all owe him reverence."

"Splendid!" thinks Napoleon. "He stands in front of his master, but lets me see he knows that the duke is a donkey. I must get this man to write my 'Cæsar's Death,' more worthily, more splendidly than in Voltaire's attempt? This might be the greatest work of your life. The aim of the tragedy would be to show how much happiness Cæsar would have conferred on the human race had he been given time to carry out his far-reaching plans. Come to Paris! I urge you to do so! Thence you will get a wider prospect of the world, and there you will find the most abundant materials for new imaginative creations."

The poet expresses his thanks for the proposal, and says he would deem himself happy were it possible to accept.

"That is as far as I had better go," thinks the Emperor, as he had thought recently in his dealings with the tsar; "if I am too insistent, he will fancy I have a strong interest in the matter. It is very strange! He wants nothing from me, not even to shine in my presence. What can charm him out of himself, this incorruptible man? He must come and see the plays we are presenting here; that will stimulate his ambition to write better ones."

Out loud: "I hope you will come to the theatre this evening. You will find a lot of princes there. Do you know the prince-primate? You'll see him in his box, fast asleep, with his head pillowed on the king of Württemberg's shoulder. Do you know the tsar? You ought to dedicate something to him in honour of Erfurt!"

Thus the Emperor gives a third hint. Will Goethe take it? But the poet only smiles civilly and candidly declares:

"I have never done anything of that sort, Sire, and therefore I have never had occasion to repent it."

A touch! A touch! The Emperor of the French cannot but feel it! Marvellous to relate, the son of the revolution tries to strengthen his position by referring to the Roi Soleil:

"In the reign of Louis XIV, our great authors held other views!"

"No doubt they did, Sire; but we do not know whether they may not have repented."

"How true!" is the Emperor's thought when he hears this sceptical answer, which is really a skirmisher's attack on the part of the German. Consequently, he makes no attempt to detain the poet when the latter, with a deprecatory gesture, himself closes the interview and bids the Emperor farewell–another breach of court traditions, with which Goethe is perfectly familiar.

Thus the amazing upshot of this uncanny conversation between the two men of genius is that the Emperor, to whom the duologue was merely interesting, had vainly solicited a favour of the poet to whom it was the greatest encounter in his life. The explanation is simple: The Emperor wanted to make use of the poet, whereas the poet did not need the Emperor. Napoleon wanted Goethe to write for him. But to Goethe, Napoleon's actions were merely the precious material which enabled him to penetrate to the heart of the other's genius; and he could do this without a journey to Paris.

Although the poet did not respond to the Emperor's invitation by so much as a poetically worded compliment, years afterward, in a tragical moment, Napoleon remembered the man whom, by three great words, he had set apart from all contemporaries.

XXI

Two months after this conversation, Napoleon is in Madrid, standing in front of the picture of Philip II. He has been over the palace, and has made a quick transit through the galleries; but here, in front of this conqueror's image, he stands so long that the members of his suite watch in dumb amazement while the Emperor seems to be holding converse with the king. The man contemplating the picture is unable to say: "Upon my realm the sun never sets." Perhaps this worldwide empire cannot be achieved without the aid of the Inquisition–which Napoleon has just suppressed, when invading Spain. Has he always been too lenient? Too democratic? Still, he has, in a dozen countries, put liberty in harness, that she may be broken in to dragging the dictator's chariot. Perhaps the trouble is that he talks and writes too much? Philip, with the unfathomable eyes, was always silent. He does not look happy. But who is happy?

A gloomy and joyless war had led the Emperor to this southern capital, for the intrigues with which the Spanish affair had been begun had wrought their own revenges. The kings and princes with whom he had dealt so high-handedly in the previous spring, had deserved no better fate; but the Emperor had failed to understand the temper of the Spanish people. When these had taken up arms in defence of their injured pride, the Emperor had regarded the insurgents as mere windbags. "They were worthy countrymen of Don Quixote. Ignorance, arrogance, cruelty, cowardice–these made up the spectacle before our eyes. Monks and inquisitors had stolen away Spanish brains.... Their soldiers were like the Arabs, and would only fight from behind the protection of walls; their peasants were no better than fellaheen; their monks were ignorant and dissolute; their grandees were degenerate, and had neither energy nor influence."

Entangled in this error, he failed to realise that, though he might conquer them today, his conquest would be for the day only.

Tomorrow the Spaniards, supported by England (which here finds its greatest rallying point), will begin to shoot once more from the houses, and who shall hinder them? The Emperor was already willing to admit it to his confidants. To Vincent, who had been a comrade in his earliest campaigns, he said:

"This is the stupidest thing I have ever done in my life! Can you think of any possible way in which I can free myself from the embarrassment?"

"You have simply to withdraw, Sire, and leave the country to itself."

"Fine words! Remember my position. I am a usurper. To gain this position, I needed to have the best head and the best sword in Europe. If I am to keep what I have won, all must be convinced of this. There must be no falling off in the prestige of my head and my sword. In face of a watchful universe it is impossible for me to say that I have made a serious mistake, and to withdraw with a defeated army. You must see for yourself that the thing can't be done. I am still asking for your advice!"

Conviction that he has made a blunder, and that it is impossible for him to retrieve it; crude admissions made to an old companion-in-arms, whose advice he asks; is this young Bonaparte, or Napoleon growing old? In a week, he had beaten Frederick's famous army. But in Spain, he effects very little in eight months. When he has to deal with armies in a country which can feed his soldiers, a country with roads and towns, he is always victorious; but when he must campaign in trackless regions, such as the desert, the plains of Poland, or the mountains of Andalusia, the tempo is too tedious for his impetuous nature, and the circumstances are too incalculable for his mathematics.

His royal brother, instead of supporting him in this perplexing situation, makes difficulties. King Joseph wants to be a Spaniard, and to win his subjects by kindness. There are scenes between the brothers. With good reason the new king feels that he had made himself ridiculous by having to run away, and because he can only return under shield of the advancing Emperor. But with even better reason does the man of iron complain to Roedérer about the king:

"Joseph wants to be loved by the Spaniards, and to make them believe in his affection. Kings cannot inspire affection through tenderness. They must make themselves feared.... He writes that he wants to retire to Morfontaine; at this busiest of moments, he proposes to leave me in the lurch.... He says that he would rather pass the time at his country-seat than in a land bought with blood unjustly shed.... The blood is that of the foes of France! If he is king of Spain today it is because he wanted to be; he could have stayed in Naples had he wished. Support me? I need no family.... My brothers are not Frenchmen, as I am.... The king of Holland, too, talks about going into private life. It seems to me that I, if any one of us three, have the best right to retire to Morfontaine!"

Why does he not break with Joseph? Here is Marshal Soult, commander in Spain, and perhaps the most highly prized among all his generals. Why does he not give Soult a crown, just as he has given one to Murat? "Joseph writes to say that if I value any one more highly than himself, that is the man I had better make king. I certainly did not make Joseph a king because I thought such a lot of him! If I distributed thrones according to merit, I should have made a very different choice! I need my family to stabilize my dynasty, for that is the system on which I am working."

Now, in Madrid, he issues decrees to establish the new order of things; which is welcomed by few, loved by no one, threatened by England, and detested by the Spanish people. Nothing can restrain him. Only last October he had written to his wife from Weimar, saying that the tsar had been dancing, but he himself would not dance, for "forty years are forty years." Moreover, he often makes fun of the way in which he is putting on fat. Yet on Christmas Eve, afoot, he crosses the Sierra de Guadarramma in a snowstorm, as if he had still been the general at Lodi. He defeats the English; but on these miry roads, deep in snow, he is no more able to follow them in retreat than he could follow the Russians after Friedlands; and he gnashes his teeth when the enemy escapes to the ships. Shall he follow up the other portion of the English forces, away there in the mountains? That would be to withdraw the nucleus of his power still farther from France. Here he is, waiting in the centre of Castille; but what is Paris saying?

He is in camp at Astorga when the courier arrives. Now he will learn what is going on at home. As he is reading one of the letters, he begins to tremble with a dumb wrath. Silently he paces up and down for an hour, without saying a word even to those who are deepest in his confidence. Then he suddenly issues order that the headquarters staff is to return. For his own part, leaving army and generals, he hastens to Valladolid, and thence to the frontier.

"King Philip was right with his unfathomable gaze!" thinks the Emperor as he drives northward in his travelling carriage. "Instead of abolishing the Inquisition in Spain, I should have set it up in France. A conspiracy in Paris, and not one organised by the enemy! Fouché and Talleyrand, whom I could only use because they hated one another, and because each watched the other and told tales, have become reconciled and have entered into an alliance. Murat in it, too!"

The warning letters, which had decided him to return, were from Eugene and from his mother. Letizia is active in spite of her years; active in playing her part when danger threatens, though she withdraws when festivals are the order of the day. She is the Corsican mother, and safeguards her children. The scope of Talleyrand's treason, and how long he has been playing a double game, can at present only be guessed. That he has advised the Austrian envoy to take the offensive against France immediately, now when the Emperor is busy elsewhere, is not known, for there are no incriminatory documents. Even if such documents were in the Emperor's possession, how could so great a master have such great servitors arrested? Slowly and invisibly has the power proceeding from himself grown in their hands, ultimately to be turned against him whom they hate. During the fortnight's journey to Paris the waters of his wrath are rising against these creatures of his making.

Arrived in the capital, the Emperor calls a Council of State composed of many senators and all his ministers, that they may be witnesses to his vengeance. The two delinquents are present. Napoleon loses no time before he begins his attack on Talleyrand: "You are a thief and a scoundrel, for whom nothing is sacred. You would sell your own father! I have showered benefactions upon you, and yet there is nothing that you would refuse to do against me. You it was who advised me to undertake the mad venture in Spain, and now you criticise it to all and sundry. It was you who informed me of the duke of Enghien's whereabouts and incited me to take ruthless measures against him.... You have intrigued with the dethroned Spaniards who were placed in your charge. Today, because you consider the Spanish affair a mistake, you have the effrontery to declare that you had always warned me against it. ....You shall restore to me the keys of your office as grand chamberlain.... I could break you like glass if I chose; I have the power! But I despise you too much to give myself the trouble! ...."

For half an hour, Napoleon holds forth in this fashion. His hearers sit petrified. Silently, Talleyrand bows, and withdraws: "What a pity," he says smilingly to a friend he meets outside, "that so great a man should be so ill-mannered!" Within the council chamber, the Emperor now proceeds to his attack on Fouché, whom he charges with having failed to work up public opinion, with having supported the enemies of the Emperor.... His hearers sit petrified. Silently, Fouché bows–and remains! The Emperor commands that the higher officials shall renounce all right of criticism; they are to become mere tools of his thoughts. He declares menacingly that doubt is the first step on the road to betrayal, which, in its turn, becomes actual as soon as it takes the forms of opposition.

Meanwhile, all Paris is convinced that both the unfaithful servants are to be banished or placed in confinement. But neither is dismissed! Fouché remains, for who could replace the man with a hundred eyes? Talleyrand, smiling as ever, continues to come to court; he has retained his official position; at the Sunday receptions, he always places himself so that his master cannot fail to see him; answers in the stead of his neighbour when the Emperor has put a question to the latter; and, in general, demonstrates the truth

Now, without a blow, he takes Vienna for the second time, and occupies the same room as of old in the palace of Schönbrunn; but the war is not over.

For what has meanwhile been happening in his wide realms is unfavourable to him, and encourages the enemy. There is bad news from Spain; in northern Italy, Eugene has been fighting unsuccessfully; and since, at this instant, Murat has to advance from Naples, the Roman Emperor makes as short work of it with Rome as the Hohenstaufen had done many centuries before. Four years ago, at the same writing table, he had penned a decree annihilating the royal house of Naples. Now he repeats the manœuvre with the Pope. Since Napoleon, at this juncture, has to strike with his sword in all directions, he no longer troubles himself about moral and political consequences, and ventures this dangerous edict for little better reason than that a junction must be effected between his armies in Italy.

But anger is a contributory cause. When he had been in Spain at the beginning of the year, he had let fall expressions showing how out of humour he was with Rome: "Last year, the Pope was impudent enough to neglect sending us the consecrated candles he sent the heads of other States. Write to Rome saying that we don't want any, not even for the three kings of our house. Say that at Candlemas I always get consecrated candles from my own clerics, and that the value of these things does not depend upon purple or the other insignia of power. In the realm of the shades, these will be priests just as good as the Popes! Thus a candle blest by one of my own clergy will be just as holy as one sent by the Pope. I won't have his candles, and none of the princes of my house may accept them."

In this way he trumped the Pope's trick, like a Protestant, like a revolutionary. Such was Napoleon's mood, in the slough of the Spanish roads and battles. Now, in Schönbrunn, he bluntly deprives the Holy Father of power as sovereign prince. The Pope is relegated to the Vatican, and assigned a revenue of two millions.

Many members of the Emperor's retinue are shocked, for some of them are good Catholics, and it is only five days from the feast of Pentecost. Is he not challenging God? Those in whom faith becomes intensified into superstition are likely enough, ere long, to find confirmation of their presentiments. In five days, at Pentecost, Napoleon will be defeated for the first time in his life.

Some regard the battle of Aspern-Essling as indecisive; at any rate, no one can consider it a success of Napoleon. When the bridge across the Danube was swept away, this was just as much and as little due to chance as were all the great happenings whereby at Lodi, Rivoli, Marengo, and on many other occasions, he had, by precisely such improvisations, wrested victory from God. A friend of his youth, Marshal Lannes, is mortally wounded, Napoleon hastens to the dying man's side, and, so the story runs, his old comrade shows hostility both in word and glance. That evening Napoleon sits long before his untasted supper, silent, and refusing to see any one,

"Conquered? Conquerable?" he muses, staring forth gloomy into the future. "Has Achilles' heel indeed been hit? That marksman aimed better than Talleyrand. No, it was my own fault. Too hazardous to cross the river in full view of the enemy! Lannes was right; he was already half way over. What is Paris saying? What will be the best way of reporting this in Paris?" In uneasy mood, he goes back to Schönbrunn, a huge, lonely palace in the midst of a hostile land. His Polish mistress! If only he had had the lovely Walewska with him. She is sitting now in a Polish castle, far away, but her thoughts fly towards him. His hopes of a child by her last year has been dashed.

He sends for her.

Strange news from Rome! To Napoleon's edicts of deposition, the Pope has promptly replied by a bull of excommunication. Does this alarm the Emperor? He laughs. He laughs at Catholic mediævalism, and the soldier, the self-made man, thinks:

"Is this vengeance for my having, in Notre Dame, snatched from him the crown which the holy man wanted to place on my head with his own hands? And what is holy? It is doubtful if Christ ever lived; the only certain thing is that we can make use of him.

But in these enlightened days, none but children and nursemaids are afraid of curses. I have been outlawed twice ere this, on the Nineteenth Brumaire, and Corsica. Such farces bring good luck!" Much refreshed by these thoughts, he prepares for the counterstroke on the Marchfeld, and at Wagram is again victorious, as in thirty battles, his excommunicated weapons being too much for the pious archduke Charles. Towards the end of his two days' battle, when all was going well, and the commander was overpowered by fatigue, he made Rustam spread a bearskin for him on the battlefield, told the Mameluke to call him in twenty minutes, lay down, and fell fast asleep for the prescribed period, to awaken fully reinvigorated. The war was finished, and a truce was agreed on. Next day, reporting the new victory to his wife, he adds: "I've been burned as brown as a berry." He has been thoroughly toned up, and his mood is rejuvenated.

Returning to Schönbrunn, he finds Walewska awaiting him. How many lovely women have glided through the secret portals and discreet chambers of this vast palace, to revivify the Habsburgs? Now the adventurer from the Mediterranean spends evening after evening to fetch the countess, who is housed near by; and again and again he warns the groom of the chambers to be careful lest the carriage should be overturned on the rough road. For the second time, the pair live three months together. He had looked forward to this in Finckenstein, and had promised her that it should happen; but the where and the when depended on the course of universal history, and not wholly on himself.

In a few weeks, she knows that she is with child. Will she this time give him the gift that he has been asking from women for twelve years, and has only once received? Thus, the idyll gains a new content; and when, at midnight on August 15th, lying in her arms, waiting for his fortieth birthday to dawn, and thinking how early next morning salutes and bell peals will hail the coming of this day, throughout France, and indeed in all the countries over which he rules, –the day to which the Pope had complacently transferred the feast of St. Napoleon– may it not seem strange to him that the first to congratulate him should be this beauty of twenty summers, who can speak but haltingly the two languages in which he is at home, and whose glances convey more meaning than her words? His thoughts may well fly back to that time ten years ago when he sailed homeward from Egypt, hazarding all to the luck of the seas, out of which the great English net could so readily have fished him. Now he is a different man, but not a happier one, for he is the slave of "the nature of things."

He is different, also, from the man he was two years ago in Finckenstein. Then he was the builder of a world empire, the potentate to whom the kings of the East and the kings of the West paid homage; now, that empire is on the defensive, and even a great victory like that he has just won, can only be turned cautiously to account.

On the day of Wagram, his people in Rome had committed a blunder of which he has only just heard:

"I am very much annoyed at the arrest of the Pope. That was an idiotic thing to do! You should have arrested Cardinal——, while leaving the Pope at his ease in Rome." He had laughed at the symbolic power of the bull of excommunication. "Excommunication" is an empty word, an airy nothing, which the French bishops can blow away; but as statesman he realises instantly that the imprisonment and deportation of the Holy Father are very serious matters. This rash action has put him in the wrong, for a banished Pope is morally stronger than a Pope fulminating bulls.

Other letters are coming to hand, from Spain this time, telling how England has made good her losses there; and how, in the forest wilds, the visible-invisible Spanish people, allied with England, is standing more stoutly to arms. The news from Paris is that Fouché has overstepped his orders, and has called up the National Guard everywhere; his obvious intention has been to intensify the dread of England throughout the country, and to fan the flames of discontent among the newly levied conscripts.

A difficult and dangerous situation, and one whose difficulties and dangers thicken as the radius widens. The dispatches from Rome and Paris are a week old, and those from more than a fortnight back. By the time fresh orders from Schönbrunn can reach Valladolid, the whole position will have changed. If only he had the power to issue his commands with the velocity of light, then he would be able to rule the world from this office on the Danube. As things are, he must cut short the negotiations, which Austria, encouraged by England and Hungary, has been protracting for weeks. When, recently, the victory demanded a third of a monarchy, with nine million souls, he was met with refusal. Now he pursues a different plan. With the splendid frankness which is so baffling to diplomats of the old school, in one of his endless conversations (this particular talk with Count Bubna lasted seven hours), he explains his own difficulties to his opponent:

"I was to blame for Aspern-Essling, and suffered for my mistake: but the confidence of my soldiers remain unshaken." In broad outline, he sketches his own tactics on the battle-field. "But I will tell you the mistake you are always making.... You draw up your plans the day before the battle, when you do not yet know your adversary's movements, or what positions you will have to occupy. But for my part, I never issue orders long in advance, and am especially cautious overnight. At peep of day, I send out my scouts, survey the field for myself, and keep my troops in mass formation as long as I am still in doubt.... Then I hurl myself on the enemy, attacking him wherever the ground makes attack most favourable.... You are right when you remind me that my free use of artillery fire causes much bloodshed. But what am I to do? My troops are weary; my men want peace. That is why I have to be sparing with the bayonet, and to use cannon more than formerly."

Later he comes to the condition of the alliances: "Today I am sure of the tsar, but what guarantee have I that he will stand by me? As regards Prussia, I have known for a long time that that county is oscillating between you and me." Suddenly he demands only half of what he had asked before, disavows his minister, and offers an alliance. Needs must, for he has to get back to Paris. A new basis for negotiation! Austria is to lose a fragment to the Confederation of the Rhine, and another to Russia; a pathway to the Balkans has to be left open for Napoleon. Several more weeks pass in negotiation. His impatience is soothed by the bright glances of Walewska.

In October, Napoleon is holding a great review in Schönbrunn. A young man forces his way into the palace. He is arrested. When searched, he is found to be carrying a long knife and the picture of a girl. Examined in the guard room, he refuses to give any information, and says he will only explain himself to the Emperor in person. Soon the lad of eighteen, a fair-haired youth, serious of aspect, frank and courageous but courteous, is confronted with Napoleon. His name is Friedrich Staps, and he is the son of a Tyrolese pastor. Napoleon questions him in French. Rapp acting as interpreter.

"Yes, I intended to kill you."

"You must be mad, young man, or ill."

"I am neither mad nor ill, but in the full possession of my faculties."

"Then why do you want to kill me?"

"Because you are ruining my country."

"Your country?"

"It is mine, as it is that of all good Germans."

"Who was the instigator?"

"No one. My heart told me that by killing you, I should do good service to Germany and to Europe."

"Have you ever seen me before?"

"In Erfurt. Then I believed you would make no more wars, and I was your greatest admirer."

The Emperor sends for his physician, in the hope that the young fellow will be declared a lunatic; but the doctor, having made his examination, says that Staps is of sound mind.

"I told you so," says Friedrich.

The Emperor is uneasy. He is loath to make an end of so frank and bold a youth. He has not to do here with a partisan, with a conspiracy, with one who is out to destroy a principle; he has not to do with an ideologue, but with an idealist. Germany has sent forth against him a Brutus with a long knife.

"You are distraught. You are bringing affliction on your family. Ask my forgiveness, and say you are sorry. Then I will grant you your life!"

Never before has Napoleon spoken thus, at any rate to an assassin. The young man remains steadfast. Has Napoleon lost the power of suggestion? "Well?"

"I do not want your forgiveness, and I am not sorry. My only regret is that I have failed."

The Emperor grows angry.

"The devil! A crime means nothing to you, then?"

"To kill you would not be a crime, but a public service," says Staps, still perfectly respectful, indeed, thoroughly well-bred.

"Hm. Whose portrait is this?"

"The girl I love."

"Will she approve this attempt of yours?"

"She will be sorry it has miscarried, for she hates you as much as I do."

"What a pretty girl," thinks the Emperor looking at the miniature in his hand. "Am I really to be baffled by this young fellow? No, I will save him, will pardon him. What does it matter to me if he hates me?" Still holding the miniature, he looks Staps squarely in the face: "If I pardon you, I suppose it will gladden the heart of this girl?"

Friedrich's blue eyes flash, and he says firmly:

"Then I shall be able to kill you after all!"

The Emperor turns away, and leaves the prisoner to his doom. To Champagny, who is present, he talks for a long time about the Illuminates. Then, with a sudden transition he says:

"We must make peace. Drive back into the town. Summon the Austrians. We are practically agreed on the main points, and the only trouble relates to the war indemnity. The difference amounts to fifty millions. Reduce the demand by half. Get the matter settled. I was satisfied with the last draft. Add whatever clauses you think necessary. I leave everything in your hands. Make peace."

So great is the impression wrought by the youth. We cannot call it alarm. Caution is too mild a word. The trouble is that a shadow has fallen across his soul. After negotiating for three months, the Emperor, simply that he may save one day, leaves the conclusion of the peace to his minister. He has Staps examined once more, but the enthusiast prefers death to recantation. Next morning at six, the minister brings the treaty which has been arranged during the night. The Emperor, well content, praises his minister.

The same morning, the assassin is shot, and the Emperor returns to the topic: "The thing is unprecedented! So young a man, a German, a Protestant, well brought up; and such a crime! How did he meet his end?" The answer is that Staps, in face of the firing squad, had cried in loud tones. "Liberty for ever! Death to the tyrant!" The Emperor holds his peace.

Napoleon commands that the long German knife shall be brought back with him to Paris.

XXII

The Empress Josephine is lying in a swoon on the floor, Napoleon summons the palace prefect, and orders him to bear her to her chamber. The Emperor goes in front, carrying a lighted candle. Since the staircase is narrow, he passes the candlestick to a servant, and helps Bausset to carry Josephine. He carefully lays her on her bed, and, in a state of great excitement, leaves the room. Hardly is he out of sight, when the empress opens her eyes; cries and fainting-fit were all the pretence! Bausset betrayed her secret later, stating that, as he carried her up the stairs, she had whispered that he was holding her too tightly, and was hurting her.

All the same, fear and sorrow are in very truth her portion, for she has been informed that she must leave the Tuileries, where, for more than a decade, she has ruled as queen. The Emperor himself has broken the news to her. Matters cannot continue as in the past; everyone is counting on his death: across the frontier are the Germans with their long knives; here at home is Fouché, colloguing with the English. Napoleon needs a son; and his son must be the child of a princess of royal blood. The scene with Josephine took place shortly after his return from Schönbrunn. Probably he was feeling sore because he could not place his Polish love, who bore his child in her womb, straight away upon the throne. For a certainty, he did not as yet know the name of his future bride.

Mother, sister, brothers, are sitting in silence, with stony face, round the table, in family conclave: Josephine is likewise present. She can detect the smothered joy in the minds of these witnesses who at last have gained their end. The "old woman" must go! With uncontrolled emotion in his voice, the Emperor declares that all hope of an heir from the empress is quenched, and that it is solely on this account that he must part from her. "God alone knows how hard a step this is for me to take.... But no sacrifice is too great for the sake of France.... For fifteen years, the empress has made my life beautiful by her presence. She was crowned by my own hands. ... I have determined that she shall preserve the rank and the title of empress; and, above all, that she shall look upon me as her lifelong friend." Josephine exercises admirable self-control, but asks the arch-chancellor to read her words of acquiescence.

The memorandum concerning the divorce is then signed by all. Napoleon's signature is more legible than usual. It is vigorous, and a long, firm flourish underlines his full name: he thus brings a very serious matter to a close, in manly fashion. Nervously, Josephine adds her signature to the right of his, quite near, as though pleading for his support. Madame Mere writes her M. as her son has written his N., and follows him, likewise, in the concluding flourish.

That night, Josephine makes an amazing entry into his room, and approaches his bed, tears streaming down her face, and her hair falling round her shoulders. Nest day, supported by Napoleon, a veritable Niobe, she quits the palace and drives to Malmaison. Before leaving, however, she has (foolishly perhaps) besought Méneval to speak of her as often as possible to the Emperor.

Napoleon went alone to Trianon, which was at this time unoccupied. There he held a death watch such as no lover had ever held before over the love from whom he was to be eternally severed; he remained there for three days, absolutely inactive–this being as great an achievement as if a Buddhist holy man had for three days done Napoleon's work! He received no one, he dictated never a word, read nothing, noted down nothing; for three days the mighty wheel stood still, the wheel which for fifteen years had rotated by the strength of its own impetus. Soon afterwards he visited his divorced lady at her house in Malmaison. Then he wrote to her:

"I found you today in a worse condition of mind than I had hoped, mon amie.... You should not give yourself up to so profound a melancholy. Take good care of your health, which is so dear to me. If you love me, then show me how strong and happy you can be. You cannot doubt my fondness, or all the tenderness I feel for you. You cannot believe that I shall ever be happy if you are unhappy.... I was very sad when I got back to the Tuileries; the great palace seemed so empty; I felt so lonely.... Farewell, chère amie; sleep soundly, and remember that I wish it thus...." After fifteen years of intimate association, the man of forty writes in so natural and so grateful a fashion–though at the same time we may detect a gentle hint of a determined will that commands.

Then come endless calculations: he will allow her three millions per annum; the set of rubies he will pay extra for: "this will cost me quite four hundred thousand francs and I will have it valued, for I do not wish to be cheated by the jeweller.... In the wardrobe at Malmaison you should find five to six hundred thousand francs. You can take this money in order to increase your silver plate and your underclothing. I have ordered a beautiful china service for you, but I have told the makers to await your commands, for I wish it to be really lovely.... The page who saw you this morning, tells me you were weeping.... I shall take my meals all by myself.... Have you really lost courage since going to Malmaison? And yet that house has been the witness of our happiness, and our feelings for one another. These feelings must never change; nor can they, at least as far as I am concerned.... I should so much like to pay you a visit; but first I must know if you are a valiant woman or a weakling. I am rather weak myself, and am suffering greatly. Farewell, Josephine. Good night."

A melting mood has once more taken possession of him. The tone resembles that of the passionate letters sent from Milan by the young general to his faithless wife in Paris. It is set in a minor key; and the same melody that surged up and soared above the whole orchestra of his senses in those days, is now played by the cello as a solo echoing through the desolate halls of the Tuileries.

Shortly after this, a masked ball was given by the arch-chancellor. Among the guests was Princess Metternich, whose husband had formerly been envoy at the court of Paris. A man clad in a green domino took her by the arm and led her aside. Everyone knew who he was, for although no one fully knew Napoleon unmasked, the masked Napoleon was impossible to mistake: the tragi-comedy of genius in this world. After a few quips, he asked her whether she thought that an archduchess would accept the offer of his hand.

"I do not know, Sire."

"Were you in the archduchess' place, would you accept the offer?"

"I should certainly refuse it," says the Viennese lady with a smile.

"How unkind! Will you write to your husband, to ask his views on the matter?"

"I think you had better say that to Prince Schwarzenberg, Sire; he is the envoy now."

Thus with one of his improvisations does Napoleon begin his new wooing after the divorce. It is a splendid return to the straightforwardness of the revolution. The same evening, he instructs Eugene, who next morning approaches the Austrian ambassador. None of the Habsburg clan understands promptness and simplicity in such campaigns; but to the Emperor these qualities come naturally. The tsar makes no sign. Vienna, beaten in four wars, must at length be pacified. What could be more obvious than this solution? Why get a divorce if you do not forthwith do your utmost to attain the unattainable?

The Corsican family feeling is at work once more. He, who so rarely holds a council of war, summons a family council before the divorce and before the marriage. There they sit just as six weeks earlier, round the oval table; all the great dignitaries are there; according to the report of one of those present, general embarrassment prevails. The Emperor announces his desire for an heir, and then speaks with an assumption of dubiety:

"Were it possible for me to be guided by personal feelings alone, I should choose my bride out of the circle of the Legion of Honour, from among the daughters of the heroes of France, and should make the worthiest of Frenchwomen empress of the French. But a man must adapt his actions to the customs of his own century, to the usage of other States, to political considerations. Many sovereigns have sought my alliance, and I do not think there is any reigning house to which I cannot propose this personal tie. Three of them have now to be considered: the Austrian, the Russian, and the Saxon, I should like to hear your views."

Thus does the curse of legitimacy break once more into the mighty dictator's private preserve. Legitimacy is the rock on which he will be shipwrecked. Why should he not choose Countess Walewska whom he loves? Or, if the empress is to be a Frenchwoman, why not a daughter of one of those heroes to whom he has given kingdoms? He has shaken the old world to its foundations; has with his own hands placed two crowns on his head; has kept kings of ancient lineage waiting in his anterooms; has dethroned one such, and placed an innkeeper's son upon the vacant throne. Has he done all these things that today, debarred from the choice of the woman of his heart, on the prowl for an heir, he must "adapt his actions to the customs of his own century" – customs which hitherto he has defied like a demigod?

But no such unconventional possibilities are discussed in these cold, imperial halls, for one and all are against a Frenchwoman. Eugene and Talleyrand are for Austria. Murat demurs, saying that Marie Antoinette had brought bad luck to France. Some voice the advantages of a Russian alliance, others favour Saxony. The Emperor listens to their views, closes the sitting, and does what he has already made up his mind to do. That same evening he sends a message to Vienna. The only one present at the council who saw clearly was the minister who had strongly urged the claims of Russia, but who did not venture to utter his real reasons except in private: "Within two years, we shall certainly be at war with both the monarchies with whose ruling house the Emperor does not ally himself by marriage–and Austria is the only one of the three a war with which would not be dangerous!"

By the Emperor's instructions, the court of St. Petersburg is informed that he has been kept waiting too long. Furthermore, it would be inconvenient to have a priest of the Russian Orthodox Church in the Tuileries. Finally, he has been informed "that Grand Duchess Anna, who is fifteen years old, is not yet ripened to womanhood, Inasmuch as, in young girls, two years elapse between the appearance of the first signs of womanhood and complete maturity, this will not suit the aims of the Emperor, who does not wish to be married for three years before he can have a child." This gynaecological excursus is the last we hear of the Russian wooing which had begun so inauspiciously in Erfurt.

But the Habsburgs are a prolific family, so that he may regard an Austrian princess as practically guaranteed against barrenness. When he learns that the mother of his chosen bride has given birth to thirteen children, that one of her ancestresses has had seventeen, and another actually twenty-six, the Emperor exclaims: "That's the kind of womb I want to marry!" There could be no doubt about the answer to his proposal; Francis would

description," writes Metternich to Vienna. At this early stage, the empress' condition is solemnly announced to the Senate and the nation; prayers for the successor to the throne are to be said; there is to be a festival of rejoicing as sumptuous as those of pagan times.

When the lovely Walewska arrives, he gives her everything she can ask for; sees the baby and fondles it; makes it a count of the Empire, with the chancellor for guardian. But nothing beyond this unites the sometime lovers. Napoleon has become a respectable married man.

In all respects, now, this man's career seems to be transcending familiar limitation, outstepping traditional horizons. Thus among the women who have crossed his path new relationships begin. The Polish countess, whose eyes Josephine would at one time have been glad to scratch out, is invited to Malmaison. Walewska brings Josephine Napoleon's son, that son whose absence from her own womb decided Josephine's fate. See the group on the terrace. One of them is a grey-headed woman, who was born in the West Indies, had a taste of prison, and then became empress of the French. The other, young and blooming, was brought up in an impoverished Polish noble family, was married off to a wealthy old man, and was then switched into a new career through Napoleon's chance glimpse of her at a ball. Between them is the child or the man who had loved both and forsaken both, that he might compel a stupid little Habsburg girl to immortalise a name which had long ere this immortalised itself.

When the empress' hour comes, he has to make a choice great as destiny itself. Paris knows, France knows, that the young wife is in labour. All are waiting for the heir; enemies are dreading him before he is born; the common people, who at such moments are always dynastically inclined, are praying for mother and child. Throughout the night Napoleon has been watching by his wife's bedside, but has withdrawn for a time. The accoucheur brings him dread tidings: "The child is in a bad position; there is danger to the life of both mother and infant!"

The whole structure of his dynastic schemes is tottering. What will he say, this man of iron, when the doctor asks whether the first thought is to be for the mother or for the child? Will he not answer that, before all, it is necessary to save the child, for whose first cry millions besides Napoleon are waiting? What does Marie Louise matter? When she has borne him a healthy boy, she will have fulfilled her earthly mission. Surely the Emperor can have no choice?

"Do exactly what you would do if an ordinary citizen's wife were in labour. The mother's life comes first!"

Two hours later, however, the baby has been born, and the mother is in good case. With rapt attention, Paris counts the cannon shots. Nineteen, twenty, twenty-one—so far, it may only be a girl. But when the twenty-second gun booms out, the whole city is in a frenzy of delight. The crowd surrounding the old Bourbon palace cheers madly. The salute is still thundering. The little lieutenant of artillery stands by the window mechanically noting the calibre of the guns from the pitch of the gun-fire, glancing down upon the mutable many without–while his thoughts reach far back into the past, and roam yet farther forward into the future.

The groom-of-the-chambers sees that there are tears in the cold, grey-blue eyes.

BOOK FOUR

THE SEA

It is essential that this man shall be ruined! ... But since, here below everything takes place by natural causes, the daimons trip him: thus, in the end, even Napoleon is overthrown.

—GOETHE

I

THE old struggle in Napoleon's mind between mathematics and fantasy had ripened. The issue of the struggle was now to decide the history of his world domination.

For now, at the climax of his career, fortified by his ties with the Habsburgs, ties for whose sake he had broken the familiar associations of years of married life; fortified by having a legitimate heir, whose birth gave firm anchorage to his adventurer's dynasty; having gained the mastery over conspiracies, and having learned to dominate all the political parties– he was once more free as he had been eleven years earlier, when the victory of Marengo had safeguarded the tranquillity he needed for the internal development of France. True, England was unconquered; but Russia seemed still friendly. True, Spain was uncoerced; but Europe from Reggio to Hammerfest was allied to France, this being a euphemism for dependence on France. For the last time in his life, he was free to make a great decision.

Had he been nothing more than a mathematician, he would have been content with his calculations within the resuscitated realm of Charlemagne, and dreams of world dominion would have yielded place before the reality of the United States of Europe under France's leadership. Had he been nothing but a visionary, he would have aimed, like a new Alexander, to march towards the Ganges; and England would have been merely a pretext for his onslaught on India. But he was both mathematician and visionary, and was therefore in danger of disavowing himself. For, as calculator, he failed to grasp an eminently real factor which could not be expressed in figures. The moods of un-uniformed men in Spain and in Germany could play no part in the cipherings of a military commander who thought in terms of army corps and big guns. Nevertheless such moods should have come within the scope of his visions as a seer!

Thus during these decisive years, after the birth of his heir, and before his next warlike designs have become active, his mind is alternately dominated by his two fundamental impulses, and the whole future depends upon which of the two will be supreme when the moment for action comes. Will his awakened fantasy warn him that it is dangerous to brave the anger of exasperated peoples, or will his calculating faculty disclose to him the danger that will await him on the distant road to the East? What will happen should he err in both respects? Then, indeed, his whole world will go up in flames.

He feels that his powers are ripening. In addition to the two energies we have been considering, a third is growing to maturity, the sense of destiny. Word unheard before, or rarely expressed, now find voice: "I feel that I am being driven towards an unknown goal. But as soon as I have reached it, as soon as I no longer have an inexorable mission an atom will suffice to overthrow me. Till then, no human powers can effect anything against me. The days are numbered."

Truly they are numbered; and through these prophetic words there already breathes the foreboding of an exit, although he does not know the way thither. Now, on the path towards the tragical catastrophe, the clarity of his inner vision is dimmed. Yet he himself speaks of the campaign against Russia as the "fifth act," though the full significance of the term is not apparent to him. Tones like those of his youthful days resound in the new harmony. "I have got to the end of everything," he had said when he was thirty, on the Nile. Now, at forty-three, he declares in the Council of State: "All this will last as long as I do, and no longer. Perhaps when I am dead, my son will think himself well off if he can be sure of an income of forty thousand francs a year."

But at the same time his ardour increases. Since those days when it seemed to him that (thanks to the acceleration of genius) he had got to the end of everything, since the days of the Egyptian campaign, he had been guided by a religious faith that it was his destiny to become a second Alexander. Now, when for the first time he is equipped with means for the carrying out of his design, is he to annihilate his dream by figures, which are not more potent in the world than dreams? When the arch-chancellor wishes him a happy new year, he answers, as if suddenly rejuvenated: "I must grow wise if you are to be able to repeat this greeting thirty years hence."

Napoleon never grew wise, but he was always clever. When he finds that his commercial warfare is reacting to the detriment of his own Country, he disregards his own prohibitions, and grants licenses for the import of certain raw materials and dyes from England, in part because they are urgently needed for French industry and in part because the articles in question are among the requirements of Parisian luxury. Soon, in all continental countries, huge sums are made by smugglers who import the very colonial produce which the Emperor wishes to prevent his chief enemy from marketing. These goods are then retailed at a great profit. Is the smartest dealer in Europe to be robbed of his gains by smugglers? He would rather have the business under his own control, so he imposes a fifty per cent duty on all the colonial produce his agents can find on the Continent, and pouches these receipts for France. Since at the same time he had all English woollen textiles that he can lay hands on burned, he opens opportunities for illicit gains which are so large that for their sake people will ignore the risks of draconian punishments. He has to carry on a guerrilla warfare, just as in Spain, though this time he is fighting the nation of shopkeepers with trade weapons.

It is likewise a war of decrees. Since Paris has prohibited all trading in English wares, London reciprocates by demanding from all neutral countries enhanced dues for permission to call at the blockaded ports. Paris counters this move by declaring that the vessels of neutrals which shall call at the ports of London or of Malta, run the risk of capture as prizes. London responds by sending her ships out under false colours, and Paris thereupon has all merchantmen trading in Mediterranean waters overhauled and searched. The American government forbids its citizens to have business dealings with Europe, or even to have any private intercourse with the Continent; but the Emperor promises all kinds of privileges to the Americans if they will cease to call at English ports. So paradoxical is the situation resulting from the endeavour to strangle overseas trade, by which Napoleon had hoped to extort the freedom of the seas!

The Emperor's hopes are rising. The English pound sterling is still quoted at seventeen francs, the English banks are failing, and in parliament the opposition is against the continuance of the war. In spite of this, his peace proposals are rejected. The disturbances in Spain are at once the cause and the consequence of England's defiant attitude.

There is still an army numbering a quarter million men stationed in Spain; and despite all endeavours, Wellington's thirty thousand are not driven out, for the bands of native insurrectionaries led by officers and monks carry on unceasing guerrilla warfare against the French invaders. The Emperor's quarrel with the Pope stiffens the antagonism of the monks. While French children on the northern slopes of the Pyrenees are being taught that Napoleon is God's vicegerent, Spanish children on the southern slopes are learning that the Emperor is the devil incarnate and that the murder of the Frenchman is a deed pleasing to the Almighty.

In so fanatical a land, where hardly any regular troops are left for the French to fight against, Napoleon's generals feel out of their element. Disunion prevails. Massena is sent against Portugal. At the same time, Napoleon deprives Joseph of four provinces. When the king journeys to Paris to demand the cancelling of the decree, the Emperor declares that his brother has ceded these lands. Napoleon places a general to administer each province, and appoints a marshal in supreme command. He carries out this Roman system of ruling through military governors thus ruthlessly and persistently because of his intense disappointment in the rule of the members of his family to whom he was allotted crowns, and, above all, in the behaviour of his brothers. Terrible battles, made more ghastly by famine and disease, are meanwhile forcing Massena to retreat. The Emperor, in a fury, recalls him.

Will Napoleon at length realise that his presence is essential? Marshals, officers, and, above all, the rank and file of the army, eagerly await his coming. Full well does he know this; and yet he does not go. Does he fear assassination at the hands of some fanatical Spaniard? Or is it treachery at home that deters him; such conspiracies as those which called him back to Paris so suddenly when he was encamped near Astorga? Is he to get enmeshed in this southern corner of his empire at the moment when the whole is at stake? What is Spain to him? He chooses the oldest of his companions-in-arms: Marmont is sent to clear up the mess and bring the campaign to an end.

The second kingly brother had, with good reason, thrown up his job. Napoleon had deprived him of all the Dutch territory on the left bank of the Rhine; had insisted upon the removal of the rest of the protective duties against France; and (this was the worst of all) had angered the Dutch, who are traders and seamen, by the measures he had compelled them to take against England. The Emperor had expected both his brothers to run counter to the currents of national feeling in their respective kingdoms, understanding alike the strength of popular sentiment and the sense of honour of the two men he had forced to become monarchs. It would have been easier for military governors to cope with the rising tide of nationalism and to dispense with a feeling of obligation towards the people they ruled, than it was for kings burdened with historic crowns.

When Louis found it impossible to put up any longer with the Emperor's tutelage, he abdicated in favour of his younger son, and fled by night from his kingdom for an unrevealed destination. Napoleon's catchpolls sought him far and wide in Europe, to discover him at length in Austria. The Emperor was greatly enraged, yet he could not but see that he was himself more to blame than Louis. He therefore made no attempt to punish, but sent his own body physician to care for the fugitive, who had excused the flight on the ground of illness. To his mother, the

Emperor wrote saying that there were tidings of Louis' whereabouts. "You need not be anxious; but his conduct has been of a kind which can only be explained by his illness. Your very affectionate son, Napoleon."

The wording of this subscription stands out among the numberless letters in which the dictator of Europe was accustomed to express his will to those who usually received these missives with trembling. The fugitive king, meanwhile, drawing a breath of relief, settled down to a literary life in Graz, writing in three volumes under the title *Marie, ou les peines d'amour* (1808), the story of the love affair which the Emperor had so ruthlessly frustrated. But when Joseph wished to follow Louis' example, feeling that he would rather retire into private life than continue to play the part of king in a pack of cards, he was restrained from abdication by the iron hand of the Emperor. Napoleon considered that his democratically inclined brother would do more mischief as an intriguer in Paris than in his position as nominal chief and military commander; so Joseph had once more to put his hand to the task of war, for which, to the Emperor's great annoyance, he was utterly unfitted.

The most frivolous members of the family, Jerome and Pauline, were amusing themselves with love affairs. Murat and Caroline were immersed over head and ears in old and new intrigues. As for Elise, she had so much printed in the Tuscan newspapers anent her reviews and hunting parties that the Emperor was even more annoyed by her craze for notoriety than by the things she actually did, and wrote to her, saying: "Europe pays very little heed to what the grand duchess of Tuscany is doing."

The most dangerous man in his family circle has not yet become an object of his menaces. Since the old king of Sweden was on friendly terms with England, the Emperor had made him abdicate in favour of an uncle; and the new ruler, who is devoted to the cause of Napoleon, has declared war against England. Being old and childless, he thinks he cannot please the Emperor better than by appointing as successor one who is closely connected with Napoleon by marriage. Thus it is that Bernadotte, Joseph's brother-in-law, who during the wars has made friends in Swedish Pomerania, is unexpectedly nominated crown prince of Sweden–as a result of a complicated intrigue, in which Fouché has played a considerable part. The Emperor would have Ffund it difficult, in any case, to object to this selection of a French general as heir to a foreign throne; and it was practically impossible for him to interfere with the promotion of his sometime rival, the man who had nearly prevented the coup d'état of the Eighteenth Brumaire, and had subsequently become the husband of the woman whom Napoleon had once thought of marrying. "A good soldier," growled the Emperor; "but with no talent for ruling; one of the old Jacobins, with a bee in his bonnet like the rest of them, and therefore he will never be able to keep his position on a throne.... Still, I could not interfere, were it only because it would be impossible to do anything more effective against the English than to set a French marshal upon the throne of Gustavus Adolphus.... I am glad to be quit of him."

Is he really so carefree? Hitherto these folk whom he cannot trust have always been kept under his own eyes in Paris.

Bernadotte triumphants! Soon, at last, he too will wear a crown, and will not even have to thank this detested Bonaparte for the gift. To Napoleon, therefore, who till yesterday was Bernadotte's supreme war lord, the crown prince of Sweden now writes a bitter-sweet letter, offering soldiers and iron, but asking for money. The Emperor smiles. He knows what is written between the lines, and makes no direct answer. He has Bernadotte informed that he does not correspond with royal princes. His old opponent will not forget the gibe. In less than two years, Bernadotte will take vengeance for it, and for all that has gone before!

Ruefully, the Emperor watches the flames that are springing up everywhere, the flames his family mania has lighted. He does not conceal from his intimates that he is disappointed with his kin and his nobles. Writing to one of them at this time, Napoleon says: "I ought never to have had Murat and my brothers crowned. Live and learn!... It was a mistake, too, to give back the confiscated estates to the émigres. I should have kept the lands as State domains, and have been content to allow the former owners a modest income. I can't stomach them, these people of the old regime; their light and airy graces are out of keeping with my serious temperament. I myself did not succeed to a heritage, but was content to take what belonged to no one. I ought to have been satisfied with the appointment of governors and viceroys. Some of my marshals, even, are beginning to dream of greatness and independence."

At length he has realised that it is dangerous to play the emperor! His troubles are the fruit of his wish to safeguard a dynasty (this meaning that the spirits of revolt and of genius, from whose union Napoleon has sprung, are to be taught to walk in the paths of legitimate mediocrity). They are the outcome of the weak moments of a man who in his hours of strength believed in the immortality of deed and of fame, of a man who in these hours of strength felt no need of the perpetuation that is achieved by means of family line. The brothers, and brothers-in-law, and marshals, who all shine by reflected light, will take vengeance ere long. When his star pales, and the skies of Europe are overcast, they will still try to shine across the Continent in the afterglow of his splendour!

Deeply ingrained in him was the illusion that his good fortune would be transmitted to his son. When, after the boy's birth, a great reception was held, and all the notables came to offer congratulations, the Schwarzenbergs were among the guests. Schwarzenberg, as Austrian envoy in Paris, had done much to promote the marriage. The Emperor, full of gratitude, went up to Princess Schwarzenberg and, taking from his coat a scarab pin, presented it to her, saying:

"I found this scarab in the tomb of an Egyptian king, and have worn it ever since as a talisman. Please accept it; I no longer need such a mascot."

He feels that the birth of his son has placed him above all possibility of danger, and that everything will go well with him in future. He can have no further need for an amulet!

These kings, these brothers, have been but a substitute for the sons that were lacking. How, when he can feast his eyes on a son of his body, he recognises his mistake, and the disastrous consequences of Josephine's barrenness are plainer than ever. Too many battles have been fought, too many years have passed, there has been too much self-restraint and self-denial, for it to be possible now to give this heir a great place in his system. The boy has been born too late. The tempo of Napoleon's life has been so rapid. The man who at two-and-twenty was still a lieutenant, had become an emperor at thirty-four. Such a man should have had his first-born son long before the age of forty-one. He has recklessly expended his vital energies, and cannot look forward confidently to many years of power. How can he reasonably expect to establish the child securely as his successor?

It is, indeed, a poignant sight. Watch this man who is now growing old with fearful speed, as he dandles the long-desired infant on his knees, tries his own hat on the baby's head, watches the child crawling on the floor while he sits at breakfast, and even (when the youngster grows a little older) allows him to run about the study. Napoleon is playing the war game, with little wooden rods representing soldiers dispersed over the floor, and is planning how to make an end of Wellington in Spain. The boy is brought to the door. According to the rule of the house, the governess may not cross the threshold, so Napoleon himself goes to the door for the child, sets him down among the mimic armies, and, with the tolerance of a grandfather, lets the child play riot with the battle. Laughing, he pulls faces at his infant son in front of the looking-glass; buckles round the body of the two-year-old sword with which he has conquered Europe; and, with his actor's instincts. feels that the boundaries between jest and earnest are being broken down. Imaginings are ripening into reality, while all that has seemed to him real is not more than an image and a parable.

He says that the child is "spirited and sensitive. Just what I want him to be.... My son is sturdy, and in splendid health. He has my lungs, my mouth, and my eyes.... I do hope he will turn out well." In such simple fashion he writes to Josephine, and to her

my sceptre from God. But I wear a worldly sword, and know how to use it! God erects thrones. I did not raise myself to my throne: God set me upon it! You poor mortals wish to resist? You will not pray for your monarch, because the priest of Rome has excommunicated him? Do you think I am the sort of man to kiss the Pope's toe? ... Prove to me, imbeciles, that Jesus has appointed the Pope his vicegerent, and that the Pope has power to excommunicate the monarch! ... Be good citizens, and sign the Concordat. You, Mr. Prefect, must take such measures as will prevent my hearing any more of these matters."

To so preposterous a travesty of his own innermost thoughts has Napoleon come. He does not believe a word of what he is here thundering out; and in private mocks at this official doctrine, as he has always done. Nonetheless, to the circlet of golden laurels with which he had crowned himself before the eyes of the priest of Rome, there now attaches a vestige of divine right which makes the crown a heavy one to wear.

II

"Kindly inform me why the price of salt in the neighbourhood of Strasburg has risen one sou."

Closely following upon the heels of this enquiry to the Ministry for War, comes a command to the Admiralty: two entire fleets are to be constructed in the course of the next three years, one Atlantic fleet and one Mediterranean fleet; the latter against Sicily and Egypt, the former against Ireland. As soon as the Spanish affair is in better case, preparations are to be made for an expedition to the Cape in 1812. An army of from sixty to eighty thousand men is to be got ready for an attack on Surinam and Martinique. "Having eluded the enemy cruisers," the expeditionary forces are to share out the two hemispheres.

We see how closely at this date, when imaginative fantasies threaten to develop into adventures, the exact observations of the father of his country are allied to the rhapsodical plans of the world conqueror. For that is what Napoleon now attempts; he is actually trying to realise his old dream of world conquest.

"You want to know whither we are going? We shall have done with Europe; then, as robbers of robbers less bold than ourselves, we shall march to the attack, seize India, over which they have made themselves masters.... I must take India... in the rear, if I am to strike successfully at England.... Just imagine Moscow occupied, the tsar conciliated or killed by his people, perhaps a new, dependent throne,–and tell me whether an army of Frenchmen, reinforced by auxiliary troops from Tiflis, cannot press forward to the Ganges, and thence, at the touch, destroy the whole structure of English commerce! ... At one blow, France would have established the independence of the West and the freedom of the seas!" A witness reports that while he was voicing these ideas "his eyes shone with a wonderful light, and he went on to point out the reasons for the adventure, all the difficulties it entailed, the means of achievement, and the prospects of success."

Shall the tsar be conciliated or killed? That is the question which troubles the Emperor the whole year round. Calculations and presentiments make him desire to have Alexander as his friend rather than his enemy. Napoleon has nothing to gain by a defeat of Russia. On the contrary! He dreads being forced into this war, and endeavours, as on former occasions, to avoid it; though only if the tsar, as previously agreed, shall participate in the great final struggle as an ally. Napoleon keeps the tsar under observation, and perceives that suggestions are having less and less effect upon Alexander. He therefore writes to a prince of the Confederation of the Rhine in these amazing terms: "This war will break out in spite of the tsar, in spite of me, and in spite of the interest of the two empires."

Never before had the Emperor or the Consul declared, in such words, that war was unavoidable. Precisely because all rational need for the campaign was lacking this time, he found it necessary to proclaim the war with the tsar to be the work of fate. At the very first handclasp, in the peace tent on the Memel, the seed of this war was sown. During the days of intimacy which followed, when the encounter blossomed into friendship, that seed invisibly took root and grew. In later days, Talleyrand's treacherous diplomacy cherished its growth; and when, at Erfurt, the emperors embraced, they could already feel between them the coils of the snake. That they did not become related by marriage was neither an accident nor the outcome of a conscious desire: it was consequent upon the mistrust which had invaded the tsar's mind, a mistrust of which he could not rid himself and which was to prove well founded. Two men wishing to divide Europe between then, could not see with complacency the half in a rival's hands. Their intentions were honourable at the outset; but they were impossible of fulfilment. The day of contest must inevitably come at last. "He alone is still weighing upon the pinnacle of my edifice. My rival is young; daily his strength is waxing, daily mine is waning." This gloomy recognition spurs him ever onward.

It is useless to try to interpret such decrees of destiny as the outcome of political causes.

Somewhat earlier, the Emperor has asked the tsar to lay an embargo on all neutral ships, as he himself has done, and thus give England the death-blow. The tsar cannot agree to this, for it would fatally injure his own sea-borne trade; he will only continue, as before, to confiscate all the prohibited goods he discovers, but he needs colonial wares from the neutrals. Being unable to stop this leak in the East, the Emperor has to exercise redoubled care on the German coast, and he therefore annexes the mouths of the Weser and the Elbe with the Hansa towns and part of Hanover. "Circumstances demand these new guarantees against England." Oldenburg is swallowed up with the rest, though the heir to this duchy has married Alexander's sister.

The Emperor's high-handed proceedings were a logical outcome of his policy, but they were necessarily an offence to the tsar. Alexander regarded them as a breach of the treaty of Tilsit, in which the integrity of Oldenburg had been guaranteed. He issued a circular to the powers protesting against this insult to his house, a remonstrance almost equivalent to a declaration of war. In this document he enquired what could be the use of alliances unless the treaties in which they were incorporated were strictly observed, so that the cabinets of Europe could not but smile at the concluding words of the circular, in which he described the alliance between Russia and France as permanent. His next step was a ukase in which he threw Russia open to colonial goods, while imposing prohibitive import duties on wine and silk, the products of French industry.

The maps lie spread on the tables in St. Petersburg and Paris. Where can either power best harass the other? The tsar proposes to make peace with Turkey. The Emperor incites Austria to seize Serbia, to advance towards Moldavia and Wallachia, promising not to interfere; this will keep Alexander busy. Metternich nods assent, but does not move. "What about Poland?" thinks Alexander. "Has not Napoleon already enlarged the duchy of Warsaw by the addition of Galicia? Is there any guarantee that he will not re-establish the kingdom of Poland?" Caulaincourt, French ambassador in Russia, who admires the tsar and wants peace, gives the desired guarantees. But the Emperor would only agree to a secret ratification. If the differences between France and Russia should culminate in war, he will need Poland for his operations against the tsar; Polish hopes must, therefore, be fostered. Penetrating this design, Alexander demands an open treaty, which shall put an end to Polish expectations.

When Masséna is defeated in Spain, the Emperor entertains fresh doubts. Caulaincourt, who is back in Paris, does his utmost to intensify these misgivings, dilates on the tsar's will-to-peace, and ventures far in his defence of Alexander. The Emperor leads him on; hears all he has to say; asks a thousand questions concerning the tsar and the court, Alexander's piety, the nobles, and the peasants; takes Caulaincourt by the ear, a sign of affability.

"You must be in love with him!"

"I am in love with peace."

"So am I. But I will not allow anyone to dictate to me. Evacuate Danzing, forsooth! Next I shall have to ask Alexander's permission before I can hold a review in Mainz. You are a fool. I am an old fox, and know the people with whom I am dealing.... We must deprive this Russian colossus and his hordes of the power to inundate the south once more.... I shall advance northwards, and re-establish there the old boundaries of Europe."

Quite unsubstantial reasons, masks, mere pretexts. Warningly Caulaincourt quotes Alexander's words: "I shall lean from his own teachings, which are those of a master. Our climate will make war for us. The French are not inured to it as we are. Miracles only happen when the Emperor is present, and he cannot be everywhere." Napoleon is greatly moved by these words; he tramps restlessly up and down the room; the conversation lasts for hours. Since he cannot refute Caulaincourt's arguments, he makes vague answers behind which his titanic wishes loom.

"A well-fought battle will put an end to the fine resolves of your friend Alexander.... He is false, ambitious, and weak; he has the character of a Greek. Believe me, it is he, not I, who wants this war, for he cherishes a hidden design..... He is out of humour because I did not take his sister." When Caulaincourt gives proofs to the contrary, Napoleon says: "I have forgotten the details." – Forgotten! This is a new word in the Emperor's mouth. He knows his position to be weak; himself a man of fact, he now brushes away those which he finds inconvenient.

He sends a more resolute envoy to the tsar. When a proposal comes from St. Petersburg that Warsaw shall be exchanged for Oldenburg, the Emperor says threateningly to the Russian ambassador, raising his voice so that everyone in the room may hear: "Not one Polish village!"

But these political incidents and discussions are merely the forms of destiny. Schemes flash like lightning through his brain; his soul is devoured by wishes: and he will rather reveal these things to a dangerous enemy like Fouché than to a shrewd adherent like Caulaincourt. He cannot rid himself of the ex-Jacobin and ex-cleric. Last year, he had cashiered the Minister of Police, for Fouché was obviously intriguing with England. But Napoleon was as lenient as he had been at the time of the conspiracy which had brought him back hot foot from Astorga. Instead of banishing the man, the Emperor had appointed him senator–at the same time writing to him words which give a glimpse into the inferno of these struggles between the monarch and the spy: "Although I do not doubt your devotion, I find it necessary to have you watched all the time. This is a fatiguing necessity, and I should not be called upon to do anything of the kind."

But though he dismisses Fouché from his ministerial post, and has the watcher watched, Napoleon cannot get on without him, and talks to him about the most private matters.

"Since my marriage, people fancy that the lion is asleep. They will soon learn whether I am asleep. I need eight hundred thousand men, and have them; I shall tow all Europe in my wake. Europe is nothing more than an old woman, and with my eight hundred thousand men I can make her do whatever I please.... Did not you yourself say to me: 'You let your genius have its way, because it does not know the word impossible.' How can I help it if a great power drives me on to become dictator of the world? You and the others, who criticise me today and would like me to become a good-natured ruler–have not you all been accessories? I have not yet fulfilled my mission, and I mean to end what I have begun. *We need a European legal code, a European court of appeal, a unified coinage, a common system of weights and measures. The same law must run throughout Europe. I shall fuse all the nations into one....* This, my lord duke, is the only solution that pleases me...." Having said this, he suddenly sends Fouché from the room.

Here we have it plainly disclosed, Napoleon's vision of the United States of Europe. The plan is recorded by one who, in his memoirs, would fain have discredited the Emperor–this plan with its extremely rational deductions and its daimonic inspiration. Europe is no longer a "mole-hill" as it was in the days of Milan and Rivoli, when he was nothing more that General Bonaparte, and when to the young man of genius all possible adversaries seemed too petty. Fifteen years later, Europe has become a plastic material; and Bonaparte is the emperor, the legislator, the great orderer, the enemy of the anarchy out of which he sprang, the modeller who would mould the clay into a splendid whole. Throughout the intervening years he has been marching along a predestined path; now he displays before us, in this statement of his aims, the productive consequences towards which he has been moving along that road of force through ever new hecatombs of slaughter. Behind him lie Charlemagne's visions of a united Europe; in front of him glide new forms, and Cæsar, half-way towards the realisation of his dream, is well aware that the spirit will ultimately overpower the sword. He has himself said this; and what he is now striving to establish by force with the aid of eight hundred thousand men, will some day come into existence as a voluntary amalgamation based upon reason and necessity. All the nations will fuse into one.

This, my lord duke, is the only solution that pleases me.

III

While Napoleon is pouring his thoughts into Fouché's ears. Alexander is pouring gold into Talleyrand's pockets, and no doubt Talleyrand is going shares with Fouché. The bank could have informed Napoleon to whom Count Nesselrode, the new secretary to the Russian embassy, was paying out such large sums of money. From month to month Talleyrand lets Russia know how the French preparations for war are advancing, and when they will be completed. The limping Mephistopheles must have smiled to himself, sometimes, when Russia paid him for his information with licences for the import of English goods into Russian harbours–documents which he could sell for hard cash in Paris!

Is the tsar richer than the Emperor? Russia is still allied to France, but the Russian market has been closed to French goods, and the famous 1811 vintage has one purchaser the less. Since England and Spain have long ceased to be customers, French industry is in a bad way. But when the Minister for Finance urges peace because tranquillity is essential to the restoration of French finances, the Emperor cuts him short by saying: "Not at all! It is true that our finances are disordered, but that is why we need war!"

This argument was valid in the past, when the general had sent from Italy the money which the indebted Directory needed, and when, as Consul and Emperor he had made money by his wars. The French State, suffering more than any other from the effects of the blockade it had itself established, showed a deficit for the first time, though the deficit amounted to hardly more than fifty millions. Yet, even now, the Emperor refused to sanction any kind of State loan; "that would be immoral, for it would lay a burden upon later generations." Nevertheless, he introduced indirect taxes and monopolies; nor did he act unwisely in doing so, since he expected to acquire fresh markets, and thereby more stable finances, from the Russian war. But victory was essential!

He enthusiastically lays his plans before the Chambers of Commerce. "England has harmed herself far more by her blockade than she has harmed any other country; she has taught us how to dispense with her products. In a couple of years' time, Europe will have adapted herself to the new ways of feeding her populations. Soon, we shall have more than enough beet sugar and shall be able to do without cane sugar.... Every year I draw only nine hundred millions revenue from my own country; three hundred millions I put away, and store in the cellars of the Tuileries. The Bank of France is full of silver; the Bank of England has none. Since the peace of Tilsit, I have received more than a milliard francs in indemnities. Austria is bankrupt. England and Russia will soon follow suit. I alone have money!"

All the same, no one has much faith in his fine words. The more the Emperor's plans for world conquest force the pace of recruiting, the more keenly does he keep watch upon the internal tranquillity of France. As the ruthlessness of his dictatorship increases, the mood of the citizens of France becomes gloomier and gloomier. Any criticism, even in the remotest corner of the realm, is immediately pounced upon and prosecuted. There are more than three thousand persons locked up in gaol without trial, because this one "hates the Emperor," or this other has certain "religious outlooks," or another has written, "in private letters, unfriendly expressions in regard to the government." A new press bureau, with the absurd name of "Bureau of Public Opinion," is established to manufacture political trends. When a Dutch newspaper publishes the statement that it is within the competence of the Pope to excommunicate kings, not only is the journal suppressed, but the author of the offending article is arrested. In a certain book, an appreciation of the English constitution has to be deleted; another work has to be rechristened "Campaigns of Napoleon the Great," whereas the author's original title had been "History of Bonaparte."

While oppression of thought is rampant, it is not inconsonant with the imperialistic spirit to find that such men as Monge and Laplace: Guérin and Gérard, are willing to accept baronial honours. And when the French version of *The robbers* is prohibited in Hamburg, the last of the republicans recall with ironical bitterness the day twenty years earlier when the revolution had conferred the right of French citizenship upon its German author.

What cares the Emperor for the mood of these ideologues? Under the spell of the evolution of his own powers, his eyes fixed upon the goal of his life's aspiration, he misjudges now, as earlier in his struggle with the Pope, the moral impression he is making upon his contemporaries. Yet in the past he had never failed to take this into account; at each step, he had questioned public opinion. Now, he allows the newfangled Bureau to manipulate public opinion: "What do I care for the opinion of the drawing-rooms and the babblers! I recognise only one opinion, that of the peasants!" Certain it is the peasants are his most faithful supporters, mainly because he rescued their lands from the dangers threatened by the revolution. Now that the Spanish war has swallowed up larger and larger armies the peasants have to pay eight thousand francs for a substitute, simply to save the few remaining sons to carry on the work of agriculture on the lands of their fathers. Many thousands of these young men are trying to evade service; and those who in the early days of the war would have joyfully rallied to the colours, have now to be rounded up by mobile columns or forced into the ranks by threats against their families and the communes to which they belong.

Why should the Emperor be surprised at such a change of mood? Had not General Bonaparte set out to carry the ideal of the revolution to the peoples groaning under the yoke of emperors and kings? Did not the First Consul go forth to repel in his one campaign, did not the Emperor likewise go forth to repel in his three wars, the ever-renewed onslaughts of the allied monarchs? That by wars thus forced upon him he won more than freedom for the land of his adoption, that by the battles of Austerlitz, Jena, and Wagram he obtained new provinces from the enemy, was the outcome of his genius, and encouraged the people's army to fresh deeds of valour. Even the rivalry with England was comprehensible to the French people; had it not been ever thus in the days of their fathers and grandfathers before them? But what could the peasant of Provence make of these purely political struggles in Spain and in Russia? The Emperor could not explain to him the plan for setting up a United States of Europe. Men had disappeared in the rivers of Andalusia, the names of which fell haltingly from a Frenchman's lips. The peasant needed the support of his son's young arm, now that the years were creeping onward. So it was that he purchased his son's freedom from military service, and growled as he paid.

What had the German peasants to say when, addressed as "contingents," they answered the call of their kings and accompanied the foreign Emperor into distant lands? Thousands of peasants from the valley of the Main were dispatched to Spain; Jerome sent thirty thousand Westphalians to the Oder; Saxons guarded the Vistula; Württembergers and Bavarians flowed in a steady stream eastward, for "if the princes of the Confederation of the Rhine" (thus writes the Emperor to one of these same princes) "give me the least cause to doubt their willingness to undertake a joint defence, then, I tell them frankly, they are lost. I prefer open enemies to untrustworthy friends." Such is the crack of the master's whip. He deals more politely with the Habsburg. All being well, Austria may even be rewarded for her aid by receiving Silesia.

Germany, composed as she is of many small and disintegrated fragments, serves Napoleon admirably in his jigsaw game with the nations. The three southern States have had their inhabitants and their lands bartered and exchanged at will; and, since Eugene has lost his throne to the Emperor's son (the baby was made "King of Rome") he is immediately installed as ruler in the hastily concocted "grand duchy of Frankfort."

What of Prussia? Why should Prussia continue to exist? Had he not, in Tilsit days, merely preserved this kingdom to please the tsar? But he is about to destroy the tsar! By notices and decrees, the Emperor announces that now, just before the war with Russia begins, Prussia is to be parcelled up. Does he not know that for the last year Prussia has been the ally of Russia, and that in a secret treaty the tsar has promised Frederick William his assistance? The Emperor hears much of defiant songs, of volunteer corps, of discontent in the universities, of the Tugendbund. Beware! Remember Spain! Do not trust to the proverbial "tolerance and coldness of these north Germans"! Surely it would be wiser to utilise the Prussian army before destroying it....

The great-hearted Scharnhorst assures Frederick William that now is the time to strike. But Metternich, in Vienna, tricks the Prussian general when he proposes an alliance, and advises him to seek alliance with Russia rather than with the Habsburg emperor. For only if the man with whom he exchanges these words of false friendship, becomes an opponent, only if Prussia enters the war as Austria's enemy, can Austria hope to enclose Silesia once more within her borders. At the same time Hardenberg bends before the Vienna wind today as always. The king, who will take no risks, and who considers Napoleon absolutely unconquerable, at last makes up his mind to enter into alliance with the Emperor, his resolution comes too late to secure favourable terms. Silesia and Poland are already alive with troops, and Prussia is surrounded. In such circumstances it is natural that she should be treated as a vassal, should have to tolerate the passage of armies, should have to put up with requisitionings, should have to look on patiently while her eastern fortresses are manned by French soldiers and her auxiliary corps commanded by foreign marshals. Metternich writes to his master in gleeful mood: "Prussia need no longer be reckoned among the powers."

And yet! And yet! Although Europe, from Capua to Tilsit, at the outset of 1812, is rallying to Napoleon's standard, although his arm reaches from Finisterre to Bukovina, he feels how uncertain is the outcome of this campaign, and, as Count Segur tells us, starts up from the conning of his interminable lists and calculations to exclaim in terror: "I am not ready to undertake a war in such far-off lands! I need three years more!"

But the machine rolls on; no master hand can stay it. An inner impulse urges him forward; the whole history of his rise to power impels him; all the shades of vanished years drive him on. He, who has built so many harbours wherein to seek refuge in times of storm and stress, is in the end tossed out upon the open sea, more roughly, more speedily than he had wished, and, with the wild determination of the adventurer, he now recklessly seizes the steering wheel which for so long he has manipulated with statesmanlike care. "Do you not see," he exclaims to his brother, "that I can only keep my seat upon this throne by means of the fame which brought me to it? That a private individual such as I, who has merely risen to beome a ruler, dare not call a halt? That such a one is constrained to mount higher and ever higher, and is doomed to perish the moment he stops climbing?"

His soul is a-flicker with excitement, so that at one moment he is eager for the final struggle, and at the next dreads it. His letter to the tsar, with which, as heretofore, he begins the campaign, still preserves a friendly tone. At the same time he says to a Russian colonel who is on spy duty in Paris: "Since the tsar is young and I have yet many years to live. I had thought to preserve the peace of Europe by means of our good feelings towards one another. My feelings have not changed. Tell him this; and say, in addition, that if the fates decree that the two greatest powers of the world are to come to blows over girlish peccadilloes, I shall enter the lists as a gallant knight, without hatred and without enmity. I suggest to him the possibility of our meeting for breakfast together

Napoleon, he needs tranquillity on his southern and his northern borders. He finds means to keep the sultan neutral; but in the case of Sweden he manages even better, for he is able to secure an alliance. He and Bernadotte meet on the frontier; and here, for the second time, the tsar of all the Russias succumbs to the charm of a French revolutionary. Sweden is in danger of English vengeance. Norway belongs to the Francophil Danes. The community of interests between Sweden and Russia secures expressions when Russia, in return for a promise of help in the coming war, guarantees that Sweden shall have Norway.

But this prospect of territorial enlargement is not the thing that spurs Bernadotte to action. He, who is king in Napoleon's despite, cares no more about his new subjects than those who had become kings by Napoleon's favour cared about theirs. But the tsar, too, has an imagination. Looking forward to the winning of this game, he sees in broad outline what lies beyond. He sees, not only the Emperor's defeat, but the Emperor's destruction; and while Napoleon, at the head of the greatest army known to history, is slowly advancing to swallow up the tsar, Alexander is promising Bernadotte, the friend of Bonaparte's youth, no less a prize than the throne of France.

To such heights, this summer, do the opposing eagles soar.

In Dresden, the Emperor treats all the princes to the spectacle of a review, just as he had done four years earlier in Erfurt. The only sovereign from among that company who is absent, is the one he is now to fight. But Alexander's place has been taken by the Habsburg ruler. Only once before have Napoleon and Francis met, on the day after Austerlitz. Twice, since then, has the victorious Emperor of the French occupied the Austrian's abandoned capital. When peace had been made between them, and the victor had wedded the daughter of the vanquished, the girl had been sent alone from Vienna to distant Paris.

Now Marie Louise sits between husband and father at the sparkling board, and to outward seeming all is well. The father-in-law is pledged in alliance, and the Emperor has appointed his wife regent of France. But vainly has he forbidden her to be so foolish that he is the first to cross the river, and he gallops several miles eastward before returning slowly to the bridge. Well, he is over now, and this time, in very truth, he has crossed the Rubicon. At his nod, three armies advance into the interior of Poland. The main army is under his immediate command, the second being commanded by Eugene, and the third by Jerome. Why does he venture to entrust a whole army to the leadership of this amateur (who made such a fool of himself in the last war), even with the safeguard of veteran generals as advisers? Napoleon thinks he can risk it. The enemy has at most three hundred thousand men.

Where is the enemy? In two armies, led by Barclay de Tolly and Bagration. They are somewhere in Lithuania, far away, and the total force is only one hundred and seventy thousand. Napoleon's overestimate of the strength of his opponents was a disastrous error, for if he had himself had fewer mouths to feed, he would have had a much better chance of getting adequate supplies for his soldiers. Why is he so keen on superiority of numbers? General Bonaparte was used, with forty thousand men, to defeat an enemy that greatly outnumbered him, his method being to crush one wing of the foe after another. The cumbrous multitude he has collected for the present campaign is symptomatic of his own increasing age, and of the lust for power which makes him pile up weight, instead of equipping the spirit with wings. Is he no longer the commander of the days of Rivoli?

In a sense, he is still that commander, for, even with this gigantic array of troops, he will be a victorious invader. His first army will march from Tilsit upon Vilna, to take up a position between the Russian detachments, so that his second and third armies can separately defeat the enemy. But the Russian distances weaken his influence. Upon a front of such vast extent, he cannot show himself everywhere. Those who command under him are too independent of one another (Davoust and Murat nearly fight a duel); and yet they are too dependent upon him. Never did he suffer more than in this campaign from the lack of speedy means of communication. His was the central brain in all his undertakings, so that a telegraph would have been far more useful to him than to his opponents.

The Russians are aware of their own weakness. Neither of the two commanders ventures to stand firm. Both of them withdraw before the invaders, at first without any, mutual understanding, to get into touch later, far in the rear. These are not the tactics of inspired leaders. Though the Russians do the right thing, it is merely because they are afraid of the forces that outnumber theirs, and because they dread the great name of Napoleon. They are but instruments in the hands of fate.

For a time, the Emperor pauses in his advance. In Vilna, he says: "If Monsieur Barclay imagines that I am going to run after him to the Volga, he is making a great mistake. We will follow him to Smolensk and the Dvina, where a good battle will provide us with quarters.... It would certainly be destruction were we to cross the Dvina this year. I shall go back to Vilna, spend the winter there, send for a troupe from the Théâter Francais, and another to play opera. We shall finish off the affair next May, unless peace is made during the winter."

News from the outer world is satisfactory. At length the United States has declared war on England, and has gained some victories at sea. In England the opposition, which wants peace, is gathering strength. Even in Spain things are not going so badly. Forward! A good battle!

But where is the enemy? The Emperor goes scouting, accompanied by only one officer; there is no trace of the Russians. Uneasiness grows. Since the invaders are marching light, and therefore too quickly, part of the army, on bad roads and amid heat and rainstorms, gets separated from its commissariat, upon which everything depends. In Vilna he fails to find the tsar, though Alexander has been there just before. At this moment, news is brought that the supplies are delayed, for the commissariat wagons have stuck fast in a morass, and the vessels that are bringing other supplies have run aground in the river; moreover, ten thousand horses have perished, through gorging themselves upon rank grass. The shortage cannot be hidden from the troops, who scatter through the town, and plunder so recklessly that there will be no supplies left for the next comers.

The Emperor can get nothing from the inhabitants of this land either by threats or cajoleries; and yet he detests rapine, which leads to chaos. The Lithuanians note that even now he has not granted the Poles the promised kingdom. They do not hail him as a liberator, as the people of Lombardy had done long years before. They give no help; they give nothing; they are hardly willing to accept in payment the forged rouble notes, millions of which he has had printed in Paris. They pray.

What is to be done? Now is the time to win over the tsar. He writes: "All that has taken place is out of keeping with Your Majesty's character, and with the personal consideration you have sometimes shown me in the past.... When I crossed the Memel, I had it in mind to send you an adjutant, as I have always done in previous campaigns." But, since the tsar had refused to receive his last envoy, "I realised that the invisible providence whose power and dominion I recognise would decide this matter, as he had decided so many others.... Nothing, therefore, is left but to conclude with the request that you will remain convinced of the steadfastness of my kindly feelings towards you."

Before writing this long and unctuous letter, in which nothing is genuine except the perplexity and the faith in destiny, he has had a conversation with a captured general who is to convey the missive. The way in which the Emperor hectors the prisoner, smacks of comic opera: "What does the tsar expect from this war? I have seized one of his best provinces without firing a shot, and neither of us knows what we are quarreling about!" Then, as his way was, he spent an hour or more pointing out the Russians' mistakes, asking why they had not defended Vilna, and talking to this captive just as if he had been berating one of his own generals in Spain. "Are you not ashamed of yourselves?" is the burden of his song. He waxes enthusiastic about the Poles, whom as a rule he frankly despises; but now it suits him to make much of their contempt for death. He says that he has thrice as many soldiers as the tsar, and much more money, so that he will be able to carry on the war for three years. These falsehoods are uttered in simulated anger, which he allows to flash out by fits and starts. The Russian meets bluff with bluff, saying that in Muscovy they have made preparations for a five years' campaign. But now the turn has come for one of the Emperor's bursts of frankness, in words suited to the ears of this officer blown him by a chance wind, but of course designed to impress the tsar, to whom they will be reported.

"I am the man of calculations. When I was in Erfurt, my reckonings convinced me that it would suit my book better to walk hand in hand with you Russians, instead of quarrelling with you. We might still have been good friends..... Then the tsar made peace with me, when his country wanted war; now he makes war on me, when his country wants peace. It puzzles me that so distinguished a man can have anything to do with such persons as some of his present advisers. How can anyone make war through a council of war? If at two in the morning a good idea enters my mind, in a quarter of an hour I have issued my orders, and half an hour later my outposts are executing it. But what happens among you?" Napoleon shows the prisoner a letter from the Russian general staff which his men have intercepted. "You can take it with you, for it will while away the tedium of your journey. Tell the tsar I pledge him my word that five hundred and fifty thousand men have already crossed the Vistula. But I am a man of calculations, not a man of passion. I am still willing to enter into negotiations. What a glorious reign he might have had, if he had not broken with me!"

The general is alarmed by this flood of confessions. But in the evening, when he dines with the Emperor and three of the marshals, he is placed on an entirely different footing, for the Emperor proceeds to cross-question him like an explorer eager for information.

"Have you any Kirghiz regiments?"

"No, but we are making experiments with Bashkirs and Tartars, who are very like the Kirghiz."

"Is it true that when the tsar was in Vilna, he went to tea everyday with a pretty lady there? Let me see, what was her name?"

"The tsar is courtly to every lady."

"Is it true that Baron vom Stein dined with the tsar?"

"All persons of note were invited to dinner."

"How can the tsar tolerate such a man as Stein at his table! Does he think the fellow can be fond of him? Angels and devils cannot be good companions.... What is the population of Moscow? How many houses? How many churches?... Why are there such a lot of churches?"

"Because our people are very pious."

"Nobody is pious nowadays. Which is the shortest way to Moscow?"

"All roads lead to Rome, Sire. You can choose your own route to Moscow. Charles XII marched by way of Pultava."

At this mischievous answer, the Emperor thought fit to turn the conversation. As for the general, he had wit enough to report in St. Petersburg that Napoleon was extremely nervous.

This nervousness increases mile after mile. The Emperor tries to join battle, but the Russians evade the issue. Barclay, who is waiting for a junction with Bagration, retreats aimlessly; Bagration does not come, for he believes that he is facing, not Jerome, but the main body of the invaders. Still, Bagration retreats. Jerome, who ought to follow him up, is too slow in his movements, so that Davoust, who is waiting for a junction with Jerome, has to let the enemy slip. The Emperor, in a rage, cashiers Jerome (who retires in dudgeon to Cassel), and gives the command to Davoust. Too late! His fondness for Jerome, the braggart, has cost him the chance of a decisive battle. As difficulties increase, the Emperor redoubles the pace of his advance; but as the tempo is quick-ended, the difficulties are redoubled. There is no means, now, of providing for the army. The retreating Russians burn their storehouses. No bread, no vegetables, nothing but meat. Dysentery breaks out. The horses eat the thatch from the roofs, and collapse in great numbers, so that their corpses line the road. During this advance in which there are no battles, the Bavarian leader estimates the losses of his corps at nine hundred men a day.

What is Paris saying?

Very little news comes to hand; hardly a word even from the empress. It seems as if the couriers were already being cut off. But here is a report from the Tuileries, written by the governess, to let him know how the child is getting on. He rejoins: "I hope to hear from you soon that the last four teeth have been out. I have seen to it that the nurse shall get everything she needs. You can assure her of this."

See the Emperor in the sun-parched steppe; before him rises the smoke of the burning villages he has yet to reach, behind him the stench of decomposing bodies. The strange food and the unaccustomed heat lead to a recurrence of his attacks of gastric spasm; he can no longer bear to ride, and, since wheeled traffic is constantly coming to grief, he covers great distances on foot, accompanied by the whole of his staff, pursued by the thought: Where is the fight to take place? Couriers arrive less frequently, and, when they do come, bring no news calculated to interest him in his present state of nervous tension. Yet here he is, pacing up and down within his tent; and the pen of his secretary, instead of, as usual, ordering masses of men to move from one place to another, hastens over the paper to record the master's concern about the four teeth which are still lacking to an infant in a forlorn palace twelve hundred miles away. Soon the Emperor will be in Vitebsk. How far is it thence to Paris?

"Too far, Sire," is re-echoed from unseen lips.

At last! We've got him! There stands Barclay, held in check for the moment by Murat! He thinks to escape to Smolensk on the morrow; such are the tidings! The hour has struck. But the Emperor is ill, irresolute. With unwonted consideration, he does not wish his exhausted army to go straight from the heat of the march into the heat of battle; with unwonted caution, he wishes to collect more troops than he really needs before beginning the attack, in order that the battle may be "another Austerlitz." He waits till morning.

The Russian laughs. Under cover of the morning mists, he makes good his retreat; and when the air clears, not a trace of the foe is to be seen, nor can a guess be made as to the direction he has taken. At midday the Emperor returns from the search, flings his sword on the table, and exclaims:

"Here I remain. Let us rally our forces. The campaign of the year '12 us at an end." When Murat urges him to continue the forward march, Napoleon answers: "In '13 I shall be at Moscow; in '14 at St. Petersburg. This war will last three years!"

It is time that the scattered army should be reorganized. Nearly a third of the forces has been struck off the lists, although no battle has taken place; the country has devoured them. Where are the auxiliaries–the Prussians under Macdonald, the Austrians under Schwarzenberg? Trustworthy news is lacking. Too far! What a country! How is one to pass the weary hours when there is no fighting? Wait? In Cario there were a hundred men of science in his train, and the country was full of unsolved riddles. –The following letter bears witness to a sense of boredom the Emperor has not known since the days of his lieutenancy:

"Send us some entertaining books," the secretary writes to the librarian in Paris. "If there are some good novels, new or old, which the Emperor has not read, or memoirs pleasantly written, we should be most grateful; for time hangs so heavily on our hands in this place."

Can we not see him standing in front of his tent in his old green coat? He takes one pinch of snuff after another, and from time to time looks through his telescope across the plain. Then a grenadier approaches with a paper in his hand; the Emperor reads it, puts it away; the two secretaries gaze dumbly from the gloom of the tent, like two tamed animals awaiting the nod of their tamer. Rustam sits apart Turk fashion; for him alone is the weather never too hot. All movement is paralysed, activity is stopped, one can go neither forward nor backward. Napoleon calls towards the tent: "Méneval! Order some novels!"

News comes at last: England has secured a treaty with the tsar and with the Spanish regent. This arouses the Emperor: he sees in it the birth of a fresh coalition; perhaps, even, encirclement. Must he really lie up here till Europe rises against him or goes to sleep? Over there is Smolensk. The two Russian armies have doubtless by now met in the town. That is where the real Russia begins: surely they will not evacuate and burn the old town of the Blessed Virgin, as they have been doing in the Polish and Lithuanian wilderness! Should victory be achieved at Smolensk, then the march on Moscow or St. Petersburg can be undertaken at will.

He questions his generals. Many of them utter words of warning. But the Emperor replies: "Russia cannot continue this sacrifice of her towns. Alexander can only begin negotiations after there has been a big battle. No blood has yet been spilled. Even if I have to march as far as the holy city of Moscow, I am determined to force a fight and win!"

At last the two Russian armies have effected a junction; they plan a systematic retreat, preceded by a stubborn resistance; wave after wave of the weary French army breaks against the walls of Smolensk. The veterans think of Acre, thirteen years gone by.... In the end, the town falls, but it falls amid the flames; a heap of ruins is all that is left in the victor's hands. Is the Emperor beginning to understand the moral strength of this people? Can he not see that day by day its mood becomes more fanatical, that it would rather burn its ancient holy things than leave them to the enemy? There remains nothing for a starving army to plunder.

The Emperor, indeed, is in sorry plight, King Lear upon the heath. Power crumbles in fragments from his body; every gesture melts in the air; from afar the laughter of the rational world comes echoing, to be lost in the void. An end must be made. A second message is sent to the tsar. No use writing, for that last letter from Vilna has remained unanswered. Once more a captured general is ushered into his presence, and once more the Emperor's secret meditations are unveiled. In conclusion he says:

"Can you write to the tsar? No? Still, you write to your brother at headquarters and tell him what I am saying to you: You will greatly oblige me if you tell him that you have seen me and that I have charged you to write to him. He would do me a real service if he himself would let the tsar know, or get the grand duke to do it for him, that my greatest wish is to conclude peace.... What are we fighting for? Of course, if you were the English, that would be a different matter! But the Russians have done nothing to me. You want to buy coffee and sugar cheaply? Very well. That can be arranged. But do you fancy it will be easy to beat me? Then get your council of war to consider the situation; if it thinks the Russians can achieve a victory, choose your battleground.... Otherwise I shall be compelled to take Moscow, and, in spite of every precaution, I shall perhaps not be able to save it from destruction. A capital which has been in the possession of the enemy, is like a woman who has lost her honour... What do you think? If the tsar wishes to conclude peace, surely none will oppose him?"

As a young lieutenant, as a young general, he had never asked a favour; he could not; he knew only how to command. Even to kings he wrote in the tone of a commander, and the word "please" had only twice passed his lips during the course of this last decade: the first time, when he asked the Pope to anoint him emperor; the second time, when he besought Francis of Habsburg for his daughter's hand. Yet today, what a tone! What thoughts must be passing through the captive's mind at the moment when his sword is given back to him!– Can this be the master of the world? Has he not begged me, a poor man, begged me and my brother, to do him a service? How came these things to be? Has he no other messenger? Coffee and sugar are to blame, it seems, for the fact that an army of hundreds of thousands of men is perishing in my land! And, as though the whole thing were some brilliant game of chess, the master player sends his challenge, while Little Mother Russia is suffering and weeping, and sees one of her cities after the other go up in flames, and the images of her saints reduced to ashes!

The letter to the captive general's brother is duly written, passes Berthier's censorship, is delivered—but is never answered. The Emperor is beside himself with rage; he passes through a period in which he makes impulsive and vacillating decisions. When Rapp asks whether the army is to go forward or to retreat, Napoleon answers: "The wine is poured out; it must be drunk to the last drop. I am for Moscow.... Too long have I played the emperor; it is time I became the general once more." The eyes of the officer light up as he recognises the old ring in the voice!–We are at the beginning of September.

On the sacred soil of the heath near Borodino, Kutusoff, Barclay's successor, must at length put up a fight. The armies now are of equal strength: this is the game the Emperor proposed. No one sleeps, for tomorrow, tomorrow at last, the battle will be joined! Then will golden Moscow lie at our feet, and all our troubles will be at an end. In the middle of the night, a courier arrives from Paris. The Emperor, bending over his maps, asks if there is anything urgent to attend to. Silently his secretary hands him a dispatch from Spain: Wellington has gained a decisive victory over Marmont in the fight near Salamanca. The Emperor reads the report, makes no comment, and resumes his interrupted work. At the eastern extremity of Europe, at the point where it loses itself in the Asiatic wastes, in a few hours he is to vanquish the Russians. This is no time to trouble his mind as to the significance of the victory of the detested Briton at the southern extremity of Europe. Day has dawned. Today, as everyday, the guards call the salute: "Vive l'Empereur!"

He shows them his son's picture, which the courier that night had brought him from Paris. There they stand, the old war-dogs, never dreaming that France has been beaten in Spain, but admiring the portrait of the beautiful boy who is their leader's very own son. When the picture is brought back to the tent, the Emperor says, speaking like a poet: "Hide it away. He is too young to look upon a battlefield."

In fierce fighting, on this day of Borodino, salient points are taken, lost, and retaken. The guards shout. They want to decide the issue, here, on the Moskva, as they have so often done before, his generals beseech him to order the advance, and his intimates urge him to action, but he will not give the word. For the first time, when the fight is on, he will not stir from his place. He is feverish, panting for breath, racked with a cough, and his legs are swelled. He sits motionless on his horse, and cannot make up his mind to order the advance of the guards, although the fate of the day seems to hang on it. "Suppose there should be another battle tomorrow? What men shall I have left to fight it with?" At night the Russians withdraw. Next day, when the fallen are counted on the field, they number seventy thousand dead or half-dead–more than in any of his previous battles. The Emperor exclaims:

"Fortune is a strumpet. I have often said so. Now the truth is coming home to me."

But the way to Moscow is open. Half a million men had been chosen for the invasion. One hundred thousand of them are still following him, when, from an elevation, with his back towards the setting sun, he first sees the city of a thousand cupolas, and upon the hill in its centre that fragment of the East, the Kremlin, Napoleon, as he gazes at the sight, is filled with weariness rather than with exultation, and he says in a low tone:

"Moscow! It is time!"

V

"Where are the keys of the city? Why are not the mayor and corporation here to hand them over?"

For the greater part of the afternoon he waits while the army marches past him, waits for the keys of the town. At Vienna and Milan, at Madrid and Berlin, he had ridden through the gates as a conqueror. Are these Tartars ignorant of the fine old Roman custom? From afar can be heard the noise made by Kutusoff's soldiers, as the half-beaten army evacuates the Eastern side of the men here. There are plenty of roofs to cover them, but what about food? The city seems to be in the middle of a desert!"

A red glare shows through the windows. Fire! Oh, well, we're used to that. There were several fires here and there yesterday evening. But orderlies rush in, and generals arrive. A hundred messengers have reported the outbreak of fires all over the city. Not accidental fires, but prearranged, for the fire-engines have been broken or removed. Do these lunatics mean that Holy Moscow should go up in flames? What will the Emperor do? Ségur, who was with him in these dark hours, tells us what happened:

"It seems as if the encircling flames have spread to the Emperor's mind. By turns, he leaps to his feet, sits down again, or tramps hastily through the rooms of the palace. His abrupt movements betray his terrible agitation. He abandons an urgent task, resumes it, abandons it once more, that he may fling the window wide. He exclaims:

"'What a dreadful sight! Their own work! So many palaces! How stupendous a decision! Who could have expected anything of the kind? What men they are! They are Scythians!"

"Suddenly we are informed that the Kremlin has been mined. Some of the servants are panic-stricken; the guard quietly awaits orders. The Emperor smiles incredulously, but he continues to pace convulsively to and fro, halting at every window to watch the raging element as it seizes the bridges and the gates, simultaneously imprisoning him and besieging him. The air is full of smoke and flying sparks; the equinoctial gale increases the fury of the conflagration.

"Murat and Eugene arrive hotfoot, force their way to the Emperor, and urge him to flee. In vain! Napoleon, master in the palace of the tsars, is steadfast. He will not yield even to devouring flame. But suddenly comes the cry: 'Fire in the Kremlin!' The Emperor is to see the danger close at hand.

"A Russian military policeman has been seized in a turret of the arsenal. Brought before the Emperor, the man admits that he has fired the Kremlin, acting under orders. The Emperor makes a sign of rage and contempt. The prisoner is led out into the courtyard and is cut down by the grenadiers. This incident decides the Emperor's action.

"We hasten down the northern staircase, and the Emperor orders us to guide him out of the town. But all the gates of the citadel are blocked by the flames. At length an alley-way leading to the Moskva is discovered between two rocks. Through this narrow passage we are able to escape from the Kremlin. But what has been gained? How can we cross the river? The soldiers, blinded by the sparks and deafened by the storm, do not know where they are, and the streets are hidden amid the smoke. The only way out of the inferno is through a winding street where the houses are on fire.

"Heedlessly the Emperor strides along this dreadful exit, undismayed by the crackle of the flaming beams and by the crash of the falling roofs.... We can hardly breathe, so intense is the heat. Our guide loses his way, and we should all have ended our lives in the flames had not some marauders belonging to the first army corps recognised the Emperor and found a way for him and the rest of us out of the smoking ruins.

"We meet Davoust. He has been injured on the Moskva, but has had himself carried back among the blazing houses, hoping to find the Emperor or perish with him. The general embraces Napoleon in a fever of delight. The Emperor responds in friendly fashion, but with that calm which never leaves him in the hour of danger."

He awaits the end of the conflagration in the Petroffsky palace, a suburban retreat. On the fourth day, he returns to the Kremlin, where very little damage has been done. On the fifth day, his patience gives out. For the third time, he writes to the tsar. Even now, when he is in possession of the capital, he feels he is grasping at the air. He is so cut off from the enemy that once more he has to make use of a Russian prisoner (this time only a captain), in order to find a contact with the tsar. Napoleon receives the man in the throne room. Does he sense the heroic grotesqueness of the fierce, he had so inflexibly made up him mind to destroy Napoleon, and he so greedily coveted the crown of France which the tsar had promised him, that he would stick at nothing.

The other was a German, the best the nation had nurtured in its downfall and in its fight for freedom. Four years had passed since Napoleon pronounced a verdict of outlawry on Baron vom Stein. The baron spent them far from his homeland; and had become the Tsar's trusted adviser. In every respect he was Napoleon's exact contrary. He was now to fight the Emperor to a decisive issue.

This time Stein would conquer.

VI

In many lands, among the many wise and energetic men who for seventeen years had pitted themselves against the General, the Consul, and the Emperor, none proved equal to the task expect Talleyrand and Stein: The former did so, because he succeeded in paralysing Napoleon's productive will by the genius of his malicious cunning; the latter, because, to Napoleon's amoral energy, he contraposed a moral energy which was wedded to fervour. Just as Stein embodied the virtues of the Germans, so Napoleon gathered into himself the talents of the Italian character; and yet, since neither Teutonic virtues nor Italian talents are mutually exclusive, but, rather, cut athwart one another, each man could understand the opponent so far, that Stein, had he been a Frenchman (Carnot's blood brother), might have proved the mainstay of the Emperor. Pride and practical good sense would have brought the two men together.

But this mutual respect could never have bridged the abyss of alienation which must have continued, in spite of everything, to hold them asunder. For, just as Napoleon lived entirely without feeling for a fatherland; just as he would gladly have made his career anywhere, and merely placed the French before other peoples because he chanced to be their emperor, so, on the other hand,

Stein lived and wrought entirely for the sake of his fatherland, and his Teutonic solidity (firmly rooted in the native soil), the whole weight of his rich soul, remained estranged from the agility, the swiftness, which was so essential a part of Napoleon's make-up, and which the Emperor utilised so adroitly. Here was a statesman whose one thought was Germany and the Germans, who wanted unity among the stocks speaking the same speech, even if such unity had to be achieved against the wishes of the weakling princes. Over the way stood the man who could only think in terms of Europe and Europeans, people whom he wished to weld together for a fight against the selfsame princes.

A baron of the empire, and therefore an independent though petty prince, Stein was a worthy son of ancestors who for seven centuries had tilled and ruled the same fragment of German soil. Having left the home of his fathers for one reason only, that he might serve the nation, he regarded with mistrust, and soon with growing contempt, the other German princes, who were so eager to barter lands and liberties–their own and their subjects'–for the favour of the world conqueror. Napoleon, sprung from an impoverished noble stock, a man who had in early youth been driven forth from the ancestral vineyard, despised these lickspittle princes as heartily as did Stein, and in secret he honoured none but the few irreconcilables.

But whereas the contempt with which he regarded the decadence of the European princes was mingled with amusement, Stein's attitude towards them was purely one of rancour. Their innate impotence, which encouraged the self-confidence of the brilliant upstart, was a challenge to the self-respect of Stein, the man who would fain believe in the knightly order to which he belonged; and just as the Corsican used his own career as an argument to strengthen his conviction that a new and splendid epoch was in the making, the German could not fail to consider the behaviour of his fellow-princes as melancholy evidence of the collapse of the old order, and must perforce regard the king of Prussia with a contempt no less hearty than the hatred he cherished for the Emperor of the French.

Thus Napoleon's pronouncement of outlawry against Stein was symbolic of the differences between the two men in respect of nationality, class, and epoch. Had the imperial baron been a king, he would, far more worthily than any Habsburg, or Hohenzollern, or other among the defeated monarchs, have embodied, in opposition to the son of the revolution, that ideas of legitimacy for which the German nation was willing to battle with no less ardour than it would display in the fight against the foreigner. Apart from the duke of Brunswick and one or two of the younger princes, Stein stood alone in those days as saviour of the pride and dignity of the German rulers.

Now his great moment has come. From Madrid, the Emperor had sent forth his decree of banishment against the Prussian minister. Twice, for this, time was to exact vengeance. Now was the first occasion. Nothing but the sentence of outlawry had brought Stein into contact with the tsar, for whose soul he was wrestling with this old enemy. In all Alexander's vacillations, no influence did more to strengthen him than the indomitable spirit of the German exile. When the Emperor, not long before, holding forth to the Russian general, had spoken with so much acerbity about Stein, it was because, from afar, he had sensed this influence, and because he was afraid of the imperial baron. He knew Stein to be a vigorous idealist, an undismayed monarchist; and he knew that in the decisive hours such a man was likely to exercise a potent suggestive influence upon the tsar, also an idealist, though irresolute and timid. Stein, knowing human character as he did, and knowing that the tsar, in a hazy fashion, was eager to live in accordance with the moral law, would dilate upon Napoleon's contempt for morality and itch for dictatorship. Stein would not tempt Alexander with countries to be annexed, but with principles to be obeyed; and would rouse to action a modern monarch who would know better than the German princes how to defend rule by right divine.

This German was the only person at the tsarist court who had no axe to grind. Driven from his own home by the homeless Napoleon, he was ready betwixt night and morning to change his present hospitable asylum for any other. The tsar knew that Stein was not a place-hunter, but an independent foreigner whose counsel was not tainted by any thought of personal advantage; for this reason, he had more trust in the German baron than in his own Francophil minister. Perhaps he had heard of the splendid words uttered by the German when the news of the burning of Moscow had arrived. Stein, sitting at table, had raised his glass, and had exclaimed: Three or four times, ere this, I have lost my baggage. We must get used to throwing away such things. Since we must die, let us be valiant."

His enemy in Moscow will soon make up his mind to the same thing. He throws away the baggage of the past, and marches on; he makes up his mind to retreat. Not a word has come from St. Petersburg. Five weeks have been wasted, and the winter draws near! He has been waiting on events, waiting and listening; this is ill-suited to his temperament, out of keeping with his energetic nature. The novels he has ordered from Paris have not yet come to hand, so he hunts up whatever can be found in the Kremlin. But he reads very little. After meals, which, contrary to his usual custom, he protracts to the uttermost, he sometimes lies for hours, book in hand, but meditating with fixed gaze.

What is there to do in a burned city where nothing is left to organize! On one or two evenings, the Emperor has some French plays performed by a troupe of actors which had remained behind at the time of the evacuation. This reminds the holiday-making ruler of the charter of the Comédie Francaise, and he sends instructions for its amendment. Half the day is whiled away in issuing army orders which by no means appear to emanate from a wearied brain, and are far from being commonplace; on the contrary, they are as crystal clear as in earlier days. But since nothing remains to be hoped for, since provisions are dwindling and the cold season is imminent, he calls a council of war in mid-October, although he knows that only one way lies open to him.

Daru counsels; make the winter quarters here; await reinforcements from liberated Lithuania; in the spring, march upon St.

Petersburg. The Emperor remains for long in a brown study. Then he says:

"That is the advice of a lion. But what will Paris say? Who can calculate the effect of six months' separation? France may grow accustomed to my absence; Germany and Austria might turn it to account." The only possible order is for the whole army to turn back. What trophies shall we bring back with us to Paris? The giant cross of gold from the church of St. John within the Kremlin walls is taken down from the cupola that it may be set up on the dome of the Invalides. But can we not devise some better revenge against the false friend? The Emperor orders the Kremlin to be blown up.

Eight miles away from Moscow he reins in, and waits for news of the explosion. The unending stream of the grand army flows steadily by the Emperor; it is flanked by the sick and the wounded; it is laden with booty, rested but undisciplined. At last come tidings: the explosion has missed fire. He is silent. But when Rapp expresses anxiety about the approach of winter, Napoleon rebukes him, saying: "Can't you see how lovely the weather is, even today, on October 19th? Do you not recognise my star?"

Such words hardly ever fall from his lips, and this day he is full of cares. He realises that the baggage train is going to cause delay, and yet he has not the heart to order his men to leave their booty behind; they must have something to take home. Russian troops have encircled the French army, and recently they pressed so heard on Murat's squadrons as to drive these back upon the town. On the eastward march, the Emperor had longed for nothing so much as a good action to take place; but now, on the westward march, there is nothing he dreads more than to have to put up a fight. Get to Smolensk as quickly as possible; we will find winter quarters there!

Is the beginning of his career falling into step with the end? Again, as in Egypt, the army marches with the baggage in the middle; again the troops have to defend themselves from the swarming enemy. Once the Emperor is saved from being made prisoner only by the presence of mind of one of his men. "Cossacks! Turn about!" cries Rapp, pointing to a thicket. The Emperor will not follow this advice. The adjutant, thereupon, seizes the bridle-rein and turns Napoleon's horse round. "You must!" Never in his whole life has he heard such an order addressed to him. What is he to do? Reason tells him to flee.

But the Emperor remains where he is, and draws his sword. Rapp, Berthier, Caulaincourt, do the same. They place themselves to the left of the road and await the riders, who are barely forty paces away. Then the officers of the suite cover Napoleon until the guard cavalry comes to the rescue and puts the Cossacks to flight.

New thoughts flit through his brain after this adventure. Shall Alexander harness him to a triumphal car? He procures a dose of poison from his physician, and wears it always in a black silk bag around his neck, in case he should be made a prisoner. Since the day when he was so nearly captured, the ambition of every Russian flying column is to procure the head of the "wicked infidel." Russian headquarters issues a warrant against the Emperor; it is embellished with is picture, and orders the corps leaders to have "every man of small stature" among the prisoners brought before them for examination: anyone of them may be Emperor Napoleon!

As in Egypt the heat of the march had killed hundreds of men, so now does the Russian cold devour them by thousands. Snow and ice bring down the horse, guns get stuck, munition wagons are blown up, cavalry soldiers must pad the hoof, frozen men line the roads.

Not more than fifty thousand reach Smolensk, one-tenth of all the invading host. They have no more supplies, and cannot winter here. The freezing army pushes forward. Thousands have thrown their weapons away; now, even the guard weaken. The Emperor comes among his grenadiers:

"You see the disorder of my army. These poor deluded men are throwing their muskets away. Are you going to follow this shameful example? If so, then there is no hope left to us. On you the whole future of the army depends!" He marches among them.

A silent procession (thus described by one who met it): first come the generals, few of whom are mounted. Ghosts in rags, in scorched cloaks, lean, grey, with matted beards, bent and silent; prisoners of fate. These are followed by the Holy Legion, a legion composed of officers, most of them leaning upon sticks, their feet swathed in remnants of sheepskin. Then come the survivors of the cavalry guard.

Last of all three men on foot: to the right, the king of Naples, no longer concerned about his peacock splendours; to the left, the viceroy of Italy. In the middle walks a little man, wearing a Polish fur coat and a cap of red fox, and helping himself along with a birchen staff. Thus in silence he wends his way through Russia

VII

What is Paris saying?

He does not know. For the first time since he was in Egypt, his calculations concerning Paris have no solid foundation in fact. Not to know what is going on in his capital: a dreadful position this, like that of a traveller who fancies that during his absence his wife may be betraying him! Writing to Maret in Vilna, he says: "For more than a fortnight I have had no courier, so that I am in the dark as to all that is going on ..... in France and Spain.... The army is terribly disorganised. It would take at least a fortnight to set things straight, but we cannot possibly spare the time. Shall we be able to maintain our position in Vilna? Only if we are not attacked during the first week. Food! Food!... Make sure that there shall be no foreign envoys in Vilna, for the army is not in a fit condition to be seen. Send them all away."

Here is the courier at last. Why does the Emperor turn pale? What terrible news can have come from Paris? Can anything have happened there worse than what he has just been living through? The fact is that, through English newspapers, through letters, and through rumour, France has long since learned the whole truth, which had been glossed over in the Emperor's bulletins. Many of the Parisians are fickle, and many of them are easily reduced to despair. A good part of Paris has already given up the Emperor for lost. Alarmist reports and spiteful quips are rife on the boulevards. But what is this item?

A coup d'état had been planned, and had been frustrated. But what a background of discontent is revealed! Malet, who had been general in the days of the republic, had years before been concerned in a conspiracy, imprisoned, and then committed to a lunatic asylum. Having received distorted news about the Emperor's disasters and the burning of Moscow, he had escaped. With a number of accomplices, he had published a forged dispatch announcing Napoleon's death. The conspirators had seized the Minister of Police; had declared a provisional government; had bamboozled the National Guard, the militia, the prefects, and even veteran generals. At length, however, two undismayed officers had seen through the cheat, had seized the conspirators, and from the balcony of the governor's residence had shouted, "Vive l'Empereur." Therewith the spectre had been laid.

In his tent, on which the snow is falling, the Emperor contemplates this document with dismay. More serious news even than that which recently arrived from Salamanca! The offenders had been shot; the whole affair had fizzled out. But for a time the conspirators had been masters of the Paris police, and one who controls the Paris police is master of France! No carriages would venture into the streets! When an elderly nobleman had asked what was afoot, a workman had laughed, saying: "Citizen, the Emperor is dead. At noon the republic will be proclaimed!" Greatly shaken by the tidings, the Emperor drops the newspaper containing these details, and says to his intimates:

"What about the dynasty? Did no one think of my wife, my son, all the institutions of the Empire? I must get back to Paris instantly!"

The dangerous possibilities revealed by this interlude, flash like lighting through his mind. "The workman who laughs–he is the people! I toil day and night for years at my great building, I break with the woman I love, and take an emperor's daughter to wife, that our heir, the pledge of earthly immortality, may grow up in our palace. Then some foolhardy officer, a man no one has ever heard of, has merely to call out that the Emperor is dead, and instantly a clamour about 'citizens' and 'republic, rises once more from the people! The regent, the heir, the Council of State–all these count for nothing? The bottomless cask of the Danaids! But I will make a bottom for it. Like the Capets, I will have my son crowned in my own lifetime, and muster my faithful supporter in Paris!"

Fortified by the approach of danger, the Emperor grips the reins firmly once more. "He is pale, but his face is calm; nothing in his features gives any sign of trouble." His health is better, too, Now the army nears the Beresina. Having received false intelligence to the effect that the auxiliary armies are close at hand, he draws his own forces more compactly together, and has the rest of the baggage train burned, that the horses may be freed to draw the remaining guns. If only the bridge is still standing! He writes: "Should the enemy have seized the bridgehead and burned the bridge in order to prevent our crossing, it would be very serious."

Next day they come to the river. No bridge, no boats; two armies outnumbering the French are waiting on the other shore; between runs the broad river with marshy banks. Is there any way out of the difficulty?

He makes a shrewd plan, like those of his early days as general. He will decoy the Russians away. Out of eighteen hundred horseless cavalry of the guard, of whom only eleven hundred still have their weapons, he forms two battalions. Then he has all the regimental eagles burned, for even in this dread hour Napoleon thinks of honour and glory, and he will not risk the loss of colours to the enemy. After midnight, he at length lies down in his tent, where he overhears Duroc and Daru, who believed him to be asleep, discussing in an undertone the possibility of a catastrophe. The phrase "State prisoner" has caught his ear. He fingers the black bag he is wearing round his neck, and sits up in bed:

"You think they would dare?"

"I would not trust the enemy's magnanimity." says Daru, composedly.

"But France! What would France do?"

Daru's answer is evasive; but when pressed, he says: "I think, Sire, the sooner you are in Paris, the better. When you are there, you will have a better chance of saving us all."

"Then you feel I am a burden on you here?"

"Yes, Sire,"

"And you don't want to be State prisoners?"

There is a long silence. Then the Emperor resumes:

"Have my ministers' reports been destroyed?"

"Hitherto you have always refrained from giving us the order."

"It must be done. Destroy the lot of them. We are in a very difficult position."

This is the only admission of the kind made by the Emperor during all the weeks of the Russian campaign. It is the voice of a man who regards himself as a moriturus. But nature is more sensible than fate, and in a few moments he is fast asleep.

Next morning, while the enemy has been lured down stream, and is being kept at a distance by artillery fire, the sappers, neck-deep in the freezing water and amid the drifting ice, hastily build two bridges. The crossing of the river takes two days more. With the cavalry, which swims the stream, the army still numbers about twenty-five thousand men. The Emperor, though the risk of his being taken prisoner is imminent, remains until all have crossed; and then, on the third day, surrounded by the old guard, he too makes his way over the river. But there are still stragglers to come, and these perish during the next few days betwixt ice and fire.

In the ensuing week the Emperor's life is twice in danger. The first peril is from a Cossack attack. On the next occasion the trouble is an assassination plot in which one of his own Frenchmen is engaged. It is early on the morning of December 5th when Major Lapie meets the officers of the Prussian guard of honour in front of the Emperor's tent. "Now then, gentlemen, the hour has come!"

Now there is something new. The Emperor embraces every one of the generals present. Is this the last coup of a trickster who wants to strengthen their waning loyalty? Is he really overcome by his feelings? Everyone of these soldiers, that evening, could feel the beating of the Emperor's heart.

He gets into the sleigh with Daru and Caulaincourt, and the three drive away. To be on the safe side, he travels under an assumed name, that of his secretary, Rayneval. This is his fifth name. The fourth had been Napoleon .

When they are driving through the snows across the Polish plain, he suddenly has the sleigh stopped at a crossroad. This must be near Countess Walewska's mansion; he wants to go there. Napoleon is on the flight from Russia, his head full of world-shaking plans; he is forsaking his army because Paris needs him and he needs Paris–and now comes this lyrical thought, the painful recollection of a frustrated idyll. But the urgent warnings of his companions, who remind him that they are alone in a couple of sledges and that Cossacks are scouring the countryside, induce him to abandon his plan. He wraps his furs around him once more and goes to sleep.

Five days afterwards he leaves the sleighs waiting on the bridge near Warsaw, and at noon goes on foot with Caulaincourt into the town, Should anyone recognise him, they will face it out, and declare that the interlocutor is seeing ghosts, or must be mad. Napoleon sends Caulaincourt to the embassy; but, in order to keep his own identity secret, he himself goes to an inn, which, of all names in the world, still calls itself the Hôtel de l'Angleterre. The low-ceilinged whitewashed room is cold; there is only green wood, and the maidservant cannot get the stove to light; he must keep on his furs, his cap, and his big boots, while he tramps up and down the room. thrashing his arms like a coachman to keep himself warm. It is thus he is found by two Polish noblemen for whom he has sent through the embassy. They can hardly believe their eyes, but the ghost laughs at their astonishment.

"How long have I been in Warsaw? A week? No, only a couple of hours. It is but one step from the sublime to the ridiculous. How are you, Monsieur Stanislas? ... Dangers? Not a bit of it. I thrive on excitement. The more I am tossed to and fro, the better I feel. The shadow kings grow fat in their palaces, but I put on flesh when riding my nag in the field.... So you've been anxious here? The army is in splendid condition. I have still one hundred and twenty thousand men! Gave the Russians a good hiding everywhere. They never ventured to stand up against me. The army will winter in Vilna. I am returning to Paris, and there I shall raise three hundred thousand soldiers! In six months I shall be back on the Memel.

"I have been through other fights! At Marengo I was beaten until six in the evening, but next day I was lord of Italy. At Aspern-Essling I made myself master of Austria, though the archduke believed he had held me in check there. It was not my fault that the Danube rose sixteen feet in one night. But for that, I should have finished off with the Habsburgs once for all. However, it was written in the stars that I was to marry an archduchess....

"The same thing in Russia. I can't prevent its freezing there. Morning after morning, the report was that ten thousand horses had perished during the night. Bon voyage! Our Normandy horses cannot endure the cold like the Russians; the same with our soldiers.... Perhaps people will say that I stayed too long in Moscow; but the weather was beautiful, and I was waiting for peace. A great political drama! Nothing venture, nothing have. One step from the sublime to the ridiculous!...Who could have foreseen the burning of Moscow?...I never felt better in my life!"...

Such is the spate of words that for two hours flows from the mouth of a man who, after unspeakable losses, wishes to give the impression of desperate courage.

Napoleon becomes an adventurer. To impress these Poles who will pass on what he says, he invents an army which has vanished long since; cold which really did nothing more than complete the destruction that other forces had begun; battles he never fought. He intersperses these figments with historical parallels of worldwide significance; treats what has just been happening as if it were ancient history; appeals to providence; and repeats no less than four times the cynically imposing aphorism about the sublime and the ridiculous, which blunts the edge of criticism. Great realist though he is, the world and what he is doing with it are becoming drama to him; and thus Napoleon, when his own fortunes are declining, is slowly mounting the ascent towards supreme irony.

The two Poles see nothing of all this. Their thoughts are concentrated upon their country's debts, and they would fain get money from this man who is still numbered among the great ones of the earth. They seize their opportunity when at length there is a pause in the torrent of speech. He gives them an order on the treasury for six millions, which he thinks will buy support for him in Poland. Then his visitors wish him a happy journey, and, with secret scorn, watch the incognito drive away hastily in his sleigh.

Day and night, night and day, they glide swiftly westward; for Germany, too, is under snow. Day and night, night and day, questions, commands, and plans are churning in his brain. "Is England really invincible? Now, the English can trade freely in the Baltic; English goods can enter Cadiz, and can make their way into the Levant." He must put off his schemes for the conquest of India, but will abate no jot of his other designs! Will the Confederation of the Rhine still answer to his nod? How will it be possible to explain this crash in Russia? The disaster cannot be hushed up indefinitely. Is there any chance of raising another hundred and twenty thousand men in France? Next year's levies must be called up in advance. Make peace with the Pope at once, and with Spain likewise, for he must feel safe at his back. A National Guard, that was the best thought of the revolution; in that way he will be able to raise a million armed citizens within three months."

Night. Change of horses. He thrusts out his head. "Where are we?"

"In Weimar. Sire."

"Weimar? How is the duchess? And how is Herr Goethe?"

will constitute a real popular representation, consisting only of experienced business men, without an ideologue among them. Then France will be satisfactorily ruled, even under a prince who is a mere figure head (and such will come), for whom the ordinary education of hereditary princes will suffice."

These Cæsarist ideas betray the monarchist, but also the sceptic. Although, when he shows people his son's portrait, they tell him that the little boy is the loveliest child in France, the flattered father knows perfectly well that dynasties last a long time whereas genius is fleeting. Foreseeing the decadence of his own blood, having studied that decadence in the annals of all princely houses, he wants to rid himself of waverers that he may fortify the position of his heir. For the very reason that he understands the contradiction inherent in monarchy, he wishes to build his own monarchy on a rock.

For the time being, his business is to buttress it anew with the power of the sword. What has been the fruit of the war games in which he moved his myriads over Europe? Those leather-bound muster rolls of his contained the death sentences of numberless youth, even though there were marshals' batons to be won by a few among the best of them! Of the old guard, four hundred men, and of the cavalry guard, eight hundred men, made their way back to Königsberg; a few thousand officers and servants, broken men most of them, have survived the storms of war. Except for the auxiliaries, who are not under France's orders, that is all that remains of the Emperor's hosts. Marshal Ney, on his flight from Russia, seems like a hero out of a Greek tragedy when he reaches Prussia, and makes his way into the first Prussian government office on his route. When old acquaintances look at him incredulously, as if questioning who this man can be, he rejoins with a superb gesture: "I am the rear guard of the Grand Army."

A new army must be made, and it must be made in a few weeks. The year 1813 will supply one hundred and forty thousand recruits, but where are the rest to come from? The Emperor has a magic wand, and can conjure up men whenever he needs them. The passing of a new law is all that is requisite for the levying of the National Guard and for the drafting of eighty thousand soldiers from the dependencies of France. Add one hundred thousand belonging to the oldest conscript levies; and call up the youngsters who should not, properly speaking, be enrolled until 1814. Soon he will have half a million under arms once more. "The French people," he says to the Prussian envoy, "will follow me whatever I do, and, if needs must, I shall arm the women!"

With unbroken will, he charms into existence the innumerable machines without which he cannot ply his trade. But how shall he explain these unexpected measures to the people? The enemy is far from the frontier.

A stroke of luck! At the close of the year, Yorck, a Prussian general, acting on his own initiative, enters into an agreement with his Russian neighbours, declares the force under his command neutral, and thus opens the door to a change in the military situation for which the German nation has long been eager. The Emperor can use the incident in order to whip up the enthusiasm of the French. For the moment, the treason of his ally costs him no more than twenty thousand men; but it serves as the text for a manifesto in Paris, and for hectoring letters to the princes of the Confederation of the Rhine. He would not, says Napoleon, need their help at all, had not Yorck's secession compelled his army to withdraw.

The summons of France is actually obeyed. The German princes, including the Habsburg ruler, once more collect money and levy troops. One of them is servile enough to send an assurance that he is "delighted to be able to give the Emperor opportunity for winning fresh laurels." The king of Prussia cashiers Yorck, and assures the Emperor of his fidelity to the alliance. But Frederick William conveys a hint to the tsar, goes to Breslau, wobbles between the parties, what time a wave of enthusiasm is spreading far beyond Prussia's borders, and threatening to sweep away the debile monarch. Youths, politicians, and poets are voicing the call of national sentiment. Stein is the man to treat with the tsar on behalf of his country, and in Königsberg the baron takes matters into his own hands.

The Emperor is ever on the watch. In a circular, he warns the princes against the intrigues of those "who by rebellion and revolution are trying to give Germany a new form. Should they succeed in infecting the Confederation of the Rhine with their doctrines, intolerable sufferings may await these territories."

He feels the stirring of the new spirit. Now, for the first time, does the Emperor seem to become aware of the growth of a national sentiment among the Germans, as among the Spaniards. Shortly before the Russian Campaign, he had said that hardly so much as a night-watchman was needed to keep the Germans quiet. "Since Germany has no America, nor yet a sea, nor yet a great number of strongholds, nor even Englishmen as there are in Spain, there is nothing to be afraid of, and would not be though the Germans were as lazy, dirty, superstitious, and monk-ridden as the Spaniards. How could there be anything to fear from such honest, reasonable, coolheaded, and patient people, who have so little inclination to violence that throughout the war not one of our soldiers has been murdered in Germany?"

A wonderfully true picture of the Germans, and yet there is a slight miscalculation. He has overlooked the romanticism by which these people can be stirred, and without a knowledge of which they cannot be understood. Of course the Italian, with his fiery imagination, cannot grasp the nature of an imagination that works slowly and lacks ardour. Napoleon, who knows how monarchical the Germans are in their sentiments, believes that when he holds the princes in his hands he must be master of the German people.

Besides, were the Germans a people? Was this realm, which ten years earlier had been formally liquidated by the abdication of the last of its emperors, really anything more than a "metaphysical concept"? Only for a moment, only for two years, will the German peoples be united. Then, as soon as the enemy's power has been broken, they will fall asunder once more. Not for half a century, and not until another Napoleon threatens them, will they at length become a nation–though even then, only a fragment. So atrophied was Napoleon's German princes made him believe that the Germans were disintegrated for all time; whereas, had he been able to understand the forces that were at work, he would have realised that the jealousies of the rival sovereign houses were the only obstacle to the reunion of these kindred stocks.

But the sublime breathing of history sometimes determines the rhythm of an epoch even in despite of the will of the genius that animates it. In sweeping curves, during these years, the spirit of liberty returns to her primal home in the hearts of the people. For, just as Bonaparte, in the name of liberty, had defeated the princes and stirred the peoples to revolt; so now, in the name of liberty, the people arose to defeat him the prince of princes. Doubtless this great movement of destiny was complicated by numerous petty wishes, and blurred by minor circles. It is not the force of legitimism which now, after twenty years, is at last gathering strength to slay the spirit of revolt. Pallid, disunited, decadent, and with never a great figure among them, are the princes in the league they form against the one man who rules in virtues of his self-made power.

But the fact that the peoples of Spain and Germany are eager to force their princes into the fight, gives to the tragical collapse of the usurper a semblance of poetical justice, and that is why we who look on find it easier to bear the sight of the slaying of the lion by the spears cast by such a legion of hunters.

IX

Letizia looks anxiously at her son. His face is clouded, though he keeps his thoughts to himself. What can she do to help him? Intimates? Many of them, she sees plainly enough, are betraying him. He needs his brothers, that he may have the support of steadfast hearts, even though he thinks them lacking in intelligence. She therefore puts her trust in her other sons, writes to London and Graz, smooths the path for reconciliation. One day, after a decade of estrangement, comes a letter from the ambitious Lucien, who says he is always at Napoleon's service.

But the Emperor cannot believe that he, the mightiest of his family, needs any assistance from the others. Though he has always regarded Lucien as the most capable of his brothers, he proposes merely a formal promotion. In imperial fashion, he answers through his mother: "Please write to let him know in my name that his letter has awakened an echo in my heart. I think of raising him to the throne of Tuscany. He loves the fine arts. It will suit him to reign in Florence, and to revive the glories of the Medicis." There is no place for Lucien at the centre of things! As for Louis, who also offers to devote his powers to the cause of France (in so far as he can honour ably do this), and who sends a copy of his last volume of verse–the ex-king of Holland is met with a rebuff: "The idea you seem to have formed about my position is quite erroneous. I have more than a million men under arms, and two hundred million francs in my war chest. Holland remains French.... Still, I am ready to greet you in the spirit of one who brought you up as if he had been your father."

The Emperor reads this answer to his mother before sending it. She tries to mitigate its harshness in a long covering letter; tells Louis how pretty his children have grown; urges him to come to Paris in any case. "The Emperor has forgotten to give me your poems. I will ask him for them, and will let you know what I think of them when next I write."

Next day, the old lady finds a savage article in the "Moniteur," in which she learns that the king of Naples will have to recall his envoy from Vienna. When she asks what this signifies, her friends reluctantly explain that Murat has been persuaded by Caroline to intrigue with the Habsburgs, so that the pair are now playing double. Letizia writes to upbraid her daughter. Joseph is out of humour, for he thinks that Napoleon is not supporting him properly in the Spanish war. She does her best to appease him through the instrumentality of his wife. Furthermore, she tries to mollify Jerome, whom the Emperor had sent home in disgrace. Finally, she gets to work on Hortense, who is doing all she can to hinder Louis' coming to Paris.

Now a woman well over sixty, she does her utmost to keep the peace between her sons, daughters, sons-in-law. But it seems to her that the greatness for which the world envies her family has brought in its train nothing but discord, jealousy, arrogance, ostracism, and betrayal. Her thoughts fly back to her native island, where her kindred always formed a united front against other clans. Moreover, her eyes, though old, are clear-sighted; and she sees that the star of the Buonaparti is paling.

The Emperor has little personal feeling about these matters. In his present situation, he regards them from a purely political outlook. No doubt he says to himself that Murat and Caroline are traitors; but his main concern is, how he can make sure of the support of Murat's soldiers. He therefore writes in a conciliatory strain to Caroline; keeps her husband informed about the impending campaign; and asks for troops, which Murat ultimately agrees to send, for both he and Caroline think that Napoleon may prove victorious after all, and are afraid of being dethroned unless they keep in his good graces. At the same time, they wish to have a secure footing in the other camp, and therefore conclude secret treaties with England and with the ex-king of Sicily (whose dominions they themselves have filched).

Napoleon even seeks to conciliate Bernadotte, though he cannot but regard the crown prince of Sweden as a treacherous kinsman and an enemy of his house. He offers Pomerania as the reward of alliance and the prize of victory. But for Bernadotte, the bid is not high enough; this Frenchman prefers to join the coalition against France. His ambition is to reign there; France is worth more than Pomerania. Bernadotte enters into especially close relationships with Prussia. In Berlin he meets Madame de Stael, and these fellow-countrymen of the Emperor, united in their detestation of him, foregather among the oppressed Prussians.

A third enemy, whom the Emperor approaches with blandishments during these feverish weeks, is the captive Pope. Pius VII has been brought to Fontainebleau, and Napoleon gets to work on him through the instrumentality of prelates devoted to the imperial cause, adding personal suggestion until the old man gives way. How great will be the power of the Church (this is the Emperor's theme) when Catholicism has been re-established throughout Germany! By trifling concessions upon matters of form, and by cunning devices, Napoleon is able to secure a new Concordat. Thanks to this reconciliation with the Church, he is able to recruit new Catholic soldiers in all the lands under his sway. When the Pope, a week after signing the Concordat, wants to revoke it, the Emperor says with a smile: "Your Holiness, being infallible, cannot have made a mistake in entering into this arrangement!"

During these weeks, a desire for peace suddenly spreads throughout Europe. The Pope wants peace on the Vistula, and Metternich wants it in London. Count Bubna, with whom Napoleon had negotiated years before in Schönbrunn, comes to Paris to advise peace, for Vienna can neither send nor refuse the troops which the Emperor has demanded. In February, peace can be had for the asking. Why does the man who needs peace most of all, make impossible stipulations?

For ten years, one war after another has been practically forced upon the Emperor as a consequence of his first victories. Now, when he is in grievous peril, and when his isolation is increasing, the will-to-war grows in him as in the early days of his career. When unconquered, he would gladly have laid aside the sword; now, after his defeat, he craves for new victories: But though his shield has been tarnished in Russia, though he would fain win fresh glories for himself and for France, these are but the pretexts of destiny. In very truth, he is stiff-necked, and will prove himself to be so at three congresses during this year 1813. The reason is that all the elements of his character are now rolling inexorably forwards; the reason is that, "in accordance with the nature of things," he is advancing along a road on which he must march to the bitter end.

Forward! Since the war must be, the allies are arming everywhere. England makes treaties with Sweden and Prussia; to conciliate the latter, the tsar renounces his claims to East Prussia; Prussia calls Germany to arms; Austria makes a truce with Russia, tries to enter into an agreement with Saxony and Bavaria and even King Jerome. Emperor Francis withdraws his troops to Cracow, ostensibly to save them for the coming campaign.

"The first step towards desertion!" exclaims Napoleon, when this news comes to hand. He must now withdraw his own forces from the Vistula to Oder. In Vienna, he once more offers Silesia. The offer is declined with thanks, for the Austrian role is to be one of armed mediation. While the whole world is thus preparing for the struggle, and when in the middle of March the first signal is given in Paris by the Prussian declaration of war, Talleyrand, in his open ambush, says with a smile: "The hour has struck; the Emperor Napoleon must become king of France."

A remarkable flash of insight, on the part of one who cannot but hope that no step so sensible as this shall be taken–and who must, none the less, at bottom, wish for it. Nevertheless matters have gone too far; not the levying of troops alone, but the preparations in the minds of men. Everyone knows that the last great combat is imminent, that nothing can avert it. The only one who could have called a halt, and will not do so, is driven onward in his own despite, and he is weary. There are new signs of this growing weariness.

First of all, there is the simplicity upon which he insists in his environment "I want my journeys to be very differently arranged. I shall not take so many people with me; fewer cooks and less table furniture; no meal to consist of more than three courses.... I shall not take any pages with me; they are of no use whatever; only two bedmakers instead of four; two tents instead of four; and so on." At the same time, he orders plans for a small palace, "a comfortable place rather than an imposing one (the two things are incompatible); ... my room must open on the garden, .. or, preferably, I must have a north room and a south room, according to the season; all arranged as in a well-to-do country gentleman's mansion.... It is to be a holiday seat, or a dwelling for a man in his declining years."

In 1805, when he was in the plenitude of his powers, he had said: "The war need not take long. I am still good for six years, but then it will be time to call a halt." Now, when he takes the field once more, four months after his return from Russia, his mien is quiet and careworn as he steps into his travelling carriage in the courtyard at Saint-Cloud. He leans back among the cushions, with his hand pressed to his forehead. To Caulaincourt, his travelling companion, he acknowledges his distress "at having so soon to leave my good Louis and my lovely boy. I envy the poorest peasant in my dominions. By the time he grows old, he has already paid his debt to his country, and can stay at home with is wife and children. I am the only person whom an inexplicable fate leads back ever and again into the field."

No more pages, he is in his declining years, wants to stay at home with wife and child–and this is only seven years after the programme just quoted! Are these fourth-act moods, these shadows that fall across his soul, merely the consequences of the Russian catastrophe? Are they not, rather, the essential causes of new defeats? The moods of a man growing prematurely old, one whose work is often interfered with by illness, one who is being increasingly mastered by the natural inclinations of a family man well on in the forties. He wants to spend at the domestic fireside the evening of a life which is not equipped for seven or eight decades like that of his mother or his brothers.

He is himself in the frame of mind with which he had reproached his marshals at Danzing less than a year ago, when he had declared they would rather have an easy life of it in their country seats than go campaigning with him. Is not such a longing natural in a man who has been working himself to death for twenty years, and who has chosen the bee for his escutcheon?

But those on whom the Parcæ bestow the ecstasies of youth, must pay for it by the oncoming of age. He has had such wonderful successes that he must not expect to garner also the joys of content in achievement. He has conjured up the gods; now they have come!

commendation: "Although I personally led all the movements of my army, and was several times within range of grape-shot, I have not had even a graze." The words and the actions are those of one who feels weak, and would fain appear strong. Henceforth the warnings of fate thicken.

True, he gains another victory at Bautzen, but does not take any prisoners. On the second day of the battle, he is riding under fire, accompanied by Caulaincourt and his friend Duroc –the latter having for a decade been his inseparable companion in the field. Men are being shot down in his immediate neighbourhood. He gallops to an adjoining elevation; adjutants follow him. Dust and smoke; a tree close at hand is smashed to splinters. He thunders past. On the hillock, a young officer comes up to him and stammers; "Marshal Duroc has been killed."

"Impossible! He was at my side a moment ago!"

"The cannon ball which struck the tree, brought down the marshal as well."

The Emperor slowly rides back into camp. He says:

"When will fate have a little discrimination? What will be the end of it all? Caulaincourt, my eagles are again victorious, but my star is setting."

Duroc has not been killed outright, but he is dying. Terrible is the aspect of this shattered comrade. Greeting and farewell, both men in tears. Duroc murmurs: "I told thee at Dresden what would happen; the inner voice ... Give me some opium."

This tone, the sudden use of "thee," the last request of a man who has no fear of death. The Emperor walks unsteadily as he leaves the cottage.

From a farmyard, he contemplates for a while the spot where his friend had fallen, and then makes his way to the place where the guard is encamped, with his own tent in the middle. That evening, wearing his grey field-coat, he sits gloomily on a campstool, apart from his suite; he listens to the sounds of the camp, where the guardsman are cooking supper and calling to one another, in the distance, the men of a yager corps are singing a song. Bivouac fires are glowing in the half-darkness of the May night; two burning villages flame like torches in the sky. An officer draws near, and hesitates to give his report. Before the words are spoken, the Emperor understands that Duroc is dead.

Next day, he orders the purchase of land where a memorial is to be erected, and he pens the inscription.. "Here died, gloriously, in the arms of his friend the Emperor, struck down on the field of battle by a cannon ball, General Duroc, Grand Marshal of the Emperor Napoleon."

General Bonaparte used to have no time for such feelings. He concealed his heartache, and stormed onward, even when he lost his wife's love. Now it behoved him to push forward into Silesia, to follow up the Russians into Poland, to take advantage of the misgivings of the allies; and, by delivering blows in rapid succession, to fetter the vacillating Austrian to his side. In later years, he said frankly that his failure to do these things had been the greatest mistake in his life. Once more, the deliberations of the emperor are impeding the activities of the general. His private letters from France are full of reports concerning the clamour for peace. "What especially determined my course of action was Austria's preparation for war, and the desire to gain time. This led me to interrupt the course of my victories." In Silesia, at the beginning of June, he agrees to a six weeks' truce, thus giving his adversaries time to attain complete unity at the congresses of Reichenbach and Prague.

Is he deceived as to the frame of mind of the wavering German princes? He knows them all. "The Saxons are just as German as the others, and would gladly follow Prussia's example. The king is faithful to me, but I do not trust his troops.... Austria's impudence is indescribable. While uttering honeyed words, she tries to snatch from me Dalmatia and Istria... There never was anything so false as the court of Vienna. If, today, I were to grant Austria's demands, she would ask tomorrow for Italy and Germany." Now, when he sees that the Habsburg ruler is about to go over to the enemy, he realises too late that his marriage has been a mistake, for he has gained nothing by it, and has lost much. His own patrician family feeling had made him believe that there must be an imperial family feeling. The old tone of contempt for hereditary monarchs is at length heard once more. To his intimates, he again and again says frankly what he thinks of the kings who are kings by birth:

"Among those who are born to sit on the throne, the ties of nature count for nothing. The interest of his daughter and his grandson will not move Emperor Francis an inch from the calculations of his cabinet. These men have no blood in their veins, nothing but frozen politics! What pygmies they are, the kings by the grace of God–and the grace of Napoleon! My leniency has been my blunder. In Tilsit I could have crushed them, but I was too generous. History should have taught me that houses so degenerate deserve neither loyalty nor faith! Now, England is filling their coffers with gold. But I shall prove myself a better statesman than these born kings who never leave their golden cages!"

In this atmosphere of intrigue, when he has to rub shoulders with princes who dare not fight either for him or against him, traitors are his best confidants.

The Emperor therefore summons Fouché, to whom he says: "Your friends Bernadotte and Metternich are my worst enemies. Your Bernadotte can do us an immense amount of harm, for he is able to give my enemies the key to our policy, and he can explain to them the tactics of our armies.... His head has been turned because legitimate princes flatter him!" There we have it once more, the word whose mystical power explains half of Napoleon's perpetual unrest. He can never refrain from a tremor when he speaks of the legitimate rulers, whom he regards with mingled contempt and envy. Whether he is mimicking them, or whether he is railing at them, he, who is an upstart, is always pondering this problem of birth.

Instead of listening to the call of the nations, which soon rises clear above the babble of the princes, he can only look on with malicious delight at the manœuvres of the chessplayers in the cabinets. He watches how England doles out subsidies to Prussia; how Alexander and Francis hold converse about the weakness of their ally, the king of Prussia; how Frederick William, in his dread of revolution, disbands the enthusiastic Landsturm, refuses to give high office of Scharnhorst the boldest and to Stein the ablest of his advisers, dismisses and banishes Schleiermacher for a speech voicing the popular sentiment. The Emperor sends Fouché on a secret mission (in plain words, as a spy) to the congress of Prague.

In Spain, meanwhile, though Napoleon in the north has been strengthening his position by two victories. Joseph has been utterly crushed by Wellington at Vittoria. The king of Spain has run away. When the princes learn in Prague that the south of France now lies open to an English invasion, their inclination to defiance is promptly strengthened. The Emperor, who had left the best of his generals to fight for Joseph in Spain, is beside himself with wrath. "He alone is to blame!" writes Napoleon to Paris. "The English reports show how utterly stupid was his command. Never was anything so absurd! Of course he is no soldier, but he is responsible... Make the king understand that he is not to see any one till I come back.... Otherwise his house in Paris will become a centre of intrigue, and I sahll have to put him under arrest, for my patience is at an end. I will no longer have my affairs imperilled out of consideration for idiots who are neither soldiers nor statesmen!"

His eldest brother is his closest intimate in the family,– and now the Emperor thinks that Joseph in a private house in Paris is more to be dreaded even than as king in Madrid! Will Napoleon at length learn his lesson, and, after this outburst, leave Joseph at peace? Hardly! For even little Jerome has an army once more, and is again making a mess of things; he gives one of the generals new marching orders, with the remark that he is acting on instructions from the Emperor. The latter hears of it too late. "I will not tell you in plain terms what I think of your conduct; enough that I will not tolerate it any longer! If you again make false representations of the kind, I shall publish an order of the day to the effect that in

The more, the merrier!" He goes on to warn Metternich against counting on Germany, whose peoples he is holding together by the presence of his soldiers and whose princes are held together by their dread of Austria. He advises armed neutrality, so long as the negotiations are going on in Prague, whereas Metternich talks of armed mediation. These finesses of the old diplomacy are to mask the gulf between them. Then, for a whole hour, they dispute about the relative strength of the opposing armies, each claiming the possession of exact information about the other side.

"I have detailed and accurate lists of your forces," says the Emperor. "I have had so many spies at work, that I know to a unit even how many drummers you have. But no one knows better than myself how much or how little value to attach to these secret service reports. My calculations are based on more exact data, upon mathematical inferences. In the last resort, no one has more than he can have." The Emperor shows the Austrian envoy the muster rolls of the Austrian army, which till yesterday had been part of the French alliance. Metternich can see for himself whether the figures are accurate. The Emperor then spends hours upon a description of the Russian campaign. When the minister remarks that the imperial troops are composed of striplings, and asks what Napoleon will do when these children, like those who have gone before them, have been swallowed up by the war, the Emperor is overcome with wrath. He turns pale, his features are distorted, and he shouts at Metternich:

"You are not a soldier. You do not know what passes in a soldier's mind. I grew to manhood on the battlefield. Such a man as I does not care a snap of the fingers for the lives of a millions men!" He flings his hat into a corner of the room. Now, there is nothing assumed about his anger, and what he has just said is the revelation of an innermost truth. The man who turns pale at the sight of a dying horse, who cannot bear to see a human being pass away, remains and must remain impassive when, in his army lists, he adds up the figures, shifts the hundreds of thousands from column to column, and erases the myriads of slain. Is not war made with human lives, and does it not end with corpses? What is the use of reproaching a craftsman for using the tools of his trade? But as far as morals are concerned, the minister has the best of the argument, and he would have been glad if all France could have heard Napoleon's words.

"France has no reason to complain," says the Emperor more calmly. "To spare France, I have sacrificed Germans and Poles. In Russia I lost three hundred thousand men, but only a tenth of them were Frenchmen!" Meanwhile, he has picked up his hat for himself, a thing he has certainly not done for the last ten years; he has acted sensibly, as if he had still been General Bonaparte. Then he plants himself in front of the Austrian and says:

"It was exceedingly stupid of me to marry an archduchess. I was trying to weld the new with the old, to make Gothic prejudices square with the institutions of my own century. Now I can see the whole extent of my error! The blunder may cost me my throne, but I will bury the world beneath its ruins!"

This tragical admission is the climax of the interview, and the turning-point of the problem of war or peace. The rancour engendered in him by his own mistake spurs him on, regardless of prudential considerations, into the fight with a coalition whose forces outnumber his by three to one. Like a great gambler who realises that he has made an irretrievable blunder he is impelled by the stubbornness characteristic of such natures as his to stake all upon a single throw. He will show that, blunder notwithstanding, he can still win.

By the time he dismisses Metternich, he has fully recovered composure. His hand on the door-handle, he says: "We shall see one another again before you leave?"

"I am at Your Majesty's service. But I have no longer any hope of succeeding in my mission."

The Emperor looks at him quizzically, and taps him gently on the shoulder: "Do you know what will happen? You will not make war on me!"

After three days' negotiation, Metternich wishes to depart, but the Emperor is afraid of the final rupture. Napoleon summons the Austrian envoy several times, and then invites him to an early interview in the garden. The two men walk up and down.

"Now then, you must not assume this injured air!" In ten minutes they arrange for a prolongation of the truce, and talk about further conversations in Prague. Everything is left hanging in the wind; and in the memorandum he signs with Metternich, the Emperor recognises his father-in-law's position of armed neutrality, which can only be a stage on the way to war. Then he drives off to Mainz, that he may see once more the wife who is daughter of that same Austrian ruler. He has appointed her regent in Paris again, but has expressly forbidden his ministers to submit certain kinds of documents for her consideration. "There are details with which a young woman's mind must not be besmirched."

Had the Habsburg archduchess been a staunch wife and an affectionate daughter, she would have journeyed on to Vienna, and would have brought about a reconciliation which there was really nothing to prevent except the two men's wounded pride. She had a passably good understanding. Only a few weeks before, the Emperor, writing to Francis, had said: "She fills the post of prime minister to my great satisfaction." We cannot for a moment suppose that now, at the height of the crisis, he can have failed to let her know all the hazards of the hour, were it only to ensure that in the event of a breach her feelings would be on his side. But the little goose made no move. Her only concern was to send costly gifts which would make an impression on her relatives.

In Prague, each party keeps the other in suspense; Fouché does his master harm by gossiping with all and sundry; Bernadotte cements his alliance with his new friends. When, at the last moment, it seems possible that the Emperor may give way, Alexander and Frederick William are so much alarmed at the prospect that they compel Metternich to make the terms more exacting, for they realise that so favourable an opportunity is not likely to recur. The Emperor now angrily draws back, and on the day after the expiry of the truce he receives his father-in-law's declaration of war. No doubt, in the interval, he has secured reinforcements; but he can no longer trust the Confederation of the Rhine, and has to keep watch upon his German auxiliaries. He stands to arms in Saxony and Silesia, faced by Schwarzenberg in command of three armies, two of them, respectively led by Blücher and Bernadotte, holding Silesia and the north. With Schwarzenberg is Moreau, who has just arrived, and who, on his last visit to Germany, had been the conqueror of that country.

Thus paradoxical is the marshalling of forces in the game of chess. Under the Emperor of the French, are fighting three German kings against a German general, who a little while back had been the Emperor's subordinate in the war against Russia. Against Napoleon, are fighting two French generals. One of them is leading Prussian troops against the man who had for years pushed him to the front; nor is this general really a royalist, for he, too, is a son of the revolution. Blücher is the only true-hearted foe, for Blücher, whom Napoleon defeated seven years earlier, has never fought on the Emperor's side, and has never espoused his cause. The one element in Napoleon's favour is that three monarchs have their fingers in Schwarzenberg's pie, three commanders who know as little about the trade of war as Brother Joseph did in Spain.

At the end of August, the Emperor opens the second Saxon campaign with a great victory near Dresden. But on the third day, when he might have followed up the allies and scattered them, he is seized by a violent attack of gastric spasm. For a whole hour he fancies he has been poisoned; his will is paralysed, and he withdraws instead of pursuing. Thereby he loses an army corps, and thus (according to the report of Daru, his daily companion) "causes the disaster of 1813." In this first battle against the hated Bonaparte, Moreau falls. Is it an omen? When the Emperor hears the news, the rivalry of his youth flames up anew, and from his very soul he cries: "Moreau is dead! My star!"

His other army has been defeated by Blücher on the Katzbach. Once more, considerations of statesmanship outweigh those of generalship. How can I divide my adversaries? It will be better to spare Bohemia for the sake of Austria, for the defeat has aroused alarm there. He will make a surprise march on Berlin, and will thus lure the Prussians out of Silesia.

But what the tsar had said years ago is still true.... Miracles only happen when the Emperor is present, and he cannot be everywhere. He is thus hampered in his great enterprise. Lack of fighting spirit, difficulties of food-supply, and the frequency of desertion, are continually making it necessary for him to visit his flanking armies; so that in popular parlance, in consequence of his rushings to and fro, he is nicknamed the "Bautzen Messenger." His armies suffer more and more from lack of food. They are so thickly set upon the ground that they have long since eaten the country bare.

Nevertheless, he has not nearly enough soldiers. Since the 1814 levies are already with the colours, he orders the Senate to call up also those of 1815, and even the men whose liability to service has nearly expired on account of advancing years–the very peasants whom, when setting forth on this campaign in a mood of self-pity, he had envied for their fortunate position. But when will the reinforcements arrive? Who will train them, and how long will it take? Vainly now, at the end of September, he sends an envoy to his father-in-law, to talk of peace; he is prepared to make great sacrifices, "if only you will listen." But Francis remains firm, and is at length able to detach an important member of the Confederation of the Rhine: the king of Bavaria falls away. Thereupon the anxious chessplayer, round whom the clouds are gathering, says to his old comrade something which he has never before been willing to admit:

"Marmont, my game is going awry."

With this admission, the Emperor's genius spreads its wings and flies away.

XI

On Düben Heath is a Saxon fortress, Düben Castle. There, one morning, the Emperor is at work; planning the march on Berlin, the defeat of Bernadotte and Blücher, smashing blows which will finish off the enemy.

Then a number of generals are announced. He comes out of his study to meet them, knowing what they want, for his intimates have kept him informed of the growing discontent among the leaders, who wish to winter quietly on the Rhine. Marshal Ney has recently reported: "I am no longer master of my army." One of the visitors begins to speak hesitatingly; a second puts forward dubious reasons; then, nodding to encourage one another, they all obsequiously beg him not to march on Berlin. Leipzing will be a better point of attack.

The Emperor listens to them in silence as he wonders: "Is my power vanishing?" At length he replies: "The secession of Bavaria is imminent. A movement on Leipzig, a backward movement, will arouse despair among the soldiers. But I will think over what you have said." He spends the rest of the day alone, refusing himself to all visitors, brooding over his maps. Caulaincourt, on duty outside, listens for sounds from within, but can only hear the windows rattling in the October gale which is howling round the castle. At length he is allowed to enter. The Emperor walks up and down, and, speaking rather to himself than to Caulaincourt, he says: "The French cannot endure reverses." Then he sinks into a reverie.

Next day he announces that they will go to Leipzig. It is October 15th: general animation; orders are issued; everyone is delighted. Discussing with Marmont the latest steps of the Habsburg ruler, Napoleon says in conclusion: "I prefer a man of honour who simply keeps his word, to a conscientious man who does what he thinks right.... Emperor Francis has done what he believes to be the best for his subjects; he is conscientious, but he is not a man of honour."

Next day begins the great "Battle of the Nations." The Emperor has only one hundred and eighty thousand men against three hundred thousand of the allies; by the evening he has won only part of the battlefield. On the second morning Bernadotte arrives with reinforcements. The Emperor sees that things are going badly, and would like to withdraw, but he cannot make up his mind to a step that would give the impression of defeat. Once more he tries negotiation. General Merveldt has been taken prisoner; his sword is restored on parole; he is to go to Emperor Francis with proposals for an armistice.

"I will retire behind the Saale, while the Russians and the Prussians withdraw beyond the Elbe, and you Austrians go back into Bohemia; Saxony must remain neutral." Then, livening up, he develops to this enemy general nothing less than a new plan for Europe. Hanover is to be returned to England; the Baltic coast is to be freed; any of the princes of the Confederation of the Rhine who wish to do so can leave the Confederation; Poland, Spain, and Holland are to be independent; the only reservation is as regards Italy, which must not become Austrian. "Be off with you! You have a splendid peace mission. Should fortune favour it, you will earn the love of a great nation. But if your side refuse peace, we shall know how to defend ourselves."

General Merveldt departs in amazement, and his report seems incredible to his master. What! The Emperor Napoleon, in the course of war, between battles, is willing to renounce half Europe and chooses a prisoner to bring this offer? We did not know he was so weak.

The Emperor is anxiously awaiting his emissary's return. Till far on into the night, therefore, he refrains from issuing orders for the morrow; he speaks of the ties of kinship, and of his wife and child. Suddenly he is attacked by his gastric trouble, and staggers against the wall of the tent, his face pale. They wish to send for his physician. "No! my tent is transparent. If I am up and about, everyone is at his post." At least lie down, Sire!"

"No, I will die standing."

"Do let me fetch the doctor, Sire."

"No, I tell you! I can send a sick soldier to hospital. But who can send me?" Terrible moments pass. "I'm getting better now. See to it that no one comes into the tent!"

Half an hour later, he issues orders, but not for a retreat. Instead, the army moves a little nearer to Leipzig. The enemy now outnumbers him by two to one.

When day comes, he takes up his headquarters in a windmill. The attack upon the French starts from three sides. It appears that, at the last moment, Bernadotte has persuaded the Saxons to turn their guns against France. "Infamous!" exclaims the Emperor, and all around echo the word. Saxon officers who remain faithful to him, break their swords. A dragoon belonging to the escort wheels his horse, and shouts: "We'll do for them yet, the scoundrels! We Frenchmen, too, are here! Vive l'Empereur!" The whole escort follows him at the charge. Soon a young officer, who has seized one of the Saxon eagles, gallops back with it to the Emperor, and collapses from his wounds as he arrives. "These sons of France!" says Napoleon softly.

On the second day of battle, he loses sixty thousand men. He is beaten, but even the German critics say of the affair: "The allies did not secure an overwhelming victory, such as might have been expected from the enormous preponderance of their forces."

During the hasty retreat of the defeated army through the town of Leipzig, the Emperor dictates orders for the withdrawal. "They had brought him a wooden stool," writes an eyewitness. "On this, he now fell into a slumber of exhaustion, his hands loosely folded in his lap. In gloomy silence the generals were standing round the fire, while the soldiers were marching past a little way off."

Next morning the pursuing enemy spread disorder in the streets; a bridge was blown up prematurely, so that the rear guard was forced to surrender; one of the marshals escaped by swimming across the river, another was drowned, several were wounded and taken prisoner. When, subsequently, Macdonald came across

and bears it lightly, as if it were a laurel crown.
Thus didst thou. What seemed so far away,
thou hast tranquilly learned to make thine own;
and whatever fierce obstacles might block the path,
thou sawest them, contemplated them, and understood them,
A joyful day dawned, it summoned thee,
thou wast summoned, and thus it came to pass...
And thou still standest despite all that has happened to thee,
despite the foe, who, with war and death,
threatens thee from without and from within....
The peoples are agape, they chatter, they are full of vain imaginings–
What do they care for, but games?....
The false world, it wooes us for our treasure,
for our favour, for our position,
and, even if one makes one's lover one's equal,
love does not suffice him, he wants the whole kingdom.
So was it with this man!–And now, declare it abroad,
even if it cost you your life:
To every man, be he whom he may,
there comes a last happiness and a last day.

At the same date, Schelling writes: "I do not believe that Napoleon's end is yet very near. If I am right, he will still be spared; and, even if all his helpers fall away from him. he will still live to drink the cup of humiliation to the dregs." When, almost immediately afterwards the Bavarians definitively changed side, Hegel wrote "In Nuremberg the mob has welcomed the incoming Austrians with the most hateful jubilation. Nothing more contemptible can be imagined than the mood and the conduct of the burghers."

Three outstanding Germans, immediately after Leipzig! Certainly, it is far from being a final defeat. Fighting, and fighting victoriously, the Emperor withdraws, In Erfurt, Murat presents himself, wishing to go back to his kingdom. The master allows him to do so, saying: "By next May, I shall have an a army of a quarter of a million on the Rhine!" Thus does his intelligence work; such is the quality of his imagination; he can still think only in hundreds of thousands. In Mainz, his troops are attacked by typhus, and he hastens to move what is left of them across the Rhine. During the retreat he works from three in the morning till eleven at night.

Meanwhile, the advancing allied headquarters are thronged by the princes who are deserting the cause of Napoleon. All is promptly forgotten and forgiven. But there is one honest man left who finds strong words to describe what is happening: "What do you think of these wretches' behaviour? .... They have had better treatment than they deserve.... All these princelets are weaklings, to whom a far more honourable existence has been conceded than their pitiful conduct would seem to justify....The retention of their sovereignty, which consists in pretentiousness, pleasure seeking, and the lust for dominion, has cost them nothing more than the blood of their subjects."

Such is Baron vom Stein's judgment concerning his peers, the German princes.

XII

Letizia is sitting by the fire. In her hand is a letter from Mainz, in which her son answers her intercession for Louis by imposing certain conditions. But this is not what troubles her; she is thinking of the Emperor's parenthetical allusion to the turn in his fortunes. He writes: "In this situation, when all Europe is rising against me, and my heart is so full of care...." She has never warned him of the impending dangers; they are both of them too proud for that, But she has often uttered her foreboding to intimates, with her phrase "Pourvou que cela doure!" She has never been disturbed by the thought of any disaster to herself. She thinks only of her dear ones. Who will help them when everything falls to pieces? To whom, she is now asking herself, can the Emperor look for support?

When he returns, she has to endure the recognition that the treachery begins among her own children. Murat, who is always led by the keener intelligence than his own (that of Caroline), signs a truce with England and enters into an alliance with Austria. Elise has an adviser. Fouché, who, keeps away from Paris until the Emperor's fall. "The only thing that could save us all would be the Emperor's death." Such are the ex-minister's words to the Emperor's sister. But Elise writes to her mother asking what dances are to be given that winter in Paris. Louis defies orders, and, being unable to stay in Austria any longer, comes to Paris without leave. Napoleon proposes to banish him to a distance of two hundred miles from Paris. The mother intercedes between the pair; there is a further interview, as a result of which Napoleon and Louis are once more estranged. Jerome has left his subjects in the lurch, and has fled incognito from Cassel. Joseph, despite the Emperor's reiterated requests, persists in his refusal to undertake the defence of Paris. Lucien keeps his distance, still in a bad humour.

Such is the gallery of brothers and sisters, the relatives upon whom for a decade the Emperor has been trying to build up his dynasty. What can be the feelings of a mother who has always cherished the most tender affection for that one of her children who happened to be suffering most keenly?

But in Morfontaine a cheerful mood prevails. The company there consists of Joseph, the Spanish king without a country; Jerome's wife, a queen in like situation, whose father has gone over to the allies; the sometime grand inquisitor of Spain says Mass in the chapel; there are two colonial bishops; German, Spanish, and Italian courtiers without a court–a brilliant company, like the audience at private theatricals, watching actors who will soon come down from the stage to take their place on the floor of the drawing-room. Only one of them hopes to draw a big fish out of the troubled waters, Bernadotte's wife, Joseph's sister-in-law, the woman to whom twenty years before the Emperor had given the go-by. She knows that her husband, commander of one of the allied armies, is already on the Rhine; she hopes that ere long, in Notre Dame, he will place Josephine's crown on her pretty brown head.

At this country-seat, more intrigues are carried on against Napoleon than Joseph is aware of; for Joseph is not himself an intriguer; he is merely easygoing and vain. The Emperor recognises this, now that it is too late, and says to Roéderer;

"That has been one of my mistakes. I fancied I needed my brothers for the dynasty, but it is safe without them. It has been brought into being the heart of the storm by the nature of things. The empress suffices.... Everything has been quiet for a year past. There is only disquiet when Joseph lives in Paris.... He cannot forget that he is the first-born. Was there ever anything more absurd? If he were talking of our father's vineyard, that would be another story!... His interests are in women, houses, furniture. He likes to go out rabbit shooting, and to play blind-man's buff with the girls. I am tied to nothing; care not a jot for houses or for women; though I do feel a little concern about my son."

Thus does his monomania make headway in these weeks of increasing peril. We see that all the rest, court included, has been nothing more than a game. He cares not a jot for anything outside the one passion of his soul—except that he is a little concerned about his son.

He now quickly makes up his mind to restore the Spanish crown to King Ferdinand, who is set at liberty; but the Cortes must approve the treaty. This is Talleyrand's advice, for Talleyrand has now been recalled to the Tuileries. Insistence on ratification by the Cortes will delay matters. The traitor's aim is to keep a French army in the south, so that France may be weakened for the benefit of the allies, for whose cause Talleyrand is now working. Joseph protests.

"My present situation makes it impossible for me to think of any sort of foreign dominion," writes the Emperor to his brother. "I shall deem myself lucky if the peace treaty will allow me to keep the old boundaries of France. Everything is crashing round me. My armies have been destroyed, and it will hardly be possible to make the losses good. Holland is gone, and Italy is uncertain.... Belgium and the Rhine province are discontented; the Spanish frontier is held by the enemy.... How is it possible, at this crisis, to think of a foreign throne?" When the prefect of police advises him to leave a larger body of National Guards in Paris, during the campaign that is now imminent, he rejoins: "Who can guarantee that they will be faithful to me? Am I to leave so large a force in my rear?"

He is in despair. Surely there is no other word for the description of these thoughts? His family, his allies, his own capital, all seem untrustworthy to him. Thus completely has his mood changed since the battle of Leipzig. Count Lavalette, Postmaster General, one of the most honest men in Paris, who often came to see him at this time, found him one evening in a condition of great depression. Napoleon received Lavalette in his bedroom, standing in front of the fire, his hands stretched out towards the blaze. The visitor, though a stout-hearted fellow, advises peace, saying that the French are mutable. But when he ventures to mention the name of the Bourbons, on whom perhaps the Emperor's mantle may fall, Napoleon turns away from the fire and silently throws himself on the bed. When, a few minutes later, the count draws near, he finds that Napoleon is sleeping.

These healthy reactions are a sign of returning courage. Napoleon's overthrow is close at hand; he foresees the catastrophe; but when people talk to him about the Bourbons, to whose throne he has mounted and who may dispossess him in turn, he cannot be bothered with the topic. It bores him, and he goes to sleep.

Awakening reinvigorated, he recognises that the Bourbon sympathies of the northern provinces are a danger; he notes that the funds have fallen to fifty, and that the shares of the Bank of France have declined to half their former value; and he finds that the new National Guard, which after all he is obliged to call up, fails to materialise. He therefore gladly accedes to a proposal that issues from the allies in Frankfort. They are a disunited as he can possibly wish. Metternich, being a statesman, thinks it will be better not to occupy Paris. The tsar, being a romanticist, wants to take vengeance for Moscow by blowing up the Tuileries. In the end, Austria gets her way. The offer to France is that the country is his legitimate heir, who is now nearly three years old, Napoleon has the child in his arms when he takes leave of the officers of the National Guard. "I entrust to you the dearest of my possessions. You are answerable!" Once more he urges tenacity on his brother; once more he leaves his wife regent of their son's realm. Next morning he quits Paris.

He will not re-enter the city for more than a year, after devious wanderings.

XIII

In a few weeks he is beaten.

His first strokes are successful. Near Brienne, where he forces Blücher to retreat, and where he himself takes so active a part in the fight that he is obliged to draw his sword in self-defence, he recognizes the tree under which "as a twelve-year-old youngster I used to sit and read Tasso." A romantic encounter which links his later life with those early days when his dreams were first dreamed! His historical feeling concerning himself grows in such circumstances to legendary proportions.

Immediately thereafter, Blücher gains a victory over him near La Rothiere. Paris is threatened. The Emperor's strength seems broken. Caulaincourt, in a letter, begs him to yield; Maret does the same by word of mouth. Napoleon pays little heed to what Maret is saying; absently, he flutters the pages of a book by Montesquieu. Then, pointing to a passage, he bids Maret read aloud. "I know of nothing nobler than the determination of a monarch of our day to prefer to bury himself beneath the ruins of a throne rather than accept proposals to which no king should ever hearken."

"I know of something nobler still!" exclaims Maret. "That you should sacrifice your glory and thereby fill the abyss wherein, otherwise, France will find her grave!"

"Very well," answers the Emperor. "Make peace

Caulaincourt can conclude it, and sign the documents. I shall bear the shame. But do not claim from me that I myself should dictate my own abasement!" Maret writes to Caulaincourt in Châtillon, where he is negotiating anew with the enemy. Caulaincourt demands confirmation. Meanwhile the Emperor has veered about. He writes to Joseph: "Hold the gates bravely. Have two guns mounted and see that the National Guard takes up its position there.... Place fifty men at each gate armed with service muskets, one hundred with pikes. Thus, each gate will be guarded by two hundred and fifty men."

Crœsus has become a beggar! Only six months ago, nay, even three months back, Napoleon would have added three noughts to the figures! But now, encircled by the conglomerated forces of so many princes, two cannon and a hundred fowling pieces must suffice to save Paris! He sees the absurdity, for the same evening Maret finds him depressed. The minister, however, tries to persuade the Emperor to dictate the conditions of peace: Belgium and the left bank of the Rhine are to be free, Italy must be yielded up, everything which Bonaparte and Napoleon conquered must be given back in order that he may keep Paris and the piece of wood covered with satin. He will sign tomorrow, he says. Those who love him, tremble at thought of that moment when with one stroke of the pen he will lose all that his warlike deeds have won.

But fate guards him from this. News comes during the night. The enemy's position is worse than it seemed the previous day. Once more the war lord's imagination gets to work. When, next morning, Maret arrives with the papers for the Emperor's signature, he finds his master brooding over the map. Napoleon hardly notices his entrance. All the minister can catch is a few hurried words:

"Other matters are to the fore! I am determined to smash Blücher!" When, at the selfsame hour, Joseph's letter arrives wherein he states that Paris is in peril, Napoleon, in the interludes of issuing army orders, dictates, from the depths of his heart, this rock-like answer:

"Should Paris be taken, I shall no longer continue to live....

I have commanded you to do all that is needful to safeguard the empress, the king of Rome, and our family.... I have the right to claim the assistance of my kin, for I have helped them so often in the past..."

"If Talleyrand considers that the empress should in any case remain in Paris, this advice is secret treachery. Do not trust him! For sixteen years I have associated with him, and have often given him favours. But nothing is more certain than that he is the greatest enemy of our house, now that luck has forsaken us. Take my advice to heart. I understand events better than the young folk. If I lose the fight and die, you will be the first to hear of it.... I fancy that Madame Mere could find asylum with the queen of Westphalia. For God's sake, do not allow the empress and the king to fall into the hands of the enemy! Austria would then lose interest in the war, and would take the empress to Vienna. England and Russia would make the French see things from their outlook, and our cause would be lost.

"Perhaps I shall conclude peace in a day or two.... Never since the world began has a sovereign allowed himself to be taken alive in an open city.... So long as I live, I must be obeyed. If I die, my reigning son and the regent his mother must not allow themselves to be taken, were it only for France's honour. On the contrary, they must withdraw with the last of their soldiers and entrench themselves in the remotest village. Otherwise it might be said that I had sacrificed my son's throne....

"I would rather know that my son had been killed than that he was being brought up in Vienna as an Austrian prince. I have never seen *Andromache* played without lamenting the fate of Astyanax, and I have always regarded it as a stroke of good fortune that his father did not live to see it. You do not know the French people. The consequences of these vast events are incalculable!"

This hunted man is panting for breath. For the first time since his youth, death or collapse seems close at hand; perhaps both. When he writes commanding Joseph to prepare for either eventuality, the two main elements of his soul are mingling, and both are scattering sparks. His calculating temperament is reckoning up the disastrous consequences that would ensue, should Austria's ambition cease to be operative; but at the same time his idea of the destiny of his nearest and dearest takes a soaring flight. Were he to fall next day, this letter would remain to show that honour and glory had been the last flames of his heroic imagination. But today, as always, everything discloses a meditation upon the historical parallels which have throughout life been his spur to greatness.

Thus the letter is the burning-cold document of a statesman and poet, and only in this frame of mind is it becoming for a Napoleon to perish.

At the same time, he is a great military commander to the last. When he divides the remnants of his army into two halves, and begins by defeating Blücher with one of them in a brilliant advance, the six battles he fights in nine days, from Champaubert to Montereau, are still in the avalanche tempo of General Bonaparte. But that the names of these battlefields are French, tells us the whole story; hitherto his victories have always borne foreign names. At Montereau he is an artillerist once more, training the guns with his own hand as at Toulon. He cries: "Forward, comrades! The cannon ball that will hit me has not been cast!"

He has settled accounts with Blücher. Now to deal with Schwarzenberg! But the Austrian is afraid of having his renown as commander dimmed, and is sedulous to avoid a decisive conflict; he actually writes direct to Berthier, suggesting that a truce be arranged in Châtillon. Enough for the Emperor to read this, and his lust for battle is redoubled. Another letter to Joseph, written with his own hand this time, breathing defiance, shrewd, bold:

"You have been talking to my wife about the Bourbons, but you should avoid such topics. I have no wish to take shelter behind my wife.... That would only sow dissension between us.... I have never tried to win the applause of the Parisians, for I am no stage puppet.... Besides, the real Paris is something very different from the passions of the three thousand persons who are raising all the clamour. Of course it would be easier to explain that one cannot levy any soldiers, than it is to make the attempt... Je vous embrasse!"

It is many, many years since he has penned these words at the close of a letter. Not since the Marengo days has he written thus to any of his brothers or to any of his commanders–and Joseph is both. His heart is beating more vigorously. Next day, writing to Savary, who has informed him about a petition to the monarchs, and about the regency and fears and intrigues, his phrasing is more incisive, and bears witness to the excitement of a campaign

"They shall learn that I am still the man of Wagram and Austerlitz! I will have no intrigues in the State.... Let me tell you that if a petition against the public authority is being circulated, I will arrest King Joseph and all the others who sign it!... I want no tribunes of the people! I myself am the great tribune!"

Meanwhile the allies are quarrelling. The tsar wants Paris to be placed under a Russian governor until the nation chooses Bernadotte or another; Austria will hear of nothing but a Bourbon restoration; Schwarzenberg wants peace to be made at once, and instead of joining battle is content to assume "a military attitude." But Blücher, who has remarshalled his forces, simply cries "Forward!" and is on the march. When the allies once more send a proposal for the re-establishment of the old frontiers of France, the Emperor is enraged, saying: "I am so angry, that I feel dishonored by the mere suggestion." Being reminded that the enemy outnumbers him by three to one, he answers heroically: "I have fifty thousand men. Add myself, and you get a hundred and fifty thousand!"

Now, at the beginning of March, when he is to attack Blücher once more, for the command of his other army he puts his trust in Marmont, his earliest companion-in-arms.

But the spirit of revolt is rising. It had shown itself to Napoleon at Düben Castle in the previous autumn; during the winter it had been fomented in his brother's circle; now it was to eventuate in treason under fire. Marmont, the first among men still above ground who had served under Napoleon, is also the first to betray him. Oudinot and Macdonald have lost the battle of Bar-sur-Aube. Now, at Laon, Marmont makes no more than a pretence of fighting, leaves his artillery in the town square, thus snatches victory from his master, and even allows himself to be surprised in his camp. "The Emperor would have been justified in cutting him down," says Berthier, "but is so fond of him that, after making a scene, he has left him in command of his corps."

What is more natural than that, during these days, his heart should go out to the friends of his youth? But Marmont is not the only traitor to whom he is lenient! Augereau, who had fought beside him at Rivoli, begins to make signals to the Austrians, fails to be at his post. The reprimand he receives is an affectionate one. Napoleon writes to him almost as if they were still brothers in the field, as of old.

"Six hours' rest were not enough for you? .... What pitiful excuses you are making, Augereau! No money! No horses! I command you to take the field within twelve hours of receiving this. If you are still the old Augereau of Castiglione, you can keep your command. But if you find the burden of your sixty years so heavy, hand over the command to the oldest of your generals. The country is in danger! ... You should be the first in the firing line. We must all put on our seven-leagued boots, and must find the reckless courage of '93.' If the French soldiers see your men whithersoever you please."

Here we have General Bonaparte once more. The red of sunset reminds us of the glories of sunrise.

Owing to Marmont's retreat, the Emperor is left unsupported at Arcis-sur-Aube, and has no more than a few thousand men with which to face a great army. Defeat is inevitable. During the height of the battle, a dust eddy sweeps across the field. A thousand dragoons are panic-stricken, and take to flight, shouting: "The Cossacks!" The Emperor gallops forward into the press. "Dragoons! Turn and fight! You are running away, but I stand firm!" He draws his sword and charges the enemy, followed only by his staff and the bodyguard. Six thousand Cossacks take to flight. It is years upon years since he has led a cavalry attack. His horse is shot under him, and he mounts another. Berthier reports that the Emperor was obviously hoping to find death on the field.

But death does not come for the asking. No more than Cæsar, Cromwell, or Frederick, is Napoleon destined for this swift, heroic end. Such men are something more than military commanders, and must live out their lives as leader of nations,—even though they have to fight against their own nation. Henceforward the blows thicken, and each blow is symbolical.

But who can wonder if, at last, men forsake the despiser of men? He has made princes of his soldiers; should it surprise us that they prefer their princedoms to a soldier's death? Need we wonder that a wife sprung from an ancient ruling house, married off to an upstart, should be quick to repudiate him and to become a Habsburg once more? That his brothers, in whom he has shown too much trust, should, when disaster comes, think of themselves rather than of the man to whom they owe everything?

When, in his last letters to Marie Louise, he asks her to write to her father, she complies with a bad grace, and, instead of following the example of Marie Theresa, she pens cold letters which can serve as hints to her father and his ministers. News reaches the allied headquarters that the English have landed in Bordeaux, and that the Bourbon flag has been hoisted there; a letter from the Emperor to his wife is intercepted, a letter in which he announces his intention to withdraw behind the Marne. It is enough; at length all are agreed for the march on Paris.

In this utmost danger, Napoleon has still a last bold shift. He will arm the peasants as a national reserve; they will be ready to his hand, for they hate the invading foreigners. But now tidings come that Marmont has allowed himself to be beaten once more, and is withdrawing to Paris with Mortier. Like one who hears that his house is on fire, the Emperor storms back towards Paris, entrusts the command of his troops to Berthier, and rides citywards and a few servants, watches them under cover of the darkness.

Then he has the carriage turned, and drives to Fontainebleau.

XIV

Next morning Talleyrand is sitting in his bedchamber, submitting to the ministrations of his valet. This statesman of the revolution still has his wig dressed in the rococo style. The door is thrown open, and almost before the servant has time to announce him, Count Nesselrode hurries in to greet the friend of many years' standing. He gets covered with powder from head to foot, Talleyrand informs us. Two hours later, the tsar himself comes to stay with his intimate friend as guest; he will not put up at the Elysée for fear of bombs. The moment for which Napoleon's minister has worked indefatigably for six years has come at last, and the smiling victors shake hands with a sense of moral righteousness: virtue has triumphed! After knocking at the gates of Paris for two and twenty years, the legitimist monarchs have at length been admitted. This is their great moment. They have ridden into the city. A small party of Bourbon supporters has hailed them as liberators; the Faubourg Saint-Germain has rallied. Elsewhere in Paris, silence reigns. Everyone is calmly waiting to see whether, on the morrow, Napoleon or Louis is to be called master.

The Emperor's fate is sealed, for Joseph, in his cowardly flight and in spite of Napoleon's warnings, has not taken Talleyrand along with him, but has left that cleverest and most dangerous of enemies in Paris. It is not fixity of purpose on the part of the nation that brings the Emperor to his doom; nor are the four allied foes unanimous as to his fate. He is ruined by the co-operation of faithless servants and treacherous friends, under the guidance of a man who is both–for Talleyrand, with the good graces of the tsar, takes upon himself the spiritual leadership of the next ten days. Now the intriguer is in his true element.

Yesterday he received another guest. Talleyrand by no

means hates the Emperor, but has from the first sign of Napoleon's decline, forsaken his master in order that he himself may climb. He has no wish to wreak vengeance on a prisoner, and, indeed, has no reason for revenge. Still, it would be convenient were the disturber of the peace quietly to disappear; and therefore he promises a goodly reward to a certain Maubreuil (a monarchist officer with an adventurous past) if this man "will carry out an important commission on the road to Fontainebleau." But the adventurer's heart fails him at the last moment, and he is content to attack Jerome's brave young wife and carry off her jewels, instead of making an attempt on Napoleon's life. Blücher, too, on his own initiative, has sent a detachment with definite orders to make an end of the Emperor.

"Well, what does France want?" asks the tsar of the abbé as a man of wide experience. Talleyrand has long had in mind the restoration of the former king, but he thinks it best to ask whom Alexander would recommend. Somewhat diffidently, the tsar mentions the name of Bernadotte. Talleyrand smiles: "France does not want any more soldiers. If we wanted one we should keep the one we have already, the finest soldier in the world. No other, in his place, would find a hundred men to follow him." Talleyrand says this to the conqueror, says it in plain words to the tsar; the defeated Emperor at Fontainebleau could have wished no greater tribute of admiration than such words from such lips in such a situation.

A day later, Talleyrand summons the Senate, and the legislature confirms the decision that the Emperor must abdicate. There is a general swing of opinion in this direction. Caulaincourt is the only one who puts up a fight for Napoleon, and tries to win over the tsar. For a moment, Alexander's impressionable heart is touched; the image of his whilom friend rises before his mind; he wavers, and says that he will do his best with his allies to save the crown for the king of Rome.

But while the impotent Caulaincourt is trying to persuade the vacillating tsar, and is doing what he can to save the house of Bonaparte, at this same hour on the third of April, Talleyrand has summoned Marshal Marmont who, with his twelve thousand men across the Seine, is still a power, since the main body of the allies has not yet reached Paris.

See them sitting there, Napoleon's companion-in-arms and senior officer, hobnobbing with the doyen of the Emperor's ministers. The diplomat reasons coldly with the soldier, who hardly needs to listen to the arguments. He is hopelessly disillusioned, tired out. His faith had been shaken three years ago in Spain. His thoughts run this wise: "What is the use of trying to march with a dead man? The king is dead; long live the king! At the military academy, we were all monarchists. His defeat is a proof that the Bourbons have the right of it. The only choice is between being stood up in front of an old wall or taking one's stand behind an old throne. The oath of allegiance? That has been abrogated. The ties of friendship? Only the other day, he was scolding me after the Laon affair." Acting on the suggestion of his old acquaintance, Marmont writes to Schwarzenberg, the allies' commander-in-chief:

"By the decree of the Senate, the army and the people have been released from their obligation of fealty to Napoleon. I am ready to promote an understanding between people and army, in order to avoid civil war." Upon this pretext, which he subsequently endeavored to fortify with the excuse of patriotism (the paltry argument of every turncoat), the Emperor's senior marshal destroys the Emperor. Augereau, in a shameful proclamation, is quick to follow Marmont's lead.

At the time when Talleyrand is winning over the marshals, the Emperor in Fontainebleau is reviewing his guards. To them he exclaims: "Never shall we allow anyone to wear in Paris the white cockade of the émigrés.... In a few days we will attack the enemy in Paris!" The officers brandish their swords enthusiastically, shouting: "À Paris! Vive l'Empereur!" He waves his hand to them, and, smiling joyfully, he briskly mounts the steps, surrounded by his last ministers in their embroidered coats.

Soon afterwards, a carriage draws up in the courtyard. Caulaincourt steps out; he is pale, having passed the night in a vigil. He approaches the Emperor. Berthier enquires: "Well, my lad, how goes it?" The minister hesitates to answer, for he does not like Berthier's tone. Are the very nearest going to fall away too? He finds the Emperor at work.

"What do they want of me?" asks Napoleon eagerly.

"Great sacrifices, that you may retain the crown for your son."

"You mean that they refuse to treat with me! They want to make a helot of me, to hold me up as a warning to all those whose genius enables them to rule men and to make the born kings tremble on their ancient thrones!"

Bonaparte's metallic tone! Such is the mood produced in the Emperor by the sight of his guards, by the perusal of his latest muster rolls, by the sight of his maps. Now the minister mentions the most moderate of the tsar's demands. Napoleon is to abdicate in favour of the king of Rome, and then the terms of a regency will be discussed. But there is talk of a Bourbon restoration. The Emperor leaps to his feet:

"They are mad! The Bourbons in France, they would not be able to hold their position for a year! Nine-tenths of the nation cannot endure them; my soldiers will never serve under them. They have lived for twenty years upon the alms of a foreigner, at war all the time with the fundamental principles of their homeland! The Senate consists entirely of regicides, or the sons of regicides. I was a newcomer, with nothing to take vengeance for; a man whose only business it was to up-build.... No doubt they can draw profit out of the crash, can exile me and my family; but the Bourbons–never!"

Thus does his work roll before his mind as in a rhapsody, lighted up by his contempt for those whom he succeeded and who are now to succeed him. He becomes the soldier once more. "They demand my abdication. Will the crown then be secure for my son? I have still fifty thousand men. They will march with me to Paris. After the victory, the people shall decide. If, then, the French want to chase me away, I will go." See the conflict in his soul. As statesman, he is willing to abdicate, that his son may reign; as soldier, he is still eager to fight, that he may retain all.

But while enthusiasm grows in the rank and file of his army, while the common soldiers are willing to give their lives for the Emperor, the marshals are malcontent. Although they have not yet heard of Marmont's defection, they cherish like wishes, and would gladly shake off their allegiance to Napoleon if they could do so decently. This marked difference between the mood of the men and that of their leaders is once more a vengeance for the system of titles and monetary rewards with whose aid the military commander, when he had become an emperor, had transformed generals into marshals. Next day, the seniors among them are of one mind. Ney, Macdonald, Oudinot, and Lefèvre, in the most subservient way possible, speak to him of the advantages of abdication.

The Emperor shows them his maps, which are again best with coloured pins; he points out to them that the enemy is in an unfavourable position, and enumerates his own resources. All is vain! The frame of mind they had shown in Düben Castle, intensified a hundredfold, blocks his way. Silently he dismisses them, for he wants to think over a plan. Mentally, he has mustered his forces, and the total of his additions does not seem to him a bad one. A conditional renunciation, therefore, will not betoken anything more than an armistice, a postponement.

A few hours after the audience of the marshals, he sends for Caulaincourt, and points to a holograph document on the table:

"There is my abdication. You can take it to Paris."

The minister reads:

"Since the allied powers have declared that Emperor Napoleon is the only obstacle to the peace of Europe, Emperor Napoleon, faithful to his oath, declares himself ready, for the welfare of his country, which is inseparable from the rights of his son, from those of the regency of the empress, and from the maintenance of the laws of the Empire, to descend from the throne, to give up France and even life itself."

What a style! A diplomatic document, involved in its phraseology, cautiously worded, ambiguous, penned for the inspection of diplomats of the old school. Nothing of Napoleon in it. The minister begs for the companionship of two of the marshals for so important a mission.

"Take Marmont and Ney." says the Emperor, adding, "Marmont is my oldest comrade."

"Marmont is not here."

"Macdonald, then."

Late that evening, three hours after the interview with Napoleon, the plenipotentiaries are at the Elysée confronting the allied princes and ministers. Most of the negotiations are carried on between the tsar and Caulaincourt. The latter's contention that the French are heartily against the Bourbons has its effect; the parleys continue far into the night. Suddenly am announcement is made in Russian; the Frenchmen do not understand. Thereupon the tsar speaks: "You are relying, gentlemen, upon the unshakable loyalty of the troops towards the imperial regime. Well, I have just been informed that the advance guard, the sixth army corps, has deserted the Emperor. It has come over to our lines."

The allies' task has become easier; they now demand instant and unconditional abdication. Meanwhile the Emperor sends one courier after another from Fontainebleau to his minister.He writes:

"If they refuse to negotiate with me, what kind of a treaty will it be? ... Bring back my act of abdication, I command you... I will sign no treaty!"

Next day at six o'clock in the morning the Emperor is at work with Berthier. A captain is introduced, an adjutant of Mortier's.

"Well, what news?"

"The sixth army corps has gone over to the enemy. It is marching to Paris."

The Emperor seizes him by the arm and shakes it.

"Marmont? Are you sure? Did the troops know where they were being led?"

more. Take the sword which Sultan Selim gave me and keep it in remembrance." While all are waiting for the signature, the Emperor sends for the gilded scimitar, and embraces the general as he presents it. Then Napoleon signs the act of abdication.

"The allied powers having declared that Emperor Napoleon is the sole obstacle to the re-establishment of peace in Europe, the Emperor, faithful to his oath, declares that he renounces, for himself and his heirs, the thrones of France and Italy, and that there is no sacrifice, not even that of life, which he is not ready to make for the interests of France."

The deed is done! All breathe freely again. The generals and the courtiers leave Fontainebleau; Maret alone remains. They hasten to Paris; even Berthier throws himself into the arms of the provisional government. Talleyrand and Fouché are at the head of things.

But the Emperor remains another nine days in his palace, and he is not alone. Around him, unshaken, his guards are encamped; they still muster twenty-five thousand men. Who else is with him? His brothers have taken to their heels. What is Josephine doing, at Malmaison? After she has wept, and sworn that she will follow the forsaken Emperor, she receives Napoleon's conqueror with sparkling eyes and adorned with all the pitiful appeal of a Niobe. The tsar wishes to play the part of a knightly cavalier, and succumbs to the renowned charms of the first empress. But Hortense, her daughter, receives the tsar's visit coldly and offhandedly. As soon as he is gone, she hastens to Fontainebleau and remains with the Emperor till his departure.

At first, his mother is with him. But, wishing to see her in safety, he persuades her to go away with Jerome. They will meet again later. When the empress says goodbye to Letizia, she utters polite commonplaces and wishes her mother-in-law well. The old lady, who sees through Marie Louise, and knows that all she cares for is security and enjoyment, answers this daughter of the Habsburgs: "That will depend upon you, and upon your future conduct."

The Emperor has no word from wife or son in reply to his numerous letters and messengers. While for himself he asks neither land nor money, for her he demands that, in addition to Parma, she should have Tuscany, or at least a strip of it which would being her lands nearer to Elba and thus set up a link between man and wife. He writes to her advising as to the best halting-places on the route; Corvisart is to decide which waters will do her health most good; she is to take her personal treasure with her. Then he writes to the palace prefect that all the diamonds which are not her or his personal property must be given back to the treasury, for they belong to France.

Meanwhile the government has sent a confidential agent to the Tuileries with orders to seize the imperial treasure. All the gold and securities, valued at one hundred and fifty millions, were taken away; in plain words, stolen. These sums had been saved by Napoleon from his civil list during the fourteen years of his rule. His silver plate, all personal articles of value, his golden snuff-boxes, and even his handkerchiefs embroidered with the initial N. were taken at the same time. The order for this bears, among others, Talleyrand's signature. The Emperor, who until yesterday was the wealthiest man in Europe, journeys to Elba with three million francs as his fortune!

He is profoundly disheartened. Can anything disillusion him further? Lucien writes to the Pope the day after the abdication, and becomes a Roman prince. Murat, acting on the advice of Fouché (who holds the net of intrigues during these last weeks), has entered Rome, has advanced his troops towards Tuscany, invading Elise's realm–always spurred on by Caroline, and always in alliance with England, which has occupied Tuscany. Elise, who at the last moment has staked on the wrong hazard, and has through a false calculation remained faithful to her brother, flees before her sister's troops, brings a child into the world while lying up at a mountain tavern, and in Bologna is taken prisoner by the Austrians. The only two of the pack who have behaved decently are Jerome and his wife.

The last days pass in sinister silence. "If a carriage drives into the palace yard, all prick up their ears. Is anyone coming to bid Napoleon farewell? No one comes while affairs are being wound up. But a day or two before the departure, a veiled lady arrives, late in the evening. No one knows her, and she is not admitted. Countess Walewska waits a whole night, and when she goes away in the morning she leaves a letter for him. He sends after her, but she has gone. He writes:

"Marie! ... The feelings which animate you touch me profoundly. They are worthy of your lovely soul and the goodness of your heart.... Think affectionately of me! Never doubt me! N."

As soon as he has recovered his old tranquillity of mind, the Emperor is promptly animated with new energy. Has he not an island as base of operations? Who knows what may come of it? Corsica, too, is an island in the Mediterranean! He orders a monograph and studies the geography and statistics of Elba. "The air is wholesome, the inhabitants are honest folk, and I hope that my good Louse will like the place well enough." He chooses his four hundred men; but the whole guard wants to go with him, though this will involve leaving wife and children. Among them are men whose hearts he had won two-and-twenty years earlier when he had been captain in Toulon, men who had followed his fortunes from Cairo to Moscow, through sixty battles.

He cheers up. Discussing predetermination with the palace prefect, and how death has passed him by during the last battles, he adds:

"A violent death is cowardice. I can see no greatness in shirking responsibility in that manner, like one who has gambled away his fortune.... Suicide is incompatible with my principles and with the position I have occupied in the world." They walk up and down the terrace in silence for a time, and then he says with a smile: "Between ourselves, a living drummer is better than a dead emperor!"

All the formalities have been accomplished; the allied commissioners who are to accompany him to Elba, four in number, have arrived; the start is fixed for noon. He writes in simple terms to tell his wife. and concludes: "Farewell, my good Louise. You can rest assured of the courage, the tranquillity, and the affection of your husband. N." He adds as a postscript: "A kiss for the little king!"

The start will be an easy matter, for no one has come to take leave.

Letter to Countess Walewska

But there are to be leave-takings after all. The old guard is waiting for him in the palace yard, drawn up in a square. As he comes down the steps, thousands of eyes are fixed on him. He must say something. What can he say? For twenty years he has only spoken to these men just before a battle and just after a victory, to inspire them or to thank them. Well, he will thank them now, though there has been no victory; he will thank them for the hundred victories of the past. He steps forward. "Vive l'Empereur!" He enters the square, and says:

"Soldiers of my old guard, I take leave of you. For twenty years I have seen you always upon the path of honour and glory. During the last few weeks, you have been models of bravery and fidelity, just as in the years of good fortune.... But there would have been civil war. That is why I sacrificed all other interests to those of the country. I am going away..... You friends, continue to serve France. Her happiness has been my only thought. My good wishes go with you. Do not mourn my fate. If I have determined to go on living, it is that I may increase your fame. I shall write the story of the great deeds we wrought together. Farewell, my children. I would gladly press you all to my heart. At least let me kiss your colours!"

The general holds out the colours. Napoleon embraces him, and kisses the flag. "Goodbye, comrades!" He gets into the carriage. "Vive l'Empereur!" He drives away.

The war-hardened veterans stand there, blubbering like children. Their father has gone away. Never had he spoken to them more movingly. The dignified pathos of ancient Rome, the ardent imagery of his manifestos, the similes and the exaltations, have vanished with the fever of battle. This Emperor spoke like a commander, this commander spoke like a company leader. His words were manly, blunt, and restrained. When he kissed the colours, it was an unparalleled gesture; never before had he done anything of the kind. They will tell their grandchildren what the great Emperor, their "petit caporal," has said to them this day. The grandchildren will tell their grandchildren in turn, and so the story will go down the generations.

But hardly has he left this soldierly atmosphere, in which he grew to manhood and then to greatness, when he has to face the mob. After the sobs of his old soldiers, come clamour, cries, and curses! As the train of carriages drives swiftly through Province, the threatening shouts of the people deafen him. "Down with the tyrant! Kill the wretch!" In the villages where the horses are changed, women rage round his carriage, screaming at him, flinging stones, trying to force the coachman to shout "Vive le Roi!" At one of these villages, the crowd has prepared an effigy, a uniform coat stuffed with straw and smeared with mire and blood. Here they hail him with the cry: "Kill the murderer!" The carriages press on at top speed and the journey becomes a flight. Napoleon's first flight.

With rigid face, the Emperor looks at the mob and listens to the cries of execration. Are these the same people who ran beside his carriage, eager to catch a glance from his eyes? They are indeed the same! What he is now experiencing, he had foreseen, with the seer's vision of the misanthrope, at his first entry into Paris when the crowd had jubilantly welcomed him as conqueror. He sits huddled in a corner of the carriage, pale and silent; at each halt, the foreign commissioners jump out to guard the windows of his coach. Will he bear all this without making a sign? Will he draw his sword? He does not wear one now. In mufti, he can get away from his county, but not in his green uniform. Only once before has he had such an experience. It was on the Nineteenth Brumaire, when the radicals were shaking their fists at him. Then he did not draw his sword. Then, as now, he was powerless against the mob, for it was not his trade to beat the mutable many, nor was it his talent to persuade them. He is not a tribune; he is an emperor. One who can command as well as he, can do nothing but command. If he fights, it must be in a battle.

Movement! Air! In a lonely road, he has the carriage stopped, and one of the post-horses taken out of the traces. He fixes a white cockade on his plain round hat, and rides in front of the carriages, outstripping them, his servant following. Thus he makes his way to Aix, but halts short of the town, enters a wayside inn, and gives circlet of little golden leaves which the foreigner from the Mediterranean island had, with the simplicity of the self-made man, placed on his own brow.

XV

How big Corsica is! How high her mountains! Bastia is an admirable harbour; its fortifications can be seen through a spy-glass. If taken from the eastern side....

When the ruler of Elba rides among the hills of his new home, the silhouette of his old home lies spread before him; everything looms larger across the water. Forty times bigger, ten times as many inhabitants; he has all the figures, to a unit, in his head. Elba is nothing more than a mole-hill.

On the clear May morning when he landed, he was welcomed by a deputation of peasants and petty burghers in Porto Ferrajo. Timidly they had paid their compliments to the man who was to reign over them. But their astonishment was great when, instead of inviting them to a banquet, he leapt into the saddle and rode of to inspect the fortifications. On the morrow, orders began to fly about the sleepy little isle: Pianosa was to have two more batteries; the mole must be lengthened; the roads improved. When first the four hundred grenadiers appeared in the land, the natives looked at them askance as men of a foreign race. Soon, however, the forces were increased by the creation of a foreign battalion, and a National Guard. Napoleon once more has an army of over a thousand men; soon he has a small flotilla likewise. What for? Just for him to see after and take care of. He has a Council of State; Bertrand and Drouot (the generals who have accompanied him into exile) and a dozen inhabitants of the island, are members; and, together with Napoleon who presides over the assembly, they discuss improvements in the iron mines and the salt pits. Have you no mulberry culture here? The silkworms bring in good money over there, in Lyons; and if the French government imposes a tariff upon our produce, we can easily sell to Italy.

Save! We are so poor, and France makes no move to pay the promised allowance. The white house is smaller than the one in Ajaccio, and very much simpler; but there is no money for building additional accommodation; and when the "grand marshal" Bertrand draws up a list of mattresses and other bedgear, his master underlines the mistakes, –for he has every detail of his establishment by heart.

Is this indefatigable man never to realise what a parody is his administration over the tiny island, the diminutive army, the small household? Never! Here in Elba, where in the best of spirits and health he throws himself whole-heartedly into his undertakings, he comes to realise that it was not the masses that had allured him. To order, to build, to press his finger into the wax of humanity, these things he must do, urged onward by the impulse of his artist's soul. But, since humanity is not as wax, and since his constructions can never be finished and are always vibrant with life; since the opposition of material forces also takes a hand in the game, even when matter seems to have been conquered–he can only fulfil his mission by coercing and conquering the human spirit, by issuing orders and bringing suggestions to bear, by constant vigilance and constant upbuilding; in a word, by ruling. He has never been a dilettante or a parvenu; and, this being so, he drives the little wheel today with just as much precision and earnestness as he had driven the earth's sphere in former days.

But soon, when most of his enterprises are in good going order, he feels he is becoming lazy, even when he is studying mathematics. This causes him to reconsider his position.

"It is by no means difficult to accustom oneself to a life of meditation," he writes, "if one possesses within oneself the necessary reserves. I work hard in my study; when I emerge I have the delightful spectacle of my old grenadiers in front of me.... Born kings must suffer terribly when they are dethroned, for pomp and etiquette are the very marrow of their lives. For my part, I have always been a soldier, and became a king only by chance, so that these things have been nothing but a burden to me, whereas wars and camps come naturally. Out of my great past, I regret naught but my soldiers. After all my treasures and my crowns, my most cherished possessions are the couple of French uniforms they have allowed me to keep"

These are the words of an unpretentious king. Do people not believe him? And does Europe laugh when, in his kingdom of Lilliput, he preserves the forms of kingship? Does Europe begin to suspect a secret in the island? The innate dignity, whereby long ago the young general had wrung respect from the bearers of inherited rank, to-day is still able to hold satirical visitors in check. Everyone admires the natural simplicity of the lonely man who, despite the exiguity of his dwelling, still holds to the title of "Majesty ". He lives in his island sans palace or fittings, sans court or ministers, only surrounded with the aureole of his deeds.

This return home brings solace to his heart–for Elba is Italy. The peasant speaks to him in the language Napolione had learned at Letizia's knee. The Mediterranean amid whose waters he was born and reared, the islands with their quiet shores, do they not all of them bring back memories of youthful days? Stone-pines, fig trees, and crags; the white houses among the vineyards; the sails, and the fishermen's nets; pride of clan and the headkerchief worn at church; all these things seem to take him gently by the hand and lead him back to the dreams of childhood. Now the storm-racked nerves relax, and at length know a spell of repose. In these wholesome months, the Emperor comes to look upon his career as a visionary flight into the land of childish imagination; and it is only when he contemplates the men of his old guard that he realises something did happen during the years that separate Corsica from Elba.

"The Emperor lives very contentedly on his island," writes one who accompanied him there. "He seems to have forgotten the past. The management of his small household gives him occupation; he is now looking out for a suitable site to build his country-seat; we ride, and drive, and sail round the coasts as much as we please."

Since he has plenty of time on his hands, and since thrift is essential, he examines everything, to the minutest details. Just as, in the Tuileries, he himself drew up the list of his clothing, so now, in Elba, he says to Bertrand: "My underlinen is in a lamentable state. Part of it has never been unpacked, and it has not been marked. Give orders that everything must be laid out in drawers and presses, and that no one is to be given anything belonging to our court without furnishing a receipt. .. There are not enough ordinary chairs. Have a sample sent from Pisa; they must not cost more than five francs apiece."

Europe laughs when it hears of this. Posterity stands bewildered before such energetic renunciation.

Once only do we hear a gentle sigh. He has climbed to the top of a hill whence he can look over the whole of his realm. Surveying the prospect, he says: "One must acknowledge that the island is very small." Like distant thunder, the fate of a man seems to rumble in these words; for an all too great imagination, confined within the narrow limits of Europe and cribbed within the circle of the folk intelligence of the nineteenth century, is doomed at the outset to be crushed.

With the summer, comes his mother. She, alone, is happy. Her son is no longer threatened with assassination or with battles. Here, all is peaceful and warm; Elba is almost as lovely as Corsica. Daily intercourse with him renews for her the good old times. It is as well that she has come; for, from the millions which she alone has put by, she now brings her son what he needs, and when he receives her banknotes, may we not picture mother and son smiling at one another? On his name-day, she invites him to a little rustic feast.

A dozen and more St. Napoleon days she has spent in Paris: the guns would fire the salute from the Invalides, Masses would be said; Senate and ministers, the court and foreign diplomats, would throng the halls of the Tuileries. When, in the evening, the rooms were filled with guests, and, amid the strains of music, there came and went all that France possessed of great names, of beauty, and of precious jewels; when the fireworks filled the August night-sky with brightness, and thousands of tiny lamps formed the initial N – Letizia, surrounded by the kings who were the fruit of her womb would stand silent and proud, thinking the old words so full of ominous warning. But today she is blithe; today she compares this jocund festivity with the little town of Ajaccio; today, for the first time, she thinks: "All the same, we achieved something fine!"

Letizia had been able, while in Rome, to heal many wounds dealt in the heat of the fray. The Pope, on his return, had pardoned the mother of his sometime foe. She was not surprised when the whole court, when even her secretary (a Corsican), speedily went over to the Bourbon king. Has she not always foretold it? Caroline, alone, is not permitted to appear before her.

Pauline, Princess Borghese, merry and brilliant, does not hang long in the wind. She has always been the most affectionate, and has been clever enough to prefer real diamonds and nights of love to uncertain thrones and crowns. She comes to the island, so that, with her mother, she may bring cheer to the Emperor. She shakes out a basketful of gossip and news for his delectation.

Hardly a word from his brothers. One letter comes from Lucien. What propositions can he be laying before his banished brother? Will he, who lives in princely fashion in Rome, with magnanimous generosity offer Napoleon money or bring his influence to bear in his imperial brother's behalf? What does the "Prince of Canino" by the Pope's grace write in his letter? He owns smelting furnaces, and Elba has iron ore wherewith to feed them: he asks his brother to provide him with the minerals. Crowns and gold, he has refused; but iron which his brother still possesses, he can make good use of: Maybe he, who is a poet, is enjoying the farce of these blast furnaces! Is it not a kindness that one still thinks of the exile? Who else writes?

Josephine is dead. A few weeks after Napoleon's departure, she died at Malmaison. No one knows if she ever wrote to him; what is certain is that she left debts amounting to three millions, which he had to pay. Hortense has been separated from her husband. She has become a duchess, and has made her most graceful curtsey before the Bourbon king, in the very room where she and her mother had held sway for so long. Little Léon, whom Letizia had for a time with her in Rome, resembles his father; he is reported to be courageous and full of pranks. These are all the members of Napoleon's family about whom he has news.

An English vessel brings the unknown lady who visited Fontainebleau to the island, In a marquee, beneath the chestnut trees, the Emperor receives Countess Walewska. For two days and two nights they are inseparable. The Emperor only issues forth to give the necessary orders, and the four-year-old boy, dressed in the Polish national costume, plays in the meadow with the tall grenadiers. The Emperor would like to keep Walewska by his side, but he does not wish to provide the empress with an excuse for not coming to live with him, Thus, for the second time, he sacrifices on the altar of the Habsburg princess, the phantom of his happiness. Walewska sails away. Her ship encounters bad weather, and the Emperor is filled with restless anxiety until he receives tidings that she has arrived safely at Leghorn.

How marvellously are the threads weaving themselves into the tissue of a legend! With wizard spells this man of forty-five links up epochs and customs. Here he is, a petty prince on a Mediterranean isle: he receives his beloved, the lady with whom he had lived in the imperial palace at Schonbrunn when he himself was an enemy and unknown to the proprietor; today he is once again this man's foe, and another woman whom he had invited to his arms from the selfsame palace has long since forsaken him; yet his natural son, born in a lonely castle in Poland, is playing beneath the trees of the southern land and wears the dress of a foreign folk which the Emperor had once promised to free. Who could believe that all this had come to pass within five years? A hundred years seemed likelier for the accomplishment of so many events. With such nets, what other fish could one expect to catch but the golden ones of the fairy tale? A thousand years ago a great emperor was banished and left forsaken on the island; but from a distant realm a beautiful, tragical woman found the way to him across the sea, and brought him his son.

In truth Napoleon is forsaken by wife and child. This loss cuts him no less, maybe even more cruelly, than the loss of power, for his conception of marriage is conservative and bourgeois.

Constantly, even during the via dolorosa of his last journey through France, he has written to Marie Louise; he has planned a new house for her. But his letters remain unanswered. Believing that his correspondence has been intercepted, he at last writes to the grand duke of Tuscany, her uncle, begging for news; for "I trust that Your Royal Highness has preserved a little friendliness towards me, in spite of the events which have changed the sentiments of so many men..... If so, I beg that you will look favourably upon the tiny commune which feels the same towards you as does Tuscany...." Ay, thus writes the prince of this diminutive isle, a prince with no more than twenty thousand subjects, to the mighty grand duke! But the grand duke keeps silence.

When Napoleon realises the sluggishness of the human heart, his old defiance regains the ascendant. It is with a sense of relief that we hear his well-known voice ring out again, after the anguish of this grovelling letter–a letter that would never have been written but for his wife's sake. He exclaims: "These sovereigns, who were wont to send me, in all solemnity, their delegations of ambassadors, who gave a daughter of their blood to share my bed, and who called me 'brother', are now cursing me as a usurper, and spit upon my picture since they cannot spit upon the original. They have bespattered the majesty of kings with mud! What is the title of emperor? Had I no other name to bequeath, posterity would laugh.... In classical days, the vanquished were robbed of their children that these might be paraded before the people when the conqueror was celebrating his triumph..."

What must be the tenor of Napoleon's thoughts when he learns how, on that shameful day of cowardice and confusion, the lad of four had refused to leave the palace of his father; of how when the little king of Rome had met his grandfather for the first time, he had uttered the innocent words: "I have seen the emperor of Austria. He is not handsome." This was precisely what Napoleon had wished to avoid. The fate of Astyanax has been prepared for the boy; and even though he is made much of, the child is well aware that he must no longer mention his father's name. Though he has received the symbolical names of Napoleon Francis and by England, is a veritable caricature of a monarch. What is Louis doing to show his goodwill towards the people?

He has granted a constitution? But soon comes news that this gracious gift exists only on paper. The old inequalities, the privileges of caste, which had cost the present king's brother his head, are quietly stealing in through the back door. The nobles are not liable to military service, and men of humble birth have no chance of rising to high office. The new nobility is made a mock of. King Louis, a good old man, reasonable enough, is led by his brother, the gloomy count of Artois. Around the latter are concentrated the vengeful émigrés, who are demanding the return of their property; but the law guarantees the rights of the actual holders. The King, therefore, gives peerages and large pensions to the émigrés.

What is this? So the clergy is rising to power once more! The priests are on the side of the old nobility, and by threats of hell-fire induce the dying to execute wills in favour of the sometime owners of confiscated property. On Sundays, though the new constitution guarantees religious freedom, all business is suspended under threat of punishment. Religious processions again make their way through the streets. But there is a reaction against ecclesiasticism. When Christian burial is refused to an actress who has lived a gay life and is a darling of the Parisians, there is a riot, the first under the restored regime.

People are beginning to see how much they owed to their foreign liberator. With intense delight, the exile contemplates a caricature showing Louis riding pillion behind a Cossack; making his way into France over French corpses. When Wellington, the conqueror of Spain, comes to Paris as British ambassador, he meets angry glances when he walks the streets. What is the new regime doing for the thousands who may no longer remain soldiers? The officers are put on half-pay, and those who are not practicing Catholics are cashiered. A new royal guard, consisting of gentlemen of noble birth, is richly endowed; the nobles' military academy is reopened; but the schools for the orphans of members of the Legion of Honour are done away with. Disillusionment spreads through France more quickly than the Emperor had expected.

But the tone in Elba is not Jacobin. Napoleon does not abandon his system, although he recognises his mistakes: "France needs an aristocracy. For its foundation, however, time and memories are requisite. I made princes and dukes, and gave them land and wealth; but they were men of low birth, so it was impossible to make noblemen of them. I tried, therefore, to unite them by marriage with old families. Had I been granted the twenty years I wanted for the establishment of France's greatness, I could have done much. Fate willed other wise."

On the whole, like a chessplayer when the game is finished, he frankly acknowledges the wrong moves that have led to his defeat. Nor is he cautious in the choice of persons to whom he pours out such confessions. He tells English visitors that he ought to have made peace after Dresden. But when they ask why he did not make peace in Châtillon, he answers proudly:

"I could not make a peace dishonourable to France. Belgium was part of France when I rose to power. Could I cede the lands I had conquered, and go back to the Bourbon frontiers? Never! .... I am a born soldier. Suddenly, I found myself in the midst of the revolution. The throne was vacant. I took it, and kept it as long as I could. Now I am once more what I was to begin with, a soldier...."

Those who know the man will recognise from such thoughts that he is still unbroken. But what amazes us is the freedom with which he speaks of the past. Never, in Elba, does he show any desire to falsify his history. And yet, during the first months, he believes his career finished, and has no thought of trying a new coup de main. He even fancies that he would like to become a justice of the peace in England. "What would happen to me if I went to England? Would people throw stones at me? The London mob is a dangerous factor." The Englishmen to whom he thus talks assure him that their country is hospitable. He makes a mental note of this assurance.

The Vienna congress is the first thing to set him in motion. Four monarchs, allied against one republic, were at length able, after a decade, to annihilate it; five monarchs, now all united, had assembled to reorganise Europe, and there was no longer an enemy worth considering to hold them in check; but four and a half conquerors (if the Bourbon ruler can be accounted as half) were soon to be disunited, thanks to the inborn jealousy with which each one of them regarded his fellows. Does the tsar want to take the whole of Poland as his share of the spoil; and does Prussia want Saxony? What will happen, then, to Galicia; and what about the worthy king of Saxony, Bourbon's ally? A split is inevitable. By New Year, three months after the opening of the congress, the coalition has been broken up. Ministers and potentates who had so recently been celebrating their victory in a series of festivities, have begun to cheat one another. The Habsburg ruler is now allied with England and France against the Russians and the Prussians, by whose side the Austrians had a few months earlier been fighting against Napoleon.

Metternich's levity, laziness, vanity, intriguing disposition (this is Stein's description), dominated the situation: "he twists our excellent and victorious monarchs round his fingers." A Saxon nobleman writes from Vienna: "The king of Prussia is the embodiment of wrath ...The king of Denmark is ... well -meaning and sometimes intelligent. The king of Bavaria looks like an uncouth and morose wagoner. The grand duke of Baden is huge, gloomy, vain, and robust.... The old duke of Weimar lives as jovially as ever he did." The hopes of the man of Elba rise as he reads and hears all this. "My time will come," he thinks, "when the congress goes up in the air!" Henceforward, he is in receipt of secret information concerning the currents of opinion in Vienna. The faithful Maret is able to arrange an intelligence service. But while the congress, a brightly lit pleasure ship, rolling for lack of ballast, is intriguing and enjoying itself, in the crow's nest sits Napoleon's old enemy, keeping anxious watch. He has his spies in Leghorn, who report every ship that sails to Elba, and tell him the names of the passengers.

Thus do the old adversaries eye one another across mountains and seas and across the documents of the diplomats, until it seems as if all these people of importance had come together in Vienna to furnish a lively setting for the game of chess the two experts are playing. Does either of them recall that night just before the Eighteenth Brumaire when they had been scared by the clatter of hoofs from the mounted patrol, and had turned pale in their dread of arrest?

This much is certain, that at Vienna Talleyrand remains a shrewd judge of men. Regarding Murat as a dangerous personality, he would like to have the king of Naples shipped off to the Azores, nearly a thousand miles from the nearest continent. But his ruling passion, avarice, comes in the way. At the congress, Murat, driven into a corner in the defence of his kingdom, promises Talleyrand a large sum of money in return for the minister's princedom of Benevento. Talleyrand therefore drops the plan against Murat, and concocts a new scheme. The Emperor is to be kidnapped. But the spies in Leghorn report that this will only be possible if one of the four captains who command his ships can be suborned.

When Napoleon gets wind of these intrigues, the adventurer's blood of his Corsican home runs swiftly through his veins. He has the defences of Elba strengthened, and his artillerymen are trained in the use of hand-grenades. "I am a soldier, and am ready to face a firing squad. But I will not be deported! Before they can do that they will have to take my citadel by storm." No attempt is made. In Vienna there is now a better understanding, and the likelihood of the rupture of negotiations diminishes. In France, however, disaffection to the Bourbons is growing. The general upshot is to stimulate the Emperor's determination. His thoughts run as follows:

"If the congress closes with a peace festival after all the documents have been signed, the phalanx will have been reconstituted. But now, when it is still imperfectly consolidated, a touch will break it to pieces. France is murmuring against the Bourbons; Paris makes fun of them; everyone detests the allies. There are a hundred signs to show that the old army is devoted to me–the Emperor. The Bourbons are fainthearts, and will run away. As soon as I regain my position, my son and heir will be sent back to me."

Calculations, only calculations; and never has he reckoned more soberly. None the less, though he considers his figures with the utmost care, in the last resort he relies upon psychological reactions. "I count upon taking them by surprise. A bold deed upsets people's equanimity, and they are dumbfounded by a great novelty." He adds: "I am the cause of France's unhappiness. I must effect a cure." In the end of February, he sends for his treasurer. "Have you plenty of money? How much does a million in gold weigh? What is the weight of a hundred francs? How much does a box filled with books weigh? ... Take a couple of packing cases, put all the gold coin you have at the bottom, and fill up the case with my books; my valet will give them to you. Discharge the present staff of servants; pack their trunks and pay them off. Everything must be kept strictly secret."

In alarm, the man hastens to General Drouot. They exchange glances, but keep their own counsel. Next day, Napoleon orders that no ships are to leave the harbour. Everything has been quietly prepared; an expedition like that to Egypt, but on a small scale.

On the eve of his departure, he plays a game of ecarte with the ladies; but he soon leaves the table and goes into the garden, whence he does not return. His mother, according to her own story, finds him sitting under a fig tree. After brief hesitation, he lays his hand on her forehead, and says, much moved:

"I will tell you all about it. No one else must know, not even Pauline."

Then he goes back to his old tone, as if he were talking to Berthier:

"I must tell you that I am leaving next evening."

"Where are you going?"

"To Paris." A pause. "I should like your advice."

His thoughts are coloured with the spirit of the time. He is a man of forty-five, with more past that future, no longer young enough to take the world by storm, but not too old for a desperate venture. Thus does Napoleon again draw near to French shores, in a mood betwixt courage and renunciation.

XVI

The mountains are calling, the valleys are echoing, as the procession of a thousand men who landed at Cannes wends its way through one Alpine village after another. An enthusiastic crowd encircles the old guard which has pursued its way along the road of history without jubilation and without sorrow, imperturbable as a rock. The peasants, these sons of the hills, in the selfsame hamlets, had once before seen him, a lean, small, unknown general; in those days he had relieved them from the burden of maintaining as undisciplined soldiery, and had led the troops over the Alps to victory. These mountain folk were the first to see the miracle he wrought; they plumed themselves on the thought that from their villages the Emperor had gone forth. And now, of a sudden, he is among them again! Surely the procession of the thousand will work a spell, and seem to be the march of prophets and saviours?

They come from their mountain fastnesses; women and children bring up the rear; songs against the king are composed and sung; in the lesser towns, the bolder spirits force the city fathers to go forth to meet the newcomer; for more than a hundred miles he encounters none but peasants.

Napoleon had reckoned upon this. He would not face a march through Aix and Avignon, through the monarchical provinces. He preferred to leave his few cannon behind in the snow-covered mountain paths, in order the quicker to reach Dauphiné. Here the peasants had received the most generous distribution of the nobles' lands. They are full of anger now against king, priest, and émigré, who, after the lapse of twenty-five years, are contesting the peasants' right to hold these lands. Was not the great revolution made to protect the poor? Was it not made by peasants in the country and workmen in the town? The Consul had not taken back anything from them; even the Emperor had only called up their sons; they have never ceased to look upon him as one of themselves, for their minds moved slowly and their hearts were constant. Now, the king had come back again, and forthwith the nobles had begun to squabble over the fields the peasant had tilled.

The souls of the countryfolk were heavy at the change of fortune. Fifteen years ago the mood had been similar when Napoleon, returning from Egypt in his little ship, had landed, and the whole of southern France had hailed him as saviour. What can have happened in the last ten months, to make these people receive with every token of joy the man whom they had so recently execrated? True, he had passed through another part of the country at that time; and the national misfortune had needed a scapegoat. His disfavour among the folk had been as brief as his defeat. But belief in him lasted as long as the years of his glory.

What will the first troops we meet do? He himself, when he took leave, had urged them to serve the fatherland. And the fatherland was the king! They wear the Bourbon's white cockade, they eat the king's bread, from the lips of patrician officers they have received a new and ugly picture of the erstwhile leader. Everything will depend on his power of suggestion. Uncertain feelings govern his heart as he strides inland from Cannes. To his left, lies the fort of Antibes. Does he recognise the tower wherein he was thrown when Robespierre fell? In just such a tower, the Bourbon will fling him, against just such a wall Europe will stand him, if he should fail on the morrow to accomplish what his glance and his word have so often succeeded in doing before.

Outside Grenoble, near La Mure, he has his first encounter with the royal troops. They have orders to exterminate him and his "band of brigands"; the officers have taken the oath to the king just as in former days they had taken the oath to the Emperor. The order to attack is given. Is the blood of brethren to be shed? That is what Napoleon has spent a lifetime in avoiding. Is this highway to be turned into a battlefield? He alights from his horse, takes ten strides towards them, and shouts:

"Soldiers of the fifth army corps! Don't you know me? If there is one among you who wishes to kill his Emperor, let him come forward and do so. Here I am!" Saying which, he throws open his grey cloak.

A terrible pause. What will happen?

Those are our brethren! This is our general! We have seen him in so many battles, standing on a hillock, or sitting over the bivouac fire, or facing the musket shots and cannon balls! Must not nature and remembrance overpower the influence of recent vows? The soldiers cry: "Vive l'Empereur!" A general running to and fro ensues, guards and soldiers mingling; caps are stuck upon bayonet points—what does one more hole in the blue cloth matter? An hour later, two thousand instead of one thousand fall in behind their leader.

This encounter on the high road to Grenoble, this moment of time, his call, his aspect, were decisive. The man of action had won back to leadership through his own deed; the middle-aged warrior had regained life, power, and realm, by a look and a word. Thus he reaches Grenoble. By a manifesto he communicates his thoughts to the people:

"Frenchmen! ... After the fall of Paris my heart was torn but my spirit remained unshaken.... My life belongs to you, and must once more be made useful to you. In my exile, I heard your plaints and your cries.... You accused me of too long a slumber, saying I was sacrificing the interests of the country to my own repose. Encompassed by dangers, I have sailed over the sea. Now I am in your midst, to demand my rights, which are also your rights.

"Soldiers! We are not conquered! ... Marmont's treachery delivered the capital into the hands of the enemy, and disorganised our army. Now I have come! Your general, who was elected to the throne by the suffrage of the people, and raised aloft on your shields, has returned to you. Rally to him! ... Wear the tricolour cockade again, the cockade of our days of victory! Let the eagles which you bore at Ulm and Austerlitz, at Jena, Eylau, and Friedland, at Eckmühl and Wagram, at Smolensk and on the Moskva, at Lützen and Montmirail, once more wave on high! Possessions, rank, and glory, for yourselves and for your children, have no worse foes than those princes who have been forced upon you by foreign powers.... Victory will guide us forward through the storms, and the eagles shall fly from one church steeple to the other until at last they alight on Notre Dame!"

Vive l'Empereur! The troops in Grenoble, together with the imperial nobles, come over. Seven thousand men follow him to Lyons. Lyons comes over, Masséna, who had been serving the king, journeys from Marseilles and pays homage to the Emperor.

"Where is Ney?" Embarrassed silence. "With the king?"

They tell him about the council of war in Paris. Since the terrible news was brought, the fat king and his lean court have sat there trembling. The "Moniteur," which had lied in Napoleon's favour for fifteen years, now lies on behalf of the king: the Emperor, it announces, is dead. Just as they are deliberating what to do, old Count Condé enters the room and asks his royal cousin whether on Maundy Thursday the king himself should not officiate at the washing of feet. The king is writing a manifesto to the army. But who is sitting by him, his mainstay, the true leader of the Bourbon army? What is the man's name?

It is Marshal Ney. When, on the retreat from Moscow he had been cut off from the main body and appeared to be lost, his master had cried: "Ney is lost! I would give the two hundred millions from my cellars in the Tuileries, if I had him again!" Now he rises from among the royal plenipotentiaries gathered round the conference table; he swears to annihilate his sometime master. But when the breeze of general enthusiasm sweeps by him, he veers; his corpse dons the tricolour cockade, and in Besançon he sends word to the Emperor that he would like to write a vindication of his conduct. But the Emperor waves the proposal aside, saying: "Tell him I love him the same as ever, and that tomorrow I shall embrace him."

What a master-stroke! True, he forgives; but he leaves Ney on tenterhooks till the morrow. Next day, the marshal stammers: "I love you, Sire; but as a son of the fatherland.... I was forced to kneel down before that fat hog to receive the cross of St. Louis! Had you not come, we should have chased him away ourselves."

"Marvellous! How vacillating he is, how pale!" These thoughts flit through the Emperor's mind as he asks his questions.

The count of Artois has fled. The very morning of the flight, the guards had sworn to die with him; by midday, they had rallied to the Emperor. Such behaviour does not please Napoleon, and he keeps this portion of the guard at arm's length. But there is one man who had remained loyal to Louis until the Bourbon was in safety; not till then does he change sides. This recruit, Napoleon welcomes, and with his own hand decorates him with the emblem of the Legion of Honour!

But what a change! The more this avalanche of soldiers grows as he marches forward towards Paris, the more peaceful do his speeches become. In one town after another, he addresses the municipal councillors and the citizens in the following words: "War is at an end. Peace and liberty! The principles of the revolution must be protected from the onslaughts of the émigrés. The treaties with Europe must be adhered to. France will win back her glory without war. We must be content to be the most esteemed nation, without trying to dominate other countries."

Does the people grasp the significance of the new tone? If the nation understands, is there belief in its genuineness? Must one be content? Glory without war? To a high official, an old acquaintance whom he meets on the march and in whom at length he finds an intelligent listener after addressing dull-witted citizens and partisan officers, he gives this political explanation:

"The spirit of the people is changed. In earlier days, the nation thought only of glory; now it thinks only of liberty In the past, I brought the nation glory; I will not withhold liberty now.

Freedom can be enjoyed in full, when power rests upon a good constitution. Only–no anarchy! That would bring us back to the days of the despotic republicans, when everyone had a finger in the pie. I shall retain only so much power as is essential for governing properly."

In the naive closing sentence lies the new problem. He has broached the question; he is determined to stabilize the basic ideas of democracy. One thing is the same as on the Eighteenth Brumaire: no party politics! "I don't want to write to them," he says, when advised to forgive the turncoats. "They would believe that I was pledged to them. How are things in the Tuileries?"

"Nothing has been changed; not even the eagles have been removed." He is gay, bubbling over with good humour. He laughs.

"I suppose King Louis found the eagles decorative! What are they playing at the theatre? How is Talma? Were you at court? I've been told that the Bourbons looked like parvenus, did not know what to talk about, nor how to behave."

How inquisitive he is! How full of malicious joy! How he yearns for the air of Paris! He seeks his revenge in mockery, he whom the others had so long held up to ridicule. He is told of the parsimony of the court. He is shown the king's effigy on a twenty-franc piece.

"Do you see? They've got it again: 'God protect the king.' My device is: 'God protect France'! They've left out those words. They were always like that: everything for themselves; nothing for France!" In the course of three minutes he enquires after twenty persons. When he is told that Hortense has been made a duchess, he answers simply:

"She should have called herself Madame Bonaparte. That name is worth more than all the rest."

His words are symbolic of the new epoch. If he calls himself Bonaparte once more, grants a constitution, allows liberty, and does not grasp at more power than he actually needs, he can make himself king of France. Then, after the failure of his attempt at the unification of Europe, he will still be able to become the happy exemplar of a modern prince by God's grace. He has always ruled as circumstances might dictate. Now, called to power for the second time, and after his imaginative flight towards far horizons, he will still prove himself a master. The road lies open.

The road to Paris is likewise open. The Bourbon king has run away, and the majority of the inhabitants are on the Emperor's side. Any one who might still have dreaded a fight with the last royal troops, must have overestimated them. When the Emperor is yet a hundred miles from the capital, the remnants of the royal guard flee from the city. The Emperor's army overtakes the king, but allows him to escape to a seaport, being content to take the silver he is carrying off with him in sixty carts, and to seize his cannon. France has a hearty laugh at this fat old gentleman, who had been escorted from England to Paris by enemy soldiers, and now makes all speed back to England with the soldiers of France chasing him.

Paris is calm. The town has long since forgotten how to take the initiative. During the twenty days between the Emperor's landing in the south and his arrival at the capital; the thermometer of the press registers the following degrees: "The monster has escaped from his place of exile."–"The Corsican werewolf has landed at Cannes."–"The tiger appeared at Gap, troops were sent against him, the wretched adventurer ended his career in the mountains."–"The fiend has actually, thanks to treachery, been able to get as far as Grenoble."–"The tyrant has reached Lyons, where horror paralysed all attempts at resistance."–"The usurper has dared to advance within a hundred and fifty miles of the capital."–"Bonaparte moves northward with rapid strides, but he will never reach Paris."–"Tomorrow Napoleon will be at our gates."–"His Majesty is at Fontainebleau."

When, at length, without having had to fire a shot, the Emperor mounts the steps of the palace he had been compelled to leave thirteen months before, Paris is overawed by his soldiers, and the émigrés have fled with the king. All is quiet. He notes the fact, listens attentively, and says: "They have let me come, just as they let the others go."

Now he has his first disappointment! The march on Paris had been glorious, and in after days he spoke of it as the most splendid experience in his life. But here, in the city which will ultimately decide his fate, the city whose favour he has wooed more assiduously than he ever fought for any realm, the city he has never wholly conquered, he encounters moral resistance. Those whose favour he courts are no longer in the arms of their new friend; but they are listless, as if, after excess of passion, their vital energy had run down. Still, here he is, and he must bestir himself.

He looks to Vienna for a sign.

A week after Napoleon's landing in France, Metternich goes to bed at three o'clock, and is awakened at six by a messenger who hands him a dispatch. He reads the inscription on the envelope, "General Consulate, Genoa," angrily turns over and goes to sleep again. He does not open the missive till several hours later, to read: "Campbell, the English commissioner, has just called to enquire whether Napoleon has been seen in Genoa. He has vanished from the island of Elba."

The bomb! Those who were yesterday still intriguing against one another, now become thick as thieves once more. The vows which have so often been broken are renewed. The first to think of declaring the man an outlaw is Baron vom Stein, whom Napoleon had outlawed five years earlier. The possibility is discussed, but father-in-law Francis of Habsburg cannot make up his mind to the step; he would like to ask Marie Louise first. Four years ago she was devoted to her husband. She has never breathed a word of complaint to her father or to any of her women friends. Why should she? Napoleon had done whatever she wanted; she had been courted and wealthy; he had been the most equable of husbands; the parents had shared in the games of the little boy. Will she now become the Emperor's advocate?

The wife of Napoleon and the mistress of the Austrian officer prefers to take up her pen and write a formal declaration to the congress. She will have nothing to do with the Emperor, and she will put herself under the protection of the allies. Such is her

ers, and court dignitaries, again flock to his levees. A count of the old aristocracy comes likewise. Napoleon had called this man back from exile and had made him senator; but at the Bourbon restoration the count had gone over to the king. Now, as the Emperor draws near, the count casts his eyes heavenward and seems to imply that his actions were dictated by God's inscrutable will. The Emperor smiles. Not a word is exchanged. But the count comes no more to court. When, on the other hand, one of Marmont's generals, a man who had delivered a decisive speech in the war council before the marshal's defection, approaches Napoleon and begins to stammer out an explanation, the Emperor does not smile. He says, in an overbearing tone: "What do you want of me? Can you not see that I do not know you?"

Here is Oudinot: for twenty years he was Bonaparte's companion-in-arms; now he comes back to the Emperor. "You see, Oudinot? You were worshipped as a god by the Lorrainers; two hundred thousands peasants were ready, even last year, to go through fire and water for your sake. Today I have to protect you against these same peasants!"

Here is Rapp. He has wavered longer than the rest, and even now comes hesitatingly to his master. "You've kept us waiting a long time! Did you really want to take up arms against me?"

Rapp is an Alsatian, half a German, and as such he is more a man of duty than a man of feeling: "My duty, Sire, constrained me."

"Diable! The soldiers would not have obeyed you; your Alsatians would have stoned you!"

But Rapp is nothing if not thorough: "You must admit Sire, the position was a difficult one. You abdicate, you leave France, you advice us to serve the king, you come again...."

"Were you often here? How did they treat you? At first, I suppose, they flattered you. Soon they'd have chucked you out of doors. That is what your fate would have been.... Have you read Chateaubriand's pamphlet? Is it true that I am a coward on the battlefield? They are always accusing me of ambition because they have nothing better to say. Does one get as fat as I, if one is constantly being spurred on by ambition? ... Once again, General, we must serve France. Then we can be gathered to our fathers."

In such a debonair and lively manner does he play with this doughty and decorous old comrade. But Rapp holds his own: "You must admit. Sire, that you made a mistake in not concluding peace after Dresden. You treated as nonsensical my reports concerning German sentiment...." The Emperor is quick with his repartee:

"You do not understand what such a peace would have meant!" Suddenly his tone changes into one more suitable to the camp than to this palace and to this hour; it is intimate and familiar, and goes home to Rapp's heart: "Or were you perhaps afraid of beginning a fresh war, you who for fifteen long years had acted as my adjutant? When you returned from Egypt you were nothing more than a soldier. I have made a man of you. Today you can have whatever you like to ask for.... I shall never forget your conduct before Moscow. At Danzing you achieved the greatest that any man could achieve. Ney and you, you belong to the tiny legion of those who have strength of character!" Then, pulling Rapp The Emperor embraces him, kisses him again and again. Then, pulling Rapp's moustache, he says:

"Eh? One of the braves of Egypt and Austerlitz–and you wanted to forsake me! You shall take command of the army on the Rhine, while I am dealing with the Prussians and the Russians. In two months, I hope you will be receiving my wife and my son in Strasburg. From today, you are my adjutant!"

"At your orders, Sire!"

Had the Emperor ever seen *Wallenstein's Death* performed on the German stage, as had, perhaps, that would-be murderer in Poland? He must have this fellow, Rapp, about him. The man is fundamentally honest, and is as brave as he is honourable; of all the Grand Army, he is the officer who was most frequently wounded. He only went over to the king from a sense of duty; he is not to be bought by the lure of promises. And yet, in a quarter of an hour, he is not only the Emperor's man once more, but has accepted the posts of army commander and adjutant, as of old. Fidelity, Napoleon realised it well, is what the Emperor most urgently needs.

Ney's case is a more difficult one. Remorse keeps Ney sleepless. With distraught countenance and extravagant words he addresses his master: "Perhaps you have heard, Sire, before I marched to Besançon, I said at the council of war–here, in the Tuileries, I promised the king–"

"Well, what did you promise?"

"To bring you in an iron cage, and place you before his throne–"

The Emperor stiffens. Then: "Foolishness! Such thoughts are unworthy of a soldier!"

"You are mistaken, Sire," exclaims the Marshal yet more excitedly; "allow me to finish. I said it, yes–but–I wanted to hide my real feelings–"

The Emperor is incensed. Ney quickly withdraws, and only after the lapse of two months takes command in the campaign. Thus near to madness had these iron warriors been brought through their struggle between duty and inclination, when the one great will which mastered them had been withdrawn. Berthier, who also rallied to Napoleon, had gone through the same experience.

"The donkey," exclaims the Emperor leniently, when talking of his old favourite. "He's a good fellow. I ask nothing of him than that he should present himself before me in the uniform of the royal guard!" But Berthier, since the Emperor's return, rushes all night through the rooms of his mansion, and at last throws himself headlong from a balcony, like Junot, to perish on the cobbles instead of dying in the battlefield.

Forwards! We have no time for loitering! Who else is there? Ah, Madame de Stael pops up again. This old opponent writes to him, admires his conduct, and promises that if he will restore the two million francs which France still owes her father, she will in future devote her literary gifts to the cause of France. The pity of it! Through making this stipulation, so splendid a woman must come down to history as beaten in the game! The Emperor mischievously replies that, to his great regret, he is not wealthy enough to fulfil her condition.

Who else is there? Marmont? Augereau? They are declared outlaws by the Emperor, because they sold the fatherland to the foreigner. And then, at long last, Talleyrand likewise! The lightning flashes that travel from Vienna to Paris and from Paris to Vienna strike a deadly blow at this hostile friendship which has lasted for eighteen years. Each man thinks in his secret heart: "A pity that so fine a brain should be working for the other side!"

What about the second of the Dioscuri? Fouché is back again! He takes up his service as Minister of Police in the twofold capacity of working for and against his master. He says of the Emperor: "Well, he's here. We none of us exactly wished him back again: now we shall have to keep close watch on him.... The man has returned even madder than when he left. I give him three months!" Meanwhile, he corresponds with Metternich; but spies soon tell the Emperor, who angrily apostrophises him: "You are a traitor!" Lavalette, who is in waiting, hears the words through the half-open door. "Why do you consent to be my minister if you mean to betray me? I know that you are exchanging letters with Metternich through the intermediation of a bank official in Basle. I could have you hanged, and all the world would applaud my action." Fouché's answer has not been recorded!

The minister owed his present position to his radical outlook, for he had been a revolutionary in theory ever since Robespierre's time. The Emperor needed him in the cabinet as a decoy for the democrats. But Fouché not only betrayed his master to Metternich, he likewise betrayed Metternich to the radicals; he wanted to set up a republic–with Fouché at the head. Carnot, who was a more violent antagonist of the king than even the Emperor himself had been, now, for the first time since the days of the Directory, entered the ministry.

people really wants freedom, I must give it.... I am no longer a conqueror; I can no longer be a conqueror. I know what is possible and what is impossible. My sole mission now is to set France on her feet once more and to give her a constitution adapted to the temperament of her people....

"I do not hate freedom, although I gave it a wide berth when I met it on my way. I understand liberty; I was nourished on this idea. The labours of fifteen years have been destroyed; if I wished to begin all over again, I should need twenty years and should have to sacrifice two million men.... I want peace; I can get it only through victory. I will not fill you with false hopes; I foresee a terrible war. In order to win through, I must have the support of the people. The people will ask for freedom in exchange for its support. Very well, the people shall have freedom.... My situation is a new one for me. I am getting older. At forty-five one is no longer the man one was at thirty. The repose of a constitutional king would suit me excellently. And I am sure that this state of things would meet with the approval of my son."

Such were the basic ideas of Emperor Napoleon on his return from Elba; he was to become king of France. That his ideas are genuine and his intentions pure, is proved by the realism of his motives. We have not to do with a man who pretends to a change of heart; this is no hero who, in commune with his maker upon an island, has become a saint. Here we have the man himself, wishful to rule as circumstances permit; a man who has ever been mindful of public opinion. He recognizes that he has to do with a new epoch. If he himself did not inaugurate such an epoch, at least, through his fall, he made its realization possible. Napoleon feels that a land which has experienced the dictatorship of genius, can no longer revert to the dictatorship of inheritance. If the spirit of the revolution has become petrified into a single huge figure, a new structure must arise from its ruins, and the stone blocks that are used in the building must be so placed as to secure wider levels and a less tapering pinnacle. In very truth, the son of the revolution, even when he becomes a tyrant, cannot be succeeded by a king who reigns by God's grace. He can only be succeeded by democracy.

For this reason, the Emperor deals more severely with the émigrés than he was wont; he confiscates estates; he disbands the royal guard; and does at the end of his career what he should have done at the start, namely, he abolishes feudal titles, thus ridding himself of the old nobility whose false compliments had cost him so dear. By these decrees he recreates the revolutionary spirit, and makes it stronger than it has been since his coronation, eleven years earlier. He issues the following declaration to the civil authorities:

"I have returned today for the same reason which brought me back from Egypt: because things are not going well with the fatherland.... I do not want to carry on any more wars. We have to forget that we were masters of the world.... In those days, I pursued the aim of creating a great United States of Europe, and I was compelled to neglect many points of home policy which would have secured the freedom of the citizens of France. Now I shall work for no other object than for France's consolidation and tranquillity, for the protection of property, for the free interchange of ideas: the prince must be the first servitor of the State." Among the hearers are many who, but a year ago, amid the thunder crashes of the catastrophe, had listened to other words uttered by these selfsame lips: "I am the State." Nevertheless they pin their faith to his new constitution, whose elaboration is entrusted to Constant.

When the constitution is placed before them, they are alarmed. "Additional Act?" Are we once more to be cheated? The democrats pour forth a hail of criticism. Simultaneously, news comes from Vienna: the powers declare war on Napoleon; no harm shall come to France. A signal! For twenty years, so the saying runs through the land, we have desired peace. At last we have got it. Is it once more to come to an end? "I cannot hide the fact from you any longer," says a councillor of State to the Emperor; "the women are your declared enemies, and these opponents are always dangerous in France." No one wants any more levies to be made. Instead of two hundred and fifty thousand men, only sixty thousand answer his call.

This decision of the powers is an expression of the mood of the princes, and not of the peoples they govern, for these, just like the French people, are eager for repose. The sentence of outlawry is not so much a political move as an insistence on a point of honour, and the expression of Emperor Francis' desire to exact moral vengeance. But it gnaws at the foundation of Napoleon's power. When he had first come back, France had been in his favour. Since, however, all the other States of Europe are against him, France will make no more sacrifices on his behalf. The funds, which had risen when he reached Paris, fall.

The Emperor is alarmed. An intimate, from whom he has asked news of the recruiting campaign, says to him: "Your Majesty will not be left unsupported." To which the Emperor replies in low tones: "I was almost afraid I should be!"

His friends find him less active than of yore; he is fatter, his features are lax, he needs many hot baths, and lies in them a long time; he takes a great deal of sleep. "He seemed full of cares," writes one of his circle. "The self-confidence of his speeches, his authoritative tone, had vanished."

Only four weeks ago, at his first advent, he appeared rejuvenated and lively. Why this relapse?

First and foremost, his wife's behaviour has shaken him. A semi-anonymous letter from Vienna, addressed to Lavalette, has fallen into his hands. Herein are described Marie Louise's scorn for the Emperor, her love for Neipperg; and a number of shameful details are added. The Emperor is surprised holding this letter, in his dimly lighted study, crouched over the fire, silent.

When Méneval, who was to have accompanied Marie Louise on her return journey to Paris, comes back from Vienna, he finds the Emperor, in the very midst of these eventful weeks, lying on a sofa, sunk deep in reverie. For many hours that day, and for half the next, the secretary has to give his master a precise account of everything that is happening over there, of all he has observed. The Emperor spoke as though "overwhelmed by a calm sorrowfulness, and seemed so resigned that I was deeply moved. He was no longer confident of victory, and I felt that his belief in his good luck, which had sustained him during the march to Paris, had forsaken him." Méneval has to describe every trait and gesture of the little son. The Emperor, an ageing man, paces to and fro in the garden on this day in May, alone; he has to rely on a stranger's word to know what his boy is like, whether the child is growing up to resemble his father or his grandfather.

These things weigh him down. Tragically, the conflicts within him are renewed. Now that he wishes to be a democrat in response to the spirit of the time, now that his will-to-peace is great, the menace from without frustrates his attempts to establish democracy or maintain peace. If no one in Europe were to lift a finger in order to replace Louis on the throne, Napoleon might content himself with ruling within the boundaries of France, might introduce the freedoms he had promised. But the powers, which have no more lands to reclaim (since they have received back all that was ever taken from them, and now possess what they had had before the revolution), come forward as they had in '92, because the wind blowing from this stormy corner of Europe threatens their inherited calm, and because none of the monarchs can sleep sound o' nights so long as their Bourbon cousin is standing on the English shore of the Channel looking plaintively across the waters towards France, the land of his fathers.

Never had Napoleon taken up arms more reluctantly than he did when this war was forced upon him by the Vienna decree. Never had the rapidity and clear-sightedness of a dictator or the sympathy of public opinion been more necessary to him than in this terrible crisis. Just now, when everyone wants peace, he is obliged to arm for war; just now, when he is to bestow liberties on the people, his actions are hampered at every turn. The struggle of the legitimists with this interloper (the upshot of which had been his own legitimization), the struggle which had placed him on the throne, is resumed when, too late, he is cured of his longing to pose as legitimate monarch. Though he is reaching out towards liberty once more, he is now to sustain his final defeat.

Thus the great renewal gets no further than the Additional Act to the Constitutions of the Empire, which, as earlier with his great decrees, he leaves to approval of the "sovereign people."

Nevertheless, the sixty-seven articles evolved out of Constant's head contain all the newer democratic elements; they are a great advance upon English constitutional law, and remain as a model for a whole of the subsequent century. No one henceforward can be imprisoned or banished without due form of law; religious belief and the press are to be free. The legislative body is changed into a lower House, the Senate becomes an Upper House without the former privileges, all deliberations are open to the public, both House may initiate legislation and reject the budget, the ministers are to be responsible to parliament, the interpretation of the law devolves upon the Chambers.

A number of new laws, each a dagger in the dictator's heart! Yet he yields in everything save two points which he carries, after a lively debate against Constant: the hereditariness of the peerage, in which "after one or two successful battles," the nobility would again pour; and his right to confiscation, for "without this right I should be defenceless against the party factions. I am not an angel, but a man who cannot allow himself to be attacked without meting out punishment."

These two concessions to him create as bad an impression as the words "Additional Act" had done. Since he will allow no discussion on the matter, but only consents to the empty form of a plebiscite, as he had done in the days when he wished to become consul for life and subsequently emperor, the democrats begin to grumble, and no one is aware how greatly the nation is to be congratulated on this latest work of its leader. Instead of the four million votes he had received of yore, his constitution receives only just over one and a half million votes, for most of the citizens abstain.

A few venture to protest. Honest Carnot says: "Your Additional Act has not pleased the people; it will not meet with acceptance. Promise me that you will amend it. I must tell you the truth, for your and our salvation hangs upon your tolerance." His tone is upright, but wholly unprecedented. Since the days when Bonaparte was a lieutenant no one had ever spoken thus to him. He makes a gesture of annoyance, and Carnot continues: "This word alarms you, Sire? Yes, you must show tolerance in the face of the national will."

"The foe is at our gates," answers the veteran soldier. "First of all, help to chase him away. Then I shall have time to occupy myself with your liberal panaceas." Even though he profoundly recognises the demands of the new age, he finds it impossible to deliberate with representatives of the people.

Napoleon knows only how to command!

XVIII

On a bright spring morning, the plain is lively as on days of high festival. The Parisians are flocking in crowds to the Champ de Mai. The whole town has come forth to this revival of the Carlovingian folk assembly. The old troops are there, and the new. The platforms are gaily decorated with tricolours. Six hundred deputies and several hundred peers are waiting for the Emperor, who is to take the oath to the new constitution before starting on his campaign. It is the first time for two or three years that the people of the gay city have had a chance of glutting their lust for merry-making. Under the king, all had been sober and staid.

Now the procession is coming forth from the town; from afar can be heard the fanfare of the trumpets, and every one is expecting the hero of the occasion, the warrior Napoleon, to be dressed as beseems the posture of affairs, seeing that within a few days he will be fighting for throne and country at the head of his troops. Rumour has run through Paris saying that he still wears his old green coat, in which people love best to see him.

But what is the pageant which unfolds itself?

First comes the guard of honour, followed by the eagles and the colours; then heralds and pages, clad in many-coloured costumes, as if in an allegorical picture; then the Emperor's coronation coach, drawn by eight horses. In it is seated a man picturesquely attend in the while silk, almost overshadowed by a hat decked with huge ostrich plumes, and burdened by his vast coronation mantle; a solitary man, glittering with gold, Is this the Emperor?

The masses are dumbfounded, for they wanted to fraternize with their ruler returned from exile; they are stupefied by the spectacle of a Cæsar whose chill splendours seem to repel the cordiality they would fain exhibit. Painful indeed in the forlorn aspect of this middle-aged man, whose wife has not returned to him and whose son is far away, as he drives among the gaping crowds in his stately chariot.

When, after High Mass, the spokesman of the new Chambers confronts the Emperor, the citizen speaks in tones which ring athwart the plain: "Trusting your pledges, the deputies will sagaciously revise our laws, and harmonize them with the constitution"–the implication being that the representatives of the people are not yet satisfied, but want more than this Additional Act. Then the spokesman of the Chambers and the citizens expressed his hopes of victory, and wishes success to the eagles.

The Emperor has to hide his vexation. He announces the new constitution, and swears to observe it faithfully. Then the soldiers must acclaim the oath. But they can hardly recognize their master in this pompously attired ruler. They want the old green coat; their hero should be wearing the tricolour cockade, not gold and plumes. Their cheers lack enthusiasm. An eyewitness writes: "These were not the cheers of Austerlitz and Wagram. The Emperor could not fail to notice it."

A week later, when he opened both Houses with a speech from the throne, he was careful to avoid everything which had put people out of humour at the Champ de Mai. The Lower House promises to devote its energies to the defence of the nation; but goes on to say: "Even the will of the victorious ruler would not induce the nation to transcend the bounds of defence." The peers in the Upper House utter a like warning in their address, saying: "The French government will never be led away by the seductions of victory." Napoleon stands there constrained to silence, but dares not even give them the lie.

Among the new peers is Lucien. He has come to join his brother after all. A glance and a handclasp have reconciled the brothers. For the first time in his life he is styled prince and imperial highness. He is the Emperor's companion, delivers speeches, even gives lectures in the Institute, and receives large sums of money. Louis is ill, and does not come. Jerome is ready and willing. Hortense must replace the missing lady of the house, and her sons have once more become important to the man without a son. Napoleon appears on the balcony with his nephews, to show the crowd, to show France, that the Emperor still has heirs. Unseen, the spirit of irony contemplates this tragical conclusion to the history of his dynastic delusion.

Once he drives with Hortense to Malmaison, but goes alone into the room where Josephine died, to come forth from it in silence:

Next day he sets out for the war, hoping it will be his last war. It is.

Carnot, to whom at this late hour he divulges his plan, strongly advises him to wait until the army has been reinforced. Neither the Russians nor the Austrians can arrive before the end of July. The English and the Prussians will not venture to attack until their allies have joined them. During these six weeks, Napoleon could double his forces, transform France into an armed camp, fortify Paris on the side whence the onslaught will come. The Emperor shakes his head:

"I know all that. But it is essential that I should win a brilliant victory without waiting so long!"

He knows what is at stake. It is his way to assume the

offensive. But the master of figures would have done well to wait awhile, and collect his forces. "I must win a brilliant victory soon!" Is not that the thought of a beaten champion? Perhaps it is; but the gloomy vaticinations of the ruined Cæsar are fortified by the memories of General Bonaparte. Not since his youth has he ventured to do what he now proposes, to advance with a small army, without reserves, mobile, swift. Such, then, is his plan. He will not give his four opponents time to get together. The two that appear to be ready must be separately attacked and defeated. That is the picture which hovers before his mind. What Napoleon, the Emperor, now begins at Charleroi, when his prospective opponents are the Prussians and the English, Bonaparte, the unknown general, had begun at Millesimo, when his prospective were the Austrians and the Piedmontese. His last battle is the parallel of his first.

But during these twenty years, all the commanders of Europe have learned the tactics of the new master of the art of war; and he, during these twenty years, has worn out his machinery. Moreover, swift though his movements are in the days before Waterloo, he no longer possesses the old tempo. As in his recent campaigns, so now, anxious considerations hamper the boldness of his attack. Having taken Charleroi, he fails next day to make a mass onslaught on Blücher, sends Ney with half the army along the Brussels road against the English, only to learn with alarm in the afternoon that he is faced by the whole of the Prussian army. He sends to recall the marshal, writing: "The fate of France is in your hands" Ney, instead of continuing his advances, must envelop the Prussian enemy. Too late! Ney has become involved in the fight with Wellington at Quatre Bras, can spare only one army corps, and sends it to a place where it can be of no use. This makes it impossible for him to gain a victory over the English, and he is driven back.

Napoleon, this same day, fighting with only half his army at Ligny, secures a victory.

The last victory! Blücher falls from his wounded horse, and is reported killed. Gneisenau retains composure, prevents the a decade it has gained a legendary force throughout the Continent. But what is imperishable? Even the eagles of Marengo are not imperishable. Is the mythical energy of this cry, Vive l'Empereur, to subside with the setting of today's sun? Yes, tomorrow it will be heard no more!

The second Prussian corps pours a deadly fire on the guard, which yields ground. The opposing force continues to grow; at eight, the third army corps appears on the scene, and a hundred and twenty thousand of the allies are now attacking half that number of Frenchmen. The battered French army takes to flight, and Bonaparte, in his last hour as a commander, is for the first time in his life commander of a routed army After an hour on horseback in the open, exposed to the British fire, the Emperor rides into the centre of one of the two remaining French squares. When these, likewise, break up, he gallops across country protected only by mounted grenadiers. Though in bodily pain, he has to stay in the saddle until five in the morning, when he is able at length to secure a few hours rest in an old cart.

Is he discouraged?

By no means! What is Paris saying? This is the thought which continually drives him onward. He does not venture, as he had done last year, to assemble the guards in Laon or Soissons, or to betake himself to one of the fortresses. He thinks only of Paris, as the place from which more soldiers can be gathered. Calculations, as of old: "I can still mobilize a hundred and fifty thousand men; with the National Guard, there will be three hundred thousand in all. That will be enough to stop the advance of the enemy." The last orders he sends to Paris end with the words: "Courage! Firmness!"

Two days later, he is once more in the Elysée, which he had left so recently. Has the whole campaign been a dream? In nine days he has lost the empire which he had fought nine years to win.

XIX

Not lost yet!

In the cabinet and in the Chambers, opinions are divided. He sits in council with his brothers and his ministers; he is worn out, but there is no sign of collapse. What does he propose? To work hand in hand with the Chambers? Far from it, he proposes dictatorship. In this national crisis, he needs, for a short time, full freedom of movement. Some of the ministers point out to him that the Chambers no longer trust him.Then Lucien takes the floor, and with all the fire of youth urges thé Emperor to dissolve the Chambers, declare Paris in a state of siege, take all power into his hands, get together the remaining troops–thus alone, now, can France be saved!

He listens. Sixteen years have passed since that November day at Saint-Cloud when this very Lucien had made the same proposal, and, with a single speech, had snatched his brother from the abyss. Then Lucien had raised Napoleon higher than he had wished. The Emperor approves the plan, but does not instantly act on it. Instead, he listens while Davoust, the Minister for War, refuses to place the remnants of the armed forces at his disposal. While they are disputing, news comes from the Chamber of Deputies. It has declared itself in permanent session, will impeach anyone who may dare to try. "I can see only one man between us and peace," said old Lafayette from the rostrum. "If we rid ourselves of him, peace will be ours for the asking!"

Is this the cry of the people? Paris is perfectly calm, so it is nothing more than the cry of a liberated democracy. But it is also the cry of a society which loves change and bears adversity badly, for the House of Peers now passes a vote identical with that of the Chamber of Deputies. The Chambers demand that the Emperor shall appear before them. Why does he not go? Who would venture to oppose him openly? "I ought to have gone," he said subsequently, "but I was tired out. I could have dissolved them, but I lacked courage; I am only a man, after all. My memories of the Nineteenth Brumaire terrified me."

Now the Chambers send for the ministers. The Emperor replies that he has forbidden them to go. The Chambers rejoin that they will depose him unless the ministers come. He gives way. He sends Lucien and the ministers to the Chamber of Deputies, and they report that he has formed a commission to negotiate with the enemy. "They have outlawed him. He must abdicate. If he refuses, we shall depose him!"

While this is going on in the Chambers, the Emperor, much agitated, is walking to and fro in the garden with Constant, At length he is roused, and flames out:

"Not my own future, but that of France is at stake! Have they considered the consequences of my abdication? The army is grouped round me. Do they think they can fight the general dissolution with ideology? I could have understood it if I had been repelled when I landed three months ago. But today, when the foe is only a hundred miles from Paris, they cannot overthrow a government without suffering for it. A fortnight back, to repudiate me would have been a bold action. Now, I am part of what the enemy is attacking, a part of France which it is their business to defend. France will sacrifice itself if it sacrifices me! It is not liberty which would fain depose me, it is Waterloo–fear! ... All I want now is to be the commander; but even if part of the troops were to fall away, I should promptly replace them by workmen, who can readily be moved to revolt."

At this moment, the two men in the garden hear shouts from the avenue, "Vive l'Empereur!" Whose are these last voices raised for Napoleon? The workers from Saint-Antoine; men whose troubles he had remembered in days of need, men who cared little about the suppression of liberty, for equality had made them free. There they were, peering through the railings which separated the son of the revolution from them just as it had separated the kings, but shouting through the bars of the cage into which he had shut himself: "Dictatorship! National Guard! Vive l'Empereur!"

The Emperor hesitates. In the morning there is another cabinet council. Much agitated, he paces the room, uttering gibes about these Jacobins, foreseeing a new Directory. Then the commandant of the Palais Bourbon arrives with a message from the Chambers. He stammers when he attempts to discharge his commission, but at length manages to get the words out. If the Emperor does not abdicate, the Chambers will outlaw him. Savary and Caulaincourt come in. All present urge him to the step, for even Lucien has given up the game. The Emperor says:

"I have accustomed them to great victories, and now they do not know how to endure a single day of adversity. What will happen to France?" He adds in low tones: "I have done what I could."

After this epilogue of six words, which tells the whole story, at noon he dictates his declaration to the people. He is making the sacrifice, his political life is at an end, he proclaims his son emperor as Napoleon II, the Chambers must establish a regency. To whom does he dictate these words? Who among his intimates can hold the pen firmly enough to write them down?

Lucien! The brother who for years from the enemy coast had gazed enviously at this city and this throne; who, if he had been a little less of a poet, might long since have collected the malcontents around him; and who might even now come to the front, not indeed as a second Napoleon, but at least as a second Bonaparte–and that would be something. Lucien sits there, a man of forty now. He had been no less ambitious than the Emperor, but had had to content himself with the modest career of a virtuoso and a Mæcenas. Four whole weeks, now, he has been an imperial prince! Smiling inwardly, he pens his great brother's abdication; writes from dictation, still a mere hodman, but this time animated with a humorous sympathy which atones for the old discords.

For, in truth, it is the eternal recurrence of the similar. As before, come cries from the Chambers, "Outlaw him!" As before, five Directors, like those Bonaparte had once deposed are appointed. They call themselves a provisional government. But when they proceed to elect from among their own number one to function as president of the Directory, who is chosen to take over the authority from Napoleon's hands? Who, by his own vote, has decided his own choice as president?

Fouché.

But the Chamber has become less turbulent. Those who, yesterday, were thirsting for Napoleon's blood, today send a deputation to thank him for his abdication. To these polite gentlemen the Emperor says: "I fear things will turn out badly, now that there is no head. I trust France will never forget that my sole object in abdicating was to promote the welfare of the nation, and that I have abdicated in favour of my son. Only under my dynasty, will France remain free and happy."

At the very time when he is saying this, Fouché and the others are considering the possibility of having one of the Orleanist Bourbons, a member of the Brunswick family, or even the king of Saxony, as Napoleon's successor. Moreover, the five Directors are appointed to form a government, not a regency; and, in his decrees, Fouché often speaks of the nation, but never of Napoleon II. The Emperor notes all this, but holds his peace. Slowly his dream of a dynasty vanishes, the dream for whose realisation he has fought half a lifetime. It has become for ever unattainable. When Lavallette comes to see him in the evening, he is in a hot bath, has been there for several hours.

"Where am I going? Why not to America?"

"Because Moreau went there."

To the Emperor this answer seems surcharged with emotion, for he has serious thoughts of seeking an asylum in the United States, and he asks the government for a frigate. But the only answer is a request that he should leave Paris, for crowds are flocking round the Elsée, clamouring for a dictatorship. He burns a number of documents, and then betakes himself to Malmaison.

In the garden there, the garden that is full of memories of Josephine, he passes two whole days in a state of reverie. The few who remain faithful to him are there: his mother, Hortense, Caulaincourt, Lavalette, Lucien, even Joseph. But when the Emperor asks who will go with him, the answers are evasive. Letizia, indeed, will go gladly, but he thinks that at her age it would be dangerous. Lavalette has a daughter growing up and his wife is expecting another child; perhaps he will follow later. Drouot, who shared the Elba exile, is wanted in France. The secretary has promised the day before to accompany Napoleon into exile, but now his mother, who is blind, has implored him not to leave her. "You are right; you must stay with your mother," says the Emperor turning away.

Pauline, before the last campaign, had pressed her jewels on him; now Hortense offers him a diamond necklace; a quixotic return of imperial gifts, a gesture suitable to the strange turn in his fortunes. He tells Hortense she will have a million, but no one knows if it will ever be paid. Lucien and Eugene get money, and he gives little Léon something for his mother –still dealing in hundreds of thousands.

But he does all these things like a man in a dream. He does not say a word about the last few weeks, but talks only of old times, and chiefly of Josephine. "I have promised the minister to go away. I shall start tonight. I am weary of myself, of France, and of Paris. Make your preparations."

Whither away? Conjectures, deliberations. Spectral is the tone of the manifesto he now adresses to the army:

"Soldiers! ... I am with you even though I am away. I know every corps. If anyone wins a victory, I shall approve his courage.... Show, in days to come, that, before all, you serve your country, show it by obeying me; and show that I have earned your affection (if indeed I have earned it) by my ardent love for our common mother. One more storm, and the coalition will be shattered! Napoleon will know you by the blows that you deal out. Save the honour and the liberty of the French. Be what you have been for twenty years, and you will be unconquerable!"

The government suppresses the document, but could have published it without risk. No one could be more aloof, no living man could have become more completely a part of history, than this man who speaks of himself as if he were speaking of a stranger. He seems to be no longer present in the flesh.

Suddenly he is startled! The old sounds assail his ears. The noise of cannon shots reaches him from the plain of Saint Denis; the foe is at the gates. Officers and soldiers, scarred and tattered, but hastily patched up, bring him the news vague and dispersed like the sound of the firing. Instantly he returns to life. "In two detachments? You must attack and defeat them separately; first one and then the other." At night he elaborates a plan for the defence of Paris. Next morning it seems as if the familiar sounds had rejuvenated him, and he writes to the five Directors as General Bonaparte had written of old:

"I offer to place myself at the head of the army. At sight of me, the soldiers will recover their courage, hurl themselves on the foe, and punish him. I pledge you my word as general, soldier, and citizen that I will not retain the command an hour after the victory has been won. I vow to conquer, not for myself but for France."

It is impossible that after such words he should fail to conquer, unless he is slain in the first onslaught. In this mood of impending death, he writes his magnificent letter. Napoleon, in the garden, surrounded by his remaining officers, restlessly awaits the answer.

Fouché's great moment has come. To this ex-master of him, to the man whom he so cordially detests, he does not even vouchsafe a written answer. The Emperor, who is trembling with eagerness to take up arms, and who has never since he grew to full manhood had to wait for another man's permission, tears the response out of the returning messenger. It is curt: The Emperor is mistaken if he thinks the members of the government are such fools as to entertain his proposal; all they ask is that he should go away as soon as possible. Napoleon says bitterly: "I ought to have hanged him long ago. Now I must leave the job to the Bourbons."

Mufti, a rapid gathering together of necessaries: Hortense sews her necklace for him into a black silk belt. For a few minutes he entertains the thought of Corsica, with Lucien as governor of the island. His mother's eyes sparkle. But he knows that the scheme is impracticable. America is his last resource. The only thing lacking is the frigate for which he has been asking. All are aware that every hour increases the risk to his liberty. It is said that Wellington has demanded his surrender, and the number of the deputies in favour of his being handed over is steadily increasing. Lavalette urges him to start, but the Emperor is stubborn.

"I cannot leave without an order from the government to the captain."

"Why not, Sire? Have the anchor weighed, promise the crew money, send the captain ashore if he won't set sail. You may be sure that Fouché has already promised to hand you over to the allies."

"Drive to the Minister for the Navy!"

The councillor drives to Decrès' and finds him in bed. Decrès refers the messenger to Fouché, saying: "I can do nothing."

Fouché cannot be found. The Councillor gets back to Malmaison at one in the morning. The Emperor is awakened, gets up, still thinks the United States will be best, but hesitates. "Over there, they will grant me land, or I will buy an estate and till it. I shall end where mankind began. I shall live upon the produce of my fields and my herds."

"But what if they propose to hand you over?" enquires the secretary.

"Then I shall go to Mexico. There I shall find patriots at whose head I can place myself."

"The leaders there might turn against you."

"All right; I shall leave them and go to Caracas. If I don't like it, I shall go on to Buenos Aires or to California. I shall sail across the seas until I find a city of refuge where I can be safe from the persecutions of my fellows."

"But what if the English catch you, Sire?"

"I must risk that. A bad government, but a great nation, noble and generous. England will treat me properly. Besides, there is no choice. Am I to allow myself, like a ninny, to be taken prisoner here by Wellington, to be led in triumph through the streets of London like King John the Good of old? Since they have no use for my services here, I must go elsewhere. Ability will do the rest."

"Your Majesty was not made for flight."

"Flight! What are you talking about?" He looks at the secretary "questioningly and proudly."

"The English must certainly be on the watch for you already. You end ought to be the worthiest possible."

"Suicide, like Hannibal? Leave that to weaklings and persons of disordered mind! Whatever fate may hold in store for me, I would never deliberately shorten my life by a single day."

"I did not mean that, Sire. But what if you were to hand over liberty and life to the enemies of France in order to save France? That is how Napoleon the Great should act."

"All very fine, but to whom am I to hand myself over? To Blücher? To Wellington? They have no plenipotentiary powers. They would simply take me prisoner, and do what they pleased with France and with me."

"The tsar, perhaps?"

"You do not know the Russians! Still, I will think the matter over. To sacrifice my own person would be easy enough. The question is, whether it would help France?"

Almost every element that goes to make the statesman seems to have been eliminated from this all-too-human dialogue. Here is an adventurer hankering after fresh voyages in every corner of the world. Here is the man without a country, the ocean traveller without any earth under his feet, always on board, always driven hither and thither, a bold pirate fearless of death. Ay, fearless of death! The dry manner in which, once again, he waves aside the idea of suicide, the sober realism of his outlook, this grasp at the flying moment, the old time dauntlessness of the islesman–what unconquerable vital energy!

Now he is to start. The last person with whom the Emperor

has a quiet talk is his mother. But a soldier rushes in; he will not let any hold him back: the soldier is Talma. The call of his heart and his love of the tragical have urged him to come for a great farewell; he feels he must be there. Later he is to represent this leave-taking between mother and son, in all its dignified simplicity, in a pathetic scene on the stage. Then the Emperor invites young General Gourgand, the scatter-brained idealist, into his dilapidated carriage. Bertrand and his wife, who had lived with him in Elba, and two others, accompany him. They drive to Rochefort, to the port where they hope to find a frigate. The pace is too slow for a fugitive. He still looks over his shoulder, listening for the call which shall summon him back at the eleventh hour. They meet two regiments marching northward. The men raise a cheer, and the Emperor discusses with the generals the possibility of overthrowing the government if he places himself at their head and marches on Paris.... Away again, at length the long drive is over, and he stands gazing at the Atlantic Ocean. Joseph is there, and urges Napoleon to charter a brig which is taking a cargo of spirits to America. The Emperor assumes the name of Muiron, his seventh name. This name calls up the vision of another coast, the Mediterranean with its many isles, and Corsica, and then Italy; and again he sees the young, small, lean general, with long hair falling on his shoulders and cold grey-blue eyes, and the bridge of Arcola where the fate of a man and a country hung in the balance; and he sees Lieutenant Muiron fling himself before the young general in the melée, he sees Muiron fall, and he knows that by this love-death the lieutenant's name will be immortalised. It would seem that once again a new epoch is opening before the genius of energy, and that across the seas, in new zones, on uninhabited prairies, the adventurer will swing himself into the saddle, will watch the increase of his herds; maybe, even, will travel to Mexico and become the leader of a band of rebels!

But God is wiser.

He sees to it that this great life shall have an epilogue such as no man has ever lived through before, an epilogue which shall fitly round off its tragical poesy. Once more the Almighty stifles the adventurous impulse in the soul of Napoleon; once more there are days of questioning, negotiation, vacillation–ten days before the final decision.

The Emperor crosses to a small island. They think of chartering two fishing smacks which the English will never dream of searching for Napoleon; but in the end he rejects the plan. There are two American ships available. Negotiations are entered into with a Danish sloop. Enthusiastic youths from the naval training school propose to carry him off in an advice-boat. Sixteen midshipmen will spirit him out of the harbour at dead of night. They sit packed together in the little room, feverishly discussing the plan with Las Cases, the Emperor's new confidant. The man to whom this madcap venture is proposed, talks over the situation coolly with his companions, asking each in turn for an opinion as to the best course. Most of them advise a return to the army, for there are still good prospects that the soldiers in the south will support him. He emphatically refuses:

"Nothing will induce me to light up a civil war. I will have no more to do with politics; I need repose; I shall go to America!"

But his self-respect makes him shrink from the thought of escaping in disguise.

News comes that the Bourbon has re-entered the land of his fathers, once more under the protection of allied troops. The path of escape seaward is now blocked by an English cruiser which bears the ominous name of "Bellerophon." The Emperor has missed his chance. Here are his thoughts: "A return to Paris is impossible. The port is blockaded. Shall I allow myself to be seized like a pirate, and taken in chains to London? England has been my foe for twenty years. Next to the French, the English nation is the greatest and the most distinguished in the world. Have I not been an Emperor? Has not, from of old, chivalry toward a fallen enemy aroused universal admiration? In Corsica, they knife anyone who violates the rights of hospitality."

Making up his mind, he dictates the following letter to the prince regent:

"Your Royal Highness, exposed to the factions which distract my country and to the enmity of the greatest powers of Europe, I have closed my political career, and I come, like Themistocles, to throw myself upon the hospitality of the British people. I put myself under the protection of their laws, and beg Your Royal Highness, as the most powerful, the most persistent, and the most generous of my enemies, to grant me this protection. Napoleon."

Eight lines, three words of respect, neither arrogance nor humility, almost courtly. There is, however, one word which embodied the pathos of the step he is taking, and assumes that his adversary will give moral guarantees; that in this century, after such a life, Napoleon with be as welcome a guest in the enemy land, as of old in Persia had been–Themistocles. It is overwhelming self-confidence, based upon historical parallels, which determines the last great step of his career, as, in youth, it had determined his first advances to Paoli. Now, this self confidence will be his ruin.

Next day, Las Cases hands the letter to the captain of the "Bellerophon," and negotiates with Maitland for Napoleon's reception on board. Admiral Hotham, Maitland's immediate superior, was not a party to the negotiations, but had long since received orders to seize the fugitive if possible. In accordance with international law, this was quite in order, for England, with the other powers in Vienna, had decreed Napoleon's outlawry. But it is an undisputed fact that Captain Maitland, supreme on his own ship, guaranteed his guest's liberty, saying: "Napoleon will receive all proper attention in England. Our people are generous and democratic."

No record was taken at the time of the terms of the under standing in accordance with which the man who had been the master of Europe went on board one of his enemy's ships. Nevertheless, it was not an affair of hours, but, rather, of days; not the outcome of haste and desperation, but the logical conclusion of a long chain of reasoning. Napoleon's own experience of the last twenty years had shown him that verbal agreements are untrustworthy, whereas written agreements are comparatively reliable. Yet he takes this last step, one of profound historical significance, without any written document having been signed, sealed, and delivered. In truth, he cannot await an answer from London. He trusts, however, not in the mere word of a captain in the navy, but in the moral effect of what he is doing. That is why, just before going on board the "Bellerophon," he writes the above-quoted heroic lines, addressed to the ruler of the land in which he seeks hospitality, and the supreme commander of all its navies.

Then, in uniform, Napoleon boards the British vessel.

XX

Maitland stands on the quarter-deck. Napoleon raises his hat, a thing he has not always done to greet princes, and addresses the captain as follows: "I come to place myself under the protection of your king and your laws." The British naval officers are introduced to him, and he asks about the sea-fights in which they have been engaged. Then, with the detachment of a man discussing ancient history, he talks about the English navy and the French, says that the English sailors are cleaner and more efficient, and argues with his host about certain punishments customary in the navy after a fight. Then he passes to generalities:

"I really cannot understand why your ships have defeated our French vessels so easily. The best of them were ours to begin with. A French ship is stronger in every respect than an English vessel of the same type. It has more and heavier guns, a larger complement."

"I have already explained that to you, Sir. Our seamen have had more experience than yours."

Napoleon does not move an eyelash. The conversation remains strictly academic; they talk of the nautical science of their respective countries.

"Instead, I came to this country as a private person. I asked the commander of one of your warships whether he was disposed to take me and my train to England. He told me he had orders to this effect from his government. If I have fallen into a trap, your government has acted dishonourably and has dishonoured your flag.... St. Helena will kill me in three months. I am used to riding twenty leagues a day. What can I do on a little rock at the world's end? I will not go! ... If your government wishes to kill me, that can be done here. ... I gave the prince regent an opportunity of performing the finest action of his life. I have been the greatest of his country's foes, and I paid you the highest compliment in the world by voluntarily entrusting myself to your protection.... What you are proposing will be an everlasting disgrace to the whole British nation!"

The most characteristic point in this protest, which he renews in writing, is the moral indignation with which it thrills, International law is but lightly touched upon, for what he claims is a hero's right. Such were the words spoken in the heat of the moment, in that small cabin, to the officers who had brought him notice of his doom and who subsequently recorded them for posterity. Though spoken in haste, they have a historical ring and some of the sentences are modelled for imperishability. A soul has been wounded, a soul that is mourning, not so much on account of its own loss of freedom, as because the world fails to recognize greatness.

Thus, in the first moment of his doom, he recognizes that which, a century later, cannot be more profoundly expressed by the great grandchildren of the men of those days, who have been brought up on contemplation of the legend of Napoleon's career. Themistocles feels that he has been betrayed. Once again, one of these legitimate princes has failed to seize the opportunity of performing the finest action of his life. A man void of imagination, a weakling in possession of brute force, he crushed the great and splendid thing which has fallen into his hands.

But from under the brutal pressure of this fist, the spirit of what he is crushing rises in a tenuous column. He upon whom the doom is enforced has acquired a power over himself, a power which sustains him in his powerlessness–stoicism. After the first outbreak, he bears the injustice with indomitable firmness, enduring for ten days the indignity of his position at Plymouth, and unruffled while England seizes his baggage and his money.

In due course, the Emperor and his companions were transferred to the "Northumberland," which set sail for St. Helena. It was on an August morning that, for the last time, Napoleon set eyes on the coast of France, looming through the mist. But what did he care about the coast? The centre of his interest lay many miles to the eastward–Paris, which he had wooed more hotly than all the rest of the world, Paris, which had rejected his suit.

By evening, he loses sight of Europe, which he has ruled. Darkling is the sea, which he has never been able to rule. He stands in the bows, not looking backwards, nor forwards either. As on the voyage to Egypt, he looks upwards towards the stars. He is seeking his own star.

A great saga is drawing to its close.

I

THE sea spreads out into the vast distance. It is like a mirror of steel. The man on the rock, hands clasped behind, stares across the watery plain. He is wearing a green coat, decorated with the star of the Legion of Honour: silk stockings; three-cornered hat in his hands. The head is large; the brownish hair makes a bush at the back; there is no sign of whitening. The short neck springs from powerful shoulders. The features are as if hewn out of stone, with a yellowish tint, like the marble of an ancient statue that has been darkened in the course of the ages; no wrinkles, but the classical profile is somewhat marred by the heaviness of the chin. The only beautiful features are the nose and the teeth. These last are perfect, and he has never lost a tooth. This hands, too, are beautiful. All through his campaigns he was scrupulous in his care for them; and, when correcting the letters and dispatches he dictated, he generally used a pencil in order that he might avoid staining his fingers with ink.

The doctors have told us a good deal about his physical condition. "Pulse never more frequent than 62; bosom well padded, almost like a woman's, and with very little hair; partes viriles exiguitates insignis sicut pueri." He himself knows much about his body, he has studied his battlefield of his life in order that here, likewise, he may utilise his forces to the best advantage.

"I have never yet heard my own heart beating; it is almost as if I had none," he says, half seriously. Moderation, he assures us, is the secret of his amazing faculty for work. "Nature has bestowed on me two valuable gifts: the capacity for sleeping whenever I want to; and the incapacity for committing excesses in drinking and eating.... However little a man may eat, he always eats too much. One can get ill from over-eating. but never from under-eating." The alternation between campaigning and sedentary life enables him again and again to escape from the air of the study, and to fortify his constitution by long rides and drives. "Water, air, and cleanliness are my favourite medicines."

With a body thus steeled, he can drive without stopping from Tilsit to Dresden, nearly five hundred miles, and be quite fresh at the journey's end: can ride fifty miles from Vienna to Semmering, breakfast there, and be back at work in Schönbrunn the same evening; can gallop in five hours from Valladolid to Burgos, a distance of about eighty miles. After long rides and marches through Poland, he reaches Warsaw at midnight and receives the new authorities at seven next morning. These are the excesses he practises to restore the balance of his natural forces. After a long spell of sedentary life, he will start off on a ride of seven days, or will go out shooting for the whole day; after great exertions, he will keep his room for twenty-four hours. He believes that his energy has saved his life. He says to Metternich: "Sometimes death only comes from lack of energy. Yesterday, when I was thrown out of my carriage, I thought I was done for. But I had just time to say to myself that I would not die. Anyone else in my place would have been killed."

His muscles are powerful, but his nerves are sensitive. Accustomed to command, he cannot endure anything in the nature of compulsion. If his coat is at all tight, he tears it off; the same with shoes that pinch him in the slightest. On these occasions, he will box his servants' ears. If he has to wear court dress, they watch out while they help him on with his coat. When his mind is busy (when is it not?) he will push away his breakfast, jump up from his chair, and stride about, talking, issuing orders. His handwriting is nothing more than a series of violent contractions of the hand which cannot keep up with the furious pace of his thoughts; a sort of involuntary shorthand, which in places has not been deciphered after a hundred years of study. He cannot endure the smell of paint or size; he always masks unpleasant odours by using eau-de-Cologne. If his nerves are utterly exhausted, he soothes them in a hot bath. When the war with England broke out, he worked continuously, with four secretaries, for three days and three nights, and then spent six hours in his bath dictating dispatches. This nervous irritability is the antithesis of his slow circulation. He thinks that, the constitution of his nerves being what it is, he would be in danger of going mad, "If it were not that my blood works so slowly."

But there is no evidence at all that his nervousness ever rose to the pitch of convulsions, that he suffered from epilepsy. This illness usually begins in childhood, and none of his schoolmates have reported that he had fits. Never was anyone's life more closely watched than Napoleon's; and the documents upon which the assertion that he was an epileptic is based are scanty, confused, and untrustworthy.

As long as his body remained healthy, he was able to endure all the tensions and shocks to which he was exposed. It was when he was approaching forty that he began to show the first symptoms of a stomach trouble which was in those days summarily diagnosed as cancerous. Beyond question, the tendency to it was inherited. During the last three years of warfare, he was put out of action in decisive hours by paroxysms of gastric spasm. His courage and resolution were practically unimpaired; had it not been for these attacks, the history of his decline would have been different.

II

The soul which governed this body was driven forward by three fundamental powers:

Self-confidence, energy, imagination.

"I am not as other men; the laws of morality and convention cannot be applied to me." In these cold words, he emphasises the "I" with which he began his first political writing in the days of his youth. They are a plain acknowledgment of a fact, by a man of thirty to whom nothing is more alien than vanity. "I alone, because of my position, know what government is," he said when he was Consul. "I am persuaded that no one save myself could govern France at this moment. Were I to die, it would be a great misfortune for the nation." He utters such words seldom, and only when he is with an intimate; but these sayings show with what scientific aloofness he could contemplate the phenomenon, Napoleon. When, during the Russian disaster, he was asked who in spite of all would defend him in France, he replied: "My name."

His contemporaries and posterity have held this fundamental feeling to be ambition. That view is mistaken. Common ambition distinguishes itself from Napoleon's self-confidence as a restless, climbing animal does from a bird of prey whose free flight, by a law of nature, assumes wider and wider circles as it swings heavenwards. Napoleon's aspiration is neither restless nor envious; it is nothing but his natural disposition which, as Consul, he once charmingly explained to his friend Roéderer:

"I have no ambition whatever; or if I have, then it is so inborn, so intimately knit up with my very life, that it is as the blood in my veins. It does not incite me to outstrip my associates....I have never had to fight for or against it; it does not urge me to greater speed than is natural to me, it comes out only when circumstances and my ideas demand."

Already in the days when he was a general, ideas and circumstances forced upon him the conviction that he was the man predestined to rebuild France. It is nothing other than the conviction of his mission which makes him say to Roéderer: "Circumstances have changed. I am now one of those who found States, not one of those who ruin States." Another time, he speaks of Corneille, but he means himself when he says: "Whence did this man acquire his antique greatness? From himself, from his soul? Very well. Do you know what that is called, My Lord Cardinal? It is called genius. Genius is a flame, which comes from heaven, but seldom finds a head ready to receive it. Corneille is a man whom the world has recognised." When his interlocutor observed that the poet had not seen the flame, so how could he recognize it, the

Emperor answered scornfully: "Precisely for that reason I consider he is a great man!"

He thus, indirectly by anticipation, announces his own genius to the world, just as Goethe had announced his own.

The will-to-power, not as an endeavour or even as a question, but, rather, as simplicity, dwells within him close at hand. He calls interest the key to ordinary deeds; the will to govern the intellect, he describes as the strongest of all the passions: and the artistic urge of genius, he depicts in the following words: "I love power, yes, I love it, but after the manner of an artist: as a fiddler loves his fiddle in order to conjure from it tone, chords, harmonies."

That is why it is his nature to command. "Wherever I may be, I command, or else I keep silence." He might have added: "I negotiate," for he had spent a quarter of his time in negotiating. Even as a young general of twenty-seven, he aroused the respect of all who came in contact with him. He never learned to obey; but to command came to him naturally at the very outset, just as a calf stands and walks in the first hour of its life. Because this power of commanding comes so naturally, he never acquires the art of asking; because he can command as no other, he is denied the gift of being able to ask favours.

His self-confidence confers on him a natural dignity that amazes and angers the legitimist world, which believes dignity to be consonant only with heredity and culture. The friends of his youth stand embarrassed when they recognize him as their commander in the field and yet realise the solitude which his position as leader entails. All his companions-in-arms speak of him with spontaneous homage. One of his intimates writes: "When he speaks, everyone listens, for he speaks as an expert; if he is silent, his silence is respected; and no one would venture to say that he was silent because of ill humour. We all felt that between him and us there lived a great thought which was wholly occupying his mind and forbade familiar accost." This statement is all the more surprising since it was made during a campaign, when tent life usually breaks down barriers. With absolute ingenuousness he once said, while playing and chatting with friends at Malmaison: "I have no sense of the ridiculous. Power is never ridiculous."

An adept at analysis, the greatest psychologist of his epoch, he knows all about his own qualities, and is therefore able, by degrees, to elaborate these instincts into principles. "The goodness of a king," he informs his brother Louis, King of Holland, "must always bear a regal stamp and must never he monkish.... The love which a king inspires should invariably be a manly love, wedded to reverence, fear, and esteem. If people speak of him as 'a good man,' his rule is a failure." This love and fear which he himself inspires has the greatest practical results.

Nevertheless, the dignity which holds people at the distance is not assumed, for a leading element in it is a bewildering naturalness, which grows with the years and with his successes. His unsophisticated and frank realism, the sterling simplicity of his character, shows itself in a hundred gestures and words, and in the freshness with which he repeatedly makes fun of his own ardency. He expresses this in a profound saying: "A truly great man will rise superior to the events which he himself has brought about." The greatest successes, whose fateful origin and consequences he fully grasps, he sums up to his intimates in a schoolboy's laugh. Many have reported this, for between the boisterous gaiety of a soldier and the most delicate curl of the lip are many shades of good humour; he possesses all.

On the eve of his coronation he exclaims: "Is the result not truly delightful, to be named brother by the kings?" Or he sends his ambassador to St. Petersburg with the words: "Our brother in Russia is fond of luxury and festivity. Very well, then, give him his fill of them!" Sometimes his simplicity of manner infringes etiquette, and the legitimists blanch: "When I was an insignificant lieutenant," he begins once at table with the kings in Dresden. General consternation! Everyone gazes into his plate. Napoleon clears his throat: "When I had the honour of serving as lieutenant in the second artillery regiment at Valence ..." Or he is sitting with the tsar in Tilsit, and since he is ever eager to learn, he asks offhandedly across the table: "How much does your tax on sugar bring in yearly?" We are told that this question places all present in a state of grave embarrassment. Why? Because, as a big man of business, he calls money by its name; whereas the kings never mention it by name, though they are glad enough to reap the harvest!

Since he was not vain, he knew when he had made mistakes. His whole lifelong he was in the habit of saying that next day he might lose a battle; he frequently consulted his friends and his experts, and was inspired with the feeling of God-given necessity. How well Napoleon could bear to be told the truth, we can learn from Marmont–who, when he praises, is one of the most trustworthy of witnesses, for he wrote his memoirs long after the Emperor had publicly stigmatised him as a traitor. "Napoleon had a strong sense of justice, and would readily forgive an improper word or other sign of anger in one who had good grounds for complaint, provided of course he was alone with the offender.... He made kindly allowance for others' weaknesses and could never resist the appeal of well-grounded sorrow. One who chose time and place, could say anything to him. He was always willing to listen to the truth. Though it did not invariably influence him, there was no danger in uttering it."

He saw through the wiles of flatterers, and they gained nothing from him. Byzantine bombast, devoid of political value, infuriated him. "How could you depict the French eagle tearing the English leopard to pieces, at a time when I cannot safely send even a fishing-smack out to sea? Break up your moulds instantly, and never show me anything of the kind again!"

On the other hand, those who fearlessly speak the truth to him, impress him. He praises Chateaubriand, who has attacked him. In the days when he was Consul he was wont, after a sitting of the Council of State, to invite to dinner the man who had most vigorously opposed his wishes. In the Russian campaign, a captive general tells him some home truths about the burning of Moscow. Napoleon dismisses the prisoner in a rage; but presently has him recalled, and shakes the Russian's hand, saying: "You are a brave man!" Méhul plays a trick on the Emperor, producing his new opera as the work of an Italian composer, and thus earning approbation. Paisiello also plays a trick by introducing into one of his own composition an aria by Cimarosa, a composer whose work Bonaparte cannot endure. The Consul applauds; and when afterwards told of the deception, he only laughs.

Madame de Stael has been a worry to him for fifteen years, voicing Europe's call for freedom. He suppresses her books, banishes her from Paris, continues to take measures against her even when he is in Russia, speaks of her as the dangerous driving-wheel which sets the salons in motion; but he pays their enemy the high compliment of dreading her, and acknowledges as much in many of his private letters.

In the Bavarian muster rolls, he comes across the name of a former regimental comrade, a declared royalist. He makes this man his military attaché. They have not met for fourteen years. Now, during the campaign, they meet, and the old companion introduces himself. The Emperor rides with him out of the press, dismounts, and sits down on a convenient stone; the other wishes to hold his horse. "Let be," says Napoleon' "that's not your business," and beckons a chasseur to take the bridle-rein. The Emperor promptly becomes reminiscent: "Do you remember how, at the lieutenants' mess in Besançon, you flung your table napkin down and shouted: 'I will not sit beside an officer who belongs to the Jacobin Club!' That is ancient history, and is of no consequence now." He beckons his attendant staff and points to his interlocutor, saying: "Look at this fellow. Ability of the old school. He and I worked at equations together." Then, coming down to practical matters: "Have you plenty of ammunition? What is your artillery like? How soon will you be ready?"

Unique, perhaps, in Napoleon's life, is the scene at Erfurt in the year of 1813, when von Müller, the Weimar chancellor, braves his anger. Two privy councillors have written letters in cipher. These have been seized at the outposts. The writers have been arrested. Müller has been sent for. The Emperor has stormed at him, threatening to burn Jena, to shoot the culprits. Müller breaks in impetuously: "No, Sire, you will not commit this abomination!

You will not tarnish your record for all time by shedding innocent blood!" In his excitement, the German presses so close that the Emperor anticipates a personal attack, and lays his hand on his sword-hilt. Müller is dragged back by a companion. A pause. "You are a bold man, but I see that you are a good friend. Berthier shall look into the matter once more." The privy councillors are pardoned.

This scene, creditable to both participants, is another proof of Napoleon's invulnerable dignity. It is invulnerable, unless the arrow is poisoned. A sense of honour is the vulnerable point of self-confidence. "If the French people expects certain advantages from me," said Bonaparte when First Consul, "it must put up with my weaknesses, and the chief of these is that I cannot endure an affront." It was he who said: "I am a man whom people may kill, but will not affront." Bourrienne tells us that from Bonaparte's earliest days he had no faith in law or morality, but always believed in honour. This compensated for his fundamental amoralism. The power exercised over him by his conception of honour distinguishes him absolutely from the condottieri of the Renaissance, with whom he ought never to have been compared. When he is Consul, betwixt night and morning he breaks off his intimacy with this very Bourrienne, who has been his private secretary for so long, because Bourrienne is involved in an unsavoury financial scandal. Years afterwards, he refuses to admit Bourrienne to the Legion of Honour, saying: "One who worships the golden calf may have money, but not honour." When a bill signed by King Jerome goes to protest, Napoleon writes: "Sell your diamonds, your silver plate, your furniture, your horses–anything to pay your debts. Honour comes first!"

He was so sensitive on this point that after his coronation he summoned to his presence a notary who had long before advised Josephine against marrying a person of doubtful character; Napoleon wished to rehabilitate himself in this man's mind. In exile at St. Helena, he remembered how his German teacher in Brienne had always treated him with contempt: "I should very much like to know whether Herr Bauer ever learned how I made good!"

He is a stickler for morality, just as he is for honour. "Nothing can be worse in a ruler than immorality. He makes it fashionable, and it poisons society." Napoleon does not say this merely because he has been warned by the example of the Bourbons and the Directors. He has an inborn sense of decency, which is part of his dignity. No one has ever recorded having heard Napoleon, the soldier, tell an obscene story. Nor did he ever listen to one complacently. When he becomes First Consul, he forbids Josephine to have anything more to do with friends of hers who are leading gay lives. Years afterwards, when the empress allows Tallien to visit her, Napoleon writes to reprimand his wife, saying: "I can see no excuses for Tallien. I know that some poor devil has married her with her eight bastards, and I despise her even more than I did before. She was an amiable cocotte; now she is nothing more than a common woman."

Talleyrand, who has had a liaison for many years, is told that he must marry his inamorata or quit Napoleon's service within twenty-four hours. Berthier is made a prince, but the same condition is imposed on him, Napoleon saying: "This passion of yours has lasted too long, and is becoming ridiculous. You are a man of fifty, but may live to be eighty, and these thirty years are left you for marriage," The revolution had encouraged nudity in mythological representations, but Napoleon wants nakedness to be draped. When, in one of the squares there is set up a fountain where there is a group of naiads with water spouting from their breasts, he has "these wet-nurses" removed as improper, and decrees that "the naiads were virgins." His own women friends must not make themselves conspicuous. He lavishes money on them; but if they are actresses, he does not allow his liaison to be used as a reason for promotion. On the other hand, like any bourgeois he boasts of sharing his wife's bedroom, saying: "It has a remarkable influence upon conjugal life, strengthens the man's influence, guarantees his faithfulness, promotes intimacy and good morals; a couple will never become estranged if they spend the whole night together. As long as Josephine and I kept this custom, she was familiar with all my thoughts."

His egotism makes him emphasise the advantage of the lack of any ancestry to an original or unusual person. When flatterers suggest that one of his Italian forebears should be canonized, he calls the suggestion an idiocy. Metternich lays before Napoleon an ancestral tree manufactured in Vienna from records of the Buonaparte family in Tuscany. The Emperor says: "Take these papers away!" In the official gazette, Napoleon has the following notice inserted: "To all questions as to when the house of Bonaparte began, the answer is simple: on the Eighteenth Brumaire. How can one show so little tact and good breeding for all one owes the Emperor as to stress the question of his ancestry?" Once he is so angry because some one has contradicted him in this matter of his genealogy that he exclaims: "I shall not suffer anyone to insult me try treating me as if I were a king!"

Then come transitions in which the cleavage begins to show itself. "I shall be the Brutus of the kings and the Cæsar of the republic": which saying is certainly ambiguous. "I know of no aristocracy but the rabble which I have created": here there is hardly any ambiguity. "Tacitus is praised because he made the tyrants fear the people and that was a very bad thing for the people": which is open to but one interpretation. No one, in the presence of such a man, can be satisfied with the facile assertion that Napoleon only pretended to believe in the principles of freedom until he attained to power, and then promptly betrayed them. On the contrary, we have here to do with a spiritual struggle. This is the one problem with which the self-confident man had to wrestle; a problem he never solved.

"I am the man of the people: its pulse beats in unison with my own.... The aristocracy remains always aloof, and never forgives." Such utterances show us the original trend of his character. Inasmuch as he overcomes this trend, never becomes an ideologue, but gets the better of his inborn sympathies, he is a statesman of genius. Of course it is ridiculous when he, who only rewards merit, decorates his baby son's cradle with the grand cordon of the Legion of Honour, or again, when he has the deposed king of Spain. who addressed him as "cousin," informed through appearance at court. He is furious: "Ah! So these people fancy that they are stronger than I? Very well, gentlemen of the old aristocracy, we shall see! We shall see!" This is on the evening after the battle of Austerlitz!

Here we see such hatred as that which a man gradually comes to feel for a woman who stubbornly resists his wooing. He must win over the spirit of tradition, cost what it may. One evening, not very long before the scene just described, he takes Roéderer from the drawing-room into the billiard-room, begins knocking the balls about, and then says, apropos of nothing in particular:

"Your Senate has no feelings for the aristocratic, no esprit de corps in favour of the imperial system."

"Sire, it is devoted to your person."

"That is not what I want. It must be devoted to my mantle no matter who wears it. The mantle ought to be enough to guarantee the safety of the wearer. This is the aristocratic spirit, which is lacking to you ideologues!"

The whole problem of hereditary succession is implicit in these considerations; it logically develops therefrom, leading to the second marriage, and thus to the tragical issue. There are only two things which Napoleon cannot create unaided children and ancestors. He therefore asks the world of legitimate rulers to enter into an alliance with him, which will settle his difficulty as far as offspring is concerned, and will also provide his children with an ancestry. He is not really a man of the people, but a nobleman; and who can complain because he regards himself as such?

"I am in a peculiar position. The genealogists want to trace my pedigree back to the deluge, while there are some who describe me as sprung from the lower middle class. Truth lies between. The Bonapartes are a good Corsican family, not celebrated, but certainly better than these coxcombs who believe themselves entitled to humiliate us."

This is the tone of the sixteen-year-old lad, scion of the lesser territorial nobility, whom a handful of counts made fun of at the military academy and slighted at the boarding school in Paris. They are the very words which the young man had used in his letters and literary sketches when the noblesse of monarchical France had mortified him. Nothing can expunge the memory of his early mortifications. It may well be that, but for these never-to-be-forgotten affronts suffered at the hands of a few silly young marquises, his whole outlook upon the question of legitimacy would have been different; his court life, his marriage, his destiny, would have been different; and therewith the course of European history would have been other than it was.

His egotism finds expression in the struggle with France, just as it does in the struggle with the noblesse. He does not wholly belong to the high nobility, and therefore throughout life he remains critical of the pretensions of birth. In the same way, though formally he was a Frenchman, he was not French by blood, and he was therefore irritably critical of the French, just as he was irritably critical of the noblesse. He conquered both, but never felt perfectly secure in either of his conquests.

But he had more success with France than with the legitimists. Because he is not really a Frenchman, France never becomes his legitimate spouse; she remains his beloved mistress. He knows this; he woos, gives himself, renounces; and from the perpetual uncertainty on his relationship to France, he derives the keenest joys of his life. "I have only one passion, only one mistress: France. I lie by her side. She has never been untrue to me; she pours out her blood for me, and lavishes her treasures upon me. If I need half a million men, she gives them!" When he chides his mistress, he does it as a jealous lover; he rules her "with an iron hand in a velvet glove"; he gratifies all her caprices; and he knows better than anyone else how to allure her by the glamour of fame and fantasy. That is why she beams on him when he comes home victorious; that is why she gives him her children.

Yet lover and mistress remain critical of one another. Mutual jealousy persists. Neither of them ever forgets the wish to master the other. Hear his exclamation in the tone of a despotic lover; "I swear that I do everything for the sake of France alone! If

I do not give her more liberty, it is because she does not need more!" He is standing in the middle of his drawing-room, scrutinizing his guests sharply as he speaks to them with raised voice. Among intimates, he will often use harsher words: "Always the same old Gauls! The same frivolity, the same vanity! When, if ever, will these be replaced by a proper pride?"

The French, likewise, remain sceptical. Must they not, in confidential talks, say of this Italian the very thing that he once wrote to his brother Louis? "Since you ascended the throne, you have forgotten that you are a Frenchman, and have strained every nerve to persuade yourself that you are a Dutchman. The foreign environment tickles your fancy, but it is still foreign." Roéderer writes of Napoleon; "He is making a mistake. They were about Lafayette (who did nothing practical of them). At bottom, they merely admire and respect him because he is useful to them."

Such a liaison cannot fail to end tragically. The mistress discards her lover when he is no longer useful to her.

Tragical, too, is the ending of another embodiment of his egotism, its noblest incorporation. "I wish I could be my own posterity, and read what such a poet as Corneille would make me feel, do, and say." From boyhood's days down to the time of his exile, in the island where he was born and in the island where he died, his self-esteem is nourished on historical parallels. History. he said, was the only true philosophy. Had he not had his peculiar feeling for history, Napoleon's career would have been very different; nay, it would have been impossible. His political calculations are fed from two sources, history and imagination; the first of these streams being intellectual, and the second passionate. It is history alone which gives him alighting places on his flight. In his own age he is unique; he travels alone; nowhere but in history can he find prototypes by whose example he can guide his impetuous progress. With Cæsar, the lieutenant begins to soar. At Rochefort, the Emperor ends the active phase of his existence by trusting too implicitly in the heroic example of Themistocles.

Between the opening and the close, we find numberless indications of the way in which his imagination remains at work, mirroring the great incidents of classical and modern history. Why is he opposed to Tacitus and Chateaubriand? Because they warn the people against tyrants. Why does he blame the assassins of Cæsar? Because he wishes to defend his own sentence upon the duke of Enghien. When he is First Consul, he actually thinks of writing a few chapters of Roman history, to prove "that Cæsar never wanted to become king, and that he was murdered because he wished to re-establish order by uniting all parties." He goes on to add that Cæsar had been killed in the Senate House, and that in the Senate were forty Pompeians, personal enemies of the dictator. Napoleon's unexpressed inference is that he must clean up the Senate, and he does so.

In the Roman style, he sketches the ideas for eight splendid bas-reliefs which, on triumphal arches, are to illustrate the doing of his region; they are to be representations of fact, devoid of self-commendation, and only in a formal sense illustrations of historical egotism. He summons historiographers and imaginative writers from all civilised lands, and converses with them for hours, in order that, through their intermediation, he may win the approval of posterity. When his portrait seems to him too crudely lifelike, he says that Alexander never sat for Apelles; David must paint him "in a tranquil attitude, mounted upon a fiery steed." It pleases him to write army orders when he is sitting in Frederick the Great's study; at Sans Souci, to invite the biographer of the former master of the house to dine with him; in Lombardy, to visit the arch of Augustus, in Egypt, the pillar of Pompey, and on these monuments to inscribe the names of those who have recently fallen; in Madrid and Moscow, to study the environment and the habits of Philip and of Catherine. But his pleasure in these things is not purely æsthetic. The hours he devotes to them are heroical; they are Napoleon's true recompense; they are realisations of his earliest dreams.

With his own hand, he is continually writing his own history. The young general records his first victories in orders of the day; with each new campaign, and after every battle, he adds to the long series; and the work is done with the hand of an artist, is wrought with an eye to immortal fame. When he is offered the crown of Italy, he surveys his own deeds of little more than five years ago as if they had come down in legend: "When, a few years later, we learned on the banks of the Nile that our aims had come to naught, we were bitterly distressed at this evil turn of fortune; but, thanks to the courage of our armies, we were able to appear in Milan at a time when Italy believed us to be still on the shores of the Red Sea." Actually, in the interim, he had, before the eyes of all the world, trampled on the Constitution of France, and even the meanest herd in the Apennines knew of his return from Egypt.

When he is carrying on a struggle with the Pope he pens a long letter, and sends it to Eugene for the latter to copy, since ostensibly it is to be a letter from Eugene to the Pope; therein Eugene is made to say that Napoleon can only be compared to Cyrus and Charlemagne.

At the height of his career, he says to his Austrian ambassador; "Don't you make any mistake, I am a Roman emperor, in the best line of the Cæsars. Chateubriand had compared me with Tiberius, who could only travel from Rome to Capri. A pretty idea! Trajan, Aurelian–that would be another story. They were self-made men, who shook the world out of old ruts. Do you not see the resemblances between my regime and that of Diocletian? The net so widely spread; the Emperor's eyes everywhere; the civil authority omnipotent throughout an empire that is fundamentally warlike.... man is born to be a Cæsar."

This is not a proclamation, not a political letter, not an attempt to seduce anyone. The words are spoken lightly, in a drawing-room, without emotion and without ulterior aim, with all the simplicity of a man aware of his own strength.

After victories and successes, this historical feeling for his own personality becomes as objective as the attitude of the chessplayer towards the pieces on his board. We seem to be contemplating a man whose fondness for the game is the only thing which makes him want to win; and who, as soon as he has won, can converse dispassionately with his defeated opponent about the mistakes they have made and the artifices to which they have had recourse. When he is talking to enemy generals whom he has taken prisoner or with whom he is negotiating, he will say: "You ought to have done this, that, or the other. There, you were in an advantageous position. That would have been an excellent move."

Immediately after his victory at Wagram, he says to Count Bubna: "I am certain that you are damnably strong, for you can deliver shrewd blows. At what figure do you estimate my forces? ... You appear to be uncommonly well informed! Would you care to have a look at my army? ... No? Well, at least you had better study my position on this map. It was my own fault when I failed to win a victory at Aspern-Essling. I got the punishment I deserved."

Only with regard to one matter does this detachment fail him–Waterloo. In St. Helena, an English surgeon ventured to say that people in England would be glad to hear his opinion of Wellington. The remark was followed by an embarrassing silence.

Fame is the supreme goal of his egotism; substantially, it is the only goat. All his energies are directed towards this end: his consciousness of his uniqueness; his historic sense; his sense of honour; his dignity; the boy's dreams, the youth's plans, the man's deeds, the prisoner's unrest. Posterity is the great confused picture which fills his imagination; and the desire of his heart would seem to be rather the Latin "gloria" which thinks of future generation, than the French "gloire" which suns itself in the smile of contemporaries. He is animated by a daimonic being's eager wish for immortality, although he knows that he must share the fate of all mortal men. "Better never to have lived, than to exist, and pass without leaving a trace."

He modifies the coronation oath by swearing, not only to protect the realm and the happiness of France, but also to rule for the glory of his people. On one of the battlefields of Henry IV in Normandy he has a column erected with the inscription. "Great men love the fame of those who resemble themselves." Frederick's sword is "more precious than all the treasures of the king of Prussia"; but it is not only when he is campaigning that his thoughts turn towards the future. When he is having houses built for the unemployed, his order to the minister to whom the task is entrusted ends with the phrase: "We must not pass out of the world without leaving traces that will commend us to the thoughts of posterity." At the close of his career as Emperor, he refuses to make peace on terms that will involve the renunciation of territories upon whose conquest part of his fame depends; and towards the end of his life he utters a melancholy parable, darkly significant, lonely as his own destiny:

"The love for glory is like the bridge which Satan tried to build across chaos in order to make his way into paradise. Glory is a connecting link between past and future, from which an abyss separates him. I leave to my son nothing but my name."

IV

Energy is the second element in Napoleon's make-up. How does this quality show itself?

First of all in calculation. Never a trace of the flash of genius; but, rather, continuous weighing, over-elaborating, discarding: "I have known myself to argue with myself over the thoughts concerning a battle, and have contradicted myself. ... When I have drawn up a plan of battle I am the most pusillanimous of men. I magnify the dangers and the incidents, am in a terrible state of excitement even when I seem cheerful; I am then like a girl who is going to have a baby." This is the mood of an artist during the conception of his work. He once described these feelings to Roéderer in even franker terms:

"I am always at work; I think a great deal. If I appeared to be ever ready and equal to any occasion, it is because I have thought over matters for long before I undertake to do the slightest thing; I have foreseen all eventualities. There exists no guardian angel who suddenly and mysteriously whispers in my ear what I have to do or to day. Everything is turned over in my mind, again and again, always, whether I am at table or at the theatre. At night, I wake up in order to work."

This constant deliberation builds up something within him which he names "the spirit of things": the precision, which penetrates all he touches; the thinking in numbers, to which he ascribes part of his success and for which he had to thank his mathematical training. There is nothing too small for this brain; for the sum total of millions of details is a plan whose scope is world embracing. If one of his officers writes to say that the Emperor's instructions have been carried out, Napoleon waves this general statement aside and demands details. Nothing is so small but he wants to know all about it and judge its importance for himself. He writes to Eugene, who is in Italy:

"How is it possible that you are distributing three million seven hundred and forty seven thousand rations of meat?...I can calculate a similar gross total for dried vegetables, wine, salt, and spirits. But I want calculations according to corps. I am robbed of fifty per cent, even as much as seventy per cent.... How can you allow them to calculate for one million three hundred and seventy-one thousand rations of hay? I should have to provide twelve thousand horses to eat it, not counting the Istrians and Dalmatians! You know I have only seven thousand.... The office charges are insane! Frs. 118,000 for four months! That equals frs. 400,000 a year! Such a sum should suffice for the whole of Italy!"

This is but one example among many. Thousands of such letters, hailing from every corner of the military and civil administration, personally dictated, are to be found in the volumes of correspondence, and must sadly disappoint those who expect to find only ideas and temperament in the letters. He is the man who, in the midst of his wars in Italy, writes home that they must concoct a letter, nominally written by a German patriot and dealing with Austrian politics, and have it circulated throughout Germany; again, in the throes of a campaign, he has to write to Murat, King of Naples, detailing how the latter is to behave at balls or when he visits the theatre, whom he is to invite and whom to exclude from his invitations. While the preparations are being made for the Erfurt gathering, he suddenly remembers that someone must be there to introduce the actresses to the gallant grand dukes. He never demonstrates more forcibly the way he formulates destinies in figures than by the following incursion into social life: "Each household should have six children, seeing that, on the average, three are sure to die. Of the three who survive, two should replace the father and mother; the third will serve for an unforeseen emergency."

His precision of thoughts goes to such grotesque lengths!

A third means for expressing this energetic faculty is his tempo. "Activity! Speed!" he writes with his own hand at the foot of an order. The king of Prussia has depicted this peculiarity with especial felicity: "We need but see him ride: he always gives his horse rein, and never troubles about what may be happening in his rear!" But Napoleon negotiated better than he rode, for he never negotiated until after long reflection. "Not a moment must be lost," is the slogan even when nothing presses for decision. The instinctive impetus of an overburdened but short life drives him forward; it seems as if he could not arrive quickly enough at the end of his career. He writes to Bernadotte, in the course of a campaign: "I have lost a whole day through you, and the fate of the world hangs upon one single day."

The drive he imposes upon himself has its reaction upon those who serve him. He drives them, not only in the field, but also in circumstances which ordinary governments would take months to decide. He demands a treaty with Russia from Talleyrand, saying it is to be drawn up and ready in a couple of hours. To explain the reasons for his second marriage, he wants a circular letter sent to all his ambassadors and consuls; this is to be drafted "In the course of the day." One night he is immersed in thoughts concerning the embellishment of Paris. Next morning he says to his Minister for Home Affairs: "I require that Paris shall have two million inhabitants by the end of ten years. I want to do something useful and great for the city. What do you suggest?"

"Provide the town with a good water-supply, Sire," and the minister expounds a plan whereby the Ourcq water can be conveyed to Paris.

"Your proposal is good. Summon G., he must send five hundred men to La Vilette tomorrow, in order to start work on the canal,"

Another of his weapons is memory. "I always know my position. I cannot remember a signal Alexandrine, but I never forget a figure relating to my military situation." This is the productive memory. Although he pronounces them abominably, he retains the names of all the important places–important from his point of view–in all the countries where he has fought. The Postmaster General reports that the Emperor is able to mention, offhand, distances which he himself has to hunt up in works of reference. On his way back to Paris from the camp at Boulogne, Napoleon encounters a troop of soldiers who have lost their way; asks the number of their regiment, whence they set out, and when. He tells them their line of march! "Your battalion will be at H. this evening." At this time, two hundred thousand men were on the march close at hand!

His technique is to arrange things in his head "as in a wardrobe." He says: "when I wish to put any matter out of my mind, I close its drawer and open the drawer belonging to another. The contents of the drawers never get mixed, and they never worry me or weary me. Do I want to sleep? I close all the drawers, and then I am asleep."

Among the numerous heraldic emblems which might have tickled the fancy of an upstart–stars, tutelary deities, saints, beasts of prey–he finds none to please him. He chooses the bee, thus emphasising once more his opinion that a man of talent who aspires and works unceasingly, can achieve everything that can otherwise be achieved through what is vaguely spoken of as genius. He declares that genius is industry; meaning, of course, that genius is industry among other things. He says that work is his element, that for which he has been created. Had he left nothing behind him, had all his works perished, still his industry and his glory would have been an emblematic stimulus to the youth of countless generations after he had passed away.

Many witnesses testify to his amazing powers of continued work. Roéderer, who was his close companion during the Consulate, writes as follows: "That which especially characterises him is the power and persistence of his attention. He can work for eighteen hours at a stretch, it may be at one piece of work, it may be at several in turn. I have never seen his mind flag, I have never seen his mind without a spring in it, not when he was physically tired, not when he was taking violent exercise, not even when he was angry. I have never seen him distracted from one affair by another, neglecting the matter in hand for one which he is about to work. Good or bad news from Egypt never interfered with the steps it was necessary to take for the safety of Egypt. No one was ever more wholly immersed in what he was doing, nor did anyone ever make a better distribution of his time among all the things he had to do. Never was anyone more stubborn in rejecting the occupation or the thought which was not appropriate to the hour or the day; nor was anyone ever more adroit in seizing an occupation or a thought when the right moment had come."

He robbed hundreds of his fellow workers of health and youth, because he demanded too much of them when he demanded from them what he exacted from himself. His private secretary would be sent for at a late hour, and would get to bed at four in the morning; at seven, the poor man would find new tasks ready for him, and would be told that they must be finished within two hours. When Napoleon and his secretary were together all day, one dictating and the other writing from dictation, at meal times the chief would order food for two, and would share with his subordinate at a corner of the work-table, just as he would have shared with his adjutant on a boundary stone. During the Consulate he would sometimes begin a sitting with his ministers at six in the evening and keep it up till five next morning. In the three months at Schönbrunn, his official correspondence comprised four hundred and thirty-five letters occupying four hundred folio pages of print. This was only his political and administrative correspondence; in addition he wrote a great many private letters, and delivered innumerable orders by word of mouth.

These are the main forms of his energy. It is with their aid that he enters upon his duel with the world, availing himself of their interplay, and speaking of his genius as a talent for combination. In his plans and orders, he is fond of the phrase "at the given moment." He is not hampered by any principle, is always willing to modify his scheme to suit the weather of destiny, to adapt his combinations to the slightest modifications of the situation. This man of iron will had a most supple intelligence. While forcing all those with whom he came in contact to bend before his resolves, he himself showed a wonderful elasticity in compliance with the will of circumstances.

"The weakness of a captain who, instead of forcing his way into port, preferred to let himself be chased on the open sea– this, and some of the trifling defects of our frigates, were the reasons why I failed to change the face of the world. Had Acre fallen, we should have made our way to Aleppo by forced marches, have enlisted Christians, Druses, and Armenians; have speedily reached the Euphrates: thence I should have gone to India, and should have established new institutions everywhere."

Whether these vaticinations were historically tenable, may remain an open question; but his belief that he could have done what he describes, bears witness to his realism. In this world of figures and magnitudes, for Napoleon everything depends upon the individual behaviour of the individual man at his post. Since the failure of any one individual may give the totality of circumstances a new trend, he is always ready to adapt the trend of his own intelligence to changing circumstances. But he does not himself attribute his successes to this, saying that they were due to his having been born at the right moment, and that under Louis XIV he would only have become a marshal like Turenne.

Napoleon's energy is very little disturbed by the passions. His self-confidence and his sense of dignity made self-command easy to him, and, being habituated to surprise, he was always fully master of himself. "Since I am used to great events, they make no impression on me at the moment when they are reported; I feel the pain an hour later." This sometimes makes him appear more

for the duties imposed by his own craft: "He who cannot look upon a battleground dry-eyed, allows many men to be killed purposelessly." This is what he wants above all to avoid. For the great aim, Europe entrusts him with a million men: his lesser aim, the taking of this trench or that bridge, must be thriftily achieved, for "he who heedlessly allows ten men to be killed where at most two need have died, is answerable for the lives of eight men."

Since most of his wars are fought from political necessity, and are always conducted without hate, as soon as the fight is finished the foe ceases to exist. He writes from Schönbrunn: "I am appalled to learn that the eighteen thousand prisoners on the island of Lobau are suffering from hunger; this is inhuman and unpardonable. Have twenty thousand rations of bread sent there immediately; a similar amount of flour for the bakehouses." But when, after the truce, soldiers are still being killed by the embittered Tyrolese, he is furious, and orders that "at least six of the larger villages are to be plundered and burned, so that the Mountain folk may not soon forget the vengeance that has been exacted."

War is for him an art, "the most noteworthy art, one which contains within itself all the other arts:" Like a true artist, he declares that, in the long run, this art cannot be taught: "You fancy that because you have read Jomini you are fitted to be a leader in war? ... I have fought in sixty fights, and I can assure you that I have learned nothing from any of them. Cæsar used the same tactics in his last battle as he had used in his first." In typical artist fashion, he contradicts himself in the definitions of those things in which he is a master. After the Spanish campaigns, he delivers the following lecture to one of his generals: "War is decided far more by the power of strategical calculation than by material force." At another time he will maintain that it is the superior numbers or the moral courage of the troops which constitutes the deciding factor. Sometimes he even goes so far as to say that inspiration decides an issue: "The result of a battle hangs on a thread and is mostly the outcome of a sudden thought. One approaches the enemy according to a prearranged plan, one comes to blows, one fights for a while, the critical moment draws near, a spark of inspiration flames up-and a small reserve division does the rest!"

More logically, but not less as the artist, he speaks of the decisive moment which, after a couple of engagements, one can find out for oneself without any difficulty. "Such moments are not more than quarter hours.... In every battle a moment comes when the bravest of soldiers would like to turn tail: it needs but a trifle, but a plea, to put heart into him again." This power of suggestion has won him many a victory, for soldiers constitute the only mass to which he can speak with effect. The soldier understands him, because Napoleon is simple. The Emperor even describes war as "a simple art like everything that is beautiful." By this contention he seems to uphold the idea that war is the highest of all arts. "The military profession is a freemasonry ... and I am the grand master of its lodge."

He draws this personal influence from the history of his own rise, which is known to every soldier. As a young general, he had learned to put up with his dependence on the civil authority; and as emperor he still commiserates his royal adversaries because their generals' activities are frustrated by civilian control. On the other hand, he knows the dangers of amateurishness, and writes to Joseph: "When the king himself commands, the soldier does not feel commanded. The army applauds him as when a queen is riding by. If one is not oneself a general, one must give the generals full power of command."

Because he is the only ruler in Europe who has risen from the ranks, from youth upwards he remains familiar with details, and always understands how things look to an officer on the fighting front. "There is nothing connected with the art of war which I cannot do with my own hand: power, siege engines, artillery." But he does not concern himself with these details unless it is necessary, and laughs at the romantic anecdote in a book where he is said, one night, to have taken over the duties of a sentry who had gone to sleep at his post: "That is a civilian's idea, the sort of thing a lawyer would think of, and was certainly not written by a soldier."

But he is a stickler for equality in the army, and in this matter remains true to the revolution until the very end of his career. No one is promoted unless his record in the service justifies the advancement. If Napoleon makes an exception in the case of his brothers, we must remember that after he has made them kings he continues to scold them as if they were subalterns. He writes to Jerome, commenting on a report from Silesia: "Besides, your letter is too clever for my taste.... What a man needs in war is precision, firmness, simplicity." When Joseph plays the prince in Boulogne, and vies with Marshal Soult in the splendour of his receptions, Napoleon scolds him. "In the army, no one must put the commander prince who must give a dinner. At a review, a royal colonel is a colonel and nothing more. Discipline can tolerate no exceptions. The army is whole. Its commander is everything. Keep to your own regiment."

Nevertheless, a wounded commander-in-chief has become a private soldier. At Eylau, where there have been heavy losses, the Emperor forbids a famous surgeon to go out of his way in order to care for a wounded general: "Your business is to attend to all the wounded, and not to anyone in particular." A German officer reports that after a fight Napoleon would often stand by the wounded and see that they were carefully lifted into the stretchers: "If this good fellow pulls through, there will be one victim the less."

In all the memoirs, we read how in camp the Emperor would foregather with his men at the bivouac fire, ask whether their food was being properly cooked, and laugh at their replies. When they confided all their troubles to him, and often said "thou" to him, this was not the assumed good fellowship of a condescending monarch, but a genuinely paternal relationship. If he calls them "my children," to them he is their "little corporal," meaning the comrade who takes the responsibility. "I have received your letter, dear comrade," he writes to a veteran grenadier who wishes to reenter the service. "You need not speak to me of your deeds, for I know you to be the bravest grenadier in the army. It will be a pleasure to see you once more. The Minister for War will send you your orders."

He never confides his plans to anyone; but when it is a question of rewarding merit, he calls in Everyman as adviser. After a fight, he often forms a circle, speaks to the officers, the non-commissioned officers, and the rankers individually, asking who were the most valiant, rewarding then and there, allotting eagles with his own hand. "The officers pointed out, the soldiers confirmed, the Emperor approved," relates Segur as eyewitness.

It is true that Napoleon loves war, but as a fine art, just as he loves power. It is true that he laughs incredulously at a traveller who tells him a tale of a Chinese island where there are no weapons.

"What do you mean? But they must have weapons?"

"No, Sire."

"Pikes, anyhow; or bows and arrows!"

"Neither the one nor the other."

"Daggers!"

"Not even daggers."

"But how the devil do they fight there?"

"There has never been a war on the island."

"What, no war?"

It sounds to the traveller as if the very existence of such people under the sun outrages the Emperor. The thought stirs a soldier's bile!

All the same, he looked forward to the coming of peaceful days, not with an ardent desire for them perhaps, but with the seer's vision. He showed his superiority to all the modern commanders against whom he fought, in that he, the greatest soldier of the new times, declared the primacy of the spirit over the sword. When Canova made a stature of him in which he was shown with a threatening mien, he said contemptuously: "Does the man think I achieved my conquests with blows of my fist?" But more, than this, he himself defined a commander as something above and beyond a soldier. When First Consul, he said in the Council of State:

"In what does the commander's superiority consist? In his mental qualities: insight, calculation, decision, eloquence, man shine in civil life.... If bodily vigour and courage sufficed the commander, any brave private could be a leader of armies. Everywhere, crude force now yields ground to moral qualities. The man with the bayonet bows before the man who possesses exceptional knowledge and understanding. ...I knew perfectly well what I was about when, as the head of the army, I bore the title of Member of the Institute; and the youngest drummer understood what I meant."

At a later date, he spoke more decisively.

"War is an anachronism. Some day, victors will be won without cannon and without bayonets.... Whoever troubles the peace of Europe, wants civil war."

Remember that these are the words of Napoleon, the military commander.

VI

His energy is concentrated on human beings. Very rarely does he come into conflict with natural forces: and whenever he does so, he is beaten. But, in general, all he has to do is to compel men to conquer, for him, the mountains and the miles. Human beings are the material in working with which the energy and the imagination of this artist are destined to become weary; them he must overcome if he is to do his work at all. No mortal ever conquered more men than did Napoleon. He subjugated, not only armies and peoples, but something more; individuals, and the best of these.

To achieve his goal, he followed the road of contempt; and used as his means, glory and money. Self-confidence and experience had convinced him that everyone acts only from self-interest: that some are driven to grasp at money through love of pleasure, or avarice, or clannishness; that others seek public recognition in order to gratify their vanity, their jealousy, or their ambition. Denying the force of ideal motives, Napoleon relied exclusively upon material means; and if the spur of ambition occasionally assumed the aspect of a desire for eternal glory, this occurred against his will, but the magic of his personality sometimes exercised a more puissant lure than the well-calculated material attractions offered by others. To quote Goethe: "Napoleon, who lived wholly for ideas, was nevertheless unable to grasp the nature of ideal motives; he repudiated the ideal, denied that there was any such thing, at the very time when he himself was eagerly trying to realise the ideal."

Yet to Napoleon the Mephistophelian conception of men was as alien as it was to Goethe. He said: "Most people bear within themselves the seeds of good and of evil, of courage and of cowardice. Thus is human nature created: upbringing and circumstance do the rest." Since, for twenty years, he needed this human nature, daily and in quantities of a hundred at a time, the subtlest knowledge of it was a primary condition of his success. Among all the materials which Napoleon bent to his uses, the human heart was the most familiar.

"I am a great friend of analysis.... 'Why' and 'How', are such useful questions, that they cannot be uttered too often." Coldly and clearly as a nerve specialist, he controls all psychical symptoms, utilizes every method for the attainment of such control, and trusts especially to physiognomy–for he knows his Lavater. He is fond of reproving people. "According as they react, I discover the pitch of their souls. If I strike brass with a glove, it gives back to tone: but if I strike with a hammer, it rings out." A person meeting Napoleon for the first time, is gripped by the magnetism of his glance.

By talking and questioning, he makes himself acquainted with the atlas of human types, an atlas he is ever enlarging.

He questions so long that a stranger grows embarrassed, confused, and alarmed; he questions until his questions become ridiculous; but he must at all costs get the information he needs, even if he is not negotiating. In what way can the twenty minutes that a doctor sits at Napoleon's table in St. Helena be put to the best use by the ex-emperor?

"How many patients suffering from ailments affecting the liver had you on board? How many cases of dysentery? What is the fee for a consultation in England? What is the pension awarded to an army surgeon? ... What is death, or how would you define it? When does the soul quit the body? When does a body first receive a soul?"

Another means is monologue. One of his intimates declares that the right of the Emperor to hold forth in Monologue was the only real pleasure his high estate awarded him! We have testimonies concerning other men of action: but who ever talked so much as Napoleon! Since he always faces the world alone, he must continually hold forth that he may convey his suggestions to the world. His conversations often lasted from five to eight hours, some of them ten or eleven hours; and during the greater part of them Napoleon took the floor. We must admit that this was more in accordance with the Italian manner than the Roman; Italian, too, were the rapidity of his utterance, and his foreign accent: but he gesticulated little; and only when much moved did he unclasp his hands–generally they were clasped behind his back, as if he wished to throw out his chest against the world.

Upon all who serve him, he lavishes money with oriental profusion. But as far as his personal expenditure is concerned, he is thrifty. During the Consulate he says:

"A man who has been through so many wars will have acquired a little property whether he will or no. I have a private income of from frs. 80, 000 to frs. 100, 000, with a house in town and a country mansion. What more do I need? If I should get out of humour with France, or France with me, I should retire from public life without a qualm.... But everyone round me is stealing; the ministers are weak. Some people must be laying by vast sums.... What is to be done about it? France is corrupt through and through. It has always been like that; as soon as a man becomes a minister, he builds himself a palace.... Do you know what they are trying to make me pay for may installation in the Tuileries? Two millions! ... It must be cut down to eight hundred thousand. I am surrounded by a pack of scoundrels."

"Your great operations," answers Roéderer, "must cost you much more than these domestic defalcations."

"All the more reason why I should watch over my personal expenditure."

This conversation tells us how the head of the State, a man of thirty, regards money. He needs nothing for himself, and complains of the venality and profusion of those by whom he is surrounded; acknowledges that he has himself made money out of the wars; rails at the tradesmen who want to charge two millions for the equipment of a palace, when, as far as his own taste is concerned, he sees no reason for spending anything at all. Amid the frightful corruption which is a heritage of the revolution, he fights with the army contractors and war profiteers; but as soon as, by drastic punishments, he has succeeded in putting an end to this scandal, he assigns preposterous incomes to his marshals, some of whom receive more than a million francs a year. As Consul, he rids the State of the thieves who are making away with the national property; and then, as Emperor, he burdens this same State with extortionate salaries.

Still, there are a few persons who make money thanks to their relationship with him, though without his aid. "When I have nothing left," he says to Talleyrand, "I shall turn to you. Tell me honestly, how much have you make out of me?"

"I am not a rich man, Sire, but all that I have is at your service."

Napoleon's way of dealing with men is modified by a hundred and one considerations. If we wish to study the variations of his technique, we must class his instruments in groups.

Generals and marshals are the easiest to keep dependent, for they have unceasing opportunities of winning military renown; and, since he pays them so liberally for their services, they grow more and more wealthy. By loading them with money, he gains two ends, spreading effulgence around himself, and keeping his most powerful officers in a state of dependence. It delights him to see these soldiers unused to money spending extravagantly, running into debt, and then turning to him for help in their difficulties. He leads them from profusion to want, and then back to profusion again. At the same time, he gives them little scope for originality, reserving important decisions for himself, so that even the commanders of armies rarely have a chance of proving themselves men of genius. He shrewdly regulates his public mention of them in his bulletins, both in respect of time and form, so that, through their vanity and jealousy, he can get his way with his generals.

The result is that their sentiments towards him are a mingling of hatred and love, whereby they are chained to his service more firmly than if the feeling had been one of pure affection. Perhaps only two of them are wholly devoted to him, Berthier and Duroc, whose love for him he compares with that of a child and a dog. Ney speaks of himself as a loaded musket which is fired when and where the Emperor orders. Napoleon, for his part, has a personal affection for those only tribute to them. He extols Desaix's mental balance. Moreau has "more instinct than genius"; whereas Lannes has "more courage than sense," though as time goes on he makes good enjoyment. Masséna is not really courageous until he is under fire. Murat "has not a spark of intelligence, but what dash! He is a duffer and a hero." Napoleon cannot break away from these witnesses of his rise, although most all of them have learned the weight of his anger. In his tent, after Wagram, Napoleon thunders at Marmont for having made a mess of things, and a quarter of an hour later appoints him marshal.

Sometimes the Emperor's misanthropy got the better of him. "In those moods, I begin to distrust even my companions-in-arms; that causes me intense suffering, and I do everything I can to rid myself of such horrible suspicions." Yet he really knew. Lannes' death touched him to the quick, but he never really uttered the moving farewell words which he publishes. Indeed, he confided to Metternich: "Lannes hated me. When I heard that, on being wounded, he had called out my name, I knew It was all up with him. He called on me as a dying atheist calls on God."

The remembrance of friendships formed in youth does not prevent him from scolding the most exalted of his marshals like schoolboys when he considers they have behave foolishly or have been wanting in courage. He says to Junot: "Your conduct was unprecedented, extraordinarily indiscreet.... You have a strange notion of your military duties. I don't recognise you!" To a general in Lombardy: "Under your command, there has been very little honesty and a great deal of avarice; but I never knew until today that you were a coward. Leave the army, and never let me see your face again!" In Spain, one of his generals capitulated in the open field. Six months later, this man ventured to appear before Napoleon at a review. The Emperor stormed at him in full hearing of the troops; would not be appeased. The witnesses say that the scene lasted a whole hour. "A man may have to surrender a fortress. The fortune of war is uncertain, and defeat is always possible. Anyone can be taken prisoner. The thing may happen to me tomorrow. But honour, before all! On the battlefield, a commander's business is to fight: and if he capitulates instead, he deserves to be shot.... A soldier must know how to die. Have we not all to face death? ... As a subject, you committed a crime in capitulating; as a general, a stupid blunder; as a soldier, your action was cowardly; but as a Frenchman, your surrender was dishonourable!"

He alarmed the diplomats of his day by a frankness which none of them trusted. "Tact, and putting all the cards on the table, will do better service in diplomacy than cunning. The tricks of the diplomats of the old school are out of date; all their rogueries have been exposed long since.... Nothing betrays weakness more than the attempt to deceive."

Just before the renewal of the ear with England, he tells the British envoy how many years it will take before France can face England at sea but he explains how quickly he can increase his army to four hundred thousand. In Schönbrunn, he says to the Austrian negotiator: "That is my last word. If you defeat me, I shall propose more favourable terms; but if I gain the victory, I shall make them harder. What I want in peace."

He studies every shade of expression when he wishes to influence the envoys of foreign powers. We see this especially when he is adapting his demeanour towards the Austrians with an eye to the Habsburg traditions. He waits for the formal reception on his birthday, and then, faced by the semicircle of the diplomats, he stops in front of Metternich to say "Well, Monsieur l'Ambassadeur, what does your emperor want? Would he like me to come to Vienna?" This is calculated to intimidate the Austrian envoy, and at the same time to advertise Napoleon's threatening attitude throughout Europe. But two days later, when Metternich comes to a private interview, the Emperor says: "Today, we won't play at being Emperor of the French and Austrian envoy. There is no audience now, so we need not make any fine speeches."

Shortly before the conclusion of the first peace with Austria he wishes to avoid meeting the defeated archduke in Schönbrunn, lest he should commit himself prematurely to peace terms. He therefore arranges that the meeting shall take place in a hunting lodge. "I shall spend only two hours there: one of them will be occupied in having dinner, and the other will be devoted to talk about the war and to mutual protestations of respect." When the First Consul receives Count Coblenz, he has personally arranged the stage in the Tuileries; writing-table in the corner; no chairs, so that they will have to sit on the sofa; only one lamp, no lights in the chandelier, although it is late in the evening. When Talleyrand ushers in the Austrian, the room seems almost dark, and the Consul, on the farther side of it, is scarcely visible; the stranger is perplexed, and has to sit exactly where his host chooses.

He is even more subtle in his dealings with the princes. During the years of his supreme power, he ceases to pay them visit. In Tilsit, he becomes the host within two days; in Dresden, though he is the king of Saxony's guest, he plays the master. He avoids having anything to do with queens. When Queen Louise pathetically implores justice, he begs her to sit down. "Nothing interrupts a tragical scene more effectually than this. When people sit down, tragedy becomes comedy."

In his dealings with the peoples he was less happy, and his only tolerable successes were secured with the French and the Italians. During the Consulate, he said in the Council of State: "My policy is to rule in accordance with the will of the majority. This, I think, implies the recognition of the sovereignty of the people. I became a good Catholic when I wanted to finish the war in Vendée; in Egypt I was Turk; when I wished to win over the Italians, I was an ultramontane. If I reigned over the Jews, I should rebuild Solomon's temple, That is why I propose to talk about freedom in that part of San Domingo where the slaves have been liberated, while maintaining slavery in the other part of the island."

His policy was not very successful in the Negro republic; he did better in Poland, which he tried to win over by festivities and phrases; and better still with the Jews. These had been granted equal rights by the revolution, and on the Rhine many of them were doing harm by the practice of usury. Napoleon, who knew their value as traders, did not have recourse to crude prohibitions. He bethought himself of Jewish laws and customs; summoned to Paris their highest council, the Sanhedrin, which had not met for centuries; left the decision to this body, and was able to arrange that the supreme Jewish authority should forbid usury as sinful. But in Spain he made a complete mess of things, overlooking the risks he was running, and advising Joseph to make himself agreeable to the whole nation "by instilling fear into the rabble."

The Germans puzzled Napoleon most of all. They had everything he lacked, and none of the things he had. He therefore, even in the midst of his successes, regarded them with a mixture of fear and admiration; they seemed to him uncanny. When he went to Erfurt and wished to influence the German princes by the drama, he told the managing director not to stage any comedies. "No one understands comedies on this bank of the Rhine. Corneille's *Cinna* might be played, for therein great interests are portrayed; then a scene depicting royal clemency, which would certainly have a good effect." He went on to misquote *Cinna.* Rémusat, having put him right said, "In this sacred office, to which God's grace has appointed the king, the past is justified and the future is free. He who is advanced to this office, cannot be held culpable; whatever he does, he remains invulnerable."

"Splendid!" exclaims the Emperor, "especially for the Germans, who always cling to the same ideas, and are still talking about the death of the duke of Enghien! We must broaden their moral outlook. That will be good for people with melancholy ideas, the sort of persons with whom Germany is filled." It is as if he were talking about German music, of which he knows practically nothing but really he is thinking of German philosophy. The one is as uncongenial to him as the other, for he is fond of Italian arias and the wisdom of Voltaire, but says that "Kant is an obscure writer." This misconception of his prevents him from foreseeing the possibility that so slow-moving a people may one day become inspired with a passionate enthusiasm.

Perhaps the reason for the misinterpretation lies in the impracticability of understanding the masses of a foreign nation. In northern Italy, he did indeed make headway, for he was a young man, his ideas were naive, the yearning of the oppressed was still fresh in him; and he was the herald of the revolution. But the dictator could no longer bring a torch to foreign peoples. Nevertheless, he continued to watch the sentiments of the masses. "A ruler should reign for the masses, without asking whether he is pleasing Mr So-and-So ... Men of mark look from above, and have no party ties; one who belongs to a party, is a slave." Such were his principles, but his actions told another story.

The masses even in France, saw a man who made himself dreaded. They feared him for a decade, but became sceptical at his first failure. "A ruler should be dignified in his demeanour towards the people," says Napoleon "But he must not flatter the crowd, which will then think itself cheated if he does not give it everything. You ask me why I make threatening speeches? I make them in order to avoid having to do the things I threaten!"

who looked forward towards an aim which was again to become an object of statesmanship a hundred years after his fall.

"There are in Europe more than thirty million Frenchmen, fifteen million Italians, thirty million Germans.... Out of each of these peoples, I wanted to make a united national whole.... That would have supplied the best chance of establishing a general unity of laws; a unity of principles and thoughts and feelings, of outlooks and interests.... Then it would have been possible to think of founding the United States of Europe after the model of the United states of America or of the Greek Amphictyonic League.... What perspective of strength greatness, and prosperity this opens up! ... For France, unity has been wrought; in Spain, it has proved unattainable; to establish the Italian nation, I should have needed twenty years; to make the Germans a nation, would have required still more patience, and all I could do was to simplify their monstrous constitution. At the same time, I wanted to pave the way for the unification of the great interests of Europe, just as I had unified the parties in France. The transient mutterings of the peoples troubled me little; they would have been reconciled to me by the result....*Europe would soon have become one nation, and any who travelled in it would always have been in a common fatherland.... Sooner or later, this union will be brought about by the force of events. The first impetus has been given; and after the fall and the disappearance of my system, it seems to me that the only way in which an equilibrium can be achieved in Europe is through a league of nations.*"

Here there is no talk of a dictatorial welding together of different stocks, or of an enthusiastic fraternization: He speaks only of interests, and of a preliminary unification of these on a national and racial basis. The work of the nineteenth century was to inaugurate the preliminaries by the establishment of the nations. The twentieth century opens with the realization of the Napoleonic idea.

VIII

The effects underlying his energy and his imagination are dominated by the clarity of his thought. Napoleon hated less and loved more, than he would have been willing to admit. In this domain, we find the converse of what happens in the matter of his sympathies in war time, when a million men are coldly sacrificed, while one man wounded and bleeding touches him to the heart. Since his fantasy needs enormous masses, he is enraged when Joseph says: "I am the only person who cares for you." Napoleon rejoins: "Nothing of the sort. I need five hundred million men to love me." In these icy words glows the volcano which one of his school masters heard rumbling long ago.

Emotionally convinced of his mission to order the affairs of the nations, he deliberately rejects anything that may distract him from this aim, and nothing sustains him but his monomania. Even in the drama, he objects to the interweaving of love stories, saying: "Love is a passion which should only be the main theme of a tragedy, and never a subsidiary motif. ... In the days of Racine, it was the whole content of a human life. That happens in a society where no great deeds are being done."

If love becomes intrusive, he annuls it. "I have no time to be bothered with feelings and to repent them like other men. ... There are two motives to action: self-interest and fear. Believe me, love is a foolish blindness! ... I love no one, not even my brothers–Joseph a little, from force of habit, and because he is the elder. I am fond of Duroc, too; he is serious and resolute; I believe the man has never shed tears in his life! ... Let us leave sensibilities to women. Men should be firm of heart and strong of will, or else they should have nothing to do with war or governance." Another time: "The only friend I have is Daru; he is unfeeling and cold; that suits me." Last of all, in St. Helena "A man of fifty has done with love.... I have an iron heart. I never really loved; perhaps Josephine, a little; but then I was only seven-and-twenty. I incline to the view of Gassion, who once said to meet that he did not love life well enough to give it to another being."

Always half ashamed of his feelings; ever ready to make excuses for them; "perhaps," "a little." Yet this is the same man who said: "I am the slave of my way of feeling and acting, for I value the heart much more than the head." This very feeling is his fantasy.

One in whom egotism is supreme, will be more inclined to jealousy than to love. His first letters to Josephine show him devoured by jealousy. Years later, as Consul, when he is inspecting his new bridge in course of construction across the Seine, he has to step aside with his companion for a moment to let a carriage pass. In the carriage sits Hippolyte, his sometime rival. That was long ago; everything has been condoned; the man's name is never mentioned in his presence. But now, at a chance encounter in the street, Bonaparte grows pale and confused, and takes a little while to recover composure.

From time to time, he shows an involuntary kindliness. On one of the Italian battlefields, he sees a dog howling over the dead body of its master. "The poor beast seemed to be asking for an avenger, or begging help. I was profoundly moved by the dog's suffering, and at that moment I should have been very much in the mood to grant quarter to an enemy. I understood why Achilles surrendered Hector's body to the weeping Priam. Such is man; so little can he count upon his moods. Impassively I had sent my soldiers into the batte; dry-eyed I had watched them marching past in an advance where thousands of them would meet their fate; then I was shaken to the depths by the howling of a dog."

Affectionate tones are to be heard in many of his letters. To Cambaceres: "I am so sorry to hear that you are not well. I hope it is only a passing trouble. If you did not take so much medicine, you be would be better already.... But anyhow, you must do your utmost to get well, if only because of my friendship for you." To Corvisart: "Dear Doctor, I wish you would see to the arch-chancellor and to Lacépede: the former has been ailing for a week, and I am afraid he is in the hands of a quack: Lacépède's wife has been ill for some time. Give them the benefit of your advice, and cure them as soon as you can. You will save the life of a man of note, and one who is very dear to me."

Chénier, who has written against him for years, is assisted by him in poverty and given a secure position. Carnot, for ten years an enemy of the Emperor, is heavily in debt; Napoleon learns this, settles the debts and refuses to hear of being given a note of hand; reckons up the pay which Carnot would have received as general in active service, makes this calculation the basis of a large pension; and when Carnot says he would like to do some work for his money, Napoleon commissions him to write a military treatise, lest his pensioner should have to undertake duties that might go against the grain.

During the Hundred Days, learning that some of the Bourbon princes are greatly distressed for lack of money, he sends them large sums anonymously. On one occasion his secretary is asleep, and he himself has nothing particular to do; he looks through a pile of begging letters, and writes in the margin of each the amount of an allowance which is to be given to the sender. Hundreds of officers whom, in fits of anger, he has sworn to have shot, remain at their posts-to forsake him in the end. When he orders Jerome to get a divorce, he is alarmed at his own harshness. After he has written to enforce his command with threats he sends a letter to his mother saying that she had better write to Jerome at once and get his sisters to write as well, " for if I have passed judgment on him, nothing can alter it, and his life will be spoiled."

From his few friends, he demands blind devotion. Never is the self-centred nature of Napoleon more plainly shown than in the words the exile speaks to Montholon, from whom he has been temporarily estranged: "I love you like a son, for I believe that you love me only; otherwise you could not love me at all. According to my way of feeling, it is not in our nature to love several persons at once. People deceive themselves in these matters; they cannot even love all their children with the same intensity. For my part, at any rate, I want to be the supreme object of affection in the case of those whom I love and honour with my confidence. I cannot bear partings. They stab me to the heart, for my disposition is too sensitive; spiritual poison affects the body more powerfully than arsenic."

Logically enough, he dislikes western views concerning the enlightenment of women. He always hankers after the East, and in this matter he is an oriental. "Nature intended women to be our slaves; and it is only because of our distorted outlooks that they venture to describe themselves as our rulers.... For one who can influence us in a good direction, there are a hundred who will only lead us into follies.... What a mad idea to demand equality for women! They are our property, we are not theirs; for they give us children, but we do not give them any. They belong to us, just as a tree which bears fruit belongs to the gardener.... In this difference, there is nothing degrading; every one has his privileges, and every one his duties. You, ladies, have beauty, attractiveness; but also dependence."

IX

Throughout life, the imagination of this creator was troubled by the thought of the Creator. This ruler of men was greatly disturbed that there should be no one who ruled all men. It was not that he ever regarded himself as divine; he laughed at all mystical interpretations of his own power; but there was one great power which remained uncoercible-no matter whether it were called God, destiny, or death. How do self-confidence and fantasy escape from this snare?

First of all by the rejection of dogma. "My firm conviction is that Jesus ... was put to death like any other fanatic who professed to be a prophet or a Messiah; there have been such persons at all times. For my part, I turn from the New Testament to the Old, and there I find one man of mark, Moses. ... Besides, how could I accept a religion which would damn Socrates and Plato? ... I cannot believe that there is a God who punishes and rewards, for I see honest folk unlucky, and rogues lucky. Look at

Talleyrand; he is sure to die in his bed! ... How could I have remained independent if I had been subject to the influence of a confessor to threaten me with the pains of hell? Think what powers a confessor who is a rascal can exercise! ..."

In this matter he is consistent; from childhood, when he would not go to Mass, until the end of his life, he rejected (for himself) all the religions. The man who, in his own life, would not recognize the existence of miracle, and ascribed everything that he was able to achieve to the working of the healthy human understanding. boldness, power of combination, knowledge of men, and imagination, could not possibly believe in the miracles recorded in the Bible. He was perfectly logical when he told one of his subordinates it was impossible that two million men could have quenched their thirst at the Wells of Moses.

Even more uncongenial to him is any dread of a great assize. He does not talk about morality; or at most, he does so with some political end in view. Only towards the last, on the island, he says once in an evening conversation with his intimates: "How happy should we be here if I could confide my troubles to God, and could expect from him happiness and salvation! Have I not a just claim to it? I, who have had so unusual a career, have never committed a crime, and need not fear to step before God's judgment seat and await his sentence. Never has the thought of committing a murder entered my mind."

For these reasons, he does not falter in the days of misfortune. Five years before the end, he expresses the hope that he will die without a confessor, but adds that no one can be certain what he will do in his last hours. In fact, this heart of steel was steadfast to the end.

Nevertheless, his ideas as to the nature of the creation development, and just as the revolutionist became a legitimist, so the materialist became a theist. But these developments were not transformations; there was simply broadening of the basis of his thought. Throughout life, he had a sense that things had come into existence by a natural process: "When out hunting, I had the deer cut open, and saw how like the beast's internal organs were to those of a human being. Man is merely a more perfect creature than a dog or a tree. The plain is the first link in a chain whose last link is mankind." It should be remembered that the Emperor had not read Goethe's *Zur Morphologie*, of Lamarck's *Philosphie zoologique*. He had actually refused to·receive Lamarck.

Still more remarkable are his deductions concerning psycho physical processes. In a Christmas discourse at St. Helena, he expresses his doubts as follows: "How can any one understand that God should sanction the caprices of a ruler who sends thousands of men into battle that they may die for him? ... Where is the soul of a child: or that of a madman? ... What are electricity, galvanism, magnetism? In these lies the great secret of nature. I am inclined to believe that man is a product of these fluids and of the atmosphere; the brain sucks them in and imparts life, and the soul is composed of them. After death, they return into the atmosphere, whence they are sucked up again by other brains." After giving utterance to these Goethean motifs, he is alarmed at his own temerity. Breaking off suddenly, he says, as a soldier among soldiers: "Oh, well, my dear Gourgaud, when we are dead, we are simply dead."

Side by side with this scepticism, there exists and expands a theism. To Laplace, who denies the existence of God, he says: "You should be more ready than anyone else to admit that God exists, for you, more than most, have seen the wonders of creation. If we cannot actually see God with our own eyes, that is because he did not wish our understanding to reach so far." On another occasion: "We believe in God because everything around us testifies to his existence." In St. Helena: "I have never doubted the existence of God, for, even if my reason were incompetent to grasp him, still my inner feelings would convince me of his reality. My temperament has always been in harmony with this feeling."

How shall such a spirit come to terms with destiny? Since his self-esteem makes it impossible for him to believe that any man can have beaten him, he is forced to ascribe his defeat to fate. But this sense of the workings of destiny is present in his mind before the final overthrow; it accompanies him throughout life, and appears to be an equivalent for the reverence, devotion, and faith by which other men live. With the aid of his belief in destiny, Napoleon wages a heroic struggle. In his strongest moments, he feels that he wears armour of proof: "I have a soul of marble. The lightnings were unable to destroy it, but broke on it in vain." Once he expresses his defiance even more poetically: "Should the heavens fall down on us, we shall hold them off with the points of our lances!"

But these defiant moods are rare. In general, he is resigned to fate. There are hundreds of his sayings to bear witness to this. Here are three: "All that happens, is written; our hour is fixed, and no one can postpone it.... No one can escape his fate." To the duchess of Weimar: "Believe me, there is a providence which guides all. I am merely its instruments." To Johannes von Muller: "Fundamentally, all things are linked together, and are subject to the unsearchable guidance of an unseen hand. I have only become great through the influence of my star." In such tropes we see awareness of God and a sense of dependence welded into pride in his own mission. At these times, a prophetical effulgence seems to radiate from him, but is obscured again and again by the self-confidence of his iron energy.

Yet Napoleon was far from believing in his star as another man may believe in a god or a talisman. He could not bear to have the greatness of his deeds minimized by insistence on his good fortune. He was, therefore, far less superstitious than other men of his type. Louis brings him a valuable knife, but hesitates to give it to him; Napoleon snatches it from his brother's hand, saying: "Don't bother, it won't cut anything but bread!" He scolds Josephine because she consults fortune-tellers; but then, being curious, asks her to tell him all about the hocus-pocus. He wants to have the signing of the peace of Pressburg postponed for a few days, that it may take place after the reintroduction of the prerevolutionary calendar; but he does not order this, being content to use the unwonted phrase, "that would please me very much." Schwarzenberg's death, in 1820, is a great relief to him; for when a fire broke out in the Schwarzenberg mansion at the ball given in honour of Napoleon's second marriage, the Emperor had interpreted this as a bad omen for himself; now Schwarzenberg's death is a derivative for his own uneasy forebodings!

Apart from these trifles, in a life so packed with important happenings, we do not hear of a single day during twenty years on which he forms, postpones, or modifies a resolution on superstitious grounds. But he makes an adroit use of his "star" and his "destiny" for political or rhetorical purposes. Since he wishes to pose before Europe as the Man of Destiny, he tries to work upon suggestible minds like Alexander's by such turns of phrase as the following: "It is wise and politic to do what fate commands, and to march on the road along which we are led by the irresistible course of events." His mind is fond of playing with the kindred notions of destiny, circumstance, and chance; and while he regards destiny as involved in more or less obscurity, he believes himself able to calculate the chances of a coming battle with almost mathematical certainty. "In these matters one must be careful not to make a slip, for an overlooked fraction can modify the whole result.... To people of mediocre intelligence, chance will always remain a mystery; but to the clear-sighted, it becomes a reality."

Sometimes he lumps them all together–talents, destiny, and power, –and shows himself an energetic fatalist when he says: "Against attempts on my life, I trust in my luck, my good genius, and my guards."

In this virile spirit, he strides resolutely along betwixt life and death.

A modern tragedy depicts a man who wishes to die, Napoleon says that the portrait is well limned, but unnatural: "A man must wish to live, and must know how to die." That is why, from youth upwards, he opposes suicide; first, in an essay then, in an order of the day; then, with the reiterated argument that suicide is cowardice, especially in hours of misfortune. A careful study of the documents shows that the story of his having attempted suicide just before the first abdication is apocryphal. The leading memoirs make no reference to the matter, and such accounts as we have are at second hand and untrustworthy. There is no doubt that during his last battles Napoleon deliberately sought a soldier's death; but he never tried to poison himself.

Yet it was not only in those last days at Fontainebleau, and after Waterloo, that he suffered from tedium vitæ. The weariness recorded in the diary of the lad of sixteen, and in the letter which the man of thirty wrote from Cairo to his brother, was little in evidence during the most energetic years of febrile activity. Those who trouble to ask whether persons of genius are happy, will have to agree that this man of genius, who was not fitted by nature for happiness, enjoyed during the climax of his career, hours of content, and even sublime moments. But there were periods of doubt:

"For the tranquillity of France," says Bonaparte at Rousseau's tomb, "it would have been better if this man had never lived."

"Why, Citizen Consul?"

"He paved the way for the revolution."

"Surely you are not the man to deplore the revolution?"

"Time will show whether it would not have been better for the peace of the world if neither Rousseau nor I had lived."

Gradually these doubts fade. But what he never loses is the sense of daimonic loneliness, which increases as his soaring flight leads him to chillier altitudes. "There are times when life is hard to bear." Since the sea has always been unfriendly to him, there is only one place where he really feels at home–the desert, which to him is the image of the infinite. The desert is the sublime vacancy which expands before him when the myriad-faceted pictures of ordinary life sink from sight.

But never was Napoleon more perfectly freed from the tyranny of his thoughts, never was he happier, than when seated alone in his box at the theatre, watching a tragedy being enacted.

Nothing else could restore his inner peace of mind; for, since he loved less than most, he was doomed to a tragical loneliness, the price he had to pay for his egotism. "There is neither happiness nor unhappiness," he said. "The life of a happy man is a picture showing black stars on a silver background. The life of an unhappy man is a picture showing silver stars on a black background." But it is not these heroic images which best characterize the loneliness of a soul. Even more poignant voices reach us from the familiar arena of the daily struggle:

"Don't you understand, Caulaincourt, what is going on here? The folk I have got together want to enjoy themselves; the poor devils don't realise that a man has to fight before he can get the repose he longs for. What about myself? Have not I a palace, a wife, a child? Do I not weary myself to the utmost with every possible kind of tension? Do I not day by day give my life to my country?

He gives his life to his work, for that is what he means when he talks of his county. A human note, gently plaintive, and fraught with the lofty irony of the finale, sounds when he says on the island:

"The whole time I was bearing the world on my shoulders. Tis rather a tiring job!"

X

A volcano made the island, which was flung up from beneath the waters thousands upon thousands of years ago. Forth from the midst of the sea, projects the gloomy mass of rock. Steep, black, and deeply furrowed are the walls of lava that run down from the heights into the waves. The chasm above the harbour looks like the gate of hell to one who first sees it from a ship; and the traveller fancies that these dark ramparts must have been built by the hands of demons. Nothing betrays the work of man but the cannon placed among the rocks. When the voyager lands, the ground crunches softly beneath his feet, for the soil is made of disintegrated lava. He is treading the road of death.

An extinct volcano in the Atlantic Ocean, two thousand

miles from Europe and nearly a thousand from Africa, guarded by British guns–such is the rock of St. Helena, on which this limitless life might have ended like a tragedy of Æschylus. But, owing to the mendacity of a moralizing century, the malice of English oligarchs, and the dry spitefulness of a colonial governor, the island becomes the stage for a tragicomedy.

The diligence of a few farmers and the energy of the East India Company had made the place pleasant enough. Hundreds of frigates had, by degrees, brought garden mould building stone, and timber. But since no one would stay long on the rock unless under compulsion, there were twelve hundred Negro slaves and Chinese to serve the five hundred white who dwelt there for a few years at a time.

No one can stay there. On this island, no one reaches the age of sixty, and very few live to be fifty; the climate is deadly. We are in sunless tropics, where the fierce heat of the equator is variegated with cloud bursts, and where within an hour a damp sultriness may give place to a cold downpour. The skin of those who, just before, were dripping with sweat, suddenly chilled by the storming south-east trade wind, whose vapours are arrested by the rock. One who, after a burning day, ventures abroad in the evening, will pant for breath as he walks. Those who stay for a year, suffer from dysentery, giddiness and fever, vomiting and palpitation. Above all, they suffer from liver disease. Whenever England tried to station a squadron at St. Helena, the sailors died by hundreds; the ships had to put out to sea, and to keep under sail. The officials and the planters fall sick. Unless they have the luck to live in one of the four or five sites protected from the wind, they and their families are soon compelled to seek some healthier place of residence.

The inhabitants will tell you that one of the most unwholesome regions is a chilly tableland seventeen hundred feet above sea level; a lonely place, on the windy side of the island, made specially insalubrious by the persistence of fogs. There grow sparse gum trees, blighted by the trade wind, gnarled and twisted, leaning away from the prevailing blast. The St. Helenians call the region Deadwood. Here is Longwood. That is the place selected by England as the one in which the sick foe can most certainly be killed. It was not a temporary asylum, chosen hastily and in an emergency; it was not originally intended for the Emperor; it was made ready for him while he was living elsewhere on the island, in poor case, but still in fairly good health.

Till yesterday, Longwood had been a stable, built fifty years before, and only at the last moment transformed into a dwelling-house. Negroes, and the carpenters of the "Northumberland," fixed a wooden floor over the mud of the interior, neglecting to clear away the cattle dung. Soon after the Emperor's entry, the planks rotted and broke, the stinking damp soaked through the flooring, and he had to move into another room. For himself and his followers, a home has been made out of a cowshed, a wash-house, and a stable. In his bedroom, a dark and narrow corner, the brown nankeen which covers the walls is stained with saltpetre; smells from the kitchen invade it. In this last point it resembles the lodging he had in a cafe thirty years ago when he was a lieutenant in Valence. But in that earlier abode his books kept dry; here they are attacked by mould. The dining-room is lighted through a glass door; the drawing-room is furnished with a worm-eaten mahogany suite; the servants' quarters are flooded by the rain, for the roof here is made of roofing-felt.

The Emperor lives in two small rooms, each about fourteen feet by twelve, and ten feet high. The bedroom boasts a threadbare carpet, muslin curtains, a fireplace, painted wooden chairs, two small tables, a wash-hand stand, and a sofa. The workroom has a bare table, under which two chairs are tucked; rough shelves closely packed with books, and an extra bed where he would rest sometimes in the daytime or which he would use on the nights when he was restless and sleepless. The bedroom contains some trophies rescued from his ruin; the little camp-bed he had used at Austerlitz, hung with green silk curtains; a silver lamp; and, on the wash-hand stand, magnificent silver ewers and basins.

These rooms, and indeed the whole premises, swarm with rats, which kill the fowls, gnaw the leg of a sick horse, bite General

can stand life on the island no more. He leaves at the end of two years. He makes friends with the English, and, when he bids farewell to Emperor and island, he sails away with letters of introduction from the governor who is the deadly foe of his master.

Count Montholon is the most loyal of the exile's companions. As a youngster of ten he had been instructed by Captain Buonaparte in mathematics. Later, he had served in two score battles under his master, and was much at the Emperor's court. Many decades after Napoleon's death, he proved his fidelity to the House of Bonaparte; for, just as now he offers up six years of his life to live with his exiled master on this rocky site, so, too, he devotes six further years to Napoleon's nephew, sharing the third Napoleon's captivity in a fortress. The only drawback in St. Helena is that the count's wife does not get on with Madame Bertrand. One day the countess declares in the hearing of all that the Bertrands' latest born is puny because the mother's milk is good for nothing.

Meanwhile Madame Bertrand is reckoning that her eldest is sure to be made grand marshal as soon as Napoleon II ascends the throne. How much jealousy rages in these breasts because, meanwhile, under Napoleon I, Bertrand remains "grand marshal," while Montholon superintends culinary affairs and Gourgaud attends to the Emperor's stable. Besides, none of them have enough to do. Their duties cannot occupy more than two hours of the endless day. At last things come to such a pass in this ramshackle palace that the members of the little court can only communicate with one another in writing. Even Countess Montholon and her children have in the end to forsake the Emperor and the island.

Who is really loyal, loyal in his heart of hearts?

Three servants. Marchand, the valet, who has attended the Emperor for the last four years; and two Corsicans who, in the hurry of departure, Napoleon had pressed into his service, thereby linking up the island of his birth with the island of his latter days. These servants never have any dealings with the English foe, who would gladly draw their secrets from them, Cipriani has a special reason for his reticence; as sergeant he had seized Capri from the governor of Capri who today is governor of St. Helena. Santini occasionally asks for a day off in order to go shooting. But his sport is soon stopped when the fact gets known that he intends to shoot "that monster, that governor," and then to put a bullet through his own head.

The Emperor sternly forbids his man to contemplate any such deed, for who in Europe would not immediately cast suspicion on himself? But when the servant has withdrawn, the master thinks indulgently: "We Corsicans are all like that!"

XI

A lean, middle-aged man with restless movements, red-haired, freckled, with a large brown patch on the cheek; his throat is stringy; he has pale golden eyebrows shading eyes which can look no one in the face; he is clad in a British uniform–such is the governor of the prison.

He lives in a fine country house, in the most sheltered part of the island, with a garden which is the oldest and most luxuriant in St. Helena. When he pays his first visit to Longwood, the Emperor says: "Execrable! A real hang-dog face, like that of a Venetian sbirro. He glared at me with the eye of a hyena caught in a trap. Perhaps he is my executioner."

It was not Sir Hudson Lowe's position which made him seem so obnoxious to the prisoner, who was on excellent terms with two or three army officers and with the admiral. But Lowe had been an English Fouché on the small scale, had been chief of the spy service in Italy, and had taken over his present delicate task in Fouché's spirit. It was true that the peace of Europe depended on his watchfulness; and since, in Europe, people loved sleep more than greatness, one section of the public was hounding Lowe on to be brutal.

The English press was describing the prisoner in atrocious terms. One of the most noted of English journals pilloried him as the murderer of the Jaffa prisoners, described his sisters as whores, and spoke of Murat as a waiter; a special law was passed to make any attempt at a rescue or an escape, or any assistance of escape on the high seas, a capital offence without benefit of clergy; the Prince Regent was said to have "besmirched his name" by presenting some fowling-pieces to Napoleon. The honour of England is saved only by the Whigs; and by the formal protest of two members of the House of Peers, the duke of Sussex and Lord Holland. Lady Holland ventures to send the Emperor books and fruit; another noblewoman, who in earlier days had wanted to raise a corps of amazons against him, now boldly espouses his cause in London; a great English lawyer writes twenty-one theses to prove that Napoleon's detention after peace has been signed is illegal; Thomas Moore and Lord Byron save England's credit before the tribunal of history. Germany's good fame is rescued by the fierce attacks upon Lowe in the German press, attacks that go on for years.

The governor is attacked because he has turned the whole island into a prison. He has issued regulations arranged in twenty-four paragraphs, informing the captains and crews of vessels that touch at St. Helena about all the things that are forbidden, under penalty; posters in the streets of Jamestown prohibit contact with the French; no one may approach Longwood without a written permit. Every movement of the prisoners is watched through a telescope; for six long years British officers keep their eyes riveted on the place of detention, but can rarely see anything more noteworthy than the lizards on the roof. Semaphores keep the governor informed as to all that is going on. They report: "General Bonaparte is out of bounds."–"He is accompanied."–"He is alone."–One flag was kept in reserve for a terrible emergency, to announce the news that General Bonaparte had vanished. This blue signal was never hoisted.

The "bounds" are a twelve-mile ring round Longwood, subsequently restricted to an eight-mile ring; at 9 p.m. (or, when the restrictions are increased, at sunset), a cordon of sentries at fifty paces' interval is posted. If Bertrand, who lives at Hutt's

Gate (a small villa about a mile away), is summoned by the Emperor after nightfall, he is escorted to Longwood by two soldiers with fixed bayonets–these bayonets, so runs the order, "must point at the Frenchman's heart."

The Emperor, who has for thirty years been accustomed to horseback exercise, may not go out of bounds unless accompanied by a British officer. He protest, "Not because I object to the red uniform more than another; after their baptism of fire, all soldiers are alike. But I refuse to do anything which involves the acknowledgment that I am a prisoner." When in high spirits, as he was sometimes in the early days of his captivity, he would defy the regulations. Once he gave the English officer the slip, rode across country with Gourgaud, burst into a private plantation, saying to the owner: "Don't let anyone know that we have been here!" But during the latter part of his stay at St. Helena he kept within bounds, and, indeed, rarely left the grounds of Longwood, Sometimes he would order his horse for a ride; and then, when all was ready for the start, overwhelmed with bitterness at sight of the officer who was to accompany him, he would countermand the order the re-enter the house.

The result of this lack of outdoor exercise is that his health suffers more and more. The climate alone would have brought premature death, but confinement to the house quickens the pace of his maladies. For lack of movement, his legs swell, Furthermore, while Sir Hudson Lowe is giving dinner parties, for weeks at a time Napoleon cannot get even fresh water or milk. His stomach trouble grows much worse. The sick man would like a wider bed, but there is no room for one; he must content himself with rigging up a sofa beside his camp-bed.

He and his companions have been deprived of their money. The letters he writes to France asking for funds are intercepted. Being positively in want, he has some of his silver plate put up to auction. When this is reported to the governor by semaphore, the inhabitants are forbidden to buy; Lowe himself purchases the articles at knock-down prices through an agent. Six months later, when the governor reads in the newspapers what Europe thinks of his conduct, he is greatly incensed, makes the regulations stricter than ever, supplies Longwood with uneatable meat and sour wine.

Like the villain in the folk-tale, Lowe is continually on the lookout for new ways of mortifying his prisoner. On the anniversary of Waterloo, he holds a great review close to Longwood. He invites "General Bonaparte" to Plantation House on the prince regent's birthday. Another invitation is "to meet the countess" (Lady Loudoun, wife of the governor general of India). When the mail brings him a new lampoon against Napoleon, the governor sends it to one of the Emperor's companions; but when a bust of the king of Rome, modelled by an admirer, arrives, he proposes to impound it, for documents may be hidden in its interior. He intercepts a letter from Napoleon to the prince regent, in which the prisoner begs for news of his wife and child; refuses to allow a Viennese traveller who has seen the little boy to visit Longwood; and when, through the kindly thought of a nurse and the loyalty of a valet, a look of the boy's hair at length reaches the Emperor by devious channels, Lowe sends home a detailed report concerning the obvious dangers of a conspiracy to liberate the caged eagle.

To begin with, the gaoler sees the prisoner a few times. "Throw away that cup of coffee," says the Emperor after one of these interviews; "the man was near it." From the first, Lowe does his utmost to shorten Napoleon's life. When the Emperor's vital energies begin to flag, the governor deprives him of the services of the English surgeon in whom Napoleon has confidence because this man, O'Meara, has refused any information beyond medical bulletins. O'Meara is one of those on whom Lowe has to keep a wary eye. It is not enough to surround Longwood with spies; the whole island is beset with them; they watch all the officers; and when they have nothing better to do, they watch one another. Soon a network of intrigue envelops the little house, whose interior is hung with yet another network—that of the jealousies which of old had been so rife in the Tuileries.

In the third year of the captivity, O'Meara reports to London that the Emperor's liver trouble has been greatly aggravated by the climate, the dampness of his dwelling, the lack of exercise, and the vexations to which the prisoner is subjected. It is amazing that the illness does not advance with more rapid strides. This would happen, were it not for the energy with which the patient bears up, and were it not that his body has not been weakened by any excesses. –Since this report is shown to the British Minister for Foreign Affairs, and presumably to the prince regent as well, and since in spite of it the Emperor is kept for three years more at St. Helena instead of being sent to the Azores or some other suitable place, the bad faith of Napoleon's custodians may be taken as proved –and Lowe was a worthy interpreter of his instructions.

The man's animus, and the craftiness of his designs, are well shown by a passage in one of his reports. Lowe says he will arrange matters so that Napoleon will be able to resume horse exercise. Otherwise the prisoner might die of apoplexy, and that would be extremely inconvenient. Death from some lingering disorder would be better, for then the British doctors would have no difficulty in certifying that death was due to natural causes.

In the early days at St. Helena, the Emperor compiles a long official protest (it occupies twelve pages of print); it contains all his grounds of objection, and he has a private copy made upon silk, hoping that he will be able to smuggle it away to Europe. In this document he reiterates his refusal to allow himself to be addressed as "General Bonaparte," for that implies a disavowal of his position as popularly elected Consul and Emperor. He remarks that he had proposed, as a reasonable compromise, to name himself Duroc or Muiron, after one of his two dead adjutants; but that England had refused to concede to him this "privilege accorded to persons of sovereign rank." The governor had even attempted to address him as General "Buonaparte."

In this tragicomical fashion, after bearing seven names, he returns with the eighth, to the first name by which he had been known.

Soon there are actual hostilities. The lust of battle glows once more in the prisoner. He displays a vigour of hatred which in former days he had hardly ever shown in words, for then he had simply annihilated the objects of his wrath. Longwood, too, inaugurates a system of signals, though a less conspicuous one than that of the British, who use flags and semaphores. When the governor approaches, the Emperor, warned by his vedettes, hastens indoors, and tells his servants to say he is "not at home," Once, however, he is taken by surprise in the garden; Lowe bluntly tells him that his establishment is too costly, and asks him to cut down expenses. The soldier flames in the Emperor.

"How dare to talk to me of such matters? You are nothing but a gaoler. You have only commanded brigands and deserters. I know the name of every English general who has won distinction. All I have ever heard of you is that you were one of Blücher's quilldrivers, and a robber captain who never had the honour of commanding real soldiers. –Don't send me any more food! I will take meals with those brave fellows of your 35th, over there; not one of them will refuse to share his rations will an old fellow-soldier. You can dispose of my life as you please, but not of my heart. That is still as proud on this rock as it was when all Europe was awaiting my orders. –You would stick at nothing. You would poison me if you had the courage, or were sent orders to do so!"

Without a word, the governor turns on his heel, mounts his horse, and gallops away. The Emperor compares past and present. "In the Tuileries, I should have blushed at such a scene."

For ever, the governor remains on the watch, negotiates about details with the Emperor's companions, but does not see the living Napoleon again. One day, however, Lowe makes another attempt, persists in spite of a refusal to admit him, wants to see with his own eyes that "General Bonaparte" is still there. The servant announces this importunacy. Then the governor hears the Emperor shout through the door:

"Tell him he can bring his executioner's axe if he likes. But if he wants to enter my room, he must do so over my dead body. Give me my pistols!"

Lowe was able to satisfy himself as to the general's presence when Napoleon lay dead.

XII

The Emperor rises as late as possible, so that the day may seem shorter. He rings; Marchand enters; Napoleon asks about the weather, slips on his white morning gown, and retains his head-gear–a red chequered Madras kerchief he has been wearing all night. The red kerchief seems to be a whimsical parody of the turban he once dreamed of donning! Cold douche and rub–but of eau-de-Cologne, alas, there is none! Then Dr. O'Meara pays a visit. He speaks Italian with the Emperor, and gossips over the ludicrous happenings on the island. Sometimes there is no sugar to sweeten the coffee. Has the mail ship come to port with fresh newspapers? Nothing as yet. Gourgaud arrives and writes from dictation. Where were we? The pyramids? The Emperor paces to and fro in the narrow room; a map of Egypt lies spread on the table.

He breakfasts with Gourgaud since the young man chances to be there. The talk is of artillery fire, and means of defence against it. In the afternoon, lounging on the sofa in the bedroom, he reads. The old home on the other island was certainly more comfortable. A couple of bound volumes of the "Moniteur" pass the hours. If he wearies of reading, his book will sink on to his knees, and his gaze will wander to Isabey's portrait of wife and child. Nearby, on the white lacquered shelf, are two eagles, candle-sticks, from Saint-Cloud. Between them is the marble bust of his son; and, hanging to the faded gilt frame of the mirror, four miniatures of the boy. There is also a picture of Josephine; and the gold watch of Rivoli, suspended by a chain made from the fair plaited hair of Marie Louise, hangs to the wall. There hangs also the silver alarum clock of Frederick the Great. Jetsam from the past, adorning his last, tiny bedroom!

He dressed for dinner in the old green coat; sported the decoration of the Legion of Honour; wore white silk stockings, and shoes with golden buckles. He was waited on at table by his Parisian servants in their rich liveries of green and gold. The table in his fusty dining-room was set with a dinner service of Sèvres depicting Napoleon's battles, branched candlesticks, glass globes crowned with eagles. Cipriani carved for His Majesty and served his master with great ceremony. Conversation was usually carried on in monosyllables; it concerned the cost of various things in Paris; the price of the throne and the sceptre. After dinner, the company would pass into the drawing-room for a reading of Corneille; the same plays over and over again; the Emperor read with too much feeling to read well. Sometimes his hearer would nod: "Madame, you are asleep!" or, "Gourgaud, wake up!"

"At your orders, Sire."

Occasionally he plays chess with Bertrand or reversi with Montholon. Then it is time to withdraw.

"What o'clock is it?"

"Eleven, Sire."

"Another victory over time. One day the less!"

Thus passed more than two thousand days and nights. His campaigns in Italy and Egypt and his coup d'état had taken half the time!

The best way of getting through the weary hours is by reading and dictating. For five-and-twenty years he had had no time for reading; in earlier days he had devoured and annotated a whole library of books. What is he reading today?

The things which the young man had not had an opportunity of reading. In those days, standing outside the closed portals of the world, he gathered materials from all sides, went to first-hand sources: a practically minded student. Now, standing on the further side of the portals of the world, which have now closed behind him, he surveys the material: a sceptical philosopher. In those days, he searched history; now, he searches the poets, and especially relishes those passages from the poets which apply to his own case. An epic lies behind him; in the epics of others, he tries to find his prototype.

First of all, the *Iliad.* He sometimes browses over this till midnight. "Now, at length, I understand Homer. He is, like Moses, a child of his epoch: poet, orator, historian, lawgiver, geographer, theologian.... I am specially struck by the rough manners of the heroes as compared with their lofty thoughts." Napoleon finds ease of heart in Homer. He cares less for the *Odyssey.* This seems to him no more than the story of an adventurer: he himself is more than that. Next in order of preference come Sophocles' *Œdipus*, a tragedy of banishment; *Æschylus' Agamemnon*; Milton's *Paradise Lost*; the Bible. Corneille and Racine depict, in the French style, the heroes of antiquity, who for thirty years have been his models; unending are his readings of *Cinna and Philoctète.* Ossian rises out of the roar of the Atlantic: this he reads in an Italian translation. In addition, the satirists of the social life of Europe: Molière, whom in the ardent years of conquest and success the Emperor had scorned; and Beaumarchais' *Figaro* and the *Barbier de Séville*. Finally, all the latest publications, whether memoirs or pamphlets, and, preferably, anything against himself.

The golden day for him was when the ship arrived with cases of books. In the course of his stay, he collected three thousand volumes; they were ranged on the bare damp shelves. Unfortunately, he reads so fast that a book hardly lasts him an hour, and the servant is kept busy carrying away armfuls of finished books which only a day before had been brought from the shelves. As soon as a book is read (or rejected) the Emperor flings it onto the floor.

In the early days on St. Helena, Napoleon's actions were performed at his erstwhile speed, a speed which was many times faster than that of any of his associates. He forgot that now it was expedient to go slower. The consequence was that the few duties the prisoner imposed upon himself came to an end too quickly.

When, on taking leave of the imperial guard, he had promised that, during his reign in Elba, he would record their deeds, this had only been thought of as a way out of the threatened idleness. In the days of his first exile, he had begun no such record. Now, during the first year of his second exile, he dictates the whole of his memoirs. This work too, like all else in his life, is begun on the inspiration of the moment. Some pamphlets have arrived. In one of them, his landing at Cannes in the year '15 is falsely described. He tells his doctor the true sequence of affairs; paces up and down, declaiming: motions to Montholon while continuing his tirade, and dictates, with a pause, the whole chapter dealing with his return from Elba. Separated from his archives by five thousand miles and more, lacking documents, from his unerring memory, and with an inspiration unsurpassed in the days of his greatest activity, he dictates the story of the Hundred Days. Then, suddenly, he breaks off. What's the use of it all?

Another day, the report of an incident in the Lower House excites him: he thereupon dictates for fourteen hours without a rest. Those who take down his words, collapse, and replace one another at the task. Napoleon laughs them to scorn, and continues his dictation. Or, again, he sends for Montholon in the middle of the night to pen his recollections of more recent times.

Since he loves above all to dwell on his early vietories, his friends at first advise him: "Perhaps Your Majesty might set about describing the Italian and Egyptian campaigns, and the days of the Consulate?" Set about describing! No one seems to notice, and least of all the Emperor, that these events are being spoken of as one might speak of the Thirty Years' War and just as, in those days, the man in whose heart and brain these things first took birth had projected his thoughts to the ends of the earth and had commanded his legions, so now, to the last instruments in his service, he communicates the details of his early campaigns, and in a few weeks describes how he conducted the ears from 1796 to1799. Up and down, up and down, the Emperor paces, noticing nothing, wholly absorbed.Without, doors bang, people talk; the amanuensis is disturbed by these noises; not so Napoleon.

Las Cases, after taking down the description of the battle of Arcola, exclaims: "That's finer than the *Iliad!*" The Emperor makes a wry face, and laughingly rejoins: "Bah! You still fancy yourself at court! I shall rewrite that chapter twenty times ere I shall be satisfied." This expostulation is only a defence against flattery, for he has no intention of writing the chapter again; all he does is to make certain emendations when it is read over to him.

On the other hand, he dictates the events of Waterloo over and over again. Since, in spite of his historical objectivity, he cannot understand the result of this battle which undid him, he is always searching for new formulations. When, through the good offices of some sympathetic Englishmen, an opportunity occurs for smuggling documents to Europe, he works laboriously at the battle of Waterloo in order to dim England's glory in the eyes of the European continent. But, he avers: "This task always makes me sad."

In these memoirs, there are errors here and there. They are not due to lapses of memory, but to the author's desire to emphasize his own place in history. Such errors are not more serious than those to be found in Cæsar's works, are not serious errors at all. When he erroneously records that in his lieutenant days he received the gold medal from the academy of Lyons for his solution of a problem, and states that the money prize was of great use to his mother; when telling the story of his battles he ascribes to himself certain deeds which, in reality, had been performed by his generals (at Marengo, for instance); when he invents a treaty in which the tsar, before the Russian campaign, is made to propose the division of Europe we have inaccurate statements regarding the individuals concerned, but the broad facts are correct. It is true that, in accordance with his conception of the hero, he formally idealizes the hero's deeds; but he seems to us to lose more than he gains thereby. Since he is describing the period of his rise to power, he cannot materially falsify the facts! The immeasurable consequences of his first victory were bound to give rise, on the one hand, to a certain boastfulness, and, on the other, to detraction. But these volumes, which deal for the most part with the exploits of the commander, furnish but little real knowledge of Napoleon. Where we have to seek for the true Napoleon is in the memoirs of those who had the privilege of recording his conversations in exile.

"I command, or else I hold my peace."

His visitors tell him interesting things. An English admiral, whose vessel had been lying of the coast during the battle of Waterloo, assures the Emperor that Wellington had already given orders to ship the English army because Blücher did not arrive. When his companions inform him of the enthusiasm with which the enemy officers were filled after their interview with the Emperor, he says, assuming the role of the revolutionary: "Of course, these people belong to us. They all come from England's third estate, and are the natural foes of their haughty aristocracy."

All the men in the services are on his side. English sailors, on shore leave for a day or two, will prowl round the place all night. At the first opportunity, they pounce upon him, stuttering incoherent words, presenting him with flowers. The Emperor claps them pleasantly on the shoulder. When the garrison is changed, he receives the members of the officers' corps, exactly as though they had been Frenchmen and he their army chief. They form a semicircle; he asks, "How many years' service; how many wounds? I was greatly pleased with the 53rd regiment. I shall always be delighted to hear of good strokes of luck coming in its way. You are sad, Admiral Bingham, that these brave soldiers are leaving you. To comfort your heart, my Lady must bear you a little Bingham!" The army men laugh. The admiral blushes. When, next day, the transport hoists sail, the men give the prisoner three hearty cheers. A few months later, all Europe is agog with the anecdote.

On another occasion, he sees a medal displayed on the chest of a captain, half raises it, and reads: Victory at Vittoria. The Emperor allows the decoration to slip from his fingers and passes without a word to the next visitor.

Each of England's allies sends a commissioner to the island. They are there merely to gratify the curiosity of their sovereigns. The prisoner refuses them access to his presence, and, though they are here on this desolate rock with the sole purpose of seeing that he is in safe custody, during all the years of their sojourn they not one soul that does not differ from all the rest. Those who fail to recognise this, make a great many mistakes. Had Tobias been a Brutus, he would have hurled himself on death; an Æsop, and he would have been governor by now; a good Christian, and he would have blessed his chains. But he is only poor Tobias, so he is none of these things, merely bows his head in his simplicity and goes on with his daily task."

The two continue their walk: "Certainly it is a long way from poor Tobias to King Richard. But the deed which brought the fellow here is no less shameful, for this man had his family, his friends, his own life. What a crime to have condemned him to slave on this island until the day of his death!" Suddenly, Napoleon stops short, and eyes Las Cases quizzically:

"I read from your face that you are thinking he is not the only sufferer of the kind on this island." Las Cases nods assent, and the Emperor bursts out with a youth's ardour. There is no warrant for such a comparison! True, the violence done to us is more refined in its cruelty, but, in compensation, we are more distinguished victims.... The world has its eyes fixed on us. We are the martyrs of an immortal cause! Millions weep for us, the fatherland sighs, the spirit of glory mourns.... Adversity, too, has its heroism and its fame. Had I died on the throne, surrounded by all the emblems of power, I should have remained a riddle to many. Today the wrappings have been stripped from me; thanks to my misfortunes, everyone can judge me in my nakedness."

Subsequently, the Emperor buys the slave, wishing to send him back to his own land and his own folk, but the governor forbids the repatriation: "It is plain to me that General Bonaparte is trying to win the hearts of the coloured population, in the hope of setting up a second Negro empire, as in San Domingo."

Tobias, therefore, remains a captive; a slave in a far country, like the Emperor.

XIII

"I am very old to make a journey of two thousand leagues. Perhaps I should die on the way; but, never mind, I should die nearer you."

Thus writes his mother. The Emperor reads the letter again and again, when it is delivered to him a year after it was penned. The powers forbade the journey; who could tell, the old lady might concoct a plan for his escape! Letizia had been banished from France when the other members of her family were expelled. For the second time in her life, she is unable to go to her island home: The first time had been long ago when Corsica was in revolt; now, Europe stands in the way. She, therefore, goes to Rome, where the moral power of the Pope upholds her; always making fresh attempts to secure her son's removal to a more healthy abiding place. Although the tsar is favourable to such a transfer, Habsburg and England are determined Napoleon shall die; so there is nothing more to be done. Neither mother nor any of the brothers and sisters is allowed to send money to the exile.

When the monarchs assemble in Aix-la-Chapelle for the congress, Letizia writes to the princes: "A mother, more bowed with grief than words can tell, has long been hoping that the meeting of your imperial and royal highnesses would give her back her life. It is impossible that the captivity of Emperor Napoleon should not come up for discussion. Your magnanimity, your power, and your memory of earlier events, will surely incline Your Imperial and Royal Majesties to work for the liberation of a prince for whom you once professed friendship. I pray to God and to you, for you are God's representatives on earth. Interests of States have their limits. Posterity, which confers immortality, admires a generous conqueror."

No answer.

Later the captive learns that his mother has been accused of fostering a conspiracy in Corsica. She is said to have provided money amounting to millions. The Pope is ordered to send his secretary of State to see the old lady and to make enquiries. Letizia gives the emissary the following message: "Tell the Pope, and may the monarchs mark my words: If I were so fortunate as to possess all these millions they have credited me with, I should certainly not spend them in buying champions for my son's cause. He has enough of them already. I would, rather, equip a fleet capable of rescuing him from the island where he is unjustly detained."

What a feeling of pride and elation fills the son's heart as he reads his mother's words! But he never hears of Letizia's bitter remark to an Austrian noble: "Why is my daughter-in-law amusing herself in Italy instead of joining her husband in St. Helena?"

Round what sun are the other planets turning? What an anticlimax!

Lucien and Joseph have gone to America, and are later joined by Jerome. They assume exotic titles. The Spanish revolutionaries have offered their ex-king the crown of Mexico. This piece of news excites the prisoner:

"Joseph will refuse. He is too fond of the pleasures of life to bother himself again with the burden of a crown—and yet, it would be a stroke of luck for England that the whole problem of Spanish America should be solved in this way. For if Joseph were to become king of Mexico a breach with France and Spain would be inevitable. For myself, his acquiescence would be weighty with consequences. He loves me and would use his position as a weapon to coerce England into treating me differently. Unfortunately, he is sure to refuse." Thus quickly and hopefully does Napoleon, in the first year of his captivity, toy with every fresh opportunity.

The other brothers and sisters retire into obscurity. Jerome alone lives to be an old man, and, in the days of the third Napoleon, appears once more at court. The Emperor receives few letters from his brothers and sisters. Caroline begs her mother to send more money. Letizia refuses: "All I have belongs to the Emperor, from whom I have received all I possess." To Lucien she writes: "When one is no longer king, one makes oneself a laughing-stock if one tries to live ostentatiously. Rings may adorn the fingers; but, if they fall off, the fingers still remain." Hortense and Pauline once more play comedy as they had done at Malmaison.

Other tidings give Napoleon food for thought. Bernadotte becomes king. And Desiree? At last Napoleon's early love wears a crown; she also lives to see the Second Empire. Countess Walewska; now a widow, marries a French nobleman. He approves the step, passes her situation in review, considers all he has done for her son, and then says complacently: "She is rich, and must have saved." The tactless Gourgaud makes answer: "Your Majesty paid Madame Walewska ten thousand francs a month." The Emperor blushes, and asks with embarrassment: "How do you know that?"

King Murat and Marshal Ney are both shot after court martial. Their master accepts their fate with soldierly fortitude. His only annoyance is that Murat should have been such a fool as to land in Calabria. He bears his brother-in-law no grudge. Even Marmont, who lives happily under the Bourbons, comes in for no more reproach than: "I am sorry for Marmont: I was really fond of him. He's not a bad fellow. They appealed to him through his feelings. He fancied he was to be saviour of his country, and behaved like a madman. He would have done better to shoot himself.... Human nature is weak."

And yet it is precisely Marmont who stifles every movement which might be of advantage to the exile. Murmurings against the Bourbon ruler spread throughout the land. But when once more, the émigrés and the members of the new nobility are placed in great positions, notwithstanding their lack of qualifications for such posts, and a Richelieu is given high office in spite of his long absence from France and his ignorance of France affairs; when Lafayette, the veteran fighter for liberty, becomes leader of the proletariat and makes ready for a new resolution, gathering his forces in the clubs and even in the schools, and preparing among the troops "the men of the coming day," to clear out the Bourbons, who can only maintain their position by the aid of foreign armies; when the radical provinces, eager to flaunt the tricolour cockade, rally in support of Napoleon II –it is Marmont, Bonaparte's eldest comrade, who crushes the movement, and thereafter becomes minister.

The Emperor composedly reads that Louis XVIII has dissolved the Chambers because many of the members favour Orleans or Napoleon. Executions for treason are the order of the day. But who is the most trusted associate of the Bourbon? A little nobody of a Corsican, whom Letizia once upon a time had made her private-secretary–a sinecure job created to provide the man with a livelihood. Since all these events take place during the first year, the Emperor is filled with hope, and meditates upon the chances of a fresh revolution.

"What a cruel decree of fate that just at this moment I should be held prisoner! Who is there to set himself at the head of things? Who will be there to save thousands of the bravest from the scaffold?" He stays alone in his room until the morrow, when he speaks absently of Elba. Soon stranger ships heave in sight, the prisoner counts the shots. What is happening? The Emperor sends his friends to gather tidings; they hear nothing; but hope is strong. "What children we are to be sure," he exclaims next day. "And I, instead of giving a good example, am no better than the rest of you. Were I in America, I should think of nothing but my garden."

Nevertheless, he would not have gone to America. He owns as much when he says: "If I were in America with Joseph, instead of suffering here, nobody would ever think of me, and my cause would be lost. I may have another fifteen years of life, but I am doomed to die here–unless France should summon me."

These hopes are not unfounded. England considers it wise to increase the garrison from two hundred men to three thousand, in order to keep guard on one individual, although the cost of the troops in St. Helena is £ 320,000 a year. Still, there are possibilities, for the soldiers are whole-heatedly on his side. On one occasion six officers were arrested. They had come from Rio de Janeiro, and had planned to get the Emperor away in a kind of submarine. Again, two captains, travellers to India on a ship which has touched at the island, make him proposals for an escape: Napoleon listens attentively, but decides not to accept. On a third occasion, Montholon breaks in on the Emperor while he is at work with Gourgaud to remind his master that the passport of a certain individual expires in an hour's time and a decision must be made. Montholon writes; "It had been proposed to take the Emperor to America for the sum of one million francs payable on landing. The Emperor's word would suffice. Unfortunately I may not divulge any more of the scheme, lest I expose the originator, for whose loyalty to the Emperor we must be eternally grateful. The Emperor listened to me, and considered all I had to say: he paced to and fro several times in silence, asked Gourgaud and myself for our opinions. He took no part in the discussion. In the end, he said: "You must decline the offer."

There he stands, he has not been captive a year as yet, passably well in health, athirst for action, goaded by the pinpricks of a mighty government and a puny governor. Before him opens out the possibility of escape, escape with the aid of English officers. The fact that risk is attached does not alarm one who is used to bold enterprises. There he is, dictating the story of his youth, when suddenly, at the end of his career, a friend makes proposals that are certainly not cobwebs of the brain. Napoleon is silent, he questions, he is silent again. Then: "You must decline the offer." Why?

Because France is once more in a state of unrest, and so he decides to stay where he is. He is so sure of a change of feeling among the people that, later, when a ship is sighted and signals to the station, the Emperor says: "Perhaps the vessel brings news of my recall. If the prince regent dies, the young queen will summon me to England. She was always against my being sent to St. Helena." When, on the outbreak of fresh revolts in Paris, his companions mention the possibility of France demanding his return, he concedes the point, adding:

"But what can they hope from my return? That I should again conduct wars? I am too old. That I should seek for fresh glories? I am sated with them.... It will be much better for, my son that I should stay here. If Christ had not died upon the cross, he would not have become the Son of God. My martyrdom will give the crown back to my son, if he lives."

Napoleon's feeling for the dynasty is as deep as ever. His preoccupation with the thought of founding a line overpowers in his maturer years, his impulse to action, to adventure, and even to win fame.

Though he is inspired with these lofty moods of hope and heroical renunciation, nevertheless despondency overwhelms him at times; then he becomes greatly depressed, and the most trifling upset in the household will seem an intolerable burden. When Bertrand stays away from dinner in a pet, the Emperor is out of sorts for days: "I know that I have fallen from my high estate, but that one of my nearest companions should rub it in is dreadful...." He groans. Las Cases offers to intervene. "No, I forbid it. I had to say that much. But now all is forgotten and I shall behave as though I had noticed nothing." If travellers should wish to see him on such days he refuses, saying: "Tell them, dead men do not receive visitors." Occasionally Napoleon broods alone for the whole evening, sends at last for one of his companions, says a word or two, and dismisses him.

A quarrel arises between Montholon and Gourgaud as to whose room shall be furnished first, the Emperor has to mediate, the countess weeps, the Emperor proposes a game of chess. Dinner. A reading from the Book of Esther. Sometimes these scenes verge on the grotesque: a cow has escaped, the Emperor shows his vexation, Gourgaud sits glum throughout dinner because he is responsible for the cow, and is feeling aggrieved by his master's anger. After dinner, the Emperor speaks of Islam and his preferences for the Mohammedan faith, then passes to a discussion of the trinity; finally he withdraws, making painful attempts to conceal his angry mood and muttering between his teeth: "Moscow! Five hundred thousand men!"

Gourgaud, who had left him overnight in an agreeable state of excitement, finds him next day in a gloomy temper: "What sort of an education will they give my son? Will they teach him to loathe his father? Hateful thought!" When Las Cases, who has copied out the chapter or Waterloo, deplores that victory should have been snatched from the Emperor's grasp, Napoleon makes no reply, but says to Las Cases' son in a voice which seems to come from a great distance: "My lad, go and fetch *Iphigenia in Aulis*; that will do us good." Or he has Racine's *Andromache* read to him.

> I am come to the place where my son
> lies captive: for one moment only,
> allow my tears to flow with his!
> This is all that is left to me
> of Hector and of Troy. Permit me, Lord,
> to visit him once on every day....

But the Emperor breaks in on the reading with the cry:

> "Enough! Leave me; I would be alone!"

XIV

With the growing inactivity and boredom, the moods of this tortured heart become more and more agonizing; this many toned instrument can no longer be controlled; discords arise.

He has been an emperor! How can he cases to play the part to which the society of a handful of courtiers and the degrading mockery of the enemy constrain him? In order to protest against the use of the title of general and against the illegality of his captivity, he drives out, at first, in full imperial grandeur, his carriage drawn by six horses, and an equerry in uniform riding at each door. His companions appear before him in general's uniform or in court dress: no one opens conversation uninvited; when he takes his walks in the garden his suite does not approach till he gives a sign; visits are announted by an adjutant general, booted, and wearing a sword. When Gourgaud rises as Countess Montholon enters the room, he is reproved for this breach of etiquette.

Meanwhile he makes fun of the whole thing, mockingly calls Gourgaud "my grand master of the horse," or announces at table: "I have been anointed by the Pope; thereby I have become a bishop, and have the power to consecrate you as priests." When he teases his friends about their all being in the "Dictionary of Weathercocks," whose pages he is at the moment fluttering. Gourgaud ventures to say that the Emperor himself deserves a place in it. "Oh; and pray why?"

"Because you first of all recognised the republic, Sire, and yet, later, you were the crown."

"You are right. Oh, well, the Empire was certainly the best of the republics!"

At the feast of Epiphany, he has a cake made for the children. Then he crowns little Napoleon Bertrand as king. When he is informed that there has been a complaint from the governor about the expenses of his household, and that, now that the price of meat has risen to forty sous, they must be more moderate in their consumption, he turns the matter off with a laugh, saying: "Parbleu! You might have answered that it costs us more than a crown."

Never before has so much self-control been forced on him. Impassively he reads Lowe's answer to a statement of grievances from Bertrand, who had said something about "the Emperor." The governor writes that he is not aware of the presence of any emperor on the island.–The prisoner asks Gourgaud to order his horse to be saddled. Gourgaud replies that he has not seen the animal for three days, since the blacksmith insists on being paid three napoleons before he will send it back. The Emperor masters his anger, and says nothing more at the time; but next day he bursts out at Gourgauds "Why did you insult me by talking to me about the blacksmith's bill?" The day before, by a superhuman effort, he had managed to restrain his wrath, but by the torturing thoughts of the intervening hours his pride had been broken. The adjutant's sullen reply had disturbed the Emperor's equanimity quite as much as Austria's desertion had done in earlier years.

A soldier and a southron, he is choked sometimes by the passion for vengeance. On one occasion, when uneatable meat is served at dinner, he contents himself with the remark: "I should trouble little about myself, if I could only feel sure that some days our humiliations would be proclaimed to the world, so that those who are responsible for them would be covered with shame!"

With a sublimity of spirit which grows in him now, he tries to moderate the natural rebelliousness of his disposition: "I am living here under a weight, so to speak; a weight which compresses the spring, but does not break it. Resignation– that is the dominion of reason, the real triumph of the soul." This masterful man does his utmost to regulate his own conduct in accordance with the foregoing axiom. Subsequently he says: "Misfortune has its good side; it teaches us truths.... For the first time, I am able to contemplate history as a philosopher."

For the first time, too, he is able to contemplate the present with a tranquil mind. During the early weeks of his stay on the island, when he was out walking with a pretty young Englishman, he conversed with her agreeably about various topics: how the climate was bad for the complexion: Ossian; the plantations. At this moment some Negro slaves carrying heavy boxes crossed the path, and the lady called to them imperiously: "Get out of the way!"

The Emperor interposed "But, Madame, please remember that the men are carrying burdens!"

Collapse of lady! Yet Napoleon Bonaparte himself would not have been so considerate in the days before he came to St. Helena.

In all matters now, except when he is playing a shadow emperor in pursuance of his feud with Lowe, Napoleon adopts a simplicity of life which outdoes that even of his poorest days as a lieutenant. When for some time there has been very little to eat, and the cook had had to eke things out with French beans, he eats them enthusiastically, praises the dish and the cooking.

"In Paris, I could get along with twelve francs a day. Dinner frs. 1.50; reading room; theatre in the evening, pit; I should hire a room for frs. 20 a month. I should only want one servant; and I should associate exclusively with people of like fortune. One can be happy in any station in life. When my mother sang lullabies over my cradle, there was not a word about what I was destined to become. I believe 'Monsieur Bonaparte' would have been quite as happy as 'Emperor Napoleon.' Everything in life is relative."

His doctor has a fainting fit. Coming to himself, he finds that he is being attended to, not a servant, but by the Emperor in person. Napoleon has lifted him on to the bed, has unfastened the collar of his shirt, and is kneeling beside him, administering vinegar. –When Cipriani, the Corsican servant, is dying, the Emperor asks the doctor whether a visit from the master would stimulate the man's flagging forces.

"The excitement would kill him."

"Oh, well, I suppose I had better not go."

When playing reversi, he establishes a bank. For whose benefit? The money is to be used to buy the freedom of the most beautiful female slave on the island. One evening, his companions find him at work beside the lamp, slowly and carefully stitching the pages of a manuscript.

Sometimes, however, his dreams reawaken, and flutter against the bars of the cage. "I wish they would transfer me to a desert island, where I could have too thousand people of my own choice, with muskets and cannon. I should found a glorious colony, and should end my days happily in that model land. There I should not find it necessary to be at grips all the time with antiquated ideas." Having said this apropos of nothing in particular, he passes on to the details of the scheme, dictating specifications–how much money and stores would be needed for the founding of his colony.

A chained sculptor, his plastic impulse must be content with such outlets in tne world of imagination; but, side by side with these capriccios, he displays a heroic simplicity. One day, during

But he will coldly reckon up the cases in which he has failed to understand men, coming at this late hour to views which the ablest observers had held while he was still on the throne. The reader who knows his story will require no comment on the remarks that follow.

"I considered Emperor Francis a good man; but he was only a blockhead, and in Metternich's hands he became an instrument for my destruction." – "I ought to have left Talleyrand at his post. What concern was it of mine that he was plundering the foreign chancelleries. I should have been content with having him closely watched. He served me well, as long as he could hope to make anything out of me. If I had kept him in office, I should still have been on the throne."–"If only that man Fulton, with his steamboat, had been right, I should have been master of the world. But those idiots of savants made fun of his invention, just as they make fun of electricity. All the same, gigantic powers are hidden in steam and electricity!"

He regrets that at Tilsit he had decided to maintain the Hohenzollern dynasty. He regrets having crossed the Memel too early; having crossed it in 1812, before he had settled matters in Spain. He regrets that, in defiance of Carnot's advice, he began the last campaign too early, and he regrets that at Waterloo he did not send the guard forward soon enough. Most of all, he regrets having, when his power was finally broken, entrusted himself to England, instead of to the tsar, or, better still, to the United States. Always, when he hears of crises in France, he regrets that he did not go to America.

"From that vantage ground I should have been able to guard France against humiliation from abroad, reaction from within; the dread of my return would have sufficed. In America I should have established the centre of a new French fatherland. Within a year, I should have had sixty thousand men grouped round me.... It would have been the most natural place of refuge–a land of vast expanses where a man can live in freedom. If I had had a fit of the blues, I should have mounted a horse, ridden hundreds of miles, enjoyed travel with the ease of a private individual, lost amid the crowd. In Europe I was too popular; bound up, in one way or another, with every nation.... As a fugitive, and disguised, I could certainly have escaped to the United States; but both expedients would have been undignified. I put my trust in the approach of danger, thinking that the nation would be forced to turn to me as its saviour; that is why I stayed as long as possible at Malmaison and in Rochefort. The destiny that brought me to St. Helena was the outcome of those feelings."

This is the most productive of his meditations. The other mistakes of his career had entailed such complicated consequences that it was impossible for him to trace what might have been had he acted otherwise. But the final resolve at Rochefort had, as its inevitable upshot, brought him to this rock. In that respect, therefore, his mind was continually busied with alternative possibilities. Although, when in fancy he roams across the American prairies, he sometimes pictures himself as founding new States there, and sometimes as galloping through the wilds, we may ascribe it to the infinite variety of human passions that he should at the same time justify his final blunder on patriotic grounds.

His critical faculty is most keenly at work when he is pondering his dynastic aspirations. In the last days of the Empire, he had confided his doubts to a few choice spirits; now, when it is too late, he freely acknowledges his error "I was a softy where my family was concerned; by sticking to their point they could get anything out of me. What terrible mistakes I made there! If my brothers had communicated a common impulse to the masses I placed under their rule, we should have been able to make our way to the ends of the earth!.... I was not so lucky as Genghis Khan, whose four sons vied with one another in their father's service. If I made any one king, he instantly regarded himself as king by divine right; the mere word was as infective as the plague. The new king was no longer my representative, but became a fresh enemy; instead of serving me, he wanted to make himself independent. I was the only stumbling block in his path. In the twinkling of an eye, they all became kings warranted genuine; under my protection, they all tasted the sweets of dominion. I alone bore the of independent character. They are sitting over a jug of porter, drinking together. Napoleon suddenly puts his question:

"What sort of a man did you think I was before you came to know me? Speak your mind frankly!"

O'Meara gives the description of an amoral chimera, a man capable of any crime to achieve his end.

"I expected as much!" exclaims the Emperor. "Probably many Frenchmen think the same. They'll be saying: Yes, he climbed to the top of the ladder of fame, by his own efforts; but in his climb he had to commit many atrocities." Thereupon he launches forth into vehement self-defence.

One night he summons Montholon in order to dictate the thoughts which throng his sleepless brain. He sets down how he was ever inclined to peace, how before a battle and after a victory he always entered negotiations. Or he compares the two revolutions, adding: "Cromwell achieved his aim when he was in the full maturity of his age, and attained to the highest rung of the ladder through cunning and hypocrisy. But Napoleon came to the fore as a stripling, and his first steps are illuminated with deeds of glory.... Whose blood have I shed? Who can boast that in my place he would have acted differently? What epoch confronted with similar difficulties has ever come through with such blameless results?.... I believe it to be without parallel in history that a plain man should have attained to such amazing power without committing a single crime. In face of death itself, I could make no other declaration."

Something now occurs which takes us wholly by surprise. Instead of, in the midst of this harangue, laying the blame for ill success on others, instead of allowing his inborn misanthropy to storm the heavens in resentment, he shows us that his days of exile have fostered his sense of justice. He who, for a lifetime, had declared that cupidity lay at the root of all men's endeavours, and had dealt with his fellows on that presupposition, now becomes a cautious analyst; the man of power becomes a philosopher; Napoleon becomes tolerant.

Now, he declares that mankind is prone to gratitude rather than to ingratitude; the only trouble is, people always expect more thanks than the deed is worth. Las Cases informs us that his greatest censure nowadays is expressed by silence. He defends even those who were faithless: Augereau, Berthier, were not equal to the magnitude of their positions; he excuses his brothers. From the altitude of these judgments, he surveys the wide perspective with a tolerant eye. We seem to be listening to the imprisoned Socrates when we read:

"It is difficult to give people their due.... Do they even know themselves? Those who forsook me would never have believed, in the days of their good fortune, that a time would come when they would deny me.... Our last trials were more than human nature could endure. As a matter of fact, I was left in the lurch rather than actually betrayed, just as Peter denied his master.... Perhaps they have already shed tears of repentance. Who ever had more friends and more adherents than I? Who has ever been more beloved? ... My fate might have been far worse!"

XVI

The Emperor's companions keep diaries. He is well aware of this; he even has a look into one of them, but he reserves his thoughts. As a realist he calculates the monetary worth of these records, and he foretells what the writers will earn when they publish their books after his death; his only mistake is that he underestimates the amount. He bequeaths to each of his secretaries those portions of his writings which he has dictated to them severally. But he is correct in his estimates of the incalculable value the diaries will have for posterity in the study of himself.

Accustomed as he is to dictate. he shapes his sentences carefully even when conversing, so that his hearers may record his sayings with advantages. The value to future generations is thus enhanced, and these summaries of his thoughts raise him above his present wearisome existence. His passionate feeling for historical events drives him to this self-expression, no less than regard for those who shall come after.

Five days pass, sometimes, without his seeing anybody; he reads and he writes nothing. The future gives him no more food for thought. But during these periods of seclusion he surveys his life as a whole. Then his soul is shaken, and his lightning glance searches through and through his personality for a hundred hours at a stretch. Never has any man before him had to submit to such a scrutiny. The tension of his being is at these moments greater than at Austerlitz, more elemental than in the Council of State; he is a bound Prometheus, one who wishes to promote human happiness; and, shackled to the rock, he groans. Yet he is but a little man in an old green coat! The visions, the dreams, which for twenty years he was able and willing to conjure into reality, he now dissects into ideas. Thus, in the end, he becomes the severest commentator upon his own life story.

A book arrives. It is a collection of his manifestoes and decrees. He reads. Then he throws the volume aside, strides to and fro, and says to Las Cases:

"Every future historian will have to allow me my share.... Facts speak for themselves. I closed up the chasm of anarchy, and put an end to chaos. I cleansed the revolution from the filth it had accumulated, I ennobled the peoples, I stabilized the thrones. I encouraged all those who had talents, rewarded every merit, and widened the boundaries of fame and glory.... Could not historians protect me against many grave charges?... If I am accused of despotism, they can claim that dictatorship was necessary in the circumstances. Is it freedom I attacked? They can answer that anarchy was still threatening on our very threshold. Love of war? I was never the aggressor. Striving for world dominion? This arose accidentally, because of the conditions of the time. Too ambitious? Yes, true indeed. But my ambition was of the sublimest; to found the kingdom of reason, with full development and unrestricted enjoyment of all the human faculties. The historian may deplore that such ambition could not wholly attain its goal." After a momentary silence, he concludes: "There, my dear fellow, in a few words, you have my entire story."

Here he is on the defensive. But neither in such moods nor in any other do we ever hear him rave enthusiastically over his battles. In all the six years of his captivity, he does not seem, even once, to have sung the praises of General Bonaparte. If he is summing up what he achieved, he says:

"My fame does not rest upon my forty victorious battles, nor does it lie in the fact that I bent the monarchs to my will. Waterloo will wipe out the memory of so many victories; the last act makes one forget the first. What will never pass away, is my book of laws, the minutes of my Council of State, my correspondence with my ministers.... Through its simplicity my code of laws has had more effect than any civil codes before it; the schools I have set up, my methods of instruction, are creating a new generation; crime has decreased during my rule, whereas in England crime has become more prevalent. ...*I wanted to found a European system, a European code of laws, a European court of appeal; there would have been but one people throughout Europe.*"

He reads in an English newspaper that Napoleon has hidden away vast treasures. He leaps to his feet, and dictates, to the man who happens to be his companion at the moment, these splendid sentences:

"Would you like to know about Napoleon's treasures? Yes, they are vast, but they are not hidden way. The harbours of Antwerp and Flushing, where there is room for the largest fleets in the world, harbours which are open all through the winter; the waterworks at Dunkirk, Havre, and Nice; the huge docks at Cherbourg; the port of Venice; the high roads form Antwerp to Amsterdam, from Mainz to Metz, and from Bordeaux to Bayonne; the passes over the Simplon, Mont Cenis, La Corniche, and Mont Genèvre, which open up the Alps in four directions, and excel all the constructions of the Romans. Then there are the roads from the Pyrenees to the Alps, from Parma to Spezia, and from Savona into Piedmont; the bridges across the Seine, and the bridges of Tours and of Lyons; ... the Rhine-Rhone canal and the draining of the Pontine marshes;... the re-establishment of the Church destroyed by the revolution; the setting up of new industries; the new Louvre; warehouses, streets, the water supply of Paris, the quays along the Seine;... the revival of the weaving mills in Lyons; more than four hundred sugar factories; the repair and embellishment of the royal palaces at the cost of frs. 50,000,000, and the refurnishing of them out of Napoleon's private fortune at a cost of frs. 60,000,000; the redemption of the only remaining crown diamond, the Regent, which had been pawned to Jews in Berlin for frs. 3,000,000; the Napoleon Museum, where all the works of art had been obtained by purchase or by the peace treaties; many millions for the support of agriculture and horse breeding ... These are the treasures of Napoleon, which represent an expenditure of milliards, and will outlast the centuries! These are the monuments which defy calumny ... Moreover, history will record that they were all erected while long wars were being waged, and without loans being raised to pay for them!"

There he is in his little room, in the narrow house, on the rock in the midst of the sea, defending his work, and with a regal gesture, shaking things together pell-mell—main roads, sugar factories, crown diamonds, and the Catholic Church! Foreseeing the criticism of history, he is fully aware of the truth about himself: though a century will elapse before posterity will begin to see in him something more than the military commander whose fame (as he says) was dimmed by the failure at Waterloo.

One evening, after dinner, the question assumes a personal aspect. An inquisitive member of his circle has asked when he was happiest, and all present give their ideas. Napoleon tells them that he was made content by his marriage and when his son was born, "I cannot say happy, but content."

"When you were First Consul?"

"I was not yet sure enough of myself."

"At the coronation?"

"In Tilsit, I think. By that time I had learned the vicissitudes of fortune; Preussisch-Eylau had been a warning to me, and nevertheless I had won a victory there; I had dictated the terms of peace; the tsar and the king of Prussia were paying court to me. But no, I am wrong, that was not the best. The happiest days I ever knew were after my first victories in Italy, when the masses surrounded me, shouting: 'Evviva il liberatore!' I was only twenty-six, but I foresaw what I might become. It was as if I were being lifted up into the air, and the world were disappearing beneath my feet!"

With a sudden transition, he hums an Italian song, and then stands up, saying: "Ten o'clock. Time for bed."

How pale do these comparisons of happy moments seem in contrast with the fiery rhapsody of his deeds! It was in the work he did that was concentrated the life happiness of the man who enjoyed nothing but the completed action. He surveys his past; doubts this suggestion and that, saying that he was no more than "content," and finally hears again the first chorus of evvivas. In imagination he is again the youth soaring upwards; and in the evening of his life, spent in this tropical exile, the vision of fame floats once more before his eyes. That was what the disciple of the classical heroes had set out to win–fame!

Fame, whose lure he had felt for the first time on the island of his birth, still allures him on the island to which he had been banished. Moreover, he knows that it is the glamour of war-like fame which has made him most widely known among men. He asks whether there can be any one in Paris who has never heard of Napoleon; he does not really mean Paris, but the world. When Las Cases tells him how, in the remotest valleys of Wales, shepherds had asked for news of the First Consul, or how yellow men in China had spoken of him in the same breath with Tamerlane, then the Emperor Napoleon forgets the shame and the weariness of his life on the rock, and knows his happiest moments. If he is in such a mood, some trifling item in the newspaper may arouse a flight of fancy:

"Yes, the reaction is doomed! Nothing can destroy great principles; they will endure for ever in the light of the wonderful deeds we have done! The first stains have been washed out in the waters of glory, and now the principles are immortal. ... Adorned with our laurels, acclaimed by the peoples, sanctified by treaties with the powers, they are breathed from all lips and hearkened to by all ears.... They will rule the world; will become the faith and the morality of all the peoples; and, say what you will, this new epoch is associated with my name. I lighted the torch; friends and foes alike will acclaim me the leading champion, the greatest representative of the new principles. After my death, for the nations I shall still be the sun of their rights; my name will be the war cry of their struggle, the slogan of their hopes!"

Still, these heroics about himself lack the right conclusion. Politically he overestimates the value of his martyrdom; it has not been able to save the dynasty; but he does not foresee the effect which this last act of the drama will have upon the hearts of men. A soldier's death looms before his eyes; he had sought it under fire on the last battle fields; again and again he turns his own story over in his mind, in search of the romantic moment which would have been the most appropriate close; he often recurs to the subject in conversation. Like a playwright he looks for the fitting climax: "I ought to have died in Moscow. Till then my fame was undiminished.... If only heaven had sent me a bullet in the Kremlin! My dynasty would have been established; history would have compared me with Alexander and Cæsar. Whereas, as things have turned out, I am practically nothing." On another occasion he thinks that death shortly before attaining the goal, would have had even more effect on posterity; "Had I fallen at Borodino, my death would have been like Alexander's. A death at Waterloo would have been a good one. But perhaps Dresden would have been better. No, no, at Waterloo would have been best. The love of the people, their mourning!"

Once he summarizes the whole as follows:

"Taking it all in all, what a ballad my life had been!"

XVII

Sunrise. A man stands at the door of a house where all the inmates are still asleep. He wears a white coat, red slippers, a broad-brimmed straw hat; he holds a spade in one hand, and rings a huge bell with the other, rousing the sleepers to work. A wall is to be raised, a ditch lengthened; land is to be reclaimed from the inroads of the sea; this is the scheme. Doors open, tent-flaps are flung back, and from all directions men flock to the master's side. They are armed with shovels, rakes, axes, and are eager to carry out the Emperor's commands.

He resembles the centenarian Faust.

The last year of his life has opened. He has made up his mind, come what may, to stay on this rock; and, since no one offers to make a verdant bower for him, he has decided, after yearlong feuds and resistance to his plans, to make a garden for himself. A half-circle of wall is to protect the growths from too much sun, from the trade wind, and from the watchful eye of the sentry. Cisterns are to store rain water; within the ramparts, earth is distributed for the flowers and the bushes, four-and-twenty large trees are planted; peaches, oranges, and, in front of his window, an oak. The trees have been imported from the Cape, and are brought to Longwood with the aid of the English artillery regiment–an old acquaintance of the Peninsular War. Chinese gardeners, Indian coolies, French servants, English stablemen, all help in the work; the doctor must take a hand too, with Montholon and Bertrand; and when the English officer on duty draws near, he see the Emperor take a turf from his grand marshal's hands, fit it into its place on the bank, and pat it down carefully. But since Napoleon knows that transplanted soldiers must be especially well treated in foreign parts, he waters the square of grass assiduously.

The work goes on for seven months; and, when it is finished, the garden, so swiftly brought into being on the rock, is regarded as a wonder. The governor's daughter comes secretly to look at it. This is the last miracle wrought by Napoleon.

It is because he has become aware of the decline in his energies, that he has decided to beautify the place in which he is to pass the remainder of his days. He is overheard murmuring to himself Voltaire's line: "See Paris once more? I cannot hope for that." When his birthday comes round, he says it will be the last, gives the children presents; "at dinner, where we were all assembled, he beamed on us like a father in the family circle."

That autumn, he takes his last ride, a long one, going out of bounds for the first time after four years.

He seldom dictates now, but has a fancy to do so sometimes at night when sleep will not come; dictates comments on the battles of Turenne, Frederick, and Cæsar; literary criticism upon Voltaire's *Mahomet* and Virgil's *Æneid*; remarks on suicide, which he had condemned long ago when he had been a lieutenant. His best secretaries, Gourgaud and La Cases, have left the island long since. For a quarter of an hour at a time, he will stand drumming with his fingers on the door of the veranda, watching the gulls, or gazing at the clouds; he no longer scrutinizes the ships through the telescope; he is only waiting for death.

The news of a fresh conspiracy against the Bourbons, originating in the army and widely supported by civilians, no longer excites him. During the last six months of his life, he rejects two schemes of rescue. "It is written in the stars that I am to die here. In America I should be assassinated, or forgotten. Nothing but my martyrdom can save my dynasty. That is why I prefer to stay in St. Helena."

His mortal illness gains on him. The climate of the island is dangerous to persons whose livers are healthy when they first come: Napoleon, at thirty-five, had foretold that he would die of liver trouble like his father, and his liver complaint is greatly aggravated. He says that his stomach burns like fire; in some of the paroxysms, he rolls on the floor in agony. He complains of a pain in the gastric region, "like the stab of a penknife." He shivers with cold, though he is burning within; when hot compresses are applied, they can never be hot enough for him.

He watches his symptoms, and studies their meaning; will not take any medicine until its action has been explained to him. He says ruefully: "I have got so fond of my bed that I would not exchange it now for a throne. What a pitiful creature I have become! I, who hardly ever needed sleep, pass my days in lethargy. It seems a desperate resolve merely to open my eyes. Often enough, I used to dictate on different topics to four secretaries at once. In those days, I was Napoleon." His mood vacillates between heroic pathos and irony. When his valet reports that a comet is visible, the Emperor rejoins: "That was the sign before the death of Cæsar." But when his doctor declares that there is no comet to be seen, the sick man says: "Well, people die without comets!"

His medical attendant is a Corsican named Antommarchi. Owing to the quarrel with the governor, the prisoner had no doctor for a year after O'Meara's departure. At length Madame Letizia, after much effort, was able to arrange for the sending of this compatriot as his physician, together with two priests, a body servant, and a cook. Thus it is that, after years of silence, the Emperor hears trustworthy details about his mother. Once, during these last days, he says in simple words what she means to him: "All that I am and was, I owe to my mother; she taught me her own principles, and encouraged in me the habit of work."

Now there are five Corsicans round the lonely man. Only two of them are any good: the body servant and the cook. Of the two priests, one is a deaf old man, partially paralysed, and unable to articulate clearly; the other, fresh from the seminary, is ignorant and uncouth. Antommarchi, too, is a young man, inexperienced but pretentious. Still, the sight of these islanders, men of his own race, revives memories of his Corsican home. Hence, towards the close, feelings reawaken which in early life he had stifled because of his determination to be a Frenchman. Napoleon dies as he was born, an Italian.

He often talks Italian, now, or intersperses his French with strange locutions literally translated from his mother tongue. When

This is a new triumph for the governor, to whom the quarrel between the great Corsican and the little is useful ammunition. Only four weeks before the Emperor's death, his gaoler once more tries to force a way into his presence, and the consequent excitement is very bad for Napoleon.

The number of the faithful diminishes, as if to justify the misanthropist at the close of his life. Now, in the very last weeks, four of the servants and the old priest set sail for Europe; two others fall sick, and the last remaining members of his suite are meditating flight: Montholon is corresponding with the countess about the possibility of a substitute; Bertrand is about to yield to the continued solicitations of his family, and return to France. Montholon, to induce him to remain, has to assure him that when the Emperor talks of being seriously ill, this is not done merely to play upon Bertrand's sympathies. When Bertrand finally decides to remain, the invalid is greatly encouraged, The only one who never thought of leaving was Marchand, the valet. The Emperor says to him: "If this goes on much longer, no one will be left here but you and me. But you will look after me till the end, and will then close my eyes for me".

What really cuts him to the heart is that the man who has been his close companion for so many years should now let long-hidden truths peep out. He has had an argument with Bertrand, who says; "It would have been the happiest day in my life if, after the deposition of the king, the Convention had raised the duke of Orleans to the throne." The Emperor makes no immediate rejoinder, but afterwards says bitterly: "Bertrand, who owes everything to me, whom I made one of the grand officers of my empire"

As his strength wanes, he looks round for something to lean on, and, for the first time in his life, he appeals to his relatives for help. Pauline is the dearest of them. Dictating a letter to her in the third person, he gives a bulletin of his condition, and ends as follows: "The Emperor earnestly hopes that Your Highness will acquaint influential Englishmen with his situation. He is dying on this dreadful rock, forsaken by all. His death struggle is terrible."

In the middle of April, three weeks before the end, behind locked doors, he dictates his will to Montholon. Then the amanuensis has to redictate the document to the Emperor, for it must be in his own handwriting, that it may be above suspicion. The Emperor sits writing for five hours, in a cold sweat. The testament is characterized alike by statesmanlike greatness and by human feelings; it represents, as it were, a survey of his whole life.

XVIII

He begins his testament by declaring that he dies in the apostolical and Roman religion, in the bosom of which he was born, –the faith which he re-established in France, which he always protected, although, in his innermost soul; he never accepted its teachings. Then his thoughts turn to the glory of a hero's grave, and, with a turn of phrase which shows that he regards himself as a Frenchman by choice rather than by birth, he writes: "It is my wish that my ashes shall be laid to rest on the bank of Seine, in the midst of the French people, which I have loved so well."

Next come thoughts of his son, upon whom are lavished all the hopes a man can entertain concerning what will happen after him own death, and for whom he wishes to concentrate such rights as he may possess, such treasures as he may own, and such teachings as he may utter. He tells his "beloved wife" that he retains for her the most tender sentiments, and beseeches her to watch over their son, since the lad is being brought up as an Austrian prince. She is never to forget that the young Napoleon was born a Frenchman. She must never allow the boy to become a tool in the hands of the triumvirs who oppress the peoples of Europe–among whom the greatest oppressor is the child's own grandfather.

Then comes a last thrust at the enemy: "I am dying before my time, murdered by the English oligarchy and its hired assassins." But, in the challenging tone of a tribune, he adds: "The English people will not be slow to avenge me." He closes this part of his will by declaring that he had been defeated "through the treachery of Marmont, Augereau, Talleyrand, and Lafayette," Though he adds, "I forgive them," behind this mask of Christian charity the warrior's steel glitters in the words: "May the France that is yet unborn forgive them as I do."

Now, quite in the patrician style, he thanks his beloved mother and his brothers and sisters for the interest they have continued to feel in him. "I pardon Louis four the libel he published in 1820: it is full of false assertions and falsified documents." Then come the actual bequests.

The main substance of what he has to leave consists of his savings out of the civil list during fourteen years, together with all the furniture, plate, etc., he had himself bought for his palaces; and also his Italian property. He estimates it as amounting to more than frs. 200,000,000, and points out that, as far as he is aware, no law has deprived him of it. Half of it is bequeathed to the surviving officers and men who had fought in the glorious campaigns from 1792 to 1815, in sums proportional to their rates of pay on active service; the other half is to go to the provincial towns and communes that had suffered in the two invasions. His aim, in this provisions, is to put the Bourbon government in the wrong for laying an embargo, at the time of his abdication, upon all his money and securities. These clauses in his will are to promote a Napoleonic sentiment among soldiers and civilians alike; his secret hope being that his testament will exercise an influence in favour of his dynasty, like Cæsar's will when disclosed to the Roman populace by Mark Antony.

Now comes legacies to ninety-seven specified individuals. The list was drawn up in the course of ten days. "His mind is continually at work discovering new objects for his liberality; day after day he recalls the names of additional old servants whom he wants to remember in his will." The bequests are to come from a special property of frs. 20,000,000, of whose ownership he feels grand collar of the Legion of Honour." Each list of items finishes with a charge to one or other of his confidants to take care of the articles named, "and to convey them to my son when he shall attain the age of sixteen years."

Here is another entry: "Marchand shall preserve my hair, and cause a bracelet to be made of it with a gold clasp, to be sent to the empress Marie Louise, to my mother, and to each of my brothers, sisters, nephews, nieces, the cardinal, and one of larger size to my son."

Various persons and places are named in which his son is likely to be interested. "I wish my executors to make a collection of engravings, pictures, books, and medals which may give my son sound ideas, and destroy the erroneous ideas which the policy of a foreign land may have tried to impress on him. I want him to be able to see things as they really were.... My memory will be the glory of his life.... I do not expect my son to benefit by my mother's will, for he is likely to be wealthier than her other children, but I hope that she will leave him some such precious legacy as her own portrait and my father's, or some trinkets which he will know have come down to him from his grandparents."

It may seen as if his life were ending with very simple thoughts, since he makes this touching reference to his parents; but in the next clause the abyss yawns. Those who are about his son, Bertrand's children perhaps, or Montholon's, are "to see to it that he resumes the name of Napoleon as soon he comes of age, and is able to do so without inconvenience."

After this sedulous care for the legitimate heir, there follows, at the very last, a clause of a few lines, §37, in which Napoleon writes: "I should not complain if little Léon were to enter the civil service, should he be so disposed. I should like Alexandre Walewski to serve France in the Army." The writer could not foresee that, some decades after the death of his legitimate son, Léon was to end his ne'er-do-well life in America as the husband of a cook; but that Count Walewski was to attain high distinction, as a diplomat under Louis Philippe, and as minister of State and senator during the second empire. By his talent and good looks, Marie's son was to show that he had, in very truth, been a love child.

But there is a second testament for the legitimate heir. Two weeks before his death, towards three in the morning, the Emperor sends for Montholon, who has been tending him faithfully for the last few weeks: "When I entered the room, I found him sitting up, and the fire glancing in his eye made me fear a fresh attack of fever. He perceived my uneasiness, and said kindly: 'I am not worse, but my mind has been roused by discussing with Bertrand what my executors ought to say to my son when they see him ... it is better, therefore, that I should, in a few words, give you a summary of the counsels which I bequeath to my son. Write:' "

There follow twelve printed pages, containing the Emperor's political testament. Not a word about war, but a great many words about pace; and, as regards Europe, we find almost all the leading thoughts of the century which opened with his rise to power. We are given a glimpse of a fancied second reign. He tells us how he would govern, loftily criticising his own previous work. He looks forward to new political forms, and, with a seer's vision, contemplates the twentieth century. From the rock, he issues an appeal for the union of Europe, a manifesto on behalf of an understanding among the peoples to promote liberty, equality, civilization, talent, and commerce. All these thoughts from themselves in the mind of the dying Napoleon during one of the last restless nights of his illness:

"My son should no think of avenging my death; he should profit by it.... The aim of all his efforts should be, to reign by peace: if he should recommence my wars out of pure love of imitation and without any absolute necessity, he would be a mere ape. To do my work over again would be to suppose that I had done nothing; ... the same thing is not done twice in a century. *I was obliged to daunt Europe by arms; in the present day, the way is to convince her reason*.... I have implanted new ideas in France and in Europe; they cannot retrograde; let my son bring into blossom all that I have sown....

"It is possible that the English, in order to efface the remembrance of their persecution, will favour my son's return to France; but in order to live in a good understanding with England it is necessary, at any cost, to favour her commercial interests: this necessity leads to one of these two consequences –war with England, or a sharing of the commerce of the world with her. This second condition is the only one possible in the present day; questions of foreign policy will, in France, for a long time, take precedence of questions of home policy. I bequeath to my son sufficient strength and sympathy to enable him to continue my work with the sole aid of a lofty and conciliatory diplomacy....

"Let not my son ever mount the throne by the aid of foreign influence: his aim should not be to fulfil a desire to reign, but to deserve the approbation of posterity. Let him cherish an intimacy with my family, whenever it shall be in his power. My mother resembles the great women of classical antiquity.... The French nation, when it is not taken the wrong way, is more easily governed than any other; its prompt and easy comprehension is unequalled; it immediately discerns who labours for, and who against it; but then it is necessary always to speak to its sense, otherwise its uneasy spite gnaws, it ferments and explodes....

"Let him despise all parties; let him only see the mass. Excepting those who have betrayed their country, he should forget the previous conduct of all men, and reward talent, merit, and services, wherever he finds them....

"France is the country where the chiefs of parties have the least influence: to rest for support on them, is to build on sand. Great things can only be done in France by having the support of the masses....

"I relied on the whole mass of the people without exception; I set the example of a government which favoured the interests of all.... To divide the interests of a nation is ... to engender civil war. A thing indivisible by nature cannot be divided; it can only be mutilated. I attach no importance to the constitution; but its fundamental principle should be universal suffrage.

"The nobility I created will not be a buttress to my son ...

"My dictatorship was indispensable, and the proof of this is that I was always offered more power than I wanted.... It will not be the same with my son: his power will be disputed; he must anticipate every desire for liberty.... The aim of a sovereign is not only to reign, but to diffuse instruction, morality, and well-being. Anything false is an untrustworthy prop....

"The French people is animated by two equally powerful passions, which seem opposed, but which, nevertheless, are derived from one and the same feeling, namely, love of liberty and love of distinction. A government can only satisfy these two wants by the most exact justice.... In order to govern, it is not necessary to pursue a more or less perfect theory, but to build with the materials which are under one's hand; to submit to necessities, and profit by them....

"The liberty of the press ought to become, in the hands of the government, a powerful auxiliary in diffusing, through all the most distant corners of the Empire, sound doctrines and good principles. To leave it to itself would be to fall asleep beside a danger.... Under pain of death, nowadays, one must either direct or hinder everything.

"My son ought to be a man of new ideas, and of the cause which I have made triumphant everywhere: ... to reunite Europe in the bonds of an indissoluble federation....

"Europe is moving towards an inevitable transformation: to endeavour to retard this progress, would be to waste strength in a useless struggle; to favour it, is to strengthen the hopes and wishes of all....

"My son's position will not be free from immense difficulties. *Let him do by general consent what circumstances forced me to work for by force of arms.* If I had remained victorious over Russia in 1812, the problem of peace would have been solved for a hundred years to come. I cut the Gordian knot of nations; at the present day it must be untied.... It is no longer in the north that great questions will be decided, but in the Mediterranean; on the shores of the Mediterranean, there is enough to content all the ambitions of the different powers, and the happiness of civilized nations may be purchased with fragments of barbarous lands. *Let the kings listen to reason; Europe will no longer provide matter for maintaining international hatreds.* Prejudices are dispersing; interests are widening and becoming fused; trading routes are being multiplied. No longer can any one nation monopolize commerce....

"All that you say to my son, or all that he learns, will be of little use to him, unless he has in the depths of his heart that sacred fire and love of good which alone can achieve great things.

"I hope, however, that he will be worthy of his destiny.

"If they refuse you permission to go to Vienna ..."

The document suddenly breaks off; Napoleon's powers have flagged; like the utterance of an oracle, the soothsaying ends in the middles of a sentence. But what this man on his deathbed designed for the instruction of his poor little son, can serve to instruct Europe a century after it was written. The political problems of our own day, however we may attempt to solve them, are in truth solved here by the sovereignty of genius.

XIX

After this brilliant outpouring, the productive spring dries up. Agreeable visions float before his mind. It seems as if fate intends him to enjoy the euthanasia. The day after writing his political testament, he lies free from pain and care, surrounded by the mist-wreaths of hope:

"When I am dead, each of you will have the sweet consolation of returning to Europe. You will see again, the one his relatives, the other his friends; but for my part, I shall meet my brave warriors in the Elysian Fields. Yes," he continued, raising his voice, "Kléber, Desaix, Bessières, Duroc, Ney, Murat, Massena, Berthier; all will come to meet me: they will talk to me of the deeds we did together. I shall recount to them the later events of my life. When they see me, they will be inspired with their old enthusiasm, their old passion for glory. We shall talk of our battles to the Scipios, to Hannibal, Cæsar, and Frederick. What a delight that will be. If only people here on earth are not terrified at seeing so many soldiers put their heads together!"

Such is the dying man's flight of fancy. In all the thousands of his recorded utterances, there is none that shows the naïveté of his mind more plainly than this reverie. He looks into a world peopled by the shades of the heroes, sees his generals there in familiar converse with those of ancient Rome, enters an idyllic paradise in which they talk of big guns. While Napoleon is speaking, the English doctor (whose ministrations the Emperor has at length consented to accept) enters the room.

At this moment, the music of flutes, to which he has, in fancy, been listening, breaks off; once more he hears the rattle of the drums. The statesman recurs to the present. Without transition, he passes into a new register, after his manner, and makes a formal oration which embodies what he wishes to be the official view of his death:

"Come nearer, Bertrand, and translate what I say word for word to this gentleman. My death is the result of injuries worthy of the hands that have inflicted them. I surrendered to the British people, that I might settle down at a British fireside. In defiance of international law, I was loaded with chains.... England overpersuaded the princes, and the world saw an unprecedented sight. Four great powers hurled themselves upon one solitary man. How shamefully you have treated me on this rock! There is no possible mortification to which you have not subjected me! ... With cold calculation, you have slowly done me to death! The vile governor has been the executioner appointed by your ministers! I end like the proud republic of Venice! I bequeath the shame of my death to the royal family of England!"

After this outburst, he sinks back upon his pillows. The doctor stands there dumbfounded, and Napoleon's companions are in little better case. What was it? An epilogue; a protest; a commination? Pure politics! In the evening, he has an account of Hannibal's campaigns read aloud to him.

Next day, April 21st, a fortnight before the end, he sends for the Corsican abbate. Since this man's coming, Napoleon has had Mass read every Sunday, but otherwise has had nothing to do with the priest. Now he says:

"Do you know what a 'chapelle ardente' is? Have you ever officiated at one before? Never? Well, now you will officiate at mine." Details follow. After my death, you will set up your altar at my bedside, and will say Mass with the usual ceremonies until I am under ground."

In the evening, the priest spends nearly an hour with him, Since, we are told, Vignali was not dressed for the occasion, he can only have conversed with Napoleon, and cannot have confessed him. Napoleon has not communicated for forty years, and does not do so now.

The sick man is much wasted; for several weeks he has not been shaved; his face is sunken and dusky. Now he has his bed carried into the drawing-room, for he finds the bedroom too confined. He is racked by terrible attacks of gastric spasm. In the intervals of calm, he continues to speak of persons to whom he wishes to leave legacies. Sometimes he dozes and dreams. In these dreams, women appear to him: Marie Louise is not one of them: "I saw my good Josephine, but she would not put her arms round me.... She was unchanged, loving as always. She said we should soon meet to part no more. She assured me– Did you see her too?" Just like the dream about his generals; from the paradise of children, from the land of faery.

When he feels better, he has the latest newspapers read aloud. An attack on him in one of them excites him, and he has his will brought to him. Breaking the seals he has laboriously affixed, without saying a word he writes with tremulous hand:

"I had the duke of Enghien arrested and brought to trial because this trial was necessary for the safety, the interest, and the honour of the French people, at a time when the count of Artois, according to his own admission, was maintaining sixty assassins in Paris."

Like two ghosts, they face one another; the dead Bourbon and the dying Bonaparte.

On the 27th, he asks for the will once more, and laboriously reseals it. He has inventories made of the contents of his boxes and cupboards; valuable documents are put into envelopes, on which he writes the inscriptions. All this is done in the intervals between attacks of vomiting. His companions have to affix their seals, and everyone of them must verify a written record of the packers. So great is his mistrust of England.

Is there anything still to do? Various articles which have not yet been dealt with are lying on the counterpane. "I am very weak; there is not much time left; we must finish things off." What is that? Hortense's diamond necklace, which used to gleam from her neck on festal occasions in the Tuileries, and was sewn into his waistband the day he left Malmaison. This he gives to Marchand. There is a plain golden snuff-box. Toilsomely, with the point of a penknife, he scratches his initial N on the lid, and gives the box to the doctor, saying:

"I expressly demand that the post-mortem shall be made, and, in especial, that the stomach shall be examined. I believe that I am dying of the same illness as my father. Ask Louis to send you the report about that, and compare it with what you find at the autopsy. Then you may at least be able to spare my son this horrible illness. Tell him how he can guard against it, and how he can be saved from the dread of it which has so afflicted me."

For six years he has been blaming the climate of the rock for his liver trouble; only a few days ago he had charged England with killing him in the unwholesome prison-house. by ordering a post-mortem examination, he is risking the collapse of this theory; indeed, this is what he expects. All is done for his son's safety. He hopes that the land can be saved from the family disorder.

Is everything ready? Can we start? Wait a moment! There is still lacking an official address to the authorities. He dictates the following letter:

"Monsieur le Gouverneur! Emperor Napoleon died on the —, after a long and painful illness. I have the honour to inform you of the fact.... Please let me know what arrangements your government has made for the conveyance of his body to Europe, and also in respect of the members of his suite."

"Count Montholon, you will sign that."

Napoleon had dictated sixty thousand political letters. Perhaps this one, the formal report of his own death with the date left open, is the most remarkable of them all; for who would have expected that destiny would leave so much time and so much tranquillity of mind in face of approaching death to a man who had faced sudden death on sixty battlefields? The line above quoted seem rather a grotesque close to his domineering career, and we feel hope that this gruesome epistle will not be his last.

It is not the last. On the 29th, after a feverish night, he dictates the drafts of two communications. One deals with the utilization of Versailles; the other with a reorganization of the National Guard. But these are not addressed, as they would have been before his abdication, to the Minister of Public Works and to the Minister for War. He dictates the superscriptions: "First Dream." Then he says: "I feel so wonderfully well now; I could go for a thirty-mile ride." Next day, he becomes icy cold and sinks into a delirium, which lasts five days till the end.

But Napoleon Bonaparte's vital energies do not subside so easily. During these five days, there is a lucid interval, and he seizes the opportunity for issuing orders and making declarations:

"When I lose consciousness, you must on no account admit an English doctor.... You will remain true to my memory, and will not do anything that might harm it. All my laws and all my actions were based upon the strictest principles. Unfortunately, the circumstances were so grave that I could not be lenient, and had to postpone many good things. Then came the disasters. I could not

"France! ... Armée! ... Tête d' armee.... Joséphine!"

This is Napoleon's last utterance.

Next moment, with amazing energy, he springs out of bed, overpowering Montholon, who is alone with him. The two fall to the floor, and he grips Montholon so fiercely that the count cannot even cry for help. Archambaud, who is in the next room, hears the noise, comes in, and releases Montholon. No one knows what enemy the Emperor was trying to strangle in this last fight.

The rest of the day he lies breathing quietly. By signs he seems to asks for water, but sine he can no longer swallow they must be content with holding a sponge moistened with vinegar to his lips. Mist and rain drive fiercely round the house. A count of the old noblesse and a man of the people watch by the camp-bed of Austerlitz.

At five o'clock, the rage of the south-east trade wind is redoubled, and two trees of the latest planting are uprooted.

At this moment, the man on the bed is in the throes of a prolonged rigor. There is no sign of pain; his eyes are widely opened, staring into vacancy; the death-rattle is in his throat. As the tropical sun sinks into the sea the Emperor's heart stops beating.

XX

On the study table, in the garish light of noon, lies the naked corpse of Napoleon. Five English surgeons, three English army officers, and the three Frenchmen, surround the extemporized post-mortem table, where Antommarchi is performing the autopsy. The Corsican doctor has removed the liver and incised it. He holds up the organs for the others' inspection, and demonstrates, as if to a class of students. "You see, gentlemen, how this ulcerated part of the stomach has become adherent to the liver. What are we to infer? That the climate of St. Helena has intensified the gastric disorder, and has thus brought about the Emperor's premature death."

A vote is taken: England against France. The majority declare the viscera to be healthy, while the Corsican is ostentatiously thrusting his finger through the perforated wall of the stomach. Medical report.

The Emperor's body was embalmed, and at the lying-in-state was covered with the gold-embroidered cloak of Marengo. The whole garrison, by its own wish, marched past. All who saw the body testify to the calm and serenity of the features. In mysterious fashion, his face, which, since the days of the coronation, had tended to assume the robust maturity of the Roman emperors, had now returned to the delicacy of youth.

The British authorities refused to allow the shipment to Europe. The grave was dug in a secluded valley, beside a spring shaded by two weeping willows. He was accorded the honours of a British general; salvos of artillery and musketry were fired over the grave, what time there fluttered in the breeze the colours on which were emblazoned the names of the English victories in Spain. The governor was present, and declared that he had forgiven the Emperor.

Six stone slabs from gun emplacements cover the tomb. A seventh was needed for the artillery officer's grave; but, since it was not available at the moment, three glazed tiles were taken from the cooking-stove of a new house. The governor would not allow the inscription "Napoleon" to be placed on the tomb, but insisted upon "Napoleon Bonaparte." There was, therefore, no inscription. The furniture of Longwood was sold by auction; the house was bought by a farmer, who turned the place into a mill; the two rooms in which the Emperor had lived for six years were restored to their former uses, becoming a byre and a pigsty.

One thing only did England do in honour of the dead: a sentry was posted at the grave. For nineteen years, the guard was relieved at the proper intervals; then the dead Emperor was brought home to Paris.

Without waiting for this, all the others return to Europe. The governor was publicly horsewhipped in London by Las Cases' son, he died in obscurity. Castlereagh, the statesman who had been predominantly responsible for the treatment of Napoleon, ultimately killed himself in an access of melancholia. All England was writing and taking about the barbarous treatment of the great exile.

The Corsican doctor goes to Italy. Lucien refuses to see him. In Parma, Marie Louise also shuts her door against him, but he sees her in her box at the theatre. In Rome, Antomarchi visits Letizia Bonaparte, and for three days she makes him tell her all his news. He leaves the silver lamp with her, and sails back to Corsica. Letizia sits by the fireside, weeping over the fate of her second son, Napoleon.

She has still fifteen years to live. She outlives Elise; outlives Pauline, who dies with a mirror in her hands; outlives several of her grandchildren, and three popes. She is half paralysed, and has become blind. But she sits there facing her sons bust, her spirit unbroken, mourning her dead. Like a princess, she welcomes to her palace all those who have remained faithful to the Emperor. Her servants are the last persons in Europe to wear his colours; her carriage is the last to bear his escutcheon. She has news at times from Vienna and her grandson, but the young man is not allowed to visit her. When he is one-and-twenty, he dies. Now, Marie Louise writes to her. She does not answer the letter. At last she is told that she may return home, but she refuses to go, since the same right is not accorded to her children.

Nine years after the Emperor's death, the Bourbon dynasty is overthrown, and the Orleans monarchy is established. The new king knows how strong the Bonaparties are, and he orders that the statue of Napoleon, which fifteen years before had been removed, shall be replaced on the Vendome column. When Jerome brings his bedridden mother these tidings, she has a renewal of health and is able to leave her bed. For the first time after a long interval she makes her way into the drawing-room, and her blind eyes turn towards the bust. She says in a toneless voice:

"Once again the Emperor is in Paris."

ENVOY

To write the history of a man, or the history of an epoch, these are two distinct undertakings, differing both in name and technique. Vain has been the attempt to combine them. Plutarch renounced the one, and Carlyle renounced the other; that is why both these masters were able to achieve their respective tasks. It would be fair to say that Plutarch's example has found no imitators; no one, after Plutarch, has made it his specific task to write the history of great minds upon a strictly historical foundation.

Such a work does not come within the domain of the historian, seeing that the search for truth demands other talents that those requisite for the art of portrayal. Artists have sometimes dramatized historical figures with a free hand; sometimes they have produced one of those horrible mishmashes which pass by the name of "historical novel"–of which Goethe, like Napoleon, said that they confuse everything.

The attempt is especially difficult when, not work, but deeds, are the milestones along the road of life. Cæsar, Frederick, and Napoleon, only became great powers through their victories in the battlefield; and yet their battles tend, more and more, to become unmeaning for posterity. Nowadays, it is only in military academies that Pharsalia, Rossbach, and Austerlitz, have a historical significance. Note one of the three great generals I have named would mean any more to us that Crassus, Seydlitz, or Masséna, had they, too, been nothing more than military commanders; it is the political genius of Cæsar, Frederick, and Napoleon, that makes these men supreme. In his highest embodiment, the statesman shapes all our destinies. Where genius and character intersect, is the focus for the searcher of the soul.

In this book, I have tried to write the inner history of Napoleon. Since his personality finds expression in every step of his political career, his ideas as founder of States and as legislator, his attitude towards revolution and legitimacy, towards the social rein to imagination, but only to him who gives himself up to the amor fati.

Thus, likewise, for the reader of these pages should be reconstructed the tragedy which once only in a millennium a mortal man has created out of his life. What a man can attain through self-confidence and courage, through passion and imagination, through industry and will, he attained. Today, in the age of the revolutions which once again are opening every path to the man of supreme ability, the ardent youth of Europe can find as an example and a warning no greater man than the one who, of all men of the West, made and suffered the most violent commotions.

THE NĀRADA-PURĀṆA

PART - IV

Translated and Annotated by

DR. G.V. TAGARE

MOTILAL BANARSIDASS
PUBLISHING HOUSE • DELHI

Email: naraina@mlbd.in • Website: www.mlbd.in

@mlbdofficial

+91 89 2999 9000

*2nd Reprint: Delhi, **2024***
First Edition: Delhi, 1982

UNESCO COLLECTION OF REPRESENTATIVE WORKS—*Indian Series*
This book has been accepted in the Indian Translation Series of the UNESCO Collection of Representative Works, jointly sponsored by the United Nations Educational, Scientific and Cultural Organization (UNESCO) and the Government of India

ISBN: 978-93-5676-126-1 (Hardcover)
ISBN: 978-93-5676-127-8 (Paperback)

Printed & Published by
Rajendra P Jain *for*
Motilal Banarsidass Publishing House
A-44, Naraina Industrial Area, Phase I,
New Delhi–110 028 (INDIA)
Email: naraina@mlbd.in Website: www.mlbd.in
Tel.: (+91-11)4751 1592
Showroom:
4637/20, F-2, Hari Sadan, First Floor, Ansari Road, Daryaganj
Delhi–110 002 (Opp. Fire Station) ***Tel.*** : (+91-11)4559 7999

ANCIENT INDIAN TRADITION AND MYTHOLOGY

Mahāpurāṇas *Translated into English*

Gen. Ed. DR. G.C. TRIPATHI

Founder Eds. LATE J.L. SHASTRI and LATE G.P. BHATT

PUBLISHED VOLUMES

Vols. 1-4	ŚIVA PURĀṆA *Tr.* J.L. Shastri
Vol. 5-6	LIṄGA PURĀṆA *Tr.* J.L. Shastri
Vol. 7-11	BHĀGAVATA PURĀṆA *Tr.* G.V. Tagare
Vol. 12-14	GARUḌA PURĀṆA *Tr.* J.L. Shastri
Vol. 15-19	NĀRADA PURĀṆA *Tr.* G.V. Tagare
Vol. 20-21	KŪRMA PURĀṆA *Tr.* G.V. Tagare
Vol. 22-26	BRAHMAṆḌA PURĀṆA *Tr.* G.V. Tagare
Vol. 27-30	AGNI PURĀṆA *Tr.* N. Gangadharan
Vol. 31-32	VARĀHA PURĀṆA *Tr.* S. Venkitasubramonia Iyer
Vol. 33-36	BRAHMA PURĀṆA *Tr.* J.L. Shastri
Vol. 37-38	VĀYU PURĀṆA *Tr.* G.V. Tagare
Vol. 39-48	PADMA PURĀṆA *Tr.* N.A. Deshpande
Vol. 49-71	SKANDA PURĀṆA *Ed.* G.P. Bhatt, *Tr. & Annot.* Shridhar Balooni & Pratosh Panda
Vol. 72-73	VĀMANA PURĀṆA *Tr. & Annot.* R.S. Shiva Ganesha Murthy
Vol. 74-76	GAṆEŚA PURĀṆA *Tr. & Annot.* Greg Bailey
Vol. 77-80	BRAHMAVAIVARTA PURĀṆA *Tr. & Annot.* G.P. Bhatt
Vol. 81-82	ŚRĪ VIṢṆU PURĀṆA *Tr. & Annot.* T.K. Narsimhan
Vol. 86	MĀRKAṆḌEYA PURĀṆA *Tr. & Annot.* I.S. Madugula

PURĀṆAS UNDER PREPARATION

Harivamśa Purāṇa • Bhavisya Purāṇa • Matsya Purāṇa
Devi Bhāgavata Purāṇa • Kālikā Purāṇa • Viṣṇudharmottara Purāṇa

ANCIENT INDIAN TRADITION AND MYTHOLOGY

Translated by
A BOARD OF SCHOLARS

and Edited by
PROF. J.L. SHASTRI

VOLUME 18

PUBLISHER'S NOTE

The purest gems lie hidden in the bottom of the ocean or in the depth of rocks. One has to dive into the ocean or delve into the rocks to find them out. Similarly, truth lies concealed in the language which with the passage of time has become obsolete. Man has to learn that language before he discovers that truth.

But he has neither the means nor the leisure to embark on that course. We have, therefore, planned to help him acquire knowledge by an easier course. We have started the series of *Ancient Indian Tradition and Mythology* in English Translation. Our goal is to universalize knowledge through the most popular international medium of expression. The publication of the Purāṇas in English translation is a step towards that goal.

PREFACE

The present book contains the *Nārada Purāṇa*, Part IV in English translation. It includes the complete fourth Pāda (chapters 92-125) and some portion of the Uttarabhāga (chs. 1-37). This is the Eighteenth Volume in the series of fifty volumes which we have planned on *Ancient Indian Tradition and Mythology*.

The project of the series was envisaged and financed in 1970 by Lala Sundar Lal Jain of Messrs Motilal Banarsidass. Hitherto seventeen volumes of the series, (comprising English translation of *Śiva*, *Liṅga*, *Bhāgavata*, *Garuḍa*, *and Nārada* (Parts I, II, III) have been published and released for sale.

This Vol., as the contents would show, is historically very important as it records the detailed contents of each Mahāpurāṇa as it stood before the final redaction of the present NP. Though as many as Sixteen chapters (92-107) deal with this subject, the problem remains the same inasmuch as they do not cover all the contents of all the Purāṇas and at the same time the information regarding interlocutors is also at variance with the published editions of these Purāṇas. Here is a scope for further research.

Beside recording information on the contents of the Purāṇas, this Vol. presents the detailed exposition of Vratas tithi-wise. The exposition covers as many as sixteen chapters (110 to 125) of the fourth Pāda and thirtyseven (1-37) chapters of the Uttarabhāga. The reader will find in this section a vivid description of Vratas, at some places very different from the one found in the Smṛti literature. Thirty-five chapters (3 to 37) of the Uttarabhāga are devoted to the glory and greatness of Ekādaśī Vrata that falls on the 11th day of the bright half and the dark half of each and every month. These chapters narrate a story in a very interesting way : how Yama, the God of Death had to close his office as all men, being compelled to observe Ekādaśī by Rukmāṅgada went straight way to heaven; how Yama approached Brahmā and requested him to lure King Rukmāṅgada to drop Ekādaśī Vrata; how Brahmā agreed, hit upon a plan, produced an enchantress to carry out the plan and how the enchantress Mohinī had finally failed. The section emphasizes the efficacy of Ekādaśī Vrata which continues to be popular among the Vaiṣṇavas even today.

The present translation is based on the Sanskrit Text of the Nārada Purāṇa as published by Messrs Kṣemarāja Śrīkṛṣṇadāsa, Veṅkaṭeśvara Press, Bombay. This text constructed on the collation of manuscripts and supported by the evidence of citations found in the Smṛti granthas is fairly accurate.

For general information about this Purāṇa, the reader is referred to Dr. G. V. Tagare's Scholarly Introduction refixed to Part I of this Purāṇa. The preliminaries prefixed to the present Part include Preface, Abbreviations and Contents. The Glossary and Index will follow this Part and be suffixed to Part V which completes the Purāṇa.

Acknowledgement of Obligations

It is our pleasant duty to put on record our sincere thanks to Dr. R. N. Dandekar and the UNESCO Authorities for their encouragement and valuable help which render this work very useful to the reader. We are extremely grateful to Dr. G. V. Tagare who has meticulously and delightfully accomplished this strenuous task of translation and annotation. We are thankful to Shri T. V. Parameshwar Iyer for his valuable assistance in the preparation of translation. We express our gratitude to all those who have offered suggestions for improving the same.

—Editor

SM	*Sādhana Mālā*—B. Bhattacharya, GOS, Baroda, 1928.
SMC	*Smṛti Candrikā*—Devanna Bhaṭṭa.
Smṛ	*Smṛti* (preceded by the author's name or simply the author's name e.g. Manu Smṛti or Manu. All GM editions in the Smṛti-Sandarbha. 1952-57.
Sv. P.	*Śiva Purāṇa,* Pandit Pustakālaya, Kashi, V.S. 2020.
Vā. P.	*Vāyu Purāṇa*, GM, 1959.
VP.	*Viṣṇu Purāṇa*, Gītā Press, Gorakhpur, V.S. 2026.
VR	Vālmīki Rāmāyaṇa, Gītā Press, V.S. 2020.
VRK	*Vālmīki Rāmāyaṇa Kośa*—Ramkumar Rai, (Chowkhamba Varanasi.)
Yaj	*Yājñavalkya* (Smṛti), etc.
YSP	*The Yoga System of Patañjali*—J. H. Wood. (MLBD)

UTTARABHĀGA

Chapters

SECTION IV[1]

CHAPTER NINETYTWO

The Brahmapurāṇa : Contents and merit accrued

Sūta said :

1. On hearing these words of Sanatkumāra joyously, the delighted Nārada who was desirous of knowing the excellent thing that is conducive to welfare, said again.

Nārada said :

2. Well done, O blessed one, Well done. The great sacred (Tantra) text, that is the most excellent among the (Tāntric) scriptural texts has been narrated by you. It renders great benefit to all the worlds.

3. Now I wish to hear the excellent narration of Purāṇas. O sage, tell me whatever (i.e. all legendary episodes) is narrated in each of the different Purāṇas, since you are considered to be omniscient.

Sūta said :

4. O Brāhmaṇa, on hearing those auspicious words of Nārada, his enquiry regarding the stories in the Purāṇas, Sanatkumāra replied.

---

1. This section is historically very important as it records the detailed contents of each *Mahāpurāṇa* as they stood before the final redaction of the present NP. As the notes below will show, the NP does *not* cover *all* the contents of *all* the Purāṇas and the information regarding interlocutors etc, is at variance with the published editions of these *Purāṇas*. But that does not mean that whatever is not recorded in the NP. is spurious. Critical editions based on all-India Mss. of the Purāṇas will be more reliable in this matter.

Sanatkumāra said :

5. O Brāhmaṇa, the stories extant in the Purāṇas are miraculous and very detailed. They have originated in the different Kalpas[1] and they include different stories and anecdotes.

6. This sage Sanātana is the most excellent among the knowers of many Kalpas. Ask him about this. No one else knows as much as he does.

7. On hearing these words of the noble-souled Sanatkumāra, Nārada bowed to Sanātana with great humility and submitted :

Nārada said :

8-9. O Brāhmaṇa, the most excellent one among the knowers of the Purāṇas, interested in the discussion of the perfect knowledge, kindly recount to me the classification of the Purāṇas in their entirety, on hearing which everything becomes heard, on knowing which everything is known. It is by following the injunctions therein that everything meritorious is done.

10-11. The duties of the different castes and stages of life are clearly understood from it. How many are the Purāṇas? What is the magnitude (extent) of each? What are the stories that they contain? O holy Lord, tell me. So also recount to me the different stories based on the four castes of people, as well as the details of the different holy observances.

12. Please reveal clearly the stories of the different races and dynasties in the order of their creation. O Holy Lord, there is no one superior to you in the knowledge of the stories contained in the Purāṇas.

13a. Hence tell me the story (i.e. the content of the Purāṇas) that dispels all doubts.

Sūta said :

13b-14a. O Brāhmaṇas, on hearing the speech (request)

1. This is a convenient plea to reconcile different versions of the same story in different *Purāṇas*.

of Nārada, Sanātana, the most excellent one among the knowers, meditated on Nārāyaṇa for a short while and said :

Sanātana said :

14b-16a. Very well ! O excellent sage, very nice ! Since your steady inclination is diverted towards the knowledge of the stories in the Purāṇas. This is conducive to the help of all the worlds. I shall tell you what had been narrated by Brahmā formerly. Urged by filial affection, he narrated to Marīci and other sages.

16b-18. Brahmā's son named Marīci is well known as one richly endowed with Vedic learning. He is the master of the Vedas and the Vedāṅgas (lores ancillary to Vedas). Once he approached his father Brahmā, the creator of the worlds. O leading sage ! O bestower of honour ! He devoutly bowed to him and asked him the same question regarding the holy narrative of the Purāṇas as you do now.

Marīci said :

19. O Lord, Lord of the chiefs of the Devas, the Creator and the annihilator of the worlds, O omniscient one, O presiding deity over all, obeisance be to you, who are gracious to all.

20. O father, I am desirous of hearing. Kindly tell me the core of the Purāṇas, their definition, their authority, the narrator and the inquirer.

Brahmā said :

21. Listen, O dear child, I shall tell you the collective account of the Purāṇas. On knowing it, all the extant literature among the mobile and the immobile beings becomes known

22. O bestower of honour, in all the Kalpas, there was only one Purāṇa[1] that was the very seed of the fourfold aims of life. It extended to a hundred crores of verses.

---

1. With due respect to P.V. Kane (H.D. V. ii.P. 829), I believe that originally there was a single text of literature called the *Purāṇa*, on account of the following reasons :

23-24. It was from the Purāṇa that all other sacred literature and sciences were evolved. As days passed by, people, could not grasp this Purāṇa properly. On realising it, Hari the highly intelligent deity, incarnated himself as Vyāsa in every age. In the course of every Dvāpara age, he reduced it to four hundred-thousand verses.

---

(1) Not only the NP here but various other Purāṇas record the tradition that originally there was one *Purāṇa, vide Brahmāṇḍa* (BdP) I.1. 40-41., LP I. 2.3., Mt. P 53. 3-11, Pd. P V. 145-52, Va. P. I. 60-61. And They have a number of common verses. For example compare, NP I.92.22-25 (our text) with the following from Mt. P. 53. 4-11. :

Purāṇam ekam evāsīt tadā Kalpāntare' nagha /
Trivarga-sādhanam puṇyaṁ śata-koṭi-pravistaram //
Pravṛttiḥ sarva-śāstrāṇām Purāṇasyā' bhavat tadā /
Kālenāgrahaṇaṁ dṛṣṭvā Purāṇasya tato nṛpa //
Vyāsa-rūpam ahaṁ kṛtvā saṁharāmi yuge yuge /
Catur-lakṣa-pramāṇena Dvāpare Dvāpare sadā //
Tad aṣṭādaśadhā kṛtvā bhūr-loke'smin prakāśyate /
Adyāpi deva-lokesmin śata-koṭi-pravistaram //

(2) All Purāṇas conform in general to a uniform structure known as *Pañca-lakṣaṇa* or claim to have the following five characteristic topics viz., the creation of the Universe (*Sarga*) after destruction or *Pralaya* (*Pratisarga*)

(3) Genealogy of Sages and Kings (*Vaṁśa*) (4) the great periods called *Manvantaras,* (5) history of dynasties both Solar and Lunar races. etc. (*Vaṁśānucarita*)

(4) Not only verses but long passages of verses are found common to a number of Purāṇas.

Thus each Purāṇa tries to follow the proto-type of that ancient text called the Purāṇa.

(5) The *Atharva Veda* (AV. XI. 7. 24 and XV. 6. 10-11) mentions *Purāṇa* which shows that there was no proliferation of Purāṇa upto the final redaction of the AV.

It was by the time of the *Dharma-Sūtras* of Āpastamba and Gautama that Purāṇas with different names came into existence "approaching in the contents to some extent at least of some of the extant Purāṇas" (HD. V. ii. 318). Writers from the 2nd to the eighth cent A.D. from Śabara to Śaṅkara show that the Purāṇa texts before those authors exhibit the same contents and characteristics as many of the extant Purāṇas.

The later proliferation does not disprove the existence of one single work called Purāṇa.

For details, vide section 1 of the *Introduction.*

25. He divides Purāṇa into eighteen books and hands it over to the people of the Earth. Even today, original in the region of the Devas, the Purāṇa extends to a hundred crores of verses.

26-28. Of course, there is a condensed version in which the essence is described briefly in four hundred thousand verses.[1] The following are the three times six (eighteen) books viz—Brāhma, Pādma, Vaiṣṇava, Vāyavīya, Bhāgavata, Nāradīya Mārkaṇḍeya, Āgneya, Bhaviṣya, Brahma Vaivarta, Liṅgaka, Vārāha, Skānda, Vāmana, Kūrma, Mātsya, Gāruḍa and Brahmāṇḍa.[2]

29. The single narrative is called the thread that binds the narrator and the listener. I shall recount briefly. Listen with great concentration.

30. It was the Brahma Purāṇa that was narrated at the outset[3] by the noble-souled Vyāsa, the Vedic scholar, for the benefit of the whole world.

31. Indeed, it is the foremost among all the Purāṇas. It bestows virtue, love, wealth and liberation from Saṁsāra. It is rich with various narratives and historical anecdotes. It consists of ten thousand verses.[4]

---

1. The total number of verses in the extant *Purāṇas* as enumerated in *Mt. P.* & *Va.P.* comes to 400600 which is approximately the same as "Four hundred thousand" as mentioned here and in other Purāṇas.

2. The list of Purāṇas given here is the same as in the Bh. P XII. 13. 4-8, VP III. 6.21.23, Mt. P. 53.11 ff Va. P. 104. 2-10, etc. But there is some difference in the serial order. For example, NP. records the *Vāyu P* as the 4th in the list, while a number of others substitute the *Śaiva* as the 4th instead of *Vāyu*. A.D. Pusalkar has however, convincingly shown that the *Vāyu* is entitled to be a Mahāpurāṇa and *Not* the Śiva Purāṇa (*Studies in the Epics & Purāṇas of India* (SEP. Ch. 2 pp. 31-41) that the VP contains this list shows that these Purāṇas existed in the Gupta Age.

3. Like the NP most *Purāṇas* give the *Brahma* the first place in their lists. But the *Vāyu* 104,3 and the *Devībhāgavata* (13.3) put the *Matsya* as the first in their list, while the *Skanda-Prabhāsa Khaṇḍa* 2. 8-9 gives that honour to the *Brahmāṇḍa*.

4. The Bh. P. XII. 13.4 agrees with the NP about the number of verses (viz 10000) in the *Brahma P* but *AP.* 272.1 credits it with 25000 verses while *Mt. P.* states 13000 as the total No. of verses therein. Actually

32. O leading sage, in it is described the origin of the Devas, *Suras and Dakṣa and other Prajāpatis.

33. Then, there is the holy narration of the race of the Sun, the Supreme Ātman, the lord of the worlds. The narrative is destructive of great sins.

34. In the course of that narrative, the incarnation of the glorious Rāmacandra[1] has been recounted, Rāmacandra of blissful form incarnating in four manifestations (vyūhas).[2]

35. Thereafter, the lunar race is described. There is the story of Kṛṣṇa, the Lord of the Universe, that is destructive of sins.

36. There is the description of all the continents and sub-continents without omitting anything. The description of the nether-worlds and the heavens is also seen (given therein).

37. There is the enumeration of the Narakas (hells). There is a hymn and a narrative of the Sun. Pārvatī's birth and marriage are described.

38. Then there is the narrative of Dakṣa. There is the description of the holy centre of 'Ekāmra'[3] (Bhuvaneśvara in Orissa). O Nārada, the first part of this Purāṇa has thus been narrated.

39. In its second part, there is the description of Puruṣottama.[4] It is explained in detail along with the injunctions as to how a pilgrimage (of Jagannātha Puri) is to be conducted.

---

the Ānandāśrama Edt. of this Purāṇa contains 13,761 verses. In the *Brahma* P, Gautamī-Māhātmya is given in 106 chapters but the NP. does not record it—a big omission.

*Probably a misprint. It should be *cāsurāṇāṁ ca* 'and of Asuras'.

1. This story of Rāma though included in the list of contents of the Brahma by the NP. is not found in the printed editions (both Ānandāśrama Poona and Gurumandal (GM) Calcutta.)

2. Obviously the *Pañcarātra* doctrine of "Four Manifestations" is implied here as Rāma is an incarnation of Viṣṇu (Vāsudeva.)

3. This is in Ch. 41 of the Bd. P. (GM. Edt). Ekāmra is Bhuvaneshvar on the river Gandhavatī in Orissa—De 59.

4. The description of Puruṣottama Kṣetra and how king Indradyumna of Avanti carved out three wooden images (of Jagannātha, Balarāma and Subhadrā) is found in Chs. 44-51 of the Bd. P. This Puruṣottama Kṣetra is Puri of Jagannātha Puri or Śrī Kṣetra in Orissa. Puri is the ancient Buddhist

40. It is here itself that the story of Kṛṣṇa[1] is explained in detail. There is the description of the region of Yama and the procedure of the Śrāddhas of the Pitṛs (manes).

41. The duties of the different castes and stages of life have been described in detail. There is the narration of Viṣṇu-Dharma and the Yugas as well as the Pralaya (dissolution of the world).

42. There is the narration of the Yogas and the Sāṅkhyas. There is the description of Brahmavāda (Philosophy of the Brahman) and the eulogy of the Purāṇa.

43. Thus the Brahma Purāṇa that consists of two parts has been described. It is destructive of all sins. It bestows all happiness.

44-46a. He who, after getting copied this Purāṇa consisting of the dialogue of Sūta and Śaunaka that yields worldly pleasure (here) and release from Saṁsāra (hereafter), donates devoutly that manuscript on the full moon day in the month of Vaiśākha, to a Brāhmaṇa well-versed in Purāṇas, alongwith gold, water and a cow, after propitiating him with garments, sweet dishes and ornaments,—(such a person) stays in the region of god Brahmā as long as the sun, the moon and the stars shine.

46b-47a. He who reads or listens to this index (table of contents) to the Brahma Purāṇa, O Brāhmaṇa, shall attain the benefit of the reciter and listener of the entire Purāṇa.

Dantapura which got its name from the shrine of Buddha's left canine tooth. The three images represent Buddha, Dharma and Saṅgha and there were car festivals of these when Fa Hian and Hiuen Tsiang visited this place—De, pp 162-163.

1. VV 40-42 give some of the main items in the Bd. P. such as the story of Kṛṣṇa (Chs. 180-211), description of the region of Yama (Chs. 214-216), *Pitṛ-Śrāddha* (219-220), Varṇāśramadharma (Ch. 222), discussion of Yoga (Chs. 234, 238), Sāṅkhya (Chs. 235, 239) and eulogy of Purāṇas (Ch. 235). But a number of chapters on sacred places and other important episodes which find a place in every Purāṇa and as such cannot be branded as 'spurious', are not mentioned in the contents of the Bd. P. as summarised in the NP.

47b-48a. He who restricts his diet to rice soaked in ghee and subdues his sense-organs through (religious) observances and listens to the whole of Brahmapurāṇa, shall attain the region of Brahmā.

48b-c. O dear one, What more needs be said ? By reciting this Purāṇa a man obtains whatever he desires.

CHAPTER NINETYTHREE

The Padma Purāṇa : Contents

God Brahmā said :

1. O son, listen. I shall tell you the story of Padma Purāṇa[1] It bestows great merit on those men who joyously read and listen to it.

2. Just as a man becomes complete with his five sense organs, so also is this Purāṇa with its five sections. It is destructive of sins.

---

1. This Vaiṣṇava Purāṇa is regarded as the heart of the Cosmic Hari (*Pd. Svarga* 62.22). There are variations in the nomenclatures of the different Sections (Khaṇḍas) and the total number of verses in this Purāṇa. The NP. gives *Sṛṣṭi, Bhūmi, Svarga, Pātāla* and *Uttara* as the names of its *Khaṇḍas* and this is borne out by the Bengal Mss of the *Padma P—another evidence to show that the author of the NP was an East Indian.* The No. of verses is 55,000 according to the NP., Bh. P., Mt. P., VaP. but the *Brahma Vaivarta* credits it with 59000 verses. The Ānandāśrama edition (Poona) mentions six *Khaṇḍas* viz. *Ādi, Bhūmi, Brahma, Pātāla, Sṛṣṭi* and *Uttara* & contains 48,425 verses. The Guru Mandal edition (Calcutta) of the Pd. P. has seven Khaṇḍas viz. *Sṛṣṭi, Bhūmi, Svarga, Brahma, Pātāla, Uttara* and *Kriyā-yoga-sāra* and they tally with the statement of the *Pd. P. Svarga-Khaṇḍa* 1.23-25 and the no. of verses is 55000. It is noteworthy that a number of topics in the published *Padma Purāṇa* such as the characteristic of heretics (Pākhaṇḍas), condemnation of the Māyā-Vāda, stories regarding wearing special Vaiṣṇava marks like *ūrdhva-Puṇḍra,* greatness of Dvaitism, etc. do not form a part of Pd. P. as describad in the NP:

17. The review of the path of activity (Karmayoga) in accordance with the castes and stages of life. The dialogue between Vyāsa and Jaimini is comprised of holy rites and stories.

18. The story of churning the ocean, thereafter, the enumeration of holy vows. The greatness of Ūrjapañcāha and the hymn that dispels all guilts.

O Brāhmaṇa, this is the section called Svarga Khaṇḍa. It is destructive of all sins.

19-21. The description of Rāma's horse sacrifice, Rāma's coronation at the outset, the arrival of Agastya and others, the narration of the family of Paulastya. The instruction regarding horse sacrifice. Then the description of rites regarding the sacrificial horse. The holy stories of many kings. The description of god Jagannātha (the Lord of the Universe) of Puri, the greatness of Vṛndāvana; it is destructive of all sins.

22. The narration of the perpetual sports of the incarnation of Kṛṣṇa, the greatness of the ablution in the month of Vaiśākha, the benefit of ablution, gifts and worship.

23. The dialogue between the Earth and Divine Boar (Viṣṇu-Varāha), the story of Yama and the Brāhmaṇa, the dialogue of the messengers of the king, review of the Hymn of Kṛṣṇa.

24. The meeting of Śiva and Śaṃbhu (?), then the story of Dadhīca, the incomparable greatness of the Bhasma, the excellent greatness of Śiva.

25. The story of the son of Devarāta, the praise of the knower of the Purāṇas, the narrative of Gautama, then the Śiva-Gītā.

26-27a. The story of Rāma in another Kalpa, the stay in the hermitage of Bhāradvāja. This is the Pātālakhaṇḍa* (The section on Pātāla). It is destructive of all the sins of those who listen and recite. It bestows all desired benefits.

---

*Some topics mentioned in the NP are found in the extant Pd. Purāṇa e.g. greatness of Bhasma (chs 105-108), Praise of the knower of Purāṇas (chs 114-115), The story of Gautama (ch. 114)—Vide *Pd. P. Pātāla* (G. M. edition) with a gold lotus. He who does so is bowed to by all the Devas. He goes to the abode of Viṣṇu. He who reads this index to Padma Purāṇa or listens to it attains the merit of listening to the whole of Padmapurāṇa.

CHAPTER NINETYFOUR

The Viṣṇu Purāṇa : The Table of Contents

Śrī Brahmā said :

1. O dear child, listen. I shall narrate the great Purāṇa of Viṣṇu.[1] It contains twenty-three thousand verses.[2] It is destructive of all sins.

2. In the first section, six divisions have been made by the descendant of Śakti i.e. Parāśara. In the first division the introduction to the Purāṇa is made to Maitreya.

3. The primordial causal creation, the origin of the Devas and others, the narrative of the churning of the ocean, the family-race of Dakṣa and others.

4. The story of Dhruva, the anecdote of Pṛthu, the narrative of Pracetas, the story of Prahlāda.[3]

---

1. Probably this is the only Purāṇa which conforms to the *Pañca-lakṣaṇa* definition of a Purāṇa. May be due to its being *Pro-pañcarātra.* Rāmānuja regards it as an authoritative text. Though I have seen the Veṇkaṭeśvara Press edition and that of Gopal Narayan & Co. with the comm, *Viṣṇucitti* and Ratnagarbha's *Vaiṣṇava-kūṭa-Candrikā,* I use here the Gita Press edition (Gorakhpur Saṁvat 2026)

2. Though the NP. and some other Purāṇas such as the *Vāyu, Matsya, Bhāgavata* and *Brahma-Vaivarta* state that VP consists of 23000 verses, the printed editions give only 6000 verses.

The Gita Press edition has 6373 verses. It appears that the NP in in verses 17b-18, regards VP and *Viṣṇudharmottara Purāṇa* as one book while Śaṅkara (800 A.D.) regards them as two separate works (PJ VIII 94-96) showing thereby that the present NP. was settled before 800 A.D.

3. In this verse the NP. mentions topics discussed in VP I. 11-22

5-6. The narration of the separate rulership and administration. These are the topics in the first division.

(The second division.) The narration of the family of Priyavrata, the review of the continents and the sub-continents, the narration of the nether worlds and hells; the review of seven heavens; the narration of the day of the week like Sunday and others alongwith their separate characteristics.

7. Then the story of Bharata, which points out the path of salvation, the dialogue between Ṛbhu and Nidāgha—these are topics in the second division.[1]

8.[2] (The Third Division.[3]) The enumeration of the Manvantaras; the incarnation of Vedavyāsa; thereafter, the rite that lifts one up from hell is mentioned.

9. The review of all the religious duties (Dharmas) in the dialogue between Sagara and Aurva; then Śrāddha Kalpa (The rituals connected with Śrāddha) is recounted; the classification of the castes and stages of life.

10. The conduct of life of the good is described; then the story of delusion due to Māyā; thus the third division that destroys all sins has been explained.

11. (The Fourth Division.) The holy story of the solar race, the narration of the lunar race. Alongwith that there are stories of different kings. O excellent sage, these are the topics in the fourth division.

12-15. (The fifth division.) The query about the incarnation of Kṛṣṇa; then the story of the family of cowherds; the death of Pūtanā during his infancy; the slaying of Agha, etc. in the course of his boyhood days; killing of Kaṁsa during the youth; the story of his life in Mathurā; then in the course of his prime of youth his sports at Dvārakā, the killing of all Daityas, the different marriages, staying at Dvārakā, the Lord of the Universe, Kṛṣṇa, the Lord of Masters of Yoga removed (lightened)

---

1. This verse refers to topics contained in VP Aṁśa II chs. 1-7, 12-16.

2. VV 8-10 mention topics described in VP *Aṁśa* II chs. 1-3, 8-9, 13-16, 17-18.

3. It appears that the NP is unaware of the chs. 21-24 which describe the future kings, in the IV Aṁśa of the VP.

the burden of the Earth through killing etc. of the enemies; the narrative of Aṣṭāvakra. The fifth division is thus recounted.[1]

16-17a. The story of Kali is mentioned, the four types of dissolution. The Knowledge of Brahman reviewed by Keśidhvaja (for the benefit) of Khāṇḍikya. So the sixth division is recounted.

17b-18. Hereafter, the perpetual virtues called Viṣṇudharmottaras are mentioned by Sūta on being respectfully asked by Śaunaka and others. Many holy stories, holy rites, observances, and restraints were also described by him.

19-20. Dharma-śāstra (Code of Laws), Arthaśāstra (Political economy) Vedānta (Metaphysics), Jyotiṣa (Astronomy and Astrology), the narration of the races, hymns according to the context; and dynasties, Manvantaras (or Manus); different vidyās (lores) that are beneficial to the worlds are described. This is verily the Viṣṇu Purāṇa which is a succinct collection of all the topics of sacred scriptures.

21-23. In this, the events of the Vārāha Kalpa[2] have been narrated by Vyāsa.[3] He who reads this with devotion and he who listens to it with respect goes to the world of Viṣṇu. Both of them enjoy all pleasures there. This Purāṇa must be written and given to a devotee of Viṣṇu who knows the meaning of the Purāṇa on the full moon day in the month of Āṣāḍha alongwith ghee and a cow. O Brāhmaṇa, he who does so goes to the abode of Viṣṇu through an aerial chariot as refulgent as the sun.

24. O Brāhmaṇa, he who hears the contents of the Viṣṇu Purāṇa shall attain the benefit of the Purāṇa itself.

---

1. VV 12-15 summarize the topics in Lord Kṛṣṇa's life and form the basis for the X Skandha of the Bh. P.

2. The device to explain different versions of the same story is to attribute it to a different Kalpa.

3. In VP., Vyāsa is not the interlocutor. It is a dialogue between Parāśara and Maitreya.

It appears that the major portion of the present day VP is known to the NP and hence it obviously precedes NP in date.

CHAPTER NINETYFIVE

The Vāyu Purāṇa : The table of contents

God Brahmā said :

1. O Brāhmaṇa, listen; I shall describe the Vāyavīya Purāṇa[1] on hearing which one attains the abode of Rudra,[2] the Supreme Soul

2. This Purāṇa is reputed to comprise of twentyfour thousand[3] verses. In the context of Śvetakalpa, holy rites (dharmas) have been described herein by the wind-god.

3-6. This Vāyavīya Purāṇa has two sections. (In the first section) the characteristics of creation etc. are mentioned in details. Kings and their dynasties in different Manvantaras have been recounted. The killing of the demon Gaya[4] is described in detail. The importance and glory of (different months and of) the month of Māgha in yielding (religious) merits is mentioned. The merit accruing from charitable gifts and the duties of the kings have been described in detail. The precise descrip-

---

1. This is called *Vāyu* as god Vāyu is the chief interlocutor. The Mt. P. (ch. 53) declares that herein Vāyu proclaimed *dharmas* pertaining to Śveta-Kalpa. This Purāṇa is published by Veṅkaṭeśvara Press Bombay, Asiatic Society Calcutta, Ānandāśram Poona and Guru Mandal Grathmālā Calcutta (to mention a few).

2. This Purāṇa belongs to the Śa iva group and is characterised by the glory of Rudra as Mt. P. puts it. The elucidation of Pāśupata Yoga and the emphasis on Śiva Māhātmya made NP declare the attainment of Rudra's abode as the fruit of listening to this Purāṇa.

3. Though Vāyu, Mt. P., Bh. P and NP declare 24000 as the total number of verses in the *Vāyu*, AP gives the 14000 as the number of verses, while according to the *Devībhāgavata* it is 24,600 verses.

Actually the Ānandāśrama edition contains 10,991 verses. It appears that sections like Revā Māhātmya and other Māhātmyas which were originally in the *Vāyu P.* when the NP wrote this chapter, later got separated as independent works (Pusalkar —*Studies in Epics and Purāṇas* (SEP).—P. 7a). Pusalkar opines that the *Vāyu* is a Mahāpurāṇa while the *Śiva Purāṇa* is an *Upa-Purāṇa* (ibid 77).

4. Kane (HD. vii p 906) and other scholars regard this Gayā Māhātmya as a later addition to counter-balance the Śaiva bias in such chapters as 20.31-35, 24.91-165 (*Sarva Stotra*), 101. 215. 33 etc.

tion of the beings wandering over the Earth, nether worlds, quarters and the firmament is made therein and all the holy vows and observances etc. are mentioned. Thus the first Section has been stated in brief.

7-9. In the latter section, there is the description of the holy river Narmadā.[1] O leading sage, Śiva's Saṁhitā (compendium) is mentioned in detail. The eternal Deity who is inscrutable to all the Devas stays perpetually on the banks of Narmadā wholeheartedly. The waters of Narmadā are identical with Brahmā, Hari, himself, the great Hara, the formless Brahman and the Kaivalya (salvation) itself.

10. Verily Revā, (this Narmadā) is a certain Śakti in the form of a river which has been brought forth from his own body by Śiva for the benefit of the worlds.

11. Those who live on its northern bank are the followers of Rudra. Those who reside on the Southern bank go to the world of Viṣṇu.

12. Beginning with Omkāreśvara and ending with the Western ocean, there are thirtyfive confluences with other rivers that destroy sins.

13. There are eleven confluences on the Northern bank (the northern side) and twentythree in the Southern bank (from the south) and the confluence of Revā with the ocean is the thirtyfifth.

14. Together on both the banks of Revā, there are four hundred famous holy centres inclusive of the confluences.

---

1. VV 7-15 : The Printed Texts (both Ānandāśrama and Guru Mandal (GM) editions) do not give the chapters pertaining to the Revā Māhātmya which might have been there when the NP was written. In stead of the division *Pūrvārdha* and *Uttarārdha* as given in the NP (of the Vāyu-Purāṇa) the *Vāyu* itself (in ch. 103.44) states that it has four sections (*Pādas*) viz. (1) *Prakriyā* (2) *Anuṣaṅga* (3) *Upodghāta* and (4) *Upasaṁhāra* and it calls the Purāṇa as 'Four-footed Purāṇa narrated by Vāyu' in the next verse (ibid 103.45)

The Ānandāśrama edition gives the following division of chapters :
1. Prakriyā (chs 1-6) (2) Anuṣaṅga (chs. 7-64) 3. Upodghāta (chs. 65-99) (Upasaṁhāra (chs. 100-112)

The contents given in the NP are to a great extent different from those in the Printed editions of the *Vāyu P.*

15. O leading sage, there are sixty crores and sixty thousand holy centres at every step on both the banks of the Revā.

16. This Saṁhitā (compendium) of Śiva, the great Ātman, is very meritorious. In this the story of the river Narmadā has been detailed by Vāyu.

17-18a. He who writes this Purāṇa and gives the manuscript with great devotion to a Brāhmaṇa householder on the full moon day in the month of Śrāvaṇa alongwith jaggery and a cow, lives in the world of Rudra as long as fourteen Indras rule over the Heaven.

18b-20. The man who narrates this Vāyavīya Purāṇa or listens to this, regularly, restricting his diet to cooked rice consecrated with ghee, is undoubtedly Rudra Himself. He who listens to or reads this index (or the contents of this Purāṇa) shall obtain the benefit of listening to the entire Purāṇa.

CHAPTER NINETYSIX

Śrīmad Bhāgavata : Contents

God Brahmā said :

1. O Marīci, listen. I shall tell you (the story of) the Purāṇa, Śrīmad Bhāgavata that has been composed by Veda-Vyāsa and which is on a par with the Vedas.

2. It consists of eighteen thousand[1] verses. It is glorified as destructive of sins. This is a veritable wish-yielding celestial tree with twelve branches (Skandhas—sections of the Bhāgavata).

3-4. O leading Brāhmaṇa therein in the first Skandha, when Sūta and the sages meet together, the Lord is mentioned

1. According to the Va. P., A.P., N.P., Br. V. & *Devībhāgavata* and the Bh. P. itself, the Bh. P. consists of 18000 verses. But actually the Gita Press edition of the Bh. P. contains 14,579 verses.

as embodying the whole of the Universe. The holy life of Vyāsa as well as that of the Pāṇḍavas (is recounted). Then the episode of Parīkṣit. This is cited as the first Skandha.

5-6. In the course of dialogue between Parīkṣit and Śuka there is the review of the two types of creation. In the course of dialogue between Brahmā and Nārada there is a nectarlike story of the Devas, the characteristics of the Purāṇa and the cause and origin of the creation. This second Skandha is thus composed by the intelligent Vyāsa.

7-8a. The anecdote of Vidura, his meeting with Maitreya : The Prakaraṇa (section) of creation from Brahman, the Supreme Soul; the Sāṅkhya doctrine propounded by Kapila : Thus the third Skandha is summarised.

8b-9. The story of Satī at the outset and that of Dhruva thereafter : There the holy story of Pṛthu as well as that of Prācīnabarhis : Thus the excellent fourth Skandha is told, while narrating the gross creation (Visarga).[1]

10-11a. The meritorious story of Priyavrata and the anecdote of the members of his family; thereafter, the description of the worlds included in the Cosmic egg. The condition of hells. This is considered (as the summary of) the fifth Skandha which is technically called Saṁsthāna or Sthiti.[2]

11b-12. The story of Ajāmila and the review of the creation by Dakṣa. The narrative of Vṛtra and thereafter, the meri-

---

1. The NP. upholds the view advocated by the Bh. P. II.90.1 that instead of the traditional five characteristics of a *Purāṇa*, the Bh. P. redefines a *Purāṇa* as possessing the following ten characteristics.

(1) Subtle creation (*Sarga*); (2) Gross creation (*Visarga*) (3) law and order ensured by God (*Sthāna*); (4) Protection—welfare of all (*Poṣaṇa*);(5) material lust for *Karmas* (*Ūti*) (6) the periods of Manus and history of that epoch (*Manvantara*); (7) accounts of the deeds of the Lord (*Īśānukathā*) (8) physical annihilation (*Nirodha*) (9) Liberation (*Mukti*); (10) the last resort of the Universe or the Ultimate reality (*Āśraya*).

These characteristics occur with some variations in the Bh. P. XII.7.9-10 but as Śrīdhara points out the terms *Vṛtti* and *Rakṣā* stand for *Sthāna* and *Poṣaṇa*. *Vaṁśānucarita* is used for *Īśānukathā*, *Saṁsthā* includes *Nirodha* and *Mukti*; and *hetu* is substituted for *Ūti*, *Apāśraya* for *Āśraya*.

2. Despite the efforts of Bopadeva in *Harilīlāmṛta* (and his able commentator Madhusūdana Sarasvati) to show how the contents of Skandha V demonstrate the characteristics of *Sthāna*, a modern reader wonders how the

torious nativity of the Maruts. This is the sixth Skandha composed by Vyāsa in the course of the section known as Pariposaṇa (or Protection and welfare of all by the Lord).

13. The holy story of Prahlāda, the review of the castes and stages of life. O dear one, thus the seventh Skandha is mentioned in the course of the narration of the desire for action as directed by past Karman. (It is technically called Ūti).

14-15a. In the course of the narration of the part known as Manvantara comes the narration of the elephant-king, the churning of the ocean and the check on the prosperity of Bali. The story of the incarnation as Fish. This is the eighth Skandha. (It comes under Manvantara).

15b. The narration of the Solar dynasty as well as the review of the lunar race. O highly intelligent one, the ninth Skandha is mentioned in the course of the narration of the dynasties.

16-17. The story of the childhood of Kṛṣṇa and his boyhood; his stay in the Vraja; his early youth and the stay in Mathurā; his later youth and stay in Dvārakā and the removal of the burden on the Earth. This is the tenth Skandha in the course of narrating the characteristic section called Nirodha or control.

18-19a. The dialogue between Nārada and Vasudeva, the meeting of Yadu with Dattātreya and that of Uddhava with Śrī Kṛṣṇa. The mutual fight and the annihilation of the Yādavas. This is the eleventh Skandha which is designated as Mukti (liberation).

---

legends of Priyavrata to Bharata (chs 1 to 15) followed by the mythological geography, ancient (mythical) astronomy and description of hells form an organic whole to be included under the characteristic *Sthiti, Saṁsthāna* or *Vṛtti*. Such doubts naturally arise when the text of the Bh. P. is stretched on the *Daśa Lakṣaṇa* bed of Procrustes.

It appears that the NP. accepts the traditional *Skandha*-wise distribution of the topics or the ten *Purāṇa lakṣaṇas* of the Bh. P. as folows :

Name of the characteristic topic.	No. of Skandha illustrating it.
1. *Sarga*	III
2. *Visarga*	IV
3. *Saṁsthāna* or *Sthiti*	V
4. *Poṣaṇa*	VI

19b-21. The future Kali is prophesied; the liberation of Parīkṣit; the composition of the branches of the Vedas; the performance of penance by Mārkaṇḍeya. The Vibhūti (elegance, glory) of Sūra (Sun-god) and thereafter, that of the Sāttvatas. The narration of the number of verses in the Purāṇa. This is the twelfth Skandha which is also called Āśraya (support). Thus the whole of Śrīmad Bhāgavata has been narrated to you, O dear one.

22. It is the bestower of devotion, worldly pleasures and salvation on the narrator, listener, instructor, supporter and the person who renders assistance.

23. The manuscript of this book is to be given with pleasure to a Brāhmaṇa devotee of the Lord alongwith a replica of a lion in gold, on the full-moon day in the month of Bhādrapada.

24. If any one desires for the devotion of the Lord, (he must give it) after duly worshipping him (the Brāhmaṇa) with clothes, gold etc.

That person too who reads or who listens to this index, attains the excellent benefit of listening to the entire Purāṇa.

5.	*Ūti*	VII
6.	*Manvantara*	VIII
7.	*Īśānucarita*	IX
8.	*Nirodha*	X
9.	*Mukti*	XI
10.	*Āśraya*	XII

This distribution is supported by later eminent writers like Bopadeva in *Harilīlāmṛta*; Śrīdhara, Vīra-rāghava, Vijayadhvaja, Vallabha and others.

As I have presented this traditional scheme and criticised it in details in my Introduction to the Bh.P. pp, xxii-xxxiv (AITM series vol. VII), I may briefly state that the claim of the Bh. P. as a *Mahāpurāṇa* with ten characteristics is tolerably justifiable within the limits of the Bh. P. as an epic of growth.

This traditional presentation of the contents of the Bh. P in the NP. shows that the major portion of the BH.P. belongs to the pre-NP. era.

CHAPTER NINETYSEVEN

The Nāradiya Purāṇa : Contents

Śrī Brahmā said :

1. O Brāhmaṇa, listen, I shall recount to you the Nāradīya Purāṇa comprising the twentyfive thousand verses,[1] based on the story of Bṛhat Kalpa.

2-3a. In the first quarter of the earlier (first) division, there is a dialogue between Sūta and Śaunaka, then there is a succinct description of Creation. Many holy religious stories connected with Pravṛtti (activity) have been narrated in the first quarter of the first division by Sanaka, the great soul.

3b-4. In the second quarter called 'Mokṣa Dharma', there is the review of the means to salvation, the detailed narration of the ancillaries of the Vedas and the birth of Śuka. All these have been recounted to the noble-souled Nārada by Sanandana.

5-7a. In the third quarter, the following have been narrated to Nārada by sage Sanatkumāra : Paśu's (individual soul's) liberation from Pāśa (bondage of Saṁsāra) as explained in Mahā Tantra; the consecration of the Mantras, the initiation, the uplift of the Mantras, the mode of worship, practical application, Kavaca (recitation of mantras as protection or coat of

---

1. According to the *Vāyu, Mt. P., Bh. P. A.P., Br. Vaivarta* and the statement of the *NP*. here, this Purāṇa consists of 25000 verses. But actually the Veṅkaṭeśvar Press edition of the NP contains 18550 verses (13144 in the I part and 5406 in the II Part) PJ. VII 2, p 349 states that it consists of 17549 verses. According to Hazra, the *Mt. P., AP* and *Sk. P.* had a different—an earlier—version of the NP before them, as that NP (according to these Purāṇas) was declared by Nārada with reference to *Bṛhat Kalpa* which is merely mentioned here. In the present NP., Nārada is a listener. Hence the present NP is different. Moreover, a number of *Nibandha*-writers quote from the NP but the quotations are untraceable in this extant Purāṇa. For example, the 47 lines quoted from the NP by Jimūtavāhana in *Kālaviveka* are not traced in this NP. It appears that an earlier edition of the NP was a bigger one when the mediaval Dharma-śāstra writers used it.

mail), the thousand names, the hymns to Gaṇeśa, Sūrya, Viṣṇu, Śiva and Śakti in due order.

7b-9. The following topics have been recounted to Nārada by Sage Sanātana in the fourth quarter : The characteristics of the Purāṇa, the authorities and means of valid knowledge, charitable gifts, etc. have been mentioned separately alongwith the proper time for the gifts. The holy vows that destroy all sins and that have to be observed on the Pratipad (first day) and other (subsequent) Tithis in all the months such as of Caitra etc.

10. Thus the first division is summarised. It is called Bṛhadākhyāna. In the second division there is the enquiry about the vowed observance of Ekādaśī.

11-18. It is a dialogue between Vasiṣṭha and Māndhātā : It contains the meritorious story of Rukmāṅgada, the origin and activities of Mohinī, the curse on Mohinī by Vasu and then the way of extrication therefrom; the holiest story of the Gaṅgā, the narration of the pilgrimage to Gayā; the incomparable greatness of Kāśī; the description of Puruṣottama, the injunctions regarding the pilgrimage to the holy centres alongwith many incidental anecdotes; the greatness of Prayāga; thereafter, that of Kurukṣetra; the description of Haridvāra; the narration of Kāmoda; the greatness of the holy centre Badarī as well as that of Kāmākṣā; the greatness of Prabhāsa; then the description of Puṣkara; the story of Gautama afterwards and then the hymn called Vedapāda; the greatness of the holy centre of Gokarṇa; the narrative of Lakṣmaṇa; the narration of the greatness of Setu (the Bridge built by Rāma from Bhārata to Laṅkā); the description of the sacred river Narmadā; the greatness of Avanti; and that of Mathurā; the greatness of Vṛndāvana; the approach of the Paśu (individual soul) near Brahman, the story of Mohinī thereafter. These are the contents of the Nāradīya Purāṇa.[1]

1. Despite the difference noted above, the division of the NP in five parts and the contents of each mentioned therein, do tally with the contents of the extant Purāṇa.

19-21. The man who hears this with devotion or narrates it with great concentration goes to the abode of Brahmā; no hesitation or doubt need be entertained in this respect. He who gives (the manuscript of) this book to an excellent Brāhmaṇa on the Iṣupūrṇā* (on the full moon day of the 5th month viz. Śrāvaṇa) alongwith seven cows, attains salvation. He who describes this index of Nāradīya Purāṇa or listens to it with concentration attains Heaven.

CHAPTER NINETYEIGHT

The Mārkaṇḍeya Purāṇa : Contents

Śrī Brahmā said :

1. O sage, henceforth, I shall narrate the Purāṇa named Mārkaṇḍeya.[1] It is highly meritorious to those who read and listen to it.

2. All the Dharmas have been reviewed therein with reference to the wise birds (in the Vindhya mountains)[2]. Mārkaṇḍeya Purāṇa is said to contain nine thousand verses.[3]

---

*The correct reading should be *Iṣā Pūrṇimā*; it will mean "Full-moon day of Āśvina (September-October).

1. This *Purāṇa* is available in two editions—B.I. (Bibliotheca Indica series) and Veṅkaṭeśvar Press. Both the editions, however, differ in the total number of chapters (viz. 137 and 134) and number of verses in many chapters. This Purāṇa is noted for the *Devī Māhātmya* or the famous *Saptaśatī* which, though an interpolation, must have taken place long before 1000 A.D., as verses from the *Saptaśatī* are quoted in the Dadhimati Mata Inscription (in former Jodhpur state dated 289 of the Gupta era (608 A.D.) vide *Epi. Ind.* XI. 299-303. This Purāṇa is assigned a date between 400-600 A.D. (Kane HD. V : 11. 903)

2. VV 2-3. This refers to the introductory part (chs 1-7) of the Mk. P. in which Mārkaṇḍeya directs Jaimini to approach the wise birds in Vindhya mountain to get answers for his Mahābhārara problems (about the Mahābhārata story such as the reason of *Nirguṇa* Vāsudeva's assumption of human form, Balarāma's token expiation for a Brāhmaṇa-slaughter etc.) I wonder why Jaimini, a direct disciple of Vyāsa, the author of the Mbh., approached Mārkaṇḍeya for problems about the Mbh and not to Vyāsa himself. The wise birds called Dharmas explain his difficulties.

3. According to the *NP.*, *Vāyu*, *Matsya*, *Agni* and *Bh.P* the Mārkaṇḍeya P. consists of 9000 verses but the Veṅkaṭeśvar edition gives only 6447 verses

4. Then the rites of fire worship, thereafter, the characteristics of the Mantras and Mudrās (gestures), etc., the injunctions regarding all initiations; the review of the procedure of ablutions.

5. The characteristics of Maṇḍala (mystic diagram) etc., then the rite of Mārjana (wiping off) with the water from Kuśa grass; the injunction regarding the wearing of the Pavitra (Kuśa grass with a loop and a tail worn like a ring), and then the instructions regarding the temples.

6-7. Then the worship of Śālagrāma etc., the separate signs and symbols of the Mūrtis, the injunctions regarding the Nyāsa rites, the worship of Vināyaka etc. alongwith their Pratiṣṭhā (installation), thereafter the rules regarding initiation of diverse kinds; the installation of all deities and the review of the Cosmic egg.

8. The greatness of the Gaṅgā and other holy rivers, the description of the continents and the sub-continents, the arrangement of the upper and the lower worlds, the review of Jyotiścakra (the circle of the luminaries.)

9. Jyotiṣa (Astrology and Astronomy) is then described and then the scripture "Yuddhajayārṇava" (Ocean of the conquests in battles), then the six holy rites are narrated and also the collections of Mantras and medicinal herbs to be used with Mantras.

10. The rites of worshipping Kubjikā (an unmarried girl of eight years) etc., then the six types of Nyāsa rites, then the injunction regarding "koṭihoma" (a crore of Homas), the review of the Manvantaras.

11. The pious rites of Brahmacarya (vow of celibacy) etc., then the rules regarding the rituals of Śrāddha, then Graha-yajña (the sacrifice for the planets) is mentioned, then the various holy rites laid down in the Vedas and the Smṛtis.

12. The narration of expiatory rites, the Vratas etc. to be performed on the various Tithis, days of the week and the constellations.

---

verses with those in the extant AP (GM;-edition) shows in majority of the topics mentioned in the NP are found in the extant AP.

13. The guidance regarding monthly Vratas, the rules regarding the charitable gifts of lamps, the worship of the Navavyūhas (the nine manifestations) and the review of hells.

14. The review of Vratas (sacred vowed observances) and charitable gifts, the direction regarding Nāḍī Cakra (circle of nerves) and the excellent rules regarding the Sandhyā prayers.

15. The stipulation regarding the meaning of the Gāyatrī, then the hymn unto the Liṅga, the specification of the Mantras for the coronation of kings; the righteous duties (and activities) of kings.

16. Then the chapter on dreams is mentioned, the review of omens, etc., the specification regarding Maṇḍala (mystic diagram) etc., then the rules regarding 'Ratna Dīkṣā'

17. The guidance in polity mentioned by Rāma, then the characteristics of Ratnas (jewels), then the science of archery is described, then the method of dealing is revealed.

18. The narrative of the conflict between the Devas and the Asuras, the review of Āyurveda (Medical Science), the Veterinary science (e. g. the treatment of elephants etc., and their pacification).

19. The treatment of cows, diagnosis and treatment of men, etc., then the different kinds of Pūjās; different kinds of Śāntis (pacificatory rites); then the science of prosody.

20. Then literature (literary criticism) and the (lexicon of) single-syllabled norms, thereafter, the enumeration of the formation of words, then lexicon according to the different groups and formations.

21. The characteristics of dissolutions; the review of the Śārīraka (limbs of the body in AP. ch. 370), description of hells, then the Yoga system of Philosophy.

22. Thereafter, the knowledge of the Brahman, the benefit of listening to the Purāṇa, O Brāhmaṇa, this is mentioned as the Agni Purāṇa.

23-25. He who writes this and gives it to a person who knows the meanings of the Purāṇa, on the full moon day in the month of Mārgaśīrṣa in accordance with the injunctions, alongwith a gold lotus and a replica of a cow in gingelly seeds, is honoured in the heavenly world. This index of topics in the Agni Purāṇa narrated to you is the bestower of salvation unto the men who read and listen to this. It benefits them both here and hereafter.

CHAPTER ONE HUNDRED

The Bhaviṣya Purāṇa : Contents

Śrī Brahmā said :

1. Henceforth, I shall recount to you the Bhaviṣya Purāṇa[1] which yields all Siddhis and which bestows the desired objects of all the worlds.

2. In it, I have come up as the primordial maker of all the Devas. For the purpose of creation, there was born the Svāyambhuva (son of the self-born) Manu formerly.

3. He bowed to me and asked me about Dharma (pious and religious duties) that is the means of achieving all objects.

---

1. This *Bhaviṣya Purāṇa* is not what is mentioned in the *Āpastamba Dharma Sūtra* (I.6.19.13) not the extant Veṅkaṭeśvara Edt. For the NP in the following verses (VV 4ff) mentions that Vyāsa divided this Purāṇa into five divisions viz. *Brāhma, Vaiṣṇava, Śaiva, Saura and Pratisarga.* But the published *Bhaviṣya Purāṇa* has only four *Parvas* viz. *Brāhma, Madhyama, Pratisarga* and *Uttara.* NP verse 5 states that the *Bhaviṣya* P. described the incidents of the *Aghora Kalpa* which is not mentioned in the Printed Edition. The NP in V 6. states that the 1st *Parvan* (Brāhma) is a dialogue between Sūta and Śaunaka which is not found in the printed edition. *Pratisarga Parvan* in the printed editions is a fabrication as it refers to the stories of Adam and Eve, Kabir, Nanak and Caitanya etc.

Thus the account regarding the extent and contents of the *Bhaviṣya* P as given in the NP., Mt. P. 53. 30-31, AP. 272. 12 does not tally with the printed editions. The number of verses in the *Bhaviṣya* P is 14500 according to Mt. P. and Vāyu. P. but 14000 according to NP. verse 13 and Agni (272. 12) but the Printed edition is much longer (25,936 verses). PJ—VII-2, p. 349. Thus the NP describes a different version of the *Bhaviṣya P.* than the published one.

Very much delighted I expounded to him the Dharmasaṁhitā (a compendium on Dharma.)

4. When the highly intelligent Vyāsa classified the Purāṇas, the sage divided that Saṁhitā (of the Bhaviṣya Purāṇa) into five divisions.

5. The incidents of Aghora Kalpa are mentioned alongwith many wonderful stories. There the first Parvan is Brāhma where the Upakrama (beginning) is mentioned.

6. In the course of the dialogue between Sūta and Śaunaka* there is the transmission of the enquiry regarding the Purāṇa. It is full of the stories of the sun and accompanied by all narratives.

7. The entire form of the scripture is endued with the characteristics of creation etc. Thereafter, the characteristics of the calligraphy of the writers of books are mentioned.

8. The characteristic features of all Saṁskāras (purificatory rites) are mentioned here. Seven rituals regarding the Tithis of the lunar fortnight are mentioned.

9-10. The Kalpas for the remaining Tithis beginning with Aṣṭamī (eighth day) are mentioned in the section called Vaiṣṇava Parvan. In the next Parvan called Śaiva Parvan those who are different in bodies are mentioned. (?) In the Saura Parvan the final stories are mentioned. The next Parvan is called Pratisarga. It contains different stories alongwith the conclusion of the Purāṇa. It is the fifth Parvan.

11-12. Among these five, in the first Parvan, the glory of Brahmā is very much greater than that of Viṣṇu or Śiva in regard to Dharma, Kāma (love) and Mokṣa (salvation). Thus the story mentioned in the second, third and the fourth section (Varga) called Saura and in the last one named Pratisarga has been recounted.

13. The Parvan alongwith the Bhaviṣya has been proclaimed by the intelligent Vyāsa. The Purāṇa consists of fourteen thousand verses.

14. The Bhaviṣya is that Parvan (Purāṇa) where the equality among all the deities is glorified. In the point of view

*Not found in the published version of this Purāṇa

of the comparison of the Guṇas, the Śruti says that "Brahman is equal."

15-16. That a learned person who being free from jealousy writes or gets written this Purāṇa and on the full moon day of the month called 'Pauṣa' (December-January) worships duly both the reader (of this Purāṇa) and the book (the manuscript of this Purāṇa) alongwith the replica of a cow made of jaggery as well as gold, clothes, garlands and ornaments.

17. Or a person who has subdued his sense-organs, observes fasts or takes only one meal per day of sacred Haviṣya food (food worthy of being oblated in sacrificial fire), hears or glorifies (recounts) this with concentrated mind becomes absolved of terrible sins and attains to the supreme region of Brahmā.

18-19. He who reads or listens to this index to Bhaviṣya Purāṇa as mentioned here shall attain worldly pleasures and liberation.

CHAPTER ONE HUNDRED AND ONE

The Brahma-Vaivarta Purāṇa : Contents

Śrī Brahmā said :

1. O dear child, I shall recount to you the tenth Purāṇa named Brahmavaivarta.[1] It points out the path of the Vedas.

---

1. This Purāṇa is *Brahma-Vaivarta* as the entire Brahman was manifested by Kṛṣṇa :

vivṛtaṁ Brahma kārtsnyena Kṛṣṇena yatra Śaunaka /
Brahma-Vaivartakaṁ tena pravadanti purā-vidaḥ //

—*Brahma-Vaivarta* 1.1-10

It is obviously a *Vaiṣṇava Purāṇa*—mainly devoted to the glorification of Rādhā and as such is very popular with Gauḍīya Vaiṣṇavas. According to Wilson this work does not deserve to be called a *Purāṇa* (*Viṣṇupurāṇa*, Intro. LXV—LXVII)

2. In it the Lord himself assumed the form of Sāvarṇa and narrated the subject matter of the Purāṇa to Nārada,[1] the divine sage. He mentioned the entire miraculous non-mundane subject matter to him.

3. The essence of virtue (dharma), wealth, love and liberation from bondage of saṁsāra is the pleasure in and love for Hari and Hara. In order to establish their non-difference is meant the excellent Brahmavaivarta (transformation of Brahman).

4. The events of Rathantara Kalpa narrated in details by me in the Purāṇa of hundred crores of verses were condensed and narrated by the knower of the Vedas (i.e. Vyāsa).

5. In the Purāṇa called Brahmavaivarta he condensed it into four parts. This Purāṇa is reputed to contain eighteen thousand verses.[2]

6. It consists of parts (sections) called Brahmā, Prakṛti, Gaṇeśa and Kṛṣṇa. There the Purāṇa starts with the dialogue between Sūta and Sages.

7. The first chapter (prakaraṇa) pertains to the creation; then there is a great verbal disputation between Nārada and Vedhas (god Brahmā) in which both of them met with a great defeat.

8-10a. Then the attainment of Śiva's world. The acquisition of perfect knowledge through the realisation of Śiva's Ātman through Śiva's exposition. Thereafter, O Marīci, Nārada

---

1. Although the NP. states that this Purāṇa is in the form of a dialogue between Lord Sāvarṇi and Nārada, in the printed edition (GM) Sauti and Śaunaka are the interlocutors in the 1st (*Brahma*) *Khaṇḍa* while Nārāyaṇa (and not Sāvarṇi) and Nārada are the interlocutors in the rest of the *khaṇḍas*.

2. This statement of NP regarding the extent of the *Brahma Vaivarta* (18000 verses) is supported by the *Vāyu, MT. P. AP., BH.P.*, and *Brahma Vaivarta* itself.

Aṣṭādaśa-sahasraṁ ca Brahma-Vaivartam īpsitam

Br. Vai. IV. 131. 16

But in the Ānandāśrama edt. there are 20,694 verses (PJ VII 2. p. 349) and GM edt. adds an additional (spurious) *khaṇḍa—Kāśīrahasya*.

goes to the hermitage of Sāvarṇi[1] which was resorted to by Siddhas for the purpose of perfect knowledge. That is an exceedingly meritorious hermitage causing wonderment in the three worlds. This is well known as Brahma Khaṇḍa. It is destructive of sins.

10b-11. Then the dialogue between Sāvarṇi and Nārada is recounted. It contains the greatness of Kṛṣṇa and a number of various different anecdotes, the greatness of the Kalās (digits) that are parts of Prakṛti is described.

12. The mode of worship in the precise manner has been described in detail. This is the well known Prakṛti Khaṇḍa that brings about prosperity.

13. The word of enquiry about the nativity of Gaṇeśa : Pārvatī's great and meritorious Vrata (holy vow) ; the birth of Vighneśa along with Kārttikeya.

14-15a. The wonderful story of Kārttavīrya and Jāmadagnya (Paraśurāma). A great dispute arises between Gaṇeśa and Jāmadagnya (Paraśurāma). This is the Vighneśa Khaṇḍa that dispels all obstacles.

15b-16. The enquiry regarding the birth of Śrīkṛṣṇa : The narration of his birth in wonderful manner, his departure to Gokula (the cowherds' colony), the miracles of killing Pūtanā, etc.; his sports during infancy and boyhood of diverse kinds, are described.

17. The Rāsa sport in the autumn alongwith the cowherdesses is mentioned; his secret dalliance with Rādhā is described in detail.

18. Thereafter, Hari goes to Mathurā accompained by Akrūra. After the killing of Kaṁsa and others Kṛṣṇa is consecrated as a twice-born (i.e. investiture with the sacred thread.)

---

1. The Printed text of *Br. Vaivarta Brahma Khaṇḍa* Ch. 28 does not mention Sāvarṇi at all. God Śaṅkara sends Nārada to Nārāyaṇa in the *Badarīvana* and the rest of the Purāṇa is a dialogue between Nārada and Nārāyaṇa (and not Sāvarṇi though Sāvarṇi in the NP. is regarded as identical with Viṣṇu).

A detailed comparison of the contents of the printed *Br. Vaivarta Purāṇa* and those given in the NP shows that the author of the NP had a different version of this Purāṇa before him.

19. The wonderful learning of all lores from Sāndīpani of Kāśi, the killing of Yavana, thereafter the departure of Hari to Dvārakā.

20. The killing of Naraka etc, was wonderfully carried out by Kṛṣṇa. O Brāhmaṇa, this is the Kṛṣṇa Khaṇḍa that cuts at the root of worldly existence of men.

21. This is read, heard, meditated upon, worshipped and saluted. Thus is the Supramundane Brahmavaivarta Purāṇa.

22. This is narrated at the outset by Vyāsa. One who reads it and listens to it is liberated from the terrible ocean of worldly existence through the acquisition of perfect knowledge and the suppression of ignorance.

23. He who writes this out and makes a gift of it on the full moon day in the month of Māgha alongwith a cow attains Brahmaloka. He is liberated from the bondage of ignorance.

24. He too, who reads or listens to this index (contents of this Purāṇa) attains the desired benefit, thanks to Kṛṣṇa's grace.

CHAPTER ONE HUNDRED AND TWO

The Liṅga Purāṇa : Contents

God Brahmā said :

1. O son, listen, I shall recount to you the Purāṇa called Liṅga.[1] It bestows worldly pleasures and salvation on those who read and listen to it.

2. It was while stationed in the huge fiery column that Hara narrated (the subject matter in the Purāṇa) named Liṅga to me in order that virtue etc, may be realised. The story refers

1. The *LP* is published by the Veṅkaṭeśvara Press, G.M. Calcutta. and MLBD, Delhi. Its translation is published in the AITM, Motilal Banarsidass, Delhi. I have used the GM. edition for reference here.

to the incidents of the Agni Kalpa.[1]

3. The same thing was described by the holy Lord Vyāsa in two parts. The Liṅga Purāṇa is mentioned to be miraculous with many narratives.

4. It comprises of eleven thousand verses.[2] It indicates the greatness of Hara. It is greater than all the other Purāṇas. It is the essence of the three worlds.

5. There is the enquiry at the start of the Purāṇa. The former creation is succinctly described. Then the Yoga system is narrated; thereafter, the Kalpa is recounted.

6. The origin of the Liṅga; then Ambā is glorified; then the holy dialogue between Sanatkumāra and Śilāda's son i.e. Nandin.

7. Thereafter, the story of Dādhīca, the review of the Yugadharma (virtue peculiar to the different Yugas), then the narrative of the Bhuvana Kośa (The globe of the world), then the Solar and the Lunar races are described.

8. Then the creation is described in detail; then the story of the Tripuras; the installation of the Liṅga and then the liberation of the Paśu (individual soul) from Pāśa (bondage i.e. from saṁsāra)

9. The holy rites of Śiva, the survey of good conduct Expiatory rites; Ariṣṭas (evil portents, harassments etc.); then the description of Kāśi and Śrī Śaila.

10. The narration of Andhaka; then the story of Varāha (The Divine Boar), the story of Nṛsiṁha and then the slaying of Jalandhara.

---

1. The NP states that the *Liṅga Purāṇa* (*LP*) refers to incidents in the *Agni Kalpa,* but LP I 2.1 states that it describes the incidents in the *Īśāna-Kalpa.*

Īśāna-Kalpa-vṛttāntam adhikṛtya mahātmanā/
Brahmaṇā kalpitam pūrvam Purāṇam Laiṅgam uttamam//

It means that the NP used a different and older version of the LP than the extant published editions.

2. This statement of the NP regarding the extent of the *LP* (viz. 11,000 verses) has been endorsed by the *Vāyu, Mt.P., Bh.P., A.P.* etc. The *LP* also states that it consists of 11000 verses ;

Asyaikādaśa-sāhasraṁ granthamānam iha dvijāḥ/

But actually the Veṅkaṭa Edt. of the LP contains 9185 verses (PJ VII—2. p. 349)

11. The thousand epithets of Śiva, the destruction of Dakṣa's sacrifice. Kāma is burnt down, then the story of the marriage of Girijā.

12. Then the story of Vināyaka, that of the kings and that of Śiva; then the story of Upamanyu. This is the summary of the first section.[1]

13. The narration of the greatness of Viṣṇu, then the story of Ambarīṣa, O sage, again there is the dialogue between Sanatkumāra and Nandīśa.

14. The greatness of Śiva, the mode of ablution and sacrificial system (yāga) etc. the injunction regarding the worship of the sun-god. Then the worship of Śiva that confers liberation from saṁsāra.

15. Many types of charitable gifts are mentioned; then the chapter on Śrāddha, the Pratiṣṭhā Tantra (the ritualistic text of installation), then the glorification of Aghora.

16. The great Vidyā of Vajreśvarī, then the glory of Gāyatrī, the greatness of Tryambaka, (the three-eyed Lord) as well as that of listening to the Purāṇa.

17. Thus the latter half of the Liṅga Purāṇa as composed by Vyāsa has been recounted by me and the greatness of Rudra is indicated.[2]

18-19a. This Purāṇa must be written and gifted to a Brāhmaṇa with devotion on the full moonday in the month of Phālguna alongwith gingelly seeds and a cow. He who does so, attains Sāyujya with Śiva. He does not have to suffer from old age or death.

19b-20a. The man who reads or listens to the Liṅga Purāṇa that dispels sins, enjoys pleasures in this world and at the end attains to Śiva's city.

---

1. Though the NP refers to a few topics in the *Pūrva Bhāga,* most of them are found in the extant editions.

2. A comparison of topics given in the NP and those found in the printed (GM) edition shows that the published LP has many topics common with the LP that was before the author of the NP.

20b-21. The man who reads the index and the man who listens to this—both of them are the devotees of Śiva. They enjoy both the worlds through the Grace of the Lord of Girijā. There is no doubt about this.

CHAPTER ONE HUNDRED AND THREE

The Vārāha Purāṇa : Contents

God Brahmā said :

1. O dear one, listen. I shall recount the Vārāha Purāṇa[1]. It is comprised of two parts and it continuously indicates the greatness of Viṣṇu.

2-3. The context of the Mānasa Kalpa composed by me before, or description of the acts I did in the Mānava Kalpa before was compiled by Vyāsa, the most excellent one among scholars in this Purāṇa that comprises twenty-four thousand verses. Vyāsa is the incarnation of Viṣṇu himself on the earth. There at the outset is the auspicious dialogue between the Earth and Varāha. (Divine Boar-Viṣṇu).

---

1. The Purāṇa is extant in two recensions—The Northern and the Southern. The Northern recension published in the B.I. (Bibliotheca Indica) series contains 217 chapters and 9654 verses (with some chapters e.g. 81-83 in prose) and *Not* 24,000 verses as stated in the NP below (verse 2) and endorsed by the *Vāyu*, *MT. P.*, *Bh. P.* and while the *Agni P* (272. 16) credits it with 14000 verses. Though the NP states that the *Vārāha* P. has two parts, the published edition has one part only, though there are indications in ch. 217 that there must have been a second part as well.

This Purāṇa is supposed to have been narrated by Viṣṇu-Varāha to the earth-goddess. Kane observes that it is remarkable that Vyāsa does not appear in this Purāṇa though Sūta figures at the beginning of several chapters (HD V.ii, p. 904).

It is obvious that the author of the NP had a different and bigger version of the *Vārāha Purāṇa* before him.

4. In the course of the incidents of the earlier period, there is the story of Rambhā and then that of Durjaya, thereafter Śrāddha Kalpa (the rituals of the Śrāddha) is described.

5. The narration of the great penance (Mahātapas)-then the origin of Gaurī, Vināyaka, the Nāgas, the commander-in-chief (i.e. Kārttikeya) and Āditya (the sun).

6. Then there is the narrative of the Gaṇas of the goddess, of Kubera and that of Vṛṣa; then the narrative of Satyatāpasa alongwith the narration of vratas.

7. Thereafter, Agastyagītā and Rudragītā are narrated; then the glory of the destruction of demon Mahiṣa (Buffalo) brought about by the three Śaktis.

8. Then is the chapter on Parvans (religious festivals), the incidental narrative of Śveta and the charitable gift of cows. All these incidents had already been pointed out by me in the section on Bhagavad Dharma (virtuous pathway to the Lord).

9-12. Thereafter, the narration of Vratas and Tīrthas, the expiatory bodily rites for thirtytwo offences. The greatness of holy centres is mentioned separately and particularly of Mathurā, thereafter, the rules of procedure regarding Śrāddha etc., the description of the world of Yama, in the context of the son of the sage, the ultimate result of Karmans and the review of Viṣṇu's Vratas, the greatness of Gokarṇa that is destructive of sins, is mentioned. Thus the early part (i.e. the first part) of the Purāṇa is reviewed.

13-14. In the latter part, in the course of the dialogue between Pulastya and the king of Kurus, the greatness of all the holy centres is mentioned in detail, severally.

All the virtues too have been mentioned. The holy Parvan pertaining to Puṣkara is mentioned. Thus the Vārāha Purāṇa. that is destructive of sins is recounted to you.

15-17. This increases devotion to the Lord, of those who read and listen to this. He who writes out this Purāṃa and gives it to a Brāhmaṇa with devotion, along with a gold replica of Garuḍa and gingelly seeds and a cow, on the full moon day in the month of Caitra, attains the abode of Viṣṇu.

He is paid obeisance by the groups of Devas and sages. He who reads or listens to this index obtains devotion to Viṣṇu that is the cause of dissolution of worldly existence.

CHAPTER ONE HUNDRED AND FOUR

The Skanda Purāṇa : Contents

God Brahmā said :

1. O dear one, listen. I shall recount Skanda Purāṇa[1] wherein Lord Mahādeva is present in every word.

2. In the Purāṇa of a hundred crores of verses, I had described the story of Śiva. In a hundred thousand verses, the essence of those topics has been described by Vyāsa.

---

1. The NP states (verse 3) that the Sk. P (*Skanda Purāṇa*) consists of 81,000 verses—a view shared by the *Sk.P.* itself and by *Mt. P.* (53-41-42) *Br. Vaivarta* and *Devī Bhāgavata.* The *Vāyu* and the *Bh. P.* credit it with 81,000 verses while *AP* (272. 17) and Skanda (elsewhere) state that the *Sk. P.* has 84,000 verses.

Caturaśīti—Sāhasraṁ Skāndaṁ Skanderitam mahat||

But the Veṅkaṭeśvar edt. contains 94,343 verses (PJ VII 2.349). According to the NP. the Sk. P. is divided in the following *Khaṇḍas—Māheśvara, Vaiṣṇava, Brahma, Kāśi, Avanti, Nāgara and Prabhāsa.* One more *Khaṇḍa*—The *Sahyādri*—is separately published. But in the *Sūta Saṁhitā* the *Skanda* consists of 6 *Saṁhitās*, fifty *Khaṇḍas* and a hundred thousand verses. The names of *Saṁhitās* being *Sanatkumāra, Sūta, Sāṅkarī, Vaiṣṇavī, Brāhmī and Saura.*

The published editions—Veṅkaṭeśvar, Bangavasi, Naval Kishor Press (Lucknow) and Gurumandal are not unanimous in contents. Thus in part I of Avantikhaṇḍa 84 chapters of the glory of 84 *Liṅgas* (*Caturaśīti liṅga māhātmya*) are not included in the Lucknow edition, while in the II Part of the Avantikhaṇḍa, the Lucknow edition gives 110 different chapters. In other words, the Lucknow and Bombay editions differ considerably in the Avanti Khaṇḍa. The GM includes the spurious *Satya-nārāyaṇa Māhātmya* in the *Revā khaṇḍa* (pp. 1122-2235)—and that too of 4 chapters while usually we find 5 chapters of the same.

27. The anecdote of Dakṣiṇāmūrti, the tale of Guṇḍiva, the arrangement for the maintenance of the chariot, the glorification of the Śayana-Utsava (the festival of Deity's going to sleep).

28. The story of Śveta is mentioned here; then the review of Pṛthūtsava (the great Festival), the Dolotsava (Festival of the Swing) of the lord and the observance called annual Vrata, the Akāmika Pūjā (worship without entertaining any desire in return) of Viṣṇu. Different kinds of Yoga and means thereto according to the teaching of Uddālaka.

29. The ten incarnations are enumerated; the rite of ablution etc. is glorified; then the greatness of Badarikā[1] that is destructive of sins.

30-32. The greatness of Agni and other holy centres situated in the rock of Vainateya; the cause for the residence of the Lord; the holy centre named Pañcadhārā, the situation of Meru. In the context of Kārttika, the glory of Madālasā.

33. The narrative of Dhūmrakeśa, the daily rites and duties in the month of Kārttika,[2] the description of "Pañca-Bhīṣma" Vrata that bestows worldly pleasures and salvation.

34. Then in the context of the greatness of Mārgaśīrṣa,[3] the rules of procedure regarding the bath, the glorification of Puṇḍra (the mark on the forehead) etc., the meritorious nature of wearing garlands, etc.

---

1. VV 29-32 adequately deal with the III section called *Badarikāśrama Māhātmya* as most of the topics like holy centres of the rocks of Vainateya (ch. 4) Kapālamocana, Pañcadhārā (ch. 7) and Meru-Saṁsthāpana (ch. 8) are mentioned herein.

2. VV 32-33 deal with the topics in the "glory of the month of Kārttika" (*Kārttika-māsa-māhātmya*). In the original Sk. P., this section contains 36 chapters. Out of them chapters connected with the glory of religious rites in this month and the *Bhīṣma pañcaka vrata* (ch. 32) are mentioned and the story of Jalandhara ignored unless we identify "Dhūmrakeśa" (mentioned in the NP) with Jalandhara.

3. VV 34-38 deal with the section *Mārgaśīrṣa Māhātmya* which consists of 17 chapters in the original. It contains the various rites regarding bath (ch. 1), the Puṇḍra mark on the forehead (ch. 2), the details of worship (chs. 5, 7, 8, 9). The importance of Ekādaśī and rules of observing that fast (chs. 11-13, 15 & 16) and the glory of Mathurā (ch. 17).

35. The merit in the ablution with Pañcāmṛta, the benefit originating from ringing the bell etc.; the benefit of worshipping with different kinds of flowers, the benefit accruing from the Tulasī leaves.

36. The greatness of Naivedya (food offering) to God, the glorification of Harivāsara (Harī's day i.e. Ekādaśī) The Akhaṇḍaikādaśī (the unbroken Ekādaśī) as well as the merit of keeping awake during Ekādaśī.

37. The rules regarding the festival thereof, the narrative of illustrious names of God, recounting of the merit of meditation, the greatness of Mathurā, etc.

38. Thereafter, the greatness of the holy centre Mathurā is separately mentioned, then the greatness of twelve forests is mentioned.

39. In this context, the greatness of Srīmad Bhāgavata[1] is mentioned in the course of dialogue between Vajra and Śāṇḍilya, the inner sports are revealed.

40. Then the greatness of the months of Māgha[2] is reviewed in ten chapters in regard to bath, charitable gifts and Japas alongwith suitable anecdotes connected therewith.

41. Then in the context of the greatness of the devotees of Viṣṇu the benefit of Śayyādāna (charitable gift of beds) is mentioned; the rules regarding the gift of water are mentioned; then the story of Kāma.

42. The story of Śrutadeva, the wonderful anecdote of the Vyādha (hunter), the special glorification of Akṣaya Tṛtīyā[3] (the everlasting Tṛtīyā i.e. the third day of the bright half of Vaiśākha)

---

1. That the SkP has a *Bhāgavata Māhātmya* is less known as generally the *Bhāgavata Māhātmya* in the *Padma P.* is printed at the beginning of different editions of the Bh. P.

2. The GM edition of the Sk. P. does not give *Māgha Māhātmya* but gives *Vaiśākha Māhātmya* instead. The *Māgha Māhātmya mentioned* in the NP consisted of 10 chapters.

3. The Sk. P. gives a section of 25 chapters for *Vaiśākha Māsa Māhātmya*. But the NP mentions only one topic viz. the glorification of *Akṣaya tṛtīyā* (ch. 23 in the original Sk. P.) and ignores all other chapters.

43. In the context of the greatness of Ayodhyā[1] the two holy Tīrthas viz. Cakratīrtha and Brahmatīrtha are mentioned. These two bring about the liberation from the sin of drinking spirituous liquor; the heavenly door with a thousand supports.

44. The description of Candrahari and Dharmahari, the anecdote of Svarṇavṛṣṭi (shower of gold); the confluence of Tilodā and Sarayū.

45. The holy pool of Sītā, the lineage of Guptahari, the confluence of Sarayū and Ghargharā; the holy centres of Gopratāra, Dugdhoda and the set of five (Tīrthas) beginning with Gurukuṇḍa.

46. Thereafter, the description of thirteen Tīrthas such as Soma, Arka etc., the greatness of Gaya-kūpa (the well of Gaya) that causes all sins to recede.

47. Thereafter, the holy spots beginning with the hermiage of Māṇḍavya, that of Ajita etc., and Mānasa etc. are mentioned.

48. Thus the second Khaṇḍa called Vaiṣṇava is explained. Hereafter, O Marīci, listen to the Brahmakhaṇḍa that bestows merit.

(The summary of Brahma Khaṇḍa)

49. In the context of the greatness of Setu (Bridge built by Rāma over the sea), the benefit resulting from bath and mere sight; the penance of Gālava, the story of Rākṣasas.

50. The greatness of Cakratīrtha etc, the greatness of Vetālatīrtha which is in Devīpattana[2] (city of the Goddess), the

---

1. VV 43-46 mention topics described in the *Ayodhyā Māhātmya*, a section of 10 chapters in the Vaiṣṇava Khaṇḍa of the Sk. P. But one wonders why the whole section called *Śrī Vāsudeva Māhātmya* in this *Khaṇḍa* of Sk. P. is completely ignored in the NP.

The first two *khaṇḍas* viz. Māheśvara and Vaiṣṇava are compared in detail with the topics mentioned in the NP. The omissions of topics in the NP shows that the author of the NP had a different and a shorter edition of the Sk. P. when he enumerated the contents of the Sk. P. As sufficient evidence for this finding is presented above, the comparison with other *khaṇḍas* of the Sk. P. is not given here.

2. This is at a distance of 12 miles from Rāmnad (Ramnath Pur). It is also called Devīpura (Sk. P. III 1. 7. 57. 63) and also Devīpurī (ibid 60). Here Durgā killed the demon Mahiṣāsura.

glorification of the holy place called Pāpanāśa (the destruction of sins).

51. The greatness of Maṅgalā etc., the description of Brahmakuṇḍa etc, the greatness of Hanumatkuṇḍa, the benefit resulting from Agastyatīrtha.

52. The narrative of Rāmatīrtha etc, the review of Lakṣmītīrtha, the greatness of Śaṅkha and other Tīrthas. So also the benefit accruing from Sādhyāmṛta etc.

53-54. The greatness of Dhanuṣkoṭi etc. and that of Kṣīra-Kuṇḍa etc., the greatness of Gāyatrī and other Tīrthas is described here; the greatness of Rāmanātha; the instruction in the perfect knowledge of Reality, the recounting of rules regarding the pilgrimage to Setu which yields salvation to men.

55. Thereafter, the greatness of Dharmāraṇya[1] (forest of Dharma) is mentioned. It was here that Lord Sthāṇu instructed Skanda in Tattva (Philosophic principles).

56. The origin of Dharmāraṇya; the glorification of its merit, the narration of Karmasiddhi (achievements of the fruit of actions, the review of the family-lines of the sages.

57. The greatness of main Apsarastīrthas (Holy centres of the divine damsels) is mentioned; the review of the principles of Dharma (duties) of the castes and stages of life.

58-59. The division of heavenly spots, the auspicious story of Bakulārka, the goddesses Chatrānandā, Śāntā, Śrīmātā, Mātaṅginī and Puṇyadā are stationed herein, the greatness of Indreśvara etc., the review of Dvārakā etc.

60. The narrative of the demon Lohāsura, the review of Gaṅgākūpa, the story of Śrī Rāma, the description of Satya Mandira.

61. The narrative of the repair to the ruins; the acceptance of seats, the mentioning of different castes, the review of the holy rites in accordance with the Smṛtis.

---

1. De. gives four locations of Dharmāraṇya but none of them is in the South. It may appear to be a mythological forest near Rāmeśvara but the association of Brāhmaṇas of 24 *gotras* with it (Sk. P. III ii. 9-27) shows the need of its correct location.

62. Then the holy rites prescribed for Vaiṣṇavas are mentioned through different narratives, thereafter, the exposition of holy rites, observances etc., in regard to the holy Cāturmāsya (the four months of the rainy season when special Vratas are observed).

63. The eulogy of charitable gifts, thereafter the greatness of Vratas, the narration of loop-holes (causes of failures) in penance and worship.

64. The narration of making amends for them (loop-holes); the review of Śālagrāma; the means for the destruction of Bhāraka, the glory of the worship of trees.

65. The cause of Viṣṇu in regard to the state of being a tree, then Pārvatī's subsequent penance, the Tāṇḍava dance of Hara, the review of the name Rāma.

66. The fall of the Liṅga of Hara, the story of Baijavana, the story of the nativity of Pārvatī, the wonderful killing of Tāraka.

67. The narration of prosperity through the Praṇava, the activities of Tāraka, the conclusion of Dakṣa's Yajña, the mantra of Twelve syllables (viz. oṁ namo bhagavate Vāsudevāya) which is its embellishment.

68. The narration of the path of knowledge and the greatness of twelve-syllabled Mantra. The merit of Śravaṇa (the means of hearing), etc. that causes happiness to men.

69. Then in the latter half of the Brahmakhaṇḍa the wonderful greatness of Śiva is narrated, then the greatness of the five-syllabled Mantra : Namaḥ Śivāya and that of Gokarṇa.

70. The greatness of Śivarātri, the glorification of Pradoṣa Vrata,[1] the Vrata on Mondays, the anecdote of Sīmantinī.

---

1. This *Vrata* is to be commenced on an auspicious day in the bright half of Caitra or Mārgaśīrṣa. Its details are given in ch. 18 of the *Brahmottara Khaṇḍa* of the Sk. P., Kane in HD V. I. 277 gives 6 varieties of this *Vrata*.

71. The narration of the origin of Bhadrāyu, the review of good conduct, the guidance of Śivavarman (?) and the description of Bhadrāyu's marriage.

72. The greatness of Bhadrāyu, the glorification of the greatness of Bhasma (Sacred ashes), the story of Śabara (Hunter), the Vrata called Umā-Maheśvara.

73. The greatness of the Rudrākṣa bead, the merit of the 'Rudrādhyāya' Mantra, the merit of Śravaṇa (hearing), etc. Thus the Brahmakhaṇḍa has been recounted.

74. Henceforth, the fourth part, the excellent Kāśi Khaṇḍa[1] (is summarised). The dialogue between Vindhya and Nārada is described.

75. The greatness of Satyaloka, the arrival of the Devas in the residence of Agastya, the story of a chaste lady, the praising of the pilgrimage to holy centres.

76. Then the narration of the seven cities, the review of Saṁyaminī, the attainment of the worlds of Budha (Mercury), Indra and Agni by Śivaśarman.

77. The origin of fire, the origin of Varuṇa from fire (?) the origin of the two cities Gandhavatī and Alakā and the nativity of Īśvarī.

78. The description of these worlds, viz., the moon, the sun, the mercury, the Mars, Jupiter, Saturn, my world, Viṣṇu's world of Dhruva's world (?) and the Tapoloka.

79. The meritorious story of the world of Dhruva, the survey of Satyaloka, the conversation between Skanda and Agastya, the origin of Maṇikarṇī.

80. The prowess of the Gaṅgā, the thousand names of the Gaṅgā, the praise of Vārāṇasī, the appearance of Bhairava.

81. Thereafter, the origin of Daṇḍapāṇi and Jñānavāpī (the well of Knowledge), then the narration of Kalāvatī and the exposition of good conduct.

82. The narration of a celibate, then the characteristics of women, the stipulation of what should be done and what should not be done, the description of Avimukteśa.

---

1. VV 74-91 summarise the main topics in the fourth *khaṇḍa* called *Kāśi khaṇḍa*. It covers the main topics found in the extant *Kāśikhaṇḍa*.

83. The duties of householders and the Yogins, then the knowledge of Kāla (Time), the holy story of Divodāsa, the description of Kāśikā.

84. The appearance on the Earth of Māyā Gaṇapati, the Universe due to Viṣṇu's Māyā, then the liberation of Divodāsa.

85. Then the origin of Pañcanada and that of Bindu Mādhava; then the enumeration of holy centres belonging to Viṣṇu, the arrival at Kāśī of the trident-bearing Lord.

86. The dialogue between Jaigīṣavya and Maheśa, the name Jyeṣṭheśa of Maheśa, the enumeration of holy temples, the origin of Kandukeśa and Vyāghreśvara.

87. The origin of Śaileśa and Ratneśvara as well as that of Kṛttivāsas; the abode of the deities; Durgā's exploit over the Asuras.

88. Durgā's victory, the description of Oṁkāreśa, then the greatness of Oṁkāra, the origin of the three-eyed Lord Śiva.

89. The narration of Kedāra, the story of Dharmeśa born of Viṣṇu's arms (?), the narrative of Vīreśvara, the glorification of the greatness of Gaṅgā.

90. The greatness of Viśvakarmeśa, the origin of Dakṣa's Yajña as well as that of Satīśa, Amṛteśa and others, the benumbing of the arms of Parāśara.

91. The group of holy centres and shrines, the dialogue in the Mukti-Maṇḍapa (The pandal of salvation) the prosperity of Viśveśa and then the circumambulatory pilgrimage.

(Thus the fourth part is summarised)

92. Hereafter, listen to the description of the fifth part called Avanti Khaṇḍa.[1] The narration of the forest Mahākāla Vana; then the chopping off of the head of Brahmā.

---

1. VV 92-141. mention the important topics in the fifth khaṇḍa—the *Avanti khaṇḍa.* One fails to understand why so much importance has been attached to this *khaṇḍa* in the NP as it devotes 49 verses to this *khaṇḍa* as compared with the meagre 17 verses to *Kāśi Khaṇḍa* which is now so popular.

It may be further added that the geographical location of each *Tīrtha* mentioned here is expected in the annotations of the *Skanda Purāṇa* proper (translation or original text) and is thus beyond the scope of *Nārada Purāṇa.*

93. The rules regarding expiatory rites; the origin of Agni; the arrival of the Devas, the initiation of the Devas; Śiva's hymn that is destructive of different kinds of sins.

94. The narration of Kapālamocana, the situation of the forest Mahākālavana, the holy centre of the Lord Kanakhala that is destructive of all sins.

95. The pool called after the Apsaras (celestial damsels) and the lake of Rudra that is meritorious, the holy centres of the Lord of Kuḍava, Vidyādhara, and Markaṭeśvara.

96. The holy waters of Svargadvāracatussindhu (the four rivers that constitute the doorways to heaven), Śaṅkaravāpikā (The tank of Śaṅkara), Śaṅkarārka, Gandhavatī Tīrtha, that is destructive of sins.

97. Daśāśvamedhika and Anaṁśa Tīrtha that bestow all Siddhis, the procession of Piśācaka, etc, Hanumadīśvara, Kavaceśvara.

98. The procession of or pilgrimage to Mahākāleśa, the holy centre of Valmīkeśvara, the circumabulations of Kuśasthalī in the fifth Tīrtha called Śukra (?).

99. The centres of Akrūra, Ekapāda and Candrārkavaibhava; the holy shrine called Karabheśa and those of Lakuṭeśa and others.

100-101. Mārkaṇḍeśa, Yajña-vāpī-someśa, Naṛakāntaka, Kedāreśvara, Rāmeśa, Saubhāgyeśa, Narārkara shrines. Then Keṣavārka, Śaktibheda, Svarṇasāra, and other shrines, the holy spots of Oṁkāreśa etc, the glorification of Andhakaśruti.

102. The number of Liṅgas in the Kālāraṇya, the shrine named Svargaśṛṅga (gold horn), the names of Kuśasthalī, Avanti and Ujjayinī.

103. The shrines named Padmāvatī, Kumudvatī, and Amarāvatī the names of Viśālā, and Pratikalpa and Amarāvatī, the subduing of fever.

104. The benefit of the names of Śiva etc., the eulogy of Śiva sung by the Nāgas (Serpents), the narrative of killing Hiraṇyākṣa, the holy centre of Sundarakuṇḍa.

105. The holy centres of Vindhyavāsin (residing in Vindhya) called Nīlagaṅgāpuṣkara, the holy centre destructive of sins, called Puruṣottama.

106. The Gomatī river, the holy pool of Vāmana, the thousand names of Viṣṇu, the lake of Vīreśvara, the shrine of Kālabhairava.

107. The greatness of Nāgapañcamī, the Jayantikā (birth anniversary) of Nṛsiṁha, the procession of Kuṭumbeśvara, the glorification of divine Sādhakas.

108. The holy shrine called Karkarāja, the bearing of Vighneśa and other Devas, the review of many holy centres in the Rudrakuṇḍa (the holy pit of Rudra) and others.

109. The holy pilgrimage of the eight holy centres, the greatness of Revā, the detachment of Dharmaputra, his meeting with Mārkaṇḍeya.

110. Narration of the most excellent experience,* the glorification of Amṛta; Different names of Narmadā in the different Kalpas.

111. The hymn of Narmadā composed by the sages, the story of Kālarātri; thereafter the prayer of Mahādeva, the wonderful stories of several Kalpas.

112. The story of Viśalyā, the story of Jāleśvara, the description of Gaurī Vrata, the burning of Tripuras.

113. The injunctions regarding the casting off of the body, then the confluence of Kāverī, the holy shrines of Dārutīrtha and Brahmāvarta, alongwith the story of Īśvara.

114-115. The following series of shrines are then described : Agni Tīrtha, Ravi Tīrtha, Meghanāda Tīrtha, Ādidāruka Tīrtha, Deva Tīrtha, Narmadeśa, Kapila Tīrtha, Karañja Tīrtha, Kuṇḍaleśa, Pippalāda, Vimaleśa and Śūlabhṛt, then the story of abduction of Śacī and killing of Abhraka. (v. l. Andhaka)

116. The Tīrtha called Śūlabhṛdudbhava where different types of charitable gifts are to be given; then the story of Dīrgha-tapas and that of Ṛṣyaśṛṅga.

---

*v.l.— *prāg-layānubhavākhyānam*—The experience of the initial dissolution (deluged universe)

117. Then the holy story of Citrasena, the characteristic feature of the kingdom of Kāśi,* then the description of Devaśilā (The rock of the lord) alongwith the holy centre of Śabarī.

118-121. Then the holy narrative of Vyādha (the hunter); then the holy centre of Puṣkariṇyarka; then the following holy pools and shrines—Āpretyeśvara Tīrtha, Śakra Tīrtha, Karoṭika, Kumāreśa, Agastyeśa, Ānandeśa, Mātṛja, Lokeśa, Dhanadeśa, Maṅgaleśa, Kāmaja, Nāgeśa, Gopāra. Gautama, Śaṅkhacūḍaka, Nāradeśa, Nandikeśa, Varuṇeśvara Tīrtha, Dadhiskanda and other holy centres; then Hanūmateśvara, Rāmeśvara and other holy centres, Someśa, Piṅgaleśvara.

122-129. Ṛṇamokṣa, Kapileśa, Pūtikeśa, Jaleśaya, Caṇḍārka, Yama Tīrtha, Kālhoḍīśa, Vanādika, (v. l. Nāndīka) Nārāyaṇa, Koṭīśa, Vyāsa Tīrtha, Prabhāsaka, Nāgeśa, Saṅkarṣaṇaka, Praśrayeśvara Tīrtha, the holy confluence of Airaṇḍī, Suvarṇaśilā Tīrtha, Karañja, Kāmaha, Bhāṇḍīra, Rohiṇībhava, Cakra Tīrtha, Dhautapāpa, Skanda, the holy place named after Aṅgiras, Koṭi Tīrtha, Tīrtha called Ayonī, Aṅgāra Tīrtha, Trilocana Tirtha, Indreśa, Kambukeśa, Someśa, Kohaneśa, Nārmada, Ārka, Āgneya, the excellent Bhārgaveśvara Brāhma, Daiva, Mārgeśa, Ādivārāhakeśvara, Rāmeśa, Siddheśa Āhalya, Kaṅkaṭeśvara, Śākra, Saumya, Nādeśa, Toyeśa, Rukmiṇībhava, Yojaneśa, Varāheśa, Dvādaśī Śiva Tīrtha, Siddheśa, Maṅgaleśa, Liṅgatīrtha, Vārāha Tīrtha, Kuṇḍeśa, Śvetavārāha, Garbhāveśa, Ravīśvara.

130-135. The holy centres of Śukla etc., Huṅkārasvāmi Tīrtha, Saṅgameśa, Nahuṣeśa, Mokṣaṇa, Pañcagopa, Nāgaśāva, Siddheśa, Mārkaṇḍatīrtha, Akrūratīrtha, Kāmodatīrtha, Śūlāropatīrtha, Māṇḍavya, Gopakeśvara, Kapileśa, Piṅgaleśa, Bhūteśa, Gaṅgā Tīrtha, Gautama Tīrtha, Āśvamedha, Bhṛgukaccha Kedāreśa, the dispeller of sins, Kālakaleśa, Jāleśa, Śālagrāma, Varāhaka, Candraprabhāsa, Āditya, Śrīpati Tīrtha, Haṁsaka, Mūlyasthāna (the original abode), Śūleśa, the Tīrtha called Ugra, Citradaivaka, Śikhīśa, Koṭi Tīrtha, Daśakanya, Suvarṇaka, Ṛṇamokṣa, (that which liberates from

---

*v.l. *Kāśi-rājasya mokṣaṇam*—Salvation of Kāśirāja

indebtedness), Bhārabhūti, Puṅkha Muṇḍi, Ḍiṇḍima (a drum), Āmaleśa, Kapāleśa, Sṛṅga Eraṇḍī Bhava, Koṭi Tīrtha and Loṭaneśa. Thereafter, there is Phalaśruti (A remark like the Vedic passage indicating the benefit) (phalastuti—praise of the benefit).

136-140. In the context of the greatness of Dṛmijaṅgala,[1] there is the story of Rohitāśva, the narration of Dhundhumāra the strategem of destroying Dhundhu; the killing of Dhundhu and the birth of Citravaha, his greatness, the prowess of Caṇḍīśa, Ratīśvara, Kedāreśa, the Lakṣatīrtha, the holy water originating from Viṣṇupadī (Firmament), Mukhāra, Cyavana, Andhāsya and the lake of Brahmā, the Tīrthas of Cakra, Lalitā, the holy centres full of cows, Rudrāvarta and Mārkaṇḍa, the holy centres that dispel sins, Śravaṇeśa, Śuddhapaṭa, Devāndhupretatīrtha, the origin of holy centre Jihvoda, Śivodbheda and their eulogy in regard to their efficacy.

141. This is the summary of the part called Avanti Khaṇḍa;[2] it is destructive of sins of those who listen. Henceforth, the sixth part named Nāgarakhaṇḍa[3] is being narrated.

The Nāgarakhaṇḍa[4]

142. The narration of the origin of Liṅga, the auspicious story of Hariścandra, the greatness of Viśvāmitra, the attainment of heaven by Triśaṅku.

---

1. The topics from *Dṛmijaṅgala* upto *Śivodbheda* mentioned in VV 136-140 are not traced in any extant edition of *Avanti Khaṇḍa* indicating that the author of Nārada Purāṇa had a different version of Sk. P. than the present printed ones.

2. The Veṅkaṭeśvara, Bangabasi and the GM editions of the Sk. P. give a big section of 84 chapters called *Caturaśīti-liṅga-māhātmya*. But the NP does not mention this whole section.

3. It is surprising that the NP does not even mention the big *Revākhaṇḍa* the Uttarārdha of *Avantikhaṇḍa*—which consists of 232 chapters and skips to the *Nāgara-khaṇḍa*.

4. VV. 142-167 give us the main topics in the *Nāgara-khaṇḍa*, many of which are found in the extant Sk. P.

143. In the context of the greatness of Hāṭakeśvara, the killing of demon Vṛtra, the description of the holy centres Nāgabila, Śaṅkha Tīrtha and Acaleśvara.

144-145a. The narration of the city of Camatkāra, that is very interesting, then the description of these holy centres—Gayaśīrṣa, Bālasākhya, Bālamaṇḍa, Mṛgāhvaya, Viṣṇupāda, Gokarṇa, Yugarūpa and Samāśraya (that is the support of the people).

145b-146. Siddheśvara, the holy pool of Nāgas, the holy centre of seven sages, of Agastya as well as that of Bhrūṇagarta, Naleśa, of Bhīṣma, Vaiḍuram, Arkaka (pertaining to the Sun-God), Śārmiṣṭha (related to Śarmiṣṭhā), Somanātha, Daurga, Ātarjakeśvara.

147-150. The story of killing of Jamadagni; the story of (Paraśurāma's vow of) making (the country) devoid of Kṣatriyas, the holy centres of Rāmahrada, Nāgapura, Ṣaḍliṅga, Yajñabhū, the three shrines of Trikārka beginning with Muṇḍīra, the marriage of Satī, the shrines of Rudraśīrṣa, Yāgeśa, Vālakhilya and Garuḍa. The curse of Lakṣmī, the twentyseven palaces of Soma; the shrine called Pāṇḍuka erected by Ambā, Āgneya (belonging to the fire God), Brahmakuṇḍa, Gomukha, the shrine called Lohayaṣṭi, the goddess Ajapāleśvarī, the shrine of Śaniścara, (Saturn), the Rājavāpī (Royal tank) Rameśa, Lakṣmaṇeśvara.

151-158. The excellentmost among the excellent Liṅgas—Kuśeśa and Laveśa. The story of Aṣṭaṣaṣṭi and that of Damayantī, the origin of the holy centre Bhaktikā Tīrtha, Kṣemaṁkarī, Kedāra, Śukla Tīrtha, Mukhārka, the narration of the shrine Satyasandheśvara, the story of Karṇotpalā, Aṭeśvara, the shrines of Yājñavalkya, Gaurī, and Gaṇeśa. Then the description of Vāstupāda, the narration of Ajāgṛha, Saubhāgyāndhu (the well of good fortune), the shrine Śūleśa, the story of Dharmarāja, the story of Lord the bestower of sweets, three shrines of Gaṇapati, the story of Jābāli and the story of Makareśa, the description of Kāleśvarī and Andhaka, the holy pool of Apsaras (celestial damsels), the shrines of Puṣyāditya and Rauhitāśva, the narrative of the origin of Nāgara, the stories of Bhṛgu Viśvāmitra, Sarasvatī,

Pippalāda, Kaṁsārīśa and Peṇḍaka, the story of the Yajña of Brahmā alongwith the narration of Sāvitrī, Raivata, Bhārata Yajña and the survey of the important holy centres.

159. The three Kṣetras (holy shrines) of Kaurava, (i. e. the descendants of Kuru) Hāṭakeśa and Prabhāsa, the three forests of Pauṣkara, Naimiṣa, and Dharma.

160. The three cities viz. Vārāṇasī, Dvārakā and Avanti, the three Vanas (Parks) viz. Vṛndāvana, Khāṇḍavavana and Advaika (?) [ta ?] vana.

161. The three excellent villages, viz. Kalpagrāma, Śālagrāma and Nandigrāma, the three Tīrthas (holy centres) viz. Asi Tīrtha, Śukla Tīrtha and Pitṛ Tīrtha.

162-63a. The three excellent Parvatas (mountains) viz. Śrī Parvata, Arbuda Parvata (mount Abu) and Raivata Parvata; the three rivers Gaṅgā, Narmadā, and Sarasvatī, each of these is glorified as yielding one and a half crore of benefits.

163b-164a. The four holy centres of Kūpikā, Saṅkhatīrtha, Amaraka and Bālamaṇḍana are said to yield the same benefit as Hāṭakeśakṣetra.

164b-165. The Śrāddhakalpa (rituals regarding Śrāddha) according to Sāmba (alongwith Ambā and Āditya ?), that of Yudhiṣṭhira and Andhaka; the holy rite of Aśūnya Śayana in the four months (of the rainy season), lying down on water., the shrine of Maṅkaṇeśa, the festival of Śivarātri, Tulāpuruṣadāna rite.

166. The gift of lands, the shrines of Vānakeśa and Kapālamocaneśvara, Pāpapiṇḍa (the lump of sins), Māsalaiṅga (the worship of Liṅga for a month), the glorification of the extent and magnitude of Yugas.

167. The narration of Nimbeśa and Śākambharī deities, the description of Rudraikādaśa (the eleven Rudras), the narration of the greatness of charitable gifts and the glorification of twelve Ādityas.

The Prabhāsa khaṇḍa[1]

168a. Thus Nāgara khaṇḍa (has been summarised). Now the part called Prabhāsa khaṇḍa is being mentioned.

1. VV. 168 to 212 give the detailed contents of the last—*Prabhāsa*

206. The greatness of Cakratīrtha, the confluence of the river Gomatī (near Dvārakā) and the ocean (the Arabian sea), the narration of the Hrada (deep pool) of Sanaka and others, then the story of Nṛgatīrtha.

207. The holy story of Gopracāra, the arrival of cowherdesses at Dvārakā, the narration of Gopīsaras (the lake of the cowherdesses); the glorification of Brahmatīrtha.

208. The narration of the advent of five rivers, alongwith different stories and the glorification of Śivaliṅga, Gadātīrtha and the worship etc. of Kṛṣṇa.

209. The story of the Mūrti (the idol) of Trivikrama, the conversation between Durvāsas and Kṛṣṇa, the benefit of the recital of death of Kuśa daitya and the special worship thereof.

210. The glorification of the advent of all the Tīrthas in Gomatī and Dvārakā, the survey of Kṛṣṇa's temple and the coronation at Dvārāvatī.

211. There the story of the residence (of all Tīrthas) that holy centre; the glorification of the merit of Dvārakā. O Brāhmaṇa, this is the summary of the seventh part called Prabhāsikā Khaṇḍa.

212-213. In the course of description of the greatness of Śiva in the Skanda Purāṇa with all the gloriousmost stories, he who writes this out and gives it to a Brāhmaṇa on the full moon day in the month of Māgha, receiving him duly and with the charitable gift of a gold trident, rejoices in the region of Śiva.

CHAPTER ONE HUNDRED AND FIVE

The Vāmana Purāṇa[1] *: Contents*

Brahmā said :

1. O dear one, listen, I shall recount to you the Purāṇa named Vāmana. It contains stories of Trivikrama and comprises ten thousand verses.

2. It contains the narratives of events of the Kūrma Kalpa; it has stories descriptive of Vargatraya (the three aims of life viz. virtue, love and wealth). It is in two parts. It is auspicious to the narrator as well as to the listener.

3. At the outset, there is the enquiry about the Purāṇa; the cutting off of the head of Brahmā, the story of Kapālamocana, the destruction of Dakṣa's Yajña.

4. The description of (and narration about) Hara in the form of Kāla, then the burning of Kāma, the fight between Prahlāda and Nārāyaṇa, the war between the Devas and the Asuras.

5. The narration of the story of Sukeśī and Arka, then the Bhuvanakośa (description of the worlds), then the description of Kāmyavratas (Vratas performed with some desired object), then the story of Śrī Durgā.

---

1. According to the NP. Vāyu, Mt. P., Bh. P. the *Vāmana* P. consists of 10,000 verses. Further the NP states that the *Vāmana* consists of two parts *Pūrvabhāga* and *Uttara bhāga* (or *Vṛddha Vāmana*) the latter containing the following *saṁhitās* viz. the *Māheśvarī, Bhāgavatī, Saurī* and *Gaṇeśvarī*, each consisting of 1000 verses (VV. 13-14). But the whole of the *Uttarabhāga* is lost leaving the Pūrvārdha of 6000 verses. But actually in Veṅkaṭeśvara edit. there are 5451 verses (chs. 26, 44 and 93 being in prose).

There is a discrepancy in the total number of chapters in the MSS of this Purāṇa e. g. Devanāgarī MSS (94 chs.), Telugu MSS (89 chs.), Śāradā code (85 chs.), Adyar Mss (67 chs.). (A. S. Gupta—PJ. V. pp. 360-66). Although many of the topics mentioned in the NP are found in the printed edition, the absence of the *Uttarārdha* and the no. of verses in the extant Purāṇa show that the NP refers to a different version of the *Vāmana Purāṇa*.

By the way it may be noted that though this was originally a Vaiṣṇava Purāṇa, Śaivism has considerably influenced it as the episodes of Śiva are also described in details. This synthetic tendency—harmonizing Vaiṣṇavism, Śaivism etc. by regarding these deities as representatives of the *Brahman*—is found practically in all Purāṇas.

6. Then the story of Tapatī, description of Kurukṣetra, the incomparable greatness of Satya, the glorification of the nativity of Pārvatī.

7. Her penance, and then the marriage, thereafter, the story of Gaurī, thereafter, the subsidiary story of Kauśikī and then the story of Kumāra.

8. Then the story of killing Andhaka, then the narrative of Sādhyas, afterwards, the story of Jābāli, the wonderful story of Arajā.

9. The fight between Andhaka and Īśvara, Andhaka given the status of a Gaṇa (attendant of Śiva), the narration of the Maruts, then the story of Bali.

10. Then Lakṣmī's story, thereafter the story of Trivikrama, then auspicious stories are being narrated in the course of pilgrimage of Prahlāda.

11. Thereafter, the story of Dhundhu; then the story of the Preta (Ghosts), the story of Nakṣatrapuruṣa (The name of a Vrata), then the story of Śrīdāma.

12. At the end of the story of Trivikrama, there is an excellent hymn composed by Brahmā. In the course of conversation between Prahlāda and Bali in Sutala (Netherworlds), Hari is praised.

13. Thus the story of the first half of this Purāṇa is mentioned to you. Hereafter, listen to its latter half called Bṛhad Vāmana.

14. There are four Saṁhitās (compendiums) therein each consisting of a thousand verses. They are Māheśvarī, Bhāgavatī, Saurī and Gaṇeśvarī.[1]

---

1. According to the NP, the Kūrma Purāṇa consists of Brāhmī, Bhāgavatī, Saurī and Vaiṣṇavi Saṁhitās and has 17,000 verses in all (verse 3), a figure endorsed by the Bh. P. (XII. 13, I). But the *Vāyu* and *Matsya* credit it with 18,003 verses, while according to AP (272-10) it has 8000 verses only. The *Kūrma B* itself states that it consists of *Brāhmī, Bhāgavatī, Saurī* and *Vaiṣṇavī Saṁhitās* and the *Brāhmī* contains 6000 verses. But actually Veṅkaṭeśvara Press edit. gives 5925 verses. The NP. gives the topical analysis of each *Saṁhitā* and states the sub-sections of each Saṁhitā e. g. the Bhāgavatī Saṁhitā has five sections (*Pañca-padī*), the Saurī, six (*ṣoḍhā*), Vaiṣṇavi, four (*catuṣpadī*). The total No. of verses in each section is given as 6000, 4000, 2000 and 5000 verses respectively. Ch. 106.

15. In the compilation called Māheśvarī, there is the glorification of Kṛṣṇa and his devotees. In the compendium Bhāgavatī, there is the wonderful story of the incarnation of the Mother of the Universe.

16. In the compendium Saurī, the glory of the Sun is spoken (praised) which is destructive of sins. In the compendium Gaṇeśvarī there is the story of Gaṇeśa and Maheśa.

17. This is a wonderful Purāṇa named Vāmana. It is narrated by Pulastya to the noble-souled Nārada.

18. Then it was acquired from Nārada by Vyāsa, a very great Ātman. From Yyāsa his disciple Romaharṣaṇa acquired this.

19. He will narrate it to the Brāhmaṇas of Naimiṣa forest. Thus the auspicious Vāmana Purāṇa has been traditionally handed down and acquired.

20-22. Those who read this or listen to this, attain the greatest goal. He who writes this out and gives it to a Brāhmaṇa Vedic scholar at the time of autumnal equinox alongwith ghee and a cow, uplifts his Pitṛs (ancestors) from hells and leads them to heaven. After enjoying all worldly pleasures and dying thereafter, he attains the great region of Viṣṇu.

All this evidence shows that the author of the NP had positively a different and a larger version than the extant KP.

The extant (both Veṅkaṭeśvara and Kāśirāja) editions of KP tally to a great extent with the *Brāhmī Saṁhitā* and the other *Saṁhitās* seem to have been lost.

Hazra notes that originally the *Kūrma* was a *Pāñcarātra Purāṇa* which was subsequently Pāśupatised. (vide PR. pp. 57. ff.)

CHAPTER ONE HUNDRED AND SIX

The Kūrma Purāṇa : Contents

God Brahmā said :

1-2. O dear child, O Marīci, listen to the Purāṇa called Kūrma. It covers the events of the Lakṣmī Kalpa. In the context of Indradyumna, the merciful Hari, assuming the form of a tortoise, proclaimed it to the sages the respective greatness of virtue, love, wealth and salvation.

3. It consists of seventeen thousand verses.[1] It is very auspicious with four Saṃhitās. O sage, many of the Brāhma dharmas (religious duties) mentioned formerly, have been explained in it.

4. They are dealt with in the context of different stories. They are the bestowers of good position (hereafter) unto men. In the first subdivision there is the usual beginning at the outset.

5. There is the dialogue between Lakṣmī and Indradyumna and the conversation between the Divine Tortoise and the groups of sages. Then is the account of the four castes (Varṇas) and stages in life (Āśramas, and their (prescribed) duties, the narration of the creation of the Universe.

6. There is a brief description about the calculation of Time (such as Yugas, Manvantaras), at the end of the dissolution, there is the eulogy of the Lord (by Siddhas), then a brief description of the creation (of the universe) and the story of Śaṅkara.

7. The thousand names of Pārvatī, the exposition of the Yoga philosophy, the description of the family of Bhṛgu, and then that of Svāyaṃbhuva (Manu).

---

1. According to the VP, Vāyu, Bh. P. (xii. 13. 4-9) and Mt. P, itself, this Purāṇa consists of 14,000 verses while AP credits it with 13000 (or 13,003 as per A. S. Gupta) the BVP with 18,000 verses. The Ānandāśrama Press edit. contains 14,062 verses and its contents agree in general with those given in the NP. This agreement is probably due to its being the best preserved and the earliest of the 18 Purāṇas (Kane—HD. vii. p. 899). Kane also notes that it has perhaps the largest number of *Smṛti* chapters among Purāṇas and assigns 200 A. D. to 400 A. D. as its probable date.

8. The origin of the Devas and others, then the destruction of Dakṣa's Yajña, the story of the creation by Dakṣa, then the narration of the lineage of Kaśyapa (containing the account of the Solar and Lunar dynasties).

9. The description of the family of Atri, the auspicious story of Kṛṣṇa, the dialogue between Kṛṣṇa and Mārtaṇḍa (The Sun-god) and the conversation between Vyāsa and the Pāṇḍavas.

10. The narration of the characteristic nature of different Yugas (Yugadharma), the glorification of Vyāsa and Jaimini, the greatness of Vārāṇasī and Prayāga.

11-12. The description of the three worlds, the review of the branches of Vedas. In the latter half of the Purāṇa there are the Īśvaragītā and the Vyāsagītā. These two illuminate the different kinds of Dharmas; the greatness of the different holy centres is mentioned separately.

13. Then there is the narration of Pratisarga (Dissolution of the Universe). This much is the summary of the first division named Brāhmī Saṁhitā. Henceforth, the compendium Bhāgavatī Saṁhitā is reviewed.

14. In this division, the separate activities of the different castes are narrated. In the first quarter of this Saṁhitā, the determination of duties etc. of the Brāhmaṇas has been narrated.

15. O dear one, it consists of good and disciplined life and it enhances their enjoyment and the happiness of worldly pleasures. In the second quarter, the functions of the profession of the Kṣatriyas are clearly enunciated.

16-19a. If a (Kṣatriya) abides by these, he shall eschew sins and go to heaven. In the third quarter, the fourfold activities of the Vaiśyas have been explained. If these are followed, one shall attain excellent salvation. In its fourth quarter, the activities of the Śūdras are explained. If these are followed, Lord Viṣṇu becomes pleased and increases the welfare of men. In the fifth quarter the duties and functions of the mixed castes are explained. If they are followed, one attains excellent state of future life.

19b. O sage, thus is narrated the second compendium (Saṁhitā) consisting of five sections (Pañcapadī).

20. The third compendium is called Saurī. It lays down the various duties of men. To men who desire (to obtain some objects), it instructs the six karmans and their Siddhis in six different ways.

21. The fourth compendium is called Vaiṣṇavī. It is glorified as the bestower of Liberation from Saṁsāra. It consists of four sections (Catuṣ-padī). It is veritable Brahma i.e. the Veda incarnate to the twice-borns.

22. The four Saṁhitās contain respectively six thousand, four thousand, two thousand and five thousand verses.

23. This Kūrma Purāṇa yields the benefit of four Vargas (the aims of life) viz. Dharma, Artha, Kāma, Mokṣa. It yields the best of all goals to the men who read and listen to it.

24. He who writes this (Purāṇa) with devotion and gives it to a Brāhmaṇa during the transit of the sun from the tropics, alongwith the replica of a tortoise in gold, attains the greatest goal.

CHAPTER ONE HUNDRED AND SEVEN

The Matsya Purāṇa : Contents

Lord Brahmā said :

1. O excellent Brāhmaṇa, I shall, henceforth, recount the Matsya Purāṇa to you. In it, all the events of the seven Kalpas in the world, have been condensed.

2. It has been composed by Vyāsa, a scholar in the Vedas, in about fourteen thousand verses.* He has begun by describing Narasiṁha.

---

*The *Vāyu*, the *Matsya* and the *Bh. P.* state this figure, but AP. gives 13000 and the Br. V. 18000 verses as the figure. Actually the Ānandāśrama edition contains 14,062 verses. The contents of that edition tally with those given by the NP. here.

3. The discussion between Manu and Matsya, then the narration (description) of the Cosmic Egg; the creation of the Devas, Asuras and the Marut (wind) from the Brahman.

4. Madana-Dvādaśī (the twelfth lunar day in honour of Madana) and the worship of the guardians of the worlds; the survey of the Manvantaras, the description of the government of the kingdom by the Vaiśyas.

5. The birth of Vaivasvata (Manu) from the sun, the contact with Budha (Mercury), the narration of the lineage of the Pitṛs; the opportune time for (performance of) Śrāddha).

6. The peregrination among the Pitṛ-Tīrthas, the origin of Soma (the moon), the glorification of the lunar race and the story of Yayāti.

7. The story of Kārttavīrya, the narration of the created race, Bhṛgu's curse to Viṣṇu to take ten births on the Earth.

8. Then the glorification of Puru's race, the race of Hutāśana (the fire), the path of activity. Thereafter, the narration of the Purāṇa.

9. The Vrata (holy rite) called Nakṣatra Puruṣa, Mārtaṇḍa-śayana, the Vrata of Kṛṣṇāṣṭamī (the eighth day of the dark half of Śrāvaṇa observance in honour of Kṛṣṇa's birth) and that of Rohiṇīcandra.

10. The greatness of constructing tanks; the gift of the trees, the Vrata called Saubhāgya and Śayana Agastya Vrata.

11. The Vrata of Anantatṛtīyā, that of Rasakalyāṇinī, that of Ānandakarī and then the Sārasvata (belonging to Sarasvatī) Vrata.

12. Uparāgābhiṣeka (Ablution at the time of eclipse Saptamī śayana, Bhīma Dvādaśī, Anaṅgaśayana rite.

13. Aśūnyaśayanavrata, Aṅgārakavrata (holy rite of Mars) Saptamī saptaka (seven Saptamīs i.e. seventh lunar day) Viśokadvādaśīvrata (holy rite on the twelfth lunar day for wiping off grief).

14. The gift of Meru, ten-fold specification of evil planets; the narration of the forms of planets, Śivacaturdaśī (the fourteenth day of Śiva).

15. The abandonment of all fruits, the holy observance of Sūryavāra (Sunday), the taking of bath at the time of

Saṅkrānti (Solar Transit from one sign of Zodiac to another), the holy rite of Vibhūti Dvādaśī.

16. The greatness of Ṣaṣṭhīvratas (holy rites on the sixth Lunar day) (leading Ṣaṣṭivratas—sixty holy rites), then the rules of procedure regarding holy baths, the greatness of Prayāga, the description of continents and the worlds.

17. The movement in the firmament, the greatness of Dhruva (Pole Star), the abodes of the leading Devas, the illumination of the three cities.

18. The greatness of leading Pitṛs, the description of Manvantaras, the creation of the set of four Yugas and the review of Yugadharma (the characteristics peculiar to the different Yugas).

19. The birth of Vajrāṅga and the nativity of Tāraka, the greatness of the demon Tāraka, the glorification of God Brahmā.

20. The nativity of Pārvatī, the penance-grove of Śiva, the burning of the body of Anaṅga (Cupid) and the grief of Rati.

21. The penance-grove of Gaurī, soothing by Śiva, the conversation between Pārvatī and the sages, the auspicious celebration of Śiva's marriage.

22. The birth of Kumāra and the victory of Kumāra, the terrible killing of Tāraka, the description of Narasiṁha.

23. The creation of the lotus-born deity; the killing of Andhaka, the greatness of Vārāṇasī as well as that of Narmadā.

24. The description of Pitṛs according to the Gotras and Pravaras, the glorification of the Pitṛgāthā (song of Pitṛs) Ubhayamukhīdānam (gift of a cow while giving birth to a calf and hence two-faced) and the gift of Kṛṣṇājina (deerskin of a black antelope).

25. Then the story of Sāvitrī, the duties of a king, the narration of different kinds of evil portents ending with eclipses.

26. The narration of omens at the time of journey, the glorification of auspicious signs in dreams, the greatness of Vāmana and that of Varāha (Boar) thereafter.

27. The churning of the ocean, the suppression (nullification) of the poison Kālakūṭa, the clash between the Devas and

the Demons; then the science of Engineering (planning the foundation and construction of a house).

28. The characteristic features of an image (idol); then (the construction) of the temple, the characteristic features of a mansion, the characteristics of a pavilion.

29. The indication of future kings, the glorification of great gifts, the narration of Kalpas—All these are narrated in this Purāṇa.

30. This Purāṇa is pure and conducive to welfare; it causes increase in longevity and fame. He who reads this or listens to it, goes to Hari's abode.

31. He who writes this and gifts it over to a Brāhmaṇa after worshipping him on the equinoctial transit, alongwith a gold fish and a cow attains the greatest region.

CHAPTER ONE HUNDRED AND EIGHT

The Garuḍa Purāṇa : Contents

God Brahmā said :

1. O Marīci, listen, I shall recount to you the auspicious Garuḍa Purāṇa.[1] On being asked, the Lord Viṣṇu, seated on Garuḍa, recounted this to Garuḍa.

---

1. The GP (*Garuḍa Purāṇa*) is an ancient encyclopaedia of Indian wisdom, though its *Preta-kalpa* section adds little to its glory. According to the NP. Bh. P. (xii. 13. 8) and BV. P., GP consists of 19,000 verses while according to the *Vāyu* and *Mt. P* the total no. of its verses is 18,000 (Kane HD. vii. 832) and according to AP 272, 21, 8000 verses. Kane's statements need revision as the Vāyu 104.8 (GM. edt.) clearly states, 19000 as its total No. of verses.

ekona-viṁśa-sāhasraṁ Vainateyam udāhṛtam/
But GP (I. 1. 35) states 8800 verses as its extent.
aṣṭau-śloka-sahasrāṇi tathā cāṣṭau śatāni ca/
Purāṇaṁ Gāruḍaṁ Vyāsaḥ purā'sau mā'bravīd idam//

2. It consists of nineteen thousand verses. The story deals with the events of the Tārkṣya Kalpa. There is the usual enquiry about the beginning of the Purāṇa, creation of the Universe is described svccinctly.

3. O Brāhmaṇa, there are rules of the procedure of the worship of the sun; thereafter, the rules regarding initiation ceremony; then there is the worship in connection with Śrāddhas, after this (injunctions regarding) the worship of nine Vyūhas (manifestations of the Lord).

4. Then the injunctions regarding the worship, the Pañjara (ritualistic cage) pertaining to Viṣṇu, the chapter on Yoga system and the glorification of Viṣṇu's thousand names.

5. The meditation on Viṣṇu, then the worship of the Sun, thereafter, the Arcanā (worship) of Mṛtyuñjaya, the Mālāmantra (Garland mantra), the worship of Śiva and then the worship of his attendants.

6. The adoration of Gopāla, the worship of Śrīdhara, the fascinator of the three worlds, the worship of Viṣṇu of the five Tattvas, the discus and the worship of the Lord.

7. The rites of Nyāsa, etc., the Upāsti, performance of Sandhyā prayers, the worship of Durgā and then the worship of the Devas, the worship of Maheśvara, and then the rite of wearing the Pavitra (Darbha grass with a loop worn in the finger like a ring) and worshipping.

8. The meditation on the idol of the Lord, the measurements of the sites of the buildings; the characteristics of palaces, the mode of installation of all the Devas with the several modes of worship.

The confusion is due to difference in Mss. or versions of the GP. available to the writer of the Purāṇa, e. g. GP. I. ch. 107 (ref. to the Parāśara Smṛti) is not known to the NP. noted by Dr. Ramshankar Bhattacharya (GP. Intro, p. 14-15)., the table of contents given in the NP agrees more closely with the Jibanand edt. of the GP. (though Veṅkaṭeśvara edt. of GP also tallies with that of the NP).

The *Pretakalpa* in the NP. differs in some respects from all the printed editions of the GP as accretions went on increasing in the Pretakalpa (R. S. Bhattacharya—ibid, p. 16).

A few slips in the readings of the NP (Veṅkaṭeśvara) edt.

NP. *Śrāddha* (verse 3) for GP. I. 10 *Śreyādi Pūjā*.

NP. *Vidhi Kriyā* (verse 9 for GP. I. 53) *Nidhi Kriyā*.

9. The Yoga with its eight ancillaries, the Dharmas regarding the charitable gifts, the activity and the rules of procedure regarding the expiatory rites, the narration of different continents and their Lords, the description of hells, the solar system (planetary system around the sun) and Jyotiṣa (Science of Astrology and Astronomy.)

10. The science of Sāmudrika (Palmistry of prediction based on the characteristic marks on the body), the knowledge of the notes, scrutiny tests of the Navaratnas (the nine precious stones) the glory of the holy centres, the excellent greatness of Gayā.

11. Then the description of the Manvantaras severally alongwith their divisions, the enumeration of the Pitṛs, the duties of the different Varṇas (castes), the purification of the materials of worship, the dedication of benefit unto God.

12. Śrāddha, worship of vināyaka, Grahayajña (sacrifice for propitiating the planets), the Āśramas (stages of life), the impurity due to birth and death (in the family), Nītiśāstra (science of Polity and Ethics), statements about the holy rites.

13. The Solar race, the lunar race, the narration of the incarnations of Hari, the story of Rāma, (the Rāmāyaṇa), the genealogical line of Hari (the Harivaṁśa) and then the story of Bhārata.

14. The science of life, pathology at the outset and (then) the treatment, then materia-medica (Dravyajā Guṇāḥ), the Kavaca (Mantras as coat of mail) that dispels ailments and which pertains to Viṣṇu and Garuḍa, the mantra pertaining to Tripura.

15. Praśna-cūḍā-maṇi (a treatise on answering astrologically problems asked) at the end, the exposition of the veterinary science branch about Horses, the enumeration of the names of drugs and then discussion about grammar.

16. The science of prosody, good conduct and discipline, and then the rules regarding ablution, the rites of Tarpaṇa Vaiśvadeva, the twilight prayers and the holy rites (offering ablutions to Pitṛs during Parvans such as the full moon and the new moon days and such other special days.

17. Nityaśrāddha (the daily Śrāddha), the description of

tion of the rites to be performed before death, the exposition of subsequent rites.

28. The 'middle' sixteen Śrāddhas, the stipulation of activities for the attainment of heaven, the reckoning of Sūtaka (period of impurity due to birth), the rite of Nārāyaṇa Bali (oblation unto Nārāyaṇa.)

29. The greatness of Vṛṣotsarga (the rite of setting a bull calf free), the avoidance of forbidden activities, statement of the rites when accidental and premature death takes place, the fruits of human action.

30. The consideration of Kṛtya and Akṛtya (what should be done and what should not be done), meditation on Viṣṇu for the purpose of Salvation, narration of the rites laid down for the attainment of heaven, the description of happiness in heaven.

31. The description of Bhūrloka, (the Earth,) the description of seven nether-worlds, the narration of five upper worlds, the description of the position of the Cosmic Egg.

32. Many stories concerning the cosmic egg, the exposition of the Brahman and the Jīva (the individual soul); the narration of the ultimate dissolution (of the Universe) and the narration of the eulogy of benefits.

33. Thus is the Purāṇa named after Garuḍa; it yields worldly pleasures and salvation; it is glorified as destructive of sins of those men who read and listen to it.

34. He who writes out this Purāṇa and gifts it to a Brāhmaṇa at the time of equinoctial transit, alongwith a pair of swans made of gold, goes to heaven.

of the noble-souled Atri, the family of Amāvasu and the wonderful story of Raji.

18. The story of Yayāti, the review of the family of Yadu; the story of Kārttavīrya, thereafter, the story of Jamadaagni and his son.

19. The description of the family of Vṛṣṇi, the birth of Sagara, the story of Bhārgava (Paraśu-Rāma) subsequent to the killing of his father.

20. The story of Sagara, the story of Bhārgava once again, the story of the battle between the Devas and Asuras, the description of the manifestation of Kṛṣṇa.

21. The meritorious hymn in praise of Indra glorified by Śukra, the narration of the greatness of Viṣṇu and the review of the family of Bali.

22. The story of the future kings after the advent of the Kali age. This is the quarter of Upodghāta in the middle section, the third quarter (in the Purāṇa).

23. I shall recount the fourth quarter viz. Upasaṁhāra (Conclusion) in the final section, the narration of Vaivasvata Manvantara precisely and in detail.

24. What has been mentioned before is mentioned here succinctly; thereafter; the story of the future Manus.

25. The specification of the Kalpas and the dissolution (then), thereafter the measurement of Time, then the fourteen worlds are mentioned along with their respective characteristics.

26. The description of hells (attained) by impious activities, the narration of Manomayapura (City of Mind) and thereafter, the Prākṛtika Laya (Dissolution within Prakṛti).

27. Thereafter, the description of Śiva's city. The threefold goal of creatures, thanks to the contact with the Guṇas, is described.

28. Thereafter, the description by means of positive and negative assertions (i. e. invariable concomitance and logical discontinuance) of the Brahman, the great Ātman, that is beyond specifications and argumentation.

29. Thus the quarter section on Upasaṁhāra has been summarised. Thus the Brahmāṇḍa Purāṇa comprising four quarters has been described to you.

30-33a. O Brāhmaṇa, this Purāṇa called Brahmāṇḍa is the eighteenth Purāṇa, the most essential of all chief (Purāṇas). What is originally composed of four hundred thousand verses has been narrated separately in eighteen books, O bestower of honour, by the sage Vyāsa the son of Parāśara who is the real instructor of all the sages of purified souls. Those sages who by nature practise religious virtues and bless the wretched ones, heard these Purāṇas from me and revealed them to the world.

33b-36a. Formerly, this Purāṇa has been narrated by me to Vasiṣṭha; it was passed on by him to his son Śakti, by him it was recounted to Jātūkarṇya. Then Vyāsa obtained it from the mouth of the Wind-God, making it authoritative in the world; he propagated this excellent Purāṇa in the Public (the world). O dear one, whoever glorifies this and listens to it with great concentration, dispels all sins and attains the world devoid of ailments.

36b-37. He who writes out this Purāṇa and gives it to a Brāhmaṇa after covering it with a cloth and placing it on a gold throne, attains the world of Brahman. No doubt need be entertained in this respect.

38. O Marīci, these eighteen Purāṇas narrated briefly by me to you should be heard in full.

39. The excellent man who listens to the eighteen Purāṇas or narrates them in accordance with the injunctions, is not born here again.

40. The Sūtra (summarised form) of the Purāṇas which has been mentioned by me to you now, should be practised everyday by one who desires the benefit out of the Purāṇas.

41. This should not be narrated to any one who is arrogant, hypocrite, sinful, malicious to the Devas and preceptors, knavish or one who hates good men.

42. It must be imparted to one who is quiescent, of tranquil mind, interested in service, devoid of indecent rivalry, is pure and is a good devotee of Viṣṇu,

CHAPTER ONE HUNDRED AND TEN

The Exposition of Vratas to be performed on Pratipads, the first day of the Lunar fortnight

Nārada said :

1. O holy sir, I have heard the full gist of all the Purāṇas, conveyed by you directly and orally in the same manner as it was narrated to Marīci by Brahmā, the highest deity.

2. O highly blessed one, now recount to me, in due order, the story of the Tithis (i. e. the details of the different lunar days) whereby the holy rites and observances can be decided upon.

3. Now please narrate to me the particular holy Vrata (vow or rite) alongwith its detailed procedure of worship etc. and enlighten me on what (particular) holy lunar day (tithi) and in what (particular) month that Vrata is to be performed.[1]

Sanātana said :

4. O Nārada, listen I shall recount to you the holy rites (Vratas) of the Tithis separately. They bring about all the Siddhis (accomplishments of objects) in the order of the Tithis and their lords.

5-6. God Brahmā created the entire Universe on the first day in the bright half of Caitra, at the time of sunrise.[2] It was in the beginning of the year and that of the spring in the kingdom of Bali (?). The Pratipad is to be taken always

---

1. Vratas are of different types. Some are to be performed on particular *tithis*, some on days, some depend on the constellation of the particular day etc. (AP. 175.I). AP later gives some general rules for observing Vratas.). Here Nārada wants to know the details of *Tithi-vratas*.

2. The belief that the Universe was created by god Brahmā at the time of sun-rise on the 1st day of the bright half of Caitra, is common to other Purāṇas. CC on Vrata, pp. 360-65, *Vrata-rāja* (VRJ.) ch. I., p. 21 quotes Bm. P and prescribes *Mahāśānti* and the worship of god Brahmā as in the NP.

when it is in conjunction with the previous Tithi, by wise persons.[1]

7. At that time, the great rite of Śānti (the pacificatory rite) should be performed. It is destructive of all sins. It subdues all evil portents. It dispels the sins of Kali.

8. It bestows longevity, causes nourishment and enhances wealth and good fortune. It is auspicious and holy and is conducive to happiness in both the worlds.

9-10. On that day, at the outset, god Brahmā who had assumed the physical body of the fire-god, should be worshipped with respectful formalities such as washing the feet with water and other respectful offerings (Pādyas, Arghyas), flowers, incense, clothes, ornaments, meals, sacrificial oblations, presents and the propitiation of the Brāhmaṇas. Thereafter, the worship of deities should be performed separately of each god.

11-12. After paying obeisance to the Oṁkāra with (the offerings of) water from the Kuśa grass, gingelly-seeds and raw rice-grains, (the devotee) shall give religious fee or gift (Dakṣiṇā) to a Brāhmaṇa who is a Vedic Scholar, alongwith clothes and gold for the purpose of complete and perfect performance of the Vrata. This Vrata that has such a special Pūjā in it, is called Saurī Vrata[2] (Vrata pertaining to the Sun).

13-14a. O Brāhmaṇa, this holy rite yields good health to men. O sage, Vidyāvrata[3] is also to be performed on that day. O sage, on the same Tithi, the holy rite called Tilaka[4] was told by Kṛṣṇa to Ajātaśatru (Yudhiṣṭhira).

14b-16. In the month of Jyeṣṭha, in the bright half, on the first day at sunrise, one should worship the pleasing Karavīra

1. VRJ. quotes this as *Vṛddha Vasiṣṭha Smṛti* and states that even if the *Pratipad* is associated with *amāvāsyā* (*pūrva-vṛddhā*), it should be taken as the proper beginning of the year.

2. Probably the same as *Ārogyapratipad vrata* (VRJ. I p, 23).

3. NP gives no details of this Vrata, for which *vide CC* on *Vrata* I. 338-40, VRJ. p. 23.

4. After worshipping Saṁvatsara (the year), the performer has to apply on his forehead a *Tilaka* with white sandal-wood paste for one year (CC on Vrata I. 348-50.

tree that grows in the temple garden.[1] It must be tied with a red thread, scents, incense and unguents must be offered alongwith the germinating seven grains, oranges and pomegranates. It must be sprinkled with water mixed with unbroken rice grain. The following Mantra should be uttered for praying for forgiveness.

17-19a. "Obeisance to you O Karavīra, the residence of meritorious acts, beloved of the sun, always liked by (one who wields thunderbolt Dambholi) i.e. Indra, Mṛḍa, (Śiva), Durgā and other deities." He should then crave forgiveness through the Vedic Mantra[2] "Ā Kṛṣṇena" etc. (ṚV. I. 35.2). After worshipping thus with great devotion and after giving due Dakṣiṇā to a Brāhmaṇa, he should circumambulate and go to his house.

19b-20. On the first day in the bright half of the month of Śrāvaṇa, there is a great Vrata[3] that yields good fortune and intellect. It is the cause of all the Puruṣārthas) viz. virtue, wealth, love and liberation.

O Brāhmaṇa, beginning on a Monday, this Vrata should be continued for three and a half months.

21-22. After observing fast on the fourteenth day in the dark half of the month of Kārttika, the devotee, earnest and interested in the Vrata, should worship Śiva on (the following) full moon day. On the Pratipad following it He should offer Vāyana (sweet-meats and other presents) alongwith a gold flute (?) to a Brāhmaṇa for the purpose of increase in the wealth. O leading sage, it is highly meritorious and it increases the pleasure of the deities.

23. On the first day in the bright half of Bhādrapada, the Vrata named 'Mahātmā' (the greatest one) should be

---

1. VV 14-19a. describe the *Karavīra-pratipad-vrata* It is observed on *Vaiśākha Śuddha Pratipad* in Tamil Nad. Cf. CC. I. 353.

2. V. 17 which is a prayer in Purāṇic SK is said to be the 'Mantra' *ā Kṛṣṇena* etc. is a Vedic Mantra in RV. I. 35. 2.

3. VV 19b-22 describe the *Roṭaka Vrata,* although NP does not disclose the name of this *mahāvrata,* Vrj., pp. 25-26 describe it as *Roṭaka Vrata*. It is also called *Bilva-roṭaka vrata.*

performed. Some call this Vrata by the name of Mauna[1] (silence). Śiva is worshipped in this rite.

24-27a. The devotee shall, in silence, cook three times sixteen fruits alongwith ground flour. He shall give one set of sixteen to a Brāhmaṇa. He shall give another set of sixteen to the Deity. One set of sixteen, he himself eats. Over the water pot, the knower of the injunctions worships a gold image of Śiva and gives everything of it to the preceptor alongwith a cow. O Brāhmaṇa, after observing this Vrata of the trident-bearing Lord of the Devas for fourteen years, the devotee enjoys worldly pleasures, till his death (thereafter), he attains to Śiva.

27b-29. O Brāhmaṇa, a man who performs Aśokavrata[2] on the first day in the bright half of the month of Āśvina, (himself) becomes Aśoka (free from grief). He is endowed with riches and grains. The Aśoka tree must be worshipped by those who are exclusively devoted to these observances and rites. At the end of the Vrata in the twelfth year, he should offer the replica of an Aśoka tree with great devotion to the preceptor. He is thereby honoured in Śivaloka.

30. One shall begin Navarātra[3] (the festival of nine nights) on this very Pratipad. He should worship the goddess in the forenoon alongwith the rite of installing the water-pot.

31. He should sow to germinate barley grains mixed with wheat. He should take only one meal once a day. The food consumed should not be one that is requested for.

32-33. In accordance with his ability, he should observe fast. The worship of the goddess, repetition of the Mantras and recitation of the holy texts (the Saptaśatī) should also be done in accordance with one's capacity. O Brāhmaṇa, the three Caritas (stories) mentioned in the Mārkaṇḍeya Purāṇa should be read for all the nine days, by one who desires to get worldly

1. VV. 23-27a detail the *Mauna Vrata*. HD V. 383-384 gives a Vrata of a similar name but the details are somewhat different.

2. VV 27-29 describe *Aśoka-vrata*. This is different from that given in CC II. 279-283. HD V. i. 295 also differs.

3. VV. 30-34 describe the *Navarātra* or *Durgā Pūjā* which is observed all over India. It is described in details in HD V. i., pp. 154-187. The *Carita* in the *Mk. P.* mentioned in V. 32 is most probably *Devī Māhātmya* (chs. 78-90) or the *Saptaśatī*.

pleasures and salvation. The worship of virgins alongwith the rite of feeding, is praised.

34. O Brāhmaṇa, after performing the Vrata thus, the man becomes a receptacle of all Siddhis on the Earth, by the grace of Durgā.

35. On the first day in the bright half in the month of Urja (Kārttika), one should perform all the rites mentioned for Navarātra. Particularly, the rite called Annakūṭa[1] (a heap of cooked articles of food) causes the increase in the delight of Viṣṇu.

36. In the course of worship of Govardhana, Annakūṭa must be made with all cooked articles and with all milk products by everyone, for achieving all objects by the worshipper.

37. In the evening the devotee should worship Govardhana mountain alongwith the cows, and offer suitable Dakṣiṇā. He shall attain worldly pleasures and liberation.

38-40a. The excellent Dhanavrata[2] is to be performed on the first day in the bright half of the month of Mārgaśīrṣa. Viṣṇu is to be worshipped at night alongwith Homas. The observer of the Vrata should give a replica in gold of the fire-god to a Brāhmaṇa after covering it with two red clothes. By performing this vrata thus, one becomes flourishing in wealth and food-grains on the Earth. With his sins burned in fire, he is honoured in the Viṣṇuloka.

---

1. VV. 35-37 describe the *Govardhana Pūjā* (in the memory of Kṛṣṇa's triumph over Indra) or *Annakūṭa*. Though v. 35 instructs "to perform all the rites mentioned for Navarātra," the essential difference is that the *Navarātra* is pertaining to Devī (Śākta) while Govardhana Pūjā is a strictly vegetarian Vaiṣṇava Vrata. Vrj. p. 33 quotes *Sanatkumāra Saṁhitā* to describe the procedure of worship of *Annakūṭa*. There are minor regional differences in performing the *Annakūṭapūjā*.

2. VV. 38-40a describe *Dhana-vrata* which is otherwise called *Dhanya-vrata* (AP. 167. 5-6) or *Dhanya pratipad Vrata*. CC I. 355-56 bases its description on the *Varāha Purāṇa* 56. 1-16 which is somewhat different from what is given here. HD. V. i. 320 lists a *Dhana-vrata* which begins on *Phālguna-Śuddha-Trayodaśī* and is concerned with Kubera and as such is different from the *Dhana-Vrata* in the NP.

40b-41a. On the first day in the bright half of the month of Pauṣa, one should worship the Sun-god with devotion. The man must restrict his diet to one meal a day. Performing the Vrata thus, that mortal being shall attain the world of the Sun.

41b-42a. On the first day in the bright half of the month of Māgha, one shall worship the Fire god as Maheśvara himself, in accordance with the injunctions. He becomes rich and flourishing on the Earth.

42b-44a. On the first day in the bright half of the month of Phālguna, one should, with water, sprinkle Digambara (the naked Lord Śiva), the Lord of the Devas, all of whose limbs have turned grey due to dust. He should sprinkle the water all over his body. Indeed, god Maheśvara is delighted even with such secular rites and activities. On being worshipped with devotion, he grants his own Sāyujya (Salvation wherein the devotee becomes one with the Deity).

44b-46.[1] On the first day in the bright half of the month of Vaiśākha, one shall worship Viṣṇu who sports in the Universe. He should worship in accordance with the injunctions. The man who observes the Vrata should feed the Brāhmaṇas. Similarly, on the first day in the bright half of the month of Jyeṣṭha and Āṣāḍha, one shall worship Brahmā, the preceptor of the worlds. Thereat, accompanied by Viṣṇu, Brahmā the Lord of the chiefs of all worlds, grants identity with himself. The devotee shall then attain all the Siddhis.

47-48.[2] O excellent Brāhmaṇa, Vratas to be observed on the first day of the twelve months—Vratas bestowing worldly pleasures here and Liberation from Saṁsāra hereafter have been recounted to you. Brahmacarya (observance of celibacy) is laid down in all these Vratas. The diet during these Vratas is prescribed as Haviṣyānna (cooked rice soaked in ghee) as common to all.

1. The last redactor of the NP seems to have rectified the missing *Vratas* on Vaiśākha Śukla 1st, by adding vv. 44b-46.

2. VV. 47-48 prescribe the general rules about observance of Vratas mentioned (vide AP. 175).

CHAPTER ONE HUNDRED AND ELEVEN

Exposition of Vratas to be observed on Dvitīyās (second Tithi in lunar fortnight)

Sanātana said :

1. O Brāhmaṇa, listen. I shall recount to you the Vratas of Dvitīyās (to be observed on the second day of the lunar fortnight). On observing them with devotion, a man is honoured in the Brahmaloka.

2-3a. On the second day in the bright half of the month of Caitra, the devotee should propitiate Brahmā alongwith his Śakti. He should eulogise the deity and propitiate him with Haviṣyānna (cooked rice soaked in ghee), scents and other things. He shall thus attain the benefit of all sacrifices. After realising all desires, he shall attain the region of the supreme spirit in the end.

3b-4a. O Brāhmaṇa, on this very day, others worship the rising crescent moon at the beginning of the night. They attain worldly pleasures and liberation.

4b-6. Or on this day, one shall devotedly worship the twin gods, Aśvins and offer gold and silver eyes to a Brāhmaṇa covering them with a pot filled with curd or ghee ? O leading Brāhmaṇa, by performing this Netravrata[1] for twelve years one becomes verily a king. He attains a comely form. He becomes valorous against the hosts of his enemies. He becomes interested in Dharma, and the chief of all kings.

7-8a. On the second day in the bright half of the month of Rādha (Vaiśākha), one shall worship Brahmā in the form of Viṣṇu in accordance with the injunction, over a pitcher containing seven kinds of grains. After enjoying all desirable worldly pleasures here one attains Viṣṇuloka thereby.

---

1. VV 4b-6 describe the *Netra-vrata* or *Cakṣu-vrate.* CC on *Vrata* I. 392-93 mentions that the *Vratin* (observer of the Vrata) is to subsist on curds and ghee on this tithi.

8b-9. On the second day in the bright half of the month of Jyeṣṭha, one should worship the Sun-god, Lord of the worlds who has assumed the form of the four-faced Lord, in accordance with the injunctions. After feeding the Brāhmaṇas with devotion, he shall attain the world of Sun-God.

10-12. The second day in the bright half of the month of Āṣāḍha is very meritorious. On that day, the observer of the Vrata takes Balarāma in procession alongwith Subhadrā. He goes round the various parts of the city, alongwith Brāhmaṇas and others. After going near a tank or a river, he should celebrate the great festival. At the end of it, he should re-instate them duly in the Lord's abode. He should feed Brāhmaṇas for completing the holy rite.

13. Prajāpati or the creator of the universe sleeps on the second day in the bright half of the month of Nabhas (Śrāvaṇa) That tithi is therefore very sacred. It is called Aśokaśayanā.[1]

14-16a. One should worship the four-faced deity lying in the bed alongwith his Śakti. After bowing down to the Lord of the worlds, one shall utter this Mantra : "O Śrīkānta (lover of Śrī) O Śrīvatsadhārin (one who bears the Śrīvatsa mark), Śrīvāsa (abode of good fortune), O Śrīpati (Lord of Śrī), O Dharmārtha-Kāmada (the bestower of virtue, wealth, and love) may not my wedded life perish." Here the charitable gift of a crescent made of gold is recommended. It brings about all Siddhis.

16b-17a. On the second day in the bright half of the month of Bhādrapada, one should worship the creator of the

---

1. VV. 13-15 describe the *Aśoka-Śayana-Vrata*, also called *Aśūnya-Śayana-Vrata*. It is meant for both men and women. NP prescribes the worship of the four-faced god Brahmā while he is lying in bed with his Śakti, in this *Vrata*. But in *Viṣṇudharmottara*. I. 145. 6-20 and AP. 177. 3-12 the worship of Viṣṇu and Lakṣmī is prescribed. Strangely enough after worshipping Brahmā the prayer is addressed to Viṣṇu in the NP (v. 15); the name of the Vrata is based on the prayer.

Lakṣmyā na śūnyaṁ varada yathā te śayanaṁ vibho/
Śayyā mamāpyaśūnyā' stu tathaiva madhusūdana//

—AP. 177. 7b-8a.

It is to be observed for four months from Śrāvaṇa,

universe in the form of Indra in accordance with the prescribed injunctions. He shall obtain the fruit of the performance of all sacrifices.

17b-21.[1] The second day in the bright half of the month Āśvina is very holy. The charitable gift made on this day is said to yield endless benefits. Formerly, Yama was fed by Yamunā in her house on the second day in the bright half of Kārttika. Hence, this is called Yamadvitīyā.[1] If one takes food in the house of one's sister on this day, it is conducive to nourishment. He must give her clothes and ornaments. It is the tithi on which Lord Yamarāja was fed by Yamunā with her own hand, out of sisterly affection. Hence, he who takes his food from the hand of his sister on that day, attains excellent jewels, wealth and food-grains.

22. Pitṛs should be worshipped through Śrāddha on the second day in the bright half of the month of Mārgaśīrṣa. Then the devotee obtains good health alongwith his sons and grandsons.

23-24. On the second day in the bright half of the month of Pauṣa, the rite of sprinkling with the water a cow's horns, is the bestower of all desires unto men. The sight of the rising moon is also conducive to the attainment of all desires. For the purpose of achieving virtue, love and wealth, the devotee should restrict his diet to cooked rice soaked in ghee and subdue his sense-organs and worship the rising moon by offering Arghya and flowers alongwith ghee.

25-29a. On the second day in the bright half of the month of Māgha, one shall duly worship Prajāpati in the form of Sun, with red flowers and red unguents. He shall make an image of the deity in gold, according to his capacity. He should take a copper vessel full of wheat or rice grains. He should dedicate all these things to the Lord and offer the same to a Brāhmaṇa. If this Vrata is thus performed, the devotee shall

---

1. VV. 18b-21 describe the *Yama dvitīyā Vrata.* It was on the 2nd day of the bright half of Kārttika that Yama, the god of Death, was fed by his sister Yamunā that people are advised to go to their sisters on this day and take meal and gift her with clothes and ornaments. The story is told in *Bs.*

observing these Vratas perfectly, a woman shall attain married bliss and good fortune.

2-5. An unmarried virgin desirous of a bridegroom, and one desirous of matrimonial bliss and good fortune for her sons and husband, should perform Gaurī Vrata.[1] The image of Gaurī is made of gold, silver, copper or clay along with that of her Lord (Śiva) on the third day in the bright half of the month of Caitra. O Brāhmaṇa, she then worships it with scents, fragrant flowers, clothes, auspicious ornaments, and bundles of Dūrvā grass. She observes fast. She propitiates Brāhmaṇa women whose husbands and sons are alive and girls with auspicious characteristics, by offering them saffron, collyrium, clothes and other things. Delighted in her mind, she should keep awake that night with the desire to fulfil the Vrata.

6. O Brāhmaṇa, she should give that image to the preceptor if it is metallic. If it is made of clay, she should immerse it in a tank or a river.

7. She should perform this auspicious Gaurī Vrata for twelve years. With the due formal resolve to donate, she should offer twelve cows also for the achievement of her desires.

8. What more needs be spoken ? There is no other bestower of good fortune and matrimonial bliss to women in all the three worlds like Gaurī.

9. A woman attains wealth, good husband, sons, learning, ability to command, fame and happiness—in fact all desired happiness, by worshipping Gaurī with devotion.

---

1. VV. 2-9 describe the *Gaurī Vrata* which if observed for twelve years, confers a good consort to the lady observer if unmarried, uninterrupted matrimonial bliss, if married, good fortune and all desired happiness. *HD* V. i. p. 296 gives five varieties of this *Vrata* some of which are to be observed in Āśvina (*Kṛtyaratnākara* 219), on the 4th day of Jyeṣṭha (Bd. p). It is similar to *Gaurī-tṛtīyā-Vrata* observed on the 3rd day of the bright half of *Caitra, Bhādrapada, Māgha*—(*Samaya-mayūkha* 36).

There is another *Gaurī Vrata* to be observed on the 4th day in the bright half of Māgha. It is also called *Ḍhuṇḍhi Vrata, Kuṇḍa Vrata, Lalitā Vrata* and *Śānti Vrata, vide infra* I. 113. 80.85.

10. The third day in the bright half of the month of Vaiśākha is glorified as Akṣaya Tṛtīyā.[1] That is the Tithi on which Tretāyuga began. Whatever holy rite is performed on this day is made everlasting (Akṣaya) by this Tṛtīyā.

11-12a. Wise men know that two inaugural days of Yugas (viz. that of Kṛta and Tretā) were in the bright half of the month, while those of the other two Yugas (viz. Dvāpara and Kali) were in the dark fortnight (of the lunar month). The two (inaugural) days in the bright fortnight are to be accepted (observed) in the earlier half of the day. Out of the Yugādi days in the dark fortnight, Dvāpara began in Māgha while the Kali Age commenced in Bhādrapada. Thus commenced the Yugas[2] on these days.

12b-13. The devotee should worship Nārāyaṇa, the preceptor of the universe accompanied by Śrī, with flowers, incense and unguents on the third day in the bright half of the month of Vaiśākha. Or if he takes his holy dip in the waters of the Gaṅgā, he is absolved of all sins.

14. He should worship Viṣṇu with unbroken rice-grains. He shall have his ablution with water mixed with unbroken

---

1. VV 10-15 describe the *Akṣaya Tṛtīyā Vrata* which falls on the 3rd day of the bright half of Vaiśākha. Any meritorious act performed on this day, becomes ever-lasting. Hence the epithet *Akṣaya.* The speciality of this day is that it marks the beginning of the *Tretā Yuga.* The rite pertains to the worship etc. of god Viṣṇu accompanied by Śrī. The performer devotee attains the region of Viṣṇu. Cf. *Viṣṇu Dh. S.* 90. 16-17: also *Bhaviṣyottara* P. 30. 2-3 & 19.

2. VV 11-12a. give the Yugādi *tithis* vide *Supra I* 56. 147-48 for the *Yugādi Tithis*—the *tithi* on which a particular Yuga began. According to the NP. the following are the *Yugādi tithis* for the following Yugas.

	Yuga		*Tithi*
1.	Kṛta	—	9th day Kārttika, Śu. (bright half) (Śuddha)
2.	Tretā	—	3rd day Vaiśākha, Śu.
3.	Dvāpara	—	15th day of Māgha (Vd—Vadya—dark half)
4.	Kali	—	13th day of Bhādrapada, Vd.

VP. III. 14. 12-13 supports this, though AP. 209. 14 differs about Kṛta-Yuga.

As *Yugādi* days are recommended for the performance of *Śrāddha* etc., the first half of the day is preferable for *Yugādi* day in the bright half of a month, while the latter half is recommended for the Yugādi days in the dark half of the month.

junctions, alongwith the rites of Pādya (viz. offering water for washing the feet, hands, worship) Arghya and Arcana.

31-32. Then the cooked rice and the Dakṣiṇā should be placed in a gold, silver, copper, bamboo or a clay vessel alongwith fruits and clothes. The same shall then be given to a Brāhmaṇa. At the end of it, she should have the Pāraṇā (break the fast) alongwith the kinsmen.

33. The woman who observes this holy rite shall enjoy all desirable pleasures. She shall become a friend and attendant of Gaurī, thanks to the efficacy of this Vrata.

34. Sixteen bamboo-baskets filled with bliss-yielding articles and clothes should be enthusiastically given to a Brāhmaṇa in accordance with the injunctions.

35-36. She should then give generous monetary gifts to the other excellent Brāhmaṇas also for the satisfaction of the goddess. The woman who performs this holy rite of Saubhāgya Vardhana (that which increases conjugal blessedness) certainly attains it, thanks to the grace of the Goddess.

37-38. When the Tṛtīyā in the month of Bhādrapada coincides with the constellation Hasta, the Vrata taught by Śauri (Kṛṣṇa ?) is called Hastagaurīvrata[1]. The Vrata called Koṭīśvarī and Lakṣeśvarī[2] has been proclaimed by Śiva the Pinākabearing Lord. Its rules of procedure are being mentioned:

V*RJ*, pp. 48-52. Sixteen wicker-baskets containing 'bliss-yielding articles (indicating *Saubhāgya*—conjugal happiness) and cloth are to be given to Brāhmaṇas. This *Vrata* increases conjugal blessedness. The term *Saubhāgya Vardhana* here does not imply a new Vrata of that name. Dr. Kane in HD. V. 1., p. 456 mentions three *Saubhāgya Vratas* but they are quite different.

1. VV 37-39 describe *Hasta-Gaurī-Vrata* which is to be observed when the constellation *Hasta* coincides with the 3rd day of Bhādrapada Śu. . Kṛṣṇa has told this *Vrata*. The *Vratārka* requires contemplation of Gauri, Hara and Gaṇeśa in this *Vrata*, for 13 years and the *Udyāpana* (conclusion) of this *Vrata* in the 14th year (HD. V. i. p. 462).

2. VV 38-45a describe the *Koṭīśvarā* alias *Lakṣeśvarī Vrata* to be observed on the 3rd day of Bhādrapada Śu. (*Śuddha Pakṣa*—The bright half). It is called Lakṣeśvarī as a paste of one hundred thousand grains of rice or Sesame seeds is used to form the image of Pārvatī. Fast is to be observed on that day. *CC on Vrata* I. 459-461 quotes the *Sk. P.* for this *Vrata.* also vide HD. V-I. p. 290.

39. On this day, the Vrata has to be taken up for four years. O Nārada, every year it has to be performed alongwith the observance of fast.

40. Unbroken rice grains or gingelly seeds should be selected, O leading sage, to the extent of one hundred thousand. They should be cleaned and put in boiling water.

41. When the grains are cooked well, a splended image of the goddess should be made. It should be embellished with scented flowers and flower garlands.

42-44. Goddess Pārvatī should be installed therein and worshipped with great devotion, with scents, fragrant flowers, incense, lights and detailed Naivedya offerings and fruits. O Brāhmaṇa, she should bow to the goddess and crave forgiveness. Then she should immerse the image of the goddess in the middle of a water-tank. Dakṣiṇā is then offered to the Brāhmaṇas who are knowers of religious rites and procedures. She should then partake of her food the next day. Thus, O Brāhmaṇa, the Koṭi Lakṣeśvarī Vrata has been narrated to you.

45a. In the end she goes to the world of Gaurī, thanks to the power of this Vrata.

45b. On the third day in the bright half of the month of Iṣa (i.e. Āśvina), the lady devotee should perform BṛhadGaurī[1] Vrata.

46. O Nārada, this Vrata is to be performed for five years in accordance with the rules of procedure mentioned above. At the end, she should worship the main preceptor and other Brāhmaṇas with cash presents etc.

47-50. Five Suvāsinīs (married women whose husband are alive) should be worshipped as Haripriyās (beloveds of Hari) with clothes, ornaments, sandal paste, bodices, earrings and necklaces; five bamboo baskets are used and they are tied round

1. VV. 45 b-53 describe the *Bṛhad-Gaurī-Vrata* to be observed on the 3rd day of Āśvina Śu. (*Śuddha*) according, to NP., but on Bhādrapada Kṛ. (*Kṛṣṇa*) *Tṛtīyā* as per VRJ. In southern Maharashtra and in Karnataka, a plant *Dorlī* or *Riṅgaṇī* (in Marathi) is brought along with its roots, fruits and branches for worship. A thread is wound round the neck in the name of Gaurī. VRJ. (pp. 53-54) narrates the story about this *Vrata* from the *Bhaviṣyottara P.*

with threads. The baskets are filled with saffron, cumin-seeds, and bliss-yielding articles. Vāyanas (presents of sweet-meats) comprising of ground wheat flour, fresh Apūpa (baked pies), fruits etc. These must be given to the Suvāsinīs who also be fed. After giving as worshipful gift half the materials gathered as Vāyanas, she shall silently take her food. For the increase of the desired objects, a fruit (out of the gift) should be worn round the neck.

51. Getting up early in the morning, bedecked in ornaments and accompanied by her friends, she should go to a river to the accompaniment of songs and instrumental music. There Gaurī image is ritualistically bidden farewell to (into the river) with the prayer :

52. "O gentle lady, you had been invoked by me and worshipped duly (as per procedure), you may be pleased to go away at will, for granting me conjugal bliss".

53. After observing the holy rite, thus, O Brāhmaṇa, and after enjoying all worldly pleasures, thanks to the grace of the goddess, she shall attain Gaurī's world after death.

54-55. On the third day in the bright half of the month of Ūrja (Kārttika), she (the lady) should perform Viṣṇugaurī-vrata.[1] After worshipping the goddess worthy of being saluted by the whole world, with different modes of worship and services and after feeding the suvāsinī (a married woman with husband alive) who has been honoured duly with auspicious articles, she should bid farewell to the goddess after bowing to her, for obtaining the grace of satisfaction of Viṣṇugaurī.

56. On the third day in the bright half of the month of Mārgaśīrṣa, a woman should perform the auspicious HaraGaurī Vrata[2] in accordance with the injunctions laid down before, in the above-mentioned Vrata and should worship Jagadambikā (Mother of the Universe).

57. As a result of the prowess of this Vrata, she shall enjoy all charming worldly pleasures. Attaining the world of the goddess, she rejoices with her.

---

1. VV. 54-55 briefly describes the *Vrata* called *Viṣṇu Gaurī*.
2. VV. 56-57 deal with *Hara-Gaurī Vrata*.

58-59a. On the third day in the bright half of the month of Pauṣa, a woman should perform the Brahmagaurīvrata[1] in accordance with the injunctions laid down above. O excellent Brāhmaṇa, on being worshipped, BrahmaGaurī shall be delighted. Thanks to her grace, the lady devotee becomes associated with the goddess and rejoices herself.

59b-60. On the third day in the bright half of the month of Māgha, (goddess) Saubhāgya-Sundarī[2] should be worshipped in accordance with the rules of procedure mentioned before, by means of offering Arghya with coconuts. Delighted and rendered pleased by means of the Vrata, the goddess grants her own world.

61. The third day in the bright half of the month of Phālguna, is the bestower of family happiness. If the goddess is worshipped with scents, fragrant flowers etc., she shall be the bestower of all auspiciousness.

62. O sage, in all these Tṛtīyās (vratas on the third days of the lunar fortnight) the rules regarding the Pūjā of the goddess, the honour to the Brāhmaṇa, the charitable gifts, Homa and the ritualistic dismissal of the goddess are the same.

63. Thus the Vratas to be performed on Tṛtīyās have been narrated to you here. If observed with great devotion, they shall bestow all desirable objects cherished in mind.

---

1. VV. 58-59a describe *Brahma-Gaurī Vrata*. It will thus be seen that the *Gaurī Vratas* are the same but are associated with each member of the Trinity of gods and are performed on the 3rd days of lunar fortnights.

2. VV. 59b-60 describe the *Saubhāgya-Sundarī Vrata* (to propitiate goddess Umā, though the NP. is silent about the name of the deity). VRJ. prescribes its performance on Mārgaśīrṣa or Māgha (Kr.) *Tṛtīyā*, especially when it is conjoined with the next (4th) *Tithi*, and not with the previous one. VRJ (pp. 54-47) quotes a long story from the *Bhaviṣyottara P.* glorifying this *Vrata*.

CHAPTER ONE HUNDRED AND THIRTEEN

The Exposition of the holy rites to be performed on Caturthīs (the fourth day in the Lunar fortnight)

Sanātana said :

1. O Brāhmaṇa listen, I shall recount to you the holy vows and rites to be observed on Caturthī days.[1] On observing them, men and women shall attain their cherished desires.

2-3a. On the fourth day in the Lunar fortnight in the month of Caitra,[2], one should duly worship Gaṇapa (i.e. Gaṇeśa) in the form of Vāsudeva and offer gold as Dakṣiṇā to a Brāhmaṇa. He will be bowed to by the Devas (thereby), and then go to Viṣṇuloka.

3b-4. On the Caturthī day in the month of Vaiśākha, the devotee should pray to the deity called Saṁkarṣaṇa. By giving a conch-shell to imporant Brāhmaṇa householders, the knower of religious injunctions shall attain the world of Saṁkarṣaṇa and rejoice there for many Kalpas.

5. On the Caturthī day in the month of Jyeṣṭha the person should worship the deity in the form of Pradyumna. By giving fruits and roots to the herds (of cattle or beasts), he shall attain heaven.

---

1. Just as all the third days in the lunar fortnights are sacred to the goddess (in any form of the Trinity), the fourth days of the lunar fortnights are sacred to god Gaṇeśa. The *Vrata* gives special merit or fruit, if the 4th *Tithi* falls on Sunday or Tuesday. (VV. 90-91 below).

2. VV. 2-6 synthesize the *Catur-vyūha* doctrine of the Pāñcarātrins with a Śaiva god like Gaṇeśa, by identifying him with Viṣṇu. This is Vaiṣṇavization, as the NP. is a Vaiṣṇava Purāṇa, while in the *Kūrma P*, we find Pāśupatization of an originally Vaiṣṇava Purāṇa

The *Gaṇeśa Vyūha* accepts the names of the Pāñcarātrins.

Thus we find :

God Gaṇeśa to be worshipped on the 4th Tithi of :	*Name of the Vyūha*
1. Caitra	Vāsudeva
2. Vaiśākha	Saṅkarṣaṇa
3. Jyeṣṭha	Pradyumna
4. Āṣāḍha	Aniruddha

This *Vrata* is to be observed for 12 years.

6. On the Caturthī day in the month of Āṣāḍha, a man should worship Aniruddha. By giving pot-gourd-vessels to ascetics, he attains the cherished desires.

7. After performing these holy rites of the four Mūrtis for twelve years, the Udyāpana rite should be performed in accordance with the injunctions, by the devotee who wishes for the benefit thereof.

8. On the Caturthī day in the month of Jyeṣṭha, there is another Vrata viz. the excellent Satīvrata. By performing it, the devotee rejoices in the world of the mother of Gaṇapati on a par with him.

9-10. There is another auspicious Vrata on the Caturthī day in the month of Āṣāḍha, since it is the day on which Kalpa called Rathantara began. The man should worship Gaṇeśa duly with his mind sanctified by faith. He shall attain the benefit inaccessible even to the Devas and others.

11-17a. On the Caturthī day in the month of Śrāvaṇa, O sage, when the moon has risen, the devotee, the most excellent among the knowers of the procedure, should offer Arghya unto Gaṇeśa. He shall meditate on Lambodara (God Gaṇeśa), the three-eyed, four-armed deity who is red-complexioned, whose face beams with pleasure, and who is bedecked in different kinds of jewels and ornaments. He should worship him with all modes of services such as invocation,. etc. He should offer Modaka (sweet meat) as Naivedya which gives pleasure to Gaṇeśa. After performing the Vrata thus, he shall partake of the Modakas. During the night, after the worship, he should gladly sleep on the bare ground. Thanks to the power of this Vrata, he shall obtain all desires cherished in his mind in this world, and (after death) shall attain the region of Gaṇeśa. In all the three worlds, there is no other Vrata like this. Hence, it must be observed with all (possible) efforts by one who wishes to attain all cherished desires.

17b-18a. O celestial sage, some wish that the holy rite called Dūrvāgaṇapativrata[1] should be performed on this very

1. VV. 17b-23 describe the *Dūrvā Gaṇapati Vrata.* VRJ (pp. 60 ff) states that it commences on the 4th day of Śrāvaṇa Śu. 4 or Kārttika Śu. 4, and quotes stories from the *Saura P.* and the SK.P. to glorify this

same day. I shall tell you the injunctions regarding its performance.

18b-23a. The devotee should make the image of Gaṇapati in gold and place it over a copper vessel after covering it with a red cloth. He should worship the (entire set) on the mystic diagram called Sarvatobhadra, with red flowers five kinds of leaves viz. Bilva, Apāmārga, Śamī, Dūrvā, and Haripriyā (i.e. Tulasī). With these leaves and other flowers he should perform worship. He shall offer fruits and sweetmeats as Naivedya. After that, O ascetic, with pleasure, he should offer the Arghya. Then, O sage, after praying to it, he should give the image of Vighneśa (gaṇeśa) alongwith the adjuncts to the preceptor who knows the rules of procedure. He should honour him befittingly and then give it to him. He should continue the Vrata for five years, after duly performing worship. After enjoying all pleasures here he will go to the world of Gaṇapati.

23b-27a. On the Caturthī day (in the dark half) of the month of Bhādrapada, is the holy rite called Bahulādhenuka. On this day, the deity cow is to be assiduously worshipped with scents, garlands, barley, and other things. After circumambulating the cow deity, he should offer charitable gifts, if he can afford. If he cannot afford it, he shall bow to it and set it free. He should continue the Vrata for five, ten or sixteen years. He shall then perform the Udyāpana rite and give a milch cow (as charitable gift). Thanks to the power of this Vrata, he shall enjoy all charming worldly pleasures, and duly honoured and greeted by groups of Devas, he shall attain Goloka (the world of cows).

27b-30. On the fourth day in the bright half (of the month of Bhādrapada) is the holy rite called Siddha-Vaināyaka-[2]

Vrata. As per SK. P., the *Vrata* is to be observed from Śrāvaṇa Śu. 4 to Māgha Śu. 4. VRJ. gives two more varieties, one allowing its commencement on any *Śukla Caturthī* if it falls on a Sunday, and another prescribing 21 days duration from Śrāvaṇa Śu. 5 to Śrāvaṇa Kr. 10.

1. VV. 23b-27 describe *Bahulā-dhenuka Vrata* to be performed on Bhādrapada Kṛ. 4, the deity being the cow.

2. 27b-39 describe the *Siddha-Vināyaka Vrata* so popular as *Gaṇeśa Caturthī* in Maharashtra and other parts of India, though with some

vrata (or 'Siddhi-Vināyāka vrata). Through invocation and all other modes of service, the worship should be performed. Concentrating the mind, he should meditate on Siddhivināyaka. He should meditate on Lord Gaṇeśa as Ekadanta (single-tusked) Śūrpakarṇa (one with winnow-like ears), Gajavaktra (elephant-faced), Caturbhuja (four-armed), Pāśāṅkuśa-Dhara (one holding in his hand, a noose and a goad), the Lord resembling molten gold (in complexion). He should offer twentyone leaves uttering the twentyone names (one by one) with devotion. Listen to those names.

31-37. Śamī-leaf should be offered to Sumukha (the good-faced Deity), the Bhṛṅga-leaf to Gaṇādhīśa, the Bilva-leaf to the son of Umā, Dūrvā-grass to the elephant-faced God, Badarī to Lambodara (the big-bellied deity), Dhattūra to the son of Hara (Śiva), Tulasī-leaf to Śūrpakarṇa (God with ears like winnowing baskets) Śami-leaf to Vakra-tuṇḍa (God with a curved trunk), Apāmārga leaf to Guhāgraja (Elder brother of Kārttikeya), Bārhata leaves (those of brinjals) to Ekadanta (Single-tusked god), Sindūra (saffron) to Heramba, leaf of the fragrant plant called Patra to Caturhotra, the leaf of the Agastya tree which is pleasing to Sarveśvara (Lord of all).

He should them take up a pair of the leaves of Dūrvā grass along with scents, fragrant flowers and unbroken rice-grains. With great devotion, he should offer worship and five Modakas as Naivedya. After the rite of Ācamana, obeisance and prayer, he should ritualistically bid farewell to the Deity.

O sage, he should give the image of Vināyaka, made of gold, to the preceptor along with adjuncts. He should then

---

different procedure than that given in the NP. VRJ (pp. 68 ff) quotes SK. P. from Hemādri (*CC-Vrata* 1.525-29). A strange restriction is that one should not look at the moon on this night, lest one should be accused of theft. It was due to this that Lord Kṛṣṇa was accused of stealing away Syamantaka jewel. If, however, one happens to catch a glimpse of the moon, he should repeat Verse No. 39 given below in the NP. recounting the Syamantaka episode. This verse is quoted from VP. IV. 13.42 and is found in the *Vāyu P.* 96. 42 and the *BR.P.* 16.36 referring to the same story.

give Dakṣiṇā (religious gifts) to Brāhmaṇas. O Nārada, one who performs worship with devotion like this for five years, shall attain all cherished desires as a result of his Upāsanā (devotion and worship) here, as well as all splendid things hereafter.

38-39. Never shall one look at the moon on this Caturthī day (i.e. night). There is no doubt about this that, if one looks at the moon, he will be falsely accused. In order to mitigate the defect thereof (i.e. of looking at the moon this night), this (following) Mantra from the Purāṇa* should be recited :

"The lion killed Prasena, the lion was killed by Jāmbavān. O gentle boy, Do not cry. This Syamantaka jewel is offered to you."

40-43a. On the Caturthī day in the bright half of the month of Āśvina, one should worship Vināyaka (Kapardīśa—the god with cowrie-like knotted hair) by means of the Puruṣa Sūkta. He should render services without any reason (i.e. without any ulterior motive). He should offer the rice grains alongwith the shell-coins to a Brāhmaṇa religious student who is worshipped with scents and fragrant flowers with prayer : "The rice grains have Viśve Devas as their deity. They are mixed with the shell coins whose presiding deity is Hara. May the leader of the Gaṇas of Śiva (Kapardin) be pleased, when (the couries) are so dedicated."

43b-44a. The holy rite called Karakavrata[1] is to be performed on the Caturthī day in the dark half of the month of Kārttika. Only women are authorised to perform this Vrata. The rules of the procedure on it are being mentioned.

---

*Like other material, the NP. seems to have borrowed this verse from the VP. IV. 13.42. The verse appears in a similar context in the *Vāyu P.* 96. 42 and Br. P. 16.36

1. VV. 43b-51a describe the *Karaka Vrata*. *Karaka* is a water-vessel for ascetics, (some times made of coconut shell also). Only women are eligible to observe this. It is to be performed on Kārttika Kṛ. Caturthī (Āśvina by *amānta* reckoning followed in VRJ., pp. 81-82 which quotes the *Vāmana* P. for its details). VRJ. (pp. 79) narrates a Daśa-*ratha Lalitā Vrata* on the same day, but does not mix up the two as is done in *Puruṣārtha Cintāmaṇi*. The NP. does not mention the picture of Gaurī (and her family) as the main deity but treats it as a *Gaṇeśa Vrata*.

44b-45. The woman should take her bath and bedeck herself. She should then worship god Gaṇeśa. In front of the deity ten bowls filled with cooked rice shall be kept and be dedicated to the Lord of the Devas with devotion and purity of the mind.

46-47. She should utter (pray) :—"May the deity be gracious unto me." Saying this she should dedicate them to God Gaṇeśa. Presents shall be given respectfully to Suvāsinīs (married women) and the Brāhmaṇas according to desire. Then at night, when the moon rises, she should duly offer Arghya and partake of sweet-meats and cooked rice for the fulfilment of the Vrata.

48. Or O sage, the bowls may be filled with milk or water alongwith a rice, a betel nut, rice-grains and jewels and gifted over to a Brāhmaṇa.

49. The woman devotee should perform this holy rite for sixteen or twelve years. After making the due presents, she should ritualistically conclude this Vrata.

50-51a. Or the holy rite shall be observed by the woman throughout her life with a desire for conjugal blessedness. There is no other Vrata like this that yields conjugal blessedness to women. Hence it should be continuously performed.

51b-53. On the fourth day in the bright half of the month of Kārttika, the holy rite Nāgavrata[1] is to be celebrated. The devotee shall perform the Saṁkalpa rite in the morning, and drink pure water from a cow's horn. After the bath, he shall worship the serpents Śaṅkhapāla and others as well as Śeṣa by means of diverse services (in worship) beginning with invocation. He should make Āpyāyana (developing and nourishing) by means of milk. This is known as Nāgavrata.

54. O leading Brāhmaṇa, if this auspicious observance of Nāgavrata is performed thus by men, poisons perish ere long, and serpents do not bite them.

55-59. O leading sage, this Vrata is to be celebrated on the fourth day in the bright half of the month of Mārgaśīrṣa.

1. VV. 51b-54 deal with the *Nāgavrata*. *CC-Vrata* I. 530 quotes this from the KP.

feed Brāhmaṇas (twenty-four in number) with sweet-meats and milk-pudding. He should then give a cow along with its calf to the preceptor, along with monetary gifts.

67-69a. He shall give cash presents to others also, according to his capacity (the more the better). After obeisance and circumambulation (around the Brāhmaṇas), the excellent Brāhmaṇas should be bidden farewell to. He should, then, with great delight in his mind, take his food along with his kinsmen. By performing this vrata, a man enjoys excellent worldly pleasures here, and attains the Liberation called Sāyujya (absorption in the Deity) with Viṣṇu, thanks to the Grace of Gaṇeśa.

69b-70a. O Nārada, some call this by the name Varavrata.[1] Its rules of procedure and benefit are the same as in the case of the former.

70b-71. On the Caturthī day in the month of Pauṣa, the devotee should pray to Vighneśa with great devotion. He should feed a single Brāhmaṇa with sweet-meats and offer monetary gifts also. O sage, if this is performed, the Vratin (the performer of the holy vow) shall become the recepient of riches.

72-73a. The holy vow Saṁkaṣṭavrata[2] is to be observed on the fourth day in the dark half of the month of Māgha. The Vratin should decide on observance of fast upto the rise of the moon, with his mind controlled.

73b-74a. After the rise of the moon, the image of Gaṇeśa, made of clay, should be placed on the pedestal alongwith his weapons and the vehicle.

74b-75. It should be worshipped with the sixteen Upacāras (modes of service) in accordance with injunctions. Modaka and ground gingelly seeds alongwith jaggery shall be offered as Naivedya. Arghya is offered in a copper vessel mixed with red-sandal paste.

1. VV. 55-70 describe the *Mahāvrata* or *Vara-Caturthī* (in the SK.P., *vide CC-Vrata,* I. 530-31). The observer gets *Sāyujya* (identity) with Viṣṇu by observing this Gaṇeśa *Vrata*--a Vaiṣṇavite tilt.

2. VV. 72-79 prescribe the *Saṅkaṣṭavrata* on the 4th day in Māgha Kṛ., but it is observed every month on Kṛ. 4 in Maharashtra. VRJ. (pp. 82-88) calls it *Saṅkaṣṭa-hara Gaṇapati Vrata* (a Gaṇeśa *Vrata* destroying extreme calamities) and attributes the illustrative story to *Nārada* P.

76-78. Kuśa grass, Dūrvā grass, flowers, raw rice grains, Śamīpatra (leaves of the Śamī tree) and curds should be mixed together and offered to the Moon (with the prayer), "O moon, the ruby in the ocean of the firmament, O Lord of Dakṣa's daughters, O representative of Gaṇeśa, kindly accept the Arghya offered by me." Uttering this he should offer the divine Arghya, that is destructive of sins to Gaṇeśa. After feeding excellent Brāhmaṇas in accordance with his capacity, he should take food himself with their formal permission.

79. O Brāhmaṇa, by performing this auspicious Vrata called Saṁkaṣṭa, he shall become flourishing with wealth and foodgrains. He shall never attain difficulty or pain.

80-82. The excellent holy vow Gaurīvrata[1] is to be observed on the fourth day in the bright half of the month of Māgha. On that day, Gaurī is to be worshipped alongwith the groups of Yoginīs by men as well as by women in particular. The articles of worship are the following : Kunda flowers, Kumkuma, red threads, red flowers, Alaktaka (the juice of red lac), incense, lights, oblations, ginger with jaggery, milk and milk puddings, salt and the greens called Pālakas.

83. Married women who are not widows and splendid Brāhmaṇas are to be worshipped for the increase in conjugal bliss. Gifts must be made. One shall take food alongwith kinsmen.

84. O Brāhmaṇa, this Gaurīvrata is conducive to the increase of conjugal blesssedness. This must be performed every year both by men and women.

85. The same holy rite is called Dhuṇḍhivrata by others. By some it is called as Kuṇḍavrata. Others call it Lalitāvrata and still others call it Śāntivrata.

---

1. VV. 80-86 describe the *Gaurī* alias *Ḍhuṇḍhi* or *Lalitā* or *Śānti Vrata*. Though observed on Magha Śu. 4, it is essentially a *Devī Vrata*, not directly connected with Gaṇeśa, though the NP. attributes its fruits to the Grace of Gaṇeśa. In VRJ. (p. 82), it is called *Gaurī Caturthī Vrata* and VRJ. quotes from *Brahma P.* from *CC—Vrata* I. 531.

86. Ablution, charitable gift, japa and homa, O sage, all these rites performed on this day shall become thousandfold, thanks to the Grace of Dantin (god Gaṇeśa).

87. On the fourth day in the month of Phālguna falls the auspicious Vrata of Dhuṇḍhirāja. Brāhmaṇas are fed with cakes of ground gingelly-seed flour. The vower should also partake of it himself.

88. One who is interested in the propitiation of Gaṇeśa shall attain Siddhi by offering religious gifts, Homa and Pūjā with gingelly seeds alone, thanks to His grace.

89. The image of the elephant-faced deity should be made of gold. After worshipping assiduously, it must be given to an excellent Brāhmaṇa, for the flourishing increase in all riches.

90. If a Caturthī day coincides with Sunday or Tuesday in any of the twelve months, O leading Brāhmaṇa, it yields special benefits.

91. In all the Caturthīs, whether of the dark half or of the bright half of the month, Vighneśa (God Gaṇeśa), the Lord of the Devas should be worshipped by those who are eagerly engaged in devotion."

CHAPTER ONE HUNDRED AND FOURTEEN

The Exposition of Holy Vratas to be performed on Pañcamī days (fifth days of Lunar fortnight)

Sanātana said :

1. O Brāhmaṇa, I shall recount to you the Vratas to be performed on Pañcamīs[1] (fifth days in the halves of Lunar months). On observing these rites with devotion, one shall attain all cherished desires.

---

1. Just as *Caturthī Vratas* are mainly concerned with god Gaṇeśa, *Vratas* on the 5th days of lunar fortnights are auspicious for the worship of

20. He shall spend the whole of the day in this activity. At sunset he shall go to Śiva's temple and worship the Lord Īśvara in the form of Liṅga.

21. After duly worshipping Maheśvara with scents, fragrant flowers, etc he shall repeat the five-syllabled Mantra (Oṁ Śivāya Namaḥ) a hundred or thousand times.

22-23a. After dedicating the benefit of Japa to Lord Śiva, the embodiment of the universe, he should eulogise the Lord with all Vedic and Paurāṇic hymns. Without agitation or perturbation, he should pray to Lord Īśāna for the sake of perpetual acquisition of cooked food.

23b-24a. "In all my births may I be richly blessed with all those foodgrains whether harvested during the autumn or during the spring."

24b-26. After praying thus to the Lord of the Devas, he should come back to his own house. He should give cooked food to the Brāhmaṇas and eat it himself silently. O Brāhmaṇa, this Annavrata (Holy rite of cooked food), if observed duly by men, is conducive to the production of all food and wealth in this world, and yields salvation in the other world.

27-29. This rite (in propitiation of serpents) is performed on the fifth day in the bright half of the month of Śrāvaṇa, by men firm in their belief in the Vedas. On either side of the door-way, figures of poisonous serpents should be drawn in cowdung. He should worship them with scents, etc. Thereafter he should worship Indrāṇī with gold, silver, etc, curds, raw rice-grains, water from Kuśa grass, scents, fragrant flowers, incense, lights and hoards of Naivedyas. After circumambulating and bowing down, he should pray with great devotion. He should give the articles of worship to leading Brāhmaṇas.

30. "In all my births, may these gold, silver, etc. that have been given to Brāhmaṇas be productive of endless benefit."

31. O Nārada, he who gifts away along with this utterance, the articles with great devotion, will delight Kubera, the presiding deity of wealth, who bestows affluence like gold, upon his devotees.

32. After observing the holy rite, the man should feed

Brāhmaṇas with devotion. Thereafter, he should partake of his food surrounded by his wife, children and friends.

33-34a. The devotee should propitiate serpents with milk on the fifth day in the dark half of the month of Bhādrapada, (thereby) the entire family upto the seventh generation shall be free from the fear of serpents.

34b. One should worship the excellent sages[1] on the fifth day in the bright half of the month of Bhādrapada.

35.37a. In the morning, he should take his bath in the river etc. and perform Nitya rites, Sandhyā prayers etc. He should then return home and make a platform with clay. He should smear and clean it with cowdung and decorate it with flowers. O Brāhmaṇa, he should then strew Kuśa grass thereon and worship the seven sages, by means of scents, different flowers, incense and splendid lights.

37b-39. The sages are Kaśyapa, Atri, Bharadvāja, Viśvāmitra, Gautama, Jamadagni and Vasiṣṭha. Arghya should be duly offered to these. The intelligent devotee should cook

1. This is the well-known *Ṛṣi-pañcamī Vrata*. The NP. records an early stage when this *Vrata* was performed both by men and women. Later on it came to be regarded as efficacious in warding off sin in 'polluting' things with their touch by women in their menses, as monthly course or menstruation came to be regarded as part of the sin of Brāhmaṇa-slaughter (*Brahmahatyā*) committed by Indra in killing Vṛtra. Naturally women (especially in Maharashtra) begin to perform it after attaining puberty. VRJ. (pp. 91-96) records a story from the *Bhaviṣyottara P.* how the sin of Brāhmaṇa-slaughter perpetrated by Indra (in killing Vṛtra) came to be equally distributed in Fire, rivers, mountains and women (viz. the menstruation of women) to expiate which women should observe this *Vrata*.

VRJ-also quotes *CC-Vrata* I. 568-572 which records the account of this *Vrata* according to the *Brahmāṇḍa P.* There are some differences in the details of the worship as given in the NP. and other works (for example non-inclusion of Arundhatī in seven sages in the NP.), prescription of this *Vrata* even to men. *Vratārka* and VRJ. specifically assert that this *Vrata* is to be observed by women only to ward off the sin of 'polluting' things by their touch during their monthly course.

The prescription to eat food that is naturally grown without ploughing the field in this *Vrata* shows that it belongs to the period of food-gathering economy. This explains why men and women were eligible for this *Vrata* in the older stage.

Śyāmāka and other grains that have not been cultivated, as Naivedya. After the food offerings, he should ritualistically bid farewell to them and eat the same cooked grains himself.

40-41. In this manner, he should perform this holy rite every year, for seven years. At the conclusion of the Vrata, he should choose seven Vedic scholars as his Ācāryas (preceptors). He should make seven images in gold, according to his capacity. They must have matted hair, rosary and water pot.

42. These images should be placed in copper vessels or clay pots and the rite of ablution is performed severally with Pañcāmṛta.

43-44. With sixteen types of services and articles of worship, they are worshipped with devotion. Arghya is offered then, and the homa is performed with gingelly seeds, grains, or barley grains etc. The Ṛk. 'Sahastomā' (ṚV X.130.7) should be used while performing homa or the names of the sages shall themselves be the Mantras. Or with other holy mantras also the homa can be performed. Then the Pūrṇāhuti is offered.

45-46. He should then give seven cows as gifts, fully bedecked in ornaments and clothes. He should worship his preceptor also with clothes, ornaments, etc. With the permission of the preceptor, he should thereafter dedicate the images unto the Brāhmaṇas. After feeding them with devotion, he should bow down to them and bid them farewell.

47. Thereafter, the food left over by the Brāhmaṇas consisting of articles of six different tastes should be taken by him along with kinsmen.

48. After performing this holy rite with its ancillaries he shall enjoy all desired worldly pleasures, thanks to the grace of seven sages. He shall go hence in an excellent aerial car.

49-52. On the fifth day in the bright half of the month of Āśvina, the holy rite of Upāṅga-Lalitā-Vrata[1] is to be observed.

---

1. VV. 49-52 briefly describe *Upāṅga-Lalitā-Vrata* popularly known in Maharashtra as *Lalitā Pañcamī*. The detailed procedure of this *Vrata* as observed in the Deccan is given in VRJ. (pp. 97-103) and the story about

O Nārada, the image of the goddess should be made in gold in accordance with one's ability. The devotee should worship her in accordance with the injunctions, with all the sixteen types of services. In order to make the Vrata perfect and complete, cooked rice alongwith fruits, ghee and monetary gifts should be given to an excellent Brāhmaṇa— "The boon-granting deity accompanied by Śakti has been worshipped by me alongwith her vehicle. O Mother, you may be pleased to go to your own abode after blessing me" (The foregoing is the final prayer).

53. O excellent Brāhmaṇa, the holy rite of the excellent Jayā vrata is to be observed on the fifth day in the bright half of the month of Kārttika with good faith, for the destruction of sins.

54-55. O Brāhmaṇa, the devotee should, with great concentration, worship Jayā according to injunction. Clean (in body and mind) and bedecked in ornaments, he should worship her with sixteen types of services. He should feed a single Brāhmaṇa and give him monetary gifts. Then he should bid farewell to him and himself partake of his food silently.

56. If any one takes his holy dip on the day of Jayā, with great devotion, all his sins perish like dear attacked by a lion.

57. O Brāhmaṇa, the fruit that has been glorified as the result of the Avabhṛtha (concluding) bath in a horse sacrifice, is attained by bath on the day of Jayā.

58. One devoid of sons gets a son, a barren woman becomes pregnant, a sick man is freed from ailments and a prisoner is released from bondage.

59. By worshipping serpents duly on the fifth day in the bright half of the month of Mārgaśīrṣa one attains fearlessness from serpents and rejoices alongwith the kinsmen.

60. In the month of Pauṣa too, on the fifth day in the bright half, one attains all cherished desires by worshipping Madhusūdana. No doubt need be entertained in this matter.

---

its importance is quoted from the SK. P. It is probably a later development.

For *Lalitā-Ṣaṣṭhī Vrata* vide *infra* Ch. 115.8-29.

61. O Nārada, the worship of the Pitṛs and the serpents on the fifth day in the bright or dark half of any month is recommended in every respect.

CHAPTER ONE HUNDRED AND FIFTEEN

The Exposition of the holy vows to be observed on Saṣṭhi (sixth) days (in lunar fortnights)

Sanātana said :

1. O Brāhmaṇa, listen. I shall recount to you the holy rites to be observed on Ṣaṣṭhī days[1] (sixth day in the lunar fortnight). On observing them perfectly, one shall obtain all cherished desires.

2-3a. On the sixth day in the bright half of the month of Caitra, the excellent holy rite of Kumāra Vrata is to be observed. By worshipping the six-faced Lord on that day in accordance with the different injunctions of worship, one shall attain a son who is endowed with all good qualities and who will live for a long time.

3b-4a. On the sixth day, in the bright half of the month of Vaiśākha, the devotee should worship Kārttika (Skanda). By doing so, one attains motherly affection and happiness. No doubt need be entertained in this respect.

4b-5a. By duly worshipping Divākara (the Sun) on the sixth day in the bright half of the month of Jyeṣṭha, one attains all desired benefits, thanks to his Grace. There is no doubt about this.

---

1. It is noteworthy that most of the sixth days in lunar fortnights are sacred to god Skanda and most of the *Vratas* have Skanda as the presiding deity, the main exception being *Lalita Ṣaṣṭhī* and *Kapilā Ṣaṣṭhī*.

5b-6. The excellent holy rite of Skanda is to be observed on the sixth day in the bright half of the month of Āṣāḍha. The devotee should observe fast and then worship the beloved son of Śiva and Umā. He attains all cherished desires and the continuation of the line of sons and grandsons.

7-8a. On the sixth day in the bright half of the month of Śrāvaṇa, the devotee, endowed with great devotion, should worship Śarajanman (i. e. Kārttikeya) with the sixteen Upacāras (types of services). Thanks to the grace of the six-faced Lord, he attains all desired objects.

8b-10. The holy vow that has to be observed on the sixth day in the month of Bhādrapada, the Lalitā Vrata[1] is being recounted. A woman devotee should take morning bath duly on that day. She should wear white cloth and white garlands. She should take the sand from the confluence of a river, in a bamboo basket. She should then make five lumps of the sandy soil and meditate on goddess Lalitā, the sportive lady of the forest.

11-12. She should then take one hundred and eight flowers of each of lotus, Karavīra Nepālī, Jasmine, blue lotus, Ketakī and Tagara and twentyeight unbroken buds. With these she should worship the goddess.

13-15. Sitting in front of the goddess, the beloved wife of Śiva, she should pray as follows : "By taking bath in Kanakhala, on the mountain Nīlaparvata, in the Kuśāvarta, in the Gaṅgādvāra and in the Bilvaka you obtained Hara as husband. O blessed goddess Lalitā, the bestower of happiness and conjugal blessedness, grant unto me endless blessedness. Obeisance, unto you again and again." Uttering this Mantra, she should worship the goddess with splendid Campaka flowers duly. She should then place the Naivedya in front of the goddess.

16-20. The Naivedya should consist of Trapuṣa (a kind of fruit) Kūṣmāṇḍa (gourd), coconut, excellent pomegranates, Tuṇḍīra, Kāravella (the gourd Momordica charantia), Cirbhaṭa

1. VV. 8b-29a describe the *Lalitā Ṣaṣṭhī Vrata*. VRJ. (pp. 103-104) quotes *Bhaviṣyottara* P. from *CC. Vrata* I. 617-620). It is popular in Gujarat according to VRJ.

(a sort of cucumber) and other seasonal fruits taken fresh. The surroundings of the image of the goddess should be beautified with rows of excellent lights and germinating food grains. There should be incense of Sargaṇaka (?) alongwith Sauhālakha and Karañjaka (?). Guḍapuṣpa (Bassia latifilia) should be placed as ornament of the ears. According to one's affluence, sweetmeats of large and small varieties of various kinds should be used as Naivedya. After worship, she should celebrate the festival of keeping awake with songs and instrumental music, as well as dances and other scenic items of various types. The chaste lady should spend the whole of that night with her female friends.

21-26a. The woman devotee shall not close her eyes throughout the four Yāmas (yāma—3 hours) (of the night). By closing her eyes, she will become sinful, barren and unhappy. After keeping awake thus, she should take (everything) to a river on the Saptamī day (i. e. seventh day) to the accompaniment of songs and instrumental music. O excellent Brāhmaṇa, she should give that Naivedya etc. to a leading Brāhmaṇa. After taking her bath, she should return home and get the Homa performed in the fire. The Devas, Pitṛs and human beings (i. e. guests) shall be worshipped. She should worship and feed married women, virgins and fifteen Brāhmaṇas with various kinds of foodstuffs and edibles. She should give them various charitable gifts as well. Saying "May Lalitā be pleased with me", she should bid farewell to them.

26b-29a. Listen to the merit of this Vrata that bestows conjugal blessedness whether performed by a man or a woman. O Nārada, of what avail is much talk ? That benefit which one desires by means of holy rites, austerities, charitable gifts and observances is attained by this holy rite. After death, the devotee attains the eternal Śivaloka and rejoices along with goddess Lalitā like her companion in the world of Śiva for a long time.

29b-30. The sixth day in the bright half of the month of Bhādrapada is called Candana Ṣaṣṭhī. By worshipping the goddess on that day, the devotee attains the same world as that of the deity. If the Ṣaṣṭhī coincides with the constellation

Rohiṇī, the astronomical division called 'Vyatipāta' and Tuesday it is called Kapilāṣaṣṭhī.[1]

31. The observer of the Vrata devoted to the observance, should worship the Sun on that day. Thanks to the grace of Sun-God, he attains cherished desires.

32. O excellent celestial sage, the charitable gift of cooked food, Japa, Homa, the rites of Tarpaṇa to the Pitṛs, Devas and sages, when performed on this day, all these should be known as everlasting.

33. After worshipping a tawny coloured cow with clothes, garlands and unguents, it shall be given to a Vedic Scholar for propitiating the sun.

34. On the sixth day in the bright half of the month of Āśvina, O Brāhmaṇa, goddess Kātyāyanī should be worshipped with scents and other auspicious articles and also with various kinds of Naivedya.

35-36a The devotee should then crave forgiveness from the goddess of the Devas, bow to her, and bid farewell to her.

---

1. One wonders why such a rare and important occasion like *Kapilā-Ṣaṣṭhī* which comes but once in 60 years, is so casually treated here. "The bright half of Bhādrapada" given in the NP. is by *amānta* reckoning *Bhādrapada Kṛṣṇa*. The occurrence of Rohiṇī Constellation in combination with other five factors (Tuesday, *Vyatīpāta yoga* etc) is possible in *amānta* reckoning. Hemādri states the following combination as *Kapilā Ṣaṣṭhī*: Bhādrapada Kṛ. 6th day, Tuesday, Vyatīpāta Yoga and Rohiṇī Nakṣatra. VRJ. confirms these by quoting from another source. But the *Karavīra Māhātmya* a *Sthala Purāṇa* of Kolhapur (regarded as a part of the *Pd. P.*) *allows even Sunday as an alternate* to Tuesday for *Kapilā Ṣaṣṭhī*. IT states:

ṣaṣṭhī bhādre ca kṛṣṇā garaja-kṛti yutā rohiṇi-pātayuktā
vāre Bhanau ca Bhaume' pyatha ca mṛga-ṣire deva-pūjyetha saṁsthe

The commentator-Dājibā Joshi Rao-quotes from *Purāṇasamuccaya*:

bhādra māsyasite pakṣe bhānau caiva kare sthite
pāte kuje ca rauhiṇyāṁ sā ṣaṣṭhī kapilā bhavet

The Com. concludes: "As the text (*Karavīra Māhātmya*) states that this (Kapilā) Saṣṭhi can fall either on Sunday or Tuesday, even Sunday is important. (*atra mūle bhānu-bhaumavārayoḥ kathanād bhānu-vāra-yogo'pi mukhyaḥ.*)

As this *Vrata* is for the propitiation of the Sun-god, Sunday might have been allowed for *Kapilā-ṣaṣṭhī* in the *Karavīra Māhātmya*. I could not trace it to any other authority. The gift of a tawny cow, being an integral part of this *Vrata*, it probably came to be known as *Kapilā Ṣaṣṭhī*.

On this day, either the image made of Sandy soil or the chaste wife of a Brāhmaṇa should be joyfully worshipped by means of clothes and auspicious ornaments, for the satisfaction of Kātyāyanī.

36b-37a. No doubt need be entertained in this respect that, thanks to the grace of Kātyāyinī,* a virgin shall attain the desired bridegroom and a woman the desired son.

37b-39. The highly blessed army of the Devas was entrusted (dedicated) to him (Skanda) by the Devas and hence acquired by the nobleminded six-faced Lord on the sixth day in the bright half of the month of Kārttika. Hence, on that day, the devotee should worship the army of the Devas consisting of excellent Devas as well as the six-faced Lord with all charming Upacāras. O excellent Brāhmaṇa, he shall achieve Siddhi mentally desired by him.

40. The worship of the fire-god is also prescribed for this day. The devotee should carry it out perfectly alongwith the worship of fire, and Homas, with different kinds of articles of worship.

41-42. The Asura Tāraka was killed on the sixth day in the bright half of the month of Mārgaśīrṣa. The Satkṛti (honour and greetings) offered by Brahmā and other gods were received by Skanda. Hence on this day, the devotee should worship Skanda with scents, fragrant flowers, raw rice grains, fruits, clothes, ornaments and diverse kinds of Naivedya.

43. If the Ṣaṣṭhī coincides with Sunday or the constellation Śatabhiṣak or Śatatāra, O excellent sage, it is called Campāṣaṣṭhī.[1]

---

*The NP uses both forms—Kātyāyanī : Kātyāyinī

1. This delimitation of the term *Campā Ṣaṣṭhī* is supported by Hemādri (*CC-Vrata* I. 590-596 wherein he quotes the SK.P.) and by *Smṛti Kaustubha* 221-222. VRJ. (p. 108) requires Vaidhṛti Yoga, Tuesday and Viśākha Nakṣatra on this day to call it *Campā Ṣaṣṭhī*. But this combination is so rare that it occurs once in 30 years or so. It is strongly recommended that god Maheśvara should be seen on this day. But in Maharashtra, Mārgaśīrṣa Śu. Saṣṭhī is called *Campā Ṣaṣṭhī* irrespective of the day or Yoga.

CHAPTER ONE HUNDRED AND SIXTEEN

The Exposition of the rites to be observed on the Saptamī (Seventh) day.

Sanātana said :

1. O Nārada, listen. I shall recount to you the holy rites to be observed on the Saptamī[1] days (seventh day of a lunar fortnight). On observing them with devotion, the man attains Sāyujya (entire identity) with the Sun-god.

2-7. One shall take external (i. e. outside the village or town in a river or well) bath on the Saptamī (seventh) day in the bright half of the month of Caitra. He should draw the mystic diagram of the eight-petalled lotus on an altar on the dry ground smeared with cowdung and strewn with white sand. Vibhāvasu (the sun-god must be placed in the pericarp. The two devas Kṛta, Dhātuka (?) should be placed in the eastern petal; the Gandharvas, Kṛta, Kāraka should be placed in the South-east petal; two Rākṣasas shall be placed in the Southern petal. O excellent sage, the two Ākṛtas (?) shall be placed in the South-west petal, the two great serpents, the sons of Kadrū, should be placed (as if they are) in motion in the Western petal, two Yātudhānas should be placed in the north-west petal, two sages shall be placed in the northern petal; O excellent Brāhmaṇa, the devotee should fix one planet in the north-east petal. Their worship is to be performed by means of scents, garlands, unguents, lights, incense, Naivedyas, petel leaves, areca nuts and other things.

8-9. After worshipping them thus, the devotee should perform Homa with ghee. He should give one hundred and eight oblations to the sun-god and offer as oblations eight Āhutis for each of the others, in due order, uttering their names as mantras. Thereafter, he should perform Pūrṇāhuti on the

1. Just as the 4th day of a lunar fortnight was sacred to god Gaṇeśa or the 6th day to god Skanda, the 7th day in a lunar fortnight has the sun as the special presiding deity. Hence the observance of *Saptamī Vratas* are said to lead to *sāyujyatā* (identity) with the sun-god. Hence in V.72 below, people are exhorted to propitiate the sun-god on all *Saptamī* days.

altar. O Brāhmaṇa, in accordance with one's capacity, monetary gifts should be given to Brāhmaṇas.

10. After carrying out all these injunctions, the devotee shall attain all happiness. At the time of death, he penetrates his way through the disc of the Sun and goes to the greatest region.

11. It was on the seventh day in the bright half of the month of Vaiśākha that Jāhnavī (the Gaṅgā) was angrily drunk up by Jahnu himself and subsequently let off through the right ear.

12. On that day, the devotee should worship Jāhnavī after taking bath in the pure water, early in the morning. He should worship with scents, fragrant flowers, unbroken rice grains and other things, with all requisite upacāras (articles of worship), etc.

13. Then, a thousand pots are to be given (as gifts) in the course of this Gaṅgāvrata. If devotedly performed, this Vrata[1] is competent to take seven generations in his family to heaven.

14-18a. The holy rite of Kamalavrata[2] is also recommended on this day.[3] Its procedure is being proclaimed. An auspicious lotus is made out of gold of the weight of a gingelly seed. It is then covered with two clothes. The devotee should then worship it with scents, incense and other things, and pray as follows : "Hail to you the lotus-handed god; obeisance to you the supporter of the universe. O Divākara, (Sun-god) salutations to you. O Prabhākara (Sun-god), homage to

---

1. Although the N.P. does not disclose the name of this *Vrata*, it is called *Gaṅgā saptamī* (VRJ, p. 110; *Smṛti Kaustubha* 112 where it quotes Br. P.). This is celebrated as Jahnu drank up the river Gaṅgā and on prayer from King Bhagīratha, let it flow through his right ear (VR. I. 35-38)

2. Although NP. prescribes this Solar *Vrata* on Vaiśākha Śu. *Saptamī*, the Mt. P. 78. 1-11 and Pd. P. V. 21. 281-290 & following them Hemādri on *Vrata* I. 640-41 prescribe them on Caitra Śu. *Saptamī*.

3. Mt. P. 77. 1-17 describe a *Kamala Vrata* to be performed on this (Vaiśākha Śu. 7 and *not* Caitra Śu 7 as Kane states in HDV. i. 422-23), but the procedure and details are different. Hemādri (*CC-Vrata* I. 642-43) quotes from Pd. P-V. 21. 263-279.

you." After praying thus to the Lord of the Devas, he should offer that lotus alongwith the water pot and a Kapilā (tawny coloured) cow to a Brāhmaṇa, after sunset. He should observe fast throughout that day and take food only on the next day. By feeding the Brāhmaṇas with devotion, he shall attain the entire benefit of the Vrata.

18b-21a. The holy rite Nimbavrata is also to be performed on this day. Listen to its injunction even as I recount it. O excellent Brāhmaṇa, the worship of the sun is to be performed with the leaves of Nimba (Margosa), uttering the Mantra 'Khakholkāya' (TĀ 10. 59. 1, TĀĀ 10. 66) etc. beginning with the Praṇava; O Nārada, he should then eat the leaves of Nimba silently and lie down on the bare ground. After feeding the Brāhmaṇas the next day, he should himself take food alongwith his kinsmen. This Nimbapatravrata bestows all happiness on those who observe it.

21b-26a. The holy rite of Śarkarāsaptamī is also to be observed on this day. Listen to its procedure also from me. While the sun was drinking nectar by means of his hand, drops of Amṛta (nectar) fell on the ground, and they grew into the plants of Śāli rice, Mudga (green gram), Yava (barley) and Ikṣu (Sugarcane). Śarkarā (sugar) is therefore the essence of sugarcane and nectar-like and so is liked by the sun. It is holy and used in Havya and Kavya. Śarkarā Saptamī yields the same benefit as the horse-sacrifice. It pacifies all miseries. It increases the line of sons and daughters. On this day sugar must be given as gift and taken alongwith food. This holy rite must be assiduously performed, as it is liked by the Sun-god. He who observes this with great devotion, shall attain the goal of the good (i.e. Heaven).

26b-27. Indra himself was born as the sun on the seventh day in the bright half of the month of Jyeṣṭha. He should be worshipped according to the injunction. The devotee observes fast and subdues his sense-organs. O Brāhmaṇa, thanks to the grace of Devendra, he attains heaven.

28-29a. On the seventh day in the bright half of the month of Āṣāḍha, the sun god became Vivasvān (the refulgent Sun). The devotee worships him separately with scents and fragrant flowers. O leading Brāhmaṇa, he (the observer of this Vrata) attains identity with the Sun.

29b-30. The auspicious holy rite called Avyaṅgavrata[1] is to be observed on the seventh day in the bright half of the month of Śrāvaṇa. At the end of the Pūjā of Gopati (sun) in order to propitiate him, he must give a cotton cloth four and a half Hastas long. This Vrata is very auspicious.

31. If this Saptamī coincides with the Hasta constellation it will be destructive of sins. Charitable gifts, Japa, Homa,—everything performed on this day shall attain everlasting status.

32-33. The holy rite of Amuktābharaṇa is to be observed on the seventh day in the bright half of the month of Bhādrapada. The worship of Maheśa accompanied by Umā is glorified on this day. He is worshipped alongwith Gaṅgā and others with the sixteen Upacāras. After the prayer and (paying) obeisance, he should ritualistically bid farewell to the deity, for the flourishing increase of all desires.

34-39. The holy rite of Phalasaptamī[2] is also to be observed on this day. Its procedure is being described: The seven fruits are—a coconut, a brinjal, an orange, a pomegranate, a white gourd, Bṛhatī and areca nut. These are placed in front of Maheśa. A thread in which seven threads are turned and seven knots are made is also placed in front of Maheśa, O excellent Brāhmaṇa, after worshipping the Lord with great devotion, the woman-devotee shall wear the thread round her left hand and the man-devotee round his right hand.

---

1. As Kane notes (HD. V. i., pp. 264), this form of sun-worship was imported from Iran (from Magas or Śākadvipiya Brāhmaṇas) or borrowed from Parsis. Sk. *Avyaṅga* here is hyper-Sanskritisation of Avestan *Aivyaṅghana* 'a girdle'. '*Aivyaṅga*' is a hollow strip made of fine white cotton thread, resembling a serpent's slough, 122 fingers in length. The Brahmanisation of this Vrata becomes complete by Japa, Homa and Dakṣiṇās.

2. This is a special variety of *Phala-Saptamī*. For other varieties vide HD. V. i, pp. 353-354. According to Pd. P. V. 21. 249-262 (quoted by Hemādri also) the Sungod, and *not* Mahādeva, is the chief deity as in the NP.

60b-62a. The holy rite of Acalāvrata is performed on the seventh day in the bright half of the month of Māgha. This is also called Trilocana Jayantī (Birth anniversary of the three-eyed Lord). It is remembered as the destroyer of all sins.

62b-64. It is also Ratha Saptami[1] that grants (even) emperorship. The devotee should worship the image of Sun made of gold. The image is placed in a chariot yoked to golden horses. Alongwith elephants, he shall give this (as gift to a deserving person). He who performs this Vrata devoutly joyfully enjoys all the pleasures in this world and goes to the region of god Śiva. This Saptamī is Bhāskarī Saptamī and is comparable to a crore of shining planets. On this day, it is laid down that one shall take one's bath at the time of Aruṇodaya (day-break). He shall place on his head seven leaves each of Arka and Badarī and take his bath for absolving the sins of seven births.

65-68. Lord Sun has himself prescribed a Putraprada[2] Vrata (holy rite that grants sons) on this day. "I shall be born with a part of mine as the son of the person who duly worships me on the seventh day in the bright half of the month of Māgha. I will be very much delighted." Hence, the devotee should conquer his sense-organs and observe fast for a day and a night. On the next day, he should perform Homa and feed the Brāhmaṇas with cooked rice mixed with curds or milk and puddings. He who performs the holy rite of Putra Saptamī according to these injunctions, shall get a good son who will be free from ailments and will live for a long time.

69-70. One should perform the rite of Arkapuṭa on the seventh day in the bright half of the month of Tapasya (Phālguna). He should worship the sun with the leaves of the Arka (the sun) plant. He shall eat the leaves of the Arka plant. He

---

1. This is an important *Vrata* in the Deccan. VRj. pp. 115-116 gives a different *Vrata* in detail and quotes *Bhaviṣyottara* P. story how Kṛṣṇa's son was restored to health thereby, *vide* HD. V. i. pp. 388-389.

2. Kane records a number of *Vratas* to be observed on different days in different months, all granting a son as their fruit (vide HD. V. i. pp. 343-345) but this one in the NP is different from the *Putra-Saptamī Vrata* in HD. V. i. 345.

shall repeat the names of the sun continuously. Thus is the holy rite called Arkapuṭavrata. It bestows sons and wealth. It destroys all sins.

71. O Brāhmaṇa, some call this holy rite Trivargada-Vrata (a Vrata that bestows Dharma, Artha and Kāma the three aims of life), others call it Yajñavrata on account of the rite of Homa duly performed in it.[1] O excellent Brāhmaṇa, it is said that the sun is to be propitiated in all the Saptamīs in all the months. It shall enable one to realise all desires.

CHAPTER ONE HUNDRED AND SEVENTEEN

The review of the Vratas to be observed on Aṣṭamī (eighth days of Lunar fortnights)

Sanātana said :

1. Bhavānī's birth is reported to have taken place on the eighth day in the bright half of the month of Caitra. The great festival of Yātrā (procession) must be performed by making a hundred circumambulations.

2. The vision of the mother of the Universe is the bestower of all joys and pleasures on men. On this very same day the holy rite of Aśoka-Kalikā-Prāśana (drinking of water mixed with the tender sprouts of the Aśoka tree) also has to be observed.

3. Those who drink (water mixed with) eight buds of the Aśoka tree on the eighth day in the bright half of

1. With exception of Vratas like *Kṛṣṇa-Janmāṣṭamī*, majority of the *Aṣṭamī Vratas* are for the propitiation of some female deity—be it Jagadambā (Pārvatī), Mahālakṣmī or Reṇukā. The Bhavānī Yātrā is given in the Kāśī Khaṇḍa of the SK.P.—VJr., P. 118.

the month of Caitra, when the constellation of Punarvasu coincides with it, never experience any sorrow.[1]

4a. This is also called Mahāṣṭamī since the worship of goddess is ordained.

4b-7a. On the eighth day in the bright half of the month of Vaiśākha, the devotee observes fast. He takes his bath (in cool) water and performs the rite of ablution to the goddess Aparājitā by means of the water from Māṁsī (Indian Spike-nard) and Bālaka (a fragrant root of the Plant Andropogom Muricatus. After worshipping with scents etc., Naivedya comprising of sugar is offered. Before performing breakfast on the following Navamī day, he should feed some virgins. O Brāhmaṇa, thanks to the grace of the goddess, he will move about in the worlds (above) in a refulgent aerial chariot, himself brilliant like the sun.[2]

7b-9a. By worshipping the three-eyed Lord on the eighth day in the dark half of the month of Jyeṣṭha, the devotee shall remain in the Śiva Loka. He will be bowed to by all the Devas. The man who worships the goddess on the eighth day in the bright half of the month of Jyeṣṭha moves about in an aerial chariot alongwith the groups of Gandharvas and Apsaras.

9b-12. On the eighth day in the bright half of the month of Āṣāḍha, the devotee takes his bath in water, mixed with turmeric powder. With the same water, he shall perform the rite of ablution of the goddess in accordance with the injunctions. After bathing the deity in pure water, subsequently, he should smear the deity with camphor and sandal paste. After offering Naivedya consisting of sugar, water for Ācamana rite should be offered. He should then feed Brāhmaṇas and give them suitable gold and monetary gifts. After bidding them farewell, he should take food himself silently. By performing this holy rite, the man shall attain to the world of the goddess.

1. The NP has omitted the *mantra* at the time of worshipping Aśoka as the worship of the Aśoka tree is deleted. But this verse (and the *mantra tvam aśoka harābhīṣṭa*) are given in the GP. I. 133. 1-2, and in the LP quoted in Hemādri's *Vrata* I. 862-63.

2. This *Vrata* is not recorded in the VRJ and in Kane (HD. V. i).

13-14* On the eighth day in the bright half of the month of Śrāvaṇa, the devotee should worship the goddess in accordance with the religious injunctions. After bathing the idol in milk, he should offer sweet cooked rice as Naivedya. He should feed Brāhmaṇas on the next day, take food himself and conclude the holy rite. This holy rite increases the progeny.

15. The holy rite called Daśāphala vrata[1] is on the eighth day in the dark half of the month of Śrāvaṇa. The devotee decides on fasting, takes his bath and performs the Nitya (usual, prescribed) rites.

16-17. With ten leaves of black-coloured Tulasī, he worships uttering (in the dative case) these ten names of the Lord—Kṛṣṇa (i.e. Kṛṣṇāya namaḥ) Viṣṇu, Ananta, Govinda, Garuḍadhvaja, Dāmodara, Hṛṣīkeśa, Padmanābha, Hari and Prabhu. One should always worship Lord Kṛṣṇa by means of these names.

18. He should then circumambulate the deity and prostrate himself before it. Thus he should perform the most excellent of all the Vratas for ten days.

19. In the beginning, in the middle and in the end, he should perform homa in accordance with the injunctions. Uttering the Mantra of (the names of) Kṛṣṇa, he should perform hundred and eight Homas with Caru (cooked rice soaked in ghee).

20-21. At the end of the Homa, the intelligent devotee should worship the preceptor duly. He should get a replica of the leaf of Tulasī exquisitely made in gold and place it in a vessel made of gold, copper, clay or bamboo. He should get an

---

*The text : *nabhomāse sitāṣṭamyām* need be emended as *nabhomāse' sitāṣṭamyām*. The *avagraha* (marked here as') before *sita* is necessary as this Vrata falls on Śravaṇa K. ṛ8th (HD. V. i. P. 311, also VRJ. p. 122 ff) If *amānta* reckoning is not taken, it will fall on Bhādrapada which is not recognised in the NP here.

1. VV. 15-26 describe the *Daśā-phala Vrata* in honour of Lord Kṛṣṇa. The *Vrata* is detailed in VRJ. P. 122 ff. and is briefiy described in HD. V. i. 312. The misprint *site* for *asite* is pointed out in a footnote to that verse.

image made in gold and worship it in accordance with the injunctions.

22. He should place the image in the vessel and offer it to the preceptor. A cow alongwith its calf, should be given fully bedecked in ornaments and clothes.

23. For ten days, he should offer ten Pūrikās (fried cakes of wheat flour) to the Lord Kṛṣṇa. The observer of the rite shall either offer these Pūrikās to a knower of the mode (of worship) or eat them himself.

24. O excellent Brāhmaṇa, a bed also should be given as gift in accordance with his capacity. On the tenth day he should give the image to the preceptor.

25-26. At the conclusion of the holy rite, ten Pūrikās should be given to each of the ten Brāhmaṇas. He should continue this rite for ten years. After performing this excellent Vrata fcr ten years and after duly observing the fast, the devotee shall realise all his cherished desires. There is no doubt in this that in the end, he will attain Sāyujya (One-ness) with Kṛṣṇa.

27-28a. This day remembered as (Kṛṣṇa-Janmāṣṭamī)[1] removes the sins of men. Merely by observing fast on this birth-

---

1. VV 27-40 describe the *Kṛṣṇa-Janmāṣṭamī Vrata,* popular all over India. Not merely the NP but other Purāṇas like Pd. P. III. Ch, 13, Mt. P. Ch. 56, AP Ch. 183 highly glorify this *Vrata.* In the *Bhaviṣyottara* P. 44. 1-60 Kṛṣṇa himself narrates this *Vrata* to Yudhiṣṭhira : Mediaeval writers on Dharma Śāstra relying on Purāṇas, other than the *Bhāgavata,* have discussed a great deal about the procedure etc. of performing this *Vrata* and brought in the Mimāṁsā and Astronomy in distinguishing between the *Janmāṣṭamī* and *Jayantī-Vratas.* But that is academic. The NP gives the main features of fast, worship, *jāgara* (remaining awake that night), though he does not mention the breaking of the fast. By the way, it may be noted that the *Varāha Purāṇa* (46.14) records that Kṛṣṇa was born on 12th day in the bright half of Āṣāḍha.

In passing, I may record a peculiar custom called *Gopāla-Vāla* or *Dahī-haṇḍī* in Maharashtra. It is based on the Bh. P. X. 5.15 where the cowherds expressed their delight (at the birth of Kṛṣṇa) by sprinkling curds, ghee etc. on each other. On this occasion, people in Maharashtra hang up earthen pots full of curds, butter milk etc. and celebrate with songs etc. the birth of Kṛṣṇa and some one breaks the pots and people vie with each other to get themselves drenched in the curds etc. falling from the holes in the pots.

day of Hari, one is undoubtedly liberated from the sins of seven births.

28b-31a. The devotee who observes fast shall take his bath with gingelly seeds mixed in the pure water of a river etc. The intelligent devotee shall make a mystic diagram on the platform erected in a good place. In its middle, a Kalaśa (vessel) made of copper or clay is placed. Over this vessel, another copper vessel is placed. Above this latter vessel, the auspicious golden image of Kṛṣṇa is placed and covered with two cloths. With a pure mind, he should then worship it with Pādya and other Upacāras.

31b-34. In the eight quarters he should worship Devakī, Vasudeva, Yaśodā, Nanda, Vraja (colony of the cowherds), cowherds, cowherdesses and cows. Ārārtika rite (waving of lights before the deity) is performed. Forgiveness is craved for, by bowing down with devotion. The devotee remains thus till midnight, when he bathes Hari with Pañcāmṛta and pure water. He should again worship the Lord with scents and other things. He should then offer the following things as Naivedya in a silver vessel : viz. Coriander, barley, ginger, sugarcandy, and ghee. O Nārada, these should be offered as Naivedya.

35. After performing the Ārārtika (waving of lights in front of the deity) rite once again, he should think of the Lord as assuming ten different forms. He should then offer Arghya to the rising moon.

36. After requesting the Lord of the Devas for forgiveness the observer of the holy rite should pass the rest of the night by reciting hymns from the Purāṇas and sing diverse songs in accompaniment of instrumental music.

37. After the daybreak, he should feed eminent Brāhmaṇas with sweet cooked rice. Delighted in his mind, he should offer Dakṣiṇā and bid them farewell.

38. Thereafter, he should give that image of Viṣṇu to the preceptor alongwith gold, cow and plot of land as well as monetary gifts. After bidding farewell to him, the devotee should partake of his food.

39. After performing thus the holy rite, the man attains Goloka itself, in the company of his wife, children, friends

and servants. He goes there, seated in an excellent aerial chariot.

40. In the whole of the three worlds, there is no other holy Vrata equal to this. By performing this, the benefit of a crore of Ekādaśī Vratas is acquired.

41-43. On the eighth day in the bright half of the month of Nabhasya (Bhādrapada) a person should perform the holy rite of Rādhāvrata.[1] As before, he should perform the worship of the gold image of Rādhā placed on the pot. At mid-day, after worshipping her, the devotee should take in a single meal. The devotee who is physically strong observes fast (for the complete day). On the next day, he feeds the Suvāsinīs in accordance with injunctions. He then offers the image to the preceptor. He shall partake of his food and formally conclude Vrata.

44. O Brāhmaṇa sage, if this holy rite is performed duly, the observer of Vrata obtains the esoteric secret of the Vraja (of Kṛṣṇa's time) and stays among the followers of Rādhā.

45-46. The holy rite of Dūrvāṣṭamī[2] too is to be observed on this day. Listen to it from me. O excellent Brāhmaṇa, the Liṅga is to be placed on the Dūrvā-grass growing in a pure and clean spot. He should then worship it with flowers, incense, scents, lights and Naivedyas, viz. curds, raw rice grains and fruits. At the end of Pūjā, he should, with great concentration, offer Arghya uttering the two Mantras.

47-49a.[2] "O Dūrvā grass, bowed to by the Devas and the Asuras, your birth is from nectar. Grant blessedness and line of children to me. Be a bestower of achievements of

1. Pd. P. III. 7. 21-23. It is performed on the 8th day in both the fortnights of Bhādrapada (HD. V-1. 392).

2. VV. 25-52 describe the *Dūrvāṣṭamī Vrata* associated with Śiva Liṅga. Women and men of all castes are eligible for this. The *Smṛti Kaustubha* 228-230 and the *Bhaviṣyottara* P. 56 give another variety in which the *Dūrvā-grass* itself (unassociated with any deity like Śiva or Gaṇeśa) is the deity—that tenacity of the Dūrvā grass for its spread and survival is prayed for the spread of one's own race. VV. 47-49a are repeated as the prayer to Dūrvā-grass,

my works. Just as you are spread over the ground with your branches and branchlets, so also grant me growing progeny that shall be immortal and unageing."

49b-50. The devotee then circumambulates it, feeds Brāhmaṇas, gives Dakṣiṇā to the Brāhmaṇas, takes food himself and returns home. Alongwith the monetary gifts, he should give Brāhmaṇas splendid, fragrant and sweet fruits.

51. Thus, O Brāhmaṇa, the holy rite of Dūrvāṣṭamī is sacred and destructive of the sins of men of all the four castes and particularly of the woman folk.

52. If any woman, out of delusion, does not worship Dūrvā duly, undoubtedly she becomes a widow for three births.

53. O Brāhmaṇa, if the Aṣṭamī coincides with the constellation Jyeṣṭhā, it should be known as Jyeṣṭhāṣṭamī.[1] If worshipped, it is destructive of sins.

54. The holy rite of Mahālakṣmī begins on this day and lasts for sixteen days. It brings about all riches.

55. "O Mahālakṣmī, I am devoted to you and I shall perform your Vrata. Hence, thanks to your grace, may it come to a conclusion (May it be completed) without any impediment."

56. After saying this, the devotee twists round sixteen threads to form a string. He ties sixteen knots therein and ties the string round his right hand.

57. The observer of the holy rite should worship Mahālakṣmī everyday, with scents and other things, upto the following Aṣṭamī in the dark half.

58a. On that day the intelligent devotee should perform the rite of Udyāpana (concluding rite).

58b. Under the canopy of cloth, the devotee makes the mystic diagram called Sarvatobhadra. The Kalaśa (vessel) is installed thereon and a lamp is lit.

---

1. VV. 53-74a describe *Jyeṣṭhāṣṭamī Vrata* which is in honour of goddess Lakṣmī. The wearing of threads with sixteen knots is still popularly practised by women in Maharashtra, but not other details of gold images, Homa etc. VRJ. (pp. 135-156) gives the details of this *Vrata*, *Pūjā* and *Udyāpana* (concluding rite) on the basis of the *Bhaviṣyottara* P. *vide* HD. V. 1 pp. 304 and 376.

Mantra : —"May Lakṣmī, born of the ocean of milk, sister of the moon and the beloved wife of Viṣṇu be pleased with this Vrata". He (the person performing this Vrata) should dedicate the four gold images to the Brāhmaṇas.

72. Thereafter, with sweet cooked rice he shall feed four Brāhmaṇas and sixteen Suvāsinīs (married women whose husbands are alive). He should bid farewell to them giving them their due Dakṣiṇās.

73-74. After concluding the observances, he should take food in the company of the affectionate ones. By performing this Vrata of Mahālakṣmī, O Brāhmaṇa, in accordance, with the injunctions, one enjoys all worldly desirable pleasures and one shall live in the world of Lakṣmī for a long time. This is called Asokāṣṭamī also, and in it the holy rite of Ramā (Śrī) is complete.

75-76a. On this day, the Aśoka tree is worshipped and only a single meal is taken every day. By performing the Aśoka Vrata, the lady, wherever she is born in this world of sorrow, becomes free from sorrow. No doubt need be entertained in this respect.

76b-78a. O Brāhmaṇa, Mahaṣṭamī[1] is to be observed in the bright half of the month of Āśvina.

On that day, Durgā is to be worshipped with all Upacāras. By observing fast or taking a single meal on the Mahāṣṭamī day, the devotee attains all round affluence and rejoices like a god for a long time.

78b-80. The holy rite of Karaka Vrata is to be observed in the dark half of the month of Kārttika. On that day, Śambhu accompanied by Umā is to be assiduously worshipped. Arghya is also to be always offered, at the time of the moon-rise, by the observers of the Vrata who wish for a son endowed with all good qualities or happiness of diverse kinds.

80b-81. Gopāṣṭamī rite is to be observed in the bright half of the month of Kārttika. On that day, one shall perform

1. VV. 76b-78a describe Mahāṣṭamī, the 8th day of Navarātra in Āśvina Śu.

the worship of cows; fodder is offered to the cows, cows are circumambulated and followed. Cows are given as gifts by those who desire all riches.

82-85. A special holy rite is performed on the eighth day in the dark half of the month of Mārgaśīrṣa. The image of a couple is made out of Darbha grass. They are named Anagha and Anaghā. They are accompanied by many sons. (images are made of these as well). On a spot scrubbed and cleaned with cow dung and made auspicious, the couple are placed and worshipped with scents, fragrant flowers, and diverse kinds of Upacāras. The devotee feeds a Brāhmaṇa couple and bids farewell to them after giving them Dakṣiṇās. A man or a woman can perform this holy rite. By performing it in accordance with the injunctions, he or she gets a son endowed with good characteristics. There is no doubt about this.

86-87. On the eighth day in the bright half of the month of Mārgaśīrṣa, the devotee observes fast in the presence of Kālabhairava. By doing so and keeping awake for that night, one is liberated from great sins. Whatever inauspicious sin has been committed by a person in his birth as a human being, is dissolved entirely by seeing Kālabhairava image;

88. The holy rite of Śrāddha called Aṣṭaka[1] is to be observed on the eighth day in the dark half of the month of Pauṣa. It makes the Pitṛs (manes) satisfied for a year. It increases the line of children in the family.

89. By worshipping Śiva devotedly on the eighth day in the bright half of the month of Pauṣa, one attains worldly pleasures and liberation by acting in pursuance of his (unflinching) devotion.

90. On the eighth day in the dark half of the month of Māgha, one should, with great devotion, worship Bhadrakālī, the destroyer of the hosts of enemies, and the bestower of all cherished desires to her devotees.

---

1. Although the NP. limited the term *Aṣṭaka* to the 8th day in Pauṣa, the *Āśvalāyana* Gr. 5. II. 4. 1. states that the 8th *tithis* in the dark halves of *Hemanta* and *Śiśira* (i.e. the months of Mārgaśīrṣa, Pauṣa, Māgha and Phālguna) are *Aṣṭakā* days.

91. O Brāhmaṇa, one who wishes for an unbroken line of children and absence of defeat in battle, should propitiate Bhīṣma on the eighth day in the bright half of the month of Māgha.

92. O Brāhmaṇa, on the eighth day in the dark half of the month of Phālguna, one should worship goddess Bhīmā. For the achievement of all cherished desires, he should be devoted to the Vrata.

93. O Brāhmaṇa, by worshipping properly with scents and other things, Śiva and Śivā on the eighth day in the bright half of the month of Phālguna, one shall become the Lord of all Siddhis (Super-natural Powers.)

94. One should worship goddess Śītalā[1] on the eighth day in the second fortnight of the month of Phālguna, with all kinds of cooked food prepared duly on the previous Saptamī (seventh) day.

95. "O Śītalā, you are the mother of the Universe. O Śītalā, you are the father of the Universe. O Śītalā, you are the support and base of the Universe. Obeisance, to you, salutations to you, O Śītalā.

96. I bow down to goddess Śītalā, who is seated on a donkey, is naked, holds the broom and the water pot and who destroys swellings.

97. Goddess Śītalā shall be the bestower of calmness and queller of swellings to those who stand in water and repeat the name "Śītalā, Śītalā".

98. O Brāhmaṇa, thanks to the grace of goddess Śītalā, he (the devotee) shall be tranquil for a year;—he who worships Śītalā by means of these Mantras of Śītalā.

99. By worshipping Śiva and Śivā on the eighth day in any of the halves and in any of the months, one attains the desired benefit.

---

1. Śītalā is the goddess of Small Pox. According to *amānta* reckoning the *Śītalāṣṭamī* is on Caitra Kṛ. 8.

CHAPTER ONE HUNDRED AND EIGHTEEN

The Exposition of the Vratas to be observed on Navamī (ninth) day (in the lunar fortnight)

Sanātana said :

1. O leading Brāhmaṇa, henceforth, I shall recount to you the Vratas to be observed on the Navamī day (i.e. ninth day in the lunar fortnight). On performing these rites, people in the world attain the desired fruit.

2. The holy rite of Śrī Rāma Navamī[1] is on the ninth day in the bright half of the month of Caitra. A devotee who is physically strong, should duly observe full fast on that day.

3. If he is incapable physically (to observe full fast), he should take a single meal on that day after the midday festival. He shall propitiate Rāma, by feeding the Brāhmaṇas with sweet cooked rice.

4-5a. By means of (gifts of) cows, plots of lands, gingelly seeds, gold etc, and by means (of gifts of) clothes and ornaments, Brāhmaṇas should be propitiated. He who devoutly performs the holy rite of Śrī Rāmanavamī shall shake off all his sins in this world and attain the region of Viṣṇu.

5b-7. The holy rite of Mātṛvrata is also to be observed on this same day. The Yoginīs, sixtyfour in number, accompanied by Bhairava, are to be propitiated by means of garlands, scents, clothes and Naivedyas. O prominent Brāhmaṇa, it was on this day that Bhadrakālī was crowned in the chieftancy of all mothers. Hence, one should worship her by observing fast and controlling his sense-organs, on this day.

8. He who worships Caṇḍikā on the ninth day in either of the fortnights of the month of Vaiśākha, in accordance with the injunctions in the matter, rejoices alongwith the Devas.

---

1. VV. 2-5a briefly state the outline of *Rāmanavamī Vrata*. We find its detailed description in works like VRJ. (pp. 149-154) where the dialogue of Sage Agasti and Sutikṣṇa (regarding the observance of this *Vrata*) from SK. P. is quoted. Hemādri's mention of the *Vrata* (CC. *Vrata* I, pp. 951-46) shows that it was popular in Maharashtra before 12th Cent. A.D. at least. NP.'s cursory treatment shows that it was not attached much importance then, though *Rāma-navamī* is now a national festival.

9-11a. On the ninth day in the bright half of the month of Jyeṣṭha, the excellent man who observes fast, should worship Umā duly and feed virgins and Brāhmaṇas in accordance with his ability. He should give them monetary gifts to the extent of his capacity. He should partake of only cooked Śāli rice along-with milk. O Brāhmaṇa, the man who duly performs this Umā Vrata[1] enjoys great pleasures in this world. In the end, he attains the goal of heaven.

11b-12. (Defective) O chief of Brāhmaṇas, he who performs (the following) holy rite on the ninth day in either of the fortnights in the month of Āṣāḍha and worships the fair-complexioned goddess Aindrī riding the elephant Airāvata and and partakes food only at night, shall become the enjoyer of pleasures in the world of the Devas. He will move about in the vehicle of the Devas or he will proceed along the path called Devayāna.

13-15. In the month of Śrāvaṇa, O leading Brāhmaṇa, the devotee should take food only at night, or he shall observe fast for two fortnights and worship Kaumārī Caṇḍikā. He should worship the goddess, the remover of sins, by means of scents, fragrant flowers, incense, lights and different Naivedyas. He should feed virgins. He who performs the excellent Kaumārī Vrata[2] devotedly in this manner, shall go to the eternal world of the goddess by means of an aerial chariot.

16-17a. The ninth day in the bright half of the month of Bhādrapada is glorified by the name of Nandā Navamī. He who worships Durgā duly with all Upacāras (articles of worship and other formalities) on that day, attains the benefit of a horse-sacrifice and is honoured in the world of Viṣṇu.

17b-20. The ninth day in the bright half of the month of Āśvina is glorified by the name Mahānavamī.[3] On this day,

---

1. VV. 9-11a describe a special *Umā Vrata* not recorded by Kane in HD V. 1.

2. VV. 13-15 describe a special *Kaumārī Vrata* with *Caṇḍikā* as the main deity. This is not noted by Kane in HD. V. i.

3. VV. 176-22 describe the Mahā-navamī in honour of Durgā. As a part of *Nava-rātra* or the *Durgā pūjā* festival, it is observed all over India. VRJ, p. 158 gives a detailed procedure on the basis of the *Bhaviṣya*, *Devī*,

2. On the tenth day, in the bright half of the month of Caitra, the devotee should worship Dharmarāja[1] by means of the seasonal flowers and fruits plucked for the nonce, and scents and other things

3. He should either observe fast or take a single meal per day. After feeding fourteen excellent Brāhmaṇas, he should give them monetary gifts according to his capacity.

4. O Brāhmaṇa, he who thus performs the worship of Dharmarāja, shall at the behest of Dharma, attain similarity with the Devas—a position from which he will not fall.

5-6. On the tenth day in the bright half of the month of Vaiśākha, a man should worship god Viṣṇu with scents and other articles of worship and formalities) as well as with white fragrant flowers. He should make hundred circumambulations, (round Viṣṇu's shrine) and assiduously feed Brāhmaṇas. He (thereby) attains to the world of Viṣṇu (Viṣṇuloka). No doubt need be entertained in this respect.

7. It was on the tenth day in the bright half of the month of Jyeṣṭha that the Jāhnavī (the river Gaṅgā), the most excellent of all the rivers, came to the Earth from the heaven. Hence, the day is remembered as the bestower of merit.

8-9. The month of Jyeṣṭha,[2] the bright fortnight, the constellation of Hasta, Wednesday, Daśamī Tithi, the Gara (Karaṇa), Ānanda (Yoga) and Vyatīpāta, the moon in the Zodiac of Virgo and the sun in the Zodiac of Taurus—the combination of all these ten, O Brāhmaṇa, is regarded to be

---

1. This and the next Vrata is not recorded in the VRJ. or HD. V. I.

2. This astronomical combination constituting Daśaharā is repeated in the Sk. P. as follows :

jyeṣṭhe māsi site pakṣe daśamyāmbudha-hastayor-
garānande Vyatīpāte kanyā candre vṛṣe raviḥ /
daśayoge naraḥ snātvā sarva-papaiḥ pramucyate //

Kane says that the *Varāha* P. accepts Tuesday instead of Wednesday (HD. V. i. P. 91) but the actual quotation of *Varāha* P. in the VRJ. p. 165, states that it was on Wednesday on 10th Jyeṣṭha Śu. that the Gaṅgā highly meritorious. It removes ten kinds of sins.[1] Hence it is called Daśahara.

10. On this day if a delighted devotee takes his holy dip in the Jāhnavī in accordance with the injunctions, he goes to Hari's abode.

11. The tenth day in the bright half of the month of Āṣāḍha is remembered by Manu and others as highly meritorious. Holy dip, Japa, charitable gift, or Homa on that day is the bestower of heavenly goal.

12. The tenth day in the bright half of the month of Śrāvaṇa is the bestower of the fulfilment of all hopes. The worship of Śiva, with scents and other articles of worship on this day, is praiseworthy.

13. Observance of fast, taking of food only at night, feeding of Brāhmaṇas, Japa, the charitable gift of gold, cow, etc. performed on this day—all these are destructive of all sins.

14-19. On the tenth day in the bright half of the month of Bhādrapada, O excellent Brāhmaṇa, the holy rite called Daśāvatāra[2] (the ten incarnations) is to be observed. After

---

descended from heaven. The NP. limits the merit of this Vrata to bath in the Gaṅgā but the *Nirṇaya Sindhu* (P. 98), on the authority of the SK.P., extends the merit of *Daśaharā* to both etc. in all big rivers. A festival of the Gaṅgā is celebrated in towns and villages in big rivers like the Krishnā and the Godāvarī in Maharashtra, though not on that big scale as found at Haradwar, Prayāga or Vārāṇasī.

1. The other derivation of Daśaharā is "that which washes off ten kinds of sins". The ten kinds of sins are given in Manu XII. 5-7 as follows :

(1) *Mental Sins* : Coveting another man's wealth, wishing evil to befall others, entertaining heretical ideas,

(2) *Vocal Sins* : harshness of speech, speaking the untruth, back-biting, irrelevent speech.

(3) *Bodily Sins* : misappropriation of another's wealth, injury to living beings, illicit intercourse with another's wife.

This efficacy of *Daśaharā* is endorsed in other Purāṇas also; *vide* Br. P. 63. 15, *Nirṇayasindhu* (p. 98) quotes the SK. P and *Varāha* P to the same effect. The VRJ. (pp. 166 ff) gives details of this *Vrata*.

2. VV. 14-19 describe the *Vrata* in honour of the currently believed ten incarnations of Viṣṇu. The inclusion of the Buddha and Kalki in the list is comparatively late when people forgot that the Buddha was the propagator of a non-Vedic faith.

taking his bath in a water-reservoir (i.e. a tank, a river etc.) and performing Sandhyā etc. and the rite of Ṭarpaṇa to the Devas, sages and Pitṛs, he should, with great concentration, worship ten incarnations (of Viṣṇu) viz. Matsya (the Divine Fish), Kūrma (the Divine Tortoise), Varāha (The boar), Narasiṁha (Man-lion), Trivikrama (the religious student Vāmana), Paraśu-Rāma, Śrī-Rāma, Kṛṣṇa, Buddha, and Kalki. O Nārada, he (the observer of the Vrata) should worship ten gold images (of these incarnations) in accordance with injunctions. He should then give them to ten excellent Brāhmaṇas after duly honouring them. After observing fast or taking one meal (on that day), he should feed the Brāhmaṇas. After bidding farewell to them, he should enjoy a meal with his friends and relatives. By performing this Vrata with devotion, he shall enjoy all excellent pleasures here. In the end he will go to the eternal Viṣṇuloka, in aerial chariot.

20-22. The tenth day in the bright half of the month of Āśvina is glorified as Vijayā.[1] In the morning the devotee places four cow-dung balls in the courtyard of the house in the form of the horizon (i.e. semicircle). In their midst he should worship the four warriors Rāma, Lakṣmaṇa, Bharata and Śatrughna. Four vessels with lids are taken and smeared with cow-dung. Grains and silver coins are put therein and closed. They are covered with white silken cloth.

Hemādri (*Vrata* I. 1158-61) instructs to begin this *Vrata* on 12th *Mārgaśīrṣa Śu.* VRJ (P. 168) on the authority of the *Bhaviṣyottara P.*, gives a different procedure though the *Vrata* commences on *Bhādrapada Śu,* 10th and the *Vrata* is to be observed for 10 years.

1. VV. 20-25a describe one variety of *Vijayā daśamī Vrata* allied with Rāma but not connected with his victory over Rāvaṇa which forms the basis of the present *Rāmalīlā* festival. This variety is not recorded by Hemādri (*Vrata* I. 970-73), *Nirṇaya sindhu* (PP. 69-70), VRJ. pp. 169-170 or by Kane (HD. V. i. pp. 188-194).

The other variety in VV 25b-31a, which is to be observed by kings or noblemen for securing conquest on the enemies, has been current all over India in slightly different forms. The worship of the *Śamī* tree, royal procession of elephants, horses etc., waving of lights (*Nīrājana*) after return from *Śamī-Pūjana* etc. have been the common features. The NP. does not include the worship of the goddess Aparājitā (recorded in *Dharma-sindhu*, pp.

23. The devotee then worships them in accordance with the injunctions with scents, fragrant flowers, Naivedyas, etc. accompanied by father, mother, brothers, sons, wife and servants.

24-25a. After paying obeisance he feeds the Brāhmaṇas who are duly honoured. By performing this holy rite, the man remains happy throughout the year. O Brāhmaṇa, he shall decisively become flourishing in wealth and grains.

25b-31a. (Another holy rite) On the previous Navamī day the devotee goes to a Śamī tree and chants Mantras : On the afternoon of the Daśamī day, O Brāhmaṇa, the devotee goes again to the Śamī tree which is on the eastern side (of the village etc) and takes mud from the foot of tree. To the accompaniment of songs and instrumental music, he brings the mud to the house. He worships the clay in accordance with the injunctions and arranges his army. He goes out of the village by means of the eastern gate without any perturbation. He should get the image of the enemy prepared by means of leaves, etc. or mentally fancy the same. He should feel mentally delighted that the deity will hit the enemy with an arrow that has its tail of gold. He should then return home at night. Or after making all these arrangements he should proceed against the enemy to curb him. O Brāhmaṇa, this Daśamī rite, performed always in accordance with the injunctions, shall bestow wealth, victory, sons, cows, elephants, horses, goats and sheep in this world. O Nārada, at death he attains heavenly world.

31b-33. One should perform the holy rite of Sārvabhauma-Vrata[1] (Vrata for Sovereignty over the world) on the tenth day

---

96 ft) though some features in Hemādri (*Vrata* I. pp. 970-971) such as despatching an arrow at the effigy of the enemy or imagining him to be facing oneself, are common.

In Maharashtra probably due to scarcity of Śamī trees, they worship the *Āptā* tree or its branch on the eastern outskirts of the village. Going out of the boundary of the village is the technical *Sīmollaṅghana* (crossing the boundary for "invading" the enemy). People return home in the evening and lights are waved round the men. (*Nīrājana*) by women in the house. They distribute the leaves of the Āptā tree as "gold coins".

1. VV. 31-47 describe the *Sārvabhauma Vrata* primarily meant for kings. A similar *Vrata* is given in the *Varāha* P. 65.1-6 and *Viṣṇudharma*

in the bright half of the month of Kārttika. The devotee either observes complete fast or takes only one meal a day. At midnight, outside the house or the city he offers oblations in all the ten directions with Apūpa (baked pie) etc. On a level spot of ground smeared with cowdung, he draws a mystic diagram of a lotus of eight petals. After worshipping Gaṇeśa and other deities he (wipes off sins) by means of these Mantras.

34. May God Indra, the king of the Devas, the granter of all desired things, destroy the sin that is to my east as a result of my own sinful actions.

35. May God Vahni (fire) the king of all splendours, the granter of all desired things quell the sin that is to my southeast as a result of my own sinful actions.

36. May Yama, the king of Pretas, ghosts, the bestower of all desired things annihilate the sin that is to my south as a result of my own actions.

37. May Nirṛti, the king of Rākṣasas, the bestower of all desired things, wipe off the sin that is to my southwest as a result of my own actions.

38. May Varuṇa, the Lord of aquatic animals, the bestower of all desired things, destroy the sin that is to my west as a result of my own actions.

39. May Vāyu, the king of Maruts (gusts of wind), the bestower of all desired things eradicate the sin that is to my north-west as a result of my own actions.

40. May Soma (Moon), the Lord of Ṛkṣas (constellations) and Yakṣas, the bestower of all desired things, quell the sin that is to my north as a result of my own actions.

41. May Īśāna, the lord of Bhūtas (goblins), the granter of all desired things, quell the sin that is to my north-east, as a result of my own actions.

42. May Brahmā (the Lord of the Prajāpatis), the granter of all desired things annihilate the sin that is above, as a result of (my own) actions.

P. III. 164. 1-7. The guardians of the quarters are at times identified with the protectors of the worlds. Manu V.96 mentions Sūrya (the Sun) as the protector of the South-West instead of Nirṛti in the NP.

43. May Ananta, the king of serpents, the granter of all desired things, quell the sin that is stationed below me as a result of my own actions.

44. After offering oblations in the ten directions thus, with great concentration, he should alertly offer oblations to Kṣetrapāla externally.

45. After having completed the rites thus the intelligent devotee should spend the remaining part of the night in mainly auspicious songs, recitation of hymns, Japas etc.

46. In the morning, he should take bath, worship guardians of the worlds (quarters), and honour and feed twelve Brāhmaṇas. He should give them Dakṣiṇā according to his ability.

47. O Brāhmaṇa, after performing the holy rite thus, the royal devotee shall enjoy all auspicious worldly pleasures. After enjoying heavenly pleasures thereafter, for the duration of a Yuga, he will become an Emperor.

48. On the tenth day in the bright half of the month of Mārgaśīrṣa, the devotee should perform the holy rite of Ārogyaka Vrata[1] (health-giving Vrata). He should worship ten Brāhmaṇas with scents and other things and drink the water with which their feet have been washed.

49-50a. After giving Dakṣiṇā to them, he should bid them farewell. He should take only a single meal. O Brāhmaṇa, after performing this Vrata the devotee attains health in this world. Thanks to the grace of Dharma-Rāja, he rejoices like a Deva in the heaven.

50b-51. On the tenth day in the bright half of the month of Pauṣa, he should worship Viśve Devas.[2] They are Kratu,

1. This is a special variety of *Vrata* in the NP. Kane records a number of *Ārogya Vratas* on different *Tithis*, but none of them prescribes the *Tīrtha* (water after washing the feet) of Brāhmaṇas. Even the *Vrata* on the Daśamī day prescribes the worship of goddess Lakṣmī and Hari.

2. These gods are supposed to be the sons of *Viśvā*. The list of their names differs e.g. Apte's SK. Dict. p. 523 and MWP. 992 give the following list :

Vasu, Satya, Kratu, Dakṣa, Kāla, Kāma, *Dhṛti*, *Kuru*, *Pururavas* and *Mādravas*—the last four are not found in the NP.-list.

Dakṣa, Vasus, Satya, Kāla, Kāma, Muni, Guru, Vipra and Rām. Keśava has identified himself with these in ten different ways.

52-54. He should make effigies of Darbha grass to represent them as seated in their seats or lying down. O Nārada, he should worship them with scents, incense, lights and Naivedyas. After giving them Dakṣiṇā separately, he should ritualistically bid farewell to them. The gifts that had been offered to them should be given to excellent Brāhmaṇas or to the preceptor. O Brahminical sage, the observer of the Vrata who performs the rite thus, taking in only one meal a day, shall be the enjoyer of pleasures of both the worlds.

55-58a. On the tenth day in the bright half of the month of Māgha, the devotee should observe fast and conquer his sense-organs. He should properly and completely worship the ten Devas called Aṅgiras after making their images in gold. He shall worship them with scents and other Upacāras. They are—Ātmā, Āyus, Manas, Dakṣa, Mada, Prāṇa, Barhiṣmān, Gaviṣṭha, Datta and Satya. O Nārada, as their representatives ten Brāhmaṇas are to be fed with sweet cooked rice. For the purpose of acquiring heavenly world, the devotee should give those Brāhmaṇas the golden image.

58b-62. On the tenth day in the bright half of the last month, the devotee should worship the fourteen Yamas. They are : Yama, Dharmarāja, Mṛtyu, Antaka, Vaivasvata, Kāla, Sarvabhūtakṣaya, Audumbara, Dadhna, Nīla, Parameṣṭhin, Vṛkodara, Citra and Citragupta. He should properly and correctly worship them with scents and other Upacāras. He shall perform Tarpaṇa three times for each with handful of water mixed with gingelly seeds. O Nārada, thereafter, with a copper vessel he should give Arghya to the sun with the mixture of red sandal, gingelly seeds, raw rice-grains and barley in the waters with the following mantra.

63. "O sun of thousand rays, come O huge mass of splendour, O Lord of the Universe, accept the Arghya given by me with devotion. Take pity on me."

64-66. The devotee should offer Arghya by uttering the above Mantra. He should feed the fourteen Brāhmaṇas and

With great concentration, he must construct an auspicious pavilion decorated with flowers of various kinds exquisitely. After taking bath perfectly in accordance with the injunctions, he should observe fast and conquer his sense-organs. With faith and great concentration he should duly worship Viṣṇu with various Upacāras, Japas, Homas and circumambulations. He should also recite different hymns in prayer to the Lord, alongwith songs and instrumental music that captivate the mind. He should glorify the Lord with charming shouts of Jaya (Be victorious). He should prostrate on the ground like a long staff. He should keep awake during the night. (By carrying out all these instructions) he attains the great region of Viṣṇu.

5-8a. On the eleventh day in the bright half of the month of Caitra, the excellent man should observe fast and maintain these observances mentioned hereinafter for these days (the previous and the subsequent days included i.e. the 10th, 11th +12th Tithis). On the Dvādaśī (twelfth) day, he should devotedly worship the eternal Vāsudeva with all the sixteen Upacāras.

Then, he should feed his kinsmen.* After giving Dakṣiṇā

11.	Bhādrapada Śu.	Padmā (Parivartinī)
12.	„ Kṛ.	Ajā (Indirā)
13.	Āśvina Śu.	Pāpāṅkuśā
14.	„ Kṛ.	Indirā (Ramā)
15.	Kārttika Śu.	Prabodhinī
16.	„ Kṛ.	Ramā (Utpatti)
17.	Mārgaśīrṣa Śu.	Mokṣā (Mokṣadā)
18.	„ Kṛ.	Utpannā (Saphalā)
19.	Pauṣa Śu.	Putradā
20.	„ Kṛ.	Saphalā (Ṣaṭ-tilā)
21.	Māgha Śu.	Jayā
22.	„ Kṛ.	Ṣaṭ-tilā (Vijayā)
23.	Phālguna Śu.	Āmalakī
24.	„ Kṛ.	Vijayā (Pāpa-mocanī)

VV. 1-4 give general instructions on the common ritual in the *Ekādaśī Vratas.*

*The wording in the next line shows that here the reading should have been *Brāhmaṇān* instead of *bāndhavān*. If the reading be *Vāḍavān* it will do as *Vāḍava*=a Brāhmaṇa.

to them he should bid farewell to them and take food himself. This holy Ekādaśī Vrata is called Kāmadā (the granter of desires). It destroys all sins. O Brāhmaṇa, if observed properly and perfectly, it yields worldly pleasures and salvation.

8b-10. On the eleventh day in the dark half of the month of Vaiṣākha, a person should observe, with all formalities (of this Vrata), fast on this Varūthinī (name of this Ekādaśī.) On the next day, he should worship Madhusūdana. The charitable gift of gold, cooked food, cow and virgin on this day is highly commendable. By performing the holy Vrata of Varūthinī (Ekādaśī), the man devoted to the regular requisite observances is liberated from all sins. He attains the region of Viṣṇu.

11-12a. On the eleventh day in the bright half of the month of Vaiśākha, the devotee observes fast on this Mohinī Ekādaśī. On the next day, he takes his bath and worships Puruṣottama with scents and other things. By feeding Brāhmaṇas, (thereafter), he shall undoubtedly be liberated from sins.

12b-14a. On the eleventh day in the dark half of the month of Jyeṣṭha (which is called Aparā,[1] he should observe fast of the Aparā Ekādaśī, O king,[2] on the Dvādaśī day, he performs the daily prescribed (Nitya) rites and worships Trivikrama. Thereafter, feeding prominent Brāhmaṇas and giving them Dakṣiṇā, he becomes liberated from all sins and goes to Viṣṇu's Region (Vaikuṇṭha).

14b-16. On the eleventh day in the bright half of the month of Jyeṣṭha, the holy rite of Nirjalā (Abstention from water) Ekādaśī is observed. O excellent Brāhmaṇa, from the sun-rise to sunrise (i. e. through-out the Ekādaśī day) (not even water is to be taken in). On the twelfth day in the morning, he performs the prescribed daily routine rites and worships Hṛṣīkeśa with all the Upacāras; (thereafter) he feeds

1. As *Aparā* is the name of Ekādaśī which follows Mohinī (HD VI. 1 p. 108 Ft. note 278), the reading in this verse should have been *Samupoṣyāparām* instead of *Samupoṣya parām*; Here *parām* is meaningless and syntactically unrelated to any substantive.

2. This is an obvious quotation, as the epithet *Nṛpa* is not applicable to Nārada

Brāhmaṇas, with devotion. By observing this holy rite, the devotee attains the benefit of twentyfour (ordinary) Ekādaśīs.

17-18. On the eleventh day in the dark half of the month of Āṣāḍha, the devotee observes the fast of Yoginī Ekādaśī. On the twelfth day, he performs his daily rites and worships Nārāyaṇa. Then, he feeds leading Brāhmaṇas and offers Dakṣiṇā to them. He attains the benefit of all charitable gifts and rejoices in the abode of Viṣṇu.

19-24. Listen to the injunctions regarding the holy rite on the eleventh day in the bright half of the month of Āṣāḍha.[1] The devotee observes fast on that day in accordance with the injunctions. He should instal the image of Viṣṇu made of gold or silver, on an auspicious pavilion. The image should be of exquisite workmanship, with the four hands shining with conch, discus, iron club and the lotus. A yellow silk-cloth should be wound round the image. O Brāhmaṇa, the image should be placed on a couch neatly covered with (silk) cloth. Uttering the Mantras he should bathe the Lord with Pañcāmṛta and pure water. The hymn 'Puruṣa Sūkta' (RV. X. 90) is recited. The Upacāras (articles and modes or details of worship) begin with Pādya (offering of water to wash the feet of the Lord) and end with Nīrājana (waving of lights in front of the Lord's image). Then he prays to Hari as follows:[2] "O Lord of the Universe, if you are asleep, this Universe too shall be asleep. When you wake up, the entire Universe consisting

---

1. For the detailed discussion of the *Vrata vide* HD. V. 109-112. The details of this *Vrata* given in NP. (VV. 19-27) are rather different from these in HD (ibid).

I doubt the Indo-European origin of this Śayanī Vrata for lack of evidence in comparative mythology. Kane's other theory viz. the monsoons causing paralysis of activities, journey etc. is more plausible.

In Maharashtra, this is treated as a *Mahā-ekādaśī* and perhaps the biggest pilgrimage is held at Pandharpur on this occasion. One wonders why farmers who are normally very busy at this time of the year, leave aside their agricultural activities and gather at Pandharpur. Is it a continuation of such gathering since the days of food-gathering economy ?

2. This verse (No. 23) is probably a quotation as we find it quoted in the *Dharma Sindhu* (P. 53) and *Nirṇaya Sindhu* (P. 102)

of the mobile and immobile being wakes up." After praying thus in the presence of the Lord, the devout man should adopt regulations (or Vratas) laid down for observance during the period of the Caturmāsya. He should adopt them to the extent of his capacity.

25-26. On the morning of the Dvādaśī day, he should worship Śeṣaśāyin (Lord Viṣṇu reposing on the couch of the body of Śeṣa) with all the sixteen types of Upacāras. He should then feed the Brāhmaṇas and propitiate them with Dakṣiṇās. After that he should take food silently. From that time onwards, O leading Brāhmaṇa, he should worship the Lord with scents and other things every day.

27. By performing this holy rite of "Śayanī-Vrata" of the Lord duly, O Brāhmaṇa, the man enjoys worldly pleasures and Salvations, thanks to the grace of Viṣṇu.

28-31a. O excellent Brāhmaṇa, the excellent man performs the holy rite of 'Kāmikā' (also known as Kāmadā) on the eleventh day in the dark half of the month of Śrāvaṇa alongwith due observances. On the twelfth day, after performing the daily routine rites, he worships Śrīdhara, Hari, with all the sixteen Upacāras.[1] He then feeds Brāhmaṇas, gives them Dakṣiṇā and bids them farewell. Thereafter, he takes his food alongwith the kinsmen. O Brāhmaṇa, he who thus performs the excellent Kāmikā (Ekādaśī) Vrata obtains

---

1. The NP. constantly refers to sixteen *Upacāras*. They are as follows : *āvāhana* (invitation), *āsana* (offering a seat), *Pādya* (water for washing feet), *arghya* (respectful offering of water with or without grains of rice, dūrvā grass, flowers mixed in it), *ācamanīya* (offering spoonfuls of water for sipping), *snāna* (*bath*), *vastra* (*cloth*), *yajñopavīta* (the sacred thread). *anulepana* or *gandha* (sandal paste or some fragrant paste), *puṣpa* (decoration with flowers) *dhūpa* (burning of incense), *dīpa* (waving of light), *naivedya* (offering of eatables, food) *tāmbūla* (offering betel-leaves, just after dinner or *naivedya*), *dakṣiṇā* (religious fee or monetary gift), *pradakṣiṇā* (clockwise circumambulation).

Many of these were current in Vedic times for receiving guests and *pitṛs* at the time of *śrāddha* and these were extended to images when idol-worship came in vogue. It is a superstition to attribute all these to Dravidians (For details vide HD. V. i PP. 33-39).

all the cherished desires in this world and attains the greatest region of Viṣṇu.

31b-33. On the eleventh day in the bright half of the month of Śrāvaṇa, the devotee performs the holy rite of "Pavitrā* (prob. an alternative name for Putradā) Ekādaśī" On the Dvādaśī day, he should worship Janārdana strictly adhering to the rules, with all the sixteen Upacāras. Thereafter, he feeds Brāhmaṇas and gives them Dakṣiṇās. He obtains a son endowed with good qualities and then attains Viṣṇu's region. He will be bowed to by all Devas.

34-36a. On the eleventh day in the dark half of the month of Bhādrapada, the devotee observes fast of the holy rite named 'Ajā-Ekādaśī'. On the Dvādaśī day, he should worship Upendra with various Upacāras. He should feed Brāhmaṇas with sweet cooked rice and bid farewell to them after giving them Dakṣiṇā. O Brāhmaṇa, he who observes the holy rite in this way with great concentration and devotion to Ajā, enjoys all worldly pleasures. In the end he attains the abode of Viṣṇu.

36b-41a. The devotee has to perform the holy rite of PadmāVrata* (Ekādaśī fast called Padmā) on the eleventh day in the bright half of the month of Bhādrapada. After finishing the daily worship, he should perform the rite of Koṭidāna (giving of a crore of things). O excellent Brāhmaṇa, the image installed before is worshipped with great festivities. The image is taken to the water-reservoir and is touched with water and is then worshipped in accordance with the injunctions. It is then brought to the platform and laid to rest on the left side. On the morning of the Dvādaśī day, he worships Vāmana with scents and other things. The Brāhmaṇas are fed, given Dakṣiṇās and bidden farewell to. O Brāhmaṇa, he who

---

*It is also called *Parivartinī* as Lord Viṣṇu is supposed to have turned on one side during his sleep on this day. (Kane—*HD* V. I. 109). The NP. subscribes to this supposition as v. 39a instructs that the image of Viṣṇu should be laid to rest on the left side.

performs the excellent holy rite of Padmāvrata thus, enjoys all worldly pleasures. In the end he attains release from Saṁsāra.

41b-44. The devotee performs the holy Ekādaśi rite called Indirā, on the eleventh day in the dark half of the month of Āśvina. He observes fast and at midday, he performs Śrāddha rite in front of a Śāligrāma stone. O Brāhmaṇa, this is highly pleasing to Viṣṇu. On the next morning of Hari's day, the intelligent devotee worships Padmanābha and feeds Brāhmaṇas. After giving them Dakṣiṇā, he bids farewell to them and takes food himself. The man who performs the holy rite thus, enjoys all desired worldly pleasures and uplifts a crore of his ancestors. In the end he goes to Viṣṇu's abode.

45-47. O Brāhmaṇa, the devotee observes the holy rite called 'Pāśāṅkuśā', on the eleventh day in the bright half of the month of Āśvina. After observing fast on this day, he should worship Viṣṇu on the day of Viṣṇu (i.e. Dvādaśī day). He then feeds prominent Brāhmaṇas, gives them Dakṣiṇā and after bowing to them devotedly, he bids farewell to them. Thereafter, he takes food himself. The man who performs the holy rite of Pāśāṅkuśa Vrata thus with devotion, enjoys excellent worldly pleasures and attains the Sālokā Mukti i.e. residence in the same region as that of Viṣṇu.

48-50. O excellent Brāhmaṇa, the devotee performs the holy rite of Ramā Ekādaśī on the eleventh day in the dark half of the month of Kārttika. After duly observing fast on that day, he worships Keśava on the morning of Dvādaśī day. He worships Keśava, the eternal Lord of the Devas, the destroyer of Keśin. He should then feed Brāhmaṇas and bid farewell to them after Dakṣiṇā has been given. O Brāhmaṇa, he who performs the holy rites thus, enjoys all desired pleasures here. He attains to the presence of Ramāpati (Viṣṇu) by means of an aerial chariot ! (This is known as samīpatā Mukti).

51-56a. On the eleventh day in the bright half of the month of Kārttika, the devotee observes the fast of Prabodhinī Ekādaśī. At night, the devotee wakens up the sleeping Keśava (Viṣṇu) with auspicious songs, with Ṛk, Yajus and Sāman Mantras and with various kinds of instrumental music. He propitiates the Lord presenting him grapes, sugarcane,

77-79. O excellent Brāhmaṇa, on the eleventh day in the bright half of the month of Phālguna, the devotee observes the holy rite of Āmalakī Ekādaśī. On the Dvādaśī day, in the morning, he should worship Puṇḍarīkākṣa with all Upacāras. With excellent cooked food, he should feed the Brāhmaṇas and give them Dakṣiṇā. By performing worship etc. duly on the eleventh day in the bright half of the month of Phālguna, that is called Āmalakī Ekādaśī, the devotee attains the greatest region of Viṣṇu.

80-82. The eleventh day in the dark half of the month of Caitra is called Pāpamocanikā (that which releases one from sins). Having observed fast on that day, the devotee worships Govinda in the morning on the Dvādaśī day, with all the sixteen Upacāras. He should feed the Brāhmaṇas, give them Dakṣiṇā and bid them farewell. Then he should take food alongwith his kinsmen. O Brāhmaṇa, he who thus performs the holy rite of Pāpamocanikā Vrata attains the world of Viṣṇu by means of a shining aerial chariot.

83. O Brāhmaṇa, thus the salvation-yielding holy rites on the Ekādaśī days in both bright and dark halves (of all the months) have been extolled to you. There is no doubt at all in this (that they are conducive to the attainment of salvation).

84. Since this Vrata is to be observed for three consecutive days, it is glorified as the most excellent of all the Vratas. Hence, it must be known as highly fruitful.

85. O Nārada, the devotee should miss four meals in the course of these three days. On the first day and the third (i.e. on Daśamī and Dvādaśī days) he shall miss one meal each (in the evening). On the day in the middle (i.e. Ekādaśī day) he should miss both the meals.

86-90. Now, I shall recount to you the restraints in regard to this Vrata in the course of these three days.[1] A true devotee

1. VV. 86-90 lay down the restraints and rules to be observed on the three days of *Ekādaśī Vrata*. It is noteworthy that the number of restraints to be observed is the same as the number of Tithi. Thirteen restraints are prescribed for the *Daśamī day* (The 10th *Tithi*), eleven ones for the *Ekādaśī* day, and twelve for the *Dvādaśī* day.

Viṣṇu should always avoid ten things on the Daśamī day :— Bell metal vessel, meat, cooked lentil, Bengal gram, Kodrava grains, greens, wine, food at others' houses, the second meal and sexual intercourse.

He should avoid these eleven things on the Ekādaśi day :- gambling, sleep, chewing the betal leaves, washing the teeth, slandering, backbiting, stealing, injury to others, sexual intercourse, anger and telling lies. He should eschew the following twelve on the Dvādasī day:— Bell metal vessel, meat, wine, honey, oil, conversation with outcaste people who remove ordure, physical exercises, journey, second meal, sexual intercourse, touching the untouchables and cooked lentil.

91-92. A Brāhmaṇa should observe fast with due observances of all the restraints, if he is physically competent. Otherwise, the intelligent devotee should take a single meal. He should not take food during the night, or he should perform the rite of Ayācitavrata (i.e. taking in what is not begged for). On no account should he miss such a Vrata as this.

CHAPTER ONE HUNDRED AND TWENTY ONE

The holy rites to be observed on Dvādaśi (Twelfth) days (in a lunar fortnight)

Sanātana said :

1. Henceforth, O sinless one, I shall recount to you the holy rites to be observed on Dvādaśī (twelfth) days (in a lunar fortnight). On observing these Vratas, in this world a man becomes more beloved of Viṣṇu.

2-10a On the twelfth day in the bright half of the month of Caitra, the devotee should perform the holy rite of Madanavrata.[1] A pot with no cracks, filled with white raw rice grains

1. VV. 2-10 describe the *Madana-dvādaśī Vrata*. This is recorded by Hemādri (*vrata* I 1194-98) and VRJ. P. 230.

is placed. Different kinds of fruits are placed nearby with stumps of sugarcane plants. White sandal-paste is applied over the pot and it is covered with two white clothes. Various dishes of foodstuffs are also kept nearby and gold according to one's ability is also placed at its side. A copper vessel containing jaggery should be placed above the pot. It is there that Lord Acyuta in the form of Kāma is worshipped with scents and other Upacāras. The devotee observes fast. On the next day in the morning, he should honour a Brāhmaṇa and give all these things to him. He should feed and give Dakṣiṇā to the Brāhmaṇas. After observing this Vrata thus for a year, the devotee should give the preceptor a bed accompanied by all the requisite adjuncts, together with ghee and a cow. A Brāhmaṇa couple should be worshipped, and presented with a gold image of Kāmadeva alongwith a white milch cow and garments. While giving the charitable gifts he should utter : "May Hari in the form of Kāma be pleased". He who observes Madana Dvādaśī Vrata thus, becomes liberated from all sins. He attains equality with Hari.

10b. It is on this very same day that Bhartṛ-Dvādaśika Vrata is also observed.

11-14. A bed is made with clean bed-sheets spread over it. A gold image of Hari accompanied by Śrī is placed over it. A pavilion is made of flowers over it. The observer of the Vrata worships the deity with scents and other things. He keeps awake at night by means of holy dances, songs, and instrumental music. On the next day, in the morning, he should gift away the gold image of Śrīhari alongwith the bed to a Prominent Brāhmaṇa. He should feed the Brāhmaṇas and give them Dakṣiṇās to their satisfaction. The married life of the person who performs the holy rite thus, becomes stable. He enjoys worldly pleasures in the course of seven births as well as the pleasures desired in both the worlds.

15-16. On the twelfth day in the bright half of the month of Vaiśākha, the devotee should observe fast and subdue his sense organs. With great devotion, he worships Mādhava with scents and other Upacāras. He should duly present sweet-cooked rice to a Brāhmaṇa till he is satisfied, along with a water-pot saying "May Mādhava be pleased".

17-19a. On the twelfth day in the bright half of the month of Jyeṣṭha, the observer of the holy rite should worship Trivikrama with scents and other things. Then he should present Brāhmaṇa with a bowl containing sweet cooked rice. Thereafter, he should take in a single meal (i.e. once in a day). Trivikrama, the Lord of the Devas, becomes pleased with this Vrata. O Nārada, he will grant him extensive pleasures and salvation in the end.

19b-21a. The devotee should feed twelve Brāhmaṇas on he twelfth day in the bright half of the month of Āṣāḍha with sweet cooked rice. He should worship them severally with scents and other things in due order. Saying "May Lord Viṣṇu be pleased with me", he should devoutly give them the following things as gifts—garments, staff, sacred thread, ridges, and vessels.

21b-23a On the twelfth day in the bright half of the month of Śrāvaṇa, the observer of holy rite should worship Śrīdhara with scents and other things. He should feed excellent Brāhmaṇas with cooked rice in curds, and give them silver coins for Dakṣiṇā. After bowing to them, he should bid them farewell saying, : "May Śrīdhara, the Lord of Devas, be pleased with this Vrata."

23b-24. On the twelfth day in the bright half of the month of Bhādrapada, the observer of the holy rite should worship Vāmana and in his presence feed twelve Brāhmaṇas with milk puddings. By giving gold as Dakṣiṇā, he delights Viṣṇu.

25-27a. On the twelfth day in the bright half of the month of Āśvina, the devotee should worship Padmanābha with scents and other Upacāras. After that in the presence of the Lord, he should feed the Brāhmaṇas with sweet cooked rice. He should present Dakṣiṇā consisting of gold and (supplement it) with clothes. O excellent Brāhmaṇa, satisfied with this Vrata, Padmanābha grants him the boon of going to Śvetadvīpa and the desired bodily pleasures.

27b-35a. On the twelfth day in the dark half of the month of Kārttika the devotee performs the holy rite of Govatsā-Dvādaśī Vrata[1] (the holy rite of cow and its calf). With fragrant sandal

1. VV. 276-35a describe a variety of *Vrata* different from the one recorded in HD, V. i i.e. in the *Bhaviṣya P.* or Hemādri (*Vrata* I. 1083-84).

paste and other things, the devotee draws the figure of a cow alongwith her calf. He then worships it with flower garlands. With flowers, raw rice-grains and gingelly seeds he prepares the Arghya in a copper vessel in accordance with the injunctions, O Nārada, the devotee should offer the Arghya at the feet of the cow uttering the following Mantra : "O Mother, O Mother of cows, born of the milk-ocean, bowed to by Devas and Asuras, O Goddess identical with the Devas, decorated by all the Devas, kindly accept the Arghya. Obeisance be to you". Then he should offer Vaṭakas (pies) prepared from black gram and other pulses, as Naivedya. Their number may be five, ten or one in accordance with one's affluence. (The Mantra for Naivedya) "O Surabhi (divine cow), you are the mother of the Universe. You are always stationed at the feet of Viṣṇu (in the region of Viṣṇu). O Goddess identical with the Devas, please accept the mouthful of morsel given by me; O Goddess identical with the Devas, decorated by the Devas, O Mother Nandinī (Divine cow), make my desire fruitful."

O excellent Brāhmaṇa, on that day the devotee should avoid foodstuffs fried in oil or cooked in mudpots; he should avoid cow milk, ghee, curds and butter-milk also.

35b-38. On the twelfth day in the bright half of the month of Bhādrapada, O Brāhmaṇa, the devotee should worship Lord Dāmodara with scents and other Upacāras. With great concentration, he should feed the Brāhmaṇas twelve in number with cooked rice in His (the Lord's) presence. Then, with great pleasure, he should offer them water pots duly worshipped, filled with water and accompanied by areca nuts, sweet-meats and gold. If the rite is performed thus, the devotee becomes a favourite of Viṣṇu. He enjoys all worldly pleasures. There is no doubt in this that on death he obtains Sāyujya (identity) with Viṣṇu.

39-42. The rite of Nīrājana vrata[1] is also recommended, to be observed on this day. Understand it from me. The devotee

---

1. The NP. gives two types of *Nīrājana Vrata*. VV. 39-43 are for common people and VV. 44-50 for Kings and nobles. It is a *Śānti Vrata*. Kane records other varieties of this *Vrata* (HD . V. 1. 334-335),

adorns (with ornaments) the Lord of the Universe, who has thus got up from his slumber. At night-fall the devotee bedecks himself and kindles fresh fires. He worships the Lord by means of Mantras and performs Homa in the fire kindled by a silver lamp that is worshipped by the people, with scents, fragrant flowers etc. O sage, the devotee should perform the Nīrājana (waving of the lights) rite to Hari with that silver lamp. There itself he should perform the Nīrājana rite for all these in the following order viz : to Lakṣmī who follows him, to Brahmāṇī, Gaurī, to Yakṣa, to Gaṇapati, to planets, to Mothers, to manes, to mountains and to all the serpents.

43. To cows, he should perform the Nīrājana (waving of lights) rite and to buffaloes etc. other Maṅgala (auspicious) rites, with shouts like namaḥ (obeisance), Jaya (be victorious) etc. and with the sounds of bells, conchs etc.

44-50. In this great festival of waving of lights, there should be tumultuous noise of the cows with their horns smeared with saffron and their limbs painted with diverse kinds of colours. The king should be accompanied by the chief priest, ministers and servants. He should duly worship horses endowed with all auspicious characteristic signs, the elephants overwhelmed by ichor in their rut, and the royal paraphernalia such as the umbrella etc. The auspicious character of atmosphere shall be increased with the sounds of conchs, and musical instruments. The king, adorned properly should occupy a newly made throne studded with various jewels. Then a courtesan or a woman of a noble family endowed with all auspicious characteristics should, slowly, perform the Nīrājana rite above the head of the king. This rite is a great Śānti (that which subdues and pacifies evils). It should be performed every year by the king or any other rich man who wishes for good health throughout the year. O Brāhmaṇa, if the excellent Śānti rite named Nīrājana is performed in any country, city or village, the ailments of the people therein are quelled and cured.

51-54a. The excellent holy rite of the Sādhya Vrata[1] is

1. This *Vrata* of semi-divine beings called *Sādhya* is recorded by Hemādri (*CC-Vrata* I. 1173)on the authority of *Viṣṇudharmottara* (III. 181.1-3)

Janārdana made in gold. He should worship it with scents and fragrant flowers as well as other things. In his presence, he should feed Brāhmaṇas, twelve in number, every month. He should take food only at night and subdue his sense-organs. At the end of the year he worships that image in accordance with the injunctions and gives it to the preceptor alongwith a cow. He should pray thus: "O Lord, if, in the previous hundred births, any Vrata performed by me is broken, may it be rendered unbroken, thanks to your Grace." Then he should feed twelve leading Brāhmaṇas with milk puddings alongwith sugar-candies. He should give gold pieces as Dakṣiṇā and make obeisance to them. O Brāhmaṇa, after observing the Vrata thus and propitiating Janārdana, he shall go to Viṣṇu's great region by means of a golden aerial car.

67b-76a. On the twelfth day in the dark half of the month Pauṣa, the holy rite Rūpavrata[1] (vrata for beauty) is said (to be observed). On the previous Daśamī day, the observer of the holy rite should duly take his bath and collect cow-dung. O Brāhmaṇa, it should be of a white cow or that of a cow of a single breast. It should be gathered from the ether itself (i.e. before it reaches the ground after being evacuated by the cow). O Nārada, he should make one hundred and eight balls out of the dung, and dry them in the sun after keeping them in a copper vessel or a mud pot. On the Ekādaśī day he should observe fast and worship the image of Viṣṇu made of gold, in accordance with the injunctions. He should keep awake during the night by means of very auspicious songs, instrumental music, recitation of hymns, japas, etc. On the Dvādaśī day, in the morning, he should place the image on a vessal full of gingelly seeds. This latter vessel should be placed on a pot full of water. He should then worship it by means of all Upacāras. By means of attrition (or friction of wooden pieces) and other methods he should kindle a fresh fire. The intelligent devotee shall worship duly and perform Homas with the cow-dung balls one by one, alongwith gingelly seeds and ghee, after uttering the twelve-

1. A special Vrata in the NP not recorded by Kane.

syllabled Mantra belonging to Viṣṇu viz. Oṁ namo Bhagavate Vāsudevāya. When hundred and eight oblations are completed he should perform Pūrṇāhuti. With an affable mind and great pleasure, he should feed Brāhmaṇas with milk puddings. He should offer the image to the preceptor alongwith the water pot. In accordance with his ability, he should give Dakṣiṇā to the Brāhmaṇas. He should bid them farewell after bowing to them. By performing the holy rite respectfully, the devotee, whether it is a man or a women, attains the blessedness of great beauty. No doubt need be entertained in this respect.

76b-85. On the twelfth day in the bright half of the month of Pauṣa, the holy rite of Sujanma-Dvādaśī Vrata,[1] (the holy rite for the attainment of good birth and pedigree) is to be observed. After taking the holy bath the devotee takes the vow of Vrata for the whole year. After drinking water from a cow's horn, at the outset, he should circumambulate the cow. Thereafter, every month, on the twelfth day in the bright half, he should offer charitable gifts (as follows) :— A Prastha measure of ghee, four Prasthas of grains and barley, two Ratikās (i.e. the weight of the seed of the Gunja plant (Abrus precatorious) of gold (1-16) grains, half an Āḍhaka of gingelly seeds, a potful of milk (or water) a Māṣa weight of silver, and sweet cooked-rice till satiety; umbrella and half a Māṣa of gold, a Prastha measure of excellent molasses; a Pola weight of Sandal, a fine thin cloth measuring five Hastas, these are the articles to be given as charitable gifts month by month. He should feed himself on the following :— cow's urine, water, ghee, four kinds of green vegetables well cooked, cooked barley grains mixed with curds, gingelly seeds with ghee and sugar, water from the Kuśa grass and milk. After performing this holy rite for a year, the devotee should get the image of the sun made in gold. He should place it on a flat copper vessel, worship it in accordance with the injunctions, and give it to the preceptor alongwith a cow. He should then bow down to him. Then

1. Hemādri recommends this vrata on the authority of *Viṣṇu-dharmottara* P. (*CC-Vrata*. 1174-75).

twelve Brāhmaṇas should be fed and presented with the due Dakṣiṇās. O Brāhmaṇa, he who performs the holy rite thus, takes his birth in a noble family. He shall be free from ailments. He shall be affluent in wealth and food-grains. His sense-organs shall be unimpaired (i.e. he shall be sound in body).

86-89a. On the twelfth day in the bright half of the month of Māgha, O Brāhmaṇa, the devotee shall duly and devoutly worship the Śālagrāma stone and place a piece of gold in its mouth. It is then placed in a silver vessel and covered with two white cloths. The devotee should then give this to a Vedic Scholar and thereafter feed him with milk-pudding along with sugar-candy and ghee (in a quantity) that is beneficial. After observing this, he should take only a single morsel a day. He should be interested in meditating on Viṣṇu. After enjoying all desired pleasures here, he attains the abode of Viṣṇu.

89b-91a. On the twelfth day in the bright half of the final month (i.e. Phālguna), the devotee should worship the golden image of Hari with scents, fragrant flowers etc. He should then give it to a Brāhmaṇa, knower of the Vedas. After feeding Brāhmaṇas, twelve in number, and giving them Dakṣiṇā, he should bid them farewell; thereafter, he should take food alongwith his kinsmen.

91b-92. The following eight Dvādaśīs are days on which one should observe fast as they remove sins. The Dvādaśīs are Trispṛśā, Unmīlinī, Pakṣavardhinī, Vañjulī, Jayā, Vijayā, Jayantī and Aparājitā.

Śrī Nārada said :

93. O holy Brāhmaṇa, what is the characteristic feature of these Dvādaśīs ? What is the benefit thereof ? Kindly explain these things to me as well as other things that may also be equally meritorious.

Sūta said :

94. On being asked thus by Nārada, Sanātana, the excellent Brāhmaṇa sage praised his brother, a great devotee of the Lord and said :

Sanātana said :

95. O brother, the question has been pertinently put by you who clear the doubts of good men. I shall recount the characteristics and the benefit of the great Dvādaśīs separately.

(1) *Tri-spṛśā* :

96. If Ekādaśī ceases to be, before the sunrise, the Dvādaśī is called Trispṛśā (touching three[1].) It is highly benevolent.

97. O Nārada, he who observes fast on this day and worships Govinda, certainly attains the benefit of a thousand horse-sacrifices.

(ii) *Un-milini* :

98. If at the Aruṇodaya time (dawn), the Ekādaśī Tithi is over-lapped by Daśamī, that day is eschewed and fast is observed on the following Dvādaśī day (This is called Unmīlinī – that which opens).

99. If on the Unmīlinī day, the devotee worships Vāsudeva perfectly in accordance with the injunctions, he derives the benefit of a thousand Rājasūya-sacrifices.

(iii) *Vañjulikā* :

100-102. When at the time of sunrise, the night touches Ekādaśī, it shall be avoided and the subsequent Dvādaśī which is called Vañjulikā[2] shall be the day on which the devotee shall fast always. On this day, the devotee should worship Lord Saṁkarṣaṇa with scents and other Upacāras devoutly. He is the great Lord who bestows fearlessness or Mokṣa on all. This great Dvādaśī yields the benefit of all Kratus i.e. sacrifices. It is said to be the remover of all sins. It bestows all riches.

---

1. Three *tithis* are 'touched' on this day: *Ekādaśi* before sunrise, *Dvādaśī* all the day and *Trayodaśī* in the last part of that night. Hence the name *Tri-spṛśā*.

2. This (*Vañjulikā*) *dvādaśī* exists the whole of one civil day (from sunrise to sunset) and extends over the next day, so that one can fast and have *pāraṇā* on the same *Tithi*—vide *Nirṇaya Sindhu*, p. 48, *Smṛti Kaustubha* 252-253.

103-104. O Brāhmaṇa, when Kuhu (new moon) and Rākā (full Moon) become increased (i.e are of a longer duration), the Dvādaśī is called Pakṣavardhanikā (that which increases the duration of fortnight) and it is highly beneficial. On that day the devotee should worship Lord Pradyumna, the Lord of the Universe, the bestower of all prosperity and the increaser of direct sons and grandsons.

105. If, in the bright half, Dvādaśī coincides with the constellation Maghā it is called Jayā.[1] It conquers all enemies.

106. On this day, the devotee should worship Lord Aniruddha, the husband of Ramā, the bestower of all cherished desires of men and the granter of all blessedness.

107-108. If, in the bright half, Dvādaśī coincides with the constellation Śravaṇa, it is called Vijayā. On that day the devotee should worship Gadādhara, the bestower of all happiness for ever, the greatest resort for all pleasures. O Brāhmaṇa, by observing fast on that day, a man shall attain the benefit of pilgrimage of all holy centres.

109. If, in the bright half, Dvādaśī coincides with the constellation of which Brahmā is the presiding deity [Rohiṇī ?] it is highly meritorious. It is remembered by the name 'Jayantī'.

110-111a. On this day the devotee should worship Lord Vāmana the bestower of Siddhis on men. O leading Brāhmaṇa, if fast is observed on this day, it yields the benefit of all Vratas.

If yields the benefit of all charitable gifts; it yields worldly pleasures and salvation.

111b-113. If, in the bright half, Dvādaśī coincides with the constellation Puṣya it is called Aparājitā. It is the

1. The NP associates the following *Dvādaśīs* in the bright halves of the month with the following *Nakṣatras* coinciding on that day :

N. of Dvādaśī	*Nakṣatra*
Jayā	Maghā
Vijayā	Śravaṇa
Jayantī	Rohiṇī
Aparājitā	Puṣya

Expert opinions differ. For example *Nirṇaya Sindhu*, p. 48 associates the constellation *Puṣya* with Jayā, *Punarvasū* with Jayantī.

bestower of all knowledge. On this day the devotee should worship Lord Nārāyaṇa, devoid of ailments, the cause of liberation (severance) from the bondage of worldly existence, the ocean of perfect knowledge. O Brāhmaṇa, by the observance of fast alone on this day, people will be liberated.

114. If, Dvādaśī in the bright half of the month of Āṣāḍha coincides with the constellation Anurādhā, two Vratas must be observed. There is no fault since the presiding deity is the same.

115. Similarly, in the bright half of the month Bhādrapada, if Ekādaśī coincides with the constellation Śravaṇa and if Dvādaśī coincides with the constellation Revatī in the bright half of the month of Kārttika, two Vratas (viz. Ekādaśī and Dvādaśī are to be observed.

116-117. O leading Brāhmaṇa, in cases other than these, only one meal is taken on Dvādaśī day. This is the natural Vrata laid down and it is destructive of sins. Since the Vrata of Ekādaśī is always in conjunction with that of Dvādaśī no rite of Udyāpana is laid down. This Vrata has to be performed throughout one's life.

CHAPTER ONE HUNDRED AND TWENTYTWO

The Vratas to be observed
on Trayodaśī (thirteenth day of the lunar fortnight)

Sanātana said :

1. Henceforth, therefore, I shall relate to you comprehensively the Vratas to be observed on Trayodaśī days (i.e. thirteenth day of lunar fortnights). On observing these Vratas with devotion, the man becomes elegant and highly blessed in the world.

2-3a. On the thirteenth day in the bright half of the month of Caitra, an image of Madana is made with sandal paste. After worshipping it assiduously, the devotee should waft it with a fan. Kāma excited thereby causes the multiplication of sons and grandsons.

3b-4. The worship of Anaṅga too is to be celebrated on this day. O leading sage, understand it. The devotee should draw the figure of Anaṅgas on a wooden plank with saffron, turmeric and red powder. He should be depicted as endowed with the love of Rati, smart and elegant and holding the flowery arrows and bow.

5. At midday, he should worship Kāmadeva, Vasanta (presiding deity of the spring), Vājivaktra (the horse-faced Lord Viṣṇu) and the bull-bannered Lord Śiva with devotion, by means of scents, garlands, ornaments and silken garments.

6-8. He should propitiate them with various kinds of foodstuffs. O Nārada, in the meantime he repeats this Mantra "Obeisance to Māra, Kāma, the deity of Kāmadeva, the exciter of the minds of Brahmā, Viṣṇu, Śiva and Indra." Then in front of him, he should worship Aṅganāpatī (the husband of a woman) with devotion, garments, garlands, ornaments and other things. He should regard that he (the Brāhmaṇa so worshipped) is Kāma himself. He should then worship a Brāhmaṇa couple with scents, garments and ornaments.

9. O Brāhmaṇa, he who performs the great festival thus, every year, becomes always delighted and well-nourished at the advent of the spring.

10-12a. Or he should worship the following (twelve forms of Kāma month by month till the year comes to a close : Madana, Hṛdbhava, Kāma, Manmatha, Ratipriya, Anaṅga, Kandarpa, (the god with the epithet) Makaradhvaja, Kusumāyudha, Manobhava, Viṣameṣu and Mālatīpriya. O Brāhmaṇa he should worship these twelve forms of Kāmadeva.

12b-13. The charitable gift of a she-goat is also recommended. After taking a holy dip in the river in accordance with the injunctions, the devotee should give milch goat to an indigent householder. Thanks to this charitable gift, he is not reborn in this world.

14. If this Trayodaśī coincides with Saturday, it is remembered as Mahāvāruṇī. If the devotee is able to get an

cloth, after bathing the image with Pañcāmṛta. He should duly worship the deity with scents and other things. After the rite of waving the light, (Ārātrika) he should make a gift of a pot of water and cooked rice. This rite is performed for three days. At the conclusion of the Vrata, he should worship the deity for a month. O Nārada, after gathering enough wealth, he should offer it as gift alongwith this Mantra :— "When the great ocean was being churned, five cows were born. Nandā is in the middle of them. Repeated Obeisance to that cow." After circumambulating the cow, he should give it to a Brāhmaṇa with this Mantra :— "May cows be in front of me. May cows be behind me. May cows be on my sides. I stay in the midst of the cows." Thereafter, he should duly honour a Brāhmaṇa couple and feed them. After honouring them suitably, the devotee should give them an image of Lakṣmīnārāyaṇa. One shall obtain from the holy rite of Gotrirātravrata, the same benefit as one obtains by performing thousands of horse-sacrifices and hundreds of Rājasūyas.

41-45. The holy rite of Tri-rātāśoka-Vrata[1] is to be observed on the thirteenth day in the bright half of the month of Āśvina. The replica of the Aśoka tree is made in gold. The woman devotee observes fast. After worshipping the image in accordance with the injunctions, she should circumambulate it for a hundred and eight times every day. O Brāhmaṇa, she should repeat this mantra with respect—"O Aśoka, formerly you have been created by Hara, the merciful deity ! You are the cause of rendering help to the whole world. O favourite one of Śiva, be gracious unto me." On the third day thereafter, she should worship the bull emblemed deity on that tree, in accordance with the injunctions. A Brāhmaṇa should be fed and given this as a gift. The woman who observed the holy rite thus, is never visited by widowhood. She will be blessed with sons, grandsons, etc. She will also be the great beloved of her husband.

---

1. This is an amalgamation of the ancient cult of tree-worship and Śaivism. This blesses one with *Saubhāgya* (life on one's husband) and progeny. Kane records a number of *Saubhāgya Vratas* (HD. V. i. 455-57) but this is not included therein.

46-47. The devotee should take only one meal on the thirteenth day in the dark half of the month of Kārttika, and with great concentration, he should light an oil lamp and assiduously worship it. Thereafter, he should keep it outside his front door saying "May Yama be pleased with me". O leading Brāhmaṇa, if this is done, one is not afflicted by Yama.

48-51 O excellent Brāhmaṇa, the devotee should take a single meal on the thirteenth day in the bright half of the month of Kārttika. At sunset, he should take bath again and observing silence, light a thousand, a hundred or a row of thirty-two lamps for Śiva. O Brāhmaṇa, he should do so with great concentration. He should light the lamp with ghee. With scents and other things he should worship Śiva. O Nārada, he should propitiate the Lord with fruits of various kinds and other items of Naivedya. Then, he should eulogise Śiva, the Lord of the Devas, with the following hundred names.[1] Those names, the bestowers of all desired benefits, are being detailed (as follows) :

52. Obeisance to Rudra, the terrible, to the bluenecked God, to the Creator, to one with matted hair, to the Lord of the Devas, bow to Vyomakeśa (one whose tresses constitute the firmament.)

53. Hail to the bull-emblemed one, to Soma (God accompanied by Umā), obeisance to Somanātha. Obeisance to Digambara (i.e. one with the quarters for garments i.e. Naked); Obeisance to Bhṛṅga; Obeisance to the deity who causes plentitude.

54. Bow to the deity full of penance (Tapas). Obeisance to the pervaded one. Obeisance to Śipiviṣṭa (pervaded by rays)

---

1. This 'Century of Rudra's names' bears a strong influence of the Fifth Prapāṭhaka in the IV Kāṇḍa of the *Taittirīya Sāṁhitā*, popularly known as *Rudrādhyāya*. The so called *Namakas* beginning with *namas te Rudra manyave* etc. have subsequently strongly influenced the 'century of names' and 'Thousand of names' of Rudra or god Śiva first, then Viṣṇu down to a river like the Gaṅgā.

It is significant that the author of the NP is not a fanatic Vaiṣṇava like his later descendants in the south. He treats fairly both the deities, as they are but two names of the Supreme Deity, *Para Brahman*.

Salutations to one fond of serpents. Obeisance to Vyāla. and to the Lord of serpents (Vyāla).

55. Hail to the supporter of the Earth, obeisance to (the god of the form of) Vyoma (ether), to the Lord of Paśus and to the lion that destroyed the three Puras (cities) (of asuras). Obeisance to Śārdūla (Tiger), Obeisance to Ṛṣabha (the bull, the chief).

56. Obeisance to Mita (the measured one), to Mitanātha (to the Lord of the measured ones); to Siddha (one who has realised the soul), to Parameṣṭhin (one stationed in the highest being), Obeisance to one who is sung about by the Vedas; to one who is concealed in the Vedas; Obeisance to one who is worthy of being kept as a secret in the Vedas.

57. Hail to the long one, to one of a long form, to one of large objects; to the greater one (than all); obeisance to the deity in whom the universe is installed; obeisance to one of the form of the sky.

58. Obeisance to one who causes welfare; obeisance to one of special nature; obeisance to Śiṣṭa (the disciplined one); to Paramātman (the reatest soul), to one who wears the elephant's hide and to one who split the demon Andhaka.

59. Obeisance to one who is blue, red and white (in complexion), to one who is the favourite of Caṇḍa and Muṇḍa; to the Lord fond of devotion, to the destroyer of the Yajña, to the unchanging one.

60. Hail to you, O Mahādeva, to Maheśa; to Hara, to the three-eyed one; obeisance to Triveda (one described in three Vedas). Repeated obeisance to one who is the embodiment of the Vedas.

61. Obeisance to the Artha (wealth), to one whose form is Artha, to one who is in the highest reality; obeisance to one whose form is the Universe, to the Universe itself, to one who is verily the Lord of the Universe.

62. Obeisance to Śaṅkara, to Kāla, to one of the form of the units of Kāla, obeisance to Arūpa (one without form), to Virūpa (the deformed), to the subtlest of the subtle.

63. Obeisance to you the resident of the cremation ground, to the wearer of the hide garment; to one with the moon for crest jewel, obeisance to one who has resorted to Rudrabhūmi (i.e. cremation ground).

64-66. Obeisance to Durga (very difficult to know), to Durgapāra (one who is on the other side of Saṁsāra), to the witness of the limbs of Durgā, obeisance to one of the form of Liṅga, to Liṅga and to the Lord of Liṅgas, obeisance to one of the form of Prowess; Obeisance to one whose object is prowess. Repeated salutes to the cause of causes, to you, the conqueror of Death, to one of the form of the self-born; obeisance to the three-eyed one; to the bluenecked, obeisance to one full of splendour; to one united to Gaurī and the cause of auspiciousness.

67. O Brāhmaṇa, this is the century of names glorifying the attributes of the Pināka-bearing Lord. The devotee should recite this, make circumambulation and go back to his own abode.

68. O Brāhmaṇa, by performing this holy rite, the devotee enjoys all worldly pleasures here, thanks to the grace of Mahādeva. In the end he shall attain the region of Śiva.

69-71. On the thirteenth day in the bright half of the month of Mārgaśīrṣa, the devotee should duly worship Anaṅga who had become so, due to his contact with Śiva. He should worship him thrice or once per day. After worshipping with scents and other Upacāras in accordance with the injunctions, he should feed a Brāhmaṇa couple in a pot or on an auspicious cloth. Then, he should give them Dakṣiṇā and take only a single meal. If this vrata is duly performed, O prominent Brāhmaṇa, the devotee becomes the object of blessedness on Earth, thanks to the grace of Mahādeva.

72. The devotee shall worship Hari—Acyuta on the thirteenth day in the bright half of the month of Pauṣa. For the achievement of everything, he should give a pot of ghee to a leading Brāhmaṇa.

73-75a. O Brāhmaṇa, the holy rite of Māgha snāna is to be observed for three days beginning with the thirteenth day in the bright half of the month of Māgha. It is conducive to the attainment of many desired benefits. On this earth even with a thousand horse-sacrifices, that benefit cannot be attained, which one gets on taking the holy dip in Prayāga for these three days in the month of Māgha. The holy dip, Japa, Homa and charitable gifts on this day yields endless benefits.

75b-84. On the thirteenth day in the bright half of the month of Phālguna, the devotee observes fast. After bowing to the Lord of the Universe at the outset, he performs the holy rite of Dhanada Vrata.[1] The picture of the great king, the Lord of the Yakṣas, is painted in colours on a cloth. The devotee worships the Lord with scents and other Upacāras with noble emotions of devotion in the mind. O excellent Brāhmaṇa, in this same manner, he should worship the deity every month on the thirteenth day in the bright half, after observing fast or taking a single meal. At the end of the Vrata he gets the image of the Lord of wealth made along with the image of the lord of Nidhis (Treasure) made in gold. O excellent Brāhmaṇa, with all the sixteen Upacāras, with the ablutions with Pañcāmṛta etc. and with different kinds of Naivedyas, he should with great concentration and devotion worship the deity. O Brāhmaṇa, thereafter, he adorns a cow with its calf by means of cloths, garlands, scents and ornaments. He then gifts it away to a knower of the Vedas. He feeds twelve or thirteen Brāhmaṇas with sweet cooked rice. The preceptor is propitiated with clothes and other things and the gold image (Kubera) is given to him. According to his ability, he should give Dakṣiṇā to the Brāhmaṇas, bow to them and bid farewell to them. The intelligent devotee, thereafter, takes his food alongwith friends and kinsmen. O Brāhmaṇa, if the Vrata is performed thus, the indigent devotee attains great wealth. He rejoices in the world. He becomes well-known on the Earth as another Rājarāja (King of Kings or Kubera).

1. This is the *Dhana Vrata* given in the *Viṣṇu-dharmottara* III. 184. 1-3 and quoted by Hemādri as *Nanda-Vrata*. What Hemādri calls *Dhanada Vrata* (Vrata I. 1161-62), begins on the 11th of Mārgaśīrṣa Śu. though both have Kubera as the deity to be propitiated.

Otherwise, he should take a single meal on that day. At sunset he should worship Nṛsiṁha, the slayer of the Daityas, with all the sixteen Upacāras and ablutions with Pañcāmṛta. Then, O Nārada, with the following Mantra, he should crave forgiveness of the Lord—"O Divine Lion with the mane resembling molten gold, with eyes shining like fire and with the touch of claws sharper than thunderbolt, obeisance be to you." After praying thus to the Lord of the Devas, the observer of holy rite should lie down on the bare ground. He should subdue his sense-organs and anger and should eschew all worldly pleasures. O Brāhmaṇa, he who duly performs this excellent holy rite every year, attains all pleasures and (after death) Hari's region.

14-15. O leading sage, the pilgrimage to Oṁkāreśvara is also to be undertaken on this day. The worship of that deity is very difficult to be obtained. The vision of deity is destructive of sins. Of what avail is much talk ? Whatever is accessible, the worship of the deity, meditation, Japa or the vision of the deity is the bestower of perfect knowledge and salvation.

16-18a. On this day, the holy rite of Liṅga-Vrata is to be performed. It is destructive of sins. Liṅga is bathed in Pañcāmṛta and saffron is smeared over it. Fruits are offered as Naivedyas. Incense, lights, clothes and ornaments are offered duly. He who worships Liṅga made of ground flour, attains worldly pleasures and salvation, thanks to the grace of Mahādeva. This Liṅga is the bestower of achievements of all objects.

18b-19a. On the fourteenth day in the bright half of the month of Jyeṣṭha, the devotee performs austerities in the midst of five fires, during the day time, at night-fall he should make a gift of a golden cow. This is called Rudravrata[1].

19b-20a. On the fourteenth day in the bright half of the month of Āṣāḍha, the devotee should worship Śiva by means of

---

1. Rudra-Vrata: This is *Pañcāgnisādhana*. Kane notes another variety HD. V. i. 393-94.

the flowers of the season and clime. The man who performs worship thus shall attain all riches.

20b-22. The holy rite of Pavitrāropaṇa is to be observed on the fourteenth day of the bright half of the month of Śrāvaṇa. O excellent Brāhmaṇa, that has to be performed in accordance with the injunctions laid down in his own branch of the Veda. He should repeat the Mantra a hundred times and dedicate it to the Goddess. By performing the rite of Pavitrāropaṇa,[1] any person, be it a man or a woman, shall attain worldly pleasures and salvation by the grace of the great Goddess (Mahādevī).

23-27. The excellent holy rite of Ananta Caturdaśī[2] is to be performed on the fourteenth day in the bright half of the month of Bhādrapada. The devotee should take only a single meal on that day. He cooks the Prastha-measure of ground wheat flour smeared with ghee and mixed with sugar and offers it to Ananta as Naivedya after worshipping him at the outset with scents. The old thread worn round the hand is taken off and thrown into the water. A new thread of silken or cotton cord is taken and fourteen knots are tied. The woman devotee wears this on her left hand and the male devotee on his right hand. After cooking the ground flour, he should give it as gift alongwith Dakṣiṇā. He himself shall take in moderate (quantity of) food. The intelligent devotee should perform this excellent Vrata for twice seven years and then perform Udyāpana (Valedictory) rite.

---

1. VV. 20b-22 mention the outline of *Pavitrāropaṇa Vrata*. For details vide HD V. i. 339-40. The NP does not clarify that *Pavitra* is the sacred thread *Yajñopavīta*.

2. VV. 23-33a describe *Ananta-caturdaśī Vrata*. Ananta is a form of Hari. It is a very popular Vrata and is described with slight variations in the procedure in AP. 192. 7-10, the *Bhaviṣyottara* and *Vratārka*. Hemādri (*Vrata* II pp, 26-36) gives an elaborate description of this Vrata quoting the story of Kauṇḍinya and his wife Sitā Kauṇḍinya losing every thing by cutting the Ananta-thread from his wife's hand and regaining it after propitiation of Ananta. Kane (HD. V. I. pp. 151-53) does not clarify how a thread could represent Kṛṣṇa. Ananta is the name of Serpent Śeṣa. Is it an assimilation of the cult of serpent-worship in Brahmanism ?

28-33a. The devotee draws the mystic diagram Sarvato-Bhadra by means of coloured power and grains. O sage, after making it splendid, the devotee places a copper pot over it. The auspicious golden image of Ananta is then placed over the Kalaśa (vessel) of copper and covered with a yellow silken cloth. He shall then worship the image in accordance with the injunctions. He should severally worship Gaṇeśa, Mothers, planets and the ten guardians of the worlds, quarters. He then performs Homa with Haviṣya (cooked rice soaked in ghee) alongwith the Pūrṇāhuti. O excellent Brāhmaṇa, to his preceptor the devotee gives a bed with all adjuncts, a cow and the image of Ananta. With great devotion he should feed fourteen other Brāhmaṇas, with sweet cooked rice, and propitiate them with Dakṣiṇās. He who thus respectfully performs the Ananta Vrata, directly enjoys worldly pleasures and attains salvation by the grace of Ananta.

33b-39a. The holy rite of Kadalī vrata[1] is also to be observed on this day. Listen to its rules of procedure from me. The devotee may be a man or a woman. He should take his bath and worship the plantain tree in the garden by means of scents, fragrant flowers, germinating grains as well as curds, Dūrvā grass, raw rice-grains, lights, clothes and diverse kinds of cooked food. After the worship, the observer of the holy rite should pray with this Mantra : "O plantain tree, who are worshipped by the Apsaras, Amara (divine) virgins and the serpent virgins, O goddess, obeisance be to you. Grant me freedom from ailment in the body and also loveliness." After the prayer the devotee should feed four virgins or Suvāsinīs (married women) ; they should be provided with silken cloth, saffron powder, collyrium and red lac juice. After bowing to them and concluding the observance, he or she should go back to the house. O Brāhmaṇa, if this Vrata is performed thus the devotee obtains excellent conjugal bliss in this world. After death, he shall go to the heavenly world in an aerial chariot.

---

1. VV 336-39a describe the *Kadalī Vrata*—wherein the plantain tree is the beauty-giving deity. Hemādri, on the authority of *Bhaviṣyottara* details it (*Vrata* II. 132-33). This is another instance of assimilation of the cult of tree worship in Brahmanism.

39b-43a. On the fourteenth day in the dark half of the month of Āśvina, the Śrāddha rites of the following categories of persons are performed viz. those who are killed by means of poison or weapons; those who are drowned in water, those who are burnt by fire, those who are bitten by serpents or mauled by beasts of prey, those who are killed by thunderbolt and those who murder Brāhmaṇas. They are performed in accordance with the rules laid down in the case of Ekoddiṣṭa Śrāddhas. Brāhmaṇas are fed with sweet cooked rice. The Tarpaṇa rite is performed, mouthfuls of fodder are given to cows and oblations are given to dogs and crows. After performing these rites and the Ācamana rite, the devotee should take his food along with his kinsmen. O Brāhmaṇa, he who performs Śrāddha in this manner alongwith the requisite Dakṣiṇās shall uplift the Pitṛs and go to the eternal world of the Devas.

43b-45. On the fourteenth day in the bright half of the month of Āśvina O excellent Brāhmaṇa, the devotee should perfectly worship the image in gold of Dharmarāja[1] with scents etc. After feeding a Brāhmaṇa, the image is given to him. O Nārada, Dharmarāja protects everyone in the world. He who thus performs the excellent rite of gifting away the image of Dharmarāja enjoys all excellent pleasures here and at the behest of Dharmarāja goes to the heaven.

46-47. On the fourteenth day in the dark half of the month of Kārttika, the devotee takes oil bath at the rise of the moon. After the bath he should worship Dharma. The devotee shall attain fearlessness from hell. For the propitiation of Yama, he should light oil lamps at night fall. With great concentration the devotee should place the lamps at the cross-roads or outside the house.

48-52. In the year called Hemalambi, on the fourteenth day in the bright half of the glorious month of Kārttika, against the dawn, Lord Viśveśvara took his bath in the holy waters at the Maṇikarṇikā Tīrtha alongwith the Devas. O leading sage, with Bhasma he applied the Tripundra (three parallel marks on the forehead). He worshipped his own self and performed

1. This is not recorded by Kane in HD. V. i.

the Pāśupata rite. Hence on that day, the devotee should perform the great worship of the Liṅga with scents and other things. He should offer worship with the flowers of Droṇa Bilva leaves, Arka flowers Ketakī flowers, fruits and different kinds of Naivedyas. If the Vrata is thus performed and only a single meal is taken on that day, it satisfies Viśveśa. O Nārada, he attains all cherished desires, both here and hereafter.

53-57. On this very day the holy rite of Brahmakūrca Vrata is to be observed by one who wishes for prosperity. Observing fast and controlling the sense-organs, the observer of the vow should drink Pañcagavya at night. The Pañcagavya is made thus :

The urine of a tawny-coloured cow; the dung of a black cow; the milk of a white cow; the curds of a red cow and the ghee of a cow of variegated colours.—all these are taken and mixed together. The devotee then takes his bath in the morning with the water sanctified by Kuśa grass and performs the Tarpaṇa rite to the Devas. After propitiating the Brāhmaṇas, he should himself take his food silently. This is the Brahmakūrca Vrata[1] that destroys all sins. The sin committed during the infancy, youth and old age, is dispelled instantaneously by means of the Brahma-Kūrca vrata and the fast on that day.

58-60a. The holy rite of Pāṣāṇa-Vrata is also to be observed on this day. Listen to it, O Nārada. The devotee observes fast during the day. He cooks ground flour in ghee, shaping it in the form of a brick. During the night, he worships Gaurī with scents and other things and offers the flour-brick cooked in ghee as Naivedya. O excellent Brāhmaṇa, after performing this holy rite in the manner mentioned above, the man attains glory, happiness, conjugal bliss and beauty of form.

60b-63. On the fourteenth day in the bright half of the month of Mārgaśīrṣa the devotee takes a single meal or abstains from food and performs the holy rite mentioned before. He should make a gold replica of a bull, worship it and give it to a Brāhmaṇa. On the next day, he should get up early in the morning,

---

1. *Brahma-Kūrca* is treated here as a *Vrata* though it is really a *Prāyaścitta*.

take his bath and worship Maheśvara accompanied by Umā, with lotus flowers, scents, fragrant garlands and unguents. He should then feed the Brāhmaṇas with sweet cooked rice and propitiate them with Dakṣiṇā etc. O Brāhmaṇa, this is called Śiva Vrata. It is the bestower of worldly pleasures and liberation to the performers, to the instructors, to those who assist, and to those who approve.

64-66a. On the fourteenth day in the bright half of the month of Pauṣa, the holy rite of Virūpākṣavrata is to be observed. The devotee should think thus "I shall attain the presence of Kapardīśvara." Having thought thus, O Brāhmaṇa, he should worship Virūpākṣa Śiva with scents, fragrant garlands, incense, lights, richly prepared cooked rice and obeisances. By giving what is contained therein, the devotee rejoices in the heaven like Deva.

66b-68. On the fourteenth day in the dark half of Māgha is prescribed the holy rite of Yamatapana.[1] Before the sunrise the devotee must take his bath and perform the rite of Tarpaṇa unto Yama with the fourteen names mentioned before (chap. 119 verses 59-90) for the purpose of liberation from all sins. The Tarpaṇa rite is to be performed by means of gingelly seeds, Darbha grass and water. Kṛśara and cooked rice constitute the meal of the Brāhmaṇas. He himself should eat the same with restricted speech in silence.

69-73a. O Brāhmaṇa, the holy rite of Śivarātrī[2] is to be observed on the fourteenth day in the dark half of the last month (i.e Phālguna). The devotee observes fast, even abjuring water, during the day, and worships the deity at night in the self-born Liṅga etc. or the Liṅga made of clay with deep concentration of mind. He worships the Lord with scents and

---

1. Kane has recorded a number of *Śiva Vratas* (HD. V. i. pp. 426-427), but this Vrata is different from them.

2. This is the famous *Mahāśivarātri-Vrata* popular all over India. The NP follows *Pūrṇimānta* reckoning and thus locates it in Phālguna. This *Vrata* is highly extolled in *Garuḍa* P. I-124, SK. P. I-1. 33, Pd. P. VI. 240 and AP. 193. The whole *Vrata* is discussed in details by Kane HD. V. 1-225-236. As compared with other Purāṇas and digests, the NP. gives a bare outline of the *Vrata*.

other Upacāras, the leaves of the Bilva, etc., water, incense, lights, recitation of hymns, Japa etc. as well as Naivedyas duly offered. On the next day too the deity is again worshipped with the Upacāras. After feeding Brāhmaṇas with sweet cooked rice, he should give them the requisite Dakṣiṇās and bid farewell to them. By performing the Vrata thus, the man obtains immortal pleasures, thanks to the grace of Mahādeva. He is well-honoured and respected by Devas.

73b-74. On the fourteenth day, in the bright half of the last month, the devotee worships Durgā with great devotion, offering scents and other Upacāras. Thereafter, he feeds the Brāhmaṇas. O Brāhmaṇa, he should take only a single meal on that day. By performing the Vrata of Durgā thus, he derives cherished desires, both here and hereafter, O Nārada.

75-76. The devotee shall observe fast on the fourteenth day in the dark half of the month of Caitra. By drinking water from a rice-field on the day one derives the benefit of a horse-sacrifice.

The general procedure regarding Udyāpana[1] (valedictory rite of conclusion) for all these holy rites is now narrated.

77-79. Fourteen pots with areca nuts, unbroken raw rice-grains and sweet-meats, may be made of copper or clay. They must be fresh and uncracked. The Dakṣiṇās and silken garments should also be placed there. Besides these the following too are to be provided as necessary viz. fourteen bamboo poles, fourteen sacred seats, fourteen vessels and fourteen sacred texts. As for the other things, they should be performed in the manner mentioned before. The devotee should not be stingy in the matter of expenses.

1. VV. 77-79 give the general procedure of the *Udyāpana* (concluding ceremony) of these *Caturdaśī Vratas*.

CHAPTER ONE HUNDRED AND TWENTYFOUR

Exposition of Vratas to be observed on the Full Moon and the New Moon days

Sanātana said :

1. Henceforth, O Nārada, I shall recount to you the holy rite to be observed on the Full Moon day. Listen. On observing these rites the performer of Vratas whether he be a man or a woman, attains series of happiness.

2. O leading Brāhmaṇa, the Full Moon day in the month of Caitra is the day of the inauguration of the Manvantara. On this day, the observer of the Vrata should give a pot of water with cooked rice, for the propitiation of Soma (the Moon).

3. On the full moon day in the month of Vaiśākha, the gift of all articles is the bestower of all things. Certainly, one attains those things which one bestows on a Brāhmaṇa.

4-5a. The holy rite of Dharmarāja Vrata is also to be performed on this day. Listen to it. One should give cooked rice and pot of water to an excellent Brāhmaṇa on the Full Moon day in the month of Vaiśākha. It is conducive to the propitiation of Dharmarāja and it yields the same benefit as the gift of a cow.

5b-7. On this very same day, one should give the hide of a deer alongwith its horn and the hoofs to a Brāhmaṇa alongwith gingelly seeds and gold. They should be covered with clothes. He who gives, in accordance with the prescribed injunctions, the hide of a deer after honouring the scholar who knows the Śāstras, is actually the donor of the whole of the earth consisting of the seven continents, and rejoices in the world of Viṣṇu as long as the moon, sun and stars shine in the firmament.

8. He who gives to prominent Brāhmaṇas pots full of water alongwith gold never meets with sorrow.

9. On the Full Moon day in the month of Jyeṣṭha the holy rite of vaṭasāvitrikā[1] is to be observed. The woman devotee

1. VV. 9-12 briefly describe the famous *Vaṭa-Sāvitrī-Vrata*, the main features of which are sprinkling water at the foot of a banyan tree,

the holy rite of Vedopākarma[1] (i.e. inauguration of Vedic studies). On this day the rite of Tarpaṇa unto the Devas, sages and the Pitṛs is to be performed through the Mantras of the Yajurveda. (The followers of the Yajurveda perform this rite of Upākarma on the day). The followers of Ṛgveda (i.e. Bahvṛcas) perform this on the Caturdaśī day and the followers of the Sāmaveda perform this in the month of Bhādrapada (on the Caturthī day). The worship of the sages is performed in the manner laid down in one's own Śākhā (branch of the Vedas). The Rakṣā (holy string) should be tied round the hand in accordance with the injunctions.

29. White Mustard seeds, unbroken raw rice-grains and black mustard are washed in water kept in a bell-metal vessel and then tied in a red silk cloth with a saffron-smeared thread. The devotee then worships Devas and prays to Viṣṇu and others. Delighted in mind, the devotee should lay down to a Brāhmaṇa and get the thread tied round his wrist by him.

30-31. Thereafter, he gives Dakṣiṇā to Brāhmaṇas and begins the study of the Vedas. After ritualistically dismissing the seven sages, he should wear a new sacred thread made by himself and coloured with saffron, etc. According to his capacity he should feed the prominent Brāhmaṇas and he himself should take only a single meal on that day.

32. O Brāhmaṇa, if this Vrata is performed, it makes atonement for all omissions and commissions in the Vedic study. If the Vedic rites are forgotten or are performed in contravention of the injunctions, this holy rite rectifies it.

33-34. The holy rite of Umāmaheśvara Vrata is to be performed on the full moon day in the month of Bhādrapada.

---

1. *Vedopākarma* is simply *upākarma* and means opening, beginning. Nārāyaṇa on *Āśvalāyana Gr. S.* III. 5.1 states that *upākarma* or *upākaraṇa* is the ceremony marking the (re-) beginning of Vedic Studies. Various dates and varieties of details of the *upārkarma* are given by Kane in HD. II. ii. pp. 807-818. Due to its performance on *Sravaṇa Nakṣatra* in the month of Śrāvaṇa, it came to be known as *Śrāvaṇo* in Marathi. The tradition of Vedic studies is lost and what the elderly people do now is to change their *Yajñopavīta* on this day with or without the performance of the rite of *Upākarma*. The ritual given by the NP is different from the traditional one prescribed in the *gṛhya sūtras*.

The devotee takes a single meal on the previous day i.e. Caturdaśī day, assiduously worships Śiva. With palms joined in reverence he should pray thus : "O Lord, I shall perform holy Vrata (vow) tomorrow." After intimating thus to the Lord, the devotee takes up the excellent Vrata.

35. At night, he sleeps near the deity and gets up in the last watch (Yāma) of the night. After carrying out the routine such as voiding of excrement and washing, etc. the devotee applies Bhasma and wears Rudrākṣa.

36. He should worship Śaṅkara correctly with different kinds of Upacāras, fragrant flowers, leaves of Bilva, incense lights and diverse kinds of Naivedya.

37. Then the scholarly devotee should observe fast till sunset. After the moonrise, he worships the deity once again and keeps awake at night.

38-41. Carefully and alertly, the devotee should perform this rite for fifteen years. In the last year, in the course of its Utsarga rite (valedictory and concluding rite), he should get two gold images made, that of Umā and that of Maheśa. He should get ready fifteen excellent posts made of gold, silver or clay. In one of the pots should be placcd the two images covered with a cloth. He should bathe them in Pañcāmṛta first and then in pure water. Thereafter he shall worship deity with the sixteen Upacāras. Then fifteen Brāhmaṇas are fed with sweet cooked rice and Dakṣiṇās too are given.

42-43a. He should give pots to the preceptor. Each of the pots is accompanied by a Mūrti (image) of the Lord. By performing this holy rite named Umā Maheśvara, the devotee becomes famous in the world and the receptacle of all riches.

43b-44. On this very same day, the holy rite of Śakra-Vrata also is to be observed. Early in the morning, the devotee takes his bath and worships the ruler of the Devas, in accordance with the injunctions, with scents and other Upacāras and diffcrent articles of Naivedya in heaps.

45. Then O, Brāhmaṇa, he should duly feed the invited Brāhmaṇas and others who had come as visitors. He shall feed the indigent and the helpless also.

46. O Brāhmaṇa, this Śakravrata must be performed every year by a king or any other rich man who wishes for plenty of food-grains.

47-48. The holy rite named Kojāgara[1] is to be observed on the full moon day in the month of Āśvina. The devotee takes the holy dip in accordance with the injunctions. He observes fast and subdues his sense-organs. A gold image of goddess Lakṣmī is placed in a pot made of copper or clay. It is covered with a cloth and worshipped with different kinds of Upacāras.

49. In the evening when the moon has risen, he should light lamps made of gold, silver or clay after filling them with ghee.

50-51. They should be a hundred thousands, fifty thousand, ten thousand, one thousand or hundred in number. Milk puddings are prepared in a huge quantity with plenty of sugar and ghee. They shall be kept in many vessels in the bright moonlight. When the night has advanced by a full Yāma (three hours), the devotee shall offer milk puddings as Naivedya to Lakṣmī.

52. With great devotion he should then feed the Brāhmaṇas with the milk puddings. All of them then keep awake for the whole of the night with songs and auspicious instrumental music and dances.

53-54. The next day before dawn, the devotee takes his bath and dedicates the gold image to the preceptor. (It is said) that on this night goddess Mahālakṣmī with the gestures of granting boon and fearlessness in her lotus-like hands moves over the Earth saying—ko jāgarti (who is keeping awake) on this Earth ? I shall give wealth to that person who keeps awake and worships me."

55. This Vrata should be performed every year. It propitiates Lakṣmī. It yields prosperity in this world and bliss in the other world after death.

---

1. VV. 47-55 describe the *Kojāgara Vrata* or Kaumudī Mahotsava mentioned in Sanskrit and Prakrit Literature, Purāṇas and mediaeval digests. The NP. does not mention dice-playing on that night.

56. On the full moon day in the month of Kārttika, Lord Kārttikeya should be visited for the attainment of Brahminhood again (i.e. in the next birth) and for the conquest of all enemies.

57. On this very same day, Tripurotsava (the festival of Tripura) should be performed by celebrating illuminations (of buildings, ghats etc.), O excellent Brāhmaṇa, this festival of light at night-fall is conducive to the happiness of all living beings.

58. Insects, locusts, mosquitoes, trees and the living beings that move about in water or dry land are not reborn after seeing these lights. They attain liberation.

59-61. O Brāhmaṇa, at the time of the moon-rise the six Kṛttikās must be worshipped. So also Kārttikeya, Khaḍgī, Varuṇa and Hutāśana (Fire-God) are to be worshipped with scents and fragrant flowers, incense, lights, extensive Naivedyas, excellent cooked rice, fruits, vegetable and by propitiation of the fire-god and the Brāhmaṇas. Thus after bowing down and worshipping the Devas, light should be offered outside the house.

62-64. Very near the lamps, a beautiful square-shaped pit fourteen Aṅgulas deep should be made and sprinkled with sandal water. After filling it with milk of cows, the devotee should put in it an image of a fish made of gold and exquisite in every limb, and with eyes constituted of pearls. Uttering the Mantra, 'Obeisance to the great Fish' the devotee should worship it with scents and other things and offer it to a Brāhmaṇa.

65. O excellent Brāhmaṇa, the charitable gift of the ocean of Milk[1] has been recounted to you by me. Thanks to the power of this charitable gift, the devotee rejoices in the presence of Hari.

66. O Nārada, by performing the rite of Vṛṣotsarga (setting a bull-calf free) during the night, the devotee attains Rudra's region. No doubt need be entertained in this respect.

1. VV. 62-65 describe the *Kṣīra-sāgara dāna* (gift of the milky ocean). The whole procedure is symbolic.

on the full moon day in the month of Phālguna. The devotee collects all types of wood and cow-dung cakes. After duly kindling fire therein, by means of extensive Mantras destructive of Rākṣasas, the devotee repeats this Mantra—"O Holi, you have been made by people of childish traits who are afraid of blood-sucking Ogresses. Hence I shall worship you. Be the bestower of prosperity on the living beings."

79. By repeating this Mantra, more and more wood is thrown in and the fire is made brighter. The devotees go round it and carry on the festivities with songs and instrumental music.

80-81. (There are two opinions about the burning of Holikā).* (one opinion) : This ogress Holikā was a terror to Prahlāda. Hence, people burn her with wood to the accompaniment of songs and instrumental music. This is the burning of the Saṁvatsara (year). In the opinion of others, it is the burning of Kāma. Thus O leading Brāhmaṇa, you shall know that there are many traditions in the world.

82. The two days of festival at the end of a fortnight are the full moon and the new moon. Hence the Amāvrata[1] (the holy rite on New Moon days) is described. O Brāhmaṇa, listen to their separate nature. This Vrata is a great favourite of the manes.

83-84. On the new moon days of the months of Caitra and Vaiśākha the worship of Pitṛs is recommended. The Śrāddha in accordance with the injunction governing festival days and in accordance with one's affluence is to be performed. The feeding of Brāhmaṇas and charitable gifts of cows etc. in particular, are highly meritorious on the new moon days, in all the months.

85. The Vrata of Sāvitrī is to be observed on the new moon day in the month of Jyeṣṭha. O Nārada, its rules of

---

*It is a very ancient festival and was called Holikā in east India (Śabara on *Pūrvamīmāṁsā* I. 3. 15-23). Hemādri calls this Hutāśanī as we do now.

1. In VV. 82-96 the NP. groups together *Amā-Vratas* i.e. Vratas to be observed on the new-moon days. As this day is specially sacred to the manes (*Pitṛs*) different *śrāddhas* are prescribed on these days.

procedure are the same as for the festival of the full moon day in the month of Jyeṣṭha.

86. O Brāhmaṇa, in the months of Āṣāḍha, Śrāvaṇa and Bhādrapada (when Pūrṇimānta or) ending with the full moon day, the following rites are to be performed, and they are endless in their benefits. The rites are Śrāddha of manes (ancestors), charitable gift, Homa and the worship of the Devas.

87-88a. O Brāhmaṇa, Kuśas grow in the fields of gingelly seeds. In the afternoon of the new moon day in the month of Bhādrapada, the devotee repeats the Mantra of Viriñci (god Brahmā) and cuts those Kuśa grasses saying 'Huṁ phaṭ'. These grasses can be used always in all holy rites. But the other Kuśa grasses can be used only once.

88b-89a. On the new moon day in the month of Āśvina, Śrāddha and Tarpaṇa of the Pitṛs are particularly recommended. They must be performed in the waters of Gaṅgā. In the holy centre of Gayā, it yields liberation.

89b-91a. On the new moon day in the month of Kārttika, lights should be offered as gifts in temples of gods, river banks, parks, tanks, cowpens, market places, monasteries and other places, Worship of Lakṣmī is performed on this day. Gold and silver whether made into ornaments or not (are dealt in on this day). Playing at dice throughout the year, predicts gain or loss exactly as one wins or loses.

91b-92a. On this day, worship of cows is laid down in the following manner viz. : the horns and other limbs are painted; barley and other grains are given; cows are bowed to and circumambulated.

92b-93a. In the month of Mārgaśīrṣa also, there is Pitṛ Pūjā (worship of the manes) by means of Śrāddhas and feeding of Brāhmaṇas, observances of the restraints of celibacy etc. as well as Japa, Homa, Arcanā and other rites.

93b-96. O leading Brāhmaṇa, in the months of Pauṣa and Māgha, the Śrāddhas performed to the Pitṛs are more efficacious. If on the New Moon Day in the month of Phālguna, the day is combined with Karṇapāta (?) and the Sun (i.e. prob. Vyatīpāta, Śravaṇā Nakṣatra and the Sun are found on that day), performance of mere Śrāddha or feeding of Brāhmaṇas is more efficacious (in giving good fruit) than even at Gayā (their performance at Gayā); charitable gifts etc. are the bestowers of all benefit if made on the new moon day. If it falls on a Monday the benefit is still more. O sage, thus in brief, I have recounted to you the duties on the different Tithis. In all these instances there are some special cases. Those are mentioned in other Purāṇas.

CHAPTER ONE HUNDRED AND TWENTYFIVE

The greatness of the Purāṇa[1]

Sūta said :

1. Having recounted thus (the matter in the foregone four Pādas of this Purāṇa) on being enquired (about it) by the sage Nārada, it is reported that the (four) Kumāras (viz. Sanat, Sanaka, Sanandana and Sanātana) who were the most excellent ones among the knowers of the sacred lore (śāstras) were worshipped by Nārada. After performing their

1. This is the concluding chapter of the original *Nārada Purāṇa* which consisted of four *pādas* (*catuṣpādasamāyuktam* V. 26). Here the interlocutors disperse as follows.

(1) The Kumāras, the reciters of the NP. are worshipped by Nārada. They went to god Śiva and learnt the *Śaiva Āgama*. After this they visited god Brahmā and lastly god Viṣṇu at the *Badari* forest (VV. 1-5).

(2) Bidding good-bye to Śaunaka and other Brāhmaṇas, Sūta went to his preceptor Vyāsa (VV. 48-49).

(3) Śaunaka and other Brāhmaṇas remained there in the Naimiṣa forest and resumed their *Satra* (sacrificial session) V. 49.

(4) VV. in this chapter 26-47 is the eulogy of the NP. and of the benefit derived form hearing NP. This is called *phalaśruti* which marks the end of a particular work.

These verses show that the original NP. was completed here at the end of this chapter.

prescribed daily routine duties, they went to the world of the Lord of Umā (i.e. god Śiva).

2. There (in the region of god Śiva) they bowed down to Ugra (i.e. Śiva), Īśa, whose feet have been worshipped by the leading sages like Śrīvāmadeva and others who resembled (in refulgence) the fire and the sun—Śiva who is worthy of being adored by the leaders of the Devas and Asuras. At his behest, they sat on the bare ground.

3. There, they heard the Śaiva Āgama which is the essence of all sacred lores, and which is conducive to the liberation of Paśu (individual soul) from Pāśa (bondage of Saṁsāra). After bowing to Purāri (Śiva) those sages who were the very concrete embodiments of Pure knowledge, went to the presence of their father (god Brahmā).

4. They bowed down to his lotus feet. They were duly honoured and welcomed by their father. Receiving his blessings they became holy and sacred. From that time onwards, they who are the embodiments of holy places, are continuously moving about in the holy centres in all the three worlds.

5. Thereafter, they went to the holy forest of Badarī, where they meditated for a long time on the immutable lotus-like feet of Lord Viṣṇu which are being resorted to by groups of leading Devas and on which the ascetics, devoid of passion, contemplate.

6. After acquiring the spiritual knowledge along with sound wisdom and discrimination so longed for by him from those Kumāras (viz. Sanaka, Sanandana and others), Nārada was highly pleased in his mind.

7. From the banks of that celestial river, he returned to his father's presence, where he was warmly welcomed by his father (god Brahmā). After bowing to him he took his seat there.

8. He described factually the spiritual wisdom along with sound knowledge that he had heard from the Kumāras. On hearing that, he (i.e. Brahmā) too rejoiced.

9. Then the excellent sage (Nārada) bowed down (to Brahmā) with his head and received his blessings. He came over to Kailāsa which is frequented by sages and Siddhas.

10-11. The place is continuously filled with different

kinds of wonderful things. It is full of trees blossoming in all the seasons—trees such as Mandāras, Pārijātas, Campakas, Aśokas, Vañjulas and many others. They are occupied by flocks of different kinds of birds. When their branches are shaken by the wind, they appear as though they are inviting the wayfarers.

12. The place is full of different herds of deer. It is thronged by the Siddhas and Kinnaras. It appears splendid, thanks to the lakes with crystal-clear water where golden lotuses bloom with splendour.

13-15a. It was reverberated with the sounds of various aquatic birds such as Sārasas, Cakravākas and swans. It was resounded with the tumultuous sound of the fall of heavenly river, by the sporting bevies of celestial damsels playing in the waters of the river Alakanandā which had turned tawny-coloured through the saffron powders from their breasts. It was teeming with joyous elephants who bathed their mates and cubs with the waters taken up by their trunks.

15b-16a. On a peak that resembled a white cloud, of that mountain, he saw a spreading banyan tree which extended over a hundred Yojanas and which appeared like a black cloud.

16b-18a. Beneath it, he saw Lord Śiva seated in the middle of a group of Yogins. The lord had matted hair and unusual number (i.e. three) of eyes. He was clad in the hide of a tiger. He had smeared ashes all over his body. He was adorned with serpents as ornaments. He was perpetually refulgent with his necklace of Rudrākṣa-beads and he had a crescent of the moon on his head.

18b-19a. On seeing (the moon-crested) Lord, O Brāhmaṇa, Nārada bent down and lowered his neck with great devotion. He bowed his head down at the feet of the Lord of the Universe.

19b-20. With a delighted mind, he eulogised the bull-bannered Lord, verbally. At the behest of Sthāṇu (Śiva), he sat down. He was greeted and honoured by the Yogins. Then the preceptor of the worlds (i.e. Lord Śiva) enquired about the health and welfare of Nārada.

21-22a. He replied—"Thanks to your Honour's grace, I am blest with everything." O Brāhmaṇas, even as all the leading Yogins were listening, (Nārada) asked Śiva about special knowledge of Śambhu, that is conducive to the liberation of the Paśu from the Pāśa.

22b-23a. Śiva was highly delighted in his mind with his respectful devotion. The Lord favourably disposed towards those who bow down to him, recounted the Yoga philosophy with all its eight subsections. (or accessories)

23b-24a. After acquiring the knowledge pertaining to Śambhu, from Śaṅkara, the benefactor of all the worlds, Nārada became delighted in his mind. After bowing to him, he went near Nārāyaṇa.

24b-25a. Nārada who was accustomed to coming to and fro frequently, propitiated Nārāyaṇa, who is served by the Yogins and the Siddhas.

25b-26. Thus, O Brāhmaṇas, the great narrative of Nārada Puraṇa has been recounted to you. It is on a par with the Vedas. It is a model for all sacred lores. It comprises four Pādas (quarters, sections). It increases the perfect knowledge of listeners.

27-29. O Brāhmaṇas, he who recites and glorifies devoutly this narrative pertaining to Nārada, in a Śiva temple, in the assembly of prominent Brāhmaṇas, in the temple of Keśava, in Mathurā, in Prayāga, in the presence of Puruṣottama (or at Jagannātha Puri), at Setu (i.e. the bridge built by Rāma on his way to Laṅkā), in Kāñcī, at Dvārakā, at Gaṅgādvāra, Kuśasthala, on the banks of the lotus tanks (or at Puṣkara), on the banks of rivers—in fact, anywhere (he pleases) shall obtain the great benefit of performance of all Yajñas and the visit of all holy centres.

30-31. He shall obtain the benefit of all charitable gifts and of performing all austerities. Both the listener and the propounder (narrator) should be devoted to Nārāyaṇa or to Śiva; He should either observe fast or take in only Haviṣya food (cooked rice soaked in ghee). He should subdue his sense-organs. Listening thus to this Purāṇa he shall attain Siddhi (Mokṣa).

32. It is in this narrative that all merits and Siddhis

originate. It is declared as destructive of all sins of those who read and listen to it.

33. It removes the defects due to Kali's harrassment; it is conducive to the increase of all riches of men. This is liked by everyone. It illuminates all knowledge.

34-37a. It sheds light on the modes of austerities, holy rites and their benefits of the followers of Śiva, Viṣṇu, Śakti, the Sun god and Gaṇapati. It explains the duties of those who adhere to the system of disciplined life in accordance with the classification of various castes and stages of life. It throws light on the Mantras, Yantras and the ancillary subjects of the Vedas with their divisions. It is a brief digest of the Āgamas, the Vedas and the Sāṁkhya tenets. He who reads this devoutly or listens to it with great concentration, shall derive all cherished desires difficult of access, even to the Devas and others.

37b-39a. After listening to this Nārada Purāṇa which is on a par with the Vedas, the devotee should worship the expounder with devotion, wealth, jewels, silk cloths, etc. and with the gifts of plots of land, cows, jewels etc. With the gifts of elephants, horses and chariots, he should ever please the preceptor.

39b-40a. O Brāhmaṇa, who else can be a preceptor other than the person who comments on the Purāṇas wherein all dharmas (religious duties) have been collected together and which bestows all the fourfold aims of human life. (viz. Dharma, Artha, Kāma and Mokṣa).

40b-41a. The devotee should always do what is pleasing to the preceptor who instructs him in religious duties. He should render him service physically, mentally and verbally as well as through cash presents.

41b-42. After listening to the Purāṇa duly and after performing Homa and worship of the Devas, the devotee should feed a hundred Brāhmaṇas, with sweet cooked rice and milk puddings. He should give them monetary gifts in accordance with his capacity. Mādhava shall be pleased with his devotion.

43-46. Just as Gaṅgā is the most excellent among the rivers, Puṣkara is the most excellent among the lakes, (and just as in their respective categories the following are the best viz.) the city of Kāśi, the mountain Meru, Lord Hari, Nārāyaṇa, the Kṛta age, the Sāma Veda, the cow, the Brāhmaṇa, the cooked rice, water, the month of Mārgaśīrṣa, the lion, the (Cosmic Man) Puruṣa, the Aśvattha (holy fig tree), Prahlāda, the face, the horse Uccaiśśravas, the season Vasanta (spring), Japa, the serpent Seṣa, Aryaman, the bow, the fire, Viṣṇu, Indra, the sage Kapila, the Lord of speech (Bṛhaspati) Kavi (poet, Śukra), Arjuna, Hanumān, Darbha grass, the mind, the gandharva Citraratha, the Lotus, the Apsaras Ūrvaśī and gold—all these are the most excellent ones in their own groups.

47. Similarly, the Nārada Purāṇa is the most excellent among all the Purāṇas. O excellent Brāhmaṇas, peace be to you; welfare be to all of you.

48. I shall now go to my preceptor Vyāsa, of unmeasured splendour. After saying this, Sūta was worshipped by Śaunaka and other noble souls.

49. Permitted by all of them, he went his way to see his preceptor Vyāsa.

All those excellent Brāhmaṇas, Śaunaka and others carried out the advice they had heard with great concentration and perfection in details. They remained there itself, performing their Satra (sacrifice).

50. He who takes (resorts) to meditating in the form of injunctions regarding the performance of Japa and worship of Hari, the destroyer of the poison of the sins of Kali, purges completely his mind of that poison (or Kali) and accomplishes Yoga and ultimately attains the ever-cherished region of Hari.

UTTARA BHĀGA[1]

CHAPTER ONE

The greatness of Ekādaśī day

Obeisance to Śrī Gaṇeśa

Obeisance to Śrī Kṛṣṇa

1. May the four arms of Hari protect you all—the arms dark like clouds in complexion, hardened by the friction (strokes) of the strings of the Śārṅga bow and which are like columns supporting the big pavilion (-like structure) of the three worlds.

2. May the lotus-like pair of Hari's feet be the bestower of desires on us—the pair of feet refulgent with the brilliance of the polished crest jewels of Devas and Asuras (as they bow to him).

Māndhātā[2] *said* :

3. O excellent Brāhmaṇa, It behoves your honour to tell me what that fire is that burns both dry and damp fuel of terrible sins.

---

1. Although the last redactor of the NP. tries to show that this Part (*Uttara Khaṇḍa*) also called *Uttara Bhāga* in colophons of chapters) is an integral part of the NP (*vide Supra* I. 97. 10-18), the whole setting of this part is different, showing that it must have been an independent work to glorify *Ekādaśī Vrata* and to illustrate it with the Rukmāṅgada-Mohinī episode. But this unification of the two parts took place before the 10th cent. A.D. (Kane HD. V. ii. pp. 892-93), An early digest writer like Devaṇa Bhaṭṭa (1200-1225 A.D.) quotes many verses from the *Uttara-Khaṇḍa* of the extant NP. in his *Smṛti-Chandrikā*. Earlier still, Aparārka (1100-1130 A.D.) quotes from it two verses on Ekādaśī (HD. V. ii. 892). Hence, though apocryphal, the *Uttara-Khaṇḍa* has been regarded as the integral part of the NP. for the last 1000 years. By any standard, it is a good story and the writer of this part is a gifted story-teller.

2. *Māndhātā*—An emperor of the solar race, son of king Yuvanāśva, He was born from his father's belly. When the problem of feeding him

24. Thus the power of Dvādaśī has been glorified by me, O king, it is called the fire that consumes the terrible fuel of sin.

25. Always the day of Hari should be observed as a day of fast by men, devoted to holiness and piety, who wish for abundant worldly pleasures as well as sons, grandsons etc.

26. The man who observes the day of Hari (Ekādaśī) with great respect, O most excellent one among men, never enters the womb of a mother even if he has committed many sins or even if he observes the fast with or without intention. He goes to the endless region of Viṣṇu, the Lord of the world.

CHAPTER TWO

Discussion on Tithis[1]

Vasiṣṭha said :

1. It was bearing on this same topic that the saintly residents of the Naimiṣa forest asked the highly intelligent Sūta, the disciple of Vyāsa.

---

1. *Tithi* is the period required by the moon to gain twelve degrees on the sun to the east (*Sūrya-siddhānta*, *Tithi Tattva* p. 2.). Due to the irregular motion of the moon, the *tithi* varies between 67 to 50 *ghaṭikās*—a finding recorded in the maxim.

Sapta-vṛddhir daśa kṣayaḥ

As a *Tithi* is not coterminus with a 'civil day' and as every religious rite, be it *Vrata*, *Dāna* etc. must be done at the exact time of the *Tithi* (otherwise it becomes fruitless), this topic has been discussed since very old times. As the word is used in the *Aitareya Brāhmaṇa* and Gṛhya and Dharma sūtras, the belief in *Tithi* exists since the 8th Cent. B.C. Works have been devoted to the discussion of the correct time on a *Tithi* for observing *Vratas*. For example, Jīmūta-vāhana's *Kāla-viveka*, Hemādri's CC., *Kāla-mādhava*, *Nīlakaṇṭha's Kāla-mayūkha*, *Dharmasindhu* and others.

But this very topic has been discussed previously in NP. I. 29 and elsewhere and the technical terms like *Pūrṇā*, *Śuddhā*, *Viddhā* etc., the *Yugma-Vākya* and rules for deciding the Ekādaśi fast etc. have been discussed in details in the annotations to those Chapters and verses. Hence, they are not repeated here.

2. On being asked, that highly pleased one recounted the greatness of Ekādaśī[1] in detail and also the rules of procedure regarding the observance of fast.

3-4a On hearing that statement of the son of Sūta, as well as the greatness of the wielder of discus (god Viṣṇu) that subdues vast multitudes of sins, O king, the excellent Brāhmaṇas again asked Sūta who is devoid of impurities and who is well versed in the Purāṇas.

4b-5. "O bestower of honour, you know the eighteen Purāṇas. Thanks to the favour of the son of virgin[2] '(i.e. Vyāsa) you know the Mahābhārata too. Hence, there is nothing in the Purāṇas or the Smṛtis which you do not know.

6-7a. A doubt is produced in our minds in the story of Raghunātha that is very extensive, containing hundred crores of verses. It behoves you to dispel it by means of factual and detailed explanation.

7b-8a. Is it the end of the Tithi that has to be taken up for the observance of fast. Or is it the root (beginning)? What is the rule regarding this in the rites pertaining to the Devas and those pertaining to the Pitṛs (manes)? Kindly narrate it as there is nothing that is unknown to you.

Sauti said :

8b. In regard to the Devas (i.e. rites pertaining to Devas) the end-period of the Tithi is to be taken for observing fast. Then it is conducive to the increase of their pleasure.

9. The root (beginning) of the Tithi is declared by the knowers of Time as pleasing to the Pitṛs. Hence, the tip is

---

1. In the previous Chs. in the NP. I discussed *Tithis* with reference to the religious rites like *Śrāddha, Vrata* etc., but this verse and the following discussion makes it clear that the object of this part is disquisition on all aspects of *Ekādaśī Vrata* only.

Another important point here is the conspicuous absence of Nārada. He is neither a listener nor a narrator of NP. Uttarārdha as contrasted with NP. Purvārdha where he is at least the listener.

2. *Kānīna*—A child born of an un-married women. *Mbh. Ādi.* 60.2 tells us that Vyāsa alias Kṛṣṇa Dvaipāyana was born of an unmarried girl (Matsyagandhā or Satyavati) on an island in the Yamunā.

taken up for the observance of fast by those who wish to obtain tenfold benefits.

10-12a. The root is to be known for being taken up (for fast) by those who desire for virtue and piety, for the purpose of propitiation of the Pitṛs. Neither Dvitīyā (the second day) nor the Aṣṭamī (the eighth day) nor Ṣaṣṭhī (the sixth day) nor Ekādaśī (the eleventh day) in a human fortnight, O king, should be taken up by those who wish for virtue, love and wealth, if it overlaps (lit. is pierced by) the previous one.

12b. O excellent Brāhmaṇas, Saptamī (the seventh day) in lunar fortnight is always to be taken up only when it overlaps the previous one. If any one eschews the following, when they overlap the previous ones, he falls into hell. Those Tithis are Darśa, (the New Moon day), Paurṇamāsa (the Full moon day) and the anniversary day of the father.

13. O king, he will be visited by misfortunes and loss of progeny. O Brāhmaṇas this has been heard by me formerly from Kṛṣṇa Dvaipāyana.

14. That Tithi is called Pūrvaviddhā (overlapping the previous one) if there is even a slight trace of it at the time of sunrise. That Tithi should be considered Prabhūta (full) (if it extends throughout) not excluding the time of sunrise.

15. In the rite of Pāraṇā (break-fast) and in the case of death of men, that Tithi is remembered which exists at that particular time. In the case of rites pertaining to Pitṛs, if there is contact of the Tithi at the time of sunset, it is called Pūrṇā (full).

16. In that case, the Tithi at the time of sunrise is not taken into account. But in the case of rites of the deities, the Tithi at the time of sunrise must be taken into account. The intelligent devotee should get the Tithi confirmed through a thoughtful astrologer.

17. O leading Brāhmaṇas, the bases for the extent of the Tithis are the sun and the moon. The knowers of the time reckon it through the movements of moon and the sun.

the next day, how is the observance of fast enjoined on that day ? O son of Sūta, pray explain to me.

Sauti said :

O Brāhmaṇas, when on Dvādaśī the previous Tithi is not at all obtainable and the day of the week is Saturday, Sunday or Monday (?) the next day is to be taken up for fasting. Even when there is the risk of contravening many Āgamas and when the Brāhmaṇas raise arguments against it, the holy Dvādaśī should be observed as the day of fast and the break fast (Pāraṇā) is on Trayodaśī (the Thirteenth day of the lunar fortnight).

31b. When Ekādaśī is Viddhā (i.e. it is overlapped by the previous Tithi) and it is the month of Śrāvaṇa, it is the holy Dvādaśī that should be observed as the day of fast, in both the fortnights. This decision, arrived at in accordance with the Śāstras (sacred lore) has been announced to you by me.

32a. What else do you wish to hear? You may be pleased to tell me the same.

The sages said :

32b-33a. O Sauti, tell us the rules regarding the observances on the inaugural days of the Yugas precisely and factually. Similarly, tell us the rules regarding the transit of the sun etc. There is nothing that cannot be understood by you.

Sauti said :

33b-34a. Wise persons know that two of the inaugural days of the Yugas fall in the bright half of the month and two in the dark half. The Tithis in the bright half are to be taken up when they exist in the forenoon, those in the dark half are to be taken up when they exist in the afternoon.

34b-35. The Ayana (the tropical transit) has the part of the day as the basis and the transit time is sixteen Palas (certain unit of time). In the southern portion (transit from the tropic of Cancer) the former one (? the forenoon) is to be taken and in the northern (transit from the tropic of Capricorn) the past one (the afternoon) is considered (for acceptance). In the middle period of Viṣuva (equinox), it is glorified as Akṣaya (imperishable).

36. O Brāhmaṇas, fast is to be undertaken after knowing precisely the Tithi mentioned for the full year. Otherwise, one is likely to fall into a hell.

37. The man observing fast when it is Pūrvaviddhā breaks Dharma. It is likely to result in death of the progeny and loss of wealth.

38. Just as one eschews the water of the Gaṅgā if it is contaminated by even a drop of liquor, O leading Brāhmaṇa, one should avoid the Ekādaśī day even if there is the overlapping of Daśamī by a single pala (a small unit of time).

39. O excellent Brāhmaṇas, just as one should throw away the Pañcagavya if it is defiled by a dog, so one should do, if Ekādaśī in both the fortnights, is defiled by Daśamī.

40. O excellent Brāhmaṇas, the Pūrvaviddhā Ekādaśī Tithi (i.e. the eleventh day with the overlapping of the tenth day) had been formerly given to the Dānavas by the scion of the family of the Yadus (i.e. Viṣṇu) for the propitiation of the noble souls.

41-44a. O excellent Brāhmaṇas the following gifts are no better than gifts offered to Asuras : the monetary gift given at the wrong time, the gift to the undeserving, what is given by the angry donor, what is given after dishonouring the recipient, the gift on a Tithi 'pierced by' the previous Tithi; the gift offered by one who is defiled by ucchiṣṭa (leavings of food), what is given unto the fallen ones, what is gifted to the hen-pecked ones, what is given without water offerings and what is offered with subsequent and frequent allusions to it. Hence, O Brāhmaṇas, the Ekādaśī Tithi should not be observed if it is Viddhā (i.e. when Daśamī overlaps it).

44b-46. Just as the paramour of Śūdra woman defiles the previous merits, Śrāddha, charitable gifts, Japas, Homas and holy dips, so also the Pūjā offered to Hari in a Tithi over-lapped by the previous one, undergoes rapid decline like darkness at sunrise. Women proud of their blooming youth and overwhelmed by the fish-bannered Lord (i.e. Kāma or sexual passion) abandon their ageing husbands. So also the learned men should eschew the Tithi that has the Vedha (overlapping). For the enhancement of Dharma they always adopt other Tithis.

CHAPTER THREE

Yama goes to the Region of Brahmā[1]

The sages said :

1. Kindly narrate in detail the rite of propitiating Viṣṇu, whereby he becomes satisfied and bounteously bestows the cherished desire.

2. The Lord of the Universe, the consort of Lakṣmī, is the destroyer of all the vast multitudes of sins. By what rite will he be pleased alongwith all the mobile and immobile creation (which he pervades through his omni-presence).

Sauti said :

3. Hṛṣīkeśa (Viṣṇu) can be captivated by devotion and not by riches. O Ruler of the Earth, Viṣṇu when duly worshipped with devotion, grants all desires.

4. Hence, O Brāhmaṇas, the devotion to the discus-bearing Lord should always be practised. The Lord of the universe worshipped even by ordinary people, shall be the destroyer of distress.

5. Just as a thirsty man immediately derives satisfaction with water, so is the Lord pleased immediately (with activities of devotion). O Brāhmaṇas, in this connection, a mythological narrative that is destructive of sins, is heard.

---

1. It is an interesting introduction to the story of Rukmāṅgada and Mohinī. This chapter emphasizes the efficacy of the *Ekādaśī Vrata* by describing how Yama has to close his Office as all men, being compelled to observe Ekādaśī by Rukmāṅgada, straightway went to Vaikuṇṭha.

6. It is in the course of conversation between Rukmāṅgada and sage Gautama.

There was a king named Rukmāṅgada.[1] He was an Emperor endowed with the quality of patience and forgiveness.

7. He was a beloved devotee of the deity lying in the Milk Ocean (i.e. Viṣṇu). He was devoted to the day of Hari (i.e. Ekādaśī). The Lord of the Earth does not see anyone other than Padmanābha (Viṣṇu), Lord of the Devas.

8-11. On the day of Hari (Ekādaśī), he used to proclaim through his servants by beating a drum kept on an elephant—"If any man (or woman) aged more than eight years and less than eightyfive years takes food on the day of Viṣṇu, that stupid fellow will be punished, killed or banished out of the city, even if it be my father, brother, son, wife or friend. The person who takes food on the day of Padmanābha (i.e. Viṣṇu) will be worthy of being punished like a robber.[2] Give gifts to leading Brāhmaṇas, have your holy dip in the waters of Jāhnavī. Listen to my words and enjoy my kingdom."

12. Thus on every day of Viṣṇu (Ekādaśī day) in the bright half of the month and especially in the dark half also, the king proclaimed thus through the drums with golden coverings.

13. O excellent Brāhmaṇas, when this was announced by the king throughout the land, the pathway leading to Hari's world (Vaikuṇṭha) was thronged by the people going there.

14. All the men who died in the realm of the king (observing Ekādaśī) whether knowingly or through error, went to the abode of Hari.

---

1. Rukmāṅgada the son of Ṛtadhvaja, the King of Vidiśā. He is the hero of this story.

2. Hemādri on *Kāla* (p. 172) quotes these verses with a slight difference, but in *Kālanirṇaya* (p. 257) a different text of the same import is quoted as from the NP. The verse is as follows :

atra Nāradaḥ

aṣṭābdād adhiko martyo hyapūrṇāśīti-hāyanaḥ |
bhuṅkte yo mānavo mohād ekādaśyāṁ sa pāpakṛt ||

15. O Brâhmaṇas, the world of Viṣṇu is definitely attained by men even if they fraudulently observe the rite of Ekādaśī that is destructive of sins.

16. He who takes food on the day of Hari consumes the sin of the whole of the Earth. He who does not eat food on the day of Hari, attains the virtue (religious merit) of the entire Earth.

17. The Smṛti following the Vedas says :
"A Brâhmaṇa should not be killed so also Food should not be taken on the Ekādaśī day in both the fortnights."

18. O excellent Brāhmaṇas, the king, the son of the Sun (i.e. Yama) became embarrassed. Citragupta[1] had ample rest in his writing activity.

19. Everything that had been written by him based on the activities of the previous births was erased and struck off by him (since) the men instantaneously went over to Viṣṇu's abode through their holy rites.

20. All the hells became devoid of sinful creatures. The pathway leading to Yama's world became scorched by the twelve Ādityas and delapidated.

21. All the people went to Hari's region riding on Garuḍa. The worlds of the Devas also became vacant and tenantless.

22. The sacrifices to the Pitṛs and the Devas, pilgrimage to holy centres, charitable gifts and other holy rites became out of vogue. Excepting Ekādaśī, men did not know any other Vrata.

23. When the heaven and the hell became empty, Nārada went to Dharmarāja (Yama) and said :—

Nārada said :

24. "O King, no cry is heard in your court-yard and in the hells. Nothing is being noted down in writing about the evil-doers.

25. This Citragupta[1] is sitting silent like a sage. What is the reason whereby no sinner comes to your abode ?

---

1. Citragupta—the record-keeper of merits and sins of human beings, in Yama's Office.

26-27a. No one engaged in wicked actions comes to your threshold. None in the grip of deception and arrogance comes to your abode."

When these words were uttered by the noble-souled Nārada, Vaivasvata (son of the Sun), the king of the world of Death said with a little disconcertedness :

Yama said :

27b-28. O Nārada, the King who is now ruling over the Earth is a great devotee of Hṛṣīkeśa (Lord Viṣṇu). This leading king instructs the people announcing on the beating of the drum.

29. "Nothing should be eaten, nothing should be eaten at all on the day of Hari. The men who take food shall be liable to punishment."

30-31. Being afraid of him, all the people observe fast on the Ekādaśī day. O excellent sage, those who even fraudulently observe fast on the Ekādaśī day, go to the world of Viṣṇu which is devoid of burning and dissolution (at the end of Kalpa). By resorting to Ekādaśī (Vrata) people go to Hari's palace.

32. O excellent Brāhmaṇa, the paths leading to my world have been made empty by that king now. The hells as well as the worlds of heaven-dwellers have been made vacant by him.

33. The writers (Yama's accountants of deeds of men) are taking rest. O excellent Brāhmaṇa, what has been already written is erased and written off, thanks to the greatness of the fast on the Ekādaśī day.

34. O Brāhmaṇa, without experiencing the fruits of Brāhmaṇa-slaughter and other sins, people go to Hari's mansion by observing fast on the day of Viṣṇu.

35. O great sage, I have become one resembling a wooden deer. I am like a person devoid of eyes and ears, like a Brāhmaṇa who has eschewed Sandhyā prayers.

36. I am like a hen-pecked husband, or like an impotent husband of a youthful woman. I have abandoned all desire for such a post of guardianship of the world.

37-38a. I shall now go to the region of Brahmā to report to him about my misery. If an employee who is to abide by the behest of his master does not work actively but goes on eating the wealth of his master, he shall certainly go to hell.

Sauti said :

38b-41. O Brāhmaṇas, after saying this, Yama went to the abode of Virañci (god Brahmā) accompanied by Nārada and followed by Citragupta. He beheld there seated the great-grand-father of all, surrounded by both embodied and bodiless people—Brahmā the seed of the universe, the support of the universe, the self-born deity, the abode of all living beings. He was free from sin, and was designated as Oṁkāra. He is Śuci (pure) and Śucipada (of pure region). Brahmā, the Supreme Soul (Haṁsa) holding Kuśa grass was being worshipped by the different guardians of the quarters and rulers of the worlds.

42-47. He was being served by all these (in person) : viz —the Epics, Purāṇas and Vedas in their embodied forms; he was served by the oceans, the rivers and the lakes that had assumed bodily forms; the trees such as the holy fig tree and others served him by taking up human bodies; so also the tanks, wells, lakes, mountains, days and nights, fortnights, months, years, Kalās, Kāṣṭhās and Nimeṣas (units of time), seasons, transits of the suns, Yugas, Manvantaras, Kalpas, closing and opening of the eyelids (the smallert unit of time) constellations, Yogas (combinations) Karaṇas (astronomical divisions), full-moon days, declines of the moon, new-moon days, Dvandvas (i.e. mutually clashing opposites such as happiness and misery, profits and loss, success and failures, truth and falsehood—all these were serving the deity. The Lord of the Devas, the sanctifier of righteousness, was surrounded by them. He was being served by persons who knew the holy rites and who were befitting him. The grandfather was being served by Sattva, Rajas. and Tamas Guṇas.

48-50. The lord was served and surrounded by the emotions such as Śānta, (calm), Mūḍha (confused) and Atighora (exceedingly terrible); by the wind, phlegm and bile (the humours), by the embodied Ātaṅka (agony) etc. and by Ānanda bliss; the soul of the universe had recourse to the greatest Dharma; the creator of the worlds himself was surrounded by other living beings not mentioned here; he was being served by the embodiments of evil words and harsh statements etc. Yama the son of the Sun, entered the place amidst them like a bashful bride.

51-55. With his head bent down and glance directed beneath to the floor, he appeared before them. On seeing Yama entering alongwith Nārada and his Kāyastha (accountant i.e. Citragupta) the people there were surprised. With surprised looks they spoke to one another—"Why ? How comes it to be that Bhāskari (son of the Sun i.e. Yama) has come here to see the Creator and the grand-sire of the worlds ? This son of Sun never remains inactive even for a moment. He is always active. Then how is it that he has come now. I hope everything is all right with the heaven-dwellers. I consider this as the wonder of wonders, that the clerk (Chitragupta) has come with his (writing) cloth completely erased and clean. He is full of great distress. No person who performs holy rites has ever erased his cloth. What has never been seen or heard is being seen now."

56-58. O Brāhmaṇa, even as they were speaking mutually thus, the son of Sun (i.e. Yama) who used to chastise all living beings, fell in front of god Brahmā, just like a tree the root of which is cut. He cried aloud "O save me, O save me, O Lord of the Devas, I have been overwhelmed and oppressed since my writing cloth has been erased clean. While you are my Lord, O Lotus-seated one, I find myself distressed." O excellent Brāhmaṇas, after saying this he became unconscious, motionless.

59-61. Then a tumultuous commotion arose in the assembly, "He who makes all the worlds consisting of the mobile and immobile beings, is himself distressed and is crying. Why is Yama, the son of the Sun, crying? Or this common saying seems to be a statement of truth—the saying "He who distresses the people ere long is distressed himself. No man who commits an evil action ever attains auspicious results."

62-64. Thereafter, knowing the view of god Brahmā, Vāyu the Wind-god, silenced the talk of those people of the same mind (i.e. holding the same opinion regarding Yama and his arrival there) The liberal-minded Vāyu raised Yama slowly with his brawny well-developed hands. He placed him on a seat even as he was agitated and was about to run away. He spoke to Yama the son of Sun, having the Ethereal form and accompanied by his Kāyastha (Accounts-clerk Citragupta).

65-67. "By whom have you been attacked? By whom have you been displaced and banished? By whom has your cloth (record) of the world, the divine cloth, been erased? Speak out everything completely. Or may this god Brahmā say? O dear one, he who is the lord of all, shall grant you the uplift. O son of Mārtaṇḍa (Sun), he will remove all the misery in your heart."

68. On being addressed thus by the Windgod, Yama, the son of the Lord of Day (the Sun), looked to the face of Nārada, the son of Brahmā and slowly uttered the following words in a voice choked with tears.

CHAPTER FOUR

An Appeal by Yama

Yama said :

1. O Lord Pitāmaha, Grandsire of the world, listen to my words. O Lord, humiliation of one's exploits is worse than death.

2. O lotus-born deity, he who is devoid of selfish motives and desire, and does not carry out his appointed task, falls into hell which is like a blind well.

3. O lotus-seated one, the employee who does not implement the direction, but continues to consume the wealth of his master, shall be a worm in the decaying wood.

4. The employee who, out of greed, consumes (i.e. misappropriates) the wealth of the common subjects or the king falls into hell for a period of three hundred Kalpas.

5. He who is interested only in selfish gains and so robs

his master, shall be a slow-witted mouse in the house for three hundred Kalpas.

6. The employee who, enjoying himself in his house, shirks his own work and compels the king's servants to do his work also, shall take the birth of a cat.

7-8a. O Lord ! It is at your behest that after due consultation with sages and texts on DharmaŚāstra that I had been administering justice and governing the subjects commending the merit of the meritorious and condemning the sin of the sinners.

8b-9. Since the beginning of the present Kalpa so long as it is your day, I can carry out my duties by dint of your command. But today I have been defeated (and overpowered) in my work by King Rukmāṅgada.[1]

10. O Lord of the Universe, afraid of that king, the entire ocean-girt Earth does not eat anything on the day of Viṣṇu (the Ekādaśī day) that is destructive of all sins.

11. People eschew all holy rites; they abandon the worship of Pitṛs, they do not worship Devas, they neglect pilgrimages, holy ablutions and other good rites.

12. O bestower of honour, they eschew both the systems of philosophy—Yoga and Sāṅkhya. They neglect the perfect knowledge and the knowable; they abandon self study of Vedas and the performance of Homas; (over and above all these) they commit many number of sins.

13-15a. Still they go to the region of Viṣṇu by observing fast on the day of Hari. They go to the world of Viṣṇu alongwith their fathers and grandfathers. Their fathers and father's fathers, mother's fathers, their fathers and their ancestors—all these go to the world of Viṣṇu.

15b-19. O Lord, this is the misery that cuts me to the quick wiping off my writings (i.e. decrees), the fathers of their beloved ones go to the abode of Viṣṇu (?). A man is born of the seed of his ancestors, he is held in the belly of the bearer (woman). He who commits any sin, has to experience the fruits

1. VV. 9-25 a: This is another way of describing the glory and efficacy of the *Ekādaśī Vrata*.

continues to abide by the holy rite of Ekādaśī, O Lord of Devas, this beloved devotee of Viṣṇu will take the entire world to the region of Viṣṇu free from ailments.

8b-9. This staff of justice and this cloth (the scroll recording details of acts of omission and commission of men) have been released by your feet (i.e. by you). My incomparable guardianship of the world has been nullified by that king Rukmāṅgada. Blessed is that lady who has borne him.

10. If the son is superior to others in good qualities, he becomes competent to destroy the miseries of his mother. Of what avail is a child that is born, if it brings distress to its mother ?

11. If the son does not harass his enemies like the sun in the month of Jyeṣṭha, the labour pain of the mother has gone in vain. O Lord, she is one having a bad son.

12-13a. That son is called the ailment or diseased part from the mother's womb born on this earth, if his fame does not shine like the lightning among the clouds, the son who does not uplift his father's side through learning or strength.

13b-16. The son who is deprived of virtue, wealth and love, though born on the Earth is only an ailment in the belly of his mother. His life is futile. O Brahmā, there is undoubtedly one heroic mother—the lady from whom is born Rukmāṅgada for the purpose of erasing my writings. Such a thing as this has never been accomplished by any king. O Lord of the Universe, even in the Purāṇas (or even since ancient times) this wiping off of the cloth has not been heard of. Seeing this king adhering to his service to Hari, proclaiming aloud by means of drum and destroying the path leading to my mansion, I cannot continue to be alive.

CHAPTER SIX

God Brahmā's Reply

Brahmā said :

1. What surprising thing has been seen by you ? Why do your feel distressed ? Distress at the good points in others is an agony that lasts till death.

2. O Sauri (Son of the Sun), how does a man not attain the highest region by observing fast on the day of the Lord, the mere utterance of whose name enables one to attain the same ?

3. A single bow offered to Kṛṣṇa is on a par with the sacred final (Avabhṛtha) ablutions in ten horse-sacrifices. Moreover, the person who performs ten horse-sacrifices may be reborn in this Saṁsāra, but the man who makes obeisance to Kṛṣṇa is never reborn.

4. If at the tip of one's tongue the two syllables HARI are present, what has one to do with the holy centres of Kurukṣetra, Kāśī and Vraja ?

5-6. A Brāhmaṇa who indulges in sexual intercourse with a Cāṇḍāla woman, especially during her monthly course, and eats food cooked in spirituous liquor, can eschew heaps of sins accumulated by perpetrating forbidden acts of eating the forbidden food and of cohabiting with a forbidden woman, if he but remembers Hari at the time of death. He (thereby) attains (Sāyujya (complete identity) with Viṣṇu and is liberated from the bondage of worldly existence.

7. If one gets salvation on uttering his name, how is it that he should not get it by observing fast on his day ? He who is sung about in it (fasting period), is the Puruṣottama who becomes contemplated.

8. Even if he were to utter the name of Lord Janārdana sportingly or listens to it, a man acquires equality with the waters of Gaṅgā in regard to sanctity and meritoriousness.

9. Puruṣottama, the Sovereign Lord of the worlds, is the cause of our birth. How can a wicked-minded fellow (like

CHAPTER SEVEN

The statement of Brahmā

Yama submitted :

1-2a. Dear grand-sire, in bowing down at the feet of the Veda, the benefit has been achieved by me. O Lord of the Universe, I shall not go again and join my duties while the king called Rukmāṅgada is ruling over the world.

2b-3. O excellent one among the deities, if when the day of Hari arrives, you are able to shake him from his courageous resolve, I shall be your servant. O Lord, he is my great foe. My cloth (account of merits and sins) has been rubbed (and erased) by him.

4. By making him take his food on the day of Kṛṣṇa (i.e. Ekādaśī), I shall feel as if I have accomplished all my objects like a person who has offered balls of rice to the manes at Gayā.

5. From today onwards, those persons cannot be restrained by me—those persons by whom Hari, the Lord of the Devas, is remembered or eulogised or by whom the fast is undertaken on his day.

6. Those men who burst into ejaculation, even fraudulently, with the word 'Hari', are liberated from the path leading to the mother's womb. They are clever people. They do not enter the sphere of writing on my cloth (of virtue and sins). They are worthy of being bowed down to by the excellent groups of heaven-walkers (i.e. gods).

Sauti said :

7. In connection with the affair (problem) of the son of Vivasvān (i.e. Yama), the Kuśa-emblemed god Brahmā had a desire to do something in his honour. He therefore pondered thus.

8-9. The Lord, adorned by the Bhūtas (living beings) pondered for a moment. The omnipresent Lord thereafter assumed a form that would terrify all living beings. He, thereafter, procreated therein a young woman who fascinated the worlds. That gentle lady, mentally created by him, the most excellent of all beautiful women, appeared splendid.

10-11. Fully bedecked in all ornaments, she stood in front of him. On seeing her fully endowed with the wealth of beauty, he (Brahmā) spoke to his own people who being deluded by lust for her, were ogling at her. Brahmā closed his eyes for fear of committing a sinful offence.

12-13. He who looks with lustful eyes or thinks about with lascivious mind, at one's own mother, or daughter, daughter-in-law or brother's wife, preceptor's wife or the king's wife falls into the terrible hell; by thinking about a Cāṇḍāla woman also, the man falls into a hell.

14. The man who becomes perturbed on seeing these young women, loses all his merits acquired in the course of various births. His merits thus become futile but not otherwise.

15. If he indulges in sexual intercourse with them, ten thousand merits of his are wasted away. As the merit goes on diminishing he becomes more and more sinful and eventually he is born as a rock-rat.

16-17. Hence no intelligent man should think about them or see them with lustful eyes. Once the sons have attained their twelfth year, they must not stroke the feet of even their mother. The mother should not get herself applied with oil over her body by sons who have reached the age of youth then. A clever son may engage his mother whose age is more than sixty, in anointing his body with oil.

18. Whether an old man or a young man, no one shall ask his daughter-in-law to massage his feet. It is proclaimed that both of them will fall into the Raurava hell full of burning coal.

19-20. O king, the daughter-in-law who shows her uncovered limbs to her father-in-law shall be knocked and kicked and will be eaten by worms therein in the hell. The same goal awaits that sinful man who gets his feet cleaned by the hands of his daughter-in-law or makes her bathe him or smear oil over him. In the hell, he shall be eaten by worms with needlelike snouts and black faces, for a period of one full Kalpa.

21. Hence no man shall glance at other's women, or one's own daughter or daughter-in-law with lustful eyes and thoughts. Immediately the man falls or incurs sins.

22-23. It was because he thought over like this that he looked at her, with a subtle, penetrating view-point. It is nothing but a mere skeleton (lit. cage) of bones covered with flesh and skin that appears a face, lofty, circular and splendid. The shining eyes seen present in women comprise suet and flesh.

24. The extremely protruding mass of flesh has been piled up over the breasts. The three folds of skin on the upper part of the belly (which are regarded as a mask of beauty) show lesser (distribution of) flesh.

25. In the buttocks again, more flesh has been stacked. This is the passage for urine. It is a private part, of which the three worlds are enamoured.

26. It is joined with the Apāna wind (i.e. this wind functions there). It is always vile (with bad odour) and contemptible always. More flesh is heaped up than the swollen bellows in the part of the buttocks.

27. Just as a log of wood is sawn into two (half way through), so also is the region of shanks (thighs ?). It (the body) is filled with semen, flesh, bone, fat and marrow. How can it be beautiful ?

28. What is there by way of essence, in the body of men wherein the main constituents are flesh, fat and marrow ? Tell me which man will be enamoured of the body, nourished and grown plump by means of faeces, urine and other dirts.

29. Viriñci (God Brahmā) pondered thus, after seeing everything with his vision of knowledge. He took courage and spoke to that lady whose gait was like that of a female elephant.

30. "O fair-complexioned lady, since you have been created by me mentally you have become a lady of beautiful limbs, competent to madden the minds of men."

31-33a. Then she bowed to the fourfaced God and said : "O Lord, see the entire universe consisting of the mobile and immobile beings deluded and falling unto senselessness. It includes even the Yogins who are totally sinless. O lotus-born deity, keeping you in the beginning (inclusive of you), there is no man in the three worlds who does not get agitated and perturbed on seeing me.

33b-34. Boasting about oneself should not be indulged in by one who wishes for one's own auspicious welfare. Even an extremely pure man falls into hell due to selfpraise. Still, O Brahmā, the glorification or self-praise must be stated to achieve some special end.

35. O Brahmā, indeed, it must be to make some one excited and perturbed that I have been created by you. O Lord of the Universe, command me. Mention who he is. I shall definitely make him excited.

36-37. O Lord, on seeing me even a mountain becomes infatuated. What then of an ordinary man endowed with consciousness who inhales and exhales ? The description of the powerful impact of a woman's glance is described in the Purāṇas. It causes madness in men and is destructive of all holy vows and rites difficult to be observed.

38. Till then the man treads the path of the good, till then the man has perfect control over his sense organs, till then he retains his humility and sense of shame, till the shaft-like glances of dalliance-minded damsels pierce his heart and destroy his fortitude. The shafts that are discharged from the well-drawn bow of the eye-brow, the eyes having blue lashes, reach up to the ears.[1]

39. Fie upon the poetry of that stupid ill-informed poet who equates the face of a lady to the moon. Is there any of these in the moon—viz. the knitting of the eyebrow, the side-glances expressing the wounding look, fury, pleasure and laughter ?

40. O Lord, only when it is drunk does the spirituous liquor cause delusion in the mind of a clever man. But a youthful maiden excites delusion even when she is seen or remembered by a man. So she is more powerful than the spirituous liquor.

41. O great grand sire of the world I have been created

1. Just as an archer bends his bow stretching the bow-string up to his ear and discharges the arrow which pierces the heart of the enemy, the shaft-like glances are discharged from the bow-like bent eye-brows of women with blue eye-lashes—eyes which are long upto the ears. Such longish eyes were traditionally regarded beautiful.

by you for fascinating men. Command me. Who is it ? I shall enchant even the three worlds.

Brahmā said :

42. O Lady with thighs like the trunk of an elephant, O fortunate one with the gait like that of an elephant in rut, the truth has been expressed by you. There is nothing that cannot be achieved by you in the three worlds.

43. O fair-complexioned lady, you are defiling even my mind also although I control and steady it by means of the goad of perfect knowledge.

44. Such being your charm how then will you not captivate the minds of people ? O large-eyed lady, truly your beauty of form is seductive.

45. I find that the entire Universe including the immortal being, is motionless. O excellent-faced lady, achieve that for which you have been created.

46. O auspicious lady, on the earth, in the city of Vidiśā[1] there is a king named Rukmāṅgada whose wife Sandhyāvalī is comparable to you in beauty.[2]

47. His son Dharmāṅgada was born of her. The son surpasses the father. He is endowed with the strength of a hundred elephants. He is like the sun in exploits.

48-52. In forbearance he is equal to the Earth; in profundity he is comparable to the ocean; like the fire, he shines with his brilliance, he is comparable to Vaivasvata Yama, God of Death in fury; he is like Bali in munificence; he is comparable to the wind god in mobility; in gentleness he is equal to the moon; he is as handsome as Manmatha the god of love; the prince is equal to Jīva (Bṛhaspati) and Bhārgava

1. A few years back (under the British) it was called Bhilsa. Now its old name Vidiśā has been adopted. In the NP. here and in the *Devī Purāṇa* (Ch. 76) it is called Vidiśā.

2. VV. 46-73 contain instructions and guidance given by god Brahmā to Mohini how to make king Rukmāṅgada break his Ekādaśī Vrata and thereby make people go to the region of Yama. This plot in a nutshell is developed in details in subsequent chapters. The denouement is very interesting.

(Śukra) (preceptors of Devas and Daityas) in statesmanship. O fair-faced lady, the entire Jambūdvīpa alone is enjoyed by his father (Rukmāṅgada). But the other Dvīpas (continents) are conquered by Dharmāṅgada. He has not yet known the thrill of a contact with a youthful maiden due to his bashfulness. Thousands of women come to him of their own accord but they are avoided by him. He does not move astray from his pledged word.

53. O fortunate lady with sweet smiles, in his father's house three hundred mothers look upon him equally without any difference in their affection, O lady with gold-like complexion !

54. O woman of beautiful limbs ! On the excellent mount Mandara, approach the King to whom Dharma is of prominent importance and who is adorned with the jewel of a son.

55. The king carried away to that place by his horse will stay there enamoured of your song, O woman of beautiful limbs, even leaving off his horse.

56-57. Climbing on to the top of the mountain he will come into contact with you. On meeting the king there, O gentle lady, you must say thus :— O king, undoubtedly, I will become your wife. But O lord, whatever I say must be definitely carried out by you.

58-62. Enamoured of your beauty the king will promise it to you. Thereupon, after a few days have elapsed you shall hold him by the right hand with imprecations. O woman of lovely eyebrows and charming limbs, when the king appears to be rapturously eager for cohabitation with you, you shall laughingly remind the king of his earlier words : "O King, you have sworn that you will abide by my word. Hence, O king, keep your promise. I think the time has now come for the same." When this is said by you, the king will certainly say thus on account of the high value and importance of the promise. "There is no doubt about it, I shall keep it. Tell me what shall I give you?" When he replies thus, O auspicious fair-faced lady, Rukmāṅgada, the king and father of Dharmāṅgada must be addressed thus by you.

63-68a. "Never should the fast be observed on the Ekādaśī day of Hari. O my darling, your fast is a hindrance to my sexual intercourse with you. He who does not attend to his own wife who is charming and who is endowed with youthful virility, he who expects another opportunity (i.e. he who postpones) is a man of wicked actions. Certainly, he goes to hell. Due to your fasting, I am abandoned by you for three nights. But actually I am incapable of staying even a moment without you. When the time of Śrāddha has come and the Brāhmaṇas sit and wait (for the performance), if the wife solicits the husband for cohabitation, she must be enjoyed at the very same time."

O woman of sweet limbs, even after being urged thus, if the king does not carry out your request, you shall say thus thereafter :

68b-69. "O King if you do not abandon your fast on the day of Hari, cut off the head of your own son Dharmāṅgada with an excellent sword, and place it on my lap.

70. O king if you do not carry out this loving wish of mine, you shall become deficient in virtue, merits and you will undoubtedly fall into hell."

71-72. O excellent lady, if, on hearing your words, he does not injure his son who is like his own vital breath unto him, he shall pay heed to the advice of the Brāhmaṇas and shall take food on the day of Ekādaśī. Thereupon, the people will go near Yama as before after being tied with ropes by the attendants. Taking the writing (of Chitragupta) as authority, there will be persons occupying hell. Thus what you do will be splendid.

73. Or if the glorious king, abiding by the promise, really kills his son he will go to the region of Padmanābha, that is worthy of being worshipped by the immortal beings wholly.

CHAPTER EIGHT

The description of Mount Mandara

Sauti said :

1. On hearing the words of Brahmā, that lotus-eyed woman said—"Give a name unto me with which I should go to Mandara mountain.

2. O Lord of the Universe, children must be named by the father. The name is said to be destructive of sins. O Kuśa-emblemed God, kindly do so."

Brahmā said :

3. Since, O beautiful woman, the entire universe is enchanted by you. O gentle lady, Mohinī (enchantress) as your name shall be true to your attributes.

4. O woman of lovely eyebrows, if he comes into a pleasure-giving contact with you, thanks to a clear vision of yours, he will have to experience all the ten states of a love-lorn lover).

5. On being thus commanded, the fair lady bowed down to the lotus-seated deity and set off to the mountain Mandara wistfully gazed at on the way by the immortal ones (gods).

6. By the third Muhūrta (one Muhurta— = 48 minutes) she reached the summit of the mountain. It had been impossible for Vāsuki to go round it once (i.e. to encircle it bodily).[1]

7. It was this mountain that was formerly lifted up by Hari (in the form of Divine Tortoise) and used for churning (the milk ocean) by the Devas and Dānavas. Sindhu (the ocean) which extends to six hundred thousand Yojanas is the deep pit made by this mountain.

---

1. This refers to the churning of the ocean by gods and demons for attaining nectar. Mount Mandara was used as the churning rod and serpent Vāsuki as the string to wind round it for churning (Mbh-*Adi*-Ch.18). The Mbh. regards mount Mandara of the Himalayan range as the real Mandara. The claim of a hill 30 miles to the south of Bhagalpur in Bhagalpur district, with grooves of artificial chiselling to indicate the impression of the coils of a serpent, disqualifies its claim of being the real Mandara—De. 124-125.

8. This great mountain was not broken even when it rubbed against the physical body of the Divine Tortoise. O leading king, when it fell into the ocean all the hidden parts of the ocean were exposed by this mountain.

9. O Brāhmaṇas, water gushed out from this mountain went up through the path of the Brahmāṇḍa (Cosmic Egg). Great fire was generated by this mountain due to attrition when it came into contact with the bony shell of the (Divine) Tortoise.

10. It is on this mountain that Lord Digambara (naked deity i.e. Śiva) resides along with his goblins, but, O exellent Brāhmaṇas, he is not visible either to the Devas or to the Dānavas.

11. It was for a great period of time viz. ten thousand years that this mountain ground and rubbed the armlets of the discus-bearing Lord.[1]

12. This is a veritable mansion of jewels equipped with many kinds of minerals.

13. It is the sporting ground of the heaven-dwellers; it is the place for penance of the sages, it enhances the zest of the divine maidens for sexual dalliance; this great mountain is the source of jewels and medicinal herbs.

14. Its girth at the root is ten thousand Yojanas, its width at the top is also that much. With the length too being as many Yojanas, it rises up as the measuring rod of the three world.

15. It illuminates the surface of the Earth and the sky by means of its golden peaks full of jewels and gems. On reaching it the son of Kaśyapa (i.e. Sun) loses his splendour. He becomes devoid of rays.

16-17. The lady of golden splendour reached the Mandara mountain whose parts are the abodes of gold (ingots). Endowed with her own splendour she made the mountain Mandara the destroyer of the brilliance of the sun, (i.e. surpass it)

---

1. The description of the churning for *Amṛta* differs slightly in the Mbh and other Purāṇas in minor details. But the object of the NP. here is to describe the glory of mount Mandara and not the churning of the nectar.

with her own lustre. For the purpose of exciting the lustful passion of the king, she sat on the rocky surface of the mountain that extended to seven Yojanas and that had a divine bluish splendour.

18. O leading king,[1] there stands on that rocky surface an adamantine Liṅga, ten Hastas in height as well as in girth.

19. It is famous by the name of Vṛṣaliṅga. It appeared like a great palace among the clouds. O excellent Brāhmaṇas that girl gave a sweet and excellent performance of music.

20. That charming lady sat near that Liṅga and played on the strings of the lute beating time harmoniously. Her songs were exquisitely destructive of tedium.

21-22. It had the Mūrcchanā (the regulated rise and fall of sounds) and the Tāla (beating time). It had the Gandhāra note in its composition. O leading king (?), when the song that heightened passionate love flowed forth from her like this, O leading sages, even the immobile beings began to desire it. Neither divine nor non-divine music had ever been like that before.

23-24. On hearing that sweet note flowing out of the mouth of Mohinī, the note that enchanted all living beings, Lord Śiva became lustful and wanted to enjoy her in that very form of Digambara (nakedness). But, on being seen by Pārvatī he felt ashamed.

---

1. We are to suppose that the words of address 'O king' in such contexts, are addressed to King Māndhātā by Vasiṣṭha.

CHAPTER NINE

A dialogue between Rukmāṅgada and Dharmāṅgada

Sauti said :

1-3. O Brāhmaṇas, the leading king Rukmāṅgada enjoyed all human pleasure. In diverse ways he worshipped the yellow-robed Lord Hari. He had already placed his feet on the heads of his enemies who dared to fight him. By making the pathway leading to Yama's land empty he conquered Yama, the son of Vivasvat (Sun). He made the path of Viṣṇu's world thronged with human beings. At the proper time, he called his son Dharmāṅgada and spoke thus :

4. "O son, protect this earth full of wealth all round, with your own might. Be firmly resolved in your own duties.

5. If the father does not hand over the kingdom when the son has become competent, there is no doubt in this that his merits and fame perish.

6. The father who does not feel happiness, thanks to his efficient son, must be certainly known as the greatest sinner in the three worlds.

7. The son who, after becoming strong enough to do so, does not take up the burden of his father, is no better than the excrement of his mother. He is a two-tongued serpent devoid of poison.

8. He is the real son who becomes more famous than the father on this Earth and illuminates the places like the sun with his rays.

9. If the father keeps awake during the night due to the sorrow resulting from the misdemeanour of the son, the son stays in hell till the final dissolution of all living beings.

10. He who honours the words of his father and carries out his behests in the house, attains Sāyujya with the deity, while he will be eulogised by the gods stationed in the heaven.

11. O son, as for me, I have been attracted by holy actions in the world for the sake of subjects. Stationed

31. After realising this, the Garuḍa-emblemed Lord (i.e. Viṣṇu) should be remembered by you all. Janārdana is to be worshipped by you after dedicating the fruit thereof to the Brahman.

32. You must eschew the sense of my-ness, and the feeling of possessiveness). You must worship in the manner laid down for your caste. Thereby, you will gain everlasting worlds. There is no doubt about this.

33. O subjects, something in addition to the path of my father has been pointed out to you, since you will be endowed with the rite of dedicating the fruit to the Brahman. May all of you be adapts in perfect knowledge.

34. You must not take food on the day of Hari. This is the permanent path in accordance with the injunction of my father. A special additional thing has been mentioned to you by me viz. abidance in the Brahman.

35. This adherence to the Brahman is to be practised by persons who know the truth. It is rare to be achieved. There is no return therefrom. As for the observance of the fast, the stipulation is that it must be observed necessarily."

36. Dharmāṅgada had no rest or sleep by day or at night. He spent his day in consoling and cajolling his subjects again and again.

37. He used to tour everywhere, through his heroic valour. He weeded the earth of all the thorns (undesirable elements). The following loud proclamation used to be announced daily with the beating of drums placed on the heads of elephants :

38-41. "O people of the world, may Hari the Lord of the Devas, be contemplated while engaged in the threefold activities (?) Refrain from taking food on the Dvādaśī day; be free from the feeling of possessiveness. The Lord partakes of oblation offered to gods and manes. He alone is the Supreme person. The Lord of the worlds is to be remembered in the Sun, in the Kṛśākāśa (in the minutest of Ethereal space) and in the Visarga (subsidiary creation) by all men who are desirous of accomplishing virtue, love and wealth. Worship of Viṣṇu has been enjoined among the duties of one's

CHAPTER TEN

The dialogue between Rukmāṅgada and Vāmadeva

Vasiṣṭha continued :

1-2. On hearing the words of her husband, the wide-eyed lady said : "O king, the truth has been spoken by you. O leading king, just as the sages say, there cannot be a greater happiness than that of a son. In this world it is equal to that of the greatest being named Viṣṇu.

3-4. The burden of responsibility arising out of the administration of the seven continents has been placed on the son by you. Abstaining from the violence to the deer, worship Janārdana by means of sacrifices; abandon desire for worldly pleasures; serve the celestial river; this is the proper and justifiable course of life to you but not the killing of the deer.

5. O king, resorting to worldly pleasures by fathers having grown up sons is like leaving the amorous marks with the nail on the breasts of an old woman.

6. O ruler of the Earth, worship Lord Hṛṣīkeśa (Viṣṇu) in the house. It is not proper on your part to kill innocent herds of deer.

7-8a. Non-violence has been glorified as the greatest virtue in the Purāṇas. One who maintains himself through violence pursues holy rites in vain. He who follows the path of violence does not gain anything, even if he follows the righteous path. O king, good men do not enjoy those things polluted and hurt by others.

8b. Violence to living beings is said to be of six types, O king.

9. The first man responsible for violence is the person who approves of it; the second one is the actual killer; the third one is the person who believes in it (who has faith in it) ; the fourth man (guilty) of violence is he who eats (the meat) ; the fifth man is the person who cooks and O king the sixth one is the person who is a participant in it. Learned men know the Dharma connected with violence is Adharma.

10. O king, a father who resorts to Dharma and who has become old in àge, does not commit sins after entrusting the burden to the son.

11. Eschew the emotional feeling connected with the violence done to the deer. O king, hundreds of kings addicted to the vice of hunting deer have perished.

12-13. Hence I consider the act of striking down deer as wickedness. Excellent deep sympathy and mercy towards deer is seen in the righteous kings. It is with the earnest desire for your welfare that you are being prevented by me." To his wife who repeatedly urged thus, the king spoke these words :

14. O gentle lady, I do not wish to hurt or kill the deer. Under the pretext of hunting deer, I will wander in the forest weeding out thorns (undesirable element) with the bow kept ready in the hand.

15. May my son be among the people, O fairfaced lady, and may I be in the forest. The subjects must be protected from both the beasts of prey and the robbers, by the king.

16. O auspicious lady, the subjects must be protected by oneself or through one's son. The king who does not protect his subjects faces downfall, though he may be virtuous or religious.

17-20. O beloved lady, it is with the protection of people in view that I will be going to the forest. I am devoid of false emotions and feelings. After saying this to her, the king climbed on to an excellent horse like the sun on the peak of the Meru mountain. The horse was defectless, lustrous like the moon, and was as it were the ornament unto the Earth. It was like the celestial horse Uccaiḥśravas in respect of its beauty; it was like the Wind God in its speed. Paying respect to the Earth the king offered his right hand (?) which had given gifts of thousands and crores, which used to press and rub the breasts of beautiful ladies, which had the shape and appearance of the tender sprouts of the Aśoka tree and which bore the marks of a thunderbolt and goad.

21. The ruler of the Earth set off on his journey making the ground quake (beneath him). The excellent king passing many lands reached the forest.

22. Elephants, horses and chariots were shaken off due to the velocity of the horse. The foot soldiers fell unconscious on the surface of the Earth.

23. O king, after traversing hundred and eight Yojanas (one Yojana = 12 kms.) that king all at once reached the great Āśrama (hermitage) of the sages.

24-27. He entered the beautiful hermitage abounding in trees such as clusters of plantain trees, Aśoka, Bakula Mimusops Elengi), Punnāga (nut-meg), Sarala (pine trees), Mātuliṅga (citron trees), Kapittha (feronia elephantum), date palms, jack trees, [coconut palms, palmyra, Ketakas, Sinduvāraṣ, Sandalwoods, Tamālas (Xanthochymus epictorius), Pippalas, Campakas, Areca palms, Dāḍimas (pomegranates), thousands of embylic myrobalans, margoas trees, mango trees, Lodhras (a tree with red-white flowers) and many other trees full of ripe fruits. They bent down due to the weight of fruits and many birds perched on them.

28-29. Sweet smelling wind gently blew, wafting the fragrance of the flowers. Searching for the sages therein the king saw Vāmadeva[1], the most excellent Brāhmaṇa who had the lustre of fire and who was surrounded by many disciples. On seeing him the king got down from his horse and bowed to him with great respect.

30. The king was honoured and greeted with Arghya and other things by that sage. Sitting on the Kuśa grass seat he said in a delighted tone :-

31. "On seeing today the lotus-like feet of yours who are ever engrossed in deep meditation, my sins have been eliminated and fruition of my meritorious deeds has been achieved."

32. On hearing the words of king Rukmāṅgada, sage Vāmadeva rejoiced much. After enquiring about his health and welfare he said thus:

---

1. This is not the Vedic seer Vāmadeva but some other sage of the same name. A number of sages of this name are mentioned in the *Mbh.* (*Sabhā.* 7. 17, *Vana.* 192. 43 H, *Śānti.* 92-94) and *VR.* (I. 7. 4. II. 67. 3 etc.)

33. O highly blessed king, my hermitage visited by you, a highly meritorious devotee of Viṣṇu, has become the most sanctified on the surface of the Earth.

34. Which other king on the Earth can attain equality with you by whom Yama has been vanquished and the path leading to his abode has been broken.

35. O king, by compelling them to observe fast on the Dvādaśī day that is destructive of sins, the entire world has been led to the imperishable region of Vaikuṇṭha.

36. After controlling and restraining the subjects on the surface of the Earth soundly through the four splendid Upāyas (means of success, viz. Sāman, dāna, daṇḍa, bheda) they have been led to the region of the slayer of Madhu (i.e. of Viṣṇu) whether they abide by their duties or carry on the duties of others.

37-38. O king, you have come within our view and we had been desirous of seeing you. O king, even a Cāṇḍāla who is a devotee of Viṣṇu is superior to a Brāhmaṇa. Even a Brāhmaṇa devoid of devotion to Viṣṇu is inferior to a Cāṇḍāla. O king, rare indeed are those kings who are devoted to Viṣṇu on the surface of this Earth.

39-40. No king who is not a devotee of Viṣṇu can be the person who embellishes the glory and splendour of the Earth. If the king is not devoted to Hari but is devoted to other Deities, that king is like a woman who has abandoned her husband and is attached to her paramour. Certainly this kind of adverse behaviour affects that king.

41-43a. His behaviour will be contrary to virtue, wealth, love, intelligence and salvation.

Hence, the worship of Viṣṇu that is reasonably laid down has been performed by you. Hence, O king, you are blessed. We too are blessed since we have seen you.

Even as Vāmadeva spoke thus to him, the excellent king, naturally endowed with humility bowed down humbly and said :

43b-45. O excellent Brāhmaṇa, I crave your forgiveness, O holy Lord, I am not like this. O Brāhmaṇa, I am not equal to even the dust of your feet. Never can even the Devas be superior to Brāhmaṇas. A creature (i.e. the individual soul) becomes devoted to Mādhava through the Brāhmaṇas who are satisfied. If they are furious he becomes worthy of being hated (by Mādhava). This is the truth that has been stated by me.

46. Vāmadeva then asked him— Tell me. What shall I give you? O king, there is nothing that cannot be given to you who have come to my house as my guest now.

47. O king, if he gives anything on the earth, it must be that which is the most pleasing to him like the announcement through drums on the day of Viṣṇu which prevents people from taking food.

48. The king thereupon joined his palms in reverence and said to him— I have achieved everything by the sight of the pair of your feet.

49. O Brāhmaṇa, I have a doubt that has persisted for a long time. I am asking you the same since you are a leading Brāhmaṇa, who dispel all doubts.

50. By what meritorious deed has my wife become the most beautiful lady in the three worlds. She looks upon me as though I am superior to Manmatha.

51. Wherever the fair-complexioned gentle lady sets her foot, the earth reveals its great treasures.

52. Her limbs are devoid of the symptoms of old age. There are neither wrinkles nor greying hairs. O excellent sage, she shines always like the lustre of the autumnal moon.

53. O Brāhmaṇa, even without fire she prepares dishes of six tastes. Crores of men take their meal out of the little quantity of food that she cooks.

54. She is a chaste woman. She is by nature munificent; she causes happiness to all living beings. O Brāhmaṇa, disrespect is not expressed by her through words even when she is asleep.

55. My son who is born of her abides by my behest always. O excellent one among the leading Brāhmaṇa, on the surface of this earth, I am the only one who have a son in the sense of the term.

56. My son is a great devotee of his father. He surpasses me by means of his attributes. It is well known

on the surface of the Earth that I am only the ruler of a single continent.

57-58a. My son has surpassed me in this respect as he is the protector of all the seven continents. O leading Brāhmaṇa, for my sake, the princess well-known by the name of Vidyullekhā, had been brought by him after conquering many kings in the battlefield.

58b-59a. In the course of six months that Lord equipped with the wealth of beauty conquered those kings and made them stripped of their weapons.

59b-60. He went to the realm of damsels and conquered them in the battle. He brought eight excellent ladies from among them with force and presented them to me with repeated obeisances.

61. Urged by his mother, my son brought and handed over to me the divine and exquisite garments and jewels on the surface of the Earth.

62. Within a day he takes a round of many Yojanas over the Earth and returns to me by nightfall for the purpose of massaging my feet.

63. After massaging my feet, he stands at the threshold at midnight with his coat of mail on. He wakens and pulls up the attendants and servants who are overwhelmed by drowsiness.

64. That is why, O excellent sage, this physical body of mine is free from sickness and ailments. My happiness is immeasurable. My beloved in the house is fully subservient to me.

65. I have numerous horses and elephants. The food-grains and riches I possess are infinite. All the people on the Earth obey my behests.

66. My present happiness is infinite. What is that meritorious action thanks to the power of which I possess it? Is it what has been performed in the course of this birth or the previous one?

67-68. O Brāhmaṇa, recount to me about my merit after pondering over it in your mind. There is no ailment in the body; the beloved wife is submissive; there is affluence in the house, devotion to Hari and reverence to scholars as well as capacity to give liberally to the Brāhmaṇas. I consider this as originating from my merits.

CHAPTER ELEVAN

Rukmāṅgada meets Mohinī

Vasiṣṭha said :

1. On hearing the words of the king, the excellent sage of sound and perfect knowledge thought for a moment. He understood its real cause and said thus :—

Vāmadeva said :

2. O king, formerly you were born of the Śūdra caste.[1] You were oppressed by poverty and harassed by a wicked wife.

3. You sustained yourself by serving others and receiving wages. O king, thus you continued to live for many years, distressed due to misery.

4-5. Thanks to your coming into contact with some Brāhmaṇas, once, your honour went on a pilgrimage to holy centres. O king, after going over all holy centres you reached the holy centre Mathurā and became interested in serving Brāhmaṇas. There, in the company of Brāhmaṇas, you took bath in the waters of the Yamunā.

6-8. At the holy centre named Viśrānti which is the most excellent of all holy centres, in the temple of the Divine

1. The motif of re-birth as an explanation of events in the present birth has been very popular in ancient and mediaeval Indian literature. The soul-denying Buddhists have extensively used it in Jātaka tales on the authority of the Buddha. Jainas used it widely in their Sanskrit-Prākrit-Apabhraṁśa narrative literature. Brahmanical Purāṇas are no exception. The NP. used it in Part-I Chs. 20, 23 with reference to *Viṣṇu Vratas*. Here too the same device is used to explain the exceptional luck of Rukmāṅgada.

Boar (Varāha), O king you heard the Puranic story being recounted. The holy rite of Aśūnya Sayana,* was being explained. As the Vrata is to be observed for four months on the 2nd tithi of the dark half of each month from Śrāvaṇa onwards, there are, for the completion of the Vrata four pāraṇās—one breaking of fast per month. Hence for its conclusion there are four Pāraṇās (breaking of the fasts). By its observance the Lord of the Devas, Hari, with the lustrous complexion like the cloud who is the Lord of the worlds and the consort of goddess Lakṣmī and the destroyer of all sins, is pleased.

9. Coming again to the temple that holy rite was performed by your honour. This observance called Aśūnya-śayana (non-vacant bed) is highly conducive to prosperity at home.

10-11a. If any one continues the life of a house-holder without observing this rite that destroys sins, O great king, his life is rendered fruitless like that of a barren woman. It appears to me that a happiness of this sort is very rare.

11b. O king, this holy rite must be undertaken on the Dvitīyā day** in the month of Śrāvaṇa. It is destructive of rebirths, death and old age.

12. O king, on this day the Lord of the Universe should be worshipped in the company of Lakṣmī with fruits, flowers, incense, sweet-smelling red unguents, charitable gifts of beds and clothes as well as by feeding Brāhmaṇas.

13. O king, everything of this Vrata has been performed by you though they were difficult. O king, this is the full fruition of the same holy rite called Aśūnya. Listen to the other sacred rites mentioned (or observed) by you in detail.

14. It is certain that these results will not have taken place, if the Lord of the Universe had been displeased. The Lord of the Devas had been worshipped by you in the previous birth through the observance of Aśunya rite.

---

*(Formerly this was mentioned as *Aśoka Śayana, vide supra* I.111.13.

**In the region of the author of the NP a month is *Pūrṇimānta*. Hence the word 'dark half' is not probably used.

15. O leading king, in this birth, you are worshipping Hari by means of the holy rite of Dvādaśī. Surely you will attain the identity with Viṣṇu.

16. O king, thus your enquiry of auspicious nature has been explained by me regarding the origin of your affluence and leading to prosperity of your kinsmen.

17. O king, what else shall I give you or do for you? By all means you are worthy of everything, as you are a devotee of Janārdana.

The king submitted :—

18. O excellent Brāhmaṇa, I am eagerly desirous of visiting the Mandara mountain. With your permission, I wish to see the various miraculous things there.

19-20. O excellent Brāhmaṇa, after transferring the weighty burden of administering the kingdom that other kings find unbearable, to my son, I have become light (less burdened). I am free to roam about as I please. My duty will be looked after by my son. On hearing the words of the king, Vāmadeva spoke thus :

21. O prominent king, this is the highest duty of the son that he should always extricate his father from distress, out of affection.

22. He who carries out the order of his father to the best of his mental, verbal and physical capacity, shall derive the benefit of having a holy dip in Gaṅgā every day.

23. It is heard mentioned in the Vedic text that if the son goes to Gaṅgā for a holy dip against the expressed desire of his father, he will not attain the usual purity and sanctity.

24. O king, you are contented and blessed. Go as you please. Thanks to the favour of Hari, a meritorious son has been born in your family.

25. After this had been spoken by the sage, the glorious king mounted his horse and rode swiftly like the Wind God himself.

26-27a. Looking at and observing all the mountains, forests, rivers and the wonderful lakes and parks, the king ere long reached the mountain Mandara.

27b-28a. On his way he went round the white mountain 'Gandhamādana',[1] crossed the Mahāmeru and saw the northern Kurus.

28b-30. He reached the Mandara mountain refulgent with the splendour of a hundred suns and covered in gold all round. On being rubbed with the hands of Hari it had generated liquid gold. The whole region there was full of trees and decorated with many metals and minerals. With many fountains over it, it was embellished with many caves. It was full of ten thousand rivers and was washed by the auspicious waters of the river Gaṅgā.

31-32a. It was frequented by bevies of youthful maidens with rendezvous for serving their lovers.

The mountain was adorned with ripe, sweet smelling, potlike big fruits of trees which resembled the breasts of youthful damsels.

32b-33. The place was resonant with the buzzing sound of the bees and was reverberating with the cooing of cuckoos. On seeing the mountain resound with the cries of many living beings all round, the king entered the great mountain.

34-35. He desired to climb on to the top of the mountain. He was curious to find out the path whereby he could climb up. As he spied all round, he saw flocks of birds from the trees moving out attracted by the charming voice of an enchanting lady. He saw the birds flying quickly over the trees and he too went swiftly alongwith them.

36-37. The enchantingly sweet sound coming out of the mouth of that bewitching beauty entered his ears also. Fascinated by it, he left off his horse that had crossed the path as if in three steps. The whole path of the moun-

1. The location of Gandhamādana is disputed. M. Ali (*The Geography of the Purāṇas*, Fig. 7—the sketch of the Hindukush Range) shows it to be the Khwaja Mohammad Range while De identifies it with Rudra Himālayas—a part of the Kailāsa range. But in either case it is difficult to understand why a traveller from India (Vidiśā, in the case of King Rukmāṅgada) need cross or visit in passing Uttara Kuru (modern Kirghizia, Samarkand and Turkemenistan-*vide* D.P. Mishra's *Studies in Proto-history of India*, pp. 17:18 and the map of Uttarakuru facing p. 17) and Mahāmeru (the Pamirs) to reach Gandhamādana. It appears that the author of the NP. had some vague ideas of the locations of these places.

tain was spell-bound by the sweet song of the enchantress. Instantaneously, the king saw a lady stationed on the mountain. She had the lustre of molten gold. She was created like the staff of Kāma.

38-40. She was worshipping the Liṅga that rose high into the sky, for the welfare of the world. She was like the embodied form of the Earth and she was as it were the culmination of beauty like a Pārvatī, the daughter of the mountain Himālaya. She had the beauteous form of the seashore. Her body could be called the very mansion of sexual pleasure. She appeared to drag even the three-eyed lord stationed in the Linga, suddenly for the pleasure of the Lord. She was the personified form of the mental wish of a meritorious person. On seeing the beautiful form of Mohinī, the king was enamoured by the enchanting arrows of the god of love and the king fell down senselessly.

41. Regaining consciousness again as if his body was seized with a very high fever, he moved swiftly to her presence. The lady of beautiful eyes noted the approaching king with her side-glances.

42-44. She stopped singing and kept lute aside. She thought of her duties for the occasion. She drove off the flocks and herds of birds and animals. She covered her cheeks and arms with a fine cloth. She shook off the bees that were attracted by the fragrance of her breath. The gentle lady then went near the king after leaving off the worship-worthy Liṅga. After going near him, the enchanting lady of elegant movements and eyes like the petals of the lotus spoke these sweet words to Rukmāṅgada who had already been scorched by the arrows of Kāma—O king, get up, I am under your control.

45-47. Why do you waste this body of yours by falling in a swoon. You are a person who bear the burden of the Earth as though it was only a blade of grass. Why do you, on seeing my enchanting form, lose sense, like a weak cow sinking beneath the mire ? Be steady and firm. You are bold. You are a brave warrior. Why do you make yourself ridiculous ? You of elegant activities. O Lord of kings, if you have any desire to have extremely pleasant and favourable sexual intercourse with me as a willing partner, after giving charitable gifts with due rites, you' can do so. You can freely enjoy me like your own slave. I am an adept in the sexual act.

CHAPTER TWELVE

Stipulation of the conditions

Vasiṣṭha said :

1-3. When these splendid words were uttered by Mohinī, the leading king opened his eyes resembling a lotus. Deluded by the sight of Mohinī, he uttered the following words in a faltering tone "O young woman, many ladies with faces like the full moon have been seen and enjoyed by me. But I have never seen such a beautiful person like yours; such personal beauty as you have, fascinates the whole world.

4. O fair-faced lady, by your sheer sight I have been struck and hit by the arrows of Cupid. I have suddenly fallen on the Earth. O gentle lady, I prattled much on being fascinated by your brilliance.

5. O lady of beautiful thighs resembling the trunk of an elephant, be favourable to me. I shall grant you whatever you have in mind. My mind has been bound by your love and as such there is nothing in the three worlds that is not worth giving to you.

6-7. O lady of beautiful eyebrows, I am ready to give you this entire Earth whose limbs are bedecked in the mountains, whose garments are the oceans, whose eyes are the moon and the sun, whose bosom are the clouds (or is supple and firm), whose body is well set with the firmament (?), whose face is a gold coin, whose nature is beautiful, whose private parts are the nether worlds, whose hair is constituted by many trees and who has seven mountain lips (?). O beautiful lady I will give you the Earth alongwith my treasury, elephants, horses and cities accompanied by the ministers and therefore hearty.

side-glances, on that mountain itself, in accordance with the (Gṛhya-sūtra) injunctions. United with her the king said smilingly :

The king said :

6b-7a. O fair-faced lady, attainment of heaven is not as much conducive to happiness as winning you, O gentle lady, on this Mandara mountain. It does not please me so much as this meeting with you.

7b-8. O gentle lady, even though I am on this Earth I consider myself superior to Purandara (god Indra) since I have obtained O fair-eyed lady, you, the most beautiful lady in the three worlds as my wife. Hence I shall do whatever is favourable to you. Command me.

9. Tell me whether you wish to sport about here itself, O young lady, or in my palace or on the Malaya mountain or on the top of the Meru or in the Nandana park.

10. On hearing the words of the king that were indicative of his close attachment to her, Mohinī spoke these sweet words that increased the pleasure of the king :—

11. O king, in your capital city I shall be the victim of wounding side-glances of my co-wives. How can I, therefore, go over to your city ?

12. Let there not be, in the whole of the Earth, any woman who will be facing the misery originating from co-wives, throughout her life (till death).

13. O king, I have been obtained by you. From the bottom of my heart, I am subservient to you. It was after understanding that there would be the misery from co-wives that you have been wooed as my husband by me.

14. I will be able to reside on the excellent mountain that contains many miraculous features. But, O leading king the only thing is you cannot stay anywhere without Sandhyāvalī.

15. On being separated from her and her son, you will be definitely unhappy. Your sadness, O king, will increase my sorrow.

16. I shall establish myself soundly wherever you will derive sufficient happiness. O king, where you are happily

diverted, I shall also be happy, feeling that your place of residence is mount Mandara to me.

17. The wife must live in the place where her husband stays, even if it is not an affluent one. They say (i.e. wise people say) that, in the proximity of her husband that place is the veritable mountain Meru of gold.

18. O Lord, where you feel happy is surely my Meru, the place of my desire. Staying in the place of one's father after eschewing that of one's husband, is to be avoided.

19. A woman interested in staying permanently in the abode of her father sinks in darkness of hell. All her holy rites shall be fruitless and she shall be born as a sow.

20. I know such evil consequences. How, then can I stay on in the Mandara mountain ? I will go along with you. You are the Lord of my happiness and misery."

21. On hearing the words of Mohinī, the king was delighted in his mind. After embracing the beautiful, lady, he spoke these words : —

22. You will be above all my wives. O lady of beautiful thighs, do not have any doubt that you will have to face misery !

23. O lady of beautiful eyebrows, in my house you will be far superior to my own life. O lady of slender frame, come on. We shall proceed to the city for our mutual happiness.

24. O my beloved wife, staying there, enjoy freely all the worldly pleasures along with me.

25. It was eventually for his own destruction that Rukmāṅgada told her thus. Mohinī whose face was as white and fair as the moon, started from there producing the tinkling sound of her anklets. It seemed that she even dragged the beauty of the mountain too after her.

CHAPTER FOURTEEN

The salvation of Godhā, (the lizard)

Vasiṣṭha continued :

1. O king, both of them set off from the top of the mountain towards the surface of the Earth, surveying the various features of the mountain that captivated their mind.

2. Some of the regions resembled corals, some were white like silver, some had the blue lustre of sapphire and some regions had golden hue.

3. Some of them were crystal-coloured and others resembled the yellow orpiment. All the immobile beings were as if closely knit together.

4. After reaching the foot of the mountain (ground level), the king saw his excellent horse scrapping the ground with his powerful hoofs that resembled the thunderbolt.

5. As it scrapped and dug up the Earth with its sharp hoofs, a domestic lizard that had been beneath the ground came out.

6. While coming out, O king (?) it was crushed beneath the hoof of the horse. The kind-hearted king saw it being crushcd.

7-8. Crying out to his beloved wife "Alas it is crushed !" he rushed to it. Then, with the tender leaf of a tree the king scrapped it from the hoof and threw it on a plot of grassy land. Seeing that it had become senseless he spoke to Mohinī :—

9. "O lady of beautiful limbs and lotus-like eyes ! Bring some water immediately so that I can sprinkle it on the lizard that has become unconscious due to its being crushed.

10. At the instance of her husband, she brought some cool water immediately. With that the king sprinkled the unconscious domestic lizard.

11-13. O king, Being sprinkled with cold water the lizard regained consciousness. In all cases of smiting blows, sprinkling with water is recommended. Or it is beneficial if it is immediately bandaged with a damp cloth. O king (?), after regaining consciousness the lizard spoke these words. Seeing the king in front of her, though it was distressed with (acute) pain it (the lizard) spoke out slowly : "O mighty-armed Rukmāṅgada, listen to my story of life.

14. O Lord, I was the wife of a Brāhmaṇa, in the beautiful city of Śākala.[1] I was endowed with beauty and youth. But I was not liked much by him.

15. O king, that husband of mine did not hate anyone else, but he was always full of hatred towards me. He invariably spoke harsh words to me.

16. I was furious on account of this. In order to attain the power of Vaśī-karaṇa (attraction), O king I consulted those young women who had been abandoned by their husbands. (but who later on controlled them).

17. O king, I was informed by them—"Your husband will be subservient. We have been convinced (because once) we too had been abandoned and slighted by our husbands.

18. Indeed our husbands became meek and submissive through the medicines and potions given by an ascetic woman. O beautiful lady, you too ask her. She will give you the auspicious medicines.

19-20. You need not entertain any doubt. Your husband will be obedient like a slave. O king, at their instance I started from the place immediately. As I asked the people on the way, they pointed out her palace consisting of hundred columns and white-washed in a shining form.

21. After entering it, I saw the brilliant woman under the vow of celibacy. She had covered herself with a long cloth. She had the tawny coloured complexion like that of the dusk.

22. The refulgent lady wore long matted hairs; a number of attendants were waiting upon her; she was being fanned gently by them.

23. With a rosary of beads in her hand, she was repeating the Mantra that was Vaśyakara (conducive to attract and subdue people), that could cause excitement which could be verified (and hence was convincing.) She had the garland of happiness giving beads (?) round her neck).

---

1. *Śākala*—Capital of Madra deśa of Mahābhārata fame, and also of Indo-Greek King Menander alias Milinda of the Buddhist work *Milinda-Pañha*. Identified with mod. Sialkot in Pakistan.

24-25. Thereafter, I placed a soft lustrous ring of fine gold with superb brilliance at her feet and bowed to her. On seeing the ring placed at her feet she become delighted. Even before being asked, she had understood the disrespect to me by my husband.

26-27. Then, O king, I was advised by the ascetic lady when I bowed to her and stood by. "This medicinal powder alongwith this amulet brings all living beings under control. The powder must be given to your husband (for being taken in) and the amulet must be worn round the neck. Certainly the husband will become submissive. He will not go to any other beautiful woman.

28. Taking the medicinal powder and the amulet, I soon reached the house of my husband. At nightfall, the powder was mixed with milk and given to my husband.

29-30. The amulet was tied round the neck and I ceased to be anxious over anything. O excellent king, when my husband drank the potion with the medicinal powder, the consumptive disease took possession of him the same day. My husband became weaker and weaker day by day. Worms originating from cuts and putrefying wounds abounded in his private parts.

31-32. Within a few days, he became pale and dim like a lamp when the sun has risen. My husband became agitated and perturbed in his sense organs. Lamenting over his lot day and night he told me : O splendid lady, I am your slave. I seek refuge in you. Save me. I will never approach another woman.

33. O king, on hearing his lamentation I became much terrified. I informed the ascetic lady about everything and asked her. How shall my husband be happy ?

34. A second course of medicine was given by her for subduing the burning sensation. When the medicine was administered, my husband attained normal health instantaneously.

35. The burning sensation originating from the previous powder was nullified by that medicine. Thereafter, my husband became subservient to me. He abided by my words and advice.

36. In due course of time, I passed away and fell into the hell called Tāmrabhrāṣṭra (Copper frying pan) where I underwent torture for the period of fifteen Yugas.

37. Pieces as subtle and minute as gingelly seeds were cut off from my body and I was tortured: When a little of my sin remained still, I was born on the Earth.

38. The form of a lizard was given to me by Yama (the son of the Sun). Thus, O king, I have been here for the last ten thousand years.

39. O king, if any young maiden were to perform Vaśīkaraṇa rite to attract and control her husband, all her holy rites will be futile; she will be considered wicked and sinful in action and she will be burned and tortured in Tāmrabhrāṣṭraka (hell).

40. To a lady the husband is the Lord, he is the goal; he is the deity and he is the preceptor. If she were to perform the Vaśīkaraṇa rite in respect of him, how can she attain happiness?

41. She is born among hundreds of species of animals and creatures including the germs of leprosy. Hence, O king, the behest of the husband must always be carried out by a woman.

42. O king, unless you redeem me who have sought refuge in you, I shall have to be born again as a despicable creature with all my sins.

43-44. You can redeem me by giving me the merit acquired by you by observing the holy rite of Vijayā Dvādaśī[1] associated with the constellation (Nakṣatra) Śravaṇa at the confluence of Gaṅgā and Sarayū. This confluence is destructive of sins. The holy rite is conducive to the redemption of ghosts. It is the bestower of all mentally cherished desires.

45. On that day, O king, even if Hari is remembered in their own house by men, there is no doubt about it that he enables them to attain the merit accrued by visiting holy centres.

46. O king, whatever meritorious act like charitable gifts, oblations to fire, worship of gods, is performed on the day of Vijayā it has ever-lasting beneficial effect.

---

1. There are eight kinds of Dvādaśīs, *Vijayā Dvādaśī* has *Śravaṇa* Nakṣatra *vide* Hemādri on Kāla, pp. 260-263, *Smṛti Kaustubha*, pp. 250-54.

47-49a Please do grant unto me that merit. If one observes fast on the Dvādaśī day and performs Pāraṇā on the Trayodaśī day, one acquires the benefit of observing fast for twelve years. O king, take pity on me and pass on that merit to me. On the Earth, you are the very physical manifestation of Dharma (virtue). You are the destroyer of the path of Yama. O save me. I am utterly miserable.

49b. On hearing the words of the lizard, Mohinī spoke these words :

50. O Lord, whether happiness or misery one experiences, it has the result of his own actions. Hence, what have you to do with this sinful creature who had been wicked to her own husband ?

51. O king, by means of amulets, medicinal powder and other things she gained control over her husband. O king, whatever is given to good men may be conducive to fame and heavenly pleasure.

52-53. What is rendered as a gift etc to the sinners causes downfall of both (the giver and the receiver). It falls off both the worlds. If milk mixed with sugar is given to a serpent, it will certainly increase its poison. Similar indeed is the help rendered to the sinners. Leave off this sinful creature. Let us go to the city.

54. If one delves into the births and dealings of others one's happiness perishes.

Rukmāṅgada said :

O daughter of Brahmā, how is it that these things were uttered by you ? O fair-faced lady, how can you say that this is not the conduct or way of life of good men?

55. O fair lady, those who are opposed to helping others are sinners. They do everything for their own happiness and harass others. They are opposed to rendering obligation to others.

56. The moon, sun, cloud, earth, fire, water, sandal, trees and good men are always for helping others.

57-58. O fair-faced lady, it is heard that there was a king named Hariścandra. Afraid of uttering a lie he experienced various miseries one after the other. He had to stay in the house of a Cāṇḍāla. He had to sell his wife and son. Thanks to his steadfast adherence to truth, Śakra and other Devas became satisfied.

59. They asked Hariścandra[1] the king to choose any boon. Brahmā and other Devas were given this reply by that truthful king—If the Devas are satisfied it behoves them to grant this boon :

60-62. May this entire city alongwith its trees, reptiles, children, young men, old men, women, and quadrupeds go to heaven. Even if it had committed sins, I shall take over the entire sins of Ayodhyā and would like to go to hell. I do not wish to go to heaven alone after leaving people on the Earth. O great Devas, this is the truth, I utter.

63. On seeing his steadfastness, Indra and others permitted it. The entire city went to the heavenly world alongwith him.

64. The king is stationed in heaven in the company of his city. He moves about in the aerial chariot that goes wherever he pleases. He is being worshipped even by the immortal beings.

65. O gentle lady, on hearing that the Devas had been defeated by the Daityas, the gift of his own bones was made by Dadhīci for helping the Devas.

66. O fair lady, his own flesh was given to the hungry vulture by king Śibi formerly, for protecting a dove.

67. Formerly, there was a king over this earth named Jīmūtavāhana[2]. O fairfaced lady, his own life was given up by him for the sake of serpents.

---

1. Son of King Triśaṅku of the solar-race. His truthfulness and harassment by Viśvāmitra mentioned here is described in details in DB. VII Chs. 20.27. The readiness of Hariścandra to go to hell for the sins of others probably discloses the influence of Buddhist ideal expressed through Bodhisattvas.

2. The story of Jimūtavāhana's self-sacrifice probably formed a part of Guṇāḍhya's *Bṛhat-Kathā*, a *Paiśācī* work now lost forever. It is recorded in its Sanskrit version *Kathāsaritsāgara* (Śaśāṅkavatī Lambaka, Taraṅga 23). Harṣa selected him as the hero of his play *Nāgānanda* for propagating the Buddhist ideal of self-sacrifice.

68. Hence, O gentle lady, a king should be kind-hearted and sympathetic. O splendid lady, the cloud showers its waters equally on an unholy and pure spot.

69-70. The moon should delight even the Cāṇḍālas and the fallen persons through his rays. Hence, O fair lady, I shall uplift this distressed lizard by means of my own merits in the same way as Nahuṣa through his daughter's descendant (?).[1] Disregarding the enchantress thus, he spoke to the lizard.

71. My merit originating from the holy rite of Vijayā is given, (I repeat) is given unto you, by me. Be free from all sins and go to the world of Viṣṇu.

72-74. O king, on his uttering this, she eschewed the old and emaciated form of the lizard and became a beautiful lady bedecked in celestial ornaments. She took leave of the king and went away brightening the ten quarters and making (as if) a wonderful boundary line to the region of Viṣṇu. It is the place approachable only by Yogins. It is an excellent region brilliant like fire. It is the greatest Ātman. Hence she is also like the lamp of fire for the illumination of the universe and was transformed by the king.

CHAPTER FIFTEEN

The dialogue between the father (Rukmāṅgada) and the son (Dharmāṅgada)

Vasiṣṭha said :

1. After setting the lizard free from the sin, the delighted king laughingly said to Mohinī—May the horse be mounted instantaneously.

1. *Dauhitraiḥ*-lit. by daughter's sons. Nahuṣa after his fall from heaven, was redeemed by Yudhiṣṭhira (*Mbh. Vana*, Chs. 179-181). Yudhiṣṭhira was not exactly his daughter's son but the term is used here loosely to express a descendant.

2-3. Like Kṛṣṇa's horse (?) this can go ten thousand Yojanas in a moment. On hearing the words of the king, Mohinī, the ardently passionate lady, climbed on to the horse which was as swift as the wind, alongwith her husband. The lady of sweet smiles spoke these words to the king her husband.

4. O king, drive this horse towards your city. My desire to see the face of your son is intense.

5. O excellent king, I am at your disposal. You may go wherever you are inclined to go. On hearing the words of Mohinī, he started towards his city.

6-9. With great delight he observed the trees, the mountains, the rivers, the different kinds of forests, the animals of various sorts, villages, forts, lands, splendid cities, lakes of variegated nature and the charming plots of lands on the way. On seeing the hermitage of Vāmadeva soon, the king who was in a hurry, bowed down from the firmament itself. Again the king proceeded on his way on his horse that was as swift as the wind-god. Observing many lands fully endowed with riches and foodgrains.

10-12. The king reached Vidiśā (a city in Madhya Pradesh) that was under his control. His son Dharmāṅgada had already heard through his spies that the king, his father, was coming. With great delight he spoke these words to the vassal kings :—O excellent kings, this northern quarter is becoming brighter on being illuminated by his splendour and on being occupied by my father's horse. Hence, let us all go to greet the king face to face.

13. If the son does not come face to face with (i.e. does not personally go to receive) his father immediately on his arrival, he falls into the terrible hell and stays there as long as fourteen Indras reign.

14. The Brāhmaṇas well-versed in the Purāṇas say that if the son goes ahead to receive his father face to face, (personally he derives the fruit of a Yajña for every step he takes).

15. Get up. I shall go to greet him lovingly surrounded by you all. He is my deity of deities.

16. When the king approved of his words saying "So be it," the prince accompanied by all of them went on foot for

a distance of a Krośa (3 km.) to greet his father personally face to face.

17. Appearing like the embodied form of Manmatha and accompanied by a thousand kings, he went a long distance and met the king on the way.

18. Meeting his father, he prostrated to him by falling at his feet on the ground affectionately. Alongwith the vassal kings, he bent his head down and made obeisance.

19-20. With great love the king observed his son falling at his feet immediately after arrival along with the vassal kings. The king got down from the horse. With his brawny arms he lifted up his son and warmly embraced him closely. Sniffing at his head the king then spoke to his son.

21. O son, I hope you are protecting your subjects. I also hope you are punishing the enemies. I presume you fill the treasury only with such amounts as are earned by justifiable means.

22. I hope, never failing maintenance amounts that are more than sufficient have been handed over to the Brāhmaṇas. I hope you practise attractive and pleasant manners, and that you do not speak harsh words.

23. I hope cows are now milked in the houses of Cāṇḍālas and sons carry out the behests of their fathers always.

24. I hope the daughter-in-law obeys the mother-in-law and her own husband. O son, I hope you never enter into verbal disputes with the Brāhmaṇas.

25. I hope the cows are not restrained in the land and are fed on different kinds of grass. I hope you scrutinise the weights and balances of foodgrains and other things.

26. O son, I hope you do not impose too much of a burden on the householder by means of taxes. I believe game of dice and over-addiction to liquor are not present in your land.

27. I hope there are people of different tastes and different opinions expressed in words in your city. I (further) hope the men do not maintain themselves on liberal gifts of others and do not wear old ragged clothes.

28. O son, I hope you personally survey the elephants and horses in your army and protect them. I hope you look after all your mothers without partiality.

29. O son, I hope men do not take food on the day of Viṣṇu (on the Ekādaśī day). I hope men are interested in performing Śrāddha when the moon is waning (on the New Moon day).

30. I hope you always eschew slumber in the latter halves of the nights. Slumber is the root of sins.

31. Slumber is the mother of poverty. It is destructive of prosperity and welfare. No king who is a slave unto slumber rules over the Earth for a long time.

32. Just as an unchaste woman destroys both the worlds of her husband so also slumber destroys both the worlds of the king.

When the father said all these things, the son spoke these words.

33. The son Dharmāṅgada bowed to the king again and again and said.

O dear father, all these things have been done by me. I shall again carry out your behests.

34. In all the three worlds those sons who carry out the instructions of their fathers, are blessed. O king, what is more sinful than not carrying out the directives of one's own father?

35. If the son disobeys his father and goes to Gaṅgā for his holy dip, he does not attain the benefit of the holy river. He who does not carry out his father's directives does not enjoy the fruits of pilgrimage to holy centres.

36. My body is subservient to you; my life is at your disposal.[1] My duty is subservient to you. You are my great deity.

37. A son cannot free himself from indebtedness to his father even by making a gift of the three worlds. O Lord, what then by means of physical strain, monetary gift and other things.

38-39. Even as his son surrounded by many kings said thus, Rukmāṅgada embraced the son and spoke these words : O

---

1. Henceforth every now and then *Dharmāṅgada* and *Sandhyāvalī* unknowingly and unintentionally hint the future tragedy—Dharmāṅgada's death at the hands of his father.

son, you have spoken the truth. You are the knower of virtue. There is no other greater deity for a son than his father. If the son disrespects the father, even the gods turn their faces from him.

40. Since you have conquered the Earth consisting of many continents and possessing many kings and since you protect that Earth, I have been held by you on your head.

41. This is the greatest happiness in the world, certainly this is the heavenly region on the surface of the Earth, that the son is superior to the father.

42. O son, I have been made contented by you who traverse the path of good qualities and who make all the kings observe holy rite on the auspicious day of Hari.

43. On hearing these words of his father, Dharmāṅgada, the son said :-

"O father, where did you go after depositing all the riches in me ?

44. At what place was this lady with the lustre of ten thousand suns attained by you? I think, after creating her Prajāpati (Brahmā) had become disgusted with the world and detached from it.

45. O king, in the whole of the three worlds there is no other woman with this form and beauty. I think she is born of the mountain or originated from the ocean.

46-47. Or she may be the Māyā (illusion) of the Daitya Maya, with the form of a young woman assumed by her. O Lord, indeed, Brahmā by whom she has been created is very clever. There is no slightest defect even to the extent of a hundred part of the tip of a hair. O Lord of the kings of the Earth, she is worthy of being the heroine of your house since she is as pure as gold. If I were to have a mother of such a type, which man is more meritorious than I ?"

bangles (i.e. sixteen) studded with diamonds for both the hands.

38-43a. They were made by men who knew their value. For each of the hands, a crore of gold coins was spent. The prince gave invaluable armlets and anklets to the beloved wife of his father as ornament. They had the refulgence of the sun. The girdle of fiery refulgence that Śarvāṇī (Pārvatī) had, fell off as she was extremely terrified in the course of the fight called Tārakāmaya (pertaining to the demon Tāraka) while Kālanemi was ruling over the kingdom. It then fell into Mūlapācana (original fire). Thereafter, it was picked up by the demon Maya who wielded his power of illusion over the whole world. Dharmāṅgada had killed that Daitya on Mount Malaya although he had been surrounded by a crore of Daityas. At the instance of his father, he had killed him in the course of a terrible war that lasted for a year (on the mountain Malaya). He got the girdle that the beloved of the king of the Daityas had on her person. The king gave that to his father's beloved great queen with his hair standing on their ends out of delight.

43b-46. Formerly, Hiraṇyakaśipu's queen who was an outstanding beauty in the world, had a crest jewel that had the refulgence of lightning. She immolated herself in her husband's funeral pyre. Before dying, the extremely distressed lady had cast her crest-jewel into the sea. The sea collected the excellent jewel and presented it to Dharmāṅgada on being delighted at his prowess. The delighted prince now gave that jewel which had the brilliance of a crore of suns to his stepmother.

47. He gave Mohinī two auspicious clothes sanctified in fire and two charming bodices, a thousand crores in value.

48-49. Dharmāṅgada then gave the gentle lady Mohinī, the divine garland and the sweet-smelling divine unguent that was very rare and had been acquired from the accomplished hands of the preceptor of all the Devas by the heroic Dharmāṅgada in the course of his conquest of all the continents. He gave her the unguent that enhanced her love.

50. After embellishing her with great devotion, he fed

her with meals consisting of dishes of six tastes and brought by his natural mother herself

51. Even before this, he had addressed his natural mother and enlightened her by means of many words. There is no doubt about this that the behest of the king must be carried out by me as well as by you.

52-53a. O gentle lady, she who is the king's beloved is a highly respectable woman for us. The wife who acts wickedly against the lady-love of the king, her husband, falls into hell and stays there till fourteen Indras reign.

53b-54. She who nurses feelings of enmity against the lady-love of her husband and tries to separate them in their love, is fried in Tāmrabhrāṣṭa hell (the frying pan made of copper.) Everything that is conducive to the happiness of her husband, should be done by the wife.

55. O fair-complexioned lady, she must view her as she views her husband. She must do what is favourable and beneficent to the lady-love of her husband.

56a. Even if she (the husband's lady-love) happens to be of a lower caste, the wife who renders service to her, goes to heaven.

56b. Afterwards she will occupy the same loving place in the mind of her husband.

57. After acceding to the wish of her husband she derives all worldly pleasures. By eschewing the feelings of malice and jealousy, she attains the region of the Lord of every one.

58. On seeing a cowife to be the most beloved of her husband, if a woman renders service to her, she will attain an eternal place in heaven.

59-60. There was a very wicked man of the Śūdra caste. He had abandoned all holy rites.[1] He had a wife and also a

---

1. VV. 59-89 give an illustration of a chaste Śūdra lady who served her depraved husband and his keep who when he was affected by fistula left him penniless. This chaste lady borrowed money from father, gave medical treatment to him, personally nursed his wound. When he died, she immolated herself on his funeral pyre and washed off her husband's sins by her merits; both of them went to heaven.

beloved lady, a prostitute whom he kept in his house. The wife who wanted to please her husband served him as well as the prostitute. She washed the feet of both of them. She partook only of the leavings of the food of both of them.

61. Though she was prevented from doing this by the prostitute, she continued her activities of service. She ever remained in the path of the good. She was engaged in what was beneficent for both of them; while both of them lay on the cot, she used to lie down beneath on the bare ground.

62. Thus she served her husband alongwith the prostitute for a long time, wading through the ocean of misery.

63-64. Without caring for the advice of the chaste wife the man committed many blunders in the matter of his diet etc. He drank the milk of the buffalo alongwith radish. The foolish fellow ate the winnowings (of corn) mixed with oil. As a result of this he had a terrible fistula in the anus.

65-66a. He was extremely distressed by day and night. The prostitute took everything valuable that the house contained and went over to another young man. The lustful woman gave him all the wealth.

66b-67. Now the Śūdra man became much ashamed. With distress evident in his face, he lamented and spoke thus to his wife. : O gentle lady, save me though I had been very cruel to you and much attached to a prostitute.

68. O beautiful lady, the sinner that I am, I have never done a good thing to you. O lady of slender waist, for many years I sported about alongwith the prostitute.

69. The sinful haughty man who does not console his wife who bows down to him, attains all inauspicious things in the course of fifteen rebirths.

70. O gentle lady, since I had disrespected you, I shall attain the despicable birth in the house of a Cāṇḍāla. But your mind has not been turbid despite insults.

71. On hearing these words of her husband, the wife spoke to the husband. It is the sins committed in the previous births that yield miseries. A learned man who bears them

with fortitude, should be known as the most excellent among men.

72. I had been sinful in the previous births. Now I experienced the fruits thereof in this birth. Hence, I have neither sorrow nor misery.

73. By saying this she consoled and cautioned her husband. The fair-complexioned lady brought some money from her father and other kinsmen.

74-75. The chaste lady considered her husband a Viṣṇu, the resident of the milk ocean. She cleaned his anus and other private parts assiduously by day as well as by night, by means of turmeric juice and water. She scraped the germs and worms in the body of her husband, by means of her nail.

76. She fanned him with peacock feathers. O gentle lady, the fair-faced lady slept neither during the day nor at night.

77-78. Distressed by the misery of her husband, she felt that the whole universe was blazing (?). She said—If there is goddess of earth, if there are manes, if there are deities, may they make my husband free from ailments. May he be free from sins. I shall give unto Goddess Caṇḍikā blood mixed with flesh.

79. I shall offer the flesh of goats, buffaloes and even human beings for the well being of my husband. With great respect I shall observe ten fasts.

80. I shall place my body on a bed of sharp-pointed thorns. I shall not take sweet things. I shall not take ghee.

81. I shall remain for days together without anointing the body externally with oil. May my husband live for a hundred years without any ailment.

82-83a. As day followed day, she blurted out like this in her agony. Within a short while, all the three humours in his system were upset. With great effort she gave her husband the three astringent medicines (black and long pepper and dry ginger).

83b-84. Once due to chilliness the man was quaking and shivering. His jaws suddenly came together and the finger of the wife was bitten off by the teeth coming together. O queen of the Lord of men, the piece of finger remained within the rigid mouth.

85. She sold off her bangle and brought a great deal of fuel. She prepared the funeral pyre. After placing her dead husband on it, she poured ghee over the pyre (fuel).

86-89. She too climbed on the funeral pyre joining her face to his face, her heart near his heart and O gentle lady, her buttocks near his buttocks. With her foot she dragged the fire. The auspicious lady of charming limbs set fire to the ailing body of the husband alongwith her body. As the fire blazed brightly, she cast off her body and went to the world of the Devas taking her husband with her after annihilating many of his sins by means of her holy rites very difficult to be performed.

CHAPTER SEVENTEEN

The statement of Mohinī

The son (Dharmāṅgada) said :

1. Hence, O Mother, eschew jealousy and feed Mohinī. A holy rite (dharma) like this cannot be attained in the three worlds.

2-3. The wife who, with her own hands, feeds the beloved lady love of her husband, the co-wife who gives a little quantity of cooked rice to the co-wife shall, O gentle lady, O dear mother, become immortal—So says god Brahmā. O Mistress (of the Mansion) be favourable to me carry out what has been related by me.

4. O fair-complexioned lady, what is conducive to the happiness of my dear father must be performed by both of us. The sins shall be exterminated perfectly. Similarly, the attainment of heaven shall be everlasting.

5-6. On hearing the words of her son then, the queen Sandhyāvalī invited* her son and embraced him again and again. She sniffed at his head and spoke these words : "O son, I shall carry out your words pregnant with dharma (virtues).

7. Eschewing jealousy and false prestige I shall feed Mohinī. I have the pleasure of being the mother of a hundred sons, O son, with you as my only son.

8. It was after observing many holy rites and restraints causing bodily exertion, that you were born. Since I observed the holiest of holy rites, the 'king' of holy rites, you were attained by me as my son.

9. In this world there is no other holy rite that is seen to be yielding benefits like this. This gives convincing proofs immediately. This is destructive of great sins.

10. Of what avail is it if many sons who cause sorrow and distress are born ? It is better to have one son, as the main prop of the family, where the entire family takes comfortable rest.

11. On attaining you as one stationed in my womb, I have reached the top of the three worlds (I am above the three worlds). O sinless one, blessed are those pains of labour whereby you are born as my son.

12. You are the son who delight both father and mother, you are the heroic son who have become the Lord of seven continents; you have carried out the words of your father.

13-15. Poets (Learned Philosophers) call only that person real son—the person who delights both the father and the mother. Others are only 'so-called' sons.

After saying these words, queen Sandhyāvalī just glanced at the pots and utensils for the purpose of a meal consisting of dishes of all the six tastes. By her very glance the utensils were full of dishes that would be pleasantly warm and that would be as tasty as Nectar, which she wished that Mohinī should partake of.

---

*A better emendation : *abhinandya* "praised", 'approved of' in stead of *abhi-mantrya* in the text.

16. She took a golden ladle studded with jewels. Smiling sweetly, she served food to Mohinī without any perturbation.

17. She slowly ate the desired and well cooked food in a polished excellent vessel, all round which beverages and edible dishes had been placed.

18-19. The gentle lady, the daughter of Brahmā, sat on an auspicious golden seat and took food that was comparable to nectar. While taking food, the fair lady was fanned with a fan of peacock feathers held by Dharmāṅgada, in accompaniment of music.

20-21. After washing with cool water (her hands and mouth gurgling four times), she accepted the fragrant Tāmbūla (chewing betel leaves) given by her (step)-son. The fair-complexioned lady took it with her hand over which excellent sandal paste had been applied. Then O king, she laughed and said slowly to Sandhyāvalī.

22. "O gentle lady, are you the mother of king Vṛṣāṅgada (i.e. Dharmāṅgada) ? O auspicious lady, due to perspiring tiredness you cauld not be recognised by me."

23. O king, while the daughter of Brahmā was speaking thus to Sandhyāvali, the son of the king bowed to her and spoke these words.

24. "I had been held in her belly (womb) by this gentle lady for three years. I flourished thanks to the favour of your husband.

25. O Beautiful lady, I have hundreds of mothers. But much milk flowing out from the breasts of this lady out of (motherly) affection has been drunk by me.

26. That severe pain which more or less amounts to old age has been endured by her. It was after giving birth to me that she had become disjointed in her limbs.

27. A son has nothing in possession in all the three worlds by giving which he can be free from the indebtedness to his mother. O lady of sweet limbs, this is the truth that has been pronounced by me.

28. I am the most blessed one in the world. No man is superior to me. Everyday I sit on the lap of groups of mothers.

29. If anywhere the son does not sit on the lap of his mother, he does not become aware of the happiness of motherly affection like a virgin who remains unaware of the love of a husband.

30. A son who has climbed on to the lap of his mother may become very proud, and wish to snatch the necklace from the excellent body of his mother, with his hand.

31. Maternal milk is so powerful that even if any body is bereft of his father, he desires to seize the whole world on being duly reared and brought up by his mother.

32-33. (?) My love toward this lady is due to the contact of the belly. My love towards the other mothers is due to the contact of the lap. If it be true that I do not cherish any difference (or partiality) between this (mother) and (my) other mothers may my father live for hundred years, thanks to that truth." When her (step) son said thus Mohini was wonder-struck.

34-37. "Ruthless as I am by nature, how can I strike him who is so humble and sinless. This would have been proper in the house of a tinner (?) If a boy is regularly rendering service to his father, there is no one on Earth on a par with him. It is for perpetrating a despicable act with regard to such a boy so superb in virtue (as compared with others) and by nature so virtuous and inclined to religion that I have become a step-mother unto him, in this world." After reflecting like this in various ways, Mohinī the most beautiful woman in the world spoke to her step-son : "Fetch my husband quickly. Without him I cannot stay even for a Muhūrta (i.e. 48 minutes).

38-39. Then, O king (?), he hastened to his father and bowed to him. He said—O dear father, the younger mother desires to see you immediately. Be favourably disposed towards her. May Brahmā's daughter be greeted and honoured" At the instance of the son the king got ready to go instantaneously.

40-42a. With pleasure evident in his face. the king entered the apartment of Sandhyāvalī and saw Mohinī the enchanting lady having the luster of molted gold lying on the bed and being served slowly by his beloved Sandhyāvalī eschewing at the advice of her son the natural anger and jealousy felt towards a co-wife.

42b-43. On seeing Rukmāṅgada come, the beautiful lady on the bed, Mohinī, delightedly said to the king who had a great deal of chivalry—" O husband, be pleased to sit here on the cot spread with soft cotton (cloth).

44. O king, the affairs of the kingdom have been looked after by you for a long time and in their entirety. Still your desire for the administration of kingdom does not cease.

45. O king, I consider you the most sinful one on the surface of the Earth since you yourself look after the royal glory (affairs of the state) although you have been aware that your son is efficient.

46-47a. Hence, there is no one more miserable than you in all the worlds. O king, the time of those fathers who have good sons passes happily and that of the experiencers of the fruits of sins, whose mind is drawn towards worldly pleasures passes in misery.

47b. All the Prakṛtis (the elements of the statecraft) (or subjects), O king, are fond of you. This is the result of your full meritoriousness.

48. When Dharmāṅgada is protecting this kingdom and the subjects, why should you also see to it now after eschewing the pleasure of your beloved wife like a weak niggardly fellow.

49. If you are going to look after the kingdom, of what use am I to you? In vain have I been brought from the head Mandara, the churning rod of the ocean of milk (?)

50a. Just as flesh is to birds I shall be turning food to faeces (?)

50b-52a. If any foolish person, too much interested in carrying out his duties, does not take to his wife endowed with blooming youth, whence can he expect to have the beloved? If the wife is not enjoyed, she may go away; if the wealth is not given in charity, it may go (disappear); if the kingdom is not protected well it may go (to ruins); if the learning is not recited and revised, it may (be forgotten and vanished).

52b-54a. Learning is not acquired by idle persons; a wife is not acquired by persons always observing holy vows; good fortune is not obtained without regular and assiduous performance (of good deeds); glory is not attained by persons who are not devotees, an industrious man does not get happiness; a person who has no wife cannot obtain children, an impure person does not attain virtue (dharma) and a Brāhmaṇa of unpleasant words does not attain wealth.

54b-56. Without asking no one understands things; without walking (i.e. moving forward) no one reaches destination; a person who is not a disciple does not understand the holy rite; a wakeful person knows no fear. Why should you, O king, leave me alone in the splendid house of Dharmāṅgada and look after the affairs of your kingdom, O lord, when your son is competent (to do it himself)?

57. When the daughter of Brahmā, who was fond of sexual intercourse and who had large charming eyes spoke thus, the king who was standing by the side of his son became ashamed. He spoke thus to his beloved.

CHAPTER EIGHTEEN

Honouring the Mothers

The king said :

1-3. "O timid lady, I did not assume authority to take up the duties of the king. Since I was very tired, I was overpowered by a pleasing slumber. I told Dharmāṅgada thus : "Take Mohinī to your apartment that is bedecked in all jewels, that could be ventilated or controlled (and protected from) wind (at will) and that is pleasing in all the seasons. O son of beautiful eyes resembling the petals of a lotus, worship her duly. She is my most beloved wife."

4. After commanding my son thus, I went to sleep after reaching the bed with great difficulty like a man of ill-luck attaining wealth.

5. The moment I woke up I have hastened to your presence at once. O gentle lady, there is no doubt about this that I shall carry out whatever you say."

Mohinī said :

6. O leading king, appease these wives of yours who are very miserable. They are dejected by your marrying me. They have lost all hopes of satisfying their passionate desire for worldly pleasures.

7-8. O king, O Lord of the subjects, If any one were to strike and pierce into the heads of the Senior wives of comely appearance, the wedge known as the younger wife, he will not have salvation nor will she attain the final beatitude. What peace can I have when I have been burnt in the scalding tears of chaste women ?

9. O king, the gentle and chaste ladies may reduce even my procreator (Brahmā) to ashes. What then about an ordinary persons like you or me ?

10. O king, there is no woman like Sandhyāvalī in all the three worlds. With all her limbs bound by love towards you, she had been feeding me with food-stuffs having all the six tastes.

11-12. Thanks to the honour and weightage given to you, she spoke pleasing and coaxing words to me. There are hundreds of women like these in your abode and O king, I am not even equal to the dust of their feet."

On hearing these words of Mohinī, the king became ashamed.

13. The king was then standing near the eldest wife who was accompanied by her son. The son who was a person understanding the inner feelings of other persons, knew that the king had gone through all the ten states of love-lorn persons.

14. He understood that his father was overwhelmed by passionate love and was fascinated by Mohinī. He called together all the mothers. (i.e. the queens of Rukmāṅgada) beginning with Sandhyāvalī.

15. With palms joined in reverence, he spoke to them these pleasing words—Mohinī, the daughter of Brahmā and the newly wedded wife (of my father) is my (step) mother.

16. O gentle ladies, she yearns for a secret meeting with the king for dalliance with him. Hence delightfully approve of it.

The Mothers said :

17. O son, who will approve of and encourage the swallowing of oneself by a serpent? O foremost one among embodied beings, who will place fire over himself and kindle it?

18. Who will swallow the terrible poison ? Who will cut off one's own head ? Who will tie a terrible stone round one's neck and try to cross the sea ?.

19. Who will enter the jaws of leopards. Who will try to pluck hairs from the manes of a fierce lion ? Who will sit over the sharp edge of a sword that dazzles in the sky.

20. Which lady will approve of the dalliance of her co-wife with her husband (?) One would rather give everything that one has than entertain thoughts about this in the mind.

21. Which woman will see with her own eyes her husband respected (and openly loved) by another woman ? It would be by far the better that her head is cut off with an excellent sharp-edged sword.

22. Who is that lady, if at all any one is like that anywhere, who will be able to bear that her husband whom she considers her own vital breath is pressing and caressing the breasts of another lady ?

23-25a. Much less who will be able to see it with her own eyes. This is the most miserable of all miseries bringing in endless grief if a woman is compelled to see with her own eyes her husband enamoured of another woman. O son, it is even better if all your mothers die simultaneously; but the king, our husband, should not be seen united with Mohinī.

Dharmāṅgada said :

25b-26a. O ladies of splendid faces, If you are not prepared to accord happiness to my father, I will mix poison and drink it. After I die you can have the happiness.

26b-27a. If any lady were to carry out anything mentally, verbally or physically causing misery to my father, she is my enemy, she deserves to be killed by me even if she were Sandhyāvalī.

27b-28a. That gentle lady Mohinī is superior to all. She is the most beloved of my father. The maiden has come from her abode on the mountain Mandara for the purpose of dalliance.

28b-29. On hearing these words of their step-son, the mother-queens trembled with grief. In a faltering tone they spoke wishing for the benefit of their step-son.

"Your statement must of necessity be executed. It is reasonable by all means.

30-32. But your father may approach Mohinī after giving gifts duly to his other wives. If any husband wishes to marry a second or a subsequent wife, he must give the eldest wife twice the amount (of dowry received from her ?) Otherwise he is a debtor. If the husband takes the permission of the eldest wife and marries another lady, he must give what the eldest wife desires and demands—so opine the persons who know the traditional customs and manners. The excellent man must perform Iṣṭāpūrta (i.e. sacrifices, digging of wells and charitable rites) in the company of the eldest wife.

33a. This is the Dharma (religious practice). Otherrwise it will be injustice and there will be complete destruction of Dharma as well.

33b-34. On hearing the words of the mothers the son (i.e. Dharmāṅgada) gave with a delightful heart each of them many presents. The prince gave them more than a crore each. He gave away a thousand cities and a thousand villages to them as well.

35. To each of them he gave eight chariots fitted with garlands of gold and yoked to four female mules.

36-37. He gave them ten thousand garments the price of each of which was more than a hundred coins. To each of his mothers the prince gave a hundred thousand pure gold pieces of everlasting (lustre) excavated from Mount Meru. The son of the king gave each of them more than a hundred men servants and women slaves.

38. To each of them he gave ten thousand cows, each of which yielded a big potfull of milk (at a time). He gave them

16. The trees were never devoid of fruits and flowers; the fields were never devoid of barley and rice grains. Cows yielded potfulls of milk sweet like sugar and productive of ghee.

17. Under his rule Milk was a good beverage, destructive of all distress, dispelling sins and increasing the development of the body. No man saved and hoarded wealth (for his selfish purpose); no wife spoke harsh or bitter words.

18. The son was humble (all sons were humble) engaged in carying out the behests of his father; the daughter-in-law remained perfectly obedient and submissive to the mother-in-law; the common people abided by the advice of Brāhmaṇas; excellent Brāhmaṇas performed holy rites mentioned in the Vedas.

19. People never took food on the day of Mādhava (Viṣṇu) i.e. on the Ekādaśī day; the rivers never went dry; riches did not get exhausted although they were enjoyed by men in the course of their enjoyment of pleasures.

20. When Dharmāṅgada engaged himself in the protection of his kingdom, the people were contented, as the Dūrvā grass flourishes when watered well and a fine grassy plain is evolved, so people flourished.

21. By observing fast etc. on the day of Hari, men enjoyed pleasures and attained the region of Hari. People, not being afraid of robbers (due to security measures and police protection prevalent then), did not bolt their doors even in dark nights.

22. Cows did not give extra trouble to the cowherds in looking after them; they went to graze according to their own wish and returned to the abodes as usual. They yielded potful of milk in plenty. They were fond of their calves and they spread peace everywhere.

23. The Earth grew plenty of grains etc. without being ploughed. All plants and trees grew up without the use of ploughshare. Infants were nourished by the breast-milk of their mothers. Young damsels were developed and nourished thanks to the activities of their husbands.

24. The people well protected by the king, were fully developed. Virtue in the company of truth was fully developed;

when the people who were endowed with devotion to Hari and who had the great interest in virtue were being protected by the king's son, time passed on causing happiness to all.

25. The king was free from ailment. He was endowed with riches; showering much (i.e. spending a great deal) he celebrated great festivals; he was much enamoured of Mohinī and all her activities gave him happiness.

26. Neither of the day nor of the night was he aware. He was not conscious of the fortnights and months that passed by; even years went by unnoticed; he was so enamoured of the sexual dalliance of the daughter of Brahmā of auspicious activities.

27. The king's virility increased with the loving union with Mohinī; the more he resorted to her with the backing of Kāma (God of Love), the sexual potency increased all the more like the moon in the bright half of the month; it never got exhausted by the frequent indulgence in sex.

28. Just as the Devas become stronger and stronger by imbibing the nectar juice, so also the more he touched her the fresher he became. Drinking charming beverages and listening to sweet songs consisting of melodious tone (he increased in virility and strength).

29-32. Even while glancing at the beauty of the (attendant) women, he touched and caressed the moon-like face of Mohinī. With delight he pressed and caressed her stout breasts resembling gold pots and covered with necklaces and other ornaments. The three curly lines of hair that grew round her navel appeared splendid and charming. On seeing the all-round beauty of the breasts of the fair-limbed lady of splendid eyes, the king thought thus (?) "No other women has a beauty like this. It is charming and pleasing to mind. The way in which the features of Mohinī have been created by Brahmā (is not found elsewhere). It is very fascinating to look at her calves that have the lustre of molten gold, that resemble the paws of a lion and that have no hair on them."

33-34. The row of her teeth had the lustre of the moon. Her hidden ankles had been created for fascinating the people. After seeing the beautiful form, from head to foot of the lady of large charming eyes, the king considered himself superior to the Devas. He was delighted and considered himself blessed much—O ! whatever this lady of slender frame and large eyes may request me should be given to her.

35-36. For the sweet and charming sexual intercourse with this splendid lady, I will give her in the end all the wealth I possess. Even rare things should be given to her, those things which cannot be given by others, I will give her even those things which should not be given. For example, my life should not be given. But if the gold-complexioned lady requests for it, I will definitely give it to her. I will never think over it hesitatingly. Excepting my son, there is nothing which should not be given to her.

CHAPTER TWENTY

Dharmāṅgada's conquest of quarters (world)

Vasiṣṭha said :

1. Thus eight years passed on happily during which king Rukmāṅgada was deluded by the sexual intercourse with Mohinī.

2-3a. In the course of the ninth year, the king's powerful son Dharmāṅgada attacked and conquered five Vidyādharas on the Malaya, the excellent mountain. He brought as booty five splendid jewels that bestowed all cherished desires.

3b-5. One of the jewels yielded crores and crores of gold pieces, and was very auspicious. The second jewel bestowed lakhs and crores of garments, ornaments etc., the third jewel exuded nectar that rejuvinated the people: the fourth jewel could erect assembly halls and present cooked accomplished food and the fifth enable one to move about anywhere in the three worlds and range through the sky.

6-7. Taking with him those five jewels, the prince instantly came near his step mother and father Rukmāṅgada accompanied by those defeated Vidyādharas and their women folk whose eyes were filled with tears. He bowed down to them and dedicated the five jewels at their feet. With the head bent down in humility he said :—

8. "O king, O dear father, these five Vidyādharas have been defeated by me in battle by the miraculous missile pertaining to Viṣṇu, on the Malaya, the excellent mountain.

9. O excellent king, these (Vidyādharas) and their women folk have come here as your servants. Please present the jewels to Mohinī as ornaments for her arms.

10-11. They are the bestowers of all cherished desires; they cause rejuvination. By wearing the jewels, old shaky teeth become stronger once again. They yield garments, mansions, gold pieces, movement through heaven and nectar. I had to fight them for a month and thanks to your brilliance, these jewels were obtained by me.

12. With great difficulty, O king, the seven island continents were won by me and thanks to your brilliance the people there are compelled to pay tributes.

13. A year elapsed since I entered into the ocean, and the city Bhogavatī surrounded by serpents has been conquered by me.

14. Serpent virgins numbering to ten thousand have been brought over by me. Necklaces and jewels are brought by me in plenty.

15-17a. Thereafter, O dear father, I went to the great city of Dānavas. After defeating them, eight thousand beautiful girls of great splendour are brought by me. O king, ten crores of jewels that carry on the duty of illumination at nightfall have been brought into your mansion.

17b-19. Then I went to the world of Varuṇa situated beneath Rasātala (netherworlds.) There Lord Varuṇa who was puffed with pride of his power and influence, although he deserves to be the servant of your feet, was intimated by me thus—"Stay under the control of my father, King Rukmāṅgada if you wish to remain alive. At my words Varuṇa was infuriated and he came to fight with me.

20. Then a fight ensued with him terribly at Rasātala and continued for a year. The leader of aquatic forces was defeated by me by means of the miraculous missile pertaining to Nārāyaṇa.

21. At the supplication of young women (his wives), he was not killed. For the protection of his life, ten thousand horses as fast as the wind were given (as tribute) by the defeated (lord).

22. These horses were white in colour with the refulgence of the moon but had one of their ears dark in colour. Without grass and water they could live for many years.

23. A beautiful and fully bedecked virgin was presented to me. Varuṇa gave her to me as my wife. That auspicious girl also has been brought by me.

24-25. The girl was brought by me alongwith much wealth. O dear, there is no spot in the three worlds which had been difficult of access to me and which had not been conquered by me because of the merit of serving your feet. Hence get up and inspect carefully the great fortune earned by me through your grace.

26-27. O Lord of the subjects, myself, all my riches, everything is subservient to you. The son who says "This fortune has been earned by me, it shall not be given to Brāhmaṇas," will fall into hell. O dear father, self-esteem should not be indulged in by the son.

28-30. In regard to the hoarded wealth, the son is like a dagger or a sickle. It is thanks to the heroism of the father that the hoards of wealth of the son increase. Taking a sharp-shining sickle, one cuts off clusters of grass.

If the cloth (mast) is filled with wind, one is enabled to cross a river etc. in a boat. (The sails filled with wind (i.e. the force of wind enables the man in the boat to cross the river (lit. water). Just as the wooden doll of a woman moves and dances in accordance with the desire of the (wire-pulling) juggler, so also the sons are instilled with brilliance and strength through the virility of the father.

31. Hence this good fortune that has been brought by me may be viewed at by you. You may distribute or preserve your riches as you wish or they may be given to the most excellent one among the groups of mothers.

CHAPTER TWENTYONE

Dharmāṅgada's marriages and his order as a Ruler

Māndhātā enquired :

1. What did the king do on hearing the words of his son ? O Brāhmaṇa, what did the daughter of the creator, Mohinī, the beloved of the king, do ?

2. A particularly wonderful and holy narrative that is comparable to the nectar and is destructive of all doubts has been told by you.

Vasiṣṭha said :

3. On hearing the words of his son, the prominent king became delighted. He got up alongwith his beloved wife and surveyed the wealth (the booty brought by Dharmāṅgada).

4-6a. Instantaneously, O king, the delighted king who was a great devotee of Viṣṇu, joyfully and lovingly gave to his son Dharmāṅgada, all those serpent-girls alongwith the daughter of Varuṇa, for the purpose of becoming his wives. All the remaining things, the king who was overwhelmed by the arrows of Kāma gave to Mohinī along with many jewels and the Dānava women (?)

6b. Thus the father distributed the wealth brought by Dharmāṅgada.

7-8. At an opportune time, the king called his priest and said this : "O Brāhmaṇa, may my son take in marriage the hands of all the virgins in accordance with religious rites.

under the ascendancy of the star propitious for marriages and on the Muhūrta that confers all cherished desires.

9. Having performed the initial religious rite of the proclamation of propitiousness (known as Svasti-Vācana) through Brāhmaṇas and after propitiating them with the gifts of cows, gold, clothes, celebrate the rite of marriage ceremony of my son Dharmāṅgada.

10. The foolish father who does not celebrate the marriage of his son, will sink down in the terrible bottomless hell and remain there for ten thousand Yugas.

11. Hence, the father endowed with (i.e. following) religious rites should celebrate the marriage of his son. He who has settled his son, has also established his own self.

12. O god on the earth (Brāhmaṇa), when the marriage of a son is celebrated, a person derives the benefit of all sacrifices irrespective of the son being endowed with good attributes or devoid of attributes.

13-15a. The marriage of the son must be celebrated by the father who wishes for gaining merit and piety. If the father does not unite (i.e. endow) his sons with wealth and a spouse, he is despised both here and hereafter, and he should not be considered a good man. Hence sons must be settled in avocations and be provided with wives, (they must be given these facilities) so that the sons are satisfied and well honoured and are able to sport (spend their life) happily."

15b-16a. On hearing these words of the king, the Brāhmaṇa his priest, exerted himself assiduously for the celebration of the marriage of Dharmāṅgada, with great. delight.

16b-17a. Though he did not crave for the happiness of contact with women, on account of his bashfulness, the son accepted the betrothal ceremony at the behest of his father.

17b-18a. The prince of mighty arms, unequalled on the Earth in beauty, married the charming serpent-virgins alongwith the daughter of Varuṇa.

18b-19. After marrying all of them in accordance with the injunctions of the sacred texts, he joyously gifted wealth, cows and jewels to the Brāhmaṇas. After the marriage rite, he joyously bowed down to the feet of his mother and father.

20. Then the son Dharmāṅgada spoke to the gentle lady Sandhyāvalī—"O gentle lady, my marriage rite has been celebrated at the instance of my father.

21. I am not retaining the memory of this fact in my mind that my marriage has already been celebrated by my father. O gentle lady, I shall serve as before my unchanging father who is a man of perfect wisdom.

22. I have nothing to do with divine enjoyment of pleasures. I don't have any use even for heaven. Service must be rendered by me to my father as well as to you both by day and at night.

Sandhyāvalī said :

23. O son, live long. Live happily. Enjoy all pleasures in accordance with your mental inclinations (i.e. as you please). May you be long-lived, thanks to the grace of your father. O my son, delight my mind.

24. O son, with you as my son of good qualities, I have become Suputriṇī (mother of a good son). I have got a special place in the hearts of all my co-wives (i.e. all of them love me)."

25. After saying this, the lady embraced him, sniffed many times the crown of his head and finally discharged him to resume his duty of looking after the administration of the kingdom.

26. After being discharged by his mother, he bowed to all the other mothers. Abiding by the advice of his father, the prince looked after the problems of government administration.

27. He chastised and restrained the wicked ones; he protected the good and the well-disciplined men of virtues; he toured over all his lands and personally looked into all affairs.

28. He inspected all the affairs in each place once in a month; he looked after the breeding and rearing of elephants and horses; he surveyed the troops of spies.

29. He observed the arguments (going on in the courts of justice); everyday he examined the measures and balances; he protected men in every house.

30. No infant in the arms accustomed to suck the breasts cried for want of breast milk; nowhere did a mother-in-law lament and complain of being disrespected by the daughter-in-law.

31. No competent and efficient son begged of his father; there was no mixing and mingling of castes in any group again.

32. No man kept any concealed income; no man blamed Dharma; no woman remained without bodice if her husband was alive.

33. "May not there be the coming out of women from their houses in my country. May not the widow keep her tresses in tact.[1] May not the ladies with their husband alive be devoid of hair on their heads.

34. May not the devotee observing holy rites be one who reviles always; may not the forest-dwellers permanently dwell in the city. Let there not be any ruthless person who does not give even ordinary maintenance.

35. Let these not stay in my kingdom—A cowherd desirous of urban life; an advisor devoid of good attributes; a Ṛtvik who has not learned the sacred texts.

---

1. This reference to tonsure of widows shows the lateness of this portion of NP. in date (not earlier than the 10th Cent. A.D.). There is no injunction or reference to such tonsure in the Vedas, the Gṛhya and Dharma Sūtras or in the old Smṛtis like Manu & Yājñavalkya. The prohibition of widows from "adorning the hair, chewing the betel-nut, using perfumes or decking in flowers and ornaments

(*keśa-rañjana-tāmbūla-gandha-puṣpādisevanam*)

in the *Vṛddha-Hārīta* VIII. 205, shows that tonsure of widows was not in vogue then. References to Kṣatriya widows of the Kaurava and Yādava families in the *Mbh.* (*Strī* 17.25, 21.6; *Mausala* 7-17) shows no reference to their tonsure. Vijñāneśvara, on Yājñavalkya III. 325, approvingly quotes in the *Mitākṣarā* Manu's prohibition of tonsure of women :

vidvad-vipra-nṛpa-strīṇām neṣyate keśa-vāpanam /

A late work or a late interpolation in the Sk. P. gives us its first indication in *Kāśī Khaṇḍa* 4·75 ff.

śiraso vapanaṁ tasmāt kāryam vidhavayā sadā)

Restriction on wearing on bodice along with this shows that both NP & Sk. P. record a period when widows came to be looked upon as *Yatis* (NP. II. 24.15). Kane conjectures that this shows a society in the 10th or 11th cent. A.D. (H.D. II. i. P. 592).

36. The man who grows the indigo plant, the man who sprinkles profusely, the blue colour; these two sinners must be banished and so also the man who brews the liquor.

37. A back-biter, a slanderer who is fond of eating the fish on the back—may he not find a residence in my kingdom. So also the man who forsakes his own wife.

38. These persons are to be punished and given capital punishment—he who eschews Viṣṇu the foremost among the gods and worships any other deity; he who cohabits with a pregnant woman and he who has sexual intercourse with a young woman who has recently delivered of a child.

CHAPTER TWENTYTWO

The glory of the month of Kārttika

Vasiṣṭha said :

1. Thus, O leading king, at the behest of his father, Dharmāṅgada ruled over the kingdom on the earth, observing fast on the day of Hari.

2. There was no such man as was not stabilised in virtue, no one was unhappy, no one was devoid of issues, O king, there was no leper in the kingdom.

3. The Earth yielded treasures to the people who were joyous and well-nourished. O king, even after the calves were fully satisfied, the cows yielded pots full of milk.

4. In every leafy cup there was honey; every tree yielded a Droṇa measure of honey ? The earth being highly delighted, all kinds of grains were produced.

5-14. It was the Dvāparayuga at the end of Tretā but it vied with Kṛta age (in piety). The danger due to clouds disappeared; the sky and the house became free from clouds or impurities. The fragrant Śāli rice grains had ripened. The star canopus (Agastya) surveyed the world (was in ascendancy).

Everywhere the rivers had medium flow of water currents (neither too much nor too little). With the white Kāśa flowers growing on the banks, the rivers appeared like whitehaired ladies, the whole world was whitened by the rays of the moon, the sun was not very fierce; the people in variegated dresses and features thronged rivers and tanks for their holy ablutions; everywhere the kings were eager to go on campaigns of conquests; at the end of Āśvina month, during the period of wakening of Viṣṇu, the preceptor of the Universe, Mohinī the beautiful lady who had delighted the king with nice feelings and different kinds of pleasures (acts of service) was oppressed by mental yearnings. She delighted the king in the forests, on the peaks of mountains, in the confluences of rivers, in the different kinds of lakes, abounding in lotus flowers, on the mountains of Malaya, Mandara, Vindhya, Mahendra, the abode of the Devas, the Sahya, the Himālayas and the auspicious mountain of the sky-clad (naked) God viz. Śiva—i.e. Śiva's mountain of Kailāsa. She gave delight to the king in the heavenly abodes, and other places. O leading king, assuming her divine form, she delighted him day by day. On obtaining Mohinī, the king forsook all holy rites but not the observance on the day of Hari (i.e. the Ekādaśī) that is destructive of births and deaths. Though excessively enamoured of her, the king did not forsake this Vrata.

15-16. The king used to eschew sexual dalliance for three days beginning with Daśamī (the tenth day). Even as he sported like this, one full year elapsed and the auspicious month of Kārttika, the most excellent one in the view of those who know time, arrived once again. This month is highly meritorious, because it puts an end to the slumber of Viṣṇu.

17. O king (Māndhātā), whatever is done in this month is meritorious; the holy rites performed by those men who are the devotees of Viṣṇu shall yield everlasting benefits; they take one to Viṣṇu's world.

18. There is no other month equal to Kārttika; there is no other Yuga equal to Kṛta; there is no other holy rite that is equal to mercifulness; there is no other Jyotis (luminary) equal to the eye.

19. There is no sacred text equal to the Vedas; there is no holy river equal to Gaṅgā; there is no other charitable gift equal to that of lands; no other pleasure is equal to that derived from one's wife.

20. There is no other valuable possession equal to agricultural lands; there is no other profitable acquisition equal to a good cow; there is no greater austerity than abstaining from taking food; there is no other auspicious thing on a par with self control.

21. No other gratification is equal to that of the palate; no one is equal to a Brāhmaṇa; there is no other friend on a par with Dharma (virtue) and there is no other fame equal to that of truthfulness.

22. No other Aiśvarya (prosperity and glory) can be equal to the freedom from ailments, no other deity greater than Keśava. The learned and wise men know of no other thing as sacred as the month of Kārttika in this world.

23-24. Kārttika is the most excellent of all months of which God Viṣṇu is always fond. He who passes this favourite month of Dāmodara without the observance of holy rites, is reborn in the wombs of animals and other creatures. He is excluded from all holy religious rites.

Māndhātā enquired :—

25-26. O sage, when the month of Kārttika arrived, how did king Rukmāṅgada enjoy Mohinī of highly fascinating features ? Tell me. The excellent king was a devotee of Viṣṇu, a follower of the Vedas and the foremost among kings. What did he do in that holiest month ?

Vasiṣṭha replied :

27. On seeing that the month of Kārttika had arrived for the awakening of Hari, the excessively enamoured prominent king spoke these words to Mohinī.

28. O gentle lady, I have had sexual dalliance with you for many years, but nothing against you had been mentioned to by me so far because I had been afraid of being disrespected by you.

Deva with an aerial chariot and he attains the highest beatitude.

39b-41a. Hence, O Mohinī, eschew your delusion and fascination over me; command me immediately. I shall perform the holy rite of Kārttika Vrata. O lotus-eyed lady, I shall desist from the worship of your breasts and I shall observe the vows for the worship of Hari.

Mohinī said :

41b-43. Narrate in detail the greatness of Kārttika. O excellent king, this month is said to be the receptacle of all merits. O highly intelligent one, what are the special features mentioned and where ? After hearing about the greatness of Kārttika, I shall perform it as desired.

Rukmāṅgada said :

44. O fair-faced lady, I shall tell you the greatness of this month,[1] whereby you will have devotion (engendered in you) for the performance of the worship of Hari.

45-46. The man who performs the Kṛcchra penance or the Prājāpatya rite[2] in the month of Kārttika or observes fast on alternate days or once in three days, or for ten days, or for a fortnight or for the whole of the month, O fair-complexioned lady attains the greatest region of Viṣṇu.

---

1. The month of Kārttika is regarded as the holiest month, holier than all *Tīrthas* (sacred places) and great sacrifices. The glory of Kārttika is detailed in Pd. P. VI. Chs. 92-95. A number of vratas are prescribed for performance in this month. *vide* CC. *Vrata* II. 769-784, *Smṛti-Kaustubha* 358-427, *Nirṇaya Sindhu* 192-208. For their alphabetic list HD V. 1. 283-285.

2. The *Prājāpatya Vrata* consists of donation of a cow at the end of *Kṛcchra* penance and feeding Brāhmaṇas according to one's ability. Fruit—a place in god Śiva's region.

Kṛcchrānte gopradaḥ kuryād bhojanaṁ śaktitaḥ padaṁ
Viprāṇāṁ Śāṅkaram yāti Prājāpatyam idaṁ vratam

- Mt. P. 100.66

It may be noted that this Vrata is different from *Prajāpati Vrata* which (according to *Praśnopaniṣad* I. 15) means 'indulging in sexual intercourse only at night'.

for the destruction of all sins and for the crease of your love".

Mohini said :

66-67. O The incomparable greatness of the month of Kārttika has been described by you. Kindly recount the rules of procedure of the concluding rites of Cāturmāsya Vratas (holy rites during the four months of the rainy season) O Lord of the earth, whereby the Vratas shall be complete and there will not be any deficiency or omission in the Vrata or in the benefit, thereof.

The king said :

68. O beloved wife, the devotee who performs the Naktavrata (i.e. taking food only at night) should feed a Brāhmaṇa with food-stuffs consisting of all the six tastes.

69. If he performs the rite of Ayācita (not begging for anything) he shall give a bull as gift along with gold. A person who does not eat flesh (meat) shall give a cow as gift alongwith Dakṣiṇā.

70. In the rite of ablution with embylic myrobalan, the man should give curds and milk-puddings. If the person observes the vow of abstaining from fruits, O lady of good eyebrows, he should make gifts of fruits.

71. If one has eschewed oil, one shall make gifts of ghee and if one has eschewed ghee, one shall make gifts of milk. If there is a vow restricting the eating of grains, one should give Śāli (rice) or the respective grains of corn.

72. If the vow is for laying down on the bare ground, he should make gift of a mattress filled with cotton along with four cowries as Dakṣiṇā. If the devotee has vowed to take food on leaves, he shall give a vessel full of ghee.

73. If the devotee has vowed silence, he should give either a bell or gingelly seeds alongwith gold. He should feed a couple and give beds for both.

74. The enjoyment of pleasures shall be alongwith Dakṣiṇās for the sake of completion of the Vrata. If the rite is regular morning ablution, he should offer a horse; if the vow is for eschewing oily stuff, he shall offer ghee and barley.

75. If the rite is for growing nails and hair he should give a mirror as a gift. If the rite is for eschewing foot-wear he should give a pair of shoes.

76. If one has vowed to forsake salt, a good cow is to be given; if one has eschewed meat eating, one should give a tawny coloured cow with its calf.

77-78. If one has vowed the offering of the lighted lamp in one's favourite temple every day, one should give a lamp made of gold or copper alongwith ghee. O beloved one, for the completion of the Vrata he should give an umbrella to a devotee of Viṣṇu alongwith a cloth. One who has undertaken fast on alternate days, should give silk-garment as a gift.

79. If one has undertaken fast once in three days one should give a fully bedecked bed accompanied by gold. In the fasts such as one for six successive days etc., one should give a palanquin alongwith umbrella.

80. If the vow is for a single meal per day, one should give stout bull alongwith a man to look after the same, or goats and sheep. If one has vowed for a fruitarian diet, one shall give gold as gift.

81. If one has vowed vegetable diet one shall give fruit as gift alongwith gold and ghee. If one has eschewed all tasty beverages, one shall give even what is not mentioned here as a gift.

82-84. One must give silver or gold vessel as gift in accordance with one's capacity. If one does not follow the injunctions in the performance of these rites or if one does give things mentioned as gifts (one will incur sin). O beautiful lady of good eyebrows, one must abide by the advice of the Brāhmaṇa priest and perform the rite with the remembrance of Viṣṇu. O auspicious lady, if one considers the statement (i.e. advice) of the Brāhmaṇa futile and does not give Dakṣiṇās, one certainly falls into hell, if there is omission or deficiency in the Vrata the man becomes a leper and a blind fellow.

85-86. The heaven-dwellers, the group of holy centres, the sacrifices of all these are well established in the words of Brāhmaṇas. O beautiful lady, who will transgress their words, if he desires welfare and if he is a sensible scholar and knowledgeable person.

87. This is the secret of Dharma (holy rites) that has been mentioned to you in the same manner as it had been mentioned to Brahmā by Lord of Śrī (Viṣṇu). It should not be divulged to others. It is beneficial and it is the cause of Mādhava's satisfaction.

CHAPTER TWENTYTHREE

The dialogue with Rukmāṅgada

Mohini said :

1. The statement made by you about the observance of fast in the month of Kārttika is quite excellent. But the observance of Vrata etc. by kings is not found anywhere in the sacred texts.

2. In fact, excepting for a Brāhmaṇa, it has not been prescribed for anyone else; not for the Śūdras and the Vaiśyas too. (As the duty) of the kings, charitable gifts, protection (of subjects) and fighting are laid down (in Smṛtis).

3. If you wish to retain me as your beloved, the Vrata should not be observed by you. O leading king, I cannot remain without · ou even for a Muhūrta.

4-5a. O dear king having the lustre of god Brahmā, how can I remain separated for a period of month? O ruler of the Earth, where you think of observing fast, food should rather be offered in lieu of it to Brāhmaṇas of noble souls. Or may the eldest of all your wives observe the Vratas.

5b-6. When this was argued by Mohinī, Rukmabhūṣaṇa (i.e. Rukāṅgada) called his auspicious and beloved wife Sandhyāvalī. The instant she was called, she came near the king who was one who had distributed religious gifts and fees in plenty.

7-8. He was seated on a divine like splendid bed clasped between the arms of Mohinī. The tip of her breasts resembled golden pitcher when rubbing against him. O king (Māndhātā) he was seated on the mattress of the lustful lady of charming eyes. With the palms joined in reverence, Sandhyāvalī stooped down her neck in bowing down to her husband.

9. She said to the king, " O darling, why have I been called? Being completely free from the jealousy usual among co-wives, I have always abided by your order.

10. There is no doubt about this, O king, that the more you indulge in sexual dalliance with Mohinī the more my pleasure increases.

11-12. O king, the woman who becomes miserable at the personal pleasure of her husband is reborn as a she-falcon for eight years (?). Command me, O king, do not get abashed due to your lustfulness.

Rukmāṅgada said :

13. O fair lady, I know your good conduct, and the nobility of your birth. It was at your instance that sexual dalliance with Mohinī for a long time was indulged in by me.

14. Many Kārttika months have gone by while I indulged in sexual dalliance. Though I have been enamoured of the happiness derived from my beloved, the day of Hari (i.e. Ekādaśī) did not slip by.

15. By my frequent enjoyment of lustful pleasures I have achieved satiety. This month of Kārttika is known to be the destroyer of all sins.

16. O gentle lady, I am desirous of observing the holy vow of Kārttika Vrata that yields great merit. But O auspicious lady, this daughter of Brahmā prevents me from observing it.

17. O fair-complexioned lady, by no means should anything displeasing to her be committed. Hence you take up my Vrata called Kṛcchra that dries up the body.

18. On being urged thus by her husband, the lady whose complexion was like that of newly burnished gold, whose breasts and other limbs were plump and whose face resembled the moon spoke these words :— "I shall observe the holy Vrata for your satisfaction."

19. O Lord of rulers of men, I shall perform only those things whereby you will have fame and renown, whereby you will have happiness without prejudice to your good reputation. I shall even cast off my tender body into the fire for your sake.

20. O king, at your instance, I will even kill my son. I will not consider it as something that should not be done. All the more, O ruler of men, I shall perform this simple holy rite."

21. After saying this and after bowing to the king who was the enemy of the son of the sun (i.e. Yama), the gentle lady of charming large eyes performed holy rite for the destruction of sins.

22. When the excellent holy penance ealled Kṛcchra was begun by his beloved wife, the king derived much pleasure. He spoke these words to the daughter of the Kuśa-emblemed deity (Brahmā)—"O lady of beautiful eyebrows, your suggestion has been carried out in accordance with your desire.

23. O beautiful lady with thighs resembling metacarpus, sport as you please with the gladness of your heart. Leave off your cares and concentrate your ambitions and desires in me. O lady of sweet eye-brows, for your sake I have eschewed my duties. There is no other woman to give me happiness."

24. On being thus addressed by her Lord, she attained great pleasure. She spoke to the king thus :— "O Lord, It was after knowing that you are exceedingly loving (and tender) that I had come to you from the heaven.

25. I had forsaken the immortal ones, the groups of Daityas, Gandharvas, Yakṣas, serpents and Rākṣasas, who were awaiting me. Overcome with love, I approached you at the mountain of Mandara.

26. The like-mindedness of both (husband and wife) is the real fruit of passion. Passionate union with the mind elsewhere is no better than the union of two corpses.

27. Fruitful is my body. Fruitful is my beauty. O lover, with you full of love towards me, I have acquired that which is very rare in the three worlds.

28-29a. When the heart clasped within plump protruding breasts does not relent (break), I think it is certainly like Indra's thunderbolt. The nectarine juice from the lips of beautiful ladies is the very ambrosia in the world. It is being drunk with the breasts pressed close to the heart."

29b-30a. After saying this, the lady of slender limbs embraced the king who was in the secluded spot and delighted him in accordance with the injunctions of Vātsyāyana[1], the author of erotic science (Kāma-sūtra).

30b-31. Even as he was diverting himself in the company of Mohinī, the sound of drums which were placed on an intoxicated elephant according to the decree of Dharmāṅgada reached his ears.

32. "O people, the day of Hari dawns tomorrow. Remain with only a single meal.[2] All shall eschew alkaline salts, taking in only Haviṣya (cooked rice soaked in ghee).

33. You must lie down on the bare ground. You must avoid sexual union with your beloved wives. Remember the Lord of the Chief of the Devas, the ancient and excellent Puruṣa.

34-35a. Either take a single meal or observe fast. You will thereby be able to go to the region of Śrī Hari without performing a series of Śrāddhas, without offering or taking Piṇḍas and even when your sons have not gone to Gayā.[3]

---

1. Vātsyāyana (Circa 300-400 A.D.) is the author of the famous treatise, *Kāma Sūtra.* The instructions on erotics mentioned here are given in the *Adhikaraṇa* (section) on *Sāmprayogika.* For details *vide Kāma sūtra* with com. *Jayamaṅgalā.* (Chowkhamba, 1912.)

2. Compare the procedure of the Ekādaśī Vrata *Supra* I. Ch. 23.

3. A famous sacred place in Bihar. It is supposed that by performing *Śrāddha* and offering *Piṇḍas* on Viṣṇupada at Gayā one redeems one thousand generations and takes them and himself to the world of Viṣṇu. The sacredness of the place and its efficacy to redeem the ancestors of the pilgrim is glorified in many other Purāṇas like *AP.*, *Vāyu* etc. Thus the *Vāyu* 105.30 states he who performs Śrāddha at Gayā repays his debts to his ancestors.

Śrāddha-kṛd yo Gayā-kṣetre pitṛṇām anṛṇo hi saḥ /

For details *vide infra* Chs. 44 to 47 with annotations.

35b-38a. This is the eleventh day in the bright half of the month of Kārttika, which dispels the slumber of Hari. The Ekādaśī dawns tomorrow. Do not take food at all. If one observes fast on the Prabodhinī Ekādaśī day, all the sins such as the slaughter of a Brāhmaṇa and the like which one might have committed wilfully, disappear. This is called Prabodhinī Ekādaśī because it enlightens virtuous persons and those who practise just activities. Also it wakens Hari from slumber.

38b-39a. The man who at least once observes the fast on this day that dispels the slumber of Hari, does not become a son once again. He is not reborn in any womb.

39b-40. O men, perform the worship of the discus-bearing Lord with your own wealth, clothes, flowers, incense, lights, excellent sandal paste, saffron, sweet fruits and scents. All of you worship the feet of Śrī Hari.

41. He who does not carry out my instructions, conducive to the attainment of piety and salvation (attainment to the vision of Viṣṇu), is liable (lit. deserves) to be killed, banished from the realm or certainly punished (otherwise) by me."

42. While the drum that had the sound of the clouds was being beaten to proclaim as before, the most excellent king dropped down the chewing betel along with camphor from his hand.

43. Withdrawing his chest that was in contact with the breasts of Mohinī, the king (though) of enhanced appetite for sexual pleasure, stood up from his bed.

44. With bland speech he consoled Mohinī who was afflicted with delusion and passion :— "O gentle lady the day of Hari that is destructive of sins dawns tomorrow.

45. I will be observing restraints. May I be forgiven. May I be excused. At your behest the Kṛcchra penance is being caused to be performed by Sandhyāvalī.

46. But this Ekādaśī vow that is called Prabodhakāraṇī should be performed by me. It cuts off bonds of all sins. It bestows salvation.

47. To all the three worlds, it is the cause of celebrating great festivities. Hence, O lady of elated gait, I will partake of only Haviṣya invariably.

48. O lady of large eyes propitiate Adhokṣaja (Viṣṇu) Hṛṣīkeśa along with me, by being engaged in the observance of fast. Thereby, you will attain salvation devoid of burning sensation and dissolution.

Mohinī said :

49. O king, you have spoken pertinently. At your behest, I shall perform the worship of the discus-bearing deity, that dispels births, deaths and old age.

50-52a. The time of fulfillment has come for that vow (promise) that had been undertaken by you formerly on the top of the Mandara mountain, along with the offering of the hand. It was marked by staking your merits. Hence, may that be given to me. If you do not grant me that boon, all the merits that you have accumulated since your birth with great difficulty, will perish instantaneously.

Rukmāṅgada said :

52b-53. Come on, O lady of charming limbs I will carry out whatever you entertain in your mind. There is nothing which should not be given to you. Even my life shall be given to you, O beautiful lady—what then of villages, wealth etc. including the earth.

Mohinī said :

54-57. O Lord, O love, O powerful king, O Lord of my life fond of sexual intercourse, if I, your beloved wife, am to be enjoyed, no fast should be observed on the day of Viṣṇu. O king, am I not your beloved wife ? I do not wish to spend even a Muhūrta without contact with you, O excellent one. So O king, devoted to truth, if you wish to enjoy me, give up this vow of fast. May food be taken on the day of Hari.

57-58a. It is this boon that should be granted to me. This is what had been requested for by me formerly. O leading king, if you do not grant it (this boon) to me, you will become a man of falsehood. You will fall into a terrible hell (and remain there as long as all living beings are dissolved. (upto the end of the world).

The king implored :

58b. O auspicious lady, please do not speak like this. This is not proper on your part ?

59. Why do you, though a daughter of god Brahmā, create obstacles in the observance of holy rites. Ever since my birth I have never taken food on the day of Hari.

60-61a. O auspicious lady, now that my hairs have begun to turn grey, how shall I take food ? Having recourse to the heavenly river (i.e. the Gaṅgā) or the worship of Hari is proper in case of a man who has gone beyond the prime of youth and the power of whose sense-organs has dwindled.

61b-62a. This (i.e. taking food on the Ekādaśī day) is what has not been committed by me whether in boyhood or in youth. It is a despicable act. How can I perform it now, when I have become feeble and am lacking in virility ?

62b-63. Be pleased, O lady of roving side-glances. be pleased, O fair-complexioned lady. Do not create obstacles in my Vrata. I shall give you the riches of the kingdom. O lady of beautiful eyes, if you do not wish for it, I shall do another thing.

64. I shall make you seated in a palanquin that is very splendid and resembling the aerial chariot. Accompanied by my wife, I shall walk on food and take you wherever you wish.

65-66. If you do not like the aerial chariot made by me, I will make two pillars of gold adorned with corals. O my beloved wife, I will prepare a swing of pearls for your sake. I shall swing you therein day and night for many months.

67-68. O my beloved lady, O beautiful one, do not create obstacles in the performance of my holy rite. If food is taken on the day of Hari, O fair-faced lady, it is more despicable than eating the flesh (from the hands) of a Cāṇḍāla or that of a dog. If one indulges in sexual intercourse when the moon dwindles (i.e. on the New Moon day), one incurs the sin of destroying the three worlds.

69-70. A man incurs sins in the following circumstances: —if he gets himself shaved on the Bhūta day (i.e. the fourteenth day in the dark half of the month of Kārttika); if he takes food on the day of Viṣṇu; if he takes oil bath on Ṣaṣṭhī (sixth day of a lunar fortnight); if he takes salt, O auspicious lady, on the Tṛtīyā (third) day and meat on the Saptamī (seventh) day if he takes in ghee on the full moon day and drinks liquor during the transit of the sun from one sign of zodiac to another.

71-73. On the day of Hari, food (to be taken in) contains the sin accrued in the following acts viz.—if one spoils the pasture-land of cows., if one commits perjury; if one misappropriates a deposit, if one causes hardships to a virgin (e.g. making her marriage impossible), if one commits breach of trust; if one milks a cow the calf of which is dead; if he does not give an excellent Brāhmaṇa what he solemnly promises to give saying 'I will give you", in Maṇikūṭa (fraud committed in regard to a precious gem), in Tulākūṭa (in using false weights), in Kanyānṛta (in uttering a lie about a virgin) and in Gavānṛta (in uttering a lie over a cow). Hence, O fair-eyed lady, how shall I take food knowing that it is a great sin?

Mohinī said :

74-77. While I was in the mountain of Mandara, Gautama told me thus : O leading king, one shall not pass an Ekādaśī day by taking in single meal throughout the day or a nocturnal meal or unsolicited food[1] or by observing fast. Observance of fast is not proper for women advanced in pregnancy, for Gṛhasthas (worshippers) of domestic sacrificial fires), Kṛśas (worn-out weaklings), sick men, Śiśu (children) and the wrinkled worne-out bodied (old people). O leading king, those who are engaged in Yajñas and their enjoyment, those who serve the Earth, those who fight and the Pativratās (chaste ladies) must not observe fast.

1. This verse is found in other Purāṇas e.g. Mk. P. quoted by Hemādri on *Kāla* p. 170, Gd, P. I. 136. 2-3. The snag in Mohinī's argument is that she applies these to an ablebodied person like Rukmāṅgada. Manu X 1.28 & 30 forbids an able-bodied capable person to resort to these alternatives. *Mbh. Śānti* 165.17 supports this. The terms *ekabhakta* or *abhukta* (taking meal after mid-day-*dinārdha-samayetīte*), *nakta* (taking food after the appearance of stars after the sun-set) and *ayācita* (subsistence on food not obtained by begging or soliciting) were used formerly with reference to *Prāyaścittas* like *Kṛcchra*. They came to be applied to fasts in Purāṇas later on.

78. O excellent man, the day of Viṣṇu must not be spent without the observance of Vrata. Those Brāhmaṇas who have maintained the sacred fire should be known as Gṛhasthas (householders).

79. Those who abide by the duties of protecting the subjects should be known as Rājas (kings). Gurviṇī is the lady who is pregnant for eight months. Śiśus are children upto their eighth year.

80. Kṣīṇas are those who observe too many fasts. Valigātras are those old men (whose body contains wrinkles) Mahotsavas are those who are busily engaged in auspicious rites such as marriage etc.

81-82. Those who are engaged in Yajñas are the persons who refrain from worldly activities. (Defective) The woman who is engaged in the welfare of her hnsband by means of the three Karaṇas(organs etc) (i.e. mind, body and speech) should be known as Pativratā (chaste lady). So also the woman who protects her vaginal passage. O king, of what avail are the many utterances I may indulge in ?

83. I will be pleased if you take food on the Ekādaśī day but I won't by pleased even if you cut off your own head and give it to me.

84. O king, if you do not take food on the day of Hari, I will not touch the body belonging to you who are untruthful in your words.

85. O leading king, truthfulness is revered among people of all stages of life and castes. O king, especially it is so among rulers of kingdom like you.

86. It is through truth that the sun blazes;[1] the moon shines through truth. O king, the Earth is established in truth. It is the truth that upholds the universe.

87. The wind blows through truthfulness and the fire burns through truth. This entire Universe consisting of the mobile and the immobile beings has truth for its support.

88. It is through truth that the ocean does not move

---

1. It appears that in VV. 86-89 the Vedic concept of *Ṛta* is extended to *Satya* (Truth).

a conch shell; one must not kill* 'tortoises' and 'pigs;' food should not be taken on the eleventh day in either half of the month. The sin of taking food on that day, O gentle lady, is the same as that of the sexual intercourse with a forbidden woman or that of eating forbidden food or that of doing a prohibited act. It is also equal to the slaughter of a thousand cows. O, gentle lady, how can I take food on the day of Hari in spite of my knowledge of this ?

6. O lady of charming thighs, when the day of Hari has dawned, even the Puroḍāśa (the sacrificial oblation of ground rice) is declared to be equal to the forbidden food. What then about the (ordinary) food taken in by way of regular meal ?

7. O fair-complexioned lady, roots, fruits, milk and water are mentioned by leading sages as favourable foodstuffs of feeble men. They can be eaten.

8-9. But taking full meal on the Ekādaśī day has not been recommended by anyone. Abstinence from food is recommended in the case of persons suffering from fever, and observance of full fast in the case of righteous persons, when the day of Hari has dawned. This is auspicious and conducive to the attainment of salvation. Even if Pathya (wholesome) food is taken in the middle of fever, it is likely to result in death.

10. If food is taken on the day of Viṣṇu (Ekādaśī) it leads only to a fall in hell. O lady of beautiful thighs, please don't insist, let there be no breaking of my holy vow. If there is anything else that appeals to you I shall undoubtedly do it.

**Khādet* should be the reading in the NP. as it is found in this verse in KP. and Devala Smṛti. For discussion vide note below.

This verse is attributed to the KP and Devala Smṛti in the *Nirṇaya Sindhu*, p. 35, and to *Viṣṇudharmottara P.* by Hemādri in *Kāla*. But those verses read

na khādet Kūrma-Śūkarau

The reading *na khādet* is better as *Kūrma* and *Śūkara* are the bulbous roots called *Kaṅgar* and *Kon* in Marathi and the question of 'killing' bulbous roots does not arise. Moreover, the reading in the NP. will amount to a license in killing other animals including cows. But the reading should be decided on the MS evidence of the NP.

Mohinī insisted :

11-12. "O king, nothing else appeals to me except your taking food. No purpose of mine is served even by your dedication of life. Moreover, the observance of fast on the day of Hari is not found in the Vedas.

13. The Brāhmaṇas maintaining the holy sacrificial fires do not accept the observance of fast. How is it that you wish to practise a rite that is outside the pale of the Vedas. ?"

14. O King (Māndhātā), on hearing the words of Mohinī, the king who was the most excellent one among the knowers of the Vedas said laughingly though he got furious in mind.

15-17. "O Mohinī, listen to my words. The performance of sacrifices has its procedure in the Veda (Kriyā Veda) and in the stage of life of a householder the Smṛtis are like the Vedas. The Vedas in the form of Smṛtis and the Kriyā Vedas are based on the Purāṇas. Just as this wonderful universe is born of Purāṇapuruṣa (the ancient Puruṣa or Being) so also the whole range of literature undoubtedly originates from the Purāṇas. O fair-faced lady, I, therefore, consider the meanings of the Purāṇas superior to the meanings of the Vedas.[1]

18. All the Vedas are ever established in the Purāṇas. The Veda is afraid of a man of deficient learning, thinking "O, this man will strike me."

---

1. VV. 15-22 establish the authoritative nature of the Pūrāṇas and their relation *vis-á-vis* the Vedas. The NP regards Purāṇas as the essence of all the Vedas (*supra* I. 1. 61-62), nay their import ss superior to the Vedas. And the NP is not the only Purāṇa to hold this view. For example, the Sk. P. repeats the very wording of these verses : e.g.

Vedāḥ pratiṣṭhitāḥ sarve purāṇe nātra saṁśayaḥ |
bibhetyalpa-śrutād Vedo mām ayam prahariṣyati ||
yan na dṛṣṭaṁ hi Vedeṣu tad dṛṣṭam smṛtibhiḥ kila |
ubhābhyāṁ yan na dṛṣṭaṁ hi tat purāṇeṣu gīyate ||
purāṇaṁ sarva-śātrāṇām prathamaṁ Brahmaṇā smṛtam|

—*Revā Khaṇḍa* I. 20-23.

The equivalence of Purāṇas with the Vedas has been stated in the *Bṛhad-āraṇyaka Up.* (11. 4. 10) where both of them are regarded as the exhalation of God. This authority of Purāṇas is confirmed by Vātsyāyana in his com. on *Nyāya Sūtra* IV. 1.62, Kumārila in *Tantra-Vārttika.* On Jaimini's *Pūrva-mīmāṁsā sūtra* I. 3. 1 and Śaṅkara on *Br. Sūtra* I.3.33.

41. The man who is devoted to other peoples' Dharma and averse to his own Dharma, sinks deep down into blinding darkness of hell and remains there as long as fourteen Indras reign.

42. It has not been mentioned anywhere that kings should abandon their legitimate duty of protecting their subjects that bestow on them the fourfold aims of life, and perform the vow of fasting.

43. (The following are the legitimate duties of the concerned persons). Service to their husbands by women; service to their parents by sons; service to the twice-born by the Śūdras and the protection of the world by the kings.

44. If out of blunder or ignorance, a person forsakes his duties and applies his efforts elsewhere, he shall undoubtedly face a downfall.

45. O Brāhmaṇas, this king of good intellect and of excellent conduct practises Dharma of ascetics and forsakes what his dharma is laid down in the Vedas.

46-47a. O Brāhmaṇas, the following fall into hell : viz.—a woman who behaves according to her own sweet will, an impudent son, a king who practises isolation, a servant who shirks work, and a person who has no steadiness and stability.

47b-48. Suppose the king is engaged in the worship of Hari and maintains all observances and also suppose some one cries out in distress. At that time, if he does not rush out leaving aside his worship of Hari, he will surely incur the sin of a Brāhmaṇa-slaughter.

49-50. n the day of Hari, if he is weak in the body, how can he restrain (his enemies) ? It is from the food that the Prāṇa (vigour) is evolved. The activities of the body are based on the Prāṇas. The destruction of the enemy is through the activities of the body. If one is devoid of them, one is harassed and overpowered. I have realised this. Though I try to enlighten the king, he does not wake up, or realise it.

51. If the king protects his subjects that alone constitutes his Vrata. O excellent Brāhmaṇas, a king has no other holy Vrata (except this).

52. Of what avail are devotion and worship of gods to a king after spreading disaffection and wrath among his subjects staying in the realm. If there is no bloodshed in his kingdom that alone is on a par with Yajñas, Homas and services to gods.

CHAPTER TWENTYFIVE

The story of Mohinī

Vasiṣṭha said :

1. On hearing the words uttered by Mohinī the Brāhmaṇas said—'True', and addressed these words to the king.

The Brāhmaṇas said :

2-3. O king, you have taken up the holy vow that food should not be taken in on the Ekādaśī day in both the fortnights (of every month). This vow is not taken from the point of view of the scriptural texts. It is evolved out of your own intellectual fancies. It has been laid down that those who maintain holy fires should take in (the food offered as oblation) during both the junctions of a day. (i.e. morning and evening.)

4. Three castes are glorified as the partakers of the leavings of Homas. Hence, how shall it be considered proper if they observe fast, particularly in the case of kings ?

5-6. The kings, O lord, are always up in arms. They are the persons who restrain the wicked. Whether with the backing of the scripture or without it, may the vow that you have taken up be concluded today through the words of the Brāhmaṇas. You will not incur (the sin of) breaking the holy vow. Eat in the company of the Brāhmaṇas.

7-8a. You need not regret or repent it. The words of a Brāhmaṇa are important (weightier) and valuable. O excellent king, he who disregards the statements of a Brāhmaṇa takes birth as a Rākṣasa fifteen times.

8b-9a. On hearing those words the king became terribly furious but with throbbing lips, he spoke to the Brāhmaṇas in soft and bland speech.

9b-11. "O Brāhmaṇas, you are the guides for all living beings. You have cited a verse regarding ascetics and widows. But when you say that observance of fasts is not laid down for kings, it is but the opinion of those who traverse the wrong path and not that of the Vaiṣṇava persons. In that connection listen to the statements in the sacred text book "Vaiṣṇavācāralakṣaṇa" (or pertaining to the characteristics of the conduct of life of a devotee of Viṣṇu)—

12. "One shall not drink water by means of a conch shell; one shall not kill "tortoises" and "pigs", in both fortnights food should not be taken on the Ekādaśī day.

13. Liquor should not be drunk; nowhere should a Brāhmaṇa be killed; a knower of Dharma shall never play the game of dice; no one should take food on the day of Hari.

14. Eating of the forbidden food is sinful; violating the chastity of another man's wife is sinful; taking food on the Ekādaśī day is definitely the cause of downfall.

15. Should any one live for a hundred years after performing an action that should not be performed. Which active man takes food on the day of Hari ?

16. Fodder should not be given even to the quadrupeds on the day of Hari by the Brāhmaṇas staying in the northern region who are devoted to the holy rites of Viṣṇu (Vaiṣṇava rites).

17. How can I eat the forbidden food today ? I am not a man physically weak and feeble.[1] O excellent Brāhmaṇas, I am not afflicted by dyspepsia.

18-19a. How can I therefore eschew the holy vow merely at the instance of the Brahmaṇa following the wrong path. When

1. In VV. 17-20, the king is perfectly right on Śāstric grounds. (vide Manu XI. 30.) He hit the week point correctly in the arguments of Gautama and Mohinī.

the whole earth is being protected by the king Dharmabhūṣaṇa (i.e. Dharmāṅgada) I am not without sufficient protection. I have no enemy.

19b-20a. After knowing all these things, O excellent Brāhmaṇas regularly practising the holy rites pertaining to Viṣṇu, it is not proper on your part to speak against me decrying my holy vow.

20b-21a. The Brāhmaṇas who observe (give) expiatory rites without carefully examining (the case) will incur sin due to the breaking (of injunctions of) the Smṛtis.

21b-23a. I will not take food on the day of Hari even if the following persons urge me to do it viz. — devas, Dānavas, Gandharvas, Rākṣasas, Siddhas, Brāhmaṇas, my own father himself, Hari, Hara, the father of Mohinī, the sun or any of the guardians of the world's quarters.

23b-25. O Brāhmaṇas, the king who is well-known on the Earth as Rukmāṅgada will never make his truthful pledge fruitless. Even the refulgence of the sun may vanish, even the Himālayas may crumble, even the ocean may dry up, even the fire may eschew its heat; still, O Brāhmaṇas, I will not break my Vrata on the day of Ekādaśī.[1]

26-28. O Brāhmaṇas, this is well-known in the three worlds. This is being proclaimed by the beating of drums —"Those who take food on the day of Hari, which is the most important of all Yajñas, which dispels sins, increases piety, bestows salvation which is called the severer of the chain of births, which is the receptacle of refulgence and is popular and established among all people in the villages and lands of Rukmāṅgada and others deserve to be killed or punished (otherwise) alongwith their sons. They will not be allowed to reside in the whole of the realm." When this has been announced loudly, if I were to take food, I would be committing a sin.

29-30a. It would be as though the drum was tarnished with filth or muffled with a blue cloth. The creature that has

---

1. VV. 21b-25 show the firm determination of Rukmāṅgada which acts as a challenge to Mohini to demand the head of his only son Dharmāṅgada.

earned renown but spoils it by itself committing sin due to the fear of life stays in the hell called Kṛmidaṁśa for sixty Yugas.

30b-31a. As soon as I break my solemn vow of the holy rite, the delivery of my mother would be futile; the Brāhmaṇas, the Pitṛs and the Devas would be disappointed and Vaivasvata (Yama) would be delighted alongwith his scribe namely Citragupta.

31b-32. Of what avail is the birth of that evil-minded being who delights the beautiful wives of his enemies (by refraining from killing their husbands). He takes delight in sins by means of evil actions; he is no better than a man of low caste; he is the destroyer of every thing. He is unclean and foolish. He does not have regard for the Vedas, Purāṇas and scriptures. In the end, he goes to the city of the son of the Lord of the day (i.e. Yama).

33-34a. He who breaks his pledged word or solemn vow is no better than one who vomits his food and eats it again. Neither the Vedas, nor the scriptures, neither the good men nor the Purāṇas and Smṛtis advocate the act of taking food on the pure day worthy of holy rites pleasing to Mādhava.

34b-35. If Śrāddha is performed on the day of Hari, the Pitṛs will not be satisfied thereby. The Ekādaśī Vrata is one that bestows the region of Viṣṇu. Only foolish persons will mention it alongwith Kṣayāha (the new moon day when Śrāddha is to be performed).

36. On hearing his words Mohinī burned within herself. With eyes turned red with anger, she retorted to her husband :-

37. "If you do not act in accordance with my advice you will be out of the pale of Dharma. A man excluded from Dharma shall be no better than dust.

38-39. The dust, at least, fills a pit whereas this sinner of a man is the digger of a pit. O king, for the purpose of granting the boon you extended your hand and offered it to me (by way of taking a pledge). You have now broken that pledge. If you do not keep up that promise my responsibility is over. I shall go away, I have obtained your Dharma (i.e. you are deprived of it.)

40. I am not your beloved wife any more. O king, you are no longer my husband. I shall have my own arms as my head-rest and not yours; (even) in case of fighting (I shall not depend on your protection.)

41. Fie upon you the destroyer of piety, the breaker of your own promise. Even among the Mlecchas (alien outcastes) a heretic like you cannot be seen.

42. I will forsake you today since you have moved away from the truth sinfully." After saying this the fair lady hurriedly stood up.

43. Just as Satī went away leaving off Hara, so also the slender-bodied lady bedecked in divine ornaments started from there accompanied by those Brāhmaṇas.

44. "Better to touch liquor than have contact with this king. Better to wear the blue cloth, rather than have the touch of this king who has swerved from virtue."

45. Lamenting thus, the infuriated Mohinī cried much and went out of the abode accompanied by Gautama and others.

46. "O father, O Lord of the Universe, the cause of creation, maintenance and dissolution (of the worlds)," cried, the mentally created daughter of Brahmā.

47. In the meantime, Dharmāṅgada who was seated on an excellent horse returned to the palace after touring over the entire Earth.

48-49. Coming in a hurry, the renowned Prince Dharmāṅgada the son of Rukmāṅgada, a prince devoid of rivalry and favourite with his father, the very embodiment of virtue came face to face. The words coming out of the mouth of Mohinī, endorsed by the words of the Brāhmaṇas reached the ears of the prince.

50. Dismounting hurriedly from the horse, he went near his father and fell at his feet. Getting up again he bowed down to the leading Brāhmaṇas with palms joined together in reverence.

51-52. Then, observing that Mohinī was mentally furious and she was hurrying out, he went over to her and with folded palms, he said to her in reverence. "O Mother, O gentle lady, O beloved wife of my father, by whom have you been insulted ? Why are you angry ? Where have you set off now alongwith these Brāhmaṇas ?"

53. On hearing the words of Dharmāṅgada, Mohinī spoke these words :

"O dear son, your father is a liar. Falsely did he offer his (right) hand (to me).

54-55. The hand that always performed holy rites, has the shape and features of red Aśoka tree, the glorious right hand wearing gold armlet and is marked with lines in the form of a banner and a goad is by your father Rukmāṅgada withdrawn—Hence I am not enthused to stay here."

Dharmāṅgada said :

56. O gentle lady, whatever you say, I shall do. There is no doubt about it. O mother, do not be angry. O beloved wife of my father, return.

Mohini said :

57. By this father of yours, I have been made his wife on the mountain Mandara with this (certain) stipulation: Śiva, the Lord of the Devas, was standing witness thereof.

58. Your father, Rukmāṅgada, has gone astray breaking those stipulations. He does not give me what should be given to me. It is not his flourishing prosperity that I am thinking about.

59. O prince, I do not beg for gold, nor for foodgrains nor for horse, elephants, villages nor clothes whereby he might incur any loss.

60. O foremost one among embodied beings, O son, only that was requested for by me whereby he could please his own body. But out of delusion, he does not give it to me.

61. O prince, the excellent king was requested for by me to help his own body for his own happiness.

62. The Lord has now landed himself in a terrible mess of falsehood on a par with imbibing liquor.

63. I will have to forsake your father who has fallen off from truthfulness, who speaks harsh words, has eschewed

and is false, roguish and base. My stay alongwith him is impossible.

64. On hearing the words of Mohinī, the son Dharmāṅgada said :

"As long as I am alive, my father cannot be false in respect of anything.

65. O fair lady, return. I shall do whatever is desired by you. O gentle lady no falsehood has ever been uttered before by my father.

66-67. How can that king speak falsehood, now that I his son, am here ? The whole world consisting of the Devas, Asuras and human beings is established in his truthfulness; the abode of Vaivasvata (Yama) has been made void of sinners and cleared of sinners by him. His fame spreads everywhere. The whole sphere of the Cosmic egg has been pervaded by his fame.

68. How can that king get involved in false utterances. I have not heard my father's words. How can I believe in an indirect (reported) statement (said to have been uttered in my absence) ?

69-70. O splendid-faced lady, take mercy on me and return."

On hearing these words of Dharmāṅgada, O king, Mohinī returned with (her hands) resting on the shoulders of her son to the place where Rukmāṅgada, as refulgent as the sun, was lying down as though dead.

71-72. She made her son sit on the bed of Rukmāṅgada which was equipped with gold, was brightly illuminated by gemset lamps, and decorated in variegated forms by corals; its extremely tender (soft-looking) legs were fashioned out of adamantine jewels. It was long and wide and charming beyond comparison.

73-75. With palms joined in reverence, he spoke to his father with bland speech. "O dear father, this mother of of mine, here says that you are a liar. How can you be, O king, a liar on this Earth ? When the kingdom consisting of the treasury hoarded with gems, possessing elephants, horses, chariots, etc., extending over the whole world containing the seven oceans is being ruled by you, O Lord, give everything to her, everything whatever has been promised to her.

76. O dear father, as long as I hold the bow who can act against you ? Give even the post of Indra to the gentle lady. Know that Indra has been defeated.

77. The region of Brahmā, which is difficult of access, is unsullied and can be approached only by Yogins. I am willing to give that too to her after propitiating the lotus-deity born by means of penance.

78. After conquering human beings, Devas and Dānavas, I will give whatever my mother wishes for in the nether worlds, on the Earth, in the heaven or in any other region.

79. O king, since I am your slave, I may even be sold. If I am considered insignificant, may I be entrusted to a sinful Cāṇḍāla.[1] I shall be his servant and be fed by him.

Or

79. O king, since I am your slave, sell me or my mother and propitiate the daughter of Kuśa-emblemed deity (i.e. Brahmā) lest there should be, O Lord of men, the (stigma) of falsehood on you in the world.

80. O Lord of the Earth, there is nothing in the three worlds, which is difficult for me to do and which hence cannot be given to her, should she like it. O leading king, give her even my life or that of my mother.

81. O Lord of kings, by that very thing, be endowed with good renown for ever. You can illuminate the groups of kings with your attributes (like the moon) that brightens the sky by means of its rays.

82. It is true what Manu has said that there will be sin in the destruction of one's reputation as killing of one's own progeny (or the subjects). But O king, how can I otherwise, wipe off the pure (stainless) fame and be happy ? Hence this course is proper.

---

1. This is an obvious reference to king Hariścandra who for sage Viśvāmitra sold his wife and son to stick to the truth.

CHAPTER TWENTYSIX

The story of Mohinī

The king said :

1. O son, may my fame perish. May I be called a liar. May I even fall into a terrible hell. But how should I take food on the day of Hari ?

2-3. O son, let this gentle lady, Mohinī go to the abode of Brahmā. This lady says to me foolishly and childishly for many times. "Excepting your taking food on the day of Hari that is destructive of sins, I do not wish for anything else such as kingdom, Earth, wealth, etc."

4. Even If I am to be born in the despicable species of a germ, I will not take food on the day of Hari.

5. This Dundubhī (drum) has loudly proclaimed (my views) and has instructed the people. How can it be made false ?

6. Is it desirable to live for a hundred years after taking the forbidden food, after approaching a forbidden woman and after drinking the prohibited beverage ?

7. Even if I were charged with falsehood and have strayed away from the royal policy and am insulted and rebuked by the people, I will not take food on the day of Hari.

8. Even if I were to die due to the separation from the lady of tremulous side-glances, that is preferable, but I will never take food on the day of Hari.

9. How can I give excessive delight to Yama by making the miserable men proceed alongwith the path leading to hell ?

10. O dear son, the rows of hell which had been made empty by me, will be filled with people if I take food.

11. Let not any lady bear in her womb such a son as would cause delight to the enemies though he is efficient enough to destroy them.

12. She requests only for this viz : taking food on the day of Viṣṇu. I shall not grant the request of Mohinī even if I am requested for it by the Devas and Asuras.

taking food by the king on the day of Hari. Let something be done so that my father does not swerve from truth and also does not take food. Let there be happiness to both.

6. O king, (Māndhātā), on hearing the words of her son the gentle lady Sandhyāvalī spoke these soft words to Mohinī, the daughter of Brahmā :

7. O beautiful lady, do not be importunate. By no means will the king taste the sinful food (cooked rice when the day of Hari has arrived.

8-9a. Closely follow the king. He is the eternal preceptor. Just as the worlds of Sāvitrī were free from impurities, so also will be the worlds of that woman who always carries out the directions of her husband.

9b-10a. O gentle lady, formerly, he was overwhelmed by passion and beguiled. If then, he had offered his hand to you, on the mountain, that should not be thought much of (no capital be made out of it). He does give what should not be given. Do not beg for what should not be given.

10b-12. Even an adversity is beneficent to one who strictly adheres to the path of the good. O blessed lady, even during his boyhood, food has not been taken by him during the day of Hari. How will he then take food now on the day of Viṣṇu (Ekādaśī). O lady of sweet and charming thighs, you may very well choose some other boon for something rare.

13-14. The king will definitely give it to you. Desist from the insistence on the taking of food. If you are convinced, O gentle lady, that it was I who brought up Dharmāṅgada, choose the kingdom alongwith our own lives, O lady of auspicious holy rites. (Choose the entire worlds) consisting of seven continents and many rivers, forests and mountains.

15. O lady of large eyes, and slender waist, for the sake of my husband I shall bow down to your feet though I am the eldest and you are the youngest.

16. The woman who traps and gets her husband involved in the faults due to the verbal pledge and makes him do what should not be done is sinful and she will stay in the hell.

17. After falling off from the terrible hell, she takes

twelve successive births as a sow. Thereafter, she is born as a Cāṇḍālī.

18. It is after knowing this aberration resulting from sins, that O gentle lady, O lady of beautiful thighs, O charming lady, you have been prevented by me with the feelings of a dear friend.

19. Good counsel must be given to an enemy by one who wishes for piety. What then, O lotus-faced lady to you who remains as a friend of mine ?

20. On hearing the words of Sandhyāvalī, Mohinī the fascinating lady spoke to the eldest wife of her husband whose complexion was lustrous like gold.

21-22. Mohinī said—"O lady of beautiful eyebrows, you are worthy of being honoured by me. I shall carry out your instructions. If the king does not wish to do what is being sung about by Nārada and other scholarly sages, viz taking food on the day of Hari, O gentle lady, may another thing, greater than your death, (?) be pursued.

23. O blessed lady, this is indeed painful to me also, but I prattle thus, thanks to divine intercession. Who likes self-slaughter? Who desires to swallow poison ?

24. Who wishes to fall down from the top of a mountain ? Who wants to play with snakes living in burrows ? Who likes to rush at lions and tigers ? Who wants to swim across the sea ?

25. Who wants to indulge in harsh words and false statements ? Who is fond of outraging the modesty of another man's wife ? Who likes to eat unwholesome food ? Who desires to eat the forbidden food in the world ?

26-27. Who wants to go hunting deer ? Who likes to play the game of dice ? Who likes to enter into risky adventure ? Who wants all these such as cutting of grass and hewing of wood; trampling and holding of clods of earth, harassing of minor deities* (?), playing in water or with fire and similar things ? Yet O beautiful lady, urged by the deity (or Fate) a man does all these things.

---

*In the reading *dehānām* instead of *devānām*, it means "minor beings (such as poor worms, etc.)

28. A man who deserves to be in the hell, does all inauspicious things that destroy his body in the form of fame and that make him fall off from the three aims of life.

29-31. I am naturally sinful and wicked in my evil[1] actions. I am desirous of saying extremely harsh words. The child is born with the same emotions and feelings as the progenitor has at the time of discharging semen into the vaginal passage. I have been created by the lotusborn deity Brahmā who had his emotions disturbed by arguments against king Rukmāṅgada. I have the form of a fair-complexioned lady but defiled in emotions. I shall be the perpetrator of some evil action in regard to the king.

32-34. O gentle lady, it is neither the Lagna nor the planet, nor the Horā (the hour, the rising of the zodiacal sign) that can indicate the future nature. The emotional feeling at that time (i.e. the time of conception) should be taken up (for consideration) The son is also born with the same emotion. In a son born with that ill feeling, there is no courtesy or kindness, there is neither shame nor affection nor any Dharma (piety) also, O gentle lady. In spite of his knowledge about his evil tendencies he pursues the same feelings.

35. I am going to say something that will take away your life, that of our husband and that of all women folk alongwith the world. It spoils my merits (dharma) and may cause slander against me. O timid lady, it is impossible to conceive mentally about it.

36. If you do according to my suggestion, your fame in the world will be great. It will cause the fame of your husband to spread; it is conducive to the attainment of heaven; your son will be praised and thereby my lot will be controversial and full of condemnation.

Vasiṣṭha said :

37. O Lord, on hearing the words of Mohini the gentle lady Sandhyāvalī (screwed up all her courage) and urged that young woman saying "Tell me, Tell me"[1].

1. This sinister confession of Mohini—the pangs of conscience (whether sincere or hypocritical) prepares the tense background for the terrible catastrophe which is impending.

61. Using it up the entire wealth of my husband was wasted by both of them. O gentle lady, by the time three years elapsed, my husband became indigent.

62. Then he requested me "Give me your ornaments". Those were not given to my husband by me as he was addicted to vice.

63-65. O blessed lady, I took everything and went to my father's abode. (He too followed me there). At my house he sold the slaves and other possessions and the money (received thereby) was given to the two courtesans. That also was exhausted. Whatever was left such as the fields, grains, etc. was sold off at throw-away-prices alongwith the garments, utensils and other personal effects. My husband thereupon entered the great ocean by means of a boat. He went oversea.

66. He went a long distance seeing wonderful things and miracles on the way. O splendid lady, he saw many animals of the sea and all their activities.

67. By the time it had gone a hundred Yojanas, the boat was caught in a violent storm. It broke into pieces and all others on the boat were killed.

68-69a. As providence would have it, and urged by his Karmans of the previous births, my husband clung to a long piece of wood. O gentle lady, led by the wind he reached a mountain bedecked with adamantine peaks.

69b-70. That mountain contained many rivulets and fountains, many birds and many trees full of fruits and flowers. With its three prominent peaks, it scraped the middle of the sky.

71. O lady of beautiful eyes, on seeing the divine, wonderfnl mountain my husbund left off the piece of wood (that brought him there) and jocously climbed on to it, as he was eager to earn some wealth.

72. He rested there for a while. When he was overwhelmed with hunger and thirst, he got up in search of food and surveyed the trees all round.

73-74. He saw ripe grape vines there and ate the grapes joyfully. He was a bit assuaged and he saw a very clean big Ṣāla tree with a thick shade and its thick foliage resembling the spreading clouds, and had the height of fifty men. Spreading his upper cloth he went to sleep under its shade.

75. Overcome by fascinating sleep his eyes began to roll. By the time the sun had set the excessively tired (Brāhmaṇa) went to sleep.

76. When the sun had set and the night had set in, a terrible Rākṣasa roaring like the cloud came there rushing in.

77. Like the ten-headed Rāvaṇa who had abducted Sītā, he had carried the slender-limbed auspicious daughter of the ruler of Kāśī, named Ratnāvalī on his lap.

78. Without washing her feet, she had gone to sleep with her head directed towards the north. The virgin of beautiful buttocks was desirous of obtaining a husband, but did not obtain one befitting her.

79. That girl was the foremost among all women. Overwhelmed by slumber she was crying. In the matter of giving her in marriage, her father had been extremely anxious day and night.

80. O lady of slender limbs, this beautiful girl, occupying a bed spread in the shadow of the lamp was seen by the sinful demon who was roaming about.

81-83. He saw her in the light of gems and jewels that were shining like lamps. She was wearing two bangles well studded with bright gems and jewels. In each bangle there were ten jewels, and in the necklace of gold coin (?) there were fifteen jewels. On the crest, there were seven jewels. On the armlets there were eight and five (thirteen) jewels. The demon abducted such a virgin bedecked in jewels and with gold-like lustrous complexion. He carried away the girl of sweet smiles from the palace of the king. Through the aerial path he reached his own abode in a moment.

84-87. He came to that mountain where my husband (was sleeping) beneath the Śāla tree. There she saw his cave that had the lustre of gold. Unable to bear the terror struck by him, she entered the cave even as he was looking on. The cave had been beautified by many jewels and it had mansions of variegated colours. Many articles lay scattered here and there. It contained beds and seats. Pots of beverages and edibles with various kinds of dishes had been kept there. After entering the cave, the demon placed that weeping girl of lily-like eyes, the excessively frightened girl of plump bosom and buttocks, on to a bed.

88. On hearing the weeping of the girl, his wife the ogress hurriedly came to the place where the demon was standing.

89. On seeing that girl whose lustre was like that of molten gold and everyone of whose limbs was beautiful, she became infuriated. Rebuking her husband she asked thus :

90. "O ruthless one, why is this girl brought here when I am alive ? Do you wish for another wife ? I will no longer be your wife then.

91. That demon joyously spoke to his beloved wife of beautiful eyes, the ogress of black eyes who had spoken to him thus.

92. "O splendid-faced lady, this pabulum (eatable) prey has been brought by me from Kāśī for your sake. A second one is standing at the gate. It has been brought to me by providence.

93. O fair-faced lady, a Brāhmaṇa is lying beneath the Śāla tree. Bring him here quickly so that I can make a meal of him.

94. On hearing the words of the Rākṣasa that virgin spoke thus :— "O Rākṣasī, out of his fear for you, your husband utters a lie.

95-96. He knows that you are old in age, hideous in form and torturous in your gait. At night when I was soundly sleeping in my father's house, he came to me passionately. O gentle lady, since I am not married he has brought me here to make me his wife in spite of my cries."

97. On hearing these words uttered by the princess, the ogress became extremely infuriated. On seeing the beautiful form (of the princess), she decided that it was the truth. In her anger she hurled words (at her husband).

98. She thought thus—"She has been brought here to be made his wife. Of necessity, this demon will strike a wedge in my head.

99. Let there not be any woman in the three worlds who undergoes the misery of having a co-wife. There will hardly be any woman in the three worlds who will survive the harassment due to the misery of being a co-wife.

100. There is no doubt about this that it is the greatest of all miseries when there is another woman to have a share in the wealth and enjoyment of pleasures."

101. After thinking much like this, she spoke these words to her husband, "This girl is mine, as this lady of charming eyes has been brought by you as food for me.

102-103a. I shall bring that Brāhmaṇa to be your prey, O Suvrata (one of holy rites)". Then the Rākṣasa urged "Go, go quickly. The corner of my mouth drips too much of saliva due to my desire to eat him."

103b-104. Thereafter, on hearing the words uttered by her husband, the terrible Rākṣasī set out with infinite hope. She saw the excellent Brāhmaṇa endowed with comely features and blooming youth as well as adorned with the jewels of learning.

105. On seeing him she was overwhelmed with love pangs in the heart. Through her Māyā (power of illusion), she became a beautiful maiden of sixteen years and approached him.

106. The maiden of large buttocks spoke to the Brāhmaṇa with great pleasure—"Who are you ? Whence have you come here ? Why do you stay here ?

107. I ask you this as I am desirous of making you my husband. I am an ogress overcome with pangs of love. I have been abandoned by my husband. I have come here to make you my husband."

108. On hearing her words my husband was frightened. O splendid lady, yet he emboldened himself. The intelligent (Brāhmaṇa) spoke these words :—

109. "O Ogress, how can there be the copulation of a Rākṣasī and a human being ? There is no doubt about this that men are remembered as the prey of Rākṣasas."

110. On hearing those words she spoke to him again respectfully—"The impossible is made possible, thanks to the intercession of the Providence.

111: This is heard in the Purāṇa. This is a future incident mentioned in the Bhārata, O Brāhmaṇa, Hiḍambā an ogress will become the wife of Bhīma.[1]

112. The son procreated by a human being will be Ghaṭotkaca. He will be one who cannot be killed by any other weapon. He will attain death through the weapon called Śakti (of Indra, hurled by Karṇa against Ghaṭotkaca).

113.. Hence, O Brāhmaṇa, do not grieve. It is through Providential intercession that I have become your wife. Fate is indeed very powerful.

114-115. When Indra went to the mortal world to meet Bali, my husband, the terrible Rākṣasa had a convenient opportunity. He stole Śakti from his abode as though it were the blazing flame. And that Śakti belonging to Indra has been kept here in the Śāla Tree.

116. O excellent Brāhmaṇa, without killing at least one it does not go back to Indra. The person for whose slaying it was hurled will perish even if he be immortal.

117. Hence, I shall climb up to the top of this Śāla tree, bring the shining Śakti to you and hand it over to you with a desire for the death of my husband.

118. If you do not hit and injure the night-prowler with this Śakti, there is no doubt that the evil-minded one will swallow you as well as me.

119. He is a great enemy of yours as well as that of me, O scorcher of enemies, since, by that foolish fellow, a virgin has been brought here for being made his wife.

120. Hence, an enmity (inimical feelings) has been generated in me against my husband of the wicked soul. If he is killed, it will be possible for both of us to have sexual dalliance.

---

1. The future tense in VV. 111 and 112 regarding Bhīma's marriage with Hiḍambā and the birth of their son Ghaṭotkaca and his death by a Śakti in the Bhārata war is used to show that this Kāṣṭhilā incident (esp. her previous birth) is more ancient than the Mahābhārata-history (mentioned only as *Bhārata* in the N.P.).

121. O Rativardhana (one who intensifies lustfulness) if I am making a false statement to you, may I not be the partaker of benefits of the merit performed by myself.

122. If this were to be a lie, may I attain that condition of a despicable nature which is attained by men on committing Brāhmaṇa slaughter.

123. O Brāhmaṇa, may I get that state, the terrible state that is laid down in the case of an evil-minded Brāhmaṇa who drinks liquor.

124. By uttering a lie, may I attain that fate, O excellent Brāhmaṇa, of that creature that is engaged in seducing the preceptor's wife and that resorts to sinful actions.

125-126. If I tell a lie, may I incur that sin which the following undergo viz :—he who steals gold and misappropriates the sum given on trust; he who forcibly occupies another man's land; he who commits suicide; he who eats meat on the Pañcamī (fifth) and Aṣṭamī (eighth) day, of a lunar fortnight.

127. The man who commits the sin of cutting off a tree or cohabiting with a woman on the new moon day, the sin acquired by taking in ghee while one is defiled by Ucchiṣṭa, the sin of sexual intercourse during the day time.

128. The householder Brāhmaṇa who does not perform the holy rite of Vaiśvadeva, the person who does not give alms to the mendicant, the widow who takes meal twice a day.[1]

129. The person who uses gingelly oil on the day of Saṁkrānti (the transit of the sun from one sign of Zodiac to another), the person who goes to the holy centre along with the cows (?), the person who takes bath in another man's tank without taking out mud therefrom.

130. The person who chews the tooth stick twig from a forbidden tree; the person who does not serve cows, but binds them; the person who treads the heretic's path.

---

1. Formerly, widows were looked upon as Yatis and all the restrictions of a Sannyāsin were imposed on them. Hence this restriction of limiting to one meal for widows.

131. The person who performs the worship of the Pitṛs and the Devas standing on a piece of wood or rock (?), the person who keeps only a buffalo without a cow also, the person who takes food off a bell metal vessel that is broken.

132. The person who performs holy rites clad in unwashed or torn clothes or those belonging to others. The person who stares at a naked woman and the person who partakes of forbidden food.

133. O Brāhmaṇa, if I tell you a lie, may I be tarnished with the same sin as that of a person who creates obstacles in the discourse about Śrīharī.

134. O Brāhmaṇa, if I tell a lie, may I be the person who incurs all these sins[1] that I have mentioned and also those I have not mentioned."

135. O gentle lady, my husband who was thus addressed by that sinful woman was deluded by the inevitable future, and he decided accordingly, saying "So be it."

136. That indigent Brāhmaṇa who had been indulging in vices and so perturbed extremely due to my harsh words spoke thus to the ogress. His words (proved to be) the bestower of all achievements.

137. "Bring that Śakti quickly. I shall carry out your directions. When the Rākṣasa is killed, all these things should be given by you to me.

138-139a It is with a keen desire for wealth that I undertook (the voyage) through the sea full of whales and sharks". On hearing these words, the ogress brought the Śakti that was on the top of the tree and that emitted brilliant lustre. She gave it to my husband for the realisation of their desire.

139b-140. In the meantime, the Rākṣasa who was overwhelmed by passion attempted to rape the virgin. She became terrified and spoke these words—"O Rākṣasa, there is a great sin in cohabiting with a virgin.

141. While I was sleeping I had been fraudulently brought here from my father's house at Kāśī. It is not your fault in this regard. My fate is evidently of this nature.

1. VV. 122-134 record a series of acts which were regarded as sins or undesirable ones in the elite Indian society of the NP-Period.

142. I am in the middle of a cave. Who will be the protector here ? It is through fate that one gets a husband. It is through fate that one gets a wife.

143. Fate alone plays the chief part in the matter of acquiring learning, house, happiness, wealth and nobility of birth. It is urged by the fate that man goes anywhere.

144. O night-prowler, of necessity you alone will be my husband. When the path is traced out by fate, what will (even) a scholar do ?

145. Hence bring that Brāhmaṇa who has resorted to that Śāla tree. Fetch ghee, water, Kuśa grass and fire. Celebrate marriage in accordance with the injunctions.

146. Even without the Darbha grass, water and fire, even without the traditional rites laid down, a marriage may be fruitful if it is blessed with the permissive statement of a Brāhmaṇa.

147. O Rākṣasa, if that Brāhmaṇa has not already been killed (bring him here quickly). When the holy rites of Homa have been performed, you will be able to eat him up.

148. When these words were addressed by that princess the Rākṣasa had full belief in his mind. He set out proudly.

149. Afflicted by pangs of love he hastened out to bring that Brāhmaṇa.

150. O gentle lady, as he was setting out he himself sneezed, his left eye throbbed and his own clothes dropped down.

151-153. Unmindful of everything, he set out from the cave. There he saw his wife in human form engaged in that form of union as is usual between a husband and a wife. She said—"I am abandoning you, a sinful Rākṣasa of ruthless action. You are enamoured of a young woman of human species. You are the defiler of my body." On hearing these terrible words uttered by his wife, the night-prowler (demon) became infuriated and malicious. He rushed at her.

154. He lifted up his arms. He kept his mouth wide open. He rushed at them to devour both of them. Uttering curses of harmful nature, he rushed at them like a violent storm, that blows in the proper season.

CHAPTER TWENTYEIGHT

Kāṣṭhilā's story (Contd.)

Kāṣṭhilā said :

1. On seeing the Rākṣasa, comparable to the black annihilator Yama, rushing at them, the Ogress became afraid and spoke thus to my husband.

2. "Hurl this Śakti that is as refulgent as fire and bedecked in gold. May this husband of mine die and become the beloved of Digambara's enemy (i.e. Yama).

3. At her instance, my husband assumed great manliness and hurled the massive Śakti at the chest of the Rākṣasa.

4-5. The Śakti that blazed brilliantly like fire and illuminated the ten quarters, the point of which was sharp and emitted divine rays and was jingling with hundreds of tinkling bells fitted into it, the body of which was smeared with red sandal paste, and was beautified with (the covering) of red cloth. It went off from the hands of the Brāhmaṇa, pierced into the heart of the Rākṣasa.

6-7. After reducing the Rākṣasa to ashes, it went up into the sky. After felling (killing) her husband through the hands of the Brāhmaṇa, the ogress considered herself as having achieved her goal. Hairs stood on end due to her delight. The delighted ogress then spoke to the splendid-eyed Brāhmaṇa.

8. "O my lover, come on, Enter freely my beautiful cave. Enjoy all the great pleasures, divine as well as human, in my company."

9. "So be it" said my husband who was extremely delighted. Then she took my husband and entered her cave joyfully.

10. Without caring to look at the ashes to which her husband's body had been reduced, she clasped my husband with her protruding breasts.

11-12. She pointed out to him that maiden of slender body who was lying down on the bed.—"O excellent Brāhmaṇa, this lady of black side-glances, with lips red like the Bimba fruit and of gold-like lustrous complexion had been brought (by thus : "O Brāhmaṇa, killing some one who has trusted in one is on a par with the slaughter of a Brāhmaṇa.

26. If, on account of this, you consider me a cruel Rākṣasī, the destroyer of her husband (my reply is) I hate my husband. How will I kill one who confides in me and believes in me?

27. The way of Dharma (virtue and piety) is very subtle. It cannot be understood by any means, by any one anywhere, whether Daitya or Rākṣasa or others. But some men are clever in thinking about the subtleties of Dharma.

28. (Those who know Dharma) attain Naiṣkarmya (freedom from the Karmans i.e. Mokṣa) through their perishable physical body. This is heard in the Purāṇas. Same thing is being mentioned here.

29. It is through the favourable nature of Dharma that Viṣṇu the powerful God could assume ten incarnations. But in them much misery was experienced by him.[1]

30. Where is Rāma, the abode of Śrī, who for the sake of Sītā, accompanied by Lakṣmaṇa lamented in the course of the events and they were bound by the serpentine nooses?

31. Where is Vasudeva's son, the lord of Devas, of the form of perfect knowledge ? And where is the fully worldly man who sheds tears saying "O what a pity ?" who makes signs and gestures with his eyes and who acts as servant unto Pārtha (i.e. Arjuna), Ugrasena and others ? (What a lot of difference there is !)

32. O Brāhmaṇa, the activities of the Lord are beyond human scrutiny[1] though he abides by the favourable Dharma. Vyāsa[2] the son of Parāśara, is himself the classifier of the Vedas. He was a man of truthful vision. His very form is worthy of being worshipped. (But) he was born of the semen virile of one who destroyed the virginity (of a woman). Hence he is called a Kānīna (son of an unmarried girl). Moreover, he had sexual intercourse with the wives of his younger brothers.[2]

---

1. VV. 29-47 give instances of *adharma* passed on as Dharma. The *Rākṣasī* describes the power of fate over all beings.

2. This refers to the births of Dhṛtarāṣṭra and Pāṇḍu from the queens of Vicitravīrya, the son of Satyavatī and Śantanu. To have a heir

33. Śantanu was a Parivettṛ (one who had married before his elder brother Devāpi). He was the second husband of a lady (Satyavatī who married twice). At first he was the husband of the heavenly river. His son was the veritable Vasu (Bhīṣma), the unmarried elder brother (whose younger brother vicitra-Vīrya was married before him); he attained death due to the arguments of a woman (Ambā) who became Śikhaṇḍin in the next birth.

34. The Pāṇḍavas were born of adultery (as each was born from a different person other than their legal father Pāṇḍu. Thus they were actually bastards. All of them cohabited with the same woman, viz. Draupadī. Still their glorification is considered holy and sacred. It is destructive of sins.

35-37. Viṣṇu whom people meditate upon and truly remember, who is called Yogamūrti (Embodiment of Yoga) and who is eternal, was enamoured of courtesans. Śrinṛsiṁha who advised Prahlāda and others and who destroyed Asuras is considered as the deity and Lord of the Devas (Defective). He is the destroyer of even the impression of worldly existence, he is the deity and Lord of the Devas. He was the destroyer of Hiraṇyākṣa (Hiraṇyakaśipu ?) but he stayed in his abode (?)

38. The son of Jamadagni (Paraśurāma) had realised his soul himself. He had destroyed his sins by means of his austerities. He was Lord himself. But he was the perpetrator of such deeds as massacres of Kṣattriyas and killing of children in the womb.

39. He himself was a leading Yogin. He was a Brāhmaṇa engaged in educating people, but acting within the perview of Dharma, he became one who brought agony into the world.

40. Nārada was a Nārada (destroyer of groups of men)[1] again and again. Nārada was devoted to Nārāyaṇa. Nāra

---

to the Throne, Satyavatī requested Vyāsa who was born of her from Parāśara, to have sons from the queens of his younger brother Vicitravīrya. (*Mbh-Ādi*). 104 and 105).

1. These different connotations of *Nārada* are peculiar.

means one who is a benefactor of men and also one who is immortal.

41. Gautama was Gotama (most timid like a cow). O Brāhmaṇa, he was devoted to the activities of a cowherd. He had written a treatise (i.e. Nyāya sūtra) the topics of which are beyond the pale of the Vedas; (but he is called) one who helps the Vedas.

42-44a Vasiṣṭha and even Agastya, who were born of Urvaśī, are considered to be masters. By Vasiṣṭha a sacred treatise of excellent nature named Vasiṣṭhasmṛti had been composed for helping the whole world. In that work the Purāṇas and the Vedas are considered to be equal. He was himself the preceptor of Śrī Rāma who was none other than the Almighty (Viṣṇu). Why was he cursed by Gādhija (Viśvāmitra) ?[1] Why was he born in the womb of a lower animal ?[2]

44b-45a The powerful Agastya had overpowered the Vindhya mountain, the demon Vātāpi and also the ocean. How is he the receiver of hire money (?)[2] He served in the way that is difficult for others to do.

45b-46a. The creator is worthy of being worshipped by the sun etc. and is the honourable grandsire of the world. How did he become enamoured of a lady of fascinating beauty and give up his body ?

46b-47a. God Śiva, the bestower of auspicious things, is the lord of Prakṛti. He is greater than the greatest. How did he carnally approach the wives of the Devas ? How does he pursue inauspicious activities in the cremation ground ?

47b-48. Hence, O Brāhmaṇa, it is the prescribed rule that good conduct must be pursued duly. He who is the foremost among the knowers of things shall not abandon good conduct by having the egotist feeling, (then) he will obtain the highest peace conducive to virtue here and hereafter.

---

1. When Vasiṣṭha learnt how Viśvāmitra persecuted his patron-disciple Hariścandra, he cursed Viśvāmitra to be a stork. In retaliation Viśvāmitra cursed him to be a kingfisher. (DB. VI. 13. 34-47).

2. This refers to Agastya's employment as a bearer of the palanquin of Nahuṣa while he was in the position of Indra. Agastya however cursed Nahuṣa who was then transformed into a serpent.
Mbh. *Udyoga* ch. 17; *Śānti* 342-51.

49. Dharma is remembered as conducive to Apavarga (salvation). Wealth is the only thing through which Dharma can be achieved. That Dharma I have achieved in the form of wealth that is the greatest of all.

50-51. O Brāhmaṇa, listen. In this connection, I shall recount to you the subtle way of Dharma. Abducting a girl, my husband was coming this way. He saw you were involved because you were brought there by your Karman. That was not his fault. He was asked by me—"Why was this girl brought ?"

52-53. Then a lie was uttered by him that it was for his food. On hearing that, the girl in bondage told me everything pointing out his desire. Those who say that in wedded life the wife is a hindrance to salvation, cannot be understood as knowers of reality. Since the wife is not an obstacle.

54. Only she is the real wife who is able to uplift a husband falling into the hell. Any other woman is like a twining creeper of Karman, the bestower of worldly bondage.

55. What is sinful in this you hear from me, O my bridegroom who have come to me by yourself. Even if the vital breaths come to the throat, falsehood should not be uttered.

56. One must always be truthful. Dharma is directly based on Truth. God Brahmā is based on Truth. All good men abide by Truth.

57. The entire universe is established in the Truth, the universe consisting of the mobile and the immobile beings is always based on Truth. The words "One shall always speak the Truth"[1] are proclaimed in the Vedāntas.

58. The Truth is of the form of Brahman. We call Brahman by the word Truth. O Brāhmaṇa, the Truth is always auspicious. It is the bestower of everything that is auspicious.

59. Untruth is the bestower of self destruction though immediately it may breed the confidence of belief. But

---

1. In various Upaniṣads such commandments are found e.g. Taittirīya I. 11.1, Kauṣitaki 1.6.

had been made miserable by him. Hence, O Brāhmaṇa, he has been killed by me.

84. O lover, since you put trust in me with all your heart and soul in every respect I shall protect you in every respect.

85. This is my binding by oath with five elements as my witness and uttered in the presence of the all-pervading person. It is the truth.

86. O excellent Brāhmaṇa, you will not alter this agreement in any respect. O bestower of honour, you must abide by me in all activities."

87. On hearing the words uttered by the ogress, the noble Brāhmaṇa carried out all instructions and she did accordingly.

88-89. Thereafter, the demoness gathered together all wealth from the cave. She assumed the form of a she-elephant and kept my husband on her back along with Ratnāvalī, the large-eyed girl. Joyously she went through the path of firmament, O lady of good eyes, towards Kāśī.

CHAPTER TWENTYNINE

The description of Kāśī

Kāṣṭhilā said :

1. Thus, O lady of beautiful eyebrows, that ogress who had assumed the form of a she-elephant, reached the temple of Viśveśa at Kāśī within three Muhūrtas.

2. On reaching that city, the lady of black eyes spoke to her husband—"O Lord, this (city) is glorified as the axe for the cutting of the tree of sin.

3. O beloved, this is said to be the dice box for the gold of six types of distresses (?) It is destructive of all seeds of Karmans, and it is the bestower of salvation on all.

4. The Purāṇas say that it was at first the abode of Viṣṇu.[1] No one can ever have salvation in a holy centre not belonging to Viṣṇu.

5. O excellant Brāhmaṇa, this was formerly a city of Viṣṇu, the bestower of salvation on all creatures and the destroyer of every one's sin.

6. Once Lord Śaṅkara went there to see Pitāmaha (god Brahmā) the sole creator of all worlds, shining with his own splendour.

7. After going there, Mahādeva bowed down to Brahmā the preceptor of the worlds. He stood in front of him listening to the recital of the Vedic lore.

8. He was delighted on seeing the Lord of the Universe joyously reciting the four Vedas by means of the four wonderful faces.

9. Thereafter, the leader of goblins saw the fifth face of Brahmā. On observing him to be impudent and arrogant, he became malicious instantaneously.

10. O leading Brāhmaṇa, the three-eyed deity, born of anger could not brook his audacity. Hence with the tip of his nail he cut off the head stationed above in the firmament (?)

11. O excellent Brāhmaṇa, the head of Brahmā that had been severed, stuck up to the sproutlike left hand (of Śiva). It did not fall off though shaken frequently.

12. Brahmā became sad. He stood there staring at Śiva. Śiva became ashamed and he hurriedly went out of the place.

13. Though he tried in many ways impatiently to cast off that head, he could not get rid of it. It was a great mystery.

14. Being perturbed and worried he remembered Viṣṇu, the Garuḍa-emblemed deity. The moment he was remembered, Viṣṇu manifested himself.

---

1. The claim that Kāśī was originally an abode of Viṣṇu and that Śiva begged of him to give that place to himself as a permanent residence as a protection against *Brahma-hatyā* is a Vaiṣṇavite tilt in the NP. The assertion that liberation in sacred place is possible only if it is presided over by Viṣṇu is a part of sectarian propaganda. It is also an explanation why a particular Tīrtha at Kāśī was called Kapāla-mocana.

15. O Brāhmaṇa, on seeing the omnipresent Viṣṇu the Lord of the chiefs of the Devas, the bull-emblemed deity who had turned pale became humble and bent down his head.

16. On seeing (Śiva) the antagonist of Brahmā, sick and frightened, Hari consoled him and spoke these words that made him satisfied.

17. "Inasmuch as the head of Brahmā had been cut off, O Śambhu, the omniscient one, you have committed a sin. Experience the fruit thereof for a short while.

18. O beloved one, a Karman performed by one, whether auspicious or inauspicious will yield its fruit which one must, of necessity, experience. Even if hundreds of births are to be taken, a Karman does not perish without being experienced.

19. What can I do ? Where shall I go ? On seeing you miserable, O Śambhu, at the sight of your misery, my Prāṇas are agitated and dispirited.

20. It is my opinion that even the most heinous of all great sins are not equal to Brāhmaṇa-slaughter.

21. You are the preceptor of the whole world. You are the instructor in Dharma. But, overpowered by the sin of Brāhmaṇa-slaughter you are incapable of remaining quiet even for a moment.

22. This extremely terrible Hatyā (the sin of Brāhmaṇa-slaughter) emits fish odour; she is senile and sick; she has put out her tongue. O Lord of Devas ! She is running after you to catch you.

23. Hence you must not stay in any single place for a while. For the sake of your benefit you have to be wandering (continuously) for twelve years, with the desire for the destruction of sins.

24-25. You must wander for twelve years with the skull, begging for alms, washing your left hand in the holy rivers and tanks. Then, O Lord of the Devas you will become pure and be liberated from this sin." O Brāhmaṇa, on being advised thus by Viṣṇu, Śiva went over all the places.

26. In order to get rid of the skull he washed his left hand in every sacred water. Wandering thus for three years he reached the penance grove of Badarikāśrama.

27. O bestower of honour, for the sake of alms he stood at the threshold of Dharmaputra,[1] the lord of the Devas and repeatedly said—"Viṣṇu, give me alms."

28. On seeing Śiva stationed at the threshold, Lord Nārāyaṇa said—"Take the alms". After saying this he offered his right hand.

29. On seeing Hari attempting to give the alms, O excellent Brāhmaṇa, Śiva struck his right hand with his trident.

30-33. Through the three wounds inflicted by (the three points of) the trident, three streamlike jets came out. They were terrifying to the worlds. They had different colours; they were twelve Hastas high. One of the streams was of blood. It fell on the skull. The second, a milky stream, reached his face; the third, a stream of water came up to Śiva in front of him, for the sake of saving Śiva. Śiva resorted to these three streams in accordance with the injunctions for the duration of three years. Becoming a little delighted, O Brāhmaṇa, he went to the holy centre of Kurukṣetra. Having gone there, he became a pillar and fell down.

34. In the holy centre of Brahma-hrada, he lay immersed in the waters of Brahmahrada. When a period of three years had elapsed he came out with half of his body wounded (?)

35. He eulogised Viṣṇu the Lord of the Devas, abiding in the cavity of the heart of everyone, for a long time. Then the Lord of the Universe who was pleased with him granted him the boon.

36-38. "O Hara, after wandering over many holy centres go to Kāśī."

Thereafter, he bowed down to Hari and circumambulating him wandered over many places. Making his pilgrimage duly he reached the city of Avimukta (Kāśī). After entering the limits of Avimukta, when Dhurjaṭi (Śiva) observed, he did not see Brahmahatyā following him. She was standing outside. Knowing that it was a holy centre belonging to Viṣṇu and

1. Nārāyaṇa was the son of Dharma and Mūrti. (Bh. P. I. 3.9, II. 7.6, Mbh. Śānti 334.9-12).

destructive of sins he became satisfied in mind and enthusiastically eulogised Viṣṇu, the Lord worthy of being saluted.

39. "Be victorious, be victorious, O Lord of the universe O Lord Viṣṇu, the storehouse of bliss of the entire universe, knowable only through the Vedas; O suppressor of demon Madhu, O Nṛsiṁha, O yellow-robed one, O One riding on Garuḍa, O Mādhava, O primordial Lord.

40. O Lord of Ramā, the lover of Vrajas, (cowherd's colony), Lord of Rādhā, Lord of the Devas, the fulfiller of the desires of all, O Kṛṣṇa, O foremost among the Devas, O ocean of kindness, O destroyer of anguish, O lotus-eyed, O Lord of the greatest beings.

41. O Ornament of the family of Yadu, O resident of the milky ocean, O Śauri, O archer, O expert in the art of uplifting the mountain (Govardhana), O deity having a pair of the lotus-feet that destroy the sin of Kali age, O deity who bestow favour on those who eulogise thee, O Kūrma (Divine Tortoise), O son of Kaśyapa (Vāmana).

42. O Paraśurāma—the fire for the forest of wicked kings, O Buddha with a saffron cloth that cleaned off blood from all sacrifices, O Kalkin, O remover of the fear of worldly existence, O deity governable by (i.e. under the influence of) the devotees, O cowherd, who lift up those who bow down to you, O Lord of sacred fame and name.

43. O remover of the burden of the Earth, O Lord worthy of being worshipped by the enemies of Asuras, O Lord of Prakṛti, O residential abode of the whole universe, O Rāma, O Lord of the mobile and immobile beings shining with many attributes, O Lord who are beyond the three Guṇas., O eternal one, O Lord worthy of being worshipped at the head of all, O Lord who protect the enemy of the annihilator Yama through your own people, O Lord with lotus-like feet, O beautiful Padmanābha, O lotus-palmed Lord, O Lord favourite of the resident of the lotus (i.e. God Brahmā), O Lord, worthy of being saluted by the destroyer of Kāma and the Lord of three worlds (?)

44. O remover of sins, O Lord of the Raghus, O Lord of the Yādavas, one who are fond of Brāhmaṇas, O greater than the greatest one, O Lord worthy of being worshipped by the immortal beings, O wielder of the ploughshare, O remover of sins, O Lord, worthy of being bowed to ; O Lord pervaded by the three Guṇas, O cleverest one in the three worlds and three units of Time.

45. O Lord with the sole duty of destroying the hosts of demons, O sinless one, O Lord lying on Śeṣa, the king of serpents, O destroyer of Kaṁsa, O Lord having the sun and the moon as eyes, O Lord of powerful activities, O Lord having the lustre of fresh clouds, O Lord of the Goddess of Fortune.

46. O sacrifice, O Lord maintaining sacrifice, O Lord who were bound with a rope by your mother, O Lord fond of fresh butter, O Lord of groups of cowherd lasses, O destroyer of demons Agha, Baka, Vṛṣa, Keśin and Pūtanā, O destroyer of Triśiras, Bāli and the ten-headed Rāvaṇa.

47. O destroyer of Naraka and Mura, O Lord who cut off the hands of Bāṇa, O Lord worthy of being worshipped by the enemy of the Tripuras, O friend of Sudāman, O Lord worthy of being served, O Lord whose lotus-like feet constitute a raft that takes one across the ocean of worldly existence, O Lord whose Aiśvarya (Lordship and prowess) is manifest, O ancient one, O One whose arms are full.

48-49. O Lord who can be attained only through the merits of many births, O Lord worthy of all auspicious things, knowable through the Vedas, O receptacle of Śrutis (Vedas), O quiescent, pure, bestower of boons, I seek refuge in your excellent pair of feet; it destroys sins, protect me.

50. There is none who can grant salvation to me other than the ancient Puruṣa. Be pleased with me with this request." The Lord of the universe, who was thus eulogised with great devotion by Lord Śambhu, Viṣṇu favourably disposed towards the devotees manifested himself suddenly.

51. On seeing Hari, Hara fell on the ground like a staff. O leading Brāhmaṇa, he got up again and with palms joined in reverence he bowed down to him.

52. Viṣṇu spoke to that leader of Bhūtas (goblins) who had bowed to him—"Choose a boon, I will give it to you. I am pleased with your eulogy."

53. On hearing the words of the Lord, Bhūteśa, Lord of the goblins who had been harassed by the evil of the slaughter of a Brāhmaṇa spoke this to Hari who is the bestower of worldly pleasures and liberation.

54. "O wielder of discus and iron club, I wish to stay in your holy centre since the 'brāhmaṇa-slaughter' is seen stationed outside the limits of your holy centre.

55. O Garuḍa-bannered deity, be merciful to me by the gift of this holy centre. On my going out, the evil of Brāhmaṇa-slaughter will harass me again.

56. Stationed in your holy centre, I will derive worship in all the three worlds."

After saying this to the Lord of the Devas the bull-bannered deity kept quiet.

57. The lover of Lakṣmī, the daughter of the milk ocean, said "So be it" and accepted the proposal. O leading Brāhmaṇa, ever since then, this place is mentioned as the holy centre pertaining to Śiva.

58-59. But poets knew this as the ancient holy centre of Keśava. O excellent Brāhmaṇa, water (tears) gushed out of the eyes of Viṣṇu overwhelmed with sympathy. Thereby the lake called Bindusaras originated. At the behest of Viṣṇu, the bull-bannered Lord took his ablution there.

60. No sooner did Hara take his holy dip therein, then the skull of Brahmā fell down from his hand. That sacred lake became famous by the name of Kapālamocana.

61. Bound by the emotional feelings of devotion of Śambhu, Viṣṇu is stationed there by the name of Bindu-Mādhava after giving his own abode to the Trident-bearing Lord.

62. He was resorted to by the Sky-clad Śiva; he had the lustre of ten thousand suns. In this manner, Brahmā and other Devas residing in Heaven ever see him.

63. O darling (husband), obstacles are put by the trident-bearing Lord (in the lives of people) so that they will serve him. People who are overwhelmed by these obstacles will eulogise Viṣṇu and then worship Śiva.

64-65. All those people dwell here thinking "Lord is Śiva: the city is Kāśī. O Brāhmaṇa, by thinking about Śiva, the devotees of Śiva are free from perturbation. They go to Siva's world devoid of old age and death. Good men endowed with many merits stay here free from ailments.

66-67. O lover of Kāśi, those who partake of the leavings of sacrifice become endowed with prosperity. O excellent Brāhmaṇa they do not extol ablution here nor Japa, nor the worship of the Devas nor charitable gifts. Excepting the abandoning of one's physical body nothing else is praised. After courting death here a man certainly becomes contented and blessed.

68. O Brāhmaṇa, such a city full of palaces, has been reached by us. It is conducive to the salvation of even those who indulge in worldly pleasures: what then of those who observe holy vows.

69. May this maiden who had been formerly separated from her parents by that wicked Rākṣasa be left in the palace of the Lord of Kāśī.

70-72. This virgin who had been practising observances had been abducted by that Rākṣasa for sexual intercourse. Thus the power of this holy centre has been described, O excellent Brāhmaṇa. All Karmans auspicious and inauspicious, of past, present and future, perpetrated knowingly or unknowingly do perish here. It is for the destruction of Karmans that this city was formerly built by (Viṣṇu). Men who die therein never experience fierce and endless misery nor the tortures of Yama.

11. Urged by her, O Lord, I have come to report the matter to you. She says "I am unravaged. May my father know that I have come back.

12-13a. O father no doubt need be entertained in respect to my good action." On hearing these wonderful words of the city Governor, the king instantaneously set off alongwith his wife, ministers and the Brāhmaṇa priest.

13b-14a After going out of the city the king saw his daughter comfortably seated on the banks of the Gaṅgā. She was as refulgent as the sun. She was accompanied by a Brāhmaṇa alongwith a woman.

14b-15. She was bedecked in her natural dress though she was fond of ornaments. She had the lustre of unfading flowers. She was refulgent like molten gold. After seeing her from a distance, the king hurriedly went near her and embraced her.

16. Over-joyed she too embraced her father and bowed down to him. Then she met her mother with great delight within her heart.

17-18. Addressing her father, the king, the large-eyed girl spoke these words. "Surrounded by my female friends I was sleeping in the Hall of Jewels. O dear father, without washing my feet I lay with my head directed towards the north on the couch anxiously pondering over a possible alliance with a husband. I was abducted during the middle of the night.

19. Taking me with him, the demon went to his city beyond the ocean on a mountain full of different kinds of jewels. I was confined in a cave.

20. There he was thinking deeply within himself about the means of a marriage with me. This lady of beautiful eyebrows and slender waist who stands here, is his wife.

21-22. She is an ogress who has assumed a human form. She had been the wife of that demon. O King, using the Śakti of god Indra intelligently she caused the death of her own husband of ruthless actions, at the hands of the Brāhmaṇa. It was through the intercession of fate that even before me the Brāhmaṇa had reached the mountain.

23-24a. This ogress found that her husband was a defiler of virtue. Moreover, she became enamoured of the handsome features of the Brāhmaṇa. Urged by her own Karman, she entered into an agreement with the Brāhmaṇa, for wedded life (with him) and brought about the death of the Rākṣasa.

24b-26. Thus, after having made the Brāhmaṇa her husband, she assumed the form of a she-elephant. The wealth got in exchange of all the articles of the house was kept on her back alongwith the Brāhmaṇa and myself. O king, she has now come here to your mansion. O king, it was by this Rākṣasī that I had been saved from that demon. Hence, honour and worship her alongwith the Brāhmaṇa.

27. With her permission give me in marriage to this Brāhmaṇa. I shared the same seat with him. Hence he has become my husband.

28. "He alone shall be the husband of a woman, with whom she shares the same seat. No one else, so we hear in the Purāṇas and Āgamas.

29. I had occupied her back with delight alongwith this Brāhmaṇa. Hence, in my opinion he must be my husband, according to Dharma.

30. Hence, dear father, console this lady and give me to the Brāhmaṇa in accordance with the injunctions in the Āgamas and other scriptural texts. I do not wish to choose any other husband."

31. On hearing these words of his daughter, Sudyumna the king, consoled the ogress in the form of the lady of slender waist. He stood bowing down with humility.

[*Sudyumna requested* :]

32. "This, my daughter, afraid of losing her merits (Dharma), has sought refuge in you alone. For that reason O chaste woman, your previous husband was killed by you.

33. Hence, O gentle lady, she has become one subservient to you. This, my daughter wishes to have as her husband the same gentleman who had been made by you your husband.

34. O Ogress, you have been requested by me by means of obeisances and gifts. O lady of beautiful eyes, give your consent to my daughter by extending your help to her.

35. At your instance, may my daughter be even the hand-maid of the Brāhmaṇa. Eschew the feelings of rivalry common among co-wives and protect my daughter.

36. There is no doubt about this that you are the mistress of myself, my daughter, my wife, my army, my people, my city and even the whole of my kingdom.

37-38. She will always abide by your instructions." On hearing these words of Sudyumna, the ogress approved his statement with a pure conscience mentally (deciding to be) her co-wife. She spoke thus to the king who was ready to give her in marriage.

39. "O excellent king, since you bowed to me with pure feelings, may this lady be the second wife of the Brāhmaṇa.

40. In the bright half of the month of Phālguna, I must be worshipped in the temple by you alongwith all the citizens.

41. Beginning with Aṣṭamī, the eighth day and ending with Caturdaśī, the festivities must be conducted by means of songs and instrumental music alongwith actors and dancers.

42-43a. Oblations of intoxicating beverages, meat, blood, etc. must be given in the course of worship. If you continue to do in this manner I shall always be the cause of your welfare. O leading king, keep your own words."

43b-44. On hearing these words of the ogress, Sudyumna, the king, accepted everything that had been proposed by that delighted lady. When it had been agreed to by the king, the ogress became satisfied.

45. She lovingly spoke to the Brāhmaṇa "O excellent Brāhmaṇa, make this splendid princess also your wife in the manner laid down in the Gṛhya texts.

46-47. I shall eschew jealousy and malice and be a sister to this large-eyed girl." At the instance of the ogress, the Brāhmaṇa, married the daughter of the king who had been endowed with much wealth. Seated on the ogress who assumed the form of a she-elephant, he went to the city of Mahodaya (Kanauj) instantaneously.

48. Then I heard thus—"O gentle lady, your husband

has returned with plenty of wealth and jewels with two wives also in the bargain."

49. Thereupon, I was rebuked and cursed by the kinsmen, parents and friends with harsh and wounding words.

50. "O lady greedy of money, how will you go to your husband who is endowed with fortune now, but who had been abandoned by you before since he was indigent and wretched ?

51. O blessed lady, in case of woman the riches inherited from parents are fickle and unsteady. It is stated that the riches earned by her husband are permanent.

52. He had once been rebuked by you with harsh words. How can you dare to speak to him now ? Your entry into his house is also difficult.

53. Granting that you are able to go there, O woman of evil actions, sharing the bed with your husband can never be conducive to your happiness.

54. If out of fear for the public censure your husband accepts you (once again), he will never have intercourse with you, because he is devoid of affection in the heart.

55. There is nothing else in the world so miserable as the coming together of a man and wife who are mentally far apart. It is exceedingly agitating and crippling."

56. I heard these and many other similar words uttered by the kinsmen. On hearing these I became extremely grief-stricken. With tears filling the eyes, I kept my face bent down.

57-58. I thought within myself thus :— "Formerly, I had been deluded by greediness. Hence neither the bangle of the hand nor the girdle round the waist nor the anklets round the legs were given up so that my husband could be satisfied. The husband is regarded in the world as the master of both wealth and life.

59. That wealth has been taken away by me. What will be my future ? How can I go to his abode ? How shall I speak to him again ?

60-62a. How can he who had been wickedly abandoned by me believe me now." Even as I was thinking thus in my perturbed mind, the palanquin surrounded by kinsmen arrived there. It was tender and elegant. It shone with an umbrella, resembling the moon in lustre. Deer skins were spread within it. Stout men bore it on their shoulders.

62b-63. Those men came in and requested me again and again: "O splendid lady, you have been invited by your husband. Hasten there with glee and joy. Your husband has returned endowed with plenty of wealth and jewels as well as two other wives.

64. O fair-faced lady, we had been sent by your husband immediately after his arrival, to fetch you who have been staying in the house of your parents."

65. O gentle lady, on noting that act of my husband I became ashamed. I did not say anything in reply to them. I remained silent.

66. Thereafter I was urged and enlightened again and again by the kinsmen. "You have been called by your husband with due honour. Hence go back to him.

67. O daughter, if the wife does not rejoin her husband when invited (to do so) she is born as a female crow for fifteen births."

68. They said thus and assuaged my grief. They took me hurriedly and made me sit in the palanquin with affection, they repeatedly said, 'Go'.

69. Thereafter those men placed the palanquin on their shoulders and started immediately with speed. They reached the city of Mahodaya where my husband was staying.

70. That his house had been surrounded by gold (i.e. full of articles, pots etc. of gold) was seen by me. It was fully equipped with furniture, foodstuffs, riches and raiments.

71. Then, O beautiful woman, that ogress and the gentle lady, the princess bowed to me with love and devotion.

72. I was befittingly greeted and honoured with love by those two ladies. Respected, and so delighted with the words of my husband, I took my bath and meal.

and other sins cry out in distress (as they are annihilated therein).

8. Rare indeed is the month of Māgha; rare indeed is the human birth; rare indeed is the ablution early in the morning and rare indeed is the opportunity to serve Kṛṣṇa.

9-12. Rare still is the day of Viṣṇu (i.e. the Ekādaśī Tithi) that is duly observed as the day of fast. Their own splendour has been cast off into the water by gods during the month of Māgha. Here water is very particularly sacred during this month. The goal that is obtained by persons who maintain regular observances by means of bathing into the water early in the morning, is the bestower of happiness, and is never attained by even heroic warriors (after death) in the battle. If one takes one's bath in the waters of rivers, lakes or tanks it is called the most excellent. If the bath is taken in the well water kept in a vessel, it is of mediocre benefit. If water that is warmed in fire is taken for bath, it is of the least benefit. Merit cannot be attained through pleasures. It is obtained only through distress and exertion.

13. Bath is taken for the purpose of observing holy and virtuous rites and not merely for the sake of purity and cleanliness of the limbs. Fire is resorted to for the purpose of performing Homas and not for removing chillness.

14. Bath should be taken before the sunrise. If the sky is overcast with clouds, one should pray and request the sun who is going to rise.

15. If rivers etc. are not available, water should be kept over-night in a fresh mud-pot. Wind must blow over it during the night. People know such water to be equal to the Gaṅgā for the purpose of holy ablution.

16. O fair lady, a person who regularly takes bath in the month of Māgha, never sees misery and misfortune. There exists no such sin as cannot be wiped off by the holy bath during the month of Māgha.

17-18. Taking the holy dip into water in the morning during the month of Māgha is better than entering fire (?) Misery is experienced if one survives (after entering fire) but if one dies one enjoys happiness. For this reason, O gentle lady the bath during the month of Māgha is of special significance Everyday gingelly seeds along (or coated ?) with sugar must be given as charitable gifts.

19. O lady of slender waist, Homa should be performed with cooked rice as white as hail or with barley grains foll wed by the oblation of cow's ghee on the full-moon day in the month of Māgha.

20. At the end of the holy observance of (pre-sunrise) bath in the month of Māgha one shall give food consisting of the six tastes (such as sweet, sour and others) and say "May the lord, the sun-god be pleased with me—Lord sun who is unsullied and the embodiment of Viṣṇu.

21. To a Brāhmaṇa couple, clothes should be given along with seven kinds of food. Thirty sweet-meats too must be given as well as gingelly seeds and cooked rice along with sugar.

22. The gingelly seeds and sugar must be in the ratio of three to one. The devotee who knows the procedure must give Tāmbūla (betel leaves) and other sources of enjoyment with devotion.

23. One should face the current when one bathes in a river, if it be in any other place (tank etc.), one should face the sun. There he must invoke Gaṅgā and other holy rivers from the disc of the sun (and then take bath).

24-25. "There are thousands of sins originating in the course of many births, some knowingly committed, some unknowingly committed. But may all those be dispelled by your brilliance, O sun, O Lord of the worlds, O Prabhākara (cause of lustre), obeisance be to you. O Acyuta, make my (observance of) holy dip in the month of Māgha well accomplished and complete."

26. O fair lady, the devotee who takes bath in the holy centres gets lesser benefit than the devotee who takes holy dip in the month of Māgha. One may go to heaven by means of baths in the holy centres. One goes to the highest region (Mokṣa) through the bath in the month of Māgha.

27. The eleventh day in the bright half of the month of Māgha is the destroyer of great sins, if it coincides with a Sunday.

28-36. Even without the conjunction of the constellation Pleiades, the eleventh day in the bright half of Māgha burns the sins of men in the same manner as a base king spoils the kingdom, or as a bad son the family, or as a vicious wife the husband, or as sin the virtue, or as the wicked minister ruins the king, or as ignorance dispels (i.e. vitiates) knowledge, or as complete uncleanliness mars purity, or as untruth dispels truth, or as a controversy spoils a conversation or as heat dispels snow or as misfortune spoils fortune, or as a sin mars fame or arrogance vitiates austerity. Just as Rasas (medicinal potions) destroy great ailments, just as Śaṅkara (fixing of rendezvous) spoils śrāddha (?), so also the Dvādaśī, if properly observed, destroys heaps of sins. The day of Hari (Ekādaśī) quickly destroys the great sins such as Brāhmaṇa-slaughter, imbibing of liquor, stealing, and outraging the modesty of the preceptor's wife. The collections of these sins are not quelled by bath in Puṣkara. Neither the holy centre of the Naimiṣa forest nor Kurukṣetra nor Prabhāsa, Gayā, Revā, Sarasvatī, Gaṅgā, Yamunā, Prayāga nor the river Devikā nor the lakes nor rivers nor Homas, gifts and austerities (can dispel these sins). Excepting the only (auspicious) day of Hari i.e. Ekādaśī no other day can destroy the multitude of sins; no other merit is clearly mentioned in the Purāṇa O lady of charming eyebrows, for the purpose of destroying aggregates of sins.

37-40. O gentle lady, by observing fast even for once, heaps of sins do perish. On one side of the balance the gift of the whole Earth and on another side the day of Hari, it is declared by Brahmā that they are not equal. The day of Hari is superior. On that day, the devotee should make a gold image of the Lord in the form of a Boar. An auspicious new copper vessel shall be kept over a jar. Into that vessel the image of the lord should be placed, so also all the seeds. It must be covered with a white cloth. Gold pieces, bright lamp etc. should be placed, and the vessel be decorated with flowers. The observer of the holy rite should worship the Lord in accordance with the injunctions and keep himself awake.

41. In the morning, the devotee should gift away the jar alongwith the Boar image and all the things within it and

also the Naivedyas and other ancillary articles to a Brāhmaṇa householder who is a devotee of Viṣṇu.

42. After feeding Brāhmaṇas, he should break his fast surrounded by his friends. O fair lady, if this observance is performed, he is never born again anywhere.

43. The sin accumulated in the course of many births whether knowingly or unknowingly committed, is wholly destroyed like the darkness at sunrise.

44. O splendid lady, the holy rite of Ekādaśī has been recounted to you by me in accordance with the (description of the same in the) scriptural texts. O gentle lady, this is the same as had been performed formerly by you in the course of another birth.

45-46. As a result of this holy rite, you have derived incomparable nourishment. It will be enhanced further later on. It is the bestower of happiness on your husband and son always. If, out of that merit a fourth part is willingly and respectfully given to me, I will become delighted and will go to the greatest region of Viṣṇu.

47. O beautiful woman, I had incurred a sin due to the denial and concealment of the wealth. In order to sanctify it (i.e. in order to dispel it and sanctify me) kindly give me one fourth part of your merit as I just now requested for.

48. The woman who deceives her husband with regard to the life or wealth undergoes hundred births in the wombs of germs and is reborn ultimately as a Pulkasī (Cāṇḍāla woman).

49. O honourable lady, the woman of perverted mind who does not yield herself up for sexual intercourse when the husband requests for the same or does not give him wealth (when he needs it) certainly is reborn as Kāṣṭhīlā (a worm ?).

50. If you have any mercy on me, give me a fourth part of your merit accruing from the observance of the holy rite of Ekādaśī for the purpose of dispelling the sin, which I had incurred.

51. O lady of good eyes, on hearing the words of that Kāṣṭhīlā, I took water in my hand and gave the (required) merit to her.

52. "By one-fourth of the merit accrued to me formerly by observing a fast on the Ekādaśī day, may this Kāṣṭhīlā be

liberated from the sins committed by her in the previous birth. What I have averred is truth and nothing but the truth."

53b-54a. When those words were uttered by me, she was seen going to the region of Viṣṇu seated in a divine aerial chariot. Her lustre was like that of lightning.

54b-55. The husband is a deity in the visible world. He should not be deceived by the wife either through her body or through her wealth, if she wishes for splendid existence (in the next birth). Hence, you speak out. I shall give you what is desired by you for the sake of our husband.

56-57. O fair-faced lady, I shall give up wealth, body, my own son or anything else (if you desire it). Who else is a deity unto the women in this world except her own husband ? O lady of beautiful eyes, the woman who sacrifices her wealth or life for his sake, is honoured in the world of Viṣṇu for the duration of a hundred crores of Kalpas and more.

58. The wife of the Brāhmaṇa saw her husband, who had wooed her with fire etc. as witness, indulging in terrible vices. So she became ruthless. Although she was requested, she did not give him wealth, as a result of that sin she became a worm.

59. During my girlhood days this flag-staff of Kāma was seen by me when I was at my father's place. After knowing that it is beneficial to the husband, I give up everything. O lady of beautiful eyebrows, take it.

CHAPTER THIRTYTWO

The Narration by Sandhyāvalī

Vasiṣṭha continued :

1. On hearing the words of Sandhyāvalī, Mohinī the daughter of Brahmā who was Mohakaraṇḍikā (a box of delusion ?) said thus, as she was interested in her own mission.

2-3. "O splendid lady, if thus you know the ways of Dharma and Adharma, and if for the sake of your husband you will readily give up your wealth and life, I beg of you then, O splendid lady, a wealth that is superior to life. Give me the head of your son which is liked by you more than the heart.

4-8a. If your husband, the king does not take food on the day of Hari (Ekādaśī), may he take the sword in his hand and cut off the beautiful head of Dharmāṅgada, which is splendid, which is comparable to the disc of the moon, which is decorated with two ear-rings and in which the moustache has not yet grown. O lady of beautiful eyes, may he cut it off and let it fall on to my lap. If he does not take food, O gentle lady, at least do this on the day of lord Viṣṇu, that is destructive of heaps of sins."

On hearing these words of Mohinī couched in bitter words, (Sandhyāvalī) the gentle lady shivered for a short while like the plantain tree blasted by chillness.

8b-14. Thereafter, Sandhyāvalī, the fair-complexioned lady mustered courage and composure and spoke these words to Mohinī, smilingly and preserving gentle expression on the face, —"O lady of beautiful eyebrows, these verses are heard mentioned in the Purāṇas. They are connected with Ekādaśī. They are the bestowers of heavenly bliss and salvation. (They are as follows :) "One should abandon wealth, one should eschew one's wife, life and house. One should abandon one's land, king, heaven, friends, and preceptor. One may leave off the holy centre, Dharma and whatever one is most fond of. One shall eschew Yoga, charitable gifts, perfect knowledge and holy rites. One should leave off austerities, Vidyā (learning), Siddhi (achievement of supernatural powers) and even salvation, O splendid lady. But one shall not leave off the holy Ekādaśī rite in both fortnights. Sons, brothers, friends and beloved ones, all are but persons with whom we come in contact only here (in this world). But Ekādaśī is remembered, O gentle lady, as the means of achievement of pleasures both here and hereafter (in this world and the other world). Thanks to the power of Ekādaśī, everything will become beneficent.

15. O blessed lady, I shall make him give you the head

of Dharmāṅgada for your satisfaction. O splendid lady, believe in my statement and be happy.

16. In this matter, O gentle lady, this traditional mythological story is heard. I shall tell you, O gentle lady, listen with attention.

17. Formerly, there was a Daitya devoted to virtuous activities. (His name was) Virocana.[1] His wife, a lady of large eyes, was interested in the worship of Brāhmaṇas.

18. O lady of beautiful eye-brows, every day in the morning, she used to worship a sage in accordance with the injunctions. With great devotion and a delighted mind, she used to drink the water with which his feet had been washed.

19-21. (Defective) The Devas became apprehensive of the son of Prahlāda (i.e. Virocana) in the same manner as they were, while Hiraṇyakaśipu of fierce valour was ruling over the kingdom. Even when he was dead, they moved about on the Earth with great anxiety when the son of Prahlāda (i.e. Virocana) was himself delighted. Once those Devas the chief of whom was Indra, consulted Bṛhaspati, the preceptor of the Devas and said : "We are oppressed by the enemies. What is it that should be done by us ?" On hearing those words of the Devas, the preceptor Bṛhaspati said :

22-23. "Viṣṇu must be respectfully informed by the Devas (gods) who have become miserable." On hearing the utterance of their preceptor, the Devas of unmeasured splendour went to Vaikuṇṭha for securing the death of Virocana. After going there, they eulogised Viṣṇu, the most excellent of all Devas, by reciting hymns.

The Devas said :

24. Obeisance to the overlord of the Devas, to Viṣṇu of unmeasured splendour. Repeated salutes to the destroyer of obstacles of devotees, to Vaikuṇṭha (Viṣṇu).

1. Virocana was Bali's father. As such he preceded Viṣṇu's incarnation as Vāmana. Strictly speaking, reference to Viṣṇu calling him by his future incarnation as Paraśurāma, Kṛṣṇa, Buddha etc. is anachronic. But the Purāṇa-writers have not developed that sense. To the author of the NP., Viṣṇu is Para-Brahman. Hence addressing him as Śiva, the universe, Kāla etc., is natural (vide VV. 30-40 below).

36. Obeisance to the deity devoid of attributes, to the deity without desires, to the deity the knower of ethics, to the Ātman devoid of motion, to Buddha, to the deity of the form of Kalki, to Kṣetrajña; obeisance to the imperishable.

37. Obeisance to Govinda; to the lord of the universe, to the infinite one, to the primordial one; obeisance to the deity having the bow Śārṅga; to the deity wielding the conch and the iron club. Bow to the deity holding the discus.

38. Hail to the deity having the sword; obeisance to the Trident-bearing deity: .obeisance to the deity striking with all weapons and missiles; Bow to the deity worthy of being a refuge; obeisance to the transcendental deity. Bow to the great Ātman.

39. Obeisance to Hṛṣīkeśa; to the deity identical with the universe; obeisance to you of the form of the universe. Hail to the deity having the Time as his umbilicus; salute to Kāla (God of Death, Time). Bow to the deity having the moon and the sunfor his eyes; obeisance to the perfect one; obeisance to the deity worthy of being served. Hail to the deity who is greater than the greatest.

40. Obeisance to the maker of the universe, to the upholder of the universe, and to the annihilator of the universe; obeisance to one who fascinates, to one who agitates, to one who assumes the form as he desires; obeisance to the unborn, to the poet (the wise one).

41. O lord, on being oppressed by the Daityas, we have sought refuge in you. Hence, O supporter of everything, do that whereby we may be happy.

42a. May we sport about accompanied by our sons, friends, wives and others."

42b.-45a. On hearing their hymn of praise, Vaikuṇṭha (god Viṣṇu) was delighted in his mind. He granted personal vision to those Devas who were distressed and harassed by the Daityas. On seeing Vaikuṇṭha (God Viṣṇu), the lord of the chiefs of the Devas very affectionate at heart, they respectfully prayed to him for the destruction of Virocana. On hearing the main task of those Devas the chief of whom was Indra, the lord who is the foremost among those who know their duties, consoled the Devas with Love and let them off fully delighted and joyous.

45.B-48. When the groups of the Devas had gone, the lord who is the foremost among the knowers of all expedients, assumed the form of an old Brāhmaṇa and went to the abode of Virocana. He, the achiever of the missions, reached the place at the time of the worship of the Brāhmaṇas. On seeing him, Viśālāksī (a lady of large eyes) became delighted in her mind. After greeting and honouring the extra-ordinary Brāhmaṇa with devotion, she gave him the seat. Without accepting the seat given by her, he told her :— "O splendid and gentle lady, I am not accepting the great seat offered by you.

49-50.A Listen. The mission for which I have come here is incomparable. O woman of honour, he who understands the task kept in my mind must agree to its fulfilment. Then, O fairfaced lady, I will accept his worship."

50.B-51.A On hearing the words of the old Brāhmaṇa the lady (though) an expert in understanding the deep significance of expressions, was deluded by the Māyā of Viṣṇu, as she was a woman. She spoke with great delight.

Viśālākṣi said :-

51-55.A "O Brāhmaṇa, I shall give you whatever may be in your mind. Take it from me. Here is the seat. Here is the water for washing the feet. Give unto me the desired object (viz. the water where-with you wash the feet)". On being requested thus, the Brāhmaṇa said, "I do not believe in the words of a woman. If your husband says it I can believe."

On hearing the words spoken by the Brāhmaṇa, the mistress of the abode of Virocana invited her husband there itself, in the presence of the Brāhmaṇa.

At the instance of the messenger, the delighted son of Prahlāda came to the harem where his wife Viśālākṣī was present.

55.B-57.A On seeing her husband arrived, the lady engaged in holy rites got up, bowed to the leading Brāhmaṇa and offered the seat. When he did not accept the seat offered respectfully, she informed her husband, the king of the Daityas.

57B-61.A. On coming to know of the incident, Virocana, the king of Daityas, was swayed by his love for his wife. With mind deluded, he accepted the (proposal of the Brāhmaṇa). After understanding the mental idea when the Daitya accepted the suggestion, the Brāhmaṇa became delighted and said, :- " Offier me your age and longevity". Then the couple became deluded due to the grief caused by themselves. After meditating for a short while and joining the hands together, they spoke to the Brāhmaṇa, "O Brāhmaṇa, accept our life. Give us the water from your feet. We shall make your utterance true, Be delighted".

61.63 A. Janārdana who was delighted by their devotion, gave her the water from his feet. Viśālākṣī became joyous by washing the feet of the Brāhmaṇa. Along with her husband, she sprinkled water with which his feet were washed, over her head.

63.B. 65. O lady of beautiful eyebrows, the couple thereupon suddenly assumed divine forms, climbed into the excellent aerial chariot and went to the region of Viṣṇu.[1] Thereafter, the lord became delighted by uprooting the cause of grief to the Devas. He went to his abode in Vaikuṇṭha. He was eulogised by all the groups of Devas. Thus, O gentle ledy, what has been promised to you must be given to you by me.

66. O gentle lady, I will not make my husband Rukmāṅgada move away from truth. It is truth alone that has been glorified as the bestower of salvation on men.

67-68. They know that the man who has fallen off from truth is baser than a Cāṇḍāla". After speaking thus to Mohinī, the daughter of the lotus-born deity (Brahmā), Sandhyāvalī as refulgent as gold, and having beautiful eyebrows touched the feet of her husband with both of her hands, the feet that were copper-coloured with red toes.

---

1. The account of the death of Virocana given here—the self-sacrifice of Virocana and queen Viśālākṣi—is not complimentary to Viṣṇu. In the *Mbh. Śānti.* 98. 49-50, he was killed by Indra in the battle with demon Tāraka. This second version of Virocana's death is supported by Mt. P., Pd. P. and Brahmāṇḍa P.

CHAPTER THIRTYTHREE

The Submission of Dharmāṅgada

Vasiṣṭha said :

1. Thereafter, O king, Sandhyāvalī clasped the feet of her husband. The gentle lady spoke these words about the (imminent) death of Dharmāṅgada (at his hands).

Sandhyāvalī said :

2. "O king, just as by you, so also by me, this lady has been advised in many ways. But nothing else appeals to Mohinī, the very embodiment of delusion.

3. She wants you to take food on the day of Viṣṇu or to kill your son. O lord striking the son down is better than violating the holy observance.

4. O king, the affliction of the father is not as severe as that of the mother in giving birth to the son.

5. Since the mother undergoes misery in holding the son in her womb, O king, her affection is excessive. O king, the affection of the father cannot be as much as that of the mother.

6. In the world, O leading king, the father is said to be the person who sows the seed, the mother is the porson who holds it within her womb. In protecting and nourishing the child, the mother is superior to the father.

7. The affection of the mother is hundred times more than that of the father. It is in view of this abundance of love and affection that they recognise that the mother is greater.

8. In spite of that, I have become devoid of affection towards the son, O leading king, because of my desire to win the other world through the maintenance of the truth of the words uttered.

9. Eschewing all your affectionate feelings O king, kill your son. Do not transgress the truthfulness of the words uttered. On my very soul, you are bound by an oath.

10-14. Hṛṣikeśa will be the bestower of fruits (after testing persons) on touch-stones (of holy rites), if, after observing them, O king, no pain is felt in the body. There is no doubt about this that it is through Adharma that a man falls off from heaven. The man who takes off his life or that of his son or sacrifices his possessions O king, and follows fate, is sung about as a great man. O king, blessed are those adversities which make men truthful. In view of their purpose of keeping up truthfulness, they may be the bestowers of salvation on men. In order to spread and guard their fame, holy rites must always be performed by men in the manner mentioned in the scriptures, without being swayed either by love or by hatred. Hence, O king, enough of your distress and anguish. Keep up the truth.

15. O king, by keeping up the truth, a man becomes united with Viṣṇu's person. This Mohinī (enchantress) is a touchstone created by the Devas for you.

16. O king, I consider that she has been made your wife (for this purpose), but you do not understand that. By your act of killing your son, the Devas will hang down their heads (in shame).

17. Placing your foot on their heads, you will attain the highest region. The Devas are the antagonists of those who have devotion towards Viṣṇu.

18-19. What has been made clear is that there will be blindness in the world. O king, the Devas along with the deities are antagonistic to you. With their activities, they break (obstruct) your path towards salvation. They cause you to drop down your resolve. Hence, O king, be steady and firm. Kill your dear son.

20-21. Carry out the directions of Mohinī by way of keeping up your own vow. O lord of kings, if the directives are unheeded, you will incur a terrible sin equal to that of Brāhmaṇa-slaughter. O ruler of the earth, you will be going to the world of Śamana (i.e. Yama) and there will be damage to your reputation on the earth."

Vasiṣṭha said :

22. O king, on hearing the words of his wife, the king Rukmāṅgada spoke those words to Sandhyāvalī in the presence of Mohinī :—

23. "O beloved wife, the slaughter of one's own son is an exceedingly sinful act. It is worse than Brāhmaṇa-

slaughter. What will be my future destiny in the world after killing my own son?

24. Wherefore did I go to the Mandara mountain? Wherefore did I meet with Mohinī? O gentle lady, this is veritable Kāla or god of death in the form of the beloved (Mohinī), for the destruction of Dharmāṅgada.

25. What will be my future state by killing my son who is conversant with Dharma, who is endowed with humility, who reconciles and delights the people and who has no issue of his own?

26-31. O gentle lady, the father incurs great misery even by killing a vicious son. What then if he happens to be by nature righteous and rendering regular service to his elders? O fair-complexioned lady, this continent of Jambūdvīpa alone is enjoyed by me. But all the seven continents are being enjoyed by your son now. O fair lady, he is a part of Viṣṇu. He will surely be superior to his father. O fair lady, this son of mine, Dharmāṅgada who has been highly extolled in Purāṇas by poets (O wise sages) is superior to all on this earth.

O lady of charming limbs, he is the bestower of honour on my family as well as on me. Alas! In this matter I am faced with a greater misery than even my son. O fair lady, with your auspicious utterances speak again to Mohinī who is deluded and so who gives me much grief."

32. After saying thus to his beloved wife Sandhyāvalī, the king came near Mohinī and spoke this :—

33-34. "O splendid lady, I will not take food on the day of Viṣṇu nor will I injure my son in any way. I would rather tear up my own self or the gentle lady Sandhyāvalī. At your behest, I may even do any other terrible deed. But, O lady of charming eyebrows, leave off your stubbornness in regard to my son.

35. What benefit will you attain by killing my son Dharmāṅgada? What do you gain by compelling me to take food on the day of Viṣṇu? Tell me.

36. O fair-faced lady, I am your servant. I am your slave. I am subservient to you. O blessed lady request for some other boon, I submit to you.

37-40. O lady of beautiful limbs, your feet are equal

61-62A. Eschew the deep overwhelming sorrow originating from killing your own son. O lord, (even if) this body is abandoned, it will lead to the creation of another body, that is devoid of all sorts of ailments and equal to that of Indra.

62B-64. Those who are killed for the cause of their fathers, or for their mothers, or for cows, Brāhmaṇas, young women, Earth, king, or the deities, or for the sake of their children or the handicapped, attain the excessively brilliant worlds. Hence enough of your worries and anxieties. Kill me with your excellent sword.

65. O leading king, stick to your vow. Do not take food on the day of Hari. O king, one may kill one's own son or wife for the sake of Dharma.

66. It is heard in the Vedic texts : A person (i.e. a king) who sits consecrated for the performance of horse-sacrifice may kill his son in that excellent sacrifice and no sin is incurred thereby.

67. O king, whatever, Mohinī, my mother, says must be carried out unhesitatingly by you.

68. O leading king, be pleased. Carry out the suggestions made by me, in regard to my own death. O king you will then release yourself from the terrible utterance of falsehood through the interference of Mohinī.

69. O king, as a result of the killing of your own son, your fame will be illuminated. Thanks to the splendour of your fame, your reputation and esteem will be very high and ever-lasting. O dear father, no doubt should be entertained in this matter."

CHAPTER THIRTYFOUR

The Visions of the Lord

Vasiṣṭha said :—

1-4. On hearing the words of his son, the king Rukmāṅgada glanced at Sandhyāvalī's face resembling a lotus and became glad. (It seemed as though her face urged) : "listening to the words of Mohinī, do not take food. Kill the boy born of your body. Do not take food. Rather kill your son". This importunity was evident in her face. In the meantime, the Lotus-eyed Lord (Viṣṇu) came there and stood in the sky but in an invisible state. He began to watch the courage and fortitude of the three persons—the heroic king, Sandhyāvalī and Dharmāṅgada. O leading king, the unsullied lord Viṣṇu having the colour of the cloud, seated himself on the Lord of birds viz. his vehicle Garuḍa.

5-9. When the words "Eat, Eat" were uttered by Mohinī, the king took up the stainless (bright) sword to kill his son Dharmāṅgada, With a delighted mind, he made obeisance to the Garuḍa-emblemed lord. On seeing his father armed with the sword, Dharmāṅgada bowed down to his parents and to the discus-bearing Lord without any feelings of sorrow, he looked at the face of his mother, O great king.*

Dharmāṅgada who was endowed with devotion to his father and who was superior to all in his devotion to his mother, kept his neck close to the ground. His neck resembled a conch-shell. It was tender with the lustre of gold. It was plump and it contained many lines. He placed his neck on the path of sword.

10. O king, (Māndhātā), when the son offered his neck with delight in the face that resembled the beautiful moon, and when the lord of the Earth (i.e. Rukmāṅgada) took up his sword, the entire Earth along with the mountains began to quake.

11. Immediately the ocean tides arose as if to submerge the three worlds. Hundreds of meteors fell on the Earth with

---

**Nṛpa-Puṅgavaḥ* in the text has no predicate, hence taken in the Voc. as *Nṛpa-Puṅgava* (Māndhātā) "O king" is repeated even out of context in this part of the NP.

violent gusts of wind and thunder-bolt's stroke from the middle of the sky.

12-14. Thinking (to herself) : "O the mission of the Devas has not been accomplished by me. My birth has been thus fruitless. It has been made so by the fate that had created the universe. My enchanting beauty has been only a fraud, since the food is not taken in by the king on the day of Hari—the day that dispels the fear of sins. In the Heaven, I will be treated as equal to grass.

He who has abundance of Sattva qualities will go along the path of salvation. But I, the sinner, will fall into the terrible hell."

15. O leading king, when the sword was lifted up by the king, Mohinī endowed with delusion over-came with swoon fell on the ground.

16-18. Shining with that sword, the king attempted to cut off the neck of his son Dharmāṅgada. When the courageous king Rukmāṅgada, with great delight, was to cut off his son's head alongwith the ear-rings the head that was beautiful, had the brilliance of the moon that was shining. But immediately the king was caught in his hand by Viṣṇu, the lord of the daughter of the Milk-ocean". I am pleased I am delighted. There is no doubt about this. O lord of the people, go to my region.

19-20. O king, establish on the Earth your fame that is worthy of being worshipped in the three worlds and that is white and pure. Set your foot on the head of Yama. O king, thereafter, accompanied by your beloved wife and son you go to my residence called after my body (i.e. Vaikuṇṭha)". The moment he was touched with the hand of the discus-bearing lord, the king became free from sins in the company of his wife and his son.

21-22. Approaching quickly, the noble-souled king entered the divine body of the lord, leaving off the Royal glory originating from the Earth abandoning the slaves, riches and treasury, elephants, horses, chariots, wives in the harem and the kinsmen. He became one with the body of Viṣṇu. Then a shower of flowers fell from the sky.

23. O king (Māndhātā), the large drums called Dundubhis were sounded by the delighted Siddhas, and the guardians of the divine world. The celestial ladies sang sweet songs and danced joyously.

24-26. The daughters of the Gandharvas were satisfied with the action of the king. The son of the sun (i.e Yama) too observed this wonderful phenomenon viz. the king entered the divine body of Viṣṇu accompanied by his wife and son after wiping off the writings of Yama. He placed all the people in the path leading to the world of Hari. The people followed the path pointed out by the king and were grateful to him. Yama became frightened again. He came to the four-faced lord Brahmā and spoke to him crying :- "O lord, I will not be a mere employee without the power to command. O lord of Devas, create another post for me. I shall do my best. Let not my baton of punishment be a thing of mere show."

CHAPTER THIRTYFIVE

Mohinī incurs a cause

Yama said :

1. "O lord of the Devas; O lord of the universe ! O lord and preceptor of the mobile and immobile beings Mohinī has become unsuccessful like a barren woman in the matter of giving birth (to childern).

2. O Kuśa-emblemed one the entire world goes to Vaikuṇṭha along the path advocated by Rukmāṅgada. No one comes to me.

3. Although the lord of kings entered the body of the discus-bearing lord (Viṣṇu), the mind of all the living beings has not changed.

4. O grand-sire of the universe, after observing fast on the day of Viṣṇu, all men including young children, go to the greatest world with their sins dispelled.

5. Your daughter, Mohinī, the gentle lady is ashamed and has been in swoon. She is not coming near you because she is despised by the world. She does not even take food.

6. I have become jobless, what am I to do? Guide me." On hearing the words of Yama the lotus-seated deity said:

7-8A "We all shall go together to bring Mohinī to consciousness. After she has got up (regained normalcy) O son of the sun, we shall perform your task. There is no doubt about it. May excitement and agitation be eschewed.

8B-9. Then all the groups of Devas led by Indra and others accompanied by Brahmā, came down to the Earth in their aerial chariots as refulgent as the sun, in order to rouse that woman to consciousness O king (Māndhātā).

10-23. With their aerial chariots they surrounded the auspicious (beautiful)-faced lady (who was in a swoon then). She was devoid of brilliance and bliss. She resembled (the following) : a river the water of which had dried up, the night without the moon, a holy rite without the Ṛtvik priest, a man who is defeated in a battle, a flower that has faded, the dais where-from the celebration of the festival has ceased, the coral that has become white and colourless, the grain-field from-where the grains have been removed, the light that is dim, the churning rod O king, when the butter is taken out,* the speech that is not refined, the army that has been crushed (severely defeated), a young woman whose husband has been killed, the subjects deprived of food grains, the sacred-rite without Mantras, the war waged in violation of its prescribed code and without mercy, the Earth without a king, the king without a minister, O excellent king, the house devoid of wealth and food-grains, the pot without water, the lordly bull stuck in mire, the householder without his wife, the king banished from his kingdom; the physician whose medical treatment has failed, the tree whose branches have been cut, the house without fire, the cloud without water, the fire with plenty of smoke, the sun without his rays, the man who has gone out of his senses, the man who indulges in sexual intercourse on Parvan

*Here the text is defective.

days (the new moon, the full moon days etc), a lover who is not satisfied with his beloved, (or with no favourable response from his beloved), the serpent deprived of its poison, the bird whose wings have been clipped, the Brāhmaṇa who has no means of sustenance; the garland that has been dropped down from the head, the mountain without metals and minerals, the scriptural text the script of which is distorted, the Ṛk and Yajus Mantra that is recited in wrong notes, the Sāman verse recited with a discordant note, a lake devoid of lotuses, the pathway overgrown with grasses, the lotus devoid of petals, knowledge (vitiated) by the feelings of egotism, the Puruṣa without Prakṛti, the Sāṅkhya philosophy minus the Tattvas (principles), and the Dharma (Virtue, piety) (tarnished) with arrogance, thus the heaven-dwellers saw Mohinī devoid of brilliance.

24-25. The Devas, on arrival, spoke to that fierce lady who was meditating (brooding) and lacking in enthusiasm; who was viewed by the people as one with (the stigma of) the murder of her son; who was criticised in cruel rebuking terms as a woman of bad conduct; who had been abandoned by the virtuous people; who had been stubborn in clinging to her own words and had been defrauded by those very words (?)

26. "O fair lady, do not feel aggrieved; you have put in manly efforts. Indeed, there is no question of wounded prestige in regard to the devotees of Viṣṇu.

27. O fawn- eyed lady, it is for the fulfilment of the work of the Devas that you have come (here). O fair lady, that is not fulfilled, now that he (king Rukmāṅgada) has attained absence of birth (i.e. salvation).

28-29. (Defective) O Mohinī, the Ekādaśī in the bright half of the month of Vaiśākha has been previously observed by Rukmāṅgada (as a day of fast). It destroys all obstacles, and it is highly meritorious. O lady of large eyes, he observed the rite continuously for a year with very great strain. The fact that he did not swerve from truth is an act without a parallel.

30-31. A woman is described as the queen of obstacles (except in your case). The king decided on killing his son without reservation in mind, thought or speech. He joyously. After placing his foot on my head, Rukmāṅgada has attained Viṣṇu.

44-47. He has attained Viṣṇu of immeasurable attributes, who is free from impurities, who is the support of pure ones, who is called Haṁsa, Śucipāda (of pure region), Vyoman (firmament), Praṇava (OM) the imperishable seed; who is formless, without any appearances; transcendental to the universe; perfectly pure and unsullied and of the nature of void (firmament), who is worthy of being meditated upon; who is beyond contemplation; whom they call both the Existent and the non-existent, who is neither far off nor close by; who is the great splendour and capable of being grasped only by the mind; who is identical with the universe and is called Puruṣa; who is abiding in the lotus of the heart; who is the embodiment of splendour and eternal. When the king has already dissolved himself in the lord, what benefit do I derive from life ?

48. The man who accepts his salary when the (appointed) work is not accomplished, goes definitely to the hell leaving off his master.

49. O heaven-dwellers, the servants who do not accomplish the tasks of their masters but still enjoy the salary, are reborn in the Earth as horses.

50. I am the destroyer of my husband as well as of my son. I am not successful in accomplishing the task. How can I accept the boon from you, the dwellers of Heaven ?"

The Devas promised :

51. "Speak out, O Mohinī, I [we] shall give what is desired by you in your heart of hearts. After helping you, we shall free ourselves from indebtedness to you.

52. O gentle lady, endeavour has been made by you in motivating the king to take food. O gentle lady, when such task has been accomplished, you deserve a share in the benefit."

53. O king (Māndhātā) ! When the Devas were speaking thus, the priest of the king (Rukmāṅgada) resplendent like fire, arrived there.

54. The sage who had been engaged in Prāṇāyāma, had been living under water. When the twelve-year-period of

this penance was completed, he came out of the water.

55. O king (Māndhātā), as soon as he came out of water, the actions of Mohinī were heard by him. The infuriated prominent sage approached that group of the Devas.

56. He condemned all those Devas who were about to grant boons to Mohinī. "Fie upon this (woman) ? Fie upon this group of Devas ! Fie upon this action that should be called a sin.

57. The boon that is desired by Mohinī and that you are about to give her is detrimental to your very existence (or feeling of devotion about you) and promotes that growth of Puruṣārtha * (Kāma ?).

58. She who has killed the son of her husband (and her husband as well) is no better than one who has killed ten thousand persons. She is like a man-eating ogress of the meanst conduct (?). O Devas, even by immolating herself into a well-kindled fire, she cannot gain in purity.

59. These three have been considered equal to one-another by the ancient excellent Brāhmaṇas, Viz. Killing ten thousand persons; slaughter of the husband, and the slaughter committed without any purpose. O Devas, even by falling into a well-kindled fire, she cannot purify herself. She had with her nectar-like sweet words deluded Rukmāṅgada, and Dharmāṅgada. Rukmāṅgada killed his son and attained salvation accompanied by his beloved wife. She (Mohinī) has made the Earth bereft of its rulers, the protectors of men.

60. She cannot have her residence even in the hells, O Devas. How can she, who is intellectually deficient (and perverse) stay in heaven ? O Devas, nor can she stay near the king; she may not attain the eternal region of Viṣṇu.

61. Nowhere in the worlds can she have her residence since she has been defiled (and condemned) by the public

---

*The text *puruṣārtha-prarohakaṁ* is obscure as *pra-rohaka* means 'causing to grow' (MW. p. 689). How could the boon to Mohini promote the germination of any Puruṣārtha except Kāma ?

censure. Fie upon the life of this lady of despicable activities who was always indulging in sinful actions, O Devas.

62. After killing her husband, after taking away the life of her son, after murdering her co-wife who was just like a mother unto her and after destroying the entire Earth, O Devas, what sort of existence or fate will she attain ?

63-64A. (Defective) O Devas, this lady is a greater sinner (than others). She has destroyed the holy observances of Hari. She always advocated "May food be taken on the day of Hari." Downfall is suffered even by those who take food (to relish it and not) for the sustenance of life. (?)

64B-65. How can one get residence in heaven by propagating "May food be eaten on the Ekādaśī day. May a cow be killed along with Brāhmaṇas. May undrinkable liquors be drunk". Such is spoken by the ignorant. This is not the decision of the learned.

66. If out of ignorance the statement viz :— "May the food be taken on the day of Hari" is made, there is an expiation for it with a hundred Prāṇāyāmas.

67-68A. O heaven-dwellers, they can atone for it by observing fast on the Ekādaśī day, or by taking a bath in the lake Puṣkara when the star under which one is born is associated with it (?), or by touching the Deity (Viṣṇu) in the Boar form or by the worship of God.

68B-69A. This expiation has been recounted by the Brāhmaṇas if the words are uttered (as mentioned before). This lady was ruthlessly engaged in sin. She insisted on food being taken on the day of Viṣṇu which is difficult of performance to sinners.

69B-70. She did not pay heed to the words of her husband. She got the favourite son killed—the son who knew the fitting words, who abided by the advice (of elders) and who was engaged in activities beneficial to his mothers. This woman has violated the Dharma of Viṣṇu. She is burdened with many sins.

71. O lords of the Devas, she is not worthy of even being touched. How then can you bestow boons on her ? Indeed your excellencies are interested in persons endowed with the qualities of justice and piety.

72. Heaven-dwellers do not accord protection to sinners. Devas are remembered as the supporters of Virtue. And Virtue (Dharma) is enshrined in the Vedas.

73. Service unto the husband is glorified as the duty of woman by the Vedas. Whatever the husband says must be carried out unhesitatingly by her.

74. If the husband says that anything is white she must also say that it is white. If he says that it is black, she must also say that it is black. This is to be known as real Śuśrūṣā (service) and mere menial action of attendance is not Śuśrūṣā.

75-77. O Devas, her husband's orders were disobeyed by her with a view of her desire to establish her own command. Hence there is no doubt that Mohinī is the most sinful of all women. In order to achieve truthfulness, the king, who had been restrained by imprecations, said different kinds of words (i.e. offered various pr oposals). But this lady, the murdress of her son, did not like them. Hence the king relegated the sins to her and attained salvation. Thus she is indeed a woman of sinful physical body responsible for ten thousand murders.

78-83. This woman of evil activities had repudiated the king who was the donor of various charitable gifts; who was a patron of Brāhmaṇas; whose deity was Hari; who invariably delighted his subjects; who regularly observed fasts on the days of Hari; who cherished no indecent Love towards the wives of others; who had no desire for worldly pleasures; who eschewed his passionate love for the sake of others; who always performed sacrifices; who continuously maintained the suppression of the wicked ones on the Earth, and who was never overwhelmed by the seven terrible vices. How can she be worthy of being granted the boons ? O excellent Devas within a trice I shall reduce to ashes the person who is likely to side with her, whether he is a Deva or Dānava. O gods, if anyone endeavours to protect Mohinī, he incurs that sin which is fixed in Mohinī."

84. O king (Māndhātā), after saying this and taking up water in his hand, the eminent Brāhmaṇa furiously looked at the daughter of Brahmā and violently hurled it on her head. The water then shone like fire.

85. O king, no sooner was the water cast on her, her body blazed like a bundle of straw licked up by the flames of fire, even as the residents of heaven were (helplessly) looking on.

86. "O Lord, check your anger; check your anger," even as these words of the Devas rose up in the sky, that (violent) fire created by the utterance of the Brāhmaṇa reduced that young woman to ashes.

CHAPTER THIRTYSIX

Brahmā intercedes for Mohinī

Vasiṣṭha continued:

1. Recovering herself from her unconscious senseless condition, Mohinī went to the mansions of the Devas, (the Heaven). She was then rebuked by the messenger of the Devas, "You are a sinning woman and you have no place here.

2. O foolish woman, a habitual sinner, O woman indulging in censuring your own husband, you have no place for staying in the heaven, since you have violated the day of Hari (the Ekādaśī Vrata).

3-5. It is in the hell that the residence of those averse to Dharma is recommended." Vāyu said thus to her in cruel and unexpected words. Beating her with a baton, he pushed her to (the place of) torture. O king, beaten thus by the celestial messenger and completely over-powered by the Brahmadaṇḍa (the baton i.e. curse of a Brāhmaṇa), Mohinī reached the hell. There, at the behest of Dharma (i.e. Yama), she was beaten by the messengers for a long time.

6-7A. She was taken to hells in the order and made to fall therein. They rebuked her, "O sinful woman, your son Dharmāṅgada had been killed by you through the hands of your husband. Hence experience here the evil effects of the sinful actions perpetrated by you.

7B-8A. You are the experiencer of such fruit as this, inasmuch as you have brought about the death of your son who was a benefactor of the subjects, whose intellect was stable and firm, who was comparable to Mahendra and Varuṇa and who was the overlord of seven continents.

8B-9A. If one violently injures even an uncultured son, one becomes the murderer of a Brāhmaṇa. What then, O sinful woman, if one injures a son like Dharmāṅgada endowed with all piety ?"

9B-10A. O excellent king, she was thus expostulated by the messengers of lord Yama. She experienced one by one all the tortures suggested by that lord.

10B-11. Since she had already been struck down by Brahmadaṇḍa (the curse of a Brāhmaṇa), the tortures (or the hells) themselves became scorched due to their contact with her. They became unable to detain her (within themselves). Then, O king, those hells approached Dharmarāja.

12. They were afflicted due to the contact with her limbs. They were frightened. With palms joined in reverence, they said, "O Lord of the Devas, O Lord of the universe, O Dharmarāja, be merciful.

13. Take away this lady from the place of tortures immediately for the sake of our relief. O lord, at her very touch, we are being instantaneously reduced to ashes.

14. Hence banish her from all hells." On hearing their words, Dharmarāja was mnch surprised.

15-16A. Dharmarāja then commanded his messengers, "This woman is to be banished from my mansion. Tortures (in my hell) do not wish to have any contact with that sinner who is burned by a Brāhmaṇa's imprecation, whether such a sinner is a man or a woman or even a thief (?)

16B. Hence banish from here this excessively sinning woman, who had disobeyed her husband's words, who had caused the death of her son; who has destroyed Dharma and who is already struck by Brahmadaṇḍa. Even my body burns at her sight".

17-18. O king, thus commanded by Dharmarāja, those emissaries struck her with weapons and missiles and threw her out of Yama's abode.

19. Thereafter, O king, the distressed woman of delusion, Mohinī went to the nether-worlds. She was prevented (from entering the region) by the people there.

20. Extremely ashamed due to this, Mohinī, the daughter of Brahmā, went to her father's presence and intimated her own grief to him.

21. "O father, there is no place of rest for me in all the three worlds consisting of mobile and immobile beings. Wherever I go they throw me out after rebuking me.

22. I have been banished by the people of the world who struck me hard with weapons. It was at your behest that I had gone to Rukmāṅgada at the outset.

23-24A. (For the same reason) this sinful activity was indulged in by me though that course of action was despicable to the entire world. I had caused distress to my husband; I had got my son killed with sword; I had made Sandhyāvalī perturbed. Hence, O father, I am reduced to this plight.

24B-25A. O lord, there is no redemption at all now, for me who am the sinner. Particularly due to the curse of the Brāhmaṇa I have had to experience the misery.

25B-26. O father, the celestial river (Gaṅgā) is the bestower of liberation to those who have been struck down by the imprecation of a Brāhmaṇa, to those who have been burnt by fire, to those who are killed by a Cāṇḍāla, to those who are eaten by animals etc. and to those who have been struck dead by lightning.

27. If out of love for me, you, accompanied by gods, can propitiate and persuade the Brāhmaṇa who had cursed me, then alone any better state of existence can be brought about."

28-29. O king, when she said thus, Brahmā, the grandfather of the worlds, started from there accompanied by Śiva Indra, Dharma, Sun, Fire, and other lords of Devas, and sages. With Mohinī at the head (of deputation) he went to the presence of the Brāhmaṇa.

29B-30. After going there, O king, god Brahmā, surrounded by gods, paid obeisance to the Brāhmaṇa with great dignity,

living being. The Earth consisting of seven continents is inhabited fully by the mobile and immobile beings for ever. The nether-worlds are occupied by the Daityas and others. The firmament has been occupied by the birds etc., heaven is occupied by the meritorious beings. Hells are teeming with persons of sinful actions. The oceans have been full of the fish and other animals. Hence it is not possible for this woman to stay in these, as she is not worthy of being touched.

53B-54A Then, O exceellent king, Brahmā took counsel with the Devas and spoke to Mohinī. "Gentle lady there is no space anywhere for you".

45B-58. On hearing the words of her father Mohinī, the obedient lady who wanted to destroy the observance of the day of Hari bowed down to all and said :- "O leading Devas, I hereby join my palms in reverence to you all including the priest, and to the Devas who are the witness of the worlds. O Devas, with delighted heart, thanks to the hundred obeisances, what has been requested for should be granted to me. It is conducive to the pleasure of everyone. Salvation of all the sinners is achieved through the power of Ekādaśī. My purpose is to increase it further. I have enabled my husband, co-wife and the son to go to Vaikuṇṭha.

59-60. I shall stay behind in the world of Earth, the widow that I am. I shall stay there for your sake, so that, O bestowers of honour, the day of Hari associated with me may not become defiled. For the sake of gaining my own selfish end I request for this. Not otherwise. Kindly grant it."

CHAPTER THIRTYSEVEN

Mohinī regains her physical body

Mohinī said :

1-2A. "O Devas, there cannot be anything else so sanctifying as the Ekādaśī (Vrata). Even great sinners go to the abode of Hari, on being sanctified by it. It seems to me proper to have my abode in its vicinity. Let this proposal be considered."

Devas said :

2B-3.[1] O Mohinī, the Vedha (overlapping of the previous Tithi) at mid-night or at the Sunrise is conducive to the help of the Devas as ordained by Hari. The breaking of the fast on the Trayodaśī day is destructive of the benefit of the fast.

4. The eight days, remembered in the Āgamas (Scriptures), of the devotees of Viṣṇu as 'Mahādvādaśīs' are those days wherein Ekādaśi is also present. They are observed as the days of fast by the devotees of Viṣṇu.

5. This observance of Ekādaśī is different in regard to the noble souls, the followers of Viṣṇu. In both the fortnights, it is observed alike for three days together.

6. In the evening of the previous (i.e. Daśamī) day and in the morning of the following (i.e. Dvādaśi) day meal is missed. (Of course, both the meals are eschewed in the middle day i.e. Ekādaśī day). But if Ekādaśī is overlapped (by the previous Tithi), the observance of full fast is on the next day. The holy rite, in that case, should be performed on the Dvādaśī

1. VV. 2B-18 discuss the proper *Tithi* for observance of Ekādaśī. This topic has been treated in detail in the *Pūrvārdha* of the NP. Shorn of mythological paddings, it means that an Ekādaśī when affected by *Aruṇodaya-Vedha* should not be observed i.e. if the 10th *Tithi*, *Daśamī*, extends on a civil day beyond 56 *ghaṭikās* from sunrise and Ekādaśī follows and continues for the whole of the next day, there is *Aruṇodaya-Vedha* and such affected or penetrated (*viddhā*) Ekādaśi is not to be observed. This period of two *muhūrtas* before the sunrise (i.e. *Aruṇodaya Vedha*) *is* assigned to Mohinī for occupation and the merit of people observing Aruṇodaya-Viddhā Ekādaśī goes to Mohini. (vv. 8-18 also V. 22).

The *Smārtas* (non-Vaiṣṇavas) however, are not governed by the doctrine of *Aruṇodaya-Vedha*.

day by fasting and even by eschewing water.

7. Those who are physically incapable of observing full fast can take water, vegetables, fruits, milk or the Naivedya offerings of Hari. In any case the quantity must not exceed a fourth of the usual diet.

8. O chaste lady, the Smārtas (those who follow Smṛtis) eschew the Ekādaśī that is overlapped (by Daśamī) at sunrise. Those who are devoid of any desire (from this Vrata) leave off (the Ekādaśī) that is overlapped by Daśamī even at midnight.

9. It is wellknown in all the worlds that the Daśamī Tithī belongs to Yama. O sinless lady, you must station yourself in its vicinity on the border.

10. O splendid lady, thanks to this, even the task of the Devas can be realised. Staying along the border of Daśamī, you will traverse along with the Sun and the Moon too.

11. In order to dispel your sins, you move about the various sacred places on the Earth. You can have the benefit of the rite of Ekādaśī within the period of time between Aruṇodaya (dawn) and sunrise.

12. If any one observes the holy rite of Ekādaśī on the day when it has been occupied by you, he will be the person assisting you, O beloved one of the Devas. The period of two Muhūrtas of the dawn should be known (as your period of occupancy).

13-14. The number of Muhūrtas of the day and of the night are remembered to be fifteen for each. They vary when the extent of time of the day and the night varies becoming short and long (by turns). This extent of time should be understood by the process of Trairāśika (Rule of Three).

15. You come (and occupy your place) after the thirteenth Muhūrta of the night. O lady of pure smiles, deriving the merit of those who observe fast on that day, be happy.

16-17 O Mohinī, the time marked by the early dawn has been assigned as the abode to you for the purpose of re-establishing Yama, to destroy the path to Vaikuṇṭha, to increase the number of heretics and to accumulate sins.

18. O splendid lady, enjoy the benefit of the merit of those persons who assiduously observe the holy rite of Ekādaśī on the day of your occupancy and overlapping. Be gracious unto this Brāhmaṇa (?)

19. Thus advised and guided by the lotus-seated deity (Brahmā) and others, Mohinī became much more delighted. She considered her life contented and blessed by the opportunity to resort to holy centers for wiping off her sins.

20. "Although my body had been reduced to ashes, this task of the Devas has been achieved. Although the body is reduced to a mere mass of ashes and consciousness of aerial nature (Liṅga-Śarīra) remains, the path made by the king is swept clean.

21. What has been stated by me when I was delighted has been carried out by myself." After thinking thus, the delighted lady bowed down to the Devas, who protected the earth as well as the priest.

22. For the delusion of the people, she stationed herself in the transition period of time of Daśamī (that is called Sūryavihīnā (devoid of the Sun or Aruṇodaya Vedha). She enjoys the whole day (?) in the form of Kṛcchrānta for the downfall into hell of men (?)

23-24. On seeing her staioned on the border (of his Daśamī Tithi) the son of Sun (Yama) became delighted as (was) evident from his face. He spoke these words :- "O lady of beautiful eyes, my re-establishment here, in this world, has been properly made by you. The sound of the drum placed on an elephant belonging to Rukmāṅgada has been silenced. (i.e. no longer do they announce the necessity of observing fast as before). Now all people place their faith only in the affairs they see.

25. If Daśamī touches Ekādaśi at the time of Sunrise what is called Sūryodaya Vedha it is always condemned. The sunrise that is not touched will be conducive to the fascination of men.

26-27. (Defective) That Daśamī day must be eschewed even if it extends to a fourth of the period and is also invisible (?) if enjoyment of the favourable Yoga is desired (?) O large-eyed lady, your name Mohinī, as people call you, is significant indeed. After deluding the people you get them recorded on the canvas (i.e. the record of their acts kept by Citragupta.)"

28A. After saying this, the son of Vivasvat (i.e. god Yama) bowed to the daughter of Brahmā. Delightfully, he went to the heavenly world along with the Devas holding his scribe, Citragupta by the hand.

28B-29. After the Devas had departed, Mohinī approached Brahmā, the lord of Devas and Asuras, and entreated him thus : O father, this priest is fiercely angry with me, O lord of the worlds, my body has been burnt by him. Do something whereby I shall regain my physical body.

30. By stationing myself on the border of Yama's Tithi, the universe has been deluded by me. O dear father, thanks to your power, Yama who had been formerly conquered by the king is now made victorious.

31. O dear father, now it is your duty that I should become one who am embodied. O lord of the universe, appease the Brāhmaṇa."

32. On hearing those words of Mohinī, god Brahmā the ordainer of the worlds, mollified the Brāhmaṇa once again for the sake of his daughter.

33. "O deer one, O Vasu, understand this that I speak which is beneficial to this lady. O blessed one, this is conducive to the benefit of all the worlds.

34. Out of anger, this Mohinī was reduced to ashes by you. She requests you for the restoration of her physical body once again. O bestower of honour, give commands for the same.

35. She is my daughter and your Yājyā (one on whose behalf you must perform Yajñas). O dear one, she has attained misfortune. This pitiable lady who has accomplished her task (assigned to her by me) must be protected by you.

36. O bestower of honour if with pure feelings you inform me, I shall, thereupon create her physical body again.

DISTANCE EDUCATION

Preface

The *DPH Education Handbook* has been created to provide access to information about contemporary topics in education. Practitioners and students at all levels in education have a need to know what is happening today, in addition to historical treatments within the literature.

Each chapter within the Handbook is designed to provide the user with needed "state-of-the-art" information as well as further sources of information. One of the significant features of each chapter is the inclusion of specific programmes, projects and activities so that the researcher can locate human resources as well as the literature.

The handbook will be of use to graduate and post graduate students in education and to practicing teachers, administrators, librarians and planners. The chapters and the further sources of information cited in each book should lead the reader to thousands of people and documents for either research or programme planning purposes.

An effort to achieve universal and effective education is based on a recognition of the rights of students to basic education that enables them to thrive in a complex society, as well as a realization the technological and economic growth is facilitated by increasing the numbers of students, even those with poor academic progresses, who are, in fact successful in learning. Thus, recent and current efforts improve education serve both private and social interests.

This series is addressed to administrators, planners and educators working in the field of education and training with a view to stimulating interest and attention in the areas of education and its related fields. It is also addressed to a growing number of teachers and instructors who will be practitioners in education and who will need to be acquainted with the modern aspects of educational practice and development. Many ideas, generalisations and discussions presented in this series should also prove useful to employing organisations committed to provide training facilities within their establishments—leading to effective mutual participation by institutions and organisations.

The editors wishes to thank the contributors, as well as those organizations that gave permission to publish their extracts, chapters etc.

Editors

Contents

1 Distance Education: A Historical, Sociological and Anthropological Interpretation

The description of distance education as a form of industrialized education will, among other things, be criticized as public opinion is a still influenced by anti-technical, or more generally, anti-industrial emotions which emerged in the context of the critique of our modern culture. 'The gospel of humanity cannot be separated from the critique of modern culture,' summarized Litt. In the second part of the nineteenth century cities of culture such as Ruskin, Hildebrandt, Nietzsche and Langbehn opposed industrialization, arguing mainly that it mechanizes and factionalizes man.

Hans Scheuerl has described the damage done to man by industrialization as set forth by critics of culture. According to these critics there is a fear that 'original individuality will decline in a mass culture' and will be summarized to mere functional efficiency, that 'the imitation, the mass production will make the deeper layers of soul waste away', that stressing external, values will result in the loss of interior values, that the materialistic attitude towards life will alienate man from spiritual contents and their requirements. Altogether, these critics believed that 'the originally wholesome nature' of man is not enriched by the artificiality of civilizatory achievements but 'alienated, endangered and suffocated'. These attacks of the critics of culture have become especially important as their fundamental attitude was mediated by the youth and school reform movements and had strong effects on the theory and practice of education in the first half of our country. The attitude of several generations of teachers towards technical achievements, the mechanization of instruction, and, therefore, towards distance education as well was influenced by their critique of culture.

In spite of this, the return to the critique of culture in order to find out the reasons for the reservations of present-day educationists to distance education seems to be a little inadequate at first glance. First of all, critical discussion of distance education has not yet started on a scientific level. And secondly, we have learnt that the opposition towards other forms of industrialized education, such as programmed learning and cybernetic pedagogy, has been less strong than was expected. In the meantime, one is often prepared to view industrialization as an irreversible process. Nevertheless, it must still be supposed that the attitude of former critics of culture was handed down by the movement of neohumanistic education and is still potent in the educational world of today, even if it is mainly found below the level of scientific discussion. This may be the reason for the widespread sacepticism, lack of interest and even disdain for distance education. As evidence for this are the critics who readily concede that 'materialistic attitude towards life' - that,is, that they strive to improve their conditions of life by obtaining higher qualifications. While this attitude may be a general one in our time, it seems, however, to be typical in a special sense for distant students.

When we consider new arguments - for instance, those of Jochen Kaltschmid, who has proved again in a profound analysis that 'the apparatus, the technicalization, mechanization, division of labour and organization' are all elements of the process of rationalization which shape the existence of man, and that the consequences of this rationalization are that our world is 'dominated by purposes', that we lose our 'inwardness', the 'immediacy of life' and the unity of our psychological faculties - then, of course, we have to see that these consequences, indeed, are very likely to be reinforced by industrialized education. In fact, its rationalized systems of teaching and learning are, as we have seen, structured in such a way that the purposes - the defined teaching goals - are achieved in the best way, the 'inwardness' of the students and the teachers, which is normally preserved by their personal interaction, is more or less lost by the objectivation of teaching behaviour, the splitting up of teaching and learning functions, and by the use of technical media. Also, the 'closeness to life' of instruction is, naturally, reduced a great deal.Teachers and students are no longer involved as whole human beings. And the unity of our psychic faculties is broken up.

There are also many current argument about the incompatibility of technical developments and education which are often emotive and relate to the concept of instrialized education, as this form of education is - as we have shown - a result of the general process technicalizing of society. Ludwig Heieck has discussed some of these arguments. According to him, education gives way to the functionalist thinking in terms of expediency in our technical age and abandons man. He says: 'Education derives from history. It is determined by the view that man is a historic being. Technical progress, however, is a historic. Instruction and education, therefore, have not participated in technical progress as they have felt threatened by it'. And he concludes : 'If man abandons himself to the world of materialistic objects, if he delivers his humanity to the functionality of set purposes-then he dehumanizes himself'.

If this treatise shows that distance education has developed so to speak unnoticeably—as industrialized education during the last 120 years, and if, over and above, it is maintained that this model of education will be of great importance for tackling important educational tasks at present and in the future, then it is necessary to comment on the reservations voiced by those critics of culture as they would otherwise underline that such a concept will be questionable, if not dangerous. The problem cannot be solved in the theoretical framework used so far in other chapters of this book. We have to face the same situation which was characterized by Paul Heimann, when he defended his contention that 'film, radio, and television are the powerful educational institutions of the present'. The objections raised to their educational use in the past also apply top distance education, especially when it employs such mass media. According to Heimann, these critics were afraid of 'the furtherance of a receptive learning behaviour, an educational and instructional impressionism, the emergence of a dangerous conformism, the immobilization of creative imagination, the artificial increase of optical and acoustical stimuli, the reduction of primary experiences in favour of secondary experiences, the depersonalization, the mechanization of the relation between teacher and taught, and the leveling out of individual instruction'. Heimann emphasized that these objections must by no means be trivialized, as some of them contain important arguments of educational philosophy. On the other hand, his reflections led to the conclusion that these objections can scarcely be refuted on the level of pure educational thinking. Therefore, he offered arguments dealing with problems of intellectual history and sociology.

In this chapter a similar avenue is followed in order to invalidate possible objections of cultural critics to distance education or other forms of industrialized education. The discussion will have four different starting points. First, the interpretation of a model of the historical development of instruction is to clarify whether distance education really distinguishes itself structurally to such a great extent from traditional education that the teacher and the students are placed in an entirely new existential situation which is not in line with the general historic trend and which must be considered as a development which fundamentally fails to reach the goal of humanity. Secondly, a number of socio-cultural preconditions of distance education and developments in the history of ideas are dealt with, in order to find out whether the objections of the critics of culture remain feasible. Thirdly, it will be proved by comparing traditional instruction in the classroom with distance education that it integrates into the process of general change of social subsystems and into the present inevitable development of society, whereby many of the norms defended by the critics of culture appear to be unreal. Fourthly, distance education is interpreted in anthropological terms. It is to be expected that dealing with it in such a way will result in further general arguments for judging the objections of the critics of culture.

Historical interpretation

If we consider the context of the origin of distance education not in a concrete socio-economic, but in a more general, far-teaching sense, then a new dimension emerges for the understanding of distance education. In order to achieve this it is, however, necessary to describe some structural elements of historical forms of instruction. If we interpret sources of ancient Indian and Egyptian education their earliest forms can be characterized by the following six aspects :

1 Usually, only a few people belonging to the ruling religious and political class participated (*elitist aspect*).

2 The imparting of knowledge and skills was mostly connected to the performance of priestly functions (*sacral aspect*).

3 The instruction was connected to special forms of the domination of the teacher who exercised his power over the student (*hierarchical aspect*).

4 The instruction took place in small groups (*familial aspect*).

5 No technical medial were used (*personal aspect*).\

6 The nature of the instruction was determined by an individual teacher, a fixed place, and a fixed time (*aspect of traditional ties*).

If one relates this initial situation of instruction to our distance education today, a historical model of instruction can be constructed which shows that instruction has fundamentally changed in a development of several thousand years. The dimensions of this change can be determined by the following extreme parameters; the elitist instruction becomes egalitarian, its sacral contents and procedures become profane, the government of the teacher is substituted by the self-government of the student, the intimate group becomes a larger and less intimate group or even an anonymous mass of students, the personal interaction between teacher and students becomes mechanized and automated, and the traditional ties of instruction to a special teacher, a special place and a special time are removed.

It is evident that developments have taken place in the dimensions referred to whereby it is not necessary to consider their division into periods or their delays in certain cultural areas. The entire extent of these changes could be demonstrated on a bipolar scale. Distance education would arrive at the extremes in all cases. However, if one also assesses the present instruction in classrooms it becomes apparent that his form of education has not developed accordingly. A closer examination will show that there is a correlation between the different stages of development and the extent to which principles of industrialization have been applied in each case.

Analogously to the historical process of the democratization of political power, which passed through several stages, there was also a process of continued democratizing of political power, which passed through several stages, there was also a process of continued democratizing of teaching and learning and of knowledge. One can ever - parallel to the political development - distinguish priestly-aristocratic, bourgeois and democratic forms of teaching and learning and of knowledge. Whereas in the beginning of the cultural development only small groups handed down their knowledge, which was often kept secret, to the chosen ones, now a phase is reached in which in many countries of the world knowledge is in principle accessible by everyone, whereby traditional ethnic, religious, social and regional boundaries, which still make education privilege to many, can be surmounted - due to the availability of industrialized education. The latest and most convincing steps in this direction have been taken by the Open University in the United Kingdom. But also the extension of the TV-College in Chicago and the plans for a University of the Air in Japan must be mentioned here. Before this, distance education techniques had been used in many universities and technical colleges of the socialist countries in eastern Europe in order to enable workers to raise their qualification by acquiring a higher education while working for a living.

Consequently, in many countries educational politicians consider distance education as a means for equalizing educational opportunities. Such a way of thinking, it is true, overlooks the enormous socio-cultural barriers on the way to education and surely underestimates the real difficulties. Nevertheless, it must be admitted that distance education provides at least necessary technical and organizational preconditions for a universal admission to continued and higher education. An analysis of statistics about distance education reveals that millions of distant students do indeed profit from this industrialized way of education. Often enough it offers them the only way towards the desired education as all other ways are barred by lack of funds or by other circumstances.

Comparison with the conditions under which face-to-face-instruction takes place in the schools of the Federal Republic of Germany as well as in those of other countries can be used to show that we are dealing with school systems organized according to class structures in which access to secondary schools and universities remains restricted, so that people continue to suffer from the inequality of educational opportunities. Ralf Dahrendorf, in his analysis of the society of the Federal Republic of Germany, has called this continued inequality a scandal.

The sacral character of instruction can be related to the fact that at the beginning of our cultural development the knowledge and skills which were handed down from one generation to the other were priestly wisdom and ritual ceremonies. Only later were the various scientific disciplines schools and colleges - still wears a gown which recalls a clergyman's vestments;

- the school continues to stick to certain rituals as, for instance, prayers at the beginning of the school day or hymns and other ceremonies during inauguration and graduation;
- school celebrations assume a special significance in the educational process.

These and other aspects of face-to-face instruction have been handed down by tradition. In distance education, however, this tradition is discontinued because of the technological revolution in the methodology of teaching. The original communicative stance of teachers and students is substituted by a technologically medicated interaction between the two of them. The process of secularization could, therefore, go further than in face-to-face teaching.

Under the aspect of hierarchy it can be stated that the structure of all early forms of instruction was characterized by the fact that the teacher assumed the role of the old man, the father, which was connected with wisdom, authority and power. His power derived often from the knowledge of the power bringing formulas and from his knowledge of the tradition. But above all, it was derived from the power of God. *Hieros* means 'holy'. Accordingly, a hierarchy was originally a 'holy rule'.

The students, who also waited on their teachers, were expected to respect and venerate them. Brunner reports on ancient Egyptian education how the power of the teachers resulted in the punishment of the students. The students were subjected to corporal punishments, were put in the stocks, threatened, admonished, but never praised.

In the Middle Ages the status symbol of the teacher was, typically enough, a rod, which he was to hold upright, as may be seen in contemporary pictures. Sometimes, the teacher was supported in his punishing activities by the *locates*, a school janitor who also carried a rod as a token of his dignity, but - for hierarchical reasons - with the tip facing downwards. Generally, people were of the opinion that, for instance, in the education of artisans as well as of knights, learning and serving went together. The master-servant relationship which was constituted during the training ceased only when the apprentice was formally released from this relationship after having qualified as a journeyman.

The development which started off with the student who was ruled and maltreated in the ways described comes to an end with a student who is able to identify his learning needs and who decides himself which learning goals he wishes to reach and in which way or with the university student who applies the concept of learning by researching. Both approaches orientate themselves to the model of the self-determined and self-governing student. Both of them advocate domination-free learning.

There are several reasons why distance education has developed structural approaches for forms of learning which are free from teacher dominance and the influence of the teacher's authority and why, hence, distance education would have its place at the end of this dimension:

- The increased availability and accessibility of distance education enables the learner for the first time to check through the learning material of a number of respective courses and make decisions himself when selecting one of them. The necessary qualification for doing so may still be lacking with most learners as, so far, usually other persons have decided what is to be studies and when and where the studying will take place. It can, however, be acquired with the help of systems of distance education and their counselling services.
- Normally, the teacher is not physically present when the student learns. He effects his learning only indirectly. In the same way as in the political sector the personal power of the king was objectified as soon as his personal exercising of power with the help of written documents which then led to bureaucracy, the personal interaction between teacher and student became objectified by the written word and the use of other media. Thus a scope of independence and freedom came into being, which, indeed, is used and appreciated by the students.
- The student takes over the control of the time, the frequency and the duration of his learning.
- Very often adults begin to study a course in distance education by their own free decision. In such cases, the relation between the teacher and the student is entirely different from the corresponding relationship in the traditional and institutionalized schools, where the teacher is usually the representative of the power which

makes students attend the school and even controls their learning behaviour and school life.

However, the simple fact that a student learns relatively independently does not allow the conclusion that distance education already gives rise to absolutely dominance-free learning. In particular, if distance education is organized as a part of compulsory general education - as, for instance, in Australia, Canada and the United States, with the military services or in vocational training - repressive effects of those who have the power are not removed, but only distributed in another way and sublimated. Their power cannot be done away with simply by replacing face-to-face instruction by distance education.

In spite of this, it must be stressed that the objectivation of learning processes offers more scope for independent learning than instruction tied to special teachers in special situations. Above all, it enables the critical cooperation of students when instruction is evaluated even if this happens only in a representative form. When, for instance, selected students are members of the course team their influence upon the intended teaching-learning process can be increased. Here, dominance-free learning might, indeed, have more scope for its development in distance education than in face-to-face instruction. At the extreme point of this dimension one can place learners who identify their learning goal themselves, select and handle the respective system of industrialized teaching expertly, and also control the outcomes of their learning themselves.

Obviously, face-to-face instruction is still far

from this extreme point, as the learning process is often not only influenced by the teachers' dominance and predilections, as A> and R. Tausch have shown so impressively in their research on the language behaviour of teachers and students, but also by traditional and institutional constraints. Criteria of repressive teaching behaviour are : corporal punishment of pupils which is still preserved in many primary schools, various forms of disciplinary action at secondary schools, and sending down from universities. In these cases the teaching-learning process is still connected to the process of disciplining the students. The double meaning of 'discipline' is, indeed, telling and applicable even today.

The social pattern of instruction was originally modelled after the social interaction in the family. Keay and Brunner agree in that in ancient times instruction began in the family on the basis of the farther-son relationship. In ancient Egypt a teacher and a student were even called father and son. If the student belonged to another family, he was, nevertheless, integrated into the teacher's family. Obviously, teaching started in the intimacy of a father-son relationship and in the form of private tuition.

Thinking in ideal types, one can assume that there was a an initial period in which private tuition dominated; for instance, when a priest introduced his successor into the procedures of secret sacral ceremonies, or when children of aristocratic families were carefully prepared for their future role in society. Our knowledge from history shows us that the subsequent periods must have been the Television Course 'Introduction into Computer Science' in Japan where 700,000 students ordered the accompanying textbooks. The traditional instruction in the classroom, however, originated at a very early period. It is, strictly speaking, still closely attached to individual instruction, as classroom instruction is basically often still merely an extended and schematized individual instruction - if one disregards the many efforts to change it into group instruction. Educational theorists, who stressed the individuality of the single pupil, Locke, Rousseau, Herbart, Weniger, Bollnow and Buber may have supported this practice. The traditional teaching and learning behaviours are obviously so stable that they resist the use of technical media and the application of principles of industrialization. The communicative structure of traditional instruction in the classroom depends on limited number of students. Probably 120 students would be the largest possible number in a lecture hall. A radical new approach was needed to overcome this limitation and to make possible the instruction of large and extremely large groups of students which appeared when the general level of education had to be raised as a consequence of industrialization. Distance education is such an approach.

The archaic forms of imparting knowledge and skills could be characterized with regard to their media structure by the negative statement that they functioned without any technical medium. This means that the teachers relied on the medium of the words spoken directly to the student. Whether the teacher was a medicine man, a prophet, a shaman or a priest, he or she always communicated knowledge orally.

The oral teaching of those priest-teachers must, however, not be understood in a modern (that means more or less abstract) sense, as the words were not yet isolated from their original context. For a long time it remained part of the redeeming actions of the priest. The student experienced his speaking as his action. This means that the student not only took in the words, but was also included in the actions. This alone shows why the students had to be taken into the teacher's house. And it becomes clear why the spoken language could not just be substituted by written language at that time as this would certainly have reduced the global context of those actions.

Therefore, the spoken language of the early forms of instruction was, so to speak, only a medal *pars pro toto*. It was connected to the personality of the teacher - who was considered to be a medium himself.

Oral instruction consisted of the teacher's saying a text and the student's repeating. A comprehensive and reliable memory was required for both of them. The oral form of instruction prevailed after writing and reading had been introduced. In ancient India they were used first for commercial and trading purposes, and it took a long time before they were accepted by the teachers. Keay assumes that the tests were considered to be too holy to be handed down in writing. Teachers might have also been afraid that such written texts could be used by unauthorized persons. He reports that in India the old forms of instruction have been preserved longest and have remained unchanged. The Veda are still handed down orally today, although they are, of course, also available in print. And it is not unusual that students succeed in learning whole textbooks by heart. Even in ancient Egypt with its comparatively more advanced written culture, memorizing was the students' main activity. The teachings were all learnt by heart although they were also available in writing.

The historical development in this dimension led to an increased used of technical media and a decreased physical presence of the teacher in the teaching-learning process. Clay tablets, wax tablets, papyrus, parchments, paper and later screen, loudspeaker and computer were placed between teacher and student in order to profit from their mediating functions. Distance education, especially in its form of integrated multimedia systems, will again have to be placed at the present end of this line of development. With regard to the decreased importance of the physical presence of the teacher it is surpassed only by programmed instruction.

Traditional face-to-face instruction, however, must be classed with an earlier stage of this development, especially when the teacher and his spoken words dominate. In spite of the use of technical media such as paper, books, blackboards, pictures or even film, the basic communicative structure has not detached itself from the original oral form of instruction.

Linking instruction to a special place is also of sacral origin. If a place had proved to be holy, because the effects of the divine power were repeated there, it became a 'special place'. This could be a grove, a grotto, but also a house or a temple. Obviously, temples were the first places where the priests accumulated wisdom, and, hence, the first places of instruction.

Just as there was - in archaic thinking - no idea of a homogeneous space, there was also no idea of a uniform time. Rather, each time had its own significance. This suggests that the early forms of instruction did not take place at fixed times in the sense of an abstract regularity. This became possible only after a first and very important phase of rationalizing in which it was considered to be possible to isolate time from its close connection to traditional places and actions which up to then were experienced as a global unit. Such an abstracting of traditional places and times became necessary when, as in ancient Egypt, one teacher had to teach several students or even larger groups of students at a time. In such a situation he was compelled to invent group instruction. It was characterized by a certain regularity and by the unity of place, time and persons. In fact, this structural unity was to become a traditional constant of all face-to-face instruction to this day.

In a second phase of rationalizing the teaching-learning process, this unity of place, time and persons disintegrated as a consequence of the application of principles of industrialization. This means that a long tradition, was discontinued. The significance of this break in the tradition of instruction may be indicated by a parallel in the arts: when dramatic presentations on the stage were substituted by dramatic presentations in film, space lost its static condition, and time its continuity. In distance education as well, the unit of place and time, constitutive of face-to-face instruction, as has been shown, ceases to exist. As the teaching is objectified in the form of course material or educational film several teachers who live far apart from each other and from the students can impart their knowledge one after the other, or even simultaneously, and in a sequence quite different from face-to-face teaching. Time as well is taken out of the context of traditional instruction. The course team can manipulate the stimuli and thus organize the presentation according to new ideas of the dramaturgy of teaching, and the students are free to develop their own learning strategy by fixing their individual times of study. Seen in this way, the break of tradition mentioned appears to be a singular event in the history of instruction.

If one assesses the described stages of development of face-to-face instruction and distance education in this sixth dimension, one cannot but see that face-to-face instruction has - on the whole - not come further than the special conditions of group instruction in ancient Egypt; that is, instruction with fixed times and places and persons. Distance education, however, developed considerably further by becoming largely independent from these ties. This opens up new perspectives which have not yet been noticed and new problems which have not yet been tackled by experts of the methodology of teaching and learning. The six lines of development show clearly that distance education is a form of instruction which reached the final stages in each dimension only because it applied principles of industrialization.

This can be specified as follows.

Distance education can be *egalitarian,* as the

application of technical media overcomes some of the traditional barriers to educational opportunity. These media enable schools and universities to extend their instructional systems in such a way that every capable citizen can profit from learning if they wish - even after their school or college years. In the present historical -economic situation of highly industrialized societies the increased availability and accessibility of education thus assumes a special importance, as the further democratizing of society will increase the educational needs of all citizens considerably. More and more of them will lay claim to their human right of education. It is safe to say that such an increased demand of education can only be satisfied with the help of industrialized forms of education.

Distance education provides for instruction in which teaching and learning have been *secularized* to a high degree, as the relation between teacher and students has been isolated from its traditional social context and objectified. Teacher and students do not interact as persons in their totality, but as special teaching and learning functions which operate only in order to reach the defined goals. The numinous, however, needs the social context in order to be able to express itself.

Distance education enables and facilitates *instruction without repressive actions* in the sense that arbitrary acts of teachers - as well as of students - are cut out as technical mediation and the required division of labour have objectified instruction. If there are institutional or direct dependencies, as, for instance, in the military services and in vocational training, they will be less effective for the same reasons.

Distance education is a form of instruction which is capable of catering for great numbers of students and even *mass audiences*. Such a form of instruction would be impossible without the techniques of industrial mass production and without the help of mass media and the computer.

Distance education is principally mediated instruction. It cannot take place without the help of *technical media*. Without the mechanization of the presentation of the contents of instruction and of the feedback activities it would not be possible to start, optimize and control it.

Distance education has *cut the three bonds which ties face-to-face instruction to special places, special times and special persons*. The industrial approach of objectifying teaching and learning behaviour and of storing, transporting and reproducing it was the required precondition for this. It has made distance education the most accessible and flexible form of teaching and learning.

On the whole, and with regard to the objections of the cultural critics referred to at the beginning, the interpretation of the historic model of instruction results in the conclusion that the tradition of instruction has not been disturbed or even neutralized by the advent of industrialized education. On the contrary, it subsequently developed along the lines of development in the history of instruction. Distance education is, therefore, not something entirely new, different and strange in the world of education. It cannot be placed beside face-to-face teaching, but rather belongs to the hitherto final stage of the developments of instruction, as it has overtaken face-to-face teaching on the six lines of development, in part even considerably and distinctly. This means that distance education is, structurally speaking, ahead of face-to-face teaching. Clearly, this is the result of its industrialization.

Socio-cultural and intellectual preconditions

In this section the hypothesis to be established and substantiated is that distance education can be assigned to the era of industrialization not only because of the availability of the necessary material and technical conditions, but also because of particular socio-cultural and intellectual developments which are imperative before distance education can emerge. If in our society many adults and adolescents decide to study at a distance and not in the traditional way, if they manage to go their own way and do not depend on the traditional educational institutions, they must have qualities which distinguish them from people who lived in earlier eras., It is elucidating to analyse these qualities.

A first precondition is a particular relationship between humans and their environment. Human consciousness of the environment has changed in along process which stated with archaic-mythological ways of thinking which were gradually replaced by empirical-realistic ideas and concepts. This process was accentuated by the Renaissance and the Enlightenment as they helped to emancipate human thinking from earlier limitations. At this point it is sufficient to indicate which of these developments were important in the context of the hypothesis presented at the beginning. In the Renaissance, many people became aware for the first time that popular motto *per aspera ad astra* was internalized by the inner-directed person. This led to a striving after vocational success never known before, and partly even to a 'passionate drive to earn and gain'. At the same time the individual in the inner-directed society 'was dissociated and sheltered from others' and became, thus, isolated and more vulnerable.

The relevance of such developments for the emergence of distance education can easily be seen. It is evident that distance education would have been unthinkable in a tradition-directed society. Only the inner-directed society provided the necessary subjective preconditions for it. Every characteristic trait used by Riesman to describe the inner-directed person can also contribute to the explanation of the situation of distant students. Their decision to enrol in a distant study course is already behaviour according to their own dir=creation. Their strongest motivation is derived from vocational career prospects. When they study a t a distance they dispose of their leisure time, make sacrifices, have many difficulties and are typically 'dissociated and sheltered from others'. Hence, it can be assumed that the phenomenon of the adult distant student is in accordance with an inner law of development of our culture in the era of industrialization. It influenced the student's socio-cultural and intellectual development in such a way that the motivation of millions of distant students became strong enough and their inner-directedness so stable that it caused them to stay outside of the institutions of traditional education and to commit themselves to an unorthodox way of teaching and learning.

Furthermore, it can be postulate that the individual's consciousness is also influenced by life in an industrialized society itself. These influences prepare the individual for being able to study at a distance in special ways, as can be illustrated by reference to the following four experiences :

1 the practice of dealing with people, who - in a given situation are charged with the performance of single functions only;

2 the adjustment to the permanent reception of coded information;

3 the development of attitudes towards substitute persons;

4 the orientation towards new basic personality types.

In agrarian society people lives in villages and had relatively few interpersonal relations, which, however, were long-lasting, emotional and integral. No matter what the reason for their interpersonal relation was, the persons involved were expected to be dealt with as total personalities. If, for instance, someone did business with someone else, it certainly mattered whether the persons involved had a liking for each other, whether they were of the same religious faith, how they had led their lives so far, whether they enjoyed a good reputation, and so on. In such a village, a teacher, for instance, played a role which exceeded that of just teaching pupils, and which affected the adults also. His impact was a unique one. Hence, he considered no exchangeable.

Man in the industrialized society is, on the other hand, typically a town-dweller and has a such usually many interpersonal relations, which, however, are relatively short, not emotional, and used for specific purposes. Even with an unusual transaction such as the purchase of an automobile the interaction between the customer and the salesman will, as a rule, no longer be influenced by their personal likings, their religious beliefs, their political leanings, their family situations or their social status. Customer and salesman interact merely as .persons who serve in a specialized function, and the two expect from each other that this function be performed well. This means that only a small fraction of one person interacts with a small fraction of another person. Each person is fragmented and consists of many functional parts. This reduction of person can be demonstrated by referring to be example of a teacher in a city school; that is, to a teacher specializing in one or two subjects. It is true he teaches pupils, but, as a rule, he cuts out his personal background in this process. He separates official and private functions sharply. As he is reduced to someone who serves certain functions only, it is easier to imagine that he could be replaced. In comparing him to the teacher in a village school it can be seen how far this process has gone. At the same time it must be seen that the teacher in a city school is still a partner in a continued process of communicative acting which induces him to perform more functions that a teacher in a system of distance education. Considering the stages of development from the teacher in a village school to a teacher in distance education, the teacher in the city school can be classed somewhere in the middle between the extremes.

As individuals in industrial society are able to make contact with many persons in order to perform special functions, they enjoy a freedom never known before. They have disentangled themselves from old bonds which involved their emotions as well, and even the totality of their persons. Now, they are principally also ready to approach complete strangers and to communicate with them - if it is necessary for objective reasons - without doubt, a new human skill. This freedom must have been a favorable precondition for readiness to teach and to learn at a distance, if a specific educational need could not be satisfied otherwise. If the individual, in doing so, did not meet 'real' teachers and 'real students, but only persons charged with the performance of often highly specialized functions, this experience was not new to them, as it was in harmony with so many patterns of interaction which are taken for granted in industrialized societies.

Individuals in industrial society distinguish themselves from persons in pre-industrial society by their ability to receive and to work with information which is technically mediated. First of all, they are reading men. The mass media with their modern methods of production and distribution enable them to take part in the doings around them and in the world in a very specific way. As oral forms of information were more or less substituted by printed ones they got used to their presentation by technical means. At the same time, in industrial society people see and listen to many things which remained closed to them in agrarian society. A permanent supply of information from radio and television has certainly an effect on them, whereby distance education the students meet, so to speak, 'vicarious teachers' whom they know only from printed texts or aural and visual presentations. This shows again that people in an industrial society are prepared for distance education to a higher degree than those in a pre-industrial society, in which corresponding relations were established by myths, legends and rumours, and remained, therefore, vagues and uncertain.

A corresponding sociological analysis shows that industrial society has also developed new models of human development. With regard to this Richard W.Behrendt speaks of a 'change of basic types of man' which was caused by the industrialization of society. Referring to pre-industrial time, he speaks, for instance, of the ruler, the subject, the patriarch, the heroic warrior, the missionary, the wise man and the scholar. In industrial society, however, these lose their importance and are substituted by types; as, for instance, the conscious man, the emancipated man, *Homo faber,* the technically competent man and the mobile man. Further types are 'the radically organizing and manipulating man' on the one hand and 'the radically organized and manipulated man' on the other.

This change of basic types of human is a profound one, and so serious in its consequences that one can consider it a major transformation in the development of mankind. This transformation has been already dealt with in regard to its relevance in intellectual history. At this point it can be postulated that only human beings who can be classed with the basic types in industrial society are ready for teaching and learning at a distance. That is to say, if one scrutinizes these basic types, one cannot but agree that all of them have a special affinity to industrial education.

Conscious man, who tries successfully 'to become aware not only of the physical and societal world around him, but also of his inner psychic structure, which is often still unconscious', is more easily ready to assess himself and his abilities and, hence, make decisions with regard to realistic educational or training goals. In addition, he is presumably also more likely to assume responsibility for his learning. Emancipated man, 'who has disentangled himself from transcendental and traditional ties' and 'claims an original and autonomous orientation in new situations of life', is certainly more easily motivated to acquire new qualifications which he needs to adjust to such new situations. Only *Homo faber*, the type of man, 'who considers the world in all its non-transcendental aspects and also man himself as producible or at least malleable', has self confidence enough to be able to change an unsatisfactory situation of life purposefully by learning. Technically competent man is 'the archetype of an era with a relatively developed technology'. He no longer carries loads and no longer eats his bread in the sweat of his brow. Instead, he operates machines, whereby his work is mostly reduced to the control of mechanical energy. This deliverance from heavy manual work and involvement with machines and technical appliances, which save time and energy, is a good precondition for learning, and especially for dealing with technical teaching-learning systems. Mobile man, who no longer accepts being rooted for his lifetime, geographically speaking, in his native country, in the spiritual sense in this religious belief, and with respect to society in specific social strata, but claims a maximum of mobility according to his abilities and opportunities is emancipated enough to be able to learn without the local, temporal, and personal ties which are usually necessary in face-to-face instruction. Finally, the negative types of Radically organizing and manipulating man and Radically organized and manipulated man can be applied to distance education organizers and to distant students too. Here it becomes evident that industrialized education brings forth dangers of its own. The structural roots of it will be dealt with later, in the discussion of the language as a medium.

On the whole, the special aspects referred to so far facilitate the formulation of the hypothesis at the beginning of this chapter in more concrete terms: the establishment of distance education and the teaching and learning in this type of industrialized education require that a certain intellectual development and the orientation to new types of man have already taken place. The ability to detach oneself from the direct guidance of a personal teacher and from the social inspiration and pressure of the learning group, and to determine oneself the time and place of study, the amount of study, and possibly even the ways in which it is controlled, is obviously based on intellectual and socio-cultural experiences which build up enough self-confidence and self-assurance in the individual learner in such a way that he or she can, indeed, 'use reason without the guidance of anyone else'.

If such a stage is reached, a barrier has been

overcome. This event can be compared with overcoming the barrier of illiteracy, as it has a similar importance in setting free intellectual potentialities and for the further development of the educational system. It may even be thought that an 'absolute threshold of culture' has been crossed.

The discussion on the intellectual and socio-cultural preconditions of distance education shows that possible reservations of the critics of culture with regard to this form of industrialized education can be modified in so far as individuals of the European-American industrial visualization are much better prepared for this form of education that people in preceding eras ever could have been. In other words: persons who teach and learn in the industrialized way are basically different human beings. In many ways - it has been possible to name only a few aspects - they are prepared and ready to benefit from abstract, objectified procedures of imparting knowledge. Furthermore, the constructed, abstract relation between teacher and student fits into z net of manifold abstract social relationships, which together form a kind of 'secondary system'. Man in industrialized societies is used to assimilating 'secondary experiences' instead of making the respective experiences himself. He does not live any longer in 'primary, organic, natural relationships, but in a produced, planned, organized, and very often manipulated world'. Those who accept the changes of man's consciousness caused by industrialization because they think that these intellectual and socio-cultural adaptations are indispensable for coping with the economical, political and cultural tasks of the future will see that the objections of the critics of culture lose some of their significance. Possibly, they will even become critics of culture the other way round, as they might think that the persistent adherence of traditional schools to preindustrial methods of teaching and learning can be considered as a serious dysfunction of the educational system - an age which is already developing structural elements of a post-industrial society.

Sociological characterization

As industrialization is at the centre of sociological research and as dealing with it has grown from the need for orientation and understanding in view of the rapid changes in our time, which were caused and accelerated exactly by this industrialization, it will be advantageous to analyse and characterize the concept of industrialized education in its sociological aspects as well.

According to Behrendt, sociology strives towards knowledge of 'generally accepted regularities of the interactive and collective behaviour of man'. As there are teachers and students in distance education as well as in face-to-face teaching who interact in special ways, the question arises where such generally accepted regularities can also be found in this particular form of instruction. In trying to answer this question, emphasis will be laid on the transition from traditional to industrialized instruction. It should be possible to characterize the social changes which have taken place in this process by means of categories of sociology more succinctly and in a more differentiated way than with categories of educational theory.

The hope for a corresponding fain in knowledge

can be founded on the fact that sociology—in contrast to theory of education—has fully understood and clearly described the 'overwhelming phenomenon of technology and industrialization and their effects on social change'. Many sociologists even think that industrialization has caused such far-reaching processes of cultural change that they interpret it as the beginning of a new cultural era in the history of mankind, quite comparable in importance with former cultural eras—for instance, those of the hunting and gathering society and the agrarian society. And—still more important—the blending of technology and the production process is considered an absolute pre-condition for the continuation of the existence of mankind. In view of such a fundamental philosophy one is not surprised to learn that the industrial production of goods is considered one of the dominant shaping powers of modern society. Helmut Schelsky emphasizes that 'there is practically no sector of life of modern man in which the industrial production has not caused decisive changes of behaviour'. The analysis of distance education has shown that the educational sector has not altogether been left out of this development.

Comparing the sociological interpretation of the industrial era with the superficial and dilatory way in which, for instance, technical media are dealt with by didactical experts - to say nothing of the rationalization of instruction by planning and organizing it professionally - the different approach of the two disciplines becomes evident. Advocates of the use of technical media for instruction have only been marginal in the theory and practice of education. Educational technology has not become a central issue in the methodology of teaching and learning, and did not even get belong the beginnings. The general attitude in this matter is that technical media are merely added to traditional instruction. The insight is lacking that in view of the changes of the consciousness of modern man, the enormous impact of the teaching capacity of industrialized mass media, which so far have only been used to a small extent, and the enormous increase of teaching and training tasks—taken altogether—will make new structural forms of teaching and learning imperative. Only such an approach would correspond with the tendencies of industrialization in our present society. Only in such a way could 'cultural lag' in this sector be reduced.

The methodology of teaching and learning has, so far, not been in position to describe the social change caused by a form of instruction in which the teaching is transported to the student, and to clarify the social conditions in it which are structurally quite different. Typically, enough, when trying to explain the teacher-student relation in programmed instruction some authors refer to old, traditional patterns of instruction such as the individual instruction is substituted by industrialized instruction. This change can be identified on several levels.

Max Weber, Ferdinand Tonnies and other representatives of the older sociology have described at an early stage the changes which took place under the dominance of purposeful, rational action and as a consequence of the scientific-technical permeation of traditional social subsystems. Jurgen Habermas summarized the results of their thinking by remarking that they characterized this change with the help of pairs of concepts, for instance, *germeinschaft* and *gesellschaft*, organic and mechanical solidarity, primary and secondary relations, and traditional and bureaucratic dominion.

Accordingly, one could understand face-to-face instruction in a classroom as a traditional social subsystem; distance education, however, as a 'modern' one. Thus, distance education would be characterized as a system based on rational planning and development just like the organization of industrialized work processes. On the other hand, face-to-face instruction in the classroom would then be a system handed down by tradition which is not, or is only slightly, affected by the consequences of industrialization.

This would mean traditional instruction in a class room could be classed with the category of *gemeinschaft*, as there is a special type of closeness or familiarity between the teacher and the students as well as among the students. The persons involved are also more or less conscious of this familiarity. They approve of it and try to deepen it in order to profit from the solidarity of *Klassengemeinschaft*. It can be assumed that in such groups of students 'archaic personal relations' are fostered. According to Tonnies, the learning group in the classroom would be founded on 'a *gemeinschaft* of place and spirit'. Subjectively experienced forms of action and their traditions and rites play an important role. In each group a balance of power is developed, a process which might become so dominant that the original objectives for bringing together teacher and students temporarily lose some of their significance.

If the concept of *gemeinschaft* is applied to teaching and learning in a class room, the following categories could be subsumed: organic solidarity which can develop in direct social interaction, informal grouping, the dominance of primary social relations, and traditional forms of control, which, for instance, are mirrored in the hierarchy of principal-teacher-student.

If, one the other hand, the concept of *gesellschaft* is applied to distance teaching, the following categories help to explain its structure: mechanical solidarity—that is, the artificial solidarity which is brought about by means of technical media: formal groups—that is, the importance of the formal organization of the learning groups in individual distance study courses; secondary relations with little intensity and without familiarity of the participants, and bureaucratic control which helps to maintain the contacts between school, teachers and students.

However, be mentioned that the characterization of distance education with the help of the category 'secondary relations' does not apply to all cases. Fairs has shown that an emotional relationship can be maintained in spite of physical separation, whereby he explicitly mentions the medium of correspondence. Therefore, elements of primary group relationships can also be found in distance education - whereas, the other way round, emotional closeness can be missing even under favorable face-to-face conditions.

Jurgen Habermas has observed that Talcott Parsons' catalogue of possible alternatives of value-orientation can also be used to characterize the these are characteristics which are of great importance for the actual achievement of the intended learning process. This tendency for clear determination corresponds with the efforts to lay down detailed definition of learning objectives and to acquire as much relevant empirical data as possible for the learning process in each case.

In an approach of his own Jurgen Habermas went beyond Max Weber, Ferdinand Tonnies and Talcott Parsons, and developed a categorization with the help of which it is possible to describe in greater detail the relevant structural changes of institutional subsystems which were caused by industrialization. He started out with Hegel's fundamental distinction between 'work' and 'interaction' in his *Phenomenology of Spirit*. Work is defined by him as 'rational acting', interaction as 'communicative acting'. By developing seven pair of categories in characterizing more closely those sectors which Tonnies called *gemeinschaft* and *gesellschaft*.

If this categorical framework is applied to instruction, the idea suggests itself that traditional face-to-face instruction could be dealt with as an institution of communicative acting, whereas industrialized instruction would be a system of rational acting using means to an end. An analysis of these two forms of instruction reveals their decisive structural differences.

Even a rough comparison shows that the two forms of instruction could, indeed, be compared with each other with the help of these seven pairs of categories. It is evident that instruction in the classroom is regulated by norms. The direct interactions of teachers and students are more or less caused by binding expectations or value concepts developed by the learning group, the school, the families and society. How much this is, indeed, the case can be seen from the fact that there are often conflicts of norms in classrooms which lead to critical intensifications of social interactions. As societal norms determine the actions of the teachers and students, their interactions are influenced by socio-cultural traditions, whereby they themselves become part of the socio-cultural life of society.

Distance education, however, is basically determined by technical rules. Most behaviour possibilities for the teachers and the students are carefully planned, calculated, formalized and standardized. Originally global and complex behaviour patterns are reduced to the setting and control of specific functions. The students are informed about the rules of the teaching-learning system, and these rules must be followed.

Instruction in the class room is a system of 'communicative acting' and uses intersubjective divided colloquial language. This language is characterized by the traits of special persons, groups of persons, places and times. Thus, in a special sense each communicative situation is experienced as being unique. Distance education, however, uses a language which is taken out of its originally associated surroundings, and is thus free of its context. The technically mediated communication of necessity remains unaffected by particular circumstance, as it addresses students everywhere.

In the classroom the communicative acting is determined by reciprocal expectations of behaviour.

This means that the teacher who acts expects the students to react in a special way and vice versa. The expected reactions take place with a higher degree of probability the more the interacting persons have internalized a role consensus and the more the expected behaviour has become ritualized by habit.

In industrialized distance education the segments of interaction are constructed on the basis of conditioned prognoses and conditioned imperatives. Again, particular sequences of a global behaviour become objectified and isolated.

In face-to-face instruction the dominant mechanism of acquisition is the internalization of roles. The students live up to expectations by internalizing the norms of the group. Knowledge and skills are transported by means of this particular role identification, role taking and role performance. In distance education, however, the teaching-learning process is reduced to the learning of skills and qualifications. Every measure in this system has the sole function of achieving this goal. Communicative action and role performance are cut out.

In face-to-face instruction the social interaction helps to maintain the institution. Teachers and students are subject to external and internal control. In distance education, however, the indirect interaction is subject to the attainment of the learning goals by using means to an end.

Correspondingly, the reactions to breaches of the rules are different in the two subsystems. In face-to-face instruction, the students are punished functionalizing and depersonalization of instruction are real. Obviously, these processes are inevitable in such a specialized system of teaching and learning. And important educational goals such as individualization and the extension of the domination-free communicative action cannot be reached.

A critic who compares distance education with face-to-face instruction will consider these deficits as really serious ones. The considerable structural difference between the two forms of instruction, however, suggests that such a comparison is not really helpful. Thus it must be regarded as inappropriate to want to use the new systems of rational thinking in instruction to achieve exactly what was possible with the system of communicative action. It would be more appropriate to ask whether the standards of communicative action must and may still be valid reference points for the evaluation of the social relationships between teacher and taught. We must also teat whether the gains in teaching capacity in the reproducible system of rational thinking are not so great that deficits in the case of certain learning objectives of the type referred to can be regarded as acceptable. In this context the basic question has to be put once again whether all mediation of knowledge and skills has to be a priori permanently connected with forms of communicative action, or whether the socialization and cultural effects—the acquisition of norms, values and symbols either consciously or unconsciously—cannot take place in other experiencing and practical contexts as well.

If, in addition, when answering this question we

start from requirements made of people living in industrial societies today, there is another aspect which plays a part. People in industrial societies have had to find their way around the secondary system referred to, and make good use of the subsystems contained in this system. This ability can obviously only be imparted by a form of instruction which is not based on communicative action alone. Exaggerating only slightly, it can be said that a form of instruction based exclusively on communicative action, which by nurturing the 'innerliness' of teachers and students enables them to develop complete, individual personalities, cannot achieve a current generally applicable learning objective, because it well not teach students how to manage the 'apparatus of existence' of the 'secondary school system' in an advanced industrial society.

Reflections of this nature can lead to the conception of a dual educational system in which it will be possible for students to relate communicative and rational actions to one another in lessons. On the other hand, it is necessary to relate the differences between the two subsystems brought out so far to a more fundamental problem. With an analysis of its particular structural elements, distance education can be seen as a system for the extension of our disposal of technical means in education. Therefore, it must be related to another analytical level than face-to-face instruction which is based on the ways groups of persons see themselves and their traditions. Following Habermas, it could be stated that the increasing application of techniques of distance education results in a variation of the general problem of how usable knowledge can be employed in a social world. Obviously, there is a clash of two different intellectual traditions: the hermeneutical interpretation of the contexts of life, and empirically obtained and technically used knowledge. In a similar context Helmut Schelsky distinguished between science as reflection and science as technology. The juxtaposition of two respective different forms of teaching and learning has not yet been theoretically incorporated. It conveys a 'life problem of our civilization' namely, how the relations between technical progress and the social world, which are today still natural, can be reflected and controlled by a rational discourse. This will become a central problem of the new didactics.

Anthropological interpretation

If one relates distance education as a form of industrialized education to anthropological terms of reference, the question arises how to interpret the phenomenon that man uses technical media in order to be able to teach and learn at a distance. To answer this question requires consideration of two general features which were very important in human development: people's attitude towards technology and their ability to be challenged by new conditions of their environment and to renew themselves through it.

On the many anthropological models of interpretation that of Arnold |Gehlen seems to be most suitable for the purpose of this discussion. Following Herder and Schemer, he sees man as a being characterized by biological deficiencies, lacking specialize4d organs and instincts, and not adapted to a particular species-specific environment. This means that he must necessarily rely on his own cautions and must make his environment himself.

In order to achieve this, people need technology, which compensates for their deficiencies in the sense of the substitution, intensification and relief of their organs. Therefore, technology had a determining influence on man's interaction with nature throughout his development. In a general sense, technology belongs to him and technology mirrors his being. Technology is, as it were, the 'great being'.

The 'continuously increasing substitution of the organic by the inorganic can be considered a relevant result of our cultural development'. This is a process which began as early as the anthropogenesis and which has accelerated increasing during the last centuries and decades. 'The development of mankind is, hence, not a purely biological one, but essentially a development of substitute organs for missing ones,' concludes Rothcker, taking Gehlen's approach. And he refers to the first important substitute organs - namely tools, language, abstraction, reason and thinking. In a long course of development man had to get used to handling these and other substitute organs and to learn how to use them; that is, how to substitute by tradition what heredity had withheld from him.

In the context of this argument it is important to note that the substitute organs are media which are also used in instruction, and that tools, language and thinking are assigned to the same categorical level. In order to stress the importance of these media, one of the first substitute human organs - language—will be discussed in a preparatory digression as it shows paradigmatically to what degree even anthropogenesis depended on a medium which first had to be created. Furthermore, with the help of this medium, effects can be identified which are comparable to those which are achieved by the mechanization and industrialization of instruction. Finally, language is chose as an example as it is certainly above suspicion for even the most severe critics of culture, as it is not considered a part of technology, but rather a part of culture which is allegedly in opposition to technology.

Marshall however, typically enough, called language a human technology. By referring to a quotation from Bergson's *L'Evolution creative*, emphasized that it enabled the human intellect to separate real objects from its environment. Without language, he explain, human intelligence would have remained totally involved in the objects of its attention. A short reflection shows, indeed, that people can distance themselves from an object only if they have found a word for it - the pre-condition of any detached consideration. Kurt Strunz characterized this development in this way: 'Man is released from the prison of the here and now of his environment'. And he added that it was only through language that man was able to give an overview and ordered analysis of reality, including past events and distant phenomena. The fundamental importance of language is further clarified by McLuhan's comparison : 'Language does for intelligence what the wheel does for the feet and the body. It enables them to move from thing to thing with greater ease and speed and ever less involvement'.

The reference to a lesser degree of involvement

can be judged positively and negatively. On looking more carefully one can see that already this early use of a medium necessarily connects the advantages mentioned with important disadvantages. As language extends and amplifies man's thinking, and as man learns to handle it as a technical extension of consciousness, it also diminishes his originally very important intuitive awareness of collective consciousness. Thus, 'speech acts to separate man from man, and mankind from the cosmic unconscious'. Strunz observes that the spoken word changes human inwardness as it objectified it. And here he sees dangerous implications. The verbal fixation of contents of the world and the inwardness blinds him with regard to the things we do not understand. His detachment alienates him from reality, its contents are 'talked to death'; and, finally, there is also the misuse of the word, in false gossip, in the distortion of the truth, and in lying. A further danger is that language tends to become independent, to develop in its own way, and thereby to assume an inadequate importance which is separated from reality. This may render communication more difficult, or block it or make it open to manipulation.

The example shows the enormous adaptations which became necessary when humans learned how to use the medium of language. Their structures of consciousness changed to a high degree. One might assume that people acquired language only reluctantly and that they refused to use it in some areas of their life altogether, as they were afraid that, for instance, religious and social relations would become stunted. Even today there are situations in which the exchange of feelings is so subtle that the persons involved believe that talking about them would destroy everything'. The use of the medium of language was, on the one hand, an important gain for the development of mankind and, on the other, a considerable loss. The same can be said about the use of newer media in instruction; namely, writing, and later print, and still later electronic media. And the same holds true for industrialized education. It must, however, be acknowledged that the losses were by far outweighed by the extraordinary and even epoch-making advantages. In all cases the use of media made it possible to solve educational tasks which so far had been insoluble.

For the interpretation of industrialized education it is important to see that there are similarities in the consequences of the use of the medium of language and of modern technical media. The following insights have been gained: (1) instruction has been removed from its close attachment to given places, times and persons; (2) teachers and students become detached from reality - that is, from the life of the learning group; (3) as the teaching behaviour is objectified the students have it practically at their disposal. They can actualize the teaching with greater case and speed whenever they wish to learn. Thus, instruction is released from the prison of the here and now and of a given environment. This opens it up for further developments in new dimensions.

Considering the structural similarities conveyed by this analogy, the question suggests itself whether industrialized instruction can release, intensify and differentiate intellectual faculties in the same way as language has done as it is also no longer tied to fixed places, times and persons.

If we follow Gehlen's approach, industrialized instruction can be understood as a complex technical system of teaching and learning which man is forced to develop as he is no longer able to cope with all the instructional and training tasks of the advanced industrial society by means of his natural organs. In the same way as technology was called 'the great teacher'. In order to be able to fulfill its tasks, the great teacher operates with the help of substitute organs which are to intensify and extend the following human organs or faculties:

- The voice of the teacher, which can scarcely fill a large auditorium, is intensified and extended by media such as audio tapes, records, television, and in a coded form as printed material. In this way it can reach practically every home of this globe - and with the help of radio waves, even out into space. Some of these media transmit the teacher's picture as well and even their gestures and body language, so that the teacher's total teaching behaviour can reach practically everyone.
- The forefinger, an organ which is so unspecified and so deficient that it had already been extended by the pointer in the pre-industrial era, is extended and intensified by graphical representations, careful camera work, and the application of multisensoric stimuli techniques. The camera, for instance, can be directed to the object to the shown in such a way that it appears more precisely than in reality. With the help of cinematographic techniques, for instance,

focusing, close-up, microscopic filming, slow motion, quick motion and trick filming, it becomes possible to present the object to the student, didactically speaking, much more effectively than it is possible in reality.

- The eyes and ears of the teacher which inform her or him about the learning behaviour of his students are substituted and intensified by the empirical collection of data and their evaluation with the help of the computer. In this way tens of thousand of students can be observed at once with regard to their particulars, their relevant previous qualifications, their entrance behaviour, their gains in knowledge and skills, the results of specific tests, and possibly also the change in their attitudes.
- The memory of the teacher, which is often not as firm and infallible as he or she might wish and which is in addition often also tied to certain situations, is extended by powerful external data banks and computer programs and thus becomes extraordinarily exact.
- The art of teaching - that is, the didactical decisions which are necessarily tied to given persons and situations in face-to-face instruction - is substituted by strategies and technologies which address all students wherever they might live.

In general, the following statement can be made: Human organs can be substituted, intensified and relieved in the ways described in an industrial society only, and the extent to which this happens will increase together with the further industrialization of society. The new possibilities for teaching and learning resulting from this development are not yet fully foreseeable.

Having interpreted the technically designed distance teaching system as equipping the teacher with artificial organs, thus enabling him or her to tackle instructional and training tasks of unprecedented magnitude, reasons why the decisive changes which industrialized instruction brings about have to be accepted now have to be given from an anthropological aspect.

Present-day man can be characterized by the fact that he is challenged in an unprecedented way by the extreme disproportion between the possibilities of his natural body and of his teaching and learning habits handed down by tradition - and the immense increase in instructional and training needs. With regard to these needs, which are very likely to increase in the future, the individual, indeed, proves to be a biological deficient being who, because of his morphological helplessness, is bound to fail in his efforts to cope with them. Since the natural teaching capacity is already at a premium in traditional forms of education and since it will be lacking even more drastically when it has to fulfil the needs of the disadvantaged in industrial as well as developing societies, the only way out is to teach and to learn in an industrialized way. This is a pre-condition for enabling as many people as possible to take part in the emerging industrial world civilization.

Heinrich Roth in his *Pedagogical Anthropology*, summed up his discussion about the biologically caused release of man from his environment by

2 On Defining Distance Education

It is easier to devise a definition than to accept someone else's. It is not the purpose of this study to devise yet another definition of distance education but to highlight those elements which are essential to any definition.

Of the many definitions of distance education which have been prepared in the last decade four have been chosen for analysis. An attempt has been made to make them as representative as possible.

Holmberg is from Sweden, works in the Federal Republic of Germany and often writes in English. The French definition is from official government sources which formulate policy on the administration of distance education. Moore has worked extensively in the United States of America and today is senior counsellor in the Southern Region of the Open University of the United Kingdom.

It will be seen at once that three of the definitions are descriptive. Peters, however, presents a new philosophical analysis of distance education as 'an industrialised form of teaching and learning'.

If Peters" definition, or any elements of it, is accepted, a radical separation of distance education from other forms of education is effected.

Holmberg

Basic to Holmberg's definition are two elements both of which can be considered essential:

— the separation of teacher and learner

— the planning of an educational organisation.

The separation of teacher and learner is fundamental to all forms of distance education whether they be print-based, audio/radio-based, video/television-based, computer-based or satellite-based. This separation differentiates distance education from all forms of conventional, face-to-face, direct teaching and learning.

The structuring of learning materials and the linking of these learning materials to effective learning by students through an educational organisation differentiates distance education from private study, learning from interesting books or cultural television programmes.

The French law

On 12 July 1971 the French Government passed a law regulating the conduct of distance education in its territories. This law contained the definition of distance education translated at the beginning of this article.

Again two elements are basic to this definition:

— the separation of teacher and learner

— the possibility of occasional seminars or meetings between student and teacher.

learning behaviours. The learner works - alone or in a group - guided by study material arranged by the instructor who together with the totors is in a location apart from the students, who however have the opportunity to communicate with a tutor/tutors with the aid of one or more media such as correspondence, telephone, television, radio. Distance education may be combined with various forms of face-to-face meetings.

This development of Moore's thought is more comprehensive and introduces the notion that the teaching role may be shared and that different study situations are possible for the learner.

Peters

The three definitions so far considered can probably be accommodated within any basic theory of education. The major theoretical formulation of distance education so far published, Otto Peters' Die didaktische Struktur des Fernunterrichts. Untersuchungen zu einer industrialisierten Form des Lehrens and Lernens takes quite a different position. It merits careful study.

Peters begins the theoretical part of his analysis with a description which coincides quite readily with the three considered so far:

Distance education is a form of indirect instruction. It is imparted by technical media such as correspondence, printed materials, teaching and learning aids, audiovisual aids, radio, television and computers.

Basic to this description are two of the elements already identified; separation between the teacher and the learner, and the use of technical media. Peters' analysis, however, proceeds much further than the others considered and leads him to the conclusion that the didactical structure of distance education can best be understood from industrial principles especially those of productivity, division of labour and mass production. The mechanisation and automation of teaching methodology and the dependence of teaching effectiveness on prior planning and organisation lead him to posit a radically different role for the teacher is distance education from that exercised in the lecture hall or seminar room.

This leads Peters to the definition quoted at the beginning of this article. The definition can be queried in the emphasis that it places on the course production process. Many would consider this as only the start of the learning process and expect some reference to tuition and teacher/learner exchanges.

Peters next considers other theories of distance education and gives a comprehensive listing of those that have been proposed:

— a fringe form of ordinary teaching

— an institutionalised form of individual study

— education through teaching aids

— expanded form of teaching by correspondence with feedback

— special type of mass education.

He is led to the conclusion that all are inadequate as explanations of the phenomenon described.

Peters concludes with an attempt to define the relationship between teacher and taught in a distance education system. He characterises this relationship as being controlled by technological rules, maintained by emotion- free language (and not interactional speech), based on a limited possibility of analysing students' needs and giving them directions (not on expectations built on personal contract) and achieving its goal by efficiency (and not through personal interaction).

In earlier writings Peters had laid the ground for his theory of distance education:

Correspondence instruction is the most industrialised form of instruction, and the usual theoretical criteria for the description of traditional instruction do not help very much in analysing correspondence instruction. This has suggested the introduction of *new categories* taken from those sciences investigating the industrial production process. It is, in fact, astounding to see how much better these criteria help to understand and describe the institutional process in correspondence instruction. Some of the suggested criteria are: division of labour (on the side of teachers); mechanisation; automation; application of organisational principles; scientific control; objectivity of teaching behaviour; mass production; concentration and centralisation.

This brief presentation cannot do justice to Peters' attempts to show that distance education is based on a new academic theory which is quite alien to traditional didactics. He is quite convinced that distance education has its own laws of didactical structure, great teaching potential, serious didactical flaws and that it presents opportunities and dangers to both teachers and students which are not yet fully studied. Anyone professionally involved in education, he maintains, must presume the existence of two forms of education which are strictly separable: traditional education based on personal communication and distance education based on industrialised and technological communication.

There have always been those who have objected to such a presentation and two of the objections will be considered briefly here.

Much confusion stems from the popular misconception that correspondence instruction is somehow different in kind from resident or institutional instruction. This simply is not so. Correspondence instruction shares the same goals and the same educational philosophy as many different methods of instruction. It differs from them primarily in the means, in the method itself.

Similar views are often encountered in Australia where an 'integrated mode' of distance education is practised in many universities and colleges. In the 'integrated mode' a lecturer is given responsibility both for a group of conventional, on-campus students and for a group of distance education students, known as external students. Learning materials are usually developed in close parallel with the lecturer's lecutre-room course and the same assignments and examinations are provided for both on-campus and external students.

It is in this context that some Australian educationalists can write of 'the blurred demarcation between on-campus and off-campus studies':

External studies, off-campus studies, or distance education, as it is variously called, is no more than a method of teaching. I believe that we shall move much more to the provision of carefully prepared learning materials and study guides for our students and to much more flexible attendance patterns. If this occurs it will become virtually impossible to designate students as on-campus or off-campus students, or to designate institutions which are teaching in the off-campus mode.

This is not the place to debate whether distance education should be integrated within or separated from conventional face-to-face programmes. The contention is, however, that what is said here of distance education should be applicable mutates mutandis to the distance education segment of an integrated programme.

The second objection to the claim of a radical separation in didactic structure between distance education and conventional education is based on the idea that Oto Peters, and many educational philosophers with him, have misinterpreted what occurs in conventional education, especially at university level.

At the culminating states of education there is little distinction between teacher and taught; they are both participating in the shared experience of exploring a participating in the shared experience of exploring a common world. The teacher is simply more familiar with its contours and more skilled in handling the tools for laying bare its mysteries and appraising its nuances. Occasionally in a tutorial this exploration takes the form of a dialogue. But more usually it is a group experience. The great teachers are those who can conduct such a shared enterprise in which all are united by a common zeal.

There is clearly a huge gulf between this statement and the industrialised process that Otto Peters describes. The counter argument runs that it is incorrect to say that in traditional education learning takes place in the lecture room and that the teacher's role is therefore of crucial importance. Good adult education, the objection claims, is essentially self-education by the learner based on private study in libraries, audio-visual carrels and laboratories. Those who support the view that distance education is radically to be differentiated from conventional education would point out that access to the university's library and carrels is not often possible for students who study at a distance from the institution and that the use of indirect teaching methods in face-to-face instruction does not make it identical with distance education.

In spite of these objections one can grant to Otto Peters that he has highlighted a characteristic of distance education that should form part of any definition:

— it is the most industrialised form of education.

Nature of distance education

It must also be conceded that Peters has attempted to get to the nature of distance education and that the two objections just quoted, and many others like them, seem to neglect certain fundamental aspects of distance education. There are five reasons for this:

1. In traditional education a teacher teaches. In

distance education an institution teaches. This is a radical difference. In traditional education the teacher is present in the lecture room with students and his success often depends on the rapport he can build up with students: personality and even idiosycracies may be central. In distance education the teacher prepares learning materials from which he himself may never teach. Another teacher may use the materials and evaluate students' work. The pedagogical structuring of the learning materials, instructional design and execution may be assigned to others. Personality needs to be played down, idiosyncracies eliminated. The teaching becomes institutionalised. Different skills are needed as even part of the content of what is taught may be contributed by others.

2. In distance education the goal of linking of learning materials to learning is at the centre of the organisational structure. In conventional education the 'inter-subjectivity that R.S. Peters saw as central to the teaching/learning process is automatically set up. In distance education this 'intersubjectivity' is lacking and there can be no guarantee that anything will happen once learning materials have been developed and dispatched to the student.

Administrators of distance education systems who consider that distance education is merely a 'fringe form of traditional education' often forget to provide this linking. They feel that once the learning materials have been developed and dispatched to the student the job is done: learning will occur. In distance education there is no basis for this unless a successful linking system is provided. Even then questions on the quantity of learning, the quality of the learning and the status of the learning remain for solution.

3 From the student's point of view there are important differences between the two systems of education. The distance system gives a radical new meaning to the concept of the independence of the audult learner. In this system he is responsible for initiating the learning process and, to a large extent, for maintaining it throughout. Questions of motivation and skill acquisition, of a specifically different kind to those required in traditional education, need to be tackled to combat the phenomena of non-starters and drop-outs that have been a feature of this type of education throughout the last one hundred years.

4 Management skills that are more akin to those found in industrialised enterprises are needed in distance education. The distance system has daily preoccupations with lead times, deadlines, print runs, job schedules, typefaces, warehousing, delivery and dispatch and planning decisions on educational priorities that must take place two, three or more years before teaching is to take place. Such pre-occupations are not normally characteristic of educational administrators.

5 Distance education is a form of education that can easily become depersonalised both for staff and students. Students are not invited to Milton Keynes nor to many of the distance education institutions throughout the world. There is little

doubt that the absence of students can create a strained atmosphere for lecturers. The constant process of writing creatively for distance students, whether alone or in a course team framework, poses problems, which are not fully resolved even in those institutions were the lecturer has some responsibilities for on-campus students as well. The marking of distance students' work, even when relieved by face-to-face seminars, telephone tuition and work for radio or television has a definite propensity for staff disillusionment.

Much has been written, from Marx to today, on alienation in the workforce. In an industrialised form of education where division of labour is necessary, where organisational planning and scheduling of a precise kind are essential and where educational decisions may be controlled by mechanised and automated processes the possibility of alienation among the workforce is real. It is even more real when the workforce is composed of academics whose qualifications and training have not prepared them for work in the most industrialised form of education.

Summary

From the examination of the four representative definitions of distance education in this section the following characteristics have been highlighted. All six are to be regarded as essential for any comprehensive definition:

— separation of teacher and student

— influence of an educational organisation especially in the planning and preparation of learning materials

— use of technical media

— provision of two-way communication

— possibility of occasional seminars

— participation in the most industrialised form of education.

The next stage is to show what forms distance education may take and why certain kinds of non-traditional education do not fall within its scope.

Forms of distance education

Distance education has been in existence for about one hundred years. The elements of a definition that have been established in the previous section do not therefore exist as abstractions; they must correspond to the reality. This section focuses on forms of education that are included within the concept of distance education; what is excluded is treated in the next.

Three different approaches to identifying the forms of distance education are presented: the medium on which the learning materials are based, institutional type and didactic model.

Choice of medium

The different forms of distance education can be identified by their

— use of technical media

— as the basis for the learning materials.

A possible presentation of the bases of the learning materials is given schematically on the previous page.

Print-based. By far the great majority of distance education programmes are print-based. The teaching basis of the Open University of the United Kingdom, for example, is approximately 80% print-based, 10% broadcasting (radio and television) and 10% face-to-face seminars and summer schools.

A real disservice has been done to the field of distance education by overemphasis on terms like 'University of the Air'. Educators, administrators and politicians, not only in developing countries but also in developed countries where finance for education is now being limited, should realise that the vast majority of distance education courses are print-based and will remain so.

Exceptions to this in the foreseeable future will come only with populations for whom literacy is a problem and perhaps in those regions where there is traditional reticience about correspondence-type programmes. Higher education in the United States of America is an area where an attempt to transfer emphasis to videotape-based or computer-based programmes might be worth considering because of the population's interest in technology and dislike of correspondence study.

An interesting variant on print-based programmes are the courses by newspaper developed under the leadership of Martin N. Chamberlain, Dean of University Extension at the University of California, San Diego. The Deutsches Institutfur Fernstudien at Tubingen has recently introduced a similar programme in the Federal Republic of Germany.

Audio-based courses in which the educational

Correspondence Colleges of the United Kingdom. Some of these institutions are non-profit making and a number receive some government support and they are found throughout the world.

Government sponsored schools, colleges and universities have played a role in distance education for the last seventy years. Many of these institutions are specially structured for distance education: Athabasca University, Edmonton; the Open College of Further Education, Adelaide; the Centre National de Tele-enseignement in France; the Fernuniversitat-Gesamthochschule in Hagen. Many other colleges and universities have a department which concentrates on the distance students : the independent study department of the University of Minnesota, Minneapolis; the external studies department of the University of Queensland, Brisbane.

The Open University at Milton Keynes in the United Kingdom founded only ten years ago, has already made an impressive contribution to research, theory and practice in the field of distance education.

This wide range of institutional type, incorporating both public and private operations, makes the defining of the limits of the educational field within which all lie a difficult task. It is felt, nevertheless, that all institutions in this area because of the separation of their students from their teachers are engaged in the planning or purchase of learning materials and possess or have access to an integrated range of technical media, by which the student is given the possibility of two-way communication, not only when beginning but coherent a structure as possible. The student is supported by a wide range of activities, most of them optional unless the course team has decided otherwise. This tends to strengthen the possibility that learning takes place and that unnecessary drop-outs are prevented.

From time to time distance education is described as 'the opposite of face-to-face education".

This statement needs to be taken further as there are many forms of what may be considered the 'opposite of face-to-face' education that are not distance education, as the following diagram shows:

Relationship of distance education to other forms of indirect education

Indirect education

This distinction is again based on an idea of Peters and merits attention because of the importance in definition of what is excluded. Each of the following forms of indirect education lacks one or more of the characteristics of distance education.

Education by letter. From Plato and Paul to Erasmus letters have been used for instructional purposes and the practice, doubtless, continues today. They lack the structuring of an educational institution that is a characteristic of distance education.

Printed education. Pamphlets, books and teach-yourself manuals fall into this category. The lack of an educational organisation is again the major factor which distinguishes these from distance education, together with the impossibility of two-way communication. It is clear that many people learn a great deal from these means, even though they may lack didactical structuring or even an educational goal.*Teaching kits.* In increasing use in face-to-face teachering are kits of various kinds containing samples, games and specimens on which students are invited to work without supervision.

Audio-visual aids. When a lecturer communicates with a student by means of audio-visual aids: slides, film, audio and video-tapes, he is teaching indirectly.

Depending on the structure of the programme within which they are being used, these forms of indirect teaching can form part either of face-to-face instruction or of a distance education programme.

Radio and Television. Many people learn a great deal from radio and television and sometimes those media are used in distance education programmes, Kenneth Clarke's Civilisation or Jacob Bronowski's The Ascent of Man were not conceived as part of a distance education programme. Nevertheless they have become part of both on-campus and distance education programmes when offered for credit with accompanying didactically structured assignment, reading and assessment materials.

Programmed learning, which was popular in the 1960s, is a form of indirect teaching which has many similarities to distance education. Both demand extensive preparation of learning materials, careful sequencing and tend towards the individualising of learning.

Computer-aided learning is a recent form of indirect education and is used extensively in many conventional teaching programmes.

Mention is made here of independent study and private study as two forms of education with similarities to the above.

Independent study. There are many forms of independent study amongst which can be classed study guided by a governess, tutor or counsellor and many contract, independent or external degree programmes in American colleges.

Private study can be seen as neither a form of direct, classroom education nor of indirect off-campus studies. It is widespread and devoid of institutional linkages, though it may be based on materials developed for use within an institution either for traditional classroom students or distance learners.

Programmes with some similarities to distance education

There are certain forms of education which have some similarities to distance education but are not identical with it. Four of the most important are here presented for consideration: extension programmes, University Without Walls, experiential learning, the external degree. Three more general terms: 'non-traditional learning', 'off-campus studies' and 'open learning' are first considered briefly.

One cannot define 'non-traditional learning' without first defining 'traditional learning' and that is clearly beyond the bounds of this article. It seems at times that in the United States any educational programme that is not a four-year, residential, university degree programme can be regarded as non-traditional learning, though there are clearly more restricted usages. "Non-traditional learning' is to be regarded as a vague, generalised term of which distance education is one example. 'Off-campus studies' is another general term for any programme which does not take place on the central university or college campus - distance education is one possibility.

Wedemeyer gives an accurate analysis of 'open learning':

> It is difficult to find a common definition for the many experimental programmes that call themselves *open*. However, all open schools have one principle in common: they are to a greater or lesser extent efforts to expand the freedoms of learners. Some are open only in a spatial sense while others provide freedoms in more significant dimensions - in admissions, selection of courses, individual adaptation of the curriculum and time, goal selection and evaluation.

'Open learning' therefore, is a term that is not to be used in an administrative context; rather its context is philosophical to describe, for instance, colleges with 'open' administration policies or a special spirit like Paris VIII at Vincennes, *l'Universite Ouverte*. Some of these are face-to-face institutions, others teach at a distance.

Extension programmes are ways of extending the expertise of a university or college to new populations. The terms can imply offering the same programmes as for full-time, day-time students by different means, at different locations or at different times. An extra-mural department usually has a similar function of extending the expertise of the university to a broader community. Some of these programmes are for credit, others not.

The range or extension and extra-mural programmes is very extensive and distance education can be regarded as one grouping of a number of possibilities of providing education outside the normal lecture room. Extension, especially as used in the United States, is a much broader term which can include part-time day or night, conventional lectures on campus.

University without walls implies the design of an individualised programme based on a learning contract for students with clear learning objectives who cannot realise their whole educational aspirations through existing programmes. A University Without Walls programme can include experiential learning credits, ordinary lectures, distance education elements, learning from community sources or job-related activities, all of which can be evaluated towards a college or university degree.

Experiential learning programmes are those which give credit for prior learning which did not take place in a lecture room setting and was not sponsored by an educational institution, but was acquired through work experience including volunteer work, co-operative education or self-study.

A degree programme which can be completed in the following manner: a student entering the programme with the minimum entrance qualifications can complete it with less than 25 percent of the required work taking the form of campus-based classroom instruction.

In the attempt to place some conceptual order around the wide range of study programmes that are associated with non-traditional and distance education, the question of whether or not the external degree should be included within the concept of distance education is the one which poses the most precise definition and research problems.

In so far as the external degree serves to describe the programmes whose primary function is to recognise education and attribute to it an appropriate qualification, it does not fall within the concept of distance education as it has been presented in this study. If, on the other hand, it is used to describe programmes whose function is to provide education for students, then it may be identified with distance education providing it agrees with the descriptors given in the first section of this article.

One hundred and eight-three college and university degree programmes are classified as external in the American study referred to above. The Ed.D. programme from Nova University, Fort Lauderdale, Florida which has been at the centre of the controversy about the external degree in the United States in recent years is not mentioned.

The Nova doctoral programme consists of class meetings known as clusters which meet for eight hours once per month; reading requirements; written assignments and a major applied research paper.

Do the Nova Ed.D. and similar external degrees lie within the field of distance education as described? When attempting to formulate an answer one is faced with the fact that any doctoral programme contains large elements of private research and little face-to-face tuition.

Clearly the dividing line between the Nova cluster system and the consultation system of the German Democratic Republic is a thin one. This study tends to exclude the former because of its lack of emphasis on the pedagogical structuring of learning materials by the educational institution and because it is a less industrialised and technological form of education and tends to include the latter.

Terminology

The term 'distance education' has been used in this article.

It is meant to designate the cluster of educational organisations which are usually referred to as *Fernstudium* in Spanish and *teleducacao* in Portuguese but for which a number of different terms are used in the English-speaking world.

Other language

In german there is an awkward status question of whether *Fernstudium* 'distance study' refers only to higher education at a distance (universities and university-oriented colleges) and *Fermanterricht* 'distance teaching' refers to further education at a distance (technical and vocationally-oriented institutions). There seems to be some indication that *Fernstudium* will become the established term for all levels in the Federal Republic of Germany, as it is in the Germany Democratic Republic.

Tele-enseignement 'distance teaching' is an influential term in French because of its use in the titles of the Centre National de Tele-enseignement, (C.N.T.E.), the Centres do Tele-enseignement Universitaire (C.T.U.) and the Tele-universite de

Quebec. There are some who would argue that *formation a distance* 'education at a distance' reflects more closely modern pedagogical theories.

The problem with *tele-enseignement* is that many do not realise that the root of *'tele'* is the Greek word *tele* 'from afar', 'from a distance' and does not refer to television. *Tele-enseignement* appears to be the generally accepted term.

The words *education a distancia* in Spanish and *teleducacao* in Portuguese seem to be gaining acceptance as terms for 'distance education', side by side with the spread of influence of this type of education in Spanish and Portuguese speaking countries.

English terminology

In English there are at least six major terms: correspondence study/education, home study, independent study, external studies, distance teaching, distance education.

Two propositions underlie what follows:

- neolgisms are unnecessary in an area where there is already a multiplicity of terms
- 'distance education', although not perfect, is the most suitable term and should be used.

Correspondence study is not a suitable word for what has been described as 'distance education' in this article. It cannot describe radio-based programmes like *Ensemble,* television-based programmes like *The Great Plaine,* computer-based programmes in the PLATO series nor the Appalachian Satellite programme.

Communications theory experts tell us that words get tired and if they do then 'correspondence study' is a tired word. It is significant that when the directors of the correspondence schools of the United States of America came together in 1926 to form an association the title chosen was the National Home Study Council and not the National Correspondence Study Council. Charles A. Wedemeyer was chairman of a committee of the International Council for Correspondence Education (I.C.C.E.) to consider a change of name as many felt its present title was inappropriate if the organisation wished to remain a major influence in the field.

'Correspondence study' is a correct designation of that subgroup of the print-based areas of distance education in which student contact is not encouraged. It should continue to be used for such programmes and only for such programmes.

'Correspondence study/education' institutions left alone', that student support services can infringe learner autonomy or the independence of the adult learner. They claim that student seminars do not add to student learning from a correspondence study system.

Home study is used mainly in the United States of America and is there confined to further and technical education. The 1979 listing of approved members of the National Home Study Council contain 94 institutions, most of them proprietary.

When the universities of the United States of American which teach at a distance wanted to form an association it is significant that they rejected the title 'Home Study' and chose instead 'Independent Study'.

'Home study' is thus unsuitable an a generic term for the wide range of teaching-learning activities which have been described.

Independent study is the term used in higher education in the U.S.A. The 1979 Guide to independent study through correspondence instruction lists 68 members of the Independent Study Division of the National University Extension Association. Nearly all of these are correspondence sections of extension departments of American universities. In addition to programmes for degree credit, may of the courses are at high school or certificate level.

Charles A. Wedemeyer has been the proponent of the term 'independent study' both in his writings and during a lecture tour of Australia which he undertook in 1977:

Independent study in the American context is a generic for a range of teaching-learning activities that sometimes go by separate names (correspondence study, open education, radio-television teaching, individualised learning). In several European countries such systems are culstered under the terms *distance education* or are still perceived as separate programmes without any basic, generic relationship.

He feels that the term 'independent study' has the capacity to encompass a wide range of activities and defines it as:

Independent study consists of various forms of teaching-learning arrangements in which teachers and learners carry out their essential tasks and responsibilities apart from one another, communicating in a variety of ways, for the purpose of freeing internal learners from inappropriate class placings or patterns or providing external learners opportunity to continue learning in their own environments, and developing in all learners the capacity to carry on self-directed learning, the ultimate maturity required of the educated person.

There are elements of a philosophy of educational maturity in this statement to which most distance educators would subscribe. The term 'independent study', nevertheless, is to be rejected as a generic term.

There are three reasons for this:

- the normal understanding of 'independent study' implies a different relationship to an educational institution (see section two)
- the ideal in distance education is not necessarily independence but, as John S. Daniel wrote, 'interaction and independence: getting the mixture right'
- in the United States of America an 'independent student' is one who sets up an individual study programme on a contract basis during an interview with a faculty member. The contract may include periods of normal lectures, unguided study or distance programmes.

External studies is the term most widely used in Australia, Its use is confined to that region where it well describes the essence of the 'integrated model' of distance education as found in many Australian institutions: 'external to' but not 'separated from' the faculty staff. It can have little claim to general acceptance because of this limitation and because of confusion with the American external degree. Whether or not the American external degree, especially those associated with Antioch and Nova universities, falls within the concept of distance education has already been discussed.

Distance teaching or teaching at a distance has been the term most commonly used by the Open University in the United Kingdom. Distance teaching is only half the process we are trying to describe: to distance teaching must be added distance learning.

out that expression helps learning and that dialogue, giving an impression of human warmth and interest, encourages it. Learning is more effective if, through dialogue between student and teacher, the student can be shown how the new matter he is learning relates to what he already knows, and relates to his environment. And dialogue has an important checking function: it enables the tutor to check the student's progress, the tutor to check her method of presentation by seeing whether the student understand her, and the student to check the tutor, in case the tutor has actually got things wrong. The strong form of the argument goes much further and claims that, unless there is dialogue, education changes to indoctrination: dialogue is here seen as a necessary condition of an education which respects the humanity of student and teacher. This view is reinforced in much out-of-school education, where it is clear that the student's knowledge of the world in which he had grown up merits respect and attention along with the tutor's knowledge of her own specialism.

If those, then, are our aims - of expanding education and of stressing the importance of dialogue - then a theory of distance teaching should illuminate the ways in which it does, or does not, lead towards them.

The ways in which distance teaching is used are, of course, politically and culturally determined. If, for example, society rewards credentials and the diploma disease is rife, then it is extremely difficult for a distance-teaching institution to set off in a different direction. In Medico, for example, *Telesecundaria*, which uses television and print to support secondary education, is successful in getting children through their examinations - but by doing so may be merely contributing to urban drift and problems of unemployment in the towns. Distance-teaching institutions inevitably reflect the values of their societies. The experience of *Telescundaria*, or of the Free University of pre-revolutionary Iran, which was seen as a device to prevent students coming together, can be contrasted with the radio campaigns of the United Republic of Tanzania, which reflect something of the political philosophy of TANU in their attempt at mass involvement. The success or failure of a distance-teaching project will, therefore, depend at least as much on its political context as on its methods. Our arguments about method inevitably rest on political assumptions.

Expanding education

Experience enables us to make five hypotheses, our first five 'statements', about the way n which distance teaching can be used to maximize education. Chu and Schramm exhaustively analysed the literature on the comparative methods of different media, seeking differences between print, radio, film, television, classroom teacher and so on. Most of the research suggests that there are no significant differences between them in their educational effectiveness. Trenaman similarly found in comparing radio, print and television that 'the three media communicate a wide variety of material with roughly equivalent efficiently.' While differences between students or audiences, and differences between subjects, have a major effect on how easily something is learned, differences between the media seem to be far less important? Making the point very broadly, then, Statement 1 is: *you can use any medium to teach anything.* Much flows from this hypothesis; it has consequences for our methodology, considered below, and for our desires to expand education. For, if we can use a variety of media secure in the knowledge that they are comparable in their effectiveness, then we can examine how to use audio-visual media like radio and television, which enable us to reach audiences who could not get to school or college. And we can go on from considering the qualities of individual media to decisions about using a variety of media, and decisions about combining print or broadcasts with some face-to-face study.

It follows from Statement 1 that the face-to-face teacher is not unique in his/her ability to teach. And so we can depose teacher: *distance teaching can break the integuments of fixed staffing ratios which limited the expansion of education when teacher and student had to be in the same place at the same time.*

Traditionally the expansion of education has demanded an expansion in the number of teachers; if that constraint is removed by distance teaching then the prospects for expanding education may be enhanced, provided that distance teaching is no more expensive than teaching through orthodox methods. The prospect would, on the other hand, be no brighter if distance teaching were necessarily more expansive than orthodox education. Economic forces would then press any reasonable person into expanding ordinary schools and colleges. But distance teaching can be cheaper. With broadcasts, as with print, one teacher's words can reach a much larger audience than world ever be possible face-to-face so that economies of scale are possible. There is empirical evidence of such economies being attained. Jamison and Orivel, for example, considered twelve distance-teaching projects for which cost data are available and found that 'most of the projects studied here are less expensive than equivalent traditional methods of education' We can then make Statement 3: *there are circumstances under which distance teaching can be cheaper than orthodox education, whether measured in terms of audience reached or of learning.*

It is not always cheaper. At primary level, most teachers are paid so little that it is difficult to find any cheaper way of educating small children. At the other extreme, tertiary education is often so expensive that it is much easier to come up with a cheaper, distance, alternative. At any level it is fairly easy for distance teaching to work out as an expensive alternative if only a handful of students follow any one course or (if we are concerned with the number of students who successfully complete a course and not just with the number of enrollments) if the drop-out rate is high. And at any level costs per student are sensitive to the choice of medium. This can vary widely, so that one could conceive of the costs, for the same programme, of print, radio and television being in the ratio of 1:10:100. Statement 4: *the economies achievable by distance education are a function of the level of education, size of audience, choice of media and sophistication of production.*

If these hypotheses are true then we have established that distance teaching can be effective and that its costs can compare favourably with those of orthodox education. Universal post, and radio with its seven-league boots, thus make it possible to increase access to education, while the social constraints on the use of telecommunications are at least slightly different from those on the use of schools. The relevance of distance teaching to the expansion of education is clear, and our key Statement 5 is: *distance teaching can reach audiences who would not be reached by orthodox means.*

Dialogue

So distance teaching may help us towards our first objective. What of the second, to encourage dialogue? We are faced with a dilemma here. If teaching through broadcasts and print is linked with face-to-face study then dialogue is, of course, possible within that face-to-face element. It is far easier to envisage dialogue, if we use the term to mean our strong form or in the sense that Freire uses it, in face-to-face discussion, than through print or broadcasts. As educators, discussion, than through print or broadcasts. An educators, therefore, we are constantly under pressure to increase the face-to-face component of distance teaching. But, as well saw, the economic attractiveness of distance teaching springs from the economies of scale which it makes possible; we are equally under pressure to limit the size of the face-to-face component. A central problem therefore, concerns the balance between economic arguments, of crucial importance to us if we wish to widen access to education, and educational arguments, of equal importance if we want to emphasize dialogue. The way that dilemma is resolved, between quantity and quality, will vary from time to time and place to place; we return to it below when considering the methods of distance teaching.

In struggling with the dilemma, it is worth remembering that much orthodox education is not based on dialogue. Children are taught to learn things by heart; much agricultural extension assumes that the farmer should simply do what the extension agent tells him. In practice we cannot learn everything, in school or out, by discovery and dialogue. The tough challenge for distance teaching, then, is provide not merely as good opportunities for dialogue as orthodox education, but more such opportunities. Distance teaching has long been criticized for encouraging rote learning. Of its nature, correspondence education demands a respect for the printed word which is at odds with the sort of scepticism implicit in our view of education. Even a distance-teaching institution as sophisticated and generously endowed with arrangements for dialogue as the British Open University has not always overcome the problem:

In far too many of the Arts assignments questions are set which it is virtually impossible for students to answer except by regurgitating the unit material ... Recently a nature student, just completing her Honours degree, wrote to me criticising a third level history course. 'When I learnt history at school', she said, 'and even when I've done the history blocks ... I've been given facts, and a sequence of events to learn. Now I'm given a series of hypotheses about which no-one seems to agree.

But many correspondence-based courses, at the Open University and elsewhere, do encourage dialogue of one kind or another. The radio campaigns of the United Republic of Tanzania and Botswana set up dialogue between village learning-group members and both educators and government; Radio Educative Senegal has used feedback from radio groups to change government policy. Students in National Extension College correspondence courses confirm that dialogue, on paper and face-to-face, forms a central part of their experience, even though they learn mainly at a distance. Despite the inherent problems, therefore, of arranging dialogue when learning is based on materials produced in advance and distributed on masse, there is empirical evidence for tour key Statement: *It is possible to organise distance teaching in such a way that there is dialogue.*

That dialogue may be on paper, or may be through occasional face-to-face sessions between tutor and student, or may be organized through group discussion of one kind or another. But its existence suggests a change in the function of the teacher, the function of a teacher working in distance education is different from that of a classroom teaching. If the distance teacher is writing lessons; or making broadcast programmes, her function can be quite easily compared with that of a teacher standing before a class. But even here there are important differences: the kind of explanation which is appropriate to a class often needs to be transformed in one way or another if it is to be recorded. In just the same way as, to turn a play into a film, you need to do more than put a cine camera in the auditorium, so the teacher producing educational material needs to do something different from recording just that she says or does before a class. Once that job of recording the factual information which is to be used by students has been done, then the role of a teacher in a face-to-face session for distance students becomes markedly different from that of an ordinary teacher. She is no longer the means of passing on information; rather she is there to help students learn information brought to them from outside. That Copernican revolution is one that many teachers in regular schools already welcome. W*here a tutor meets distance students face-to-face, her role is changed from being a communicator of information to that of a facilitator of learning.*

Dialogue between a student and tutor is only one kind of dialogue. There is extensive evidence that, where distance teaching materials are available, students can help each other to solve problems which in an ordinary class they would put to their teacher. This is the normal method of working for distant students in farm forums or radio schools; more surprisingly, perhaps, children learning from television in Niger found that they could and would solve each other's learning problems when there was no adult present. In formal education, then, there is a place for class work or group work, along with distance study. Group work looks even more important in adult education. A whole range of group-learning projects, from the radiophonic schools of Latin America to the farm forums of Africa and India, confirm that group learning can be effective, and can lead to group activity. The finding is buttressed by communication theory: the two-step and multi-step theories of human communication suggest that we are more likely to adopt an innovation if we discuss it with friends or colleagues than if we simply learn about it individually and passively. The combination of local interest and knowledge, possessed by a group of people meeting together, and information from scholars recorded in print or on tape, is a potent one: *group discussion is an effective method of learning when distance teaching is used to bring relevant information to the group.*

Distance teaching, then, can be effective and can stimulate dialogue. Linked with group study, it can extend education far beyond the confines of schools or colleges and can be related to community needs and interests. It can do all these things cheaply. But it will not do so cheaply if we have to provide anew the schools, the libraries or the network of teachers or extension agents which orthodox education and extension requires. We need to use what is already there. And experience of many projects suggests that, in many communities, there are resources which are under-used. Tevec, a distance teaching project in a poor area of Quebec, for example, had as an explicit aim to enable its students to make use of its resources in the community, nominally available to them, which they lacked the knowledge or confidence to take advantage of. Obviously the resources available will vary immensely from place to place, from time to time, and in their relevance to any particular educational programme. I*n most communities there are resources which can be used to support distance learning, to its educational and economic advantage.*

Methods

We started with 'method' in order to establish that distance teaching could face the major educational problems of access and of dialogue. But considerations of 'method' lead in another direction, too, into decisions about the best way of organizing distance teaching. If Statement is accepted, and a range of media are available to us, then there is no easy way of deciding which medium to use, in what way, for which purpose. But there is evidence to believe that several media are better than one. This may simply mean that to use more than one medium makes learning more fun, and therefore, perhaps, more effective, or that it enables information presented in one medium to reinforce that in another, or that individuals learn more easily from one rather than another. There is evidence that, in the United Kingdom, if we measure the proportion of people following a course, a multi-media approach is superior to one that relies on a single medium. A *multi-media programme is likely to be more effective than one which relies on a single medium.*

This does not solve our problems of choice. Distance teaching remains, for many educators and scholars, an uncharted area. We have very few years' experience of combining print, broadcasts and face-to-face learning in contrast with the centuries of experience of orthodox teachers, working with schools and books. We cannot - for better or worse - teach just as we were taught if we are to teach in a new medium; we need to plan to do something different. Experience so far suggests Statement 11: *a systems approach is helpful in planning distance education.*

The problems of students at a distance drive us on to three further statements.

We have already stressed the importance of dialogue to the student. But the benefits to the tutor are also important, and the problems for the tutor separated from her students are different from those of classroom teachers. Unless the tutor has some means of knowing how her students are working, she has no means of helping them and she cannot discover how successful are the materials she has created. *Feedback is a necessary part of a distance-learning system.*

Feedback can be of various kinds: the term embraces both feedback to the student, showing where he has understood or misunderstood, and feedback to the tutor or course writer. Some of the feedback to the student is immediate - if answers to questions in a correspondence course are printed at the back of the book, for example. But some is necessarily delayed and the distant student faces particular problems in learning by himself. It is peculiarly easy not to learn when studying by correspondence, or by following broadcasts. One can concentrate on the material, feeling that one is working hard, but remembering little of what one experiences. Even with generous opportunities for face-to-face learning, most distance study involves individuals working their way through material, and we cannot assume that tutorials will ensure learning. To help the student learn, the materials he is to use must be designed so that he does more than read or listen to them or watch them. *To be effective, distance-teaching materials should ensure that students undertake frequent and regular activities over and above reading, watching or listening.*

Feedback and active learning, the, are necessary for effective distance education, but a concentration on them does not answer the opening question about which medium to use for which purpose. If we group the media roughly into three - print, broadcasts (including recordings) and face-to-face meetings of any kind—then face-to-face communication has two qualities which differentiate it from the others. It makes possible immediate feedback between student and tutor, or dialogue between student and student, and its costs rise proportionately with the number of students, whereas economies of scale are possible with both print and broadcasts. It is this which, as we saw above, leads to central problems for us in reconciling the demands of education and economy. And it therefore suggests a paradoxical criterion for choice - to concentrate on the non-distant elements in order to design good distance teaching, and make wise use of all elements in multi-media education. Statement 14 therefore claims: *in choosing between media, the key decision on which the rest depend concerns the use of face-to-face learning.*

Another approach

We can look at all this another way, and state the argument more 'succinctly or set it out diagramatically, as in the figure. Educational media are similar in their effectiveness, but differ in the ways they can readily be distributed. This makes it possible to move away from the fixed staffing ratios necessary to face-to-face study, thereby changing the role of the teacher and making possible a reduction in costs. It is then possible to reach audiences different from the traditional ones, through distance teaching, and to do so at a reasonable cost. The equivalence of the media, however, presents us with problems of choice, best resolved by a multi media approach which allows for feedback and encourages active learning. In working out the approach to be used, the organization of any face-to-face element is of key importance and leads us to consider how to use distance teaching to ensure dialogue—something which is facilitated if a concern with new audiences and a new relation between education and the community lead to the use of groups as a basis for adult learning.

What is the use of it? And what is to be done? Is the construction of this sort of theory of any use? I'd suggest two tests for it. First, does it help anyone to see where and how distance teaching might be useful, or useless, for a particular educational job? Second, does the formulation of fourteen hypotheses suggest ways of testing them which would yield useful knowledge for practical educators?

country in the same way as other forms of higher learning, it is difficult to describe the distant students in unified, general terms. However, it is possible to distinguish three types of them according to the goals and the duration of their studies. There are undergraduate, part-time and postgraduate distant students.

Undergraduate distant students tale courses in order to prepare themselves for graduation. We find them, for instance, in England, South African, the Soviet Union, Poland, Czechoslovakia, Hungary, Romania, Bulgaria and East Germany. As they usually have also to work for a living they must extend their study time considerably. Often they have to carry this double burden for five to seven years, and in many cases even longer.

Part-time distant student are to be found among the regular students of a university. They enrol for recourses the contents of which are normally delivered by professors or lecturers in one semester. This type of student emerged especially in the United States, but also in Sweden, Norway and the Netherlands. It includes regular students who had to discontinue their studies for health, family of financial reasons or had to go into the armed forces but wish to use their free time for studying single course at a distance until they are able to resume their regular studies.

Post-graduate distant students are graduate students employed in the professions who wish to enrol in distance education courses in order to continue their education. Up to now this group has been comparatively small. But there are signs that it will grow considerably in the years to come.

Distance education will mean different things for the distant students of these three groups, and this will affect their motivation and commitment. For undergraduate students, studying at a distance is a central life task which determines their way of living for a long time in specific way. If they drop out, their plans for a professional future have failed and they have to dispense with the vocational promotion they had in mind. For the regular students who enrol in only one or in several single course, the new learning experience might merely be an interesting episode. And for the professional employees who are continuing their education, distance study will be considered as an additional task which will not bind them very much, especially if they volunteered to study at a distance and think that they can postpone it for any length of time.

A surprisingly large portion of the distant students are teachers or future teachers. In East Germany, for instance, there were more than 10,000 teachers enrolled in distance education in 1965. In the USSR, there were more than 261,000 distant students enrolled in teachers training college in 1961. Large groups of teachers can also be found among distant students in the Netherlands, the France, in the United States and Australia, in South Africa and India. In Cuba, Costa Rica, Mexico and in the Lebanon all distant students are teachers - as distance education was introduced in these countries just for them. The teachers studying at a distance can also be allotted to the three types described. In East Germany and eastern European countries they study mainly in order to pass the prescribed state examinations. In the United States younger teachers enrol in supplementary single courses. Postgraduate courses for senior teachers have been developed in Sweden, England and Australia. The number of distant students studying technical subjects is even larger. A third large group which has become more important in recent years consists of those persons who are studying economics at a distance.

Distant students are generally older than day students. In South Africa their average age is twenty-seven years, which means that on average they are seven years older. In the United States the average age is between 26.3 and 29.4 years. Most distant students belong to the age group up to thirty five years, but many of them are considerably older. In eastern countries there is an age limit. In western countries, however, it is possible to become a distant student if you are considerably older even that. At the University of Wisconsin, for instance, they have enrolled a seventy-year-old man and at the University of South Africa the oldest student was seventy-two years old.

As distance students are generally older than day students s greater portion of them are married and responsible for children. Experience has shown that married distant students are 'better' students. However, the years before and after their marriage are reported to be rather unfavourable for their studies. Female students often have to discontinue their studies for longer periods because they have had children.

The disadvantages of higher age, however, are compensated for b higher motivation. As distant students are more experienced in the world of work and in life, it is easier for them to judge the importance of graduation and continuing education for their professional development. Tutors, in particular, confirm that their maturity is obviously a favourable conditions for the learning process and the general progress of their studies. If their study programme is related to their vocational work, their motivation can be supported in a unique way.

For universities and colleges the higher age of their distant students means that they are in the process of slowly becoming institutes of adult education as will, which will make considerable adjustments necessary.

As there are only a few distant students in the Federal Republic of Germany, misunderstandings are likely regarding their image. In this country it could happen that the traditional concept of the working student will be transferred to the distant student. This would, however, be wrong, as this concept refers to the exceptional case and to a low social prestige, neither of which applies to distant students in most cases. In the United States, the second large group, this concept would be wrong, as many distant students do not work at all whereas many of the day students are compelled to work for a living.

People often think that distance education is preferred mainly by outsiders. There cannot possibly be so many outsiders. In western countries, however, one can often observe that distant students do indeed take a special course, and differ from the majority of students. However, in the United States nobody has any objection whatsoever to distant students, as this form of teaching and learning has a long tradition in that country. Distant students are even more likely to be respected than scorned, although group life is highly regarded on the campus. The students and the university teachers hold that distance education is 'more difficult' and compels the distant students to deal with the subject matter longer and more intensely than is the case with day students. If they have successfully finished their course, their achievements are duly acknowledged - in spite of their special way of studying.

The status of distant students is also different in East and West, as the respective societies judge the importance of vocational work quite differently - mainly for ideological reasons. Whereas the necessity of working for a living is considered to be rather an impediment to university studies in western countries, it is appreciated as a necessary precondition for successful university study in eastern countries. Typical of the western attitude is the remark of a Canadian professor who said, 'Every encouragement should be given to all persons who desire to become better educated and more highly trained, particularly those who have sufficient zeal and ambition to learn while they earn.' Apart from the view that vocational work is such a great, but unavoidable, burden that it could be carried only by distant students with special qualities, these works convey an attitude towards distance students which still suggests a philanthropic benevolence. It would be worth examining whether this attitude is disappearing in western industrialized countries.

In eastern European countries distant students are systematically made conscious of the fact that they have an obligation to society which they are expected to live up to, an din government and communist party reports they are called the 'pioneers of a new socialist intelligentsia'. In addition, they enjoy considerable financial privileges, and this is the reason why the image of the distant student is much more clear-cut and positive in these countries.

Teachers

Whereas commercial correspondence schools are sometimes criticized because of the doubtful qualifications of their teachers, university distance education can rely on the high academic standard of their teachers as they usually have to have the same credentials as the teachers on the campus.

Because distance education can take place only when special teaching functions are performed and because it is organized at regular universities as well as at special institutes, it is possible to subdivide teachers in distance education into five groups, each representing a special type.

Type 1: University teachers who are responsible for their day students as well as for distant students. Their traditional field of activities, which is already very complex, is extended by the additional functions of being an author of teaching material and a tutor of distant students. Many of them like these new functions and endeavour to become excellent in performing them. Writing teaching material for distant students is new for them as it differs decisively from writing down their lectures. They no longer write for the day student in the class or the auditorium, but for the student who sits at home and tries to reach his goals by reading the texts. As it is necessary to use their limited time necessary to use their limited time economically, such teachers will have to calculate their approach very carefully and thereby realize the importance of new didactical perspectives which induce them to separate the two groups of students and deal with them to separate the two groups of students and deal with them in different ways. The function of a tutor of distant students is also new to such a teacher. It will call for developing further those guiding and counselling functions which are used when talking with the day students about their tests and seminar papers—a considerable educational task.

- *Type 2*: Teachers at distance teaching colleges and at departments for distance education in universities. They deal with distant students only, which changes the profile of their work. It consists mainly of writing teaching material and tutoring. As they can specialize in these activities, they are more likely to develop new concepts of distance teaching of their own.

In the Federal Republic of Germany, professors and lectures who deal exclusively with distant students are still unknown and do not correspond with the current idea of university teachers. In other countries, however, there are university teachers who even prefer this new form of teaching, as it certainly does not exclude research activities. This remains true, although an American professor for distance teaching, when asked about the difference between teaching day students and distant students, said frankly: 'I have to write more, to telephone more, to deal with more visitors and have less time for research.'

- *Type 3:* University teachers who conduct seminars for distant students regularly. A typical representative of this type I the *Konsulent* in East Germany, where a considerable amount of distance education consists of obligatory face-to-face teaching. Generally, they are lecturers and readers working under the supervision of a professor. they perform a very demanding job as they have to combine and adjust principles of face-to-face teaching with those of distance teaching, which is difficult as there are no traditional patterns for this special teaching approach.
- *Type 4*: A professor who typically does not write any teaching material and does not correct assignments at all, but exchanges letters with a number of advanced students in order to guide and conduct their doctoral studies. There students usually live far away from the university and are working in the production process. At this level of university education the work of a student is already so specialized and individualized that regular courses will no longer do. Furthermore, these students are already so self-reliant and have become able to master the techniques of acquiring knowledge b methodical reading that they need professional advice which is given to them by their academic mentor. An experiment at the National Extension College in the United Kingdom shows that this type of

distance duration can also be tried out and be successful at a lower level.

- *Type 5*: University teachers who assume responsibility for the management of distance teaching departments of institutions. They are confronted with tasks differing decisively from the corresponding tasks at conventional universities. Vice-chancellors and presidents, for instance, do not normally deal with teaching problems, as this task is dealt with by the individual professors or lecturers. The heads of distance teaching universities or departments, however, have to see to it that the contributions of all departments and sections can be guided and adapted in such a way that they fit together and elicit the intended learning effects. Furthermore, they have to keep complex technical systems going as the success of distance teaching relies on them entirely.

The programmes of study of distance teaching departments and universities show that university teachers of all academic ranks contribute to it. Often the proportion of full professors is higher than at traditional universities, as they are responsible for the courses and often like to write them themselves. In addition professors from other universities are invited to participate in writing the courses. This indicates that distance education is by no means something which is accomplished merely at the level of lecturers and readers.

Often the question is discussed whether teachers in distance education should have qualities different from teachers on the campus. Ossian Mackenzie of the University of Pennsylvania thinks different from teachers on the campus. Ossian Mackenzie of the University of Pennsylvania thinks that they should combine scientific knowledge and intellectual capabilities with the rare gift to motivate and to guide. Charles Wedemeyer of the University of Wisconsin said that the distance teacher must be able to write efficiently, have a good sense of humour and, above all, be a good teacher. One might wish to attribute these qualities to every university teacher. It is, however, striking that opinions like these can be met very often. Presumably, particularly good teaching is expected from the teacher in distance education as a compensation for not having the students in the classroom. People might think that this 'handicap' can be overcome by special personal and methodical qualities. Perhaps teachers in distance education are also expected to be particularly good as they have to deal with adults calling for new and therefore unusual approaches to teaching.

Models of university-level distance education

If we examine university-level distance education in various countries of the world we can see that the special educational traditions and socio-economic conditions of these countries have led to individual models of distance education in each case. In spite of this, it is possible to identify two distinct, supra-national models of distance education if we disregard some particular developments and minor exceptions: a western and an eastern one. They differ with regard to their rank in national educational policy, the competent and responsible persons for it in the hierarchy of the university, the degree of their organizational integration into the university, and the methods of teaching and learning employed.

Rank in national educational policy

The rank of the two models in the national educational policy can be easily identified when we consider the reasons for establishing distance education. In western countries the universities originally intended to help certain fringe groups to take part in university studies. Here, they were very much in the tradition of private correspondence schools or colleges. They were aimed at the individual person who was prevented from attending university by adverse circumstances. The number of distant students was, therefore, usually relatively small. Hence, distance education was not an important issue with educational politicians. As a rule it was neglected in the same way as correspondence education.

In eastern European countries the situation was entirely different. Here, distance education was introduced and developed systematically by the respective ministries of higher education in order to increase the number of qualified specialists in many branches of the economic and political system. At the same time, the governments intended to provide for additional access to the professions for wider sections of the working people. Finally, the governments believed that distance education was a good example for reaffirming the ideological concept of the close connection of theory and practice. Such a high degree of political motivation and, above all, the enormous demand of highly qualified specialists meant that the number of distant students increased so dramatically in the fifties and sixties that they made up a considerable percentage of the students in the universities - that is, 20 to 50 per cent, and in some disciplines even more. Only recently have these high numbers of students been somewhat reduced. This does not, however, detract from the great political importance of distance education at universities in eastern European countries. Experts assure us that this form of university study has become a permanent part of higher education. Legally, it is entirely on a par with that of traditional university study.

Areas of responsibility

The different goals of distance education have also led to different areas of responsibility. In the western model the establishment of distance education rests usually with the departments of university extension or adult education. These departments decide the contents and procedures of their distance education themselves. The result can be highly differentiated programmes, as, for instance, at the University of Wisconsin and the University of Nebraska. On the other hand, one can also find meagre programmes with a small number of accidental and unrelated correspondence courses often administered by only one secretary.

The relative autonomy of these departments has a special negative effect, in that they do not coordinate their programmes with those of other universities. For instance, American universities have developed fifty-eight different courses for distance education under the title *Survey of the history of the USA*. Clearly, this goes against important principles of distance education, especially against those of rationalization and centralization.

The eastern European model of distance study, however, can usually rely on centralized planning and coordination by the respective ministries of higher education,which also adapt the distant study programmes to the requirements of the economic system. Sometimes central institutes have been established to prepare and distribute the necessary teaching and study material and to examine problems of teaching at a distance for the benefit of all universities.

Integration into the hierarchy of the university

The way in which distance education is integrated into the hierarchy of the university sheds some light on its relative institutional importance.

As has already been mentioned,in western countries distance education is usually organized by a section of the department of university extension or adult education. As these departments lack the academic reputation and the weight and power of the classical faculties or departments, this organizational structure is bound to be detrimental to the healthy development of distance education. The same can be said about universities which cooperate with correspondence colleges outside the university by using their course material as,for instance, the University of Lund. There,distance education is even less integrated. An extreme form of this non-integration of distance education can be found when the university limits itself to conducting final examinations only and relies on private correspondence colleges for the teaching of the courses. For a very long time the University of London was a good example of this approach.

medium—the correspondence course—to bi-or multimedia teaching activities. The new technical media force them to objectify longer sequences of their teaching. Careful, time-consuming and expensive preparations have now become inevitable. All the problems of planning the teaching-learning process, especially the division of labour between the teachers and media experts, and the organization and control of learning activities, assume a new importance.

Fortunately, the new model of distance study can profit from the 'technological turn' in the methodology of teaching which can at present be identified - mainly as a consequence of experiments with programmed learning. Today, it is easier to recognize the characteristic outlines of the emerging new model of distance education and to further its progressive elements than it would have been only a few years ago, because the newly developed 'educational technology' already provides us with a number of categories necessary for analysing and describing it.

Such assistance, though, cannot be expected from an educational technology which regards itself as the technical or instrumental side of the teaching-learning process only and attempts to reinforce it. Rather, we will have to look out for an educational technology which concentrates on the use of scientific methods and procedures for the planning, development and evaluation of teaching-learning projects. A. A. Lumsdaine, who described such an educational technology for the first time, said that it depends on the scientific disciplines related it in the same way as, for instance, the technology of engineering depends physics and the technology of medicine on biology. In short, the technological turn in the methodology of teaching and learning means that those process are to be explored and manipulated which can help to influence the learning situation.

Flechsing has pointed out that the technological turn in the methodology of teaching is brought about in five phases. In the first phase, the technical medium is used to stimulate the teacher, in the second phase this approach is given up and teaching techniques are developed in a rational way, which are optimized in the third phase. In the fourth phase, teaching techniques are coordinated with the help of systems approach, and in the last phase the development work is based on curriculum research and the duplication of teaching techniques.

It is important to investigate how the western and eastern models of distance education relate to these phases, and what the possible features of the coming technological model of distance education will be...

If we analyse the relationship of distance education to the five phases of the technological development we can conclude that it had a remarkable affinity to some of these phases long before this concept was developed. and, on the other hand, we can identify several features which do not yet correspond to these phases. In other words, distance education is partly a forerunner of educational technology and in part still lacks the specific technological development.

Such a partial delay need not concern or

discourage distance education experts. It can already be considered to be remarkable progress that study can be improved as the technological model displays the standards of future developments in distance education. Only ten years ago the improvement of projects of distance education took lace more or less arbitrarily at best based on conjectures or according to the principle of trail and error. Even if money was available, one could not really identify the critical factors in the system of distance education which needed purposeful changes. The real contribution of the new educational technology is that now things have changed. It provides us with a system of scientific instruments and procedures which enable us to improve distance education systematically and also verify the outcomes. Even more: if we match a given project of distance education with the five phases of the technological turn its structural advantages and deficits become clearly visible. This is very favourable precondition for slowly raising the development of distance education to higher levels of accomplishment.

An additional advantage of the new technological model of distance education is that the techniques of planning, designing and optimizing projects in distance education can be favourable for the further development of distance study at university level.

Which of the three models of distance education will become dominant? We believe that the western and eastern models will continue for a considerable time, as they have already become a matter of routine and have also become a tradition. The technological model is much more demanding, as special experts, very expensive media and organizational systems will be required. For this reason, only a slow development can be predicted. In the long run, however, this model will permeate all endeavours of the teaching at a distance at university level.

5 Distance Education Curriculum

This chapter represents the results of our reflection on a specific innovation in distance education: the Deakin University Master of Education course 'ECS 802 Curriculum Theory'. As the reader will soon discover, the course was informed by a particular view of education and curriculum, but practice turned out to be something other than our theory envisaged, giving us the opportunity to improve the theory and our practice. In the following pages we give a brief outline of the structure of the course and offer an interpretation of some of the issues it has raised for those working on it over its five-year history. The chapter is organized in two major sections with a brief conclusion. The first section is a descriptive account, giving the background, rationale and brief history of the course from 1983 to 1987. The second provides an analysis of several issues which emerge out of the self-understanding of the course - a perspective which attempts to place the work and ideas of the course in a general curriculum context. In the conclusion we return to some of the central concerns which have structured, and continue to structure, the nature of the course as an examination of the curriculum problem.

The 'Curriculum Theory course is one of the about eighteen courses available within the Deakin University Master of Education and Master of Education Administration degree programmes. It is a whole-year course, valued are two semester units. The handbook outline for the course reads as follows:

This course distinguishes theories of curriculum from theories of curriculum development, and introduces students to an approach to curriculum theory. Students read monographs introducing some 'conceptual furniture' for thinking about curriculum.

The course is modeled on a professional association: the main work of the course is expressed through professional reading in curriculum (guided by a course bibliography), writing for other students in a course journal, and carrying out a project. Through this collaboration, the course community develops a critical perspective on contemporary curriculum theorizing and the conceptual furniture proposed in the monographs.

This outline introduces several point about the course: its particular view about curriculum as dynamic the idea of students learning as part of a community of scholars, and the idea that students should develop a critical perspective. These were initial aspirations about the course and after five years they provide a basis for a critical review. In order to do this, it will necessary at times to reflect on issues in a wider frame of social change, away from the specifics of curriculum and the course itself.

General background: 'The hope...'

To make a sense of the idea of a Masters level

course taught in the distance education mode, it is first necessary to know something of Deakin University and its character as a provider of distance education. Of the four distinguishing features of the University noted in the 1988 *Handbook,* the following is given them most emphasis: 'but perhaps the most singular distinction is that it provides the option of either on-campus or off-campus study, being considered a leader in the field of distance education'. Established in 1977, Deakin University was invested with a charter for providing courses in a distance education mode; a model that had already been developed in the Open University in Britain. Deakin University started at a time of dramatic expansion of the tertiary education sector in Australia; thus its formative years were in a period of relative luxury for tertiary education.

In the late 1970s and early 1980s the School Education at Deakin University became involved in the development of postgraduate courses that were innovative in two senses: first, they were to be offered solely in the distance education mode; and second, they involved offering a range of fresh interpretations of the areas of curriculum, classroom process and educational administration. The course 'Curriculum Theory' aimed to be innovative in both these senses. In its development phase it was conceptualized as a key unit in a sequence of courses in curriculum in the Masters programme - one that would not only introduce students to curriculum as a field of study, but which would also help students explore recent developments in thinking about curriculum issues - the forms of theorizing and of as appropriate to content, problems and issues of the field.

The initial ideas about the 'Curriculum Theory course were inspired by an increasing concern to explore the general patterns of thinking in the field of curriculum. Yet course team members found themselves caught in a unique dilemma: the course they offered was not only *about* curriculum, at the same time it *was* a curriculum. To avoid contradiction, the course would have to be quite explicit in exemplifying any curriculum ideas and principles it chose to advocate. Course team members realized that they could not offer just a guided tour of the literature of curriculum - a reading course which left questions of the 'livid curriculum' of the course to chance. It had to model a set of curriculum principles in its practice. The issue of theory and practice in curriculum was thus a real and compelling one for the makers of the 'Curriculum Theory' curriculum. Their own curriculum and curriculum development practice should provide a model of the practice of curriculum theorizing, and the course should construct a set of tasks for students in such a way that they, too, could encounter and engage issues of the relationships between theory and practice in their own curriculum work.

But the problem was not only one of exemplifying an agreed or accepted theory of curriculum in practice. As the recent literature of curriculum had shown, new views of curriculum theory were emerging in the field. The idea of 'theory' also needed to be made problematic. It was recognized that students might well find this unfamiliar and difficult; it could not be assumed that many, let alone most, had previously encountered the idea that, to construct a theory, one actually needs a theory of what 'theory' is—a *meta-theory*. In curriculum this means having a theory about the nature of curriculum theory. It means being able to distinguish different kinds of curriculum theories in terms of their theories of curriculum. In identifying the need for a discussion of meta-theory, the course team was acknowledging that presumption about the nature of curriculum theory and theorizing are potentially invidious, carrying sometimes unrecognized and unexamined assumptions about the nature of curriculum itself. Particularly at the time when the course was first mooted, the course team was aware that the terms of curriculum theory were changing - that the field was entering a new phases. These changes could be understood in terms of meta-theory so the course team regarded it as important to focus on meta-theory in order to offer an interpretation of the quite concrete, changing patterns of assumptions that characterized contemporary trends in the field.

A first aspect of the change in curriculum theory and theorizing could be discerned in its view of the central role of teachers in curriculum theorizing—in addition to their role in curriculum planning, curriculum change and curriculum realization. The emergence of a strong professional consciousness in the teaching service had been given structure be the trend toward school-based curriculum development and away from the central control of the curriculum processes by state education departments. In Australia this trend was the producer of a struggle be Victorian teacher unions for greater influence in curriculum matters as a 'terms and conditions' issue through the late 1960s and earl 1970s. They saw curriculum issues as of similar importance to other industrial issues, since curriculum matters so directly affected the nature and conditions of teachers' work. Outside Australia the trend had been fostered by British arguments for the centrality of teachers in curriculum research and development, for example, in the work of Lawrence Stenhouse, and in the United States by arguments for curriculum deliberation by teachers as a mode of curriculum theorizing, for example, by Joseph Schwab and Decker Walker. An awareness of these theoretical arguments and political struggles has led various Deakin researchers to work on the development of 'action research' as a modus operandi for those people at the front line of curriculum actualization - an approach which recognized the exigencies of specific social sites and the importance or the active participants in the work at those sites having control in the planning processes.

A second set of changes in the understanding of curriculum in the literature was the emergence of 'critical' theorizing about curriculum. At the time the 'Curriculum Theory' course was being planned, course team members were grappling with some of the implications of this view of curriculum theorizing in their own work. One source of this new 'critical' view drew on the insights of the new sociology of education' and the Marxian/structuralist work of people such as Bowles and Gintis in North America. Another source was more local; Deakin theorists of curriculum were beginning to explore the ramifications of the Frankfurt School of critical theory which had produced a critique of 'scientific' reasoning in contemporary social life; they had begun to make new connections between action research and ideology-critique in a conception of a critical educational science. These developing theoretical perspectives on curriculum, based on work at Deakin and elsewhere, when combined with the awareness of the impact of the school-based curriculum development trend, provided some fundamental ideas for a course about curriculum.

In 1981-1982 the course team began serious work in preparation for teaching 'Curriculum Theory' for the first time in 1983. They were assisted in their work by consultants appointed to bring particular expertise to the development of the course. These consultants were the late Professor Lawrence Stenhouse and Dr Jean Rudduck, 5 at that time members of the Centre for Applied Research of the University of East Anglia in England, and Professor Ulf Lundgren from the Department of Educational Research of the Stockholm Institute of Education in Sweden. Stenhouse and Rudduck brought with them a great deal of experience and insight into the matters related to thinking about the roles of teachers in curriculum research and development; Lundgren brought with him ideas emerging from the Marxian inspired theorist of social reproduction. These three people provided perspectives which, when combined, picked up on two of the major trends in thinking about the curriculum of the time.

In a deliberations with the course team Stenhouse Rudduck explored ideas related to students thinking about curriculum within the context of their particular forms of teaching practice.6. This notion developed from the attempt to hold the theory/practice relationship together and to avoid the separation of these elements which characterizes many postgraduate courses. From the outset the course aspired to develop approaches which helped teachers and others to articulate and elaborate ideas and issues based on actual teaching situations. Stenhouse and Rudduck thus provided a subtle but significant shift in the self understanding of the course - a shift 'theory' to *'theorizing'*. On the basis of Stenhouse's previous work developing the nation of the teacher as an 'extended professional'. the course team began to explore ways in which the course could support the development of extended professionalism in its students.

The action-based approach to studying one's won work context provided a fundamental statement of principle and a practical basis for the development of the pedagogy of the course. One of the ways this orientation to action came to be enacted in the course design was in the notion that students would conduct *projects* in which they explored their own work and working situations. it was also to be enacted by making the theorizing required by these projects public. Research is systematic enquiry made public. It is made public for criticism and utilization within a particular research tradition. In keeping with this definition Stenhouse and Rudduck advocated the development of an information exchange forum within the course and, given the nature of the distance education situation, in which students would not have direct contact with either their peers or tutors, the idea turned out to be extremely important for the *annual conference* at which they read and discussed papers face-to-face. The ideas of the journal and the annual course conference thus became central to the pedagogical design of the course.

Ulf Lundgren's contribution occurred after that of Stenhouse and Rudduck. As noted previously, he brought with him an interest in understanding the curriculum in terms of relationship between schooling and society. Lundgren's work had left into a way of thinking about the structure of the curriculum in terms of its relationship to the economic mode of production in a society. In this sense his was a classic Marxian approach one that formulated a way of thinking about social instructions in terms of their relative positions in the base/superstructure framework of Marxian thinking. His analysis was fresh and powerful. It built on emerging tradition of a critical or conflict approach to thinking about the structure of the curriculum. While Rudduck and Stenhouse had greatly influenced the course teams's ideas about the pedagogy of the course, Lundgren's contribution was especially important in giving focus to the content of the course. It was agreed that he would write a monograph for the course as a statement of his theoretical ideas about curriculum which could, on the one hand, problematize the field and the notion of 'curriculum' for students, and, on the other, provide a common point of reference for students and the course team in their own projects, reflection and writing.

Curriculum is to be understood as part of the social and historical process by which the social relationships necessary for production are reproduced.

then the task of curriculum theory is to develop general theories capable of understanding and explaining the specific theories which inform specific curricula. In this sense Lundgren regards the study of curriculum theory as meta-theoretical.

Lundgren's ideas, when placed beside those of Stenhouse and Rudduck, helped provide a general conceptual framework for the course. Stenhouse and Rudduck had provided the basis for the primary pedagogical considerations of the course, while Lundgren had provided the primary theoretical questions. At the same time the course could also understand itself in the terms of Lundgren's theoretical framework as aiming to produce — or reproduce — a different kind of teaching force in Australia: one committed to what Stenhouse described as 'extended professionalism'. The course team understood itself to be selecting the critical curriculum theorizing and practice of some teachers and teachers' organizations, and preparing a pedagogy capable of reproducing this extended professionalism among its students as a rising generation of curriculum theorist-practitioners. The way these two dimensions came together can be seen in an image provided by a short comment in the *Study Guide* produced for the first offering of the course in 1983. The statement read: 'The long term aim of the course is to help you change the way you do things in the light of what you know. This major aspiration of the course was given a structure by the ideas and suggestions of Rudduck, Stenhouse and Lundgren, but it is equally important to recall that the perspectives of these people were set against a stream of research and theorizing by

Deakin researchers over the preceding years. That is, the ideas built up in the planning phase of the course were set down on a foundation of several years of work that related to different aspects of the problem of the curriculum. This point is clearly demonstrated in the following extract from the 1983 *Study Guide:*

In terms of historical and political processes which produced the *Curriculum Theory* course, it is a product of a continuous line of development in the work of Deakin staff interested in curriculum — a development which has taken place over the last few years. It has involved research on teacher action research, long-term in-service work with teachers helping them to develop a critical perspective on their own practices, and a great deal of critical reflection on our own teaching practices.

At a more concrete level the work of the course team, in the planning phase, can be characterized in terms of the agreement reached on the key ideas or propositions of the course and the actual structural components of the pedagogy of the course. These were described in the first *Study Guide* which presented students with four key propositions and one supporting theme, a composite list which provided the surface text of the theoretical aspirations of the course:

1 Any curriculum (text *for* pedagogy) or any curriculum theory (text *about* pedagogy) is a unique product of the *historical and political circumstances* and processes which produced it.

2 Any curriculum or curriculum theory expresses particular values and value systems; implicitly or

explicitly, it expresses a social and moral philosophy. By examining these value commitments and the social relationships which support them, we may identify the *ideological* aspect of the curriculum or theory.

3 Any curriculum or curriculum theory likewise takes an implicit or explicit stand on the nature of knowledge. By examining its perspective on subject-matter (of learning or of curriculum theory) we may identify the *epistemological* aspects of curriculum theory.

4 Any curriculum or curriculum theory expresses, implicitly or explicitly, a view about the organization of teaching and learning. A curriculum theory therefore, is also a theory about *pedagogical* action.

A fifth point, which emerges out of these four, was that a dialectical conception of theory and practice could assist students to develop a platform for *critique* in which action and understanding could be seen as mutually constitutive, constantly and critically informing one another.

The pedagogical structure of other course was designed to permit students to explore these five points critically and self-critically in their own day-to-day practice as well as in the work of the course. It included:

1 the production of a *course journal* based on contribution from all course participants (students and course team) in several distinct 'departments' (*theoretical articles* addressing the 'conceptual furniture' of the Lundgren

monograph, *activity reports* through which students reported on their explorations of the key propositions of the course in their own practice, contributed *abstracts* of reading done for the course, and *correspondence* with other course members about their contributions);

2 the holding of an *annual course conference* at which papers would be presented and discussed;

3 *project work* by course participants which would permit actual curriculum theorizing undertaken in participants' own curriculum settings, with a major project to be conducted throughout the year and reported on in a project report, and smaller-scale investigative activities (perhaps contributing to the major project) to be carried out along the way and reported in the *Course Journal* and at the conference; and

4 engagement in a wide range of *reading and reflection* on curriculum as a basis for reflection both on one's own practical activities and on theoretical ideas being discussed in the *Journal*.

Being constructed on these pedagogical principles, the 'Curriculum Theory' course set itself against the view that it is the task of teachers to present a 'correct' view of the subject matter of a course, or a variety of competing but more-or-less adequate views. In this way it challenged a conventional liberal view, widely held in universities since the Enlightenment, that a variety of competing, more or less adequate, views of a subject should be presented so that students can choose among them. This Enlightenment view may seem to be important in any course which aims to be 'critical'. In practice, however, the presentation of alternative views in many higher education courses if frequently no more than a manifestation of the 'marketplace' notion of debate criticized by Maclntyre. On the 'marketplace' notion staff frequently present views without sufficiently engaging the arguments between them and sometimes distort their presentations s o that their theoretical preferences are clearly implied even though insufficiently justified by argument). Similarly students are not compelled to argue the strengths and weaknesses of competing theories; a choice between them is regarded as a matter of private conviction, not public justification. In such cases the substance of points of view is regarded as separate from the substance of arguments for and against them ; by this means the process of debate itself, through which the compulsion to support or reject views is secured, is made secondary, and 'holding' views is treated as more significant than sustaining them through argument . For such reasons the 'Curriculum Theory' course constructed itself as a 'community' of enquirers', creating a journal and a conference, and requiring correspondence between students. For such reasons also it prescribed the Lundgren monograph as a focus for debate— as a proto-theory to be tested against students' views and the views of the literature of curriculum. The course was thus to be constructed through critical and self-critical debate in which students would be required to argue about the strengths and limitations of Lundgren's views, the views of the course team and each other's views. Their commitment to the debate would be secured by making their own practice a source for and an object of their enquiries.

The description of 'Curriculum Theory' so far has given some background to the development of the course for its first offering in 1983, illustrating some of its major assumptions and its strong sense that it should be explicit about its own pedagogy as a curriculum about curriculum. It describes features of the course that were themselves to undergo change in the light of experience of the course in practice, when its 'hopes' became — or did not become — 'happenings'.

A Description of Five Years of ECS 802: 'The Happening...'

The first number of the *Course Journal* was prepared by the course team and some other people, such as David Hamilton from Glasgow, who might be described as an 'outer circle' of 'associate members' of the course. It was a primer, one to be set up as a starting point for the sort of contributions which were anticipated from all course members. The protocol for student publication involved submission of articles to a tutor who would determine if the pieces satisfied explicitly stated course requirements for journal submissions. If there was any doubt about the standard of the work submitted, it was to be second-checked by another tutor and returned to the student with recommendations for rectifying the particular problems. In this sense the course team was to function as an editorial board. The difficulty in entering into the sort of public exchange anticipated by the *Journal* structure is captured in the words of one of the first contributions in Volume 1, Number. The statement commenced with the following remark:

It is not clear if this statement represented the view

and emotions of other course participants. People wrote articles about theoretical issues, about their attempts to interpret the curriculum activities they were engaged in, about the books and papers they were reading *and* about their reactions to other people's ideas (as reported in previous *Journals).* The *Journals* came out on a regular basis and information started to filter across the various departments (theoretical articles, activity reports, abstracts, correspondence). People wrote about Lundgren's monograph and started to move around the various pieces of his 'conceptual furniture'. Lundgren's proto-theory provided the common reference point for placing curriculum issues in a wider context. In August 1983 a course conference was conducted in which people who had known each other only abstractly, through their journal writing, met each other and talked in person. Fifteen people attended, including some invited speakers. Those people unable to attend submitted 'display papers'. The forum provided a significant extension to the theme of the course, giving it a moment of life and vitality that is important in all forms of education.

Looking back at the entries in the *Journal* in 1983, one can detect a sense of the long-term patterns of concerns which were to emerge time and again in subsequent years. The following comments lifted from Volume 1, Number 4 (the final issue of the first year of the course) are indicative of trends and concerns which were to become consolidated in subsequent years. For example, with regard to the Lundgren monograph: 'The more I am working through this course the more restricted I am beginning to feel having to use Lundgren's furniture.

I feel the meanings of some of the terms he uses are too narrow, or fluctuate'. A different type of comment, but one that clearly related to the philosophical underpinnings of the course, noted the following concern:

To my mind the real reason for the reactionism emanating from the course developers is their inability to appreciate that although this course is based in materialism (which they acknowledge) they have been prepared to accept material from participants who do not utilize materialism's philosophical underpinnings. This does not mean that course participants must believe in materialism, rather I am expressing the view that argument put forward in course material must be based in support or attack of that philosophy. However, what has been obvious from the first articles in the Journals is writing based in Platonic idealism but lacking a perspective critical of the Marxist materialist view.

Comments like these raise questions about the epistemological framework of the course and its pedagogy, especially its notion of the course as a 'professional association'.

At a different level other comments point to a different type of reaction, one that aligned more closely with the *hope* of the course team and, in particular, to the ideals espoused by Stenhouse and Rudduck. This point relates to the opportunity afforded by the course structure to take apart and reassemble one's particular context of work.

What has appealed to me is the valuing and recognition of my everyday knowledge about curriculum by the course team and other course participants. This affirmation via the journal, curriculum conference and tutor's comments has encouraged me to lay out more of my practice for scrutiny and in so doing has given me greater control over it.

Not all students had such a positive reaction to 'Curriculum Theory', of course, and course team members were not uniformly satisfied with the quality of students' work.

In the latter part of 1985 a review of the course was conducted by Terry Evans from the Deakin University Distance Education Unit. This evaluation provided insights into both the theoretical scope and the pedagogy of the course. Evans discovered a high degree of confusion and apprehension amongst the students he interviewed. In his words, '... the most important single point about the students was that they were not expecting the sort of course that they received'. The largest cause of this confusion, in his opinion, was students' lack of familiarity with the neo-Marxist perspective and/or the history of educational thought. This particular concern was most manifest in having to work with the Lundgren monograph. Evans noted that 'the monograph represents the central component of the course and is also the location of most of the problems for the students'.

Staff were running into difficulties too. In the area of the course pedagogy there were many concerns associated with the trials and tribulations of turning course material around in sufficient detail and time to be meaningful. The process required that tutors read and check submissions against course requirements, decide whether they could be published as they stood or whether resubmission should be required, hand over material to be published to a course assistant who would collate, paginate and index the material, send it off to the University's Printery for reproduction, and ensure that it was sent out promptly to students. The process, while administratively routine, was easily disrupted. Tutors much be away at the time material was received, arranging the first check of material against course requirements might take longer than the few days allowed in planning the process, second checking adds time to the process, compiling the material might be held up by late student submissions, and occasionally delays could occur when the University's Printery or mail-out facilities were unable to process the material speedily. Alongside this production process, tutors were expected to respond to students' work individually, offering suggestions, advice and evaluative comment. This assessment process was also demanding, since students' work varied greatly with their individual interests and work settings, so no marking could be considered 'routine'. Through the year students were submitting as many as fifteen pieces of work, varying from one-paragraph abstracts of *Journal* articles to substantial project reports. The assessment load was thus substantial in quantity and demanding because of the rather relentless course schedule.

One of Evans' concluding comments provides a summary for the first few years of operation:

The task of constructing a critical community at a distance is no mean challenge. From the evidence of the present group of students it has not been achieved, but there has been some progress. For example, almost all the students said that they did not feel that they were members of a *Curriculum Theory* critical community—one said that the feeling was of a 'sense of loneliness on the course'—but several students did feel that they were more involved with each other than in other distance education courses at Deakin or elsewhere. These points are worthy of some elaboration, for they pull into sharp relief the different elements of this course. The substance of Evans' analysis will be developed further through the ideas and observations of one of the students of the course who, in the pages of the *Course Journal*, provided some telling insights into the life of 'Curriculum Theory' as a course for students.

In 1986 one of the students, Rigmor George, conducted a continuing critique of both the course in general and the Lundgren monograph in particular. He comments neatly encapsulated concerns expressed by some students and the course team:

Critical meta-theories
Now it is this context that ECS 802 is presented. Not only is it dealing with meta-theories of education, it is itself a product of one of them. Not only is it altering us to the ideological implications of curricula, it carries with it its own ideological message.

George notes that a 'critical theory approach to curriculum' is one that'... maintains the issues are political and related to the much wider and more pervasive social theory which is capitalistic'.

relationships. Perhaps personal individual relationships would work better—phone calls, in person conversations, and letters between students might be a good idea.

The idea expressed here has been the concern of a number of students other than Rigmor George; and their concerns are legitimate. What comes into question is the very frame we use to think about this issue. Using ideas lifted from the times and places when education was always intimate and face-to-face does not help in our understanding of the form of social relationships which are increasingly separated and distant. This is the substantive curriculum question of '*Curriculum theory*' and other distance education courses. Among the course team, at least initially, there was a tendency to see the issue as a problem of a 'theory/practice gap'; one in which theorizing is done in one context and practice in another. Some may see this as a technical issue in which the challenge is to find a technical and bureaucratic solution to the delivery of educational ideas. This approach accepts as fundamental a distinction between theory and practice. Others, however, regard a distinction between theory and practice as committing one to false dichotomy. Such people attempt to demonstrate in the design of courses that theory and practice are mutually constitutive. On this latter view the so-called 'gap' is treated as a matter of logical inconsistency. Many of the arguments associated with 'Curriculum Theory' have been set within the limits of one or other of these positions, embracing different dimensions of arguments that have held away in earlier times. Lundgren's insight into the 'representation problem' is one way of characterizing the parameters of the theory/practice issue, at least to the extent that Lundgren's view of meta-theory puts the theory/practice issue on the agenda of curriculum debates. The debates in the pages of the *Course Journal* have generally utilized a limited range of perspectives for thinking about the substantive problem of the curriculum, but in doing so they have remained wedded to the ideas of a bygone era. They have accepted as fundamental the distinction between theory and practice in ways characteristic of the curriculum, theorizing that developed and tool root in an earlier period of curriculum theory. What is required now is a fresh perspective on the curriculum issue. In words reminiscent of Geothe's views of 150 years before, the contemporary Australian curriculum theorist Doug White wrote: "Thought and action, intellectual and material production are inextricably linked in the modern world ... The issue before us is not whether intellect and action are combined, but on what terms'. The final part of this section will highlight the attempts within the course to move towards such an understanding.

In 1986, partly as a result of the survey conducted by Terry Evans, we decided to introduce a second monograph, *Between Hope and Happening*. This second monograph developed an argument about the changing the meta-theoretical commitments of several key curriculum theorists of the last forty years, to illustrate how and why the 'critical' position of some contemporary curriculum theorists had emerged. The importance of this new position, it was argued, is that it has not only put new issues on the curriculum agenda, but it has also required new social relations and forms of spheres. In this sense the course has staked a genuine claim in the territory of curriculum theory and as a component of the idea of distance education. A brief elaboration of the different perspectives developed, highlighting an emerging thread which has held the practice of the course together, would confirm this point. Yet to do so risk remaining on the surface of the activities of the course and taking different participants' views of the course at face value; beneath this surface, between rather than on the lines of its next, however, an unfolding logic can be discerned. This unfolding logic shaped, and continuous to shape, the cultural foundations on which the ideas of the course are constructed. As we have attempted to show, the course strove to make students aware and active in their roles as curriculum workers, not simply as cogs in the machine of social reproduction, but as the producers of curriculum, and through show, the course was only partially successful in achieving this aim. The 'hope' was yet unrealized in the 'happening'.

Nevertheless, the course team retained the 'hope' of enacting the view of curriculum workers as the producers of history in a communitarian practice.

This is no easy task. Changing social relationships to allow curriculum workers to enact this emancipatory ideal requires not only changes in the social relations of schooling but also new kinds of interpretation of curriculum work and the social condition. these changes must occur not only in schooling but also in the construction of courses about curriculum. Reflecting on our emancipatory aspirations in the light of our analysis of the 'Curriculum Theory' course, we have come to an understanding of a new dilemma confronting the course: the dilemma of creating *a communitarian* practice in *distance education*. This is a dilemma to be faced by a variety of groups aiming to enact a critical view of distance education, not just for members of the Deakin 'Curriculum Theory' course.

Our account of the first five years of the 'Curriculum Theory' course has highlighted concerns about the course which point to a confusion about expectations about the nature of distance education generally and the study of curriculum specifically. The analysis to this point has concentrated on establishing a warrant for a new perspective on the nature of the curriculum problem for people whose work is the production of curricula and, through curricula, of the social relations and social life of society. Through the course is still far from exemplary in achieving its aims, we have attempted to argue that its steps towards a collaborative, communitarian practice of curriculum critique and curriculum production are at least suggestive of models of curriculum work appropriate for a society in which people can legitimately see themselves as the producers, not just the products, of history. Our reflection on the history of the course has revealed a potential contradiction between the practice of distance education and the collaborative, communitarian practice which the course aimed to foster.

In the modern world absence and presence, the concrete and abstract, are united in radically new forms. The global satellite network, new innovations in telecommunications and the spread of computer technology have collapsed the time and space boundaries that previously structured social interaction. Modern jet transport permits travel to most corners of the globe in a relatively short time. The geographic and cultural divisions between north and south, east and west have altered dramatically during the latter part of this century. This new level of social exchange has been called the emergence of the 'information society', 'Curriculum Theory', as a distance education course, is itself an expression of the expansion and diversification of the 'information society', attenuating and straining the social relations of education as they have been understood in previous times. The new cultural situation is one in which ideas and action become radically reconstituted and produce the opportunity for new forms of social interaction *and* the need for new forms of theoretical interpretation. In what follows we attempt to sketch the outlines of an interpretive alternative.

The general curriculum problem introduced here holds the clues for an interpretation of ECS 802 'Curriculum Theory'. The monograph is at pains to point out that a number of theoretical perspectives collide and confront one another in contemporary educational debate and in contemporary curriculum theorizing. But this image of contested positions actually begs the question as to which theoretical position provides the greatest interpretive power.

The 'post-industrial' or information society is constituted around the convergence of new social associations. We need think no further than the course described here to understand how this new level of associations comes into being. Distance education works on an assumption of establishing and maintaining continuing contact despite the 'class' members being thousands of miles apart. The assumptions here are supported materially by the capacity to exchange information quickly and over vast distances. The long distance associations of the modern world are directly linked to the extended market relationships that stretch relationships away from the former face-to-face relations that characterized the clan and kin associations of former times, the village relationships of pre-industrial society, and the class relationships that existed in the industrial communities of the late nineteenth and early twentieth centuries. The extended market logic of contemporary Western society envelops the predominantly concrete relationships of family and neighbourhood and school, and locates them in a matric of abstracted functional relationships characteristic of the modern state and its increasingly transnational economic structures. Increasingly, in our formation as persons, we carry our sense of primary attachment to others in our families and neighhourhoods into this more abstracted realm of functional associations—for example, through informal relationships with others in the workplace, through our use of the new telecommunications media and through the identifications we make with political and cultural identities known to us only through television. The data highlighting the time that children spend watching television provide just one example of evidence to support this trend.

Education has become directly involved in the transformation being discussed here. Schools, colleges and universities have become an aspect of the 'information revolution', in helping to provide the skills and develop the predispositions associated with the more complex juxtaposition of abstract/ concrete relationships. The increasing stress on exposure to different forms of print media and computer hardware and software, coupled with the contemporary return to pedagogues of problem-solving and discovery learning, are indicators of education's role in the new level of social transformation. The changes in social relationships in education (and elsewhere in society) are not confined to the development of these new communication technologies but also appear in technologies of social and educational administration. The trend has been recognized since Weber. In bureaucratic models of social organization and management, persons are construed not as common bearers of a shared culture and shared circumstances, but as 'individuals' dominated by the pursuit of private modes of consumption and gratification. While 'autonomy' is lauded as a primary social value, in fact people find themselves cast as objects (rather than subjects) - as employees, to be managed and controlled like other elements in production processes. In his eloquent critique of the rise of modern, bureaucratized forms of consciousness and morality, Maclntyre expressed it this way: 'the society in which we live is one in which bureaucracy and individualism are partners as well as antagonists'.

Maclntyre argues that contemporary social life does not perspectives on the world characteristic of a sense of 'community'. Our moral and intellectual debates can no longer presuppose the forms of sharing on which fundamental agreements can be based, sufficient to sustain us through debate to mutually agreed conclusions. Instead, contemporary culture takes a 'marketplace' view of debate, in which people feel free to select the premises and conclusions which best suit their views and interests—and suffer the consequences in interminable disagreements. The burden of MacIntyre's argument is that we need to re-establish such forms of community. To do so, he argues, three things are necessary: (1) a sense that our social (and educational) practice are cooperatively agreed, embodying shared values and excellences, (2) a common sense of tradition against which the excellence of practice may be judged, and (3) a sense of 'the narrative unity of a human life'—the sense that a person's life can only be judged from the perspective of her or his death as having embodied a striving to enact particular values. The unity of these three features in the social life of earlier times, he argues, has been fragmented be contemporary conditions. Referring to the great theorist of bureaucracy, Max Weber, he says, 'We are all Weberians now'—meaning that our sense of being and belonging through communities in civil society has been replaced by a sense of being and belonging through the bureaucratic institutions of the modern state.

It is our contention that many debates relating to the form and substance of current education practices are related to a misinterpretation or misrepresentation of the changed nature of contemporary social life. The current debate about the nature of tertiary education in the new struggle for national renovation is an example of the confusion and conflict engendered by the bureaucratized form of social life. Within the more restricted context of distance education it is essential that the radically altered nature of social life is made problematic and placed on the agenda of considerations for students of curriculum.

The 'Curriculum Theory' course, as described in this chapter, brings into question any static view of the relationship between education and society. By its practice it clearly brings into question more conventional assumptions about the relationship between the university and society. In its substance and its pedagogy it challenges the view that it is the task of the teachers of the course to present a 'correct' view of theory to be implemented by students of the course in their curriculum practice. Yet it must confront its own role and agency in the production of more bureaucratized and abstracted social relations.

Many of the articles which have been written in this *Journal* as well as the earlier editions highlight the impact of this transformation. It is relevant for all of us to read the different articles with a strong sense of the new logic which is at work. It is here that our separate contexts and problems can help inform us of the bigger picture which is being etched on the ground on which we all stand. This approach of critical exchange is also part of a practice which maintains a sense of the ideal of education as an aspect of the cultural heritage; and not just as an appendage of the instrumental demands of the new breed of political managers. That is where curriculum issues can be debated as an aspect of long term traditions and practices in particular settings and not simply according to the quantifying logic of performance indicators.

The changing ideas, practices and social relations of society in general can be read in the life of the 'Curriculum Theory' course, just as they can be read in other parts of social life, despite the aspirations of the course to challenge at least some of them. It would be at least uncharitable to assert that the course did nor (or does not) challenge some taken-for-granted assumptions about curriculum and pedagogy for example, by changing the role of the reacher, by establishing direct communication between students through the medium of the *Course Journal,* by taking some steps towards establishing a critical community in which students together make critical analyses of their own curriculum work and of contemporary curriculum theoretic ideas. But the very modes of relationship possible in the course are ones which bedevil contemporary social life, including the abstraction of ideas and interpersonal relationships. The need and demand for distance education is in a sense an expression of what some might see as a social pathology—the isolation of people from the sites and people in which and with whom they can become educated. We are less certain than we were when first we designed the course about whether distance education is an expression of the problem or part of its resolution. In the case of the 'Curriculum Theory' course there is a certain irony in creating a 'course community' in which members interact almost wholly through a journal, with very limited access to one another as persons, and in a highly deliberate, careful, written form. The appearance of the *Journal* only four times a year. also gives the interaction an attenuated, stylized quality which mitigates against the kind of 'suck it and see' interchange which helps people develop confidence and competence in critical discourse.

It is not simply that the "Curriculum Theory' course is limited in achieving its aspirations by the attenuation of relationships characteristic of distance education. It is also that, by its very operation, it models these attenuated relationships and thus creates conditions for their reproduction. To the extent that it is successful it may even encourage participants to believe that distance relationships are as 'normal' and as 'real'—even as 'critical'—as face-to-face relationships can be. There is little doubt that such relationships are increasingly typical of the abstracted social relationships characteristic of contemporary society, but the course aims to treat such relationships critically rather than to take them for granted. If such relationships are part of the means by which societies are able not only to coordinate action across vast spaces but also to keep the operation of certain economic and cultural interests invisible and thus contain the expression of critical thought and the development of solidarity (for example, in social movements), then a profound question is raised for any course which attempts to create a 'critical community' through distance education. Can such a course be 'critical' in ways which challenge the presumptions of the very means by which it is offered? Can it be 'critical' in ways which reveal the ownership and control of the means of communication which make it possible? Does such a course reveal the attenuation of social relationships in technologized, bureaucratized societies, or does it simply exploit and symbolize them?

Of course, these questions do not apply to Deakin's Curriculum Theory' course alone. Nor do they apply only to courses with an explicitly 'critical' intent. The trends to abstraction are apparent in institutionalized education in general. What is apparent in innovation in distance education as a field (especially given its fascination for the potential of new information technologies like computer-based teaching and learning, the use of satellite communication, and the like) is the emergence of new patterns of social interaction based on the increasing acceptance of abstraction—abstraction not only in the realm of ideas, but also in our modes of social relationship (increasingly mediated by organizations and technologies of communication), and even our understanding of our own identities. This trend towards abstraction requires interpretation and it requires attempts to invoke alternative practices—interpretations and practices capable of relocating us as agents in the production of our own identities, our social relationships and our society.

Our argument is that the forms of social life which previously shaped education and schooling have changed markedly. Some argue that education should 'keep up with' the shifts in our forms of social life which the changing technology of communications has wrought by mimicking and extending the new communicative forms in schooling (for example, by increased use of computers as if this were necessarily a contribution to the development of the 'information society' as a better

When people lack such competence, social action that transcends the struggle for justice within the empirically given rules of social organization and discourse is impossible.

On this analysis it is inappropriate for distance educators to continue thinking about their curricula and pedagogies in terms of criteria associated with a form of education and social life that has been superseded. The challenge now appears to be to find alternative ways to think about the new social contradictions associated with the turn towards the abstract mode of ideational, social and economic exchange characteristic of contemporary social life — a trend of which distance education is manifestly a part. This requires a form of theorizing that views culture in a comprehensive sense—one that moves beyond the different kinds of interpretation noted in the 'Preface' to the course monograph in which ideas about social consensus played such an important theoretical role. At the current historical juncture there is a need to offer a theoretical alternative to narrow, consensulaist, bureaucratic and technicist approaches to thinking about education. In curriculum theory significant steps were taken in this direction by the development of reproduction theory as a means of understanding education in relation to society, at first in its 'correspondence' form and later in its 'contestation' and 'resistance' theory forms. In their turn certain of the key ideas and assumptions of reproduction theory which persist from the theoretical frameworks of earlier times need to be challenged. For example, ideas about the determination of the cultural superstructure by the economic base (which tended to survive in the correspondence theory of reproduction) must be replaced by more dialectrical understandings of the mutual determination of base and superstructure, and there is a need to move beyond outmoded ideas about the nature and significance of social class which fail to acknowledge that the social relations of advanced capitalism are very different from the class relations of nineteenth century capitalism.

Developing such new forms of interpretation and new practices is the permanent problem of social theorizing, including curriculum theorizing. In the Kemmis/Fitzclarence monograph we argued that 'the central problem of curriculum theory is to be understood as double problem of the relationship between theory and practice, on the one hand, and of the relationship between education and society, on the other'. Moreover, 'curriculum theories are social theories not only in the sense that they reflect the history of the societies in which they arose, but also in the sense that they entail ideas about social change and, in particular, about the role of education in the reproduction and transformation of society'. We hold the view that these are the abiding concerns of curriculum theory and curriculum theorizing. We are as aware as ever that our own theory and practice, and the reproductive and transformative relationships created by the 'Curriculum Theory' course, are as much objects for critical and self-critical scrutiny as are any other educational institutions and practices. We remain conscious that both our theories and our curricula are, and must be, both the products of their times and limited by the blindnesses and partialities of the historically bound people who develop them.

Yet the curriculum problem confronted in the early days of planning the 'Curriculum Theory' course remains fresh and compelling —the problem of making a curriculum for a course about curriculum. It is even more culturally pointed as in 1988 the course team considers the problem of remaking the course — a *distance education* course about curriculum for students whose lives are increasingly characterized by abstracted and 'distanced' social relationships. The analysis is far from complete; the task is unfinished. Despite changing to meet its changing analysis and changing circumstances, the course team — and the students of the course—still stand at the threshold of the possibility of making a course which is what the original course team intended it to be: an introduction to the problems of theory and practice in curriculum which reveals these problems through a self-disclosing pedagogy, and a view of the substance of the course as both a product of the history of the field and a model for future practice.

disciplines—can and often has outstripped the supply of teachers and we can see, for example, in the United Kingdoms that the government is now beginning to use the expertise of the open University in the area of continuing education and for updating in subjects such as computer science and the use of computing in management where the advances have been so rapid as to deny the opportunity for training a large cohort of teachers.

Freedom and restrictions on distance students

Teaching at a distance liberates the student/teacher interface from the strait - jacket of the lecture hall or tutorial room. The student may learn when he wants, whatever the hour of the day or night; he may learn wherever he wants; he may learn at his own pace. Because of this 'freedom' allowed to the student learning at a distance, we might consider that teaching at a distance is inherently a more individualized system than the conventional face-to-face method as far as the student is concerned. In the conventional system, teaching is directed to a group and the group must learn together within the restrictions placed upon it by the abilities of those who form its membership. Its learning will therefore approximate to the mean between the extremes of the abilities of its members, and the needs and potential of the individual in learning will tend to be subservient to this mean. However, the student learning at a distance normally does so as an individual. He learns, therefore, in the way and at the pace which is most suitable to him since he controls his own learning situation. On the debit side, however, it is clear that the student learning alone and at a distance lacks the supportive atmosphere of the tutorial class. He has no-one against whom he can measure himself in the development of his learning. He does not know if he is doing well in relation to his learning. Indeed he has no framework against which to judge 'doing well'. He can of course expect to receive comments on and perhaps grading for, this work from his tutor, but this interaction is strictly between teacher and student, and the student is therefore always at a disadvantage. No comparison with the peer group is possible and the student learning at a distance lacks the usual bench marks for his self-assessment.

A variety of educational packages

Any system of teaching at a distance must concern itself with what it is teaching and how it is teaching. The variety of systems of teaching at a distance and the level of study which they embrace are now almost legion. Most of the systems contain a package of attractively presented self-instructional materials. Printed material invariably forms the basis of this package, but it is often supplemented by audio-visual material, normally on cassettes but sometimes offered through open circuit broadcasting. n all cases a great deal of though t is customarily put into the assembly of this package and it is made as attractive as possible for the student learning at a distance. The production of such packages is usually seen as the basis on which economic calculations are made and, since the production demands complex resources, both material and human, and requires long-term planning, it often dominates the system of teaching at a distance to the exclusion of all other activities. Indeed there is a beguiling temptation to assume that the problems of teaching at a distance can all be solved by the production of an as yet merely hypothetical perfect package of material.

This excessive concentration on the package is the institution-based approach to teaching at a distance and indeed it is characterized in the very use of the word 'teaching'. The student-based approach involves a more rigorous examination learning at a distance. It is, of course, inherently more difficult since, whereas the teaching approach can start from a fixed standard package—a unified, concrete and controllable phenomenon—and tacitly assume the subordination of the needs of the individual to that package, the student approach requires a consideration of the needs of the individual in relation to the package and must involve an examination of an almost infinitely variable base which cannot be controlled or completely variable base which cannot be controlled or completely stabilized within a specially de-limited area.

A student-based versus institution-based approach

Yet why is it necessary to consider the student-based approach? Can we not seek to arrive more closely at the theoretically perfect teaching package of material? Before we can begin to arrive at any answer to this question, we institution to the student and the flow of contacts or interchange between both parties, the one attempting to teach and the other to learn at a distance. In a simple civilization there can be a personal relationship between the individual and those who stand for the religious or secular authority. In a complex civilization, such as our own, this personal relationship, of necessity, disappears. There is a gulf between the systems and the individual. Within this gulf in the complex civilization there has grown up a group of intermediaries—social workers, broadcasters, teachers, counsellors, etc. - who seek to adapt a system to the individual needs of people. The primary concern of the intermediaries is not for the system itself, but rather for the individuals and, although they are normally employees of the system, they seek to represent individual needs to such as extent that they force the system to take cognisance of these needs. In education this function of intermediary is embraced within a variety of roles which we refer to as teacher, tutor, advisor, counsellor, etc. The intermediary is concerned with the general welfare and support of students, but the various applications of this concern, both in breadth and depth, are almost infinite. On the one hand he may provide information on basic administrative functions; on the other hand he may offer psychological and medical advice. The reason for the variety of roles and duties lies in the variety of education itself. For each system of education we may posit a distinct supportive role.

Why are intermediaries necessary?

In examining a system of teaching at a distance we must analyse the requirements of an intermediary function. To pose the question in more concrete terms we must ask ourselves whether these requirements can be met by a package of materials, that is whether the package can take the place of every essential facet of the teacher in the conventional teaching situation.

Even a cursory examination of the learning process will lead to the conclusion that the needs of the student are not wholly related to the subject that is being studied. That is not to say that such needs are solely of a psychological nature and completely unconnected with the content of his study. His needs are of an educational kind, even of an academic kind, but they are not strictly related to a subject. This phenomenon is observable in education at all levels. The word 'teaching' is a simple definition of a complex interactive process and we might begin by dividing teaching from the point of view of the institution into the subject matter and advice/support. The subject matter would embrace the strictly academic content of the course and advice/support would embrace general study problems arising from the individual circumstances of the student or the system of teaching peculiar to the institution? We might look at this in another way by saying that the subject matter is information or knowledge and the advice/support covers the way in which the student as an individual fits this new knowledge into his own peculiar pre-existing frame-work and into his everyday life style.

Limitations of the package

What part does the teaching package in a system of teaching at a distance play in the intermediary role? Does it or could it provide both subject matter and advice/support for individuals? While not wishing to exclude the theoretical possibility that the teaching package could perform all these functions, there are a number of reasons for suggesting that in practice it will always fall a good way short of this ideal, if only for reasons of complexity and cost. While it is possible to define and de-limit the subject matter through an institutionally centred analysis in a way which might receive general assent within the institution, advice/support, being student-centred, is by comparison almost infinitely variable. It follows therefore that nay package of materials which seems to embrace advice/support must admit of almost infinite variation. Moreover, if we were to posit the existence of such a hypothetical package of materials, the cost of production and delivery would render it completely impractical. Clearly however, a package of material need not be limited to the subject matter. It may cover some aspects of advice/support which are judged to be universal or at least common. While economic considerations will of course be of importance in that area of the package which deals with the subject matter, it is likely in practice that general agreement can be obtained on the various limits of the subject matter and therefore on its cost. The same is unlikely to be true in the case of advice/support and here the cost-benefit approach will begin to operate. All students need the subject matter, therefore this element is 'cost-effective'. Not all students can easily be seen to need some/all of what can be offered in terms of advice/support; consequently it is by comparison far less cost-effective.

It does not seem unfair to suggest that there is an overwhelming tendency within the field of teaching at a distance to offer systems from the standpoint of the institution teaching at a distance, rather than from the standpoint of the student learning at a distance. The response to the individual needs of the student learning alone and at a distance has often become lost in the overriding requirement to produce a grand lose package of materials.

Contexts of distance and conventional students

Perhaps this failure to recognize and concentrate on individual needs arises out of a failure adequately to appreciate the difference between the conventional student and the student learning at a distance. Conventional students, in digesting the academic pabulum of their chosen study, exist within a highly artificial and wholly supportive framework. For most of them their study is merely a further stage in an unbroken linear development which began when they were infants. The infant school class and the university lecture are generically similar in offering a group learning situation with a face-to-face teacher/student contact and the subsequent possibility for instant feedback of an oral and visual nature. The group learning situation is itself supportive of the learning process, not only because of the potential interaction between students in relation o the academic content of the course learning through discussion with one's peers - but also because the group learning offers a bench mark to the individual members of the group. The students might naturally expect to fall short of the comprehension of a particular subject which is demonstrated by their teacher. The benchmark of how short or 'how much of this are we expected to understand?' is provided by the group, and through the group a common denominator of success or achievement is established for all its members.

The situation of students learning at a distance is wholly different. Often they are returning to study after a number of years. For such people the concept and practice of their previous learning i somewhat clouded. They have an experience of life and work and hence a framework into which their new learning has to be set. Often the students learning at a distance are part-timers. Their work and families are of prime importance. It is not open to them as it is open to the conventional students to devote themselves entirely and with singular purpose to learning. Moreover, the process of learning at a distance is generically different from the face-to-face learning model is almost entirely absent. The supportive environment of the per group is lacking and the bench mark of achievement and, deriving from this, the maintenance of the individual's confidence, is difficult to establish.

A division of roles

It is elements of this sort, fundamental to the student learning at a distance, which the package of materials either cannot influence at all or can only influence in a marginal way. The teaching package is the raw academic pabulum of the institution for teaching at a distance; for the student learning at a distance there is need of another element, an advisor/supportive role. In conventional education the teacher can and often does preform the advisory/supportive role while acting as the source of academic knowledge. In a system of teaching at a distance we normally find the separation of the source of academic knowledge and the advisory/support role, the former being contained in the teaching package. The separation of these activities does not, in itself, create problems. Problems will however arise if the two elements are not balanced;

if the teaching package predominates to the virtual or complete exclusion of the intermediary role; if the existence of these two activities is not constantly in the minds of those involved in teaching at a distance.

Drop-out as a measure of effectiveness

No-one who has given even a cursory glance to the literature of distance teaching will have failed to note a preoccupation, almost at times approaching hysteria, with the phenomenon variously described as drop-out, wastage, withdrawal, attrition, etc. This phenomenon exists in all forms of teaching, but in distance teaching it is a major characteristic since its incidence in often many times as great as in any form of conventional teaching, and its very existence threatens the 'cost-effectiveness' which is so often listed as an advantage. The hypothesis that the face-to-face teacher and the student's peer group could not be adequately replaced in distance teaching received, until recently, almost universal credence and this belief was 'substantiated' by reference to drop-out statistics. In the last decade and particularly in the last two or three years the hypothesis has received a practical challenge from the success of the Open University in the United Kingdoms. Here, instead of the ninety per cent drop-out confidently predicted in the educational press when the University first began to offer courses, we find that up to sixty per cent of finally registered students are graduating, and, moreover, that a very significant proportion of the forty per cent of 'drop-outs' is in any case unavoidable, ranging from the obvious cases of death, through movement outside the United Kingdom, significant changes in domestic quasi-mathematical terms through the use of a paradigm of the Open University. The Fernuniversitat in Hagen falls within the same broad ambit of Western European culture and tradition as the Open University in the United Kingdom. While the countries are not identical in geographical, cultural and economic terms they are, nevertheless, very similar. The students of the Fernuniversitat are highly motivated, being self-selecting as in the Open University. In general, however, they are far better qualified than Open University students, since they must normally have achieved the Abitur, whereas forty per cent Open University students in the last three years have less than the minimal requirements for normal entry to a degree course at universities and polytechnics in the United Kingdom.

The teaching package of the Fernuniversitat does not contain open circuit broadcasting, although audio and video material is often available in cassette form.

Bases of Open University support services

If we accept that, for all practical purposes, the advice/support function cannot be supplied through the teaching package, but see it as a vital element in the system, we can go on to consider the ways in which this might be supplied.

In practice, Open University support services are offered through tutor-counsellors in some two hundred and sixty local study centers throughout the United Kingdom. In addition, students are attached to specialist tutors to deal with the specific academic content of the course and to mark their assignments. The function of the tutors is exclusively related to the teaching package. What then is the rationale behind the us of study centres and tutor-counsellors?

The use of study centres in a system of teaching at a distance might not unreasonably been seen s a contradiction in terms. Study at a distance is normally depicted as independent of time and place and these are normally claimed as characteristics and advantages for the system. But study centres impose a restriction in place; they also impose a restriction in time to a greater or lesser extent as they are not open all day for every day of the year. Are study centres per se an essential part of teaching at a distance, if it is to be successful, or are they not essential at all? If the latter is true, why do many systems of teaching at a distance use them and in particular the Open University? Since they almost invariably offer a facility for face-to-face interaction, do they therefore deny on this account the practical viability of teaching at a distance?

Radio, television and telephone supplementing print

In our earlier analysis we defined the teaching process as the transmission of subject matter and advice/support. Until the sixteenth century, the transmission of subject matter or at any rate its wide dissemination—was through a verbal medium. Cost and time factors inherent in copying by hand placed out of court the provision of a text for students. The professors and the lecturers communicated verbally with their students as the very root of these words implies. The introduction of print brought a dramatic change. The professors and lecturers continued to lecture to their students, but no longer was the student limited exclusively to the time and space of a lecture room. He could have as a supplement - or even as a substitute - a text book written by someone to whom he would, perhaps not otherwise have access. Moreover, he could study this in his own time an at his own pace, re-reading whenever and wherever he thought fit. However, the text book had none of the interaction of face-to-face teaching. Teaching at a distance relies now, and for. the foreseeable future will continue to rely, upon the technology of printing. Other more recent technologies have supplemented this, but none have replace it. The telephone has offered a direct substitute for student/tutor interaction. The student can receive an immediate response to his question through the telephone as in the lecture room. He lacks the non-verbal signs of normal communication, but this is not usually seen as a vital loss. However, the telephone is limited in time, since tutors and students must have their interchange at the same time and it is limited in space both by the requirement of an installation and by the cost of the link. Furthermore, telephone lectures or tutorials between one tutor and a number of students, while fearless costly in tutor time, being to pose some of the disadvantages of radio in that tutors, deprived of on-verbal signals, teach at their own pace, and their students, unwilling to contribute to a technological anarchy, refrain from interrupting. There are certain similar disadvantages attached to the use of radio. While open circuit broadcasting is restrictive in time and space, the use of audio and video cassettes can ameliorate, to some extent, these problems by offering the student an opportunity to view and listen at his own pace and in his own time, the availability of a re-play facility being the only restriction. However, the possibility of interaction between tutor and student is the virtually non-existent within this medium. Printed material, radio and television can be used for the simple transmission of subject matter. Assuming re-play facilities, all can be used by the student in his own time and, with the wide dissemination of equipment in recent years, all are, or could be, independent of space. They are however the tools of *teaching* at a distance, not necessarily of *learning* at a distance, since they are not susceptible of an interactive mode: only the telephone offers this facility.

Education is about learning more than teaching

The view that education is primarily a learning process on the part of the student rather than a instrumental process on the part of the teacher has achieved almost universal acceptance in recent years. The fact that the Ministry of Education in Italy is till called the Department of Public Instruction and that *enseignement* is still used in France can be seen as anachronisms. In Germany the use of *Fern unterricht* for 'distance teaching' has been superseded at all levels by the term *Fernstudium* (distance learning) which had originally only been used for degree level study. While recognizing this trend in educational thinking, distance teaching systems have found difficulty in its practical application. One solution has been to develop, for the printed medium highly structured se,f-instructional materials in which the student is required to respond at regular intervals to the text and there follows a discussion of a variety of potential responses. Because of the wide range of where the origin of the study centre system is shrouded in complex educational politics, and study centres are seen as a tangible link between the otherwise amorphous distance teaching institution and the local community.

Can we then say that the study centre is the dustbin of teaching at a distance? Is it the repository into which are emptied those functions or parts of functions which seem to be too difficult or too expensive to carry out? Is it there because we cannot feel completely confident as yet in our combination of teaching materials and correspondence tuition, because it is particularly useful in the provision of the advice/support function in which the necessity for individualization is paramount? Is the presence of study centres a denial of the practical possibility, as yet, of teaching at a distance? Might we so 'improve' teaching at a distance as to be able to dispense with study centres entirely?

We might construct cogent arguments against the use of study centres. Clearly they are a costly element. As far as can be ascertained in all systems of teaching at a distance, students falls a long way short of the use and need projected by the institution. It is clear that a large number of students either are not able, or choose not to, attend a study centre. Clearly, many students choose to study by distance teaching methods because they prefer or require, for domestic or work purpose, to be freed from the time an space constraints of conventional teaching methods.

Continuingly changing functions

We would suggest that we are being over-simplistic,

if we take the view that the study centre in the Open University s merely a dustbin wherein we can deposit all the difficult functions of teaching at a distance, which we intend ultimately to carry out by other means. Indeed, we would suggest that it is entirely wrong to see study centres in the Open University solely against the background of traditional education, as placed in which conventional face-to-face contact between teachers and students takes place. Within the Open University our concept of a study centre is blinkered by our adherence to the objectives of study centres seen in the original report of the Planning Committee of the Open University. The Planning Committee had initially seen two purposes for study centres. They were to be used as viewing centres and as places in which tutorials would take place. Such tutorials were envisaged as an essential element in this system of teaching at a distance. The reality, almost from the beginning, proved to be different. Over two hundred and sixty study centres were created, but within the first three years it became apparent that they were not being and could not be used as originally intended. The open circuit broadcasting of radio and television did not always match the evening opening times for study centres. Furthermore, the store of audio and video tapes, particularly the latter, became too expensive to maintain, and the replay facility provided through technicolour machines and audio-cassette devices lapsed. The increase in the number of courses after foundation level was not and could not be matched by increases the student numbers. The average post-foundation course population rapidly fell below two students per study centre. The idea of local tutorials, other than of the high population foundation level courses thus disappeared. Thus the conception of study centres as viewing centres and locations for essential tuition was not even the case, in practice, in the University's first year of operation. It is even less the case today. Yet the Open University has failed to re-define the role of study centres in its formal publications, although a significant element of their role is implicit in the functions of the tutor-counsellors.

A focus for the tutor-counsellor

Tutor-counsellors are seen in the Open University as the local and continuing support for students. The description of this support as local is given a physical presence in the study centre which is seen as the base for a tutor-counsellor's activities. The local study centre is a place in which the foundation level tutor-counsellor is able to offer face-to-face support of a strictly academic and of an advisory/supportive nature to his first year students, all of whom live in the vicinity. The tutor-cousellor is seen as weaning students from the traditional methods of face-to-face group teaching to the Open University's methods of individual and independent study. The study centre is, in reality, a traditional phase for the students in this process. For the student it has much of the appearance of the traditional classroom is that it is a physical location in which an authoritative fugue, the tutor-counsellor, is present. If the similarity between the traditional and non-traditional teaching methods holds good for the physical situation, it certainly does not hold good for the educational rationale. The tutor-counsellor does not lecture or profess a subject in the traditional way. Instead he takes the academic content as given in the shape of the course units and broadcasts and sets out instead he takes the academic content as given in the shape of the course units and broadcasts and sets out instead to help the student to learn from the material, either by himself or in groups. As such, therefore, we might describe the study centre as an important element for most new students in the painful early steps of adapting to learning at a distance. It is a stepping stone from group learning of the traditional sort to individual and/or group learning of the non-traditional sort. While it is possible that some students do not need such a stepping stone, it seems clear from the attendance of students themselves that most students still require this element. Moreover, the needs of the individual can be met by the service of the tutor-counsellor in the study centre. The student may take advantage of what is offered whenever and as often as he pleases. He may feel no need to attend for some time but later develop a need. Such a need is met by the regular presence of the tutor-counsellor in the study centre.

A local resource centre

It might be alleged that this argument does not hold equally true for post-foundation level tuition and this is almost certainly true. For post-foundation level students the tuition is unlikely to be as 'local', but the study centre with its face-to-face tutorials - and by this we mean tutorials in the Open University sense—does satisfy a need. The face-to-face contact provides for a large of students a stimulus, both social and educational, to the continuing process of study. The initial strong 'local' support of the tutor-counsellor is not totally withdrawn after the first year. It exits in more rarefied form thereafter but can be tapped into by the student as an when he thinks fit.

The study centre is a place in which tutorials, day schools and self-help goods take place. Students do not us these facilities as often as the institution makes them available, but they are nevertheless essential. We know that students do not read every word of the course units or even all the course units. They sometimes—perhaps often—do not read the set books. Some students omit the radio and television broadcasts entirely, most are extremely selective. Some students do not complete all their home experiment kit activities and, indeed, a few do not even open up the boxes. It is certainly over-simplistic to try to use student usage as the sole determinant of the value of an element in the system, unless of course the use is that of a careful. It is the richness and variety, the multiplicity of provision, which attracts and sustains our students. Study centres and what is offered in them are part of this richness of provision.

Are study centres an anomaly?

Are we to say that study centres are a contradiction of the feasibility of teaching at a distance? The answer for the Open University is certainly no. The confusion rests with the definition of teaching at a distance. If we consider the variety of teaching and learning processes we might see at one extreme the continuous face-to-face dialogue between one teacher and one student, a totally supportive learning situation. Further along the spectrum we find the conventional primary school in which the authoritative figure of the teacher provides a continuous contact throughout the day with a group of students. Much further along the spectrum we find a traditional university teaching system in which the authoritative figure of the teacher appears only occasionally and the students are more independent in their learning situation. At the other rend of the spectrum we find a pure system of teaching at a distance in which the student is learning at a distance from those who have prepared the material and learns at his own pace, wherever he wishes to study. The Open University, like the conventional universities, falls somewhere between the two ends of the spectrum, although it is clearly further towards the end of pure distance teaching. Its position in the system has been determined by a number of elements. These include the varying entry qualifications of its students, their domestic and work circumstances as adults learning part-time, their previous experience of learning and their perception of what they are capable of and the support that they require. The study centres and what is provided in them are part of the total package of the Open University teaching system to which we ascribe overall the generic term of teaching at a distance. There is no contradiction between the notion of study centres and teaching at a distance. For some students who do not attend study centres, the Open University might come close to 'pure' teaching at a distance. For others it will come less close. More important, however, from the student's point of view, the Open University offers a richness of variety in opportunities for learning, such that its appeal is catholic. It is from this that its success follows, and if the University ever seeks to alter the balance of this provision or removes specific elements from the rich variety of this provision, it must do so only with extreme care and mindful of the fact that in doing so it will almost certainly be detracting somewhat from its present universal appeal.

7 Distance Education: An Interpretation

The more one attempts to grasp and explain the phenomenon of distance teaching, and especially the more one tries to identify the particular educational opportunities distinguishing this form of teaching from other forms of imparting academic knowledge, the clearer it becomes that the conventional range of educational terminology is not sufficiently comprehensive. Distance study represents facts new to education in several aspects. Compared with other forms of study it was novel in the form in which it made its first breakthrough over ninety years ago. With even greater justification it can be called novel in its present form in which it is currently spreading throughout the world, contributing towards the discovery of the educational opportunities provided by the modern media, such as radio and television. It is, above all, novel and pointing towards the future when it makes use of electronic data-processing equipment and wide-band cable transmission techniques. It is no coincidence that university study at a distance, in its early form of correspondence teaching, began its development only about 130 years ago, as it requires conditions that only existed from then on. One from all previous epochs. It is without example in history, above all, on account of the basic changes in most spheres of human existence. Academic teaching alone seems to have remained largely unscathed by industrialization—with the exception of distance study, for this form of study is remarkably consistent with the principles and tendencies of industrialization. For this reason, experimentally, structural elements, concepts and principles derived from the theories of industrial production are used here to interpret the distance study phenomenon. This does not mean that the teaching and learning processes occurring in distance study are equated with processes in industrial production. The comparison is purely heuristic.

A comparison of this kind between a form of teaching and processes from another sphere of life is legitimate and not without example in the history of educational theory. Amos Comenius, the 'founder and virtuoso of the method of parallel comparison' in his *Didactical Magna,* for example, compared the 'art of teaching' in unusual detail with the art of printing, also a technical process. Theodor Litt identified the nature of pedagogic thinking by comparing it with artistic creativity, technology and the processes of growth. In the sixties, experiments were carried out which tried to explain the teaching and learning processes using the technical model of the feedback control system, in order to find approaches to a 'cybernetic pedagogy'. Most impressive, however, was the achievement of Gottfried Hausmann who, in 1959, condensed the analogy between the dramatic arts and education into a 'dramaturgy of teaching'. In it he interprets the educational structure of teaching and learning processes in detail using the terms and principles of the dramatic are in the theatre. Paul Heimann saw the merit of this comprehensive and detailed comparison in the possibility that 'it might give rise to a complete revision of our teaching and learning models'.

Furthermore, it may not be without significance for this planned interpretation that for another important aspect of university or college work, namely research, comparisons with the production process already exist. In 1919, Max Weber defined structural similarities between research institutes and capitalistic organizations and, in 1924, Helmut Plessner pointed out that the 'mechanization, methodization and depersonalization of the manufacturing process equally dominate the production of economic as well as cultural goods'. The following comparison between distance study and the industrial production process will prove similar consistencies.

From the start, distance study has a special relationship with the industrial production process in so far as the production of study materials in itself is an industrial process built into the whole teaching process as a constituent part, quite unlike the production of textbooks, for example. In the case of commercial distance teaching establishments the further question of selling the printed or otherwise duplicated study units adds calculations of applied economics to the teaching process. Even the distance teaching departments of government-financed universities are not entirely free from these considerations. It would be interesting to examine how far these facts have already influenced the structure of distance teaching.

In order to facilitate the discovery of further relationships between distance teaching and the production process, the following structural changes - essentially brought about by industrialization - in the development of the production of goods should be noted:

1 According to the principle of rationalization, individual work as was traditional in the craftsmen's trades changes at an early stage to a production based on the division of labour, and this later leads to the development of assembly lines and mass production.

2 Work processes initially characterized by the use of tools are increasingly restructured by mechanization and, later, automation.

3 In detail, these changes lead to the following results:

- The preparatory phase becomes increasingly important.
- Success depends, among other things, on systematic planning and organization. Scientific measures of control are needed.
- Work processes must be formalized and products standardized. The production process is objectified.
- Each developmental step towards increased mechanization leads to changes in the function of those involved in the production process.
- Small concerns are no longer able to raise the investment needed for developmental work and technical equipment. A strong tendency towards concentration and centralization becomes noticeable.

The terms used in business studies to describe these facts will be outlined briefly and - where possible - applied to distance teaching.

Rationalization

By rationalization we mean all 'methodical' 'measures' with the purpose of achieving 'output with a comparatively lower input of power, time and money'. Scientific discoveries should 'be evaluated for practical use in such a way as to achieve the best possible results in view of the continually necessary development and redevelopment of economic and technical processes'.

Applied to the practical example of the production process this means that 'the entire production line, from raw material to end product, is carefully analysed to allow each single work process to be planned so as to make the most effective contribution possible towards achieving clearly formulated business tasks.

Georges Friedmann emphasizes that this is a dynamic process aiming at continuous improvement in quality through continuous progress in the study of materials, accuracy and precision'. Rationalisation of this type has only started to develop with increasing industrialization at the end of the nineteenth century.

Management science holds that the reason for the considerable obstacles to rationalization lies in human nature itself, because 'human inadequacy inhibits the motivation to gain unprejudiced views and the willingness to act according to rational convictions'. Further obstacles are considered to be tradition, convention, habits and fashion. In education, a rationalizing way of thinking is nothing new. In a general form, it influences the reasoning for numerous educational decisions. For example, the introduction of lectures to larger groups of students, the use of printed books and the specialization of university lecturers were considerable steps towards the rationalization of the academic teaching process. Every university teacher will, when planning a lecture, choose those subjects that will best help him or her to fulfil the purpose of that particular lecture. In distance teaching, however, ways of thinking, attitudes and procedures can be found which only established themselves in the wake of an increased rationalization in the industrialization of production processes. The characteristic details are, among others, as follows:

1 In distance study the teaching process is based on the division of labour and detached from the person of the university lecturer. It is therefore independent from a subjectively determined teaching situation, thus eliminating part of the earlier mentioned obstacles to rationalization. The division of labour and the objectification of the teaching process allow each work process to be planned in such a way that clearly formulated teaching objectives are achieved in the most effective manner. Specialists may be responsible for a limited area in each phase.

2 The use of technical equipment (duplicating machines, organization systems, transporting devices) makes it possible to convey the knowledge, ability and teaching skills of a university lecturer, by means of the detached objectivity of a distance study course of constant

basic functions of the university teacher, that of conveying information and that of counselling, were allocated as separate responsibilities in distance teaching departments of universities or colleges. Both functions, above all however that of transmitting information, are now even further divided. If, for example, the number of students enrolled on a distance study course is high, regular assessment of performance is not carried out by those academics who developed the course. The recording of results is the responsibility of yet another unit; and the development of the course itself is divided into numerous phases, in each of which experts in particular fields are active.

This specialization may bring the following advantages:

- Materials required for the development of the distance study course can be assembled by leading experts in the specialist fields concerned.
- Having completed the manuscript, the author can then be freed from the time-consuming processes of exact source references and of lecturing.
- Educationists and experienced practitioners of distance teaching are able to revise the manuscripts of study units in order to make the planned teaching process more effective.
- Colleagues from the 'academic middle tier' may be involved in the correction of exercises carried out by students. There are cases where even senior students have taken or such tasks especially where they are concentrating on marking the exercises from a limited number of

correspondence units. As in the industrial manufacturing process, the level of previous training may be lower on account of the division of labour and, as there, 'more people are able to carry out the work'. Since with extensive specialization of this type the number of scripts one university teacher is able to mark may be much higher, this process is also cheaper.

Mechanization

Mechanization means the use of machines in a work process. These machines replace the work done by the muscles of men or animals. In part they even take over elements of brain work. There are varying degrees of mechanization. The pre-industrial stage is characterized mainly by craftwork making use of tools. The first level of industrialization was reached with the use of 'dependent machines'. The second level of industrialization led to mass production as a result of the use of 'semi-independent machines' and assembly lines. Finally, the third level of industrialization is characterized by the spread of automation. The changes occurring at each level are so great that, in this context, one author has spoken about a first, second and third technical or industrial revolution .

In order to stay with this analogy, distance study could be ascribed to be industrial levels, as it cannot take place without the use of machines. Duplicating machines and transport systems are prerequisites, and later forms of distance teaching have the additional facilities of modern means of communication and electronic data processing installations.

In contrast, when considering the framework of conventional study, one cannot help thinking that its forms of teaching belong to the pre-industrial level. There the university teacher is comparable to a craftsman as he uses 'tools' (pictures, objects, books), without these changing the structure of the teaching process to any considerable degree.

Assembly line

Buckingham referred to the importance of the assembly-line principle in connection with the use of machines. Both these factors, among others, had made mass production possible. Assembly-line work is characterized by the fact that the worker remains at his place of work whilst the workpieces travel past him.

The formal similarity between distance teaching and the production process becomes particularly noticeable here. In the development of the distance study course the manuscript is passed from one area of responsibility to another and specific changes are made at each stage. The study units are printed on a large scale, stored, sent to the distance learner, who completes them, sent to the script marker who checks the work, and finally submitted to the administration, where the performance of the distance learner and the effort of the script marker are recorded. The rationalization effect achieved by the fact that many university teachers and thousands of students do not have to meet in one place in order to participate in teaching events is at least the same as that which a car manufacturer tries to achieve when, instead of sending the worker to the vehicle to be built, he transports the necessary parts to the worker. In both cases-the production process as well as distance teaching-time, energy and money are saved.

Mass production

In modern sociology the term 'mass trend' has rid itself of its negative cultural connotation, making it a largely neutral expression. Mass trend nowadays merely denotes a structural characteristic of an advanced industrial society and indicates 'that in a pure consumer society such as ours, the rise in the standard of living is due purely to the fact that industry produces certain consumer goods and commodities in large quantities. thus making them generally accessible'.

Mass production is by its nature only possible where there is a sufficiently large 'mass of consumers'. This, in turn, requires an efficient transport system providing a connection between producer and consumer who, as is typical in today's system, are geographically distant. In order to work profitably, producers need to research consumer requirements and find standards acceptable to all consumers for their products. They must continually improve their goods (aim at perfection), as each shortcoming is multiplied by the number of items produced.

If one equally rids the term 'consumer' of its negative cultural connotation, one can speak of the student as a 'consumer of academic education'. Quite obviously, 'demand' outstrips 'supply' at universities and colleges, and this had led to the large-scale operation at our universities and colleges. As traditional forms of academic teaching originally envisaged small groups of students, and today's practice of applying methods designed for small groups to large groups must be seen as a perversion f an educational concept, one can, one can understand it if various governments see distance teaching, on account of its similarity with the mass-production process, as a means of providing very large groups of students more adequately with academic teaching than conventional methods would allow.

Indeed, the multiplication effect achieved by technology and the postal delivery system means that the university teacher and the distance learner - like producer and consumer -no longer need to live in the same geographical location.

From an economic point of view, the production of distance study courses represents mass production. Apart from reasons of profitability, the large number of courses produced forces distance teaching organizations to analyse the requirements of potential distance learners far more carefully than in conventional teaching and to improve the quality of the courses. For example, in the USSR the Public Accounts Authority complained at one time that too many students dropped out of distance study, and it is suspected that this might have been the reason that led to an examination of the study materials. Most American distance study courses are revised and re-issued at regular intervals. As American universities charge fees to cover the greatest part of the budget allocated to distance teaching departments, the quality of distance study courses must not be allowed to deteriorate. When, on account of mass production, the University of California has more distance study courses to offer than there is demand for them, it occasionally places advertisements for students in newspapers.

Statistics prove that the number of graduates in areas without a university is lower than in areas near universities. It is possible that, according to the principle of mass production, distance teaching will one day equalize the opportunities to study, just as industrial mass production has assimilated consumer patterns in town and country. Analogous to the increase in the standard of living, this would make a general increase in the level of education possible, which might not otherwise have been achieved.

Preparatory work

In a production situation where a division of labour prevails, economy, quality and speed of the work process depend on the right type of preparation. This is necessary in industries producing a type of preparation. This is necessary in industries producing a variety of articles and needs to be carried out by senior specialist staff in special departments, as workers, foremen and masters involved in the production process lack the necessary knowledge and experience. During the preparatory stages one determines how workers, machines and materials can usefully relate to one another during each phase of the production process. In addition, there are developmental and constructional tasks. The more thorough the preparation, the less is a successful production process dependent on the particular abilities of the workers involved. Consequently, workers can easily be exchanged. Normally, considerably larger sums of investment are required for preparatory work than was the case previously in the manufacture of goods.

As distance teaching institutions have to develop a great variety of distance teaching courses, the comparison with a firm producing a variety of goods comes to mind. In distance teaching too success depends decisively on a 'preparatory phase'. It concerns the development of the distance study course involving experts in the various specialist fields with qualifications also often higher than those of other teachers involved in distance study. Here, too, each section of the course can be carefully planned. The use of technical support and a suitable combination of this with individual contributions from distance tutors and advisers play an important role here. Compared to university teachers in conventional study, who are responsible for the entire teaching process, distance tutors and advisers are more easily exchangeable on account of the thorough preparatory work. Finally, the development of distance study courses also requires investment to an extent that has never before been considered at establishments of higher education.

The separation of preparatory work and individual instruction and the distribution of these function among several persons is a particularly clear example of analogy with the production process.

Planning

An essential element of preparation is planning, which needs to be far more comprehensive and detailed in the industrial manufacturing process

In all these efforts to predetermine and arrange the course of teaching processes as far as possible, we are dealing with effective planning. Intervention by advisers and tutors during the course of distance study, however, is regarded as contingency planning, which supplements effective planning.

Organization

Planning largely concerns itself with the organization of the production cycle. In organizational management terms, organization means 'creating general or permanent arrangements for purpose-orientated activity'. As a consequence of the division of labour, the production process has to be rationally ordered according to organizational principles and with specially developed organizational means, since 'the continuous interacting of numerous people towards a specific purpose requires organization'. Furthermore, productivity depends on the type and degree of organization. Distinguished from organization are improvisation and disposition.

In distance study, likewise, there is an immediate connection between the effectiveness of the teaching method and rational organization. Organization, for example, makes it possible for students to receive exactly predetermined documents at appointed times, for an appropriate university teacher to be immediately available for each assignment sent in, for consultations to take place at fixed locations at fixed times, or for examinations to be held, or for counsellors to inform themselves at any time of the progress of a student or a group of students. Organization becomes easier in large distance teaching establishments, as trained personnel and modern means of organization are available. These enable them to supplement the organization of distance teaching with improvisation and disposition.

The importance of organization in distance teaching can be assessed by the fact that it is often difficult to distinguish between the operational (technical organization of distance study and the methodical organization of the actual academic contents.

Formalization

On account of the division of labour and mechanization in the manufacturing process there is a much greater need to predetermine the various phases formally than in manual production. It is only the emphasis on formality which makes the cooperation of all those involved in the production process possible, as each of them has to rely on previous work having been carried out according to plan. Most activities and interactions in an industrial set-up must therefore be determined according to agreed rules.

In distance study, likewise, all the points in the cycle, from student to distance teaching establishment to the academics allocated, must be determined exactly. Communication is standardized by the use of forms. Authors of correspondence units are recommended to consider the incorporation of standard formalized aspects that have proved to be of advantage. Lecturers marking assignments also work to standard guidelines. Assessment is, in parts, largely formalized through the frequent use of multiple choice questions, where the student only has to place a cross against the right answer. In the most modern forms of distance teaching, formalization goes as far as students marking the results of their learning on a punch card in coded form, and this is then input to a computer.

Standardization

It is characteristic of a production situation involving the division of labour and high technology that manufacture is limited to a number of types of one product, in order to make these more suitable for their purpose. cheaper to produce and easier to replace. Georages Friedmann pointed out that this does not at all represent a threat of dullness and uniformity. On the contrary, the elementary parts produced could be combined in extremely diverse ways.

The application of the principle of the division of labour and the use of machines, as well as the duplication of correspondence units in often large numbers, force distance teaching institutions likewise to adopt a greater degree of standardization than is required in conventional teaching. Not only is the format of the correspondence units standardized, so also is the stationery for written communication between student and lecturer, and the organizational support, as well as each single phase of the teaching process, and even the academic contents.

Whereas the academic giving a conventional lecture may indulge in an interesting deviation, because he sees educational advantages in this at a particular time with a certain group of students, the distance study lecturer has to be aware that he is, when writing a correspondence unit, addressing such a large group of students that situation-dependent improvisation becomes impossible. Instead he has to find a standard adequate, as far as possible, for every student admitted to the distance study course in question. This is achieved by developing a model for the course, perfecting it through the involvement of several experts and then approximating it to the required standard by testing it on a representative group of students before printing large number of copies. Just as the production of a branded article can only remain economical if its quality is continuously adapted to the constant needs of a large group of consumers, a distance teaching institution has to standardize the academic contents of its courses in such a way that it can be sure they appeal to all distance learners as equally as possible. The adaptation to any number of students, however large, forces the lecturer more strongly than in conventional study to consider the necessary standard that is, at the same time, realistic for as many students as possible.

Consequently, the choice of contents of a distance study course is less likely to be a reflection of the particular interest of an academic giving conventional lectures, than of the objective requirements of the total course profile.

Change of function

On account of the division of labour and the use of various types of machines, the function of the worker in the production process has changed considerably. Whereas it was typical for the craftsman to plan the production of a piece of work as well as acquire the necessary materials, carry out the work and finally sell the finished piece of work himself, industrialization led to a more marked functional differentiation. When preparatory work and selling became separate from production and, within these three phases, many individual functions were allocated to different individual, a loss of function naturally occurred for each single worker. On the other hand, new roles were created and new achievements became possible. For example, 'in jobs where, due to mechanization, the processing of the material has been taken out of the worker's hand, speed and energy of execution are no longer required: they have been replaced by accuracy and diligence; the work no longer shows quantitative but qualitative criteria'.

As a result of the division of labour, the function of the lecturer teaching at a distance also changes. The original role of provider of knowledge in the form of the lecturer is split into that of study unit author and that of marker; the role of counsellor is allocated to a particular person or position. Frequently, the original role of lecturer is reduced to that of a consultant whose involvement in distance teaching manifests itself in periodically recurrent contributions. In order to ensure the effectiveness of the four functions mentioned, numerous support functions of an operational-technical type are particularly important, as, without them, distance study could not take place.

As tutors and consultants have largely been relieved of the task of conveying course matter, they are able to devote themselves to a considerable degree to more demanding tasks, such as aiding motivation, providing individual support, structuring course contents for students, identifying problems, establishing connections and so on. Here, too, a loss of function is compensated for by a gain in function whereby, at the same time, an otherwise almost unattainable level of quality can be achieved.

Objectification

The more the production process is determined by machines and organizational principles, the more it loses its subjective element which used to determine craftsmen's work to a considerable degree. Hermann Schmidt pointed out that this process already started when man began to substitute tools provided by nature, such as hands, fists and teeth, with tools taken from his surroundings. Objectification was not possible until the item to be objectified had become the subject of reflection.Considering that, since Frederick Winslow Taylor, there has been a changeover to analysing each single phase of the industrial production process with scientific means and to organizing purposefully the contribution of workers and machines accordingly, it becomes clear what a high degree of objectification has been achieved. This development has found a climax in automated production where man's involvement in the course of the production process has largely been eliminated.

In this respect too, the relationship between distance study and conventional study is the same as between industrial production and mechanical fabrication. The university lecturer who lectures from his chair or leads a seminar discussion has the freedom and the opportunity to allow his subjectivity to influence his way of teaching: he is free to decide how and how much to prepare, he determines his own academic aims and methods and monopoly-like positions do not hinder free competition.

The possible consequences of a rigorous concentration and centralization of distance teaching were hinted at, for the first time in 1966, in a memorandum from the British government concerning the then proposed University of the Air. In future, universities would no longer pursue the same objectives in all subjects, but specialize in some disciplines and cater for the national requirements for distance study in these.

8 Distance Teaching and Industrial Production

The more one attempts to grasp and explain the phenomenon of distance teaching, and especially the more one tries to identify the particular educational opportunities distinguishing this form of teaching from other forms of imparting academic knowledge, the clearer it becomes that the conventional range of educational terminology is not sufficiently comprehensive. Distance study represents facts new to education in several aspects. Compared with other forms of study it was novel in the form in which it made its first breakthrough over ninety years ago. With even greater justification it can be called novel in its present form in which it is currently spreading throughout the world, contributing towards the discovery of the educational opportunities provided by the modern media, such as radio and television. It is, above all, novel and pointing towards the future when it makes use of electronic data-processing equipment and wide-band cable transmission techniques. It is no coincidence that university study at a distance, in its early form of correspondence teaching, began its development only about 130 years ago, as it requires conditions that only existed from then on. One necessity, for example, is a relatively fast and regular postal and transport service. The first railway lines and the first correspondence schools were established around the same time. When one further realizes how much technical support distance teaching establishment need nowadays in order to cater effectively for large groups of students, it becomes clear that distance study is a form of study complementary to our industrial and technological age. Lectures, seminars and practice sessions, on the other hand, have developed from forms of teaching derived from ancient rhetoric and were practised at medieval universities; the colloquium originates from the dialogic teaching methods of the humanistic era. These forms of teaching have changed little in their basic structure since the beginning of the nineteenth century. They proved almost completely resistant to combination with technical support facilities. In this context they can therefore be described as pre-industrial forms of study.

On account of these differences, distance study can only be described and analysed to a limited extent using traditional educational terms. They are not wholly adequate for this new form of study. This is understandable in so far as these terms developed from pre-industrial forms of teaching. If one applies them to distance study one will think in conventional concepts. To emphasize the point, one looks at a new form of study from an old perspective and has one's view of the essential structural characteristics distorted.

Industrialization is the symbol of a new epoch in the development of man fundamentally different from all previous epochs. It is without example in history, above all, on account of the basic changes in most spheres of human existence. Academic teaching alone seems to have remained largely unscathed by industrialization - with the exception of distance study, for this form of study is remarkably consistent with the principles and tendencies of industrialization. For this reason, experimentally, structural elements, concepts and principles derived from the theories of industrial production are used here to interpret the distance study phenomenon. This does not mean that the teaching and learning processes occurring in distance study are equated with processes in industrial production. The comparison is purely heuristic.

A comparison of this kind between a form of teaching and processes from another sphere of life is legitimate and not without example in the history of educational theory. Amos Comenius, the 'founder and virtuoso of the method of parallel comparison' in his *Didactical Magna*, for example, compared the 'art of teaching' in unusual detail with the art of printing, also a technical process. Theodor Litt identified the nature of pedagogic thinking by comparing it with artistic creativity, technology and the processes of growth. In the sixties, experiments were carried out which tried to explain the teaching and learning processes using the technical model of the feedback control system, in order to find approaches to a 'cybernetic pedagogy' . Most impressive, however, was the achievement of Gottfried Hausmann who, in 1959, condensed the analogy between the dramatic arts and education into a 'dramaturgy of teaching'. In it he interprets the educational structure of teaching and learning processes in detail using the terms and principles of the dramatic are in the theatre. Paul Heimann saw the merit of this comprehensive and detailed comparison in the possibility that 'it might give rise to a complete revision of our teaching and learning models'.

Furthermore, it may not be without significance for this planned interpretation that for another important aspect of university or college work, namely research, comparisons with the production process already exist. In 1919, Max Weber defined structural similarities between research institutes and capitalistic organizations and, in 1924, Helmut Plessner pointed out that the 'mechanization, methodization and depersonalization of the manufacturing process equally dominate the production of economic as well as cultural goods'. The following comparison between distance study and the industrial production process will prove similar consistencies.

From the start, distance study has a special relationship with the industrial production process in so far as the production of study materials in itself is an industrial process built into the whole teaching process as a constituent part, quite unlike the production of textbooks, for example. In the case of commercial distance teaching establishments the further question of selling the printed or otherwise duplicated study units adds calculations of applied economics to the teaching process. Even the distance teaching departments of government-financed universities are not entirely free from these considerations. It would be interesting to examine how far these facts have already influenced the structure of distance teaching.

In order to facilitate the discovery of further relationships between distance teaching and the production process, the following structural changes - essentially brought about by industrialization - in the development of the production of goods should be noted:

1 According to the principle of rationalization, individual work as was traditional in the craftsmen's trades changes at an early stage to a production based on the division of labour (e.g., in factories), and this later leads to the development of assembly lines and mass production.

2 Work processes initially characterized by the use of tools are increasingly restructured by mechanization and, later, automation.

3 In detail, these changes lead to the following results:

- The preparatory phase becomes increasingly important.
- Success depends, among other things, on systematic planning and organization. Scientific measures of control are needed.
- Work processes must be formalized and products standardized. The production process is objectified.
- Each developmental step towards increased mechanization leads to changes in the function of those involved in the production process.
- Small concerns are no longer able to raise the investment needed for developmental work

human nature itself, because 'human inadequacy inhibits the motivation to gain unprejudiced views and the willingness to act according to rational convictions'. Further obstacles are considered to be tradition, convention, habits and fashion. In education, a rationalizing way of thinking is nothing new. In a general form, it influences the reasoning for numerous educational decisions. For example, the introduction of lectures to larger groups of students, the use of printed books and the specialization of university lecturers were considerable steps towards the rationalization of the academic teaching process. Every university teacher will, when planning a lecture, choose those subjects that will best help him or her to fulfil the purpose of that particular lecture. In distance teaching, however, ways of thinking, attitudes and procedures can be found which only established themselves in the wake of an increased rationalization in the industrialization of production processes. The characteristic details are, among others, as follows:

1 In distance study the teaching process is based on the division of labour and detached from the person of the university lecturer. It is therefore independent from a subjectively determined teaching situation, thus eliminating part of the earlier mentioned obstacles to rationalization. The division of labour and the objectification of the teaching process allow each work process to be planned in such a way that clearly formulated teaching objectives are achieved in the most effective manner. Specialists may be responsible for a limited area in each phase.

2 The use of technical equipment (duplicating

machines, organization systems, transporting devices) makes it possible to convey the knowledge, ability and teaching skills of a university lecturer, by means of the detached objectivity of a distance study course of constant quality, to a theoretically unlimited number of students. The rationalization effect of mass production becomes apparent here.

3 The rigorous application of organizational principles and means saves teachers as well as students unnecessary effort.

4 At some of the newer distance teaching establishments, modern means of technical support, such as film, television and electronic data-processing installations, have replaced teaching staff in certain areas of their work, in particular, in the fields of giving information and assessing performance.

5 Student work through a course which has been tested prior to going to print. This prevents misunderstandings and stops students from going in the wrong direction.

6 The quality of a distance study course can be improved, because its effectiveness can be monitored at any time by scientific methods.

If the number of students required in a society outgrows the number of university teachers available, rational thinking should be able to find ways and means of changing teaching methods in such a way that the teaching resources of the university teachers available are used to the best effect, quantitatively as well as qualitatively. Distances study can be regarded as a result of such endeavours.

The division of labour

The division of labour has played an important role in the sociological theories of the last 100 years. Applied to the production processes it means that the work is split in the sense of 'dividing one complete work process into a number of elementary procedures', as described by Adam Smith at an early stage. With an extensive division of labour 'training periods become shorter, more people are able to carry out the work and wages can be lowered.

A result of the advanced division of labour is increased specialization. The following statement, by Adam Smith in 1776, applies to everyone involved in a production process where a division of labour exists:

> Men are much more likely to discover easier and readier methods of attaining any object, when the whole attention of their minds is directed towards that single object then when it is dissipated among a great variety of things. It is naturally to be expected therefore that some one or other of those who are employed in each particular branch of labour should soon find out easier and readier methods of performing their own particular work, whenever the nature of it admits of such improvement.

Just as the division of labour is a precondition for the mechanization of work processes and for industrialization as a whole, it has made university study at a distance possible. The division of labour is the main prerequisite for the advantages of this new form of teaching to become effective. The principle of the division of labour is thus a constituent element of distance teaching.

The 'complete work process', which is split in distance teaching, consists of the teaching activity of the university lecturer: namely, the entirety of the measures he takes in order to initiate and guide learning processes in students. Initially, the two basic functions of the university teacher, that of conveying information and that of counselling, were allocated as separate responsibilities in distance teaching departments of universities or colleges. Both functions, above all however that of transmitting information, are now even further divided. If, for example, the number of students enrolled on a distance study course is high, regular assessment of performance is not carried out by those academics who developed the course. The recording of results is the responsibility of yet another unit; and the development of the course itself is divided into numerous phases, in each of which experts in particular fields are active.

This specialization may bring the following advantages:

- Materials required for the development of the distance study course can be assembled by leading experts in the specialist fields concerned.
- Having completed the manuscript, the author can then be freed from the time-consuming processes of exact source references and of lecturing.
- Educationists and experienced practitioners of distance teaching are able to revise the manuscripts of study units in order to make the planned teaching process more effective.
- Colleagues from the 'academic middle tier' may

be involved in the correction of exercises carried out by students. There are cases where even senior students have taken or such tasks especially where they are concentrating on marking the exercises from a limited number of correspondence units. As in the industrial manufacturing process, the level of previous training may be lower on account of the division of labour and, as there, 'more people are able to carry out the work'. Since with extensive specialization of this type the number of scripts one university teacher is able to mark may be much higher, this process is also cheaper.

Mechanization

Mechanization means the use of machines in a work process. These machines replace the work done by the muscles of men or animals. In part they even take over elements of brain work. There are varying degrees of mechanization. The pre-industrial stage is characterized mainly by craftwork making use of tools. The first level of industrialization was reached with the use of 'dependent machines'. The second level of industrialization led to mass production as a result of the use of 'semi-independent machines' and assembly lines. Finally, the third level of industrialization is characterized by the spread of automation.

In order to stay with this analogy, distance study vould be ascribed to be industrial levels, as it cannot take place without the use of machines. Duplicating machines and transport systems are prerequisites, and later forms of distance teaching have the additional facilities of modern means of communication and electronic data processing installations.

In contrast, when considering the framework of conventional study, one cannot help thinking that its forms of teaching belong to the pre-industrial level. There the university teacher is comparable to a craftsman as he uses 'tools' (pictures, objects, books), without these changing the structure of the teaching process to any considerable degree.

Assembly line

Buckingham referred to the importance of the assembly-line principle in connection with the use of machines. Both these factors, among others, had made mass production possible. Assembly-line work is characterized by the fact that the worker remains at his place of work whilst the workpieces travel past him.

The formal similarity between distance teaching and the production process becomes particularly noticeable here. In the development of the distance study course the manuscript is passed from one area of responsibility to another and specific changes are made at each stage. The study units are printed on a large scale, stored, sent to the distance learner, who completes them, sent to the script marker who checks the work, and finally submitted to the administration, where the performance of the distance learner and the effort of the script marker (to calculate fees) are recorded. The rationalization effect achieved by the fact that many university teachers and thousands of students do not have to meet in one place in order to participate in teaching events is at least the same as that which a car manufacturer tries to achieve when, instead of sending the worker to the vehicle to be built, he transports the necessary parts to the worker. In both cases-the production process as well as distance teaching-time, energy and money are saved.

Mass production

In modern sociology the term 'mass trend' has rid itself of its negative cultural connotation, making it a largely neutral expression. Mass trend nowadays merely denotes a structural characteristic of an advanced industrial society and indicates 'that in a pure consumer society such as ours, the rise in the standard of living is due purely to the fact that industry produces certain consumer goods and commodities in large quantities. thus making them generally accessible'.

Mass production is by its nature only possible where there is a sufficiently large 'mass of consumers'. This, in turn, requires an efficient transport system providing a connection between producer and consumer who, as is typical in today's system, are geographically distant. In order to work profitably, producers need to research consumer requirements and find standards acceptable to all consumers for their products. They must continually improve their goods, as each shortcoming is multiplied by the number of items produced.

If one equally rids the term 'consumer' of its negative cultural connotation, one can speak of the student as a 'consumer of academic education'. Quite obviously, 'demand' outstrips 'supply' at universities and colleges, and this had led to the large-scale operation at our universities and colleges. As traditional forms of academic teaching originally envisaged small groups of students, and today's practice of applying methods designed for small success depends decisively on a 'preparatory phase'. It concerns the development of the distance study course involving experts in the various specialist fields with qualifications also often higher than those of other teachers involved in distance study. Here, too, each section of the course can be carefully planned. The use of technical support and a suitable combination of this with individual contributions from distance tutors and advisers play an important role here. Compared to university teachers in conventional study, who are responsible for the entire teaching process, distance tutors and advisers are more easily exchangeable on account of the thorough preparatory work. Finally, the development of distance study courses also requires investment to an extent that has never before been considered at establishments of higher education.

The separation of preparatory work and individual instruction and the distribution of these function among several persons is a particularly clear example of analogy with the production process.

Planning

An essential element of preparation is planning, which needs to be far more comprehensive and detailed in the industrial manufacturing process than in manual production, as it requires the coordination of many interacting factors. By planning we mean that 'system of decisions which determines an operation prior to it being carried out'. In more detail this means that 'all measures necessary for the economical execution of an order - from placement to delivery—must be introduced according to plan.

Management science distinguishes two methods of planning. Effective planning consists of choosing the most advantageous of several alternatives and forecasting the future development of data. Contingency planning is applied where marked situations suddenly change.

In the developmental phase of a distance study course planning plays an important role, as the contents of correspondence units, from the first to the last, must be determined in detail, adjusted in relation to each other and represented in a predetermined number of correspondence units. Where instance study is supplemented by residential weeks on campus or weekend seminars, planning becomes even more important; these supplementary teaching events are not intended to repeat academic contents already offered, nor have an 'enrichment' function, but should be structurally integrated in the distances study course. When combining distance teaching with other media, one has to consider carefully which type of contents suits what medium. Finally, where computers are used in distance study, preparatory planning is most advanced and demands by far the greatest expenditure, as the teaching activity of the computers needs to be programmed.

In all these efforts to predetermine and arrange the course of teaching processes as far as possible, we are dealing with effective planning. Intervention by advisers and tutors during the course of distance study, however, is regarded as contingency planning, which supplements effective planning.

Organization

Planning largely concerns itself with the

organization of the production cycle. In organizational management terms, organization means 'creating general or permanent arrangements for purpose-orientated activity'. As a consequence of the division of labour, the production process has to be rationally ordered according to organizational principles and with specially developed organizational means, since 'the continuous interacting of numerous people towards a specific purpose requires organization'. Furthermore, productivity depends on the type and degree of organization.

In distance study, likewise, there is an immediate connection between the effectiveness of the teaching method and rational organization. Organization, for example, makes it possible for students to receive exactly predetermined documents at appointed times, for an appropriate university teacher to be immediately available for each assignment sent in, for consultations to take place at fixed locations at fixed times, or for examinations to be held, or for counsellors to inform themselves at any time of the progress of a student or a group of students. Organization becomes easier in large distance teaching establishments, as trained personnel and modern means of organization are available. These enable them to supplement the organization of distance teaching with improvisation and disposition.

The importance of organization in distance teaching can be assessed by the fact that it is often difficult to distinguish between the operational (technical organization of distance study and the methodical organization of the actual academic contents.

Formalization

On account of the division of labour and mechanization in the manufacturing process there is a much greater need to predetermine the various phases formally than in manual production. It is only the emphasis on formality which makes the cooperation of all those involved in the production process possible, as each of them has to rely on previous work having been carried out according to plan. Most activities and interactions in an industrial set-up must therefore be determined according to agreed rules.

In distance study, likewise, all the points in the cycle, from student to distance teaching establishment to the academics allocated, must be determined exactly. Communication is standardized by the use of forms. Authors of correspondence units are recommended to consider the incorporation of standard formalized aspects that have proved to be of advantage. Lecturers marking assignments also work to standard guidelines. Assessment is, in parts, largely formalized through the frequent use of multiple choice questions, where the student only has to place a cross against the right answer. In the most modern forms of distance teaching, formalization goes as far as students marking the results of their learning on a punch card in coded form, and this is then input to a computer.

Standardization

It is characteristic of a production situation involving the division of labour and high technology that manufacture is limited to a number of types of one product, in order to make these more suitable for their purpose. Cheaper to produce and easier to replace. Georages Friedmann pointed out that this does not at all represent a threat of dullness and uniformity. On the contrary, the elementary parts produced could be combined in extremely diverse ways.

The application of the principle of the division of labour and the use of machines, as well as the duplication of correspondence units in often large numbers, force distance teaching institutions likewise to adopt a greater degree of standardization than is required in conventional teaching. Not only is the format of the correspondence units standardized, so also is the stationery for written communication between student and lecturer, and the organizational support, as well as each single phase of the teaching process, and even the academic contents.

Whereas the academic giving a conventional lecture may indulge in an interesting deviation, because he sees educational advantages in this at a particular time with a certain group of students, the distance study lecturer has to be aware that he is, when writing a correspondence unit, addressing such a large group of students that situation-dependent improvisation becomes impossible. Instead he has to find a standard adequate, as far as possible, for every student admitted to the distance study course in question. This is achieved by developing a model for the course, perfecting it through the involvement of several experts and then approximating it to the required standard by testing it on a representative group of students before printing large number of copies. Just as the production of a branded article can only remain economical if its quality is longer required: they have been replaced by accuracy and diligence; the work no longer shows quantitative but qualitative criteria'.

As a result of the division of labour, the function of the lecturer teaching at a distance also changes. The original role of provider of knowledge in the form of the lecturer is split into that of study unit author and that of marker; the role of counsellor is allocated to a particular person or position. Frequently, the original role of lecturer is reduced to that of a consultant whose involvement in distance teaching manifests itself in periodically recurrent contributions. In order to ensure the effectiveness of the four functions mentioned, numerous support functions of an operational-technical type are particularly important, as, without them, distance study could not take place.

As tutors and consultants have largely been relieved of the task of conveying course matter, they are able to devote themselves to a considerable degree to more demanding tasks, such as aiding motivation, providing individual support, structuring course contents for students, identifying problems, establishing connections and so on. Here, too, a loss of function is compensated for by a gain in function whereby, at the same time, an otherwise almost unattainable level of quality can be achieved.

Objectification

The more the production process is determined by machines and organizational principles, the more it loses its subjective element which used to determine craftsmen's work to a considerable degree. Hermann Schmidt pointed out that this process already started when man began to substitute tools provided by nature, such as hands, fists and teeth, with tools taken from his surroundings. Objectification was not possible until the item to be objectified had become the subject of reflection.

In this respect too, the relationship between distance study and conventional study is the same as between industrial production and mechanical fabrication. The university lecturer who lectures from his chair or leads a seminar discussion has the freedom and the opportunity to allow his subjectivity to influence his way of teaching: he is free to decide how and how much to prepare, he determines his own academic aims and methods and is able to change them spontaneously during a lecture, whereby not all the changes in his teaching method need to be reflected. In distance teaching, however, most teaching functions are objectified as they are determined by the distance study courses as well as technical means. Only in written communications with the distance learner or possibly in a consultation or the brief additional face-to-face events on campus has the teacher some individual scope left for subjectively determined variants in his teaching method. In cases where a computer is used in distance study, even this opportunity is limited further.

The advantages of objectifying the teaching process in the form of a distance study course lie in the fact that the teaching process can then be reproduced, thus making it available at any time and, above all, that it can be manipulated. Without objectification distance study courses could not take place anywhere and at any time and be continuously improved.

The objectification of teaching practice in distance study is of particular importance in societies where, on account of an hierarchic structure of universities and colleges, the function of the provider of knowledge is combined in many academic with that of a holder of very great authority. As a result of this the relationship between student and lecturer is similar to that of subordinate and superior. As distance study has largely been freed from subjectivity, the process of providing knowledge is hardly affected by situations of this kind. In this context, distance study is particularly suitable for the further education of adults.

Concentration and centralization

The investment required for mechanized mass production involving the division of labour has led to large industrial concerns with a concentration of capital, a frequently Centralized administration, and a market that is not seldom monopolized.

In this context it is significant that some distance teaching establishments cater for very large groups of students. The largest universities teaching at a distance in the Russia and in South Africa have over 40,000 students, and the Open University in England has more than 70,000. Each of these three establishments - as well as their Spanish equivalent - caters for the national demand. Obviously, a minimum number of students is necessary to make the technical installations and the establishment of an efficient organization feasible. Economically, it is therefore more worthwhile to create a large central distance study establishment rather than ten or twenty small regional institutions. Just as the industrial markets for certain products have long expended beyond narrow regional frontiers, such centralized distance teaching establishments must cross the traditional areas of the responsibility of universities and the educational administration.

If all the said principles of distance teaching are rigorously applied, monopoly-like prestige positions in teaching activity are created for leading experts in various disciplines. Just as no record producer would use a mediocre singer when he can engage a Fischer Dieskau, a distance teaching institution has to try and gain the best lecturers in their field for the development of its distance study courses. Just as in industry, however, one must ensure that such monopoly-like positions do not hinder free competition.

The possible consequences of a rigorous concentration and centralization of distance teaching were hinted at, for the first time in 1966, in a memorandum from the British government concerning the then proposed University of the Air. In future, universities would no longer pursue the same objectives in all subjects, but specialize in some disciplines and cater for the national requirements for distance study in these.

9 Distance Education by Correspondence Schools

Definitions

The term 'distance education' is predominantly used in its narrower meaning. It then refers to instruction by the exchange of letters between teacher and student, a process in which the contributions of both are usually based on specially prepared and methodically developed printed course material. This form of distance education is practised in most of the correspondence schools.

The wider meaning of the term is derived from the word 'distance'. It indicates more generally any form of instruction in which it is necessary to bridge a distance between teacher and student, which can be achieved not only with the help of letters and printed course material, but also by other technical media such as telephone, radio, television, audio and video cassettes, as well as by newer electronic media.

In both definitions-and this is of great importance, as it separates distance education from other forms of influencing people by giving information - *instruction* means a methodical process of imparting knowledge with the following characteristics.

- The contents of the instruction are chosen taking into account didactical and methodical considerations.
- The indirect contact between teacher and students is continued until the end of the instruction.
- There are possibilities for the teacher to influence the learning behaviour of the students.
- The learning of the students is measured and graded.

Self-instruction and *self-study,* which have been often used as synonyms for distance education, have none of these characteristics. There is, however, an intermediate stage between distance education and self-instruction, if, for instance, a student reads a series of methodically developed study materials. Such a form of instruction corresponds to face-to-face teaching in which only the teacher speaks - limiting himself or herself exclusively to the presentation of teaching material.

Supervised distance education has been used by schools which lacked teachers of certain subjects. In this case a student sits in the classroom at regular hours, studies course units and communicates with his teacher in the correspondence school somewhere else. The student - and others who might be studying different courses - is supervised by a teacher who, as a rule, does not interfere with the teaching-learning processes which are taking place under his eyes.

Students

As distance education is practised in many subject

areas and in many countries it is difficult to describe features which are common to all students. However, if one tries to find out why they decide to enroll in distance study courses it is easy to see that most of them do so because they are prevented from attending regular day schools. If we categorize the respective impediments the distance students can be assigned to the following groups:

Group 1: Students who have to work for a living in order to support themselves and often also their family: workers who want to complete their primary or secondary school education; workers, skilled workers, and technicians who want to improve their vocational qualification: agricultural labourers who intended to move into a town and therefore wish to prepare themselves for a new occupation; workers in occupations which come to an end and who, therefore, need retraining; immigrants who wish to obtain the citizenship of their new country and have to acquire specific knowledge about it.

Group 2: Students who live in sparsely settled areas: children of farmers in isolated areas, for instance in Canada and Australia.

Group 3: Students who live too far away from the nearest day school of their own nationality: children of diplomats, missionaries, military personnel abroad, children of experts employed in developing countries, children of persons in itinerant trades, sailors, boatmen, children of immigrants who are to be instructed in their mother tongues.

Group 4: Persons who are unable to attend regular schools for health reasons: sick persons who are bedridden, handicapped persons, children who have to stay in hospital for some time.

Group 5: Persons who are hindered from attending regular schools by the state: prisoners children and juveniles in reformatories.

Apart from these five groups, there are distance students who do not come into this category. They might well be able to attend regular schools but prefer to enrol in distance education courses. Some do it in order to supplement the instruction of their regular school or to raise their level of general education; gifted students do it in order to reach an advanced level and still other students do it in order to find out whether they fit into a specific vocational pattern so as to clarify vocational options. Finally, there are also teachers who study courses at a distance in order to inspire and prepare themselves for teaching.

Usually there are fewer students who wish to complete their secondary education in order to obtain entrance qualification for institutes of higher learning. Many more students intend to improve their vocational qualifications. Generally speaking, both groups belong to the higher ranks of workers and the middle ranks of salaried staff - those wide, intermediate sections of the population in industrialized countries which wish to improve their conditions of life and to climb socially. They are interested in information and eager for knowledge. Many of them can be characterized by the fact that *The Reader's Digest* recruits its readers among them. It is not coincidental that many correspondence schools like to place their advertisements in this magazine, where they have proved to be most successful.

Students who enrol in distance education do not

country, and depends on the achievements of the correspondence schools and the social structures and traditions of a given country - whether they are, for instance, capitalist or socialist. The scale of possible attitudes reaches from condescending pity and derision for the poor guys who turn themselves into drudges in order to climb the social ladder, to the firm conviction that the economic future of society depends on the qualification of numerous distant students who work and study at the same time. In the first case, distant students appear to be strange characters and outsiders, showing all the disadvantages of the self-educated: in the second case, they are considered the blue-eyed boys of the nation.

An attitude has also emerged which is located midway between these two extremes. Thus distant students are persons who take the initiative in the planning and pursuit of their careers, who have considerable will-power and perseverance in mastering a difficult task, and who are often praised for their stamina.

Teachers

In distance education, courses are usually written for an arbitrary number of students. This shows the importance of the qualification of the teachers. A bad course written by one teacher which will be studied by 10,000 students will do more harm that the oral instruction of the same teacher in a classroom. Therefore, correspondence schools try to employ teacher whose competence is higher than average. Large correspondence schools with highly differentiated course programmes employ teachers who have not only studied their subjects at a university but who also teach at institutes of higher learning: graduate engineers, businessmen, and teachers. On the other hand, they also employ experienced practitioners, leading experts and managers coming directly from the world of work.

Little is known about the educational qualifications of these teachers. Generally speaking, their competencies are mainly subject-orientated. Often they are experts in a limited field only. Educational and didactical knowledge are, as a rule, missing. Some correspondence schools like to employ experts with a special reputation or persons who have become popular—mainly for advertising purposes. A correspondence school in Paris, for instance, took pride in employing a general as well as an opera singer, and in the United States 'famous artists' founded a correspondence school in order to offer tuition in painting and writing.

On the other hand, there are correspondence schools in which teachers have not passed the examinations for which they prepare their students. As there are often no public regulations about the educational training of teachers at correspondence schools, these institutes may become places in which ambitious outsiders can stand the test as well as in which arrogant know-nothings can do a lot of harm.

As a rule, a correspondence school has a small staff of full-time and a great number of part-time employees. Many of the part-time employees are teachers in the state school system. They work as authors of course material and as correctors of assignments. Correspondence schools are happy with this arrangement as they can tell their students that they are taught by 'real' teachers. And the state schools profit from it as well, as their teachers gain new insights in the methodology of teaching when writing course material and communicating with the distant students after having corrected the assignments. Experienced teachers can often also be found in the permanent staff of correspondence schools. Usually they are unable to work in state schools because they are retired, ill or have had to leave their schools for other reasons. Among them is also a number of younger, well-trained teachers who found that they could not cope with a normal class situation as they cannot get along with larger groups of students. They find teaching at a distance much easier and more rewarding.

The work of the teacher in distance education differs from face-to-face teaching in a classroom through the increased division of labour. This principle is fundamental in industrialized production processes. Its application to the process of instructions has therefore caused considerable resistance and, mainly emotional, opposition. Division of labour, however, is not alien to our schools and universities, although they postulate a special pedagogical relationship between teacher and student and deduce from this a holistic concept of instruction. Usually the long-and medium-term plans for instruction are developed by special teams of experts, special subjects are taught by special teachers and the final evaluation of the learning outcomes of the students is often decided upon by meetings of all teachers in a given school. Nobody objects to a professor who conducts a seminar himself but asks his assistants to read and mark the papers of the students.

Although the principle of division of labour has already influenced the teaching and learning of our day schools, the job of the teacher remains extremely complex, as it consists of a number of different activities. At large correspondence schools, however, this complexity is reduced by splitting the job into several functions which are assigned to several departments:

- *Preparation of the instruction 1*: selection of the contents of instruction by the author in cooperation with the directorate of the school.
- *Preparation of the instruction 2*: development of manuscripts by an editorial staff according to the special requirements of distance teaching.
- *Presentation*: typographical design of the teaching material by layout specialists and designers.
- *Assessment and marking*: correction of the assignments by specialized correctors.
- *Interaction*: exchange of letters between the student and various persons in the correspondence school.
- *Administration and supervision*: control of the whole process of instruction, registering of the corrected assignments, card filings by specialists in the office.
- *Counselling*: Passing on information about courses and examinations and writing of letters reminding the students to send in the assignments by the information section and the respective distant teachers.

student's file and photograph when sending the assignments. Their task is difficult, indeed. While they correct, mark, explain and comment they must endeavour to individualize the course material which is, necessarily, the same for thousands of students. This can be attained by inspiring, encouraging and advising the student in such a way as is necessary in this particular teaching-learning situation. Correctors are able to devote more of their time to performing these important functions as the schools free them from written routine work. Often they use computers which print out long and very individualized letters according to the key numbers which the corrector has indicated. This very often enables them to comment upon a mistake comprehensively and to give just those hints which are required by the particular teaching-learning situation.

Some correspondence schools work with 'travelling teachers' who visit groups of distant students more or less regularly. They need special teaching skills, as they must not waste the short time available by lecturing on the topics exhibited in the course units, but must use it for identifying the most important learning difficulties and showing ways of overcoming them. This means again that the instruction is to be individualized. Furthermore, it suggests that the precious time to face-to-face instruction is also used for motivational purposes.

If the importance of correspondence schools and their possible advantages are more and more recognized their teachers will attract more public attention. It is certainly imaginable that special training courses for this group of persons will be established at teacher training colleges and at universities. For the time being, correspondence schools have to train their teachers themselves. The bigger the schools are, the easier it might be to cease improvising and to develop elaborated training procedures. The American giant correspondence school ICS, for instance, has set up a special training department which is connected fifteen schools. Applicants are selected by tests and interviews. then their educational and vocational backgrounds are considered. The training is strictly practice-oriented and has similarities to an apprenticeship. Trainees are assigned to a teacher who acquaints them with a course unit and demands that they study it in the same way as a student is expected to. This also means that the trainees have to pass the prescribed examinations. Their assignments are discussed and evaluated with the teacher, who will dwell upon typical mistakes and the best ways of dealing with them. Then the future teachers start practising themselves. They are asked to correct further assignments of the same course unit, but still under supervision of their trainees increase the number of course units they are able to correct.

Part-time teachers and often full-time teachers work at home. A correspondence school may, therefore, employ hundreds of teachers without providing offices. The teachers need not live near the correspondence school, as contacts between them and their school can be secured by mail. At a correspondence school in the Paris the teachers are obliged to be present once a week to deliver the correct assignments and to obtain new ones. This gives the teachers an opportunity to meet their colleagues and to discuss their experiences.

Objections are often raised against the depersonalizing of the teacher-student relationship in distance education. Teachers of correspondence schools, however, like to stress that they devote much more time to each individual student than could possibly be the case in the classroom. Quite often this leads, they say, to sustained personal relationships which result in distant students sending postcards from their vacations or announcements of engagements, weddings and births. When Hamburg was deluged by a big flood, a correspondence school there received many letters expressing concern for the well-being of their teachers.

10 Teaching Distance Education

There were expressions of interest in a professional qualification for distance educators at the Fourth Biennial Forum of the Australian and South Pacific External Studies Association. The South Australian College of Advanced Education made the first move and proposed a Graduate Diploma in Distance Education which the Forum endorsed. This was subsequently developed by the College and submitted to its local accrediting authority in April 1981. The course enrolled its first students in February 1983.

It is probably helpful to put the cart before the horse for a moment. The focus here is on the development process, but some introduction to the product will provide a point of reference in the following discussion.

Description of the graduate diploma

The course is the equivalent of one year of full-time study. It is only available externally and is normally taken part-time over three years. This is acknowledged in the course structure which consists of three year-long units, comprising between them some eight discrete modules. The modules where initially conceived and taught as separate units and were combined into their present form to accommodate changes to the College's academic calendar. The annual units and their modular components are:

Development and Design in Distance Education, incorporating

Introduction to Distance Education

Programme Development in Distance Education

Instrumental Design in Distance Education

Technology and Student Support in distance Education, incorporating

Communication Technology in Distance Education

Administration of Distance Education

Student Support in Distance Education

Evaluation and Project in Distance Education, incorporating

Evaluation in Distance Education

Distance Education Project

The final modular component is double-weighted, in that expectations of students are twice those which apply in each other module and it is normally taken over two-thirds of the final year of the course. Each of these modules will be discussed separately, as they were designed and developed, but first some attention will be given to more general issues concerning the steps taken in developing the programme which, from an unsteady beginning, has enjoyed considerable success. Part of the purpose here is to chart that unsteady beginning. This is in keeping with the strongly held view of the small group who were responsible for the Graduate Diploma that the experience of distance educators should be documented and shared.

The Core Team

The term 'core team' had no status within SACAE and was a matter of self-designation. Although many others were involved in preparation of the Graduate Diploma course, it was always the case that a small group took responsibility for managing the process, determining not only what would happen but how their purposes would be met, and arguing for their standards with others they persuaded to work with them. Despite a change in membership and the absence of one member on leave for several months, the ore maintained their control over the course development process throughout. The members of this group were initially Gray Willmott, Rosemary Luke, Ian Mitchell and the present author. Anne Forster subsequently joined the team.

Willmott and the author had enjoyed a close professional relationship since 1975 as the two lectures in curriculum studies at the City Campus of the College. Their educational perspectives were very similar, to the point where either worked easily with course materials developed by the other. They joined the distance education group, having been responsible for a Graduate Diploma in Curriculum Development which was largely taught by working with teachers *in situ* as they undertook various practical projects. Both lectures had considerable experience in producing external teaching materials with a strong applied focus, and drew heavily on adult learning theories, and contemporary British approaches to curriculum, theory, their work. Willmott was the first Coordinator of the distance education programme and assumed major responsibility for it, both academically and administrately. He felt the College in mid-1984 to take up a senior administrative position within another institution; the present author was appointed Head: External Studies within SACAE in August of the same year, but continued to work in the team until the course materials were completed early in 1985.

Rosemary Luke entered the programme on a short-term research contract, having previously lectured in English and librarianship. Her early responsibilities included the compilation and authorship of an annotated bibliography on distance education. Although intended to assist course planning, this was eventually distributed to students as part of the first set of course materials. Luke quickly acquired a comprehensive knowledge of current and available sources on distance education and assumed the role of editor within the group. Her incisiveness and authority on matters of presentation and style were accepted, and she was given final editorial authority over all written contributions to the course. Over her own objections, Luke was pressed into both writing course materials and teaching in the programme and was appointed to a lectureship in distance education in 1984. At the end of 1985 she left the College to become a teacher librarian.

Most of the team were newcomers to the

distance education fraternity in Australia. Ian Mitchell provided the link with the personalities and practices of those we came to see as our colleagues. As Head of External Studies in one of the colleges subsequently amalgamated as SACAE, he had initiated the proposal for a distance education course and participated in the planning process since 1979. His knowledge of the field was drawn both from an extensive range of personal contacts and several years as the foundation and executive editor of *Distance Education*. Although involved in the writing process, Mitchell moved quickly into organizing the teaching of the course and worked closely with tutors drawn from outside the core team. He is now the Course Coordinator of the programme.

During early 1984 Rosemary Luke was on leave, and Anne Forster was appointed as the first Lecturer in Distance Education within the College. Her background included research at the Institute of Educational Technology at the Open University of the United Kingdom and involvement in external programmes in the New South Wales Department of Technical and Further Education, and at the Royal Melbourne Institute of Technology. Following Willmott's departure, Forster exercised a shaping influence in the philosophy of the course team, drawing both on her formal studies in evaluation and on a passionate commitment to the liberating power of external study for students. In late 1984 she became Course Coordinator, holding the position until the end of 1985 when she moved to Canada.

The course team process

In the planning which preceded accreditation it was

agreed that the Graduate Diploma would be produced using a course team approach. Two things need to be said about this decision: first, it marked a significant shift in practice for SACAE, in that hitherto most external materials were prepared by individual academics, working alone; second, the group was initially conceived of as being quite large, involving all who would make a contribution to a given unit, including personnel from outside the College.

The group process prevailed, but it tended to be dominated by the personalities and commitment of the core team. Planning for the first unit began with a larger group which fragmented after the firs one or two meetings. The core team quickly came to reject the notion of drawing on a wide range of expertise across and outside the College and preferred to make their own way, consulting with others over quite specific contributions which were then incorporated into the materials by members of the core.

There was a number of reasons for this. First, the core argued that all those in the courses team should accept a collective responsibility for the course. Some who had expressed initial interest did not share the commitment or academic orientation of those who became the core and were not prepared to assume the responsibility being offered.

Second, both Willmott and the present author rejected conventional approaches to instructional design and asserted their views from the earliest meetings. This may well have caused those with different views to lose interest in the proposed course. The particular arguments will be discussed later.

The writing and review process involved the following steps:

1 a team would be gathered to prepare and individual unit;

2 one member would assume responsibility for managing the meetings, for example, convening the group, arranging photocopying, etc.;

3 there would be an attempt to take decisions on the structure and general approach of the unit;

4 individuals would nominate for (or be pressured into) writing tasks;

5 at subsequent meetings the group would review and comment on drafted materials (and this was frequently done at first sighting);

6 the writer would rewrite the materials in the light of comments made, or another team member would take over the redrafting;

7 the materials as improved would be subjected to a further review, although sometimes at this point they were rejected;

8 there would be a further tight edit undertaken outside the group and, depending on available time, the manuscript would be either bought back to the group for a final review or sent straight for typesetting.

From what has been said above, and because of its nature, the process generated a degree of conflict, although less than might have been expected because of the cohesiveness in the core team. The judgment of those involved was that the approach adopted was successful on at least two other counts:

the course materials produced were very well received and the process was a most powerful professional development exercise.

There were drawbacks, however. Conflict and the difficulties associated with new members have been mentioned. Perhaps the most persistent was fatigue, the product of too much to do, too little time to do it, and the knowledge that with the completion of every unit it had to be taught as the next cycle of development began. On two occasions, when preparing the *Administration and Student Support* units, core members were almost too tired to function properly yet were driven by timeliness which could not be exceeded. Considerable time was wasted in each instance as the team sought, without success, for a fresh approach to structuring the new unit.

Part of the trouble was that staff were over committed. At SACAE staff workloads are based on students taught, and no allowance is made for the development of teaching materials. Such overload may be inevitable in periods of limited resources, particularly if one accepts that people with the necessary energy or enthusiasm for development projects are likely not to be underemployed when new ventures are proposed.

The fatigue problem was most evident when the core team faced the last major undertaking, preparation of the unit *Student Techniques in Distance Education*. There was no real agreement on what we should attempt to cover and a total lack of ideas for some conceptual framework. The group faced a real tension between our theoretical perspective and confidence in our students and the weariness and sense that we just could not do it all again. The resolution of this dilemma is discussed later.

The relationship between the course team process and the membership of the core group was very close. Because of this, change was to be expected when its membership altered. Comment has already been made on the difficulties facing new members of the course team. The hegemony of the core group was such that newcomers tended to adapt to the existing process or be bypassed by it. On one occasion at least 'outsiders' joined together in a de facto sub-group in an attempt to maintain a degree of control over their intellectual product, and so manage their contribution to the course development process.

Furthermore, there was a discernible shift in emphasis when Anne Forster replaced Gary Willmott in 1984. Forster brought a new perspective to the award and was a significant influence on the rest of the group. Her specific contributions included the advocacy of a much stronger and more applied focus on evaluation within the course, both as content and process, and a deep personal commitment to supporting students towards the personal liberation and goals realization distance education affords. The team would have contended that these were both major emphases in the award from the beginning, but this would have reckoned without Forster's commitment and advocacy. She moved team from an intellectual commitment to distance education and a p4occupation with developing a course which would be favorably received towards better, practical and interactive part of the core group to involving students in the course development process. This was never realized to the level of our aspirations, but steps were taken in the right direction. First, the course planning process involved serious consideration of feedback from students on a unit-by-nit basis. It was possible in some instances to address a specific point of concern, such as assignment work, in the subsequent unit. This process was largely reactive, although the team actively sought student comment. For example, a telephone conference was run in the third unit and staff met with almost half of the first cohort of students at the ASPESA Forum at Toowoomba in 1983. Second, contributions to content were sought from students who were experienced practitioners, for instance, one student was interviewed as part of a group of expert practicing instructional designers. Third, there were student representatives on the Planning Committee of the award throughout, who acted as sounding boards for course development suggestions. Fourth, a comprehensive unit monitoring instrument was incorporated into the materials for the *Evaluation* unit, which afforded very specific feedback thereon.

These steps notwithstanding, the core team wished to share the development process in some more substantial manner. Considerable scope given to students to pursue their own professional interests through applied assignment work and a high degree of interactive sharing of experience were created in the *Student Support* unit by using part of the course development process as content, and by allowing students to determine their own purposes for the unit and achieve this 5through one-to-one dialogue with their tutors. This is described in more detail below.

Both prior to accreditation and in the early weeks of planing the *Introduction to Distance Education* unit, decisions were taken which affected the whole award. In retrospect it is difficult to explain some of them. Often quite pragmatic arguments prevailed, yet the decisions were consistent with the educational stance of the course team members. This may be explained in part y the sometimes unspoken but nonetheless shared understandings we had about what the group was trying to achieve.

The three most important determinants of the decisions taken were: the political judgment that an in-service rather than pre-service course would receive widest support in the field; a view of our likely clientele, informed by a perspective on adult learners; and a commitment to producing course materials which were of very high quality. The last of these was very much a product of the group's desire for legitimacy; we shared the view that a potentially critical professional community would determine the success of the award very much on the basis of the quality of the first set of teaching material produced. Our collected fear was the judgment that the College had taken upon itself the task of providing in-service for the field and then failed to match the quality of course materials emanating from other institutions.

Three is a tension between these three shaping elements and the group was very conscious of this at the time, for instance, the potential conflict between our preoccupation with the course materials and the commitment to students shaping their own study goals through the programme. The tension was not resolved. Our stance was that curriculum development necessarily involves an accommodation of the ideal to the practical, that the quest for perfect solutions to developmental problems is misconceived, and that our approach should be as defensible as possible.

Equally there were positive relationships between the three areas. For example, in considering potential students, it appeared likely that enrollees would bring very different levels of sophistication as distance educators to the programme. This was consonant with our view of an in-service course providing opportunities for students to meet a range of professional needs of their own determination. Further, it related to design decisions about the course materials, including the need to provide alternative study pathways and responsiveness to students' proposals to vary aspects of their programme. Thus the major determinants of design decisions existed in a dynamic tension, reflecting the need to marry practical and educational considerations without conceding some overall coherence and defensibility.

Some of the decision taken were:

1 *in relation to the quality of materials*

a materials would be print-based, typeset, and packaged in coordinated set of purpose designed loose-leaf binders;

b each modular unit would be structured differently, to demonstrate a range of presentational, methodological and assessment techniques;

c the course materials would be conceived as a set of professional resources, t be retained by the student, and embodying exercises and models which could be applied in a variety of distance education settings;

d the print materials would be a complemented with a range of non-print media; and

e materials would be visually attractive, accessible to readers, and provide a production standard within the field;

2 in relation to perceptions of students

a students would be distance education practitioners with a diversity of special interests, in fields like teaching, administration, graphic art, instructional design;

b students would reflect the range of distance education applications, e.g., schools of the air, primary and secondary correspondence education, universities and colleges, technical and further education;

c students would have very different levels of understanding skills in distance education;

d students as experienced practitioners would wish to be valued, have their expertise acknowledged, and be trusted to exercise autonomy and professional responsibility in relation to their own study programmes;

c traditional power relations between staff and students should be broken down as much as possible;

f each student should be expected to develop professionally through the programme and, while no status or exemption would be granted, could negotiate study outside that provided in the course materials, or pursue different paths within them;

g students would be encouraged to contribute to the course materials; and

h attempts would be made to engage with students beyond conventional tutor-student relationship, for example, in organizing conference participation, assisting with publications, and encouraging open dialogue with students as professional equals;

3 *in relation to the in-service nature of the course:*

a the course materials should provide both flexibility and support such that students could pursue interests at levels commensurate with their professional experience;

b the experience of practitioners at all educational levels should be valued and acknowledged within the course;

c the course would be available only to practitioners;

d all practitioners would be exposed to the experience of being an external student through the course;

e students would be encouraged to undertake applied assignments within their own professional contexts;

f students would not be required to attend on-campus at any point in the programme or in any other way cut across their vocational and personal commitments beyond the necessary allocation of time and energy demanded by their chosen study programme;

g assessment requirements would be varied to meet the needs, interests and previous experience of individual students; and

h the course would provide opportunities for students to clarify their personal learning goals and reflect on their progress towards achieving them.

Development of the modules

There were three notable features of the development of this unit: first, the course team was conscious that many of the decisions they were taking related not only to the unit, but to the whole programme; second, the process of course team activity for the programme was established through the development of the first unit; and third, the notion of contracting authors to prepare unit materials, which had been strongly argued for during accreditation, broke down in practice.

Much of the course team work for the first unit was also about planning for the Graduate Diploma as a whole. A number of the design decisions discussed above were rested immediately. For instance, having determined that the course would be prepared for people currently employed as distance education practitioners, our conception of the range of professional activities which might be covered in the course was challenged. Would we, for example, accept public radio broadcasters or tutors based on remote cattle stations as students? Conversely, additional commitments were entered into which locked the course team into particular approaches for the rest of the programme. For example, the decision to package course materials in a series of four specially designed ring-binders involved graphic art, structural and purchasing considerations to cover a three-year period.

The need to be conscious of the entire process of development was a source of chronic stress. Despite the range of decisions already made, members had considerable uncertainty about the approach and likely content of most of the proposed modules. It is not going too far to say that the team commenced the development process for almost every unit with no clear notion of what they intended to produce. This was offset by a confidence, at least on the part of Willmott and King, that it was all manageable. this may have been unduly arrogant, but their stance was essentially that the Graduate Diploma was not more than another curriculum development exercise, and if specialist expertise were required, it could and would be found. What was not foreseen was how quickly the contracting and brokering processes for obtaining course content foreshadowed during accreditation would break down.

The group development process was established at this point. The personnel, the ways of working, the roles individuals played within the group, were all being sorted through with the knowledge that we would be doing these things for some time together. What should be noted is that there was a political as well as an educational dimension to the decision to proceed using a course team. The educational argument was centrally concerned with staff development and the coherence which could be attained through collective endeavour. The political dimension, and 'political' is used here in a very broad sense, reflected a concern by the dominant group to protect their own view of the standards and course orientation necessary within the award. The collectivity allowed the core group to vet all contributions and propose amendments to, or even reject, material from individual authors about which they had reservations. The group's legitimacy came from educational arguments and notions of participatory democracy; in fact, it was an oligarchy which drew upon others only on its own terms. The members of the core were prepared to be judged on the quality of their product and to triumph or be damned.

As indicated earlier, there was some reinforcement for the concentration of control in the hands of core team by the early breakdown of the proposed contracting system for producing materials. The most serious criticism was that the material presented was heavily didactic and did not fit at all well with the commitments made to respecting the experience and expertise of students. Our view was that the students should be able to locate themselves personally and professionally within the course through the first unit, and be assisted to develop their own strategies for using the Graduate Diploma to meet their own legitimate needs. As a result, a new section was planned, the 'Autobiography of a Distance Learner', which came to comprise the first third of the module. This provided a series of structured activities to assist students to reflect on their personal and professional circumstances, reasons for taking the course, learning styles, vocational goals and strategies they intended to adopt for achieving success — however they defined it—throughout the programme.

The course team quickly realized that the time available for the development of each unit module did not allow for such reworking of proposed content. Further, there were some aspects of the proposed course on which they had a considerable agreement and about which they would rather take on additional workload than compromise. An important dimensions of this understanding was the recognition that agreement on process, on the approach to be taken in the module, was more important than being clear about the content.

Programme development in distance education

Willmott and King undertook the drafting of the module, as other course team members turned their attention to teaching *Introduction to Distance Education*. The result was their attempt to apply the work they had been doing in curriculum studies to distance education, and in some ways it is the most conventional section of the Graduate Diploma programme. This is particularly so in relation to its structure and presentation.

The content was more interesting and constituted something of an assault on the field. It drew on a series of five propositions which have been discussed elsewhere and can be restated in the following manner:

1 There is no coherent general theory or broad paradigm of programme development in distance education. The field needs to develop conceptual

schemes for drawing together its fragmented literature and guiding research and practice.

2 The literature on programme development in distance education draws upon the limiting traditions of instructional design and educational technology. The field would be better served in this regard by a curriculum theory which embraces a wider range of concerns and treats them as problematic.

3 Programme development in distance education is characterized by a series of myths and untested assumptions which most analysis fails to acknowledge and examine. There are important questions about the legitimation and justification of distance education which should be of concern to programme developers.

4 Existing analyses of programme development in distance education fail to acknowledge the significance of post-implementation procedures characteristic of successful innovation.

5 To a large degree the literature on course design in distance education is either unknown or ignored by practitioners, probably because it fails to recognize the realities they face.

Using the propositions as points of departure, the authors proposed a conceptual framework as one possible way of making explicit the critical tasks, problems and relationships which exist in programme development in distance education. Its rationale will not he rehearsed here.

The conceptual framework provided the structural basis for the module. In retrospect the

Students were given the option of doing specified assignments from any two of the sections or negotiating a single assessment on any matter of interest to them generally relevant to the area. Within the specified assignments there were both opportunity for directly applied study and considerable difference in the level of sophistication required, although all assignments were equally weighted.

The materials responded to the diverse experience of students of providing quite separate study pathways through the module; thus individuals could complete the requirements by studying quite difference things, and by rewarding accomplishment at the student's own self-nominated level of expertise. These were significant departures from existing external practices at SACAE.

This module also marked the end of attempts to contract authors from outside the College. The problems encountered might have been predicted: failure to meet time-lines, incompatibility of what was provided with the orientation of the in-College course team members, and obstacles to participation by the external author created by his own institution. The decision not to use the contracted materials created substantial problem for the team, all of whom found themselves unexpectedly pressed into designing and drafting sections of the course.

In part the burden was one of the team's own creation.The decision to contract authors had been taken before the core team had emerged and asserted their control over the programme. It was very much a matter of unwillingness to compromise with their own standards. The delays in submission also enabled the core to consider strategies for dealing with the diversity of student experience in the area. The failure of the contracting process had two consequences: first, the core was left to develop the rest of the programme, and second, it could no longer avoid more conscious planning of the modules before drafting commenced.

Communication technology in distance education

This module is remarkable for the fact that the course team agreed to present the instructional content on video-tape, which may have been the worst design decision taken. It has been subject to the greatest modification following its initial offering and is in the process of major revision.

The decision to base the module on a three-hour video tape was in keeping with a determination to model a range of delivery techniques, a desire to be innovative, and the availability of a staff member with considerable professional expertise in video production. The core team was very inexperienced with the medium, however, and unaware of the constraints involved. There were communication problems, arising both from the difficulties of the inexperienced trying to control the technically expert and the obstacles to close contact between staff working on different campuses. Further, the core were unaware of the limited opportunities for editorial revision of a complex video production and the time involved in post-production and tape duplication. In short, the core lost control over the teaching materials. Our difficulties were compounded by the nature of the content (for example, a section on computers rapidly became embarrassingly out-of-date) and overestimating the weariness, was clearly affecting their efficiency. The strategy belatedly adopted was born of desperation. Those wishing to contribute were asked to draft material without considering how their sections might relate to the module overall. This reflected concern that, as time was running out, we should have something on paper, if only to provide an impetus in some other direction.

The components prepared covered: an introduction to administrative theory, the impact of governmental enquiries on distance education, financial management and planing, staff development, the administration of policy development and change, and staff and jab management. The orientation of these discrete section was very different. The problem for the course team was how might be brought together and appropriate study paths created for students with different expertise and interests.

This did not afford an easy solution and, after time, the group opted for the non-solution of passing the problem on to students. The decision was taken to make no attempt to bring the six components into some coherent whole, but to emphasize their separate concerns. Students were invited to select any two areas and to undertake an applied exercise in each. Despite their different emphases, levels of sophistication and demands made on readers, the six sections were treated as equal. This decision was not taken as casually as it might seem. Members recognized that the areas had equal potential to allow students to pursue matters of interest and professional relevance to themselves.

Subsequent evaluation supports the design decisions taken. Students where not bothered by our lack of conceptual clarity. Without wishing to diminish the force of that support, it is worth emphasizing that at best the design of this module was the result of a search for a way to capitalize on educational difficulties.

Evaluation in distance education

This module review heavily on the expertise of other College staff who had not previously worked in the graduate Diploma programme, but was shaped and tightly controlled by the core team. It is more coherent than the section which precede, it and models the view of the *Programme Development* module that evaluation is central to planning and teaching.

A particular strength is the assessment activity, which is embedded in the substance of the module and establishes an unambiguous connection between content and process. Student's reactions to the module are more rigorously sought through an in built monitoring instrument. The centrality of evaluation in course planning is highlighted by a recapitulation of·activities undertaken by students in each earlier module which were evaluative in nature. In essence, there is a movement from the stance of the course thus far, which might be characterized as opening up issues and providing opportunities for students to engage with them both reflecting and in application, to obliging students to identify and come to terms with issues as they arise from their own practice. The difference is one of degree but it is there.

There were excellent contributions from staff outside the core who entered into the course team process wholeheartedly. However, the review process became too daunting and two of the outsiders formed a sub-group, preferring to work on one aspect of the module on their own. Another felt unable to make deletions from an analysis of theories of evaluation which the core felt unbalanced the module through its length. The Section was reduced by about one third by the present author, but the original contributor was clearly dismayed by this aspect of the group process.

The assessment activity guides students through the planning of an evaluation exercise in their own field, and is possibly the guest example of teaching by involving students in process offered in the course.

Student support in distance education

This may well be the most satisfactory module in the course. Yet the core team was so over stressed at the point where its development was scheduled that it was decided to produce the *Evaluation* unit first, out of sequence, using the expertise of other staff.

The support module is notable for the following: considerable time was again expended in attempting to find a structure for the materials; the orientation of some of the course team changed markedly during the development process; working on the materials became so engrossing that we had consciously to avoid recommitting the contents of earlier modules; it was during the development process that many of our own ideas and practices were clarified; and finally, the module is so different from where the programme started that it would be better located at the beginning of the Graduate Diploma.

If we had experienced problems in finding a coherent framework for earlier modules, they were as nothing to the difficulties which now confronted the group. The team met for hours over several days in an attempt to find a structural framework and orientation for the module. There were quite different perspectives on what we should be doing. Unfortunately, the view which ultimately prevailed was not clearly understood in the early weeks and for some time members talked at cross purposes.

In introducing the module to the first group of students, we outlined some of the matters which had been important during our discussions:

1 we wanted to reflect adult learning theory in our own teaching to the greatest possible degree;

2 we had a commitment to modelling quite different approaches to written materials with each module;

3 we had been very conscious of the different interests of our students, some of whom worked with children and other with adults, and our concern was to maximize flexibility;

4 we wanted an approach to the materials which allowed us to raise issues without having to treat them in an equally through manner; and

5 we wished to avid the suggestion that the area lent itself easily to some comprehensive theoretical overview.

This suggests a greater clarity than initially existed. At first we had sought an overview and wanted to provide students with a comprehensive and up-to-date perspective on student support. It was also the case that wile team members were not complacent about the degree to which the Graduate Diploma had been responsive to meeting students' perceptions of their own professional needs, most were proud of what had been achieved in the programme and believed its general orientation was sound. Anne Forster challenged us to take a more radical stance, Her view was that members had not yet grappled with their own conceptions of distance education and that this was evident in the way students were regarded. Further, if there was to be any change, this module provided the last opportunity.

The difficulties in finding some direction became so acute that, as Course coordinator, I attempted an assumption clarification exercise which was referred to above under the heading "The Course Team Process". While this made some of our attitudes to the programme more explicit, it did not resolve the block members were experiencing.

Progress was first achieved with a decision on the nature of assessment within the module. The team had been impressed by the work of Barbara Comber, from the College's Graduate Diploma in Reading and language, who had experimented with assessmented based on correspondence with individual students. We agreed students would be asked to establish areas of interest for themselves and to write their tutors four letters during the teaching period about what they were learning and any other related matters. The tutors would write individual responses, and participation in this correspondence would be the sole basis for determining assessment, which would be in the form of a non-graded pass.

Secondly, and soon afterwards, the group began to understand Forster's criticisms. In module 2, *Programme Development,* we had argued against adopting deficit approaches to distance education, for example, by assuming that the course materials were the sole determinants of the learning experience and had there fore to be as near perfect as possible. This was very close to the stance we were taking with the present module. We decided to require students to become more self-directed than earlier modules had encouraged or allowed. Further, we wanted to alter the staff-student relationship to make it more collaborative and exploratory than before. These decisions have been discussed elsewhere. There was still the problem of how to present the various resources we believed students should receive. We adopted the approach taken in relation to assessment for the rest of the module. All the content would be in the form of letters to the general student group from individual staff. There would be no attempt to present comprehensive treatments for various issues, or to relate the letters one to another. In some instances this would happen, but only because the author concerned chose to do so. Contributions would vary in length, focus and approach, depending on the interest of the lecturer concerned.

This was a new stance for the group. Previously all materials had been presented as products of the course team. Members would this time be exposing themselves as individuals. The group review process was still retained however, although the attention given previously to consistency of style and approach no longer applied. The approach liberated members of the course team. There was no attempt to produce the definitive contribution; rather, as individuals we took chances and tried to communicate our interests and enthusiasms to students. Often the substance of a letter from another member of the team would stimulate each of us to write something else. There is little doubt that the team found the module easier to write for than had previously been the case, once this stance was adopted.

Two things happened as a result. First, some of us began to realize the satisfactions of a new approach to distance education. Despite long-standing involvement with external students, the genuinely interactive approach had both intellectual and social rewards which some had not previously found in their distance teaching. Second, without initially realizing the implications of our stance, and as a result of Forster's gentle insistence, the group was reconceiving distance education as support for students who faced a particular set of problems in achieving their personal study goals.

Another aspect of this approach was that it contributed to the breaking down of battiers between staff and students. By writing as individuals rather than a group, a personal dimension was added to the course materials. This brought the core team closer to the collaboration with students as equals it desired and espoused, but had found difficult to achieve. Further, it was a much distance course writing is: 'As your tutor, I have a thorough grasp of the field, which we presenting here in a form you will be able to manage, and with exercises and assignments at points which will reveal to me how well you are mastering and applying the material we are opening up for you.' The message of the materials in this module was closer to: 'we think this item is relevant to the general topic of the module. What do you think? Do you want to purpose it any further?' This may overstate each position, but the team felt they were closer to the second stance.

We tried to be honest about our own uncertainties and described the difficulties we had been having in our attempt to establish a conceptual framework, including the reasons for ultimately rejecting it as a legitimate undertaking, including the reasons for ultimately rejecting it as a legitimate undertaking. The assumption clarification exercise had not solved our problem, but it did make clear a number of attitudes team members had to our students and as such seemed potentially useful. It was described in one of the letters, and students were invited to reflect on its possible application in their own situation.

Distance education project

This double-weighted module had been the subject of longest planning in the award, having been the subject of considerable discussion during the accreditation process. The course materials are briefer than for any other section yet they represent the culmination of the educational intentions of the programme.

It had been agreed from the very early stages of course planning that a substantial part of student's work in the Graduate Diploma would be in the form of an applied project in an area of professional interest of their own nomination. The Assessment Committee during accreditation had been concerned about the degree of supervision possible in the distance mode, and the group had agreed to adopt a process of regular reporting to meet such concerns, although at the time the module was prepared our emphasis was more on negotiation and collaboration than supervision.

Three factors in particular shaped the approach taken. First, the evaluation module provided a successful module of structured and supportive guidance through project planning activities. Second, one student had already completed the project under special arrangement, having taken an overload in other modules to complete the course ahead of schedule. In determining the approach to be taken with him, the team had already considered the emphasis to be given to research methodology, the range of approaches which might be acceptable, likely areas for investigation and the methods of assessment. Finally, the very positive response of students to the high degree of interaction with tutors in the *Student Support* module give staff good reason to think that communication and negotiation would be a strength rather than a difficulty in this final course component.

Each student's proposal was vetted by an approvals group, comprising members of the core team, who then assigned a supervisor competent to support the individual in the nominated field. In some instances, where the intended project required specialist expertise outside the scope of members of the course team, and additional external supervisor was nominated. The final project reports were assessed by the supervisor and an external assessor, who reported to the approvals groups. Reports were then forward to the students concerned.

Reflection on the development process

In retrospect the rationale for course development in the Graduate Diploma in Distance Education appears to have been based on:

— a concern to improve practice, both through modelling a range of strategies in the delivery of the course and providing opportunities for students to reflect on their practice and attempt modifications of it;

— a rejection of the familiar, rule-based instructional design approach to course development;

— adoption of a curriculum model which identified a broad range of areas which would impact upon course development decisions;

— an acknowledgment that the broader range of issues which thus became a concern in course development should be treated as problematic;

— a determination to apply precepts from adult learning theories in the design and delivery of the course, particularly in the acknowledgment of the expertise of our students; and a commitment to taking decisions which, in the language of Stenhouse, were intelligent, thus making best use of the information available to us at the time.

Course team members were aware of each of these elements during the development process and saw their stance as differing from much of the practice and precept of the field. What was missing, I suspect, was an acknowledgment that one teacher-dominated model had been replaced by another, albeit one which was more liberal and open to student concerns. In this there was a disjunction between the aspirations of the group and the practical consequences of the approach adopted, and members were not initially aware of this. We were unintentionally taking a decisions on the basis of a two limited perspective. The course development strategy altered about two-thirds of the way through the process. Course team members may not have fully appreciated how they were changing the 'curriculum; model they had initially adopted. The change in strategy began during the drafting of the *Evaluation* module, but had a significant impact on the group's practice when, during its delivery to students, tutor-student interaction became more genuinely interactive. This coincided with the development phase for *Student Support,* during which the team came to terms with the altered directions in which they were moving. The difficulties experienced at that time within the team may have resulted from a basic misunderstanding of what was happening. Those who had been with the awarded longest regarded the changes going proposed as extensions of the stance they had already taken, that is, more 'freedom' would be extended to students. But this was not what was being suggested, and it took some of us several weeks to understand that what was sought was a new basis for legitimating the course development decisions we were taking.

11 Computer Education–At a Distance

Introduction

This chapter is concerned with two home-computing issues: the kinds of problems and difficulties that people have when they are learning to use computers by means of distance-teaching materials, and the design of instruction for learners in this position. These two issues are intimately connected: in order to design effective teaching materials students can use on their own, it is essential to find out about the kinds of problems students have in learning about computers and the kinds of errors they make. Problems to do with learning to use the computer and computer application are the next hurdle after the problem of gaining access to the computer itself has been solved.

There are now research findings in two important areas related to student computing. Firstly there are studies of learning to use computer applications in commercial environments, and on designing self-instructional training materials for these applications. Many of the same issues arise in producing distance-education materials for teaching practical computing as in designing self-instructional minimalist approach is to obstruct as little as possible the learner's self-initiated efforts to find meaning in the activities of learning.

On the face of it, this approach would also seem to address some of the fundamental issues for students learning to use information technology at a distance. This section will discuss the problems Carroll's learners experienced, before going on to consider his proposed instructional model.

In an early study the participants, who were temporary office staff, learnt one of two text-processing systems. They used self-study manuals for about 12 hours over four half days, and in the testing phase they were asked to type and revise a letter. They were asked to think aloud while they worked and all their interactions with the computer were recorded.

The learners had a lot of difficulties with the task. They often attempted to carry out tasks, such as logging on to the system, without reading the manual, and complained about the amount of material to read and remember. They lacked basic knowledge and had problems with terms such as parameter, queue and pagination. Some of these were problems in misinterpreting words the participants were familiar with but which, in the context of the computer application they were learning to use, now had a different specialised meaning. For example, one of Carroll's learners wondered who the printer was. Another problematic term was 'default', which elsewhere is a legal term.

They did not know what was relevant and so were influenced by superficial connections between what they did or perceived and the problems they were trying to solve. They were also very active in their learning: 'Complementary to learners' lack of knowledge about what is relevant is their ability to go beyond the information given by constructing and elaborating ad hoc interpretations of experiences. In explaining away puzzles, learners can convince themselves that all is well when the odd happenings they have noticed are really evidence of disaster'. For example, one learner was attempting to enter her password when she made a typing mistake which caused the system to stop and await correction. An indicator light marked 'input inhibited' came on. The learner attributed both the delay and light to a heavy workload on the system. Another learner had made an error in issuing a 'file' command and wondered whether her work had been filed. She interpreted the message, '*input mode 1 file*' as meaning that it had.

In another paper such explanations are described as abductive reasoning, where a hypothesis is generated to account for one or more observation. One implication of abduction is that the consequences of errors are explained away and learners do not realise they have made a mistake. They are influenced by superficial resemblances between what they think they need to know and what they see or do. Such abductions are often wrong and are not tested out. Lewis and Mack suggest that such reasoning has value in interpreting future events where there is no alternative to abductive reasoning. Often such complex learning is characterised by incomplete and ambiguous information and if learners are to try to understand the process that might lie behind what they experience then they have to use abductions. What Lewis and Mack are in fact talking about is learners *building up mental models,* which will often be wrong, as they are based on fragmented, ambiguous information. This notion of mental models will be taken up a little further on in the chapter.

One response to problems such as those experienced by the learners Carroll studied is to consider them as the teething problems of introducing new technology into the office for the first time. If this is the case, then it should be expected that later systems would benefit from the experience of earlier ones. However, Carroll cities similar problems in learning the later Macintosh-like Lisa system. The Lisa was, at the time, a new user interface with a high-resolution display, a reliance on graphic presentation and applications and was mouse driven. It was highly regarded and highly acclaimed in a review: 'Lisa has made giant steps in saving the user both time and frustration'.

In the study of learners using the Lisa, there were six volunteers drawn from various professions. These participants were not computer professionals but did have a reasonable amount of computer experience and, furthermore, they had experience of different systems. As in the previous study, the participants worked on their own, using the self-9instructional manuals. These included an online tutorial, although not all the participants tried this. Carroll concluded that overall there was a rather lower level of success than expected. The participants did not finish all the tasks suggested and the same types of problems occurred that had been seen in the previous study. They also took far longer than estimated on the instructional materials: for example, the five who tried the online tutorial spent over an hour and three-quarters on it: three times the time estimated by Apple. One complaint made by all the participants was that the tutorial placed them in too passive a role.

These participants said that they were going to read the manual carefully before doing anything - but none of them maintained this strategy for long; instead, they started to try out activities on the computer. When they did read they had trouble finding what they were looking for in the manuals and in co-ordinating the display with what they were reading in their books.

Designing minimalist instruction for teaching wordprocessing

The learners in these studies can be viewed as being active in their learning, making use of their prior knowledge, and having great difficulty in recovering from errors. The problems experienced by the learners in these studies led to a critical analysis of the design of the self-instructional materials.

The style of the self-instructional material the participants had used throughout the studies was very structured. The design followed a standard systems approach which involves hierarchical decomposition of learning objectives. However, Carroll argues that learners have problems because such materials do not relate to their own goals, and because learners are very active in the learning process. He argues that the systems approach does not work and describes how

Systematic drill and practice materials present learners with a motivational double bind with respect to meaningful interaction. If they succeed at following the steps..the success is hollow. They have little control over the situation and cannot feel seriously responsible for the outcomes. However if they eschew the prescribed path - for example, correcting a real typo - they are likely to become snarled in a tangle of errors, which the system and training do not anticipate and recovery from which they do not support. The learner will fail in some sense no matter what the choice.

On this basis, the idea of minimalist instruction was developed, which aims to avoid these problems, first, any allowing learners to start immediately on meaningfully realistic tasks; second, by reducing the amount of reading and other passive activity in training; and, third, by helping to make errors ad error recovery less problematic and more pedagogically productive.

The minimal instruction approach was first tried out by producing a set of cards which replaced the self-instruction manual and which adopted a 'guided exploration' approach. These were tried out with a group of learners. Although the cards worked well, and this group did better than a group using the standard training manual, it did not ameliorate all of the standard problems. In particular, the learners wanted a more traditionally structured manual, and so a self-instructional manual was designed, based on the minimalist model. It attempted to have topics of interest to the learners - for example, chapters had headings such as 'Typing Something'—and learners were able to start learning to use the system.

Two experiments carried out on the use of the 'minimal manual' indicated that it was substantially and reliably better than the commercial self-instruction manual. An important concern to those designing distance or self-teaching material for students using computers is the best way of carrying out the design process itself. Interestingly, the design process for the minimalist manual described by Carroll is similar to the standard process adopted for OU teaching material which is described in the next section. It is an interactive design process where the material is designed, empirically evaluated and then redesigned. In particular, producing the minimal manual involved three states of different empirical testing. Pilot testing was incorporated into a design-analysis stage which drew on knowledge of how users went about tasks and their typical errors. Following this, particular design elements were empirically tested in qualitative detail by observing typical users at work with the manual. The final version of the manual was tested in the two experiments described earlier.

In earlier chapters we saw that the very structured approach to distance learning offered by the 'industrial model', of which the OU is an example, was criticised for being too prescriptive and didactic and for promoting a one-way model of teaching, where the students has little opportunity to engage in a real dialogue. Such criticism is consistent with Carrolls's data where learners felt they were cast in too passive a role. one alternative to this kind of approach for practical work is a more student-centred 'discovery' model. Such an approach has often been used with children learning the language LOGO. Some of the claims made for LOGO are that it can teach people to reason, problem solve and plan, or rather, help people to learn these things for themselves. The best exposition of this LOGO philosophy is given by Papert in his book *Mindstorms,* where he says:

> In my vision the child programs the computer, and in doing so, both acquires a sense of mastery over a piece of the most modern and powerful technology and establishes an intimate contact with some of the deepest ideas from science, from mathematics, and from the art of intellectual model building.

This philosophy assumes an open approach to learning where the sequence of concepts learnt will depend largely on the learner, and the judgement of the teacher.

One manual produced to accompany a version of LOGO developed by the OU did adopt such an approach, where the learner is invited to explore and discover LOGO. In line with LOGO philosophy, the manual adopts a style which is rather less structured than many programming instructional manuals. However, a study of adult learners using this booklet showed that some problems arose because it was *not* prescriptive enough. For how long were they supposed to explore? Had they got a 'right' answer? The adult learners in this study found learning LOGO hard and the difficulties they had led to problems with the exploratory 'diagnose your bugs' style of the tutorial manual. Where they have made more than one mistake, and these may interact in a programming language, and their processing models are faulty, students are unlikely, themselves, to diagnose the problems. In this style of teaching, programming is not taught because the learner is supposed to discover it.

Too unstructured an approach can feel very uncomfortable for adults who are not used to working in this way: moreover, in practical work at a distance, it can leave them without sufficient support when things go wrong as, when students explore, things inevitably will! The LOGO curriculum, in attempting not to be prescriptive, failed to meet the needs of the intended audience, and was criticised both for misjudging the audience and for therefore presenting both inappropriate material and for using an inappropriate style. It is interesting that Carroll's learners also found the unstructured style of the guided exploration cards uncomfortable, and asked for a more traditional manual.

To a large extent, the kind of interactive process employed by Carroll *et al.* is already built into the production cycle of most OU materials. Courses are produced by a course team which will typically include academics, a course administrator, a member of the academic computing service, a television audio producer, an editor and designer and an educational technologist. Drafts of particular parts of the course are produced and circulated around the members for comment. Typically a unit of course material will undergo three full drafts before it is finalised and handed over to the editor. In addition to this internal commenting, there will be one or more external assessors who will also receive and comment on all the drafts. Depending on the course, it may also undergo formative evaluation, which usually involves a number of students working through the course materials and commenting on them. The stage at which this happens is quite critical: if it is too early, the materials will have gaps and they will not resemble the final product closely enough to be a realistic simulation; if it is too late, then there will be insufficient time to make changes following the feedback.

Designing practical work for trainings teachers to use computers

The formative evaluation process described above is not applied to every course. However, it is particularly important to test out any element of practical work, whether it is a laboratory-style home experiment or the use of a computer, as students will be on their own if and when any problems occur. We know that learners are likely to have difficulties when starting to use computers for the first time, and in developing one set of materials for novice computer users, the course team adopted a particular design process to ensure that the material was as accessible as possible for students. In this case what was being developed was training materials for teachers as part of the 'Microcomputers in Schools' project. The project team responsible for these materials decided that the empirical evaluation process was so important that it should be carried out twice. Before describing the process it is necessary to describe the courses and their design.

The 'Microcomputers in Schools' project produced five standalone but linked 'packs' of course materials aimed at teachers, ranging from complete novices to those with some experience of computers.

Its background, aims and design process are described in more detail elsewhere by the project director. At the time, the early 1980s, it was clear that there were teachers who were very frightened by the idea of using computers, and the first pack produced was the 'awareness pack' which assumed that the student had no knowledge whatsoever of computers and, moreover, might be very nervous. To help students with the very real problem of getting the computer they were using connected up in order to start, different-coloured and coded labels were provided which could be attached to the leads and their connections.

In the text material, all the practical work was laid out in a three-column format, where the first column gave the keypress required, the second gave a photograph of the screen display that appeared as a result of that action, and the third column provided a commentary. Clearly in this style of very structured instruction it is imperative for the text and the screen photograph to match exactly what was happening on the student's screen. For the courses in the 'Microcomputers in Schools" project, the empirical testing was extensive. External 'critical readers' were employed to comment on the first drafts of materials in addition to the project members. The second draft, which incorporated the feedback from the first, was evaluated by students working through the whole course in detail. Following comments from other team and project members and the evaluation feedback, a third draft was produced. Before this was handed over to the editor, a final round of testing was carried out to ensure that all the steps in the practical work corresponded to the screen photographs and that these, in turn, were an accurate representation. This final round of testing came to be known as 'catastrophe testing'!

This formula proved to be very successful for complete novices, and was also appreciated by students with some experience. It is quite structured, and allows the student relatively little freedom to decide what to do in the practical hands-on material, although in other parts of the course there is much more open-ended work where the student applies what he or she has learnt to his or her own situation and carries out project work.

These two figures illustrate how exploration, and the learner's own goals, can be encompassed within this model: it does not need to be the kind of step-by-step approach criticised by Carroll for leading to passive learning, and which seemed to contain a lot of drill-and-practice.

There was also an attempt to avoid the problems of the step-by-step approach, where students lose the global view and can end up recipe-following with little understanding by including the third 'commentary' column which provides some rationale and an overview.

The three-column style of the activities book, along with the case study and project book which accompanied it, appears to fulfil the same criteria as Carroll's minimalist instruction. Students are quickly in a position where they are engaged in hands-on activities; the guided exploration which happens in some places encourages students to be active and to engage in the activities they want to;

and recovery from the errors they make should be supported by the troubleshooting guide supplied in the appendix. As far as keeping the reading down is concerned, the booklets are quite slim with little extra verbiage or repetition and little in the way of overviews and prefaces, etc. In fact, the OU has a built-in disincentive against producing too much reading material because of the high cost of extra print - and the extra study time required of students.

This approach is not completely successful in all cases, however, A study of students carrying out practical work with such an approach, on quite a different course, indicated that, for these students, the problem of learners operating at too low a level (taking a micro-level approach, like the surface-level processing) has not altogether been avoided. The course was analysed as part of a study in which four different curricula for teaching novices to program were evaluated. Three of these texts guide the student quite closely by structuring the material very carefully, two of which adopted the three-column format discussed above. It would seem that in some cases, however, this style of instruction, although it does provide an overview, may still encourage the learner to adopt an over-dependent attitude towards the text.

The experiment book for one of the courses examined in the study, *Microcomputers for Managers*, adopts a step-by-step 'recipe'-type approach and contains relatively little work of a less structured and open-ended nature. Students instead carry out 'experiments' and are working in assembler, a low-level programming language where

increasingly coming to believe that people deal with complex interactive devices by making use of a conceptual model of the device, and that the fostering of this model is an important consideration for the designer. The notion of a user's 'conceptual model' is a rather hazy one, but central to it is the assumption that the user will adopt some more or less definite representation or metaphor which guides his actions and helps him interpret the device's behaviour. Such a model, when appropriate, can be helpful, or perhaps even necessary for dealing with the device, but when inappropriate or inadequate can lead to misconceptions and errors.

This then is the idea of the mental learners use when operating a device. It has also been argued that the system itself should be taught using a similar model. This idea applies throughout learning complex devices or domains, and when teaching about computer systems or applications it is particularly important to consider how they are presented and represented to the learner, especially given that learners will be active in their interpretation. Du Boulay, O'Shea and Monk, for example, argue that a major problem in teaching voices programming is describing the machine the novice is learning to use at the right level—as the novice usually does not know what the machine can be instructed to do or how it does it. They suggest overcoming this problem by basing the teaching on a 'notional machine', which is an idealised model of the computer based on the programming language. The notional machine helps learners by providing a descriptive model which they can use to plan programs and to interpret the machine's response. As this idea, and similar ones, are usually referred to as 'conceptual models' by other researchers, this is the terminology that will be used here from now on.

Criteria for designing conceptual models for novices

Du Boulay, O'Shea and Monk advocate two principles upon which to base the conceptual model: *simplicity* and *visibility*. One aspect of simplicity is that there should be a set of instructions and commands which is small enough to be learnt readily by a novice. Another example of simplicity is that the language is suited to the task in hand. Syntactic simplicity 'is achieved by ensuring that the rules for writing instructions are uniform, with few special cases to remember, and have well chosen names'.

Visibility means that wherever possible, methods should be provided for the learner to see the workings of the conceptual model in action, for instances the effects of commands. One way of doing this is by means of a commentary, a 'glass box' through which novices can see the workings of the machine. As the area they discuss is programming, it is not surprising that most of the examples of visibility which are given concern highlighting flow of control. Help for novices to decide what state the machine is in is also mentioned, and the importance of choosing names that do not conflict with novices' previous knowledge. In the context of distance education where learners have little support, it is clearly important to consider how to make learning such skills as easy possible.

To help illustrate these ideas, an example of a conceptual model will be discussed which embodies the principles of both simplicity and visibility. The discussion is necessarily rather more technical than previous sections of this chapter, and readers who don't want to follow through the example in detail should miss this section and go on to the last part of the chapter, the conclusions. The conceptual model is a for a microcomputer, 'DESMOND'. The conceptual model is essentially provided by the machine itself - it is its own model and has been designed so that its workings, at the appropriate level, are visible. DESMOND is the name given to the microcomputer used as part of two OU study packs: *Inside Microcomputers* and *Learning about Microelectronics*, and was in fact sent out to students as a home experiment kit.

DESMOND can be operated in three different 'modes'. In the first, monitor mode, the user can inspect different memory locations and change the contents. In order to increase the machine's simplicity, there is an attempt to make the workings of each mode easy to understand. In monitor mode, for example, the display is divided into three parts, each giving different information: the first part gives the address of the memory location, and the second and third parts give the contents in two different forms. Arrow keys are used to move backwards and forwards through memory locations.

To fulfil the criterion of visibility, all the circuitry and chips are visible, and devices are grouped together according to their function. The battery box is on the top right. On the top left are various switches and below these are the sensors. Together these make up input devices. The output devices are grouped together on the right. On the right, below the battery box, are five different-coloured lamps; below these are a buzzer and a motor. The keypad has two sections: the left side contains digits from 0 to 9, and the right has two rows of keys, of which the top four are keys for changing *mode,* for example, going into assembly mode where programs can be entered in assembly language, or into run mode by pressing R for running a program.

A detailed analysis of the design of DESMOND in terms of visibility, simplicity and additional criteria is given by Jones. Here, one further example will help to illustrate the attempt to make the conceptual machine as visible as possible and to help the learner keep track of where he or she is. This is visibility by making the contents of memory locations visible, for example by making it easy to inspect the 'address' of a memory location and its contents. An earlier example was given of how in one mode, monitor, the display shows the address of the location and its contents; in another mode, assembly, we see the program line, and the two parts of the instruction. In run mode, when programs are being executed, the contents of different locations are not usually shown, but there is a facility for running a program step by step and being able to inspect the contents of the relevant memory locations after each step has been executed by the computer. This helps the user to see what changes are happening at each step.

Keypresses are given for most of the experiments in the practical book, except for the final experiments where it is assumed that this level of guidance is not needed. The instructions are given in the three-column format described previously where the first column gives the keypress, the second shows what will appear in the screen and the third gives the commentary.

The criteria for designing conceptual models in use

One important problem with such criteria is that there may not be a clear correspondence between what appears to be good design, according to the principle of simplicity, and how easy such systems are to use in practice. Mayer has carried out empirical work demonstrating the value of conceptual models, but prior to a study carried out by one of the authors, du Boulay, O'Shea and Monk's criteria had not been empirically tested, although the three examples of systems they give have all been in use.

A further principle for conceptual models is introduced by Jones—the principle of consistency. Consistency is the extent to which the behaviour of various parts of the conceptual machine is related. An example of this would be whether a particular command can be inferred from another. In LOGO, having learnt the *left* instruction, one can reasonably infer that there will be a *right* instruction. This principle applies in environments other than programming and may even be more important in such application in that, if there is consistency, then one application can be used by analogy with another. The Apple Macintosh provides a good illustration of this principle, as it enables users to transfer between applications. For example, when using an unknown piece of software, a user can assume that he or she can take the mouse to one of the headings at the top (many of which stay constant across applications), click to obtain the menu, drag the mouse down to where he or she wants and release to activate the appropriate action. In other words, using a new application is done by analogy with a previously known application. There is also another more general type of consistency, which is whether the conceptual model is always presented in a consistent way. The conceptual model is not solely presented through one channel, such as the instructional text, but through error messages, what appears on the screen, etc. All these should be consistent.

It has recently been argued that the criteria offered by due Boulay, O'Shea and Monk are not sufficient for evaluating conceptual models for novice programmers as they do not give enough emphasis to what happens when novices are learning programming languages. Jones's argument is that, for an analysis which is helpful in designing conceptual models for novices, and which also has some predictive power, it is necessary to combine such criteria with a different approach, which categorises the conceptual model in terms of state, function and procedure. the analysis she advocates combines three criteria for a conceptual model (simplicity, consistency and visibility) with the identification of which of three views of the system (function, state and description) are most prevalent in practice, and this is described next.

Views of the machine

The three different views or descriptions of the system are given briefly below. A full description is given by Jones:

State description This is the state of the machine at any point in time, and will include for example, the values of variables, or in the case of DESMOND, the contents of particular memory locations.

Functional description A description of the system in terms of the goals of the task and a description of the methods for achieving the goals. The goal could be expressed at various levels of detail. In some languages such a goal might be to 'add 2 numbers', and the method for achieving it would be described in terms of the contents of particular 'registers' or memory locations. In another language the goal might be to sort to unordered sequence of numbers into ascending order and the way to do this might be to use a SORT routine. Some goals might be achieved by a single statement or command, e.g. a LOGO repeat statement has the function of repeating commands.

Procedural description A description of the machine in terms of the set of operators and their pre-conditions for carrying out a task. In LOGO examples include the commands for moving the turtle or for printing on the screen. In order to have a complete procedural description for drawing a square, the necessary pre-conditions include the position of the turtle on the screen. In a low level language an example is the command for incrementing the contents of a register.

A conceptual model is unlikely to give equal emphasis to these three different views. Which of the three views is emphasised will depend on a number of factors which include the language, the types of examples given, the style of the instruction and the representation used.

There may well be examples for which it is difficult to decide which view is being given. This is not a serious problem: what is important is which aspect is emphasised or highlighted. So, for example, a functional description emphasises the function or role of the code whereas a procedural description gives the steps for carrying it out. This emphasis is important for the novice. The usefulness of the categorization lies in identifying the different kinds of knowledge which are necessary to understand the conceptual model. It provides a way of assessing whether the conceptual model offered gives these different views, or whether it is emphasising only one or two views. For example, a conceptual model offering only a state description will not be helpful, because the steps for carrying out the solution are not fully specified - through listing the intermediate states which presenting a procedural model may be helpful since it gives the learner confirmation that his or her mental model is correct.

For the example considered earlier, DESMOND, it was the functional view which was the weakest. For example, the two main problems for students learning to use DESMOND were identifying the appropriate 'plans' to use, and flow of control. This is consistent with the lack of a functional view of the machine: students were required to use such plans as counting routines or testing thekeyboard, yet such plans were not acquired by most of the students and even the simplest was not given in the DESMOND manual. Instead, the instruction manual gives examples of the plans in the form of short programs but does not give the plan themselves.

The indications, therefore, are that it is important for the novice to have a functional view of the machine, as this will help in developing programming plans. However, in the conceptual model studied it was this view which was often missing. fortunately, such a deficit is not too hard to remedy. Whenever possible, a functional description could be displayed in addition to the state descriptions and procedural descriptions.

In a language such as DESMOND, the best way to give a functional description of the conceptual model is to give the plans. By giving the description of the conceptual model is to give the plans. By giving the learners a functional model, their task would be made less demanding, and their chances of successful learning increased.

In spite of the concern that learners become too dependent on them, it is clear that of the students in the study mentioned above were active in their learning - interpreting the next and making connections. It seems, therefore, that the designer of distance-learning or self-instructional material for the programming novice is faced with a dilemma. The material needs to be structured and much support provided such that the novice can confidently negotiate the material, but it should not lead the novice to place too much problems that will undoubtedly occur, and have faith in his or her ability to do so. However, encouraging (and indeed requiring) students to interpret the text actively means allowing them to make their own mistakes, form misinterpretations and incorrect models. The issue is not about preventing them from doing this, which is neither possible nor desirable, but about how to support them when they have made mistakes.

Index

CATAPULTING INDIA AS GLOBAL LEADER
Crisis as Paradigm Shifter

About the Author

Dr. Jyotsna R. Bapat is a trained Cultural Anthropologist from Poona University, with a Doctoral degree from Indian Institute of Technology. She has over 35 years of experience in environment and social science sector, with specialization in infrastructure projects. She started her career as a faculty in Department of Sociology and Cultural Anthropology, in Mumbai University. In 2000 she relocated to Delhi following her spouse Dr. Subir V. Gokarn. Once in Delhi, she chose to maintain a balance between short term consultancies, teaching and academic research along with family responsibilities. She had the honor to lead and consult in a few funded programmes, on physical infrastructure and its impact on social systems. Following her spouse to the International Monetary Fund in Washington DC, USA (2014-2019), she was privileged to be exposed to an international perspective to her interests and specialization mainly through biannual "Bank Fund Meetings". On her return to Delhi, after the demise of her spouse in 2019, she has chosen to jump right back into reflections on India, in this international arena dictated by foreign policy. The book is an outcome of these insights and reflections.

CATAPULTING INDIA AS GLOBAL LEADER
Crisis as Paradigm Shifter

Jyotsna R. Bapat

CONCEPT PUBLISHING COMPANY PVT. LTD.
NEW DELHI - 110059

ISBN: 978-93-5594-668-3

First Published 2024

Published and Printed by

Concept Since 1974

Concept Publishing Company Pvt. Ltd.
A/15-16, Commercial Block, Mohan Garden
New Delhi-110059 (India)
T: +91-11-41101460
E: publishing@conceptpub.com, *W*: www.conceptpub.com

Cataloging in Publication--Courtesy: D.K. Agencies (P) Ltd. <docinfo@dkagencies.com>

Bapat, Jyotsna R., author.
Catapulting India as global leader : crisis as paradigm shifter / Jyotsna R. Bapat.
pages cm
Includes bibliographical references and index.
ISBN 9789355946683

1. India--Foreign relations--21st century. 2. India--Foreign economic relations. 3. COVID-19 Pandemic, 2020- --Political aspects--India. I. Title.

LCC DS449.B37 2023 | DDC 327.54 23

...always counting that the worst will happen, because it may happen, to these I say, how much pain have cost us the evils which have never happened!

–Thomas Jefferson

Contents

Preface

> *How you got there is not important, what you do there once you got there is what matters.*

Being spouse of a Diplomat offers a unique perspective from the boundaries of an event happening in front of you. As an anthropologist the best position for me – being a non-participant observer. Being curious and present to all the biannual meetings of the World Bank and International Monetary Fund called Annual Bank Fund Meetings since 2015 till 2019 and attending the Open meetings and listening, is what I did from that position. Often grappling with my ethical perspective, offered by existential ethics. The Development debates in various sectors and the new and emerging areas in development funding has a charm of its own to a curious development anthropologist like myself.

This resulted in a lot of critical reflection on my part on this entire talk about the 'financial sector reforms and development in private funding, to corporate sector and Non Banking Financial Sector (NBFC) related new initiatives through the IMF sessions. The World Bank sessions were more focused on development funding issues and mainly, infrastructure funding through the World Bank (IBRD) towards sovereign Governments with the caviar of poverty, climate change and green funding. New and emerging technologies 'Corners' was the most fascinating sessions related to Big Data, Green Technologies, Internet Technology, bit coins (and controlling this currency by central financial institutions), and cyber technology impacts. It was very creative guessing game of future impacts from people who are working on it.

Finally, there were always very interesting people to interact for in-depth conversations about their perspectives off the table, on these developments. These were always success stories, no one ever talked of 'what did not work', best they were lessons learnt.

The global level country dynamics and various groups and associations of countries was one dimension of interest. During that time India focus occupied only a small corner in country reviews or regional focus on South Asia. It was a fascinating kaleidoscope of ideas sectors and regions in which the economic and finance, sector dominated.

Another interesting space for interaction were the various embassy events, for building solidarity among 'appointees' from different countries and connecting up with unknown strangers. The best way of communication was based on sharing cultural traditions and social histories with the hosts. The conversation took the turn towards exchange of myths, appreciation of paintings, other displays and statues, in the Resident Commissioner houses or the locale of the event, with the hosts. These exchanges, during these events, the traditional foods they served, the cultural activities about their culture like *Mehendi* event in India or the dance performances in Bangladesh or Russian Balle, or calligraphy in Japanese event to name a few off the cuff. We as spouses had the privilege of attending these events and I took full advantage of it.

Experiencing this and the thinking it prompted, especially the absence of India, on the global stage was an interesting insight that prompted my publications since homecoming in 2019. This is the context for the time line that I have covered in the book. I am using a little hyperbole here, pardon me for that; the transition of India from being nothing, even though the economic growth was substantial during the early decade plus, to becoming something, and being counted as a major economic power on the world stage

Acknowledgements

First and foremost I acknowledge my respected teacher Prof. R.K. Mutatkar, from Pune University. He is a stalwart in his own field of Medical Anthropology and has a long list of achievements. But he never lost sight of his students wherever in their life they were. He was always there for them. He encouraged us to keep in touch with each other and include us in all his activities.

For me he has been a beacon of encouragement. Ever since I was his student, he always encouraged me to follow my interests and opportunities, quite different than his own. He never once suggested that I follow his field of interest. Whenever possible he has supported me and showed me the path to take the next step in my journey in the field of anthropology—in environment and development.

It is solely because of him that I have written this book after such a long break and in a completely new field of research.

Second, I acknowledge my spouse Dr. Subir V. Gokarn. A famous economist, a stalwart in his field and who truly encourage me to get into interdisciplinary research. It was his encouragement during his last posting with the International Monetary Fund in Washington DC that I got exposed to International Relations in development sector, and particularly India's prominent and emerging role as a new and equally formidable player in the Asian arena. Because of his encouragement and opportunities and insights assumption of free and open trade got challenged. It was easy to assume that opposite that must be true in crisis, that is how the world reacted by a shut down. The lesson of a crisis is, what new paradigm will emerge, is completely unpredictable. It depends on how a crisis is seen and interpretated by the actors involved in it. In International relationships the space for global leadership position, in the dominant paradigm was seen to be a steady upward movement towards financial growth through GDP and each state had to strive towards that goal. Along with that security was the other sector to gain global leadership position. Security seen as conventional military security and energy security, through conventional energy and nuclear capability balancing both military and energy security through it was the other sub-sectors in security indicator. This crisis COVID-19, has proven that GDP growth and security—military and energy security, are not the only two sectors through which global leadership positions can be gained, and friendships re-enforced.

India over the last decade has been showing a stable economic growth following this Sustainable Development paradigm promoted by free movement of goods services and human resources. 'Full Year GDP Growth in India averaged 6.12 per cent from 2006 until 2023, reaching an all time high of 8.70 per cent in 2022 and a record low of -6.60 per cent in 2021.[1] This is a stable economic growth over different political parties and Prime Ministers. It resulted in high exports and high number of migrants to other countries for employment.

India's Foreign Policy so far

The dominant history about India was that India was constrained in its foreign policy and therefore, Global Leadership position. South Asia is considered an insecure region, and India is surrounded on all sides by unstable democracies, conflict-ridden countries, militant activity, authoritarian leaders or weak governments. These are the countries with which India has historically acrimonious relations. India's foreign policy is, therefore, driven by five principal considerations since its independence and this is one way of looking at it.

1. **Conventional Security:** Boarders with China and Pakistan where India's military skirmishes have been called upon very frequently over the last few years, India has ensured used of soft power with other nations in neighbourhood. India uses its diplomatic and economic leverage and soft power to help mitigate the conflicts with its neighbours, particularly Nepal, Sri Lanka, and Bangladesh.
2. **Economic Growth:** India's second principal foreign policy goal is economic growth. Over the last decade plus India has been able to grow well over 6 per cent GDP the best growth rate globally in spite of pandemic.
3. **Energy Security:** In order to sustain present economic growth at around India must ensure energy security, its third major area of focus. India currently imports 70 per cent of its oil and 50 per cent of its gas; by 2025 it is projected that India will import 80 per cent of its energy needs.
4. **Nuclear Capability and Non-proliferation:** India's nuclear weapon status today is unknown, but it is a signatory to non-proliferation treaty. It has even recently, taken Russian aid for providing Nuclear power to Bangladesh for a power plant as is illustrated in the example quoted in the chapter. India remains extremely concerned regarding the addition of any new nuclear powers as demonstrated by casting their two UNSC votes against Iran's nuclear programme in recent years.
5. **Prestige Security:** India recognizes the importance of building its strategic stature and leadership by purchasing weapons strengthening its Navy and continuing to be non-aligned by involving in Military exercises with USA and Russia in Indo-Pacific and Indian Ocean.[2]

These principal considerations as the Security studies tend to emphasize for foreign policy for a country are Security (military and energy—including nuclear), economic growth and political leadership, constrain the International Relations of a country. Therefore, by implication had constrained that the possibility of India graining a politically significant leadership position in the region. Though India has steadily grown economically in nature and volumes over the last three governments since its economic reforms and particularly since 2004 till 2022, the impact of this growth is rarely taken into account, nor are impacts of changing leadership in India taken into account while studying its International Relations.

Strategic Vision Shift

Post-2014 and after 2014 national elections, there was a change in political leadership. A defining characteristic of the leadership was its willingness to take risk and take bold steps, that questioned the *status quo*. Its willingness to test new and transformed strategies in foreign policy for the first time, was done without fundamentally rocking the global growth and development paradigm dictated by Sustainable Development by the macro financial institutions.

Do note that before 2014, there were issues of increasing terrorist attacks, the more famous of these were the Mumbi terrorist attack in 2008 and the Kashmir Kargil war of 1999 where the skirmishes persisted, along with steady economic growth due to economic liberalisation since 1991, helped India improve its GDP through economic development. Indian economy grew with an 8-9 per cent economic growth rate. In 2007, India achieved its highest GDP growth rate of 9 per cent and became the second fastest growing major economy in the world. Actions were taken by the then Manmohan Singh's government to strengthened anti-terror laws with amendments to Unlawful Activities (Prevention) Act (UAPA). National Investigation Agency (NIA) was also created soon after the November 2008 Mumbai terror attacks, as need for a central agency to combat terrorism was realized. But India never actually invested in defence security capital or human investment in conventional security, substantively.

While the trend towards economic development was set two decades ago by the then political leaders, the bold political leadership and clear strategies in foreign policy towards International Relationship adopted since 2014 is a major driving force for the transformation its development aid profile—from aid receiver to aid giver and bilateral to multilateral infrastructure projects. This stable economic growth alone cannot be enough for a value shift. Though it resulted in the enhanced economic status, along with China, globally (Menon, S., May, 2020). India along with China and others, created The Asian Infrastructure Bank as founder member by contributing funds to its creation. Without the shift in vision, India would have continued on these non-assertive lines of growth.

There was a shift in IR, in three areas of political leadership, economics and security. The newly elected political leadership took risks. International strategy shifted from economic aid to cooperation, from receiver to donor in connectivity and infrastructure projects, and from associate members in various forums into being a global leader in governance with its unique ideology and followings. Encouraging Indian private sector investors in multilateral connectivity projects and creating a captive energy market, all supported India's own growth and faster development, while creating its leadership position in South and South Asia and East Africa.

The new Government in 2014 made direct investment in military air and naval capital. India engaged in more regional security partnerships, while taking on leadership initiatives in these partnerships.

India discontinued bilateral aid it was receiving till 2014 and since has reduced its loan obligations steadily. India created a Development Partnership Administration to provide development aid funding for investing in multilateral infrastructure projects multilaterally. India is more actively engaged in International Governance role as a leader, UN Security Council, in G-20 and other economic regional forums. India took independent stand when decision making was required.

Military and Regional Security Partnerships

The Act East Policy, Gulf Engagement, Central Asia Initiatives and Sagar Outlook, as titled, are targeted at strategies corresponding to the geographical location of those countries, in relation to India.

The Act East Policy was to develop strategic relationships with countries in the Asia-Pacific region by providing enhanced connectivity to the States of the North Eastern Region including Arunachal Pradesh with other countries in our neighbourhood. There is an ongoing connectivity project with Myanmar, Thailand and India to ensure enhanced land trade. When needed surgical strike was used to curtail terrorists in that region in 2016.

Gulf engagement: India's sphere of influence has expanded to include the Gulf region. India has signed defence and security agreements with several Gulf countries. Apart from anti-piracy efforts, these include: a defence cooperation deal with Qatar, a maritime pact that provides access to Oman's Duqm Port, joint naval exercises with the United Arab Emirates (UAE) and Saudi Arabia, a counter-terrorism arrangement with the UAE, and a commitment to fight terrorism and contribute to regional security in March 2020.

SAGAR Outlook: SAGAR stands for Security and Growth for All in the Region and covers in both the Indian Ocean and Indo-Pacific for India's foreign policy geo-strategically and involves maritime security vision and currently joint naval exercises in that area are carried out. It is a vision still evolving since 2014.

India's foreign policy has seen a dramatic shift over the last seven years since 2014, as an outcome of major changes, in leadership, in defence security, in energy security, and in economy. Post-elections, a new leadership took charge since 2014, with a clear vision towards its partner countries in neighbourhood—'Neighbourhood First'. The actions it took strengthened its 'Neighbourhood First' in multilateral physical infrastructure projects—in economics (through Development Partnership Administration within the Ministry of External Affairs) both regularly and in time of crisis. Finally, a firm action to indicate a strong security stand and defence procurement and joint exercises both with its Western and Pacific Ocean allies and Russia.

Actions Taken by India on Ground

Post-2014 elections, the role that India's foreign policy was supported by action on ground, in India gaining a leadership position globally in today's geopolitics is significant. These new leaders were bold willing to take risks, and take actions on ground, has resulted in some implied stand and clear message India sent to all countries globally. These corresponding actions are listed here.

- India will not tolerate overt or covert aggression by hostile neighbours.

India has taken a more aggressive and clear stands in situations of conflict, against its hostile countries like Pakistan and China. Most recent examples are listed here. Balakot Airstrike was a bombing raid conducted by Indian warplanes on February 26, 2019, in Balakot[3], (Wikipedia, Article 2019). Pakistan against an alleged terrorist training camp and there was a retaliation by Pakistan and an Indian warplane shot, the Indian pilot was recovered by India through negotiations with Pakistan later. In Doclam region with China after the initial aggressive skirmishes India was able to push back China to its old LAC in 2017 and maintain a no man's land between the two, through diplomatic negotiations. In addition Indian and Myanmar troops carried out jointly Operation Sunrise and Operation Sunrise 2 in 2019 in their respective territories to destroy several insurgent camps. India has also supported Myanmar in its efforts to combat Rohingya (Wikipedia, Article 2017), insurgent groups like the Arakan Rohingya Salvation Army (ARSA) and Aqa Mul Mujahideen (AMM), after Indian intelligence agencies found the ARSA and AMM to have links with terror groups like the Lashkar-e-Taiba (LeT) and Jaish-e-Mohammed (JeM) as well as reported Rohingya terrorists fighting alongside Pakistani extremists in Kashmir.Thus India's security and therefore, geo-political stand in any given situation is based on its own merit. It is clear and is independent of other nations involved in a given situation.

India has a clear anti-China stand militarily[4]. India has with USA along with Australia and Japan carried out joint Naval exercises in Indian Ocean, to curtail China. On 7 August, 2014 India and Russia held a joint counter-terrorism exercise near Moscow, on the boundary with China and Mongolia. But does not blindly support the West. During the 2014 Crimean crisis[5] India refused to support American sanctions against Russia. Simultaneously it has also maintained friendly ties with USA, EU and other West leaning nations.

Thus far India has been involved in supporting partner countries, to militarily fight insurgency groups with international links as in case of Myanmar. India took on a more aggressive stand against hostile countries like China and Pakistan. When there was military aggression by China, in the past, as in case of Bhutan, India supported Bhutan on ground, militarily. Skirmishes in Arunachal Pradesh continue to be resisted by India.

This has reflected in India's foreign policy. The Policy since the last seven/eight years has engaged the world intensively. As of January 2018, India has become member of Wassenaar Arrangement, Australia Group and Missile Technology Control Regime. India has been a member of the UN Security Council for eight terms and a total of 16 years.

- India is participating actively in global governance agencies, organizations, associations, and forms related to economic trade and security issues.

India has acted with a clear objective of taking on a global leadership role whenever the opportunity arose. These opportunities are reflected in economically and militarily spheres over the last seven years. Economic arrangements involved helping partner countries in South Asia and Africa, who needs financial help with no reciprocal expectations and forming associations with others partnership countries on a mutually beneficial arrangement in transport and energy sectors projects supporting trade and commerce.

- For India, interest of its citizens in foreign countries comes first, particularly in situation of crisis.

India has put the economic interests of its citizens abroad in establishing businesses and supporting their employment abroad. As many as 44 million people of Indian origin live and work abroad and constitute an important link with the mother country. An important role of India's foreign policy has been to ensure their welfare and well-being within the framework of the laws of the country where they live. India is committed in protecting the interest and security of its own citizens living and working in other countries, which includes student studying abroad (Minister of External Affairs, 7 June, 2022). While drawing benefits for its own people, India also contributed in greater measure to global welfare, development and security. Indian foreign policy thinking is displaying greater conceptual and operational clarity. Neighbourhood First, for example, it is now clearly associated with a generous and non-reciprocal approach to our immediate neighbours for both financial and development project aid. This includes providing Line for Credit for neighbours in Africa or providing Infrastructure project to promote better transport, energy, connectivity, and for improving supply chains, with its South Asian, South East Asian and Middle Eastern partner counties.

- India puts National interest and economic priorities first.

Various policies like Act East Policy, a Sagar outlook, a Gulf engagement and a Central Asia initiative need to be noted for resource use, humanitarian aid as well as defence. Building on national defence and providing maritime security in Indian Ocean and Arabian Sea with its partner countries in joint exercises is now common. In addition by making more investments in defence preparedness and restructuring its defence organization India is now better prepared to defend boundaries and its national security. India also takes on the role when required by its partner countries, as first responder for countries in need, e.g. in case of Disaster Management be it natural or manmade. Over last few years we have taken on leadership of global south and engaged with United Nations including its Security Council as temporary member, and hosting G-20. (Minister of External Affairs, 7 June, 2022).

An economically stronger India expresses its deep belief of the world being a family through greater development partnerships prioritizing its neighbourhood partner countries. The last eight years have witnessed a tripling of our Lines of Credit commitments to our friendly nations, over the previous eight-year period. The value of project completion also went up by 38 per cent. Our immediate neighbourhood and our African partners were the main beneficiaries, even as we expanded projects into new areas. In the coming years, we intend to focus even more on green growth, on digital delivery and on health capacities. India has taken on independent actions in the face of actions taken by Developed Country Blocks against its partner countries in various occasions. Getting exemption to purchase oil after major oil sanctions were imposed by USA in case of Iran is an example. Or not supporting USA sanctions against Russia when Crimea crisis took place in 2014 is another example.

Structure of the Book

The book discusses the micro history of IR strategy over past six/ seven years. The methods and motives of these ruling leaders and the vision they followed, post-2014 has brought about a strategic shift in India's Foreign Policy. India from being a receiver of bilateral funds became a donor of bilateral funds, line of credit, and conducting multilateral development projects as partners with its neighbours. The development projects were in line with the UN agenda of sustainable development goals focusing on the decade's emphasis of transport connectivity and energy.

Then COVID-19 Crisis happened. Crisis theory predicts that when a system level crisis emerges the outcome is unpredictable. That provides the opportunity for transformation of the system. This is what happened and India could take advantage of the crisis to its advantage. This crisis created a possibility of new and independent leadership position for India in Global governance successfully because India took actions, that were different from most other countries in the G7 + 2 group. This Indian leadership asserted non-alignment and peace globally. But ensured India's security first. Just by way of an observation, this is the first time that these ruling leaders, Central Ministers in Finance, Home Affairs, Defence, External Affairs and Prime Minister, are all born post- Independent India.

As the introduction chapter highlights the shift in India's foreign policy began in 2014 post-elections where there was shift in the party ruling the country. This shift towards foreign policy, was not just on paper but explicitly stated by the leadership. The main thing that they did was to discontinue bilater aid coming into India and promoted its own aid model by extending line of credit, direct aid and partnership projects in infrastructure. Chapter 2 covers this transition.

This emerging foreign policy was practiced in infrastructure projects created in partnership with more than one country with a clear vision and the parameters that Development Partner Administration, with MEA, as the implementing ministry. These kinds of development projects, involve multiple ministries and need a co-ordinating administrative agency to ensure timely implementation of projects. India should follow to handle its development funds and using Development Aid Partnership (DAP) to carry them out as is elaborated in Chapter 3.

2
India's Future Development Assistance Partnerships

Introduction

Government of India since 1950 has been providing foreign aid or development assistance as it now called, through bilateral aid to its friendly neighbourhood countries. India's major quantum of foreign aid is given to neighbouring countries. (According to India's Budget in 2021-22, it's direct overseas aid stood at Rs. 18,154 crore (US$2.3 billion).[1] That apart, India also extended a direct line of credit worth $30.66 billion dollars to several foreign countries for developmental projects. [2] The way of providing a much larger share of aid in the form of concessional loans is quite similar to that of China.[3] India has set up 'Indian Agency for Partnership in Development' as a part of Ministry of External Affairs (India) to channelize aid to recipient nations. India also received bilateral foreign aid till 2014. Government of India's foreign aid is budgeted in its annual budget and routed through Ministry of External Affairs (MEA). In 2012, MEA created a Development Partnership Administration (DPA) The DPA has set up an online Performance Dashboard that gives details on its partnership projects under three heads: (a) Lines of Credit; (b) Grants and Loans; and (c) Capacity Building.

This kind of country to country development assistance is referred to as Official Development Assistance (ODA) and it is defined as *government aid designed to promote the economic development and welfare of developing countries.* There is a forum of countries that monitor this kind of development assistance called Organization for Economic Co-operation and Development (OECD), located in Paris. It is a unique forum where the governments of 37 democracies with market-based economies collaborate to develop policy standards to promote sustainable economic growth. India is one of the many non-member economies with which the OECD has working relationships in addition to its member countries. The OECD has been co-operating with India since 1995. India chooses to be a non-member partner because India is being cautious about what kind of signal its membership in OECD would give to other emerging countries located in South Asian Continent.

Government of India had also been receiving development assistance through bilateral aid from other developed countries: G7, namely France, United States, United Kingdom, Germany, Japan, Italy and Canada plus a few others like Australia. This aid was routed through Ministry of Finance and monitored by Development Partnership Administration created in 2012 to monitor the development assistance both incoming and outgoing.

In 2015 Government of India brought about a shift in its foreign policy and took a decision to stopped taking bilateral foreign aid, or overseas development assistance (ODA) from the advanced countries. This chapter begins with the justification given by India for stopping bilateral foreign aid in 2015. The reason was, as India became a net surplus contributor to ODA, it did not need foreign aid. The MEA then sought to learn from the experiences of various other prominent models for ODA.[4] This chapter then explores the impact of this discontinuation of bilateral foreign aid on India. The nature of India investing its net surplus into (a) Lines of Credit; (b) Grants and Loans; and (c) Capacity Building, was in helping its neighbour in Indian Ocean rim countries. The projects that emerged out of capacity building component of ODA are discussed in more details in the next chapter.

Shift in India's Foreign Policy

In 2015-16, there was a shift that happened when India refused bilateral financial aid from most of the Group of Seven (G7) countries. Soon after in 2017, the government declared that India had been a net donor to the ODA. The Indian Government's budget for the year 2019-20 had allocated US$ 1.32 billion (INR 8415 crore) to India's foreign aid programme. which was 0.3 per cent of the overall budget. However, there is no fixed budget that is approved by the parliament as part of the Development Partnership Fund (DPF) routed through the MEA in India called Development Partnership Assistance (DPA).

India is not alone in this foreign aid or Official Development Assistance (ODA). In this recent decade from 2010-2020, nineteen countries, mostly middle-income countries with emerging economies, have reported investment with other countries through the development assistance initiative. This is a new trend among middle income countries to be involved in South-South dialogue and to be broadly categorised into three: providers of South-South Cooperation members, Arab donors, and Emerging EU donors (within the EU, some donors are newly formed countries and some are old EU countries reviving development initiatives). Together, their contribution is estimated to be 9-10 per cent of ODA[5].

Development Partnership Administration (DPA)

Within a few years of its independence, India has been participating in bilateral development assistance particularly by providing grants to its immediate neighbours in South Asia. Indian grants have funded transport infrastructure like roads and railways, dams for power and agriculture, and trade and investment. However, funding of multilateral development projects is relatively new. In the year 2019-20, India allocated foreign aid through within the Ministry of Foreign Affairs (MEA). The MEA sought to learn

As of today, only Japan provides ODA to India. The total amount provided by Japan is approximately 203 billion JPY or 240 billion INR (1.48 JPY=1 INR) in 2019-20. India has been the largest recipient of the Japanese ODA Loan for several years now since 2010. The cumulative amount of Japanese ODA Loan to India amounts to approximately 3, 600 billion JPY. More recently France is following suit.

As per the RBI public documents, the overall external debt from all sources at the end of June 2020 is placed at 554.5 billion USD[12]. As the annual long-term debt for 2019-20 is 449.5USD, 105 billion USD is settled in 2019-20. Of the 449.5 billion USD, India's bilateral debt is placed at 27.5 billion USD, while multilateral debt is placed at 64.8 billion USD. Together, these form 20.5 per cent of annual loans, with bilateral debts forming only 6.11 per cent of the debts that India owes to the world, including part capital and part interest.

Table 2.1: External Debt—Outstanding and Variation 2020

(*USD billion*)

Component	**Outstanding as at end of**			**Absolute variation**		**Percentage variation**	
	June 2019 PR	**March 2020 PR**	**June 2020 P**	**Jun-20 over Jun-19**	**Jun-20 over Mar-20**	**Jun-20 over Jun-19**	**Jun-20 over Mar-20**
1	2	3	4	5	6	7	8
1. Multilateral	59.0	60.0	64.8	5.8	4.8	9.8	8.0
2. Bilateral	26.5	27.2	27.5	0.9			

(PR—Partially revised, P—provisional) Publication: India Economic Review 2020-21 by GoI.

More recently, all independent bilateral aid agencies have merged their ODA and commercial loan funding agencies under one ministry, except the USA. The strategies they now employ can serve as a guide for the DPA's investment strategies for future projects.

There was a structural transformation that happened over the last few years in the ODA agencies that were providing aid to developing countries with focus on India. Following is a table (Table 2.2) that indicates the transformation, whereby the ODA agencies merged with the parent ministry, namely the Foreign Affairs, Investment and Trade Ministry that oversees these aspects in the G7 countries. Except for Japan, which continues to have ODA with India, the other countries involved have ceased their ODA. Japan has an ODA through the Japan Bank for International Cooperation (JBIC) in FY 2018-19, which was at 522.405 billion JPY in two major mega projects in connectivity, hitherto the highest ODA. Japan's bilateral trade with India, for FY 2019-20 (April-December) was 11.87 billion USD[13] in 2019-20.

Table 2.2: Transition in ODA agencies to Developing Countries

Country	Old name	New name	Status	Current Focus in India
Canada	CIDA	GAC	Merged	Gender equity
France	FDA	FDA	Merged	Multimodal transport and water infrastructure
Germany	GTZ	GIZ	Merged	Science and technology
Italy	IADC	IADC	Merged	Trade and investment
Japan	JAICA	JBIC	Merged	Transport and water infrastructure
UK	DFID	FCDO	Merged	Fintech
USA	USAID	USAID	Separate	Disaster proofing urban infrastructure

(Data is compiled using ODA country-wise websites and newspaper articles).

The strategy of all the G7 countries is to accept the host country's grant-in-aid and work around it. The fact remains that ODA are 'loans' that are to be returned to the bilateral donor country eventually, albeit long term low interest loans. These are relatively safe investments for the donor country as there is a sovereign guarantee against the loans given by the bilateral donor. However, they are a liability for the host country. Thus, while the interest may be low the risk is minimal to the donor as the host takes on the burden of returning the loan.

Outstanding 'concessional debt' or development aid loans by bilateral and even multilateral aid agencies to India remained by and large, range-bound for many years. The concessional debt marginally rose by 1.6 per cent to 48.2 billion USD as at the end of March 2020. As a share in the total debt, it declined significantly from around 20 per cent as at the end of March 2008 to around 9 per cent as at the end of March 2020[14]. Principal repayments constitute the bulk of sovereign external debt servicing. While the absolute amount of principal repayments rose over the years, the share of principal payments in the total sovereign external debt service payments declined post-2015-16. This can be mainly attributed to the 2017 'no bilateral aid' policy. In 2017, General V.K. Singh, the then Minister of State for External Affairs, informed the parliament that India had been a net donor in 2015-16 by donating 7,719.65 crore INR (1.1 billion USD) as aid and receiving only Rs. 2,144.77 crore (300 million USD) in 2015-16 from foreign countries and global banks[15].

Singh indicated that India could donate much more than it was receiving in concessional debts. The reduction in concessional debt over time could be substantially attributed to the cessation of ODA from bilateral donors. Thus, when these loans were stopped, the impact on sovereign finances was a positive one.

Interestingly, the G7 countries now have a substantial FDI in India (Table 2.3), which is a higher risk investment to India and G7 than a sovereign loan with a concessional finance would have been and interesting the fincial investments are from Non-Banking Financial Companies (NBFC). The following table indicates the FDI. They are in the forms of NBFC such as pension funds, insurance funds etc. which can be moved in and out of India relatively easily. This is a risk that India is willing to take.

Table 2.3: FDI by G7 countries in 2020

Country Name	**US$ in Billions**
Canada	32.60
France	6.59
Germany	11.90
Italy	–
Japan	32.06
UK	28.32
USA	45.9
Total FDI in India 2020	157.43

Data compiled from Country-wise details about past trade and aid which is available on MEA website e.g. https://mea.gov.in/Portal/ForeignRelation/India-Japan_Bilateral_Brief_feb_2020.pdf for details on Japan-India details, and so on.

As a result of theis shift in foreign policy in India, the G7 members no longer donated development aid to the GOI but to registered NGOs within India. Second the private industry in G7 invested directly in India and partnered with Indian companies. Finally, GoI invested in multilateral physical infrastructure projects with friendly countries along Indian Ocean rim counties.

Data indicated that three different relations emerged after this shift in foreign policy, between advance county industry with Indian Industry on Indian soil through direct investment, Development Aid from advance country to Indian NGOs and India giving development funds to other developing countries. This has been beneficial to India.

What India did

Since 2015 the DPA indicated that India's development assistance funding was in the form of on grant-in-aid, line of credit and capacity building and technical assistance. The focus of this aid was on friendly, Indian Ocean rim countries as per the new focus in foreign policy of 2015. The projects that supported on lines of the model used IBRD, of the World Bank, with a difference, as discussed in details in the next chapter. These projects are physical infrastructure projects in capacity building and technical assistance. Here funding for, DPA is available and routed through MEA, to support these projects in other countries.

As can be seen from the profile of FDI projects coming to India mentioned earlier, India possesses the technical skills, capacity for competence, and even the ability to provide rolling stocks and equipment needed for projects. This bodes well, for the future investment of infrastructure development projects in other countries for India through private industry and commercial banks.

Future DPA Projects Through MEA

The sectors in which future development assistance by India can be invested are climate change, energy, connectivity, sustainable development, and fintech—namely the new verticals. These projects would be in sectors such as new and renewable energy, disaster risk proofing infrastructure, and fintech in the financial and service sector.

Despite these positive conclusions, India lacks the large funds that are required for mega projects that G7 countries, or even China, can invest. However, the gap between the mega projects that a developing country desires and the projects that a developing country can afford to undertake within its budget can potentially be filled with medium sized projects. This is a point of entry for India.

As per its foreign policy, India's primary focus is on its neighbour countries, i.e. Asia and the Indian Ocean rim countries. Any project selection will always have to take into account other strategic calculations besides the economic ones, namely those of energy security, defence, geopolitical security and environmental security. South-South Cooperation has created the opportunity to invest in countries that qualify these criteria. This is a new area in which India is taking a leadership role to create funds, such as the India-UN fund for South-South cooperation, which was created for disaster risk proofing infrastructure in urban areas. USAID is willing to contribute to it. Thus, the DPA, MEA appears to be on a developmentally-soundtrack.

Improving Development Assistance Partnership

A mature view would acknowledge successes and constraints, the job done and remaining to be done. India, while being a middle-incom country and an emerging market—has retained Third World developing country characteristics in both its bilateralism and in its multilaterally funded development projects. The same urbanisational structure and functions that allow for the development projects not to succeed, also have the capacity to respond to crisesand to operate effectively on a mission mode or through Special Purpose Vehicles (SPV). To quote an example, the same DPA has shown grit and persistence in pushing for the India-Myanmar-Thailand (IMT) trilateral highway that will provide connectivity from Thailand to India, across Myanmar, thus linking the three countries effectively. When Myanmar backed out of its commitment to the four-lane Mandalay (Myanmar) to Moreh (India) connection, India stepped in. Through the DPA, it mobilised funding through Exim Bank and hired private contractors through a global tendering process to plan, initiate, and construct a road connectivity project[16] (*ibid*: Bapat, J., 2020).

Thus, India has the capability to operate in mission mode and respond to crises effectively. Institutional and industrial capabilities when they function in mission mode, however, the "Normal" is a snafu[17]. There is no accountability for finishing a project on time and within budget. The IMT project from Moreh to Mandalay was not carried out within the timeline and therefore, extending the budget is an inevitable consequence. However, the current unstable geopolitical situation renders its future uncertain.

One feature of the 'third world /developing country' is lack of accountability[18] (*ibid.*). There is no fear of action being taken against those responsible for the failure. There is no incentive to keep to the established timeline of the project or to complete the project within the allotted budget. It is only when raising international funds and when the international markets demand rigorous economic, financial, and environmental viability standards and reports do Indian funding agencies perform their duties rigorously.

This rigorous accounting and the presence of systemic checks in projects is a resounding feature of all the projects carried out by the G7 countries, both within India and outside India. These systemic checks and processes of accountability are still missing in the Indian projects undertaken abroad. In India, projects favoured by the Prime Minister obtain special sanctions, a feature that is characteristic of a developing country[19] (*ibid.*).

Future challenges are going to be projects that are in new vertical sectors with no set rules or laws to guide them apart from 'best practices'. They are likely to have uncertain outcomes, with low probability and high risk of success. Therefore, accountability and transparency in the processes followed becomes all the more crucial for the development projects that India funds bilaterally and multilaterally in its neighbour countries in the future.

A proof of success of this shift is in the recent events (2021 April), more than 40 countries have committed to providing India with the medical resources and pharmaceutical products that the country urgently needs to battle the sudden surge of COVID-19 cases, ongoing since the start of the second phase around 4th April 2021. 'They have come forward on their own. We have assisted and we are getting assistance, it shows an interdependent world', said the foreign Secretary'[20].

Notes

1. Official Development Assistance: Definition and Coverage. https:// www.oecd.org/development/financing-sustainable-development/development-finance-standards/officialdevelopment assistancedefinitionandcoverage.htm
2. Smith, Kimberly. Yamashiro Fordelone, Talita. and Zimmermann, Felix. OECD Development Co-operation Directorate. "Beyond the DAC: The Welcome Role of Other Providers of Development Co-operation" May 2016 https://www.oecd.org/dac/beyondthedacthew elcomeroleofotherprovidersofco-operation.htm
3. Raghavan, P.S. SS (DP) on Development Partnership Administration (DPA) "Talk" 18 July 2013 https://idsa.in/event/ TalkbyShriPSRaghavan

4. *Op. cit.*
5. *Op. cit.*
6. *Op. cit.*
7. Overview of India Development Partnership https://mea.gov.in/Overview-of-India-Development-Partnership.htm
8. Prime Minister's speech. https://mea.gov.in/Overview-of-India-Development-Partnership.htm
9. Official Development Assistance: Definition and Coverage. https://www.oecd.org/development/financing-sustainable-development/development-finance-standards/officialdevelopment assistancedefinitionandcoverage.htm
10. Official development assistance ODA https://www.oecd-ilibrary.org/development/official-development-assistance-oda/indicator-group/english_5136f9ba-en
11. Department of Economic Affairs Press release repayment of bilateral loans https://dea.gov.in/press-release/Issuance of Press Release- /Repayment of 7.94 per cent (download file/ STATUS%20 REPORT%202018-19.pdf) /GS 2021
12. India's External Debt as at the end of June 2020 https://www.rbi.org.in/Scripts/BS_PressReleaseDisplay.aspx?prid=50440
13. India Japan Bilateral Brief Feb 2020 https://mea.gov.in/Portal/ForeignRelation/India-Japan_Bilateral_Brief_feb_2020.pdf
14. India External Debt: status report 2019-2020 (https://dea.gov.in/sites/default/files/India%27s%20External%20Debt%20-%20A%20Status%20Report%202019-20.pdf)
15. Inaugural Speech RIS seminar, Post-Pandemic Indian Ocean Regional Economic Cooperation—way forward. https://mea.gov.in/Speeches-Statements.htm?dtl/33237/speech+by+mos+at+the+inaugural+of+ris+seminar+on+postpandemic+indianocean+regional+economic+cooperation+way+forward+in+context+of+iora
16. *Op cit.* Bapat, J., 2020.
17. *Ninan, T.N., Editorial, Business Standard,* 1 May, 2021.
18. *Ibid.*
19. *Ibid.*
20. Secretary, Ministry of External Affairs (MEA), India in a press note released on 4 April, 2021.

3
Multilateral Infrastructure
Projects by India[1]

Briefly[2]

India, till 2014, had bilateral trade and infrastructure agreement treaties with its Asian neighbours. India, through the Ministry of External Affairs (MEA), has been investing in trilateral and multilateral infrastructure projects since 2014, with its littoral (coastal) and inland neighbours in Asia. While it demonstrates the growing potential of infrastructure diplomacy, it also puts India in direct competition with China, which through its own infrastructure initiative, has been involved in building physical infrastructure in India's neighbours.

This chapter argues that taking into account environmental security as a parameter for developing cross-border sustainable infrastructure, during signing of MoUs in these multilateral treaties, will provide a unique opportunity for India to develop norms for environmental and social security framework/policy, training assistance, and capacity building in its funded projects in other countries.

Introduction

With the breakdown of bipolarity, by 2010, international politics saw a rise in regional powers. Infrastructure diplomacy became a

India's programmes, is an Environmental and Social Security (ESS) Framework/Policy (ESSF/P) as funding criteria for these projects. Such an ESSF/P is essential to ensure sustainable infrastructure development.

Proposed by the author here are norms for social and environmental sustainability in infrastructure projects built or planned by India and partner countries as transnational projects. It is important to have these environmental and social security (ESS) criteria because there is an ethical principle about the future survival of humankind involved, (survival of future of humankind-footnote)[5] linked to the issue of sustainable development.

For this chapter, physical infrastructure refers to projects that cover connectivity in transport and energy. These projects involve India and at least two other countries, pooling resources. These can be linear projects cutting across two or more nations, or they could be localised projects, like ports or nuclear power plants, located in one nation. But all these projects involve agreements with more than two countries. The physical infrastructure projects, supported by India in South Asia, are of medium-sized projects, in roads, power, irrigation dams or multipurpose projects.

Development Assistance Partnership (DAP) projects are funded by India to increase goodwill with its partners and neighbours, and as part of the multilateral economic diplomacy. Most of these are financial assistance projects, implemented in the countries of East Africa and South Asia.

Given that these projects are aimed at specific infrastructure sectors and regional economic growth and development, for the countries involved in the project, financial resources are pooled with the better-off countries contributing larger share in the project, rather than taking aid or loans from bilateral or multilateral funding agencies. India as a partner in such projects has made financial contributions and has Indian private infrastructure companies, create infrastructure projects, on Build Own Operate and Transfer (BOOT) and Build Operate and Transfer (BOT) basis.

India, through its experience in infrastructure development projects, should evolve its own norms for Environmental and Social Security Impact Assessment (ESSIA) in the multilateral projects it funds. India has competence to develop such norms. It has developed, through the Ministry of Environment, Forest and Climate Change (MoEFCC), domestic ESSIA norms related to community consultation, Resettlement and Rehabilitation (R&R), bio-conservation and heritage conservation projects carried out within the country, both in urban and rural areas.

These norms are essential for long-term environmental and social sustainability of projects. It minimises the negative impacts of the projects on local ecology and the livelihoods of local people and communities, thereby ensuring that positive impacts altogether outweigh or neutralise the negative.

Objective

As mentioned earlier, MEA's DAF funds the DAP projects to increase India's goodwill with its partners and neighbours, and furthers its multilateral economic diplomacy. While these projects consider financial and economic viability along with other strategic considerations, they do not take into account ESSIA dimension, as part of the agreement. Moreover, India does not have a ESSF/P fully spelt out for its DAP infrastructure projects.

Firstly, this chapter will review the existing ESSF/P and ESSIA guidelines followed by the multilateral and international organisations in different parts of Asia. It will cover United Nations Environment Programme (UNEP) guidelines and initiatives by three relevant multilateral aid agencies: the World Bank (WB), Asian Development Bank (ADB) and Asia Infrastructure Investment Bank (AIIB). This will help in crafting the policy/ framework for ESS and ESSIA clauses that would be relevant for India.

Secondly, the chapter will look at the governance challenges that arise out of such projects, especially as the DAF projects are not implemented as direct transfer of funds from donor government to receiving government. The new trend is that donor countries transfer funds through special purpose banks to private construction companies, for the implementation of projects in overseas territories.

Finally, the chapter will review, through four case studies, where projects have been implemented or are being implemented by India, in partnership with two or more countries. These case studies pertain to two sectors: transport and power. The projects selected are:

- Chabahar project, a transport corridor involving India, Iran and Afghanistan;
- Friendship Road project, involving India, Myanmar and Thailand;
- Rooppur nuclear power project involving India, Bangladesh and Russia; and
- Power trading initiative involving the Bay of Bengal Initiative for Multi-Sectoral Technical and Economic Cooperation (BIMSTEC) countries.

Drawing on the experience of these case studies, insights would be gleaned on lessons to be learnt. These would be valuable inputs for future investments by DAP, along with the suggested ESSF/P for India.

Global Environment and Social Security Framework/Policy (ESSF/P) Trends

United Nations Environment Programme

UNEP is a global environmental programme that provides the framework for implementing an environmental agenda in development projects across the world. A theme is set for every decade by UNEP to help achieve its environmental agenda. UNEP's work for 'Agenda 2030' has focused on:

1. Green economy in the context of sustainable development and poverty eradication, and

2. Institutional framework for sustainable development. It has successfully created the framework for environmental governance in the form of ministry of environment in Asian countries in almost all its member countries.[6]

UN Agenda 2030's theme focuses, among other things, on Goal 9 of the Sustainable Development Goal (SDG) 'Industry Infrastructure and Research' with emphasis on sub-theme 'connectivity.'[7]

Five cross-cutting UN sustainable development goals set the base for connectivity projects globally. These goals are to be incorporated in any connectivity projects, namely poverty eradication (Goal 1), hunger eradication (Goal 2), gender equity (Goal 5), decent labour conditions (Goal 8), and indigenous community (Goal 11), while ensuring environmental sustainability.

Therefore, the global multilateral funding agencies including the WB, ADB and AIIB, have incorporated these environmental dimensions in their Environmental and Social Sustainability Assessments (ESSA) for sustainable development projects funded by them, with some variations.

ESSA Policies

All the three multilateral funding agencies reviewed here, namely the WB, the ADB, and the AIIB, have invested in a large number of projects in Asia. All three have incorporated ESSA in their policy documents with some differences and under different titles:

- WB calls it Environment and Social Framework (ESF) providing the policy framework for the WB as a whole with regional banks adopting their own additional norms relevant to the region they operate in, like Latin America, Africa, Asia etc.
- ADB calls it Environment and Social Protection, and Safeguard Policy Statement (SPS).
- AIIB calls it Environmental and Social Security Policy (SSP) and exclusion list.

- Involuntary Resettlement Policy,
- Policy on Indigenous Peoples, and
- Environment Policy.

These assessments are based on equator principles of risk assessment. Equator principles were first used in finance as a risk management technique, for minimum due diligence, required to support responsible risk decision making.

Environmental and Social Governance

To ensure proper implementation of policy and borrower compliance, additional training and capacity building is provided by ADB to members of staff in environment governance institutions of member countries. If the standards and laws exist for due diligence, they can be implemented according to member country procedures or upgraded, with mitigation measures through knowledge sharing.

Due to the unpredictability of the three risks related to environment—physical environment, affected people and indigenous people—preparing a flexible action plan in advance and constant reviews of mitigation measures, are needed through project life cycles.[9]

Asian Infrastructure Investment Bank

The Asian Infrastructure Investment Bank provides a multilateral regional financing and investment platform for infrastructure development and enhanced inter-connectivity in Asia. It has as its clients both public and private sector companies for project or sub-project funding.

Vision: AIIB's vision for environmental and social development, in addition to sustainable development goals, is to support infrastructure and inter-connectivity to promote economic growth and improve the lives of people in Asia—economically, socially and environmentally.

ESIA: Every project, based on its category, will have an ESIA.

ESSF/P: At policy level it has an appropriate ESSF/P. Each project is treated as unique, and bank approval is needed for every ESSF/P before the project begins. For impact risks that cannot be predicted with certainty, flexibility in mitigation measures is adopted.

Environmental and Social Security Policy (ESP)

An environmental and social policy (ESP) sets forth mandatory environmental and social requirements for each project:

1. **Environmental and Social Standards.** The following three associated environmental and social standards (ESSs) set out more detailed mandatory environmental and social requirements relating to the following:

- **ESS 1:** Environmental and Social Assessment and Management (ESS 1); impact assessment and its management plan to be part of the Environmental and Social Management Plan (ESMP) covering both environment and social aspects of a project.
- **ESS 2:** Involuntary Resettlement (ESS 2); including the option of change of location before the project and a financial feasibility study of the actions proposed to look at the viability of the project.
- **ESS 3:** Indigenous Peoples (ESS 3); including the definition of and emphasis on free, prior and informed consent, and an Indigenous People Plan that is unique to every group impacted by the projects.

2. **Environmental and Social Exclusion List.** The list reflects banned social practices related to indentured labour and child labour and the production of banned substances – according to international treaties – that are harmful to public health, environment and bio-ecologies.[10]

ESS Governance Strategy

Environment and social policies of the host government are imposed on the project so far as they are consistent with the AIIB policies.

Additionally, AIIB training and capacity building is conducted, for borrowing governments and involved corporations, to update their policies and make them consistent with AIIB policies.

Other Commercial Banks

Other commercial banks funding infrastructure projects – like China Construction Bank, Exim Bank of China and India's commercial banks including Exim Bank of India–have been following global trends like CSR and raising green financing since 2014. Global funds supporting infrastructure projects, like insurance companies, also demand environmental reports before investing funds in developing countries' infrastructure projects.

Procedure for Implementation

Local governance mechanisms of the borrower, set environmental standards and social standards for the projects, as long as they are consistent with the multilateral funding agencies' ESP. Where not consistent, the inclusion of bank policies in projects are mandatory requirements that apply to borrowers, as a conditionality for the finance. Any additional standards that are relevant to country specific needs may be added, if the borrower so desires, so long as they do not contradict these five cross-cutting SDGs mentioned earlier.

End of Project Review

Thus, while the technical terms and procedures used by different multilateral funding agencies to plan and implement environmental and social assessment are different, there is a common feature across all of them. This common ensures that the implementation is done by the host country and its governance agency, and there is an end of project review by specialist consultants, not directly associated with the day to day implementation of the project. This is in addition to creating a grievance addressal mechanism which is more a mitigative or adaptive measure, used by the implementing governance agency.

India's ESSIA F/P and Governance Policy for Multilateral Projects

India and its Asian neighbours have a long-shared history, culture, people contacts, and similar ecosystems and environments. Till recently India had assisted its neighbours in bilateral projects with federal government partnership for middle level physical infrastructure projects. Therefore, arriving at mutual understanding of project ESSIA, action plan implementation and consultation of local communities is relatively straight forward. For specific infrastructure projects the ESSF/P has to narrow down to specific regional uniqueness, and India's experience in similar projects domestically, is important.

As India now enters into tri-party treaties for physical infrastructure projects, ESSIA and its implementation becomes more complex. Drawing from ESSIA P/F of multilateral aid agencies, and following their examples of implementation of ESIA and their policy frameworks, and their good practices, India can create its own ESSIA P/F, ESSIA standards, and exclusion list.

Suggested Framework for ESS Policy, Standards and Governance Policy

India's framework for ESS Policy, standards and governance policy is suggested below:

Environmental and Social Standards:

- **ESS 1:** Environmental and Social Assessment and Management (ESS 1); impact assessment and its management plan to be part of the ESMP.
- **ESS 2:** Involuntary Resettlement (ESS 2); including the option of change of location before the project is finalised and a financial feasibility study of the actions proposed to look at the viability of the project.
- **ESS 3:** Indigenous Peoples (ESS 3); including the definition of and emphasis on free prior and informed consent and

Indigenous People Plan that is unique to every group impacted by the projects.

In addition, unique to India's neighbours India could add a clause on heritage conservation.

- **ESS 4:** Heritage conservation (ESS 4). The region where India has been funding projects in Asian countries have a number of bio-diversity forest commons that the local people consider as sacred—groves, sacred water bodies: like rivers, ponds, and tanks that may or may not be linked with religious sites. In addition, these regions have long socio-cultural history and there are man-made heritage monuments and regionally held important heritage sites.

Environmental and Social Exclusion List

The list reflects banned social practices related to indentured labour and child labour and production of banned substances according to international treaties that are harmful to environment and bio-ecologies.

Since the projects considered involve multilateral treaties, such an ESSF/P[11] criteria would have to be consistent with India's foreign policy approach of mutual non-interference in the internal (political) affairs, intervention on request of the countries' government, India to deal with the government-of-the-day.

The project agreement has conditionalities at the signing of MoU. These can include ESS risk assessment along with financial and environmental risk assessment. The ESS risk assessment can be done at the pre-planning stage of the project, by the host countries' environment department, or corporations involved in the project with technical assistance and capacity building (TA and CB) by India, if needed.

When the ESS risk assessment document is drawn up, along with an action plan by the host government, it amounts to non-interference by India. End of project review when India's project funding ends, will ensure feedback and new knowledge for similar projects by EDP in future. An end-of-project review by independent ESS specialists will ensure neutrality of review.

Including these clauses in project agreements, when the MoU is signed, is a suggested ESSF/P for India. Ensuring that the existing ESS policies of the borrower government are consistent with these policies is mandatory. India's own project experiences of similar projects can be shared with borrower countries and corporations involved as part of TA and CB.

ESS Governance Policy for India

The complexity of implementing an ESS policy for a project in lands over which India has no sovereign authority is difficult and tricky. Adding an explicit governance policy in ESSIA consistent with India's foreign policy of equal partnership, is, therefore, recommended for India.

A recommended governance policy is listed below:

- *Adopt territorial approach*: For implementation of ESSIA action plans, clearly demark the project impact boundaries.
- *Clarify involvement of local stakeholders and the role they will play*: List who would be local stakeholders in the specific project with the local governance authority and make the project plan, project impact social and ecological environment, and compensation or restoration plans, transparent to them.
- *List, data monitoring and implementation of action plans*: Local authority will be responsible for listing of data, monitoring parameters and supervising implementation of action plans.
- *Support action of local authorities by federal authorities*: Local authorities involved in the project must be fully supported by federal authorities to ensure funding allocations through the lifetime of the project.
- *Training and capacity building*: Staff of local authorities, project implementing corporations and funding agencies involved in carrying out the project must all be and their capacity built for carrying out its duties related to ESSIA.

End of Project Review for India

A mid-term review with the borrowing countries and an end of project review by specialist consultants from the donor country (India), not directly associated with the day to day implementation of the project, is a SoP for all externally funded projects. This will provide lessons for India's future projects.

India's Environment Policy and Competence

ESSIA is a mandatory process requirement for India's MoEFCC to predict the social and environmental consequences of any development project. In India, it is a statutory requirement mandated by Environment Protection Act (EPA) in 1986. It is initiated at a very early stage at the time of project negotiations, through ESSIA scoping, while examining the economic and financial viability of the project. An ESSIA report is a continuous process that takes into account social and environmental impacts at every stage of the project. Mitigative measures are suggested right at the planning stage, along with risk analysis. These mitigation measures are implemented as the project proceeds.

India has a very comprehensive domestic environment policy, published in 2006, that fills the gaps between six different policies passed in the past. The MoEFCC is the nodal agency that has the power to sanction industrial, infrastructural, forest, and wildlife projects in the country. Depending on the financial investment required for the project, decision-making is done at either the central or state government level.

India has accumulated experience in planning and implementing infrastructure projects with environmental clearance. EIA and SIA are techniques used to predict thethe environment and social consequences of any development project. This impact assessment provides a regional approach to sustainable development. The impact assessmentsare policy tools, a systematic process of identifying and mitigation impacts. These reports of EIA and SIA are made available to the general public, to identify the public objections to a project prior to decision making.

Physical connectivity infrastructure projects in port, road transport, power production and power transmission have been implemented by India and the processes and procedures to be followed through the life cycles[12] of projects are well-known.

The MoEFCC has created handbooks to be followed for ESSIA in domestic infrastructure projects. India can, therefore, create training and capacity building programmes, if needed, to share its experience with other countries. Thus, India has the necessary competence in all the projects it has taken on, multilaterally, to fill in the missing policies, if any, for partner governments' environment and social security departments.[13]

Case Studies

Given the UN 2030 Agenda on transport and power connectivity, India has supported multilateral projects with its neighbourhood countries. The four case studies take into account security concerns of India and China, before reviewing the details of the projects. It then elaborates on the missing dimension of ESSIA and India's competence to provide it in each of the case studies that follow.

Chabahar Multimodal Transport Project

India

India's primary interest in its investment mission is to safeguard India's geopolitical security, economic security and energy security. India's total trade with Iran in 2018 was $17.03 billion and $900 million with Afghanistan. India imported crude oil from Iran and exported wheat to Afghanistan. Iraq accounted for 23 per cent of India's crude imports.

After American troops started to withdraw from Afghanistan on 31 December, 2016, India has exported wheat to the country on humanitarian grounds. It also has plans for developing trade with Afghanistan in the future. But India faces a logistical challenge in this, as the distance between India and Afghanistan is 990 km. India has repeatedly asked Pakistan to grant permission to supply wheat to Afghanistan *via* road, but to no avail.

transport and transit corridor that connects port of Chabahar in Iran, to Afghanistan. Chabahar port is to be used as one of the regional hubs for sea transportation in Iran. An elevated road from Chabahar through Tehran to Zaranjon the Afghanistan border, into Kandahar and Kabul, facilitates multi-modal transport of goods (vehicles) and passengers (visa, passport, papers for travel, cargo services) across the three nations.

India has signed the contract to operate five berths of the Shahid Beheshti port of Chabahar, commencing in 2019 for 18 months. India has invested $85.21 million in this project contract to be operated by a private company (Interview with Senior MEA official, 21/4/2020).

ESSIA

Adding an environmental and social sustainability policy in the tri-party treaties is not very difficult. Iran has a Department of Environment (www.doe.ir), and the necessary organisational structure and process for impact assessment needed for any infrastructure project. It is also signatory to major environmental conventions including CRZ. In addition, local governance of these policies is considered an equally important aspect of implementation of ESS. Afghanistan is in the process of establishing its own organisational structure introduced in 1994 (Ref: website). India could follow the example of other multilateral aid agencies for ESS, in its DAF projects, and ensure that and ESSIA is prepared and shared by Iran for this project. Gaps can be filled though TA and CB by India.

India's ESSIA Responsibility for the Project

India is entering an operations and maintenance phase in the trans-border connectivity project. This mainly involves operating the facility and data management related to traffic parameters. Additional environmental impacts due to the increased traffic in sea and on road of the project at point of entry and exit of the trans-border connections can be monitored and mitigative actions predicted.

The corresponding local governance authority across which the trans-border road passes can be involved in data collection and monitoring of traffic and monitoring environmental parameters. Hence, India's ESSIA is limited to an increase in air and sea water pollution due to increased traffic.

Possible Environment Impacts

At a macro level a status document for the Chabahar port project and its possible environmental impacts may have been listed with Iran's department of environment,[14] which India can use. Chabahar is the first deep sea port on the west coastline of Iran, created in 1983. The marine biota was undisturbed till the port was created. Based on similar studies and drawing on the status of the region before the port possible environmental impacts it may have had are:

Tribal fishing villages and related marine biota: Along the coast there are poor tribal fishing villages where fish is their main source of living. The port is located along fishing villages sparsely populated by a community called Meids (To Author: Please Give Reference), an indigenous tribal fishing community, along the south-western coastline of Iran. These are very poor communities using boats for fishing within 20 km of the coastline. With a deep sea port already in place, fish processing is a major industry at the economic zone at Chabahar.

With increased large ship activity and large mechanised trawler fishing, 'if the fishing takes place too close to the coastline the fish breeding grounds get destroyed. With dredging, oil spills, and the depletion of the fish catch, the communities' only known source of livelihood will be destroyed. The big issue is loss of income, due to reduced fish catch. This is the only major source of livelihood known to the community in its neighbourhood. This would lead to displacement of the villages, leading to an increase in urban migration out of desperation.

Dredging and marine pollution and oil spills: Dredging of the sea bed for shipping, and oil spills have two major impacts on marine biota. Dredging destroys the sand bed which supports different types of marine biota like molluscs, sea weeds and corals. Oil spills leave behind a thin film of oil that makes the sea water turbid and depletes oxygen in the sea water, bleaching corals and killing all life forms like fish, crabs, oysters, and molluscs.

Magasi slums: There are many tribes in the upper and lower middle level of socio-cultural hierarchy, but at the bottom are former slaves from Eastern Africa that had been brought by colonialists and Arab traders, especially Omanis, to the Makran Coastal area. These tribes are known as *Darzada, Nokar, Sheedi and Gholams. But very little is known about them or their status in the city.*[15] They, most likely, live in the slum surrounding the city. These settlements have very little basic services like drinking water, sanitation and garbage collection. Some have moved into the free economic zone (FEZ) that has not yet developed, and sell smuggled goods. This further encourages piracy, causing a security issue for the ships sailing to the port.

Increase in urban air pollution: Increased heavy vehicle traffic due to cargo movement on the elevated highway is inevitable. With increased traffic there will be increase in air pollution in major cities like Tehran. This leads to increased health hazards, mainly due to increased upper respiratory track infection related morbidity. This requires strict monitoring of air pollution and strict implementation of pollution control norms.

Ruins of archaeological importance: Iran is discovering eco-tourism as a form of development and Chabahar has developed some resorts along its coast line between Chabahar and the nearby ancient settlement of Tis. Tis has heritage resources, including ruins (ref. 20). It was a major trading port before Chabahar. Since 2300 BC it had traded with India (To Author: Reference Required Here) and is of historical archaeological importance. With increasing eco and heritage tourism Tis could become a major economic development centre. But if not managed sustainably, it could destroy the heritage resource.

India's Competence

India has experience of over ten years for managing deep sea ports and over twenty years of building highways, which has resulted in EIA handbooks by the DOEFCC. Deep sea ports had similar impacts like oil spill, marine biota conservation, and fishing villages of poor fish-workers for which DOEFCC has suggested EIA, with mitigation and adaptation measures. These are implemented in Indian ports in Tadadi, Karwar district, Karnataka[16] and in Dharma Port, Bhadrak district, in Odisha which can be used for training programmes.

Urban air pollution and its mitigation has been implemented in major metropolitan cities in India. Through various development aid funds provided by World Bank, various missions for providing basic services to rural villages and urban slums, are implemented though the Atal Mission for Rejuvenation and Urban Transformation (AMRUT) and the Swachh Bharat Mission in India.

Various success stories in environmental improvements and governance strategies from India, can be shared with the recipient countries for their capacity building through tailored training and capacity building programmes for specific needs for this project and future similar projects, specific to the stage in project cycle the development assistance is provided. A review of ongoing project at fixed intervals, in addition to end of project review would benefit trilaterally.

Friendship Road

India

India shares 1643 km of border with Myanmar. The North Eastern border is extremely porous due to the mountainous terrain. India's total trade with Myanmar was US $194.6 million and $12.46 billion with Thailand in 2018, as per the MEA website (http:// meadashboard.gov.in/indicators/92 country-wise breakup).

Land-based trade and connectivity between Myanmar and Thailand, not only gives India, an alternative to the sea route to ASEAN, but also has the potential to provide an Indian strategic counter to development projects promoted by China, which has always maintained a friendly relationship with the military junta.

China

China shares a 2, 129 km border and is a major trading partner with Myanmar. Access to Myanmar's ports and naval installations provide China with strategic influence in the Bay of Bengal, in the wider Indian Ocean region and in South East Asia. As China is landlocked on its south-western and western borders, these are important. China recently funded road construction linking the New Yangon City project and the deep-sea port at Kyaukpyu, providing the shortest route from landlocked Yunnan province from southern China to the Indian Ocean. China had trade worth $4.44 billion with Myanmar in 2011.

With the new democratic government in Myanmar post-2015, all the major Chinese mega-projects related to hydro-power Myitsone, Sittwe port projects were halted, but the gas pipelines from Sittwe and Kyaukpu to Yunnan province in China are functional. Some projects have been reviewed. A case in point is the Yangon city project as per media report. Myanmar government has decided to open up the New Yangon city project to other foreign firms besides China Communications Construction Company (CCCC), as it is not keen that one single company dominate the mega project according to recent media reports.

The Project

The Friendship *Highway* between Myanmar and Thailand, not only gives India, an alternative to the sea route to ASEAN, but also has the potential to promote in land trade for Myanmar with a free economic zone along the road's connectivity. *India, Myanmar and Thailand have a trilateral agreement to construct a* 1360 km *Friendship Highway*[17] so as to upgrade road connectivity – to vulnerable to the criticism of not managing its DAF projects in an environmentally sustainable manner.

ESSIA during the project that will need monitoring, mitigation and action plans:

Myanmar has a Ministry of Natural Resources and Environmental Conservation combined with Ministry of Mines. It has the necessary organisational structure and processes required for any infrastructure project impact assessment. It is capable of status documentation and environmental impact assessment of the road project across India and Thailand. Therefore, the ESSIA monitoring and mitigation and action plans can be prepared by them with the help of additional TA and CB, as needed, by India.

Air pollution: Increase in particulate matter and carbon dioxide due to heavy machine operations in construction phase – Monitoring and Mitigation.

Water pollution: Given the heavy rainfall in the tropical rainforest surrounding the road way, mud and silt over-flowing from construction site polluting small and large water streams – Monitoring and Mitigation.

Land slide risks: During the various phases of construction and subsequent operation phase of the road project, landslides are often inevitable due to road widening in the hilly regions. The road is widened towards the slope of the hills. Mountain ranges are also subject to earthquakes – Monitoring and Mitigation.

Social security of indigenous communities: Indigenous communities along North-Eastern part of India, northern belt of Myanmar and Northern Thailand, described as Zoomia or Zoram, are neither primitive nor backward nor underdeveloped, as per academic scholars.[22] They live mainly in the forested hills practicing slash and burn agriculture along with a hunting and gathering lifestyle. This lifestyle is a conscious choice by these indigenous communities, to resist domination by Myanmar. They, even now, continue to resist Chinese mega projects and are responsible for halting these projects, as per media reports.

Of interest, for the current project, are the Rakhine and Chin communities occupying territories along the road projects. Displacement and resettlement due to infrastructure projects is a serious issue as their lifestyles are dependent on the hilly forests they occupy. Their demand is much more than just resettlement and rehabilitation, they want autonomy, territorial protection and an equal share in profits from the project.

For example, in the Kalewa-Yagyi road section the local community demanded realignment of the road, once the project work had already begun. The demand could not be met, as the new alignment of road would pass through protected forests. But the demand had to be reviewed by both the countries, which caused a delay (MEA Official interviewed, March 2020).Thus, a detailed action plan in consultation with the impacted indigenous people, and their settlements boundaries, could have avoided project such delays.

Forest impact: Forest and indigenous communities are intertwined in a complex way. The forest area (% of land area under forest) in Myanmar, as per media reports, was 43.63 as of 2016 and housed over 30 species of wild life. These primary forests, in particular tropical moist forests, include the most species-rich, diverse terrestrial ecosystems in Myanmar, with minimal human activity. There are five national parks, 30 conservation parks, and four nature parks, in Myanmar.

Deforestation and smuggling of teak wood, is a major cause of loss of biodiversity. Habitat conservation is vital for stemming this loss. Conservation efforts have focused on protecting areas of high biodiversity. Efforts are made to conserve these forests but with the unstable political situation in the region, it is difficult to reverse the rapid ongoing deforestation.

Strict adherence to the boundaries that cover the core areas and the buffer zones is essential to ensure their protection. Ensuring forest protection will require a 'forest action plan' in consultation with the impacted indigenous people of those regions. These negotiations, which require diplomatic handling, often cause project delays.

India's Competence

India has, since its independence, been dealing with the indigenous tribal communities living in similar ecosystems, in states in its North Eastern regions. India has dealt with tribal unrest and arrived at peaceful negotiations in these states. Mizoram with Khasi tribes has been supporting the Friendship Road connectivity. Moreh, in the state of Manipur, is the last stop on India's side of the road.

India has a large forest reserve, a National Forest Conservation Policy, 1988, and a Ministry (MoEFCC) that deals with forest conservation. It also has a website created to deal with acts, rules, protected species etc. including user manuals for environment forest and wild life (single window) clearance for projects (http://parivesh.nic.in/acts.aspx?id=FC). India has nature parks, protected forest and biodiversity conservation areas that it has taken care of. Issues of shared benefits with local communities in buffer zones are dealt with through community forestry plans. Profit sharing with local communities through CSR of major infrastructure projects in India by private companies investing in these projects, is now a best practice.

Negotiating with tribal communities (Ministry of Tribal Affairs, GoI (https://tribal.nic.in/), along with non-state actors (NGOs), and ensuring willing participation at the EIA stage, results in an action plan, that is implemented throughout the project lifetime. These action plans include indigenous communities and are recognised and accepted by tribal communities, where relevant. India has ensured this across multiple projects, in the states of Odisha, Maharashtra, Madhya Pradesh and the NE states, in its public sector iron and steel industry, trans-state highways, and oil and gas projects.

Thus, India has experience in dealing with forest conservation and dealing with indigenous communities in its domestic projects, over the last several decades. These experiences can be shared to train officials and stakeholders in Myanmar and Thailand, through capacity building training programmes and ongoing project reviews, in addition to an end of project review.

Rooppur Nuclear Power Plant

India

Besides geopolitical security, ensuring energy security is an important aspect of India's security strategy. Energy security is defined as uninterrupted supply of energy sources, at affordable prices. This involves creating multiple resources mix, reducing cost by using energy efficient technologies, and creating indigenous competence in technologies imported into the country—nuclear energy is one of them.

For years, India has been trying to make a mark in the global nuclear commerce market that is worth multi-billion dollars without a lot of success, since it is not a member of the Nuclear Suppliers Group (NSG). Entering the international nuclear energy trade is important for India's rising ambition of being an emerging power in Asia.

China/Pakistan

China is a recognised as a 'nuclear weapon state' as per the nuclear non-proliferation treaty. Media reports state that China desired to cultivate Pakistan as a strategic partner in South Asia as part of its regional balance of power strategy *vis-à-vis* India. In 2015, China offered to fund and build a nuclear power plant in Bangladesh, but the project did not go through. Media reports now say that China is offering Bangladesh a second nuclear power plant, to be built and funded by China.

China has the technology to produce nuclear power plants and nuclear weapons. It helped Pakistan to set up its nuclear power plants. In 1991, China agreed to supply Pakistan with its indigenously developed Qinshan-1 nuclear power plant. Construction on Chashma Nuclear Power Plant-1 (CHASNUPP-1 or C-1) began in 1993, and the 300 M. We reactor became operational in May 2000. Since then three more units in Chasma are under construction in Karachi and are scheduled to be operational in 2021 with that Pakistan will be producing 3,346 MWe of nuclear energy by 2022.[23]

The Project

With the Rooppur project India gains a foothold in the nuclear commerce. This is the first joint initiative by India and Russia to undertake atomic energy projects in developing countries. India is not a member of the Nuclear Suppliers Group (NSG) and hence cannot participate directly in the construction of atomic power reactors. This will also be the first time Indian companies will be able to participate in a nuclear power project, in another country.

Bangladesh has framework agreements for peaceful *nuclear energy* applications with the US, France and China. India's investments and development projects are based on the development priorities of the country concerned and these, stand firmly on their own merits. India, has regularly extended financial and development assistance to Bangladesh.

A third Line of Credit (LOC) of $4.5 billion to Bangladesh was announced in April 2017 during Bangladesh PM Sheikh Hasina's visit to India. This $4.5 LOC was the biggest LOC that India has so far extended to any country. This covers a wide range of areas, such as power supply, port development, connectivity (rail and road), civil nuclear energy etc.[24]

The three-country treaty was signed on 1 March 2018 between India, Russia and Bangladesh. According to Rosatom, the Russian company providing the reactor for the power plant, the agreement allows Indian firms in construction and installation works in the "non-critical"category for the Rooppur plant.[25]

The plant with the capacity for power production of 2.4 GW is being set up in Rooppur, in the Ishwardi sub-district of Pabna district, on the bank of the river Padma, 121 km west of Dhaka, in northwest Bangladesh. Construction began in 2017 and the first unit is expected to complete by 2023 and the second unit by 2024. The total estimated investment is of $12.65 bn and is developed by Bangladesh Atomic Energy Commission. As mentioned earlier, the reactor is being supplied by Rosatom, a Russian State Corporation, headquartered in Moscow that specialises in nuclear energy[26].

Environmental Social Security Impact

Here, the focus is only on possible environmental impacts 'onsite', and will not take into account fuel milling, mining, and manufacture of fuel elements, and its environmental impacts, before the fuel arrives at the reactor site in Bangladesh. ESSIA is taken very seriously hence listed in details below[27]:

Advantages

There are certain advantages to own a nuclear power plant in comparison with coal fired plant producing same amount of energy a nuclear power plan has certain possible advantages as listed below.

For generation of 1000-MWe of electricity generated by a coal-fired plant—a nuclear power plant:

	Coal fired power plant	Nuclear power plant:Light Water Breeder Reactor (LWBR)
Effluent (waste water generated)	Millions of tons	1500 t/a
Land use	330 to 400 acres	70 to 140 acres
Per unit water consumed (in Cubic Meters per second Cu.Sec)	100 Cu. Sec	140 Cu. Sec

Thus, there is reduced land use in a nuclear plant and reduced effluent discharge in the environment in a nuclear power plant. Bangladesh, with high density of population of 1, 115.62 people per square kilometre (2020 Census Data), power projects needing less land is a preference. Given that the Ganga and its tributaries are perennial rivers and crisscross the country, the extra water requirement for the project is not a concern.

Possible Disadvantages of a Nuclear Plant

There are International Atomic Energy Agency (IAEA) guidelines for a nuclear power plant to which strict adherence is expected.[28] With India partnering and being more familiar with development and environment issues, certain mitigation measures are possible for Bangladesh, against such a strict adherence. These are listed below:

Exclusion Zone area: These exclusion zone areas are marked in concentric circles of 2.5 km radius, 5 km radius and 30 km radius from the site of the nuclear plant. No population habitation is allowed between a 5–30 km radius other than plant employees who are allowed within a 2.5 km radius.[29]

Given the high density of population in Bangladesh, such an exclusion zone restriction would imply displacement and relocation of 10, 000, 000 people living in the surrounding areas, as rescuing them in case of disaster will be very difficult. These zonal restrictions of habitation are revised by India, a densely populated country. Bangladesh can adopt these revised norms given similar geoclimatic regions.[30]

Disposal of spent water into the water body: Hot water generated out of cooling of the nuclear reactors and steam used for turbines is about 30 to 40 degrees Celsius when disposed into the water body, in this case the Padma river —a tributary of the Ganges river. This causes thermal pollution in water body, leading to a rise in pH levels and a reduction in dissolved oxygen, killing fish and other aquatic life forms leading to eutrophication, that does not support any life forms other than algae and aerobic microbes.[31]

Natural disasters: Earthquakes are a major risk factor. An earthquake beyond 7 on the Richter scale can cause serious damage but the Rooppur plant site is seismically quiet. Tsunamis are a major threat to nuclear power plants. A powerful tsunami in the sea could launch enough water through a major river to flood a power plant. But the Padma river is a tributary of the Ganga and not a very big river.[32]

Disposal of spent fuel nuclear waste: Around 20-30 tons of high-level waste is produced per month per nuclear reactor. Radioactive waste generates gamma ray radiation—a direct radiation hazard. Such radioactive fission products could pose a direct radiation hazard, contaminate soil and vegetation, and be ingested by humans and animals. Human exposure at high enough levels can cause

Bangladesh, India has the competence to take on the ESSIA and implement it.[33]

In addition, in case of Bangladesh, there would be training and capacity development (T & CD). This will be for the staff that would be operating the nuclear power plant as well as awareness creation for information sharing, and preventive practices for disaster management, for the local community around the nuclear plant. Since Bengali, the national language of Bangladesh, is also one of the state languages in India, such a training would be facilitated further. (Interview with MEA officials, May 2020). Thus, India will play a significant role in the tri-party nuclear power agreement.

BIMSTEC Electricity Sharing

India

All the well-established examples of regional energy cooperation, like the European Union, the South African Power Pool, or the Gulf Cooperation Council, have the underlying foundation of regional stability and peace as one of their enablers and drivers. "The South Asian Association for Regional Cooperation (SAARC) Framework Agreement for Energy Cooperation (Electricity)" was signed by all SAARC member-states including India on 27 November, 2014 during the 18th SAARC Summit, held in Nepal for cross-border electricity trade, with the underlying foundation of regional stability and peace.[34]

Under this framework, the High Voltage DC (HVDC) station in Bheramara, in Bangladesh was inaugurated on September 2018, to provide a safe and reliable inter-connection of the power grids of India and Bangladesh, which will enable supply of 500 MW of power from India to Bangladesh.[35] This marked a new beginning in cross-border trading of electricity, which will take care of peak demands in Bangladesh. The alternative is, increasing generation costs to peak capacity, as most of these power plants are old and ageing or build new power plants.

China

Concurrent with 2014 SAARC framework agreement, China has invested in new projects producing power in Nepal, Myanmar, Sri Lanka, and Bangladesh, with loans from its China Exim Bank and using its own construction company.

According to media[36] reports on 18 November, 2019, Nepal's China-funded 60MW Hydropower Project in Upper Trishuli 3A Hydropower Project was inaugurated. The project which was developed by Nepal Electricity Authority (NEA), and constructed by China Gezhouba Group Company, is located at the border of Rasuwa and Nuwakot districts in the central region of Nepal. NEA is to repay the concessional loan of around $116 million from China Exim Bank, of the total cost of $125 million, over 25 years at 1.2 per cent interest per month.

The media also reported on 13 March, 2020 that China had been negotiating with Myanmar for a power transmission connection from its Yunnan province to Kachin district in Myanmar, and an MoU has been signed for new power projects across Myanmar, enabling China to export surplus electricity concessional rates. This would reduce the need for power imports from Thailand through the grid inter-connection that already exists under BIMSTEC.[37]

In April 2019 and October 2019, respectively, Payra 1320 MW Thermal (Coal) Power Plant Project (1 and 2 Phases) were commissioned in Bangladesh as a joint venture created on a turnkey basis between Bangladesh-China Power Company (Pvt.) Limited (BCPCL) with an investment of $500 million by the Chinese government. The project faced environmental protests.[38] China is negotiating with Thailand for a future renewable energy project. By providing the capital and technology, China is helping these countries achieve 100 per cent energy coverage, thus eliminating the need for trading energy within the region as initiated by India.

The Project

Bay of Bengal Initiative for Multi Sectoral Technical and Economic Cooperation (BIMSTEC) is a regional organisation consisting of seven members located in the littoral and adjacent areas of the Bay of Bengal—Bangladesh, Bhutan, India, Myanmar, Nepal, Sri Lanka and Thailand. The MoU signed among these nations is to provide a broad framework for parties to cooperate over grid inter-connections for the trade of electricity, with a view to promote rational and optimal power transmission in the BIMSTEC region.

An MoU signed on 8 August, 2018, provides a broad framework for "Plan of Action for Energy Cooperation in BIMSTEC", ensuring grid inter-connection in electricity, across nations. It provides a broad framework for "Plan of Action for Energy Cooperation in BIMSTEC", ensuring grid inter-connection in electricity, across nations.[39]

India is the largest country in the region in terms of geography (67%), population (80%) and GDP (74%), followed by Thailand in terms of GDP, Myanmar in terms of area, and Bangladesh in terms of population. India is, therefore, playing key role in driving energy trade in the region. Except for Thailand and Bhutan, none of these countries have 100 per cent access to electricity.[40]

The justification for power trading is that it helps the socio-economic development of nations. Bangladesh offers the best illustration of relationship between, electricity access per capita consumption and economic growth. Between FY2015-FY2019 it has increased its power access from 75 per cent to 95 per cent, its per capita power consumption from 251-375 MWhrs (Mega Watt hours) and its GDP growth rate increased from 6.55 per cent to 8.13 per cent in five years.[41]

Environmental and Social Security Impacts

In a power trading project, cross-border inter-connections have already been established between India-Bangladesh, India-Bhutan, India-Nepal, India-Myanmar, and Myanmar-Thailand. The biggest environmental impact of a grid inter-connection is the building of additional transmission lines if needed and power sub-stations where needed.

The ESSIA for these multilateral treaties need to incorporate resettlement impacts and indigenous community impacts for grid connectivity. Special sensitivity is needed to right of way for animals and communities during the laying of transmission lines and the construction phase. Terrestrial and biological biodiversity mitigation measures must also be taken into account while laying the High Voltage Transmission Lines (HVTL).

Disaster risks due to tower construction, and high-tension wire breaking away, mainly during natural disasters, is another risk. These environmental risks are of particular importance and need to be taken into account, as there would be new construction of transmission lines and sub-stations created for such trading and hence, should be an important part of power transmission agreements. This needs to be worked out in consultation with local governance authorities that the communities accept and respect, especially when dealing with indigenous communities.

A common environmental code across borders is important when cross-border trading is established, as each country is allowed to retain their local codes and laws within the country. The legal details are being worked out under BIMSTEC for creating a common minimum grid code to further this grid connectivity. India can take lead in this ESSIA common minimum code for environmental and social safety impact assessment with partner countries' department of environment.

India's Competence

MoEFCC has recommended a hand book for power transmission that can be used as a guideline for environmental impacts of high voltage transmission lines and HVDC sub-stations to be laid for grid inter-connections across different countries. India has the relevant experience in ESSIA for transmission lines to produce connections across HVDC sub-stations. India has put up these lines across the country while conducting ESSIAs across all aspects, including social impact assessment, and passage way for terrestrial animals and human communities along the transmission lines.[42] This is a very relevant for TA and CB in grid connection projects.

Modern technology applications, like fuel cells, clean coal technologies, energy storage, energy integration with biofuels, smart grids etc. are new solutions emerging specific to a fuel use, in developing local markets for energy.

Conclusion

As the case studies indicate, none of the projects are 'green field' projects. They involve intervention in different phases of ongoing projects, making skilful diplomacy a critical element in each task, as follows:

- Operation and Maintenance phase in multimodal transport project in the Chabahar treaty with Iran and Afghanistan.
- Construction phase, in two sub-projects in the tri-party road connectivity project with Myanmar and Thailand.
- Construction of non-critical construction and installation works for the nuclear reactor in Bangladesh.
- Detailed pre-planning and planning phase, and operation phase of BIMSTEC.

It is possible to add an appropriate ESSF/P at the MoU stage, along with financial and economic criteria in India's DAP projects. While other security and strategic concerns for selecting the countries and projects may be the prime motive for project selection, ensuring best practices in ESSF/P in India's funded projects will be a good strategy in the long run. This is consistent with India's foreign policy as well as with the globally signed treaties, for environmental sustainability. It is also a best practice adopted by other multilateral banks. Insurance and pension funds, and more recently, commercial banks lending for infrastructure projects, are also moving in that direction. It would be the next step in DAP project funding for India.

Notes

1. This is an inter-disciplinary research, in an evolving area of funding provided by India, in trilateral and multilateral projects. Therefore, certain base knowledge of physical infrastructure projects, environmental impacts of physical infrastructure, international relations, India's foreign policy, and Development Assistance Fund of Ministry of External Affairs (MEA) and MEA's organisation of structure, is assumed.
2. I gratefully acknowledge the larger context for the paper provided by retired Ambassadors Mr. A.R. Deo, Mr. S.T. Devare and Mr. G. Parthsarathy and Ex Chief Secretary of State, GoI who wishes not to be named. They were posted to these case study countries in the past. The present context for the paper is provided by present Secretary of MEA and his colleagues and MD EXIM Bank and member of his board of directors. They do not wish to be named. Last but not the least Dr. Jyoti Parikh of IRADE, for her support.
   The views expressed in the paper are my own. I take full responsibility for them.
3. Khilnani *et al.* Non-Alignment 2: http://www. Cprindia. org>tdf>policy-brief>non Alignment2.pdf
4. Lines of Credit for Development Projects, https://www.mea.gov.in/Lines-of-Credit-for-Development-Projects.htm
5. Survival of humankind. We humans are totally dependent for our survival upon the continued functioning of natural systems. Sustainable development, involves environmental sustainability and social sustainability. Environmental sustainability is *defined* as responsible interaction with the *environment* to avoid depletion or degradation of natural resources and allow for long-term *environmental* quality. Social sustainability is defined as the ability of a community to develop processes and structures, which meet the needs of its current generation, and does not compromise the needs of the future generations.
   Rasmus Øjvind Nielsen, Agata M. Gurzawska and Philip Brey, 'Ethical Impact Assessment and Conventional Impact Assessment' June 2015. This deliverable and the work described in it is part of the project "*Stakeholders Acting Together on the Ethical Impact Assessment of Research and Innovation"—SATORI—*funded by the European Commission's Seventh Framework Programme *(FP7/2007-2013)* under grant agreement # 612231

26. (https://www.power-technology.com/projects/rooppur-nuclear-power-plant-ishwardi/)
27. Essam E. El-Hinnawi. 'Review of the Environmental Impact of Nuclear Energy' May 1977.
    https://inis.iaea.org/search/search.aspx?orig_q=RN:8303221)
28. *Ibid.*
29. *Ibid.*
30. Tausif Ali, Mohammad Shidujaman *et al.* (6 others) 'Feasibility Study of RNPP Rooppur Nuclear Power Project in Bangladesh'. January 2013 https://www.researchgate.net/publication/276421020_Feasibility_Study_of_RNPP_)
31. (Md. Mosaddequr Rahman Ferdous Ahamed 'Biodiversity in the Padma Distributary of the Ganges River, Northwestern Bangladesh: Recommendations for Conservation'. December 2012)
    https://www.researchgate.net/publication/234065251 Biodiversity in Padma Distributary.
32. *Ibid.*
33. Rapid Environmental Impact Assessment of Proposed Nuclear Power Plant (Units 1 & 2), Kudankulam, T.N. (Sponsor: Nuclear Power Corporation (I) Ltd, Mumbai,) National Environmental Engineering Research Institute. Nehru Marg, Nagpur 440020 (India) May 2002
34. (SAARC Framework Agreement for Energy Cooperation (Electricity) 27November 2014 https://powermin.nic.in/en/content/saarc-framework-agreement-energy-cooperation-electricity
35. (Remarks by Prime Minister at the Inauguration of India-Bangladesh Grid Inter-connection, Bheramara & Laying of Foundation Stone of Thermal Power Project, Rampal, Bangladesh, September 2018
    https://mea.gov.in/Speeches-Statements.htm/dtl/22289/remarks+by+prime+minister+at+the+inauguration+of+indiabangladesh+grid+inter-connection+bheramara+amp+laying+of+foundation+stone+of+thermal+power+project+rampal+bangladesh
36. 'Nepali prime minister inaugurates China funded hydro project in Nepal'. *Source*: Xinhua| 2019-11-18 23:28:24|Editor: yanhttp://www.xinhuanet.com/english/2019-11/18/c_138564821.htm
37. Chinese electricity blessing or curse? https://www.irrawaddy.com/opinion/analysis/chinese-electricity-blessing-curse-myanmar.html
38. Payra Power Plant https://www.nsenergybusiness.com/projects/payra-power-plant/
39. Memorandum of Understanding for establishment of the BIMSTEC Grid Inter-connection 8 August, 2018.

https://powermin.nic.in/en/content/memorandum-understanding-establishment-bimstec-grid-inter-connection

40. Prospects for Regional Energy Cooperation and Cross Border energy Trading in the BIMSTEC region.
https:/BIMSTEC+background+paper&rlz=1C1CHBF_enUS753US753&oq=BIMSTEC+background+paper&aqs=chrome..69i57j33.17873j0j7&sourceid=chrome&ie=UTF-8
41. Prospects for Regional Energy Cooperation and Cross-Border Energy Trading in the BIMSTEC region.
https:/BIMSTEC+background+paper&rlz=1C1CHBF_enUS753US753&oq=BIMSTEC+background+paper&aqs=chrome..69i57j33.17873j0j7&sourceid=chrome&ie=UTF-8
42. Environmental and Social Impact Assessment of 220 kV Power Transmission line: Manali to Nalagarh, Himachal Pradesh India 2014, for AD Hydro Power Ltd. WWW. Erm.com

4
Covid-19
A Systems Crisis

When UN-WHO declared on February 2020 COVID-19 as a pandemic, India's international relations strategies were continuing to be consistent with the dominant development paradigm of Sustainable Development accepted globally for economic development related interventions. India's emphasis on 'Neighbourhood First' had a focus on ocean rim countries, in Indo-Pacific Ocean and Indian Ocean. It covered countries in West Africa, West Asia and South East Asia. The development projects that Indian Government undertook were consistent with the dominant paradigm and the UN Sustainable Development goals as per the theme of the decade – energy and transport connectivity. Specific project level Memorandum of Understanding (MoU) were signed between multiple countries since 2015. The projects implemented in connectivity, capacity building and maritime operations were undertaken with partner countries. Given the increasing salience of the Indian Ocean region and Indo-Pacific region in the global discourse, the Ministry of External Affairs established a new Division for the Indo-Pacific in April 2019. Both bilateral and especially multilateral projects, were signed and undertaken since 2014 as the previous chapter has covered in details. India would have probably continued its efforts with other partner countries, on these lines—negotiating for new multilateral infrastructure projects with partner countries and providing grant-in-aid and providing Line of credit (LoC) for less well-off partners seeking help according to their needs.

Dynamics of Crisis

Then the COVID-19 pandemic struck the world. A crisis challenges a *status quo*. The Dynamics of a crisis event like COVID-19 pandemic needs to be understood in details, to fully understand what happened. UN-WHO declared on February 2020 that COVID-19 was a global pandemic, with high morbidity and mortality rates, that infections were spreading across countries very rapidly and had very high death rates among infected. There was no known treatment or cure for it then. There is no agreed upon definition of a pandemicor when COVID-19 became a pandemic. Hence, when WHO declared COVID-19 as a pandemic, we will take it as a start date.

Any epidemic is a disease that spreads very quickly across population over a given geographic region. A Pandemic is an epidemic that has spread globally, both over population and geographies, and therefore, has the same impacts like an epidemic, but over geographies across nations. A Dashboard of the pandemic macro graph over a given time period[1] indicates three phases, the initial phase of high morbidity mortality rates, then a middle phase of declining mortality rates, while the infections continue and finally when the pandemic is not a threat. The disease persists globally as a long tail, but at relatively low rates of mortality and morbidity. Typically, a pandemic in a region, lasts for about two to three years, it has multiple peaks and troughs. But a macro graph will indicate a very high morbidity and mortality rate in the first two peaks combined, that reaches very high numbers, then it decline at the middle range and the graph then shows low rates but persistence as indicated by a long tail, with low peaks indicating low morbidity and mortality in the population in that region, over time.[2] In case of COVID-19 the outbreak as a pandemic with high global death was in 2020, then come another high peak in global deaths in 2021 and now a slow decline into 2022 onwards persists.

A key part of managing an infectious disease outbreak is trying to decrease the epidemic peak, known as "flattening the curve"[3]. This helps decrease the risk of health services being overwhelmed and provides more time for a vaccine and treatments to be developed. A broad group of the non-pharmaceutical interventions, may be taken to manage the outbreak. The most extreme management of the disease is a complete isolation, a shutdown of the global cross-border transactions, across countries and across states within a country as it happened in case of COVID-19.

The basic strategies in the control of an outbreak are three—prevention, containment and mitigation. Ideal strategy is prevention. But in early stage prevention may not be available as the vaccine may not exist. Without it containment and mitigation need to go hand in hand. Containment is mainly non-pharmaceutical in nature and may be undertaken in the early stages of the outbreak, including contact tracing and isolating infected individuals, to stop the disease from spreading to the rest of the population, too quickly. Also reducing spread helps from over burdening of the medical facilities till a cure is found. In the meantime when infection does happen, mitigation measures, at treatment levels need to be explored, including relief measures like availability of Oxygen, and medicines for fighting the infection, that are needed for treatment. Finally, find a prevention measure – a vaccine from the disease spreading agents, so the disease is prevented from happening. Mitigation measures have two dimensions, paramedical and non-paramedical interventions. Paramedical measures involve Contact tracing through RTPCR tests, while preventive measures are pharmaceutical and medical in nature, requiring hospitalisation.

While three things were happening simultaneously in 2020, vaccine creation actions for prevention of the virus, mitigation actions had to be tried and tested and then shared immediately for pharmaceuticals and other medicines' treatment that worked at paramedic levels and non-paramedic levels measures. A World Health Organization study indicated that the world continents have confirmed a total of 1,202,320 confirmed COVID-19 cases as early as February 2020: (51.2%) in Europe, (27.7%) in North America, (17.9%) in Asia, (1.96%) in South America and a smaller number of confirmed COVID-19 cases in Africa and Australia which was accounted 0.8 per cent and 0.5 per cent, respectively in January 2020. With a disclaimer that these statistics are still changing and the morbidity and mortality is dramatically increasing from time to time as given in.[4]

Since 31/12/2020, when the first Emergency use listing of vaccine was sanctioned for pharmaceutical companies, Pfizer (USA), Astra Zenca (Britian) was sanction on 16/4/2021 and Serum Institute (COVI-shield) (India) vaccine was sanctioned on 23/12/2021. While with Russia and China Phase III trial results were awaited by WHO. But it must be noted that "in line with their national regulations and legislation, countries have the autonomy to issue emergency use authorizations for any health product. Domestic emergency use authorizations are issued at the discretion of countries and not subject to WHO approval."[5] So countrycan immunise their domestic populations.

Thus, a country has choices to be made for controlling the pandemic. These are choices based on political decisions to be taken rationally based on 'common sense understanding' and history of similar pandemics from the past. Remember COVID-19 was an unknown pandemic. To put it harshly, nobody knew nothing about prevention for sure. The strategies were evolving. Without going details of choices and the risks and benefits of each choice I will focus on what India did here.

Challenging the Dominant Paradigm

COVID-19 led to a global shutdown of international trade, only slow opening of the trade as the epidemic progressed. Resulting in a dramatic shifted in the balance between the input-output model of world trade and therefore, the way the World Economic System was operating. Each state was left to defend for itself during the crisis. This was partially because, the multilateral World Health Organization (WHO) had declared that the pandemic had arrived, such a world order. All these corollaries were called into question subsequently.

What India Did

India took a political decisions related to COVID-19: to immediately 'shut down' of the country for thirty days, to control population movements and slowly 'open up'. It started monitoring spread of the disease through the RTPCR 'testing', and supported efforts for research for indigenous vaccine and get international approval for Indians the vaccine, which it could manufacture and export.

Since India's foreign policy is the focus, of the book, hence India's actions in the context of its partner countries and therefore, its international relations during the pandemic is the focus here. In India, Ministry of External Affairs (MEA) deals with India's international relations. MEA adopted actions that were in line with the actions taken globally and by other developed countries. In addition India immediately within days of declaration of epidemic reached out to the partner countries along the Ocean rim and continued it at all the three stages of the pandemic. India sent technical help to train paramedics to train its partners in preventive measures supported medical inventions, for both prevention and mitigation measures through pharmaceutical aid and exports. Finally, once the emergency use was authorised India started reaching out to its neighbouring partner countries for vaccination. This is when, the first mass vaccine for Indian Ocean Rim countries that asked for help, were covered by India. India at the same time did not ignore needs of its own large population, domestically. Once Emergency Use Listing (EUL) was authorized, India had to take measures related to pricing and volume of vaccine to be made available to different countries. These were also political decisions, that the political leadership had to take immediately, and they took some confident decision towards these actions consistent with the 'neighbourhood first' foreign policy.

MEA Actions

Thus, a structured response to COVID-19 pandemic was put together and implemented systematically by MEA. It required urgent action at multiple levels. Action directly related to COVID-19 are mentioned above. India has a large number of emigrant population living in different global regions. Bringing back citizens was urgent and ensuring their safe return post-pandemic equally important. Then India had a Second wave of COVID-19 that required immediate medical help including imports of vaccine and pharmaceuticals from other countries, due to the size of India's population. On all these levels, MEA was the coordinating ministry. MEA officials stepped in to take the responsibility for coordinating all these actions across different departments across different ministries.

India immediately put a Rapid Response Teams of medical and paramedical specialists that went to Comoros, Kuwait, Maldives and Mauritius to assist in pandemic response[6] to set up training and information sharing programmes for them. The SAARC Covid-19 Emergency Fund was created with India contributing USD 10 million. Subsequently, India shared medicine supplies with these countries that were supplied partially free and partially charged[7].

Further Supportive Actions

During this period, the Ministry of External Affairs continued its structured response to Covid-19 challenges at multiple levels, which it had never done at this scale and urgency before. As the global arm of the Government of India, the Ministry was involved in coordinating a wide range of Covid-19 response mechanisms – special cell for 24×7 operations, procurement operations, sourcing technologies, coordinating vaccines supplies and distribution coordinating returning citizens (repatriates) and now by end 2022, citizens wanting to go back to their place of work abroad[8] (Table 4.1).

Table 4.1: Indicating returning Indians from six gulf countries.

S.No.	Name ofEmigration Clearance Required (ECR) Countries	Estimated No. of Indian workers
1.	UAE	3,30,058
2.	Saudi Arabia	1,37,900
3.	Kuwait	97,802
4.	Oman	72,259
5.	Qatar	51,190
6.	Bahrain	27,453
	Total	**7,16,662**

Special COVID-19 Cell

A Covid-19 cell was immediately created and senior officers deployed on Covid related duties. A Control Room manned 24×7 was set up to deal with emergency requests from stranded Indians and to disseminate information. It has received more than 1,10,000 emails and 33,000 telephone calls.

In addition continuous daily updates were providing during the peak pandemic in India in 2021 on their website for returning citizens to take decisions of travel[9].

Returning Citizens

A large-scale coordinated effort, the '*Vande Bharat* Mission'- Solute to India mission, involving Indian Missions and Posts abroad and all concerned organisations in India was launched. More than 3 million Indians, some repatriated by the host countries others volenterily, have returned to India under this mission from different parts of the world. As India began unlocking, air bubble agreements (direct flight across countries) were negotiated with 24 countries that restored mobility between India and these destinations. Returns took place by air, by sea and by land. The evacuation of more than 1,10,000 foreign nationals from different parts of India to 123 countries was facilitated. As well as returning nationals from Bhutan Nepal Bangladesh were also accommodated in the air bubble arrangement on their way home. As per Government's estimates, about 7,16,662 workers returned from the six Gulf countries alone under the *Vande Bharat* Mission.[10]

By 2021-22 as the Pandemic infections reduced and the epidemic was brought under control, so the number of Indians wanting to return to their jobs and thus the need for issuing new visas is also rising which is the core responsibility of MEA in India.

Table 4.2: MEA has issued new visas since 2021-22

MEA was required to take actions since the onset of pandemic 2021	70,26,960
MEA was required to take actions since the onset of pandemic 2022	82,48,870

Medical Supplies Procurement Operations

India provided Covid-related medical supplies to over 154 countries. Medications such as Hydroxychloroquine and Paracetamol, supplies were transported in spite of lockdowns and logistical challenges. India from 2020 to 2022 has airlifted another 6.2 tons of medicines under Operation *Sanjeevani* to its partner countries.[11]

Testing kits, ventilators, PPEs and masks and also appropriate technologies were sourced on a worldwide basis since 2020. The second wave of the pandemic in April-June 2021 caused enormous stresses on our health care systems. Regular PIB Covid-19 Updates through bulletins on Covid-19 started from May 2, 2021, corresponding to when the vaccine drive had commenced, till July 6 2021 at the peak of infection wave, as it is known. There were shortages of critical medical supplies such as oxygen cylinders and concentrators. Procurement and logistics during the second wave proved to be much more daunting because the number of infections, critically ill patients and deaths were much higher. The Ministry mounted a global effort, for imports of equipment under emergency, to speedily source critical supplies to fight the second wave in May-June 2022. Indian Missions and Posts abroad were at the forefront of this mammoth exercise. The Special Control

Room functioning 24×7 for these operations. Critical supplies that included Liquid Medical Oxygen (LMO), oxygen generation plants, concentrators, ECMO machines, vaccines and essential medicines were procured from all over the world. More than 50 countries extended support to India during this difficult time by donating essential medical supplies. Indian Missions and Posts also reached out to non-governmental organizations and individual donors who were keen to assist India at the peak of the pandemic.

Table 4.3: Critical equipments, drugs and others imported by India 2020-22[12]

	2020	2021	2022
Indicating critical equipment			
Oxygen Cylinders	18,326	16,550	34,876
Oxygen Concentrators	13,826	16,051	29,877
Oxygen PSA Plant	47	1	48
Ventilator/BIPAP/Cpap	17,120	2,440	19,560
Metric Tonnes of LMO	635	210	845
Drugs			
Favipiravir	13,30,107	20,00,080	33,30,187
Remdesivir	7,01,578	4,05,362	11,06,940
Tocilizumab	1,000	50,024	51,024
Others			
Mask	84,93,000	13,39,274	98,32,274
Rapid Diagnostic Kit	19,78,800	10,185	19,88,985

Vaccine Related

India coordinated with global regulatory agencies for expediting approvals for 'Made in India' vaccines. Covishield was approved by the World Health Organisation in February 2021 and Covaxin in November 2021. India worked with global and domestic stakeholders for the introduction of foreign vaccines in India along with emphasis on domestic vaccine research and production. During the Second Wave of COVID-19, the supply of critical pharmaceutical items was a major challenge for bulk vaccine production in India. The Ministry coordinated with US and European counterparts for easing imports of pharmaceutical ingredients. Resulting in rapid production of much needed vaccine. World leaders publicly commended India's efforts to rapidly expand vaccine production and supplies at critical junctures of the pandemic.

India provided vaccines to Afghanistan, Bhutan, Maldives, Bangladesh, Nepal, Myanmar, Mauritius, Mexico, Seychelles, Sri Lanka, the UAE, Brazil, Morocco, Bahrain, Oman, Egypt, Algeria, Kuwait and South Africa. The supplies have been made under grant assistance as well as on a commercial basis very early during the pandemic. As on 31 December, 2021, India has supplied more than 110 million vaccine doses to 97 countries. The Ministry also has worked out travel arrangements based on mutual recognition of vaccine certificates with over 100 countries in a bid to expeditiously normalize international travel.[13]

Grant-in-Aid and Assistance

India specially helped its partner countries in immediate neighbourhood[14], Bangladesh, Bhutan, Mauritius, Afghanistan with financial support and vaccines.

Bilateral trade between India and Afghanistan has crossed the USD 1.5 billion mark in 2020-21. India extended Covid-19 related assistance to Afghanistan including more than 20 MT of life-saving medicines and humanitarian assistance of 75,000 MT of wheat through Chabahar Port to strengthen the food security situation. 500,000 doses of Covishield vaccine, were sent to Afghanistan in February 2021 as grant assistance.

India has provided three tranches of Covid related assistance to Bangladesh. Over 2 million doses of Covishield vaccine were sent to Bangladesh in January 2021 as grant assistance. 1,50,000 doses of Covishield vaccine were sent to Bhutan in January 2021 as grant assistance etc. Thus total of 2915 lakh vaccines were sent to 101 countries.

Global Governance Initiative

India accelerated its diplomatic engagements at the highest levels in this rapidly evolving international environment. During 2021-22, Prime Minister participated at the Summit Level meetings of G7, G20 and COP-26. Prime Minister also chaired a United Nations Security Council session in August 2021, the BRICS Summit and the Shanghai Cooperation Organisation Council of Heads of Government, and hosted the first meeting of the India Central Asia Summit, in virtual format. He also delivered a virtual message at the Eastern Economic Forum; and at the Global Covid-19 Summit. During these events, Prime Minister reiterated India's commitment to reformed multilateralism and reaffirmed India's emerging role as "force for the good" in contributing global solutions to global problems.

This also demonstrated India's digital capacities in fighting the pandemic. This was further re-enforced in July 2021, in the 'CoWin Global Conclave' organized to showcase India's digital capacity during the pandemic. What is now identified as 'Corona-era diplomacy' using virtual tools was rapidly activated. Multilateral, plurilateral and bilateral meetings have taken place at all levels using virtual platforms.

Thus, the COVID-19 pandemic was a crisis event and no one could be prepared to handle it. India could have just looked inwards and taken care of itself. India has had very structured response and took actions adhering to its commitments and missions to its neighbourhood countries, it has declared since 2014. India has explored new ways to support its partner countries by re-enforcing its 'Neighbourhood First' policy in action even in crisis. India has proven its competence in bio-medical and pharmaceutical sector in addition to demonstrate its competence in Communication technology through 'COVID-19 Diplomacy.' All this is expanding India's initiative in broad vision of Security and Growth for All in the Region (SAGAR) relations have been augmented with partners in the region in defence and security, trade, development partnership projects, training and capacity building and vaccine and medical supplies. In addition GoI has sustained high level contacts throughout the pandemic across all countries through MEA.

major powers' economic hubs and influential regional players, while practising the foreign policy maxim of *Sabka Sath, Sabka Vikas, Sabka Vishwas*, (Everyone Together, Everyone's Development and Everyone's Trust)[1]. A common engagement with major powers has resulted in multiple quadrilateral, trilateral and regional arrangements as well as in 2+2 meetings. As such, India's evolving and ambitious foreign policy, with corresponding actions on ground, has helped send clear messages to other countries over the last eight years. The priorities and strategies of these policies are consistent with India's economic growth and defence.[2] While India could take an aggressive stand against its hostile neighbours, it supports its partner countries in their development without reciprocal expectations. For instance, it has contributed to a large extent to the relatively-developed nations in the Middle East and South East Asia to create connectivity in transport and power.[3] The actions taken by the Ministry of External Affairs (MEA) in the context of the COVID-19 pandemic are also examples of how India is practising its policies as per its priorities while interacting with its partner countries.

COVID-19: A Global Event

On March 11, 2020, COVID-19, was declared a pandemic by the World Health Organization. India took both military and non-military action in order to control population and commodity movements across international and national borders, which were sealed for over a few months and re-opened gradually. More specifically, the Indian government adopted two measures to manage the disease: containment and mitigation. Containment was undertaken in the early stages of the outbreak, including contact tracing and isolating infected individuals to stop the disease from spreading to the rest of the population. This helped decrease the risk of health services being overwhelmed more than they already were and provided more time for vaccines and treatments to be developed. Mitigation measures were medical, paramedical, and non-paramedical or non-pharmaceutical interventions.

Non-pharmaceutical interventions such as wearing masks, social distancing, and avoiding public transport were taken to manage the outbreak. An extreme measure taken to contain the spread of the disease was to completely shutdown global cross-border transactions, both international and intra-national ones. The impact of lockdowns of entire nations on a global scale have been multi-fold. Considering this context, this paper focuses on India's intervention to help its partner nations.

India's international interventions take place through the Ministry of External Affairs (MEA) and as such, India had engaged with its partner countries in South Asia by sending trained doctors and nurses experienced in managing epidemics. India also exported domestically-developed vaccines to its friendly nations and continues to do so till date. Along with this, India provided safe transport of those Indians and partner country citizens abroad who wished to return. At the national level, India organized a massive vaccination campaign through effective coordination across ministries. India counts 'Vaccine *Maitri*' (Vaccine Friendship) as one of its key diplomatic achievements of this period, not just for reasons of health but as a statement of solidarity.[4]

Paradigm to Understand COVID-19

How does one understand an event which has the potential to change the global system as we know it? Where do we look for its impact in a global system? A Systems Approach based paradigm by the Centre for Strategic and International Studies CSIS (www.CSIS.org), a policy research organisation is proposed here. It considers seven major global issues called Resolutions. Each Resolution consists of major indicators and for each indicator, the short and long-term trends are documented. Each indicator is represented by experts in making predictions over the next 15 years. The experts are supported by the latest data, research, and technologies. They are encouraged to think outside the box and make possible predictions in each of the seven global trends to understand global events such as COVID-19[5]. This is an ongoing research initiative to identify the most important macrotrends defining our world from now until 2050. This is the paradigm we review now.

The Annexure 1 gives the details of "The seven global macro trends or the seven revolutions according to the paradigm are (Annexure 1: Seven Revolutions) population, resources, technology, information, economics, governance, and security" each revolution and its details. A catastrophic event such as the COVID-19 pandemic has the potential to change the current global system. CSIS's directors of the global health policy centre, J. Stephen Morrison and Anna Carroll, observed that 'pandemics change history by transforming populations, states, societies, economies, norms, and governing structures'[6]. Four months into the declaration of the pandemic, an analysis was conducted to think systematically about the pandemic and list out potentially fundamental changes in the seven major global trend lines. This research was conducted through the analytic framework of the Seven Revolutions initiative, a macro-trends assessment that is continually updated with a 30-year horizon. The net assessment is that COVID-19 is highly disruptive in the near term and highly unpredictable in the medium to long term across every macro trend line. The study viewed COVID-19 as an accelerant, an irritant, and a stress test[7]. Its effects will ebb and flow and hit various nations and populations in different ways and on different timescales. This prediction has proven true two years into the pandemic given the virus mutations and the consequent struggle to control it globally. Here we will review in detail only the dominant trends in each Resolution relevant to India. Brannan's report provides a detailed global analysis of COVID-19[8]. A very brief overview of the other trends areprovided here to demonstrate the application of the paradigm to India. The main focus is the Resolution of Security and its trends.

The impact of COVID-19 on the Resolution 'population' and the trend from the MEA perspective is the return migration of Indian citizens and their families living abroad. Introducing direct flights across continents was a major short-term impact co-ordinated by the MEA.

The COVID-19 impact on the Resolution 'resources' as well as the supply chain trend is also documented and relevant to India in terms of the shutdown of both sea and land transport. Both imports and exports had ceased and have not yet been fully restored, resulting in global inflation of up to 10 per cent even in developed countries. The 'Technology' Resolution and especially the internet technology trend is also noteworthy. The speed with which the use of internet technology was adopted and implemented is a favourable sign of the impact of COVID-19. Most relevant was the large data generation and the monitoring that was required for the returning migrants. The other Resolutions and their global impacts listed in the report[9] are not directly related to India's foreign policy.

The seventh global trend line is Security, whose immediate and long-term impacts are considered in more detail here. Further, as conflicts between nations escalate, the war between Russia and Ukraine is explored with a focus on India's actions and gains in this context. The seven Resolutions mentioned above are the first order outcomes of the pandemic and can be easily identified. The second order outcomes are events that are just unfolding, the specifics of which canonly begin to be anticipated. For example, while the authors of this report predicted in April 2020 that COVID-19 would likely accelerate the governance impact trend line, and global protest movements as immediate impact was assessed, the specific countries, patterns, and situations were never anticipated. By late May 2020, the United States became the epicentre of a global protest movement against police brutality and systemic racism. In the trend line of economic impact, breakdown in the global supply chain as a secondary outcome could be anticipated, however, the delay in restoring the USA-China supply chain due to the extended COVID-19 impact on China could never have been anticipated.

Table 5.1: Paradigm to understand the impact of COVID-19 on security

Revo-lution	Indicator	Immediate Impacts	Long-term Impacts
Security	Expanding National Security	Health security elevated as core to national security	Growing debt pressures reduce defence spending
	Fragmen-tation	U.S. and Chinese leadership failures deepen global fragmentation	Future organizing principles for the international system unclear
	Gray Zone	Countries intensify gray zone actions as they avoid conventional conflict and seek advantages	Low defence budgets and increased fragmentation drive even more gray zone activities
	Return to Terror	Increased activity by violence extremist organization (VEOs)	VEOs prey on weakened states, economic vulnerability to push ideology and influence

Source: CSIS Risk and Foresight Group.

(Ref: Brannen, Samuel, Ahmed, Habiba, and Newton, Henry, 2020. 'COVID-19 Reshapes the Future', Centre for Strategic and International Studies (CSIS).)

Under the security trend line, the Russia-Ukraine Conflict could have played out as an immediate impact[10] in the 'grey zone' (refer Fig. 5.1) where the land ownership or line of control between the two nations is contested. However, the conflict has now blown up to the level of a global event by way of a prolonged war. It may cause a re-emergence of a bipolar world and all countries currently have national security concerns about future security boundaries and increasing defence budgets.

The pandemic has entered the second phase of low mortality and morbidity heading towards a long tail. A spate of studies emerged anticipating the relationship between COVID-19, conflict and security issues. The policy brief 'Taking Stock'[11] states that the COVID-19 pandemic shattered global health security, devastated the world economy, and accelerated great-power rivalry between the USA and China. It provides details about the origin of the novel coronavirus and how it spread around the world. It also examines how COVID-19 exacerbated or created pressure points in the global order, highlights uncertainties ahead, and provides

The present Russia-Ukraine conflict is one possible outcome of the waning of the pandemic. It began in the grey area as the paradigm describes (*see* Annexure 1). It was a result of a necessity for Russia to resolve hostilities with Ukraine and the chance taken by the Russian President Vladimir Putin to send troops into Ukraine territory, along the shared Eastern borders with Ukraine. The pro-West government in Ukraine post-their 2019 elections was threatening Russia's power of influence over Ukraine[14]. The chance that Russia took was to send troops into the Eastern border with Ukraine in February 2022 as a special military operation, another grey zone activity, dividing Ukraine along the centre. The stated intention was to control terrorist groups attacking Russians in Ukraine. At the very least, Russia wanted to capture the city of Mariupol, currently in Ukraine, and complete its land bridge to Crimea. This would give Russia control over more than 80 per cent of the Ukrainian Black Sea coastline, and cuts off Ukraine's maritime trade.

When Russian troops finally crossed Ukraine's Northern and Eastern borders, they met with massive resistance. Ukraine's President, Volodymyr Zelenskyy, quickly approached the EU and the USA for military help. The strategy that the USA employed was to escalate the Russia-Ukraine conflict into a global issue. It chose to draft a resolution at the United Nations Security Council (UNSC) on ending the Ukraine crisis. The draft was to hold the Russian Federation accountable for the refugee crisis caused by military operations initiated by Russia. The resolution ordered Russia to withdraw Russian forces immediately from inside Ukraine's boundaries and to allow for humanitarian aid to be made available to people in need. Passing such a resolution would mean that UN peacekeeping forces would have been deployed between the two countries to stop the conflict and UN trade sanctions against Russia would be applied for ensuring its compliance. The draft resolution, submitted by Albania and the United States, was filed in the UNSC, and the Security Council met on 25 February, 2022 to pass this resolution. This garnered support from 11 members but was vetoed by the Russian Federation. China, India and the United Arab Emirates all abstained. Amid the unfolding crisis in Ukraine, the Security Council rejected the resolution.[15]

As a result, the USA and the EU countries imposed progressive trade sanctions against Russia in a phased manner. The most important impact is the energy sanctions imposed by Russia in retaliation to European trade sanctions. Natural gas, considered clean from a climate change perspective, is the most important energy export from Russia to the European countries. Russia had established major gas pipelines with European countries including the United Kingdom (UK) and its own neighbourhood of Eastern European countries. In 2021, Russian gas met 40 per cent of European energy requirements. European countries then decided to reduce their dependence on Russian gas. In reaction, Russia turned off its pipeline to various gas companies. Besides the UK and Germany, the other large Russian gas importers in the European Union are France, Hungary, the Czech Republic, Poland, Austria and Slovakia. The largest non-EU importers of Russian natural gas are Turkey and Belarus.[16]

India's Position

These sanctions are expected to have an impact on the global economy through the disruption of supply chains. The impact on energy and commodity prices is already visible. The disruption of the global supply chain is expected to significantly impact the movement of goods and the import-export trade, particularly food grains, fertilizers, and petroleum. India has substantial dealings with both Russia and Ukraine; an assessment in this regard by the Indian government is underway.[17] India is in the process of analysing its impact on India-Russia bilateral trade and economic cooperation, in consultation with all stakeholders. India's stance is that its relations with Russia stand on their own merit.[18]

While India abstained from voting in the UNSC meeting, it has not violated any UN charter in maintaining friendships with all nations and with its commitment to peace. The Indian Prime

Minister Narendra Modi's statement in different forums since 25 February, 2022, is to express deep concern at the worsening situation in Ukraine, to extend humanitarian assistance and to call for the immediate cessation of violence. India has asserted that a path of diplomacy and dialogue be followed to resolve differences internationally. India has emphasised to all member states of the UN that the UN Charter be respected for territorial integrity and the sovereignty of states.

For India, the interests of its citizens in foreign countries in situations of crisis is a priority. Indian students studying abroad and Indian businesses expanding into the Balkans and Russia is a new reality that at the height of the crisis, required prompt action. Operation Ganga involved contacting Indian students studying in Ukraine, releasing advisories everyday, and organising flights to India by the embassy in Ukraine. The support that India received from Ukraine's neighbours during Operation Ganga was also very valuable. On India's part, it is by now an established tradition that any rescue and relief effort also include citizens of other neighbouring countries. As a result of Indian advisories and Operation Ganga, around 22,500 Indian citizens have returned to India safely since February 24, 2022. India since then has sent and continues to send humanitarian aid[19] (Minister of External Affairs April 1, 2022)[20]. It has also offered to help neighbouring and developing countries who may ask for assistance.[21]

The impact of EU and USA sanctions on Russia due to the conflict has had a positive impact on India-Russia bilateral trade and economic cooperation on account of India choosing to abstain in the UNSC vote. India's relations with Russia stand on their own merit. India's trade has risen with Russia from 75.8 million USD over the last five years to 6.4 billion USD in April 2022. This is almost twice as much as for the same period last year. If India maintains these volumes throughout the year, it will have a turnover of more than 19 billion USD by the end of 2022.[22]

Since February 2022, India has taken quick action to protect its interests and the interests of its partner developing countries. India will ensure that the long-term unrest due to shortages is avoided in the partner countries. While being the second largest wheat exporting country, India has banned wheat exports in anticipation of food shortages in the future due to the Russia-Ukraine conflict and with the intention of helping neighbourhood partner countries when needed.[23] India also focuses on the availability of fertilizers, and has kept the value chains of fertilizers smooth at a global scale. India is trying to increase the production of fertilizers within its borders and seek cooperation from the G7-countries in this regard.[24]

Conclusion

India's clearly-stated foreign policy asserts its stand in international situations of stress. In the case of COVID-19, as soon as the global shutdown was declared, India mobilized its human resource team from scratch to assist its partner countries who needed help. In the case of the Russia-Ukraine conflict, India's commitment to peace and non-alignment, while respecting the UN Charter and territorial integrity, was seen in its emphasis on the restoration of peace immediately. India has emphasised that the path of diplomacy and dialogue be followed to resolve differences internationally.

India's interests are put first. India used this opportunity to promote its interest by creating an indigenous vaccine and exporting it to 101 countries.[25] India promoted special trade with Russia, because it was in India's national interest to do so. India's commitment to the safety of its citizens was also asserted through safe travel during both the COVID-19 and the Russia-Ukraine crisis.

India has also offered assistance to its partner countries in need of medical support, and transport for their citizens. Humanitarian assistance is also provided for countries in crisis when needed.

India has respected and participated in global governance institutions and organisations. In the case of the COVID-19 crisis, the WHO guidelines were followed. In the case of international security, the set procedures of the UNSC were adhered to and in the case of trade with Russia, international trade rules were followed.

In conclusion, the four principles on which the policies and strategies are based are clear, and the corresponding actions are implemented on ground effectively. This has helped India now emerge as a global leader. This leadership believes in global peace and an independent and autonomous position of leadership that is truly non-aligned, protecting and taking care of India: its economic and defence interest and its citizens' interests first and subsequently taking every partner country along with India, while participating in global governance.

Annexure 1

Populattion

Revolution	Indicator	Immediate	Long-term Impacts
Population	Aging	Elderly highly vulnerable to disease	Greater use of biosecurity and technology to protect and connect elderly in the future
		Rapid adoption of remote work	Possible changes in urbanization and settlement patterns in some countries/regions
	Urbanization	Emergency measures taken by city governments to extend services and social safety nets during lockdowns; rapid infrastructure adaption a to health crisis	Expansion of universal public services (health,cash transfers, electricity)
			Data-driven city management
			Increasing urban public areas, greenspace,and bike lanes
	Migration	Migrant labor shortages	Increasing urban public areas, greenspace,and bike lanes
		Broad border, travel, and immigration restrictions	labor-saving innovations Loss of immigrant talent to advanced economies; increased South-South migration
		Severe decline in Global remittances	Economic crisis in emerging markets; potential political instability

Resources

Revolution	Indicator	Immediate	Long-term Impacts
Resources	Energy	Severe energy market disruption; steep decline in energy demand; collapsed energy investment	Possible permanent slowdowns in fossil fuel demand and supply (early "peak oil" demand) bolstered by renewables investment.

Revolution	Indicator	Immediate	Long-term Impacts
		Decreased commuting;	Delayed deployment of electric vehicles
	Climate	Climate activism slowed	Increased activist ambition for significant global climate policy post-Covid 19
			Multiple national "green recovery" economic policies
	Food	Global food system shocks	Lasting supply chain and consumer changes (shortened; reduced meat demand}
		Labor shortages	Increasing agricultural automation
		Food price and supply protests	Increasing local food production, urban farming
			Greater government involvement in supply chains

Technology

Revolution	Indicator	Immediate	Long-term Impacts
Technology	Robotics	Heightened interest in robotics due to public health and labor shortage	Accelerated replacement of human labor across sectors (especially health, food and agriculture)
	Additive Manufacturing	Rapid production of medical components at points of needs	Accelerated replacement of traditional manufacturing processes with additive technologies (especially in health sector)
	Internet of Things	loT usage remains high, with certain sectors reporting huge increases in data flows	Increased reliance on loT in everyday use, especially for health monitoring and surveillance

Revolution	Indicator	Immediate	Long-term Impacts
	Artificial Intelligence	Rapid adoption of AI chatbots and other applications to fill surrge needs	Increased R&D spending related to and overall digitalization pushes up adoption timeline across sectors
	Biotechnology	Surge of investment in synthetic biology in pursuit of therapeutics and vaccines	Growing global competition for leadership in biotech; sustained high levels of national investment

Information

Revolution	Indicator	Immediate	Long-term Impacts
Information	Access/Privacy	Broad use of digital surveillance to track Covid-19	Expanded digital surveillance by
	Data Growth	Large scale digitalization of commercial and social activities	Faster growth in data volume; shift to online-first culture
	False News and Social Media	"Infodemic" races ahead of the pandemic	Intensified geopolitical competition in misinformation/dis-information
	Knowledge and Learning	Widescale adoption of online learning	The digital divide within societies increases inequity

Economics

Revolution	Indicator	Immediate	Long-term Impacts
Economics	Globalization	Synchronized recessions in deve-loped and developing countries	Gradual global economic recovery globalization recedes further
	Supply Chains	Export restrictions on medical supplies and pharmaceuticals	Fragmentation and rationalization of supply chains; acceleration of U.S. China decoupling in certain industries.

6. *Ibid.*
7. *Ibid.*
8. *Ibid.*
9. *Ibid.*
10. Matsaberidze, David. (2015) 'Russia vs. EU/US through Georgia and Ukraine, Connections', Vol. 14, No. 2 (Spring 2015), pp. 77-86 Published by: Partnership for Peace Consortium Of Defence Academies and Security Studies Institutes Stable URL: https://www.jstor.org/stable/10.2307/26326399
11. Cimmino, Jeffry. Kroenig Mathew. and Pavel Barry. 2020 'Taking Stock: Where Are Geopolitics Headed in the COVID-19 Era?' Atlantic Council (2020) Stable URL: http://www.jstor.com/stable/resrep24633)
12. *Op. cit.*
13. Russia developed its own vaccine and greatly controlled the spread of COVID-19 by late 2021.
14. Allison Roy, November 2014. 'Russian deniable' intervention in Ukraine: how and why Russia broke the rules International Affairs Vol. 90, No. 6, pp. 1255-1297. Published by Oxford University Press on behalf of The Royal Institute of International Affaris. URL: htpps://www.jstore.org/stable/24538666
15. UN Press, February 25, 2022. 'Security Council Fails to Adopt Draft Resolution on Ending Ukraine Crisis, as Russian Federation Wields Veto' https://www.un.org/press/en/2022/sc14808.doc.htm
16. Fisher, Jonah, June 22, 2022. 'Europe told to prepare for Russia turning off gas' (https://www.bbc.com/news/science-environment-61899509#:~:text=France%20says%20it%20has%20received, to%20pay%20in%20Russian%20roubles
17. Minister of External Affairs, March 15, 2022. 'Suo-Motu Statement by External Affairs Minister, Dr. S. Jaishankar' in the Rajya Sabha on the "Situation in Ukraine".
(https://www.mea.gov.in/Speeches-Statements.htm?dtl/34952)
18. *Ibid.*
19. *Ibid.*
20. Minister of External Affairs, April 1, 2022. Lok-Sabha Question # 4973. INDIANS REPATRIATED UNDER VANDE BHARAT MISSION'.
https://www.mea.gov.in/lok-sabha.htm?dtl/35127/question+no4973+indians+repatriated+under+vande+bharat+mission
QUESTION NO. 4973, April 01, 2022

21. NDTV India-News, July 6, 2022. 'India Russia trade will continue despite western sanctions—Russian Envoy'. https://www.ndtv.com/india-news/india-russia-trade-will-continue-despite-western-sanctions-russian-envoy-3131308
22. Chakraborty, Debashish. June 13, 2022. 'A closer look at India's wheat export ban'. East Asia Forum. www.eastasianforum.org
23. Ministry of External Affairs, Prime Minister, June 27, 2022. English Translation of Prime Minister's remarks at the session on 'Stronger Together: Addressing Food Security and Advancing Gender Equality' at G7 Summit in Germany https://www.mea.gov.in/Speeches-Statements.htm?dtl/35451/English_Translation_of_Prime_Ministers_remarks_at_the_session_on_Stronger_Together_Addressing_Food_Security_and_Advancing_Gender_Equality_at_G7_Summit
24. Vaccine Supply/August 25, 2022. (Vaccine Maitri Initiative, https//www.mea.gov.in/vaccine supply.htm
25. Vaccine Supply: Supplies so far (in lakhs) (As on June 15, 2023 at 1000 hrs). www.mea.gov.in/vaccine-supply.htm

6
Discussion and Conclusion

India had followed Sustainable Development Paradigm. The book traces last six/seven years micro-history of India's foreign policy, post-2014 elections. The leadership post-2014 had a clear ideology, was brave and willingness to take risk. This new leadership in India since 2014 had been trying to gain global leadership position, by tweaking the paradigm of sustainable development and its various components to India's advantage and steer the 'ship of development' in direction favourable to India through India initiated and funded the divisions of Development Partnership Administration of Ministry of External Affairs for development projects. Then COVID-19 crisis happened, followed by Russia-Ukraine conflict. Over both these events India took actions that were based on the Neighbourhood first commitment. It took action in defence and energy security, to take risks and ensure its self-interest, when opportunity arose.This is what the case studies demonstrate in the book. But the simplest explanation is often not the most probable reason and need to be set aside. I focused on all the others. The prominent one was the one related to crisis of a system. When a system undergoes a crisis, the Crisis challenges an existing paradigm, what will emerge is not known, but it has to be robust to replace the existing paradigm.

From Economic Development to Sustainable Development

International Relations is interdisciplinary in nature, and all of us scholars, have our grounding in different social science disciplines. Hence there is a need to have a common context. Here is a brief 'common sense history' of the world that brought us to this point of COVID-19 crisis. This will ensure all of us are on the same page to fully appreciate emergence of India as a global leader post-COVID-19 pandemic.

The three important sectors, economics, security and leadership of a state even today determine the position of a country in the world today. The consensus post-World War II was, a common pool of funding was needed to ensure reconstruction of the devastation caused by the war. Founded in 1944, the International Bank for Reconstruction and Development—soon called the World Bank—has expanded to a closely associated group of five development institutions. Originally, its loans helped rebuild countries devastated by World War II. In time, the focus shifted from reconstruction to development, with a heavy emphasis on infrastructure such as dams, electrical grids, irrigation systems, and roads[1]. Thus a global bank to fund development projects was created.

As World War II was about to end in 1945, nations were in ruins, and the world wanted peace. Representatives of 50 countries gathered at the United Nations Conference on International Organization in San Francisco, California from 25 April to 26 June, 1945. For the next two months, they proceeded to draft and then sign the UN Charter, which created a new international organization, the United Nations, which, it was hoped, would prevent another world war like the one they had just lived through. Thus a Global governance institution was created. The United Nations officially began, on 24 October, 1945, when it came into existence after its Charter had been ratified by China, France, the Soviet Union, the United Kingdom, the United States and by a majority of other signatories.[2] These five founding members have Veto power to which two more temporary members were added subsequently. Subsequently these organizations have expanded to by the United Kingdom, the United States, the Soviet Union, and 59 other states. A non-proliferation of Nuclear Weapons was a commitment by the three countries who possessed nuclear weapons to not share with other countries. This deterrence kept the two super powers, Soviet Union and USA on two sides of cold war. In 1990 the breakdown of the Soviet Union into east Europe boarder nations and Russia happened. Current war between Russia and Ukraine can be traced to these events.

Questioning the Paradigm

Over 1990 terrorist attacks across the globe were increasing. In 2001 September 11, 5:44 pm the terrorist attack against USA where it was firmly established that the nature of 'conventional war' could be shifted to targeted attacks through terrorist groups or other defence strategies, as mentioned in the introduction.

Then in 2008 financial crisis happened where the financial institutions that were 'Too big to Fail' had to be bailed out to ensure that a global recession will not set in by the USA Central Bank. This had a Dominos effect and other countries started questioning the economic development paradigm which was promoted as the way to ensure development and growth for developing countries. The economic development paradigm had the promise that if the countries followed this free trade and open supply chain model one day developing countries will match up with developed countries economically.

COVID-19 pandemic in 2019 has illustrated, a serious questioning of bilateral governance institution and global funding institution to support individual countries in the face of an unprecedented global crisis.

Challenges of a Crisis

A crisis can be interpreted as a risk or an opportunity by different countries. A crisis challenges an existing paradigm, what will emerge is not known, but it has to be robust to replace the existing paradigm. This COVID-19 crisis has proven that Economy and

Security in defence and energy are not the only two sectors that determine leadership positions for a country that get recognised in Global Governance (Please note: we are using the developed, developing and least developed, categories here as accepted currently). What is emerging is a new paradigm, where regional hubs of developing and least developed countries are emerging as new pressure points that cannot be manipulated by security and economicsby developed countries.

India has been competing with China for a global leadership position especially since 2014. It had taken a firm stand in defence security, in energy security and putting neighbourhood first in its IR. Most countries chose to treat COVID-19 crisis as a threat and were looking inwards. China interpreted this crisis as a major threat and adopted "Zero Tolerance" policy. This meant shut down of regions and cities as soon as the pandemic virus was detected in any location. It led to shut down, of its economy and playing down, its defence security.

While India saw COVID-19 as an opportunity. Actions taken by the Ministry of External Affairs (MEA) during the last two years in the context of COVID-19 are an example of India putting its neighbourhood first, and consolidating its role of 'Early Responder' and stepping into a leadership role that was demanded of it. India interpreted this crisis of COVID-19, as an opportunity and re-asserted the values of *Vasudhaiv Kutambakam* (the world is one family) supported by its Neighbourhood First strategy in its international relations, in actions it took during COVID-19 crisis. India continues to do so and these actions have benefitted India economically and got a lot of support and goodwill. COVID-19 crisis has shown both medical plus paramedical interventions and all the non-paramedical interventions can be equally powerful means to gain global leadership and not just economy and security sectors. For India it has proven to be an opportunity to assert its role, as a global leader. The non-alignment and peace commitment that India re-asserted has attracted enough support and following from its partner countries in Indian Ocean rim and Indo-Pacific region. Other developed countries now pay attention to India's opinion. Especially after the Russia-Ukraine conflict, India has ensured energy security.

The crisis is an opportunity for a paradigm shift, when sustainable development paradigm was seen as the only way to gain and consolidate political leadership in global governance. India could have stopped at focusing inwardly and consolidating its energy security. But the search for new avenues to consolidate its global leadership coming out of an ideological value commitment, has opened a space for global leadership for India.This Global Leadership India assumed is consistent with India's Non-alignment Stand and peace commitment. It is also not pro-West nor pro-Russia but unique. COVID-19 crisis has led to a paradigm shift, by creating new spaces for a Global Leadership position for India. Taking care of its neighbours first matters, and being non-aligned matters, while able to consolidate its energy security and now looks like military security through negotiations. With the slowing down of global growth rate to GDP is 3 per cent in 2023 as per Spring Meeting of the World Bank and International Monetary Fund held in (April 10-16, 2023) prediction. With 80 per cent of the countries not able service they have taken from Multilateral Banks and their financial institutions the time seem to be right to truly re-examine the Sustainable development strategies dictated by developed countries. As these multilateral funding agencies "Too big to fail" hence will be salvaged by the primary donors, that is a question. Salvaging these Multinational Development Financial institutions will ensure US Dollar supremacy. Will the paradigm shift push for a basket of curries or other forms of funding? Who knows. Will India be able to consolidate this leadership in the long run? It is too early to tell.

Notes

1. 1946-1967, The World Bank as Builder and Engineer https://www.worldbank.org/en/archive/history
2. 'History of United Nations' https://www.un.org/en/about-us/history-of-the-un)

Index

CONTRACT FARMING & FARMERS IN INDIA

Contract Farming & Farmers in India

D.P. Sarda

ABD PUBLISHERS
Jaipur ■ New Delhi

ABD PUBLISHERS

Regd. Off. "Bony Residency", Gate No. 2
Opp. Tilak Public School, Vishweswariya Nagar,
Gopalpura Road, Jaipur - 302018, India
Ph: 0141 - 2761280, Telefax: 2761381
Email: abdpublishersjpr@gmail.com

Delhi Office: 102, 1st Floor, Satyam House,
4327/3, Ansari Road, Darya Ganj,
New Delhi - 110002, India
Ph: 011-45652440

visit us: www.oxfordbookcompany.com

Published in India, 2024

ISBN : 9788183762007

Price : ₹ 1550/-

Typeset by Shivangi Computer, Jaipur

Printed and bound in India by Thomson Press Ltd.,
New Delhi

Preface

Agriculture provides foodgrains to the growing population, supplies raw material to industries, generates purchasing power and demand for consumer goods in rural areas and also plays a significant role in exports. It continues single largest occupation providing livelihood to more than 60 per cent population. While presenting the budget for 2004-05 in the Parliament, Hon'ble Union Minister for Finance has announced about his intention to double the flow of agricultural credit in three years. Lending to agriculture by banks should be increased without impairing the health of credit delivery system.

Keeping in view the above objective, I have made an humble attempt to prepare this handbook covering practical aspects relating to appraisal and follow up of lending to agriculture and allied activities. It is primarily meant to serve as a practical guide to bank officials working at grass root level. My rural background and practical experience gained while working in Rural Planning and Credit Department of a Premier Bank has induced me to write this book. I hope it will help the banks to increase their finance to agriculture not only to meet their social commitments, but also to raise their profitability. If necessary precautions are taken, lending to agriculture may prove the best retail lending for banks, particularly for banks having large number of semi-urban and rural branches.

I wish to express my sincere thanks to Shri A.K. Pandya and my colleagues, particularly Shri S.R. Narayanan, for giving valuable suggestions.

I may mention that the views expressed in the book are my personal views and are not be attributed to any bank/ institution.

I shall welcome suggestions for improving future editions of the book.

D.P. Sarda

Contents

1 Introduction

Credit is an important instrument required for national development and it should be utilised according to the national priorities. Till late sixties, commercial banks in India were mainly financing trade, commerce and industry. The flow of credit towards agriculture and weaker sections of the community was quite low. In order to ensure equitable distribution of credit, keeping in view the relative priorities of development needs, 14 major Indian scheduled commercial banks were nationalised on 19th July, 1969. The main objectives of nationalisation were "to control the heights of the economy and to meet progressively, and serve better, the needs of development of the economy in conformity with national policy and objectives." The nationalised banks were advised to open branches in rural and semi-urban areas and provide funds for all productive activities irrespective of the size and social status of the borrower, particularly to those in the weaker sections of the economy. Six more private sector banks were nationalised on 15th April, 1980 extending further the area of public control over the country's banking system.

Certain sectors of the economy were declared as priority sectors for the purpose of providing bank credit to them. The concept of priority sector lending has been evolved to ensure that bank credit flows in an increasing measure to certain vital sectors of the economy which are included in the priority sector for the purpose of lending by banks. The concept has been reviewed from time to time to make necessary changes according to national planning priorities. In November, 1974, public sector banks were advised that their priority sector lending should reach a level of not less than one-third of their outstanding credit by March, 1979. Private sector banks were also advised in November, 1978 to undertake similar responsibilities and lend at least one-third of their total advances to the priority sector by the end of March, 1980. It was further decided in March 1980 that banks should raise the proportion of their advances to priority sector to 40 per cent by March 1985.

Target for Agricultural Finance

Agriculture occupies a very important place in the Indian economy. It provides food grains to the growing population, supplies raw material to industries, generates purchasing power and demand for consumer goods in rural areas and also plays a significant role in exports. The agriculture sector sustains livelihood of about 60 per cent population of the country, but it contributes just 22 per cent of gross domestic product. It shows that per capita income and productivity is low in agriculture which has to be raised to reduce disparity. In order to achieve this, bank credit for agriculture should be increased. Demand for credit to meet requirements of agriculture will continue to rise for use of modern technology, increase in use of fertilizers, insecticides and pesticides, increase in irrigation facilities and increase in coverage under high yielding varieties programme. Besides, it is also necessary to encourage activities allied to agriculture for increasing the income of poor farmers and providing full employment to them.

With a view to increase the flow of credit to agriculture, banks were advised to step up finance to agriculture (including allied activities) so as to reach a level of at least 16 per cent of their total outstanding credit by March 1987, 17 percent by March 1989 and 18 per cent by March, 1990 within the overall target of 40 per cent for priority sector lending. Although most of the banks have achieved the target of 40 the lendings under the 'direct' and 'indirect' categories of agricultural advances are clubbed for the purpose of computing performance of banks vis-a-vis the target of 18 per cent for agricultural lending. However, with a view to ensure that the focus of the banks on the 'direct' category of agricultural advances does not get diluted, it has been stipulated that agricultural lendings under the 'indirect' category should not exceed one-fourth of the agricultural lendings target of 18 per cent i.e. 4.5 per cent of adjusted net bank credit.

Advances under the 'indirect' category in excess of 4.5 per cent of adjusted net bank credit should not be reckoned in computing performance under the target of 18 per cent for agricultural lending. However, all agricultural advances under the categories 'direct' and 'indirect' are reckoned in computing performance under the overall priority sector target of 40 per cent of the adjusted net bank credit.

Annexure

Activities Included in Direct and Indirect Finance to Agriculture

1. Agriculture

Direct Finance

1.1 Finance to individual farmers [including Self Help Groups (SHGs) or Joint Liability Groups (JLGs) i.e. groups of individual farmers, provided banks maintain disaggregated data of such finance] for agriculture and Allied Activites (dairy, fishery, piggery, poultary, bee-keeping, etc.)

1.1.1. Short-term loans for raising crops i.e. for crop loans. This will include traditional/non-traditional plantations and horticulture.

1.1.2. Advances up to Rs. 10 lakhs against pledge/hypothecation of agricultural produce (including warehouse receipts) for a period not exceeding 12 months, irrespective of whether the farmers were giving crop loans for raising the produce or not

1.1.3. Working capital and term loans for financing production and investment requirements for agriculture and allied activities.

1.1.4. Loans to small and marginal farmers for purchase of land for agricultural purpose.

1.1.5. Loans to distressed farmers indebted to non-institutional lenders, against appropriate collateral or group security.

1.1.6. Loans granted for pre-harvest and post-harvest activities such as spraying, weeding, harvesting, grading, sorting, processing and transporting undertaken by individuals, SHGs and co-operatives in rural areas.

1.2. Finance to other [such as corporates, partnership firms and institutions] for Agriculture and Allied Activites (dairy, fishery, piggery, polutry, bee-keeping, etc.)

1.2.1 Loans granted for pre-harvest and post harvest activities such as spraying, weeding, harvesting, grading, sorting and transporting.

1.2.2. Finance up to an aggregate amount of Rs. one Crore per borrower for the purpose listed at 1.1.1, 1.1.2, 1.1.3 and 1.2.1 above.

1.2.3. One-third of loans in excess of Rs. one crore in aggregate per borrower for agriculture and allied activities.

Indirect Finance

1.3. Finance for Agriculture and Allied Activities

1.3.1 Two-third of loans for entities covered under 1.2 above in excess of Rs. one crore in aggregate per borrower for agriculture and allied activites.

1.3.2. Loans to food and agro-based processing units with investments in plant and machinery upto Rs. 10 crore, undertaken by those other than 1.1.6 above.

1.3.3 (i) Credit for purchase and distribution of fertilisers, pesticides, seeds, etc.

(ii) Loans up to Rs. 40 lakh granted for purchase and distribution of inputs for allied activities such as cattle feed, polutry feed etc.

1.3.4. Finance for setting up of Agriclinics and Agribusiness Centres.

1.3.5. Finance for hire-purchase schemes for distribution of agricultural machinery and implements.

1.3.6. Loans to farmers through Primary Agricultural Credit Socities (PACS), Farmers' Service Societies (FSS) and Large-sized Adivasi Multi Purpose Societies (LAMPS).

1.3.7. Loans to co-operative Societies of farmers for disposing of the produce of members.

1.3.8. Financing the farmers indirectly through the co-operative system (otherwise than by subscription to bonds and debenture issues).

1.3.9. Existing investments as on March 31, 2007, made by banks in special bonds issued by NABARD with the objective of financing exclusively agriculture/allied activities may be classified as indirect finance to agriculture till the date of maturity of such bonds or March 31, 2010, whichever is earlier. Fresh investments in such special bonds made subsequent to March 31, 2007 will, however, not be eligible for such classification.

1.3.10. Loans for construction and running of storage facilities (warehouse, market yards, godowns, and silos), including cold storage units designed to store agriculture produce/products, irrespective of their location.

If the storage unit is registered as SSI units/micro or small enterprise, the loans granted to such units may be classified under advances to Small Enterprises sector.

1.3.11. Advances to Custom Service units managed by individuals, institutions or organisation who maintain a fleet of tractors, bulldozers, well-boring equipment, threshers, combines, etc. and undertake work for farmers on contract basis.

1.3.12. Finance extended to dealers in drip irrigation/ sprinkler irrigation system/agricultural machinery, irrespective of their location, subject to the following conditions :

(a) The dealer should be dealing exclusively in such items or if dealing in other products, should be maintaining separate and distinct records in respect of such items.

(b) A ceiling of up to Rs. 30 lakh per dealer should be observed.

1.3.13. Loans to *Arthias* (commission agents in rural/semi-urban areas functioning in markets/*mandies*) for extending credit to farmers, for supply of inputs as also for buying the output from the individual farmers/SHGs/JLGs.

1.3.14. Fifty per cent of the credit outstanding under loans for general purposes under General Credit Cards (GCC).

1.3.15. The deposits placed in RIDF with NABARD by banking on account of non-achievement of priority sector lending targets/sub-tragets and outstanding as on the date of circular would be eligible for classification as indirect finance to agriculture sector till the date of maturity of such deposits or March 31, 2010, whichever is earlier.

1.3.16. Loans already disbursed and outstanding as on the date of this circular to State Electricty Boards (SEBs) and power distribution corporations/companies, emerging out of bifurcation/restructuring of SEBs, for reimbursing the expenditure already incurred by them for providng low tension connection from step-down point to individual farmers for energising their wells and for System Improvement Scheme under special Project Agriculture (SI-SPA), are eligible for classification as indirect finance till the dates of their maturity/repayment or March 31, 2010, whichever is earlier. Fresh advances will however, not be eligible for classification as indirect finance to agriculture.

1.3.17. Loans to National Co-operative Development Corporation (NCDC) for on-lending to the co-operative sector for purposes coming under the priority sector will be treated as indirect finance to agriculture till March 31, 2010.

1.3.18. Loans to Non-Banking Finance Companies (NBFCs) for on-lending to individual farmers or their SHGs/JLGs.

1.3.19. Loans granted to NGOs/MFIs for on-lending to individual farmers or their SHGs/JLGs.

□□□

3 Common Guidelines for Lending to Agriculture

In order to have uniformity and smooth functioning, the Reserve Bank of India issues guidelines from time to time regarding various aspects of lending to agriculture and also other segments of priority sector. The guidelines provided by the Reserve Bank cover definition/classification of different activities included for lending to agriculture, simplification of loan application forms, expeditious disposal of loan proposals, rate of interest, service charges to be levied, requirement of margin money, security norms, period of repayment, follow-up, recovery of loans, etc. The present position of important guidelines can be summarized as under:

1. Activities included for lending to agriculture

While fixing the target for financing agriculture, it is necessary to provide a list of activities which are included in agriculture and allied activities. Accordingly, the Reserve Bank has circulated a list of activities divided into two parts, viz., 'Direct finance to agriculture' and 'Indirect finance to agriculture'. A few additions have been made in the list of activities from time to time to meet the emerging requirements. The present position of the list of activities has been given in the previous chapter of this book. Finance provided for these activities may be counted as finance provided to agriculture for the purpose of achieving the target of financing to agriculture.

2. Completion of application forms

In areas covered by special schemes, the concerned project authorities should arrange for completion of application forms received from borrowers. In areas not covered by specific schemes, bank staff should help the borrowers in filling up the application form.

3. Acknowledgement of applications

The banks should give acknowledgement for loan applications received from weaker sections. Towards this purpose, while getting fresh stocks of application forms printed, it may be ensured that these forms have a perforated portion for acknowledgement to be completed and issued by the receiving branch. Each branch may give a running serial number on the main application form as well as the corresponding portion for acknowledgement. Till the new stock of forms is printed, existing stock of application forms may be used and an acknowledgement may be given separately for each application. It may be ensured that serial number given on the acknowledgement is also recorded on the main application.

4. Disposal of applications

All loan applications upto a credit limit of Rs. 25,000/- should be disposed of within a fortnight and those applications which are for over Rs.25,000/- should be disposed of within 8 to 9 weeks.

5. Discretionary powers for sanction of loans

In order to have quick disposal of loan applications, it is necessary that all branch managers of banks should be vested with discretionary powers to sanction proposals from weaker sections without reference to any higher authorities. If there are difficulties in extending such powers to all the branch managers, such powers should exist at least at the district level and arrangements may be made to ensure that credit proposals from weaker sections are cleared promptly. The weaker sections include the following:-

(i) Small and marginal farmers with land holding of 5 acres and less and landless labourers, tenant farmers and share croppers.

(ii) Artisans, village and cottage industries where individual credit limits do not exceed Rs.50,000/-.

(iii) Beneficiaries of Swarnjayanti Gram Swarojgar Yojana (SGSY).

(iv) Scheduled Castes and Scheduled Tribes.

(v) Beneficiaries of Differential Rate of Interest (DRI) Scheme.

(vi) Beneficiaries under Swarna Jayanti Shahari Rojgar Yojana (SJSRY).

(vii) Beneficiaries under the Scheme for Liberation and Rehabilitation of Scavangers (SLRS).

(viii) Advances to Self Help Groups.

6. Rejection of proposals

Branch managers may reject applications except in respect of scheduled castes/tribes provided the cases of rejection are verified subsequently by the Divisional/Regional Managers. In the case of proposals from scheduled castes/tribes, rejection may be done at a level higher than that of branch manager.

7. Register of applications rejected

A register should be maintained at branches in which the date of applications received, sanction/rejection, the reasons for rejection, etc., should be recorded. The register should be made available to all inspecting agencies. This register will help the Divisional/Regional Managers to verify the rejected cases.

8. Rate of Interest

Interest rate on loans up to Rs.2 lakhs should not exceed the prime lending rate of the bank. For loans above Rs.2 lakhs, banks can charge interest as per the policy approved by their Board. The Indian Banks' Association has advised all public sector banks to reduce their lending rate to a single digit rate of not more than 9 per cent per annum on crop loans up to a ceiling of Rs. 50,000/-.

9. Penal Interest

(i) No penal interest should be charged for loans up to Rs.25,000/-.

(ii) For loans exceeding Rs.25,000/-, the issue of charging penal interest for reasons such as default in repayment, non-submission of financial statements, etc., has been left to the Board of each bank. Banks have been advised to formulate policy for charging such penal interest with the approval of their Boards, to be governed by well accepted principles of transparency, fairness, incentive to service the debt and due regard to difficulties of customers.

10. Photographs of borrowers

Banks may take photographs of the borrowers for the purpose of identification. However, banks themselves should make arrangements for the photographs and also bear the cost of photographs of borrowers coming in the category of weaker sections. It should also be ensured that the photographs are taken in time and disbursement of loan is not delayed on account of photographs.

11. Service charges and Inspection charges

Bank should not levy any service charges or inspection charges on advances up to Rs.25,000/-. In the case of loans above this limit, banks are free to prescribe service charges with the prior approval of their Boards.

12. Mode of disbursement of loan

As far as possible, disbursement of loan amounts should be made directly to the suppliers of inputs/assets, such as fertilizers, seeds, raw materials, implements, trucks, machinery, etc.

With a view to provide wider choice to farmers and eliminate undesirable practices, banks may disburse loans for agricultural purposes in cash which will facilitate dealer choice to borrowers and foster an environment of trust. However, banks may continue the practice of obtaining receipts from borrowers.

13. Repayment Schedule

Repayment programme should be fixed taking into account the sustenance requirements, surplus generating capacity, the break-even point, the life of the asset, etc., and not in an "ad hoc" manner.

(i) In case of default on account of natural calamities like floods, drought, etc., crop loans may be converted into medium-term loans of 3 to 5 years and extension/rephasement may be allowed in the case of term loans.

(ii) In the case of other borrowers affected by natural calamities, banks may convert drawings in excess of the value of security into a term loan repayable over a reasonable period of time and may also provide further working capital and extend/rephase the instalments due under term loans.

14. Margin and security

Banks may waive margin/security requirements for agricultural loans up to Rs.50,000/- and in case of Agriclinics and Agribusiness Centres for loans upto Rs.5 lakhs.

15. Machinery to look into complaints

The Regional Offices of banks should have a machinery to entertain complaints from the borrowers if the branches do not follow the guidelines issued by RBI for lending to priority sector. The Regional Offices should also verify periodically that the guidelines issued by RBI in this regard are implemented by the branches in actual practice.

The names and addresses of the officers with whom complaints can be lodged should be displayed on the notice board of every branch.

16. Conclusion

The guidelines issued by Reserve Bank are very useful not only to the beneficiaries, but also to banks and government agencies. All the concerned parties are made aware about their responsibilities and also facilities available to them. With the help of these guidelines, a uniform policy is followed in the field of lending to agriculture.

❑❑❑

4 Kisan Credit Card

Under the crop loan system, crop-wise limits for credit on the basis of the scale of finance fixed by District Level Technical Committee are provided by banks in cash and/or kind in one or two instalments according to the seasonality of crops. The loan is recovered after the harvesting and marketing of crops. It has been observed that this system does not have the desired flexibility in availing of loan as per the actual needs of farmers and also there is no adequate discretion to decide the repayment schedule depending upon the repaying capacity. Therefore, the Hon'ble Union Minister for Finance in his budget speech for the year 1998-99 had desired that banks should issue Kisan Credit Card (KCC) to farmers on the basis of their land holdings. Accordingly, a model scheme prepared by NABARD for issue of Kisan Credit Cards to farmers was circulated to commercial banks, regional rural banks and co-operative banks during August, 1998 for introducing Kisan Credit Cards. A few changes have been suggested from time to time to improve the scheme in the light of the experience gained. The present position is as under:-

1. Objectives of the Scheme

Its main objective is to provide adequate and timely support to the farmers to meet their short term credit requirements. It also gives flexibility to farmers to withdraw and deposit as per their convenience.

2. Eligibility

Initially, the scheme was introduced for those farmers who were eligible for sanction of credit limits of Rs. 5000/- and above. In the light of the representations received, it was decided in June, 2000 to issue Kisan Credit Cards for limits below Rs. 5000/- also to have wider coverage under the scheme.

3. Issue of Cards

The beneficiaries under the scheme are issued with a credit card and a pass book or a credit card cum pass book incorporating the name, address, particulars of land holding, borrowing limit, validity period, etc. It serves the purpose of an identity card. It also facilitates recording of the transactions on an ongoing basis. The card also provides for a passport size photograph of the holder. The borrower is required to produce the card cum pass book whenever he operates the account. The credit extended under the KCC Scheme is in the nature of a revolving cash credit and provide for any number of drawals and repayments within the limit. Such an approach provides flexibility to the farmer in choosing the appropriate time to repay his loan and reduce the interest burden besides being in a position to draw on the card to meet his urgent credit requirements.

4. Fixation of Credit Limit:

(i) The credit limit under the card may be fixed on the basis of the operational land holding, cropping pattern and scale of finance as recommended by the District Level Technical Committee (DLTC)/ State Level Technical Committee (SLTC). Wherever the DLTC/SLTC have not recommended scale of finance for any crops or in the opinion of the bank, has recommended lower than the required amount, the bank may fix appropriate scale of finance for the crop. While fixing the scale of finance, banks should keep in view the credit needs of capital intensive agriculture using new technologies and very good quality of inputs. The scale of finance suggested by DLTC/SLTC is an indicative scale during the period from 10th to the last day of each calendar month.

10. Personal Accident Insurance Scheme for KCC Holders

Hon'ble Minister for Finance in his budget speech for the year 2001-2002 has desired to introduce Personal Accident Insurance Scheme for KCC holders. Accordingly, in consultation with the representatives of insurance companies, banks and Govt. of India, NABARD has finalised the Personal Accident Insurance Scheme to cover all the existing and prospective KCC holders. The procedure for collection of insurance premium, issue of master insurance policy, extension of insurance cover, settlement of insurance claims etc. have been simplified and made hassle-free. The salient features of the Scheme are as under:

(i) The servicing of the insurance business is undertaken by the four insurance companies on zone-wise basis so as to cover entire country.

(ii) The insurance company for each zone designates an office at the district level as the nodal office for co-ordinating the implementation of personal accident insurance scheme for KCC holders in the district.

(iii) A Master Insurance Policy is issued by the nodal office of the insurance company to each Zonal/ Regional office of the bank covering all its KCC holders.

(iv) The premium payable for a one year policy is Rs. 15/- while the same for 3 year policy is Rs. 45/-.

(v) The insurance coverage is available under the Policy, only from the date of receipt of premium by the insurance company.

(vi) The premium payable to the insurance company under the Scheme is shared between the KCC issuing bank and the KCC holder in the ratio of 2:1.

(vii) It covers KCC holders up to the age of 70 years and whose names are declared by the banks and in respect of whom the premium is paid by the banks to the Insurance Company.

Sl.No.	Issues	Clarification
		the date of commencement of cover under the scheme. For example, a borrower at the age of 69 can be covered for three years by payment of Rs. 45/- as premium.
(vi)	Effective date of cover	As per the Insurance Act, liability of the Insurance company begins on the receipt of the premium. There is provision for advance payment under the master policy. Banks may, therefore, pay premium in advance to take care of time gap of debit to farmer's account and payment of premium to insurance company to avoid embarrassment and complications in the event of any mishap during the interregnum.
(vii)	Is it possible to choose insurance company from out of the four mentioned in the scheme?	It is a joint managed scheme with the risk and returns shared equally by all the four insurance companies. The nodal agencies are specified area-wise for operational convenience and this arrangement cannot be disturbed:
(viii)	Will the KCC holder who has already claimed the benefit for partial disability continue to get the benefit of cover under the scheme?	Upper limit is fixed at Rs. 25,000/- for partial disability. The remaining limit of Rs. 25,000/- will also be available to farmer for certain risk during the period of insurance. However, maximum risk covered under the scheme would not exceed Rs. 50,000/-.

12. Check-list for Issue of Kisan Credit Cards

A banker may study following aspects while considering applications received for issue of Kisan Credit Cards:

(i) It may be ensured that the farmer possesses necessary land as shown in the proposed crop plan. For fixation of credit card limits, operational land holdings may include the land taken on lease for cultivation and exclude the land given on lease to other parties.

(ii) The credit limit may be fixed annually on the basis of the production plan submitted by the farmers. The production plans should indicate the following points to work out the limits on the basis of the scale of finance for the concerned crops:

(a) crops to be cultivated and the cropping intensity

(b) area under cultivation

(c) irrigation facilities available.

(d) details of allied and off-farm activities, if any.

(iii) If the borrower is undertaking any allied activities and/or non-farm activities to supplement his income, credit limits required for the same may also be added to the limits required for crops.

(iv) It may be ascertained whether the crops proposed to be cultivated are generally raised in the area. If not, is there any recommendation from the department of agriculture suggesting such crops? It may be ensured that the soil and climatic conditions are suitable for the proposed crops.

(v) Scale of finance may be taken as recommended by District Level Technical Committee (DLTC)/ State Level Technical Committee (SLTC). If in the opinion of the bank, the scale of finance recommended by DLTC/SLTC is lower than the required amount, the bank may fix higher scale of finance.

(vi) It may be ascertained whether the applicant has adequate experience to manage the size of the farm proposed in the plan.

(vii) The applicant may need technical advice at various stages of cultivation of crops. Advice from concerned government agency should be readily available.

(viii) It may be ensured that facilities for procurement of inputs (seeds, fertilisers, pesticides, etc.) required for the proposed crops are available in the area.

(ix) It may be ensured that the farmer has adequate agricultural implements and machinery required for cultivation of the proposed crops. If not, they should be available on hire at the appropriate time.

(x) Farmer should have adequate irrigation facilities required for the proposed crop plan.

(xi) It may be examined whether the farmer and members of his family will be able to do the entire work. If not, necessary additional labour should be available in the area.

(xii) It may be ensured that the yield estimated by the farmer is in accordance with the normal yield for such crops in the area. Total expected yield may be multiplied with expected sale price to know the total sale proceeds of the farmer.

(xiii) It may be ensured that the farmer will be able to sell the produce at a reasonable price. If possible, the recovery of loan may be linked with a marketing organisation and/or a processing industry.

(xiv) Estimated net increase in income from the proposed crops should be sufficient to repay the amount of crop loan with interest on it.

(xv) In case of default on account of natural calamities like floods, drought, etc. outstanding limits may be converted into medium term loans.

Conclusion

The encouraging progress in the implementation of the Kisan Credit Card Scheme indicates that it has been found beneficial not only by farmers, but also by banks. It has several advantages over the conventional system of crop loans for meeting the working capital requirements of the farmers. The banks should ensure coverage of all eligible agricultural farmers under this scheme. Kisan Credit Cards may be issued even to those farmers who approach a bank for production credit for the first time. All the farmers who are eligible to get crop loans may be issued Kisan Credit Cards as this scheme has several advantages over crop loan system for farmers as well as banks.

❑❑❑

5 Dairy Farming

India occupies first position in the world for milk production with its share of about 14 per cent of total world milk production. While buffaloes contribute about 55 per cent of milk production, indigenous cows contribute 24 per cent and crossbred cows contributes 16 per cent of milk production. Remaining 5 per cent of milk production is contributed by goats. Dairy farming has national importance for India due to the following reasons:-

(i) As agriculture is seasonal, dairy farming provides employment opportunities throughout the year.

(ii) Agricultural by-products which are unfit for human consumption like rice straw, wheat straw, etc. are gainfully utilised for feeding the animals.

(iii) It provides additional income to agricultural labourers and small/marginal farmers. More than 50% of milk production comes from landless labourers and small farmers. They rear one or two milch animals mainly on crop residues with the help of under-employed and unemployed family members, especially the female work force.

(iv) Dairy farming provides regular cash flow throughout the year in contrast to income from crops which comes only at the end of the season.

(v) Waste products such as cow-dung and urine of animals is used as manure for farms.

(vi) The gobar gas from the dung can be used as fuel for domestic purposes and as also as a source of energy for running engines to draw water from wells.

(vii) Demand for milk and milk products is continuously increasing due to population growth, increasing urbanisation, increase in income level, increasing awareness about the nutritive value of milk, changing preference for vegetarian diets, etc.

(viii) Although income generation by keeping one or two milch animals is low, it is still cost effective for landless labourers and small farmers because use of family labour and agricultural waste. In the absence of any alternative employment opportunities, dairy farming is an important source of supplementary income and nutrition to the poor families.

(ix) Dairy farming can also be taken as a main occupation around towns and cities where the demand for milk is gradually increasing.

Financial Assistance for Dairy Farming

In case of small loans, applications should be made to the nearest branch of the bank in the prescribed application form which is available in the branches of financing banks. In case application is made under any special scheme, the concerned project authorities help in completion of the application forms. In other cases, bank staff should help the borrowers for completing the application forms.

In case of dairy schemes for large outlays, detailed reports have to be prepared by the beneficiary with the help of technical persons of state animal husbandry department/ District Rural Development Agency or any other expert in the field. The project report should provide information on land, livestock markets, availability of water, feeds, fodders, veterinary aid, breeding facilities, training facilities, experience of the promoters and the assistance available from State

Government. It should also provide details regarding proposed marketing arrangements. The cost of the project may include following items:-

(i) Cost of purchasing milch animals
(ii) Cost of land and its development
(iii) Construction of sheds
(iv) Essential labour quarters and godowns
(v) Digging of well, if necessary
(vi) Electricity connections
(vii) Transport vehicle
(viii) Milk processing facilities
(ix) Other miscellaneous fixed assets depending on the requirements of the project
(x) Feeding cost of initial period of one or two months.

The project report should also give projections of sales realisation and expenditures. The amount of loan to be sanctioned is decided on the basis of the cost of the project and margin money to be provided by the beneficiary. The repayment period is decided on the basis of future profitability estimates.

While considering the applications for financial assistance, following points may be considered depending upon the size of the scheme and finance required:

(i) Farmers and agricultural labourers can take up dairy farming as an allied activity and get supplementary income. The main sources of income are from sale of milk, manure and calves.
(ii) Dairy farming can also be undertaken as full-time occupation and it may be a small unit with five to ten animals or a large size unit.
(iii) It may be ensured that the borrower has necessary accommodation for keeping the animals.
(iv) It may be ascertained whether animals of good quality/breed are available in the area. If not, arrangements may be made to purchase them from outside.
(v) The sources of getting fodder and other feed required for animals may be ascertained. If the applicant does not have his own land to grow

fodder, it may be ascertained whether sufficient fodder is available in the area.

(vi) It may be ascertained whether necessary veterinary services are readily available.

(vii) It may be ascertained whether the beneficiary has any experience in dairy farming. The expertise of the beneficiary should be studied in relation to the size of the proposed dairy.

(viii) Marketing facilities available for the disposal of milk and milk products may be studied carefully. It may be ensured that the beneficiary will be able to sell milk/milk products and get reasonable profit on the basis of existing sale price. If an arrangement is made to market milk through the organised system, the bank may make arrangements with the milk collection agencies for recovery of loan out of sale proceeds.

(ix) Loan should be provided for the purchase of at least 2 milch animals for every beneficiary (one animal to be purchased initially and the second one after an interval of 6 to 8 months) unless the beneficiary already owns at least one animal. It will ensure continuity in milk production because when the first animal goes dry, the second is in lactation.

(x) For the purpose of deciding the loan amount, cost of the animal may be decided keeping in view the unit cost indicated by the State Level Unit Cost Committee constituted by the regional office of NABARD and the actual availability in the area. It is not obligatory to follow the unit cost decided by the Committee. Banks can take their view depending on the actual situation in the area.

(xi) After release of the loan, animal(s) should be purchased from a reliable breeder or from nearest livestock market.

(xii) With the help of bank's technical officer, veterinary/ animal husbandry officer of State Government/ Zilla Parishad, etc., healthy animals should be purchased.

(xiii) It is better to purchase freshly calved animals in their second/third lactation.

(xiv) Before purchasing, actual milk yield by milking the animal three times consecutively may be ascertained.

(xv) Newly purchased animal may be identified by giving suitable identification mark.

(xvi) Newly purchased animal should be vaccinated against disease.

(xvii) As far as possible; second animal may be purchased when the first animal is in its late stage of lactation and is about to become dry. This will maintain continuity in milk production and ensure availability of adequate funds for maintaining the dry animals.

(xviii) Arrangements may be made for insurance of the cattle and the insurance policy may be assigned in favour of the bank.

(xix) Repayment period should be sufficiently long to enable the beneficiary to repay from the income earned from the investment. The repayment period of the loan given for 2 animals may be fixed at 4-5 years (spread over 2-3 lactations). It may be longer for medium and large projects depending on their profitability estimates.

Conclusion

Banks can help small and marginal farmers and landless labourers in supplementing their income by providing credit for dairy farming. It can be viable inspite of low price realisations due to involvement of family labour without any additional cost and use of agricultural by-products for feeding the animals. Independent dairy units may also be financed if proper marketing arrangements are available. In order to get repayment in time, repayment period should be sufficiently long according to expected profitability estimates. If proper follow-up is done, banks can receive repayment without creating any non-performing assets.

❑❑❑

6 Poultry Farming

India is the second largest egg producer and one of the top ten broiler producers in the world. Poultry has emerged as the fastest growing segment of agriculture. Poultry industry in India has been transformed from a backyard activity into a modern, scientific and technology driven industry during the last three decades. Poultry farming has become very popular in the country due to following reasons:

(i) India has developed necessary technology and capability to produce all the essential inputs required for successful poultry farming.

(ii) Indigenous research and development has taken place to supply superior high-yielding breeding stock which is totally acclimatized to our agro-climatic condition. Today's genetically superior chicken lays about 270-290 eggs in a year which is about 9 to 10 times its own weight.

(iii) Network of breeding farms and hatcheries has been developed in various parts of the country.

(iv) Wide range of vaccines and medicines to provide adequate health care have been developed within the country.

be ensured that medicines and vaccines against poultry diseases are easily available.

(x) It may be ascertained whether the supply of poultry feed is available from close proximity at a reasonable price.

(xi) It may be examined whether the marketing arrangements proposed for selling eggs and disposal of birds are sufficient and can be reasonably executed.

(xii) It may be ascertained whether the applicant has knowledge/experience in raising poultry. If not, services of a person qualified/experienced in poultry raising may be made available. It would be desirable if arrangements are made to give training to the applicants at Government Institutes so that they are well qualified to give the vaccines at the right time as well as do the debeaking.

(xiii) It may be ensured that the equipments (brooders nests, feeders, waterers, egg-trays, etc.) proposed to be purchased are adequate and their prices are reasonable.

(xiv) Estimated cost of construction of poultry sheds should be reasonable.

(xv) Adequate arrangements should be made in the scheme for working capital.

(xvi) The amount of loan should be sufficient to meet the requirement of funds after deducting margin money.

(xvii) Arrangements may be made for insurance of birds and the insurance policy may be assigned in favour of the bank.

(xviii) An assessment may be made to find out the expected income from the proposed poultry farm. Income may be generated mainly from following sources:-

(a) sale of eggs
(b) sale of manure
(c) sale of culled birds
(d) sale of gunny bags

(xix) An assessment may also be made to find out expected expenditure on following items:-

(a) Purchase of chicks/layers

(b) Feed

(c) Medicines

(d) Depreciation

(e) Interest on Loans

(f) Overheads

(xx) Expected annual net income may be ascertained after making estimates of income and expenditure as mentioned above. The repayment should be fixed according to the surplus available with the borrower.

In case of medium and large projects, various techniques discussed in the book regarding technical, commercial, financial and management appraisal should be used to judge viability of the project.

❑❑❑

7 Minor Irrigation and Land Development Schemes

India has about 2.4 per cent of land mass and 4 per cent fresh water resources of the world to support 17 per cent of the world population. With the increase in population, per capita land and water availability is declining. Further, the demand of water is increasing for domestic and industrial use. Therefore, availability of irrigation water for agriculture has been under pressure. Banks can play an important role in improving irrigation facilities by providing loans for construction and deepening of wells, boring of wells, purchase of oil engines, installation of electric motor and pumps, construction of field channels, installation of sprinkler irrigation system, construction of lift irrigation project, etc.

1. Check-list for Minor Irrigation Schemes

While considering the applications for financial assistance for minor irrigation schemes, banks may examine the following points to judge viability of the proposal:-

(i) It may be ascertained whether any geological underground water survey has been taken up in that area to assess the underground water potentiality. It may be ensured that adequate ground water suitable for irrigation purposes is

(l) Length, number and diameter of sprinkler lateral lines

(m) Cost of various items with total unit cost

(n) Details of technical guidance and government support/extension service available.

(xiii) It may be ascertained whether the applicant has necessary funds to meet the difference between the cost of the project and the amount of proposed loan.

(xiv) New cropping pattern proposed to be adopted with the additional irrigation facility should be suitable for the soil and climate of the area and must be recommended by agriculture department.

(xv) It may be ensured that the applicant has made adequate provision for working capital requirements for the new cropping pattern to be adopted with the irrigation facilities to be created. If not, Kisan Credit Card may be issued to the applicant to provide finance for raising the crops.

(xvi) Net income from the crops proposed to be grown with the additional irrigation facilities should be sufficient to repay the loan instalments and the accrued interest within the period prescribed for the loan.

(xvii) Ground water potential available in the Eastern States (Arunachal Pradesh, Assam, Manipur, Mizoram, Bihar, Jharkhand, Orissa, Chattisgarh and certain districts of UP and West Bengal) have not been utilized to a great extent. They hold high potential and prospects for irrigation development. Banks may consider providing financial assistance for using ground water.

While finance provided to the farmers is considered 'Direct financing to agriculture', the finance extended to dealers in drip irrigation/sprinkler irrigation system/agricultural machinery upto a ceiling of Rs.20 lakhs per dealer is considered 'Indirect finance to agriculture'.

Check-list for Land Development Schemes

India has about 24.5 million hectares of wasteland and 16.6 million hectares of fallow land. Sizeable part of this land can be converted into cultivable land through development of irrigation potential, efficient use of water, adoption of watershed approach and selection of appropriate crops. For this purpose, State Government and the banking sector may have to prepare a long term plan. Sometimes, individual farmers may also approach banks for financial assistance to carry out land developments in their farms. Banks may consider following points to judge viability of such proposals:-

(i) Details regarding the proposed land developments may be obtained and their cost may be estimated.

(ii) It may be ascertained whether the plans and estimates for undertaking the proposed developments are prepared by recognized agencies like agriculture department, soil conservation department, irrigation department or any other department of the State Government. If the proposed developments are to be done under any scheme of NABARD, its details may be obtained.

(iii) It may be ensured that various phases of proposed land developments are arranged in proper sequence.

(iv) It may be ensured that necessary equipment will be available for carrying out the proposed land developments if the same are to be undertaken by the beneficiary himself.

(v) It may be ascertained whether any assistance from any contractor or government agency is required for carrying out the proposed land developments. If so, it may be ensured that it will be available at the appropriate time.

(vi) It may be ascertained whether sufficient water is available for the proposed crops after land developments.

(vii) Soil and climatic conditions should be suitable for the proposed crops.

(viii) Increase in income likely to be generated by adopting new crop plan, after carrying out the proposed land development work, should be sufficient to repay the loan.

While providing term loan for irrigation facilities/land development schemes, it is necessary to issue Kisan Credit Card for production credit (working capital) to take advantage of improved irrigation facilities/land development schemes. Term loans provided for investment in fixed assets cannot give full benefit without working capital for raising crops with improved inputs (fertilizers, seeds, pesticides, etc.).

❑❑❑

8 Farm Mechanisation Programme

In view of the importance of mechanization in increasing the agricultural production, banks may provide finance for purchasing new tractors, second hand tractors, trailer without tractor, trailers in sugarcane areas, renovation/ repairs/ replacement of parts of tractors, combine harvesters, power tillers and power threshers, sprayers and other farm machinery. While considering the applications for financial assistance for farm mechanization, following points may be considered by banks to judge viability of the proposal:-

(i) It may be ascertained whether the beneficiary has his own farm for the use of the tractor. If so, does he possess adequate area to justify the economic use of a tractor? If not, whether there is sufficient scope for doing custom service in that area? It may be ensured that the tractor or other farm machinery proposed to be financed will have minimum hours of use as under:-

Type of Machinery	Minimum hours of use
(a) New tractor	A minimum of 1000 hours of productive work in agriculture per

	year on own-farm or both own farm and custom services.
(b) Second hand tractor	A minimum of 550 hours of productive work in agriculture per year on own-farm or both own-farm and custom services.
(c) Power tiller	A minimum of 600 hours of productive work in agriculture per year on own-farm or both own-farm and custom services.
(d) Power thresher	A minimum of 315 hours of use per annum.
(e) Sprayer	A minimum of 250 hours of use per annum.

(ii) The tractor proposed to be purchased should have necessary Commercial Test Report (CTR) as per BIS Code issued by the Central Farm Machinery Training and Testing Institute (CFMTTI), Budni, Madhya Pradesh. It may also be examined whether the tractor proposed to be purchased is in common use in the area. If the beneficiary proposes to purchase an unusual make, an enquiry may be made to know the reasons for preferring an unusual make and also the facilities available for its servicing.

(iii) The capacity of the tractor in terms of horse power should be appropriate for the type of soil and the nature of operations required to be carried out.

(iv) It may be ensured that the tractor-drawn implements proposed to be purchased with the tractor are suitable for the make and type of the tractor and nature of operations to be carried out.

(v) In case of second hand tractors, it may be ensured that they are in good condition. Generally, bank finance may not be provided if tractor is more than 7 years old. The price of tractor may be assessed by approved surveyor or calculated by applying 10 per cent depreciation, whichever is lower. Bank finance should be provided only in respect of first resale of tractors.

(vi) It may be enquired whether the applicant possesses adequate knowledge of operating the tractor. If not, the services of an experienced tractor operator to drive and maintain it, should be available.

(vii) It may be ascertained whether adequate arrangements for servicing the tractor/machinery are available.

(viii) It may be ensured that a shed is available to house the tractor/machinery. If it is not already available with the beneficiary, provision may be made in the cost of the proposal for construction of the shed.

(ix) Banks may satisfy themselves regarding actual cost of tractor/power tiller/combine harvester/thresher/sprayer by verification of invoices/quotations/vouchers/bills before sanctioning/disbursing loan under the programme.

(x) Selection of tractor/power tiller/combine harvester/ thresher/sprayer may be made by farmers having regard to the terrain, soil conditions and their use.

(xi) Banks may ensure that arrangements exist/have been made by manufacturers/dealers for supply of spare parts, after sale service and repair facilities to the beneficiaries in the scheme area or that these are generally available in the area.

(xii) The cost of the other accessories should also be added to the cost of tractor for arriving at the total financial requirement.

(xiii) It may be ascertained whether the beneficiary has enough resources to meet the difference between the total finance required and the amount of loan to be provided for it.

(xiv) For financing second tractor, it may be ensured that a minimum period of three years has elapsed since financing the borrower for purchase of a tractor earlier and the previous loan has been fully repaid.

(xv) Loan may be given for renovation/repairs/ replacement of spare parts of tractors to those farmers who had repaid earlier loan. The tractor should be more than 5 years old but not older than 12 years from the date of manufacture. Bank loan for this purpose may be given once only.

(xvi) An assessment may be made to find out the incremental income to be derived out of mechanization of borrower's farm. Income from custom service for various uses of tractors, viz. ploughing, leveling, threshing, chaffing, winnowing, transport, etc., may be added to it to find out the total expected income.

(xvii) An assessment may also be made to find out expected expenditure on (a) Salary of the operator, (b) Cost of lubricants, (c) Cost of fuel, (d) Cost of repairs and maintenance (e) Insurance charges, (f) Registration fees and other taxes (g) Interest on term loan and cash-credit and (h) Depreciation.

(xviii) Expected annual net income may be ascertained after making estimates of income and expenditure as mentioned above. The amount of depreciation may be added back to assess the repaying capacity as this does not involve cash out-flow.

Repayment schedule should be fixed after providing for contingency and consumption needs of the borrower. Provision should also be made for repayment of existing liabilities, if any, before fixing the repayment schedule. Maximum repayment period of loans provided for purchase of tractors and other farm machinery may be as under:-

	Type of Machinery	Repayment period (years)
1.	Tractor	9
2.	Trailer/Two trailers in sugarcane growing areas	5
3.	Renovation/repairs/replacement of spare parts of tractor (should be fixed on a case-by-case basis)	5

4.	Power Thresher and Sprayers	5
5.	Combine Harvester	5
6.	Power Tiller	7

(xix) Banks should make payment directly to the suppliers in respect of farm machinery and implements purchased by the borrower.

(xix) It may be ensured that the tractor is registered with R.T.O. with bank's name as financier. The bank s name plate indicating its lien should be fixed on the tractor.

(xx) Comprehensive insurance cover should be obtained in respect of the assets acquired by the borrower from the loan amount. It may be ensured that such insurance cover is available during the currency of the loan. The relative policy should be assigned in bank's favour, and the assignment should also be registered with the insurance company. The financing banks may, at their discretion, agree for a third party insurance with "Theft Clause" keeping in view their own risk perception in this regard.

Conclusion

Banks may provide loans for purchase of tractors and other farm machinery after ascertaining their use for certain minimum hours. Necessary safeguards as mentioned above may be observed. A few banks have entered into agreement with major tractor and farm machinery manufacturers for financing their products. Such arrangements help the farmers in purchasing the tractors at a discounted price and obtaining enhanced warranty for the maintenance of the tractors. This also ensures proper utilization of the loan amount. While entering into a tie-up arrangement with the tractor and farm machinery manufacturer, banks should take necessary precautions to ensure that farmers are able to receive the tractor or other farm machinery at the minimum possible price.

❑❑❑

(iii) The processing firms are able to get agricultural products according to their specific requirements. A risk of non-availability of raw material is reduced with assured supply of quality goods from the farmers.

While in some cases of contract farming the farmer takes production related risk and transfers price related risk to the company, in certain contract farming the production risk is also taken by the company.

3. Advantages of Contract Farming for Bankers

Banks can recover their advances through the agribusiness firms. As the agribusiness firms supply inputs and provides technology support, the chances of post harvest losses of agricultural/horticulture products would be much less. This will reduce the risk of the banks.

The increased productivity and improved quality of fruits, vegetables, superior grains, etc. produced under contract farming may result in realisation of remunerative prices by the farmers for their products. The higher surplus with the farmers will not only help the banks in realising their loans, but also to increase their deposits which may help the farmers at the time of difficulties.

4. Agri Exports Zones and Contract Farming

With a view to increase agri exports, the concept of Agri-Export Zones (AEZ) has been introduced in 2001. Under the concept of AEZ, a geographically contiguous area is identified for a particular product for increasing its production and processing/packaging leading to final exports. On behalf of Govt. of India, the Agricultural and Processed Food Products & Export Development Authority (APEDA) acts as nodal agency for AEZ. In consultation with State Governments, it identifies and makes notification declaring an area as AEZ. for certain product/products. A Memorandum of Understanding is signed by the concerned State Government and APEDA (on behalf of Govt. of India) defining the role of each agency. A list of Agri-Export Zones already approved by APEDA is given as Annexure at the end of this chapter. In view of the popularity of the scheme, many proposals for setting up similar Agri-Export Zones are under consideration of APEDA. After identifying the area and product for AEZ, necessary efforts are made to promote the identified crop in that zone.

The contract farming can play an important role in supplying sufficient quantity of the product as per the quality standard prescribed by the exporters. Banks can play an important role in financing contract farming in AEZ as under:-

(i) Banks may finance farmers directly for crop production under tripartite agreement.

(ii) Banks may provide finance to processors/exporters who in turn would provide all inputs including the technical know how with a buy-back arrangement to farmers.

As the farmers may use improved technology and inputs for identified commodities in AEZ, banks may provide higher than the normal scale of finance. Banks may ensure that adequate credit support is provided to the farmers covered under the AEZ scheme.

An integrated approach adopted in AEZ by processing units/exporters, farmers, banks and concerned Government agencies may go a long way not only for increasing agro-exports but also raising income level of farmers.

5. Constraints of Contract Farming

Sometimes, processing firm or agribusiness firm is not an exclusive buyer of a commodity. In such cases, farmers may behave opportunistically. For example, tomatoes produced by the farmers for a processing firm under contract in Punjab were sold in the open market when the market price was high and the farmers supplied the entire quantity to the firm when market price was low. Similarly, agribusiness firm may give some excuses for not taking delivery if price in the open market is low. For example, a chocolate manufacturer introduced cocoa farming in Kerala promising certain price and a paper unit entered into contract with farmers in Karnataka for bamboo production. As the farmers entered into contract with huge investments, these firms tried to exploit the farmers by withdrawing from their commitment.

The imposition of quality standards and grading provides an opportunity to exploit the farmers. If proper precautions are not taken at the time of the contract, certain problems may be faced under contract farming.

6. Precautions to be taken under Contract Farming

It is necessary to have clear terms under the contract farming. It is better to involve banks, govt. organisations and voluntary organisations in the contract farming. Third party assistance in resolving disputes has many advantages over litigation to solve the problems of dispute, if any. Involvement of local community organisations at the time of contract may help in preventing exploitation of the farmers. These organisations may monitor the implementation of the contract and take necessary action, if any violation takes place. This may prevent re-occurance of such violation and avoid litigation. The firm may include certain innovative pricing policy in the contract to prevent diversion of the product. It may reward loyal farmers by introducing bonus schemes which may encourage them to supply certain quantities as per the specification of the quality. Agribusiness firm should treat the farmers as partners rather than mere suppliers of raw materials. The farmers must feel that the firm will reward them appropriately for their efforts. A few firms have even given a small payment in case of natural disasters to encourage the farmers to continue in the subsequent season.

7. Conclusion

The demand for processed food is increasing in recent years due to rapid urbanisation and changing life styles. With the introduction of globalisation, developing countries are able to increase their export of processed food. A special farm produce scheme called Vishesh Krishi Upaj Yojana (VKUY) has been introduced in the Foreign Trade Policy announced on 31st August, 2004 for the next 5 years (2004-09) to boost agro exports. This scheme allows duty free credit entitlement of 5 per cent of free-on-board (f.o.b.) value of the export of fruits, vegetables, flowers, minor forest produce and their value-added products. The measures announced in Foreign Trade Policy may help increasing agricultural exports.

Bharti Enterprises, at present engaged in telecom business, has recently entered into an agreement with foreign collaborators to diversify in the area of exports of vegetables and fruits. The new venture called "Field Fresh Foods", aims to link Indian farms with markets of developed countries. With an initial investment of Rs.250 crores, it will commence its operations in North India and open a model farm and agriculture research centre in Punjab. It Will link farmers of Punjab, Haryana, Himachal Pradesh, Jammu & Kashmir, Uttaranchal and Western Uttar Pradesh to the research centre and the model farm that will help them for improving the yield. It will provide seeds and other emerging technical facilities to farmers. It is looking for contract farming and direct procurement from farmers in that region. It will gradually move to other parts of the country in the field of procurement and processing of vegetables and fruits. With the growing demand of processed foods and increasing emphasis on agro-exports, it is hoped that new units will be set up gradually in this field. Contract farming may help processing firms and exporters in procuring agricultural products according to specific quality required by them. It may also help farmers in increasing their income by adopting improved seeds and other inputs.

Banks can play an important role in encouraging the contract farming by initiating discussions with the processing firms, concerned govt. agencies and voluntary organisations. Contract farming has potential for expanding credit to farmers, especially to the small/marginal farmers, share croppers and tenant farmers. However, necessary precautions mentioned in the above paragraph should be taken for its success.

Annexure

Agri-Export Zones approved by APEDA

Sr. No.	Product	State and date of approval	District/Area notified
1	2	3	4
1	Pineapple	West Bengal 7th Sept 2001	Darjeeling, Uttar Dinajpur, Cooch Bihar and Jalpaiguri
2	Gherkins	Karnataka 7th Sept 2001	Tumkur, Bangalore Urban, Bangalore Rural, Hassan, Kolar, Chitradurga, Dharwad and Bagalkot
3	Lychee	Uttranchal 7th Sept 2001	Udhamsingh, Nagar, Nainital and Dehradun
4	Vegetables	Punjab 11th Oct 2001	Fatehgarh Sahib, Patiala, Sangrur, Ropar & Ludhiana
5	Potatoes	Uttar Pradesh 11th Oct 2001	Agra, Hathras, Farrukhabad, Kannoj, Meerut, Aligarh and Bagpat
6	Mangoes	Uttar Pradesh 11th Oct 2001	Lucknow, Unnao, Hardoi, Sitapur & Barabanki
7	Potatoes	Punjab 27th Nov 2001	Singhpura, Zirakpur (Patiala), Rampura Phul, Muktsar, Ludhiana, Jallandhar

1	2	3	4
25	Flowers	Karnataka 13th Jun 2002	Bangalore (Urban), Bangalore (Rural), Kolar, Tumkur, Kodagu and Belgaum
26	Mango & Grapes	Andhra Pradesh 23rd Apr 2002	Districts of Rangareddy, Medak & Parts of Mahaboobnagar Districts
27	Flowers (Orchids) & Cherry Pepper	Sikkim 13th Jun 2002	East Sikkim
28	Ginger	Sikkim 13th Jun 2002	North, East, South & West Sikkim
29	Apples	Himachal Pradesh 28th Aug 2002	Shimla, Sirmour, Kullu, Mandi, Chamba and Kinnaur
30	Basmati Rice	Punjab 28th Aug 2002	Districts of Gurdaspur, Amritsar, Kapurthala, Jalandhar, Hoshiarpur and Nawanshahar
31	Mangoes	Andhra Pradesh 28th Aug 2002	Krishna District
32	Flowers	Tamilnadu 28th Aug 2002	Nilgiri District
33	Onion	Maharashtra 18th Nov 2002	Districts of Nasik, Ahmednagar, Pune, Satara and Solapur

1	2	3	4
34	Ginger and Turmeric	Orissa 18th Nov 2002	Kandhamal District
35	Vegetables	Jharkhand 18th Nov 2002	Ranchi, Hazaribagh and Lohardaga
36	Seed Spices	Madhya Pradesh 18th Nov 2002	Guna, Mandsaur, Ujjain, Rajgarh, Ratlam, Shajapur and Nimuch
37	Basmati Rice	Uttaranchal 18th Nov 2002	Udham Singh Nagar, Nainital, Dehradun and Haridwar
38	Mango	West Bengal 18th Nov 2002	Malda and Murshidabad
39	Vegetables	West Bengal 18th Nov 2002	Nadia, Murshidabad and North 24 Parganas
40	Mangoes	Tamil Nadu 18th Nov 2002	Districts of Madurai, Theni, Dingidul, Virudhunagar and Tirunelveli
41	Wheat	Madhya Pradesh 28th Aug 2002	Three distinct and contiguous zones:- Ujjain Zone comprising of Neemach, Ratlam, Mandsaur and Ujjain / Indore Zone comprising of Indore, Dhar, Shajapur and Dewas/ Bhopal Division, comprising of Sehore, Vidisha Raisen, Hoshangabad, Harda, Narsinghpur and Bhopal

1	2	3	4
42	Fresh and Processed Ginger	Assam 5th May 2003	Kamrup, Nalbari, Barpeta, Darrang, Nagaon, Morigaon, Karbi Anglong and North Cachar.
43	Horticulture Products	Kerala 3rd Feb 2003	Districts of Thrissur, Ernakulam, Kottayaam, Alappuzha, Pathanumthitta, Kollam, Thiruvananthapuram, Idukki and Pallakad
44	Fresh & Processed Ginger	Assam 3rd Feb 2003	Kamrup, Nalbari, Barpeta, Darrang, Nagaon, Morigaon, Karbi Anglong and North Cachar districts
45	Basmati Rice	Uttar Pradesh 3rd Feb 2003	Districts of Bareilly, Shahajahanpur, Pilibhit, Rampur, Badaun, Bijnor, Moradabad, J B Phulenagar, Saharanpur, Mujjafarnagar, Meerut, Bulandshahar, Ghaziabad
46	Medicinal & Aromatic Plants	Uttaranchal 3rd Feb 2003	Districts of Uttarkashi, Chamoli, Pithoragarh, Dehradun and Nainital
47	Onion and Garlic	Gujarat 5th May 2003	Districts of Bhavnagar, Surendranagar, Amreli, Rajkot, Junagadh and Jamnagar
48	Gherkins	Andhra Pradesh 5th May 2003	Districts of Mahboobnagar, Rangareddy, Medak, Karimnagar, Warangal, Ananthpur and Nalgonda
49	Pomegranate	Maharashtra 5th May 2003	Districts of Solapur, Sangli, Ahmednagar, Pune, Nasik, Osmanabad, Latur

❑❑❑

10 Agriclinics and Agribusiness Centres

Farmers should use best possible technologies to maximize their income. They may receive necessary expertise and guidance for this purpose from their fellow progressive farmers, State Agencies, Agricultural Consultants, Para Technicians, Farmers' Organisations/ Co-operatives, Non-governmental Organisations (NGOs), Krishi Vigyana Kendras (KVKs), Input Dealers, Agribusiness Companies, Newspapers, Agricultural Magazines, Television Channels, Internet, Donor Agencies, etc. With a view to supplement these sources, it has been felt necessary to encourage establishment of Agriclinics and Agribusiness Centres to provide necessary services to farmers for adopting best possible technologies. NABARD introduced in July, 2001 a refinance scheme for financing setting up of Agriclinics and Agribusiness Centres by agricultural graduates. The scheme prepared by NABARD can be summarized as under:

1. Concept and Objectives

Agriclinics are envisaged to provide expert services and advice to farmers on cropping practices, technology dissemination, crop protection from pests & diseases, market trends and prices of various crops in the markets and also clinical services for animal health etc. which would enhance productivity of crops/animals.

Agribusiness Centres are envisaged to provide input supply, farm equipments on hire and other services.

Objectives of setting up Agriclinics and Agribusiness Centres are as under:-

(i) To supplement the efforts of government extension system

(ii) To make available supplementary sources of input supply and services to needy farmers

(iii) To provide gainful employment to agriculture graduates in new emerging areas in agricultural sector.

2. Eligibility.

Agriculture Graduates/Graduates in subjects allied to agriculture like horticulture, animal husbandry, forestry, dairy, veterinary, poultry farming, pisciculture and other allied activities may be financed for setting up Agriclinics and Agribusiness Centres. It can be set up by Agricultural Graduate individually or on joint / group basis involving maximum five entrepreneurs. One of the group entrepreneurs may be a management graduate or person with experience in business development and management.

3. Activities

Agriclinics and Agribusiness Centres may take up following activities:-

(i) Soil and water quality cum inputs testing laboratories (with Atomic Absorption Spectrophotometers)

(ii) Pest surveillance, diagnostic and control services

(iii) Maintenance, repairs and custom hiring of agricultural implements and machinery including micro irrigation systems (sprinkler and drip)

(iv) Agri Service Centres including the three activities mentioned above (Group Activity)

(v) Seed Processing Units

(vi) Micro-propagation through Plant Tissue Culture Labs and Hardening Units

(vii) Setting up of Vermiculture units, production of bio-fertilisers, bio--pesticides, bio-control agents.

(viii) Setting up of Apiaries (bee-keeping) and honey & bee products' processing units.

(ix) Provision of Extension Consultancy Services

(x) Facilitation and agency of agricultural insurance services

(xi) Hatcheries and production of fish finger-lings for aquaculture

(xii) Provision of livestock health cover, setting up veterinary dispensaries & services including frozen semen banks and liquid nitrogen supply

(xiii) Setting up of Information Technology Kiosks in rural areas for access to various agriculture related portals

(xiv) Feed Processing and testing units

(xv) Value Addition Centres

(xvi) Setting up of Cool Chain from the farm level onwards (Group Activity)

(xvii) Post Harvest Management Centres for sorting, grading, standardization, storage and packaging

(xviii) Setting up of Metallic / Non-Metallic Storage Structures (Group Activity)

(xix) Retail marketing outlets for processed agri-products

(xx) Rural marketing dealerships of farm inputs and outputs.

The above list is an illustrative list. The combination of two or more than two activities may also be taken to make the project viable. In order to enhance viability of the ventures, Agricultural Graduates may take other commercial activity in the field of agriculture and allied areas along with the Agriclinics/Agribusiness Centre.

4. Model Project Profiles

NABARD has circulated a few model projects in respect of following activities:-

(i) Soil, Water Quality and Input Testing Laboratory Service Centre

11 Appraisal of Medium and Large Projects

It is necessary to finance medium and large projects in the field of agriculture and allied activities to generate employment opportunities and increase income level. With the introduction of globalisation policies, financing of medium and large projects is necessary to increase agricultural exports. The target of 18 per cent to outstanding credit fixed by the Reserve Bank can be achieved by financing to various activities included in the field of agriculture. A list of activities included in agriculture are given in the second chapter of this book.

Banks may receive medium and large projects for financing in following areas included in agriculture:-

(i) Dairy development schemes

(ii) Fisheries schemes

(a) Marine Fisheries Schemes

(b) Inland Fisheries Schemes

(iii) Poultry Farming

(iv) Stallfed goat farming

(v) Projects in horticulture

(a) Captive farms for production of flowers/ fruits /vegetables/spices/medicinal and aromatic plants

(b) Tissue culture
(c) Mushroom production
(d) Processing of fruits and vegetables

(vi) Land development schemes
(vii) Irrigation schemes
(viii) Development of market yards
(ix) Construction of godowns and silos
(x) Cold storage schemes
(xi) Agri export zones under contract farming
(xii) Production and marketing of seeds
(xiii) Agriclinics and Agribusiness centres

The above list is illustrative and not exhaustive to indicate medium and large projects which may require finance from banks under agriculture. Projects can be identified and formulated by progressive entrepreneurs, govt. agencies, consultancy organisations, etc. Project profiles on several agricultural activities may be obtained from NABARD. Sometimes, banks also may have to help the entrepreneurs to identify and formulate the projects. After receiving a project for financing, the banker should make a preliminary study to find out whether it will be possible for the bank to finance the same according to its credit policy. Preliminary discussions between the officials of the bank and the borrowing concerns are necessary to reduce avoidable expenses and facilitate expeditious disposal of proposals received for financing.

A project may be considered for detailed scrutiny if it satisfies following criteria on the preliminary scrutiny:-

(i) It has priority according to bank's policy and Govt. guidelines.
(ii) The technology to be adopted is well proven
(iii) The product to be manufactured has market potential and units already working in this field are performing well
(iv) Capital cost of the project is not unreasonably high
(v) Promoters are having good reputation or at least have necessary knowledge/experience in the field

(vi) The promoter's contribution is not unduly low

(vii) On preliminary scrutiny, profitability estimates are reasonable indicating chances of repayment of the loan within the period stipulated in the bank's policy

A project may not be taken for detailed appraisal if it has some of the following features:-

(i) The concerned bank has already financed a large number of units in this field and it has decided not to finance new units for the present due to excessive involvement already committed

(ii) Reputation of promoters is not good and reported to have indulged in illegal and anti-social activities

(iii) Financial position of the promoters is not satisfactory

(iv) Capital cost of the project is unduly high

(v) Promoter's contribution unusually low and promoters decline to increase it

(vi) Location of the proposed unit has apparent disadvantages

(vii) Performance of the equipments supplied by the proposed machinery suppliers to some other units has not been satisfactory

(viii) Process know-how/technology has become obsolete

(ix) Availability of raw material in adequate quantity is doubtful

(x) Products to be manufactured do not have sufficient market potential or units already working in this field are not performing well due to lack of demand

While having informal discussions with the borrowing concerns, if they agree to take corrective steps for the above basic adverse features noticed at the preliminary scrutiny, the project may be taken up for a detailed scrutiny.

A project can be taken up for detailed appraisal if prima facie it appears viable. The lending institution has to ensure that the project will generate sufficient return on the resources invested in it. The viability of a project depends on technical feasibility, marketability of the products at a profitable price, availability of financial resources in time and proper management of the unit. Various aspects of project appraisal which are discussed in subsequent chapters can be summarised as under:-

(I) Technical appraisal

(II) Commercial appraisal - Marketing at profitable price

(III) Financial appraisal,

- (i) Capital cost of projects and sources of finance
- (ii) Financial Projections - Profitability and cash flow estimates
- (iii) Ratio Analysis
- (iv) Break-even Point
- (v) Discounted Cash Flow Techniques - Net Present Value and Internal Rate of Return

(IV) Appraisal of management.

All the above aspects of project appraisal are discussed in subsequent chapters. A chart showing various techniques of project appraisal is also given at the end of the chapter as an Annexure.

Annexure

Project Appraisal - An Overview

Technical Appraisal	Commercial Appraisal Marketing	Financial Appraisal	Management Appraisal
1. Production process/ technology 2. Arrangements for technical know-how 3. Size of the plant 4. Product-mix 5. Selection of plant and machinery 6. Procurement of plant and machinery 7. Plant layout 8. Location of the project (a) Land (b) Raw material (c) Market	1. Depth of competition 2. Pricing policy 3. Brand name for the product 4. Packing and transport 5. Distribution channels 6. Advertising and sales promotion 7. Steps for commercial appraisal	1. Capital cost of projects (a) Land and site developments (b) Buildings (c) Plant and machinery (d) Engineering and consultancy fees (e) Miscellaneous fixed assets (f) Preliminary and pre-operative expenses (g) Provision for contingencies (h) Margin money for working capital 2. Sources of finance 3. Financial projections	1. Qualities of an entrepreneur. (a) Honesty & integrity (b) Involvement in the project (c) Financial resources (d) Competence (e) Initiative (f) Intelligence (g) Drive and energy (h) Self confidence (i) Frankness (j) Patience

(d) Labour (e) Utilities such as water, power, fuel, etc. (f) Transport facilities (g) Effluent disposal 9. Schedule of project implementation	(a) Profitability estimates (b) Cash flow estimates (c) Projected balance sheets 4. Ratio analysis (a) Debt-equity ratio (b) Current ratio (c) Debt-service coverage ratio (d) Margin of security (e) Other ratios 5. Break-even point 6. Discounted cash flow techniques (a) Net present value (b) Internal rate of return	2. Organisational set up 3. Management problems

❑❑❑

12 Technical Appraisal of Medium and Large Projects

Technical appraisal of a project is essential to ensure that necessary physical facilities required for production will be available and the best possible alternative is selected to procure them. The technical appraisal of different types of agriculture projects has to be different depending upon their requirement. Technical appraisal of a project relating to horticulture may be different than that of dairy development, fishery development or poultry development. Technical appraisal includes the study of production process, size of the farm/plant, product mix, selection and procurement of plant and machinery, plant layout, schedule of project implementation and location of the project with reference to availability of various inputs required for production. In case of a project of horticulture, it may be necessary to study the location of the farm, agro climatic conditions of the area, sources of irrigation and other relevant factors relating to the crops to be grown. Although a banker may not have technical qualifications, he can examine the following basic points relating to technical appraisal with his common sense, experience and discussions with the promoter and their technical personnel.

The total capacity of the plant in above case will be considered as 60 units because the capacity in the third stage of process is only 60 units. If the capacity in third stage is increased, the total capacity of the plant can be raised upto 80 units without increasing the capacity of other stages. Perfect balancing of all stages may not be possible in many cases due to non-availability of certain machines of specific size. However, as far as possible, a unit should have balance of capacity in different stages. Equipments for utilities (power, water, fuel, etc.) should also have sufficient capacity to meet the requirement of main plant and machinery. While determining capacity of the equipment, necessary provision may be made for process time, idle time and shutdown time required for it. It may also be examined that the list of machines (both imported and indigenous) is comprehensive and it includes all the items required for production. If necessary, stand-by arrangements may be made for critical equipment. Adequate provision may also be made for tools and spares.

6. Procurement of Plant and Machinery

Plant and machinery can be procured by giving a contract on turnkey basis or by placing orders for different items of machinery with different machinery suppliers. The procurement can be done through agents or through direct negotiation or by formal quotations. It is always not necessary to procure from suppliers whose quotations are the lowest. The machinery suppliers should be decided keeping in view the quality of the machine, the reputation of the suppliers, delivery schedule, payment terms, performance guarantee and other relevant matters. Many machinery suppliers undertake the job of installation and give performance guarantee for a specified period.

If performance guarantee is given by the machinery supplier, the terms and conditions of the performance guarantee should be studied. Generally, the performance guarantee provides for repairing the machines free of charge during guarantee period. But no performance guarantee compensates for the loss caused due to closure of the plant. Therefore, performance guarantee is not a substitute for appraisal to be done about the quality of the machines and reputation of machinery suppliers.

If promoters propose to fabricate any machine instead of purchasing it from machinery suppliers, it should be ensured that promoters will be able to provide necessary technical expertise to fabricate machines of good quality and the cost of fabrication will be lower than the price quoted by machinery suppliers.

In order to have uninterrupted production, it should be ensured that satisfactory arrangements for repairs have been made and necessary spare parts will be available in time.

7. Plant Layout

The efficiency of manufacturing operation also depends on the layout of the plant and machinery. Plant layout may be done in such a way that minimum time is taken in handling equipment, raw material, consumables, goods-in-process and finished goods. Proper plant layout can reduce manufacturing cost by saving time and money. Building plan should be prepared according to the proposed plant layout.

8. Location of the Project

Study of the location includes selection of general location (city/town/village) and also particular site within the general location. It may be decided keeping in view the relative importance of various requirements of production, i.e. land, climatic conditions, raw materials/inputs, market, labour, utilities, effluent disposal, etc.

It is always not possible to have all the above facilities at one place. Relative importance of each factor for a project should be studied and location should be decided keeping in view the availability of basic or major inputs required for the project. A comparative study may be done to choose a place where the cost of production is minimum.

(i) Land

Land should be sufficient for the proposed project and the future expansion plans. The requirement of land can be assessed from the nature of the project, plant layout and the building to be constructed. Expenses for site development, if necessary, should be added to the cost of land.

(ii) Raw Materials/Inputs

The requirement of total raw material/inputs at full capacity should be ascertained and it should be ensured that they will be available at reasonable price. If imported raw material is required for the project, evaluation of the government policy in this regard as well as the prospects for its production within the country should be studied. If necessary, arrangements may be made for testing raw materials/inputs regarding their suitability for process requirements and yields. Arrangement may also be made for storage of raw materials/inputs depending on their requirement and availability. More storage capacity may be required, if supply is seasonal.

(iii) Market

While deciding location of a project, a comparative study regarding transportation cost of inputs received and finished product should also be done. If transportation of finished product is more difficult than its inputs, it may be better to set up such projects near the market.

(iv) Labour

Labour in terms of unemployed people is available in plenty in our country. But sometimes skilled labour may not be available at a particular place. If a project is taken up in an area where skilled labour is not available, necessary arrangements should be made to get labour from outside and training facilities for the local labour should be provided. If labour has to be obtained from outside, arrangements may have to be made to provide housing facilities.

(v) Utilities (power, water, fuel, etc.)

A unit requiring high power consumption should be located at a place where regular power supply may be ensured at reasonable rates. It may be a safe policy to keep generators where the power supply is not regular and the nature of project is such that sudden power failure may disturb the manufacturing activities considerably causing heavy losses as in the case of cold storage unit. If power requirement is above a certain level, cost of transformers and other facilities may be included in the capital cost of the project. If water requirement is high, the water table in the area of the proposed site and availability of enough water may be checked. Quality of water may have to be tested. If the water is not suitable, necessary arrangement (such as water softening plant) may be made to make it suitable for the manufacturing process. The co-operation of state and other local authorities, which control supply of power, water, etc. may be ensured. If municipal connection for water is not available, necessary provision may be made in the cost of the project to dig tube-wells.

(vi) Transport facilities

If the proposed site is not connected with the main roads, an approach road may have to be laid from the site to the main road. The quality of road may be decided keeping in view the quantum of goods to be transported. If the unit proposes to buy a vehicle, its cost benefit analysis may be done. If depreciation, interest and other expenses of maintaining a vehicle are less than the transportation charges to be paid to hired vehicles, it may be worthwhile to buy it. If a unit has to export major portion of its production, it is better to locate it near a place from where the exports can be done without much difficulty.

(vii) Effluent disposal

The problem of effluent disposal differs from project to project depending on the nature and quantity of effluents. It should be ensured that necessary treatment is provided to the effluents before they are discharged and permission is also taken from concerned authorities to discharge the effluents.

Major Headings	Information needed
1. Demand	Products, uses, the consumers, actual consumption, likely consumption in future and export prospects.
2. Supply	Production capacity, actual production, capacity utilization, imports and likely future capacity.
3. Distribution	Channels of distribution involved, the cost of distribution and the mode of transport.
4. Pricing	Domestic and international price trends, control of prices, duties and taxes.
5. External Forces	Government policies regarding exports, imports, foreign collaboration, plan outlay, etc.

1. Check-list for verification of various aspects of marketing

Information supplied by the entrepreneurs has to be checked by banks. Ascertaining the demand alone is not sufficient to study the commercial feasibility of a project. Many times, although uncatered demand is available in the market, a unit may not be able to sell its product. Knowledge of proper pricing policy, distribution policy, advertising policy and many other aspects of marketing is also essential to sell products. An illustrative check-list is given below to study the depth of competition, pricing policy, distribution channels, brand name for the product, packing and transportation, advertising and sales promotion

I. Depth of Competition

(i) What is the size of the total market for the product? What are the changes in the size of the market during last few years? Is it growing, constant or shrinking? Is there any significant trend suggesting a shift in demand?

(ii) Who are the main suppliers to the market?

(iii) What are the strengths and weaknesses of existing producers?

(iv) What is the likelihood of other producers entering in the field with similar products?

(v) What is the extent of brand recognition/ preferences or insistence on competitive brands? What is the number of brands - national, regional and local? What are the characteristics of the leading brands?

(vi) What steps will be necessary for the proposed unit to cope with existing producers?

(vii) In case of cash crops, position of user industry may be ascertained. It may also be ascertained whether the firm is able to enter into a contract to supply its product to any user industry.

II. Pricing Policy

(i) Taking note of all items of cost, at what price can the product be marketed?

(ii) What are the taxes and duties levied on the product in the domestic market?

(iii) What are the margins/discounts that have to be given to the trade?

(iv) Adding distribution cost and taxes/duties, at what price can the product be offered in the domestic market?

(v) What are the prices of imported products and that of domestic manufacturers of similar products and substitutes

(vi) What type of pricing would be appropriate for this product keeping in view the depth of competition and existing price?

(vii) In the light of existing trade customs, what would be the policy in areas such as trade credit facilities and acceptance of returned goods?

III. Distribution Channels

(i) What are the normal channels through which the consumers are accustomed to getting this type of product?

(ii) What is the usual arrangement made by competitors to sell this kind of product?

(iii) If the product is to be distributed directly through retailers, what kind of retail stores are best suited and likely to sell it?

(iv) Is it better to sell through wholesalers or directly to retailers or directly to consumers or users?

(v) Is it necessary to have exclusive dealership arrangements for various areas?

IV. Brand Name of the Product

(i) Is it necessary to have a brand name for the product?

(ii) Is the brand name proposed will be appropriate with reference to memory value, suggestiveness, pleasantness, family expression, legal protection and goodwill value?

(iii) What are the legal problems relating to obtaining patent rights and protection of trade marks?

V. Packaging and Transportation

(i) What type of packing will be necessary for the product and how does it compare with that of competitors in terms of attributes of protection, convenience, attractiveness, easy identification, economy and adaptability to retail outlets?

(ii) How do the firm's packaging and physical transport methods compare with the competitors in terms of cost, speed, liability to damage and vulnerable to pilferage?

VI. Advertising and Sales Promotion

(i) To what type of advertising media are consumers/users and potential consumers/users exposed?

(ii) What methods of advertising and sales promotion are used by competitors?

(iii) What will be the strategy to enter into the market and promote sales?

(iv) What will be the cost of advertising and sales promotion?

Advertising and sales promotion techniques should be decided keeping in view the size of the firm, competition in market, distribution channels and other relevant factors.

At the time of appraisal of a new project or expansion/ diversification project of an existing unit, banks should invariably take into account the marketing expenditure as an item of project cost. If existing units have to incur large special expenditure towards marketing of their product and such expenditure can not be written off from the profit and loss account in that year, it may have to be treated as deferred revenue expenditure recoverable over a reasonable period during which the benefits of such expenditure will be reaped. Banks may sanction appropriate amount of assistance for the purpose on merits of each case taking into account various factors like working of the unit, market potential, reasonableness of the expenditure, security and repayment period.

2. Conclusion-Steps for Commercial Appraisal

All the information required as per the above check-list may not be available, particularly with an entrepreneur of a small project. It is not necessary to get complete information on all the items mentioned in the check-list. A discussion with the promoters keeping in view the check-list will help the appraising officer to form an opinion whether the promoters will be able to sell their products. The above check-list will also help the promoters to decide proper marketing policy for their products. It will also help in selecting proper product-mix to suit the requirement of the market. Banks may have to take the following steps to analyse marketing prospects for a product:-

Sr. No.	Steps	Remarks
I	Discuss with the client about the details of the proposed product specification, prospective demand, depth of competition, pricing policy, marketing organisation sales promotion policy, etc.	The client is the best source of information on these aspects. However, data given by the client needs further checking.
II	Collect data, within the financial Institution/bank	Internal sources can be as under: (i) Any proposal of similar or substitute product financed in the past and its performance regarding marketing, if production has already started. (ii) Past studies on the market about similar or substitute products. (iii) Data Bank of the market research department, (if any). (iv) Library of the organization for publications, newspaper clippings etc.
III	Assess the adequacy of the data from internal sources. If data is not available or found inadequate:- (i) Determine the data that needs to be collected (ii) Assess the sources of information	The determination of the data that needs to be collected can be decided keeping in view the size of the project, time and personnel available for the study and the information already available within the organization.
IV	Collect and analyse the information	The information can be collected from primary and/or secondary sources. Primary sources are

Sr. No.	Steps	Remarks
		those sources which can directly provide all or part of the information and include consumers, traders, trader's organizations/ associations, manufacturers, manufacturers' associations, Government departments and agencies, research institutions, knowledgeable circles, other financial institutions, competing banks and consultancy organizations, and last but not the least the client himself who in many instances has prior knowledge and even experience in the marketing of the product under review. Following steps may be taken to collect information from primary sources:- (i) Determine the type of information required. (ii) Determine the source(s) of information (iii) Design the sample and select the parties to be contacted (iv) Prepare the data collection form or questionnaire (v) Give prior information to the concerned parties regarding purpose of the visit and the information required. An assurance may have to be given to treat the information as confidential. (vi) Collect the information (vii) Analyse the information collected and prepare the market report.

Sr. No.	Steps	Remarks
		It is difficult to collect information from primary sources for all projects and an appraising officer may have to depend on secondary sources of information which include published material pertaining to the product and the market for it. It may be published by Government, research institutions, manufacturers' associations, consultancy organizations, international agencies and even other financial institutions/ banks. Many newspapers, journals and company balance sheets also give information about marketing prospects of many commodities. Information can be obtained from Internet also.
V	Evaluate the marketing strategy proposed by the client in the background of the market information analysed.	Discuss with the client. If necessary, change the original product-mix and marketing strategy proposed by the client.
VI	Prepare a market report	Market reports need to be clear, precise, as brief as possible, logical and adequate for decision making.
VII	Code, classify and preserve market report.	Preservation of market reports will be helpful for evaluation of marketing strategy for future projects and follow-up of present projects.

While preparing profitability estimates, price of the product and selling expenditure should be estimated keeping in view the price structure in the market, firm's position in the market, its distribution system and other relevant matters.

The gateway to profit is sales. A unit with excellent facilities of production may also incur losses if it is not able to sell its product. Therefore, a proper study of demand, market environment, pricing policy, distribution system, packing, sales promotion, etc. should be done before sanctioning the loan. Even after the commencement of production, a close watch on the market is necessary to take corrective steps, whenever necessary.

❑❑❑

14 Capital Cost of Projects and Sources of Finance

Estimation of the capital cost of a project provides the basic information to decide its pattern of financing and viability. If cost of the project is not estimated correctly, the preparation of cash flow and profitability estimates will be futile exercise because the amount of depreciation, interest and dividend will change with the change in the capital cost of the project. An entrepreneur has to tie up the resources according to the estimates of the cost of the project. If there is an overrun in the cost of a project, the entrepreneur may find it difficult to arrange for additional resources and it may delay the implementation of the project which will lead to further overrun in the capital cost. Banks are taking an undertaking from entrepreneurs to meet cost of overrun, if any, in the implementation of the project. But such an undertaking does not have much practical meaning. Many a times, an entrepreneur is not in a position to bring additional resources to finance the overrun and ultimately financial institutions and banks have to provide additional resources to safeguard the money already invested in the project. Over-estimation of the cost of the project is also equally bad as under-estimation. If the cost of a project is over-estimated,

	III. Sales-tax IV. Transportation and installation charges	hinery suppliers III. Cross-check with some reputable potential suppliers from whom the promoters could have asked, but have not asked, to bid or quote. IV. Selection should be done from various quotations on the basis of not only price but also technical sophistication, reputation of suppliers, delivery dates, credit terms, etc. V. Orders for machinery, if placed VI. Contract entered with the machinery suppliers
D. Engineering and Consultancy fees	I. Expenses of foreign technicians II. Expenses of training for Indian technicians III. Technical know-how fee IV. Expenses on drawings V. Consultancy fees for preparing project report	I. Contract with the foreign collaborators II. Contract with the consultants III. A note on past record of consultants IV. Relationship, if any, between Promoters of a project and Consultants

E. Miscellaneous Fixed Assets	I. Furniture II. Office machinery and equipment III. Vehicles-cars, trucks, etc. IV. Cost of electric installation V. Equipment and pipes for distribution of water, air and steam VI. Laboratory equipment VII. Workshop equipment VIII. Fire fighting equipment IX. Effluent collection, treatment and disposal arrangement X. Miscellaneous fixed assets	I. Details of various items of furniture, various office machinery, equipment, etc. and cost thereof II. Ascertain whether it is necessary to invest in vehicles for the project. Estimate cost of maintaining vehicle(s) and compare with transportation charges to be paid, if outside vehicles are hired. III. Contract regarding electric installation, piping, etc. IV. Price list of laboratory equipment, workshop equipment, etc.
F. Preliminary and Pre-operative expenses	I. Capital issue expenses if capital issue is to be made II. Commitment charges III. Interest on term loans during construction period IV. Mortgage expenses V. Miscellaneous expenses during construction period	I. Find the total amount of capital issue and calculate charges thereon II. Find the construction period and calculate interest for that period III. Calculate the amount of mortgage expenses IV. Calculate the other expenses during construction period

promoters' background, etc. Higher debt-equity ratio is allowed for projects promoted by technocrats, large-sized capital intensive projects and also projects located in backward areas. The details of debt-equity ratio are discussed later in the chapter on Ratio Analysis.

Sufficient finance should be provided to complete the implementation of the project after deducting the margin money. Under-financing of a project leads to dependence on outside sources and delay in implementation of the project.

❑❑❑

15 Financial Projections

Financial projections include profitability estimates (estimates of working results), cash flow estimates and projected balance sheets. They are inter-related and prepared on the basis of cost of the project, sources of finance and various assumptions of profitability estimates.

1. Profitability Estimates

Profitability estimates are estimates of expected sales realisations and expenses to be incurred by the unit. Excess of sales realisation over expenses indicates the expected profit of the unit. The borrower may be tempted to give a bright picture of his project to enable him to get finance from banks and financial institutions. The appraising officer should verify the figures given by the borrower. Mere checking of arithmetical calculations of various figures is not sufficient. The basis of various figures should be ascertained and checked to satisfy that profits shown in the profitability estimates are realistic.

Various items included in profitability estimates can be verified according to the check-list given below:

I. Sales Realisations

(i) Check the project implementation schedule to ascertain whether it is realistic and production will start according to estimates.

(ii) Assume only 40-60% of installed capacity as production in first year, 60-80% in second year and 80-100% in third year depending on the type of activity.

(iii) Assume that entire production is sold and stocks are maintained at the same level.

(iv) Take present sale price (it is presumed that if there is any change in sale price, cost of production will also change in the same proportion).

(v) If a percentage of production is controlled, take control price for the portion.

(vi) Multiply expected production with sale price to ascertain total sales realisations.

(vii) Deduct excise duty, if any, from sales realisations and take net price.

(viii) Add other income, if any.

II. Raw Material and Consumable Stores

(i) Check the requirement of each raw material and other inputs for expected production taken for sales realisations.

(ii) Take the present price of each component (raw materials and consumable stores) as we have taken sales price at present level.

(iii) Add transportation and other expenses to be incurred for procuring raw materials and consumable stores.

III. Utilities (Power, fuel, water, etc.)

(i) Calculate requirement of power keeping in view the manufacturing process.

(ii) Multiply the total power requirement with the tariff structure of the power supplying company or State Electricity Board.

(iii) Fuel consumption is based on the specifications of the equipments. Find out the fuel price and add the transportation cost for delivery at plant.

(iv) If water is to be purchased, find the price being charged by water supply undertaking. If water is to be obtained from wells, streams, etc., it is necessary to build up its costs considering power, labour, chemicals, etc., used for supply of water.

IV. Repairs and Maintenance

Take low charges for repairs and maintenance in first year and increase them every year. It may be taken in first year about 0.5% for building and from 0.5% to 5% for plant and machinery depending on the nature of machinery. Increase these charges every year over the figure of previous year because longer the life of fixed assets, higher will be the repairs and maintenance charges.

V. Wages and Salaries

(i) Check the requirements of production staff and workers.

(ii) Check the wage structure in the area of factory.

(iii) Provide 5% increase in wages and salaries every year over the figure of previous year to cover routine increments to be granted to staff.

VI. Rent, Insurance, etc.

(i) Find the area and type of space to be taken on rent and rates of rent.

(ii) The cost of insurance will depend on the nature of property to be insured, the risk proposed to be covered and the value of property. Take the insurance rates and find out the total insurance expenditure on the property to be insured.

VII. Depreciation

Take 5% depreciation on building, 10% depreciation on plant and machinery and 10% depreciation on miscellaneous fixed assets. Depreciation on plant and machinery should be raised by 5% for every shift. In other words, take depreciation at 15% on the two shifts basis and 20% on the three shifts basis on plant and machinery.

VIII. Administrative Expenses

If the entrepreneur is working full time and depends for his expenses on the proposed unit only, provide a reasonable amount as remuneration payable to him. Salary of administrative staff, audit fees and other miscellaneous expenditure to be incurred on administration are included in this cost. Take the total requirement of the administrative staff and their salary structure to ascertain administrative cost. The quantum of administrative expenses depends on the nature and magnitude of the administrative set-up.

IX. Selling expenses

Presume a percentage of sales as selling expenses. The percentage should be decided keeping in view the type of product, packing charges, distribution system and other market conditions prevailing in the industry. The marketing strategy to be adopted by the unit should be taken into consideration while verifying the estimates of selling expenses.

X. Interest on Term Loan

(i) Interest on term loan is calculated according to the present rate of interest charged by the banks and institutions which propose to grant term loan.

(ii) Interest amount will be reduced according to the repayment schedule of term loan.

XI. Interest on Bank Borrowings

(i) Find out the total requirement of working capital

(ii) Take the bank borrowings likely to be made available against the total working capital requirement.

(iii) Take the rate of interest to be charged by the bank and calculate the interest charges.

XII. Profit

After deducting the above expenditures from the sales realisations, the profit before tax can be ascertained. Tax may be calculated according to present tax structure. Tax concessions, if any, available to the unit should be considered while calculating the amount of tax. After deducting the amount of tax the net profit is ascertained.

Although the actual profit of the unit will be different than the estimated figure, the above scrutiny may ensure that the variation is minimum possible. In the case of existing companies, separate profitability estimates should be prepared for the projects to be financed by bank/institutions and also combined profitability estimates of the existing operations and proposed new operations.

Cash Flow Estimates

Cash flow estimates are prepared to ensure that the unit will have necessary cash with it and it will not face liquidity problem. The cash flow estimates include sources of funds and their deployment (uses). While profitability estimates are prepared only from the year in which the unit is likely to commence production, cash flow estimates are necessary for the construction period also to ensure availability of cash according to the requirements of the project.

Sources of funds may include the following items:-

(i) Share capital
(ii) Term loans/Debentures
(iii) Net profit after depreciation and writing off preliminary expenses but before interest and taxes
(iv) Depreciation
(v) Preliminary expenses written off
(vi) Deferred credits
(vii) Trade credits
(viii) Bank borrowings
(ix) Capital Subsidy from Central Government on any other agencies
(x) Development loans/Sales tax loans in notified areas
(xi) Unsecured loans and deposits
(xii) Any other sources

While examining the sources of funds, we must ascertain the period in which the unit is likely to raise share capital, term loans, deferred credits, development loans, capital subsidy, unsecured loans, etc. and it should match with the requirements of the project according to its implementation schedule. Net profit is shown as a source of funds after providing for depreciation and writing off preliminary expenses, but before interest and taxes. As the amount of depreciation and preliminary expenses written off remains within the business, it is shown separately as a source of funds. The payment of interest and taxation is shown as deployment of funds because net profit is taken as a source of funds before interest and taxes. The figures of net profit, depreciation, preliminary expenses written off, if any, interest and taxation are taken from profitability estimates.

Deployment or use of funds may include the following items:-

(i) Capital expenditure
(ii) Preliminary expenses
(iii) Current assets - Increase in level of inventories and book debts
(iv) Decrease in term loans/debentures/deferred credit
(v) Decrease in secured loans/public deposits
(vi) Repayment of bank borrowings
(vii) Interest
(viii) Taxation
(ix) Dividends
(x) Any other payments

Use of funds for capital expenditure and preliminary expenses should be shown according to the requirements of the project estimated while examining the capital cost of the project. The level of inventories and book debts will increase in first 2-3 years with the increase in the level of production. Decrease in term loans/ debentures/ deferred credit/ unsecured loans is shown according to the proposed repayment schedule. The amount of interest, taxation and dividend can be taken from profitability estimates.

The difference between sources and deployment of funds indicates the net cash surplus or deficit arising out of movement of funds in that year.

Projected Balance Sheets

Projected balance sheets are prepared on the basis of profitability estimates and cash flow estimates. The position of share capital, term loans, sundry creditors, bank borrowings, current assets etc. is ascertained at the end of each year, according to the movements shown in cash flow and profitability estimates. Fixed assets are taken after deducting depreciation provided in profitability estimates. Preliminary expenses are taken after deducting the amount which is already written off from the expected profit of the unit. Cumulative surplus shown in profitability estimates represents the position of reserves at the end of each year. Closing balance shown in cash flow estimates represents the position of cash and bank balances at the end of each year. It should be remembered that balance sheet is a snap shot picture of the financial position at the end of each year and the total of its assets side will be equal to the total of its liabilities side.

Sensitivity Analysis

It is impossible to have the actual results exactly according to projections. If actual results are plus or minus 10 per cent of projections, it can be considered that the work of projections has been done very well. Debt-service coverage ratio, break-even point and many other ratios are calculated on the basis of financial projections. In fact, even the repayment schedule of term loans is drawn on the basis of surplus shown in financial projections. If financial projections go wrong and expected surplus is not available with the unit, the repayment of term loan may face difficulties.

Although actual results will be different than the figures shown in projections, proper verification of various assumptions will ensure that variation between actual results and projections is minimum and a project which is considered viable may not become unviable. Projected profit may change owing to changes in the cost of project, cost of production, volume of production or selling price. The appraising officer should ascertain the most sensitive areas of the project. If working results of a project are highly sensitive to a particular variable, sufficient study should be made to find out the probability of a change in that variable. If it is felt that a particular assumption which is important for the project is likely to change, sensitivity analysis should be done and separate profitability estimates should be prepared with the change in assumption. For example, if it is felt that sale price may go down by 10 per cent without any reduction in cost of production, separate profitability estimates should be prepared with 10 per cent reduction in sale price to find out whether the project will be viable even after the reduction in sale price. Similarly, separate profitability estimates can be prepared with the expected changes in other assumptions to find out whether the project remains viable even after these changes in assumptions. This type of analysis is called sensitivity analysis and it indicates the degree of cushion available in the profitability of a project to withstand changes in assumed conditions and shortfall in expected results. It should be done for such projects where proper assumptions cannot be made regarding important variables.

❑❑❑

16 Ratio Analysis for Medium and Large Projects

Ratio indicates the relationship between two or more than two variables. Many important items like sales, profit, net profit, debt, equity, current assets, current liabilities, etc. do not give much information if each figure is studied in isolation. If a ratio is calculated between the related items, a banker can get meaningful information about the borrowing unit. Ratios are useful for comparative study of various units and also of various years' working of the same unit.

Ratio can be calculated for the past record as well as for the future. Past record can be studied only in case of the existing undertakings by analysing their balance sheets. Future records can be studied for existing undertakings as well as new undertakings by analysing their financial projections. Ratios should be calculated from the figures of balance sheets to study past record and from figures of financial projections to study the future.

Many ratios can be calculated to study financial position and working of a unit by applying different formulae. In order to have comparative study of several units and also several years of the same unit, it is necessary to follow uniform formula for calculating a particular ratio. Ratio analysis helps in appraisal of projects as well as their follow-up to take corrective steps, whenever necessary. Important ratios calculated by banks are as follows:

I. **Loan Safety Ratios or Appraisal Ratios**

(i) Debt-equity ratio (Term liabilities to owned funds)
(ii) Current ratio (Current assets to current liabilities)
(iii) Debt-service coverage ratio
(iv) Fixed assets coverage ratio
(v) Break-even point (Discussed in a separate chapter)
(vi) Internal rate of return (Discussed in a separate chapter)

II. **Profitability Ratios**

(i) Profit before interest, lease rentals and depreciation (PBILD) to total income
(ii) Operating profit to total income
(iii) Return on capital employed
(iv) Earnings per share (EPS)
(v) Interest coverage ratio

III. **Turnover Ratios**

(i) Current assets holding ratio
(ii) Raw materials holding ratio
(iii) Stores holding ratio
(iv) Work-in-process holding ratio
(v) Finished goods holding ratio
(vi) Collection ratio
(vii) Total income to net fixed assets ratio
(viii) Capital turnover ratio

IV. **Operating Ratios**

(i) Raw materials to total cost
(ii) Consumable stores to total cost
(iii) Power, fuel and water to total cost
(iv) Salaries and wages to total cost
(v) Marketing and selling expenses to total cost
(vi) Interest on lease rentals to total cost

financed from long term funds (owned funds and term borrowings) and it gives a minimum current ratio of 1.3:1. Therefore, while estimating the total requirement of long term funds for new projects, margin money for working capital should be calculated at 25 per cent of the expected total current assets. The requirement of margin money for working capital should be included in the capital cost of the project and long term resources should be provided to finance it like other fixed assets.

If the current ratio of any unit is less than 1.33, efforts should be made to raise the long term sources (owned funds and term borrowings) to provide sufficient margin to the banker for working capital requirements.

3. Debt-service Coverage Ratio

The ratio indicates the capacity of the unit to repay term loan and interest thereon. The formula for calculating this ratio is as under:-

$$\frac{\text{Profit after tax} + \text{Depreciation} + \text{Interest on term debt} + \text{Lease rentals, if any}}{\text{Repayment of term loan} + \text{Interest on term debt} + \text{Lease rentals, if any}}$$

The above ratio should be calculated during the entire repayment period separately for each year and also as an average for the entire repayment period. The average debt-service coverage ratio (DSCR) should be computed by taking the total of all values of the numerator and denominator for the entire repayment period and not by taking an average of DSCRs for each year. This ratio should be generally about two. As this ratio indicates the capacity of a unit to repay the term loan, it is a very important ratio for a term lending institution. A term loan may not be repaid if the concerned unit does not generate profit. Repayment of term loan without generating profit will lead to reduction in working capital, tight liquidity position and further deterioration in the working of the unit. Therefore, repayment schedule should be drawn on the basis of profitability estimates.

4. Fixed Assets Coverage Ratio

Term loans are generally sanctioned against the security of fixed assets. The excess of fixed assets over term loans secured by them provides margin on security. In order to find out the available security cover, fixed assets coverage ratio may be calculated by the following formula:

$$\frac{\text{Net fixed assets + Capital work-in-process}}{\text{Deferred credits + Term loans + Debentures secured by First charge over fixed assets + other loans having pari passu charge on fixed assets}}$$

In case of existing units, fixed assets to be created for implementation of the project are added to the present net assets (gross fixed assets minus depreciation). Similarly, proposed term loans are added to existing term loans if both have pari passu charge on fixed assets. If any fixed asset is having specific charge for a particular loan, the amount of such fixed asset and the loan should be excluded. If the amount of existing fixed assets includes any addition by revaluation, it should be deducted to find out the present net fixed assets.

In case of new units, proposed fixed assets will cover the proposed term loans. Proposed fixed assets will be equal to the entire capital cost of the project except those preliminary expenses which will not be capitalised. It may be clarified that the provision for contingencies provided while estimating the capital cost of a project forms a part of fixed assets because the amount of the provision will be utilised, if necessary, for creation of fixed assets.

The fixed assets coverage ratio depends on debt-equity ratio. Higher the debt equity ratio, lower will be the margin available because the amount of term loans will be higher for creation of fixed assets. As now-a-days emphasis is more on purpose-oriented advances than security-oriented advances, higher emphasis is given on debt-service coverage ratio to ensure repayment of term loans. Sometimes, banks are asking for collateral security or personal guarantee of promoters, if they find the risk involved in the project is very high.

5. Conclusion

It may be observed from the above that various ratios are calculated to study various aspects of a unit. However, all ratios do not have equal importance to a term lending institution. Debt equity ratio and debt-service coverage ratio are vital for a term lending institution. Profits earned by a unit and repayment schedule of the term loan are reflected in debt-service coverage ratio. Similarly, debt-equity ratio indicates the amount of cushion available to the term lending institution. Current ratio is very important for a bank providing working capital finance.

It may also be mentioned that a ratio by itself does not have much significance unless it is compared with an appropriate standard. The comparison can be done between different units engaged in the same activity and also one year to other years of the same unit depending on the nature of the ratio, object of the study and availability of data.

17 Break-even Point

Break-even Point is the point at which a unit neither earns profit nor incurs losses. The cost of production is just recovered at the break-even point. The cost of production can be divided into two categories, viz., Fixed Cost and Variable Cost.

Division of total cost into fixed cost and variable cost is a difficult task because a few expenses can be counted under both the categories. They neither remain fixed nor change in the same proportion in which the level of production changes. Therefore, a banker should follow the uniform policy to divide the total cost into fixed and variable cost to enable him to compare the break-even point of one unit with another unit.

Fixed Cost (Including Semi-fixed Cost)

A certain amount of cost has to be incurred by a unit irrespective of level of production. It will not change with the change in the level of production. Since in the short run, the semi-fixed cost may not vary materially with the level of output, the entire semi-fixed cost is added to the fixed cost for the purpose of calculating break-even point. Cost incurred on following items may be included into fixed and semi-fixed cost :-

(i) Salaries and wages
(ii) Repairs and maintenance
(iii) Administrative and miscellaneous expenses
(iv) Fixed portion of selling expenses
(v) Fixed royalty and know-how payments
(vi) Interest on term debt
(vii) Depreciation on straight line basis (not to be included for cash break-even calculation)

Variable Cost or Marginal Cost

Variable cost or marginal cost varies with the variation in the level of production. It is presumed that it changes in the same proportion in which the level of production changes. The cost incurred on following items may be included into variable cost:-

(i) Raw materials
(ii) Outside purchases
(iii) Purchase of goods for re-sale
(iv) Consumable stores and spares
(v) Packing materials
(vi) Power, fuel and water
(vii) Royalty payments linked to sales
(viii) Variable selling expenses
(ix) Interest on working capital
(x) Other variable expenses varying directly in proportion to output

Selling Price

Selling price is the price at which the unit is selling its product. It should be taken after excluding excise duty, if any. If sale price is taken gross and excise duty is also counted in the selling price, the excise duty should be included as an item of variable cost. It is better to take selling price (net of excise duty) and avoid excise duty as an item of expenditure. Other incomes like import entitlements, export incentives, etc. should be included in selling price. In the case of units having multi-products, it is presumed that the same product mix will be continued.

Contribution and Break-even Point

Difference between sale price and variable cost is called contribution. The contribution helps a unit to recover its fixed cost. The level of production at which the contribution recovers entire fixed cost is called break-even point. For example, if fixed cost is Rs.6,000, sale price is Rs.12 per unit and variable cost is Rs.6 per unit, the break-even point will be at the production of 1,000 unit because the contribution of Rs.6 per unit (sale price-variable cost) will recover the entire fixed cost of Rs.6,000 at the production of 1,000 units. It can be calculated by using the following formula:-

$$\text{Break-even Point} = \frac{\text{Fixed Cost}}{\text{Sale Price - Variable Cost}} = \frac{\text{Fixed Cost}}{\text{Contribution}}$$

Break-even point can be calculated from figures of financial statements of previous years to study past record and from figures of profitability estimates to study future. While calculating break-even point from profitability estimates, it is better to calculate it on the basis of figures when the unit is likely to achieve the normal level of production.

Break-even point can be expressed in terms of

(a) volume of production, or
(b) a percentage of installed capacity, or
(c) amount of sales

Utility of Break-even Point for Appraisal

Break-even point indicates the level of production which is necessary to avoid losses. Break-even point can be called bread earning point because a unit earns profit from sales above break-even point. Sales above break-even point indicate the margin of safety available to a unit. Break-even point should be low for units likely to have difficulties regarding marketing or non-availability of raw materials or shortage of power or any other difficulties in achieving utilisation of full capacity. But a unit can have high break-even point if raw material, power and market for finished product are assured.

A private entrepreneur will prefer to close his plant when variable cost is more than sales price and the situation is not likely to improve in near future. He will lose only fixed cost by closing such plant, but if he runs the plant he will lose not only fixed cost but also excess of variable cost over sale price. Whenever banks consider any proposal for rehabilitation of a sick unit, they must ensure that sale price will be higher than variable cost and some contribution will be available to recover the fixed cost and unit will achieve the break-even point.

Break-even point can be calculated with sensitivity analysis also by assuming increase/decrease in fixed cost or variable cost or sale price. Break-even point can be used for comparative study of various proposals.

❑❑❑

18 Evaluation of Profitability for Medium and Large Projects

A project should earn sufficient return which should be at least equal to the cost of the funds invested in it. If many alternative proposals are available for the investment, the investor should make a comparative study of the return on various proposals. Following methods have been suggested for evaluating the profitability of projects:-

(1) Pay-Back Method
(2) Average Rate of Return Method
(3) Net Present Value Method
(4) Internal Rate of Return

Pay Back Method

The object of this method is to ascertain the period required for recovering the entire investment made in a project. The cash inflow includes net operating profit after adding back to it the amount of depreciation on fixed assets and amortisation of intangible assets, if any, less income-tax payable during the year. The cash inflow is accumulated, year by year, until it equals the original investment. The length of time required for total cash inflow to recover the original investment is called the pay-back period. For example. a project needs original investment of Rs.1000 and its estimated cash inflow (net operating profit + depreciation and other non-cash write offs added back less income tax) is as follows:

Original Investment: Rs.1000

Year	Cash inflow of each year	Cumulative Cash Inflow
1	100	100
2	150	250
3	250	500
4	300	800
5	300	1100

Pay back period to recover original investment of Rs.1000 comes to 4 years and 8 months [Rs. 800 is recovered in 4 years and to recover balance amount of Rs. 200, 8 months are required because the rate of recovery is Rs. 25/- per month (300÷12) in fifth year].

Although the calculation of pay back period is simple, it ignores the time value of money and does not take into account the income which may be received beyond the pay back period. Sometimes, a project having higher pay back period may be better than lower pay back period owing to higher return after pay back period. For example, two projects having original investment of Rs.1,000/- each are having cash inflow as under:-

Comparison of Two Projects by Pay Back Method

Year	Project A-Original Investment Rs.1000		Project B-Original Investment Rs.1000	
	Annual Cash Inflow	Cumulative	Annual Cash Inflow	Cumulative
1	200	200	100	100
2	400	600	150	250
3	300	900	200	450
4	100	1000	250	700
5	-	-	300	1000
6	-	-	250	1250
7	-	-	250	1500
8	-	-	150	1650
9	-	-	100	1750

Pay Back Period 4 years 5 years

According to pay back method, project A is better because the entire investment is recovered in 4 years against 5 years required for project B. But project A recovers only original investment and it does not have earning capacity after 4 years, whereas project B earns much more than its original investment. Pay back method ignores the cash inflow received after crossing the pay back period and does not give the rate of return. However, this method can be used where emphasis is on avoidance of long term risk or on the liquidity value of investment. For example, while investing in a foreign country where political stability cannot be forecasted for a long period or while investing in a plant which is likely to be obsolete shortly, this method can be used to judge suitability of investment.

Average Rate of Return Method

Under this method, the entire life of a project is taken into account, unlike the pay-back period. An average of the annual net operating profits (after depreciation) for the entire life of the project is taken and rate of return on original investment and average investment is calculated. Average investment of one year can be ascertained by taking the average of opening and closing book value of investments in the year. The grand average of such average investments of all the years is obtained to know the average investment for the project. Average profit is divided by original investment and average investment to get the rate of return on them.

An example giving comparison of three projects by average rate of return method is given below:-

Comparison of three projects by Average Rate of Return Method

(Amount in Rs.)

Net operating profit (after depreciation)	Project 'A'	Project 'B'	Project 'C'
Year I	300	50	300
Year II	400	150	300
Year III	400	200	300

Net operating profit (after depreciation)	Project 'A'	Project 'B'	Project 'C'
Year IV 300	200	800	
Year V	200	300	300
Year VI	-	-	300
Total Profit	1500	1500	1800
Life of project	5 years	5 years	6 years
Average annual Profit	300	300	300
Original investment	2000	2000	2000
Return on original Investment	15%	15%	15%
Return on average Investment (presuming average investment at Rs.1000)	30%	30%	30%

It may be observed from the above example that income received in earlier years is more for project 'A' as compared to project 'B'. But this method does not give any importance to the time value of money. Further, total income of project 'C' is more than project 'A' and 'B'. But its annual average is same because the life of the project is longer than that of the other two projects. This method does not take into account the life differential of projects.

Time Value of Money-Discounting Technique

Pay back method and average rate of return method do not consider the time value of money. This initial amount incurred for acquisition of assets to implement a project and income received from the project in future is given equal importance under the above two methods. But in fact the value of money received in future is not equivalent to the value of money invested today. In other words, a rupee in hand now is more valuable than a rupee to be received in future because cash in hand can be invested elsewhere and interest can be earned on it. For example, if Rs.100 is invested at the annual interest of ten per cent, it will increase as follows:-

Rs.100 today is equal to

Rs.110 after one year	(Rs.100 + Rs.10 of interest)
Rs.121 after two years	(Rs.110 + Rs.11 of interest)
Rs.133.1 after three years	(Rs.121 + Rs.12.1 of interest), and so on.

The above example gives an idea of the compounding increase of the present value in future. The opposite of compounding is called discounting. If we want to know the present sum from the future sum, we have to discount the future sum. Taking the above example, it can be said that Rs.110 after 1 year is equal to Rs.100 today or Rs.121 after two years is equal to Rs.100 today or Rs.133.1 after three years is equal to Rs.100 today. It can be expressed as under:

Rs.110 after 1 year is equal to Rs.100 today,

Or Rs.1 after 1 year is equal to Rs. $\frac{100}{110}$

= Rs.0.909 today

Rs.121 after 2 years is equal to Rs.100 today

Or Rs.1 after 2 years is equal to Rs. $\frac{100}{121}$

= Rs.0.826 today

Rs.131.1 after 3 years is equal to Rs.100 today

Or Rs.1 after 3 years is equal to Rs. $\frac{100}{133.1}$

= Rs.0.751 today.

If rate of return is 10 per cent, 0.909, 0.826 and 0.751 are the discounting factors to know the present value of future sums after 1, 2 and 3 years respectively. If we multiply the future sum with discounting factor, we can get the present value, the discounting factors are given in discounting tables according to the different rates of return and different periods (years). While calculating present value of future sum, take the discounting factor from discounting tables according to the period and rate of return and multiply the future sum by discounting factor to get the present value.

This relationship between present and future values can be expressed as follows:-

Multiply by compounding factor

Present	---------------------->	Future
Amount	<----------------------	Amount

Multiply by discounting factor

Net Present Value Method

After understanding discounting technique, we shall now discuss the net present value method. Under this method, the cash flows of all the years during the expected life of the project are discounted at a pre-determined cut-off rate and net present value is obtained. The cut-off rate should be either equal to or more than the cost of funds. A positive net present value at the cut-off rate indicates that the investment in the project gives profits greater than the marginal investment rate or cost of capital and hence the proposal can be accepted. If net present value is zero, it indicates that the total earnings from the project are equal to marginal investment rate. If net present value is negative, it indicates that total earnings from the project are less than the marginal investment rate or cost of capital. An example showing calculation of net present value of two projects at 15% discount rate is given on the next page.

(1) It is presumed that life of both the projects is 5 years.

(2) Investment in both the projects is Rs.1000 each. Entire investment is done in one year of construction period. The first year construction period, is considered as zero year and no discounting is necessary for zero year. Therefore, present value of investment remains at Rs.1000 each for both the projects.

(3) The cash inflow has been discounted at the rate of 15% presuming that the cost of funds or cut-off rate is 15.

(4) Discounting factors at 15% have been taken from discounting tables for 1st year to 5th year.

(5) Present value of cash inflow has been obtained by multiplying the inflow by its respective discounting factors.

To test the validity of the above formula, if we discount the cash flows at 21%, the net present value will be almost negligible as under—

(Amount in Rs.)

	Cash Flow	Discounting Factor at 21 %	Present Value
Year 0	-1000	-	-1000
Year 1	+300	0.826	+247.8
Year 2	+400	0.683	+273.2
Year 3	+400	0.564	+225.6
Year 4	+300	0.467	+140.1
Year 5	+300	0.386	+115.8
Net Present Value			+2.5

The present value of 2.5 is too small and can be ignored. The internal rate of return for above example comes to 21%.

It may be mentioned that we should not try to interpolate between a range of more than 5 per cent. In other words, while using the interpolation formula, we should ensure that the difference between lower discount rate on which the net present value comes positive and higher discount rate on which the net present value comes negative, is not more than 5. If the difference is more than 5, it is better to use the discounting tables and reduce the difference between the two discounting rates for calculating the internal rate of return with the help of interpolation formula.

Information needed for Calculation of Net Present Value and Internal Rate of Return

It may be observed from the earlier discussions that the following information is required for calculation of net present value or internal rate of return :

1. Life of the Project
2. Cash Outflow (amount of investment for capital expenditure and working capital)
3. Cash inflow (benefits of the project)

4. Residual or terminal value of the project
5. Net cash receipt and calculation of internal rate of return
6. Pre-determined cut-off rate or minimum rate of return

1. Life of the Project

The life of the project means the estimated period (in terms of number of years) during which it will be economically productive. It should be shortest of (a) physical life or (b) technological life (equipment obsolescence) or (c) product market life (product obsolescence) because a project will become unproductive due to any of the above reasons. The life of a project should not be based on the rate of depreciation used in the books of accounts. A few agricultural projects like growing coconuts, construction of irrigation dams, etc. may have life of 40-50 years. But the present value of the future amount goes on decreasing with an increase in number of years. If we take 50 years as project life, the present value of the income received at 50th year will be almost negligible. Therefore, while calculating internal rate of return, life of a project is generally not taken above 25 years.

2. Cash Outflow

Resources are used in a project for acquisition of two kinds of assets, viz., fixed assets and current assets. Fixed assets mean project cost minus margin for working capital and interest during construction period. Any expenditure which is incurred after commencement of production for maintaining the life and productivity of fixed assets should be charged to repairs and maintenance. However, expenditures incurred on additions to fixed assets, if any, should be shown in cash outflow of the year in which they are incurred.

In addition to the cost of fixed assets, the requirement of working capital (current assets minus current liabilities other than bank borrowings) is shown in cash outflow. The requirement of working capital increases with the increase in the level of production in the initial years and expected to remain at the level of normal year of operations when maximum production is achieved.

Implementation period or construction period of a project is considered as zero year. However, if implementation period of a project exceeds one year, the first year of the implementation should be treated as zero year, the second as first year and so on. The first year of operations may therefore become the second or the third year depending on the implementation period. The life of the project should be taken after implementation of the project. For example, if implementation of a project takes three years and life of the project is taken for twelve years, the cash flow may have to be prepared from zero year to 14 years to indicate the cash flow position of 3 years of project implementation and 12 years of the project life.

3. Cash Inflow

Cash inflow includes the profit earned from operations of the project during life of the project and residual or terminal value of the project in the last year of operations. Profit should be taken before interest, lease rentals, depreciation and tax for each year during the estimated life of the project. As interest and lease rentals represent the return of funds employed, profit should be taken before their payment. Similarly, profit is taken before depreciation also because the amount of depreciation remains within the unit and it does not involve cash outflow.

As the purpose of calculating internal rate of return is to find out the income generating capacity of the total funds invested in the project, we should avoid distortions caused by changing the pattern of financing. The amount of interest and direct tax depends on debt-equity position. If the debt-equity ratio is high, the amount of interest will also be high and direct tax may be low because interest is a deductable item of expenditure for the purpose of direct tax. The amount of interest and direct tax will change with the change in debt-equity ratio. Therefore, while calculating internal rate of return for the purpose of comparative study of various projects regarding their income generating capacity, profit should be taken before payment of tax. In other words, interests, lease rentals and depreciation are added back to the profit before tax while taking cash inflow for calculating internal rate of return of various projects.

If we wish to calculate internal rate of return from the point of view of equity holders, benefits of the project should be taken after deduction of the tax. Net profits (Profit after deduction of the tax) should be taken in the cash inflow. In other words, profit after tax should be taken and interest, lease rentals and depreciation should be added back to it.

If we want to calculate economic rate of return from the point of view of economy, we may have to recast the cash flow on the basis of shadow prices which may reflect socially desirable use of each input and output and calculate internal rate of return from the recasted cash flow.

4. Residual or Terminal Value of the Project

Assets will have some value even at the end of the estimated life of the project. The residual value of assets should be added to cash inflow of the last year of the project life. The value of land can be taken at its cost price shown in cash outflow because it does not depreciate. The salvage value of the fixed assets (other than land) can be taken at 5% of cash outflow shown for them. Recovery of current assets used for working capital may be taken at the amount shown for their investment in the cash outflow.

5. Net Cash Receipt and Calculation of Internal Rate of Return

The difference between cash outflow and cash inflow is called net receipt. It may show negative figures in initial years owing to high outflow on investment in fixed assets and working capital assets. It may start showing positive figures when the level of production and profitability is increased. The net cash receipt may be discounted on various discounting rates to know the present value till a rate is ascertained on which the sum of positive present value is almost equal to the sum of negative present value or in other words, the net present value comes to almost zero. The rate of discounting on which the net present value comes to almost zero is called internal rate of return.

6. Pre-determined Cut-off Rate or Minimum Rate of Return

Although pre-determined cut-off rate is not required to calculate internal rate of return, it is necessary to compare the internal rate of return with the pre-determined cut-off rate to take a decision regarding financing a project. A project is generally accepted if the internal rate of return is higher than the pre-determined cut-off rate. The cut-off rate is decided on the basis of availability of capital in the economy and the desired growth rate. A relaxation in the cut-off rate can be allowed if a project is considered highly useful for the economy due to other considerations like increase in employment, distribution of income in favour of weaker sections, development of backward areas or saving/earning of foreign exchange.

❑❑❑

19 Appraisal of Management

A project which is considered technically feasible, commercially viable and financially sound may run into difficulties if it is not backed by sound and efficient management. The man behind the project is very important. It is said that a second rate project in the hands of first rate management is better than a first rate project in the hands of second rate management. Therefore, proper evaluation of management is a highly essential part of appraisal of a project.

A project is promoted by proprietary concern or partnership firm or private/public company or a co-operative society with all major management functions being done by one or two/three persons. It is essential to assess their knowledge, experience, integrity and organisational ability. In addition to obtaining information from the entrepreneur himself on his age, education, training, experience, involvement in any other business, financial resources, etc., informal enquiries may be made from other persons on his personal habits, living style, family history and social life. Each promoter has to come in contact with the banker for discussions regarding the project. The banker should make efforts to judge the competence of the promoter while discussing the proposal with him. The banker should just guide the discussion and encourage the entrepreneur to talk freely and frankly on the subject. Sometimes, the banker may ask indirect questions to get correct information. The competence of the entrepreneurs may be judged on the basis of following qualities in an entrepreneur:-

	Excellent	Good	Poor
1. Character	Honest and keeps his word under all circumstances	Makes sincere efforts to honour his word	Does not bother much to honour his word
2. Involvement in the Project	Highly involved - only source of income	Has other sources of income	Does as part-time work
3. Financial Resources	Has enough financial resources to meet not only the requirement of promoters contribution but also to finance small overrun in the cost of project	Has sufficient financial resources to meet the requirement of promoters' contribution	May have to borrow to meet the requirement of promoters' contribution
4. Competence	Has knowledge and experience relating to the project	Has either knowledge or experience relating to the project	Has neither knowledge nor experience relating to the project
5. Initiative	Highly alert to opportunities	Performs work with general guidance	Routine worker awaiting directions
6. Intelligence	Very quick in understand-	Understands the problem	Takes time to understand

	ing pertinent points of a problem	after reasonable explanation	the implications of any action
7. Drive and Energy	Always highly energetic	Fairly energetic	Avoids hard work
8. Self-Confidence	Believes strongly in himself and his abilities	Has faith in his abilities	Believes in luck
9. Frankness	Talks frankly about the weak points of the project	Prepared to talk on weak point of the project	Avoids talking on weak points of the project.
10. Patience	Has patience and does not expect quick results	Appreciates the time taken by lending institutions in appraisal	Wants quick results.

It is very difficult to get an entrepreneur having all the qualities. Even when a small entrepreneur is quite competent, he may not have proficiency in all the functions. Promoters having technical expertise may not have knowledge regarding finance and marketing. Similarly, promoters having knowledge regarding finance and marketing may not have necessary technical expertise with them. However, overall assessment of entrepreneur may be done on the basis of the above qualities. Every project has some critical areas. It may be ensured that the management has necessary key expertise required for the project. Banks may also provide necessary guidance to the entrepreneurs particularly in those areas where the entrepreneurs are not having sufficient expertise. Some banks have recruited agricultural experts to provide necessary guidance to the entrepreneurs. Concerned government departments, universities, research organisations, consultants, NABARD, etc. may also provide necessary guidance to entrepreneurs.

If the main person behind the unit is old and does not have good health, necessary arrangements may be made to train the second person. In the case of partnership firms, an assessment may also be made whether partners will be able to maintain good relations among them. In case of corporate sector/co-operative sector, necessary appraisal should be done regarding composition of Board of Directors, constitution and powers of Management Committee, Chief Executive and other Executives.

It may be ascertained in the beginning itself whether promoters will be able to bring a minimum percentage of promoters contribution stipulated for them. Banks should encourage small entrepreneurs. But a small man should promote a small enterprise. If a person is allowed to take up a project much higher than his capacity, he may have difficulties afterwards to run the unit.

□□□

20 Disbursement, Supervision, Follow-up and Recovery of Non-Performing Advances

Sanction of financial assistance after proper appraisal of the proposal alone is not sufficient. Prompt disbursement of funds for the creation of the proposed assets and close supervision and follow-up are also equally essential for successful implementation of the project and for the recovery of the loan.

After sanction of loan and execution of related documents, loan should be disbursed according to the requirements of funds for implementation of the project. Delay in disbursement may cause delay in implementation of the project which in turn may lead to overrun in the cost of the project and sometimes may even defeat the very purpose of the loan. For example, crop loan disbursed after the sowing season is over, will not serve its purpose and on the contrary, is more likely to be misutilised. If the project is small and the entire amount is required at one time only, the disbursement can be done in one installment. On the other hand, if the project is large and the requirements of funds are likely to be at varying intervals depending on the

4. Recovery under special Acts by State Government

Banks should take advantage of the legislation enacted by the State Government for speedy recovery of banks overdues. They should promptly file cases against willful defaulters with the concerned authorities. While filing the cases, they may ensure that necessary details and statements are submitted. The monetary ceiling of the cases to be referred to Lok Adalats, organized by the Civil Courts, has been enhanced recently from Rs.5 lakhs to Rs.20 lakhs. Representatives of banks should also attend the court on the fixed dates. The matters relating to recovery of advances should be discussed in the meetings of State Level Bankers' Committee (SLBC) and District Consultative Committee (DCC) and efforts should be made to obtain necessary help from State Government authorities. Proper co-ordination between banks and state authorities is necessary for the recovery of banks' dues.

5. Recovery campaign

It is necessary to organize recovery camps for effecting speedy recovery of banks' dues. A list of defaulters may be prepared for each village before the organization of the camp, with which Revenue Officers, Block Development Officers, Patwaris, Gram Sewaks, etc., may be closely associated. It is the moral responsibility of the Government agencies to assist the banks in recovery. It is suggested that recovery of loans should also be pursued at the time of loaning camps, especially for the loans advanced under Government sponsored programmes. In these camps, certificates may be awarded to those beneficiaries who have been prompt in repaying their loans. Efforts may be made to infuse the spirit of enthusiasm among the loanees for the prompt repayment of loans. Banks may also give special preference to those beneficiaries who have been regular in making repayment of loan.

6. Action regarding false affidavits and misutilisation of loans and subsidies

In order to simplify the procedure, production of no-dues certificate is not insisted upon from the borrowers and banks believe in affidavits filed by them. Similarly, banks do not make detailed enquiry about the eligibility of the borrowers as they put faith on the affidavits given by them. Therefore, it is necessary to create an atmosphere in which people are deterred from giving false affidavits. Strong action may be taken against borrowers for filing false affidavits. This would create an impact in the area against giving false affidavits and misutilising loan and subsidy.

7. Approaching debt recovery tribunals

An Act has been passed by the Parliament for setting up Debt Recovery Tribunals for expeditious adjudication and recovery of debts due to banks and financial institutions. The provisions of this act titled as "The Recovery of Debts due to Banks and Financial Institutions Act 1993", are applicable where the amount of debt due to any bank or financial institution or to a consortium of banks or financial institutions is not less than Rs.10 lakhs. The Central Government have, however, been empowered to reduce the lower limit of Rs.10 lakhs but not below Rs.1.00 lakh by issuing a Notification.

The "Debt Recovery Tribunals" are set up in various States and an Appellate Tribunal has also been set up at Mumbai to hear the appeals against the decisions of the Debt Recovery Tribunals. In order to discourage unnecessary delay in settlement of case, a provision has been made in the Act to deposit 75 per cent of the decretal amount before going for appeal. Banks should take following steps to ensure fast disposal of their claims lodged with debt recovery tribunals.

(i) In case of default, a decision to lodge an application with the Tribunal should be taken on commercial consideration without wasting time. Many borrowers try to gain time by making false promise of settlement/payment. In fact, filing the case before the Tribunal may induce the borrowers to enter into a reasonable compromise.

(ii) Recovery Department/Law Department should be given all relevant papers in the first instance itself.

(iii) Affidavits filed on behalf of the banks should be self-contained giving complete details of the case.

the borrower has to repay Rs.1000/- each year. If any extension has been given in the past due to natural calamities, the period of repayment can be further extended taking into account such extension.

(II) Shorter grace period

A borrower cannot repay the term loan till the income from the proposed investment materialises. It is necessary to allow grace period till the investment has fructified. NABARD has suggested minimum grace period to be given for various agricultural activities. Where the borrower has been given shorter grace period and, in consequence, has committed default, he may be allowed necessary grace period now. If necessary, total repayment period may also be extended in his case by the period now allowed as additional grace period. In case of projects where NABARD has not indicated grace period, banks should allow grace period according to the project implementation period and expected income. If implementation of the project is delayed, the grace period may also be suitably extended by banks.

(III) Incomplete investments

Banks should identify, on a case to case basis, the reasons for incomplete investments. If it is felt that such investment can be completed by providing further financial assistance, banks should provide supplementary finance after taking into consideration the technical requirements and viability of the proposal. In all such cases, banks should refix the loan repayment period after aggregating the old loan outstanding against the borrower, interest accrued thereon and the supplementary loan now given.

(IV) Infructuous investments

In case of infructuous investments, which cannot be rehabilitated by fresh induction of capital such as failed wells, banks may receive payment either from the insurance company or from failed wells relief scheme, if any, operating in the State. Similarly, in case of death of cattle, banks may receive payment from the insurance company. In such cases, banks may persuade the borrower to purchase another animal from the insurance amount instead of just adjusting it against the outstanding loan. If the beneficiary does not want to purchase another animal, banks can adjust the outstanding loan amount from the insurance money.

(V) Natural Calamities

In the case of natural calamities such as, droughts and floods, government authorities declare Annawari to indicate the extent to which the crops are damaged. Where such declaration is not made, banks may provide conversion facilities, provided the District Collector gives a certificate that crop yield is below 50 per cent of the normal yield and it is approved at the meeting of the District Consultative Committee. Short-term production loans, under such circumstances, may be converted into term loans on the due date of repayment. The repayment period of converted term loans may be fixed having regard to the intensity of crop loss/calamity and the overall repaying capacity of the borrower. For small and marginal farmers, interest on short-term loan which has been converted may be postponed and recovered in full at the time of next harvesting/marketing season without compounding of interest. The rate of interest on converted loans should be the same as that of charged on short-term loans. The scheme of crop insurance has been introduced for certain crop loans. If such a scheme is available in the area, the amount received from the insurance company may be utilized for repayment of the crop loans. Pending finalization of conversion/rescheduling/receipt of amount against crop insurance, the eligible cultivators should be disbursed fresh crop loans for the current season also. The instalments fixed for repayment of existing term loans may also have to be rescheduled/postponed keeping in view the repaying capacity of borrowers and the nature of the calamity. In case of droughts, floods, cyclones, etc., where only crop for that year is damaged and productive assets are not damaged, banks may postpone payment of instalments due in the year of natural calamity and extend the loan period by one year.

In case of floods or cyclones, where the productive assets are totally damaged, banks may have to provide fresh loans to the affected farmers of all categories for various development purposes, i.e., repairs to wells, pumpsets, shelters, etc., purchase of agricultural equipments, purchase of animals under dairy, poultry, piggery, goatery, etc., purchase/repairs of fishing boats, nets and other equipments, etc. Repayment of fresh term loans may be determined taking into account repayment commitment on the old term-loans and also the converted loans on account of postponement of repayment of crop loans. In such cases, the repayment period of total loan may be fixed after giving due regard to the repaying capacity of the borrower, nature of investment and economic life of the new assets financed.

(VI) Relief to farmers affected by natural calamities for at least two successive years

Reserve Bank issued a circular to banks in June, 2004 to provide relief to those farmers who have suffered production and income losses for two or more successive years on account of natural calamities such as drought/flood or other calamities which might have occurred in the districts for two or more successive years during the past five years, provided such districts had been declared as "calamity affected" by the State Government concerned. The relief may be provided as follows:-

(i) The outstanding in crop loans and agricultural term loans as on March 31, 2004 alongwith interest accrued may be converted into a term loan repayable over a period of five years with an initial moratorium of two years. It may be clarified that in respect of agricultural term loan account, only the overdue instalments including interest thereon receivable/accrued upto March 31, 2004 should be taken into account for the proposed restructuring. The repayment commitments in respect of instalments which have not fallen due will continue as originally scheduled.

(ii) In respect of crop loans and agricultural term loans which have already been restructured in the past on account of natural calamities, only the overdue instalments including interest thereon as on March 31, 2004 may be taken into account if they fall under the eligibility criteria of two or more successive years of natural calamities mentioned above. Overdue instalments including interest thereon as on March 31, 2004 in respect of existing restructured loan will be converted into a separate funded account. The repayment of this funded loan may be effected over the next five years with a moratorium of two years.

(iii) Interest may be charged on the restructured loan at the current rate of interest applicable for such loans.

(iv) List of districts eligible for coverage under this scheme may be circulated by the Convenor of State Level Bankers' Committee (SLBC) on the basis of the information gathered from respective State Governments.

On restructuring as indicated above, the concerned farmers would become eligible for fresh loans. The rescheduled/restructured loans as also the fresh loans issued to the farmers should be treated as current dues and should not be classified as non-performing assets (NPA). The fresh loans would be governed by the NPA norms as applicable to agricultural loans. In the case of rescheduled/restructured loans, the NPA norms would be applicable from the third year onwards, i.e., on expiry of the initial moratorium period of two years.

(VII) Relief to farmers in distress due to factors other than natural calamities

Sometimes farmers suffer production and income losses due to factors other than natural calamities declared by the State Government which result in their inability to meet repayment commitments. Pest attack, serious illness to self or dependents, failed well, theft of farm equipments, etc., may be some such instances. Default may lead to the loan accounts being declared NPAs by banks. Without continued financial support by banks, their future operations may suffer leading to further losses. They may be forced to borrow from non-institutional lenders at exorbitant interest rates. If the banking system is able to provide relief by way of restructuring of loans/rephasing of instalments and provide further funding for carrying on with their farming operations, the farmers may be able to recoup their losses and repay their loans to banks. Keeping in view this objective, Indian Banks' Association prepared a scheme for providing relief to farmers in arrears and circulated the same among banks on 7th July 2004. The details of the scheme are as follows:-

(i) Restructuring/rephasing of loans may be done subject to the bank being satisfied about the genuineness of the difficulties faced by the farmers leading to default. Farmers who have misutilised the finance provided or diverted the funds to other purposes may not be eligible for relief.

(ii) Accounts which are classified as standard, sub-standard or doubtful category may be eligible for relief under the scheme.

(iii) It is expected that the farmers seeking relief under the scheme should have displayed their willingness to repay the loan by making part payment say 20-30 per cent for instalments and interest, which had fallen due for payment.

(iv) The default should normally be attributable to one or more of the following causes:

(a) Failure of crop due to localized reasons

(b) Loss/theft of assets financed

(c) Failure of asset financed (say, failed well)

(d) Serious illness to self or dependents.

(v) The amount in arrears i.e. overdue principal and interest in respect of production loan and investment credit granted to the farmers may be converted into a term loan repayable over a period of 3 to 5 years depending on the income generation and repaying capacity. It may be clarified that repayment commitments in respect of term loan instalments, which have not fallen due, will continue as scheduled. While fixing repayment of the restructured loan, banks may, at their discretion, provide for an initial moratorium period in individual cases on merit taking into account the income generation and repayment capacity.

(vi) For the purpose of NPA norms, the existing classification of the accounts restructured should be continued. However, fresh loans issued by banks to such farmers may be treated as standard assets.

Banks may frame a policy, with the approval of their Board of Directors, on the basis of above model scheme circulated by Indian Banks' Association to provide relief to farmers in arrears.

9. Compromise with borrowers

A compromise may be called a negotiated settlement in which the borrower agrees to pay a certain amount to the banker after getting certain concessions. A large number of compromise proposals are being approved by banks with a view to reducing the NPAs and recycling the funds instead of resorting to expensive recovery proceedings spread over a long period. The advantages and disadvantages of a compromise proposal are given as under:

Compromise Proposals

Advantages	Disadvantages
(i) Reduction in NPAs	(i) Loss suffered by the bank as a result of difference between loan outstanding and the amount actually received.
(ii) Recycling of funds	
(iii) Savings in time and expenses involved in legal proceedings	(ii) While calculating the loss, unapplied interest for the period upto which payment is likely to be received after compromise and other notional waivers, if any, should be added to the outstanding balance.
(iv) Tax relief due to writing-off the unrealised portion of the outstanding.	

In view of the advantages and disadvantages of the compromise proposals, it is necessary to have proper scrutiny of the proposals. While entering into the compromise proposals, following points should be taken into consideration:

(i) Compromise proposals should be accepted by a bank keeping in view the guidelines given in its Loan Recovery Policy.

(ii) A proper distinction should be made between willful defaulters and the borrowers defaulting in repayments due to circumstances beyond their control. Normally, compromise proposals should be accepted from non-willful defaulters only. If any compromise is done with a willful defaulter, compelling reasons for resorting to the same should be spelt out in the note/memorandum prepared for its approval.

(iii) Where security is available, its realizable value should be assessed taking into consideration its location, present condition, marketable title and possession.

(iv) Worth of a guarantor, if any, should be assessed. Many a time banks may be able to recover the amount with the help of the guarantee available.

(v) Borrower's credibility and his repaying capacity should be assessed if recovery is to be made in instalments as per the compromise proposal.

(vi) Staff accountability should be examined expeditiously and completed within a time frame.

(vii) All compromise proposals approved by any functionary should be promptly reported to the next higher authority for post-facto scrutiny.

It may be observed from the above that compromise has to be done with great care after taking into consideration various factors. As no standard formula can be prescribed for entering into a compromise proposal, banks should consider the above points while taking a decision on a compromise proposal. .

10. One time settlement scheme for small and marginal farmers

Reserve Bank has advised banks to formulate guidelines with the approval of their Board of Directors on one-time settlement (OTS) for small and marginal farmers, who have been declared as defaulters as on June 24, 2004 and have become ineligible for fresh credit.

Accordingly, banks have formulated OTS guidelines with the approval of their Boards giving details of settlement formula, sanctioning authority and procedure to be followed. All applications for OTS received from defaulters should be processed within one month of their receipt. Banks should ensure that the settlement is done without discrimination and in a transparent manner so that farmers can access fresh credit.

11. Non-Performing Advances

A proper system for recognition of income, classification of assets and provisioning for bad-debts on prudential basis is necessary if balance sheet of a bank is to reflect its actual financial health. The Committee on Financial system under the Chairmanship of Shri M Narasimham has examined this issue and recommended that a policy of income recognition should be objective and based on record of recovery rather than on any subjective considerations. Similarly, the classification of assets and provisioning for them should be done on the basis of certain objective criteria which would ensure a uniform and consistent application of norms. On the basis of the recommendations of the Narasimham Committee in this regard, the Reserve Bank had issued guidelines to banks in April 1992 which have been revised from time to time on the basis of the experience gained and suggestions received from banks. The present position of the guidelines for identification of Non-Performing Assets (NPAs) regarding direct advances to agriculture is as under:

In order to align the repayment dates with the harvesting of crops, the Reserve Bank has decided that with effect from September 30, 2004 the following revised norms would be applicable to all direct agricultural advances:

(i) A loan granted for short duration crops would be treated as NPA, if the instalment of principal or interest thereon remains overdue for two crop seasons.

(ii) A loan granted for long duration crops would be treated as NPA, if the instalment of principal or interest thereon remains overdue for one crop season.

For the above purpose, "long duration" crops would be crops with crop season longer than one year and crops, which are not "long duration" crops, would be treated as "short duration" crops.

The crop season for each crop, which means the period up to harvesting of the crops raised, would be as determined by the State Level Bankers' Committee (SLBC) in each state.

Depending upon the duration of crops raised by an agriculturist, these NPA norms would also be applicable to agricultural term loans availed of by him.

The above norms will be applicable only in respect of direct finance to farmers for following agricultural purposes:

may be adopted wherever group pressure on borrowers may be required.

(vii) Recovery action may start with a reminder letter to be sent to a borrower. A diary note may be kept to send second reminder if no response is received. Reminders may continue to be sent until the recovery is made. The contents of the letters may be such that the reader is motivated to come to the branch for the payment of instalment. The language may be hard gradually with subsequent reminders.

(viii) All borrowers may not respond to the reminder and therefore it is essential to meet them personally. During the visit, the branch staff should enquire about the difficulties of the borrower in payment of instalments and request him to co-operate with the branch by even making a small payment.

(ix) Small borrowers may be advised to open a "pigmy deposit" or "daily deposit scheme" towards the payment of loan instalment. Visit to a borrower's premises helps in recovery. Sometimes, it may be necessary to make more than one visit to convince the borrower to repay the bank dues.

(x) Wherever the borrowers are not convinced by the branch staff, it may be necessary to bring pressure on them. Such pressures may be brought from friends and relatives, co-borrowers, social workers, etc. If it is necessary to pressurize borrowers with a visit by a group of branch staff, it may also be tried out. Efforts may be made to take assistance from the development agencies such as Block Development Officer, Revenue Officer, Gram Panchayat, etc.

(xi) During the visit to the borrower's premises/ discussions with the borrower, if it is felt that the borrower has genuine difficulties in payment of interest and loan instalments, the repayment period may be rescheduled in such a way that unpaid dues may be paid the way it suits the borrower's liquidity position. If necessary, rehabilitation programme may be initiated so that recovery can take place after sometime. The branch may co-operate with the borrowers who are honest and hardworking.

(xii) In case of willful defaulters, the branch should recall the advances and send a legal notice. In that case, the recovery will be made through legal process of the court which is time consuming.

(xiii) To avoid time consuming legal process, compromise can be considered within the guidelines issued by the Regional Office/Zonal Office.

(xiv) The meeting of the Recovery Team should be held frequently to monitor the action plan and make changes in the original plan, wherever found necessary.

Various steps to be taken by the branch for reducing NPAs, can be summarized in the chart given below:

Various steps of Recovery Strategy of a Branch

↓

Organise staff meeting and form recovery team

↓

Decide recovery strategy of the branch

↓

Issue reminders to the defaulters

↓

Frequent visit to borrowers

↓

Bringing pressure on borrowers

↓

Reschedulement of loan instalments, if necessary

↓

Rehabilitation programme in deserving cases

↓

Approaching the Lokadalat

↓

Recovery through legal process

Recovery performance of the branch may improve considerably, if the above steps are seriously taken by its manager and other staff members.

Conclusion

Effective supervision and follow-up is necessary for ensuring proper utilization of assets and recovery of loans. The experience gained during supervision and follow-up also helps in understanding the problems at the grass root level and improving the lending procedures. Proper co-ordination between banks and various government agencies is necessary for the effective supervision and follow-up and recovery of banks' loans. Problems of co-ordination, if any, may be discussed in the various meetings being conducted under the Lead Bank scheme to find a solution. If any borrower has genuine difficulties, banks may adopt a sympathetic attitude and make all possible efforts to solve his problems. Wherever necessary, rephasing of repayment schedule may be done. However, strong action should be taken against willful defaulters. The success of lending to agriculture is attained not only by achieving the targets of sanction and disbursement but also by getting prompt repayment of loans which is essential for recycling of funds and further advances to this sector. Sanction, disbursement, supervision and follow-up are inter-related and it is necessary to give equal importance to all these aspects.

*Repayment instalments fixed should be adequate to repay the portion of pumpset loan with interest fully within a period of nine years i.e. the maximum period allowed for repayment of a loan for pumpset.

❑❑❑

Annexure

Repayment Period Schedule for Term Loans provided to Small Farmers

Sr. No	Nature of Investment	Minimum & Maximum Repayment Period in years (including gestation Period)	Duration of Loan Instal-ments	Gestation Grace Period
(1)	(2)	(3)	(4)	(5)
1.	Dugwell with or without pumpset	11-15*	Yearly	23 months
2.	Deepening of well	5	Yearly	Nil
3.	Pumpset	9	Yearly	Nil
4.	Filter point+ pumpset	11-15*	Yearly	11 months
5.	Borewell	11-15	Yearly	11 months
6.	Shallow Tubewells	11-15	Yearly	11 months
7.	Persian wheels/ Rahat	5	Yearly	Nil
8.	Sprinkler/drip irrigation	10-15	Yearly	11 months
9.	Land Development	9-15	Yearly	23 months
10.	Soil conservation	9-15	Yearly	23 months
11.	Ravine Reclamation	9-15	Yearly	23 months
12.	Lift Irrigation	11-15	Yearly	23 months
13.	Lining of Water Courses	9-15	Yearly	11 months
14.	OFD under CAD Project	11-15	Yearly	23 months
15.	Cross-bred Cow(s)	5	Monthly/ Quarterly	Repayment to be lin-ked with lactation period

(1)	(2)	(3)	(4)	(5)
40.	Casurina Plantation	7-12	Yearly	6 Years
41.	Coconut Plantation	14-15	Yearly	8-9 Years
42.	Grape Cultivation	7-9	Yearly	3 Years
43.	Orange Plantation	10-15	Yearly	5- 7 Years
44.	Betelvine Plantation	5-10	Yearly	1 Year
45.	Arecanut replantation	13-15	Yearly	7-8 Years
46.	Pineapple Cultivation	4-5	Yearly	1-2 Years
47.	Gobar Gas (Upto 5 M3)	7	Yearly	-
48.	Farm Forestry	7-10	Yearly	6 Years
49.	Storage Bins	3-5	Half Yearly	-

NB: If desired by the beneficiary farmer, he may repay the loan amount earlier than the prescribed period depending on his incremental income/ability.

21 Suggestions for Increasing Credit Flow to Agriculture

Many banks have not achieved the target of 18 per cent of net bank credit stipulated by the Reserve Bank for lending to agriculture. While presenting the budget for 2004-05 in the Parliament, Hon'ble Union Minister for Finance has announced about his intention to double the flow of agricultural credit in 3 years. In order to achieve the target announced by the Finance Minister, banks should achieve a minimum 30 per cent annual growth in disbursements under agricultural credit. Several steps have been taken by the Reserve Bank from time to time to increase the flow of credit to agriculture. The Reserve Bank äppointed a "High Level Committee on Agricultural Credit (Chairman.: Shri R V Gupta) which submitted its report in April 1998. On the basis of the recommendations of this committee, the Reserve Bank advised banks for several improvements in credit delivery system to agriculture. With a view to further improve the flow of credit to agriculture, the Reserve Bank appointed "Advisory Committee on Flow of Credit to Agriculture and Related Activities from the Banking System" (Chairman: Prof. V S Vyas) which submitted its report in June 2004. On the basis of the recommendations of this Committee, certain modifications have been done in the guidelines issued by the Reserve Bank of India on flow of credit to agriculture.

Banks may consider following suggestions to increase credit to agriculture and recovering the same for recycling the funds and avoiding increase in NPAs:

1. Financing emerging activities included in agriculture

Certain emerging activities have been included in agriculture for the purpose of providing finance to them. Banks may finance these new activities to enable them to increase their lending to agriculture. For example, financing to Agriclinics and Agribusiness Centres has been included as an activity for direct finance to agriculture. Financing to dealers in drip irrigation/sprinkler irrigation/agricultural machinery upto Rs.20 lakhs per dealer is considered as financing to agriculture, irrespective of their location. Similarly, financing for construction and running of storage facilities (including cold storage units) designed to store agricultural produce/products are counted as finance to agriculture, irrespective of their location. Investment by banks in securitized assets representing direct/indirect lending to agriculture is now treated as their direct/indirect lending to agriculture. Banks may take necessary steps to finance these activities which have been included in financing to agriculture for the purpose of achieving the target.

2. Financing cultivation of vegetables

India is the second largest (next to China) producer of vegetables in the world accounting for about 10 per cent of the world's production of vegetables. Vegetables can be grown quickly, provides more jobs and generates higher income compared to cereals. Vegetables can be grown on small land area. Tremendous progress has been made in the development of hybrids in tomato, brinjal, chilli, bell pepper, cabbage, cauliflower, cucumber, muskmelon, watermelon, carrot and onion to provide higher yield to farmers. Availability of good quality seeds is very important for increasing production of vegetables. As the cost of seeds is only a very small fraction of total cost of inputs involved in growing vegetables, availability of good quality seeds may not be a problem. But vegetables are perishable and their markets are less developed. As the demand for vegetables is growing fast for internal consumption and exports, banks can finance for cultivation of vegetables wherever the problem of marketing is solved. For example, demand for mushrooms is increasing at 7 per cent per annum resulting in widening gap between demand and supply which gives an opportunity to capitalize on the gap.

3. Financing production of fruits

India is the second largest producer of fruits after Brazil contributing more than 10 per cent of the world production. A wide variety of tropical fruits (mango, banana, citrus fruits, papaya, guava, sapota and grapes), temperate fruits (apple, pear, peach and walnut) and arid zone fruits (anola, ber, pomegranate, annona, fig, phalsa, etc.) are produced in the country. Diverse agro climate across the country provides for extending period of availability and differential quality. Extended harvesting season for the export oriented fruits like mangoes, grapes and pomegranates can be a strength for us in exploiting the export markets. Banks generally hesitate to finance for fruit plantations due to long gestation period involved in it. However, if land is taken as security, banks may provide finance for fruit plantations. The long gestation period should not create a problem after having land as security. While financing fruit plantations, disbursement of loan may be done in instalments depending on growth of fruit plants.

4. Financing of cultivation of medicinal plants

Cultivation of medicinal and aromatic plants has great scope due to their increasing demand from pharmaceutical, perfumery, flavour, cosmetic and food industries. Collection of medicinal plants from wild/forest sources is not sufficient according to the quantity and quality required. In order to meet the growing demand, it is necessary to develop cultivation of medicinal and aromatic plants. Sarpgandha (Rauvolfia serpentina), periwinkle (Catharanthus rosells), safed musli (Chlorophytum borivilianum), ashwagandha (Withana sornnifera), isabgol (Plantago ovata), senna (Cassta senna) and aloe (Aloe vera) are some of the medicinal plants cultivated on a larger scale for the regular supply of raw material to pharmaceutical industries. Central Institute of Medicinal and Aromatic Plants (CIMAP) has developed technology package for cultivation of several medicinal and aromatic plants. The high yielding varieties of menthol mint (mentha arvensis) developed by CIMAP has got wide acceptability from the farmers due to higher returns and also from industries due to its quality. Many small and marginal farmers in north Indian plains have earned very good income by adopting this crop. Similarly, cultivation of several medicinal and aromatic plants can be undertaken depending on the agro-climatic conditions of the area. Banks may provide finance for cultivation of these plants wherever marketing support is available from user industries/traders/exporters. They may finance directly to the farmers or through user industries/traders. Whenever banks finance through user industries/traders, they may ensure that interest of the farmers is protected and their products are sold at a reasonable price.

5. Prompt decision on loan applications

As per the guidelines issued by the Reserve Bank, all loan applications upto a credit limit of Rs.25,000/- should be disposed off within a fortnight and those applications which are for above Rs.25,000/- should be disposed off within 8-9 weeks. However, in practice, banks are taking longer time in disposing off the loan applications. Most of the banks have simplified the application form and delegated powers to branch managers/regional managers. However, the procedure adopted by them is time consuming. Sometimes, applications are collected and disposed off in the last quarter of the year to achieve the target. Bunching of applications is not proper for the banks as well as borrowers. Appraisal techniques or check-lists given in this book should be used as an aid with discretion rather than as routine tool. The appraisal of a proposal regarding a small loan may need lesser information as compared to a proposal relating to a large amount. Sometimes a particular information may not be readily available. In such cases, judgement should be applied to determine the most suitable alternative. After sanction, disbursement should be done promptly. As the banks have already standardized the documentation, disbursement should not be delayed without valid reasons.

6. Adequate financial assistance

Banks should provide adequate financial assistance after deducting the margin money, if any, for the proposals approved by them. Under-financing of a proposal leads to dependence on outside sources and delay in implementation of the project. If adequate financial assistance is not given, the farmer may be forced to borrow from moneylenders or other non-institutional sources at a high rate of interest which may reduce his income and repaying capacity.

7. Reasonable repayment schedule

The repayment schedule may be fixed according to the expected surplus available with the beneficiaries after providing for their consumption needs instead of an adhoc manner. Repayment capacity can be worked out as under:

$$R = Y - (C+L+K+M)$$

R = Repayment capacity
Y = Expected income after the proposed investment
C = Existing family expenditure
L = Repayment due on existing liabilities
K = Expected increase in family expenditure owing to increase in income
M = Margin for unforeseen events

While calculating expected income, sale price of the product and various expenses should be estimated on realistic basis. Necessary gestation period should be allowed keeping in view the time to be taken in commencement of production and earning surplus from the project. If the repayment schedule is not fixed according to the repaying capacity, the bank may have a bad loan from the beginning itself. A small farmer may need a longer repayment period than a large farmer because surplus available with him after meeting his expenditures may be lower than that with the large farmer.

8. Sanction of sufficient limits under Kisan Credit Card Scheme

While fixing the limits under the Kisan Credit Card Scheme, banks should take into account the entire production credit requirement for full year including the credit requirement of farmers for ancillary activities. Scale of finance taken by banks should be sufficient to meet the requirements of capital intensive agriculture, using improved technologies and superior inputs. Banks should not have rigid approach to follow the scale of finance/unit cost suggested by District Level Technical Committee (DLTC)/State Level Technical Committee (SLTC). The scale suggested by DLTC/SLTC is only indicative and bankers should have freedom to increase or decrease the same depending on the local conditions. Adverse remarks made by branch inspectors and statutory auditors leads to rigidity of the bankers in adhering to scale of finance suggested by DLTC/SLTC. Therefore, operating staff and other concerned officials should be provided clarity on the subject to meet the need-based requirements of the farmees.

9. Tie up arrangements with major tractor and farm machinery manufacturers

Banks may enter into agreements with tractor and farm machinery manufacturers for financing their products. While entering into such an arrangement, banks should take necessary precautions to ensure that farmers are able to receive the tractor or other farm machinery at the minimum possible price. One public sector bank has entered into an agreement with a tractor manufacturer which enables the farmers to purchase the tractors at a discounted price and obtain enhanced warranty for the maintenance of the tractors. Such arrangements may help the farmers in getting loans easily and ensures proper utilization of the loan amount.

10. Tie up arrangements for contract farming

Contract farming has potential of extending credit to farmers, especially to the small/marginal farmers, share croppers and tenant farmers. As the demand for processed food is increasing in recent years, banks can play an important role for encouraging contract farming by initiating discussions with the processing firms, concerned govt. agencies and voluntary organizations.

electric motors, installing drip/sprinkler irrigation system, purchase or replacement of tractors and farm equipment, purchase of dairy animals, etc. While providing term loans, banks should also consider issue of Kisan Credit Card to meet the requirement of production credit. It may help the farmers in taking full advantage of their investments. Banks can expand the flow of credit to agriculture. It may also help them in proper supervision and follow-up to recover the advance.

16. Linking of credit with marketing

Banks may finance post-harvest operations which may help the farmers to get higher price of their products. Advances upto Rs.5 lakhs to farmers against pledge/hypothecation of agricultural produce (including warehouse receipts) are considered as direct finance to agriculture. Such type of finance links crop loans with marketing which may help the banks in recovering the credit provided for raising crops.

17. Branch wise targets for new accounts

Banks should fix branch wise targets for its rural and semi-urban branches to finance new accounts. This will help to finance even those farmers who hesitate to approach banks. Targets should be fixed not only for total disbursements by the branch but also for financing new accounts. These targets may be fixed on the basis of the size of the branch and potentiality of the area served by the branch.

18. Improvement in working of specialized agricultural branches

Banks have set up specialized agricultural finance branches at several places. The working of these branches should be improved to finance innovative high technical projects in agriculture and allied activities like aquaculture, horticulture, tissue culture, etc. These branches may be used to disseminate information relating to agricultural operations. They should be able to provide guidance to other branches of the bank and also farmers regarding cultivation of high value crops and using new technologies.

19. One-time settlement scheme

As advised by the Reserve Bank in June 2004, banks have formulated one-time settlement scheme for small and marginal farmers. All applications received under this scheme should be processed within one month of their receipt so that the problem of NPAs is solved on one side and the farmers covered under this scheme may be able to receive fresh finance in due course on the other side.

20. Effective supervision and follow-up

After sanction and disbursement of the loan, supervision and follow-up is highly essential to recover the advance. Various techniques mentioned in the chapter of supervision and follow-up should be applied for recovering the advances and avoiding NPAs. Sometimes, banks are giving higher importance to sanction of loans than supervision and follow-up which is not correct. Supervision and follow-up is equally important for success of any loan scheme.

21. Human Resources Development

As training given for a short period cannot be a substitute of education received at graduation/post-graduation level, banks may recruit agricultural officers having necessary qualifications in agriculture/allied activities to be posted in head office, regional offices and critical rural branches. A few banks have already initiated action in this direction. It is also necessary to change the mindset of those branch managers who consider agricultural lending as highly risky proposition. In fact, lending to agriculture can prove a very good source of retail lending in our country. If it is felt that approaching large number of small borrowers is costly, banks may outsource certain activities to other agencies operating at the village level like Self-Help Groups, panchayat raj institutions, input suppliers, tractor manufacturers, corporate bodies involved in contract farming, post-office, etc. Banks may take help of unemployed youth in rural areas on job work basis. Such type of approach has been adopted by a few banks for retail lending in the area of financing consumer durables and houses. Such approach may also be tried for retail lending to agriculture.

Conclusion

Above suggestions may help banks in increasing their lending to agriculture which is highly necessary for the development of our economy and raising the income level of farmers. Credit is required to improve the process of agricultural development through the creation of irrigation facilities, energisation of pumpsets, land development, moisture conservation, farm mechanization, plantation and forestry development, creation of agriclinics and agribusiness centres, etc. The credit provided through Kisan Credit Cards helps in using improved inputs and technology resulting into increase in per hectare productivity. Financing of dairy, poultry, fishery development and other allied activities may help in increasing the income of farmers and reducing unemployment, rural poverty, rural-urban migration and income disparities.

If necessary precautions are taken for sanction, disbursement, supervision and follow-up, financing to agriculture can be a profitable activity for banks, particularly for banks having large number of semi-urban and rural branches. Banks should increase their finance to agriculture not only to meet their social commitments but also to raise their profitability. This Handbook may help the banks' staff working at grass root level in accomplishing this noble task.

❑❑❑

Index

Index

But the story was not finished—such was the implied menace that sounded, with a metallic ring, from the concluding words of the statesman hidden in the soldier. The Directors understood his meaning, knew that the threat was for them. But Barras pulled himself together, delivered a fulsome speech, and then, for the first and last time embraced the little general, whose wife he would infinitely rather have held in his arms.

Josephine, where was Josephine? Why was she absent on the great occasion? No one knows with certainty how or where she spent these weeks. She did not reach Paris until a month after Napoleon. When she came, she was serene, charming, rather tired. In Paris, she promptly resumed her old life, and took up the threads of some of her old amours.

Meanwhile, another woman had entered Napoleon's orbit. She was handsome, but was too intelligent to please him. This was Necker's daughter, Madame de Staël. An influential woman, as well as interesting; it was at her suggestion that Talleyrand had been appointed Minister for Foreign Affairs. She besieged Bonaparte with letters; she would fain have harnessed him to her chariot wheels, but he jibbed at the prospect. Now, when she had met him in the flesh, he parried her advances with a few civilities; but he could not prevent this talented woman from seeing further into his mind than most men had succeeded in doing. Here is her pen picture of the commander, an early impression:

"His face is thin and pale, but not unpleasing. Being short of stature, he looks better on horseback than on foot. In social life, he has rather awkward manners, though he is by no means shy. When he is on the alert, he is a little contemptuous in his bearing; whereas his natural demeanour is a trifle common. The contemptuous pose suits him better... When he is speaking, I am enthralled by an impression of his pre-eminence, though he has none of the qualities of the men of the study and of society. If he recounts his personal experiences, he often discloses the lively imagination of an Italian.... But I always become aware of a profound irony, which nothing escapes, neither the sublime, nor the beautiful, nor even his own fame..... I have known not a few men of note, some of restore the morale of the others. After a brief pause, he was ready with encouraging words: "So we are cut off in Egypt. Good. We must keep our heads above the stormy waters; the sea will soon be smooth once more. –Perhaps we are predestined to change the face of the East. Here we must remain, or achieve a grandeur like that of the ancients!"

A terrible reverse! What will Paris say? He is not admiral of the fleet, and was not present at the battle of the Nile, but the disaster will certainly affect his prestige. How are we to get home again? On Turkish ships? But will the sultan remain neutral any longer? He has been wavering between Russia and France, and will be likely, now, to turn against the French. England, too. The fleet annihilated; thirteen battleships gone. How many years will it be before we can again face England on the high seas? A decade, perhaps. Allah is Allah, but behind what cloud was my star hidden?

No, not my star! For, when he reports the defeat, he conceals nothing, but is careful to explain in his official dispatches that fortune had delayed Nelson's return until the French had been able to secure their footing in Egypt.

Weeks of uncertainty. This is a new phase in Bonaparte's life. He must remain inactive, while he waits for news that will throw light upon the state of affairs in Europe. If England keeps good watch, perhaps no letter will be able to cross the seas. For the first time in his career, he begins to wonder how he can kill time. The administration of a whole army, the suppression of disturbances, the rehabilitation of crumbling fortresses-these are no more than variants of idleness. The hours hand heavily, and he becomes more nervous, more fanciful than of yore. Bourrienne tries to tranquillize the commander's mind, saying: "Let us wait till we hear what the Directory proposes to do!"

"The Directory? A dung-heap! The Directors hate me, and will leave me here to rot!"

If he could only ride! But it is too hot, at any rate to ride in uniform, and an attempt to wear Arab clothing has been aban-

These and similar items catch Bonaparte's eyes as he flutters the newspapers. Day by day he can read an abundance of details, mingled truth and falsehood, concerning his aspect, demeanour, and dress. Even the opposition press pins its hopes on him: "His Egyptian campaign has miscarried; but what does it matter? He is satisfied with having undertaken it, and it is difficult to say whither his rashness may lead. All the same, his bold ventures restore our courage." He is received with acclamation, and his plans are consolidated.

But his wife is away. When the news that he had landed reached Paris, she was dining with Gohier, the first of the five Directors. She, and her host were equally alarmed. Both had uneasy consciences, and now the volcano was rumbling beneath them. Some time ago, Barras (who during this period seems still to have been an occasional recipient of her favours) had advised her to procure a divorce from the absent and almost vanished adventurer, and to marry handsome Hippolyte. She had received no letters from Napoleon. If he had written any, they must have miscarried. But her brother-in-law's hostile attitude showed her what was in the wind. Barras was right. She would do well to act first. — Then Paris was electrified by the news of Napoleon's great victory over the Turks. Perhaps it would be wiser, after all, to stay in her present safe harbourage. Unstable and frivolous, she had of late been conquetting with the thought of reconciliation. A glance at her own image in the mirror, a knowledge of the way she could turn men's heads, sufficed to convince her of the possibility.

Now, at Gohier's table she pulls herself together, and her host tries to outdo her in self-command. They drink to the General's return. She hurries home, packs up all that can set off her beauty to the best advantage, and in a trice is driving southward. As her carriage rattles past the barrier, she thinks: "Act promptly, and take the enemy by surprise—is not that the secret of his military success? On the return journey, I shall be with him day and night, and shall win him over before the tale-bearers can get at him!"

But she misses him, learns that he has passed her, and hastens back to Paris. She has lost three precious days, during quickly, he makes for the back room.

During the Italian campaign, Bonaparte was under fire in the front ranks on several occasions. At Lodi, and again at Arcola, he had been in imminent peril. But here, he was for the first time involved in a rough-and-tumble affray where firearms and cold steel are against the rules. Towards the close of his career, he was to have a similar experience. In such a chance medley, he could not draw his sword. He must assume his antagonists to be unarmed, though some of them were in truth armed. To use his sword seemed to be in hopeless conflict with the fundamental principles of the coup d'état—as he envisaged it.

But at length he has to abandon these principles of his. In person, he has been rescued from the blows of his adversaries, but their fists have shattered his doctrine. Force has been used against him. He strides furiously up and down the room; his pride is touched to the quick; in his anger, he scratches his cheek till his finger-nails are bloody. Blood? In an instant he has recovered his composure. This blood will be most useful! Attempted assassination in the council chamber! He will show his soldiers how these villains have manhandled the commander of Paris! The pretence that the other side had been the first to break the law, frees him from the tyranny of his principles.

In the assembly hall, meanwhile, Lucien is fighting for him. "Hors la loi! Outlaw him!" cry most of the deputies. Lucien tries to still the clamour with voice and bell. The attempt is in vain. A formal demand is made for a vote on Bonaparte's outlawry, and everyone knows what that means in revolutionary Paris. Since there is no other way out of the difficulty, Lucien, whose pose today is that of the defender of law and order, with an imposing gesture throws off his toga and storms out of the hall. None too soon!

He finds his brother with the troops. Napoleon had turned pale when the news had been brought of the vote of outlawry. Then, running to the window, he called to the troops: "To arms!" Going out, he mounted, and was quick to notice that the soldiers

"In these sittings," says Roéderer, "the First Consul manifested those remarkable powers of attention and precise analysis which enabled him for ten hours at a stretch to devote himself to one object, or to several, without ever allowing himself to be distracted by memory or by errant thoughts."

Bonaparte is filled with respect for the logicality and mental energy of the octogenarian Tronchet; and the old lawyer responds with admiration for the analytical faculty and the sense of justice of the young Consul, who, in the case of every ordinance, asks: "Is it just?" and "Is it useful?" He is never tired of enquiring how predecessors have solved the problems under consideration, paying special attention to Roman law and to the legal institutions of Frederick the Great.

Not only are thirty-seven laws discussed at this table; furthermore, the Consul propounds question after question concerning other matters. How is bread made? How shall we make new money? How shall we establish security? He makes all his ministers send detailed reports, and this is a great tax upon their energies. But he affects not to notice that they are overworked, and when they get home they often find letters from him requiring an immediate answer. On of his collaborators writes: "Ruling, administering, negotiating—with that orderly intelligence of his, he gets through eighteen hours work every day. In three years he has ruled more than the kings ruled in a century." He spoke to every expert in the phraseology of the craft, so that none of them could ever plead in excuse that his questions had not been understood. Even the most hidebound royalists were amazed at the technical accuracy of his enquiries.

His unfailing memory was the artillery wherewith he defended the fortress of his brain. Ségur, returning from an official inspection of the fortifications on the north coast, sends in a report. "I have read your report," says the First Consul. "It is accurate, but you have forgotten two of the four guns in Ostend. They are on the high road behind the town." Ségur is astonished to find that Napoleon is right. His report deals with thousands of guns, scattered all over the place, but the chief pounces on the omission of two.

"If the cold should be sharp, as it was in 1789, you must have fires kept alight in the churches and market-places, so that as many people as possible can warm themselves."–"The winter is very severe, meat is dear, we must provide work in Paris. Get on with the cutting of the Ourcq canal with the construction of the Quai Desaix with the paving of the back streets."–"The law directs that all beggars shall be laid by the heels. Were we to do nothing more than this, our conduct would be barbarous and absurd. Arrest them, certainly, that you may give them work and food. We must have several homes of refuge in every department." – "There are a great many out-of-work shoemakers, hatters, tailors, and saddlers. See to it that five hundred pairs of shoes are made every day." He writes to the Minister for War saying that special orders for supplies for the artillery are to be issued. To the Minister for Home Affairs: "We must provide work, especially this month before the holidays. Issue an order that in May and June two thousand of the Saint Antoine workmen are to supply chairs, chest of drawers, armchairs, etc.... Send me your proposals tomorrow, so that a beginning may be made promptly."

He reads a by-law that no one wearing a workman's blouse is to walk through the Tuileries garden. Instantly he has the regulation cancelled, and gives express permission for such people to go through. He leans of a proposal to close the public reading-rooms: "I won't allow anything of the kind. I have not forgotten my own experience, how useful it was to know of a well-warmed room where I could read the newspapers and recent pamphlets. I will not allow others who are as poor as I was then to be robbed of these comforts." In the Théâtre Francais, the stalls are to be very cheap on Sundays, "so that the people may enjoy the performance." There are to be no gambling hells in France: "They bring families to ruin and I should set a bad example were I to tolerate them."

By his new education law, he establishes public elementary schools, middle schools, lycées, and technical colleges, throughout the country. There are to be six thousand free scholarships, and a third of these are to be reserved for the sons of specially deserving own future, advises court martial and the severest measures, knowing that the moral reprobation thus aroused will, in the end, prove disastrous to Napoleon. Brother Joseph is alarmed at the same thought. He reminds Napoleon of the veneration they had shared for the great Condé during their cadet days; of the verses they had recited about the hero of the seventeenth century. Was the only remaining descendant of that famous man to be slaughtered?

"I have made up my mind to pardon him," answers the Consul. "But that is not sufficient. I feel that I am strong enough to have him fighting on my side."

Joseph returns home, able to reassure Madame de Staël and his other guests.

The duke, who was two years younger than Napoleon, and who would probably have won renown but for the peculiar political circumstances which had brought Napoleon fame and power, was tried by court martial the same evening. With a brave and knightly bearing, he faced the twelve staff officers who formed the court, while a member of the Council of State, acting as prosecutor, asked the question that had been drafted by Napoleon.

"Did you never have any dealings with English agents?"–"No."–"Was it not your intention, if Pichegru's conspiracy had been successful, to cross the Rhine and invade Alsace?"–"No"–"Have you been in receipt of an English pension?"–"Yes"–"Did you wish to enter the English service?"–"Yes, in order to free my country."–"This means that you placed yourself at England's disposal in order to take up arms against France?"–"How can a Condé return to his homeland except under arms?"

A death sentence follows, and next day at dawn the Duke of Enghien is shot.

In one respect the treatment of the Duke of Enghien was definitely illegal. The French had no right to kidnap him in foreign territory and to bring him across the frontier. Once he was on French soil, there was legal warrant for condemning him to death as a person who (according to his own admission) desired by force of arms to overthrow the extant form of State. With the primary his motives must be mixed; in part obscurely felt, in part coldly calculated.

He is half an oriental, and it tickles his fancy to bestow diadems as he used to bestow sword and snuff-boxes; but all the same, he warily contrives that power shall be given to those only on whom he can rely. Well, what is thicker than blood? Even his companions-in-arms seem to him less trustworthy than his relatives; but for his trust in them, his relatives will repay him with ingratitude, and in the end his sister will betray him. Because in this one respect he infringes his own principle of equality and departs from his determination to choose only the efficient, because he appoints brothers and nephews to high office and looks upon them as his heirs, he cannot give them the free hand which it is his way to give all his generals within the limits of their commissions. But treating his relatives as an all-powerful minister treats princes who are still under tutelage, he enrages them, and lays up a store of bitterness for himself.

Joseph is already animated by a mocking spirit. He tells his daughter to address His Majesty as "Consul"; holds disputations in democratic circles; refuses to become a minister of State; but accepts an allowance of two millions as an imperial prince, and lives at the Luxembourg, which his brother hands over to him. At length Napoleon loses patience. The ostensible cause of his anger is a trifle, but all the rage of his heart is now vented in this complaint:

"What on earth is Joseph thinking about? Does he imagine that he has been made prince in order to hobnob with my enemies and walk up and down the streets of Paris in brown surtout and round hat? I have sacrificed my own personal pleasures in order to become what I am. I am as well fitted as another to shine in society! ... But things of that sort do not help a man to rule. Does he dream of disputing with me for the supreme power? My strength is built on a rock!

"Do you know what he ventured to say to me recently in the presence of two others? I ought not to have my wife crowned; the all this two months before the events, and at a distance of six or seven hundred miles from the scene of action."

Austria had good reason for taking up arms once more. On the knob of the new king of Italy's sceptre, the lion of Venice was grave. This, and the seizure of Genoa, were urgent warnings to the Habsburg ruler not to venture across the Alps a third time. Francis must be content to fight the matter out on German soil. England was liberal with proffers of money; and the inexhaustible forces of Russia were again available for the coalition, as they had been when it was victorious during Bonaparte's absence in Egypt. The new tsar was determined to overcome European's old prejudice against Russia, and, with an exchange of roles, to draw his sword against the tyrant of the West. The secret of Napoleon's fighting technique had been learned, and this time the engineer should be hoist with his own petard.

But the soldier of genius can evolve new methods of victory, By forced marches he encircles the Austrians before they realise what is afoot, encloses them in an iron ring at Ulm, and compels the capitulation of an army which has not even a chance to fire a shot. "I have attained my end, and have annihilated the Austrian army by simple marches. Now I shall turn against the Russians. They are lost."

The habit of success is making him thrifty of his words. "I had a rough time of it, rougher than necessary," he writes to Josephine; "wet through day after day for a week, and my feet very cold." Among the gold-bedizened marshals, who are for the first time parading their splendours on foreign soil, stands Napoleon to receive the capitulation of Ulm. He wears the uniform of a private soldier, a mantle weather-worn at elbows and skirt, a hat without a cockade. His arms are locked behind. Of the imperial purple there is no sign.

Once more, as on the evening after Marengo, he offers peace, sends an admonitory letter to the defeated Austrian emperor, writing as usual with the frankness which is so annoying to the diplomats of Europe: "You will understand that it is only right and proper if I take advantage of my good luck to impose, as

Holland and Italy, ideas of self-government were by no means new. But as far as concerned the princes of the Confederation of the Rhine, although, acting under orders, they could introduce the new legal codes, they lacked the traditions and the talents that might have made it possible to initiate such changes from within. We can now understand the historic mission of the youngest of the Bonapartes. He was to make a great experiment in democracy; he was to transform four million Germans from subjects into citizens. Had this impetus been successful, the whole nation might have been spare resubjugation to princely arrogance after the War of Liberation.

But the young man of twenty-three who, coming at the end of this long family, had been reared as a prince, regarded his kingship as a gallant adventure, in which money and vital energy could be squandered. Youth was like champagne, which bubbles when the cork is drawn. He forsook the arms of his Württemberg consort for those of innumerable mistresses; ran into debt, became involved in manifold scandals, and procreated children all over the place; amused himself more than his subjects; and, by this traditional deportment of one born in the purple, succeeded for decades to come in discrediting the fine notion of the choice of the fittest. There was something to be said for the German view that, if they must have a prince to ride across fields and men, they would like him to be one who had inherited the position. Jerome, however, laughed at the world's mockery, and even laughed at his great brother's exhortations.

Napoleon has a predilection for his youngest brother, the sort of weakness that fathers are apt to have for the latest born of their sons. The brio of the young's man life was in keeping with his own tempo. Besides, Jerome was always amiable, took nothing amiss. For instance, on one occasion he asked Napoleon to make him commander-in-chief, and showed no offence at a refusal couched in the following terms: "Are you serious? After you have been through six campaigns, and after you have had a half a dozen horses shot under you, you can ask me again!"

Emperor is in a quandary. He wants the help of a man whom he cannot coerce, and one who in certain respects is his equal. In the light thrown by Lucien, Napoleon's character becomes positively transparent. He develops himself under our very eyes, showing us all the interplay of his motives.

He lavishes temptation in the endeavour to overpersuade his adversary. Every move is carefully thought out, that it may exercise its appropriate influence upon the ambition of his interlocutor, whom he tries to win by the studied gradations of the dialogue. The visitor finds him brooding over the map of Europe, and is greeted in a way which is to alarm and to inspire confidence by turns. The wife, the bone of contention is first vilified and then extolled. Napoleon goes back to the phraseology of the Jacobin Club, calls his brother "citizen" pulls out one emotional stop after another. He reminds Lucien that they are both Corsicans; says with a challenging irony that Europe is too small for the pair of them; talks of Mamma and Pauline, of Joseph and Louis, using names that carry with them reminiscences of the nursery in which the Bonaparte children had played together. Thus he spins his web round Lucien.

And yet–this is the marvel–we are shown the bubbling up of his nature, the beating of his heart, the quivering of his brain. Again and ever again, imagination and passion seem to carry him beyond the limits of self-restraint. Though his brother is a declared opponent, he makes all kinds of confessions: about Josephine and the countess; about his step-children and his generals; about his own blunders and his new, far-reaching plans. There is a flood of confidential admission. Why?

Because this Lucien, though an adversary, though no less gifted than Talleyrand, is a brother, and therefore, to the clannish Napoleon, is, in spite of everything, worthy of confidence. It moves us to see the way in which Napoleon detains him in private talk for hours, till midnight is long past; how he presses Lucien to stay for a few days, that they may thrash matters out; and how Lucien insists on going, not because he really needs to, but materials, the Emperor was able, without periphrases, to come direct to the topics which must interest every historian, and were especially interesting to this one. Within three minutes, the pair were deep in the profoundest problems of history.

The Emperor spoke of Tacitus. Then he sketched the main epochs of intellectual life, and waxed enthusiastic concerning the wonderful manner in which Greek culture was renovated by Christianity when Roman culture was decaying. How adroit had been the Greek tactic, when Greece, conquered by the Roman sword, had found a way to reassert her dominance over the things of the spirit. These words, addressed by Napoleon so soon after the battle of Jena to a man of learning in Prussian service, convey both recognition and a challenge. The Emperor showed himself even more affable by going on to advise Müller to write a history of the Napoleonic exploits–advice he had never given to any Frenchman. Then he spoke of the basis of all religions, and of the need for religion " The conversation was a long one," writes Müller. "It embraced nearly all lands and nations in its scope.... The more interesting he became, the more did he drop his voice, so that at length I had to come very close to him, and no one else in the room can have heard what he was saying, Much of it, indeed, I shall never disclose."

From this remarkable conclusion to a bald report, we may infer, not only the discretion of the grave historian, but also the splendid frankness which the Emperor could show when holding forth in monologue to a man of mark.

Now, in Weimar, he pays especial attention to old Wieland, compares him to Voltaire, but asks him rather critically why he mixes up romance and history. "A man of outstanding intelligence, like you, should know how to keep them apart. Running them together is apt to lead to confusion."

Something more serious than literary criticism is involved, for when Wieland ably defends his misuse of history, and goes on to speak of virtue as an example, the Emperor pulls him up with customary bluntness, saying: "But don't you know what happens to people who are always expounding virtue in the realm of fable different places he must pass through, including where relays of horses are awaiting him. Should a courier reach him. Berthier, or another official who happens to be at hand, must take down the more pressing orders, while the carriage goes jolting on its way. Before long, orderlies are to be seen flying off in every direction.

On the box seat, the Mameluke is enthroned in solitary grandeur. Two postilions whip up the six horses. The carriage is surrounded by a crowd of equerries, pages, and light cavalrymen; when the procession sets forward, the road is all too narrow to accommodate it. The peasants stand aside to set the tornado pass; they are agape with wonderment and firmly believe that the devil is hiding inside the great Napoleon. He leaves behind him a trail like that of a paper-chase: for he throws out of the windows of the carriage, not only all the envelopes and other useless paper, but all the reports he does not wish to file (torn into tiny fragments); all the newspapers he had read; and, finally, books, which he glances at when he has a moment to spare, and then consigns to their fate in the mud of the highway.

Wherever he gets out of his carriage, a hot bath is ready for him. Then, at two in the morning, he will dictate till four, snatch three hours' sleep, and start off again at seven. At his halts, four light cavalrymen surround him in a square, and follow him in all his movements, if, for instance, in the daytime he studies the country through his small telescope. Should he need the large telescope, he uses the shoulder of the page in waiting as a rest. Whether his halt be short or long, in wartime the map is always ready to his hand, in carriage or tent, in camp and by the watch-fire. Any member of his escort who fails to show him in the map the precise point where the halt has been made, the area he now wishes to study, receives a volley of abuse–be it Berthier himself, Prince of Neuchâtel. Through all countries, for the whole duration of his life, the map follows him, pierced with coloured pins, illuminated at night by twenty or thirty candles, and with a pair of compasses lying on it. This is his altar, before which he offers up his prayers. It is the real home of the man who has no home.

The Emperor, meanwhile, gives more attention to clothing and furniture than to affairs of State; orders for Marie Louise a trousseau to the tune of five millions, for what she is bringing with her has cost only half a million; studies all the details of Marie Antoinette's journey, lest the Habsburgs should be able to plume themselves on breaches of etiquette; orders fashionable coats from his tailor, and buckled shoes from his shoemaker; goes out hunting, rides vigorously, in the hope of sweating off his fat; even finds that his dancing days are not yet over.

While on her way to Paris, Marie Louise receives a love letter, quite illegible, for all she can make out is the capital N. of the signature; flowers greet her wherever she halts for the night; in Compiègne she is expecting to be received by the terrible man whom she is to wed; he is waiting there for her with all his family.

But suddenly, with a surge of vigorous youth, the firm will and the fierce impatience of the revolutionist break through this hedge of antiquated formalities. Laying aside his new embroidered coat, and donning his old uniform, he jumps into a calash undecorated with armorial bearings, and drives to meet the bridal procession. There it is; the horses are being changed in a downpour of rain. He wants to take Marie Louise by surprise, but her master-of-the-horse, recognising him, exclaims, "His Majesty": so the little coup fails to come off. In a moment he is in the carriage beside her, dismisses the lady-in-waiting, kisses his bride, laughing the while, for he is wet through. In her embarrassment, she finds a pretty phrase: "Your portrait does not flatter you, Sire!"

"She is by no means beautiful," he meditates, as he takes stock of her. "Marked with smallpox, though not badly, thick lips; watery blue eyes; full-bosomed for her years; but fresh and young."

With disgust, that evening, the masters of the ceremonies see their whole programme, which has been rehearsed for weeks in advance, torn to tatters. The meeting with the imperial family has been effected with scant formality; all come and go as they please; the girls who present bouquets must cut their compliments short for everyone is wet and cold, supper is improvised, with Caroline only. He insists upon her keeping up the old tone of comradeship, and scolds her when, after the divorce, she writes to him as "Your Majesty." "You have written me an unkind letter. I am always the same; my feelings do not change.... I shall say no more until you have compared this letter with yours. Then you can judge for yourself which of us two is more friendly, you or I." To no one else can he speak so simply, unless it be to Berthier, whom he often calls his "wife." The only thing that annoys him with Josephine is that she is always running into debt. He thinks that she ought to be able to save half of her allowance of three millions. "Then in ten years you would have put by fifteen mullions for your grandsons.... Let me know that you are quite well again. I am told that you are getting as stout as one of our good Norman peasant women." But when Josephine continues to be spendthrift, he tells the steward of her property not to make her any further payments till evidence is forthcoming that she is no longer squandering money.

He sees very little more of her, however; and he will have nothing to do with the lady friends of earlier years. His attitude towards marriage is that of a respectable citizen, and that of an Italian. Besides, as a sovereign prince he wishes to set a good example to his subjects. Since Marie Louise makes no nationalist pretensions (for, being of a dull, easygoing, and fickle temperament, she has promptly come to regard herself as a Frenchwoman), the two get on very well together. He has always time to spare for her. When she is learning to ride, he walks patiently at her bridle. He, who has never waited before, will even wait when she is late for dinner. She is not afraid of him, and is saucy enough to tell the Austrian envoy that she thinks her husband is a little afraid of her. It is important to the Emperor that he should make a good impression upon the Hofburg. Regarding it as politically expedient that a report of his wife's happiness shall be sent to Vienna, he brings Metternich to see the empress, and tells the envoy to stay until someone fetches him. Napoleon goes away, locking the door of the room after him. He does not release the prisoners, for an hour, and then, with a sly laugh, asks Metternich whether he is satisfied, now, that the empress is happy.

between our respective outposts. I still hope that we shall not spill the blood of hundreds of thousands of brave men, simply because we cannot agree as to the colour of a ribbon!"

How his own unrest vibrates through these brilliant subterfuges, which he specially adapts to cajole Alexander's feminine disposition! A grey gauntlet of steel is hurled from one world power to the other; the great fight between birth and genius is now to take place in all its grandeur. And he who, after two decades of dreaming, sees his dream descending out of the clouds earthwards, talks as if nothing more were at stake than a girl's quarrel or the colour of a piece of ribbon–when in reality the fate of the world hangs in the balance!

IV

What is passing in Alexander's mind? Estranged from the Russian nobility, railed at by his mother, cheated out of his hopes of setting up the cross once more on St. Sophia, deeply concerned about Poland (which his adversary threatens to liberate) –there are reasons enough, both in political and court life, why he should no longer regard Napoleon as his friend. After Tilsit, Metternich had said that it would take five years for the tsar's feelings to swing to the opposite pole. That period had now elapsed, and although the tsar's was one of those nervous temperaments in which moods decide actions, on his side, too, the struggle could assume allegorical greatness. But he lacked a grand aim and a lofty thought. He was not even fighting to win warlike renown against the master craftsman in the art of war. The impulses that drove him to the fight were merely the outcome of a confused mysticism, in whose waters he had drowned his old veneration for the magician of Tilsit.

Politically, he makes two successful moves in the game, one of these being intimately adapted to the peculiarities of human character, and therefore weighty with consequence. To cope with town, while Napoleon's men are streaming in from the west. The advance guard of the French and the rear guard of the Russians are almost in touch. It is a silent entry, for the town is like a city of the dead; the houses are empty. "Still, there are plenty of houses," think the weary campaigners; "we shall find food, and be able to sleep at our ease."

The Emperor and his staff ride slowly through the streets whose silence is so ominous. The Kremlin is their destination. Here is the ancient fortress. The newcomers look with astonishment at its walls. All the gates are open, but there is no one there to act as guide. The golden and red halls are forsaken, as in the vision of a dream. The invaders make their way into a huge room where the windows are boarded up. The grenadiers knock the boards away with the butt ends of their muskets, and the Emperor recognises by the canopy that he is in the coronation room of the tsars of Muscovy; but the throne is veiled.

Peace is the only thing lacking to him in this moment of fulfilment. Where is the peace? He has nothing but a victory. Who has cheated him of its fruits? Only the vast, strange land; the steppe has cheated him today, as the desert cheated him thirteen years ago. Why did he not free the serfs in Lithuania, and thus win guides and new soldiers, as he had planned to do aforetime with the liberated Arabs? What if he were to adopt this policy now? The town is deserted, but there are peasants in the surrounding countryside. Why not summon them, make terms with them? We are masters here; this enigmatic realm can still offer much of what we desire!

Night comes, but sleep is coy. "Let us do some work, then, to distract our minds," he says to Caulaincourt. He opens the map of Poland; satisfies himself that it was impossible to stay there; in six weeks he can be in St. Petersburg. The muster rolls (they are his Bible, which he always takes with him on a journey, and perpetually cons even in peace time) show him what forces are still at his disposal. His spirits rise as he looks at the columns of figures. "In a few weeks I could get together a quarter of a million

The senior captain is to cut down the Mameluke, and then to make an end of Napoleon. Presumably the conspirators have seen Schiller's *Wallenstein* on the German stage! The Prussian wants the Frenchman to do the deed, but Lapie says he is not sure of his men. Then Caulaincourt, to whom the conspirators' behaviour seems suspicious, comes forward, claps his hand, and says: "Now, gentlemen, it is time to start!"

That evening the Emperor, who has not heard a word of the affair, summons his marshals. "I shall be stronger when I can speak from my throne in the Tuileries than I am at the head of an army which has been destroyed by the cold.... Had I been a Bourbon, born to rule, it would have been easy for me to avoid making mistakes." He takes the marshals aside by turns, asking each for his advice; he flatters, praises, and encourages; he smiles and charms. Obviously his design is to counteract the possibility of revolt.

Next, he tells Eugene to read them his latest bulletin, the first in which he admits disaster. "Men who had not been sufficiently steeled by nature to rise superior to all vicissitudes of fate and fortune, lost courage and equanimity, and could dream of nothing but misfortune and defeat. But those who were equal to the occasion were able to keep up their spirits, and regarded every fresh difficulty as a fresh opportunity for glory." The only reason why the army had wasted away was the rigour of the climate. "His Majesty has never been in better health."

The unfeeling, metallic tone! Again we are listening to General Bonaparte who, having recovered confidence in his destiny, and having regained health, is able to use the old language. The incisive sentence at the close is, of course, added for the special benefit of Paris, which for several weeks has had no news as to his state of health. But, on the whole, the mood in which he ends the Russian campaign, exactly six months after it had begun, is one of heroic cynicism. The command of the army is handed over to Murat, who is to lead the survivors home. There are still nine thousand men under arms.

X

At the first review in Mainz, there are only one hundred and eighty thousand men instead of the three hundred thousand he had hoped to assemble there. The army is very short of cavalry; the equipment is inadequate, for it has been far too hastily got together; the best guns have been lost in Russia, or are tied up in Spain; the general staff has been decimated; the ambulance service is defective. He sees all that is amiss, but even this imperfect army reminds him of old times and old happiness. He recalls the April days in Cannes and Nice, seventeen years before, when he had taken over the command of half-starved and ragged soldiers, that he might lead them through the mountains to victory. With these memories surging up in his mind, he gathers his energies, and utters the darkly challenging words: "I shall conduct this war as General Bonaparte."

Such is the signal, a mingling of impetus and self-restraint, with which he launches himself into the first battle. At Lützen he exposes himself more than he has done for years. During the first day's fighting, he does not sleep at all; on the second day, when everything is going well, he has his bearskin spread on the ground in the middle of Marmont's corps; and when, an hour later, they wake him to let him know that all is going on well, he leaps to his feet with the ironical remark: "You see, the best things come to one while one is asleep."

But hardly has the general won his victory than the emperor-politician resumes the ascendant. He sends letters in all directions; forces the vacillating king of Saxony to a decision, talks to the princes of the Confederation of the Rhine about providence and the fortune of war, that he may keep them up to the scratch; sends his ministers to the Russian outposts; abruptly and informally offers the tsar Poland in exchange for Prussia, and suggests other territorial rearrangements, until Alexander weakens; and he writes to Emperor Francis in terms of unusual self-

Augereau, for whose corps he had been waiting, Augereau laughed him to scorn: "Do you think me such a fool as to let myself be slaughtered in a Leipzig suburb? I won't do that for a madman's sake!"

Here we have it for the first time, a sign that one of Napoleon's oldest companions-in-arms has become completely indifferent to the Emperor's fame; is animated by the mere will-to-live, reasonable enough in a private soldier, but unworthy of a marshal of France. On the very same day, another friend of Bonaparte's youth writes to the Emperor, complaining that in the report of the previous day's fighting his services have been overlooked, although for ten hours he had held a part of the plain for whose defence another man is now given the credit. "Never in my life have I served you more faithfully than I did on this occasion.. Sire, I could not suffer anything worse than to be forgotten at such a time." The letter is signed, "Marmont."

These two utterances on the day after Leipzig are the shadows of coming events. Marmont and Augereau will both desert the Emperor in the decisive hour.

Fifty miles away, Goethe is sitting in his room at Weimar. Napoleon's picture has fallen from its nail. The poet has heard the sound of the Leipzig guns. The first news of the French defeat has arrived. Though none of the allied generals can say, yet, whether the Emperor may not be able to collect his forces once more, and to resume his career of victory Goethe, who only a few months earlier had declared Napoleon to be invincible, already realises the full extent of the disaster. On the day of the retreat, as everything had happened hundred years before, and the whole matter had become legendary, he writes the following verses:

He who feels courage in his royal breast
knows no shudderings, treads gladly
the undermined road leading to the steps of the throne,
knows the danger and nevertheless mounts confidently.
The golden circlet's tremendous burden,
he does not try its weight; resolute and calm,
he presses it gladly on his bold brow,

with his bodyguard. Then, leaving everything behind, he jumps with Caulaincourt into a post-chaise, hoping it will not be too late to seize the reins of power. After how many victories has he not driven in such a carriage through the gates of his capital? Always his thoughts have circled round the problem, "What is Paris saying? How shall I find things there?" But now there is only one idea pulsing in his brain: Will three persons stand firm till I come; three to whom I can entrust the safety of the realm? The empress as regent, Joseph as governor of Paris, Marmont as leader of the strongest corps!

Night. Change of horses. A squad of soldiers led by an officer. The officer reports "I am under Marshal Mortier's orders, and am seeking quarters for the troops that are being withdrawn."

"Troops being withdrawn? Where is the empress? Where is King Joseph?"

"Her Majesty, with the king of Rome, fled yesterday to Blois. King Joseph left Paris today."

"Where is Marmont?"

"I don't know, Sire."

Beads of sweat form on the Emperor's forehead; his lips twitch nervously; he is horrified at the news. He breaks out: "Forward! Tomorrow the guards will be here. The National Guard is on my side. Once within the walls of Paris, I shall only leave the town as a conqueror or as a dead man!"

With difficulty, Caulaincourt persuades him to renounce this foolhardy design. The Emperor orders that Marmont's corps is to take up its position behind the Essonne. Then he says to his minister: "Hasten to Paris! Go on negotiating for a treaty. I have been betrayed and sold. You have full powers. I will wait for you here. It is not far. Forward!"

He drives a hundred paces nearer, and can see the waters of the Seine. But what is mirrored therein? The enemy's watchfires! At the outposts, the invaders are cooking supper and singing songs; while the Emperor, on the left bank with two post-chaises his name there as Campbell, a British colonel. This is his sixth name.

The little Provençal maid who waits at table prattles:" They'll finish him off before he reaches the sea!" "Colonel Campbell" nods, saying "Of course, of course!" to all her utterances. Then, when he is left alone with his servant, his head droops on the man's shoulder, he has a nap to make up for two sleepless nights. Kindly nature, this is your gift to the greatest of your warriors! When he wakes, the recent sounds and sights recur to his mind. With a shudder, he says in low tones:

"Never again! I shall be happier in Elba than ever before. The sciences now, nothing more. I do not want to wear another European crown. You have seen what the people really is. Was I not right to despise man?"

When the carriages reach the inn, he thinks it wise, warned by his previous experiences, to change his clothes once more. Since time presses, he puts on the uniform of an Austrian general which belongs to Commissioner Koller; surmounts it with the cap of Truchsess, the Prussian colonel; and has a Russian cloak hung round his shoulders by Shuvaloff. Thus bedecked in a carnival costume, pieced together from garments belonging to the three allied powers, a fool on the heath, does Emperor Napoleon escape from his country.

Fréjus at last! This is the port where he landed on his return from Egypt, a beaten commander, who had lost all the battleships of France, and ought to have been tried by court martial! But how enthusiastic, then, had been his reception by this leaderless people, for the memory of his successful Italian campaign was still fresh. Then, he had driven through triumphal arches on the journey to Paris; the journey he had now been making in the reverse direction, in danger of being stoned, and escaping murder only by a mummer's disguise! Fifteen years lie between, the rebirth of a State, the glory of a nation. Europe lies between, the clash of arms, dead soldiers rotting in their graves, the returning hero received with frenzied acclamations, a marshal rising from pothouse to palace, men of genius taking sides for and against the conquering nation–and a

"You see?" said Napoleon to Constant. "I never loaded those fellows with honours. What have they got to thank me for? I left them poor men, just as I had found them. Nothing but instinct leads them to me. If I liked, these rebellious Chambers would be dissolved within the hour. ... I need merely say the word, and all the deputies who oppose me would be butchered! But for one man, the price is too high. Blood must not flow in Paris!"

This mood of renunciation, which is akin to justice, this refusal to employ brute force in his extremity, just as he had refused (to begin with) sixteen years earlier, resembles the mood of Brumaire. But what was then the prudence of a statesman who did not wish to tarnish the origins of his long career of power, is now a prudence which does not beseem the adventurer he is today. Nevertheless, his unwillingness to use the bayonets with which, today, he could again have cleared the Chambers, is one more sign of his recognition of the new epoch which wants more freedom and less force.

Meanwhile, the Chamber of Deputies is in secret session. Lucien has presented the imperial message. The deputies are willing to discuss matters. Some of them speak, in civil terms, of the abdication as a sacrifice necessary for France. Honest Carnot mounts the rostrum, and, in this moment of disaster, is almost alone in espousing the cause of the Emperor whom almost alone he had openly attacked in the days when all others had been subservient to the man of the hour. But now Sieyes, too, speaks in favour of the Emperor, speaks like a Roman of old: "Napoleon has lost a battle.... Let us help him to drive the barbarians from our country, for no one else is equal to the task. If, when he has done it, he wants to play the despot, we can hang him. But today we must march with him shoulder to shoulder!"

Lafayette springs to the rostrum once more: "Have you forgotten where the bones of our sons and our brothers whiten? in Africa, on the Tagus, on the Vistula, amid the snows of Russia. Two million have been the victims of this one man who wanted to fight all Europe! Enough! In the small hours, the Chamber demands Napoleon's abdication.

BOOK FIVE

THE ROCK

On Judgement Day, before God's throne,
There stood at last, Napoleon.
The Devil had his list begun
Of crimes the Bonapartes had done,
When God the Father, or God the Son,
Cut Satan short before God's throne:
"Don't bore us all to death with reading
A German professorial pleading!
If you're bold enough to face him,
In your kingdom you may place him."

–GOETHE

the intermediation of Talleyrand that the Emperor must be addressed as "Sire." These weaknesses are grotesque, and yet they are superficial; he himself recognizes them and spurns them if the mood is upon him. When he is hesitating whether he shall send Eugene, or perhaps better still Talleyrand (a man sprung from the old noblesse), to prepare the ground for the "imperial diet" at Erfurt. he suddenly, in virile fashion, ceases to bother about the question: "After all, what does it matter to me whether I am criticized? I will show them that I do not care."

A more serious problem, both for him and for us, is when the origin and the laws of the right of succession to throne come up for discussion. "It is false to call me a usurper; I have simply taken the unoccupied place which Louis could not keep for himself. Had I been Louis I should have hindered the revolution in spite of the amazing progress which has accrued to thought because of the change.... My strength is in my good luck; I am as new as the Empire." Yet, in spite of this somewhat confused reasoning, he ventures a step farther, and writes to Brother Louis: "I hold myself responsible for everything that has happened since Clovis' days down to the days of the Committee of Public Safety; and I shall consider everything that is deliberately said against the government as an attack on myself."

Thus we see that his egotism reaches so paradoxical an intensity in the championship of legitimacy, and that he sails so near the serious acceptance of rule by divine right (which in otherwise only used by him as a political formula), that he makes himself responsible for the actions of those very kings whose dethronement has opened the way to his rise!

All his life he restlessly hovered round this question of status. At Kaunitz Castle, during the night after Austerlitz, while at every minute Austrian and Russian colours, captive generals, and dispatches from the beaten commanders, are being brought to him, he thrusts everything aside because the courier from Paris has entered the room. Then he does the same with all the tidings from the capital, in order to read a letter full of gossip from a lady, who tells how the Fronde of the Faubourg has sworn never to put in an

V

Napoleon's energy is most conspicuous in his role of conqueror. But in this case it finds a more spiritual expression than one would be led to anticipate from a soldier. "I have seldom drawn my sword; I won my battles with my eyes, not with my weapons." To gain a knowledge of his soul, it is not important to understand the new forms of his art of war; of importance is to understand the way in which his whole being vibrated before, during, and after a fight. In this, too, he is wholly original.

Even courage, that fundamental virtue of the soldier, assumes in Napoleon a form peculiar to himself. During his youthful days, and again during the last campaigns he displayed so much personal courage that he can venture to say, "no soldier is proof against cowardice": but such moments of panic fear must be utilised against the foe. What he believes himself almost alone to possess is "two-o'clock in-the-morning courage": courage in face of the unforeseen, the sudden; courage which demands presence of mind and power of determination. But he despises the "chivalrous" courage of the duel, which he crushingly describes as "cannibal courage."– "Since you have both fought at Marengo and Austerlitz you do not need to give any further proofs of your courage. Women are fickle, and so is good luck. Go back to your regiments and become comrades again."

The commander of armies clearly recognises the line of demarcation between humaneness and coldness. The same man who, in his study, could exclaim to Mettenich: "Such a man as I does not care a snap of the fingers for the lives of a million men"; will say on the field of battle: "If the kings of the world could contemplate such a sight as this, they would hanker less after wars and conquests." Another time he writes to Josephine: "The earth is strewn with dead and bleeding men; this is the obverse of war; the heart is tortured at the sight of so many victims." Calculation and feeling are at cross purposes in this case, and he excuses himself plating the princes to contemplating the masses, his contempt for his fellows diminishes, but not enough. The masses like the princes, are to be used for his own ends. He says: "The men of intelligence who have changed the world, have never done so by influencing the leaders, but have always set the masses in motion. He who influences princes is only an intriguer, and his results are second rate; but he who moves the masses, changes the face of the earth." Democracy came between him and the people; and what he has to say about parliamentarism is not creative but critical:

"The republic is the political form which elevates the soul and contains the germ of great things: but, precisely because of its greatness, it will sooner or later perish, for it needs a unified authority to maintain its power, and this must lead either to despotism or to a patriciate. The latter is the worst of despotisms: Rome, Venice, England, and even France are instances. If the republic wishes to attain greatness, the central authority must be established upon a permanent parliamentary majority; ... but this can be secured only by corruption, which is the cancer of the peoples, and a terrible weapon in the hands of the central authority. The liberals have discovered the expedient of constitutional monarchy. That is, a mezzo termine, which has its advantages, but only when the popular assembly, whose business it is to bridle the monarchical authority, is elected by universal suffrage."

Napoleon recognized the existence of all the problems that confronted the nineteenth century; but he never understood the social problem, with which his own story began.

VII

Imagination, the third element of his personality, is the real driving force of his self-confidence and his energy. Continually at war with the calculating part of his nature, fantasy, in the end, brings this harbourer of opposites to destruction. The imaginative power, which links the poet to the statesman (enabling both unceasingly to dwell in the affective world of strangers as well as

Bertrand in the hand, and spring out of Napoleon's three-cornered hat as he takes it from the sideboard.

Who lives in the house besides the rats? Three counts and one baron with their families (all of them officers, and accustomed to court life), two valets, and the rest of the Emperor's staff with their dependents; nearly forty persons in all, when they first land. After six years, at the end of Napoleon's life, the number has been reduced by half.

Las Cases and his young son hold out for a year. Marquis and émigré, older than the Emperor, a sprig of the Faubourg, count of the empire, it was not until the Hundred Days that Las Cases became one of Napoleon's close associates. He was a man of the world, author of some works on geography; later he was to write his *Memorial of St. Helena*, which is said to have brought him thousands of pounds. He was shorter than the Emperor, and as lean as General Bonaparte had been. He was cultured, pleasant of temper, always ready to serve: certainly the most agreeable companion and secretary the prisoner had. He entertained the Emperor with witticisms the Parisians had made at Napoleon's expense, thereby unfolding the comic obverse of a tragic career. Las Cases taught the Emperor English, thus widening the scope of the exile's reading. When the two men exchanged notes in English, the count would underscore the Emperor's mistakes. Las Cases, under various pretexts, finally abandoned the island, and left a vacant place which during the last years of the Emperor's life was never to be filled.

For Bertrand, sometime governor of Illyria, and devoted to the Emperor, is touchy, and is too proud to write from dictation; in other respects, he observes a faultless passivity, except when he shows fear of offending his wife. This lady, a beautiful Creole, half-English, with the head of a young lord had been loath to share Napoleon's exile. At Plymouth, she had tried to throw herself overboard; she is miserable, thinks of Paris, and weeps over her youth; consorts much with the enemy. One day her place is empty at the Emperor's board. Napoleon says that his house is not an inn; Bertrand is aggrieved at the reproach, and does not put in an

Soon, indeed, his pleasure in dictation evaporates. Though he had intended to dictate in a few weeks the campaign of 1800 which had lasted but that amount of time, he postpones this labour, and tells Gourgaud to collect material bearing upon the Russian campaign. Then the young general, who had himself participated in the campaign of 1812, sets to work to read–not a Russian work dealing with the campaign, but an English work dealing with the life of the Emperor who is there, three rooms away, and could probably furnish full particulars!

Napoleon, the movement of whose mind was from events to ideas, and very rarely from thought to deed, is still true to type. When he reads news from Paris, he dictates rejoinders which demonstrate his expertise, and he compiles financial schemes. From his rock, from his little room, he answers the sounds coming from the outer world, although the sounds are no summons and his answer dies away into the void. He often proposes to write a treatise on the art of war. But he gives the notion up, "for the generals who in days to come get beaten will blame me, and say they were following my principles.... I could instruct them, for I am a good teacher; but I cannot have my principles of warfare set down in print." He mistrusts every systematization, for he is essentially a man who has learned by experience, by the unexpected. But if an isolated problem crops up in the course of a book he is dictating, then he deals with it in the precisest of terms. Thus, he makes Gourgaud calculate how much water a fire-hose can deliver, for he wants to introduce the fire-hose to combat the consequences of artillery fire.

Congenial society occasionally shortens the day. Or visitors come to see the Emperor. English travellers, men of learning, colonial magnates, are admitted to audience. On their return to Europe, they bear witness to his mental alertness. Napoleon himself desires such reports to be spread abroad, for they can do nothing but good to his cause now that Las Cases' diary has aroused fresh sympathy for his plight.

"Scatter your complaints throughout Europe! I myself do not complain." And he adds the orphic saying:

the early weeks at St. Helena, he is out riding with Las Cases "We came to a field that was being ploughed. The Emperor dismounted, and took the handles of the plough. With incredible speed, he drove a long and perfectly straight furrow. All this without saying a word until he had finished, when he told me to give the ploughman a napoleon. We remounted, and rode on our way."

XV

"No one but myself can be blamed for my fall. I have been my own greatest enemy, the cause of my own disastrous fate."

This admission, the profoundest of all those made by the exile shows that Napoleon has completely outgrown the cloudy Cæsarist fancies of his middle period. Had he been a believing Christian, the confession would have rounded off his atonement upon the rock. His sense of responsibility, however, is not directed towards God but only towards himself, and therefore the utterance represents a great man's final settlement of accounts with destiny. But, at the same time, it is a last outburst of defiance, for his overweening self-esteem made it impossible for him to admit that there were any greater forces in the world than his own. Napoleon alone could overthrow Napoleon.

The remark was not the outcome of transient depression. During the closing years of his power, he had again and again spoken to his intimates about his faults and errors; now, upon the island, such admissions are frequent. Some of them are ardent, and some of them are cold; for even in these self-examinations there is an alternation between fantasy and realism. From time to time, we have the heartfelt cry of a penitent: "When I close my eyes, all my mistakes parade themselves before me, like figures in a nightmare." Or, again: "I wanted too much.... I strung the bow too tightly, and trusted too much in my good fortune."

he reads an attack made on him by a senator who declares that in the day of the Empire France had chosen her master from among a people whom the Romans did not consider good enough to use as slaves, Napoleon's comment is that it is a great compliment to the Corsicans, "for the Romans knew that this people could not be forced to serve.... Besides, Corsica, lying between France and Italy, was an appropriate, birthplace for a man who was to rule both."

Then, suddenly, it is again his fatherland. "Ah, Doctor, where are the lovely skies of Corsica? If only I could have fled thither, the people would have received me with open arms, and would have become my family. Do you think that the allies could have mastered me in Corsica? You know our mountaineers, their courage and their pride! I am familiar with every ravine in the island, every stream!" He declares that he would fain have made much of this island (about which he never troubled after leaving it), would have signalized his love for it before all France. Only his misfortunes had prevented his carrying out these plans. He speaks of the spiritual greatness of the islanders, of their veneration for honour, of the blood feuds they hand down from generation to generation; he speaks of Paoli. "Everything is better there, the very smell of the ground. If my eyes were shut, I should recognize it; I have never come across it anywhere else.... No longer to own the house where one was born, to be homeless-this is to be without a fatherland!" Thus late, thus painfully, and thus indirectly, does this man without a fatherland make his great discovery; or thus late does he acknowledge his true feelings.

The Corsican doctor has no great sympathy with the Emperor; he does not credit Napoleon's sufferings; he believes them to be simulated for political ends, in the hope of a removal to Europe; and is absent during the worst paroxysms. Thus the political use the Emperor has made of his ailments works out its own revenge; for now, when he is really dying, his own compatriot regards his sufferings as spurious. There is ample record of these differences between doctor and patient. Napoleon wishes to get rid of Antommarchi, and asks Lowe to have him sent back to Europe.

string the bow more tightly; ... that was why France never secured the liberal institutions I had intended to introduce. But the country credits me with my good intentions; it loves my name and my victories. You will do the same! Be true to our principles and to our fame!"

His thoughts are still circling round his work: With the mournful glance of a dying sculptor, he sees before him nothing but a fragment; and with his last breath he tells those around him what he had designed to fashion.

Next day, his mind is wandering once more amid memories of youth and of Corsica. But still, from time to time, there revives the wish to be useful to his son. His fantasy creates possessions on the island, and the faithful Marchand takes down from dictation these mind-wanderings that are so precise in their details:

"I leave to my son my house in Ajaccio with its outbuildings; two houses adjacent to the saltpits with their gardens: and all my estates in the Ajaccio district. These will bring him an income of frs. 50,000. I bequeath...."

This is Napoleon's last command. He has won and lost half the world; but in his dying visions he sees the Corsican home of his ancestors, together with the son to whom he had intended to leave half the world as heirlooms. The strains mingle; to keep his son from want, he bequeaths the lad a house which he does not own. Then his mind turns back from his kin. He is once more the soldier, on his first campaign, in Italy. Around him flit the wraiths of his earliest comrades. He shouts:

"Desaix! Masséna! Victory is ours! Quick! Forward! We have them....

Next day the abbate goes to him unsummoned. Beneath a layman's dress, the priest carries something he seeks to hide. He demands to be left alone with the dying man. After a while he comes out, saying: "I have given him extreme unction. Owing to the condition of the stomach, no other sacrament was possible."

A terrible last night. Towards morning, when he is murmuring in delirium, Montholon hears the words:

CONTENTS

TRANSLATION AND NOTES

27b-28. The story of Parvata originally recounted to Gaurī by Śiva; then the story of Jālaṇdhara, the narration of Śrī-Śaila etc.; thereafter, the meritorious story of Sagara is narrated.

29. The merit of Gaṅgā, Prayāga, Kāśi and the special merit of Gayā, the greatness (in efficacy) of the gift of cooked rice etc, the holy rite of Mahādvādaśī (12th Tithi of Bhādrapada (Śuddha) with Śravaṇa Nakṣatra.)

30. The greatness of twentyfour Ekādaśīs (eleventh day) in each fortnight is described severally, the narration of Viṣṇu-dharma, the thousand names of Viṣṇu.

31. The greatness of Kārttikavrata, the benefit of ablution in the month of Māgha. The greatness of the holy centres of the continent Jambūdvīpa, which destroys sins.

32. The greatness of Sābhramatī, the description of the origin of Nṛsiṁha, the narration of the story of Devaśarmā and others, the description of the greatness of Gītā.*

33. The description of devotion and the greatness of Śrīmad Bhāgavata,** the greatness of Indraprastha with the stories of many holy centres.

34. The mentioning of Mantraratna, the description of Tripādbhūti; thereafter, the holy stories of the incarnation of Matsya (fish) etc.

35-37. The hundred divine names of Rāma, O Brāhmaṇa; thereafter, its greatness is described; then the testing of the greatness of Śrī Viṣṇu by Bhṛgu. This is the holy fifth section called Uttarakhaṇḍa. The excellent man who listens to the Padma Purāṇa comprising of five Khaṇḍas attains the abode of Viṣṇu after enjoying all pleasures here that he desires. This Purāṇa contains fiftyfive thousand verses. It is called Padma Purāṇa.

38. This must be written in full and handed over to a Brāhmaṇa well versed in the Purāṇas after honouring him suitably on the full moon day in the month of Jyeṣṭha along-

*Vide Pd. P. Uttara Khaṇḍa, chs. 175-192.

**Vide ibid. chs. 193-198.

CHAPTER NINETYNINE

The Agni Purāṇa : Contents

Śrī Brahmā said :

1. Henceforth, I shall describe to you the Agni Purāṇa. The Fire-god recounted the events of Īśāna Kalpa[1] to Vasiṣṭha.

2. It comprises fifteen thousand[2] verses of various wonderful stories. It dispels all the sins of men who listen to this.

3. At the outset is the enquiry about the Purāṇa, then the story of all incarnations, then the chapter on the Creation and then the (mode of) worship of Viṣṇu and other things.[3]

---

1. This Purāṇa is an encyclopaedia of the mediaeval India as stated by it : *Āgneye hi purāṇe'smin sarvā vidyāḥ pradarśitāḥ*

AP. 383.52

Although the *NP* is supported by the *Mt.P.* and *Sk.P.* in connecting the events in the *AP* to *Īśāna Kalpa*, the extant AP does not mention that Kalpa or that the incidents therein belong to that Kalpa. This is quite natural, as Hazra points out that the genuine *Āgneya Purāṇa* was forced to travel to the south and came to be known as the *Vahni Purāṇa* and is awaiting publication. Hazra states that it is considerably free from the influence of Tantrism while the extant AP is a spurious *Āgneya Purāṇa* written under the influence of Tantrism in the 9th cent. A.D. He states that the extant *Agni Purāṇa* is different from the AP which was before the writer of the NP. The Sk. P. states that glorification of the *Agni* is the aim of the AP but that is not found in the present text of the AP. Moreover, a number of verses said to be quotations from the AP in Ballālasena's *Dānasāgara* are not traced in the present text of the AP.

Hence, it is held that the published text of the AP is different from the text available to the writer of the NP (vide Hazra : 'Present Agni Purāṇa" —*IHQ*.XII 683-691, '*Our Heritage*' Vol. I.ii 209. 45).

2. The NP. is supported by the Bh. P, and Br. Vaivarta in claiming 15000 verses to the AP. The AP also calls itself to be *Pañcadaśa-sāhasram* (382.64). The statements that it contains 16000 verses (*the Vāyu, Mt.P Sk.P*) shows that those Purāṇas refer to a different version. The Ānandāśrama edition has 11,457 verses. But Hazra has shown that the Ānandāśrama edition is not the original *Purāṇa* but a late compilation, the original *Āgneya* or *Vahni* Purāṇa is unpublished (Hazra—"Discovery of genuine Āgneya Purāṇa", *Journal, Oriental Institute Baroda* V. pp.411-416.

3. VV 3-22 give the list of various topics described in the AP. As the *Vahni Purāṇa* is not available in print, nothing can be said about the contents of that genuine AP. But a comparison of the topics mentioned in these

8. The narration of churning the ocean, then the story of Indra, the ruler of the Devas; the narrative of Pārvatī and her subsequent marriage.

9. The birth of Kumāra (Skanda) is narrated thereafter, then the battle with Tāraka, then the narration of Paśupati, alongwith that of Caṇḍa.

10. The narration of being engaged in the game of dice, the meeting with Nārada. Then in the context of the greatness of Kumāra, the story of five Tīrthas (holy centres).

11. The anecdote of king Dharmavarman; the enumeration of rivers and oceans; thereafter, the story of Indradyumna alongwith the story of Nāḍī-jaṅgha.

12. The appearance of the Earth, the story of Damanaka, the contact between the Earth and the ocean, then the story of Lord Kumāra.

13. Then the fight with Tāraka alongwith various anecdotes, the killing of Tāraka, the installation of five Liṅgas.

14. The holy narration of the continents, the orderly arrangement of the upper worlds, the situation and magnitude of the Cosmic Egg, the story of Varkareśa.

15. The origin of Mahākāla and his extremely miraculous story, the greatness of Vāsudeva, thereafter the Koṭi Tīrtha.

16. The narration of different holy centres, Gupta Kṣetra (near the confluence of the Mahī with the sea) the holy story of the Pāṇḍavas and the achievement of great Vidyā.

17. The wonderful conclusion of pilgrimage to holy centres by Kumāra; the greatness of Aruṇācala, the conversation between Sanaka and Brahmā.

18. The description of Gaurī's penance, the review of different holy centres, the narrative of demon Mahiṣa and his wonderful death.

Actually we find that the NP touches a fringe of this part of the SkP and a great number of topics are not even mentioned.

The same is the case with other *Khaṇḍas*. One wonders whether a shorter version of the Sk. P. was used by the NP or a casual mention of a few chapters was looked upon as a table of contents in those days. Many of the topics not mentioned by the NP are found in other *Purāṇas* also and as such one should think thrice before branding them spurious.

168b-169. The shrines Someśa and Viśveśa, the great and meritorious holy centre called Arkasthala, the narration of Siddheśvara etc., is made here separately; the shrines of Agni-Tīrtha, Kapardīśa and Kedāreśa and the bestowers of goals (heavenly abodes).

170. The different forms of Hara—viz. Bhīma, Bhairava, Caṇḍīśa, etc., the planets viz. the Sun, Moon, Mars, Mercury, Jupiter, Venus, Saturn, Rāhu and Śikhin (Ketu).

171. Then five others Siddheśvara and the forms of Rudra, are stationed there. The goddesses of excellent beauty—Ajā, Pālā, Maṅgalā and Laliteśvarī.

172-74. Then the shrines of Lakṣmīśa, Yādaveśa, Urvīśa, Kāmeśvara, Gaurīṣa, Varuṇeśa, Durvāseśa, Gaṇeśvara, Kumāreśa, Caṇḍakalpa and Śakulīśvara. Then the holy story of Koṭīśa, Bālabrahma, etc., then the stories of Narakeśa, Saṁvarteśa and Nidhīśvara, then that of Balabhadreśvara, Gaṅgā and Gaṇapa.

175. Then the good story of the river named Jāmbavatī and the well called Pāṇḍukūpa, the story of Śatamedha (hundred sacrifices), Lakṣamedha (hundred-thousand sacrifices) and Koṭimedha (a crore of sacrifices.)

176-177a. The prominent story of Durvāsas, Arka, Ghaṭasthāna (place of Water pot) and Hiraṇyasaṅgama (confluence of the Hiraṇya), the separate stories of Nagarārka, Kṛṣṇa, Saṅkarṣaṇa and Samudra (sea), Kumārī (Virgin), Rṣetrapāla (the guardian of the fields) and Brahmeśa.

177b-178. The glorification of Piṅgalā and Saṅgameśa, Śaṅkara, Arkeśa, Ghaṭeśa, the holy centre Ṛṣitīrtha, Nandārka-tritakūpa, the wonderful story of Parṇārka and Nyaṅkumatī with Sopāna.

179. The news (or the details) of Varāhasvāmin and that of Chāyāliṅga and Gulpha, the story of Kanakanandā as well as that of Kuntī and Gaṅgeśa.

180. Then the story of Camasa, Udbheḍa, Vidura and Trilokeśa (Lord of the three worlds), then the stories of Maṅkaṇeśa, Traipureśa and Ṣaṇḍa-Tīrtha.

Khaṇḍa which agrees with the extant published Sk. P., showing the degree of authenticity of the *Khaṇḍa*.

Sapiṇḍa rite, the essence of Dharma, the atonement of sins, the secondary creation, the dissolution and the particular characteristics of the Yugas are narrated, the benefit of religious rites.

18. The system of Yoga philosophy, the devotion to Viṣṇu, the benefit of obeisance to Hari, the greatness of Viṣṇu, the excellent hymn to Narasiṁha.

19. The nectar of perfect knowledge, the set of eight verses in praise of Guha (Kārttikeya), the eulogy of Viṣṇu, the principal tenets of Vedānta and Sāṁkhya, the knowledge of the Brahman and the Ātman.

20. The gist of the Bhagavadgītā, glorification of the fruit thereof—these are the topics mentioned in the first section. Then in the second section Pretakalpa (the rituals after the death) is narrated.

21. O Brāhmaṇa, on being asked by Tārkṣya (Garuḍa) the lord communicated all these things, the revelation of Dharmas, the cause of salvation of the Yogins.

22. The benefit of charitable gifts etc. is mentioned and then the Mantras for the rites of obsequies, then the description of the path leading to the world of Yama.

23. The details (regarding the performance) are stated alongwith the fruit of sixteen Śrāddhas. Expiatory rites in regard to the path of Yama, then the greatness of Dharmarāja.

24. Specific mention of the harassment of the Pretas (ghosts), review of the characteristic signs of the Pretas, the narration of the stories of the Pretas; the cause of ghosthood.

25. Consideration of religious rites for the ghosts; statements regarding Sapiṇḍīkaraṇa (the rite regarding the offerings of the balls of rice to the departed), the description of the release from ghost-hood, the charitable gifts for the purpose of salvation (of the ghosts).

26. The indispensable excellent charitable gift; the inference of things causing happiness to the ghosts; the description of the embodied soul, the description of Yama's world.

27. The narration of the uplift from ghosthood; the specification regarding the holy rites and the doer, the narra-

be like the rising sun. The man will be unapproachable and unthwartable in the world. After enjoying all excellent worldly pleasures here, he attains Brahmā's region in the end. He will be seated in an excellent aerial chariot, eulogised frequently by the Devas.

29b-31. An excellent Brāhmaṇa should worship Śiva with white and fragrant flowers on the second day in the bright half of the month of Phālguna. He should make a canopy and decorate it with flowers and ornamental fittings. He should propitiate the Lord with Naivedyas of various kinds. He should offer incense and lights. He should perform Nīrājana rite (waving of lights). Prostrating on the ground with eight limbs touching it, he shall make obeisance to the Lord.

32. Worshipping the Lord of the Devas thus, the man becomes free from all sickness. With plenty of wealth and food-grains, he shall certainly live for a hundred years.

33. The injunctions regarding the Dvitīyās of the bright half of the month should be followed in the case of those of the dark half of the month also, by the people clever in the matter of procedures.

34. It is the fire-god alone that is worshipped separately in the different months. He assumes different forms and so is worshipped on the Dvitīyās. The vow of celibacy etc. are to be observed as before.

CHAPTER ONE HUNDRED AND TWELVE

Enumeration of Vratas to be observed on Tṛtīyās (third day of a lunar fortnight

Sanātana said :

1. O Nārada, listen. I shall recount to you the Vratas pertaining to Tṛtīyā (third day in the lunar fort-night). On

P. Uttara 14. 18-23. It is also known as *Bhrātṛ-dvitīyā* (*Bhaiyyā-dūja* and people make it a point to go to their sister's place and offer her some gift. *Vrj.* quotes *CC.* wherein the *Bṣ. P.* mentioned above is quoted. *Vrj.* quotes from the *Sanatkumāra Saṁhitā*, LP & Pd. P. in support of this *Vrata* which is an act of fraternal affection.

The full extent of the holy observance is for a period of four years, beginning with this Caturthī day. He must spend the first year, taking only a single meal per day. He must spend the second year by taking meal only at night every day. He shall spend the third year by taking in only the food obtained without solicitation. He shall spend the fourth year also similarly. If no food is offered, he observes a fast. After completing the vrata at the end of the fourth year, he should perform the rite of ablution. He is then a Mahāvratin (a man of great Vratas). He shall then make the replica of the 'mouse-chariot' of Vighneśvara (i.e. god Gaṇeśa) made of gold. If he cannot afford this, he should make the mystic diagram of a lotus with good petals, by means of colours. The jar is placed over it alongwith a copper vessel, that is filled with raw rice-grains. Image of Gaṇeśvara (i.e. Gaṇeśa) is placed over it covered with two clothes. The devotee should worship the deity with scents and other things.

60-61. Modaka is to be offered as Naivedya saying : "May Gaṇeśa be pleased." The night shall be spent by keeping awake through songs and instrumental music as well as in the narration of the Purāṇas. After the day has dawned, he should take bath and perform Homa in accordance with injunctions, with gingelly seeds, rice grains, barley grains and white mustard along with ghee and sugar-candy.

62-64. The following sixteen names of the deity should be uttered in the dative case. Om is prefixed to them and Namaḥ is added at the end. (For example, here the 1st name is Gaṇa. It should be uttered and addressed as : Om Gaṇāya namaḥ).

The names of the god are : Gaṇa, Gaṇādhipa, Kūṣmāṇḍa, Tripurāntaka, Lambodara, Ekadanta, Rukma-daṁṣṭra, Vighnahā, Brahmā, Yama, Varuṇa, Soma, Sūrya, Hutāśana, Gandhamādin and Parameṣṭhin.

With the utterance of each name, one oblation is offered into the fire. A hundred and eight Homas are performed with the utterance of 'Vakra-tuṇḍa' and 'Varman' in the dative case (i.e. Vakra-tuṇḍāya and Varmaṇe.

65-66. Thereafter, he performs Homas with Vyāhṛtis to the extent of his capacity and then the Pūrṇāhuti is performed. After worshipping the guardians of the quarters, he should

44. On that day, Lord Viśveśvara, the destroyer of sins, should be seen, worshipped, known and remembered by one who wishes for happiness.

45a. Holy dip, charitable gift etc., performed on this day are proclaimed to be everlasting.

45b-47. O Brāhmaṇa, it was on the sixth day in the bright half of the month of Pauṣa that Dinapati (the Sun) manifested himself in the form of eternal Viṣṇu, the protector of the Universe. Hence, on this day, he is to be worshipped with scents and other articles of worship, Naivedyas, clothes and ornaments by those who desire for all kinds of happiness.

48-50a. The sixth day in the bright half of the month of Māgha is called Varuṇa[1] Ṣaṣṭhī. On that day, one should worship god Varuṇa who has the eternal form of Viṣṇu, with scents, red silken garments, flowers, Naivedyas, incense and lights. By worshipping thus in accordance with the injunctions, the man obtains whatever he desires. After attaining all the fruits he rejoices, thanks to his grace.

50b-51. On the sixth day in the bright half of the month of Phālguna, O Brāhmaṇa, the devotee should make an image of Lord Paśupati duly in clay and worship it with Upacāras (sixteen articles and modes). He should bathe the image with water or Pañcāmṛta while uttering Śatarudra mantra.

52-53. While unguents shall be smeared over the image, the deity should be worshipped with raw rice-grains, white flowers and fruits. Different kinds of Naivedya should be offered. Nīrājana (waving of lights) is duly performed. After bowing to and craving forgiveness of the Lord, he should be ritualistically sent to Kailāsa.

54. O sage, whether he is a man or a woman, whoever performs the worship of Śiva thus, enjoys all worldly pleasures here and in the end attains the goal of Śiva

---

1. This seems to be a contribution of the NP. as Kane does not mention it in HD.V. i.

59-62. He should take off strings from the arm and keep it below the water pot. Four images in the form of the deity are made in gold, and they are bathed in water and Pañcāmṛta. After worshipping them in accordance with the injunctions, with the sixteen types of Upacāras, the devotee keeps awake till midnight, to the accompaniment of songs and instrumental music. At midnight, when the nectar-rayed moon rises, Arghya is offered to Mahālakṣmī stationed in the middle of the moon's disc, in accordance with the injunctions, together with Śrīkhaṇḍa (sandal) and other material. The string is also offered.

[The following Mantras are utterred]

63. "O Moon, born of the ocean of milk, brother of Mahālakṣmī, O storehouse of nectar, accompanied by Rohiṇī, accept my Arghya."

64. "O Kamalā, born of the ocean of milk, a resident of the Lotus, resting on the chest of Viṣṇu, be the bestower of all the cherished desires on me."

65. "O gentle lady Reṇukā, O beloved wife of Jamadagni, O Mistress of the Universe, having only a single Lord, O unchanging one, O mother of Paraśurāma, do what is auspicious to me".

66-69. The devotee should pray to the goddess Mahālakṣmī with the above Mantras. He should worship Brāhmaṇa women duly with scents, lac juice and collyrium and feed them. He should perform Homa oblating in the fire Bilva, lotus and milk puddings. If they are not available O Brāhmaṇa, homa is performed with ghee. For acquiring houses, homa is performed with sacrificial twigs or gingelly seeds. For conquering (i. e. averting) death and for subduing ailments the following articles are offered as gifts viz.—sandal paste, palmyra leaf, flower-garland, raw unbroken rice grains, Dūrvā grass, thread with saffron applied, two coconuts and foodstuffs. The food-stuffs should be placed in a new winnowing basket. There must be sixteen of them in each item.

70-71. The observer of the holy rite shall cover it with another winnowing basket and present it uttering the following give them silver coins as Dakṣiṇā. After bidding farewell to them, he should partake of his own food. O Brāhmaṇa, the devotee who performs the holy rite thus, enjoys all worldly pleasures, inaccessible to the Devas, such as sons and riches. At the death of his body, he occupies excellent aerial chariot and attains to Viṣṇu's Loka.

CHAPTER ONE HUNDRED AND TWENTY

The exposition of the Vratas to be observed on Ekādaśi (eleventh) days[1] *(of the lunar fortnight)*

Sanātana said :

1-4. On the eleventh day in either of the fortnights of (any month), O sage, the devotee must desist from taking food.

1. The NP. being a Vaiṣṇava Purāṇa gives full details of Ekādaśi Vrata. It has devoted the whole of *Uttarārdha* in glorification of this Vrata.

The NP. follows *Pūrṇimānta* reckoning. Hence the Ekādaśi in the dark half is treated first. It is not known why *Caitra Ekādaśis* should be an exception and why *Ekādaśi* in *Caitra* Śu. and *Kṛ* are so much bifurcated (*Caitra* Śu in VV 5-8a and *Caitra* Kṛ in VV 80-82)

The following is the Tabular statement of Ekādaśis and the month and fortnight for their performance. The difference of name in the list in HDV. i P. 108 Note 278 is noted in the bracket.

	N. of the lunar Fortnight and month	*N. of the Ekādaśī Vrata*
1.	Caitra Śu.	Kāmadā
2.	,, Kṛ.	Pāpamocanī (Varūthinī)
3.	Vaiśākha Śu.	Mohinī
4.	,, Kṛ.	Varūthinī (Aparā)
5.	Jyeṣṭha Śu.	Nirjalā
6.	,, Kṛ	Aparā (Yoginī)
7.	Āṣāḍha Śu.	Śayanī
8.	,, Kṛ.	Yoginī (Kāmikā or Kāmadā)
9.	Śrāvaṇa Śu.	Putradā
10.	,, Kṛ.	Kāmikā (Ajā)

to be observed on the twelfth day in the bright half of the month of Mārgaśīrṣa. The Sādhyas are twelve in number. They are stated as follows : Manobhava, Prāṇa, Nara, Yāta (v.l. Apāna) Vīryavān, Citi, Haya, Nṛpa (v.l. Naya) Haṁsa, Nārāyaṇa, Vibhu and Prabhu. These shall be represented by raw rice grains and worshipped with scents, fragrant flowers etc. He should then feed twelve leading Brāhmaṇas. Good Dakṣiṇās are to be given to them. He should then bid farewell to them saying, 'May Nārāyaṇa be pleased.'

54b-61a. On the very same day, the holy rite of Dvādaśāditya Vrata[1] is known to be observed. The intelligent devotee should worship the twelve Ādityas viz : Dhātā, Mitra, Aryamā, Pūṣā, Śakra, Aṁśa, Varuṇa, Bhaga, Tvaṣṭṛ, Vivasvān, Savitṛ and Viṣṇu. Every month, on the twelfth day in the bright half, he should assiduously worship them and spend the year thus. At the conclusion of the holy rite, he should worship twelve gold images in accordance with the injunctions. He should feed twelve excellent Brāhmaṇas with sweet cooked rice. The observer of the holy rite should honour them separately and offer the gold image to each. By performing the Vrata, called Dvādaśāditya Vrata thus, the devotee attains the world of the sun and enjoys the pleasures therein for a long time. Then, he is born on the Earth among human beings as a pious soul, devoid of ailments. Thereafter, thanks to the merit of the Vrata, he shall accomplish the Vrata again (i.e. he shall perform it successfully again) O excellent Brāhmaṇa, thanks to its merit, he pierces the orb of the sun and attains the Brahman which is unsullied, formless and free from mutually clashing pairs (e.g. pleasure, pain etc).

61b-67a. On this very same day is to be observed the Akhaṇḍa Dvādaśī Vrata.[2] The devotee gets the replica of

1. Also called *Kāmadeva Vrata* in HD. V. i., P. 318 on the authority of *CC. Vrata* I. 1173.

2. Hemādri on the authority of *Viṣṇudharmottara* extends this efficacy of removing the *Vaikalya* (deficiency) in performing penance or even sacrifices (*Vrata* I. 1117-1124). AP. Ch. 190 limits the efficacy to seven births only (VV. 3 & 6), a view endorsed by *Garuḍa* P. 118.

Hemādri recommends another *Vrata* of the same name for the same purpose, but it starts on *Āśvina Śu* 11. (Ibid. *Vrata* I. 1103-1105).

CHAPTER ONE HUNDRED AND TWENTYTHREE

Description of the Vratas to be observed on Caturdaśi (fourteenth day in a lunar fortnight)

Sanātana said :

1. O Nārada, listen. I shall recount to you the holy rites to be observed on the Caturdaśī (fourteenth) days (of lunar fortnights). On observing these holy rites, a man shall attain his cherished desires in this world.

2-4a. On the fourteenth day in the bright half of the month of Caitra, magnificent worship of Śiva should be performed with saffron, agallochum, sandal paste, scents, and other things, clothes and ornaments. Erecting the canopy, the banner and the umbrellas, the mothers are to be worshipped. O Brāhmaṇa, by performing the worship thus alongwith the observance of fast or taking a single meal on that day, the man obtains merit more than that of a horse-sacrifice, on this Earth.

4b-5a. On this very same day, the devotee should perform Damanārcā (worship by means of Damanaka leaves and fragrant flowers). When the Vrata is concluded the devotee should dedicate the fruit to Śiva of auspicious form.

5b-8a. On the fourteenth day in the dark half of the month of Vaiśākha, the intelligent devotee should observe fast. At sunset he should take bath and wear clean white clothes and worship Liṅga with scents and other Upacāras and the leaves of a Bilva tree. After giving invitation to a prominent Brāhmaṇa, he should take food on the next day. O excellent Brāhmaṇa on all Caturdaśīs in the dark halves of the months, the holy rites Śivarātra Vrata should be performed by one who wishes for wealth and progeny.

8b-13. The devotee should observe the holy Vrata of Śrī-Nṛsiṁha[1] on the fourteenth day in the bright half of the month of Vaiśākha. If he is physically capable, he should observe fast.

---

1. VV. 8b-13 describe what is popularly known as Nṛsiṁha Jayanti as Viṣṇu manifested himself on Vaiśākha Śu 14 as Narasiṁha in the evening on Svāti Nakṣatra. The NP. calls this simply as *Nṛsiṁha-Vrata*. a confusing designation, as we have Nṛsiṁha Vratas on 8th, 12th and the 13th *Tithis* of different months (vide HD. V. I, pp. 328-329).

you) chastise the person who observes fast on his (Viṣṇu's) day ?

10. That you have not been ground down into powder, that you have not been tightly bound by them, is due to the honour bestowed on us. You are not trying to understand the real point from me.

11. The employee who does not know the most excellent and loyal devotees of the king on the Earth is subjected to arduous exertion and is again kept captive by them.

12. Persons favourite with the king should not be apprehended as culprits by an employee (a servant of a king). Achieving their objects through the favour of the master, they may get the employee dismissed.

13. Similar is the position of the sinners who bow down to Janārdana. How will you restrain them out of foolhardiness, O son of Bhāskara ?

14. O son of Divākara (Sun-god), O son of Bhāskara I may help you with the devotee of Śiva or Bhāskara (Sun-god) or my own devotees, but never with the devotees of Hari.

15. Puruṣottama is the Primordial deity among all Devas.

16. Restraining the devotees of Madhusūdana (God Viṣṇu) is not proper even if they fraudulently observe the holy rite of Ekādaśī during the lunar fortnight.

17-18. If they have slighted you, I cannot help you. O son of the Sun, if any help is rendered to you that will be injustice to me. It may even destroy my body. There may even be reversion from the post of Brahmā that is attained through high merit which I have achieved during the course of my life in the company of Viṣṇu's devotees.

own caste. It is in the path of the good. Mādhava himself is the Enjoyer and (the object of enjoyment. He alone is the supreme Man (Puruṣottama). Employment of him alone in all holy rites is the proper thing.

42-43. Thus it proclaimed to the people by means of beating of drums with the rumbling sound of the cloud, O leading Brāhmaṇas. Thus the father of Dharmāṅgada realised the virtue of his son. O Brāhmaṇas, on realising that his son was equipped with the practical holy rites even more than himself, the delighted king said to his wife who stood there like another Lakṣmī.

44. "O fair-complexioned Sandhyāvalī, I am blessed. You too are blessed. To both of us is born as son white as the moon on the Earth.

45. Salvation has never been seen by anyone anywhere. Much about it has been heard by the ears. But the birth of our good son is the super-salvation that has been attained by us.

46. O fair lady, if the son is richly endowed with humility, good conduct and heroism, if he is valorous, certainly it is salvation obtained by the father in his very house.

47-48. Bliss is the form of the Brahman. Hundred such blisses are acquired by the father through his son, O woman of beautiful limbs, by his auspicious and holy rites.

49. O gentle lady, there is nothing on a par with this in the whole world consisting of mobile and immobile beings, if the good son takes over the burden of his father and lifts it himself.

50. So, I am delighted now. I shall go to the forest for hunting the deer and have some good sports. O woman of wide eyes, I am freed of my sins by affording protection to the people. I shall now freely move about.

31-32. Paśupati (god Śiva) is satisfied with it and has immediately granted me the boon. You, the king of the Earth have been attained by me and this was what I had liked. O king you are loved by me and I am loved by you.

33. After saying thus to him, Mohinī caught hold of the hand of the king and quickly lifted him up even as he was lying on the ground like the thunderbolt of Indra.

CHAPTER THIRTEEN

The Fascination of Mohinī

Vasiṣṭha said :

1. Lifting up the king, Mohinī spoke these words : O leading king, do not entertain any doubt. Know me to be a virgin without sins.

2-3a. O king, marry me in accordance with the injunctions laid down in the Gṛhyasūtras. If an unmarried virgin becomes pregnant, she delivers of a son of ill fame who will be despised by the people of all castes.

3b-4. In the Purāṇa, the wise know (i. e. say) that there are three types of Cāṇḍālas. One is the child born of an unmarried virgin; the second type is the progeny of Sagotra marriage (i.e. marriage between a man and a woman of the same Gotra or lineage). O leading king, the third type of Cāṇḍāla is the progeny of a Brāhmaṇa lady begot by a Śūdra.[1]

5-6a. For this reason, O king marry me a virgin." Thereafter, King Rukmāṅgada married that lady of tremulous

---

1. Cf *Veda-Vyāsa Smṛti* I. 9-10
Kumārī-Sambhavas tvekaḥ sagotrāyāṁ dvitīyakaḥ |
Brāhmaṇyāṁ śūdra-janitaś cāṇḍālas trividhaḥ smṛtaḥ ||

12-13. Accompanied by many kings I make obeisance to my mother. On seeing the son prostrating on the ground and thanks to the chivalry of her husband, the king, Mohinī got down from the horse, raised up the son and embraced him with her hands.

14-16a. Embraced by his mother, he saluted her once again. He adorned her with nice clothes and charming ornaments. Dharmāṅgada, the son with eyes like lotus, requested her to place her legs on his back and mount the horse. In the same manner, he made his father too mount the horse.

16b-17a. He himself walked on foot surrounded by the vassal kings. On looking at his step-mother he was delighted and had his hair standing on their ends. Praising himself in a resonant voice like the rumbling sound of the cloud he said.

17b-21a. Blessed is the son who has many mothers in the world, new, fresh and charming beloved wives of his father. If one has only one mother, one's father is miserable. If the father is miserable what happiness can the son have in the heart ? By saluting one mother the son has only the merit of bowing to one earth. By saluting many mothers I will have greater benefit day by day.

21b-22. Saying thus he entered the city surrounded by the vassal kings. He entered the beautiful city of Vaidiśa endowed with (i.e. abounding in) all prosperity. Seated on the horse alongwith Mohinī the king too followed instantaneously.

23. Then he entered the excellent mansion. On being greeted and honoured by the people, the king got down from the horse and spoke these words to Mohinī.

24. O charming one, go to the house of Dharmāṅgada our son. In accordance with his attributes, he will render service to you as befitting an elderly person.

25. Neither a chaperon nor a servant can render such a willing service ! On being thus advised by her husband, she started for the mansion of their son.

26-27. She was seen entering the mansion by Dharmāṅgada, at the instance of her husband's words. He thereupon left the vassal kings saying—"All of you stay here. At the a thousand good poles to which the yokes are to be fixed, severally.

39. The son of the king gave each of them ten kinds of grains. Laughingly he gave a hundred thousand gardens.

40. He gave ten thousand pots of ghee and oil separately. To each of them he offered inumerable goats and ewes.

41. The highly devoted son presented them (the queen-mothers) thousands of gold ornaments studded with diamonds (and precious stones).

42. He gave them necklaces made of brilliant pearls of the size of embylic myrobalan fruits. He gave them five and seven (a dozen) bangles each.

43. Sandhyāvalī was already wearing on her person two hundred and fifty pearls resembling the moon.

44. The son presented each of them two necklaces that captivated the mind. He gave them Prastha measures of Saffron, sandal paste and camphor.

45-46. The son gave them huge quantity of musk. Desirous of the happiness of his father he impartially distributed to them different kinds of vessels, water pots, ghee pots, milk pots, and pots for different kinds of beverages.

47. The prince gave them gold plates, pots and vessels one thousand and fourteen hundred in number (?)

48. To each of them he gave three hundred to five hundred she-elephants of great speed with muscular and fleshy shoulders.

49. He gave them twenty she-camels each and hundred palanquins with brawny men with excellent dress (uniform).

50-51. To the mothers he gave seventy horses of happy pleasing trot. After giving thus to them much wealth, the blessed prince who had the affluence and brilliance of Kubera circumambulated them. With palms joined in reverence he addressed these words.

52-53. I bow down to you with my head bent low. It is my importunity to you all that all of you should say thus to my father.— O king, enjoy Mohinī freely. We have no trace of malice towards you nor should you be malicious towards us. Sport with Mohinī the good natured daughter of Brahmā, with hundreds of secret pleasures from her.

29. I am desirous of telling you now. O splendid fair-faced lady, know it. O gentle lady, many Kārttika months have gone by since my infatuation over you.

30. I did not observe any holy rite except the single holy vow of the day of Hari. But now I wish to observe the holy vow of the month of Kārttika.

31. If mortal beings spend the Kārttika month without observing the holy vows, O daughter of Brahmā, all their righteous activities and the Iṣṭāpūrtas (charitable rites such as digging wells, tanks etc. and sacrificial rites) are futile.

32. O blessed lady, even those kings, who are addicted to non-vegetarian diet and who are too much engaged in hunting have eschewed meat in the month of Kārttika and have gone to Viṣṇu's abode.

33. If the aspirant abstains from those foodstuffs to which he is addicted in the month of Kārttika, certainly he attains the form of Viṣṇu.

34. O fair-complexioned lady, let alone the charitable gifts involving the expense of great amounts of wealth and causing great mental strain, one can go to heaven merely by means of the charitable gift of lamps.

35. If that is not available, O blessed lady, one shall kindle the lights offered by others with great devotion. It is superior to all charitable gifts.

36. If one were to weigh all the charitable gifts placed on one side and the charitable gift of lamps on the other side, Lord Kārttikeya has said that the charitable gifts of lamps and the kindling of lamps are on a par with each other.

37-38a. This kindling of lights must be performed with the feelings of devotion. Then it is superior to all kinds of charitable gifts. There is no doubt about this that, by observing the holy rite (by fasting etc.) on the full moon day in the month of Kārttika, in the holy centre of the umbilical lotus of Viṣṇu (i.e. Puṣkara), one is liberated from the sins committed ever since the birth.

38b-39a. He who observes holy vows, fasts and other restraints throughout the month of Kārttika shall become a (away from its place). O king (for the same reason) the Vindhya mountain does grow (rise) up. Never does a yonng woman carry the child in her crossing the time limit (i.e. beyond a stipulated period of about ten months, she does not hold it.)

89. It is only when they are abiding by truthfulness that trees put forth flowers and fruits. O king, the means of Divine judgement, etc. of men has for its basis, truthfulness alone.

90. Truthfulness surpasses thousands of horse-sacrifices. Through falsehood you will be tainted with such a sin as that of drinking liquor.

CHAPTER TWENTYFOUR

Questions of Mohinī[1]

The king said :

1-2. You mention that it had been recounted to you by Gautama on the excellent mountain Mandara that food be taken on the day of Hari. But this is contrary to the opinion of the Purāṇas. O fair-faced lady, it has been mentioned by that Brāhmaṇa who indulges in spreading the insignificant sacred texts out of greed.

3-5. The following decisions have been proclaimed in the Purāṇas by learned men viz—one should not drink water with

1. This chapter describes a typical conflict between parochical Vedists and *Vaiṣṇavas*. This part of the NP. is meant for the glorification of the Ekādaśī Vrata. Though this topic is discussed in Part I Ch. 23 (and elsewhere), a detailed description and importance of this Vrata is found (sometimes repeated in this part also. This chapter emphasizes the importtance of complete fasts of Ekādaśī and the acceptance of the authority of Purāṇas in interpreting the Vedas. The medieval writers who compiled treatises on Ekādaśī (e.g. Śūlapāṇi's *Ekādaśī Viveka*, Raghunandana's *Ekādaśītattva*) and on *Kāla* (e.g. *Hemādri* on *Kāla*, *Mādhava* on *Kālanirṇaya*) have profusely quoted the NP as an authority on Ekādaśī. Hence the importance of these chapters.

13-14. He may even drink poison, he may enter fire, he may jump down from a lofty mountain; he may cut off his head with an excellent sword that brightens the sky; but king Rukmāṅgada will never take food on the day of Hari, on this Earth. My name Rukmāṅgada is famous in the three worlds.

15. How can I, by taking food on the Ekādaśī day, destroy the reputation earned by me—accumulated by me through the observance of fast on the Ekādaśī day.

16. Even if it dies, goes off, falls down, perishes, breaks into pieces, my heart shall not desist from this for the sake of Mohinī.

17. I may even forsake my life alongwith the worlds, my wives and servants. But I will never resort to the taking of food on the auspicious day of Viṣṇu.

CHAPTER TWENTYSEVEN

*The story of Kāṣṭhilā**

Vasiṣṭha said :

1-2. On hearing the words of his father, the son Dharmāṅgada called his mother named Sandhyāvalī who was auspicious, lustrous like ten thousand suns, of beautiful breasts and who protected the entire earth by the pacing of her steps over it.

3. At the instance of her son, she immediately reached the presence of the king. The words of Mohinī as well as those of his father were repeated to her.

4-5. Get an agreement effected between these two—console Mohini who tenaciously clings to (the stipulation of)

*Standard dictionaries like SKD, MW, give a 'plantain tree" as the meaning of *Kāṣṭhilā* but the story shows it to be a worm in the wood.

my husband) to make her his wife, from Varanasi, the city whose limits are not transgressed by all sins.

13. That city is called Śakti Kṣetra (the sacred place of Divine Power) and is holy and destructive of sins. It is the abode of Tripurāri (God Śiva) and it extends to five Gavyūtis (i.e. fifteen Kilometers).

14. Men who die therein are never reborn into any womb. Kindly take this lady of bright eyes to her father's house.

15. These jewels, beds and seats are at your disposal. If you wish you can sell all these things including myself.

16. O Brāhmaṇa, for your sake the terrible Rākṣasa was slain by me who am enamoured of your comely features. He has been sent to the abode of Yama.

17. Hence, O Lord, have confidence in me. O large-eyed one, I am your devotee. I can assume any form I like. 'Enjoy me.'

18. O lady of beautiful eyes, on hearing these words of the love-lorn ogress, my husband spoke these words to the Rākṣasī in the presence of that virgin.

19. As he was guarded and suspicious he spoke sweet words—

"O blessed lady, (it is mentioned) in the treatises on polity and ethics that women should not be trusted.

20-21. How will she not injure me, she who kills her husband ever since her girlhood days ? Considering another man more handsome, this lascivious woman (may cause my death). O fair-faced lady, still I continue to believe in you.

22. O beautiful woman, I have sought refuge in you, kill me, if you please, to-day or tomorrow or after a fortnight or a month or a year.

23-24. This must be done by you only thus (as though) I have not helped you today (?) For the sake of vengeance (help in return ?) the soul must be offered by you. (You must give yourself up). Since you unhesitatingly killed your husband for my sake, O lady of good eyes, I do not say anything more."

25. On hearing the words of my husband, she spoke

CHAPTER THIRTY

The story of Kāṣṭhilā (*Contd.*)

Kāṣṭhilā said :

1. On hearing these words based on (and approved by) Dharma of his wife, the ogress, the Brāhmaṇa and girl descended from the back of the ogress who had assumed the form of a she-elephant.

2. When the Brāhmaṇa got down, that ogress became once again a beautiful young woman with her face resembling the moon and with plump and protruding breasts.

3. On reaching the splendid city of her own father, that virgin spoke to the city governor who had come there in the course of his duty of guarding the exterior limits of the city.

4-7. O city Governor, go to my father the king Sudyumna and tell him that I Ratnāvalī alias Ratnaśālā* who had been abducted from his city, from my bed, have come back. O Brāhmaṇa, (you remember) that I had been abducted though I had been considered the jewel of the king Sudyumna. His daughter has come back alive and safe and sound. (You tell him as though I say) "O dear father, be consoled. Do not feel sorry on my account, O leading king, I have never been ravaged. I am like the pure water of the Gaṅgā. I have brought about your fame (I have not marred your fame). I am the index of the good nature of my mother."

8. On hearing the words of the virgin, the city-governor who was well known as Abāhu reached the presence of Sudyumna in a hurry.

9-10. He made obeisance and on being asked spoke to the king respectfully. "O king, O bestower of honour, your daughter well known as Ratnāvalī, who had been lost has come back. She is accompanied by a Brāhmaṇa in the company of a woman. She was seen by me standing outside the city limits but could not be recognized.

**Ratna-śālām* in the Text. It should have been rather *Ratna-śālāyāḥ* who was abducted from *Ratna-śālā*. She was sleeping in Ratnaśālā. The Accusative is used for Ablative in the text. [*vide* v. 17 below]

25. Obeisance to Hari, the miraculous lion. Hail to the noble-souled Vāmana. Bow to the deity of the form of a Boar. Obeisance to the Divine Fire, the resident of the ocean (at the time) of dissolution of the universe.

26. Obeisance to the Tortoise, the upholder of the Mandara mountain. Hail to Bhārgva; obeisance to the deity lying in the ocean; Bow to Rāma the lord of all; obeisance to the lord of the universe, the cosmic witness.

27. Obeisance to Dattātreya, the pure one; obeisance to Kapila, the remover of distress; Bow to the sacrifice the upholder of Dharma; obeisance to the deity of the form of Sanaka and others.

28. Hail to the deity who granted boons to Dhruva; to Pṛthu of plenty of activities; to Ṛṣabha the pure one; obeisance to the Ātman bearing horse's head.

29. Bow to Haṁsa (the swan), the embodiment of Āgama, to the deity holding the vessel of nectar; obeisance to Kṛṣṇa, to Vāsudeva, to the deity who assumes the form of Saṁkarṣaṇa.

30. Obeisance to Pradyumna, to Aniruddha, to Brahmā, Śaṅkara, to Kumāra, to Gaṇeśa, to Nandin, to Bhṛṅgin.

31. Obeisance to the deity staying on the mountain Gandhamādana, obeisance to Nara and Nārāyaṇa. Bow to the lord of the universe; obeisance to Rāmeśvara.

32. Hail to the resident of Dvārakā; obeisance to the resident of Tulasī grove. Obeisance to the deity having the lotus in umbilicus. Bow to you the lotus-footed.

33. Obeisance to the Lotus-handed deity; obeisance to you, the Lotus-eyed one. Hail to the protector of Kamalā (Lakṣmī). Repeated obeisance to Keśava.

34. Bow to the deity having the form of the Sun; obeisance to the deity assuming the form of the moon; obeisance to the deity having the form of the guardians of the worlds (quarters). Hail to the deity assuming the form of Prajāpati.

35. Obeisance to the deity of the form of the groups of elements (or mass of living beings); obeisance to the splendour in the form of the Jīva (individual soul); obeisance to the Victory, to the victorious, to the leader, to the deity in the form of observances and holy rites.

cast off his affection and lifted his sword. The lord Viṣṇu observed that (the king's steadfastness had been proved) on that touch-stone.

32-33. For he was prepared to kill his son but he would not take food on the day of Hari. Hari (Viṣṇu) saw the real feelings of the king, his wife and his son. He was extremely pleased (with them) and so all the three were taken to his own abode along with their physical bodies like coals deposited (ignited) with fire, as their Karmans were exhausted.

34. O blessed and gentle lady, if the work is begun in earnest and performed assiduously but the fruit is not derived, what is your fault in it now ?

35. For this reason, O splendid lady, Devas have come as granters of boon. Whether it fructifies or not, one should engage oneself in an activity. One must not remain idle.

36-38. All his attendants must be properly maintained by a king, who wishes for piety. If, even after an honest effort, the servant is not able to accomplish the task, at least the remuneration must be paid. There may not be any gratuity. If a man (i.e. the master) does not give the (servant) living sustenance, he attains the sin of a cow-slaughter. There is no doubt about this. Hence, O fair lady, O excellently beautiful woman, what is desired by you must be given.

39-40A. (Defective) the task of heaven-dwellers had been to create the obstacle. Since you have endeavoured with sincerity what is it that the Devas will not do. But O fair-faced lady, along with you, they toó have been frustrated by the brilliance of fast which they call the destroyer of obstacles."

40B-41. On being told thus by the Devas, Mohinī the enchantress of the worlds, who was bereft of her husband and so was cheerless and extremely distressed, spoke thus :- "Fie upon this life of mine, inasmuch as the entrusted work was not achieved.

42-43. O lords of the immortal beings, the path of the world of Yama has not been rendered thronging with people. The vow of the day of Hari was not violated. Food was not taken by that king. His own son was executed by that hero

37. But she became a sinner inasmuch as she was antagonistic to Viṣṇu's day. O leading Brāhmaṇa may something be done immediately so that she is sanctified."

38. On hearing god Brahmā's words of request, the sacrificial priest (of Mohinī's family) delightfully passed orders for reunion of the physical body (after its creation) with (the jīva) of his Yājyā.

39. On hearing the words of the Brāhmaṇa, Brahmā, the grandfather of the worlds, sprinkled water from his waterpot on the ashes of the body of Mohinī.

40. When the ashes were sprinkled with water by Brahmā, the maker of the worlds, Mohinī was endowed with a physical body. After bowing down to her father, she humbly bowed down to Vasu, the priest and grasped his feet.

41. Then Vasu, the Yājaka (priest) of the king, became joyous. He spoke these words to (Mohinī) who was the wife of his Yājya (one on whose behalf he had to perform a Yajña), whose prowess was wellknown and who had been abandoned by her husband and son.

42. Vasu said:- "O gentle lady, anger has been abandoned by me at the instance of Brahmā. I shall facilitate your salvation by means of such rites as visiting holy centres and taking holy dips".

43. After saying this to Mohinī, the Brāhmaṇa joyously bowed down to Brahmā, the lord of the worlds, and the father of Mohinī, and bade goodbye to him.

44. Bidden farewell by Mohinī and Vasu out of affection Brahmā went to the world beyond darkness through the unmanifest path.

45-46. Vasu the excellent Brāhmaṇa who was the priest of Rukmāṅgada considered Mohinī worthy of being blessed and pondered. After meditating for a Muhūrta he understood the way to her salvation.[1]

1. This chapter serves as a background for the *Tīrtha-Yātrā* (Pilgrimage to holy places) section that follows.

industrialization is, indeed, an irrevocable development, but at the same time consider it dangerous and disastrous. Judgements of this kind can be heard from modern critics of culture in the conservative camp to the anti-authoritarian and progressive Marxist camp - where they are growing in numbers. Progressive Marxist examples are mainly the attacks on the cultural industry by Theodor W. Adorno, on the consciousness industry by Hans Magnus Enzensberger and Herbert Marcuse's description of the consequences of advanced industrialization on man.

There is no doubt that many of the arguments set forth by critics of culture in three different historical periods apply also to industrialized education. One is, for instance in line with the critics of culture of the second part of the nineteenth century when saying that the original individuality of the teacher and also of the students cannot express itself and is even lost over long periods of the teaching-learning process because of the use of technical media and of fixed goals and procedures of instruction. Teachers and students do not meet as fully developed individuals, but only as reduced and specialized functionaries. Distance education produces neither funny teaching characters nor notoriously annoying types of students, as is often the case in face-to-face instruction. The systems of distance education are, it is true, 'standardized in order to raise their functionality', and 'production in series', 'mechanization', and 'functionalization' and 'functionalization' are their important structural traits. Finally, it should be mentioned that the motivation of many distant students derives from a characterized by the following communication structures between teachers and students :

- group instruction;
- classroom instruction;
- large group instruction;
- instruction of mass audience.

It must be added that each period continued to exist and could even assume new importance in later periods. The changes, however, which came to pass when one period replaced the other must have been considerable, and were, obviously, caused by certain societal necessities. Brunner, for instance, reported that in ancient Egypt private tuition changed to classroom instruction as early as the beginning of the second millennium - that is, at a time when a rigid administration was established and a technically and ethically well-educated civil service was highly valued. The ability to rationalize instruction with the help of better organization is obviously a precondition for proceeding from one period to the next one.

If one asks how distance education relates to these periods, and especially distance education in the multimedia form which has developed during the last fifteen years and which has already integrated radio and television, the answer can only be that it belongs to the final period. The extreme of mass education has been reached fully. Some projects of this kind provided tuition for groups counted in tens of thousands and even a hundred thousand students - for instance, the Quadriga-Funkkolleg in the Federal Republic of Germany and the same information can be coded in different ways; for instance, by newspaper, radio or television.

In order to acquire the ability to study at a distance - that is, to work with mediated instruction - it may be very important that people have already gained the experience of receiving many pieces of coded information which are independent from the persons and occurrences in their immediate neighborhood. This experience is new, for pre-industrial man received typically only relatively few pieces of information, which were accidental, not coded, and connected to persons and events. The difference is obvious. Through his daily experience, industrial man has learnt to use purposeful (that is, constructed) communications which tend to be concentrated and concise. Such communications are intentional to a high degree, they avoid unnecessary repetitions, and try each time to reach the highest level of information. Evidently, experiences of this kind are better preconditions for learning at a distance than oral communication as practised nearly exclusively in agrarian societies.

The ideas and the behaviour of persons in industrial society are not formed and shaped by their interaction with their primary and secondary groups only, but also by their relations to human beings whom they know exclusively from the mass media: sports idols, film stars, politicians, scholars, authors. They learn about their developments and their life style, observe how they react to actual occurrences, and even develop a lasting attitude towards them. Thus, they are already used to dealing with 'substitute persons' and have accumulated a considerable skill in this respect. In by conventional sanctions; they fail because of the authority of the institution. In distance education, however, they fail because of lack of success; that is, they fail because of reality.

Finally, the two subsystems also differ with regard to their particular ways of 'rationalizing'. Face-to-face instruction leads to the emancipation of the student, to his individuation, and to the extension of 'dominance-free communication'. Distance education leads to an increase of effectiveness by using technical devices.

In the result of this comparison are summarized.

On the basis of this sociological analysis the following definition of distance education can be give:

> *Distance education is a system of rational actions for the imparting of knowledge, skills and attitudes, whereby the originally direct social relationships between teacher and students are substituted to a great extent by indirect relations which are characterized by technical rules and prescriptions, a context-free language, conditioned prognoses and conditioned instructions, goal attainment with the help of target-means relations, and the systematical increase of effectivity.*

With regard to the objections of cultural critics it must be stated here that the described change of behaviour is, indeed, a deep one, and therefore, full of consequences for the didactical structure of distance education. The fears of negative consequences, for instance, the mechanization,

The separation of teacher and taught is underlined as it is in Holmberg's definition and it can be accepted that no one in Holmberg's definition and it can be accepted that no one would wish to propose a definition of distance education which did not include the possibility of face-to-face contact 'on occasion or for selected tasks'. The wording of the law can be challenged in that it is so broad that it could encompass certain forms of conventional education.

Moore

Moore's definition highlights three elements:

— the separation of teaching behaviours and learning behaviours

— the use of technical media

— the possibility of two-way communication.

His analysis separates teaching into two areas: in normal face-to-face teaching the teacher's preparation is done apart from his students and he teaches in the presence of students. In distance education both the preparation and the teaching are done apart from students.

The emphasis on technical media and two-way communication are valuable additions to what has already been presented. It is important for Moore that the system should allow the learner to initiate this communication.

Moore-s definition was further elaborated by Rune Flinck who presents it as follows:

Distance education is a learning system where the teaching behaviours are separate from the throughout the course. These institutions are representatives of the most industrialised form of education.

Didactic model

Three forms of didactic structure characterise distance education institutions, especially when considered under the headings:

— provision for two-way communication and

— possibility of occasional seminars.

Variations of the three models presented here are to be found employed by the different institutional types considered above in their effort to link learning materials to learning.

The correspondence schools send learning materials by post to the student, the student studies the materials and posts assignment back to the institution which marks and comments upon them and posts them back to the student.

The correspondence element in distance education is here reduced to a minimum and once the learning materials have been developed and distributed to the students, the emphasis is placed on compulsory fortnightly two-to-three hour consultations. At these, groups of students meet their tutor for evaluation of their home study and for explanation and preparation of the next stage of learning materials. In the third and fourth year of study the frequency of the consultations is greatly diminished.

In a system similar to that of the Open University of the United Kingdom the link between learning materials and learning is promoted by as

Man. The same is true of education. Its purpose is the liberation of man from the restraints and limitation of ignorance and dependency. Education has to increase men's physical and mental freedom - to increase their control over themselves, their own lives, and the environment in which they live.

The ideas imparted by education, or released in the mind through education, should therefore be liberating ideas; the skills acquired by education should be liberating skills. Nothing else can properly be called education.

We went onto argue:

In other words, education is to do with power. People without education are at the mercy of those with it, who can use what they know to their advantage and to the disadvantage of the ignorant around them. Education is a means of gaining power, and not simply the right of the better-educated minority. On this showing the case for expanding education is a simple egalitarian one.

My starting point is, therefore, expansion - the need to expand education.

But the way in which education is expanded is also important. Expansion of schooling is of limited value if it simply reinforces the ideas that learning is a valuable possession, held by the teacher or shut within the covers of a textbook, that can be acquired provided the student listens or reads diligently and respectfully. Instead, with many educators, we would stress the importance of dialogue. There are, however, both weak and strong forms of the argument for making it central to a theory of education. The weak form of the argument points

Another important distinctive attribute of distance study is the *indirect* interaction between the university teachers and their students. This must be stressed, as many people believe that there is not communication between them at all. It is accomplished by means of letters, printed material, telephone calls, video and audio from lectures and classes at a university where this interaction usually takes place *indirectly*, that is, face-to-face.

There are four fundamental types of distance education in higher learning:

- *Type 1*: Distance education is accomplished by studying the printed material sent to the students by their university teachers, as well as by means of an exchange of letters between them, whereby the university teachers and their assistants correct the assignments and guide the further work of the students. This type was developed out of the traditional correspondence instruction and can be found especially in countries with long experiences in this field; for instance, England, France, the United States, Canada, Australia and South Africa.
- *Type 2*: Here, distance education type 1 is supplemented by regular and obligatory teaching-learning activities which take place face-to-face. It was developed in the Soviet Union and later introduced in eastern Germany. Variations of this type can be found in Japan, Sweden, Cuba, Mexico and Costa Rica. In extreme cases the face-to-face periods become so important that it becomes doubtful whether one can still speak of distance education.

In *Eastern* European countries the organizational structure of distance education provides that most professors, deans and reactors of the universities have to be responsible for their distant students in the same way as for their day students. Quite often the universities even have special pro-rectors for distance study. In this way, distance education is fully integrated not only into the general teaching programme, but also into the hierarchy of the university.

A total integration is achieved in seventeen higher educational institutions in the USSR and in China. There, the entire faculty of the college caters exclusively for distant students. If we want to find out what a similar set-up would look like in a western county, we need only examine the University of South Africa, where there is a whole university which takes care of distant students only.

Methods of teaching and learning

There are also fundamental differences between the two models of distance education with regard to the methods of teaching and learning employed. A first structural difference can be derived from the fact that western correspondence schools have contributed considerable experience to the development of printed teaching material. It was taken over by universities and adapted to their special purposes. Over the last hundred years private correspondence colleges have accumulated special knowledge of how to teach at a distance, which could easily be systematized into a methodology of teaching by writing. However, the value of this methodology should not be assessed as pedagogy of the course. It took concrete form with the development of the idea of a *Course Journal*.

The idea of the 'Curriculum theory' *Course of Journal* was regarded as significant not only because it could provide a medium for students to exchange ideas. It also offered the possibility of enacting Stenhouse's notion of 'academia as a social system for the production and utilization of knowledge through research'. A journal offered the prospect of collaborative exchange in which course team members teaching the course could enter the forum on a more equal basis with students. For this reason there was some spirited discussion in the course team about whether and how it should operate as an 'editorial board' for the journal. Would it accept all student submissions? Would only those submissions be published which seemed particularly meritorious? In the end it was agreed that all student work should be published, but that all work should be checked against explicitly stated criteria of acceptability. Work which did not meet these requirements would be returned to students for resubmission. On this model of the journal, with the course team operating as this particular kind of editorial board, it was thought that the journal could become a medium for declaration and dialogue between students and course team members. On this basis, perhaps staff and students could exchange ideas as a *community of enquirers*.

Working from this image of the course as a community of enquirers, the course team began to consider the course on the model of a professional association, in which members contributed to and received a journal, but also participated in an

Her comment exposes a major point of contention about the way the theory and pedagogy of the course are interrelated. Her concern was that the critical meta-theory, as represented by Lundgren, failed to say enough about the complexity and richness of human experience. She opens up this concern with the question, 'What is this proto-theory saying about human beings?' She expressed the more substantive point thus:

> The most fundamental question - What is the nature of our 'humanness'? — will determine the direction our education 'system' will take. It is at this level we see a basic problem with the theory. Society's views on humanity and the means used to assist the growth and development of that quality are so divergent that it is not possible to provide educational curricula which can openly and honestly accommodate the different world views which generate them.

The full implication of this concern goes back to the point made earlier about the expression of humanness. The critical meta-theoretical position calls forth a communication ideal — the idea that the course can be in some concrete sense a living community. But such an ideal usually rests on the notion that members of the community can interact face-to-face. Distance education challenges this basic assumption. The attenuation, intangibility and transience of relationships in the distance education mode make the communitarian ideal highly problematic.

> We need to learn a new role of relating to each other as colleagues. Relationships of any sort are delicate, complex affairs.... Let's build on the

society for all people). Others are less sanguine about such developments, seeing in them the possibility that an extension or expansion of these technologies of communication in schooling may threaten the practice of education, undermining the very possibility of critical thought. The problem was well articulated by Stanley Aronowitz, writing about Max Horkheimer:

In his book *The Eclipse of Reason*, Max HOrkheimer, founder of the Frankfurt Institute for Social Research, provide one of the most succinct formulations of the problem engendered by mass culture. According to Horkheimer, the significance of the challenge posed by the massified culture industry to civilisation as such consisted in its assault on the capacity to engage in critical thought as a meaningful form of social discourse. Horkheimer cared deeply about the content of critical thought, but with the rise of fascism he became more concerned with the spectre of the end of reason itself. In his view, the capacity of humans to distance themselves from the object in order to gain a perspective on their social world can no longer be taken for granted. The restricted language and thought codes produced by the reduction of all thought to its technical dimensions reach for into the culture, encompassing schools as well as communications, the public as well as the private spheres of discourse. It is no longer a question of whether ordinary discourse is able to deal with specific ideological and social content. As Jurgen Habermas expressed it, the new situation raises the question of the competence of people to effectively communicate ideational content. The issue is the capacity for theoretical or conceptual thought itself.

circumstances and satisfaction with the completion of a part rather than the whole of a particular programme. The success of the Open University has brought it an international reputation and many attempts have been made to transplant this success to other countries and other continents. So far it would appear that none have managed to improve upon the drop-out rate and thus, in popular terms, the 'success'. Indeed the opposite seems to be the truth. None have come anywhere near reaching a success rate approaching sixty per cent. There are a number of reasons for this but, we would suggest, only one of major significance. This popular conception of the Open University, even by those who have made a careful study of it, is of a system dominated by a highly structured package of correspondence texts and broadcasts.

The method of preparation of this package by a course team has been seen as a unique development and a major contributory factor to the quality of the package. The package - particularly the course units and its method of production, are extensively and variously copied. Yet, we would contend that this analysis of the Open University does not rest wholly or entirely on the highly structure teaching package. It rests rather on the inter-relationships of that package with the student as an individual through the agency of the counselling and tuition functions peculiar to the Open University. It is the combination of these elements on which the comparative success of the Open University is based. Neither is sufficient in itself.

Contracting the Open University with Fernuniversitat

The truth of this hypothesis might be supported in

and technical equipment. A strong tendency towards concentration and centralization becomes noticeable.

The terms used in business studies to describe these facts will be outlined briefly and - where possible - applied to distance teaching.

Rationalization

By rationalization we mean all 'methodical' (that is, rationally guided) 'measures' with the purpose of achieving 'output with a comparatively (compared to earlier situations) lower input of power, time and money'. Scientific discoveries should 'be evaluated for practical use in such a way as to achieve the best possible results in view of the continually necessary development and redevelopment of economic and technical processes'.

Applied to the practical example of the production process this means that 'the entire production line, from raw material to end product, is carefully analysed to allow each single work process to be planned so as to make the most effective contribution possible towards achieving clearly formulated business tasks.

Georges Friedmann emphasizes that this is a dynamic process aiming at continuous improvement in quality through continuous progress in the study of materials, accuracy and precision'. Rationalisation of this type has only started to develop with increasing industrialization at the end of the nineteenth century.

Management science holds that the reason for the considerable obstacles to rationalization lies in continuously adapted to the constant needs of a large group of consumers, a distance teaching institution has to standardize the academic contents of its courses in such a way that it can be sure they appeal to all distance learners as equally as possible. The adaptation to any number of students, however large, forces the lecturer more strongly than in conventional study to consider the necessary standard that is, at the same time, realistic for as many students as possible.

Consequently, the choice of contents of a distance study course is less likely to be a reflection of the particular interest of an academic giving conventional lectures, than of the objective requirements of the total course profile.

Change of function

On account of the division of labour and the use of various types of machines, the function of the worker in the production process has changed considerably. Whereas it was typical for the craftsman to plan the production of a piece of work as well as acquire the necessary materials, carry out the work and finally sell the finished piece of work himself, industrialization led to a more marked functional differentiation. When preparatory work and selling became separate from production and, within these three phases, many individual functions were allocated to different individual, a loss of function naturally occurred for each single worker. On the other hand, new roles were created and new achievements became possible. For example, 'in jobs where, due to mechanization, the processing of the material has been taken out of the worker's hand, speed and energy of execution are no

- *Evaluation*: Examination of the learning results of all course students, recommendations of changes to the instructions and further developmental of courses, taking into consideration new findings by educational experts of the research unit.

The most important functions are the writing of course material and the correction of papers sent in by the students. This is what most of the teachers do. The division of labour frees them from the more bothersome extra functions which can be carried out by specialists in the various departments of the school. It stands to reason that these specialists can do their job more thoroughly, reliably and effectively.

Generally, the qualities of the persons teachings at a distance must be the same as in face-to-face instruction. As their functions are, however, reduced to course writing as well as correcting and marking assignments, and as they have to specialize in these fields, they need additional qualifications. The *course writer* must have the ability to envisage the teaching-learning situation they want to create and to foresee possible difficulties of comprehending and learning, and must be able to write instead of instructing orally or lecturing—which is quite a different thing. Even more, the course writer must be able to write short, concise and succinct sentences which are understandable—a gift which is certainly not found very often.

The *corrector* must be able to react as if he or she were in a virtual instructional situation with a single student. Some correspondence schools help correctors to do so by supplying them with the distance teaching. That she did so, and maintained the close ties of friendship in the group, further underscores her considerable personal and professional strengths.

If one may be permitted a generalization which both oversimplifies individual contributions and reveals a major truth about he course team process, Willmott and King provided the focus and determination which were necessary to get the Graduate Diploma up and running, while Forster and Luke modelled how we should work with our students.

Ian Mitchell's role was rather different. he was the one member of the group who had any standing or was even known in the distance education community when the course was mooted, and we relied on his knowledge and extensive personal connections. It was very much in keeping with his personality and commitment to the field that he both accepted and supported others shaping the course; indeed, his commitment to delivery of the prepared units made the continuing development process possible. Mitchell understood that the rest f the team did not know as much about distance education as might have been expected of them, given the tasks they were undertaking. By gently seeking to extend the boundaries of what was being addressed, in particular in relation to the academic and research expectations we had of students, and avoiding obtrusive reference to mistakes being made, he both influenced and gave licence to others who helped in bringing his initial conception to reality.

Finally, there was a serious commitment on the

accessibility of the materials to students (for instance, nearly all students had indicated they had access to a video-recorder, but the team failed to recognize that this did not mean regular or convenient access).

The module was the least satisfactory overall. Core members were reinforced in the belief that if their view of necessary standards were to prevail, control of the process could not be allowed to move outside the group again. One does not need the wisdom of hindsight to be aware of the objections which could be raised to such assertions of the need for control. The stance of the core team was very much that of the need to maintain control to avoid prescription of content and inflexibilities for students. We saw a necessary disjunction between ends and means.

Administration of distance education

This module was largely written before the course team could find and intellectual framework within which to structure to teaching materials. The final product reflects the course team as its most pragmatic, attempting to make virtue out of necessity. The course team was expanded to include other College staff with expertise in educational administration, and various members had views on desirable content. What was missing was any sense of the overall structure or intellectual framework for the module. There is some irony in this, given the determination of the core to exercise greater control over the direction and substance of course components, although the frustration members felt over the development and late delivery of *Communication Technology,* together with a general materials; in both cases the learner is almost completely reliant on the packaged teaching material. This material, therefore, has a crucial role and will affect the ease with which the student is able to learn. Secondly there is research on learning to program, including a study of learners using OU instructional materials carried out by one of the authors. The studies on wordprocessing and learning programming at a distance are both important for informing the design of instructional material for carrying out home-computer-related activities at a distance. The remainder of this chapter will draw on these areas, and on past and current practice in instructional design for practical home-computing work to consider issues of learnability and instructional design.

Learning to use wordprocessors and text editors

Several studies have been carried out on learning to use such applications as wordprocessing in commercial environments using self-instructional materials. As with distance teaching, learners are largely on their own in this situation. Carroll and his colleagues have carried out a number of studies in this area starting in the early 1980s, the results of which were used to inform the design of a manual for self-instruction. Carroll explains his approach and goals in his preface:

> One of my professional concerns has been to understand how people acquire competence at using new technology. Our analysis of specific learner problems exposed fundamental flaws in the standard systems approach to instruction and exposed an alternate instructional model, which we call the minimalist model. The essence of the

listening to the tape although of course there are place where he or she will need to pause the tape in order to try out some activity and then re-start it when finished. Some students have found this way of introducing them to the practical work invaluable. Others have used it in ways that were certainly not anticipated by the course team, e.g. listening to the tapes whilst driving to work! However, once students have worked through the tapes, they are not a good vehicle for reference. Trying to find where particular commands are dealt with on an audio-tape is not easy and, similarly, for students who are not complete beginners, using tapes is not so helpful, as what they need is a quick and easy reference system that reminds them about particular

Another important factor in distance learning and practical work the three column format may not take fully into account is that learners actively interpret the text and form mental models. This is inevitable and necessary in order for them to learn and assimilate the material they are encountering Carroll's studies provide examples of how learners will seek to be active in their learning even when discouraged from doing so.

In the previous sections, the term 'mental model' has been used to describe how learners represent the system they are learning to use. The idea of learners using such mental models has been around for some time, although different researchers have used different terms. It can probably be traced back to at least 1981 to a statement made by Young:

System designers and applied psychologists are

of international relations is this fascinating story. It obviously did not happen overnight and the future is unknown.

My academic, philosophical and methodological grounding has given me the ability to be creative and think outside the Box. For this, I am eternally grateful for my teachers and mentors. But this book is about me, giving myself a second chance.

22 July, 2023 **Jyotsna R. Bapat**

This is when the COVID-19 Crisis happened. This crisis was an unprecedented situation that indicated a complete breakdown of the Sustainable Development paradigm where the trade and supply chains were shut down and so were movements of passengers across countries. The actions that India took in the crisis were consistent with the vision of the new leadership as elaborated in Chapter 4. These actions created trust and the space for a new global leadership position that India stepped into.

Chapter 5 indicated the Russia-Ukraine conflict. Special operations as referred by Russia and War by Ukraine, provided an opportunity for India to take in independent decisions in global governance institutions and take on a clear leadership role as a non-aligned nation that believes in principal of Non-Alignment and Peace' and benefit from it, by ensuring its energy security and that of its neighbours when needed. Sri Lanka support, most recently (2020) is an example. This goes on to show that a Global leadership is gained by India, with a following of nations it had assisted and continues to assist post-Covid.

The discussion and conclusion chapter, Chapter 7 discusses these outcomes in a larger context of international relations, grow of the world economy growing conflict and energy and food security threats. The future for India consolidating its as global leader is yet too early to tell.

Notes

1. India fiscal Year GDP Growth 2022 data (accessed on 2/23/2023) http:// tradingeconomics.com>india).
2. Dormandy, Xenia, November 5, 2007, India's foreign policy. https://www.belfercenter.org/publication/indias-foreign-policy
3. 2019 Balakot air strike. https://en.wikipedia.org/wiki/2019_Balakot_airstrike
4. A border dispute between India and China is getting more serious https://www.economist.com/asia/2020/05/28/a-border-dispute-between-india-and-china-is-getting-more-serious?utm
5. Annexation of Crimea by the Russian Federation 2014. https://en.wikipedia.org/wiki/Annexation_of_Crimea_by_the_Russian_Federation

new instrument of power and influence for many nations especially when engaged in building infrastructure projects in neighbouring countries and other partner countries. Successful and on-time completion of these projects added to the regional powers' influence.

India and China emerged as growing players in this field with infrastructure investments in South Asian counties. Both have followed similar policy based on building economicties with regional actors, regardless of existing rivalries, among themselves. This engagement with neighbouring countries is driven not just by economic factors, but also by security considerations. India's strategy is to enhance its strategic autonomy and pursue its development goals in volatile and uncertain global circumstances.[3]

Over the last few decades, another trend of countries pool financial resources to build mega infrastructure projects, that cut across nations, became evident. Since 2014, India has been drawn into this trend, with investments in trilateral and multilateral infrastructure projects, in its neighbourhood.

For example: the North South Corridor (involving India, Iran, Afghanistan, Azerbaijan and Russia), Bay of Bengal Initiative for Multi-Sectoral Technical and Economic Cooperation (BIMSTEC) electricity trade (involving Bangladesh, Bhutan, India, Myanmar, Nepal, and Sri Lanka), LNG terminal built for downstream customers by private companies (involving Russia, India and Bangladesh). While considering these infrastructure projects, India has adopted, economic investment as a geopolitical policy, for achieving its strategic interests.

Meanwhile, China through its own physical infrastructure initiative is involved with multiple Asian and European nations to build power plants, road, and rail links.

India contributes financially, to these trilateral and multilateral projects, through Development Assistance Funds (DAF) set up by the MEA (organisation chart available at the MEA website) through its Lines of Credit for Development Assistance Partnership (DAP) projects.[4] This, however, covers only the financial and economic criteria for funding these projects. What is missing currently in

According to media reports, after the UN imposed sanctions against Iran for its nuclear programme in 2018, India managed to get a special waiver or "carve-out" and continued to import oil from Iran but volumes crashed 79 per cent y-o-y in 2019 to 5.4 mln. tonnes, from 25.5 mln. tonnes in 2018 (https://www.meg.gov.in).

Given the territorial conflicts with Pakistan and China, India needed an alternate route for energy and economic security. A major trade and connectivity hub on Iran's southern coast in the form of Chabahar port in the Hormuz strait not only gives India an alternative route to Afghanistan, bypassing Pakistan, but also has the potential to provide an Indian strategic counter to Pakistan's Gwadar port, being developed by China about 70 km east of Chabahar. As for Afghanistan—which, crucially, imports half of its oil from Iran, Chabahar port can connect it to the Arabian Sea *via* Iran, thus relieving its dependence on Pakistan.

China

As mentioned earlier, China has developed Gwadar port in Pakistan about 70 km east of Chabahar port. Gwadar Port is owned by the government-owned Gwadar Port Authority and operated by China Overseas Port Holding Company (COPHC), a state-run Chinese firm. Media reports claim Pakistan owes a $10 billion debt for the construction of the Gwadar port and other projects built by China under the aegis of the China-Pakistan Economic Corridor (CPEC).

Gwadar is a key transshipment hub linking China to Central Asia and the Persian Gulf. An estimated $54 billion worth of infrastructure projects have been planned for this stretch under the China-Pakistan Economic Corridor, which is part of China's Belt and Road Initiative. China now has a direct access to the Arabian Sea after its 3200 km long road connection from Xinjiang to Gwadar port became partly operational in 2020.

The Project

In May 2016 India Iran and Afghanistan signed the Chabahar Treaty. The treaty is signed to establish and operate a multimodal both short, and long term illness and exposure to radiation can affect multiple generations. At present this waste is stored safely on-site.

Terrorism: There is a serious risk of weapons-grade plutonium being stolen, and providing an opportunity and motive for nuclear blackmail. This risk has been mitigated by protecting the site *via* a series of physical barriers, employing strict security measures, a trained security force and making pre-hiring investigation and training mandatory. If a nuclear power plant accident occurs, the environment and surrounding people could be exposed to high levels of radiation and could be sick for generations due to gamma ray radiation.

India's Competence

India has set up its nuclear power plants in the past with Russia. The most recent, Kudankulam Nuclear Power Plant (KNPP), in Tamil Nadu, is one of two AES-92 design VVER-1000 units under construction under the aegis of the Russia-India project, and commissioned in two phases, in 2013 and 2016 respectively. These are similar in design and technology to the ones developed by Russia for Bangladesh. They use boiling water to cool the core reactor when operational.

Indian companies have participated in construction and installation works in the "non-critical" category for nuclear the KNPP power plant. This includes every construction outside the main core reactor building, such as the setting up of a compound wall, building roads, some security systems, residential areas and office blocks, and subsequently constructions for storage and disposal of spent fuel etc. as well as creating and maintaining a green buffer zone.

India is familiar with the ESSIA planning and implementation procedures which require a very detailed risk analysis that covers the risk of weapons-grade plutonium being stolen, and a detailed disaster management plan. Armed with this experience, and with a similar socio-cultural, economic and environmental profile to but specific actions to be taken against it, was left at the discretion of individual states and not dictated by WHO. Therefore, different countries tried different actions against the pandemic. For example, Scandinavia had 'no mask' policy for a while in the initial stage of the pandemic, most countries chose masks, constrained movement of people and social distancing. All countries followed a short period of complete shutdown, followed by slowly opening of the economy. While China took zero tolerance policy till 2022. Global events change unpredictably. By 2022 February China was facing a fourth wave of COVID-19 and with its 'zero tolerance' policy, had chosen complete lockdown major cities reducing or even shutting down industrial production and disrupting supply chain to the world including USA. While USA after its elections in 2021, was recovering from the previous government's anti-containment and mitigations policies also adopted shut down for a short period. This severely impacted the trade between USA and China. Mainly due to China's very stringent measures to eliminate COVID-19 from its country domestically, put pressure on China to focus internally, rather than on economic production, defence and security initiatives externally. In 2020 when this was becoming a global problem, most countries had adopted economic shut down across nations, in trade and passenger transport followed by slow opening up.

COVID-19 was a system level crisis. Having to deal with it, challenged the *status quo*, namely, globally accepted paradigm of Sustainable Development. This paradigm is based on the assumption that finance and economics not security not politics, is a solution to development of the world. Economics of free trade and globalisation. Development of a country is based on its economic growth. Being part of a global supply chain for goods and services, will ensure interdependence between countries. The corollaries, are just that corollaries. First corollary is economic growth would be 'growth for all' in a country. Another is, such a world order will sustain peace and prosperity and prevent war. Yet another is, democratically elected political governance structure is essential for recommendations to the USA and its partners for shaping the post-COVID world. The following pressure points are identified: global economic downturn due to shut down to contain the virus; conflict between China and the USA over soft power control; tensions between Russia and NATO; trans-Atlantic tension between the USA and its European allies during COVID-19 due to travel bans; and an Indo-Pacific alliance that excludes the EU and partnership with multilateral institutions and global health.

However, global events change unpredictably. By February 2022, China was facing a fourth wave of COVID-19 and with its zero-tolerance policy, had implemented a complete lockdown of major cities, reducing and even shutting down industrial production and disrupting the supply chain to the USA. The USA was recovering from the previous Trump government's anti-containment and anti-mitigation policies. This severely impacted the trade between USA and China. Mainly due to China's very stringent measures to eliminate COVID-19 from its country, the pressure on China was to focus internally, rather than on defence and security initiatives externally till recently. The supply-side constraints causing delivery delays in consumer goods and in semiconductor chips that were mainly produced in China, were quoted as high inflation and slow economic recovery. Both these economies, seen as global leaders, had to deploy their armed forces towards COVID-19 containment and mitigation on account of their large populations and geographies. The main focus was to reduce death rates and reduce hospitalization through COVID-19 vaccination.

Opportunity for Russia

In the face of the pandemic, along with the USA and China, Russia remains a key player in the global landscape. It has intervened militarily in Georgia, Ukraine, and Syria[12]. While Russia is not a rising power and its economy is smaller than those of Brazil, Italy, and India, the disorder caused by a global pandemic served Russia's interest as the impact of the pandemic became manageable.[13]

create new agencies. Over time, the United Nations is doing new work not envisioned for it in 1945 by its founders. The United Nations has set sustainable development goals for 2030, in order to achieve a better and more sustainable future for us all. UN Member-States have also agreed to climate action to limit global warming.

The global bank was created for economic development of countries through infrastructure projects. The economic development paradigm was created, to ensure funding according to goals sent by the UN global governance. When the outcome of this paradigm, namely the impact of these infrastructure projects on social and environmental consequences, started becoming clear, Sustainable Development as a concept began to gather momentum following the 1987 Brundtland Report, Our Common Future, and the 1992 UN Conference on Environment and Development (UNCED), also known as the Earth Summit. UM set nine goals to a common future for the world.

This paradigm supported the assumption that economic development through global financial institutions will ensure global growth. Then in 2008 financial crisis happened in USA that had a Dominos effect and other countries on their path to economic development started questioning the paradigm as the way to ensure development and growth for developing countries in 'Annual Bank Fund Meetings' as late as 2016.

Security and Defence

Post World War II the fear of nuclear war after Japan's nuclear strike, was the other deciding factor to ensure strategies to avoid war, especially a nuclear war globally. Deterrence is a core element of overall strategy to prevent conflict and war. This was a result of the mounting tensions between the then Soviet Union and the United States gave rise to a cold war between them and countries supporting these two Super powers. Nuclear weapons were being created by more and more nations for defence purpose. Treaty on the Non-Proliferation of Nuclear Weapons, also called Nuclear Non-Proliferation Treaty, agreement of July 1, 1968, was signed a separate chapter is devoted on it. A large number of term loans are given for dairy farming, poultry farming, minor irrigation, land developments and farm mechanization. Therefore, separate chapters are devoted on them. With a view to increase agricultural exports, contract farming may become popular. Therefore, a separate chapter is devoted on contract farming to explain its concept. As Agriclinics and Agribusiness Centres may play an important role to encourage farmers for adopting best possible technologies to maximize their income, a separate chapter has been devoted on this subject.

It is necessary to finance medium and large projects in the field of agriculture and allied activities for increasing agricultural finance by banks. Attempts have been made to explain technical, commercial, financial and management appraisal to judge viability of the projects. It may be emphasized that all the appraisal techniques mentioned in various chapters of this book are not essential for appraisal of each and every proposal. The appraisal of a proposal regarding a small loan may need lesser information as compared to a proposal relating to a large amount. Sometimes a particular information may not be readily available. In such cases, judgement should be applied to determine the most suitable alternative. Appraisal techniques given in various chapters of this book should be used as an aid with discretion rather than as routine tools.

The task of banks does not end with the proper appraisal and sanction of financial assistance. Prompt disbursement, close supervision and follow-up is necessary not only during the project implementation but also afterwards to anticipate the problems in advance and take corrective steps, before they take a serious turn. Therefore, after discussing all the aspects of appraisal, a chapter has also been included on disbursement, supervision and follow-up. Problems of recovery of overdues have also been discussed in this chapter.

After explaining various aspects of appraisal and follow-up, several suggestions have been given in the last chapter of the book to increase flow of credit to agriculture.

Utility of the Book

It may be observed from the above-mentioned coverage of the book that an attempt has been made to cover, in brief, almost all the important aspects of lending to agriculture. In order to meet the changing requirements, the Reserve Bank has been issuing various instructions from time to time regarding agricultural advances. Efforts have been made to incorporate relevant instructions and give present position regarding various aspects relating to agricultural finance. In addition to explaining the present position of instructions, various techniques to be followed for appraisal and supervision of agricultural advances have been incorporated in the book. It is needless to say that proper knowledge at the grass root level regarding appraisal and supervision of advances relating to agriculture may go a long way in avoiding non-performing assets. It is hoped that this Handbook will serve as a practical guide to officers in banks not only for knowing the present instructions regarding lending to agriculture, but also assist them in proper appraisal and follow-up of the advances to have recovery in time and avoid non-performing assets. It may help agricultural officers working in banks after having formal education in agriculture and allied subjects, to know financial aspects of lending to agriculture. Similarly, it may help other officers of banks to understand technical aspects of agricultural finance. It may serve as a practical guide to bankers for increasing their finance to agriculture without increasing non-performing assets. Proper appraisal and regular follow-up may ensure recovery of advances.

❑❑❑

and deviations from it may be done keeping in view the requirement of improved farming.

(ii) Banks may at their discretion, fix appropriate sub-limits within the overall credit limits sanctioned, taking into account the seasonality in credit requirements.

(iii) While fixing the limit, banks may take into account the entire production credit requirement for full year including the credit requirement of farmers for ancillary activities related to crop production such as maintenance of agricultural machinery / implements, electricity charges etc. The credit limit may also provide for allied activities and non-farm credit needs of borrowers.

5. Validity / Renewal

(i) Card should normally be valid for 3 years subject to an annual review. Renewal/enhancement / cancellation of limit depends on the performance.

(ii) The review may result in continuation of the facility, enhancement of the limit or cancellation of the limit/withdrawal of the facility, depending upon the performance of the borrower.

(iii) The aggregate credit into account during 12 months period should alteast be equal to maximum outstanding in the account. No drawal in the account should remain outstanding for more than 12 months.

(iv) As a measure of incentive for card holders with good performance, banks may at the time of review, enhance credit limit suitably to take care of increase in cost of inputs, labour charges, etc.

6. Maintenance and operations in the account

(i) The issuing branch should maintain the ledger account in respect of each KCC account. All the operations in the account are generally done through the issuing branch. However, banks may, at their discretion permit operations through other designated branches, taking into account the convenience of the clientele.

(ii) Withdrawal in the card account may be through withdrawal slips/cheques accompanied by the Kisan Credit Card and Pass Book. Withdrawal slips/cheques of a different colour may be issued to distinguish the KCC account holders.

Opening of a Savings Bank Account should not be precondition for issue of Kisan Credit Card. However, if a Kisan Credit Card holder desires to open a Savings Bank Account, he should not be discouraged to do so.

7. Disposal of applications

(i) Brochure of bank should display the benefits of Kisan Credit Card Scheme and requirements to be fulfilled to become eligible for it.

(ii) Applications complete in all respects should be promptly accepted. A Kisan Credit Card should be issued to eligible borrower within 15 days of the receipt of the application.

8. Security, margin, rate of interest, etc.

(i) Instruction given by the Reserve Bank/NABARD regarding security, margin and rate of interest for crop loans may be followed for Kisan Credit Cards also. These instructions have been given in the chapter of general guidelines for advances to agriculture.

(ii) Charges for issuing KCCs should be commensurate with the actual expenses and it should not be considered as a source of income. A fee charged, if any, for issue of a laminated photo card should not exceed Rs.50/-.

(iii) No service charges or inspection charges should be levied by banks on KCCs with limits upto Rs.25,000/-.

9. Payment of interest on credit balance

Banks have been advised by the Reserve Bank in June, 2000 that they may, at their discretion, pay interest at a rate based on their perception and other relevant factors on the minimum credit balance in the accounts of Kisan Credit Cards

(v) Disease diagnostic and monitoring laboratories and technical service centres have been set up in various parts of the country.

(vi) Several large and small poultry feed manufacturing units have been set up in public and private sectors for production and supply of ready-made balanced poultry feed.

(vii) Sophisticated equipment for hatchery and environment control systems are manufactured in the country.

(viii) Training centres have been set up to provide professional training to entrepreneurs.

(ix) Demand for poultry products is increasing due to their high nutritious value.

(x) As poultry can be taken up either full-time or part-time occupation, it reduces under-employment/ unemployment in rural India.

Financial Assistance for Poultry Farming

In case of small loans, banks receive maximum loan applications for the activity of egg production. One day old inoculated female chicks are purchased direct from hatcheries. The chicks are reared for egg laying and they start laying eggs after about 6 months when they are called layers. On an average, each layer gives about 250 eggs in a year after it commences laying eggs. A bird requires 10-11 kg. feed for the first six months when it does not give any production. It requires 40-42 kg. feed for the next one year. After about a year of egg laying, the birds are culled off for table purposes. To have an uninterrupted supply of eggs, fresh stocks of chicks have to be purchased after one year of original supply so that by the time the original stocks of chicks complete their economic period of egg production and are culled off for table purposes, the second stock of chicks will complete their rearing period of six months and start laying eggs. As laying of eggs start after about 6 months from the date of purchase of chicks, the feeding and other requirements of this period should be capitalized for calculating loan requirement and repayment can be expected only after this period. While financing poultry proposals for eggs production, the following points may be taken into consideration:-

(i) It may be ensured that the climate of the place where poultry farm is proposed to be located is suitable for poultry farming. Existence of any poultry farm in the area may be taken as an indication of suitability of the area for establishing a poultry farm. It may, however, be clarified that non-existence of another farm in the area should not be a bar for consideration of the proposal.

(ii) Selected site should be free from water logging conditions. It must be away from main roads having heavy traffic and aerodrome because the birds do not like noise.

(iii) The size of the poultry shed proposed to be constructed should be adequate to accommodate the number of birds to be raised.

(iv) It may be enquired whether the services of experienced contractor for constructing the poultry house are available. If not, it may be ensured that proposed construction will be according to standard requirements. The poultry house should give proper protection to birds from sun, rain, wind and predators.

(v) It may be ensured that electric supply will be made available and adequate arrangements are made for it.

(vi) Sufficient clean water should be available for birds.

(vii) It may be ensured that suitable arrangements are made for purchase of one day old chicks or layers from reputed sellers at reasonable price.

(viii) It may be ensured that necessary hygienic conditions are maintained in poultry farms because birds are highly susceptible to diseases such as cocodiosis, worms, foulpox, bronchitis, coryza, etc.

(ix) It may be ascertained whether the services of officials of the Veternary Department/Block Development Agency are readily available. It may

9 Contract Farming

Diversification of agriculture has been considered necessary to increase income of farmers and generate additional employment for rural masses. Contract farming may help in diversification of agriculture by providing financial support, technology and assured market to farmers. Several agricultural and horticultural crops such as tomatoes, potatoes, chillies, gherkin, baby corn, onions, cotton, wheat, basmati rice, groundnut, flowers, medicinal plants, etc., are produced in some form of contractual arrangements with the farmers in India. In addition to many small players, many large sized companies undertake contract farming for many crops.

A processing firm has to obtain agricultural products with certain specifications to meet the demand of its buyers. It may procure its requirement of agriculture products either from the open market or produce itself (corporate farming) or produce under contract farming. If necessary agricultural products are available in open market at a reasonable price, the processing firm need not go for corporate farming or contract farming. However, sometimes it may not be possible for certain processing firms to get right quality and right quantity at the appropriate time from the market. Therefore, they have to opt for either corporate farming or contract farming. Corporate farming is quite expensive because family labour is not available for it like family farms. Therefore, in such cases, processing firms may have to opt for contract farming.

1. Main Features of Contract Farming

Under contract farming, selected crops are grown by farmers under a buy-back arrangement with an agency engaged in trading or processing. The essence of such contracts is a commitment made by the producer to provide an agricultural commodity of a particular type to a known buyer who commits to buy the same. The contracts may be of three types:

(i) Procurement contracts under which only sale and purchase conditions are specified.

(ii) Partial contracts wherein only some of the inputs are supplied by the contracting firm and the produce is bought at pre-agreed prices.

(iii) Total contracts under which the contracting firm supplies and manages all the inputs and the farmer becomes just a supplier of land and labour requirements.

Banks provide finance for supply of inputs and repayment is received by them through the buyers from the amount payable to the farmers. Contract farming may be by bilateral contract arrangement between the buyers and farmers or it may be by tripartite/multipartite arrangements depending on the requirements.

2. Advantages of Contract Farming for Farmers and Processing Firms

Contract farming is a dynamic partnership between processing firms/agribusiness firms and small farmers. It benefits both of them as under:

(i) It helps small farmers to participate in the production of high value crops like fruits, vegetables, flowers, etc., which may give better income than the conventional crops.

(ii) It helps the small farmers to take advantage of the technological support. The farmers can improve their production by using new technologies and inputs.

(ii) Plant Protection Service Centre
(iii) Vermicomposting Unit
(iv) Horticulture Clinic and Business Centre
(v) Agroservice Centre - Farm Machinery
(vi) Agroservice Centre - Farm Machinery and Primary Processing
(vii) Private Veterinary Clinic
(viii) Private Veterinary Clinic with Retail Outlet for Feed and Medicine
(ix) Private Veterinary Clinic with Small Dairy Unit
(x) Private Artificial Insemination Centre
(xi) Eco-Hatchery for Crop Seed Production and Extension Services

The project profiles circulated by NABARD for above activities are only indicative and banks may finance other similar activities also for which project profiles are not circulated by NABARD. Banks may use their discretion for selection of borrowers/entrepreneurs and activities depending on the potential of the area. The cost of the projects and expected income generation depends on the location and combination of activities. Activities should be selected keeping in view the location and needs of that area. Income from Agriclinics and Agribusiness Centres may be low in the initial years of operation. They may be able to increase their income gradually on gaining popularity in the area. If considered necessary to enhance viability of the proposal, the Agricultural Graduates may be allowed to undertake other commercial activity in agriculture and allied activities alongwith the Agriclinics/Agribusiness Centres. Banks should ensure that the proposals are technically feasible, commercially viable, financially sound and the beneficiaries are having necessary competence to implement them. The repayment period should be decided according to expected income generation. It may vary between 5 years to 10 years depending on the activity and expected income. The repayment period may include grace period of a maximum of 2 years. Keeping in view the importance of Agriclinics and Agribusiness Centres, banks may waive margin/security requirement for loans given to them up to Rs. 5 lakhs.

Conclusion

Agriclinics and Agribusiness Centres play an important role in improving technology adopted for farming. Farmers may increase their income by improving productivity of their farms by taking necessary guidance from Agriclinics and Agribusiness Centres. At the time of introduction of this scheme, the Reserve Bank advised banks in August 2001 to include financing of Agriclinics and Agribusiness Centres under the "Indirect Finance to Agriculture". Subsequently, in order to encourage banks to finance Agriclinics and Agribusiness Centres, the Reserve Bank issued a circular in August 2002 advising banks that financing Agriclinics and Agribusiness Centres will qualify for inclusion under "Direct Finance to Agriculture". Banks should encourage Agriculture Graduates to set up Agriclinics and Agribusiness Centres. In consultation with Agricultural Universities, Krishi Vigyana Kendras (KVKs) and other concerned agencies, banks may guide agricultural graduates to set up Agriclinics and Agribusiness Centres. If necessary precautions are taken in selecting the area and activities to be undertaken by Agriclinics and Agribusiness Centres, they can be viable units not only for improving farming techniques in the area but also for repayment of the loan granted to them.

❑❑❑

9. Schedule of Project Implementation

The Project Evaluation and Review Technique (abbreviated at PERT) or Critical Path Method (abbreviated as CPM) helps the promoters in proper planning, scheduling and controlling various activities essential for the execution of a project. All possible activities from project identification to commencement of production should be listed. If the project is small and it is not possible for the promoters to prepare PERT/CPM diagram, time taken in each activity can be shown in a bar-chart indicating the activities which should be done simultaneously. The preparation of such a chart will help the promoters to undertake various activities at proper time.

The appraising officer should verify whether all the activities have been included and time schedule given by the promoters is reasonable. Such assessment gives an idea about the probable date of commencement of production. It also helps in disbursement of funds according to the requirements of the project and supervision of project implementation. Delay in the schedule of implementation often leads to overrun in the cost of the project and consequential problems. Therefore, proper evaluation of implementation schedule is necessary for estimation of capital cost (including provision for contingencies) and preparation of cash-flow and profitability estimates.

10. Conclusion

The above discussion gives an idea for judging the feasibility of a project to produce goods. It is not only sufficient to ensure that necessary physical facilities will be available for production but it should also be ensured that the best possible alternative is selected to procure them to keep the cost at the minimum possible. Study of different alternatives and selecting the best possible among them makes the technical appraisal more meaningful and relevant. It may be noted that although a project may be technically feasible in terms of availability of physical facilities required for production, it does not justify its implementation unless the benefits obtained from the project are more than its cost and it is found suitable after commercial, financial and managerial appraisals which are discussed in subsequent chapters.

❑❑❑

13 Commercial Appraisal – Marketing at Profitable Price

Many entrepreneurs come to the bank and financial institutions with a proposal to produce whatever they can without giving due consideration to the marketability of the proposed product. They do not provide any information about marketing and even if they provide the information, it may not be sufficient and reliable. In most of the cases, very vague and general statements like "market is good" or "competition is normal and not very much" are made.

Fortunately, the lending institutions are becoming increasingly aware of the situation and beginning to take the steps required for the proper evaluation of the demand for the different products proposed to be manufactured by entrepreneurs approaching them. The old style of selling "whatever we produce" should be converted into "produce whatever we can sell".

In order to have proper appraisal of the demand forecast made by borrowers, banks require information regarding demand, supply, distribution, pricing and external forces. The information required by them can be classified under 5 major headings as mentioned as follows:-

	VI. Cash losses if any	
G. Provision for Contin-gencies	I. Probable increase in cost due to new additions II. Probable increase in cost due to rise in prices, sales-tax, excise duty, transportation charges, fluctuation in foreign exchange rates, etc.	I. Divide total cost estimates into two groups - considered firm and non- firm II. Make provision for contingencies on non-firm items of cost at the rate of 5% to 10% depending on inflationary trend and period of project implementation. Longer the implementation period, higher the contingencies required.
H. Margin Money for Working Capital	I. Indigenous raw materials II. Imported raw materials III. Consumable stores IV. Stock of goods-in-process V. Stock of finished goods VI. Outstanding debtors	Calculate total requirement of working capital and provide 25% of it as margin money for working capital to be brought from long term sources.

Each project is different from the other projects and cost of one project should not be blindly followed for other similar projects. However, it is worthwhile to have a cross-check with previous data on hand or other sources (other financial institutions and banks, government institutions, consultancy organisations, trade associations, etc). If a major difference is observed regarding cost of any particular item,

(xii) Payment to be received from contracted sale of fixed assets during the next 12 months

Following items should be included in the current liabilities:-

(i) Short-term borrowings (including bills purchased and discounted) from (a) banks and (b) others

(ii) Unsecured loans

(iii) Public deposits maturing within one year

(iv) Sundry creditors (trade) for raw materials and consumable stores and spares

(v) Interest and other charges accrued but not due for payment

(vi) Advance/progress payment from customers

(vii) Deposits from dealers, selling agents, etc. However, if such deposits are payable only when the dealership/agency is terminated, they may be treated as term liabilities

(viii) Installments of term loans, deferred payment credits, debentures, redeemable preference shares and long term deposits payable within one year.

(ix) Statutory Liabilities
- (a) Provident Fund dues
- (b) Provision for taxation
- (c) Sales Tax, excise, etc.
- (d) Obligations towards workers considered as statutory
- (e) Any other statutory liability payable within one year

(x) Miscellaneous Current Liabilities
- (a) Dividends
- (b) Liabilities for expenses
- (c) Gratuity payable within one year
- (d) Other provisions
- (e) Any other payments due within one year.

Current assets should be more than current liabilities to provide necessary margin to the banker for working capital finance. About 25 per cent of total current assets should be

Comparison of Two Projects by Net Present Value Method

Project A				Project B		
Investment in 0 year cash inflow in other years		Discounting Factor at 15%	Present Value	Investment in 0 year cash inflow in other years	Discounting Factor at 15%	Present Value
Year	-1000	-	-1000	-1000	-	-1000
Year 1	+300	0.870	+261.0	+200	0.870	+174.0
Year 2	+400	0.756	+302.4	+300	0.756	+226.8
Year 3	+400	0.658	+263.2	+500	0.658	+329.0
Year 4	+300	0.572	+171.6	+400	0.572	+228.8
Year 5	+300	0.497	+149.1	+300	0.497	+149.1
Total Inflow	+1700		+1147.3	+1700		+1107.7
Total Outflow	-1000		-1000.0	- 1000		-1000.0
Net Present Value		+147.3			+107.7	

(6) Although total cash inflow in 5 years is same (Rs.1700) for both the projects, project A has higher net present value because cash inflow in initial years is more in project A as compared to that in project B. As discounting is just opposite of compounding, the discounting factor to find present value from future value gets reduced with the increase in years. The timing of cash flow makes all the difference in favour of project A.

If investment in both the projects is same, the project with higher net present value is preferred. But two projects having different investment outlay should not be compared by net present value because it indicates the excess amount in absolute terms. For example projects X and Y are having initial investment of Rs.5,000 and Rs.10,000 respectively. Their net present value is as under:

(Amount of Rs.)

	Project X	**Project Y**
Present value of investments (costs)	-5000	-10000
Present value of cash inflows (benefits)	+6000	+11,000
Net present value	+1,000	+1,000

If we see the absolute figure of net present value, project Y appears better than project X. But in fact project X is better because in project X, an investment of Rs.5,000 provides a net present value of Rs.1,000, whereas in project Y, an investment of twice that amount provides a net present value of only Rs.1000. In such a situation, profitability index should be calculated by using the following formula to compare the two projects having different investment outlays:-

$$\text{Profitability Index} \; \frac{\text{Present Value of cash inflows}}{\text{Present Value of cash outflows}}$$

$$\text{Profitability Index of Project X} = \frac{6,000}{5,000} = 1.20$$

$$\text{Profitability Index of Project Y} = \frac{11,000}{10,000} = 1.10$$

progress in implementation of the project, the disbursement of funds should be done in installments only. In such cases, it is necessary to ascertain up-to-date progress of the project before disbursement of the second and subsequent installments. As far as possible, disbursement of the loan should be done directly to the suppliers of the assets. However, banks should not insist on the borrowers to purchase the assets from a particular supplier alone. With a view to provide wider choice to farmers and eliminate undesirable practices, banks may disburse loans for agricultural purposes in cash which will facilitate dealer choice to borrowers and foster an environment of trust. However, banks may continue the practice of obtaining receipts from borrowers.

Acquisition of assets is only a beginning. Supervision and follow-up is necessary to maintain proper relations with the borrowers and anticipate the problems in advance. Bankers should periodically visit the beneficiaries to ascertain whether the assets exist physically and are being used properly. They may also make enquiries about problems, if any, faced by the beneficiaries and assist them in taking appropriate corrective steps before they take a serious turn. The following suggestions may be considered for effective follow-up and recovery of loans:-

1. Suitable and adequate field staff

Suitable and adequate field staff should be posted to keep in touch with the borrowers to ensure proper utilization of credit and assist the borrowers in sorting out their problems. Schematic approach or lending to clusters of borrowers in a village may facilitate effective supervision. The field staff can contact the borrowers easily to solve their problems and recover the bank loan. Banks should post, in a phased manner, at least one Agricultural Field Officer, qualified or trained in agricultural financing, at each branch dealing in agricultural finance. It is better to appoint graduates in agriculture because they would be better equipped to provide technical advice than those who have merely undergone some training programme in agricultural financing.

2. Approaching borrowers before due date

Due date for repayment of the loan should be fixed in such a way that it coincides with the time when the beneficiary generally sells his produce and is likely to be in possession of funds. On the lines of Kisan Credit Card, each borrower should be provided a loan pass book for term loans also recording the date and amount of disbursement, details of repayments received under interest and principal, charges debited to account and the balance due. It should also indicate the repayment schedule to be followed by the borrower. The bank staff should educate the borrowers regarding the amount of loan instalments, interest, due dates of the repayment, etc. A close liaison should be maintained and the borrower should get the feeling that the banker is not only the financier but also his friend. Banks which have built up good rapport and intimate the borrowers about repayment one or two weeks before the due date will be able to show better recovery performance than those who have merely waited for the borrower to walk in and make the repayment. Harvesting seasons should be effectively used for recovery of dues. Banks should make efforts to inculcate the habit of regular repayment among borrowers so that a tendency of default does not develop.

3. Branch-wise analysis of overdues

Controlling offices should constantly and closely review recovery performance of each branch. They may make branch-wise analysis of overdues and try to find out the reasons for heavy overdues in a particular branch. Separate recovery cells should be created in those branches where overdues exceed 50 per cent of demand and total advances are sizeable. These cells may ensure continuous and effective supervision for recovery of not only overdues but also current dues to avoid further overdues. Senior officers from controlling offices should visit these branches frequently and have a meaningful dialogue with the manager and other officials regarding the problems pertaining to the area. This will instill a sense of responsibility and they would make special efforts to improve their recovery performance.

I. Short-term loans for raising crops i.e. for crop loans. In addition, advances upto Rs.5 lakh to farmers against pledge/hypothecation of agricultural produce (including warehouse receipts) for a period not exceeding 12 months, where the farmers were given crop loans for raising the produce, provided the borrowers draw credit from one bank.

II. Medium and long-term loans (Provided directly to farmers for financing production and development needs)

(i) Purchase of agricultural implements and machinery

(ii) Development of irrigation potential

(iii) Reclamation and Land Development Schemes

(iv) Construction of farm buildings and structures, etc.

(v) Construction and running of storage facilities

(vi) Production and processing of hybrid seeds for crops

(vii) Payment of irrigation charges, etc.

(viii) Other types of direct finance to farmers

a. Short-term loans

(1) To traditional/non-traditional plantations and horticulture

b. Medium and long term loans

(1) Development loans to all plantations, horticulture, forestry and wasteland

(2) Financing of small and marginal farmers for purchase of land for agricultural purposes

The details of items (i) to (vii) are given in Chapter 2 of the book while explaining the activities included in agriculture. In respect of agricultural loans other than the above and term loans given to non-agriculturists, identification of NPAs should be done on the same basis as non-agricultural advances which, at present, is the 90 days delinquency norm.

12. Recovery Strategy for a bank's branch

A branch may take following steps to improve its recovery performance:

(i) Organise a staff meeting to discuss about recovery performance of the branch and the position of NPAs.

(ii) Explain importance of recovery to the staff by sharing statistics. At the end of the meeting, the branch managers should seek full support from the staff for the recovery drive.

(iii) In consultation with the staff, the branch manager may form a recovery team. The members of the team may be chosen carefully keeping in view skills for performing recovery functions and aptitude for field visits. In small branches, all members of the staff may be involved in recovery and become members of the team. Attempts may be made to educate and motivate the recovery team adequately by quoting examples of those branches which succeeded in the recovery drive.

(iv) The recovery team may study the NPAs and classify into three categories viz., (a) area wise, (b) amount wise and (c) strategy wise (reschedulement of term loan, rehabilitation, compromise, recalled advances, suit filed, decreed cases, write-off, etc.). Those NPAs wherein the recovery is possible immediately and also the amount involved is large, may be taken up first. Similarly, cases wherein the documents are likely to become time-barred and pending execution of decreed cases may be given preference.

(v) After proper classification, each member of the team may be given a certain target for recovery after consulting the concerned member keeping in view the target set for the branch by the Zonal Office.

(vi) After the targets are set, each member may decide the course of action to be followed. Group approach

11. Assistance to farmers indebted to non-institutional lenders

Loans taken by farmers from money lenders and other non-institutional lenders at a high rate of interest leads to reduction in their income due to heavy payment of interest. With a view to reduce their hardship, the Reserve Bank issued a circular in June, 2004 advising banks that they may finance the farmers to provide them relief from such indebtedness. The broad guidelines for providing such loans may be approved by their Board of Directors.

Banks may provide loans for this purpose under Kisan Credit Card scheme. Income generation and repaying capacity of the farmers may be considered while determining the amount which could be included as part of assessment of limits under Kisan Credit Card scheme. If necessary, banks may consider even granting term loan for this purpose. Savings in interest may help the farmers in repaying the loan. In many cases, payment of interest itself takes heavy burden and the farmer is not able to repay the loan. As the rate of interest charged by the banks will be much lower than that of moneylenders, the repayment of principal and interest may be easy for the farmer.

Banks may take appropriate collateral security, if considered necessary, while providing loans for this purpose. Charge over assets and documents pledged with the moneylenders may also be taken as security after the dues are cleared. In respect of tenant farmers and other small farmers, banks may adopt group approach (self-help groups or joint liability groups) for granting loans to repay the borrowings from non-institutional borrowers.

Loans provided for the above purpose may be treated as part of direct finance to agriculture.

12. Review of the cases denied assistance

As per the guidelines issued by the RBI in June 2004, banks should review all cases of small and marginal farmers where credit has been denied on the sole ground that a loan account was settled through compromise or write-offs. Banks should consider giving financial assistance to such farmers, if their proposals are viable.

13. Financing through Self-Help Groups

In case of small and marginal farmers, share croppers and tenant farmers who are not able to provide security, banks may finance them through Joint Liability Group (JLG) or Self-Help Group (SHG) Schemes. The group as a whole commits repayment of the loan to the bank. As moral pressure is extended on the borrowing members for repayment of loan, the recovery percentage is very high for the loans given under the Schemes of Joint Liability Group or Self-Help Group.

As per the instructions issued by the Reserve Bank in June 2004, banks may finance the farmers to repay the loans taken from moneylenders and other non-institutional lenders and such finance may be treated as part of direct finance to agriculture. Joint Liability Groups or Self-help Groups of farmers having outstanding loans taken from non-institutional lenders may be formed. Such Joint Liability Groups/Self-help Group may prove helpful in coming out of loans taken at high rate of interest by saving the difference between the interest charged by moneylenders and banks. Banks may encourage this process because it will not only help in reducing poverty, but also in recovering banks' loan as a result of savings in interest amount and moral pressure extended by members of the Group.

14. Banker-Farmers meet

Banker-Farmers meet is an effective tool for generating wide awareness about the various schemes of financing to agriculture. This meet may also be used for emphasizing about cultivating savings habit and repaying the loan in time. Such meetings may be arranged either by the branch individually or collectively by the branches of the same bank or different banks. Representatives of other concerned agencies may also be invited to attend such meetings. Such meetings may induce those farmers also, who often shy away from formal institutions, to approach banks.

15. Integrating term loans with production credit

Banks provide term loans for various activities like digging/deepening of wells, installing diesel pump sets or a detailed study should be done to identify the reasons for difference and to ascertain whether the difference is desirable.

Sources of Finance

After assessing the capital cost of the project, the entrepreneurs and banks have to decide the pattern of financing the capital cost. A project can be financed by anyone or more than one of the following sources:-

(i) Issue of ordinary/preference shares
(ii) Issue of secured debentures
(iii) Issue of convertible debentures and bonds
(iv) Term loans from financial institutions and banks
(v) External commercial borrowings
(vi) Foreign investments
(vii) Special schemes formulated by certain institutions/govt. agencies
(viii) Deferred credits from equipment suppliers including those under bill rediscounting scheme
(ix) Leasing finance
(x) Unsecured loans and deposits
(xi) Capital subsidy or development loans/sales tax loans
(xii) Internal accruals for existing undertakings.

The various sources can be broadly classified into two categories, equity capital and borrowed capital. The proportion between these two categories of funds may vary considerably from project to project depending upon the nature of the project, its size, location, background of promoters and expected profitability.

Equity capital does not involve any fixed charge like loan for repayment of principal and payment of interest. It serves as a cushion in the event of unfavourable conditions and operational difficulties. Banks will not commit to provide the entire finance by term loan because they will not have any cushion and asset coverage for the loan to be provided by them. The debt-equity ratio is generally allowed about 1.5:1 depending on the nature of the project, its location, developed/backward areas. It can also be high for certain projects like dairy farming where gestation period is very short.

In case of modernization/rehabilitation assistance, flexible approach is adopted for debt equity ratio depending upon the profitability of the individual project.

It may be observed from the above that banks adopt flexible approach in regard to debt-equity ratio depending on various relevant factors.

In order to find out overall debt position and capital gearing of the unit, banks have recently started calculating total debt-equity ratio where the total liabilities - both short-term and long term - are compared with the equity. However, no norms have been suggested for this ratio so far.

2. Current Ratio (Current Assets to Current Liabilities)

This ratio indicates the liquidity position of a unit. Following items should be included in current assets:-

(i) Cash and bank balances

(ii) Investments

(a) Government and other Trustee Securities (other than for long-term purposes eg., Sinking Fund, Gratuity Fund, etc.)

(b) Fixed Deposits with banks

(iii) Receivables arising out of sales other than deferred receivables (including bills purchased and discounted by banks)

(iv) Installments of deferred receivables due within one year

(v) Raw materials and components used in the process of manufacture including those in transit

(vi) Stock-in-process including semi-finished goods

(vii) Finished goods including goods in transit

(viii) Other consumable spares

(ix) Advance payment for tax

(x) Pre-paid expenses

(xi) Advances for purchase of raw materials, components and consumable stores